FINLAND
Helsinki
St. Petersburg
Tallinn
ESTONIA
Pärnu
Riga
LATVIA
LITHUANIA
Kaunas
Vilnius
Minsk
BELARUS
Warsaw
Brest
Gomel
Moscow
RUSSIAN FEDERATION
URAL MTS.
Ural R.
Volga R.
KAZAKHSTAN
Kharkiv
Kiev
Dnieper R.
UKRAINE
CARPATHIAN MTS.
Miskolc
Cluj
MOLDOVA
Chisinau
Tiraspol
Odessa
Timisoara
ROMANIA
Bucharest
Danube R.
BULGARIA
Sofia
Plovdiv
Pristina
Skopje
Salonica
Istanbul
Black Sea
Caspian Sea
CAUCASUS MTS.
GEORGIA
Tbilisi
Baku
ARMENIA
Yerevan
AZERBAIJAN
Tehran
IRAN
Ankara
TURKEY
Aegean Sea
GREECE
Izmir
Athens
Tigris R.
SYRIA
Baghdad
IRAQ
Euphrates R.
Nicosia
Crete
CYPRUS
Beirut
LEBANON
Damascus
ISRAEL
Tel Aviv
Jerusalem
Amman
JORDAN
Kuwait City
KUWAIT
SAUDI ARABIA
Alexandria
Cairo
Nile R.
EGYPT
D0603909

Learn how this book can improve your performance on tests and exams.

See pages xli–xliii.

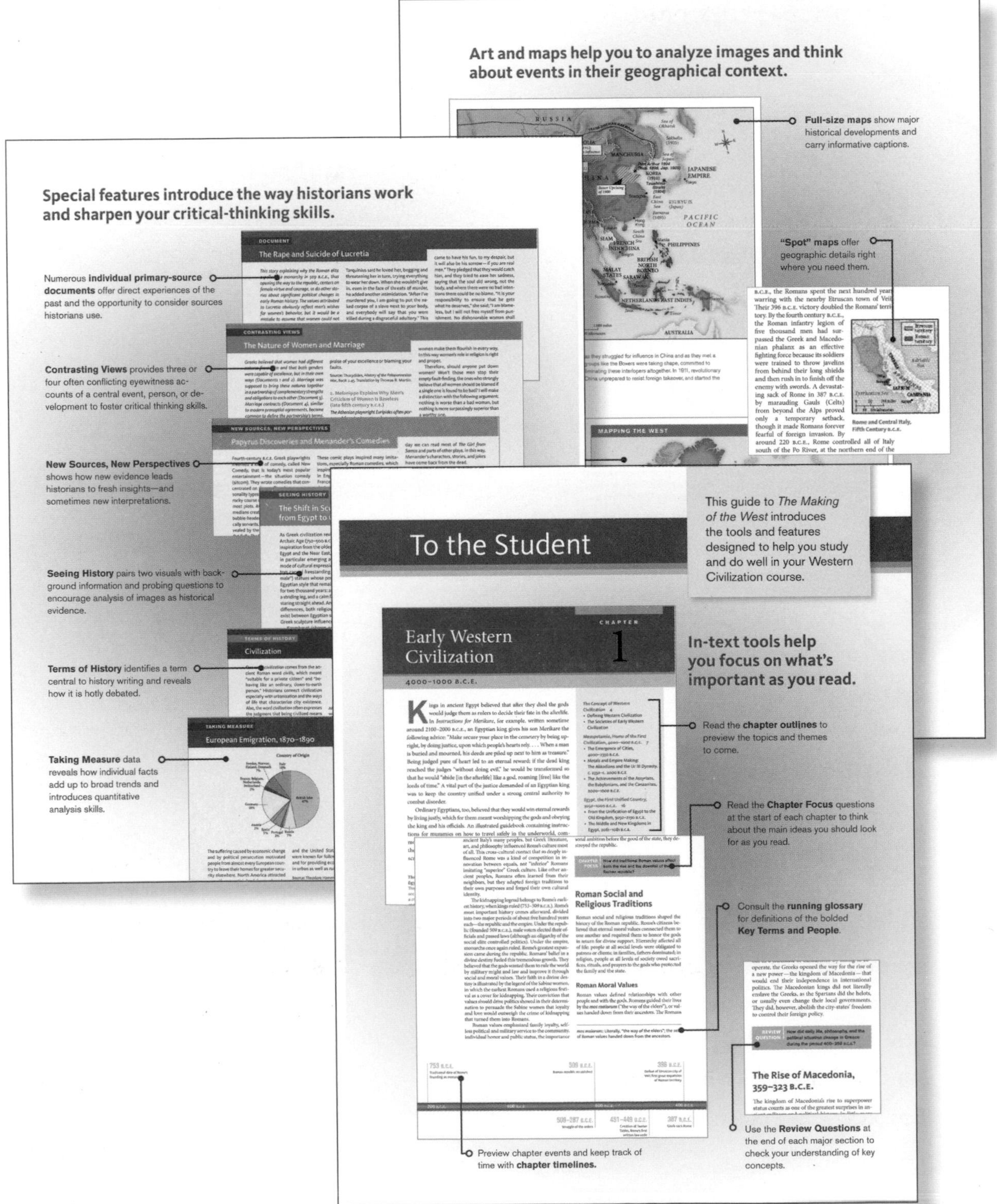

FOURTH EDITION

The Making of the West

PEOPLES AND CULTURES

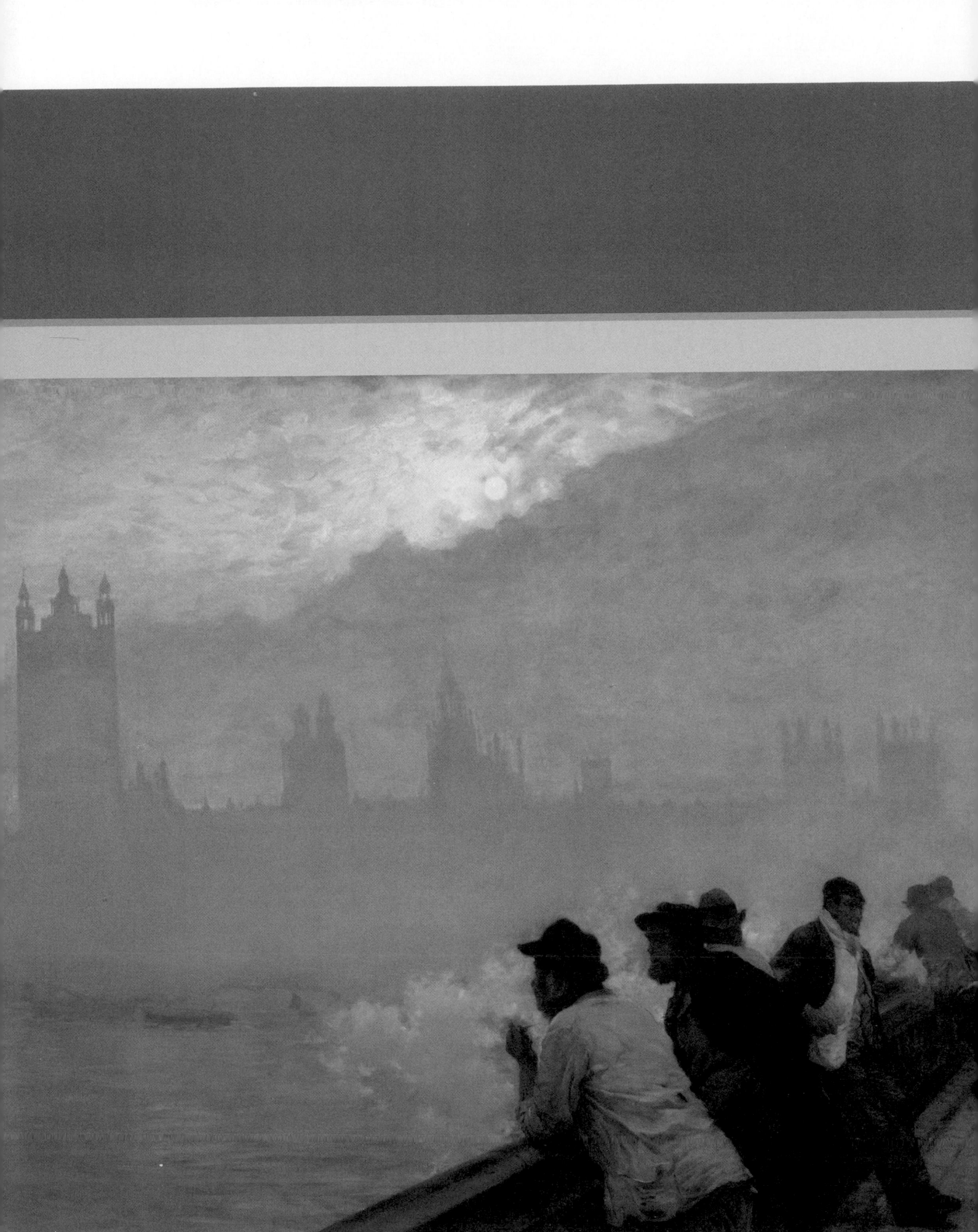

FOURTH EDITION

The Making of the West

PEOPLES AND CULTURES

Lynn Hunt
University of California, Los Angeles

Thomas R. Martin
College of the Holy Cross

Barbara H. Rosenwein
Loyola University Chicago

Bonnie G. Smith
Rutgers University

BEDFORD/ST. MARTIN'S
Boston ♦ New York

For Bedford/St. Martin's

Publisher for History: Mary Dougherty
Director of Development for History: Jane Knetzger
Developmental Editor: Danielle Slevens
Senior Production Editor: Karen S. Baart
Production Editor: Marcy Ross
Senior Production Supervisor: Jennifer L. Peterson
Senior Executive Marketing Manager: Jenna Bookin Barry
Associate Editor: Robin Soule
Production Assistants: Elise Keller and Victoria Royal
Copyeditor: Janet Renard
Indexer: Leoni Z. McVey, McVey & Associates, Inc.
Cartography: Mapping Specialists Limited
Photo Researcher: Bruce Carson
Permissions Manager: Kalina K. Ingham
Senior Art Director: Anna Palchik
Text Designer: Lisa Buckley
Page Layout: Boynton Hue Studio
Cover Designer: Billy Boardman
Cover Art: Giuseppe De Nittis (1846–1884). *Westminster,* 1875. Private Collection. Cameraphoto Arte, Venice/Art Resource, NY.
Composition: Jouve
Printing and Binding: RR Donnelley and Sons

President: Joan E. Feinberg
Editorial Director: Denise B. Wydra
Director of Marketing: Karen R. Soeltz
Director of Production: Susan W. Brown
Associate Director, Editorial Production: Elise S. Kaiser
Managing Editor: Elizabeth M. Schaaf

Library of Congress Control Number: 2011939727

Manufactured in the United States of America.

1 2 3 4 5 6 15 14 13 12 11

For information, write: Bedford/St. Martin's, 75 Arlington Street, Boston, MA 02116 (617-399-4000)

ISBN: 978-0-312-67268-3 (Combined Edition)
ISBN: 978-0-312-57571-7 (Loose-Leaf Edition)
ISBN: 978-0-312-58343-9 (High School Edition)
ISBN: 978-0-312-67269-0 (Volume I)
ISBN: 978-0-312-57569-4 (Loose-Leaf Edition, Volume I)
ISBN: 978-0-312-67271-3 (Volume II)
ISBN: 978-0-312-57570-0 (Loose-Leaf Edition, Volume II)
ISBN: 978-0-312-58340-8 (Volume A)
ISBN: 978-0-312-58341-5 (Volume B)
ISBN: 978-0-312-58342-2 (Volume C)

Acknowledgments: *Acknowledgments and copyrights are printed at the back of the book on pages C-1–C-3, which constitute an extension of the copyright page. It is a violation of the law to reproduce these selections by any means whatsoever without the written permission of the copyright holder. At the time of publication all Internet URLs published in this text were found to accurately link to their intended Web site. If you do find a broken link, please forward the information to* history@bedfordstmartins.com *so that it can be corrected for the next printing.*

Preface

History requires constant rethinking and rewriting, because current events make us see the past in a new light. The fall of the Berlin Wall in 1989; the attacks of September 11, 2001; and the world economic crisis that began in 2008 are dramatic examples of how events shift our perspective. As a result of these events, communism, Islam, and globalization all took on different meanings — not just for the present, but also in ways that compel us to reconsider the past. To take just one example, Islam has been part of the history of the West since its founding as a religion in the seventh century, and yet until the last two decades most textbooks of the history of the West gave it relatively little attention. No one would think of limiting its coverage now.

As this book goes into its fourth edition, we authors feel confident that our fundamental approach is well suited to incorporating changes in perspective. We have always linked the history of the West to wider developments in the world. A new edition gives us the opportunity to make those links even stronger and more global, and thereby help students better understand the world in which they live. Instructors who have read and used our book also confirm that the synthesis of approaches we offer — from military to gender history — enables them to bring the most up-to-date conceptualizations of the West into their classroom. We aim to integrate different approaches rather than privileging any one of them.

Our primary goal has been to create a text that demonstrates that the history of the West is the story of an ongoing process, not a finished result with one fixed meaning. We wanted also to make clear that there is no one Western people or culture that has existed from the beginning until now. Instead, the history of the West includes many different peoples and cultures. To convey these ideas, we have written a sustained story of the West's development in a broad, global context that reveals the cross-cultural interactions fundamental to the shaping of Western politics, societies, cultures, and economies. Indeed, the first chapter opens with a section on the origins and contested meaning of the term *Western civilization*.

Equally valuable to instructors has been the way our book is organized in a chronological framework to help students understand how political, social, cultural, and economic histories have influenced one another over time. We know from our own teaching that introductory students need a solid chronological framework, one with enough familiar benchmarks to make the material easy to grasp. Each chapter treats the main events, people, and themes of a period in which the West significantly changed; thus, students learn about political and military events and social and cultural developments as they unfolded. This chronological integration also accords with our belief that it is important, above all else, for students to see the interconnections among varieties of historical experience — between politics and cultures, between public events and private experiences, between wars and diplomacy and everyday life. Our chronological synthesis provides a unique benefit to students: it makes these relationships clear while highlighting the major changes of each age. For teachers, our chronological approach ensures a balanced account and provides the opportunity to present themes within their greater context. But perhaps best of all, this approach provides a text that reveals history as a process that is constantly alive, subject to pressures, and able to surprise us.

Cultural borrowing between the peoples of Europe and their neighbors has characterized Western civilization from the beginning. Thus, we have insisted on an expanded vision of the West that includes the United States and fully incorporates Scandinavia, eastern Europe, and the Ottoman Empire. Latin America, Africa, China, Japan, and India also come into the story. We have been able to offer sustained treatment of crucial topics such as Islam and provide a more thorough examination of globalization than any competing text. Study of Western history provides essential background to today's events, from debates over immigration to conflicts in the Middle East. Instructors have found this synthesis essential for helping students understand the West amid today's globalization.

In this edition, we have enhanced our coverage of Western interactions with other parts of the world and the cross-cultural exchanges that influenced the making of the West. Chapter 2, for example, demonstrates that despite the Dark Age, Greek civilization stayed in contact with civilization in the Near East as it reinvented itself — and that this cultural interaction produced a reemergence with profound differences from the social and political traditions that had existed in Greece before. Chapter 14 shows how the gold and silver discovered in the New World combined with growing confrontations over religion within Europe to reshape the long-standing rivalries among princes, treating these topics together to illustrate how earlier forms of globalization influenced daily life, religious beliefs, and the ways wars were fought. Chapter 27 features a revised, updated discussion of decolonization and the end of empire in Asia, Africa, and the Middle East, including a new document on torture in Algeria. Chapter 29 includes current coverage of recent events in the Middle East, the global economic crisis, the rise of economies in the Pacific and the Southern Hemisphere, and globalized culture and communications.

As always, we have also incorporated the latest scholarly findings throughout the book so that students and instructors alike have a text on which they can confidently rely. In the fourth edition, we have included new and updated discussions of topics such as fresh archaeological evidence for the possible role of religion in stimulating the major changes of the Neolithic Revolution; the dating of the Great Sphinx in Egypt, the scholarly debate that could radically change our ideas of the earliest Egyptian history; the newest thinking on the origins of Islam; the crucial issues in the Investiture Conflict between pope and emperor; the impact of the Great Famine of the fourteenth century; the slave trade, and especially its continuation into the nineteenth century; and, in a brand-new epilogue, the ways in which scholars are considering recent events within the context of the new digital world.

Aided by a fresh and welcoming design, new pedagogical aids, and new multimedia offerings that give students and instructors interactive tools for study and teaching (see "Versions and Supplements" on page xi), the new edition is, we believe, even better suited to today's Western civilization courses. In writing *The Making of the West: Peoples and Cultures*, we have aimed to communicate the vitality and excitement as well as the fundamental importance of history. Students should be enthusiastic about history; we hope we have conveyed some of our own enthusiasm and love for the study of history in these pages.

Pedagogy and Features

We know from our own teaching that students need all the help they can get in absorbing and making sense of information, thinking analytically, and understanding that history itself is often debated and constantly revised. With these goals in mind, we retained the class-tested learning and teaching aids that worked well in the previous editions, but we have also done more to help students distill the central story of each age and give them more opportunities to develop their own historical skills.

Compared with previous editions, the fourth edition incorporates more aids to help students sort out what is most important to learn while they read. Completely redesigned Chapter Review sections feature new, dynamic activities asking students to identify and discuss the chapter's key terms, encouraging students to go beyond rote memorization and consider each term's importance in context. We have also added questions in three different places: to the documents (which are described more fully below), to the end-of-chapter timelines, and to the Making Connections sections. Posed at the end of the documents, questions help focus students' attention on the main themes and concepts expressed in them. The questions at the end of the timelines encourage students to think about possible links between political, economic, social, and cultural events. We have added more questions to the Making Connections feature because instructors find these questions to be useful in prompting students to think across the sections of any given chapter. To further help students as they read, we have worked hard to ensure that chapter and section overviews outline the central points of each section in the clearest manner possible, and we have condensed some material to better illuminate key ideas.

The study tools introduced in the previous editions continue to help students check their understanding of the chapters and the periods they cover. Boldface key terms and names have been updated to concentrate on likely test items. Those terms and people are defined in a running glossary at the bottom of pages and collected in a comprehensive glossary at the end of the book. Review questions, strategically placed at the end of each major section, help students recall and assimilate core points in digestible increments. Vivid chapter-opening anecdotes, timelines, and conclusions further reinforce the central developments covered in the reading.

To reflect the richness of the themes in the text and offer further opportunities for historical investigation, we include a rich assortment of single-source documents (two to three per chapter), 30 percent of them new to this edition. Nothing can give students a more direct experience of the past than original voices, and we have endeavored to let those voices speak, whether it is Frederick

Barbarossa replying to the Romans when they offer him the emperor's crown, Marie de Sévigné's description of the French court, or an ordinary person's account of the outbreak of the Russian Revolution.

Accompanying these primary-source documents are our five unique skill-building features. Reviewed with users and revised for the fourth edition, these features extend the narrative by revealing the process of interpretation, providing a solid introduction to historical argument and critical thinking, and capturing the excitement of historical investigation.

- ***Seeing History*** features guide students through the process of reading images as historical evidence. Each of the ten features provides a pair of images for comparison and contrast, with background information and questions that encourage visual analysis. Examples include comparisons of pagan and Christian sarcophagi, Persian and Arabic coins, Romanesque and Gothic naves, pre- and post–French Revolution attire, and portrayals of soldiers in World War I.
- ***Contrasting Views*** features provide three or four often conflicting primary-source accounts of a central event, person, or development— such as Julius Caesar, Charlemagne, Magna Carta, Martin Luther, the English Civil War, and late-nineteenth-century migration— enabling students to understand history from a variety of contemporaneous perspectives.
- ***New Sources, New Perspectives*** features show students how historians continue to develop fresh insights using new kinds of evidence about the past, from tree rings to Holocaust museums.
- ***Terms of History*** features explain the meanings of some of the most important and contested terms in the history of the West— *civilization*, *nationalism*, and *progress*, for example— and show how those meanings have developed and changed over time.
- ***Taking Measure*** features introduce students to the intriguing stories revealed by quantitative analysis. Each feature highlights a chart, table, graph, or map of historical statistics that illuminates an important political, social, or cultural development.

The book's map program has been widely praised as one of the most comprehensive and inviting of any survey text. In each chapter, we offer three types of maps, each with a distinct role in conveying information to students. Four to five full-size maps show major developments, two to four "spot" maps— small maps positioned within the discussion right where students need them— serve as immediate locators, and "Mapping the West" summary maps at the end of each chapter provide a snapshot of the West at the close of a transformative period and help students visualize the West's changing contours over time. For this edition, we have added new maps and carefully considered each of the existing maps, simplifying where possible to better highlight essential information, and clarifying and updating borders and labels where needed.

We have striven to integrate art as fully as possible into the narrative and to show its value for teaching and learning. Over 430 illustrations— 30 percent of which are new— were carefully chosen to reflect this edition's broad topical coverage and geographic inclusion, reinforce the text, and show the varieties of visual sources from which historians build their narratives and interpretations. All artifacts, illustrations, paintings, and photographs are contemporaneous with the chapter; there are no anachronistic illustrations. Substantive captions for the maps and art help students learn how to read visuals, and we have frequently included specific questions or suggestions for comparisons that might be developed. Specially designed visual exercises in the Online Study Guide supplement this approach. A new page design for the fourth edition supports our goal of intertwining the art and the narrative, and makes the new study tools readily accessible.

Acknowledgments

In the vital process of revision, the authors have benefited from repeated critical readings by many talented scholars and teachers. Our sincere thanks go to the following instructors, whose comments often challenged us to rethink or justify our interpretations and who always provided a check on accuracy down to the smallest detail.

Robert Beachy, *Goucher College*
William E. Burns, *George Washington University*
Kevin W. Caldwell, *Blue Ridge Community College*
Patricia G. Clark, *Westminster College*
Oliver Griffin, *St. John Fisher College*
Rebecca K. Hayes, *Northern Virginia Community College–Manassas*
Anne Huebel, *Franklin Pierce University*
Steven Kale, *Washington State University*
Jeff Kleiman, *University of Wisconsin–Marshfield*
John Leazer, *Carthage College*

Charles Levine, *Mesa Community College*
Mauro Magarelli, *William Paterson University*
Kelly Obernuefemann, *Lewis & Clark Community College*
Ann Ostendorf, *Gonzaga University*
Maryanne Rhett, *Monmouth University*
Sarah Shurts, *Montclair State University*
Mark Stephens, *Chabot College*
Frank Van Nuys, *South Dakota School of Mines and Technology*

Many colleagues, friends, and family members have made contributions to this work. They know how grateful we are. We also wish to acknowledge and thank the publishing team at Bedford/St. Martin's who did so much to bring this revised edition to completion: president Joan Feinberg, editorial director Denise Wydra, publisher for history Mary Dougherty, director of development for history Jane Knetzger, developmental editor Danielle Slevens, freelance editors Jim Strandberg and Debra Michals, associate editor Robin Soule, senior executive marketing manager Jenna Bookin Barry, senior production editor Karen Baart, freelance production editor Marcy Ross, managing editor Elizabeth Schaaf, art researcher Bruce Carson, text designer Lisa Buckley, page makeup artist Cia Boynton, cover designer Billy Boardman, and copyeditor Janet Renard.

Our students' questions and concerns have shaped much of this work, and we welcome all our readers' suggestions, queries, and criticisms. Please contact us at our respective institutions or via **history@bedfordstmartins.com**.

Versions and Supplements

Adopters of *The Making of the West* and their students have access to abundant extra resources, including documents, presentation and testing materials, the acclaimed Bedford Series in History and Culture volumes, and much much more. See below for more information, visit the book's catalog site at **bedfordstmartins.com/hunt/catalog**, or contact your local Bedford/St. Martin's sales representative.

Get the Right Version for Your Class

To accommodate different course lengths and course budgets, *The Making of the West* is available in several different formats, including three-hole punched loose-leaf Budget Books versions and e-books, which are available at a substantial discount.

- Combined edition (Chapters 1–29) — available in hardcover, loose-leaf, and e-book formats
- Volume 1: To 1750 (Chapters 1–17) — available in paperback, loose-leaf, and e-book formats
- Volume 2: Since 1500 (Chapters 14–29) — available in paperback, loose-leaf, and e-book formats
- Volume A: To 1500 (Chapters 1–13) — available in paperback format
- Volume B: 1340–1830 (Chapters 13–20) — available in paperback format
- Volume C: Since 1750 (Chapters 18–29) — available in paperback format

The online, interactive **Bedford e-Book** can be examined at **bedfordstmartins.com/hunt** or purchased at a discount there. Your students can also purchase *The Making of the West* in other popular e-book formats for computers, tablets, and e-readers.

Online Extras for Students

The book's companion site at **bedfordstmartins.com/hunt** gives students a way to read, write, and study, and to find and access quizzes and activities, study aids, and history research and writing help.

FREE **Online Study Guide.** Available at the companion site, this popular resource provides students with quizzes and activities for each chapter, including multiple-choice self-tests that focus on important concepts; flashcards that test students' knowledge of key terms; timeline activities that emphasize causal relationships; and map quizzes intended to strengthen students' geography skills. Instructors can monitor students' progress through an online Quiz Gradebook or receive email updates.

FREE **Research, Writing, and Anti-plagiarism Advice.** Available at the companion site, Bedford's **History Research and Writing Help** includes **History Research and Reference Sources**, with links to history-related databases, indexes, and journals; **More Sources and How to Format a History Paper**, with clear advice on how to integrate primary and secondary sources into research papers and how to cite and format sources correctly; **Build a Bibliography**, a simple Web-based tool known as The Bedford Bibliographer that generates bibliographies in four commonly used documentation styles; and **Tips on Avoiding Plagiarism**, an online tutorial that reviews the consequences of plagiarism and features exercises to help students practice integrating sources and recognize acceptable summaries.

Resources for Instructors

Bedford/St. Martin's has developed a wide range of teaching resources for this book and for this course. They range from lecture and presentation materials and assessment tools to course management options. Most can be downloaded or ordered at **bedfordstmartins.com/hunt/catalog**.

HistoryClass for The Making of the West. HistoryClass, a Bedford/St. Martin's Online Course Space, puts the online resources available with this textbook in one convenient and completely customizable course space. There, you and your students can access an interactive e-book and primary sources reader; maps, images, documents, and links; chapter review quizzes; interactive multimedia exercises; and research and writing help. In HistoryClass you can get all of our premium content and tools and assign, rearrange, and mix them with your own resources. For more information, visit **yourhistoryclass.com**.

Bedford Coursepack for Blackboard, WebCT, Desire2Learn, Angel, Sakai, or Moodle. We have free content to help you integrate our rich content into your course management system. Registered instructors can download coursepacks with no hassle and no strings attached. Content includes our most popular free resources and book-specific content for *The Making of the West.* Visit **bedfordstmartins.com/coursepacks** to see a demo, find your version, or download your coursepack.

Instructor's Resource Manual. The instructor's manual offers both experienced and first-time instructors tools for preparing for lecture and running discussions. It includes chapter review material, teaching strategies, and a guide to chapter-specific supplements available for the text.

Guide to Changing Editions. Designed to facilitate an instructor's transition from the previous edition of *The Making of the West* to the current edition, this guide presents an overview of major changes as well as changes in each chapter.

Computerized Test Bank. The test bank includes a mix of fresh, carefully crafted multiple-choice, matching, fill-in-the-blank, short-answer, and essay questions for each chapter. It also contains the Chapter Focus, Review, Important Events, and Making Connections questions from the textbook and model answers for each. The questions appear in Microsoft Word format and in easy-to-use test bank software that allows instructors to easily add, edit, re-sequence, and print questions and answers. Instructors can also export questions into a variety of formats, including WebCT and Blackboard.

PowerPoint Maps, Images, Lecture Outlines, and i>clicker Content. Look good and save time with *The Bedford Lecture Kit.* These presentation materials are downloadable individually from the Instructor Resources tab at **bedfordstmartins.com/hunt/catalog** and are available on *The Bedford Lecture Kit* Instructor's Resource CD-ROM. They include ready-made and fully customizable PowerPoint multimedia presentations built around lecture outlines with embedded maps, figures, and selected images from the textbook and detailed instructor notes on key points. Also available are maps and selected images in JPEG and PowerPoint formats; content for i>clicker, a classroom response system, in Microsoft Word and PowerPoint formats; the Instructor's Resource Manual in Microsoft Word format; and outline maps in PDF format for quizzing or handing out. All files are suitable for copying onto transparency acetates.

***Make History*—Free Documents, Maps, Images, and Web Sites.** *Make History* combines the best Web resources with hundreds of maps and images, to make it simple to find the source material you need. Browse the collection of thousands of resources by course or by topic, date, and type. Each item has been carefully chosen and helpfully annotated to make it easy to find exactly what you need. Available at **bedfordstmartins.com/makehistory**.

Videos and Multimedia. A wide assortment of videos and multimedia CD-ROMs on various topics in Western civilization is available to qualified adopters through your Bedford/St. Martin's sales representative.

Package and Save Your Students Money

For information on free packages and discounts up to 50%, visit **bedfordstmartins.com/hunt/catalog**, or contact your local Bedford/St. Martin's sales representative.

Bedford e-Book. The e-book for this title, described above, can be packaged with the print text at a discount.

***Sources of The Making of the West*, Fourth Edition.** This companion sourcebook provides written and visual sources to accompany each chapter of *The Making of the West.* Political, social, and cultural documents offer a variety of perspectives that complement the textbook and encourage students to make connections between narrative history and primary sources. Over thirty new documents and visual sources highlight the diversity of historical voices that shaped each period. To aid students in approaching and interpreting documents, each chapter contains an introduction, document headnotes, and questions for discussion. Available free when packaged with the print text.

***Sources of The Making of the West* e-Book.** The reader is also available as an e-book. When packaged with the print or electronic version of the textbook, it is available for free.

The Bedford Series in History and Culture. More than one hundred titles in this highly praised series combine first-rate scholarship, historical narrative, and important primary documents for undergraduate courses. Each book is brief, inexpensive, and focused on a specific topic or period. For a complete list of titles, visit **bedfordstmartins.com/history/series**. Package discounts are available.

Rand McNally Atlas of Western Civilization. This collection of over fifty full-color maps highlights social, political, and cross-cultural change and interaction from classical Greece and Rome to the postindustrial Western world. Each map is thoroughly indexed for fast reference. Available for $3.00 when packaged with the print text.

The Bedford Glossary for European History. This handy supplement for the survey course gives students historically contextualized definitions for hundreds of terms — from *Abbasids* to *Zionism* — that they will encounter in lectures, reading, and exams. Available free when packaged with the print text.

Trade Books. Titles published by sister companies Hill and Wang; Farrar, Straus and Giroux; Henry Holt and Company; St. Martin's Press; Picador; and Palgrave Macmillan are available at a 50% discount when packaged with Bedford/St. Martin's textbooks. For more information, visit **bedfordstmartins.com/tradeup**.

A Pocket Guide to Writing in History. This portable and affordable reference tool by Mary Lynn Rampolla provides reading, writing, and research advice useful to students in all history courses. Concise yet comprehensive advice on approaching typical history assignments, developing critical reading skills, writing effective history papers, conducting research, using and documenting sources, and avoiding plagiarism — enhanced with practical tips and examples throughout — have made this slim reference a best seller. Package discounts are available.

A Student's Guide to History. This complete guide to success in any history course provides the practical help students need to be effective. In addition to introducing students to the nature of the discipline, author Jules Benjamin teaches a wide range of skills, from preparing for exams to approaching common writing assignments, and explains the research and documentation process with plentiful examples. Package discounts are available.

The Social Dimension of Western Civilization. Combining current scholarship with classic pieces, this reader's forty-eight secondary sources, compiled by Richard M. Golden, hook students with the fascinating and often surprising details of how everyday Western people worked, ate, played, celebrated, worshipped, married, procreated, fought, persecuted, and died. Package discounts are available.

The West in the Wider World: Sources and Perspectives. Edited by Richard Lim and David Kammerling Smith, this first college reader to focus on the central historical question "How did the West become the West?" offers a wealth of written and visual source materials to reveal the influence of non-European regions on the origins and development of Western civilization. Package discounts are available.

Brief Contents

Contents

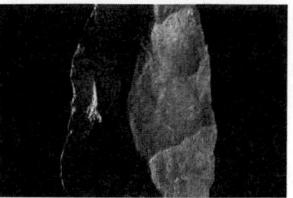

CHAPTER 1
Early Western Civilization

4000–1000 B.C.E. 3

CHAPTER 2
Near East Empires and the Reemergence of Civilization in Greece

1000–500 B.C.E. 37

CHAPTER 3 The Greek Golden Age

CHAPTER 4 From the Classical to the Hellenistic World

CHAPTER 5
The Rise of Rome and Its Republic

753–44 B.C.E. 139

CHAPTER 6
The Creation of the Roman Empire

44 B.C.E.–284 C.E. 171

CHAPTER 7

The Transformation of the Roman Empire

CHAPTER 8

The Heirs of Rome: Islam, Byzantium, and Europe

CHAPTER 9 From Centralization to Fragmentation

CHAPTER 10 Commercial Quickening and Religious Reform

CHAPTER 11

The Flowering of the Middle Ages

1150–1215 345

CHAPTER 12

The Medieval Synthesis—and Its Cracks

1215–1340 381

CHAPTER 13

Crisis and Renaissance

1340–1492 411

CHAPTER 14

Global Encounters and the Shock of the Reformation

1492–1560 451

CHAPTER 15

Wars of Religion and the Clash of Worldviews

CHAPTER 16

Absolutism, Constitutionalism, and the Search for Order

CHAPTER 17

The Atlantic System and Its Consequences

1700–1750 551

CHAPTER 18

The Promise of Enlightenment

1750–1789 587

CHAPTER 19

The Cataclysm of Revolution

1789–1799 619

CHAPTER 20

Napoleon and the Revolutionary Legacy

1800–1830 651

CHAPTER 21

Industrialization and Social Ferment

1830–1850 685

CHAPTER 22

Politics and Culture of the Nation-State

1850–1870 721

CHAPTER 23

Empire, Industry, and Everyday Life

1870–1890 759

CHAPTER 24

Modernity and the Road to War

1890–1914 797

CHAPTER 25

World War I and Its Aftermath

1914–1929 835

CHAPTER 26

The Great Depression and World War II

1929–1945 873

CHAPTER 27

The Cold War and the Remaking of Europe

1945–1960s 913

CHAPTER 28

Postindustrial Society and the End of the Cold War Order

1960s–1989 949

CHAPTER 29

A New Globalism

EPILOGUE

The Making of the West Continues in the Digital Age

Maps and Figures

Maps

Prologue

Chapter 1

Chapter 2

Chapter 3

Chapter 4

Chapter 5

Chapter 6

Chapter 7

Chapter 8

Chapter 9

Chapter 10

Chapter 11

Chapter 12

Chapter 13

Chapter 14

Chapter 15

Chapter 16

Chapter 17

Chapter 18

Chapter 19

Chapter 20

Chapter 21

Chapter 22

Chapter 23

Chapter 24

Chapter 25

Chapter 26

Chapter 27

Chapter 28

Chapter 29

Epilogue

Figures

Special Features

Documents

Contrasting Views

New Sources, New Perspectives

Terms of History

Seeing History

Taking Measure

To the Student

This guide to *The Making of the West* introduces the tools and features designed to help you study and do well in your Western Civilization course.

In-text tools help you focus on what's important as you read.

Read the **chapter outlines** to preview the topics and themes to come.

Read the **Chapter Focus** questions at the start of each chapter to think about the main ideas you should look for as you read.

Consult the **running glossary** for definitions of the bolded **Key Terms and People**.

Use the **Review Questions** at the end of each major section to check your understanding of key concepts.

Preview chapter events and keep track of time with **chapter timelines**.

CHAPTER 1

Early Western Civilization

4000–1000 B.C.E.

Kings in ancient Egypt believed that after they died the gods would judge them as rulers to decide their fate in the afterlife. In *Instructions for Merikare*, for example, written sometime around 2100–2000 B.C.E., an Egyptian king gives his son Merikare the following advice: "Make secure your place in the cemetery by being upright, by doing justice, upon which people's hearts rely. . . . When a man is buried and mourned, his deeds are piled up next to him as treasure." Being judged pure of heart led to an eternal reward; if the dead king reached the judges "without doing evil," he would be transformed so that he would "abide [in the afterlife] like a god, roaming [free] like the lords of time." A vital part of the justice demanded of an Egyptian king was to keep the country unified under a strong central authority to combat disorder.

Ordinary Egyptians, too, believed that they would win eternal rewards by living justly, which for them meant worshipping the gods and obeying the king and his officials. An illustrated guidebook containing instructions for mummies on how to travel safely in the underworld, com-

ancient Italy's many peoples, but Greek literature, art, and philosophy influenced Rome's culture most of all. This cross-cultural contact that so deeply influenced Rome was a kind of competition in innovation between equals, not "inferior" Romans imitating "superior" Greek culture. Like other ancient peoples, Romans often learned from their neighbors, but they adapted foreign traditions to their own purposes and forged their own cultural identity.

The kidnapping legend belongs to Rome's earliest history, when kings ruled (753–509 B.C.E.). Rome's most important history comes afterward, divided into two major periods of about five hundred years each—the republic and the empire. Under the republic (founded 509 B.C.E.), male voters elected their officials and passed laws (although an oligarchy of the social elite controlled politics). Under the empire, monarchs once again ruled. Rome's greatest expansion came during the republic. Romans' belief in a divine destiny fueled this tremendous growth. They believed that the gods wanted them to rule the world by military might and law and improve it through social and moral values. Their faith in a divine destiny is illustrated by the legend of the Sabine women, in which the earliest Romans used a religious festival as a cover for kidnapping. Their conviction that values should drive politics showed in their determination to persuade the Sabine women that loyalty and love would outweigh the crime of kidnapping that turned them into Romans.

Roman values emphasized family loyalty, selfless political and military service to the community, individual honor and public status, the importance

sonal ambition before the good of the state, they destroyed the republic.

CHAPTER FOCUS: How did traditional Roman values affect both the rise and the downfall of the Roman republic?

Roman Social and Religious Traditions

Roman social and religious traditions shaped the history of the Roman republic. Rome's citizens believed that eternal moral values connected them to one another and required them to honor the gods in return for divine support. Hierarchy affected all of life: people at all social levels were obligated to patrons or clients; in families, fathers dominated; in religion, people at all levels of society owed sacrifices, rituals, and prayers to the gods who protected the family and the state.

Roman Moral Values

Roman values defined relationships with other people and with the gods. Romans guided their lives by the ***mos maiorum*** ("the way of the elders"), or values handed down from their ancestors. The Romans

mos maiorum: Literally, "the way of the elders"; the set of Roman values handed down from the ancestors.

753 B.C.E.	509 B.C.E.	396 B.C.E.
Traditional date of Rome's founding as monarchy	Roman republic established	Defeat of Etruscan city of Veii; first great expansion of Roman territory

700 B.C.E. — 600 B.C.E. — 500 B.C.E. — 400 B.C.E.

509–287 B.C.E.	451–449 B.C.E.	387 B.C.E.
Struggle of the orders	Creation of Twelve Tables, Rome's first written law code	Gauls sack Rome

operate, the Greeks opened the way for the rise of a new power—the kingdom of Macedonia—that would end their independence in international politics. The Macedonian kings did not literally enslave the Greeks, as the Spartans did the helots, or usually even change their local governments. They did, however, abolish the city-states' freedom to control their foreign policy.

REVIEW QUESTION: How did daily life, philosophy, and the political situation change in Greece during the period 400–350 B.C.E.?

The Rise of Macedonia, 359–323 B.C.E.

The kingdom of Macedonia's rise to superpower status counts as one of the greatest surprises in an-

Special features introduce the way historians work and sharpen your critical-thinking skills.

Numerous **individual primary-source documents** offer direct experiences of the past and the opportunity to consider sources historians use.

DOCUMENT

The Rape and Suicide of Lucretia

This story explaining why the Roman elite expelled the monarchy in 509 B.C.E., thus opening the way to the republic, centers on female virtue and courage, as do other stories about significant political changes in early Roman history. The values attributed to Lucretia obviously reflect men's wishes for women's behavior, but it would be a mistake to assume that women could not

Tarquinius said he loved her, begging and threatening her in turn, trying everything to wear her down. When she wouldn't give in, even in the face of threats of murder, he added another intimidation. "After I've murdered you, I am going to put the naked corpse of a slave next to your body, and everybody will say that you were killed during a disgraceful adultery." This

came to have his fun, to my despair, but it will also be his sorrow—if you are real men." They pledged that they would catch him, and they tried to ease her sadness, saying that the soul did wrong, not the body, and where there were no bad intentions there could be no blame. "It is your responsibility to ensure that he gets what he deserves," she said; "I am blameless, but I will not free myself from punishment. No dishonorable woman shall

Contrasting Views provides three or four often conflicting eyewitness accounts of a central event, person, or development to foster critical-thinking skills.

CONTRASTING VIEWS

The Nature of Women and Marriage

Greeks believed that women had different natures from men and that both genders were capable of excellence, but in their own ways (Documents 1 and 2). Marriage was supposed to bring these natures together in a partnership of complementary strengths and obligations to each other (Document 3). Marriage contracts (Document 4), similar to modern prenuptial agreements, became common to define the partnership's terms.

praise of your excellence or blaming your faults.

Source: Thucydides, *History of the Peloponnesian War*, Book 2.45. Translation by Thomas R. Martin.

2. Melanippe Explains Why Men's Criticism of Women Is Baseless (late fifth century B.C.E.)

The Athenian playwright Euripides often por-

women make them flourish in every way. In this way women's role in religion is right and proper.

Therefore, should anyone put down women? Won't those men stop their empty fault-finding, the ones who strongly believe that all women should be blamed if a single one is found to be bad? I will make a distinction with the following argument: nothing is worse than a bad woman, but nothing is more surpassingly superior than a worthy one.

New Sources, New Perspectives shows how new evidence leads historians to fresh insights—and sometimes new interpretations.

NEW SOURCES, NEW PERSPECTIVES

Papyrus Discoveries and Menander's Comedies

Fourth-century B.C.E. Greek playwrights invented a kind of comedy, called New Comedy, that is today's most popular entertainment—the situation comedy (sitcom). They wrote comedies that concentrated on ... sonality types ... rocky course ... most plots. A... medians creat... bubble-headed ... cally servants, ... vealed by the...

These comic plays inspired many imitations, especially Roman comedies, which inspired William Shakespeare (1564–1616) in England and Molière (1622–1673) in France. Their comedies, in turn, led to to-

day we can read most of *The Girl from Samos* and parts of other plays. In this way, Menander's characters, stories, and jokes have come back from the dead.

Recovering plays from papyrus is difficult. The handwriting is often difficult to make out, there are no gaps between

Seeing History pairs two visuals with background information and probing questions to encourage analysis of images as historical evidence.

SEEING HISTORY

The Shift in Sculptural Style from Egypt to Greece

As Greek civilization revived during the Archaic Age (750–500 B.C.E.), artists took inspiration from the older civilizations of Egypt and the Near East, with sculpture in particular emerging as an important mode of cultural expression. Greek sculptors carved freestanding *kouros* ("young male") statues whose poses recalled the Egyptian style that remained unchanged for two thousand years: an erect posture, a striding leg, and a calm facial expression staring straight ahead. And yet important differences, both religious and stylistic, exist between Egyptian statuary and the Greek sculpture influenced by it.

ralism and idealization of the human body that would characterize the later Greek classical style (see the illustration on page 93). What evidence do you see of that in the differences between the two sculptures?

Question to Consider

■ **What cultural factors do you think could account for Egyptian statues keeping the same style over time, while the style of Greek statues changed?**

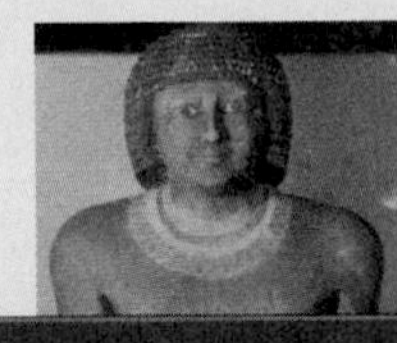

Terms of History identifies a term central to history writing and reveals how it is hotly debated.

TERMS OF HISTORY

Civilization

Our word *civilization* comes from the ancient Roman word *civilis*, which meant "suitable for a private citizen" and "behaving like an ordinary, down-to-earth person." Historians connect civilization especially with urbanization and the ways of life that characterize city existence. Also, the word *civilization* often expresses the judgment that being civilized means

and intellectual refinement. **6.** cities or populated areas in general, as opposed to unpopulated or wilderness areas. **7.** modern comforts and conveniences, as made possible by science and technology.

All these definitions imply that *civilization* means an "advanced" or "refined" way of life compared to a "savage" or

lization has become so accepted that it can even be used in nonhuman contexts, such as in the following startling comparison: "some communities of ants are more advanced in civilization than others."[1]

Sometimes *civilization* is used without much definitional content at all, as in the Random House dictionary's third definition. Can the word have any deep meaning if it can be used to mean "any type of culture, society, etc. of a specific place,

Taking Measure data reveals how individual facts add up to broad trends and introduces quantitative analysis skills.

TAKING MEASURE

European Emigration, 1870–1890

Country of Origin

Sweden, Norway, Finland, Denmark 7%; Italy 10%; France, Belgium, Netherlands, Switzerland 2%; Germany 18%; Austria 2%; Spain 5%; Portugal 2%; Russia 7%; British Isles 47%

Destinations

Asiatic Russia 6%; New Zealand 2%; Australia 5%; British West Indies 1%; Uruguay 2%; Brazil 6%; Argentina 10%; Canada 5%; United States 63%

The suffering caused by economic change and by political persecution motivated people from almost every European country to leave their homes for greater secu-

and the United States. Both countries were known for following the rule of law and for providing economic opportunity in urban as well as rural areas.

Question for Consideration

■ **Where did the majority of these migrants originate? What historical factors prompted them to leave their**

Art and maps help you to analyze images and think about events in their geographical context.

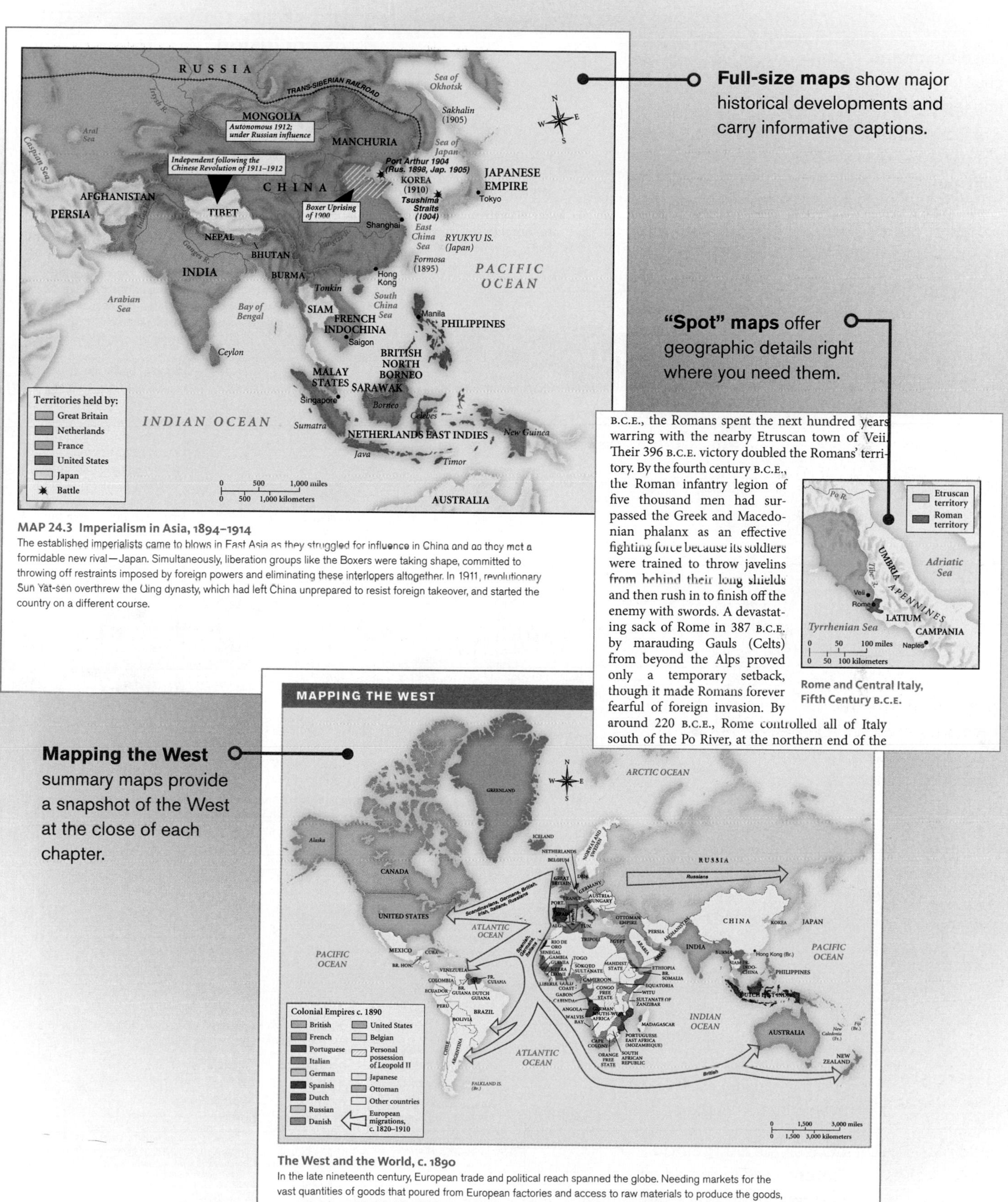

MAP 24.3 Imperialism in Asia, 1894–1914
The established imperialists came to blows in East Asia as they struggled for influence in China and as they met a formidable new rival—Japan. Simultaneously, liberation groups like the Boxers were taking shape, committed to throwing off restraints imposed by foreign powers and eliminating these interlopers altogether. In 1911, revolutionary Sun Yat-sen overthrew the Qing dynasty, which had left China unprepared to resist foreign takeover, and started the country on a different course.

B.C.E., the Romans spent the next hundred years warring with the nearby Etruscan town of Veii. Their 396 B.C.E. victory doubled the Romans' territory. By the fourth century B.C.E., the Roman infantry legion of five thousand men had surpassed the Greek and Macedonian phalanx as an effective fighting force because its soldiers were trained to throw javelins from behind their long shields and then rush in to finish off the enemy with swords. A devastating sack of Rome in 387 B.C.E. by marauding Gauls (Celts) from beyond the Alps proved only a temporary setback, though it made Romans forever fearful of foreign invasion. By around 220 B.C.E., Rome controlled all of Italy south of the Po River, at the northern end of the

Rome and Central Italy, Fifth Century B.C.E.

The West and the World, c. 1890
In the late nineteenth century, European trade and political reach spanned the globe. Needing markets for the vast quantities of goods that poured from European factories and access to raw materials to produce the goods, governments asserted that the Western way of life should be spread to the rest of the world and that resources would

End-of-chapter materials enable you to synthesize what you've learned and provide ideas for further research.

Read the **chapter conclusions** to review how the chapters' most important themes and topics fit together and learn how they connect to the next chapter.

Consult the **For Further Exploration** boxes at the end of each chapter, which guide you to additional primary-source materials and related Web resources.

Visit the **free online study guide**, which provides quizzes and activities to help you master the chapter material.

Test your knowledge of the important concepts and historical figures in the **Key Terms and People** grids by identifying each term and explaining its significance.

Answer the **Review Questions**, which repeat the chapter's end-of-section comprehension prompts.

Answer the analytical **Making Connections** questions, which will help you link ideas within or across chapters.

Review the **Important Events** chronologies and answer the chronology question to make sure you understand the sequence of and relationships between major events in the chapter.

Consult the **Suggested References** to find additional Web and print sources for further research.

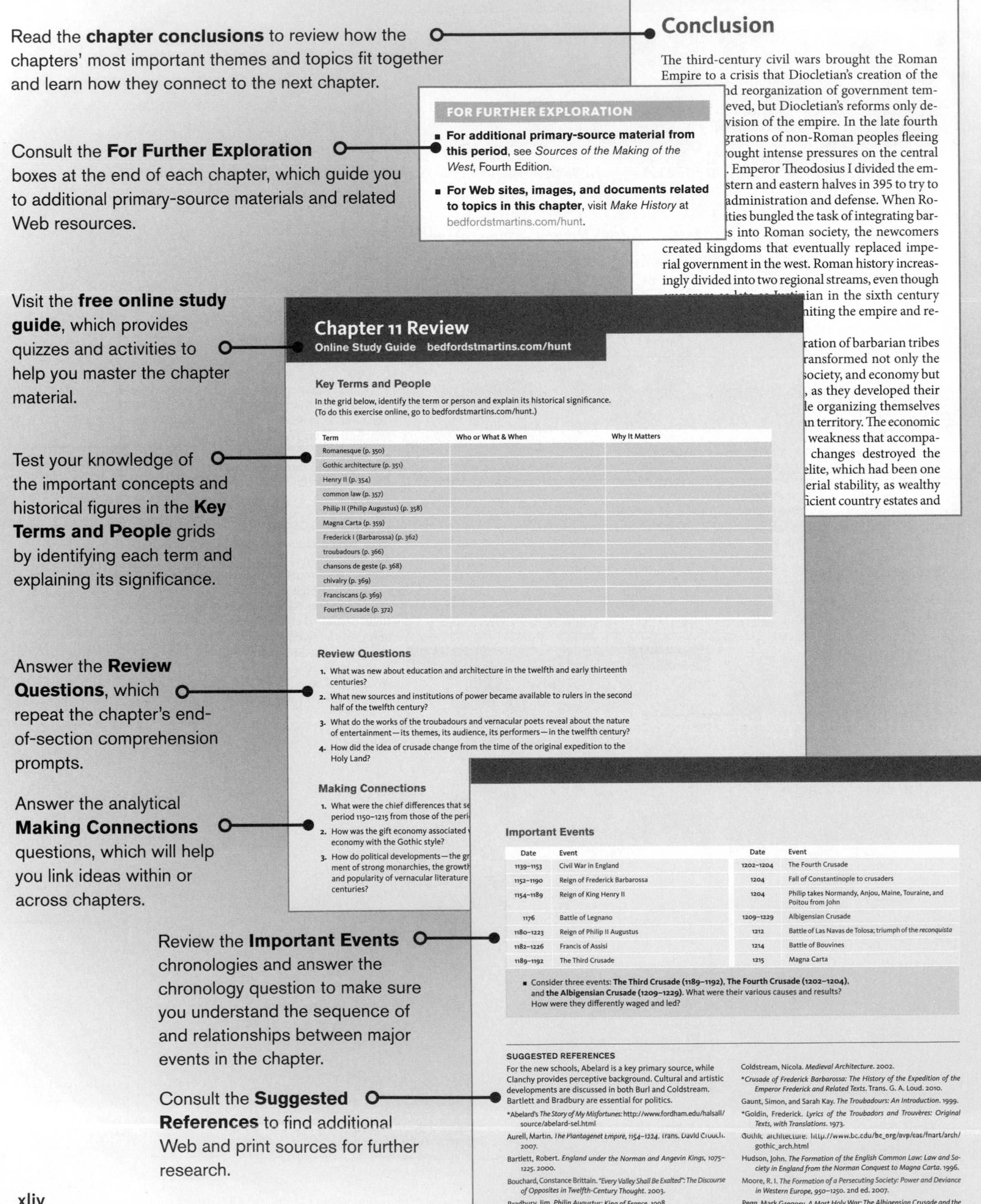

Conclusion

The third-century civil wars brought the Roman Empire to a crisis that Diocletian's creation of the
nd reorganization of government tem-
eved, but Diocletian's reforms only de-
vision of the empire. In the late fourth
grations of non-Roman peoples fleeing
ought intense pressures on the central
. Emperor Theodosius I divided the em-
stern and eastern halves in 395 to try to
administration and defense. When Ro-
ities bungled the task of integrating bar-
s into Roman society, the newcomers
created kingdoms that eventually replaced imperial government in the west. Roman history increasingly divided into two regional streams, even though
ian in the sixth century
niting the empire and re-
ration of barbarian tribes
ransformed not only the
society, and economy but
, as they developed their
le organizing themselves
n territory. The economic
weakness that accompa-
changes destroyed the
elite, which had been one
erial stability, as wealthy
ficient country estates and

FOR FURTHER EXPLORATION

- **For additional primary-source material from this period**, see *Sources of the Making of the West*, Fourth Edition.
- **For Web sites, images, and documents related to topics in this chapter**, visit *Make History* at bedfordstmartins.com/hunt.

Chapter 11 Review

Online Study Guide bedfordstmartins.com/hunt

Key Terms and People

In the grid below, identify the term or person and explain its historical significance. (To do this exercise online, go to bedfordstmartins.com/hunt.)

Term	Who or What & When	Why It Matters
Romanesque (p. 350)		
Gothic architecture (p. 351)		
Henry II (p. 354)		
common law (p. 357)		
Philip II (Philip Augustus) (p. 358)		
Magna Carta (p. 359)		
Frederick I (Barbarossa) (p. 362)		
troubadours (p. 366)		
chansons de geste (p. 368)		
chivalry (p. 369)		
Franciscans (p. 369)		
Fourth Crusade (p. 372)		

Review Questions

1. What was new about education and architecture in the twelfth and early thirteenth centuries?
2. What new sources and institutions of power became available to rulers in the second half of the twelfth century?
3. What do the works of the troubadours and vernacular poets reveal about the nature of entertainment—its themes, its audience, its performers—in the twelfth century?
4. How did the idea of crusade change from the time of the original expedition to the Holy Land?

Making Connections

1. What were the chief differences that se period 1150–1215 from those of the peri
2. How was the gift economy associated economy with the Gothic style?
3. How do political developments—the gr ment of strong monarchies, the growth and popularity of vernacular literature centuries?

Important Events

Date	Event	Date	Event
1139–1153	Civil War in England	1202–1204	The Fourth Crusade
1152–1190	Reign of Frederick Barbarossa	1204	Fall of Constantinople to crusaders
1154–1189	Reign of King Henry II	1204	Philip takes Normandy, Anjou, Maine, Touraine, and Poitou from John
1176	Battle of Legnano	1209–1229	Albigensian Crusade
1180–1223	Reign of Philip II Augustus	1212	Battle of Las Navas de Tolosa; triumph of the *reconquista*
1182–1226	Francis of Assisi	1214	Battle of Bouvines
1189–1192	The Third Crusade	1215	Magna Carta

- Consider three events: **The Third Crusade (1189–1192), The Fourth Crusade (1202–1204),** and **the Albigensian Crusade (1209–1229).** What were their various causes and results? How were they differently waged and led?

SUGGESTED REFERENCES

For the new schools, Abelard is a key primary source, while Clanchy provides perceptive background. Cultural and artistic developments are discussed in both Burl and Coldstream. Bartlett and Bradbury are essential for politics.

*Abelard's *The Story of My Misfortunes*: http://www.fordham.edu/halsall/source/abelard-sel.html

Aurell, Martin. *The Plantagenet Empire, 1154–1224*. Trans. David Crouch. 2007.

Bartlett, Robert. *England under the Norman and Angevin Kings, 1075–1225*. 2000.

Bouchard, Constance Brittain. *"Every Valley Shall Be Exalted": The Discourse of Opposites in Twelfth-Century Thought*. 2003.

Bradbury, Jim. *Philip Augustus: King of France*. 1998.

Burl, Aubrey. *Courts of Love, Castles of Hate: Troubadours and Trobairitz in Southern France, 1071–1321*. 2008.

Cheyette, Fredric L. *Ermengard of Narbonne and the World of the*

Coldstream, Nicola. *Medieval Architecture*. 2002.

**Crusade of Frederick Barbarossa: The History of the Expedition of the Emperor Frederick and Related Texts*. Trans. G. A. Loud. 2010.

Gaunt, Simon, and Sarah Kay. *The Troubadours: An Introduction*. 1999.

*Goldin, Frederick. *Lyrics of the Troubadors and Trouvères: Original Texts, with Translations*. 1973.

Gothic architecture: http://www.bc.edu/bc_org/avp/cas/fnart/arch/gothic_arch.html

Hudson, John. *The Formation of the English Common Law: Law and Society in England from the Norman Conquest to Magna Carta*. 1996.

Moore, R. I. *The Formation of a Persecuting Society: Power and Deviance in Western Europe, 950–1250*. 2nd ed. 2007.

Pegg, Mark Gregory. *A Most Holy War: The Albigensian Crusade and the Battle for Christendom*. 2008.

Robson, Michael. *The Franciscans in the Middle Ages*. 2006.

Stephensen, David. *Heavenly Vaults: From Romanesque to Gothic in Euro-*

Primary documents help you to understand history through the voices of those who lived it.

In each chapter of this textbook you will find many primary sources to broaden your understanding of the development of the West. Primary sources refer to firsthand, contemporary accounts or direct evidence about a particular topic. For example, speeches, letters, diaries, song lyrics, and newspaper articles are all primary sources that historians use to construct accounts of the past. Nonwritten materials such as maps, paintings, artifacts, and even architecture and music can also be primary sources. Both types of historical documents in this textbook — written and visual — provide a glimpse into the lives of the men and women who influenced or were influenced by the course of Western history.

To guide your interpretation of any source, you should begin by asking several basic questions, listed below, as starting points for observing, analyzing, and interpreting the past. Your answers should prompt further questions of your own.

1. **Who is the author?** Who wrote or created the material? What was his or her authority? (Personal? institutional?) Did the author have specialized knowledge or experience? If you are reading a written document, how would you describe the author's tone of voice? (Formal, personal, angry?)

2. **Who is the audience?** Who were the intended readers, listeners, or viewers? How does the intended audience affect the ways that the author presents ideas?

3. **What are the main ideas?** What are the main points that the author is trying to convey? Can you detect any underlying assumptions of values or attitudes? How does the form or medium affect the meaning of this document?

4. **In what context was the document created?** From when and where does the document originate? What was the interval between the initial problem or event and this document, which responded to it? Through what form or medium was the document communicated? (For example, a newspaper, a government record, an illustration.) What contemporary events or conditions might have affected the creation of the document?

5. **What's missing?** What's missing or cannot be learned from this source, and what might this omission reveal? Are there other sources that might fill in the gaps?

Now consider these questions as you read "Columbus Describes His First Voyage (1493)," the document on the next page. Compare your answers to the sample observations provided.

DOCUMENT

Columbus Describes His First Voyage (1493)

In this famous letter to Raphael Sanchez, treasurer to his patrons, Ferdinand and Isabella, Columbus recounts his initial journey to the Bahamas, Cuba, and Hispaniola (today Haiti and the Dominican Republic), and tells of his achievements. This passage reflects the first contact between native Americans and Europeans; already the themes of trade, subjugation, gold, and conversion emerge in Columbus's own words.

Indians would give whatever the seller required; . . . Thus they bartered, like idiots, cotton and gold for fragments of bows, glasses, bottles, and jars; which I forbad as being unjust, and myself gave them many beautiful and acceptable articles which I had brought with me, taking nothing from them in return; I did this in order that I might the more easily conciliate them, that they might be led to become Christians, and be inclined to entertain a regard for the King and Queen, our Princes and all Spaniards, and that I might induce them to take an interest in seeking out, and collecting, and delivering to us such things as they possessed in abundance, but which we greatly needed. They practise no kind of idolatry, but have a firm belief that all strength and power, and indeed all good things, are in heaven, and that I had descended from thence with these ships and sailors, and under this impression was I received after they had thrown aside their fears. Nor are they slow or stupid, but of very clear understanding; and those men who have crossed to the neighbouring islands give an admirable description of everything they observed; but they never saw any people clothed, nor any ships like ours. On my arrival at that sea, I had taken some Indians by force from the first island that I came to, in order that they might learn our language, and communicate to us what they know respecting the country; which plan succeeded excellently, and was a great advantage to us, for in a short time, either by gestures and signs, or by words, we were enabled to understand each other. These men are still travelling with me, and although they have been with us now a long time, they continue to entertain the idea that I have descended from heaven.

Source: Christopher Columbus, *Four Voyages to the New World*, trans. R. H. Major (New York: Corinth Books, 1961), 8–9.

Question to Consider

- **In what ways were Columbus's early impressions of native Americans both respectful and condescending?**

1. **Who is the author?** The title and headnote that precede each document contain information about the authorship and date of its creation. In this case, the Italian explorer Christopher Columbus is the author. His letter describes events in which he was both an eyewitness and a participant.
2. **Who is the audience?** Columbus sent the letter to Raphael Sanchez, treasurer to Ferdinand and Isabella — someone who Columbus knew would be keenly interested in the fate of his patrons' investment. Because the letter was also a public document written to a crown official, Columbus would have expected a wider audience beyond Sanchez. How might his letter have differed had it been written to a friend?
3. **What are the main ideas?** In this segment, Columbus describes his encounter with the native people. He speaks of his desire to establish good relations by treating them fairly, and he offers his impressions of their intelligence and naiveté — characteristics he implies will prove useful to Europeans. He also expresses an interest in converting them to Christianity and making them loyal subjects of the crown.
4. **In what context was the document created?** Columbus wrote the letter in 1493, within six months of his first voyage. He would have been eager to announce the success of his endeavor.
5. **What's missing?** Columbus's letter provides just one view of the encounter. We do not have a corresponding account from the native Americans' perspective nor from anyone else traveling with Columbus. With no corroborating evidence, how reliable is this description?

Note: You can use these same questions to analyze visual images. Start by determining who created the image — whether it's a painting, photograph, sculpture, map, or artifact — and when it was made. Then consider the audience for whom the artist might have intended the work and how viewers might have reacted. Consult the text for information about the time period, and look for visual cues such as color, artistic style, and use of space to determine the central idea of the work. As you read, consult the captions in this book to help you evaluate the images and to ask more questions of your own.

Authors' Note

The B.C.E./C.E. Dating System

"When were you born?" "What year is it?" We customarily answer questions like these with a number, such as "1987" or "2012." Our replies are usually automatic, taking for granted the numerous assumptions Westerners make about how dates indicate chronology. But to what do numbers such as 1987 and 2012 actually refer? In this book the numbers used to specify dates follow a recent revision of the system most common in the Western secular world. This system reckons the dates of solar years by counting backward and forward from the traditional date of the birth of Jesus Christ, over two thousand years ago.

Using this method, numbers followed by the abbreviation B.C.E., standing for "before the common era" (or, as some would say, "before the Christian era"), indicate the number of years counting backward from the assumed date of the birth of Jesus Christ. B.C.E. therefore indicates the same chronology marked by the traditional abbreviation B.C. ("before Christ"). The larger the number following B.C.E. (or B.C.), the earlier in history is the year to which it refers. The date 431 B.C.E., for example, refers to a year 431 years before the birth of Jesus and therefore comes earlier in time than the dates 430 B.C.E., 429 B.C.E., and so on. The same calculation applies to numbering other time intervals calculated on the decimal system: those of ten years (a decade), of one hundred years (a century), and of one thousand years (a millennium). For example, the decade of the 440s B.C.E. (449 B.C.E. to 440 B.C.E.) is earlier than the decade of the 430s B.C.E. (439 B.C.E. to 430 B.C.E.). "Fifth century B.C.E." refers to the fifth period of 100 years reckoning backward from the birth of Jesus and covers the years 500 B.C.E. to 401 B.C.E. It is earlier in history than the fourth century B.C.E. (400 B.C.E. to 301 B.C.E.), which followed the fifth century B.C.E. Because this system has no year "zero," the first century B.C.E. covers the years 100 B.C.E. to 1 B.C.E. Dating millennia works similarly: the second millennium B.C.E. refers to the years 2000 B.C.E. to 1001 B.C.E., the third millennium to the years 3000 B.C.E. to 2001 B.C.E., and so on.

To indicate years counted forward from the traditional date of Jesus's birth, numbers are followed by the abbreviation C.E., standing for "of the common era" (or "of the Christian era"). C.E. therefore indicates the same chronology marked by the traditional abbreviation A.D., which stands for the Latin phrase *anno Domini* ("in the year of the Lord"). A.D. properly comes before the date being marked. The date A.D. 1492, for example, translates as "in the year of the Lord 1492," meaning 1492 years after the birth of Jesus. Under the B.C.E./C.E. system, this date would be written as 1492 C.E. For dating centuries, the term "first century C.E." refers to the period from 1 C.E. to 100 C.E. (which is the same period as A.D. 1 to A.D. 100). For dates C.E., the smaller the number, the earlier the date in history. The fourth century C.E. (301 C.E. to 400 C.E.) comes before the fifth century C.E. (401 C.E. to 500 C.E.). The year 312 C.E. is a date in the early fourth century C.E., while 395 C.E. is a date late in the same century. When numbers are given without either B.C.E. or C.E., they are presumed to be dates C.E. For example, the term *eighteenth century* with no abbreviation accompanying it refers to the years 1701 C.E. to 1800 C.E.

No standard system of numbering years, such as B.C.E./C.E., existed in antiquity. Different people in different places identified years with varying names and numbers. Consequently, it was difficult to match up the years in any particular local system with those in a different system. Each city of ancient Greece, for example, had its own method for keeping track of the years. The ancient Greek historian Thucydides, therefore, faced a problem in presenting a chronology for the famous Peloponnesian War between Athens and Sparta, which began (by our reckoning) in 431 B.C.E. To try to explain to as many of his readers as possible the date the war had begun, he described its first year by three different local systems: "the year when Chrysis was in the forty-eighth year of her priesthood at Argos, and Aenesias was overseer at Sparta, and Pythodorus was magistrate at Athens."

A Catholic monk named Dionysius, who lived in Rome in the sixth century C.E., invented the system of reckoning dates forward from the birth of Jesus. Calling himself *Exiguus* (Latin for "the little" or "the small") as a mark of humility, he placed

Jesus's birth 754 years after the foundation of ancient Rome. Others then and now believe his date for Jesus's birth was in fact several years too late. Many scholars today calculate that Jesus was born in what would be 4 B.C.E. according to Dionysius's system, although a date a year or so earlier also seems possible.

Counting backward from the supposed date of Jesus's birth to indicate dates earlier than that event represented a natural complement to reckoning forward for dates after it. The English historian and theologian Bede in the early eighth century was the first to use both forward and backward reckoning from the birth of Jesus in a historical work, and this system gradually gained wider acceptance because it provided a basis for standardizing the many local calendars used in the Western Christian world. Nevertheless, B.C. and A.D. were not used together as a system until the end of the eighteenth century. B.C.E. and C.E. became common in the late twentieth century.

The system of numbering years from the birth of Jesus is far from the only one in use today. The Jewish calendar of years, for example, counts forward from the date given to the creation of the world, which would be calculated as 3761 B.C.E. under the B.C.E./C.E. system. Under this system, years are designated A.M., an abbreviation of the Latin *anno mundi*, "in the year of the world." The Islamic calendar counts forward from the date of the prophet Muhammad's flight from Mecca, called the Hijra, in what is the year 622 C.E. The abbreviation A.H. (standing for the Latin phrase *anno Hegirae*, "in the year of the Hijra") indicates dates calculated by this system. Anthropology commonly reckons distant dates as "before the present" (abbreviated B.P.).

History is often defined as the study of change over time; hence the importance of dates for the historian. But just as historians argue over which dates are most significant, they disagree over which dating system to follow. Their debate reveals perhaps the most enduring fact about history—its vitality.

FOURTH EDITION

The Making of the West

PEOPLES AND CULTURES

Prologue

The Beginnings of Human Society

To c. 4000 B.C.E.

In 1997, archaeologists working in the East African nation of Ethiopia discovered fossilized skulls that dated from at least 160,000 years ago. These bones are the oldest remains ever found from the species *Homo sapiens* ("wise human being")—people whose brains and appearances were similar though not identical to ours. This discovery excited scientists because it supported the "out of Africa" theory about human origins, which claims that *Homo sapiens* first appeared in Africa perhaps as early as two hundred thousand years ago and then spread from that continent all over the world. In contrast, recent discoveries of human remains in Asia have reignited debate over the "out of Africa" theory, bringing back the once-discarded idea that human beings arose independently in different parts of the earth.

The innovations that early human beings made in technology, trade, religion, and social organization formed the basis of our modern way of life. They also led to the emergence of war. As the discoveries of the skulls in Ethiopia and the human remains in Asia show, researchers continue to find evidence that adds to our knowledge about the past and therefore our thinking about how the past relates to the present. This process of discovery always involves questioning and debate. When we study history, therefore, we have to expect uncertainty and disagreements, especially about how to interpret past events, what those events meant then, and what they mean today.

Stone Age Handaxe
Archaeologists regard stone cutting tools like this one, called a handaxe, as the first great invention. Stone Age peoples made handaxes for hundreds of thousands of years, probably using hammers made from bone or wood to chip off flakes from the stone to create knifelike edges for cutting and scraping. This sharp tool would have been especially useful for butchering animals, such as the hippopotamuses that African hunter-gatherers killed for meat. Shown here at its full size (about seven and three-quarter inches top to bottom), this handaxe was, like all others, shaped to fit the human palm; users probably wrapped the tool in a piece of hide to protect their hands from cuts. *(© The Trustees of The British Museum/Art Resource, NY.)*

Scientists studying fossilized bones and those studying human mitochondrial DNA (the type inherited from the mother) have shown that it took millions of years for the earliest human species to emerge. According to the "out of Africa" theory, human beings exactly like us first developed in sub-Saharan Africa more than fifty thousand years ago. Starting about forty-five thousand years ago, those human beings began moving out of Africa, first into the Near East[1] and then into Europe and Asia.

This migration took place in the period commonly called the Stone Age, during which human beings made their most durable tools from stones, before they learned to work metals. Human society began in the Stone Age, which archaeologists divide into two parts to mark the greatest turning point in human history: the invention of agriculture and the domestication of animals and the enormous changes in human society that these innovations brought. The first part, the **Paleolithic** ("Old Stone") **Age**, dates from about 200,000 B.C.E. to about 10,000 B.C.E. The second part, the **Neolithic** ("New Stone") **Age**, dates from about 10,000 B.C.E. to about 4000 B.C.E.

Archaeology—the study of physical evidence from the past—is our only source of information about the Stone Age; there are no documents to inform us about the lives of early human beings because people did not invent writing until about 4000–3000 B.C.E. Historians sometimes label the time before the invention of writing *prehistory*, because *history* traditionally means having written sources about the past. Historians also usually do not apply the word *civilization* to human society in the Stone Age because people then had not yet begun to live in cities or form **political states** (people living in a defined territory and organized under a central authority). The first cities and political states emerged about the same time as writing, as we will see in Chapter 1.

It was in the Neolithic Age that, instead of only hunting and gathering food in the wild, people learned how to produce their own food by raising crops and domesticating animals. The technological innovations of agriculture and animal husbandry produced lasting changes in human society, especially in strengthening social hierarchies, supporting gender inequality, and encouraging war for conquest. Historians continue to debate what was positive and what was negative in the consequences, intentional and unintentional, that this turning point produced for human society.

CHAPTER FOCUS What were the positive and the negative consequences for human life when people learned how to produce their food by farming instead of only hunting and gathering food in the wild?

The Paleolithic Age, 200,000–10,000 B.C.E.

Human society began during the Paleolithic Age and was organized to suit a mobile way of life because human beings in this early period roamed around in small groups to hunt and gather food in the wild. The most notable feature of early Paleo-

[1]The term *Near East*, like *Middle East*, has undergone several changes in meaning over time. Both terms reflect the geographical point of view of Europeans. Today, the term *Middle East*, more commonly employed in politics and journalism than in history, usually refers to the area encompassing the Arabic-speaking countries of the eastern Mediterranean region as well as Israel, Iran, Turkey, Cyprus, and much of North Africa. Historians, by contrast, generally use the term *ancient Near East* to designate Anatolia (often called Asia Minor, today occupied by the Asian portion of Turkey), Cyprus, the lands around the eastern end of the Mediterranean, the Arabian peninsula, Mesopotamia (the lands north of the Persian Gulf, today Iraq and Iran), and Egypt. In this book we will observe the common usage of the term *Near East* to mean Egypt and southwestern Asia.

Paleolithic Age: The "Old Stone" Age, dating from around 200,000 to 10,000 B.C.E.

Neolithic Age: The "New Stone" Age, dating from around 10,000 to 4000 B.C.E.

political states: People living in a defined territory with boundaries and organized under a system of government with powerful officials, leaders, and judges.

50,000–45,000 B.C.E. *Homo sapiens sapiens* migrate from Africa into southwest Asia and Europe

8000 B.C.E. Walled settlement at Jericho (in modern Israel)

200,000 B.C.E. — 50,000 B.C.E. — 10,000 B.C.E. — 0

200,000–160,000 B.C.E. Beginning of Paleolithic ("Old Stone") Age

10,000–8000 B.C.E. Neolithic ("New Stone") Revolution in the Fertile Crescent and the Sahara

7000–5500 B.C.E. Farming community thrives at Çatalhöyük (in modern Turkey)

lithic society was that the group probably made important decisions in common, with all adult men and women having a more or less equal say. Over time, however, Paleolithic peoples created a more complex social organization as they developed trade to acquire goods from long distances, technology such as fire for heat and cooking, religious beliefs to express their understanding of the divine and of the mystery of death, and social hierarchies to denote differences in status.

The Life of Hunter-Gatherers

The characteristics of human society in the Paleolithic period originally reflected the conditions of life for **hunter-gatherers,** the term historians use for people who roamed all their lives, hunting wild animals and foraging edible plants. They never settled permanently in one place. Although they knew a great deal about how to survive in the natural environment, they had not yet learned to produce their own food by growing crops and raising animals. Instead, they hunted game for meat; fished in lakes and rivers; collected shellfish along the shore; and gathered edible plants, fruits, and nuts.

Archaeology reveals that a change in weather patterns apparently motivated hunter-gatherers of the modern type of human being, ***Homo sapiens sapiens***, to begin wandering out of Africa around 50,000–45,000 B.C.E. (*Homo sapiens sapiens* means "wise, wise human being"; the repeated *wise* is meant to distinguish this later type from the earlier and slightly different type, called simply *Homo sapiens.*) Long periods without rain drove game animals into southwestern Asia and then Europe to find water, and at least some of the mobile human populations who hunted them in African lands followed this moving food into new continents. There is no evidence to explain why some hunter-gatherers left Africa in the Paleolithic period while others stayed behind.

When *Homo sapiens sapiens* hunter-gatherers reached Europe and Asia, they met earlier types of human beings who had already migrated out of Africa, such as the heavy-browed, squat-bodied Neanderthal type (named after the Neander valley in Germany, where their fossil remains were first found; their body type is often used to represent "cavemen" in popular art). Eventually, after walking across then-existent land bridges to reach the Americas and Australia, *Homo sapiens sapiens* replaced all earlier types of people around the globe.

Archaeological excavations of hunter-gatherers' campsites tell us about their lives on the move, showing that over time they invented new forms of tools, weapons, and jewelry and began burying their dead with special care. Anthropologists have also reconstructed the lives of ancient hunter-gatherers from comparative study of the few groups who lived on as hunter-gatherers into modern times, such as the !Kung San of southern Africa's Kalahari Desert, the Aborigines in Australia, and the Coahuiltecans in the American Southwest. These two categories of evidence suggest that Paleolithic hunter-gatherers banded together in groups numbering around twenty or thirty to hunt and gather food that they shared among themselves. Their life expectancy was about twenty-five to thirty years for both men and women. Since they had not learned to domesticate animals or to make wheels for carts, they walked everywhere. Because women of childbearing age had to carry and nurse their babies, it was difficult for them to roam long distances. They and the younger children therefore gathered plants, fruits, and nuts close to camp and caught small animals such as frogs and rabbits. The plant food that they gathered provided the majority of the group's diet. Men did most of the hunting of large animals, which frequently took them far from camp to kill prey at close range with rocks and spears; butchered hippopotamus bones found near the skulls in Ethiopia show that early humans hunted these dangerous animals. Women probably participated in hunts when the group used nets to catch wild animals.

Each band of Paleolithic hunter-gatherers moved around searching for food, usually ranging over an area that averaged roughly sixty miles across in any one direction. They tended not to intrude on other bands' areas, but there were no set boundaries or central settlements to identify a band's territory. To judge from battles observed between surviving tribes of hunter-gatherers, conflicts between Paleolithic bands were more skirmishes than total battles, and there was as much display as serious fighting; for ancient hunter-gatherers, there was nothing to take from another group that one's own group did not already possess, except other people. Hunter-gatherers' constant walking, bending, and lifting kept them in fine physical shape, but they counted on their knowledge as much as their strength for both hunting and the occasional battle. Most important, they planned ahead for cooperative hunts at favorite spots, such as river crossings or lakes with shallow banks, where experience taught they were

---

hunter-gatherers: Human beings who roam to hunt and gather food in the wild and do not live in permanent, settled communities.

***Homo sapiens sapiens*:** The scientific name (in Latin) of the type of early human being identical to people today; it means "wise, wise human being."

Building with Bones
This reconstruction shows how Paleolithic people built shelters using bones from mammoths they hunted. Dating from about fifteen thousand years ago and found in Ukraine in east-central Europe, this closely fitted structure reveals how hunter-gatherers made the maximum use of the bodies of dead animals. *(C. M. Dixon / Ancient Art & Architecture Collection, Ltd.)*

likely to find herds of large animals fording the stream and drinking water.

Paleolithic hunter-gatherers also used their knowledge to establish camps year after year in particularly good spots for gathering plants. They took shelter from the weather in caves or temporary dwellings made from branches and animal skins. On occasion, they built sturdier shelters, such as the dome-like hut found in Ukraine that was constructed from the bones of mammoths. They never built permanent homes, however; they had to roam to survive.

Hunter-gatherers probably lived originally in egalitarian societies, meaning that all adults enjoyed a general equality in making decisions for the group. This cooperation reflected the fact that men and women both worked hard to provide food for the group, even if they tended to divide this labor by gender, with men doing more hunting and women more gathering. At some point, however, differences in social status began to emerge. Most likely, age was the first basis of social status: older people of both genders won prestige and probably positions of leadership because of the wisdom gained from long experience of life in an era when most people died of illness or accidents before they were thirty years old. Women past childbearing age who helped out in multiple ways and strong, clever men who hunted dangerous animals also likely held high status.

Innovations in Paleolithic Life

Paleolithic people made changes in their lives that turned out to be important for the later development of civilization. In technology, learning how to create ever sharper edges and points in stone, bone, and wood led to better weapons for hunting and tools for digging out roots and making clothes from animal skins, thereby increasing the chances for survival. The discovery of how to make fire was especially important because Paleolithic people had to endure the cold of extended ice ages, when the northern European glaciers moved much farther south than usual. The coldest part of the most recent

Bison Painting in the Cave at Lascaux
Stone Age people painted these bison (European bison) on the rock walls of a large cave at Lascaux in central France around 15,000 B.C.E., to judge from radiocarbon dating of charcoal found on the floor. Using black, red, yellow, and white pigments, the artists made the deep cave into an art gallery by filling it with pictures not only of these bison but also of horses, deer, bears, and wooly rhinoceroses. Some scholars have suggested that the scenes symbolized the importance of hunting to the people who painted them, but this guess seems wrong because the bones from butchered animals found in the cave are 90 percent reindeer, while no reindeer pictures exist in the cave. *(Caves of Lascaux, Dordogne, France / The Bridgeman Art Library International.)*

ice age started about twenty thousand years ago and created a harsh climate in much of Europe for nearly ten thousand years. Hunter-gatherers' knowledge of how to control fire led to the invention of cooking. This was a crucial innovation because it turned indigestible plants, such as grains, into edible and nutritious food.

Long-distance trade also began in the Stone Age. When hunter-gatherers encountered other bands, they exchanged things they had made, such as blades and jewelry, as well as natural objects such as flint or seashells. Trade could move valuable objects great distances: for example, ocean shells worn as jewelry made their way far inland through repeated swaps.

Archaeological discoveries suggest that Paleolithic hunter-gatherers developed religious beliefs, a crucial factor in the evolution of human society, and reveal that ancient peoples saw religion as necessary for living a successful and just life. Some late Paleolithic cave paintings found in Spain and France hint at hunter-gatherers' religious ideas as well as display their artistic ability. Using strong, dark lines and earthy colors, Paleolithic artists painted on the walls of caves that were set aside as special places, not used as day-to-day shelters. The paintings, which primarily depict large animals, suggest that these powerful beasts played a significant role in the religion of Paleolithic hunter-gatherers. Still, there remains a great deal we do not yet understand about their beliefs, such as the meaning of the dots, rectangles, and hands that they often drew beside their paintings of animals.

Important evidence for early religious beliefs also comes from the discovery of specially shaped female figurines at late Paleolithic sites all over Europe. Modern archaeologists call these statuettes of women with extra-large breasts, abdomens, buttocks, and thighs Venus figurines, after the Roman goddess of sexual love (see the illustration on the right). The oversized features of these sculptures suggest that the people who made them had a special set of beliefs and rituals regarding fertility and birth.

Anthropologists study Paleolithic burial sites to find clues to what these early peoples believed about the mystery of death and the possibility of an afterlife. The early skulls found in Ethiopia have missing jaws and marks in the bone, hints that the living cut away the flesh from the heads of the dead to prepare their remains for a new future after burial (and not for cannibalism, as some have said). More evidence for Paleolithic ideas on fundamental questions about life and death come from the care with which corpses were decorated with red paint, flowers, and seashells. Some researchers conclude that these careful preparations for burial mean that early

Prehistoric Venus Figurine

This limestone statuette, four and a half inches high, was found at Willendorf, in Austria. Carved in the later Paleolithic period and originally colored red, it probably was meant to have symbolic power expressing the importance of women's fertility. The emphasis on the woman's breasts, hips, and pubic area have led scholars to call such statuettes Venus figurines, after the Roman goddess of love and sex; archaeologists have uncovered many of them all across Europe. Since no written records exist to explain the significance of such figurines' hairstyle, obesity, and prominent sexual characteristics, we can only speculate about the complex meanings that early peoples attributed to them. How would you explain this figurine's appearance? *(Museum of Natural History, Vienna, Austria, photo SuperStock.)*

human beings already had complex religious ideas about what happened to them after they died.

Burials reveal more than religious beliefs; they also show that, by late Paleolithic times, hunter-gatherer society had begun to mark significant differences in status among people. Those who were buried with valuable items such as weapons, tools, animal figurines, ivory beads, and bracelets likely had special social standing. These object-rich burials reveal that late Paleolithic groups had begun organizing their society according to a **hierarchy**, a ranking system identifying certain people as having more status and authority than others. This is the earliest evidence for social differentiation, the marking of certain people as more respected, richer, or more powerful than others in their society.

Despite their varied status, knowledge, and technological skill, prehistoric hunter-gatherers lived precarious lives dominated by the relentless search for something to eat. Survival was a risky business. The groups that survived were those that cooperated in finding food and shelter; profited from innovations such as fire, tools, and trade; and taught their children the knowledge, beliefs, and social traditions that had helped them endure in a harsh world.

REVIEW QUESTION What were the most important activities, skills, and beliefs that helped Paleolithic hunter-gatherers survive?

hierarchy: The system of ranking people in society according to their status and authority.

The Neolithic Age, 10,000–4000 B.C.E.

By around 10,000–8000 B.C.E., people in the Near East had opened the way to a different kind of society by learning to grow their own food and build permanent farming settlements that housed larger populations than the twenty- to thirty-member bands of hunter-gatherers. In this new society, dominance by men replaced the general equality in status and decision making between men and women that likely existed in earlier times. In addition, war became a prominent part of human life.

The inventions of agriculture and permanent settlements in the Neolithic Age occurred over a long time, but once established they changed forever the way human beings lived; eventually, these changes would make civilization possible. Daily life as we know it still depends on farming and the domestication of animals, developments that began at the beginning of the Neolithic Age. These radical innovations in food acquisition caused such fundamental changes in human life that they are called the **Neolithic Revolution**.

Neolithic Revolution: The invention of agriculture, the domestication of animals, and the consequent changes in human society that occurred about 10,000–8,000 B.C.E. in the Near East.

The Neolithic Revolution and the Production of Food

Revolutionary change took place in human history in the Neolithic Age when hunter-gatherers learned to sow and harvest crops and to raise animals for food. Exactly how they gained this knowledge remains mysterious. Recent archaeological research, however, indicates that it took thousands of years for people to develop agriculture. The process began in the part of the Near East that we call the Fertile Crescent, whose hilly regions happened to have the right combination of soil, water, climate, and wild mammals for the invention of farming and the domestication of animals. The Fertile Crescent stretches in an arc, or crescent, along the foothills and lowlands that run northward from modern Israel across southeastern Turkey and Syria and then turn in a southeasterly direction down to the plain of the lower stretches of the Tigris and Euphrates Rivers in what is now southern Iraq (Map 1).

The slow trial-and-error process through which former hunter-gatherers developed agriculture had complex origins. Recent archaeological excavations at Göbekli Tepe, a site in southeastern Turkey whose name means "stomach-shaped little hill," have revealed stone-lined rooms in the earth decorated with stone pillars eight or more feet tall that are carved to depict boars, bears, birds, snakes, and other animals. Freestanding sculptures of animals seem to have been placed atop the rooms' walls. Radiocarbon dating suggests these rooms were built around 9300 B.C.E., which would make them contemporary

Stone Structures in the Neolithic Revolution
These ruins of stone-built structures from around 9300 B.C.E., many decorated with incised drawings of animals, were found at Göbekli Tepe in Turkey. Since their construction would have required many workers for a long time, archaeologists speculate that people's desire to build these large structures led to them developing agriculture so they could stay in one place long enough to accomplish their goal. *(Marcia Chambers/© dbimages/Alamy.)*

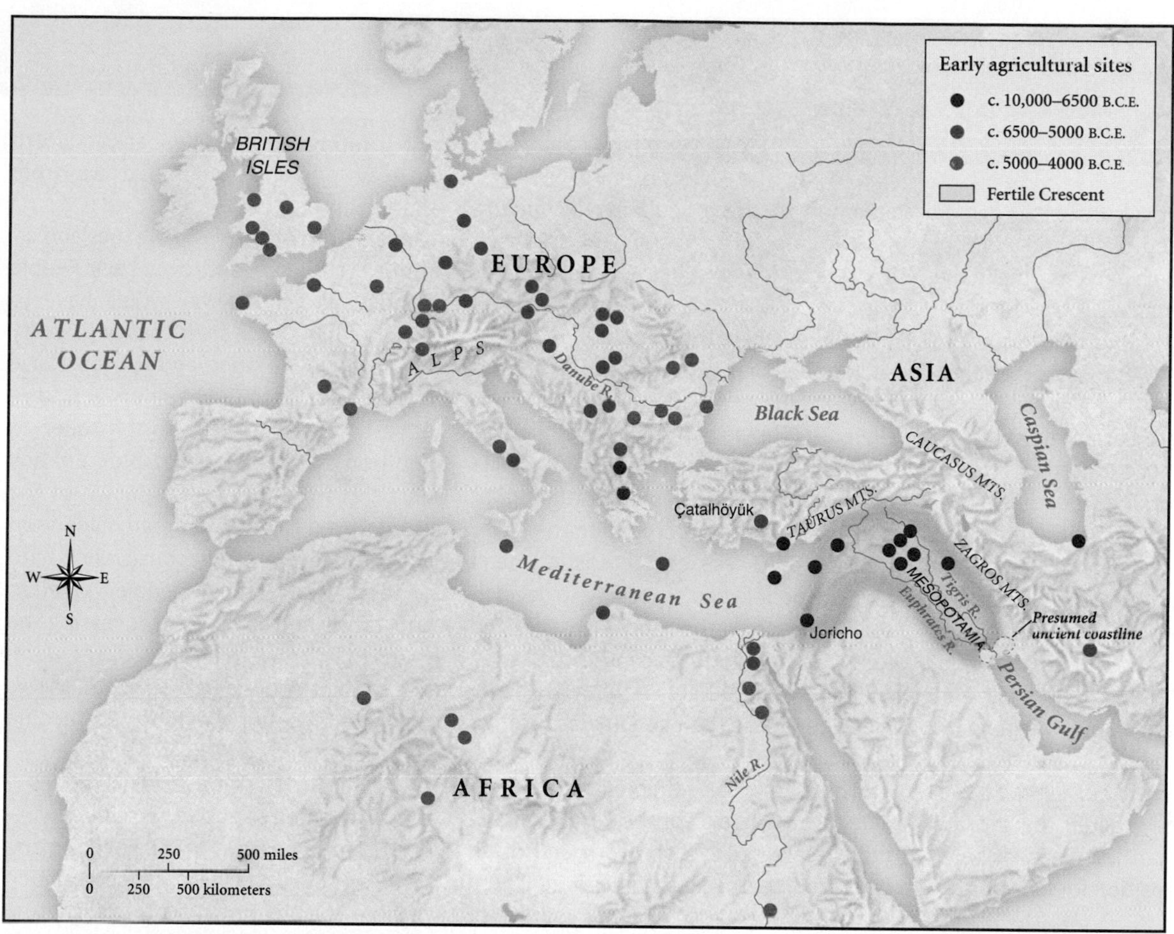

MAP 1 The Development of Agriculture
From around 10,000 to 8000 B.C.E., people learned to plant seeds to grow nourishing plants and to domesticate animals in the Fertile Crescent, the foothills of the semicircle of mountains that curved up and around from the eastern end of the Mediterranean down to Mesopotamia, where reliable rainfall and moderate temperatures prevailed. At about the same time, domestication of animals took place in the grasslands then flourishing in the Sahara region of Africa. The invention of irrigation in the Fertile Crescent allowed farmers to grow lush crops in the region's arid plains, providing resources that eventually spurred the emergence of the first large cities by about 4000 B.C.E.

with the first attested agriculture or perhaps even earlier. Some scholars speculate that hunter-gatherers built these monuments to express their religious beliefs. According to this theory, since a large group had to remain in one place for a long time to complete such elaborate structures and art, they had to develop agriculture to feed themselves. In this way, farming was a consequence of this new, concrete expression of religious ideas.

Only further archaeological research can reveal whether Stone Age religious activity was a cause of the Neolithic Revolution or vice versa. What seems certain is that climate change contributed significantly to the Neolithic Revolution. About ten to twelve thousand years ago, the long-term weather pattern in the Fertile Crescent became milder and rainier than it had been during the ice age that had just ended. This change promoted the growth of abundant fields of wild cereal grains. Similarly, recent archaeological research reveals that increased rain in the Sahara Desert, in central Africa, created there lush grasslands called savannahs that attracted hunter-gatherer nomads from the southern part of the continent; in a slow process of change, these people built settlements, domesticated cattle instead of only hunting wild animals, and created intricate pottery suited to their new way of life.

The hunter-gatherers living in the Fertile Crescent began to gather more and more of their food from the now easily available wild grains. This regular supply of food in turn promoted human fertility, which led to a growth in population, a process that might have already begun as a result of the milder climate. The more children that were born, the greater the need to exploit the food supply efficiently. Over centuries, people learned to plant part of the seeds from one crop of grain to produce another crop. Since Neolithic women did most of the gather-

NEW SOURCES, NEW PERSPECTIVES

Daily Bread, Damaged Bones, and Cracked Teeth

The invention of agriculture helped people produce a more predictable and plentiful supply of food, which in turn allowed the population to expand. This change came at a price. Recent scientific research in biological anthropology and osteological archaeology (the study of ancient bones and teeth) has uncovered dramatic evidence of the physical stress endured by some of the individuals working in early agriculture. Excavators at Tell Abu Hureyra in Syria have found bones and teeth from people living around 6000 B.C.E. that reveal the pain that the new technology could cause. The big toes of these ancient people especially show proof of extreme and prolonged dorsiflexion—bending the front of the foot up toward the shin. Dorsiflexion made the ends of the toe bones become flatter and broader than normal through the constant pressure of being bent in the same position for long periods of time.

What activity could the people have been pursuing so doggedly that it deformed their bones? The only posture that creates such severe bending of the foot is kneeling for extended periods. Osteologists confirmed that kneeling was common in this population by finding several cases of arthritic changes in knee joints and lower spines in skeletons at the site.

But why were the people kneeling for so long? Other bone evidence offered the first clue to solving this mystery. The skeletons showed strongly developed attachment points for the deltoid muscle on the humerus (the bone in the upper arm) and prominent growth in the lower arm bones. These characteristics mean that the people had especially strong deltoids for pushing their shoulders back and forth and powerful biceps for rotating their forearms. Whatever they were doing made them use their shoulders and arms vigorously.

The skeletons' teeth provided the next clue. Everyone except the very youngest individuals had deeply worn and often fractured teeth. This damage indicated that they regularly chewed food full of rock dust, which probably resulted from grain being ground in rock bowls.

The final clue came from art. Later paintings and sculptures from the region show people, usually women, kneeling down to grind grain into flour by pushing and rotating a stone roller back and forth on heavy grinding stones tilted away from them. This posture is exactly what would cause deformation of the big toes and arthritis in the knees and lower back. People grinding grain this way would have to push off hard from their toes with every stroke down the stone, and vigorously use the muscles of their shoulders and forearms to apply pressure to the roller. In addition, the flour would pick up tiny particles from the wearing down of the stones used to grind it; bread made from it would have a sandy consistency hard on teeth. That Neolithic people worked so constantly and so hard at processing the grain they grew, regardless of the damage to their bones and their teeth, shows how vital this supply of food had become to them.

At this Syrian site, everyone's bones—men's, women's, and even children's—show the same signs of the kneeling and grinding activity. Evidently the production of flour for bread was so crucial that no gender division of this labor was possible or desirable, as it seems to have become in later times. Regardless of who used it, this new technology that provided essential food for the community took its toll in individual pain and hardship.

ing of plant food, they had the greatest knowledge of plant life and therefore probably played the major role in the invention of agriculture and the fashioning of tools needed to turn grains into food, such as grinding stones for making flour. At this early stage in the development of agriculture, women and children did most of the agricultural labor, using hand tools to grow and harvest crops, while men continued to hunt to obtain meat.

During the early Neolithic Age, people also learned to breed and herd animals that they could eat, a development that helped replace the meat previously acquired by hunting large mammals, many of which had by now been hunted to extinction. Fortunately for the people in the Fertile Crescent, their region was home to surviving large mammals that could be domesticated. Unlike the zebra or the hippopotamus found in Africa, the wild sheep, goats, and cattle of the Fertile Crescent could, over the span of generations, be turned into animals accustomed to live closely and interdependently with human beings. The sheep was the first animal to be domesticated as a source of meat, beginning about 8500 B.C.E. (The dog had been domesticated much earlier but was not usually eaten.) By about 7000 B.C.E., domesticated animals had become common throughout the Near East. In this early period of domestication, some people lived as pastoralists, meaning they obtained their food mainly from the herds of animals they kept, frequently moving around to find fresh grazing land. They also cultivated small temporary plots from time to time when they found a suitable area. Other people, relying more and more on growing crops for their livelihood, kept small herds close to their settlements. Men, women, and children alike could therefore

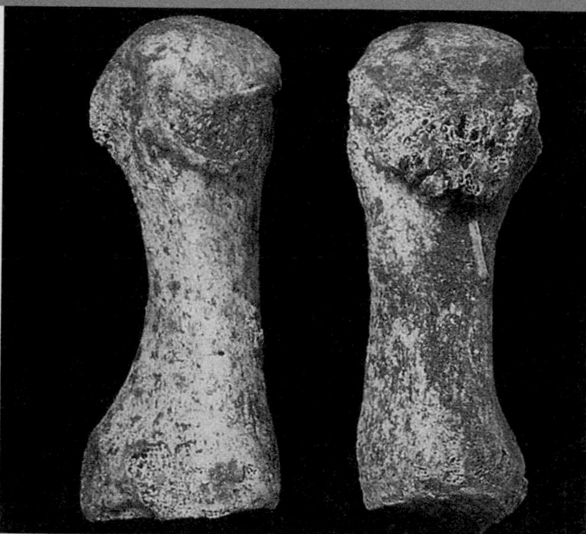

Bones from Tell Abu Hureyra, Syria
These big toes from a middle-aged man reveal severe arthritic changes to the joint. Osteologists interpret this damage as evidence of extreme and prolonged dorsiflexion, or bending of the foot. *(© Natural History Museum, London.)*

Sculpture from Giza, Egypt
In this statuette, a woman grinds grain into flour. The sculptor shows her rubbing her severely flexed left foot with the toes of her right foot, probably trying to ease the throbbing resulting from hours of kneeling. *(Courtesy of the Oriental Institute of the University of Chicago.)*

Questions to Consider

1. **What other new technologies that have increased productivity and bettered human life have also involved new pains and stresses?**
2. **How do you decide what price—financial, physical, emotional—is worth paying for new technology? Who will make those decisions?**

Further Reading

Abu Hureyra: http://www.mnsu.edu/emuseum/archaeology/sites/middle_east/abuhureyra.html

Hillman, G. "Traditional Husbandry and Processing of Archaic Cereals in Recent Times: The Operations, Products, and Equipment Which Might Feature in Sumerian Texts." *Bulletin on Sumerian Agriculture* 1 (1984): 114–52.

Molleson, Theya. "Seed Preparation in the Mesolithic: The Osteological Evidence." *Antiquity* 63 (1989): 358.

Moore, A. M. T. "The Excavation of Tell Abu Hureyra in Syria: A Preliminary Report." *Proceedings of the Prehistoric Society* 41 (1975): 50–71.

tend the animals. These earliest domesticated herds seem to have been used only as a source of meat, not for products such as milk or wool. Hunting never completely disappeared, but it evolved into an activity mainly for establishing men's masculinity and prestige—something that would be increasingly important as humans moved toward civilization.

The Neolithic Origins of Civilization

The Neolithic Revolution laid the foundation for civilization and our modern way of life. The remarkable new knowledge of how to produce food and the consequent division and specialization of labor emerged through innovative human responses to the link between environmental change and population growth (see "New Sources, New Perspectives," above). Furthermore, the Neolithic Revolution reveals the importance of **demography**—the study of the size, growth, density, distribution, and vital statistics of the human population—to the study of history.

Two central features of Neolithic farming villages helped create conditions that eventually led to urban-based civilization: they were permanent, and they supported larger populations than were characteristic of hunter-gatherer society. First, to be able to raise crops, people had to stop roaming and settle in one place with adequate land and water. Farming communities thus sprang up in the Fertile

---

demography: The study of the size, growth, density, distribution, and vital statistics of the human population.

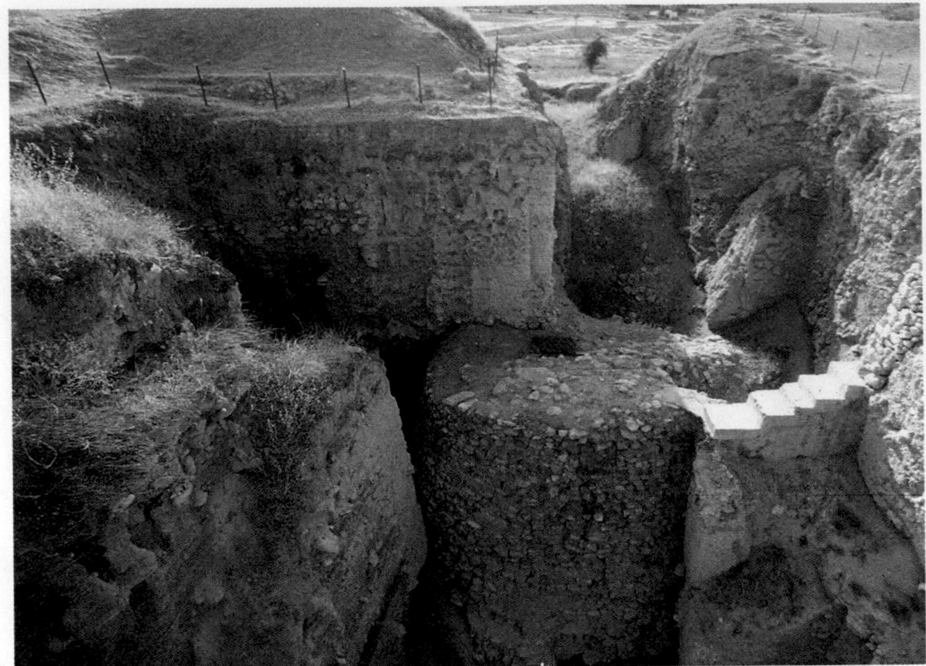

Tower in the Stone Wall of Neolithic Jericho

The circular mass in the center of this photograph is the base of a tower in the stone wall that the people of Jericho (today in Israel) built to protect their community around 8000–7000 B.C.E. This is one of the earliest defensive walls ever discovered; most of the people in this era still lived in unwalled collections of mud huts, but the inhabitants of Jericho had reached a more complex level of social organization that allowed them to collaborate on major building projects. The agricultural fields that lay outside the walls supplied the overwhelming majority of Jericho's economy, while the wall surrounding their settlement provided security for the residents' homes and storehouses and thus protected their improving standard of living. *(Photo © Zev Radovan/The Bridgeman Art Library International.)*

Crescent starting around 10,000 B.C.E., sharing the region with pastoralists. Second, parents began to have more children because agriculture required a great deal of labor and because the fields and herds supplied readily available food. At the same time, living in close quarters with domesticated animals, which might well be penned right next to or even inside the house, exposed people to new epidemic diseases transmitted from animals to humans. Hunter-gatherers had largely escaped this danger because they had no groups of animals around them every day, although they could sometimes become infected by eating diseased wild animals. Since many viruses that afflict people today—for example, the avian influenza (bird flu) virus—originated in domesticated animals, we are still living with this unintended consequence of the Neolithic Revolution.

Much bigger and more densely packed than the temporary settlements of the Paleolithic Age, early farming communities built sturdy houses of mud brick and used containers made of pottery (whose broken remains provide evidence for chronology and cultural development). The first homes were apparently circular huts, like those known in Jericho (in what is today Israel). Around two thousand people had settled in Jericho by 8000 B.C.E., their huts sprawling over about twelve acres.

Jericho's remains also reveal that war became a prominent part of life during the Neolithic Revolution. The most remarkable part of the village was the massive fortification wall surrounding the community. Ten feet thick, the wall was crowned with a thirty-foot-diameter stone tower enclosing a flight of stairs; this massive structure shows that the inhabitants of Jericho feared attacks by their neighbors (see the illustration above). The presence of the tower suggests that growing prosperity brought by the Neolithic Revolution had also spurred war for conquest and acquisition. Religion remained central to the lives of the Neolithic inhabitants of Jericho, as evidenced by the human skulls that they covered with plaster and paint, perhaps to honor their ancestors.

Neolithic people from the Fertile Crescent opened the way for civilization to develop in other regions by gradually spreading their knowledge of agriculture abroad. Farmers looking for more land migrated westward from the Near East and brought the new technology of farming into areas where it was not previously known. Although recent scholarship argues that human beings in other areas, especially Asia, independently developed agriculture and the domestication of animals, migrants from the Near East were the ones who spread this knowledge across Europe by 4000 B.C.E.

Daily Life in the Neolithic Village of Çatalhöyük

An archaeological site northwest of the Fertile Crescent, in present-day Turkey, provides vital evidence for the vast changes in human life brought on by the spread of knowledge during the Neolithic Age, especially how agriculture's efficiency in providing food led to the division and specialization of labor.

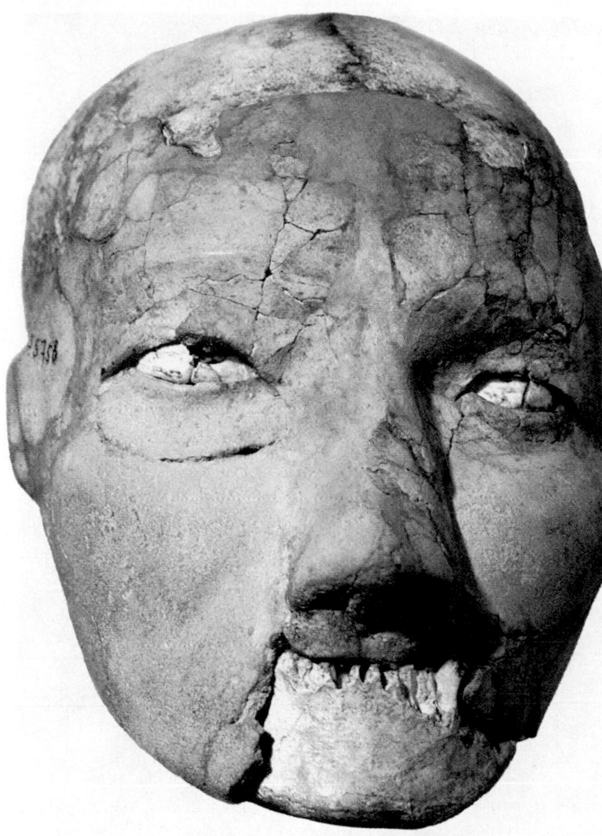

Decorated Human Skull
The inhabitants of Jericho buried human skulls under the floors of buildings in their Neolithic town. They made the skulls look more lifelike by applying plaster and shells. It seems possible that these carefully decorated remains expressed respect and religious awe for ancestors. *(Archeological Museum, Amman, Jordan / Giraudon / The Bridgeman Art Library International.)*

At this site a large mound rises from a plain near a river. Known to us only by its modern Turkish name, Çatalhöyük (meaning "Fork Mound"), the site reveals what daily life was like in a Neolithic farming community. By 7000 to 6500 B.C.E., the farmers of Çatalhöyük had erected a settlement of mud-brick houses sharing common walls. They constructed their dwellings in the rectangular shape still used for most homes today, with one striking difference: they had no doors in their outer walls. Instead, they entered their homes by climbing down a ladder through a hole in the flat roof. Since this hole also served as a vent for smoke from the family fire, getting into a house at Çatalhöyük could be a grimy experience. But the absence of exterior doors also meant that the walls of the community's outermost houses served as the village's fortification wall to defend it against attacks.

The people of Çatalhöyük fed themselves by growing wheat, barley, and vegetables such as field peas; they diverted water from the nearby river to irrigate their fields to increase their harvests. They also kept domesticated cattle to provide their main supply of meat and, by this time, hides and milk. They continued to hunt, too, as we can tell from the hunting scenes they drew on the walls of some of their buildings, recalling the cave paintings of much earlier times. Unlike hunter-gatherers, however, these villagers no longer had to depend on the hit-or-miss luck of the hunt or risk being killed by wild animals to acquire meat and leather. The village's population reached perhaps six thousand at its height, and its inhabitants practiced a wide array of occupations.

The diversity of occupations at Çatalhöyük reveals a significant change from earlier times, anticipating the division of labor characteristic of the later cities of the first fully developed civilizations. Since the community could produce enough food to support itself without everyone having to work in the fields or herd cattle, some people could develop crafts full-time. Just as others in the community produced food for them, craft specialists produced goods for those who provided the food. Craft specialists continued to fashion tools, containers, and ornaments in the traditional way—from wood, bone, hide, and stone—but they now also worked with the material of the future: metal. So far, archaeologists are certain only that metalworkers at Çatalhöyük knew how to fashion lead into pendants and to hammer naturally occurring lumps of copper into beads and tubes for jewelry. But traces of slag, the scum that floats on molten metal, have been found on the site, suggesting that the workers may have begun to develop the technique of smelting metal from ore. This tricky process—the basis of true metallurgy and an essential technology of civilization—required temperatures of 700 degrees centigrade and took centuries for metalworkers to perfect. Other workers at Çatalhöyük specialized in weaving textiles, and the scraps of cloth discovered there are the oldest examples of this craft ever found. Like other early technological innovations, metallurgy and the production of cloth apparently also developed independently in other places.

Trade—another central aspect of human existence that became increasingly prominent in the Neolithic Age—also figured in the economy of this early farming community. The trading contacts the Neolithic villagers made with other settlements increased the level of economic interconnection among far-flung communities that had begun in the Paleolithic Age. Trade allowed the people of Çatalhöyük to acquire goods from far away, such as shells from the Mediterranean Sea to wear as ornaments and a special flint from far to the east to shape into ceremonial daggers. The villagers acquired these prized materials by offering obsidian in exchange, a local volcanic glass whose glossy luster and capacity to hold a sharp edge made it valuable.

Model of a House at Çatalhöyük

Archaeologists built this model of a house to show how Neolithic villagers lived in Çatalhöyük (today in central Turkey) from around 6500 to 5500 B.C.E. The wall paintings and bull-head sculpture had religious meaning, perhaps linked to the graves that the residents dug under the floor for their dead. The main entrance to the house was through the ceiling, as the houses were built right next to one another without streets in between, only some space for dumping refuse; the roofs served as walkways. Why do you think the villagers chose this arrangement for their settlement? *(Çatalhöyük Research Project.)*

Just as members of the community saw trade as vital to their economic prosperity, they saw religion as essential for their spiritual needs. The shrines and burial sites uncovered by archaeologists offer us hints about these beliefs and practices. The villagers outfitted their shrines with paintings and sculptures of bulls' heads and female breasts, perhaps as symbols of male and female elements in their religion. Like the hunter-gatherers before them, they sculpted figurines depicting large-breasted, large-hipped women who perhaps represented goddesses of birth, although some figurines recently found with skeletal designs suggest they were also related to ideas about death. The villagers' deep interest in the mystery of death is demonstrated by the skulls displayed in their shrines and by wall paintings of vultures devouring headless corpses. They buried their dead, some holding skulls decorated with painted plaster, under the floors of their houses. Perhaps they, too, believed their dead ancestors had power and therefore wanted to keep them close by. A remarkable wall painting also suggests that the people of Çatalhöyük regarded the volcano looming over their settlement as an angry god whom they needed to please. As it turned out, a volcanic eruption overwhelmed Çatalhöyük about fourteen hundred years after its foundation, and the settlement never recovered.

Along with religion, hierarchy was also important to the people of Çatalhöyük. They had a clear social hierarchy, another example of the lasting changes that occurred in the Neolithic Age and influenced the development of civilization. The villagers developed a hierarchical society because they needed leaders to plan and regulate irrigation, trade, the exchange of food and goods between farmers and crafts producers, and the defense of the community against enemies. These leaders held more authority than had been required to maintain peace and order in Paleolithic hunter-gatherer bands because their responsibilities were more complicated. Furthermore, households that were successful in farming, herding, crafts production, and trade generated surpluses in wealth that set them apart from those whose efforts proved less fortunate.

The Emergence of Gender Inequality in the Neolithic Age

As hierarchy became increasingly important, the social equality between men and women that had existed in hunter-gatherer bands dwindled during the Neolithic Age. By about 4000 B.C.E., when the first political states had begun to emerge in the Near East, **patriarchy** was the rule. (Patriarchal political states also emerged at various other distant places around the world, including India, China, and the Americas—whether through independent development or some process of mutual influence we cannot yet say.) The reasons for the appearance of patriarchy remain uncertain, but they perhaps involved gradual changes in agriculture and herding over many centuries. After about 4000 B.C.E., farmers used plows pulled by large animals to cultivate land that was difficult to sow. Men apparently operated this new technology of plowing, probably because it required much more physical strength than digging with sticks and hoes, as women had done with hand tools in the earliest period of agriculture. Men also looked after the larger herds that had become more common in settled communities; people were now keeping cattle as sources of milk and raising sheep for wool. The herding of a community's large groups of animals tended to take place at a distance from the home settlement because the animals continually needed new grazing land. Free from having to nurse children, men took on this task, as they had with hunting in hunter-gatherer populations.

As agriculture became more intensive and therefore required more and more labor than had food gathering or the earliest forms of farming, the increasing pressure to bear and raise children probably tied women to the central settlement. Women also took responsibility for the new labor-intensive tasks needed to process the secondary products of larger herds. For example, they now turned milk into cheese and yogurt and made cloth by spinning and weaving wool. Men's predominant role in agriculture and herding in the late Neolithic period, combined with women's lessened mobility and increasingly home-based tasks, apparently led to women's loss of equality with men in these early times of human society.

patriarchy: Dominance by men in society and politics.

REVIEW QUESTION What benefits and what drawbacks did the Neolithic Revolution bring to human life?

Conclusion

Permanent homes, fairly reliable food supplies from agriculture and domesticated animals, specialized occupations, hierarchical patriarchies, and war characterized Western history from the Neolithic period forward. For this reason, the broad outlines of the life of Neolithic villagers might seem unremarkable to us today. But the Neolithic way of life in built environments surrounded by cultivated fields and herds would have seemed astounding, we can guess, to Paleolithic hunter-gatherers such as the roaming hippopotamus hunters of Africa who now rank as the earliest known *Homo sapiens*. The Neolithic Revolution was the most important change in the early history of human beings; it overturned the ways in which people interacted with the natural environment and with one another. Now that farmers and herders could produce a surplus of food to support other people, specialists in art, architecture, crafts, religion, and politics could emerge. Hand in hand with these developments came a new division of labor by gender that saw men begin to take over agriculture and herding while women took up new tasks at home, leading to a loss of gender equality. At the same time, war between newly prosperous communities became common. These changes altered the course of human history and spurred the development of Western civilization as we know it today.

FOR FURTHER EXPLORATION

- **For additional primary-source material from this period**, see *Sources of the Making of the West*, Fourth Edition.
- **For Web sites, images, and documents related to topics in this chapter**, visit *Make History* at bedfordstmartins.com/hunt.

Prologue Review

Online Study Guide bedfordstmartins.com/hunt

Key Terms and People

In the grid below, identify the term or person and explain its historical significance. (To do this exercise online, go to bedfordstmartins.com/hunt.)

Term	Who or What & When	Why It Matters
Paleolithic Age (p. P-2)		
Neolithic Age (p. P-2)		
political states (p. P-2)		
hunter-gatherers (p. P-3)		
Homo sapiens sapiens (p. P-3)		
hierarchy (p. P-5)		
Neolithic Revolution (p. P-6)		
demography (p. P-9)		
patriarchy (p. P-13)		

Review Questions

1. What were the most important activities, skills, and beliefs that helped Paleolithic hunter-gatherers survive?
2. What benefits and what drawbacks did the Neolithic Revolution bring to human life?

Making Connections

1. Explain whether you think human life was more stressful in the Paleolithic period or the Neolithic period.
2. What do you think are the most important differences and similarities between Stone Age life and modern life? Why?
3. How might historians draw conclusions about religious beliefs of Stone Age people, given that there are no written records?

Important Events

Date	Event
200,000–160,000 B.C.E.	Beginning of Paleolithic ("Old Stone") Age
50,000–45,000 B.C.E.	*Homo sapiens sapiens* migrate from Africa into southwest Asia and Europe
10,000–8000 B.C.E.	Neolithic ("New Stone") Revolution in the Fertile Crescent and the Sahara
8000 B.C.E.	Walled settlement at Jericho (in modern Israel)
7000–5500 B.C.E.	Farming community thrives at Çatalhöyük (in modern Turkey)

■ How might the changes characterizing the **Neolithic Revolution (10,000–8000 B.C.E.)** relate to the creation of the **walled settlement at Jericho (8000 B.C.E.)**?

SUGGESTED REFERENCES

Çatalhöyük: Excavations of a Neolithic Anatolian Höyük: http:// www .catalhoyuk.com/

Clark, J. Desmond, et al. "Stratigraphic, Chronological and Behavioural Contexts of Pleistocene *Homo Sapiens* from Middle Awash, Ethiopia." *Nature* 423 (June 12, 2003): 747–52.

Diamond, Jared M. *Guns, Germs, and Steel: The Fates of Human Societies.* 2005.

Ehrenberg, Margaret. *Women in Prehistory*. 1989.

Fagan, Brian M. *People of the Earth: An Introduction to World Prehistory*. 13th ed. 2009.

Hodder, Ian. *The Leopard's Tale. Revealing the Mysteries of Çatalhöyük.* 2006.

Klein, Richard G. *The Human Career. Human Biological and Cultural Origins*. 3rd ed. 2009.

Lewis-Williams, David, and David Pearce. *Inside the Neolithic Mind: Consciousness, Cosmos and the Realm of the Gods*. 2005.

Mithen, Steven. *After the Ice: A Global Human History 20,000–5000 BC*. 2004.

Moore, A. M. T. *Village on the Euphrates: From Foraging to Farming at Abu Hureyra*. 2000.

Renfrew, Colin. *Prehistory: The Making of the Human Mind*. 2009.

Scarre, Chris. *The Human Past: World Prehistory and the Development of Human Societies*. 2009.

Wenke, Robert J. *Patterns in Prehistory: Humankind's First Three Million Years*. 5th ed. 2006.

White, Tim D., et al. "Pleistocene *Homo Sapiens* from Middle Awash, Ethiopia." *Nature* 423 (June 12, 2003): 742–47.

CHAPTER

1

Early Western Civilization

4000–1000 B.C.E.

Kings in ancient Egypt believed that after they died the gods would judge them as rulers to decide their fate in the afterlife. In *Instructions for Merikare*, for example, written sometime around 2100–2000 B.C.E., an Egyptian king gives his son Merikare the following advice: "Make secure your place in the cemetery by being upright, by doing justice, upon which people's hearts rely. . . . When a man is buried and mourned, his deeds are piled up next to him as treasure." Being judged pure of heart led to an eternal reward; if the dead king reached the judges "without doing evil," he would be transformed so that he would "abide [in the afterlife] like a god, roaming [free] like the lords of time." A vital part of the justice demanded of an Egyptian king was to keep the country unified under a strong central authority to combat disorder.

Ordinary Egyptians, too, believed that they would win eternal rewards by living justly, which for them meant worshipping the gods and obeying the king and his officials. An illustrated guidebook containing instructions for mummies on how to travel safely in the underworld, commonly called the *Book of the Dead*, explained that on the day of judgment the jackal-headed god Anubis would weigh the dead person's heart on a scale against the goddess Maat and her feather of Truth, with the bird-headed god Thoth carefully writing down the result. Pictures in the *Book of the Dead* also show the Swallower of the Damned—a hybrid monster with a crocodile's head, a lion's body, and a hippopotamus's hind end—who crouched behind Thoth ready to eat the heart of anyone who failed the test of purity. Egyptian mythology thus taught that living a just life was the most important human goal because it was the key to winning the gods' help for a blessed existence after death.

The Afterlife in Egyptian Religion
This illustration comes from the ancient Egyptian *Book of the Dead*, a collection of illustrated instructions and magic spells buried with dead people to help them in the afterlife. It shows the deceased standing in front of offerings made to Osiris, the god of the underworld. He is seated on a throne with his sister and wife, the goddess Isis, and her sister standing behind him. The myth of Osiris, who died and was cut up into pieces but then reassembled and resurrected by Isis, expressed Egyptians' belief in an eternal life after death. *(The Art Archive/Egyptian Museum, Cairo/Alfredo Dagli Orti.)*

The earliest examples of Western civilization arose in Mesopotamia, Egypt, Anatolia (today Turkey), Crete and other Aegean islands, and Greece. Each of these societies believed in the need for a centralized authority, but the forms of that authority differed. In Egypt, a single central authority united the country; in the others, smaller independent states competed with one another. All believed that religion and justice were basic building blocks for organizing human life. They believed that many gods existed, but their particular religious beliefs and practices differed. In contrast to the Egyptians, for example, the Greeks believed that most people could expect only a gloomy, shadowlike existence following their deaths.

Trade and war brought these societies, with their sometimes differing religious beliefs and practices, into frequent contact. They exchanged not only goods and technologies but also ideas. Thus cultural diversity has always characterized Western civilization. The question arises, then, of what historians mean by the concept *Western civilization*. What defines it in particular, as compared to other civilizations?

CHAPTER FOCUS What changes did Western civilization bring to human life?

The Concept of Western Civilization

It is difficult to give a precise definition of *Western civilization* because the concept involves three hotly debated topics: the concept of civilization in general, the vagueness of the idea of the West geographically, and—most controversial of all—the nature and the value of the West's ideas and ways of life. The history of Western civilization, in any case, begins with the history of Sumer in Mesopotamia and of Egypt in Africa and extends to the present day. The early history of the West focuses on the peoples who lived in and around the Mediterranean Sea in southwestern Asia, northern Africa, and southern Europe.

Defining Western Civilization

To define *Western civilization*, it is necessary first to define **civilization** in general (see "Terms of History," page 5). Historians traditionally define it as a way of life based in cities governed as political states under a central authority, with a complex organization of labor, trade, religion, and other central aspects of human life. The definition of *city* is also imprecise, but the word certainly refers to a densely settled urban area with large buildings and a population governed by a system of political authority. Other characteristics of civilization are also identified as a diverse economy generating surplus resources, strong social hierarchies, a sense of local identity, some knowledge of writing, and a military force for defense and, perhaps, conquest of the land and property of others.

We generally use *civilization* and related terms such as *civilized behavior* as if everyone agreed that the development of civilization brought progress, giving people opportunities for greater prosperity and creating more complex but nevertheless advantageous interactions. Some historians, however, deny that civilization represents a better way of life than the way human beings lived before civilization. They argue that people were healthier, more

---

civilization: A way of life based in cities with dense populations organized as political states, large buildings constructed for communal activities, the production of food, diverse economies, a sense of local identity, and some knowledge of writing.

4000–1000 B.C.E. Bronze Age in southwestern Asia, Egypt, and Europe

3050 B.C.E. Narmer (Menes) unites Upper and Lower Egypt into one kingdom

4000 B.C.E. | 3500 B.C.E. | 3000 B.C.E.

4000–3000 B.C.E. Mesopotamians invent writing and establish first cities

2687–2190 B.C.E. Old Kingdom in Egypt

TERMS OF HISTORY

Civilization

Our word *civilization* comes from the ancient Roman word *civilis*, which meant "suitable for a private citizen" and "behaving like an ordinary, down-to-earth person." Historians connect civilization especially with urbanization and the ways of life that characterize city existence. Also, the word *civilization* often expresses the judgment that being civilized means achieving a superior way of life. Consider, for example, these definitions from *The Random House Webster's College Dictionary* (1997), p. 240:

> *civilization*: **1.** an advanced state of human society, in which a high level of culture, science, and government has been reached. **2.** those people or nations that have reached such a state. **3.** any type of culture, society, etc. of a specific place, time, or group: *Greek civilization*. **4.** the act or process of civilizing or being civilized. **5.** cultural and intellectual refinement. **6.** cities or populated areas in general, as opposed to unpopulated or wilderness areas. **7.** modern comforts and conveniences, as made possible by science and technology.

All these definitions imply that *civilization* means an "advanced" or "refined" way of life compared to a "savage" or "rude" way. Ancient peoples often drew this sort of comparison between themselves and those whom they saw as crude. Much later, this notion of superiority became prominent in European thought after voyagers to the Americas reported on what they saw as the barbarian life of the peoples they called Indians. Because these Europeans saw Native American life as lacking discipline, government, and above all Christianity, it seemed to them to be "uncivilized." Today, this sense of comparative superiority in the word *civilization* has become so accepted that it can even be used in nonhuman contexts, such as in the following startling comparison: "some communities of ants are more advanced in civilization than others."[1]

Sometimes *civilization* is used without much definitional content at all, as in the Random House dictionary's third definition. Can the word have any deep meaning if it can be used to mean "any type of culture, society, etc. of a specific place, time, or group"? This broad definition reveals that studying civilization and deciding what it does—and should—mean still presents difficult challenges to students of history today. Should it not be their task to make *civilization* a word with intellectual content and a reality with meaning for improving human life, as those who first used the word thought that it was?

[1] Sir John Lubbock, *On the Origin and Metamorphoses of Insects*, 2nd ed. (London, 1874), 13.

equal in power, and more peaceful before they created cities, political states, and complex economies. Such comparisons are hard to make because there is so little evidence about early human life (see the Prologue). If there truly was less war before the emergence of civilization, the reason might simply be that many fewer people existed in early times and they were spread much farther apart—but it also probably matters that early peoples lacked the surpluses to finance long or distant wars. In any case, human beings all over the world chose to develop civilization, and no peoples have yet decided to reject it in favor of a simpler life.

Ancient peoples developed the idea that different civilizations are defined by their geography and their particular ideas and practices (their culture). The Greeks invented the geographic notion of the West. Building on ideas they probably learned from

2350 B.C.E. Sargon, king of Akkad, establishes the world's first empire

2300–2200 B.C.E. Enheduanna, princess of Akkad, composes poetry

2200 B.C.E. Minoans build their first palaces

2112–2004 B.C.E. Ur III dynasty rules in Sumer

2061–1665 B.C.E. Middle Kingdom in Egypt

2000 B.C.E.

1792–1750 B.C.E. Hammurabi rules Babylon and issues his law code

1750 B.C.E. Hittites establish their kingdom in Anatolia

1569–1081 B.C.E. New Kingdom in Egypt

1500 B.C.E.

1400 B.C.E. The Mycenaeans build their first palaces in Greece and take over Minoan Crete

1274 B.C.E. Battle of Kadesh in Syria between the Egyptians and the Hittites

1200–1000 B.C.E. Period of violence ends many kingdoms

1000 B.C.E.

their Near Eastern neighbors, they created the term *Europe* to indicate the West (where the sun sets), as distinct from the East (where the sun rises). The Greeks, like modern historians, were not sure exactly where to draw the boundaries of the West because its geographical meaning was then, as it remains now, vague. The boundaries shift depending on what period is being described, and the word *Western* in *Western civilization* sometimes refers to peoples and places beyond Europe, and sometimes not. For example, the region that is today Turkey was certainly part of Western civilization at the time of the Roman Empire; yet now in the twenty-first century, Europeans and Turks alike are debating what changes in Turkish life and politics it would take—and what the financial and cultural costs would be—for Turkey to be judged Western enough to join the European Union.

Because it is difficult to identify precisely what set of ideas and customs makes up the culture of a particular civilization, the most controversial questions about any given civilization are "What are its particular ideas and practices?," "Are those ideas and practices different from those of other civilizations?," and "If so, are they inferior or superior to those of other civilizations?" For example, Mesopotamian religion and Egyptian religion were both forms of **polytheism** (belief in many gods). The Mesopotamians in the region called Sumer, who built the world's first cities, believed that the deities were unpredictable and often harsh to humans, and that people had to ward off divine anger by serving the gods obediently, building them temples, worshipping them, and bringing them gifts. The Egyptians also believed that they had to respect the gods to find happiness, but they thought that their gods lovingly provided them with life's delights and that, if their king fulfilled his duties, the divinity Maat would bless them with justice. As we will see in Chapters 2 and 3, the Israelites made **monotheism** (belief in one god) a distinctive feature in Western civilization.

The Greeks inherited from their neighbors in the Near East the idea that regional differences meant that one people's culture was better than another's. Merikare's father, for instance, sternly warned him, "[Beware of the] miserable Asiatic [Near Easterner], wretched because of where he's from, a place with no water, no wood. . . . He doesn't live in one place, hunger propels his legs. . . . He doesn't announce the day of battle, he's like a thief darting around a crowd." The Greeks also later contributed to Western civilization new and unique ideas about alternative types of central political authority not involving kings and about the importance of reason for human thought.

In every known civilization, people have insisted on establishing social hierarchies. The invention of increasingly sophisticated metallurgy (the technology of working metals), for example, led to the creation of ever better tools and weapons, but it also turned out to be another factor prompting more visible differences in social status: people constructed status for themselves in part by acquiring metal objects, from jewelry to finely decorated weapons. Some contemporary scientists claim that this development was inevitable because human beings are by nature "status-protecting organisms."

It would be misleading, however, to define Western civilization by a simple list of characteristics: we have to find the nature and value of Western civilization by studying its history. As we shall see, Western civilization evolved to a large extent through cultural interaction provoked by trade and war. Contact with unfamiliar ways and technologies spurred people to learn from one another and to adapt for themselves the inventions and beliefs of others. Western civilization therefore developed in a mixing of different cultures. In the long run, the story of Western civilization expanded to include not only cultural and political interaction among the West's diverse peoples themselves but also between them and the peoples of the rest of the globe. It is clearly a mistake to understand the word *Western* to mean "fenced off in the West from the rest of the world."

The Societies of Early Western Civilization

Under the definition of *civilization* outlined here, civilization in the West locates its deepest foundations in two societies: (1) Mesopotamia, where the people of Sumer had developed separate cities and political states by 4000–3000 B.C.E., and (2) Egypt, in northeastern Africa, whose civilization emerged beginning around 3050 B.C.E., when a strong ruler made the country into a unified political state stretching along the Nile River. Both societies waged frequent wars to protect their civilization, to demonstrate their superiority over outsiders, and to seize resources through conquest.

The story of Western civilization next spreads beyond Mesopotamia and Egypt. By around 2000–1900 B.C.E., civilization had also appeared in

polytheism: The belief in and worship of multiple gods.

monotheism: The belief in and worship of only one god, as in Judaism, Christianity, and Islam.

Anatolia, Crete and other islands in the eastern Mediterranean Sea, and Greece. All these peoples learned from the older civilizations of Mesopotamia and Egypt, shared the sense that nothing in life was more important than religion, and waged war for defense and conquest. Comparably complex societies also emerged in India, China, and the Americas in different eras starting around 2500 B.C.E.; however, these societies pursued independent paths of development. Their direct connections to the West began only much later.

Since studying the history of Western civilization seems the best way to understand its definition, it is important to trace the interactions of its diverse peoples and regions in commerce, war, and ideas. We will follow that story here beginning with the Mesopotamians, the Egyptians, the Minoans on Crete and the Aegean islands, and the Mycenaeans in Greece. The insecurity of what we traditionally call civilization will become apparent when we come to the mysterious era of widespread violence that lasted from about 1200 to 1000 B.C.E. and threatened to destroy civilization in the West.

REVIEW QUESTION What are the challenges in defining the term *Western civilization*?

Mesopotamia, Home of the First Civilization, 4000–1000 B.C.E.

The Neolithic Revolution (see the Prologue, pages P-6–P-9) created the economic basis of civilization by providing enough surplus agricultural resources to allow many people to work full-time at occupations other than farming and by encouraging permanent settlements that could grow into cities. These changes in the physical conditions of life in turn generated changes in society. The first place where farming villages gradually became cities was Mesopotamia, in southwestern Asia (the ancient Near East). There, climate change had promoted agriculture and domestication of animals in the region called the Fertile Crescent. Sumer, the name for southern Mesopotamia, developed the first cities. By 4000–3000 B.C.E., the Sumerians had built large urban communities, each controlling its surrounding territory as a separate political state. Archaeological and textual evidence has revealed the interlocking physical and social conditions of the first civilization: cities, successful agriculture on arid plains made possible by complex irrigation, religion as the guide to life, a social hierarchy with kings at the top and slaves at the bottom, the invention of writing to keep track of economic transactions and record people's stories and beliefs, and war to demonstrate cultural superiority and gain land and riches from others.

The riches for which people now fought had a new component: metal. Items made of metal had become central to wealth and power after craft workers invented the technology of metallurgy about 4000 B.C.E. Historians label the period from about 4000 to 1000 B.C.E. the Bronze Age because at this time bronze, an alloy of copper and tin, was the most important metal for weapons and tools; iron was not yet in common use. The ownership of metal objects strengthened visible status divisions in society between men and women and rich and poor. Long-distance commerce increased to satisfy people's desire for resources and goods not available in their homelands and stimulated the invention of the alphabet to supplement earlier forms of writing. Rulers created systems of law to regulate the complex economic and social activities of their society, instruct their subjects to be obedient to their rulers, and show the gods that they were fulfilling the divine command to maintain order by dispensing justice.

The Emergence of Cities, 4000–2350 B.C.E.

The first cities, and therefore the first civilization, emerged in Sumer when its inhabitants figured out how to raise crops on the fertile but dry plains between and around the Euphrates and Tigris Rivers (Map 1.1). This flat region was spacious enough for the growth of cities, but it was not ideal for agriculture: little rain fell, temperatures soared to 120 degrees Fahrenheit, and devastating floods occurred, caused by heavy precipitation that fell in unpredictable patterns in the faraway northern mountains where the Euphrates and Tigris originated. First Sumerians and then other Mesopotamians turned this marginal environment into rich farmland by diverting water from the Tigris and Euphrates to irrigate the plains. The complex system of canals, which provided irrigation and also helped limit flooding, required constant maintenance. The need to organize workers to maintain the many canals promoted the growth of centralized authority in Mesopotamian city-states, which led to the

---

Anatolia: The large peninsula that is today the nation of Turkey.

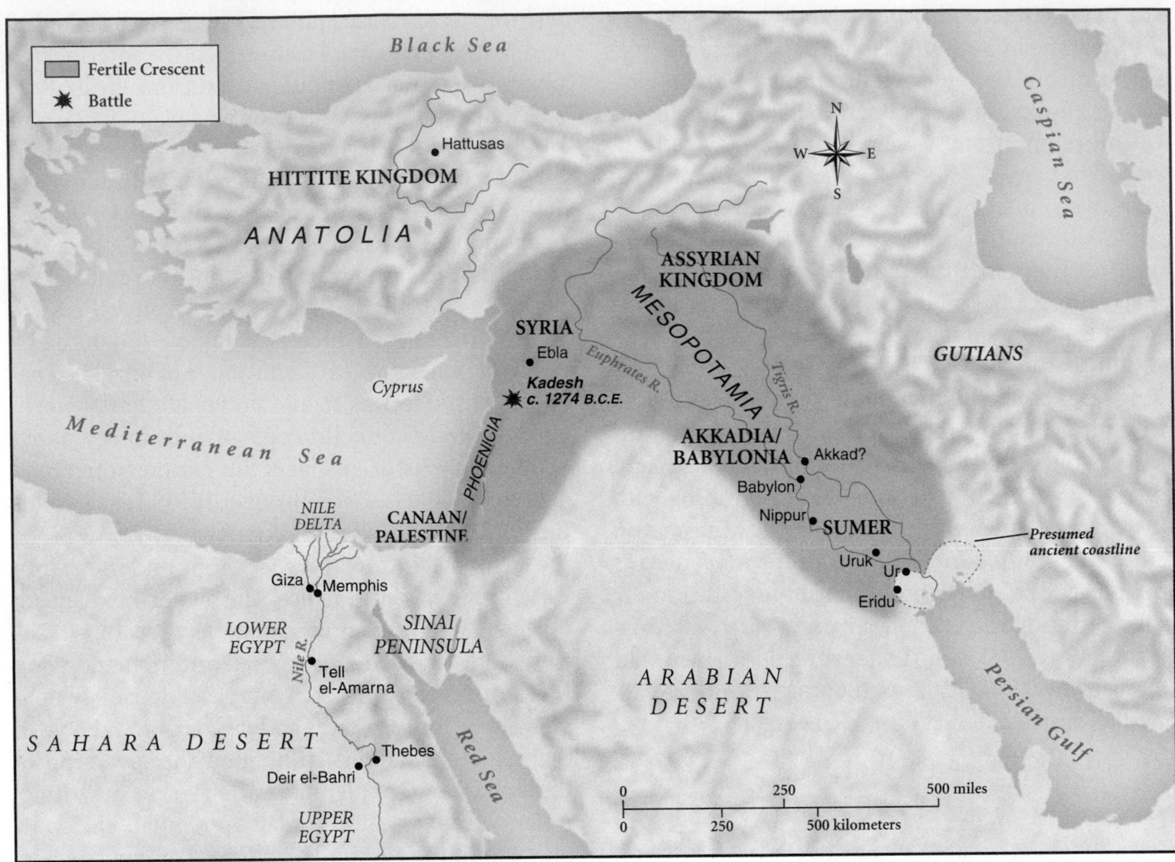

MAP 1.1 The Ancient Near East, 4000–3000 B.C.E.
The diverse region we call the ancient Near East included many different landscapes, climates, peoples, and languages. Kings ruled its independent city-states, the centers of the world's first civilizations, beginning around 4000–3000 B.C.E. Trade by land and sea for natural resources, especially metals, and wars of conquest kept the peoples of the region in constant contact and conflict with one another. | **How did geography facilitate—or hinder—the development of civilization in the Near East?**

emergence of kings as rulers. In this way, civilization created monarchy as a political system.

Food surpluses produced by Mesopotamian farmers stimulated population growth, increased the number of craft producers, and led to the emergence of cities. Each city controlled agricultural land outside its fortification walls and built large temples inside them. Historians call this arrangement—an urban center exercising political and economic control over the countryside around it—a **city-state**. Mesopotamia became a land of independent city-states, each with its own central political authority.

The Cities of Sumer | The origins of the Sumerians remain a mystery, and the background of the language they spoke remains obscure. What is known, however, is that by around 3000 B.C.E. the Sumerians had established twelve independent city-states—including Uruk, Eridu, and Ur—which remained fiercely separate communities warring over land and natural resources. By around 2500 B.C.E., each of the Sumerian cities had expanded to twenty thousand residents or more.

These first city-states had similar layouts. Irrigated fields filled their outlying territories, with villages housing agricultural workers closer to the urban center. A fortress wall surrounded the city itself. Outside the city's gates, bustling centers of trade developed, either at a harbor on the river or in a marketplace along the overland routes leading to the city. Inside the city, the most prominent buildings were the **ziggurats** (see the illustration on page 9), temples of a stair-step design that soared up to ten stories high.

city-state: An urban center exercising political and economic control over the surrounding countryside.

ziggurats (ZIH guh ratz): Mesopotamian temples of massive size built on a stair-step design.

The Ziggurat at Ur in Sumer
Sumerian royalty built this massive temple (called a ziggurat) in the twenty-first century B.C.E. To construct its three huge terraces (placed one above another and connected with stairways), workers glued bricks together with tar around a central core. The walls had to be more than seven feet thick to hold the weight of the building, whose original height is uncertain. The first terrace reached forty-five feet above the ground. Still, the Great Pyramid in Egypt dwarfed even this large monument. *(© Michael S. Yamashita/Corbis.)*

Cities were crowded, though some space was left open for parks. Urban dwellers lived in mud-brick houses constructed around an open court. Most houses had only one or two rooms, but the wealthy constructed two-story dwellings that had a dozen or more rooms. Rich and poor alike could become ill from the water supply, which was often contaminated by sewage because no system of waste disposal existed. Pigs and dogs scavenged in the streets and areas where garbage was dumped before it could be cleared away.

Still, agriculture and trade made Sumerian city-states prosperous. They bartered grain, vegetable oil, woolens, and leather with one another and with foreign regions, from which they acquired natural resources not found in Sumer, such as metals, timber, and precious stones. Sailing for weeks, Sumerian traders traveled as far east as India, where the Indus civilization's large cities emerged about five hundred years after Sumer's. Technological innovation further strengthened the early Mesopotamian economy, especially beginning around 3000 B.C.E., when Sumerians invented the wheel in a form sturdy enough to be used on carts for transport.

Religious officials predominated in the early Sumerian economy because they controlled large farms and gangs of laborers, whose work for the gods supported the ziggurats and their related activities. Priests and priestesses supervised a large amount of property and economic activity. By around 2600 B.C.E., however, kings dominated the economy because their leadership in Mesopotamia's frequent wars won them control of their territories' resources; some private households also amassed significant wealth by working large fields.

Kings in Sumer Kings and their royal families were the highest-ranking people in the Sumerian social hierarchy. A king formed a council of older men as his advisers and praised the gods as his rulers, who made his power secure. This claim to divinely justified power gave priests and priestesses political influence. Although a Sumerian queen was respected as the wife of the king and the mother of the royal children, the king held supreme power in the patriarchal city-states of Mesopotamia. Still, women had more legal rights under Sumerian law than they would in later Mesopotamian societies; only Egypt would give women greater legal standing than Sumer did.

The king's supreme responsibility was to ensure justice, which meant pleasing the gods, developing law, keeping order among the people, and fighting wars against other city-states both for defense and for conquest. In return, the king extracted surpluses from the working population as taxes to support his

Gold Helmet from the Sumerian Royal Tomb at Ur
This helmet sculpted from gold was among the costly treasures placed in a grave in the royal cemetery at Ur in Sumer about 2600–2400 B.C.E. It was meant for ceremonial use rather than protection in war. The Sumerians buried such expensive goods with their kings and queens so that their royalty could maintain after death the position at the top of the social hierarchy that they had possessed while alive. *(The Granger Collection, New York/All rights reserved.)*

family, court, palace, army, and officials. If the surpluses came in regularly, the king mostly left the people alone to live their daily lives; from time to time, he released the poor from their debts as part of his divine mission to fight injustice.

To demonstrate their status atop the social hierarchy, Sumerian kings and their families lived in luxurious palaces that rivaled the size of the great temples. The palace served as the city-state's administrative center and the storehouse for the ruler's enormous wealth. Members of the royal family dedicated a significant portion of the community's economic surplus to displaying their superior status. Archaeological excavation of the immense royal cemetery in Ur, for example, has revealed the dazzling extent of the rulers' riches — spectacular possessions included crowns, weapons, tableware, and cosmetics sets crafted in gold, silver, and precious stones. The graves in Ur also yielded more gruesome evidence of the exalted status of the king and queen: the bodies of servants sacrificed to serve their royal masters after death. The spectacle of wealth and power that characterized Sumerian kingship reveals the enormous gap between the upper and lower ranks of Sumerian society.

Slaves in Sumer Just as it created monarchy, civilization also created slavery. Scholars dispute precisely how and why people began enslaving other people, but a rigid system of ranking people by status was slavery's foundation. Slaves were those confined to the bottom of this hierarchy. No single description of Mesopotamian slavery covers all its diverse forms or its social and legal consequences. Both the gods (through their temple officials) and private individuals could own slaves. People lost their freedom by being captured in war, by being born to slaves, by voluntarily selling themselves or their children to escape starvation, or by being sold by their creditors to satisfy debts. Foreigners enslaved as captives in war or in raids were considered inferior to citizens who fell into slavery to pay off debts. Children whose parents dedicated them as servants to the gods counted as slaves, but they could rise to prominent positions in the temple administrations.

In general, slaves worked without pay and lacked nearly all rights; they existed as property rather than people. Slave owners could demand sex from, beat, or even kill their slaves with impunity. Although slaves frequently married among themselves, had families, and sometimes formed relationships with free persons, masters could buy and sell slaves at will. Sumerians, like later Mesopotamians, apparently accepted slavery as a fact, and there is no evidence of any sentiment for abolishing it.

Slaves worked as household servants, craft producers, and farm laborers, but historians dispute their economic significance compared with that of free workers. Most labor for the city-state seems to have been performed by free persons who paid their taxes through work rather than with money (which consisted of measured amounts of food or precious metal; coins were not invented until around 700 B.C.E. in Anatolia). Under certain conditions slaves could gain their freedom: masters' wills could liberate them, or they could purchase their freedom with earnings they were sometimes allowed to save.

The Invention of Writing Writing was also a creation of civilization. Beginning around 3500 B.C.E., the Sumerians invented writing to do accounting because expanding populations and commerce had increased the complexity of economic transactions. Before writing, people drew small pictures on clay tablets to represent objects. At first, these pictographs symbolized concrete objects only, such as a cow. Over several centuries of development, nonpictorial symbols and marks were added to the pictographs to stand for the sounds of spoken language. The final version of Sumerian writing was not an alphabet, in which a symbol (a letter) represents one or more designated sounds, but rather a mixed system of phonetic symbols and pictographs that represented entire syllables or entire words.

Archaeologists call the Sumerians' fully developed script **cuneiform** (from *cuneus*, Latin for "wedge") because the writers used wedge-shaped marks pressed into clay tablets to record spoken language (Figure 1.1). Other Mesopotamian peoples subsequently adopted cuneiform to write their own languages. For a long time, only a few professionally trained men and women, known as scribes, mastered the new technology of writing. Schools sprang up to teach aspiring scribes, who could then find jobs as accountants. Kings, priests, and wealthy landowners employed scribes above all to record who had paid their taxes and who still owed.

Writing soon created a new way to hand down stories and beliefs previously preserved only in memory and speech. The scribal schools extended their curriculum to cover nature lore, mathematics, and foreign languages. Written literature provided a powerful new tool for passing on a culture's traditions to later generations. Enheduanna, an Akkadian woman of the twenty-third century B.C.E., is considered the world's first known author of written poetry. She was a priestess, prophetess, and princess, the daughter of King Sargon of the city of Akkad. Her poetry, written in Sumerian, praised the awesome power of the life-giving and life-taking goddess of love and war, Inanna (also known as Ishtar): "I great gods scattered from you like fluttering bats, unable to face your intimidating gaze . . . knowing and wise queen of all the lands, who makes all creatures and people multiply." Later princesses—who wrote love songs, lullabies, songs of mourning, and prayers—continued the Mesopotamian tradition of royal women as authors and composers.

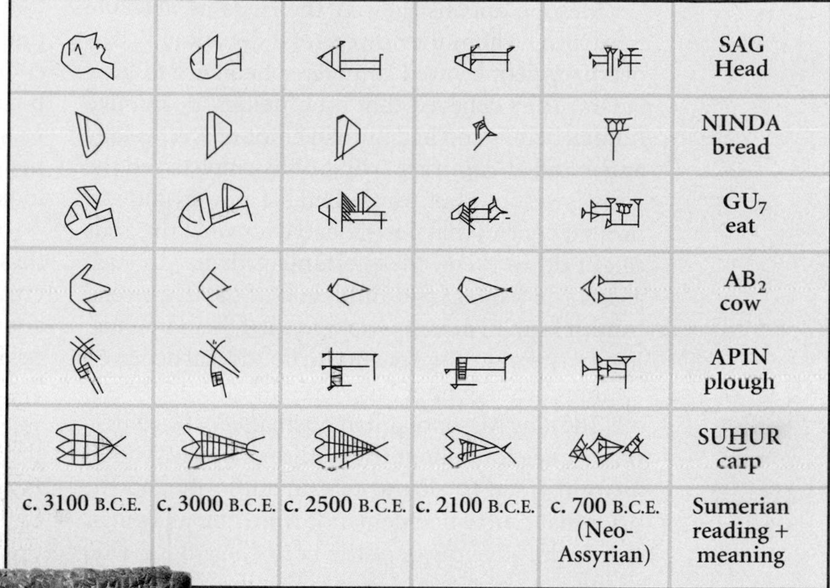

SAG
Head
NINDA
bread
GU$_7$
eat
AB$_2$
cow
APIN
plough
SUHUR
carp
c. 3100 B.C.E.
c. 3000 B.C.E.
c. 2500 B.C.E.
c. 2100 B.C.E.
c. 700 B.C.E. (Neo-Assyrian)
Sumerian reading + meaning

FIGURE 1.1 Cuneiform Writing
The earliest known form of writing developed in different locations in Mesopotamia in 4000–3000 B.C.E. when people began linking meaning and sound to signs such as those shown in the chart. Some scribes who mastered the system used sticks or reeds to press dense rows of small wedge-shaped marks into damp clay tablets; others used chisels to engrave them on stone. Cuneiform was used for at least fifteen Near Eastern languages and continued to be written for three thousand years. Written about 1900 B.C.E., the cuneiform text records a merchant's complaint that a shipment of copper contained less metal than he had expected. His letter, impressed on a clay tablet several inches long, was enclosed in an outer clay shell, which was then marked with the sender's private seal. This envelope protected the inner text from tampering or breakage. *(© The Trustees of The British Museum/Art Resource, NY.)*

Mesopotamian Myths and Religion

Writing developed into a crucial technology for supporting civilization because it provided a new way to record the traditions that helped hold communities together, especially myths (legendary stories about the gods and the origins of civilization that people saw as teaching important truths about the conditions of life) and religion (people's individual beliefs and group practices in worshipping the gods). Mesopotamians believed that the gods had created the universe as a hierarchy requiring that social inferiors obey their superiors. They also believed that the gods controlled all areas affecting human existence, from war to fertility to the weather. The more power over people's well-being that a divinity was believed to have, the more important the god. Each city-state honored a particular major deity as its special protector.

---

cuneiform (kyoo NEE uh form): The earliest form of writing, invented in Mesopotamia and done with wedge-shaped characters.

Mesopotamians viewed the gods as absolute masters to whom they owed total devotion, just as ordinary people owed complete obedience to their rulers. They believed that their deities looked like human beings and had human emotions, especially anger and an arbitrary will. Myths emphasized the gods' awesome but unpredictable power and the limited control that people had over what the gods might do to them. Mesopotamian divinities such as Inanna (Ishtar) and Enlil, god of the sky, would punish human beings who offended them by causing disasters like the destructive floods that occurred at unpredictable intervals.

The long Mesopotamian poem *Epic of Gilgamesh* poses questions about the nature of civilization in a world ruled by divine central authority and the price that civilization demands from human beings. It tells the adventures of the hero Gilgamesh, who as king of the city of Uruk forces the city's young men to construct a temple and a fortification wall, and its young women to sleep with him. When the distressed inhabitants beg Anu, lord of the gods, to grant them a rival to Gilgamesh, Anu calls on Aruru, the mother of the gods, to create a wild man, Enkidu, "hairy all over . . . dressed as cattle are." A week of sex with a prostitute tames this brute, preparing him for civilization: "Enkidu was weaker; he ran slower than before. But he had gained judgment, was wiser." After wrestling to a draw, Enkidu and Gilgamesh become friends and set out to conquer Humbaba (or Huwawa), the ugly, giant monster of the Pine Forest. Gilgamesh later insults the goddess Ishtar, who sends the Bull of Heaven to challenge him and Enkidu. The two comrades prevail, but when Enkidu makes matters worse by hurling the dead bull's haunch at Ishtar, the gods condemn him to death. In despair over human failure and weakness, Gilgamesh tries to find the secret of immortality, only to have his quest ended by a thieving snake. He realizes that immortality for human beings comes only from the fame of their achievements, above all building a great city such as Uruk, which spreads to "three square miles and its open ground." Only memory and gods live forever, Gilgamesh discovers.

A later version of the *Epic of Gilgamesh* includes a description of a huge flood that covers the earth, recalling the devastating deluges that often killed people and damaged the economy of Mesopotamia. Before sending the flood, the gods warn one man, Utnapishtim, of the coming disaster, telling him to build a boat. He loads his vessel with his relatives, his possessions, artisans, and domesticated and wild animals—"everything there was." After a week of drowning rains, he and his passengers land to repopulate the earth. This story shows that ancient Mesopotamians realized their civilization might be flawed—after all, it angered the gods enough to want to destroy it. The themes of Mesopotamian mythology, which lived on in poetry and song, powerfully influenced the mythology of distant peoples, especially the Greeks. The flood story also looks forward to the biblical account of Noah's ark.

Religion lay at the heart of Mesopotamian civilization because people believed that the divinely created hierarchy of the universe determined the conditions of their lives. As a result, the priest or priestess of a city's chief deity enjoyed high status. The most important duty of Mesopotamian priests was divination, the ritual process for discovering the gods' will and predicting the future. In performing divination, priests searched for divine messages by tracking the patterns of the stars, interpreting dreams, and cutting open animals to examine their organs for shapes signaling trouble ahead. These inspections helped people decide how to behave to persuade their unpredictable gods to give them a better future. Ordinary people joined priests in donating gifts to the gods and celebrating festivals to please their many deities. During the New Year holiday, for example, the reenactment of the mythical marriage of the goddess Inanna and the god Dumuzi was believed to ensure successful reproduction by the city's humans, animals, and plants for the coming year.

Metals and Empire Making: The Akkadians and the Ur III Dynasty, c. 2350–c. 2000 B.C.E.

The growth of agriculture and trade strengthened city-states in Mesopotamia. Their prosperity led them into competition and conflict, as rulers led armies on brutal campaigns to conquer their neighbors and win glory and wealth. Although agricultural production remained the greatest source of wealth, the desire to acquire metals pushed the kings of the city-state of Akkad to wage war to create the world's first **empire** (a political state in which one or more formerly independent territories or peoples are ruled by a single sovereign power).

Early metallurgy presents a clear example of a regular theme in history since the Neolithic Revolution: technological change leading to changes in social customs and values. In the case of metal, craftsmen invented ways to smelt ore and to make

---

empire: A political state in which one or more formerly independent territories or peoples are ruled by a single sovereign power.

metal alloys at high temperatures. Pure copper, which people had been using for some time, easily lost its shape and edge. The invention of bronze, a copper-tin alloy hard enough to hold a razor edge, enabled smiths to produce durable and deadly swords, daggers, and spearheads. The new technology of metallurgy led kings and the social elite of the Akkadian Empire to want new and more expensive luxury goods in metal; improved tools for agriculture and construction; and, above all, bronze weapons for war.

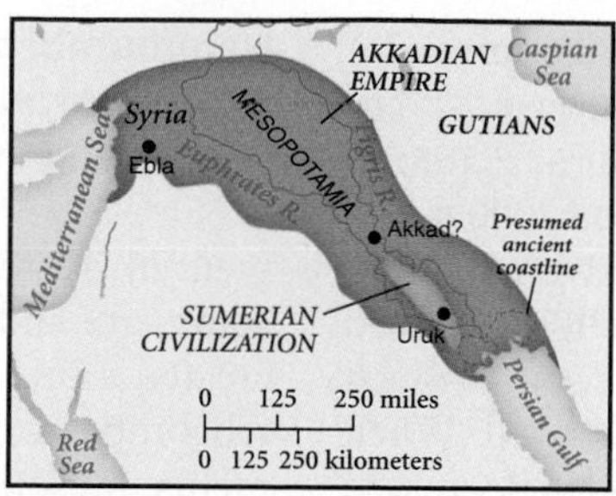

The Akkadian Empire, 2350–2200 B.C.E.

The desire to accumulate wealth and to possess status symbols stimulated demand for lavishly adorned weapons and exquisitely crafted jewelry. Rich men, especially, paid skilled metalworkers to make bronze swords and daggers decorated with expensive inlays, as on costly guns today. Such weapons increased visible social differences between men and women because they marked the status of the masculine roles of hunter and warrior.

Ambitious rulers chose to acquire metals by conquest rather than by trade, and they started wars to capture territory containing ore mines. The first empire began around 2350 B.C.E., when Sargon, king of Akkad, launched invasions far to the north and south of his homeland in mid-Mesopotamia. Through violent wars he conquered Sumer and the regions all the way westward to the Mediterranean Sea. Since Akkadians expressed their ideas about their own history in poetry and believed that the gods determined their fate, it was fitting that a poet of around 2000 B.C.E. credited Sargon's success to the favor of the god Enlil: "To Sargon the king of Akkad, from below to above, Enlil had given him lordship and kingship."

Sargon's grandson Naram-Sin continued the family tradition of conquering distant places to gain valuable resources, especially metals, and to prove the king's worthiness to rule. By around 2250 B.C.E., he had severely damaged Ebla, a large city whose site has been discovered in modern Syria, more than five hundred miles from his home base in Mesopotamia. Archaeologists have unearthed many cuneiform tablets at Ebla, some of them in more than one language. These discoveries suggest that the city thrived as an early center for learning and for trade.

The process of building an empire by force had the unintended consequence of spreading Mesopotamian literature and art throughout the Near East. The Akkadians spoke a language unrelated to Sumerian, but in conquering Sumer they took on most of the characteristics of that region's religion, literature, and culture. The other peoples whom the Akkadians conquered were then exposed to Sumerian beliefs and traditions, which they in turn adapted to suit their own purposes. In this way, war promoted cultural interaction.

Violence ended the Akkadian Empire. The traditional explanation for the empire's fall has been that the Gutians, a neighboring hill people, overthrew the Akkadian dynasty around 2200 B.C.E. by attacking from, in the words of a poet, "their land that rejects outside control, with the intelligence of human beings but with the form and stumbling words of a dog." Research has revealed, however, that civil war is a more likely explanation for the Akkadian Empire's fall. A newly resurgent Sumerian dynasty called Ur III (2112–2004 B.C.E.) then seized power in Sumer and presided over a flourishing of Sumerian literature. The Ur III rulers created a centralized economy, published the earliest preserved law code, and justified their rule by proclaiming their king to be divine. The best-preserved ziggurat was built in their era. Royal hymns, a new literary form, glorified the king; one example reads: "Your commands, like the word of a god, cannot be reversed; your words, like rain pouring down from heaven, are without number."

Mesopotamia remained politically unstable, and the development of civilization based on the centralized authority of kings did little to change that fact. The Ur III kings could not protect their dynasty from monarchy's fatal weakness — its tendency to inspire powerful and ambitious internal rivals to conspire to overthrow the ruling dynasty and take power themselves. When civil war weakened the regime, Amorite marauders from nearby saw their opportunity to conduct damaging raids. The Ur III dynasty collapsed after only a century of rule.

The Achievements of the Assyrians, the Babylonians, and the Canaanites, 2000–1000 B.C.E.

New kingdoms emerged in Assyria and Babylonia in the second millennium B.C.E. following the fall of the Akkadian Empire and the Sumerian Ur III dynasty. Assyrian innovations in long-distance commerce, Babylonian achievements in law, and the Canaanite invention of the alphabet were important contributions to the development of Western civilization. Such accomplishments are especially remarkable because they occurred while Mesopotamia

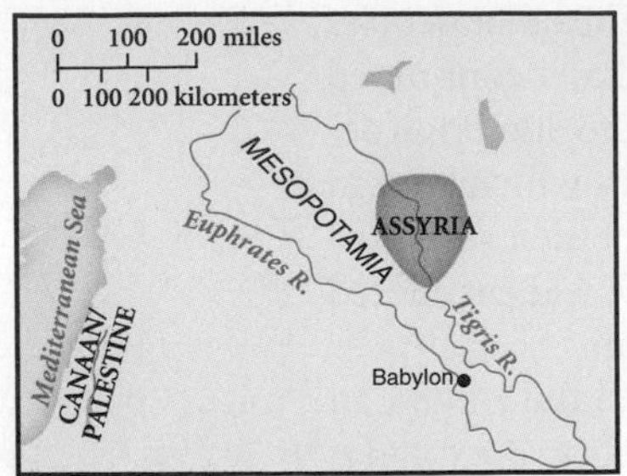

The Kingdom of Assyria, 1900 B.C.E.

was experiencing long-term economic troubles caused by climate change and agricultural pollution. By around 2000 B.C.E., the region's intensive irrigation had unintentionally increased the salt level of the soil so much that crop yields declined. When an extended period of decreased rainfall, especially in southern Mesopotamia, made the situation worse, the resulting economic stress generated political instability that lasted for centuries. In Canaan (ancient Palestine), on the eastern Mediterranean coast, strong trade by sea with many diverse regions and the export of timber from inland supported the growth of prosperous and independent city-states.

The Assyrians and Long-Distance Commerce The Assyrians inhabited northern Mesopotamia, just east of Anatolia. They took advantage of their geography to build an independent kingdom whose rulers permitted long-distance trade conducted by private entrepreneurs. The city-states of Anatolia were rich sources of wood, copper, silver, and gold for many Mesopotamian states. By acting as intermediaries in this trade between Anatolia and Mesopotamia, the Assyrians became the leading merchants of the Near East. They exported woolen textiles to Anatolia in exchange for its raw materials, which they in turn sold to the rest of Mesopotamia.

The economies of Mesopotamian city-states had previously been dominated by centralized state monopolies in which the king's officials controlled international trade and redistributed goods according to their ideas of who needed what. This kind of **redistributive economy** managed by the state never disappeared in Mesopotamia, but by 1900 B.C.E. the Assyrian kings were allowing individuals to transact large commercial deals on their own initiative. This system allowed private entrepreneurs to maximize profits as a reward for taking risks in business. Private Assyrian investors, for example, provided funds to traders to purchase an export cargo of cloth. The traders then formed donkey caravans to travel hundreds of miles to Anatolia, where, if they survived the dangerous journey, they could make huge profits to be split with their investors. Royal regulators settled any complaints of trader fraud or losses in transit.

Hammurabi of Babylon and Written Law To maintain social order, Mesopotamians established written laws that were made known to the people, an important development in Western civilization. The growth of private commerce and property ownership in Mesopotamia created a pressing need to guarantee fairness and reliability in contracts and other business agreements. Mesopotamians believed that the king had a sacred duty to make divine justice known to his subjects by rendering judgments in all sorts of cases, from commercial disputes to crime. Once written down, the record of the king's decisions amounted to what historians today call a law code. **Hammurabi** (r. c. 1792–c. 1750 B.C.E.), king of Babylon, a great city on the Euphrates River in what is today Iraq, became the most famous lawgiver in Mesopotamia (see Document, "Hammurabi's Laws for Physicians," page 15). In making his laws, he drew on earlier Mesopotamian legal traditions, such as the laws of the Sumerian Ur III dynasty.

In his code, Hammurabi proclaimed that his goals as ruler were to support "the principles of truth and equity" and to protect the less powerful members of society from exploitation. He gave a new emphasis to relieving the burdens of the poor as a necessary part of royal justice. The code legally divided society into three categories: free persons, commoners, and slaves. We do not know exactly how the first two categories differed, but they reflected a social hierarchy in which some people were assigned a higher value than others. An attacker who caused a pregnant woman of the free class to miscarry, for example, paid twice the fine levied for the same offense against a commoner. In the case of physical injury between social equals, the code specified "an eye for an eye" (an expression still used today). But a member of the free class who killed a commoner was not executed, only fined.

Many of Hammurabi's laws concerned the king's interests as a property owner who leased tracts of land to tenants in return for rent or services. The laws imposed severe penalties for offenses against property, including mutilation or a gruesome death for crimes ranging from theft to wrongful sales and careless construction. Women had only limited legal rights in this patriarchal society, but they could make business contracts and appear in court. A wife could divorce her husband for cruelty; a husband could divorce his wife for any reason. The law protected the wife's interests, however, by requiring a husband to restore his wife's property to her in the case of divorce.

---

redistributive economy: A system in which state officials control the production and distribution of goods.

Hammurabi (ha muh RAH bee): King of Babylonia in the eighteenth century B.C.E., famous for his law code.

DOCUMENT

Hammurabi's Laws for Physicians

In Hammurabi's collection of 282 laws, the following decisions set the fees for successful operations and the punishment for physicians' errors. The prescription of mutilation of a surgeon as the punishment for mutilation of a patient from the highest social class (law number 218) squares with the legal principle of equivalent punishment ("an eye for an eye") that occurs throughout Hammurabi's law code—a principle applied differently to patients of lower social classes.

215. If a physician performed a major operation on a freeman with a bronze scalpel and has saved the freeman's life, or he opened up the eye-socket of a freeman with a bronze scalpel and has saved the freeman's eye, he shall receive ten shekels[1] of silver.

216. If it was a commoner, he shall receive five shekels of silver.

217. If it was a freeman's slave, the owner of the slave shall give two shekels of silver to the physician.

218. If a physician performed a major operation on a freeman with a bronze scalpel and has caused the freeman's death, or he opened up the eye-socket of a freeman and has destroyed the freeman's eye, they shall cut off his hand.

219. If a physician performed a major operation on a commoner's slave with a bronze scalpel and has caused his death, he shall make good slave for slave.

220. If he opened up [the slave's] eye-socket with a bronze scalpel and has destroyed his eye, he shall pay half his value in silver.

Source: Adapted from James B. Pritchard, *Ancient Near Eastern Texts Relating to the Old Testament*, 3rd ed. with supplement (Princeton, NJ: Princeton University Press, 1969), 175.

[1]A shekel is a measurement of weight (about three-tenths of an ounce), not a coin. A hired laborer earned about one shekel per week. The average price of a slave was about twenty shekels.

Question to Consider

- **What does the nature of these punishments reveal about the different social worth of the physician and his patients?**

Hammurabi's law code was based on an ideal of justice. For example, under the eye-for-an-eye principle, the penalty was meant to match the crime as literally as possible. In this same spirit, the code protected people from bad-faith prosecutions by imposing the death penalty on anyone who made a serious accusation but did not prove his case. It also relied on what might be called nature-decided justice by allowing an accused person to leap into a river to receive a judgment: if the accused person sank, he was guilty; if he floated, he was innocent.

In everyday practice, however, Hammurabi's laws apparently were not always followed to the letter. Babylonian documents show that legal penalties were often less severe than the code specified. The people themselves assembled in courts to determine most cases by their own judgments. Why, then, did Hammurabi have his laws written down? He announces his reasons at the beginning and end of his code: to show Shamash, the Babylonian sun god and god of justice, that he had fulfilled the moral responsibility imposed on him as a divinely installed monarch—to ensure justice and the moral and material welfare of his people: "So that the powerful may not oppress the powerless, to provide justice for the orphan and the widow . . . let the victim of injustice see the law which applies to him, let his heart be put at ease." The king's responsibility for his society's welfare corresponded to the strictly hierarchical and religious vision of society accepted by all Mesopotamian peoples.

Mesopotamian City Life and Learning Hammurabi's code offers glimpses into the daily life of Bronze Age Mesopotamian city dwellers. It suggests that crimes of burglary and assault were common in cities, for example, and it reveals that marriages were arranged by the bride's father and the groom, and sealed with a legal contract. The detailed laws on surgery make clear that doctors practiced in the cities. Because people believed that angry gods or evil spirits caused serious diseases, Mesopotamian medicine included magic: a doctor might prescribe an incantation along with potions and diet recommendations. Magicians or exorcists offered medical treatment that depended primarily on spells and on interpreting signs, such as the patient's dreams or hallucinations.

Archaeological evidence adds to the information on urban life found in Hammurabi's code. That cities had many taverns and wine shops, often run by women proprietors, indicates that Babylonians enjoyed having alcoholic drinks in a friendly setting. Contaminated drinking water caused many illnesses because sewage disposal was rudimentary. Citizens could find relief from the odors and crowding of the streets in the city's open spaces. The world's oldest known map, an inscribed clay tablet showing the outlines of the Babylonian city of Nippur about 1500 B.C.E., indicates a substantial area set aside as a city park.

Having large numbers of people living and interacting in cities helped stimulate intellectual developments. Mesopotamian achievements in mathematics and astronomy had a tremendous effect that endures to this day. Creating maps, for example, required sophisticated techniques of measurement and knowledge of spatial relationships. Mathematicians invented algebra, including the derivation of roots of numbers, to solve complex problems. They invented place-value notation, which makes a numeral's position in a number indicate ones, tens, hundreds, and so on. The system of reckoning based on sixty, still used in the division of hours and minutes and in the degrees of a circle, also comes from Mesopotamia. Mesopotamian expertise in recording the paths of the stars and planets probably arose from the desire to make predictions about the future, in accordance with the astrological belief that the movement of celestial bodies directly affects human life. The charts and tables compiled by Mesopotamian stargazers laid the foundation for later advances in astronomy.

Canaanites, Commerce, and the Alphabet The people of Canaan expanded their population by absorbing merchants from many lands. Some scholars believe that the political structure of the Canaanite communities even provided inspiration for the city-states of Greece. The interaction of traders and travelers from many different cultures in Canaanite cities encouraged innovation in the recording of business transactions. This multilingual business environment produced an overwhelmingly important writing technology about 1600 B.C.E.: the alphabet. In this new system of writing, a simplified picture — a letter — stood for only one sound in the language, a dramatic change from complicated scripts such as cuneiform. The alphabet developed in Canaanite cities later became the basis for the Greek and Roman alphabets and, from there, of modern Western alphabets. The Canaanite alphabet therefore ranks as one of the most important contributions to the history of Western civilization.

REVIEW QUESTION How did life change for people in Mesopotamia when they began to live in cities?

Egypt, the First Unified Country, 3050–1000 B.C.E.

Alongside Mesopotamian civilization, the other earliest example of Western civilization arose in Egypt, in northeastern Africa. The Egyptians built a wealthy, profoundly religious, and strongly centralized society ruled by kings. Unlike the Mesopotamian city-states, Egypt became a unified country, the world's first large-scale territorial state, whose prosperity and stability depended on the king's success in maintaining strong central authority and defeating enemies. Egypt was located close enough to Mesopotamia to learn from peoples there but was geographically protected enough to develop its own distinct culture, which Egyptians believed was superior to any other. Like the Mesopotamians, the Egyptians believed that a just society respected the gods, was structured in a hierarchy, and had a supreme ruler who made law for the rest of the people. The Egyptian rulers' belief in the soul's immortality and the possibility of a happy afterlife motivated them to construct the most imposing tombs in history, the pyramids. Egyptian architecture, art, and religious ideas influenced later Mediterranean peoples, especially the Greeks.

From the Unification of Egypt to the Old Kingdom, 3050–2190 B.C.E.

When climate change dried up the grasslands of the Sahara region of Africa about 5000–4000 B.C.E., people slowly migrated from there to the northeast corner of the continent, settling along the Nile River. They had formed a large political state by about 3050 B.C.E., when King Narmer (also called Menes)[1] united the previously separate territories of Upper (southern) Egypt and Lower (northern) Egypt. (*Upper* and *Lower* refer to the direction of the Nile River, which begins south of Egypt and flows northward to the Mediterranean.) The Egyptian ruler therefore referred to himself as King of the Two Lands. By around 2687 B.C.E., the monarchs had created a strong centralized state in these large territories. Historians refer to this first great unified Egyptian state as the Old Kingdom. It lasted until around 2190 B.C.E. (Map 1.2). Unlike their Mesopotamian counterparts, who ruled independent city-

[1]Representing ancient Egyptian names and dates presents serious problems. Since the Egyptians did not include vowel sounds in their writing, we are not sure how to spell their names. The spelling of names here is taken from *The Oxford Encyclopedia of Ancient Egypt*, edited by Donald B. Redford (2001), with alternate names given in cases where they might be more familiar. Dates are approximate and uncertain, and scholars bitterly disagree about them. (For an explanation of the problems, see Redford, "Chronology and Periodization," *The Oxford Encyclopedia*, vol. 1, 264–68.) The dates appearing in this book are compiled with as much consistency as possible from articles in *The Oxford Encyclopedia* and in the "Egyptian King List" given at the back of each of its volumes.

states in a divided land, Egyptian kings built only a few large cities in their united country. The first capital of the united country, Memphis (south of modern Cairo), grew into a metropolis packed with mammoth structures in and near its urban center. The most spectacular—and most mysterious—of the Old Kingdom architectural marvels is the so-called Great Sphinx. The oldest monumental sculpture in the world, this statue carved from stones has a human head on the body of a lion lying on its four paws. It is nearly 250 feet long and almost 70 feet high. A temple was built in front of it, perhaps to worship the sun as a god. The precise date and the purpose of this huge monument remain hotly contested issues. A thousand years later, Egyptians apparently regarded the Sphinx as a divinity, but no records exist to explain its original meaning. Most scholars believe that this enormous statue was erected in the Old Kingdom (although they disagree about exactly when to date it within that period). A few, however, citing weathering and erosion patterns on the stone of the statue, have argued that it is much older, indeed as old as 5000 B.C.E. If clear evidence supporting this date is ever discovered, then the history of early Egypt will have to be completely rewritten. This is just one of the many controversies about ancient Egypt that archaeological science may someday settle.

The Old Kingdom's costly architectural marvels indicate the prosperity and power that Narmer's unified state gradually acquired. That state's central territory consisted of a narrow strip of fertile land on either side of the Nile River. This ribbon of green fields zigzagged along the river's banks for seven hundred miles southward from the Mediterranean Sea. The great desert flanking the fields on the west and the east protected Egypt from invasion, except through the northern Nile delta and from Nubia in the south. The deserts also were sources of wealth because they contained large deposits of metal ores. Egypt's geography additionally contributed to its prosperity by supporting seaborne commerce in the Mediterranean sea to the north and the Indian Ocean to the east, as well as overland trade with peoples in central Africa to the south.

The most important sector of Egypt's economy was agriculture. Under normal weather conditions, the Nile River overflowed its channel for several weeks each year, when melting snow from the mountains of central Africa swelled its waters. This annual flood, which usually happened at a predictable time in the year, enriched the soil with nutrients from the river's silt and diluted harmful mineral salts, thereby making farming much more productive and supporting strong population growth. In sharp contrast to the unpredictable floods that harmed Mesopotamian peoples, the regular flooding of the Nile benefited Egyptians. Trouble came in Egypt only if the usual flood did not take place, as occasionally happened when not enough winter precipitation fell in the African mountains.

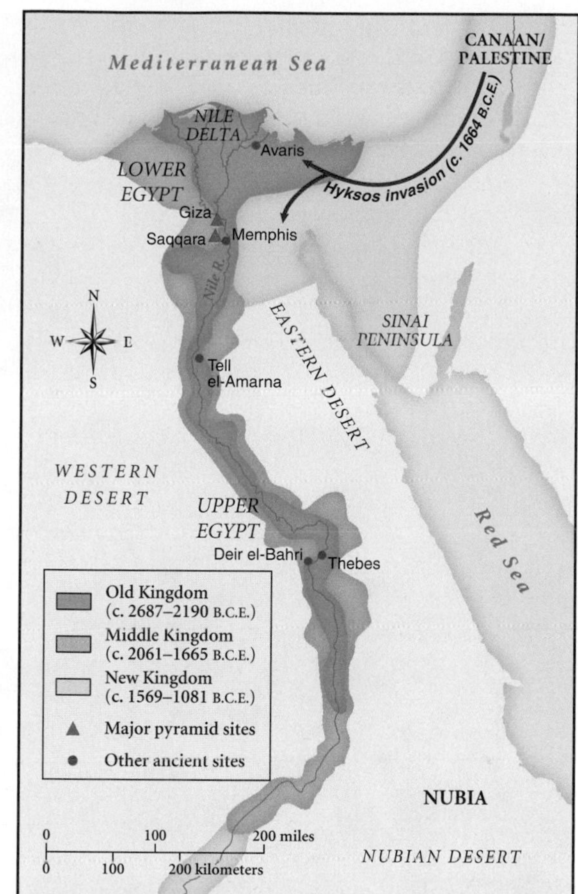

MAP 1.2 Ancient Egypt
Large deserts enclosed the Nile River on the west and the east. The Nile provided Egyptians with water to irrigate their fields and a highway for traveling north to the Mediterranean Sea and south to Nubia. The only easy land route into and out of Egypt lay through the northern Sinai peninsula into the coastal area of the eastern Mediterranean; Egyptian kings always fought to control this region to secure the safety of their land.

The plants and animals raised by Egypt's farmers on the flood-nourished lands fed a population that grew faster than in Mesopotamia. Egypt had expanded to perhaps several million people (the exact size is uncertain) by the time of the New Kingdom. Date palms, vegetables, grass for pasturing animals, and grain grew in abundance. From their ample supplies of grain, the Egyptians made bread and beer, the country's most popular beverage for people of all ages. Thicker and more nutritious than the modern version, ancient Egyptian beer was such an important food that it was sometimes used to pay workmen's wages. Egyptians, like other ancient societies, often flavored and sweetened their beer with fruits, usually dates.

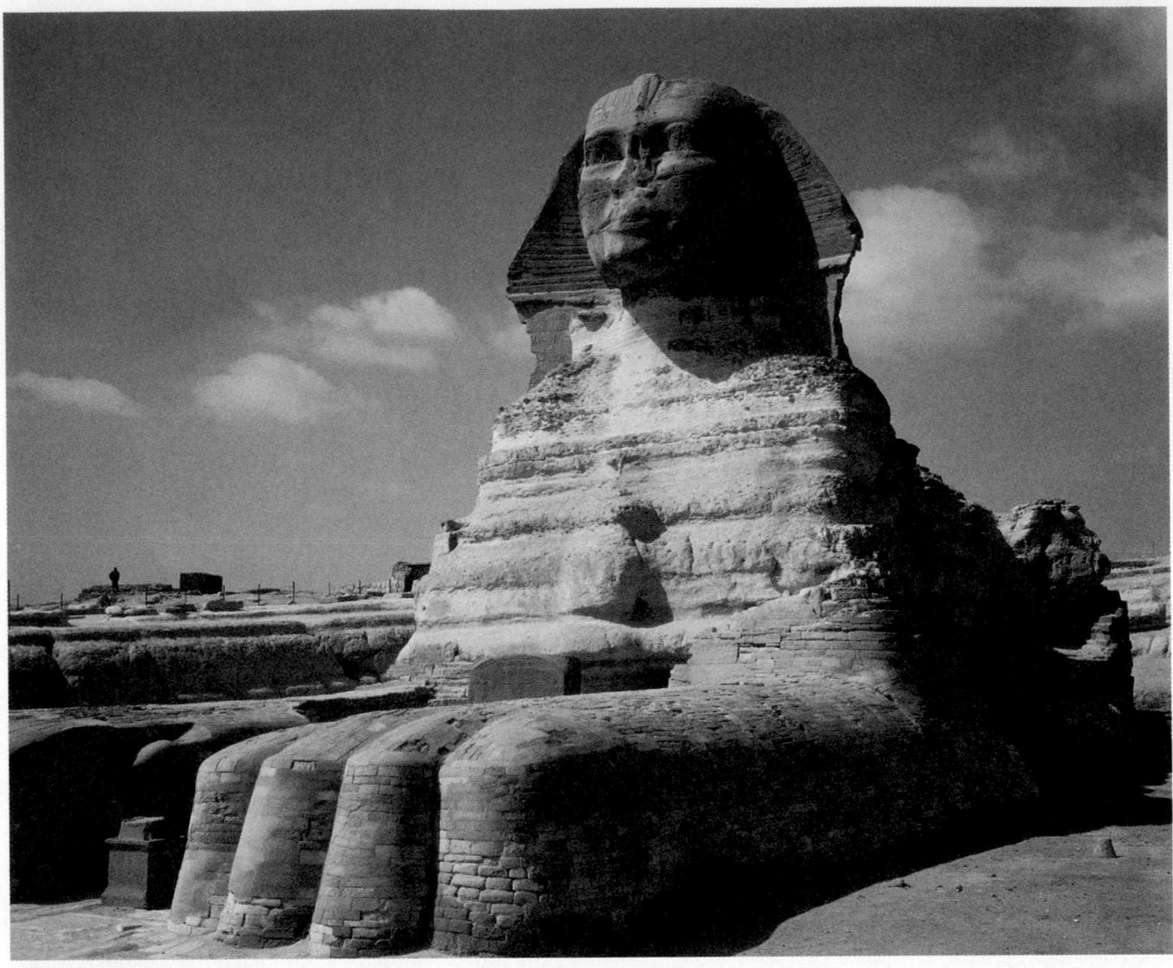

The Great Sphinx of Egypt
This enormous stone sculpture of a sphinx, a mythical female creature with a human head and torso and lion's body, was built near the Great Pyramid in Egypt. Since no inscriptions tell us which king or kings ordered it built, or when or why, scholars still debate its place in ancient Egyptian history and thought. It remains the largest stone monument in the world. *(The Art Archive/Gianni Dagli Orti.)*

Egypt's diverse population included people whose skin color ranged from light to dark. Although many ancient Egyptians would be regarded as black by modern racial classification, ancient peoples did not observe such distinctions. The modern controversy over whether Egyptians were people of color is therefore not an issue that ancient Egyptians would have considered. If asked, they would probably have identified themselves by geography, language, religion, or traditions rather than skin color. Like many other ancient groups, the Egyptians called themselves simply The People. Later peoples, especially the Greeks, recognized the ethnic and cultural differences between themselves and the Egyptians, but they deeply admired Egyptian civilization for its long history and strongly religious character. The Greeks above all recognized that they had received many ideas about the gods from the traditions of the Egyptians, which they respected for their great age.

Although early Egyptians absorbed knowledge from both the Mesopotamians and their African neighbors to the south, the Nubians, they developed their own written scripts rather than using cuneiform. To write formal and official texts they used an ornate pictographic script known as **hieroglyphic** (Figure 1.2, page 19). They also developed other scripts for everyday purposes.

But some scholars believe that of all the outside influences, Nubian society was the one that most deeply influenced early Egypt. A Nubian social elite lived in dwellings much grander than the small

hieroglyphic: The ancient Egyptian pictographic writing system for official texts.

FIGURE 1.2 Egyptian Hieroglyphs
Ancient Egyptians used pictures such as these to develop their own system of writing around 3000 B.C.E. Egyptian hieroglyphs include around seven hundred pictures in three categories: ideograms (signs indicating things or ideas), phonograms (signs indicating sounds), and determinatives (signs clarifying the meaning of the other signs). Because Egyptians employed this formal script mainly for religious inscriptions on buildings and sacred objects, Greeks referred to it as *ta hieroglyphica* ("the sacred carved letters"), from which comes the modern word *hieroglyphic*, used to designate this system of writing. Eventually, Egyptians also developed the handwritten cursive script called demotic (Greek for "of the people"), a much simpler and quicker form of writing. The hieroglyphic writing system continued until about 400 C.E., when it was replaced by the Coptic alphabet. Compare hieroglyphs with cuneiform shapes (see page 11).
(Victor R. Boswell Jr./National Geographic Stock.)

Hieroglyph	*Meaning*	*Sound value*
	vulture	glottal stop
	flowering reed	consonantal I
	forearm and hand	ayin
	quail chick	W
	foot	B
	stool	P
	horned viper	F
	owl	M
	water	N
	mouth	R
	reed shelter	H
	twisted flax	slightly guttural
	placenta (?)	H as in "loch"
	animal's belly	slightly softer than h
	door bolt	S
	folded cloth	S
	pool	SH
	hill	Q
	basket with handle	K
	jar stand	G
	loaf	T

huts housing most of the population. Egyptians interacted with Nubians while trading for raw materials such as gold, ivory, and animal skins, and scholars argue that Nubia's hierarchical political and social organization influenced the development of Egypt's politically centralized Old Kingdom. Eventually, however, Egypt's greater power led it to dominate its southern neighbor.

Religion and the Authority of the King

Although the Egyptians carved a new path for civilization by creating a large unified country under a central authority, keeping the country unified and politically stable turned out to be difficult. When the kings were strong, as during the Old Kingdom, the country was peaceful and rich, with flourishing international trade, especially by sea along the eastern Mediterranean coast. However, when regional governors became rebellious and the king was weak, political instability resulted.

The king derived power and success from the fulfillment of his religious obligations. Like the Mesopotamians, Egyptians centered their lives on religion. They worshipped a great variety of gods, who were often shown in paintings and sculptures as creatures with both human and animal features, such as the head of a jackal or a bird atop a human body. This style of representing deities did not mean that people worshipped animals, but rather that they believed the gods each had a particular animal through which they revealed themselves to human beings. At the most basic level, Egyptian gods were associated with powerful natural objects, emotions, qualities, and technologies — examples are Re, the sun god; Isis, the goddess of love and fertility; and Thoth, the god of wisdom and the inventor of writing. People worshipped the gods with rituals, prayers, and festivals that expressed their respect and devotion to these divine powers.

Modern historians' generalizations about religions should never be taken as adequate descriptions of an ancient people's beliefs, but it seems worth asking the question: Did Egyptians in general consider their gods as more kindly and helpful to human beings than did Mesopotamians, whose deities seem more harsh and even sometimes cruel? If this is indeed a significant difference between the religions of Egypt and Mesopotamia, one might ask whether it could reflect the difference in the two regions' natural environments: as noted above, the annual flooding of the Nile benefited the Egyptians, while the random flooding of the Euphrates and Tigris Rivers brought disaster to Mesopotamian peoples. Given that both Egyptians and Mesopotamians believed that the gods were responsible for the weather and the good or the bad that it brought to human beings, it seems possible that these cultures' respective environments played a role in their understanding of their deities.

In any case, the Egyptians regarded their king as a helpful divinity in human form, identified with the hawk-headed god Horus. In the Egyptian view, the king's rule was divine because he helped generate *maat* ("what is right"), the supernatural force that brought order and harmony to human beings if they maintained a stable hierarchy. The goddess **Maat** embodied this force, which was the source of justice in a world that would, the Egyptians believed, fall into violent disorder if the king did not rule properly. To fulfill his religious obligation to rule according to maat and therefore maintain the goodwill of the gods toward the people, the king had the duties of making law, keeping the forces of nature in balance for the benefit of his people, and waging war on Egypt's enemies.

To express the king's legitimacy as ruler, official art represented him carrying out his religious and military duties. The requirement for the king to show piety (proper religious belief and behavior) demanded strict regulation of his daily activities: he had specific times to take a bath, go for a walk, and make love to his wife. Most important, he had to ensure the country's fertility and prosperity. Above all, the king was supposed to guarantee a proper flooding of the Nile by performing his duties justly and in accordance with traditional order. Any failure of the flood to happen, which would devastate the country's economy and leave many people hungry, seriously weakened the king's authority and encouraged rebellions by rivals for power.

Pyramids and the Afterlife

Successful Old Kingdom rulers used expensive building programs to demonstrate their piety and exhibit their status atop the social hierarchy. In the desert outside Memphis, the Old Kingdom rulers erected stunning monuments displaying their status and their religious belief: their huge tombs. These tombs — the pyramids (see the illustration on page 21) — formed the centerpieces of elaborate groups of temples and halls for religious ceremonies and royal funerals. Although the pyramids were not the first monuments built from enormous worked stones (that title goes to a set of temples, admittedly much smaller in scale, on the Mediterranean island of Malta), they rank as the grandest, much larger even than the Great Sphinx.

Old Kingdom rulers spent vast resources on these huge complexes to proclaim their divine status and protect their mummified bodies for existence in the afterlife. King Khufu (r. 2609–2584 B.C.E.; also known as Cheops) commissioned the hugest monument of all — the Great Pyramid at Giza. At about 480 feet high, it stands taller than a forty-story skyscraper. Covering more than thirteen acres and 760 feet long on each side, it required more than two million blocks of limestone, some of which weighed fifteen tons apiece. Its exterior blocks were quarried along the Nile and then floated to the site on barges. Free workers (not slaves) dragged the blocks up ramps into position using rollers and sleds.

The Old Kingdom rulers' expensive preparations for death reflected their strong belief in an

---

Maat (MAH aht): The Egyptian goddess embodying truth, justice, and cosmic order. (The word *maat* means "what is right.")

eternal afterlife. A hieroglyphic text addressed to the god Atum expresses the hope that the ruler will have a safe existence after death: "O Atum, put your arms around King Neferkare Pepy II [r. c. 2300–2206 B.C.E.], around this construction work, around this pyramid. . . . May you guard lest anything happen to him evilly throughout the course of eternity." The royal family equipped their tombs with loads of comforts to use when they joined the world of the dead. Gilded furniture, sparkling jewelry, exquisite objects of all kinds — the dead kings had all this and more placed alongside their coffins, in which rested their mummies. Archaeologists have even uncovered two full-sized cedar ships buried next to the Great Pyramid, meant to carry King Khufu on his journey into eternity.

Hierarchy and Order in Egyptian Society The Old Kingdom ranked Egyptians in a tightly structured hierarchy to preserve their kings' authority and therefore support what they regarded as the proper order of a just society. Egyptians believed that their ordered society was superior to any other, and they despised foreigners, such as the Near Easterners criticized by Merikare's father.

The king and queen headed the hierarchy. Brothers and sisters in the royal family could marry each other, perhaps because such matches were believed necessary to preserve the purity of the royal line and to imitate the marriages of the gods. The priests, royal administrators, provincial governors, and commanders of the army ranked next in the hierarchy. Then came the free common people, most of whom worked in agriculture. Free workers had heavy obligations to the state. For example, in a system called corvée labor, the kings commanded commoners to work on the pyramids during slack times in farming. The state fed, housed, and clothed the workers while they performed this seasonal work, but their labor was a way of paying taxes. Rates of taxation reached 20 percent on the produce of free farmers. Slaves captured in foreign wars served the royal family and the priests in the Old Kingdom, but privately owned slaves working in free persons' homes or on their farms did not become numerous until after the Old Kingdom. The king hired mercenaries, many from Nubia, to form the majority of the army.

Hierarchy seemed less important when it came to gender. Egypt preserved more of the gender equality of the early Stone Age than did its neighbors, for reasons not easy to discover. Egyptian religion gave great respect to female divinities, but so did Mesopotamian religion. Perhaps the Egyptian myth of the goddess Isis, who restored life to her husband Osiris after he had been torn into pieces, expressed a special belief in the ability of women to restore order to life in times of great loss. Whatever

The Pyramids at Giza in Egypt

The kings of the Egyptian Old Kingdom constructed massive stone pyramids for their tombs, the centerpieces of large complexes of temples and courtyards stretching down to the banks of the Nile or along a canal leading to the river. The inner burial chambers lay at the end of long, narrow tunnels snaking through the pyramids' interiors. The biggest pyramid shown here is the so-called Great Pyramid of King Khufu (Cheops), erected at Giza (in the desert outside what is today Cairo) in the twenty-sixth century B.C.E. and soaring almost 480 feet high, several times taller than the famous Parthenon temple in fifth-century B.C.E. Athens (see page 85). *(Travel Pix Ltd./SuperStock.)*

the explanation, women in ancient Egypt generally enjoyed the same legal rights as free men. They could own land and slaves, inherit property, pursue lawsuits, transact business, and initiate divorces. Old Kingdom portrait statues show the equal status of wife and husband: each figure is the same size and sits on the same kind of chair. Men dominated public life, while women devoted themselves mainly to private life, managing their households and property. When their husbands went to war or were killed in battle, however, women often took on men's work. Women could serve as priestesses, farm managers, or healers to maintain stability and order in times of crisis.

The formal style of Egypt's art illustrates how much the civilization valued order and predictability. Almost all Egyptian sculpture and painting comes from tombs or temples, testimony to its people's deep desire to maintain proper relations with the gods by honoring them with appropriate art. Old Kingdom artists excelled in stonework, from carved ornamental jars to massive portrait statues of the kings. These statues represent the subject either standing stiffly with the left leg advanced or sitting on a chair or throne, stable and poised. The concern for decorum (suitable behavior) also appears in the Old Kingdom literature the Egyptians called instructions, known today as **wisdom literature**. These texts gave instructions for appropriate behavior by officials. In the *Instruction of Ptahhotep*, for example, the royal minister Ptahhotep instructs his son, who will succeed him in office, to seek advice from ignorant people as well as the wise and not to be arrogant or overconfident just because he is well educated. This kind of literature had a strong influence on later civilizations, especially the ancient Israelites.

The Middle and New Kingdoms in Egypt, 2061–1081 B.C.E.

The Old Kingdom began to disintegrate in the late third millennium B.C.E. The reasons remain mysterious. One suggestion is that climate changes caused the annual Nile flood to shrink and the ensuing agricultural failure discredited the regime—people believed the kings had betrayed Maat. Economic hard times probably fueled rivalry for royal rule between ambitious families, and civil war between a northern and a southern dynasty then ripped apart the Kingdom of the Two Lands. This destruction of the Old Kingdom's unity allowed regional governors to increase their power. Some governors, who had previously supported the kings while times were good, now seized independence for their regions. It was the troubles of this period that made Merikare's father's advice so pressing: famine and civil unrest during the so-called First Intermediate Period (2190–2061 B.C.E.) prevented the reestablishment of political unity.

The Middle Kingdom The kings of what historians label the Middle Kingdom (2061–1665 B.C.E.) gradually restored the strong central authority their Old Kingdom predecessors had lost. They waged war to extend the southern boundaries of Egypt, while to the north they expanded diplomatic and trade contacts in the eastern Mediterranean region and with the island of Crete.

Middle Kingdom literature reveals that the reclaimed national unity contributed to a deeply felt pride in the homeland. The Egyptian narrator of *The Story of Sinuhe*, for example, reports that he lived luxuriously during a forced stay in Syria but still longed to return: "Whichever god you are who ordered my exile, have mercy and bring me home! Please allow me to see the land where my heart dwells! Nothing is more important than that my body be buried in the country where I was born!" For this lost soul, love for Egypt outranked personal riches and comfort in a foreign land.

From Hyksos Rule to the New Kingdom The Middle Kingdom lost its unity during the Second Intermediate Period (1664–1570 B.C.E.), when the kings proved too weak to control aggressive foreigners who had migrated into Egypt and gradually set up independent communities. By 1664 B.C.E., diverse bands of a Semitic people originally from the eastern Mediterranean coast took advantage of the troubled times to become Egypt's rulers. The Egyptians called these foreigners Hyksos ("rulers of the foreign countries"). Recent archaeological discoveries have emphasized the role of Hyksos settlers in transplanting elements of foreign culture to Egypt: their capital, Avaris, boasted wall paintings done in the Minoan style current on the island of Crete. Some historians think the Hyksos also introduced such innovations as bronze-making technology, new musical instruments, humpbacked cattle, and olive trees; they certainly promoted frequent contact between Egypt and other Near Eastern states. Hyksos rulers also strengthened Egypt's capacity to make war by expanding the use of chariots on the battlefield and more powerful bows in the army.

After a long struggle with the Hyksos, the leaders of Thebes, in southern Egypt, reunited the kingdom. The series of royal dynasties they founded is called the New Kingdom (1569–1081 B.C.E.). Recent

---

wisdom literature: Texts giving instructions for proper behavior by officials.

archaeological discoveries reveal that Thebes may have drawn some of the strength that allowed it to reunite Egypt from its connections with prosperous settlements that emerged far out in the western desert, such as at Kharga Oasis. Oases featured abundant water from underground aquifers in the middle of an otherwise dry and scorching environment. An oasis settlement could flourish because it provided an essential stopping point for the caravans of merchants who endured dangerously harsh desert conditions to profit from commerce. Thebes seems to have benefited from access to trade provided by good relations with the peoples settled in the western desert. This expansion of contact is a clear sign that Egyptian society did not remain unchanged over time, shutting itself off behind its natural boundaries along the Nile. Similarly, contacts with peoples to the east across the Red Sea and along the Indian Ocean increased in the New Kingdom.

The kings of the New Kingdom, known as pharaohs, rebuilt central authority by restricting the power of regional governors and promoting a renewed sense of national identity. To prevent invasions, the pharaohs followed up the Hyksos innovations in military technology by creating a standing army, another significant change in Egyptian society. These kings still employed many mercenaries, but they formed an Egyptian military elite to command national defense. Recognizing that knowledge of the rest of the world was necessary for safety, the pharaohs engaged in regular diplomacy with neighboring monarchs to increase their international contacts. In fact, the pharaohs regularly exchanged letters on matters of state with their "brother kings," as they called them, in Mesopotamia, Anatolia, and the eastern Mediterranean region.

Warrior Pharaohs The New Kingdom pharaohs sent their reorganized military into foreign wars to gain territory and show their superiority. They waged many campaigns abroad and presented themselves in official propaganda and art as the incarnations of warrior gods. They invaded lands to the south to win access to gold and other precious materials, and they fought up and down the eastern Mediterranean coast to control that crucial land route into Egypt. Their imperialism has today earned them the title *warrior pharaohs.*

Hatshepsut as Pharaoh Offering Maat

This granite statue, eight and a half feet tall, portrayed Hatshepsut, queen of Egypt in the early fifteenth century B.C.E., as pharaoh wearing a beard and male clothing. She is performing her royal duty of offering *maat* (the divine principle of order and justice) to the gods. Egyptian religion taught that the gods "lived on maat" and that the land's rulers were responsible for providing it. Hatshepsut had this statue, and many others, placed in a huge temple she built outside Thebes, in Upper Egypt. Compare her posture to that of the statue of a woman grinding grain on page P-9. Why do you think Hatshepsut is shown as calm and relaxed, despite having her toes severely flexed? *(Egypt, eighteenth dynasty, ca. 1473–1458 B.C.E. Granite, H. 261.5 cm. [102 15/16 in.]; w. 80 cm. [31½ in.]; d. 137 cm. [53 15/16 in.]. Rogers Fund, 1929 [29.3.1]. The Metropolitan Museum of Art, New York, NY, U.S.A. Image copyright © The Metropolitan Museum of Art/Art Resource, NY.)*

Massive riches supported the power of the warrior pharaohs. Egyptian traders exchanged local fine goods, such as ivory, for foreign luxury goods, such as wine and olive oil transported in painted pottery from Greece. Egyptian rulers displayed their wealth most conspicuously in the enormous sums spent to build stone temples. Queen Hatshepsut (r. 1502–1482 B.C.E.), for example, built her massive mortuary temple at Deir el-Bahri, near Thebes, including a temple dedicated to the god Amun (or Amen), to express her claim to divine birth and the right to rule. After her husband (who was also her half brother) died, Hatshepsut proclaimed herself "female king" as co-ruler with her young stepson. In this way, she got around the restrictions of Egyptian political tradition, which did not recognize the right of a queen to reign in her own right. Hatshepsut also often had herself represented in official art as a king, with a royal beard and male clothing. Hatshepsut succeeded in her unusual rule because she demonstrated that a woman could ensure safety and prosperity by maintaining the goodwill of the gods toward the country and its people.

Religious Tradition and Upheaval Egyptians believed that their gods oversaw all aspects of life and death. Many large temples honored the traditional gods, and by the time of the New Kingdom, the gods' cults (that is, the traditions and rituals used in worship) enriched the religious life of the entire population. The principal festivals of the gods featured large public celebrations. A calendar based on the moon governed the dates of religious ceremonies. (The Egyptians also developed a calendar for administrative and fiscal purposes that had 365 days, divided into 12 months of 30 days each, with the extra 5 days added before the start of the next year. Our modern calendar comes from this source.)

The early New Kingdom pharaohs from Thebes promoted their state god Amun-Re (a combination of Thebes's patron god and the sun god) so energetically that he became far more important than the other gods. This Theban cult took in and subordinated the other gods, without denying their existence or the continued importance of their priests. The pharaoh Akhenaten (r. 1372–1355 B.C.E.) went a step further, however: he proclaimed that official religion would concentrate on worshipping Aten, who represented the sun. Akhenaten made the king and the queen the only people with direct access to the cult of Aten; ordinary people had no part in it. Some scholars identify Akhenaten's religious reform as a step toward monotheism, with Aten meant to be the state's sole god. Whatever may have been Akhenaten's attitude toward the question of whether the universe was ruled by one god or many, his main goal was to use religion to strengthen his personal rule as king.

To showcase the royal family and the concentration of power that he sought, Akhenaten built a new capital for his favorite god at Tell el-Amarna (see Map 1.2). He tried to force his revised religion on the priests of the old cults, but they resisted. Historians have blamed Akhenaten's religious zeal for leading him to neglect practical affairs and thus weaken his kingdom's defense, but recent research on international correspondence found at Tell el-Amarna has shown that the pharaoh tried to use diplomacy to turn foreign enemies against one another so that they would not become strong enough to threaten Egypt. His policy failed, however, when the Hittites from Anatolia defeated the Mitanni, Egypt's allies in eastern Syria. Akhenaten's religious reform also died with him. During the reign of his successor, Tutankhamun (r. 1355–1346 B.C.E.)—famous today through the discovery in 1922 of his rich, unlooted tomb—the cult of Amun-Re reclaimed its leading role. The crisis created by Akhenaten's attempted reform emphasizes the overwhelming importance of religious conservatism in Egyptian life and the control of religion by the ruling power.

Life and Belief in the New Kingdom Most Egyptians' daily lives under the New Kingdom still revolved around their labor and the annual flood of the Nile. During the months when the river stayed between its banks, they worked their fields, rising early in the morning to avoid the searing heat. When the flooding halted agricultural work, the king required them to work on his building projects. They lived in workers' quarters erected next to the construction sites. Although slaves became more common as household workers in the New Kingdom, free workers, performing labor instead of paying taxes in money, did most of the work on this period's mammoth royal construction projects. Written texts reveal that workers lightened their burden by singing songs, telling adventure stories, and drinking a lot of beer. They accomplished a great deal with their labors: the majority of the ancient temples remaining in Egypt today were built during the New Kingdom.

Ordinary people worshipped many different gods, especially deities they hoped would protect them in their daily lives. They venerated Bes, for instance, a dwarf with the features of a lion, as a protector of the household. They carved his image on amulets, beds, headrests, and mirror handles. By the time of the New Kingdom, ordinary people believed that they, too, could have a blessed afterlife and therefore put great effort into preparing for it. Those who could afford it arranged to have their tombs outfitted with all the goods needed for the journey to their new existence. Most important, they paid burial experts to turn their corpses into mummies so that they could have a complete body in the afterlife. Making a mummy required removing the brain (through the nose with a long-handled spoon), cutting out the internal organs to store separately in stone jars, drying the body with mineral salts to the consistency of old leather, and wrapping the shrunken flesh in linen soaked with ointments.

Every mummy had to travel to the afterlife with a copy of the *Book of the Dead*, which included magical spells for avoiding dangers along the way as well as instructions on how to prepare for the judgment-day trial before the gods. To prove that they deserved a good fate after death, the dead had to convincingly recite claims such as the following: "I have not committed crimes against people; I have not mistreated cattle; I have not robbed the poor; I have not caused pain; I have not caused tears" (see Document, "Declaring Innocence on Judgment Day in Ancient Egypt," page 25). Only if the gods believed the dead person was he or she allowed to live a blessed afterlife.

DOCUMENT

Declaring Innocence on Judgment Day in Ancient Egypt

The Egyptian collection of spells and instructions for the dead—known today as the Book of the Dead*—instructed the dead person how to make a declaration of innocence to the gods judging the person's fate on the day of judgment. The declaration listed evils that the person denied having committed; presumably the divine judges could tell whether the deceased was speaking truthfully. This selection of denials, each directed to a specific deity, reveals what Egyptians regarded as just and proper behavior.*

Wide-of-Stride who comes from On: I have not done evil.
Flame-grasper who comes from Kheraha: I have not robbed.
Long-nosed who comes from Khmun: I have not coveted.
Shadow-eater who comes from the cave: I have not stolen.
Savage-faced who comes from Rostau: I have not killed people.
Lion-Twins who come from heaven: I have not trimmed the measure.
Flint-eyed who comes from Kehm: I have not cheated.
Fiery-one who comes backward: I have not stolen a god's property.
Bone-smasher who comes from Hnes: I have not told lies.
Flame-thrower who comes from Memphis: I have not seized food.
Cave-dweller who comes from the west: I have not sulked.
White-toothed who comes from Lake-land: I have not trespassed.
Blood-eater who comes from slaughter-place: I have not slain sacred cattle.
Entrail-eater who comes from the tribunal: I have not extorted.
Lord of Maat who comes from Maaty: I have not extorted.
Wanderer who comes from Bubastis: I have not spied.
Pale-one who comes from On: I have not prattled.
Villain who comes from Anjdty: I have contended only for my goods.
Fiend who comes from slaughterhouse: I have not committed adultery.
Examiner who comes from Min's temple: I have not defiled myself.
Chief of the nobles who comes from Imu: I have not caused fear.
Wrecker who comes from Huy: I have not trespassed.
Disturber who comes from the sanctuary: I have not been violent.
Child who comes from On: I have not been deaf to Maat.
Foreteller who comes from Wensi: I have not quarreled.
Bastet who comes from the shrine: I have not winked.
Backward-face who comes from the pit: I have not copulated with a boy.
Flame-footed who comes from the dusk: I have not been false.
Dark-one who comes from darkness: I have not reviled.

Source: Translation from Miriam Lichtheim, *Ancient Egyptian Literature* (Berkeley: University of California Press, 1978), vol. 2, 126–27.

Question to Consider

■ **What do the crimes enumerated here reveal about the values embraced by Egyptian society?**

Magic played a large role in the lives of Egyptians. Professional magicians sold them spells and charms, both written and oral, they could use to promote their eternal salvation, protect themselves from demons, smooth the rocky course of love, exact revenge on enemies, and find relief from disease and injury. Egyptian doctors knew many medicinal herbs (knowledge they passed on to later civilizations) and could perform major surgeries, including opening the skull. Still, no doctor could cure severe infections; as in the past, sick people continued to rely on the help of supernatural forces through prayers and spells.

REVIEW QUESTION How did religion guide the lives of both rulers and ordinary people in ancient Egypt?

The Hittites, the Minoans, and the Mycenaeans, 2200–1000 B.C.E.

The first examples of Western civilization to emerge in the central Mediterranean region were located in Anatolia, dominated by the warlike Hittite kingdom (see Map 1.1); on the large island of Crete and nearby islands, home to the Minoans; and on the Greek mainland, where the Mycenaeans grew rich from raiding and trade (Map 1.3). As early as 6000 B.C.E., people from southwestern Asia, especially Anatolia, began migrating westward and southward to inhabit islands in the Mediterranean Sea. From this migration, the rich civilization of the Minoans gradually emerged on the island of Crete and other islands in

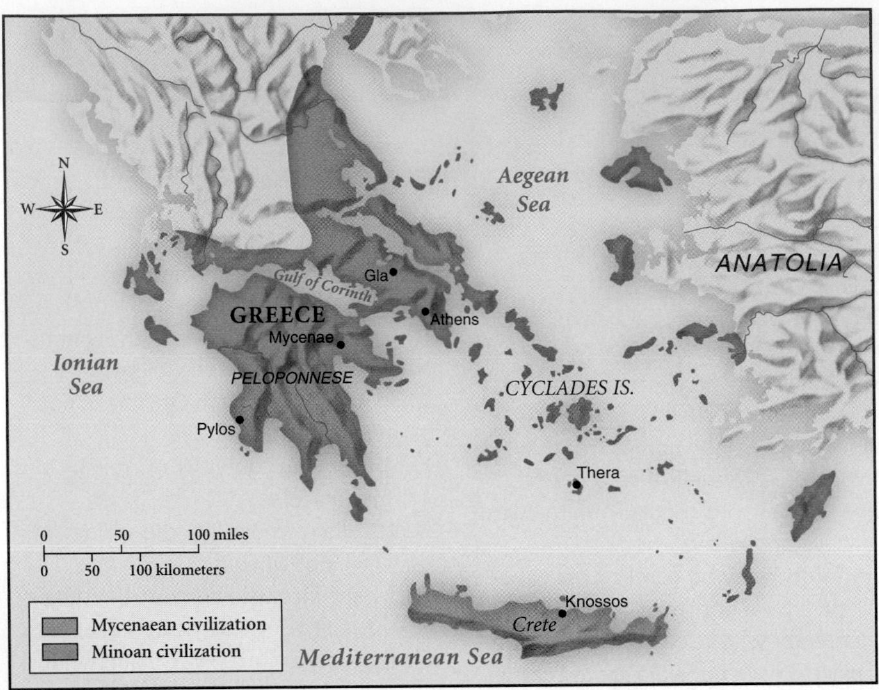

MAP 1.3 Greece and the Aegean Sea, 1500 B.C.E.
A varied landscape of mountains, islands, and seas defined the geography of Greece. The distances between settlements were mostly short, but rough terrain and seasonally stormy sailing made travel a chore. The distance from the mainland to the largest island in this region, Crete, where Minoan civilization arose, was sufficiently long to keep Cretans isolated from the wars of most of later Greek history.

the Aegean Sea by around 2200 B.C.E. In mainland Greece, civilization eventually arose among peoples who had moved into the area thousands of years before, again most likely from southwestern Asia.

The Hittites, the Minoans, and the Mycenaeans had advanced military technologies, elaborate architecture, striking art, a marked taste for luxury, and extensive trade contacts with Egypt and the Near East. The Hittites, like the Egyptians, created a unified state under a single central authority. The Minoans and the Mycenaeans, like the Mesopotamians, established separate city-states. All three peoples inhabited a dangerous world in which repeated raids and violent disruptions lasting from around 1200 to 1000 B.C.E. ultimately destroyed their prosperous cultures. Nevertheless, their accomplishments paved the way for the later civilization of Greece, which would greatly influence the history of Western civilization.

The Hittites, 1750–1200 B.C.E.

By around 1750 B.C.E. the Hittites had made themselves the most powerful people of central Anatolia. They had migrated from the Caucasus area, between the Black and Caspian Seas, and overcome indigenous Anatolian peoples to set up their centralized kingdom. It flourished because they inhabited a fertile upland plateau in the peninsula's center, excelled in war and diplomacy, and controlled trade in their region and southward. The Hittites' southward-knifing military campaigns eventually threatened Egypt's possessions on the eastern Mediterranean coast, bringing them into conflict with the warrior pharaohs of the New Kingdom.

Since the Hittites spoke an Indo-European language, they belonged to the linguistic family that over time populated most of Europe. The original Indo-European speakers, who were pastoralists and raiders, had migrated as separate groups into Anatolia and Europe, including Greece, most likely from western Asia. Recent archaeological discoveries in that general region have revealed graves of women buried with weapons. These burials suggest that women in these groups originally occupied positions of leadership in war and peace alongside men; the prominence of Hittite queens in documents, royal letters, and foreign treaties perhaps sprang from that tradition.

As in other early civilizations, rule in the Hittite kingdom depended on religion for its justification and structuring of authority. Hittite religion combined worship of Indo-European gods with worship of deities inherited from the original Anatolian population. The king served as high priest of the storm god, and Hittite belief demanded that he maintain a strict purity in his life as a demonstration of his justice and guardianship of social order. His drinking water, for example, always had to be strained. So strong was this insistence on purity that the king's water carrier was executed if so much as one hair was found in the water. Like Egyptian kings, Hittite rulers felt responsible for maintaining the gods' goodwill toward their subjects. King Mursili II (r. 1321–1295 B.C.E.), for example, issued a set of prayers begging the gods to end a plague: "What is this, o gods, that you have done? Our land is dying. . . . We have lost our wits, and we can do nothing right. O gods, whatever sin you behold, either let a prophet come forth to identify it . . . or let us see it in a dream!"

The kings conducted many religious ceremonies in their capital, Hattusas, which grew into one of the most impressive cities of its era. Ringed by massive defensive walls and stone towers, it featured huge palaces aligned along straight, gravel-paved streets. Sculptures of animals, warriors, and, especially, the royal rulers decorated public spaces. Hit-

Chariots in the Ancient Near East
Chariots appear frequently in hunting and war scenes in Assyrian, Egyptian, Hittite, and Persian art. The scenes often show a rider, usually a king or noble, shooting a bow at an animal or an enemy, with a charioteer to guide the charging horse. Textual evidence confirms that chariots were important weaponry in the ancient Near East, but scenes such as this one were primarily intended to impress viewers with the skill and majesty of the hunter or warrior rather than to give an exact picture of the battlefield or hunting ground. *(© C. M. Dixon/HIP/The Image Works.)*

tite kings maintained their rule by forging personal alliances—cemented by marriages and oaths of loyalty—with the noble families of the kingdom.

These rulers aggressively employed their troops to expand their power. In periods when ties between kings and nobles remained strong and the kingdom therefore preserved its unity, they launched extremely ambitious military campaigns. In 1595 B.C.E., for example, the royal army raided as far southeast as Babylon in Mesopotamia, destroying that kingdom. Scholars no longer accept the once popular idea that the Hittites owed their success in war to a special knowledge of making weapons from iron, although their craftsmen did smelt iron, from which they made ceremonial implements. (Weapons made from iron did not become common in the Mediterranean world until well after 1200 B.C.E.—at the end of the Hittite kingdom.) The Hittite army excelled in the use of chariots, and perhaps this skill gave it an edge.

The economic strength of the Hittite kingdom came from control over long-distance trade routes for essential raw materials, especially metals. The Hittites worked mightily to dominate the lucrative trade moving between the Mediterranean coast and inland northern Syria. The Egyptian New Kingdom pharaohs fiercely resisted Hittite expansion and power in this region. The Anatolian kingdom proved too strong, however, and in the bloody battle of Kadesh, around 1274 B.C.E., the Hittites fought the Egyptians to a standstill in Syria, leading to a political stalemate in that region. Fear of neighboring Assyria eventually led the Hittite king to negotiate with his Egyptian rival, and the two war-weary kingdoms became allies sixteen years after the battle of Kadesh by agreeing to a treaty that is a landmark in the history of international diplomacy. Remarkably, both Egyptian and Hittite copies of the treaty survive. In it, the two monarchs pledged to be "at peace and brothers forever." The alliance lasted, and thirteen years later the Hittite king gave his daughter in marriage to his Egyptian "brother."

The Minoans, 2200–1400 B.C.E.

Study of early Greek civilization traditionally begins with the people today known as Minoans, who inhabited Crete and other islands in the Aegean Sea by the late third millennium. The word *Minoan* was applied after the archaeologist Arthur Evans (1851–1941) searched the island for traces of King Minos, famous in Greek myth for building the first great navy and keeping the half-human/half-bull Minotaur in a labyrinth at his palace. Scholars today are not sure whether to count the Minoans as the earliest Greeks because they are uncertain whether the Minoan language, whose decipherment remains controversial, was related to Greek or belongs to another linguistic tradition.

Minoans apparently had no written literature, only official records. They wrote these records in a script today called Linear A. If further research confirms a recent suggestion that Minoan was a member of the Indo-European family of languages (the ancestor of many languages, including Greek, Latin, and, much later, English), then Minoans can be seen as the earliest Greeks. Regardless of how the Minoans' language is classified, their interactions with the mainland deeply influenced later Greek civilization.

By around 2200 B.C.E., Minoans on Crete and nearby islands had created what scholars call a **palace society**, in recognition of its sprawling multichambered buildings that apparently housed not only the rulers, their families, and their servants but also the political, economic, and religious administrative offices of the state. Minoan rulers combined the functions of ruler and priest, dominating both politics and religion. The palaces seem to have been largely independent, with no single Minoan community imposing unity on the others. The general population clustered around each palace in houses adjacent to one another; some of these settlements reached the size and density of small cities. The Cretan site Knossos, which Evans thought had been Minos's headquarters, is the most famous such palace complex. Other, smaller settlements dotted outlying areas of the island, especially on the coast. The Minoans' numerous ports supported extensive international trade, above all with the Egyptians and the Hittites.

The most surprising feature of Minoan communities is that they did not build elaborate defensive walls. Palaces, towns, and even isolated country houses apparently saw no need to fortify themselves. The remains of the newer palaces—such as the one at Knossos, with its hundreds of rooms in five stories, indoor plumbing, and colorful scenes painted on the walls—have led some historians to the controversial conclusion that Minoans avoided war among themselves, despite their having no single central authority over their independent settlements. Others object to this vision of peaceful Minoans as overly romantic, arguing that the most powerful Minoans on Crete dominated some neighboring islands. Recent discoveries of tombs on Crete have revealed weapons caches, and a find of bones cut by knives has even raised the possibility of human sacrifice. The prominence of women in palace frescoes and the numerous figurines of large-breasted goddesses found on Minoan sites have also prompted speculation that women dominated Minoan society, but no texts so far discovered have verified this. Minoan art certainly depicts women prominently and respectfully, but the same is true of contemporary civilizations that we know were controlled by men. More archaeological research is needed to resolve the controversies concerning gender roles in Minoan civilization.

Scholars agree, however, that the development of **Mediterranean polyculture**—the cultivation of olives, grapes, and grains in a single, interrelated agricultural system—greatly increased the health and wealth of Minoan society. This innovation made the most efficient use of a farmer's labor by combining crops that required intense work at different seasons. This system of farming, which still characterizes Mediterranean agriculture, had two major consequences. First, the combination of crops provided a healthy way of eating (the Mediterranean diet, as doctors call it today), which in turn stimulated population growth. Second, agriculture became both more diversified and more specialized, increasing production of the valuable products olive oil and wine.

Just as they had in Mesopotamia and Egypt, agricultural surpluses on Crete and nearby islands spurred the growth of specialized, often related crafts. To store and transport surplus food, Minoan artisans manufactured huge storage jars (the size of a modern refrigerator), in the process creating another specialized industry. Craft workers, producing sophisticated goods using time-consuming techniques, no longer had time to grow their own food or make the things, such as clothes and lamps, they needed for everyday life. Instead, they exchanged the products they made for food and other goods. In this way, Minoan society experienced increasing economic interdependence.

---

palace society: Minoan and Mycenaean social and political organization centered on multichambered buildings housing the rulers and the administration of the state.

Mediterranean polyculture: The cultivation of olives, grapes, and grains in a single, interrelated agricultural system.

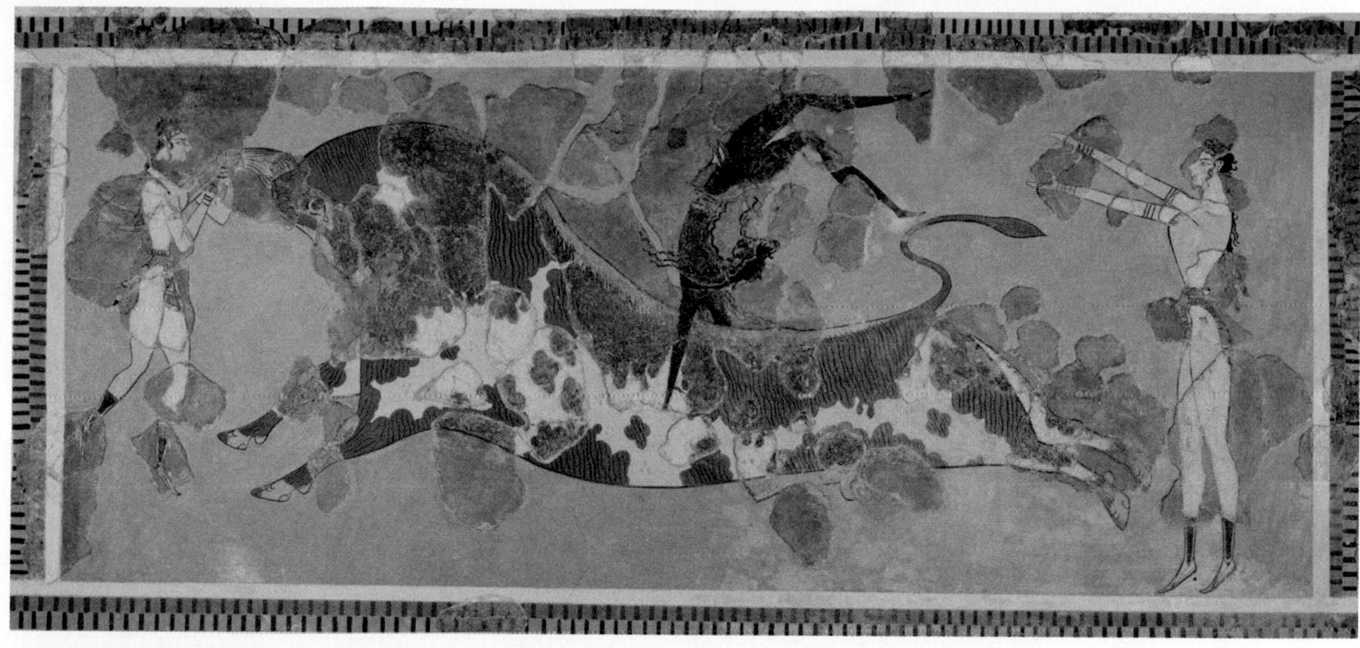

Wall Painting from Knossos, Crete
Minoan artists painted with vivid colors on plaster to enliven the walls of buildings. Unfortunately, time and earthquakes have severely damaged most Minoan wall paintings, and the versions we see today are largely reconstructions painted around surviving fragments of the originals. This painting from the palace at Knossos depicted an acrobatic performance in which a youth leaped in an aerial somersault over the back of a charging bull. Some scholars speculate this dangerous activity was a religious ritual instead of just a circus act. If it was a part of Minoan religion, what do you think this performance could symbolize? *(Archeological Museum of Heraklion, Crete, Greece/Bernard Cox/The Bridgeman Art Library International.)*

The vast storage areas in Minoan palaces suggest that the rulers, like some Mesopotamian kings before them, controlled this interdependence through a redistributive economic system. The Knossos palace, for example, held hundreds of gigantic jars capable of storing 240,000 gallons of olive oil and wine. Bowls, cups, and dippers crammed storerooms nearby. Palace officials would have decided how much each farmer or craft producer had to contribute to the palace storehouse and how much of those contributions would then be redistributed to each person in the community for basic subsistence or as an extra reward. In this way, people gave the products of their labor to the central authority, which redistributed them according to its own priorities.

The Mycenaeans, 1800–1000 B.C.E.

Ancestors of the Greeks had moved into the mainland region of Greece by perhaps 8000 B.C.E., yet the first civilization definitely identified as Greek because of its Indo-European language arose only in the early second millennium B.C.E., about the same time as the Hittite kingdom. These first Greeks are called Mycenaeans, a name derived from the hilltop site of Mycenae, famous for its multichambered palace, rich graves, and massive fortification walls. Located in the Peloponnese (the large peninsula forming southern Greece; see Map 1.3), Mycenae dominated its local area, but neither it nor any other settlement ever ruled all of Bronze Age Greece. Instead, the independent communities of Mycenaean civilization vied with one another in a fierce competition for natural resources and territory.

The nineteenth-century German millionaire Heinrich Schliemann was the first to discover treasure-filled graves at Mycenae. The burial objects revealed a warrior culture organized in independent settlements and ruled by aggressive kings. Constructed as stone-lined shafts, the graves contained entombed dead, who had taken hordes of valuables with them: golden jewelry, including heavy necklaces loaded with pendants, gold and silver vessels, bronze weapons decorated with scenes of wild animals inlaid in precious metals, and delicately painted pottery.

In his excitement at finding treasure, Schliemann proudly announced that he had found the grave of Agamemnon, the legendary king who commanded the Greek army against Troy, a city in northwestern Anatolia, in the Trojan War. Homer, Greece's first and most famous poet, immortalized this war in his epic poem *The Iliad*. Archaeologists now know the shaft graves date to around 1700–1600 B.C.E., long before the Trojan War could have taken place. Schliemann, who paid for his own excavation at Troy to prove to skeptics that the city had really existed, infuriated scholars with his self-promotion. But his passion to confirm that Greek myth preserved a kernel of historical truth motivated him to excavate at Mycenae. His discoveries provided the most spectacular evidence for mainland Greece's earliest civilization.

Mycenaean Interaction with Minoan Crete

Since the hilly terrain of Greece had little fertile land but many useful ports, settlements tended to spring up near the coast. Mycenaean rulers enriched themselves by dominating local farmers, conducting naval raids, and participating in seaborne trade. Palace records inscribed on clay tablets reveal that the Mycenaeans operated under a redistributive economy. On the tablets scribes made detailed lists of goods received and goods paid out, recording everything from chariots to livestock, landholdings, personnel, and perfumes, even broken equipment taken out of service. Like the Minoans, Mycenaeans apparently did not use writing to record the oral literature that scholars believe they created.

The existence of *tholos* tombs—massive underground burial chambers built in beehive shapes with closely fitted stones—shows that some Mycenaeans had become very rich by about 1500 B.C.E. The architectural details of the tholos tombs and the style of the burial goods placed in them testify to the far-flung expeditions for trade and war that Mycenaean rulers conducted throughout the eastern Mediterranean. Above all, however, their many decorative patterns clearly inspired by Minoan art indicate a close connection with Minoan civilization.

Underwater archaeology has revealed the influence of international commerce during this period in (unintentionally) promoting cultural interaction. Divers have discovered, for example, that a late-fourteenth-century B.C.E. shipwreck off Uluburun in Turkey carried a mixed cargo and varied personal possessions from many locations in the eastern Mediterranean, including Canaan, Cyprus, Greece, Egypt, and Babylon. The variety confirms that merchants and consumers involved in this sort of trade were exposed directly to the goods produced by others and indirectly to their ideas.

The sea brought the Mycenaean and Minoan civilizations into close contact, but they remained different in significant ways. The Mycenaeans spoke Greek and made burnt offerings to the gods; the Minoans did neither. The Minoans extended their religious worship outside their centers, establishing sacred places in caves, on mountaintops, and in country villas, while the mainlanders concentrated the worship of their gods inside their walled communities. When the Mycenaeans started building palaces in the fourteenth century B.C.E., they (unlike the palace society Minoans) designed them around *megarons*—rooms with prominent ceremonial hearths and thrones for the rulers. Some Mycenaean palaces had more than one megaron, which could soar two stories high with columns to support a roof above the second-floor balconies.

Documents found in the palace at Knossos reveal that by around 1400 B.C.E. the Mycenaeans had acquired dominance over Crete, possibly in a war over commerce in the Mediterranean. The documents were tablets written in **Linear B**, a pictographic script based on Minoan Linear A, an earlier writing system used for the Minoan language (which scholars still cannot fully decipher). The twentieth-century architect Michael Ventris proved that Linear B was used to write not Minoan, but in fact Greek. Because the Linear B tablets date from before the final destruction of Knossos in about 1370 B.C.E., they show that the palace administration had been keeping its records in a foreign language for some time and therefore that Mycenaeans were controlling Crete well before the end of Minoan civilization. By the middle of the fourteenth century B.C.E., then, the Mycenaeans had displaced the Minoans as the Aegean region's preeminent civilization.

War in Mycenaean Society

By the time Mycenaeans took over Crete, war at home and abroad was the principal concern of well-off Mycenaean men, a tradition that they passed on to later Greek civilization. Contents of Bronze Age tombs in Greece reveal that no wealthy man went to his grave without his war equipment. Armor and weapons were so central to a Mycenaean man's identity that he could not do without them, even in death. Warriors rode into battle on revolutionary transport—lightweight two-wheeled chariots pulled by horses. These expensive vehicles, perhaps introduced by Indo-Europeans migrating from Central Asia, first appeared in various Mediterranean and Near Eastern societies not long after 2000 B.C.E.; the first picture of such a chariot

---

Linear B: The Mycenaeans' pictographic script for writing Greek.

Decorated Dagger from Mycenae
The hilltop fortress and palace at Mycenae was the capital of Bronze Age Greece's most famous kingdom. The picture of a lion hunt inlaid in gold and silver on this sixteenth century B.C.E. dagger expressed how wealthy Mycenaean men saw their roles in society: as courageous hunters and warriors overcoming the hostile forces of nature. The nine-inch blade was found in a circle of graves inside Mycenae's walls, where the highest-ranking people were buried with their treasures as evidence of their status. *(Nimatallah/Art Resource, NY.)*

in the Aegean region occurs on a Mycenaean grave marker from about 1500 B.C.E. Wealthy people evidently desired this new and costly equipment not only for war but also as proof of their social status.

The Mycenaeans seem to have spent more on war than on religion. In any case, they did not construct any giant religious buildings like Mesopotamia's ziggurats or Egypt's pyramids. Their most important deities were male gods concerned with war. The names of gods found in the Linear B tablets reveal that Mycenaeans passed down many divinities to the Greeks of later times, such as Dionysus, the god of wine.

The Violent End to Early Western Civilization, 1200–1000 B.C.E.

A state of political equilibrium, in which kings corresponded with one another and traders traveled all over the area, characterized the Mediterranean and Near Eastern world around 1300 B.C.E. Within a century, however, violence had destroyed or weakened almost every major political state in the region, including Egypt, some kingdoms of Mesopotamia, and the Hittite and Mycenaean kingdoms. Neither the civilizations united under a single central authority nor the ones with independent states survived. This period of international violence from about 1200 to 1000 B.C.E. remains one of the most fascinating and disturbing puzzles in the history of Western civilization.

The best clue to what happened comes from Egyptian and Hittite records. They document many foreign attacks in this period, especially from the sea. According to an inscription, in about 1190 B.C.E. a warrior pharaoh defeated a powerful coalition of seaborne invaders from the north, who had fought their way to the edge of Egypt. These **Sea Peoples**, as historians call them, were made up of many different groups operating separately. No single, unified group of Sea Peoples originated the tidal wave of violence starting around 1200 B.C.E. Rather, many different bands devastated the region. A chain reaction of attacks and flights in a recurring and expanding cycle put even more bands on the move. Some were mercenary soldiers who had deserted the rulers who had employed them; some were raiders by profession. Many may have been Greeks. The famous story of the Trojan War probably recalls this period of repeated violent attacks from abroad: it portrays an army from Greece crossing the Aegean Sea to attack and plunder Troy and the surrounding region in coastal Anatolia. The attacks also reached far inland. As a result, the Babylonian kingdom collapsed, the Assyrians were confined to their homeland, and much of western Asia and Syria was devastated.

It remains mysterious how so many attackers could be so successful over such a long time, but the consequences for the eastern Mediterranean region are clear. The once mighty Hittite kingdom fell around 1200 B.C.E., when raiders cut off its trade routes for raw materials. Invaders razed its capital city, Hattusas, which never revived. Egypt's New Kingdom turned back the Sea Peoples after a tremendous military effort, but the raiders destroyed

---

Sea Peoples: The diverse groups of raiders who devastated the eastern Mediterranean region in the period of violence 1200–1000 B.C.E.

the Egyptian long-distance trade network. By the end of the New Kingdom, around 1081 B.C.E., Egypt had shrunk to its original territorial core along the Nile's banks. These problems ruined the Egyptian state's credit. For example, when an eleventh-century B.C.E. Theban temple official traveled to Phoenicia to buy cedar for a ceremonial boat, the city's ruler demanded cash in advance. Although the Egyptian monarchy hung on, power struggles between pharaohs and priests, made worse by frequent attacks from abroad, prevented the reestablishment of centralized authority. No Egyptian dynasty ever again became an aggressive international power.

In Greece, homegrown conflict apparently led to the tipping point for Mycenaean civilization at the time when the Sea Peoples became a threat. The Mycenaeans reached the zenith of their power around 1400–1250 B.C.E. The enormous domed tomb at Mycenae, called the Treasury of Atreus, testifies to the riches of this period. The tomb's elaborately decorated front and soaring roof reveal the pride and wealth of the Mycenaean warrior princes. The last phase of the extensive palace at Pylos on the west coast of the Peloponnese also dates from this time. It boasted vivid wall paintings, storerooms bursting with food, and a royal bathroom with a built-in tub and intricate plumbing. But these prosperous Mycenaeans did not escape the widespread violence that began around 1200 B.C.E. Linear B tablets record the disposition of troops to the coast to guard the palace at Pylos from raids from the sea. The palace inhabitants of eastern Greece constructed defensive walls so massive that the later

MAPPING THE WEST

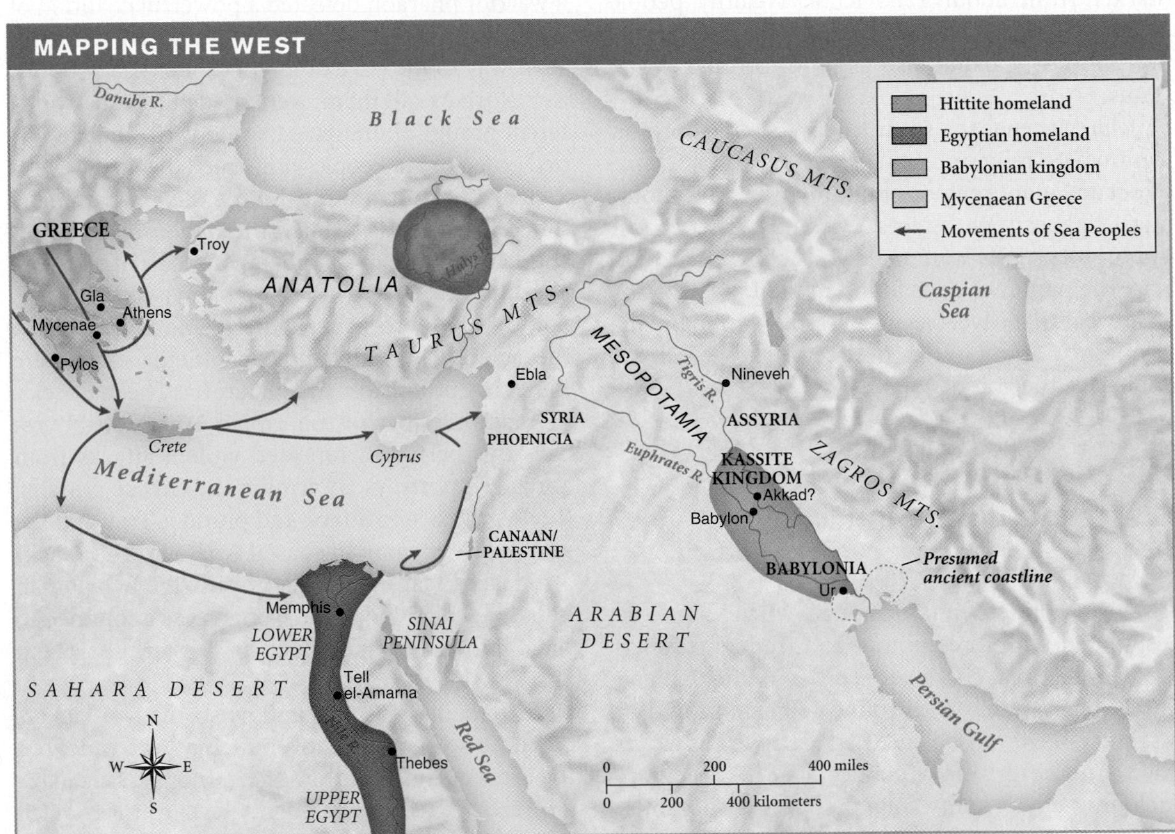

The Violent End to Early Western Civilization, 1200–1000 B.C.E.
Bands of wandering warriors and raiders set the eastern Mediterranean aflame at the end of the Bronze Age. This violence displaced many people and ended the power of the Egyptian, Hittite, and Mycenaean kingdoms. Even some of the Near Eastern states well inland from the eastern Mediterranean coast felt the effects of this period of unrest, whose causes remain mysterious. The Mediterranean Sea was a two-edged sword for the early civilizations that grew up around and near it: as a highway for transporting goods and ideas, it was a benefit; as an easy access corridor for attackers, it was a danger. The raids of the Sea Peoples that smashed the prosperity of the eastern Mediterranean region around 1200–1000 B.C.E. also set in motion the forces that led to the next step in our story, the reestablishment of civilization in Greece. Internal conflict among Mycenaean rulers turned the regional unrest of those centuries into a local catastrophe; fighting each other for dominance, they so weakened their monarchies that their societies could not recover from the effects of battles and earthquakes.

Greeks thought giants had built them. These fortifications would have protected coastal palaces against seafaring attackers, who could have been either outsiders or Greeks. The wall around the inland palace at Gla in central Greece, however, which foreign raiders could not easily reach, confirms that Mycenaean communities also had to defend themselves against other Mycenaean communities.

The internal conflict probably did more damage to Mycenaean civilization than the raids of the Sea Peoples. Major earthquakes also struck at this time, spreading further destruction among the Mycenaeans. Archaeology offers no evidence for the ancient tradition that Dorian Greeks invading from the north caused this damage. Rather, near-constant civil war by jealous local Mycenaean rulers overburdened the complicated administrative balancing system necessary for the palaces' redistributive economies and hindered recovery from earthquake damage. The violence killed many Mycenaeans, and the disappearance of the palace-based redistributive economy put many others on the road to starvation. The destruction of central authority left most Greeks with no organized way to defend or feed themselves and forced them to wander abroad in search of new places to settle and learn to farm. Like people from the earliest times, they had to move to build a better life.

REVIEW QUESTION How did war determine the fate of early Western civilization in Anatolia, Crete, and Greece?

Conclusion

The best way to create a meaningful definition of Western civilization is to study its history, which begins in Mesopotamia and Egypt; early societies there influenced the later civilization of Greece. Cities first arose in Mesopotamia around 4000 to 3000 B.C.E. Hierarchy had characterized society to some degree from the very beginning, but it, along with patriarchy, grew more prominent once civilization and political states with centralized authority became widespread.

Trade and war were constants, both aiming in different ways at profit and glory. Indirectly, they often generated cultural interaction by putting civilizations into close contact to learn from one another. Technological innovation was also a prominent characteristic of this long period. The invention of metallurgy, monumental architecture, mathematics, and alphabetic writing greatly affected people's lives. Religion was at the center of society; people believed that the gods demanded everyone, from king to worker, to display just and righteous conduct.

FOR FURTHER EXPLORATION

- **For additional primary-source material from this period**, see *Sources of the Making of the West*, Fourth Edition.
- **For Web sites, images, and documents related to topics in this chapter**, visit *Make History* at bedfordstmartins.com/hunt.

Chapter 1 Review

Online Study Guide bedfordstmartins.com/hunt

Key Terms and People

In the grid below, identify the term or person and explain its historical significance. (To do this exercise online, go to bedfordstmartins.com/hunt.)

Term	Who or What & When	Why It Matters
civilization (p. 4)		
polytheism (p. 6)		
monotheism (p. 6)		
Anatolia (p. 7)		
city-state (p. 8)		
ziggurats (p. 8)		
cuneiform (p. 11)		
empire (p. 12)		
redistributive economy (p. 14)		
Hammurabi (p. 14)		
hieroglyphic (p. 18)		
Maat (p. 20)		
wisdom literature (p. 22)		
palace society (p. 28)		
Mediterranean polyculture (p. 28)		
Linear B (p. 30)		
Sea Peoples (p. 31)		

Review Questions

1. What are the challenges in defining the term *Western civilization*?
2. How did life change for people in Mesopotamia when they began to live in cities?
3. How did religion guide the lives of both rulers and ordinary people in ancient Egypt?
4. How did war determine the fate of early Western civilization in Anatolia, Crete, and Greece?

Making Connections

1. Compare and contrast the environmental factors affecting the emergence of the world's first civilizations in Mesopotamia and Egypt.
2. What were the advantages and disadvantages of living in a unified country under a single central authority compared to living in a region with separate city-states?
3. Which were more important in influencing the development of early Western civilization: the intentional or the unintentional consequences of change?

Important Events

Date	Event
4000–1000 B.C.E.	Bronze Age in southwestern Asia, Egypt, and Europe
4000–3000 B.C.E.	Mesopotamians invent writing and establish first cities
3050 B.C.E.	Narmer (Menes) unites Upper and Lower Egypt into one kingdom
2687–2190 B.C.E.	Old Kingdom in Egypt
2350 B.C.E.	Sargon, king of Akkad, establishes the world's first empire
2300–2200 B.C.E.	Enheduanna, princess of Akkad, composes poetry
2200 B.C.E.	Minoans build their first palaces
2112–2004 B.C.E.	Ur III dynasty rules in Sumer
2061–1665 B.C.E.	Middle Kingdom in Egypt
1792–1750 B.C.E.	Hammurabi rules Babylon and issues his law code
1750 B.C.E.	Hittites establish their kingdom in Anatolia
1569–1081 B.C.E.	New Kingdom in Egypt
1400 B.C.E.	The Mycenaeans build their first palaces in Greece and take over Minoan Crete
1274 B.C.E.	Battle of Kadesh in Syria between the Egyptians and the Hittites
1200–1000 B.C.E.	Period of violence ends many kingdoms

- Consider three events: **Mesopotamians invent writing and establish first cities (4000–3000 B.C.E.)**, **Sargon establishes the world's first empire in Akkadia (2350 B.C.E.)**, and **Enheduanna composes poetry (2300–2200 B.C.E.)**. How might the invention of writing have promoted the growth of stronger city-states and the first empire? How might the creation of the Akkadian empire have fostered the development of literature?

SUGGESTED REFERENCES

The combination of archaeological and linguistic research informs scholarship on the history of the ancient Near East, Egypt, and Greece. New discoveries and new ideas both help historians achieve a clearer understanding of these earliest societies of Western civilization.

Baines, John. *Religion and Society in Ancient Egypt*. 2003.

Bertman, Stephen. *Handbook to Life in Ancient Mesopotamia*. 2003.

Bryce, Trevor. *Life and Society in the Hittite World*. 2004.

——, and Adam Hook. *Hittite Warrior*. 2007.

*Chavalas, Mark W., ed. *The Ancient Near East. Historical Sources in Translation*. 2006.

Cline, Eric H. *Oxford Handbook of the Bronze Age Aegean*. 2010.

Crouch, Carly L. *War and Ethics in the Ancient Near East*. 2009.

*Dalley, Stephanie, trans. *Myths from Mesopotamia: Creation, the Flood, Gilgamesh, and Others*. 1991.

Ikram, Salima. *Ancient Egypt: An Introduction*. 2010.

Mieroop, Marc Van De. *King Hammurabi of Babylon: A Biography*. 2005.

——. *A History of the Ancient Near East ca. 3000–323 B.C.* 2nd ed. 2007.

Partridge, Robert B. *Fighting Pharaohs: Weapons and Warfare in Ancient Egypt*. 2002.

Podany, Amanda H. *Brotherhood of Kings: How International Relations Shaped the Ancient Near East*. 2010.

Sanders, N. K. *The Sea Peoples: Warriors of the Ancient Mediterranean, 1250–1150 B.C.* Rev. ed. 1985.

Shelmerdine, Cynthia. *The Cambridge Companion to the Aegean Bronze Age*. 2008.

*Simpson, William Kelly, ed. *The Literature of Ancient Egypt. An Anthology of Stories, Instructions, and Poetry*. 3rd ed. 2003.

Szapakowska, Kasia. *Daily Life in Ancient Egypt: Recreating Lahun*. 2008.

Thebes in ancient Egypt: http://www.thebanmappingproject.com/

Tyldesley, Joyce. *Hatchepsut: The Female Pharaoh*. 1998.

*Primary source.

CHAPTER 2

Near East Empires and the Reemergence of Civilization in Greece

1000–500 B.C.E.

The Greek poet Homer in the eighth century B.C.E. told emotion-filled stories recalling the period of violence in 1200–1000 B.C.E. that had wrecked Greek civilization. In his epic poem *The Iliad*, he narrated bloody tales of the Trojan War that were rich with legends born from combined Greek and Near Eastern traditions, such as the story of the Greek hero Bellerophon. Driven from his home by a false charge of sexual assault, Bellerophon had to serve as "enforcer" for a foreign king, combating the king's most dangerous enemies. He had to fight—and kill—fierce tribesmen, Amazons, and even the king's own warriors, but his most famous contest pitted him against a monster. As Homer tells it, Bellerophon was ordered "to defeat the Chimera, an inhuman freak created by the gods, horrible with its lion's head, goat's body, and dragon's tail, breathing fire all the time." Riding on the winged horse Pegasus, Bellerophon triumphed by swooping down on the Chimera in an aerial attack. For such amazing heroics, the king gave Bellerophon his daughter in marriage and half his kingdom.

Black-Figure Vase from Corinth
This vase was made in Corinth about 600 B.C.E., painted in the so-called black-figure style in which artists carved details into the dark-baked clay. In the late sixth century B.C.E., this style gave way to red-figure, in which artists painted details in black on a reddish background instead of engraving them; the result was finer detail (compare this vase painting with that on page 5). The animals and mythical creatures on the vase shown here follow Near Eastern models, which inspired Archaic Age Greek artists to put people and animals into their designs again after their absence during the Dark Age. Why do you think the artist depicted the animal at the lower right with two bodies but only one head? *(© The Trustees of the British Museum/Art Resource, NY.)*

Homer's story provides evidence for the intercultural contact between the Near East and Greece that supported the reemergence of civilization in Greece after 1000 B.C.E. Both the Chimera and the horse-headed, hawk-bodied, lion-footed beast painted on the vase from Corinth shown in the chapter-opening illustration were creatures from Near Eastern myth taken over by Greeks. Greece's geography—countless ports on its long coastline and many islands—promoted contacts by sea through trade, travel, and war with its richer and stronger Near Eastern neighbors. In the centuries from

1000 to 500 B.C.E., these contacts—combined with the Greeks' value of competitive individual excellence, their sense of a communal identity, and their belief that people in general (and not just rulers) were responsible for maintaining justice and the goodwill of the gods toward the community—helped Greeks reestablish their prosperity and reinvent their civilization with a radically new concept of central authority: city-states governed not by kings but by groups of citizens.

Despite the violence and consequent economic failure that had destroyed so many Bronze Age communities in the eastern Mediterranean region by around 1000 B.C.E., people's desire for trade and cross-cultural contact endured and increased as conditions improved over the following centuries. The Near East, retaining monarchy as its traditional form of social and political organization, recovered more quickly than Greece. Near Eastern kings in this period extracted surpluses from subject populations to fund their palaces and their armies. They also continually sought new conquests to win glory, exploit the labor of conquered peoples, seize raw materials, and conduct long-distance trade.

Attacks of the Sea Peoples, internal wars, and earthquakes had destroyed the political and social organization of Minoan and Mycenaean Greece in 1200–1000 B.C.E. During Greece's initial recovery from poverty and depopulation around 1000 to 750 B.C.E., there emerged new political and social institutions and traditions rejecting the rule of kings. In this period, Greeks sailed the Mediterranean Sea to maintain trade and cross-cultural contact with the older civilizations of the Near East. Their mythology, as in Homer, and their art, as on the Corinthian vase, reveal that Greeks imported ideas and technology from that part of the wider world as they remade their lives during this difficult era.

By the eighth century B.C.E., Greeks had begun to create their own kind of city-state, the polis, as a new form of political and social organization. The polis was a radical innovation because it made citizenship—not subjection to kings—the basis for society and politics, and included the poor as citizens. It gave legal—though not political—rights to women, but no rights to slaves. With the exception of occasional tyrannies, Greek city-states governed themselves by having male citizens share political power. The extent of the power sharing varied, with small groups of upper-class men dominating in some places. In other places, however, the polis shared power among all free men, even the poor, eventually creating the world's first democracy. The Greeks' invention of democratic politics, limited though it might have been by modern standards, stands as a landmark in the history of Western civilization.

Religion and philosophy also changed greatly in this period. Leaders and thinkers in the Near East and Greece gradually created new ways of belief and thought that slowly filtered down to the mass of people and deeply influenced the development of Western civilization. In religion, the Persians developed beliefs that saw human life as a struggle between good and evil, and the Israelites evolved their monotheism. In philosophy, the Greeks began to use reason and logic to replace mythological explanations of nature.

CHAPTER FOCUS How did the forms of political and social organization that Greece developed after 1000 B.C.E. differ from those of the Near East?

From Dark Age to Empire in the Near East, 1000–500 B.C.E.

The widespread violence in 1200–1000 B.C.E. had weakened or obliterated many communities and populations in the eastern Mediterranean. Although

1000–750 B.C.E. Greece experiences its Dark Age

800 B.C.E. Greeks learn to write with an alphabet

750 B.C.E. Greeks begin to create the polis

1000 B.C.E. — 900 B.C.E. — 800 B.C.E.

900 B.C.E. Neo-Assyrian Empire emerges

776 B.C.E. Olympic Games founded in Greece

recent archaeological research shows that people in this era were still actively pursuing trade and intercultural contacts, historians have traditionally used the term *Dark Age* to refer to the times immediately following the period of violence, both because economic conditions were so gloomy for so many people and because our knowledge of what happened is so limited. The Dark Age in the Near East lasted less than a century, while in Greece it lasted over two hundred years.

By 900 B.C.E., a powerful centralized Assyrian kingdom had once again gained power in Mesopotamia. From this base, the Assyrians carved out a new empire even larger than the preceding one. The riches and power of this Neo-Assyrian Empire inspired first the Babylonians and then the Persians to build their own empires when Assyrian power collapsed. The traditional striving for empire remained constant in the Near East. In comparison, the Israelites had little military power, but they established a new path for civilization during this period by changing their religion. They developed monotheism and produced the Hebrew Bible (as it is known today), called the Old Testament by Christians.

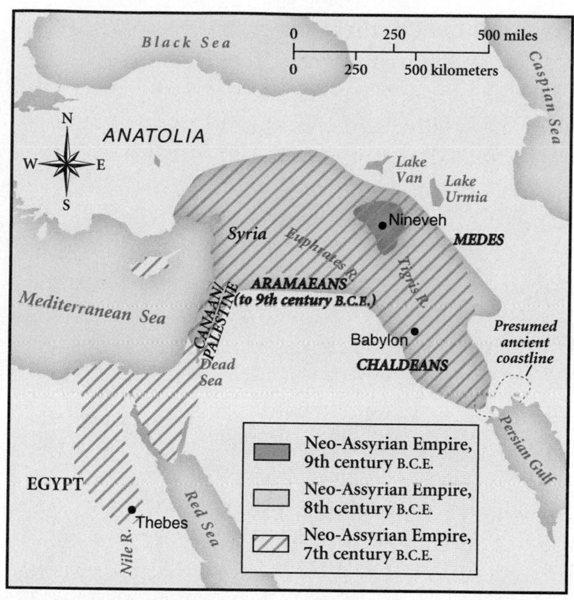

MAP 2.1 Expansion of the Neo-Assyrian Empire, c. 900–650 B.C.E.
Like their Akkadian, Assyrian, and Babylonian predecessors, the Neo-Assyrian kings dominated a vast region of the Near East to secure a supply of metals, access to trade routes on land and sea, and imperial glory. In this way, they built the largest empire the world had yet seen. Also like their predecessors, they treated disobedient subjects harshly and intolerantly to try to prevent their diverse territories from rebelling.

The New Empire of Assyria, 900–600 B.C.E.

When the Hittite kingdom fell around 1000 B.C.E., the Assyrians gained power by seizing supplies of metal—much prized by rulers—and controlling trade routes in the eastern Mediterranean (Map 2.1). By 900 B.C.E., Assyrian armies had punched westward all the way to the coast. The Neo-Assyrian kings conquered Babylon, in southern Mesopotamia, in the eighth century B.C.E., and they added Egypt to their empire in the seventh century. These kings proclaimed their pride at having restored and expanded the imperial power that Assyria had possessed in the past.

Neo-Assyrian Militarism and Imperial Brutality

A warrior culture provided the foundation for the military strength that established the Neo-Assyrian Empire. A tactical innovation made Assyrian armies unstoppable: foot soldiers, not cavalry, were the Assyrians' main strike force. These infantrymen excelled in using military technology such as siege towers and battering rams, while swift chariots carried archers. Wars against foreign lands brought in revenues supplementing the domestic economy, which centered on agriculture, animal husbandry, and long-distance trade.

700 B.C.E. Spartans conquer Messenia and enslave its inhabitants as helots

657 B.C.E. Cypselus becomes tyrant in Corinth

597 and 586 B.C.E. Israelites exiled to Babylon

546–510 B.C.E. Peisistratus's family rules Athens as tyrants

508–500 B.C.E. Cleisthenes' reforms extend democracy in Athens

700 B.C.E. — 600 B.C.E. — 500 B.C.E.

700–500 B.C.E. Ionian philosophers invent rationalism

630 B.C.E. The lyric poet Sappho is born

594 B.C.E. Solon's reforms promote early democracy in Athens

539 B.C.E. Persian king Cyrus captures Babylon and permits Israelites to return to Canaan

Assyrian Warfare
The Assyrians relied on technology and bravery to attack walled cities. This sculpture shows a covered and wheeled battering ram and warriors climbing up a siege ladder to defeat their enemies. The crucified victims above and the bodies below reveal the brutal fate awaiting anyone who resisted the Assyrian army. The king and his entourage are shown as much larger than others to express their supreme status in society and to emphasize their rule. *(Ancient Art & Architecture Collection, Ltd.)*

Neo-Assyrian kings kept order by treating conquered peoples brutally. Those allowed to stay in their homelands had to pay annual tributes to the Assyrians: these payments included raw materials and luxury goods such as incense, wine, dyed linens, glasswork, and ivory. Worse was the fate of the large number of defeated people whom the kings routinely deported to Assyria for work on huge building projects—temples and palaces—in main cities. One unexpected consequence of this harsh policy was the undermining of the kings' native language: so many Aramaeans, for example, were deported from Canaan to Assyria that Aramaic had largely replaced Assyrian as the land's everyday language by the eighth century B.C.E.

Neo-Assyrian Life and Religion

When not making war, Neo-Assyrian men displayed their status and masculinity by hunting wild animals; the more dangerous the prey, the better. The king hunted lions to demonstrate his vigor and power and thus his capacity to rule. Royal lion hunts provided a favorite subject for sculptors, who carved long relief sculptures that narrated a connected story. Practical technology apparently also mattered to the kings. One, for example, boasted that he invented new irrigation equipment and a novel method of metal casting. The Neo-Assyrian kings also proclaimed that they were following the historical example of their ancestors in building an empire, and they prided themselves as authorities on that past. As one boasted, "I have read complicated texts, whose versions in Sumerian are obscure and in Akkadian hard to understand. I do research on the cuneiform texts on stone from before the Flood." Women of the social elite probably had a chance to become literate, but they were excluded from the male dominions of war and hunting.

Public religion, which included deities adopted from Babylonia, reflected the prominence of war in Assyrian culture: the cult of Ishtar, the goddess of love and war, glorified warfare, as it had in Babylonia. The Neo-Assyrian rulers' desire to demonstrate their respect for the gods motivated them to build huge and costly temples. These shrines' staffs of priests and slaves grew so numerous that the revenues from temple lands were insufficient to support them; the kings had to supply extra funds from the spoils of conquest.

The Neo-Assyrian kings' demand for revenue and generally harsh rule made their own people, especially the social elite, resent their regimes. Rebellions therefore became common throughout the history of the kingdom; a seventh-century B.C.E. revolt fatally weakened it. The Medes, an Iranian people, and the Chaldeans, a Semitic people who had driven the Assyrians from Babylonia, combined forces to invade the kingdom. Recent research has disproved the long-standing assumption that the attackers completely destroyed the Assyrian capital at Nineveh in 612 B.C.E., but their invasion nevertheless ended the Neo-Assyrian Empire.

The Neo-Babylonian Empire, 600–539 B.C.E.

As leaders of the allies who overthrew the Neo-Assyrian Empire, the Chaldeans seized the lion's share of territory. Originating among semi-nomadic herders along the Persian Gulf, by 600 B.C.E. the Chaldeans had established the Neo-Babylonian Empire, the most powerful in Babylonian history, though the shortest-lived: it fell to the Near East's next great empire, that of the Persians, in 539 B.C.E. The Neo-Babylonians spent great sums to increase the architectural splendor of Babylon, rebuilding the great temple of Marduk, the chief god, and constructing an elaborate city gate dedicated to the goddess Ishtar. Blue-glazed bricks and lions molded in yellow, red, and white decorated the gate's walls, which soared thirty-six feet high.

The Neo-Babylonians adopted ancestral Babylonian culture and preserved much Mesopotamian literature, such as the *Epic of Gilgamesh*. They also created many new works of prose and poetry, which the educated minority would often read aloud publicly for the enjoyment of the illiterate. Particularly popular were fables, proverbs, essays, and prophecies teaching morality and proper behavior. This so-called wisdom literature, a tradition going back at least to the Egyptian Old Kingdom, was a Near Eastern tradition that also was prominent in the religious writings of the Israelites.

The Neo-Babylonians passed their knowledge to others outside their region. Their advances in astronomy became so influential that the Greeks later used the word *Chaldean* to mean "astronomer." The primary motivation for observing the stars was the belief that the gods communicated their will to humans through natural phenomena, such as celestial movements and eclipses, abnormal births, patterns of smoke curling upward from a fire, and the trails of ants. The interpretation of these phenomena as messages from the gods exemplified the mixture of science and religion characteristic of ancient Near Eastern thought.

The Persian Empire, 557–500 B.C.E.

Cyrus (r. 557–530 B.C.E.) founded the Persian Empire in what is today Iran through his skills as a general and a diplomat who saw respect for others' religious practices as good imperial policy. He continued the region's tradition of kings waging war

Cyrus: Founder of the Persian Empire.

The Great King of Persia
Like their Assyrian predecessors, the Persian kings decorated their palaces with large relief sculptures emphasizing royal dignity and success. This one from Persepolis shows officials and petitioners giving the king proper respect when entering his presence. To symbolize their elevated status, the king and his son, who stands behind the throne, are shown larger than everyone else, as also in other Near Eastern royal art. Do you think the way the sculptors portrayed the figures from the side is more or less artistic than the technique used by the Egyptian painters in the image from the *Book of the Dead* on page 2. Why? *(Courtesy of the Oriental Institute of the University of Chicago.)*

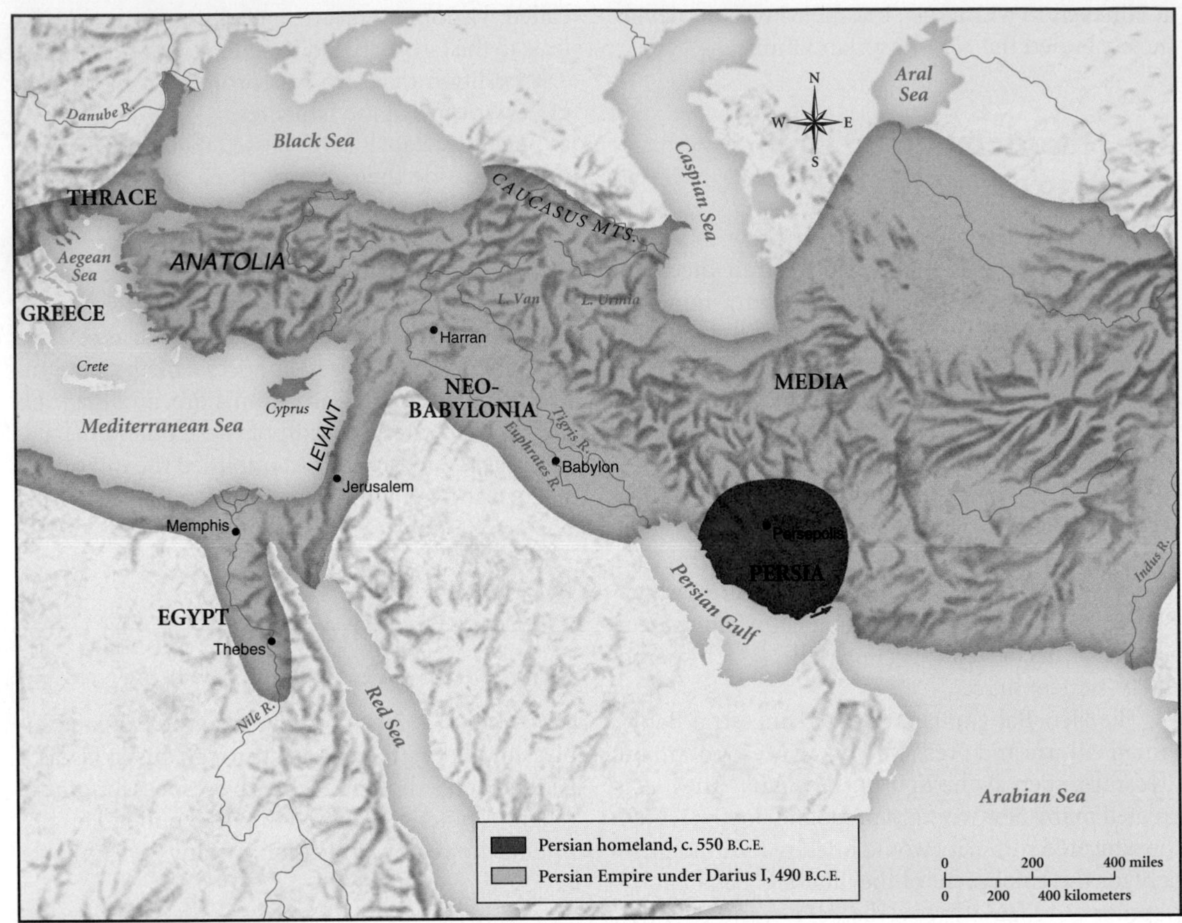

MAP 2.2 Expansion of the Persian Empire, c. 550–490 B.C.E.
Cyrus (r. 557–530 B.C.E.) founded the Persian Empire, which his successors expanded to be even larger than the Neo-Assyrian Empire that it replaced. The Persian kings made war outward from their inland center to gain coastal possessions for access to seaborne trade and naval bases. By late in the reign of Darius I (r. 522–486 B.C.E.), the Persian Empire had expanded eastward as far as the western edge of India, while to the west it reached Thrace, the eastern edge of Europe. Unlike their imperial predecessors, the Persian kings won their subjects' loyalty with tolerance of local customs and religion, although they treated rebels harshly.

to gain territory when he conquered Babylon in 539 B.C.E. Cyrus won local support there by presenting himself as the restorer of traditional religion. An ancient inscription has him proclaim: "I returned the statues of the gods [of Babylon] to their places. . . . Obeying the order of Marduk, the great lord, I put the gods of Sumer and Akkad in their homes."

Cyrus's successors expanded Persian rule via the same principles of military strength and cultural tolerance as foundations for maintaining order in an empire. At its height, the Persian Empire extended from Anatolia (today Turkey), the eastern Mediterranean coast, and Egypt on the west to present-day Pakistan on the east (Map 2.2). Since Persian kings believed that they had a divine right to rule everyone in the world, they never stopped trying to expand their empire.

Persian Royal Magnificence and Decentralized Rule

The Persian monarchy's revenues produced enormous wealth, and everything about the king emphasized his magnificence. His robes of purple outshone everyone else's; only he could step on the red carpets spread for him to walk on; his servants held their hands before their mouths in his presence so that he would not have to breathe the same air as they. As in other Near Eastern royal art, the Persian king was shown as larger than any other person in the sculpture adorning his immense palace at Persepolis. To display his concern for his loyal subjects as well as the gigantic scale of his resources, the king provided meals for fifteen thousand nobles and other guests every day—although he himself ate hidden from their view. Those who committed serious offenses against his laws or his

DOCUMENT

Excerpt from a Gatha

This excerpt from a Gatha *(one of the seventeen hymns believed to have been composed by Zarathustra) comes from the* Avesta, *the sacred scripture of Zoroastrianism. The dates of composition of the various parts of the Avesta are uncertain, but this text reflects Zoroastrians' belief in the divine power of their supreme god and creator of the world, Ahura Mazda, and in his loving and protective care for his worshippers.*

I announce and [will] complete [my worship] to Ahura Mazda, the creator, the radiant and glorious, the greatest and the best, the most beautiful, the most firm, the wisest, and the one of all whose body is the most perfect, who attains His ends the most infallibly, because of His Righteous Order, to Him who puts our minds in right order, who sends His joy-creating grace far and wide; who made us, and has fashioned us, and who has nourished and protected us, who is the most bounteous Spirit!

I announce and I (will) complete (my worship) to the Good Mind, and to Righteousness the Best, and to the Sovereignty which is to be desired, and to Piety the Bountiful, and to the two, the Universal Well-Being and Immortality. . . .

And I announce and complete my worship to all the stars . . . to the Moon . . . to the resplendent Sun . . . to Ahura Mazda . . . to the guardian spirits of the saints. . . .

And I announce and complete my worship to you, the Fire, O Ahura Mazda's son, together with all the fires, and to the good waters, even to all the waters made by Mazda, and to all the plants which Mazda made.

O all you lords, the greatest one, holy lords of the ritual order, if I have offended you by thought, or word or deed, whether with my will, or without intending error, I praise you [now the more] for this.

Source: *The Zend Avesta*, translated by James Darmesteter and L. H. Mills. Copyright © 1880, Oxford University Press.

Question to Consider

- **How does this song demonstrate the worshipper's understanding of his relationship to the supreme god?**

dignity the king punished brutally, mutilating their bodies and executing their families. Contemporary Greeks, in awe of the Persian monarch's power and his luxurious lifestyle, called him the Great King.

So long as his subjects—numbering in the millions and of many different ethnicities—remained peaceful, the king left them alone to live and worship as they pleased. The empire's smoothly functioning administrative structure sprang from Assyrian precedents: satraps (regional governors) ruled enormous territories with little interference from the kings. In this decentralized system, the governors' duties included keeping order, enrolling troops when needed, and sending revenues to the royal treasury.

Darius I (r. 522–486 B.C.E.) extended Persian power eastward to the western edge of India and westward to Thrace, northeast of Greece. This expansion created the Near East's greatest empire. Organizing this vast territory into provinces, Darius assigned each region taxes payable in the way best suited to its local economy—precious metals, grain, horses, slaves. He also required each region to send soldiers to the royal army. A network of roads and a courier system for royal mail provided communication among the far-flung provincial centers. The Greek historian Herodotus reported that neither snow, rain, heat, nor darkness slowed the couriers from completing their routes as swiftly as possible, a claim transformed centuries later into the U.S. Postal Service motto.

Persian Religion

Ruling as absolute autocrats, the Persian kings believed themselves superior to everyone. They claimed to be not gods but rather the agents of Ahura Mazda, the supreme god of Persia. As Darius I said in his autobiography, carved into a mountainside in three languages, "Ahura Mazda gave me kingship. . . . By the will of Ahura Mazda the provinces respected my laws."

Persian religion made Ahura Mazda the center of its devotion and took its doctrines from the teachings of the legendary prophet Zarathustra. (The religion is called Zoroastrianism today from Zoroaster, the Greek name for this holy man.) Zarathustra proclaimed Ahura Mazda to be "the father of Truth" and "creator of Good Thought," who demanded purity from his worshippers and promised help to those who lived with truthfulness and justice (see Document, "Excerpt from a Gatha," above). The most important doctrine of Zoroastrianism was **moral dualism**. This belief saw the world as the arena

---

moral dualism: The belief that the world is the arena for an ongoing battle for control between divine forces of good and evil.

for an ongoing battle between the two opposing divine forces of good and evil. Ahura Mazda, as the embodiment of good and light, constantly struggled against the evil darkness represented by the Satan-like figure Ahriman. Human beings had to choose between the way of the truth and the way of the lie, between purity and impurity. As in the judgment of the dead in ancient Egyptian religion, so too in Persian religion only those judged righteous after death made it across "the bridge of separation" to heaven and avoided falling from its narrow span into hell. Persian religion's emphasis on ethical behavior and on a supreme god had a lasting influence on others, especially the Israelites.

The Israelites, Origins to 539 B.C.E.

The Israelites' development of a monotheistic religion makes them a principal building block in the foundations of Western civilization, even though they never rivaled the political and military power of the great empires in the Near East. Their religion, known as Judaism, developed over a long time. It reflected influences from the Israelites' polytheistic neighbors in Canaan (ancient Palestine), but its ideas on the nature of a monotheistic divinity became a turning point in the history of religions.

Israelite Origins and the Bible The influence of the Israelites on Western civilization came from the impact of the book that became their sacred scripture, the Hebrew Bible. This book deeply affected not only Judaism but also Christianity and, later, Islam. Unfortunately, no source provides definitive information on the historical background of the Israelites or their religion. The Bible tells stories to explain God's moral plan for the universe, not to give a full account of Israelite origins, and archaeology has not yielded a clear picture.

According to the Bible's account, the patriarch Abraham and his followers migrated from the Mesopotamian city of Ur to Canaan, perhaps around 1900 B.C.E. Once there, the Israelites continued to live as semi-nomads, tending flocks of animals on the region's scraggly grasslands and living in temporary tent settlements. They occasionally planted barley or wheat for a season or two and then moved on to new pastures. Traditionally believed to have been divided into twelve tribes, they never settled down or formed a political state in this period. The Canaanites remained the political and military power in the region.

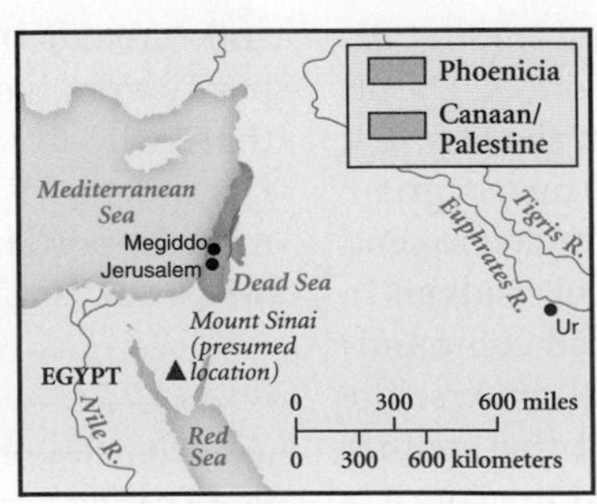

Phoenicia and Canaan/Palestine

Abraham's son Isaac moved his pastoral people to various locations to try to avoid disputes with local Canaanites over grazing rights. Isaac's son Jacob, the story continues, moved to Egypt late in life when his son Joseph brought Jacob and other relatives there to escape famine in Canaan. Joseph had previously used his intelligence and charisma to rise to an important position in the Egyptian administration. The biblical story of the movement of a band of Israelites to Egypt represents a crucial event in their early history, possibly reflecting a time when drought forced some Israelites to migrate gradually into the Nile delta of Egypt. They probably drifted in during the seventeenth or sixteenth century B.C.E. as part of the movement of peoples into Egypt at the time of Hyksos rule. By the thirteenth century B.C.E., the pharaohs had forced the Israelite men into slave-labor gangs for farming and for construction work on large building projects.

Although historians have found no secure evidence for the story, according to the biblical Book of Exodus, the Israelite deity, Yahweh, instructed Moses to lead the Israelites out of bondage in Egypt against the will of the king, perhaps around the mid-thirteenth century B.C.E. Yahweh sent ten plagues to compel the pharaoh to free the Israelites, but the king still tried to recapture them during their flight. Yahweh therefore miraculously parted the sea to allow them to escape eastward; the water swirled back together and drowned the pharaoh's army as it tried to follow.

Covenant, Monotheism, and Israelite Law Next in the biblical narrative after the story of the exodus from Egypt comes the crucial event in the history of the Israelites: the formalizing of a contractual agreement (called a covenant in religious terminology) between them and their deity, who revealed himself to Moses on Mount Sinai in the desert northeast of Egypt. This contract between the Israelites and Yahweh specified that, in return for their worshipping him exclusively as their only god and living by his laws, Yahweh would make them his chosen people and lead them into a promised land of safety and prosperity. The form of the covenant with Yahweh followed the ancient Near Eastern tradition of treaties between a superior and subordinates, but its content differed from that of other ancient

Near Eastern religions because it made Yahweh the exclusive deity of his people.

This binding agreement demanded human obedience to divine law and promised punishment for unrighteousness. Yahweh described himself to Moses as "compassionate and gracious, patient, ever constant and true . . . forgiving wickedness, rebellion, and sin," yet he also declared that he was "one who punishes sons and grandsons to the third and fourth generation for their fathers' iniquity" (Exod. 34:6–7).

Because the earliest parts of the Hebrew Bible were probably composed about 950 B.C.E., more than three hundred years after the date implied in the Bible for the Israelites' exodus from Egypt, this narrative of the Israelite covenant and laws deals with a distant time for whose history there is no indisputable documentation. It is clear, however, that the early Israelites, like their neighbors in Canaan, originally worshipped a variety of gods, including spirits believed to reside in natural objects such as trees and stones. Yahweh may have originally been the deity of the tribe of Midian, to which Moses's father-in-law belonged. In the time of Moses, some Israelites, ignoring their leaders' instructions, continued to worship other local gods, such as Baal of Canaan.

The Hebrew Bible sets forth the religious and moral code the Israelites had to follow. The **Torah** (the first five books of the Hebrew Bible, called the Pentateuch by Christians) recorded numerous laws for righteous living. Most famous are the Ten Commandments, which required Israelites to worship Yahweh exclusively; make no idols; keep from misusing Yahweh's name; honor their parents; refrain from work on the seventh day of the week (the Sabbath); and abstain from murder, adultery, theft, lying, and covetousness. Many of the Israelites' laws shared the traditional form and content of earlier Mesopotamian laws, such as those of Hammurabi in Mesopotamia: if someone did a certain thing to another person, then a specified punishment was imposed on the perpetrator. For example, both Hammurabi's laws and Israelite law covered the case of an ox that had gored a person; the owner was penalized only if he had been warned about his beast's tendency to gore and had done nothing to restrain it. Also like Hammurabi's laws, Israelite law expressed an interest in the welfare of the poor as well as the rich. In addition, it secured protection for the lower classes and people without power, such as strangers, widows, and orphans. The correspondence between the Pentateuch and Hammurabi's laws, which date from centuries before the imputed date of the exodus, is of course an indication that Israelite legal traditions were not created in isolation from long-standing ideas about justice in Near Eastern societies.

Torah: The first five books of the Hebrew Bible, also referred to as the Pentateuch. It contains early Jewish law.

Goddess Figurines from Judah
Many small statues of this type, called Astarte figurines after a goddess of Canaan, have been found in private houses in Judah dating from about 800 to 600 B.C.E. Israelites evidently kept them as magical tokens to promote fertility and prosperity. The prophets fiercely condemned the worship of such figures as part of the development of Israelite monotheism and the abandoning of polytheism. Compare the shape of these figurines to the body shape of the Venus figurine on page P-5. What do you think these shapes represented? *(Collection of the Israel Antiquities Authority and Collection of The Israel Museum, Jerusalem. Photo © The Israel Museum, Jerusalem.)*

Israelite law and thus Israelite justice differed significantly from their Mesopotamian precedent, however, in applying the same rules and punishments to everyone, without regard to social rank. Israelite law also eliminated eye-for-an-eye punishment—a Mesopotamian tradition ordering, for example, that a rapist's wife be raped, or that the son of a builder be killed if his father's negligent work caused the death of someone else's son. Crimes against property did not carry the death penalty, as they frequently did in other Near Eastern societies. Israelite women and children had reduced legal rights compared to men: for example, wives had less freedom to divorce their husbands than husbands had to divorce their wives, much as in the laws of Hammurabi. Israelite laws also protected slaves against flagrant mistreatment by their masters. Slaves who lost an eye or a tooth from a beating were to be freed. Like free people, slaves enjoyed the right to rest on the Sabbath.

According to the Bible, the Israelites who fled from Egypt with Moses made their way back to Canaan, joining their relatives who had remained there and somehow carving out separate territories for themselves. The twelve Israelite tribes remained

Solomon's Walls at Megiddo
Rulers in the Near East often fought to control the city of Megiddo because it controlled an important pass along a main north-south route near the eastern Mediterranean coast. The Israelite king Solomon built strong fortification walls for it in the tenth century B.C.E., as recalled in the Hebrew Bible (1 Kings 9:15). A tunnel reaching hundreds of feet through rock to a spring hidden in a cave supplied water during a siege. Despite these defenses, the city later fell to the Egyptians and the Assyrians. *(Erich Lessing/Art Resource, NY.)*

politically distinct under the direction of separate leaders, called judges, until the eleventh century, when according to tradition their first monarchy emerged. Their monotheism gradually developed over the succeeding centuries.

The Consolidation of Israelite Monotheism Again, controversy rages among historians about the accuracy of the biblical account, according to which the Israelites achieved their first national organization with the creation of a monarchy in the late eleventh century B.C.E. Saul became their first king, and his successors David (r. 1010–970 B.C.E.) and Solomon (r. c. 961–922 B.C.E.) brought the Israelite kingdom to the height of its prosperity. The kingdom's wealth, based on international commerce conducted through its cities, was displayed above all in the great temple richly decorated with gold leaf that Solomon built in Jerusalem to be the house of Yahweh. Whatever one thinks about the truth of the details of these stories, the temple in Jerusalem and the sacrifices that took place there did become the center of the Israelites' religion.

The Israelites' initial unity and prosperity were short-lived. After Solomon's death, the monarchy split into two kingdoms: Israel in the north and Judah in the south. The Assyrians destroyed Israel in 722 B.C.E. and deported its population to Assyria. In 597 B.C.E., the Babylonians conquered Judah and captured its capital, Jerusalem. In 586 B.C.E., they destroyed the temple to Yahweh and banished the Israelite leaders, along with much of the population, to Babylon.

During their period of exile in Mesopotamia, the Israelites came into close contact with Zoroastrianism. Scholars strongly dispute the extent of influence that the religious ideas of this religion had on the beliefs of the exiled Israelites. Some argue that in reality the ideas of the Israelites influenced Zoroastrian religion. It is clear, however, that the religions of these two groups eventually (the timing is uncertain) came to share crucial concepts, such as the existence of God and Satan, angels and demons, God's day of judgment, and the arrival of a messiah. Even if we cannot make out the exact details of the effect on the Israelites of their exile in Babylon, it seems likely that this forced experience of living in a foreign culture would have altered their worldview.

When the Persian king Cyrus overthrew the Babylonians in 539 B.C.E., he permitted the Israelites to return to their part of Canaan. The Bible proclaimed Cyrus a messiah of the Israelites chosen by Yahweh as his "shepherd . . . to accomplish all his purpose" in restoring his people to their previous home (Isa. 44:28–45:1). This region was called Yehud, from the name of the southern Israelite kingdom, Judah. From this geographical term came the word *Jew*, a designation for the Israelites after their Babylonian exile. Cyrus allowed them to rebuild their main temple in Jerusalem and to practice their religion. After returning from exile, the Jews were forever a people subject to the political domination of various Near Eastern powers, except for a period of independence during the second and first centuries B.C.E.

Jewish prophets, both men and women, preached that their defeats were divine punishment for neglecting the Sinai covenant and mistreating their poor. Some prophets also predicted the coming end of the present world following a great crisis, a judgment by Yahweh, and salvation leading to a new and better world. This apocalypticism ("uncovering," or revelation), reminiscent of Babylonian prophetic wisdom literature, would later provide the worldview of Christianity. Yahweh would save the Israelite nation, the prophets thundered, only if Jews strictly observed divine law.

Jewish leaders therefore developed complex religious laws to maintain ritual and ethical purity in all aspects of life. Marrying non-Jews was forbidden, as was working on the Sabbath. Fathers had legal power over the household, subject to intervention by the male elders of the community; women gained honor as mothers. Only men could initiate divorce proceedings. Ethics applied not only to obvious crimes but also to financial dealings; cheating in business transactions was condemned. Jews had to pay taxes and offerings to support and honor the sanctuary of Yahweh, and they had to forgive debts every seventh year.

The Jews' hardships had taught them that their religious traditions and laws gave them the strength to survive even when separated from their homeland. Gradually, they created their monotheism by accepting their leaders' preaching that Yahweh was the only god and that they had to adhere to his divine will by obeying his laws. Jews retained their identity by following this religion, regardless of their personal fate or their geographical location. A remarkable outcome of these religious developments was that Jews who did not return to their homeland, instead choosing to remain in Babylon or Persia or Egypt, could maintain their Jewish identity by following Jewish law while living among foreigners. In this way, the **Diaspora** ("dispersion of population") came to characterize the history of the Jewish people.

Israelite monotheism made the preservation and understanding of a sacred text, the Bible, the center of religious life. The chief priests compiled an authoritative scripture by adding to the Torah the books of the prophets, such as Isaiah, and other writings, including Psalms and wisdom literature. Making scripture the focus of religion proved the most crucial development for the history not only of Judaism but also of Christianity and Islam, because these later religions made their own sacred texts—the Bible and the Qur'an, respectively—the centers of their belief and practice.

Although the ancient Israelites never formed a militarily powerful nation, their monotheistic religion created a new path for Western civilization. Through the continuing vitality of Judaism and its impact on the doctrines of Christianity and Islam, the early Jews passed on ideas—chiefly monotheism and the notion of a covenant bestowing a divinely ordained destiny on a people if they obey divine will—whose effects have endured to this day. These religious concepts constitute one of the most significant legacies to Western civilization from the Near East in the period 1000–500 B.C.E.

REVIEW QUESTION In what ways was religion important in the Near East from c. 1000 B.C.E. to c. 500 B.C.E.?

The Reemergence of Greek Civilization, 1000–750 B.C.E.

During the period of violence in 1200–1000 B.C.E., the Greeks lost the distinguishing marks of civilization: they no longer had unified states, prosperous large settlements, or writing. Thus, during their Dark Age (c. 1000–750 B.C.E.), they had to remake their civilization. Trade, cultural interaction, and technological innovation led to recovery: contact with the Near East promoted intellectual, artistic, and economic revival, while the introduction of metallurgy for making iron made farming more efficient. As conditions improved, a social elite distinguished by wealth and the competitive pursuit of individual excellence described in Homeric poetry replaced the hierarchy of Mycenaean times. In the eighth century B.C.E., the creation of the Olympic Games and the emphasis on justice in the poetry of Hesiod promoted the communal values that fueled the re emergence of Greek civilization. It also laid the foundation for a radically new form of political organization in which central authority was based on citizenship rather than on subjection to kings.

The Greek Dark Age

The fall of Mycenaean civilization brought to Greece the depressed economic conditions that so many people in other regions experienced during the worst years of their Dark Ages. One of the most startling indications of the severity of life in the Dark Age in Greece is that Greeks apparently lost their knowledge of writing when Mycenaean civilization fell. The Linear B script they had used to write Greek was difficult to master and probably known only by a few scribes, who used writing exclusively to track the flow of goods in and out of the palaces. When the Mycenaean states collapsed, the Greeks no longer needed scribes or writing.

Diaspora (die ASS por a): The dispersal of the Jewish population from their homeland.

The Greek Dark Age, 1000–750 B.C.E.

1000 B.C.E.	Almost all important Mycenaean sites except Athens destroyed by now
1000–900 B.C.E.	Greatest depopulation and economic loss
900–800 B.C.E.	Early revival of population and agriculture; beginning use of iron tools and weapons
800 B.C.E.	Greek trading contacts initiated with Al Mina in Syria
776 B.C.E.	First Olympic Games held
775 B.C.E.	Euboeans found trading post on island in the Bay of Naples
750 B.C.E.	Homeric poetry recorded in writing after Greeks learn to write again; Hesiod composes his poetry

MAP 2.3 Dark Age Greece, 1000–750 B.C.E.
During their Dark Age, Greeks lived in many fewer and smaller settlements than in the Bronze Age. It took centuries for the region as a whole to revive. Recent archaeological research, however, indicates that Greece was not as impoverished or as depopulated after the fall of the Mycenaean kingdoms as sometimes assumed. The many small ports along Greece's jagged coastline and the short distances between its islands allowed seafaring trade and communication to continue. By island-hopping, boats could make it safely across the Aegean Sea and beyond, keeping the routes open to the Near East.

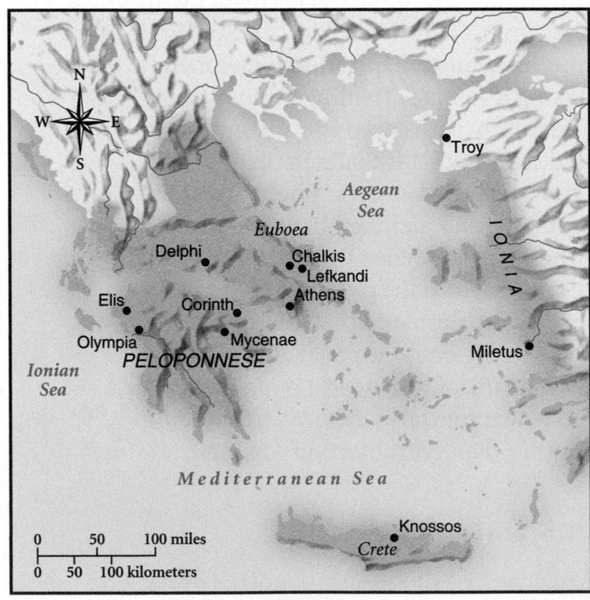

Only oral transmission kept Greek cultural traditions alive.

Archaeology reveals that the Mycenaean collapse meant that Greeks in the early Dark Age, although spread across roughly the same geographical area as before, cultivated much less land and had many fewer settlements (Map 2.3). No longer did powerful rulers sheltered in stone fortresses control redistributive economies. The number of ships carrying Greek adventurers, raiders, and traders dwindled. Large political states ceased to exist; people scratched out an existence as herders, shepherds, and subsistence farmers bunched in tiny settlements — as few as twenty people in many cases. The smaller population could not produce as much food as before, causing its numbers to drop still further as hunger and starvation killed many people. These two processes reinforced each other in a vicious circle, multiplying their negative effects.

With the decline of agriculture in their Dark Age, more Greeks than ever before made their living by herding animals. These herders necessarily no longer lived in permanent settlements: they needed to move their herds to new pastures once the animals had overgrazed their current location. Lucky ones might find a new spot where they could grow a crop of grain if they stayed long enough. In this transient lifestyle, people built only simple huts and kept few possessions. Unlike their Bronze Age ancestors, Greeks in the Dark Age had no monumental architecture, and they even lost an old tradition in their everyday art: they stopped including people and animals in their principal art form — paintings on ceramics — putting only nonfigural designs on their pots.

Trade, Innovation, and Recovery in Greece

Geography allowed the Greeks to continue seaborne trade with the civilizations of the eastern Mediterranean even during their Dark Age. Trade promoted cultural interaction, and the Greeks learned to write again about 800 B.C.E. They adopted the alphabet from the Phoenicians, seafaring traders from Canaan. Greeks changed and added letters to achieve independent representation of vowel sounds so that they could express their language and record their literature, beginning with Homer's and Hesiod's poetry in the eighth century B.C.E. Near Eastern art inspired Greeks to resume the production of ceramics with figural designs (as on the Corinthian vase on page 36). Seaborne commerce encouraged better-off Greeks to produce agricultural surpluses and goods they could trade for luxuries such as gold jewelry and gems from Egypt and Syria.

Most important, trade brought the new technology of iron metallurgy. The violence of 1200–1000 B.C.E. had interrupted the traditional trading routes for tin. Without tin, metalworkers could not forge bronze weapons and tools. To make up for this loss, smiths in the eastern Mediterranean devised technology to smelt iron ore. Greeks then learned this skill through their eastern trade contacts and mined their own iron ore, which was common in Greece. Iron eventually replaced bronze in many uses, above all for agricultural tools, swords, and spear points. The Greeks still used bronze for shields and armor, however, because it was easier to shape into thin, curved pieces.

The iron tools' lower cost allowed more people to acquire them. Because iron is harder than bronze, implements kept their sharp edges longer. Better and more plentiful farming implements of iron helped increase food production, which sustained population growth. In this way, technology imported from the Near East improved people's chances for survival and thus helped Greece recover from the Dark Age's depopulation.

The Greek Social Elite and the Homeric Ideal

With the Mycenaean rulers gone, leadership became an open competition in Dark Age Greece. Individuals who proved themselves excellent in action, words, charisma, and religious knowledge joined the social elite, enjoying higher prestige and authority in society. Competition as a social value defined Greek life. Excellence—***aretê*** in Greek—was earned by competing. Men competed with others for aretê as warriors and persuasive public speakers. Women won their highest aretê by being seen to manage a household of children, slaves, and storerooms that was more successful than those of struggling families. Members of the elite accumulated wealth by controlling agricultural land, which people of lower status worked for them as tenants or slaves.

The poems of **Homer**, Greece's first and most famous author, reflect the social elite's ideals, especially the competition for aretê. The Greeks believed that Homer was a blind poet from Ionia (today Turkey's western coast) who composed the epic poems *The Iliad* and *The Odyssey*. Most modern scholars believe that Homer was the last in a long line of poets who, influenced by Near Eastern mythology, had been singing these stories for centuries, orally transmitting cultural values from one generation to the next. *The Iliad* tells the story of the Greek army in the Trojan War. Camped before the walls of Troy for ten years, the heroes of the army compete for glory and riches by raiding the countryside, dueling Troy's best fighters, and quarreling with one another over prestige and booty. The greatest Greek warrior is Achilles, who proves his aretê by choosing to die in battle rather than accept the gods' offer to return home safely but without glory. *The Odyssey* recounts not only the hero Odysseus's ten-year adventure sailing home after the fall of Troy but also the struggle of his wife, Penelope, to protect their household from the schemes of rivals. Penelope proves her aretê by outwitting jealous neighbors to preserve her family's prosperity for her husband's return.

aretê **(ah reh TAY):** The Greek value of competitive individual excellence.

Homer: Greece's first and most famous author, who composed *The Iliad* and *The Odyssey*.

A Rich Woman's Model Granary from the Dark Age
This clay model of storage containers for grain was found in a woman's tomb in Athens from about 850 B.C.E. It apparently symbolizes the surpluses that the woman and her family were able to accumulate and indicates that she was wealthy by the standards of her time. The geometric designs painted on the pottery are characteristic of Greek art in this period, when human and animal figures were not used. By the Archaic Age, figures returned to Greek art, the result of Near Eastern influence. Contrast the lively animals painted some two hundred years later on the Corinthian vase illustrated at the opening of this chapter (page 36). *(American School of Classical Studies at Athens: Agora Excavations.)*

Homer reveals that the white-hot emotions inflamed by the competition for excellence could provoke a disturbing level of inhumanity. Achilles, in preparing to duel Hector, the prince of Troy, brutally rejects the Trojan's proposal that the winner return the loser's corpse to his family and friends: "Do wolves and lambs agree to cooperate? No, they hate each other to the roots of their being." The victor, Achilles, mutilates Hector's body. When Hecuba, the queen of Troy, sees this outrage, she bitterly shouts, "I wish I could sink my teeth into his liver in his guts to eat it raw." The endings of Homer's poems suggest that the gods could sometimes help people achieve reconciliation after violent conflict, but the amount of human suffering in his stories makes it clear that the pursuit of excellence can come at a high price.

As in Homer, the real world of the Greek Dark Age had a small but wealthy social elite. On the island of Euboea, for example, archaeologists have discovered the tenth-century B.C.E. grave of a couple who took such enormous riches with them to the next world that the woman's body was covered in gold ornaments. They had done well in the competition for prestige and wealth; most people of the time were, by comparison, desperately poor. Those who scratched out a hard living could only dream of

Athletic Competition
Greek vase painters often showed male athletes in action or training, perhaps in part because athletes were customers who would buy pottery with such scenes. As in this painting of an Athenian foot race from around 530 B.C.E., the athletes were usually shown nude, which is how they competed, revealing their superb physical condition and strong musculature. Being in excellent shape was a man's ideal for several reasons: it was regarded as beautiful, it enabled him to compete for individual glory in athletic contests, and it allowed him to fulfill his community responsibility by fighting as a well-conditioned soldier in the city-state's citizen militia. Why do you think the figure at the far left does not have a full beard? (See the caption on page 69 for a hint.) *([Euphiletos Painter [sixth century B.C.E.], Panathenaic prize amphora, ca. 530 B.C.E. Reverse. Terracotta, H. 24½ in. [62.2 cm.]. Archaic Greek, Attic. Rogers Fund, 1914. [14.130.12]. The Metropolitan Museum of Art, New York, U.S.A. Image copyright © The Metropolitan Museum of Art/Art Resource, NY.)*

the luxurious life and rich goods they heard about in Homer's poems.

The Values of the Olympic Games

Greece had recovered enough population and prosperity by the eighth century B.C.E. to begin creating new forms of social and political organization. The most vivid evidence is the founding of the Olympic Games, traditionally dated to 776 B.C.E. This international religious festival showcased the competitive value of aretê.

Every four years, the games took place in a huge sanctuary dedicated to Zeus, the king of the gods, at Olympia, in the northwestern Peloponnese. Male athletes from elite families vied in sports, imitating the aretê needed for war: running, wrestling, jumping, and throwing. Horse and chariot racing were added to the program later, but the main event remained a two-hundred-yard sprint, the *stadion* (hence our word *stadium*). The athletes competed as individuals, not on national teams as in the modern Olympic Games. Winners received not money but rather a garland made from wild olive leaves to symbolize the prestige of victory.

The Olympics illustrate Greek notions of proper behavior for each gender: crowds of men flocked to the games, but women were prohibited on pain of death. Women had their own separate Olympic festival on a different date in honor of Hera, queen of the gods. Only unmarried women could compete. These separate games existed because most Greeks believed it was not proper for men and women to observe nonslave strangers of the opposite gender wearing no or little clothing. In later times, professional athletes dominated the Olympics, earning their living from appearance fees and prizes at games held throughout the Greek world. The most famous winner was Milo, from Croton in Italy. Six-time Olympic wrestling champion, he stunned audiences with demonstrations of strength such as holding his breath until his veins expanded to snap a cord tied around his head.

Although the Olympics existed to glorify individual competitive excellence by identifying winners and losers, the games' organization reveals an important trend under way in Greek society: they were open to any socially elite Greek male good enough to compete and to any male spectator who could journey there. These rules represented beginning steps toward a concept of collective Greek identity. Remarkably for a land so often torn by internal wars, once every four years an international truce of several weeks was declared so that competitors and fans from all Greek communities could safely travel to and from Olympia. The Olympic Games, then, helped channel the competition for individual excellence into a new context of social cooperation and community values, essential preconditions for the creation of Greece's new political form, the city-state ruled by citizens.

Homer, Hesiod, and Divine Justice in Greek Myth

The Greeks' belief in divine justice inspired them to develop the cooperative values that remade their civilization. This idea came not from scripture—Greeks had none—but from poetry that told myths about the gods and goddesses and their relationships to humans. Myths could seem fantastically unrealistic, but at the same time they taught lessons about the nature of life in a world that Greeks saw as under the control of gods whose purposes were difficult to understand. Different myths often provided different lessons, teaching that human beings could not expect to have a clear understanding of the gods and had to make choices on their own about how to live.

Homer's poems reveal that the gods had plans for human existence. Zeus's will, for example, motivated the Trojan War's tragic events. This myth did not specify, however, that Zeus's purpose was just. Bellerophon, for example, the wronged hero whose brave efforts won him a princess bride and a kingdom, ended up losing everything. He became, in Homer's words, "hated by the gods and wandering the land alone, eating his heart out, a refugee fleeing from the haunts of men." The poem gives no explanation for this tragedy and therefore no reason to believe that a concern for justice motivated the gods in this case.

Hesiod's poetry, by contrast, reveals how other myths describing divine support for justice contributed to the feeling of community that motivated the creation of Greece's new social and political organization. Hesiod's vivid stories, which originated in Near Eastern creation myths, show that existence, even for deities, always involved struggle, sorrow, and violence. These stories also reveal, however, that the divine order of the universe could sometimes include a concern for justice.

Hesiod's epic poem *Theogony* (whose title means "genealogy of the gods") recounted the birth of the race of gods—including Sky and numerous others—from the intercourse of primeval Chaos and Earth. Hesiod explained that when Sky began to imprison his siblings, Earth persuaded her fiercest son, Kronos, to overthrow him violently because "Sky first schemed to do shameful things." When Kronos later began to swallow his own children to avoid sharing power with them, his wife, Rhea (who was also his sister), had their son Zeus violently force his father from power.

In *Works and Days*, his poem on conditions in his own time, Hesiod identified Zeus as the source of justice in human affairs, a force that punished evildoers: "Zeus commanded that fishes and wild beasts and birds should eat each other, for they have no justice; but to human beings he has given justice, which is far the best." People, however, were responsible for administering justice, and in the eighth century B.C.E. this meant the male social elite. They controlled their family members and household servants. Hesiod insisted that a leader should demonstrate aretê by employing persuasion instead of force: "When his people in their assembly get on the wrong track, he gently sets matters right, persuading them with soft words."

Hesiod complained that many elite leaders in his time failed to exercise their power in this way, instead creating conflict between themselves and the peasants—free proprietors of small farms owning a slave or two, oxen to work their fields, and a limited amount of goods acquired by trading the surplus of their crops. Hesiod warned "bribe-devouring chiefs," who used "crooked judgments" to settle disputes among their followers and neighbors, to fear divine justice. The outrage that peasants felt at not receiving equal treatment helped push the gradual movement toward a new form of social and political organization in Greece.

REVIEW QUESTION What factors proved most important in the Greek recovery from the troubles of the Dark Age?

The Creation of the Greek City-State, 750–500 B.C.E.

The Greek Dark Age led to what historians call the Archaic Age (c. 750–500 B.C.E.). This new era saw the creation of the Greek city-state—the **polis**—an independent community of citizens inhabiting

polis: The Greek city-state, an independent community of citizens not ruled by a king.

a city and the countryside around it. Greece's geography, dominated by mountains and islands, promoted the creation of hundreds of independent city-states in its heartland in and around the Aegean Sea. From these original locations, Greeks dispersed widely around the Mediterranean to settle hundreds more trading communities that often grew into new city-states. Individuals' drive for profit from trade, especially in raw materials, and for free farmland probably started this process of founding new settlements.

Though it took varying forms, the Greek polis differed from the Mesopotamian city-state primarily in being a community of citizens making laws and administering justice among themselves versus being a collection of inhabitants subject to a king. Another difference was that poor citizens of Greek city-states enjoyed a rough legal and political equality with the rich. Not different, however, were the subordination of women and the subjugation of slaves. Also, though this new direction in social and political organization gave the poor a share of power in the community, it was never able to eliminate tension between the interests of the social elite and those of ordinary people.

The Physical Environment of the Greek City-State

Culturally, Greeks identified with one another because they spoke the same language and worshipped the same gods. Still, the ancient Greeks never became a nation in the political sense because their many city-states never unified. Their homeland lay in and around the Aegean Sea, a section of the Mediterranean between modern Greece and Turkey dotted with large and small islands (Map 2.4).

The mountainous geography of Greece tended to isolate its communities and contributed to the city-states' often hostile relations. A single island could be home to multiple city-states; Lesbos, for example, had five. Because few city-states had enough farmland to support many people, most of them had populations of only several hundred to several thousand. Some that had revenues from international trade, like Athens or Corinth, grew to be much larger.

Only the sea offered practical long-distance transportation in Greece. Greek rivers were little more than creeks, while land travel was slow and expensive because rudimentary dirt paths and dry riverbeds provided the only roads. The most plentiful resource was timber from the mountains for building houses and ships. Deposits of metal ore were scattered throughout Greek territory, as were clays suitable for pottery and sculpture. Various quarries of fine stone such as marble provided material for special buildings and works of art. The uneven distribution of these resources meant that some areas were considerably wealthier than others.

None of the mountains wrinkling the Greek landscape rose higher than ten thousand feet, but their steep slopes limited agriculture. Only 20 to 30 percent of the total land area could be farmed. The scarcity of level terrain in most areas made it impossible to raise large herds of cattle and horses. Pigs, sheep, and goats were the common livestock, and the domestic chicken had been introduced from the Near East by the seventh century B.C.E. The Mediterranean climate (intermittent heavy rain during a few months and hot, dry summers) limited a farmer's options, as did the fragility of the environment. Grazing livestock, for example, could be so hard on plant life that winter downpours would wash away the shallow topsoil. Because the amount of annual precipitation varied greatly, farming was a precarious business of boom and bust. People preferred wheat, but since that grain was expensive to cultivate, the cereal staple of the Greek diet became barley. Wine grapes and olives were the other most important crops.

Trade and "Colonization," 800–580 B.C.E.

A desire for greater prosperity led Greeks to engage in long-distance trade by sea throughout the Mediterranean region. Greece's jagged coastline made sea travel practical: almost every community lay within forty miles of the Mediterranean Sea. But sailors faced dangers from pirates and, especially, storms. Seasonal winds and fierce gales almost ruled out sea travel during winter. Sailors tried to hug the coast, hopping from island to island and putting in to shore at night, but sometimes the drive for profit required long, nonstop voyages over open waters. As Hesiod commented, merchants took to the sea "because an income means life to poor mortals, but it is a terrible fate to die among the waves."

The search for metals and other scarce resources took traders far from home, and also brought them into frequent contact with other cultures. *The Odyssey* describes the basic strategy of this commodity trading, when the goddess Athena appears disguised as a metal trader: "I am here . . . with my ship and crew on our way across the wine-dark sea to foreign lands in search of copper; I am carrying iron now." By 800 B.C.E., the Mediterranean swarmed with entrepreneurs of many nationalities. The Phoenicians established settlements as far west as Spain's Atlantic coast to gain access to inland mines there. Their

North African settlement at Carthage (modern Tunis) would become one of the Mediterranean's most powerful cities in later times, dominating commerce west of Italy.

Greeks energetically joined this seaborne competition for profit as the scale of trade soared near the end of the Dark Age: archaeologists have found only two tenth-century B.C.E. Greek pots that were carried abroad, but eighth-century pottery has turned up at more than eighty foreign sites. By 750 B.C.E. (or earlier—the evidence is hard to date), Greeks had begun to settle far from their homeland, sometimes living in others' settlements, especially those of the Phoenicians in the western Mediterranean, and sometimes establishing trading posts of their own, as on an island in the Bay of Naples. Everywhere they traded with the local populations, such as the Etruscans in central Italy, who imported large amounts of Greek goods, as the vases found in their tombs reveal. Greeks staying abroad for the long term would also cultivate vacant land, gradually building permanent communities. Traders were not the only Greeks to leave home. As the population expanded following the Dark Age, a shortage of farmland in Greece drove some poor farmers abroad to find fields they could work. Apparently only males left home on trading and land-hunting expeditions, so they had to find wives wherever they settled, either through peaceful negotiation or by kidnapping.

MAP 2.4 Archaic Greece, 750–500 B.C.E.
The Greek heartland lay in and around the Aegean Sea, in what is today the nation of Greece and the western edge of the nation of Turkey (ancient Anatolia). The "mainland," where Athens, Corinth, and Sparta are located, is the southernmost tip of the mountainous Balkan peninsula. The many islands of the Aegean area were home mainly to small city-states, with the exception of the large islands just off the western Anatolian coast, which were home to populous ones.

By about 580 B.C.E., Greek settlements had spread westward to Spain, present-day southern France, southern Italy, and Sicily; southward to North Africa; and eastward to the Black Sea coast (Map 2.5). The settlements in southern Italy and Sicily, such as Naples and Syracuse, eventually became so large and powerful that this region was called Magna Graecia ("Great Greece"). Its communities became rivals of Carthage for commercial dominance in the western Mediterranean.

Fewer Greeks settled in the eastern Mediterranean, perhaps because the monarchies there restricted immigration. Still, a Greek trading station had sprung up in Syria by 800 B.C.E., and in the seventh century B.C.E. the Egyptians permitted Greek merchants to settle in a coastal town. These close contacts with eastern Mediterranean peoples paid cultural as well as economic dividends. In addition to inspiring Greeks to reintroduce figures into their painting, Near Eastern art gave them models for statues: they began sculpting images that stood stiffly and stared straight ahead, imitating Egyptian statuary. (See "Seeing History," page 55.) When the improving economy of the later Archaic Age allowed Greeks again to afford monumental architecture in stone, their rectangular temples on platforms with columns reflected Egyptian architectural designs.

Historians have traditionally called the Greeks' settlement process in this era colonization, but recent research questions this term's accuracy because the word *colonization* implies the process by which modern European governments officially installed dependent settlements and regimes abroad. The evidence for these Greek settlements suggests rather that private entrepreneurship created most of them. Official state involvement was minimal, at least in the beginning. Most commonly, a Greek city-state in the homeland would establish ties with a settlement originally set up by its citizens privately and then claim it as its colony only after the community had grown into an economic success. Few instances are clearly recorded in which a Greek city-state sent out a group to establish a formally organized colony abroad.

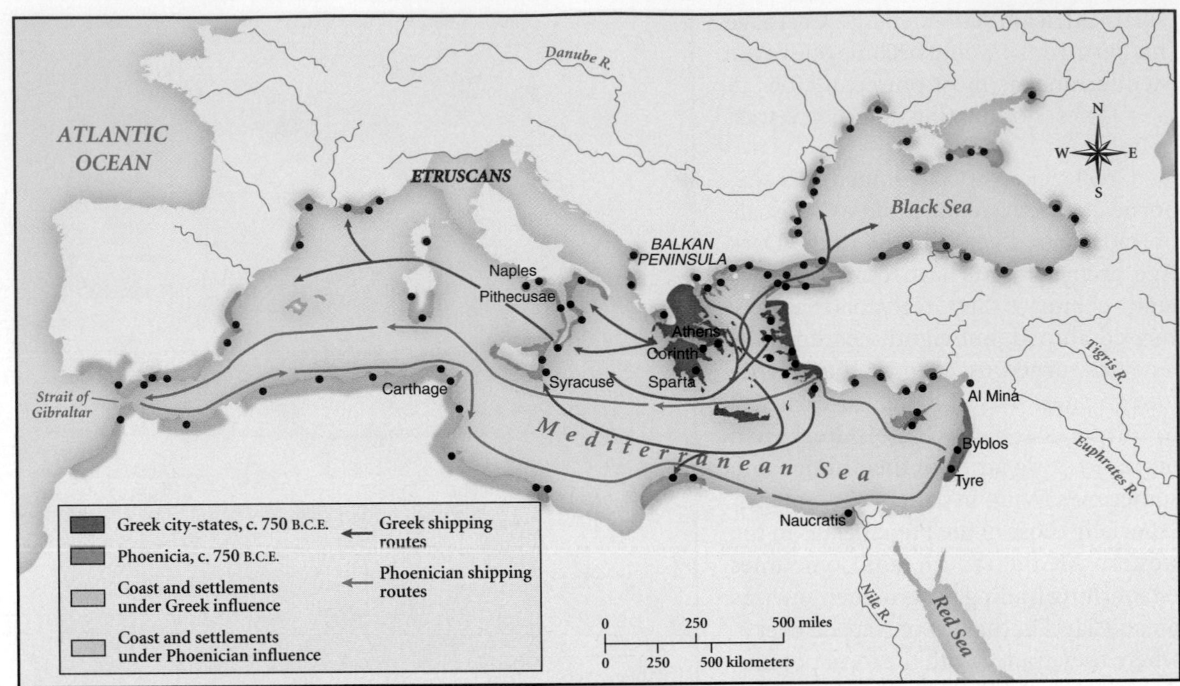

MAP 2.5 Phoenician and Greek Expansion, 750–500 B.C.E.
The Phoenicians were early explorers and settlers of the western Mediterranean. By 800 B.C.E. they had already founded the city of Carthage, which would become the main commercial power in the region. During the Archaic Age, groups of adventurous Greeks followed the Phoenicians' lead and settled all around the Mediterranean, hoping to improve their economic prospects by trade and farming. Sometimes they moved into previously established Phoenician settlements; sometimes they founded their own. Some Greek city-states established formal ties with new settlements or sent out their own expeditions to try to establish loyal colonies. | **Where did Phoenicians predominantly settle, and where did Greeks?**

Citizenship and Freedom in the Greek City-State

The creation of the polis filled the political vacuum left by Mycenaean civilization's fall. The Greek city-state was unique because it was based on the concept of citizenship for all its free inhabitants, rejected monarchy as its central authority, and made justice the responsibility of the citizens. Moreover, except in tyrannies (in which one man seized control of the city-state), at least some degree of shared governing was normal. This principle was manifest as early as the seventh century B.C.E., when the polis of Dreros on Crete inscribed on stone a law setting a term limit on its head judicial office, thereby ensuring that no single individual could dominate this crucial position.

Power sharing reached its widest form in democratic Greek city-states. Some historians argue that knowledge of the older cities on Cyprus and in Phoenicia influenced the Greeks in creating their new political systems. Since monarchs dominated their subjects in those eastern states, however, this theory cannot explain the origin of citizenship in all Greek city-states and the sharing of power in most. The most famous ancient analyst of Greek politics and society, the philosopher Aristotle (384–322 B.C.E.), insisted that the forces of nature had created the city-state: "Humans are beings who by nature live in a city-state." Anyone who existed outside such a community, Aristotle remarked, must be either a simple fool or superhuman. The polis's innovation in making shared power the basis of government did not immediately change the course of history—monarchy later became once again the most common form of government in ancient Western civilization—but it was important as proof that power sharing was a workable system of political organization.

Religion in the Greek City-State Like all earlier ancient communities, Greek city-states were officially religious communities. As well as worshipping many deities, each city-state honored a particular god or goddess as its special protector, such as Athena at Athens. Different communities could choose the same deity: Sparta, Athens's chief rival in later times, also chose Athena as its defender. Greeks envisioned the twelve most important gods banqueting atop Mount Olympus, the

SEEING HISTORY

The Shift in Sculptural Style from Egypt to Greece

As Greek civilization revived during the Archaic Age (750–500 B.C.E.), artists took inspiration from the older civilizations of Egypt and the Near East, with sculpture in particular emerging as an important mode of cultural expression. Greek sculptors carved freestanding *kouros* ("young male") statues whose poses recalled the Egyptian style that remained unchanged for two thousand years: an erect posture, a striding leg, and a calm facial expression staring straight ahead. And yet important differences, both religious and stylistic, exist between Egyptian statuary and the Greek sculpture influenced by it.

Kaemheset (shown on the left) held a high government position during the Old Kingdom as Egypt's chief architect and supervisor of sculptors. Croesus (on the right) was a warrior from Athens who died in battle; the inscription on the base of his statue proclaimed: "Stand and mourn at this monument of Croesus, now dead; raging Ares [the Greek war god] destroyed him as he battled in the front ranks." Both statues were painted in bright colors (traces of red survive on Croesus's statue); Kaemheset's lively decoration remains because it stood inside his closed tomb, while Croesus's stood outside. Croesus's statue differs from Kaemheset's in that it portrays him nude, even though warriors went into battle wearing armor. What do you think could have been the reasons for placing statues inside or outside tombs and for portraying their subjects clothed or nude?

Look more closely at the details of the figures—musculature, hair, hands, facial expression, stride. What stylistic similarities do you see? Art historians have argued that, despite the similarities, the *kouros* statues of Greece's Archaic period already show signs of the increasing naturalism and idealization of the human body that would characterize the later Greek classical style (see the illustration on page 93). What evidence do you see of that in the differences between the two sculptures?

Question to Consider

- **What cultural factors do you think could account for Egyptian statues keeping the same style over time, while the style of Greek statues changed?**

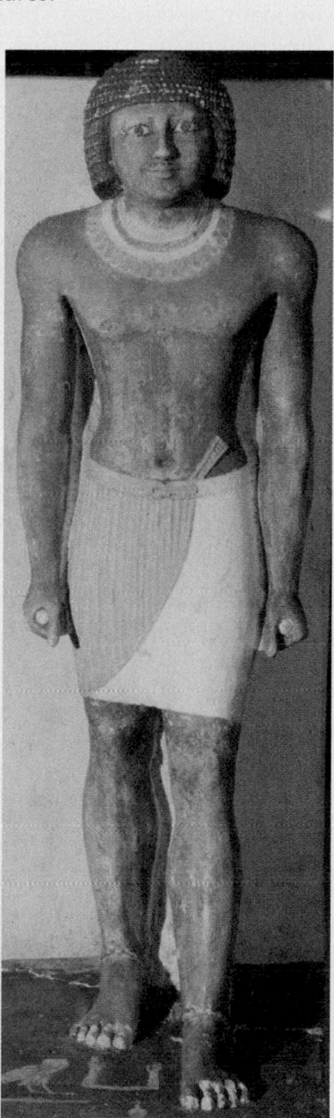

Limestone Statue of Kaemheset, Old Kingdom Egypt, c. 2400 B.C.E. *(Borromeo/Art Resource, NY.)*

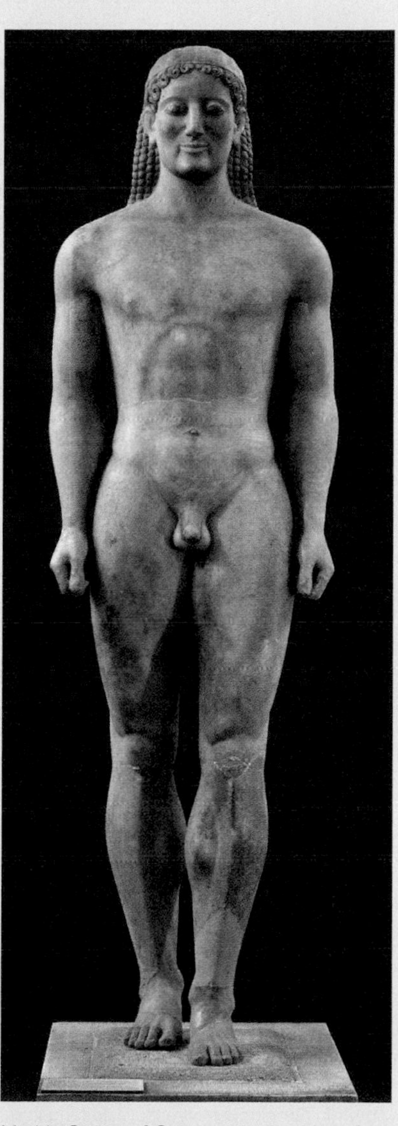

Marble Statue of Croesus, Archaic Age Greece, c. 530–520 B.C.E. *(The Art Archive/National Archeological Museum, Athens/Gianni Dagli Orti.)*

highest peak in mainland Greece. Zeus headed this pantheon; the others were Hera, his wife; Aphrodite, goddess of love; Apollo, sun god; Ares, war god; Artemis, moon goddess; Athena, goddess of wisdom and war; Demeter, earth goddess; Dionysus, god of pleasure, wine, and disorder; Hephaestus, fire god; Hermes, messenger god; and Poseidon, sea god. Like Homer's warriors, the Olympian gods were competitive, both with one another and with human beings, and they punished any disrespect. "I am well aware that the gods are competitively jealous and disruptive towards humans," remarked the sixth-century Athenian statesman Solon. The Greeks believed that their gods occasionally experienced temporary pain or sadness in their dealings with one another but were immune to permanent suffering because they were immortal.

Greek religion's core belief was that humans, both as individuals and as communities, must honor the gods to thank them for blessings received and to receive more blessings in return. Furthermore, the Greeks believed that the gods sent both good and bad into the world. The relationship between gods and humans generated sorrow as well as joy, punishment in the here and now, and only a limited hope for favored treatment in this life and in the underworld after death for the gods' favorites. Ordinary Greeks did not expect the gods to take them to a paradise at some future time when evil forces would be eliminated forever.

The idea of reciprocity between gods and humans underlay the Greek understanding of the nature of the gods. Deities did not love humans. Rather, they protected people who paid them honor and did not offend them. Gods could punish offenders by sending disasters such as floods, famines, earthquakes, epidemic diseases, and defeats in battle.

City-states honored gods by sacrificing animals such as cattle, sheep, goats, and pigs; decorating their sanctuaries with works of art; and celebrating festivals with songs, dances, prayers, and processions. A seventh-century B.C.E. bronze statuette, which a man named Mantiklos gave to a sanctuary of Apollo, makes clear why individuals offered such gifts. On its legs the donor inscribed his understanding of the transaction, using one of the god's titles: "Mantiklos gave this from his share to the Far Darter of the Silver Bow; now you, Apollo, do something for me in return."

People's greatest religious difficulty came in anticipating what might offend a deity. Mythology hinted at the gods' expectations of proper human behavior. For example, the Greeks told stories of the gods demanding hospitality for strangers or proper burial for family members. Other acts such as performing a sacrifice improperly, violating the sanctity of a temple area, or breaking an oath or sworn agreement also counted as disrespect for the gods. People believed that the deities were generally not concerned with most other crimes, which humans had to police themselves. Homicide, however, was such a serious offense that the gods were thought to punish it by casting a miasma (ritual contamination) on the murderer and on all those around him or her. Unless the members of the affected group purified themselves by punishing the murderer, they could all expect to suffer divine punishment, such as bad harvests or disease. In this way, the divine penalty for failing to punish the crime was extended to the entire community.

Oracles, dreams, divination, and the interpretations of prophets provided clues about what hu-

A Greek Woman at an Altar

This red-figure vase painting (contrast the black-figure vase on page 36) from the center of a large drinking cup shows a woman in rich clothing pouring a libation to the gods onto a flaming altar. In her other arm, she carries a religious object that has not been securely identified. This scene illustrates the most important and frequent role of women in Greek public life: participating in religious ceremonies, both at home and in community festivals. Greek women (and men) commonly wore sandals; why do you think they are usually depicted without shoes in vase paintings? *(Attributed to Makron [painter] and Hieron [potter], [Greek, from Athens], Kylix [Drinking Vessel], detail, Tondo:* Woman Sacrificing at an Altar, *ca. 490-480 B.C.E., wheel-thrown, slip-decorated earthenware, red-figure technique, h. 4 7/16 in. [11.3 cm.]; diam. at lip 11 5/16 in. [28.7 cm.]; diam. with handles 14¼ in. [36.2 cm.]. Toledo Museum of Art [Toledo, Ohio], Purchased with funds from the Libbey Endowment, Gift of Edward Drummond Libbey [1972.55].)*

DOCUMENT

Zaleucus's Law Code for a Greek City-State in Seventh-Century B.C.E. Italy

Zaleucus from the Greek city-state of Locri, in southern Italy, became the most famous early Greek lawmaker for his creation of a new law code for his community around 650 B.C.E. He founded his law code on belief in the gods as benefactors of human life. Some of his laws imposed harsh penalties for crimes, literally incorporating the eye-for-an-eye principle of equivalent punishment known from much earlier Mesopotamian law codes. Other laws took a different approach, as shown below. The Locrians respected Zaleucus's lawgiving so highly that three hundred years later they still required anyone who wished to change a law to make the proposal with a noose around his neck. If his proposal failed, he was strangled on the spot.

As you read, consider this: Do you think that fear of public shame or humiliation is a strong enough deterrent for certain crimes? If so, is it acceptable to use such a fear to change people's behavior?

Zaleucus's family came from Locri in Italy, and he was from the upper class. He was a student of the philosopher Pythagoras. Gaining a high reputation in his homeland, he was chosen as lawmaker. Creating a new law code from the foundation up, he began, first of all, with the gods of the heavens.

Immediately in the introduction to the entire code he said that the inhabitants of the city first of all must accept and believe that gods exist, and that, using their minds to inspect the heavens and their beautiful arrangement and order, they should judge that these things had been arranged not by chance or by human beings. Also, the inhabitants must worship the gods as being responsible for everything fine and good in life. They must keep their souls pure from every kind of wrongdoing, believing that the gods rejoice not at the sacrifices or expensive gifts of bad people, but at the just and fine ways of life of good men.

After urging the citizens in this introduction to pious worshipping and justice, he added the command that they should not regard a fellow citizen as an enemy with whom they could never be reconciled. Serious conflict should be conducted in such a way that they could come to a settlement and friendship. Anyone who behaves contrary to this should be considered by the citizens to be savage and wild in his soul. He instructed the officials not to be self-willed or arrogant, and not to give legal judgments based on hatred or friendship.

Among his various laws he came up with many on his own very wisely and extraordinarily. For, although everywhere else women who behaved badly were made to pay fines in money, Zaleucus corrected their out-of-control behavior with an ingenious penalty. He wrote the following: a freeborn woman may not be accompanied by more than one female slave, unless she is drunk; she may not leave the city during the night, unless she is committing adultery; she may not wear gold jewelry or clothing with a woven purple border, unless she is a hired "companion." A man may not wear a ring gleaming with gold or a cloak in the luxurious style of the city-state of Miletus unless he is partying with a "companion" or committing adultery.

In this way, with his (on the surface) shameful removal of penalties, he easily turned people away from harmful luxury and out-of-control habits. For no one wanted to be the object of ridicule among the citizens by seeming to approve of shameful out-of-control behavior.

He made other fine laws, such as those on contracts and other sources of disputes in life.

Source: Diodorus Siculus, *Library of History*, Book 12, chapter 20. Translation by Thomas R. Martin.

Question to Consider

■ **What presumptions about appropriate behavior for women and men are embedded in these laws? Why do you think this is so?**

mans might have done to anger the gods. The most important oracle was at Delphi, in central Greece, where a priestess in a trance provided Apollo's answers—in the form of riddles that had to be interpreted—to questions posed by city-states as well as individuals, who paid a fee for the information. Competition to consult the Delphic oracle concerning the will of the gods could be fierce because the priestess gave answers only on a limited number of days each year.

City-states and individuals alike paid respect to each god and goddess through a **cult**, a set of official, publicly funded religious activities for each deity overseen by priests and priestesses. To fulfill their religious obligations, people prayed, sang hymns of praise, offered sacrifices, and presented gifts at the deity's sanctuary. In these holy places a person could honor and thank the deities for blessings and beg them for relief when misfortune struck the community or the individual. People could also offer sacrifices at home with the household gathered around; sometimes the family's slaves were allowed to participate.

---

cult: In ancient Greece, a set of official, publicly funded religious activities for a deity overseen by priests and priestesses.

Priests and priestesses chosen from the citizen body performed the sacrifices of public cults; they did not use their positions to influence political or social matters. Their special knowledge consisted in knowing how to perform traditional religious rites. They were not guardians of correct religious thinking because Greek polytheism had no scripture or uniform set of beliefs and practices. It required its worshippers only to support the community's local rituals and to avoid religious pollution.

Citizenship for Rich and Poor In the Greek city-state, the concept of citizenship meant free people agreeing to form a political community that was a partnership of privileges and duties in common affairs under the rule of law (see Document, "Zaleucus's Law Code for a Greek City-State in Seventh-Century B.C.E. Italy," page 57). Citizenship was a remarkable political concept because, even in Greek city-states organized as tyrannies or oligarchies (rule by a small group), it meant a basic level of political equality among citizens. Most important, it carried the expectation (if not always the fulfillment) of equal treatment under the law for male citizens regardless of their social status or wealth. The degree of power sharing varied. In oligarchic city-states, where the social elite had a stranglehold on politics, small groups or even a single family could dominate the process of legislating. Women had the protection of the law, but they were barred from participation in politics on the grounds that female judgment was inferior to male. Regulations governing sexual behavior and control of property were stricter for women than for men.

In the most egalitarian version of the polis, all free adult male citizens shared in governing by attending and voting in a political assembly, where the laws and policies of the community were decided. In this direct democracy, all free men had the right to make proposals to be voted on in the assembly and to serve on juries. Even in democratic city-states, however, citizens did not enjoy perfect political equality. The right to hold office, for example, could be restricted to citizens possessing a certain amount of property. Equality prevailed most strongly in the justice system, in which all male citizens were treated the same, regardless of wealth or status.

Because monarchy and legal inequality had characterized the history of the ancient Near East and Greece in earlier times, making equality of male citizens the principle for the reorganization of Greek society and politics in the Archaic Age was a radical innovation. The polis—with its emphasis on equal protection of the laws for rich and poor alike—remained the preeminent form of political and social organization in Greece until the beginning of Roman control six centuries later.

How the poor originally gained the privileges of citizenship remains a mystery. The population increase in the late Dark Age and the Archaic Age was greatest among the poor. These families raised more children to help farm more land, which had been vacant after the depopulation brought on by the worst of the Dark Age. (See "Taking Measure," page 59.) There was no precedent in Western civilization for extending even limited political and legal equality to the poor, but the Greek city-states did so even as the number of poor people grew.

Historians have customarily believed that a hoplite revolution was the reason for expanded political rights, but recent research has undermined this interpretation. A **hoplite** was an infantryman who wore metal body armor and attacked with a thrusting spear. Hoplites made up the main strike force of the militia that defended each city-state; there were no permanent Greek armies at this period. Hoplites marched into combat arrayed in a rectangular formation called a phalanx. Staying in line and working together were the secrets to successful phalanx tactics. Greeks had fought in phalanxes for a long time, but only the elite could afford hoplite equipment. In the eighth century B.C.E.,

Grave Monument of a Greek Warrior
This inscribed flat pillar stood above the grave of a Greek warrior from Athens who died in the late sixth century B.C.E. An inscription preserves his name for future generations to remember: Aristion. The sculpture shows him with the muscular build that Greek hoplites (heavily armed infantry) worked to develop so that they could fight effectively while wearing metal armor. He holds the thrusting spear that was a hoplite's main battle weapon. *(AISA / Everett Collection.)*

hoplite: A heavily armed Greek infantryman. Hoplites constituted the main strike force of a city-state's militia.

TAKING MEASURE

Greek Family Size and Agricultural Labor in the Archaic Age

Using archaeological surveys and estimates of population size, modern demographers have calculated the changing relationship in the Archaic Age between the number of people in a farming family and the amount of land that the family could cultivate successfully. The graph shows how valuable healthy teenage children were to the family's prosperity. For example, when the family had two children old enough to work in the fields, it could farm over 50 percent more land, increasing its productivity significantly and thus making the family better off.

Source: Adapted from Thomas W. Gallant, *Risk and Survival in Ancient Greece: Reconstructing the Rural Domestic Economy* [1991], Fig. 4.10.

Question to Consider

■ Given the information in this chart, what do you think childhood and adolescence looked like in this era?

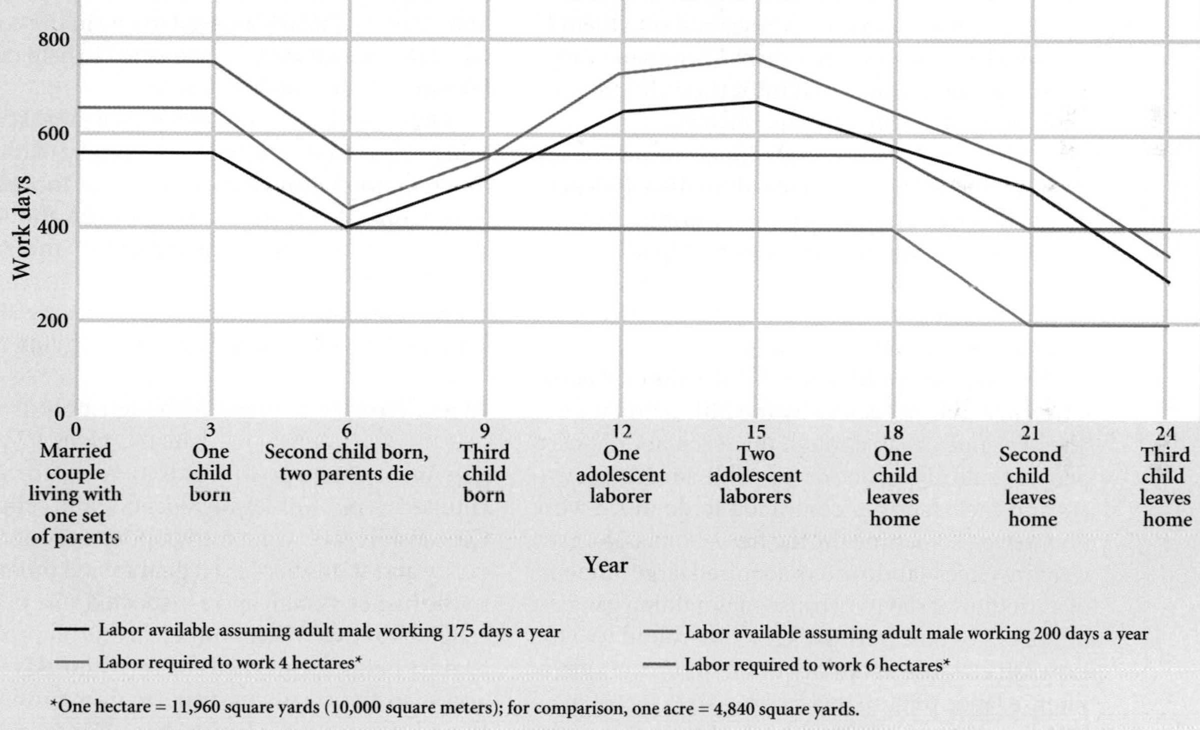

however, a growing number of men had become prosperous enough to buy metal weapons, especially because the use of iron had made such weapons more readily available.

According to the hoplite revolution theory, these new hoplites—feeling that they should enjoy political rights in exchange for buying their own equipment and training hard—forced the social elite to share political power by threatening to refuse to fight, which would cripple military defense. This interpretation correctly assumes that the hoplites had the power to demand and receive a voice in politics but ignores that hoplites were not poor. Furthermore, archaeology shows that not many men were wealthy enough to afford hoplite armor until the middle of the seventh century B.C.E., well after the earliest city-states had emerged. How then did poor men, too, win political rights?

The most likely explanation is that the poor earned respect by fighting to defend the community, just as hoplites did. Fighting as so-called light troops (that is, lightly armed), poor men could disrupt an enemy's heavy infantry by slinging barrages of rocks or shooting arrows. It is also possible that tyrants—sole rulers who seized power for their families in some city-states (see "Tyranny in the

City-State of Corinth," page 65)—boosted the status of poor men. Tyrants may have granted greater political rights to poor men as a means of gathering popular support. No matter how the poor became citizens who possessed a rough equality of political freedom and legal rights with the rich, this unprecedented change was Greek society's most remarkable innovation in the Archaic Age.

The Expansion of Greek Slavery The growth of freedom and equality for citizens in Greece produced a corresponding expansion of slavery, as free citizens protected their status by drawing harsh lines between themselves and slaves. Many slaves were war captives. Pirates or raiders also seized people from non-Greek regions to the north and east to sell into slavery in Greece. The fierce bands in these areas also captured members from one another and sold them to slave dealers. Rich families prized educated Greek-speaking slaves, who could tutor their children (no public schools existed in this period).

City-states as well as individuals owned slaves. Publicly owned slaves enjoyed limited independence, living on their own and performing specialized tasks. In Athens, for example, special slaves were trained to detect counterfeit coinage. Temple slaves belonged to the deity of the sanctuary, for whom they worked as servants.

Slaves made up about one-third of the total population in some city-states by the fifth century B.C.E. They became cheap enough that even middle-class people could afford one or two. Still, small landowners and their families continued to do much work themselves, sometimes hiring free laborers. Not even wealthy Greek landowners acquired large numbers of agricultural slaves because maintaining gangs of hundreds of enslaved workers year-round was too expensive. Most crops required short periods of intense labor punctuated by long stretches of inactivity, and owners did not want to feed slaves who had no work.

Slaves did all kinds of jobs. Household slaves, often women, cleaned, cooked, fetched water from public fountains, helped the wife with the weaving, watched the children, accompanied the husband as he did the marketing, and performed other domestic chores. Neither female nor male slaves could refuse if their masters demanded sexual favors. Owners often labored alongside their slaves in small manufacturing businesses and on farms, although rich landowners might appoint a slave supervisor to oversee work in the fields. Slaves toiling in the narrow, landslide-prone tunnels of Greece's silver and gold mines had the worst lot: many died doing this dangerous, dark, backbreaking work.

Since slaves existed as property, not people, owners could legally beat or even kill them. But injuring or executing slaves would have made no economic sense—the master would have been crippling or destroying his own property. Under the best conditions, household workers could live free of violent punishment. They sometimes were allowed to join their owners' families on excursions and attend religious rituals. However, without families of their own, without property, and without legal or political rights, slaves remained alienated from regular society. In the words of an ancient commentator, slaves lived lives of "work, punishment, and food." Sometimes owners freed their slaves, and some promised freedom at a future date to encourage their slaves to work hard. Those slaves who gained their freedom did not become citizens in Greek city-states but instead mixed into the population of noncitizens officially allowed to live in the community. Freed slaves were still expected to help out their former masters when called on.

Greek slaves rarely rebelled on a large scale, except in Sparta, because they were usually of too many different origins and nationalities and too scattered to organize. No Greeks called for the abolition of slavery. The expansion of slavery in the Archaic Age reduced more and more unfree persons to a state of absolute dependence. As Aristotle later described their condition, slaves were "living tools."

Greek Women's Lives Although only free men had the right to participate in city-state politics and to vote, free women counted as citizens legally, socially, and religiously. Citizenship gave women an important source of security and status because it guaranteed them access to the justice system and a respected role in official religious activity. Free women had legal protection against being kidnapped for sale into slavery and access to the courts in disputes over property, although they usually had to have a man speak for them. The traditional paternalism of Greek society required that all women have male guardians who acted as "fathers" to regulate their lives and safeguard their interests (as defined by men). Before a woman's marriage, her father served as her legal guardian; after marriage, her husband took over that duty.

The expansion of slavery made households bigger and added new responsibilities for women. While their husbands farmed, participated in politics, and met with their male friends, well-off wives managed the household: raising the children, supervising the preservation and preparation of food, keeping the family's financial accounts, weaving fabric for clothing, directing the work of the slaves, and tending them when they were ill. Poor women worked outside the home, laboring in the fields or selling produce and small goods such as ribbons and trinkets in the market that occupied the center of every settlement. Women's labor ensured the family's economic self-sufficiency and allowed male citizens the time to participate in public life.

Women's religious functions gave them prestige and freedom of movement. Women left the home to attend funerals, state festivals, and public rituals. They had access, for example, to the initiation rights of the popular cult of Demeter at Eleusis, near Athens. Women had control over cults reserved exclusively for them and also performed important duties in other official cults. In fifth-century B.C.E. Athens, for example, women officiated as priestesses for more than forty different deities, with benefits including salaries paid by the state.

Marriage Marriages were arranged, and everyone was expected to marry. A woman's guardian — her father or, if he was dead, her uncle or her brother — would often engage her to another man's son while she was still a child, perhaps as young as five. The engagement was a public event conducted in the presence of witnesses. The guardian on this occasion repeated the phrase that expressed the primary aim of the marriage: "I give you this woman for the plowing [procreation] of legitimate children." The wedding took place when the girl was in her early teens and the groom ten to fifteen years older. Hesiod advised a man to marry a virgin in the fifth year after her first menstruation, when the man was "not much younger than thirty and not much older."

A legal wedding consisted of the bride moving to her husband's dwelling; the procession to his house served as the ceremony. The bride's father bestowed on her a dowry (a certain amount of family property a daughter received at marriage); if she was wealthy, this could include land yielding an income as well as personal possessions that formed part of her new household's assets and could be inherited by her children. Her husband was legally obliged to preserve the dowry, use it to support his wife and their children, and return it in case of a divorce.

Except in certain cases in Sparta, monogamy was the rule in ancient Greece, as was a nuclear family (husband, wife, and children living together without other relatives in the same house). Citizen men, married or not, were free to have sexual relations with slaves, foreign concubines, female prostitutes, or willing pre-adult citizen males. Citizen women, single or married, had no such freedom. Sex between a wife and anyone other than her husband carried harsh penalties for both parties.

Greek citizen men placed Greek citizen women under their guardianship both to regulate marriage and procreation and to maintain family property. According to Greek mythology, women were a necessary evil. Zeus supposedly ordered the creation of the first woman, Pandora, as a punishment for men in retaliation against Prometheus, who had stolen fire from Zeus and given it to humans. To see what

A Bride's Preparation

This special piece of pottery was designed to fit over a woman's thigh to protect it while she sat down to spin wool. As a woman's tool, it appropriately carried a picture from a woman's life: a bride being helped to prepare for her wedding by her family, friends, and servants. The inscriptions indicate that this fifth-century B.C.E. piece shows the mythological bride Alcestis, famous for sacrificing herself to save her husband and then being rescued from Death by the hero Herakles. *(Deutsches Archeologisches Institut-Athens, Neg. Nr. DAI-ATHEN-NM 5126. Photo: E. M. Czako.)*

was in a container that had come as a gift from the gods, Pandora lifted its lid and accidentally released into a previously trouble-free world the evils that had been locked inside. When she finally slammed the lid back down, only hope still remained in the container. Hesiod described women as "big trouble" but thought any man who refused to marry to escape the "troublesome deeds of women" would come to "destructive old age" alone, with no heirs. In other words, a man needed a wife so that he could father children who would later care for him and preserve the family property after his death. This paternalistic attitude allowed Greek men to control human reproduction and consequently the distribution of property.

REVIEW QUESTION How did the physical, social, and intellectual conditions of life in the Archaic Age promote the emergence of the Greek city-state?

New Directions for the Greek City-State, 750–500 B.C.E.

Greek city-states developed three forms of social and political organization based on citizenship: oligarchy, tyranny, and democracy. Sparta provided Greece's most famous example of an oligarchy, in which a small number of men dominated policymaking in an assembly of male citizens. For a time Corinth had the best-known tyranny, in which one man seized control of the city-state, ruling it for the advantage of his family and loyal supporters, while acknowledging the citizenship of all (thereby distinguishing a tyrant from a king, who ruled over subjects). Athens developed Greece's best-known democracy by allowing all male citizens to participate in governing. Although assemblies of men had influenced some ancient Near Eastern kings (see "Contrasting Views," page 63), Greek democracies gave their male citizens an unprecedented degree of equality and political power.

The Archaic Age polis is justly famous as the incubator for democratic politics; it also provided the environment in which Greeks created new forms of artistic expression and new ways of thought. In this period they developed innovative ways of using reason to understand the physical world, their relations to it, and their relationships with one another. This intellectual innovation laid the foundation for the gradual emergence of scientific thought and logic in Western civilization.

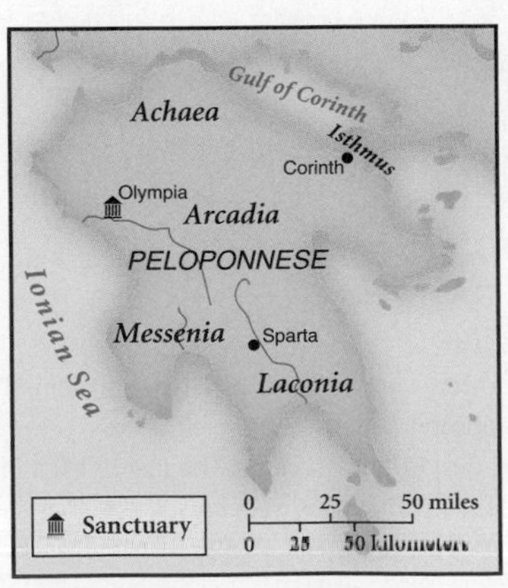

Sparta and Corinth, 750–500 B.C.E.

Oligarchy in the City-State of Sparta, 700–500 B.C.E.

Uniquely among the Greek city-states, Sparta organized its society with laws directed at a single purpose: military readiness. This oligarchic city-state developed the mightiest infantry force in Greece during the Archaic Age. Its citizens were famous for their militaristic self-discipline. Sparta's urban center nestled in an easily defended valley on the Peloponnesian peninsula twenty-five miles from the Mediterranean coast. This separation from the sea kept the Spartans from becoming skilled sailors; their strength lay on land.

The Spartan oligarchy included three components of rule. First came the two hereditary, prestigious military leaders called kings, who served as the state's religious heads and the generals of its army. Despite their title, they were not monarchs but just one part of the ruling oligarchy. The second part was a council of twenty-eight men over sixty years old (the elders), and the third part consisted of five annually elected officials called *ephors* ("overseers"), who made policy and enforced the laws.

In principle, legislation had to be approved by an assembly of all Sparta's free adult males, who were called the Alike to stress their common status and purpose. The assembly had only limited power to amend the proposals put before it, however, and the council would withdraw a proposal when the assembly's reaction proved negative. "If the people speak crookedly," according to Spartan tradition, "the elders and the leaders of the people shall be withdrawers." The council would then resubmit the proposal after gaining support for its passage.

Spartan society demanded strict obedience to all laws. When the ephors took office, for example, they issued an official proclamation to Sparta's males: "Shave your mustache and obey the laws." The laws' importance was emphasized by the official story that the god Apollo had given them to Sparta. Unlike other Greeks, the Spartans never wrote down their laws. Instead, they preserved their system with a unique, highly structured way of life. All Spartan citizens were expected to put service to

CONTRASTING VIEWS

Persians Debate Democracy, Oligarchy, and Monarchy

According to the Greek historian Herodotus, after a group of seven eminent Persians overthrew a false king in 522 B.C.E., they debated what would be the best type of government to establish in Persia. Otanes argued for democracy (or, as he calls it, "putting things in the middle"), Megabyzus for oligarchy, and Darius for monarchy. Four of the seven voted in favor of monarchy, and Darius became the new, legitimate king. Herodotus also says that some Greeks refused to believe that the debate ever took place, perhaps because there was no evidence that any system other than monarchy had ever been possible in Persia. In any case, these speeches present the earliest recorded contrasting views on systems of government, with special attention to the characteristics of monarchy.

Otanes recommended to the Persians to put things in the middle by saying this: "It doesn't seem right to me that one of us should be the monarch. There is nothing sweet or good about it. You know to what lengths violent arrogance [hubris] carried our former king Camybses, and you experienced that violent arrogance under the recent false king. How could monarchy be a suitable thing, when it allows the ruler to do whatever he wishes without any official accountability? Even the best of men would change his usual ideas if he had such a position of rule. Violent arrogance comes to him from the good things that he possesses, and jealousy has been part of human nature from the start. In having these two characteristics he has total bad character. Sated with his violent arrogance and jealousy, he does many outrageous things. A ruler with tyrannical power ought to be free of envy, for he possesses every good thing. But the opposite is true of his relations with the citizens. He is jealous if the best ones stay alive, delighted if the worst ones do; he's the best at listening to accusations. He is most difficult of men to deal with: if you only praise him in moderation, he gets angry because he is not being energetically flattered, but if someone flatters him energetically, he gets angry because the person is a flatterer. And now I am going to say the worst things of all: he overturns traditional customs, he rapes women, and he kills people without a trial. When the people are the ruler, the government has the best name: equality before the law. It does nothing of the things that a monarch does. It fills offices by lottery, its rule is subject to official accountability, and it has the community make all decisions. My judgment is that we should get rid of the monarchy and increase the power of the masses. For in the many is everything."

Otanes offered this judgment, but Megabyzus said they should entrust the government to an oligarchy, saying this: "What Otanes said about not having tyranny, I agree with, but as for giving power to the masses, he has missed the best judgment. There is nothing less intelligent or more violently arrogant than a useless crowd. It is certainly intolerable for men to flee the violent arrogance of the tyrant, only to fall victim to the violent arrogance of the people, who have no restraints upon them. If a tyrant does something, he does it from knowledge, but there is no knowledge in the people. How could someone have knowledge when he hasn't been taught anything fine and doesn't know it innately? He rushes into things without thought, like a river in its winter flood. Let those who intend evil to the Persians push for democracy, but let us choose a group of the best men and endow them with power. For we will be part of this group, and it is likely that the best plans will come from the best men."

Megabyzus offered this judgment, and Darius was the third to reveal his judgment, saying: "Megabyzus seems to me to speak correctly in what he says about the masses, but not correctly about oligarchy. For if we consider for argument's sake that all three systems are the best they can be—the best democracy, the best oligarchy, the best monarchy—then monarchy is far superior. For clearly nothing is better than the one best man. Relying on judgment that is the best he would direct the masses faultlessly, and he would be especially good at making plans against hostile men without them being divulged. In an oligarchy, where many men want to use their excellence for common interests, intense private hatreds tend to arise. For each one wants to be the head man and to win with his judgments, and they create great hatreds among themselves. From this come violent factions, and from factions comes murder, and from murder the system turns to monarchy. And in this one sees by how much monarchy is the best. Again, when the people rule, it is impossible that there not be evildoing. Moreover, when there is evildoing for the common interests, hatred doesn't arise among the evildoers; instead, strong friendships arise. For the evildoers act together to corrupt the common interests. This sort of thing happens until one man becomes the head of the people and stops these evildoers. With these actions he amazes the people, and being the object of amazement he clearly becomes a monarch. So, in this way, too, it is clear that monarchy is the strongest. To say it all together in one word: from where did our [i.e., Persian] freedom come, and who gave it to us? From the people, or an oligarchy, or a monarch? It is my judgment that, having obtained our freedom through one man, we should maintain our freedom in the same way, and we should also not do away with our sound traditional customs; for this is not better."

Source: Herodotus, *The Histories*, Book 3, chapters 80–82. Translation by Thomas R. Martin.

Question to Consider

- **Which arguments do you think are the most persuasive, and why?**

their city-state before personal concerns because their state's survival was continually threatened by its own economic foundation: the great mass of Greek slaves, called helots, who did almost all the work for citizens.

The Helots A **helot** was a slave owned by the Spartan city-state. They were Greeks captured in neighboring parts of Greece that the Spartans defeated in war. Most helots lived in Messenia, to the west, which Sparta had conquered by around 700 B.C.E. The helots outnumbered Sparta's free citizens. Harshly treated by their Spartan masters, helots constantly looked for chances to revolt.

Helots had some family life because they were expected to produce children to maintain their population, and they could own some personal possessions and practice their religion. They labored as farmers and household slaves so that Spartan citizens would not have to do such nonmilitary work. Spartan men wore their hair very long to show they were warriors rather than laborers, for whom long hair was inconvenient.

Helots lived under the constant threat of officially approved violence by Spartan citizens. Every year the ephors formally declared war between Sparta and the helots, allowing any Spartan to kill a helot without legal penalty or fear of offending the gods by committing murder. By beating the helots frequently, forcing them to get drunk in public as an object lesson to young Spartans, and humiliating them by making them wear dog-skin caps, the Spartans emphasized their slaves' "otherness." In this way Spartans created a justification for their harsh abuse of fellow Greeks. Contrasting the freedom of Spartan citizens from ordinary work with the ceaseless labor of the helots, a later Athenian observed, "Sparta is the home of the freest of the Greeks, and of the most enslaved."

Spartan Communal Life With helots to work the fields, male citizens could devote themselves full-time to preparation for war, training to protect their state both from hostile neighbors and its own slaves. Boys lived at home until their seventh year, when they were sent to live in barracks with other males until they were thirty. They spent most of their time exercising, hunting, practicing with weapons, and learning Spartan values by listening to tales of bravery and heroism at shared meals, where adult males in groups of about fifteen usually ate instead of at home. Discipline was strict, and the boys were purposely underfed so that they would learn stealth tactics by stealing food. If they were caught, punishment and disgrace followed immediately. One famous Spartan tale shows how seriously boys were supposed to fear such failure: having stolen a fox and hidden it under his clothing, a Spartan youth died because he let the panicked animal rip out his insides rather than letting himself be detected in the theft. A Spartan male who could not survive the tough training was publicly disgraced and denied the status of being an Alike.

Spending so much time in shared quarters schooled Sparta's young men in their society's values. The community took the place of a Spartan boy's family when he was growing up and remained his main social environment even after he reached adulthood. There he learned to call all older men Father to emphasize that his primary loyalty was to the group instead of his biological family. This way of life trained him for the one honorable occupation for Spartan men: obedient soldier. A seventh-century B.C.E. poet expressed the Spartan male ideal: "Know that it is good for the city-state and the whole people when a man takes his place in the front row of warriors and stands his ground without flinching."

An adolescent boy's life often involved what in today's terminology would be called a homosexual relationship, although the ancient concepts of heterosexuality and homosexuality did not match modern notions. An older male would choose a teenager as a special favorite, in many cases engaging him in sexual relations. Their bond of affection was meant to make each ready to die for the other, at whose side he would march into battle. Numerous Greek city-states included this form of homosexuality among their customs, although some made it illegal. The physical relationship could be controversial; the Athenian author Xenophon (c. 430–355 B.C.E.) wrote a work on the Spartan way of life denying that sex with boys existed there because he thought it a stain on the Spartans' reputation for virtue. However, other sources testify that such relationships did exist in Sparta and elsewhere. (The first modern histories of Greece suppressed discussion of this topic because their writers saw it as a form of child abuse.)

In such relationships the elder partner (the "lover") was supposed to help educate the young man (the "beloved") in politics and community values, and not just exploit him for physical pleasure. The relationship would not be lasting or exclusive: beloveds would grow up to get married, as lovers were, and would eventually become the older mem-

---

helot: A slave owned by the Spartan city-state; such slaves came from parts of Greece conquered by the Spartans.

ber of a new pair. Sex between adult males was considered disgraceful, as was sex between females of all ages (at least according to men).

Spartan women were known throughout the Greek world for their personal freedom. Since their husbands were so rarely at home, women controlled the households, which included servants, daughters, and sons who had not yet left for their communal training. Consequently, Spartan women exercised even more power at home than did women elsewhere in Greece. They could own property, including land. Wives were expected to stay physically fit so that they could bear healthy children to keep up the population. They were also expected to drum Spartan values into their children. One mother became legendary for handing her son his shield on the eve of battle and sternly telling him, "Come back with it or [lying dead] on it."

Demography determined Sparta's long-term fate. The population of Sparta was never large. Adult males—who made up the army—numbered between eight and ten thousand in the Archaic period. Over time, the problem of producing enough children to keep the Spartan army from shrinking became desperate, probably because losses in war far outnumbered births. Men became legally required to marry, with bachelors punished by fines and public ridicule. A woman could legitimately have children by a man other than her husband, if all three agreed.

Because the Spartans' survival depended on the exploitation of enslaved Greeks, they believed changes in their way of life must be avoided because any change might make them vulnerable to internal revolts. Some Greeks criticized the Spartan way of life as repressive and monotonous, but the Spartans' discipline and respect for their laws gained them widespread admiration.

Tyranny in the City-State of Corinth, 657–585 B.C.E.

In some city-states, competition among the social elite for political leadership became so bitter that a single family would suppress all its rivals and establish itself in rule for a time. The family's leader thus became a tyrant, a dictator who gained political dominance by force and was backed by his relatives and other supporters. Tyrants usually rallied support by promising privileges to poor citizens in city-states where they lacked full citizenship or felt disfranchised in political life. Successful tyrants kept their elite rivals out of power by cultivating the goodwill of the masses with economic policies favoring their interests, such as public employment schemes. Since few tyrants successfully passed their popularity on to their heirs, tyrannies tended to be short-lived.

Tyrants usually preserved their city-states' existing laws and political institutions. If a city-state had an assembly, for example, the tyrant would allow it to continue to meet, expecting it to follow his direction. Although today the word *tyrant* indicates a brutal or unwanted leader, tyrants in Archaic Greece did not always fit that description. Ordinary Greeks evaluated tyrants according to their behavior, opposing the ruthless and violent ones but welcoming the fair and generous ones.

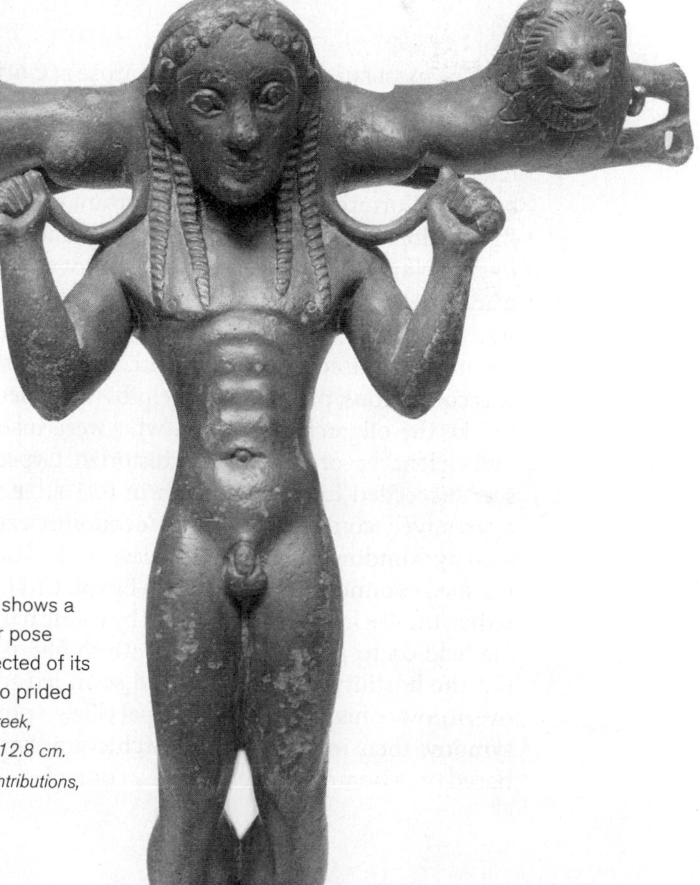

Bronze Sculpture of a Spartan Youth

This sculpted handle of a bronze water jar from sixth-century B.C.E. Sparta shows a young male holding two lions by the tail on his shoulders. That spectacular pose portrayed the fearlessness and control over fierce nature that Sparta expected of its citizens. His hair is long in the self-conscious style of Spartan warriors, who prided themselves on not having the short hair that was common for laborers. *(Greek, Archaic, about 540 B.C.E. Place of manufacture: Greece, Laconia, Sparta. Bronze. H: 12.8 cm. [5 1/16 in.]. Museum of Fine Arts, Boston; Museum purchase with funds donated by contributions, 85.515. Photograph © 2011 Museum of Fine Arts, Boston.)*

The Temple of Apollo at Corinth
Built at Corinth in southern Greece to honor the god Apollo in the sixth century B.C.E., this temple exemplifies what is called the Doric architectural style. This called for fluted columns resting directly on the foundation and topped by flattened disks. Just as the worship of Apollo was meant to ensure divine protection for Corinth, the towering stone hill in the background served as its emergency fortress on an acropolis (central highpoint of a Greek city-state). *(The Art Archive/Gianni Dagli Orti.)*

The most famous early tyranny arose at Corinth in 657 B.C.E., when the family of Cypselus rebelled against the city's harsh oligarchic leadership. This takeover attracted wide attention in the Greek world because Corinth was such an important city-state. Its location on the isthmus controlling land access to the Peloponnese and a huge amount of seaborne trade made it the most prosperous city-state of the Archaic Age (see Map 2.4). Cypselus "became one of the most admired of Corinth's citizens because he was courageous, prudent, and helpful to the people, unlike the oligarchs in power, who were insolent and violent," according to a later historian. Cypselus's son succeeded him at his death in 625 B.C.E. and aggressively continued Corinth's economic expansion by founding colonies to increase trade. He also pursued commercial contacts with Egypt. Unlike his father, the son lost popular support by ruling harshly. He held on to power until his death in 585 B.C.E., but the hostility he had provoked soon led to the overthrow of his own heir. The social elite, to prevent tyranny, then installed an oligarchic government based on a board of officials and a council.

Democracy in the City-State of Athens, 632–500 B.C.E.

Only democracy, which the Greeks invented, instituted genuine political power sharing in the polis. Athens, located at the southeastern corner of central Greece, became the most famous of the democratic city-states because its government gave political rights to the greatest number of people; financed magnificent temples and public buildings; and, in the fifth century B.C.E., became militarily strong enough to force numerous other city-states to follow Athenian leadership in a maritime empire. Athenian democracy did not reach its full development until the mid-fifth century B.C.E., but its first steps in the Archaic Age allowed all male citizens to participate meaningfully in making laws and administering justice. Democracy has remained so important in Western civilization that understanding why and how Athenian democracy worked remains a vital responsibility for historians.

Athens's early development of a large middle class was a crucial factor in opening this new path for Western civilization. The Athenian population apparently expanded at a phenomenal rate when economic conditions improved rapidly from about 800 to 700 B.C.E. The ready availability of good farmland in Athenian territory and opportunities for seaborne trade along the long coastline allowed many families to achieve modest prosperity. These hard-working entrepreneurs evidently felt that their self-won economic success entitled them to a say in government. The democratic unity forged by the Athenian masses was evident as early as 632 B.C.E., when the people rallied "from the fields in a body," according to Herodotus, to block the attempt by an elite Athenian to install a tyranny.

By the seventh century B.C.E., all freeborn adult male citizens of Athens had the right to vote on public matters in the assembly, whose meetings regularly attracted several thousand participants. They also elected high officials called archons, who ran the judicial system by rendering verdicts in disputes and criminal accusations. Members of the elite dominated these offices; because archons received no pay, poor men could not afford to serve.

An extended economic crisis beginning in the late seventh century B.C.E. almost destroyed Athens's infant democracy. The first attempt to solve the crisis was the emergency appointment around 621 B.C.E. of a man named Draco to revise the laws. Athens's leaders hoped that reforming and clarifying the laws would bring social harmony through justice. Unfortunately, Draco's changes, which made death the penalty for even minor crimes, proved too harsh to work. Later Greeks said Draco (whose harshness inspired the word *draconian*) had written his laws in blood, not ink. By 600 B.C.E., economic conditions had become so terrible that poor farmers had to borrow constantly from richer neighbors and deeply mortgage their land. As the crisis grew worse, impoverished citizens were sold into slavery to pay off debts. Civil war seemed next.

Solon's Democratic Reforms

Desperate, Athenians appointed another emergency official in 594 B.C.E., a war hero named **Solon**. To head off violence, Solon gave both rich and poor something of what they wanted, a compromise called the "shaking off of obligations." He canceled private debts, which helped the poor but displeased the rich; he decided not to redistribute land, which pleased the wealthy but disappointed the poor. He banned selling citizens into slavery to settle debts and liberated citizens who had become slaves in this way. His elimination of debt slavery was a significant recognition of what today would be called citizen rights. Solon celebrated his success in poetry: "To Athens, their home established by the gods, I brought back many who had been sold into slavery, some justly, some not."

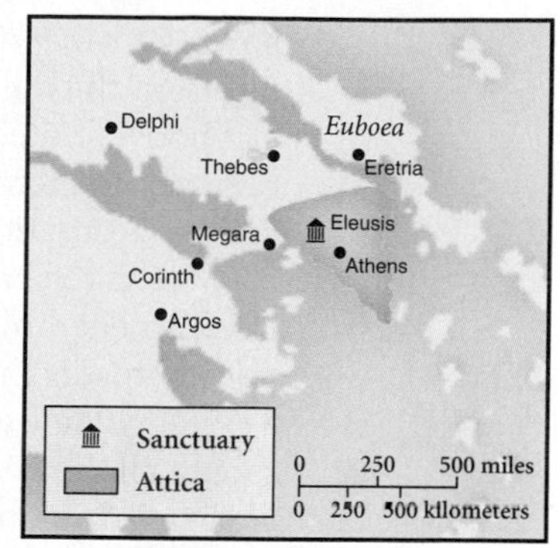

Athens and Central Greece, 750–500 B.C.E.

Solon was able to balance political power between rich and poor by reordering Athens's traditional ranking of citizens into four groups. Most important, he made the top-ranking division depend solely on wealth, not birth. This change eliminated inherited aristocracy at Athens. The groupings did not affect a man's treatment at law, only his eligibility for government office. The higher a man's ranking, the higher the post to which he could be elected, but higher also was the contribution he was expected to make to the community with his service and his money. Men at the poorest level, called laborers, were not eligible for any office. Solon did, however, confirm the laborers' right to vote in the legislative assembly. His classification scheme was consistent with democratic principles because it allowed for upward social mobility: a man who increased his wealth could move up the scale of eligibility for office.

Because the process of making decisions by persuasion can be glacially slow in large groups, the creation of a smaller council to prepare the agenda for the assembly was a crucial development in making Athenian democracy efficient. Solon may have been the one who created the council of four hundred men that decided what the assembly needed to discuss (though some evidence suggests it was instituted after his rule). The council members were chosen annually from the adult male citizenry by lottery—the most democratic method possible—which prevented the social elite from capturing too many seats.

Even more than his changes to the government, Solon's two reforms in the judicial system promoted democratic principles of equality. First, he directed that any male citizen could start a prosecution on behalf of any crime victim. Second, he gave people the right to appeal an archon's judgment to the assembly. With these two measures, Solon empowered ordinary citizens in the administration of justice. Characteristically, he balanced these democratic reforms by granting broader

Solon: Athenian political reformer whose changes promoted early democracy.

powers to the Areopagus Council ("council that meets on the hill of the god of war Ares"). This select body, limited to ex-archons, held great power because its members judged the most important cases — accusations against archons themselves.

Solon's reforms broke the traditional pattern of government limited to the elite. They extended power broadly through the citizen body and created a system of law that applied more equally than before to all the community's free men. A critic once challenged Solon, "Do you actually believe your fellow citizens' injustice and greed can be kept in check this way? Written laws are more like spiders' webs than anything else: they tie up the weak and the small fry who get stuck in them, but the rich and the powerful tear them to shreds." Solon replied that communal values ensure the rule of law: "People abide by their agreements when neither side has anything to gain by breaking them. I am writing laws for the Athenians in such a way that they will clearly see it is to everyone's advantage to obey the laws rather than to break them."

Some elite Athenians wanted oligarchy and therefore bitterly disagreed with Solon. The unrest they caused opened the door to tyranny at Athens. Peisistratus, helped by his upper-class friends and the poor whose interests he championed, made himself tyrant in 546 B.C.E. Like the Corinthian tyrants, he promoted the economic, cultural, and architectural development of Athens and bought the masses' support. He helped poorer men, for example, by hiring them to build roads, a huge temple to Zeus, and fountains to increase the supply of drinking water. He boosted Athens's economy and its image by minting new coins stamped with Athena's owl (a symbol of the goddess of wisdom; see the illustration on page 112) and organizing a great annual festival honoring the god Dionysus that attracted people from near and far to see its musical and dramatic performances.

Peisistratus's family could not maintain public goodwill after his death. Hippias, his eldest son, ruled harshly and was denounced as unjust by a rival elite family. These rivals convinced the Spartans, the self-proclaimed champions of Greek freedom, to "liberate" Athens from tyranny by expelling Hippias and his family in 510 B.C.E.

Cleisthenes, "Father of Athenian Democracy" Peisistratus's support of ordinary people evidently had the unintended consequence of making them think that they deserved political equality. Tyranny at Athens thus opened the way to the most important step in developing Athenian democracy, the reforms of Cleisthenes. A member of the social elite, Cleisthenes found himself losing against rivals for election to office in 508 B.C.E. He turned his electoral campaign around by offering more political participation to the masses; he called his program "equality through law." Ordinary people so strongly favored his plan that they spontaneously rallied to repel a Spartan army that Cleisthenes' bitterest rival had convinced Sparta's leaders to send to block his reforms.

By about 500 B.C.E., Cleisthenes had engineered direct participation in Athens's democracy by as many adult male citizens as possible. First he created constituent units for the city-state's new political organization by grouping country villages and urban neighborhoods into units called **demes**. The demes chose council members annually by lottery in proportion to the size of their populations. To allow for greater participation, Solon's Council of Four Hundred was expanded to five hundred members. Finally, Cleisthenes required candidates for public office to be spread widely throughout the demes.

Cleisthenes helped his reforms succeed by grounding them in existing social conditions favorable to democracy. The creation of demes, for example, suggests that democratic notions stemmed from traditions of small-community life, in which each man was entitled to his say in running local affairs and had to persuade — not force — others to agree. Athenians remembered Cleisthenes as the father of their democracy. It took another fifty years of political struggle, however, before Athenian democracy reached its full development with the democratization of its judicial system.

New Ways of Thought and Expression in Greece, 630–500 B.C.E.

The idea that persuasion, rather than force or status, should drive political decisions matched the spirit of intellectual change rippling through Greece in the late Archaic Age. In city-states all over the Greek world, artists, poets, and philosophers pursued new ways of thought and new forms of expression. Through their contacts with the Near East, the Greeks encountered traditions to learn from and, in some cases, to alter for their own purposes.

---

demes (DEEMZ): The villages and city neighborhoods that formed the constituent political units of Athenian democracy in the late Archaic Age.

Vase Painting of a Music Lesson

This sixth-century B.C.E. red-figure vase shows a young man (seated on the left, without a beard) holding a lyre and watching an older, bearded man play the same instrument, while an adolescent boy and an older man listen. They all wear wreaths to show they are in a festive mood. The youth is evidently a pupil learning to play. Instruction in performing music and singing lyric poetry was considered an essential part of an upper-class Greek male's education. The teacher's lyre has a sounding board made from a turtle shell, as was customary for this instrument. *(Foto Marburg/Art Resource, NY.)*

Archaic Art and Literature

Early in the Archaic period Greek artists took inspiration from the Near East, but by the sixth century B.C.E. they had introduced innovations of their own. In ceramics, painters experimented with different clays and colors to depict vivid scenes from mythology and daily life. They became expert at rendering three-dimensional figures in an increasingly realistic style. Sculptors gave their statues balanced poses and calm, smiling faces.

Building on the Near Eastern tradition of poetry expressing personal emotions, Greeks created a new poetic form. This poetry, which sprang from popular song, was performed to the accompaniment of a lyre (a kind of harp) and thus called lyric poetry. Greek lyric poems were short, rhythmic, and diverse in subject. Lyric poets wrote songs both for choruses and for individual performers. Choral poems honored gods on public occasions, celebrated famous events in a city-state's history, praised victors in athletic contests, and enlivened weddings.

Solo lyric poems generated controversy because they valued individual expression and opinion over conventional views. Solon wrote poems justifying his reforms. Other poets criticized traditional values, such as strength in war. **Sappho**, a lyric poet from Lesbos born about 630 B.C.E. and famous for her poems on love, wrote, "Some would say the most beautiful thing on our dark earth is an army of cavalry, others of infantry, others of ships, but I say it's whatever a person loves." In this poem Sappho was expressing her longing for a woman she loved, who was now far away. Archilochus of Paros, who probably lived in the early seventh century B.C.E., became famous for poems mocking militarism, lamenting friends lost at sea, and regretting love affairs gone wrong. He became infamous for his lines about throwing away his shield in battle so that he could run away to save his life: "Oh, the hell with it; I can get another one just as good." When he taunted a family in verse after the father had ended Archilochus's affair with one of his daughters, the power of his ridicule reportedly caused the father and his two daughters to commit suicide.

Aegean Sea
Lesbos
GREECE
Chios
IONIA
Athens
Colophon
Samos
Miletus
Paros
0 50 100 miles
0 50 100 kilometers
Rhodes

Ionia and the Aegean, 750–500 B.C.E.

Greek Philosophy and Science

The study of philosophy ("love of wisdom") began in the seventh and sixth centuries B.C.E. when Greek thinkers created prose writing to express their innovative ideas, in particular their radically new explanations of the human world and its relation to the gods. Most of these philosophers lived in Ionia, on Anatolia's western coast, where they came in contact with Near Eastern knowledge in astronomy, mathematics, and myth. Because there were no formal schools in the Archaic Age, philosophers communicated their ideas by teaching privately and giving public lectures. Some also

---

Sappho (SAF oh): The most famous woman lyric poet of ancient Greece, a native of Lesbos.

composed poetry to explain their theories. People who studied with these philosophers or heard their presentations helped spread the new ideas.

Working from Babylonian discoveries about the regular movements of the stars and planets, Ionian philosophers such as Thales (c. 625–545 B.C.E.) and Anaximander (c. 610–540 B.C.E.), both of Miletus, reached the revolutionary conclusion that unchanging laws of nature (rather than gods' whims) governed the universe. Pythagoras, who emigrated from the island of Samos to the Greek city-state Croton in southern Italy about 530 B.C.E., taught that numerical relationships explained the world. He began the Greek study of high-level mathematics and the numerical aspects of musical harmony.

Ionian philosophers insisted that natural phenomena were neither random nor arbitrary. They applied the word *cosmos*—meaning "an orderly arrangement that is beautiful"—to the universe. The cosmos included not only the motions of heavenly bodies but also the weather, the growth of plants and animals, and human health. Because the universe was ordered, it was knowable; because it was knowable, thought and research could explain it. Philosophers therefore looked for the first or universal cause of all things, a quest that scientists still pursue. These first philosophers believed they needed to give reasons for their conclusions and to persuade others by arguments based on evidence. That is, they believed in logic. This new way of thought, called **rationalism**, became the foundation for the study of science and philosophy. This rule-based view of the causes of events and physical phenomena contrasted sharply with the traditional mythological view. Naturally, many people had difficulty accepting such a startling change in their understanding of the world, and the older tradition of explaining events as the work of deities lived on alongside the new approach.

These early Greek philosophers deeply influenced later times by being the first to clearly separate scientific thinking from myth and religion. Their idea that people must give reasons to justify their beliefs, rather than simply make assertions that others must accept without evidence, was their most

rationalism: The philosophic idea that people must justify their claims by logic and reason, not myth.

MAPPING THE WEST

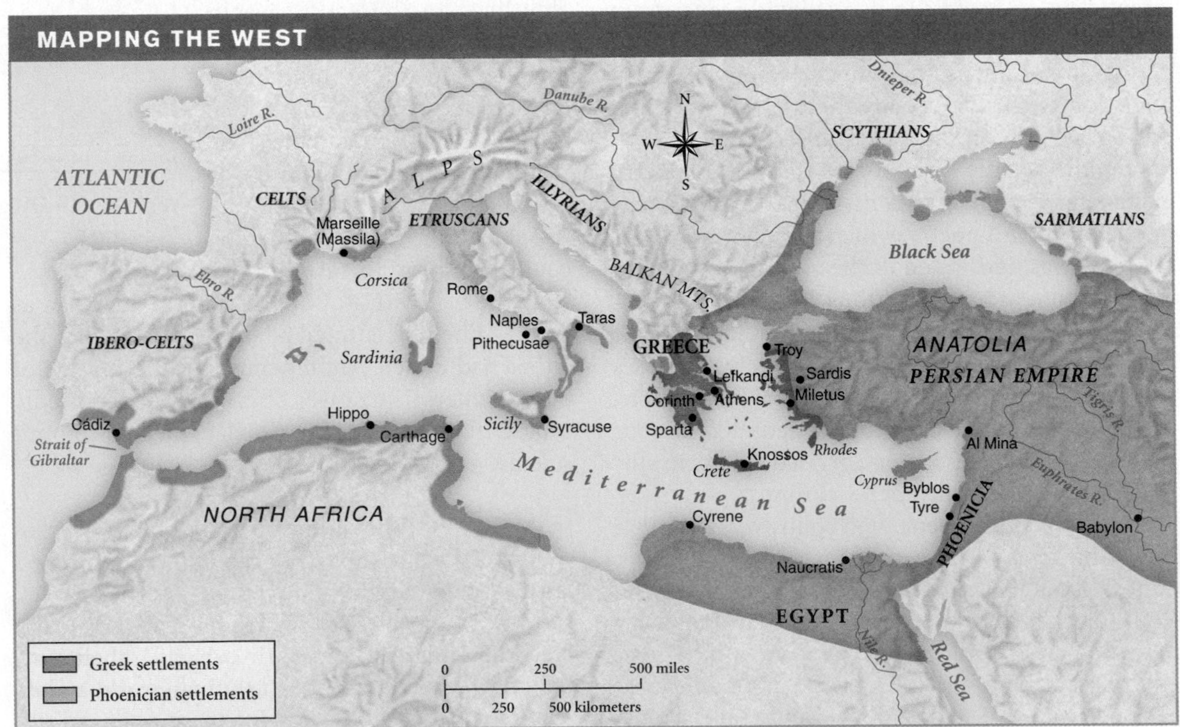

Mediterranean Civilizations, c. 500 B.C.E.

At the end of the sixth century B.C.E., the Persian Empire was by far the most powerful civilization touching the Mediterranean. Its riches and its unity gave it resources that no Phoenician or Greek city could match. The Phoenicians dominated economically in the western Mediterranean, while the Greek city-states in Sicily and southern Italy rivaled the power of those in the heartland. In Italy, the Etruscans were the most powerful civilization; the Romans were still a small community struggling to replace monarchy with a republic.

important achievement. This insistence on rationalism, coupled with the belief that the world could be understood as something other than the plaything of the gods, gave people hope that they could improve their lives through their own efforts. As Xenophanes of Colophon (c. 570–c. 478 B.C.E.) concluded, "The gods have not revealed all things from the beginning to mortals, but, by seeking, human beings find out, in time, what is better." This saying expressed the value Archaic Age philosophers gave to intellectual freedom, corresponding to the value that citizens gave to political freedom in the city-state. Even though these early concepts of freedom were not as complete as some modern thinkers believe that they should have been, they nevertheless represent a significant development in the history of Western civilization.

REVIEW QUESTION What were the main differences among the various forms of government in the Greek city-states?

Conclusion

Over different spans of time and with different results, both the Near East and Greece recovered from their Dark Ages brought on by the violence of the period 1200–1000 B.C.E. The Near East quickly revived its traditional pattern of social and political organization: empire with a strong central authority (monarchy). The Neo-Assyrians, the Neo-Babylonians, and the Persians succeeded one another as imperial powers. The moral dualism of Persian religion, Zoroastrianism, influenced later religions. The Israelites' development of monotheism based on scripture changed the course of religious history in Western civilization.

Greece's recovery from its Dark Age produced a new form of political and social organization: the polis, a city-state based on citizenship and shared governance. The rapidly growing population of the Archaic Age developed the sense of communal identity, personal freedom, and divine justice instituted by citizens that underlay the city-state. The degree of power sharing and the form of the political system varied in the Greek city-states. Some, like Sparta, were oligarchies; in others, like Corinth, rule was by tyranny. Over time, Athens developed the most extensive democracy, in which political power extended to all male citizens.

Just as revolutionary as the invention of democracy were the new methods of artistic expression and new ways of thought that Greeks developed. Building on Near Eastern traditions, Greek poets created lyric poetry to express personal emotion. Greek philosophers argued that laws of nature controlled the universe and that humans could discover these laws through reason and research, thereby establishing rationalism as the conceptual basis for science and philosophy.

The political and intellectual innovations of the Greek Archaic Age, which so profoundly affected later Western civilization, were almost lost to history. By about 500 B.C.E., Persia's awesome empire threatened the Greek world and its new values.

FOR FURTHER EXPLORATION

- **For additional primary-source material from this period**, see *Sources of the Making of the West*, Fourth Edition.
- **For Web sites, images, and documents related to topics in this chapter**, visit *Make History* at bedfordstmartins.com/hunt.

Chapter 2 Review

Online Study Guide   bedfordstmartins.com/hunt

Key Terms and People

In the grid below, identify the term or person and explain its historical significance. (To do this exercise online, go to bedfordstmartins.com/hunt.)

Term	Who or What & When	Why It Matters
Cyrus (p. 41)		
moral dualism (p. 43)		
Torah (p. 45)		
Diaspora (p. 47)		
aretê (p. 49)		
Homer (p. 49)		
polis (p. 51)		
cult (p. 57)		
hoplite (p. 58)		
helot (p. 64)		
Solon (p. 67)		
demes (p. 68)		
Sappho (p. 69)		
rationalism (p. 70)		

Review Questions

1. In what ways was religion important in the Near East from c. 1000 B.C.E. to c. 500 B.C.E.?
2. What factors proved most important in the Greek recovery from the troubles of the Dark Age?
3. How did the physical, social, and intellectual conditions of life in the Archaic Age promote the emergence of the Greek city-state?
4. What were the main differences among the various forms of government in the Greek city-states?

Making Connections

1. What characteristics made the Greek city-state differ in political and social organization from the Near Eastern city-state?
2. How were the ideas of the Ionian philosophers different from mythic traditions?
3. To what extent were the most important changes in Western civilization in this period intentional or unintentional?

Important Events

Date	Event	Date	Event
1000–750 B.C.E.	Greece experiences its Dark Age	657 B.C.E.	Cypselus becomes tyrant in Corinth
900 B.C.E.	Neo-Assyrian Empire emerges	630 B.C.E.	The lyric poet Sappho is born
800 B.C.E.	Greeks learn to write with an alphabet	597 and 586 B.C.E.	Israelites exiled to Babylon
776 B.C.E.	Olympic Games founded in Greece	594 B.C.E.	Solon's reforms promote early democracy in Athens
750 B.C.E.	Greeks begin to create the polis	546–510 B.C.E.	Peisistratus's family rules Athens as tyrants
700 B.C.E.	Spartans conquer Messenia and enslave its inhabitants as helots	539 B.C.E.	Persian king Cyrus captures Babylon and permits Israelites to return to Canaan
700–500 B.C.E.	Ionian philosophers invent rationalism	508–500 B.C.E.	Cleisthenes' reforms extend democracy in Athens

- Consider three events: **Ionian philosophers develop rationalism (700–500 B.C.E.)**, **The lyric poet Sappho is born (630 B.C.E.)**, and **Solon's reforms promote early democracy in Athens (594 B.C.E.)**. How did the development of the Greek city-state (polis) encourage new modes of thinking and expression in science, philosophy, and literature?

SUGGESTED REFERENCES

Scholars today emphasize the importance of contact and intercultural influence among different peoples around the Mediterranean in helping us understand the history of the region as it recovered from the economic troubles and depopulation of the Dark Age.

Ancient Olympic Games: http://www.perseus.tufts.edu/Olympics/

Balot, Ryan K. *Greek Political Thought*. 2005.

*Barnes, Jonathan. *Early Greek Philosophy*. Rev. ed. 2002.

*Boyce, Mary, trans. *Textual Sources for the Study of Zoroastrianism*. 1990.

Bright, John. *A History of Israel*. 4th ed. 2000.

Brosius, Maria. *The Persians*. New ed. 2006.

Bryce, Trevor. *Life and Society in the Hittite World*. 2004.

*Dalley, Stephanie, trans. *Myths from Mesopotamia: Creation, the Flood, Gilgamesh, and Others*. Rev. ed. 2009.

Finkelstein, Israel, and Amihai Mazar. *The Quest for the Historical Israel: Debating Archaeology and the History of Early Israel*. Brian B. Schmidt, ed. 2007.

Hales, Shelley, and Tamar Hodos, eds. *Material Culture and Social Identities in the Ancient World*. 2009.

Hall, Jonathan M. *A History of the Archaic Greek World: ca. 1200–479 B.C.E.* 2006.

Hurwitt, Jeffrey M. *The Art and Culture of Early Greece, 1100–480 B.C.* 1985.

Kugel, James. *The God of Old: Inside the Lost World of the Bible*. 2003.

Lewis, John. *Solon the Thinker: Political Thought in Archaic Athens*. 2008.

*Malandra, William W. *An Introduction to Ancient Iranian Religion: Readings from the Avesta and the Achaemenid Inscriptions*. 1983.

Osborne, Robin. *Greece in the Making, 1200–479 B.C.* 2nd ed. 2009.

Shapiro, H. A. *The Cambridge Companion to Archaic Greece*. 2007.

*Primary source

The Greek Golden Age

CHAPTER

3

C. 500–C. 400 B.C.E.

A failure in international negotiations led to the greatest foreign danger ever to threaten Greece. In 507 B.C.E., Athens feared an attack from Sparta, its more powerful rival. The Athenian assembly therefore sent ambassadors to the Persian king, Darius I (r. 522–486 B.C.E.), to plead for a defensive alliance. The Athenian diplomats arranged for a meeting with the king's governor in Ionia (the western coast of modern Turkey), who controlled the Greeks living in that region. After the Athenians made their plea, the governor asked, "But who in the world are these people and where do they live that they are begging for an alliance with the Persians?" The mutual misunderstandings that resulted from this confused exchange helped start a prolonged conflict between mainland Greece and Persia in the early fifth century B.C.E.

This incident reveals external and internal reasons why war dominated Greece's history throughout that century, first with Greeks fighting Persians and then with Greeks fighting Greeks. The Persian king was eager to make more Greek city-states his subjects (those in Ionia had been his subjects for forty years) because their trade and growing wealth made them desirable prizes and because Persian kings believed it was their duty to expand their empire whenever possible. Unity seemed the Greeks' best defense, but the mainland city-states were so intensely competitive and suspicious of one another that they had never yet been able to come together to combat the Persians, not even to try to liberate the Greek city-states in Ionia from Persian control. Athens and Sparta so mistrusted each other that the Athenians appealed to foreigners for help against fellow Greeks.

Conflicting interests and mutual misunderstandings between Persia and Greece ignited a great conflict at the

Greek against Persian in Hand-to-Hand Combat (detail)
This red-figure painting appears on the interior of a Greek wine cup. Painted about 480 B.C.E. (during the Persian Wars), it shows a Greek hoplite (armored infantryman) striking a Persian warrior in hand-to-hand combat with swords. The Greek has lost his principal weapon, a spear, and the Persian can no longer shoot his, the bow and arrow. The Greek artist designed the painting to express multiple messages: the Persian's colorful outfit with sleeves and pants stresses the "otherness" of the enemy in Greek eyes, and their serene expressions at such a desperate moment dignify the horror of killing. Greek warriors often had heroic symbols painted on their shields, such as the winged horse Pegasus, an allusion to the brave exploits of Bellerophon. *(© National Museums of Scotland/The Bridgeman Art Library International.)*

start of the fifth century B.C.E.: the so-called Persian Wars (499–479 B.C.E.), in which Persia invaded Greece. The Persian invasions threatened the independence of the Greek mainland and Aegean islands. So dangerous was the threat that thirty-one Greek states (out of hundreds) temporarily laid aside their traditional competition to form an alliance to defeat the Persians. In victory, however, they lost their unity and fell to fighting one another. In the midst of nearly constant warfare spanning the century, Greeks (especially in Athens) created what later ages judged to be their most famous innovations in architecture, art, and theater. These cultural achievements have led historians to call this period from around 500 to around 400 B.C.E. the Golden Age. This Golden Age is the first part of the period called the Classical Age of Greece, which lasted from around 500 B.C.E. to the death of Alexander the Great in 323 B.C.E.

Most of the cultural achievements of the Golden Age took place in Athens, and only limited details about other important city-states, such as Corinth and Syracuse, emerge from the surviving literary and archaeological sources from this period. Many famous plays, histories, inscriptions, buildings, and sculptures survive from fifth-century B.C.E. Athens. For these reasons, studying the Greek Golden Age primarily means studying the Athenian Golden Age.

The confidence the Greeks gained from defeating the Persian invaders, combined with their traditional competitiveness, produced brilliant innovations in art, architecture, literature, education, and philosophy in the Golden Age. The new ideas in education and philosophy were hotly controversial at the time but have had a lasting influence on Western civilization. The controversy arose because many people saw the changes as attacks on ancient traditions, especially religion; they feared the gods would punish their communities for abandoning ancestral beliefs.

Political change also characterized the Athenian Golden Age. First, Athenian citizens made their city-state government more democratic than ever. Second, Athens also grew internationally powerful by using its navy to establish rule over other Greeks in a system dubbed "empire" by modern scholars. This naval power also promoted seaborne trade, and revenues from rule and trade brought Athens enormous prosperity. Athens's citizens voted to use the funds to finance new public buildings, art, and competitive theater festivals, and to pay for poorer men to serve as officials and jurors in an expanded democratic government.

The Golden Age ended when Sparta defeated Athens in the Peloponnesian War (431–404 B.C.E.) and the Athenians then fought a brief but bloody civil war (404–403 B.C.E.). The fifth century B.C.E., so famous for its cultural innovation, thus both began and ended with fierce wars, with Greeks standing together in the first one and tearing each other apart in the concluding one. Losing the Peloponnesian War bankrupted and divided Athens, turning its Golden Age to lead.

CHAPTER FOCUS **Did war bring more benefit or more harm—politically, socially, and intellectually—to Golden Age Athens?**

Wars between Persia and Greece, 499–479 B.C.E.

The Persian Wars had their roots in Athens's request for help from Persia in 507 B.C.E. The Athenian ambassadors agreed to the standard Persian requirement for an alliance: presenting tokens of earth and water to acknowledge submission to the Persian king. The Athenian assembly erupted in outrage at their diplomats' submitting to Persian authority but failed to inform King Darius that it rejected his terms; he continued to believe that Athens had agreed to obey him in return for his support. This misunderstanding planted the seed for two Persian attacks on Greece, one small and one huge. Since

500–323 B.C.E. Classical Age of Greece

480–479 B.C.E. Xerxes' invasion of Greece

451 B.C.E. Pericles restricts Athenian citizenship to children whose parents are both citizens

500 B.C.E. — 475 B.C.E. — 450 B.C.E.

499–479 B.C.E. Wars between Persia and Greece

490 B.C.E. Battle of Marathon

480 B.C.E. Battle of Salamis

461 B.C.E. Ephialtes reforms Athenian court system

Early 450s B.C.E. Pericles introduces pay for officeholders in Athenian democracy the Persian Empire far outstripped the Greek city-states in soldiers and money, the conflict pitted the equivalent of a huge bear against a pack of under-sized dogs.

From the Ionian Revolt to the Battle of Marathon, 499–490 B.C.E.

The lead-up from the Ionian Revolt to the Persian Wars is an example of a smaller conflict sparking a greater one—a common occurrence in the history of war. In 499 B.C.E., the Greek city-states in Ionia revolted against their Persian-installed tyrants, who were ruling harshly and unjustly, and ignored the demand of Darius I that the Ionians send more soldiers for his army. The Spartans refused to help the Ionian rebels, but the Athenians sent troops because they regarded the Ionians as close kin. A Persian counterattack sent the Athenians fleeing home and crushed the revolt by 494 B.C.E. (Map 3.1, page 79). Darius exploded in anger when he learned that the Athenians had attacked in Ionia. After all, he thought they were faithful allies. So bitter to him was this perceived betrayal that, according to the historian Herodotus, Darius ordered a slave to repeat three times at every meal, "Lord, remember the Athenians."

In 490 B.C.E., Darius sent a small fleet to punish Athens and install a puppet tyrant. He expected Athens to surrender without a fight. The Athenians refused to back down, however, confronting the invaders near the village of Marathon. The Athenian soldiers were stunned by the Persians' strange garb—colorful pants instead of the short tunics and bare legs that Greeks regarded as proper dress (see the chapter-opening photo)—but the Greek commanders in a tactical innovation had the hoplites (armored infantry) charge the enemy at a dead run instead of their usual slow advance. Running cut the time that the Athenians were exposed to the enemy's archers. The Greek soldiers, each wearing heavy metal armor, clanked across the Marathon plain through a hail of Persian arrows. In the hand-to-hand combat, the Greek hoplites used their heavier weapons to overwhelm the Persian infantry.

The Athenian infantry then hurried the twenty-six miles from Marathon to Athens to guard the city against the Persian navy. (Today's marathon races commemorate the legend of a runner speeding ahead to announce the victory and then dropping dead.) When the Persians sailed home, the Athenians rejoiced in disbelief. Thereafter, a family's greatest honor was to have a "Marathon fighter" among its ancestors.

Their unexpected success at Marathon evidently strengthened the Athenians' sense of community. When a fabulously rich strike was made in Athens's publicly owned silver mines in 483 B.C.E., a far-sighted leader named **Themistocles** convinced the assembly to spend the money on doubling the size of the navy to defend against possible foreign attack instead of distributing the money to the citizens to spend on themselves.

The Great Persian Invasion, 480–479 B.C.E.

Themistocles' foresight proved valuable when Darius's son Xerxes I (r. 486–465 B.C.E.) assembled an immense force to invade Greece to avenge his father's defeat and add the mainland city-states to the many lands paying him taxes. The Persians spared no expense, even digging a great canal through a peninsula in northern Greece to give their fleet safe passage. So huge was Xerxes' army, the Greeks claimed, that when the invasion began in 480 B.C.E. it took seven days and seven nights for the entire force to cross the Hellespont, the strip of sea between Anatolia and Greece, which Xerxes had bridged.

Themistocles (thuh MIST uh kleez): Athens's leader during the great Persian invasion of Greece.

450 B.C.E. Protagoras and other Sophists begin to teach in Athens

446–445 B.C.E. (winter) Peace treaty between Athens and Sparta; intended to last thirty years

441 B.C.E. Sophocles presents the tragedy *Antigone*

431–404 B.C.E. Peloponnesian War

425 B.C.E.

420s B.C.E. Herodotus finishes *Histories*

415–413 B.C.E. Enormous Athenian military expedition against Sicily

411 B.C.E. Aristophanes presents the comedy *Lysistrata*

404–403 B.C.E. Rule of the Thirty Tyrants at Athens

403 B.C.E. Restoration of democracy in Athens

400 B.C.E.

A Cylindrical Signet of Persia's King Darius
Like other kings in the ancient Mediterranean region, the Persian king hunted lions to show his courage and his ability to overcome nature's threats. Here on this cylindrical signet, used to impress the royal seal into wet clay to verify documents, King Darius (r. 522–486 B.C.E.) shoots arrows from a chariot driven for him by a charioteer. He is depicted wearing his crown so that his status as ruler would be obvious. The symbol of Ahura Mazda, the chief god of Persian religion, hovers in the sky to indicate that the king enjoys divine favor. *(The British Museum/akg-images.)*

Xerxes thought the Greek city-states would immediately surrender. Some did, but thirty-one made a decision new in Greek history: to unite as allies to defend their city-states' political freedom.

Their coalition became known as the Hellenic League, but it hardly represented the entire Greek world. The allies desperately wanted the major Greek city-states in Italy and Sicily to join the league because these western states were rich naval powers, but they refused. Syracuse, for example, the most powerful Greek state at the time, controlled a regional empire built on agriculture in Sicily's plains and seaborne commerce through its harbors on the Mediterranean's western trading routes. The tyrant ruling Syracuse rejected the league's appeal for help because he was fighting his own war against Carthage, a Phoenician city in North Africa, over control of the trade routes.

The Hellenic League chose Sparta to lead because of its reputation for military excellence. The Athenians swallowed their competitive desire for honor and agreed to follow. The Spartans demonstrated their courage in 480 B.C.E. when three hundred of their infantry (and a few hundred other troops) blocked Xerxes' army for several days at the narrow pass called Thermopylae ("gate of hot springs") in central Greece. When told the Persian archers were so numerous that their arrows darkened the sun, one Spartan reportedly remarked, "That's good news; we'll get to fight in the shade." They did—to the death. Their tomb's memorial proclaimed, "Go tell the Spartans that we lie buried here obedient to their orders."

When the Persians marched south, the Athenians, knowing they could not defend the city, evacuated their residents to the Peloponnese rather than surrender. The Persians then burned Athens. The panicked allies decided to retreat to the Peloponnese, but in the summer of 480 B.C.E. Themistocles and his Athenian political rival Aristides cooperated to win a tough argument with the other city-states' generals, convincing them to stay and fight a naval battle. Themistocles then tricked the Persian king into sending his ships into battle against the Greek fleet in the channel between the island of Salamis and the west coast of Athens: the narrowness of the channel prevented Xerxes from sending all his fleet (twice or more the size of the Greeks') into battle at the same time. The heavier Greek warships won the battle by ramming the flimsier Persian craft in the tight space. The battle of Salamis turned the tide of the war, and Xerxes retreated to Persia. The following summer (479 B.C.E.), the Spartans led the Greek infantry to dual victories over the remaining Persian land forces on the Greek mainland and, now on the offensive against the enemy,

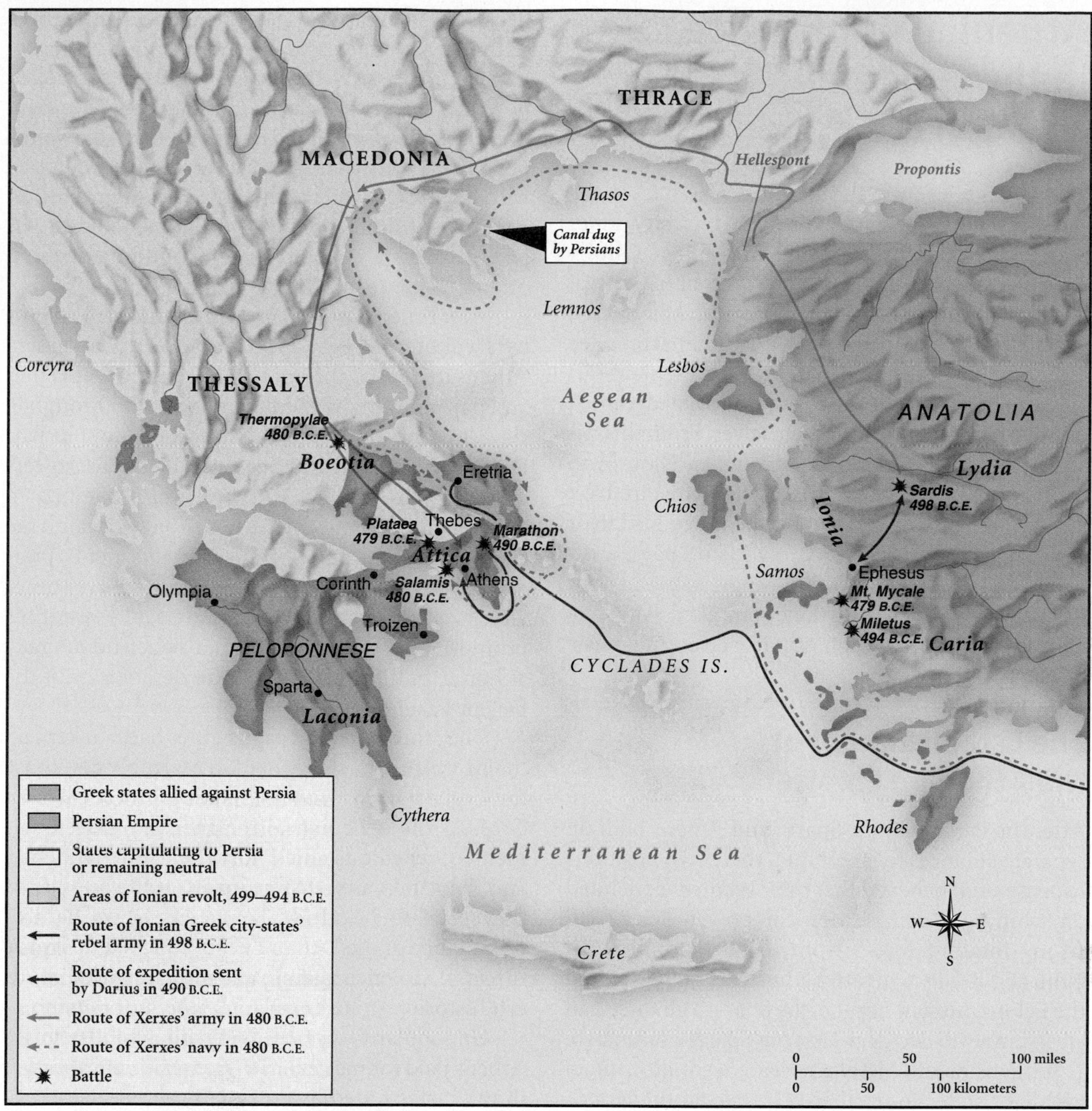

MAP 3.1 The Persian Wars, 499–479 B.C.E.
Following the example of King Cyrus (r. 557–530 B.C.E.), the founder of the Persian Empire, King Cambyses (r. 530–522 B.C.E.) and King Darius I (r. 522–486 B.C.E.) expanded the empire eastward and westward. Darius invaded Thrace more than fifteen years before the conflict against the Greeks that we call the Persian Wars. The Persians' unexpected defeat in Greece put an end to their attempt to extend their power into Europe.

on the Anatolian coast. Superior generalship and the Greek competitive spirit of aretê ("excellence") underlay these successes. When the victorious allies met to award a prize to the war's best Greek commander, Themistocles won the competition—every general voted for himself first and Themistocles second!

The Greeks won their battles against the Persians because their generals, especially Themistocles, had better strategic foresight, their soldiers had stronger body armor, their warships were more effective in close combat, and their tactics minimized the Persian advantage in numbers of troops and ships. Above all, the Greeks won the war because enough of them took the innovative step of uniting to fight together to keep their independence. Because the Greek forces included not only the social elites but also thousands of poorer men who rowed the warships, the victory over the Persians showed that rich and poor Greeks alike treasured the ideal of political freedom for their city-states that had emerged during the Archaic Age.

REVIEW QUESTION How did the Greeks overcome the dangers of the Persian invasions?

Athenian Confidence in the Golden Age, 478–431 B.C.E.

The struggle against the Persians was one of the rare occasions when at least some Greek city-states cooperated. Victory fractured this alliance, however, because the allies resented the harshness of Spartan command and the Athenians had gained the confidence to compete with the Spartans for leadership of Greece. No longer were Athenians satisfied to be followers of Sparta; now they dreamed of a much grander role for themselves. From this desire arose the so-called Athenian Empire. The growth of Athens's power over other Greeks inspired yet more confidence in its citizens, who broadened their democracy and spent vast amounts on pay for officials and jurors, public buildings, art, and religious festivals in which they competed with one another for public recognition in presenting music and drama.

The Establishment of the Athenian Empire

After the Persian Wars, Sparta and Athens built up separate alliances to strengthen their own positions because each believed that their security depended on winning a competition for power. Sparta led strong infantry forces from the Peloponnese region, and its ally Corinth had a sizable navy. Called the Peloponnesian League, the Spartan alliance had an assembly to decide policy, but Sparta dominated.

Athens, with Aristides as lead negotiator, allied with city-states in northern Greece, on the islands of the Aegean Sea, and along the Ionian coast — the places most in need of protection from Persian retaliation. This alliance, whose treasury was originally located on the Aegean island of Delos, was built on naval power and today is called the **Delian League**. The Delian League started out as a democratic alliance for collective security, but Athens came to control it through the allies' willingness to allow the Athenians to command and to set the financing arrangements for the league's fleet. At its height, the league included some three hundred city-states. Each paid dues according to its size; Athens as the league's leader controlled how the dues were used. Larger city-states paid their dues by sending **triremes** — warships propelled by 170 rowers on three levels and equipped with a battering ram at the bow (see Figure 3.1 on page 81) — complete with trained crews and their pay. Smaller states could share in building one ship or contribute cash instead.

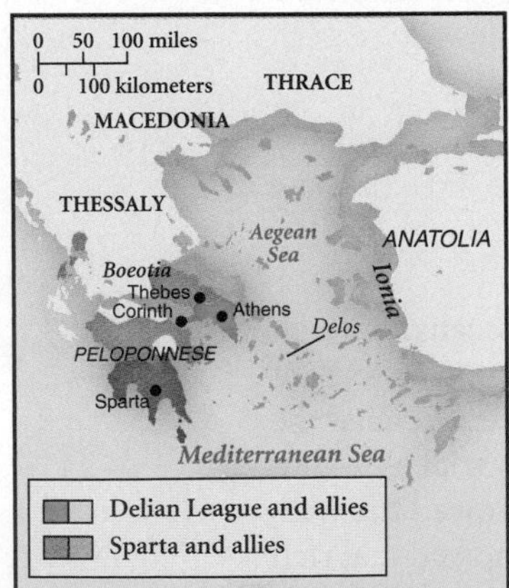

The Delian and Peloponnesian Leagues

Over time, more and more Delian League members voluntarily paid cash because it was easier. Athens then used this money to construct triremes and pay men to row them; oarsmen who brought a slave to row alongside them earned double pay. Drawn primarily from the poorest citizens, rowers gained both income and political influence in Athenian democracy because the navy became the city-state's main force. These benefits made poor citizens eager to expand Athens's power over other Greeks. The increase in Athenian naval power thus promoted the development of a wider democracy at home, but it undermined the democracy of the Delian League.

Since most Delian League allies had not kept up their own navies, the Athenian assembly could use the league fleet to force disobedient allies to pay cash dues. As the Athenian historian Thucydides commented, rebellious allies "lost their independence, and the Athenians became no longer as popular as they used to be." It was Athens's heavy-handed dominance of the Delian League, backed up by the threat of violence against allies, that has led modern historians to use the label *Athenian Empire*.

Unpopularity among many allies was the price Athens paid for making itself the major naval power in the eastern Mediterranean: by about 460 B.C.E., the Delian League's fleet had expelled remaining Persian garrisons from northern Greece and driven the enemy fleet from the Aegean Sea. This sweep eliminated the Persian threat for the next fifty years and proved the effectiveness of Athenian leadership.

Military success made Athens prosperous by bringing in spoils and cash dues from the Delian League, making seaborne trade safe, and benefiting rich and poor alike — the poor men who rowed the league's navy earned good pay, while elite commanders enhanced their chances for election to high office by spending their spoils on public festivals and buildings. The Athenian assembly debated how Athens should treat its league allies, but the majority consistently rejected complaints on the grounds that

---

Delian (DEE lee un) League: The naval alliance led by Athens in the Golden Age that became the basis for the Athenian Empire.

triremes (TRY reems): Greek wooden warships rowed by 170 oarsmen sitting on three levels and equipped with a battering ram at the bow.

the league was fulfilling its original duty by protecting everyone from Persian attack. In this way, there were direct links in Golden Age Athens among democracy for its own citizens, pay, and imperialism.

Radical Democracy and Pericles' Leadership, 461–431 B.C.E.

As the Delian League grew, the Athenian fleet's oarsmen realized that they provided the cornerstone for Athens's new power and prosperity. In the late 460s B.C.E., they decided that the time had come to increase their political power by making the court system of Athens just as democratic as the legislative assembly, in which all free adult male citizens could already participate. They wanted laws and political institutions that would finally make Cleisthenes' promise of equality through law a reality for everyone so that they would no longer be liable to unfair verdicts at the hands of the elite in criminal cases and civil suits. Members of the elite led this push for judicial reform, hoping to win popular support for election to high office by speaking out for the interests of the masses. A member of one of Athens's most distinguished families, **Pericles** (c. 495–429 B.C.E.), became Golden Age Athens's dominant politician by spearheading reforms to democratize its judicial system and provide pay for many public offices.

Creating Radical Democracy

The changes to Athenian democracy in the 460s and 450s B.C.E. have led historians to label the system *radical* ("from the roots") because it gave direct political power in the assembly and participation in the court system to all adult male citizens, not just elites. The government consisted of the assembly open to all these men, the Council of Five Hundred chosen annually by lottery, the Council of the Areopagus of ex-archons serving for life, an executive board of ten annually elected "generals," nine archons (now chosen by lottery every year), hundreds of other annual minor officials (most chosen by lottery), and the court system.

Athens's **radical democracy** balanced two competing goals: (1) participation by as many ordinary male citizens as possible in direct (not representative) democracy and (2) selective leadership by elite citizens. To achieve the first goal, Athenian voters established (1) random selection by lottery for most public offices, term limits, shared power, and salaries for most officials and members of the Council of Five Hundred (which prepared the assembly's agenda and supervised public matters); (2) open investigation and punishment of corruption; (3) equal protection under the law for citizens regardless of wealth; and (4) payment for and random selection of jurors. To achieve the second, the highest-level officials were elected, rather than chosen by lottery. The top officials (the board of ten generals, who oversaw military and financial affairs) ran for election every year, could be reelected an unlimited number of times, and received no pay so that they would not

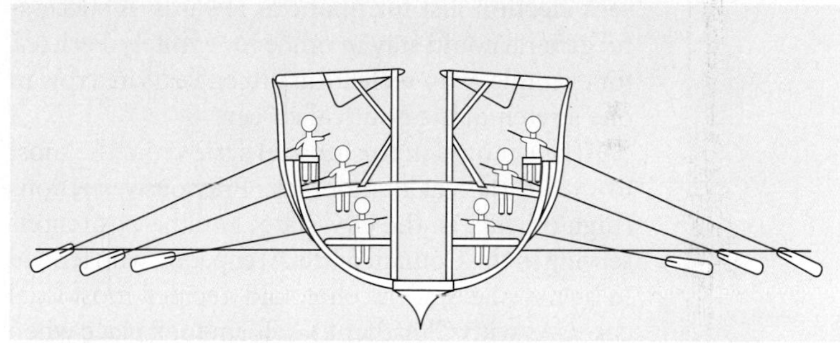

FIGURE 3.1 Triremes, the Foremost Classical Greek Warships
Innovations in military technology and training propelled a naval arms race in the fifth century B.C.E. when Greek shipbuilders designed larger and faster ramming ships powered by 170 rowers seated in three rows, each above the other. (See the line illustration of the rowers from behind.) Called triremes, these ships were expensive to build and required extensive crew training. Only wealthy and populous city-states such as Athens could afford to build and man large fleets of triremes. The relief sculpture found on the Athenian acropolis and dating from about 400 B.C.E. gives a glimpse of what a trireme looked like from the side when being rowed into battle. (Sails were used for power only when the ship was not in combat.) *(The Art Archive/Acropolis Museum, Athens/Gianni Dagli Orti.)*

Pericles (PEHR uh kleez): Athens's political leader during the Golden Age.

radical democracy: The Athenian system of democracy established in the 460s and 450s B.C.E. that extended direct political power and participation in the court system to all adult male citizens.

Potsherd Ballots for Ostracism
These two shards (*ostraka*) were broken from the same pot (as the breakage line shows) and inscribed for use as ballots in an ostracism at Athens. The lower fragment carries the name of Themistocles, the leader who engineered the Greek fleet's success against the Persian navy off the island of Salamis in 480 B.C.E. The upper one has the name of Cimon, the Delian League's most famous general. Political competition led to Themistocles' ostracism sometime in the late 470s B.C.E. and Cimon's in 461 B.C.E. Therefore, if these two ballots were intended for the same ostracism, it must have been that of Themistocles, or an earlier one when he was still in Athens. *(American School of Classical Studies at Athens: Agora Excavations.)*

seek election just for financial rewards. A successful general could stay in office indefinitely. Pericles, for example, won reelection fifteen years in a row in one stretch of his political career.

The changes in the judicial system did the most to create radical democracy. Previously, archons (high officials in the city-state) and the ex-archons serving in the Council of the Areopagus, who tended to be members of the elite, had decided most legal cases. As with Cleisthenes, reform took place when an elite man proposed it to support ordinary men's political rights and simultaneously win their votes against his rivals: in 461 B.C.E. Ephialtes won popular support by getting the assembly to establish a new system that took away jurisdiction from the archons and gave it to courts manned by citizen jurors. To make it more democratic and prevent bribery, jurors were selected by lottery from male citizens over thirty years old. They received pay to serve on juries numbering from several hundred to several thousand members. No judges or lawyers existed, and jurors voted by secret ballot after hearing speeches from the persons involved. As in the assembly, a majority vote decided matters; no appeals of verdicts were allowed.

Ostracism and Majority Rule

Athenian radical democracy included notions of privacy and legal protection for individuals, but the majority could overrule those protections on matters of public policy. A striking example was **ostracism** (from *ostrakon*, a piece of broken pottery used as a ballot). Once a year, all male citizens could cast a ballot on which they scratched the name of one man they thought should be exiled for ten years. If at least six thousand ballots were cast, the man whose name appeared on the greatest number was expelled from Athens. He suffered no other penalty; his family and property remained undisturbed.

Usually a man was ostracized because he had become so popular that a majority feared he would overthrow the democracy to rule as a tyrant. Sometimes a leader was ostracized when his political competitors ganged up to vote against him. This happened to Themistocles, who in a great irony ended up living in Persia as a favorite of King Xerxes, who valued his former enemy's intelligence. There was no guarantee of voters' motives in an ostracism, as a story about Aristides illustrates. He was nicknamed "the Just" because he had proved himself so fair-minded in setting the original level of dues for Delian League members. On the day of an ostracism, an illiterate citizen handed him a pottery fragment and asked him to scratch a name on it:

> "Certainly," said Aristides. "Which name shall I write?" "Aristides," replied the man. "All right," said Aristides as he inscribed his own name, "but why do you want to ostracize Aristides? What has he done to you?" "Oh, nothing. I don't even know him," sputtered the man. "I just can't stand hearing everybody refer to him as 'the Just.'"

True or not, this tale demonstrates that most Athenians believed the right way to support democracy was to trust a majority vote, regardless of its possible injustice to a particular individual.

Not all citizens approved of the equality of radical democracy. Some socially elite citizens bitterly criticized what they saw as its disregard for social merit in giving political power to the poor. Opponents of democracy blamed it for promoting the interests of those whom they called the "wicked" (i.e., the poor) over the interests of "useful" citizens (i.e., themselves, the rich). These critics became particularly vocal when Athens's democracy suffered periods of crisis, as at certain points in the great war with Sparta that was to erupt at the end of the Golden Age. They insisted that oligarchy—the rule of the few—was morally superior to radical democracy because they believed that the poor lacked the education and moral values needed for leadership and would use their majority rule to

---

ostracism (AHS truh sizm): An annual procedure in Athenian radical democracy by which a man could be voted out of the city-state for ten years; its purpose was to prevent tyranny.

strip the rich of their wealth by passing laws to make them pay for expensive public programs.

Pericles' Leadership Still, Pericles used his political vision and spellbinding public-speaking skills to convince the assembly to pass reforms that would strengthen the equality prized by poor citizens. These efforts contributed to his popularity and helped him become the most influential leader of his era. Pericles began his career by supporting Ephialtes' reform of the court system. Then, in the early 450s B.C.E., he boosted mass participation in democracy by introducing pay for service in the public offices filled by lottery. This reform used public funds to pay men for serving in numerous government posts, on the Council of Five Hundred, and on juries. Previously, because these offices had been unpaid, only wealthy men could afford to fill them. Now poor citizens could serve.

Pericles' citizenship reforms not only boosted the status of native-born Athenians from all classes but also recast who constituted a citizen. In 451 B.C.E., Pericles sponsored a law restricting citizenship to those whose mother and father were both Athenian by birth. Previously, wealthy men had often married foreign women from elite families. This change both increased the status of Athenian women, rich or poor, as potential mothers of citizens and made Athenian citizenship more valuable by reducing the number of people eligible for its legal and financial benefits. In another effort to enforce exclusiveness, officials reviewed everyone's identity and, some sources report, revoked the citizenship of thousands.

Pericles also convinced the assembly to launch naval campaigns (and thus provide poor Athenians an income as rowers) when war with Sparta broke out in the 450s B.C.E. over Athenian actions against Peloponnesian League states. He supported sending the fleet against Persian garrisons in Cyprus, Egypt, and the eastern Mediterranean to expand the Delian League's power and win war spoils. The voters in the assembly were so eager to compete for international power against both Persians and other Greeks that they authorized up to three major expeditions at a time. This large-scale militarism slowed in the late 450s B.C.E. after a large naval force sent to aid an Egyptian rebellion against Persian rule, in an effort to weaken Persian power in the eastern Mediterranean, suffered a horrendous defeat in which the Persian forces killed tens of thousands of oarsmen. In the winter of 446–445 B.C.E., Pericles arranged a peace treaty with Sparta with the goal of stabilizing the balance of power in Greece for thirty years and thus preserving Athenian control of the Delian League.

The Urban Landscape in Athens

Golden Age Athens prospered from Delian League dues, war plunder, and taxes on booming international seaborne trade. Its harbor in Piraeus promoted cross-Mediterranean commerce, its navy made its empire's numerous ports safe for merchants and travelers, and its courts resolved legal disputes. Its artisans produced goods traded far and wide; the Etruscans in central Italy, for example, imported countless painted vases for wine drinking at Greek-style dinner parties. The economic activity and international traffic of the mid-fifth century B.C.E. boosted Athens to its greatest prosperity ever.

Athenians spent their new riches not just on pay for citizens to participate in democratic government but also on their city's public buildings, art, and religious festivals. In private life, rich urban dwellers splurged on luxury goods influenced by Persian designs, but most houses retained their traditional modest size and plainness. Farmhouses could cluster in villages or stand isolated, while houses and apartments in the city wedged tightly against one another along narrow, winding streets. Recent archaeological study of the city of Olynthus in northeastern Greece shows that urban one-family homes were built on varying patterns, but one favorite plan grouped bedrooms, storerooms, and dining rooms around open-air courtyards. Poor city residents rented small apartments. Wall paintings or decorative artworks were rare, furnishings sparse. Toilets consisted of pots and a pit outside the front door. The city paid collectors to dump the dung outside its fortification walls.

Generals who wanted to display their excellence and also win the people's favor spent their war spoils on running tracks, shade trees, and public buildings. A popular building project was a stoa, a narrow structure open along one side that offered shelter from the weather. The super-rich commander Cimon, for example, paid for the Painted Stoa to be built on the edge of Athens's **agora**, the central market square. There, crowds of shoppers could admire the stoa's bright paintings depicting Cimon's family's military achievements, especially his father's leadership in the battle of Marathon. This sort of contribution was voluntary, but the laws required wealthy citizens to pay for festivals and equipping warships. This financial obligation on the rich was essential because Athens, like most other Greek city-states, had no regular property or income taxes.

---

agora (AH gore uh): The central market square of a Greek city-state, a popular gathering place for conversation.

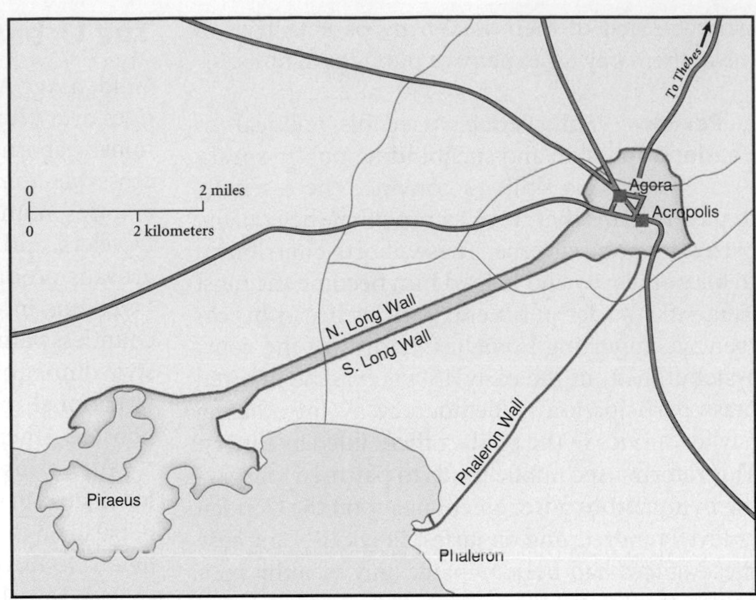

MAP 3.2 Fifth-Century B.C.E. Athens
The urban center of Athens, with the agora and acropolis at its heart, measured about one square mile; it was surrounded by a stone wall with a circuit of some four miles. Gates guarded by towers and various smaller entries allowed traffic in and out of the city. Much of the Athenian population lived in the many demes (villages) of the surrounding countryside. Most of the city's water supply came from wells and springs inside the walls, but, unusual for a Greek city, Athens also had water piped in from outside. The Long Walls provided a protected corridor connecting the city to its harbor at Piraeus, where the Athenian navy was anchored and grain was imported to feed the people.

The Parthenon On Athens's acropolis (the rocky hill at the city's center, Map 3.2), Pericles had the two most famous buildings of Golden Age Athens erected during the 440s and 430s B.C.E.: a mammoth gateway and an enormous marble temple of Athena called the **Parthenon**. Comparing a day's wage then and now, we can estimate that these buildings together cost more than the equivalent of a billion dollars, a phenomenal sum for a Greek city-state. Pericles' political rivals slammed him for spending too much public money on the project and diverting Delian League funds to beautify Athens.

The Parthenon ("virgin goddess's house") has become the foremost symbol of Athens's Golden Age. The Parthenon honored Athena, the city's patron deity, as the divine champion of Athenian military power and demonstrated her visible presence in the city. Inside the temple, a gold-and-ivory statue nearly forty feet high depicted the goddess in armor, holding in her outstretched hand a six-foot statue of Nike, the goddess of victory.

Like all Greek temples, the Parthenon was meant as a house for its divinity, not as a gathering place for worshippers. Its design followed standard temple architecture: a rectangular box on a raised platform lined with columns, a plan the Greeks probably derived from the stone temples of Egypt. The Parthenon's soaring columns fenced in a porch surrounding the interior chamber on all sides. They were carved in the simple style called Doric, in contrast to the more elaborate Ionic and Corinthian styles often imitated in columns on modern buildings (Figure 3.2).

The Parthenon's massive size and innovative style proclaimed the self-confidence of Golden Age Athens and its competitive drive to build a monument more spectacular than any other in Greece. Constructed from twenty thousand tons of Attic marble, the temple stretched some 230 feet long and 100 feet wide, with eight columns across the ends instead of the six normally found in Doric style and seventeen instead of thirteen along the sides. The temple's complex architecture demonstrated the

Parthenon (PAR thuh non): The massive temple to Athena as a warrior goddess built atop the Athenian acropolis in the Golden Age of Greece.

FIGURE 3.2 Styles of Greek Capitals
The Greeks decorated the capitals, or tops, of columns in these three styles to fit the different architectural "canons" (their word for precise mathematical systems of proportions) that they devised for designing buildings. These styles were much imitated in later times, as on many U.S. state capitols and the U.S. Supreme Court Building in Washington, D.C.

Athenian ambition to use human skill to improve nature: because perfectly rectilinear architecture appears curved to the human eye, subtle curves and inclines were built into the Parthenon to produce an illusion of completely straight lines and emphasize its massiveness.

The Parthenon's many sculptures communicated confident messages: the gods ensure triumph over the forces of chaos, and Athenians enjoy the gods' goodwill more than any other city-state's citizens do. The sculptures in each pediment (the triangular space atop the columns at either end of the temple) portrayed Athena as the city-state's benefactor. The metopes (panels sculpted in relief above the outer columns around all four sides) portrayed victories over hostile centaurs (creatures with the body of a horse but torso and head of a man) and other enemies of civilization. Most strikingly of all, a frieze (a continuous band of figures carved in relief) ran around the top of the walls inside the porch and was painted in bright colors to make it more visible. The Parthenon's frieze was special because usually only Ionic-style buildings had one. Although it had no inscription to state its subject, the frieze most likely portrayed Athenian men, women, and children on parade in the presence of the gods, the procession shown in motion like the pictures in a graphic novel or cartoon today.

The Parthenon frieze made a bold statement about how Athenians perceived their relationship to the gods — no other Greeks had ever adorned a temple with representations of themselves. Its sculpture staked a claim of unique closeness between the city-state and the gods, reflecting the Athenians' confidence after helping turn back the Persians, achieving leadership of a powerful naval alliance, and accumulating great wealth. Their success, the Athenians believed, proved that the gods were on their side, and their fabulous buildings displayed their gratitude.

Sculpture's New Message Like the unique Parthenon frieze, the innovations that Golden Age artists made in representing the human body shattered tradition. By the time of the Persian Wars, Greek sculptors had begun replacing the stiffly balanced style of Archaic Age statues with statues in motion in new poses. This style of movement in stone expressed an energetic balancing of competing forces, echoing a theme evident in radical democracy's principles.

Sculptors also began carving anatomically realistic but perfect-looking bodies, suggesting that humans could be confident in their potential for beauty and perfection. Female statues, for example, now displayed the shape of the curves underneath clothing,

The Acropolis of Athens

Most Greek city-states, including Athens, sprang up around a prominent rocky hill, called an acropolis ("height of the city"; compare the picture of Corinth on page 66). The summit of the acropolis usually housed sanctuaries for the city's protective deities and could serve as a fortress for the population during an enemy attack. Athens's acropolis boasted several elaborately decorated marble temples honoring the goddess Athena; the largest one was the Parthenon, seen here from its west (back) side. Recent research suggests that the ruins of a temple burned by the Persians when they captured Athens in 480 B.C.E. remained in place right next to the Parthenon. The Athenians left its charred remains to remind themselves of the sacrifices they had made in defending their freedom. (The walls in the lower foreground are from a theater built in Roman times.) *(akg-images.)*

Scene from the Parthenon Frieze
The Parthenon, the Athenian temple honoring Athena as a warrior goddess and patron of the Delian League, dominated the summit of the city's acropolis. A frieze (band of sculpture in relief), of which this is a small section, ran around the top of the temple's outside wall. Here, riders line up in the Pan-Athenaic festival's procession to the Parthenon; the artist layered the horses' legs to show depth. The original blazed with bright colors and details fashioned from metal, such as the horses' bridles. The elaborate folds of the riders' garments display the rich style characteristic of clothed figures in Classical Age sculpture. How would you compare the style of this relief to that of the Persian relief on page 41? *(The Art Archive/Acropolis Museum, Athens/Gianni Dagli Orti.)*

while male ones showed bodybuilders' muscles. The faces showed a more relaxed and self-confident look in place of the rigid smiles of archaic statues.

As with relief sculptures on temples, freestanding Golden Age statues were erected to be seen by the public, whether they were paid for with private or government funds. Privately commissioned statues of gods were placed in sanctuaries as symbols of devotion. Wealthy families paid for statues of their deceased relatives, especially if they had died young in war, to be placed above their graves as memorials of their excellence and signs of the family's social status.

REVIEW QUESTION What factors produced political change in fifth-century B.C.E. Athens?

Tradition and Innovation in Athens's Golden Age

Golden Age Athens's prosperity and international contacts created unprecedented innovations in architecture, art, drama, education, and philosophy, but central aspects of the city-state's social and religious customs remained traditional, as they did elsewhere throughout Greece. This contrast between cultural change and social continuity generated tension between the desire to innovate and the pressure to preserve traditional ways, especially concerning the conduct of women and the practice of religion. In keeping with tradition, Athenian women, along with other Greek women, were expected to limit their public role to participation in religious ceremonies. In private life they were to manage their households and, if they were poor, work to help support their families. The startling new ideas of competitive philosophers and teachers called Sophists and the Athenian philosopher Socrates' views on personal morality and responsibility caused many people to fear that the gods would become angry at the community. The most famous response to the clash between innovation and tradition was the development of publicly funded drama festivals, whose contests for tragic and comic plays examined problems in city-state life, especially the social and personal hardships caused by war.

Religious Tradition in a Period of Change

Greeks maintained religious tradition publicly by participating in the city-state's sacrifices and festivals, and privately by seeking a personal relationship with the gods in the rituals of hero cults and mystery cults. Each cult had its own rituals, including everything from large-animal sacrifices to bloodless offerings of fruits, vegetables, and small cakes. The speechwriter Lysias (c. 445–380 B.C.E.), a Syracusan residing in Athens, explained the reason for publicly funded sacrifices:

> Our ancestors handed down to us the most powerful and prosperous community in Greece by

> performing the prescribed sacrifices. It is therefore proper for us to offer the same sacrifices as they, if only for the sake of the success which has resulted from those rites.

The public slaughter of a large animal provided an occasion for the community to reaffirm its ties to the divine world and for the worshippers to benefit by feasting on the roasted meat of the sacrificed beast. For poor people, the free food provided at religious festivals might be the only meat they ever tasted.

Golden Age Athens used its riches to pay for more religious festivals than any other city-state; nearly half the days of the year included one. The biggest festivals featured parades as well as contests with valuable prizes in music, dancing, poetry, and athletics. Laborers' contracts specified how many days off they received to attend such ceremonies. Some festivals were for women only, such as the three-day festival for married women in honor of Demeter, goddess of agriculture and fertility.

Privately, people took a keen interest in affirming their personal relations with the divine. Families marked significant events such as birth, marriage, and death with prayers, rituals, and sacrifices. They honored their ancestors with offerings made at their tombs, consulted seers about the meanings of dreams and omens, and paid magicians for spells to improve their love lives or curses to harm their enemies. Particularly important were hero cults and mystery cults. Hero cults included rituals performed at the tomb of an extraordinarily famous man or woman. Heroes' remains were thought to retain special power to reveal the future by inspiring oracles, healing sickness, and providing protection in battle. The strongman Herakles (or Hercules, as the Romans spelled his name) had cults all over the Greek world because his superhuman reputation gave him international appeal. **Mystery cults** involved a set of prayers, hymns, ritual purification, sacrifices, and other forms of worship that initiated members into secret knowledge about the divine and human worlds. Initiates believed that they gained divine protection from the cult's god or gods.

The Athenian mystery cult of Demeter and her daughter Persephone attracted worshippers from all parts of the world because it offered hope for protection on earth and in the afterlife. The cult's central rite was the Mysteries, a series of initiation ceremonies into secret knowledge. So important were the Mysteries that the Greek states observed an international truce—as with the Olympic Games—to allow travel even from distant corners of the world to attend them. The Mysteries were open to any free Greek-speaking individuals—women and men, adults and children—if they were clear of ritual pollution (for example, if they had not committed sacrilege, been convicted of murder, or had recent contact with a corpse or blood from a birth). Some slaves who worked in the sanctuary were also eligible to participate. The main stage of initiation took almost two weeks, culminating in the revelation of Demeter's central secret after a day of fasting. So seriously did Greeks take the initiation that no one ever revealed the secret during the cult's thousand-year history. Being initiated promised a better fate on earth and after death. A sixth-century B.C.E. poem read, "Richly blessed is the mortal who has seen these rites; but whoever is not an initiate and has no share in them, that one never has an equal portion after death, down in the gloomy darkness."

Mystery cults reveal that ancient Greeks thought their gods required action from their worshippers to receive blessings. Preserving religious tradition mattered deeply to most people because they saw it as a safeguard against the precariousness of life.

Women, Slaves, and Metics

Women, slaves, and **metics** (foreigners granted permanent residence status in return for paying taxes and serving in the military) made up the majority of Athens's population, but they lacked political rights. Women who were citizens enjoyed legal privileges and social status denied slaves and foreigners, and they earned respect through their roles in the family and in religion. Upper-class women managed their households, visited female friends, and participated in religious cults at home and in public. Poor women worked as small-scale merchants, crafts producers, and agricultural laborers. Slaves and metics also contributed much to Athens's prosperity, but they always remained outsiders in the city-state.

Property, Inheritance, and Marriage Bearing children in marriage earned women status because it was literally the source of family—the heart of Greek society. To defend this fundamental social institution, men were expected to respect and support their wives. Childbirth was dangerous under the medical conditions of the time. In *Medea*, a play of 431 B.C.E. by Euripides, the heroine shouts in anger at her husband, who has selfishly betrayed her: "People say that

---

mystery cults: Religious worship that provided initiation into secret knowledge and divine protection, including hope for a better afterlife.

metic: A foreigner granted permanent residence status in Athens in return for paying taxes and serving in the military.

CONTRASTING VIEWS

The Nature of Women and Marriage

Greeks believed that women had different natures from men and that both genders were capable of excellence, but in their own ways (Documents 1 and 2). Marriage was supposed to bring these natures together in a partnership of complementary strengths and obligations to each other (Document 3). Marriage contracts (Document 4), similar to modern prenuptial agreements, became common to define the partnership's terms. In reading these passages, consider whether you think they would have been different if they had been written by women instead of men.

1. Pericles Addresses the Athenians in the First Year of the Peloponnesian War (431–430 B.C.E.)

According to Thucydides, Pericles concluded his Funeral Oration, a solemn public occasion commemorating the valor of soldiers killed in battle and the excellences expected of citizens, with these terse remarks to the women in the audience. His comments reveal not only the assumption that women had a different nature from men but also the assumption that women best served social harmony by not becoming subjects of gossip. He kept these comments to a bare minimum in his long speech.

If it is also appropriate now for me to say something about what excellence means for women, I will signal all my thinking with this short piece of advice to those of you present who are now widows of the war dead: your reputation will be great if you don't fall short of your innate nature and men talk about you the least whether in praise of your excellence or blaming your faults.

Source: Thucydides, *History of the Peloponnesian War*, Book 2.45. Translation by Thomas R. Martin.

2. Melanippe Explains Why Men's Criticism of Women Is Baseless (late fifth century B.C.E.)

The Athenian playwright Euripides often portrayed female characters denouncing men for misunderstanding and criticizing women. The heroine of his tragedy Melanippe the Captive *is a mother who overcomes hardship and treachery to save her family. Preserved only on damaged papyrus scraps, Melanippe's speech unfortunately breaks off before finishing.*

Men's blame and criticism of women are empty, like the twanging sound a bow string makes without an arrow. Women are superior to men, and I'll demonstrate it. They make contracts with no need of witnesses [to swear they are honest]. They manage their households and keep safe the valuable possessions, shipped from abroad, that they have inside their homes. Without a woman, no household is elegant or happy. And then in the matter of people's relationship with the gods—this I judge to be most important of all—there we have the greatest role. For women prophesy the will of Apollo in his oracles [at Delphi], and at the hallowed oracle of Dodona by the sacred oak tree a woman reveals the will of Zeus to all Greeks who seek it. And then there are the sacred rites of initiation performed for the Fates and the Goddesses Without Names: these can't be done with holiness by men, but women make them flourish in every way. In this way women's role in religion is right and proper.

Therefore, should anyone put down women? Won't those men stop their empty fault-finding, the ones who strongly believe that all women should be blamed if a single one is found to be bad? I will make a distinction with the following argument: nothing is worse than a bad woman, but nothing is more surpassingly superior than a worthy one.

Source: Euripides, *Melanippe the Captive*, fragment 660 Mette. Translation by Thomas R. Martin.

3. Socrates Discusses Gender Roles in Marriage (late fifth century B.C.E.)

In this passage written by his follower and famous soldier Xenophon, Socrates discusses family life because it reveals the qualities of women as well as men. His analysis is part of his quest to discover the nature of human excellence. Socrates' upper-class friend Ischomachus has, as was common, married a young woman (whose name is not given), and the philosopher is quizzing him about their marriage. The new husband explains that it was a partnership based on the complementary natures of male and female.

Ischomachus: I said to her: . . . I for my sake and your parents for your sake [arranged our marriage] by considering who would be the best partner for forming a household and having children. I chose you, and your parents chose me as the best they could find. If God should give us children, we will then plan how to raise them in the best possible way. For our partnership provides us this good: the best

we women lead a safe life at home, while men have to go to war. What fools they are! I would much rather fight in battle three times than give birth to a child even once."

Athenian wives were expected to be partners with their husbands in owning and managing the household's property to help the family thrive. (See "Contrasting Views," above.) Rich women acquired property, including land—the most valued possession in Greek society because it could be farmed or rented out for income—through inheritance and dowry. A husband often had to put up valuable land of his own as collateral to guarantee repayment to his wife of the amount of her dowry if he mutual support and the best maintenance in our old age. We have this sharing now in our household, because I've contributed all that I own to the common resources of the household, and so have you. We're not going to count up who brought more property, because the one who turns out to be the better partner in a marriage has made the greater contribution.

Ischomachus's wife: But how will I be able to partner you? What ability do I have? Everything rests on you. My mother told me my job was to behave with thoughtful moderation.

Ischomachus: Well, my father told me the same thing. Thoughtful moderation for a man, as for a woman, means behaving in such a way that their possessions will be in the best possible condition and will increase as much as possible by good and just means. . . . So, you must do what the gods made you naturally capable of and what our law requires. . . . With great forethought the gods have yoked together male and female so that they can form the most beneficial partnership. This yoking together keeps living creatures from disappearing by producing children, and it provides offspring to look after parents in their old age, at least for people. [He then explains that human survival requires outdoor work — to raise crops and livestock — and indoor work — to preserve food, raise infants, and manufacture clothing.] . . . And since the work both outside and inside required effort and care, God, it seems to me, from the start fashioned women's nature for indoor work and men's for outdoor. Therefore he made men's bodies and spirits more able to endure cold and heat and travel and marches, giving them the outside jobs, while assigning indoor tasks to women, it seems, because their bodies are less hardy. . . .

But since both men and women have to manage things, [God] gave them equal shares in memory and attentiveness; you can't tell which gender has more of these qualities. And God gave both an equal ability to practice self-control, with the power to benefit the most from this quality going to whoever is better at it—whether man or woman. Precisely because they have different natures, they have greater need of each other and their yoking together is the most beneficial, with the one being capable where the other one is lacking. And as God has made them partners for their children, the law makes them partners for the household.

Source: Xenophon, *Oeconomicus* 7.10–30. Translation by Thomas R. Martin.

4. Greek Marriage Contract from Egypt (311–310 B.C.E.)

Greeks living abroad customarily drew up written contracts to define the duties of each partner in a marriage because they wanted their traditional expectations to remain legally binding regardless of the local laws. The earliest surviving such contract comes from Elephantine, the site of a Greek military garrison far up the Nile.

Marriage contract of Heraclides and Demetria. Heraclides [of Temnos] takes as his lawful wife Demetria of Cos from her father Leptines of Cos and her mother Philotis. He is a free person; she is a free person. She brings a dowry of clothing and jewelry worth 1,000 drachmas. Heraclides must provide Demetria with everything appropriate for a freeborn wife. We will live together in what ever location Leptines and Heraclides together decide is best.

If Demetria is apprehended doing anything bad that shames her husband, she will forfeit all her dowry. Heraclides will have to prove any allegations against her in the presence of three men, whom they both must approve. It will be illegal for Heraclides to bring home another wife to Demetria's harm, or to father children by another woman, or to do anything bad to Demetria for any reason. If he is caught doing any of these things and Demetria proves it in the presence of three men whom they both approve, Heraclides must return her dowry in full and pay her 1,000 drachmas additional. Demetria and those who help her in getting this payment will have legal standing to act against Heraclides and all his property on land and sea. . . . Each shall have the right to keep a personal copy of this contract. [A list of witnesses follows.]

Source: O. Rubensohn, ed., *Elephantine Papyri* (Berlin: 1907), no. 1. Translation by Thomas R. Martin.

Questions to Consider

1. **What evidence and arguments for differing natures for men and women do these documents offer?**
2. **Do you think Athenian women would have found these arguments convincing? Why or why not?**

squandered it through bad investments or reckless spending.

Like fathers, mothers were expected to hand down property to their children to keep it in the family through male heirs, since only sons could maintain their father's family line; married daughters became members of their husband's family. The goal of keeping property in the possession of male heirs shows up most clearly in Athenian law about heiresses (daughters whose fathers died without any sons, which happened in about one of every five families): the closest male relative of the heiress's father — her official guardian after her father's death — was required to marry her. The goal was to produce a son to inherit the father's property. This rule applied regardless of whether either party was already married (unless the heiress had sons); the heiress and the male relative were both supposed to divorce their present spouses and marry each other. In real life, however, people often used legal technicalities to get around this requirement so that they could remain with their chosen partners.

Requiring property to be passed down in this way therefore met two traditional goals of male-dominated Greek society: continuing the father's bloodline and preventing property from piling up in the hands of unmarried women (and therefore out of the control of men). At Sparta, the famous scholar Aristotle (384–322 B.C.E.) reported, the inheritance laws were different (and, in his opinion, flawed); he claimed that women came to own 40 percent of Spartan territory.

Women's Daily Lives Tradition restricted women's freedom of movement in public; men claimed that this restriction protected women by limiting opportunities for seducers and rapists. Men wanted to ensure that their children were truly theirs, that family property went only to genuine heirs, and that the city had only legitimate citizens. Well-off women in the city were expected to avoid contact with male strangers and mainly to spend their time at home or with women friends in their houses. Recent research has discredited the idea that Greek homes had a defined "women's quarter" to which women were confined. Rather, women were granted privacy in certain rooms. If the house included an interior courtyard, women could walk there in the open air and talk with other members of the household, male and female. In the safety of her home, a well-to-do woman would spin wool for clothing, converse with visiting friends, direct her children, supervise the slaves, and present her opinions on various matters, including politics, to the men of the house as they came and went. Poor women had little time for such activities because they—like their husbands, sons, and brothers—had to leave the house, usually a crowded rental apartment, to set up small stalls to sell bread, vegetables, simple clothing, or trinkets they had made.

An elite woman careful of her reputation left home only for appropriate reasons, such as religious festivals, funerals, childbirths at the houses of relatives and friends, and trips to workshops to buy shoes or other domestic articles. Often her husband escorted her, but sometimes she took only a slave, setting her own itinerary.

Most upper-class women probably viewed their limited contact with men outside the household as a badge of superior social status. For example, a pale complexion, from staying inside so much, was much admired as a sign of an enviable life of leisure and wealth. Many women, unaware of the health risk, used powdered white lead as makeup to give themselves a fashionable lack of color in their skin.

Staying close to home and safeguarding one's reputation could afford some advantages. Women who bore legitimate children gained increased respect and freedom, as an Athenian man explained in his speech (written by Lysias) defending himself for having killed his wife's lover:

> After my marriage, I at first didn't interfere with my wife very much, but neither did I allow her too much independence. I kept an eye on her. . . . But after she had a baby, I started to trust her more and put her in charge of all my things, believing we now had the closest of relationships.

Vase Painting of a Woman Buying Shoes (detail)
Greek vases frequently displayed scenes from daily life instead of mythological stories. Here, a woman is being fitted for a pair of custom-made shoes by a craftsman and his apprentice. Her husband has accompanied her, as was often the case for shopping, and he appears to be participating in the discussion of the purchase. This vase was painted in so-called black-figure technique, in which the figures are dark and have their details incised on a background of red clay. *(The Plousios Painter, Two-handled jar [amphora], Greek, Late Archaic Period, about 500–490 B.C.E. Place of manufacture: Greece, Attica, Athens. Ceramic, Black Figure. H: 36.1 cm. [14 3/16 in.]; diameter: 25.9 cm. [10 3/16 in.]. Museum of Fine Arts, Boston, Henry Lillie Pierce Fund, 01.8035. Photograph © 2011 Museum of Fine Arts, Boston.)*

Vase Painting of a Symposium
Upper-class Greek men often spent their evenings at a symposium, a drinking party that always included much conversation and usually featured music and entertainers. Wives were not included. The discussions could range widely, from literature to politics to philosophy. The man on the right is about to fling the dregs of his wine, playing a messy game called *kottabos*. The nudity of the female musician indicates she is a hired prostitute. *(Detail, Foundry Painter—Red-figured cup with symposium scene. Reproduced by permission of the Syndics of the Fitzwilliam Museum, Cambridge.)*

Bearing male children brought a woman special honor because sons meant security. Sons could appear in court to support their parents in lawsuits and protect them in the streets of Athens, which for most of its history had no regular police force. By law, sons were required to support elderly parents. So intense was the pressure to produce sons that stories circulated of women who smuggled in male babies born to slaves and passed them off as their own.

Extraordinary Women A few women in Athens escaped traditional restrictions by working as what Greeks called a **hetaira** ("companion"). Hetairas, usually foreigners, were unmarried, physically attractive, witty in speech, and skilled in music and poetry. Men might hire them to entertain at a symposium (a drinking party to which wives were not invited) with their playful conversation. Their much-admired skill at clever teasing and verbal insults allowed companions a freedom of speech denied to "proper" women. Hetairas nevertheless lacked the social status and respectability that wives and mothers possessed.

Sometimes hetairas also sold sex for a high price, and they could control their own sexuality by choosing their clients. Athenian men (but not women) could buy sex as they pleased without legal hindrance. "Certainly you don't think men father children out of sexual desire?" wrote the upper-class author Xenophon. "The streets and the brothels are swarming with ways to take care of that." Men (but, again, not women) could also have sex freely with female or male slaves, who could not refuse their masters.

Less successful hetairas lived precarious lives of exploitation and even violence at the hands of their male customers, but the most skilled of them attracted admirers from the highest levels of society and earned enough to live in luxury on their own. The most famous hetaira in Athens was Aspasia from Miletus, who became Pericles' lover and bore him a son. She dazzled men with her brilliant talk and wide knowledge. Pericles fell so deeply in love with her that he wanted to marry her, despite his own law of 451 B.C.E. restricting citizenship, which said that their children would not be citizens without a special law passed by the assembly.

Great riches could also free a woman from tradition, allowing her to speak to men openly and bluntly. The most outspoken Athenian woman of wealth was Elpinike, Cimon's sister. When controversy erupted over a speech in which Pericles supported Athens's attack on a rebellious Delian League ally, Elpinike publicly criticized him by sarcastically remarking in front of a group of women who were praising him, "This really is wonderful, Pericles. . . . You have caused the loss of many good citizens, not in battle against Phoenicians or Persians . . . but in suppressing an allied city of fellow Greeks."

Other sources, especially comic drama and fourth-century B.C.E. oratory, imply that not-so-rich women, too, had strong opinions about politics. They customarily expressed their views to their husbands and male relatives at home in private.

---

hetaira (heh TYE ruh): A witty and attractive woman who charged fees to entertain at a symposium.

Slaves and Metics Traditional social and legal restrictions in Golden Age Athens meant slaves and metics counted as outsiders, despite all the work they did in and for the city-state. Individuals and the city-state alike owned slaves, who could be purchased from traders or bred in the household. Unwanted newborns abandoned by their parents (an accepted practice called infant exposure) were often picked up by others and raised as slaves. Athens's commercial growth in this period increased the demand for slaves, who in Pericles' time made up around 100,000 of the city-state's total of perhaps 250,000 inhabitants (the numbers are extremely uncertain estimates from ancient reports of the army's numbers and probable household sizes). Slaves worked in homes, on farms, and in crafts shops; rowed alongside their owners in the navy; and, if they were really unlucky, toiled in Athens's dangerous silver mines. Unlike those at Sparta, Athens's slaves almost never rebelled, probably because they originated from too many different places to be able to unite. Many mining slaves did run away to the Spartan base established in Athenian territory during the Peloponnesian War; the Spartans probably resold them.

Golden Age Athens's wealth and cultural activities attracted many metics, who streamed to the city from all around the Mediterranean, hoping to make money as importers, crafts producers, entertainers, and laborers. By the start of the Peloponnesian War in 431 B.C.E., metics constituted perhaps 50,000 to 75,000 of the estimated 150,000 free men, women, and children in the city-state. Metics paid for the privilege of living and working in Athens through a special foreigners' tax and military service. Athenians valued metics' contributions to the city's prosperity, but their insistence on exclusive citizenship meant they were unwilling to share its legal and financial benefits with immigrants.

Innovative Ideas in Education, Philosophy, History, and Medicine

Building on the intellectual foundation of rationalism that emerged in the Archaic Age, thinkers in the Greek Golden Age developed innovative ideas in education, philosophy, history, and medicine. These innovations delighted some fifth-century Greeks, but they deeply upset others, who feared that these drastic changes from older ways of life and thought would undermine the traditions that held society together, especially religion, thereby provoking punishment from the angry gods. These controversial changes opened the way to the development of scientific study as an enduring characteristic of Western civilization.

Education and philosophy provided the hottest battles between tradition and innovation. Earlier, education had stressed the preservation of old ways. Parents controlled what children learned at home and from hired tutors (there were still no public schools). Controversy erupted when men known as Sophists appeared in the mid-fifth century B.C.E. and offered, for pay, classes to teenage and young-adult males that taught nontraditional philosophy and religious doctrines, as well as novel techniques for public speaking. Some philosophers' ideas about the nature of the cosmos challenged traditional religious views. The philosopher Socrates, who did not work as a Sophist, expressed such strict views on personal morality and responsibility that he provoked an equally fierce controversy. In history writing and medicine, innovators created models of interpretation and scientific method that stimulated argument over how to understand human experience and the body.

Disagreement over whether these changes in intellectual life were dangerous for Athenian society added to the political tension that had arisen at Athens by the 430s B.C.E. concerning Athens's harsh treatment of its own allies and its economic sanctions against Sparta's allies. This interaction occurred because the political, intellectual, and religious dimensions of life in ancient Athens were closely intertwined. Athenians would connect philosophic ideas about the nature of justice with their decisions about the city-state's domestic and foreign policy, while also being concerned about the attitude of the gods toward the community. (See Document, "Athenian Regulations for a Rebellious Ally," page 93.)

Education The only formal education available came from private teachers, to whom well-to-do families sent their sons to learn to read, write, play a musical instrument or sing, and develop athletic skills suitable for war. Physical training was considered a vital part of men's education because it both made their bodies beautiful and prepared them for service in the militia (to which they could be summoned anytime between ages eighteen and sixty). Therefore, men exercised nude every day in gymnasia, public open-air facilities paid for by wealthy families. Men frequently discussed politics and exchanged news at a gymnasium. The daughters of wealthy families usually received instruction at home from educated slaves, who were expensive because they were rare. The young girls learned reading, writing, and arithmetic so that they would be ready to help their future husbands by managing the household.

DOCUMENT

Athenian Regulations for a Rebellious Ally

The city-state of Chalcis on the island of Euboea rebelled from the Athenian-dominated Delian League in 446 B.C.E. After defeating the rebels, the Athenians forced the Chalcidians to swear compliance with new regulations, which were inscribed on stone in both cities. The text reveals that the terms were not the same for the two sides.

The Athenian Council and the jurors shall swear an oath in this form: "I will not expel Chalcidians from Chalcis nor will I reduce the city to ruins nor deprive any individual of his citizen rights nor punish him with exile nor imprison him nor kill him nor take property from anyone who has not had a trial without approval from the People [i.e., the assembly] of the Athenians, nor will I have a vote taken against the community or any single individual without their being called to trial, and when their representatives arrive, I will introduce them to the Council and People within ten days when I am in charge of the procedure, so far as I am able. These things I will guarantee the Chalcidians if they obey the People of the Athenians."

The Chalcidians shall swear an oath in this form: "I will not rebel from the People of the Athenians either by cunning or by any way at all either by word or by deed, and I will not obey anyone who rebels, and if anyone does rebel, I will denounce him to the Athenians, and I will pay the dues to the Athenians which I persuade the Athenians [to levy on me], and as an ally I will be the best and most just that I am able, and I will give support to and defend the People of the Athenians, if anyone wrongs the People of the Athenians, and I will obey the People of the Athenians."

Source: *Inscriptiones Graecae*, 3rd ed. (1981), no. 40. Translation by Thomas R. Martin.

Question to Consider

- **Would you regard the terms of the oaths each side was required to swear as harsh, given the circumstances?**

Poor girls and boys received no formal education; they learned a trade and perhaps a little reading, writing, and calculating by assisting their parents in their daily work or by serving as apprentices to skilled crafts workers. Scholars disagree about how many people could read well, but most likely they were a minority. Those with weak reading skills, however, could always find someone to read aloud any written text. In fact, oral communication was at the center of Greek life, whether in political speeches or in songs, plays, and stories from literature and history.

After their early education, young men from prosperous families would learn how to participate in public life, and especially Athenian democracy,

The Masculine Ideal

This sculpture of a male warrior/athlete, found in a shipwreck off the coast of Riace in southern Italy, was cast in bronze in the mid-fifth century B.C.E. Greeks preferred bronze over marble for top-rank statues, but few have survived because they were usually melted down and their metal reused (e.g., to make guns in later ages). The figure's relaxed pose displays the asymmetry—the head looking to one side, the arms in different positions, the torso tilted—that made Greek statues from the Classical Age appear less stiff than Archaic Age ones. The cap on his head was what warriors wore to cushion their helmet. The body displays the ideal build that Greek men strove to achieve through daily workouts. For male statues, nudity indicated a heroic ideal. *(Eric Lessing/Art Resource, NY.)*

not by taking formal lessons but by observing their fathers, uncles, and other older men as they debated in the Council of Five Hundred and the assembly, served in public office, and spoke in court. Often an older man would choose an adolescent boy as his special favorite to educate. The teenager would learn about public life by spending time with the older man. During the day the boy would listen to his mentor talking politics in the agora, help him perform his duties in public office, and work out with him in a gymnasium. They would spend their evenings at a symposium, whose agenda could range from serious political and philosophical discussion to riotous partying.

This older mentor/younger favorite relationship could lead to sexual relations between the youth and the older male, the latter of whom was usually married. Sex between mentors and favorites was considered acceptable in elite circles in many city-states, including Athens, Sparta, and Thebes. Other city-states banned this behavior because they believed, as the Athenian author Xenophon suggests, that it sprang from an adult man's shameful inability to control his lustful desires.

Sophists and Philosophers as a Threat to Tradition

By the time of radical democracy in Athens, young men eager to develop the essential political skill of public speaking could obtain higher education in a new way: by paying an expensive professional teacher to train them. These teachers, called **Sophists** ("men of wisdom"), sparked controversy because they strongly challenged traditional beliefs by teaching new skills of persuasion in speaking and new ways of thinking based on rational arguments. The term *sophist* later acquired a negative connotation (preserved in the English word *sophistry*) because clever Sophists could use complex reasoning to make deceptive arguments.

Starting about 450 B.C.E., Athens's booming economy and lively intellectual environment attracted Sophists from around the Greek world. These individual entrepreneurs competed with one another to attract pupils who could pay the hefty prices they charged for their innovative courses. As in every part of Greek intellectual life, the competition for prominence was intense. Sophists strove for excellence by offering specialized training in rhetoric—the skill of speaking persuasively. Every ambitious man wanted rhetorical training because it promised power in Athens's assembly, councils, and courts. The Sophists alarmed many tradition-minded Athenians, who feared their teachings would undermine established social and political traditions. Speakers trained by silver-tongued Sophists, they believed, might be able to mislead the assembly while promoting their private interests.

Prominent older leaders, Pericles among them, often joined the Sophists for discussions. The most notorious Sophist was Protagoras, a contemporary of Pericles from Abdera, in northern Greece. Protagoras moved to Athens around 450 B.C.E., when he was around forty, and spent most of his career there. His views on the nature of truth and morality outraged many Athenians: he argued that rationally there could be no absolute standard of truth because every issue had two irreconcilable sides. For example, if one person feeling a breeze thinks it warm whereas another person thinks it cool, neither judgment can be absolutely correct because the wind simply is warm to one and cool to the other. Protagoras summed up this subjectivism—the belief that there is no absolute reality behind and independent of appearances—in his work *Truth*: "The human being is the measure of all things, of the things that are that they are, and of the things that are not that they are not."

The subjectivism of Protagoras and other Sophists contained two main ideas: (1) human institutions and values are only matters of convention, custom, or *nomos* ("law") and not creations of *physis* ("nature"), and (2) since truth is subjective, speakers should be able to argue either side of a question with equal persuasiveness and rationality. The first view implied that traditional human institutions were arbitrary and changing rather than natural and permanent, while the second seemed to many people to make questions of right and wrong irrelevant. (See Document, "Sophists Argue Both Sides of a Case," page 95.)

The Sophists' critics therefore accused them of teaching moral relativism and threatening the shared public values of the democratic city-state. Aristophanes, author of comic plays, satirized Sophists for harming Athens by instructing students in persuasive techniques "to make the weaker argument the stronger." Protagoras, for one, energetically responded that his doctrines were not hostile to democracy, arguing that every person had a natural capability for excellence and that human society depended on the rule of law based on a sense of justice. Members of a community, he explained, must be persuaded to obey the laws, not because laws were based on absolute truth, which did not exist,

---

Sophists (SAH fists): Competitive intellectuals and teachers in ancient Greece who offered expensive courses in persuasive public speaking and new ways of philosophic and religious thinking beginning around 450 B.C.E.

DOCUMENT

Sophists Argue Both Sides of a Case

The Sophist Protagoras taught his students to argue both sides of any case, but he insisted he did not teach this skill for immoral purposes. Some teachers following in his footsteps were less ethical. This excerpt comes from an anonymous handbook of the late fifth century B.C.E. entitled Double Arguments, *which provided examples of how Sophists could make arguments in the fashion of Protagoras.*

Greek philosophers put forward double arguments concerning the good and the bad. Some say that the good is one thing and the bad another, but others say that they are the same, and that a thing might be good for some persons but bad for others, or at one time good and at another time bad for the same person. I myself agree with those who hold the latter opinion, which I shall examine using as an example human life and its concern for food, drink, and sexual pleasures: these things are bad for a man if he is sick but good if he is healthy and needs them. And, further, overindulgence in these things is bad for the one who overindulges but good for those who make a profit by selling these things. And again, sickness is bad for the sick but good for the doctors. And death is bad for those who die but good for the undertakers and makers of grave monuments. . . . Shipwrecks are bad for the ship owners but good for the ship builders. When tools are blunted and worn away it is bad for others but good for the blacksmith. And if a pot gets smashed, this is bad for everyone else but good for the potter. When shoes wear out and fall apart it is bad for others but good for the shoemaker. . . . In the *stadion* race for runners, victory is good for the winner but bad for the losers.

Source: *Dissoi Logoi* 1.1–6. Translation adapted from Rosamund Kent Sprague, ed., *The Older Sophists* (Columbia: University of South Carolina Press, 1972), 279–80.

Question to Consider

■ **Do you think it is impossible ever to reach a firm conclusion about whether something is good or bad? Why or why not?**

but because rationally it was advantageous for everyone to be law-abiding. A thief, for example, who might claim that stealing was a part of nature, would have to be persuaded by reason that a man-made law forbidding theft was to his advantage because it protected his own property and the community in which he, like all humans, had to live in order to survive.

Even more disturbing to Athenians than the Sophists' ideas about truth were their ideas about religion. Protagoras angered people with his agnosticism (the belief that supernatural phenomena are unknowable): "Whether the gods exist I cannot discover, nor what their form is like, for there are many impediments to knowledge, [such as] the obscurity of the subject and the brevity of human life." His implication that even religious belief must be based on knowledge acquired through evidence was in keeping with the development of Greek rationalism and scientific thought, but it upset those who thought he was saying that conventional religion had no meaning. They worried that his words would provoke divine anger against the community that gave him a home.

Other fifth-century B.C.E. philosophers and thinkers, although not working as Sophists, also proposed new scientific theories about the nature of the cosmos and the origin of religion that offended believers in traditional religion. A philosopher friend of Pericles, for example, argued that the sun was a lump of flaming rock, not a god. Another philosopher invented an atomic theory of matter to explain how change was constant in the universe. Everything, he argued, consisted of tiny, invisible particles in eternal motion. Their random collisions caused them to combine and recombine in an infinite variety of forms, with no divine purpose guiding their collisions and combinations. These ideas seemed to invalidate traditional religion, which explained events as governed by the gods' will. Even worse was the idea advanced by the wealthy aristocrat Critias, who wrote a play in which religion was denounced as a clever but false system invented by powerful men to fool ordinary people into obeying moral standards through fear of divine punishment.

The Sophists' techniques of persuasion and ways of thought based on rational arguments helped their students forcefully advance their political opinions and defend themselves in court. But because only wealthy men could afford their classes, the Sophists threatened Athenian democracy by giving yet another advantage to the rich in the assembly's debates or speeches in court. In addition, moral relativism and the physical explanation of the universe struck many Athenians as dangerous: they feared that such teachings, by offending the gods, would destroy the divine goodwill they believed Athens enjoyed. These ideas so infuriated some Athenians that in the 430s B.C.E. they sponsored a law allowing citizens to bring charges of impiety against "those who fail to respect divine things or teach theories about the cosmos." Not even Pericles could prevent his philosopher friend from being convicted on this charge and expelled from Athens.

Socrates on Ethics Socrates (469–399 B.C.E.), the most famous philosopher of the Golden Age, became well known in his home state of Athens during this troubled time of the 430s, when people were anxious not just about the Sophists but also about the growing threat of war with Sparta. Socrates devoted his life to questioning people about their beliefs, but he insisted he was not a Sophist because he offered no courses and took no pay. Above all, he fought against the view that justice should be equated with power over others. By insisting that true justice was better than injustice under any and all circumstances, he gave a new direction to Greek philosophy: an emphasis on ethics (the study of ideal human values and moral duties). Although other thinkers before him (especially poets and authors of plays) had dealt with similar issues, Socrates was the first philosopher to make ethics his central concern.

Statuette of the Philosopher Socrates
The controversial Socrates, the most famous philosopher of Athens in the fifth century B.C.E., joked that he had a homely face and a bulging stomach. This small statue is an artist's impression of what Socrates looked like; we cannot be sure of the truth. Socrates was renowned for his irony, and he may have purposely exaggerated his physical unattractiveness to show his disdain for ordinary standards of beauty and his own emphasis on the quality of one's soul as the true measure of one's worth. Compare his body to that of the athletes shown in the vase painting on page 50 or of the statue of the warrior/athlete on page 93. *(Erich Lessing/Art Resource, NY.)*

Socrates lived an eccentric life that attracted constant attention. Sporting a stomach, in his words, "a bit too big to be convenient," he wore the same cheap cloak summer and winter and always went barefoot no matter how cold the weather. His physical stamina—including both his tirelessness as a soldier in Athens's infantry and his ability to outdrink anyone at a symposium—was legendary. Unlike the high-priced Sophists, he lived in poverty and disdained material possessions, though somehow he managed to support a wife and several children. He probably inherited some money and also accepted gifts from wealthy admirers.

Socrates spent his time in conversations all over Athens: participating in symposia, strolling in the agora, or watching young men exercise in a gymnasium. In this behavior he resembled his fellow Athenians, who placed great value on the importance and pleasure of speaking with one another at length. He wrote nothing. Our knowledge of his ideas comes from others' writings, especially those of his famous follower Plato (c. 428–348 B.C.E.). Plato portrays Socrates as a relentless questioner of his fellow citizens, foreign friends, and leading Sophists. Socrates' questions had the goal of making his conversational partners examine the basic assumptions of their way of life. Giving few answers, Socrates never directly instructed anyone. Instead, he led people to draw conclusions in response to his probing questions and refutations of their cherished assumptions. Today this procedure is called the **Socratic method**.

Socrates frequently upset and even outraged people because his method made them feel ignorant and baffled. His questions forced them to admit that they did not in fact know what they had assumed they knew very well. Even more painful to them was Socrates' fiercely argued view that the way they lived their lives—pursuing success in politics or business or art—was merely an excuse for avoiding the hard work of understanding and de-

---

Socratic method: The Athenian philosopher Socrates' method of teaching through conversation, in which he asked probing questions to make his listeners examine their most cherished assumptions.

veloping genuine aretê ("excellence"). Socrates insisted that he was ignorant of the best definition of excellence and what was best for human beings, but that his wisdom consisted of knowing that he did not know. He vowed he was trying to improve, not undermine, people's ethical beliefs, even though, as a friend put it, a conversation with Socrates made a man feel numb—as if a jellyfish had stung him.

Socrates especially wanted to use reasoning to discover universal, objective standards that justified individual ethics. He attacked the Sophists for their relativistic claim that conventional standards of right and wrong were merely "the chains that handcuff nature." This view, he protested, equated human happiness with power and "getting more."

Socrates insisted that the only way to achieve true happiness was to behave in accordance with a universal, transcendent standard of just behavior that people could understand rationally. Essentially, he argued that just behavior and excellence were identical to knowledge, and that true knowledge of justice would inevitably lead people to choose good over evil. They would therefore have truly happy lives, regardless of how rich or poor they were. Since Socrates believed that ethical knowledge was all a person needed for the good life, he argued that no one knowingly behaved unjustly and that behaving justly was always in the individual's interest. It was simply ignorant to believe that the best life was the life of unlimited power to pursue whatever one desired. The most desirable human life was concerned with excellence and guided by reason, not by dreams of personal gain.

Though very different from the Sophists' doctrines, Socrates' ideas proved just as disturbing because they rejected the Athenians' traditional way of life. His ridicule of commonly accepted ideas about the importance of wealth and public success angered many people. Unhappiest of all were the fathers whose sons, after listening to Socrates' questions reduce someone to utter bewilderment, came home to try the same technique on their parents, employing rational arguments to criticize as old-fashioned and worthless the values their family held dear. Men who experienced this reversal of the traditional educational hierarchy—the father was supposed to educate the son—felt that Socrates was undermining the stability of society by making young men question Athenian traditions. Socrates evidently did not teach women, but Plato portrays him as ready to learn from exceptional women, such as Pericles' companion Aspasia.

The worry that Socrates' ideas presented a danger to conventional society inspired Aristophanes to write his comedy *The Clouds* (423 B.C.E.). This play portrays Socrates as a cynical Sophist who, for a fee, offers instruction in Protagoras's technique of making the weaker argument the stronger. When the curriculum of Socrates' school, The Thinkery, transforms a youth into a public speaker who argues that a son has the right to beat his parents, his father burns the place down. None of these plot details seems to have been real; what was genuine was the fear that Socrates' radical views on individual morality endangered the city-state's traditional practices. This anxiety only grew worse as the Peloponnesian War dragged on with ever more casualties, and many citizens began to feel that their best hope for victory lay in strengthening tradition, not weakening it.

History Writing | Just as the Sophists and Socrates antagonized many people with their new ideas, the inventors of history writing drew attention because they took a critical attitude in their descriptions of the past. Herodotus of Halicarnassus (c. 485–425 B.C.E.) and Thucydides of Athens (c. 455–399 B.C.E.) became Greece's most famous historians and established Western civilization's tradition of history writing. The fifth-century B.C.E.'s unprecedented events—a coalition Greek victory over the world's greatest power and then the longest war ever between Greeks—apparently inspired them to create history as a subject based on strenuous research. They explained that they wrote histories because they wanted people to remember the past and to understand why wars had taken place.

In the 420s B.C.E., Herodotus finished a long, groundbreaking work called *Histories* ("inquiries" in Greek) to explain the Persian Wars as a clash between the cultures of the East and West. A typically competitive Greek intellectual, Herodotus—who by Roman times had become known as the Father of History—made the justifiable claim that he surpassed all those who had previously recorded the past by taking an in-depth and investigative approach to evidence, examining the culture of non-Greeks as well as Greeks, and expressing explicit and implicit judgments about people's actions. Because Herodotus recognized the necessity (and the delight) of studying other cultures with respect, he pushed his inquiries deep into the past, looking for long-standing cultural differences to help explain the Persian-Greek conflict. He showed that Greeks and non-Greeks were equally capable of good and evil. Unlike poets and playwrights, he focused on human psychology and interactions, not the gods, as the driving forces in history.

Thucydides redirected historical inquiry—and competed with Herodotus—by writing contemporary history and inventing the kind of analysis of power that today informs political science. His *History of the Peloponnesian War*, published after the end of the war, made power politics, not divine intervention, history's primary force. Deeply affected by the war's brutality, he used his experiences as a politician and failed military commander (he was exiled for losing a key outpost) to make his narrative vivid and frank in describing human moral failings. His insistence that historians should energetically seek out the most reliable sources and evaluate their testimony with objectivity set a high standard for later writers. Like Herodotus, he challenged tradition by revealing that Greek history was not just a story of glorious achievements but also had its share of shameful actions (such as the Athenian punishment of the Melians in the Peloponnesian War — see page 103).

Hippocrates and the Birth of Scientific Medicine

Hippocrates of Cos, a fifth-century B.C.E. contemporary of Thucydides, challenged tradition by grounding medical diagnosis and treatment in clinical observation. His fame continues today in the oath bearing his name that doctors swear at the beginning of their professional careers. Previously, medicine had depended on magic and ritual. Illness was believed to be caused by evil spirits, and various cults in Greek religion offered healing to patients through divine intervention. Competing to refute these earlier doctors' theories, Hippocrates insisted that only physical factors caused disease. He may have been the author of the view, dominant in later medicine, that four humors (fluids) made up the human body: blood, phlegm, black bile, and yellow bile. Health depended on keeping the proper balance among them; being healthy was to be in "good humor." This system for understanding the body corresponded to the division of the inanimate world into four parts: the elements earth, air, fire, and water.

Hippocrates taught that the physician's most important duty was to base his knowledge on careful observation of patients and their response to different treatments. Clinical experience, not abstract theory or religious belief, was the proper foundation for establishing effective cures. By putting his innovative ideas and practices to the test in competition with those of traditional medicine, Hippocrates established the truth of his principle, which later became a cornerstone of scientific medicine.

The Development of Greek Tragedy

Along with history and philosophy, Greek ideas about the problematic relationship between gods and humans inspired Golden Age Athens's most prominent cultural innovation: tragic drama. Plays called tragedies were presented over three days at the major annual festival of the god Dionysus in a contest for playwrights, in keeping with the competitive spirit characteristic of Greek life. Tragedies presented shocking stories involving fierce conflict and characters representing powerful forces, usually from myth but occasionally from recent history, that could be related to controversial issues in contemporary Athens. Therefore, these plays stimulated their large audiences to ponder the danger that ignorance, arrogance, and violence presented to the city-state's democratic society. Following the tradition of Homer and Hesiod, Golden Age playwrights explored top-

Divine Healing

This relief sculpture shows the god Asclepius healing Archinus (his name is inscribed at the bottom). Patients sought Asclepius's help by going to sleep and dreaming in his sanctuary, as shown at right. The god in the form of a snake is licking the patient's shoulder to heal it. At left, the god's power is symbolized by showing him as a heroic-sized figure, who is directly treating the injured shoulder. The Athenians brought Asclepius's cult from abroad to their city in 420 B.C.E. during the Peloponnesian War to try to alleviate epidemic disease and war injuries. The famous doctor and medical theorist Hippocrates challenged tradition by rejecting this kind of divine healing. *(The Art Archive/National Archeological Museum, Athens/Gianni Dagli Orti.)*

ics ranging from the roots of good and evil to the nature of individual freedom and responsibility in the family and the political community. As with other ancient texts, most of the Greek tragedies have not survived: only thirty-three still exist of the hundreds that were produced at Athens.

Athenian tragedy was a competitive public art form subsidized by tax revenues and mandatory contributions by the rich. The competition took place every year, with an official choosing three authors from a pool of applicants. Each of these finalists presented four plays during the festival: three tragedies in a row (a trilogy), followed by a semicomic play featuring satyrs (mythical half-man, half-animal beings) to end the day on a lighter note. Tragedies were written in verses of solemn language, and many were based on stories about the violent possibilities when gods and humans interacted. The plots often ended with a resolution to the trouble—but only after enormous suffering.

The performances of tragedies in Athens, as in many other cities in Greece, took place during the daytime in an outdoor theater. The theater at Athens was sacred to the god Dionysus and built into the southern slope of the acropolis; it held about fourteen thousand spectators overlooking an open, circular area in front of a slightly raised stage. A tragedy had eighteen cast members, all of whom were men: three actors to play the speaking roles (both male and female characters) and fifteen chorus members. Although the chorus leader sometimes engaged in dialogue with the actors, the chorus primarily performed songs and dances in the circular area in front of the stage, called the orchestra.

A successful tragedy offered a vivid spectacle. The chorus wore elaborate costumes and performed intricate dance routines. The actors, who wore masks, used broad gestures and booming voices to reach the upper tier of seats. A powerful voice was crucial to a tragic actor because words represented the heart of the plays, in which dialogue and long speeches predominated over physical action. Special effects were part of the spectacle. For example, a crane allowed actors playing the roles of gods to fly suddenly onto the stage. The actors playing lead roles, called the protagonists ("first competitors"), competed against one another for the designation of best actor. So important was a first-rate protagonist to a play's success that actors were assigned by lottery to the competing playwrights to give all three an equal chance to have a winning cast. Great protagonists became enormously popular, although they were not usually members of the social elite.

Playwrights were from the elite because only men of some wealth could afford the amount of time and learning this work demanded. They served as author, director, producer, musical composer, choreographer, and sometimes even actor. As citizens, playwrights also fulfilled the normal military and political obligations of Athenian men. The best-known Athenian tragedians—Aeschylus (525–456 B.C.E.), Sophocles (c. 496–406 B.C.E.), and Euripides (c. 485–406 B.C.E.)—all served in the army, and Sophocles was elected to Athens's highest public office. Authors of plays competed from a love of honor, not money. The prizes, determined by a board of judges, awarded high prestige but little cash. The competition was regarded as so important that any judge who took a bribe to award a prize was put to death.

Tragedy's plots explored the difficulties of telling right from wrong when humans came into conflict in the city-state and the gods became involved. Even though most tragedies were based on stories that referred to a legendary time before city-states existed, such as the period of the Trojan War, the moral issues pertained to the society and obligations of citizens in a city-state. For example, Aeschylus's trilogy *Oresteia* (458 B.C.E) uses the story of how the gods stop the murderous violence in the family of Orestes, son of Agamemnon, the Greek leader against Troy, to explain the divine origins of democratic Athens's court system. The plays suggest that human beings learn only by suffering but that the gods provide justice in the long run.

Sophocles' *Antigone* (441 B.C.E.) presents the story of the cursed family of Oedipus of Thebes as a drama of harsh conflict between a courageous woman, Antigone, and the city-state's stern male leader, her uncle Creon. After her brother dies in a failed rebellion, Antigone insists on her family's moral obligation to bury its dead in obedience to divine command, while Creon takes harsh action to preserve order and protect community values by prohibiting the burial of his nephew the traitor. In a horrifying story of raging anger and suicide that features one of the most famous heroines of Western literature, Sophocles exposes the right and wrong on each side of the conflict. His play offers no easy resolution of the competing interests of divinely sanctioned moral tradition and the state's political rules.

Ancient sources tell us that the audiences reacted strongly to the messages of the tragedies presented in the drama competition of the Dionysian festival. For one thing, they could see that the central characters of the plays were figures who fell into disaster even though they held positions of power and prestige. The characters' reversals of fortune came about not because they were absolute villains but because, as humans, they were susceptible to a lethal mixture of error, ignorance, and **hubris** (vio-

hubris (HYOO bris): The Greek term for violent arrogance.

lent arrogance that, according to the Greeks, drove the competitive spirit to excess). The Athenian Empire was at its height when audiences at Athens attended the tragedies written by competing playwrights. Thoughtful spectators could reflect on the possibility that Athens's current power and prestige, managed as they were by humans, might fall victim to the same kind of mistakes and conflicts that brought down the heroes and heroines of tragedy. Thus, tragedies not only entertained through their spectacle but also educated through their stories and words. In particular, they reminded male citizens — who governed the city-state in its assembly, council, and courts — that success created complex moral problems that self-righteous arrogance never solved.

The Development of Greek Comedy

Golden Age Athens developed comedy as its second distinctive form of public theater. Like tragedies, comedies were written in verse, performed in Dionysus festivals, and subsidized with public funds and contributions from the rich. Unlike tragedies, comedies commented directly on public policy and criticized current politicians and intellectuals. They did this with plots and casts presenting outrageous fantasies of contemporary life. For example, comic choruses, which had twenty-four dancing singers, could be colorfully costumed as talking birds or dancing clouds, or an actor could fly on a giant dung beetle to visit the gods.

Comic playwrights competed to win the award for the festival's best comedy by creating beautiful poetry, raising laughs with constant jokes and puns, and mocking self-important citizens and political leaders. Much of the humor concerned sex and bodily functions, delivered in a stream of imaginative profanity. Well-known men of the day were targets for insults as cowards or weaklings. Women characters portrayed as figures of fun and ridicule seem to have been fictional, to protect the dignity of actual female citizens.

Athenian comedies often made fun of political leaders. As the leading politician of radical democracy, Pericles came in for fierce criticism in comedy. Comic playwrights ridiculed his policies, his love life, even the shape of his skull ("Old Turnip Head" was a favorite insult). Aristophanes (c. 455–385 B.C.E.), Athens's most famous comic playwright, so fiercely satirized Cleon, the city's most prominent leader early in the Peloponnesian War, that Cleon sued him. A citizen jury ruled in Aristophanes' favor, upholding the Athenian tradition of free speech.

In several of Aristophanes' comedies, the main characters are powerful women who force the men of Athens to change their policy to preserve family life and the city-state. These plays even criticize the assembly's policy during wartime. Most famous is *Lysistrata* (411 B.C.E.), named after the female lead character of the play. In this fantasy, the women of Athens and Sparta unite to force their husbands to end the Peloponnesian War. To make the men agree to a peace treaty, they first seize the acropolis,

Greek Vase Painting of the Murder of King Agamemnon

This Greek vase from the fifth century B.C.E. shows Queen Clytemnestra (left) and her lover Aegisthus murdering her husband, King Agamemnon, after he returns home from leading the Greek army in its ten-year war against Troy. The painting shows Agamemnon as defenseless because he was ensnared in a gauzy robe that his wife gave him after he took a bath. The other side of the vase shows Agamemnon's son murdering Clytemnestra, his mother, in revenge. Greek mythology had many stories of murderous vengeance that emphasized how difficult it was to regulate human passions with social norms and laws. *(Greek, Early Classical Period, about 460 B.C.E. Place of manufacture: Greece, Attica, Athens. Ceramic, Red Figure. H: 51 cm. [20 1/16 in.]; diameter: 51 cm. [20 1/6 in.]. Museum of Fine Arts, Boston; William Francis Warden Fund, 63.1246. Photograph © 2011 Museum of Fine Arts, Boston.)*

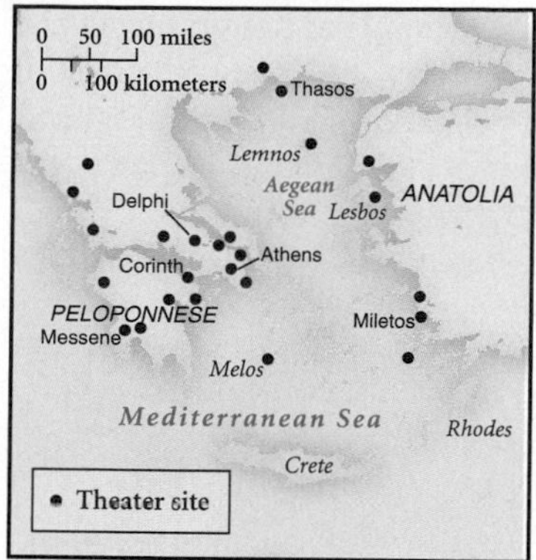

Theaters of Classical Greece

Statuettes of Comic Actors
Although these little statues are dressed in the kinds of masks and costumes that came into vogue later than the style of comedy that Aristophanes and his contemporaries wrote in the fifth century B.C.E. (for which no such pieces exist), they give a vivid sense of the exaggerated buffoonery that characterized the acting in Greek comedy. In Aristophanes' day, the grotesque unreality of comic costumes would have been even more striking because the male actors wore large leather phalluses (penises) attached below their waists that could be props for all sorts of ribald jokes. The use of masks in certain kinds of theater performances continued into Roman times. *(bpk, Berlin/Antikensammlung, Staaliche Musen, Berlin, Germany/photo by Johannes Laurentius/Art Resource, NY.)*

where Athens's financial reserves are kept, to prevent the men from squandering them further on the war. They then use sarcasm and pitchers of cold water to beat back an attack on their position by the old men who have remained in Athens while the younger men are out on campaign. Above all, the women steel themselves to refuse to sleep with their husbands when they return from battle. The effects of their sex strike on the men, portrayed in a series of explicit episodes, finally drive the warriors to make peace.

Lysistrata presents women acting bravely and aggressively against men who seem bent on destroying traditional family life — they are staying away from home for long stretches while on military campaigns and are ruining the city-state by prolonging a pointless war. Lysistrata insists that women have the intelligence and judgment to make political decisions: "I am a woman, and, yes, I have brains. And I'm not badly off for judgment. Nor has my education been bad, coming as it has from my listening often to the conversations of my father and the elders among the men." Her old-fashioned training and good sense allow her to see what needs to be done to protect the community. Like the heroines of tragedy, Lysistrata is a conservative, even a reactionary. She wants to put things back the way they were before the war ruined family life. To do that, however, she has to act like an impatient revolutionary. That irony sums up the challenge that fifth-century B.C.E. Athens faced in trying to resolve the tension between the dynamic innovation of its Golden Age and the importance of tradition in Greek life.

The remarkable freedom of speech of Athenian comedy allowed frank, even brutal, commentary on current issues and personalities. It cannot be an accident that this energetic, critical drama emerged in Athens at the same time as radical democracy, in the mid-fifth century B.C.E. The feeling that all citizens should have a stake in determining their government's policies evidently fueled a passion for using biting humor to keep the community's leaders from becoming arrogant and aloof.

REVIEW QUESTION How did new ways of thinking in the Golden Age change traditional ways of life?

The End of Athens's Golden Age, 431–403 B.C.E.

A war between Athens and Sparta that lasted a generation (431–404 B.C.E.) ended the Golden Age. Today it is called the Peloponnesian War because it matched Sparta's Peloponnese-based alliance against Athens and the Delian League. The war started, according to Thucydides, because the growth of Athenian power alarmed the Spartans, who feared that their interests and allies would fall to the Athenians' restless drive. Pericles, the most powerful politician in Athens at the time, persuaded its assembly to take a hard line when the Spartans demanded that Athens ease restrictions on city-states allied with Sparta. Corinth and Megara, crucial Spartan allies, complained bitterly to Sparta about Athens.

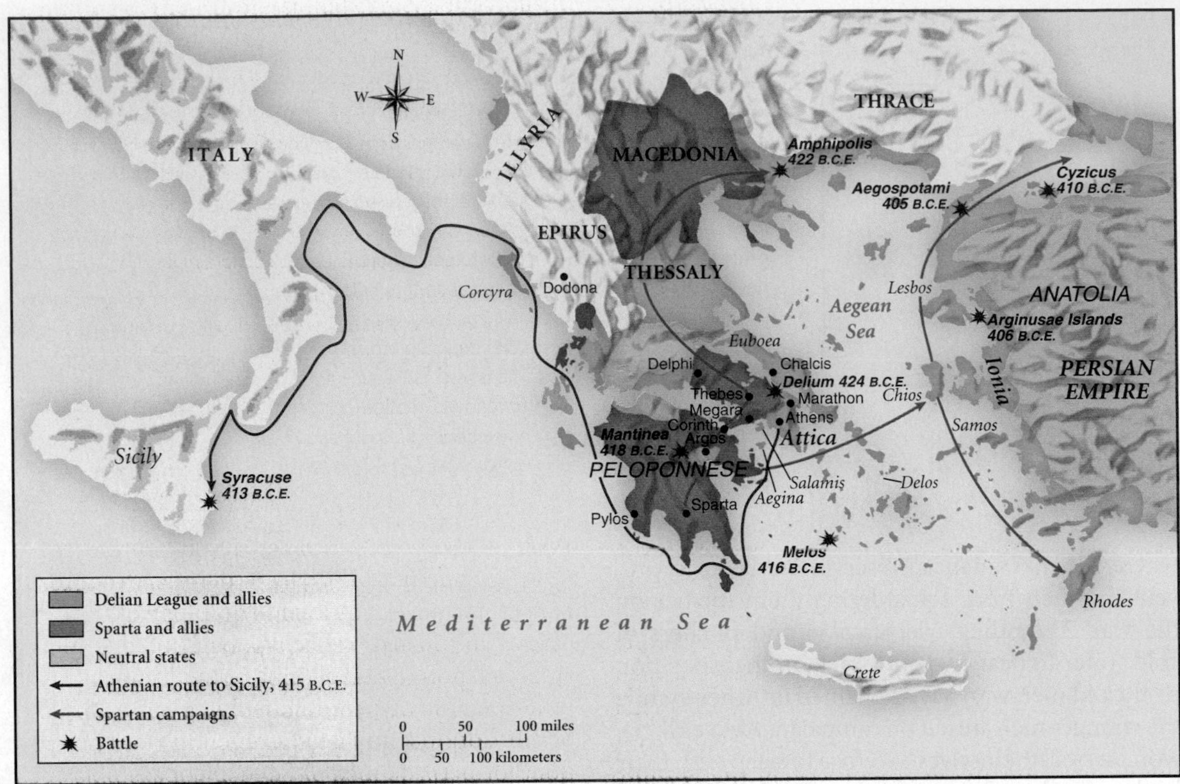

MAP 3.3 The Peloponnesian War, 431–404 B.C.E.
For the first ten years, the Peloponnesian War's battles took place largely in mainland Greece. Sparta, whose armies usually avoided distant campaigns, shocked Athens when its general Brasidas led successful attacks against Athenian forces in northeast Greece. Athens stunned the entire Greek world in the war's next phase by launching a huge naval expedition against Spartan allies in far-off Sicily. The last ten years of the war saw the action move to the east, on and along the western coast of Anatolia and its islands, on the boundary of the Persian Empire. Feeling threatened, the Persian king helped the Spartans build a navy there to defeat the famous Athenian fleet. | **Look at the route of Athens's expedition to Sicily; why do you think the Athenians took this longer voyage, rather than a more direct route?**

Finally, Corinth told Sparta to attack Athens, or else Corinth and its navy would change sides to the Athenian alliance. Sparta's leaders therefore gave Athens an ultimatum — stop mistreating our allies. Pericles convinced the Athenian assembly to reject the ultimatum on the grounds that Sparta had refused to settle the dispute through the third-party arbitration process called for by the 446–445 B.C.E. treaty. Pericles' critics claimed he was insisting on war against Sparta to revive his fading popularity. His supporters replied that he was defending Athenian honor and protecting foreign trade, a key to the economy. By 431 B.C.E. these disputes had shattered the peace treaty between Athens and Sparta negotiated by Pericles fifteen years before.

The Peloponnesian War, 431–404 B.C.E.

Lasting longer than any previous war in Greek history, the Peloponnesian War (Map 3.3) took place above all because Spartan leaders believed they had to fight now to keep the Athenians from using their superior long-distance offensive power — the Delian League's naval forces — to destroy Sparta's control of the Peloponnesian League. (See "Taking Measure," page 103) Sparta made the first strike of the war, but the conflict dragged on so long because the Athenian assembly failed to negotiate peace with Sparta when it had the chance and because the Spartans were willing to deal with Persia for money to build a fleet to win the war.

Dramatic evidence for the angry feelings that fueled the war comes from Thucydides' version of Pericles' stern oration to the Athenian assembly about not yielding to Spartan pressure:

> If we do go to war, have no thought that you went to war over a trivial affair. For you this trifling matter is the assurance and the proof of your determination. If you yield to their demands, they will immediately confront you with some larger demand, since they will think that you only gave way on the first point out of fear. But if you stand firm, you will show them that they

have to deal with you as equals. . . . When our equals, without agreeing to arbitration of the matter under dispute, make claims on us as neighbors and state those claims as commands, it would be no better than slavery to give in to them, no matter how large or how small the claim may be.

When Sparta invaded Athenian territory, Pericles advised a two-pronged strategy to win what he saw would be a long war: (1) use the navy to raid the lands of Sparta and its allies, and (2) avoid large infantry battles with the superior land forces of the Spartans, even when the enemy hoplites plundered the Athenian countryside outside the city. Athens's citizens could retreat to safety behind the city's impregnable walls, massive barriers of stone that encircled the city and the harbor, with the fortification known as the Long Walls protecting the land corridor between the urban center and the port (see Map 3.2). He insisted that Athenians should sacrifice their vast and valuable country property to save their population. In the end, he predicted, Athens, with its superior resources, would win a war of attrition, especially because the Spartans, lacking a base in Athenian territory, could not support long invasions.

Pericles' strategy and leadership might have made Athens the winner in the long run, but chance intervened to deprive Athens of his guidance: an epidemic struck Athens in 430 B.C.E. and killed Pericles the next year. This plague ravaged Athens's population for four years, killing thousands as it spread like wildfire among the people packed in behind the walls to avoid Spartan attacks. Despite their losses and the fears of many that the gods had sent the disease to punish them, the Athenians fought on. Over time, however, they abandoned the disciplined strategy that Pericles' prudent plan had required. The generals elected after his death, especially Cleon, pursued a much more aggressive strategy. At first this succeeded, especially when a group of Spartan hoplites surrendered after being blockaded by Cleon's forces at Pylos in 425 B.C.E. Their giving up shocked the Greek world and led Sparta to ask for a truce, but the Athenian assembly wanted more. When the daring Spartan general Brasidas captured Athens's possessions in northern Greece in 424 and 423 B.C.E., however, he turned the tide of war in the other direction by crippling the Athenian supply of timber and precious metals from this crucial region. When Brasidas and Cleon were both killed in 422 B.C.E., Sparta and Athens made peace in 421 B.C.E. out of mutual exhaustion.

Athens's most innovative and confident new general, Alcibiades, soon persuaded the assembly to reject the peace and to attack Spartan allies in 418 B.C.E. In 416–415 B.C.E., the Athenians and their allies overpowered the tiny and strategically meaningless Aegean island of Melos because it refused to abandon its allegiance to Sparta. Thucydides dramatically represents Athenian messengers telling the Melians they had to be conquered to show that Athens permitted no defiance to its dominance. Following their victory the Athenians executed the

TAKING MEASURE

Military Forces of Athens and Sparta at the Beginning of the Peloponnesian War (431 B.C.E.)

This chart compares the military forces of the Athenian side and the Spartan side when the Peloponnesian War broke out in 431 B.C.E. The numbers come from ancient sources, above all the Athenian general and historian Thucydides, who fought in the war. The bar graph starkly reveals the different characteristics of the competing forces: Athens relied on its navy of triremes and its archers (the fifth-century B.C.E. equivalent of artillery and snipers), while Sparta was superior in the forces needed for pitched land battles—hoplites (heavily armed infantry) and cavalry (shock troops used to disrupt opposing phalanxes). These differences dictated the differing strategies and tactics of the two sides: Athens in guerrilla fashion launching surprise raids from the sea, and Sparta trying to force decisive confrontations on the battlefield.

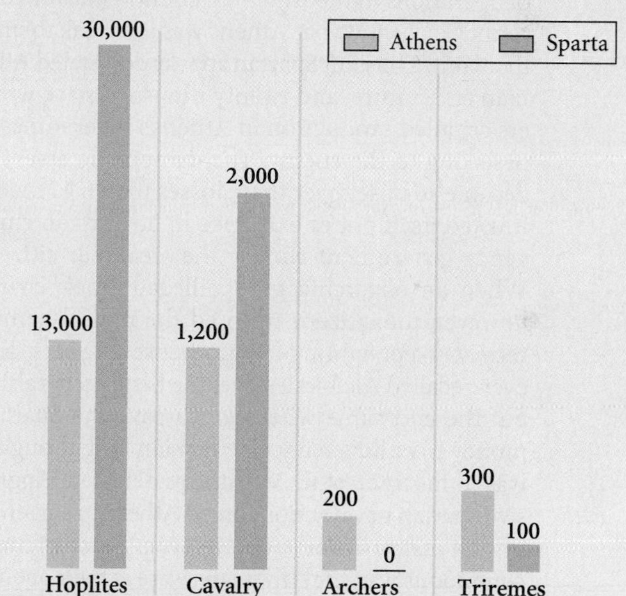

Question to Consider

■ Given these figures, who at the start of the war would you have predicted would be the winner?

Source: From Pamela Bradley, *Ancient Greece: Using Evidence* (Melbourne: Edward Arnold, 1990), 229.

Melian men, sold the women and children into slavery, and colonized the island.

The turning point in the war came soon thereafter when, in 415 B.C.E., Alcibiades persuaded the Athenian assembly to launch the greatest and most expensive campaign in Greek history. The expedition of 415 B.C.E. was directed against Sparta's allies in Sicily, far to the west. Alcibiades had dazzled his fellow citizens with the dream of conquering that rich island and especially its greatest city, Syracuse. Alcibiades' political rivals had him removed from his command, however, and the other generals blundered into catastrophic defeat in Sicily in 413 B.C.E. (see Map 3.3). The victorious Syracusans destroyed the allied invasion fleet and packed the survivors like human sardines into quarries under the blazing sun, with no toilets and only half a pint of drinking water and a handful of grain a day.

On the advice of Alcibiades, who had deserted to their side in anger at having lost his command, the Spartans in 413 B.C.E. seized a permanent base of operations in the Athenian countryside for year-round raids, now that Athens was too weak to drive them out. Constant Spartan attacks devastated Athenian agriculture, and twenty thousand slave workers crippled production in Athens's silver mines by deserting to the enemy. The democratic assembly became so upset over these losses that in 411 B.C.E. it voted itself out of existence in favor of an emergency government run by the wealthier citizens. When an oligarchic group illegally took charge, however, the citizens restored the radical democracy and kept fighting for another seven years. They even recalled Alcibiades, seeking better generalship, but the end came when Persia gave the Spartans money to build a navy. The Persian king thought it was in his interest to see Athens defeated. Aggressive Spartan naval action forced Athens to surrender in 404 B.C.E. After twenty-seven years of near-continuous war, the Athenians were at their enemy's mercy.

Athens Defeated: Tyranny and Civil War, 404–403 B.C.E.

Following Athens's surrender, the Spartans installed a regime of antidemocratic Athenians known as the Thirty Tyrants who were willing to collaborate with the victors. The collaborators were members of the social elite, and some, including their notoriously violent leader Critias, notorious for his criticism of religion, had been well-known pupils of the Sophists. Brutally suppressing democratic opposition, these oligarchs embarked on an eight-month period of murder and plunder in 404–403 B.C.E. The speechwriter Lysias, for example, reported that Spartan henchmen murdered his brother in order to steal the family's valuables, even ripping the gold rings from the ears of his brother's wife. Outraged at the violence and greed of the Thirty Tyrants, citizens who wanted to restore democracy banded together outside the city to fight to regain control of Athens. Fortunately for them, a feud between Sparta's two most important leaders paralyzed the Spartans, and they failed to send help to the Athenian collaborators. The democratic rebels defeated the forces of the Thirty Tyrants in a series of bloody street battles in Athens.

Democracy was thereby restored, but the city-state still seethed with anger and unrest. To settle the internal strife that threatened to tear Athens apart, the newly restored democratic assembly voted the first known amnesty in Western history, a truce agreement forbidding any official charges or recriminations stemming from the crimes of 404–403 B.C.E. Agreeing not to pursue grievances in court was the price of peace. As would soon become clear, however, some Athenians harbored grudges that no amnesty could dispel. In addition, Athens's financial and military strength had been shattered. At the end of the Golden Age, Athenians worried about how to remake their lives and restore the reputation that their city-state's innovative accomplishments had produced.

REVIEW QUESTION What factors determined the course of the Peloponnesian War?

Conclusion

When at the beginning of the fifth century B.C.E. some Greek city-states temporarily united to resist the Persian Empire, they surprised themselves by defeating the Persian invaders, who threatened their political independence. When the Persians retreated, however, so too did Greek unity. Following the Greek victory, Athens competed with Sparta for power. The Athenian Golden Age that followed the Persian Wars was based on empire and trade, and the city's riches funded the widening of democracy and brilliant cultural accomplishments.

As the money poured in, Athens built glorious and expensive temples, legislated pay for service in many government offices to strengthen democracy, and assembled the Mediterranean's most powerful navy. The poor men who rowed the ships demanded greater democracy; such demands led to political and legal reforms that guaranteed fairer treatment

MAPPING THE WEST

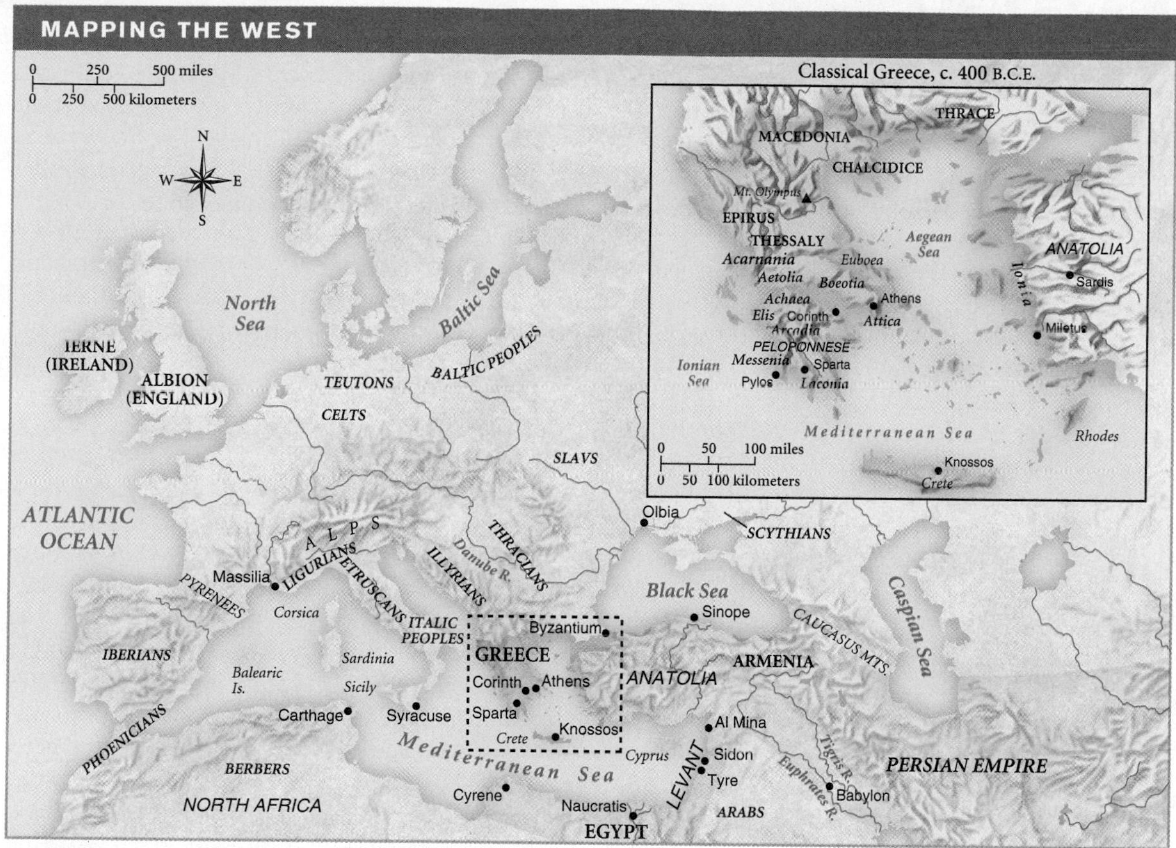

Greece, Europe, and the Mediterranean, 400 B.C.E.

No single power controlled the Mediterranean region at the end of the fifth century B.C.E. In the west, the Phoenician city of Carthage and the Greek cities on Sicily and in southern Italy were rivals for the riches to be won by trade. In the east, the Spartans, confident after their recent victory over Athens in the Peloponnesian War, tried to become an international power outside the mainland for the first time in their history by sending campaigns into Anatolia. This aggressive action aroused stiff opposition from the Persians because it was a threat to their westernmost imperial provinces. There was to be no peace and quiet in the Mediterranean even after the twenty-seven years of the Peloponnesian War.

for all. Pericles became the most famous politician of the Golden Age by leading the drive for radical democracy.

Religious practice and women's lives reflected the strong grip of tradition on everyday life, but dramatic innovations in education and philosophy created social tension. The Sophists' relativistic views disturbed tradition-minded people, as did Socrates' definition of virtue, which questioned ordinary people's love of wealth and success. Art and architecture broke out of old forms, promoting an impression of balanced motion rather than stability, while medicine gained a more scientific basis. Tragedy and comedy developed at Athens as public art forms commenting on contemporary social and political issues.

Wars framed the Golden Age. The Persian Wars sent Athens soaring to imperial power and prosperity, but the Athenians' high-handed treatment of allies and enemies combined with Spartan fears about Athenian power to bring on the disastrous Peloponnesian War. Nearly three decades of battle brought the stars of the Greek Golden Age crashing to earth: by 400 B.C.E. the Athenians found themselves in the same situation as in 500 B.C.E., fearful of Spartan power and worried whether the world's first democracy could survive. As it turned out, the next great threat to Greek stability and independence would once again come from a neighboring monarchy, this time not from Persia (to the east) but from Macedonia (to the north).

FOR FURTHER EXPLORATION

- **For additional primary-source material from this period**, see *Sources of the Making of the West*, Fourth Edition.
- **For Web sites, images, and documents related to topics in this chapter**, visit *Make History* at bedfordstmartins.com/hunt.

Chapter 3 Review

Online Study Guide bedfordstmartins.com/hunt

Key Terms and People

In the grid below, identify the term or person and explain its historical significance. (To do this exercise online, go to bedfordstmartins.com/hunt.)

Term	Who or What & When	Why It Matters
Themistocles (p. 77)		
Delian League (p. 80)		
triremes (p. 80)		
Pericles (p. 81)		
radical democracy (p. 81)		
ostracism (p. 82)		
agora (p. 83)		
Parthenon (p. 84)		
mystery cults (p. 87)		
metic (p. 87)		
hetaira (p. 91)		
Sophists (p. 94)		
Socratic method (p. 96)		
hubris (p. 99)		

Review Questions

1. How did the Greeks overcome the dangers of the Persian invasions?
2. What factors produced political change in fifth-century B.C.E. Athens?
3. How did new ways of thinking in the Golden Age change traditional ways of life?
4. What factors determined the course of the Peloponnesian War?

Making Connections

1. What were the most significant differences between Archaic Age Greece and Golden Age Greece?
2. For what sorts of things did Greeks of the Golden Age spend public funds? Why did they believe these things were worth the expense?
3. What price, in all senses, did Athens and the rest of Greece pay for the Golden Age? Was it worth it?

Important Events

Date	Event
500–323 B.C.E.	Classical Age of Greece
499–479 B.C.E.	Wars between Persia and Greece
490 B.C.E.	Battle of Marathon
480–479 B.C.E.	Xerxes' invasion of Greece
480 B.C.E.	Battle of Salamis
461 B.C.E.	Ephialtes reforms Athenian court system
EARLY 450S B.C.E.	Pericles introduces pay for officeholders in Athenian democracy
451 B.C.E.	Pericles restricts Athenian citizenship to children whose parents are both citizens
450 B.C.E.	Protagoras and other Sophists begin to teach in Athens

Date	Event
446–445 B.C.E. (WINTER)	Peace treaty between Athens and Sparta; intended to last thirty years
441 B.C.E.	Sophocles presents the tragedy *Antigone*
431–404 B.C.E.	Peloponnesian War
420S B.C.E.	Herodotus finishes *Histories*
415–413 B.C.E.	Enormous Athenian military expedition against Sicily
411 B.C.E.	Aristophanes presents the comedy *Lysistrata*
404–403 B.C.E.	Rule of the Thirty Tyrants at Athens
403 B.C.E.	Restoration of democracy in Athens

- Consider three events: **Ephialtes reforms Athenian court system (461 B.C.E.)**, **Protagoras and other Sophists begin to teach in Athens (450 B.C.E.)**, and **Aristophanes presents the comedy *Lysistrata* (411 B.C.E.)**. How did the principles of radical democracy during the Athenian Golden Age help to make possible these different events?

SUGGESTED REFERENCES

The Greek city-states, especially Athens, reached the height of their political, economic, and military power in the fifth century B.C.E. following the defeat of the Persian invasion of mainland Greece; scholars continue to investigate how the frequent wars of this period influenced not only the democracy of Athens but also the famous dramatists and philosophers of this so-called Golden Age.

Blundell, Sue. *Women in Ancient Greece*. 1995.

Briant, Pierre. *From Cyrus to Alexander: History of the Persian Empire*. Translated by Peter Daniels. 2006.

Brunschwig, Jacques, and G. E. R. Lloyd, eds. *Greek Thought: A Guide to Classical Knowledge*. 2000.

Camp, John M. *The Archaeology of Athens*. 2004.

*Dillon, John, and Tania Gergel. *The Greek Sophists*. 2003.

*Grene, David, and Richmond Lattimore, eds. *The Complete Greek Tragedies*. 1992.

Hanson, Victor Davis. *A War Like No Other: How the Athenians and Spartans Fought the Peloponnesian War*. 2005.

Herman, Gabriel. *Morality and Behavior in Democratic Athens*. 2006.

*Herodotus. *The Histories*. Trans. Aubrey de Sélincourt. Revised by John Marincola. Rev. ed. 2003.

Mitchell-Boyask, Robin. *Plague and the Athenian Imagination: Drama, History, and the Cult of Asclepius*. 2008.

Papazarkadas, Nikolaus, et al., eds. *Interpreting the Athenian Empire*. 2009.

Parker, Robert. *Athenian Religion: A History*. 1996.

Parthenon: http://www.perseus.tufts.edu/cgi-bin/vor?x=16&y=13&lookup=parthenon

Patterson, Cynthia B. *The Family in Greek History*. 1998.

*Strassler, Robert B., ed. *The Landmark Thucydides. A Comprehensive Guide to the Peloponnesian War*. 1996.

Strauss, Barry. *The Battle of Salamis: The Naval Encounter That Saved Greece—and Western Civilization*. 2005.

Thorley, John. *Athenian Democracy*. 2004.

Wees, Hans van, ed. *War and Violence in Ancient Greece*. 2000.

Winkler, John J., and Froma I. Zeitlin, eds. *Nothing to Do with Dionysus? Athenian Drama in Its Social Context*. 1992.

*Primary source.

CHAPTER

4

From the Classical to the Hellenistic World

400–30 B.C.E.

About 255 B.C.E., an Egyptian camel trader far from home paid a scribe to write his Greek employer, Zeno, back in Egypt, to protest how Zeno's assistant, Krotos, was cheating him:

> You know that when you left me in Syria with Krotos I followed all your instructions concerning the camels and behaved blamelessly towards you. But Krotos has ignored your orders to pay me my salary; I've received nothing despite asking him for my money over and over. He just tells me to go away. I waited a long time for you to come, but when I no longer had life's necessities and couldn't get help anywhere, I had to run away . . . to keep from starving to death. . . . I am desperate summer and winter. . . . They have treated me like dirt because I am not a Greek. I therefore beg you, please, command them to pay me so that I won't go hungry just because I don't know how to speak Greek.

The trader's need for help from a foreigner holding power in his homeland reflects the changes in the eastern Mediterranean world during the Hellenistic Age (323–30 B.C.E.). The movement of Greeks into the Near East and their contacts with local peoples increased the cultural interaction of the Greek and the Near Eastern worlds to the highest level ever, forging a multicultural synthesis that set a new course for Western civilization in politics, art, philosophy, science, and religion. The first stage of this movement came after the Peloponnesian War, when thousands of Greeks became mercenary soldiers serving Near Eastern rulers. Alexander the Great (356–323 B.C.E.) then changed the course of history by conquering the Persian Empire, leading an army of Greeks and Macedonians to the border of India, taking Near Easterners into his army and imperial administration, and planting colonies of Greeks as far

The Rosetta Stone
Dug out of the wall of a fort in 1799 by a soldier in Napoleon's army near Rosetta, in the Nile River delta, this Hellenistic inscription in two different languages and three different forms of writing unlocked the lost secrets of how to read Egyptian hieroglyphs. The bands of text repeat the same message (priests praising King Ptolemy V in 196 B.C.E.) in hieroglyphs, demotic (a cursive form of Egyptian invented around 600 B.C.E.), and Greek. Bilingual texts were necessary to reach the mixed population of Hellenistic Egypt. Scholars deciphered the hieroglyphs by comparing them to the Greek version. They started with the hieroglyphs surrounded by an oval, which they guessed were royal names. *(Art Resource, NY.)*

east as Afghanistan. His amazing expedition—with its almost superhuman exploits—shocked the world and acted like a cultural whirlwind to give new creative energy to Western civilization by combining Near Eastern and Greek traditions as never before.

Politics changed in the Greek world when Alexander's successors revived monarchy by taking over territories to rule as their personal kingdoms. These new kingdoms, which became the dominant powers of the Hellenistic Age, restricted the freedom of Greece's city-states. The city-states retained local rule but lost their independence to compete with one another in foreign policy. The Hellenistic kings now controlled international affairs. They imported Greeks to fill royal offices, man their armies, and run businesses. This demographic change created tension with the kings' non-Greek subjects. Immigrant Greeks, such as Zeno in Egypt, formed a social elite that lorded it over the kingdoms' local populations. Egyptians, Syrians, or Mesopotamians who wanted to rise in society had to win the support of these Greeks and learn their language. Otherwise, they were likely to find themselves as powerless as the hungry camel merchant.

Over time, the Near East's local cultures interacted with the Greek overlords' culture to spawn a multicultural synthesis. Locals married Greeks, shared their artistic and religious traditions with the newcomers, passed along their agricultural and scientific knowledge, and learned Greek to win administrative jobs. Although Hellenistic royal society always remained hierarchical, with Greeks at the top, and never eliminated tension between rulers and ruled, its kings and queens did finance innovations in art, philosophy, religion, and science that combined Near Eastern and Greek traditions. The Hellenistic kingdoms fell in the second and first centuries B.C.E. when the Romans overthrew them one by one.

All this happened during an era of constant warfare. Cultural interaction, a characteristic of Western civilization from the beginning, reached a new level of intensity as an unintended consequence of Alexander's military campaigns. The new contacts between diverse peoples and the emergence of new ideas strongly influenced Roman civilization and therefore later Western civilization. In particular, Hellenistic artistic, scientific, philosophical, and religious innovations persisted even after the glory of Greece's Golden Age had faded, especially since Hellenistic religion provided the background for Christianity.

CHAPTER FOCUS What were the major political and cultural changes in the Hellenistic Age?

Classical Greece after the Peloponnesian War, 400–350 B.C.E.

The Greek city-states gradually regained their economic and political stability after the Peloponnesian War (431–404 B.C.E.), but daily life remained hard, especially for working people. The war's aftermath dramatically affected Greek philosophy. At Athens, citizens who blamed Socrates for inspiring the worst of the Thirty Tyrants brought him to trial; the jury condemned him to death. His execution helped persuade the philosophers Plato and Aristotle to detest democracy and develop new ways of thinking about right versus wrong and how human beings should live.

Although the city-states recovered after the war, their continuing competition for power in the fourth century B.C.E. drained their resources. After failing to control defeated Athens, the Spartans tried to expand their power into central Greece and Anatolia

399 B.C.E. Execution of Socrates

386 B.C.E. In King's Peace, Sparta surrenders control of Anatolian Greek city-states to Persia; Plato founds Academy

400 B.C.E.

362 B.C.E. Battle of Mantinea leaves power vacuum in Greece

338 B.C.E. Battle of Chaeronea allows Macedonian Philip II to become the leading power in Greece

350 B.C.E.

335 B.C.E. Aristotle founds Lyceum

334–323 B.C.E. Alexander the Great leads Greeks and Macedonians to conquer Persian Empire

307 B.C.E. Epicurus founds his philosophical group in Athens

306–304 B.C.E. Successors of Alexander declare themselves kings

300 B.C.E.

c. 300 B.C.E. Euclid teaches geometry at Alexandria

300–260 B.C.E. Theocritus writes poetry at Ptolemaic court

250 B.C.E.

by collaborating with the Persians. This policy stirred up violent resistance from Thebes and from Athens, which had rebuilt its naval empire. By the 350s B.C.E., the strife among the Greek city-states so weakened all of them that they were unable to prevent the Macedonian kingdom (Alexander the Great's homeland) from gaining control of Greece.

Athens's Recovery after the Peloponnesian War

Athens provides the most evidence for Greek life after the Peloponnesian War. The devastation of Athens's rural economy by Spartan raids and the overcrowding in the wartime city produced friction between refugees from the countryside and city dwellers. Life became difficult for middle-class women whose husbands and brothers had died during the conflict. Traditionally, they had woven cloth at home for their families and supervised the household slaves, but the men had earned the family's income by farming or working at a trade. Now, with no man to provide for them and their children, many war widows had to work outside the home. The only jobs open to them — such as wet-nursing, weaving, or laboring in vineyards—were low-paying.

Resourceful Athenians found ways to profit from women's skills. The family of one of Socrates' friends, for example, fell into poverty when several widowed sisters, nieces, and female cousins moved in. The friend complained to Socrates that he was too poor to support his new family of fourteen plus their slaves. Socrates replied that the women knew how to make men's and women's cloaks, shirts, capes, and smocks, "the work considered the best and most fitting for women." He suggested they begin to sell the clothes outside the home. This plan succeeded financially, but the women complained that Socrates' friend was the household's only member who ate without working. Socrates advised the man to reply that the women should think of him as sheep did a guard dog — he earned his share of the food by keeping the wolves away.

Athens's postwar economy recovered because small-business owners and households engaged in trade and produced manufactured goods. Greek businesses, usually family-run, were small; the largest known was a shield-making company with 120 slave workers. Some changes occurred in occupations formerly defined by gender. For example, men began working alongside women in cloth production when the first commercial weaving shops outside the home sprang up. Some women made careers in the arts, especially painting and music, which men had traditionally dominated.

The rebuilding by 393 B.C.E. of Athens's destroyed Long Walls, which protected the transportation

Vase Painting of Women Fetching Water (detail)
This vase painting shows women filling water jugs at a public fountain to take back to their homes. Both freeborn and slave women fetched water for their households; few Greek homes had running water. Cities built attractive fountain houses such as the one depicted here, which dispensed fresh water from springs or piped it in through small aqueducts (compare the large Roman aqueduct on page 152.) Women often gathered at fountains for conversation with people from outside their household. *(The Priam Painter, Water jar [hydria], Athens, Attica, Greece. Place of manufacture: Athens, Attica, Greece. H. 53 cm. [20⅞ in.]; diameter: 37 cm. [14 9/16 in.]. Ceramic, Black Figure, Museum of Fine Arts, Boston, William Francis Warden Fund, 61.195. Photograph © 2011 Museum of Fine Arts, Boston.)*

30 B.C.E. Cleopatra VII dies and Rome takes over Ptolemaic Empire

200 B.C.E. | 150 B.C.E. | 100 B.C.E. | 50 B.C.E.

195 B.C.E. Seleucid queen Laodice endows dowries for girls

167 B.C.E. Maccabee revolt after Antiochus IV turns temple in Jerusalem into a Greek sanctuary

Silver Coins of Athens
The city-state of ancient Athens owned rich silver mines that financed its silver coinage, famous around the Greek world for purity and reliability. This coin from the fifth century B.C.E. was a tetradrachm ("four drachmas"), which was the amount that a worker or rower in the Athenian navy earned in four days. The images show Athena, the city-state's main goddess, and an owl with an olive branch, also symbols of Athena. The style of the images was kept old-fashioned and mostly unchanging so as not to harm the trust that people in foreign lands had in accepting Athenian coins in trade and commerce as a form of international currency. *(© C. M. Dixon/Ancient Art & Architecture Collection. Ltd.)*

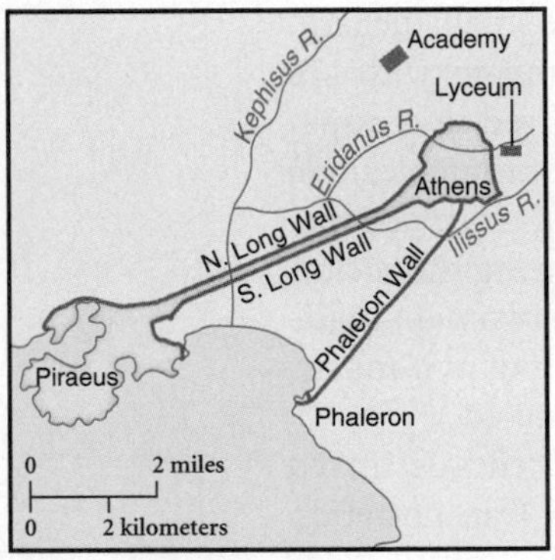

Athens's Long Walls as Rebuilt after the Peloponnesian War

corridor from the city to the port, gave evidence of a recovering economy. Exports of grain, wine, and pottery resumed, as did exports of silver from Athens's mines. The refortified harbor also allowed Athens to begin to rebuild its navy, which increased employment opportunities for poor men.

Even in an improving economy, daily life remained difficult for working people. Most workers earned barely enough to feed and clothe their families. They ate two meals a day, a light one at midmorning and a heavier evening meal. Bread baked from barley provided their main food; only rich people could afford wheat bread. A family bought bread from small bakery stands, often run by women, or made it at home, with the wife directing the slaves in grinding the grain, shaping the dough, and baking it in a clay oven heated by charcoal. People topped their bread with greens, beans, onions, garlic, olives, fruit, and cheese. The few households rich enough to afford meat boiled or grilled it over a fire. Everyone of all ages drank wine, diluted with water, with every meal.

The Execution of Socrates, 399 B.C.E.

Socrates, Athens's most famous philosopher in the Golden Age, fell victim to the bitterness many Athenians felt about the rule of the Thirty Tyrants following the Peloponnesian War. Since the amnesty proclaimed by the restored democratic assembly prohibited prosecutions for crimes committed under the tyrants' reign of terror, angry citizens had to bring other charges against those they hated. Some prominent Athenians hated Socrates because his follower Critias had been one of the Thirty Tyrants' most violent leaders.

These prominent citizens charged Socrates with impiety, a serious crime, claiming that he had angered the gods with his ideas and therefore threatened the city with divine punishment. In 399 B.C.E., they argued their case to a jury of 501 male citizens. They presented religious and moral arguments: Socrates, they claimed, rejected the city-state's gods, introduced new divinities, and lured young men away from Athenian moral traditions. Speaking in his own defense, Socrates refused to beg for sympathy, as was customary in trials. Instead, he repeated his dedication to goading his fellow citizens into examining their preconceptions about how to live justly. He vowed to remain their stinging gadfly no matter what.

When the jurors narrowly voted to convict the philosopher, Athenian law required them to decide between the penalty proposed by the prosecutors and that proposed by the defendant. The prosecutors proposed death. Everyone expected Socrates to offer exile as an alternative and the jury to accept it. The philosopher, however, said that he deserved a reward rather than punishment, until his friends made him propose a fine as his penalty. The jury chose death, requiring him to drink a poison concocted from powdered hemlock. Socrates accepted his sentence calmly, saying that "no evil can befall a good man either in life or in death." Ancient sources report that many Athenians soon came to regret Socrates' punishment as a tragic mistake and a severe blow to their reputation.

The Philosophy of Plato

Socrates' death made his follower and Greece's most famous philosopher, **Plato** (429–348 B.C.E.), hate democracy. From a well-to-do family and related to the infamous Critias, whom he wrote about favorably, Plato started out as a political consultant promoting the rule of philosopher-tyrants as the best form of government. He traveled to Sicily to advise Dionysius, tyrant of Syracuse, but when he failed to turn Dionysius into an ideal ruler, Plato gave up hope that political action could stop violence and greed. Instead, he turned to talking and writing about philosophy as the guide to life and established a philosophical school, the Academy, in Athens around 386 B.C.E. The Academy was an informal as-

Plato: A follower of Socrates who became Greece's most famous philosopher.

sociation of people who studied philosophy, mathematics, and theoretical astronomy under the leader's guidance. It attracted intellectuals to Athens for the next nine hundred years, and Plato's ideas about the nature of reality, ethics, and politics have remained central to philosophy and political science to this day.

Plato's Ethical Thought Plato's intellectual interests covered astronomy, mathematics, political philosophy, **metaphysics** (ideas about the ultimate nature of reality beyond the reach of the human senses), and ethics. His radical views on reality underlay his ethics. He presented his ideas in dialogues, which usually featured Socrates conversing with a variety of people. Plato wrote to provoke readers into thoughtful reflection, not to prescribe a set of beliefs. Nevertheless, he always maintained one essential idea based on his view of reality: ultimate moral qualities are universal, unchanging, and absolute, not relative. He thus rejected the relativism that the Sophists had taught.

Plato's dialogues explore his theory that justice, goodness, beauty, and equality exist on their own in a higher realm beyond the daily world. He used the word *Forms* (or *Ideas*) to describe the abstract, invariable, and ultimate realities of such ethical qualities. According to Plato, the Forms are the only genuine reality. All things that humans perceive with their senses on earth are only dim and imperfect copies of these metaphysical, ultimate realities. Forms are not defined by human experience of them—any earthly examples can always display the opposite quality. For example, returning a borrowed item might seem like justice. But what if the borrowed item is a weapon and the lender wants it back to commit murder? Returning the borrowed item would then support injustice. Therefore, every ethical quality is relative in the world that humans experience. But, Plato insists, they are absolute in the ultimate reality. Human experiences are like shadows of the absolutes cast on the wall of a cave. The difficult notion of Forms made metaphysics an important issue in philosophy.

Plato's ideas about the soul also deeply influenced later thought. He believed that humans possess immortal souls distinct from their bodies; this idea established the concept of **dualism**, a separation between soul (or mind) and body. Plato further explained that the human soul possesses preexisting knowledge put there by a god. The world has order because a rational deity created it. The god wanted to reproduce the Forms' perfect order in the material world, but the world turned out imperfect because matter is imperfect. Humans' present, impure existence is only a temporary stage in cosmic existence because, while the body does not last, the soul is immortal.

Mosaic Depicting Plato's Academy
This Roman-era mosaic shows philosophers talking at Plato's school in Athens, the Academy. Founded about 386 B.C.E., the Academy became one of Greece's longest-lasting institutions, attracting scholars and students for more than nine hundred years. The columns and the tree in the mosaic express the harmonious blend of the natural and built environment of the Academy, which was meant to promote discussion. What message do the philosophers' bare chests convey? *(Erich Lessing/Art Resource, NY.)*

Building on earlier Greek rationalism, Plato argued that people must seek perfect order and purity in their souls by using rational thought to control irrational and therefore harmful desires. People who yield to irrational desires fail to consider the future of their body and soul. The desire to drink too much alcohol, for example, is irrational because the binge drinker fails to consider the painful hangover that will follow.

Plato's Republic Plato presented his most famous ideas on politics in his dialogue *The Republic*. This work, whose Greek title means "system of government," discusses the nature of

---

metaphysics: Philosophical ideas about the ultimate nature of reality beyond the reach of human senses.

dualism: The philosophical idea that the human soul (or mind) and body are separate.

justice and the reasons people should never commit injustice. Democracy, Plato wrote, cannot create justice because people on their own cannot rise above narrow self-interest to knowledge of the ultimate reality of universal truth. Justice can come only under the rule of an enlightened oligarchy or monarchy. Therefore, a just society requires a strict hierarchy.

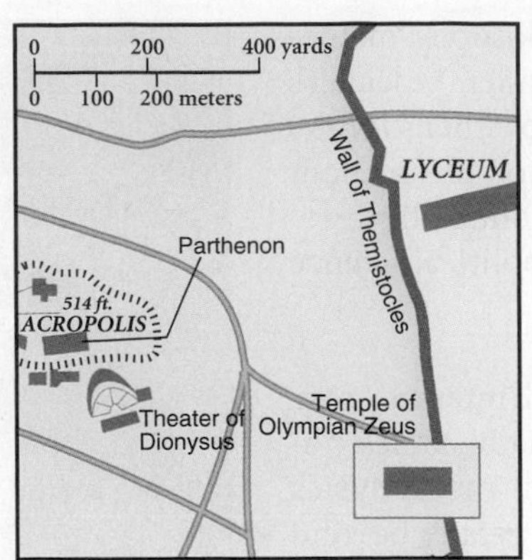

Aristotle's Lyceum, established 335 B.C.E.

Plato's *Republic* describes an ideal society with a hierarchy of three classes distinguished by their ability to grasp the truth of Forms. The highest class is the rulers, or "guardians," who must be educated in mathematics, astronomy, and metaphysics. Next come the "auxiliaries," who defend the community. "Producers" make up the bottom class; they grow food and make objects for everyone.

Women can be guardians because they possess the same virtues and abilities as men, except that the average woman has less physical strength than the average man. To minimize distraction, guardians are to have neither private property nor nuclear families. Male and female guardians are to live in houses shared in common, eat in the same dining halls, and exercise in the same gymnasia. They are to have sex with various partners so that the best women can mate with the best men to produce the best children. The children are to be raised together by special caretakers, not their parents. Guardians who achieve the highest level of knowledge can rule as philosopher-kings. Plato did not think humans could actually create the ideal society described in *The Republic*, but he did believe that imagining it was an important way to help people learn to live justly. For Plato, philosophy was an essential guide to human life.

Aristotle, Scientist and Philosopher

Aristotle (384–322 B.C.E.) was another Greek thinker who believed in the importance of philosophy as a guide to life. At age seventeen, he joined Plato's Academy. From 342 to 335 B.C.E., he earned a living by tutoring the teenage Alexander the Great in Macedonia. Returning to Athens in 335 B.C.E., Aristotle founded his own school, the **Lyceum**, and taught his own life-guiding philosophy, based on logic, scientific knowledge, and practical experience. Like Plato, he thought Athenian democracy was a bad system because it did not restrict decision making to the most educated and moderate citizens. His vast writings made him one of the world's most influential thinkers.

Aristotle's reputation rests on his scientific investigation of the natural world, development of rigorous systems of logical argument, and practical ethics. He regarded science and philosophy as the disciplined search for knowledge in every aspect of everyday life. That search brought the good life and genuine happiness. Aristotle lectured with dazzling intelligence on biology, medicine, anatomy, psychology, meteorology, physics, chemistry, mathematics, music, metaphysics, rhetoric, literary criticism, political science, and ethics. He also invented a system of logic for precise argumentation. By creating ways to identify valid arguments, Aristotle established grounds for determining whether an argument was logically valid or merely persuasive.

Aristotle required explanations to be based on strict rationality and common sense rather than metaphysics. He rejected Plato's theory of Forms because, he said, the separate, ultimate existence Plato postulated for Forms was not subject to demonstrable proof. Aristotle believed that the best way to understand anything was to observe it in its natural setting. He coupled detailed investigation with careful reasoning in biology, botany, and zoology. He was the first investigator to try to collect and classify all available information on animal species, recording facts and advancing knowledge about more than five hundred different kinds of animals, including insects. His recognition that whales and dolphins are mammals, for example, was overlooked by later writers on animals and not rediscovered for another two thousand years.

Not all of Aristotle's observations were accurate, and some of his views justified inequalities characteristic of his time. He regarded slavery as natural, arguing that some people were slaves by nature because their souls lacked the rational part

Aristotle: Greek philosopher famous for his scientific investigations, development of logical argument, and practical ethics.

Lyceum: The school for research and teaching in a wide range of subjects founded by Aristotle in Athens in 335 B.C.E.

DOCUMENT

Aristotle on the Nature of the Greek Polis

Aristotle's book Politics *discussed the origins of political states and the different ways to organize them. Reflecting on his research into many fields in science, Aristotle connected his theories on the structures of politics to his ideas that emerged from his investigations of the fundamental principles of the natural world. In this excerpt, Aristotle explains that the polis (city-state) was a creation of nature.*

Since we see that every city-state is a type of partnership and that every partnership is established for the sake of some good, for everything that everyone does is motivated by what seems to them to be a good, it is clear that, with all partnerships aiming at some good, the most authoritative partnership, which includes all other partnerships, does this the most of all and aims at the most authoritative of all goods. This is what is called the city-state, that is, the political partnership. . . .

If one looks at things as they grow from the beginning, one will make the best observations, on this topic and all others. Necessity first brings together those who cannot exist without each other, that is, on the one hand, the female and the male for the purpose of reproduction, and this is not a matter of choice, but just as with the other animals and with plants, it is a matter of nature to desire to leave behind another of the same kind. On the other hand, [necessity brings together] the ruler and the one who is naturally ruled for the sake of security, for the one who is able to foresee things with his mind is by nature a ruler and by nature a master, while the one who is able to do things with his body is the one who is ruled and is by nature a slave. For this reason the same thing benefits master and slave. . . .

From these two partnerships comes first the household, and Hesiod spoke correctly, saying, "First of all, [get yourself] a house and a wife and an ox for plowing,"[1] because the ox is a household slave for a poor man. Therefore, the partnership that is established first by nature for everyday purposes is the household. . . .

The partnership that first arises from multiple households for the sake of more than everyday needs is the village. The village seems by nature to be a colony from the household. . . .

The final partnership of multiple villages is the city-state, which possesses the limit of self-sufficiency, so to speak. It comes into being for the sake of living, but it exists for the sake of living well. Every city-state therefore exists by nature, if it is true that the first partnerships do. . . . It is clear that the city-state belongs to the things existing by nature, and that humans are beings who by nature live in a city-state, and that the one who has no city-state by nature and not by chance is either a fool or a superhuman.

Source: Aristotle, *Politics*, Book 1.1–2, 1252a1–1253a19. Translation by Thomas R. Martin.

[1]A quotation from *Works and Days*, line 405.

Question to Consider

- **On what specific ideas does Aristotle base his explanation of the origins and character of the city-state as a form of political and social organization? Does he make a convincing argument? Why or why not?**

that should rule in a human. He also concluded, on the basis of faulty biological observations, that nature made women inferior to men. He wrongly believed, for example, that in procreation the male's semen actively gave the fetus its design, whereas the female passively provided its matter. Mistaken biological information led Aristotle to evaluate females as incomplete males, a conclusion with disastrous results for later thought. At the same time, he believed that human communities could be successful and happy only if women and men both contributed. (See Document, "Aristotle on the Nature of the Greek Polis," above.)

In ethics, Aristotle emphasized the need to develop practical habits of just behavior to achieve happiness. People should achieve self-control by training their minds to win out over instincts and passions. Self-control meant finding "the mean," or balance, between denying and indulging physical pleasures. Aristotle claimed that the mind must rule in finding the balance leading to true happiness because the intellect is the finest human quality and the mind is the true self—indeed, the godlike part of a person.

Aristotle influenced ethics by insisting that standards of right and wrong have merit only if they are grounded in character and aligned with the good in human nature. They cannot work if they consist of abstract reasons for just behavior. That is, an ethical system must be relevant to real human situations. He argued that the life of the mind and experience of the real world are inseparable in defining a worthwhile and happy existence.

Greek Political Disunity

In the same period that Plato and Aristotle were developing their philosophies as guides to life, the Greek city-states were in a constant state of war. Sparta, Thebes, and Athens competed to dominate

Greece. None succeeded. Their endless fighting weakened their morale and their finances, leaving Greek independence vulnerable to external threat.

The Spartans provoked the competition by trying to conquer other city-states in central Greece and in Anatolia in the 390s B.C.E. Thebes, Athens, Corinth, and Argos then formed an anti-Spartan coalition. The Spartans checkmated the alliance by negotiating with the Persian king. Betraying their traditional claim to defend Greek freedom, the Spartans acknowledged the Persian ruler's right to control the Greek city-states of Anatolia—in return for permission to wage war in Greece without Persian interference. This agreement of 386 B.C.E., called the King's Peace, sold out the Greeks of Anatolia, returning them to submission to the Persian Empire, just as before the Persian Wars.

The Athenians rebuilt their military to compete with Sparta. The Long Walls restored Athens's invulnerability to invasion, and a new kind of light infantry—the *peltast*, armed with a small leather shield, a sword, and several javelins—fighting alongside hoplites gave Athenian ground forces greater tactical mobility and flexibility. Most important, Athens rebuilt its navy so that by 377 B.C.E. it had again become the leader of a naval alliance of Greek city-states. Members of this alliance insisted that their rights be specified in writing to prevent a repeat of Athenian domination as in the Delian League of the fifth century B.C.E.

The Thebans became Greece's main power in the 370s B.C.E. through brilliant generalship. They crushed the Spartan invasion of Theban territory in 371 B.C.E. and then invaded the Spartan homeland in the Peloponnese. They greatly weakened Sparta by freeing many helots. Since Thebes was only forty miles from Athens, the Thebans' success alarmed the Athenians, who allied with their hated enemies, the Spartans. The armies of Athens and Sparta confronted the Thebans in the battle of Mantinea in the Peloponnese in 362 B.C.E. Thebes won the battle but lost the war when its best general was killed and no capable replacement could be found.

The battle of Mantinea left the Greek city-states disunified and weak. As a commentator said, "Everyone had supposed that this battle's winners would become Greece's rulers and its losers their subjects; but there was only more confusion and disturbance in Greece after Mantinea than before." This judgment was confirmed when the Athenian naval alliance fell apart in a war between Athens and its allies over the negotiations some allies were conducting with Persia and Macedonia.

By the 350s B.C.E., no Greek city-state had the power to rule anything except its own territory. The city-states' competition for supremacy finally died out in a stalemate of exhaustion. By failing to cooperate, the Greeks opened the way for the rise of a new power—the kingdom of Macedonia—that would end their independence in international politics. The Macedonian kings did not literally enslave the Greeks, as the Spartans did the helots, or usually even change their local governments. They did, however, abolish the city-states' freedom to control their foreign policy.

REVIEW QUESTION How did daily life, philosophy, and the political situation change in Greece during the period 400–350 B.C.E.?

The Rise of Macedonia, 359–323 B.C.E.

The kingdom of Macedonia's rise to superpower status counts as one of the greatest surprises in ancient military and political history. In little more than a generation, the Macedonian kingdom, located just north of central Greece, took advantage of the Greek city-states' disunity to rocket from being a minor state to ruling the Greek and Near Eastern worlds. Two aggressive and charismatic Macedonian kings produced this transformation: Philip II (r. 359–336 B.C.E.) and his son **Alexander the Great** (r. 336–323 B.C.E.). Their conquests ended the Greek Classical Age and set in motion the Hellenistic Age's cultural changes.

The Roots of Macedonian Power

The Macedonians' power sprang from the characteristics of their monarchy and their people's ethnic pride. Macedonian kings had to listen to their people, who had freedom of speech. The king governed by maintaining the support of the elite, who ranked as his social equals and controlled many followers. Men spent their time training for war, hunting, and drinking heavily. The king had to excel in these activities to show that he deserved to lead the state. Queens and royal mothers received respect because they came from powerful families or the ruling houses of neighboring regions. In the king's absence these royal women exercised power at court.

Alexander the Great: The fourth-century B.C.E. Macedonian king whose conquest of the Persian Empire led to the greatly increased cultural interactions of Greece and the Near East in the Hellenistic Age.

Macedonian kings thought of themselves as ethnically Greek; they spoke Greek as well as they did their native Macedonian. Macedonians as a whole, however, looked down on the Greeks as too soft to survive life in their northern land. The Greeks returned this contempt. The famed Athenian orator Demosthenes (384–322 B.C.E.) mocked Philip II as "not only not a Greek nor related to the Greeks, but not even a barbarian from a land worth mentioning; no, he's a pestilence from Macedonia, a region where you can't even buy a slave worth his salt."

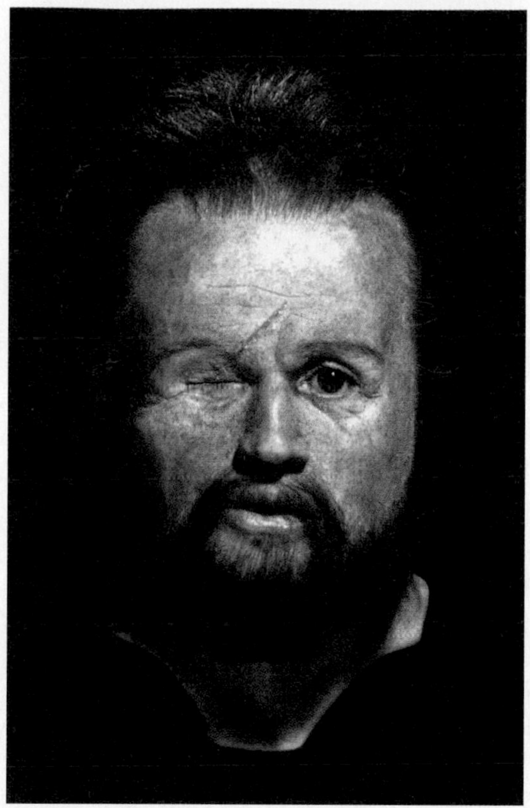

Reconstruction of the Head of King Philip II of Macedonia

Forensic archaeologists have reconstructed this head in wax to show what they think Philip II, King of Macedonia in the mid-fourth century B.C.E. and father of Alexander the Great, looked like. Philip's right eye was destroyed by an arrow, which left him disfigured but did not keep him out of battle as he went on to win the military and political leadership of mainland Greece. *(Reconstruction by Richard Neave/Photograph courtesy of the University of Manchester.)*

The Rule of Philip II, 359–336 B.C.E.

King Philip II forged Macedonia into an international power against heavy odds. Before his reign, the kingdom remained weak because of frequent strife between royals and the elite, and attacks from hostile neighbors. Princes married young, soon after the age of twenty, and possibly more than one wife, to try to produce male heirs to provide strong rule protecting the kingdom.

A military disaster in 359 B.C.E. brought Philip to the throne at a desperate moment. The Illyrians, neighbors to the west, had slaughtered the previous king and four thousand troops. Philip restored the Macedonian army's confidence by teaching his troops an unstoppable new tactic with their thrusting spears, which reached a length of sixteen feet and took two hands to wield: arranging them in the traditional phalanx formation, he created deep blocks of soldiers whose front lines bristled with outstretched spears like a lethal porcupine. Then he trained them to move around in battle in different directions without losing their formation. By moving as a unit, a mobile phalanx armed with such long spears could splinter the enemy's infantry. Deploying cavalry as a strike force to soften up the enemy while also protecting the infantry's flanks, Philip used his reorganized army to rout the Illyrians in the field, while at home he eliminated his local rivals for kingship.

Philip next moved southward into Greece, employing diplomacy, bribery, and military action to bulldoze the city-states into following him. A Greek contemporary labeled Philip "insatiable and extravagant; he did everything in a hurry . . . he never spared the time to reckon up his income and expenses." By the late 340s B.C.E., Philip had persuaded or forced most of northern and central Greece into alliance with him. Seeking glory for Greece and fearing the instability his strengthened army would create in his kingdom if the soldiers had nothing to do, he decided to lead a united Macedonian and Greek army to conquer the Persian Empire.

Philip justified attacking Persia as revenge for its invasion of Greece 150 years earlier. Some Greeks remained unconvinced. At Athens, Demosthenes bitterly criticized Greeks for not resisting Philip. They stood by, he thundered, "as if Philip was a hailstorm, praying that he would not come their way, but not trying to do anything to head him off." Moved by Demosthenes' words, Athens and Thebes rallied a coalition of southern Greek city-states to combat Philip, but in 338 B.C.E. the Macedonian king and his Greek allies crushed the coalition's forces at the battle of Chaeronea in Boeotia (Map 4.1). The defeated city-states retained their internal freedom, but Philip forced them to join his alliance. The battle of Chaeronea marked a turning point in Greek history: never again would the city-states of Greece be independent agents in foreign policy. City-states re-

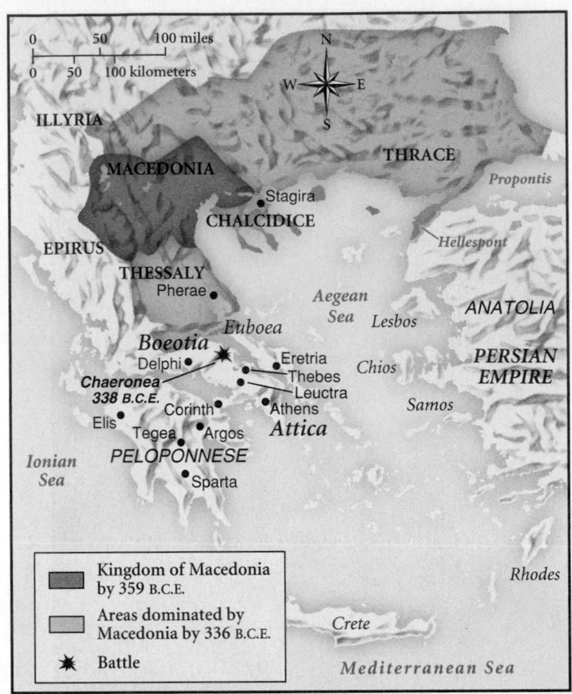

MAP 4.1 Expansion of Macedonia under Philip II, 359–336 B.C.E.
King Philip II expanded Macedonian power southward; mountainous terrain and warlike people blocked the way northward. The Macedonian royal house saw itself as ethnically Greek, and Philip made himself the leader of Greece by defeating a Greek coalition led by Athens at the battle of Chaeronea in 338 B.C.E. Sparta, far from Macedonia in the southern Peloponnese, did not join the coalition. Philip ignored it; Sparta's declining number of citizens made it too weak to matter.

mained Greece's central social and economic units, but they were always looking over their shoulders, worrying about the powerful kings who wanted to control them.

The Rule of Alexander the Great, 336–323 B.C.E.

If Philip had not been murdered by a Macedonian acquaintance in 336 B.C.E., we might be calling him Philip the Great. Instead, his assassination brought his son Alexander III to power. Rumors swirled that the son and his mother, Olympias, had arranged Philip's murder to seize the throne for the twenty-year-old Alexander, but our best guess is that the murderer acted out of personal anger at the king. Alexander secured his rule by killing his internal rivals and defeating Macedonia's enemies to the west and north in several lightning-fast strikes. Finally, Alexander forced the southern Greeks, who had defected from the alliance at the news of Philip's death, to rejoin. To demonstrate the price of disloyalty, in 335 B.C.E. Alexander destroyed Thebes for having rebelled.

Conquering the Persian Empire In 334 B.C.E., Alexander launched the most astonishing military campaign in ancient history by leading a Macedonian and Greek army against the Persian Empire to fulfill Philip's dream of avenging Greece. Alexander's conquest of all the lands from Turkey to Egypt to Uzbekistan while still in his twenties led later peoples to call him Alexander the Great. In his own time, he became a legend by motivating his men to victory after victory in hostile regions far from Macedonia.

Alexander inspired his troops by exhibiting reckless disregard for his own safety in battle. He often led the charge against the enemy's front line, riding his warhorse Bucephalas ("oxhead"). Everyone saw him speeding ahead in his plumed helmet, polished armor, and vividly colored cloak. He was so intent on conquest that he rejected advice to delay the war until he had fathered an heir. He gave away nearly all of his land to strengthen ties with his army officers. "What," one adviser asked, "do you have left for yourself?" "My hopes," Alexander replied. Alexander's hopes centered on making himself a warrior as famous as Achilles; under his pillow he always kept a copy of Homer's *Iliad*—and a dagger.

Alexander displayed his heroic ambitions as his army advanced. In Anatolia, he visited Gordion, where an oracle had promised the lordship of Asia to whoever could untie a massive knot of rope tying the yoke of an ancient chariot. Alexander, so the story goes, cut the Gordian knot with his sword. When Alexander later captured the Persian king's wives and daughters, he treated the women with respect. His honorable behavior toward the Persian royal women enhanced his claim to be the legitimate king of all Asia.

Building on Near Eastern traditions of siege technology and Philip's innovations, Alexander developed better military technology. When Tyre, a heavily fortified city on an island off the eastern Mediterranean coast, refused to surrender to him in 332 B.C.E., he built a massive stone pier as a platform for artillery towers, armored battering rams, and catapults flinging boulders to breach Tyre's walls. The successful use of this siege technology against Tyre showed that walls alone could no longer protect city-states. The knowledge that Alexander's army could overcome their fortifications made enemies much readier to negotiate a deal.

In his conquest of Egypt and the Persian heartland, Alexander revealed his strategy for ruling a vast empire: keeping an area's traditional administrative system in place while sprinkling cities of Greeks and Macedonians in conquered territory. In Egypt, he established his first new city, naming it Alexandria after himself. In Persia, he proclaimed himself the king of Asia and left the existing governing units intact, retaining selected Persian administrators. For local populations, Alexander's becoming their king changed their lives not a bit. They continued to send the same taxes to a remote master.

To India and Back Alexander led his army past the Persian heartland farther east into territory hardly known to the Greeks (Map 4.2). He aimed to outdo the heroes of legend by marching to the end of the world. Shrinking his army to reduce the need for supplies, he marched northeast into what is today Afghanistan and Uzbekistan. On the Jaxartes River, he founded a city called Alexandria the Furthest to show that he had penetrated deeper into this region than even Cyrus, the founder of the Persian Empire. Unable to subdue the local guerrilla forces, Alexander settled for an alliance sealed by his marriage to the Bactrian princess Roxane.

Alexander then headed east into India. Seventy days of marching through monsoon rains extinguished his soldiers' fire for conquest. In the spring of 326 B.C.E., they mutinied on the banks of the Hyphasis River and forced Alexander to turn back. The return journey through southeastern Iran's deserts cost many casualties from hunger and thirst; the survivors finally reached safety in the Persian heartland in 324 B.C.E. Alexander immediately began planning an invasion of the Arabian peninsula and, after that, of North Africa.

Alexander ruled more harshly after his return and began treating the Greeks as subjects instead of allies. He ordered the city-states to restore citizenship to the many exiles created by war, whose status as stateless persons was causing unrest. Even more striking was Alexander's announcement that he wished to receive the honors due a god. Most Greek city-states obeyed by sending religious delegations to him. A Spartan expressed the only prudent position on Alexander's deification: "If Alexander wishes to be a god, then we'll agree that he be called a god."

Personal motives best explain Alexander's announcement. He had come to believe he was truly the son of Zeus; after all, Greek myths said Zeus had mated with many human females who produced children. Since Alexander's superhuman accomplishments demonstrated that he had achieved godlike power, he must be a god himself. Alexander's divinity was, in ancient terms, a natural consequence of his power.

Alexander's premature death from a fever and heavy drinking in 323 B.C.E. aborted his plan to conquer Arabia and North Africa. His death followed months of depression provoked by the death of his best friend, Hephaistion. Some modern historians conclude that Alexander and Hephaistion were lovers, but no surviving ancient source reports this. Unfortunately for the stability of Alexander's immense conquests, by the time of his death he had not fathered an heir who could take over his rule. Roxane gave birth to their son only after Alexander's death. The story goes that, when at Alexander's deathbed his commanders asked him to whom he left his kingdom, he replied, "To the most powerful."

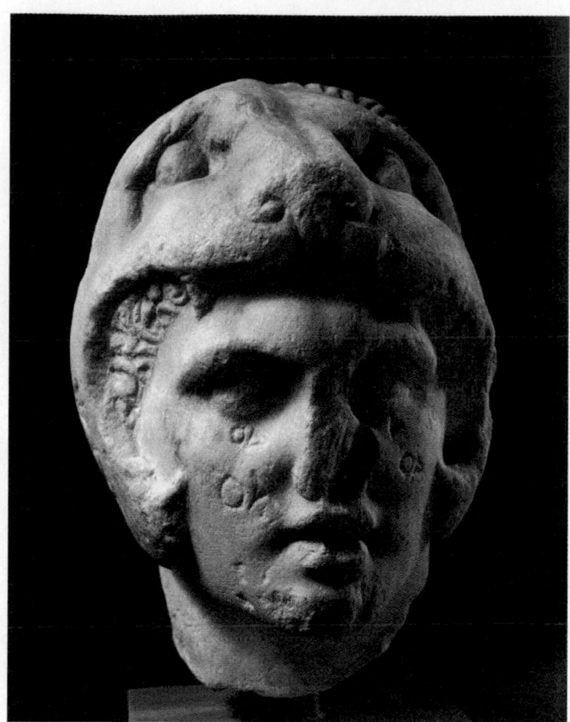

Alexander the Great
This marble portrait of Alexander (a copy of a bronze original) has him wearing a lion's head as a helmet to recall the hero Herakles (Hercules), whose myth said he killed the fiercest beast in Greece and wore its head as proof. Alexander gazes into the distance; he commanded that his portraits show him with this visionary expression. Why do you think he wanted the world to see him with these attributes? *(The Art Archive/National Archeological Museum, Athens/Dagli Orti Collection.)*

Alexander's Impact Scholars disagree on almost everything about Alexander, from whether his claim to divinity was meant to justify his increasingly authoritarian attitude toward the Greek city-states, to what he meant to achieve through conquest, to the nature of his character. Was he a bloodthirsty monster obsessed with war, or a romantic visionary intent on creating a multiethnic world open to all cultures? The ancient sources suggest that Alexander had interlinked goals reflecting his restless and ruthless nature: both to conquer and administer the known world and to explore and colonize new territory beyond.

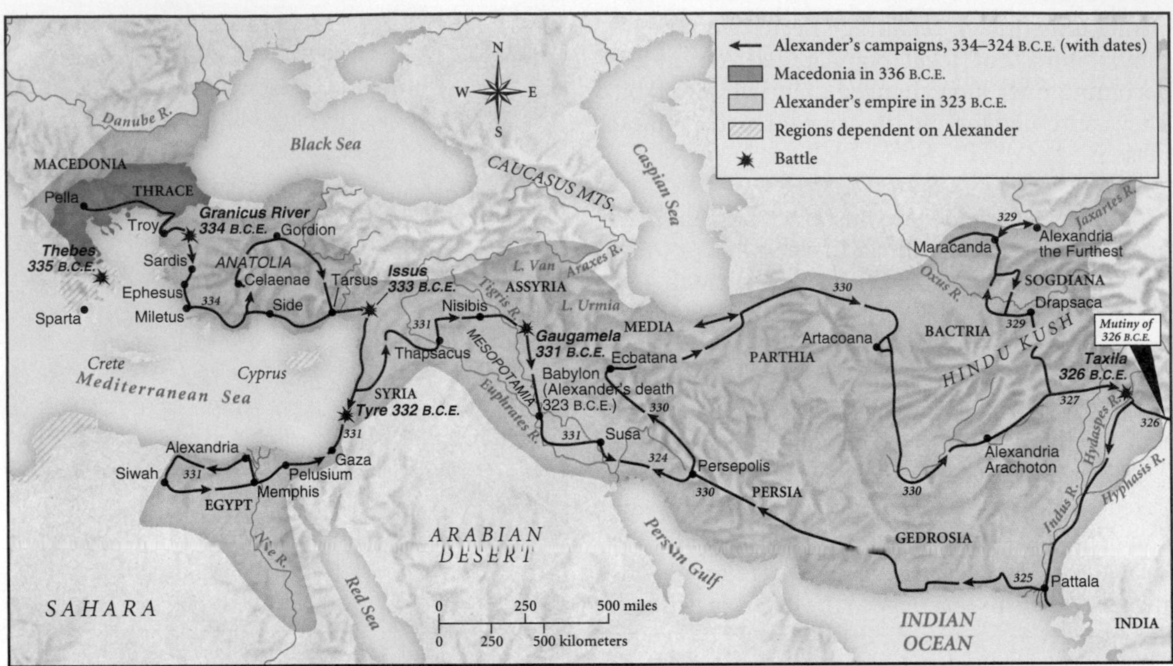

MAP 4.2 Conquests of Alexander the Great, 336–323 B.C.E.
From the time Alexander led his army against Persia in 334 B.C.E. until his death in 323 B.C.E., he was continually fighting military campaigns. His charismatic and fearless generalship, combined with effective intelligence gathering about his targets, generated an unbroken string of victories and made him a legend. His founding of garrison cities and preservation of local governments kept his conquests largely stable during his lifetime.

The ancient world agreed that Alexander was a marvel. An Athenian orator expressed the bewilderment many people felt over the events of Alexander's lifetime: "What strange and unexpected event has not occurred in our time? The life we have lived is no ordinary human one, but we were born to be an object of wonder to posterity." Alexander's fame increased after his death. Stories of reality-defying exploits attributed to him became popular folktales throughout the ancient world, even in distant regions such as southern Africa, where Alexander never set foot.

Alexander's conquests had consequences in many areas. His explorations benefited scientific fields from geography to botany because he took along knowledgeable writers to collect and catalog new knowledge. He had vast quantities of scientific observations dispatched to his old tutor Aristotle. Alexander's new cities promoted trade between Greece and the Near East. Most of all, his career brought these cultures into closer contact than ever before. This contact represented his career's most enduring impact.

REVIEW QUESTION What were the accomplishments of Alexander the Great, and what were their effects both for the ancient world and for later Western civilization?

The Hellenistic Kingdoms, 323–30 B.C.E.

Alexander's empire fragmented after his death, and new kingdoms arose. The period that extends from Alexander's death in 323 B.C.E. to the death of Cleopatra VII, the last Macedonian queen of Egypt, in 30 B.C.E. is known as the Hellenistic Age, a name given it by modern scholars. The word **Hellenistic** ("Greek-like") conveys the most significant characteristic of this period: the emergence in the eastern Mediterranean world of a mixture of Near Eastern and Greek traditions that generated innovations in politics, literature, art, philosophy, and religion. War stirred up this cultural mixing, and tension persisted between conquerors and subjects. The process promoted regional diversity: Greek ideas and practices had their greatest impact on the urban populations of Egypt and southwestern Asia, while the many people who farmed in the countryside had much less contact with Greek ways of life.

Hellenistic: An adjective meaning "Greek-like" that is today used as a chronological term for the period 323–30 B.C.E.

New kingdoms formed the Hellenistic period's dominant political structures. They reintroduced monarchy into Greek culture, there having been no kings in Greece since the fall of Mycenaean civilization nearly a thousand years earlier. Commanders from Alexander's army created the kingdoms after his death by seizing portions of his empire and proclaiming themselves kings in these new states. This process of state formation took more than fifty years of war. The self-proclaimed kings — called Alexander's successors — had to transform their families into dynasties and accumulate enough power to force the Greek city-states to give control of foreign policy to these new overlords. This process of transformation reinforced the hierarchical nature of Hellenistic society. Eventually, wars with the Romans brought all the Hellenistic kingdoms to an end.

Creating New Kingdoms

Alexander's early death left his succession an open question. His only legitimate son was born a few months later. Alexander's mother, Olympias, tried to protect her grandson, but Alexander's former commanders executed Olympias in 316 B.C.E. and later murdered the boy, Alexander IV, and his mother, Roxane. Having wiped out the royal family, the successors divided Alexander's conquests among themselves. Antigonus (c. 382–301 B.C.E.) took over Anatolia, the Near East, Macedonia, and Greece; Seleucus (c. 358–281 B.C.E.) seized Babylonia and the East as far as India; and Ptolemy (c. 367–282 B.C.E.) grabbed Egypt. These successors had to create their own form of monarchy based on military power and personal prestige because they did not inherit their positions legitimately: they were self-proclaimed rulers with no connection to Alexander's royal line. Several years after the elimination of Alexander's line, however, they announced that they were now kings.

In the beginning, the new kings' biggest enemies were one another. They fought constantly in the decades after Alexander's death, trying to annex more territory to their individual kingdoms. By the middle of the third century B.C.E., the three Hellenistic kingdoms had established their home territories (Map 4.3). The Antigonids had been reduced to a kingdom in Macedonia, but they also compelled the mainland Greek city-states to follow royal foreign policy. The Seleucids ruled in Syria and Mesopotamia, but they had to cede their easternmost territory to the Indian king Chandragupta (r. 323–299 B.C.E.). They also lost most of Persia to the Parthians, a northern Iranian people. The Ptolemies ruled the rich land of Egypt.

These territorial arrangements were never completely stable because the Hellenistic monarchs never stopped competing. Conflicts repeatedly arose over border areas. The Ptolemies and the Seleucids, for example, fought to control the eastern Mediterranean coast, just as the Egyptians and Hittites had

Greek-Style Buddha
The style of this statue of the founder of Buddhism, who expounded his doctrines in India, shows the mingling of eastern and western art. The Buddha's appearance, gaze, and posture stem from Indian artistic traditions, while the flowing folds of his garment recall Greek traditions. Compare the garment that Socrates is wearing on page 96. This combination of styles is called Gandhara, after the region in northwestern India where it began. What do you think are the possible motives for combining different artistic traditions? *(Borromeo/Art Resource, NY.)*

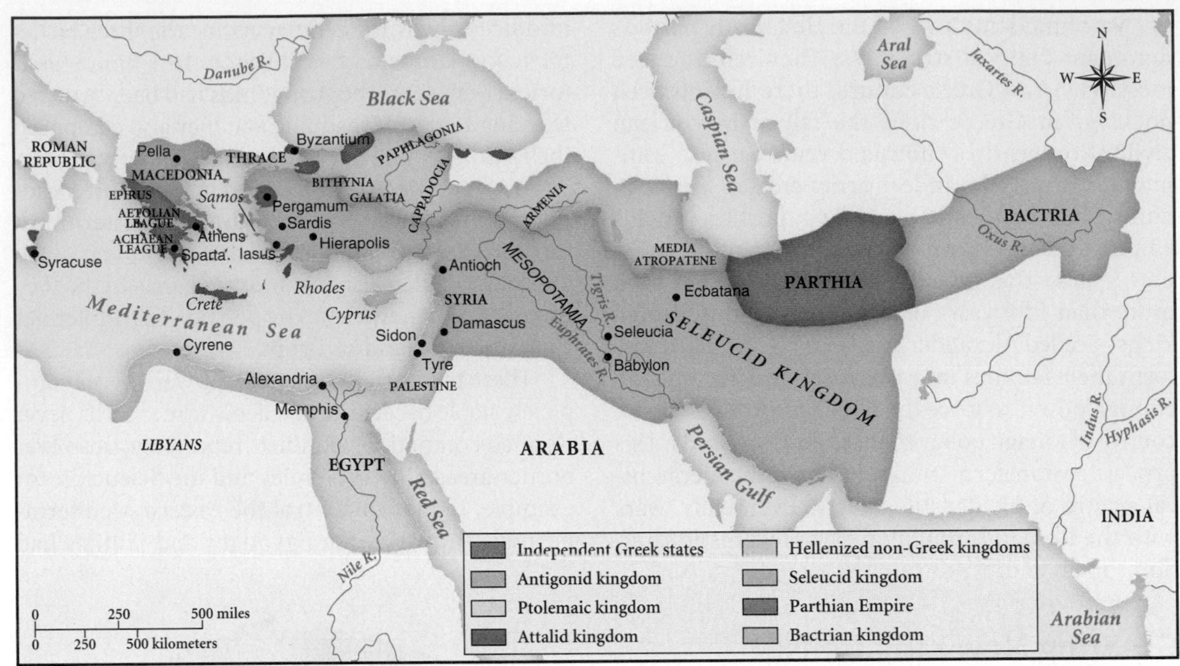

MAP 4.3 Hellenistic Kingdoms, 240 B.C.E.
Monarchy became the dominant political system in the areas of Alexander's conquests. By about eighty years after his death, the three major kingdoms established by his successors had settled their boundaries, after the Seleucids gave up their easternmost territories to an Indian king and the Attalids carved out their kingdom in western Anatolia.

done centuries earlier. The wars between the major kingdoms left openings for smaller, regional kingdoms to establish themselves. The most famous of these was the kingdom of the Attalids in western Anatolia, with the wealthy city of Pergamum as its capital. In Bactria in Central Asia, the Greeks—originally colonists settled by Alexander—broke off from the Seleucid kingdom in the mid-third century B.C.E. to found their own regional kingdom, which flourished for a time from the trade in luxury goods between India and China and the Mediterranean world.

Royal Silver Coin of Bactria
Bactria in central Asia (today part of Afghanistan, Pakistan, and Tajikistan) had been a province of the Persian Empire and then of the empire of Alexander the Great. After the fragmentation of Alexander's empire in the century after his death, Greeks established what scholars call Indo-Greek kingdoms there. This coin of King Demetrius I shows him wearing an elephant headdress, a symbol of his ambitions to conquer India. The other side shows the Greek mythological hero Heracles, who was said to have been the first Greek to visit this part of the world. *(The Granger Collection, New York—All rights reserved.)*

The Structure of Hellenistic Kingdoms

The Hellenistic kingdoms imposed foreign rule by Macedonian kings and queens on indigenous populations. The kings incorporated local traditions into their rule to build legitimacy. The Seleucids combined Macedonian with Near Eastern traditions, while the Ptolemies mixed Macedonian with Egyptian ones. The Ptolemaic royal family, for example, observed the Egyptian royal tradition of brother-sister marriage. Royal power was the ultimate source of control over the kingdoms' subjects, in keeping with the Near Eastern monarchical tradition that Hellenistic kings adopted. This tradition persisted above all in defining justice. Seleucus justified his rule on what he claimed as a universal truth of monarchy: "It is not the customs of the Persians and other people that I impose upon you, but the law which is common to everyone, that what is decreed by the king is always just." Hellenistic kings had to do more to survive than simply assert a right to rule, however. The survival of their dynasties depended on their ability to create strong armies, effective administrations, and close ties to urban elites. A letter from a Greek city summed up the situation while praising the Seleucid king Antiochus I (c. 324–261 B.C.E.): "His rule depends above all on his own excellence [aretê], and on the goodwill of his friends, and on his forces."

Royal Military Forces and Administration

Hellenistic royal armies and navies provided internal and external security. Professional soldiers manned these forces. To develop their military might, the Seleucid and Ptolemaic kings encouraged immigration by Greeks and Macedonians, who received land grants in return for military service. When this source of manpower gave out, the kings had to employ more local men as troops. Military competition put tremendous financial pressure on the kings to pay growing numbers of mercenaries and to purchase expensive new military technology. To compete effectively, a Hellenistic king had to provide giant artillery, such as catapults capable of flinging a 170-pound projectile up to two hundred yards. His navy cost a fortune because warships were now huge, requiring crews of several hundred men. War elephants, whose bellowing charges frightened opposing infantry, became popular after Alexander's encounters with them in India, and they were extremely costly to maintain.

Hellenistic kings needed effective administrations to collect revenues. Initially, they recruited mostly Greek and Macedonian immigrants to fill high-level posts. Following Alexander's example, however, the Seleucids and the Ptolemies also employed non-Greeks for middle- and lower-level positions, where officials had to be able to deal with the subject populations and speak their languages. Local men who wanted a government job bettered their chances if they could read and write Greek in addition to their native language. Bilingualism qualified them to fill positions communicating the orders of the highest-ranking officials, all Greeks and Macedonians, to local farmers, builders, and crafts producers. Non-Greeks who had successful government careers were rarely admitted to royal society because Greeks and Macedonians saw themselves as too superior to mix with locals. Greeks and non-Greeks therefore tended to live in separate communities.

Hellenistic royal administrations resembled those of the earlier Assyrian, Babylonian, and Persian Empires. Administrators' principal responsibilities were to maintain order and to direct the kingdoms' tax systems. Officials mediated disputes whenever possible, but they could call on soldiers to serve as police. The Ptolemaic administration used methods of central planning and control inherited from earlier Egyptian history. Its officials continued to administer royal monopolies, such as that on vegetable oil, to maximize the king's revenue. They decided how much land farmers could sow in oil-bearing plants, supervised production and distribution of the oil, and set prices for every stage of the oil business. The king, through his officials, also often entered into partnerships with private investors to produce more revenue.

Cities and Urban Elites

Cities were the Hellenistic kingdoms' economic and social hubs. Many Greeks and Macedonians lived in new cities founded by Alexander and the Hellenistic kings in Egypt and the Near East, and they also immigrated to existing cities there. Hellenistic kings promoted this urban immigration by adorning their new cities with the features of classical Greek city-states, such as gymnasia and theaters. Although these cities often retained the city-state's political institutions, such as councils and assemblies for citizen men, the need to follow royal policy limited their freedom; they made no independent decisions on foreign policy. In addition, the cities taxed their populations to send money demanded by the king.

Monarchy's reemergence in the Greek world also created a new relationship between rulers and the social elites, because the crucial element in the Hellenistic kingdom's political and social structure was the system of mutual rewards by which the kings and their leading urban subjects became partners in government and public finance. Wealthy people in the cities had the crucial responsibility of collecting taxes from the surrounding countryside as well as from their city and sending the money on to the royal treasury; the royal military and the administration were too small to perform these duties themselves. The kings honored and flattered the cities' Greek and Macedonian social elites because they needed their cooperation to ensure a steady flow of tax revenues. When writing to a city's council, the king would express himself in the form of polite requests, but the recipients knew he was giving commands.

This system thus continued the Greek tradition of requiring the wealthy elite to contribute to the common good. Cooperative cities received gifts from the king to pay for expensive public works like theaters and temples or for reconstruction after natural disasters such as earthquakes. Wealthy men and women in turn helped keep the general population peaceful by subsidizing teachers and doctors, financing public works, and providing donations and loans to ensure a reliable supply of grain to feed the city's residents.

The system of mutual rewards also required the kings to establish relationships with well-to-do non-Greeks living in the old cities of Anatolia and the Near East to keep their vast kingdoms peaceful and profitable. In addition, non-Greeks and non-Macedonians from eastern regions began moving westward to the new Hellenistic Greek cities in increasing numbers. Jews in particular moved from their ancestral homeland to Anatolia, Greece, and Egypt. The Jewish community eventually became an influential minority in Egyptian Alexandria, the most important Hellenistic city. In Egypt, as the Rosetta stone shows, the king also had to build good relationships with the priests who controlled the temples of the traditional Egyptian gods because the temples owned large tracts of rich land worked by tenant farmers.

The Layers of Hellenistic Society

Hellenistic monarchy reinforced social hierarchy. At the top were the royal family and the king's friends. The Greek and Macedonian elites of the major cities ranked next. Then came indigenous urban elites, leaders of large minority urban populations, and local lords in rural regions. Merchants, artisans, and laborers made up the free population's bottom layer. Slaves remained where they had always been, without any social status.

The kingdoms' growth increased the demand for slave labor throughout the eastern Mediterranean; the island of Delos established a market where up to ten thousand slaves a day were bought and sold. The fortunate ones were purchased as servants for the royal court or elite households and lived physically comfortable lives, so long as they pleased their owners. The luckless ones labored, and often died, in the mines. Enslaved children could be taken far from home to work. For example, a sales contract from 259 B.C.E. records that Zeno, to whom the camel trader wrote, bought a girl about seven years old named Gemstone to work in an Egyptian textile factory. Originally from an eastern Mediterranean town, she had previously labored as the slave of a Greek mercenary soldier employed by a Jewish cavalry commander in the Transjordan region.

The Poor Like slaves, poor people—who made up the majority of the population—lived their lives as workers, most of them as laborers in agriculture, the foundation of the Hellenistic kingdoms' economies. There were some large cities, above all Alexandria in Egypt, but the majority of the population had their homes in country villages. Many of the poor were employed on the royal family's huge estates, but free peasants still worked their own small fields in addition to laboring for wealthy landowners. Rural people rose with the sun and began working before the heat became unbearable, raising the same kinds of crops and animals as their ancestors had, using the same simple hand tools. Perhaps as many as 80 percent of all adult men and women had to work the land to produce enough food to sustain the population. Poverty often meant hunger, even in fertile lands such as Egypt. In cities, poor women and men could work as small merchants, peddlers, and artisans, producing and selling goods such as tools, pottery, clothing, and furniture. Men could sign on as deckhands on the merchant ships that sailed the Mediterranean Sea and Indian Ocean.

Many country people in the Seleucid and Ptolemaic kingdoms existed in a state of dependency between free and slave. The peoples, as they were called, were tenants who farmed the estates belonging to the king. Although they could not be sold like slaves, they were not allowed to move away or abandon their tenancies. They owed a large quota of produce to the king, and this compulsory rent gave these tenant farmers little chance to escape poverty.

Emotion in Hellenistic Sculpture
Hellenistic sculptors introduced a new style into Greek art by depicting people's emotions. This statue of an elderly woman, for example, shows an expression of pain, disheveled clothing, and a body stooped from age and from carrying a basket of chickens and vegetables. The statue probably portrays a poor woman trying to survive by hawking food in the street. It is probably a later copy of a Hellenistic original. What sort of emotional response do you think this new style was meant to produce in the audience for such art? *(Statue of an old woman. Roman. Early Imperial, Julio-Claudian, 14–68 C.E. Marble, Pentelic, h. 49⅝ in. [125.98 cm.], Rogers Fund, 1909 [09.39]. The Metropolitan Museum of Art, New York, NY, U.S.A. Image copyright © The Metropolitan Museum of Art / Art Resource, NY.)*

Women's Lives Hellenistic women's social and political status depended on their rank in the kingdom's hierarchy. Hellenistic queens commanded enormous riches and honors. The kingdoms based their legitimacy on the female as well as the male side. Hellenistic queens exercised power as the representatives of distinguished families; the mothers of a line of royal descendants; and patrons of artists, thinkers, and even cities. Later Ptolemaic queens essentially co-ruled with their husbands. Queens ruled on their own when no male heir existed. For example, Arsinoe II (c. 316–270 B.C.E.), the daughter of Ptolemy I, first married the Macedonian successor Lysimachus, who gave her four towns as her personal domain. After his death she married her brother Ptolemy II of Egypt and exerted at least as much influence on policy as he did. The excellences publicly praised in a queen reflected traditional Greek values for women. A city decree from about 165 B.C.E. honored Queen Apollonis of Pergamum by praising her piety toward the gods, reverence toward her parents, distinguished conduct toward her husband, and harmonious relations with her "beautiful children born in wedlock."

Some queens paid special attention to the condition of women. About 195 B.C.E., for example, the Seleucid queen Laodice gave a ten-year endowment to a city to provide dowries for needy girls. That Laodice funded dowries shows that she recognized the importance to women of controlling property, the surest guarantee of respect in their households.

Most women remained under the control of men. "Who can judge better than a father what is to his daughter's interest?" remained the dominant belief of fathers. Once a woman married, the words *husband* and *wife* replaced *father* and *daughter*. Most of the time, elite women continued to be separated from men outside their families, while poor women still worked in public. Greeks continued to abandon infants they did not want to raise—girls more often than boys—but other populations, such as the Egyptians and the Jews, did not practice infant exposure. Exposure differed from infanticide in that the parents expected someone to find the child and rear it, usually as a slave. A third-century B.C.E. comic poet overstated the case by saying, "A son, one always raises even if one is poor; a daughter, one exposes, even if one is rich." Daughters of wealthy parents were not usually abandoned, but scholars have estimated that up to 10 percent of other infant girls were.

Depending on their social class, women could sometimes achieve greater control over their lives in the Hellenistic period than before. A woman of exceptional wealth could enter public life by making donations or loans to her city and in return be rewarded with an official post in local government. In Egypt, women of all classes acquired greater say in married life as the marriage contract (see Chapter 3, "Contrasting Views," page 88) evolved from an agreement between the bride's parents and the groom to one in which the bride made her own arrangements with the groom.

The Wealthy Rich people showed increasing concern for the welfare of the less fortunate during the Hellenistic period. They were following the lead of the royal families, who emphasized philanthropy to build a reputation for generosity that would support their legitimacy in ruling. Sometimes wealthy citizens funded a foundation to distribute free grain to eliminate food shortages, and they also funded schools for children in various Hellenistic cities, the first public schools in the Greek world. In some places, girls as well as boys could attend school. Many cities also began sponsoring doctors to improve medical care: patients still had to pay, but at least they could count on finding a doctor.

The donors funding these services were repaid by the respect and honor they earned from their fellow citizens. Philanthropy even touched international relations. When an earthquake devastated Rhodes, many cities joined kings and queens in sending donations to help the residents recover. In return, they showered honors on their benefactors by appointing them to prestigious municipal offices and erecting inscriptions expressing the city's gratitude. In this system, the masses' welfare depended more and more on the generosity of the rich. Lacking democracy, the poor had no political power to demand support.

The End of the Hellenistic Kingdoms

All the Hellenistic kingdoms eventually lost their great riches and power, mostly through internal disunity in their ruling families. In their weakened condition, Hellenistic states could not prevent takeovers by the Romans, who over time intervened more and more forcefully in conflicts among kingdoms and Greek city-states in the eastern Mediterranean. Roman foreign policy was meant to protect their growing interests in this part of the world and ward off any danger to their own territory.

These interventions caused wars. Rome first established dominance over the Antigonid kingdom by the middle of the second century B.C.E. Next, the Seleucid kingdom fell to the Romans in 64 B.C.E. The Ptolemaic kingdom in Egypt survived a bit longer; by the 50s B.C.E., its royal family had split into warring factions, and the resulting weakness forced the rivals for the throne to seek Roman support. The end came when the famous queen Cleopatra, the last Macedonian to rule Egypt, chose the losing side in the civil war between Mark Antony and the future emperor Augustus in the late first century B.C.E. An invading Roman army ended Ptolemaic rule in 30 B.C.E. Rome thus became the heir to all the Hellenistic kingdoms (see Mapping the West, page 135).

REVIEW QUESTION How did the political and social organization of the new Hellenistic kingdoms compare with that of the earlier Greek city-states?

Seated Boxer
This Hellenistic-era sculpture in bronze shows an obviously tired boxer after a bout. He is still wearing the hard-edged leather gloves that made Greek and Roman boxing so brutal and dangerous. His pose, showing him looking up at the sky in weariness, or perhaps listening to his trainer or a fan, is characteristic of the tendency of Hellenistic artists to portray people in realistic rather than idealized ways. *(Museo Nazionale Romano delle Terme/akg-images/Jürgen Raible.)*

Hellenistic Culture

Hellenistic culture reflected three principal influences: the overwhelming impact of royal wealth, increased emphasis on private life and emotion, and greater interaction of diverse peoples. The kings drove developments in literature, art, science, and philosophy by deciding which scholars and artists to put on the royal payroll. The obligation of authors and artists to the kings meant that they could not criticize public policy; their works therefore concentrated on everyday life and individual emotion.

Cultural interaction between Near Eastern and Greek traditions occurred most prominently in language and religion. These developments deeply influenced the Romans as they took over the Hellenistic world. The Roman poet Horace (65–8 B.C.E.) described the effect of Hellenistic culture on his own by saying that "captive Greece captured its fierce victor."

The Arts under Royal Support

Hellenistic kings became the supporters of scholarship and the arts on a vast scale, competing with one another to lure the best scholars and artists to their capitals with lavish salaries. They funded intellectuals and artists because they wanted to boost their reputations by having these famous people produce books, poems, sculptures, and other prestigious creations at their courts.

The Ptolemies turned Alexandria into the Mediterranean's leading arts and sciences center, establishing the world's first scholarly research institute and a massive library. The librarians were instructed to collect all the books in the world. The library grew to hold half a million scrolls, an enormous number for the time. Linked to it was the building in which the hired research scholars dined together and produced encyclopedias of knowledge such as *The Wonders of the World* and *On the Rivers of Europe*. We still use the name of the research institute's building, the Museum ("place of the Muses," the Greek goddesses of learning and the arts), to designate institutions preserving knowledge. The Alexandrian scholars produced prodigiously. Their champion was the scholar Didymus (c. 80–10 B.C.E.), nicknamed "Brass Bowels" for writing nearly four thousand books commenting on literature. Sadly, not a single one has survived; the library was later destroyed by fire in wartime.

Literature at Court The writers and artists paid by Hellenistic kings had to please their paymasters with their works. The poet Theocritus (c. 300–260 B.C.E.) spelled out the deal

DOCUMENT

Epigrams by Women Poets

Anyte, Nossis, and Erinna were three of the most famous women poets of the Hellenistic period. They composed short poems about death, love, and sex, often centered on women. They also invented the tradition of writing poems about speaking animals. None of them was hired by a Hellenistic king to be a resident poet at court, so they had to create their poetic masterpieces on their own. We lack documentary evidence to tell us why women authors worked in this genre of creative literature, as opposed to writing longer works of epic or history; they may have preferred shorter poems for aesthetic and literary reasons, but it may also be because they lacked the financial backing to complete bigger projects.

Anyte on Mourning a Young Woman

The virgin Antibia I mourn for; many
young men came to her father's house seeking to marry her,
drawn by the fame of her beauty and wisdom. But everyone's
hopes deadly Fate tossed away.

Anyte on a Dolphin Speaking after Death

No longer taking joy in surging seas
will I stretch out my neck as I leap from the depths,
no longer around the lovely bows of the ship
will I jump, delighting in the figurehead, my likeness.
No, the purple surge of the sea cast me onto the land;
here I lie on this narrow strip of beach.

Nossis on the Joy of Sex

Nothing is sweeter than sexual passion; every other blessing is second;
I spit out from my mouth even honey.
This is what Nossis says: anyone that Aphrodite has not kissed
doesn't know what kind of flowers her roses are.

Nossis on a Woman's Present to Aphrodite

The picture of herself Callo dedicated in the temple of blond Aphrodite,
having her portrait made to look exactly like herself.
How gracefully it stands; see how great is the grace that blooms on it.
Best wishes to her! For she has no blame in her life.

Erinna on the Death of the Bride Baukis

I am the grave marker of the bride Baukis. As you pass by
this most wept-for pillar, say this to Hades in the underworld:
"You are jealous of Baukis, Hades!" The lovely letters that you see
announce the brutal fate Chance brought to Baukis,
how with the pine-torches from the wedding that they were using to worship Hymenaeus [the god of marriage]
the groom's father set afire her funeral pyre.
And you, Hymenaeus, the tuneful song of the wedding
converted to the sad cries of lamentation.

Source: *Palatine Anthology*, 7.490, 7.215, 5.170, 9.605, 7.712. Translations by Thomas R. Martin.

Question to Consider

- **What do these women's poems reveal about women's lives and concerns in the Hellenistic age?**

underlying royal support in a poem flattering King Ptolemy II: "The spokesmen of the Muses [that is, poets] celebrate Ptolemy in return for his benefactions." Poets such as Theocritus avoided political topics and stressed the social gap between the intellectual elite—to which the kings belonged—and the uneducated masses. They filled their new poetry with erudite references to make it difficult to understand and therefore exclusive. Only people with a deep literary education could appreciate the mythological allusions that studded these authors' elaborate poems.

Theocritus was the first Greek poet to express the divide between town and countryside, a poetic stance corresponding to a growing Hellenistic reality. His *Idylls* emphasized the discontinuity between urban life and the country bumpkins' bucolic existence, reflecting the Ptolemaic social division between the food consumers in the town and the food producers in the countryside. Theocritus presented a city dweller's idealized dream that country life was peaceful and stress-free, a fiction that deeply influenced later literature.

No Hellenistic women poets seem to have enjoyed royal financial support; rather, they created their art independently. They excelled in writing **epigrams**, a style of short poem originally used on tombstones to remember the dead. Highly literary poems by women from diverse regions of the Hellenistic world still survive (see Document, "Epigrams by Women Poets," above). Many epigrams were about women, from courtesans to respectable matrons, and the writer's personal feelings. No other

epigrams: Short poems written by women in the Hellenistic Age; many were about other women and the writer's personal feelings.

Hellenistic literature better conveys the depth of human emotion than the epigrams of women poets.

Hellenistic comedies also emphasized stories about emotions and stayed away from politics. Comic playwrights presented plays concerning the troubles of fictional lovers. These comedies of manners, as they are called, became enormously popular because, like modern situation comedies, they offered humorous views of daily life. Papyrus discoveries have restored comedies of Menander (c. 342–289 B.C.E.), the most famous Hellenistic comic poet, noted for his skill in depicting human personality (see "New Sources, New Perspectives," page 129). Hellenistic tragedy could take a multicultural approach: Ezechiel, a Jew living in Alexandria, wrote *Exodus*, a tragedy in Greek about Moses leading the Hebrews out of captivity in Egypt.

Emotion in Sculpture Hellenistic sculptors and painters also featured emotions in their works. Classical artists had given their subjects' faces an idealized serenity, but now sculptures depicted personal feelings. A sculpture from Pergamum, for example, commemorating the Attalid victory over invading Gauls (one of the Celtic peoples from what is now France), showed a defeated Celtic warrior stabbing himself after having killed his wife to prevent her enslavement by the victors.

The artists created their works mainly on order from royalty, and from the urban elites who wanted to show they had the same artistic taste as their royal superiors. The increasing diversity of subjects that emerged in Hellenistic art presumably represented a trend approved by kings, queens, and the elites. Sculpture best reveals this new preference for depicting people never before appearing in art: heartbreaking victims of war, drunkards, battered athletes, wrinkled old people. The female nude became common. A statue of Aphrodite by Praxiteles, which portrayed the goddess completely nude for the first time, became renowned as a religious object and tourist attraction in the city of Cnidos, which had commissioned it. The king of Bithynia offered to pay off the citizens' entire public debt if he could have the work of art. They refused.

Philosophy for a New Age

New philosophies arose in the Hellenistic period, all asking the same question: What is the best way to live? They recommended different paths to the same answer: individuals must achieve inner personal tranquillity to achieve freedom from the blows of outside forces, especially chance. It is easy to see why these philosophies had appeal: outside forces—the Hellenistic kings—had robbed the Greek city-states of their independence in foreign policy, and their citizens' fates ultimately rested in the hands of unpredictable monarchs. More than ever, human life seemed out of individuals' control. It therefore was appealing to look to philosophy for personal, private solutions to the unsettling new conditions of Hellenistic life.

Hellenistic philosophers concentrated on **materialism**, the doctrine that only things made of matter truly exist. Materialism denied Plato's metaphysical concept of the soul and indeed of all nonmaterial phenomena, following up Aristotle's doctrine that only things identified through logic or observation exist. Hellenistic philosophy was divided into three areas: (1) logic, the process for discovering truth; (2) physics, the fundamental truth about the nature of existence; and (3) ethics, how humans should achieve happiness and well-being through logic and physics. Materialism greatly influenced Roman thinkers and the many important Western philosophers who later read those thinkers' works.

---

materialism: A philosophical doctrine of the Hellenistic Age that denied metaphysics and claimed instead that only things consisting of matter truly exist.

Dying Barbarians
Hellenistic artists excelled in portraying emotional scenes, such as this murder-suicide of a Celtic warrior who is slaying himself after killing his wife, to prevent their capture by the enemy. (Celtic women followed their men to the battlefield.) The original was in bronze, forming part of a large sculptural group that Attalus I (r. 241–197 B.C.E.) erected at Pergamum to commemorate his victory over these barbarian raiders. Why did Attalus celebrate his victory by erecting a monument portraying the defeated enemy as brave, noble, and sympathetic? *(Erich Lessing/Art Resource, NY.)*

NEW SOURCES, NEW PERSPECTIVES

Papyrus Discoveries and Menander's Comedies

Fourth-century B.C.E. Greek playwrights invented a kind of comedy, called New Comedy, that is today's most popular entertainment—the situation comedy (sitcom). They wrote comedies that concentrated on the conflicts between personality types in everyday situations. The rocky course of love and marriage drove most plots. Avoiding political satire, comedians created type characters such as bubble-headed lovers, cranky fathers, rascally servants, and boastful soldiers, as revealed by their titles: *The Country Boob*, *Pot-Belly*, *The Stolen Girl*, *The Bad-Tempered Man*, and so on. Confusions of identity leading to hilarious misunderstandings were frequent, as were jokes about marriage, such as this one:

First Man: "He's married, you know."

Second Man: "What's that you say? Actually married? How can that be? I just left him alive and walking around!"

These comic plays inspired many imitations, especially Roman comedies, which inspired William Shakespeare (1564–1616) in England and Molière (1622–1673) in France. Their comedies, in turn, led to today's sitcoms.

The most famous author of this kind of comedy was Menander (343–291 B.C.E.) of Athens. Despite antiquity's "two thumbs up," none of Menander's comedies survived into modern times. Works of Greek and Roman literature had to be copied over and over by hand for centuries if they were to survive. For unknown reasons, people at some point stopped recopying New Comedy. So scholars knew Menander had been a star, but they had never read any of his plays—until archaeologists began finding ancient paper in Egypt.

The Egyptians made paper from the papyrus plant, and their super-dry climate preserved the paper that people used to wrap mummies or simply threw away after writing on it. The French emperor Napoleon's conquest of Egypt in 1798–1801 inspired a European craze for collecting papyrus. By unwrapping mummies and excavating ancient trash dumps, scholars have discovered thousands of texts of all kinds.

Incredibly, some of Menander's comedies turned up in these discoveries, beginning with *The Bad-Tempered Man*. Further detective work has yielded more, and today we can read most of *The Girl from Samos* and parts of other plays. In this way, Menander's characters, stories, and jokes have come back from the dead.

Recovering plays from papyrus is difficult. The handwriting is often difficult to make out, there are no gaps between words, punctuation is minimal, changes in speakers are indicated by colons or dashes rather than by names, and there are no stage directions. Sometimes the papyrus has been chewed by mice and insects, burned, or torn. One part of a play can turn up in the wrapping of one mummy and another part in a different one. However, the collaboration of archaeologists, historians, and literary scholars has brought back to life the ancestors of what remains our most crowd-pleasing form of comedy.

Questions to Consider

1. What makes situation comedy so appealing?
2. Why would Greeks living in the fourth century B.C.E. prefer situation comedy to political satire or darker forms of humor?

Further Reading

Bagnall, Roger. *Reading Papyri, Writing Ancient History*. 1995.

Menander: Plays and Fragments. Translated with an introduction by Norma Miller. 1987.

Parkinson, Richard, and Stephen Quirke. *Papyrus*. 1995.

Pompeian Wall Painting of Menander

A wealthy Roman had this painting of Menander put on a wall in his house at Pompeii. The owner appears to have loved Greek plays—he had the room's other walls decorated with images of the tragedian Euripides and possibly the Muses of Tragedy and Comedy. The faded lettering on the scroll identified the playwright: "Menander: he was the first to write New Comedy." The ivy wreath on his head symbolizes the poet's victory in the contests of comedies presented at the festivals of the god Dionysus, the patron of drama. *(Scala/Art Resource, NY.)*

Epicureanism One of the two most significant new Hellenistic philosophies was **Epicureanism**, named for its founder, Epicurus (341–271 B.C.E.), who settled his followers around 307 B.C.E. in an Athenian house surrounded by greenery—hence, his school came to be known as the Garden. Epicurus broke tradition by admitting both women and slaves to study philosophy in his group.

Epicureanism (eh puh KYUR ee uh nizm): The philosophy founded by Epicurus of Athens to help people achieve a life of true pleasure, by which he meant "absence of disturbance."

Praxiteles' Statue of Aphrodite
The fourth-century B.C.E. Athenian sculptor Praxiteles excelled at carving stone to resemble flesh and producing perfect surfaces, which he had a painter make lively with color. His masterpiece was the Aphrodite made for the city-state of Cnidos in southwestern Anatolia; the original is lost, but many Hellenistic-era copies like this one were made. Praxiteles was the first to show the goddess of love nude, and rumor said his lover was the model. Given that there was a long tradition of nude male statues, why do you think it took until the Hellenistic period for Greek sculptors to produce female nudes? *(Nimatallah/Art Resource, NY.)*

Epicurus's key idea was that people should be free of worry about death. Because all matter consists of tiny, invisible, irreducible pieces called atoms ("indivisible things") in random movement, he said, death is nothing more than the painless separating of the body's atoms. Moreover, all human knowledge must be empirical, that is, derived from experience and perception. Phenomena that most people perceive as the work of the gods, such as thunder, do not result from divine intervention in the world. The gods live far away in perfect tranquillity, ignoring human affairs. People therefore have nothing to fear from the gods, in life or in death.

Epicurus believed people should pursue pleasure, but by true pleasure he meant an "absence of disturbance." Thus, people should live free from the turmoil, passions, and desires of ordinary existence. A sober life spent with friends and separated from the cares of the common world provided Epicurean pleasure. Epicureanism therefore represented a serious challenge to the Greek tradition of political participation by citizens.

Stoicism The other important new Hellenistic philosophy, **Stoicism**, prohibited an isolationist life. Its name derives from the Painted Stoa in Athens, where Stoic philosophers discussed their doctrines. Stoics believed that fate controls people's lives but that individuals should still make the pursuit of excellence (that is, virtue) their goal. Stoic excellence meant putting oneself in harmony with the divine, rational force of universal nature by cultivating good sense, justice, courage, and temperance. These doctrines applied to women as well as men. In fact, some Stoics advocated equal citizenship for women, unisex clothing, and abolition of marriage and families.

The Stoic belief in fate raised the question of whether humans have free will. Stoic philosophers concluded that purposeful human actions do have significance even if fate rules. Nature, itself good, does not prevent evil from occurring, because excellence would otherwise have no meaning. What matters in life is striving for good. A person should therefore take action against evil by, for example, participating in politics. To be a Stoic also meant to shun desire and anger while calmly enduring pain and sorrow, an attitude that yields the modern meaning of the word *stoic*. Through endurance and self-control, adherents of Stoic philosophy gained inner tranquillity. They did not fear death because they believed that people live the same life over and over again. This repetition occurred because the world is periodically destroyed by fire and then re-formed.

Competing Philosophies Several other Hellenistic philosophies competed with Epicureanism and Stoicism. Some of these philosophies built on the work of earlier giants such as Pythagoras and Plato. Others struck out in new directions. Skeptics, for example, aimed at the same state of personal calm as did Epicureans, but from a completely different basis. They believed that secure knowledge about anything was impossible because the human senses perceive contradictory information about the world. All people can do, they insisted, is depend on perceptions and appearances while suspending judgment about their ultimate reality. These ideas had been influenced by the Indian ascetics (who practiced self-denial as part of their spiritual discipline) encountered on Alexander the Great's expedition.

For their part, Cynics rejected every convention of ordinary life, especially wealth and material comfort. The name *Cynic*, which means "like a dog,"

Stoicism: The Hellenistic philosophy whose followers believed in fate but also in pursuing excellence (virtue) by cultivating good sense, justice, courage, and temperance.

came from the notion that dogs had no shame. Cynics believed that humans should aim for complete self-sufficiency and that whatever was natural was good and could be done without shame before anyone. Therefore, public bowel movements and sexual intercourse were fine. Women and men alike should be free to follow their sexual inclinations. Above all, Cynics rejected life's comforts. The most famous early Cynic, Diogenes (d. 323 B.C.E.), wore borrowed clothing and slept in a storage jar. Also notorious was Hipparchia, a female Cynic of the late fourth century B.C.E. who once defeated a philosophical opponent named Theodorus the Atheist with the following remarks: "That which would not be considered wrong if done by Theodorus would also not be considered wrong if done by Hipparchia. Now if Theodorus punches himself, he does no wrong. Therefore, if Hipparchia punches Theodorus, she does no wrong."

Philosophy in the Hellenistic Age reached a wider audience than ever before. Although the working poor were too busy to attend philosophers' lectures, well-off members of society studied philosophy in growing numbers. Kings competed to attract famous philosophers to their courts, and Greek settlers took their interest in philosophy with them to even the most remote Hellenistic cities. Archaeologists excavating a city in Afghanistan — thousands of miles from Greece — uncovered a Greek philosophical text and inscriptions of moral advice recording Apollo's oracle at Delphi as their source. Sadly, this site, called Ai-Khanoum, was devastated in the twentieth century during the Soviet war in Afghanistan.

Gemstone Showing Diogenes in His Jar
This engraved gem from the Roman period shows the famous philosopher Diogenes (c. 412–c. 324 B.C.E.) living in a storage jar and talking with a man holding a scroll. Diogenes was born at Sinope on the Black Sea but was exiled in a dispute over monetary fraud. He then lived at Athens and Corinth, becoming infamous as the founder of Cynic ("doglike") philosophy. To defy social convention, he lived as shamelessly as a dog, hence the name given to his philosophical views and the dog usually shown beside him in art. What kind of person do you think would have wanted this gemstone as a piece of jewelry? *(Inv. No. I 977, Diogenes in his pithos, in dispute with a seated man. Roman Republican ringstone, 100 B.C.E.–30 B.C.E. Thorvaldsens Museum.)*

Scientific Innovation

Scientific investigation was separated from philosophy in the Hellenistic period. Science so benefited from this divorce that historians have called this era ancient science's golden age. Scientific innovation flourished because Alexander's expedition had encouraged curiosity and increased knowledge about the world's extent and diversity, royal families supported scientists financially, and the concentration of scientists in Alexandria promoted the exchange of ideas.

Advances in Geometry and Mathematics The greatest advances in scientific knowledge came in geometry and mathematics. Euclid, who taught at Alexandria around 300 B.C.E., made revolutionary discoveries in analyzing two- and three-dimensional space. The utility of Euclidean geometry still endures. Archimedes of Syracuse (287–212 B.C.E.) calculated the approximate value of pi and invented a way to manipulate very large numbers. He also invented hydrostatics (the science of the equilibrium of fluid systems) and mechanical devices, such as a screw for lifting water to a higher elevation and cranes to disable enemy warships. Archimedes' shout of delight when he solved a problem while soaking in his bathtub has been immortalized in the modern expression "Eureka!" meaning "I have found it!"

Advances in Hellenistic mathematics energized other fields that required complex computation. Early in the third century B.C.E. Aristarchus was the first to propose the correct model of the solar system: the earth revolving around the sun. Later astronomers rejected Aristarchus's heliocentric model in favor of the traditional geocentric one (with the earth at the center) because conclusions drawn from his calculations of the earth's orbit failed to correspond to the observed positions of celestial objects. Aristarchus had assumed a circular orbit instead of an elliptical one, an assumption not corrected until much later. Eratosthenes (c. 275–194 B.C.E.) pioneered mathematical geography. He calculated the circumference of the earth with astonishing accuracy by simultaneously measuring the length of the shadows of widely separated but identically tall structures. Together, these researchers gave Western scientific

Tower of the Winds
This forty-foot octagonal tower, built in Athens about 150 B.C.E., used scientific knowledge developed in Hellenistic Alexandria to tell time and predict the weather. Eight sundials (now missing) carved on the walls displayed the time of day all year; a huge interior water clock showed hours, days, and phases of the moon. A vane on top showed wind direction. The carved figures represented the winds, which the Greeks saw as gods. Each figure's clothing predicted the typical weather from that direction, with the cold northern winds wearing boots and heavy cloaks, while the southern ones have bare feet and gauzy clothes. What were the goals, do you imagine, in erecting such a large clock in a public place? *(The Art Archive/Gianni Dagli Orti.)*

thought an important start toward its fundamental procedure of reconciling theory with observed data through measurement and experimentation.

Discoveries in Science and Medicine Hellenistic science and medicine made gains through royal support, especially in Alexandria, although rigorous experimentation was impossible because no technology existed to measure very small amounts of time or matter. The science of the age was as quantitative as it could be given these limitations. Ctesibius invented pneumatics by creating machines operated by air pressure. He also built a working water pump, an organ powered by water, and the first accurate water clock. Hero continued this development of mechanical ingenuity by building a rotating sphere powered by steam. As in most of Hellenistic science, these inventions did not lead to usable applications in daily life. The scientists and their royal patrons were more interested in new theoretical discoveries than in practical results, and the technology did not exist to produce the pipes, fittings, and screws needed to build metal machines.

Hellenistic science produced impressive military technology, such as more powerful catapults and huge siege towers on wheels. The most famous large-scale application of technology for nonmilitary purposes was the construction of the Pharos, a lighthouse three hundred feet tall, for the harbor at Alexandria. Using polished metal mirrors to reflect the light from a large bonfire, the Pharos shone many miles out over the sea. Awestruck sailors called it one of the wonders of the world.

Medicine also benefited from the Hellenistic quest for new knowledge as medical researchers worked on understanding human health. Increased contact between Greeks and people of the Near East made Mesopotamian and Egyptian medical knowledge better known in the West and promoted research on what made people ill. Hellenistic medical researchers discovered the value of measuring the pulse in diagnosing illness and studied anatomy by dissecting human corpses. It was rumored that they also dissected condemned criminals still alive; they had access to these subjects because the king authorized the research. Some of the terms then invented are still used, such as *diastolic* and *systolic* for blood pressure. Other Hellenistic advances in anatomy included the discovery of the nerves and nervous system.

Cultural and Religious Transformations

Along with scientific innovations, cultural transformations also shaped Hellenistic society. Wealthy non-Greeks increasingly adopted a Greek lifestyle to conform to the Hellenistic world's social hierarchy. Greek became the common language for international commerce and cultural exchange. The widespread use of the simplified form of the Greek language called **Koine** ("shared" or "common") reflected the emergence of an international culture based on Greek models; this was the reason the Egyptian camel trader stranded in Syria (recall the

---

Koine (koy NAY): The "common" or "shared" form of the Greek language that became the international language in the Hellenistic period.

story at the beginning of this chapter) had to communicate in Greek with a high-level official in Egypt. The most striking evidence of this cultural development comes from Afghanistan. There, King Ashoka (r. c. 268–232 B.C.E.), who ruled most of the Indian subcontinent, used Greek as one of the languages in his public inscriptions. These texts announced his plan to teach his subjects Buddhist self-control, such as abstinence from eating meat. Local languages did not disappear in the Hellenistic kingdoms, however. In one region of Anatolia, for example, people spoke twenty-two different languages. This sort of diversity was common in the Hellenistic world.

Changes in Greek and Egyptian Religion

Diversity and interaction in religion also grew. Traditional Greek cults remained popular, but new cults, especially those deifying kings, reflected changing political and social conditions. Preexisting cults that previously had only local significance gained adherents all over the Hellenistic world. In many cases, Greek cults and local cults from the eastern Mediterranean influenced each other. Their beliefs meshed well because these cults shared many assumptions about how to remedy the troubles of human life. In other instances, local cults and Greek cults existed side by side and even overlapped. Some Egyptian villagers, for example, continued worshipping their traditional crocodile god and mummifying their dead according to the old ways but also paid honor to Greek deities. Since they were polytheists (believers in multiple gods), people could worship in both old and new cults.

New cults incorporated a prominent theme of Hellenistic thought: concern for the relationship between the individual and what seemed the arbitrary power of divinities such as Tychê ("chance" or "luck"). Since advances in astronomy had furthered earlier Mesopotamian science on the mathematical precision of the movement of the universe's celestial bodies, religion now had to address the disconnect between heavenly uniformity and the shapeless chaos of earthly life. One increasingly popular approach to bridging that gap was to rely on astrology for advice based on the movement of the stars and planets, thought of as divinities. Another very common choice was to worship Tychê in the hope of securing good luck in life.

The most revolutionary approach in seeking protection from Tychê's unpredictable tricks was to pray for salvation from deified kings, who expressed their divine power in what are now called **ruler cults**.

---

ruler cults: Cults that involved worship of a Hellenistic ruler as a savior god.

Various populations established these cults in recognition of great benefactions. The Athenians, for example, deified the Macedonian Antigonus and his son Demetrius as savior gods in 307 B.C.E., when they liberated the city and bestowed magnificent gifts on it. Like most ruler cults, this one expressed the populations' spontaneous gratitude and a desire to flatter the rulers in the hope of obtaining additional favors, and the rulers' wish to have their power made clear. Many cities in the Ptolemaic and Seleucid kingdoms set up ruler cults for their kings and queens. An inscription put up by Egyptian priests in 238 B.C.E. concretely described the qualities appropriate for a divine king and queen:

> King Ptolemy III and Queen Berenice, his sister and wife, the Benefactor Gods, . . . have provided good government . . . and [after a drought] sacrificed a large amount of their revenues for the salvation of the population, and by importing grain . . . they saved the inhabitants of Egypt.

As these words make clear, the Hellenistic monarchs' tremendous power and wealth gave them the status of gods to the ordinary people who depended on their generosity and protection. The idea that a human being could be a god, present on earth to save people from evils, was now firmly established and would prove influential later in Roman imperial religion and Christianity.

Healing divinities offered another form of protection to anxious individuals. Scientific Greek medicine had rejected the notion of supernatural causes and cures for disease ever since Hippocrates in the fifth century B.C.E. Nevertheless, the cult of the god Asclepius, who offered cures for illness and injury at his many shrines, grew popular during the Hellenistic period. Suppliants seeking Asclepius's help would sleep in special locations at his shrines to await dreams in which he prescribed healing treatments. These prescriptions emphasized diet and exercise, but numerous inscriptions commissioned by grateful patients also testified to miraculous cures and surgery performed while the sufferer slept. The following example is typical:

> Ambrosia of Athens was blind in one eye. . . . She . . . ridiculed some of the cures [described in inscriptions in the sanctuary] as being incredible and impossible. . . . But when she went to sleep, she saw a vision; she thought the god was standing next to her. . . . He split open the diseased eye and poured in a medicine. When day came she left cured.

People's faith in divine healing gave them hope that they could overcome the constant danger of illness, which appeared to strike at random; there was no knowledge of germs as causing infections.

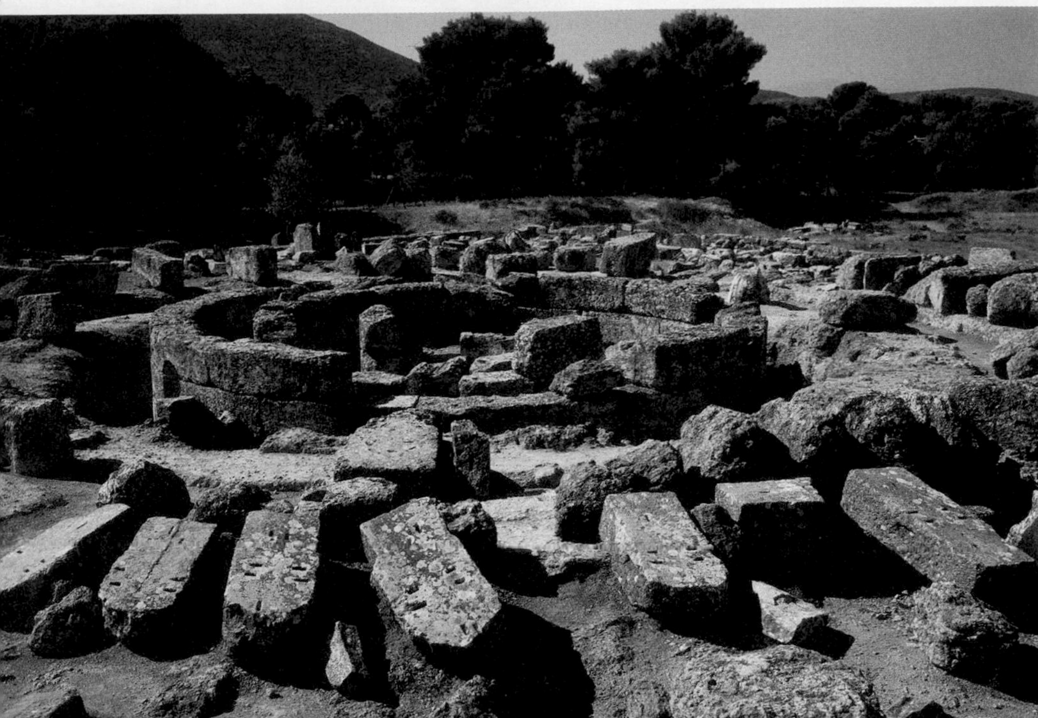

Underground Labyrinth for Healing
This underground stone labyrinth formed part of the enormous healing sanctuary of the god Asclepius at Epidaurus in Greece. Patients flocked to the site from all over the Mediterranean world. They descended into the labyrinth, which was covered and dark, as part of their treatment, which centered on reaching a trance state to receive dreams that would provide instructions on their healing and, sometimes, miraculous surgery. Do you think such treatment could be effective? *(The Art Archive / Dagli Orti.)*

Mystery cults promised secret knowledge to initiates as a key to worldly and physical salvation. The cults of the Greek god Dionysus and, in particular, the Egyptian goddess Isis attracted many people to their initiations in this period. Isis was beloved because her powers protected her worshippers in all aspects of their lives. King Ptolemy I boosted her popularity by establishing a headquarters for her cult in Alexandria. The cult of Isis, who became the most popular female divinity in the Mediterranean, involved extensive ceremonies, rituals, and festivals incorporating features of Egyptian religion mixed with Greek elements. Disciples of Isis hoped to achieve personal purification, as well as the aid of the goddess in overcoming the demonic power of Tychê. That an Egyptian deity like Isis could achieve such popularity among Greeks (and, later, Romans) is the best evidence of the cultural interaction of the Hellenistic world.

Hellenistic Judaism Cultural interaction between Greeks and Jews produced important changes in Judaism during the Hellenistic period. King Ptolemy II made the Hebrew Bible accessible to a wide audience by having his Alexandrian scholars produce a Greek translation — the Septuagint. Many Jews, especially those in the large Jewish communities that had grown up in Hellenistic cities outside their homeland, began to speak Greek and adopt Greek culture. These Greek-style Jews mixed Jewish and Greek customs, while retaining Judaism's rituals and rules and not worshipping Greek gods.

Internal conflict among Jews erupted in second-century B.C.E. Palestine over how much Greek tradition was acceptable for traditional Jews. The Seleucid king Antiochus IV (r. 175–164 B.C.E.) intervened to support Greek-style Jews in Jerusalem, who had taken over the high priesthood that ruled the Jewish community. In 167 B.C.E., Antiochus converted the great Jewish temple in Jerusalem into a Greek temple and outlawed the practice of Jewish religious rites, such as observing the Sabbath and circumcision. This action provoked a revolt led by Judah the Maccabee, which won Jewish independence from Seleucid control after twenty-five years of war. The most famous episode in this revolt was the retaking of the Jerusalem temple and its rededication to the worship of the Jewish god, Yahweh, commemorated by the Hanukkah holiday. That Greek culture attracted some Jews in the first place provides a striking example of the transformations that affected many — though far from all — people of the Hellenistic world. By the time of the Roman Empire, one of those transformations would be Christianity, whose theology had roots in the cultural interaction of Hellenistic Jews and Greeks and their ideas on apocalypticism (religious ideas revealing the future) and divine human beings.

REVIEW QUESTION How did the political changes of the Hellenistic period affect art, science, and religion?

MAPPING THE WEST

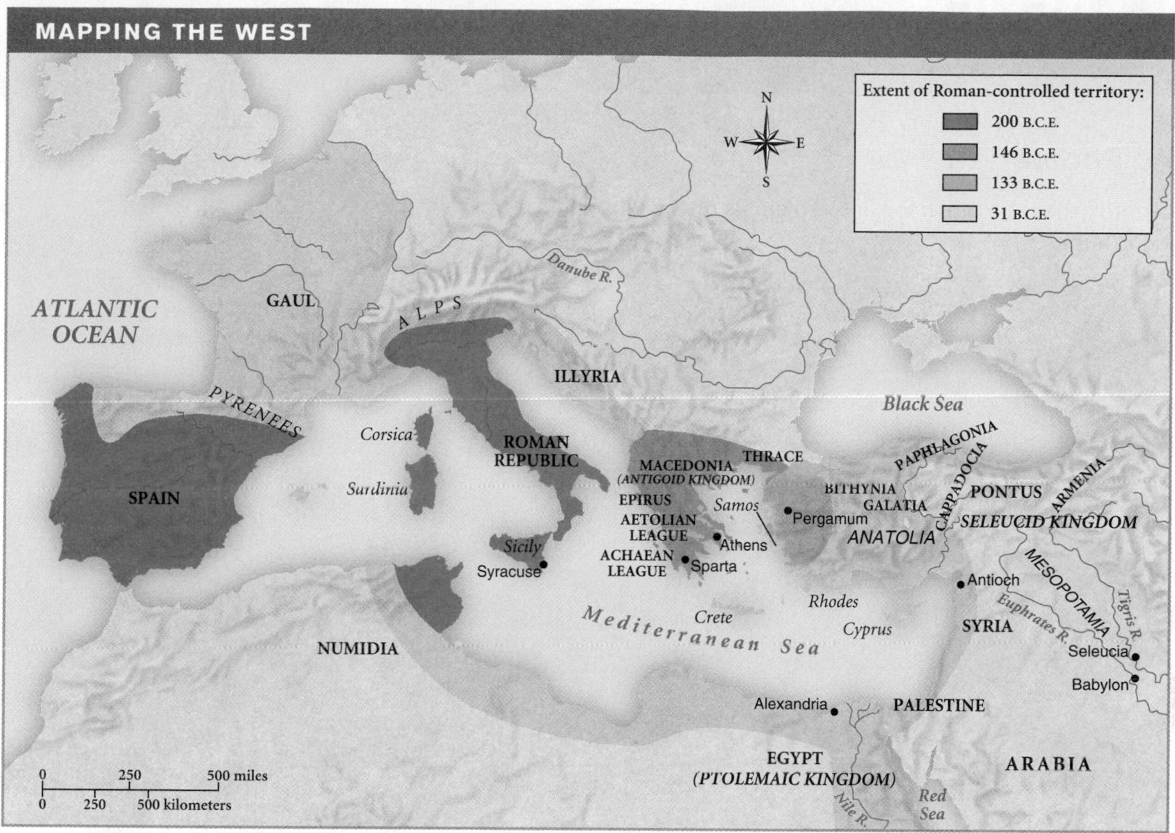

Roman Takeover of the Hellenistic World, to 30 B.C.E.
By the death of Cleopatra VII of Egypt in 30 B.C.E., the Romans had taken over the Hellenistic kingdoms of the eastern Mediterranean. This territory became the eastern half of the Roman Empire. Compare the political divisions on this map with those on the map at the end of Chapter 3 to see the differences from the Classical Age.

Conclusion

The aftermath of the Peloponnesian War led ordinary people as well as philosophers like Plato and Aristotle to question the basis of morality. The disunity of Greek international politics allowed Macedonia's aggressive leaders Philip II (r. 359–336 B.C.E.) and Alexander the Great (r. 336–323 B.C.E.) to make themselves the masters of the competing city-states. Inspired by Greek heroic ideals, Alexander the Great conquered the Persian Empire and set in motion the Hellenistic period's enormous political, social, and cultural changes.

When Alexander's commanders transformed themselves into Hellenistic kings after his death, they reintroduced monarchy into the Greek world, adding an administrative layer of Greek and Macedonian officials to the conquered lands' existing governments. Local elites cooperated with the new Hellenistic monarchs in governing and financing their hierarchical society, which was divided along ethnic lines, with the Greek and Macedonian elite ranking above local elites. To enhance their own reputations, Hellenistic kings and queens funded writers, artists, scholars, philosophers, and scientists, thereby energizing intellectual life. The traditional city-states continued to exist in Hellenistic Greece, but their freedom extended only to local governance; the Hellenistic kings controlled foreign policy.

Increased contacts between diverse peoples promoted greater cultural interaction in the Hellenistic world. What changed most of all was the Romans' culture once they took over the Hellenistic kingdoms' territory and came into close contact with their diverse peoples' traditions. Rome's rise to power took centuries, however, because Rome originated as a tiny, insignificant place that no one except Romans ever expected to amount to anything in the wider world.

FOR FURTHER EXPLORATION

- **For additional primary-source material from this period**, see *Sources of the Making of the West*, Fourth Edition.
- **For Web sites, images, and documents related to topics in this chapter**, visit *Make History* at bedfordstmartins.com/hunt.

Chapter 4 Review

Online Study Guide bedfordstmartins.com/hunt

Key Terms and People

In the grid below, identify the term or person and explain its historical significance. (To do this exercise online, go to bedfordstmartins.com/hunt.)

Term	Who or What & When	Why It Matters
Plato (p. 112)		
metaphysics (p. 113)		
dualism (p. 113)		
Aristotle (p. 114)		
Lyceum (p. 114)		
Alexander the Great (p. 116)		
Hellenistic (p. 120)		
epigrams (p. 127)		
materialism (p. 128)		
Epicureanism (p. 129)		
Stoicism (p. 130)		
Koine (p. 132)		
ruler cults (p. 133)		

Review Questions

1. How did daily life, philosophy, and the political situation change in Greece during the period 400–350 B.C.E.?
2. What were the accomplishments of Alexander the Great, and what were their effects both for the ancient world and for later Western civilization?
3. How did the political and social organization of the new Hellenistic kingdoms compare with that of the earlier Greek city-states?
4. How did the political changes of the Hellenistic period affect art, science, and religion?

Making Connections

1. What made ancient people see Alexander as "great"? Would he be regarded as "great" in today's world?
2. What are the advantages and disadvantages of governmental support of the arts and sciences? Compare such support in the Hellenistic kingdoms to that in the United States today (e.g., through the National Endowment for the Humanities, National Endowment for the Arts, and the National Science Foundation).
3. Is inner personal tranquillity powerful enough to make a difficult or painful life bearable?

Important Events

Date	Event	Date	Event
399 B.C.E.	Execution of Socrates	306–304 B.C.E.	Successors of Alexander declare themselves kings
386 B.C.E.	In King's Peace, Sparta surrenders control of Anatolian Greek city-states to Persia; Plato founds Academy	300–260 B.C.E.	Theocritus writes poetry at Ptolemaic court
362 B.C.E.	Battle of Mantinea leaves power vacuum in Greece	c. 300 B.C.E.	Euclid teaches geometry at Alexandria
338 B.C.E.	Battle of Chaeronea allows Macedonian Philip II to become the leading power in Greece	195 B.C.E.	Seleucid queen Laodice endows dowries for girls
335 B.C.E.	Aristotle founds Lyceum	167 B.C.E.	Maccabee revolt after Antiochus IV turns temple in Jerusalem into a Greek sanctuary
334–323 B.C.E.	Alexander the Great leads Greeks and Macedonians to conquer Persian Empire	30 B.C.E.	Cleopatra VII dies and Rome takes over Ptolemaic Empire
307 B.C.E.	Epicurus founds his philosophical group in Athens		

- Consider three events: **Alexander the Great leads Greeks and Macedonians to conquer Persian Empire (334–323 B.C.E.), Epicurus founds his philosophical group in Athens (307 B.C.E.)**, and **Euclid teaches geometry at Alexandria (c. 300 B.C.E.)**. How might Alexander's expeditions have influenced developments in politics, philosophy, and science?

SUGGESTED REFERENCES

After the Peloponnesian War, the structure of international relations changed radically in the Greek world as the city-states became secondary in political power, first to the kingdom of Macedonia and then to the kingdoms of the Hellenistic period. Long-lasting cultural changes accompanied this political transformation.

*Aristotle. *Complete Works*. Ed. Jonathan Barnes. 1985.

Briant, Pierre. *Alexander the Great and His Empire: A Short Introduction*. Trans. Amélie Kuhrt. 2010.

Chaniotis, Angelos. *War in the Hellenistic World*. 2005.

Collins, John Joseph. *Between Athens and Jerusalem: Jewish Identity in the Hellenistic Diaspora*. 1999.

Dahmen, Karsten. *The Legend of Alexander the Great on Greek and Roman Coins*. 2006.

Empereur, Jean-Yves. *Alexandria: Jewel of Egypt*. 2002.

Evans, J. A. S. *Daily Life in the Hellenistic Age: From Alexander to Cleopatra*. 2008.

Hornblower, Simon. *The Greek World 479–323 B.C.* 4th ed. 2011.

Mikalson, Jon D. *Religion in Hellenistic Athens*. 1998.

*Plato. *The Collected Dialogues*. Ed. Edith Hamilton and Huntington Cairns. 1963.

*Plutarch. *The Age of Alexander*. Trans. Ian Scott-Kilvert. 1973.

Pollitt, J. J. *Art in the Hellenistic Age*. 1986.

Ptolemaic Egypt: http://www.houseofptolemy.org/

Rogers, Guy MacLean. *Alexander: The Ambiguity of Greatness*. 2004.

Sharples, R. W. *Stoics, Epicureans, and Sceptics: An Introduction to Hellenistic Philosophy*. 1996.

Shipley, Graham. *The Greek World after Alexander 323–30 B.C.* 1999.

Snyder, Jane M. *The Woman and the Lyre: Women Writers in Classical Greece and Rome*. 1989.

*Primary source.

CHAPTER

5

The Rise of Rome and Its Republic

753–44 B.C.E.

The Romans treasured legends about their state's transformation from a tiny village to a world power. They especially loved stories about their first king, Romulus, famous as a hot-tempered but shrewd leader. According to the tale later called "The Rape of the Sabine Women," Romulus's Rome needed more women to bear children to increase its population and build a strong army. The king therefore begged Rome's neighbors for permission for Romans to marry their women. Everyone turned him down, mocking Rome's poverty and weakness. Enraged, Romulus hatched a plan to use force where diplomacy had failed. Inviting the neighboring Sabines to a religious festival, he had his men kidnap the unmarried women. The Roman kidnappers immediately married the Sabine women, promising to cherish them as beloved wives and new citizens. When the Sabine men attacked Rome to rescue their kin, the women rushed into the midst of the bloody battle, begging their brothers, fathers, and new husbands either to stop slaughtering one another or to kill them to end the war. The men made peace on the spot and agreed to merge their populations under Roman rule.

This legend emphasizes that Rome, unlike the city-states of Greece, expanded by absorbing outsiders into its citizen body, sometimes violently, sometimes peacefully. Rome's growth became the ancient world's greatest expansion of population and territory, as a people originally housed in a few huts gradually created a state that fought countless wars and relocated an unprecedented number of citizens to gain control of most of Europe, North Africa, Egypt, and the eastern Mediterranean lands. The social, cultural, political, legal, and economic traditions that Romans developed in ruling this vast area created closer interconnections between many diverse peoples than ever before or since. Unlike the Greeks and Macedonians, the

The Wolf Suckling Romulus and Remus
This bronze statue relates to the myth that a she-wolf nursed the twin brothers Romulus and Remus, the offspring of the war god Mars and the future founders of Rome. Romans treasured this story because it meant that Mars loved their city so dearly that he sent a wild animal to nurse its founders after a cruel tyrant had forced their mother to abandon the infants. The myth also taught Romans that their state had been born in violence: Romulus killed Remus in an argument over who would lead their new settlement. The wolf is an Etruscan sculpture from the fifth century B.C.E.; the babies were added in the Renaissance. *(Scala/Art Resource, NY.)*

Romans maintained the unity of their state for centuries. Its long existence allowed many Roman values and traditions to become essential components of Western civilization.

Roman values and traditions originated with ancient Italy's many peoples, but Greek literature, art, and philosophy influenced Rome's culture most of all. This cross-cultural contact that so deeply influenced Rome was a kind of competition in innovation between equals, not "inferior" Romans imitating "superior" Greek culture. Like other ancient peoples, Romans often learned from their neighbors, but they adapted foreign traditions to their own purposes and forged their own cultural identity.

The kidnapping legend belongs to Rome's earliest history, when kings ruled (753–509 B.C.E.). Rome's most important history comes afterward, divided into two major periods of about five hundred years each—the republic and the empire. Under the republic (founded 509 B.C.E.), male voters elected their officials and passed laws (although an oligarchy of the social elite controlled politics). Under the empire, monarchs once again ruled. Rome's greatest expansion came during the republic. Romans' belief in a divine destiny fueled this tremendous growth. They believed that the gods wanted them to rule the world by military might and law and improve it through social and moral values. Their faith in a divine destiny is illustrated by the legend of the Sabine women, in which the earliest Romans used a religious festival as a cover for kidnapping. Their conviction that values should drive politics showed in their determination to persuade the Sabine women that loyalty and love would outweigh the crime of kidnapping that turned them into Romans.

Roman values emphasized family loyalty, selfless political and military service to the community, individual honor and public status, the importance of the law, and shared decision making. Unfortunately, these values conflicted with one another in the long run. By the first century B.C.E., power-hungry leaders such as Sulla and Julius Caesar had plunged Rome into civil war. By putting their personal ambition before the good of the state, they destroyed the republic.

CHAPTER FOCUS How did traditional Roman values affect both the rise and the downfall of the Roman republic?

Roman Social and Religious Traditions

Roman social and religious traditions shaped the history of the Roman republic. Rome's citizens believed that eternal moral values connected them to one another and required them to honor the gods in return for divine support. Hierarchy affected all of life: people at all social levels were obligated to patrons or clients; in families, fathers dominated; in religion, people at all levels of society owed sacrifices, rituals, and prayers to the gods who protected the family and the state.

Roman Moral Values

Roman values defined relationships with other people and with the gods. Romans guided their lives by the ***mos maiorum*** ("the way of the elders"), or values handed down from their ancestors. The Romans

mos maiorum: Literally, "the way of the elders"; the set of Roman values handed down from the ancestors.

753 B.C.E. Traditional date of Rome's founding as monarchy

509 B.C.E. Roman republic established

396 B.C.E. Defeat of Etruscan city of Veii; first great expansion of Roman territory

700 B.C.E. — 600 B.C.E. — 500 B.C.E. — 400 B.C.E.

509–287 B.C.E. Struggle of the orders

451–449 B.C.E. Creation of Twelve Tables, Rome's first written law code

387 B.C.E. Gauls sack Rome

preserved these values because, for them, *old* equaled "tested by time," while *new* meant "dangerous." Roman morality emphasized virtue, faithfulness, and respect. Being seen to behave morally was crucial to Romans because it earned them the respect of others.

Virtus ("manly virtue") was a primarily masculine quality comprising strength, loyalty, and courage, especially in war. It also included wisdom and moral purity, qualities that the social elite were expected to display in their public and private lives. In this broader sense, women, too, could possess virtus. In the second century B.C.E., the Roman poet Lucilius defined it this way:

> *Virtus* is to know the human relevance of each thing,
> To know what is humanly right and useful and honorable,
> And what things are good and what are bad, useless, shameful, and dishonorable. . . .
> *Virtus* is to pay what in reality is owed to honorable status,
> To be an enemy and a foe to bad people and bad values,
> But a defender of good people and good values. . . .
> And, in addition, *virtus* is putting the country's interests first,
> Then our parents', with our own interests third and last.

Fides (FEE dehs, "faithfulness") meant keeping one's obligations no matter the cost. Failing to meet an obligation offended the community and the gods. Faithful women remained virgins before marriage and monogamous afterward. Men demonstrated faithfulness by keeping their word, paying their debts, and treating everyone with justice—which did not mean treating everyone equally, but rather treating each person appropriately, according to whether he or she was a social superior, an equal, or an inferior.

Religion was part of faithfulness. Showing respect and devotion to the gods and to one's family was the supreme form of this value. Romans respected the superior authority of the gods and of the elders and ancestors of their families. Performing religious rituals properly was crucial: Romans believed they had to worship the gods faithfully to maintain the divine favor that protected their community.

Roman values required that each person maintain self-control and limit displays of emotion, to show other people that they respected themselves and their status in society. So strict was this value that not even wives and husbands could kiss in public without seeming emotionally out of control. It also meant that a person should never give up no matter how hard the situation. Persevering and doing one's duty were instilled from a young age.

The reward for living these values was respect from others. Women earned respect by bearing legitimate children and educating them morally; their reward was a good reputation among their families and friends. Respected men relied on their reputations to help them win election to government posts. A man of the highest reputation commanded so much respect that others would obey him regardless of whether he held an office with formal power over them. A man with this much prestige was said to possess authority.

The concept of authority based on respect reflected the Roman belief that some people were by nature superior to others and that society had to be hierarchical to be just. Thus, they determined status both by family history and by wealth. Romans believed that aristocrats, or people born into the best families, automatically deserved high respect. In return, aristocrats were supposed to live strictly by the highest values and serve the community.

264–241 B.C.E. Rome and Carthage fight First Punic War

220 B.C.E. Rome controls Italy south of Po River

218–201 B.C.E. Rome and Carthage fight Second Punic War

168–149 B.C.E. Cato writes *The Origins*, first history of Rome in Latin

149–146 B.C.E. Rome and Carthage fight Third Punic War

146 B.C.E. Carthage and Corinth destroyed

133 B.C.E. Tiberius Gracchus elected tribune; assassinated in same year

91–87 B.C.E. Social War between Rome and its Italian allies

60 B.C.E. First Triumvirate of Caesar, Pompey, and Crassus

49–45 B.C.E. Civil war, with Caesar the victor

45–44 B.C.E. Cicero writes his philosophical works on *humanitas*

44 B.C.E. Caesar appointed dictator with no term limit; assassinated in same year

300 B.C.E. — 200 B.C.E. — 100 B.C.E. — 0

In Roman legends about the early days, a person could be poor and still remain a proud aristocrat. Over time, however, money became overwhelmingly important to the Roman elite, for spending on showy luxuries, large-scale entertaining, and extremely costly gifts to the community. In this way, wealth became necessary to maintain high social status. By the later centuries of the Roman republic, ambitious men often trampled on other values to acquire riches and high status.

The Patron-Client System

The **patron-client system** underlay status in Roman society. It was an interlocking network of personal relationships that obligated people to one another. A patron was a man of superior status who could provide benefits, as they were called, to lower-status people; these were his clients, who in return owed him duties and paid him special attention. In this hierarchical system, a patron was often himself the client of a higher-status man.

patron-client system: The interlocking network of mutual obligations between Roman patrons (social superiors) and clients (social inferiors).

Sculpted Tomb of a Family of Ex-Slaves
The inscription on this tomb monument from, probably, the first century B.C.E. reveals that the couple started life as slaves but became free and thus Roman citizens. Their son (his head has been knocked off) is shown in the background holding a pet pigeon. This family had done well enough financially to afford a sculpted tomb, and the tablets the man is holding and the woman's hairstyle are meant to show that their family was literate and stylish. Compare the man's realistically lined face with the woman's softer, more idealized one. *(German Archeological Institute/Madeline Grimoldi.)*

Benefits and duties centered on mutual exchanges of financial and political help. Patrons would help their clients get started in making a living by giving them a gift or a loan and putting them in touch with others who could help them. In politics, a patron would jump-start a client's career by promoting his candidacy for elective office and providing money for campaigning and doing favors for influential supporters. A patron's most important obligation was to support a client and his family if they got into legal trouble.

Clients had to aid their patrons' campaigns for public office by swinging votes their way. They also had to lend money when patrons had huge expenses to provide public works and to fund their daughters' dowries. A patron expected his clients to gather at his house at dawn to accompany him to the forum, the city's public center, because it was a mark of great status to have numerous clients thronging around. A Roman leader needed a large house to hold this throng and to entertain his social equals. A crowded house indicated social success.

Patrons' and clients' mutual obligations endured for generations. Ex-slaves, who became the clients for life of the masters who freed them, often passed this relationship on to their children. Romans with contacts abroad could acquire clients among foreigners; Roman generals sometimes had entire foreign communities obligated to them. The patron-client system demonstrated the Roman idea that social stability and well-being were achieved by faithfully maintaining established ties.

The Roman Family

The family was Roman society's bedrock because it taught values and determined the ownership of property. Men and women shared the duty of teaching their children values, though by law the father possessed the ***patria potestas*** ("father's power") over his children—no matter how old—and his slaves. This power made him the sole owner of all his dependents' property. As long as he was alive, no son or daughter could officially own anything, accumulate money, or possess any independent legal standing. Unofficially, however, adult children did control personal property and money, and favored slaves could build up savings. Fathers also held legal power of life and death over these members of their households, but they rarely exercised this power except, like the

patria potestas **(PAH tree uh po TEHS tahs):** Literally, "father's power"; the legal power a Roman father possessed over the children and slaves in his family, including owning all their property and having the right to punish them, even with death.

Sculpture of a Woman Running a Store
This sculpture portrays a woman selling food from a small shop while customers make purchases or chat. Since Roman women could own property, it is possible that the woman is the store owner. The man standing behind her could be her husband or a servant. Much like malls of today, markets in Roman towns were packed with small stores. *(Art Resource, NY.)*

Greeks, through exposure of newborns, an accepted practice to limit family size and dispose of physically imperfect infants.

Patria potestas did not allow a husband to control his wife because "free" marriages—in which the wife formally remained under her father's power as long as the father lived—became common. But in the ancient world, few fathers lived long enough to oversee the lives of their married daughters or sons; four out of five parents died before their children reached age thirty. A Roman woman without a living father was relatively independent. Legally she needed a male guardian to conduct her business, but guardianship was largely an empty formality by the first century B.C.E. Upper-class women could even demonstrate publicly to express their opinions. In 195 B.C.E., for example, a group of women blocked Rome's streets for days, until the men abolished a wartime law meant to reduce tensions between rich and poor by limiting the amount of gold jewelry and fine clothing women could wear and where they could ride in carriages. A later legal expert commented on women's freedom of action: "The common belief, that because of their instability of judgment women are often deceived and that it is only fair to have them controlled by the authority of guardians, seems more false than true. For women of full age manage their affairs themselves."

A Roman woman had to grow up fast to assume her duties as teacher of values to her children and manager of her household's resources. Tullia (c. 79–45 B.C.E.), daughter of Rome's most famous politician and orator, Cicero, was engaged at twelve, married at sixteen, and widowed by twenty-two. Like every other wealthy married Roman woman, she managed the household slaves, monitored the nurturing of the young children by wet nurses, kept account books to track the property she personally owned, and accompanied her husband to dinner parties—something a Greek wife never did.

A mother's responsibility for shaping her children's values constituted the foundation of female virtue. Women like Cornelia, a famous aristocrat of the second century B.C.E., won enormous respect for loyalty to family. When her husband died, Cornelia refused an offer of marriage from King Ptolemy VIII of Egypt so that she could continue to oversee the family estate and educate her surviving daughter and two sons. (Her other nine children had died.) The boys, Tiberius and Gaius Gracchus, grew up to be among the most influential political leaders in the late republic. The number of children Cornelia bore reveals the fertility and stamina required of a Roman wife to ensure the survival of her husband's family line. Cornelia also became famous for her stylishly worded letters, which were still being read a century later.

Roman women had no official political role, but wealthy women like Cornelia could influence politics indirectly through expressing their opinions to their male relatives and friends in conversations at their homes and at dinner parties. Marcus Porcius Cato (234–149 B.C.E.), a famous politician and author, described this clout: "All mankind rule their wives, we [Roman men] rule all mankind, and our wives rule us."

Women could acquire property through inheritance and entrepreneurship. Archaeological discoveries reveal that by the end of the republic some women owned large businesses. Because both women and men could control property, prenuptial agreements determining the property rights of husband and wife were common. Divorce was legally simple, with fathers usually keeping the children, a reflection of the father's power over the members of his household. Most poor women, like poor men, had to toil for a living as field laborers or hawkers selling trinkets in cities. Women and men both worked in manufacturing, which mostly happened in the home. The men worked the raw materials — cutting, fitting, and polishing wood, leather, and metal — while the women sold the finished goods. The poorest women earned money through prostitution, which was legal but considered disgraceful.

Education for Public Life

Roman education aimed to make men and women effective speakers and exponents of traditional values. Most children received their education at home; there were no public schools, and only the rich could afford private teachers. Wealthy parents bought literate slaves (pedagogues) to educate their children; by the late republic, they often chose Greek slaves so that their children could learn to speak Greek and read Greek literature. Lessons emphasized memorization, and teachers used physical punishment to keep pupils attentive. In upper-class families, both daughters and sons learned to read. The girls were also taught literature and perhaps some music, and how to make educated conversation at dinner parties. The principal aim of women's education was to prepare them to teach traditional social and moral values to their children.

Sons received physical training and learned to fight with weapons, but rhetorical training dominated an upper-class Roman boy's education because a successful political career depended on the ability to speak persuasively in public. A boy would learn winning techniques by listening to speeches in political meetings and arguments in court cases. As the orator Cicero said, young men must learn to "excel in public speaking. It is the tool for controlling men at Rome."

Public and Private Religion

Romans followed Greek models in religion. Their chief deity, Jupiter, corresponded to the Greek god Zeus and was seen as a powerful, stern father. Juno (Greek Hera), queen of the gods, and Minerva (Greek Athena), goddess of wisdom, joined Jupiter to form the state religion's central triad. These three deities shared Rome's most revered temple.

Protecting Rome's safety and prosperity was the gods' major function. They were supposed to help Rome defeat enemies in war, but divine support for agriculture was also essential. Official prayers requested the gods' aid in growing abundant crops, healing disease, and promoting reproduction for animals and people. In times of crisis, Romans sought foreign gods for help, such as when the government imported the cult of the healing god Asclepius from

Household Shrine from Pompeii
This shrine stood inside the entrance to a house at Pompeii owned by successful businessmen, who spent heavily to decorate their home with 188 colorful wall paintings. This type of shrine housed statuettes of the deities protecting the household, shown here also in a painting, flanking a figure representing the spirit of the family's father. What do you think it signifies that the deities are dancing? The snake below, which is about to drink from a bowl probably holding milk, also symbolizes a protective force. The scene sums up the role Romans expected their gods to play: protecting people against harm and bad luck. *(Scala/Art Resource, NY.)*

Greece in 293 B.C.E., hoping he would save Rome from an epidemic.

The republic supported many other cults, including that of Vesta, goddess of the hearth and therefore protector of the family. Her shrine housed Rome's official eternal flame, which guaranteed the state's permanent existence. The Vestal Virgins, six unmarried women sworn to chastity and Rome's only female priests, tended Vesta's shrine. Their chastity was considered crucial to preserving Rome. They earned high status and freedom from their fathers' control by performing their most important duty: keeping the flame from going out. If the flame went out, the Romans assumed that one of the Vestal Virgins had had sex and buried her alive.

Religion was important in Roman family life. Each household maintained small indoor shrines housing statuettes of the spirits of the household and those of the ancestors, who were believed to protect the family's health and morality. Upper-class families kept death masks of ancestors hanging in the main room and wore them at funerals to commemorate the family's heritage and the current generation's responsibility to live up to the ancestors' values.

Because Romans believed that divine spirits participated in crucial events such as birth, marriage, and death, they performed many rituals seeking protection. Rituals also accompanied everyday activities, such as breast-feeding babies or fertilizing crops. Many public religious gatherings promoted the community's health and stability. For example, during the February 15 Lupercalia festival (whose name recalled the wolf, *luper* in Latin, that legend said had reared Romulus and his twin, Remus), near-naked young men streaked around the Palatine hill, lashing any woman they met with strips of goatskin. Women who had not yet borne children would run out to be struck, believing this would help them become fertile.

Like the Greeks, the Romans did not regard the gods as guardians of human morality. Cicero's description of Jupiter's titles explained public religion's closer ties to security and prosperity than to personal behavior: "We call Jupiter the Best and Greatest not because he makes us just or sober or wise but, rather, healthy, unharmed, rich, and prosperous." Roman officials preceded important actions with the ritual called taking the auspices, in which they sought Jupiter's approval by observing natural signs such as birds' flight direction or eating habits, or the appearance of thunder and lightning. Action proceeded only if the auspices were favorable.

Romans linked values and religion by regarding values as divine forces. *Pietas* ("piety"), for example, meant devotion and duty to family, friends, the state, and the gods; a temple at Rome held a statue personifying pietas as a female divinity. The personification of abstract moral qualities provided a focus for cult rituals.

The duty of Roman religious officials was to maintain peace with the gods. Socially prominent men served as priests, conducting sacrifices, festivals, and prayers. They were not professionals devoting their lives to religious activity; they were citizens performing public service. The chief priest, the *pontifex maximus* ("greatest bridge-builder"), served as the head of state religion and the ultimate authority on religious matters affecting government. The political powers of this priesthood motivated Rome's most ambitious men to seek it.

Disrespect for religious tradition brought punishment. Admirals, for example, took the auspices by feeding sacred chickens on their warships: if the birds ate energetically, Jupiter favored the Romans and an attack could begin. In 249 B.C.E., the commander Publius Claudius Pulcher grew frustrated when his chickens, probably seasick, refused to eat. Determined to attack, he finally hurled the birds overboard in a rage, sputtering, "Well then, let them drink!" When he promptly suffered a huge defeat, he was fined heavily.

REVIEW QUESTION What common themes underlay Roman values? How did Romans' behavior reflect those values?

From Monarchy to Republic

Romans' values and their belief in a divine destiny fueled their astounding growth from a tiny settlement into the Mediterranean's greatest power. The surviving evidence for the first five hundred years of Roman history down to the wars against Carthage is very limited, and therefore much remains uncertain about the development of Roman society, politics, and military power. The Romans spilled much blood as they gradually expanded their territory through war. From the eighth to the sixth century B.C.E., they were ruled by kings, but the later kings' violence provoked members of the social elite to overthrow the monarchy and create the republic, which lasted from the fifth through the first century B.C.E. The republic — from the Latin ***res publica*** ("the people's matter" or "the public business") —

res publica (REHS POOB lih kuh): Literally, "the people's matter" or "the public business"; the Romans' name for their republic and the source of our word *republic*.

distributed power by electing officials and making laws in open meetings of male citizens. This model of republican government, rather than Athens's direct democracy, influenced the founders of the United States in organizing their new nation as a federal republic. Rome gained land and population by winning aggressive wars and by absorbing other peoples. Its economic and cultural growth depended on contact with many other peoples around the Mediterranean.

Roman Society under the Kings, 753–509 B.C.E.

Legend taught that Rome's original government had seven kings, ruling from 753 to 509 B.C.E. The kings created Rome's most famous and enduring government body: the Senate, a group of distinguished men chosen as the king's personal council. This council played the same role — advising government leaders — for a thousand years, as Rome changed from a monarchy to a republic and back to a monarchy (the empire). It was always a Roman tradition that one should never make decisions by oneself but only after consulting advisers and friends.

The kings began Rome's expansion by taking in outsiders whom they conquered, as reflected in the story of Romulus's assimilating the Sabines. This inclusionary policy of making others into citizens, which contrasted sharply with the exclusionary laws of the Greeks, proved crucial for Rome's growth and promoted ethnic diversity. Even more remarkably, Romans, unlike Greeks, granted citizenship to freed slaves. Though freedmen and freedwomen owed special obligations to their former owners and could not hold elective office or serve in the army, they enjoyed all other citizens' rights, such as legal marriage. Their children possessed citizenship without any limits. By the late republic, many Roman citizens were descendants of freed slaves.

Expansion and Cross-Cultural Contact By approximately 550 B.C.E., Rome had grown to between thirty and forty thousand people and, through war and diplomacy, had won control of three hundred square miles of surrounding territory. Rome's geography propelled its further expansion. The Romans originated in central Italy, a long peninsula with a mountain range down its middle like a spine and fertile plains on either side. In addition to possessing rich farmland, Rome controlled a river crossing on a major north–south route. Most important, Rome was ideally situated for international trade: the Italian peninsula stuck so far out into the Mediterranean

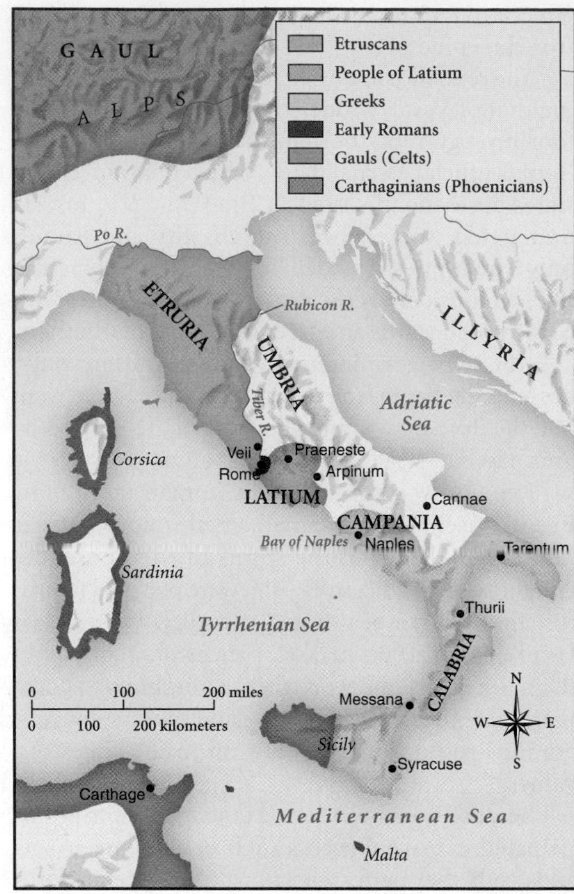

MAP 5.1 Ancient Italy, 500 B.C.E.
When the Romans removed the monarchy to found a republic in 509 B.C.E., they inhabited a relatively small territory in central Italy. Many different peoples lived in Italy at this time, with the most prosperous occupying fertile agricultural land and sheltered harbors on the peninsula's west side. The early republic's most urbanized neighbors were the Etruscans to the north and the Greeks in the city-states to the south, including on the island of Sicily. Immediately adjacent to Rome were the people of Latium, called Latins. | **How did geography aid Roman expansion?**

that east–west seaborne traffic naturally encountered it (Map 5.1), and the city had a good port nearby.

The Romans' predecessors in Italy were peoples whose languages belonged to what linguists call the Indo-European family of related languages, which are found from Europe to India. Our only material evidence for these ancestors of the Romans comes from archaeological excavation of ninth- and eighth-century B.C.E. tombs. The Italian pre-Romans lived by herding animals, farming, and hunting. They became skilled metalworkers, especially in iron.

The earliest Romans' closest neighbors in central Italy were poor villagers, too, and spoke the same Indo-European language, Latin. Greeks lived to the south in Italy and Sicily, however, and contact with them had the greatest effect on Roman cultural development. Greek culture reached its most famous flowering in its fifth-century B.C.E. Golden Age, at the time when the Roman republic was taking shape and centuries before Rome had its own literature, theater, or monumental architecture. Romans developed a love-hate relationship with Greece, admiring its literature and art but looking down on its lack of military unity. They adopted many elements from Greek culture—from deities for their national cults to models for their poetry, prose, and architectural styles.

The Etruscans The Etruscans, a people to the north, also influenced Roman culture. Brightly colored wall paintings in tombs, portraying funeral banquets and games, reveal the splendor of Etruscan society. In addition to producing their own art, jewelry, and sculpture, the Etruscans also imported luxurious objects from Greece and the Near East. Most of the intact Greek vases known today were found in Etruscan tombs, and Etruscan culture was deeply influenced by that of Greece.

The relationship between the Etruscan and Roman cultures remains a controversial topic. Scholars long believed that the Etruscans completely reshaped Roman culture during a period of supposed political domination in the sixth century B.C.E. New research, however, shows the Romans' independence in developing their own cultural traditions: they borrowed from the Etruscans, as from the Greeks, whatever appealed to them and adapted these borrowings to their own circumstances.

Romans adopted ceremonial features of Etruscan culture, such as musical instruments, religious rituals, and lictors (attendants who walked in front of the highest officials carrying the fasces, a bundle of rods around an axe, symbolizing the officials' right to command and punish). The Romans also borrowed from the Etruscans the ritual of divination—determining the will of the gods by examining organs of slaughtered animals. The custom of wives joining husbands at dinner parties may also have come from the Etruscans.

Etruscan Painting of a Musician

This Etruscan painting, characteristically done with bright colors (now faded), shows a man playing the double pipe, a reed wind instrument with holes in both tubes that the player fingered simultaneously. This instrument originated in Greece, as did the designs above and below the central figure. The Etruscans adopted many cultural traditions from the Greeks, some of which they then passed on to the Romans. *(Italic, Etruscan, Late Archaic period or early Classical period, about 470 B.C.E. Terracotta, overall dimensions: 112.5 x 52 cm. [44 5/16 x 20½ in.]. Museum of Fine Arts, Boston, William Francis Warden Fund, 62.363. Photograph © 2011 Museum of Fine Arts, Boston.)*

Other features of Roman culture formerly seen as deriving from Etruscan influence were probably part of the ancient Mediterranean's shared practices. The organization of the Roman army—a citizen militia of heavily armed infantry troops fighting in formation—reflected the practice of many other peoples. The alphabet, which the Romans first learned from the Etruscans, was actually Greek; the Greeks had gotten it through their contact with the earlier alphabets of eastern Mediterranean peoples. Foreign trade and urban planning are other features of Etruscan life that Romans are said to have assimilated, but it is too simplistic to assume these cultural developments resulted from a superior culture instructing a less developed one. Rather, at this time in Mediterranean history, similar cultural developments were under way in many places.

DOCUMENT

The Rape and Suicide of Lucretia

This story explaining why the Roman elite expelled the monarchy in 509 B.C.E., thus opening the way to the republic, centers on female virtue and courage, as do other stories about significant political changes in early Roman history. The values attributed to Lucretia obviously reflect men's wishes for women's behavior, but it would be a mistake to assume that women could not hold the same views. The historian Livy wrote this document in the late first century B.C.E., at another crucial point in Roman history—the violent transition from republic to empire—when Romans were deeply concerned with the values of the past as a guide to the present.

Sextus Tarquinius, the son of Rome's king (Tarquin the Proud, r. 534–510 B.C.E.), came to Lucretia's home. She greeted him warmly and asked him to stay [as Roman hospitality demanded for such a high-status visitor]. Crazy with lust, he waited until he was sure the household was sleeping. Drawing his sword, he snuck into Lucretia's bedroom and placed the blade against her left breast, whispering, "Quiet, Lucretia; I am Sextus Tarquinius, and I am holding a sword. If you cry out, I'll kill you!" Rudely awakened, the desperate woman realized that no one could help her and that she was close to death. Sextus Tarquinius said he loved her, begging and threatening her in turn, trying everything to wear her down. When she wouldn't give in, even in the face of threats of murder, he added another intimidation. "After I've murdered you, I am going to put the naked corpse of a slave next to your body, and everybody will say that you were killed during a disgraceful adultery." This final threat defeated her, and after raping her he left, having stolen her honor.

Lucretia, overwhelmed by sadness and shame, sent messengers to her husband, Tarquinius Conlatinus, who was away, and her father at Rome, telling them, "Come immediately, with a good friend, because something horrible has happened." Her father arrived with a friend, and her husband came with Lucius Junius Brutus. . . . They found Lucretia in her room, overcome with grief. When she saw them, she started weeping. "How are you?" her husband asked. "Very bad," she replied. "How can anything be fine for a woman who has lost her honor? Traces of another man are in our bed, my husband. My body is defiled, though my heart is still pure; my death will be the proof. But give me your right hand and promise that you will not let the guilty escape. It was Sextus Tarquinius who returned our hospitality with hostility last night. With his sword in his hand, he came to have his fun, to my despair, but it will also be his sorrow—if you are real men." They pledged that they would catch him, and they tried to ease her sadness, saying that the soul did wrong, not the body, and where there were no bad intentions there could be no blame. "It is your responsibility to ensure that he gets what he deserves," she said; "I am blameless, but I will not free myself from punishment. No dishonorable woman shall hold up Lucretia as an example." Then she grabbed a dagger hidden underneath her robe and stabbed herself in the heart. She fell dead, as her husband and father cried out.

Brutus, leaving them to their tears, pulled the blade from Lucretia's wound and held it up drenched in blood, shouting, "By this blood, which was completely pure before the crime of the king's son, I swear before you, O gods, to drive out the king himself, his criminal wife, and all their children, by sword, fire, and everything in my power, and never to allow a king to rule Rome ever again, whether from that family or any other."

Source: Livy, *From the Foundation of the City*, 1.57–59. Translation by Thomas R. Martin.

Question to Consider

- **What notions of honor for men and for women are reflected in Livy's tale?**

The Early Roman Republic, 509–287 B.C.E.

The Roman social elite's hatred of monarchy motivated the creation of the republic. The upper class believed that power would inevitably corrupt a sole ruler. This belief was enshrined in the most famous legend about the fall of the Roman monarchy: the rape of the virtuous Roman woman Lucretia by the king's son and her subsequent suicide (see Document, "The Rape and Suicide of Lucretia," above). Declaring themselves Rome's liberators from tyranny, in 509 B.C.E. Lucretia's relatives and friends from the social elite drove out the king and founded the republic. Thereafter, the Romans prided themselves on having created a political system freer than that of many of their neighbors.

The Struggle of the Orders The Romans struggled for nearly 250 years to shape a stable government for the republic. Roman social hierarchy split the population into two **orders**: the **patricians** (a small group of the most aristocratic families) and the **plebeians** (the rest of the citizens). Bitter striving for power pitted the orders

---

orders: The two groups of people in the Roman republic—**patricians** (aristocratic families) and **plebeians** (all other citizens).

against each other; historians call this turmoil the struggle of the orders. The conflict finally ended in 287 B.C.E. when plebeians won the right to make laws in their own assembly.

Social and economic disputes underlay the struggle of the orders. Patricians constituted a tiny percentage of the population—numbering only about 130 families—but their inherited status entitled them to control public religion. Soon after the republic's founding, they used this power to monopolize political office. In this early period, many patricians were much wealthier than most plebeians. Some plebeians, however, were also rich, and they resented the patricians' dominance, especially their ban on intermarriage with plebeians. Patricians inflamed tensions by wearing special red shoes to set themselves apart; later they changed to black shoes adorned with a small metal crescent.

The struggle began when rich plebeians insisted on the right to marry patricians as social equals, while poor plebeians demanded farmland and relief from crushing debts. To pressure the patricians, the plebeians periodically refused military service. This tactic worked because Rome's army depended on plebeian manpower; the patricians were too few to defend Rome by themselves.

In response, between 451 and 449 B.C.E., the patricians agreed to the earliest Roman law code, guaranteeing greater equality and social mobility. This code, known as the **Twelve Tables**, formalized early Rome's legal customs in simply worded laws such as "If plaintiff calls defendant to court, he shall go," or "If a wind causes a neighbor's tree to be bent and lean over your farm, action may be taken to have that tree removed." The Twelve Tables prevented the patrician public officials who judged most legal cases from giving judgments only according to their own wishes. They became so important a symbol of the commitment to justice for all citizens that children were required to memorize them. The Roman belief in fair laws as the best protection against social unrest helped keep the republic united until the late second century B.C.E.

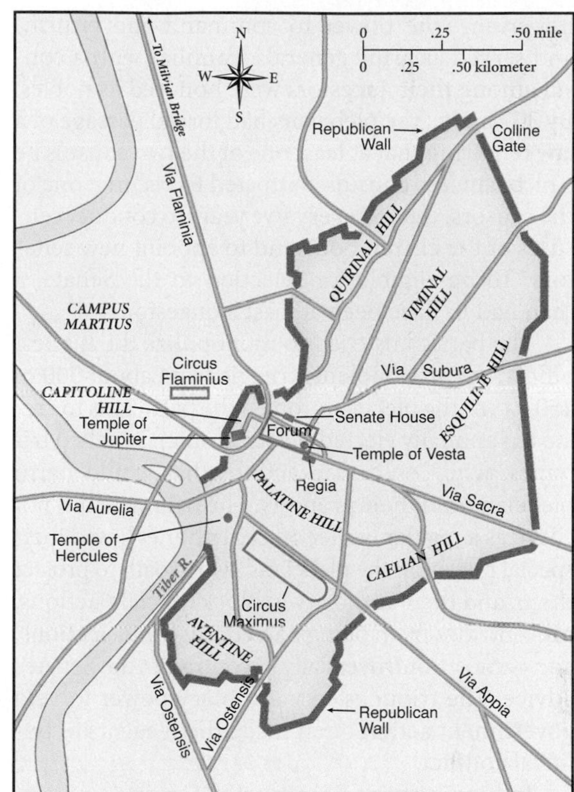

MAP 5.2 The City of Rome during the Republic

Roman tradition said that a king built Rome's first defensive wall in the sixth century B.C.E., but archaeology shows that the first wall encircling the city's center and seven hills on the east bank of the Tiber River belongs to the fourth century B.C.E.; this wall covered a circuit of about seven miles. By the second century B.C.E., the wall had been extended to soar fifty-two feet high and had been fitted with catapults to protect the large gates. Like the open agora surrounded by buildings at the heart of a Greek city, the forum remained Rome's political and social heart. | **How might modern cities benefit from having a large public space at their center?**

The Consuls, the Ladder of Offices, and the Senate

Elected officials ran Roman republican government; voting took place in and near the forum in the center of the city (Map 5.2). All officials joined committees, numbering from two to more than a dozen members, in accordance with the Roman value that rule should be shared. The highest officials, two elected each year, were called consuls. Their most important duty was commanding the army.

To be elected consul, a man had to win elections all the way up a **ladder of offices** (*cursus honorum*). Before politics, however, came ten years of military service from about ages twenty to thirty. The ladder's first step was getting elected quaestor, a financial administrator. The second step was getting elected as an aedile (supervisors of Rome's streets, sewers, aqueducts, temples, and markets). Few men reached the next step, election as praetor. Praetors performed judicial and military duties. The most successful praetors competed to be one of the two consuls elected each year. Praetors and consuls held

---

Twelve Tables: The first written Roman law code, enacted between 451 and 449 B.C.E.

ladder of offices: The series of Roman elective government offices from quaestor to aedile to praetor to consul.

imperium (the power to command and punish) and served as army generals. Families with a consul among their ancestors were honored as nobles. By 367 B.C.E., the plebeians had forced passage of a law requiring that at least one of the two consuls be a plebeian. Ex-consuls competed to become one of the censors, elected every five years to conduct censuses of the citizen body and to appoint new senators. To be eligible for selection to the Senate, a man had to have been at least a quaestor.

The patricians tried to monopolize the highest offices, but after violent struggle from about 500 to 450 B.C.E., the plebeians forced the patricians to create ten annually elected plebeian officials, called tribunes, who could stop actions that would harm plebeians and their property. The tribunate did not count as a regular ladder office. Tribunes based their special power on the plebeians' sworn oath to protect them, and their authority to block officials' actions, prevent laws from being passed, suspend elections, and—most controversially—contradict the Senate's advice. The tribunes' extraordinary power to veto government action often made them agents of political conflict.

In keeping with Roman values, men were supposed to compete for public office to win respect and glory, not money. Only well-off men could run for election because officials earned no salaries. In fact, they were expected to spend a great deal of their own money to win popular support by paying for expensive public shows featuring gladiators and wild animals, such as lions imported from Africa. Financing such exhibitions could put a candidate deeply in debt. Once elected, a magistrate had to pour his private funds into building and maintaining roads, aqueducts, and temples.

Early republican officials' only reward was the respect they earned for public service. As Romans conquered more and more overseas territory, however, the desire for money to finance electoral campaigns overcame many men's adherence to traditional Roman values of faithfulness and honesty. By the second century B.C.E., military officers enriched themselves not only legally by seizing booty from foreign enemies but also illegally by extorting bribes as administrators of newly conquered territories. Over time, acquiring money became more important than serving the public.

The Senate retained the role it had played under the monarchy: directing government policy by giving advice to its highest officials. Strictly speaking, the Senate did not make law, but the senators' high social standing gave their opinions the moral force of law. If a consul rejected or ignored the Senate's advice, a political crisis resulted. The Senate thus guided the republic in every area: decisions on war, domestic and foreign policy, state finance, official religion, and all types of legislation. To make their status visible, the senators wore black high-top shoes and robes with a broad purple stripe.

The Assemblies | Male citizens meeting in three different assemblies decided legislation, government policy, election outcomes, and judgment in certain trials. The Centuriate Assembly, which elected praetors and consuls, was dominated by patricians and richer plebeians. The Plebeian Assembly, which excluded patricians, elected the tribunes. In 287 B.C.E., its resolutions, called **plebiscites**, became legally binding on all Romans. The Tribal Assembly mixed patricians with plebeians and became the republic's most important assembly for making policy, passing laws, and, until separate courts were later created, holding trials.

Assemblies met outdoors and were only for voting, not debates. Discussions of a sort took place before assembly meetings when orators gave speeches about the issues. Everyone, including women and noncitizens, could listen to these pre-vote speeches. The crowd expressed its agreement or disagreement with the speeches by applauding or hissing. This process mixed a small measure of democracy with the republic's oligarchic government. A significant restriction on democracy in the assemblies, however, was that voting took place by group, not by individuals. Each assembly was divided into groups with different numbers of men determined by status and wealth; each group had one vote.

The Judicial System | The Roman republic's judicial system developed overlapping institutions. Early on, the praetors decided many legal cases; especially serious trials could be transferred to the assemblies. A separate jury system arose in the second century B.C.E., and senators repeatedly clashed with other upper-class Romans over whether these juries should consist exclusively of senators.

As in Greece, Rome had no state-paid prosecutors or defenders. Accusers and accused had to speak for themselves in court or have friends speak for them. Priests dominated in legal knowledge until the third century B.C.E., when senators with legal expertise began to offer legal advice. Called jurists, these senators operated as private citizens, not as officials. Developed over centuries and gradually incorporating laws from other peoples, Roman law,

---

plebiscites (PLEH buh sites): Resolutions passed by the Plebeian Assembly; such resolutions gained the force of law in 287 B.C.E.

especially on civil matters, became the basis for European legal codes still in use today.

The republic's complex system of political and judicial institutions evolved in response to conflicts over power. Laws could emerge from different assemblies, and legal cases could be decided by various institutions. Rome had no single highest court, such as the U.S. Supreme Court, to give final verdicts. The republic's stability therefore depended on maintaining the mos maiorum. Because they defined this tradition, the most socially prominent and richest Romans dominated politics and the courts.

REVIEW QUESTION How and why did the Roman republic develop its complicated political and judicial systems?

Roman Imperialism and Its Consequences

Expansion through war made military service central to Romans' lives; it also caused a huge number of citizens to migrate to communities that the government established as anchors in newly conquered areas. From the fifth to the third century B.C.E., the Romans fought war after war in Italy until Rome became the most powerful state on the peninsula. In the third and second centuries B.C.E., Romans warred far from home in every direction, above all against Carthage to the south. Their success in these campaigns made Rome the premier power in the Mediterranean by the first century B.C.E.

Fear of attacks and the desire for wealth propelled Roman imperialism. The senators' worries about national security made them advise preemptive attacks against potential enemies, while everyone longed to capture plunder and new farmland. Poor soldiers hoped to pull their families out of poverty; the elite, who commanded the armies, wanted to strengthen their campaigns for office by acquiring glory and greater wealth.

The wars in Italy and abroad transformed Roman life. Astonishingly, Rome had no literature until around 240 B.C.E.; the contact with others that conquest brought stimulated the first Roman written works of history and poetry. War's harshness also influenced Roman art, especially portraiture. On the social side, endless military service away from home created stresses on small farmers and undermined the stability of Roman society; so too did the relocation of numerous citizens and the importation of countless war captives to work as slaves on rich people's estates. Rome's great conquests thus turned out to be a two-edged sword: they brought expansion and wealth, but their unexpected social and political consequences disrupted traditional values and the community's stability.

Expansion in Italy, 500–220 B.C.E.

After defeating their Latin neighbors in the 490s B.C.E., the Romans spent the next hundred years warring with the nearby Etruscan town of Veii. Their 396 B.C.E. victory doubled the Romans' territory. By the fourth century B.C.E., the Roman infantry legion of five thousand men had surpassed the Greek and Macedonian phalanx as an effective fighting force because its soldiers were trained to throw javelins from behind their long shields and then rush in to finish off the enemy with swords. A devastating sack of Rome in 387 B.C.E. by marauding Gauls (Celts) from beyond the Alps proved only a temporary setback, though it made Romans forever fearful of foreign invasion. By around 220 B.C.E., Rome controlled all of Italy south of the Po River, at the northern end of the peninsula.

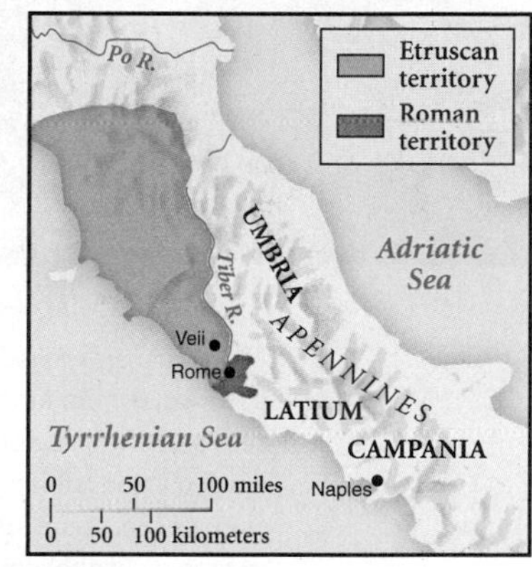

Rome and Central Italy, Fifth Century B.C.E.

The Romans combined brutality with diplomacy to control conquered people and territory. Sometimes they enslaved the defeated or forced them to surrender large parcels of land. Other times they struck generous peace terms with former enemies but required them to render military aid against other foes, for which they received a share of the booty, chiefly slaves and land. In this way, the Romans co-opted opponents by making them partners in the spoils of conquest.

To increase homeland security, the Romans planted numerous colonies of relocated citizens and constructed roads up and down the peninsula to allow troops to march faster. By connecting Italy's diverse peoples, these roads promoted a unified culture dominated by Rome.

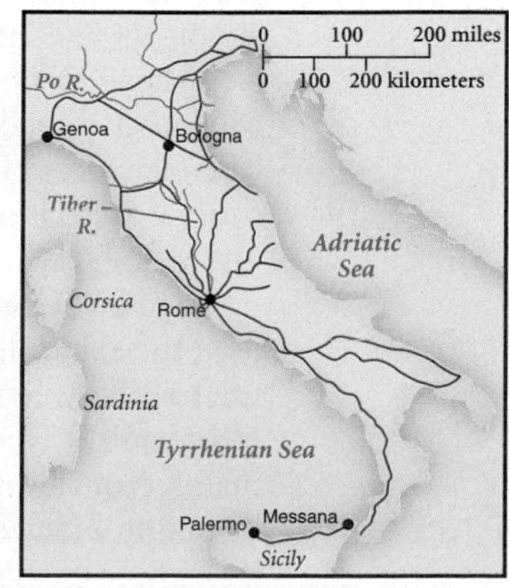

Roman Roads, 110 B.C.E.

Aqueduct at Nîmes in France
The Romans excelled at building complex delivery systems of tunnels, channels, bridges, and fountains to transport fresh water from far away. Compare the Greek city fountain shown in the vase painting on page 111. One of the best-preserved sections of a major aqueduct is the so-called Pont-du-Gard near Nîmes (ancient Nemausus) in France, erected in the late first century B.C.E. to serve the flourishing town there. Built of stones fitted together without clamps or mortar, the span soars 160 feet high and 875 feet long, carrying water along its topmost level from thirty-five miles away in a channel constructed to fall only one foot in height for every three thousand feet in length so that the flow would remain steady but gentle. What sort of social and political organization would be necessary to construct such a system? *(Hubertus Kanus/Photo Researchers, Inc.)*

Latin became the common language, although local tongues lived on, especially Greek in the south.

The wealth that the Roman army captured in the first two centuries of expansion attracted hordes of people to the capital because it financed new aqueducts to provide fresh, running water—a treasure in the ancient world—and a massive building program that employed the poor. By 300 B.C.E., about 150,000 people lived within Rome's walls (see Map 5.2). Outside the city, around 750,000 free Roman citizens inhabited various parts of Italy on land taken from local peoples. Much conquered territory was declared public land, open to any Roman for grazing cattle.

Rich plebeians and patricians cooperated to exploit the expanding Roman territories; the old distinction between the orders had become largely a technicality. This merged elite derived its wealth mainly from agricultural land and plunder acquired during military service. Since Rome had no regular income or inheritance taxes, families could pass down their wealth from generation to generation.

Wars with Carthage and in the East, 264–121 B.C.E.

Rome's leaders, remembering the Gauls' attack on the city in 387 B.C.E., feared foreign invasions and also saw imperialism as the route to riches. The republic therefore fought its three most famous wars against the wealthy city of Carthage in North Africa, which Phoenicians had founded around 800 B.C.E. In the third century B.C.E., Carthage, governed like Rome as a republic, controlled a powerful empire rich from farming in Africa and seaborne trade in the Mediterranean. Geography meant that an expansionist Rome would sooner or later come into conflict with Carthage. To Romans, Carthage seemed both a dangerous rival and a fine prize because it had grown so prosperous from agriculture and international commerce. Horror at the Carthaginians' alleged tradition of incinerating infants to placate their gods in times of trouble also fed Romans' hostility against people they saw as barbarians.

TAKING MEASURE

Census Records during the First and Second Punic Wars

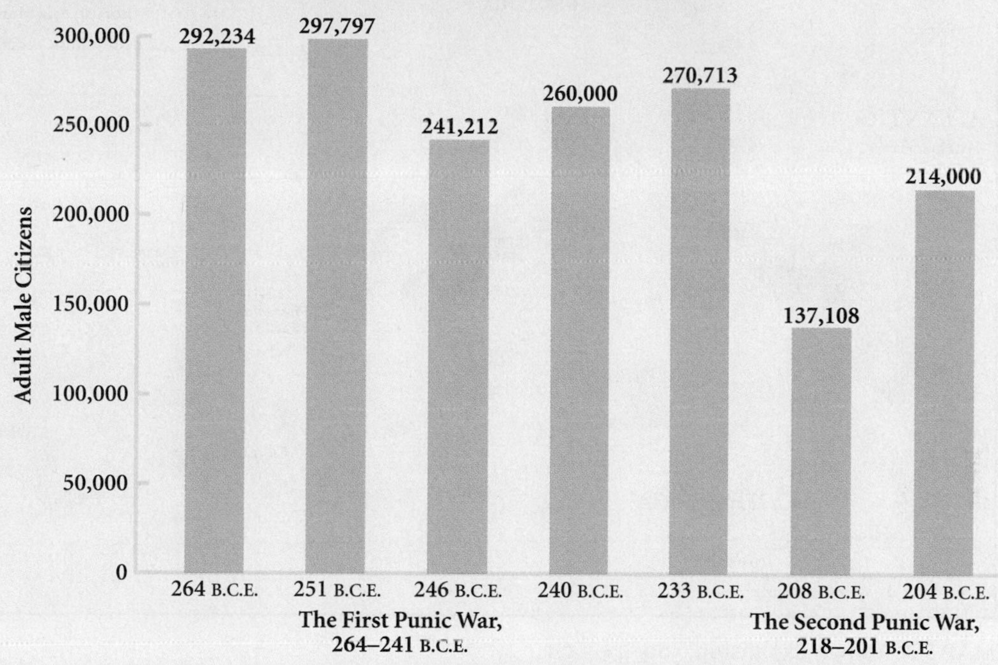

Writing hundreds of years apart, Livy (59 B.C.E.–17 C.E.) and Jerome (c. 347–420 C.E.) provide these numbers from Rome's censuses, which counted only adult male citizens (the men eligible for Rome's regular army), conducted during and between the first two wars against Carthage. Since the census did not include the Italian allies fighting on Rome's side, the census numbers understate the wars' total casualties; scholars estimate that they took the lives of nearly a third of Italy's adult male population, which would have meant perhaps a quarter of a million soldiers killed.

Source: Tenney Frank, *An Economic Survey of Ancient Rome*, vol. 1 (New York: Farrar, Straus and Giroux, 1959), 56.

Question to Consider

- **What effects do you think the population changes shown in this graph might have had on Roman society?**

First Wars Abroad Rome's three wars with Carthage are called the Punic Wars (from the Latin word for "Phoenician"). The first one (264–241 B.C.E.) erupted over Sicily, where Carthage wanted to preserve its trading settlements and Rome wanted to prevent Carthaginian troops from being close to their territory. This long conflict revealed why the Romans won wars: the large Italian population provided deep manpower reserves, and the Roman government was prepared to sacrifice as many troops, spend as much money, and fight as long as it took to defeat the enemy. Previously unskilled at naval warfare, the Romans expended vast sums to build warships to combat Carthage's experienced navy; they lost more than five hundred ships and 250,000 men while learning how to win at sea. (See "Taking Measure," above.)

The Romans' victory in the First Punic War made them masters of Sicily, where they set up their first province (a foreign territory ruled and taxed by Roman officials). This innovation proved so profitable that they soon seized the islands of Sardinia and Corsica from the Carthaginians to create another province. These first successful foreign conquests increased the Romans' appetite for expansion outside Italy (Map 5.3). Fearing a renewal

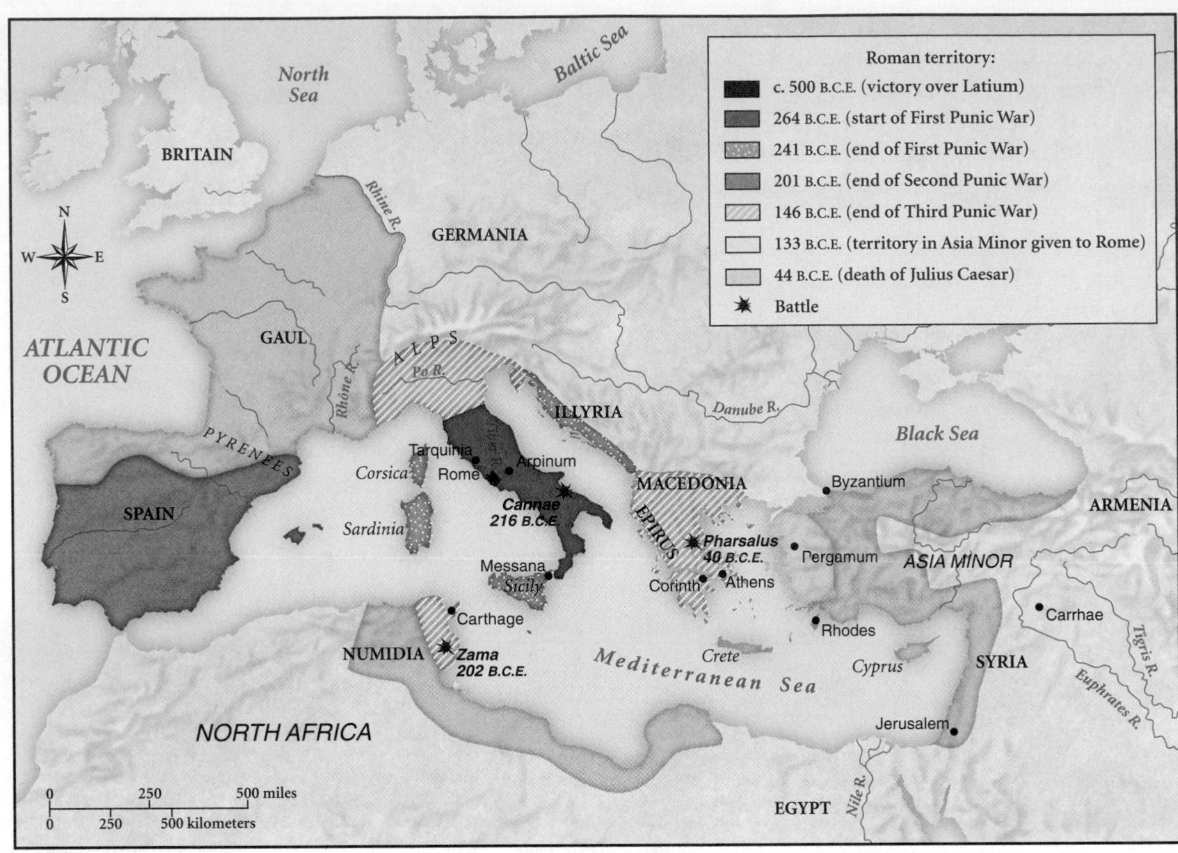

MAP 5.3 Roman Expansion, 500–44 B.C.E.
During its first two centuries, the Roman republic used war and diplomacy to extend its power north and south in the Italian peninsula. In the third and second centuries B.C.E., conflict with Carthage in the south and west and the Hellenistic kingdoms in the east extended Roman power outside Italy and led to the creation of provinces from Spain to Greece. The first century B.C.E. saw the conquest of Syria by Pompey and of Gaul by Julius Caesar (d. 44 B.C.E.).

of Carthage's power, the Romans cemented alliances with local peoples in Spain, where the Carthaginians were expanding from their southern trading posts.

A Roman ultimatum forbidding further expansion convinced the Carthaginians that another war was inevitable, so they decided to strike back. In the Second Punic War (218–201 B.C.E.), the daring Carthaginian general Hannibal terrified the Romans by marching troops and war elephants over the Alps into Italy. Slaughtering more than thirty thousand at Cannae in 216 B.C.E. in the bloodiest Roman loss ever, Hannibal tried to convince Rome's Italian allies to desert, but most refused to rebel. Hannibal's alliance in 215 B.C.E. with the king of Macedonia forced the Romans to fight on a second front in Greece. Still, they refused to crack despite Hannibal's ravaging of Italy from 218 to 203 B.C.E. Then the Romans turned the tables: invading the Carthaginians' African homeland, the Roman army prevailed at the battle of Zama in 202 B.C.E. The Senate imposed a punishing settlement on the enemy in 201 B.C.E., forcing Carthage to scuttle its navy, pay huge war indemnities, and hand over its lucrative holdings in Spain, which Rome made into provinces prosperous from their mines.

Dominance in the Mediterranean

The Third Punic War (149–146 B.C.E.) began when the Carthaginians, who had revived financially, retaliated against the aggression of the king of Numidia, a Roman ally. After winning the war, the Romans heeded the crusty senator Cato's repeated opinion, "Carthage must be destroyed!" They obliterated the city and converted its territory into a province. This disaster did not destroy Carthaginian culture, however, and under the Roman Empire this part of North Africa flourished economically and intellectually, creating a synthesis of Roman and Carthaginian traditions.

The Punic War victories extended Roman power beyond Spain and North Africa to Macedonia, Greece, and western Asia Minor. Hannibal's alliance with the king of Macedonia had brought Roman troops east of Italy for the first time. After defeating the Macedonian king for revenge and to prevent any threat of his invading Italy, the Roman commander proclaimed the "freedom of the Greeks" in 196 B.C.E. to show respect for Greece's glorious past. The Greek cities and federal leagues understood the proclamation to mean that they, as "friends" of Rome, could behave as they liked. They misunderstood. The Romans expected them to behave as clients and follow their new patrons' advice.

The Romans repeatedly intervened to make the kingdom of Macedonia and the Greeks observe their obligations as clients. The Senate in 146 B.C.E. ordered Corinth destroyed for asserting its independence and converted Macedonia and Greece into a province. In 133 B.C.E., the Attalid king increased Roman power with a stupendous gift: in his will he bequeathed his Asia Minor kingdom to Rome. In 121 B.C.E., the Romans made the lower part of Gaul across the Alps (modern southern France) into a province. By the late first century B.C.E., then, Rome governed and profited from two-thirds of the Mediterranean region; only the easternmost Mediterranean lay outside its control (see Map 5.3).

Comparison of Ancient Greek and Roman Developments, c. 750 B.C.E.–146 B.C.E.

	Greece	Rome
753 B.C.E.		Traditional date for the founding of Rome
750 B.C.E.	Polis begins to develop	
750–700 B.C.E.	First Greek poetry (Homer and Hesiod)	
509 B.C.E.		Overthrow of monarchy and establishment of the republic
508–500 B.C.E.	Cleisthenes' reforms to strengthen Athenian democracy	
500–450 B.C.E.		Struggle to establish office of tribune to protect the people
461 B.C.E.	Ephialtes' reforms to democratize Athens's courts	
451–449 B.C.E.		Rome's first law code established (Twelve Tables)
420s B.C.E.	The first Greek history (Herodotus)	
240–210 B.C.E.		First poetry in Latin (translation of Homer's *Odyssey*)
200 B.C.E.		First Roman history in Greek
168–149 B.C.E.		First Roman history in Latin (Cato)
146 B.C.E.	Rome makes Greece a province	

Greek Influence on Roman Literature and the Arts

Roman imperialism generated extensive cross-cultural contact with Greece. Although Romans looked down on Greeks for their military weakness, Roman authors and artists found inspiration in Greek literature and art. About 200 B.C.E., the first Roman historian used Greek to write his narrative of Rome's foundation and the wars with Carthage. The earliest Latin poetry was a translation of Homer's *Odyssey* by a Greek ex-slave, composed sometime after the First Punic War.

Roman literature combined the foreign and the familiar. Many famous early Latin authors were not native Romans but came from different regions of Italy, Sicily, and even North Africa. All found inspiration in Greek literature. Roman comedies, for example, took their plots and stock characters from Hellenistic comedy such as that of Menander, which featured jokes about family life and stereotyped personalities, such as the braggart warrior and the obsessed lover. (See the sculpture on page 156.)

Some Romans distrusted the effect of Greek culture on their own. In the mid-second century B.C.E., Cato, although he studied Greek himself, thundered against the influence of the "weakling" Greeks on the "sturdy" Romans. His history of Rome, *The Origins*, and his instructions on running a large farm, *On Agriculture*, established Latin prose. Cato predicted that if the Romans ever adopted Greek values, they would lose their power. In truth, despite its debt to Greek literature, early Latin literature reflected traditional Roman values. For example, the pathbreaking Latin epic *Annals*, a poetic version of Roman history by the poet Ennius, shows the influence of Greek epic but praises ancestral Roman traditions, as in this famous line: "On the ways and the men of old rests the Roman state."

Later Roman writers also took inspiration from Greek literature in both content and style. The first-century B.C.E. poet Lucretius wrote *On the Nature of Things* to persuade people not to fear death, a terror that only inflamed "the running sores of life." His ideas reflected Greek philosophy's "atomic theory," which said that matter was composed of tiny, invisible particles. Dying, the poem taught, simply meant the dissolving of the union of atoms, which had come together temporarily to make up a person's body. There could be no eternal punishment or pain after death, indeed no existence at all, because a person's soul, itself made up of atoms, perished along with the body.

Hellenistic Greek authors inspired Catullus in the first century B.C.E. to write witty poems ridiculing prominent politicians for their sexual behavior (see Document 2 in "Contrasting Views," page 162)

Actors in a Comedy

This sculpture from the first century C.E. shows actors portraying characters in one of the several kinds of comedy popular during the Roman republic. In this variety, which derived from Hellenistic comedy, the actors wore exaggerated masks designating stock personality types and acted broad, slapstick comedy. The plots ranged from burlesques of famous myths to stereotypes of family problems. Here, on the right, a son returns home after a night of binge drinking, leaning on his slave and accompanied by a hired female musician. On the left, his enraged father is being restrained by a friend from beating his drunken son with a cane. *(Scala/Art Resource, NY.)*

and lamenting his own disastrous love life. His most famous love poems revealed his obsession with a married woman named Lesbia, whom he begged to think only of immediate pleasures:

> Let us live, my Lesbia, and love; the gossip of stern old men is not worth a cent. Suns can set and rise again; we, when once our brief light has set, must sleep one never-ending night. Give me a thousand kisses, then a hundred, then a thousand more.

The orator and politician **Cicero** (106–43 B.C.E.) wrote speeches, letters, and treatises on political science, philosophy, ethics, and theology. He adapted Greek philosophy to Roman life and stressed the need to appreciate each person's uniqueness. His doctrine of ***humanitas*** ("humaneness, the quality of humanity") expressed an ideal for human life based on generous and honest treatment of others and a commitment to morality based on natural law (the rights that belong to all people because they are human beings, independent of the differing laws and customs of different societies). The spirit of humanitas that Cicero passed on to later Western civilization was one of the ancient world's most attractive ideals.

Greece also influenced Rome's art and architecture, from the style of sculpture and painting to the design of public buildings. Romans adapted Greek models to their own purposes, as portrait sculpture reveals. Hellenistic sculptors had pioneered a realistic style showing the ravages of age and infirmity on the human body. They portrayed only stereotypes, however, such as the "old man" or the "drunken woman," not specific people. Their portrait sculpture presented actual individuals in the best possible light, much like an airbrushed photograph today.

Roman artists applied Greek realism to male portraiture, as contemporary Etruscan sculptors also did. They sculpted men without hiding their unflattering features: long noses, receding chins, deep wrinkles, bald heads, careworn looks. Portraits of women, by contrast, were more idealized, probably representing the traditional vision of the bliss of family life (see the image of the sculpted family tomb on page 142). Because the men depicted in the portraits (or their families) paid for the busts, they must have wanted their faces sculpted realistically—showing the damage of age and effort—to emphasize how hard they had worked to serve the republic.

Stresses on Society from Imperialism

The wars of the third and second centuries B.C.E. proved disastrous for small farmers, confronting the republic with grave social and economic difficulties. The long deployments of troops abroad disrupted Rome's agricultural system, the economy's foundation. Before this time, Roman warfare had followed a pattern of short campaigns timed not to interfere with farmers' work. Now, however, a farmer absent during a protracted war had two unhappy choices: rely on a hired hand or slave to manage his crops and animals, or have his wife perform farmwork in addition to her usual domestic tasks.

The story of the consul Regulus, who won a great victory in Africa in 256 B.C.E., revealed the problems prolonged absence caused. When the man who managed Regulus's farm died while the consul was away fighting, a worker stole all the farm's tools and livestock. Regulus begged the Senate to send a replacement fighter so that he could return to save his wife and children from starving. The senators instead sent help to preserve Regulus's family and

---

Cicero (SIH suh roh): Rome's most famous orator and author of the doctrine of *humanitas*.

humanitas: The Roman orator Cicero's ideal of "humaneness," meaning generous and honest treatment of others based on natural law.

property because they wanted to keep him on the battle lines.

The Poor Ordinary soldiers could expect no special aid, and economic troubles hit their families particularly hard when, in the second century B.C.E., for reasons that remain unclear, there was not enough farmland to support the population. Scholars have usually concluded that the rich had deprived the poor of land, but recent research suggests that the problem stemmed from an unexplained increase in the number of births of young people. Not all regions of Italy suffered as severely as others, and some impoverished farmers and their families managed to survive by working as agricultural laborers for others. Still, the number of poor people with no way to make a living created a social crisis by the late second century B.C.E. Many homeless people relocated to Rome, where the men begged for work as day laborers and women sought piecework making cloth but often had to become prostitutes to survive.

This flood of desperate people increased the poverty-level population of Rome, and the landless poor became an explosive swing element in Roman politics. They backed any politician who promised to address their need for food, and the government had to feed them to avert riots. Like Athens in the fifth century B.C.E., Rome by the late second century B.C.E. needed to import grain to feed its swollen urban population. The poor's demand for low-priced (and eventually free) food distributed at state expense became one of the most divisive issues in late republican politics.

The Rich While the landless poor struggled, imperialism brought Rome's elite ample political and financial rewards. The need for commanders to lead military campaigns abroad created opportunities for successful generals to enrich their families. The elite enhanced their reputations by using their gains to finance public works that benefited the general population. Building new temples, for example, was thought to increase everyone's security because the Romans believed it pleased their gods to have many shrines. In 146 B.C.E., a victorious general paid for Rome's first marble temple, finally bringing this Greek style to the capital city.

Bedroom in a Rich Roman House

This bedroom from about 40 B.C.E. was in the house of a rich Roman family near Naples; it was buried—and preserved—by the eruption of the volcano Vesuvius in 79 C.E. The bright paintings showed a dazzling variety of outdoor scenes and architecture. The stone floor helped create a sensation of coolness in the summer. *(Cubiculum [bedroom] from the Villa of P. Fannius Synistor at Boscoreale, ca. 50–40 B.C.E. Fresco, Room: 8 ft. ½ in. x 10 ft. 11½ in. x 19 ft. 7⅛ in. [265.4 x 334 x 583.9 cm.] Rogers Fund, 1903 [03.14.13a-g]. Location: the Metropolitan Museum of Art, New York, NY, U.S.A. Image copyright © The Metropolitan Museum of Art/Art Resource, NY.)*

The economic distress of small farmers benefited rich landowners because they could buy bankrupt farms to create large estates. They further increased their holdings by illegally occupying public land carved out of the territory seized from defeated enemies. The rich worked their huge farms, called *latifundia*, with free laborers as well as slaves, a ready supply of which were available from the huge numbers taken captive in the same wars that displaced so many farmers. Thus, the victories won by free but poor Roman citizens created a slave workforce with which they could not compete. The growing size of the slave crews working on latifundia was a mixed blessing for their wealthy owners. Although the owners did not have to pay these laborers, the presence of so many slave workers in one place led to periodic revolts that required military intervention.

The elite profited from Rome's expansion by filling the governing offices in the new provinces. Some governors ruled honestly, but others used their power to squeeze the provincials. Since provincial officials ruled by martial law, no one in the provinces could curb a greedy governor's appetite for graft, extortion, and landgrabbing. Often such offenders faced no punishment because their colleagues in the Senate excused their crimes.

The new opportunities for rich living strained the traditional values of moderation and frugality. Previously, a man could become legendary for his life's simplicity: Manius Curius (d. 270 B.C.E.), for example, boiled turnips for his meals in a humble hut despite his glorious military victories. Now, in the second century B.C.E., the elite acquired showy luxuries, such as large country villas for entertaining friends and clients. Money had become more valuable to them than the ancestral values of the republic.

REVIEW QUESTION What advantages and disadvantages did Rome's victories over foreign peoples create for both rich and poor Romans?

Civil War and the Destruction of the Republic

Beginning in the late second century B.C.E., members of the Roman upper class set in motion a series of events that for the next century turned politics into a violent competition. This conflict exploded into civil wars in the first century that destroyed the republic. Senators introduced violence to politics by murdering the tribunes Tiberius and Gaius Gracchus when the brothers pushed for reforms to help the poor by giving them land. When a would-be member of the elite, Gaius Marius, opened military service to the poor to boost his personal status, his creation of "client armies" undermined faithfulness to the general good of the community. The people's unwillingness to share citizenship with Italian allies sparked a damaging war in Italy. Finally, the out-of-control competition for leadership and power by the "great men" Sulla, Pompey, and Julius Caesar peaked in destructive civil wars.

The Gracchus Brothers and Violence in Politics, 133–121 B.C.E.

Tiberius and Gaius Gracchus based their political careers on pressing the rich to make concessions to strengthen the state. They came from the cream of Roman society: their grandfather had defeated Hannibal, and their mother was the Cornelia whom the king of Egypt had courted. Their policies supporting the poor angered many of their fellow members of the social elite. Tiberius explained the tragic circumstances that motivated them politically:

> The wild beasts that roam over Italy have their dens. . . . But the men who fight and die for Italy enjoy nothing but the air and light. They wander about homeless with their wives and children. . . . They fight and die to protect the wealth and luxury of others. They are called masters of the world, and have not a lump of earth they call their own.

When Tiberius won election as a tribune in 133 B.C.E., his opponents blocked his attempts at reform. He then took the radical step of disregarding the Senate's advice by having the Plebeian Assembly pass reform laws to redistribute public land to landless Romans. He again broke with tradition by ignoring the Senate in financing his farming reforms: he convinced the people pass a law to use the Attalid king's gift of his kingdom to equip new farms on the redistributed land.

Tiberius next announced he would run for reelection as tribune for the following year, violating the prohibition against consecutive terms. His opponents had had enough: Tiberius's cousin, an ex-consul, led a band of senators and their clients in a sudden attack on him, shouting, "Save the republic." Pulling up their togas over their left arms so they would not trip in a fight, they clubbed the tribune to death, along with many of his supporters and clients.

Gaius, whom the people elected tribune for 123 B.C.E. and, contrary to tradition, again for the next year, also pushed measures that outraged his fellow elite: more farming reforms, subsidized prices for grain, public works projects to employ the poor, and colonies abroad with farms for the landless. His most revolutionary measures proposed Roman citizenship for many Italians and new courts to try senators accused of corruption as provincial governors. The new juries would be manned not by senators but by ***equites*** ("equestrians" or "knights"). These were elite landowners who, in the earliest republic, had been men rich enough to provide horses for cavalry service but were now wealthy businessmen, whose careers in commerce instead of government made their interests different from the senators'. Because they did not serve in the Senate, the equites could convict senators for crimes without having to face peer pressure. Gaius's proposal marked the equites' emergence as a political force in Roman politics, angering the Senate.

When in 121 B.C.E. the senators blocked Gaius's plans, he assembled an armed group to threaten them. They responded by advising the consuls "to take all measures necessary to defend the republic," meaning the use of force to kill anyone identified, rightly or wrongly, as a threat to public order. When his enemies came to murder him, Gaius robbed them of their prize and proved his courage by committing suicide in dramatic fashion: he had one of his slaves cut his throat. The senators then killed hundreds of his supporters and their servants.

The violence from this conflict introduced factions (strongly aggressive interest groups) into Roman politics. From that point on, members of the elite identified themselves as either supporters of the people, the ***populares*** faction, or supporters of "the best," the ***optimates*** faction. Some chose a faction from genuine allegiance to its policies; others supported whichever side better promoted their own political advancement. The elite's splintering into bitterly hostile factions remained a source of murderous political violence until the end of the republic.

---

equites (EHK wih tehs): Literally, "equestrians" or "knights"; wealthy Roman businessmen who chose not to pursue a government career.

populares (poh poo LAH rehs): The Roman political faction supporting the common people; established during the late republic.

optimates (op tee MAH tehs): The Roman political faction supporting the "best," or highest, social class; established during the late republic.

Marius and the Origin of Client Armies, 107–100 B.C.E.

The republic needed innovative commanders to combat slave revolts and foreign invasions in the late second and early first centuries B.C.E. A new kind of leader arose to meet this need: the "new man," an upper-class man without a consul among his ancestors, who relied on sheer ability and often political violence to force his way to fame, fortune, and—his ultimate goal—the consulship.

Gaius Marius (c. 157–86 B.C.E.), who came from the equites class, set the pattern for this new kind of leader. Ordinarily, a man of Marius's status had no chance to crack the ranks of Rome's ruling oligarchy. Gaining fame for his brilliant military record as a junior officer and relying on voters' anger at the current war leadership, Marius won election as a consul for 107 B.C.E. In Roman terms this election made him a "new man"—that is, the first man in his family's history to become consul. Marius's continuing success as a commander, first in North Africa and next against German tribes who attacked southern France and then Italy, led the people to elect him consul six times, breaking all tradition.

For his victories, the Senate voted Marius a triumph, Rome's ultimate military honor. In the ceremony, huge crowds cheered him as he rode in a chariot through the streets of Rome. His soldiers shouted obscene jokes about him, to ward off the evil eye at this moment of supreme glory. For a former small-town member of the equites class like Marius, this honor was a supreme social coup. Yet, despite Marius's triumph, the optimates never accepted him as one of them. His support came from the common people, whom he had won over with his revolutionary reform of entrance requirements for the army. Previously, only men with property could usually enroll as soldiers. Marius opened the ranks to **proletarians**, men who had no property and could not afford weapons on their own. For them, serving in the army meant an opportunity to better their lot by acquiring booty and a grant of land. (See Document, "Polybius on Roman Military Discipline," page 160.)

Marius's reform changed Roman history by creating armies more loyal to their commander than to the republic. Proletarian troops felt immense goodwill toward a commander who led them to victory and then divided the spoils with them generously. The crowds of poor Roman soldiers thus began to behave like an army of clients following

---

proletarians: In the Roman republic, the mass of people so poor they owned no property.

DOCUMENT

Polybius on Roman Military Discipline

Polybius, a Greek commander who spent years on campaign with Roman armies in the second century B.C.E., describes the ideal centurion (an experienced soldier appointed to discipline the troops). He also notes the importance of harsh punishments and the fear of disgrace and shame for maintaining military discipline.

The Romans want centurions not so much to be bold and eager to take risks but rather to be capable of leadership and steady and solid in character. Nor do they want them to start attacks and start battles. They want men who will hold their position and stay in place even when they are losing the battle and will die to hold their ground. . . . Soldiers [convicted of neglecting sentry duty] who manage to live [after being beaten or stoned as punishment] don't thereby secure their safety. How could they? For they are not permitted to return to their homeland, and none of their relatives would dare to accept such a man into their households. For this reason men who have once fallen into this misfortune are completely ruined. . . . Even when clearly at risk of being wiped out by enormously superior enemy forces, troops in tactical reserve units are not willing to desert their places in the battle line, for fear of the punishment that would be inflicted by their own side. Some men who have lost a shield or sword or another part of their arms in battle heedlessly throw themselves against the enemy, hoping either to recover what they lost, or to escape the inevitable disgrace and the insults of their relatives by suffering [injury or death].

Source: Polybius, *Histories*, Book 6.24, 37. Translation by Thomas R. Martin.

Question to Consider

- **What purpose does punishment serve in the maintenance of a fighting army, according to Polybius?**

their commander as patron. In keeping with the patron-client system, they supported his personal ambitions. Marius was the first to promote his own career in this way. He lost his political importance after 100 B.C.E. when, no longer consul, he tried but failed to win the backing of the optimates. Commanders after Marius used client armies to advance their political careers more ruthlessly than he had, thereby accelerating the republic's destruction.

Sulla and Civil War, 91–78 B.C.E.

One such commander, Lucius Cornelius Sulla (c. 138–78 B.C.E.), took advantage of uprisings by non-Romans in Italy and Asia Minor in the early first century B.C.E. to use his client army to seize Rome's highest offices and force the Senate to support his policies. His career revealed the dirty secret of politics in the late republic: traditional values no longer restrained commanders who—above peace and the good of the community—prized their own advancement and the enriching of their troops.

The Social War The uprisings in Italy occurred because many of Rome's Italian allies lacked Roman citizenship and therefore had no vote in decisions concerning their own interests. They became increasingly unhappy as wealth from conquests piled up in the late republic. Their upper classes wanted a greater share of the prosperity that war had brought to the citizen elite. The Roman people rejected the allies' demand for citizenship, from fear that sharing such status would lessen their own privileges.

The Italians' discontent erupted in 91–87 B.C.E. in the Social War (so named because the Latin word for "ally" is *socius*). Forming a confederacy to fight Rome, the allies demonstrated their commitment by the number of their casualties—300,000 dead. Although Rome's army prevailed, the rebels won the political war: the Romans granted citizenship and the vote to all freeborn people in Italy south of the Po River. The Social War's bloodshed therefore reestablished Rome's tradition of strengthening the state by granting citizenship to outsiders. The war's other significant outcome was that Sulla's successful generalship won him election as consul for 88 B.C.E.

Plunder Abroad and Violence at Home Sulla gained supreme power by taking advantage of events in Asia Minor in 88 B.C.E., when Mithridates VI (120–63 B.C.E.), king of Pontus on the Black Sea's southern coast, rebelled against Roman control. The peoples of Asia Minor hated Rome's tax collectors, who tried to make provincials pay much more than was required. Denouncing the Romans as "the common enemies of all mankind," Mithridates persuaded the locals to kill all the Italians there—tens of thousands of them—in a single day.

The Senate advised a military expedition to punish this treachery. Victory would mean capturing unimaginable booty from Asia Minor's wealthy cities. Born to a patrician family that had lost much of its status and all of its money, Sulla craved the command. When the Senate gave it to him, his jealous rival Marius, now an old man, immediately plotted to have it transferred to himself by plebiscite. Outraged, Sulla did the unthinkable: he marched his client army against Rome itself. All his officers except one deserted him in horror at this shameful attack, but his common soldiers followed him to a man. Neither they nor their commander shrank from starting a civil war. After capturing Rome, Sulla killed or exiled his opponents. He let his men rampage through the city and then led them off to Asia Minor, ignoring a summons to stand trial and sacking Athens on the way. In Sulla's absence, Marius embarked on his own reign of terror in Rome to try to regain his former power. In 83 B.C.E., Sulla returned victorious, having allowed his soldiers to plunder Asia Minor. Civil war erupted for two years until Sulla crushed his enemies at home.

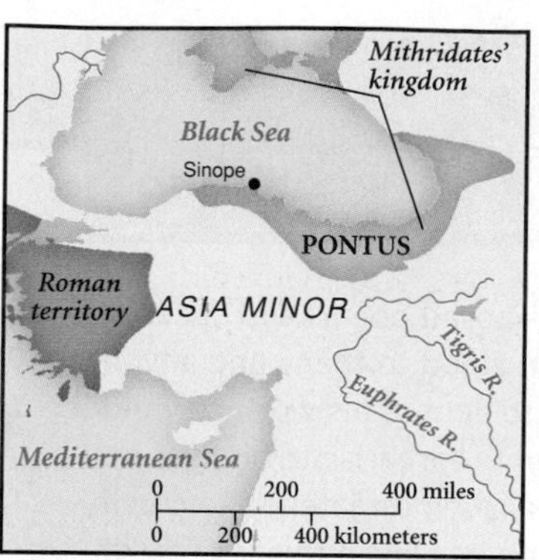

The Kingdom of Mithridates VI, 88 B.C.E.

Sulla then exterminated everyone who had opposed him. To speed the process, he devised a procedure called proscription—posting a list of people accused of being traitors so that anyone could hunt them down and execute them. Because proscribed men's property was confiscated, the victors fraudulently added to the list anyone whose wealth they coveted. The terrorized Senate appointed Sulla dictator—an emergency office supposed to be held only temporarily—and gave him permanent immunity from prosecution. As dictator, Sulla reorganized the government to favor the optimates—his social class—by making senators the only ones allowed to judge cases against their colleagues and forbidding tribunes from sponsoring legislation or holding any other office after their term.

The Effects of Sulla's Career Sulla died before he could remake the republic's government, but his murderous career revealed the strengths and weaknesses of Roman values. First, the purpose of war had changed from defending the community to accumulating plunder for common soldiers as well as commanders. Second, the patron-client system led proletarian soldiers to feel stronger ties of obligation to their generals than to the republic.

Finally, the traditional competition for status worked both for and against political stability. When that value motivated men to seek office to promote the community's welfare—the traditional ideal of a public career—it exerted a powerful force for social unity and prosperity. But pushed to its extreme, as in the case of Sulla, the contest for individual prestige and wealth pulled the republic apart.

Julius Caesar and the Collapse of the Republic, 83–44 B.C.E.

Powerful generals after Sulla took him as their model: while declaring their loyalty to the community, they ruthlessly pursued their own advancement. Two Roman aristocrats' competition for power and money led to the civil war that brought the final destruction of the republic and opened the way for the return of monarchy. Those competitors were Gnaeus Pompey and Julius Caesar. (See "Contrasting Views," page 162.)

Pompey's Tradition-Shattering Career Pompey (106–48 B.C.E.) was a better general than a politician. In his early twenties he won victories supporting Sulla. In 71 B.C.E., Pompey won the mop-up battles defeating a massive slave rebellion led by a fugitive gladiator named Spartacus, stealing the glory from the real victor, Marcus Licinius Crassus. (Spartacus had terrorized southern Italy for two years and defeated consuls with his army of 100,000 escaped slaves.) Pompey shattered tradition by demanding and receiving a consulship for 70 B.C.E., even though he was nowhere near the legal age of forty-two and had not been elected to any lower post on the ladder of offices. Three years later, he received a command with unlimited powers to exterminate the pirates then infesting the Mediterranean, a task he accomplished in a matter of months. This success made him wildly popular with many groups: the urban poor, who depended on a steady flow of imported grain; merchants, who depended on safe sea lanes; and coastal communities, which were vulnerable to pirates' raids. In 66 B.C.E., he defeated Mithridates, who was still stirring up trouble in Asia Minor. By annexing Syria as a province in 64 B.C.E., Pompey ended the Seleucid kingdom and extended Rome's power to the Mediterranean's eastern coast.

People compared Pompey to Alexander the Great and added *Magnus* ("the Great") to his name.

CONTRASTING VIEWS

What Was Julius Caesar Like?

Julius Caesar provoked strong reactions among people: some loved him, some hated him, some ridiculed him (Document 2), and some changed their minds (Document 3)—but only fools failed to recognize his extraordinary energy and will (Document 1). These excerpts, including one in his own words (Document 4), offer sample assessments of what different sources said this most famous Roman was like. The biographer Suetonius described both Caesar's strengths and faults (Document 5).

1. Caesar and the Pirates

About a century and a half after Caesar's death, the Greek scholar Plutarch wrote a biography to reveal the famous leader's character. He tells this story of Caesar as an eighteen-year-old (well before he became famous) refusing the dictator Sulla's politically motivated order to divorce his wife. When the teenage Caesar fled Rome to escape being murdered by Sulla's henchmen, he was captured by pirates while trying to get to safety in Asia Minor.

[To escape Sulla], Caesar sailed to King Nicomedes in Bithynia (in Asia Minor). On his voyage home, pirates from Cilicia captured him and held him on an island. When they demanded twenty talents [a huge sum] for his ransom, he laughed at them for not knowing who he was, and spontaneously promised to give them fifty talents instead. Next, after he had dispatched friends to various cities to gather the money, he had only one friend and two attendants left while a captive of the most murderous men in the world. Nevertheless, he felt so superior to them that whenever he wanted to sleep, he would order them to be quiet.

For thirty-eight days, as if the pirates were not his kidnappers but rather his bodyguards, he participated in their games and exercises with a carefree spirit. He also composed poems and speeches that he read aloud to them, and anyone who failed to admire his work he would call an illiterate barbarian to his face, and often with a laugh threatened to crucify them. The pirates loved this, and attributed his free speech to simplemindedness and youthful spirit.

After Caesar had paid the ransom and was released, he immediately manned ships and put to sea against the pirates. He caught them still anchored, and captured most of them. He took their loot as his booty and threw the men into prison, telling the Roman provincial governor that it was his job to punish them. But since the governor had his eyes on the pirates' rich loot and kept saying that he would consider their case when he had time, Caesar took the pirates out of prison and crucified them all, just as he had often warned them on the island that he was going to do, when they thought he was joking.

Source: Plutarch, *Life of Julius Caesar*, 1–2 (excerpted). Translation by Thomas R. Martin.

2. A Poet Mocks Caesar about Sex

*In about 58 B.C.E., the twenty-something Catullus ridiculed Caesar (in his early forties) and his follower Mamurra in several acid-tongued poems. The biographer Suetonius (*Life of Julius Caesar *73) reports that Caesar said the ridicule inflicted a permanent blot on his name, but that when Catullus apologized, Caesar invited the poet to dinner that very same day.*

They're a pretty good match, those fags,
Mamurra and that queer, Caesar.
And no wonder. They've both got the
  same stains,
One of them a City guy and the other
  from Formiae,
And they won't wash out.
One's just as sick as the other, those
  twins,
Two little brainiacs on the same little
  couch,
This one's just as greedy an adulterer as
  the other,
They're allies competing even for little
  girlies;
So, they're a pretty good match,
  those fags.

Source: Catullus, Poem 57. Translation by Thomas R. Martin.

3. Cicero Writes to a Friend about Caesar

Cicero, Rome's most famous orator, wrote many private letters that have survived. In this one, written to his friend Atticus a few days after Caesar began the civil war by crossing the Rubicon River in January 49 B.C.E., Cicero worriedly expresses his opinion of Caesar at the time.

What's going on? I'm in the dark. . . . That awful fool Caesar, who has never had even the slightest thought of "the good and the fair"! He claims he's doing all this for the sake of honor? But how can you have honor if you have no ethics? Is it ethical to lead an army without official confirmation of your command, to capture cities of Roman citizens to force your way more easily to our mother city, to plot abolition of debts and the recall of exiles, a thousand outrages, "all to obtain the greatest of divinities, sole rule"?

In this letter, written on March 1 of the same year, Cicero offers a different opinion.

Just look at the kind of man who has taken over the republic: clear thinking, sharp, on the ball. By god, if he doesn't murder anyone and doesn't take away people's property, the very people who lived in fear of him will worship him the most.

Source: Cicero, *Letters to Atticus*, 7.11, 8.13. Translation by Thomas R. Martin.

4. Caesar Explains Why He Fought the Civil War

In his memoirs, Caesar provided his own account of the civil war that made him Rome's most powerful man. Here he reports what he said to the Senate on April 1, 49 B.C.E., after Pompey left the capital and Caesar took it without a struggle. In his own writings Caesar refers to himself in the third person (i.e., the he *in this excerpt is Caesar).*

A meeting of the Senate convened, and he spoke about the wrongs his enemies had done him. He explained that he had only wanted a usual office [i.e., consul] . . . and was content with what any citizen could obtain. . . . He emphasized his moderation in asking on his own initiative that both his army and Pompey's be disbanded [to prevent war], a concession that would have cost him both status and office. He talked about how bitter his enemies had been . . . and how they had not laid down their command and armies, even at the cost of anarchy. He stressed how unfair they had been to try to deprive him of his legions, and how savage and arrogant in putting restrictions on the tribunes [who favored him]. He spoke about the offers he had made, the meeting that he had suggested but they had rejected. Given all this, he encouraged, he asked the Senators to take responsibility for the state and govern it together with him. But, he added, if they ran away out of fear, he would not run away from the job and would govern the state by himself. His opinion was that the Senate should send delegates to Pompey to arrange a settlement; he was not cowed by Pompey's recent remark in the Senate that to receive a delegation implied authority but sending it implied fear. That sort of thought revealed a weak and superficial spirit. He, by contrast, wished to win the competition to be just and fair in the same way in which he had striven to excel in his achievements.

Source: Julius Caesar, *The Civil War*, 1.32. Translation by Thomas R. Martin.

5. A Biographer Describes Caesar's Character

These excerpts about Caesar's character and behavior come from Suetonius's biography, written about 150 years after Caesar's assassination.

Caesar was somewhat overly concerned with how he looked, and he always had a careful haircut and shave, and even had excess hair removed. . . . His baldness embarrassed him because his enemies made fun of it. He therefore used to comb his little remaining hair forward, and more than any other honor bestowed by the Senate and people he treasured and used the right to wear a wreath of laurel leaves on his head all the time. . . .

The only sexual impropriety in his reputation was his relationship with the king of Bythinia, but that accusation was serious and lasted; everybody insulted him about it. . . . He seduced lots of women . . . and had love affairs with queens. . . . He drank only very little.

Both as a military commander and as a public official at Rome he used every trick to accumulate money. . . . As a public speaker and a general he either equaled or outstripped the fame of the most outstanding men of the past. . . . He wrote memoirs . . . which Cicero says "deserve the highest praise—they're simple and elegant at the same time."

On military campaigns he showed incredible endurance. . . . It's hard to say whether as a commander he relied more on caution or boldness because he never led his army into a spot where it could be ambushed without first making a careful scouting of the territory. . . . He never let concern for religious scruples deter him from action or slow him down. . . . Whenever his troops started to retreat, he often rallied them himself, using his body to block their way . . . even grabbing them by the throat and making them turn around to face the enemy. . . . He judged his soldiers not by their character or luck but only by how skilled they were, and he treated them all with the same strictness and the same indulgence. . . . He would sometimes overlook their mistakes and didn't punish them strictly according to the rules, but he always kept careful watch for soldiers deserting or mutinying, and these he punished with great harshness. . . . So, he made his men very devoted to him and also very brave.

Even as a young man he treated his clients faithfully. . . . He was always kind to his friends. . . . He never became so much of an enemy to anyone that he couldn't make them a friend when the chance came. . . . Even in seeking revenge he was naturally very merciful . . . and he certainly showed wonderful self-restraint and mercy while fighting the civil war and after he won. . . .

In the end, however, his other words and deeds outbalance all this, and there is the opinion that he abused his rule and that it was justice that he was murdered.

Source: Suetonius, *Life of Julius Caesar*, 45–76. Translation by Thomas R. Martin.

Questions to Consider

1. **How and why do a leader's personal characteristics matter for political success?**
2. **What methods can historians use to evaluate a leader when the evidence is inconsistent or conflicting?**

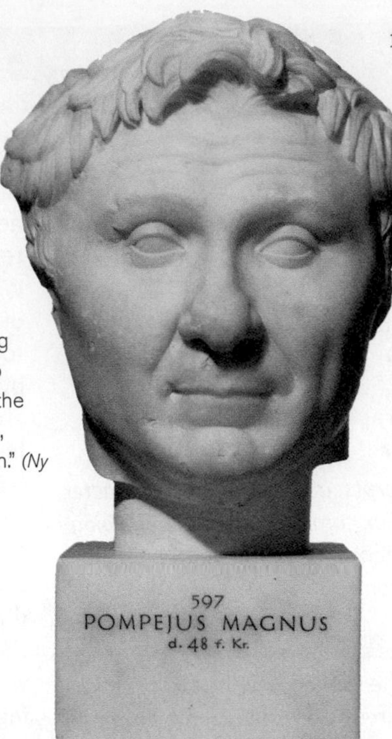

Bust of Pompey

Gnaeus Pompey (106–48 B.C.E.) became Julius Caesar's main political opponent, until Caesar defeated him in the civil war that destroyed the Roman republic. Pompey was a brilliant general, even when young. At twenty-three he raised a client army to fight on Sulla's side. So frightening was Pompey's power that Sulla could not refuse the youth's astonishing demand for a triumph—the ultimate military honor. Awarding the supreme honor to such a young man, who had held not a single public office, shattered the republic's traditions. But as Pompey told Sulla, "People worship the rising, not the setting, sun." *(Ny Carlsberg Glyptotek, Copenhagen, Denmark/The Bridgeman Art Library International.)*

His actions show the degree to which Roman foreign policy had become the personal business of "great men." He ignored the tradition of commanders consulting the Senate about conquering and administering foreign territories, behaving like an independent king rather than a Roman official. He summed up his attitude by replying to some foreigners who criticized his actions as unjust: "Stop quoting the laws to us," he told them. "We carry swords."

Pompey's enemies at Rome worked to undermine his popularity by seeking the people's support, proclaiming their concern for the problems of citizens in financial trouble. By the 60s B.C.E., Rome's urban population had soared to more than half a million. Hundreds of thousands of the poor lived crowded together in slum apartments, surviving on subsidized food distributions. Jobs were scarce. Danger haunted the streets because the city had no police force. Even many formerly wealthy property owners were in trouble: Sulla's confiscations had caused land values to plummet and produced a credit crunch by flooding the real estate market with properties for sale. Overextended investors were trying to borrow their way back to financial security, without success.

The First Triumvirate The senators, who saw the glory that Pompey won from his great military successes as posing a threat to their traditional status as the most important leaders at Rome, were especially eager to cut his power. They therefore blocked his reorganization of the former Seleucid kingdom and his distribution of land to his army veterans. Pompey therefore negotiated with his fiercest political rivals, Crassus and Caesar (100–44 B.C.E.). In 60 B.C.E., they formed an unofficial arrangement that historians call the **First Triumvirate** ("group of three"). Pompey then forced through laws confirming his earlier plans, thus reinforcing his status as a great patron. Caesar got the consulship for 59 B.C.E. and a special command in Gaul, where he could seize booty to build his own client army. Crassus received financial breaks for the Roman tax collectors in Asia Minor, who supported him politically and financially.

This coalition of political rivals revealed how private relationships had largely replaced communal values in politics. To cement their political bond, Caesar arranged to have his daughter, Julia, marry Pompey in 59 B.C.E., even though she had been engaged to another man. Pompey soothed Julia's jilted fiancé by offering the hand of his own daughter, who had been engaged to yet somebody else. Through these marital machinations, the two powerful antagonists now had a common interest: the fate of Julia, Caesar's only daughter and Pompey's new wife. (Pompey had earlier divorced his second wife after Caesar allegedly seduced her.) Pompey and Julia apparently fell deeply in love in their arranged marriage. As long as Julia lived, Pompey's affection for her kept him from breaking his alliance with her father.

Civil War During the 50s B.C.E., Caesar won his soldiers' loyalty with victories and plunder in Gaul, which he added to the Roman provinces, and he awed his troops with his boldness by crossing the channel to campaign in Britain. His political enemies in Rome dreaded him even more as his military successes mounted, and the bond allying him to Pompey shattered in 54 B.C.E. when Julia died in childbirth. The two leaders' rivalry then exploded into violence: gangs of their supporters battled each other in the streets of Rome. The violence became so bad in 53 B.C.E. that it was impossible to hold elections. The First Triumvirate soon dissolved, and in 52 B.C.E. Caesar's enemies convinced the Senate to make Pompey consul by himself, breaking the Republic's long tradition of two consuls sharing power at the head of the state.

First Triumvirate: The coalition formed in 60 B.C.E. by Pompey, Crassus, and Caesar. (The word *triumvirate* means "group of three.")

Escape from Troy on a Coin of Julius Caesar
This coin minted for Julius Caesar in 47/46 B.C.E. shows the hero Aeneas escaping from Troy, which the victorious Greeks were burning down. He carries his elderly father on his shoulder and the city's wooden statue of the goddess Athena in his right hand. This myth was a famous example of the Roman value of faithfulness, a quality that Caesar wanted to claim for himself at the time, when he was still fighting other Romans for control of the state as the republic was being torn apart by the violent conflict among upper-class leaders. *(bpk, Berlin/Muenzkabinett, Staaliche Museen, Berlin, Germany/Art Resource, NY.)*

Civil war exploded when the Senate ordered Caesar to surrender his command. Like Sulla, Caesar led his army against Rome. As he crossed the Rubicon River, the official northern boundary of Italy, in early 49 B.C.E., he uttered the famous words signaling that there was now no turning back: "Let's roll the dice." His troops followed him without hesitation, and the people in the countryside cheered him on. He had many backers in Rome, too: not only the masses counting on his legendary generosity for handouts but also impoverished members of the elite hoping to regain their fortunes through proscriptions of the rich.

The support for Caesar convinced Pompey and most senators, including the famous politician and orator Cicero, to flee to Greece. Caesar entered Rome peacefully, left to defeat the enemies he had in Spain, and then sailed to Greece. There he nearly lost the war when his supplies ran out, but his soldiers stayed loyal even when they were reduced to eating bread made from roots. When Pompey saw what Caesar's men were willing to live on, he cried, "I am fighting wild beasts." Caesar's nail-hard troops defeated the army of Pompey and the Senate at the battle of Pharsalus in central Greece in 48 B.C.E. Pompey fled to Egypt, where the ministers of the teenaged pharaoh Ptolemy XIII (63–47 B.C.E.) treacherously murdered him.

Relief Carving of Cleopatra and Her Son Caesarion
This relief carving appears on the wall of a temple at Dendera in Egypt. It depicts Cleopatra VII, queen of Egypt, and her son by Julius Caesar, Caesarion ("Little Caesar"). They are shown wearing the traditional ceremonial clothing and crowns of Egyptian pharaohs, a sign of the claim of the Ptolemaic ruling family to be the legitimate rulers of Egypt despite their Macedonian ethnic origins. Both died in 30 B.C.E. when Octavian, the adopted son of Julius Caesar and soon to become Augustus and the ruler of Rome, conquered Egypt and made it a Roman province. *(© Ancient Art and Architecture Collection, Ltd.)*

Caesar next invaded Egypt, winning a difficult campaign that ended when he restored Cleopatra VII (69–30 B.C.E.) to the throne of Egypt. As ruthless as she was intelligent, Cleopatra charmed Caesar into sharing her bed and supporting her rule. Their love affair shocked the general's friends and enemies alike: they thought Rome should seize power from foreigners, not share it with them.

Caesar's Dictatorship and Murder

By 45 B.C.E., Caesar had won the civil war. He now had to decide how to rule a shattered republic. He apparently believed that only a sole ruler could end the chaotic violence of the factions, but the republic's oldest tradition prohibited

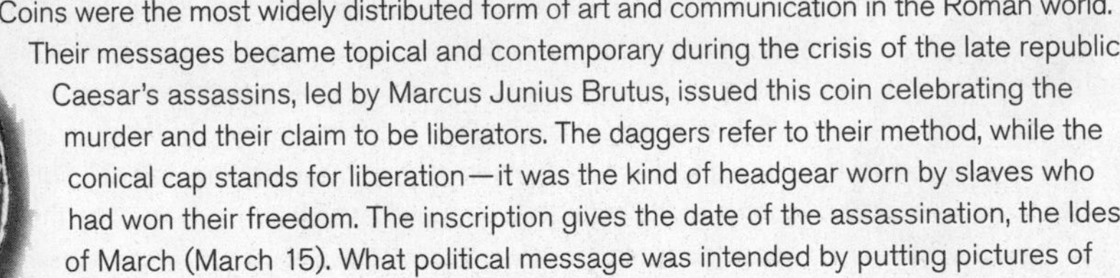

Ides of March Coin Celebrating Caesar's Murder
Coins were the most widely distributed form of art and communication in the Roman world. Their messages became topical and contemporary during the crisis of the late republic. Caesar's assassins, led by Marcus Junius Brutus, issued this coin celebrating the murder and their claim to be liberators. The daggers refer to their method, while the conical cap stands for liberation—it was the kind of headgear worn by slaves who had won their freedom. The inscription gives the date of the assassination, the Ides of March (March 15). What political message was intended by putting pictures of murder weapons on a coin? *(© The Trustees of the British Museum/Art Resource, NY.)*

monarchy. Still, Caesar decided to rule as a king, but without the title, taking instead the traditional Roman title of *dictator*, used for a temporary emergency ruler. In 44 B.C.E., he announced he would continue as dictator without a term limit. "I am not a king," he insisted. The distinction, however, was meaningless. As ongoing dictator, he controlled the government. Elections for offices continued, but Caesar manipulated the results by recommending candidates to the assemblies, which his supporters dominated.

Caesar's policies as dictator were meant to improve the financial situation and reward his supporters. As sole ruler, he offered them a moderate cancellation of debts; a cap on the number of people eligible for subsidized grain; a large program of public works, including public libraries; colonies for his veterans in Italy and abroad; plans to rebuild Corinth and Carthage as commercial centers; and citizenship for more non-Romans.

Unlike Sulla, Caesar did not proscribe his enemies. Instead, he treated them mildly, thereby obligating them to become his grateful clients. For example, he allowed Cicero to return to Rome without punishment. Caesar's decision not to seek revenge earned him unheard-of honors, such as a special golden seat in the Senate house and the renaming of the seventh month of the year after him (July). He also regularized the Roman calendar by having each year include 365 days, a calculation based on an ancient Egyptian calendar that forms the basis for our modern one.

Caesar's dictatorship satisfied the people but outraged the optimates. (See "Contrasting Views," page 162.) They resented being dominated by one of their own, a "traitor" who had deserted to the people's faction. Some senators, led by Caesar's former close friend Marcus Junius Brutus (85–42 B.C.E.) and inspired by the memory of the ancestor of Brutus who led the overthrow of Rome's first monarchy five hundred years before, conspired to murder him. They stabbed Caesar repeatedly in a shower of blood in the Senate house on March 15 (the Ides of March in the Roman calendar), 44 B.C.E. When Brutus struck him, Caesar gasped his last words—in Greek: "You, too, son?" He collapsed dead at the foot of a statue of Pompey.

The liberators, as they called themselves, had no new plans for government. They apparently expected the traditional republic to revive automatically after Caesar's murder, ignoring the political violence of the past century and the deadly imbalance in Roman values, with "great men" placing their competitive private interests above the community's well-being. The liberators were stunned when the people rioted at Caesar's funeral to vent their anger against the upper class that had robbed them of their generous patron. Instead of then forming a united front, the elite resumed their personal vendettas. The traditional values of the republic failed to save it.

REVIEW QUESTION What factors generated the conflicts that caused the Roman republic's destruction?

Conclusion

The two most remarkable features of the Roman republic's history were its phenomenal expansion and its violent disintegration. Rome expanded to control vast territories because it incorporated outsiders, its small farmers produced agricultural surpluses to support a growing population and army, and its leaders respected the traditional values stressing the common good. The Romans' willingness to endure great loss of life and property—the proof of their faithfulness—made their army unstoppable in prolonged conflicts: Rome might lose battles, but never wars. Because wars of conquest brought profits to leaders and the common people alike, peace seemed a wasted opportunity.

MAPPING THE WEST

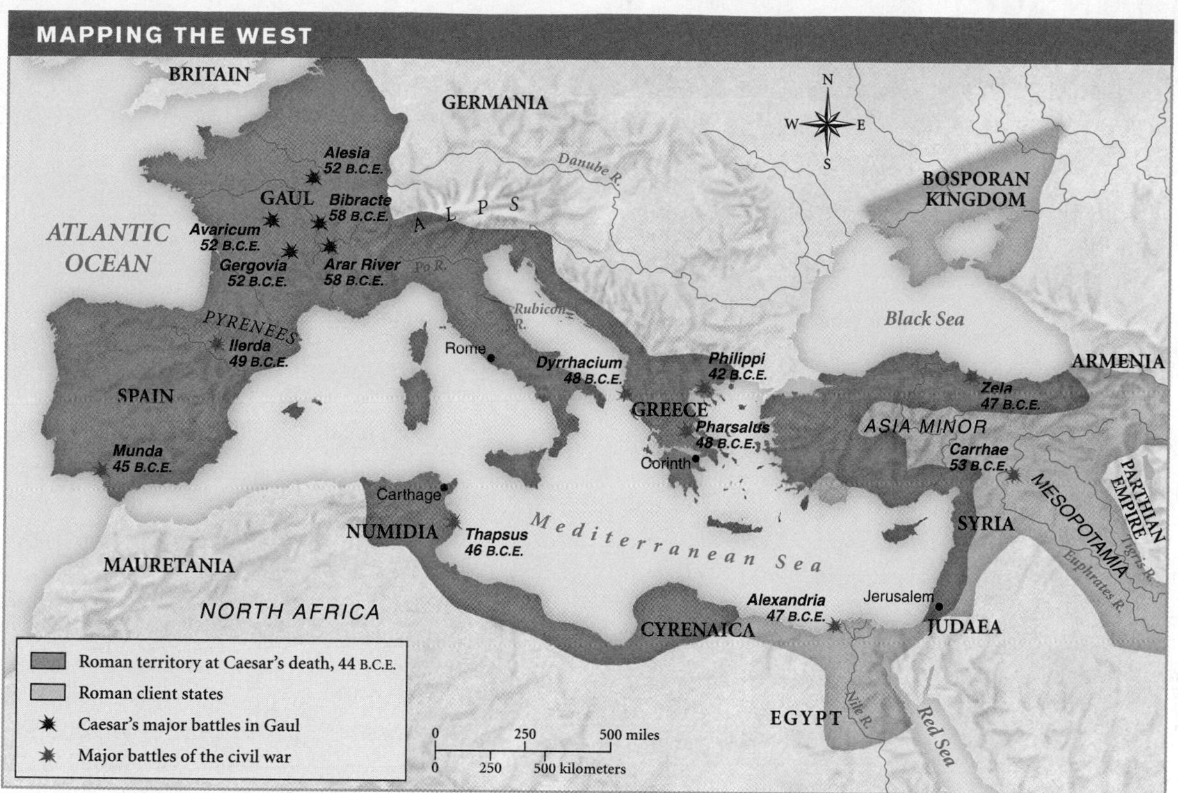

The Roman World at the End of the Republic, 44 B.C.E.

By the time of Julius Caesar's assassination in 44 B.C.E., the territory that would be the Roman Empire was almost complete. Caesar's young relative Octavian (the future Augustus) would conquer and add Egypt in 30 B.C.E. Geography, distance, and formidable enemies were the primary factors inhibiting further expansion—which Romans never stopped wanting, even when lack of money and political discord rendered it purely theoretical. The deserts of Africa and the once again powerful Persian kingdom in the Near East worked against expansion southward or eastward, while trackless forests and fierce resistance from local inhabitants made expansion into central Europe and the British Isles impossible to maintain.

But the republic's victories against Carthage and in Macedonia and Greece had unexpected consequences. Long military service ruined many farming families, and poor people flocked to Rome to live on subsidized food, becoming an unstable political force. Members of the upper class increased their competition with one another for the career opportunities presented by constant war. These rivalries became dangerous to the state when successful generals began acting as patrons to client armies of poor troops. In this dog-eat-dog atmosphere, violence and murder became the preferred means for settling political disputes. Communal values were drowned in the blood of civil war. No reasonable Roman could have been optimistic about the chances for an enduring peace following Caesar's assassination in 44 B.C.E. It would have seemed an impossible dream to imagine that Caesar's grandnephew and adopted son, Octavian—a teenage student at the time of the murder—would eventually bring peace by creating a new political system disguised as the restoration of the old republic.

FOR FURTHER EXPLORATION

- **For additional primary-source material from this period**, see *Sources of the Making of the West*, Fourth Edition.
- **For Web sites, images, and documents related to topics in this chapter**, visit *Make History* at bedfordstmartins.com/hunt.

Chapter 5 Review

Online Study Guide bedfordstmartins.com/hunt

Key Terms and People

In the grid below, identify the term or person and explain its historical significance. (To do this exercise online, go to bedfordstmartins.com/hunt.)

Term	Who or What & When	Why It Matters
mos maiorum (p. 140)		
patron-client system (p. 142)		
patria potestas (p. 142)		
res publica (p. 145)		
orders: patricians and plebeians (p. 148)		
Twelve Tables (p. 149)		
ladder of offices (p. 149)		
plebiscites (p. 150)		
Cicero (p. 156)		
humanitas (p. 156)		
equites (p. 159)		
populares (p. 159)		
optimates (p. 159)		
proletarians (p. 159)		
First Triumvirate (p. 164)		

Review Questions

1. What common themes underlay Roman values? How did Romans' behavior reflect those values?
2. How and why did the Roman republic develop its complicated political and judicial systems?
3. What advantages and disadvantages did Rome's victories over foreign peoples create for both rich and poor Romans?
4. What factors generated the conflicts that caused the Roman republic's destruction?

Making Connections

1. How do the political and social values of the Roman republic compare to those of the Greek city-state in the Classical Age?
2. What were the positive and the negative consequences of war for the Roman republic?
3. How can people decide what is the best balance between individual advancement and communal stability?

Important Events

Date	Event
753 B.C.E.	Traditional date of Rome's founding as monarchy
509 B.C.E.	Roman republic established
509–287 B.C.E.	Struggle of the orders
451–449 B.C.E.	Creation of Twelve Tables, Rome's first written law code
396 B.C.E.	Defeat of Etruscan city of Veii; first great expansion of Roman territory
387 B.C.E.	Gauls sack Rome
264–241 B.C.E.	Rome and Carthage fight First Punic War
220 B.C.E.	Rome controls Italy south of Po River
218–201 B.C.E.	Rome and Carthage fight Second Punic War
168–149 B.C.E.	Cato writes *The Origins*, first history of Rome in Latin
149–146 B.C.E.	Rome and Carthage fight Third Punic War
146 B.C.E.	Carthage and Corinth destroyed
133 B.C.E.	Tiberius Gracchus elected tribune; assassinated in same year
91–87 B.C.E.	Social War between Rome and its Italian allies
60 B.C.E.	First Triumvirate of Caesar, Pompey, and Crassus
49–45 B.C.E.	Civil war, with Caesar the victor
45–44 B.C.E.	Cicero writes his philosophical works on *humanitas*
44 B.C.E.	Caesar appointed dictator with no term limit; assassinated in same year

- Consider two events: **Cato writes *The Origins* (168–149 B.C.E.)** and **Carthage and Corinth are destroyed (146 B.C.E.)**. What attitudes prompted Cato's writings, and how were similar ideas reflected in the destruction of Carthage and Corinth?

SUGGESTED REFERENCES

Scholars continue to debate the causes and the effects of the rise and fall of the Roman republic, focusing in particular on the intended and unintended political, social, and cultural consequences of the many wars that the Romans fought in this period.

Beard, Mary, et al. *Religions of Rome*. 2 vols. 1998.

Billows, Richard. *Julius Caesar: The Colossus of Rome*. 2008.

Bradley, Keith. *Slavery and Society at Rome*. 1994.

*Caesar. *The Civil War*. Trans. John Carter. 1997.

*Cicero. *On the Good Life*. Trans. Michael Grant. 1971.

Cornell, Tim. *The Beginnings of Rome: Italy and Rome from the Bronze Age to the Punic Wars* (c. 1000–264 B.C.). 1995.

Daily life (and more): http://www.vroma.org/~bmcmanus/romanpages.html

Earl, Donald. *The Moral and Political Tradition of Rome*. 1967.

Flower, Harriet. *Roman Republics*. 2009

Gardner, Jane. *Women in Roman Law and Society*. 1986.

Goldworthy, Adrian. *The Punic Wars*. 2000.

Haynes, Sybill. *Etruscan Civilization: A Cultural History*. 2005.

Hoyos, Dexter. *The Carthaginians*. 2010.

Keaveney, Arthur. *Sulla: The Last Republican*. 2nd ed. 2005.

Lancel, Serge. *Carthage: A History*. Trans. Antonia Nevill. 1995.

*Plutarch. *The Fall of the Roman Republic*. Trans. Rex Warner. Rev. ed. 2006.

Ramage, Nancy H., and Andrew Ramage. *Roman Art*. 2008.

Roller, Duane W. *Cleopatra: A Biography*. 2010.

*Primary source.

CHAPTER 6

The Creation of the Roman Empire

44 B.C.E.–284 C.E.

In 203 C.E., Vibia Perpetua, wealthy and twenty-two years old, sat in a Carthage jail, nursing her infant while awaiting execution. She had received the death sentence for refusing to sacrifice to the gods for the Roman emperor's health and safety. One morning the jailer dragged her off to the city's main square, where a crowd had gathered. Perpetua described in her prison journal what happened when the local governor tried to persuade her to save her life:

> My father came carrying my son, shouting "Perform the sacrifice; take pity on your baby!" Then the governor said, "Think of your old father; show pity for your little child! Offer the sacrifice for the imperial family's well being." "I refuse," I answered. "Are you a Christian?" asked the governor. "Yes." When my father would not stop trying to change my mind, the governor ordered him thrown to the earth and whipped with a rod. I felt sorry for my father; it seemed they were beating me. I pitied his pathetic old age.

The brutality of Perpetua's punishment failed to break her: gored by a wild cow and stabbed by a gladiator, she died professing her faith.

Perpetua went to her death because she believed that Christianity required her not only to disregard the traditional Roman value of faithfulness to her family obligations but also to refuse the state's demand to show loyalty. Her decision to put her personal religious commitment ahead of her civic duty was a different version of the civil wars fought by the Roman republic's commanders because they valued their individual success above service to the common good.

Following Julius Caesar's assassination in 44 B.C.E., his grandnephew and adopted son, Octavian (the future Augustus), eventually brought peace by transforming Roman government and creating what is today called the

Mosaic of Chariot Racing
Racing four-horse chariots was the most popular—and most expensive—sport in the Roman Empire. This mosaic, a picture made from thousands of tiny colored tiles put together like a giant jigsaw puzzle, shows a driver holding a branch signifying that he has just won a big race. Two attendants or race officials are in the background. Hundreds of thousands of spectators attended the largest races at the Circus Maximus in Rome, but many cities across the empire had tracks. Romans loved the races' action and potential violence, as chariots swerved at top speed around and around the tight turns of the track and sometimes collided in bloody accidents. *(National Museum of Archeology, Madrid, Spain/ullstein bild/AISA.)*

Roman Empire. Ever after, Rome's rulers feared disloyalty above all because it threatened to reignite the civil wars that had destroyed the Roman Republic. The refusal of Christians such as Perpetua to perform traditional sacrifice was considered treason—the ultimate disloyalty—because Romans believed the gods would punish the entire community for sheltering people who refused to worship them.

This period of political transformation opened with a bloodbath: seventeen years of civil war followed Caesar's funeral. Finally, in 27 B.C.E., Augustus created a disguised monarchy to end the violence, ingeniously masking his creation as a restoration of the old Roman republic. Romans continued to call their new system by this old name throughout the long history of what in modern times is usually referred to as the Roman Empire. Augustus's system retained traditional institutions for sharing power—the Senate, the consuls, the courts—but in reality he and his successors governed like kings ruling an empire. More than a thousand years would pass before government under a true republic reappeared in Western civilization.

The challenge for Romans under the new system was to maintain political stability and prosperity. Augustus's political system brought peace for two hundred years, except for a struggle between generals for rule in 69 C.E. This **Pax Romana** ("Roman Peace") allowed agriculture and trade to flourish in the provinces, but war still determined Rome's long-term future because of its financial consequences. Under the republic, foreign wars had won huge amounts of land and money for Romans, but now the distances were too great, the adjoining lands too rough, and the foreign enemies too strong for continued conquest. The army became no longer an offensive weapon for expansion bringing in new taxes but instead a defense force protecting the frontier regions that had to be paid for out of current revenues. This change during the Pax Romana slowly created a financial crisis that weakened the principate and destabilized the government. The emergence of Christianity created a new religion that would over centuries transform the Roman world, but this change also created tension because the growing presence of Christians made other Romans worry about punishment from the gods. In the third century C.E., a crisis developed when generals competing to rule reignited prolonged civil war. By the 280s C.E., Roman government was once more on the brink of disintegration.

Pax Romana: Literally "Roman Peace"; the two centuries of relative peace and prosperity in the Roman Empire under the early principate begun by Augustus.

CHAPTER FOCUS How did Augustus's "restored republic" successfully keep the peace for more than two centuries, and why did it fail in the third century?

From Republic to Empire, 44 B.C.E.—14 C.E.

Inventing tradition takes time. Augustus created his new political system gradually; in keeping with one of his favorite sayings, Augustus "made haste slowly." He succeeded because he reinvented government, guaranteed the army's support, did not hesitate to use violence to win power, and built political legitimacy by communicating an image of himself as a dedicated leader and patron. His announced respect for tradition and his reign's length established his disguised monarchy as Rome's political system and saved the state from anarchy. Succeeding where Caesar had failed, he did it by making the new look old.

30 B.C.E. Octavian (the future Augustus) conquers Ptolemaic Egypt

27 B.C.E. Augustus inaugurates the principate

30 C.E. Jesus crucified in Jerusalem

64 C.E. Great fire in Rome; Nero blames Christians

69 C.E. Civil war after death of Nero

70 C.E. Titus captures Jerusalem and destroys the Jewish temple

70–90 C.E. New Testament Gospels are written

80s C.E. Domitian leads campaigns against multiethnic invaders on northern frontiers

50 B.C.E. | 0 | 50 C.E.

Civil War, 44–27 B.C.E.

Members of the social elite competing for power after Caesar's assassination in 44 B.C.E. started a civil war that lasted until 30 B.C.E. The main competitors were Caesar's friend Mark Antony and Caesar's eighteen-year-old grandnephew and adopted son, Octavian (the future Augustus). Octavian won over Caesar's soldiers by promising them money from their murdered general's wealth, which he had inherited. Marching these troops to Rome, the teenager forced the Senate to make him consul in 43 B.C.E., disregarding the rule that a man had to climb the ladder of offices before becoming consul.

Octavian and Antony put aside their differences—for a time—and with a general named Lepidus joined forces against Caesar's assassins and anyone else they thought dangerous. In late 43 B.C.E., the trio formed the so-called Second Triumvirate and forced the Senate to recognize them as an official panel for restoring the government. They then conducted a murderous proscription of their enemies, including some of their own relatives, and confiscated their property.

Octavian and Antony next forced Lepidus into retirement and began fighting each other. Antony controlled the eastern provinces by allying with the ruler of Egypt, Queen Cleopatra VII (69–30 B.C.E.), who had earlier allied with Caesar. Dazzled by her intelligence and personal magnetism, Antony, who was married to Octavian's sister, fell in love with Cleopatra. Octavian rallied support by claiming that Antony planned to make this foreign queen Rome's ruler. He made the residents of Italy and the western provinces swear allegiance to him. His victory in the naval battle of Actium in northwest Greece in 31 B.C.E. won the war. Cleopatra and Antony fled to Egypt, where they committed suicide in 30 B.C.E. The general first stabbed himself, bleeding to death in his lover's embrace. The queen then allowed a poisonous snake to bite her. Octavian's revenues from the capture of Egypt made him Rome's richest citizen.

The Creation of the Principate, 27 B.C.E.–14 C.E.

After distributing land to army veterans and creating colonies in the provinces, in 27 B.C.E. Octavian, in his own words, "gave back the state from [his] own power to the control of the Roman Senate and the people" and announced they should decide how to preserve it. Recognizing Octavian's overwhelming power, the senators asked him to safeguard the state, granted him special civil and military powers, and bestowed on him the honorary title **Augustus**, meaning "divinely favored." From this point Augustus became his name.

Inventing the Principate In reality, Augustus changed Rome's political system, but he kept up the appearance and the name of government under a republic. Citizens elected consuls, the Senate gave advice, and the assemblies met. Augustus occasionally served as consul, but mostly he let others hold that office. While making himself sole ruler, he concealed his monarchy by referring to himself not as a *rex* ("king") but only with the honorary title *princeps*, meaning "first man" (among social equals), a term from the republic indicating general agreement about who was the leading individual of the time or who was the most distinguished Roman senator. Princeps is thus the position we call emperor, and the Roman government in the early empire after 27 B.C.E. is best described as a ***principate***. Each new princeps was supposed to be chosen only with the Senate's approval, but in practice each ruler chose his own

---

Augustus: The honorary name meaning "divinely favored" that the Roman Senate bestowed on Octavian; it became shorthand for "Roman imperial ruler."

***principate*:** Roman political system invented by Augustus as a disguised monarchy with the *princeps* ("first man") as emperor.

161–180 C.E. Marcus Aurelius battles multiethnic bands attacking northern frontiers

230s–280s C.E. Third-century financial and political crisis

100 C.E. — 150 C.E. — 200 C.E. — 250 C.E.

212 C.E. Caracalla extends Roman citizenship to almost all free inhabitants of the provinces

249–251 C.E. Decius persecutes Christians

Cameo Celebrating Augustus
This cameo, about eight by nine inches, was carved early in the Roman Empire from a stone with layers of blue and white. Interpretations of the scenes vary, but the upper scene probably shows a standing female figure representing the Inhabited World who is crowning Augustus for rescuing Roman citizens. The seated female figure represents Rome and resembles Augustus's wife, Livia, his partner in rule. The man stepping out of a chariot is Tiberius, Augustus's choice to succeed him as princeps. Why do you think Tiberius carries a scepter like that held by Augustus? The lower scene shows defeated enemies subjected to Roman power. How do you think the lower scene relates to the upper scene? *(Erich Lessing/Art Resource, NY.)*

successor, like kings with a royal family. To preserve the tradition that no official should hold more than one post at a time, Augustus as princeps had the Senate grant him the powers, though not the office, of a tribune. That is, he possessed the legal power to act and to veto as if he were a tribune protecting the rights of the people, but he left all the positions of tribune open for other men to occupy. In 23 B.C.E., the Senate agreed that Augustus should also have a consul's power to command (*imperium*)—with the crucial addition that his power would be superior to that of the actual consuls.

Holding the power of a tribune and the "superior power" of a consul meant that Augustus could rule the state without filling any formal executive political office. He did not take the office of dictator that Sulla and Julius Caesar had used to rule. Augustus proclaimed that people obeyed him not because of his powers but because they so respected his *auctoritas* ("moral authority"). The truth was that Augustus and the rulers of the Roman Empire who followed him were able to exercise supreme power because they controlled the army and the treasury. Augustus knew, however, that symbols affect people's perception of reality, so he dressed and acted modestly, like a regular citizen in a republic, not an arrogant king. Livia, his wife, played a prominent role under his regime as his political adviser and partner in upholding old-fashioned values.

Augustus's choice of *princeps* as his public, though unofficial, title was a brilliant symbolic move because it used tradition to give legitimacy to a political revolution. He invented the principate to disguise a monarchy as a corrected and restored republic. Roman emperors after Augustus continued this same arrangement and proclaimed the same propaganda: they continued to refer to the state as the Roman republic, the senators and the consuls continued to exist, and the princeps continued to pretend to respect their positions. In truth, Augustus revolutionized the underlying power structure of Rome's government: no one previously could have exercised the powers of both tribune and "superior" consul simultaneously while also controlling the state's money and troops.

Augustus made the military the foundation of his power by turning the republic's citizen militia into a professional, full-time army and navy. He established regular lengths of service and substantial retirement benefits, changes that made the emperor the troops' patron and solidified their loyalty to him. To raise money for the added costs, Augustus imposed Rome's first inheritance tax on citizens, angering the rich. His other major military innovation was to station several thousand soldiers in Rome for the first time ever. These soldiers—the **praetorian guard**—would later play a crucial role in imperial politics by selecting the next emperor when the current one died. Augustus meant them to provide security for him and prevent rebellion in the capital by serving as a visible reminder that the superiority of the princeps was backed by the threat of armed force.

---

praetorian guard: The group of soldiers stationed in Rome under the emperor's control; first formed by Augustus.

Communicating the Emperor's Image In keeping with his policy of using both force and symbols, Augustus constantly communicated his image as patron and public benefactor (see Document, "Augustus, *Res Gestae* [My Accomplishments]," page 176). He used media as small as coins and as large as buildings. As the only mass-produced medium for official messages, Roman coins functioned like modern political advertising. They proclaimed slogans such as "Father of His Country" to remind Romans of Augustus's moral authority, or "Roads have been built" to emphasize his generosity in paying for highway construction.

Augustus used his personal fortune to erect spectacular public buildings in Rome. The huge Forum of Augustus, dedicated in 2 B.C.E., best illustrates his skill at sending messages through architecture (Figure 6.1). This public gathering space centered on a temple to Mars, the Roman god of war; Julius Caesar's sword was preserved there as a national treasure. Two-story colonnades extended from the temple like wings, sheltering statues of famous Roman heroes to serve as inspirations to future leaders. Augustus's forum provided space for religious rituals and the coming-of-age ceremonies of upper-class boys, but it also stressed his justifications for his rule: peace and security restored through military power, the foundation of a new age, devotion to the gods who protected Rome, respect for tradition, and generosity in spending money for public purposes.

Augustus's Motives Augustus never revealed his motives for establishing the principate, but his challenge was the one every Roman leader faced—balancing his own ambition with Rome's need for peace and its traditional commitment to its citizens' freedom of action. Augustus's solution was to employ traditional values to justify changes, as with his reinvention of the meaning of the word *princeps*. Above all, he transferred the traditional paternalism of social relations—the patron-client system—to politics by making the princeps everyone's most important patron, with the moral authority to guide their lives. This process reached its peak in 2 B.C.E. when the Senate joined the Roman people in formally proclaiming Augustus "Father of His Country" (a title that Cicero and Julius Caesar had also received). The title emphasized that the principate gave Romans a sole ruler who governed them like a father: stern but caring, expecting obedience and loyalty from his children, and obligated to take care of them in return. The goal of this arrangement was a combination of stability and order, not political freedom.

Augustus ruled until his death at age seventy-five in 14 C.E. The length of his reign — forty-one years — gave his transformation of Roman government time to become accepted. As the historian Tacitus (c. 56–120 C.E.) remarked, by the time Augustus died, "almost no one was still alive who had seen the republic." Through his longevity, command over the army, good relations with the capital's urban masses, and manipulation of political symbols and language to mask his power, Augustus restored political stability and created imperial Rome.

Daily Life in the Rome of Augustus

Archaeological and literary sources reveal a composite picture of life in Rome at the time of Augustus. Although some of the sources refer to times after Augustus and to cities other than Rome, they help us understand the Augustan period because economic and social conditions remained essentially unchanged in Roman cities during the early Roman Empire.

Augustan Rome's population of nearly one million was vast for the ancient world. No European city would have this many people again until London in the 1700s. Many people had no regular jobs and too little to eat. The streets were packed: "One man jabs me with his elbow, another whacks me with a pole; my legs are smeared with mud, and big feet step on me from all sides" was how one poet de-

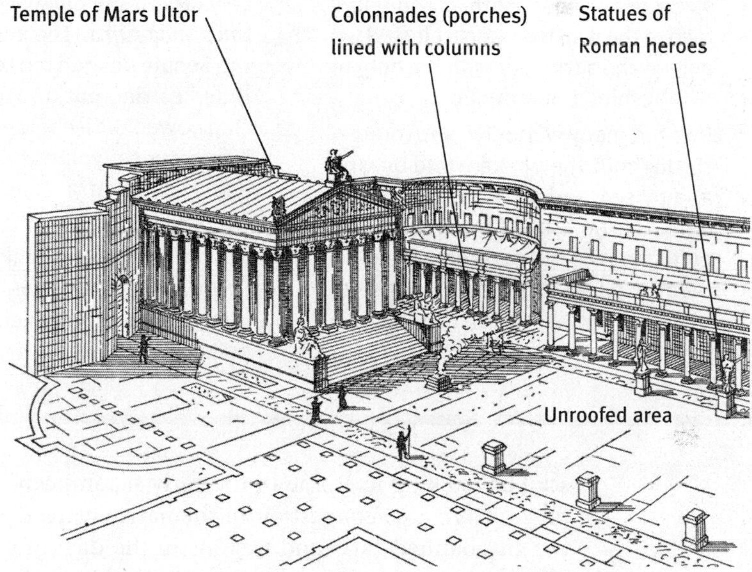

FIGURE 6.1 Cutaway Reconstruction of the Forum of Augustus
Augustus built this large forum (120 × 90 yards) to commemorate his victory over the assassins of Julius Caesar. The centerpiece was a marble temple to Mars Ultor ("Mars the Avenger"), and inside the temple were statues of Mars, Venus (the divine ancestor of Julius Caesar), and Julius Caesar (as a god), as well as works of art and Caesar's sword. The two spaces flanking the temple featured statues of Aeneas and Romulus, Rome's founders. The high stone wall behind the temple protected it from fire, a constant threat in the crowded neighborhood just behind.

DOCUMENT

Augustus, *Res Gestae* (My Accomplishments)

Augustus, the first Roman emperor, had an autobiographical report of his accomplishments displayed around the empire. These excerpts reveal his justifications for his rule, especially the peace and financial benefits that he had brought to Roman citizens, thereby making him their patron and morally obligating them to be loyal clients. Many of the sections not included here list his numerous and expensive personal payments for public works.

1. At the age of nineteen, on my own initiative and at my own expense, I raised an army, which I used to liberate the republic, which had been oppressed by the tyranny of a faction. For this reason the Senate passed honorary votes for me and made me a member [in 43 B.C.E.], at the same time granting me the rank of a consul in its voting, and it gave me the power of military command [imperium]. It ordered me as propraetor to see to it, along with the consuls, that no harm came to the state. Moreover, in the same year, when both consuls had died in the war, the people elected me consul and a triumvir with the duty of establishing the republic. . . .

3. I waged many wars, civil and foreign, throughout the whole world by land and by sea, and as victor I spared all citizens who asked for pardons. Foreign peoples who could safely be pardoned I preferred to spare rather than destroy. Approximately 500,000 Roman citizens swore military oaths to me. A little more than 300,000 of these, when their terms of service were ended, I settled in colonies or sent back to their own municipalities; I allotted lands or granted money to all of them as rewards for military service. . . .

5. I refused to accept the dictatorship offered to me [in 22 B.C.E.] by the people and by the Senate, both in my absence and my presence. During a severe scarcity of grain I accepted the supervision of the grain supply, which I so administered that within a few days I freed the whole people from imminent panic and danger by my expenditures and effort. The consulship, too, which was offered to me at that time as an annual office for life, I refused to accept.

6. [In 19, 18, and 11 B.C.E.], although the Roman Senate and people in unison agreed that I should be elected sole guardian of the laws and morals with supreme power, I refused to accept any office offered to me that was contrary to our ancestors' traditions [*mos maiorum*]. The measures that the Senate desired me to take at that time I carried out under the tribunician power. While holding this power I five times voluntarily requested and was given a colleague by the Senate.

7. . . . I have been ranking senator [*princeps senatus*] for forty years, up to the day on which I wrote this document. . . .

34. In my sixth and seventh consulships [28 and 27 B.C.E.], after I had put an end to the civil wars, having gained possession of everything through the consent of everyone, I returned the state from my own power [*potestas*] to the control of the Roman Senate and the people. As reward for this meritorious service, I received the title of Augustus by vote of the Senate, and the doorposts of my house were publicly decked with laurels, the civic crown was affixed over my doorway, and a golden shield was set up in the Julian Senate house, which, as the inscription on this shield testifies, the Roman Senate and people gave me in recognition of my valor, clemency, justice, and devotion. After that time I excelled all in authority [*auctoritas*], but I possessed no more power [*potestas*] than the others who were my colleagues in each magistracy.

35. When I held my thirteenth consulship [2 B.C.E.], the Senate, the equestrian order, and the entire Roman people gave me the title of "father of the country" [*pater patriae*]. . . . At the time I wrote this document I was in my seventy-sixth year.

Source: Herbert W. Benario, ed., *Caesaris Augusti Res Gestae et Fragmenta*, 2nd ed. (1990). Translation by Thomas R. Martin.

Question to Consider

- **Why do you think Augustus ends this justification of his rule with a list of his personal and moral qualities as officially recognized by the Roman Senate and people?**

scribed walking in Rome in the early second century C.E. To ease congestion in the narrow streets, the city banned carts and wagons in the daytime. This regulation made nights noisy with the creaking of axles and the shouting of drivers caught in traffic jams.

The Conditions of City Life Most urban residents lived in small apartments in multistoried buildings called islands. Outnumbering private houses by more than twenty to one, the islands' first floors housed shops, bars, and restaurants. Graffiti of all kinds — political endorsements, the posting of rewards, personal insults, and advertising — covered the exterior walls. The higher the floor, the cheaper the rent. Well-off tenants occupied the lower stories, while the poorest people lived in single rooms rented by the day on the top floors. Aqueducts delivered a plentiful supply of fresh water to public fountains, but apartment dwellers had to lug heavy jugs up the stairs. The wealthy few had piped-in water at ground level. Most tenants lacked bathrooms and had to use the public latrines or pots for toilets at home. Some buildings had cesspits, but most people had to carry buckets of excrement down to the streets to be emptied by sewage collectors. Lazy tenants flung these containers' foul-smelling contents out the window. Sanitation was an enormous problem in a city that generated sixty tons of human waste every day.

To keep clean, residents used public baths. Because admission fees were low, almost everyone could afford to bathe daily. Baths existed all over the city; like modern health clubs, they served as centers for exercising and socializing (see Document, "The Scene at a Roman Bath," page 178). Bathers progressed through a series of increasingly warm, humid areas until they reached a sauna-like room. They swam naked in their choice of hot or cold pools. Women had access to the public baths, but men and women bathed apart. Since bathing was thought to be helpful for sick people, the public baths unintentionally contributed to the spread of communicable diseases.

Augustus's care for citizens' everyday lives helped them accept his political changes. He did all he could to improve Rome's public safety and health. Since fire presented a constant danger, Augustus gave Rome the first public fire department in Western history. He also established the first permanent police force, despite his fondness for watching the frequent brawls in Rome's crowded streets. There were challenges in urban life, however, that not even his power and money could overcome. He greatly enlarged the city's main sewer, but its contents still emptied untreated into the Tiber River. The technology for sanitary disposal of waste did not exist. People often left human and animal corpses in the streets, to be gnawed by vultures and dogs. The poor were not the only people affected by such conditions: a stray mutt once brought a human hand to the table where Vespasian, who would be emperor from 69 to 79 C.E., was eating lunch. Flies everywhere and a lack of refrigeration contributed to frequent gastrointestinal ailments: the most popular jewelry of the time was supposed to ward off stomach trouble. Although the wealthy could not avoid such problems, they made their lives more pleasant with luxuries such as snow rushed from the mountains to ice their drinks and slaves to clean their houses, which were built around courtyards and gardens.

City residents faced hazards beyond infectious disease. Apartment dwellers often hurled debris out their windows, where it rained down on pedestrians. "If you are walking to a dinner party in Rome," a poet warned, "you would be foolish not to make out your will first. For every open window is a source of potential disaster." Roman architects built public structures from concrete, brick, and stone that lasted centuries, but crooked contractors cut costs by cheating on materials for private buildings; therefore, apartment buildings sometimes collapsed. Augustus imposed a height limit of seventy feet on new apartment buildings to limit the danger.

A Roman Street
Like Pompeii, the town of Herculaneum on the Bay of Naples was frozen in time by the volcanic eruption of Mount Vesuvius in 79 C.E. Mud from the eruption buried the town and preserved its buildings. Herculaneum's straight roads paved with flat stones and sidewalks were typical for a Roman town. Balconies jutted from the houses, offering a shady viewing point for life in the streets. Roman houses often enclosed a garden courtyard instead of having yards in front or back. Why do you think urban homes had this arrangement? *(Scala/Art Resource, NY.)*

As the people's patron, Augustus used his own money to import grain to feed the urban poor. State distribution of grain had long been a tradition in the capital, but Augustus extended his welfare plan to reach 250,000 recipients. Counting the recipients' families, more than 700,000 people depended on the princeps to survive. Poor Romans cooked this grain into bread or soup — if they were lucky, they might add beans, leeks, or cheese — and they washed down their meals with cheap wine. The rich ate more costly food, such as roast pork or crayfish, flavored with sweet-and-sour sauce concocted from honey and vinegar.

Wealthy Romans increasingly spent money on luxuries and political careers instead of raising

DOCUMENT

The Scene at a Roman Bath

Life in the streets of Roman cities could be loud and crowded. People sought relaxation in public baths—which could, however, be just as hectic. In this letter, the Roman philosopher Seneca (4 B.C.E.–65 C.E.) wrote to a friend describing his experience living in a rented apartment located above one of the large and busy bathing and exercise establishments that existed in every sizable community in the Roman Empire.

I am staying in an apartment directly above a public bath. Imagine all the kinds of voices that I hear, enough to make me hate having ears! When the really strong guys are working out with heavy lead weights, when they are working hard or at least pretending to work hard, I hear their grunts. Whenever they let out the breath they've been holding in, I hear them hissing and panting loudly. When I happen to notice some sluggish type getting a cheap rubdown, I hear the slap of the hand pounding his shoulders, changing its sound according to whether it's a blow with an open or a closed fist. If a serious ball-player comes along and starts keeping score out loud, then I'm done for. Add to this the bruiser who likes to pick fights, the pickpocket who's been caught, and the man who loves to hear the sound of his own voice in the bath. And there are those people who jump into the swimming pool with a tremendous splash and lots of noise. Besides all the ones who have awful voices, imagine the "armpit hair plucker-outer" with his high, shrill voice—so he'll be noticed—always chattering and never shutting up, except when he is plucking armpits and making his customer yell instead of yelling himself. And there are also all the different cries from the sausage seller, and the fellow selling pastries, and all the food vendors screaming out what they have to sell, all of them with their own special tones.

Source: Seneca, *Moral Epistles*, 56.1–2. Translation by Thomas R. Martin.

Question to Consider

- **What do the sounds described by the Roman philosopher reveal about the kinds of people frequenting the bath and the nature of the community itself?**

families. Fearing that the falling birthrate would destroy the social elite on whom Rome relied for public service, Augustus granted legal privileges to the parents of three or more children. To strengthen marriages, he made adultery a crime and supported this reform so strongly that he exiled his own daughter—his only child—and a granddaughter for sex scandals. His legislation had little effect, however, and the prestigious old families dwindled over the coming centuries. Recent research suggests that up to three-quarters of senatorial families either lost their official status by spending all their money or died out every generation by failing to have children. Equites and provincials who won the emperor's favor filled the open places in the social hierarchy and the Senate.

Roman Slavery In a remarkable departure from the practice of other ancient states, Rome gave citizenship to freed slaves. All slaves—and there were many in Roman society—had the hope of someday becoming a free Roman citizen, regardless of whether they had originally become enslaved by being captured in wars against Romans, had been carried off from their home region by slave traders in raids in non-Roman territory and then sold to Roman owners, or had been born to slave women and therefore started life as the property of the mother's owner. Slaves' descendants, if they became wealthy, could become members of the social elite. This policy gave slaves reason to cooperate with their masters, as an owner might reward a slave's dutiful work with emancipation. Scholars lack the evidence to calculate precisely what percentage of Roman slaves were freed in their lifetimes, but it is clear that the tradition of giving citizenship to former slaves did eventually lead to most Romans having slave ancestors in their family history.

The harshness of slaves' lives varied widely. Slaves in agriculture and manufacturing lived a grueling existence. Most such workers were men, although women might assist the foremen who managed gangs of rural laborers. A second-century C.E. novelist described the grim situation of slaves in a flour mill: "Through the holes in their ragged clothes you could see all over their bodies the scars from whippings. Some wore only loincloths. Letters had been branded on their foreheads [to show they were slaves and should be captured and returned to their owners, if they escaped] and irons manacled their ankles." Worse than the mills were the mines, where the foremen whipped the miners to keep them working in such a dangerous environment.

Household slaves lived better. Most Romans owned slaves as home servants; modestly well-off families had one or two, while rich houses and the imperial palace owned large numbers. Domestic slaves were often women, working as nurses, maids, kitchen helpers, and clothes makers. Some male slaves ran businesses for their masters, and they were often allowed to keep part of the profits as an incentive; they saved to purchase their freedom someday. Women had less opportunity to earn money, though masters sometimes granted tips for sexual favors to female and male slaves. Many female prostitutes were slaves working for their owner in a brothel. Slaves with savings would sometimes buy other slaves, especially to have a mate; they were barred from legal marriage, because they and their children remained their master's property, but they could live as a shadow family. Fortunate slaves could buy themselves from their masters or be freed in their masters' wills. Some masters' tomb inscriptions record their affection for a slave, but even household slaves could experience painful treatment from cruel masters. Slaves had no right to bring legal charges against their owners. If slaves attacked their owners, the punishment was death.

Violence in Public Entertainment While potential violence defined slaves' lives, actual violence featured in much Roman public entertainment, revealing that many Romans felt comfortable watching the suffering of other people and of animals. The emperors regularly provided shows featuring hunters killing fierce beasts, wild African animals mangling condemned criminals, mock naval battles in flooded arenas, blood-drenched gladiatorial combats, and wreck-filled chariot races. Spectators packed arenas for these shows, seated according to their social rank and gender following an Augustan law. The emperor and senators sat close to the action, while women and the poor were seated in the upper seats, to display the hierarchy that Romans believed necessary to social stability.

War captives, criminals, and slaves could be forced to fight as gladiators, but free people also voluntarily became gladiators, hoping to become sports celebrities and win rich prizes if they survived. Most gladiators were men, though women could also fight other women if they wished. The first female gladiators were the daughters of gladiators in the time of the Roman republic, trained by their fathers to compete in the arena. Women continued to fight each other in bloody spectacles until the emperor Septimius Severus (r. 193–211 C.E.) banned their appearance.

Gladiatorial shows had originated as part of rich funerals, but Augustus made them popular entertainment. Gladiators were often wounded or killed because the fights were so dangerous, but their contests rarely required a fight to the death, unless they were captives or criminals. Professional fighters could have extended careers and win riches and celebrity. To make the fights unpredictable, pairs of gladiators often competed with different weapons. One favorite bout pitted a lightly armored "net man," who used a net and a trident, against a more heavily armored "fish man," so named from the design of his helmet crest. Betting was popular, the crowds rowdy. As a Christian commentator complained: "Look at the mob coming to the show—already they're out of their minds! Aggressive, thoughtless,

Gladiator after a Kill
This first-century C.E. mosaic covered a villa floor in North Africa. It shows a gladiator staring at the opponent he has just killed. What feelings do you think his expression conveys? Gladiatorial combats originated as part of wealthy people's funeral ceremonies, symbolizing the human struggle to avoid death. Training an expert gladiator took many years and great expense. Like boxers today, gladiators fought only a couple of times a year. Because it cost so much to replace a dead gladiator, most fights were not to the death intentionally; however, kills often happened in the fury of combat. *(Photo courtesy Helmut Ziegert/University of Hamburg.)*

already in an uproar about their bets! They all share the same suspense, the same madness, the same voice."

Public entertainment served as two-way communication between ruler and ruled. Emperors provided gladiatorial combats, chariot races, and theater productions for the masses, and ordinary citizens staged protests at these festivals to express their wishes to the emperors, who were expected to attend. Poor Romans, for example, rioted to protest shortfalls in the free grain supply.

Changes in Education, Literature, and Art in Augustus's Rome

Elite culture changed in the Augustan period to serve the same goal as public entertainment: legitimizing the transformed political system. Oratory—the highest attainment of Roman education—lost its freedom. Under the republic, the ability to make frank speeches criticizing political opponents had been such a powerful weapon that it could catapult a "new man" like Cicero to a leadership role. Now, the emperor's supremacy ruled out honest political debate. Ambitious men required rhetorical skills only to praise the emperor. Criticism of the established political system in both oratory and the arts was too risky.

Literacy and Social Status
This two-foot-high wall painting of a woman and her husband was found in a comfortable house in Pompeii, buried by twelve feet of ash from Mount Vesuvius's volcanic eruption in 79 C.E. The couple may have owned the bakery that adjoined the house. Both are holding items showing that they were literate and therefore deserving of social status. She has the notepad of the time, a hinged wooden tablet filled with wax for writing on with the stylus (thin stick) that she touches to her lips. He holds a scroll of papyrus or animal skin, the standard form for books at the time. Her hairstyle was one popular in the mid-first century C.E. *(Erich Lessing/Art Resource, NY.)*

Education Education in oratory remained a privilege of the wealthy. Since Rome had no free public schools, the poor received no formal education. Most people had time for learning only practical skills. A character in a Roman satirical novel expresses this utilitarian attitude: "I didn't study geometry and literary criticism and worthless junk like that. I just learned how to read the letters on signs and how to work out percentages, and I learned weights, measures, and the values of the different kinds of coins."

Servants took care of rich boys and girls, who attended private elementary schools from ages seven to eleven to learn reading, writing, and basic arithmetic. Some children went on to the next three years of school, in which they studied literature, history, and grammar. Only a few boys then proceeded to the study of rhetoric. Advanced studies concerned literature, history, ethical philosophy, law, and dialectic (reasoned argument). Mathematics and science were rarely studied as separate subjects, but engineers and architects became proficient at calculation despite the difficulty of using Roman numerals for complex math.

Ideals in Literature and Sculpture So much famous literature comes from the Augustan period that scholars call it the Golden Age of Latin literature. The emperor, himself an author, served as a patron for writers and artists. His favorites were Horace (65–8 B.C.E.) and Virgil (70–19 B.C.E.). Horace entranced audiences with the rhythms and irony of his poems on public and private subjects. His poem celebrating Augustus's victory at Actium became famous for its opening line: "Now we have to drink!"

Virgil became the most admired Roman poet for his long poem *The Aeneid*, which both praised Augustus's new system and—very indirectly—alluded to problems in it. Inspired by Homer's epics,

The Aeneid told the story of the Trojan Aeneas, the legendary founder of Rome. Virgil balanced his praise for Roman civilization with recognition of the price in freedom to be paid for peace. *The Aeneid* thus revealed the complex mix of gain and loss created by Augustus's transformation of Roman politics.

Authors with a more independent streak had to be careful. The historian Livy (54 B.C.E.–17 C.E.) composed a history of Rome in which he recorded Augustus's ruthlessness in the civil war after Caesar's murder. The emperor scolded but did not punish Livy because his work proclaimed that stability and prosperity depended on traditional values of loyalty and self-sacrifice. The poet Ovid (43 B.C.E.–17 C.E.), however, wrote *Art of Love* and *Love Affairs* to mock the emperor's moral legislation with witty advice for conducting sexual affairs and picking up other men's wives. His work *Metamorphoses* undermined the idea of hierarchy as natural by telling bizarre stories of supernatural shape-changes, with people becoming animals and confusion between the human and the divine. In 8 B.C.E., after Ovid became embroiled in the scandal involving Augustus's granddaughter, the emperor exiled him.

Changes in public sculpture also reflected the emperor's influence. When Augustus was growing up, portraits were starkly realistic. The sculpture that Augustus ordered displayed an idealized style based on classical Greek models. In works such as the Prima Porta statue, Augustus had himself portrayed as serene and dignified, not careworn and sick, as he often was. As with architecture, Augustus used sculpture to project a calm and competent image of himself as the "Restorer of the Roman Republic" and founder of a new age for Rome.

Marble Statue of Augustus from Prima Porta

At six feet eight inches high, this statue of Augustus stood a foot taller than he did. Found at his wife Livia's country villa at Prima Porta ("First Gate"), the portrait was probably done about 20 B.C.E., when Augustus was in his forties; however, it shows him as younger, using the idealizing techniques of classical Greek art. Compare his smooth face to the realistic portraiture in Chapter 5. The statue's symbols communicate Augustus's image: his bare feet hint he is a near-divine hero, the Cupid refers to the Julian family's descent from the goddess Venus, and the breastplate's design shows a Parthian surrendering to a Roman soldier under the gaze of personified cosmic forces admiring the peace Augustus's regime has created. *(Scala/Art Resource, NY.)*

REVIEW QUESTION How did the peace gained through Augustus's "restoration of the Roman republic" affect Romans' lives in all social classes?

Politics and Society in the Early Roman Empire

Augustus made political changes to promote not only his personal glory but also stability and prosperity—above all by preventing civil war—but his new system lacked a way to block struggles for power when the princeps died. Since Augustus claimed not to have created a monarchy, no successor could automatically inherit his power without the Senate's approval. Augustus therefore decided to identify an heir whom he wished the senators to recognize as princeps after his death. This strategy succeeded and kept rule in his family, called the **Julio-Claudians**, until the death in 68 C.E. of Augustus's last descendant, the infamous Nero. It established the tradition that family dynasties ruled the "restored republic" of imperial Rome.

Under the principate, the emperor's main goals were preventing unrest, building loyalty, and financing the administration while governing the diverse provinces. Augustus set the pattern for effective imperial rule: take special care of the army, communicate the emperor's image as a just ruler and generous patron, and promote Roman law and culture as universal standards. The citizens, in

---

Julio-Claudians: The ruling family of the early principate from Augustus through Nero, descended from the aristocratic families of the Julians and the Claudians.

return for their loyalty, expected the emperors to be generous patrons—but the difficulties of long-range communication imposed practical limits on imperial support of or intervention in the lives of the residents of the provinces.

The Perpetuation of the Principate after Augustus, 14–180 C.E.

Augustus's claim that the republic continued meant that he needed the Senate's cooperation to give legitimacy to his successor and perpetuate his disguised monarchy. He had no son, so he adopted Livia's son by a previous marriage, Tiberius (42 B.C.E.–37 C.E.). Since Tiberius had a brilliant career as a general, the army supported Augustus's choice. Augustus had Tiberius granted the power of a tribune and the power of a consul equal to his own so that he would be recognized as emperor after Augustus's death. The senators did just that when Augustus died in 14 C.E., allowing the Julio-Claudian dynasty to begin.

The First Dynasty: The Julio-Claudians, 14–68 C.E. Tiberius (r. 14–37 C.E.) was able to stay in power for twenty-three years because he had the most important qualification for succeeding as emperor: the army's loyalty. He built the praetorian guard a fortified camp in Rome so that its soldiers could better protect the emperor. This change had the unintended consequence of guaranteeing the guards a role in determining all future successions—no emperor could come to power without their support. Tiberius described his position by saying, "I am the master of the slaves, the commander of the soldiers, and the princeps of the rest."

Tiberius's long reign provided the extended transition period that the principate needed to endure, establishing the compromise on power between the elite and the emperor essential for political stability. The traditional offices of consul, senator, and provincial governor continued, with elite Romans filling them and enjoying their prestige, but the emperors decided who received the offices and controlled law and government policy. In this way, the social elite performed valuable service, especially by keeping the peace and overseeing the collection of taxes while governing provinces that the emperor assigned them. (The emperor used his own assistants to govern the provinces that housed strong military forces.) Everyone saved face by pretending that the republic's political offices retained their original power.

Tiberius paid a bitter price to rule. To strengthen their family tie, Augustus forced Tiberius to divorce his beloved wife, Vipsania, to marry Augustus's daughter, Julia—and the marriage proved disastrously unhappy. When Tiberius's sadness led him to spend his reign's last decade in seclusion far from Rome, his neglect of the government permitted abuses in the capital and kept him from training a decent successor for the Senate to approve.

Tiberius designated Gaius, better known as Caligula (r. 37–41 C.E.), to be the next emperor because the young man was Augustus's great-grandson and Tiberius's uncritical supporter, not because he had leadership qualities. The third Julio-Claudian emperor might have been successful because he knew about soldiering: *Caligula* means "baby boots," the nickname the soldiers gave him as a child because he wore little leather shoes like theirs when he was growing up in the military garrisons his father commanded. Unfortunately, Caligula's enormous appetites outweighed his feeble virtues. Cruel and violent, he bankrupted the treasury to satisfy his desires. His biographer labeled him a monster for his murders and sexual crimes, which some said included incest with his sisters. He outraged the elite by fighting in mock gladiatorial combats and appearing in public in women's clothing or costumes imitating gods. He once said, "I'm allowed to do anything." The praetorian commanders murdered him in 41 C.E. to avenge personal insults.

The senators then debated the idea of truly restoring the republic by refusing to approve a new emperor. They backed down, however, when Claudius (r. 41–54 C.E.), Augustus's grandnephew and Caligula's uncle, bribed the praetorian guard to back him. The soldiers' insistence on there being an emperor so that they would have a patron to pay them indicated that the old republic was never coming back.

Claudius was an active emperor, commanding a successful invasion of Britain in 43 C.E. that made much of the island into a Roman province. He opened the way for provincial elites to expand their participation in government by enrolling men from Gaul in the Senate. In return for keeping their regions peaceful and ensuring tax payments, they would receive offices at Rome and the emperor's support. Claudius also transformed imperial bureaucracy by employing freed slaves as powerful administrators; since they owed their positions to the emperor, they could be expected to be loyal.

Power corrupted Claudius's teenage successor, Nero (r. 54–68 C.E.). Emperor at sixteen, he loved music and acting, not governing. The public entertainments he sponsored and the cash he distributed kept him popular with Rome's poor. His generals put down the revolt in Britain led by the woman commander Boudica in 60 C.E. and fought the Jewish rebels who tried to throw off Roman rule in Judaea in 66 C.E., but he himself had no military career. A giant fire in 64 C.E. (the event behind the legend that Nero fiddled while Rome burned) aroused suspicions that he ordered the city burned to make space for a new palace. Nero scandalized the senatorial class by appearing onstage to sing, and he emptied the treasury by building a palace called the Golden House. To raise money, he faked treason charges against senators and equites to seize their property. When his generals toppled his regime, Nero had a servant help him cut his own throat as he dug his grave, wailing, "I'm dying reduced to the status of a laborer!"

The Flavian Dynasty and the Imperial Cult, 69–96 C.E.

Nero's death sparked a year of civil war in 69 C.E. during which four generals competed for power. Vespasian (r. 69–79 C.E.) won. His victory showed that the elite and the army wanted the principate to continue. To give legitimacy to his new dynasty (called Flavian, from his family name), Vespasian had the Senate grant him the same powers as previous emperors, pointedly leaving Caligula and Nero off the list. He encouraged the spread of the imperial cult (worship of the emperor as a living god and sacrifices for his household's welfare) in the provinces but not in Italy, where this innovation would have disturbed traditional Romans. The imperial cult communicated the same image of the emperor to the provinces as Rome's architecture and sculpture did: he was superhuman, provided benefactions, and deserved loyalty. Vespasian reportedly did not believe in his own divinity, to judge from his joking remark on his deathbed: "Oh me! I think I'm becoming a god."

Vespasian's sons, Titus (r. 79–81 C.E.) and Domitian (r. 81–96 C.E.), conducted hardheaded fiscal policy and high-profile military campaigns. Titus had become famous by finally suppressing the Jewish revolt and capturing Jerusalem in 70 C.E. He sent relief to Pompeii and Herculaneum when, in 79 C.E., Mount Vesuvius's volcanic eruption buried these towns. He built a state-of-the-art site for public entertainment by finishing Rome's **Colosseum**, outfitting the amphitheater seating fifty thousand spectators with awnings to shade the crowd. The Colosseum was deliberately constructed on the site of the former fishpond in Nero's Golden House to demonstrate the Flavian dynasty's commitment to the well-being of the people.

When Titus died suddenly after only two years as emperor, his brother Domitian stepped in. Domitian balanced the budget and campaigned against Germanic tribes threatening the empire's northern frontiers, a sign of the greater troubles to come for the empire from this region. Domitian's arrogance turned the senators against him; once he sent them a letter announcing, "Our lord god, myself, orders you to do this." Alarmed by an elite general's rebellion, Domitian executed numerous upper-class citizens as conspirators. Fearful that they, too, would become victims, his wife and members of his court murdered him in 96 C.E.

The Five "Good Emperors," 96–180 C.E.

As Domitian's murder showed, the principate had not solved monarchy's inevitable weakness: rivalry among the elite for rule. The danger of civil war persisted, whether generated by ambitious generals or the emperor's jealous heirs. No one could predict whether a good ruler or a bad one would emerge. As Tacitus commented, emperors were like the weather: "We just have to wait for bad ones to pass and hope for good ones to appear."

Fortunately for Rome, fair weather dawned with the next five emperors: Nerva (r. 96–98 C.E.), Trajan (r. 98–117 C.E.), Hadrian (r. 117–138 C.E.), Antoninus Pius (r. 138–161 C.E.), and Marcus Aurelius (r. 161–180 C.E.). Historians call this period the Roman political Golden Age because it had peaceful successions for nearly a century. Nevertheless, it saw ample war and strife: Trajan fought to expand Roman control across the Danube River into Dacia (today Romania) and eastward into Mesopotamia (Map 6.1); Hadrian executed several senators as alleged conspirators, punished a Jewish revolt by turning Jerusalem into a military colony, and withdrew Roman forces from Mesopotamia; and Marcus Aurelius, who wanted to be a philosopher instead of an emperor, nevertheless faithfully did his duty by spending difficult years fighting off invaders from the Danube region as the dangers to imperial territory along the northern frontiers kept increasing.

Still, the five "good emperors" did preside over a political and economic Golden Age. They succeeded one another without murder or conspiracy—the first four, having no surviving sons, used adoption to find the best possible successor. The economy provided enough money to finance building projects such as the fortification wall Hadrian built across Britain. Most important, they kept the army

---

Colosseum: Rome's fifty-thousand-seat amphitheater built by the Flavian dynasty for gladiatorial combats and other spectacles.

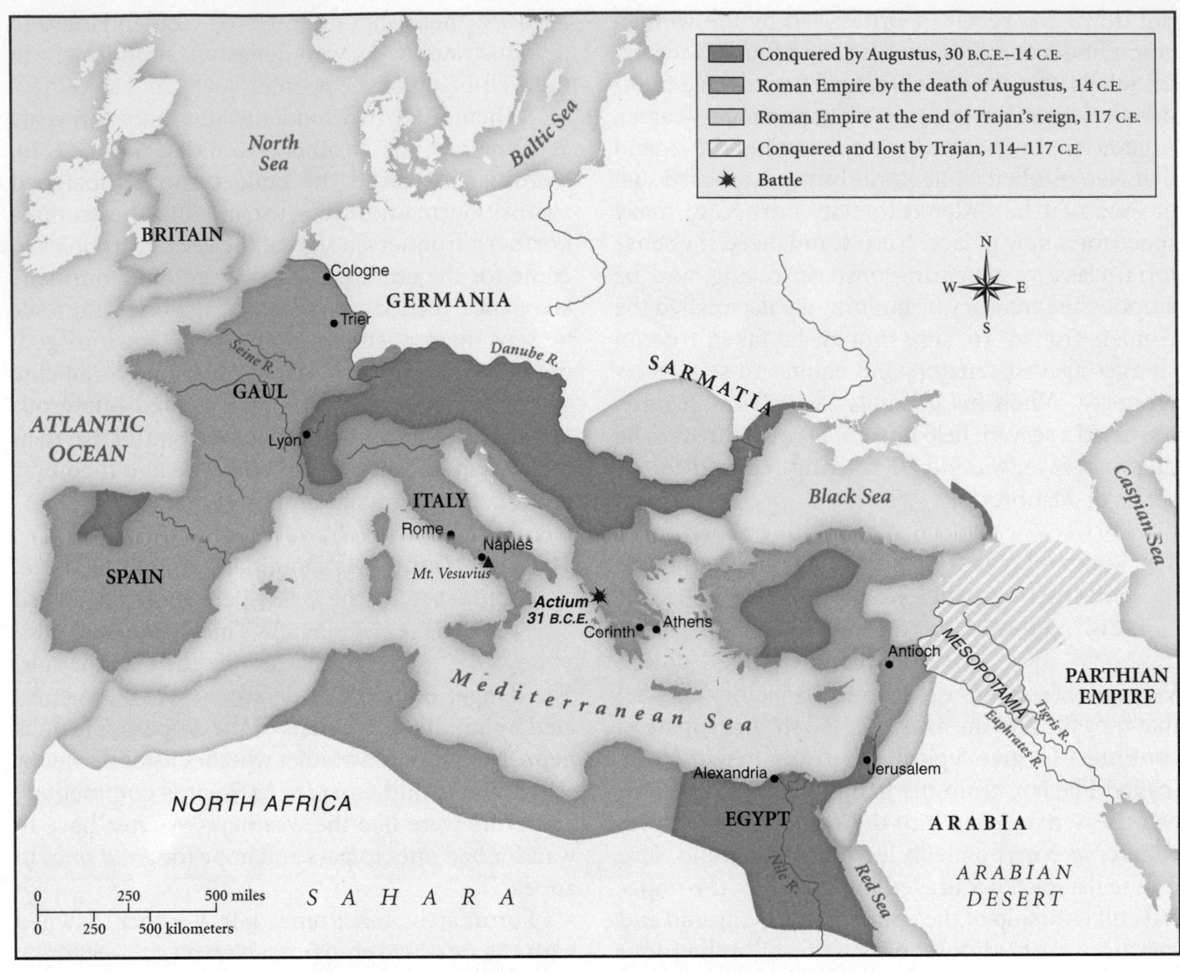

MAP 6.1 The Expansion of the Roman Empire, 30 B.C.E.–117 C.E.
When Octavian (the future Augustus) captured Egypt in 30 B.C.E. after the suicides of Mark Antony and Cleopatra, he greatly boosted Rome's economic strength. The land produced enormous amounts of grain and metals, and Roman power now almost encircled the Mediterranean Sea. When Emperor Trajan took over the southern part of Mesopotamia in 114–117 C.E., imperial conquest reached its height; Rome's control had never extended so far east. Egypt remained part of the empire until the Arab conquest in 642 C.E., but Mesopotamia was immediately abandoned by Hadrian, Trajan's successor, probably because it seemed too distant to defend. | **How did territorial expansion both strengthen and weaken the Roman Empire?**

obedient. Their reigns marked Rome's longest stretch without a civil war since the second century B.C.E.

Life in the Roman Golden Age, 96–180 C.E.

Peace and prosperity in Rome's Golden Age depended on defense by a loyal military, service by provincial elites in local administration and tax collection, common laws enforced throughout the empire, and a healthy population reproducing itself. The empire's vast size and the relatively small numbers of soldiers and imperial officials in the provinces meant that emperors had only limited control over these factors.

The Army in the Early Roman Empire

In theory, Rome's military goal remained perpetual expansion because conquest brought land, money, and glory. Virgil expressed this idea in *The Aeneid* by describing Jupiter, the king of the gods, as promising Rome "imperial rule without limit." In reality, the emperors lacked the resources to expand the empire permanently much beyond what Augustus had controlled and had to concentrate on defending imperial territory.

Most provinces were peaceful and had no need for garrisons. Even Gaul, which had originally fiercely resisted Roman control, was, according to one witness, "kept in order by 1,200 troops—hardly more soldiers than it has towns." Most legions (units of five thousand troops) were stationed on frontiers to prevent invasions from barbarians to the north and Persians to the east. The long period of peace supported the Golden Age's prosperity and promoted long-distance trade to import luxury goods, such as spices and silk, from as far away as India and China. Roman merchants in search of profits took advantage of the patterns of the winds to sail from Egypt to India and back every year.

The army, which included both Romans and noncitizens from the provinces, reflected the population's diversity. Serving under Roman officers, the non-Romans could learn to speak Latin and to live by Roman customs. Upon discharge, they received Roman citizenship. Thus the army helped spread a common way of life.

Paying for Government and Defense

Paying for imperial government became an insoluble problem. In the past, foreign wars had brought in huge amounts of revenue from booty and prisoners of war sold into slavery. Conquered territory also provided regular income from taxes. Now the army was no longer making big conquests, but the soldiers had to be paid well to maintain discipline. As the army's patrons, emperors at their accession and other special occasions supplemented soldiers' regular pay with substantial bonuses. These rewards made a soldier's career desirable but cost the emperors dearly.

A tax on agriculture in the provinces (Italy was exempt) now provided the principal source of revenue for the imperial government and the army. The administration itself required relatively little money because it was small compared with the size of the territory being governed: no more than several hundred top officials governed a population of about fifty million. Most locally collected taxes stayed in the provinces to pay expenses there, especially legionnaires' pay. Senatorial and equestrian governors with small staffs ran the provinces, which eventually numbered about forty. In Rome, the emperor employed a large staff of freedmen and slaves, while equestrian officials called prefects managed the city.

The government's finances depended on tax collection carried out by provincial elites. Serving as **decurions** (members of municipal Senates), these wealthy men were required personally to guarantee that their area's financial responsibilities were met. If there was a shortfall in tax collection or local finances, the decurions had to make up the difference from their own pockets. Wise emperors kept taxes moderate. As Tiberius put it when refusing a request for tax increases from provincial governors, "I want you to shear my sheep, not skin them alive." The financial liability in holding civic office made that honor expensive, but the accompanying prestige made the elite willing to take the risk. Rewards for decurions included priesthoods in the imperial cult, an honor open to both men and women, although few women had the wealth to pay for the expected public sacrifices and other priestly responsibilities of the post.

The system worked because it observed tradition: the local elites were their communities' patrons and the emperor's clients. As long as there were enough rich, public-spirited provincials participating, the principate functioned by fostering the old ideal of community service by the upper class in return for respect and social status.

The Impact of Roman Culture on the Provinces

The provinces contained diverse peoples who spoke different languages, observed different customs, dressed in different styles, and worshipped different divinities (Map 6.2). In the countryside, Roman conquest only lightly affected local customs. In new towns that sprang up around Roman forts or settlements of army veterans, Roman influence predominated. Modern cities such as Trier and Cologne in Germany started as such towns. Roman culture had the greatest effect on western Europe, permanently rooting Latin (and the languages that would emerge from it) as well as Roman law and customs there. Over time, social and cultural differences lessened between the provinces and Italy. Eventually, emperors came from citizen-families in the provinces; Trajan, from Spain, was the first of those emperors.

Romanization, as historians call the spread of Roman law and culture in the provinces, raised the standard of living for many by providing roads and bridges, increasing trade, and establishing peaceful conditions for agriculture. The army's need for supplies created business for farmers and merchants. The prosperity that provincials enjoyed under Roman rule made Romanization acceptable. In addition, Romanization was not a one-way street. In western regions as diverse as Gaul, Britain, and North Africa, interaction between the local people and Romans produced mixed cultural traditions, especially in religion and art. Therefore, the process led to a gradual merging of Roman and local culture, not a mere imposition of the conquerors' way of life. (See the illustration on page 187.)

---

decurions (dih KYUR ee uhns): Municipal Senate members in the Roman Empire responsible for collecting local taxes.

Romanization: The spread of Roman law and culture in the provinces of the Roman Empire.

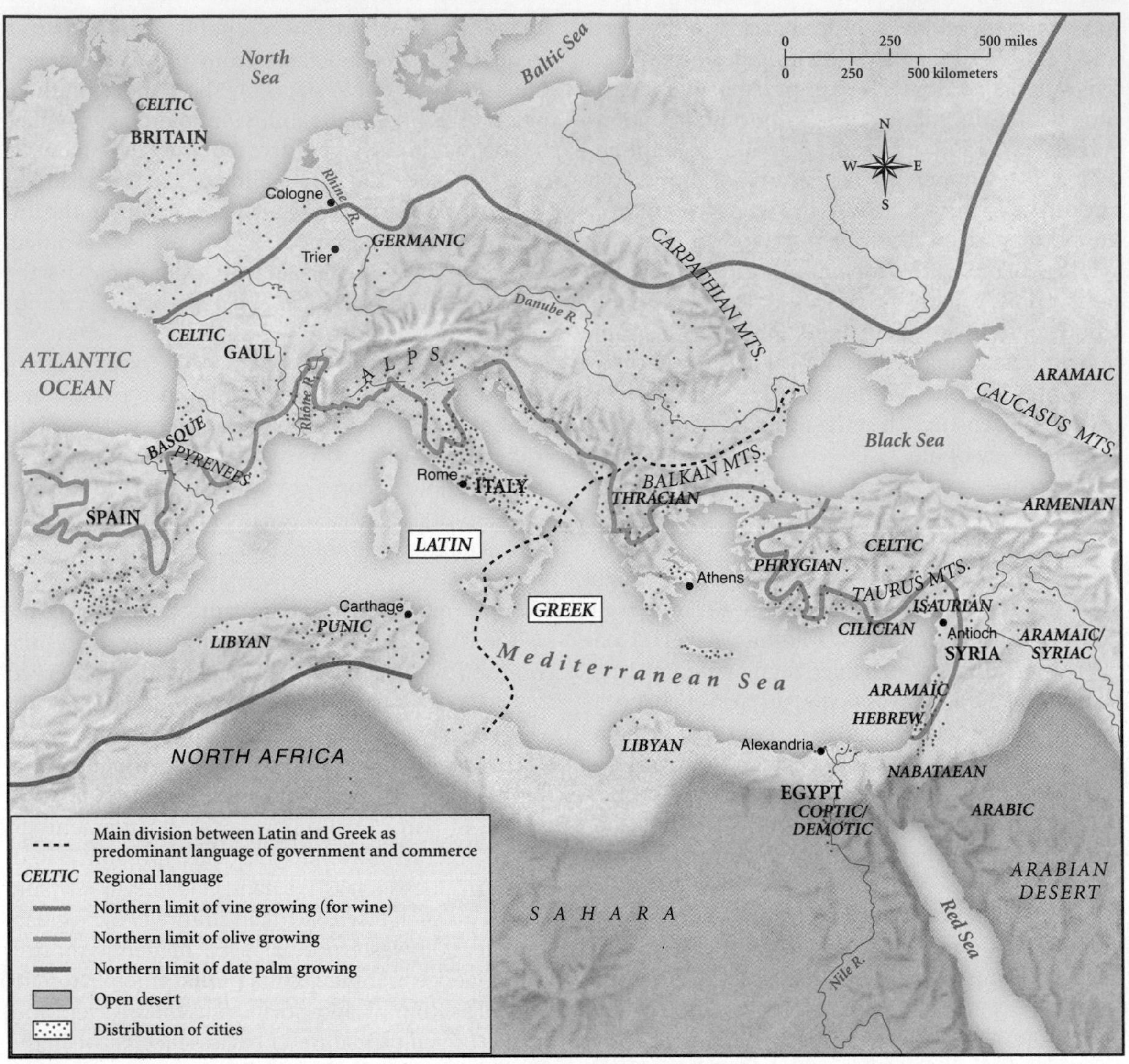

MAP 6.2 Natural Features and Languages of the Roman World
The environment of the Roman world included a large variety of topography, climate, and languages. The inhabitants of the Roman Empire, estimated to have numbered as many as fifty million, spoke dozens of different tongues, many of which survived well into the late empire. The two predominant languages were Latin in the western part of the empire and Greek in the eastern. Latin remained the language of law even in the eastern empire. Vineyards and olive groves were important agricultural resources because wine was regarded as an essential beverage, and olive oil was the principal source of fat for most people as well as being used to make soap, perfume, and other products for daily life. Dates and figs were popular sweets in the Roman world, which had no refined sugar.

Romanization affected the eastern provinces less, and they largely retained their Greek and Near Eastern characteristics. Huge Hellenistic cities such as Alexandria (in Egypt) and Antioch (in Syria) rivaled Rome in size and splendor. The eastern provincial elites readily accepted Roman governance because Hellenistic royal traditions had prepared them to see the emperor as their patron and themselves as his clients.

New Trends in Literature The continuing vitality of Greek language and culture contributed to new trends in Roman literature. Lucian (c. 117–180 C.E.) composed satirical dialogues in Greek mocking stuffy and superstitious people. The essayist and philosopher Plutarch (c. 50–120 C.E.) also used Greek to write paired biographies of Greek and Roman men. His exciting stories made him favorite reading for centuries; William Shakespeare based several plays on Plutarch's biographies.

As for literature in Latin, modern scholars call the late first century and early to mid-second century C.E. its Silver Age, second only to the Augustan Golden Age. Tacitus (c. 56–120 C.E.) wrote historical works that exposed the Julio-Claudian emperors'

Roman Theater at Sabratha in North Africa
This theater, with its three-story scene building at the back of the stage, was built in the late third century C.E. at the coastal city of Sabratha in Libya. Phoenicians had founded Sabratha as a trading station some eight hundred years earlier; it was still flourishing under the Roman Empire. The size of this very expensive building shows the importance that Romans attached to public entertainment for large numbers of people. *(Frans Lemmens/The Image Bank/Getty Images.)*

ruthlessness. Juvenal (c. 65–130 C.E.) wrote poems ridiculing pretentious Romans while complaining about living broke in the capital. Apuleius (c. 125–170 C.E.) excited readers with his *Golden Ass*, a sexually explicit novel about a man turned into a donkey who regains his body and his soul through the kindness of the Egyptian goddess Isis.

Law and Order through Equity Romans prided themselves on their ability to order their society through law. As Virgil said, their divine mission was "to establish law and order within a framework of peace." Roman law influenced most modern European legal systems. Its foundation was the principle of equity, which meant doing what was "good and fair" even if that required ignoring the letter of the law. This principle taught that the intent in a contract outweighed its words, and that accusers should prove the accused guilty because it was unfair to make defendants prove their innocence. The emperor Trajan ruled that no one should be convicted on the grounds of suspicion alone because it was better for a guilty person to go unpunished than for an innocent person to be condemned. (See "Contrasting Views," page 188.)

The importance of hierarchy led Romans to create formal distinctions in society based on wealth. The elites constituted a tiny portion of the population. Only about one in every fifty thousand had enough money to qualify for the senatorial order, the highest-ranking class, while about one in a thousand belonged to the equestrian order, the second-ranking class. Different purple stripes on clothing identified these orders. The third-highest order consisted of decurions, the local Senate members in provincial towns.

Under the republic, Roman law had made a legal distinction between patricians and plebeians. This division became even stricter under the early Roman Empire. "Better people" included senators, equites, decurions, and retired army veterans. Everybody else — except slaves, who counted as property, not people — made up the vastly larger group of "humbler people." The law imposed harsher penalties on them than on "better people" for the same crime. "Humbler people" convicted of serious crimes were regularly executed by being crucified or torn apart by wild animals before a crowd of spectators. "Better people" rarely received the death penalty, and those who did were allowed a quicker and more dignified execution by the sword. "Humbler people" could also be tortured in criminal investigations, even if they were citizens. Romans regarded these differences as fair on the grounds that an elite per-

CONTRASTING VIEWS

Christians in the Empire: Conspirators or Faithful Subjects?

Romans worried that new religions would disrupt the "peace with the gods" that guaranteed their national safety and prosperity. Groups whose religious beliefs seemed likely to anger the traditional deities could therefore be accused of treason, but Christians insisted that they were loyal subjects who prayed for the safety of the emperors (Document 1). The early emperors tried to form a policy on religion that was fair both to Christian subjects and to those citizens who feared them (Document 2).

1. Tertullian's Defense of His Fellow Christians, 197 C.E.

A theologian from North Africa, Tertullian insisted that Christians supported the empire. He explained that even though Christians refused to pray to the emperor, they prayed for him and thus for the community's health and safety.

So that is why Christians are public enemies—because they will not give the emperors vain, false, and reckless honors; because, being men of a true religion, they celebrate the emperors' festivals more in heart than in a festival mood. . . .

On the contrary, the name faction may properly be given to those who join to hate the good and honest, who shout for the blood of the innocent, who use as a pretext to defend their hatred the absurdity that they take the Christians to be the cause of every disaster to the state, of every misfortune of the people. If the Tiber reaches the walls, if the Nile does not rise to water the fields, if the sky does not move [i.e., if there is no rain] or the earth does, if there is famine, if there is plague, the cry at once arises: "The Christians to the lions!"

For we do pray to the eternal God, the true God, the living God, for the safety of the emperors. . . . Looking up to heaven, the Christians—with hands outspread because innocent, with head bare because we do not blush, yes!, and without a prompter because we pray from the heart—are ever praying for all the emperors. We pray for a fortunate life for them, a secure rule, a safe house, brave armies, a faithful Senate, a virtuous people, a peaceful world. . . .

Should not our sect [i.e., Christianity] have been listed among the legal associations, when it commits no such actions as are commonly feared from unlawful associations? For unless I am mistaken, the reason for prohibiting associations clearly lay in care for public order—to save the state from being torn into factions, a thing very likely to disturb election assemblies, public gatherings, local Senates, meetings, even the public games, with the clashing and rivalry of partisans. . . . We, however, whom all the passion for glory and rank leave cold, have no need to combine; nothing is more foreign to us than the state. One state we recognize for all—the universe.

Source: Tertullian, *Apology*, 30.1, 30.4; 35.1; 38.1–3; 40.1–2. Translation (modified) by T. R. Glover, 1931.

2. Pliny on Early Imperial Policy toward Christians, 112 C.E.

As governor of the province of Bithynia, Pliny had to decide the fate of Christians accused of crimes by their neighbors. Knowing of no precedent to guide him, he tried to be fair and wrote to the emperor Trajan to ask if he had acted correctly. The emperor's reply set out official policy concerning Christians in the early empire.

[Pliny to the emperor Trajan]

It is my habit, my lord, to refer to you all matters concerning which I am in doubt. For who can better give guidance to my hesitation or inform my ignorance? I have never participated in trials of Christians. I therefore do not know what offenses it is the practice to punish or investigate, and to what extent. . . .

In the case of those who were denounced to me as Christians, I have observed the following procedure: I interrogated these as to whether they were

son's higher status required of him or her a higher level of responsibility for the common good. As one provincial governor expressed it, "Nothing is less equitable than mere equality itself."

Marriage and Reproduction Although competition for social status drove many aspects of Roman life, nothing mattered more to the empire's strength than steady population levels. The upper-class government official Pliny, for example, sent the following report to the grandfather of his third wife, Calpurnia: "You will be very sad to learn that your granddaughter has suffered a miscarriage. She is a young girl and did not realize she was pregnant. As a result she was more active than she should have been and paid a high price."

Concerns about marriage and reproduction thus filled Roman society; remaining single and childless represented social failure for both women and men. The propertied classes usually arranged marriages between spouses who hardly knew each other, although husband and wife could grow to love each other in a partnership devoted to family. As in earlier times, girls often married in their early teens, to have as many years as possible to bear children. Because so many babies died young, families had to produce numerous offspring to keep from disappearing. The tombstone of Veturia, a soldier's wife,

Christians; those who confessed I interrogated a second and a third time, threatening them with punishment; those who persisted I ordered executed. For I had no doubt that, whatever the nature of their religion, stubbornness and inflexible obstinacy surely deserve to be punished. There were others possessed of the same madness; but because they were Roman citizens, I signed an order for them to be transferred to Rome.

Soon accusations spread, as usually happens, because of the proceedings going on, and several incidents occurred. An anonymous document was published containing the names of many persons. Those who denied that they were or had been Christians, when they called on the gods in words dictated by me, offered prayer with incense and wine to your image, which I had ordered to be brought for this purpose together with statues of the gods, and moreover cursed Christ—none of which those who are really Christians, it is said, can be forced to do—these I thought should be set free. Others named by the informer declared that they were Christians, but then denied it, asserting that they had been but had ceased to be, some three years before, others many years, some as much as twenty-five years. They all worshipped your image and the statues of the gods, and cursed Christ.

They asserted, however, that the sum and substance of their fault or error had been that they were accustomed to meet on a fixed day before dawn and sing responsively a hymn to Christ as to a god, and to bind themselves by oath, not to some crime, but not to commit fraud, theft, or adultery, not to break their word, nor to refuse to return a trust when called upon to do so. When this was over, it was their custom to depart and to assemble again to eat together—but ordinary and innocent food. Even this, they affirmed, they had stopped doing after my edict by which, in accordance with your instructions, I had forbidden political associations. Accordingly, I judged it all the more necessary to find out what the truth was by torturing two female slaves who were called attendants. But I discovered nothing else except depraved, excessive superstition.

I therefore postponed the investigation and hastened to consult you. For the matter seemed to me to require consulting you, especially because of the numbers involved. For the infection of this superstition has spread not only to the cities but also to the villages and farms. But it seems possible to check and cure it. It is certainly quite clear that the temples, which had been almost deserted, have begun to be frequented, that the established religious rites, long neglected, are being resumed, and that from everywhere sacrificial animals are coming, for which until now very few purchasers could be found. Hence it is easy to imagine what a multitude of people can be reformed if an opportunity for repentance is given.

[Emperor Trajan to Pliny]

You followed proper procedure, my dear Pliny, in handling the cases of those who had been denounced to you as Christians. For it is not possible to lay down any general rule to serve as a kind of fixed standard. They are not to be searched for; if they are denounced and proved guilty, they are to be punished, with this reservation, that whoever denies that he is a Christian and really proves it—that is, by worshipping our gods—even though he was under suspicion in the past, shall obtain pardon through repentance. But anonymously posted accusations ought to have no place in any prosecution. For this is both a dangerous kind of precedent and out of keeping with [the spirit of] our age.

Source: Pliny, *Letters*, Book 10, nos. 96 and 97. Translation (modified) by Betty Radice, 1969.

Questions to Consider

1. **Do you think that Pliny's procedure in dealing with the accused Christians respected the Roman legal principle of equity? Explain.**
2. **How should a society treat a minority of its members whose presence severely disturbs the majority?**

tells a typical story: "Here I lie, having lived for twenty-seven years. I was married to the same man for sixteen years and bore six children, five of whom died before I did."

While the emphasis on childbearing brought status to mothers, the social pressure to bear numerous children also created many health hazards for women. The biology of reproduction was not well understood. Gynecologists erroneously recommended the days just after menstruation as the best time to become pregnant, when the woman's body was "not congested." Doctors possessed metal instruments for surgery and physical examinations, but many were freedmen (former slaves) from the provinces, usually with only informal training. There was no official licensing of medical personnel, and most people considered being a doctor a job with low status and therefore fit for ex-slaves. Complications in childbirth could easily lead to the mother's death because doctors could not stop internal bleeding or cure infections. When Romans did want to control family size, they practiced contraception (by obstructing the vagina or by administering drugs to the female partner) or they abandoned unwanted infants.

The emperors tried to support reproduction. They gave money to feed needy children in the hope they would grow up to have families. Following the

Midwife's Sign
Childbirth carried the danger of death from infection or internal hemorrhage. This terra-cotta sign from Ostia, the ancient port city of Rome, probably hung outside a midwife's room to announce her expertise in helping women give birth. It shows a pregnant woman clutching the sides of her chair, with an assistant supporting her from behind and the midwife crouched in front to help deliver the baby. Why do you think the woman is seated for delivery instead of lying down? Such signs were especially effective for people who were illiterate; a person did not have to read to understand the services that the specialist inside could provide. *(Scala/Art Resource, NY.)*

emperors' lead, wealthy people often adopted children in their communities. One North African man supported three hundred boys and three hundred girls each year until they grew up.

REVIEW QUESTION In the early Roman Empire, what was life like in the cities and in the country for the elite and for ordinary people?

The Emergence of Christianity in the Early Roman Empire

Christianity began as what scholars call "the Jesus movement," a Jewish splinter group in Judaea (today Israel and the Palestinian Territories). There, as elsewhere under Roman rule, Jews were allowed to worship in their ancestral religion. The emergence of the new religion was gradual: three centuries after the death of Jesus, Christians were still a minority in the Roman Empire. Moreover, Christians' beliefs created official suspicion and hostility. Christianity grew because of the attraction of Jesus's charismatic career, its message of salvation, its early members' sense of mission, and the strong bonds of community it inspired. Ultimately, Christianity's emergence proved the most significant development in Roman history.

Palestine in the Time of Jesus, 30 C.E.

Jesus and His Teachings

Jesus (c. 4 B.C.E.–30 C.E.) grew up in a troubled region. Harsh Roman rule in Judaea had angered the Jews, and Rome's provincial governors worried about rebellion. Jesus's execution reflected the Roman policy of eliminating any threat to social order. In the two decades after his crucifixion, his followers, particularly Paul of Tarsus, developed and spread his teachings beyond his region's Jewish community to the wider Roman world.

Jewish Apocalypticism and Christianity Christianity offered an answer to a difficult question about divine justice raised by the Jews' long history of oppression under the kingdoms of the ancient and Hellenistic Near East: If God was just, as Hebrew monotheism taught, how could he allow the wicked to prosper and the righteous to suffer? Nearly two hundred years before Jesus's birth, persecution by the Seleucid king Antiochus IV (r. 175–164 B.C.E.) had provoked the Jews into revolt, a struggle that generated the concept of apocalypticism (see Chapter 2, page 46). According to this doctrine, evil powers controlled the world, but God would end their rule by sending the Messiah ("anointed one," *Mashiach* in Hebrew, **Christ** in Greek) to conquer them. A final judgment would soon follow, punishing the wicked and rewarding the righteous for eternity. Apocalypticism especially influenced the Jews living in Judaea under Roman rule and later inspired Christians and Muslims.

During Jesus's life, Jews disagreed among themselves about what form Judaism should take in such troubled times. Some favored getting along with the Romans, while others preached rejection of the non-Jewish world and its spiritual corruption. The local ruler, installed by the Romans, was Herod the Great (r. 37–4 B.C.E.). He was a Jew, but his Greek

---

Christ: Greek for "anointed one," in Hebrew *Mashiach* or in English *Messiah*; in apocalyptic thought, God's agent sent to conquer the forces of evil.

style of life ignored Jewish law and made him unpopular, despite his magnificent rebuilding of the great Jewish temple in Jerusalem. When a decade of unrest followed Herod's death, Augustus installed a Roman administration to suppress disorder. Life in Judaea was tense during Jesus's early life.

The Life and Ministry of Jesus

Jesus began his career as a teacher and healer during the reign of Emperor Tiberius. The books that would later become the New Testament Gospels, composed around 70 to 90 C.E., offer the earliest accounts of his life. Jesus wrote nothing down, and others' accounts of his words and deeds are often inconsistent. He taught not through direct instruction but through stories and parables that challenged his followers to reflect on what he meant.

Jesus's public ministry began with his baptism by John the Baptist, who preached a message of repentance before the approaching final judgment. The Jewish ruler Herod Antipas, a son of Herod the Great, executed John because he feared that John's apocalyptic preaching might cause riots. After John's death, Jesus continued his mission by traveling around Judaea's countryside teaching that God's kingdom was coming and that those who heard him needed to prepare spiritually for it. Some saw Jesus as the Messiah, but his apocalypticism did not call for immediate revolt against the Romans. Instead, he taught that God's true kingdom was to be found not on earth but in heaven. He stressed that this kingdom was open to believers regardless of their social status or apparent sinfulness. His emphasis on God's love for humanity and people's responsibility to love one another reflected Jewish religious teachings, such as the scriptural interpretations and moral teachings of the scholar Hillel, who lived in the time of Jesus.

Realizing that he had to reach more than country people to make an impact, Jesus took his message to the Jewish population of Jerusalem, the region's main city. His miraculous healings and exorcisms, combined with his powerful preaching, created a sensation. So popular was he that his followers created the Jesus movement; it was not yet Christianity but rather a Jewish sect, of which there were several, such as the Saduccees and Pharisees, competing for authority at the time. Jesus attracted the attention of Jewish leaders, who assumed that he wanted to replace them. Fearing Jesus might lead a Jewish revolt, the Roman governor Pontius Pilate ordered his crucifixion in Jerusalem in 30 C.E.

The Mission of Paul of Tarsus

Jesus's followers reported that they had seen him in person after his death, proclaiming that God had raised him from the dead. They convinced a few other Jews that he would soon return to judge the world and begin God's kingdom. At this time, his closest disciples, the twelve Apostles (Greek for "messengers"), still considered themselves faithful Jews and continued to follow the commandments of Jewish law. Their leader was Peter, who won acclaim as the greatest miracle worker of the Apostles, an ambassador to Jews interested in the Jesus movement, and the most important messenger proclaiming Jesus's teachings in the imperial capital. The later Christian church called him the first bishop of Rome.

A turning point came with the conversion of Paul of Tarsus (c. 10–65 C.E.), a pious Jew and a Roman citizen who had violently opposed Jews who accepted Jesus as the Messiah. A spiritual vision on the road to Damascus in Syria, which Paul interpreted as a divine revelation, inspired him to become a follower of Jesus as the Messiah, or Christ—a Christian, as members of the movement came to be known. Paul taught that accepting Jesus as divine and his crucifixion as the ultimate sacrifice for the sins of humanity was the only way of becoming righteous in the eyes of God. In this way alone could one expect to attain salvation in the world to come. Paul's new mission opened the way for Christianity to become a new religion separate from Judaism.

Seeking converts outside Judaea, Paul traveled to preach to Jews and Gentiles (non-Jews) who had adopted some Jewish practices in Asia Minor (today Turkey), Syria, and Greece. Although he stressed the necessity of ethical behavior as defined by Jewish tradition, especially the rejection of sexual immorality and polytheism, Paul also taught that converts did not have to live strictly according to Jewish law. To make conversion easier, he did not require male converts to undergo the Jewish initiation rite of circumcision. He also told his congregations that they did not have to observe Jewish dietary restrictions or festivals. These teachings generated tensions with Jewish authorities in Jerusalem as well as with followers of Jesus living there, who still believed that Christians had to follow Jewish law. Roman authorities arrested Paul as a troublemaker, and he was executed in about 65 C.E.

Hatred of Roman rule provoked Jews to revolt in 66 C.E. After crushing the rebels in 70 C.E., the Roman emperor Titus destroyed the Jerusalem temple and sold most of the city's population into slavery. In the aftermath of this catastrophe, in which Jews lost their religious center, Christianity began to separate more and more clearly from Judaism.

Paul's importance in early Christianity shows in the number of letters—thirteen—attributed to him among the twenty-seven Christian writings that were eventually put together as the New Testament. Christians came to regard the New Testament as having equal authority with the Jewish Bible, which they then called the Old Testament. Since teachers like Paul preached mainly in the cities to reach large crowds, congregations of Christians sprang up in urban areas. In early Christianity, women in some locations could be leaders — such as Lydia, a businesswoman who founded the congregation in Philippi in Greece — but many men, including Paul, opposed women's leadership.

Growth of a New Religion

Christianity faced serious obstacles as a new religion. Imperial officials, suspecting Christians such as Vibia Perpetua (mentioned in the opening of this chapter) of being traitors, could prosecute them for refusing to perform traditional sacrifices. Christian leaders had to build an organization from scratch to administer their growing congregations. Finally, Christians had to decide whether women could continue as leaders in their congregations.

The Rise of Persecution and Martyrdom The Roman emperors found Christians baffling and troublesome. Unlike Jews, Christians professed a new faith rather than their ancestors' traditional religion. Roman law therefore granted them no special treatment. Most Romans feared that Christians' denial of the old gods and the imperial cult would bring down divine punishment upon the empire. Secret rituals in which Christians symbolically ate the body and drank the blood of Jesus during communal dinners, called Love Feasts, led to accusations of cannibalism and sexual promiscuity.

For these reasons, Romans were quick to blame Christians for disasters. Nero declared that Rome's great fire in 64 C.E. was caused by Christian arsonists, whom he had covered in wild animal skins to be torn to pieces by dogs or fastened to crosses and set on fire to light the streets at night. Nero's cruelty, however, earned Christians sympathy from Rome's population.

Persecutions like Nero's were infrequent. There was no law against Christianity, but officials could punish Christians, as they could anyone, to protect public order. Pliny's actions as a provincial governor in Asia Minor illustrated the situation. (See "Contrasting Views," page 188.) In about 112 C.E., Pliny asked a group of people accused of following this new religion if they were really Christians. When some said yes, he asked them to reconsider. He freed those who denied Christianity, so long as they sacrificed to the gods, swore loyalty to the imperial cult, and cursed Christ. He executed those who refused these actions. Christians argued that Romans had nothing to fear from their faith. Far from spreading immorality and subversion, they insisted, Christianity taught morality and respect for authority. It was not a foreign superstition but the true philosophy, combining the best features of Judaism and Greek rational thought.

The occasional persecutions in the early empire did not stop Christianity. Christians like Perpetua regarded public executions as an opportunity to be-

Catacomb Painting of Christ as the Good Shepherd
Catacombs (tunnels with underground rooms), cut deep into soft rock outside major cities in the Roman Empire, served as meeting places and burial chambers for Jews and Christians. Rome had 340 miles of catacombs. This painting from the catacomb at Rome named after Priscilla, who was probably a Christian from the first century C.E., shows Jesus as the Good Shepherd (John 10: 10–11). He is carrying an animal back to the flock, symbolizing his role as savior; he is dressed in the traditional fashion for a Roman man on a special occasion. Catacomb paintings such as this one were the earliest form of Christian art. *(Catacomb of Priscilla, Rome, Italy/photograph by Erich Lessing/Art Resource, NY.)*

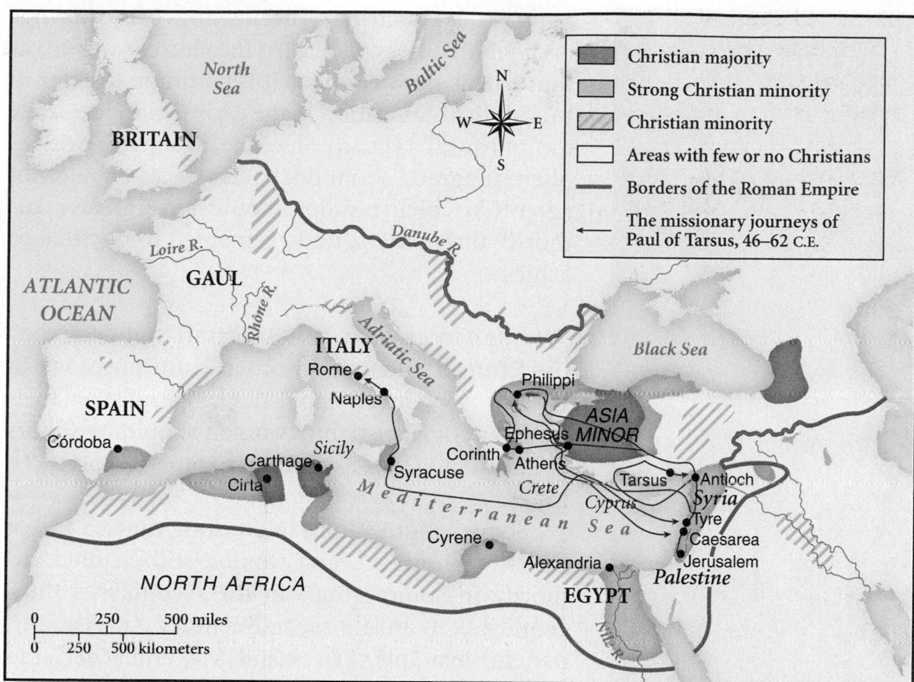

MAP 6.3 Christian Populations in the Late Third Century C.E.
Christians were still a minority in the Roman world three hundred years after Jesus's crucifixion. However, certain areas of the empire—especially Asia Minor, where Paul had preached—had a concentration of Christians. Most Christians lived in cities and towns, where the missionaries had gone to find crowds to hear their message. *Paganus*, a Latin word for "country person" or "rural villager," came to mean a believer in traditional polytheistic cults—hence the word *pagan* that modern historians sometimes use to indicate traditional polytheism. Paganism lived on in rural areas for centuries.

come a **martyr** (Greek for "witness"), someone who dies for his or her religious faith. Martyrs' belief that their deaths would send them directly to paradise allowed them to face torture. Some Christians actively sought to become martyrs. Tertullian (c. 160–240 C.E.) proclaimed that "martyrs' blood is the seed of the Church." Ignatius (c. 35–107 C.E.), bishop of Antioch, begged Rome's congregation, which was becoming the most prominent Christian group, not to ask the emperor to show him mercy after his arrest: "Let me be food for the wild animals [in the arena] through which I can reach God," he pleaded. "I am God's wheat, to be ground up by the teeth of beasts so that I may be found pure bread of Christ." Stories reporting the martyrs' courage inspired the faithful to accept hostility from non-Christians and helped shape the new religion as one that gave its believers the spiritual power to endure suffering.

Bishops and Christian Hierarchy

First-century C.E. Christians expected Jesus to return to pass judgment on the world during their lifetimes. When that did not happen, they began transforming their religion from an apocalyptic Jewish sect expecting the immediate end of the world into one that could survive indefinitely. This transformation was painful because early Christians fiercely disagreed about what they should believe, how they should live, and who had the authority to decide these questions. Some insisted Christians should withdraw from the everyday world to escape its evil, abandoning their families and shunning sex and reproduction. Others believed they could follow Christ's teachings while living ordinary lives. Many Christians worried they could not serve as soldiers without betraying their faith because the army participated in the imperial cult. This dilemma raised the further issue of whether Christians could remain loyal subjects of the emperor. Disagreement over these doctrinal questions raged in the many congregations that arose in the early empire around the Mediterranean, from Gaul to Africa to the Near East (Map 6.3).

The need to deal with such tensions and to administer the congregations led Christians to create an official hierarchy, headed by bishops meant to provide the connection of spiritual communion between congregations and Christ that promised salvation to believers. Bishops possessed authority both to define Christian doctrine and to administer the practical affairs of a growing religion. The emergence of bishops became the most important institutional development in early Christianity. Bishops received their positions according to the principle later called **apostolic succession**, which states that the Apostles appointed the first bishops as their successors, granting these new officials the author-

martyr: Greek for "witness," the term for someone who dies for his or her religious beliefs.

apostolic (ah puh STAH lihk) succession: The principle by which Christian bishops traced their authority back to the apostles of Jesus.

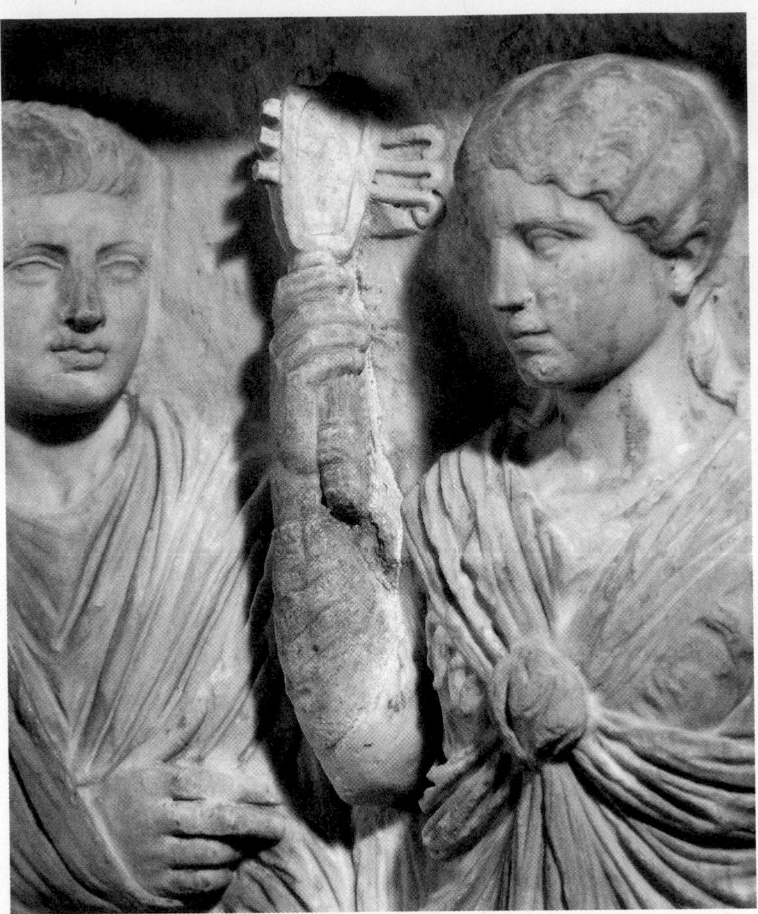

Woman Holding a Religious Musical Instrument
This sculpture dating from the early Roman Empire shows a woman standing next to her husband and holding a musical instrument called a *sistrum*. This percussion instrument consisted of a frame with rods piercing it that made a rattling sound when shaken. It was used especially in rituals in the worship of Isis, the Egyptian goddess whose cult as a mother figure/savior became widespread around the Mediterranean in Roman imperial times. *(© akg-images/Pietro Baguzzi/The Image Works.)*

ity Jesus had originally given to the Apostles. Those designated by the Apostles in turn appointed their own successors. Bishops had authority to ordain ministers with the holy power to administer the sacraments, above all baptism and communion, which believers regarded as necessary for achieving eternal life. Bishops also controlled their congregations' memberships and finances. The money financing the early church came from members' donations.

The bishops tried to suppress the disagreements that arose in the new religion. They used their authority to define **orthodoxy** (true doctrine) and **heresy** (false doctrine). The meetings of the bishops of different cities constituted the church's organization in this period. Today it is common to refer to this loose organization as the early Catholic (Greek for "universal") church. Since the bishops themselves often disagreed about doctrine and also could not agree on which bishops should have greater authority than others, unity remained impossible to achieve.

Women in the Church When bishops came to power, they demoted women from positions of leadership. This change reflected their view that in Christianity women should be subordinate to men, just as in Roman imperial society in general.

Some congregations took a long time to accept this shift, however, and women still claimed authority in some groups in the second and third centuries C.E. In late-second-century C.E. Asia Minor, for example, Prisca and Maximilla declared themselves prophetesses with the power to baptize believers in anticipation of the coming end of the world. They spread the apocalyptic message that the heavenly Jerusalem would soon descend in their region.

Excluded from leadership posts, many women chose a life without sex to demonstrate their devotion to Christ. Their commitment to celibacy gave these women the power to control their own bodies. Other Christians regarded women who reached this special closeness to God as holy and socially superior. By rejecting the traditional roles of wife and mother in favor of spiritual excellence, celibate Christian women achieved independence and status otherwise denied them.

Competing Religious Beliefs

Three centuries after Jesus's death, traditional polytheism was still the religion of the overwhelming majority of the Roman Empire's population. Polytheists, who worshipped a variety of gods in different ways in diverse kinds of sanctuaries, often reflecting regional religious rituals and traditions, never created a unified religion. Nevertheless, the stability and prosperity of the early empire gave traditional believers confidence that the old gods and the imperial cult protected them. Even those who preferred religious philosophy, such as Stoicism's idea of divine providence, respected the old cults because they embodied Roman tradition. By the third century C.E., the growth of Christianity, along with the persistence of Judaism and polytheistic cults, meant that people could choose from a number of competing beliefs. Especially appealing were beliefs that offered people hope that they could change their

---

orthodoxy: True doctrine; specifically, the beliefs defined for Christians by councils of bishops.

heresy: False doctrine; specifically, the beliefs banned for Christians by councils of bishops.

Mithras Slaying the Bull
Hundreds of shrines to the mysterious god Mithras have been found in the Roman Empire. Scholars debate the symbolic meaning of the bull slaying that is prominent in art connected to Mithras's cult, as in this wall painting of about 200 C.E. from the shrine at Marino, south of Rome. Here, a snake and a dog lick the sacrificial animal's blood, while a scorpion pinches its testicles as it dies in agony. The ancient sources do not clarify the scene's meaning. What do you think could be the explanation for this type of sacrifice? *(Scala/Art Resource, NY.)*

present lives for the better and also look forward to an afterlife.

Polytheistic religion had as its goal winning the goodwill of all the divinities who could affect human life. Its deities ranged from the state cults' major gods, such as Jupiter and Minerva, to spirits thought to inhabit groves and springs. International cults such as the Mysteries of Demeter and Persephone outside Athens remained popular; the emperor Hadrian traveled there to be initiated.

Isis and Mithras The cults of Isis and Mithras demonstrate how polytheism could provide a religious experience arousing strong emotions and demanding a moral way of life. The Egyptian goddess Isis had already attracted Romans by the time of Augustus, who tried to suppress her cult because it was Cleopatra's religion. But the fame of Isis as a kind, compassionate goddess who cared for her followers made her cult too popular to crush: the Egyptians said it was her tears for starving humans that caused the Nile to flood every year and bring them good harvests. Her image was that of a loving mother, and in art she was often depicted nursing her son. Her cult's central doctrine concerned the death and resurrection of her husband, Osiris. Isis also promised her believers a life after death.

Isis required her followers to behave righteously. Many inscriptions expressed her high moral standards by listing her own civilizing accomplishments: "I broke down the rule of tyrants; I put an end to murders; I caused what is right to be mightier than gold and silver." The hero of Apuleius's novel *The Golden Ass* shouts out his intense joy after his rescue and spiritual rebirth through Isis: "O holy and eternal guardian of the human race, who always cherishes mortals and blesses them, you care for the troubles of miserable humans with a sweet mother's love. Neither day nor night, nor any moment of time, ever passes by without your blessings." Other cults also required worshippers to lead upright lives. Inscriptions from Asia Minor, for example, record people's confessions to sins such as sexual transgressions for which their local god had imposed severe penance.

Archaeology reveals that the cult of Mithras had many shrines under the Roman Empire, but no texts survive to explain its mysterious rituals and symbols, which Romans believed had originated in Persia. Mithras's legend said that he killed a bull in a cave, apparently as a sacrifice for the benefit of his worshippers. As pictures show (see the illustration on page 195), this was no ordinary sacrifice because the animal was allowed to struggle as it was killed. Initiates in Mithras's cult proceeded through rankings named, from bottom to top, Raven, Male Bride, Soldier, Lion, Persian, Sun-runner, and Father—the latter a title of great honor.

Philosophy as the Science of Living In addition to following their religious beliefs, many upper-class Romans guided their lives by Greek philosophy. The most popular choice was Stoicism, which presented philosophy as the "science of living" and required self-discipline and duty from men and women alike. (See Chapter 4, page 130, and see Document, "A Roman Stoic Philosopher on the Capabilities of Women," page 197.) Philosophic individuals put together their own set of beliefs, such as those on duty expressed by the emperor Marcus Aurelius in his memoirs, entitled *To Myself* (or *Meditations*).

Christian and polytheist intellectuals debated Christianity's relationship to Greek philosophy. Origen (c. 185–255 C.E.) argued that Christianity was superior to Greek philosophical doctrines as a guide to correct living. At about the same time, Plotinus (c. 205–270 C.E.) developed the philosophy that had the greatest influence on religion. His spiritual philosophy was influenced by Persian religious ideas and, above all, Plato's philosophy, for which reason this new philosophy is called **Neoplatonism**. Plotinus's ideas deeply influenced many Christian thinkers as well as polytheists. He wrote that ultimate reality is a trinity of The One, Mind, and Soul. By turning away from the life of the body and relying on reason, individual souls could achieve a mystic union with The One, who in Christian thought would be God. To succeed in this spiritual quest required strenuous self-discipline in personal morality and spiritual purity as well as in philosophical contemplation.

REVIEW QUESTION **Which aspects of social, cultural, and political life in the early Roman Empire supported the growth of Christianity, and which opposed it?**

Neoplatonism: Plotinus's spiritual philosophy, based mainly on Plato's ideas, which was very influential for Christian intellectuals.

From Stability to Crisis in the Third Century C.E.

In the third century C.E., military expenses provoked a financial crisis that fed a political crisis lasting from the 230s to the 280s C.E. Invasions on the northern and eastern frontiers had forced the Roman emperors to expand the army for defense, but no new revenues came in to meet the additional costs. The emperors' desperate schemes to finance defense costs damaged the economy and infuriated the population. This anger at the regime encouraged generals to repeat the behavior that had destroyed the republic: commanding client armies to seize power. They created a civil war that lasted fifty years. Earthquakes and regional epidemics added to people's misery. By 284 C.E., this combination of troubles had destroyed the Pax Romana of the early empire.

Threats to the Northern and Eastern Frontiers of the Early Roman Empire

Emperors since Domitian in the first century had combated invaders. The most aggressive attackers were the multiethnic bands from northern Europe that crossed the Danube and Rhine Rivers to raid Roman territory. One theory is that these attacks were the result of a ripple effect of pressure on the northerners caused by wars in central Asia that disrupted trade and normal economic conditions like falling dominoes from east to west. Whatever motivated their incursions into the Roman Empire, these originally poorly organized northerners developed military discipline through their frequent fighting against the Roman army. They mounted especially damaging invasions during the reign of Marcus Aurelius (r. 161–180 C.E.). A major threat also appeared at the eastern edge of the empire, when a new Persian dynasty, the Sasanids, defeated the Parthian Empire and fought to re-create the ancient Persian Empire. By the early third century C.E., Persia's renewed military power forced the emperors to deploy a large part of the army to protect the rich eastern provinces, which took troops away from defense of the northern frontiers.

Recognizing the northern warriors' bravery, the emperors had begun hiring them as auxiliary soldiers for the Roman army in the late first century C.E. and settling them on the frontiers as buffers against other invaders. By the early third century, the army had expanded to enroll perhaps as many as 450,000 troops (the size of the navy remains unknown). Training constantly, soldiers had to be able to carry

DOCUMENT

A Roman Stoic Philosopher on the Capabilities of Women

Musonius Rufus was a Roman philosopher in the first century C.E. who lectured (in Greek) on Stoicism as "the science of living." Leading citizens in Rome became his students. He put his teaching to work by trying to serve as a mediator between the warring forces in the civil war that followed the emperor Nero's death. His ideas were regarded as subversive enough to be threatening to those in power: two different emperors expelled him from Rome, hoping to eliminate his influence. These excerpts reveal his views on the natural capacities of women, education in philosophy, and marriage. His arguments in favor of opportunities and greater equality for women expressed philosophical ideas first explored by earlier Greek philosophers; they did not reflect actual changes in Roman society under the empire.

The gods have given women the same ability to use their minds as men. . . . Women have the same senses as men: vision, hearing, smell, and everything else. . . . Women as well as men have an eagerness and a natural tendency towards excellence (virtue). . . . Therefore, why is it proper for men to investigate and examine to live rightly, that is, to study philosophy and live by its guidance, but not for women? Is it appropriate for men to be good, but not women?

To begin with, a woman must manage her household and pick out what is helpful for her home and take charge of the household slaves. I claim that philosophy is especially helpful for these actions, since each of them is a part of life, and philosophy is nothing other than the science of living. . . . Next, a woman must be chaste, and capable of keeping herself free from illegal love affairs, and pure in other self-indulgent pleasures. She must not delight in quarreling, not be extravagant, or overly concerned with her appearance. . . . She must control her anger, and not be overcome by grief, and stronger than every kind of emotion.

[A woman who is guided by philosophy knows to] love her children more than her own life. What woman could be more just than someone who behaves like that? Therefore, it follows that an educated woman will have more courage than an uneducated woman . . . because neither fear of death nor any concern about suffering would lead her to do anything shameful, and she would not be afraid of anyone just because he was from an important family or powerful or rich. . . .

It is easy to recognize that there are not different types of excellences for men and women. First, men and women both need to have common sense. . . . Second, both need to live just lives. An unjust man can not be a good citizen, and a woman can not run her household well, if she does not run it justly. . . . Third, a wife ought to be chaste, and so should a husband, for the laws punish both sides in cases of adultery. . . .

You might argue that only men need courage, but that is false. The best sort of woman must have the courage of a man and purge herself of cowardice, so that she will not give in to suffering or fear. If she can't do that, then how can she be chaste, if someone by threatening her or torturing her can force her to act disgracefully? . . . That women are able to use weapons, we know from the Amazons, who fought many peoples in battle. . . .

Well then, suppose someone asks, "Do you think that men should learn to work wool like women and that women should work out in the gymnasium like men?" No, that is not what I recommend. I say that, since in the case of human beings the males are naturally stronger . . . , appropriate work ought to be assigned to men and women, with the physically heavier tasks given to the stronger, and the lighter ones to the less strong. . . . Nevertheless, some men might fittingly undertake some of the lighter work and work regarded as more suitable for women, when the conditions of their body or necessity or time require it. For all human work is a common responsibility for men and women, and nothing is necessarily prescribed for one gender or the other. . . .

It is reasonable, then, for me to think that women should be educated like men concerning excellence, and they must be taught, beginning in their childhood, that this is good and that is bad, and that they are the same for both genders, and that this is beneficial and that harmful, and that an individual must do this, and not do that. Such lessons develop reasoning in both girls and boys, and there is no distinction between them. . . .

[In marriage], husband and wife join together to live their lives in common and to have children. . . . They should consider all their property to be shared, and nothing to belong only to themselves, not even their bodies. . . . There must be complete companionship and concern for each other by both husband and wife, in health and in sickness and at all times, because they entered upon the marriage for this reason, as well as to have children. When such caring for one another is perfect, and the married couple provide it for each another, and each works to outdo the other, then this is marriage as it ought to be. . . . But when one partner looks to their own interests alone and neglects the other's concerns . . . or is unwilling to pull together with their partner or to cooperate, then inevitably the marriage is destroyed, and although the two live together, their common interests do poorly, and finally they get a divorce, or they live on in an existence that is worse than loneliness.

Source: Musonius Rufus 3, 4, 13A, Lutz edition. Translation by Thomas R. Martin.

Question to Consider

- **What arguments does the Stoic philosopher make about the benefits of women studying philosophy?**

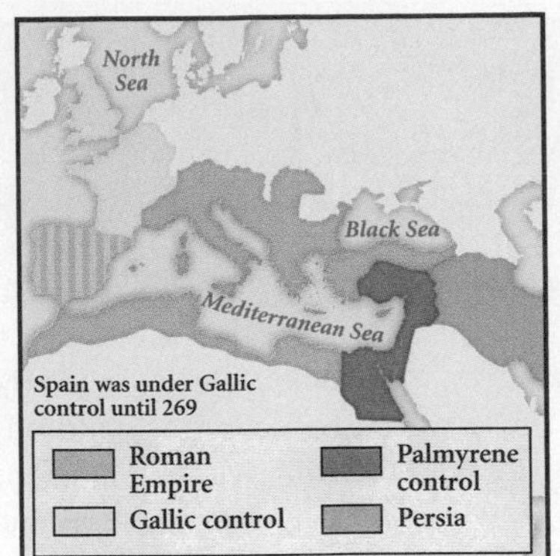

The Fragmented Roman Empire of the Third Century

forty-pound packs twenty miles in five hours, swimming rivers on the way. Since the early second century C.E., the emperors had built many stone camps for permanent garrisons, but on the march an army constructed a fortified camp every night; soldiers transported all the makings of a wooden walled city everywhere they went. As one ancient commentator noted, "Infantrymen were little different from loaded pack mules." At one temporary fort in a frontier area, archaeologists found a supply of a million iron nails—ten tons' worth. The same encampment required seventeen miles of timber for its barracks' walls. To outfit a single legion with tents required fifty-four thousand calves' hides.

The increased demand for pay and supplies strained imperial finances because successful conquests had become rare. The army had become a source of negative instead of positive cash flow to the treasury, and the economy had not expanded to make up the difference. To make matters worse, inflation had driven up prices. A principal cause of inflation may have been, ironically, the principate's long period of peace, which increased demand for goods and services to a level that outstripped the supply.

In desperation, some emperors attempted to curb inflation by debasing imperial coinage to cut government costs. **Debasement of coinage** meant putting less silver in each coin without changing its face value. In this way, the emperors created more cash from the same amount of precious metal. (See "Taking Measure" on page 199.) But merchants soon raised prices to make up for the debased coinage's reduced value; this in turn produced more inflation. By the early third century, the furious spiral of rising prices had spun into a financial tornado. Still, the soldiers demanded that their patrons, the emperors, pay them well. This pressure drove imperial finances into collapse by the 250s C.E.

Uncontrolled Spending, Natural Disasters, and Political Crisis, 193–284 C.E.

The emperors Septimius Severus (r. 193–211 C.E.) and his son Caracalla (r. 211–217 C.E.) made financial crisis unavoidable when they drained the treasury to satisfy the army and their own dreams of glory. A soldier's soldier who came from North Africa, Severus became emperor when his predecessor's incompetence caused a government crisis and civil war. To restore imperial prestige and acquire money through foreign conquest, Severus pursued successful campaigns beyond the frontiers of the provinces in Mesopotamia and Scotland.

Since inflation had reduced their wages to almost nothing, soldiers expected the emperors, as their patrons, to provide gifts of extra money. Severus spent large sums on gifts and raised their regular pay by a third. The army's expanded size made this raise more expensive than the treasury could handle. This out-of-control spending did not bother Severus in the least. His deathbed advice to his sons Caracalla and Geta in 211 C.E. was to "stay on good terms with each other, be generous to the soldiers, and pay no attention to anyone else."

Caracalla and Civil War

Severus's sons followed his advice only on the last two points. Caracalla, after murdering his brother, ended the Roman Golden Age of peace

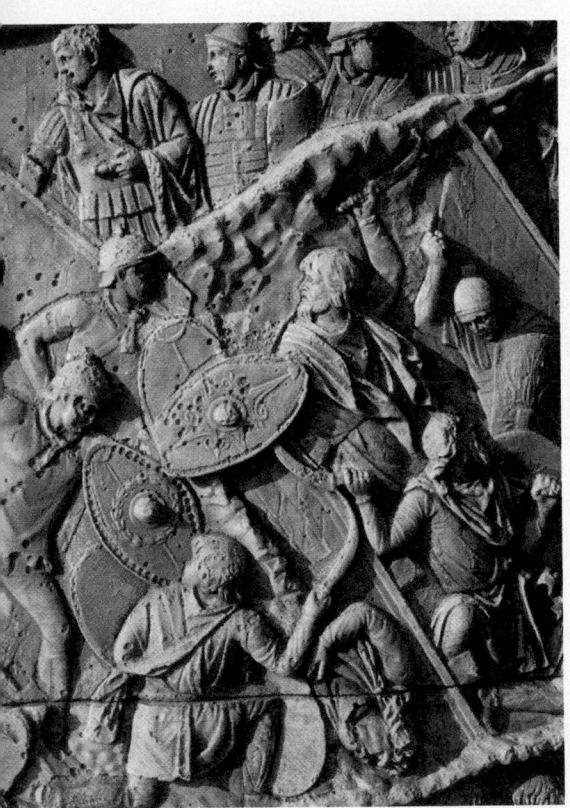

War Scene on Trajan's Column
The emperor Trajan erected a hundred-foot-tall column carved with some twenty-five hundred figures to show his conquest of Dacia (territory north of the Danube River). Our knowledge of Roman military equipment largely comes from the pictures on the column. The scenes spiral up the column in a continuing story, showing Trajan leading his troops and making sacrifices to the gods, with his soldiers preparing to march, crossing the river, building camps, and (as here) fighting hand-to-hand battles with the Dacians, who fought with no armor except shields. (*© Vittoriano Rastelli/Corbis.*)

debasement of coinage: Putting less silver in a coin without changing its face value; a failed financial strategy during the third-century C.E. crisis in Rome.

and prosperity with his uncontrolled spending and cruelty. He increased the soldiers' pay by another 40 to 50 percent and spent gigantic sums on building projects, including the largest public baths Rome had ever seen, covering blocks and blocks of the city. These huge expenses put unbearable pressure on the local provincial officials responsible for collecting taxes and on the citizens, whom the officials in turn squeezed for ever larger payments.

In 212 C.E., Caracalla took his most famous step to try to fix the budget: he granted Roman citizenship to almost every man and woman in imperial territory except slaves. Since only citizens paid inheritance taxes and fees for freeing slaves, an increase in citizens meant an increase in revenues, most of which was earmarked for the army. But too much was never enough for Caracalla, whose cruelty to anyone who displeased him made contemporaries whisper that he was insane. His attempted conquests of new territory failed to bring in enough funds, and he wrecked imperial finances. Once when his mother reprimanded him for his excesses he replied, as he drew his sword, "Never mind, we won't run out of money as long as I have this."

The financial crisis generated political instability that led to a half century of civil war. This period of violent struggle broke the back of the principate. For fifty years, a parade of emperors and pretenders fought to rule. More than two dozen men, often several at once, held or claimed power in that time. Their only qualification was their ability to command a frontier army and to reward the troops for loyalty to their general instead of to the state.

The civil war devastated the population and the economy. Violence and hyperinflation made life miserable in many regions. Agriculture withered as farmers could not keep up normal production when armies searching for food ravaged their crops. City council members faced constantly escalating demands for tax revenues from the swiftly changing emperors. The endless financial pressure destroyed members' will to serve their communities.

Historians dispute how severely natural disaster worsened the empire's financial and political crisis, but earthquakes and epidemics did strike some of the provinces in the mid-third century. In some regions, the population declined significantly as food supplies became less dependable, civil war killed soldiers and civilians alike, and infection raged. The loss of population meant fewer soldiers for the army, whose strength as a defense and police force had been gutted by political and financial chaos. This weakness made frontier areas more vulnerable to raids and allowed roving bands of robbers to range unchecked inside the borders.

TAKING MEASURE

The Value of Roman Imperial Coinage, 27 B.C.E.–300 C.E.

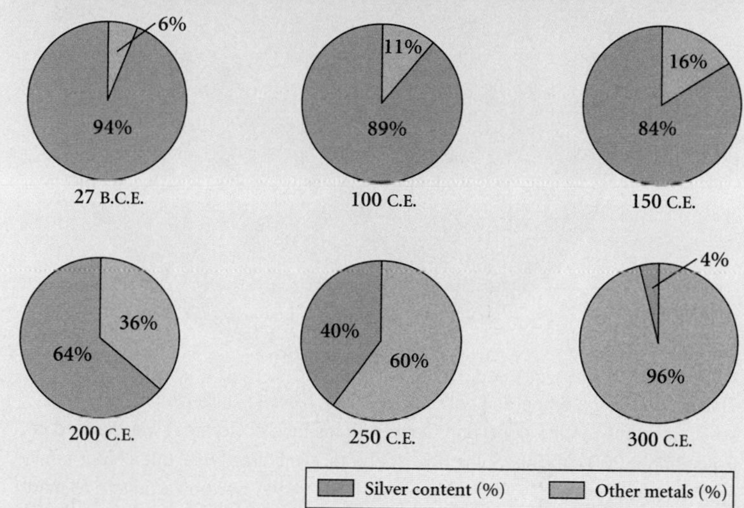

Ancient silver coinage got its value from its metallic content; the less silver in a coin, the less the coin was worth. When government and military expenses rose but revenues fell because no conquests were being made, emperors debased the coinage by reducing the amount of silver and increasing the amount of other, cheaper metals in each coin. These pie charts reveal that devaluation of the coinage was gradual until the third century C.E., when military expenses skyrocketed. By 300 C.E., coins contained only a trace amount of silver. Debasement fueled inflation because merchants and producers had to raise their prices for goods and services when they were paid with currency that was increasingly less valuable.

Source: Adapted from Kevin Greene, *The Archeology of the Roman Economy* (London: B. T. Batsford, Ltd., 1986), 60.

Question to Consider

- **How might the increasing devaluation have affected the lives of citizens at all levels in the Roman Empire?**

Foreign enemies to the north and east took advantage of the third-century crisis to attack. Roman fortunes hit bottom when Shapur I, king of the Sasanid Empire of Persia, invaded the province of Syria and captured the emperor Valerian (r. 253–260 C.E.). By this time, imperial territory was in constant danger of being captured. Zenobia, the warrior queen of Palmyra in Syria, for example, seized Egypt and Asia Minor. Emperor Aurelian (r. 270–275 C.E.) won back these provinces only with great difficulty. He also had to encircle Rome with a larger wall to ward off attacks from northern raiders, who were smashing their way into Italy.

Emperor Severus and His Family

This portrait of the emperor Septimius Severus; his wife, Julia Domna; and their sons, Caracalla (on the right) and Geta (with his face obliterated) was painted in Egypt about 200 C.E. The males hold scepters, symbolic of rule, but all four family members wear bejeweled golden crowns fit for royalty. Severus arranged to marry Julia without ever meeting her because her horoscope predicted she would become a queen, and she served as her husband's valued adviser. They hoped their sons would share rule, but when Severus died in 211 C.E., Caracalla murdered Geta so that he could rule alone. Why do you think the portrait's owner rubbed out Geta's face? *(bpk, Berlin/Antikensammlung, Staaliche Museen, Berlin, Germany/photo by Johannes Laurentius/Art Resource, NY.)*

Persecution of Christians Polytheists explained the third-century crisis in the traditional way: the state gods were angry about something. But what? The obvious answer was the presence of Christians, who denied the existence of the Roman gods and refused to worship them. Emperor Decius (r. 249–251 C.E.) therefore launched a systematic persecution to eliminate Christians and restore the goodwill of the gods. He proclaimed himself Restorer of the Cults while declaring, "I would rather see a rival to my throne than another bishop of Rome." He ordered all the empire's inhabitants to prove their loyalty to the state's well-being by sacrificing to its gods. Christians who refused were killed. This persecution did not stop the civil war, economic failure, and natural disasters that threatened Rome's empire, and Emperor Gallienus (r. 253–268 C.E.) ordered Christians to be left alone and their property restored. The crisis in government continued, however, and by the 280s C.E. the principate had reached a political dead end.

REVIEW QUESTION What were the causes and the effects of the Roman crisis in the third century C.E.?

Conclusion

Augustus created the principate and the Pax Romana by constructing a disguised monarchy as princeps while insisting that he was restoring the Roman republic. He succeeded because he ensured the loyalty of the army and the people by becoming their patron. He bought off the upper class by letting them keep their traditional offices and status. Provincials found this arrangement acceptable because it resembled the kind of top-down government that they had grown used to before Roman conquest. The imperial cult provided a focus for building and displaying loyalty to the emperor.

So long as the emperors had enough money to keep their millions of clients satisfied, stability prevailed. They provided food to the poor, built baths and arenas for public entertainment, paid their troops well, and helped out members of the elite when they needed it. The emperors of the first and second centuries expanded the military to protect their distant territories stretching from Britain to North Africa to Syria. By the second century, peace and prosperity had created an imperial Golden Age. Long-term financial difficulties set in, however, because the army, now concentrating on defense, no longer brought money in through frequent conquests. Severe inflation made the situation desperate. Since the provincial elites could no longer meet the demand for increased taxes without draining their fortunes, they lost their public-spiritedness and avoided their communal responsibilities. Loyalty to the state became too expensive.

The emergence of Christianity added to the instability because Roman officials doubted the loyalty of the Christians. The new religion evolved from Jewish apocalypticism to a hierarchical organization. Its

Sasanid Silver Plate with Royal Hunting Scene

This silver plate, plated with gold, shows the ruler of the Sasanid Empire hunting with a bow and arrow while riding a camel. The Sasanids ruled the territory of the ancient Persian Empire, centered in Iran, for four hundred years beginning in the third century C.E. The Roman emperors treated the Sasanid emperors as their equals, respecting their wealth and fearing their military power. *(© Ancient Art and Architecture Collection, Ltd.)*

MAPPING THE WEST

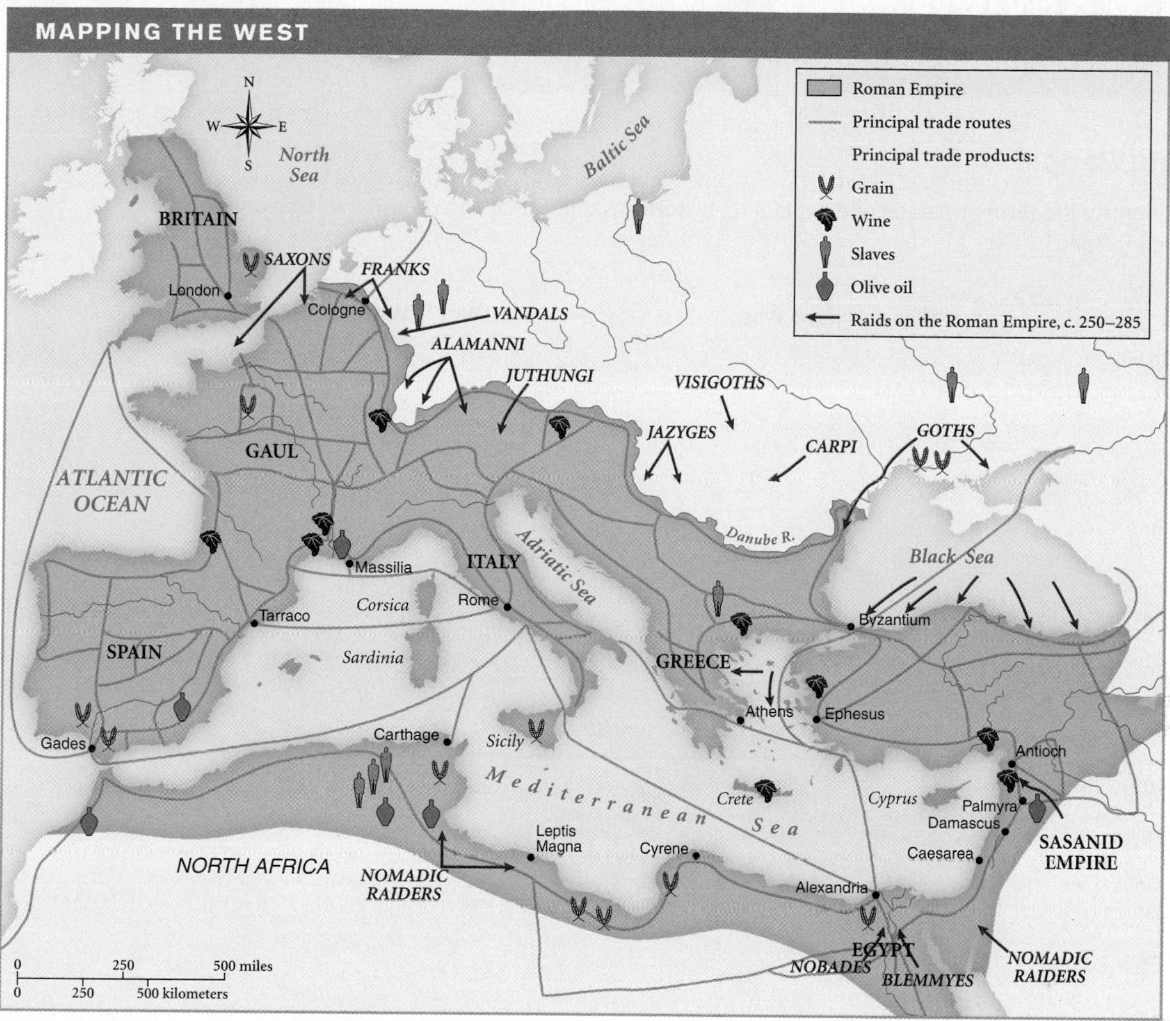

The Roman Empire in Crisis, 284 C.E.

By the 280s C.E., fifty years of civil war had torn the principate apart. Imperial territory retained the outlines inherited from the time of Augustus (compare Map 6.1 on page 184), except for the loss of Dacia to the Goths a few years before. Attacks from the north and east had repeatedly penetrated the frontiers, however. Long-distance trade had always been important to the empire's prosperity, but the decades of violence had made transport riskier and therefore more expensive, contributing to the crisis. | **What do you think would have been the greatest challenges in ruling such a vast empire in an age without swift communications or fast travel?**

believers argued with one another and with the authorities. Martyrs such as Vibia Perpetua worried the government with the depth of their beliefs; citizens placing loyalty to a single divinity ahead of loyalty to the state was a new and inexplicable phenomenon for Roman officialdom.

When financial ruin, natural disasters, and civil war combined to create a political crisis for the principate in the mid-third century C.E., the emperors lacked the money and the popular support to solve their problems. Not even persecutions of Christians could convince the gods to restore Rome's good fortunes. Threatened with the loss of peace, prosperity, and territory, the empire needed a political transformation to survive. That process began under the emperor Diocletian (r. 284–305 C.E.). Under his successor, Constantine (r. 306–337 C.E.), the Roman Empire also began the slow process of becoming officially Christian.

FOR FURTHER EXPLORATION

- **For additional primary-source material from this period**, see *Sources of the Making of the West*, Fourth Edition.
- **For Web sites, images, and documents related to topics in this chapter**, visit *Make History* at bedfordstmartins.com/hunt.

Chapter 6 Review

Online Study Guide bedfordstmartins.com/hunt

Key Terms and People

In the grid below, identify the term or person and explain its historical significance. (To do this exercise online, go to bedfordstmartins.com/hunt.)

Term	Who or What & When	Why It Matters
Pax Romana (Roman Peace) (p. 172)		
Augustus (p. 173)		
principate (p. 173)		
praetorian guard (p. 174)		
Julio-Claudians (p. 181)		
Colosseum (p. 183)		
decurions (p. 185)		
Romanization (p. 185)		
Christ (p. 190)		
martyr (p. 193)		
apostolic succession (p. 193)		
orthodoxy (p. 194)		
heresy (p. 194)		
Neoplatonism (p. 196)		
debasement of coinage (p. 198)		

Review Questions

1. How did the peace gained through Augustus's "restoration of the Roman republic" affect Romans' lives in all social classes?
2. In the early Roman Empire, what was life like in the cities and in the country for the elite and for ordinary people?
3. Which aspects of social, cultural, and political life in the early Roman Empire supported the growth of Christianity, and which opposed it?
4. What were the causes and the effects of the Roman crisis in the third century C.E.?

Making Connections

1. What were the similarities and differences between the crisis in the first century B.C.E. that undermined the Roman republic and the crisis in the third century C.E. that undermined the principate?
2. If you had been a first-century Roman emperor under the principate, what would you have done about the Christians and why? What if you had been a third-century emperor?
3. Do you think that the factors that caused the crisis in the Roman Empire could cause a similar crisis in the Western world of today?

Important Events

Date	Event	Date	Event
30 B.C.E.	Octavian (the future Augustus) conquers Ptolemaic Egypt	70–90 C.E.	New Testament Gospels are written
27 B.C.E.	Augustus inaugurates the principate	80s C.E.	Domitian leads campaigns against multiethnic invaders on northern frontiers
30 C.E.	Jesus crucified in Jerusalem	161–180 C.E.	Marcus Aurelius battles multiethnic bands attacking northern frontiers
64 C.E.	Great fire in Rome; Nero blames Christians	212 C.E.	Caracalla extends Roman citizenship to almost all free inhabitants of the provinces
69 C.E.	Civil war after death of Nero	230s–280s C.E.	Third-century financial and political crisis
70 C.E.	Titus captures Jerusalem and destroys the Jewish temple	249–251 C.E.	Decius persecutes Christians

- Consider three events: **Great fire in Rome; Nero blames Christians (64 C.E.), New Testament Gospels are written (70–90 C.E.)**, and **Decius persecutes Christians (249–251 C.E.)**. How were these persecutions similar to and different from one another, and what attitudes did they illustrate? How might polytheist and Christian ideas have contributed to these events?

SUGGESTED REFERENCES

Scholars continue to debate the nature and the significance of the many social, cultural, and (especially) religious changes that occurred under the early Roman Empire. Perhaps the most difficult question to answer is to what extent life became better or worse for most people—and indeed how to define *better* and *worse* in this context—once the empire stopped expanding into new territories.

Ando, Clifford. *The Matter of the Gods: Religion and the Roman Empire*. 2008.

Crossan, Dominic, and Jonathan Reed. *In Search of Paul: How Jesus's Apostle Opposed Rome's Empire with God's Kingdom*. 2005.

Denzey, Nicola. *The Bone Gatherers: The Lost Worlds of Early Christian Women*. 2007.

*Futrell, Allison. *The Roman Games: Historical Sources in Translation*. 2006.

Galinsky, Karl, ed. *The Cambridge Companion to the Age of Augustus*. 2005.

Goldsworthy, Adrian. *The Complete Roman Army*. 2003.

Green, Bernard. *Christianity in Ancient Rome: The First Three Centuries*. 2010.

Harris, W. V. *Rome's Imperial Economy*. 2010.

*Kraemer, Ross Shephard. *Her Share of the Blessings: Women's Religion among Pagans, Jews, and Christians in the Greco-Roman World*. 1992.

MacMullen, Ramsay. *Christianizing the Roman Empire (A.D. 100–400)*. 1984.

Mattingly, David J. *Imperialism, Power, and Identity: Experiencing the Roman Empire*. 2010.

Matz, David. *Life of the Ancient Romans: Daily Life through History*. 2008.

Roman emperors: http://www.roman-emperors.org/startup.htm

Roth, Roman, and Johannes Keller, eds. "Roman by Integration: Dimensions of Group Identity in Material Culture and Text." Special issue, *Journal of Roman Archaeology* (suppl. no. 66). 2007.

*Suetonius. *Lives of the Caesars*. Trans. Catharine Edwards. 2009.

Syme, Ronald. *The Roman Revolution*. 1939; repr. 2002.

*Tacitus. *The Complete Works*. Trans. Alfred John Church and William Jackson Brodribb. 1964.

*Primary source.

CHAPTER

7

The Transformation of the Roman Empire

284–600 C.E.

In 376, bands of Visigoths, desperate to escape the deadly attacks of the Huns, begged the Roman emperor Valens (r. 364–378) to let them cross the Danube River from their northern homelands into Roman territory.[1] Like emperors before him, Valens admitted them into the empire because he wanted to use their warriors in place of Romans, who could buy their way out of military service by paying for barbarian—that is, northern foreign—mercenaries to substitute for them. Roman officers charged with helping the barbarians instead greedily extorted bribes. They even forced the starving refugees to sell some of their own people into slavery to buy dogs to eat.

Furious, the barbarians massacred Valens's army at the battle of Adrianople in Thrace in 378. Valens trampled on the bleeding corpses of his men as he tried to escape. He did not make it, and his body was never found. Some said he was burned to death while hiding in a farmhouse, fulfilling the wish of citizens who often expressed their unhappiness with his reign by rioting in the streets and yelling, "We want to set Valens on fire alive!" Theodosius I (r. 379–395), Valens's successor, then had to allow the barbarians to settle permanently inside the borders in a kingdom under their own laws and give them annual "gifts" of money, in return for their fighting alongside Romans as federates (allies) protecting the empire.

The battle of Adrianople, Rome's bloodiest defeat since Hannibal invaded Italy six hundred years earlier,

Vandal General Stilicho and His Family

This ivory diptych ("folding tablet") from around 400 C.E. shows Stilicho, the top general in the Roman army in Europe and close adviser to the western Roman emperor, with his wife, Serena, and their son Eucherius. Stilicho's life reveals the mixing of cultures in the later Roman Empire: his father was from the Vandal tribe in Germany and his mother was Roman; he himself rose to prominence in Roman imperial government and society. Serena was the adoptive daughter of the emperor, and Stilicho and Serena's daughter Maria married the emperor's son. Stilicho is shown dressed in the richly decorated clothing appropriate for a member of the Roman elite, and he wears a metal clasp to fasten his robe, a symbol of his father's ethnicity. The images on his shield of the two emperors then ruling the divided Roman Empire proclaim his loyalty even as they point to the political and geographic fragmentation of the time. *(Basilica di San Giovanni Battista, Monza, Italy/The Bridgeman Art Library International.)*

[1]From this point on, dates are C.E. unless otherwise indicated.

illustrates the conflicted relationship that the emperors had with the peoples north and east of the Danube and Rhine Rivers in Europe: for centuries, Rome's rulers, recognizing the barbarians' bravery, had hired them as soldiers and let them bring their families into the empire, while at the same time looking down on them for their non-Roman ways and often allowing imperial officials to exploit them so cruelly that they rebelled. The unintended consequences of this relationship helped change the course of history by pushing the Roman Empire toward division into two halves with different destinies.

Competition between ambitious generals and would-be emperors had driven the empire's third-century political crisis. The emperor Diocletian (r. 284–305) finally restored temporary political stability. Tough enough to impose peace, he was also flexible enough to reorganize the administration by appointing a co-emperor and two assistant emperors. Regaining social stability proved more difficult because of suspicion between Christians and followers of traditional polytheistic cults concerning who was responsible for the divine anger that, they all believed, had sent the crisis. Diocletian convinced his co-rulers to persecute the Christians, whom he blamed. His successor Constantine (r. 306–337) ended the persecution by converting to Christianity and supporting his new faith with imperial funds and a policy of religious freedom. Even with official support, however, it took nearly a hundred years more for Christianity to become the state religion, and the church from early on was rocked by fierce disagreements over doctrine. The social and cultural transformations produced by the Christianization of the Roman Empire settled in even more slowly because many Romans clung to their traditional beliefs; Christian emperors had to employ non-Christians if they wanted to get the best possible administrators and generals.

Diocletian's reform of government only postponed the division of imperial territory: less than twenty years after the battle of Adrianople, Theodosius I split the empire in two, with one of his sons ruling the west and the other the east. The two emperors were supposed to cooperate, but in the long run this system of divided rule could not cope with the different pressures affecting the two regions.

In the western Roman empire, military and political events provoked social and cultural change when barbarian newcomers began living side by side with Romans. Both sides changed, with the barbarians creating kingdoms and laws based on Roman traditions yet adopting Christianity, while wealthy Romans increasingly fled from cities to seek safety in country estates when the western central government became ineffective. These changes in turn transformed the political landscape of western Europe in ways that

Coin Portrait of Emperor Constantine
Constantine had these special, extra-large coins minted to depict him for the first time as an overtly Christian emperor. The jewels on his helmet and crown, the fancy bridle on the horse, and the scepter indicate his status as emperor, while his armor and shield signify his military accomplishments. He proclaims his Christian rule with his scepter's new design—a cross with a globe—and the round badge sticking up from his helmet that carries the monogram signifying "Christ" that he had his soldiers paint on their shields to win God's favor in battle. *(The Art Archive.)*

293 Diocletian creates the tetrarchy

301 Diocletian issues edict on maximum prices and wages

303 Diocletian launches Great Persecution of Christians

312 Constantine wins battle of the Milvian Bridge and converts to Christianity

313 Religious freedom proclaimed in the Edict of Milan

323 Pachomius in Upper Egypt establishes the first monasteries

324 Constantine wins civil war and refounds Byzantium as Constantinople, the "new Rome"

325 Council of Nicaea defends Christian orthodoxy against Arianism

300 C.E. — 350 C.E. — 400 C.E.

361–363 Julian the Apostate tries to reinstate polytheism as official state religion

378 Barbarian massacre of Roman army in battle of Adrianople

391 Theodosius I makes Christianity the official state religion

395 Theodosius I divides empire into western and eastern halves

410 Visigoths sack Rome

foreshadowed Europe's later political states. In the east, the empire, economically vibrant and politically united, lived on for a thousand years beyond its disintegration and transformation in the west and helped pass on the memory of classical traditions to later Western civilization by preserving much ancient Greek and Roman literature. Despite financial pressures and the gradual loss of territory, the eastern half endured as the continuation of the Roman Empire until Turkish invaders conquered it in 1453.

CHAPTER FOCUS What were the most important sources of unity and of division in the Roman Empire from the reign of Diocletian to the reign of Justinian, and why?

From Principate to Dominate in the Late Roman Empire, 284–395

Diocletian and Constantine pulled Roman government from its extended crisis by increasing the emperors' authority, reorganizing the empire's defense, restricting workers' freedom, and changing the tax system to try to raise the money for all these changes. The two emperors also believed that they had to win back divine favor to ensure their people's safety. However, the effort to regain the gods' goodwill was complicated by worry about the growing number of Christians in the empire.

Diocletian and Constantine believed that they had to resolve the empire's problems by becoming more autocratic. Since for Romans strength had to be visible to be effective, they transformed their appearance as rulers to make their power seem awesome beyond compare, taking ideas from the self-presentation of the kings of the powerful contemporary Persian Empire. They hoped that their assertion of supremacy would help keep the empire united. In the long run and for multiple reasons, however, it proved impossible to preserve the empire on the scale once ruled by Augustus.

The Political Transformation and Division of the Roman Empire

The man to make the first attempt to restore and secure the empire was Diocletian. No one could have predicted his rise to power: he began life as an uneducated peasant in the Balkans, far from the center of power in Rome. In the third-century crisis, however, military talent counted for more than connections. Diocletian's leadership, courage, and intelligence propelled him through the ranks until the army made him emperor in 284. He ended a half a century of civil war by imposing the most autocratic system of rule in Roman history.

Inventing the Dominate The foremost symbol of Diocletian's new system was the title that he used after becoming emperor: *dominus*, meaning "lord" or "master"— what slaves called their owners. Historians refer to Roman rule from Diocletian onward as the ***dominate***. Like the emperors before them, the emperors of the dominate continued to refer to their government

dominate: The openly authoritarian style of Roman rule from Diocletian (r. 284–305) onward; the word was derived from *dominus* ("master" or "lord") and contrasted with *principate.*

426 Augustine publishes *The City of God*

451 Council of Chalcedon attempts to forge agreement on Christian orthodoxy

476 German commander Odoacer deposes the final western emperor, the boy Romulus Augustulus ("fall of Rome")

540 Benedict devises his rule for monasteries

450 C.E. 500 C.E. 550 C.E.

475 Visigoths publish law code

493–526 Ostrogothic kingdom in Italy

507 Clovis establishes Frankish kingdom in Gaul

527–565 Reign of eastern Roman emperor Justinian

529–534 Justinian publishes law code and handbooks

as the Roman republic (see, for example, the first line in the document "Diocletian's Edict on Maximum Prices and Wages," page 211), but they ruled autocratically. This new system eliminated the principate's ideal of the princeps ("first man") as the social equal of the senators, with whom he shared political power—the emperors of the dominate recognized no equals. The offices of senator, the consul, and so on from the ancient republic continued to exist but only as posts of honor. These officials had the responsibility to pay for public services, especially chariot races and festivals, but no power to govern. Imperial administrators were increasingly chosen from lower ranks of society according to their competence and their loyalty to the emperor.

The grandiose style of the dominate recalled the monarchies of the Near East rather than the modest manner of Augustus's principate. In particular, the dominate's emperors took ideas for emphasizing their superiority from the Sasanids in Persia, whose empire (224–651) they recognized as equal to their own in power and whose king and queen they addressed as "our brother" and "our sister." The Roman Empire's masters now broadcasted their majesty by surrounding themselves with courtiers and ceremony, presiding from a raised platform, and sparkling in jeweled crowns, robes, and shoes. Constantine took from Persia the tradition that emperors set themselves apart by wearing a diadem, a purple gem-studded headband, as a visible boast of supremacy that recalled the decorated ribbon Alexander the Great put on his head after conquering the Persian king. In another echo of Persian monarchy, a series of veils separated the palace's waiting rooms from the interior room where the emperor listened to people's pleas for help or justice, further emphasizing the difference between the emperor and ordinary people. Officials marked their rank in the rigidly hierarchical administration by wearing special shoes and belts and claiming grandiose titles such as "most perfect."

The dominate's emperors also asserted their supreme power through laws and punishments. Their word alone made law. Indeed, they came to be above the law because they were not bound by anyone else's decisions, not even those of their predecessors. To impose order, they raised punishments to often brutal levels. Violent criminals were executed in traditional fashion: tied in a leather sack with poisonous snakes and drowned in a river. New punishments included Constantine's order that the "greedy hands" of officials who took bribes "shall be cut off by the sword." The guardians of a young girl who allowed a lover to seduce her were executed by having molten lead poured into their mouths. Penalties

The Empire's Four Rulers
This sculpture shows the four rulers of the tetrarchy, the system of shared rule that the emperor Diocletian created in the 290s C.E. to try to administer and defend the Roman Empire more effectively. The sculptor divided the rulers into two pairs, each showing an emperor and a co-emperor (the junior member of the pair). Their gestures symbolize the closeness that the pairs were supposed to display in the tetrarchy, while their nearly identical faces imply that individuality was secondary to cooperation in the new system of governing. Their hands on swords emphasize that they were ready to use force to defend Roman territory and tradition. Originally erected in Constantinople, the capital of the eastern empire, the sculpture was probably looted when crusaders sacked that city in 1204. It was then carried back to Venice, where it was built into the wall of St. Mark's cathedral. *(Basilica di San Marco, Venice, Italy / The Bridgeman Art Library International.)*

grew ever harsher for the majority of the population, legally designated as "humbler people" to indicate they could be punished more severely than the "better people" for comparable offenses. In this way, the dominate strengthened the divisions between ordinary people and the rich.

Subdividing Imperial Rule Diocletian realized that he needed to reform imperial rule to prevent civil war and defend against invaders from the north and the east. The principle underlying his reforms — subdivide the government's power to strengthen it — was daring because it increased the chance of more civil war between ambitious leaders. By 293, he had put the first part of his plan into practice. He divided imperial territory into four loosely defined administrative districts, two in the west and two in the east. He then appointed three "partners" (a co-emperor, Maximian, and two assistant emperors, Constantius and Galerius, who were the designated successors) to join him in this new subdivision of power, called a **tetrarchy** ("rule by four"). Each ruler controlled one of the four districts. Diocletian served as supreme ruler and was supposed to receive the loyalty of the others. This system was Diocletian's attempt to put imperial government into closer contact with the empire's frontier regions, where the dangers of invasion and rebellious troops loomed.

Diocletian also subdivided the territory of the provinces themselves, thereby doubling their number to almost a hundred. He then grouped these smaller administrative units into twelve regions (dioceses) under separate governors, who reported to the four emperors' assistants, the praetorian prefects (Map 7.1). Finally, he tried to prevent provincial

tetrarchy: The "rule by four," consisting of two co-emperors and two assistant emperors/designated successors, initiated by Diocletian to subdivide the ruling of the Roman Empire into four regions.

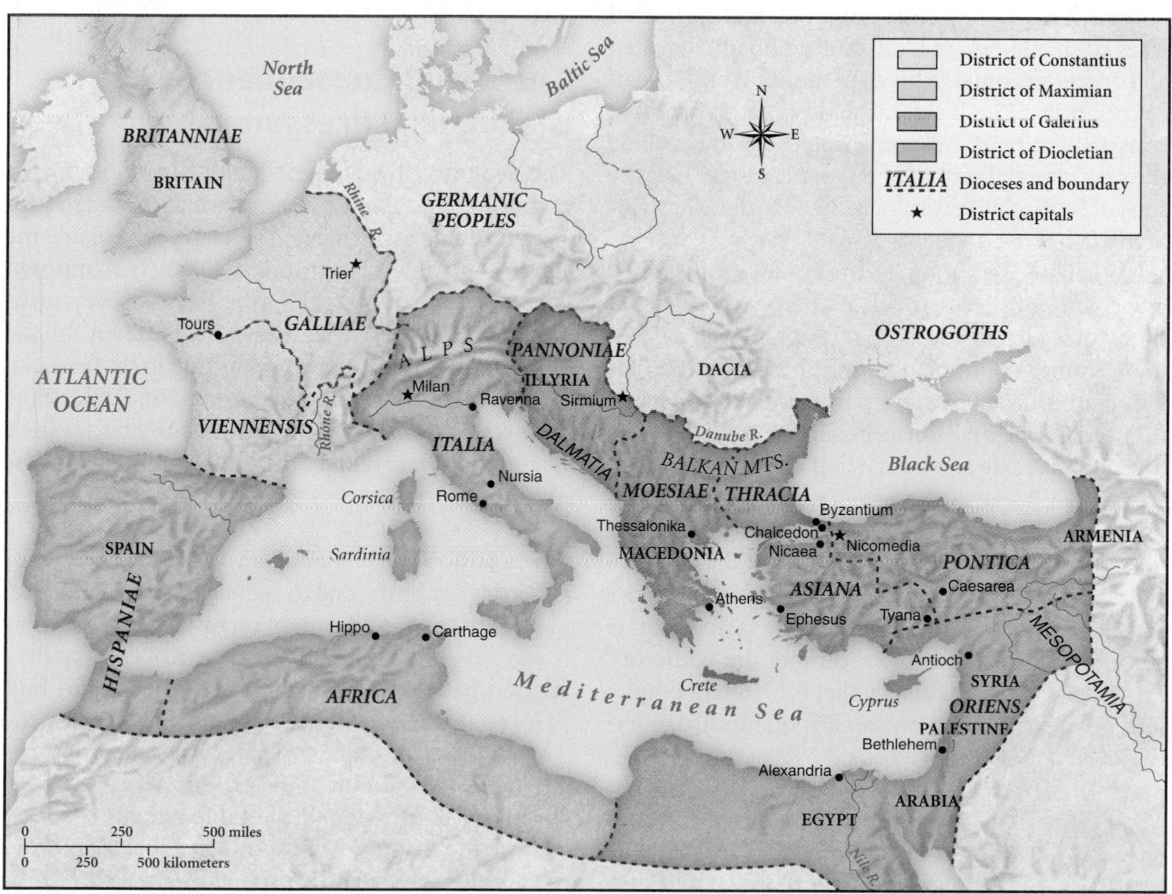

MAP 7.1 Diocletian's Reorganization of 293
Trying to prevent civil war, Emperor Diocletian reorganized Rome's imperial territory into a tetrarchy, to be ruled by himself, his co-emperor Maximian, and assistant emperors Constantius and Galerius, each the head of a large district. He subdivided the preexisting provinces into smaller units and grouped them into twelve dioceses, each overseen by a regional administrator. The four districts as shown here reflect the arrangement recorded by the imperial official Sextus Aurelius Victor in about 360. | **What were the advantages and disadvantages of subdividing the empire?**

administrators from rebelling by separating their civil and military authority—granting them control only of legal and financial affairs while entrusting defense to separate commanders, a process that Constantine completed.

Diocletian's successors dropped the tetrarchy, but his reforms mattered because appointing co-emperors continued to be tried in later times as a way to prevent political instability. His reforms also ended Rome's thousand years as the empire's most important city. Diocletian—who lived in Nicomedia, in Asia Minor—did not even visit Rome until 303, nearly twenty years after becoming emperor. Italy became just another section of the empire, on an equal footing with the other provinces and subject to the same taxation system, except for the district of Rome itself—the last trace of the city's traditional preeminence.

The Creation of the Eastern and Western Empires

Diocletian failed to bring long-lasting political stability to the Roman Empire. He resigned in 305 for unknown reasons, after which rivals for power fought off and on in civil wars until 324, when Constantine finally defeated all contenders outside his own family. At the end of his reign in 337, Constantine designated his three sons as joint heirs, admonishing them to continue the new imperial system of co-emperorship. Like the sons of Septimius Severus a century earlier, they violently failed to cooperate.

When the wars among Constantine's sons ruined any chance of successful co-emperorship, they put their forces in positions that roughly split the Roman Empire on a north–south line along the Balkan peninsula. In 395, Emperor Theodosius made this territorial division official. He intended this division to create an eastern half and a western half of the empire that would be co-ruled and cooperate politically and militarily, but in the long run the empire's halves would be governed largely as de facto separate territories despite the emperors' insistence that the Roman Empire had not been split into two different states.

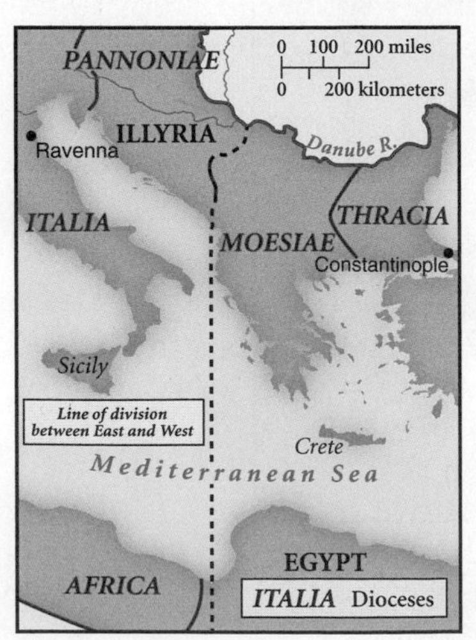

The Empire's East/West Division, 395

Each half had its own capital city. Constantinople ("Constantine's City")—formerly the ancient city of Byzantium (today Istanbul, Turkey)—was the eastern capital. Constantine—who had renamed it after himself in 324, boasting that it was a "new Rome"—had made it his capital because of its strategic military and commercial location: it lay at the mouth of the Black Sea on an easily fortified peninsula astride principal routes for trade and troop movements. To recall the glory of Rome and thus claim for himself the political legitimacy of the old capital, Constantine constructed a forum, an imperial palace, a hippodrome for chariot races, and monumental statues of the traditional gods in his refounded city. Constantinople grew to be the most important city in the Roman Empire.

Geography determined the site of the western capital as well. Honorius, Theodosius's son and successor in the west, wanted his palace in a city that he believed was easy to defend. In 404, he chose the port of Ravenna, an important commercial center on Italy's northeastern coast that housed a main naval base. Great marshes and walls protected it from attack by land, while access to the sea kept it from being starved out in a siege. Though the emperors enhanced it with churches covered in multicolored mosaics, Ravenna never rivaled Constantinople in size or splendor.

The Social Consequences of Financial Pressures

Diocletian's reforms carried high costs, both financial and social. To try to control inflation and to support the huge army needed to keep peace inside the empire and defend its frontiers, Diocletian imposed not only price and wage controls but also a new taxation system. These measures failed, except for the unintended consequence of putting great financial pressures on both rich and poor. Also, Diocletian's new restrictions on people's rights to choose their occupations curtailed freedoms for many in the empire.

Price and Wage Controls and Tax Increases

Diocletian realized it was crucial to reduce the hyperinflation brought on by the third-century civil wars. As prices rose ever higher, people hoarded whatever they could buy. "Hurry and spend all my money you have; buy me any kinds of goods at whatever prices they are available," wrote one official to his servant, trying to salvage something of the value of his savings by converting his money into things. Hoarding, however, only worsened the problem.

In 301, the inflation was so severe that Diocletian imposed harsh price and wage controls in the worst-hit areas (see Document, "Diocletian's Edict on Maximum Prices and Wages," page 211). This mandate, which blamed high prices not on government

DOCUMENT

Diocletian's Edict on Maximum Prices and Wages

In an effort to control high inflation caused by soaring government spending, Diocletian and his co-emperors issued an edict in 301 C.E. setting maximum prices and wages for the first time in Roman history. Their orders proved impossible to enforce across the vast empire. The chances for success were small in any case, as setting fixed prices tends to lead people to reduce production of goods and hoard those that are available. The high-sounding language was typical of imperial bureaucracy under the dominate.

Recalling the wars that we have successfully waged, it is to the fortune of our republic, next to the immortal gods, that we owe the peaceful state of our world, located in the lap of the deepest tranquillity, and the benefits of peace, which we worked for with great effort. Our honorable public and Rome's respectability and majesty long for this fortune to be faithfully established and suitably adorned. Therefore, we, who with the kind support of the gods in the past overcame the blazing raids of the barbarian peoples by slaughtering those nations, must fortify the tranquillity that we established for eternity with the necessary defenses of justice. . . .

It is agreed that we [the co-emperors], who are the parents of the human race, are to bring decisive justice to the situation, so that what humanity has long hoped for but not been able to provide will be conferred by the solutions of our foresight for the common improvement of everyone. . . .

Who then could be unaware that audacity lies in wait to attack the public interest wherever the common well-being of everyone demands that our armies be directed, not only in villages or towns but on every march, jacking up prices for goods for sale not four or eight times, but to such a height that the system of human speech cannot find names for this pricing and this deed. And so the result is that the sale of a single item deprives the soldier of his bonus and his pay, and that all the taxes paid by the entire world to support the armies fall victim to this detestable profit seeking. . . .

It is our decision that, if anyone makes an effort through daring to go against this edict, he shall be subject to capital punishment. . . .

Listed below are the prices for the sale of individual items; no one may exceed them. *[These examples are selections from the edict's long list of maximum allowed prices and wages. A sextarius was about half a liter. The Roman pound was about three-quarters of a U.S. pound. The silver coin was the denarius. A soldier at this date earned eighteen hundred silver coins per year.]*

Prices for food

Sextarius of first-quality old wine, 24 silver coins
Sextarius of country wine, 8 silver coins
Sextarius of beer from Gaul, 4 silver coins
Sextarius of beer from Egypt, 2 silver coins
Pound of pork, 12 silver coins
Pound of goat or sheep, 8 silver coins
Fattened pheasant, 250 silver coins
Pair of chickens, 60 silver coins
Pound of second-quality fish, 16 silver coins

Wages for workers

Daily pay for a farm laborer, with food, 25 silver coins
Daily pay for a finish carpenter, with food, 50 silver coins
Baker, with food, 50 silver coins
Mule doctor, for trimming and preparing hoofs, 6 silver coins per animal
Scribe, for first-quality writing, 25 silver coins per 100 lines
Scribe, for second-quality writing, 20 silver coins per 100 lines
Elementary teacher, 50 silver coins per student per month
Greek, Latin, or geometry teacher, 200 silver coins per student per month
Public speaking teacher, 250 silver coins per student per month
Legal expert or speaker in court, 1,000 silver coins per case

Source: *Diocletiani edictum de pretiis rerum venalium*. Translation by Thomas R. Martin.

Question to Consider

- **What do the maximum prices set reveal about what society most valued in the late Roman Empire?**

spending but on profiteers' "unlimited and frenzied avarice," forbade hoarding of goods and set ceilings on what could legally be charged or paid for about one thousand goods and services. Merchants refused to cooperate, however, and government officials were unable to enforce the mandate, despite the threat of death or exile as the penalty for violations. Diocletian's price and wage controls therefore only increased the financial pressures on the population.

The civil wars that followed Diocletian's resignation stoked the government's insatiable appetite for revenue. The emperors increased taxes mostly to support the army, which required enormous amounts of grain, meat, salt, wine, vegetable oil, horses, camels, and mules. The major sources of revenue were a tax on land, assessed according to its productivity, and a head tax on individuals. To supplement taxes paid in coin, the emperors began collecting some payments in goods and services.

The empire was too large to enforce the tax system uniformly. In some areas both men and women ages twelve to sixty-five paid the full tax, but in others women paid only half the tax assessment or none at all. The reasons for such differences are not

TAKING MEASURE

Peasants' Use of Farm Produce in the Roman Empire

This graph offers a speculative model (precise statistics have not survived) of how peasants during the Roman Empire perhaps used what they produced as farmers and herders to maintain their families, pay rent and taxes, and buy things they did not produce themselves. Individual families would have had widely varying experiences and there were definitely strong regional differences in the vast empire, but it is nevertheless likely that most families had to use most of their production just to maintain a subsistence level—a description of poverty by modern standards.

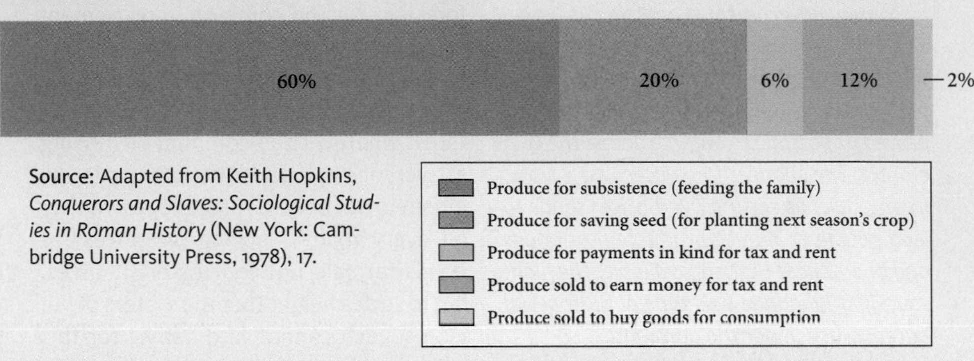

Source: Adapted from Keith Hopkins, *Conquerors and Slaves: Sociological Studies in Roman History* (New York: Cambridge University Press, 1978), 17.

Question to Consider

- **What does the distribution of farmers' produce reveal about priorities, as well as the nature of their life and existence?**

recorded, so we cannot tell whether women were being granted a privilege (perhaps to recognize their role as caregivers for children) or being regarded as less valuable than men and therefore liable to a lower rate. Workers in cities probably owed taxes only on their property, perhaps to encourage crafts production; they periodically paid "in kind," that is, by laboring without pay on public works projects such as cleaning municipal drains or repairing buildings. People in commerce, from shopkeepers to prostitutes, still paid taxes in money, while members of the senatorial class were exempt from ordinary taxes but had to pay special levies.

Social Consequences The new tax system could work only if agricultural production remained stable and the government kept track of the people liable for the head tax (see "Taking Measure," above). Diocletian therefore restricted the movement of tenant farmers, called ***coloni*** ("cultivators"), whose work provided the empire's economic base. Coloni had traditionally been free to move from farm to farm as long as their debts were paid. Now male coloni, as well as their wives in areas where women were assessed for taxes, were increasingly tied to a particular plot of land. Their children were also bound to the family plot, making farming a hereditary obligation.

The government also regulated other occupations deemed essential. Bakers, who were required to produce free bread for Rome's many poor, a tradition begun under the republic to prevent food riots, could not leave their jobs, and anyone who acquired a baker's property had to assume that occupation. From Constantine's reign on, the military was another hereditary lifetime career: the sons of military veterans were obliged to serve in the army. As usual, however, conditions were not the same everywhere in the empire. Free workers earning wages apparently remained important in the economy of Egypt in the late Roman Empire, and archaeological evidence suggests that some regions may actually have become more prosperous. As always, no single or simple description can cover the varieties in the conditions of life in such a vast extent of territories and over long periods of time.

The emperors also decreed oppressive regulations for the **curials**, the social elite in the cities and towns. During this period, many men in the curial class were obliged to serve as decurions (un-

coloni (kuh LOH ny): Literally, "cultivators"; tenant farmers in the Roman Empire who became bound by law to the land they worked and whose children were legally required to continue to farm the same land.

curials (KYUR ee uhls): The social elite in Roman empires' cities and towns, most of whom were obliged to serve as decurions on municipal Senates and collect taxes for the imperial government, paying any shortfalls themselves.

salaried members of their city Senate) and to spend their own funds to support the community. Their financial responsibilities ranged from maintaining the water supply to feeding troops, but their most expensive duty was paying for shortfalls in tax collection. The emperors' demands for more and more revenue made this duty a crushing obligation, compounding the damage that the third-century crisis had inflicted on local elites. Scholars debate how effective imperial regulations were in forcing curials to take on burdensome public service and how deep dissatisfaction with the central government became, but it is clear that the emperors tried hard to squeeze more out of the curials.

For centuries, the empire's welfare had depended on a steady supply of property owners filling local offices in return for honor and the emperor's favor. Now this tradition broke down as some wealthy people avoided public service to escape financial ruin. So distorted had the situation become that service on a municipal council could be imposed as punishment for a crime. Eventually, to prevent curials from escaping their obligations, imperial policy decreed that they could not move away from the town where they had been born. Members of the elite sought exemptions from public service by petitioning the emperor, bribing imperial officials, or taking up an occupation that freed them from curial obligations (the military, imperial administration, or church governance). The most desperate simply fled, abandoning home and property to avoid fulfilling their traditional duties.

The restrictions on personal freedom caused by the pressures for higher taxes contributed to the erosion of communal values that had long motivated wealthy Romans. The drive to increase revenues also produced social discontent among poorer citizens: the tax rate on land eventually reached one-third of the land's gross yield, impoverishing small farmers. Financial troubles, especially severe in the west, kept the empire overall from ever regaining the prosperity of its Golden Age.

From the Great Persecution to Religious Freedom

Diocletian concluded that the gods' anger had caused the empire's third-century crisis. To win back divine goodwill, he called on citizens to follow the ancient gods who had guided Rome to power and virtue in the past: "Through the providence of the immortal gods, eminent, wise, and upright men have in their wisdom established good and true principles. It is wrong to oppose these principles or to abandon the ancient religion for some new one." Christianity was the new faith he meant.

Diocletian's Great Persecution and the Conversion of Constantine

To eliminate what he saw as a threat to national security, Diocletian in 303 launched the so-called **Great Persecution** to please the gods by suppressing Christianity. He expelled Christians from official posts, seized their property, tore down churches, and executed anyone who refused to participate in official religious rituals. His three partners in the tetrarchy applied the policy unevenly. In the western empire, official violence against Christians stopped after about a year; in the east, it continued for a decade. The public executions of Christians were so gruesome that they aroused the sympathy of some polytheists. The Great Persecution, like the edict on prices and wages, ultimately failed: it undermined social stability without destroying Christianity.

Constantine changed the world's religious history forever by converting to the new faith. He had learned to have a favorable view of Christians from his father, one of the empire's co-rulers, and believed that the Christian God brought him victory in a crucial battle that secured his political power. During the civil war that Constantine fought after Diocletian stepped down, before the battle of the Milvian Bridge in Rome in 312, Constantine reportedly experienced a dream promising him God's support and saw Jesus's cross in the sky surrounded by the words "In this sign you will be the victor." Constantine ordered his soldiers to paint "the sign of the cross of Christ" on their shields and won a great victory that ended the civil war. He attributed his success to the Christian God's miraculous power and goodwill, and declared himself a Christian.

Edict of Milan of 313

Following his conversion to the new faith, Constantine did not make polytheism illegal and did not make Christianity the official state religion. Instead, he forced his co-rulers to allow religious freedom, a policy that, following his father's lead, he had put into practice in the west as early as 306. The best evidence for this change survives in the so-called **Edict of Milan** of 313 (see Document, "The Edict of Milan on Religious Freedom," page 214). It proclaimed that Constantine and his polytheist co-emperor Licinius decreed free choice of religion for everyone under

---

Great Persecution: The violent program initiated by Diocletian in 303 to make Christians convert to traditional religion or risk confiscation of their property and even death.

Edict of Milan: The proclamation of Roman co-emperors Constantine and Licinius decreeing free choice of religion in the empire.

DOCUMENT

The Edict of Milan on Religious Freedom

In 313 C.E., Constantine, recently converted to Christianity, and his co-emperor, Licinius, a follower of traditional Roman religion, met to discuss official policy on religion. They agreed to abolish restrictions on Christianity and proclaim religious freedom in the eastern parts of the empire; Constantine had done this as early as 306 in the west. The document contains the letter of instructions later sent to governors in the eastern provinces; it is the best surviving evidence for the new policies. The long sentences (which are shortened here) and lofty language reflect the official imperial style.

When I, Constantine Augustus, and I, Licinius Augustus, had a successful meeting at Milan and discussed everything pertaining to the public benefit and security, among other things that we regarded as going to be of use to many people, we believed that first place should go to those matters having to do with reverence for divinity, so that we might give the Christians and everyone the free power of worshipping in the religion that they wish. In this way, whatever divinity exists in the heavenly seat may be appeased and be kind to us and to all those who are established under our power. And thus, believing that we should initiate this policy on a wholesome and most upright basis, we thought that to no one whatsoever should the opportunity be denied, whether he dedicates his mind to the worship of the Christians or to that religion, which he felt best suited him. Our purpose is so that the highest divinity, whose religion we follow with free minds, may provide his customary favor and kindness in all things. Wherefore it has pleased us for your Devotedness [the provincial governor] to know that all the restrictions on the Christian name set forth in letters given to your office previously are completely removed and that whatever seemed utterly sinister and foreign to our clemency should be repealed, and that now any person of those also wishing to observe the religion of the Christians may strive to do so freely and plainly without any worry or interference. We believed that these things should be made completely clear to your Solicitude so that you would know that we have given a free and absolute permission to these Christians to practice their religion. When you see that we have granted this to them, your Devotedness will know that we have likewise conceded an open and free power to others to practice their religion for the sake of the tranquillity of our age, so that each person may have free permission to worship in the manner he has chosen. We did this so that we shall not seem to have detracted from any observance or religion.

[The emperors next order people who bought or received Christians' property confiscated in the Great Persecution to return it at no cost and then to apply to an imperial representative for reimbursement through the emperors' "clemency."]

On all these matters you will be obligated to provide your most effectual aid to the body of Christians mentioned above, so that our orders may be carried out more quickly, whereby public tranquillity may be served also by our clemency. In this way it will happen, as was explained above, that divine favor toward us, which we have experienced in so many things, will endure for all time to give prosperity to our successes in company with the public happiness. Moreover, so that the content of this ordinance and of our kindness may come to everyone's attention, it should be put up everywhere above an announcement of your own and brought to the knowledge of everyone, so that this ordinance of our kindness shall not be concealed.

Source: Lactantius, *On the Deaths of the Persecutors*, 48, and Eusebius, *Ecclesiastical History*, 10.5.2–14. Translation by Thomas R. Martin.

Question to Consider

■ **What reasons do Constantine and Licinius give for instituting this new policy of religious freedom?**

their rule and referred to protection of the empire by "the highest divinity"—an imprecise term meant to satisfy both polytheists and Christians.

Constantine tried to avoid angering traditional polytheists, who still greatly outnumbered Christians, but he also promoted his newly chosen religion. These conflicting goals called for a careful balancing act that continued the principle of subdividing power to try to maintain order and stability. In this case, he subdivided official support and respect for religion. For example, he returned all property confiscated from Christians during the Great Persecution, but he had the treasury compensate those who had bought it. When in 321 he made the Lord's Day of each week a holy occasion on which no official business or manufacturing work could be performed, he called it Sunday to blend Christian and traditional notions in honoring two divinities, God and the sun. He decorated his new capital of Constantinople with statues of traditional gods. Above all, he respected tradition by continuing to hold the office of *pontifex maximus* ("chief priest"), which emperors had filled ever since Augustus.

REVIEW QUESTION What were Diocletian's policies to end the third-century crisis, and how successful were they?

The Official Christianization of the Empire, 312–c. 540

Constantine's conversion in 312 set the empire on the path to official Christianization. The process was gradual: not until the end of the fourth century was Christianity proclaimed the state religion, and even after that many people for a long time continued to worship the traditional gods in private. Eventually, however, Christianity became the religion of the overwhelming majority by attracting converts among women and men of all classes, assuring believers of personal salvation, offering the social advantages and security of belonging to the emperors' religion, nourishing a strong sense of shared identity and community, developing a hierarchy to govern the church, and creating communities of devoted monks (male and female). The transformation from polytheist empire into Christian state was the Roman Empire's most important influence on Western civilization.

Polytheism and Christianity in Competition

Since almost everyone in the Roman Empire believed that religion was fundamental to the safety and prosperity of the community and the individual, polytheism and Christianity were in a serious competition for people's faith. (See "Seeing History," page 216.) Polytheists and Christians shared some similar beliefs. Both, for example, regarded spirits and demons as powerful and ever-present forces in life. Over time, the two competing faiths influenced each other to a limited degree. Some polytheists focused their beliefs on a supreme god who seemed almost monotheistic; some Christians took ideas from Neoplatonist philosophy. Some people perhaps merged the two faiths: a silver spoon used in the worship of the polytheist forest spirit Faunus, for example, has been found engraved with the outline of a fish, the common symbol whose Greek spelling (*ichthys*) was taken as an acronym for the Greek words "Jesus Christ the Son of God, the Savior." Some scholars think this image indicates a combination of pagan and Christian beliefs in the same cult.

The Persistence of Polytheism

Unbridgeable differences remained, however, between the beliefs of traditional polytheists and Christians. People disagreed over whether there was one God or many, and what degree of interest the divinity (or divinities) paid to the human world. Most polytheists participated in frequent festivals and sacrifices to many different gods. Why, they wondered, were these joyous occasions not enough to satisfy everyone's need for contact with divinity?

Polytheists also could not accept a divine savior who promised eternal salvation for believers but had apparently lacked the will or the power to overthrow Roman rule and prevent his own execution as a rebel. The traditional gods, by contrast, had given their worshippers a world empire. Moreover, polytheists could say, cults such as that of the goddess Isis and philosophies such as Stoicism insisted that only the pure of heart and mind could be admitted to their fellowship. Christians, by contrast, embraced sinners. Why, wondered perplexed polytheists, would anyone want to associate with such people? In short, as the Greek philosopher Porphyry argued, Christians had no right to claim they possessed the sole version of religious truth, for no one had ever discovered a doctrine that provided "the sole path to the liberation of the soul."

The slow pace of Christianization revealed how strong polytheism remained in this period, especially at the highest social levels. In fact, the emperor known as **Julian the Apostate** (r. 361–363) rebelled against his family's Christianity—the word *apostate* means "renegade from the faith"—by trying to reverse official support of the new religion in favor of his own less

Julian the Apostate: The Roman emperor (r. 361–363), who rejected Christianity and tried to restore traditional religion as the state religion. *Apostate* means "renegade from the faith."

Relief Sculpture of Saturn from North Africa

This pillar depicts the solar divinity known to Romans as Saturn and to Carthaginians as Ba'al Hammon, from the cult of the Phoenician founders of Carthage. This syncretism (identifying deities as the same even though they carried different names in different places) was typical of ancient polytheism and allowed Roman and non-Roman cults to merge. The inscription dates the pillar to 323. Other objects testify to the prevalence of polytheistic cults in the Roman Empire until the end of the fourth century. What in this sculpture indicates that it depicts a god? *(© Martha Cooper/Peter Arnold, Inc./photolibrary.)*

SEEING HISTORY

Changing Religious Beliefs: Pagan and Christian Sarcophagi

Christianity became Rome's state religion in 391 when the emperor Theodosius I banned polytheist sacrifices, but the Christianization of the empire had begun long before. Over time, Christians found ways to testify publicly to their beliefs, often making creative use of methods previously employed to honor Rome's traditional gods. We can see this process in action by comparing scenes from two sarcophagi (stone coffins), one from the first century and one from the mid-fourth century. These decorated coffins were meant to be seen, not hidden in the ground, to make a statement about their owner's beliefs.

The left-hand image, from a pagan Roman sarcophagus, shows a religious procession by members of the cult of the god Dionysus. The worship of Dionysus as god of wine and theater was so complex

Scene of a Procession in Honor of the God Dionysus. Marble Sarcophagus, Roman, First Century C.E. *(Erich Lessing/Art Resource, NY.)*

traditional and more philosophical interpretation of polytheism. Like Christians, he believed in a supreme deity, but he based his religious beliefs on Greek philosophy when he said, "This divine and completely beautiful universe, from heaven's highest arch to earth's lowest limit, is tied together by the continuous providence of god, has existed ungenerated eternally, and is imperishable forever."

Making Christianity Official

Julian was killed in a military expedition against Persia, and the succeeding emperors were Christians. They provided financial support for their religion while denying it to traditional cults. They dropped the title *pontifex maximus* and ceased government-funded sacrifices. Symmachus (c. 340–402), a polytheist senator who also served as prefect (mayor) of Rome, objected to this suppression of religious diversity. In a last public plea for religious freedom, he echoed Porphyry: "We all have our own way of life and our own way of worship. . . . So vast a mystery cannot be approached by only one path."

Christianity officially replaced polytheism as the state religion in 391 when **Theodosius I** enforced a

Theodosius I: The Roman emperor (r. 379–395) who made Christianity the state religion by ending public sacrifices in the traditional cults and closing their temples. In 395 he also divided the empire into western and eastern halves to be ruled by his sons.

as even to seem contradictory, ranging from violent passion to peaceful rest; it showed both the good that could come from pleasure and the evil that resulted from going too far. Lively processions in his honor, some led by women, were popular. Dionysus is shown here in one of his many different forms: a chubby, lusty, old drunkard, whom the Romans called Bacchus. He reclines on a cart with a jar of wine, pulled by a horse and some kind of half man, half beast, perhaps a centaur. His entourage also includes female musicians, who dance along playing horns and beating tambourines. What other details can you make out? Do they offer hints about the values of the cult of Dionysus?

Compare this scene with the one shown on the right, a detail from the most spectacular surviving example of an early Christian sarcophagus. This coffin, from 359, held the remains of Junius Bassus, a prominent Roman official. Carved from marble in a classical style, the scenes are all taken from the Bible and center on the story of Christ. The absence of references to polytheistic mythology, which had been standard on earlier Christian sarcophagi, illustrates Christians' growing confidence in their own religious traditions, which they display in the same way that pagans had previously done. What accounts for the position of Adam's and Eve's hands? What do the scenes suggest about the roles of women in pagan and Christian religion?

Adam and Eve on the Sarcophagus of Junius Bassus, 359 C.E. *(Erich Lessing/Art Resource, NY.)*

Question to Consider

■ **What similarities and differences do you see in these two images, and what do they suggest about the religious traditions by which they are inspired?**

ban on polytheist sacrifices, even if private individuals paid for the animals. He also announced that all polytheist temples had to close. Nevertheless, some famous shrines, such as the Parthenon in Athens, remained open for a long time. Pagan temples were gradually converted to churches during the fifth and sixth centuries. Non-Christian schools were not forced to close — the Academy, founded by Plato in Athens in the early fourth century B.C.E., endured for 140 years after Theodosius's reign — but Christians received advantages in official careers.

Jews posed a special problem for the Christian emperors. They seemed entitled to special treatment because Jesus had been a Jew. Previous emperors had allowed Jews to practice their religion, but the Christian emperors now burdened them with legal restrictions. Imperial decrees banned Jews from holding government posts but still required them to assume the financial burdens of curials without the status. By the late sixth century, the law barred Jews from marrying Christians, making wills, receiving inheritances, or testifying in court.

These restrictions began the long process that made Jews into second-class citizens in later European history, but they did not destroy Judaism. Magnificent synagogues had appeared in Palestine, where some Jews still lived, though most had been dispersed throughout the cities of the empire and the lands to the east. Jewish scholarship flourished in this period, culminating in the vast fifth-century C.E.

texts known as the Palestinian and the Babylonian Talmuds (learned opinions on the Mishnah, a collection of Jewish law) and the Midrash (commentaries on parts of Hebrew Scripture). These extremely detailed records of centuries of argument over everything from philosophical ideas to the rules for daily life eventually became authoritative for many Jews in medieval and modern Europe.

Christianity's Growing Appeal By the end of the fourth century, Christianity had been finding converts outside the Jewish community for three hundred years. Now that the faith had an official status, it attracted even more new believers, especially in the military. Since their emperors were now Christian, soldiers could convert and still serve in the army; previously, Christians had sometimes created disciplinary problems by renouncing their military oath. At his court-martial in 298 for refusing to continue his duties, one senior infantryman had said, "A Christian serving the Lord Christ should not serve the affairs of this world." Once the emperors had become Christians, however, soldiers saw military duty as serving Christ's regime.

Christianity's social values contributed to its appeal by offering believers a strong sense of shared identity and community in this world. Since the time of Paul, when Christians traveled, they could find a warm welcome in the local congregation (Map 7.2). The faith had also won converts from early on by promoting the tradition of charitable works characteristic of Judaism and some polytheist cults, which emphasized caring for poor people, widows, and orphans. By the mid-third century, for example, Rome's Christian congregation was supporting fifteen hundred widows and poor people. Fellowship and philanthropy to support believers in need contributed to the faith's growth.

Women were deeply involved in the new faith. **Augustine** (354–430), bishop of Hippo, in North Africa, and perhaps the most influential theologian in Western civilization, recognized women's contribution to the strengthening of Christianity in a letter he wrote to the unbaptized husband of a baptized woman: "O you men, who fear all the burdens imposed by baptism! Your women easily best you. Chaste and devoted to the faith, it is their presence in large numbers that causes the church to grow." Women could win a high reputation by giving their property to their congregation or by renouncing marriage to dedicate themselves to Christ. Consecrated virgins who chose not to marry and widows who chose not to remarry thus joined large donors as especially respected women. These women's choices challenged the traditional social order, in which women were supposed to devote themselves to raising families. Even these sanctified women, however, were largely excluded from leadership positions as the church's hierarchy came more closely to resemble the male-dominated world of imperial rule. There were still some women leaders in the church even in the fourth century, but they were a small minority.

Jesus as Sun God

This heavily damaged mosaic, perhaps from the mid-third century, depicts Jesus like the Greek god of the sun, Apollo, riding in a chariot pulled by horses with rays of light shining forth around his head. This symbolism—God is light—reached back to ancient Egypt. Christian artists used it to portray Jesus because he had said, "I am the light of the world" (John 8:12). The mosaic artist arranged the sunbeams to suggest the shape of the Christian cross. The cloak flaring from Jesus's shoulder suggests the spread of his motion across the heavens. *(Scala / Art Resource, NY.)*

Augustine: Bishop in North Africa whose writings defining religious orthodoxy made him the most influential theologian in Western civilization.

Hierarchy in the Church The need to organize believers to support the Christianization of the Roman Empire led to the creation of a hierarchy based on the authority of male bishops in charge of groups of congregations in different regions. That hierarchy replaced early Christianity's relatively loose communal organization, in which many women held leadership posts. Over time, the bishops replaced the curials as the emperors' partners in local rule, in return earning the right to control the distribution of imperial subsidies to the people. Regional councils of bishops appointed new bishops and addressed doctrinal disputes. There were regional differences concerning whether some bishops should outrank other bishops in the area, but bishops in the largest cities eventually became the most powerful leaders in the church. The main bishop of Carthage, for example, oversaw at least a hundred local bishops in the surrounding area. The bishop of Rome eventually emerged as the church's supreme leader in the western empire, claiming for himself a title previously applied to many bishops: pope (from *pappas*, a child's word for "father" in Greek), the designation still used for the head of the Roman Catholic church. Christians in the eastern empire never conceded this title to the bishop of Rome, however.

The bishops of Rome claimed they had leadership over other bishops on the basis of the New Testament, where Jesus addresses Peter, his head apostle: "You are Peter, and upon this rock I will build my church. . . . I will entrust to you the keys of the kingdom of heaven. Whatever you bind on earth shall be bound in heaven. Whatever you loose on earth shall be loosed in heaven" (Matt. 16:18–19). Noting that Peter's name in Greek means "rock" and that Peter had founded the Roman church, bishops in Rome eventually argued that they had the right to command the church as Peter's successors.

Portrait of Augustine
This fresco (painting on plaster) from the Lateran Basilica in Rome is the oldest surviving portrait of Augustine. It shows him reading a book in the form of a codex (that is, as books are made today, with bound pages instead of one long scroll of paper). This was an appropriate pose since Augustine was one of the most widely read scholars of the Roman Empire, as well as perhaps its most productive author, writing countless works on Christian thought and doctrine. *(The Granger Collection, NY—All rights reserved.)*

The Struggle for Clarification in Christian Belief

Jesus himself left no written teachings, and early Christians frequently argued over what their savior had meant them to believe. The church's expanding hierarchy struggled to establish clarity concerning what Christians should believe to ensure its members' spiritual purity. Bishops as well as rank-and-file believers often disagreed about theology, however, and doctrinal disputes repeatedly threatened the unity of the church.

Controversy centered on what was orthodoxy and what was heresy. (See Chapter 6, page 194.) After Christianity became official, the emperor was ultimately responsible for enforcing orthodox creed (a summary of correct beliefs) and could use force to compel agreement when disputes led to violence.

Arguing about God: Arianism Theological questions about the nature of the Christian Trinity—Father, Son, and Holy Spirit, three seemingly separate deities nevertheless conceived by orthodox believers to be a unified, co-eternal, and identical divinity—proved the hardest to clarify. The doctrine called **Arianism** generated fierce controversy for centuries. Named after its founder, Arius (c. 260–336), a priest from Alexandria, it maintained

---

Arianism: The Christian doctrine named after Arius, who argued that Jesus was "begotten" by God and did not have an identical nature with God the Father.

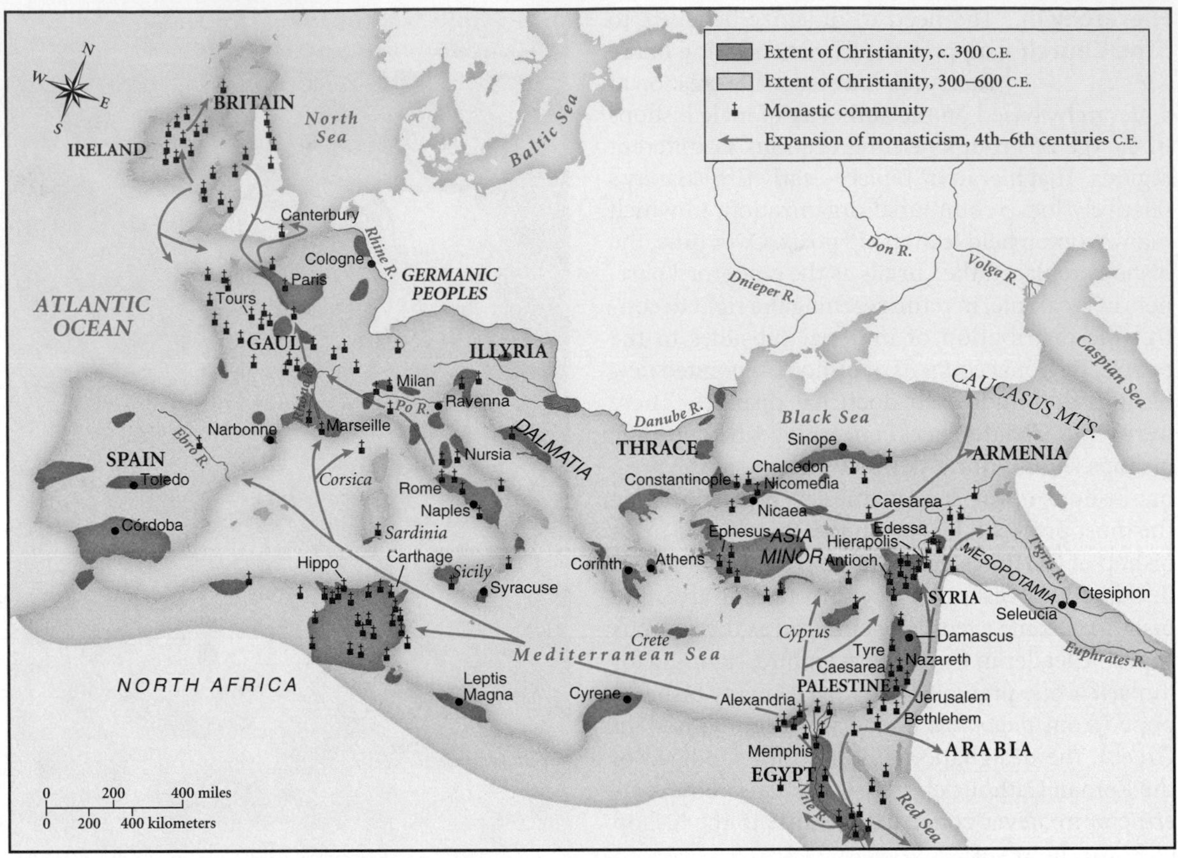

MAP 7.2 The Spread of Christianity, 300–600

Christians were a minority in the Roman Empire in 300, although congregations existed in many cities and towns, especially in the eastern provinces. The emperor Constantine's conversion to Christianity in the early fourth century gave a boost to the new religion. It gained further strength during that century as the Christian emperors supported it financially and eliminated subsidies for the polytheist cults that had previously made up the religion of the state. By 600, Christians were numerous in all parts of the empire. *(From Henry Chadwick and G. R. Evans,* Atlas of the Christian Church *[Oxford: Andromeda Oxford Ltd., 1987], 28. Reproduced by permission of Andromeda Oxford Limited.)*

that God the Father begot (created) his son Jesus from nothing and gave him his special status. Thus, Jesus was not identical with God the Father and was, in fact, dependent on him. This view of Jesus as secondary did not fit with others' ideas about the nature of the Holy Trinity. Arianism found widespread support — the emperor Valens and his barbarian opponents were Arian Christians. Many people found this doctrine appealing because it eliminated the difficulty of understanding how a son could be the equal of his father and because its subordination of son to father corresponded to the norms of family life. Arius used popular songs to make his views known, and people everywhere became engaged in the controversy. "When you ask for your change from a shopkeeper," one observer remarked in describing Constantinople, "he harangues you about the Begotten and the Unbegotten. If you inquire how much bread costs, the reply is that 'the Father is superior and the Son inferior.'"

Disputes such as this led Constantine to try to restore ecclesiastical peace and lead the bishops in clarifying religious truth. In 325, he convened 220 bishops at the Council of Nicaea to discuss Arianism. The majority of bishops voted to come down hard on the heresy: they banished Arius to Illyria, a rough Balkan region, and declared in the **Nicene Creed** that the Father and the Son were *homoousion* ("of one substance") and co-eternal. So difficult were the issues, however, that Constantine later changed his mind twice, first recalling Arius from exile and then reproaching him again not long after. The doctrine lived on: Constantine's third son, Constantius II

Nicene Creed: The doctrine agreed on by the council of bishops convened by Constantine at Nicaea in 325 to defend orthodoxy against Arianism. It declared that God the Father and Jesus were *homoousion* ("of one substance").

Mosaic of a Family from Edessa
This mosaic, found in a cave tomb from c. 218–238 C.E., depicts an elite family from Edessa in the late Roman Empire. Their names are given in Syriac, the dialect of Aramaic spoken in their region, and their colorful clothing reflects local Iranian traditions. The mosaic's border uses decorative patterns from Roman art, illustrating the combining of cultural traditions in the Roman Empire. Edessa was the capital of the small kingdom of Osrhoëne, annexed by Rome in 216. It became famous in Christian history because its king Abgar (r. 179–216) was the first monarch to convert to Christianity, well before Constantine. The eastern Roman emperors proclaimed themselves the heirs of King Abgar. *(Photo by J. B. Segal, one of the authors, from* Vanished Civilizations: Forgotten Peoples of the Ancient World, *ed. by Edward Bacon, 1967. London: Thames and Hudson.)*

(r. 337–361), favored Arianism, and his missionaries converted many of the non-Roman peoples who later poured into the empire.

Monophysitism, Nestorianism, and Donatism Numerous other disputes about the nature of Christ divided believers. The orthodox position held that Jesus's divine and human natures commingled within his person but remained distinct. Monophysites (a Greek term for "single nature believers") argued that the divine took precedence over the human in Jesus and that he therefore had essentially only a single nature. They split from the orthodox hierarchy in the sixth century to found independent churches in Egypt (the Coptic church), Ethiopia, Syria, and Armenia.

Nestorius, who became the bishop of Constantinople in 428, argued that Mary in giving birth to Jesus produced the human being who became the temple for the indwelling God. Nestorianism therefore offended Christians who accepted the designation of *theotokos* (Greek for "bearer of God") for Mary. The bishops of Alexandria and Rome had Nestorius deposed and his doctrines officially rejected at councils held in 430 and 431; they condemned his writings in 435. Refusing to accept these decisions, Nestorian bishops in the eastern empire formed a separate church centered in Persia, where for centuries Nestorian Christians flourished under the tolerance of non-Christian rulers. They later became important agents of cultural diffusion by establishing communities that still endure in Arabia, India, and China.

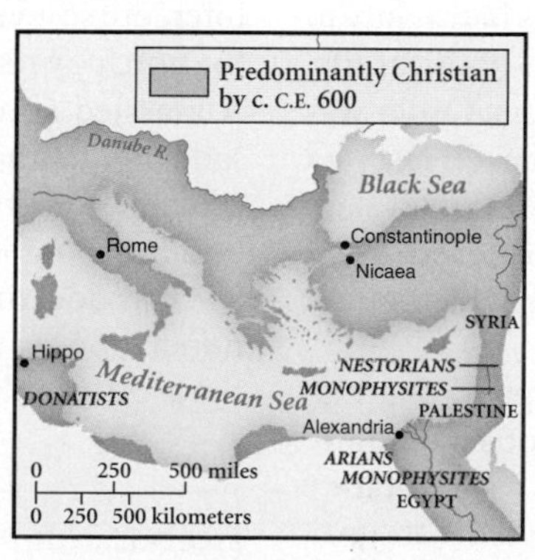

Original Areas of Christian Splinter Groups

Donatism best illustrates the level of ferocity that Christian disputes could generate. A conflict erupted in North Africa not over theology but over whether to readmit to their old congregations Christians who had cooperated with imperial authorities during the Great Persecution. The Donatists (followers of the North African priest Donatus) insisted that the church should not be polluted with such "traitors." So bitter was the clash that it even broke apart Christian families. One son threatened his mother, "I will join Donatus's followers, and I will drink your blood."

With emotions at a fever pitch, the church promoted orthodoxy as religious truth. A council organized in Chalcedon (a suburb of Constantinople) in 451 to settle the still-raging disagreement over Nestorius's views was the most important attempt to clarify orthodoxy. The conclusions of the Council of Chalcedon form the basis of what most Christians in the West still accept as doctrine. At the time, however, it failed to create unanimity, especially in the eastern empire, where Monophysites flourished.

Augustine on Order

The ideas of Augustine contributed largely to Christian orthodoxy in the western empire. By around 500, Augustine and other influential theologians such as Ambrose (c. 339–397) and Jerome (c. 345–420) earned the informal title *church fathers* because their views were cited as authoritative in disputes over orthodoxy. Augustine became the most famous of this group of patristic (from *pater*, Greek for "father") authors, and for the next thousand years his works would be the most influential texts in western Christianity except the Bible. He wrote so prolifically about religion and philosophy that a later scholar was moved to declare: "The man lies who says he has read all your works."

Augustine deeply affected later thinkers with his views on order in human life, expressed in *The City of God*, a "large and arduous work," as he called it, published in 426 after thirteen years of writing. In it, Augustine asserted that the basic dilemma for humans lay between the desire for earthly pleasures and the desire for spiritual purity. Emotion, especially love, was natural and commendable, but only when directed toward God. Humans were misguided to look for any value in life on earth. Only life in God's eternal city at the end of time had meaning.

Nevertheless, Augustine wrote, law and government are required on earth because humans are imperfect. God's original creation was perfect, but after Adam and Eve disobeyed God, humans lost their initial perfection and inherited a permanently flawed nature. According to this doctrine of original sin—a subject of theological debate since at least the second century—Adam and Eve's disobedience passed down to human beings a hereditary moral disease that made the human will a divisive force. This corruption necessitated governments that could suppress evil. The state therefore had a duty to compel people to remain loyal to the church, by force if necessary.

For Augustine, the purpose of secular authority was to maintain a social order based on a moral order. To help maintain order, Christians had a duty to obey the emperor and participate in political life. Soldiers, too, had to follow their orders. Order was so essential, Augustine argued, that it even justified what he admitted was the unjust institution of slavery. Although detesting slavery, he believed it was a lesser evil than the social disorder that he thought its abolition would create.

In *The City of God*, Augustine argued that history has a divine purpose, even if people could not see it. All that Christians could know with certainty was that history progressed toward an ultimate goal, but only God could know the meaning of each day's events:

> To be truthful, I myself fail to understand why God created mice and frogs, flies and worms. Nevertheless, I recognize that each of these creatures is beautiful in its own way. For when I contemplate the body and limbs of any living creature, where do I not find proportion, number, and order exhibiting the unity of concord? Where one discovers proportion, number, and order, one should look for the craftsman.

The repeated *I* in this passage indicates the intense personal engagement Augustine brought to matters of faith and doctrine. Many other Christians shared this intensity, a trait that energized their disagreements over orthodoxy and heresy.

Augustine and Sexual Desire

Next to the nature of Christ, the question of how to understand and regulate sexual desire presented Christians with the thorniest problem in the search for religious truth. Augustine became the most influential source of the idea that sex trapped human beings in evil and that they should therefore strive for **asceticism**, the practice of self-denial, especially through spiritual discipline. Augustine knew from personal experience how difficult it was to accept this doctrine. In his autobiographical work *Confessions*, written about 397, he described the deep conflict he felt between his sexual desires and his religious beliefs. Only after a long period of reflection and doubt, he wrote, did he find the inner strength to commit to chastity as part of his conversion to Christianity.

He advocated sexual abstinence as the highest course for Christians because he believed that Adam and Eve's disobedience had forever ruined the perfect harmony God created between the human will and human passions. According to Augustine, God punished his disobedient children by making sexual desire a disruptive force that human will would always struggle to control. He reaffirmed the value of marriage in God's plan, but he insisted that sexual intercourse even between loving spouses carried the unhappy reminder of humanity's fall from grace. A married couple should "descend with a certain sadness" to the task of procreation, the only acceptable reason for sex; sexual pleasure could never be a human good.

This doctrine ennobled virginity and sexual renunciation as the highest virtues; in the words of the ascetic biblical scholar Jerome, they counted as

---

asceticism (uh SEH tuh sih zuhm): The practice of self-denial, especially through spiritual discipline; a doctrine for Christians emphasized by Augustine.

"daily martyrdom." By the end of the fourth century, Christians valued virginity as an ascetic virtue so highly that congregations began to call for virgin ministers and bishops.

The Emergence of Christian Monks

Christian asceticism reached its peak with the emergence of monks: men and women who withdrew from everyday society to live a life of extreme self-denial imitating Jesus's suffering, while praying for divine mercy on the world. In this movement, called monasticism, monks at first lived alone, but soon they formed communities for mutual support in the pursuit of holiness.

The Appeal of Monasticism Polytheists and Jews had strong ascetic traditions, but Christian monasticism was distinctive for the huge numbers of people drawn to it and the high status that they earned in the Christian population. Monks' fame came from their rejection of ordinary pleasures and comforts. They left their families and congregations, renounced sex, worshipped almost constantly, wore rough clothes, and ate so little they were always starving. To achieve inner peace detached from daily concerns, monks fought a constant spiritual battle against fantasies of earthly delights—plentiful, tasty food and the joys of sex.

The earliest monks emerged in Egypt in the second half of the third century. Antony (c. 251–356), the son of a well-to-do family, was among the first to renounce regular existence. After hearing a sermon stressing Jesus's command to a rich young man to sell his possessions and give the proceeds to the poor (Matt. 19:21), he left his property in about 285 and withdrew into the desert to devote the rest of his life to worshipping God through extreme self-denial.

Antony achieved fame for his ascetic life, illustrating a main appeal of monasticism: the chance to achieve excellence and recognition, a traditional ideal in the ancient Western world. This opportunity seemed especially valuable after the end of the Great Persecution. Becoming a monk—a living martyrdom—not only served as the substitute for dying a martyr's death but also emulated the sacrifice of Christ. Hermit monks went to great lengths to attract attention to their dedication. In Syria, "holy women" and "holy men" sought fame through feats of pious endurance; Symeon (390–459), for example, lived atop a tall pillar for thirty years, preaching to the people gathered at the foot of his perch. Egyptian Christians came to believe that their monks' supreme piety made them living heroes who ensured the annual flooding of the Nile, an event once associated with the pharaohs' religious power.

The influence of ascetics with reputations for exceptional holiness continued after their deaths. In a Christian tradition that had originated with martyrs, the relics of dead holy men and women—body parts or clothing—became treasured sources of protection and healing. Projecting the enduring power of saints (people venerated after their deaths for their holiness), relics gave believers faith in divine favor. Christian reverence for relics continued a more long-standing tradition: the fifth-century B.C.E. Athenians, for example, had believed that good fortune followed from the recovery of bones identified as the remains of Theseus, their legendary founder.

The Rise of Monastic Communities In about 323, an Egyptian Christian named Pachomius organized the first monastic community, establishing the tradition of single-sex settlements of male or female monks helping one another along the harsh path to holiness. This communal monasticism dominated Christian asceticism ever after. Communities of men and women were often built close together to share labor, with women making clothing, for example, while men farmed.

Some monasteries imposed military-style discipline, but there were large differences in the degree of control of the monks and the extent of contact allowed with the outside world (see the illustration on page 224). Some groups strove for complete self-sufficiency to avoid transactions with outsiders. The most isolationist groups lived in the eastern empire, but the followers of Martin of Tours (c. 316–397), an ex-soldier famed for his pious deeds, founded communities in the west as austere as any. Basil of Caesarea (c. 330–379), in Asia Minor, started an alternative tradition of monasteries in service to society. Basil (later dubbed "the Great") required monks to perform charitable deeds, especially ministering to the sick, a development that led to the foundation of the first hospitals, attached to monasteries.

A milder code of monastic conduct became the standard in the west beginning about 540. Called the Benedictine rule after its creator, Benedict of Nursia (c. 480–553), in central Italy, it mandated the monastery's daily routine of prayer, scriptural readings, and manual labor. This was the first time in Greek and Roman history that physical work was seen as noble, even godly. The rule divided the day into seven parts, each with a compulsory service of prayers and lessons, called the office. Unlike the harsh regulations of other monastic communities, Benedict's code did not isolate the monks from the outside world or deprive them of sleep, adequate food, or warm clothing. Although it gave the abbot (the head monk) full authority, it instructed him to listen to other members of the community before deciding important matters. He was not allowed to beat disobedient monks, as sometimes happened under other systems. Communities of women, such as those founded by Basil's sister Macrina and Benedict's sister Scholastica, generally followed the rules of the male monasteries, with an emphasis on the decorum thought necessary for women.

The thousands upon thousands of Christians who joined monasteries from the fourth century onward abandoned the outside world for social as well as theological reasons. Monastic piety held special appeal for women and the rich, as women could achieve greater status and respect for their holiness than ordinary life allowed them, while the rich could win fame on earth and hope for favor in heaven by endowing monasteries with large gifts of money. Jerome wrote, "[As monks,] we evaluate people's virtue not by their gender but by their character, and deem those to be worthy of the greatest glory who have renounced both status and riches." Some monks did not choose their life; monasteries took in children from parents who could not raise them or who, in a practice called oblation, gave them up to fulfill pious vows. Jerome once advised a mother who decided to send her young daughter to a monastery:

> Let her be brought up in a monastery, let her live among virgins, let her learn to avoid swearing, let her regard lying as an offense against God, let her be ignorant of the world, let her live the angelic life, while in the flesh let her be without the flesh, and let her suppose that all human beings are like herself.

When the girl reached adulthood as a virgin, he added, she should avoid the baths so that she would not be seen naked or give her body pleasure by dipping in the warm pools. Jerome emphasized tradi-

Monastery of St. Catherine at Mount Sinai

The sixth-century eastern Roman emperor Justinian built a wall to protect this monastery in the desert at the foot of Mount Sinai (on the peninsula between Egypt and Arabia). Justinian fortified the monastery to promote orthodoxy in a region dominated by Monophysite Christians. The monastery gained its name in the ninth century when the story was circulated that angels had recently brought the body of Catherine of Alexandria there. Catherine was said to have been martyred in the fourth century for refusing to marry the emperor because, in her words, she was the bride of Christ. *(Erich Lessing/Art Resource, NY.)*

tional values favoring males when he promised that God would reward the mother with the birth of sons in compensation for the dedication of her daughter.

Since monasteries were self-governing, they could find themselves in conflict with the church leadership. Bishops resented members of their congregations who withdrew into monasteries, especially because they then gave money and property to their new community instead of to their local churches. Moreover, monks represented a threat to bishops' authority because holy men and women earned their special status not by having it bestowed from the church hierarchy but through their own actions; strengthening the bishops' right to discipline monks who resisted their authority was one of the goals of the Council of Chalcedon. At bottom, however, bishops and monks shared a spiritual goal—salvation and service to God.

REVIEW QUESTION How did Christianity both unite and divide the Roman Empire?

Non-Roman Kingdoms in the Western Roman Empire, c. 370–550s

The residents of the western empire had special reason to pray for God's help because their territory came under great pressure from the many incursions of non-Roman peoples—barbarians, the Romans called them, meaning "brave but uncivilized"—that took place in the fourth and fifth centuries. The emperors had traditionally admitted some multiethnic groups from east of the Rhine River and north of the Danube River into the empire to fight in the Roman army, but eventually other barbarians fought their way in from the northeast. The barbarians had two strong motivations to move westward: to flee attacks by the Huns (nomads from central Asia) and to share in Roman prosperity. By the 370s, this human tide had swollen to a flood, provoking violence and a loss of order in the western empire.

Over the coming decades, the immigrants transformed themselves from loosely organized tribes into kingdoms with newly defined identities. By the 470s, one of their commanders ruled Italy—the political change that has been said to mark the so-called fall of the Roman Empire. However, the interactions of these non-Roman peoples with the empire's residents in western Europe and North Africa are better understood as causing a political, social, and cultural transformation—admittedly based on force more than cooperation—that made the immigrants the heirs of the western Roman Empire and led to the formation of medieval Europe.

Non-Roman Migrations into the Western Roman Empire

The non-Roman peoples who flooded into the empire had diverse origins; scholars in the past referred to them generically as Germanic peoples, but this label misrepresents the variety of languages and customs among these multiethnic groups. What we must remember is that the diverse barbarian peoples had no previously established sense of ethnic identity, and that many of them had had long-term contact with Romans through trade across the frontiers and service in the Roman army. By encouraging this contact, the emperors unwittingly set in motion forces that they could not in the end control. By late in the fourth century, attacks by the Huns had destabilized life for these bands across the Roman frontiers, and the families of warriors followed them into the empire seeking safety. Hordes of men, women, and children crossed into the empire as refugees. They came with no political or military unity and no clear plan. Loosely organized into tribes that often warred with one another, they shared only their terror of the Huns and their custom of conducting raids for a living in addition to farming small plots.

The inability to prevent immigrants from crossing the border or to integrate them into Roman society once they had crossed put great stress on the western central government. Persistent economic weakness rooted in the third-century crisis worsened this pressure. Tenant farmers and landlords fleeing crushing taxes had left as much as 20 percent of farmland unworked in the most seriously affected areas. The loss of revenue made the government unable to afford enough soldiers to control the frontiers. Over time, the immigrating non-Roman peoples forced the Roman government to grant them territory in the empire. Remarkably, they then began to develop separate ethnic identities and create new societies for themselves and the Romans living under their control.

Immigrant Traditions The traditions the newcomers brought with them from their barbarian homelands poorly prepared them for ruling others. There they had lived in small settlements whose economies depended on farming, herding, and ironworking; they had no experience with running kingdoms built on strong central authority (see "Contrasting Views," page 226).

CONTRASTING VIEWS

Debate: Did Romans or Huns Better Protect Life, Law, and Freedom?

In 448, a Roman named Priscus went as a diplomat to the court of Attila the Hun at a location north of the Danube River. His firsthand report of what he learned about life among the Huns during this visit includes this conversation with a stranger he met there. They exchanged contrasting views of whether life, law, and freedom were better protected among the Romans or the Huns (called Scythians here). According to descriptions of the Huns by other authors (such as the fourth-century historian and military man Ammianus Marcellinus), Romans recognized these barbarians as fearless and proud, and they respected them for their fierce dedication to their way of life. As a writer, Priscus could have been influenced by having read the bitter criticism of Roman society that Tacitus, the famous first-century C.E. Roman historian, put into the mouths of non-Romans in his works. But the details that Priscus gives about the stranger's personal appearance and life story perhaps increase the likelihood that he is reporting, in this document, a conversation held with a real person.

A man who I assumed was a barbarian from his Scythian-style clothes came up to me and said "Hello!" in Greek. I was surprised by a Scythian speaking Greek. For the subjects of the Huns, swept together from various lands, speak, in addition to their native barbarian languages, either Hunnic or Gothic, or—since many of them do business with the western Romans—Latin. None of them usually speak Greek, except captives from the Thracian or Illyrian coast; anyone who meets them easily recognizes, from their ripped clothing and the poor appearance of their heads, that they are individuals whose lives have taken a turn for the worse. This man, on the other hand, was well dressed in fancy Scythian clothes and a circular mullet-style haircut.

Returning his greeting, I asked him who he was and where he had come from into a barbarian land and chosen the Scythian lifestyle. When he asked me why I was eager to know, I told him that his speaking Greek had made me curious. Then he laughed and said that he was a Greek by birth and had gone as a merchant to trade in Viminacium, in the region of Moesia on the Danube River. He had lived there a long time and married a very rich wife. But barbarians captured the city, and his property was taken away. On account of his riches he was allotted as a captive to [the Hun] Onegesius in the division of the spoils, since it was customary that, after Attila, the chiefs of the Scythians, because they commanded many men, would keep the rich prisoners for themselves. He later fought bravely [in attacks by the Huns] against the Romans and the Acatiri tribe. Following the Scythian custom, he gave the spoils that he won to his master, and so got his freedom. He then married a barbarian wife and had children.

Since he had the privilege of eating at the table of Onegesius, he considered his new life among the Scythians better than his old life among the Romans. For he explained that once a war is over, the Scythians live at ease, each enjoying what he has got, with no, or only a little, bothering of others or being bothered themselves. The Romans, on the other hand, are very likely to be destroyed by war, as they have to pin their hopes of safety on other people: their tyrants do not permit everyone to use weapons. And Romans who do use them are harmed by the cowardly actions of their generals, who cannot stand up to the stresses of war. But the condition of Roman subjects in peacetime is far more burdensome than the evils of war, on account of the harshness of tax collection and the harm done by wrongdoers, since the laws do not apply to everyone. A member of the upper class who breaks the law does not face punishment. If a man is poor, however, and doesn't understand how to handle things, he suffers the penalty imposed by the law, if he doesn't leave this life before he gets to the trial, given how long lawsuits are dragged out and how much money has to be spent. The most painful thing of all is to have to pay in order to try to get justice. For no one will give his day in court to the man who has been treated unjustly unless he pays money to the judge and the judge's clerks.

As he was saying many other things like this, I calmly asked him to hear what I had to say. I insisted that the founders of the Roman Republic were wise and good

In their homelands the barbarians had lived in chiefdom societies, whose members could only be persuaded, not ordered, to follow the chief. Chiefs maintained their status by giving gifts to their followers and leading raids to capture cattle and slaves. They led clans—groups of households organized on kinship lines, following maternal as well as paternal descent. Members of a clan were supposed to keep peace among themselves, and violence against a fellow clan member was the worst possible offense. Clans in turn grouped themselves into tribes—fluctuating coalitions that anyone could join. Tribes differentiated themselves by their clothing, hairstyles, jewelry, weapons, religious cults, and oral stories.

Family life was patriarchal: men headed households and held authority over women, children, and slaves. Warfare preoccupied men, as their ritual men. To prevent things from being done randomly, they arranged for some people to be guardians of the laws, while others were tasked with skill in weapons and to train for war, focused on nothing else but being ready for battle and having the spirit to go to war as if going to their usual exercises, having gotten rid of their fear ahead of time through their training. The founders arranged for others to do farming and care for the land, to feed both themselves and those who fought for them by contributing the tax that consists of the grain supply for the army. They arranged for others to pay attention to people who have been treated unjustly and to conduct rightful prosecutions for people who are too weak to advance their own case. Others they set up as judges to guard what the law wishes.

Since the founders were concerned for those involved in the judicial process, they also arranged for others whose job it is to make sure that a person who wins a judgment in court will in fact receive the damages that have been awarded, as well as that the person who was found guilty does not pay more than the legal judgment specified. If no one existed who would pay attention to such things, then the motivation for a second case at law would arise from the first one, because either the winner in the case would apply too much pressure, or the person who lost the case would continue to act unjustly.

There is indeed an amount of money that these officials are paid by those involved in court cases, just as the farmers pay a set amount to the soldiers. Isn't it proper to support those who help you and reward their good will, in the same way that feeding a horse helps a horseman . . . ? Whenever court costs have to be paid even though we've lost the case, shouldn't we blame our own unjust action instead of attributing the harm to someone else?

If it does happen that it takes too long to try a case, that's the result of a concern for justice, to prevent judges from judging cases carelessly and making mistaken judgments. For they believe that it is better to finish a case late than to wrong someone by hurrying and thereby committing an offense against God, the founder of justice. The laws do apply to everyone, so that even the Roman emperor obeys them. And it's not true, as was said in his accusation, that the rich use force against the poor without any risk, unless someone escapes prosecution because he never got caught. The poor can get away with things this way, too. Criminals under these circumstances get away because of the lack of evidence, something that happens among all peoples and not just the Romans.

You ought to thank chance for the freedom you enjoy, not the master who led you into war, where as a result of your inexperience you could have been killed by the enemy or punished by the one who possessed you if you ran away from the battlefield. The Romans usually treat even their household slaves better than this. They act like fathers or teachers to them, to restrain them from behaving stupidly and to get them to do what is considered right, and they teach them self-control when they make mistakes, just as with the children in their families. It is not legal for them to punish them with death, as the Scythians do.

There are many ways to freedom among the Romans. Not just the living but even those who have died gladly give it, arranging their estates however they wish. The law is that whatever each person wishes to happen to his possessions when he dies is valid.

In tears, he said that the laws were excellent and the Roman Republic [as the Romans still called the Empire] was good, but the officials were corrupting it by not living up to the same moral standards that the officials of the past did.

Source: Priscus, fr. 11.2 Müller *Fragmenta Historicorum Graecorum* (= *Exc. de Leg. Rom.* 3). Translation by Thomas R. Martin.

Questions to Consider

1. **Do you think that this is a fabricated account written by Priscus to demonstrate a point, a documentation of an actual exchange, or a combination of both? What evidence from the document supports your argument?**
2. **Do you think Priscus, in his reply, adequately answers the points raised by the stranger? Why or why not?**
3. **What do you think is the intended effect of Priscus's giving the stranger the last word in this exchange?**

sacrifices of weapons preserved in northern European bogs have shown. Women were valued for their ability to bear children, and rich men could have more than one wife and perhaps concubines as well. A division of labor made women responsible for growing crops, making pottery, and producing textiles, while men worked iron and herded cattle. Women enjoyed certain rights of inheritance and could control property, and married women received a dowry of one-third of their husband's property.

Assemblies of free male warriors made major decisions in the tribes. Their leaders' authority was restricted mostly to religious and military matters. Tribes could be unstable and prone to internal conflict—clans frequently feuded, with bloody consequences. Tribal law tried to determine what forms of violence were and were not acceptable in seeking revenge, but laws were oral, not written, and thus open to wide dispute.

Fleeing the Huns The migrations avalanched when the Huns invaded eastern Europe in the fourth century. The Huns arrived on the Russian steppes shortly before 370 as the vanguard of Turkish-speaking nomads moving west. Their warriors' appearance terrified their victims, who reported skulls elongated from having been bound between boards in infancy, faces grooved with decorative scars, and arms fearsome with elaborate tattoos. Huns excelled as raiders, launching cavalry attacks without warning. Skilled as horsemen, they could shoot their powerful bows accurately while riding full tilt and stay mounted for days, sleeping atop their horses and carrying snacks of raw meat between their thighs and the animal's back.

By later in the fourth century the Huns had moved as far west as the Hungarian plain north of the Danube, terrifying the peoples there and launching raids southward into the Balkans. The emperors in Constantinople began paying the Huns to spare their territory, so the most ambitious Hunnic leader, Attila (r. c. 440–453), pushed his domain westward toward the Alps. He led his forces as far west as central France and into northern Italy. At Attila's death in 453, the Huns lost their fragile unity and faded from history. By this time, however, the terror that they had inspired in the peoples living in eastern Europe had provoked the migrations that eventually transformed the western empire.

Visigoths: The First New Society The first non-Roman group that created a new identity and society for themselves inside the empire were the barbarians who defeated Valens at Adrianople (Map 7.3). Their history illustrates the pattern of the migrations: desperate barbarians in barely organized groups with no uniform

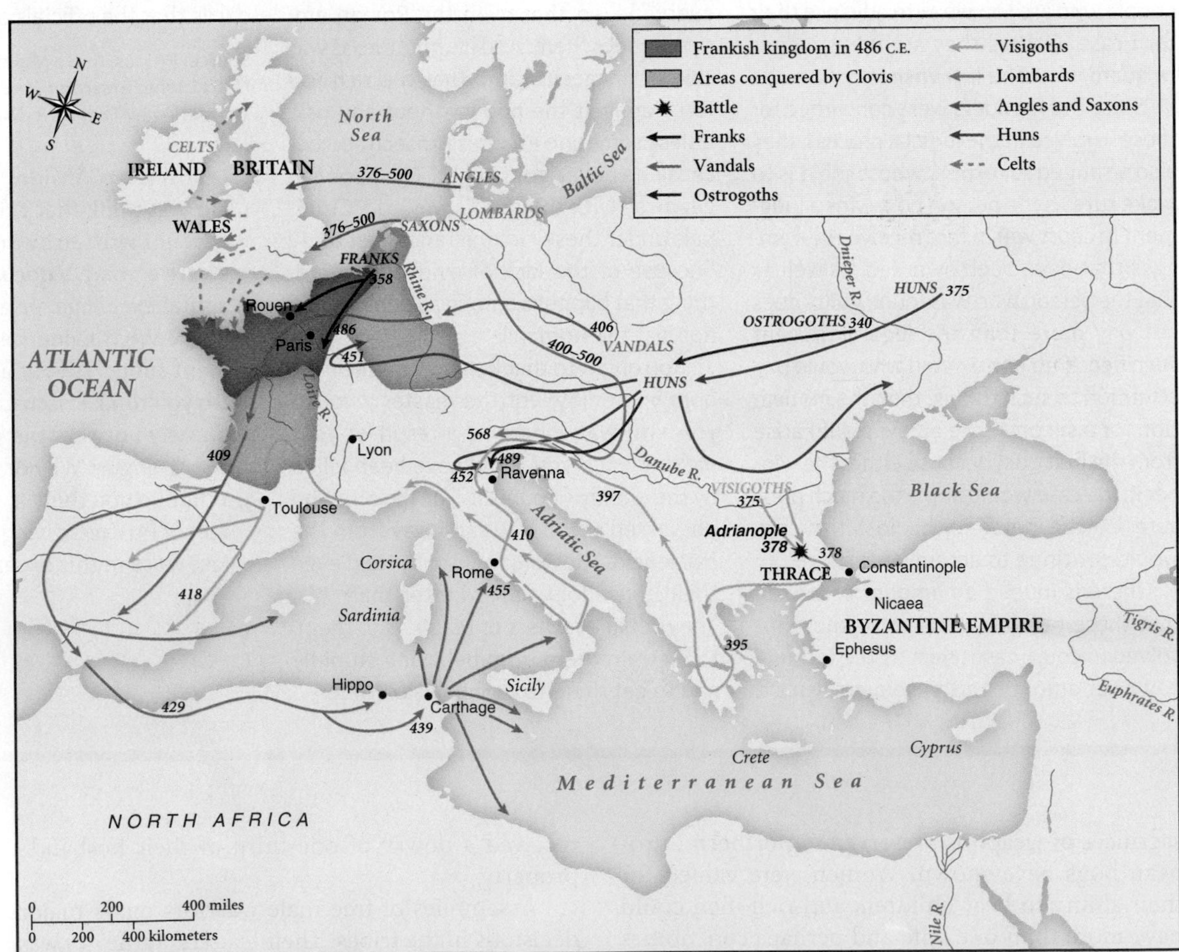

MAP 7.3 Migrations and Invasions of the Fourth and Fifth Centuries
The movements of non-Roman peoples into imperial territory transformed the Roman Empire. These migrations had begun as early as the reign of Domitian (r. 81–96), but in the fourth century they increased greatly when the Huns' attacks pushed numerous barbarian bands into the empire's northern provinces. Print maps offer only a static representation of dynamic processes such as movements of populations, but this map helps illustrate the variety of peoples involved, the wide extent of imperial territory that they affected, and their prominence in the western empire.

ethnic identity, seeking protection in the Roman Empire in return for military service but being mistreated, and then rebelling to form their own, new kingdom.

When the emperor Theodosius died in 395, the barbarians whom he had allowed to settle in the empire rebelled. United by Alaric into a tribe known as the **Visigoths**, they fought their way into the western empire. In 410, they stunned the world by sacking Rome itself. For the first time since the Gauls eight hundred years before, a foreign force occupied the ancient capital. They terrorized the population: when Alaric demanded all the citizens' goods, the Romans asked, "What will be left to us?" "Your lives," he replied.

Too weak to fend off the invaders, the western emperor Honorius in 418 reluctantly agreed to settle the newcomers in southwestern Gaul (present-day France), where they completed their unprecedented transition from tribe to kingdom, organizing a political state and creating their identity as Visigoths. In this process they followed the only model available: Roman tradition, especially having a code of law. They established mutually beneficial relations with local Roman elites, who used time-tested ways of flattering their new superiors to gain advantages. Sidonius Apollinaris (c. 430–479), for example, a well-connected noble from Lyon, once purposely lost a backgammon game to the Visigothic king as a way of winning a favor.

How the new non-Roman kingdoms raised revenues has become a much-debated question. Did the newcomers become landlords by forcing Roman property owners to redistribute a portion of their lands, slaves, and movable property as "ransom" to them? Or did Romans directly pay the expenses of the kingdom's soldiers, who lived mostly in urban garrisons? Whatever the new arrangements were, the Visigoths found them profitable enough to expand into Spain within a century of establishing themselves in southwestern Gaul.

The Vandals and the Spiral of Violence

The western government's concessions to the Visigoths led other groups to seize territory and create new kingdoms and identities. In 406, the Vandals, fleeing the Huns, crossed the Rhine into Roman territory. This huge group cut a swath through Gaul all the way to the Spanish coast. (The modern word *vandal*, meaning "destroyer of property," perpetuates their reputation for warlike ruthlessness.)

In 429, eighty thousand Vandals ferried to North Africa, where they soon broke their agreement to become federate allies and captured the region. They crippled the western empire by seizing North Africa's tax payments of grain and vegetable oil and disrupting the importation of food to Rome. They threatened the eastern empire with their strong navy and in 455 sailed to Rome, plundering the city. In Africa the Vandals caused tremendous hardship for local people by confiscating property rather than (like the Visigoths) allowing owners to make regular payments on the land. As Arian Christians, they persecuted North African Christians whose doctrines they considered heresy.

The Anglo-Saxons at the Empire's Western Edge

Small non-Roman groups took advantage of the disruption caused by bigger bands to break off distant pieces of the weakened western empire. The most significant group for later history was the Anglo-Saxons. Composed of Angles from what is now Denmark and Saxons from northwestern Germany, this mixed group invaded Britain in the 440s after the Roman army had been recalled from the province to defend Italy against the Visigoths. The Anglo-Saxons captured territory from the local Celtic peoples and the remaining Roman inhabitants. Gradually, their culture replaced the local traditions of the island's eastern regions. The Celts there lost most of their language, and Christianity gave way to Anglo-Saxon beliefs, surviving only in Wales and Ireland.

The Fall of Rome and the Ostrogoths

Another barbarian group, the Ostrogoths, carved out a kingdom in Italy in the fifth century. By the time the Ostrogothic king Theodoric (r. 493–526) came to power, there had not been a western Roman emperor for nearly twenty years, and there never would be again — the change that has traditionally, but simplistically, been called the fall of the Roman Empire. The story's details reveal the complexity of the political transformation of the western empire under the new kingdoms. The weakness of the western emperors' army had obliged them to hire foreign officers to lead the defense of Italy. By the middle of the fifth century, one non-Roman general after another decided who would serve as puppet emperor under his control. The employees were running the company.

The last such unfortunate puppet was only a child. His father, a former aide to Attila, tried to establish a royal house by proclaiming his young son as western emperor in 475. He gave the boy ruler the name Romulus Augustulus ("Romulus the Little

---

Visigoths: The name given to the barbarians whom Alaric united and led on a military campaign into the western Roman Empire to establish a new kingdom; they sacked Rome in 410.

Augustus") to match his young age and to recall both Rome's founder and its first emperor. In 476, following a dispute over pay, the boy emperor's non-Roman soldiers murdered his father and deposed him. Pitied as an innocent child, Little Augustus was given safe refuge and a generous pension. The rebels' leader, Odoacer, did not appoint another emperor. Instead, he had the Roman Senate petition Zeno, the eastern emperor, to recognize his leadership in return for his acknowledging Zeno as sole emperor over west and east. Odoacer thereafter oversaw Italy nominally as the eastern emperor's viceroy, but in fact he ruled as he liked.

Zeno later plotted to rid himself of an ambitious non-Roman general then resident in Constantinople—Theodoric—by sending him to fight Odoacer, whom the emperor had found too independent. Successfully eliminating Odoacer by 493, Theodoric then established his own Ostrogothic kingdom, ruling Italy from the capital at Ravenna.

Theodoric and his Ostrogothic nobles wanted to enjoy the luxurious life of the empire's elite, not destroy it, and to preserve the empire's prestige and status. They therefore left the Senate and consulships intact. An Arian Christian, Theodoric followed Constantine's example by announcing a policy of religious freedom. Like the other non-Romans, the Ostrogoths adopted and adapted Roman traditions that supported the stability of their own rule. For these reasons, some scholars consider it more accurate to speak of the western empire's "transformation" than of its "fall."

The Enduring Kingdom of the Franks Among the groups reshaping the western Roman Empire politically, socially, and culturally, the Franks were especially significant because they were the people who transformed Roman Gaul into Francia (from which comes the name *France*). Roman emperors had allowed some of the Franks to settle in a rough northern border region (now in the Netherlands) in the early fourth century; by the late fifth century they were a major presence in Gaul. In 507, their king Clovis (r. 485–511), with support from the eastern Roman emperor, overthrew the Visigothic king in Gaul. When the emperor named Clovis an honorary consul, Clovis celebrated this ancient honor by having himself crowned with a diadem in the style of the emperors since Constantine.

Eagle Brooches from Gothic Spain

Wealthy Gothic women used brooches like these to fasten their clothes at the shoulder. The costly materials from which they were made displayed the wearer's status in society. The eagle design pointed both to the respect that those predator birds enjoyed in Gothic ideas about the natural world and to Roman power and majesty (the eagle had long been depicted on the standards carried in front of the Roman army's legions). In this way, the ornaments emphasized Gothic women's pride in their own heritage as well as their adaption to what was best (in their eyes) in Roman society. (Eagle Fibula, Anonymous, Visigothic, sixth century, gold over bronze with gemstones, glass and meerschaum. Object 54.421–422, photo *© The Walters Art Museum, Baltimore.)*

He established western Europe's largest new kingdom in what is today mostly France, overshadowing the neighboring and rival kingdoms of the Burgundians and Alemanni in eastern Gaul. Probably persuaded by his wife, Clotilda, a Christian, to believe that God had helped him defeat the Alemanni, Clovis proclaimed himself an orthodox Christian and renounced Arianism, which he had reportedly embraced previously. To build stability, he carefully fostered good relations with the bishops as the regime's intermediaries with the population.

Clovis's dynasty, called Merovingian after the legendary Frankish ancestor Merovech, endured for another two hundred years, foreshadowing the kingdom that would emerge much later as the forerunner of modern France. The Merovingians survived so long because, better than any other kingdom, they successfully combined their own traditions of military bravery with Roman social and legal traditions. In addition, their location in far western Europe kept them out of the reach of the destructive invasions sent against Italy by the eastern emperor Justinian in the sixth century to reunite the Roman world.

Social and Cultural Transformation in the Western Roman Empire

Western Europe's political transformation—the gradual replacement of imperial government by the new kingdoms—set in motion social and cultural transformations as well (Map 7.4). The newcomers and their Roman subjects created novel ways of life by combining old traditions, as the Visigoth

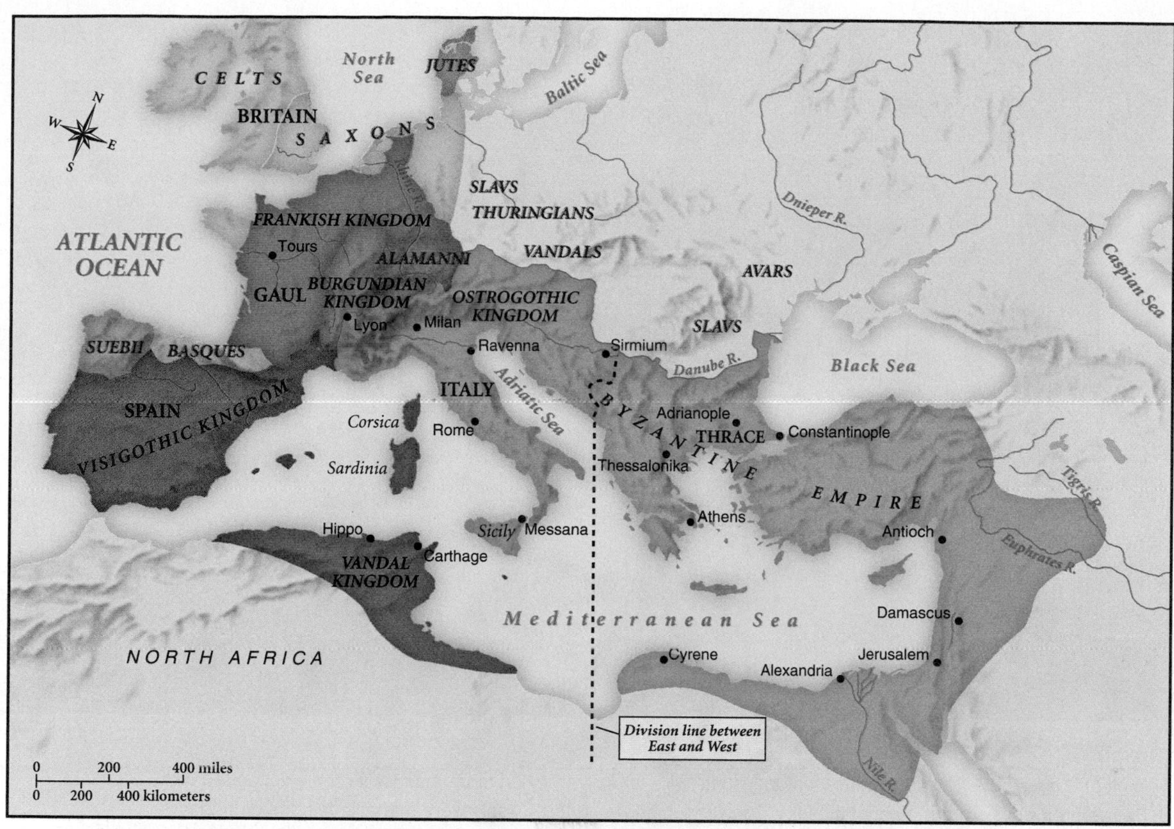

MAP 7.4 Peoples and Kingdoms of the Roman World, 526

The provinces of the Roman Empire had always been home to a population diverse in language and ethnicity. By the early sixth century, the territory of the western empire had become a mixture of diverse political units as well. Italy and most of the former western provinces were ruled by kingdoms organized by different non-Roman peoples, who had moved into former imperial territory over several centuries. The eastern empire remained under the political control of the emperor in Constantinople.

king Athaulf (r. 410–415) explained after marrying a Roman noblewoman:

> At the start I wanted to erase the Romans' name and turn their land into a Gothic empire, doing myself what Augustus had done. But I have learned that the Goths' freewheeling wildness will never accept the rule of law, and that state with no law is no state. Thus, I have more wisely chosen another path to glory: reviving the Roman name with Gothic vigor. I pray that future generations will remember me as the founder of a Roman restoration.

This process of social and cultural transformation promoted stability by producing new law codes but undermined long-term security by weakening the economic situation.

Visigothic and Frankish Law

Roman law was the most influential precedent for the new kings in their efforts to construct stable states. Their original tribal societies never had written laws, but their new states required legal codes to create a sense of justice and keep order. The Visigothic kings were the first to issue a written law code. Published in Latin in about 475, it made fines and compensation the primary method for resolving disputes. Clovis also emphasized written law for the Merovingian kingdom. His code, also published in Latin between about 507 and 511, promoted social order through clear penalties for specific crimes. In particular, he formalized a system of fines intended to defuse feuds and vendettas between individuals and clans. The most prominent component of this system was **wergild**, the payment a murderer had to make as compensation for his crime, to prevent feuds of revenge. The king received about one-third of the fine, with the rest paid to the victim's family.

Since laws indicate social values, the differing amounts of wergild in Clovis's code suggest the relative values of different categories of people in his kingdom. Murdering a woman of childbearing age,

---

wergild: Under Frankish law, the payment that a murderer had to make as compensation for the crime, to prevent feuds of revenge.

Mosaic of Women Exercising
This picture covered a floor in a fourth-century country villa in Sicily that had more than forty rooms decorated with thirty-five hundred square meters of mosaics. The women shown in this mosaic were perhaps dancers getting in shape for public appearances or athletes performing as part of a show. Members of the Roman elite built such enormous and expensive houses as the centerpieces of estates meant to insulate them from increasingly dismal conditions in cities and protect them from barbarian attack. In this case, the strategy apparently failed: the villa was likely seriously damaged by Vandal invaders. *(Erich Lessing/Art Resource, NY.)*

a boy under twelve, or a man in the king's retinue brought a massive fine of six hundred gold coins, enough to buy six hundred cattle. A woman past childbearing age (specified as sixty years), a young girl, or a freeborn man was valued at two hundred. Ordinary slaves rated thirty-five. Obviously these laws did not support true equality among people, but they did make clear that appropriate compensation had to be paid for the damage done by crimes, a requirement that was surely meant to help prevent an endless cycle of revenge in society. This feature of the so-called barbarian law codes had a long influence in later legal history.

A Transformed Economic Landscape

Law codes promoted social stability in the new kingdoms of the transformed western Roman Empire, but the migrations that had brought the new groups into Roman territory had the unintended consequence of harming the empire's already weakened economy. The Vandals' violent attacks severely damaged many towns in Gaul, hastening a decline in urban population. In the countryside, now beyond the control of any central government, wealthy Romans built sprawling villas on extensive estates, staffed by tenants bound to the land like slaves. These establishments aimed to operate as self-sufficient units by producing all they needed, defending themselves against barbarian raids, and keeping their distance from any authorities. The owners shunned municipal offices and tax collection, the public services that had supplied the lifeblood of Roman administration. Provincial government disappeared, and the new kingdoms never fully replaced its duties.

The situation only grew grimmer as the effects of these changes multiplied. In some areas now outside reach of the central government, the infrastructure of trade — roads and bridges — fell into disrepair with no public-spirited elite to maintain them. The elite holed up in their fortress-like households. They could afford to protect themselves: the annual income of the richest of them rivaled the revenue of an entire province in the old western empire.

In some cases, these fortunate few helped pass down Roman learning to later ages. Cassiodorus (c. 490–585), for one, founded a monastery on his ancestral estate in Italy in the 550s after a career in imperial administration. He gave the monks the task of copying manuscripts as old ones disintegrated. His own book, *Institutions*, summed up what he saw as the foundation of ancient Greek and Roman culture by listing the books an educated person should read; it included ancient classical literature as well as Christian texts. The most lasting effort to keep classical traditions alive, however, came in the eastern empire.

REVIEW QUESTION How did their migrations and invasions change the barbarians themselves and the Roman Empire?

The Roman Empire in the East, c. 500–565

The eastern Roman Empire (later called the Byzantine Empire — see Chapter 8) avoided the massive transformations that reshaped western Europe. Trade and agriculture kept the eastern empire from poverty, while its emperors used force, diplomacy, and bribery to prevent invasions from the north and repel attacks by the powerful Sasanid Empire in Persia, which was still making periodic strikes against the eastern empire.

The eastern emperors believed it was their duty to rule a united Roman Empire and prevent barbarians from degrading its culture. The most famous eastern Roman emperor, **Justinian** (r. 527–565), and his wife and partner in rule, **Theodora** (500–548), took this mission so seriously that for decades the eastern empire waged war against the barbarian kingdoms in the west, aiming to reunite the empire and restore the imperial glory of the Augustan period. Like Diocletian, Justinian increased imperial authority and tried to purify religion to provide what he saw as the strong leadership and divine favor necessary in troubled times. He and his successors in the eastern empire also contributed to the preservation of the memory of classical Greek and Roman culture by preserving a great deal of earlier literature, non-Christian and Christian.

Imperial Society in the Eastern Roman Empire

The sixth-century eastern empire enjoyed a vitality that had vanished in the west. Its social elite spent freely on luxuries such as silk, precious stones, and pepper and other spices imported from India and China. Markets in its large cities teemed with merchants from far and wide. Its churches' soaring domes testified to its confidence in the Christian God as its divine protector.

In keeping with Roman tradition, the eastern emperors sponsored religious festivals and entertainments on a massive scale to rally public support. Rich and poor alike crowded city squares, theaters, and hippodromes on these lively occasions. Chariot racing aroused the hottest passions. Constantinople's residents divided themselves into competitive factions called Blues and Greens after the racing colors of their favorite charioteers. Emperors sometimes backed one gang or the other to intimidate potential rivals.

Preserving "Romanness" The eastern emperors worked to maintain Roman tradition and identity, believing that "Romanness" was the best defense against what they saw as the barbarization of the western empire. They hired many foreign mercenaries, but they also tried to keep their subjects from adopting foreign ways. Styles of dress figured largely in this struggle. Ignoring the favored clothing of the chariot factions, eastern emperors ordered Constantinople's residents not to wear barbarian-style clothing (especially heavy boots and furs) instead of traditional Roman attire (sandals or light shoes and cloth robes).

The quest for cultural unity was hopeless because society in the eastern empire was thoroughly multilingual and multiethnic. The eastern empire's inhabitants regarded themselves as the heirs of ancient Roman culture: they referred to themselves as Romans, even though most of them spoke Greek as their native language and used Latin only for government and military communication. Many people retained their traditional languages, such as Phrygian and Cappadocian in western Asia Minor, Armenian farther east, and Syriac and other Aramaic dialects along the eastern Mediterranean coast. The streets of Constantinople reportedly rang with seventy-two languages.

Romanness definitely included Christianity, but the eastern empire's theological diversity rivaled its ethnic and linguistic complexity. Bitter controversies over doctrine divided eastern Christians; neither the emperors nor the bishops succeeded in imposing orthodoxy. Emperors used violence against heretics when persuasion failed. They had to resort to extreme measures, they believed, to save lost souls and preserve the empire's religious purity and divine goodwill. The persecution of Christian subjects by Christian emperors illustrates the disturbing consequences of the quest for a unitary identity.

Justinian and Theodora: Sixth-century emperor and empress of the eastern Roman Empire, famous for waging costly wars to reunite the empire.

Theodora and Her Court in Ravenna
This mosaic shows the empress Theodora and members of her court presenting a gift to the church at San Vitale in Ravenna. It faced the matching scene of her husband Justinian and his attendants (page 235). Theodora wears the jewels, pearls, and rich robes characteristic of eastern Roman monarchs. (Compare the style of the clothes in these two mosaics to those shown in the cameo from Augustus's time on page 174. What were the different styles of dress meant to convey about the leaders in each period?) Theodora extends in her hands a gem-encrusted wine cup as her present. Her gesture imitates the gift-giving of the Magi to the baby Jesus, the scene illustrated on the hem of her garment. The circle around her head, called a nimbus (Latin for "cloud"), indicates special holiness. *(Scala / Art Resource, NY.)*

Women in Society and at Court

Most women in eastern Roman society lived according to ancient Mediterranean tradition: they concentrated on their households and minimized contact with men outside that circle. Law barred them from performing many public functions, such as witnessing wills. Subject to the authority of their fathers and husbands, women veiled their heads (though not their faces) to show modesty. The strict views of Christian theologians on sexuality and reproduction made divorce more difficult and discouraged remarriage even for widows. Sexual offenses carried harsher legal penalties. Female prostitution remained legal and common, but emperors raised the penalties for those who forced girls or female slaves under their control into prostitution.

Women in the imperial family could achieve prominence unattainable for ordinary women. Empress Theodora demonstrated the influence high-ranking women could have in the eastern empire. Uninhibited by her humble origins (she was the daughter of a bear trainer and had been an actress with a scandalous reputation), she came to rival anyone in influence and wealth (see the illustration above). She had a hand in every aspect of Justinian's rule, advising him on personnel for his administration, pushing for her religious views in disputes over Christian doctrine, and rallying his courage at times of crisis. John Lydus, a contemporary government official and high-ranking administrator, judged her "superior in intelligence to any man."

Social Class and Government Services

Government in the eastern empire increased social divisions because it provided services according to people's wealth. Officials received fees for countless activities, from commercial permits to legal grievances. Some scholars argue that these arrangements actually promoted more effective action by government officials. People with money and status certainly found the situation useful: they relied on their social connections to get a hearing from the right official, and on their wealth to make payments to move matters along quickly. Whether seeking preferential treatment or just spurring administrators to do what they were supposed to do, the rich could make the system work. The poor, by contrast, had trouble affording the payments that government officials expected.

This fee-based system allowed the emperors to pay their civil servants tiny salaries and spend imperial funds for other purposes. John Lydus, for example, reported that he earned thirty times his annual salary in payments from people seeking services during his first year in office. To keep the sys-

Justinian and His Court in Ravenna
This mosaic scene dominated by the eastern Roman emperor Justinian stands opposite Theodora's mosaic (page 234) in San Vitale's Church in Ravenna. The emperor is shown presenting a gift to the church. Justinian and Theodora finished building the church, which the Ostrogothic king Theodoric had started, to commemorate their successful campaign to restore Italy to the Roman Empire and reassert control of the western capital, Ravenna. The inclusion of the portrait of Maximianus, bishop of Ravenna, standing on Justinian's left and identified by name, stresses the theme of cooperation between bishops and emperors in ruling the world. What do you think the inclusion of the soldiers at the left is meant to indicate? *(Scala/Art Resource, NY.)*

tem from destroying itself through extortion, the emperors published an official list of the maximum fees that their employees could charge.

The Reign of Emperor Justinian, 527–565

Justinian became the most famous eastern emperor by waging war to reunite the empire as it had been in the days of Augustus, making imperial rule more autocratic, constructing costly buildings in Constantinople, and instituting legal and religious reforms. Also the most intellectual emperor since Julian the Apostate two centuries earlier, Justinian had the same aims as all his predecessors: to preserve social order based on hierarchy and maintain divine goodwill (see the illustration above). Unfortunately, the cost of his plans forced him to raise taxes, generating civil strife.

Taxes and Social Unrest Justinian faced bitter resistance to his plans and their enormous cost. His unpopular taxes provoked a major riot in 532. Known as the Nika Riot, it arose when the Blue and Green factions, gathering to watch chariot races, unexpectedly united against the emperor, shouting "Nika! Nika!" ("Win! Win!") as their battle cry. After nine days of violence that left much of Constantinople in ashes, Justinian was ready to abandon his throne and flee in panic. But Theodora sternly rebuked him: "Once born, no one can escape dying, but for one who has held imperial power it would be unbearable to be a fugitive. May I never take off my imperial robes of purple, nor live to see the day when those who meet me will not greet me as their ruler." Her husband then sent in troops, who ended the rioting by slaughtering thirty thousand rioters trapped in the racetrack.

Justinian's most ambitious goal was to restore the empire to a unified territory, religion, and culture. Invading the former western provinces, his generals defeated the Vandals and Ostrogoths after campaigns that in some cases took decades to complete. At an enormous price in lives and money, Justinian's armies restored the old empire's geography, with its territory stretching from the Atlantic to the western edge of Mesopotamia.

Justinian's success in reuniting the western and eastern empires had unintended consequences: severe damage to the west's infrastructure and the east's finances. Italy endured the most physical destruction, while the eastern empire suffered because Justinian squeezed even more taxes out of his already overburdened population to finance his wars and pay the Persian kingdom not to attack while his home defenses were weakened. The tax burden crippled the economy, leading to constant banditry in the countryside. Crowds poured into the capital from rural areas, seeking relief from poverty and robbers.

Natural disaster compounded Justinian's problems. In the 540s, a horrific epidemic killed a third of his empire's inhabitants; a quarter of a million, half the capital's population, died in Constantinople alone. This was only the first of many pandemics that erased millions of people in the eastern empire over the next two centuries. Serious earthquakes, always a danger in this region, increased the death toll. The loss of so many people created a shortage of army recruits, requiring the emperor to hire expensive mercenaries, and left countless farms vacant, reducing tax revenues.

Strengthening Central Authority Justinian craved stability, which he sought by strengthening his authority in two ways: emphasizing his closeness to God and increasing the autocratic power of his rule. These traits became characteristic of eastern Roman emperors. Moreover, Justinian proclaimed the emperor the "living law," recalling the Hellenistic royal doctrine that the ruler's decisions defined law.

His building program in Constantinople communicated his overpowering supremacy and piety. Most spectacular of all was his reconstruction of Hagia Sophia (Church of the Holy Wisdom). Creating a new design for churches, Justinian's architects erected a huge building on a square plan capped by a dome 107 feet across and 160 feet high. Its interior walls glowed like the sun from the light reflecting off their four acres of gold mosaics. Imported marble of every color added to the sparkling effect. When he first entered his masterpiece, dedicated in 538, Justinian exclaimed, "I have defeated you, Solomon," claiming to have bested the glorious temple that the ancient king built for the Hebrews.

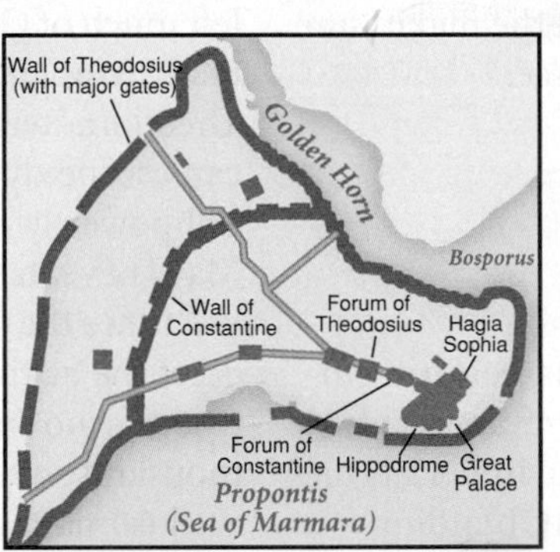

Constantinople during the Rule of Justinian

Justinian's autocratic rule reduced the autonomy of the empire's cities. Their councils ceased to govern; imperial officials took over instead. Provincial elites still had to ensure full payment of their area's taxes, but no longer could they decide local matters. Now the central government determined all aspects of decision making and social status. Men of property from the provinces who aspired to power and prestige could satisfy their ambitions only by joining the imperial administration in the capital.

Legal and Religious Reform To solidify his authority and bring uniformity to the confusing mass of decisions that earlier emperors had made, Justinian codified the laws of the empire. His *Codex* appeared in 529, with a revised version completed in 534. A team of scholars also condensed millions of words of regulations to produce the *Digest* in 533, intended to expedite legal cases and provide a syllabus for law schools. This collection, like the *Codex* written in Latin and therefore readable in the western empire, influenced legal scholars for centuries. Justinian's legal experts also compiled a textbook for students, the *Institutes*, which appeared in 533 and remained on law school reading lists until modern times.

To fulfill the emperor's sacred duty to secure the welfare of his people, Justinian acted to enforce their religious purity. Like the polytheist and Christian emperors before him, he believed his world could not flourish if its god became angered by the presence of religious offenders. As emperor, Justinian decided who the offenders were. Zealously enforcing laws against polytheists, he compelled them to be baptized or forfeit their lands and official positions. He also relentlessly purged heretical Christians who rejected his version of orthodoxy.

Justinian's laws made male homosexual relations illegal for the first time in Roman history. Earlier, same-sex unions between men had apparently been allowed, or at least officially ignored, until they were prohibited in 342 after Christianity became the emperors' religion. There had never before been any civil penalties imposed on men engaging in homosexual activity, perhaps because previous rulers considered it impractical to regulate men's sexuality, given that adult men lived their private lives free of direct oversight. All the previous emperors had, for example, simply taxed male prostitutes. The legal status of homosexual activity between women is uncertain, but women's restricted freedom made it easier for men to think that women's sexuality could and should be controlled. Homosexual activity between married women probably counted as adultery and thus as a crime. In reality, Justinian probably had limited success in changing people's sexual behaviors, but he saw his strengthened emphasis on greater purity of life as an important demonstration of his commitment to fulfilling his responsibilities as a Christian emperor with the duty of preserving God's favor toward his rule and his subjects.

A brilliant theologian in his own right, Justinian tried to reconcile orthodox and Monophysite Christians by revising the creed of the Council of Chalcedon. But the church leaders in Rome and Constantinople had become too bitterly divided and too jealous of one another's prominence to agree on a unified church. The eastern and western churches were by now firmly launched on the diverging courses that would result in formal schism five hundred years later. Justinian's own ecumenical council in Constantinople ended in conflict in 553 when it jailed Rome's defiant Pope Vigilius while also managing to alienate Monophysite bishops. Probably no one could have done better, but Justinian's efforts to impose religious unity only drove Christians further apart and undermined his vision of a restored Roman world.

The Preservation of Classical Traditions in the Late Roman Empire

Since knowledge of a culture can disappear if its texts are not preserved, Christianization of the late Roman Empire endangered the memory of classical traditions. The greatest danger to the survival of the plays, histories, philosophical works, poems, speeches, and novels of classical Greece and Rome — which were polytheist and therefore potentially subversive of Christian belief — stemmed not so much from active censorship as simple neglect. As Christians became authors, which they did in great numbers, their works displaced ancient Greek and Roman texts as the most important literature of the age. Fortunately for later times, however, the eastern empire played a crucial role in passing on intellectual achievements from the past to later Western civilization.

Classical texts survived because Christian education and literature depended on non Christian models, Latin and Greek. In the eastern empire, the region's original Greek culture remained the dominant influence, but Latin literature continued to be read because the administration was bilingual, with official documents and laws published in Latin along with Greek translations. Latin scholarship in the east received a boost when Justinian's Italian wars caused Latin-speaking scholars to flee for safety to Constantinople. There they helped conserve many works that might otherwise have disappeared. Scholars preserved classical literature because they regarded it as a crucial part of a high-level education. In other words, much of the classical literature available today survived because it formed part of an elite curriculum for Christians. At least some knowledge of some pre-Christian classics was required for a successful career in government service, the goal of every ambitious student. An imperial decree from 360 stated, "No person shall obtain a post of the first rank unless it shall be shown that he excels in long practice of liberal studies, and that he is so polished in literary matters that words flow from his pen faultlessly."

Another factor promoting the preservation of classical literature was that the principles of classical rhetoric provided the guidelines for the most effective presentation of Christian theology. When Ambrose, bishop of Milan from 374 to 397, composed the first systematic description of Christian ethics for young ministers, he consciously imitated the great classical orator Cicero. Theologians refuted heretical Christian doctrines by employing the dialogue form pioneered by Plato, and polytheist traditions of biography praising heroes inspired the hugely popular genre of saints' lives. Choricius, a Christian who held the official position of professor of rhetoric in Gaza, wrote works based on subjects from pre-Christian Greek mythology and history, such as the Trojan War or the Athenian general Miltiades. Similarly, Christian artists incorporated polytheist traditions in communicating their beliefs and emotions in paintings, mosaics, and carved reliefs. A favorite artistic motif of Christ with a sunburst surrounding his head, for example, took its inspiration from polytheist depictions of the radiant Sun as a god. (See the illustration on page 218.)

The growth of Christian literature generated a technological innovation used also to preserve classical literature. Polytheist scribes had written books on sheets of parchment (made from thin animal skin) or paper (made from papyrus). They then glued the sheets together and attached rods at both ends to form a scroll. Readers faced an awkward task in unrolling scrolls to read. For ease of use, Christians produced their literature in the form of the codex — a book with bound pages that not only stood up better to use but also held text more efficiently than scrolls. Eventually the codex became the standard form of book production.

Despite its continuing importance in education and rhetoric, classical Greek and Latin literature barely survived the war-torn world dominated by Christians. Knowledge of Greek in the west faded so drastically that by the sixth century almost no one there could read the original versions of Homer's *Iliad* and *Odyssey*, the traditional foundations of a classical literary education. Latin fared better, and scholars such as Augustine and Jerome knew Rome's ancient literature extremely well. But they also saw its classics as potentially too seductive for a pious Christian because the pleasure that came from

An Author or Scribe at Work
This illustration from a book produced in late Roman/early medieval times shows either an author writing a book or a scribe making a copy of a book by hand. This was the painstaking and slow process necessary to produce books in antiquity; mechanical printing had not yet been invented, and therefore mass production of books was not possible. As a result, books were expensive and precious objects, as indicated in the painting by their being carefully placed on their sides in the cabinet behind the writer to keep their weight from warping their spines and pages. *(The Granger Collection, NY—All rights reserved.)*

reading them could be a distraction from the worship of God. Jerome in fact once had a nightmare of being condemned on Judgment Day for having been more dedicated to Cicero than to Christ.

The closing around 530 of the Academy, founded in Athens by Plato more than nine hundred years earlier, demonstrated the dangers for classical learning in the later Roman Empire. This most famous of classical schools finally went out of business when many of its scholars emigrated to Persia to escape Justinian's tightened restrictions on polytheist teachers and its revenues dwindled because the Athenian elite, its traditional supporters, were increasingly Christianized. The Neoplatonist school at Alexandria, by contrast, continued. Its leader John Philoponus (c. 490–570) was a Christian. In addition to Christian theology, Philoponus wrote commentaries on the works of Aristotle. Some of his ideas anticipated those of Galileo a thousand years later. With his work, he achieved the kind of synthesis of old and new that was one of the fruitful possibilities in the cultural transformation of the late Roman world—he was a Christian subject of the eastern Roman Empire in sixth-century Egypt, heading a school founded long before by polytheists, studying the works of an ancient Greek philosopher as the inspiration for his forward-looking scholarship. The strong possibility that present generations could learn from the past would continue as Western civilization once again remade itself in medieval times.

REVIEW QUESTION What policies did Justinian undertake to try to restore and strengthen the Roman Empire?

Conclusion

The third-century civil wars brought the Roman Empire to a crisis that Diocletian's creation of the dominate and reorganization of government temporarily relieved, but Diocletian's reforms only delayed the division of the empire. In the late fourth century, migrations of non-Roman peoples fleeing the Huns brought intense pressures on the central government. Emperor Theodosius I divided the empire into western and eastern halves in 395 to try to improve its administration and defense. When Roman authorities bungled the task of integrating barbarian tribes into Roman society, the newcomers created kingdoms that eventually replaced imperial government in the west. Roman history increasingly divided into two regional streams, even though emperors as late as Justinian in the sixth century retained the dream of reuniting the empire and restoring its glory.

The large-scale immigration of barbarian tribes into the Roman Empire transformed not only the western empire's politics, society, and economy but also the tribes themselves, as they developed their own ethnic identities while organizing themselves into kingdoms inside Roman territory. The economic deterioration and political weakness that accompanied these often violent changes destroyed the public-spiritedness of the elite, which had been one of the foundations of imperial stability, as wealthy nobles retreated to self-sufficient country estates and shunned municipal office.

The eastern empire fared better economically than the western and avoided the worst violence of the migrations. Eastern emperors attempted to pre-

MAPPING THE WEST

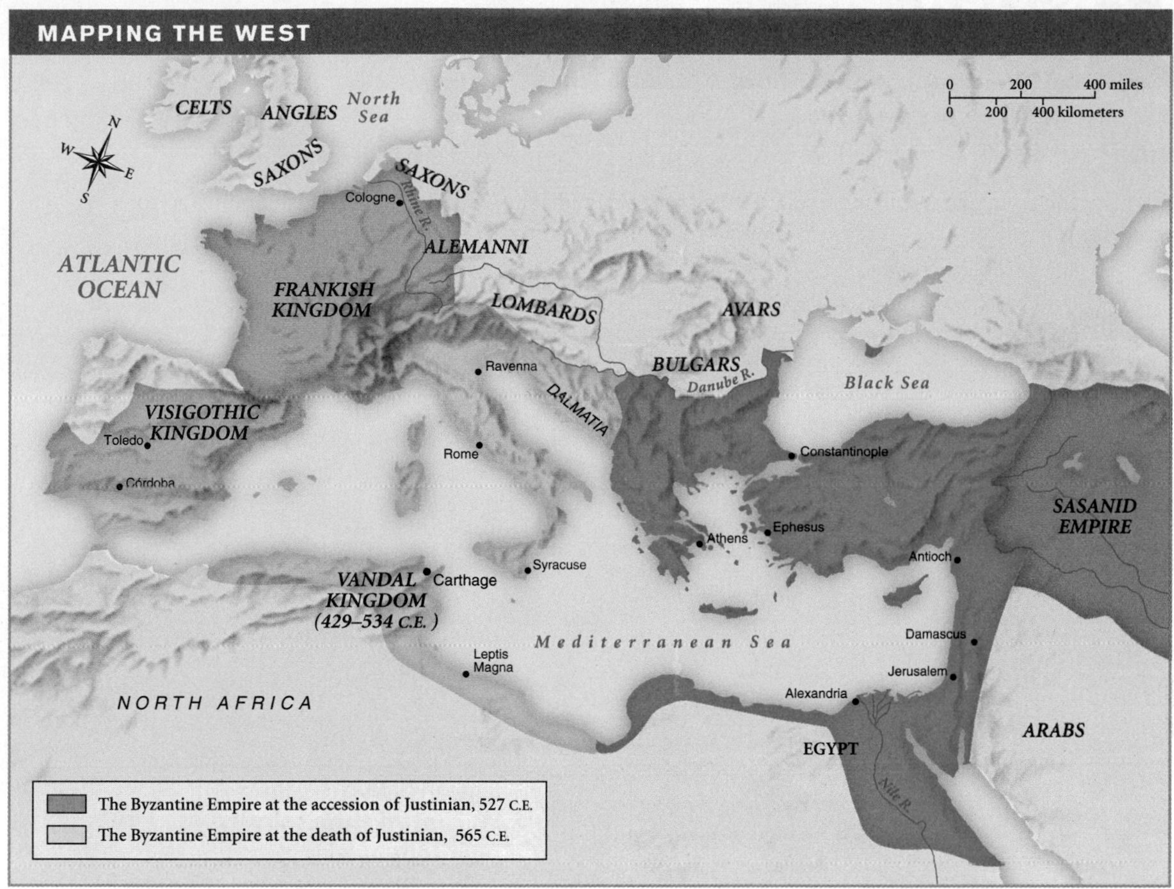

Western Europe and the Eastern Roman Empire, c. 600

The eastern Roman emperor Justinian employed brilliant generals and expended huge sums of money to reconquer Italy, North Africa, and part of Spain to reunite the western and eastern halves of the former Roman Empire. His wars to regain Italy and North Africa eliminated the Ostrogothic and Vandal kingdoms, respectively, but at a huge cost in effort, time—the war in Italy took twenty years—and expense. The resources of the eastern empire were so depleted that his successors could not maintain the reunification. By the early seventh century, the Visigoths had taken back all of Spain. Africa, despite serious revolts by indigenous Berber tribes, remained under imperial control until the Arab conquest of the seventh century. Within five years of Justinian's death, however, the Lombards had set up a new kingdom controlling a large section of Italy. Never again would anyone in the ancient world attempt to reestablish a universal Roman Empire.

serve "Romanness" by maintaining Roman culture and political traditions. The financial drain of trying to reunite the empire by wars against the new kingdoms increased social discontent by driving tax rates to unbearable levels, while the concentration of authority in the capital weakened local communities.

Constantine's conversion to Christianity in 312 marked a turning point in Western history. Christianization of the empire occurred gradually, and it was not until 391 that it became the official state religion and public polytheist worship was completely banned. Christians disagreed among themselves over fundamental doctrines of faith, even to the point of deadly violence. Many Christians attempted to come closer to God by abandoning everyday society to live as monks. Monastic life redefined the meaning of holiness by creating communities of God's heroes who withdrew from this world to devote their service to glorifying the next. In the end, then, the imperial vision of unity faded in the face of the powerful effects of political and social transformation. Nevertheless, the memory of Roman power and culture remained potent and present, providing an influential inheritance to the peoples and states that would become Rome's heirs in the next stage of Western civilization.

FOR FURTHER EXPLORATION

- **For additional primary-source material from this period**, see *Sources of the Making of the West*, Fourth Edition.
- **For Web sites, images, and documents related to topics in this chapter**, visit *Make History* at bedfordstmartins.com/hunt.

Chapter 7 Review

Online Study Guide bedfordstmartins.com/hunt

Key Terms and People

In the grid below, identify the term or person and explain its historical significance. (To do this exercise online, go to bedfordstmartins.com/hunt.)

Term	Who or What & When	Why It Matters
dominate (p. 207)		
tetrarchy (p. 209)		
coloni (p. 212)		
curials (p. 212)		
Great Persecution (p. 213)		
Edict of Milan (p. 213)		
Julian the Apostate (p. 215)		
Theodosius I (p. 216)		
Augustine (p. 218)		
Arianism (p. 219)		
Nicene Creed (p. 220)		
asceticism (p. 222)		
Visigoths (p. 229)		
wergild (p. 231)		
Justinian and Theodora (p. 233)		

Review Questions

1. What were Diocletian's policies to end the third-century crisis, and how successful were they?
2. How did Christianity both unite and divide the Roman Empire?
3. How did their migrations and invasions change the barbarians themselves and the Roman Empire?
4. What policies did Justinian undertake to try to restore and strengthen the Roman Empire?

Making Connections

1. How did the principate and the dominate differ with regard to political appearance versus political reality?
2. What were the main similarities and differences between polytheism and Christianity as official state religions in the late Roman Empire?
3. What developments in the late Roman Empire would support the idea that it is possible for a state to be too large to be well governed and to remain united indefinitely?

Important Events

Date	Event
293	Diocletian creates the tetrarchy
301	Diocletian issues edict on maximum prices and wages
303	Diocletian launches Great Persecution of Christians
312	Constantine wins battle of the Milvian Bridge and converts to Christianity
313	Religious freedom proclaimed in the Edict of Milan
323	Pachomius in Upper Egypt establishes the first monasteries
324	Constantine wins civil war and refounds Byzantium as Constantinople, the "new Rome"
325	Council of Nicaea defends Christian orthodoxy against Arianism
361–363	Julian the Apostate tries to reinstate polytheism as official state religion
378	Barbarian massacre of Roman army in battle of Adrianople
391	Theodosius I makes Christianity the official state religion
395	Theodosius I divides empire into western and eastern halves
410	Visigoths sack Rome
426	Augustine publishes *The City of God*
451	Council of Chalcedon attempts to forge agreement on Christian orthodoxy
475	Visigoths publish law code
476	German commander Odoacer deposes the final western emperor, the boy Romulus Augustulus ("fall of Rome")
493–526	Ostrogothic kingdom in Italy
507	Clovis establishes Frankish kingdom in Gaul
527–565	Reign of eastern Roman emperor Justinian
529–534	Justinian publishes law code and handbooks
540	Benedict devises his rule for monasteries

- Consider three events: **Augustine publishes *The City of God* (426)**, **Council of Chalcedon attempts to forge agreement on Christian orthodoxy (451)**, and **Justinian publishes law code and handbooks (529–534)**. What connections can be drawn between these events in terms of the attitudes that informed them, their goals, and their effects on society?

SUGGESTED REFERENCES

Some scholars regard the political, social, and cultural changes in the late Roman Empire as evidence of a sad "decline and fall"; others judge them to have had mixed positive and negative consequences. The rise of Christianity to the status of an official religion also changed Roman life in complex ways that are still being investigated.

Brown, Peter. *The Body and Society: Men, Women, and Sexual Renunciation in Early Christianity*. 1988.

Cameron, Alan. *The Last Pagans of Rome*. 2010.

Daryaee, Touraj. *Sasanian Iran (224–651 C.E.): Portrait of a Late Antique Empire*. 2008.

*Drew, Katherine Fischer, ed. *The Laws of the Salian Franks*. 1991.

Elsner, Jas. *Imperial Rome and Christian Triumph: The Art of the Roman Empire, A.D. 100–450*. 1998.

*Grubbs, Judith Evans. *Women and Law in the Roman Empire: A Sourcebook on Marriage, Divorce, and Widowhood*. 2002.

Halsall, Guy. *Barbarian Migrations and the Roman West, 376–568*. 2008.

Heather, Peter. *Empires and Barbarians: The Fall of Rome and the Birth of Europe*. 2010.

Kelly, Christopher. *Ruling the Later Roman Empire*. 2006.

*Lee, A. D. *Pagans and Christians in Late Antiquity: A Sourcebook*. 2000.

Little, Lester K., ed. *Plague and the End of Antiquity: The Pandemic of 541–750*. 2006.

MacMullen, Ramsay. *Christianity and Paganism in the Fourth to Eighth Centuries*. 1997.

Odahl, Charles. *Constantine and the Christian Empire*. 2nd ed. 2010.

*Procopius. *The Secret History*. Trans. G. A. Williamson and Peter Sarris. 2007.

*Procopius. *The Wars*. Vols. I–V. Trans. H. B. Dewing. 1914–1928.

Rosen, William. *Justinian's Flea: The First Great Plague and the End of the Roman Empire*. 2008.

Southern, Pat, and Karen R. Dixon. *The Late Roman Army*. 1996.

Wickham, Chris. *Framing the Early Middle Ages: Europe and the Mediterranean*. 2007.

*Primary source.

CHAPTER

8

The Heirs of Rome: Islam, Byzantium, and Europe

600–750

In the eighth century, a Syrian monk named Joshua wrote about the first appearance of Islam in Roman territory. "The Arabs conquered the land of Palestine and the land as far as the great river Euphrates. The Romans fled," he marveled, and then continued:

> The first king was a man among them named Muhammad, whom they also called Prophet because he turned them away from cults of all kinds and taught them that there was only one God, creator of the universe. He also instituted laws for them because they were much entangled in the worship of demons.

Joshua was wrong about Muhammad leading the conquest of Palestine — Muhammad died in 632, six years before the fall of Palestine. But he was right to see the Arab movement as a momentous development, for in the course of a few decades the Arabs conquered much of the Persian and Roman Empires. Joshua was also right to emphasize Muhammad's teachings, for it was the fervor of Islam that brought the Arabs out of the Arabian peninsula and into the regions that hugged the Mediterranean in one direction and led to the Indus River in the other.

In the sixth century, as the western and eastern parts of the Roman Empire were going their separate ways, a third power — Arab and Muslim — was forming. These three powers have continued in various forms to the present: the western Roman Empire became western Europe; the eastern Roman Empire (occupying what is now Turkey, Greece, and some of the Balkans) became part of eastern Europe and helped create Russia; and the Arab world endures in North Africa and the Middle East (the ancient Near East).

As diverse as these cultures are today, they share many of the same roots: All were heirs of Rome. All adhered to monotheism. The western and eastern

The Dome of the Rock at Jerusalem (691)
Rivaling the great churches of Christendom, the mosque in Jerusalem called Dome of the Rock borrowed from late Roman and Byzantine forms even while asserting its Islamic identity. The columns and the capitals atop them, the round arches, the dome, and the mosaics are all from Byzantine models. In fact, the columns were taken from older buildings at Jerusalem. But the strips of Arabic writing on the dome itself — and in many other parts of the building — assert Islamic doctrine. *(Erich Lessing/Art Resource, NY.)*

halves of the Roman Empire had Christianity in common, although they differed at times in interpreting it. Adherents of Islam, the Arab world's religion, believed in the same God as the Jews and Christians. They understood Jesus, however, as God's prophet rather than his son.

The history of the seventh and eighth centuries is a story of the Roman Empire's persistence and transformation. Historians consider the changes in the eastern empire so important that they use a new term — Byzantine Empire — to describe it. They also speak of the end of antiquity and the beginning of the Middle Ages. (See "Terms of History," page 245.) Use of the term *Byzantine Empire* or *Byzantium*, which comes from the old Greek name for Constantinople, rightly implies that the center of power and culture in the eastern Roman Empire was now concentrated in this one city. Over the centuries, the Byzantine Empire shrank, expanded, and even nearly disappeared — but it hung on in one form or another until 1453.

During the period 600–750, all three heirs of the Roman Empire combined elements of their heritage with new values, interests, and conditions. The divergences among them resulted from disparities in geography and climate, material and human resources, skills, beliefs, and local traditions. But these differences should not obscure the fact that the Byzantine, Muslim, and western European cultures were related.

CHAPTER FOCUS What three cultures took the place of the Roman Empire, and to what extent did each of them both draw on and reject Roman traditions?

Islam: A New Religion and a New Empire

In the sixth century, a religion that called on all to believe in one God began in Arabia (today Saudi Arabia). Islam ("submission to God") emerged under **Muhammad** (c. 570–632), a merchant turned holy man from the city of Mecca. While many of the people living in Arabia were polytheists, Muhammad recognized one God, the same one worshipped by Jews and Christians. He understood himself to be God's last prophet and thus came to be called the Prophet — the person who received and in turn repeated God's final words to humans. Invited by the quarreling tribes of Medina to act as a mediator for them, Muhammad exercised the powers of both a religious and a secular leader. This dual role became the model for his successors, known as caliphs. Through a combination of persuasion and force, Muhammad and his co-religionists, the Muslims ("those who submit to Islam"), converted most of the Arabian peninsula. By the time Muhammad died in 632, conquest and conversion had begun to move northward into Byzantine and Persian territories. In the next generation, the Arabs conquered most of Persia and all of Egypt and were on their way across North Africa to Spain. Yet within the territories they conquered, daily life went on much as before.

Nomads and City Dwellers

In the seventh century, the vast deserts of the Arabian peninsula were populated by both sedentary and nomadic peoples. The sedentary peoples, who lived in one place, far outnumbered the nomads, who were often on the move. Some of the sedentary groups lived in oases, where they raised dates, a highly prized food. Some oases were prosperous enough to support merchants and artisans. The nomads were known as Bedouins; they lived in the desert, where they herded goats, camels, or sheep, surviving largely on the products of their animals: leather, milk, and meat. (The richer nomads herded camels and called themselves Arabs.) The Bedouins

Muhammad: The prophet of Islam (c. 570–632). He united a community of believers around his religious tenets, above all that there was one God whose words had been revealed to him by the angel Gabriel. Later, written down, these revelations became the Qur'an.

c. 486–751 Merovingian dynasty

572 Lombards conquer northern Italy

587 Conversion of Visigothic king Reccared

r. 590–604 Papacy of Pope Gregory the Great

603–623 War between Byzantium and Persia

622 Hijra to Medina; year 1 of the Islamic calendar

550 — 575 — 600 — 625

c. 570–632 Life of Muhammad, prophet of Islam

r. 573–c. 594 Bishop Gregory of Tours

c. 590 Arrival of Irish monk Columbanus in Gaul

624 Muhammad and Meccans fight battle of Badr

were warriors; valuing honor and bravery, Bedouin tribes raided one another to capture slaves or wives and to take belongings. Although they lacked written literature, their oral tradition of poetry expressed many things, including the bravado of a boast, the trials of a journey, and longing for a lost love, as in the following verse:

> To remember Salma! to recall
> times spent with her
> is folly, conjecture about the other side,
> a casting of stones.

The "follies of love" were part of a culture in which men practiced polygyny (having more than one wife at a time).

Islam began as a religion of the city dwellers, but it soon found support and military strength among the nomads. It had its start in Mecca, an important commercial center near the coast of the Red Sea. Mecca was also a religious center, the home of the Ka'ba, a shrine that contained the images of many gods. The Ka'ba was a sacred place within which war and violence were prohibited. The tribe that dominated Mecca, the Quraysh, controlled access to the shrine, taxing the pilgrims who flocked there and selling them food and drink. Visitors, assured of their safety, bartered on the sacred grounds, transforming the plunder from raids into trade.

The Prophet Muhammad and the Faith of Islam

Muhammad was born in Mecca. Orphaned at the age of six, he lived two years with his grandfather and then came under the care of his uncle, a leader of the Quraysh tribe. Eventually, Muhammad became a trader. At the age of twenty-five, he married Khadija, a rich widow who had once employed him. They had at least four daughters and lived (to all appearances) happily and comfortably. Yet Muhammad sometimes left home and spent a few days in a nearby cave in prayer and contemplation, practicing a type of piety similar to that of the early Christians.

In about 610, on one of these retreats, Muhammad heard a voice and had a vision that summoned him to worship the God of the Jews and Christians, Allah ("the God" in Arabic). He accepted the call as coming from God. Over the next years, he received messages that he understood to be divine revelations. Later, when these messages had been written down and compiled—a process completed in the seventh century, but after Muhammad's

TERMS OF HISTORY

Medieval

How did the word *medieval* come into being, and why is it a derogatory term today? No one who lived in the Middle Ages thought of himself or herself as "medieval." People did not say they lived in the "Middle Ages." The whole idea of the Middle Ages began in the sixteenth century. At that time, writers decided that their own age, known as the Renaissance (French for "rebirth"), and the ancient Greek and Roman civilizations were much alike. They dubbed the period in between—from about 600 to about 1400—with a Latin term: the *medium aevum*, or the "middle age." It was not a flattering term. Renaissance writers considered the *medium aevum* a single unfortunate, barbaric, and ignorant period.

Only with the Romantic movement of the nineteenth century and the advent of history as an academic discipline did writers begin to divide that middle age into several ages. Often they divided it into three periods: Early (c. 600–1100), High (c. 1100–1300), and Late (c. 1300–1400). Today there is no hard-and-fast rule about this terminology: Chapter 11 of this book, for example, covers the period 1150–1215 as the High Middle Ages.

The period before the High Middle Ages was sometimes called the Dark Ages, a term that immediately brings to mind doom and gloom. However, recent research disputes this view of the period, stressing instead its creativity, multiethnicity, and localism.

Newspaper reporters and others still sometimes use *medieval* as a negative term: for example, by calling a primitive prison system "medieval." Little do they know that when they do that, they are stuck in the sixteenth century.

661–750 Umayyad caliphate

664 Synod of Whitby; English king opts for Roman form of Christianity

680–754 Life of Boniface, who reformed the Frankish church

r. 717–741 Emperor Leo III the Isaurian

726–787 Period of iconoclasm at Byzantium

650 — 675 — 700 — 725

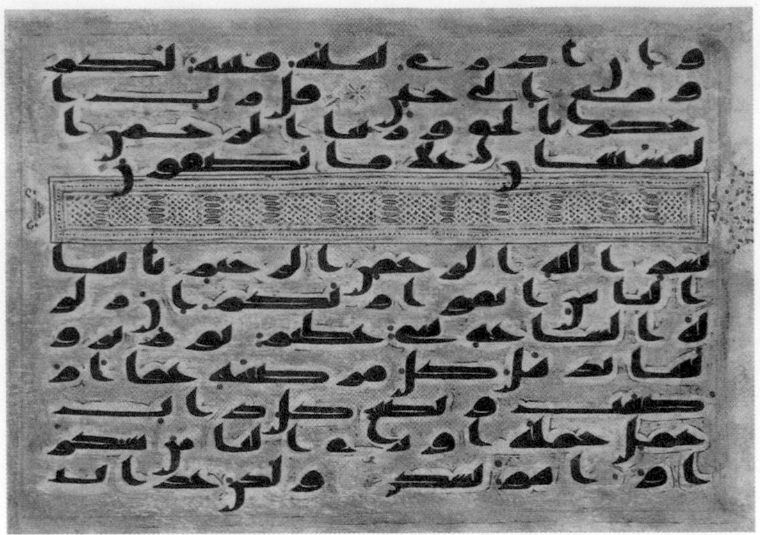

Qur'an
More than a holy book, the Qur'an represents for Muslims the very words of God that were dictated to Muhammad by the archangel Gabriel. In the Umayyad period, the Qur'an was written, as here, on pages wider than long. The first four lines on the top give the last verses of Sura 21. *(Freer Gallery of Art, Smithsonian Institution, Washington, DC, Purchase F1945.16.)*

death—they became the **Qur'an**, the holy book of Islam. *Qur'an* means "recitation"; each of the book's parts, or suras, is understood to be God's revelation as told to Muhammad by the archangel Gabriel—the very Gabriel of the Hebrew and Christian Bibles—and then recited by Muhammad to others. Written entirely in verse, the Qur'an changed the focus of traditional Bedouin poetry, which had emphasized the here and now. The Qur'an focuses on the divine, the "one of great power." In an early sura, Muhammad has a vision of this power:

> This is a revelation
> taught him by one of great power
> and strength that stretched out over
> while on the highest horizon—
> then drew near and came down
> two bows' lengths or nearer

Here the object of Muhammad's vision never quite reveals itself; nevertheless, it teaches him about its great power and strength, its astonishing ability to stretch to the horizon, and its willingness at the same time almost to touch him.

Beginning with the Fatihah ("opening"; see Document, "The Fatihah of the Qur'an," page 247), frequently also said as an independent prayer, the Qur'an continues with suras of gradually decreasing length. They cover the gamut of human experience and the life to come. For Muslims, the Qur'an contains the foundations of history, prophecy, and the legal and moral code by which men and women should live: "Do not set up another god with God. . . . Do not worship anyone but Him, and be good to your parents. . . . Give to your relatives what is their due, and to those who are needy, and the wayfarers." The Qur'an emphasizes the family—a man, his wife (or wives), and children—as the basic unit of Muslim society. For its adherents, Islam replaced the identity and protection of the tribe with a new identity as part of the *ummah*, the community of believers, who share both a belief in one God and a set of religious practices.

Stressing individual belief in God and adherence to the Qur'an, Islam had no priests or sacraments, though in time it came to have authoritative religious leaders who interpreted the Qur'an and related texts. The Ka'ba, with its many gods, had attracted tribes from the surrounding vicinity. Muhammad, with his one God, forged an even more universal religion.

Growth of Islam, c. 610–632

The first convert to Muhammad's faith was his wife, Khadija. A few friends and members of their immediate family joined them. Eventually, as Muhammad preached the new faith, others became adherents. Soon the new faith polarized Meccan society. Muhammad's insistence that the cults of all other gods be abandoned in favor of one brought him into conflict with leading members of the Quraysh tribe, whose control over the Ka'ba had given them prestige and wealth. Perceiving Muhammad as a threat, they insulted him and harassed his adherents.

Hijra: Muhammad's Journey from Mecca to Medina

Disillusioned with the people of Mecca, Muhammad looked elsewhere for a place and a population receptive to his message. In particular, he expected support from Jews, whose monotheism, in Muhammad's view, prepared them for his own faith. When a few of Muhammad's converts from Medina, an oasis about two hundred miles north of Mecca, promised to protect him if he would join them there, he eagerly accepted the invitation, in part because Medina had a significant Jewish population. Muhammad's journey to Medina—called the **Hijra**—proved to be a crucial event for the new faith. Although he was disappointed not to find much

Qur'an (Kur AN/Koo RAHN): The holy book of Islam, considered the word of Allah ("the God") as revealed to the Prophet Muhammad.

Hijra (HIJ ruh): The emigration of Muhammad from Mecca to Medina. Its date, 622, marks year 1 of the Islamic calendar.

support among the Jews at Medina, Muhammad did find others there ready to listen to his religious message and to accept him as the leader of their community. They expected him to act as a neutral and impartial judge in their interclan disputes. Muhammad's political position in the community set the pattern by which Islamic society would be governed afterward; rather than simply adding a church to political and cultural life, Muslims made their political and religious institutions inseparable. After Muhammad's death, the year of the Hijra, 622, was named the first year of the Islamic calendar; it marked the beginning of the new Islamic era.[1]

Although successful at Medina, Muhammad and his Muslim followers felt threatened by the Quraysh at Mecca, who actively opposed the public practice of Islam. For this reason, Muhammad led raids against them. At the battle of Badr in 624, the Muslims killed forty-nine of the Meccan enemy, took numerous prisoners, and confiscated rich booty. Thus, from the time of this conflict, the Bedouin tradition of plundering was grafted onto the Muslim duty of **jihad** ("striving in the way of God").

The battle of Badr was a great triumph for Muhammad, who was able to secure his position at Medina, gaining new adherents and silencing all doubters, including Jews. When the Jews of Medina did not convert to Islam as expected, Muhammad suspected them of supporting his enemies; he expelled two Jewish tribes from Medina and executed the male members of another. Although Muslims had originally prayed in the direction of Jerusalem, the center of Jewish worship, Muhammad now had them turn in the direction of Mecca.

DOCUMENT

The Fatihah of the Qur'an

The Fatihah is the prayer that begins the Qur'an. It emphasizes God's compassion for the believer, who needs to be guided "along the road straight"—God's highway. To convey the fluid nature of the phrases, which relate to one another in many ways and have no one meaning, the translation here uses no punctuation.

In the name of God
 the Compassionate the Caring
Praise be to God
 lord sustainer of the worlds
the Compassionate the Caring
master of the day of reckoning
To you we turn to worship
 and to you we turn in time of need
Guide us along the road straight
the road of those to whom you are giving
 not those with anger upon them
 not those who have lost the way

Source: *Approaching the Qur'an: The Early Revelations*, intro. and trans. Michael Sells (Ashland, OR: White Cloud Press, 1999), 42.

Question to Consider

- **According to this passage from the Fatihah, what are the attributes of God—and the corresponding attributes of those who believe in him?**

Defining the Faith

As Muhammad broke with the Jews, he instituted new practices to define Islam as a unique religion. Among these were the *zakat*, a tax on possessions to be used for alms; the fast of Ramadan, which took place during the ninth month of the Islamic year, the month in which the battle of Badr had been fought; the *hajj*, the pilgrimage to Mecca during the last month of the year, which each Muslim was to make at least once in his or her lifetime; and the *salat*, formal worship at least three times a day (later increased to five). The salat could include the *shahadah*, or profession of faith: "There is no divinity but God, and Muhammad is the messenger of God." Detailed regulations for these practices, sometimes called the **Five Pillars of Islam**, were worked out in the eighth and early ninth centuries.

Meanwhile, Muhammad sent troops to subdue Arabs north and south. In 630, he entered Mecca with ten thousand men and took over the city, assuring the Quraysh of leniency and offering alliances with its leaders. As the prestige of Islam grew, clans elsewhere converted. Through a combination of force, conversion, and negotiation, Muhammad was able to unite many, though by no means all, Arabic-speaking tribes under his leadership by the time of his death in 632.

Muhammad was responsible for social as well as religious change. The ummah included both men and women; Islam thus enhanced women's status. At

---

[1]Thus, 1 anno Hegirae (1 A.H.) on the Muslim calendar is equivalent to 622 C.E.

jihad: In the Qur'an, the word means "striving in the way of God." This can mean both striving to live righteously and striving to confront unbelievers, even through holy war.

Five Pillars of Islam: The five essential practices of Islam, namely, the *zakat* (alms); the fast of Ramadan; the *hajj* (pilgrimage to Mecca); the *salat* (formal worship); and the *shahadah* (profession of faith).

first, Muslim women joined men during the prayer periods that punctuated the day, but beginning in the eighth century, women began to pray apart from men. Men were allowed to have up to four wives at one time but were obliged to treat them equally; wives received dowries and had certain inheritance rights. Islam prohibited all infanticide, a practice that Arabs had long used largely against female infants. Like Judaism and Christianity, however, Islam retained the practices of a patriarchal society in which women's participation in community life was limited.

Even though the Islamic ummah was a new sort of community, it functioned in many ways as a tribe, or rather a "supertribe," obligated to fight common enemies, share plunder, and peacefully resolve any internal disputes. Muslims participated in group rituals, such as the salat and public recitation. The Qur'an was soon publicly sung by professional reciters, much as the old tribal poetry had been. Most significant for the eventual spread of Islam was that Bedouin converts to Islam turned their traditional warrior culture to its cause. Along the routes once taken by caravans to Syria, Muslim armies reaped profits at the point of a sword. But this differed from intertribal fighting; it was the jihad of people who were carrying out God's command against unbelievers as recorded in the Qur'an: "Strive, O Prophet, against the unbelievers and the hypocrites, and deal with them firmly. Their final abode is Hell: And what a wretched destination!"

The Caliphs, Muhammad's Successors, 632–750

In the new political community he founded in Arabia, Muhammad reorganized traditional Arab society by cutting across clan allegiances and welcoming converts from every tribe. He forged the Muslims into a formidable military force, and his successors, the caliphs, used this force to take the Byzantine and Persian worlds by storm.

War and Conquest After Muhammad's death, the Muslims moved to the north and west, quickly taking Byzantine territory in Syria and Egypt (Map 8.1). To the east, they invaded the Sasanid Empire, conquering the whole of Persia by 651. During the last half of the seventh century and the beginning of the eighth, Islamic warriors extended their sway westward to Spain and eastward to India.

How were such widespread conquests possible, especially in so short a time? First, the Islamic forces

MAP 8.1 Expansion of Islam to 750
In little more than a century, Islamic armies conquered a vast region that included numerous different people, cultures, climates, and living conditions. Yet under the Umayyads these disparate territories were administered by one ruler from the capital city at Damascus. The uniting force was the religion of Islam, which gathered all believers into one community, the *ummah.*

DOCUMENT

The Pact of Umar

Treaties such as the one excerpted here regulated the relations between Muslims and other monotheists in the regions conquered by the Muslims. The Muslims wished both to safeguard those who practiced other "religions of the book [the Bible]" and at the same time protect themselves and their religion from contamination by non-Muslims. The treaties also imposed a tax on non-Muslims. Historians used to think that this tax was simply a token, but recent studies argue that it was a considerable burden on many. The treaty given here is specifically for Christians, but those for Jews were similar. The numbering of the provisions here differs from the original.

1. If any of you [Christians] says of Muhammad or God's book or His religion something which is inappropriate for him to say, the protection of God, the commander of the faithful and all Muslims is removed from him; the conditions under which security was given will be annulled and the commander of the faithful will put that person's property and life outside the protection of the law, like the property and lives of enemies.
2. If one of you commits adultery with or marries a Muslim woman, or robs a Muslim on the highway, or turns a Muslim away from his religion . . . he has broken this agreement, and his life and property are outside the protection of the law. . . . We shall examine your every dealing between yourself and Muslims, and if you have had a part in anything that is unlawful for a Muslim, we shall undo it and punish you for it. . . . You will not give a Muslim any forbidden thing to eat or drink, and you will not allow him to marry in the presence of your witnesses, nor to partake in a marriage we consider illegal. [On the other hand] we shall not scrutinize nor inquire into a contract between you and any other unbeliever. . . .
3. You shall not display the cross nor parade your idolatry in any Muslim town, nor shall you build a church or place of assembly for your prayers, nor sound your bells. You will not use your idolatrous language about Jesus, son of Mary, or anyone else to any Muslim. . . .
4. For every free adult male of sound mind, there will be on his head a poll-tax of one dinar of full weight, payable at new year. He will not leave his land until he has paid the tax. . . .
5. These terms are binding on you and those who accept them; we have no treaty with those who reject them. We will protect you and your property which we deem lawful against anyone, Muslim or not, who tries to wrong you, just as we protect ourselves and our own property.

Source: "'Umar II and the 'protected people'" in *Classical Islam: A Sourcebook of Religious Literature*, ed. and trans. Norman Calder, Jawid Mojaddedi, and Andrew Rippin (London: Routledge, 2003), 90–92.

Question to Consider

- **In what ways does this pact protect Christians, and in what ways does it coerce them?**

came up against weakened empires. The Byzantine and Sasanid states were exhausted from fighting each other, and the cities they fought over were depopulated and demoralized. Second, discontented Christians and Jews welcomed Muslims into both Byzantine and Persian territories. The Monophysite Christians in Syria and Egypt, for example, who had suffered persecution under the Byzantines, were glad to have new, Islamic overlords. The so-called Pact of Umar, which set out the terms by which Christians and Jews were to be integrated into the new Islamic empire, made clear that Christianity and Judaism could be practiced so long as Islam was accorded special honor (see Document, "The Pact of Umar," above).

There were also internal reasons for Islamic success. Arabs had long been used to intertribal warfare; now united as a supertribe, inspired by religious fervor, and fighting under the banner of jihad, they exercised their skills as warriors against unbelievers. Fully armed and mounted on horseback, using camel convoys to carry supplies and provide protection, they conquered with amazing ease. To secure their victories, they built garrison cities from which their soldiers requisitioned taxes and goods. Sometimes whole Arab tribes, including women and children, were resettled in conquered territory, as happened in parts of Syria. In other regions, such as Egypt, one small Muslim settlement sufficed to gather the spoils of conquest.

The Politics of Succession Muhammad died quietly at Medina in 632. The question of who should succeed him as leader of the new Islamic state was the origin of the tension between the two main Muslim factions — Shi'ite and Sunni — that continues today. The caliphs who followed Muhammad came not from the traditional tribal elite but rather from the inner circle of men who had participated in the Hijra and remained close to the Prophet. The first two caliphs ruled without serious opposition, but the third caliph,

Uthman (r. 644–656), a member of the Umayyad clan and son-in-law of Muhammad, aroused discontent among other members of the inner circle and soldiers unhappy with his distribution of high offices and revenues. Accusing Uthman of favoritism, they supported his rival, Ali, a member of the Hashim clan (to which Muhammad had belonged) and the husband of Muhammad's only surviving child, Fatimah. After a group of discontented soldiers murdered Uthman, civil war broke out between the Umayyads and Ali's faction. It ended when Ali was killed by one of his own former supporters, and the caliphate remained in Umayyad hands from 661 to 750.

Despite defeat, the Shi'at Ali ("Ali's faction"), did not fade away. Ali's memory lived on among **Shi'ite Muslims**, who saw in him a symbol of justice and righteousness. For them, Ali's death was the martyrdom of the only true successor to Muhammad. They remained faithful to his dynasty, shunning the mainstream caliphs of Sunni Muslims (whose name derived from the word *sunna*, the practices of Muhammad). The Shi'ites awaited the arrival of the true leader — the imam — who in their view could come only from the house of Ali.

Shi'ite: A Muslim of the "party of Ali" and his descendants. Shi'ites are thus opposed to the Sunni Muslims, who reject the authority of Ali.

Peace and Prosperity in Islamic Lands

Ironically, the definitive victories of the Muslim warriors in the seventh and early eighth centuries ushered in times of peace. While the conquerors stayed within their fortified cities or built magnificent hunting lodges in the deserts of Syria, the conquered went back to work, to study, to play, and — in the case of Christians and Jews, who were considered protected subjects — to live in accordance with the provisions of the Pact of Umar. Under the **Umayyad caliphate**, which lasted from 661 to 750, the Muslim world became a state. Its capital was at Damascus, in Syria.

Borrowing from institutions well known to the civilizations they had just conquered, the Muslims issued coins and hired Byzantine and Persian officials as civil servants (see "Seeing History," page 251). They made Arabic a tool of centralization, imposing it as the language of government on regions not previously united linguistically. At the same time, the Islamic world was startlingly multireligious and multiethnic, including Arabs, Syrians, Egyptians, Iraqis, and many other peoples.

Taking advantage of the vigorous economy in both the cities and the countryside, the Umayyads presided over a new literary and artistic flowering. At Damascus, local artists and craftspeople worked on the lavish decorations for a mosque that used Roman motifs. At Jerusalem, the mosque called the Dome of the Rock used Christian building models for its octagonal form and its interior arches,

Umayyad caliphate (oo MAH yuhd KAY luhf ayt): The caliphs (successors of Muhammad) who traced their ancestry to Umayyah, a member of Muhammad's tribe. The dynasty lasted from 661 to 750.

Mosaic from the Great Mosque at Damascus
Like the Dome of the Rock, the Umayyad mosque at Damascus in Syria, built at the beginning of the eighth century, drew on Byzantine forms. In this mosaic, which is one of many that decorate the interior of the mosque, the style is Byzantine. But the harmonious intertwining of trees, buildings, rocks, and water picks up on an Islamic theme: the new faith's conquest over both civilization and nature. *(© Umayyad Mosque, Damascus, Syria / Bildarchiv Steffens / The Bridgeman Art Library International.)*

SEEING HISTORY

Who Conquered Whom? A Persian and an Arabic Coin Compared

Do you see any differences between the two coins shown here? One is Persian; the other is Arabic and comes from a later period. Both were minted for use in Iran and Iraq, but at different times, when these lands were under different rule. The coin on the top is Persian and shows the image of a Sasanid King of Kings. In the margin are three crescents, each encompassing stars. It was minted under Chosroes II (r. 591–628), the ambitious conqueror of Jerusalem. The coin on the bottom was minted by an Umayyad provincial governor in 696/697, after Islamic armies had conquered Persia. True, one branch of Islam barred depicting the human form, but the early Ummayads were less condemning and saw nothing wrong with imitating traditional numismatic models. Although the image on the Arabic coin is still of a Sasanid ruler, the governor had his own name added in Arabic—it's in the right half of the central roundel, perpendicular to the nose. He also added in the margin of the coin an Arabic inscription that mentions Allah several times.

Consider these coins in conjunction with supplemental evidence. The Arabic word for this type of coin, *dirham*, comes from the Greek *drachma*, a monetary unit used under the Byzantines. In areas that had been under Byzantine rule, the early Umayyad rulers adopted Byzantine coin forms, reusing *their* images—just as here they used the face of a Sasanid ruler. In general, the Umayyad fiscal system, which preserved the Byzantine land taxes, was administered by Syrians, who had often served Byzantine rulers in the same capacity. What advantages did the Arabs derive from adopting these institutions? From this evidence, how might you argue that both Greek and Persian institutions captured the conquering Arabs?

Question to Consider

- **What do the images and history of these two coins suggest about how much the Islamic world borrowed from the Persian Empire that it conquered?**

Persian Silver Coin (minted 606). (*© The Trustees of the British Museum/Art Resource, NY.*)

Umayyad Silver Dirham (minted 696/697). (*© The Trustees of the British Museum/Art Resource, NY.*)

which rested on columns and piers (see the chapter-opening photo).

During the seventh and eighth centuries, Muslim scholars turned Arabic, previously an oral language primarily, into a written language as well. They determined the definitive form for the Qur'an and compiled pious narratives about Muhammad, called hadith literature. A literate class—consisting mainly of the old Persian and Syrian elites, now converted to Islam—created new forms of prose writing in Arabic, producing official documents and essays on every sort of topic. They also wrote poetry, exploring new worlds of thought and feeling. Supported by the caliphs, for whom written poetry served as an important source of propaganda and reinforcement for their power, the poets also reached a wider audience that delighted in their clever use of words, their satire, and their verses celebrating courage, piety, and sometimes erotic love:

> I spent the night as her bed-companion, each enamored of the other,
> And I made her laugh and cry, and stripped her of her clothes.
> I played with her and she vanquished me; I made her happy and I angered her.
> That was a night we spent, in my sleep, playing and joyful,
> But the caller to prayer woke me up.

Such poetry scandalized conservative Muslims, brought up on the ascetic tenets of the Qur'an. But this love poetry was a by-product of the new urban civilization of the Umayyad period, during which wealth, cultural mix, and the confidence born of conquest inspired diverse and experimental literary forms. By the time the Umayyad caliphate ended in 750, Islamic civilization was multiethnic, urban, and sophisticated—a true heir of Roman and Persian traditions.

REVIEW QUESTION How and why did the Muslims conquer so many lands in the period 632–750?

Byzantium Besieged

The Byzantines saw themselves as the direct heirs of Rome. In fact, as we have seen, Emperor Justinian (r. 527–565) had tried to re-create the old Roman Empire and, on the surface, had succeeded. His empire once again included Italy, North Africa, and the Balkans. Vestiges of the old Roman society persisted: an educated elite maintained its prestige, town governments continued to function, and old myths and legends were retold in poetry and depicted in works of art. Around 600, however, the eastern half of the Roman Empire began to undergo a transformation as striking as the one that had earlier remade the western half.

Almost constant war, beginning in the last third of the sixth century and continuing through the seventh century, shrank the eastern empire's territory drastically. Cultural and political change came as well. Cities decayed, and the countryside became the focus of governmental and military administration. In the wake of these shifts, the old elite largely disappeared and classical learning gave way to new forms of education, mainly religious in content. The traditional styles of urban life, dependent on public gathering places and community spirit, faded away. Historians have good reason to stop speaking of the eastern Roman Empire and call this something new—the Byzantine Empire.

At the same time, the transformations should not be exaggerated. A powerful emperor continued to rule at Constantinople. Roman laws and taxes remained in place. The cities, while shrunken, nevertheless survived, and Constantinople itself had a flourishing economic and cultural life even in Byzantium's darkest hours. The Byzantines continued to call themselves Romans. For them, the empire never ended: it just moved to Constantinople.

Wars on the Frontiers, c. 570–750

From about 570 to 750, the Byzantines waged war against invaders. One key challenge came from an old enemy, Persia. Another involved many new groups—Lombards, Slavs, Avars, Bulgars, and Muslims. In the wake of these onslaughts, Byzantium became smaller but tougher.

Invasions from Persia In the sixth century, before the Muslims came on the scene, the principal challenge to Byzantine power came from the Sasanid Empire of Persia (Map 8.2). From their capital city at Ctesiphon, where they built a grand palace complex, the Sasanid kings promoted an exalted view of themselves: they took the title *King of Kings* and gave the men at their court titles such as *priest of priests* and *scribe of scribes*. Dreams of military and imperial glory accompanied the display of splendor. Using the revenues from new taxes to strengthen the army, the Sasanids decided to invade major areas of the Roman Empire. Between 611 and 614, King Chosroes II (r. 591–628) took Syria and Jerusalem; he conquered Egypt in 620. The fall of Jerusalem particularly shocked the pious Byzantines, since Chosroes took as plunder the relic of the Holy Cross (on which Jesus was said to have died).

Responding to this affront, the Byzantine emperor **Heraclius** reorganized his army and inspired his troops to avenge the sack of Jerusalem. By 627, the Byzantines had regained all their lost territory. But the wars had changed much: Syrian, Egyptian, and Palestinian cities had grown used to being under Persian rule, and Christians who did not adhere to the orthodoxy at Byzantium preferred their Persian overlords. Even more important, the constant wars and plundering sapped the wealth of the region and the energy of its people.

Attack on All Fronts Preoccupied by war with the Sasanids, Byzantium was ill equipped to deal with other groups who were pushing into parts of the empire at about the same time. The **Lombards**, a Germanic people, entered northern Italy in 568 and by 572 were masters of the Po valley and some inland regions in Italy's south. In addition to Rome, the Byzantines retained only Bari, Calabria, Sicily, and a narrow swath of land through the middle called the Exarchate of Ravenna.

The Byzantine army could not contend anymore with the Slavs and other peoples just beyond the Danube River. The Slavs conducted lightning

---

Heraclius (her uh KLY uhs): The Byzantine emperor who reversed the fortunes of war with the Persians in the first quarter of the seventh century.

Lombards: The people who settled in Italy during the sixth century, following Justinian's reconquest. A king ruled the north of Italy, while dukes ruled the south. In between was the papacy, which felt threatened both by Lombard Arianism and by the Lombards' geographical proximity to Rome.

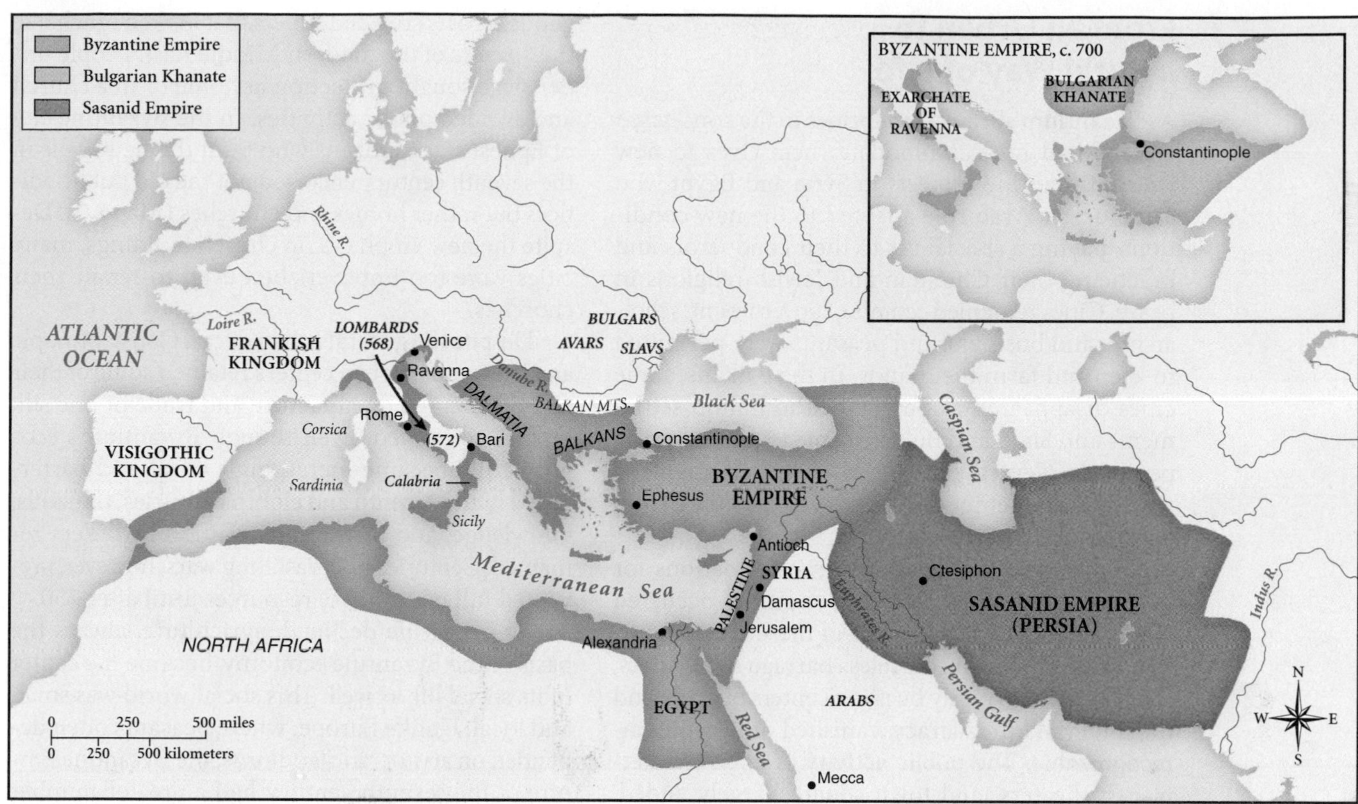

MAP 8.2 Byzantine and Sasanid Empires, c. 600
The emperor Justinian (r. 527–565) hoped to re-create the old Roman Empire, but just a century after his death Italy was largely conquered by the Lombards. Meanwhile, the Byzantine Empire had to contend with the Sasanid Empire to its east. In 600, these two major powers faced each other uneasily. Three years later, the Sasanid king attacked Byzantine territory. The resulting wars, which lasted until 627, exhausted both empires and left them open to invasion by the Arabs. By 700, the Byzantine Empire was quite small. | **Compare the inset map here with Map 8.1, on page 248. Where did the Muslims made significant conquests of Byzantine territory?**

raids on the Balkan countryside (part of Byzantium at the time); joined by the Avars, they attacked Byzantine cities as well. Meanwhile, the Bulgars entered what is now Bulgaria in the 670s, defeating the Byzantine army and in 681 forcing the emperor to recognize their new state.

Even as the Byzantine Empire was facing military attacks on all fronts, its power was being whittled away by more peaceful means. For example, as Slavs and Avars, who were not subject to Byzantine rulers, settled in the Balkans, they often intermingled with the native peoples there, absorbing local agricultural techniques and burial practices while imposing their language and establishing religious cults.

Consequences of Constant Warfare

Byzantium's loss of control over the Balkans meant the shrinking of its empire (see Map 8.2 inset). More important, the Balkan peninsula could no longer serve, as it had previously, as a major link between Byzantium and Europe. The loss of the Balkans exacerbated the growing separation between the eastern and western parts of the former Roman Empire. The political division between the Greek-speaking and Latin-speaking halves had begun in the fourth century; the events of the seventh century, however, made the split both physical and cultural. Avar and Slavic control of the Balkans effectively cut off trade and travel between Constantinople and the cities of the Dalmatian coast, while the Bulgarian khanate threw up a political barrier across the Danube. Perhaps as a result of this physical separation, historians in the East ceased to be interested in the western part of Europe, and Byzantine scholars no longer bothered to learn Latin. The two halves of the former Roman Empire communicated very little in the seventh century.

Byzantium's wars with the Sasanid Empire exhausted both Persian and Byzantine military strength. Both empires were now vulnerable to attack by the Muslim Arabs, whose military conquests created a new empire and introduced a new religion.

From an Urban to a Rural Way of Life

As Byzantium shrank, Byzantines in the conquered regions had to accommodate themselves to new rulers. Byzantine subjects in Syria and Egypt who came under Arab rule adapted to the new conditions, paying a special tax to their conquerors and practicing their Christian and Jewish religions in peace. Cities remained centers of government, scholarship, and business, and peasants were permitted to keep and farm their lands. In the Balkans, some cities disappeared as people fled to hilltop settlements and Slavs and Bulgars came to dominate the peninsula. Nevertheless, the newcomers recognized the Byzantine emperor's authority, and they soon began to flirt with Christianity.

Some of the most radical transformations for seventh- and eighth-century Byzantines occurred not in the territories lost but in the shrunken empire itself. Under the ceaseless barrage of invaders, many towns, formerly bustling centers of trade and the imperial bureaucracy, vanished or became unrecognizable. The public activity of open marketplaces, theaters, and town squares largely ended. City baths, once places where people gossiped, made deals, and talked politics and philosophy, disappeared in most Byzantine towns—with the significant exception of Constantinople. Warfare reduced some cities to rubble, and the limited resources available for rebuilding went to construct thick city walls and solid churches instead of spacious marketplaces and baths. Traders and craftspeople sold their goods on overcrowded streets that looked much like the bazaars of the modern Middle East. People under siege sought protection at home or in a church and avoided public activities. In the Byzantine city of Ephesus, the citizens who built the new walls in the seventh century enclosed not the old public edifices but rather homes and churches (Map 8.3). Despite the new emphasis on church buildings, many cities were too impoverished even to repair their churches.

Despite the general urban decay, Constantinople and a few other urban centers retained some of their old vitality. The manufacture and trade of fine silk textiles continued. Even though Byzantium's economic life became increasingly rural and barter-based in the seventh and eighth centuries, the skills, knowledge, and institutions of urban workers remained. Centuries of devastating wars, however, prevented full use of these resources until after 750.

As urban life declined, agriculture, always the basis of the Byzantine economy, became the center of its social life as well. This social world was small and local. Unlike Europe, where peasants often depended on aristocratic landlords, the Byzantine Empire of the seventh century had a greater number of free peasants who grew food, herded cattle, and tended vineyards on their own small plots of land. Farmers interacted mostly with members of their families or with monks at local monasteries; two or three neighbors were enough to ratify a land transfer. As Byzantine cities declined, the curials (town councilors), the elite who for centuries had mediated between the emperor and the people, disappeared. Now on those occasions when farmers came into contact with the state—to pay taxes, for example—they felt the impact of the emperor or his representatives directly. There were no local protectors any longer.

Emperors, drawing on the still-vigorous Roman legal tradition, promoted local, domestic life with new imperial legislation. The laws strengthened the nuclear family by narrowing the grounds for divorce and setting new punishments for marital infidelity. Husbands and wives who committed adultery were to be whipped and fined, and their noses slit. Abortion was prohibited, and new protections were set in place against incest. Mothers were given equal power with fathers over their offspring; if widowed, they became the legal guardians of their minor children and controlled the household property.

Silver Censer from Cyprus
This small dish, used for burning incense (and thus called a censer), was used during the Christian church service; it was carried and swung on three chains attached to the round rings on the lip of the censer. Each of the six sides shows a holy figure; pictured here is the Virgin Mary flanked by Saints John and James. By the seventh century, such precious objects were common in churches throughout the Byzantine Empire. *(© The Trustees of the British Museum/Art Resource, NY.)*

New Military and Cultural Forms

The shift from an urban-centered society to a rural one meant changes not only in daily life and the economy but also in the empire's military and cultural institutions. The Byzantine navy fought successfully at sea with its powerful weapon of "Greek fire," a mixture of crude oil and resin that was heated and shot via a tube over the water, engulfing enemy ships in flames. Determined to win wars on land as well, the imperial government tightened its control over the military by wresting power from other elite families and encouraging the formation of a middle class of farmer-soldiers. One seventh-century emperor, possibly Heraclius, divided the empire into military districts called ***themes*** and put all civil as well as military matters in each district into the hands of one general, a *strategos*. Landless men were lured to join the army with the promise of land and low taxes; they fought side by side with local farmers, who provided their own weapons and horses. The new organization effectively countered frontier attacks.

The disappearance of the old cultural elite meant a shift in the focus of education. Whereas the curial class had cultivated the study of the pagan classics, hiring tutors or sending their children (primarily their sons) to school to learn to read the works of Greek poets and philosophers, eighth-century parents showed far more interest in giving their children, both sons and daughters, a religious education. Even with the decay of urban centers, cities and villages often retained an elementary school. There teachers used the Book of Psalms (the Psalter) as their primer. Secular, classical learning remained decidedly out of favor throughout the seventh and eighth centuries; dogmatic writings, biographies of saints, and devotional works took center stage.

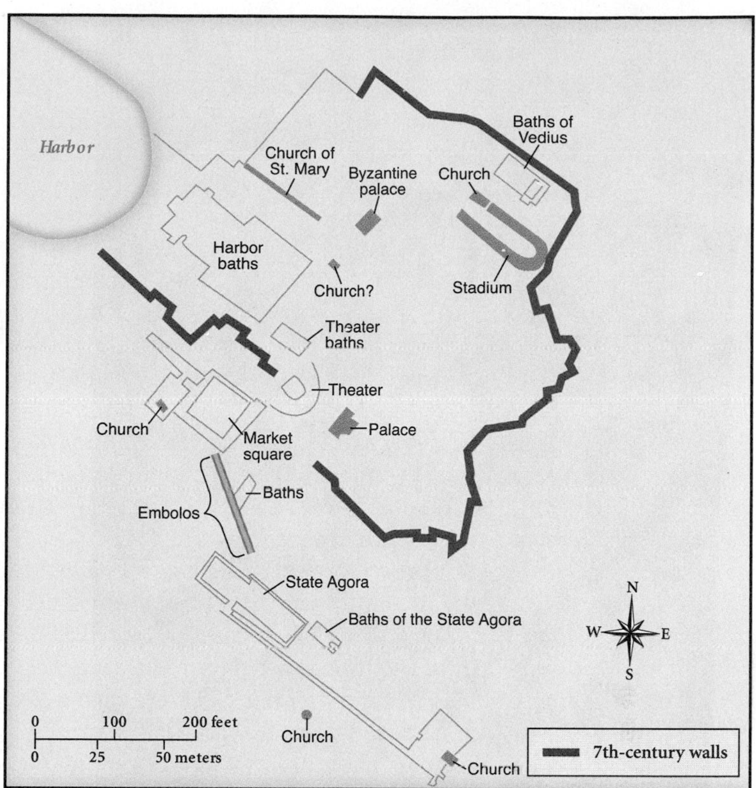

MAP 8.3 Plan of the City of Ephesus
Before the seventh century, Ephesus sprawled around its harbor. Nearest the harbor were baths and churches including, by 500, the bishop's Church of St. Mary. To the south was the Embolos—a long, marble-paved avenue adorned with fountains, statues, and arcades and bordered by well-appointed homes. Earthquakes, plague, and invasions changed much in the seventh century. Ephesians built a new wall to embrace the area around the harbor. The Embolos was neglected, and even within the narrow precinct protected by the new wall, baths were allowed to go to ruin, while people made their homes within the debris. After the Arabs invaded, the bishop moved out of the city altogether.

Religion, Politics, and Iconoclasm

The importance of religious learning and piety in the seventh century complemented both the autocratic imperial ideal and the powers of the bishops. While in theory imperial and church powers were separate, in practice they were interdependent. The emperor exercised considerable power over the church: he influenced the appointment of the chief religious official, the patriarch of Constantinople; he called church councils to determine dogma; and he regularly used bishops as local governors. Beginning with Heraclius, the emperors considered it one of their duties to baptize Jews forcibly, persecuting those who would not convert. In the view of the imperial court, this was part of the ruler's role in upholding orthodoxy.

Bishops and Monks Jostling for Power

At the same time, although the curial lay elite had disappeared, bishops and their clergy formed a rich and powerful upper class, even in declining cities. They served as judges and tax collectors. They distributed food in times of famine or siege, provisioned troops, and set up military fortifications. As part of their charitable work, they cared for the sick and the needy. Byzantine bishops were part of a three-tiered system: they were appointed by metropolitans (bishops who headed an entire province), and the metropolitans were in turn appointed by the patriarchs (bishops with authority over whole regions).

Theoretically, monasteries were under the limited control of the local bishop, but in practice they were enormously powerful institutions that often defied the authority of bishops and even emperors. Because monks commanded immense prestige as

theme: A military district in Byzantium. The earliest themes were created in the seventh century and served mainly defensive purposes.

Icon of the Virgin and Child
Surrounded by two angels in the back and two soldier-saints at either side, the Virgin Mary and the Christ Child are depicted with still, otherworldly dignity. The sixth-century artist gave the angels transparent halos to emphasize their spiritual natures, while depicting the saints as earthly men, with hair and beards, and feet planted firmly on the ground. Icons like this were used for worship both in private homes and in Byzantine monasteries. *(Erich Lessing / Art Resource, NY.)*

the holiest of God's faithful, they could influence the many issues of doctrine that racked the Byzantine church.

Conflict over Icons The most important doctrinal issue of the Byzantine church in this period revolved around **icons**—images of holy people, such as Jesus; his mother, Mary; and the saints (see the illustration above). To Byzantine Christians, icons were far more than mere representations: they were believed to possess holy power that directly affected people's daily lives as well as their chances for salvation.

Many seventh-century Byzantines made icons the focus of their religious devotion. To them, the images were like the incarnation of Christ in that they turned spirit into material substance. That is, they believed that an icon manifested in physical form the holy person it depicted. Some Byzantines actually worshipped icons; others, particularly monks, considered icons a necessary part of Christian piety. Protected by his Muslim overlords, the Christian Syrian St. John of Damascus wrote a thundering defense of icons (see Document, "On Holy Images," page 257).

Other Byzantines abhorred icons. Most numerous of these were the soldiers on the frontiers. Unnerved by Arab triumphs, they attributed their misfortunes to disregard of the biblical command against graven (carved) images: "You shall not make for yourself a graven image, or any likeness of anything that is in heaven above, or that is in the earth beneath, or that is in the water under the earth" (Exod. 20:4). When they compared their defeats to Muslim successes, Byzantine soldiers could not help but notice that Islam prohibited all visual images of the divine. To these soldiers and others who shared their view, icons revived pagan idolatry and desecrated Christian divinity. As the movement toward **iconoclasm** ("icon breaking") grew, some churchmen became outspoken in their opposition to icons.

Byzantine emperors shared these religious objections, and they also had important political reasons for opposing icons. One reason was that the issue of icons became a test of their authority. Icons diluted loyalties, creating intermediaries between worshippers and God that undermined the emperor's exclusive place in the divine and temporal order. In addition, the emphasis on icons in monastic communities made the monks potential threats to imperial power; the emperors hoped to use this issue to weaken the monasteries. Above all, though, the emperors opposed icons because the army did, and they needed to retain the loyalty of their troops.

After Emperor Leo III the Isaurian (r. 717–741) defeated the Arabs besieging Constantinople at the beginning of his reign, he turned his attention to consolidating his political position. Officers of the

---

icons: Images of holy people such as Jesus, Mary, and the saints. Controversy arose in Byzantium over the meaning of such images. The iconoclasts considered them "idols," but those who adored icons maintained that they manifested the physical form of those who were holy.

iconoclasm: Literally, "icon breaking"; referring to the destruction of icons, or images of holy people. Byzantine emperors banned icons from 726 to 787; a modified ban was revived in 815 and lasted until 843.

DOCUMENT

On Holy Images

At Constantinople, no one could publicly oppose iconoclasm. But Christians in the Arab world had more freedom. John of Damascus (c. 675–749) was born in Syria after it came under Islamic rule. His father, though Christian, worked for the Arab governor there, and John soon did so as well. John wrote this ringing defense of icons shortly before he joined a monastery near Jerusalem. To be sure, the iconoclasts condemned his work, but he was vindicated in 787, when the ban was lifted (for a time).

I believe in one God, the source of all things, without beginning, uncreated, immortal, everlasting, incomprehensible, bodiless, invisible, uncircumscribed [i.e., in no one place], without form. I believe in one supersubstantial being [i.e., beyond all substance], one divine Godhead in three entities, the Father, the Son, and the Holy Ghost, and I adore Him alone with the worship [due God alone]. I adore one God, one Godhead but three Persons, God the Father, God the Son made flesh, and God the Holy Ghost, one God. I do not adore creation more than the Creator, but I adore the creature created as I am, adopting creation freely and spontaneously that He might elevate our nature and make us partakers of His divine nature. Together with my Lord and King I worship Him clothed in the flesh, not as if it were a garment or He constituted a fourth person of the Trinity—God forbid. That flesh is divine, and endures after its assumption. Human nature was not lost in the Godhead, but just as the Word made flesh remained the Word, so flesh became the Word remaining flesh, becoming, rather, one with the Word through union. Therefore I venture to draw an image of the invisible God, not as invisible, but as having become visible for our sakes through flesh and blood. I do not draw an image of the immortal Godhead. I paint the visible flesh of God, for if it is impossible to represent a spirit, how much more God who gives breath to the spirit.

Source: *St. John Damascene on Holy Images*, trans. Mary H. Allies (London: Thomas Baker, 1898), 1 (slightly modified).

Question to Consider

- **How does John's view of the nature of the Son (Jesus Christ) support his argument in favor of icons?**

imperial court tore down the great golden icon of Christ at the gateway of the palace and replaced it with a cross. In 726, Leo ordered all icons destroyed, a ban that remained in effect until 787. This is known as the period of iconoclasm in Byzantine history. A modified ban would be revived in 815 and last until 843.

Iconoclasm had an enormous impact on Byzantium. At home, where people had their own portable icons, the devout had to destroy their icons or worship them in secret. Iconoclasts (who were especially numerous at Constantinople itself) whitewashed the walls of churches, erasing all the images. They smashed portable icons. Artists largely ceased depicting the human form, and artistic production in general dwindled during this time. The power and prestige of the monasteries, which were associated with icons, diminished. As the tide of battle turned in favor of the Byzantines, imperial supporters and soldiers credited iconoclasm for their victories.

REVIEW QUESTION What stresses did the Byzantine Empire endure in the seventh and eighth centuries, and how was iconoclasm a response to those stresses?

Western Europe: A Medley of Kingdoms

In contrast to Byzantium—where an emperor still ruled as the successor to Augustus and Constantine, drawing on an unbroken chain of Roman legal and administrative traditions—western Europe saw a dispersal of political power in the seventh and eighth centuries. With the end of Roman imperial government in the western half of the empire, the region was divided into a number of kingdoms: various monarchs ruled in Spain, Italy, England, and Gaul. The primary foundations of power and stability in all of these kingdoms were kinship networks, church patronage, royal courts, and wealth derived from land and plunder. There were kings, to be sure, but in some places churchmen and rich magnates were even more powerful than royalty. Icons were not very important in the West, but in their place was the power of the saints as exercised through their relics—the bodies and body parts, even clothes and dust from the tombs of holy people. These represented and wielded the divine forces of God. Although the patterns of daily life and the procedures of government in western Europe remained recognizably Roman, they were also in the process of

TABLE 8.1 The Three Monotheistic Religions, c. 750*

Religion	Founder/ Prophet	Chief Religious Head(s)	Place of Worship	Important Elements of Worship	Key Religious Texts	Material Aids to Worship
Christianity *Roman Catholic*	Jesus	Bishops, increasingly pope at Rome	Church	Mass, prayer, fasting	Bible, especially the Psalms	Relics
Byzantine	Jesus	Patriarch of Constantinople	Church	Mass, prayer, fasting	Bible, especially the Psalms	Icons
Judaism	Abraham	Rabbis	Synagogue	Prayer, fasting	Hebrew Scriptures and rabbinic legal literature (Talmud)	Torah (first five books of the Bible)
Islam	Muhammad	Caliphs or, increasingly, religious scholars	Mosque	Prayer, fasting	Qur'an and commentaries on it	Qur'an

*None of these religions remained fixed in the form they had in 750.

change, borrowing from and adapting to local traditions and to the very powerful role of the Christian religion in every aspect of society.

Frankish Kingdoms with Roman Roots

The most important kingdoms in post-Roman Europe were Frankish. During the sixth century, the Franks had established themselves as dominant in Gaul, and by the seventh century the limits of their kingdoms roughly approximated the eastern borders of present-day France, Belgium, the Netherlands, and Luxembourg (Map 8.4). Moreover, the Frankish kings who constituted the **Merovingian dynasty** (c. 486–751) subjugated many of the peoples beyond the Rhine, foreshadowing the contours of the western half of modern Germany. Where there were cities, there were reminders of Rome. Elsewhere, the Roman heritage was less obvious.

Blending the Roman Past with the Frankish Present Imagine travelers going from Rome to Trier (near what is now Bonn, Germany) in the early eighth century, perhaps to visit its bishop and check up on his piety. No doubt they would have relied on river travel, even though some Roman roads were still in fair repair. Water routes were preferable because land travel was slow and because even large groups of travelers on the roads were vulnerable to attacks by robbers (see Taking Measure, page 260). Like the roads, other structures in the landscape would have seemed familiarly Roman. Traveling northward on the Rhône River, our voyagers would have passed Roman walled cities and farmlands neatly and squarely laid out by Roman land surveyors. The great stone palaces of villas would still have dotted the countryside. Once at Trier, the travelers would have felt at home seeing the city's great gate (now called the Porta Nigra; see the illustration on page 259), its monumental baths (some still standing today), and its cathedral, built on the site of a Roman palace. Being in Trier was almost like being in Rome.

Nevertheless, travelers would have had to have been unobservant not to notice that the cities that they passed through were not what they had once been in the heyday of the Roman Empire. True, cities still served as the centers of church administration. Bishops lived in them, and so did clergymen, servants, and others who helped the bishops. Cathedrals (the churches presided over by bishops) remained within city walls, and people were drawn to them for important rituals such as baptism. Nevertheless, many urban centers had lost their commercial and cultural vitality. Largely depopulated, they survived as skeletons of their former selves.

Whereas the chief feature of the Roman landscape had been cities, the Frankish landscape was characterized by dense forests, acres of marshes and bogs, patches of cleared farmland, and pasturage for

Merovingian (mehr oh VIN jian) dynasty: The royal dynasty that ruled Gaul from about 486 to 751.

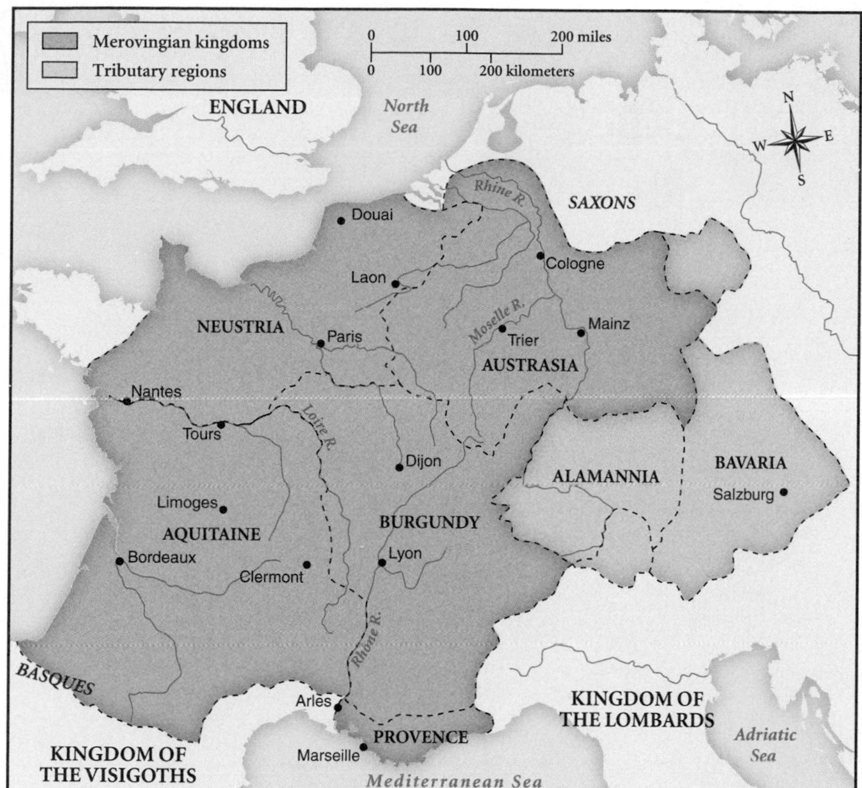

MAP 8.4 The Merovingian Kingdoms in the Seventh Century

By the seventh century, there were three powerful Merovingian kingdoms: Neustria, Austrasia, and Burgundy. The important cities of Aquitaine were assigned to these major kingdoms, while Aquitaine as a whole was assigned to a duke or other governor. Kings did not establish capital cities; they did not even stay in one place. Rather, they continually traveled throughout their kingdoms, making their power felt in person.

animals. These areas were not much influenced by Rome; they represented far more the farming and village settlement patterns of the Franks.

On the vast plains between Paris and Trier, most peasants were only semi-free. They were settled—in family groups—on small holdings called manses, which included a house, a garden, and cultivable land. The peasants paid dues and sometimes owed labor services to a lord (an aristocrat who owned the land). Some of the peasants were descendants of the *coloni* (tenant farmers) of the late Roman Empire; others were the sons and daughters of slaves, now provided with a small plot of land; and a few were people of free Frankish origin who for various reasons had come down in the world. At the lower end of the social scale, the status of Franks and Romans had become identical.

Romans (or, more precisely, Gallo-Romans) and Franks had also merged at the elite level. Although people south of the Loire River continued to be called Romans and people to the north Franks, their cultures—their languages, their settlement patterns, their newly military way of life—were strikingly similar (see "New Sources, New Perspectives," page 261).

The Porta Nigra at Trier

Although in Germania, Trier became one of Rome's capitals in the fourth century. The Porta Nigra was originally the northern gate of the city. During the course of the fifth century, the Porta Nigra came to be considered at best useless and at worst pagan, so bits and pieces of it were pillaged to be used in other building projects. However, this practice stopped when a hermit named Simeon moved into its eastern tower. After Simeon's death in 1035, the Porta Nigra was turned into a two-story church, which it remained until the early nineteenth century, when Napoleon, who conquered Trier, ordered the church to be dismantled and the site returned (more or less) to its original shape. *(The Art Archive/Gianni Dagli Orti.)*

TAKING MEASURE

Papal Letters Sent from Rome to Northern Europe, c. 600–c.700

Between 600 and 700, the pope at Rome sent many letters to kings, queens, aristocrats, and members of the clergy in northern Europe. But he didn't send the same number every month. This graph shows that papal communications were never sent in January and February, whereas their numbers peaked in June and July. The explanation? Very likely the popes had to wait for fine sailing weather to get their letters to their destination, since land routes were too uncertain.

Source: Adapted from Michael McCormick, *Origins of the European Economy: Communications and Commerce, AD 300–900* (Cambridge: Cambridge University Press, 2001), chart 3.1, 80.

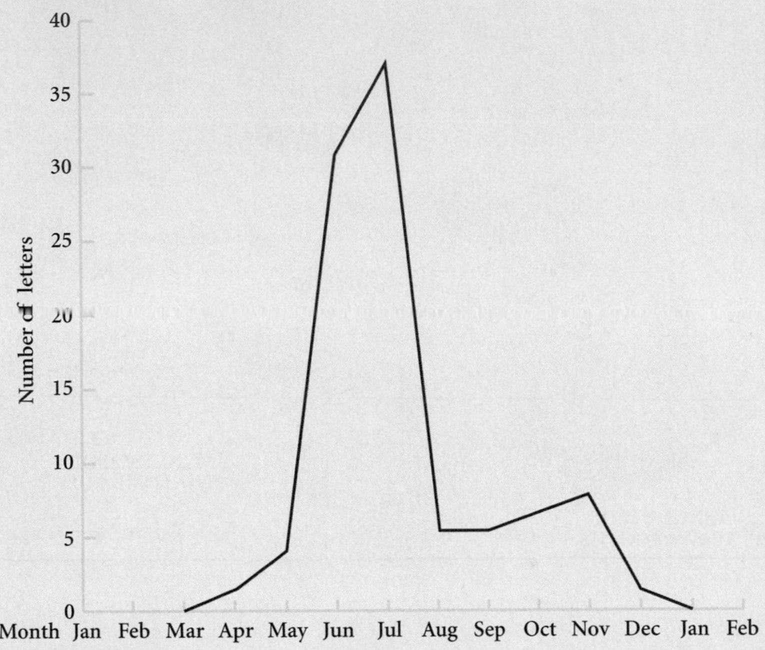

Question to Consider

- **How might the seasonal limitations on communication have affected the relationship between the pope and his church?**

The language that aristocrats spoke and (often) read depended on their location, not their ethnicity. Among the many dialects in the Frankish kingdoms, some were Germanic, especially to the east and north, but most were derived from Latin, yet no longer the Latin of Cicero. At the end of the sixth century, Bishop **Gregory of Tours** (r. 573–c. 594), wrote, "Though my speech is rude, . . . to my surprise, it has often been said by men of our day, that few understand the learned words of the rhetorician but many the rude language of the common people." This beginning to Gregory's *Histories*, a valuable source for the Merovingian period, testifies to Latin's transformation; Gregory expected that his "rude" Latin—the plain Latin of everyday speech—would be understood and welcomed by the general public.

The Frankish elites, like Frankish peasants, tended to live in the countryside rather than in cities. In fact, peasants and aristocrats tended to live together in villages. In many cases, these consisted of a large central building (probably for the aristocratic household to use), sometimes with stone foundations. It was surrounded by smaller buildings, some of which were no doubt houses for peasant families along with their livestock, which provided warmth in the winter. Such villages might boast populations a bit over a hundred.

The elites of the Merovingian period cultivated military—rather than civilian—skills. They went on hunts and wore military-style clothing: the men wore trousers, a heavy belt, and a long cloak; both men and women bedecked themselves with jewelry. As hardened warriors, or wanting to appear so, aristocrats no longer lived in grand villas, choosing instead modest wooden structures without baths or heating systems. That explains why the village great house and the smaller ones nearby looked very much alike.

Saints and Relics

Sometimes villages formed around old villas. In other instances they clustered around sacred sites. Tours—where Gregory was bishop—exemplified this new-style settlement. In Roman times, Tours was a thriving city; around 400, its population diminished (as happened elsewhere in Gaul) and it constructed walls

Gregory of Tours: Bishop of Tours (in Gaul) from 573 to 594, the chief source for the history and culture of the Merovingian kingdoms.

NEW SOURCES, NEW PERSPECTIVES

Anthropology, Archaeology, and Changing Notions of Ethnicity

At the end of the nineteenth century, scholars argued that ethnicity was the same as race and that both were biological. They measured skeletal features and argued that different human groups—blacks, whites, Jews, and Slavs, for example—were biologically distinct and that some were better than others according to "scientific" criteria. This same view was shared by historians, who spoke of the various groups who entered the Roman Empire—Franks, Visigoths, Saxons, Lombards—as if these people were biologically different from Romans and from one another. They thought, for example, that there was a real biological group called the Lombards who had migrated into the Roman Empire and set up the "Lombard kingdom" in Italy by conquering another real biological group called the Romans.

Some anthropologists challenged this view. In the early 1900s, for example, the anthropologist Franz Boas showed that American Indians were not biologically different from any other human group; their "ethnicity" was cultural. Boas meant that the characteristics that made Indians "Indian" were not physical but rather a combination of practices, beliefs, language, dress, and sense of identity. Soon archaeologists came to realize that no physical difference distinguished a Frankish skeleton from a Lombard or a Roman or a Slav skeleton. It was only the artifacts associated with skeletons in grave excavations—jewelry, weapons—that revealed to what ethnicity a person belonged.

If ethnicity were biological, it would be fixed. No one could be a Lombard unless he or she had been born into the group. But since ethnicity is cultural, "outsiders" can join, while "insiders" can be shed. Historians—especially those associated with the University of Vienna—have shown in detail how this was the case with the peoples that the Romans called barbarians. Walter Pohl, for example, has demonstrated how ethnic groups like the Lombards and Franks were made up of men and women from all sorts of backgrounds. Their sense of being Lombard or Frankish was a product of common myths that they accepted about themselves. The Lombards, for example, thought that their name came from a trick played by their women, who tied their long hair around their chins, humoring the war god Woden into calling them "Longbeards" and giving their men victory in battle. The Avars, for their part, were held together by their loyalty to their leader, the *khagan*. Avars who broke away from the khagan's political dominance were no longer considered part of the group—they were considered Bulgarians instead. In contrast, the less centrally organized Slavs recognized all sorts of people living in their territory as Slavs; their ethnicity was based on language and other cultural traditions, which could be learned even by newcomers.

Seeing ethnicity as cultural allows us to understand the origins of European states not as the result of the conquest of one well-defined group by another but rather as a historical process. France, Germany, and England were not created by fixed entities known for all time as, respectively, the Franks, the Germans, and the Angles. Rather, they were created and shaped by the will and imagination of men and women who intermingled, interacted, and adapted to one another over time.

The benefits of this view depend, to be sure, on whether the evidence bears it out. Recent critiques, by Andrew Gillett and others, point out that the primary sources for the discussion of Germanic identity are in Latin. These scholars suggest that France, Germany, and England were created not by ethnic groups but by Roman administrative structures and categories of thought that automatically associated peoples with geographical regions.

Pohl and others respond that there is no one foundation for ethnic identity. Rather, identities are the result of a series of acts: individuals identify themelves with a group that has an ethnic name for itself; groups identify themselves with an ethnic term; and outsiders identify groups with an ethnic epithet that sets them off from others. This view does not deny the contribution of Roman categories, but it views them as just one factor in a complex process of identification.

Questions to Consider

1. **The society of the United States has been called a melting pot. In what ways might the same be said about European societies?**
2. **How do common myths nourish contemporary notions of ethnicity?**
3. **Does the language of a primary source matter in assessing its value for discussions of ethnicity?**

Further Reading

Geary, Patrick J. *The Myth of Nations: The Medieval Origins of Europe*. 2002.

Gillett, Andrew. "Ethnogenesis: A Contested Model of Early Medieval Europe," *History Compass* 4/2 (2006): 241–60.

Pohl, Walter, and Gerda Heydemann, eds. *Strategies of Identification*. 2011.

around its now smaller acreage. By Gregory's day, however, it had gained a new center *outside* of the city walls. There a church had been built to house the remains of the most important and venerated person in the locale: St. Martin. This fourth-century soldier-turned-monk was long dead, but his relics remained at Tours, where he had served as bishop. The population of the surrounding countryside was pulled to his church as if to a magnet. Seen as a miracle worker, Martin acted as the representa-

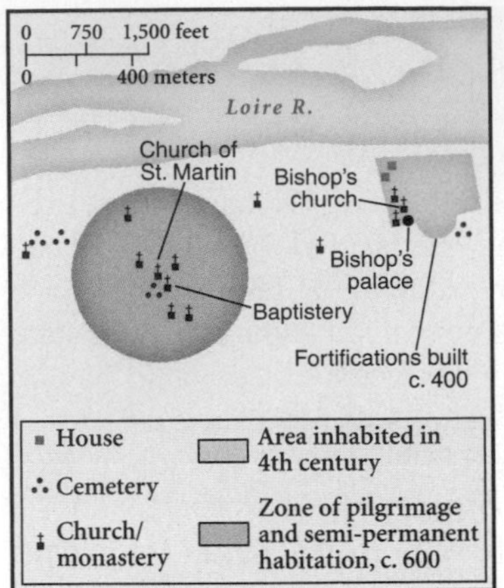

Tours, c. 600

(Nancy Gauthier and Henri Galinié, eds., Gregoire de Tours et l'espace gaulois [Tours: Actes du congrès internationale, 1997], 70.)

tive of God's power: a protector, healer, and avenger. In Gregory's view, Martin's relics (or rather God *through* Martin's relics) not only cured the lame and sick but even prevented armies from plundering local peasants. Martin was not the only human thought to have such great power; all saints were miracle workers.

The veneration of dead saints and their relics marked a major departure from practices of the classical age, in which the dead had been banished from the presence of the living. In the medieval world, the holy dead held the place of highest esteem. The church had no formal procedures for proclaiming saints in the early Middle Ages, but holiness was "recognized" by influential local people and the local bishop. When, for example, miracles were observed at the supposed tomb of the martyr Benignus in Dijon, the common people went there regularly to ask for help. But only after the martyr himself appeared to the local bishop in a vision, thus dispelling doubts about the tomb, was Benignus accorded saintly status. No one at Tours doubted that Martin had been a saint, however, and to tap into the power of his relics, the local bishop built a church directly over his tomb. For a man like Gregory of Tours and his flock, the church building was above all a home for the relics of the saints.

Reliquary

The cult of relics necessitated housing the precious parts of the saints in equally precious containers. This reliquary—made of cloisonné enamel (bits of enamel framed by metal), garnets, glass gems, and a cameo—is in the shape of a miniature sarcophagus. It was made in honor of St. Maurice, a venerated martyr, and was given to a monastery dedicated to Maurice, Saint-Maurice d'Agaune (today in Switzerland). Note the side hinges, which allowed the casket to be worn on a chain. No doubt the abbot of Saint-Maurice wore it when he traveled outside the monastery, to ensure him of the power and protection of the saint. *(Erich Lessing/Art Resource, NY.)*

Economic Activity in a Peasant Society

As a bishop, Gregory was aware of some sophisticated forms of economic activity that existed in early medieval Europe, such as long-distance trade, which depended on surpluses. Most people, however, lived on the edge of survival. Studies of Alpine peat bogs show that from the fifth to the mid-eighth century glaciers advanced and the mean temperature in Europe dropped. This climatic change spelled shortages in crops. Chronicles, histories, and biographies of saints also describe crop shortages, famines, and diseases as a normal part of life. For the year 591 alone, Gregory reported that

> a terrible epidemic killed off the people in Tours and in Nantes. . . . In the town of Limoges a number of people were consumed by fire from heaven for having profaned the Lord's day by transacting business. . . . There was a terrible drought which destroyed all the green pasture. As a result there were great losses of flocks and herds.

Subsistence and Gift Economies An underlying reason for the calamities of the Merovingian period was the weakness of the agricultural economy. Even the meager population of the Merovingian world was too large for the land's productive capacities. Farmers could easily till the light, dry soil of the Mediterranean region with wooden implements. But the heavy, wet soils of northern Europe were difficult to turn and aerate. Technological limitations meant a limited food supply, and agricultural work was not equitably or efficiently allocated and managed. A leisure class of landowning warriors and churchmen lived off the work of peasant men, who tilled the fields, and peasant women, who wove cloth, gardened, brewed, and baked.

Occasionally surpluses developed, either from good harvests in peacetime or from plunder in warfare, and these changed hands, although rarely in an impersonal, commercial manner. Most economic transactions of the seventh and eighth centuries were part of a gift economy, a system of give-and-take: the rich took booty, demanded tribute, hoarded harvests, and minted coins—all to be redistributed to friends, followers, and dependents. Kings and other powerful men and women

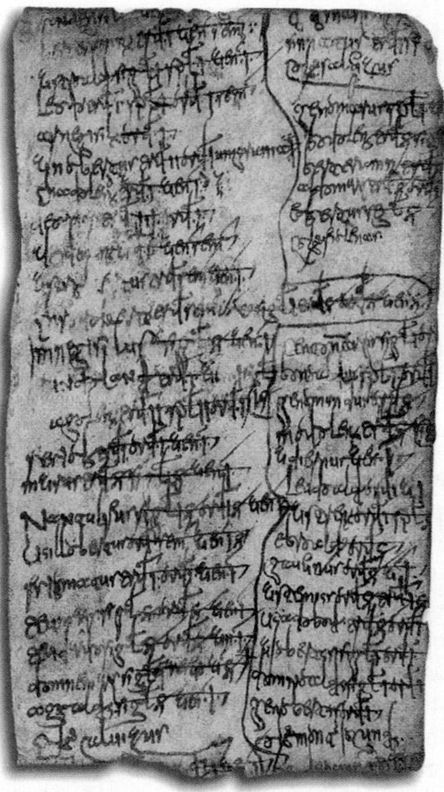

Early Medieval Accounting
In the seventh century, peasants in western Europe were lucky to produce more grain than they sowed. To make sure that it got its share of this meager production, the monastery of Saint-Martin at Tours kept a kind of ledger. This parchment sheet, dating from the second half of the seventh century, lists the amount of grain and wood that tenants owed to the monastery. It is one of the few such early accounts that have survived the ages. *(Bibliothèque nationale de France.)*

amassed gold, silver, ornaments, and jewelry in their treasuries and grain in their storehouses to mark their power, add to their prestige, and demonstrate their generosity. Those reaping benefits from the gifts of the rich included religious people and institutions: monks, nuns, bishops, monasteries, and churches. We still have a partial gift economy today; at holidays, for example, goods change hands for social purposes: to consecrate a holy event, to express love and friendship, to show off wealth and status. In the Merovingian world, the gift economy was the dynamic behind most of the exchanges of goods and money.

Trade and Traders However, some economic activity in this period was purely commercial and impersonal, especially long-distance trade. In these transactions, Europe supplied slaves and raw materials such as furs and honey. In return, it received luxuries and manufactured goods such as silks and papyrus. Byzantine, Islamic, and western European descendants of the Roman Empire kept in tenuous contact with one another by making voyages for trade, diplomatic ventures, and pilgrimages. Seventh- and eighth-century sources speak of Byzantines, Syrians, and Jews as the chief intermediaries of any long-distance trade that existed. Many of these intermediaries lived in the still-thriving port cities of the Mediterranean. Gregory of Tours associated Jews with commerce, complaining that they sold things "at a higher price than they were worth."

Although the population of the Merovingian world was overwhelmingly Christian, Jews were integrated into every aspect of secular life. They used Hebrew in worship, but otherwise they spoke the same languages as Christians and used Latin in their legal documents. Jews often gave their children the same names as Christians (and, in turn, Christians often took Old Testament names); they dressed as everyone else dressed; and they engaged in the same occupations. Many Jews planted and tended vineyards, in part because of the importance of wine in synagogue services and in part because they could easily sell the surplus. Some Jews were rich landowners, with slaves and dependent peasants working for them; others were independent peasants of modest means. Some Jews lived in towns with a small Jewish quarter that included both homes and synagogues, but most Jews, like their Christian neighbors, lived on the land. Only much later, in the eleventh century, would the status of Jews change, setting them markedly apart from Christians.

The Powerful in Merovingian Society

Monarchs and aristocrats held political power in Merovingian society. The Merovingian elite—who included monks and bishops as well as laypeople—obtained their power through hereditary wealth, status, and personal influence.

The Aristocrats Many aristocrats of the period were extremely wealthy. The will drawn up by a bishop and aristocrat named Bertram of Le Mans, for example, shows that he owned estates—some from his family, others given him as gifts—scattered over much of Gaul.

Along with administering their estates, many male aristocrats spent their time honing their proficiency as warriors. To be a great warrior in Merovingian society, just as in the otherwise very different world of the Bedouins, meant more than just fighting: it meant perfecting the virtues necessary for leading armed men. Merovingian warriors affirmed their skills and comradeship in the hunt; they proved their worth in the regular taking of booty; and they rewarded their followers afterward at generous banquets. At these feasts, as they gave abundantly to their dependents in keeping with the gift economy, the lords combined fellowship with the redistribution of wealth.

Merovingian aristocrats also spent time with their families. The focus of marriage was procreation. Important both to the survival of aristocratic families and to the transmission of their property and power, marriage was an expensive institution. It had two forms: in the most formal, the man gave a generous dowry of clothes, livestock, and land to his bride; after the marriage was consummated, he gave her a "morning gift" of furniture. Very wealthy men also might support one or more concubines, who enjoyed a less formal type of marriage, receiving a morning gift but no dowry. Churchmen in this period had many ideas about the value of marriages, but in practice they had little to do with the matter. Marriage was a family decision and a family matter; no one was married in a church.

Some sixth-century aristocrats still patterned their lives on those of the Romans, teaching their children classical Latin poetry and writing to one another in phrases borrowed from Virgil. But already in the seventh century their spoken language had come to diverge from literary Latin. Some still learned Latin, but they cultivated it mainly to read the Psalms. Just as in Byzantium, a religious culture that emphasized Christian piety over the classics was developing in Europe.

The arrival on the continent around 590 of the Irish monk St. Columbanus (c. 543–615) energized this heightened emphasis on religion. Columbanus's brand of monasticism — which stressed exile, devotion, and discipline — found much favor among the Merovingian elite. The monasteries St. Columbanus established in both Gaul and Italy attracted local recruits from the aristocracy, some of them grown men and women. Others were young children, given to the monastery by their parents in the ritual called oblation. This practice was not only accepted but also often considered essential for the spiritual well-being of both the children and their families. Irish monasticism introduced Merovingian aristocrats to a deepened religious devotion. Those aristocrats who did not join or patronize a monastery still often read (or listened to others read) books about penitence, and they chanted the Psalms.

Bishops ranked among the most powerful men in Merovingian society. Gregory of Tours, for example, considered himself the protector of "his citizens." When representatives of the king came to collect taxes in Tours, Gregory stopped them in their tracks, warning them that St. Martin would punish anyone who tried to tax his people. "That very day," Gregory reported, "the man who had produced the tax rolls caught a fever and died." Little wonder that Frankish kings let the old Roman land tax die out.

Like other aristocrats, many bishops chose to marry, even though church councils demanded celibacy. As the overseers of priests and guardians of morality, however, bishops were expected to refrain from sexual relations with their wives. Since bishops were ordinarily appointed late in life, long after they had raised a family, this restriction did not threaten the ideal of a procreative marriage.

Women of Power Noble parents generally decided whom their daughters would marry, for such unions bound together not only husbands and wives but entire extended families as well. Brides received a dowry — often land, over which they had some control; if they were widowed without children, they were allowed to sell, give away, exchange, or rent out their dowry estates as they wished. Moreover, men could give property to their women kinfolk outright in written testaments. Because fathers often wanted to share their property with their daughters, an enterprising author created a formula for scribes to follow when drawing up wills in such cases. It began:

> For a long time an ungodly custom has been observed among us that forbids sisters to share with their brothers the paternal land. I reject this impious law: I make you, my beloved daughter, an equal and legitimate heir in all my patrimony [inheritance].

Praying Man

This incised brick, formed in the shape of a church, was a decorative element in an edifice (perhaps itself a church) built in the eighth century. The figure is a bearded man in prayer. Prior to the tenth or eleventh century, people did not pray with hands pressed together but rather with hands raised up on either side of the head. Here the artist gave the gesture special importance by exaggerating the man's arms and hands; his legs and feet hardly matter. *(Musée de l'Hôtel Goüin de la Société Archéologique de Touraine, France, n° d'inventaire HG 856.007.)*

Bequests, dowries, and other such gifts made many aristocratic women very rich. Childless widows frequently gave generous gifts to the church from their vast possessions. But a woman need not have been a widow to control enormous wealth. In 632, for example, the nun Burgundofara, who had never married, drew up a will giving her monastery the land, slaves, vineyards, pastures, and forests she had received from her two brothers and her father. She bequeathed other property that she owned to her brothers and sister.

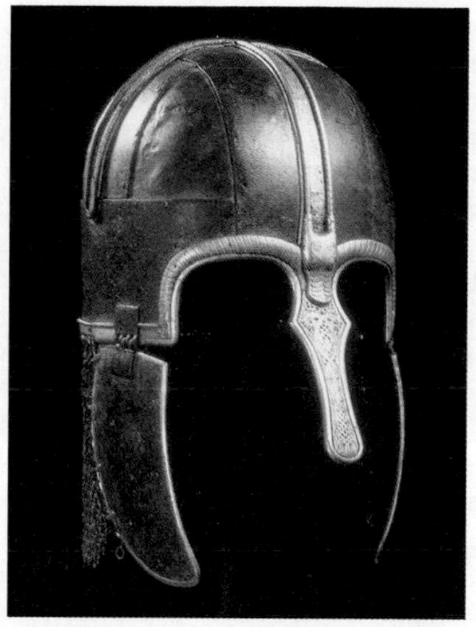

York Helmet
This fine helmet—which belonged to a wealthy warrior named Oshere who lived near York, England, in the second half of the eighth century—was intended for both display and battle. The helmet, made of iron, and the back flap, made of flexible chain mail, gave excellent protection against sword blades. The cheek pieces were probably originally pulled close to the warrior's face by a leather tie. The nose piece is decorated with interlaced animals. Over the top, two bands of copper meet at the middle. They were inscribed "In the name of our Lord Jesus, the Holy Spirit, God, and with all, we pray. Amen. Oshere. Christ." What do the features of this helmet imply about the relationship between the Christian religion and the profession of warrior? *(York Museums Trust [Yorkshire Museum].)*

Though legally under the authority of her husband, a Merovingian woman often found ways to exercise some power and control over her life. Tetradia, wife of Count Eulalius, left her husband, taking all his gold and silver, because, as Gregory of Tours describes to us,

> he was in the habit of sleeping with the women-servants in his household. As a result he neglected his wife. . . . As a result of his excesses, he ran into serious debt, and to meet this he stole his wife's jewelry and money.

A court of law ordered Tetradia to repay Eulalius four times the amount she had taken from him, but she was allowed to keep and live on her own property.

Other women were able to exercise behind-the-scenes control through their sons. A woman named Artemia, for example, used the prophecy that her son Nicetius would become a bishop to prevent her husband from taking the bishopric himself. After Nicetius did become a bishop (thus fulfilling the prophecy), he remained at home with his mother well into his thirties, working alongside the servants and teaching the younger children to read the Psalms.

Some women exercised direct power. Rich widows with fortunes to bestow wielded enormous influence. Some Merovingian women were abbesses, rulers in their own right over female monasteries and sometimes over "double monasteries," with separate facilities for men and women. Monasteries under the control of abbesses could be substantial centers of population: the convent at Laon, for example, had three hundred nuns in the seventh century. Because women lived in populous convents or were monopolized by rich men able to support several wives or mistresses at one time, unattached aristocratic women were scarce.

The Power of Kings

Atop the aristocracy were the Merovingian kings, rulers of the Frankish kingdoms. The Merovingian dynasty (c. 486–751) owed its longevity to good political sense: it had allied itself with local lay aristocrats and ecclesiastical (church) authorities. The kings relied on these men to bolster the power they derived from other sources, such as their leadership in war, their access to the lion's share of plunder, and their takeover of the public lands and legal framework of Roman administration. The kings' courts functioned as schools for the sons of the elite, tightening the bonds and loyalties between royal and aristocratic families. When kings sent officials—counts and dukes—to rule in their name in various regions of their kingdoms, these regional governors worked with and married into the aristocratic families who had long controlled local affairs.

Both kings and aristocrats had good reason to want a powerful royal authority. The king acted as arbitrator and intermediary for the competing interests of the aristocrats while taking advantage of local opportunities to appoint favorites and garner prestige by giving out land and privileges to supporters and religious institutions. Gregory of Tours's history of the sixth century is filled with stories of bitter battles between Merovingian kings, as royal brothers fought continuously. Yet what seemed to the bishop like royal weakness and violent chaos was in fact one way the kings contained local aristocratic tensions, organizing them on one side or another and preventing them from spinning out of royal control. By the beginning of the seventh century, three relatively stable Frankish kingdoms had emerged: Austrasia to the northeast; Neustria to the west, with its capital city at Paris; and Burgundy, incorporating the southeast (see Map 8.4). In an age that depended on local face-to-face contact, these divisions were so useful to aristocrats and Merovingian kings alike that even when royal power was united in the hands of one king, Clothar II (r. 613–623), he made his son the independent king of Austrasia.

As the power of the kings in the seventh century increased, however, so did the might of their chief court official, the mayor of the palace. As we shall see, one mayoral family allied with the Austrasian aristocracy would in the following century displace the Merovingian dynasty and establish a new royal line, the Carolingians.

Christianity and Classical Culture in the British Isles

The Merovingian kingdoms exemplify some of the ways in which Roman and non-Roman traditions combined; the British Isles show others. Ireland had never been part of the Roman Empire, but the Irish people were early converts to Christianity, as were people in Roman Britain and parts of Scotland. Invasions by various Celtic and Germanic groups—particularly the Anglo-Saxons, who gave their name to England, "the land of the Angles"—redrew the religious boundaries. Ireland, largely free of invaders, remained Christian; Scotland, also relatively untouched by invaders, had been slowly Christianized by the Irish from the west and in early years by the British from the south; England, which emerged from the invasions as a mosaic of about a dozen kingdoms ruled by separate Anglo-Saxon kings, became largely pagan until it was actively converted in the seventh century.

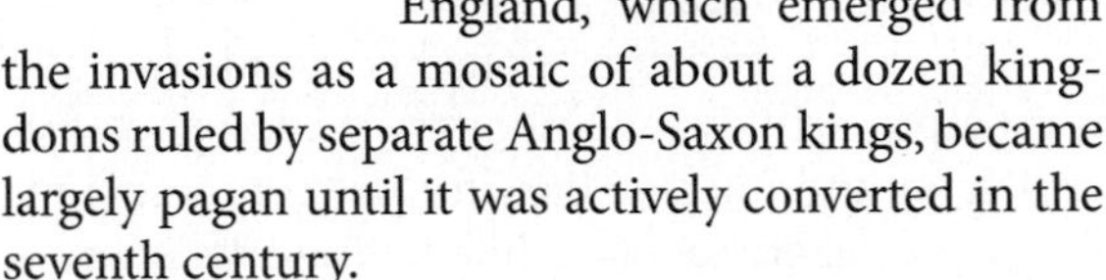

The British Isles

Competing Church Hierarchies in Anglo-Saxon England Christianity was introduced to Anglo-Saxon England from two directions. In the north of England, Irish monks brought their own brand of Christianity. Converted in the fifth century by St. Patrick and other missionaries, the Irish had evolved a church organization that corresponded to its rural clan organization. Abbots and abbesses, generally from powerful dynasties, headed monastic *familiae*, communities composed of blood relatives, servants, slaves, and of course monks or nuns. Bishops were often under the authority of abbots, since the monasteries rather than cities were the centers of population in Ireland. The Irish missionaries to England were monks, and they set up monasteries modeled on those at home.

In the south of England, Christianity came in 597 via missionaries sent by the pope known as **Gregory the Great** (r. 590–604). The missionaries, under the leadership of Augustine (not the same Augustine as the bishop of Hippo), intended to convert the king and people of Kent, the southernmost kingdom, and then work their way northward. But Augustine and his party brought with them Roman practices at odds with those of Irish Christianity, stressing ties to the pope and the organization of the church under bishops rather than abbots. Using the Roman model, they divided England into territorial units, called dioceses, headed by an archbishop and bishops. Augustine, for example, became archbishop of Canterbury. Because he was a monk, he set up a monastery right next to his cathedral; thus having a community of monks attached to the bishop's church became a characteristic of the English church. Later a second archbishopric was added at York.

A major bone of contention between the Roman and Irish churches involved the calculation of the date of Easter, celebrated by Christians as the day on which Christ rose from the dead. The Roman church insisted that Easter fall on the first Sunday following the first full moon after the vernal equinox. The Irish had a different method of determining when Easter should fall, and therefore they celebrated Easter on a different day. Because everyone agreed that believers could not be saved unless they observed Christ's resurrection properly and on the right date, the conflict was bitter. It was resolved by Oswy, king of Northumbria, who organized a meeting of churchmen, the **Synod of Whitby**, in 664. Convinced by the synod that Rome spoke with the voice of St. Peter, who was said in the New Testament to hold the keys of the kingdom of heaven, Oswy chose the Roman date. His decision paved the way for the triumph of the Roman brand of Christianity in England.

Literary Culture The authority of St. Peter was not the only reason for favoring Roman Christianity. For many English churchmen, Rome had great prestige because it was a treasure trove of knowledge, piety, and holy objects. Benedict

---

Gregory the Great: The pope (r. 590–604) who sent missionaries to Anglo-Saxon England, wrote influential books, tried to reform the church, and had contact with the major ruling families of Europe and Byzantium.

Synod of Whitby: The meeting of churchmen and King Oswy of Northumbria in 664 that led to the adoption of the Roman brand of Christianity in England.

Biscop (c. 630–690), the founder of two important English monasteries, made many difficult trips to Rome, bringing back relics, liturgical vestments, and even a cantor to teach his monks the proper melodies in a time before written musical notation. Above all, he went to Rome to get books. At his monasteries in the north of England, he built up a grand library. In Anglo-Saxon England, as in Scotland and Ireland, all of which lacked a strong classical tradition from Roman times, a book was considered a precious object, to be decorated as finely as a garnet-studded brooch. (See the illustration on the right.)

The Anglo-Saxons and Irish Celts had a thriving oral culture but extremely limited uses for writing. Books became valuable only when these societies converted to Christianity. Just as Islamic reliance on the Qur'an made possible a literary culture under the Umayyads, so Christian dependence on the Bible, liturgy, and the writings of the church fathers helped make England and Ireland centers of literature and learning in the seventh and eighth centuries. Archbishop Theodore (r. 669–690), who had studied at Athens and was one of the most learned men of his day, founded a school at Canterbury where students studied Latin and even some Greek in order to comment on biblical texts. Men like Benedict Biscop soon sponsored other centers of learning, using the texts from the classical past. Although women did not establish famous schools, many abbesses ruled over monasteries that stressed Christian learning. Here, as elsewhere in the British Isles, Latin writings, even pagan texts, were studied diligently, in part because Latin was so foreign a language that mastering it required systematic and formal study. One of Benedict Biscop's pupils was Bede ("the Venerable"; 673–735), an Anglo-Saxon monk and a historian of extraordinary breadth. Bede in turn taught a new generation of monks who became advisers to eighth-century rulers.

Page from the Lindisfarne Gospels

The lavishly illuminated manuscript known as the Lindisfarne Gospels, of which this is one page, was probably produced in the first third of the eighth century. For the monks at Lindisfarne (a tidal island off the northeast coast of England) and elsewhere in the British Isles, books were precious objects, to be decorated much like pieces of jewelry. (Compare the treatment of the figure here with the decoration of the eagle brooches on page 230, both of which rely on flat areas of color.) The page shown here depicts the Evangelist St. Mark, writing while also holding a book. Above his halo is his symbol, a winged lion; it is blowing a trumpet while its front paws rest on a book. What books might St. Mark and the lion be holding? *(© The British Library/HIP/The Image Works.)*

Much of the vigorous pagan Anglo-Saxon oral tradition was adapted to Christian culture. Bede encouraged and supported the use of the Anglo-Saxon language, urging priests, for example, to use it when they instructed their flocks. In contrast to other European regions, where Latin was the primary written language in the seventh and eighth centuries, England made use of the vernacular—the language normally spoken by the people. Written Anglo-Saxon (or Old English) was used in every aspect of English life, from government to entertainment.

The decision at the Synod of Whitby to favor Roman Christianity tied the English church to the church of Rome by doctrine, friendship, and conviction. The Anglo-Saxon monk and bishop Wynfrith even changed his name to the Latin Boniface to symbolize his loyalty to the Roman church. Preaching on the continent, Boniface (680–754) set up churches in Germany and Gaul that, like those in England, looked to Rome for leadership and guidance. Boniface was one of those travelers from Rome who went to Trier to check on the bishop's piety. He found it badly wanting! Boniface's efforts to reform the Frankish church gave the papacy new importance in Europe.

Unity in Spain, Division in Italy

In contrast to the British Isles, southern Gaul, Spain, and Italy had long been part of the Roman Empire and preserved many of its traditions. Nevertheless, as they were settled and fought over by new peoples, their histories diverged dramatically. When the Merovingian king Clovis (r. 485–511) defeated the Visigoths in 507, the Visigothic kingdom, which had sprawled across southern Gaul into Spain, was dismembered. By midcentury, the Franks had come into possession of most of its remnants in southern Gaul.

In Spain, the Visigothic king Leovigild (r. 569–586) established territorial control by military might. But no ruler could hope to maintain his position in Visigothic Spain without the support of the Hispano-Roman population, which included both the great landowners and leading bishops; and their backing was unattainable while the Visigoths remained Arian Christians (maintaining that Christ was not identical with God; see page 219). Leovigild's son Reccared (r. 586–601) took the necessary step in 587, converting to Roman Catholic Christianity. Two years later, at the Third Council of Toledo, most of the Arian bishops followed their king by announcing their conversion to Catholicism.

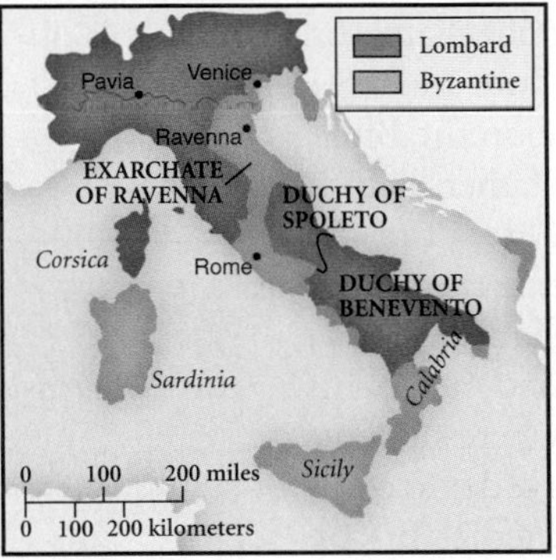

Lombard Italy, Early Eighth Century

Thereafter, the bishops and kings of Spain cooperated to a degree unprecedented in other regions. While the king gave the churchmen free rein to set up their own hierarchy (with the bishop of Toledo at the top) and to meet regularly at synods to regulate and reform the church, the bishops in turn supported their Visigothic king, who ruled as a minister of the Christian people. Rebellion against him was tantamount to rebellion against Christ. The Spanish bishops reinforced this idea by anointing the king, daubing him with holy oil in a ritual that paralleled the ordination of priests and demonstrated divine favor. Toledo, the city where the highest bishop presided, was also where the kings were "made" through anointment. While the bishops in this way made the king's cause their own, their lay counterparts, the great landowners, helped supply the king with troops, allowing him to maintain internal order and repel his external enemies.

Ironically, it was precisely the centralization and unification of the Visigothic kingdom that proved its undoing. When the Arabs arrived in 711, they needed only to kill the king, defeat his army, and capture Toledo to take the kingdom.

By contrast, in Italy the Lombard king constantly faced a hostile papacy in the center of the peninsula and virtually independent dukes in the south. Theoretically royal officers, the dukes of Benevento and Spoleto in fact ruled on their own behalf. Although many Lombards were Catholics, others, including important kings and dukes, were Arian. The "official" religion of Lombards in Italy varied with the ruler in power. Rather than signal a major political event, the conversion of the Lombards to Catholic Christianity occurred gradually, ending only around the mid-seventh century. Partly as a result of this slow development, the Lombard kings, unlike the Visigoths, Franks, or even the Anglo-Saxons, never enlisted the full support of any particular group of churchmen.

Although lacking united religious support, Lombard royal power still had strengths. Chief among these were the traditions of leadership associated with the royal dynasty, the kings' military ability and their control over large estates in northern Italy, and the Roman institutions that survived in Italy. The Italian peninsula had been devastated by the wars between the Ostrogoths and the Byzantine Empire, but the Lombard kings took advantage of the still-urban organization of Italian society and the economy, assigning dukes to city bases and setting up a royal capital at Pavia. Recalling emperors like Constantine and Justinian, the kings built churches, monasteries, and other places of worship in the royal capital; they maintained the city walls, issued laws, and minted coins. Revenues from tolls, sales taxes, port duties, and court fines filled their treasuries, although their inability to revive the Roman land tax was a major weakness. The greatest challenge for the Lombard kings came from sharing the peninsula with Rome. As soon as the kings began to make serious headway into southern Italy against the duchies of Spoleto and Benevento, the pope began to fear for his own position and called on the Franks for help.

Political Tensions and the Power of the Pope

In the year 600, the pope's position was ambiguous: he was both a ruler and a subordinate. On the one hand, believing he was the successor of St. Peter and head of the church, he wielded real secular power. Pope Gregory the Great in many ways laid the foundations for the papacy's spiritual and temporal ascendancy. During Gregory's reign, the papacy became the greatest landowner in Italy. Gregory organized the defenses of Rome and paid for its army; he heard court cases, made treaties, and

Mosaic from Sant'Agnese

The church of Sant'Agnese was founded by Constantine and rebuilt by Pope Honorius I (625–638). It has been much restored and reworked since then, but the apse mosaic is almost as it was when commissioned by Honorius. The mosaic shows St. Agnes flanked by two popes (one of them Honorius, holding a church) against a background of heavenly bands of gold. *(akg-images/Andrea Jemolo.)*

provided welfare services. The missionary expedition Gregory sent to England was only a small part of his involvement in the rest of Europe. He also maintained close ties with the churchmen in Spain who were working to convert the Visigoths from Arianism to Catholicism. He wrote letters to the Byzantine emperor and to European kings and queens. He admonished Brunhild, a Frankish queen well known to Gregory of Tours, to reform the church in Gaul:

> Evil priests cause ruin for the people . . . [so] see that you send us a letter of yours, and we shall send over a person with the assent of your authority, if you give the order, who together with other priests should inquire into these acts with great care, and correct them according to God's will.

A prolific author of spiritual works and biblical commentaries, Gregory digested and simplified the ideas of church fathers like St. Augustine of Hippo, making them accessible to a wider audience. His book *Pastoral Rule* was used as a guide for bishops throughout Europe.

Yet the pope was not independent. He was only one of many bishops in the Roman Empire, which was now ruled from Constantinople, and he was therefore subordinate to the emperor at Byzantium. For a long time the emperor's views on dogma, discipline, and church administration prevailed at Rome. This authority began to unravel in the seventh century. In 691, Emperor Justinian II convened a council that determined 102 rules for the church, and he sent them to Rome for papal endorsement. Most of the rules were unobjectionable, but Pope Sergius I (r. 687 or 689–701) was unwilling to agree to all of them because they permitted priests to marry (which the Roman church did not want to allow) and prohibited fasting on Saturdays in Lent (which the Roman church required). Outraged by Sergius's refusal, Justinian tried to arrest him, but Italian armies (theoretically under the emperor) came to the pope's aid, while Justinian's arresting officer cowered under the pope's bed. As this incident reveals, some local forces were already willing to rally to the side of the pope against the emperor. Constantinople's influence and authority over Rome was dwindling. Sheer distance, as well as diminishing imperial power in Italy, meant that the popes were, in effect, the leaders of the parts of Italy not controlled by the Lombards.

The gap between Byzantium and Rome widened in the early eighth century as Emperor Leo III tried to increase the taxes on papal property to pay for his war against the Arab invaders. The pope responded by leading a general tax revolt. Meanwhile, Leo's fierce policy of iconoclasm collided with the pope's tolerance of images. In Italy, as in other European regions, Christian piety focused more on relics than on icons. Nevertheless, the papacy would not allow sacred images and icons to be destroyed. The pope argued that holy images should be respected, though not worshipped. His support of images reflected popular opinion as well. A later commentator wrote that iconoclasm so infuriated the inhabitants of Ravenna and Venice that "if the pope had not prohibited the people, they would have attempted to set up a [different] emperor over themselves."

These difficulties with the emperor were matched by increasing friction between the pope and the Lombards. The Lombard kings had gradually managed to bring under their control the duchies of Spoleto and Benevento as well as part of the Exarchate of Ravenna. By the mid-eighth century, the popes feared that Rome would fall to the Lombards, and Pope Zachary (r. 741–752) looked northward for friends. He created an ally by giving his approval to the removal of the last Merovingian king and his replacement by the first Carolingian king, Pippin III (r. 751–768). In 753, Pope Stephen II (r. 752–757) called on Pippin to march to Italy with an army to fight the Lombards. Thus, events at Rome had a major impact on the history not only of Italy but of the Frankish kingdom as well.

REVIEW QUESTION What were the similarities and differences among the kingdoms that emerged in western Europe, and how did their histories combine and diverge?

MAPPING THE WEST

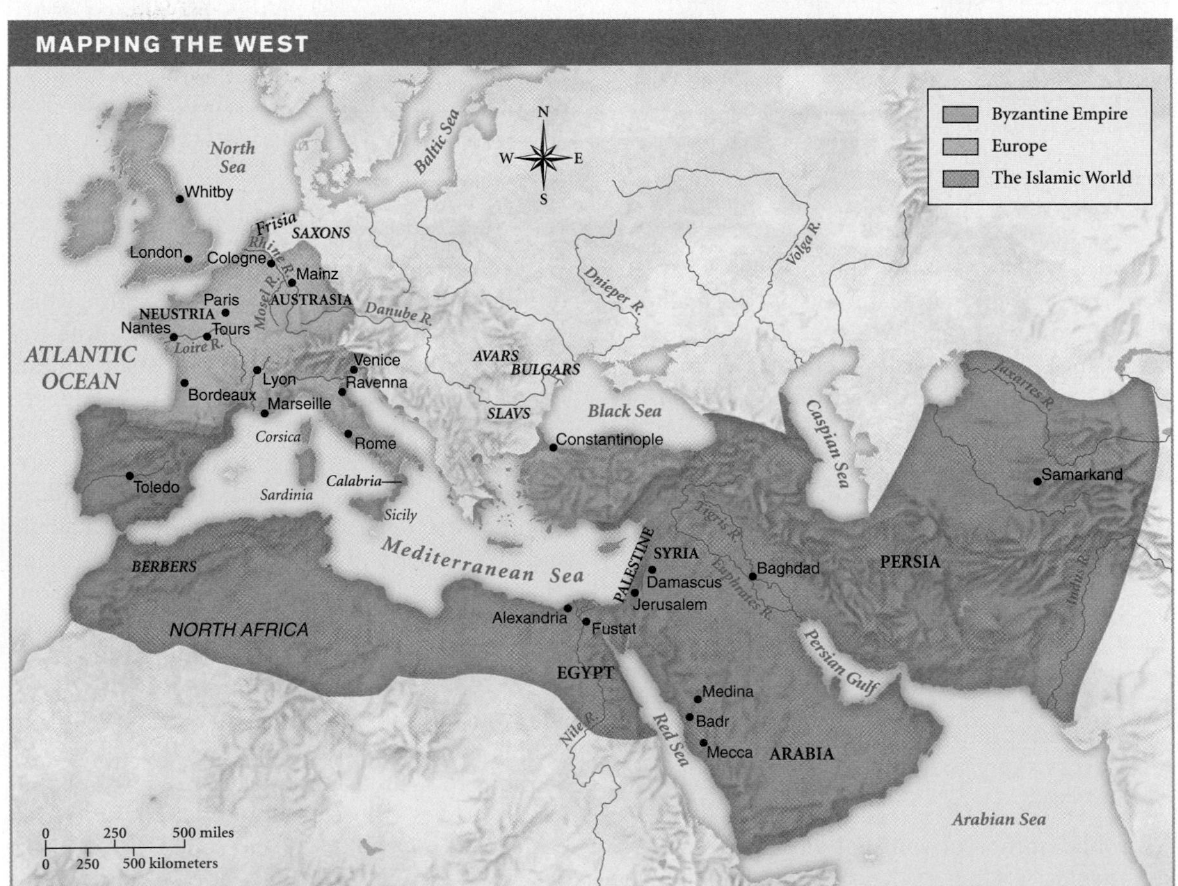

Rome's Heirs, c. 750

The major political fact of the period 600–750 was the emergence of Islam and the creation of an Islamic state that reached from Spain to the Indus River. The Byzantine Empire, once a great power, was dwarfed—and half swallowed up—by its Islamic neighbor. To the west were fledgling European kingdoms, mere trifles on the world stage. The next centuries, however, would prove their resourcefulness and durability.

Conclusion

The Islamic world, Byzantium, and western Europe were heirs of the Roman Empire, but they built on its legacies in different ways. Muslims were the newcomers to the Roman world, but their religion, Islam, was influenced by both Jewish and Christian monotheism, each with roots in Roman culture. Under the guidance of Muhammad the Prophet, Islam became both a coherent theology and a tightly structured way of life. Once the Muslim Arabs embarked on military conquests, they became the heirs of Rome in other ways: preserving Byzantine cities, hiring Syrian civil servants, and adopting Mediterranean artistic styles. Drawing on Roman and Persian traditions, the Umayyad dynasty created a powerful Islamic state, with a capital city in Syria and a culture that generally tolerated a wide variety of economic, religious, and social institutions so long as the conquered paid taxes to their Muslim overlords.

Byzantium directly inherited the central political institutions of Rome: its people called themselves Romans; its emperor was the Roman emperor; and its capital, Constantinople, was considered to be the new Rome. Byzantium also inherited the taxes, cities, laws, and religion — Christianity — of Rome. The changes of the seventh and eighth centuries — contraction of territory, urban decline, disappearance of the old elite, and a ban on icons — whittled away at this Roman character. By 750, Byzantium was less Roman than it was a new, resilient political and cultural entity, a Christian state on the borders of the new Muslim empire.

Western Europe also inherited — and transformed — Roman institutions. The Frankish kings built on Roman traditions that had earlier been modified by provincial and Germanic custom. In Anglo-Saxon England, once the far-flung northern outpost of the Roman Empire, parts of the Roman legacy — Latin learning and the Christian religion — had to be reimported in the seventh century. In Spain, the Visigothic kings converted from Arian to Roman Christianity and allied themselves with a Hispano-Roman elite that maintained elements of the organization and intellectual traditions of the late empire. In Italy and at Rome itself, the traditions of the classical past endured. The roads remained, the cities of Italy survived (although depopulated), and both the popes and the Lombard kings ruled according to the traditions of Roman government.

Muslim, Byzantine, and western European societies all suffered the ravages of war. In each one, the social hierarchy became simpler, with the loss of "middle" groups like the curials at Byzantium and the near suppression of tribal affiliations among Muslims. All tied politics to religion more tightly than ever before. In Byzantium, the emperor was a religious force, presiding over the destruction of icons. In the Islamic world, the caliph was the successor to Muhammad, a religious and political leader. In western Europe the kings allied with churchmen in order to rule. Despite their many differences, all these leaders had a common understanding of their place in a divine scheme: they were God's agents on earth, ruling over God's people. In the next century they would consolidate their power. Little did they know that, soon thereafter, local elites would be able to assert greater authority than ever before.

FOR FURTHER EXPLORATION

- **For additional primary-source material from this period**, see *Sources of the Making of the West*, Fourth Edition.
- **For Web sites, images, and documents related to topics in this chapter**, visit *Make History* at bedfordstmartins.com/hunt.

Chapter 8 Review

Online Study Guide bedfordstmartins.com/hunt

Key Terms and People

In the grid below, identify the term or person and explain its historical significance. (To do this exercise online, go to bedfordstmartins.com/hunt.)

Term	Who or What & When	Why It Matters
Muhammad (p. 244)		
Qur'an (p. 246)		
Hijra (p. 246)		
jihad (p. 247)		
Five Pillars of Islam (p. 247)		
Shi'ite (p. 250)		
Umayyad caliphate (p. 250)		
Heraclius (p. 252)		
Lombards (p. 252)		
theme (p. 255)		
icon (p. 256)		
iconoclasm (p. 256)		
Merovingian dynasty (p. 258)		
Gregory of Tours (p. 260)		
Gregory the Great (p. 266)		
Synod of Whitby (p. 266)		

Review Questions

1. How and why did the Muslims conquer so many lands in the period 632–750?
2. What stresses did the Byzantine Empire endure in the seventh and eighth centuries, and how was iconoclasm a response to those stresses?
3. What were the similarities and differences among the kingdoms that emerged in western Europe, and how did their histories combine and diverge?

Making Connections

1. What were the similarities and the differences in political organizations of the Islamic, Byzantine, and western European societies in the period 600–750?
2. Compare and contrast the roles of religion in the Islamic, Byzantine, and western European worlds in the period 600–750.
3. Compare the material resources of the Islamic, Byzantine, and western European governments in the period 600–750.

Important Events

Date	Event	Date	Event
c. 486–751	Merovingian dynasty	622	Hijra to Medina; year 1 of the Islamic calendar
c. 570–632	Life of Muhammad, prophet of Islam	624	Muhammad and Meccans fight battle of Badr
572	Lombards conquer northern Italy	661–750	Umayyad caliphate
r. 573–c. 594	Bishop Gregory of Tours	664	Synod of Whitby; English king opts for Roman form of Christianity
587	Conversion of Visigothic king Reccared	680–754	Life of Boniface, who reformed the Frankish church
c. 590	Arrival of Irish monk Columbanus in Gaul	r. 717–741	Emperor Leo III the Isaurian
r. 590–604	Papacy of Pope Gregory the Great	726–787	Period of iconoclasm at Byzantium
603–623	War between Byzantium and Persia		

- Consider three events: **Papacy of Pope Gregory the Great (r. 590–604); Hijra to Medina, year 1 of the Islamic calendar (622)**; and **Emperor Leo III the Isaurian (r. 717–741)**. How did these events reshape religious faith? What were the broader implications of those changes for social and political life?

SUGGESTED REFERENCES

Donner's book is insightful on the origins of Islam. Herrin gives a dazzling overview of Byzantine history. Smith's and Wickham's books are essential for understanding the early medieval West.

Ahmed, Leila. *Women and Gender in Islam: Historical Roots of a Modern Debate*. 1992.

*Bede. *A History of the English Church and People*. Trans. Leo Sherley-Price. 1991.

Berkey, Jonathan P. *The Formation of Islam: Religion and Society in the Near East, 600–1800*. 2003.

*Byzantine Sourcebook: http://www.fordham.edu/halsall/sbook1c.html

Cameron, Averil. *The Byzantines*. 2006.

Connor, Carolyn L. *Women of Byzantium*. 2004.

Donner, Fred McGraw. *Muhammad and the Believers: At the Origins of Islam*. 2010.

*Geanakoplos, Deno John, ed. and trans. *Byzantium: Church, Society, and Civilization Seen through Contemporary Eyes*. 1984.

Geary, Patrick. *Before France and Germany: The Creation and Transformation of the Merovingian World*. 1988.

*Gregory of Tours. *The History of the Franks*. Trans. Lewis Thorpe. 1976.

Haldon, J. F. *Byzantium in the Seventh Century: The Transformation of a Culture*. 1990.

Hen, Yitzhak. *Roman Barbarians: The Royal Court and Culture in the Early Medieval West*. 2007.

Herrin, Judith. *Byzantium: The Surprising Life of a Medieval Empire*. 2007.

Hodgson, Marshall G. S. *The Venture of Islam: Conscience and History in a World Civilization*. Vol. 1, *The Classical Age of Islam*. 1974.

*Islamic Sourcebook: http://www.fordham.edu/halsall/islam/islamsbook.html

Kennedy, Hugh. *The Prophet and the Age of the Caliphates: The Islamic Near East from the Sixth to the Eleventh Century*. 2nd ed. 2004.

Smith, Julia M. H. *Europe after Rome: A New Cultural History 500–1000*. 2005.

Whittow, Mark. *The Making of Byzantium, 600–1025*. 1996.

Wickham, Chris. *Framing the Early Middle Ages: Europe and the Mediterranean, 400–800*. 2005.

*Primary source.

IHC
XPC

CHAPTER

9

From Centralization to Fragmentation

750–1050

In 841, a fifteen-year-old boy named William went to serve at the court of Charles the Bald, king of the Franks. William's father, Bernard, was an extremely powerful noble. His mother, Dhuoda, was a well-educated, pious, and able woman; she administered the family's estates in the south of France while her husband was occupied with politics at court. In 841, however, politics had become a dangerous business. King Charles was fighting with his brothers over his portion of the Frankish Empire, and he doubted Bernard's loyalty. In fact, William was sent to Charles's court as a kind of hostage, to ensure Bernard's fidelity. Anxious about her son, Dhuoda wrote a handbook of advice for William, outlining what he ought to believe about God; about politics and society; about obligations to his family; and, above all, about his duties to his father, which she emphasized even over loyalty to the king:

> In the human understanding of things, royal and imperial appearance and power seem preeminent in the world, and the custom of men is to account those men's actions and their names ahead of all others. . . . But despite all this . . . I caution you to render first to him whose son you are special, faithful, steadfast loyalty as long as you shall live. . . . So I urge you again, most beloved son William, that first of all you love God. . . . Then love, fear, and cherish your father.

The Kiss of Judas
According to the Gospels, Judas, one of the original twelve Apostles, betrayed Jesus by giving him a kiss, in that way identifying him to the Roman and Hebrew authorities. In this depiction of the scene from the late tenth century, Judas is almost dancing with Jesus. Soldiers and the servants of the Hebrew high priest grab Jesus's arms from both sides. Meanwhile, St. Peter, the chief of the Apostles, has grabbed one of the priest's servants and is cutting off his ear. In the tenth century, people knew a great deal about loyalty and betrayal. Most of the institutions of government relied on oaths of fidelity, but these turned out to be fragile instruments for cohesion. *(Stadtbibliothek / Stadtarchiv, Trier.)*

William heeded his mother's words, with tragic results: when Bernard ran afoul of Charles and was executed, William died in a failed attempt to avenge his father.

Dhuoda's handbook reveals the volatile political atmosphere of the mid-ninth century, and her advice to her son points to one of its causes: a crisis of loyalty. Loyalty to emperors, caliphs, and kings — all of whom were symbols of unity cutting across regional and family ties — competed with allegiances to local authorities; and those, in turn, vied with family loyalties. The period 600–750 had seen the startling rise of Islam, the whittling away of Byzantium, and the beginnings of stable political and economic development in an impoverished Europe. The period 750–1050 would see all three societies contend with internal issues of diversity even as they became increasingly conscious of their unity and uniqueness. At the beginning of this period, rulers built up and dominated strong, united political communities. By the end, these realms had fragmented into smaller, more local units. While men and women continued to feel some loyalty toward faraway emperors and caliphs, their most powerful allegiances often focused on local lords closer to home.

In Byzantium, military triumphs brought emperors enormous prestige. A renaissance (French for "rebirth")—that is, an important revival—of culture and art took place at Constantinople. Yet at the same time new elites began to dominate the Byzantine countryside. In the Islamic world, a dynastic revolution in 750 ousted the Umayyads from the caliphate and replaced them with a new family, the Abbasids. The Abbasid caliphs moved their capital from Damascus to Baghdad, in the area formerly called Persia. Even though the Abbasids' power began to ebb as regional Islamic rulers came to the fore, the Islamic world, too, saw a renaissance. In western Europe, Charlemagne—a Frankish king from a new dynasty, the Carolingians—forged a huge empire and presided over yet another cultural renaissance. Yet this newly unified kingdom was fragile, disintegrating within a generation of Charlemagne's death. In western Europe, even more than in the Byzantine and Islamic worlds, power fell into the hands of local lords.

Along the borders of these realms, new political entities began to develop, shaped by the religion and culture of their more dominant neighbors. The ancestor of Russia grew up in the shadow of Byzantium, as did Bulgaria and Serbia. Western Europe cast its influence over central European states. In the west, the borders of the Islamic world remained stable or were pushed back. (By contrast, Muslim expansion to the east changed the shape of central Asia.) By the year 1050, the contours of what were to become modern Europe and the Middle East were dimly visible.

CHAPTER FOCUS What forces led to the dissolution—or weakening—of centralized government in the period 750–1050, and what institutions took their place?

The Byzantine Emperor and Local Elites

Between 750 and 850, Byzantium staved off Muslim attacks in Asia Minor and began to rebuild. After 850, it went on the attack. Military victories brought new wealth and power to the imperial court, and the emperors supported a vast program of literary and artistic revival—the Macedonian renaissance—at Constantinople. But while the emperor dominated at the capital, a new landowning elite began to control the countryside. On its northern frontier, Byzantium helped create new Slavic realms.

Imperial Power

While the *themes*, with their territorial military organization, took care of attacks on Byzantine territory, *tagmata*—new mobile armies made up of the best troops—moved aggressively outward, beginning around 850. By 1025, the Byzantine Empire extended from the Danube in the north to the Euphrates in the south (Map 9.1). The Byzantines had not controlled so much territory since their wars with the Sasanid Persians four hundred years earlier.

750–c. 950 The Abbasid caliphate

751 Pippin III becomes king of the Franks, establishing Carolingian rule

768–814 Charlemagne rules as king of the Franks

786–809 Caliphate of Harun al-Rashid

800 Charlemagne crowned emperor at Rome

843 Treaty of Verdun

871–899 Reign of King Alfred of England

750 — 800 — 850

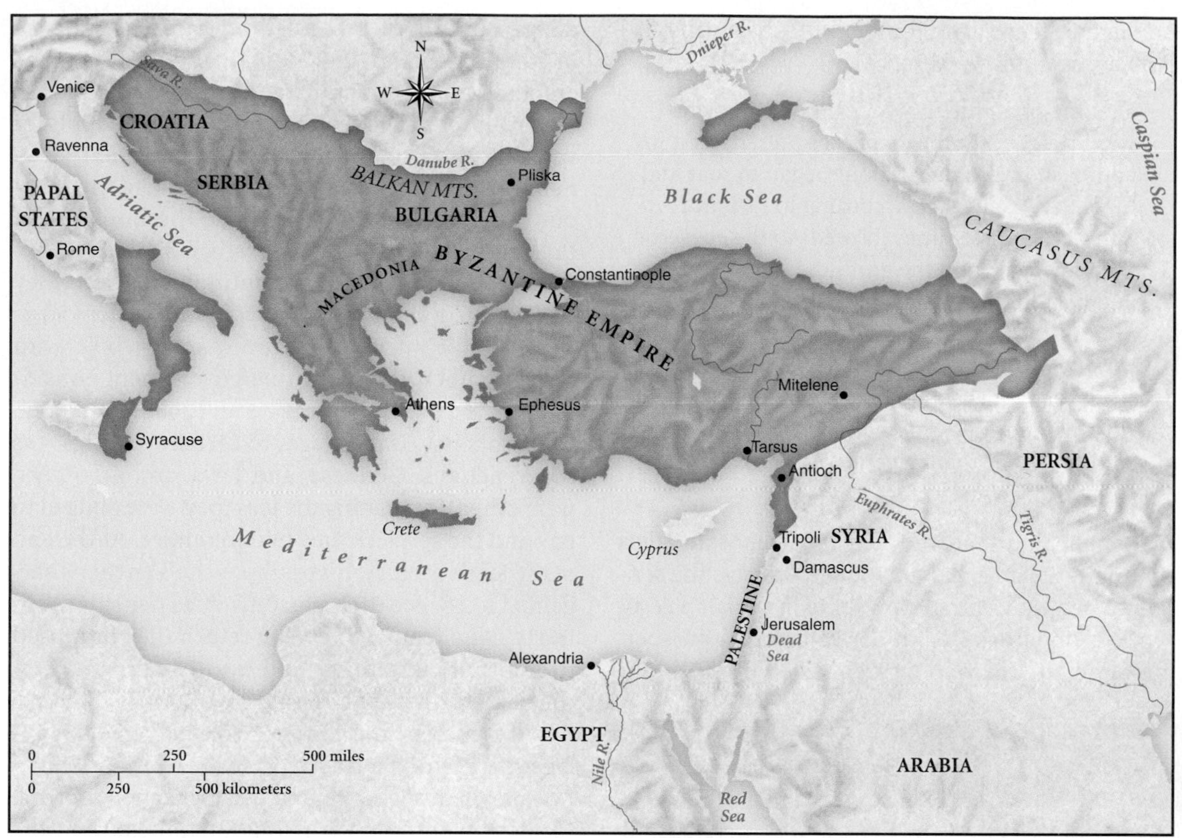

MAP 9.1 The Byzantine Empire, 1025

Under Emperor Basil II, the Byzantine Empire once again embraced the entire area of the Balkans, while its eastern arm extended around the Black Sea and its southern fringe reached nearly to Tripoli. The year 1025 marked the Byzantine Empire's greatest size after the rise of Islam.

Military victories gave new prestige and wealth to the army and to the imperial court. The emperors drew revenues from vast and growing imperial estates. They could demand services and money from the general population at will—requiring citizens to build bridges and roads, to offer lodging to the emperor and his attendants, and to pay taxes in cash. Emperors used their wealth to create a lavish court culture, surrounding themselves with servants, slaves, family members, and civil servants. Eunuchs (castrated men who could not pose a threat to the imperial line) were entrusted with some of the highest posts in government. From their powerful position, the emperors negotiated with other rulers, exchanging ambassadors and receiving and entertaining diplomats with elaborate ceremonies. One such diplomat, Liutprand, bishop of the northern Italian city of Cremona, reported

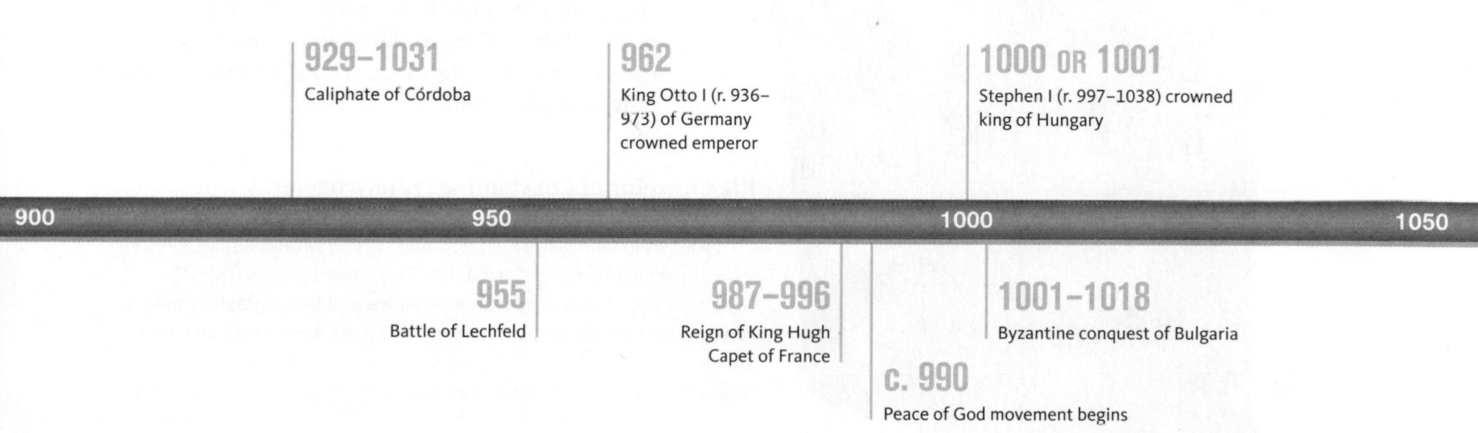

on his audience with Emperor Constantine VII Porphyrogenitos (r. 913–959):

> Leaning upon the shoulders of two eunuchs I was brought into the emperor's presence. At my approach [mechanical] lions began to roar and birds to cry out, each according to its kind. . . . After I had three times [bowed] to the emperor with my face upon the ground, I lifted my head, and behold! the man whom just before I had seen sitting on a moderately elevated seat had now changed his [clothing] and was sitting on the level of the ceiling. How it was done I could not imagine, unless perhaps he was lifted up by some such sort of device as we use for raising the timbers of a wine press.

Although Liutprand mocked this elaborate court ceremony, it had a real function: to express the serious, sacred, concentrated power of imperial majesty.

The emperor's wealth derived from a prosperous agricultural economy organized for trade. Byzantine commerce depended on a careful balance of state regulation and individual enterprise. The emperor controlled craft and commercial guilds to ensure imperial revenues and a stable supply of valuable and useful commodities, while entrepreneurs organized most of the markets held throughout the empire (see Document, "The Book of the Prefect," page 279). Foreign merchants traded within the empire, either at Constantinople (where they were lodged at state expense) or in border cities. Because this international trade intertwined with foreign policy, the Byzantine government considered trade a political as well as an economic matter. Emperors issued privileges to certain "nations" (as the Venetians, Genoese, and Jews, among others, were called), regulating the fees they were obliged to pay and the services they had to render. At the end of the tenth century, for example, the Venetians bargained to reduce their customs dues per ship from thirty *solidi* (coins) to two; in return they promised to transport Byzantine soldiers to Italy whenever the emperor wished.

At the same time, the emperors negotiated privileges for their own traders in foreign lands. Byzantine merchants were guaranteed protection in Syria, for example, while the two governments split the income on sales taxes. Thus, Byzantine trade flourished in the Middle East and, thanks to Venetian intermediaries, with western Europe. Equally significant was trade to the north; from the Kievan Rus the Byzantines imported furs, slaves, wax, and honey.

The Macedonian Renaissance, c. 870–c. 1025

Flush with victory and recalling Byzantium's past glory, the emperors revived classical intellectual pursuits. Basil I (r. 867–886) from Macedonia founded the imperial dynasty that presided over the so-called Macedonian renaissance. This renaissance was made possible by an intellectual elite who came from families that—even in the anxious years of the eighth century—had persisted in studying the classics in spite of the trend toward a simple religious education.

The Crowning of Constantine Porphyrogenitos
This ivory relief was carved at Constantinople in the mid-tenth century. The artist wanted to emphasize hierarchy and symbolism, not nature. Christ is shown crowning Emperor Constantine Porphyrogenitos (r. 913–959). What message do you suppose the artist wanted to telegraph by making Christ higher than the emperor and by having the emperor slightly incline his head and upper torso to receive the crown? *(Pushkin Museum, Moscow, Russia / The Bridgeman Art Library International.)*

DOCUMENT

The Book of the Prefect

Claiming to control all aspects of Byzantine life, emperors issued rules and regulations for every sort of profession. The Book of the Prefect, a decree issued in 911 or 912 by the emperor, shows the emperor's concern to implement God's harmonious intentions by making sure that no group infringed on the activities or duties of any other. Thus the book regulated numerous traders and craftspeople, including silk merchants, perfume dealers, candle makers, butchers, bakers, and—as illustrated here—notaries and jewelers. The prefect was the chief city official at Constantinople.

Preface

God, after having created all things that are and given order and harmony to the universe, with his own finger engraved the Law on the tables and published it openly so that men, being well directed thereby, should not shamelessly trample upon one another and the stronger should not do violence to the weaker but that all things should be apportioned with just measure. Therefore it has seemed good for Our Serenity [i.e., the emperor] also to lay down the following ordinances based on the statutes in order that the human race may be governed fittingly and no person may injure his fellow.

I. The Notaries

1. Whoever wishes to be appointed a notary [a writer of legal or official documents] must be elected by a vote and decision both of the *primicerius* [the chief of the guild of notaries] and the notaries acting with him to ensure that he has a knowledge and understanding of the laws, that he excels in handwriting, that he is not garrulous [overly talkative] or insolent, and that he does not lead a corrupt life, but on the contrary is serious in his habits, guileless in his thoughts, eloquent, intelligent, a polished reader, and accurate in his diction, to guard against his being easily led to give a false meaning in places to what he writes or to insert deceptive clauses. And if at any time a notary is found to be doing something contrary to the law and the authorized written regulations, those who have acted as his witnesses shall be responsible.
2. The candidate must know by heart the forty titles of the *Manual of Law* [a short compilation of imperial laws] and must also know the sixty books of the Basilika [a much longer compilation]. He shall also have received a general education so that he may not make mistakes in formulating his documents and be guilty of errors in his reading. He shall also have abundant time to give proof of his ability both mental and physical. Let him prepare a handwritten document in a meeting of the guild, so that he may not later commit unforeseen errors; but if he should then be detected in any, let him be expelled, from the order. . . .

II. The Jewelers

1. We ordain that the jewelers may, if any one invites them, buy the things that pertain to them, such as gold, silver, pearls, or precious stones; but not bronze and woven linens or any other materials which others should purchase rather than they. However, they are not hereby prevented from buying anything they wish for private use.
2. They must not depreciate or increase the price of things for sale to the detriment of the vendors, but shall appraise them at their just value. If anyone acts deceitfully in this, he shall forfeit the appraised value of the things to the vendor. . . .
4. If a jeweler discovers a woman offering for sale objects of gold or silver, or pearls, or precious stones, he shall inform the Prefect of these things to prevent their being exported to foreign peoples.
5. If anyone adulterates uncoined metal and manufactures things for sale from it, he shall have his hand cut off.

Source: A. E. R. Boak, "Notes and Documents: The Book of the Prefect," *Journal of Economic and Business History* 1 (1929): 600–602, 604 (slightly modified).

Question to Consider

- **What sort of legal training did notaries have to have? How does modern legal training compare? What does this tell us about Byzantine life and society?**

Now, with the empire slowly regaining its military eminence and with icons permanently restored in 843, this scholarly elite thrived again. Byzantine artists produced new works, and emperors and other members of the new court society, liberated from the sober taboos of the iconoclastic period, sponsored lavish artistic productions. Emperor Constantine Porphyrogenitos wrote books of geography and history and financed the work of other scholars and artists. He even supervised the details of his craftspeople's products, insisting on exacting standards: "Who could enumerate how many artisans the Porphyrogenitos corrected? He corrected the stonemasons, the carpenters, the goldsmiths, the silversmiths, and the blacksmiths," wrote a historian supported by the same emperor's patronage.

The emperors were not alone in their support of the arts. Other members of the imperial court also sponsored writers, philosophers, and historians. Scholars wrote summaries of classical literature, encyclopedias of ancient knowledge, and commentaries on classical authors. Some copied manuscripts of religious and theological commentaries, such as homilies, liturgical texts, Bibles, and Psalters. The

A Depiction of David from the Macedonian Renaissance
This manuscript illumination, made at Constantinople in the mid-ninth century, combines Christian and classical elements in a harmonious composition. David, author of the Psalms, sits in the center. Like the classical Orpheus, he plays music that attracts and tames the beasts. In the right-hand corner, a figure labeled "Bethlehem" is modeled on a lounging river or mountain god. *(Bibliothèque nationale, Paris, France/The Bridgeman Art Library International.)*

merging of classical and Christian traditions is clearest in manuscript illuminations (painted illustrations or embellishments in hand-copied manuscripts). For example, to depict King David, the supposed poet of the Psalms, an artist illuminating a Psalter turned to a model of Orpheus, the enchanting musician of ancient Greek mythology. (See the illustration above.) Both in Byzantium and in the West, artists chose their subjects by considering the texts they were to illustrate and the ways in which previous artists had handled particular themes. As with the illustration of King David, they drew on traditional models to make their subjects identifiable. Like modern illustrators of Santa Claus who rely on a tradition dictating a plump man with a bushy white beard (Santa's "iconography"), medieval artists used particular visual cues to alert viewers to the identity of their subjects.

The *Dynatoi*: A New Landowning Elite

At Constantinople the emperor reigned supreme. But outside the capital, especially in the border regions of Anatolia, where leaders of the tagmata became famous as military heroes, extremely powerful military families began to compete with imperial power. The ***dynatoi*** ("powerful men"), as this new hereditary elite was called, got rich on booty and new lands taken in the aggressive wars of the tenth century. They took over or bought up whole villages, turning the peasants' labor to their benefit. For the most part they exercised their power locally, but they also sometimes occupied the imperial throne.

The Phocas family exemplifies the strengths as well as the weaknesses of the dynatoi. Probably originally from Armenia, they possessed military skills and exhibited loyalty to the emperor that together brought them high positions in both the army and at court in the last decades of the ninth century. In the tenth century, with new successes in the east, the Phocas family gained independent power. After some particularly brilliant victories, Nicephorus Phocas was declared emperor by his armies and ruled (as Nicephorus II Phocas) at Constantinople from 963 to 969. But opposing factions

dynatoi **(DY nuh toy):** The "powerful men" who dominated the countryside of the Byzantine Empire in the tenth and eleventh centuries, and to some degree challenged the authority of the emperor.

of the dynatoi brought him down. The mainstay of Phocas family power, as of that of all the dynatoi, was outside the capital, on the family's great estates.

As the dynatoi gained power, the social hierarchy of Byzantium began to resemble that of western Europe, where land owned by aristocratic lords was farmed by peasants bound by tax and service obligations to the fields they cultivated.

The Formation of Eastern Europe and Kievan Rus

What would become modern eastern Europe was shaped during the period 850–950. By 800, Slavic settlements dotted the area from the Danube River down to Greece and from the Black Sea to Croatia. The ruler of the Bulgarians, called a *khagan*, presided over the largest realm, northwest of Constantinople. Under the khagan Krum (r. c. 803–814) and his son, Bulgarian rule stretched west to the Tisza River in modern Hungary. At about the same time as Krum's triumphant expansion, however, the Byzantine Empire began its own campaigns to conquer, convert, and control these Slavic regions, today known as the Balkans.

Bulgaria and Serbia

The Byzantine offensive to the north and west began under Emperor Nicephorus I (r. 802–811), who waged war against the Slavs of Greece in the Peloponnese, set up a new Christian diocese there, organized it as a new military theme, and forcibly resettled Christians in the area to counteract Slavic paganism. The Byzantines followed this pattern of conquest as they pushed northward. By 900, Byzantium ruled all of Greece.

Still under Nicephorus I, the Byzantines launched a massive attack against the Bulgarians, took the chief city of Pliska, plundered it, burned it to the ground, and then marched against Krum's encampment in the Balkan Mountains. Krum, however, attacked the imperial troops, killed Nicephorus, and brought home the emperor's skull in triumph. Cleaned out and lined with silver, the skull served as the victorious Krum's drinking goblet. In 816, the two sides agreed to a peace that lasted for thirty years. But hostility remained, and intermittent skirmishes between the Bulgarians and Byzantines gave way to longer wars throughout the tenth century.

Emperor **Basil II** (r. 976–1025) led the Byzantines in a slow, methodical conquest. Aptly called the Bulgar-Slayer, Basil brought the entire region under Byzantine control and forced its ruler to accept the Byzantine form of Christianity. Around the same time, the Serbs, encouraged by Byzantium to oppose the Bulgarians, began to form the political community that would become Serbia.

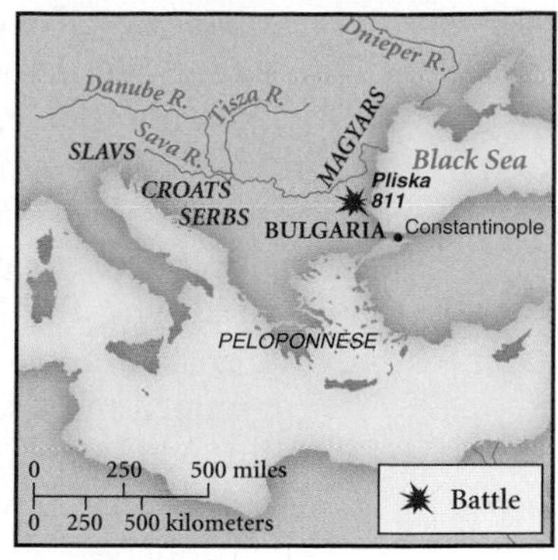

The Balkans, c. 850–950

Religion played an important role in the Byzantine conquest of the Balkans. In 863, the brothers Cyril and Methodius were sent as Christian missionaries from the Byzantines to the Slavs. Well educated in both classical and religious texts, they spoke one Slavic dialect fluently and devised an alphabet for Slavic (until then an oral language) based on Greek forms. It was the ancestor of the modern Cyrillic alphabet used in Bulgaria, Serbia, and Russia today.

Kievan Rus

The region that would eventually become Russia lay outside the sphere of direct Byzantine rule in the ninth and tenth centuries. Like Serbia and Bulgaria, however, it came under increasingly strong Byzantine influence. In the ninth century, the Vikings—Scandinavian adventurers who ranged over vast stretches of ninth-century Europe seeking trade, booty, and land—penetrated the region below the Gulf of Finland, where they imposed their rule. By the end of the century they had moved southward, taking in the region around Kiev, a key commercial emporium. There the Rus, as they were called, adopted some of the ceremonial trappings of the nearby Khazar state, a formidable power at the mouth of the Volga River. From Kiev, which today is the capital of Ukraine, enterprising Rus sailed the Dnieper River and crossed the Black Sea in search of markets for their slaves and furs.

The relationship between Rus and Byzantium began with trade, continued with an interlude of war, and was soon sustained by a common religion. Already at the start of the tenth century the Rus had special trade privileges at Constantinople, where they were allowed to enter in groups of fifty, though only if unarmed. In 911, the Rus and the Byzantines drew up a detailed treaty that proclaimed

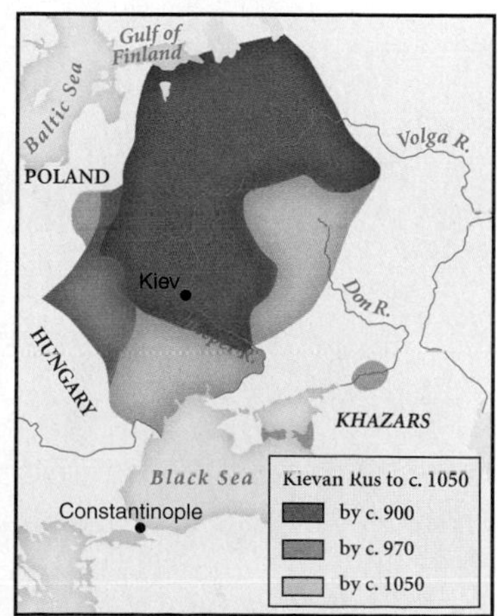

The Formation of Kievan Rus

Basil II: The Byzantine emperor (r. 976–1025) who presided over the end of the Bulgar threat (earning the name Bulgar-Slayer) and the conversion of Kievan Russia to Christianity.

their "amity" and "love." It regulated relations between the two peoples at Constantinople. "If a Rus kill a Byzantine, or a Byzantine a Rus, let him die where the murder has been committed," read one typical provision. But when the Byzantines tried to use the Rus to attack the Khazars, their plan backfired, and the Khazars forced the Rus to attack Constantinople in 941. Soon, however, the Rus regrouped and resumed trading with Byzantium. They brought home not only money but also Byzantine silks, some of which have survived in the burial chambers of well-to-do Rus women.

Few Rus were Christian (most were polytheists, others Muslims or Jews), but that changed at the end of the tenth century, when good relations between the Rus and the Byzantines were sealed by the conversion of the Rus ruler Vladimir (r. c. 978–1015). Emperor Basil II, in need of military help in 988, sent his sister Anna to marry Vladimir in exchange for an army of Rus. To seal the alliance, Vladimir was baptized and took his brother-in-law's name. The general population seems to have quickly adopted the new religion.

Mosaic of Mary in the Cathedral of St. Sophia
Imitating Justinian's Hagia Sophia at Constantinople, the cathedral of St. Sophia in Kiev was built by Rus ruler Iaroslav the Wise (r. 1019–1054) around 1050. Here the Virgin Mary, who looms at the very center of the cathedral, is portrayed praying in the position of the praying man figure shown on page 264. Compare her to the icon of the Virgin and Child on page 256 to see how much the Russian artists borrowed from Byzantine styles. *(Cathedral of St. Sophia, Kiev, Russia/Vadim Gippenreiter/The Bridgeman Art Library International.)*

Vladimir's conversion represented a wider pattern: the Christianization of Europe. In the southeast, orthodox Byzantine Christianity was decisive, while in the west and northwest, Roman Catholicism tended to be most important. Slavic realms such as Moravia, Serbia, and Bulgaria adopted the Byzantine form of Christianity, while the rulers and peoples of Poland, Hungary, Denmark, and Norway were converted under the auspices of the Roman church. The conversion of the Rus was especially significant, because they were geographically as close to the Islamic world as to the Christian and could conceivably have become Muslims. By converting to Byzantine Christianity, the Rus made themselves heir to Byzantium and its church, customs, art, and political ideology. The adoption of Christianity linked Rus to the Christian world, but choosing the Byzantine form, rather than the Roman Catholic, later served to isolate the region from western Europe, as in the course of the centuries the Byzantine (Greek-speaking) and Roman (Latin-speaking) churches became estranged.

Wishing to counteract this isolation, Rus rulers at times sought to cement relations with central and western Europe, which were tied to Catholic Rome. Prince Iaroslav the Wise, who became sole ruler in 1034 or 1036, forged such links through his own marriage and those of his sons and daughters to rulers and princely families in France, Hungary, and Scandinavia. Iaroslav encouraged intellectual and artistic developments that would connect Russian culture to the classical past. At his own church of St. Sophia, in Kiev, which copied the one at Constantinople, Iaroslav created a major library.

When Iaroslav died in 1054, his kingdom was divided among his sons. Civil wars broke out between the brothers and eventually between cousins, shredding what unity Rus had known. Massive invasions by outsiders, particularly from the east, further weakened the Kievan rulers, who were eventually displaced by princes from the north. At the crossroads of East and West, Rus could meet and absorb a great variety of traditions; but its geographical position also opened it to unremitting military pressures.

REVIEW QUESTION In what ways did the Byzantine emperor expand his power, and in what ways was that power checked?

The Rise and Fall of the Abbasid Caliphate

A new dynasty of caliphs—the Abbasids—first brought unity and then, in their decline, fragmentation to the Islamic world. Caliphs ruled in name only, as regional rulers took over the actual government in Islamic lands. Local traditions based on religious and political differences played an increasingly important role in people's lives. Yet, even in the eleventh century, the Islamic world had a clear sense of its own unity, based on language, commerce, and artistic and intellectual achievements that transcended regional boundaries.

The Abbasid Caliphate, 750–936

In 750, a civil war ousted the Umayyads and raised the **Abbasids** to the caliphate. The Abbasids found support in an uneasy coalition of Shi'ites (the faction of Islam loyal to Ali's memory) and non-Arabs who had been excluded from the Umayyad government and now demanded a place in political life. With the new regime, the center of Islamic rule shifted from Damascus, with its roots in the Roman tradition, to Baghdad, a new capital city built by the Abbasids right next to Ctesiphon, which had been the Sasanid capital. Here the Abbasid caliphs adhered even more firmly than the Umayyads to Persian courtly models. Their administration grew more and more centralized: the caliph's staff grew, and he controlled the appointment of regional governors.

From Baghdad, the Abbasid caliph Harun al-Rashid (r. 786–809) presided over a flourishing empire. His contemporary Frankish ruler, Charlemagne, was impressed with the elephant Harun sent him as a gift, along with monkeys, spices, and medicines. Such items were mainstays of everyday commerce in Harun's Iraq. A mid-ninth-century catalog of imports listed "tigers, panthers, elephants, panther skins, rubies, white sandal[wood], ebony, and coconuts" from India as well as "silk, chinaware, paper, ink, peacocks, racing horses, saddles, felts [and] cinnamon" from China.

The Abbasid dynasty began to decline after Harun's death. For eight years, his two sons waged war against each other, splintering the caliphate. During the war, the caliphs lost control over many regions, including Syria and Egypt. They needed to recruit an army that would be loyal to them alone. This they found in "outsiders," many of them Turks from east of the Caspian Sea (today Kazakhstan). Many of the Turks, later called Mamluks, were bought as slaves. One slave trader reported, "[The caliph sent me] to purchase Turks. Each year I would bring him a certain number such that . . . [he] accumulated some three thousand young men." Once purchased, the Turks were freed and paid a salary. They were crackerjack troops because they knew how to fire arrows while riding horseback. But to keep them employed, the Abbasids needed a good tax base, and this they did not have. Even in Iraq itself, serious uprisings just south of Baghdad kept huge swaths of territory outside the control of the caliphs. Other regions of the Islamic world easily went their own way. In the tenth century the caliphs became figureheads only, while independent regional rulers collected taxes and hired their own armies.

Thus, in the Islamic world, as in the Byzantine, new regional lords challenged the power of the central ruler. But the process was soon much more advanced in Islamic than in Byzantine territories. Map 9.1 (see page 277) correctly omits any indication of regional dynatoi because the key center of power in the Byzantine Empire continued to be Constantinople. Map 9.2, on the other hand, shows the fragmentation of the Abbasid caliphate, as local dynasties established themselves.

Regional Diversity in Islamic Lands

A faraway caliph could not command sufficient allegiance from local leaders once he demanded more in taxes than he gave back in favors. The forces of fragmentation were strong in the Islamic world, which was, after all, based on the conquest of many diverse regions, each with its own deeply rooted traditions and culture. The Islamic religion, with its Sunni/Shi'ite split, also became a source of polarization.[1] Western Europeans knew almost nothing about Muslims, calling all of them Saracens (from the Latin word for "Arabs") without distinction. But, like today, Muslims were of different ethnicities, practiced different customs, and identified with different regions. With the fragmentation of political and religious unity, each of the tenth- and early-eleventh-century Islamic states built on local traditions under local rulers.

Abbasids (A buh sihds): The dynasty of caliphs that, in 750, took over from the Umayyads in all of the Islamic realm except for Spain (al-Andalus). From their new capital at Baghdad, they presided over a wealthy realm until the late ninth century.

[1] The Shi'ites, originally followers of Ali, had by this time come to practice Islam differently from the Sunni. Each faction adhered to its own interpretation of the Prophet Muhammad's life and message.

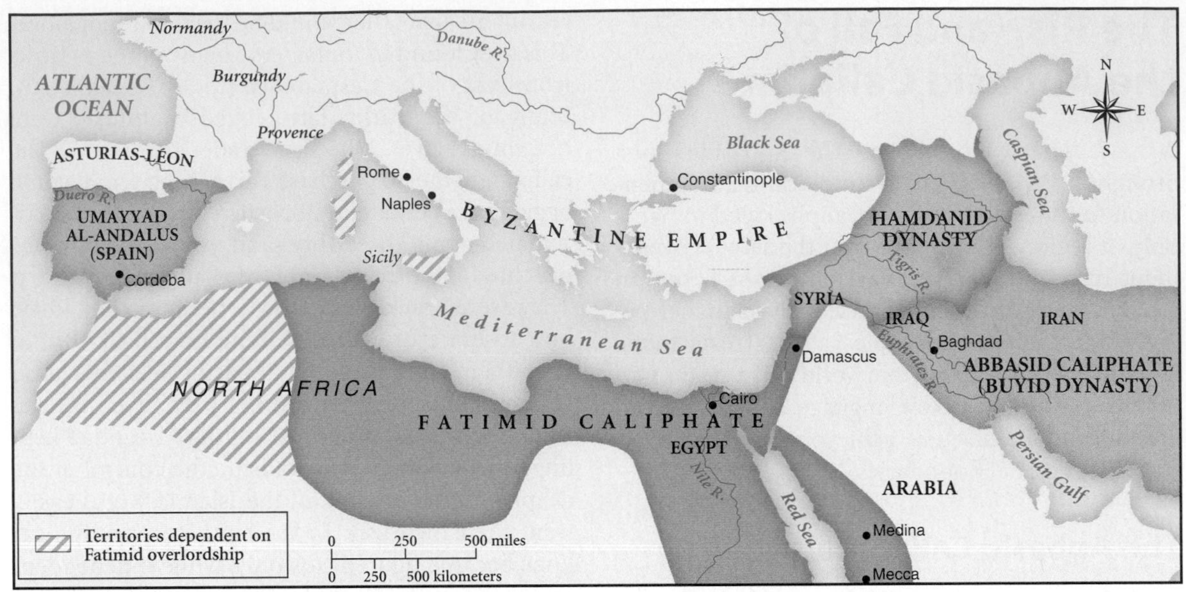

MAP 9.2 Islamic States, c. 1000
Comparing this map with Map 8.1 on page 248 will quickly demonstrate the fragmentation of the once united Islamic caliphate. In 750, one caliph ruled territory stretching from Spain to India. In 1000, there was more than one caliphate as well as several other ruling dynasties. The most important of those dynasties were the Fatimids, who began as organizers of a movement to overthrow the Abbasids. By 1000, the Fatimids had conquered Egypt and claimed hegemony over all of North Africa.

The Fatimid Dynasty In the tenth century, one group of Shiʿites, calling themselves the **Fatimids** (after Fatimah, daughter of Muhammad and wife of Ali), allied with the Berbers in North Africa and established themselves in 909 as rulers in the region now called Tunisia. The Fatimid Ubayd Allah claimed to be not only the true imam—the descendant of Ali—but also the *mahdi*, the "divinely guided" messiah, come to bring justice on earth. In 969, the Fatimids declared themselves rulers of Egypt. Their dynasty lasted for about two hundred years. Fatimid leaders also controlled North Africa, Arabia, and even Syria for a time. They established a lavish court culture that rivaled the one at Baghdad, and they supported industries such as lusterware (see the illustration on the right), that had once been a monopoly of the Abbasids.

Fatimids (FAT ih mihds): Members of the tenth-century Shiʿite dynasty who derived their name from Fatimah, the daughter of Muhammad and wife of Ali; they dominated in parts of North Africa, Egypt, and even Syria.

The Spanish Emirate Whereas the Shiʿites dominated Egypt, Sunni Muslims ruled al-Andalus, the Islamic central and southern heart of Spain. Unlike the other independent Islamic states, which were forged during the ninth and tenth centuries, the Spanish emirate of Córdoba (so called because its ruler took the secular title *emir*, "commander," and fixed his capital at Córdoba) was created near the start of the Abbasid

Fatimid Tableware
The elites under the Fatimid rulers cultivated a luxurious lifestyle that including dining on porcelain tableware, which was glazed and fired several times to produce the effect seen here. Trade contacts with China inspired the Islamic world to mimic Chinese pottery. *(Museum of Fine Arts, Cleveland/photo © Werner Forman/HIP/The Image Works.)*

caliphate. During the Abbasid revolution of 750, Abd al-Rahman—a member of the Umayyad family—fled to Morocco, gathered an army, invaded Spain, and after only one battle was declared emir in 756, becoming Abd al-Rahman I. He and his successors ruled a broad range of peoples, including many Jews and Christians. After the initial Islamic conquest of Spain, the Christians adopted so much of the new Arabic language and so many of the customs that they were called Mozarabs, that is, "like Arabs." The Arabs allowed them freedom of worship and let them live according to their own laws. Some Mozarabs were content with their status, others converted to Islam, and still others intermarried—most commonly, Christian women married Muslim men and raised their children as Muslims, since the religion of the father determined that of the children.

A Princely Pyxis

A pyxis is a small container, and this one, about six inches high and carved out of ivory, was made for the younger son of Abd al-Rahman III, the caliph of Córdoba. The prince is depicted in a decorative lozenge, sitting on a rug and holding a bottle and a flower. One servant sits beside him to cool him with a fan; another stands and plays the lute. Underneath the rug are lions, symbols of power. Outside the princely enclosure, falconers stand by, ready to accompany the prince to the hunt. The whole scene suggests order, skill, and elegance, all important features of the Islamic renaissance. *(Louvre, Paris, France/Peter Willi/The Bridgeman Art Library International.)*

Abd al-Rahman III (r. 912–961) was powerful enough to take the title of caliph, and the caliphate of Córdoba, which he created, lasted from 929 to 1031. Under Abd al-Rahman III's rule, members of all religious groups in al-Andalus enjoyed not only freedom of worship but also equal opportunity to rise in the civil service. The caliph also initiated diplomatic contacts with Byzantine and European rulers, ignoring the weak and tiny Christian kingdoms squeezed into northern Spain. Yet under later caliphs, al-Andalus experienced the same political fragmentation that was occurring everywhere else. The caliphate of Córdoba broke up in 1031, and rulers of small, independent regions, called *taifas*, took power.

Unity of Commerce and Language

Although the regions of the Islamic world were culturally and politically diverse, they maintained a measure of unity through trade networks and language. Their principal bond was Arabic, the language of the Qur'an. At once poetic and sacred, Arabic was also the language of commerce and government from Baghdad to Córdoba. Moreover, despite political differences, borders were open: an artisan could move from Córdoba to Cairo; a landowner in Morocco might very well own property in al-Andalus; a young man from North Africa would think nothing of going to Baghdad to find a wife; a young girl purchased as a slave in Mecca might become part of a prince's household in Baghdad. With few barriers to commerce (though every city and town had its own customs dues), traders regularly dealt in various, often exotic, goods.

The primary reason for these open borders was Islam itself, but the openness extended to non-Muslims as well. The commercial activities of the Tustari brothers, Jewish merchants from southern Iran, were typical in the Arabic-speaking world. By 1026, the Tustaris had established a flourishing business in Egypt. Although they did not have "branch offices," informal contacts with friends and family allowed them to import fine textiles from Iran to sell in Egypt and to export Egyptian fabrics to sell in Iran. Dealing in fabrics could yield fabulous wealth, for cloth was essential not only for clothing but also for home decoration: textiles covered walls; curtains separated rooms. The Tustari brothers held the highest rank in Jewish society and had contacts with Muslim rulers. The son of one of the brothers converted to Islam and became vizier (chief minister) to the Fatimids in Egypt.

The sophisticated Islamic society of the tenth and eleventh centuries supported commercial networks even more vast than those of the Tustari family. Muslim merchants brought tin from England; salt and gold from Timbuktu in west-central Africa; amber, gold, and copper from Rus; and slaves from every region. Equally widespread was the reach of the Islamic renaissance.

DOCUMENT

When She Approached

The tenth and eleventh centuries marked the golden age of Arabic poetry in al-Andalus. In the first of these centuries, the poets' patron was the caliph at Córdoba. In the eleventh century, as al-Andalus broke up into taifas *(see page 285), each taifa ruler supported his own artists. Ibn Darraj al-Quastali (958–1030) revealed his most intimate feelings when he wrote in this poem about leaving his wife and child behind to find employment at the court of a taifa ruler.*

When she approached to bid me farewell,
her sighs and moans breaking down my endurance,
reminding me of the times of love and joy,
while in the crib a little one gurgles,
unable to talk, but the sounds he makes
firmly lodge in the heart's whims. . . .
I disobeyed the promptings of my heart to stay with him,
led on by a habit of constant travel day and night,
and the wing of parting took off with me, while the fear
of parting flew high with many wings.

Source: Salma Khadra Jayyusi, "Andalusi Poetry: The Golden Period," in *The Legacy of Muslim Spain*, ed. Salma Khadra Jayyusi, 2 vols. (Leiden: Brill, 1994), 1:335.

Question to Consider

- **What image of family life does this poem project? What does it tell us about the different attractions of career and family in the Islamic world?**

The Islamic Renaissance, c. 790–c. 1050

Unlike the Macedonian renaissance, which was concentrated in Constantinople, the Islamic renaissance occurred throughout the Islamic world. The dissolution of the caliphate into separate political entities multiplied the centers of learning and intellectual productivity. The Islamic renaissance was particularly dazzling in capital cities such as Córdoba, where tenth-century rulers presided over a brilliant court culture, patronizing scholars, poets, and artists. The library at Córdoba contained the largest collection of books in Europe at that time (see Document, "When She Approached," above).

Elsewhere, already in the eighth century, the Abbasid caliphs endowed research libraries and set up centers for translation where scholars culled the writings of the ancients, including the classics of Persia, India, and Greece. Many scholars read, translated, and commented on the works of ancient philosophers. Some studied astronomy while others wrote on mathematical matters. Al-Khwarizmi (c. 780–c. 850) wrote a book on algebra (the word itself is from the Arab *al-jabr*) and another on the Indian method of calculation, using the numbers 1, 2, and 3. He introduced the zero, essential for differentiating 1 from 10, for example. When these numerals were introduced into western Europe in the twelfth century, they were known as Arabic, as they are still called today.

The newly independent Islamic rulers supported science as well as mathematics. Ibn Sina (980–1037), known in Christian Europe as Avicenna, wrote books on logic, the natural sciences, and physics. His *Canon of Medicine* systematized earlier treatises and reconciled them with his own experience as a physician. Active in the centers of power, he served as vizier to various rulers. In his autobiography, he spoke with pleasure and pride about his intellectual development:

> One day I asked permission [of the ruler] to go into [his doctors'] library, look at their books, and read the medical ones. He gave me permission, and I went into a palace of many rooms, each with trunks full of books, back-to-back. In one room there were books on Arabic and poetry, in another books on jurisprudence, and similarly in each room books on a single subject. . . . When I reached the age of eighteen, I had completed the study of all these sciences.

Long before there were universities in Europe, there were institutions of higher learning in the Islamic world. Rich Muslims, often members of the ruling elite, demonstrated their piety and charity by establishing schools. Each school, or madrasa, was located within or attached to a mosque. Sometimes visiting scholars held passionate public debates at these schools. More regularly, professors held classes throughout the day on the interpretation of the Qur'an and other literary or legal texts. Students, all male, attended the classes that suited their achievement level and interest. Most students paid a fee for learning, but there were also scholarship students. One tenth-century vizier was so solicitous of the welfare of the scholars he supported that each day he set out iced refreshments, candles, and paper for them in his own kitchen.

The use of paper, made from flax and hemp or rags and vegetable fiber, points to a major difference among the Islamic, Byzantine, and (as we shall see) Carolingian renaissances. Byzantine scholars worked to enhance the prestige of the ruling classes. Their work, written on expensive parchment (made from animal skins), kept manuscripts out of the hands of all but the very rich. This was true of scholarship in Europe as well. By contrast, Islamic scholars had goals that cut across all social classes: to be physicians to the rich, teachers to the young, and contributors to passionate religious debates. Their writings, on paper (less expensive than parchment), were widely available.

REVIEW QUESTION What forces contributed to the fragmentation of the Islamic world in the tenth and eleventh centuries, and what forces held it together?

The Carolingian Empire

Just as in the Byzantine and Islamic worlds, in Europe the period 750–1050 saw first the formation of a strong empire, ruled by one man, and then its fragmentation as local rulers took power into their own hands. A new dynasty, the Carolingians, came to rule in the Frankish kingdom at almost the very moment (c. 750) that the Abbasids gained the caliphate. Charlemagne, the most powerful Carolingian monarch, conquered new territory, took the title of emperor, and presided over a revival of Christian classical culture known as the Carolingian renaissance. He ruled at the local level through counts and other military men. Nevertheless, the unity of the Carolingian Empire — based largely on conquest, a measure of prosperity, and personal allegiance to Charlemagne — was shaky. Its weaknesses were exacerbated by attacks from Viking, Muslim, and Magyar invaders. Charlemagne's successors divided his empire among themselves and saw it divided further as local leaders took defense — and rule — into their own hands.

The Rise of the Carolingians

The Carolingians were among many aristocratic families on the rise during the Merovingian period, but they gained exceptional power by monopolizing the position of "palace mayor" — a sort of prime minister — under the Merovingian kings. Charles Martel ("Charles the Hammer"), mayor 714–741, gave the name **Carolingian** (from *Carolus*, Latin for "Charles") to the dynasty. Renowned for defeating an invading army of Muslims from al-Andalus near Poitiers in 732, he also contended vigorously against other aristocrats who were carving out independent lordships for themselves. Charles Martel and his family turned aristocratic factions against one another, rewarded supporters, crushed enemies, and dominated whole regions by supporting monasteries that served as focal points for both religious piety and land donations.

The Carolingians also allied themselves with the Roman papacy and its adherents. They supported Anglo-Saxon missionaries like Boniface (see page 267) who went to areas on the fringes of the Carolingian realm as the pope's ambassador. Reforming the Christianity that these regions had adopted, Boniface set up a hierarchical church organization and founded monasteries dedicated to the Benedictine rule. His newly appointed bishops were loyal to Rome and the Carolingians.

Pippin III (d. 768), Charles Martel's son, turned to the pope even more directly. When he deposed the Merovingian king in 751, taking over the kingship himself, Pippin petitioned Pope Zachary to legitimize the act; the pope agreed. The Carolingians returned the favor a few years later when the pope asked for their help against hostile Lombards. That papal request signaled a major shift. Before 754, the papacy had been part of the Byzantine Empire; after that, it turned to Europe for protection. Pippin launched a successful campaign against the Lombard king that ended in 756 with the so-called Donation of Pippin, a peace accord between the Lombards and the pope. The treaty gave back to the pope cities that had been taken by the Lombard king. The new arrangement recognized what the papacy had long before created: a territorial "republic of St. Peter" ruled by the pope, not by the Byzantine emperor. Henceforth, the fate of Italy would be tied largely to the policies of the pope and the Frankish kings to the north, not to the eastern emperors.

Partnership with the Roman church gave the Carolingian dynasty a Christian aura, expressed in symbolic form by anointment. Bishops rubbed holy oil on the foreheads and shoulders of Carolingian kings during the coronation ceremony, imitating the Old Testament kings who had been anointed by God.

Charlemagne and His Kingdom, 768–814

The most famous Carolingian king was Charles, called the Great (*le Magne* in Old French) by his contemporaries — thus, **Charlemagne** (r. 768–814). (See "Contrasting Views," pages 290–291.) Mod-

Carolingian: The Frankish dynasty that ruled a western European empire from 751 to the late 800s; its greatest vigor was in the time of Charlemagne (r. 768–814) and Louis the Pious (r. 814–840).

Charlemagne (SHAR luh mayn): The Carolingian king (r. 768–814) whose conquests greatly expanded the Frankish kingdom. He was crowned emperor on December 25, 800.

Charlemagne's Chapel
Charlemagne was the first Frankish king to build a permanent capital city. He decided to do so in 789 and chose Aachen because of its natural warm springs. There he built a palace complex that, besides a grand living area for himself and his retinue, included a chapel (a small semiprivate church). Today the entire chapel is enclosed within Aachen's cathedral. *(© Aachen Cathedral, Aachen, Germany/Bildarchiv Steffens/The Bridgeman Art Library International.)*

ern historians are less dazzled than his contemporaries were, noting that Charlemagne was complex, contradictory, and sometimes brutal. He loved listening to St. Augustine's *City of God* as it was read aloud, and he supported major scholarly enterprises, yet he never learned to write. He was devout, building a beautiful chapel at his major residence at Aachen (see the illustration above), yet he flouted the advice of churchmen when they told him to convert pagans rather than force baptism on them. He admired the pope, yet he was furious when a pope placed the imperial crown on his head. He waged many successful wars, yet he thereby destroyed the buffer states surrounding the Frankish kingdoms, unleashing a new round of invasions even before his death.

Behind these contradictions, however, lay a unifying vision. Charlemagne dreamed of an empire that would unite the martial and learned traditions of the Roman and Germanic worlds with the legacy of Christianity. This vision lay at the core of his political activity, his building programs, and his support of scholarship and education.

Territorial Expansion

During the early years of his reign, Charlemagne conquered lands in all directions (Map 9.3). He invaded Italy, seizing the crown of the Lombard kings and annexing northern Italy in 774. He then moved northward and began a long and difficult war against the Saxons, concluded only after more than thirty years of fighting, during which he forcibly annexed Saxon territory and converted the Saxon people to Christianity through mass baptisms at the point of the sword. To the southeast, Charlemagne fought the Avars. Charlemagne's courtier and biographer Einhard described this campaign as follows: "All the money and treasure that had been amassed over many years was seized, and no war in which the Franks have ever engaged within the memory of man brought them such riches and such booty." To the southwest, Charlemagne led an expedition to al-Andalus. Although suffering a defeat at Roncesvalles in 778 (immortalized later in the medieval epic *The Song of Roland*), he did set up a march, or military buffer region, between al-Andalus and his own realm.

By the 790s, Charlemagne's kingdom stretched eastward beyond the Elbe River (today in Germany), southeast to what is today Austria, and south to Spain and Italy. Such power in the West was unheard of since the time of the Roman Empire. Charlemagne began to imitate aspects of the imperial model: he sponsored building programs to symbolize his authority, standardized weights and measures, and acted as a patron of intellectual and artistic efforts. He built a capital city at Aachen, complete with a chapel that was patterned on Justinian's church of San Vitale (see pages 234–35) at Ravenna.

To discourage corruption, Charlemagne appointed special officials, called *missi dominici* ("those sent out by the lord king"), to oversee his regional governors — the counts — on the king's behalf. The missi — lay aristocrats or bishops — traveled in pairs throughout the kingdom. As one of Charlemagne's capitularies (summaries of royal decisions) put it, the missi "are to make diligent inquiry wherever people claim that someone has done them an injustice, so that the missi fully carry out the law and do justice for everyone everywhere, whether in the holy churches of God or among the poor, orphans, or widows."

MAP 9.3 Expansion of the Carolingian Empire under Charlemagne
The conquests of Charlemagne temporarily united almost all of western Europe under one ruler. Although this great empire broke apart (see the inset showing how the empire was divided by the Treaty of Verdun), the legacy of that unity remained, even serving as one of the inspirations behind today's European Union.

Imperial Coronation While Charlemagne was busy imitating Roman emperors through his conquests, his building programs, his legislation, and his efforts at church reform, the papacy was beginning to claim imperial power for itself. At some point, perhaps in the 760s, members of the papal chancery (writing office) created a document called the Donation of Constantine, which declared the pope the recipient of the fourth-century emperor Constantine's crown, cloak, and military rank along with "all provinces, palaces, and districts of the city of Rome and Italy and of the regions of the West." (The document was much later proved a forgery.) The tension between the imperial claims of the Carolingians and those of the pope was heightened by the existence of an emperor at Constantinople who also had rights in the West.

Pope Leo III (r. 795–816) upset the delicate balance among these three powers. In 799, accused of adultery and perjury by a faction of the Roman aristocracy, Leo narrowly escaped being blinded and having his tongue cut out. He fled northward to seek Charlemagne's protection. (See an anonymous poet's account of this event in Document 2 in "Contrasting Views," page 290.) Charlemagne had the pope escorted back to Rome under royal protection, and he soon arrived there himself to an imperial welcome orchestrated by Leo. On Christmas Day, 800, Leo put an imperial crown on Charlemagne's head, and the clergy and nobles who were present acclaimed the king Augustus, the title of the first Roman emperor. The pope hoped in this way to exalt the king of the Franks, to downgrade the Byzantine ruler, and to claim for himself the role of "emperor maker."

About twenty years later, when Einhard wrote about this coronation, he said that the imperial title at first displeased Charlemagne "so much that he

CONTRASTING VIEWS

Charlemagne: Roman Emperor, Father of Europe, or the Chief Bishop?

Charlemagne was crowned emperor, but was he really one of the successors of Augustus? Einhard (Document 1) thought so. An anonymous poet at Charlemagne's court claimed still more (Document 2): the king was the "father of Europe." Even while these secular views of Charlemagne were being expressed, other people—both in and outside the court—were stressing the king's religious functions and duties. Later on, these views became even more grandiose, as Notker the Stammerer's statement (Document 3) reveals.

1. Charles as Emperor

Probably at some point in the mid-820s, Einhard, who had spent time at the Carolingian court and knew Charlemagne well, wrote a biography of the emperor that took as its model the Lives of the Caesars *by Suetonius (c. 70–130). Although he did not emphasize Charlemagne's imperial title per se, Einhard stressed the classical moral values of his hero, including his "greatness of spirit" and steadfast determination. (See pages 140–41 for the traditional Roman virtues.)*

It is widely recognized that, in these ways [i.e., through conquests, diplomacy, and patronage of the arts], [Charlemagne] protected, increased the size of, and beautified his kingdom. Now I should begin at this point to speak of the character of his mind, his supreme steadfastness in good times and bad, and those other things that belong to his spiritual and domestic life.

After the death of his father [in 768], when he was sharing the kingdom with his brother [Carloman], he endured the pettiness and jealousy of his brother with such great patience, that it seemed remarkable to all that he could not be provoked to anger by him. Then [in 770], at the urging of his mother [Bertrada], he married a daughter of Desiderius, the king of the Lombards, but for some unknown reason he sent her away after a year and took Hildegard [758–783], a Swabian woman of distinct nobility. . . .

[Charlemagne] believed that his children, both his daughters and his sons, should be educated, first in the liberal arts, which he himself had studied. Then, he saw to it that when the boys had reached the right age they were trained to ride in the Frankish fashion, to fight, and to hunt. But he ordered his daughters to learn how to work with wool, how to spin and weave it, so that they might not grow dull from inactivity and [instead might] learn to value work and virtuous activity. . . .

Source: *Charlemagne's Courtier: The Complete Einhard*, ed. and trans. Paul Edward Dutton (Peterborough, Ont.: Broadview Press, 1998), 27–28.

2. The "Father of Europe"

Shortly after Pope Leo III fled northward to seek Charlemagne's help (799), an anonymous poet at the royal court composed an extremely flattering poem about the king. Here Charlemagne's virtues became larger than life.

The priests and the joyful people await
 the pope's advent.
Now father Charles [i.e., Charlemagne]
 sees his troops arrayed on the wide
 field;
He knows that Pepin [his son] and the
 highest pastor [the pope] are fast
 approaching;
He orders his people to wait for them.
He divides his troops into a ring-like
 shape,
In the center of which, he himself, that
 blessed one, stands,
Awaiting the advent of the pope, but
 higher up than his comrades
On the summit of the ring; he rises
 above the assembled [Franks].

stated that, if he had known in advance of the pope's plan, he would not have entered the church that day." For more than a year after getting the imperial crown, Charlemagne used no title but *king*. However, it is unlikely that he was completely surprised by the imperial title; his advisers certainly had been thinking about it for him. He might have hesitated to adopt the title because he feared the reaction of the Byzantines, as Einhard went on to suggest, or he might have objected to the papal role in his crowning rather than to the crown itself. When Charlemagne finally did call himself emperor, after establishing a peace with the Byzantines, he used a long and revealing title: "Charles, the most serene Augustus, crowned by God, great and peaceful Emperor who governs the Roman Empire and who is, by the mercy of God, king of the Franks and the Lombards." According to this title, Charlemagne was not the Roman emperor crowned by the pope, but rather God's emperor who governed the Roman Empire along with his many other duties.

The Carolingian Renaissance, c. 790–c. 900

Charlemagne inaugurated—and his successors continued to support—a revival of learning designed to enhance the glory of the kings, educate their officials, reform the liturgy, and purify the faith. Like

Now Pope Leo approaches and crosses
the front line of the ring.
He marvels at the many peoples from
many lands whom he sees,
At their differences, their strange
tongues, dress, and weapons.
At once Charles hastens to pay his reverent respects,
Embraces the great pontiff, and
kisses him.
The two men join hands and walk
together, speaking as they go.
The entire army prostrates itself three
times before the pope,
And the suppliant throng three times
pays its respects.
The pope prays from his heart for the
people three times.
The king, the father of Europe, and Leo,
the world's highest pastor,
Walk together and exchange views,
Charles inquiring as to the pope's case
and his troubles.
He is shocked to learn of the wicked
deeds of the [Roman] people.
He is amazed by the pope's eyes which
had been blinded,
But to which sight had now returned,
And he marveled that a tongue mutilated with tongs now spoke.

Source: Paul Edward Dutton, ed., *Carolingian Civilization: A Reader*, 2nd ed. (Peterborough, Ont.: Broadview Press, 2004), 64–65.

3. The Chief Bishop

A monk at the Swiss monastery of St. Gall, Notker the Stammerer, wrote a biography of Charlemagne in 884 at the request of Charlemagne's great-grandson Charles the Fat. Here the emphasis is on Charlemagne's religious authority.

The Devil, who is skilful in laying ambushes and is in the habit of setting snares for us in the road which we are to follow, is not slow to trip us up one after another by means of some vice or other. The crime of fornication was imputed to a certain princely bishop—in such a case the name must be omitted. This matter came to the notice of his congregation, and then through tale-tellers it eventually reached the ears of the most pious Charles, the chief bishop of them all. . . . Charlemagne, that most rigorous searcher after justice, sent two of his court officials who were to turn aside that evening to a place near to the city in question and then come unexpectedly to the bishop at first light and ask him to celebrate Mass for them. If he should refuse, then they were to compel him in the name of the Emperor to celebrate the Holy Mysteries in person. The bishop did not know what to do, for that very night he had sinned before the eyes of the Heavenly Observer [God], and yet he did not dare to offend his visitors. Fearing men more than he feared God, he bathed his sweaty limbs in ice-cold springwater and then went forward to offer the awe-inspiring sacraments. Behold, either his conscience gripped his heart tight, or the water penetrated his veins, for he was seized with such frosty chill that no attention from his doctors was of use to him. He was brought to his death by a frightful attack of fever and compelled to submit his soul to the decree of the strict and eternal Judge.

Source: *Einhard and Notker the Stammerer: Two Lives of Charlemagne*, trans. Lewis Thorpe (Harmondsworth, England: Penguin, 1969), 121–22.

Questions to Consider

1. **How does the anonymous poet describe the relationship between Charlemagne and the pope?**
2. **According to Notker, how important is the Mass?**
3. **What did Einhard consider to be the chief imperial virtues?**

the renaissances of the Byzantine and Islamic worlds, the Carolingian renaissance resuscitated the learning of the past. Scholars studied Roman imperial writers such as Suetonius and Virgil, read and commented on the works of the church fathers, and worked to establish complete and accurate texts of everything they read and prized.

The English scholar Alcuin (c. 732–804), a member of the circle of scholars whom Charlemagne recruited to form a center of study, brought with him the traditions of Anglo-Saxon scholarship that had been developed by men such as Benedict Biscop and Bede. Invited to Aachen, Alcuin became Charlemagne's chief adviser, writing letters on the king's behalf, counseling him on royal policy, and tutoring the king's household, including the women and girls. He also prepared an improved edition of the Vulgate, the Latin Bible used by the clergy in all church services.

The Carolingian renaissance depended on an elite staff of scholars such as Alcuin, yet its educational program had broader appeal. In one of his capitularies, Charlemagne ordered that the cathedrals and monasteries of his kingdom teach reading and writing to all who were able to learn. Some churchmen expressed the hope that schools for children would be established even in small villages and hamlets. Although this dream was never realized, it shows that, at just about the same time as the Islamic world was organizing its madrasas, the Carolingians

David in the Carolingian Renaissance
In this sumptuous illustration from a Bible made for Charlemagne's grandson Charles the Bald, the central figure is David, the composer of the Psalms, who is playing the harp and dancing on a cloud. Above and below him are his musicians with their instruments. The influence of earlier models is clear in the two figures flanking David, who are dressed like soldiers in the late Roman Empire. Compare this depiction of David with the one painted during the Macedonian renaissance on page 289. *(Scala/White Images/Art Resource, NY.)*

were thinking about the importance of religious education for more than a small elite.

Art, like scholarship, served Carolingian political and religious goals. Carolingian artists turned to models from Byzantium (perhaps some refugees from Byzantine iconoclasm joined them) and Italy to illustrate Bibles (see the illustration above), Psalters, scientific treatises, and literary manuscripts.

The ambitious educational program endured, even after the Carolingian dynasty had faded to a memory. The work of locating, understanding, and transmitting models of the past continued in a number of monastic schools. In the twelfth century, scholars would build on the foundations laid by the Carolingian renaissance. The very print of this textbook depends on one achievement of the period: modern letter fonts are based on the clear and beautiful letter forms, called Caroline minuscule, invented in the ninth century to standardize manuscript handwriting—and make it more readable—across the whole empire.

Charlemagne's Successors, 814–911

When Charlemagne died (of a fever at age sixty-six), his son Louis the Pious (r. 814–840) took his role as leader of the Christian empire even more seriously than his father did. He brought the monastic reformer Benedict of Aniane to court and issued a capitulary in 817 imposing a uniform way of life, based on the Benedictine rule, on all the monasteries of the empire. Although some monasteries opposed this legislation, and in the years to come the king was unable to impose his will directly, this moment marked the effective adoption of the Benedictine rule as the monastic standard in Europe.

In a new development of the coronation ritual, Louis's first wife, Ermengard, was crowned empress by the pope in 816. In 817, their firstborn son, Lothar, was given the title emperor and made co-ruler with Louis. Their other sons, Pippin and Louis (later called Louis the German), were made subkings under imperial rule. Louis the Pious hoped in this way to ensure the unity of the empire while satisfying the claims of all his sons. Should any son die, only his firstborn could succeed him, a measure intended to prevent further splintering. But Louis's hopes were thwarted by events. Ermengard died, and Louis married Judith, reputed to be the most beautiful woman in the kingdom. In 823, she and Louis had a son, Charles (later known as Charles the Bald, to whose court Dhuoda's son William was sent). The sons of Ermengard, bitter over the birth of another royal heir, rebelled against their father and fought one another for more than a decade.

Finally, after Louis the Pious's death in 840, the **Treaty of Verdun** (843) divided the empire among his three remaining sons (Pippin had died in 838)—in an arrangement that would roughly define the future political contours of western Europe (see the inset in Map 9.3). The western third, bequeathed to Charles the Bald (r. 843–877), would eventually become France, and the eastern third, handed to Louis the German (r. 843–876), would become Ger-

Treaty of Verdun: The treaty that, in 843, split the Carolingian Empire into three parts; its borders roughly outline modern western European states.

many. The "Middle Kingdom," which was given to Lothar (r. 840–855) along with the imperial title, had a different fate: parts of it were absorbed by France and Germany, and the rest eventually formed what were to become the modern states of the Netherlands, Belgium, Luxembourg, Switzerland, and Italy.

By 843, Charlemagne's European-wide empire had dissolved. Forged by conquest, it had been supported by a small group of privileged aristocrats with lands and offices stretching across its entire expanse. Their loyalty—based on shared values, friendship, expectations of gain, and sometimes formal ties of vassalage and fealty (see page 298)—was crucial to the success of the Carolingians. The empire had also been supported by an ideal, shared by educated laymen and churchmen alike, of conquest and Christian belief working together to bring good order to the earthly state. But powerful forces operated against the Carolingian Empire. Once the empire's borders were fixed and conquests ceased, the aristocrats could not hope for new lands and offices. They put down roots in particular regions and began to gather their own followings. Powerful local traditions such as different languages also undermined imperial unity. Finally, as Dhuoda revealed in the handbook she wrote for her son, some people disagreed with the imperial ideal. By asking her son to put his father before the emperor, Dhuoda demonstrated her belief in the primacy of the family and the personal ties that bound it together. Her ideal represented a new sensibility that saw real value in the breaking apart of Charlemagne's empire into smaller, more intimate local units.

Land and Power

The Carolingian economy, based on trade and agriculture, contributed to both the rise and the dissolution of the Carolingian Empire. At the onset, the empire's wealth came from land and plunder. After the booty from war ceased to pour in, the Carolingians still had access to money and goods. To the north, in Viking trading stations such as Haithabu (today Hedeby, in northern Germany), archaeologists have found Carolingian glass and pots alongside Islamic coins and cloth, evidence that the Carolingian economy intermingled with that of the Abbasid caliphate. Silver from the Islamic world probably came north up the Volga River through Russia to the Baltic Sea. There the coins were melted down and the silver was traded to the Carolingians in return for wine, jugs, glasses, and other manufactured goods. The Carolingians turned the silver into coins of their own, to be used throughout the empire for small-scale local trade. The weakening of the Abbasid caliphate in the mid-ninth century, however, disrupted this far-flung trade network and contributed to the weakening of the Carolingians at about the same time.

Land provided the most important source of Carolingian wealth and power. Like the landholders of the late Roman Empire and the Merovingian period, Carolingian aristocrats held many estates, scattered throughout the Frankish kingdoms. In the Merovingian period these estates were rare, but in the Carolingian period they became more common and better organized for production. We also know much more about them than about their predecessors because their tenants and the dues and services they owed were carefully noted down in registers. Modern historians often call these estates manors.

A typical manor was Villeneuve Saint-Georges, which belonged to the monastery of Saint-Germain-des-Près (today in Paris) in the ninth century. Villeneuve consisted of arable fields, vineyards, meadows where animals could roam, and woodlands, all scattered about the countryside rather than connected in a compact unit. Peasant families tilled the fields, and each family had its own manse, which consisted of a house, a garden, and small sections of the arable land. Besides farming the land that belonged to them, the families—which ordinarily lived in households of no more than two generations: a mother, a father, and their minor children—also worked the demesne, the very large manse of the lord, in this case the abbey of Saint-Germain. Grown children would found their own families, and their parents' land would be subdivided to give them a share. In many ways, the peasant household of the Carolingian period was the precursor of the modern nuclear family.

Peasants at Villeneuve practiced the most progressive sort of plowing, known as the three-field system, in which they farmed two-thirds of the arable land at one time (see Figure 9.1). They planted one-third of their arable land in the fall with winter wheat and one-third in the spring with summer crops, leaving the remaining third fallow to restore its fertility. The crops sown and the fallow field then rotated so that land use was repeated only every three years. This method of organizing the land produced larger yields (because two-thirds of the land was cultivated each year) than the still-prevalent two-field system, in which only half of the arable land was cultivated one year while the other half lay fallow.

All the peasants at Villeneuve were dependents of the monastery and owed dues and services to Saint-Germain. Their status and obligations varied enormously. One family, for example, owed four silver coins, wine, wood, three hens, and fifteen eggs every year, and the men had to plow the fields of

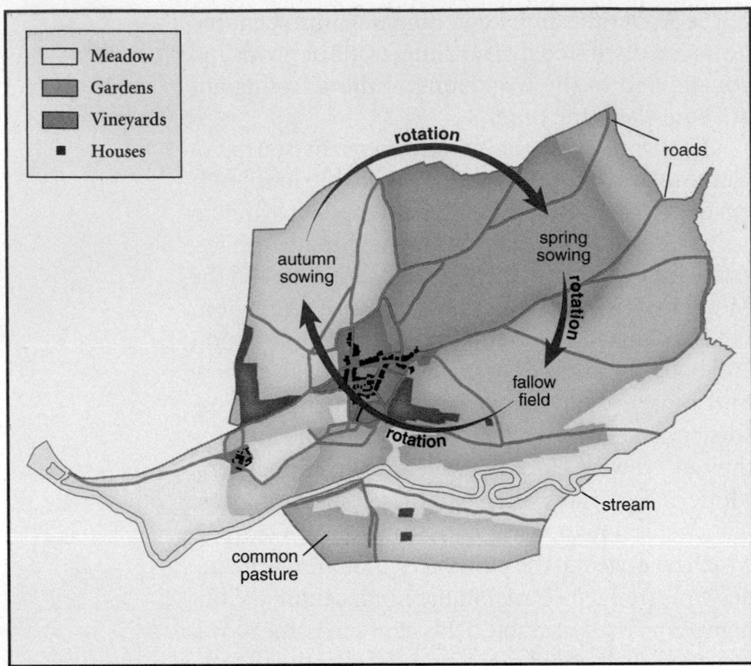

FIGURE 9.1 Diagram of a Manor and Its Three-Field System
This schematic diagram of a manor shows that peasants lived clustered together in a village that consisted of houses and gardens. One of the buildings was a church. Nearby were vineyards. A bit beyond were the fields, pastureland, and meadows, well connected by dirt roads. The field sown with spring crops (such as oats) this year would have been sown with winter wheat the next year, while the fallow field would get a spring crop. *(Based on Map IV in Marc Bloch,* French Rural History: An Essay on Its Basic Characteristics. *Berkeley: University of California Press, 1966.)*

the demesne. Another family owed the intensive labor of working the vineyards. One woman was required to weave cloth and feed the chickens. Peasant women spent much time at the lord's house in the *gynaeceum*—the workshop where women made and dyed cloth and sewed garments—or in the kitchens, as cooks. Peasant men spent most of their time in the fields.

Manors organized on the model of Villeneuve were profitable. Like other lords, the Carolingians benefited from their extensive manors. Nevertheless, farming was still too primitive to return great surpluses, and as the lands belonging to the king were divided up in the wake of the partitioning of the empire and new invasions, the Carolingians' dependence on manors scattered throughout their kingdom proved to be a source of weakness.

Viking, Muslim, and Magyar Invasions, c. 790–955

Beginning around the time of Charlemagne's imperial coronation and extending to the mid-tenth century, new groups—Vikings, Muslims, and Magyars—confronted the Carolingian Empire and many of the other kingdoms of Europe (Map 9.4). Some rulers fought off the invaders; others allied with the newcomers. By around the year 1000, the Vikings and Magyars had largely been integrated into European politics and society, while the Muslims were largely pushed out, except in Sicily and, of course, al-Andalus.

Vikings About the same time as they made their eastward forays into the region below the Gulf of Finland, the Vikings moved westward as well. The Franks called them Northmen; the English called them Danes. They were, in fact, much less united than their victims thought. When they began their voyages at the end of the eighth century, they did so in independent bands. Both merchants and pirates, Vikings followed a chief, seeking profit, prestige, and land. Many traveled as families: husbands, wives, children, and slaves.

The Vikings perfected the art of navigation. They crossed the Atlantic in their longships, not only settling Iceland and Greenland but also (in about the year 1000) landing on the coast of North America. Other Viking bands navigated the rivers of Europe. The Vikings were pagans, and to them monasteries and churches—with their reliquaries, chalices, and crosses—were simply storehouses of booty.

Parts of the British Isles were especially hard hit. In England, for example, the Vikings raided regularly in the 830s and 840s; by midcentury, they were spending winters there. The Vikings did not just destroy. In 876, they settled in the northeast of England, plowing the land and preparing to live on it. The region where they settled and imposed their own laws was later called the Danelaw. (See England in the Age of King Alfred, page 303.)

In Wessex, the southernmost kingdom of England, King Alfred the Great (r. 871–899) bought time and peace by paying tribute and giving hostages. Such tribute, later called Danegeld, eventually became the basis of a relatively lucrative taxation system in England. In 878, Alfred led an army that, as his biographer put it, "gained the victory through God's will. He destroyed the Vikings with great slaughter and pursued those who fled, . . . hacking them down." Thereafter, the pressures of invasion eased as Alfred reorganized his army, set up strongholds, and deployed new warships.

On the continent, too, Viking invaders set up trading stations and settled where originally they had raided. Beginning about 850, their attacks became well-organized expeditions for regional control. At the end of the ninth century, one contingent settled in the region of France that soon took the name Normandy ("land of the Northmen"). In

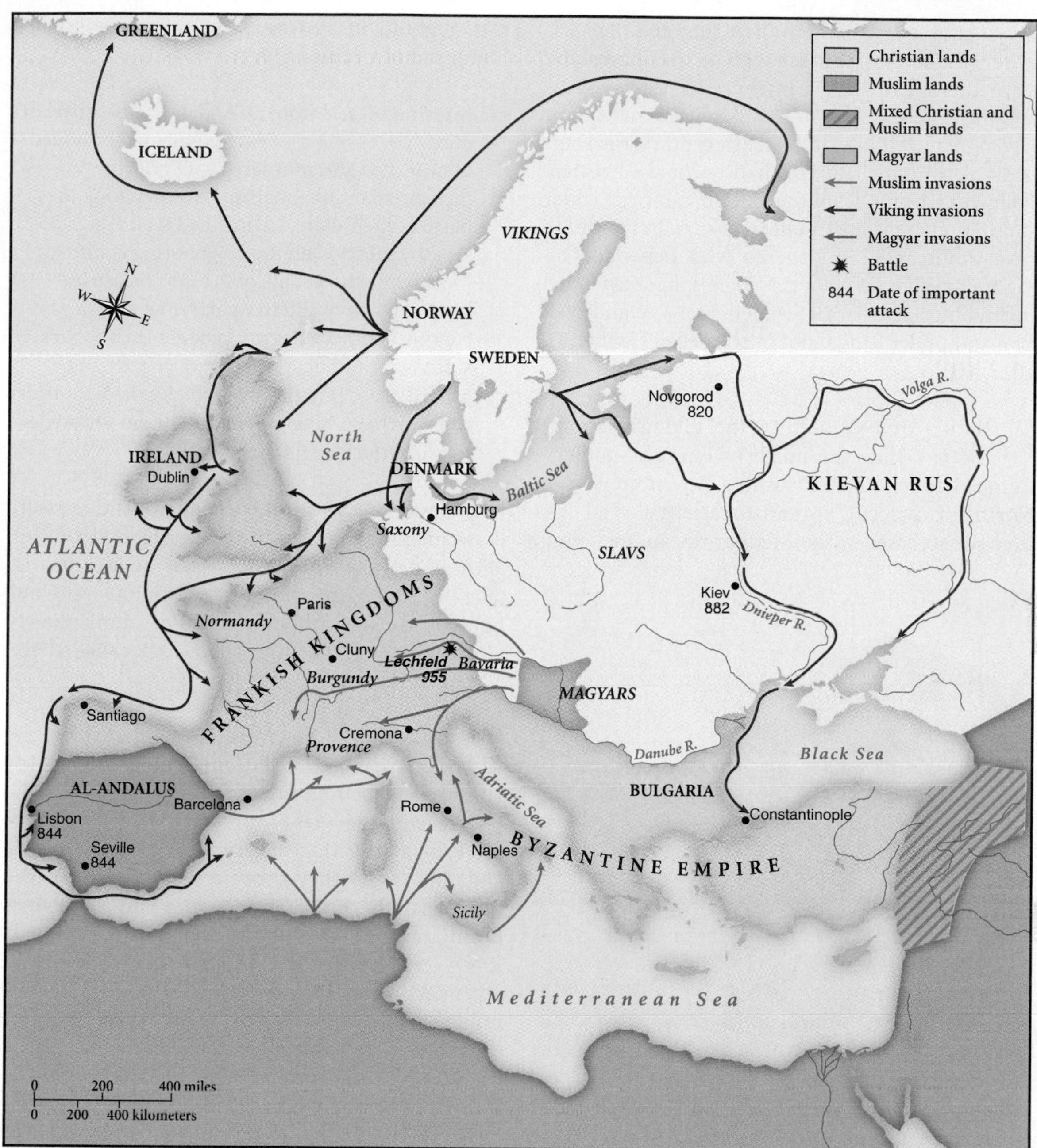

MAP 9.4 Muslim, Viking, and Magyar Invasions of the Ninth and Tenth Centuries
Bristling with arrows of different colors, this map suggests that western Europe was continually and thoroughly pillaged by invaders for almost two centuries. That impression, only partially true, must be offset by several factors. First, not all the invaders came at once. The Viking raids were nearly over when the Magyar attacks began. Second, the invaders were not entirely unwelcome. The Magyars were for a time enlisted as mercenaries by an Italian ruler, and some Muslims were allied to local lords in Provence. Third, the invasions, though widespread, were local in effect. Note, for example, that the Viking raids were largely limited to rivers or coastal areas. | **Why might the Vikings have raided primarily in these areas?**

911, the Frankish king Charles the Simple ceded the region to Rollo, the Viking leader there. In turn, Rollo converted to Christianity.

Normandy was not the only new Christian polity created in the north during the tenth and eleventh centuries. Scandinavia itself was transformed with the creation of the powerful kingdom of Denmark. There had been kings in Scandinavia before the tenth century, but they had been weak, their power challenged by nearby chieftains. The Vikings had been led by these chieftains, each competing for booty to win prestige, land, and power back home.

During the course of their raids, they and their followers came into contact with new cultures and learned from them. Meanwhile the Carolingians and the English supported missionaries in Scandinavia. By the middle of the tenth century, the Danish kings and their people had become Christian. Following the model of the Christian kings to their south, they built up an effective monarchy, with a royal mint and local agents who depended on them. By about 1000, the Danes had extended their control to parts of Sweden, Norway, and even England under King Cnut (also spelled Canute) (r. 1017–1035).

Muslims Around the time the Vikings were invading the north of Europe, southern Europe was attacked by Muslims. Adventurers from North Africa, Sicily, and northeastern al-Andalus, they set up bases in the Mediterranean, including a stronghold in Provence (in southern France). Liutprand of Cremona was outraged:

> [Muslim pirates from al-Andalus], disembarking under cover of night, entered the manor house unobserved and murdered—O grievous tale!—the Christian inhabitants. They then took the place as their own . . . [fortified it and] started stealthy raids on all the neighboring country. . . . Meanwhile the people of Provence close by, swayed by envy and mutual jealousy, began to cut one another's throats, plunder each other's substance, and do every sort of conceivable mischief. . . . [Furthermore, they called upon the Muslims] and in company with them proceeded to crush their neighbors.

In this way the Muslims, although outsiders, were drawn into local Provençal disputes. However, when, at the end of the tenth century, they made the mistake of kidnapping the most prestigious religious figure of the age, Abbot Maiolus of Cluny, the regional elites rescued the abbot and expelled the Muslims.

Magyars While the Muslims remained on the fringes of Europe, the Magyars (or Hungarians) settled in its very center. A nomadic people from the Ural Mountains (today northeastern Russia), the Magyars arrived around 899 in the Danube basin. They drove a wedge between the Slavs near the Frankish kingdom and those bordering on Byzantium. The Bulgarians, Serbs, and Rus were forced into the Byzantine orbit, while the Slavs nearer the Frankish kingdom came under the influence of Germany.

From their bases in present-day Hungary, the Magyars raided far to the west, attacking Germany, Italy, and even southern Gaul frequently between 899 and 955. Then in 955 the German king Otto I (r. 936–973) defeated a marauding party of Mag-

Viking Picture Stone
Picture stones—some elaborate, others with simple incisions—were made on the island of Gotland, today part of Sweden, from the fifth to the twelfth century. This one, dating from the eighth or ninth century, has four interrelated scenes. The bottom scene is a battle between people defending a farm and archers outside. The woman in the enclosure above is either Gudrun mourning her brother Gunnar, who was thrown into a snake pit, or Sigyn, the faithful wife of the god Loke, catching in a bowl the venom that a snake pours down on her chained husband. The ship in the next scene is the ship of death that takes heroes to Valhalla (heaven). At the very top is Valhalla, where the heroes hunt and feast for all eternity. *(The Granger Collection, NY—All rights reserved.)*

yars at the battle of Lechfeld. Otto's victory, his subsequent military reorganization of his eastern frontiers, and the cessation of Magyar raids around this time made Otto a great hero to his contemporaries. However, historians today think the containment of the Magyars had more to do with their internal transformation from nomads to farmers than with their military defeat. Soon they converted to the Roman form of Christianity. Hungary's position between East and West made it a frontier region, vulnerable to invasion and immigration, but also open to new experiments in assimilation and integration.

The Viking, Muslim, and Magyar invasions were the final onslaught western Europe experienced from outsiders. In some ways they were a continuation of the invasions that had rocked the Roman Empire in the fourth and fifth centuries. Loosely organized in war bands, the new groups entered western Europe looking for wealth but stayed on to become absorbed in the region's post-invasion society.

REVIEW QUESTION What were the strengths and weaknesses of Carolingian institutions of government, warfare, and defense?

After the Carolingians: The Emergence of Local Rule

The Carolingian Empire was too diverse to cohere. Although Latin was the language of official documents and most literary and ecclesiastical texts, few people spoke it; instead they used a wide variety of different languages and dialects. The king demanded loyalty from everyone, but most people knew only his representative, the local count. The king's power ultimately depended on the count's allegiance, but as the empire ceased to expand and came under attack by outsiders, the counts and other powerful men stopped looking to the king for new lands and offices and began to develop and exploit what they already had. Commanding allegiance from vassals, controlling the local peasantry, building castles, setting up markets, collecting revenues, and keeping the peace, they regarded themselves as independent regional rulers. In this way, a new warrior class of lords and vassals came to dominate post-Carolingian society.

Not all of Europe, however, came under the control of rural leaders. In northern and central Italy, where cities had never lost their importance, urban elites ruled over the surrounding countryside. Everywhere kings retained a certain amount of power; in some places, such as Germany and England, they were extremely effective. Central European monarchies formed under the influence of Germany.[2] Still, throughout this period, it was local allegiance—lord and vassal, castellan and peasant, bishop and layman—that mattered most to the societies of Europe.

Public Power and Private Relationships

Both kings and less powerful men commanded others through institutions designed to ensure personal loyalty. In the ninth century, the Carolingian kings had their *fideles* ("faithful men"), among whom were the counts. In addition to a share in the revenues of their administrative district—known as the county—counts received benefices, later also called **fiefs**, temporary grants of land given in return for service. These short-term arrangements often became permanent when a count's son inherited the job and the fiefs of his father. By the end of the ninth century, fiefs could often be passed on to heirs.

Vassals, Lords, and Ladies In the wake of the Viking, Magyar, and Muslim invasions, more and more warriors were drawn into networks of dependency, but not with the king: they became the faithful men—the vassals—of local lords. From the Latin *feodum* ("fief") comes the word *feudal*, and some historians call the social and economic system created by the relationship among vassals, lords, and fiefs **feudalism**. (See "Terms of History," page 298.)

Medieval people often said that their society consisted of three groups: those who prayed, those who fought, and those who worked. People of all these groups were involved in a hierarchy of depen-

---

[2]Names such as *Germany*, *France*, and *Italy* are used here for the sake of convenience. They refer to regions, not to the nation-states that would eventually become associated with those names.

fiefs: Grants of land, theoretically temporary, from lords to their noble dependents (*fideles* or, later, vassals) given in recognition of services, usually military, done or expected in the future; also called *benefices*.

feudalism: The whole complex of lords, vassals, and fiefs (from the Latin *feodum*) as an institution. The nature of that institution varied from place to place, and in some regions it did not exist at all.

TERMS OF HISTORY

Feudalism

Feudalism is a modern word, like *capitalism* and *communism*. No one in the Middle Ages used it, or any of its related terms, such as *feudal system* or *feudal society*. Many historians today think that it is a misleading word and should be discarded. The term poses two serious problems. First, historians have used it to mean different things. Second, it implies that one way of life dominated the Middle Ages, when in fact social, political, and economic arrangements varied widely.

Consider the many different meanings that *feudalism* has had. Historians influenced by Karl Marx's powerful communist theory used (and still use) the word *feudalism* to refer to an economic system in which nobles dominated subservient peasant cultivators. When they speak of feudalism, they are speaking of manors, lords, and serfs. Other historians, however, call that system *manorialism*. They reserve the word *feudalism* for a system consisting of vassals (who did no agricultural labor but only military service), lords, and fiefs. For example, in *Feudalism*, an influential book written in the mid-1940s, F. L. Ganshof considered the tenth to the thirteenth centuries to be the "classical age of feudalism" because during this period lords regularly granted fiefs to their vassals, who fought on their lord's behalf in return.

But, writing around the same time as Ganshof, Marc Bloch included in his definition of feudalism every aspect of the political and social life of the Middle Ages, including peasants, fiefs, knights, vassals, the fragmentation of royal authority, and even the survival of the state.

Today some historians argue that talking about feudalism distorts the realities of medieval life. The fief—whose Latin form, *feodum*, gave rise to the word *feudalism*—was by no means important everywhere. And even where it was important, it did not necessarily have anything to do with lords, vassals, or military obligations. For such historians, feudalism is a myth. Other historians, however, think that the term is extremely useful as long as its multiple forms are recognized. These historians are now starting to speak of "feudalisms"—in the plural.

dency and linked by personal bonds, but the upper classes—those who prayed (monks) and those who fought (knights)—were free. Their brand of dependency was prestigious, whether they were vassals, lords, or both. In fact, a typical warrior was lord of several vassals even while serving as the vassal of another lord. Monasteries normally had vassals to fight for them, and their abbots in turn were often vassals of a king or other powerful lord.

Vassalage served both as an alternative to public power and as a way to strengthen what little public power there was. Given the impoverished economic conditions of western Europe, its primitive methods of communication, and its lack of unifying traditions, kings relied on vassals personally loyal to them to muster troops, collect taxes, and administer justice. When in the ninth century the Carolingian Empire broke up politically and power fell into the hands of local lords, those lords, too, needed "faithful men" to protect them and carry out their orders. And vassals needed lords. At the low end of the social scale, poor vassals depended on their lords to feed, clothe, house, and arm them. They hoped that they would be rewarded for their service with a fief of their own, with which they could support themselves and a family. At the upper end of the social scale, landowning vassals looked to lords to give them still more land.

Many upper-class laywomen participated in the society of those who fought as wives and mothers of vassals and lords. A few women were themselves vassals, and some were lords (or, rather, ladies). Other women entered convents and joined the group of those who prayed. Through its abbess or a man standing in for her, a convent often had vassals as well. Many elite women engaged in property transactions, whether alone, with other family members, or as part of a group such as a convent. (See "Taking Measure," page 299.)

Becoming a vassal involved both ritual gestures and verbal promises. In a ceremony witnessed by others, the vassal-to-be knelt and, placing his hands between the hands of his lord, said, "I promise to be your man." This act, known as homage, was followed by the promise of fealty—fidelity, trust, and service—which the vassal swore with his hand on relics or a Bible. Then the vassal and the lord kissed. In an age when many people could not read, a public ceremony such as this represented a visual and verbal contract. Vassalage bound the lord and vassal to one another with reciprocal obligations, usually military. Knights, as the premier fighters of the day, were the most desirable vassals.

Lords and Peasants

At the bottom of the social scale were those who worked—the peasants. In the Carolingian period, many peasants were free; they did not live on a manor or, if they did, they owed very little to its lord. (Manors like Villeneuve were the exceptions.) But as power fell into the hands of local rulers, fewer and fewer peasants remained free. Rather, they were made dependent on lords, not as vassals but as serfs. A serf's dependency was completely unlike that of a vassal. Serfdom was not voluntary but rather inherited. No serf did homage or fealty to his lord; no serf kissed his lord as an equal. Whereas vassals served their

TAKING MEASURE

Sellers, Buyers, and Donors, 800–1000

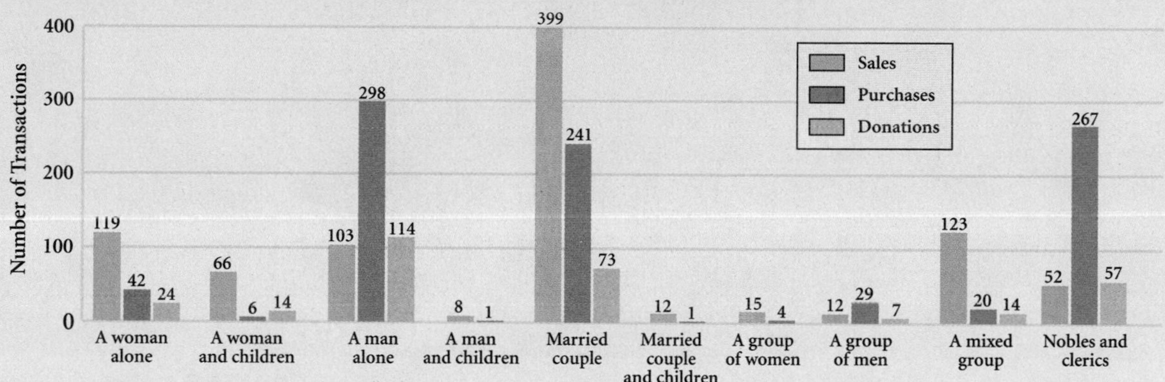

How did ladies get their wealth, and what did they do with it? Two counties in northeastern Spain, Osona and Manresa, are particularly rich in documentation for the period 880–1000. We have 2,121 charters (legal documents) attesting to sales, purchases, and donations of land from this period. As the graph shows, few women purchased property, which suggests that they gained their lands mainly through inheritance. As for what they did with it: by themselves they were more likely to sell property than men alone, and as part of a married couple, they were often involved in sales. They were less likely than men to make donations, many of which went to churches or monasteries.

Source: Lluís to Figueras, "Dot et douaire dans la société rurale de Catalogne," in *Dots et douaires dans le haut moyen âge*, ed. F. Bougard, L. Feller, and R. Le Jan (École française de Rome, 2002), 193, Table 1.

Question to Consider

■ **How do you account for the differences between the ways in which women and men inherited and used their property?**

lords as warriors, serfs worked as laborers on their lord's land and paid taxes and dues to their lord. Peasants constituted the majority of the population, but unlike knights, who were celebrated in song, they were barely noticed by the upper classes—except as a source of revenue. While there were still free peasants who could lease land or till their own soil without paying dues to a lord, serfs—who could not be kicked off their land but who were also not free to leave it—became the norm.

New methods of cultivation and a slightly warmer climate helped transform the rural landscape, making it more productive and thus able to support a larger population. Along with a growing number of men and women to work the land, however, population increase meant more mouths to feed and the threat of food shortages. Landlords began reorganizing their estates to run more efficiently. In the tenth century, the three-field system became more prevalent; heavy plows that could turn wet, clayey northern soils came into wider use; and horses (more effective than oxen) were harnessed to pull the plows. The results were surplus food and a better standard of living for nearly everyone. (See the illustration on page 300.)

In search of greater profits, some lords lightened the dues and services of peasants to allow them to open up new lands by draining marshes and cutting down forests. Some landlords converted dues and labor services into money payments, a boon for both lords and peasants. Rather than getting hens and eggs they might not need, lords now received money to spend on what they wanted. Peasants benefited because their dues were fixed despite inflation. Thus, as the prices of their hens and eggs went up, they could sell them, reaping a profit in spite of the payments they owed their lords.

By the tenth century, many peasants had begun living in populous rural settlements, true villages. Surrounded by arable lands, meadows, woods, and wastelands, villages developed a sense of community. Boundaries—sometimes real fortifications,

Peasants at the Plow

When peasants used the three-field system, the month of January, which this illumination illustrates, was the month in which to start spring crops. The peasant at the plow guides it as the blade cuts into the soil. Behind him is another peasant, sowing seeds. Four oxen pull the plow, and a peasant ahead of the animals keeps them in line. *(akg-images/The British Library.)*

sometimes simple markers—told nonresidents to stay away or to find shelter in huts located outside the village limits.

The church often formed the focal point of village activity. There people met, received the sacraments, drew up contracts, and buried their dead. Religious feasts and festivals joined the rituals of farming to mark the seasons. The church dominated the village in another way: men and women owed it a tax called a tithe (one-tenth of their crops or income, paid in money or in kind), which was first instituted on a regular basis by the Carolingians.

Village peasants developed a sense of common purpose based on their interdependence, as they shared oxen or horses for the teams that pulled the plow or turned to village craftsmen to fix their wheels or shoe their horses. A sense of solidarity sometimes encouraged people to band together to ask for privileges as a group. Near Verona, in northern Italy, for example, twenty-five men living around the castle of Nogara joined together in 920 to ask their lord, the abbot of Nonantola, to allow them to lease plots of land, houses, and pasturage there in return for a small yearly rent and the promise to defend the castle. The abbot granted their request.

Village solidarity could be compromised, however, by conflicting loyalties and obligations. A peasant in one village might very well have one piece of land connected with a certain manor and another piece on a different estate; and he or she might owe several lords different kinds of dues. Even peasants of one village working for one lord might owe him varied services and taxes.

Obligations differed even more strikingly across the regions of Europe than within particular villages. The principal distinction was between free peasants—such as small landowners in Saxony and other parts of Germany, who had no lords—and serfs, who were especially common in France and England. In Italy, peasants ranged from small independent landowners to leaseholders (like the tenants at Nogara); most were both, owning a parcel in one place and leasing another nearby.

As the power of kings weakened, the system of peasant obligations became part of a larger system of local rule. When landlords consolidated their power over their manors, they collected not only dues and services but also fees for the use of their flour mills, bake houses, and breweries. Some built castles, fortified strongholds, collected taxes, heard court cases, levied fines, and mustered men for defense.

In France, for example, as the king's power waned, political control fell into the hands of counts and other princes. By 1000, castles had become the key to their power. In the south of France, power was so fragmented that each man who controlled a castle—a **castellan**—was a virtual ruler, although

---

castellan (KAS tuh luhn): The holder of a castle. In the tenth and eleventh centuries, castellans became important local lords. They mustered men for military service, collected taxes, and administered justice.

often with a very limited reach. In northwestern France, territorial princes, basing their rule on the control of many castles, dominated much broader regions. For example, Fulk Nera, count of Anjou (987–1040), built more than thirteen castles and captured others from rival counts. By the end of his life, he controlled a region extending from Blois to Nantes along the Loire valley.

Castellans extended their authority by subjecting everyone near their castle to them. Peasants, whether or not they worked on his estates, had to pay the castellan a variety of dues for his "protection" and judicial rights over them. Castellans also established links with wealthy landholders in the region, tempting or coercing them to become vassals. Lay castellans often supported local monasteries and controlled the appointment of local priests. But churchmen themselves sometimes held the position of territorial lord, as did, for example, the archbishop of Milan in the eleventh century.

The development of virtually independent local political units, dominated by a castle and controlled by a military elite, marks an important turning point in western Europe. Although this development did not occur everywhere simultaneously (and in some places it hardly occurred at all), the social, political, and cultural life of Europe was now dominated by landowners who were both military men and regional rulers.

Warriors and Warfare

Not all medieval warriors were alike. At the top of this elite group were the kings, counts, and dukes. Below them, but on the rise, were the castellans; and still further down the social scale were ordinary knights. Yet all shared in a common lifestyle.

Knights and their lords fought on horseback. High astride his steed, wearing a shirt of chain mail and a helmet of flat metal plates riveted together, the knight marked a military revolution. The war season started in May, when the grasses were high enough for horses to forage. Horseshoes allowed armies to move faster than ever before and to negotiate rough terrain previously unsuitable for battle. Stirrups, probably invented by nomadic Asiatic tribes, allowed the mounted warrior to hold his seat and thrust at the enemy with heavy lances. The light javelin of ancient Roman warfare was abandoned.

Lords and their vassals often lived together. In the lord's great hall they ate, listened to entertainment, and bedded down for the night. They went out hunting together, competed with one another in military games, and went off to the battlefield as a group. Some powerful vassals—counts, for example—lived on their own fiefs. They hardly ever saw their lord (probably the king), except when doing homage and fealty—once in their lifetime—or serving him in battles, for perhaps forty days a year (as was the custom in eleventh-century France). But they themselves were lords of knightly vassals who were not married and who lived and ate and hunted with them.

No matter how old they might be, unmarried knights who lived with their lords were called youths by their contemporaries. Such perpetual bachelors were something new, the result of a profound transformation in the organization of families and inheritance. Before about 1000, noble families had recognized all their children as heirs and had divided their estates accordingly. In the mid-ninth century, Count Everard and his wife, for example, willed their large estates, scattered from Belgium to Italy, to their four sons and three daughters (although they gave the boys far more than the girls, and the oldest boy far more than the others).

By 1000, however, adapting to diminished opportunities for land and office and wary of fragmenting the estates they had, French nobles changed both their conception of their family and the way property passed to the next generation. Recognizing the overriding claims of one son, often the eldest, they handed down their entire inheritance to him. (The system of inheritance in which the heir is the eldest son is called **primogeniture**.) The heir, in turn, traced his lineage only through the male line, backward through his father and forward through his own eldest son. Such **patrilineal** families left many younger sons without an inheritance and therefore without the prospect of marrying and founding a family; instead, the younger sons lived at the courts of the great as youths, or they joined the church as clerics or monks. The development of territorial rule and patrilineal families went hand in hand, as fathers passed down to one son not only manors but also titles, castles, and the authority of the ban.

Patrilineal inheritance tended to bypass daughters and so worked against aristocratic women, who lost the power that came with inherited wealth. In families without sons, however, widows and daughters did inherit property. And wives often acted as lords of estates when their husbands were at war. Moreover, all aristocratic women played an important role in this warrior society, whether in the

---

primogeniture: An inheritance practice that left all property to the oldest son.

patrilineal: Relating to or tracing descent through the paternal line (for example, through the father and grandfather).

monastery (where they prayed for the souls of their families) or through their marriages (where they produced children and helped forge alliances between their own natal families and the families of their husbands).

Efforts to Contain Violence

The rise of the castellans meant an increase in violence. Supported by their knights, castellans were keen to maintain their new authority over the peasants in their vicinity in the face of older regional powers, like counts and dukes. Threatened from below, those higher-ranking authorities looked to the bishops for help. The bishops, themselves resentful of local castellan claims and, moreover, generally members of the same elite families as counts and dukes, were glad to oblige. To do so, they enlisted the lower classes—peasants who were tired of wars that destroyed their crops or forced them to join regional infantries. The result was the **Peace of God**, which united bishops, counts, and peasants in an attempt to contain local violence. The movement began in the south of France around 990 and by 1050 had spread over a wide region. At impassioned meetings of bishops, lords, and crowds of enthusiastic men and women, the clergy set forth the provisions of this peace. "No man in the counties or bishoprics shall seize a horse, colt, ox, cow, ass, or the burdens which it carries. . . . No one shall seize a peasant, man or woman," ran the decree of one early council. Anyone who violated this peace was to be excommunicated: cut off from the community of the faithful, denied the services of the church and the hope of salvation.

The Peace of God proclaimed at local councils like this limited some violence but did not address the problem of conflict between armed men. A second set of agreements, the Truce of God, soon supplemented the peace. The truce prohibited fighting between warriors at certain times: on Sunday because it was the Lord's day, on Saturday because it was a reminder of Holy Saturday, on Friday because it symbolized Good Friday, and on Thursday because it stood for Holy Thursday. Enforcement of the truce fell to the local knights and nobles, who swore over saints' relics to uphold it and to fight anyone who broke it.

The Peace of God and the Truce of God were only two of the mechanisms that attempted to contain or defuse violent confrontations in the tenth and eleventh centuries. At times, lords and their vassals mediated wars and feuds at grand judicial assemblies. In other instances, monks or laymen tried to find solutions to disputes that would leave the honor of both parties intact. Rather than establishing guilt or innocence, winners or losers, these methods of adjudication often resulted in compromises on both sides.

Peace of God: A movement begun by bishops in the south of France around 990, first to limit the violence done to property and to the unarmed, and later, with the Truce of God, to limit fighting between warriors.

Political Communities in Italy, England, and France

The political systems that emerged following the breakup of the Carolingian Empire were as varied as the regions of Europe. In northern and central Italy, cities were the centers of power, still reflecting, if feebly, the political organization of ancient Rome. In England, strong kings came to the fore. In France, where the king was relatively weak, great lords dominated the countryside.

Urban Power in Northern and Central Italy

Unlike their counterparts in France, where great landlords built their castles in the countryside, Italian elites tended to construct their family castles within the walls of cities such as Milan and Lucca. Also built within the city walls were churches—as many as fifty or sixty—the proud work of rich laymen and laywomen or of bishops. Although residing in the city, these elites normally controlled the land and people in the surrounding countryside.

Italian cities also served as marketplaces where peasants sold their surplus goods, artisans and merchants lived, and foreign traders offered their wares. These members of the lower classes were supported by the wealthy elite, who depended, here more than elsewhere, on cash to satisfy their desires. In the course of the ninth and tenth centuries, the peasants in the countryside became renters who paid in currency, helping meet their landlords' need for cash.

Family organization in Italy was quite different from that of the patrilineal families of France. To stave off the partitioning of its properties among heirs, the Italian family became a kind of economic corporation in which all male members shared the profits of the family's inheritance and all women were excluded. In the coming centuries, this successful model would also serve as the foundation of most early Italian businesses and banks.

Alfred and His Successors: Kings of All the English

Whereas much of Italy was urban, most of England was rural. Having successfully repelled the Viking invaders, **Alfred the Great**, king of Wessex (r. 871–899), developed new mechanisms of royal government, instituting reforms that his successors continued. He fortified settlements throughout Wessex and divided the army into two parts, one with the duty of defending these fortifications, the other operating as a mobile unit. Alfred also started a navy. The money to pay for these military innovations came from assessments on peasants' holdings.

Along with its regional fortifications, Alfred sought to strengthen his kingdom's religious integrity. In the ninth century, people interpreted invasions as God's punishment for sin. Hence, Alfred began a program of religious reform by bringing scholars to his court. Above all, Alfred wanted to translate key religious works from Latin into Anglo-Saxon (or Old English). He was determined to "turn into the language that we can all understand certain books which are the most necessary for all men to know." Alfred and the scholars under his guidance translated works by church fathers such as Gregory the Great and St. Augustine. Even the Psalms, until now sung only in Hebrew, Greek, and Latin, were rendered into Anglo-Saxon. In most of ninth- and tenth-century Europe, Latin remained the language of scholarship, government, and writing, separate from the language people spoke. In England, however, the vernacular—the common spoken language—was also a literary language. With Alfred's reign giving it greater legitimacy, Anglo-Saxon came to be used alongside Latin for both literature and royal administration.

Alfred's reforms strengthened not only defense, education, and religion but also royal power. He consolidated his control over Wessex and fought the Danish kings, who by the mid-870s had taken Northumbria, northeastern Mercia, and East Anglia. Eventually, as he successfully fought the Danes who were pushing south and westward, he was recognized as king of all the English not under Danish rule. He issued a law code, the first by an English king since 695. Unlike earlier codes, which had been drawn up for each separate kingdom of England, Alfred drew his laws from and for all of the English kingdoms. In this way, Alfred became the first king of all the English.

Alfred's successors rolled back the Danish rule in England. "Then the Norsemen departed in their nailed ships, bloodstained survivors of spears," wrote one poet about a battle the Vikings lost in 937. But many Vikings remained. Converted to Christianity, their great men joined Anglo-Saxons in attending the English king at court. As peace returned, new administrative subdivisions for judicial and tax purposes were established throughout England: shires (the English equivalent of counties) and hundreds (smaller units). The powerful men of the kingdom swore fealty to the king, promising to be enemies of his enemies, friends of his friends. England was united and organized to support a strong ruler.

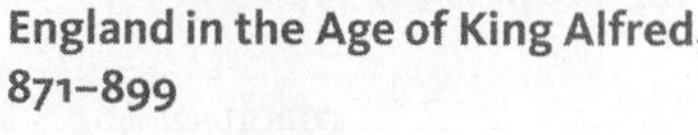

England in the Age of King Alfred, 871–899

Alfred's grandson Edgar (r. 957–975) commanded all the possibilities early medieval kingship offered. He was the sworn lord of all the great men of the kingdom. He controlled appointments to the English church and sponsored monastic reform. In 973, following the continental fashion, he was anointed king. The fortifications of the kingdom were in his hands, as was the army, and he took responsibility for keeping the peace by proclaiming certain crimes—arson and theft—to be under his special jurisdiction and by mobilizing the machinery of the shire and the hundred to find and punish thieves.

Despite its apparent centralization, England was not a unified state in the modern sense, and the king's control was often tenuous. Many royal officials were great landowners who (as on the continent) worked for the king because it was in their best interest. When it was not, they allied with different claimants to the throne. This political fragility may have helped the Danish king Cnut to conquer England. As king there from 1017 to 1035, Cnut reinforced the already strong connections between England and Scandinavia while keeping intact much of the administrative, ecclesiastical, and military apparatus already established in England by the Anglo-Saxons. By Cnut's time, Scandinavian traditions had largely merged with those of the rest of Europe and the Vikings were no longer an alien culture.

Capetian Kings of Franks: Weak but Prestigious

French kings had a harder time than the English coping with invasions because their realm was much larger. They had no chance to build up their defenses slowly from one powerful base. During most of the tenth century, Carolin-

---

Alfred the Great: King of Wessex (r. 871–899) and the first king to rule over most of England. He organized a successful defense against Viking invaders, had key Latin works translated into the vernacular, and wrote a law code for the whole of England.

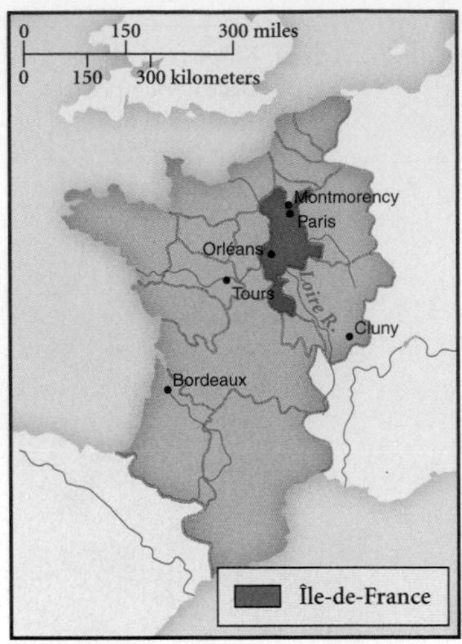

The Kingdom of the Franks under Hugh Capet, 987–996

gian kings alternated on the throne with kings from a family that would later be called the Capetian. As the Carolingian dynasty waned, the most powerful men of the kingdom—dukes, counts, and important bishops—came together to elect as king Hugh Capet (r. 987–996), a lord of great prestige yet relatively little power. His choice marked the end of Carolingian rule and the beginning of the **Capetian dynasty**, which would hand down the royal title from father to son until the fourteenth century.

In the eleventh century, territorial lordships limited the reach of the Capetian kings. The king's scattered but substantial estates lay in the north of France, in the region around Paris—the Île-de-France ("island of France"). His castles and his vassals were there. Independent castellans, however, controlled areas nearby. In the sense that he was a neighbor of castellans and not much more powerful militarily than they, the king of the Franks—who would only later take the territorial title of king of France—was just another local leader. Yet the Capetian kings had considerable prestige. They were anointed with holy oil, and they represented the idea of unity inherited from Charlemagne. Most of the counts, at least in the north of France, became their vassals. They did not promise to obey the king, but they did vow not to try to kill or depose him.

Emperors and Kings in Central and Eastern Europe

In contrast to the development of territorial lordships in France, Germany's fragmentation had hardly begun before it was reversed. The **Ottonian kings** of Germany consolidated their rule there; took the title *emperor*; and then, hand in hand with the papacy, fostered the emergence of new Christian monarchies. Aligned with the Roman church, these new kingdoms were the ancestors of today's Czech and Slovak Republics, Poland, and Hungary.

Ottonian Power in Germany

Five duchies (regions dominated by dukes) emerged in Germany in the late Carolingian period, each much larger than the counties and castellanies of France. When Louis the Child, the last Carolingian king in Germany, died in 911, the dukes elected one of themselves as king. Then, as the Magyar invasions increased, the dukes gave the royal title to the duke of Saxony, Henry I (r. 919–936), who proceeded to set up fortifications and reorganize his army, crowning his efforts with a major defeat of a Magyar army in 933.

Otto I (r. 936–973), the son of Henry I, was an even greater military hero. In 951, he marched into Italy and took the Lombard crown. His defeat of the Magyar forces in 955 at Lechfeld gave him prestige and helped solidify his dynasty. Against the Slavs, with whom the Germans shared a border, Otto created marches (border regions specifically set up for defense) from which he could make expeditions and stave off counterattacks. After the pope crowned him emperor in 962, Otto claimed the Middle Kingdom carved out by the Treaty of Verdun and cast himself as the agent of Roman imperial renewal. His kingdom was called "the Empire," as if it were the old Roman Empire revived. Some historians call it the "Holy Roman Empire" to distinguish it from the Roman Empire. But Otto and his successors never distinguished it from the Roman Empire; they considered it a continuation. In this book, it will be called the Empire.

Otto's victories brought tribute and plunder, ensuring him a following but also raising the German nobles' expectations for enrichment. He and his successors—including Otto II (r. 973–983) and Otto III (r. 983–1002), for which reason the dynasty is called the Ottonian—were not always able or willing to provide the gifts and inheritances their family members and followers expected. To maintain centralized rule, for example, the Ottonians did not divide their kingdom among their sons: like castellans in France, they created a patrilineal pattern of inheritance. But the consequence was that younger sons and other potential heirs felt cheated, and disgruntled royal kin led revolt after revolt against the Ottonian kings. The rebels found followers among the aristocracy, where the trend toward the patrilineal family prompted similar feuds and thwarted expectations.

Relations between the Ottonians and the German clergy were more harmonious. With a ribbon of new bishoprics along his eastern border, Otto I

Capetian (kuh PAY shuhn) dynasty: A long-lasting dynasty of French kings, taking their name from Hugh Capet (r. 987–996).

Ottonian (ah TOH nee uhn) kings: The tenth- and early-eleventh-century kings of Germany; beginning with Otto I (r. 936–973), they claimed the imperial crown and worked closely with their bishops to rule a vast territory.

Otto III Receiving Gifts
This triumphal image is in a book of Gospels made for Otto III (r. 983–1002). The crowned women on the left are personifications of the four parts of Otto's empire: Sclavinia (the Slavic lands), Germania (Germany), Gallia (Gaul), and Roma (Rome). Each offers a gift in tribute and homage to the emperor, who sits on a throne holding the symbols of his power (orb and scepter) and flanked by representatives of the church (on his right) and of the army (on his left). Why do you suppose the artist separated the image of the emperor from that of the women? What does the body language of the women indicate about the relations Otto wanted to portray between himself and the parts of his empire? Can you relate this manuscript, which was made in 997–1000, to Otto's conquest over the Slavs in 997? *(bpk, Berlin/Bayerische Staasbibliothek, Munich, Germany/Art Resource, NY.)*

appointed bishops, gave them extensive lands, and subjected the local peasantry to their overlordship. Like Charlemagne, Otto believed that the well-being of the church in his kingdom depended on him. The Ottonians placed the churches and many monasteries of Germany under their control. They gave bishops the powers of the ban, allowing them to collect revenues and call men to arms. Answering to the king and furnishing him with troops, the bishops became royal officials, while also carrying out their religious duties. German kings claimed the right to select bishops, even the pope at Rome, and to "invest" them (install them in their office) by participating in the ceremony that made them bishops. The higher clergy joined royal court society. Most came to the court to be schooled; in turn, they taught the kings, princes, and noblewomen there.

Like all the strong rulers of the day, whether in Europe or in the Byzantine and Islamic worlds, the Ottonians presided over a renaissance of learning. For example, the tutor of Otto III was Gerbert, the best-educated man of his time. Placed on the papal throne as Pope Sylvester II (r. 999–1003), Gerbert knew how to use the abacus and to calculate with Arabic numerals. He spent "large sums of money to pay copyists and to acquire copies of authors," as he put it. He studied the Latin classics as models of rhetoric and argument, and he reveled in logic and debate. Not only did churchmen and kings support Ottonian scholarship, but to an unprecedented extent noblewomen in Germany also acquired an education and participated in the intellectual revival. Aristocratic women spent much of their wealth on learning. Living at home with their kinfolk and servants or in convents that provided them with comfortable

The Ottonian Empire, 936–1002

private apartments, noblewomen wrote books and occasionally even Roman-style plays. They also supported other artists and scholars.

Despite their military and political strength, the kings of Germany faced resistance from dukes and other powerful princes, who hoped to become regional rulers themselves. The Salians, the dynasty that succeeded the Ottonians, tried to balance the power among the German dukes but could not meld them into a corps of vassals the way the Capetian kings tamed their counts. In Germany, vassalage was considered beneath the dignity of free men. Instead of relying on vassals, the Salian kings and their bishops used ministerials (specially designated men who were legally serfs) to collect taxes, administer justice, and fight on horseback. Ministerials retained their servile status even though they often rose to wealth and high position. Under the Salian kings, ministerials became the mainstay of the royal army and administration.

Supported by their prestige, their churchmen, and their ministerials, the German kings expanded their influence eastward, into the region from the Elbe River to Russia. Otto I was so serious about expansion that he created an extraordinary "elastic" archbishopric: it had no eastern boundary, so it could extend as far as future conquests and conversions to Christianity would allow.

The Emergence of Catholic Bohemia, Poland, and Hungary

Hand in hand with the popes, German kings insisted on the creation of new, Catholic polities along their eastern frontier. The Czechs, who lived in the region of Bohemia, converted under the rule of Václav (r. 920–929), who thereby gained recognition in Germany as the duke of Bohemia. He and his successors did not become kings, remaining politically within the German sphere. Václav's murder by his younger brother made him a martyr and the patron saint of Bohemia, a symbol around which later movements for independence rallied.

The Poles gained a greater measure of independence than the Czechs. In 966, Mieszko I (r. 963–992), the leader of the Slavic tribe known as the Polanians, accepted baptism to forestall the attack that the Germans were already mounting against pagan Slavic peoples along the Baltic coast and east of the Elbe River. Busily engaged in bringing the other Slavic tribes of Poland under his control, Mieszko adroitly shifted his alliances with various German princes to suit his needs. In 991, he placed his realm under the protection of the pope, establishing a tradition of Polish loyalty to the Roman church. Mieszko's son Boleslaw the Brave (r. 992–1025) greatly extended Poland's boundaries, at one time or another holding sway from the Bohemian border to Kiev. In 1000, he gained a royal crown with papal blessing.

Hungary's case was similar to that of Poland. As we have seen, the Magyars settled in the region known today as Hungary. Under Stephen I (r. 997–1038), they accepted Roman Christianity. According to legend, the crown placed on Stephen's head at his coronation (in late 1000 or early 1001) was sent to him by the pope. Stephen was canonized in 1083, and to this day the crown of St. Stephen remains the most hallowed symbol of Hungarian nationhood.

Symbols of rulership such as crowns, consecrated by Christian priests and accorded a prestige almost akin to saints' relics, were among the most vital sources of royal power in central Europe. The economic basis for the power of central European rulers was largely agricultural. As happened elsewhere, here too centralized rule gradually gave way to regional rulers.

REVIEW QUESTION **After the dissolution of the Carolingian Empire, what political systems developed in western, northern, eastern, and central Europe, and how did these systems differ from one another?**

Conclusion

In 800, the three heirs of the Roman Empire all appeared to be organized like their parent: centralized, monarchical, imperial. Byzantine emperors writing their learned books, Abbasid caliphs holding court in their new resplendent palace at Baghdad, and Carolingian emperors issuing their directives for reform all mimicked the Roman emperors. Yet leaders in the three realms confronted tensions and regional pressures that tended to put political power into the hands of local lords. Byzantium felt this fragmentation least, yet even there the emergence of a new elite, the *dynatoi*, weakened the emperor's control over the countryside. In the Islamic world, quarrels between Abbasid heirs, army disloyalty, economic weakness, and the ambitions of powerful local rulers decisively weakened the caliphate and opened the way to separate successor states. In Europe, powerful independent landowners strove with greater or lesser success (depending on the region) to establish themselves as effective rulers. By 1050, most of the states of modern Europe — western, central, and eastern — had begun to form.

In western Europe, local conditions determined political and economic organizations. Between 900

MAPPING THE WEST

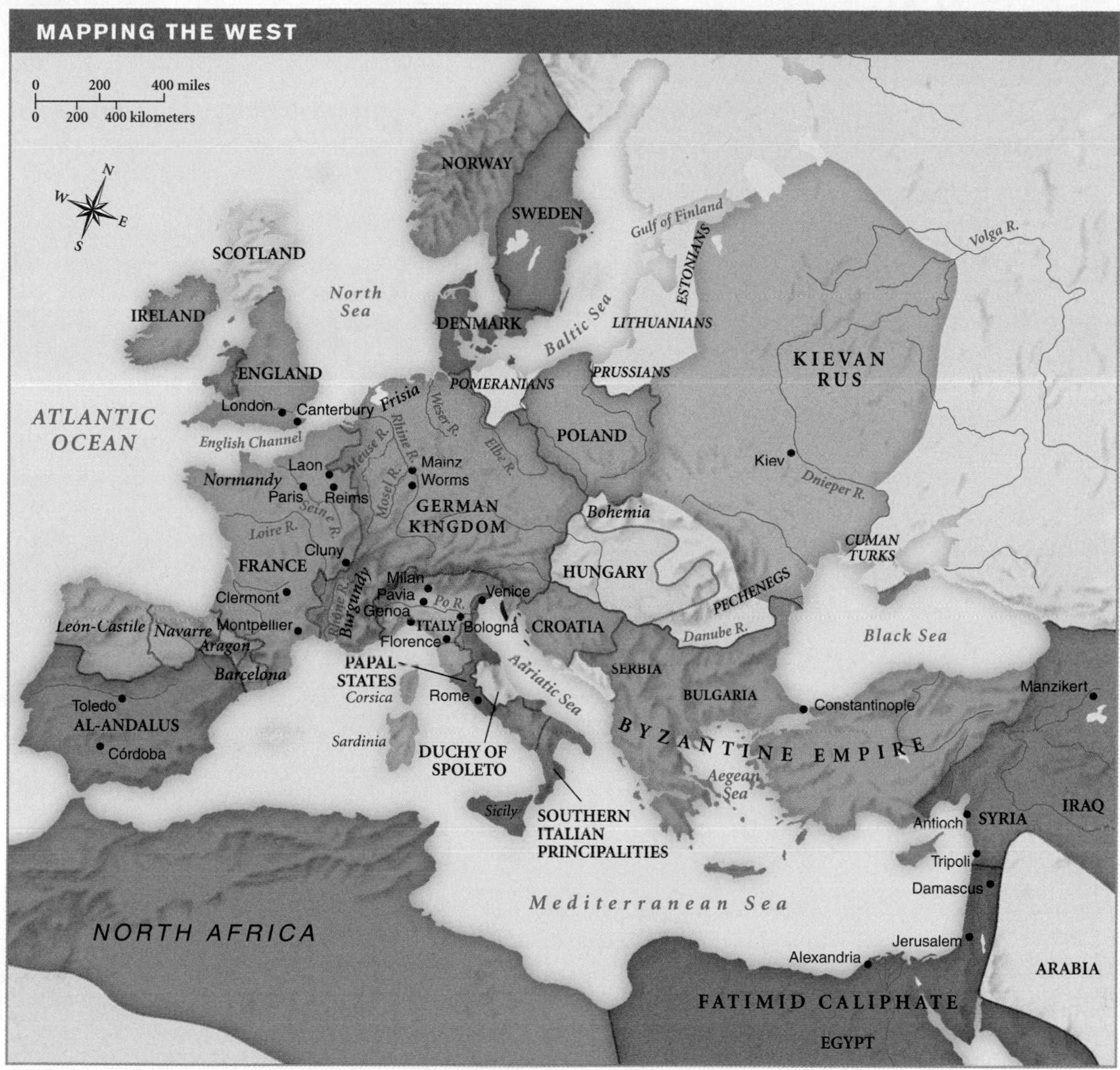

Europe and the Mediterranean, c. 1050

The clear borders and distinct colors of the "states" on this map distort an essential truth: none of the areas shown had centralized governments that controlled whole territories, as in modern states. Instead, there were numerous regional rulers within each, and there were often competing claims of jurisdiction and conflicting allegiances. Consider Sicily: it was conquered by Muslims in the tenth century, but by 1060 it had been taken over by the Normans—adventurers from Normandy (in France). Its predominantly Greek-speaking population, however, was Greek Orthodox in religion, a legacy of its Byzantine past.

and 1000, for example, French society was transformed by the rise of castellans, the formation of patrilineal families, and the spread of ties of vassalage. These factors figured less prominently in Germany, where a central monarchy remained, buttressed by churchmen, ministerials, and conquests to the east.

After 1050, however, the German king would lose his supreme position as a storm of church reform whirled around him. The economy changed, becoming more commercial and urban, and the papacy asserted itself with new force in the life of Europe.

FOR FURTHER EXPLORATION

- **For additional primary-source material from this period**, see *Sources of the Making of the West*, Fourth Edition.
- **For Web sites, images, and documents related to topics in this chapter**, visit *Make History* at bedfordstmartins.com/hunt.

Chapter 9 Review

Online Study Guide bedfordstmartins.com/hunt

Key Terms and People

In the grid below, identify the term or person and explain its historical significance. (To do this exercise online, go to bedfordstmartins.com/hunt.)

Term	Who or What & When	Why It Matters
dynatoi (p. 280)		
Basil II (p. 281)		
Abbasids (p. 283)		
Fatimids (p. 284)		
Carolingian (p. 287)		
Charlemagne (p. 287)		
Treaty of Verdun (p. 292)		
fiefs (p. 297)		
feudalism (p. 297)		
castellan (p. 300)		
primogeniture (p. 301)		
patrilineal (p. 301)		
Peace of God (p. 302)		
Alfred the Great (p. 303)		
Capetian dynasty (p. 304)		
Ottonian kings (p. 304)		

Review Questions

1. In what ways did the Byzantine emperor expand his power, and in what ways was that power checked?
2. What forces contributed to the fragmentation of the Islamic world in the tenth and eleventh centuries, and what forces held it together?
3. What were the strengths and weaknesses of Carolingian institutions of government, warfare, and defense?
4. After the dissolution of the Carolingian Empire, what political systems developed in western, northern, eastern, and central Europe, and how did these systems differ from one another?

Making Connections

1. How were the Byzantine, Islamic, and European economies similar? How did they differ? How did these economies interact?
2. How did the powers and ambitions of castellans compare with those of the dynatoi of Byzantium and of Muslim provincial rulers?
3. Compare the effects of the barbarian invasions into the Roman Empire with the effects of the Viking, Muslim, and Magyar invasions into Carolingian Europe.

Important Events

Date	Event	Date	Event
750–c. 950	The Abbasid caliphate	929–1031	Caliphate of Córdoba
751	Pippin III becomes king of the Franks, establishing Carolingian rule	955	Battle of Lechfeld
768–814	Charlemagne rules as king of the Franks	962	King Otto I (r. 936–973) of Germany crowned emperor
786–809	Caliphate of Harun al-Rashid	987–996	Reign of King Hugh Capet of France
800	Charlemagne crowned emperor at Rome	c. 990	Peace of God movement begins
843	Treaty of Verdun	1000 or 1001	Stephen I (r. 997–1038) crowned king of Hungary
871–899	Reign of King Alfred of England	1001–1018	Byzantine conquest of Bulgaria

- Consider two events: **Peace of God movement begins (c. 990)** and **Stephen I (r. 997–1038) crowned King of Hungary (1000 or 1001)**. How do these events illustrate Christianity's ability to unify and mobilize people in this era?

SUGGESTED REFERENCES

A few books, like Brubaker and Smith's, try to bridge the divides between the Byzantine, Islamic, and western European worlds. Nevertheless, for the most part these regions are treated separately. For Byzantium, Whittow is essential. For insight into the Islamic world, see especially Cooperson. For the Carolingian world, De Jong provides a new approach. For the post-Carolingian West, see Head and Landes, who value fragmentation and the diversity of developments that it permitted.

Becher, Matthias. *Charlemagne*. 2003.

Berend, Nora. *At the Gate of Christendom: Jews, Muslims, and "Pagans" in Medieval Hungary, c. 1000–c. 1300*. 2001.

Brubaker, Leslie, and Julia M. H. Smith. *Gender in the Early Medieval World: East and West, 300–900*. 2004.

**Chronicle of Zuqnin, Parts III and IV, A.D. 488–775*. Trans. Amir Harrak. 1999.

Cooperson, Michael. *Al Ma'mun*. 2005.

De Jong, Mayke. *The Penitential State: Authority and Atonement in the Age of Louis the Pious, 814–840*. 2009.

Duby, Georges. *The Early Growth of the European Economy: Warriors and Peasants from the Seventh to the Twelfth Century*. Trans. H. B. Clark. 1974.

*Dutton, Paul Edward, ed. *Carolingian Civilization: A Reader*. 1993.

*——, ed. and trans. *Charlemagne's Courtier: The Complete Einhard*. 1998.

*Einhard and Notker the Stammerer. *Two Lives of Charlemagne*. Trans. Lewis Thorpe. 1969.

Fine, Jon V. A., Jr. *The Early Medieval Balkans: A Critical Survey from the Sixth to the Late Twelfth Century*. 1983.

Franklin, Simon, and Jonathan Shepard. *The Emergence of Rus, 750–1200*. 1996.

Garver, Valerie L. *Women and Aristocratic Culture in the Carolingian World*. 2009.

Head, Thomas, and Richard Landes, eds. *The Peace of God: Social Violence and Religious Response in France around the Year 1000*. 1992.

Jones, Anna Trumbore. *Noble Lord, Good Shepherd: Episcopal Power and Piety in Aquitaine, 877–1050*. 2009.

Kennedy, Hugh. *The Armies of the Caliphs: Military and Society in the Early Islamic State*. 2001.

Maguire, Henry, ed. *Byzantine Court Culture from 829 to 1204*. 1997.

*Psellus, Michael. *Fourteen Byzantine Rulers: The Chronographia*. Trans. E. R. A. Sewter. 1966.

Sweeney, Del, ed. *Agriculture in the Middle Ages: Technology, Practice, and Representation*. 1995.

Whittow, Mark. *The Making of Byzantium, 600–1025*. 1996.

*Primary source.

CHAPTER

10

Commercial Quickening and Religious Reform

1050–1150

In the middle of the twelfth century, a sculptor was hired to add some friezes depicting scenes from the Old and New Testaments to the facade of the grand new hilltop cathedral at Lincoln, England. He portrayed in striking fashion the deaths of the poor man Lazarus and the rich man Dives. Their fates could not have been more different. While Lazarus was carried to heaven by two angels, a contented-looking devil poked Dives and two other rich men straight into the mouth of hell—headfirst.

The sculptor's work reflected a widespread change in attitude toward money. In the Carolingian and post-Carolingian period (up to, say, 1050), wealth was considered, in general, a very good thing. Rich kings were praised for their generosity; expensively produced manuscripts, illuminated with gold leaf and precious colors, were highly prized; and splendid churches like Charlemagne's chapel at Aachen were widely admired. Such views changed over the course of the eleventh century.

The most striking feature of the period 1050–1150 was the rise of a money economy in western Europe. Agricultural production swelled, fueling the growth of trade and the expansion of cities. A new class of well-heeled merchants, bankers, and entrepreneurs emerged. These developments were met with a wide variety of responses. Some people fled the cities and their new wealth altogether, seeking isolation and poverty. Others, even the participants in the new economy, condemned it and emphasized its corrupting influence: Lincoln's new cathedral was built right next to a marketplace, and its twelfth-century bishops—who were themselves rich men—wanted to warn moneymaking parishioners about the perils of wealth. Most people embraced the new money economy, however—some eagerly, others cautiously.

Dives and Lazarus
At the time this sculpted depiction of Dives and Lazarus was made, the town of Lincoln was expanding both within and without its Roman walls. Within the walls were the precincts of the fishmongers, the grain sellers, and the poultry merchants. Outside the walls were the bakers, the soapmakers, and the salt sellers. The town was highly attuned to moneymaking—both its pleasures and its dangers. *(Conway Library, The Courtauld Institute of Art, London.)*

The development of a profit-based economy quickly transformed the landscape and lifestyles of western Europe. Many villages and fortifications became cities where traders, merchants, and artisans conducted business. In some places, town dwellers began to determine their own laws and administer their own justice. Although most people still lived in sparsely populated rural areas, their lives were touched in many ways by the new cash economy. Economic concerns helped drive changes within the church, where a movement for reform gathered steam and exploded in three directions: the Investiture Conflict, new monastic orders emphasizing poverty, and the crusades. Money even helped popes, kings, and princes redefine the nature of their power.

CHAPTER FOCUS How did the commercial revolution affect religion and politics?

The Commercial Revolution

As the population of Europe continued to expand in the eleventh century, cities, long-distance trade networks, local markets, and new business arrangements meshed to create a profit-based economy. With improvements in agriculture and more land in cultivation, the great estates of the eleventh century produced surpluses that helped feed—and therefore make possible—a new urban population.

Commerce was not new to the history of western Europe, but the **commercial revolution** of the Middle Ages spawned the institutions that would be the direct ancestors of modern businesses: corporations, banks, accounting systems, and, above all, urban centers that thrived on economic vitality. Whereas ancient cities had primarily religious, social, and political functions, medieval cities were centers of production and economic activity. Wealth meant power: it allowed city dwellers to become self-governing.

commercial revolution: A term for the western European development (starting around 1050) of a money economy centered in urban areas but affecting the countryside as well.

Fairs, Towns, and Cities

The commercial revolution took place in three venues: markets, fairs, and permanent centers. In some places, markets met weekly to sell local surplus goods. In others, fairs—which lasted anywhere from several days to a few months—took place once a year and drew traders from longer distances (Map 10.1). Some fairs specialized in particular goods: at Skania, in southern Sweden, the chief product was herring. At Saint-Denis, a monastery near Paris that had had a fair since at least the seventh century, the star attraction was wine. Most fairs offered a wide variety of products: at six different fairs in Champagne, merchants arrived from Flanders with woolen fabrics, from Lucca with silks, from Spain with leather goods, from Germany with furs. Bankers attended as well, exchanging coins from one currency into another—and charging for their services. (Sometimes, the currency was in peppercorns or other spices; see Document, "Peppercorns as Money," page 314.) Local inhabitants did not have to pay taxes or tolls, but traders from the outside—protected by guarantees of safe conduct—were charged stall fees as well as entry and exit fees. Local landlords reaped great profits, and as the fairs came under royal control, kings did so as well.

Permanent commercial centers—cities and towns—developed around castles and monasteries and within the walls of ancient Roman towns.

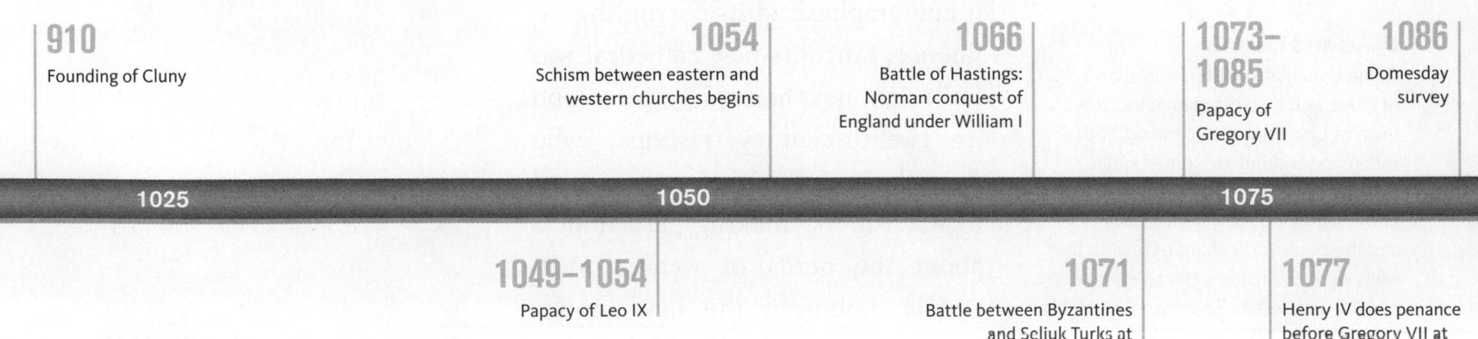

910
Founding of Cluny
1054
Schism between eastern and western churches begins
1066
Battle of Hastings: Norman conquest of England under William I
1073–1085
Papacy of Gregory VII
1086
Domesday survey
1025
1050
1075
1049–1054
Papacy of Leo IX
1071
Battle between Byzantines and Seljuk Turks at Manzikert
1077
Henry IV does penance before Gregory VII at Canossa; war breaks out

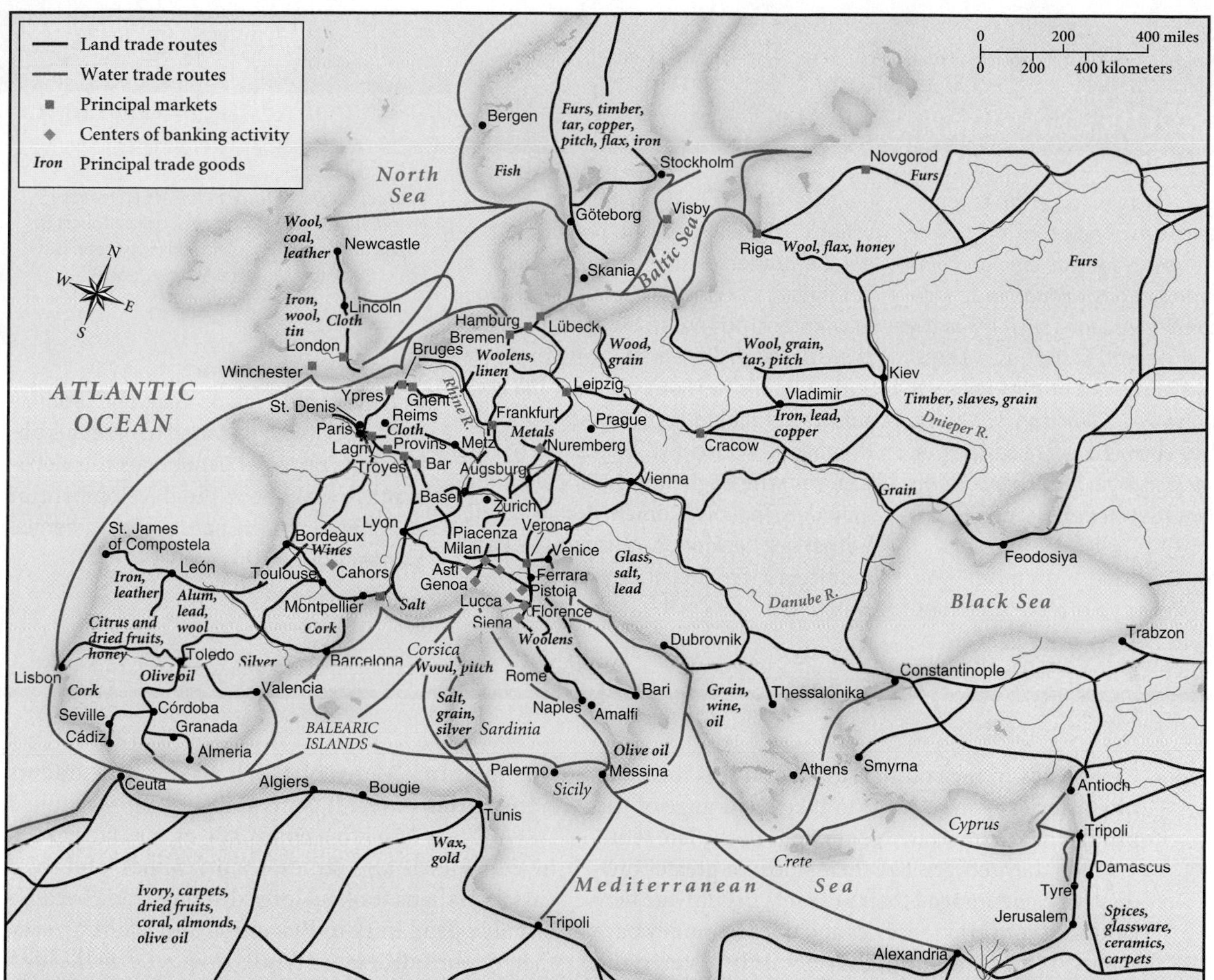

MAP 10.1 Medieval Trade Routes in the Eleventh and Twelfth Centuries
In the medieval world, bulk goods from the north (furs, fish, and wood) were traded for luxury goods from the south (ivory, spices, medicines, perfumes, and dyes). Already regions were beginning to specialize. England, for example, supplied raw wool, but Flanders (Ypres, Ghent) specialized in turning that wool into cloth and shipping it farther south, to the fairs of Champagne (whose capital was Troyes) or Germany. Italian cities channeled goods from the Muslim and Byzantine worlds northward and exported European goods southward and eastward.

1095
Council of Clermont;
Pope Urban II calls First Crusade

1108–1137
Reign of Louis VI

1122
Concordat of Worms ends Investiture Conflict

c. 1140
Gratian's *Decretum* published

1100 — 1125 — 1150

1097
Establishment of commune at Milan

1109
Establishment of the crusader states

1096–1099
First Crusade

1147–1149
Second Crusade

DOCUMENT

Peppercorns as Money

The commercial revolution, with its growing dependence on money, took off so fast that there simply were not enough coins for all the transactions taking place. Peppercorns, which have a long shelf life and a fairly uniform weight, served as a useful substitute. The document printed here was a contract drawn up in Genoa on January 14, 1156, to make a payment before Easter in either pepper or coin. A pound of peppercorns was equivalent to a monetary pound.

I, Rinaldo Gauxone, promise you, Lamberto Grillo, or your accredited messenger, £6½ in pepper or in coin [to be delivered any time] up to next Easter; otherwise [I will pay] the penalty of the double, under pledge of my orchard in Sozziglia [a region of Genoa]. And you may enter into [possession] of it for the principal and the penalty on your own authority and without order by the consuls [the chief judges of Genoa]. Done in the chapter house, 1156, on the fourteenth day from the beginning of January, third indiction [an old Roman dating term]. Witnesses: Sismondo Muscula, B. Papa Canticula Macobrio, notary, Baldo Rubeo, watchman.

Source: *Medieval Trade in the Mediterranean World: Illustrative Documents*, trans. Robert S. Lopez and Irving W. Raymond (1955; repr. New York: Columbia University Press, 2001), 145.

Question to Consider

- **Why would Rinaldo Gauxone promise to pay double if he failed to meet his obligations on time? What does this document reveal about the development of commerce and the nature of commercial transactions in this era?**

Great lords in the countryside—and this included monasteries—were eager to take advantage of the profits that their estates generated. In the late tenth century, they reorganized their lands for greater productivity, encouraged their peasants to cultivate new land, and converted services and dues to money payments. With ready cash, they not only fostered the development of local markets and yearly fairs, where they could sell their surpluses and buy luxury goods, but also encouraged traders and craftspeople to settle down near them. For example, at Bruges (today in Belgium), the local lord's castle became the magnet around which a city formed. As a medieval chronicler observed:

> To satisfy the needs of the people in the castle at Bruges, first merchants with luxury articles began to surge around the gate: then the winesellers came; finally the innkeepers arrived to feed and lodge the people who had business with the prince. . . . So many houses were built that soon a great city was created.

Other commercial centers clustered around monasteries and churches. Still other markets formed just outside the walls of older cities; these gradually merged into new and enlarged urban communities as town walls were built around them to protect their inhabitants. Sometimes informal country markets were housed in permanent structures. Along the Rhine and in other river valleys, cities sprang up to service the merchants who traversed the route between Italy and the north.

The Jews in the Cities Many of the long-distance traders were Italians and Jews. They supplied the fine wines, spices, and fabrics beloved by lords and ladies, their families, and their vassals. Italians took up long-distance trade because of Italy's proximity to Byzantine and Islamic ports, their opportunities for plunder and trade on the high seas, and their never entirely extinguished urban traditions. The Jews of Mediterranean regions—especially Italy and Spain—had been involved in commerce since Roman times. That trade had centered on the Mediterranean; now it extended to the north as well. For Jews living in the port cities of the old Roman Empire, little had changed. But for many Jews in northern Europe, the story was different. They had settled on the land alongside other peasants, and during the Carolingian period their properties bordered those of their Christian neighbors. As political power fragmented in the course of the tenth century—and the countryside was reorganized under the ban (controlling powers) of local lords—many Jews were driven off the land. They found refuge in the new towns and cities. Some became scholars, doctors, and judges within their communities; many became small-time pawnbrokers; and still others became moneylenders and financiers.

By the eleventh century, most Jews lived in cities but were not citizens. They were, in general, serfs of the king or, in the Rhineland, under the safeguard of the local bishop. This status was ambiguous: they were "protected" but also exploited, since their protectors constantly demanded steep taxes. Regular town trade groups, craft organizations, and town governments often rested on a conception of the common good sealed by an oath among Christians — and thus, by definition, excluded Jews. Nevertheless, Jews had their own institutions, centered on the synagogue, their place of worship (see the illustration on the right). Although they often lived in a "Jewish quarter," they were not forcibly segregated from other townspeople. In many cities they lived near Christians, purchased products from Christian craftspeople, and hired Christians as servants. In turn, Christians purchased luxury goods from Jewish long-distance traders and often borrowed money from Jewish lenders.

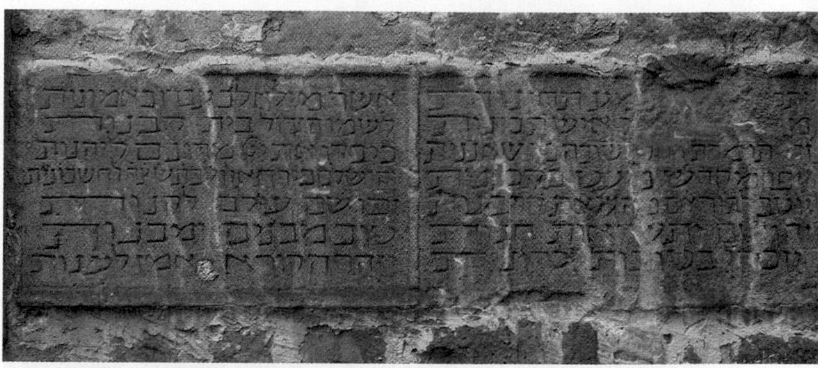

Synagogue Inscription from the City of Worms
This inscription is the oldest artifact we have from a synagogue in Europe. It says that Jacob ben David and his wife, Rahel, used their fortune to construct and furnish the synagogue, which was completed in 1034. They express the belief that this act of piety is as pleasing to God as having children. *(Jüdisches Museum im Raschihaus, Worms, Germany.)*

The "Unplanned" Town The fact that Jews and Christians could live side by side had less to do with tolerance than with lack of planning. Most towns in medieval Europe grew haphazardly. Typically, towns had a center, where the church and town governments had their headquarters, and around this were the shops of tradespeople and craftspeople, generally grouped by specialty. Around the marketplace at Reims, for example, was a network of streets whose names (many of which still exist) revealed their commercial functions: Street of the Butchers, Street of the Wool Market, Street of the Wheat Market.

The look and feel of such developing cities varied enormously, but nearly all cities included a marketplace, a castle, and several churches. The streets — made of packed clay or gravel — were often narrow, dirty, dark, and winding. Most people had to adapt to increasingly crowded conditions. Archaeologists have discovered, for example, that at the end of the eleventh century in Winchester, England, city plots were still large enough to accommodate houses parallel to the street; but the swelling population soon necessitated destroying those houses and building instead long, narrow, hall-like tenements, constructed at right angles to the thoroughfare. These were built on a frame made from strips of wood filled with wattle and daub — twigs woven together and covered with clay. If they were like the stone houses built in the late twelfth century (a period about which we know a good deal), they had two stories: a shop or warehouse on the lower floor and living quarters above. Behind this main building was the kitchen and perhaps also enclosures for livestock. As this building style demonstrates, even city dwellers clung to rural pursuits, living largely off the food they raised themselves.

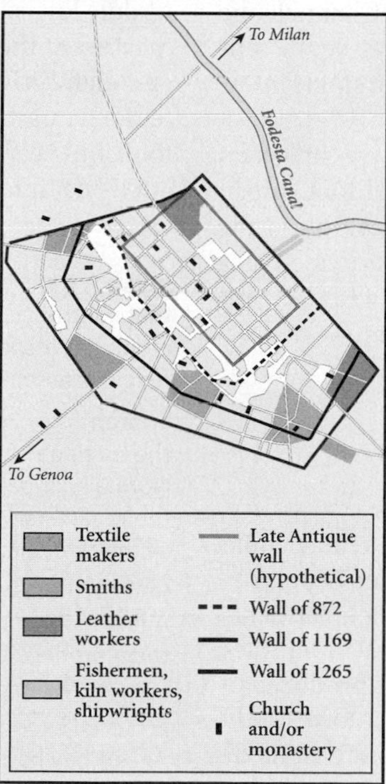

The Walls of Piacenza

The construction of houses and markets was part of a building boom that began in the tenth century and continued at an accelerated pace through the thirteenth. Towns put up specialized buildings for trade and city government — charitable houses for the sick and indigent, city halls, and warehouses. They also expanded their walls. Workers at Piacenza, for example, first pulled down the late antique wall and replaced it with a more extensive one in 872. Then, in 1169, Piacenzans took down the ninth-century wall and replaced it with one that was still more expansive. (See The Walls of Piacenza, left.)

Outside the cities, new bridges spanned the rivers. Before the eleventh century, Europeans had depended on boats and waterways for bulky long-distance transport; in the twelfth century, carts could haul items overland because new roads through the countryside linked the urban markets and because strengthened governments could protect overland travelers. Still, although commercial centers developed throughout western Europe, they grew fastest and most densely in

Baptismal Font at Liège, 1107–1118
This detail from a large bronze baptismal font cast at Liège (a city today in Belgium) illustrated the words of Luke 3:12–14: "Tax collectors also came to be baptized, and said to [Jesus], 'Teacher, what shall we do?' And he said to them, 'Collect no more than is appointed you.' Soldiers also asked him, 'And we, what shall we do?' And he said to them, 'Rob no one . . . and be content with your wages.'" In this representation, the tax collectors are dressed like twelfth-century city dwellers, while a soldier is dressed like a knight of the period. *(akg-images.)*

regions along key waterways: the Mediterranean coasts of Italy, France, and Spain; northern Italy along the Po River; the Rhône-Saône-Meuse river system; the Rhineland; the English Channel; the shores of the Baltic Sea. During the eleventh century, these waterways became part of a single interdependent economy.

What did townspeople look like? We can get an idea from a twelfth-century baptismal font cast in Liège (see above). It shows Jesus speaking to the soldiers and publicans: the soldier is dressed as a medieval knight, while the publicans wear the caps and clothes of well-to-do city dwellers.

Organizing Crafts and Commerce

In modern capitalism, there are few craftspeople: machines weave textiles, for example, and people sew pieces (a collar, perhaps) rather than whole garments. Piecework was just beginning in the Middle Ages, when most manufactured goods were produced by hand or with primitive machines and tools (see the illustration on page 317). Nevertheless, most medieval industries, though not mechanized, were highly organized. The fundamental unit of organization was the guild, a sort of club for craftspeople and tradespeople. Similarly, the ancestors of modern business corporations—which rely on capital pooled from various sources—originated in the Middle Ages.

Guilds | It was not by chance that city streets were named for various occupations: in a medieval city, crafts and trades were collective endeavors. Each was organized as a **guild**. Originally these were religious and charitable associations of people in the same line of trade. In Ferrara, Italy, for example, the shoemakers' guild started as a prayer confraternity, an association whose members gathered and prayed for one another. But soon guilds became professional corporations defined by statutes and rules. They charged dues, negotiated with lords and town governments, set the standards of their trade, and controlled their membership.

The manufacture of finished products often required the cooperation of several guilds. The production of wool cloth, for example, involved numerous guilds—shearers, weavers, fullers (who thickened the cloth), dyers—generally working under the supervision of the merchant guild that imported the raw wool. Some guilds were more prestigious than others: in Florence, for example, professional guilds of notaries and judges ranked above craft guilds. Within each guild of artisans, merchants, or professionals existed another kind of hierarchy. **Apprentices** were at the bottom, **journeymen** and **journeywomen** (that is, male or female day laborers—the word comes from the Middle English for "a day's work") in the middle, and **masters** at the top. Apprentices were boys (and occasionally girls) placed under the tutelage of a master for a number of years to learn a trade. At Paris, it took four years of apprenticeship to become a baker; at Genoa, it took ten to become a silversmith.

---

guild: A trade organization within a city or town that controlled product quality and cost and outlined members' responsibilities. Guilds were also social and religious associations.

apprentices: Boys (and occasionally girls) placed under the tutelage of a master craftsman in the Middle Ages. Normally unpaid, they were expected to be servants of their masters, with whom they lived, at the same time as they were learning their trade.

journeymen/journeywomen: Laborers in the Middle Ages whom guildmasters hired for a daily wage to help them produce their products.

masters: Men (and occasionally women) who, having achieved expertise in a craft, ran the guilds in the Middle Ages. They had to be rich enough to have their own shop and tools and to pay an entry fee into the guild. Often their positions were hereditary.

Learning a trade was not the same as becoming a master. A young person would spend many years as a day laborer hired by a master who needed extra help. Masters occupied the top of the guild hierarchy, dominating the offices and policies of the guild. They drew up the guild regulations and served as its chief overseers, inspectors, and treasurers. Because the number of masters was few and the turnover of official posts frequent, most masters eventually had a chance to serve as guild officers. Occasionally they were elected, but more often they were appointed by town governments or local rulers.

Partnerships, Contracts, and the Rise of Industry In the course of the eleventh and twelfth centuries, people created new kinds of business arrangements through partnerships, contracts, and large-scale productive enterprises—the ancestors of modern **capitalism**. Although they took many forms, all of these business agreements had the common purpose of bringing people together to pool their resources and finance larger initiatives. Short-lived partnerships were set up for the term of one sea voyage; longer-term partnerships were created for land trade. In northern and central Italy, for example, long-term ventures took the form of a family corporation formed by extended families. Everyone who contributed to this corporation bore joint and unlimited liability for all losses and debts. This provision enhanced family solidarity, because each member was responsible for the debts of all the others, but it also risked bankrupting everyone in the family.

The commercial revolution also fostered the development of contracts for sales, exchanges, and loans. Loans were the most problematic. In the Middle Ages, as now, interest payments were the chief inducement for an investor to supply money. To circumvent the church's ban on usury (lending money at interest), a contract often disguised interest as a "penalty for late payment." The new willingness to finance business enterprises with loans signaled a changed attitude toward credit: risk was acceptable if it brought profit.

Contracts and partnerships made large-scale productive enterprises possible. In fact, light industry began in the eleventh century. One of the earliest products to benefit from new industrial technologies was cloth. Water mills powered machines such as presses to extract oil from fibers, and flails to clean and thicken cloth. Machines also exploited raw materials more efficiently: new deep-mining technology provided Europeans with hitherto untapped sources of metals. At the same time, forging techniques improved, and iron was for the first time since antiquity regularly used for agricultural tools and plows. Iron tools—which were more durable than wood—made farming more productive, which in turn fed the commercial revolution. People also fashioned metals into objects ranging from weapons and armor to ornaments and coins.

capitalism: The modern economic system characterized by an entrepreneurial class of property owners who employ others and produce (or provide services) for a market in order to make a profit.

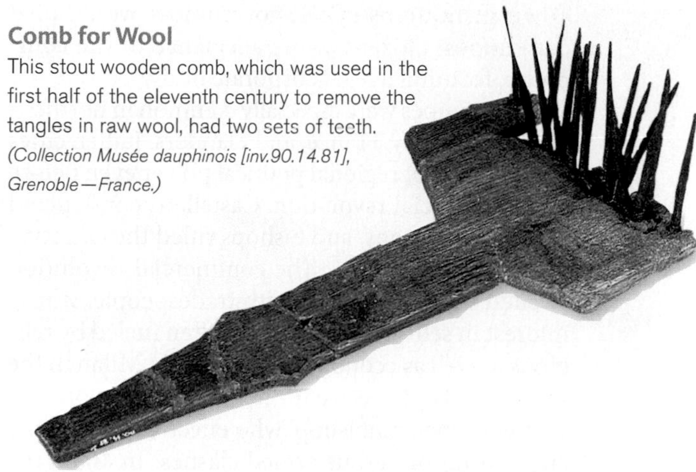

Comb for Wool
This stout wooden comb, which was used in the first half of the eleventh century to remove the tangles in raw wool, had two sets of teeth. *(Collection Musée dauphinois [inv.90.14.81], Grenoble—France.)*

Communes: Self-Government for the Towns

In the eleventh and twelfth centuries, townspeople—traders, artisans, ship captains, innkeepers, and money changers—did not fit into the old categories of medieval types as those who prayed, those who fought, or those who labored on the land. Just knowing they were different from those groups gave townspeople a sense of solidarity. But practical reasons also contributed to their feeling of common purpose: they lived in close quarters, and they shared a mutual interest in reliable coinage, laws to facilitate commerce, freedom from servile dues and duties, and independence to buy and sell as the market dictated. Already in the early twelfth century, the king of England granted to the citizens of Newcastle-upon-Tyne the privilege that any unfree peasant who lived there unclaimed by his lord for a year and a day would thereafter be a free person. This privilege became general. To townspeople, freedom meant having their own officials and law courts. They petitioned the political powers that ruled them—bishops, kings, counts, castellans—for the right to govern themselves. Often they had to fight for this freedom and, if successful, paid a hefty sum for it.

Town institutions of self-government were called **communes**; citizens swore allegiance to the commune, forming a legal corporate body.

Communes were especially common in northern and central Italy, France, and Flanders. Italian cities were centers of regional political power even before the commercial revolution. Castellans constructed their fortifications, and bishops ruled the countryside from such cities. The commercial revolution swelled the Italian cities with tradespeople, whose interest in self-government was often fueled by religious as well as economic concerns. At Milan in the second half of the eleventh century, popular discontent with the archbishop, who effectively ruled the city, led to numerous armed clashes. In 1097, the Milanese succeeded in transferring political power from the archbishop and his clergy to a government of leading men of the city, who called themselves consuls. The title recalled the government of the ancient Roman republic, affirming the consuls' status as representatives of the people. As the archbishop's power had done, the consuls' rule extended beyond the town walls into the *contado*, the outlying countryside.

Outside Italy, movements for city independence took place within the framework of larger kingdoms or principalities. Such movements were sometimes violent, as at Milan, but at other times they were peaceful. For example, William Clito, who claimed the county of Flanders (today in Belgium), willingly granted the citizens of St. Omer the privileges they asked for in 1127 in return for their support of his claims: he recognized them as legally free, gave them the right to mint coins, allowed them their own laws and courts, and lifted certain tolls and taxes. Whether violently or peacefully, the men and women of many towns and cities gained a measure of self-rule.

The Commercial Revolution in the Countryside

The countryside, too, was caught in the new networks of trade. Country people brought local products to markets and fairs. By 1150, rural life in many regions was organized for the marketplace. The commercialization of the countryside opened up opportunities for both peasants and lords, but it also burdened some with unwelcome obligations.

commune: In a medieval town, a sworn association of citizens who formed a legal corporate body. The commune appointed or elected officials, made laws, kept the peace, and administered justice.

Great lords hired trained, literate agents to administer their estates, calculate their profits and losses, and make marketing decisions. Aristocrats needed money not only because they relished luxuries but also because their honor and authority continued to depend on their personal generosity, patronage, and displays of wealth. In the twelfth century, when some townsmen could boast fortunes that rivaled the riches of the landed aristocracy, the economic pressures on the nobles increased as their extravagance exceeded their income. Many went into debt.

The lord's need for money integrated peasants, too, into the developing commercial economy. The increase in population and the resultant greater demand for food required bringing more land under cultivation. By the middle of the twelfth century, the cultivation of new land had changed from a sporadic activity to a planned program. Great lords offered special privileges to peasants who would do the backbreaking work of plowing marginal land or draining marshes. For example, in Flanders, where land was regularly inundated by seawater, the great monasteries sponsored drainage projects. Canals linking the cities to the agricultural districts let boats ply the waters to virtually every nook and cranny of the region. With its dense population, Flanders provided not only a natural meeting ground for long-distance traders from England and France but also numerous markets for local traders.

Sometimes free peasants acted on their own to clear land and relieve the pressure of overpopulation, as when the small freeholders in England's Fenland region cooperated to build banks and dikes to reclaim the land that led out to the North Sea. Villages were founded on the drained land, and villagers shared responsibility for repairing and maintaining the dikes even as each peasant family farmed its new holding individually.

On old estates the rise in population strained to the breaking point the Carolingian period's manse organization, in which each household had been settled on the land that supported it. Now, in the twelfth century, twenty peasant families might live on what had been, in the tenth century, the manse of one family. With the manse supporting so many more people, labor services and dues had to be recalculated, and peasants and their lords often turned services and dues into money rents, payable once a year. Peasants sometimes formed commune-like collectives to buy their liberty for a high price, paid out over many years to their lord. Like town citizens, they gained a new sense of identity and solidarity as they bargained with a lord keen to increase his income at their expense.

The commercial revolution and the resulting money economy brought both benefits and burdens to peasants. They gained from rising prices, which made their fixed rents less onerous. They had access to markets where they could sell their surplus and buy what they lacked. Increases in land under cultivation and the use of iron tools meant greater productivity. Peasants also gained increased personal freedom as they shook off direct control by lords. Nevertheless, these advantages were partially canceled out by their cash obligations. Peasants touched by the commercial revolution ate better than their forebears had eaten, but they also had to spend more money.

REVIEW QUESTION What new institutions resulted from the commercial revolution?

Church Reform

The commercial revolution affected the church no less than it affected other institutions of the time. Bishops ruled over many cities, and many bishops were appointed by kings or powerful local lords. This transaction involved gifts: churchmen gave gifts and money to secular leaders in return for their offices. Soon these transactions were being condemned by the same sorts of people who appreciated the fates of Dives and Lazarus. The impulse to free the church from "the world"—from rulers, wealth, sex, money, and power—was as old as the origins of monasticism; but, beginning in the tenth century and increasing to fever pitch in the eleventh, reformers demanded that the church as a whole remodel itself and become free of secular entanglements.

This freedom was, from the start, as much a matter of power as of religion. Most people had long believed that their ruler—whether king, duke, count, or castellan—reigned by the grace of God and had the right to control the churches in his territory. But by the second half of the eleventh century, more and more people saw a great deal wrong with secular power over the church. They looked to the papacy to lead the movement of church reform. The matter came to a head during the so-called Investiture Conflict, when Pope Gregory VII clashed with Emperor Henry IV (whose empire embraced both Germany and Italy). The Investiture Conflict ushered in a major civil war in Germany and a great upheaval in the distribution of power across western Europe. By the early 1100s, a reformed church—with the pope at its head—was penetrating into areas of life never before touched by churchmen. Church reform began as a way to free the church from the world, but in the end the church was thoroughly involved in the new world it had helped create.

Beginnings of Reform

The project of freeing the church from the world began in the tenth century with no particular plan and only a vague idea of what it might mean. Local reformers—both clerical and lay—took some early steps to make the clergy not only celibate but also independent of the laity. But church reform did not take final shape until the papacy embraced it and turned it into a blueprint for reorganizing the church under papal leadership. The movement to "liberate the church" in fact began in unlikely circles: with the very rulers who were controlling churches and monasteries, appointing churchmen, and using bishops as their administrators.

Cluniac Reform The Benedictine monastery of Cluny (today in France) may serve to represent the early phases of the reform. The duke and duchess of Aquitaine founded Cluny in 910 and endowed it with property. Then they did something new: instead of retaining control over the monastery, as other monastic founders did, they gave it and its worldly possessions to Saints Peter and Paul. In this way, they put control of the monastery into the hands of heaven's two most powerful saints. They designated the pope, as the successor of St. Peter, to be the monastery's worldly protector if anyone should bother or threaten it.

The whole notion of "freedom" at this point was vague. But Cluny's prestige was great because of its status as St. Peter's property and the elaborate round of prayers that the monks carried out there with scrupulous devotion. The Cluniac monks fulfilled the role of "those who pray" in a way that dazzled their contemporaries. Through their prayers, they seemed to guarantee the salvation of all Christians. Rulers, bishops, rich landowners, and even serfs (if they could) donated land to Cluny, joining their contributions to the land of St. Peter and the fate of their souls to Cluny's efficacious prayers. Powerful men and women called on the Cluniac monks to reform other monasteries along the Cluniac model.

The abbots of Cluny came to see themselves as reformers of the world as well. They advocated clerical celibacy, arguing against the prevailing norm in which parish priests and even some bishops were married. They thought that the laity could be reformed, become more virtuous, and cease its oppression of the poor. In the eleventh century, the Cluniacs began to link their program of internal monastic and external worldly reform to the papacy. When bishops and laypeople encroached on their lands, they appealed to the popes for help. At the same time, the papacy itself was becoming interested in reform.

Church Reform in the Empire Around the time the Cluniacs were joining their fate to that of the popes, a small group of clerics and monks in the Empire, the political entity created by the Ottonians, began calling for systematic reform within the church. They buttressed their arguments with new interpretations of canon law—the laws decreed over the centuries at church councils and by bishops and popes. They concentrated on two breaches of those laws: clerical marriage and **simony** (buying church offices).[1] Later they added the condemnation of **lay investiture**—the installation of clerics into their offices by lay rulers. In the investiture ritual, the emperor or his representative symbolically gave the church and the land that went with it to the priest or bishop or archbishop chosen for the job.

Many of the men who promoted the reform lived in the highly commercialized regions of the empire—Italy and the regions along the northern half of the Rhine River. Familiar with the impersonal practices of a profit economy, they regarded the gifts that churchmen usually gave in return for their offices as no more than crass purchases.

Emperor Henry III (r. 1039–1056) supported the reformers. Taking seriously his position as the anointed of God, Henry felt responsible for the well-being of the church in his empire. He denounced simony and refused to accept money or gifts when he appointed bishops to their posts. When in 1046 three men, each representing a different faction of the Roman aristocracy, claimed to be pope, Henry, as ruler of Rome, traveled to Italy to settle the matter. The Synod of Sutri (1046), over which he presided, deposed all three popes and elected another. In 1049, Henry appointed a bishop from the Rhineland to the papacy as Leo IX (r. 1049–1054). But this appointment did not work out as Henry had expected, for Leo set out to reform the church under his own, not the emperor's, control.

Leo IX and the Expansion of Papal Power During Leo's tenure, the pope's role expanded. Leo traveled to France and Germany, holding councils to condemn bishops guilty of simony. He sponsored the creation of a canon law textbook—*Collection in 74 Titles*—that emphasized the pope's power. To the papal court, Leo brought the most zealous reformers of his day, including Humbert of Silva Candida and Hildebrand (later Pope Gregory VII).

At first, clergy and secular rulers alike ignored Leo's claims to new power over the church hierarchy. Only a few bishops attended the Council of Reims, which Leo called in 1049; the king of France boycotted it entirely. Nevertheless, the pope turned the council into a forum for exercising his authority. Placing the relics of St. Remigius (the patron saint of Reims) on the altar of the church, he demanded that the attending bishops and abbots say whether or not they had purchased their offices. A few confessed, some did not respond, and others gave excuses. New and extraordinary was the fact that all present felt accountable to the pope and accepted his verdicts.

In 1054, his last year as pope, Leo sent Humbert of Silva Candida to Constantinople on a diplomatic mission to argue against the patriarch of Constantinople on behalf of the new, lofty claims of the pope. Furious at the contemptuous way he was treated by the patriarch, Humbert excommunicated him. In retaliation, the patriarch excommunicated Humbert and his party, threatening them with eternal damnation. Clashes between the two churches had occurred before and had been patched up, but this one, the schism between the eastern and western churches, (1054), proved insurmountable.[2] Thereafter, the Roman Catholic and the Greek Orthodox churches were largely separate.

Leo also had to confront a new power to his south. Under Count Roger I (c. 1040–1101), the Normans created a county that would eventually stretch from Capua to Sicily (see the map on page 322). Leo, threatened by this great power, tried to curtail it: in 1053 he sent a military force to Apulia, but it was soundly defeated. Leo's successors were obliged to change their policy. In 1058, the reigning pope "invested"—in effect, gave—Apulia, nearby

---

[1]The word *simony* comes from the name Simon Magus, the magician in the New Testament who wanted to buy the gifts of the Holy Spirit from St. Peter.

simony (SY muh nee): The sin of giving gifts or paying money to get a church office.

lay investiture: The installation of clerics into their offices by lay rulers.

[2]The mutual excommunications led to a permanent breach between the churches that largely remained in effect until 1965, when Pope Paul VI and Patriarch Athenagoras I made a joint declaration regretting "the offensive words" and sentences of excommunication on both sides, deploring "the effective rupture of ecclesiastical communion," and expressing the hope that the "differences between the Roman Catholic Church and the Orthodox Church" would be overcome in time.

Leo IX

This eleventh-century manuscript shows not so much a portrait of Pope Leo IX as an idealized image of his power and position. What might the halo signify? Why do you suppose Leo stands at least three heads taller than the other figure in the picture, Warinus, the abbot of St. Arnulf of Metz? What is Leo doing with his right hand? With his left hand he holds a little church (symbol of a real one) that is being presented to him by Warinus. What did the artist intend to convey about the relationship of this church to papal power? *(Burgerbibliothek Bern, Cod. 292, f. 73r.)*

Calabria, "and in the future, with the help of God and St. Peter," even Sicily to Roger's brother, even though none of this was the pope's to give. The papacy was particularly keen to see the Normans conquer Sicily. Once part of the Byzantine Empire, the island had been taken by Muslims in the tenth century; now the pope hoped to bring it under Catholic control. Thus, the pope's desires to convert Sicily nicely meshed with the territorial ambitions of Roger and his brother. The agreement of 1058 included a promise that all of the churches of southern Italy and Sicily would be placed under papal jurisdiction. No wonder that when the Investiture Conflict broke out, Roger and his army played an important role as a military arm of the papacy.

The popes were in fact becoming more and more involved in military enterprises. They participated in wars of expansion in Spain, for example. There, political fragmentation into small and weak *taifas* (see page 285) made al-Andalus fair game for the Christians to the north. Slowly the idea of the ***reconquista***, the Christian "reconquest" of Spain from the Muslims, took shape, fed by religious fervor as well as by greed for land and power. In 1063, just before a major battle, the pope issued an indulgence to all who would fight—a grant that, if it did not go so far as to forgive all sins, nevertheless lifted the knights' obligation to do penance. (For such penances, see Document: "Penances for the Invaders," page 338).

The Gregorian Reform and the Investiture Conflict, 1075–1122

Historians associate the papal reform movement above all with Gregory VII (r. 1073–1085) and therefore often call it the **Gregorian reform**. Beginning as a lowly Roman cleric named Hildebrand, with the job of administering the papal estates, he rose slowly through the hierarchy. A passionate advocate of papal primacy (the theory that the pope was the head of the church), Gregory was not afraid to clash head-on with **Henry IV** (r. 1056–1106), ruler of Germany and much of Italy, over leadership of the church. As his views crystallized, Gregory came to see an anointed ruler as just another layman who had no right to meddle in church affairs. At the time, this was an astonishing position, given the traditional religious and spiritual roles associated with kings and emperors.

Gregory was, and remains, an extraordinarily controversial figure. He certainly thought that as pope he was acting as the vicar, or representative, of St. Peter on earth. Describing himself, he declared, "I have labored with all my power that Holy Church, the bride of God, our Lady Mother, might come again to her own splendor and might remain free, pure, and Catholic." He thought that the reforms he advocated and the upheavals he precipitated were necessary to free the church from the evil rulers of

---

reconquista **(ray con KEE stuh):** The collective name for the wars waged by the Christian princes of Spain against the Muslim-ruled regions to their south. These wars were considered holy, akin to the crusades.

Gregorian reform: The papal movement for church reform associated with Gregory VII (r. 1073–1085); its ideals included ending three practices: the purchase of church offices, clerical marriage, and lay investiture.

Henry IV: King of Germany (r. 1056–1106), crowned emperor in 1084. From 1075 until his death, he was embroiled in the Investiture Conflict with Pope Gregory VII.

the world. But his great nemesis, Henry IV, had a very different view of Gregory. He considered him an ambitious and evil man who "seduced the world far and wide and stained the Church with the blood of her sons." Not surprisingly, modern historians are only a bit less divided in their assessment of Gregory. Few deny his sincerity and deep religious devotion, but many speak of his pride, ambition, and single-mindedness. He was not an easy man.

Henry IV was less complex. He was raised in the traditions of his father, Henry III, a pious church reformer who considered it part of his duty to appoint bishops and even popes to ensure the well-being of both church and state. Henry IV believed that he and his bishops—who were, at the same time, his most valuable supporters and administrators—were the rightful leaders of the church. He had no intention of allowing the pope to become head of the church; he didn't see that new religious ideals were sweeping away the old traditions. (See Contrasting Views, page 324.)

The World of the Investiture Conflict, c. 1070–1122

The Investiture Conflict

The great confrontation between Gregory and Henry that historians call the **Investiture Conflict**[3] began in 1075 over the appointment of the archbishop of Milan and a few other Italian prelates. When Henry insisted on appointing these clergymen, Gregory admonished the king. Henry responded by calling on Gregory to step down as pope. In turn, Gregory called a synod that both excommunicated and suspended Henry from office:

> I deprive King Henry [IV], son of the emperor Henry [III], who has rebelled against [God's] Church with unheard-of audacity, of the government over the whole kingdom of Germany and Italy, and I release all Christian men from the allegiance which they have sworn or may swear to him, and I forbid anyone to serve him as king.

It was this last part of the decree that made it politically explosive; it authorized everyone in Henry's kingdom to rebel against him. Henry's enemies, mostly German princes (as German aristocrats were called), now threatened to elect another king. They were motivated partly by religious sentiments, as many had established links with the papacy through their support of reformed monasteries, and partly by political opportunism, as they had chafed under the strong German king, who had tried to keep their power in check. Some bishops joined forces with Gregory's supporters. This was a great blow to royal power because Henry desperately needed the troops supplied by his churchmen.

Attacked from all sides, Henry traveled to intercept Gregory, who was journeying northward to visit the rebellious princes. In early 1077, king and pope met at a castle belonging to Matilda, countess of Tuscany, at Canossa, high in central Italy's snowy Apennine Mountains. Gregory remained inside the fortress there; Henry stood outside as a penitent, begging forgiveness. Henry's move was astute, for no priest could refuse absolution to a penitent; Gregory had to lift the excommunication and receive Henry back into the church. But Gregory now had the advantage of enjoying the king's humiliation before the majesty of the pope.

Although Henry was technically back in the church's fold, nothing of substance had been resolved. The princes elected an antiking (a king chosen illegally), and Henry and his supporters elected an antipope. From 1077 until 1122, papal and imperial armies and supporters waged intermittent war in both Germany and Italy.

Outcome of the Investiture Conflict

The Investiture Conflict was finally resolved long after Henry IV and Gregory VII had died. The **Concordat of Worms** of 1122 ended the fighting with a compromise. Henry V, the heir of Henry IV, gave up the right in the investiture ceremony to confer the ring and the pastoral

---

[3] This movement is also called the Investiture Controversy, Investiture Contest, or Investiture Struggle. The epithets all refer to the same thing: the disagreement and eventually war between the pope and the emperor over the right to invest churchmen in particular and power over the church hierarchy in general.

Investiture Conflict: The confrontation between Pope Gregory VII and Emperor Henry IV that began in 1075 over the appointment of prelates in some Italian cities and grew into a dispute over the nature of church leadership. It ended in 1122 with the Concordat of Worms.

Concordat of Worms: The agreement between pope and emperor in 1122 that ended the Investiture Conflict.

Matilda of Tuscany

How often is a woman the dominant figure in medieval art? In this illustration made around 1115, Matilda, countess of Tuscany, towers above the king (Henry IV) and upstages the abbot of Cluny (Hugh). Matilda was a key supporter of Pope Gregory VII. It was at her castle at Canossa that Henry IV did penance. The words underneath the picture emphasize Henry's abjection. They read: "The king begs the abbot and supplicates Matilda as well." *(Biblioteca Apostolica Vaticana, The Vatican, Italy/Flammarion/The Bridgeman Art Library International.)*

staff—symbols of spiritual power. But he retained, in Germany, the right to be present when bishops were elected. In effect, he would continue to have influence over those elections. In both Germany and Italy he also had the right to give the scepter to the churchman in a gesture meant to indicate the transfer of the temporal, or worldly, powers and possessions of the church—the lands by which it was supported.

Superficially, nothing much had changed; the Concordat of Worms ensured that secular rulers would continue to have a part in choosing and investing churchmen. In fact, however, few people would now claim that a king could act as head of the church. Just as the concordat broke the investiture ritual into two parts—one spiritual, with ring and staff, the other secular, with the scepter—so too it implied a new notion of kingship that separated it from priesthood. The Investiture Conflict did not produce the modern distinction between church and state—that would develop slowly—but it set the wheels in motion.

The most important changes brought about by the Investiture Conflict, however, were on the ground: the political landscape in both Italy and Germany was irrevocably transformed. In Germany, the princes consolidated their lands and their positions at the expense of royal power. In Italy, the emperor lost power to the cities. The northern and central Italian communes were formed in the crucible of the war between the pope and the emperor. In fierce communal struggles, city factions, often created by local grievances but claiming to fight on behalf of the papal or the imperial cause, created their own governing bodies. In the course of the twelfth century, these Italian cities became accustomed to self-government.

The Sweep of Reform

Church reform involved much more than the clash of popes, emperors, and their supporters. It penetrated into the daily lives of ordinary Christians, inspired new ways to think about church institutions such as the sacraments, brought about a new systemization of church law, changed the way the papacy operated, inspired new monastic orders dedicated to poverty, and led to the crusades.

New Emphasis on the Sacraments According to the Catholic church, the **sacraments** were the regular means by which God's heavenly grace infused mundane existence; they included rites such as baptism, the Eucharist (communion), and marriage. But this did not mean that Christians were clear about how many sacraments there were, how they worked, or even what their significance was. Eleventh-century church reformers began the process—which would continue into the thirteenth century—of emphasizing the importance of the sacraments and the special nature of the priest, whose chief role was to administer them.

Marriage, for example, became a sacrament only after the Gregorian reform. Before the twelfth century, priests had little to do with weddings, which were family affairs. After the twelfth century, however, priests were expected to consecrate marriages. When the knight Arnulf of Ardres got married in 1194, for example, priests blessed and sprinkled him and his wife with holy water as the couple lay in their nuptial bed. Churchmen also began to assume jurisdiction over marital disputes, not simply in cases involving royalty (as they had always done) but also in those involving lesser aristocrats. Because the no-

---

sacraments: In the Catholic church, the institutionalized means by which God's heavenly grace is transmitted to Christians. Examples of sacraments include baptism, the Eucharist (communion), and marriage.

CONTRASTING VIEWS

Henry IV

Henry III was a church reformer in the old mold: he had ensured the well-being of the church by appointing excellent prelates. When he died in 1056, he left his six-year-old son, Henry IV, as his heir. Document 1 is a sympathetic account of the young king, whose minority gave many powerful groups in Germany a chance to exploit him. When he turned fifteen and was therefore no longer legally a minor, Henry freed himself from their grasp and began to restore royal power. This meant, in part, asserting his right to appoint bishops and archbishops, as he did in 1075 to the sees of Milan, Fermo, and Spoleto. In Document 2, Gregory VII scolds Henry for these appointments and demands that he heed the pope, or rather St. Peter, in whose place the pope stands. In Gregory's view, Henry was disobeying God. Henry's response to Gregory's scolding letter is in Document 3: there he portrays himself as the ordained of God and calls on Gregory to resign the papacy. Gregory reacted to this letter by excommunicating Henry, declaring him no longer king, and releasing all his subjects from their obedience to him. Suddenly Henry found himself nearly abandoned. To regain his position, he needed Gregory to lift the excommunication. In January 1077, Henry stood barefoot in the snow at Canossa, acting as a penitent. Document 4 describes that moment.

1. Anonymous Account of Henry's Minority

A biographer of Henry IV wrote this account shortly after the emperor's death in 1106. By then, the Investiture Conflict had raged for decades, and most people had taken sides. This biographer was on Henry's side.

But since immature age inspires too little fear, and while awe languishes, audacity increases, the boyish years of the king excited in many the spirit of crime. Therefore everyone strove to become equal to the one greater than him, or even greater, and the might of many increased through crime; nor was there any fear of the law, which had little authority under the young boy-king.

And so that they could do everything with more license, they first robbed of her child the mother [Empress Agnes, wife of Henry III] whose mature wisdom and grave habits they feared, pleading that it was dishonorable for the kingdom to be administered by a woman (although one may read of many queens who administered kingdoms with manly wisdom). But after the boy-king, once drawn away from the bosom of his mother, came into the hands of the princes to be raised, whatever they prescribed for him to do, he did like the boy he was. Whomever they wished, he exalted; whomever they wished, he set down; so that they may rightly be said not to have ministered to their king so much as to have given orders to him. When they dealt with the affairs of the kingdom, they took counsel not so much for the affairs of the kingdom as for their own; and in everything they did, it was their primary concern to put their own advantage above everything else. . . .

But when [at the age of fifteen] he passed into that measure of age and mind in which he could discern what was honorable, what shameful, what useful, and what was not, he reconsidered what he had done while led by the suggestion of the princes and condemned many things which he had done. And, having become his own judge, he changed those of his acts which were to be changed. He also prohibited wars, violence, and rapine; he strove to recall peace and justice, which had been expelled to restore neglected laws, and to check the license of crime.

Source: "The Life of the Emperor Henry IV" in *Imperial Lives and Letters of the Eleventh Century*, trans. Theodor E. Mommsen and Karl F. Morrison (New York: Columbia University Press, 2000), 106.

2. Gregory VII Admonishes Henry (1075)

Gregory had written letters to Henry before 1075, but this was the first one that scolded him. The issue was Henry's attempt to appoint prelates to three Italian sees (the seat, jurisdiction, or office of a bishop). Gregory complained that Henry's candidates were unknown and inappropriate. He did not yet object to royal investiture.

We marvel exceedingly that you have sent us so many devoted letters and displayed such humility by the spoken words of your legates . . . and yet in action showing yourself most bitterly hostile to the canons and apostolic decrees in those duties especially required by loyalty to the Church. Not to mention other cases, the way you have observed your promises in the Milan affair, made through your mother and through bishops, our colleagues, whom we sent to you, and what your intentions were in making them is evident to all. And now, heaping wounds upon wounds, you have handed over the sees of Fermo and Spoleto—if indeed a church may be given over by any human power—to persons entirely unknown to us, whereas it is not lawful to consecrate anyone except after probation and with due knowledge.

It would have been becoming to you, since you confess yourself to be a son of the Church, to give more respectful attention to the master of the Church, that is, to Peter, prince of the Apostles. To him, if you are of the Lord's flock, you have been committed for your pasture, since Christ said to him: "Peter, feed my sheep" (John 21:17), and again: "To thee are given the keys of Heaven, and whatsoever thou shalt bind on earth shall be bound in Heaven and whatsoever thou shalt loose on earth shall be loosed in Heaven" (Matt. 16:19). Now, while we, unworthy sinner that we are, stand in his place of power, still whatever you send to us, whether in writing or by word of mouth, he [Peter] himself receives, and while we read what is written or hear the voice of those who speak, he discerns with subtle insight from what spirit the message comes.

Source: *The Correspondence of Pope Gregory VII*, trans. Ephraim Emerton (New York: W. W. Norton, 1969), 87.

3. Henry's Response to Gregory's Admonition (early 1076)

A meeting called by Henry and attended by nobles and bishops in Germany produced two documents in response to Gregory's scolding letter: a harsh retort meant to be circulated in Germany as propaganda for Henry, and a gentler version to be sent to Gregory himself. Both called on Gregory to step down as pope. The harsh letter, part of which is printed here, makes clear Henry's exalted view of his own role in the church.

Henry, King not by usurpation, but by the pious ordination of God, to Hildebrand, now not Pope, but false monk:

You have deserved such a salutation as this because of the confusion you have wrought; for you left untouched no order of the Church which you could make a sharer of confusion instead of honor, of malediction instead of benediction.

For to discuss a few outstanding points among many: Not only have you dared to touch the rectors of the holy Church—the archbishops, the bishops, and the priests, anointed of the Lord as they are—but you have trodden them under foot like slaves who know not what their lord may do. . . .

And we, indeed, bore with all these abuses, since we were eager to preserve the honor of the Apostolic See. But you construed our humility as fear, and so you were emboldened to rise up even against the royal power itself, granted to us by God. You dared to threaten to take the kingship away from us—as though we had received the kingship from you, as though kingship and empire were in your hand and not in the hand of God.

Our Lord, Jesus Christ, has called us to kingship, but has not called you to the priesthood.

Source: *Imperial Lives and Letters of the Eleventh Century*, trans. Theodor E. Mommsen and Karl F. Morrison (New York: Columbia University Press, 2000), 150.

4. Lampert of Hersfeld Describes Henry at Canossa (c. 1077)

Lampert of Hersfeld was a German monk whose monastery, Hersfeld, supported Henry. However, in his Annales, *from which this excerpt is taken, Lampert emphasizes how weak the king had become as he awaited the pope's absolution at Canossa.*

Leaving Speyer a few days before Christmas with his wife and infant son, the journey [to Canossa] was begun. That noble man [Henry IV] left the realm accompanied by not a soul from Germany save one notable neither for his lineage nor his wealth. Since he needed resources for so long a journey, Henry sought aid from many men he had often benefited when his kingdom was intact. There were very few, however, who relieved his necessity to any extent, moved either by memory of past favors or by the present spectacle of human events. And thus the king descended suddenly from the height of glory and greatest wealth to such distress and calamity! . . .

Henry came [to the walls of Canossa], as he was ordered to, and since that castle had been enclosed by a triple wall, having been received within the space of the second wall, his band of retainers having been left outside, his regalia laid aside, displaying nothing pertaining to the kingship, showing no ceremony, with bare feet and fasting from morning until vespers, he waited for the decision of the Roman Pontiff. He did this a second day, and then a third. On the fourth day, finally having been admitted into the pope's presence, after many opinions were voiced on each side, he was finally absolved from the excommunication under these conditions: that on the day and at the place designated by the pope, he promptly call a general council of the German princes . . . [and there] it would be decided according to ecclesiastical law whether Henry should retain the realm.

Source: Maureen C. Miller, ed., *Power and the Holy in the Age of the Investiture Conflict: A Brief History with Documents* (Boston: Bedford/St. Martin's, 2005), 91–97.

Questions to Consider

1. **How important was Henry's minority in weakening royal authority?**
2. **Why did Gregory consider Henry impious when he appointed churchmen?**
3. **Why did Henry consider Gregory a false pope?**
4. **If the events at Canossa led to the king's absolution, why did Lampert and others consider it a sign of royal weakness?**

bility kept its inheritance intact by transferring it to a single male heir, the heir's marriage was crucial to the family strategy. The clergy's prohibition of marriage partners as distant as seventh cousins (since marriage between cousins was considered incest) had the potential to control dynastic alliances.

At the same time, churchmen began to stress the sanctity of marriage. Hugh of St. Victor, a twelfth-century scholar, dwelled on the sacramental meaning of marriage:

> Can you find anything else in marriage except conjugal society which makes it sacred and by which you can assert that it is holy? . . . Each shall be to the other as a same self in all sincere love, all careful solicitude, every kindness of affection, in constant compassion, unflagging consolation, and faithful devotedness.

In other words, Hugh saw marriage as a matter of Christian love.

The reformers also proclaimed the special importance of the sacrament of the Eucharist (holy communion), received by eating the wafer (the body of Christ) and drinking wine (the blood of Christ) during the Mass. Gregory VII called the Mass "the greatest thing in the Christian religion." No layman, regardless of how powerful, and no woman of any class or status at all could perform anything equal to it, for the Mass was the key to salvation.

Clerical Celibacy The new emphasis on the sacraments, which were now more thoroughly and carefully defined, along with the desire to set priests clearly apart from the laity (all who were not part of the clergy) led to vigorous enforcement of an old element of church discipline: the celibacy of priests. The demand for a celibate clergy had far-reaching significance for the history of the church. It distanced western clerics even further from their eastern Orthodox counterparts (who did not practice celibacy), exacerbating the east-west church schism of 1054. It also broke with traditional local practices, as clerical marriage was customary in some places. Gregorian reformers exhorted every cleric from the humble parish priest to the exalted bishop to refrain from marriage or to abandon his wife. Naturally, many churchmen resisted. The historian Orderic Vitalis (1075–c. 1142) reported that one zealous archbishop in Normandy

> fulfilled his duties as metropolitan [bishop] with courage and thoroughness, continually striving to separate immoral priests from their mistresses [and wives]: on one occasion when he forbade them to keep concubines he was stoned out of the synod.

Undaunted, the reformers persisted, and in 1123 the pope proclaimed all clerical marriages invalid. With its new power, the papacy was largely able to enforce the rule.

The Papal Monarchy Some of the new powers of the papacy rested on the consolidation and imposition of canon, or church, law. These laws had begun simply as rules determined at church councils. Later they were supplemented with papal declarations. Churchmen had made several attempts to gather together and organize these laws before the eleventh century. But the proliferation of rules during that century, along with the desire of Gregory's followers to clarify church law as they saw it, made a systematic collection of rules even more necessary. Around 1140, a teacher of canon law named Gratian achieved this goal with a landmark synthesis, the *Decretum*. Collecting nearly two thousand passages from the decrees of popes and councils as well as the writings of the church fathers, Gratian intended to demonstrate their essential agreement. In fact, his book's original title was *Harmony of Discordant Canons*. If he found any discord in his sources, Gratian usually imposed the harmony himself by arguing that the passages dealt with different situations. A bit later, another legal scholar revised and expanded the *Decretum*, adding ancient Roman law to the mix.

Even while Gratian was writing, the papal curia (government), centered in Rome, resembled a court of law with its own collection agency. In the course of the eleventh and twelfth centuries, the papacy developed a bureaucracy to hear cases, such as disputed elections of bishops. Churchmen not involved in litigation went to the papal curia for other purposes as well: to petition for privileges for their monasteries or to be consecrated by the pope. All these services were expensive, requiring lawyers, judges, hearing officers, notaries, and collectors. The lands owned by the papacy were not sufficient to support the growing cost of its administrative apparatus, and the petitioners and litigants themselves had to pay, a practice they resented. A satire written about 1100, in the style of the Gospels, made bitter fun of papal greed:

> There came to the court a certain wealthy clerk, fat and thick, and gross. . . . He first gave to the dispenser, second to the treasurer, third to the cardinals. But they thought among themselves that they should receive more. The Lord Pope, hearing that his cardinals had received many gifts, was sick, nigh unto death. But the rich man sent to him a couch of gold and silver and immediately he was made whole. Then the Lord Pope called his cardinals and ministers to him and said to them: "Brethren, look, lest anyone deceive you

with vain words. For I have given you an example: as I have grasped, so you grasp also."

The pope, with his law courts, bureaucracy, and financial apparatus, had become a monarch.

New Monastic Orders of Poverty

Like the popes, the monks of Cluny and other Benedictine monasteries were reformers. Unlike the popes, they spent nearly their entire day in large and magnificently outfitted churches singing a long and complex liturgy consisting of Masses, prayers, and psalms. These "black monks"—so called because they dyed their robes black—reached the height of their popularity in the eleventh century. Their monasteries often housed hundreds of monks, though convents for Benedictine nuns were usually less populated. Cluny was one of the largest monasteries, with some four hundred brothers in the mid-eleventh century.

In the twelfth century, the black monks' lifestyle came under attack by groups seeking a religious life of poverty. They considered the opulence of a huge and gorgeous monastery like Cluny to be a sign of greed rather than honor. (See the illustration below.) The Carthusian order founded by Bruno of Cologne in the 1080s was one such group. Each monk took a vow of silence and lived as a hermit in his own small hut. Monks occasionally joined others for prayer in a common prayer room, or oratory. When not engaged in prayer or meditation, the Carthusians copied manuscripts. They considered this task part of their religious vocation, a way to preach God's word with their hands rather than their mouths. The Carthusian order grew slowly. Each monastery was limited to only twelve monks, the number of the Apostles.

The Cistercians, by contrast, expanded rapidly. Their guiding spirit was **St. Bernard** (c. 1090–1153), who arrived at the Burgundian monastery of Cîteaux (in Latin, Cistercium, hence the name of the monks) in 1112 along with about thirty friends and relatives. Soon he became abbot of Clairvaux, one of a cluster of Cistercian monasteries in Burgundy. By the mid-twelfth century, more than three hundred monasteries spread throughout Europe were following what they took to be the customs of Cîteaux. Nuns too—as eager as monks to live the life of simplicity and poverty that they believed the Apostles had enjoyed and endured—adopted Cistercian cus-

St. Bernard: The most important Cistercian abbot (early twelfth century) and the chief preacher of the Second Crusade.

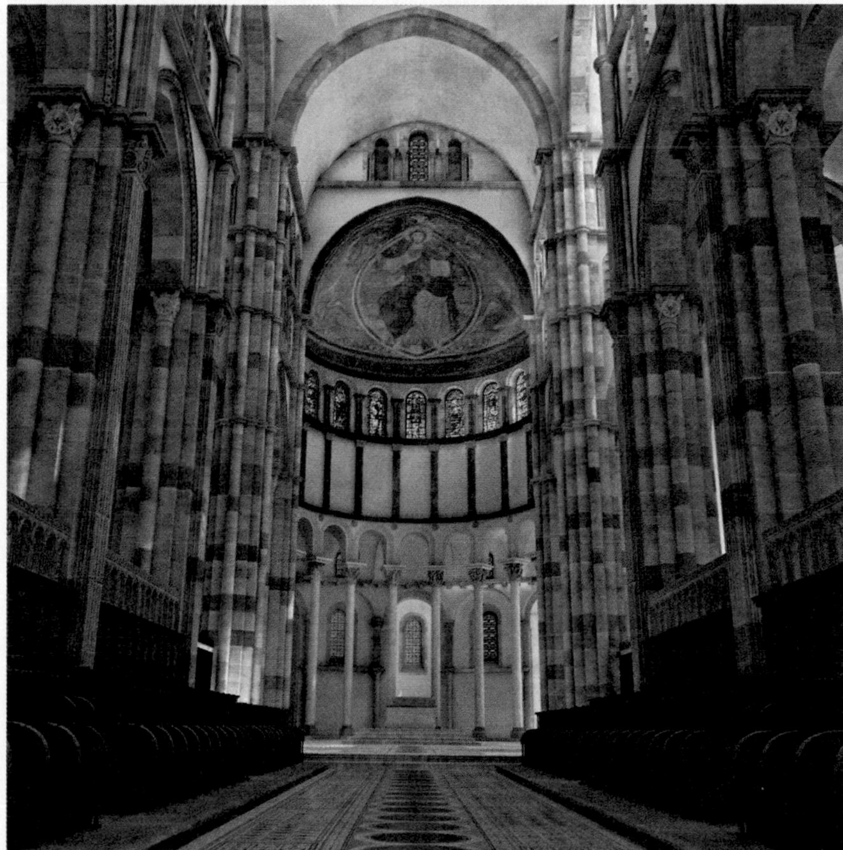

Cluny (twelfth century)
The church of the monastery of Cluny, built under the abbot Hugh (who appears with Matilda on page 323), was the largest and grandest in all of Christendom in the twelfth century. In its cavernous stone building, the sounds of the liturgy echoed throughout the day. Unfortunately, much of the church was torn down after the French Revolution in 1789. The depiction here is an image of the interior that relies on the best archaeological insights combined with computer-enhanced technologies. *(Major Ecclésia © on-situ/Arts et Metiers ParisTech/Centre des Monuments Nationaux—2010.)*

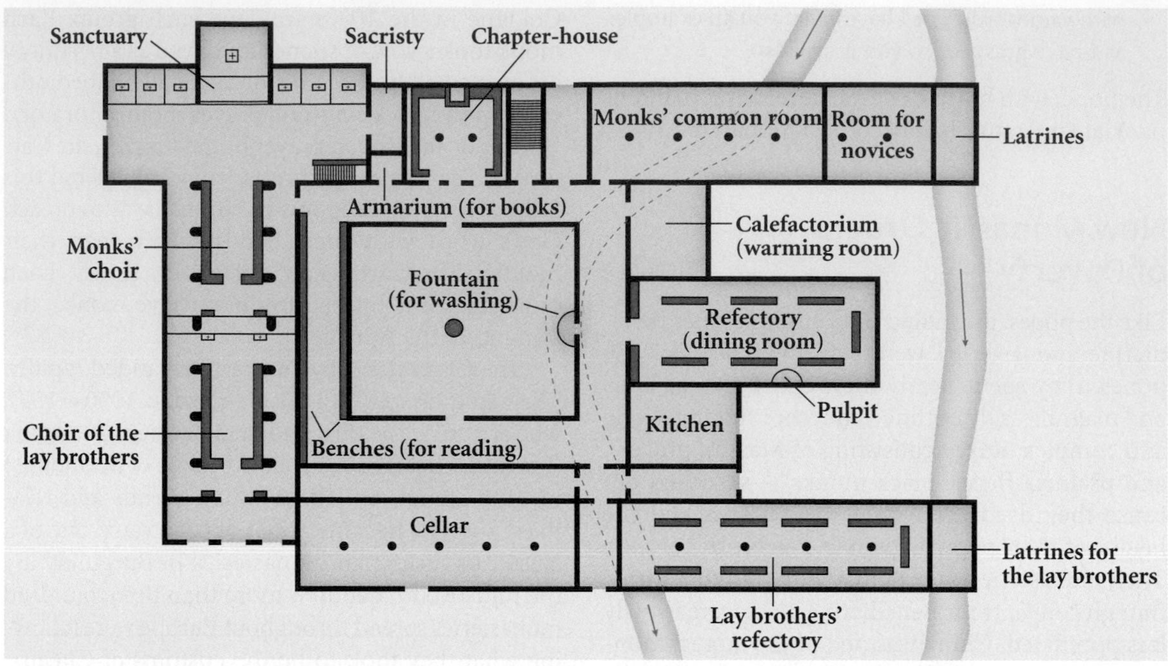

FIGURE 10.1 Floor Plan of a Cistercian Monastery
Cistercian monasteries seldom deviated much from this standard plan, which perfectly suited their dual nature—one half for the lay brothers, who worked in the fields, the other half for the monks, who performed the devotions. This plan shows the first floor. Above were the dormitories. The lay brothers slept above their cellar and refectory, the monks above their chapter house, common room, and room for novices. No one had a private bedroom, just as the rule of St. Benedict prescribed. *(Adapted from Wolfgang Braunfels,* Monasteries of Western Europe *[Princeton, NJ: Princeton University Press, 1972], 75.)*

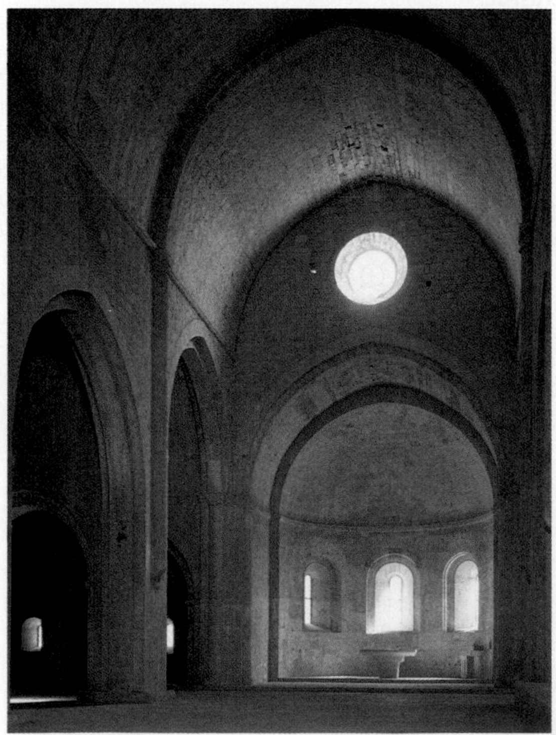

Le Thoronet
Le Thoronet, a Cistercian monastery founded in 1136, boasted a small and plain church devoid of any wall paintings, ornaments, or sculpture. Nothing was to interfere with the contemplative inner lives of the monks worshipping there. *(Giraudon/The Bridgeman Art Library International.)*

toms. By the end of the twelfth century, the Cistercians were an order: all of their houses followed rules determined at the General Chapter, a meeting at which the abbots met to hammer out legislation.

Although they held up the rule of St. Benedict as the foundation of their monastic life, the Cistercians created a lifestyle all their own, largely governed by the goal of simplicity. Rejecting even the conceit of blackening their robes, they left them undyed (hence their nickname, the "white monks"). Cistercian monasteries were remarkably standardized. As shown in Figure 10.1, there were two halves to each monastery: the eastern half was for the monks, and the western half was for the lay brothers. The lay brothers did the hard manual labor necessary to keep the other monks—the "choir" monks—free to worship.

Cistercian churches reflected the order's emphasis on poverty. The churches were small, made of smoothly hewn, undecorated stone. Wall paintings and sculpture were prohibited. St. Bernard wrote a scathing attack on the sort of decorative sculpture shown in this chapter's opening illustration, the frieze depicting Dives and Lazarus:

> What is the point of ridiculous monstrosities in the cloister where there are brethren reading—I mean those extraordinary deformed beauties

> and beautiful deformities? What are those lascivious apes doing, those fierce lions, monstrous centaurs, half-men and spotted leopards? . . . It is more diverting to decipher marble than the text before you.

The Cistercians had no such visual diversions, but the simplicity of their buildings and of their clothing also had its beauty. Illuminated by the pure white light that came through clear glass windows, Cistercian churches like the one at Le Thoronet (see the illustration on page 328) were bright, cool, and serene.

True to this emphasis on purity, the communal liturgy of the Cistercians was shorn of the many additions found in the houses of the black monks. The white monks dedicated themselves to monastic administration as well as to private prayer and contemplation. Each house had large and highly organized farms and grazing lands called granges. Cistercian monks spent much of their time managing their estates and flocks, both of which were yielding handsome profits by the end of the twelfth century. Although they reacted against the wealth of the commercial revolution, the Cistercians became part of it, and managerial expertise was an integral part of their monastic life.

At the same time, the Cistercians emphasized a spirituality of intense personal emotion. St. Bernard said:

> Often enough when we approach the altar to pray our hearts are dry and lukewarm. But if we persevere, there comes an unexpected infusion of grace, our breast expands as it were, and our interior is filled with an overflowing love.

The Cistercians emphasized not only human emotion but also Christ's and Mary's humanity. While pilgrims continued to stream to the tombs and reliquaries of saints, the Cistercians dedicated all their churches to the Virgin Mary (for whom they had no relics) because for them she signified the model of a loving mother. Indeed, the Cistercians regularly used maternal imagery (as St. Bernard's description invoking the metaphor of a flowing breast illustrates) to describe the nurturing care that Jesus provided to humans. The Cistercian Jesus was approachable, human, protective, even mothering.

Many who were not members of the Cistercian order held similar views of God; their spirituality signaled wider changes. For example, around 1099, St. Anselm wrote a theological treatise entitled *Why God Became Man*, arguing that since man had sinned, only a sinless man could redeem him. St. Anselm's work represented a new theological emphasis on the redemptive power of human charity, including that of Jesus as a human being. As Anselm was writing, the crusaders were heading for the very place of Christ's crucifixion, making his humanity more real and powerful to people who walked in the holy "place of God's humiliation and our redemption," as one chronicler put it. Yet this new stress on the loving bonds that tied Christians together also led to the persecution of non-Christians, especially Jews and Muslims.

REVIEW QUESTION What were the causes and consequences of the Gregorian reform?

The Crusades

The crusades were the culmination of two separate historical movements: pilgrimages and holy wars. As pilgrimages to the Holy Land, the place where Jesus had lived and died, they drew on a long tradition of making pious voyages to sacred shrines to petition for help or cure. The relics of Jesus's crucifixion in Jerusalem, and even the region around it, attracted pilgrims long before the First Crusade was called in 1095.

As holy wars blessed by church leaders, the crusades had a prehistory. The Truce of God, begun in the late tenth century, depended on knights ready to go to battle to uphold it. The Normans' war against Sicily had the pope's approval. Already, as we have seen, the battle of 1063 in the reconquista of Spain was fought with a papal indulgence.

European crusaders established states in the Middle East that lasted for two hundred years. A tiny strip of crusader states along the eastern Mediterranean survived—perilously—until 1291. Although the crusades ultimately failed, in the sense that the crusaders did not succeed in permanently retaining the Holy Land for Christendom, they were a pivotal episode in Western civilization, marking the first stage of European overseas expansion.

Calling the Crusade

The events leading to the First Crusade began with the entry of the Seljuk Turks into Asia Minor (Map 10.2). As noted in Chapter 9, the Muslim world had splintered into numerous small states during the 900s. Weakened by disunity, those states were easy prey for the fierce Seljuk Turks—Sunni Muslims inspired by religious zeal to take over both Islamic and infidel (unbeliever) regions. By the 1050s, they had captured Baghdad, subjugated the Abbasid caliphate, and begun to threaten Byzantium.

The difficulties the Byzantine emperor Romanus IV had in pulling together an army to attack the Turks reveal how weak his position had become. Unable to muster Byzantine troops—which

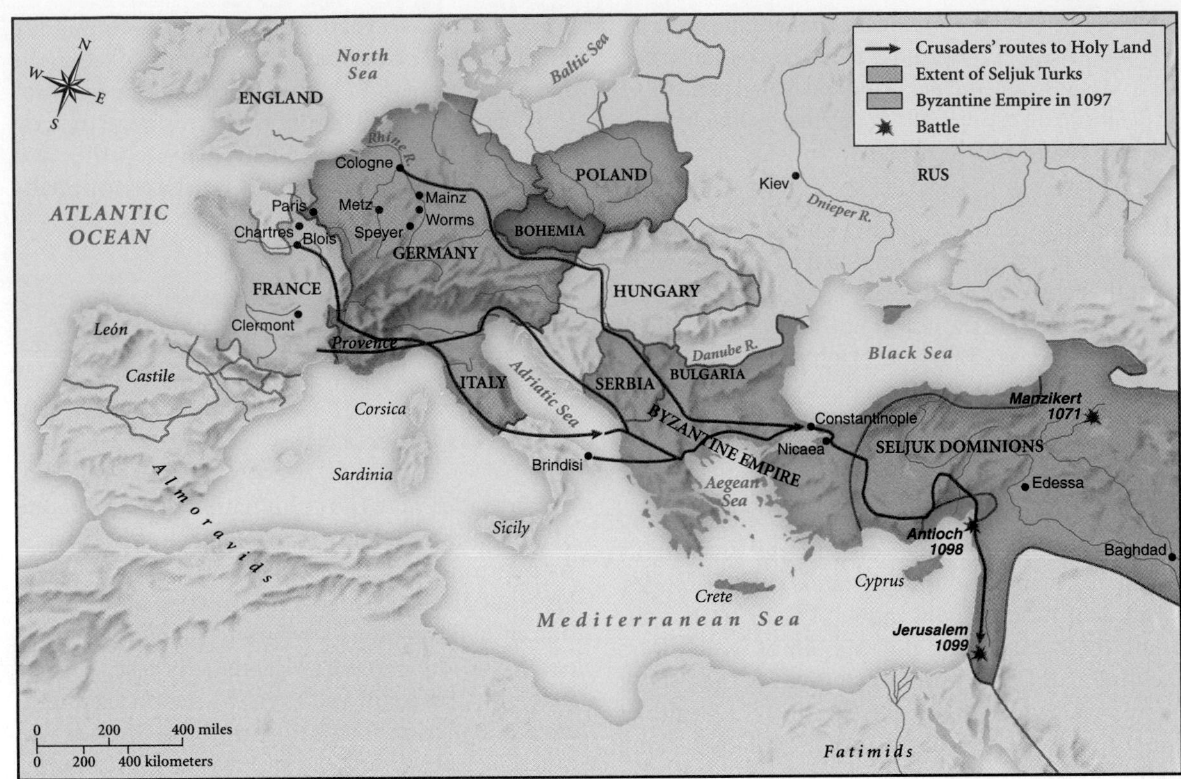

MAP 10.2 The First Crusade, 1096–1099

The First Crusade was a major military undertaking that required organization, movement over both land and sea, and enormous resources. Four main groups were responsible for the conquest of Jerusalem. One began at Cologne, in northern Germany; a second group started out from Blois, in France; the third originated just to the west of Provence; and the fourth launched ships from Brindisi, at the heel of Italy. All joined up at Constantinople, where their leaders negotiated with Alexius Comnenus for help and supplies in return for a pledge of vassalage to the emperor.

were either busy defending their own districts or were under the control of *dynatoi* (see page 280) wary of sending support to the emperor—Romanus had to rely on a mercenary army made up of Normans, Franks, Slavs, and even Turks. This motley force met the Seljuks at Manzikert in what is today eastern Turkey. The battle was a disaster for Romanus: the Seljuks routed the Byzantine army and captured the emperor. The battle of Manzikert (1071) marked the end of Byzantine domination in the region.

Gradually settling in Asia Minor, the Turks extended their control across the empire and beyond, all the way to Jerusalem, which had been under Muslim control since the seventh century and most recently had been under the rule of the Shi'ite Fatimids. In 1095, the Byzantine emperor **Alexius I (Alexius Comnenus)** (r. 1081–1118) appealed for help to Pope Urban II, hoping to get new mercenary troops for a fresh offensive.

Urban II (r. 1088–1099) chose to interpret the request in his own way. He made a long voyage through France, consecrating churches, cemeteries, and other holy places. In 1095 he attended a church council in Clermont; after the council had finished the usual business of proclaiming the Truce of God and condemning simony among the clergy, Urban moved outside the church and addressed an already excited throng:

> Oh, race of Franks, race from across the mountains, race beloved and chosen by God. . . . Let hatred depart from among you, let your quarrels end, let wars cease, and let all dissensions and controversies slumber. Enter upon the road to the Holy Sepulcher; wrest that land from the wicked race, and subject it to yourselves.

Alexius I (Alexius Comnenus): The Byzantine emperor (r. 1081–1118) whose leadership marked a new triumph of the *dynatoi*. His request to Pope Urban II for troops to fight the Turks turned into the First Crusade.

Urban II: The pope (r. 1088–1099) responsible for calling the First Crusade in 1095.

The crowd reportedly responded with one voice: "God wills it." Urban offered all who made the difficult trek to the Holy Land an indulgence—the forgiveness of sins. The pains of the trip would substitute for ordinary penance.

Historians remain divided over Urban's motives for his massive call to arms. Certainly he hoped to win Christian control of the Holy Land. He was also anxious to fulfill the goals of the Truce of God by turning the entire "race of Franks" into a peace militia dedicated to holy purposes, an army of God. Just as the Truce of God mobilized whole communities to fight against anyone who broke the truce, so the First Crusade mobilized armed groups sworn to free the Holy Land of its enemies. Finally, Urban's call placed the papacy in a new position of leadership, one that complemented in a military arena the position the popes had gained in the church hierarchy.

Inspired by local preachers, men and women, rich and poor, young and old, laypeople and clerics heeded Urban's call to go on the **First Crusade** (1096–1099). Between 60,000 and 100,000 people abandoned their homes and braved the rough journey to the Holy Land to fight for God. They also went to gain land; this was especially true of younger sons of aristocrats, who because of the tradition of primogeniture (whereby the oldest son alone was heir) could not expect an inheritance. Some knights went because they were obligated to follow their lord. Others hoped for plunder.

Although women were discouraged from going, some crusaders were accompanied by their wives. Other women went as servants; a few may have been fighters. Children and old people, not able to fight, made the cords for siege engines—giant machines used to hurl stones at enemy fortifications. As Christians undertook more crusades during the twelfth century, the transport and supply of these armies became a lucrative business for the commercial classes of maritime Italian cities such as Venice, strategically located on the route eastward.

The First Crusade

The armies of the First Crusade were organized not as one military force but rather as separate militias, each commanded by a different individual. Fulcher of Chartres (c. 1059–c. 1127), an eyewitness, reported: "There grew armies of innumerable people coming together from everywhere. Thus a countless multitude speaking many languages and coming from many regions was to be seen." Fulcher was describing the armies led by nobles and authorized by the pope. There were also irregular armies with their own agendas; most were soon decimated. The main forces, despite numerous difficulties, managed to achieve their goal to take Jerusalem.

First Crusade: The massive armed pilgrimage to Jerusalem that lasted from 1096 to 1099. It resulted in the massacre of Jews in the Rhineland (1095), the sack of Jerusalem (1099), and the setting up of the crusader states.

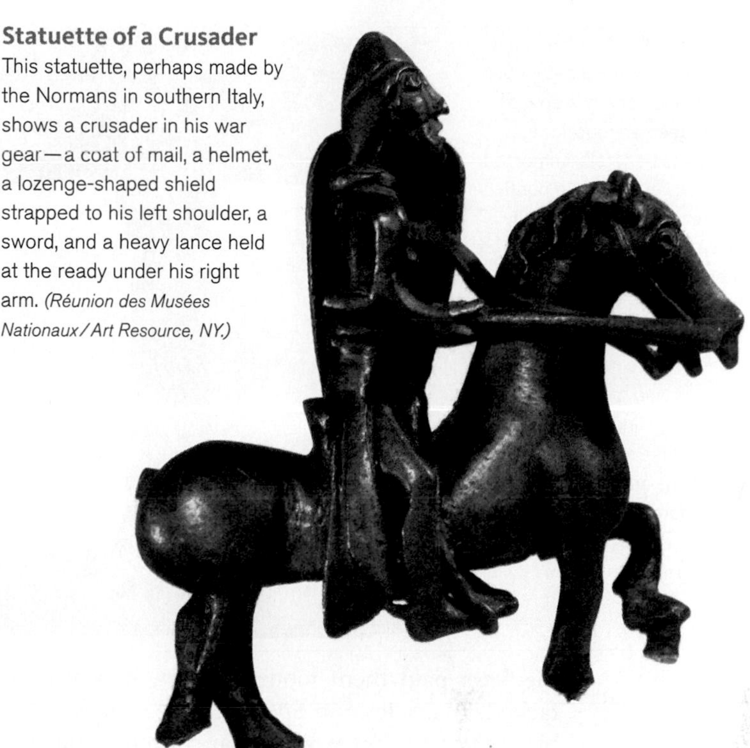

Statuette of a Crusader
This statuette, perhaps made by the Normans in southern Italy, shows a crusader in his war gear—a coat of mail, a helmet, a lozenge-shaped shield strapped to his left shoulder, a sword, and a heavy lance held at the ready under his right arm. *(Réunion des Musées Nationaux/Art Resource, NY.)*

Attacking the Jews A number of armed groups, not heeding the pope's official departure date in August, took off in late spring. Historians have called these loosely affiliated groups the People's (or Peasants') Crusade. Some of the participants were peasants, others knights. Inspired by the fiery and charismatic orator Peter the Hermit and others like him, they took off for the Holy Land via the Rhineland. This unlikely route was no mistake: the crusaders took it to kill Jews. By 1095, three cities of the Rhineland—Speyer, Worms, and Mainz—had especially large and flourishing Jewish populations. (See the illustrations on pages 315 and 332.) They had long-established relationships with the local bishops, and in 1090 Emperor Henry IV had granted the Jews of Speyer and Worms a privilege of special protection.

It was against such Jewish communities that the People's Crusade—joined by local nobles, knights, and townspeople—vented its fury. As one commentator put it, the crusaders considered it ridiculous to attack Muslims when other infidels lived in their own backyards: "That's doing our work backward." The Rhineland Jews faced either forced conversion or death. Some of their persecutors relented when

Window from a Mikvah
A mikvah is a ritual bathhouse. Within each one is a pool of water deep enough for a person to be totally immersed. The mikvah is used in purification rituals, most typically when Jewish women purify themselves in the pool after their menstrual period. This mikvah window at Speyer was carved by the same stonemasons who made the Speyer Cathedral windows, attesting to the close relations between Christians and Jews in that city before the attacks of the First Crusade. *(Historisches Museum der Pfalz, Speyer.)*

the Jews paid them money; others, however, attacked. Many Jews in Speyer found refuge in the bishop's castle, but at Worms and Mainz hundreds were massacred. Similar pogroms—systematic persecutions of the Jews—took place a half century later, when the preaching of the Second Crusade led to new attacks on the Jews.

Miserable as it was to die, Jews believed, it was glorious to be a martyr. The Rhineland Jews met their persecutors with uncustomary fervor, preferring to kill themselves and their children rather than be polluted by the enemy's sword. A new kind of Hebrew literature was created, celebrating the "beautiful death" of those who died in this way:

> Youths like saplings pleaded with their fathers:
> "Hurry! Hasten to do our Maker's Will!
> The One God is our portion and destiny
> Our days are over, our end has come."

Taking the Holy Land Some members of the People's Crusade died or dropped out; the rest continued through Hungary to Constantinople, where Alexius Comnenus promptly shipped them across the Bosporus—most to meet their death in Asia Minor. In the autumn, the main armies of the crusaders began to arrive, their leaders squabbling with Alexius as their expectations and his clashed. Eventually, they promised that whatever they conquered they would return to the Byzantine Empire. They didn't keep the promise.

Considering them too weak to bother with, the Turks spared the arriving crusaders, who made their way south to the Seljuk capital at Nicaea. At first, their armies were uncoordinated and their food supplies uncertain, but soon the crusaders organized themselves, setting up a "council of princes" that included their best leaders, while the Byzantines supplied food at a nearby port. The crusaders managed to defeat a Turkish army that attacked from nearby; then, surrounding Nicaea and besieging it with catapults and other war machines, they took the city on June 18, 1097, dutifully handing it over to Alexius.

Gradually, the crusaders left the Byzantine orbit. Most of them went toward Antioch, which stood in the way of their conquest of Jerusalem, but one led his followers to Edessa, where they took over the city and its outlying area, creating the first of the crusader states: the county of Edessa. Meanwhile, the main body of crusaders remained stymied for eight months before the thick and heavily fortified walls of Antioch. Then, in a surprise turnaround, they entered the town and found themselves besieged by Turks from the outside. Their mood grim, they rallied when a peasant named Peter Bartholomew reported that he had seen buried in the main church in Antioch the Holy Lance that had pierced Christ's body. (Antioch had a flourishing Christian population even under Muslim rule.) After a night of feverish digging, the crusaders found an object they believed to be the Holy Lance and prepared for a decisive confrontation with the Turks. "Then with God's right hand fighting with us," wrote Fulcher of Chartres, "we forced them to drive together to flee, and to leave their camps with everything in them."

From Antioch, it was only a short march to Jerusalem. But disputes among the leaders delayed that next step for over a year. One crusader claimed Antioch. Another eventually took charge—provisionally—of the expedition to Jerusalem. Quarrels among Muslim rulers eased his way, and an alliance with one of them allowed free passage through what would have been enemy territory. In early June 1099, a large force of crusaders amassed before the walls of Jerusalem and set to work building siege engines—some an astonishing three stories high. In mid-July they attacked, breached the walls, and entered the city. "Now that our men had possession of the walls and towers, wonderful sights were to be seen," wrote Raymond d'Aguiliers, a priest serving one of the crusade leaders. He continued:

> Some of our men (and this was the more merciful) cut off the heads of their enemies; others shot them with arrows, so that they fell from the towers; others tortured them longer by casting them into the flames. Piles of heads, hands, and

> feet were to be seen in the streets of the city. . . . In the Temple and porch of Solomon, men rode in blood up to their knees and bridle reins. Indeed, it was a just and splendid judgment of God that this place should be filled with the blood of the unbelievers, since it had suffered so long from their blasphemies.

The Crusader States

The main objective of the First Crusade—to wrest the Holy Land from the Muslims and subject it to Christian rule—had now been accomplished. The leaders of the expedition did not give the conquered territories to Alexius but held onto them instead. By 1109 they had carved out several tiny states in the Holy Land.

Because the crusader states were created by conquest, they were treated as lordships. The rulers granted fiefs to their own vassals, and some of these men in turn gave portions of their holdings as fiefs to their own vassals. Many other vassals simply lived in the households of their lords. Since most Europeans went home after the First Crusade, the rulers who remained learned to coexist with the indigenous population, which included Muslims, Jews, and Greek Orthodox Christians (see "New Sources, New Perspectives," page 334). They encouraged a lively trade at their ports, visited by merchants from Italy, Byzantium, and Islamic cities.

The main concerns of these rulers, however, were military. They set up castles and recruited knights from Europe. So organized for war was this society that it produced a new and militant kind of monasticism: the Knights Templar. The Templars vowed themselves to poverty and chastity. But unlike monks, the Templars, whose name came from their living quarters in the area of the former Jewish Temple at Jerusalem, devoted themselves to warfare. Their first mission to protect the pilgrimage routes from Palestine to Jerusalem—soon diversified. They manned the town garrisons of the crusader states, and they transported money from Europe to the Holy Land. In this way, the Order of the Templars became enormously wealthy (even though individual monks owned nothing), with branch "banks" in major cities across Europe.

The Disastrous Second Crusade

The presence of the Knights Templar did not prevent the Seljuks from taking the county of Edessa in 1144. This was the beginning of the slow but steady shrinking of the crusader states, and it sparked the Second Crusade (1147–1149). Called by Pope Eugenius III (r. 1145–1153), it attracted, for the first time, ruling monarchs to the cause: Louis VII of France and Emperor Conrad III in Germany. (The First Crusade had been led by counts and dukes.) St. Bernard, the charismatic and influential Cistercian abbot, was its tireless preacher. But Bernard and the pope were equally interested in other ventures. Eugenius supported Alfonso VI of Castile in his bid to continue the reconquista of Spain. He also encouraged German nobles to turn their interest in crusading not toward the Holy Land but rather northeastward—to conquer the pagans on the Baltic coast. St. Bernard inspired Flemings and Germans to attack the Portuguese city of Lisbon, aiding the king of Portugal in his own bid to expand into Muslim territory.

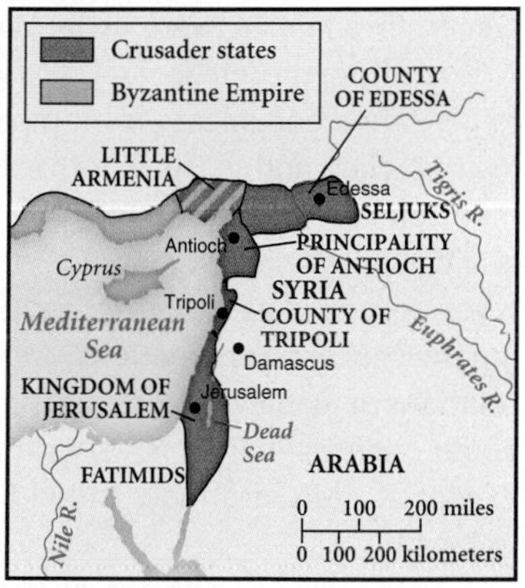

The Crusader States in 1109

Little organization or planning went into the Second Crusade. The emperor at Byzantium was hardly involved. Louis VII and Conrad had no coordinated strategy, and after Conrad had crossed the Bosporus to Asia Minor, it was too late for Louis to beg him to wait. As a chronicler of the crusade remarked, "Those whose common will had undertaken a common task should also use a common plan of action."

In fact, the Germans themselves had no clear plan, breaking into two groups that went their separate ways. All the armies—both French and German—were badly hurt by Turkish attacks. Furthermore, they largely acted at cross-purposes with the Christian rulers still in the Holy Land.

At last the leaders met at Acre and agreed to storm Damascus, which was under Muslim control and a thorn in the side of the Christian king of Jerusalem. On July 24, 1148, they were on the city's outskirts, but, encountering a stiff defense, they abandoned the attack after five days, suffering many losses as they retreated. The crusade was over.

The Second Crusade had one decisive outcome: it led Louis VII to divorce his wife, Eleanor, the heiress of Aquitaine. He was already primed to do this, since she had provided him with a daughter but no son. During the crusade, on which she accompanied her husband, he came to suspect her of infidelity, and after she gave birth to yet another daughter, their marriage was "dissolved" by the pope—that is, found to have been uncanonical in the first place. Eleanor promptly married Henry, count of Anjou and duke of Normandy. This marriage had far-reaching consequences, as we shall see, when Henry became King Henry II of England in 1154.

NEW SOURCES, NEW PERSPECTIVES

The Cairo Geniza

What do historians know about the daily life of ordinary people in the Middle Ages? Generally speaking, very little. We have writings from the intellectual elite and administrative documents from monasteries, churches, and courts. But these rarely mention ordinary folk, and if they do, it is always from the standpoint of those who are not ordinary themselves. Glimpsing the concerns, occupations, and family relations of medieval people as they went about their daily lives is very difficult—except at old Cairo (now called Fustat), in Egypt.

Cairo is exceptional because of a cache of unusual sources that were discovered in the *geniza* ("depository") of the Jewish synagogue near the city. Because their writings might include the name of God, members of the Jewish community left everything that they wrote, including their notes, letters, and even shopping lists, in the geniza to await ceremonial burial. Cairo was not the only place where this was the practice. But by chance at Cairo, the papers were left untouched in the depository and not buried. In 1890, when the synagogue was remodeled, workers tore down the walls of the geniza and discovered literally heaps of documents.

Many of these documents were purchased by American and English collectors and ended up in libraries in New York, Philadelphia, and Cambridge, England, where they remain. As is often the case in historical research, the questions that scholars ask are just as important as the sources themselves. At first, historians did not ask what the documents could tell them about everyday life. They wanted to know how to transcribe and read them; they wanted to study the evolution of their handwriting (a discipline called paleography). They also needed to organize the material. Dispersed among various libraries, the documents were a hodgepodge of lists, books, pages, and fragments. For example, the first page of a personal letter might be in one library, the second page in a completely different location. For decades, scholars were busy simply transcribing the documents with a view to printing and publishing their contents. Not until 1964 was a bibliography of these published materials made available.

Only then, when they knew where to find the sources and how to piece them together, did historians, most notably S. D. Goitein, begin to work through the papers for their historical interest. What Goitein learned through the remains of the geniza amplified historians' understanding of the everyday life of much of the Mediterranean world. He discovered a cosmopolitan community occupied with trade, schooling, marriages, divorces, poetry, litigation—all the common issues and activities of a middle-class society. For example, some documents showed that middle-class Jewish women disposed of their own property and that widows often reared and educated their children on their own.

More recently, Mark R. Cohen has looked at the underclass—the poor and needy—represented in the geniza documents. He has discovered workers down on their luck, starving children, and refugees in need of aid. At moments of crisis, these people wrote letters appealing for help. These were private messages, usually addressed to wealthier individuals or a small group: "I have been earning a livelihood, just managing to get by," wrote a man named Yahya sometime around 1100 to a hoped-for benefactor. He continued:

> I have responsibility for children and a family and an old mother advanced in years and blind. I incurred losses because of debts owed to Muslims in Alexandria. I remained in hiding. . . . Unable to go out, I began watching my children and old mother starve. . . . I heard that your excellency has a heart for his fellow Jews and is a generous person, who acts to receive reward from God and seeks to do good works, so I throw myself before God and you to help me.

In the last few years, the Friedberg Genizah Project (FGP) has begun digitizing, transcribing, and posting on the Web all of the geniza documents along with an exhaustive bibliography. A demo is readily available online at http://www.genizah.org/.

So think twice the next time you throw away a piece of paper. If a historian of the year 3000 were to read your notes, lists, or letters, what would he or she learn about your culture?

Questions to Consider

1. **What do the documents in the geniza tell us about Muslim as well as Jewish life in medieval Cairo?**
2. **What new questions might historians explore with the geniza documents?**
3. **How might digitization and Web access change the questions that historians ask?**

Further Reading

Cohen, Mark R. *The Voice of the Poor in the Middle Ages: An Anthology of Documents from the Cairo Geniza.* 2005.

Goitein, S. D. *A Mediterranean Society: The Jewish Communities of the Arab World as Portrayed in the Documents of the Cairo Geniza.* 6 vols. 1967–1983.

http://www.genizah.org/

Source: Quote is from Mark R. Cohen, *The Voice of the Poor in the Middle Ages: An Anthology of Documents from the Cairo Geniza* (Princeton: Princeton University Press, 2005), 22–23.

The Long-Term Impact of the Crusades

The success of the First Crusade was a mirage. The European toehold in the Middle East could not last. Numerous new crusades were called, and eight major ones were fought between the first in 1096 and the last at the end of the thirteenth century. But most Europeans were not willing to commit the vast resources and personnel that would have been necessary to maintain the crusader states, which fell to the Muslims permanently in 1291. In Europe, the crusades to the Holy Land became a sort of myth—an elusive goal that receded before more pressing ventures nearer to home. Yet they inspired far-flung expeditions like Columbus's in 1492. Although the crusades stimulated trade a bit, especially enhancing the prosperity of Italian cities like Venice, the commercial revolution would have happened without them. On the other hand, modern taxation systems may well have been stimulated by the machinery of revenue collection used to finance the crusades.

In the Middle East, the crusades worsened—but did not cause—Islamic disunity. Initially, the Muslims were perplexed by Europeans meddling in a region that had had only peripheral importance to them as a place of pilgrimage. Before the crusades, Muslims had a complex relationship with the Christians in their midst—taxing but not persecuting them, allowing their churches to stand and be used, permitting pilgrims into Jerusalem to visit the holy sites of Christ's life and death. In many ways, the split between Shi'ite and Sunni Muslims was more serious than the rift between Muslims and Christians. The crusades, and especially the conquest of Jerusalem, which was extraordinarily brutal, shocked and dismayed Muslims: "We have mingled blood with flowing tears," wrote one of their poets, "and there is no room left in us for pity."

REVIEW QUESTION How and why was the First Crusade a success, and how and why was it a failure?

The Revival of Monarchies

Even as the papacy was exercising its new authority by annulling marriages and calling crusades, kings and other rulers were, for the most part, enhancing and consolidating their own power. They created new ideologies and dusted off old theories to justify their hegemony (dominating influence), they

Alexius Comnenus Stands before Christ
In this twelfth-century manuscript illumination, the Byzantine emperor Alexius is shown in the presence of Christ. Note that both are almost exactly the same height, and the halos around their heads are the same size. What do you suppose is the significance of Christ sitting on a throne while the emperor is standing? Compare this image of the emperor with that on page 278. What statement is the twelfth-century artist making about the relationship between Christ and Alexius? *(© Biblioteca Apostolica Vaticana [Vatican Library] Vat. Lat.)*

hired officials to work for them, and they found vassals and churchmen to support them. Money gave them greater effectiveness, and the new commercial economy supplied them with increased revenues. The exception was the emperor in Germany, weakened by the Investiture Conflict.

Reconstructing the Empire at Byzantium

Ten years after the disastrous battle at Manzikert, Alexius Comnenus became the Byzantine emperor. He was an upstart—from a family of dynatoi—who saw the opportunity to seize the throne in a time of crisis. The people of Constantinople were suffering under a combination of high taxes and rising living costs. In addition, the empire was under attack on every side—from Normans in southern Italy, Seljuk Turks in Asia Minor, and new groups in the Balkans. (It is no wonder that an artist of his time hopefully pictured Alexius receiving Christ's blessing [see the illustration on page 335].) However, the emperor managed to avert the worst dangers. We have already seen how astutely he handled the crusaders who arrived on his doorstep.

To wage all the wars he had to fight, Alexius relied on mercenaries and allied dynatoi, armed and mounted like European knights and accompanied by their own troops. In return for their services, he gave these nobles lifetime possession of large imperial estates and their dependent peasants. Meanwhile, Alexius satisfied the urban elite by granting them new offices. He normally got on well with the patriarch and Byzantine clergy, for emperor and church depended on each other to suppress heresy and foster orthodoxy. The emperors of the Comnenian dynasty (1081–1185) thus gained in prestige and military might, but at the price of significant concessions to the nobility.

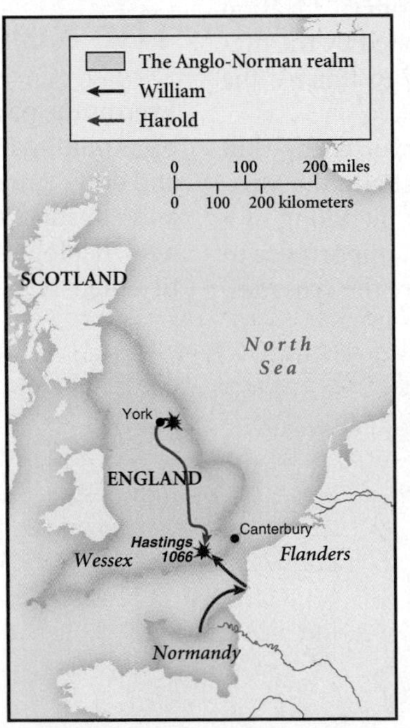

Norman Conquest of England, 1066

England under Norman Rule

In the twelfth century, the kings of England were the most powerful monarchs of Europe in large part because they ruled their whole kingdom by right of conquest. When the Anglo-Saxon king Edward the Confessor (r. 1042–1066) died childless in 1066, three main contenders vied for the English throne: Harold, earl of Wessex, an Englishman close to the king but not of royal blood; Harald Hardrada, the king of Norway, who had unsuccessfully attempted to conquer the Danes and now turned hopefully to England; and William, duke of Normandy, who claimed that Edward had promised him the throne fifteen years earlier. On his deathbed, Edward had named Harold of Wessex to succeed him, and a royal advisory committee that had the right to choose the king had confirmed the nomination.

The Norman Invasion, 1066 When he learned that Harold had been anointed and crowned, William (1027–1087) prepared for battle. Appealing to the pope, he received the banner of St. Peter and with this symbol of God's approval launched the invasion of England, filling his ships with warriors recruited from many parts of France. Just before William's invasion force landed, Harold defeated Harald Hardrada at Stamford Bridge, near York, in the north of England. When he heard of William's arrival, Harold turned his forces south, marching them 250 miles and picking up new soldiers along the way to meet the Normans.

The two armies clashed at the **battle of Hastings** on October 14, 1066, in one of history's rare decisive battles. Both armies had about seven or eight thousand men, Harold's in defensive position on a slope, William's attacking from below. All the men were crammed into a very small space as they began the fight. Most of Harold's men were on foot, armed with battle-axes and stones tied to sticks, which could be thrown with great force. William's army consisted of perhaps three thousand mounted knights, a thousand archers, and the rest infantry.

At first William's knights broke rank, frightened by the deadly battle-axes thrown by the English; but then some of the English also broke rank as they pursued the knights. William removed his helmet so his men would know him, rallying them to surround and cut down the English who had

---

battle of Hastings: The battle of 1066 that replaced the Anglo-Saxon king with a Norman one and thus tied England to the rest of Europe as never before.

broken away. Gradually Harold's troops were worn down, particularly by William's archers, whose arrows flew a hundred yards, much farther than an Englishman could throw his battle-ax. (Some of the archers are depicted on the lower margin of the Bayeux "Tapestry," below.) By dusk, King Harold was dead and his army utterly defeated. No other army gathered to oppose the successful claimant. (See Document, "Penances for the Invaders," page 338.)

Some people in England gladly supported William, considering his victory a verdict from God and hoping to gain a place in the new order themselves. But William — known to posterity as William the Conqueror — wanted to replace, not assimilate, the Anglo-Saxons. During William's reign, families from the continent almost totally supplanted the English aristocracy. Although the English peasantry remained — now with new lords — they were severely shaken. A twelfth-century historian claimed to record William's deathbed confession:

> I have persecuted [England's] native inhabitants beyond all reason. Whether gentle or simple, I have cruelly oppressed them; many I unjustly disinherited; innumerable multitudes, especially in the county of York, perished through me by famine or the sword.

Modern historians estimate that one out of five people in England died as a result of the Norman conquest and its immediate aftermath.

Institutions of Norman Kingship Although the Normans destroyed a generation of English men and women, they preserved and extended many Anglo-Saxon institutions. For example, the new kings used writs — terse written instructions — to communicate orders, and they retained the old administrative divisions and legal system of the shires. However, the Norman kings also drew from continental institutions. They set up a graded political hierarchy, culminating in the king, whose strength was reinforced by his castles and made visible to all. Because all of England was the king's by conquest, he could treat it as his booty; William kept about 20 percent of the land for himself and divided the rest, distributing it in large but scattered fiefs to a relatively small number of his barons and family members, lay and ecclesiastical, as well as to some lesser men, such as personal servants and soldiers. In turn, these men maintained their own vassals; they owed the king military service—and the service of a fixed number of their vassals—along with certain dues, such as reliefs (money paid upon inheriting a fief) and aids (payments made on important occasions).

Bayeux "Tapestry" (detail)

This famous "tapestry" is misnamed; it is really an embroidery, 230 feet long and 20 inches wide, created to tell the story of the Norman conquest of England from William's point of view. In this detail, the Norman archers are lined up along the lower margin, in a band below the armies. In the central band, the English warriors are on foot (the one at the farthest right holds a long battle-ax), while the Norman knights are on horseback. Who seems to be winning?

(Detail of the Bayeux Tapestry—eleventh century. By special permission of the City of Bayeux.)

DOCUMENT

Penances for the Invaders (1070)

Although William's conquest of England took place with papal blessing, nevertheless the church still insisted that the shedding of blood was a sin requiring penance. This explains why the indulgence (forgiveness of sins) offered by the pope to those who fought in Spain against the Muslims in 1063 or to those went on the First Crusade in 1096 was so important. Such an indulgence was not given to those who participated in the invasion of England. In this document the Norman bishops impose penances on those who participated in the invasion and conquest.

This is an institution of penance according to the decrees of the bishops of the Normans, confirmed by the authority of the pope through his legate Ermenfrid, bishop of [Sion, Switzerland]. It is to apply to those men whom William, duke of the Normans [commanded], and who gave him military service as their duty.

Anyone who knows that he killed a man in the great battle [of Hastings] must do penance for one year for each man that he killed.

Anyone who wounded a man, and does not know whether he killed him or not, must do penance for forty days for each man he thus struck (if he can remember the number), either continuously or at intervals.

Anyone who does not know the number of those he wounded or killed must, at the discretion of his bishop, do penance for one day in each week for the remainder of his life; or, if he can, let him redeem his sin by a perpetual alms [charity], either by building or by endowing a church.

The [churchmen] who fought, or who were armed for fighting, must do penance as if they had committed these sins in their own country, for they are forbidden by the canons [church law] to do battle.

Source: David C. Douglas and George W. Greenaway, eds., *English Historical Documents*, vol. 2: *1042–1189*, 2nd ed. (London: Routledge, 1981), 649.

Question to Consider

- **What impact would the imposition of penance have on the daily life of an ordinary warrior?**

Domesday Apart from the revenues and rights expected from the nobles, the king of England commanded the peasantry as well. Twenty years after his conquest, in 1086, William ordered a survey and census of England, popularly called Domesday because, like the reckoning Christians expected at doomsday, it provided facts that could not be appealed. It was the most extensive inventory of land, livestock, taxes, and population that had ever been compiled in Europe (see "Taking Measure," page 339). According to a contemporary observer, the king

> sent his men over all England into every shire and had them find out how many hundred hides [a measure of land] there were in the shire, or what land and cattle the king himself had in the country, or what dues he ought to receive every year from the shire. . . . So very narrowly did he have the survey to be made that there was not a single hide or yard of land, nor indeed . . . an ox or a cow or a pig left out.

The king's men conducted local surveys by consulting Anglo-Saxon tax lists and by taking testimony from local jurors, men sworn to answer a series of formal questions truthfully. From these inquests, scribes wrote voluminous reports filled with facts and statements from villagers, sheriffs, priests, and barons. These reports were then summarized in Domesday itself, a concise record of England's resources that supplied the king and his officials with information such as how much and what sort of land England had, who held it, and what revenues—including the lucrative Danegeld, which was now in effect a royal tax—could be expected from it.

England and the Continent The Norman conquest tied England to the languages, politics, institutions, and culture of the continent. Modern English is an amalgam of Anglo-Saxon and Norman French, the language the Normans spoke. English commerce was linked to the wool industry in Flanders. St. Anselm, the archbishop of Canterbury and author of *Why God Became Man*, was born in Italy and served as the abbot of a monastery in Normandy before crossing the Channel to England.

The barons of England retained their estates in Normandy and elsewhere, and the kings of England often spent more time on the continent than they did on the island. When William's son Henry I (r. 1100–1135) died without male heirs, civil war soon erupted: the throne of England was fought

TAKING MEASURE

English Livestock in 1086

Domesday provided important data for the English king in 1086, and those data remain important for historians today. Although relatively few Domesday records discuss livestock—apart from the oxen that pulled the plows—documents from East Anglia and the southwest are exceptions to this rule. They show that the great preponderance of animals raised was sheep. These were grazed on the marshes of both regions. Apart from milk and meat, sheep provided wool. It is no wonder that England soon became the great exporter of raw wool to textile manufacturers in Flanders.

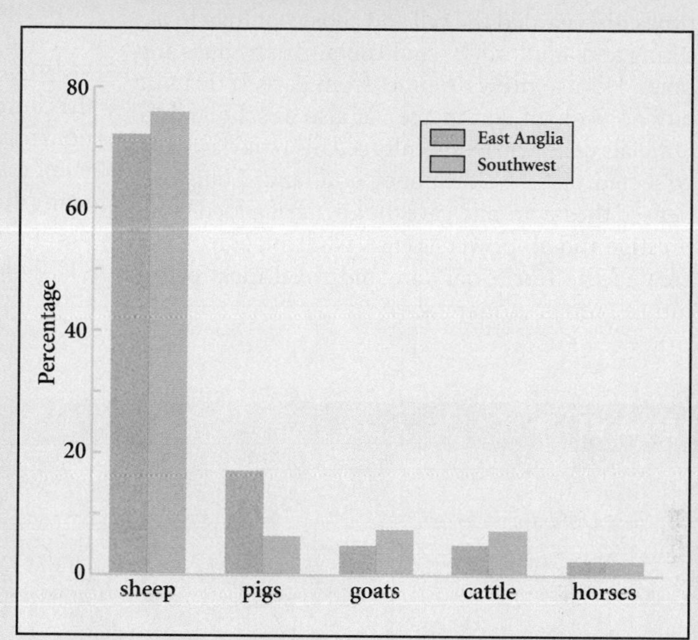

Source: Robert Bartlett, *England Under the Norman and Angevin Kings, 1075–1225* (Oxford: Clarendon Press, 2000), Fig. 7, 306).

Question to Consider

- **Why do you suppose the people of East Anglia concentrated on raising sheep instead of other types of livestock?**

over by two French counts, one married to Henry's daughter, the other to his sister. The story of England after 1066 was, in miniature, the story of Europe.

Praising the King of France

The twelfth-century kings of France were much less obviously powerful than their English and Byzantine counterparts. Yet they, too, took part in the monarchical revival. Louis VI, called Louis the Fat (r. 1108–1137), so heavy that he had to be hoisted onto his horse by a crane, was a tireless defender of royal power. We know a good deal about him and his reputation because a contemporary and close associate, Suger (1081–1152), abbot of Saint-Denis, wrote Louis's biography.

Although a churchman, Suger was a propagandist for his king. When Louis set about consolidating his rule in the Île-de-France, Suger portrayed him as a righteous hero. He thought that the king had rights over the French nobles because they were his vassals. He believed that the king had a religious role as the protector of the church and the poor. He saw Louis as another Charlemagne, a ruler for all society, not merely an overlord of the nobility. In Suger's view, Louis waged war to keep God's peace.

To be sure, the Gregorian reform had made its mark: Suger did not claim Louis was the head of the church. But he nevertheless emphasized the royal dignity and its importance to the papacy. When a pope arrived in France, Louis, not yet king, and his father, Philip I (r. 1052–1108), bowed low, but (Suger wrote), "the pope lifted them up and made them sit before him like devout sons of the apostles. In the manner of a wise man acting wisely, he conferred with them privately on the present condition of the church." In this passage Suger shows the pope in need of royal advice. Meanwhile, Suger stressed Louis's piety and active defense of the faith:

> Helped by his powerful band of armed men, or rather by the hand of God, he abruptly seized the castle [of Crécy] and captured its very strong tower as if it were simply the hut of a peasant. Having startled those criminals, he piously slaughtered the impious.

When Louis VI died in 1137, Suger's notion of the might and right of the king of France reflected reality in an extremely small area. Nevertheless, Louis laid the groundwork for the gradual extension of royal power in France. As the lord of vassals, the king could call on his men to aid him in times of war, though the most powerful among them sometimes disregarded the call and chose not to help. As a king and landlord, he could obtain many dues and taxes. He also drew revenues from Paris, a thriving city not only of commerce but also of scholarship. Officials called provosts enforced his royal laws and collected taxes. With money and land, Louis dispensed the favors and gave the gifts that added to his prestige and his power. Louis VI and Suger together created the territorial core and royal ideal of the future French monarchy.

Surviving as Emperor

As we have seen, Henry IV, king of Germany and emperor-to-be, began his reign as a child. Taken advantage of by powerful princes, he lost much of the power over the church and over Italy that his father had wielded. The Investiture Conflict thwarted his attempts to revive it: he could no longer control the church hierarchy in Germany and northern Italy, nor could he depend on bishops to work as government officials. The rebellion of the princes of Germany during the conflict was a symptom of his lack of support there, and the growing independence of the Italian cities ended his control over them and their revenues.

MAPPING THE WEST

Europe and the Mediterranean, c. 1150
A comparison with Mapping the West on page 307 reveals the major changes wrought during the century 1050–1150. England was politically tied to the continent with the Norman invasion of 1066. Soon the Seljuk Turks settled most of Anatolia, and the eastern wing of Byzantium was tightly wedged around Constantinople. At the end of the eleventh century, a narrow ribbon of crusader states was set up in the Holy Land. Meanwhile, Sicily and southern Italy came under Norman rule.

When Henry IV died and his son, Henry V (r. 1105–1125), came to the throne, the Investiture Conflict was still raging. Years of fruitless negotiations and numerous wars ended only in 1122 with the Concordat of Worms. This conceded considerable power within the church to the king, since he was understood to invest the bishops with their temporal goods—including the church buildings, estates, and taxes that belonged to them. But the concordat said nothing about the ruler's relations with the German princes or the Italian cities. When Henry V died childless in 1125, the position of the emperor was extremely uncertain.

When a German king died childless, the great bishops and princes would meet together to elect the next emperor. In 1125, numerous candidates were put forward; the winner, Lothar III (r. 1125–1137), was chosen largely because he was *not* the person designated by Henry V. Lothar had little time to reestablish royal control before he, too, died childless, leaving the princes to elect Conrad III. It was Conrad's nephew, Frederick Barbarossa, who would have a chance to find new sources of imperial power in a post-Gregorian age.

REVIEW QUESTION Which ruler—Alexius Comnenus, William the Conqueror, or Louis VI—was the strongest, which the feeblest, and why?

Conclusion

The commercial revolution and the building boom it spurred profoundly changed Europe. New trade, wealth, and business institutions became common in its thriving cities. Merchants and artisans became important people. Mutual and fraternal organizations like the guilds and communes expressed and reinforced the solidarity and economic interests of city dwellers. The countryside became reorganized for the market.

Sensitized by the commercial revolution to the corrupting effects of money and inspired by the model of Cluny, which seemed to "free the church from the world," reformers at the papal court began to demand a new and purified church. They were joined by ordinary laypeople, who feared that their immortal souls were jeopardized by priests who married or committed simony. Under Pope Gregory VII, the reform asserted a new vision of the church with the pope at the top. But too many people—especially rulers—depended on the old system, in which kings and bishops together kept the temporal and spiritual peace. Henry IV was particularly affected, and for him the Gregorian reform meant war: the Investiture Conflict. Although officially ended by a compromise, the conflict in fact greatly enhanced the power of the papacy and weakened that of the emperor.

The First Crusade was both cause and effect of the new power of the papacy. But the crusades were not just papal projects. They were fueled by enormous popular piety as well as the ambitions of European rulers. They resulted in a ribbon of crusader states along the Eastern Mediterranean that lasted until 1291.

Apart from the emperor, rulers in the period after the Investiture Conflict gained new prestige and, with the wealth of the commercial revolution, the ability to hire civil servants and impose their will as never before. The Norman ruler of England is a good example of the new-style king; William the Conqueror was interested not only in waging war but also in setting up the most efficient possible taxation system in times of peace. The successes of these rulers signaled a new era: the flowering of the Middle Ages.

FOR FURTHER EXPLORATION

- **For additional primary-source material from this period**, see *Sources of the Making of the West*, Fourth Edition.
- **For Web sites, images, and documents related to topics in this chapter**, visit *Make History* at bedfordstmartins.com/hunt.

Chapter 10 Review

Online Study Guide bedfordstmartins.com/hunt

Key Terms and People

In the grid below, identify the term or person and explain its historical significance. (To do this exercise online, go to bedfordstmartins.com/hunt.)

Term	Who or What & When	Why It Matters
commercial revolution (p. 312)		
guild (p. 316)		
apprentices (p. 316)		
journeymen/journeywomen (p. 316)		
masters (p. 316)		
capitalism (p. 317)		
commune (p. 318)		
simony (p. 320)		
lay investiture (p. 320)		
reconquista (p. 321)		
Gregorian reform (p. 321)		
Henry IV (p. 321)		
Investiture Conflict (p. 322)		
Concordat of Worms (p. 322)		
sacraments (p. 323)		
St. Bernard (p. 327)		
Alexius I (Alexius Comnenus) (p. 330)		
Urban II (p. 330)		
First Crusade (p. 331)		
battle of Hastings (p. 336)		

Review Questions

1. What new institutions resulted from the commercial revolution?
2. What were the causes and consequences of the Gregorian reform?
3. How and why was the First Crusade a success, and how and why was it a failure?
4. Which ruler—Alexius Comnenus, William the Conqueror, or Louis VI—was the strongest, which the feeblest, and why?

Making Connections

1. What were the similarities—and what were the differences—between the powers wielded by the Carolingian kings and those wielded by twelfth-century rulers?
2. In what ways was the movement for church reform a consequence of the commercial revolution?
3. How may the First Crusade be understood as a consequence of the Gregorian reform?

Important Events

Date	Event
910	Founding of Cluny
1049–1054	Papacy of Leo IX
1054	Schism between eastern and western churches begins
1066	Battle of Hastings: Norman conquest of England under William I
1071	Battle between Byzantines and Seljuk Turks at Manzikert
1073–1085	Papacy of Gregory VII
1077	Henry IV does penance before Gregory VII at Canossa; war breaks out
1086	Domesday survey
1095	Council of Clermont; Pope Urban II calls First Crusade
1096–1099	First Crusade
1097	Establishment of commune at Milan
1108–1137	Reign of Louis VI
1109	Establishment of the crusader states
1122	Concordat of Worms ends Investiture Conflict
c. 1140	Gratian's *Decretum* published
1147–1149	Second Crusade

- Consider three events: **Papacy of Gregory VII (1073–1085), Concordat of Worms ends Investiture Conflict (1122)**, and **Gratian's *Decretum* published (c. 1140)**. How did these events serve to enhance the power of the papacy? How might the papacy have looked different had any of these events not occurred?

SUGGESTED REFERENCES

Lopez was the first to recognize the importance of the commercial revolution, and Little makes crucial connections between the new commerce and religious reform. Miller's running narrative and primary sources provide the best introduction to the Investiture Conflict and its aftermath. Asbridge offers a vivid account of the crusades, while Nicholson gives a quick overview along with primary sources. The new western monarchies are well covered by Hallam, Fuhrmann, Waley, and Huscroft.

Akbari, Suzanne Conklin. *Idols in the East: European Representations of Islam and the Orient, 1100–1450*. 2009.

Asbridge, Thomas. *The Crusades: The Authoritative History of the War for the Holy Land*. 2010.

*Bayeux Tapestry: http://www.bayeuxtapestry.org.uk/Index.htm

Clanchy, Michael. *From Memory to Written Record: England 1066–1307*. 3rd ed. 2006.

Epstein, Steven A. *An Economic and Social History of Later Medieval Europe, 1000–1500*. 2009.

Fuhrmann, Horst. *Germany in the High Middle Ages, c. 1050–1200*. 2002.

Hallam, Elizabeth M., and Judith Everard. *Capetian France, 987–1328*. 2nd ed. 2001.

Huscroft, Richard. *The Norman Conquest: A New Introduction*. 2009.

*Kerak (crusader) castle: http://www.vkrp.org/studies/historical/town-castle

Little, Lester K. *Religious Poverty and the Profit Economy in Medieval Europe*. 1978.

Lopez, Robert S. *The Commercial Revolution of the Middle Ages, 950–1350*. 1976.

*———, and Irving W. Raymond. *Medieval Trade in the Mediterranean World*. 1955.

Melve, Leidulf. *Inventing the Public Sphere: The Public Debate during the Investiture Contest (c. 1030–1122)*. 2 vols. 2007.

*Miller, Maureen C. *Power and the Holy in the Age of the Investiture Conflict*. 2005.

Moore, Robert I. *The First European Revolution, c. 970–1215*. 2000.

Morris, Colin. *The Papal Monarchy: The Western Church from 1050 to 1250*. 1989.

Nicholson, Helen. *The Crusades*. 2004.

*Peters, Edward, ed. *The First Crusade: The Chronicle of Fulcher of Chartres and Other Source Materials*. 1971.

Robinson, Ian S. *Henry IV of Germany*. 2000.

*Suger. *The Deeds of Louis the Fat*. Trans. Richard C. Cusimano and John Moorhead. 1992.

Tyerman, Christopher. *God's War: A New History of the Crusades*. 2006.

Waley, Daniel. *The Italian City-Republics*. 1969.

*Primary source.

CHAPTER 11

The Flowering of the Middle Ages

1150–1215

In 1194 a raging fire burned most of the town of Chartres, in France—including its cathedral. Worried citizens feared that their most prized relic, the sacred tunic worn by the Virgin Mary when Christ was born, had gone up in flames as well. Had the Virgin abandoned the town? Suddenly the bishop and his clerics emerged from the cathedral crypt, carrying the sacred tunic, which had remained unharmed. Not only had the Virgin *not* abandoned her city, but she had made clear that she wanted a new and more magnificent cathedral to house her relic. The town dedicated itself to the task; the bishop, his clerics, and the town guilds all gave generously to pay for stonecutters, carvers, glaziers, countless other workmen, and a master builder. Donations poured in from the counts and dukes of France and from the royal house. The new cathedral was finished in an incredible twenty-six years—in an age when such churches usually took a century or more to build. Its vault soared 116 feet high; its length stretched more than one hundred yards, longer than a modern football field. Its western portals, which had been spared the flames, retained the sculptural decoration—carved around 1150—of the old church: three doorways surrounded and surmounted by figures that demonstrated the close relationship between the truths of divine wisdom, the French royal house, and the seven liberal arts—grammar, rhetoric, logic, arithmetic, geometry, music, and astronomy. The rest of the church was built in a new style: Gothic.

The rebuilt cathedral at Chartres sums up in stone the key features that characterized the period 1150–1215 and would mark the rest of the Middle Ages. Its Gothic style—with its high vault, flying buttresses, and enormous stained-glass windows—became the quintessential style of medieval architecture. The celebration of the liberal arts on one of its doorways mirrors the new schools that flourished in the twelfth century and culminated in the universities of the thirteenth. The twenty-four statues of Old Testament figures flanking its western portals were meant to prefigure the kings of France; they

Chartres Cathedral
Rebuilt after a fire in 1194, the cathedral of Chartres reconciled old and new. The three doorways of its west end (shown here) were remnants of the former church. But they were crowned by a rose window, a form newly in vogue. *(The Art Archive / Neil Setchfield.)*

demonstrate the extraordinary importance of powerful princes in this period, when monarchies and principalities ceased to be the personal creation of each ruler and became—with varying success in different places—permanent institutions, with professional bureaucratic staffs. The outpouring of popular support that culminated in the building of the cathedral is evidence of a vibrant vernacular (non-Latin-speaking) culture, which expressed itself not only in stone but in literature as well. Finally, the emphasis at Chartres on the divine wisdom echoes the age's fervor about Christian truths, a zeal that led to the creation of new religious movements even as it stoked the fires of the crusade movement.

CHAPTER FOCUS What tied together the cultural and political achievements of the late twelfth century?

New Schools and Churches

Key to the flowering of the Middle Ages was a new emphasis on learning and a new form of church architecture—the Gothic style. In many ways, these developments laid the foundation for other trends of the period. The princely bureaucrats who kept governments running efficiently even when the ruler himself was absent were literate men trained in the schools; theological speculation and debate, a product of the schools as well, fed the new religious fervor—and dissent. The new architectural style gave special luster to its rich patrons, the increasingly powerful rulers of the time. At the same time, without the support of these rulers, neither the new institutions of learning nor the new style of architecture would have had a chance to flourish.

The New Learning and the Rise of the University

Schools had been connected to monasteries and cathedrals since the Carolingian period. They served to train new recruits to become either monks or priests. Some were better endowed with books and masters (or teachers) than others; a few developed a reputation for a certain kind of theological approach or specialized in a particular branch of learning, such as literature, medicine, or law. By the end of the eleventh century, the best schools were generally in the larger cities: Reims, Paris, and Montpellier in France and Bologna in Italy.

Eager students sampled nearly all of them. The young monk Gilbert of Liège was typical: "Instilled with an insatiable thirst for learning, whenever he heard of somebody excelling in the arts, he rushed immediately to that place and drank whatever delightful potion he could draw from the master there," wrote a contemporary observer. For Gilbert and other students, a good lecture had the excitement of theater. Teachers at cathedral schools found themselves forced to find larger halls to accommodate the crush of students. Other teachers simply declared themselves "masters" and set up shop by renting a room. If they could prove their mettle in the classroom, they had no trouble finding paying students (see the illustration on page 347).

Wandering scholars like Gilbert were probably all male, and because schools hitherto had been the training ground for clergymen, all students were considered clerics, whether or not they had been ordained. Wandering became a way of life as the consolidation of castellanies, counties, and kingdoms made violence against travelers less frequent. Markets, taverns, and lodgings sprang up in urban centers to serve the needs of transients.

Using Latin, Europe's common language, students could drift from, say, Italy and Spain to France

1125 — 1150 — 1175

1139–1153 Civil War in England

1152–1190 Reign of Frederick Barbarossa

1154–1189 Reign of King Henry II

1176 Battle of Legnano

1180–1223 Reign of Philip II Augustus

1182–1226 Francis of Assisi

and England, wherever a noted master had settled. Students joined crusaders, pilgrims, and merchants to make the roads of Europe crowded indeed. What the students sought, above all, was knowledge of the seven liberal arts. Grammar, rhetoric, and logic (or dialectic) belonged to the beginning arts, the so-called trivium. Logic, involving the technical analysis of texts as well as the application and manipulation of mental constructs, was a transitional subject leading to the second part of the liberal arts, the quadrivium. This comprised four areas of study that we might call theoretical math and science: arithmetic, geometry, music (theory), and astronomy.

Of all these arts, logic appealed the most to twelfth-century students. Medieval students and masters were convinced that logic could bring together, order, and clarify every issue, even questions about the nature of God. St. Anselm, a major theologian as well as an abbot and archbishop, saw logic as a way for faith to "seek understanding." Emptying his mind of all ideas except that of God, he attempted to use the tools of logic to prove God's existence.

After studying the trivium, students went on to schools of medicine, theology, or law. Paris was renowned for theology, Montpellier for medicine, and Bologna for law. All of these schools trained men for jobs. The law schools, for example, taught men who went on to serve popes, bishops, kings, princes, and communes. Scholars interested in the quadrivium, by contrast, tended to pursue those studies outside of the normal school curriculum, and few gained their living through such pursuits. With books expensive and hard to find, lectures were the chief method of communication. Students committed the lectures to memory.

The remarkable renewal of scholarship in the twelfth century had an unexpected benefit: we know a great deal about the men involved in it—and a few of the women—because they wrote so much,

A Teacher and His Students
This miniature, which illustrates the hierarchical relationship between students and teachers in the twelfth century, appears in a late-twelfth-century manuscript of a commentary written by Gilbert (d. 1154), bishop of Poitiers. Some considered Gilbert's ideas in this commentary to be heretical. Nevertheless, Gilbert escaped condemnation. The artist asserts Gilbert's orthodoxy by depicting Gilbert with a halo, in the full dress of a bishop, speaking from his throne. Below Gilbert are three of his disciples, also with halos. The artist's positive view of Gilbert is echoed by modern historians, who recognize Gilbert as a pioneer in his approach to scriptural commentary. *(Erich Lessing/Art Resource, NY.)*

1189–1192 The Third Crusade

1202–1204 The Fourth Crusade

1204 Philip takes Normandy, Anjou, Maine, Touraine, and Poitou from John

1204 Fall of Constantinople to crusaders

1209–1229 Albigensian Crusade

1212 Battle of Las Navas de Tolosa; triumph of the reconquista

1214 Battle of Bouvines

1215 Magna Carta

1200 — 1225

often about themselves. Three important figures may serve to typify the scholars of the period: Abelard and Heloise, who were early examples of the new learning; and Peter the Chanter, the product of a slightly later period.

Abelard and Heloise | Born into a family of the lower nobility in Brittany and destined for a career as a warrior and lord, Peter Abelard (1079–1142) instead became one of the twelfth century's greatest thinkers. In his autobiographical account, *The Story of My Misfortunes*, Abelard described his shift from the life of the warrior to the life of the scholar:

> I was so carried away by my love of learning, that I renounced the glory of a soldier's life, made over my inheritance and rights of the eldest son to my brothers, and withdrew from the court of Mars [war] in order to kneel at the feet of Minerva [learning].

Arriving eventually at Paris, Abelard studied with one of the best-known teachers of his day, William of Champeaux. Soon he began to lecture and to gather students of his own. Around 1122–1123, he composed a textbook for his students, *Sic et Non* (*Yes and No*). It consisted of opposing positions on 156 subjects, among them "That God is one and the contrary," "That all are permitted to marry and the contrary," and "That it is permitted to kill men and the contrary." Arrayed on both sides of each question were passages from the Bible, the church fathers, the letters of popes, and other sources. The juxtaposition of authoritative sources was nothing new; what was new was calling attention to their contradictions. Abelard's students loved the challenge: they were eager to find the origins of the quotes, consider the context of each one carefully, and seek to reconcile the opposing sides by using the tools of logic.[1]

Abelard's fame as a teacher was such that a Parisian cleric named Fulbert gave Abelard room and board and engaged him as tutor for Heloise (c. 1100–c. 1163/1164), Fulbert's niece. Heloise is one of the few learned women of the period who left written traces. Brought up under Fulbert's guardianship, Heloise had been sent as a young girl to a convent school, where she received a thorough grounding in a literary education. Her uncle had hoped to continue her education at home by hiring Abelard. Abelard, however, became Heloise's lover as well as her tutor. "Our desires left no stage of love-making untried," wrote Abelard in his *Misfortunes*.

At first their love affair was secret. But Heloise became pregnant, and Abelard insisted they marry. They did so clandestinely to prevent damaging Abelard's career, for the new emphasis on clerical celibacy meant that Abelard's professional success and prestige would have been compromised if news of his marriage were made public. After they were married, Heloise and Abelard rarely saw one another; Abelard's sister took in their child, Astrolabe. Fulbert, suspecting that Abelard had abandoned his niece, plotted a cruel revenge against him: he paid a servant to castrate Abelard. Soon after, Abelard and Heloise entered separate monasteries.

For Heloise, separation from Abelard was a lasting blow. Although she became a successful abbess, carefully tending to the physical and spiritual needs of her nuns, she continued to call on Abelard for "renewal of strength." In a series of letters addressed to him, she poured out her feelings as "his handmaid, or rather his daughter, wife, or rather sister":

> You know, beloved, as the whole world knows, how much I have lost in you, how at one wretched stroke of fortune that supreme act of flagrant treachery robbed me of my very self in robbing me of you. . . . You alone have the power to make me sad, to bring me happiness or comfort.

For Abelard, however, the loss of Heloise and even his castration were not the worst disasters of his life. The heaviest blow came later, and it was directed at his intellect. He wrote a book that applied "human and logical reasons" (as he put it) to the Trinity; the book was condemned at the Council of Soissons in 1121, and he was forced to throw it, page by page, into the flames. Bitterly weeping at the injustice, Abelard lamented, "This open violence had come upon me only because of the purity of my intentions and love of our Faith, which had compelled me to write."

Peter the Chanter | By the second half of the twelfth century, masters like Abelard had become far more common. Many of them were at Paris, though others taught at Montpellier, Bologna, and Oxford in England. Peter the Chanter (d. 1197) was one of the most influential and prolific. Like Abelard, he came from a family of

---

[1]Abelard's students did not yet have the sophisticated rules of logic that had been worked out by the ancient philosopher Aristotle (see page 114). Until the middle of the twelfth century, very little of Aristotle's work was available in Europe because it had not been translated from Greek into Latin. By the end of the century, however, that situation had been rectified by translators who traveled to cities such as Córdoba in Spain and Syracuse in Sicily, where they found Islamic scholars who had already translated Aristotle's Greek into Arabic and could help them translate from Arabic to Latin.

the lower nobility. He studied at the cathedral school at Reims and was given the honorary title of chanter of Notre Dame in Paris in 1183. The chant, as we shall see, consisted of the music and words of the church liturgy. But Peter had his underlings work with the choir singers; he himself was far more interested in lecturing, disputing, and preaching.

Peter's lectures followed the pattern established by other masters. The lecture began with the recitation of a passage from an important text. The master then explained the text, giving his comments. He then "disputed"—mentioning other explanations and refuting them, often drawing on the logic of Aristotle, which by Peter's time was fully available. Sometimes masters held public debates on their interpretations.

Peter chose to comment on biblical texts. There were many ways to interpret the Bible. Some commentators chose to talk about it as an allegory; others preferred to stress its literal meaning. Peter was interested in the morals it taught. While most theology masters commented on just the Psalms and the New Testament, Peter taught all the books of the Bible. He wrote two important treatises and was particularly interested in exploring social issues and the sacrament of penance.

Peter also took the fruits of his classroom experience to the people. His sermons have not survived, but he inspired a whole group of men to preach in and around Paris. One of his protégés, for example, was renowned for turning prostitutes, usurers, and immoral clerics from their sinful ways.

Universities Around 1200, the pope wrote to the masters of theology, church law, and the liberal arts at Paris. He called them a *universitas*—the Latin word for a corporation or guild. The pope was right: universities were guilds. Like guilds, they evolved from earlier institutions (schools, in the case of universities; religious associations, in the case of craft guilds). Universities were schools that had become corporations and issued regulations for themselves. They had apprentices (students) and masters (schoolmasters). They issued rules to cover their trade (the acquisition and dissemination of knowledge). They had provisions for disciplining, testing, and housing students. They regulated the masters in similar detail. For example, masters at the University of Paris were required to wear long black gowns, follow a particular order in their lectures, and set the standards by which students could become masters themselves. The University of Bologna was unique in having two guilds, one of students and one of masters. At Bologna, the students participated in the appointment of masters and paid their salaries.

The University of Bologna was unusual because it was principally a school of law, where the students were often older men, well along in their careers and used to wielding power. The University of Paris, however, attracted younger students, drawn particularly by its renown in the liberal arts and theology. The universities of Salerno and Montpellier specialized in medicine. Oxford, once a sleepy town where students clustered around one or two masters, became a center of royal administration, and its university soon developed a reputation for teaching the liberal arts, theology, and—extraordinarily—science.

University curricula differed in content and duration. At the University of Paris in the early thirteenth century, for example, a student had to spend at least six years studying the liberal arts before he could begin to teach. If he wanted to continue his studies with theology, he had to attend lectures on the subject for at least another five years.

With few exceptions, masters and students were considered clerics. This had two important consequences: first, it meant that there were no university women, and second, it ensured that university men would be subject to church courts rather than to the secular jurisdiction of towns or lords. Many universities received generous privileges from popes and kings, who valued the services of scholars. Thus, for example, in 1200 the king of France promised that "neither our provost nor our judges shall lay hands on a student [at the University of Paris] for any offense whatever."

The combination of clerical status and special privileges made universities virtually self-governing corporations within the towns. This sometimes led to friction. For example, when a student at Oxford was suspected of killing his mistress and the townspeople tried to punish him, the masters protested by refusing to teach and leaving town. Incidents such as this explain why historians speak of the hostility between "town" and "gown." Yet, as in our own time, university towns depended on scholars to patronize local restaurants, shops, and hostels. Town and gown normally learned to negotiate with each other to their mutual advantage.

Architectural Style: From Romanesque to Gothic

While Peter the Chanter lectured at Notre Dame, the cathedral itself was going up around him—in Gothic style. At the time, this was a new architectural fashion, attempted only in the Île-de-France and nearby cities. It was associated with the luster of the Capetian kings of France. Elsewhere—in

Painted Vault
This fresco of Christ as ruler of the universe, his hand raised in a gesture of blessing, is one of many paintings in the Romanesque church of San Isidore de León, built in northwest Spain in the eleventh century. Surrounding Christ are the symbols of the four evangelists: the ox for Luke, the lion for Mark, the eagle for John, and the man for Matthew. *(The Art Archive / Real Collegiata San Isidoro León / Collection Dagli Orti.)*

France, Germany, Italy—the reigning style was Romanesque. But in the course of the thirteenth century Gothic style took Europe by storm, and by the fourteenth it was the quintessential cathedral style.

Romanesque Solidity

Romanesque is the term art historians use to describe the massive church buildings making up eleventh-century monasteries like Cluny. Heavy, serious, and solid, Romanesque churches were decorated with brightly colored wall paintings and sculpture. (See the illustration above.) The various parts of the church—the chapels in the *chevet*, or apse (the east end), for example—were handled as discrete units, with the forms of cubes, cones, and cylinders (Figure 11.1). Inventive sculptural reliefs, both inside and outside the church, enlivened these pristine geometrical forms. Emotional and sometimes frenzied, Romanesque sculpture depicted themes ranging from the beauty of Eve to the horrors of the Last Judgment. (See the frieze depicting Dives and Lazarus on page 310 for an example.)

Romanesque churches were above all houses for prayer, which was neither silent nor private. Prayer was sung in a musical style called plainchant, or Gregorian chant. Plainchant melodies were sung in unison and without instrumental accompaniment. Although rhythmically free, lacking a regular beat, chant's melodies ranged from extremely simple to highly ornate and embellished. By the twelfth century, a large repertoire of melodies had grown up, at first through oral composition and transmission and then, starting in the ninth century, in written notation. Echoing within the stone walls and the cavernous choirs, plainchant worked well in a Romanesque church.

Gilded reliquaries (where sacred relics were housed) and altars made of silver, precious gems, and pearls were considered the fitting accoutrements of worship in Romanesque churches. The prayer, decoration, and music complemented the gift economy of the period before the commercial revolution: wearing vestments of the finest materi-

---

Romanesque: An architectural style that flourished in Europe between about 1000 and 1150. It is characterized by solid, heavy forms and semicircular arches and vaults. Romanesque buildings were often decorated with fanciful sculpture and wall paintings.

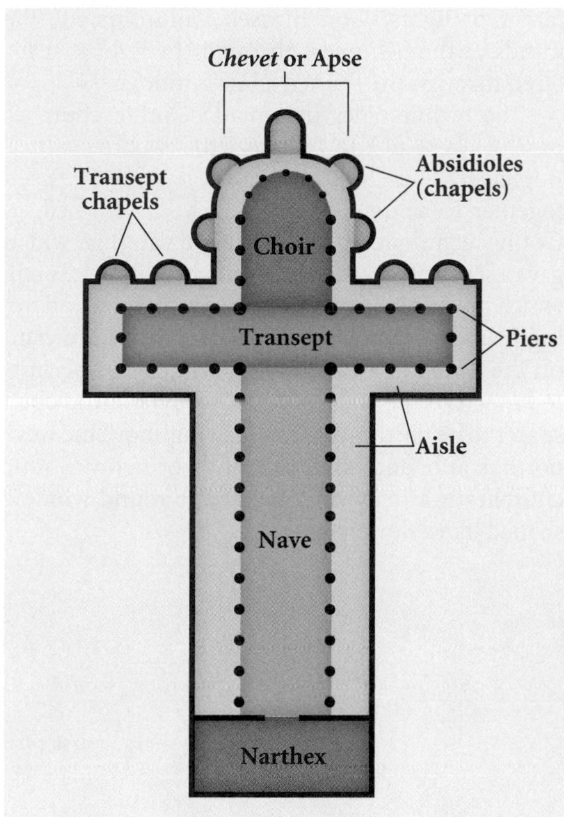

FIGURE 11.1 Floor Plan of a Romanesque Church
As churchgoers entered a Romanesque church, they passed through the narthex, an anteroom decorated with sculptures depicting scenes from the Bible. Walking through the portal of the narthex, they entered the church's nave, at the east end of which—just after the crossing of the transept and in front of the choir—was the altar. Walking down the nave, they passed tall, massive piers leading up to the vault (the ceiling) of the nave. Each of these piers was decorated with sculpture, and the walls were brightly painted. Romanesque churches were both lively and colorful (because of their decoration) and solemn and somber (because of their heavy stones and massive scale).

als, intoning the liturgy in the most splendid of churches, monks and priests offered up the gift of prayer to God, begging in return the gift of salvation of their souls and the souls of all the faithful.

Gothic Style **Gothic architecture**, to the contrary, was a style of the cities, reflecting the self-confidence and wealth of merchants, guildspeople, bishops, and kings.[2] Usually a cathedral—the bishop's principal church—rather than a monastic church, the Gothic church was the religious, social, and commercial focal point of a city. The style, popular from the twelfth to fifteenth centuries, was characterized by pointed arches, ribbed vaults, and stained-glass windows. The arches began as architectural motifs but were soon adopted in every art form. Gothic churches appealed to the senses the way that Peter the Chanter's lectures and disputations appealed to human logic and reason: both were designed to lead people to knowledge that

[2]*Gothic* is a modern term, originally meant to denigrate the style's "barbarity" but now used admiringly.

Gothic architecture: The style of architecture that started in the Île-de-France in the twelfth century and eventually became the quintessential cathedral style of the Middle Ages, characterized by pointed arches, ribbed vaults, and stained-glass windows.

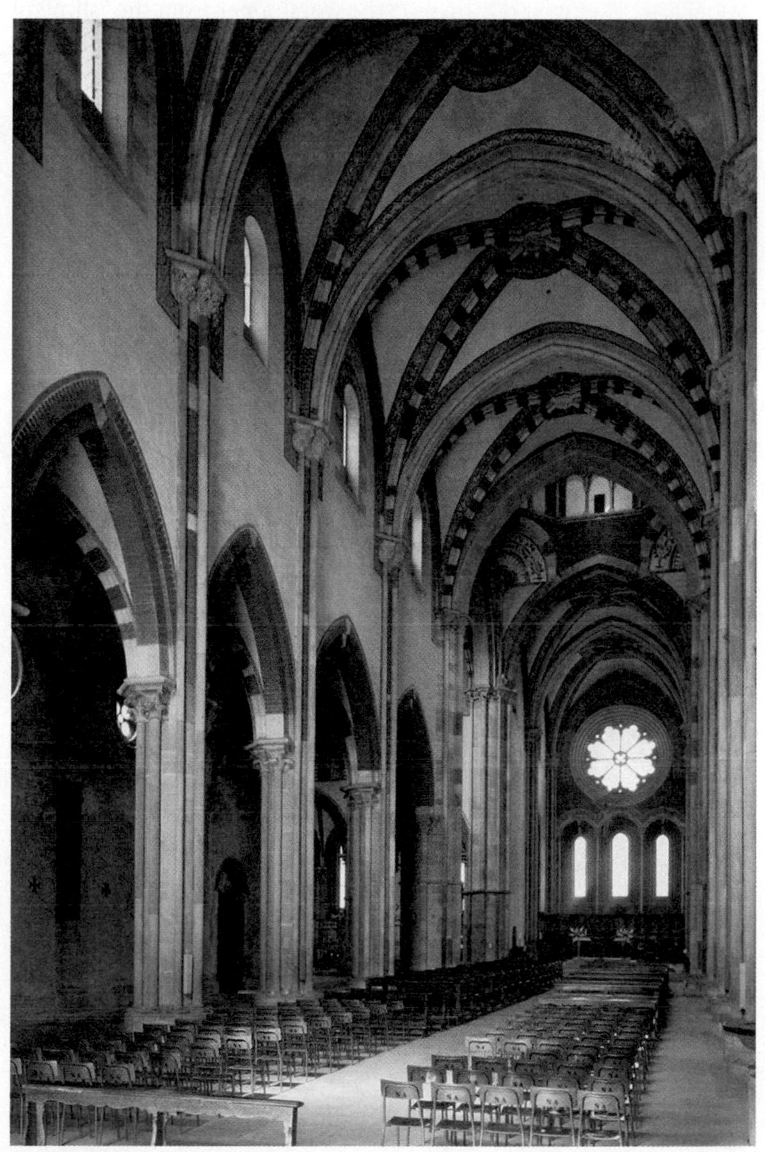

Sant'Andrea
The church of Sant'Andrea at Vercelli suggests that Italian church architects and patrons adopted what they liked of French Gothic, particularly its pointed arches, while remaining uninterested in soaring heights and grand stained-glass windows. The real interest of the interior of Sant'Andrea is its inventive and lively use of contrasting light and dark stone. *(Scala/Art Resource, NY.)*

touched the divine. The atmosphere of a Gothic church was a foretaste of heaven.

The style had its beginnings around 1135, with the project of Abbot Suger, the close associate of King Louis the Fat of France (see page 339), to remodel portions of the church of Saint-Denis. Suger's rebuilding was part of the fruitful melding of royal and ecclesiastical interests and ideals in the north of France. At the west end of his church, the place where the faithful entered, Suger decorated the portals with figures of Old Testament kings, queens, and patriarchs, signaling the links between the present king and his illustrious predecessors. At the eastern end, behind the altar, Suger used pointed arches and stained glass to let in light, which Suger believed would transport the worshipper from the "slime of earth" to the "purity of Heaven." Suger said that the father of lights, God himself, "illuminated" the minds of the beholders through the light that filtered through the stained-glass windows.

The technologies that made Gothic churches possible were all known before the twelfth century. But Suger's church showed how they could be used together to achieve a particularly dazzling effect. Gothic techniques included ribbed vaulting, which gave a sense of precision and order; the pointed arch, which produced a feeling of soaring height; and flying buttresses, which took the weight of the vault off the walls (Figure 11.2). The buttresses permitted much of the wall to be cut away and the open spaces to be filled with glass. Soaring above the west, north, south, and often east ends of many Gothic churches is a rose window: a large round window shaped like a flower.

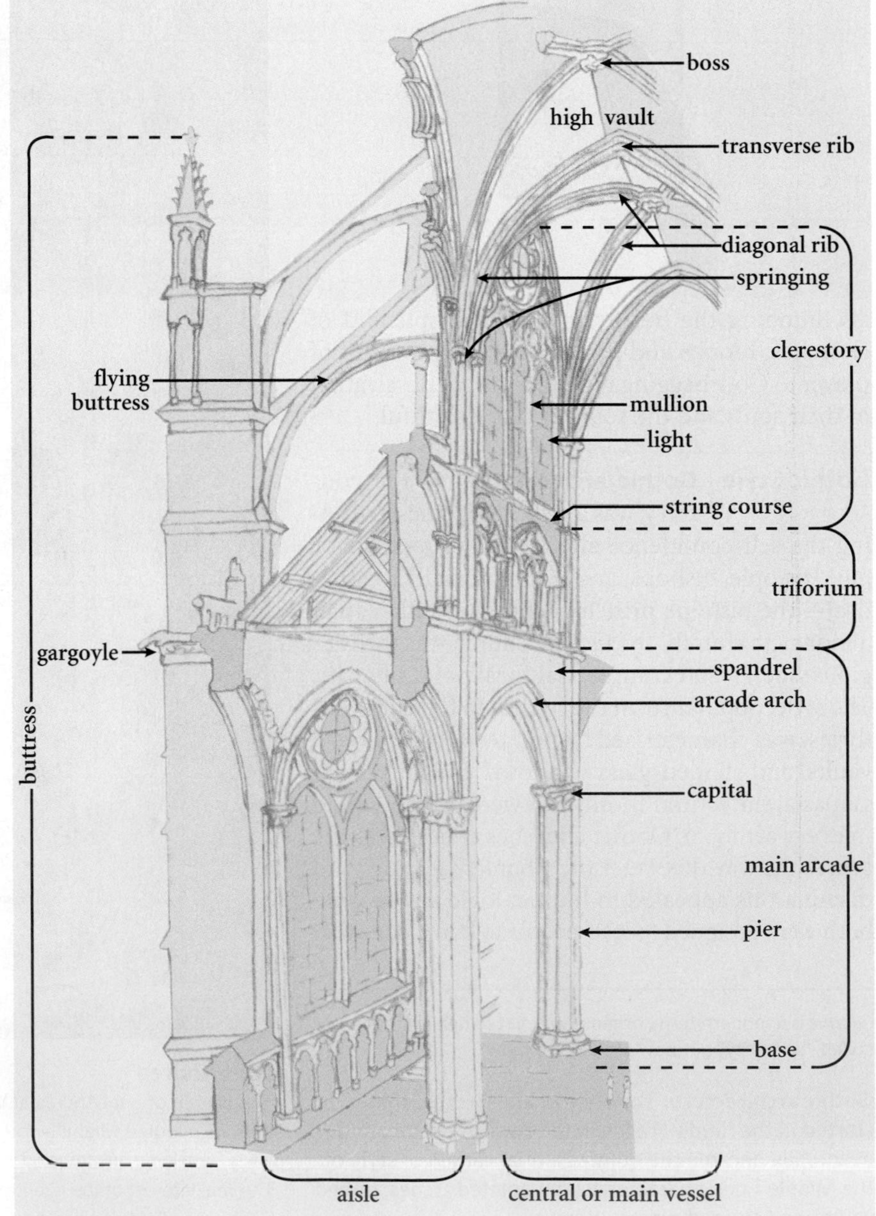

FIGURE 11.2 Elements of a Gothic Cathedral
Bristling on the outside with flying buttresses of stone, Gothic cathedrals were lofty and serene on the inside. The buttresses, which held the weight of the vault, allowed Gothic architects to pierce the walls with enormous windows. Thick piers anchored on sturdy bases became thin columns as they mounted over the triforium and clerestory, blossoming into ribs at the top. Whether plain or ornate, the ribs gave definition and drew attention to the high pointed vault. *(Figure adapted from Michael Camille,* Gothic Art: Glorious Visions *[New York: Abrams, 1996].)*

SEEING HISTORY

Romanesque versus Gothic: The View Down the Nave

When you enter a church, which, in the Middle Ages, you always did from the west end, you find yourself looking down its nave, toward the choir and the altar (the focal points of the church). That view changed over time, and the change tells us a lot about new architectural tastes in the Middle Ages. The church on the left, Saint-Savin, built near Poitiers, in France, in the early twelfth century, is a representative Romanesque church. The one on the right is Bourges, a Gothic church built (about a hundred miles to the east of Saint-Savin) around a century later. Comparing the views down the nave systematically will allow us to discover what makes the Romanesque and Gothic styles distinctive. You might first consider the vaults. Which one is more like a tunnel, and what contributes to that effect? Does one interior create more of a soaring effect? How? What elements of the architecture contribute to this impression? Which one has paintings? Which one lets in the most light? What architectural features make this possible? In which church are the capitals of the columns (the very tops) elaborately carved? In which one are the columns themselves highly articulated, with multiple pillars? From these considerations, name the features that make a Gothic church "Gothic."

Question to Consider

- **What twelfth-century social and cultural trends are reflected in the shift from Romanesque to Gothic?**

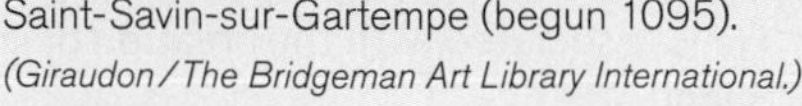

Saint-Savin-sur-Gartempe (begun 1095). *(Giraudon/The Bridgeman Art Library International.)*

Bourges (begun 1195). *(Scala/Art Resource, NY.)*

Unlike Romanesque churches, whose exteriors prepare visitors for what they will see within them, Gothic cathedrals surprise. The exterior of a Gothic church has an opaque, bristling, and forbidding look owing to the dark surface of its stained glass and its flying buttresses. The interior, however, is just the opposite. All is soaring lightness, harmony, and order. (See "Seeing History," page 353.)

By the mid-thirteenth century, Gothic architecture had spread from France to other European countries. The style varied by region, most dramatically in Italy. At Sant'Andrea in Vercelli, shown on page 351, for example, there are only two stories, and light filters in from small windows. Yet with its pointed arches and ribbed vaulting, Sant'Andrea is considered a Gothic church. At its east end is a rose window.

REVIEW QUESTION What was new about education and church architecture in the twelfth and early thirteenth centuries?

Governments as Institutions

Around the same time that architects, workers, patrons, theologians, and city dwellers were coming together to produce Gothic cathedrals, and masters and students were incorporating themselves as universities, rulership was becoming institutionalized. By the end of the twelfth century, western Europeans for the first time spoke of their rulers not as kings of a people (for example, the king of the Franks) but as kings of a territory (for example, the king of France). This new designation reflected an important change in medieval rulership. However strong earlier rulers had been, their political power had been personal (depending on ties of kinship, friendship, and vassalage) rather than territorial (touching all who lived within the borders of their state). Renewed interest in Roman law, a product of the schools, served as a foundation for strong, central rule. Money allowed kings to hire salaried professionals — talented, literate officials, many of whom had been schooled in the new universities cropping up across Europe — to carry out the new ideology. The process of state building had begun.

In England, the governmental system was institutionalized early, with royal officials administering both law and revenues. In other regions, such as France and Germany, bureaucratic administration did not develop so far. In eastern Europe, it hardly existed at all. At Byzantium, the bureaucracy that had long been in place frayed badly, leaving the state open to conquest by western crusaders.

England: Unity through Common Law

In the mid-twelfth century, the government of England was by far the most institutionalized in Europe. The king hardly needed to be present: royal government functioned smoothly without him, since officials handled all the administrative matters and record keeping. The very circumstances of the English king favored the growth of an administrative staff— the king's frequent travels to and from the continent meant that officials needed to work in his absence, and his enormous wealth meant that he could afford them. **Henry II** (r. 1154–1189) was the driving force in extending and strengthening the institutions of English government.

Accession of Henry II, 1154 Henry II became king in the wake of a terrible civil war. Henry I (r. 1100–1135), son of William the Conqueror, had no male heir. Before he died, he called on the great barons to swear that his daughter Matilda would rule after him. The effort failed; the Norman barons could not imagine a woman ruling over them. Many were glad to see Stephen of Blois (r. 1135–1154), Henry's nephew, take the throne. With Matilda's son, the future Henry II, only two years old when Stephen took the crown, the struggle for control of England during Stephen's reign became part of a larger territorial contest between the house of Anjou (Henry's family) and the house of Blois (Stephen's family) (Figure 11.3). Continual civil war (1139–1153) in England benefited the English barons and high churchmen, who gained new privileges and powers as the monarch's authority waned. Newly built private castles, already familiar on the continent, now appeared in England as symbols of the rising power of the English barons. Stephen's coalition of barons, high clergymen, and townsmen eventually fell apart, and he agreed to the accession of Henry of Anjou. Thus began what would be known as the Angevin (from Anjou) dynasty.[3]

---

[3]Henry's father, Geoffrey of Anjou, was nicknamed "Plantagenet" from the *genet*, a shrub he liked. Historians sometimes use the name to refer to the entire dynasty, so Henry II was the first Plantagenet as well as the first Angevin king of England.

Henry II: King of England (r. 1154–1189) who ended the period of civil war there and affirmed and expanded royal powers. He is associated with the creation of common law in England.

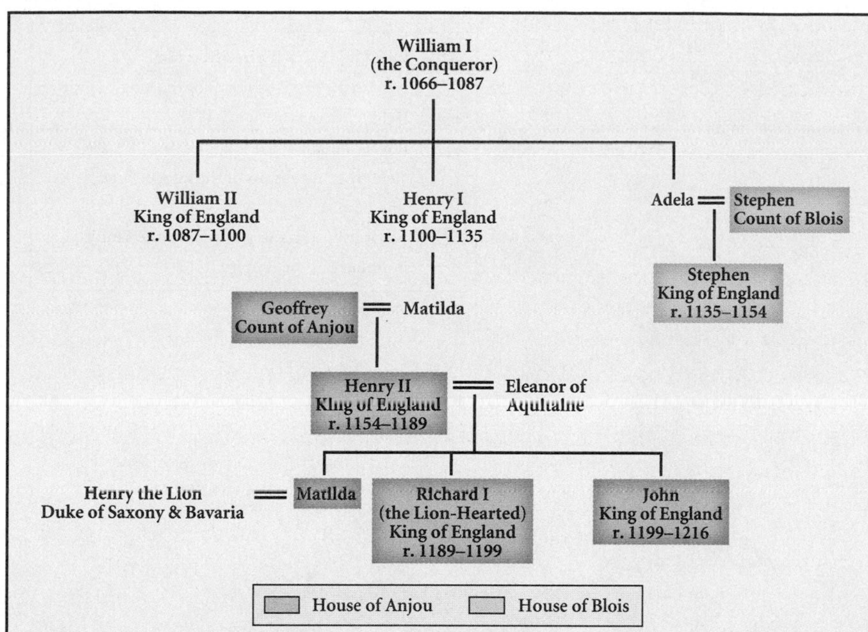

FIGURE 11.3 Genealogy of Henry II
King William I of England was succeeded by his sons, William II and Henry I. When Henry I died, the succession was disputed by two women and their husbands. One was William I's daughter, Adela, married to Stephen, count of Blois; the other was Henry's daughter, Matilda, wife of the count of Anjou. Although the English crown first went to the house of Blois, it reverted in 1154 to the house of Anjou, headed by Matilda's son, Henry. Henry II thus began the Angevin dynasty in England.

Henry's marriage to Eleanor of Aquitaine in 1152, after her marriage to Louis VII of France was annulled, brought the enormous inheritance of the duchy of Aquitaine to the English crown. Although he remained the vassal of the king of France for his continental lands, Henry in effect ruled a territory that stretched from England to southern France (Map 11.1).

Eleanor brought Henry not only an enormous inheritance but also the sons he needed to maintain his dynasty. He gave her much less. As queen of France, Eleanor had enjoyed an important position: she disputed with St. Bernard, the Cistercian abbot who was the most renowned churchman of the day, and when she accompanied Louis on the Second Crusade, she brought more troops than he did. Of independent mind, she determined to separate from Louis even before he considered leaving her. But with Henry, she lost much of her power, for he dominated her just as he came to dominate his barons. Turning to her offspring in 1173, Eleanor, disguised as a man, tried to join her eldest son, Henry the Younger, in a plot against his father. But the rebellion was put down, and she spent most of her years

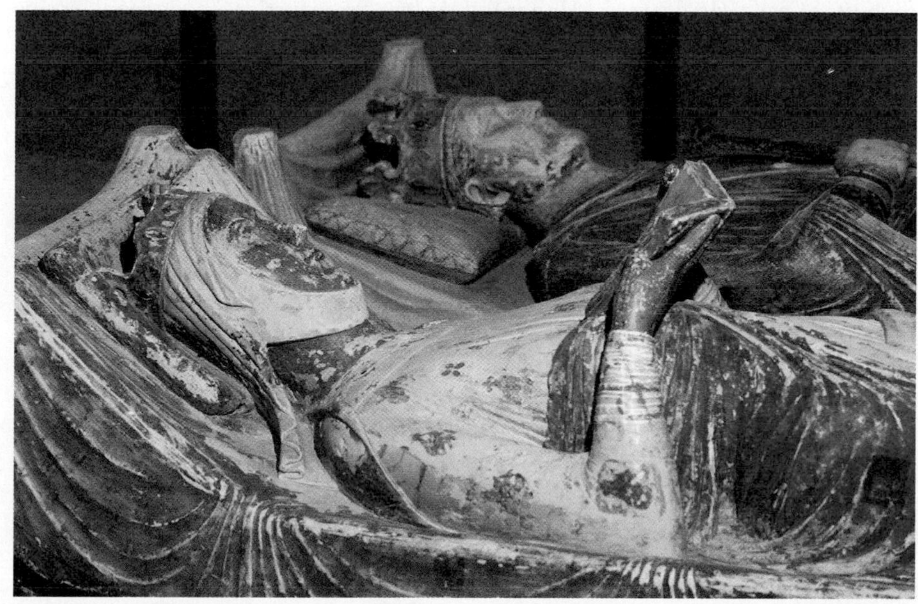

Eleanor and Henry
Nothing about their side-by-side tombs suggests the stormy relationship of Eleanor of Aquitaine and King Henry II of England. Their effigies, carved of limestone and walnut, suggest peace and piety. How does Eleanor's book help project this image? What do you suppose she is reading? The placement of the couple's tombs also attests to their religious fervor: they were buried in the powerful monastery of Fontevraud, a "double monastery" consisting (in separate quarters) of both monks and nuns. An abbess presided over all. *(Hervé Champollion/© Cephas Picture Library/Alamy.)*

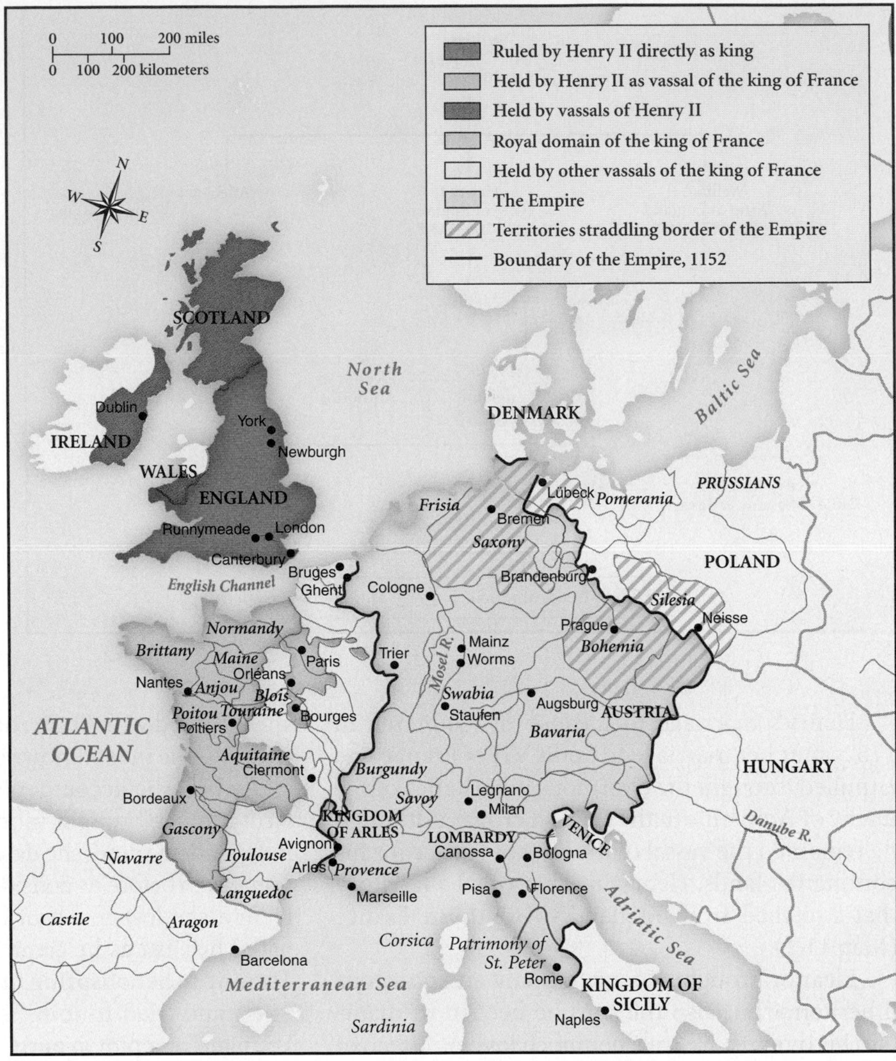

MAP 11.1 Europe in the Age of Henry II and Frederick Barbarossa, 1150–1190
The second half of the twelfth century was dominated by two men, King Henry II and Emperor Frederick Barbarossa. Of the two, Frederick seemed to control more land, but this was deceptive. Although he was emperor, he had great difficulty ruling the territory that was theoretically part of his empire. Frederick's base was in central Germany, and even there he had to contend with powerful vassals. Henry II's territory was more compact but also more surely under his control.

thereafter, until her husband's death in 1189, confined under guard at Winchester Castle. (In death, however, she gained dignity, with her tomb next to Henry's. See the illustration on page 355.)

Royal Authority and Common Law

When Henry II became king of England, he immediately set about to undo the damage to the monarchy caused by the civil war. He destroyed or confiscated the new castles and regained crown land. Then he proceeded to extend monarchical power, above all by imposing royal justice.

Henry's judicial reforms built on an already well-developed English system. The Anglo-Saxon kings had royal district courts: the king appointed sheriffs to police the shires, muster military levies, and haul criminals into court. The Norman kings retained these courts, which all the free men of the shire were summoned to attend. To these established institutions, Henry II added a system of judicial visitations called eyres (from the Latin *iter*, "journey"). Under this system, royal justices made regular trips to every locality in England. Henry declared that some crimes, such as murder, arson, and rape, were so heinous that they violated the "king's peace" no matter where they were committed. The king required local representatives of the knightly class to meet during each eyre and either give the sheriff the names of those suspected of committing crimes in the vicinity or arrest the suspects themselves and hand them over to the royal justices.

During the eyres, the justices also heard cases between individuals, today called civil cases. Free men and women (that is, people of the knightly class or above) could bring their disputes over such matters as inheritance, dowries, and property claims to the king's justices. Earlier courts had generally relied on duels between litigants to determine verdicts. Henry's new system offered a different option, an inquest under royal supervision.

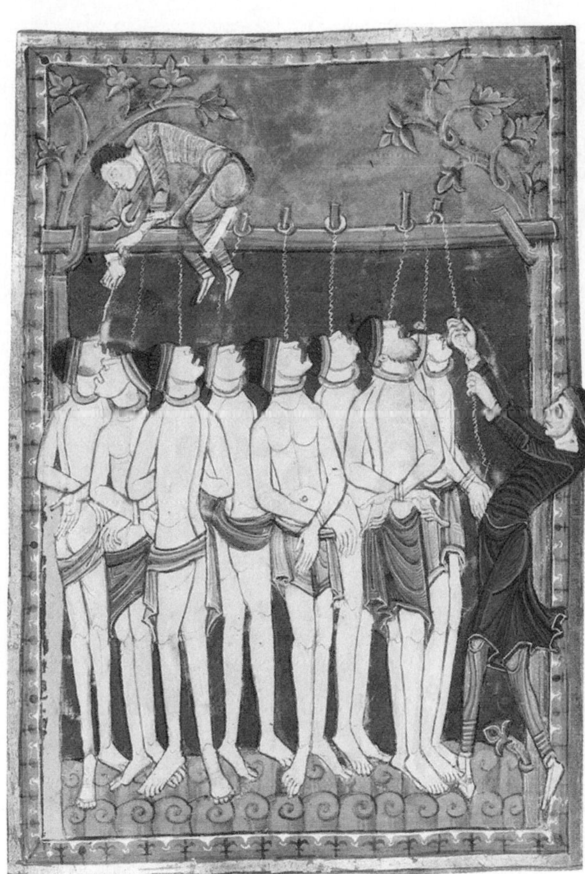

Hanging Thieves
The development of common law in England meant mobilizing royal agents to bring charges and arrest people throughout the land. In 1124, the royal justice Ralph Basset hanged forty-four thieves. It could not have been very shocking in that context to see, in this miniature from around 1130, eight thieves hanged for breaking into the shrine of St. Edmund. Under Henry II, all cases of murder, arson, and rape were considered crimes against the king himself. The result was not just the enhancement of the king's power but also new definitions of crime, more thorough policing, and more systematic punishments. Even so, hanging was probably no more frequent than it had been before. (The Thieves Are Hanged. *From* The Life, Passion, and Miracles of St. Edmund, King and Martyr, *in Latin. Bury St. Edmund's, c. 1130. MS. M.736, f. 19v. The Pierpont Morgan Library/Art Resource, NY.)*

The new system of **common law**—law that applied to all of England—was praised for its efficiency, speed, and conclusiveness in a twelfth-century legal treatise known as *Glanvill* (after its presumed author): "This legal institution emanates from perfect equity. For justice, which after many and long delays is scarcely ever demonstrated by the duel, is advantageously and speedily attained through this institution." *Glanvill* might have added that the king also speedily gained a large treasury. The exchequer, as the financial bureau of England was called, recorded all the fines paid for judgments and the sums collected for writs. The amounts, entered on parchment sewn together and stored as rolls, became the Receipt Rolls and Pipe Rolls, the first of many such records of the English monarchy and an indication that writing had become a mechanism for institutionalizing royal power in England.

The stiffest opposition to Henry's extension of royal courts came from the church, where a separate system of trial and punishment had long been available to the clergy and to others who enjoyed church protection. The punishments for crimes meted out by church courts were generally quite mild. Protective of their special status, churchmen refused to submit to the jurisdiction of Henry's courts. Henry insisted, and the ensuing contest between Henry II and his archbishop, Thomas Becket (1118–1170), became the greatest battle between the church and the state in the twelfth century. The conflict simmered for six years, with Becket refusing to allow "criminous clerics"—clergy suspected of committing a crime—to come before royal courts. Then Henry's henchmen murdered Thomas, right in his own cathedral. The desecration unintentionally turned Becket into a martyr. Although Henry's role in the murder remained ambiguous, he was forced by the general outcry to do public penance for the deed. In the end, both church and royal courts expanded to address the concerns of an increasingly litigious society. (See the illustration on page 358.)

Henry II was an English king with an imperial reach. He was lord over almost half of France, though much of this territory was in the hands of his vassals, and he was, at least theoretically, vassal to the French king (see Map 11.1). In England, he made the king's presence felt everywhere through his system of traveling royal courts. On the conti-

---

common law: Begun by Henry II (r. 1154–1189), the English royal law carried out by the king's justices in eyre (traveling justices). It applied to the entire kingdom and thus was "common" to all.

The Murder of Thomas Becket
Almost immediately after King Henry II's knights murdered Archbishop Thomas Becket in his church at Canterbury, Becket was viewed as a martyr. In this early depiction of the event, one of the murderers knocks off Becket's cap, while another hits the arm of Becket's supporter, who holds the bishop's cross-staff. *(British Library, London, UK/© British Library Board. All Rights Reserved./The Bridgeman Art Library International.)*

nent, he maintained his position through a combination of war and negotiation, but rebellions begun by his own sons with help from the king of France dogged him throughout his life.

Henry's Successors Under Henry II and his sons Richard I (r. 1189–1199) and John (r. 1199–1216), the English monarchy was omnipresent and rich. Its omnipresence derived largely from its eyre system of justice and its administrative apparatus. Its wealth came from court fees, income from numerous royal estates both in England and on the continent, taxes from cities, and customary feudal dues (reliefs and aids) collected from barons and knights. These dues were paid on such occasions as the knighting of the king's eldest son and the marriage of the king's eldest daughter. Enriched by the commercial economy of the late twelfth century, the English kings encouraged their knights and barons not to serve them personally in battle but instead to pay the king a tax called scutage in lieu of service. The monarchs preferred to hire mercenaries both as troops to fight external enemies and as police to enforce the king's will at home.

Richard I was known as the Lion-Hearted for his boldness. Historians have often criticized him for being an "absentee" king, yet it is hard to see what he might have done differently. He went on the Third Crusade the very year he was crowned; on his way home, he was captured and held for ransom by political enemies for a long time; and he died defending his possessions on the continent. Richard's real tragedy was that he died young.

Richard's successor, John, has also been widely faulted. Even in his own day, he was accused of asserting his will in a highhanded way. To understand John, it is necessary to appreciate how desperate he was to keep his continental possessions. In 1204, the king of France, **Philip II (Philip Augustus)** (r. 1180–1223), confiscated the northern French territories held by John. Between 1204 and 1214, John did ev-

---

Philip II (Philip Augustus): King of France (r. 1180–1223) who bested the English king John and won most of John's continental territories, thus immeasurably strengthening the power of the Capetian dynasty.

erything he could to add to the crown revenues so that he could pay for an army to win back the territories. He forced his vassals to pay ever-increasing scutages and extorted money in the form of new feudal dues. He compelled the widows of his vassals to either marry men of his choosing or pay him a hefty fee. Despite John's heavy investment in this war effort, his army was defeated in 1214 at the battle of Bouvines. The defeat caused discontented English barons to rebel openly against the king. At Runnymede in June 1215, John was forced to agree to the charter of baronial liberties that has come to be called **Magna Carta** ("Great Charter").

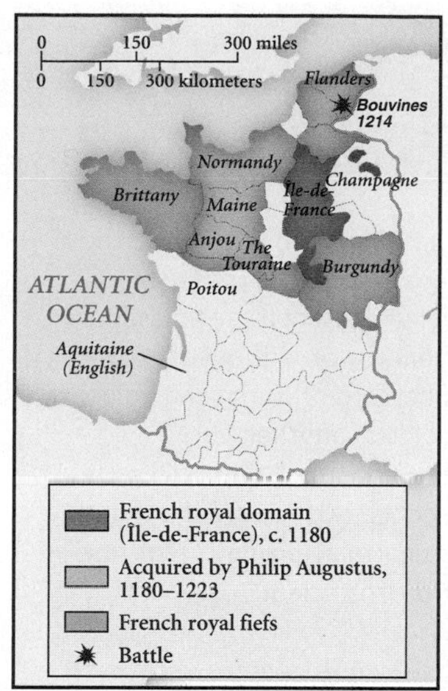

The Consolidation of France under Philip Augustus, 1180–1223

Magna Carta, 1215 The English barons intended Magna Carta to be a conservative document defining the "customary" obligations and rights of the nobility and forbidding the king to break from these customs without consulting his barons. It also maintained that all free men in the land had certain rights that the king was obligated to uphold. (See "Contrasting Views," pages 360–61.) In this way, Magna Carta implied that the king was not above the law. The growing royal power was matched by the self-confidence of the English barons, certain of their rights and eager to articulate them. In time, as the definition of *free men* expanded to include all the king's subjects, Magna Carta came to be seen as a guarantee of the rights of Englishmen (and eventually Englishwomen) in general.

France: Consolidation and Conquest

Whereas the power of the English king led to a baronial movement to curb it, the weakness of the French monarchy ironically led to its expansion. In 1180, the French crown passed from the Capetian king Louis VII (first husband of Eleanor of Aquitaine) to his fourteen-year-old son, Philip Augustus. When the new king came to the throne, the royal domain, the Île-de-France, was sandwiched between territory controlled by the counts of Flanders, Champagne, and Anjou. By far the most powerful ruler on the continent was King Henry II of England. He was the count of Anjou and the duke of Normandy, and he held the duchy of Aquitaine through his wife and also controlled Poitou and Brittany (see Map 11.1, page 356).

Henry and the counts of Flanders and Champagne vied to control the youthful new king of France. Philip, however, quickly learned to play off the three rulers against one another, in particular by setting the sons of Henry II against their father. Contemporaries were astounded when Philip successfully gained territory: he wrested land from Flanders in the 1190s and Normandy, Anjou, Maine, the Touraine, and Poitou from King John of England in 1204. No wonder he was given the epithet *Augustus*, after the first Roman emperor.

After Philip's army confirmed its triumph over most of John's continental territories in 1214, the French monarch could boast that he was the richest and most powerful ruler in France. Most important, Philip had sufficient support and resources to keep a tight hold on Normandy.[4] He received homage and fealty from most of the Norman aristocracy, and his officers carried out their work there in accordance with Norman customs. For ordinary Normans, the shift from English duke to French king brought few changes.

Wherever he ruled, Philip instituted new administrative practices, run by officials who kept accounts and files. Before Philip's day, most French royal arrangements were committed to memory rather than to writing. If decrees were recorded at all, they were saved by the recipient, not by the government. The king did keep some documents, which he generally carried with him in his travels like personal possessions. But in 1194, in a battle with the king of England, Philip lost his meager cache of documents along with much treasure when he had to abandon his baggage train. After 1194, the king had all his decrees written down,

---

Magna Carta: Literally "Great Charter"; the charter of baronial liberties that King John was forced to agree to in 1215. It implied that royal power was subject to custom and law.

[4]Philip was particularly successful in imposing royal control in Normandy; later French kings gave most of the other territories to collateral members of the royal family.

CONTRASTING VIEWS

Magna Carta

Magna Carta ("Great Charter"), today considered a landmark of constitutional government, began as a demand by English barons and churchmen for specific rights and privileges. Reacting to King John's "abuses," they forced him in 1215 to affix his seal to a "charter of liberties" (Document 1). It set forth the customs that the king was expected to observe and, in its sixty-first clause, in effect allowed the king's subjects to declare war against him if he failed to carry out the charter's provisions. In 1225, Henry III, John's son, issued a definitive version of the charter. By then, it had become more important as a symbol of liberty than for its specific provisions. It was, for example, invoked by the barons in 1242 when they were summoned to one of the first Parliaments (Document 2).

1. Magna Carta, 1215

In these excerpts, the provisions that were dropped by Henry III in the definitive version of 1225 are starred. Explanatory notes are in brackets. The original charter had sixty-three clauses. In every clause John refers to himself by the royal "we."

1. First of all [we, i.e., John] have granted to God, and by this our present charter confirmed for us and our heirs for ever that the English church shall be free, and shall have its rights undiminished and its liberties unimpaired. . . .

8. No widow shall be forced to marry so long as she wishes to live without a husband, provided that she gives security [pledges] not to marry without our consent if she holds [her land] from us, or without the consent of her lord of whom she holds, if she holds of another.

9. Neither we nor our bailiffs will seize for any debt any land or rent, so long as the chattels [property] of the debtor are sufficient to repay the debt. . . .

*10. If anyone who has borrowed from the Jews any sum, great or small, dies before it is repaid, the debt shall not bear interest as long as the heir is under age, of whomsoever [lord] he holds [his land]; and if the debt falls into our hands [which might happen, as Jews were serfs of the crown], we will not take anything except the principal mentioned in the bond.

*12. No scutage or aid [money payments owed by a vassal to his lord] shall be imposed in our kingdom unless by common counsel of our kingdom, except for ransoming our person, for making our eldest son a knight, and for once marrying our eldest daughter; and for these only a reasonable aid shall be levied. . . .

30. No sheriff, or bailiff of ours, or anyone else shall take the horses or carts of any free man [for the most part, a member of the elite] for transport work save with the agreement of that freeman.

31. Neither we nor our bailiffs will take, for castles or other works of ours, timber which is not ours, except with the agreement of him whose timber it is. . . .

39. No free man shall be arrested or imprisoned or disseised [deprived of his land] or outlawed or exiled or in any way victimized, neither will we attack him or send anyone to attack him, except by the lawful judgment of his peers or by the law of the land. . . .

*61. Since . . . we have granted all these things aforesaid . . . we give and grant [the barons] the underwritten security, namely, that the barons shall choose any twenty-five barons of the kingdom they wish, who must with all their might observe, hold, and cause to be observed, the peace and liberties which we have granted and confirmed to them by this present charter of ours, so that if we, or our justiciar [the king's chief minister], or our bailiffs or any one of our servants offend in any way against anyone or transgress any of the articles of the peace or the security . . . , [the barons] shall come to us . . . and laying the transgression before us, shall petition us to have that transgression corrected without delay. And if we do not correct the transgression . . . within forty days . . . those twenty-five bar-

and he established permanent repositories in which to keep them.

Like the English king, Philip relied largely on members of the lesser nobility — knights and clerics, many of whom were masters educated in the city schools of France. They served as officers of his court, tax collectors, and overseers of the royal estates, making the king's power felt locally as never before.

Germany: The Revived Monarchy of Frederick Barbarossa

Theoretically, Henry V and his successors were kings of Germany and Italy, and at Rome they received the crown and title of emperor from the popes as well. But the Investiture Conflict (see page 322) had reduced their power and authority. Meanwhile, the German princes strengthened their position, enjoy-

ons together with the community of the whole land shall distrain and distress us in every way they can, namely, by seizing castles, lands, possessions, and in such other ways as they can, saving [not harming] our person.

Source: Harry Rothwell, ed., *English Historical Documents*, vol. 3 (London: Eyre & Spottiswoode, 1975), 317–23.

2. The Barons at Parliament Refuse to Give the King an Aid, 1242

Henry III convoked the barons to a meeting (parliament), expecting them to ratify his request for money to wage war for his French possessions. According to the writer of this document, Matthew Paris (a monk, artist, and chronicler of his time), the barons considered his request an excessive imposition. Magna Carta was a justification for their flat rejection of the king's request.

Since he had been their ruler they had many times, at his request, given him aid, namely, a thirteenth of their movable property, and afterwards a fifteenth and a sixteenth and a fortieth. . . . Scarcely, however, had four years or so elapsed from that time, when he again asked them for aid, and, at length, by dint of great entreaties, he obtained a thirtieth, which they granted him on the condition that neither that exaction nor the others before it should in the future be made a precedent of. And regarding that he gave them his charter. Furthermore, he then [at that earlier time] granted them that all the liberties contained in Magna Carta should thenceforward be fully observed throughout the whole of his kingdom. . . .

Furthermore, from the time of their giving the said thirtieth, itinerant justices have been continually going on eyre [moving from place to place] through all parts of England, alike for pleas of the forest [to enforce the king's monopoly on forests] and all other pleas, so that all the counties, hundreds, cities, boroughs, and nearly all the vills of England are heavily amerced [fined]; wherefore, from that eyre alone the king has, or ought to have, a very large sum of money, if it were paid, and properly collected. They therefore say with truth that all in the kingdom are so oppressed and impoverished by these amercements and by the other aids given before that they have little or no goods left. And because the king had never, after the granting of the thirtieth, abided by his charter of liberties [namely, Magna Carta], nay had since then oppressed them more than usual . . . they told the king flatly that for the present they would not give him an aid.

Source: Harry Rothwell, ed., *English Historical Documents*, vol. 3 (London: Eyre & Spottiswoode, 1975), 355–56.

John's Seal on Magna Carta

King John did not sign Magna Carta; he sealed it. From the thirteenth through the fifteenth century, kings, queens, and many other individuals and groups at all levels of society used seals to authenticate their charters—what we would call legal documents. The seal itself was made of wax or lead that was melted and pressed with a matrix of hard metal, such as gold or brass, that was carved in the negative, to produce a raised image. These seals reminded the public of the status as well as the name of the sealer. What image did John wish to project? *(The British Library/ Ancient Art & Architecture Collection, Ltd.)*

Questions to Consider

1. **What do the clauses of Magna Carta that say what will henceforth *not* be done suggest about what the king *had been* doing?**
2. **How did the barons of 1242 use Magna Carta as a symbol of liberty?**
3. **Why didn't John sign Magna Carta?**

ing near independence as they built castles on their properties and established control over whole territories. When they elected a new king, the princes made sure that he would give them new lands and powers. The German kings were in a difficult position: they had to balance the many conflicting interests of their royal and imperial offices, their families, and the German princes, and they had to contend with the increasing influence of the papacy and the Italian communes, which made alliances with one another and with the German princes. All this prevented the consolidation of power under a strong German monarch during the first half of the twelfth century.

During the Investiture Conflict, the two sides (imperial and papal) were represented by two noble families. Leading the imperial party were the Staufer, or Hohenstaufen, clan; opposing them were the

Welfs. (Two later Italian factions, the Ghibellines and the Guelphs, corresponded, respectively, to the Hohenstaufens and the Welfs.) The enmity between these families was legendary, and warfare between the groups raged even after the Concordat of Worms in 1122. Decades of constant battles exhausted all parties, who began to long for peace. In an act of rare unanimity, they elected **Frederick I (Barbarossa)**. In Frederick (r. 1152–1190) they seemed to have a candidate who could end the strife: his mother was a Welf, his father a Staufer. Contemporary accounts of the king's career represented Frederick in the image of Christ as the cornerstone that joined two houses and reconciled enemies.

Frederick I (Barbarossa): King of Germany (r. 1152–1190) and emperor (crowned 1155) who tried to cement the power of the German king through conquest (for example, of northern Italy) and the bonds of vassalage.

New Foundations of Power

Frederick's appearance impressed his contemporaries — the name *Barbarossa* referred to his red-blond hair and beard. But beyond appearances, Frederick impressed those around him by what they called his firmness. He affirmed royal rights, even when he handed out duchies and allowed others to name bishops, because in return for these political powers Frederick required the princes to concede formally and publicly that they held their rights and territories from him as their lord. By making them his vassals, although with nearly royal rights within their principalities, Frederick defined the princes' relationship to the German king: they were powerful yet personally subordinate to him. In this way, Frederick hoped to save the monarchy and to coordinate royal and princely rule, thus ending Germany's chronic civil wars. Frederick used the lord–vassal relationship to give him a free hand to rule while placating the princes.

Frederick Barbarossa

In this image of Frederick, made during his lifetime, the emperor is dressed as a crusader, and the inscription tells him to fight the Muslims. The small figure on the right is the abbot of the Monastery of Schäftlarn, who gives Frederick a book that contains an account of the First Crusade. *(HIP/Art Resource, NY.)*

DOCUMENT

Frederick I's Reply to the Romans

Frederick I's conception of his rights and powers is well illustrated by the speech that he reportedly gave upon his entry into Rome in 1155 for his imperial coronation. The pope considered it his right to confer the crown on the king. But when Frederick came to Rome, envoys from the new city government that had been established there greeted him with an offer to give him the crown instead. Frederick reacted forcefully: the crown was not theirs to give; it was his by right. The gist of his reply to the Romans was recorded by his counselor and chronicler, Bishop Otto of Freising.

We have heard much heretofore concerning the wisdom and the valor of the Romans, yet more concerning their wisdom. Wherefore we cannot wonder enough at finding your words insipid with swollen pride rather than seasoned with the salt of wisdom. You set forth the ancient renown of your city. You extol to the very stars the ancient status of your sacred republic. Granted, granted! To use the words of your own writer, "There was, *there was once*, virtue in this republic." "Once," I say. And oh that we might truthfully and freely say "now"! Your Rome—nay, ours also—has experienced the vicissitudes of time. She could not be the only one to escape a fate ordained by the Author of all things for all that dwell beneath the orb of the moon. What shall I say? It is clear how first the strength of your nobility was transferred from this city of ours to the royal city of the East [Constantinople], and how for the course of many years the thirsty Greekling sucked the breasts of your delight. Then came the Frank, truly noble, in deed as in name, and forcibly possessed himself of whatever freedom was still left to you. Do you wish to know the ancient glory of your Rome? The worth of the senatorial dignity? The impregnable disposition of the camp? The virtue and the discipline of the equestrian order, its unmarred and unconquerable boldness when advancing to a conflict? Behold our state. All these things are to be found with us. All these have descended to us, together with the empire.

Source: Brian Tierney, *The Crisis of Church and State, 1050–1300: With Selected Documents* (Englewood Cliffs, NJ: Prentice Hall, 1964), 103–4.

Question to Consider

- **Why did Frederick think that Germany had inherited the Roman Empire along with all its power and glory?**

As the king of Germany, Frederick had the traditional right to claim the imperial crown. When, in 1155, he marched to Rome to be crowned emperor, the fledgling commune there protested that it alone had the right to give him the crown. Frederick interrupted them, asserting that the glory of Rome, together with its crown, came to him by right of conquest (see Document, "Frederick I's Reply to the Romans," above). He was equally insistent with the pope, who wrote to tell him that Rome belonged to St. Peter. Frederick replied that his imperial title gave him rights over the city. In part, Frederick was influenced by the revival of Roman law—the laws of Theodosius and Justinian—that was taking place in the schools of Italy. In part, too, he was convinced of the sacred—not just secular—origins of the imperial office. Frederick called his empire *sacer* ("sacred"), asserting that it was in its own way as precious, worthwhile, and God-given as the church.

Frederick buttressed this high view of his imperial right with worldly power. He married Beatrice of Burgundy, whose vast estates in Burgundy and Provence enabled him to establish a powerful political and territorial base centered in Swabia (today southwestern Germany).

Frederick and Italy | Frederick Barbarossa then looked south to Italy. Its flourishing commercial cities could make him rich. Taxes on agricultural production there alone yielded thirty thousand silver talents annually, an incredible sum equal to the annual income of the richest ruler of the day, the king of England. Swabia and northern Italy together would give Frederick a compact and centrally located territory.

Some historians have faulted Frederick for "entangling" himself in Italy, but no emperor could leave Italy alone. The very title came from the Roman emperor, who had controlled the city of Rome and all of Italy. It would have seemed laughable to be "emperor" without holding at least some of this territory.

Nevertheless, Frederick's ambitions in Italy were problematic. Since the Investiture Conflict, the emperor had ruled Italy in name only. The communes of the northern cities guarded their liberties jealously, while the pope considered Italy his own sphere of influence. Frederick's territorial base just north of Italy threatened those interests (see Map 11.1, page 356). In 1157, soon after Frederick's imperial coronation, the pope's envoys arrived at a meeting called by the emperor with a letter detailing the dignities, honors, and other *beneficia* the papacy had showered on Frederick. The word *beneficia* angered Frederick and his supporters because it meant not only "benefits" but also "fiefs," casting Frederick as the pope's vassal. The incident opened old wounds from the Investiture Conflict and revealed the gulf between papal and imperial conceptions of worldly authority.

Despite the opposition of the cities and the pope, Frederick was determined to conquer northern Italy, which he managed to do by 1158. Adopting an Italian solution for governing the communes — appointing outsiders as magistrates — Frederick appointed his own men to these powerful positions. But that was where Frederick made his mistake. He chose German officials who lacked a sense of Italian communal traditions. The heavy hand of Frederick's magistrates created enormous resentment. For example, the magistrates at Milan immediately ordered an inventory of all taxes due the emperor and levied new and demeaning labor duties, even demanding that citizens carry the wood and stones of their plundered city to Pavia, twenty-five miles away, for use in constructing new houses there. By 1167, most of the cities of northern Italy had joined with the pope to form the Lombard League against Frederick. Defeated by the league at the battle of Legnano in 1176, Frederick made peace and withdrew most of his forces from Italy. The battle marked the triumph of the city over the crown in Italy, which would not have a centralized government until the nineteenth century; its political history would instead be that of its various regions and their dominant cities.

Frederick was the victim of traditions that were rapidly being outmoded. He based much of his rule in Germany on the bond of lord and vassal at the very moment when rulers elsewhere were relying less on such personal ties and more on salaried officials. He lived up to the meaning of *emperor*, with all its obligations to rule Rome and northern Italy, when other leaders were consolidating their terri-

Henry the Lion and Matilda

In this illustration from a deluxe manuscript of a liturgical book made for Henry the Lion, the duke and his wife are shown being crowned from heaven. Behind them are their royal and ducal forefathers. *(IAM/akg/World History Archive.)*

torial rule bit by bit. In addition, as "universal" emperor, he did not recognize the importance of local pride, language, customs, and traditions; he tried to rule Italian communes with his own men from Germany, and he failed.

Henry the Lion: Lord and Vassal Frederick Barbarossa also had problems in Germany, where he had to contend with princes of near-royal status who acted as independent rulers of their principalities, though acknowledging Frederick as their feudal lord. One of the most powerful was Henry the Lion (c. 1130–1195). Married to Matilda, daughter of the English king Henry II and Eleanor of Aquitaine, Henry was duke of Saxony and Bavaria, which gave him important bases in both the north and the south of Germany. (See the illustration on page 364.) A self-confident and aggressive ruler, Henry dominated his territory by investing bishops (usurping the role of the emperor as outlined in the Concordat of Worms), collecting dues from his estates, and exercising judicial rights over his duchies. He also actively extended his rule, especially in Slavic regions, pushing northeast past the Elbe River to reestablish dioceses and to build the commercial city of Lübeck.

Henry was lord of many vassals and ministerials (people of unfree status but high prestige). He organized a staff of clerics and ministerials to collect taxes and tolls and to write up his legal acts. Here, as elsewhere, administration no longer depended entirely on the personal involvement of the ruler.

Yet like kings, princes could fall. Henry's growing power so threatened other princes and even Frederick that in 1179 Frederick called Henry to the king's court for violating the peace. When Henry chose not to appear, Frederick exercised his authority as Henry's lord and charged him with violating his duty as a vassal. Because Henry refused the summons to court and avoided serving his lord in Italy, Frederick condemned him, confiscated his holdings, and drove him out of Germany in 1180.

Late-twelfth-century kings and emperors often found themselves engaged in a balancing act of ruling yet placating their powerful vassals. The process was almost always risky. Successfully challenging one recalcitrant prince/vassal meant negotiating costly deals with the others, since their support was vital. Frederick wanted to retain Henry's duchy for himself, as Philip Augustus had managed to do with Normandy. But Frederick was not powerful enough to do so and was forced to divide and distribute it to the supporters he had relied on to enforce his decrees against Henry.

Eastern Europe and Byzantium: Fragmenting Realms

The importance of governmental and bureaucratic institutions such as those developed in England and France is made especially clear by comparing the experience of regions where they were not established. In eastern Europe, the characteristic pattern was for states to form under the leadership of one great ruler and then to fragment under his successor. For example, King Béla III of Hungary (r. 1172–1196) built up a state that looked superficially like a western European kingdom. He married a French princess, sent his officials to Paris to be educated, and built his palace in the French Romanesque style. The annual income from his estates, tolls, dues, and taxes equaled that of the richest western monarchs. But he did not set up enduring governmental institutions, and in the decades that followed Béla's death, wars between his sons splintered his monarchical holdings and aristocratic supporters divided the wealth.

Rus underwent a similar process. Although twelfth-century Kiev was politically fragmented, autocratic princes to the north constructed Vladimir (also known as Suzdalia), the nucleus of the later Muscovite state. Within the clearly defined borders of this principality, well-to-do towns prospered and monasteries and churches flourished; one chronicler wrote that "all lands trembled at the name [of its ruler]." Yet early in the thirteenth century this nascent state began to crumble as princely claimants fought one another for power, much as Béla's sons had done in Hungary. Soon Rus would be conquered by the Mongols (see page 402).

Although the Byzantine Empire was already a consolidated, bureaucratic state, after the mid-twelfth century it gradually began to show weaknesses. Traders from the west — the Venetians especially — dominated its commerce. The Byzantine emperors who ruled during the last half of

Eastern Europe and Byzantium, c. 1200

the twelfth century downgraded the old civil servants, elevated imperial relatives to high offices, and favored the military elite, who nevertheless rarely came to the aid of the emperor. As Byzantine rule grew more personal and European rule became more bureaucratic, the two gradually became more alike.

The Byzantine Empire might well have continued like this for a long time. Instead, its heart was knocked out by the warriors of the Fourth Crusade (1202–1204). At the instigation of Venice, the crusaders made a detour to Constantinople on their way to the Holy Land, capturing the city in 1204. Although one of the crusade leaders was named "emperor" and ruled in Constantinople and its surrounding territory, the Byzantine Empire itself continued to exist, though disunited and weak. It retook Constantinople in 1261, but it never regained the power that it had had in the eleventh century.

REVIEW QUESTION What new sources and institutions of power became available to rulers in the second half of the twelfth century?

The Growth of a Vernacular High Culture

With their consolidation of territory, wealth, and power in the last half of the twelfth century, kings, barons, princes, and their wives and daughters supported new kinds of literature and music. For the first time on the continent, though long true in England, poems and songs were written in the vernacular, the spoken language, rather than in Latin. They celebrated the lives of the nobility and were meant to be read or sung aloud, sometimes with accompanying musical instruments. They provided a common experience for aristocrats at court. Whether in the cities of Italy or the more isolated courts of northern Europe, patrons and patronesses spent the profits from their estates and commerce on the arts. Their support helped develop and enrich the spoken language while it heightened their prestige as aristocrats.

The Troubadours: Poets of Love and Play

Already at the beginning of the twelfth century, Duke William IX of Aquitaine (1071–1126), the grandfather of Eleanor, had written lyric poems in Occitan, the vernacular of southern France. Perhaps influenced by Arabic and Hebrew love poetry from al-Andalus, his own poetry in turn provided a model for poetic forms that gained popularity through repeated performances. The final four-line stanza of one such poem demonstrates the composer's skill with words:

Per aquesta fri e tremble,	For this one I shiver and tremble,
quar de tan bon' amor l'am;	I love her with such a good love;
qu'anc no cug qu'en nasques semble	I do not think the like of her was ever born
en semblan de gran linh n'Adam.	in the long line of Lord Adam.

The rhyme scheme of this poem appears to be simple—*tremble* goes with *semble*, *l'am* with *n'Adam*—but the entire poem has five earlier verses, all six lines long and all containing the *-am*, *-am* rhyme in the fourth and sixth lines, while every other line within each verse rhymes as well.

Troubadours, lyric poets who wrote in Occitan, varied their rhymes and meters endlessly to dazzle their audiences with brilliant originality. Most of their rhymes and meters resemble Latin religious poetry of the same time, indicating that the vernacular and Latin religious cultures overlapped. Such similarity is also evident in the troubadours' choice of subjects. The most common topic, love, echoed the twelfth-century church's emphasis on the emotional relationship between God and humans.

The troubadours invented new meanings for old images. When William IX sang of his "good love" for a woman unlike any other born in the line of Adam, the words could be interpreted in two ways: they reminded listeners of the Virgin Mary, a woman unlike any other, but they also referred to William's lover, recalled in another part of the poem, where he had complained

If I do not get help soon
and my lady does not give me love,
by Saint Gregory's holy head I'll die
if she doesn't kiss me in a chamber or under a tree.

His lady's character is ambiguous: she is like the Virgin Mary, but she is also his mistress.

Troubadours, both male and female, expressed prevalent views of love much as popular singers do

---

troubadours: Vernacular poets in southern France in the twelfth and early thirteenth centuries who sang of love, longing, and courtesy.

today. The Contessa de Dia (flourished c. 1160) wrote about her unrequited love for a man:

> So bitter do I feel toward him
> whom I love more than anything.
> With him my mercy and *cortesia* [fine manners]
> are in vain.

The key to troubadour verse is the idea of *cortesia*. The word refers to courtesy (the refinement of people living at court) and to the struggle to achieve an ideal of virtue.

Historians and literary critics used to use the term *courtly love* to emphasize one of the themes of courtly literature: overwhelming love for a beautiful married noblewoman who is far above the poet in status and utterly unattainable. But this theme was only one of many aspects of love that the troubadours sang about: some of the songs boasted of sexual conquests, others played with the notion of equality between lovers, and still others preached that love was the source of virtue. The real overall theme of this literature is not courtly love; it is the power of women. No wonder Eleanor of Aquitaine and other aristocratic women patronized the troubadours: they enjoyed the image that troubadour verse gave them of themselves. Until recently, historians thought that the image was a delusion and that twelfth-century aristocratic women were valuable mainly as heiresses to marry and as mothers of sons. But new research has revealed that there were many powerful female lords in southern France. They owned property, had vassals, led battles, decided disputes, and entered into and broke political alliances as their advantage dictated. Both men and women appreciated troubadour poetry, which recognized and praised women's power even as it eroticized it.

Troubadour poetry was not read; it was sung, typically by a *jongleur*, a medieval musician. No written troubadour music exists from before the thirteenth century, and even for poems written thereafter we have music for only a fraction. This music was written on four- and five-line staves, so scholars can at least determine relative pitches, and modern musicians can sing some troubadour songs with the hope of sounding reasonably like the original. This popular music is the earliest that can be re-created authentically (Figure 11.4).

FIGURE 11.4 Troubadour Song: "I Never Died for Love"
This music is the first part of a song written by troubadour poet Peire Vidal sometime between 1175 and 1205. It has been adapted here for the treble clef. There is no time signature, but the music may easily be played by calculating one beat for each note, except for the two-note slurs, which fit into one beat together. *(From Samuel N. Rosenberg, Margaret Switten, and Gerard Le Vot, eds.,* Songs of the Troubadours and Trouvères. *Copyright © 1997 by Samuel N. Rosenberg, Margaret Switten, and Gerard Le Vot. Reprinted by permission of Taylor & Francis/Garland Publishing, http://www.taylorandfrancis.com.)*

From southern France, the troubadours' songs spread to Italy, northern France, England, and Germany. Similar poetry appeared in other vernacular languages: the *minnesingers* ("love singers") sang in German; the *trouvères* sang in the Old French of northern France. One trouvère was the English king Richard the Lion-Hearted. Taken prisoner on his return from the Third Crusade, Richard wrote a poem expressing his longing not for a lady but for the good companions of war, the knightly "youths" he had joined in battle:

> They know well, the men of Anjou and Touraine,
> those bachelors, now so magnificent and safe,
> that I am arrested, far from them, in another's
> hands.
> They used to love me much, now they love me
> not at all.
> There's no lordly fighting now on the barren
> plains,
> because I am a prisoner.

Clearly some troubadour poetry was about war rather than love. (See Document: "Bertran de Born, 'I love the joyful time of Easter,'" page 368.)

The Birth of Epic and Romance Literature

War was not as common a topic in lyric poetry as love, but long narrative poems appeared frequently

DOCUMENT

Bertran de Born, "I love the joyful time of Easter"

The troubadours mainly sang of love. But they also sometimes wrote about war. Bertran de Born, whose poems date from the second half of the twelfth century, celebrated warfare. In "I love the joyful time of Easter," he satirized the many poems that proclaimed springtime to be the moment for lovers.

I love the joyful time of Easter,
that makes the leaves and flowers come forth,
and it pleases me to hear the mirth
of the birds, who make their song
resound through the woods,
and it pleases me to see upon the meadows
tents and pavilions planted,
and I feel a great joy
when I see ranged along the field
knights and horses armed for war.

And it pleases me when the skirmishers
make the people and their baggage run away,
and it pleases me when I see behind them coming
a great mass of armed men together,
and I have pleasure in my heart
when I see strong castles besieged,
the broken ramparts caving in,
and I see the host [army] on the water's edge,
closed in all around by ditches,
with palisades, strong stakes close together.

And I am as well pleased by a lord
when he is first in the attack,
armed, upon his horse, unafraid,
so he makes his men take heart
by his own brave lordliness.

Source: Frederick Goldin, ed. and trans., *Lyrics of the Troubadours and Trouvères: An Anthology and a History* (Garden City: Anchor Books, 1973), 243–45.

Question to Consider

- **In what ways was war like love for Bertran?**

in vernacular writing. Such poems, called **chansons de geste** ("songs of heroic deeds"), followed a long oral tradition and appeared at about the same time as love poems. Like the songs of the troubadours, these epic poems implied a code of behavior for aristocrats, in this case on the battlefield.

By the end of the twelfth century, warriors wanted a guide for conduct and a common identity. Nobles and knights had begun to merge into one class as they felt threatened from below by newly rich merchants and from above by newly powerful kings. Their ascendancy on the battlefield, where they unhorsed one another with lances and long swords and took prisoners rather than killing their opponents, was also beginning to wane in the face of mercenary infantrymen who wielded long hooks and knives that ripped easily through chain mail. A knightly ethos and sense of group solidarity emerged in the face of these social, political, and military changes. The protagonists of heroic poems yearned for battle:

> The armies are in sight of one another. . . . The cowards tremble as they march, but the brave hearts rejoice for the battle.

chansons de geste (shahn SOHN duh ZHEST): Epic poems of the twelfth century about knightly and heroic deeds.

Examining the moral issues that made war both tragic and inevitable, poets played on the contradictory values of their society, such as the conflicting loyalties of friendship and vassalage or a vassal's right to a fief versus a son's right to his father's land.

These vernacular narrative poems, later called epics, focused on war. Other long poems, later called romances, explored the relationships between men and women. Romances reached their zenith of popularity during the late twelfth and early thirteenth centuries. The legend of King Arthur inspired many of them. For example, in a romance by the poet Chrétien de Troyes (c. 1150–1190) the heroic knight Lancelot, who is in love with King Arthur's wife, Queen Guinevere, comes across a comb bearing some strands of her radiant hair:

> Never will the eye of man see anything receive such honor as when [Lancelot] begins to adore these tresses. . . . Even for St. Martin and St. James he has no need.

Chrétien was evoking the familiar imagery of relics, such as bits of hair or the bones of saints, as items of devotion. Making Guinevere's hair an object of adoration not only conveyed the depth of Lancelot's feeling but also poked a bit of fun at him. Like the troubadours, the romantic poets enjoyed the interplay between religious and amorous feelings. Just as the ideal monk merges his will in God's will, Lancelot loses his will to Guinevere. When she sees him—the greatest knight in Christendom—fighting in a tournament, she tests him by asking him to do his "worst." The poor knight is obliged to lose all his battles until she changes her mind.

Lancelot was the perfect chivalric knight. The word **chivalry** derives from the French word *cheval* ("horse"); the fact that the knight was a horseman marked him as a warrior of the most prestigious sort. Perched high on his horse, his heavy lance couched in his right arm, the knight was an imposing and menacing figure. Chivalry made him gentle—except to his enemies on the battlefield. The chivalric hero was a knight constrained by a code of refinement, fair play, piety, and devotion to an ideal. Historians debate whether real knights lived up to the codes implicit in epics and romances, but there is no doubt that knights saw themselves mirrored there. They were the poets' audience; sometimes they were the poets' subject as well. For example, when the knight William the Marshal died, his son commissioned a poet to write his biography. In it, William was depicted as a model knight, courteous with the ladies and brave on the battlefield.

REVIEW QUESTION What do the works of the troubadours and vernacular poets reveal about the nature of entertainment—its themes, its audience, its performers—in the twelfth century?

Religious Fervor and Crusade

The new vernacular culture was merely one sign of the growing wealth, sophistication, and self-confidence of the late twelfth century. New forms of religious life were another. Unlike the reformed orders of the early half of the century, which had fled the cities, the new religious groups embraced (and were embraced by) urban populations. Rich and poor, male and female joined these movements. They criticized the existing church as too wealthy, impersonal, and spiritually superficial. Intensely interested in the life of Christ, men and women in the late twelfth century made his childhood, agony, death, and presence in the Eucharist—the bread and wine that became the body and blood of Christ in the Mass—the emotional focus of their own lives.

Religious fervor mixed with greed in new crusades that had little success in the Holy Land but were victorious on the borders of Europe and, as we have already seen, at Constantinople. These were the poisonous flowers of the Middle Ages.

New Religious Orders in the Cities

The quick rebuilding of the cathedral at Chartres reveals the religious fervor of late-twelfth-century city dwellers. New religious orders in the cities speak to that fervor as well. Appealing to people who did not want to leave urban society but who nevertheless wished to deepen their religious lives, the new orders—including the Franciscans and the Beguines—had enormous success. Some of these urban movements, however, so threatened established doctrine and church hierarchy that they were condemned as heresies.

Francis and the Franciscans St. Francis (c. 1182–1226) founded the most famous orthodox religious movement—the **Franciscans.** Francis was a child of city life and commerce. Expected to follow his well-to-do father in the cloth trade at Assisi in Italy, Francis began to experience doubts, dreams, and illnesses that spurred him to religious self-examination. Eventually, he renounced his family's wealth, dramatically marking the decision by casting off all his clothes and standing naked before his father, a crowd of spectators, and the bishop of Assisi. Francis then put on a simple robe and went about preaching penance to anyone who would listen.

Clinging to poverty as if, in his words, "she" were his "lady" (and thus borrowing the vocabulary of chivalry), he accepted no money, walked without shoes, and wore only one coarse tunic. Francis brought religious devotion out of the monastery and into the streets. Intending to follow the model of Christ, he received, as his biographers put it, a miraculous gift of grace: the stigmata, bleeding sores corresponding to the wounds Christ suffered on the cross.

By all accounts Francis was a spellbinding speaker, and he attracted many followers. Because they went about begging, those followers were called

chivalry: An ideal of knightly comportment that included military prowess, bravery, fair play, piety, and courtesy.

Franciscans: The religious order founded by St. Francis (c. 1182–1226) and dedicated to poverty and preaching, particularly in towns and cities.

mendicants, from the Latin verb *mendicare* ("to beg"). Recognized as a religious order by the pope, the Brothers of St. Francis (or friars, from the Latin term for "brothers") spent their time preaching, ministering to lepers, and doing manual labor. Eventually they dispersed, setting up fraternal groups throughout Italy and then in France, Spain, the Holy Land, Germany, and England. The friars sought town society, preaching to crowds and begging for their daily bread.

St. Francis converted both men and women. In 1212, an eighteen-year-old noblewoman, Clare, formed the nucleus of a community of pious women, which became the Order of the Sisters of St. Francis. At first, the women worked alongside the friars; but both Francis and the church hierarchy disapproved of their activities in the world, and soon Franciscan sisters were confined to cloisters under the rule of St. Benedict.

Beguine Psalter
Although emphasizing labor and caring for others, most Beguines were also literate. The Psalter (book of Psalms) illustrated here was probably made by Beguines. The painting focuses on Mary: in the bottom tier is the Annunciation, when she learns that she will give birth to the Savior. At the top she reigns as Queen of Heaven, with a crown on her head and the baby Jesus on her lap.

The Beguines Clare was one of many women who sought a new kind of religious expression. Some women joined convents; others became recluses, living alone, like hermits; still others sought membership in new lay sisterhoods. In northern Europe at the end of the twelfth century, laywomen who lived together in informal pious communities were called Beguines. Without permanent vows or an established rule, the Beguines chose to be celibate (though they were free to leave and marry) and often made their living by weaving cloth or tending to the sick and old. Some of them may have prepared and illustrated their own reading materials. (See the illustration on the left.) Although their daily occupations were ordinary, the Beguines' spiritual lives were often emotional and ecstatic, infused with the combined imagery of love and religion so pervasive in both monasteries and courts. One renowned Beguine, Mary of Oignies (1177–1213), who like St. Francis was said to have received stigmata, felt herself to be a pious mother entrusted with the Christ child. As her biographer, Jacques de Vitry, wrote, "Sometimes it seemed to her that for three or more days she held [Christ] close to her so that He nestled between her breasts like a baby, and she hid Him there lest He be seen by others."

Heresies In addition to the orthodox religious movements that took off at the end of the twelfth century, there was a veritable explosion of ideas and doctrines that contradicted those officially accepted by church authorities and were therefore labeled heresies. Heresies were not new in the twelfth century. But the eleventh-century Gregorian reform had created for the first time in the West a clear church hierarchy headed by a pope who could enforce a single doctrine and discipline. Clearly defined orthodoxy meant that people in western Europe now perceived heresy as a serious problem. When intense religious feeling led to the fervent espousal of new religious ideas, established authorities often felt threatened and took steps to preserve their power.

Among the most visible heretics were dualists who saw the world as being torn between two great forces—one good, the other evil. Already important in Bulgaria and Asia Minor, dualism became a prominent ingredient in religious life in Italy and the Rhineland by the end of the twelfth century. Another center of dualism was Languedoc, an area of southern France; there the dualists were called Albigensians, a name derived from the town of Albi.

Calling themselves "Christ's poor"—though modern historians have given them the collective name Cathars (from a Greek word meaning "pure")—these men and women believed that the devil had created the material world. Therefore, they renounced the world, abjuring wealth, meat, and sex. Their repudiation of sex reflected some of the attitudes of eleventh-century church reformers (whose orthodoxy, however, was never in doubt), while their rejection of wealth echoed the same concerns that moved St. Francis to embrace poverty. In many ways, the dualists simply took these attitudes to an extreme; but unlike orthodox reformers, they also challenged the efficacy and legitimacy of the church hierarchy. Attracting both men and women, young and old, literate and unlettered, and giving women access to all but the highest positions in their church, the dualists saw themselves as followers of Christ's original message. But the church called them heretics.

The church also condemned other, nondualist groups as heretical, not on doctrinal grounds but because these groups allowed their lay members to preach, challenging the authority of the church hierarchy. In Lyon (in southeastern France) in the 1170s, for example, a rich merchant named Waldo decided to take literally the Gospel message "If you wish to be perfect, then go and sell everything you have, and give to the poor" (Matt. 19:21). The same message had inspired countless monks and would worry the church far less several decades later, when St. Francis established his new order. But when Waldo went into the street and gave away his belongings, announcing, "I am not really insane, as you think," he scandalized not only the bystanders but the church as well. Refusing to retire to a monastery, Waldo and his followers—men and women who called themselves the Poor of Lyon but were called Waldensians by their enemies—lived in poverty. They spent their time preaching, quoting the Gospel in the vernacular so that everyone would understand. But the papacy rebuffed Waldo's bid to preach freely, and his community—denounced, excommunicated, and expelled from Lyon—wandered to Languedoc, Italy, northern Spain, and the Mosel valley in Germany. Most were persecuted and eventually exterminated, but a few remnants survived and their descendants were absorbed into the sixteenth-century Protestant Reformation.

Disastrous Crusades to the Holy Land

Did religious fervor also inspire the new crusades of the later twelfth century? At least some Europeans thought so. The pope called the Third Crusade "an opportunity for repentance and doing good." A poet in Bavaria wrote, "If any man now will not have pity upon [Christ's] cross and his Sepulcher [in Jerusalem], then he will not be given heavenly bliss."

In the twelfth century, the Seljuk Empire fell apart. Following the crushing defeat of the crusaders in the Second Crusade, the Muslim hero Nur al-Din united Syria and presided over a renewal of Sunni Islam. His successor, Saladin (1138–1193), fought the Christian king of Jerusalem over Egypt, which Saladin ruled, together with Syria, by 1186. Caught in a pincer, Jerusalem fell to Saladin's armies in 1187. The Third Crusade, an unsuccessful bid to retake Jerusalem from Saladin, marked a military and political turning point for the crusader states. The European outpost survived, but it was reduced to very little. Christians could continue to enter Jerusalem as pilgrims, but Islamic hegemony over the Holy Land would remain a fact of life for centuries.

The Third Crusade, 1189–1192 Led by the greatest rulers of Europe—Emperor Frederick I (Barbarossa), Philip II of France, Leopold of Austria, and Richard I of England—the Third Crusade reflected political tensions among the European ruling class. Richard, in particular, seemed to cultivate enemies. The most serious of these was Leopold, whom he offended at the siege of Acre. But the apparent personal tensions indicated a broader hostility between the kings of England and France. In this, Leopold was Philip's ally. On his return home, Richard was captured by Leopold and held for a huge ransom. He had good reason to write his plaintive poem bemoaning his captivity and the lost "love" of former friends.

The Third Crusade accomplished little and exacerbated tensions with Byzantium. Frederick Barbarossa went overland on the crusade, passing through Hungary and Bulgaria and descending into the Byzantine Empire (Map 11.2). Before his untimely death by drowning, he spent most of his time harassing the Byzantines.

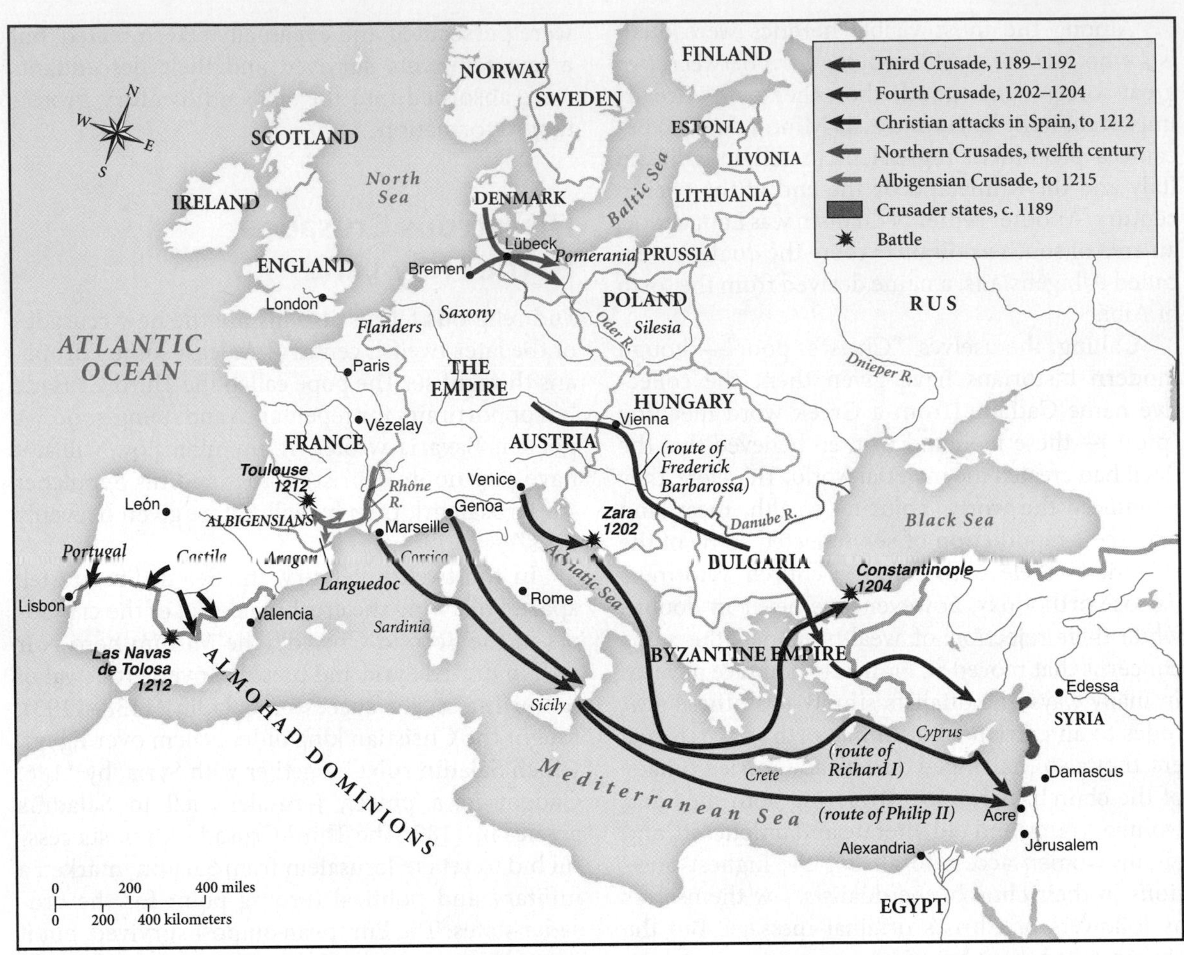

MAP 11.2 Crusades and Anti-Heretic Campaigns, 1150–1215
Europeans aggressively expanded their territory during the second half of the twelfth century. To the north, knights pushed into the Baltic Sea region. To the south, warriors pushed against the Muslims in al-Andalus and waged war against the Cathars in southern France. To the east, the new crusades were undertaken to shore up the tiny European outpost in the Holy Land. Although most of these aggressive activities had the establishment of Christianity as at least one motive, the conquest of Constantinople in 1204 had no such justification. It grew in part out of general European hostility toward Byzantium but mainly out of Venice's commercial ambitions.

The Fourth Crusade, 1202–1204

The hostilities that surfaced during the Third Crusade made it a dress rehearsal for the Fourth. Resentment had built up against the Byzantine Greeks ever since the First Crusade, when they had abandoned the crusaders after the battle of Nicaea (see page 332). During the **Fourth Crusade** prejudice and religious zeal combined to persuade many of the crusaders to change their plans and capture Constantinople rather than Jerusalem (see Map 11.2). (Some were disgusted by the new goal and went home.)

Fourth Crusade: The crusade that lasted from 1202 to 1204; its original goal was to recapture Jerusalem, but the crusaders ended up conquering Constantinople instead.

The Venetians instigated the change of plans. After the pope called the crusade, the Venetians fitted out a fine fleet of ships and galleys for the expedition. But when the crusaders arrived in Venice, there were far fewer fighters to pay for the transport than had been anticipated. To defray the costs of the ships and other expenses, the Venetians convinced the crusaders to do them some favors before taking off against the Muslims. First, they had the crusaders attack Zara, a Christian city in Dalmatia (today's Croatia) that was Venice's competitor in the Adriatic. Then they urged the army to attack Constantinople itself, where they hoped to gain commercial advantage over their rivals. Convinced of the superiority of their brand of Christianity over that of the Byzantines, the crusaders killed the inhabitants of Constantinople and ransacked the city for treasure and relics. "Never," wrote a contemporary, "was so great

DOCUMENT

The Children's Crusade (1212)

In some regions, intense lay piety led groups of unarmed young people, accompanied by priests and other adults, to attempt to free the Holy Sepulcher at Jerusalem. Chroniclers recorded their activities, some with dismay, others with amusement or admiration. The account below comes from the Ebersheim Chronicle, *written in Germany.*

Unheard-of events appeal to us from their outset, challenging us to preserve their memory. A certain little boy named Nicholas, who came from the region of Cologne, spurred on a great gathering of children through some unknown counsel, claiming that he could walk across the waves of the sea without wetting his feet and could provide sufficient provisions for those following him. The rumor of such a marvelous deed resounded through the cities and towns, and however many heard him, boys or girls, they abandoned their parents, marked themselves as crusaders, and prepared to cross the sea. And so throughout all Germany and France an infinite number of serving-boys, handmaids, and maidens followed their leader and came to Vienne, which is a city by the sea.[1] There they were taken on board some ships, carried off by pirates, and sold to the Saracens. Some who tried to return home wasted away with hunger; and many girls who were virgins when they left were pregnant when they returned. Thus, one can clearly see that this journey issued from the deception of the devil because it caused so much loss.

[1]Vienne isn't by the sea, but the child crusaders did get to various Mediterranean port cities.

Source: John Shinners, ed., *Medieval Popular Religion 1000–1500: A Reader*, 2nd ed. (Peterborough, Ontario: Broadview Press, 2007), 418–19.

Question to Consider

- **What factors help to explain the phenomenon of a mass crusade of young people?**

an enterprise undertaken by any people since the creation of the world." When one crusader discovered a cache of relics, a chronicler recalled, "he plunged both hands in and, girding up his loins, he filled the folds of his gown with the holy booty of the Church."

The pope decried the sack of Constantinople, but he also took advantage of it, ordering the crusaders to stay there for a year to consolidate their gains. Plans to go on to the Holy Land were never carried out. The crusade leaders chose one of themselves—Baldwin of Flanders—to be emperor, and he, the other princes, and the Venetians divided the conquered lands among themselves.

Popes continued to call crusades to the Holy Land until the mid-fifteenth century, but the Fourth Crusade marked the last major mobilization of men and leaders for such an enterprise. Working against these expeditions were the new values of the late twelfth century, which placed a premium on the interior pilgrimage of the soul and valued rulers who stayed home and cared for their people. (See Document, "The Children's Crusade [1212]," above.)

Victorious Crusades in Europe and on Its Frontiers

Armed expeditions against those perceived as infidels were launched not only to the Holy Land but also much nearer to home. In the second half of the twelfth century, the Spanish reconquista continued with increasing success and virulence, new wars of conquest were waged at the northern edge of Europe, and a crusade was launched against the Albigensians living in Europe itself.

The War in Spain In the second half of the twelfth century, Christian Spain achieved a political configuration that would last for centuries, dominated to the east by the kingdom of Aragon; in the middle by Castile, whose ruler styled himself emperor; and in the west by Portugal, whose ruler similarly transformed his title from *prince* to *king*. The three leaders competed for territory and power, but above all they sought an advantage against the Muslims to the south (Map 11.3).

Muslim disunity aided the Christian reconquest of Spain. The Muslims of al-Andalus were themselves beset from the south by new waves of Berber Muslims from North Africa. Claiming religious purity, these North African zealots declared their own holy war against the Andalusians. Threatened from both north and south, the Muslim leaders of Spain tried to negotiate with their Christian neighbors, sometimes even swearing vassalage to them.

But the crusading ideal held no room for such subtleties. The reconquista was set back by Berber victories, and competition between the Christian Spanish states prevented a coordinated effort. Nevertheless, piecemeal conquests—followed by the granting of law codes to regulate relations among

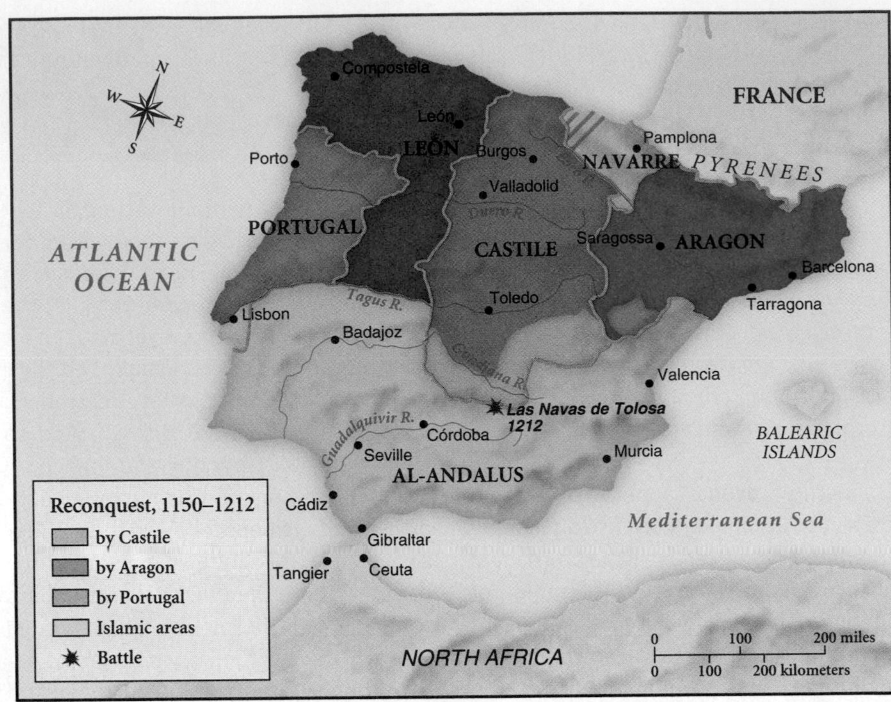

MAP 11.3 The Reconquista, 1150–1212
Slowly but surely the Christian kingdoms of Spain encroached on al-Andalus, taking Las Navas de Tolosa, deep in Islamic territory, in 1212. At the center of this activity was Castile. It had originally been a tributary of León, but in the twelfth century it became a power in its own right. (In 1230, León and Castile merged into one kingdom.) Meanwhile, the ruler of Portugal, who had also been dependent on León, began to claim the title of king, which was recognized officially in 1179, when he put Portugal under the protection of the papacy. Navarre was joined to Aragon until 1134, when it became, briefly, an independent kingdom. (In 1234, the count of Champagne came to the throne of Navarre, and thereafter its history was as much tied to France as to Spain.)

new Christian settlers as well as the Muslims, Mozarabs (Christians who had lived under the Muslims), and Jews who remained — gradually brought more territory under the control of the north. In 1212, a crusading army of Spaniards led by the kings of Aragon and Castile defeated the Muslims decisively at the battle of Las Navas de Tolosa. "On their side 100,000 armed men or more fell in the battle," the king of Castile wrote afterward, "but of the army of the Lord . . . incredible though it may be, unless it be a miracle, hardly 25 or 30 Christians of our whole army fell. O what happiness! O what thanksgiving!" The decisive turning point in the reconquista had been reached, though all of Spain came under Christian control only in 1492.

The Northern Crusades Christians flexed their military muscle along Europe's northern frontiers as well. By the twelfth century, the peoples living along the Baltic coast — partly pagan, mostly Slavic- or Baltic-speaking — had learned to glean a living and a profit from inhospitable soil and climate. Through fishing and trading, they supplied the rest of Europe and Russia with slaves, furs, amber, wax, and dried fish. Like the earlier Vikings, they combined commercial competition with outright raiding, so that the Danes and the Germans of Saxony both benefited and suffered from their presence. As noted in Chapter 10 (page 333), during the Second Crusade a number of campaigns had been launched against the people on the Baltic coast. Thus began the Northern Crusades, which continued intermittently until the early fifteenth century.

The Danish king Valdemar I (r. 1157–1182) and the Saxon duke Henry the Lion led the first phase of the Northern Crusades. Their initial attacks on the Slavs were uncoordinated — in some instances, the Danes and Saxons even fought each other. But in key raids in the 1160s and 1170s, the two leaders worked together briefly to bring much of the region west of the Oder River under their control. They took some land outright — Henry the Lion apportioned conquered territory to his followers, for example — but more often the Slavic princes surrendered and had their territories reinstated once they became vassals of the Christian rulers. Meanwhile, churchmen arrived: the Cistercians came long before the first phase of fighting had ended, confidently building their monasteries to the very banks of the Oder River. Slavic peasants surely suffered from the conquerors' fire and pillage, but the Slavic ruling classes ultimately benefited from the northern crusades. Once converted to Christianity, they found it advantageous for both their eternal salvation and their worldly profit to join new crusades to areas still farther east.

Meanwhile German traders, craftspeople, and colonists poured in, populating new towns and cities along the Baltic coast and dominating the shipping that had once been controlled by non-Christians. The leaders of the crusades gave these townsmen some political independence but demanded a large share of the cities' wealth in return.

Although less well known than the crusades to the Holy Land, the Northern Crusades had far more lasting effects: they settled the Baltic region with German-speaking lords and peasants and forged a permanent relationship between northeastern Europe and its neighbors to the south and west. With the Baltic dotted with churches and monasteries and its peoples dipped into baptismal waters, the region would gradually adopt the institutions of western medieval society—cities, guilds, universities, castles, and manors. The Livs (whose region was eventually known as Livonia) were conquered by 1208, and their bishop sent knights northward to conquer the Estonians. A cooperative venture between the Polish and German aristocracy conquered the Prussians, and German peasants eventually settled Prussia. Only the Lithuanians managed to resist western conquest, settlement, and conversion.

The Albigensian Crusade The first crusade to be launched within Europe itself was against the Cathars in southern France. It began with papal missions to preach to the people there, convert the heretics, and, if necessary use force. The Dominican Order had its start in this way. Its founder, St. Dominic (1170–1221), recognized that preachers of Christ's word who came to the region on horseback, followed by a crowd of servants and wearing fine clothes, had no moral leverage with their audience. Dominic and his followers, like their heretical adversaries, rejected material riches and instead went about on foot, preaching and begging. They resembled the Franciscans, both organizationally and spiritually, and were also called friars.

The missions did not have the success anticipated, however, and in 1208, the murder of a papal

Almourol Castle

In the early twelfth century, the papacy recognized the reconquista as equivalent to a crusade, and the rulers of Portugal, Castile, and Aragon persuaded the Templars and other military orders to help them hold on to regions that had formerly been Muslim. When the Portuguese ruler conquered the western end of the Tagus River valley in the mid-twelfth century, he entrusted some of the Muslim strongholds there to the Templars. They rebuilt one of them as Almourol castle, using it to defend Portugal's new frontier. *(© Patrick Frilet/Hemis/Corbis.)*

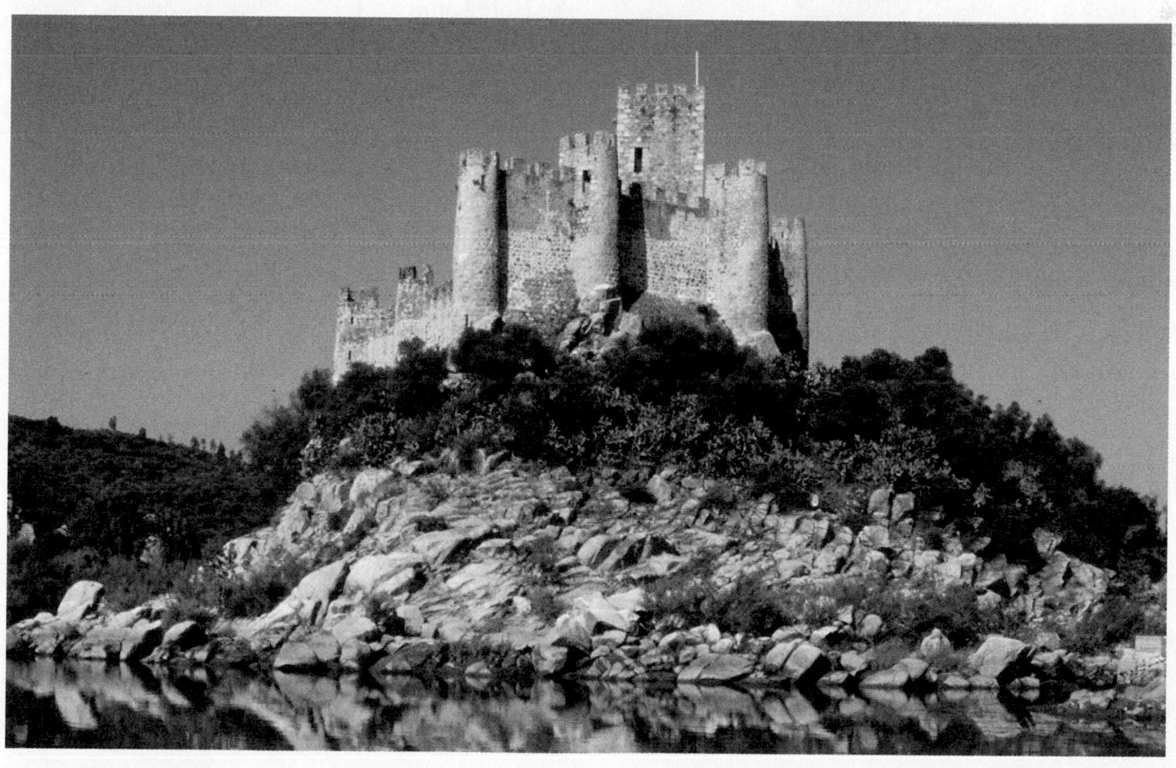

legate in southern France prompted the pope to demand that northern princes take up the sword, invade Languedoc, wrest the land from the heretics, and populate it with orthodox Christians. The Albigensian Crusade (1209–1229) marked the first time the pope offered warriors fighting an enemy within Christian Europe all the spiritual and temporal benefits of a crusade to the Holy Land. The crusaders' monetary debts were suspended, and they were promised that their sins would be forgiven after forty days' service. Like all other crusades, the Albigensian Crusade had political as well as religious dimensions. It pitted southern French princes, who often had heretical sympathies, against northern leaders eager to demonstrate their piety and win new possessions. After sixteen years of warfare, the Capetian kings of France took over leadership of the crusade. By 1229, all resistance was broken, and Languedoc was brought under the French crown.

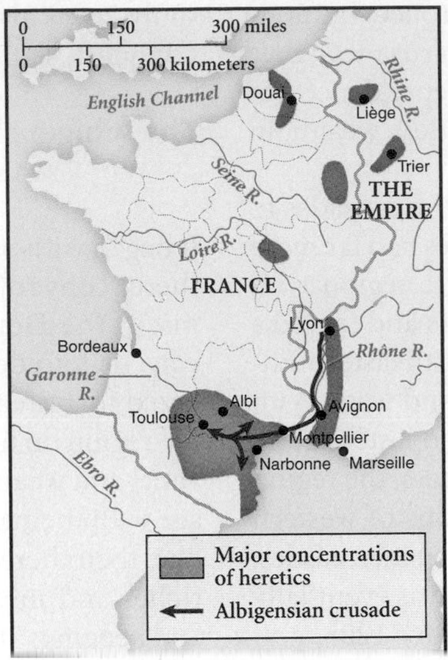

The Albigensian Crusade, 1209–1229

REVIEW QUESTION How did the idea of crusade change from the time of the original expedition to the Holy Land?

Conclusion

In the second half of the twelfth century, Christian Europe expanded from the Baltic Sea to the southern Iberian peninsula. European settlements in the Holy Land, by contrast, were nearly obliterated. When western Europeans sacked Constantinople in 1204, Europe and the Islamic world became the dominant political forces in the West.

Powerful territorial kings and princes established institutions of bureaucratic authority. They hired staffs to handle their accounts, record acts, collect taxes, issue writs, and preside over courts. A money economy provided the finances necessary to support the personnel now hired by medieval governments. Cathedral schools and universities became the training grounds for the new administrators. A new lay vernacular culture celebrated the achievements and power of the ruling class, while Gothic architecture reflected above all the pride and power of the cities.

New religious groups blossomed — Beguines, Franciscans, Dominicans, and heretics. However dissimilar the particulars, their beliefs and lifestyles all reflected the fact that people, especially city dwellers, yearned for a deeper spirituality.

Intense religiosity helped fuel the flames of crusades, which were now fought more often and against an increasing variety of foes, not only in the Holy Land but also in Spain, in southern France, and on Europe's northern frontiers. With heretics voicing criticisms and maintaining their beliefs, the church, led by the papacy, now defined orthodoxy and declared dissenters its enemies. The peoples on the Baltic coast became targets for new evangelical zeal; the Byzantines became the butt of envy, hostility, and finally enmity. European Christians still considered Muslims arrogant heathens, and the deflection of the Fourth Crusade did not stem the zeal of popes to call for new crusades to the Holy Land.

Confident and aggressive, the leaders of Christian Europe in the thirteenth century would attempt to impose their rule, legislate morality, and create a unified worldview impregnable to attack. But this drive for order would be countered by unexpected varieties of thought and action, by political and social tensions, and by intensely personal religious quests.

FOR FURTHER EXPLORATION

- **For additional primary-source material from this period**, see *Sources of the Making of the West*, Fourth Edition.
- **For Web sites, images, and documents related to topics in this chapter**, visit *Make History* at bedfordstmartins.com/hunt.

MAPPING THE WEST

Europe and Byzantium, c. 1215

The major transformation in the map of the West between 1150 and 1215 was the conquest of Constantinople and the setting up of European rule there until 1261. The Byzantine Empire was now split into two parts. Bulgaria once again gained its independence. If Venice had hoped to control the Adriatic by conquering Constantinople, it must have been disappointed, for Hungary became its rival over the ports of the Dalmatian coast.

Chapter 11 Review

Online Study Guide bedfordstmartins.com/hunt

Key Terms and People

In the grid below, identify the term or person and explain its historical significance. (To do this exercise online, go to bedfordstmartins.com/hunt.)

Term	Who or What & When	Why It Matters
Romanesque (p. 350)		
Gothic architecture (p. 351)		
Henry II (p. 354)		
common law (p. 357)		
Philip II (Philip Augustus) (p. 358)		
Magna Carta (p. 359)		
Frederick I (Barbarossa) (p. 362)		
troubadours (p. 366)		
chansons de geste (p. 368)		
chivalry (p. 369)		
Franciscans (p. 369)		
Fourth Crusade (p. 372)		

Review Questions

1. What was new about education and architecture in the twelfth and early thirteenth centuries?
2. What new sources and institutions of power became available to rulers in the second half of the twelfth century?
3. What do the works of the troubadours and vernacular poets reveal about the nature of entertainment—its themes, its audience, its performers—in the twelfth century?
4. How did the idea of crusade change from the time of the original expedition to the Holy Land?

Making Connections

1. What were the chief differences that separated the ideals of the religious life in the period 1150–1215 from those of the period 1050–1150?
2. How was the gift economy associated with Romanesque architecture and the money economy with the Gothic style?
3. How do political developments—the growth of bureaucratic institutions, the development of strong monarchies, the growth of city governments—help explain the rise and popularity of vernacular literature and song in the twelfth and thirteenth centuries?

Important Events

Date	Event
1139–1153	Civil War in England
1152–1190	Reign of Frederick Barbarossa
1154–1189	Reign of King Henry II
1176	Battle of Legnano
1180–1223	Reign of Philip II Augustus
1182–1226	Francis of Assisi
1189–1192	The Third Crusade
1202–1204	The Fourth Crusade
1204	Fall of Constantinople to crusaders
1204	Philip takes Normandy, Anjou, Maine, Touraine, and Poitou from John
1209–1229	Albigensian Crusade
1212	Battle of Las Navas de Tolosa; triumph of the reconquista
1214	Battle of Bouvines
1215	Magna Carta

- Consider three events: **The Third Crusade (1189–1192)**, **The Fourth Crusade (1202–1204)**, and the **Albigensian Crusade (1209–1229)**. What were their various causes and results? How were they differently waged and led?

SUGGESTED REFERENCES

For the new schools, Abelard is a key primary source, while Clanchy provides perceptive background. Cultural and artistic developments are discussed in both Burl and Coldstream. Bartlett and Bradbury are essential for politics.

*Abelard's *The Story of My Misfortunes:* http://www.fordham.edu/halsall/source/abelard-sel.html

Aurell, Martin. *The Plantagenet Empire, 1154–1224*. Trans. David Crouch. 2007.

Bartlett, Robert. *England under the Norman and Angevin Kings, 1075–1225*. 2000.

Bouchard, Constance Brittain. *"Every Valley Shall Be Exalted": The Discourse of Opposites in Twelfth-Century Thought*. 2003.

Bradbury, Jim. *Philip Augustus: King of France*. 1998.

Burl, Aubrey. *Courts of Love, Castles of Hate: Troubadours and Trobairitz in Southern France, 1071–1321*. 2008.

Cheyette, Fredric L. *Ermengard of Narbonne and the World of the Troubadours*. 2001.

*Chrétien de Troyes. *Yvain: The Knight of the Lion*. Trans. Burton Raffel. 1987.

Christiansen, Eric. *The Northern Crusades*. 2nd ed. 1998.

Clanchy, Michael. *Abelard: A Medieval Life*. 1997.

Coldstream, Nicola. *Medieval Architecture*. 2002.

**Crusade of Frederick Barbarossa: The History of the Expedition of the Emperor Frederick and Related Texts*. Trans. G. A. Loud. 2010.

Gaunt, Simon, and Sarah Kay. *The Troubadours: An Introduction*. 1999.

*Goldin, Frederick. *Lyrics of the Troubadors and Trouvères: Original Texts, with Translations*. 1973.

Gothic architecture: http://www.bc.edu/bc_org/avp/cas/fnart/arch/gothic_arch.html

Hudson, John. *The Formation of the English Common Law: Law and Society in England from the Norman Conquest to Magna Carta*. 1996.

Moore, R. I. *The Formation of a Persecuting Society: Power and Deviance in Western Europe, 950–1250*. 2nd ed. 2007.

Pegg, Mark Gregory. *A Most Holy War: The Albigensian Crusade and the Battle for Christendom*. 2008.

Robson, Michael. *The Franciscans in the Middle Ages*. 2006.

Stephensen, David. *Heavenly Vaults: From Romanesque to Gothic in European Architecture*. 2009.

Troubadour poetry:
http://globegate.utm.edu/french/globegate_ mirror/occit.html

*Primary source.

CHAPTER

12

The Medieval Synthesis— and Its Cracks

1215–1340

In the second half of the thirteenth century, a wealthy patron asked a Parisian workshop specializing in manuscript illuminations to decorate Aristotle's *On the Length and Shortness of Life*. Most Parisian illuminators knew very well how to illustrate the Bible, liturgical books, and the writings of the church fathers. But Aristotle was a Greek who had lived before the time of Christ, and he was skeptical about the possibility of an afterlife. His treatise on life ended with death. The workshop's artists did not care about this fact. They illustrated Aristotle's work as if he had been a Christian and had believed in the immortal soul. As shown in the illustration opposite this page, the artists decorated one of the opening letters of the text with a depiction of the Christian Mass for the dead, a rite that is performed for the eternal salvation of Christians. In this way, the artists subtly but surely incorporated the pagan Aristotle into Christian belief and practice.

In the period 1215–1340, Europeans at all levels, from workshop artisans to kings and popes, thought that they could harmonize all ideas with Christianity, all aspects of this world with the next, and all of nature with revelation. Sometimes, as in the case of the illumination made for Aristotle's work, or in the writings of scholars seeking to bring together faith and reason, the synthesis seemed to work. But often it was forced, fragile, or elusive: not all people were willing to subordinate their beliefs to the tenets of Christianity; kings and popes debated without resolution the limits of their power; and theologians fought over the place of reason in matters of faith. Discord continually threatened expectations of unity and harmony.

New institutions of power and control were created to ensure the medieval synthesis. In 1215, the church set forth a comprehensive set of laws for

Christianizing Aristotle
This illumination was created for a thirteenth-century Latin translation of Aristotle's *On the Length and Shortness of Life*. Although Aristotle did not believe in the eternity of the soul, the artists nevertheless placed a depiction of the Christian Mass for the dead in one of the book's initials, in this way revealing their conviction that the ancient teachings of Aristotle and Christian practice worked together. (*© Biblioteca Apostolica Vaticana [Vatican Library] Vat. Lat. 2071, f. 297.*)

both clergy and laity. Designed to create an orderly Christian society, these laws sought to regulate lay life and suppress heresy. They led to the establishment of courts of inquisition designed to find and punish heretics—those who dissented from church teachings and authority. Ironically, the Inquisition called attention to divergence even as it intended to enforce unity.

Around the same time, many Christian laypeople spontaneously sought new ways to express their religious zeal. This resulted in new devotional practices. It also led to the persecution of others—such as Jews and lepers—who were seen as contaminating the purity of a newly fervent Christian life.

On the whole, however, people did not so much seek to stamp out opposition as to reconcile opposites and find common ground in differences. Medieval thinkers, writers, musicians, and artists attempted to reconcile faith and reason and to find the commonalities in the sacred and secular realms. At the level of philosophy, this quest led to a new method of inquiry and study known as scholasticism. Yet even some scholastic thinkers pointed out cracks and disjunctions in the syntheses achieved.

To impose greater order and unity, kings and other rulers found new ways to extend their influence over their subjects. They used the tools of taxes, courts, and even representative institutions to control their realms. Yet the laws did not prevent dissent, and rulers often did not gain all the power they wanted. During this period the Empire weakened, the papacy was forced to move out of Rome, and the Mongols challenged Christian rulers. Soon natural disasters—crop failures and famine—added to the tension.

CHAPTER FOCUS **In what areas of life did thirteenth-century Europeans try to find harmony and impose order, and how successful were these attempts?**

The Church's Mission

The church had long sought to reform the secular world. In the eleventh century, during the Gregorian reform, such efforts focused on the king. In the thirteenth century, however, the church hoped to purify all of society. It tried to strengthen its institutions of law and justice to combat heresy and heretics, and it supported preachers who would bring the official views of the church to the streets. In this way, the church attempted to reorder the world in the image of heaven, with everyone following one rule of God in harmony. To some degree, the church succeeded in this endeavor; but it also came up against the limits of control, as dissident voices and forces clashed with its vision.

Innocent III and the Fourth Lateran Council

Innocent III (r. 1198–1216) was the most powerful, respected, and prestigious of medieval popes. As pope, he allowed St. Francis's group of impoverished followers to become a new church order, and he called the Fourth Crusade, which mobilized a large force drawn from every level of European society. The first pope to be trained at universities, Innocent studied theology at Paris and law at Bologna. From theology, he learned to tease new meaning out of canonical writings to magnify papal authority: he thought of himself as ruling in the place of Christ the King, with kings and emperors existing to help the pope. From law, Innocent gained his conception of the pope as lawmaker and of law as an instrument of moral reformation.

Innocent III: The pope (r. 1198–1216) who called the Fourth Lateran Council; he was the most powerful, respected, and prestigious of medieval popes.

1188 King Alfonso IX summons townsmen to the *cortes*

1215 Fourth Lateran Council

1232 Frederick II finalizes Statute in Favor of the Princes

1175 — 1200 — 1225 — 1250

1212–1250 Reign of Frederick II

1226–1270 Reign of Louis IX (St. Louis)

1240 Mongols capture Kiev

Innocent used the traditional method of declaring church law: a council. Presided over by Innocent, the **Fourth Lateran Council** (1215) attempted to regulate all aspects of Christian life. The comprehensive legislation it produced aimed at reforming both the clergy and the laity. Innocent and the bishops who met at the council hoped in this way to create a society united under God's law. They expected that Christians, lay and clerical alike, would work together harmoniously to achieve the common goal of salvation. They did not anticipate either the sheer variety of responses to their message or the persistence of those who defied it altogether.

The Laity and the Sacraments

For laypeople, perhaps the most important canons (church laws) of the Fourth Lateran Council concerned the sacraments, the rites the church believed Jesus had instituted to confer sanctifying grace. Building on the reforms of the eleventh century, the council made the obligations that the sacraments imposed on the laity more precise and detailed. One canon required Christians to attend Mass and to confess their sins to a priest at least once a year. The increasing importance of the Eucharist as God's powerful instrument of salvation was reinforced by the council's definition:

> [Christ's] body and blood are truly contained in the sacrament of the altar under the forms of bread and wine, the bread and wine having been changed in substance [transubstantiated], by God's power, into his body and blood, so that in order to achieve this mystery of unity we receive from God what he received from us. Nobody can effect this sacrament except a priest who has been properly ordained according to the church's keys, which Jesus Christ himself gave to the apostles and their successors.

The council's emphasis on this moment of transformation, which it termed transubstantiation, gave the host—the bread taken at communion—new importance.

Other canons of the Fourth Lateran Council codified the traditions of marriage. The church declared that it had the duty to discover any impediments to a union (such as a close relationship by blood), and it claimed jurisdiction over marital disputes. The canons further insisted that children conceived within clandestine or forbidden marriages be declared illegitimate; they were not to inherit from their parents or become priests.

The impact of these provisions was perhaps less dramatic than church leaders hoped. Well-to-do London fathers still included their bastard children in their wills. On English manors, sons conceived out of wedlock regularly took over their parents' land. Men and women continued to marry in secret, and even churchmen had to admit that the consent of both parties made any marriage valid. Nevertheless, many men and women accepted the obligation to take communion and confess once a year, and priests proceeded to call out the banns (announcements of marriages) to discover any impediments to them.

Labeling the Jews

Innocent III had wanted the Fourth Lateran Council to condemn Christian men who had sexual intercourse with Jewish women and then claimed ignorance as their excuse. But, building on the anti-Jewish feelings that had been mounting throughout the twelfth century, the council went even further, requiring all Jews to advertise their religion by some outward sign: "We decree that [Jews] of either sex in every Christian province at all times shall be distinguished

---

Fourth Lateran Council: The council that met in 1215 and covered the important topics of Christianity, among them the nature of the sacraments, the obligations of the laity, and policies toward heretics and Jews.

1265 English commons summoned to Parliament

1273 Thomas Aquinas publishes the *Summa Theologiae*

1275

1302 First Meeting of the French Estates General

1300

1309–1378 Avignon papacy

1313–1321 Dante writes *Divine Comedy*

1315–1322 Great Famine

1325

Jewish Couple
In this illustration from a Hebrew prayer book, a couple sits in a garden of lilies under a starry sky, illustrating the Bible's Song of Solomon 4:8: "come with me from Lebanon my bride." Hebrew commentators interpreted the bride as standing for Israel, while the speaker, the groom, was God. The groom wears a traditional Jewish hat, while the bride, Israel, wears a crown. There is an irony here: Christians portrayed the church as a crowned female. However, in this case the woman wears a blindfold, making her like the Christian depiction of the allegorical figure of the Jewish synagogue. Thus, this seemingly innocuous illustration gives the synagogue the status and dignity of the church. *(Staats- und Universitätsbibliothek Hamburg Carl von Ossietzky, Cod. Levy 37, fol. 169.)*

from other people by the character of their dress in public."

As with all church laws, these took effect only when local political powers enforced them. In many instances, rulers did so with zeal, not so much because they were eager to humiliate Jews but rather because they could make money selling exemptions to Jews who were willing to pay to avoid the requirements. Nonetheless, sooner or later Jews almost everywhere had to wear a badge as a sign of their second-class status. In southern France and in a few places in Spain, Jews were supposed to wear round badges. In England, Oxford required a rectangular badge, while Salisbury demanded that Jews wear special clothing. In Vienna and Germany, they were told to put on pointed hats. (See the illustration above.)

The Suppression of Heretics The Fourth Lateran Council's longest decree blasted heretics: "Those condemned as heretics shall be handed over to the secular authorities for punishment." If the secular authority did not carry out the punishment, the heretic was to be excommunicated. If he or she had vassals, they were to be released from their oaths of fealty. The lands of heretics were to be taken over by orthodox Christians.

Rulers heeded these declarations. Already some had taken up arms against heretics in the Albigensian Crusade (1209–1229). As a result of this crusade, southern France, which had been the home of most Albigensians, came under French royal control. The continuing presence of heretics there and elsewhere led church authorities inspired by the Fourth Lateran Council to set up a court of papal inquisitors. The Inquisition became permanent in 1233.

The Inquisition

The word *inquisition* simply means "investigation"; secular rulers had long used the method to summon people together, either to discover facts or to uncover and punish crimes. In its zeal to end heresy and save souls, the thirteenth-century church used the Inquisition to ferret out "heretical depravity." Calling suspects to testify, inquisitors, aided by secular authorities, rounded up virtually entire villages and interrogated everyone. (See "New Sources, New Perspectives," page 386.)

Typically, the inquisitors first called the people of a district to a "preaching," where they gave a sermon and promised clemency to those who promptly confessed their heresy. Then, at a general inquest, they questioned each man and woman who seemed to know something about heresy: "Have you ever seen any heretics? Have you heard them preach? Attended any of their ceremonies? Adored heretics?" The judges assigned relatively lenient penalties to those who were not aware that they held heretical beliefs and to heretics who quickly recanted. But unrepentant heretics were punished severely because the church believed that such people threatened the salvation of all.

In the thirteenth century, for the first time, long-term imprisonment became a tool to repress heresy, even if the heretic confessed. "It is our will," wrote one tribunal, "that [Raymond Maurin and Arnalda, his wife,] because they have rashly transgressed against God and holy church . . . be thrust into perpetual prison to do [appropriate] penance, and we command them to remain there in perpetuity." The inquisitors also used imprisonment to force people to recant, to give the names of other heretics, or to admit a plot. As the quest for religious control spawned wild fantasies of conspiracy, the inquisitors pinned their fears on real people.

Lay Piety

The church's zeal to reform the laity was matched by the desire of many laypeople to become more involved in their religion. They flocked to hear the preaching of friars and took what they heard to heart. Some women found new outlets for their piety by focusing on the Eucharist.

Preaching Friars and Receptive Townspeople The friars made themselves a permanent feature of the towns. At night they slept in their friaries, but they spent their days preaching. So, too, did other men, often trained in the universities and willing to take to the road to address throngs of townsfolk. When Berthold, a Franciscan who traveled the length and breadth of Germany giving sermons, came to a town, a high tower was set up for him outside the city walls. A pennant advertised his presence and let people know which way the wind would blow his voice. St. Anthony of Padua preached in Italian to huge audiences that had lined up hours in advance to be sure they would have a place to hear him.

Townspeople flocked to hear such preachers because they wanted to know how the Christian message applied to their daily lives. They were concerned, for example, about the ethics of moneymaking, sex in marriage, and family life. In turn, the preachers represented the front line of the church. They met the laity on their own turf, spoke in the vernacular that all could understand, and taught them to shape their behaviors to church teachings.

Laypeople further tied their lives to the mendicants, particularly the Franciscans, by becoming tertiaries. They adopted the practices of the friars—prayer and works of charity, for example—while continuing to live in the world, raising families and tending to the normal tasks of daily life, whatever their occupation. Even kings and queens became tertiaries.

The Piety of Women All across Europe, women in the thirteenth century sought outlets for their intense piety. As in previous centuries, powerful families founded new nunneries, especially within towns and cities. On the whole, these were set up for the daughters of the very wealthy. Ordinary women found different modes of religious expression. Some sought the lives of quiet activity and rapturous mysticism of the Beguines, others chose the lives of charity and service of women's mendicant orders, and still others decided on domestic lives of marriage and family punctuated by religious devotions. Elisabeth of Hungary, who married a German prince at the age of fourteen, raised three children. At the same time, she devoted her life to fasting, prayer, and service to the poor.

Many women were not as devout as Elisabeth. In the countryside, they cooked their porridge, brewed their ale, and raised their children. They attended church only on major feast days or for churching—the ritual of purification after a pregnancy. In the cities, working women scratched out a meager living. They sometimes made pilgrimages to relic shrines to seek help or cures. Religion was a part of these women's lives, but it did not dominate them.

For some urban women, however, religion was the focus of life, and the church's attempt to define and control the Eucharist had some unintended results. The new emphasis on the holiness of the transformed wine and bread induced some of these pious women to eat nothing but the Eucharist. One such woman, Angela of Foligno, reported that the consecrated bread swelled in her mouth, tasting sweeter than any other food. For these women, eating the Eucharist was truly eating God: they believed that Christ's crucifixion was the literal sacrifice of his body, to be eaten by sinful men and women as the way to redeem themselves and others. Renouncing all other foods became part of a life of service, because many of these devout women gave the poor the food they refused to eat.

Such women both accepted and challenged the pronouncements of the Fourth Lateran Council about the meaning of the Eucharist. They agreed that only priests could say Mass, but some of them bypassed their own priests, receiving the Eucharist (as they explained) directly from Christ in the form of a vision. Although men dominated the institutions that governed political, religious, and economic affairs, these women found ways to control their own lives and to some extent the lives of those around them, both those whom they served and those they lived with. Typically involved with meal preparation and feeding, like other women of the time, these holy women found a way to use their control over ordinary food to gain new kinds of social and religious power.

Jews and Lepers as Outcasts

While Christian women found new roles for themselves, non-Christians were pushed further into the category of "outsiders." To be sure, the First and Second Crusades gave outlet to anti-Jewish feeling. Nevertheless, they were abnormal episodes in the generally stable if tense relationship between Christians and Jews in Europe up to the middle of the

NEW SOURCES, NEW PERSPECTIVES

The Peasants of Montaillou

While historians can learn from material evidence how medieval peasants lived and worked, it is nearly impossible to find out what peasants thought. Almost all of our written sources come from the elite classes, who, if they noticed peasants at all, certainly did not care about their ideas. How, then, can historians hear and record the voices of peasants themselves? Until the 1960s, historians cared little about hearing those voices. They wanted to know about economic structures rather than peasant mentalities.

For that reason, historians did not notice an extremely important source of peasant voices, the Inquisition register made at the command of Bishop Fournier of Pamiers in the years 1318–1325. Fournier was a zealous anti-heretic, and when he became bishop of a diocese that harbored many Albigensians, he put the full weight of his office behind rounding them up. He concentrated on one particularly "heretic-infested" village, Montaillou, in the south of France near the Spanish border. Interrogating 114 people (including 48 women) over seven years, he committed their confessions and testimony to parchment with a view to punishing those who were heretics. Fournier was not interested in the peasants' voices; he simply wanted to know their religious beliefs and every other detail of their lives and thoughts. However, the long-term result of Fournier's zealous inquest—though he would not be happy to hear it—was to preserve the words of a whole village of peasants, shepherds, artisans, and shopkeepers. Fournier's register gathered dust in the Vatican archives for centuries, until it was transcribed and published in 1965. Only in 1975 was its great potential for peasant history made clear; in that year, Emmanuel Le Roy Ladurie published *Montaillou: The Promised Land of Error*, which for the first time brought a medieval peasant village to life.

Le Roy Ladurie's book reveals the myths, beliefs, rivalries, tensions, love affairs, tendernesses, and duplicities of a small peasant community in which all the people, even those who were relatively well off, worked with their hands; in which wealth was calculated by the size of a family's herd of livestock; and in which the church's demands for tithes seemed outrageously unfair.

The register shows a community torn apart by the opportunities the Inquisition gave to informers. The village priest, from a well-off family, was very clear about why he was denouncing his parishioners. He liked the Albigensians, he said (he was probably one himself), but he added: "I want to be revenged on the peasants of Montaillou, who have done me harm, and I will avenge myself in every possible way." However, the register also shows a community united by love: parents cared about their children, husbands and wives loved one another, and illicit lovers were caught up in passion. One affair took place between the village priest and a woman of somewhat higher rank. The priest courted the woman, Béatrice, for half a year, and after she gave in they met two or three nights a week. In the end, though, Béatrice decided to marry someone else and left the village.

Béatrice was not the only person of independent mind in Montaillou. Many people there were indeed heretics in the sense that their beliefs defied the teachings of the church. But they called themselves "good Christians." Other villagers remained in the Catholic fold. And still others in the region had their own ideas, as may be seen from Raimond de l'Aire's testimony, on the right.

twelfth century. Then things changed dramatically, as kings became more powerful, popular piety deepened, and church law singled Jews out for particular discrimination.

Jews were not alone in this new segregation. Lepers, too, had to wear a special costume, were forbidden to touch children, could not eat with the unafflicted, and were kept in leper houses.

Jews Exploited and Expelled As noted in Chapter 10, when Christian lords came to dominate the countryside, most Jews were forced off the manors and into the cities. Their opportunities narrowed with the growing monopoly of guilds, which prohibited Jewish members. Thus in many places Jews were barred from the crafts and trades. In effect, many were compelled to become usurers (moneylenders) because other fields were closed to them. Even with Christian moneylenders available (for some existed despite the Bible's prohibition against charging interest for loans), lords, especially kings, borrowed from Jews and encouraged others to do so because, along with their newly asserted powers, European rulers claimed the Jews as their serfs and Jewish property as their own. In England, where Jews had arrived with the Norman conquest in 1066, a special royal exchequer of the Jews was created in 1194 to collect unpaid debts due after the death of a Jewish creditor.

Even before 1194, the king of England had imposed new and arbitrary taxes on the Jewish community. Similarly in France, persecuting Jews and confiscating their property benefited both the treasury and the authoritative image of the king. In 1198, the French king declared that Jews must be mon-

Fournier's register became a "new" source because Le Roy Ladurie had new questions and sought a way to answer them, treating his evidence the way ethnographers treat reports by native peoples they have interviewed. Today, some historians question Le Roy Ladurie's approach, arguing that an Inquisition record cannot be handled in the same way that ethnographers consider information from their informants. For example, they point out that the words of the peasants were translated from Occitan, the language they spoke, to Latin for the official record. What readers hear are not the voices of the peasants but rather their ideas filtered through the vocabulary and summaries of the elite. Moreover, the peasants called before the tribunal were held in prison, feared for their lives, and were forced to talk about events that had taken place ten or more years earlier. In light of these circumstances, to what extent is their testimony a direct window onto their lives? Nevertheless, the register remains a precious source for learning at least something about what ordinary people thought and felt in a small village about seven hundred years ago.

Raimond de l'Aire's Testimony

One witness Fournier recorded was Raimond de l'Aire, who was not from Montaillou but rather from Tignac, a small town in Fournier's diocese. An older man had told [Raimond de l'Aire] that a mule has a soul as good as a man's, and, Fournier wrote,

> from this belief he [Raimond] had by himself deduced that his own soul and those of other men are nothing but blood, because when a person's blood is taken away, he dies. He also believed that a dead person's soul and body both die, and that after death nothing human remains. . . . From this he believed that the human soul after death [is] neither good nor evil, and that there is no hell or paradise in another world where human souls are rewarded or punished.

Source for Raimond de l'Aire: *Heresy and Authority in Medieval Europe: Documents in Translation*, ed. Edward Peters (Philadelphia: University of Pennsylvania Press, 1980), 253.

Further Reading

Boyle, Leonard. "Montaillou Revisited: *Mentalité* and Methodology." In J. A. Raftis, ed., *Pathways to Medieval Peasants*. 1981.

Le Roy Ladurie, Emmanuel. *Montaillou: The Promised Land of Error*. 1978. The original French version was published in 1975.

Resaldo, Renato. "From the Door of His Tent: The Fieldworker and the Inquisitor." In James Clifford and George E. Marcus, eds., *Writing Culture: The Poetics and Politics of Ethnography*. 1986.

Questions to Consider

1. **In what ways are modern court cases like Fournier's Inquisition register? In what ways are they unlike such a source? Could you use modern court cases to reconstruct the life of a community?**
2. **What are the advantages and the pitfalls of using a source such as the register for historical research?**
3. **Do you think that Raimond might have made up his testimony? Why or why not?**
4. **What does this testimony suggest about the impact of church doctrines in the French countryside?**

eylenders or money changers exclusively. Their activities were to be taxed and monitored by royal officials.

Limiting Jews to moneylending in an increasingly commercial economy clearly served the interests of kings. But lesser lords who needed cash also benefited: they borrowed money from Jews and then, as happened in York (England) in 1190, they orchestrated an attack to rid themselves of their debts and of the Jews to whom they owed money. Churchmen, too, used credit in a money economy but resented the fiscal obligations it imposed. With their drive to create centralized territorial states and their desire to make their authority known and felt, powerful rulers of Europe—churchmen and laymen alike—exploited and coerced the Jews while drawing on and encouraging a wellspring of elite and popular anti-Jewish feeling.

Attacks against Jews were inspired by more than resentment against Jewish money and the desire for power and control. They also, ironically, grew out of the codification of Christian religious doctrine and the anxiety of Christians about their own institutions. For example, in the twelfth century, the newly rigorous definition of the Eucharist represented by the word *transubstantiation* meant to many pious Christians that the body of Christ literally lay on the altar. Reflecting this unsettling view, sensational stories, originating in clerical circles but soon widely circulated, told of Jews who secretly sacrificed Christian children in a morbid revisiting of the crucifixion of Jesus.

In 1144, in one of the earliest instances of this charge, the body of a young boy named William was found in the woods near Norwich (England). His uncle, a priest, accused local Jews of killing the

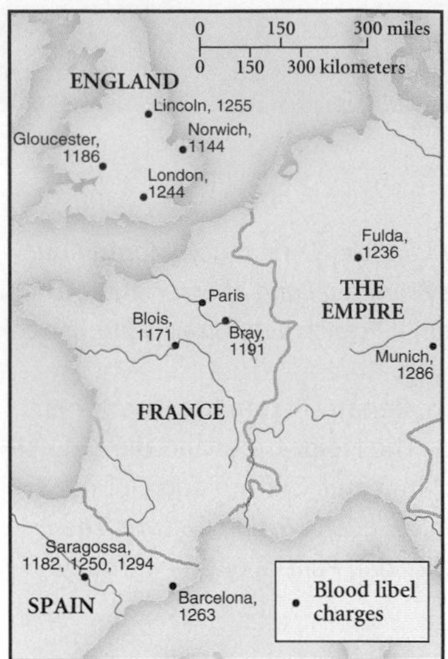

Blood Libel Charges in Europe, c. 1100–1300 *(Adapted from David Ditchburn, Simon MacLean, and Angus MacKay, eds.,* Atlas of Medieval Europe, *2nd ed. [London: Routledge, 2007].)*

child. A monk connected to the cathedral at Norwich, Thomas of Monmouth, took up the cause. He had visions that told him to exhume the body from the cemetery and bring it into the monastery. Miracles followed, and soon Thomas wrote *The Life and Martyrdom of St. William of Norwich.* According to his account, the Jews carefully prepared at Passover for the horrible ritual slaughter of the boy, whom they had chosen "to be mocked and sacrificed in scorn of the Lord's passion." This charge, which historians have called **blood libel**, was made frequently about other "martyrs" and led to massacres of Jews in cities in England, France, Spain, and Germany. (In truth, however, Jews had no rituals involving blood sacrifice at all.)

Some communities simply expelled Jews. At Bury-Saint-Edmunds, which was under the jurisdiction of the abbot of the monastery, a chronicler of the time described one such expulsion:

> And when they had been sent forth and conducted under armed escort to other towns [in England], the abbot ordered that all those who from that time forth should receive Jews or harbor them in the town of St. Edmund should be solemnly excommunicated in every church and at every altar.

Eventually, in 1291, the Jews were cast out from the entire kingdom of England. Most dispersed to France and Germany, but to a sad welcome. In 1306, for example, King Philip the Fair had them driven from France, though they were allowed to reenter, tentatively, in 1315.

Fearing the Contamination of Lepers

People attacked by **leprosy**—a disease that causes skin lesions and attacks the peripheral nerves—were an unimportant minority in medieval society until the eleventh century. Then, beginning around 1075 and extending to the fourteenth century, lepers, though still a small minority, became the objects of both charity and disgust. Houses for lepers were set up both to provide for them and to segregate them from everyone else.

Leprosy delivered three blows: it was horribly disfiguring; it was associated with sin in the Bible; and it was contagious. In 1179, the Third Lateran Council took note of the fact that "lepers cannot dwell with the healthy or come to church with others" and asked that, where possible, special churches and cemeteries be set aside for them. No doubt this inspired a boom in the foundation of leper houses, which peaked between 1175 and 1250.

Before the leper went to such a house, he or she was formally expelled from the community of Christians via a ceremony of terrible solemnity. In northern France, for example, the leper had to stand in a cemetery, his or her face veiled. Mass was intoned, and the priest threw dirt on the leper as if he or she were being buried. "Be dead to the world, be reborn in God," the priest said, continuing:

> I forbid you to ever enter the church or monastery, fair, mill, marketplace, or company of persons. I forbid you to ever leave your house without your leper's costume [usually gloves and a long robe], in order that one recognize you and that you never go barefoot. I forbid you to wash your hands or any thing about you in the stream or in the fountain.

In 1321, the prohibition against drinking in the stream or fountain gained more sinister meaning as false rumors spread that Muslims had recruited both Jews and lepers to poison all the wells of Christendom.

REVIEW QUESTION How did people respond to the teachings and laws of the church in the early thirteenth century?

Reconciling This World and the Next

Just as the church wanted to regulate worldly life in accordance with God's plan for salvation, so contemporary thinkers, writers, musicians, and artists sought to harmonize the secular with the sacred realms. Scholars wrote treatises that reconciled faith with reason, poets and musicians sang of the links between heaven and human life on earth, and artists expressed the same ideas in stone and sculpture and on parchment. In the face of many contradictions, all of these groups were largely successful in communicating an orderly image of the world.

---

blood libel: The charge that Jews used the blood of Christian children in their Passover ritual; though false, it led to massacres of Jews in cities in England, France, Spain, and Germany in the thirteenth century.

leprosy: A bacterial disease that causes skin lesions and attacks the peripheral nerves. In the later Middle Ages, lepers were isolated from society.

The Achievement of Scholasticism

Scholasticism was the culmination of the method of logical inquiry and exposition pioneered by masters like Peter Abelard and Peter the Chanter (see Chapter 11). In the thirteenth century, the method was used to summarize and reconcile all knowledge. Many of the thirteenth-century scholastics (those who practiced scholasticism) were members of the Dominican and Franciscan orders and taught in the universities. On the whole, they were confident that knowledge obtained through the senses and reason was compatible with the knowledge derived from faith and revelation.

One of the scholastics' goals was to demonstrate this harmony. The scholastic summa, or summary of knowledge, was a systematic exposition of the answer to every possible question about human morality, the physical world, society, belief, action, and theology. Another goal of the scholastics was to preach the conclusions of these treatises. As one scholastic put it, "First the bow is bent in study, then the arrow is released in preaching": first you study the summa, and then you hit your mark—convert people—by preaching. Many of the preachers who came to the towns were students and disciples of scholastic university teachers.

The method of the summa borrowed much of the vocabulary and many of the rules of logic long ago outlined by Aristotle. Even though Aristotle was a pagan, scholastics considered his coherent and rational body of thought the most perfect that human reason alone could devise. Because they had the benefit of Christ's revelations, the scholastics believed they could take Aristotle's philosophy one necessary step further and reconcile human reason with Christian faith. Confident in their method and conclusions, scholastics embraced the world and its issues.

Some scholastics considered questions about the natural world. Albertus Magnus (c. 1200–1280) was a major theologian who also contributed to the fields of biology, botany, astronomy, and physics. His reconsideration of Aristotle's views on motion led the way to distinctions that helped scientists in the sixteenth and seventeenth centuries arrive at the modern notion of inertia.

St. Thomas Aquinas (1225–1274) was perhaps the most famous scholastic. A hefty man who was renowned for his composure in scholastic disputation, Thomas came from a noble Neapolitan family that had hoped to see him become a powerful bishop rather than a poor university professor. When he was about eighteen years old, he thwarted his family's wishes and joined the Dominicans. Soon he was studying at Cologne with Albertus Magnus. At thirty-two, he became a master at the University of Paris.

Like many other scholastics, Thomas considered Aristotle to be "the Philosopher," the authoritative voice of human reason, which he sought to reconcile with divine revelation in a universal and harmonious scheme. In 1273, he published his monumental *Summa Theologiae* (sometimes called the *Summa Theologica*), intended to cover all important topics, human and divine. He divided these topics into questions, exploring each one thoroughly and concluding with a decisive position and a refutation of opposing views. Yet even Thomas departed from Aristotle, who had explained the universe through human reason alone. In Thomas's view, God, nature, and reason were in harmony, so even though Aristotle's arguments could be used to explore both the human and the divine order, there were some exceptions. "Certain things that are true about God wholly surpass the capability of human reason, for instance that God is three and one," Thomas wrote. But he thought these exceptions were rare.

Many of Thomas's questions spoke to the keenest concerns of his day. He asked, for example, whether it was lawful to sell something for more than its worth. (See the illustration on page 390.) Thomas arranged his argument systematically, first quoting authorities that seemed to declare every sort of selling practice, even deceptive ones, to be lawful; this was the *sic* ("yes") position. Then he quoted an authority that opposed selling something for more than its worth; this was the *non*. Following that, he gave his own argument, prefaced by the words "I answer that." Unlike Abelard, who had not supplied answers, Thomas came to clear conclusions that harmonized both the yes and the no responses. In the case of selling something for more than it was worth, he pointed out that price and worth depended on the circumstances of the buyer and seller. He concluded that charging more than a seller had originally paid could be legitimate at times, as, for example, "when a man has great need of a certain thing, while another man will suffer if he is without it."

For townspeople engaged in commerce and worried about biblical admonitions against greed, Thomas's ideas about selling practices addressed burning questions. Hoping to go to heaven as well as to reap the profits of their business ventures, laypeople listened eagerly to preachers who delivered

---

scholasticism: The method of logical inquiry used by the scholastics, the scholars of the medieval universities; it applied Aristotelian logic to biblical and other authoritative texts in an attempt to summarize and reconcile all knowledge.

Friars and Usurers
Although clerics sometimes borrowed money, the friars had a different attitude. St. Francis, son of a merchant, refused to touch money altogether. In this illumination from about 1250, a Franciscan (in light-colored robes) and a Dominican (in black) reject offers from two usurers, whose profession they are thus shown to condemn. Other friars, including Thomas Aquinas, worked out justifications for some kinds of moneymaking professions, though not usury. *(bpk, Berlin/Bibliothèque Nationale, Paris, France/photo by Gerard Le Gall/Art Resource, NY.)*

their sermons in the vernacular but who based their ideas on the Latin summae (the plural of *summa*) of Thomas and other scholastics. Thomas's conclusions aided townspeople in justifying their worldly activities.

Scholastics like Thomas were enormous optimists. They believed that everything had a place in God's scheme of things, that the world was orderly, and that human beings could make rational sense of it. Their logical arguments filled the classrooms, spilled into the friars' convents, found their way into the shops of artisans, and even crept between the sheets of lovers. (See Document: "Thomas Aquinas Writes about Sex," page 391.) Scholastic philosophy helped give ordinary people a sense of purpose and a guide to behavior.

Yet even among scholastics, unity was elusive. In his own day, Thomas was accused of placing too much emphasis on reason and relying too fully on Aristotle. Later scholastics argued that reason could not find truth through its own faculties and energies. In the summae of John Duns Scotus (c. 1266–1308), for example, the world and God were less compatible. John, whose name Duns Scotus reveals his Scottish origin, was a Franciscan who taught at both Oxford and Paris. For John, human reason could know truth only through the "special illumination of the uncreated light," that is, by divine illumination. But unlike his predecessors, John believed that this illumination came not as a matter of course but only when God chose to intervene. John—and others—experienced God as sometimes willful rather than reasonable. Human reason could not soar to God; God's will alone determined whether or not a person could know him. In this way, John separated the divine and secular realms, and the medieval synthesis cracked.

New Syntheses in Writing and Music

Thirteenth-century writers and musicians, like scholastics, presented complicated ideas and feelings as harmonious and unified syntheses. Writers explored the relations between this world and the next, whereas musicians found ways to bridge sacred and secular forms of music.

Vernacular Literature Comes of Age Vernacular literature may be said to have reached its full development with the work of Dante Alighieri (1265–1321), who harmonized the mysteries of faith with the poetry of love. Born in Florence in a time of political turmoil, Dante incorporated the major figures of history and his own day into his most famous poem, *Commedia*, written between 1313 and 1321. Later known as *Divina commedia* (*Divine Comedy*), Dante's poem describes the poet taking an imaginary journey from hell to purgatory and finally to paradise.

The poem is an allegory in which every person and object must be read at more than one level. At the most literal level, the poem is about Dante's travels. At a deeper level, it is about the soul's search for meaning and enlightenment and its ultimate discovery of God in the light of divine love. Just as Thomas Aquinas employed Aristotle's logic to reach important truths, so Dante used the pagan poet Virgil as his guide through hell and purgatory. And just as Thomas believed that faith went beyond reason to even higher truths, so Dante found a new guide representing earthly love to lead him through most of paradise. That guide was Beatrice, a Florentine girl with whom Dante had fallen in love as a boy and whom he never forgot. But only faith, in the form of the divine love of the Virgin Mary, could bring Dante to the culmination of his journey—a blinding and inexpressibly awesome vision of God:

> What I then saw is more than tongue can say.
> Our human speech is dark before the vision. The
> ravished memory swoons and falls away.

DOCUMENT

Thomas Aquinas Writes about Sex

Glad to broach every topic, human and divine, the scholastic Thomas Aquinas (1225–1274) took up the issue of sex in his Summa against the Gentiles. *He wrote this work around 1260 to provide arguments against the scientific views of—among others—elite Muslim scholars of ancient Greek learning, such as Averroes. The section on sex came when Thomas took up issues involved in living a moral life. As usual, he first offered arguments [here 1–3] for the position that he disagreed with: that sex outside of marriage ("fornication") was not a sin. Then he offered a long rebuttal [excerpted here as 4–6].*

The Reason Why Simple Fornication Is a Sin According to Divine Law, and That Matrimony Is Natural

[1] . . . We can see the futility of the argument of certain people who say that simple fornication is not a sin. For they say: Suppose there is a woman who is not married, or under the control of any man, either her father or another man. Now, if a man performs the sexual act with her, and she is willing, he does not injure her, because she favors the action and she has control over her own body. Nor does he injure any other person, because she is understood to be under no other person's control. So, this does not seem to be a sin.

[2] Now, to say that he injures God would not seem to be an adequate answer [against this argument]. For we do not offend God except by doing something contrary to our own good, as has been said. But this does not appear contrary to man's good. Hence, on this basis, no injury seems to be done to God.

[3] Likewise, it also would seem an inadequate answer to say that some injury is done to one's neighbor by this action, inasmuch as he may be scandalized. Indeed, it is possible for him to be scandalized by something which is not in itself a sin. In this event, the act would be accidentally sinful. But our problem is not whether simple fornication is accidentally a sin, but whether it is so essentially.

[4] Hence, we must look for a solution in our earlier considerations. We have said that God exercises care over every person on the basis of what is good for him. Now, it is good for each person to attain his end, whereas it is bad for him to swerve away from his proper end. Now, this should be considered applicable to the parts, just as it is to the whole being; for instance, each and every part of man, and every one of his acts, should attain the proper end. Now, though the male semen is superfluous in regard to the preservation of the individual, it is nevertheless necessary in regard to the propagation of the species. Other superfluous things, such as excrement, urine, sweat, and such things, are not at all necessary; hence, their emission contributes to man's good. Now, this is not what is sought in the case of semen, but, rather, to emit it for the purpose of generation, to which purpose the sexual act is directed. But man's generative process would be frustrated unless it were followed by proper nutrition, because the offspring would not survive if proper nutrition were withheld. Therefore, the emission of semen ought to be so ordered that it will result in both the production of the proper offspring and in the upbringing of this offspring.

[5] It is evident from this that every emission of semen, in such a way that generation cannot follow, is contrary to the good for man. And if this be done deliberately, it must be a sin. Now, I am speaking of a way from which, in itself, generation could not result: such would be any emission of semen apart from the natural union of male and female. For which reason, sins of this type are called contrary to nature. But, if by accident generation cannot result from the emission of semen, then this is not a reason for it being against nature, or a sin; as for instance, if the woman happens to be sterile.

[6] Likewise, it must also be contrary to the good for man if the semen be emitted under conditions such that generation could result but the proper upbringing would be prevented. We should take into consideration the fact that, among some animals where the female is able to take care of the upbringing of offspring, male and female do not remain together for any time after the act of generation. This is obviously the case with dogs. But in the case of animals of which the female is not able to provide for the upbringing of offspring, the male and female do stay together after the act of generation as long as is necessary for the upbringing and instruction of the offspring. Examples are found among certain species of birds whose young are not able to seek out food for themselves immediately after hatching. In fact, since a bird does not nourish its young with milk, made available by nature as it were, as occurs in the case of quadrupeds, but the bird must look elsewhere for food for its young, and since besides this it must protect them by sitting on them, the female is not able to do this by herself. So, as a result of divine providence, there is naturally implanted in the male of these animals a tendency to remain with the female in order to bring up the young. Now, it is abundantly evident that the female in the human species is not at all able to take care of the upbringing of offspring by herself, since the needs of human life demand many things which cannot be provided by one person alone. Therefore, it is appropriate to human nature that a man remain together with a woman after the generative act, and not leave her immediately to have such relations with another woman, as is the practice with fornicators.

Source: Thomas Aquinas, *Summa contra Gentiles*, book 3, Part II. Translated by Vernon J. Bourke at http://dhspriory.org/thomas/ContraGentiles3b.htm#122.

Question to Consider

- **Why might Thomas have based his arguments against fornication on what is good for man rather than on citations from the Bible?**

DOCUMENT

The Debate between Reason and the Lover

Jean de Meun (d. c. 1305) was the continuator of the Romance of the Rose, *a poem about a lover's quest for his beloved. Jean organized his part of the poem as a series of dialogues between the lover and various figures he encountered on his journeys. Meeting with the figure of Reason, the lover hears the following jaundiced definition of love.*

[Reason says:]
If I know anything of love, it is
Imaginary illness freely spread
Between two persons of opposing sex,
Originating from disordered sight,
Producing great desire to hug and kiss
And see enjoyment in a mutual lust.
[To which the Lover responds:]
Madam, you would betray me; should I scorn
All folk because the God of Love now frowns?
Shall I no more experience true love,
But live in hate? Truly, so help me God,
Then were I moral sinner worse than thief!

Source: Guillaume de Lorris and Jean de Meun, *The Romance of the Rose*, trans. Harry W. Robbins (New York: Dutton, 1962), 97, 102.

Question to Consider

■ **Whose point of view—Reason's or the lover's—do you think Jean de Meun agrees with, and why do you think so?**

Dante's poem electrified a wide audience. By elevating one dialect of Italian—the language that ordinary Florentines used in their everyday life—to a language of exquisite poetry, Dante was able to communicate an orderly and optimistic vision of the universe in an even more exciting and accessible way than the scholastics had. So influential was his work that it is no exaggeration to say that modern Italian is based on Dante's Florentine dialect.

Other writers of the period used different methods to express the harmony between heaven and earth. The anonymous author of the *Quest of the Holy Grail* (c. 1225), for example, wrote about the adventures of some of the knights of King Arthur's Round Table to convey the doctrine of transubstantiation and the wonder of the vision of God. In *The Romance of the Rose*, begun by one poet and finished by another, a lover seeks the rose, his true love. In the long dream that the poem describes, the narrator's search for the rose is thwarted by personifications of Love, Shame, Reason, Abstinence, and so on. They present him with arguments for and against love. In the end, sexual love is made part of the divine scheme—and the lover plucks the rose. (See Document, "The Debate between Reason and the Lover," at left.)

Polyphony and the Motet Just as some writers asserted the harmony of heavenly and earthly things, so musicians experimented at this time with combining sacred and secular music. This was quite new. The music before this time, plainchant (see Chapter 11), had a particular sequence of notes for a given text. It is true that sometimes a form of harmony was achieved when two voices sang exactly the same melody an interval apart. This was the first form of polyphony, the simultaneous sounding of two or more melodies. In the twelfth century, musicians experimented with freer melodies. One voice might go up the scale, for example, while the other went down, achieving even so a pleasing harmony. Or one voice might hold a pitch while the other danced around it.

Now, in the thirteenth century, some musicians put secular and sacred tunes together. This form of music, which probably originated in Paris, was called the motet (from the French *mot*, meaning "word"). The typical thirteenth-century motet had two or three melody lines, or "voices". The lowest, usually from a chant melody that was used in a church service, had only one or two words; sometimes, it was played on an instrument rather than sung. The remaining melodies had different texts, either Latin or French (or one of each), which were sung simultaneously. Latin texts were usually sacred, whereas French ones were secular, dealing with themes such as love and springtime. The motet thus wove the sacred (the chant melody in the lowest voice) and the secular (the French texts in the upper voices) into a sophisticated tapestry of words and music.

Like the scholastic summae, motets were written by and for a clerical elite. (See the illustration on page 393.) Yet they incorporated the music of ordinary people, such as the calls of street vendors and the boisterous songs of students. In turn, they touched the lives of everyone, for polyphony influenced every form of music, from the Mass to popular songs that entertained laypeople and churchmen alike.

Complementing the motet's complexity was the development of a new notation for rhythm. A primitive form of musical notation had been created in the ninth century; by the eleventh century, composers could indicate pitch but had no way to show the duration of the notes. Music theorists of the thirteenth century, however, developed increasingly

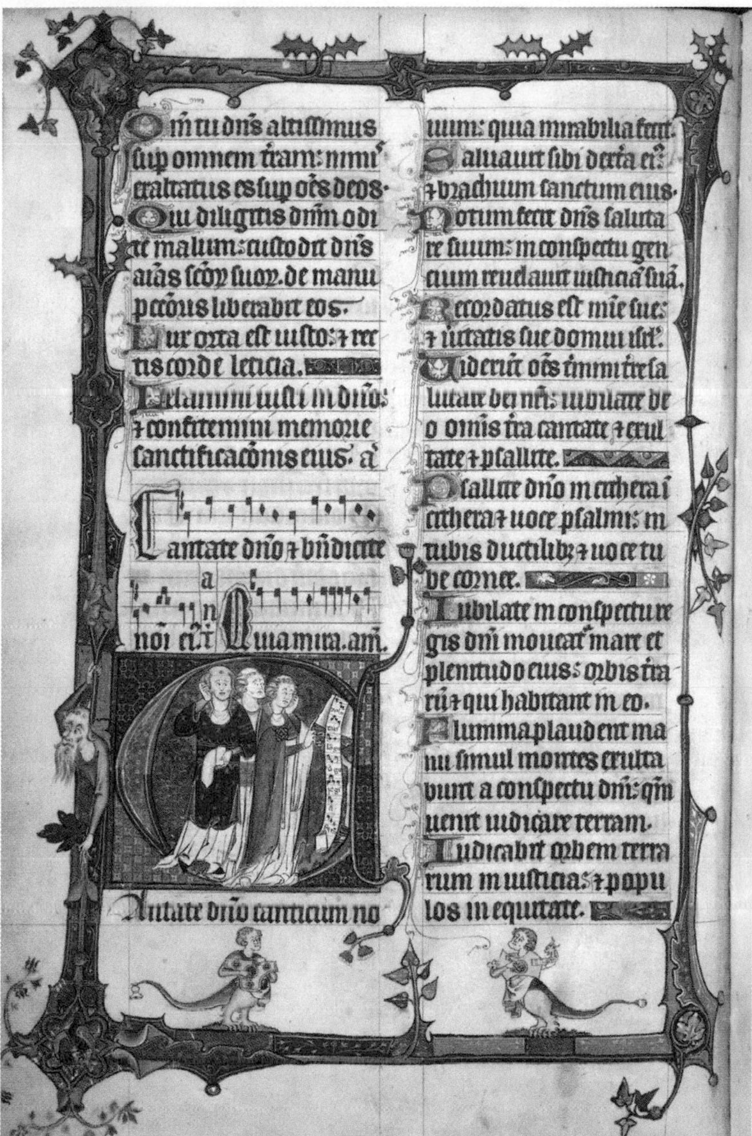

Singing a Motet
In this fourteenth-century English Psalter, the artist has illustrated the first letter of Psalm 96, which begins, "O sing to the Lord a new song," with a depiction of three clerics singing a motet. Its words and musical notation are written on a scroll draped over a lectern. *(© The British Library Board, All Rights Reserved. Arundel 83, fol. 63v.)*

precise methods to indicate rhythm. Franco of Cologne, for example, in his *Art of Measurable Song* (c. 1280), used different shapes to mark the number of beats each note should be held. His system became the basis of modern musical notation. Because each note could now be allotted a specific duration, written music could express new and complicated rhythms. The music of the thirteenth century reflected both the melding of the secular and the sacred and the possibilities of greater order and control.

Gothic Art

Gothic architecture—like philosophy, literature, and music—melded the sacred and the secular. By the end of the thirteenth century, the Gothic style, which had its beginnings at Saint-Denis and Chartres (see Chapter 11), had spread across most of Europe. Elements of Gothic style began to appear as well in other forms of art: stained glass, sculpture, painting, and the decorative motifs in manuscript illuminations.

Stained Glass Because pointed arches and flying buttresses allowed the walls of a Gothic church to be pierced with large windows, stained glass became a newly important art form. (See the illustrations on page 394.) To make this colored glass, workers added chemicals to sand, heated the mixture until it was liquid, and then blew and flattened it. Adding cobalt produced blue glass; copper oxide made red. Yellow, a rare color, was produced by painting clear glass with silver nitrate, then firing it in a kiln. Artists cut shapes from these colored glass sheets and held them in place with lead strips. They painted details right on the glass. As the sun shone through the finished windows, they glowed like jewels.

Last Judgment
Stained glass could illustrate complex theological truths. In this thirteenth-century depiction of the Last Judgment from Bourges Cathedral in France, two colorful devils force two naked sinners into the toothy mouth of hell. Licks of red flame greet them. While the devils enjoy their task (the green one is smiling), the sinners grimace and seem to cry out in pain. *(Saint-Etienne Cathedral, Bourges, France/The Bridgeman Art Library International.)*

The size of the windows allowed glaziers to depict complicated themes. The windows at Sainte-Chapelle, for example, tell the story of salvation in 1,134 scenes, starting with events of the Old Testament and ending with the Apocalypse. (All such windows must be read from bottom to top.) Themes ranged from heaven to hell. (See the illustration at left.)

Sculpture Gothic cathedrals were decorated with sculpture. This was not new: Romanesque architecture had also featured sculpture (see the opening illustration for Chapter 10, page 310). But Gothic figures were separated from their background and sculpted in the round. The figures evoked motion—turning, moving, and interacting; at times, they even smiled. (See the illustration on page 395, bottom left.) Taken together, they were often meant to be "read" like a scholastic summa. The south portal of Chartres cathedral is a good example of the way in which Gothic sculpture could be used to sum up a body of truths. The sculptures in each massive doorway have related themes: the left doorway depicts the martyrs, the right the confessors, and the center the Last Judgment. Like Dante's *Divine Comedy*, these portals tell the story of the soul's pilgrimage from the suffering of this world to eternal life.

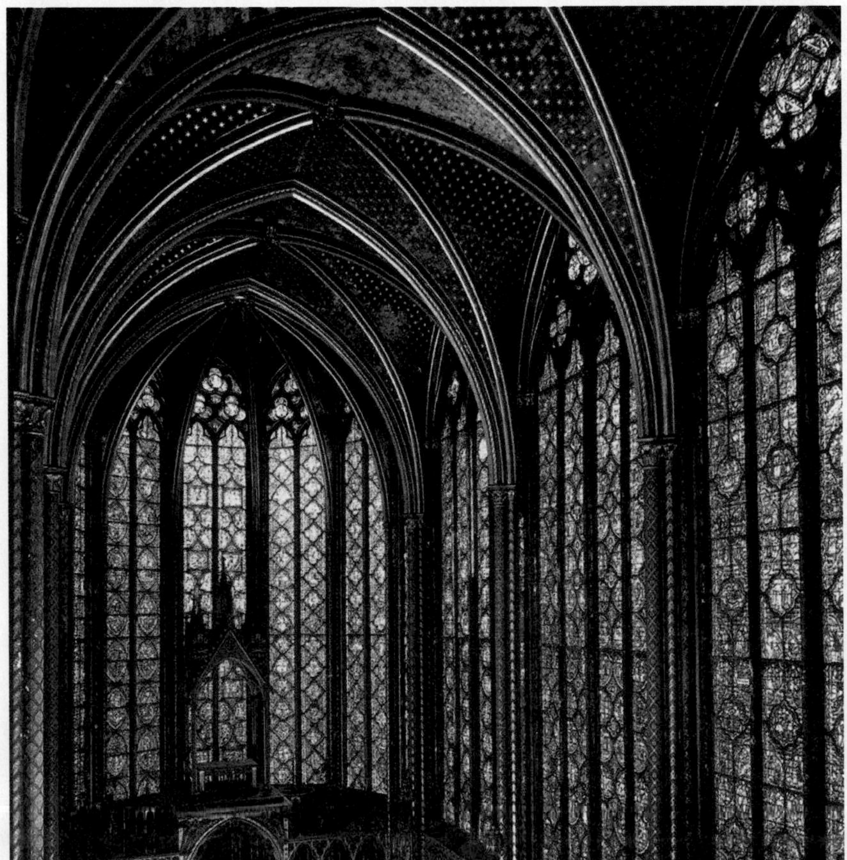

Sainte-Chapelle
Gothic architecture opened up the walls of the church to windows, as may be seen at Sainte-Chapelle, the private chapel of the French king Louis IX (St. Louis). Consecrated in 1248, it was built to house Christ's crown of thorns and other relics of the Passion. This photo shows the interior of the upper chapel looking east. *(Giraudon/The Bridgeman Art Library International.)*

Gothic sculpture began in France and was adopted, with many variations, elsewhere in Europe during the thirteenth century. The Italian sculptor Nicola Pisano (c. 1220–1278?), for example, crafted dignified figures inspired by classical forms. German sculptors created excited, emotional figures that sometimes gestured dramatically to one another.

Painting By the early fourteenth century, the naturalistic sculptures so prominent in architecture were reflected in painting as well. This new style is evident in the work of Giotto (1266–1337), a Florentine artist who changed the emphasis of painting, which had been predominantly symbolic, decorative, and intellectual. When Giotto filled the walls of a private chapel at Padua with paintings depicting scenes of Christ's life, he experimented with the illusion of depth. Giotto's figures, appearing weighty and voluminous, express a range of emotions as they move across interior and exterior spaces. (See the illustration below.) In bringing sculptural naturalism to a flat surface, Giotto stressed three-dimensionality, illusional space, and human emotion. By fusing earthly forms with religious meaning, Giotto found yet another way to fuse the natural and divine realms.

Gothic style also appeared in paintings as a decorative motif. Manuscript illuminations feature the shape of stained-glass windows and pointed vaults as common background themes. (See the illustration on page 396 for one example.) The colors of Gothic manuscripts echoed the rich hues of stained glass.

REVIEW QUESTION How did artists, musicians, and scholastics try to link the physical world with the divine?

The Annunciation
Figures decorating Gothic churches, such as this one at Reims (in northern France), were carved in the round. Here the angel Gabriel (on the left) turns and smiles joyfully at Mary, who looks down modestly as he announces that she will give birth to Jesus. *(Scala/Art Resource, NY.)*

Giotto's *Birth of the Virgin*
This depiction of the Virgin Mary's birth pays attention to the homey details of a thirteenth-century Florentine aristocratic household. Those details portray a sequence: the baby is bathed and swaddled by maidservants in the bottom tier, while above she is handed to her mother, St. Anne, who reaches out eagerly for the child. *(The Art Archive/Scrovegni Chapel, Padua/Dagli Orti.)*

Louis IX and Blanche of Castile
This miniature shows St. Louis, portrayed as a young boy, sitting opposite his mother, Blanche of Castile. Blanche served as regent twice in Louis's lifetime, once when he was too young to rule and a second time when he was away on crusade. The emphasis on the equality of queen and king may be evidence of Blanche's influence on and patronage of the artist. *(Detail from* Moralized Bible, *France, c. 1230. MS. M. 240, F.8. The Pierpont Morgan Library/Art Resource, NY.)*

The Politics of Control

The quest for order, control, and harmony also became part of the political agendas of princes, popes, and cities. These rulers and institutions imposed—or tried to impose—their authority ever more fully and systematically through taxes, courts, and sometimes representative institutions. Vestiges of these systems live on in modern European parliaments and in the U.S. Congress.

Louis IX of France is a good example of a ruler whose power increased during this period. In contrast, the emperor—who once claimed both Germany and Italy—gave up most of his power in Germany and lost it in Italy as well, while the papacy moved from Rome to Avignon, a real blow to its prestige. In Italy the rise of *signori* (lords) meant that the communes, which had long governed many cities, gave way to rule by one strong man.

A new political entity, the Mongols, directly confronted the rulers of Russia, Poland, and Hungary. Installing themselves in Russia, the Mongols became a new fixture in the West. In the end, they vitalized European trade, opening up routes to the East. But just as this was taking place, a challenge to the political and economic order came in the form of the calamities known collectively as the Great Famine, a period of devastating food shortages that lasted from 1315 to 1322.

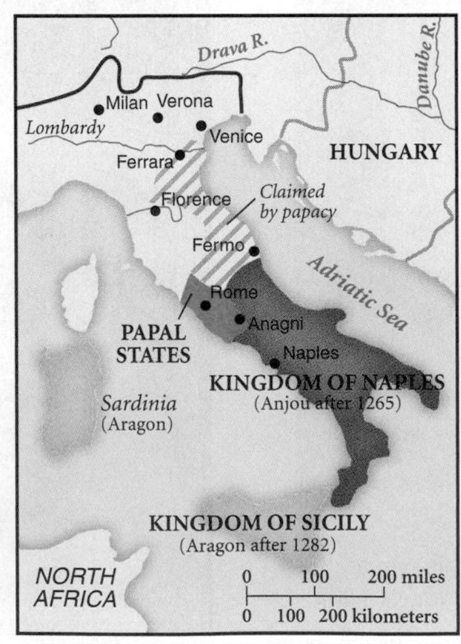

Italy at the End of the Thirteenth Century

The Weakening of the Empire

During the thirteenth century, both popes and emperors sought to dominate Italy. The clash of the German emperor and the papacy had its origins in Frederick Barbarossa's failure to control northern Italy, which was crucial to imperial policy. The model of Charlemagne required his imperial successors to exercise hegemony there. Moreover, Italy's prosperous cities beckoned as rich sources of income. When Barbarossa failed in the north, his son tried a new approach to gain Italy: he married Constance, the heiress of Sicily. From this base near the southern tip of Italy, he hoped to make good his imperial title. But he died suddenly, leaving his three-year-old son, Frederick II, to take up his plan. It was a perilous moment.

While Frederick was a child, the imperial office became the plaything of the German princes and the papacy. Both wanted an emperor, but a virtually powerless one. Therefore, when Frederick's uncle attempted to become interim king until Frederick reached his majority, many princes and the papacy blocked the move. They supported Otto of Brunswick, the son of Henry the Lion and an implacable foe of Frederick's family. Otto promised the pope that he would not intervene in Italy, and Pope Innocent III crowned him emperor in return.

But Innocent had miscalculated. No emperor worthy of the name could leave Italy alone. Almost immediately after his coronation, Otto invaded Sicily, and Innocent excommunicated him in 1211. In 1212, Innocent gave the imperial crown to **Frederick II** (r. 1212–1250), now a young man ready to take up the reins of power.

Frederick was an amazing ruler: *stupor mundi* ("wonder of the world") his contemporaries called him. Heir to two cultures, Sicilian on his mother's side and German on his father's, he cut a worldly and sophisticated figure. In Sicily, he moved easily within a diverse culture of Jews, Muslims, and Christians. Here he could play the role of all-powerful ruler. In Germany, he was less at home. There Christian princes, often churchmen with ministerial retinues, were acutely aware of their crucial role in royal elections and jealously guarded their rights and privileges.

Both emperor and pope needed to dominate Italy to maintain their power and position. The papacy under Innocent III was expansionist, gathering money and troops to make good its claim to the Papal States, the band of territory stretching from Rome to Ferrara in the north and Fermo in the east. The pope expected dues and taxes, military service, and the profits of justice from this region. To ensure its survival, the pope refused to tolerate any imperial claims to Italy.

Frederick, in turn, could not imagine ruling as an emperor unless he controlled Italy. He attempted to do this throughout his life, as did his heirs. Frederick had a three-pronged strategy. First, he revamped the government of Sicily to give him more control and yield greater profits. His *Constitutions of Melfi* (1231), an eclectic body of laws, set up a system of salaried governors who worked according to uniform procedures. The *Constitutions* called for nearly all court cases to be heard by royal courts, regularized commercial privileges, and set up a system of taxation. Second, to ensure that he would not be hounded by opponents in Germany, Frederick granted them important concessions in his **Statute in Favor of the Princes**, finalized in 1232. These concessions allowed the German princes to turn their principalities into virtually independent states. Third, Frederick sought to enter Italy through Lombardy, as his grandfather had done.

Each of the four popes who ruled after the death of Innocent, in 1216, followed Frederick's every move and excommunicated the emperor a number of times. The most serious of these condemnations came in 1245, when the pope and other churchmen assembled at the Council of Lyon and excommunicated and deposed Frederick, absolving his vassals and subjects of their fealty to him and, indeed, forbidding anyone to support him. By 1248, papal legates were preaching a crusade against Frederick and all his followers. Frederick's death, in 1250, ensured their triumph.

The fact that Frederick's vision of the empire failed is of less long-term importance than the way it failed. His concessions to the German princes meant that Germany would not be united until the nineteenth century. The political entity now called Germany was simply a geographical expression, divided among many independent princes. Between 1254 and 1273, the princes kept the German throne empty. Splintered into factions, they elected two different foreigners, who spent their time fighting each other. In one of history's great ironies, it was during this low point of the German monarchy that the term *Holy Roman Empire* was coined to denote the empire that had begun with the crowning of Charlemagne in 800. In 1273, the princes at last united and elected a German, Rudolf (r. 1273–1291), whose family, the Habsburgs, was new to imperial power. Rudolf used the imperial title to help him consolidate control over his own principality, Swabia, but he did not try to fulfill the meaning of the imperial title elsewhere. For the first time, the word *emperor* was freed from its association with Italy and Rome. For the Habsburgs, the title *Holy Roman Emperor* was a prestigious but otherwise meaningless honorific.

The failure of Frederick II in Italy meant that the Italian cities would continue their independent course. To ensure that Frederick's heirs would not continue their rule in Sicily, the papacy called successively on other rulers to take over the island—first Henry III of England and then Charles of Anjou. Forces loyal to Frederick's family turned to the king of Aragon (Spain). The move left two enduring claimants to Sicily's crown—the kings of Aragon and the house of Anjou—and it spawned a long war that impoverished the region.

The popes won the war against Frederick, but at a cost. Even the king of France criticized the popes for doing "new and unheard-of things." By making its war against Frederick part of its crusade

---

Frederick II: The grandson of Barbarossa who became king of Sicily and Germany, as well as emperor (r. 1212–1250), who allowed the German princes a free hand as he battled the pope for control of Italy.

Statute in Favor of the Princes: A statute finalized by Frederick II in 1232 that gave the German princes sovereign power within their own principalities.

against heresy, the papacy came under attack for using religion as a political tool.

Louis IX and a New Ideal of Kingship

In hindsight, we can see that Frederick's fight for an empire that would stretch from Germany to Sicily was doomed. The successful rulers of medieval Europe were those content with smaller, more compact, more united polities. "National" states, like France and England, were in the future. (However, the existence of such states, too, may just be one phase of Western civilization.) In France, the new ideal of a stay-at-home monarch started in the thirteenth century with the reign of **Louis IX** (r. 1226–1270). Louis's two crusades to the Holy Land made clear to his subjects just how much they needed him in France, even though his place was ably filled the first time by his mother, Blanche of Castile. The two are pictured on page 396.

Louis was revered not because he was a military leader but because he was an administrator, a judge, and a "just father" of his people. On warm summer days, he would sit under a tree in the woods near his castle at Vincennes on the outskirts of Paris, hearing disputes and dispensing justice personally. Through his administrators, he vigorously imposed his laws and justice over much of France. At Paris he appointed a salaried chief magistrate, who could be supervised and fired if necessary. During Louis's reign, the influence of the parlement of Paris (the royal court of justice) increased significantly. Originally a changeable and movable body, part of the king's personal entourage when he dealt with litigation, the parlement was now permanently housed in Paris and staffed by professional judges who heard cases and recorded their decisions.

Unlike his grandfather Philip Augustus, Louis did not try to expand his territory. He inherited a large kingdom that included Poitou and Languedoc (Map 12.1), and he was content. Although at first Henry III, the king of England, attacked France continually to try to regain territory lost under Philip Augustus, Louis remained unprovoked. Rather than prolong the fighting, he conceded a bit and made peace. At the same time, Louis was a zealous crusader. He took seriously the need to defend the Holy Land when most of his contemporaries were weary of the idea.

Louis was respectful of the church and the pope; he accepted limits on his authority in relation to the church and never claimed power over spiritual matters. Nevertheless, he vigorously maintained the dignity of the king and his rights. He expected royal and ecclesiastical power to work in harmony, and he refused to let the church dictate how he should use his temporal authority. For example, French bishops wanted royal officers to support the church's sentences of excommunication. But Louis declared that he would authorize his officials to do so only if he was able to judge each case himself, to see if the excommunication had been justly pronounced or not. The bishops refused, and Louis held his ground. Royal and ecclesiastical power would work side by side, neither subservient to the other.

It would be easy to fault Louis for his policies toward Jews. His hatred of them was well known. He did not exactly advocate violence against them, but he sometimes subjected them to arrest, canceling the debts owed to them (but collecting part into the royal treasury) and confiscating their belongings. In 1253, he ordered them to live "by the labor of their hands" or leave France. He meant that they should no longer lend money, in effect taking away their one means of livelihood. Louis's contem-

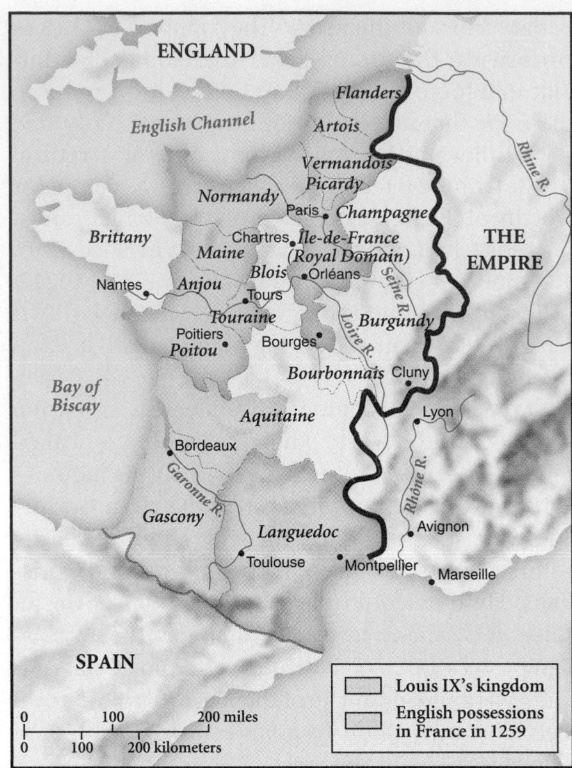

MAP 12.1 France under Louis IX, r. 1226–1270
Louis IX did not expand his kingdom as dramatically as his grandfather Philip Augustus had done. He was greatly admired, nevertheless, for he was seen by contemporaries as a model of Christian piety and justice. After his death, he was recognized as a saint and thus posthumously enhanced the prestige of the French monarchy.

Louis IX: A French king (r. 1226–1270) revered as a military leader and a judge; he was declared a saint after his death.

poraries did not criticize him for his Jewish policies. If anything, his hatred of Jews enhanced his reputation.

In fact, many of Louis's contemporaries considered him a saint, praising his care for the poor and sick, the pains and penances he inflicted on himself, and his regular participation in church services. In 1297, Pope Boniface VIII canonized him as St. Louis. The result was enormous prestige for the French monarchy. This prestige, joined with the renown of Paris as the center of scholarship and the repute of French courts as the hubs of chivalry, made France the cultural model of Europe.

The Birth of Representative Institutions

As thirteenth-century monarchs and princes expanded their powers, they devised a new political tool to enlist more broadly based support: all across Europe, from Spain to Poland, from England to Hungary, rulers summoned parliaments. These grew out of the ad hoc advisory sessions kings had held in the past with men from the two most powerful classes, or orders, of medieval society — the nobility and the clergy. In the thirteenth century, the advisory sessions turned into solemn, formal meetings of representatives of the orders to the kings' chief councils — the precursor of parliamentary sessions. Eventually these bodies became organs through which people not ordinarily present at court could articulate their wishes.

In practice, thirteenth-century kings did not so much command representatives of the orders to come to court as they simply summoned the most powerful members of their realm — whether clerics, nobles, or important townsmen — to support their policies. In thirteenth-century León (part of present-day Spain), for example, the king sometimes called only the clergy and nobles; sometimes he sent for representatives of the towns, especially when he wanted the help of town militias. As townsmen gradually began to participate regularly in advisory sessions, kings came to depend on them and their support. In turn, commoners became more fully integrated into the work of royal government.

Spanish Cortes | The ***cortes*** of Castile-León were among the earliest representative assemblies called to the king's court and the first to include townsmen. Enriched by plunder, fledgling villages soon burgeoned into major commercial centers. Like the cities of Italy, Spanish towns dominated the countryside. Hence, it was no wonder that King Alfonso IX (r. 1188–1230) summoned townsmen to the cortes in the first year of his reign, getting their representatives to agree to his plea for military and financial support and for help in consolidating his rule. Once convened at court, the townsmen joined bishops and noblemen in formally counseling the king and assenting to royal decisions. Beginning with Alfonso X (r. 1252–1284), Castilian monarchs regularly called on the cortes to participate in major political and military decisions and to assent to new taxes to finance them.

English Parliament | The English Parliament also developed as a new tool of royal government.[1] In this case, however, the king's control was complicated by the power of the barons, manifested, for example, in Magna Carta. In the twelfth century, King Henry II had consulted prelates and barons at Great Councils, using these parliaments as his tool to ratify and gain support for his policies. Although Magna Carta had nothing to do with such councils, the barons thought the document gave them an important and permanent role in royal government as the king's advisers and a solid guarantee of their customary rights and privileges. Henry III (r. 1216–1272) was crowned at the age of nine and was king in name only for the first sixteen years of his reign. Instead, England was governed by a council consisting of a few barons, university-trained administrators, and a papal legate. Although not quite "government by Parliament," this council set a precedent for baronial participation in government.

A parliament that included commoners came only in the midst of war and as a result of political weakness. Once in power, Henry III so alienated nobles and commoners alike by his wars, debts, choice of advisers, and demands for money that the barons threatened to rebel. At a meeting at Oxford in 1258, they forced Henry to dismiss his foreign advisers; rule with the advice of the Council of Fifteen, chosen jointly by the barons and the king; and limit the terms of his chief officers. However, this new government was itself riven by strife among the barons, and civil war erupted in 1264. At the battle

cortes **(kawr TEHZ):** The earliest European representative institution, called initially to consent to royal wishes; first convoked in 1188 by the king of Castile-León.

[1]Although *parlement* and *Parliament* are similar words, both deriving from the French word *parler* ("to speak"), the institutions they named were very different. The parlement of France was a law court, whereas the English Parliament, although beginning as a court to redress grievances, had by 1327 become above all a representative institution. The major French representative assembly, the Estates General, first convened at the beginning of the fourteenth century (see page 401).

of Lewes in the same year, the leader of the baronial opposition, Simon de Montfort (c. 1208–1265), routed the king's forces, captured the king, and became England's de facto ruler.

Because only a minority of the barons followed him, Simon sought new support by convening a parliament in 1265, to which he summoned not only the earls, barons, and churchmen who backed him but also representatives from the towns, the "commons"—and he appealed for their help. Thus, for the first time the commons were given a voice in English government. Even though Simon's brief rule ended that very year and Henry's son Edward I (r. 1272–1307) became a rallying point for royalists, the idea of representative government in England had emerged, born out of the interplay between royal initiatives and baronial revolts.

The Weakening of the Papacy

In contrast with England, representative institutions developed in France out of the conflict between Pope **Boniface VIII** (r. 1294–1303) and King Philip IV (r. 1285–1314), known as Philip the Fair. At the time, this confrontation seemed to be just one more episode in the ongoing struggle between medieval popes and secular rulers for power and authority. Throughout the thirteenth century the papacy confidently asserted its prerogatives. (See the illustration at right.) In fact, however, kings were gradually gaining ground. The conflict between Boniface and Philip signaled the turning point, when royal power trumped papal power.

Portrait of a Pope
Celebrating the power of the papacy, Pope Nicholas III (r. 1277–1280) sponsored a thorough redecoration of Rome's ancient basilica of St. Paul's Outside the Walls (the burial place of St. Paul). In the space above each of the columns running down the nave, he had his artists paint portraits of the popes, linking all to one another and ultimately to St. Peter (whose portrait was nearest the altar). In this image of Anacletus (c. 79–c. 91), the artist asserted the pope's gravity, solemnity, and otherworldliness. Anacletus wears a pallium, a white scarf symbolizing papal power, even though the pallium did not exist in the first century. *(Nimatallah/Art Resource, NY.)*

Taxing the Clergy | For centuries, the clergy had maintained a special status within the medieval state. Since the twelfth century, popes had declared the clergy under their jurisdiction. Clerics were not taxed except in the case of religious wars; they were not tried except in clerical courts. At the end of the thirteenth century, royal challenges to these principles provoked angry papal responses. The clashes began over taxing the clergy. Philip the Fair and the English king Edward I both financed their wars (mainly against one another) by taxing the clergy along with everyone else. The new principle of national sovereignty that they were claiming led them to assert jurisdiction over all people, even churchmen, who lived within their borders. For the pope, however, the principle at stake was his role as head of the clergy. Thus, Pope Boniface VIII declared that only the pope could authorize taxes on clerics. Threatening to excommunicate kings who taxed prelates without papal permission, he called on clerics to disobey any such royal orders.

Edward and Philip reacted swiftly. Taking advantage of the role English courts played in protecting the peace, Edward declared that all clerics who refused to pay his taxes would be considered outlaws—literally "outside the law." Clergymen who were robbed, for example, would have no recourse against their attackers; if accused of crimes, they would have no defense in court. Relying on a different strategy, Philip forbade the exportation of precious metals, money, or jewels—effectively sealing the French borders. Immediately, the English clergy cried out for legal protection, while the papacy itself cried out for the revenues it had long enjoyed from French pilgrims, litigants, and travelers. Boniface was forced to back down, conceding

Boniface VIII: The pope (r. 1294–1303) whose clash with King Philip the Fair of France left the papacy considerably weakened.

in 1297 that kings had the right to tax their clergy in emergencies. But this concession did not end the confrontation.

The King's New Tools: Propaganda and Popular Opinion In 1301, Philip the Fair tested his jurisdiction in southern France by arresting Bernard Saisset, the bishop of Pamiers, on a charge of treason for slandering the king by comparing him to an owl, "the handsomest of birds which is worth absolutely nothing." Saisset's imprisonment violated the principle, maintained both by the pope and by French law, that a clergyman was not subject to lay justice. Boniface reacted angrily, and Philip seized the opportunity to deride and humiliate him, orchestrating a public relations campaign against Boniface. Philip convened representatives of the clergy, nobles, and townspeople to explain, justify, and propagandize his position. This new assembly, which met in 1302, was the ancestor of the French representative institution, the Estates General. The pope's reply, the bull[2] *Unam Sanctam* (1302), intensified the situation to fever pitch by declaring bluntly "that it is altogether necessary to salvation for every human creature to be subject to the Roman Pontiff." At meetings of the king's inner circle, Philip's agents declared Boniface a false pope, accusing him of sexual perversion, various crimes, and heresy.

Papal Defeat In 1303, French royal agents, acting on Philip's orders, invaded Boniface's palace at Anagni (southeast of Rome) to capture the pope, bring him to France, and try him. Fearing for the pope's life, however, the people of Anagni joined forces and drove the French agents out of town. Yet even after such public support for the pope, the king made his power felt. Boniface died very shortly thereafter, and the next two popes quickly pardoned Philip and his agents for their actions.

Just as Frederick II's failure revealed the weakness of the empire, so Boniface's humiliation demonstrated the limits of papal control. The two powers that claimed "universal" authority had very little weight in the face of new, limited, but tightly controlled national states such as France and England. After 1303, popes continued to denounce kings and emperors, but their words had less and less impact. In the face of newly powerful medieval states—undergirded by vast revenues, judicial apparatuses, representative institutions, and even the loyalty of churchmen—the papacy could make little headway. The delicate balance between church and state, reflecting a sense of universal order and harmony and a hallmark of the reign of St. Louis, broke down at the end of the thirteenth century.

The Avignon Papacy In 1309, forced from Rome by civil strife, the papacy settled at Avignon, a city then belonging to the Angevin rulers of Naples and very close to—and influenced by—France. Here the popes remained until 1378, and thus the period 1309–1378 is called the **Avignon papacy**. Europeans ashamed that the pope lived so far from Rome called it the Babylonian captivity. They were thinking of the Old Testament story of the Hebrews captured and brought into slavery in ancient Babylon.[3] The Avignon popes, many of them French, established a sober and efficient organization that took in regular revenues and gave the papacy more say than ever before in the appointment of churchmen. Slowly, they abandoned the idea of leading all of Christendom, tacitly recognizing the growing power of the secular states to regulate their internal affairs.

The Rise of the *Signori*

During the thirteenth century, new groups, generally made up of the non-noble classes—the ***popolo*** ("people"), who fought on foot—attempted to take over the reins of power from the nobility in many Italian communes. The popolo incorporated members of city associations such as craft and merchant guilds, parishes, and the commune itself. In fact, the popolo was a kind of alternative commune. Armed and militant, the popolo demanded a share in city government, particularly to gain a voice in matters of taxation. In 1223 at Piacenza, for example, the popolo's members and the nobles worked out a plan to share the election of their city's government. Such power sharing was a typical result of the popolo's struggle. In some cities, however, nobles dissolved the popolo, while in others the popolo virtually excluded the nobles from government. Such factions turned northern Italian cities into centers of civil discord.

[2]An official papal document is called a bull, from the *bulla*, or seal, that was used to authenticate it.

[3]See 2 Kings 24–25.

Avignon (AH vee NYAW) papacy: The period (1309–1378) during which the popes ruled from Avignon rather than from Rome.

***popolo*:** Literally, "people"; a communal faction, largely made up of merchants, that demanded (and often obtained) power in thirteenth-century Italian cities.

Weakened by this constant friction, the communes were tempting prey for great regional nobles who, allying with one or another urban group, often succeeded in establishing themselves as *signori* (singular *signore*, "lord") of the cities, keeping the peace at the price of repression. Thirteenth-century Piacenza was typical: first dominated by nobles, the popolo gained a voice by 1225; but then by midcentury both the nobles and the popolo were eclipsed by the power of a signore.

The Mongol Takeover

Europeans were not the only warring society in the thirteenth century: to the east, the Mongols (sometimes called Tatars or Tartars) created an aggressive army under the leadership of Chingiz (or Genghis) Khan (c. 1162–1227) and his sons. In part, economic necessity drove them out of Mongolia: changes in climate had reduced the grasslands that sustained their animals and their nomadic way of life. But they were also inspired by Chingiz's hope of conquering the world. By 1215, the Mongols held Beijing and most of northern China. Some years later, they moved through central Asia and skirted the Caspian Sea (Map 12.2).

The Golden Horde in Russia In the 1230s, the Mongols began concerted attacks in Russia, Poland, and Hungary, where native princes were weak. Only the death of the Great Khan, Chingiz's son Ogodei (1186–1241), and disputes over his succession prevented a concentrated assault on Germany. In the 1250s, the Mongols took Iran and Iraq.

The Mongols' sophisticated military tactics contributed to their overwhelming success. They devised two- and three-flank operations. The invasion of Hungary, for example, was two-pronged, with divisions arriving from Russia, Poland, and Germany. The Mongols—fighting mainly on horseback with heavy lances and powerful bows and arrows whose shots traveled far and penetrated deeply—crushed the Hungarian army of mixed infantry and cavalry.

In the West, the Mongol rule in Russia lasted the longest. Their most important victory there was the capture of Kiev in 1240. Making the mouth of the Volga River the center of their power in Russia, the

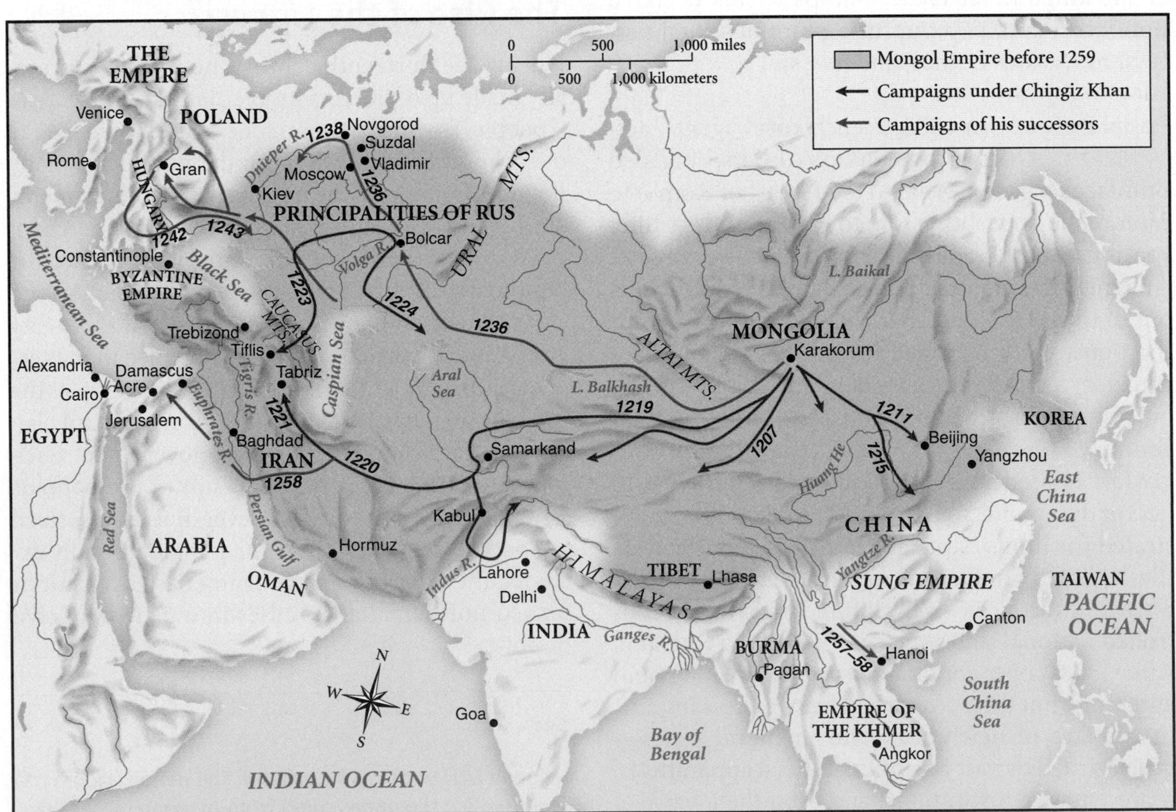

MAP 12.2 The Mongol Invasions to 1259
The Mongols tied East Asia to the west. Their conquest of China, which took place at about the same time as their invasions of Russia and Iran, created a Eurasian economy. | **Compare this map with the Mapping the West map on page 377. Why were the Mongol invasions a threat to the Muslim world?**

Mongols dominated all of Russia's principalities for about two hundred years. The Mongol Empire in Russia, later called the **Golden Horde** (*golden* probably from the color of their leader's tent; *horde* from a Turkish word meaning "camp"), adopted much of the local government apparatus and left many of the old institutions in place. They allowed Russian princes to continue ruling as long as they paid homage and tribute to the khan, and they tolerated the Russian church, exempting it from taxes. The Mongols' chief undertaking was a series of population censuses on the basis of which they recalculated taxes and recruited troops.

The Opening of China to Europeans The Mongol invasion changed the political configuration of Europe and Asia. Because the Mongols were willing to deal with Westerners, one effect of their conquests was to open China to European travelers for the first time. Missionaries, diplomats, and merchants went to China over land routes and via the Persian Gulf. Some of these voyagers hoped to enlist the aid of the Mongols against the Muslims; others expected to make new converts to Christianity; still others dreamed of lucrative trade routes.

The most famous of these travelers was Marco Polo (1254–1324), son of a merchant family from Venice. Marco's father and uncle had already made the round trip to China once when Marco joined them on a second expedition. He stayed in China for nearly two years. Others stayed even longer. In fact, evidence suggests that an entire community of Venetian traders lived in the city of Yangzhou in the mid-fourteenth century.

Merchants paved the way for missionaries. Friars (preachers to the cities of Europe) became missionaries to new continents as well. In 1289, the pope made the Franciscan John of Monte Corvino his envoy to China. Preaching in India along the way, John arrived in China four or five years after setting out, converting one local ruler, and building a church. A few years later, now at Beijing, he boasted that he had converted six thousand people, constructed two churches, and translated the New Testament and Psalms into the native language.

The long-term effect of the Mongols on the West was to open up new land routes to the East that helped bind together the two halves of the known world. Travel stories such as Marco Polo's account of his journeys stimulated others to seek out the fabulous riches—textiles, ginger, ceramics, copper—of China and other regions of the East. In a sense, the Mongols initiated the search for exotic goods and missionary opportunities that culminated in the European "discovery" of a new world, the Americas.

The Great Famine

While the Mongols stimulated the European economy, natural disasters coupled with political ineptitude brought on a terrible period of famine in northern Europe. The **Great Famine** (1315–1322) left many hungry, sick, and weak while it fueled social antagonisms.

Hunger and Its Effects An anonymous chronicler looking back on the events of 1315 wrote:

> The floods of rain have rotted almost all the seed, so that the prophecy of Isaiah might seem now to be fulfilled, . . . and in many places the hay lay so long under water that it could neither be mown nor gathered. Sheep generally died and other animals were killed in a sudden plague. . . . [In the next year, 1316,] the dearth of grain was much increased. Such a scarcity has not been seen in our time in England, nor heard of for a hundred years. For the measure of wheat sold in London and the neighboring places for forty pence [a very high price], and in other less thickly populated parts of the country thirty pence was a common price.

Thus did the writer chronicle the causes and effects of the famine: uncommonly heavy rains, a disease that killed farm animals important not only for their meat and fleeces but also for their labor; and, finally, the economic effects, as scarcity drove up the prices of ordinary foods. All of these led to hunger, disease, and death.

Had the rains gone back to normal, the European economy would no doubt have recovered. But the rains continued, and the crops kept failing. In many regions, the crisis lasted for a full seven years. Hardest hit were the peasants and the poor. In rural areas, wealthy lords, churches, monasteries, and well-to-do peasants profited from the newly high prices they could charge. (See Taking Measure, "Grain Prices during the Great Famine," page 404.) In the cities, some merchants and ecclesiastical institutions benefited as well. But on the whole, even

---

Golden Horde: The political institution set up by the Mongols in Russia, lasting from the thirteenth to the fifteenth century.

Great Famine: The shortage of food and accompanying social ills that besieged northern Europe between 1315 and 1322.

TAKING MEASURE

Grain Prices during the Great Famine

Famine was caused not just by a shortage of food but also by spikes in prices that made it impossible for the poor to buy enough to eat. The graph shown here represents the prices of grain produced on the English manor of Hinderclay between 1272 and 1324. It is clear that prices fluctuated greatly and that during the period of the Great Famine, 1315–1322, they rose dramatically, with the years 1316–1317 particularly striking. Note that the price of wheat was always higher than the prices of barley and rye, which were considered inferior grains. (That notion would change as beer, which is made with barley, gained favor.) The spikes in prices suggest that very little charitable distribution of grain was taking place on Hinderclay manor.

Source: Based on Phillipp R. Schofield, "The Social Economy of the Medieval Village in the Early Fourteenth Century," *Economic History Review* 61 (2008): 44, Figure 1.

Question to Consider

- **What explains the extraordinary price fluctuations shown on this graph?**

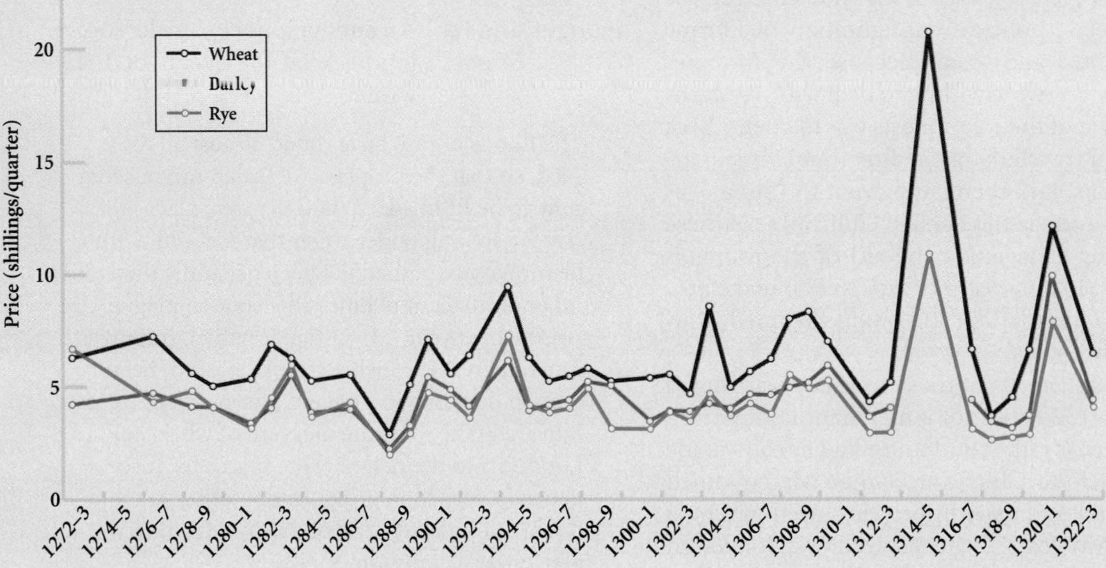

the well-to-do suffered, as both rural and urban areas lost fully 5 to 10 percent of their population. The impact was enormous, for loss of population meant erosion of manpower and falling productivity.

People did attempt to cope with and contain these disasters. The clergy offered up prayers and urged their congregations to do penance, for the famine was seen as God's punishment for the sins of humanity. In the countryside, charitable monasteries gave out food; conscientious kings tried to control high interest rates on loans; and hungry peasants migrated from west to east—to Poland, for example, where land was more plentiful. In the cities, where starving refugees from rural areas flocked for food, wealthy men and women sometimes opened their storehouses or distributed coins. Other rich townspeople founded hospitals for the poor. Town councils sold municipal bonds at high rates of interest, gaining some temporary solvency. These towns became the primary charitable institutions of the era, importing grain and selling it at or slightly below cost.

Social Causes and Consequences of the Great Famine

Contributing to the crop failure was population growth that challenged the productive capabilities of the age. The exponential leap in population from the tenth to the twelfth century slowed to zero around the year 1300, but all the land that could be cultivated had been settled by this time. No new technology had been developed to increase crop yields. The swollen population demanded a lot from the productive capacities of the land. Just a small shortfall could dislocate the whole system of distribution.

The policies of rulers added to the problems of too many people and too little food. The anonymous chronicler who considered "floods of rain" the cause of the famine also observed "that in Northumbria [the north of England] dogs and horses and other unclean things were eaten. For there, on account of the frequent raids of the Scots, work is more irksome, as the accursed Scots despoil the people daily of their food." Scottish troops were not the only ones who destroyed the crops. The king of England sent his soldiers to ravage Scotland in turn. The kings of Norway, Denmark, and Sweden regularly fought one another. The king of France was at war with rebellious Flemings to control Flanders. These wars not only ruined the crops but also diverted manpower and resources to arms and castles, at the same time disrupting normal markets and trade routes.

In order to wage wars, rulers imposed heavy taxes and, as the famine became worse, requisitioned grain to support their troops. Consequently, the effects of the famine grew worse, and in many regions people rose up in protest. In France, the merchants were enraged to see their grain taken off the open market, where they could hope to profit. The king tried to mollify them. In England, peasants resisted tax collectors. In a more violent reaction, poor French shepherds, outcasts, clerics, and artisans entered Paris to storm the prisons. They then marched southward—burning royal castles and attacking officials, Jews, and lepers. They were pursued by the king, who succeeded in putting down the movement. But the limits of the politics of control were made clear in this confrontation, which exacerbated the misery of the famine while doing nothing to contain it.

REVIEW QUESTION How did the search for harmony result in cooperation—and confrontation—between secular rulers and other institutions, such as the church and the towns?

A Famine in Florence
Starvation did not end with the last year of the Great Famine. This miniature from a manuscript detailing grain prices shows the effects—and the artist's interpretation—of a famine in 1329. The scene is the Orsanmichele, the Florentine grain market. The market was dominated by an image of the Virgin Mary, here depicted on the right-hand side. Extending beyond the margin on the far left, a mother with two children raises her hands and eyes to heaven in prayer. In the back, soldiers guard the market's entrance. The market itself bustles with rich buyers, who hand over their money and pack their bags with grain. Above flies an angel with broken trumpets, while a demon takes center stage and says, among other things, "I will make you ache with hunger and high prices." *(Biblioteca Laurenziana, Florence, Italy/Scala/Art Resource, NY.)*

Conclusion

The thirteenth century sought harmony and synthesis but discovered how elusive these goals could be. Theoretically, the papacy and empire were supposed to work together; instead they clashed in bitter warfare, leaving the government of Germany to the princes and northern Italy to its communes and *signori*. Theoretically, faith and reason were supposed to arrive at the same truths. They sometimes did so in the hands of scholastics, but not always. Theoretically, all Christians practiced the same rites and followed the teachings of the church. In practice, local enforcement determined which church laws took effect—and to what extent. Moreover, the search for order was never able to bring together all the diverse peoples, ideas, and interests of thirteenth-century society. Heretics and Jews were set apart.

Synthesis was more achievable in the arts. Heaven, earth, and hell were melded harmoniously together in stained glass and sculpture. Musicians wove disparate melodic and poetic lines into motets. Writers melded heroic and romantic themes with theological truths and mystical visions.

Political leaders also aimed at harmony. Via representative institutions, they harnessed the various

MAPPING THE WEST

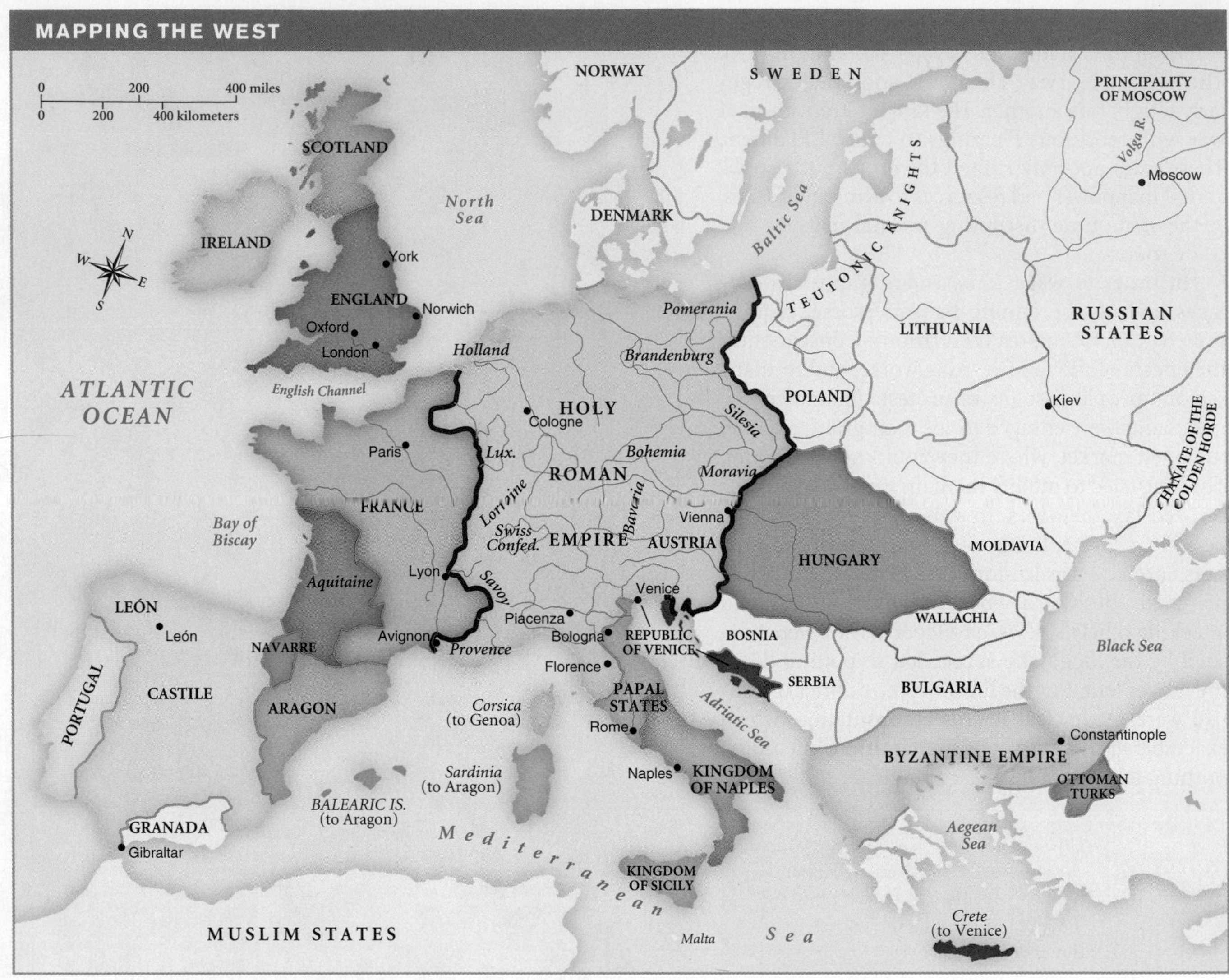

Europe, c. 1340

The Empire, which in the thirteenth century came to be called the Holy Roman Empire, still dominated the map of Europe in 1340, but the emperor himself had less power than ever. Each principality—often each city—was ruled separately and independently. To the east, the Ottoman Turks were just beginning to make themselves felt. In the course of the next century, they would disrupt the Mongol hegemony and become a great power.

social orders to their quest for greater order and control. They asserted sovereignty over all the people who lived in their borders, asserting unity while increasing their revenues, expanding their territories, and enhancing their prestige. The kings of England and France and the governments of northern and central Italian cities largely succeeded in these goals, while the king of Germany failed miserably. Germany and Italy remained fragmented until the nineteenth century. Ironically, the Mongols, who began as invaders in the West, helped unify areas that were far apart by opening trade routes.

Events at the end of the thirteenth century thwarted the search for harmony. The mutual respect of church and state achieved under St. Louis in France disintegrated into irreconcilable claims to power under Pope Boniface VIII and Philip the Fair. The carefully constructed tapestry of St. Thomas's summae began to unravel in the teachings of John Duns Scotus. An economy stretched to the breaking point resulted in a terrible period of famine. Disorder and anxiety—but also extraordinary creativity—would mark the next era.

FOR FURTHER EXPLORATION

- **For additional primary-source material from this period**, see *Sources of the Making of the West*, Fourth Edition.
- **For Web sites, images, and documents related to topics in this chapter**, visit *Make History* at bedfordstmartins.com/hunt.

Chapter 12 Review

Online Study Guide bedfordstmartins.com/hunt

Key Terms and People

In the grid below, identify the term or person and explain its historical significance. (To do this exercise online, go to bedfordstmartins.com/hunt.)

Term	Who or What & When	Why It Matters
Innocent III (p. 382)		
Fourth Lateran Council (p. 383)		
blood libel (p. 388)		
leprosy (p. 388)		
scholasticism (p. 389)		
Frederick II (p. 397)		
Statute in Favor of the Princes (p. 397)		
Louis IX (p. 398)		
cortes (p. 399)		
Boniface VIII (p. 400)		
Avignon papacy (p. 401)		
popolo (p. 401)		
Golden Horde (p. 403)		
Great Famine (p. 403)		

Review Questions

1. How did people respond to the teachings and laws of the church in the early thirteenth century?
2. How did artists, musicians, and scholastics try to link the physical world with the divine?
3. How did the search for harmony result in cooperation—and confrontation—between secular rulers and other institutions, such as the church and the towns?

Making Connections

1. Why was Innocent III more successful than Boniface VIII in carrying out his objectives?
2. How did the growth of lay piety help bolster the prestige and power of kings like Louis IX?
3. Comparing the goals and methods of Abelard's scholarship with those of Thomas Aquinas, explain the continuities and the differences between the twelfth-century schools and the scholastic movement.

Important Events

Date	Event	Date	Event
1188	King Alfonso IX summons townsmen to the *cortes*	1265	English commons summoned to Parliament
1212–1250	Reign of Frederick II	1273	Thomas Aquinas publishes the *Summa Theologiae*
1215	Fourth Lateran Council	1302	First Meeting of the French Estates General
1226–1270	Reign of Louis IX (St. Louis)	1309–1378	Avignon papacy
1232	Frederick II finalizes Statute in Favor of the Princes	1313–1321	Dante writes *Divine Comedy*
1240	Mongols capture Kiev	1315–1322	Great Famine

- Consider three events: **Fourth Lateran Coucil (1215), Dante writes *Divine Comedy* (1313–1321),** and **Thomas Aquinas publishes the *Summa Theologiae* (1273).** How did the papacy, vernacular literature, and scholastic philosophy represent different aspects of the medieval search for order?

SUGGESTED REFERENCES

For the church's mission, see Bynum, Sayers, and Kessler and Zacharias. The Inquisition and other forms of persecution are the subjects of the books by Given, Jordan (on the Jews), and Nirenberg. Colish's collected essays discuss the many forms of scholasticism. Abulafia, Jones, Le Goff, Maddicott, and O'Callaghan each helpfully cover the political developments of the period.

Abulafia, David. *Frederick II: A Medieval Emperor*. 1988.

Bynum, Caroline Walker. *Holy Feast and Holy Fast: The Religious Significance of Food to Medieval Women*. 1987.

Colish, Marcia L. *Studies in Scholasticism*. 2006.

*Fourth Lateran Council: http://www.fordham.edu/halsall/source/ lat4-select.html

Gaposchkin, M. Cecilia. *The Making of Saint Louis: Kingship, Sanctity, and Crusade in the Later Middle Ages*. 2008.

Given, James Buchanan. *Inquisition and Medieval Society*. 2001.

Jackson, Peter. *The Mongols and the West*. 2005.

*Joinville, Jean de, and Geoffroy de Villehardouin. *Chronicles of the Crusades*. Trans. M. R. B. Shaw. 1963.

Jones, Philip. *The Italian City-State: From Commune to Signoria*. 1997.

Jordan, William Chester. *The French Monarchy and the Jews: From Philip Augustus to the Last Capetians*. 1989.

———. *The Great Famine: Northern Europe in the Early Fourteenth Century*. 1996.

Kessler, Herbert L., and Johanna Zacharias. *Rome 1300: On the Path of the Pilgrim*. 2000.

Le Goff, Jacques. *Saint Louis*. Trans. Gareth Evan Gollrad. 2009.

Maddicott, J. R. *Simon De Montfort*. 1994.

Nichols, Aidan. *Discovering Aquinas: An Introduction to His Life, Work and Influence*. 2003.

Nirenberg, David. *Communities of Violence: Persecution of Minorities in the Middle Ages*. 1996.

O'Callaghan, Joseph F. *The Cortes of Castille-León, 1188–1350*. 1989.

Panofsky, Erwin. *Gothic Architecture and Scholasticism*. 1951.

Richardson, H. G., and G. O. Sayles. *The English Parliament in the Middle Ages*. 1981.

Sayers, Jane. *Innocent III: Leader of Europe, 1198–1216*. 1994.

*Thomas Aquinas: http://www.newadvent.org/summa

Strayer, Joseph R. *The Reign of Philip the Fair*. 1980.

*Primary source.

CHAPTER

13

Crisis and Renaissance

1340–1492

In 1453, the Ottoman Turks turned their cannons on Constantinople and blasted the city's walls. The fall of Constantinople, which spelled the end of the Byzantine Empire, was an enormous shock to Europeans. Some, like the pope, called for a crusade against the Ottomans; others, like the writer Lauro Quirini, sneered, calling them "a barbaric, uncultivated race, without established customs, or laws, [who lived] a careless, vagrant, arbitrary life."

But the Turks didn't consider themselves uncultivated or arbitrary. In fact, they saw themselves as the true heirs of the Roman Empire, and they shared many of the values and tastes of the very Europeans who were so hostile to them. Sultan Mehmed II employed European architects to construct his new palace—the Topkapi Saray—in the city once known as Constantinople and now popularly called Istanbul. He commissioned the Venetian artist Gentile Bellini to paint his portrait, a genre invented in Burgundy to celebrate the status and individuality of important and wealthy patrons.

Mehmed's actions and interests sum up the dual features of the period of crisis and Renaissance that took place from the middle of the fourteenth century to the late fifteenth century. What was a crisis from one point of view—the fall of the Byzantine Empire—was at the same time stimulus for what historians call the Renaissance. Both to confront and to mask the crises of the day, people discovered new value in ancient, classical culture; they created a new vocabulary drawn from classical literature as well as astonishing new forms of art and music based on ancient precedents. The classical revival provided the stimulus for new styles of living, ruling, and thinking.

Along with the fall of the Byzantine Empire, other crises marked the period from 1340 to 1492. These were matched by equally significant gains. The plague, or Black Death, tore at the

Portrait of Mehmed II
The Ottoman ruler Mehmed II saw himself as a Renaissance patron of the arts, and he called upon the most famous artists and architects of the day to work for him. The painter of this portrait, Gentile Bellini, was from a well-known family of artists in Venice and served at Mehmed's court in 1479–1480. The revival of portraiture, so characteristic of Renaissance tastes, was as important to the Turkish sultans as to European rulers. *(Erich Lessing/Art Resource, NY.)*

fabric of communities and families; but the survivors and their children reaped the benefits of higher wages and better living standards. The Hundred Years' War, fought between France and England, involved many smaller states in its slaughter and brought untold misery to the French countryside; but it also helped create the glittering court of Burgundy, patron of new art and music. By the war's end, both the French and the English kings were more powerful than ever. Following their conquest of Constantinople, the Ottoman Turks penetrated far into the Balkans; but this was a calamity only from the European point of view. Well into the sixteenth century, the Ottomans were part of the culture that nourished the artistic achievements of the Renaissance. A crisis in the church overlapped with the crises of disease and war as a schism within the papacy—pitting pope against pope—divided Europe into separate camps; but a church council, whose members included Renaissance humanists, eventually resolved the papal schism reestablishing the old system: a single pope who presided over the church from Rome.

CHAPTER FOCUS How were the crises of 1340–1492 and the Renaissance related?

Crisis: Disease, War, and Schism

In the mid-fourteenth century, a series of crises shook the West. The Black Death swept through Europe and decimated the population, especially in the cities. Two major wars redrew the map of Europe between 1340 and 1492. The first was the Hundred Years' War, fought from 1337 to 1453 (thus actually lasting 116 years). This war turned a dynastic struggle over the kingdom of France into a military confrontation that transformed the nature of warfare itself. The second war began with the Ottoman domination of Byzantium in the 1360s and culminated in the Ottoman conquest of Constantinople in 1453—the same year the Hundred Years' War ended. Because Constantinople was the last buffer between Europe and the Islamic world, its fall marked a major shift in global power. The Ottomans now had a secure base from which to move into Europe. As the wars raged and attacks of the plague came and went, a crisis in the church also weighed on Europeans. Attempts to return the papacy from Avignon to Rome resulted in the Great Schism (1378–1417), when first two and then three rival popes asserted universal authority. In the wake of these crises, many ordinary folk sought solace in new forms of piety, some of them condemned by the church as heretical.

The Black Death, 1347–1352

The **Black Death**, so named by later historians, was a calamitous disease. It decimated the population wherever it struck and wreaked havoc on social and economic structures. Yet in the wake of this plague, those fortunate enough to survive benefited from an improved standard of living through greater access to jobs and resources. Unprofitable farms were abandoned, and a more diversified agriculture developed. Birthrates climbed, and new universities were established to educate the post-plague generations.

A "Pestilential Disease" A harbinger of the Black Death was noted in 1346, perhaps in the region between the Black and Caspian Seas. A year later, the Byzantine scholar Nicephorus Gregoras was already familiar with it.

Black Death: The term historians give to the disease that swept through Europe in 1347–1352.

1337–1453	Hundred Years' War
1347–1352	Black Death in Europe
1358	Jacquerie uprising in France
1378	Ciompi Revolt in Florence
1378–1417	Great Schism divides papacy
1381	Wat Tyler's Rebellion in England
1386	Union of Lithuania and Poland

1325 1350 1375 1400

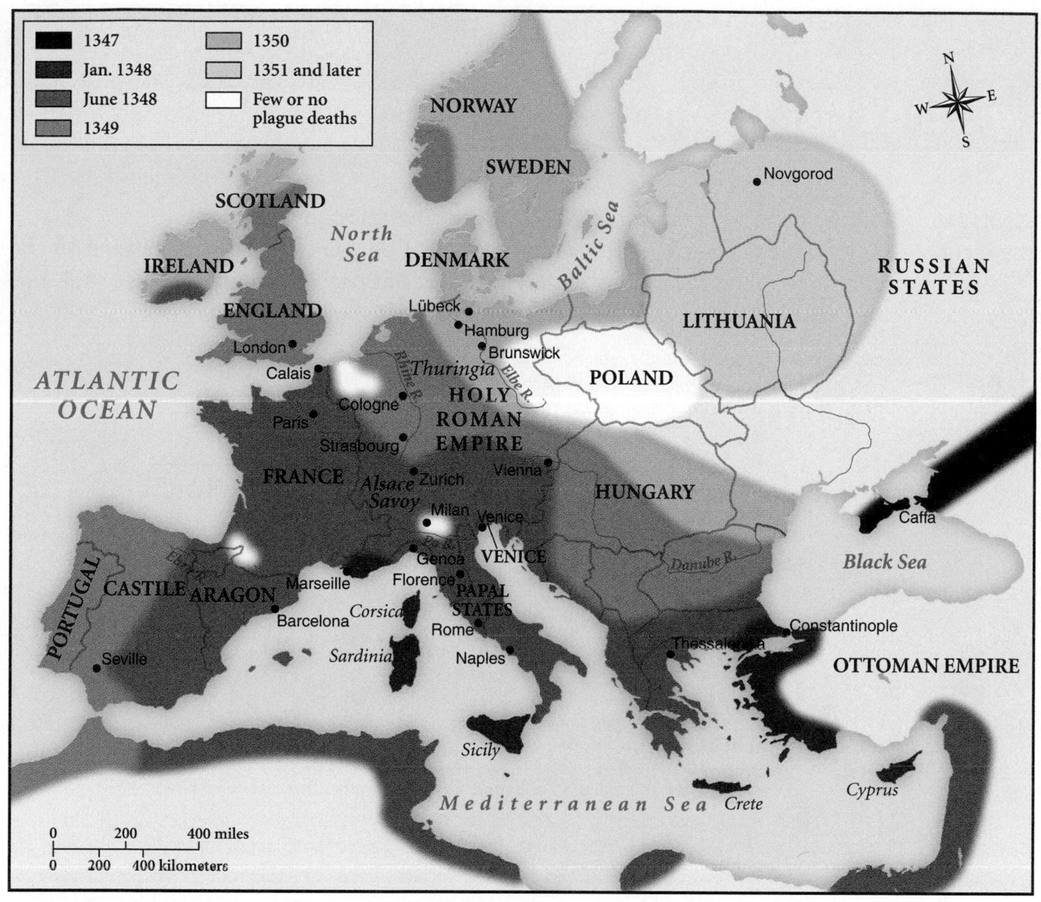

MAP 13.1 Advance of the Black Death, 1346–1352
Hitting the West in 1346, the Black Death quickly worked its way across the Mediterranean and then northward. Its path generally followed waterways and roads. With the exception of a few regions that were spared, it killed between one-third and one-half of the population of western Europe. However, in eastern Europe its impact was far less. The plague recurred—at first every ten to twelve years and then at longer intervals.

Calling it a "pestilential disease," he described its symptoms: "The prominent signs of this disease, signs indicating early death, were tumorous outgrowths at the roots of thighs and arms and simultaneously bleeding ulcerations." The Black Death was almost certainly caused by the bacterium *Yersinia pestis*, the same organism responsible for outbreaks of plague today. From its breeding ground, it traveled westward to the Middle East, the North African coast, and Europe (Map 13.1).

Probably carried by fleas traveling on the backs of rats, it hitched boat rides with spices, silks, and

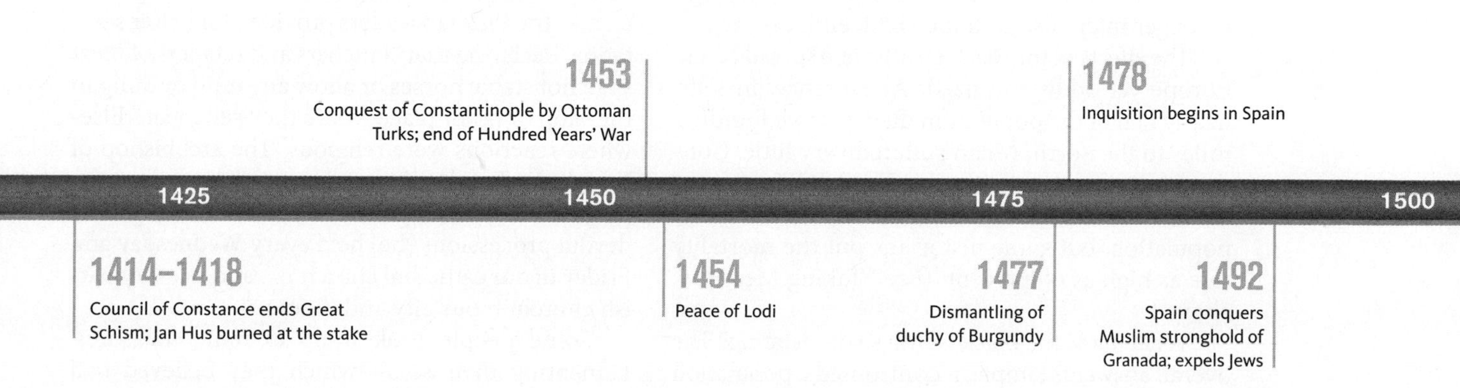

TAKING MEASURE

Population Losses and the Black Death

The bar chart dramatically represents the impact of the Black Death and the recurrent epidemics that hit Europe between 1340 and 1450. More than a century after the Black Death, none of the regions of Europe had made up for the losses of population. The population of 1450 stood at about 75–80 percent of the pre-plague population. The areas hardest hit were France and the Low Countries, which also suffered from the devastation of the Hundred Years' War.

Source: From Carlo M. Cipolla, ed., *Fontana Economic History of Europe: The Middle Ages* (Great Britain: Collins/Fontana Books, 1974), 36.

Question to Consider

- **Can you suggest explanations for the variations in population loss that this chart shows?**

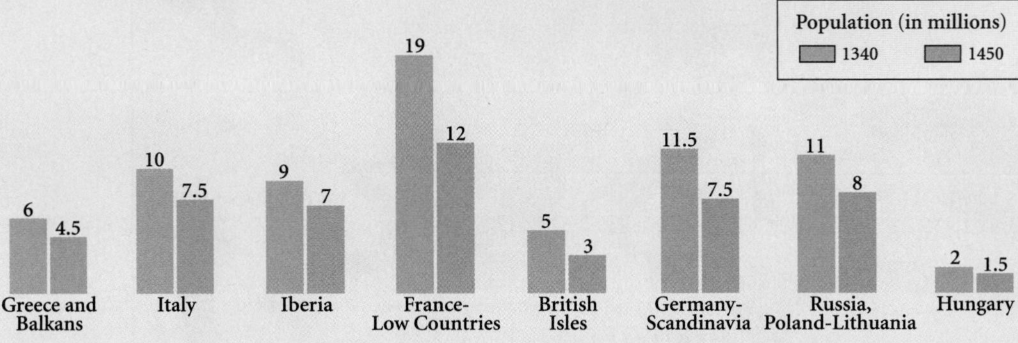

porcelain. In 1347, people in the Genoese colony in Caffa, on the north edge of the Black Sea, contracted the disease. Soon after that, it arrived in Constantinople and at the same time in Europe — in Sicily, Sardinia, Corsica, and Marseille. Within a few months it spread to Aragon, all of Italy, the Balkans, and most of France. It then crept northward to Germany, England, Scandinavia, and Russia. Meanwhile, it attacked the Islamic world as well — Baghdad, North Africa, and the bit of al-Andalus that remained. This was just the beginning. The disease recurred every ten to twelve years throughout the fourteenth century (though only the outbreak of 1347–1352 is called the Black Death), and it continued, though at longer intervals, until the eighteenth century.

The effects of the Black Death were spread across Europe yet oddly localized. At Florence, in Italy, nearly half of the population died, yet two hundred miles to the north, Milan suffered very little. Conservative estimates put the death toll in Europe anywhere between one-third and one-half of the entire population, but some historians put the mortality rate as high as 60 percent. (See "Taking Measure," above.)

What made the Black Death so devastating? The overall answer is simple: it confronted a population already weakened by disease or famine. The Great Famine that began in 1315 may have been over by 1322, but it was followed by local famines such as the one that hit Italy in 1339–1340. Epidemic diseases followed the famines: smallpox, influenza, and tuberculosis all took their toll.

Consequences of the Black Death

Some responses came from local governments. The government of the Italian city of Pistoia, for example, decreed in 1348 that no citizen could go to nearby Pisa or Lucca, nor could people from those cities enter Pistoia; in effect, Pistoia set up a quarantine. Thinking that "bad air" brought the plague, the Pistoian leaders provided for better sanitation, declaring that "butchers and retailers of meat shall not stable horses or allow any mud or dung in the shop or other place where they sell meat." Elsewhere reactions were religious. The archbishop of York in England, for example, tried to prevent the plague from entering his diocese by ordering "that devout processions [be] held every Wednesday and Friday in our cathedral church . . . and in every parish church in our city and diocese."

Some people took more extreme measures. Lamenting their sins — which they believed had

Dance of Death
Figures meant to represent all the "types" in medieval society are depicted in this fresco, painted in 1474 on a wall of a cemetery church in Croatia. It should be read from right to left. Not pictured here, but first in line, is the pope, followed by a cardinal and a bishop. The portion shown here comes next: the king, who holds a scepter; the queen; and a landlord, carrying a small barrel. At the far left is a child. Even farther to the left (but not shown here) come a beggar, a knight, and a shopkeeper. All the figures are flanked by gleeful, dancing skeletons. The message is clear: everyone, even the most exalted, ends up in the grave. *(Alfredo Dagli Orti/Art Resource, NY.)*

brought on the plague—and attempting to placate God, men and women wandered from city to city with whips in their hands. Entering a church, they took off their shirts or blouses, lay down one by one on the church floor, and, according to the chronicler Henry of Hervordia (d. 1370),

> one of them would strike the first with a whip, saying, "May God grant you remission [forgiveness] of all your sins. Arise." And he would get up, and do the same to the second, and all the others in turn did the same. When they were all on their feet, and arranged two by two in procession, two of them in the middle of the column would begin singing a hymn in a high voice, with a sweet melody.

The church did not approve of this practice. Only members of the clergy were supposed to determine acts of penance, but the flagellants—as the people who whipped themselves were called (from the Latin *flagellum*, meaning "whip")—imposed penance on themselves. To Henry, the flagellants were "a race without a head," with neither sense nor a leader.

Yet Henry also thought that "a man would need a heart of stone to watch [the flagellants] without tears." They aroused enormous popular feeling wherever they went. This religious enthusiasm often culminated in violence against the Jews, as rumors circulated that the Jews were responsible for the Black Death. Christians revived old charges that Jews were plotting to "wipe out all the Christians with poison and had poisoned wells and springs everywhere," as one Franciscan friar put it. In Germany, especially, thousands of Jews were slaughtered. Many Jews fled to Poland, where the epidemic affected fewer people and where the authorities welcomed Jews as productive taxpayers. In western and central Europe, however, the persecutions impoverished the Jews.

Preoccupation with death led to the popularity of a theme called the Dance of Death as a subject of art, literature, and performance. It featured a procession of people of every age, sex, and rank mak-

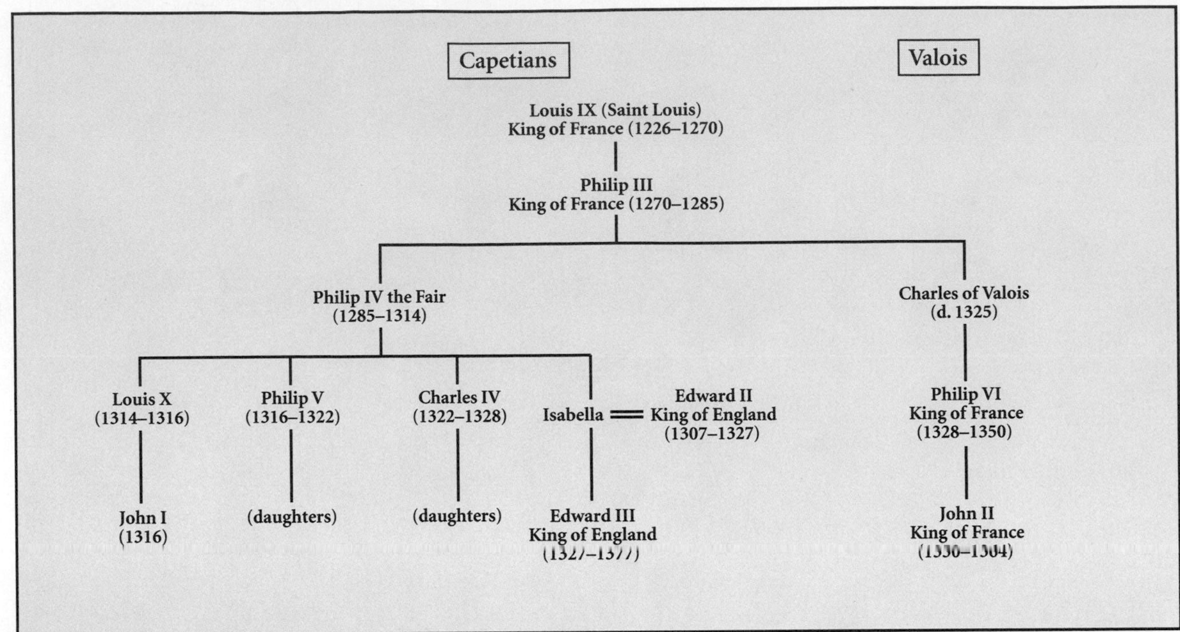

FIGURE 13.1 The Valois Succession
When Capetian King Charles IV died in 1328, his daughter was next in line for the French throne, but prejudice in France against female succession was so strong that the crown went to the Valois branch of the family. Meanwhile English King Edward III, as son of the French princess Isabella, claimed to be the rightful king of France.

ing their way to the grave. In works of art, skeletal figures of Death, whirling about, laughed as they abducted their prey. These were often life-size paintings that ran horizontally for many feet. They were meant to be "mirrors" in which viewers could see themselves. The Dance of Death was also sometimes performed—in a church or at a princely court. Preachers talked about the theme; poets wrote dialogues between Death and his victims. "Thus Death takes us all; that is certain," one poet concluded.

At the same time that it helped inspire this bleak view of the world, the Black Death brought new opportunities for those who survived its murderous path. With a smaller population to feed, less land was needed for farming. Marginal land that had been cultivated was returned to pasture, meadow, or forest. Landlords diversified their products. Wheat had been the favored crop before the plague, but barley—the key ingredient of beer—turned out to be more profitable afterward. Animal products continued to fetch a high price, and some landlords switched from raising crops to raising animals.

These changes in agriculture meant a better standard of living. The peasants and urban workers who survived the plague were able to negotiate better conditions or higher wages from their landlords or employers. With more money to spend, people could afford a better and more varied diet that included beer and meat.

A few years after each attack of the disease came a slight jump in the birthrate. It is unlikely that women became more fertile. Rather, the cause of the increased birthrate was more subtle: with good employment opportunities, couples married at younger ages and with greater frequency than they had previously. For example, before the Black Death, about seventeen couples per year married at Givry, a small town in Burgundy. But once the plague hit, an average of forty-seven couples there wed each year. "After the end of the epidemic," one chronicler wrote, "the men and women who stayed alive did everything to get married."

The Black Death also affected patterns of education. The post-plague generations needed schooling. The pestilential disease spared neither the students nor the professors of the old universities. As the disease ebbed, survivors built new local colleges and universities, partly to train a new generation for the priesthood and partly to satisfy local donors—many of them princes—who, riding on a sea of wealth left behind by the dead, wanted to be known as patrons of education. Thus, in 1348, in the midst of the Black Death, Holy Roman Emperor Charles IV chartered a university at Prague. The king of Poland founded Cracow University, and a Habsburg duke created a university at Vienna. Rather than traveling to Paris or Bologna, young men living east of the Rhine River now tended to study nearer home.

The Hundred Years' War, 1337–1453

Adding to people's miseries during the Black Death were the ravages of war. One of the most brutal was the **Hundred Years' War**, which pitted England against France. Since the Norman conquest of England in 1066, the king of England had held land on the continent. The French kings continually chipped away at it, however, and by the beginning of the fourteenth century England retained only the area around Bordeaux, called Guyenne. In 1337, after a series of challenges and skirmishes, King Philip VI of France (whose dynasty, the Valois, took over when the Capetians had no male heir) declared Guyenne to be his. In turn, King Edward III of England, son of Philip the Fair's daughter, declared himself king of France (Figure 13.1). The Hundred Years' War had begun.

The war had two major phases. In the first, the English gained ground, and a new political entity, the duchy of Burgundy, allied itself with England. This phase culminated in 1415, when the English achieved a great victory at the battle of Agincourt and took over northern France. In the second phase, however, fortunes reversed entirely: the French, after a major victory at the battle of Formigny, ousted the English (Map 13.2).

Joan of Arc | How did the French achieve this turnaround? The answer lies partly in the inspiration of a sixteen-year-old peasant girl who presented herself at the court of the dauphin (the man who had been designated as king but had not yet been anointed and crowned) as the heaven-sent savior of France. Inspired by visions in which God told her to lead the war against the English, and calling herself "the Maid" (a virgin), **Joan of Arc** (1412–1431) arrived at court in 1429 wearing armor, riding a horse, and leading a small army. Full of charisma and confidence at a desperate hour, Joan was carefully questioned and examined (to be sure of her virginity) before her message was accepted. She convinced the French that she had been sent by God when she fought courageously (and was wounded) in the successful battle of Orléans. With Joan at his side, the dauphin traveled deep into enemy territory to be anointed and crowned as King Charles VII at the cathedral in Reims, following the tradition of French monarchs.

Portrait of Charles VII
The French artist who created this portrait of King Charles VII, Jean Fouquet (d. 1481), studied in Italy and knew about the new, naturalistic styles that were coming into vogue there (see the discussion of Renaissance art beginning on page 430). His portrait of Charles shows a broad-shouldered and serious man. The only hints of the monarch's royal status are his hat of blue and gold (reminiscent of the French crown) and the words that frame him above and below: "The Very Victorious King of France, Charles, Seventh of the Name." *(Louvre, Paris, France/ Giraudon/The Bridgeman Art Library International.)*

The victory at Orléans and the anointing of Charles began the French about-face, but Joan herself suffered greatly. A promise to take Paris proved empty, and she was captured and turned over to the English. Tried as a witch, she was burned at the stake in 1431. (See "Contrasting Views," page 418.)

The Hundred Years' War as a World War | The Hundred Years' War, although directly fought by England and France, drew people from other states of Europe into its vortex. Both the English and the French hired mercenaries from Germany, Switzerland, and the Netherlands; the best crossbowmen came from Genoa. Since the economies of England and Flanders (for Flanders, see Map 13.2) were interdependent, with England

---

Hundred Years' War: The long war between England and France, 1337–1453 (actually 116 years); it produced numerous social upheavals yet left both states more powerful than before.

Joan of Arc: A peasant girl (1412–1431) whose conviction that God had sent her to save France in fact helped France win the Hundred Years' War.

CONTRASTING VIEWS

Joan of Arc: Who Was "the Maid"?

The figure of Joan of Arc gives shape to the confused events and personalities of the Hundred Years' War. But who was this young woman? Joan herself emphasized her visions and divine calling (Document 1). The royal court was unsure whether to consider her a fraud (or, worse, the devil's tool) or a gift from heaven (Document 2). A neighbor of the young Joan recalled her as an ordinary young country girl (Document 3).

1. Joan the Visionary

Joan first referred to her visions at length after her capture by her enemies, who were eager to prove that she was inspired by the devil. The light and voices that she testified to echoed the experiences of many medieval visionaries. But we do not have Joan's exact words; her account was written up by her examiners, who composed it in Latin even though Joan spoke in French.

She confessed that when she was aged thirteen, she had a voice from God to help her to guide herself. And the first time she was greatly afraid. And this voice came around noon, in summer, in the garden of her father, and Joan had not fasted on the preceding day. She heard the voice on the right-hand side, towards the church, and she rarely heard it without a light. This light came from the same side that she heard the voice, but generally there was a great light there. And when Joan came to France [Lorraine, where Joan was raised, was not considered part of France], she often heard this voice. . . .

She said, in addition, that if she was in a wood, she clearly heard the voices coming to her. She also said that it seemed to her that it was a worthy voice and she believed that this voice had been sent from God, and that, after she had heard this voice three times, she knew that this was the voice of an angel. She said also that this voice had always protected her well and that she understood this voice clearly.

Asked about the instruction that this voice gave to her for the salvation of her soul, she said that it taught her to conduct herself well, to go to church often, and that it was necessary that she should travel to France. Joan added that her interrogator would not learn from her, on this occasion, in what form that voice had appeared to her. . . . She said moreover that the voice had told her that she, Joan, should go to find Robert de Baudricourt in the town of Vaucouleurs [a tiny holdout in eastern France that was not under English control], of which he was captain, and that he would provide her with men to travel with her. Joan then replied that she was a poor girl who did not know how to ride on horseback or to lead in war. [But she obeyed the voice, met with Robert de Baudricourt, and in the end got the escort that she needed to go to the court of the dauphin, the future Charles VII.]

Source: *Joan of Arc: La Pucelle*, trans. and annotated by Craig Taylor (Manchester: Manchester University Press, 2006), 141–42.

2. Messenger of God?

When Joan appeared at the court of the dauphin, her reputation as the messenger of God had preceded her. The French court received her with a mixture of wonder, curiosity, and skepticism. The dauphin's counselors debated about whether Joan should be taken seriously, and the dauphin referred the case to a panel of theologians to determine whether Joan's mission was of divine origin. The following account of Joan's first visit to the dauphin was given by Simon Charles, president of the royal Chamber of Accounts, at an investigation begun in 1455 to nullify Joan's sentence of 1429.

Questioned first on what he could depose and testify . . . [Simon Charles] said and declared upon oath that he only knew what follows: . . . that when Joan arrived at the town of Chinon, the council discussed whether the King should hear her or not. She was first asked why she had

exporting the wool that Flemish workers turned into cloth, it was inevitable that Flanders would be drawn into the conflict. In fact, once the war broke out, Flemish townsmen allied with England against their count, who supported the French king.

The duchy of Burgundy became involved in the war when the marriage of the heiress to Flanders and the duke of Burgundy in 1369 created a powerful new state. Calculating shrewdly which side—England or France—to support and cannily entering the fray when it suited them, the dukes of Burgundy created a glittering court, a center of art and culture. Had Burgundy maintained its alliance with England, the map of Europe would be entirely different today. But, sensing France's new strength, the duke of Burgundy broke off with England in 1435. The duchy continued to prosper until its expansionist policies led to the formation of a coalition against it. The last duke, Charles the Bold, died fighting in 1477. His daughter, his only heir, tried to save Burgundy by marrying the Holy Roman Emperor, but the move was to little avail. The duchy broke up, with France absorbing its western bits.

come and what she wanted. Although she did not wish to say anything except to the King, she was nevertheless forced on behalf of the King to reveal the purpose of her mission. She said that she had two commands from the King of Heaven, that is to say one to raise the siege of Orléans, and the other to conduct the King to Reims for his coronation and consecration. Having heard this, some among the King's councilors said that the King should not have any faith in this Joan, and the others said that, since she declared that she had been sent by God and that she had certain things to say to the King, the King should at least hear her. But the King decided that she should first be examined by the clerks and churchmen, which was done.

Source: *Joan of Arc: La Pucelle*, trans. and annotated by Craig Taylor (Manchester: Manchester University Press, 2006), 317–18.

3. Normal Girl?

At the same trial, various inhabitants in and near Domremy, Joan's village, recalled her as a normal young girl. The following account was given by Jean Morel, a laborer from a town near Joan's. He knew her as Jeannette.

He declared upon oath that the Jeannette in question was born at Domremy and was baptized at the parish church of Saint-Rémy in that place. Her father was named Jacques d'Arc, her mother Isabelle, both laborers living together at Domremy as long as they lived. They were good and faithful Catholics, good laborers, of good reputation, and of honest behavior. . . .

He declared upon oath that from her earliest childhood, Jeannette was well brought up in the faith as was appropriate, and instructed in good morals, as far as he knew, so that almost everyone in the village of Domremy loved her. Just like the other young girls she knew the *Credo*, the *Pater Noster*, and the *Ave Maria* [all three basic texts of Christian belief].

He declared that Jeannette was honest in her behavior, just as any similar girl is, because her parents were not very rich. In her childhood, and right up to her departure from her family home, she followed the plow and sometimes minded the animals in the fields; she did the work of a woman, spinning and making other things.

He declared upon oath that, as he saw, this Jeannette often went to church willingly to the extent that sometimes she was mocked by the other young people. . . .

He declared upon oath that on the subject of the tree called "of the Ladies," he once heard it said that women or supernatural persons—they were called fairies—came long ago to dance under that tree. But, so it is said, since a reading of the gospel of St. John, they did not come there any more. He also declared that in the present day . . . the young girls and lads of Domremy went under this tree to dance [on a particular Sunday in Lent], and sometimes also in the spring and summer on feast days; sometimes they ate at that place. On their return, they went to the spring of Thorns, strolling and singing, and they drank from the water of this spring, and all around they had fun gathering flowers. He also declared that Joan the Pucelle ["the Maid"] went there sometimes with the other girls and did as they did; he never heard it said that she went alone to the tree or to the spring, which is nearer to the village than the tree, for any other reason than to walk about and to play just like the other young girls.

Source: *Joan of Arc: La Pucelle*, trans. and annotated by Craig Taylor (Manchester: Manchester University Press, 2006), 267–68.

Questions to Consider

1. **Given the norms of the time, in what ways was Joan ordinary?**
2. **What do you suppose was the royal court's reaction to the testimony of Simon Charles? And to the testimony of Jean Morel?**

From Chivalry to Modern Warfare

When he first started to write about the Hundred Years' War, the chronicler Jean Froissart (d. c. 1405) considered it a chivalric adventure—chivalry being the medieval code of refinement, fair play, and piety followed by knights. He expected it to display the gallantry and bravery of the medieval nobility. He said that he was writing his account

> in order that the honorable enterprises, noble adventure, and deeds of arms which took place during the wars waged by France and England should be fittingly related and preserved for posterity, so that brave men should be inspired thereby to follow such examples.

Froissart described knights like the Englishman Walter de Manny, who was so eager to show off his prowess that he privately gathered a group of followers and attacked a French town in order to fulfill a vow made "in the hearing of ladies and lords that, 'If war breaks out, . . . I'll be the first to arm myself and capture a castle or town in the kingdom of France.'"

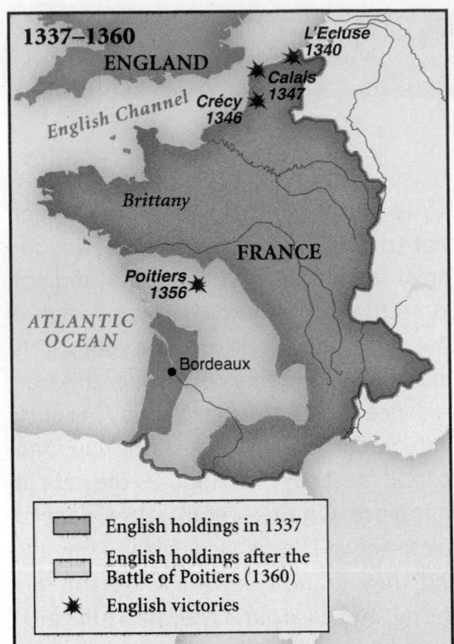

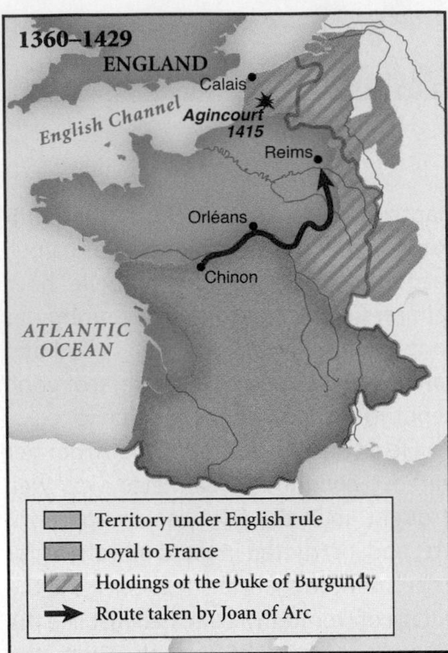

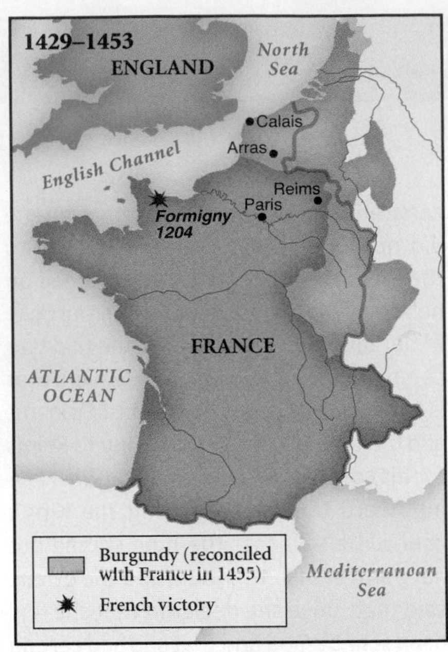

MAP 13.2 The Hundred Years' War, 1337–1453
During the Hundred Years' War, English kings—aided by the new state of Burgundy—contested the French monarchy for the domination of France. For many decades, the English seemed to be winning, but the French monarchy prevailed in the end.

But even Froissart could not help but notice that most of the men who went to battle were not wealthy knights on a lark like Walter de Manny. Nor were they ordinary foot soldiers, who had always made up a large portion of all medieval armies. The soldiers of the Hundred Years' War were primarily mercenaries: men who fought for pay and plunder, heedless of the king for whom they were supposed to be fighting. During lulls in the war, these so-called Free Companies lived off the French countryside, terrorizing the peasants and exacting "protection" money. Froissart wrote of "men-at-arms and irregulars from various countries, who subdued and plundered the whole region between the Seine and the Loire. . . . They roamed the country in troops of twenty, thirty, or forty, and they met no one capable of putting up a resistance to them."

The ideal chivalric knight fought on horseback with other armed horsemen. But in the Hundred Years' War, foot soldiers and archers were far more important than swordsmen. The French tended to use crossbows, whose heavy, deadly arrows were released by a mechanism that even a townsman could master. (See the illustration on page 421.) The English employed longbows, which could shoot five arrows for every one launched on the crossbow. Large groups of English archers could wreak havoc with a volley of arrows. Meanwhile, gunpowder was slowly being introduced and cannons forged. Handguns were beginning to be used, their effect about equal to that of crossbows.

By the end of the war, chivalry was only a dream—though one that continued to inspire soldiers even up to the First World War. Heavy artillery and foot soldiers, tightly massed together in formations of many thousands of men, were the face of the new military. Moreover, the army was becoming more professional and centralized. In the 1440s, the French king created a permanent army of mounted soldiers. He paid them a wage and subjected them to regular inspection. Private armies—such as the one Walter de Manny recruited for his own ambitions—were prohibited.

The War's Progeny: Uprisings in Flanders, the Jacquerie, and Wat Tyler's Rebellion

The outbreak of the Hundred Years' War led to revolts in Ghent and other great textile centers in Flanders. Dependent on England for the raw wool they processed, Flemish cities could not afford to have their count, Louis I, side with the French. The cities revolted and succeeded for a time in ousting the count, who fled to France in 1339. But discord among the cities and within each town allowed Louis I's successor, count Louis II, to return in 1348. Revolts continued to flare up thereafter, but Louis allowed a measure of self-government to the towns, maintained some distance from French influence, and managed on the whole to keep the peace.

In France, the Parisians chafed against the high taxes they were forced to pay to finance the war.

Crossbows at a Siege
This manuscript illumination from the fifteenth century shows city defenders using hand bows and arrows to fight against armed attackers. One of the besiegers uses a hand bow while another shoots a crossbow. Two of the attackers are in the process of spanning their crossbows, using a device to draw back the string. The heavy bolts (as crossbow arrows were called) were deadly, but crossbows were not ideal weapons because spanning took up precious time. *(© The British Library/HIP/The Image Works.)*

When the English captured the French king John at the battle of Poitiers in 1358, Étienne Marcel, provost of the Paris merchants, and other disillusioned members of the estates of France (the representatives of the clergy, nobility, and commons) met in Paris to discuss political reform, the incompetence of the French army, and taxes. Under Marcel's leadership, a crowd of Parisians killed some nobles and for a short while took control of the city. But troops soon blockaded Paris and cut off its food supply. Later that year, Marcel was assassinated and the Parisian revolt came to an end.

Also in that year, peasants weary of the Free Companies (who were ravaging the countryside) and disgusted by the military incompetence of the nobility rose up in protest. The French nobility called the peasant rebellion the **Jacquerie**, probably taken from a derisive name for male peasants: Jacques Bonhomme ("Jack Goodfellow"). Froissart was scandalized by the peasants' behavior:

> They banded together and went off . . . unarmed except for pikes and knives, to the house of a knight who lived near by. They broke in and killed the knight with his lady and his children, big and small, and set fire to the house. Next they went to another castle and did much worse.

If the peasants were in fact guilty of these atrocities, the nobles soon gave as good as they got. The Jacquerie was put down with exceptional brutality. Froissart described the moment with relish: "They [the nobles] began to kill those evil men [the peasants] and to cut them to pieces without mercy."

Similar revolts took place in England. The movement known as Wat Tyler's Rebellion, for example, started as an uprising in much of southern and central England when royal agents tried to collect poll taxes (a tax on each household) to finance the Hundred Years' War. Refusing to pay and refusing

---

Jacquerie (zhah kuh ree): The 1358 uprising of French peasants against the nobles amid the Hundred Years' War; it was brutally put down.

DOCUMENT

Wat Tyler's Rebellion (1381)

An anonymous chronicler wrote about Wat Tyler's Rebellion shortly after it took place in 1381. The author was hostile to the rebels yet understood their motives quite well. After converging on London from various parts of southern England, the rebels, led by men like Wat Tyler, demanded that the king end the unjust taxes collected by local officials. The fourteen-year-old King Richard II (r. 1377–1399) eventually met with them and seemed to give in to their demands, but another meeting the next day led to Tyler's death and the dispersal of the demonstrators. The excerpt here chronicles the very beginning of the movement, before the march on London.

Because in the year 1380 the subsidies [taxes] were over lightly granted at the Parliament of Northampton and because it seemed to divers lords and to the commons that the said subsidies were not honestly levied, but commonly exacted from the poor and not from the rich, to the great profit and advantage of the tax-collectors, and to the deception of the king and the commons, the Council of the King ordained certain commissions to make inquiry in every township how the tax had been levied. Among these commissions, one for Essex was sent to one Thomas Bampton [one of the tax collectors]. . . . He had summoned before him the townships of a neighboring hundred, and wished to have from them new contributions. . . .

Among these townships was Fobbing, whose people made answer that they would not pay a penny more, because they already had a receipt from himself for the said subsidy. On which the said Thomas threatened them angrily. . . . And for fear of his malice the folks of Fobbing took counsel with the folks of Corringham, and the folks of these two places . . . sent messages to the men of Stanford. . . . Then the people of these three townships came together to the number of a hundred or more, and with one assent went to the said Thomas Bampton, and roundly gave him answer that they would have no traffic with him, nor give him a penny. . . .

And afterwards the said commons assembled together . . . to the number of some 50,000, and they went to the manors and townships of those who would not rise with them, and cast their houses to the ground or set fire to them. At this time they caught three clerks of Thomas Bampton, and cut off their heads, and carried the heads about with them for several days stuck on poles as an example to others. For it was their purpose to slay all lawyers, and all jurors, and all the servants of the king whom they could find.

Source: Charles Oman, *The Great Revolt of 1381* (Oxford: Clarendon Press, 1906), 186–88.

Question to Consider

- **What did the author consider to be the main causes of the rebellion?**

to be arrested, the commons—peasants and small householders—rose up in rebellion in 1381. They massed in various groups, vowing "to slay all lawyers, and all jurors, and all the servants of the King whom they could find," as one chronicler put it. Marching to London to see the king, whom they professed to support, they began to make a more radical demand: an end to serfdom. Although the rebellion was put down and its leaders executed, the death knell of serfdom in England had been sounded, as peasants returned home to bargain with their lords for better terms. (See Document, "Wat Tyler's Rebellion," above.)

The Ottoman Conquest of Constantinople, 1453

The end of the Hundred Years' War coincided with an event that was even more decisive for all of Europe: the conquest of Constantinople by the Ottoman Turks. The Ottomans, who were converts to Islam, were one of several tribal confederations in central Asia. Starting as a small enclave between the Mongol Empire and Byzantium, and taking their name from a potent early leader, Osman I (r. 1280–1324), the Ottomans began to expand in the fourteenth century in a quest to wage holy war against infidels, or unbelievers.

During the next two centuries, the Ottomans took over the Balkans and Anatolia by both negotiations and arms (Map 13.3). Under Murad I (r. 1360–1389), they reduced the Byzantine Empire to the city of Constantinople and treated it as a vassal state. At the Maritsa River in 1364, Murad defeated a joint Hungarian-Serbian army, setting off a wave of crusading fervor in Europe that led (in the end) to only a few unsuccessful expeditions. In 1389, Murad's forces won the battle of Kosovo—still invoked in Serbia today as a great struggle between Christians and Muslims, even though a number of Serbian princes fought on the Ottoman side.

After a lull, when the Ottoman thrust was stopped, Sultan Mehmed I (r. 1410–1421) resumed the conquests; eventually, his grandson **Mehmed II** (r. 1451–1481) determined to take the city of Constantinople itself. Preparations began about a year in advance, when Mehmed II built an enormous fortress near the capital and fitted it out with a large number of soldiers and several brass cannons. In March 1453, he launched the attack. Perhaps eighty thousand men confronted some three thousand defenders (the entire population of Constantinople was no more than fifty thousand) and a fleet from Genoa. The city held out until the end of May, when Mehmed's forces attacked by both land and sea. The decisive moment came when the sultan's cannons breached the city's land walls. Mehmed's troops entered the city and plundered it thoroughly, killing the emperor and displaying his head in triumph.

The conquest of Constantinople marked the end of the Byzantine Empire. But that was not the way Mehmed saw the matter. He conquered Constantinople in part to be a successor to the Roman emperors—a Muslim successor, to be sure. He turned Hagia Sophia, the great church built by the emperor Justinian in 538, into a mosque, as he did with most of the other Byzantine churches. He retained the city's name, the City of Constantine—Qustantiniyya in Turkish—though it was popularly referred to as Istanbul, meaning, simply, "the city."

Like the French and English kings after the Hundred Years' War, the Ottoman sultans were centralizing monarchs who guaranteed law and order. The core of their army consisted of European Christian boys, who were requisitioned as tribute every five years. Trained in arms and converted to Islam, these young fighters made up the Janissaries—a highly disciplined military force also used to supervise local administrators throughout formerly Byzantine regions. Building a system of roads that crisscrossed their empire, the sultans made long-distance trade easy and profitable.

Once Constantinople was his, Mehmed embarked on an ambitious program of expansion and conquest. He brought all of Serbia under Ottoman control in 1458; he crossed the Aegean Sea and took over Athens and the Peloponnese by 1460; six years later, he gained Bosnia. By 1500, the Ottoman Empire was a new and powerful state bridging Europe and the Middle East.

The Great Schism, 1378–1417

Even as war and disease threatened their material and physical well-being, a crisis in the church, precipitated by a scandal in the papacy, tore at Europeans' spiritual life. The move of the papacy from Rome to Avignon in 1309 had caused an outcry, especially among Italians, distraught by the election of French popes and anxious to see the papacy return to Rome. Some critics, such as Marsilius of Padua, became disillusioned with the institution of the papacy itself. Marsilius, a physician and lawyer by training, argued in *The Defender of the Peace* (1324) that the source of all power lay with the people: "the law-making power or the first and real effective source of law is the people or the body of citizens or the prevailing part of the people according to its election or its will expressed in general convention by vote." Applied to the papacy, Marsilius's argument meant that Christians themselves formed the church and that the pope should be elected by a general council representing all Christians.

William of Ockham (c. 1285–1349), an English Franciscan who was one of the most eminent theologians of his age, was an even more thoroughgoing critic of the papacy. He believed that church power derived from the congregation of the faithful, both laity and clergy, not from the pope or a church council. Rejecting the confident synthesis of Christian doctrine and Aristotelian philosophy by Thomas Aquinas, Ockham believed that universal concepts had no reality in nature but instead existed only as mere representations, names in the mind—a philosophy that came to be called nominalism. Perceiving and analyzing such concepts as "man" or "papal infallibility" offered no assurance that the concepts expressed truth. Observation and human reason

Mehmed II: The sultan under whom the Ottoman Turks conquered Constantinople in 1453.

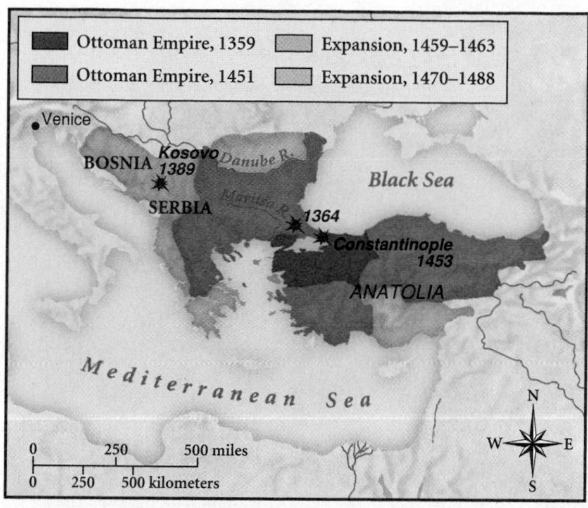

MAP 13.3 Ottoman Expansion in the Fourteenth and Fifteenth Centuries

The Balkans were the major theater of expansion for the Ottoman Empire. The Byzantine Empire was reduced to the city of Constantinople and surrounded by the Ottomans before its final fall in 1453.

Martin V at the Council of Constance

The events at the Council of Constance (1414–1418) were important both locally and across Europe. That is why a citizen of Constance, Ulrich von Richental, wrote a chronicle of the council. It was full of details about every event and richly illustrated. On this page, the bareheaded and newly elected Oddo di Colonna is led to the altar by two cardinals to gain the papal tiara as Martin V. *(akg-images/Interfoto/Bildarchiv Hansmann.)*

were limited tools with which to understand the universe and to know God. The principle that simple explanations were superior to complex ones became known as Ockham's razor (to suggest the idea of shaving away unnecessary hypotheses). Imprisoned by Pope John XXII for heresy in 1328, Ockham escaped within the year and found refuge with Emperor Louis of Bavaria.

Stung by his critics, Pope Gregory XI (r. 1370–1378) left Avignon to return to Rome in 1377. The scandal of the Avignon papacy seemed to be over. But Rome itself presented a problem. Glad to have the papacy back, the Romans were determined never to lose it again. When the cardinals — many of whom came from Spain, Italy, and France — met to elect Gregory's successor, the *popolo*, the communal faction who controlled the city, demanded that they choose a Roman: "A Roman! A Roman! A Roman or at least an Italian! Or else we'll kill them all." Expecting to gain an important place in papal government, the cardinals chose an Italian, who took the name Urban VI. But Urban had no intention of kowtowing to the cardinals: he exalted the power of the pope and began to reduce the cardinals' wealth and privileges. The cardinals from France decided that they had made a big mistake. Many left Rome for a meeting at Anagni, where they claimed that Urban's election had been irregular and called on him to resign. When he refused, they elected a Frenchman as pope; he took the name Clement VII and soon moved his papal court to Avignon, but not before he and Urban had excommunicated each other. The **Great Schism** (1378–1417), which split the loyalties of all of Europe, had begun.

The king of France supported Clement; the king of England favored Urban. Some European states — Burgundy, Scotland, and Castile, for example — lined up on the side of France. Others — the Holy Roman Empire, Poland, and Hungary — supported Urban. Portugal switched sides four times, depending on which alliance offered it the most advantages. Each pope declared that those who followed the other were to be deprived of the rights of church membership; in effect, everyone in Europe was excommunicated by one pope or the other.

The Conciliar Movement

Contrary to the ideas of Marsilius, church law said that only a pope could summon a general council of the church — a sort of parliament of high churchmen. But given the state of confusion in Christendom, many intellectuals argued that the crisis justified calling a general council to represent the body of the faithful, even against the wishes of an unwilling pope — or popes. They spearheaded the conciliar movement — a movement to have the cardinals or the emperor call a council.

In 1408, long after Urban and Clement had passed away and new popes had followed, the conciliar movement succeeded when cardinals from both sides met and declared their resolve "to pursue the union of the Church . . . by way of abdication of both papal contenders." With support from both England and France, the cardinals called for a

Great Schism: The papal dispute of 1378–1417 when the church had two and even (between 1409 and 1417) three popes. The Great Schism was ended by the Council of Constance.

council to be held at Pisa in 1409. Both popes refused to attend, and the council deposed them, electing a new pope.

But the "deposed" popes refused to budge, even though most of the European powers abandoned them. There were now three popes. The successor of the newest one, John XXIII, turned to the emperor to arrange for another council.

The Council of Constance (1414–1418) met to resolve the papal crisis as well as to institute church reforms. The delegates deposed John XXIII and accepted the resignation of the pope at Rome. After long negotiations with rulers still supporting the Avignon pope, all allegiance to him was withdrawn and he was deposed. The council then elected Martin V, who was recognized as pope by every important ruler of Europe. Finally, the Great Schism had come to an end.

Book of Hours
This illustration for June in a Book of Hours made for the duke of Berry was meant for the contemplation of a nobleman. In the background is a fairy-tale depiction of the duke's palace and the tower of a Gothic church, while in the foreground graceful women rake the hay and well-muscled men swing their scythes. *(Réunion des Musées Nationaux, Art Resource, NY.)*

New Forms of Piety The Great Schism, no doubt abetted by the miseries of the plague and the distresses of war, caused enormous anxiety among ordinary Christians. Worried about the salvation of their souls now that the church was fractured by multiple popes, pious men and women eagerly sought new forms of religious solace. The church offered the plenary indulgence — full forgiveness of sins, which had been originally offered to crusaders who died while fighting for the cause — to those who made a pilgrimage to Rome and other designated holy places during declared Holy Years. People could wipe away their sins through confession and contrition, but they retained some guilt that they could remove only through good deeds or in purgatory. The idea of purgatory — the place where sins were fully purged — took precise form at this time, and with it **indulgences** became popular. These remissions of sin were offered for good works to reduce the time in purgatory. Thus, for example, the duchess of Brittany was granted a hundred days off of her purgatorial punishments when she allowed the Feast of Corpus Christi to be preached in her chapel. Lesser folk might obtain indulgences in more modest ways.

Both clergy and laity became more interested than ever in the education of young people as a way to deepen their faith and spiritual life. The Brethren of the Common Life — laypeople, mainly in the Low Countries (the region comprising today's Belgium, Luxembourg, and the Netherlands) who devoted themselves to pious works — set up a model school at Deventer. In Italy, humanists (see page 428) emphasized primary school education. Priests were expected to teach the faithful the basics of the Christian religion.

Home was equally a place for devotion. Portable images of Mary, the mother of God, and of the life and passion of Christ proliferated. They were meant

indulgence: A step beyond confession and penance, an indulgence (normally granted by popes or bishops) lifted the temporal punishment still necessary for a sin already forgiven. Normally, that punishment was said to take place in purgatory. But it could be remitted through good works (including prayers and contributing money to worthy causes).

to be contemplated by ordinary Christians at convenient moments throughout the day. People purchased or commissioned copies of Books of Hours, which contained prayers to be said on the appropriate day at the hours of the monastic office. Books of Hours included calendars, sometimes splendidly illustrated with depictions of the seasons and labors of the year. (See the illustration on page 425.) Other illustrations reminded their users of the life and suffering of Christ.

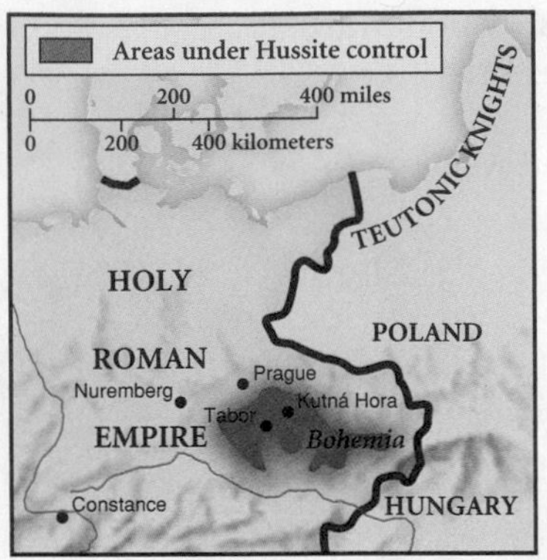

The Hussite Revolution, 1415–1436

On the streets of towns, priests marched in dignified processions, carrying the sanctified bread of the Mass—the very body of Christ—in tall and splendid monstrances that trumpeted the importance and dignity of the Eucharistic wafer. (See the illustration below.) Like images of the Lord's life and crucifixion, the monstrance emphasized Christ's body. Christ's blood was perhaps even more important. It was thought of as "wonderful blood," the blood that brought man's redemption. Thus, the image of a bleeding, crucified Christ was repeated over and over in depictions of the day. Viewers were meant to think about Christ's pain and feel it themselves, mentally participating in his death on the cross. Flagellants, as we have seen, literally drew their own blood.

New Heresies: The Lollards and the Hussites

Religious anxieties, intellectual dissent, and social unrest combined to create new heretical movements in England and Bohemia. In England were the Lollards, a term that was derogatory in the hands of their opponents and yet a proud title when used by the Lollards themselves. The Lollards were initially inspired by the Oxford scholar John Wycliffe (c. 1330–1384), who, like Marsilius of Padua and William of Ockham in an earlier generation, came to believe that the true church was the community of believers rather than the clerical hierarchy. Wycliffe criticized monasticism, excommunication, and the Mass. He emphasized Bible reading in the vernacular, arguing that true believers, not corrupt priests, formed the church.

The Lollard movement included scholars and members of the gentry (lesser noble) class as well as artisans and other humbler folk. Women were able and enthusiastic participants. Although suffering widespread hostility and persecution into the sixteenth century, the Lollards were extremely active, setting up schools for children (girls as well as boys), translating the Bible into English, preaching numerous sermons, and inspiring new recruits, clerical as well as lay.

On the other side of Europe were the Bohemian Hussites—named after one of their leaders,

Monstrance

Elaborate vessels such as the one held by angels in this woodcut became popular church furnishings in the fifteenth century. The monstrance, a term that comes from a Latin word meaning "to show," displayed the consecrated bread of the Eucharist to the laity in fitting splendor, as if it were a relic. *(© The Trustees of the British Museum/Art Resource, NY.)*

Jan Hus (1372?–1415), an admirer of Wycliffe. Their central demand—that the faithful receive not just the bread (the body) but also the wine (the blood) at Mass—brought together several passionately held desires and beliefs. The blood of Christ was particularly important to the devout, and the Hussite call to allow the laity to drink the wine from the chalice reflected this focus on the blood's redemptive power. Furthermore, the call for communion with *both* bread and wine signified a desire for equality. Bohemia was an exceptionally divided country, with an urban German-speaking elite, including merchants, artisans, bishops, and scholars, and a Czech-speaking nobility and peasantry that was beginning to seek better opportunities. (Hus himself was a Czech of peasant stock who became a professor at the University of Prague.) When priests celebrated Mass, they had the privilege of drinking the wine. The Hussites, who were largely Czech laity, wanted the same privilege and, with it, recognition of their dignity and worth.

The Bohemian nobility protected Hus after the church condemned him as a heretic, but the Holy Roman Emperor Sigismund lured him to the Council of Constance "to justify himself before all men." Though promised safe conduct, Hus was arrested when he arrived at the council. When he refused to recant his views, the church leaders burned him at the stake.

Hus's death caused an uproar, and his movement became a full-scale national revolt of Czechs against Germans. Sigismund called crusades against the Hussites, but all of his expeditions were soundly defeated. Radical groups of Hussites organized several new communities in southern Bohemia at Mount Tabor, named after the New Testament spot where the Transfiguration of Christ was thought to have taken place (Matt. 17:1–8). Here the radicals attempted to live according to the example of the first apostles. They recognized no lord, gave women some political rights, and created a simple liturgy that was carried out in the Czech language. Negotiations with Sigismund and his successor led to the Hussites' incorporation into the Bohemian political system by 1450. Though the Hussites were largely marginalized, they had won the right to receive communion in "both kinds" (wine and bread) and they had made Bohemia intensely aware of its Czech, rather than German, identity.

REVIEW QUESTION **What crises did Europeans confront in the fourteenth and fifteenth centuries, and how did they handle them?**

The Renaissance: New Forms of Thought and Expression

Some Europeans confronted the crises they faced by creating the culture of the Renaissance (French for "rebirth"). The period associated with the Renaissance, about 1350 to 1600, revived elements of the classical past—the Greek philosophers before Aristotle, Hellenistic artists, and Roman rhetoricians. (See "Terms of History," page 428.) Disillusioned with present institutions, many people looked back to the ancient world; in Greece and Rome they found models of thought, language, power, prestige, and the arts that they could apply to their own circumstances. Humanists modeled their writing on the Latin of Cicero, architects embraced ancient notions of public space, artists adopted classical forms, and musicians used classical texts. In reality, Renaissance writers and artists built much of their work on medieval precedents, but they rarely acknowledged this fact. They found great satisfaction in believing that they were resuscitating the glories of the ancient world—and that everything between them and the classical past was a contemptible "Middle Age."

Renaissance Humanism

Three of the delegates at the Council of Constance—Cincius Romanus, Poggius Bracciolinus, and Bartholomaeus Politianus—reveal the attitudes of the Renaissance. Although busy with church work, they decided to take time off for a "rescue mission." Cincius described the escapade to one of his Latin teachers back in Italy:

> In Germany there are many monasteries with libraries full of Latin books. This aroused the hope in me that some of the works of Cicero, Varro, Livy, and other great men of learning, which seem to have completely vanished, might come to light, if a careful search were instituted. A few days ago, [we] went by agreement to the town of St. Gall. As soon as we went into the library [of the monastery there], we found *Jason's Argonauticon*, written by C. Valerius Flaccus in verse that is both splendid and dignified and not far removed from poetic majesty. Then we found some discussion in prose of a number of Cicero's orations.

Cicero, Varro, Livy, and Valerius Flaccus were pagan Latin writers. Even though Cincius and his friends were working for Pope John XXIII, they loved the writings of the ancients, whose Latin was, in their

TERMS OF HISTORY

Renaissance

The word *renaissance* was first used in the sixteenth century to refer to a historical moment. At that time it meant the rebirth of classical poetry, prose, and art of that period alone. Only later did historians borrow the word to refer to earlier rebirths. One of the first persons to herald the fifteenth-century Renaissance was the Italian painter and architect Giorgio Vasari (1511–1574) in his *Lives of the Most Excellent Italian Architects, Painters, and Sculptors* (1550). Vasari argued that Greco-Roman art declined after the dissolution of the Roman Empire, to be followed by a long period of barbarity. Only in the past generations had Italian artists begun to restore the perfection of the arts, according to Vasari, a development he called *rinascita*, the Italian for "rebirth." It was the French equivalent—*renaissance*—that stuck.

Referring initially to a rebirth in the arts and literature, the word *renaissance* came to mean a new consciousness of modernity and individuality. Prizing the ancient world, Renaissance humanists were convinced that they lived in a new age that recalled that lost glory. They called the period between their age and the ancient one "the Middle Age." (That's why today we call it the Middle Ages.) They reveled in their human potential and their individuality.

The Renaissance was an important movement in Italy, France, Spain, the Low Countries, and central Europe. The word itself acquired widespread recognition with the 1860 publication of Jakob Burckhardt's *The Civilization of the Renaissance in Italy*. A historian at the University of Basel, Burckhardt considered the Renaissance a watershed in Western civilization. For him, the Renaissance ushered in a spirit of modernity, freeing the individual from the domination of society and creative impulses from the repression of the church; the Renaissance represented the beginning of secular society and the preeminence of individual creative geniuses.

Although very influential, Burckhardt's ideas have also been strongly challenged by many recent scholars. Some point out the various continuities between the Middle Ages and the Renaissance, others argue that the Renaissance was not a secular but a profoundly religious age, and still others see the Renaissance as only the beginning of a long period of transition from the Middle Ages to modernity. The consensus among scholars today is that the Renaissance represents a distinct cultural period lasting from the fourteenth to the sixteenth century, centered on the revival of classical learning. Historians disagree about its significance, but they generally understand it to represent some of the complex changes that characterized the passing from medieval society to modernity.

view, "splendid and dignified," unlike the Latin used in their own time, which they found debased and faulty. They saw themselves as the resuscitators of ancient language, literature, and culture. Cincius continued:

> When we carefully inspected the nearby tower of the church of St. Gall in which countless books were kept like captives and the library neglected and infested with dust, worms, soot, and all the things associated with the destruction of books, we all burst into tears. . . . Truly if this library could speak for itself, it would cry loudly: ". . . Snatch me from this prison. . . ." There were in that monastery an abbot and monks totally devoid of any knowledge of literature. What barbarous hostility to the Latin tongue! What damned dregs of humanity!

The monks were barbarians, in Cincius's view, while he and his companions were heroic raiders swooping in to liberate the captive books. **Humanism** was a literary and linguistic movement—an attempt to revive classical Latin (and later Greek) as well as the values and sensibilities that came with the language. It began among men and women living in the Italian city-states, where many saw parallels between their urban, independent lives and the experiences of the city-states of the ancient world. Humanism was a way to confront the crises—and praise the advances—of the fourteenth through sixteenth centuries. Humanists wrote poetry, history, moral philosophy, and grammar books, all patterned on classical models, especially the writings of Cicero.

That Cincius was employed by the pope yet considered the monks of St. Gall barbarians was no oddity. Most humanists combined sincere Christian piety with a new appreciation of the pagan past. Besides, they needed to work in order to live, and they took employment where they found it. Some humanists worked for the church, others were civil

---

humanism: A literary and linguistic movement cultivated in particular during the Renaissance (1350–1600) and founded on reviving classical Latin and Greek texts, styles, and values.

Petrarch
About seventy-five years after Petrarch's death, the artist Andrea del Castagno was commissioned to decorate the walls of a villa near Florence with a cycle of nine famous men and women. The three women he illustrated were drawn from the Bible or legend; one of them was Queen Esther. Three of the men were well-known Florentine military heroes. The three remaining men were poets whom Florence claimed as its own: Dante, Boccaccio, and (shown here) Petrarch. The monumentality, seriousness, and dignity of this portrait conveyed the importance of humanists, who in the eyes of contemporaries were equal to the most praiseworthy heroes and heroines. *(Galleria degli Uffizi, Florence, Italy/Giraudon/The Bridgeman Art Library International.)*

servants, and still others were notaries. A few were rich men who had a taste for literary subjects.

The first humanist, most historians agree, was **Francis Petrarch** (1304–1374). He was born in Arezzo, a town about fifty miles southeast of Florence. As a boy, he moved around a lot (his father was exiled from Florence), ending up in the region of Avignon, where he received his earliest schooling and fell in love with classical literature. After a brief flirtation with legal studies at the behest of his father, Petrarch gave up law and devoted himself to writing poetry, both in Italian and in Latin. When writing in Italian, he drew on the traditions of the troubadours, dedicating poems of longing to an unattainable and idealized woman named Laura; who she really was, we do not know. When writing in Latin, Petrarch was much influenced by classical poetry.

On the one hand, a boyhood in Avignon made Petrarch sensitive to the failings of the church: he was the writer who coined the phrase "Babylonian captivity" to liken the Avignon papacy to the Bible's account of the Hebrews' captivity in Babylonia. On the other hand, he took minor religious orders there, which gave him a modest living. Struggling between what he considered a life of dissipation (he fathered two children out of wedlock) and a religious vocation, he resolved the conflict at last in his book *On the Solitary Life*, in which he claimed that the solitude needed for reading the classics was akin to the solitude practiced by those who devoted themselves to God. For Petrarch, humanism was a vocation, a calling.

Less famous, but for that reason perhaps more representative of humanists in general, was Lauro Quirini (1420–1475?), the man who (as we saw at the start of this chapter) wrote disparagingly about

---

Francis Petrarch: An Italian poet (1304–1374) who revived the styles of classical authors; he is considered the first Renaissance humanist.

the Turks as barbarians. Educated at the University of Padua, Quirini eventually got a law degree there. He wrote numerous letters and essays, corresponding with other humanists on topics such as the nature of the state and the character of true nobility. He spent the last half of his life in Crete, where he traded various commodities — alum, cloth, wine, Greek books. Believing that the Ottomans had destroyed the libraries of Constantinople, he wrote to Pope Nicholas V: "The language and literature of the Greeks, invented, augmented, and perfected over so long a period with such labor and industry, will certainly perish." But the fact that he himself participated in the lively trade of Greek books proves his prediction wrong.

If Quirini represents the ordinary humanist, Giovanni Pico della Mirandola (1463–1494) was perhaps the most flamboyant. Born near Ferrara of a noble family, Pico received a humanist education at home before going on to Bologna to study law and to Padua to study philosophy. Soon he was picking up Hebrew, Aramaic, and Arabic. A convinced eclectic (one who selects the best from various doctrines), he thought that Jewish mystical writings supported Christian scriptures, and in 1486 he proposed that he publicly defend at Rome nine hundred theses drawn from diverse sources. The church found some of the theses heretical, however, and banned the whole affair. But Pico's *Oration on the Dignity of Man*, which he intended to deliver before his defense, summed up the humanist view: the creative individual, armed only with his (or her) "desires and judgment," could choose to become a boor or an angel. Humanity's potential was unlimited.

Christine de Pisan (c. 1365–c. 1430) exemplifies a humanist who chose to fashion herself into a writer and courtier. Born in Venice and educated in France, Christine was married and then soon widowed. Forced to support herself, her mother, and her three young children, she began to write poems inspired by classical models, depending on patrons to admire her work and pay her to write more. Many members of the upper nobility supported her, including Duke Philip the Bold of Burgundy, Queen Isabelle of Bavaria, and the English earl of Salisbury. But this cast of characters did not mean she sided with the English during the Hundred Years' War. On the contrary, she lamented the violence on all sides, and Joan of Arc's early victories inspired her to write a hymn to the Maid:

> We've never heard
> About a marvel quite so great,
> For all the heroes who have lived
> In history can't measure up
> In bravery against the Maid.

The Arts

The lure of the classical past was as strong in the visual and performing arts as in literature — and for many of the same reasons. Architects and artists admired ancient Athens and Rome, but they also

The Renaissance Facade at Santa Maria Novella
When Italians wished to transform their churches into the Renaissance style, they did not tear them down; they gave them a new facade. At Santa Maria Novella in Florence, the architect Leon Battista Alberti designed a facade that was inspired by classical models — hence the round-arched entranceway and columns. At the same time he paid tribute to the original Gothic church by including a round window. *(Scala/Art Resource, NY.)*

Pietro Perugino, *Christ Giving the Keys to St. Peter*
In this fresco on one of the side walls of the Sistine Chapel in the papal palace at Rome (now the Vatican), the artist Perugino depicted the transfer of power in Christ's church. Inspired by the architecture of the ancient world, Perugino set the action in a large piazza flanked by Roman triumphal arches. *(Vatican Museums and Galleries, Vatican City, Italy/The Bridgeman Art Library International.)*

modified these classical models, melding them with medieval artistic traditions. In music, Renaissance composers incorporated classical texts and allusions into songs that were based on the motet and other forms of polyphony. Working for patrons—whether churchmen, secular rulers, or republican governments—Renaissance artists and musicians used both past and present to express the patriotism, religious piety, and prestige of their benefactors.

From Agora to Piazza Medieval cities had grown without planning. Streets turned back on themselves. Churches sat cheek-by-jowl with private houses. Renaissance architects, however, reimagined the whole city as a place of order and harmony. The Florentine architect Leon Battista Alberti (1404–1472) proposed that each building in a city be proportioned to fit harmoniously with all the others and that city spaces allow for all necessary public activities—there should be market squares, play areas, grounds for military exercises. In Renaissance cities, the agora and the forum (the open, public spaces of the classical world) appeared

Lorenzo Ghiberti, *The Sacrifice of Isaac*
This bronze relief, which was entered into the competition to decorate the doors of the San Giovanni Baptistery in Florence, captures the dramatic moment (on the right-hand side) when the angel intervenes as Abraham prepares to kill Isaac, a story told in the Hebrew Scriptures. *(Museo Nazionale del Bargello/akg-images/Rabatti-Domingie.)*

once again, but in a new guise: the piazza — a plaza or open square. Architects carved out spaces around their new buildings, and they built porticoes — graceful covered walkways of columns and arches. The artist Pietro Perugino (1445–1523) depicted Christ giving the keys of the kingdom of heaven to the apostle Peter in an idealized city piazza, at the center of which was a perfectly proportioned church (see the illustration on the top of page 431).

The same principles applied to the architecture of the Renaissance court. At Urbino, Duke Federico, a great patron of humanists and artists, commissioned a new palace. The architect, probably Luciano Laurana, designed its spacious and airy courtyard as a public space, a sort of piazza within a palace. Later the courtier Baldassare Castiglione reminisced about this building: "[Duke Federico] built on the rugged site of Urbino a palace thought by many the most beautiful to be found anywhere in all Italy, and he furnished it so well with every suitable thing that it seemed not a palace but a city in the form of a palace." A city had both public and private spaces; similarly, public rooms at the ducal palace gave way to a modest space for the duke's private quarters, a bedroom, a bathroom, a chapel, and, most important, his study, filled with books.

The Gothic cathedral of the Middle Ages was a cluster of graceful spikes and soaring arches. Renaissance architects appreciated its vigor and energy, but they tamed it with regular geometrical forms inspired by classical buildings. Classical forms were applied to previously built structures as well as new ones. Florence's Santa Maria Novella, for example, had been a typical Gothic church when it was first built. But when Alberti, the man who believed in public spaces and harmonious buildings, was commissioned to replace its facade, he drew on Roman temple forms. (See the illustration on page 430.)

Sculpture and Painting

In 1400, the Florentines sponsored a competition for new bronze doors for their baptistery. The entry of Lorenzo Ghiberti (1378?–1455) depicted a scene from the Old Testament story in which God tested Abraham's faith by ordering him to sacrifice his son Isaac (see the illustration on page 431). Cast in one piece, a major technological feat at the time, it shows a young, nude Isaac modeled on the masculine ideal of ancient Greek sculpture. At the same time, Ghiberti drew on medieval models for his depiction of Abraham and for his

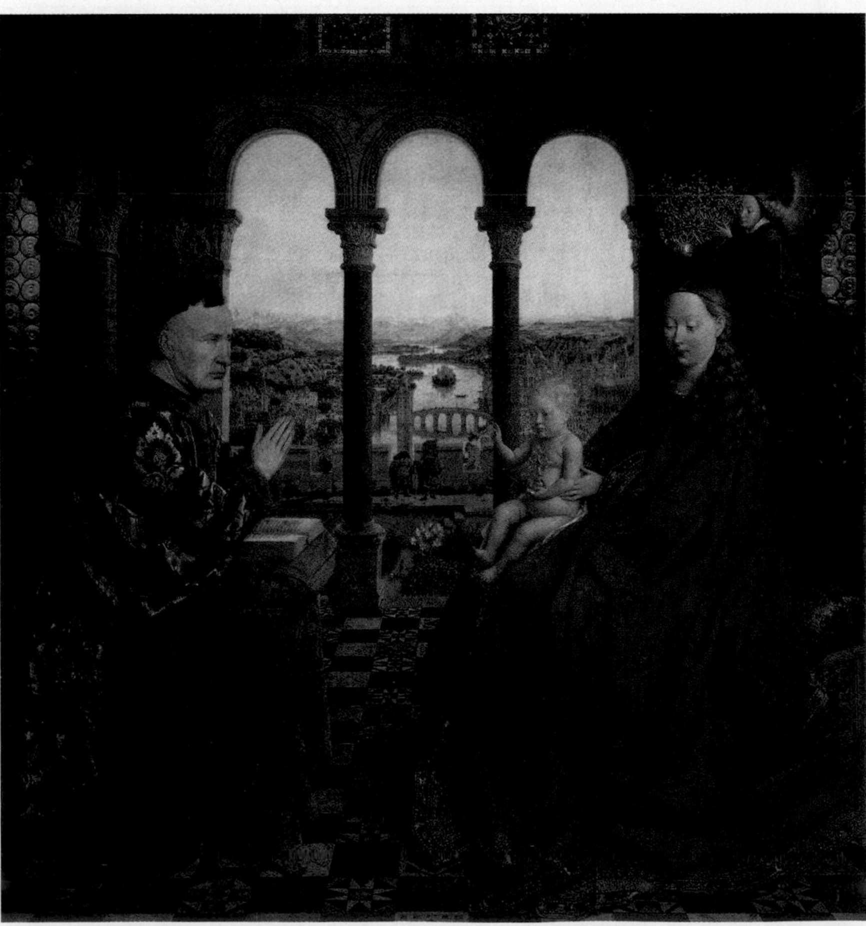

Jan van Eyck, *The Virgin of Chancellor Rolin*
Van Eyck portrays the Virgin and Chancellor Nicolas Rolin as if they were contemporaries sharing a nice chat. Only the angel, who is placing a crown on the Virgin's head, suggests that something out of the ordinary is happening. *(Erich Lessing/Art Resource, NY.)*

Sandro Botticelli, *The Birth of Venus*
Other artists had depicted Venus, but Botticelli was the first since antiquity to portray her in the nude. *(Galleria degli Uffizi, Florence, Italy/The Bridgeman Art Library International.)*

Leonardo da Vinci, *The Annunciation*
Working with a traditional Christian theme—the moment when the angel Gabriel announced to the Virgin Mary that she would give birth to Christ—Leonardo produced a work of great originality, drawing the viewer's eye from a vanishing point in the distance to the subject of the painting. The ability to subordinate the background to the foreground was the key contribution of Renaissance perspective. *(Scala/Ministero per i Beni e le Attività culturali/Art Resource, NY.)*

quatrefoil frame. In this way, he gracefully melded old and new elements—and won the contest.

In addition to using the forms of classical art, Renaissance artists also mined the ancient world for new subjects. Venus, the Roman goddess of love and beauty, had numerous stories attached to her name. At first glance, *The Birth of Venus* by Sandro Botticelli (c. 1445–1510) seems simply an illustration of the tale of Venus's rise from the sea (see page 433). A closer look, however, shows that Botticelli's work is complicated, drawing on the ideas of the humanist philosopher Marsilio Ficino (1433–1499) and the poetry of Angelo Poliziano (1454–1494). According to Ficino, Venus was *humanitas*—the essence of the humanities. For Poliziano, she was

> fair Venus, mother of the cupids.
> Zephyr bathes the meadow with dew
> spreading a thousand lovely fragrances:
> wherever he flies he clothes the countryside
> in roses, lilies, violets, and other flowers.

In Botticelli's painting, Zephyr (one of the winds) blows while Venus herself is about to be clothed in a fine robe embroidered with leaves and flowers.

The Sacrifice of Isaac and *The Birth of Venus* show some of the ways in which Renaissance artists used ancient models. Other artists perfected perspective—the illusion of three-dimensional space—to a degree that even classical antiquity had not anticipated. The development of the laws of perspective accompanied the introduction of long-range weaponry, such as cannons. In fact, some of perspective's practitioners—Leonardo da Vinci (1452–1519), for example—were military engineers as well as artists. In Leonardo's painting *The Annunciation*, sight lines meeting at a point on the horizon open wide precisely where the angel kneels and Mary responds in surprise (see the illustration at the bottom of page 433).

Ghiberti, Botticelli, and Leonardo were all Italian artists. While they were creating their works, a northern Renaissance was taking place as well. At the court of Burgundy during the Hundred Years' War, the dukes commissioned portraits of themselves—sometimes unflattering ones—just as Roman leaders had once commissioned their own busts. Soon it was the fashion for everyone who could afford it to have a portrait made, as naturalistically as possible. Around 1433, the chancellor Nicolas Rolin, for example, commissioned the Dutch artist Jan van Eyck to paint his portrait (see page 432). Though opposite the Virgin and the baby Jesus, Rolin, in a pious pose, is the key figure in the picture. The grand view of a city behind the figures was meant to underscore Rolin's prominence in the community. In fact Rolin *was* an important man: he worked for the duke of Burgundy and was also the founder of a hospital at Beaune and a religious order of nurses to serve it. Van Eyck's portrait emphasized not only Rolin's dignity and status but also his individuality. The artist took pains to show even the wrinkles of his neck and the furrows on his brow.

New Harmonies in Music

Using music to add glamour and glory to their courts and reputations, Renaissance rulers spent as much as 6 percent of their annual revenue to support musicians and composers. The Avignon papacy, in its own way one such court, was a major

Music in the Streets

Music in the Renaissance was as important in public places—even in the streets—as it was in the courts. In this satirical woodcut, one of many illustrating a book by Sebastian Brant called *The Ship of Fools* (1494), musicians dressed as fools serenade a nude lady. She is attempting to get rid of them by emptying her chamber pot on their heads. The picture makes fun of courtly gallantry even as it depicts the sort of thing that could really happen on a town street.

sponsor of sacred music. People appreciated music, whether secular or religious, for its ability to express their innermost feelings.

Every proper court had its own musicians. Some served as chaplains, writing music for the ruler's private chapel—the place where his court and household heard Mass. When Josquin Desprez (1440–1521) served as the duke of Ferrara's chaplain, he wrote a Mass that used the musical equivalents of the letters of the duke's name (the Italian version of *do re mi*) as its theme. Isabella d'Este (1474–1539), the daughter of the duke, employed her own musicians—singers, woodwind and string players, percussionists, and keyboard players—while her husband, the duke of Mantua, had his own band. Bartolomeo Tromboncino was Isabella's favorite musician. When her brother sent her poems to recopy, she had Tromboncino set them to music. This was one of the ways in which humanists and musicians worked together: the poems that interested Tromboncino were of the newest sort, patterned on classical forms. He and Isabella particularly favored Petrarch's poems.

The church, too, was a major sponsor of music. Every feast required music, and the papal schism inadvertently encouraged more musical production than usual, as rival popes tried to best one another in the realm of pageantry and sound. Churches needed choirs of singers, and many choirboys went on to become composers, while others sang well into adulthood: in the fourteenth century, the men who sang in the choir at Reims received a yearly stipend and an extra fee every time they sang the Mass and the liturgical offices of the day.

Isabella d'Este as Patron of the Arts

At the beginning of the sixteenth century, Isabella d'Este commissioned Lorenzo Costa to make five paintings to decorate her "little studio"—her special retreat—at the Mantuan ducal palace. In this painting, he depicted a "coronation," perhaps of Isabella herself. Cupid, held by his mother, Venus, places a laurel wreath on the lady's head. A battle rages far away, but the chief figures—personifications at one and the same time of music and poetry and the virtues—bask in peace and harmony. Pleased by the painting, Isabella made Costa the official painter of the court. *(Louvre, Paris, France/Giraudon/The Bridgeman Art Library International.)*

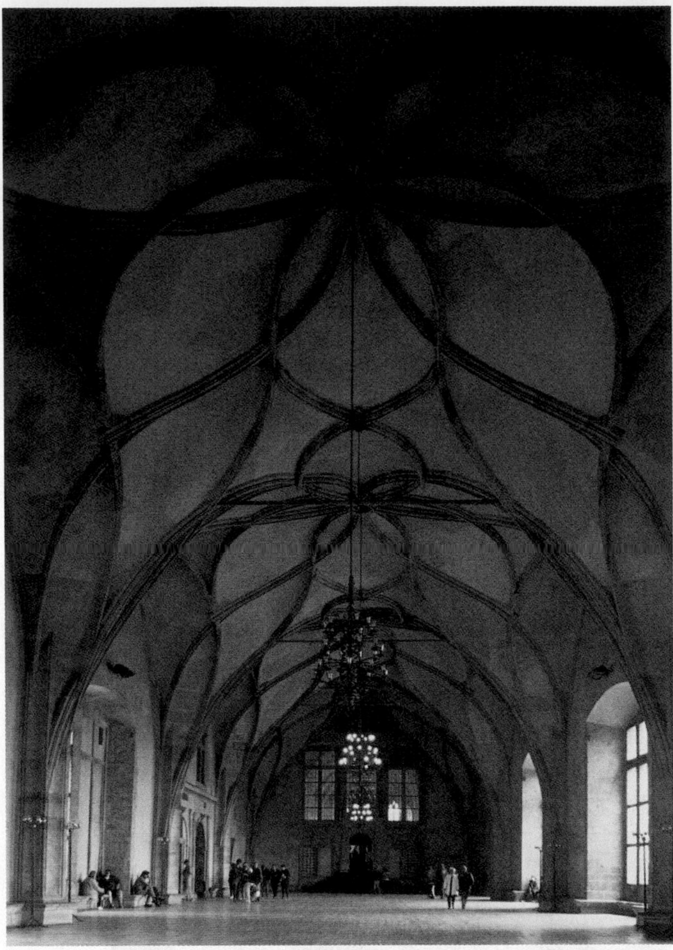

Vladislav Hall
The interior of this hall, built by Bohemian king Vladislav to house grand tournaments, is largely based on Gothic forms. Note, for example, the elaborate ribs of the vault. But the rectangular windows echo Renaissance architecture, the first such borrowing north of the Alps. *(© Franz-Marc Frei/Corbis.)*

When the composer Johannes Ockeghem—chaplain for three French kings—died in 1497, his fellow musicians vied in expressing their grief in song. Josquin Desprez was among them, and his composition illustrates how the addition of classical elements to very traditional musical forms enhanced music's emotive power. Josquin's work combines personal grief with religious liturgy and the feelings expressed in classical elegies. The piece uses five voices. Inspired by classical mythology, four of the voices sing in the vernacular French about the "nymphs of the wood" coming together to mourn. But the fifth voice intones the words of the liturgy: *Requiescat in pace* ("May he rest in peace"). At the very moment in the song that the four vernacular voices lament Ockeghem's burial in the dark ground, the liturgical voice sings of the heavenly light. The contrast makes the song more moving. By drawing on the classical past, Renaissance musicians found new ways in which to express emotion.

REVIEW QUESTION How and why did Renaissance humanists, artists, and musicians revive classical traditions?

Consolidating Power

The shape of Europe changed between 1340 and 1492. In Eastern Europe, the Ottoman Empire took the place (though not the role) of Byzantium. The capital of the Holy Roman Empire moved to Prague, bringing Bohemia to the fore. Meanwhile, the duke of Lithuania married the queen of Poland, uniting those two states. In western Europe, a few places organized and maintained themselves as republics; the Swiss, for example, consolidated their informal alliances in the Swiss Confederation. Italy, which at the beginning of the period was dotted with numerous small city-states, was by the end dominated by five major powers: Milan, the papacy, Naples, and the republics of Venice and Florence. Most western European states—England and France, for example—became centralized monarchies. The union of Aragon and Castile via the marriage of their respective rulers created Spain. Whether monarchies, principalities, or republics, states throughout Europe used their new powers to finance humanists, artists, and musicians—and to persecute heretics, Muslims, and Jews with new vigor.

New Political Formations in Eastern Europe

In the eastern half of the Holy Roman Empire, Bohemia gained new status as the seat of the Luxembourg imperial dynasty, whose last representative was Emperor Sigismund. This development led to a religious and political crisis when the Hussites clashed with Sigismund (see page 427). The chief beneficiaries of the violence were the nobles, both Catholic and Hussite, but they quarreled among themselves, especially about who should be king. No Joan of Arc appeared to declare the national will, and most of Europe considered Bohemia a heretic state. Countering this isolation from the rest of Europe, the Bohemian king Vladislav Jagiello (r. 1471–1516) borrowed some Renaissance architectural motifs for his palace.

Cracow in the Fifteenth Century
In the fifteenth century, Poland, united with Lithuania, was growing both in population and diversity. Relatively untouched by the plague, towns like Cracow were part of thriving trade networks, while Cracow itself boasted a university established along the lines of the one at Paris. No wonder that when Michael Wohlgemut's workshop was commissioned to make woodcuts for Hartmann Schedel's *World Chronicle* in 1493 (an early printed book), Cracow was depicted as not only densely packed but even spilling beyond its walls. *(Interfoto/Ancient Art & Architecture Collection, Ltd.)*

Farther north, it was the cities rather than the landed nobility that held power. Allied cities, known as *Hanse*, were common. The most successful alliance was the **Hanseatic League**, a loose federation of mainly north German cities formed to protect their mutual interests in defense and trade—and art. The Dance of Death, for example, painted at the Hanse town of Reval (see page 415), was made by the artist Bernt Notke, who hailed from Lübeck, another Hanse town. The Hanseatic League linked the Baltic coast with Russia, Norway, the British Isles, France, and even (via imperial cities like Augsburg and Nuremberg) the cities of Italy. When threatened by rival powers in Denmark and Norway in 1367–1370, the league waged war and usually won. But in the fifteenth century it confronted new rivals and began a long, slow decline.

Hanseatic League: A league of northern European cities formed in the fourteenth century to protect their mutual interests in trade and defense.

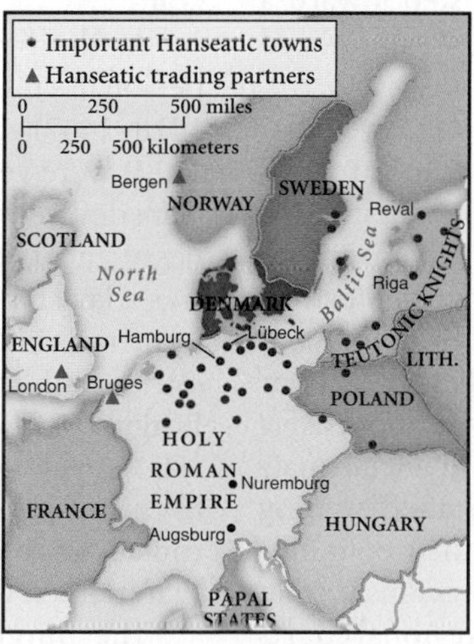

The Hanseatic League

To the east of the Hanseatic cities, two new monarchies took shape in northeastern Europe: Poland and Lithuania. Poland had begun to form in the tenth century. Powerful nobles soon dominated it, and Mongol invasions devastated the land. But recovery was under way by 1300. Unlike almost every other part of Europe, Poland expanded demographically and economically during the fourteenth century. Jews migrated there to escape persecutions in western Europe, and both Jewish and German settlers helped build thriving towns like Cracow. Monarchical consolidation began thereafter.

On Poland's eastern flank was Lithuania, the only major holdout from Christianity in eastern Europe. But as it expanded into southern Russia, its grand dukes flirted with both the Roman Catholic and Orthodox varieties. In 1386, Grand Duke Jogailo (c. 1351–1434), taking advantage of a hiatus in the Polish ruling dynasty, united both states when he married Queen Jadwiga of Poland, received a Catholic baptism, and was elected by the Polish nobility as King Wladyslaw II Jagiello. As part of the negotiations prior to these events, he promised to convert Lithuania, and after his coronation he sent churchmen there to begin the long, slow process. The union of Poland and Lithuania lasted, with some interruptions, until 1772. (See Mapping the West, page 445.)

Powerful States in Western Europe

Four powerful states dominated western Europe during the fifteenth century. The kingdom of Spain and the duchy of Burgundy were created by marriage; the newly powerful kingdoms of France and England were forged in the crucible of war. By the end of the century, however, Burgundy had disappeared, leaving three exceptionally powerful monarchies.

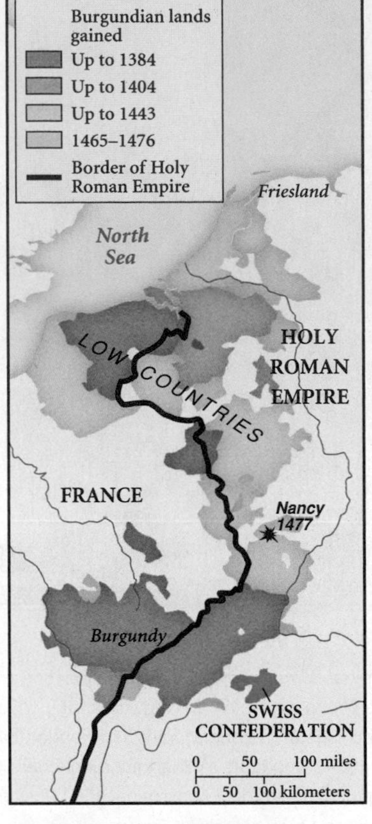

The Expansion of Burgundy, 1384–1476

Spain | Decades of violence on the Iberian peninsula ended when Isabella of Castile and Ferdinand of Aragon married in 1469 and restored law and order in the decades that followed. Castile was the powerhouse, with Aragon its lesser neighbor and Navarre a pawn between the two. When the king and queen joined forces, they ruled together over their separate dominions, allowing each to retain its traditional laws and privileges. The union of Castile and Aragon was the first step toward a united Spain and a centralized monarchy there.

Spain before Unification, Late Fifteenth Century

Relying on a lucrative taxation system, pliant meetings of the *cortes* (the representative institution that voted on taxes), and an ideology that glorified the monarchy, Ferdinand and Isabella consolidated their power. They had an extensive bureaucracy for financial matters and a well-staffed writing office. They sent their own officials to rule over towns that had previously been self governing, and they established regional courts of law.

Burgundy | The duchy of Burgundy—created when the duke of Burgundy and heiress of Flanders married in 1369—was disunited linguistically and geographically. Its success and expansion in the fifteenth century resulted from military might and careful statecraft.

Part of the French royal house, the Burgundian dynasty expanded its power rapidly by acquiring land, primarily in the Netherlands. Between 1384 and 1476, the Burgundian state filled the territorial gap between France and Germany, extending from the Swiss border in the south to Friesland (Germany) in the north. Through purchases, inheritance, and conquests, the dukes ruled over French-, Dutch-, and German-speaking subjects, creating a state that resembled a patchwork of provinces and regions, each jealously guarding its laws and traditions. The Low Countries, with their flourishing cities, constituted the state's economic heartland, while the region of Burgundy itself, which gave the state its name, offered rich farmlands and vineyards. Unlike England, whose island geography made it a natural political unit; or France, whose borders were forged in the national experience of repelling English invaders; or Spain, whose national identity came from centuries of warfare against Islam, Burgundy was an artificial creation whose coherence depended entirely on the skillful exercise of statecraft.

At the heart of Burgundian politics was the personal cult of its dukes. Philip the Good (r. 1418–1467) and his son Charles the Bold (r. 1467–1477) were very different kinds of rulers, but both were devoted to enhancing the prestige of their dynasty and the security of their dominion. Philip was a lavish patron of the arts who commissioned numerous illuminated manuscripts, chronicles, tapestries, paintings, and music in his efforts to glorify Burgundy. Charles, by contrast, spent more time on war than at court. Renowned for his courage (hence his nickname), he died in 1477 when his army was routed by the Swiss at the town of Nancy, a loss that marked the end of Burgundian power.

The Burgundians' success depended in large part on their personal relationship with their sub-

Philip the Good's *History of Alexander the Great* Tapestries
In 1459 Duke Philip of Burgundy bought a series of tapestries that told the story of Alexander's adventures. These had been recounted in popular vernacular romances; now they were illustrated in silk, gold, and silver threads. In this detail, Alexander flies in the sky in a decorated cage held by winged mythical creatures known as griffons. Just to the right of that, he appears on the ground, surrounded by his courtiers. Next, he is inside a glass bell; you can just barely see him behind the white scrim made of sea creatures. *(Partial view, from* Episodes in the Life of Alexander: Flight of Alexander *and* Alexander Plumbs the Depths of the Oceans, *Galleria Doria Pamphilij. Rome/photo: akg-images/Pirozzi.)*

jects. Not only did the dukes travel constantly from one part of their dominion to another, but they also staged elaborate ceremonies to enhance their power and promote their legitimacy. Their entries into cities and their presence at weddings, births, and funerals became the centerpieces of a "theater state" in which the dynasty provided the only link among diverse territories. (See Document, "The Ducal Entry into Ghent," page 440.) New rituals became propaganda tools. Philip's revival of chivalry at court transformed the semi-independent nobility into courtiers closely tied to the prince. But, as mentioned earlier in this chapter (page 418), when Charles the Bold died in 1477, the duchy was parceled out to France and the Holy Roman Empire.

France | Because of its quick recovery from the Hundred Years' War, France was powerful enough to take a large bite out of Burgundy. Under Louis XI (r. 1461–1483), the French monarchy both expanded its territory and consolidated its power. Soon after Burgundy fell to him, Louis inherited most of southern France after the Anjou dynasty died out. When the French king inherited claims to the duchy of Milan and the kingdom of Naples, he was ready to exploit other opportunities in Italy. By the end of the century, France had doubled its territory, assuming boundaries close to its modern ones, and was looking to expand even further.

To strengthen royal power at home, Louis promoted industry and commerce, imposed permanent salt and land taxes, maintained western Europe's first standing army (created by his predecessor), and dispensed with the meetings of the Estates General, which included the clergy, the nobility, and representatives from the major towns of France. The French kings had already increased their power with important concessions from the papacy. The Pragmatic Sanction of Bourges (1438) asserted the superiority of a general church council over the pope. Harking back to a long tradition of the high Middle Ages, the Pragmatic Sanction established what would come to be known as Gallicanism (after Gaul, the ancient Roman name for France), in which the French king would effectively control ecclesiastical revenues and the appointment of French bishops.

England | In England the Hundred Years' War led to intermittent civil wars that came to be called the Wars of the Roses. Those wars ended

DOCUMENT

The Ducal Entry into Ghent (1458)

The dukes of Burgundy made numerous ceremonial entries into the cities of their duchy. Such events, elaborately planned and exactingly executed, enhanced the duke's prestige as well as the standing of those who participated in or contributed to the performance. Entries cemented (or repaired) ties with townspeople even as they cost the cities an enormous amount of money. In the case of Ghent, the entry of 1458 marked a reconciliation: several years before this time, the town had unsuccessfully rebelled against the duke. The description here is from the Chronicle of Flanders; *it presents the point of the view of the townspeople.*

The Joyous Entry of my most redoubted [awesome] lord and prince Philip [the Good] . . . which he made into his city of Ghent on the feast of St. George, Sunday, April 23, 1458, and which was organized by the aldermen and others of the same city of Ghent in the following manner. . . .

Outside the Walpoort [one of the gates of Ghent], on the outskirts of the city along both sides of the street to the end of the Waldamme [near the Walpoort] as far as the ramparts [city walls], the deacons and all the sworn members of the weavers [guild] were spread as far out as possible, each finely dressed in his long cloak of office down to the ground and as many as 500 in number, each bearing a lit torch in his hand. When they became aware of the approach of my redoubted lord, they fell to their knees and removed their hats in fine and graceful order. . . .

Between the crenellations of the gate there were many trumpeters and minstrels who played most agreeably from the arrival of my redoubted lord until he was led far into the city, and they were all richly dressed in the [coat of] arms [the heraldic devices] of my said lord and of the city as befitted the occasion. . . . All of the parish priests and other priests of the city, people in minor orders, and the beguines of both the beguinages were present within the city close by the gate each in their most precious copes, habits, and chasubles [names for various liturgical garments] of their churches in the manner of a fine procession. . . .

Inside the said Walpoort, opposite the house called *De Roze*, there was a stage covering the street next to the ca-

with the victory of Henry Tudor, who took the title of Henry VII (r. 1485–1509). Though long, the Wars of the Roses caused relatively little damage; the battles were generally short and, in the words of one chronicler, "neither the country, nor the people nor the houses, were wasted, destroyed or demolished, but the calamities and misfortunes of the war fell only upon the soldiers, and especially on the nobility."

As a result, the English economy continued to grow during the fifteenth century. The cloth industry expanded considerably, and the English used much of the raw wool that they had been exporting to the Low Countries to manufacture goods at home. London merchants, taking a vigorous role in trade, also assumed greater political prominence, not only in governing London but also as bankers to kings and members of Parliament. In the countryside the landed classes — the nobility, the gentry (the lesser nobility), and the yeomanry (free farmers) — benefited from rising farm and land-rent income as the population increased slowly but steadily. The Tudor monarchs took advantage of the general prosperity to bolster both their treasury and their power.

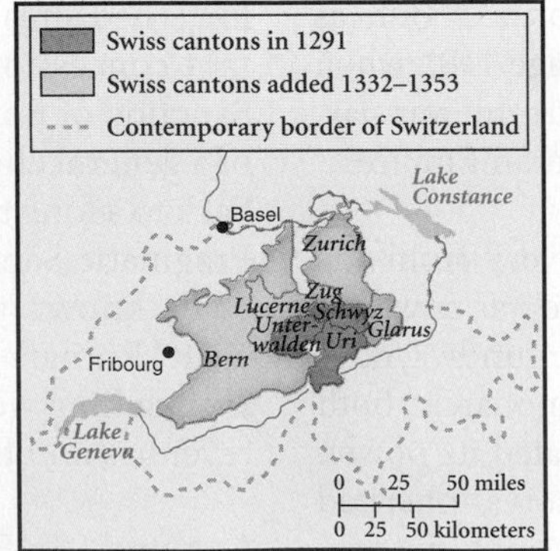

The Growth of the Swiss Confederation, to 1353

Power in the Republics

Within the fifteenth-century world of largely monarchical power were three important exceptions: Switzerland, Venice, and Florence. Republics, they prided themselves on traditions of self-rule. At the same time, however, they were in every case dominated by elites — or even by one family.

The Swiss Confederation The cities of the Alpine region of the Holy Roman Empire, like those of the Hanseatic League in the Baltic, had long had alliances with one another. In the fourteenth century, their union became more binding, and they joined with equally well organized communities in rural and forested areas in nal, and upon it stood the figure of the Prodigal Son who had ignobly squandered his portion, finely presented in the following manner. The father wore a long hooded gown and a small hat with a red brim, with three servants dressed in black behind him. The son was poorly dressed, his doublet in tatters, his stockings rent at the knee, and the father met him in this pitiful state and pardoned him as a result of the son acknowledging his misdeeds. Beneath the said stage were written the words, "Father, I have sinned against Heaven and against you. Luke [15:21]." . . .

Across the Holstraat there stood a stage which bore a great black lion with its jaws gaping as if it was roaring. In its paw the lion held a fine standard bearing the [coat of] arms of our most redoubted lord. Opposite this lion there was another, a beautiful white female meekly stretched out, and between them lay three white lion cubs which seemed to be half-dead. When the black lion roared, they awoke and were brought back to life. Everything was masterfully crafted and lifelike. On the edge of this stage was written "He will roar like a lion and the children will be afraid. Hosea [11:10]." . . .

In front of the gate of the residence of my redoubted lord . . . children sweetly sang a new song that had been composed for the Entry of my redoubted lord . . . :

Long live Burgundy! That's our cry.
We sing from the heart. I prithee,
On this, his joyous Entry,
Let us spare no expense.
Since he has come to his land,
All our sadness is gone. . . .

[After a speech by an important official of Ghent] the prince [Duke Philip] made a gracious reply and all returned to their homes or lodgings. It was fully nine in the evening, and my lord had spent more than four hours passing between the gate and his palace.

Source: Andrew Brown and Graeme Small, eds., *Court and Civic Society in the Burgundian Low Countries, c. 1420–1530* (Manchester: Manchester University Press, 2007), 176–86, slightly modified.

Question to Consider

■ **Considering that Ghent and the duke had recently been at war against one another, what might be the symbolic meanings of the various staged dramas?**

the region. Their original purpose was to keep the peace, but soon they also pledged to aid one another against the Holy Roman Emperor. By the end of the fourteenth century, they had become an entity: the Swiss Confederation. While not united by a comprehensive constitution, they were nevertheless an effective political force.

Wealthy merchants and tradesmen dominated the cities of the Swiss Confederation, and in the fifteenth century they managed to supplant the landed nobility. At the same time, the power of the rural communes gave some ordinary folk political importance. No king, duke, or count ever became head of the confederation. In its fiercely independent stance against the Holy Roman Empire, it became a symbol of republican freedom. On the other hand, poor Swiss foot soldiers made their living by hiring themselves out as mercenaries, fueling the wars of kings in the rest of Europe.

The Republic of Venice | By the fifteenth century, Venice, a city built on a lagoon, ruled an extensive empire. Its merchant ships plied the waters stretching from the Black Sea to the Mediterranean and out to the Atlantic Ocean. It had an excellent navy. Now, for the first time in its career, it turned to conquer land in northern Italy. In the early fifteenth century, Venice took over Brescia, Verona, Padua, Belluno, and many other cities, eventually coming up against the equally powerful city-state of Milan to its west. Between 1450 and 1454, two coalitions, one led by Milan, the other by Venice, fought for territorial control of the eastern half of northern Italy. Financial exhaustion and fear of an invasion by France or the Ottoman Turks led to the Peace of Lodi in 1454. Italy was a collection no longer of small cities, each with its own *contado* (surrounding countryside), but of large territorial city-states.

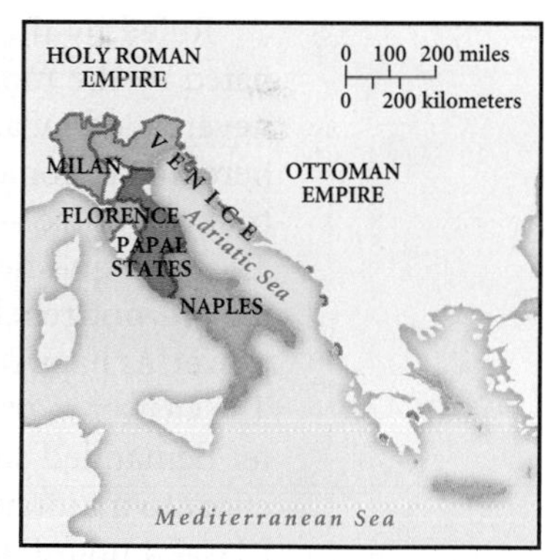

Italy at the Peace of Lodi, 1454

It is no accident that the Peace of Lodi was signed one year after the Ottoman conquest of Constantinople: Venice wanted to direct its might against the Turks. But the Venetians also knew that peace was good for business; they traded with the Ottomans, and the two powers influenced each other's art and culture: Gentile Bellini's portrait of Mehmed (see the chapter-opening illustration) is a good example of

Gentile Bellini, *Procession in Piazza San Marco*
After he returned to Venice from Istanbul, Bellini was commissioned by a prestigious confraternity—the Grand School of St. John—to paint a large canvas of the procession of the Holy Cross for the school's new Renaissance-style Great Hall. Bellini set the scene in the Piazza San Marco, Venice's central square. *(Erich Lessing/Art Resource, NY.)*

the importance of the Renaissance at the Ottoman court.

Ruled by the Great Council, which was dominated by the most important families, Venice was never ruled by a *signore* ("lord"). Far from being a hereditary monarch, the doge—the leading magistrate at Venice—was elected by the Great Council. The great question is why the lower classes at Venice did not rebel and demand their own political power, as happened in so many other Italian cities. The answer may be that Venice's foundation on water demanded so much central planning, so much effort to maintain buildings and services, and such a large amount of public funds to provide the population with necessities that it fostered a greater sense of common community than could be found elsewhere.

While Venice was not itself a center of humanism, its conquest of Padua in 1405 transformed its culture. After studying rhetoric at the University of Padua, young Venetian nobles returned home convinced of the values of a humanistic education for administering their empire. Lauro Quirini was one such man; his time at Padua was followed by a long period on Crete, which was under Venetian control.

Like humanism, Renaissance art also became part of the fabric of the city. Because of its trading links with Byzantium, Venice had long been influenced by Byzantine artistic styles. As it acquired a land-based empire in northern Italy, however, its artists adopted the Gothic styles prevalent elsewhere. In the fifteenth century, Renaissance art forms began to make inroads as well. Venice achieved its own unique style, characterized by strong colors, intense lighting, and sensuous use of paint—adapting the work of classical antiquity for its own purposes. Most Venetian artists worked on commission from churches, but lay confraternities—lay religious organizations devoted to charity—also sponsored paintings. (For one of these, see the illustration above.)

Florence | Florence, like Venice, was also a republic. But unlike Venice, its society and political life were turbulent, as social classes and political factions competed for power. The most important of these civil uprisings was the so-called Ciompi Revolt of 1378. Named after the wool workers (*ciompi*), laborers so lowly that they had not been allowed to form a guild, the revolt led to the creation of a guild for them, along with a new distribution of power in the city. But by 1382, the upper classes were once again monopolizing the government, and now with even less sympathy for the commoners.

By 1434, the **Medici** family had become the dominant power in this unruly city. The patriarch of this family, Cosimo de' Medici (1389–1464), founded his political power on the wealth of the Medici bank, which handled papal finances and had numerous branch offices in Italian and northern European cities. Backed by his money, Cosimo took over Florentine politics. He determined who could take public office, and he established new committees made up of men loyal to him to govern the city. He kept the old forms of the Florentine constitution intact, governing behind the scenes not by force but through a broad consensus among the ruling elite.

Cosimo's grandson Lorenzo "the Magnificent" (1449–1492), who assumed power in 1467, bolstered the regime's legitimacy with his patronage of the humanities and the arts. He himself was a poet and an avid collector of antiquities. He intended to build a grand library made of marble at his palace but died before it was complete. More successful was his sculpture garden, which he filled with ancient works and entrusted to the sculptor Bertoldo di Giovanni to tend. Serving on various Florentine committees in charge of building, renovating, and adorning the churches of the city, Lorenzo employed important artists and architects to work on his own palaces. He probably encouraged the young Michelangelo; he certainly patronized the poet Angelo Poliziano, whose verses inspired Botticelli's *Venus*. No wonder humanists and poets sang his praises.

But the Medici family also had enemies. In 1478, Lorenzo narrowly escaped an assassination attempt, and his successor was driven out of Florence in 1494. The Medici returned to power in 1512, only to be driven out again in 1527. In 1530, the republic fell for good as the Medici once again took power, this time declaring themselves dukes of Florence.

Venetian Art

When he was commissioned in the 1490s to depict the legend of Saint Ursula, Vittore Carpaccio chose Venice as the backdrop. Found in the very popular thirteenth-century *Golden Legend* by Jacobus de Voragine, the tale begins in England, where a pagan king is so inspired by hearing of the virtue of Ursula, daughter of the Christian king of Brittany, that he sends his ambassadors to ask for her hand for his son. In this detail, Carpaccio shows the English ambassadors arriving in a gondola. Note the glass-like colors and the evocation of atmosphere, both characteristic of Venetian style. *(Detail from the Ursula Cycle, 1490–96 (oil on canvas), Vittore Carpaccio, Galleria dell' Accademia, Venice, Italy/Cameraphoto Arte Venezia/The Bridgeman Art Library International.)*

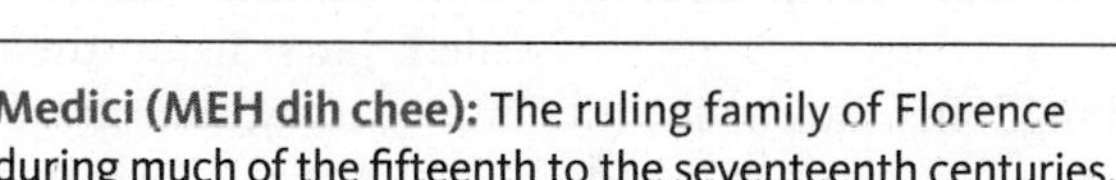

Medici (MEH dih chee): The ruling family of Florence during much of the fifteenth to the seventeenth centuries.

Lorenzo's "Gardener"

Bertoldo di Giovanni presided over the antiquities collected by the Medici and exhibited in their sculpture garden. He was himself a fine artist, pioneering small bronze statuettes such as this one, which drew upon Homer's *Iliad* for its subject. It shows the hero Bellerophon capturing the winged horse Pegasus as part of his quest to defeat the Chimera, a ferocious monster. The underside of the base explains that Bertoldo was the designer, while Adriano Fiorentino cast it in bronze. Bertoldo found the model for his design in Roman art of the classical period, some of which was still where it had originally been placed. *(Kunsthistorisches Museum, Vienna, Austria/Erich Lessing/Art Resource, NY.)*

The Tools of Power

Whether monarchies, duchies, or republics, the newly consolidated states of the fifteenth century exercised their powers more thoroughly than ever before. Sometimes they reached into the intimate lives of their subjects or citizens; at other times they persecuted undesirables with new efficiency.

New Taxes, New Knowledge A good example of the ways in which governments peeked into the lives of their citizens—and picked their pockets—is the Florentine *catasto*. This was an inventory of households within the city and its outlying territory made for the purposes of taxation in 1427. The Domesday survey conducted in England in 1086 had been the most complete census of its day. But the catasto bested Domesday in thoroughness and inquisitiveness. It inquired about names, types of houses, and animals. It asked people to specify their trade, and their answers revealed the levels of Florentine society, ranging from agricultural laborers with no land of their own to soldiers, cooks, grave diggers, scribes, great merchants, doctors, wine dealers, innkeepers, and tanners. The list went on and on. The catasto inquired about private and public investments, real estate holdings, and taxable assets. Finally, it turned to the sex of the head of the family, his or her age and marital status, and the number of mouths to feed in the household. An identification number was assigned to each household.

The catasto showed that in 1427 Florence and its outlying regions had a population of more than 260,000. Although the city itself had only 38,000 inhabitants (about 15 percent of the total population), it held 67 percent of the wealth. Some 60 percent of the Florentine households in the city belonged to the "little people" (a literal translation from the Italian term; it referred to artisans and small merchants). The "fat people" (what we would call the upper middle class) made up 30 percent of the urban population and included wealthy merchants, leading artisans, notaries, doctors, and other professionals. At the very bottom of the hierarchy were slaves and servants, largely women from the surrounding countryside employed in domestic service. At the top, a tiny elite of wealthy patricians, bankers, and wool merchants controlled the state and owned more than one-quarter of its wealth. This was the group that produced the Medici family.

Most Florentine households consisted of at least six people, not all of whom were members of the family. Wealthier families had more children, while childless couples existed almost exclusively among the poor. The rich gave their infants to wet nurses to breast-feed, while the poor often left their children to public charity. Florence was rightly proud of its orphanage: it both provided for the city's poor children and was built in the newest and finest Renaissance style.

Driving Out Muslims, Heretics, and Jews European kings had long fought Muslims and expelled Jews from their kingdoms. But in the fifteenth century, their powers became concentrated and centralized. Newly rich from national taxes, buttressed by political theo-

Alfonso de Espina and the Jews

As a Franciscan friar and university rector, Alfonso de Espina was an influential man. His *The Fortress of Faith against the Jews, Muslims, and Other Enemies of the Christian Faith* devoted a whole chapter to "the cruelties of the Jews." It included a plan to ferret out heretical conversos, called for an Inquisition, and recommended the expulsion of the Jews from Spain. In this woodcut, made c. 1474 to illustrate the book, a well-armed Alfonso walks by a fortress. Ahead of him are devils. Behind are blindfolded Jews. What do you suppose the blindfolds were meant to signify? *(© Topham/The Image Works.)*

MAPPING THE WEST

Europe, c. 1492
By the end of the fifteenth century, the shape of early modern Europe was largely fixed as it would remain until the eighteenth century. The chief exception was the disappearance of an independent Hungarian kingdom after 1529.

ries that glorified their power, masters of the new expensive technologies of war (like cannons and mercenary armies), fifteenth-century kings in western Europe — England, France, Spain — commanded what we may call modern states. They used the full force of their new powers against their internal and external enemies.

Spain is a good example of this new trend. Once Ferdinand and Isabella established their rule over Castile and Aragon, they sought to impose religious uniformity and purity. They began systematically to persecute the *conversos* (converts); these were Jews who converted to Christianity in the aftermath of vicious attacks on Jews at Seville, Cordova, Toledo, and other Spanish towns in 1391. During the first half of the fifteenth century they and their descendants (still called conversos, even though their children were born and baptized in the Christian faith) took advantage of the opportunities open to educated Christians, in many instances rising to high positions in both the church and the state and marrying into so-called Old Christian families.

The conversos' success bred resentment, and their commitment to Christianity was questioned as well. Local massacres of conversos began. In Toledo in 1467, two conversos were caught and hanged "as traitors and captains of the heretical conversos." The terms *traitors* and *heretics* are telling. Conversos were no longer Jews, so their persecution was justified by branding them as heretics who undermined the monarchy. In 1478, Ferdinand and Isabella set up the Inquisition in Spain to do on behalf of the crown what the towns had started. Treating the conversos as heretics, the inquisitors imposed harsh sentences, expelling or burning most of them. That was not enough (in the view of the monarchs) to purify the land. In 1492, Ferdinand and Isabella decreed that all Jews in Spain must convert or leave the country. Some did indeed convert, but the experiences of the former conversos soured most on the prospect, and a large number of Jews—perhaps 150,000—left Spain, scattering around the Mediterranean.

Meanwhile, Ferdinand and Isabella determined to rid Spain of its last Muslim stronghold, Granada. Disunity within the ruling family at Granada allowed the conquest to proceed, and in January 1492—just a few months before they expelled the Jews—Ferdinand and Isabella made their triumphal entry into the Alhambra, the former residence of the Muslim king of Granada. While they initially promised freedom of religion to the Muslims who chose to remain, the royal couple also provided a fleet of boats to take away those who chose exile. In 1502, they demanded that all Muslims adopt Christianity or leave the kingdom.

REVIEW QUESTION How did the monarchs and republics of the fifteenth century use (and abuse) their powers?

Conclusion

The years from 1340 to 1492 marked a period of crisis in Europe. The Hundred Years' War broke out in 1337, and ten years later, in 1347, the Black Death hit, taking a heavy toll. In 1378, a crisis shook the church when first two and then three popes claimed universal authority. Revolts and riots plagued the cities and countryside. The Ottoman Turks took Constantinople in 1453, changing the very shape of Europe and the Middle East.

The revival of classical literature, art, architecture, and music helped men and women cope with these crises and gave them new tools for dealing with them. The Renaissance began mainly in the city-states of Italy, but it spread throughout much of Europe via the education and training of humanists, artists, sculptors, architects, and musicians. At the courts of great kings and dukes—even of the sultan—Renaissance music, art, and literature served as a way to celebrate the grandeur of rulers who controlled more of the apparatuses of government (armies, artillery, courts, and taxes) than ever before.

Consolidation was the principle underlying the new states of the Renaissance. Venice absorbed nearby northern Italian cities, and the Peace of Lodi confirmed its new status as a power on land as well as the sea. In eastern Europe, marriage joined together the states of Lithuania and Poland. A similar union took place in Spain when Isabella of Castile and Ferdinand of Aragon married. The Swiss Confederation became a permanent entity. The king of France came to rule over all of the area that we today call France. The consolidated modern states of the fifteenth century would soon look to the Atlantic Ocean and beyond for new lands to explore and conquer.

FOR FURTHER EXPLORATION

- **For additional primary-source material from this period**, see *Sources of the Making of the West*, Fourth Edition.
- **For Web sites, images, and documents related to topics in this chapter**, visit *Make History* at bedfordstmartins.com/hunt.

Chapter 13 Review

Online Study Guide bedfordstmartins.com/hunt

Key Terms and People

In the grid below, identify the term or person and explain its historical significance. (To do this exercise online, go to bedfordstmartins.com/hunt.)

Term	Who or What & When	Why It Matters
Black Death (p. 412)		
Hundred Years' War (p. 417)		
Joan of Arc (p. 417)		
Jacquerie (p. 421)		
Mehmed II (p. 423)		
Great Schism (p. 424)		
indulgences (p. 425)		
humanism (p. 428)		
Francis Petrarch (p. 429)		
Hanseatic League (p. 437)		
Medici (p. 443)		

Review Questions

1. What crises did Europeans confront in the fourteenth and fifteenth centuries, and how did they handle them?
2. How and why did Renaissance humanists, artists, and musicians revive classical traditions?
3. How did the monarchs and republics of the fifteenth century use (and abuse) their powers?

Making Connections

1. How did the rulers of the fourteenth century make use of the forms and styles of the Renaissance?
2. On what values did Renaissance humanists and artists agree?
3. What tied the crises of the period (disease, war, schism) to the Renaissance (the flowering of literature, art, architecture, and music)?

Important Events

Date	Event	Date	Event
1337–1453	Hundred Years' War	1414–1418	Council of Constance ends Great Schism; Jan Hus burned at the stake
1347–1352	Black Death in Europe	1453	Conquest of Constantinople by Ottoman Turks; end of Hundred Years' War
1358	Jacquerie uprising in France	1454	Peace of Lodi
1378–1417	Great Schism divides papacy	1477	Dismantling of duchy of Burgundy
1378	Ciompi Revolt in Florence	1478	Inquisition begins in Spain
1381	Wat Tyler's Rebellion in England	1492	Spain conquers Muslim stronghold of Granada; expels Jews
1386	Union of Lithuania and Poland		

- Consider two events: **Hundred Years' War (1337–1453)** and the **Black Death in Europe (1347–1352)**. How did these events represent both major crises and new opportunities? How was the Renaissance both a crisis itself and a response to the crises of this period?

SUGGESTED REFERENCES

Aberth provides a good overview of the crises. Blumenfeld-Kosinski and Bynum each explore various aspects of late medieval piety. Nauert treats the many ramifications of Renaissance humanism, and Hale gives a useful overview of political developments.

Aberth, John. *From the Brink of the Apocalypse: Confronting Famine, War, Plague, and Death in the Later Middle Ages*. 2001.

*Beg, Tursun. *The History of Mehmed the Conqueror*. Trans. Halil Inalcik and Rhoads Murphey. 1978.

**The Black Death*. Ed. and trans. Rosemary Horrox. 1994.

Blumenfeld-Kosinski, Renate. *Poets, Saints, and Visionaries of the Great Schism, 1378–1417*. 2006.

Bynum, Caroline. *Wonderful Blood: Theology and Practice in Late Medieval Northern Germany and Beyond*. 2006.

Byrne, Joseph P. *The Black Death*. 2004.

Cohn, Samuel K., Jr. *Lust for Liberty: The Politics of Social Revolt in Medieval Europe, 1200–1425*. 2006.

Grendler, Paul F. *The Universities of the Italian Renaissance*. 2002.

Hale, J. R. *Renaissance Europe, 1480–1520*. 2nd ed. 2000.

Herlihy, David, and Christiane Klapisch-Zuber. *Tuscans and Their Families: A Study of the Florentine Catasto of 1427*. 1985.

Imber, Colin. *The Ottoman Empire, 1300–1650: The Structure of Power*. 2002.

**Joan of Arc: La Pucelle*. Trans. and ed. Craig Taylor. 2006.

Kent, F. W. *Lorenzo de' Medici and the Art of Magnificence*. 2004.

Kirkpatrick, Robin. *The European Renaissance: 1400–1600*. 2002.

Knecht, Robert. *Valois: Kings of France, 1328–1589*. 2004.

Lambert, Malcolm. *Medieval Heresy: Popular Movements from the Gregorian Reform to the Reformation*. 3rd ed. 2002.

Nauert, Charles G. *Humanism and the Culture of the Renaissance Europe*. 2nd ed. 2006.

**The Renaissance in Europe: An Anthology*. Ed. Peter Elmer, Nick Webb, and Roberta Wood. 2000.

Rollo-Koster, Joëlle, and Thomas M. Izbicki, eds. *A Companion to the Great Western Schism (1378–1417)*. 2009.

**Selections from English Wycliffite Writings*. Ed. and trans. Anne Hudson. 1978.

*Primary source.

Global Encounters and the Shock of the Reformation

CHAPTER

14

1492–1560

In 1539 in Tlaxcala, New Spain (present-day Mexico), Indians newly converted to Christianity performed a pageant organized by Catholic missionaries. The festivities celebrated a truce recently concluded between the Habsburg emperor Charles V and the French king Francis I. *The Conquest of Jerusalem*, as the drama was called, featured a combined army from Spain and New Spain fighting to protect the pope, defeat the Muslims, and win control of the holy city of Jerusalem. In the play, after a miracle saves the Christian soldiers the Muslims give up and convert to Christianity. Although it is hard to imagine what the Indians made of this celebration of places and people far away, the event reveals a great deal about the Europeans: still preoccupied with battling the Muslims and still fighting among themselves, Europeans now pursued their interests worldwide. Yet even as their explorations and conquests transformed the New World, disputes over the "true" religion divided Europeans into hostile camps back home. Catholic missionaries saw their success in converting Indians as a sign of God's favor in the struggle against the Protestant reformers, who had begun to spread their message in Europe not long before the pageant in Tlaxcala took place.

Cortés
In this Spanish depiction of the landing of Hernán Cortés in Mexico in 1519, the ships and arms of the Spanish are a commanding presence, especially in comparison to the nakedness of the Indians and the kneeling stance of their leader. A Spanish artist painted this miniature, which measures only 6⅛ inches by 4¼ inches. It probably accompanied an account of the Spanish conquest of Mexico. On the back of the picture is a small map of the west coast of Europe and Africa and the east coast of Central America. Europeans relied on such images, and especially on maps, to help them make sense of all the new information flooding into Europe from faraway places. Many Spaniards viewed Cortés's conquests as a sign of divine favor toward Catholicism in a time of religious division. Some even believed that Cortés was born the same day, or at least the same year, as Martin Luther, the German monk who had initiated the Protestant Reformation just two years before Cortés's landing (in fact, Luther was born two years before Cortés). *(Erich Lessing/Art Resource, NY.)*

Led first by the Portuguese and then Spanish explorers, Europeans sailed into contact with peoples and cultures previously unknown to them. Motivated by the desire to find gold, win personal glory, extend the reach of Christianity, and chart the unknown, European voyagers subjugated native peoples, declared their control over vast new lands, and established a new system of slavery linking Africa and the New World. Millions of Indians died of diseases unknowingly imported by the Europeans. The discovery of new crops—corn, potatoes, tobacco, coffee, and cocoa—and of gold and silver mines brought new patterns of consumption, and new objects of conflict, to Europe. This spiral of changes in ecology, agriculture, and social patterns is so momentous that historians now call it the Columbian exchange, after Christopher Columbus, who started the process. Both Europe and the New World would be utterly transformed.

While the Spanish were conquering lands in the New World, an equally momentous but very different kind of change challenged the hold of the Catholic church in central and western Europe. Religious reformers attacked the leadership of the pope in Rome and formed competing religious groups called Protestants (so-called because they protested against some beliefs of the Catholic church). The movement began when the German Catholic monk Martin Luther criticized the sale of indulgences in 1517. His challenge to the authority of the pope gained greater credibility when leading nobles and many city dwellers came over to his side. Other reformers raised their voices in the wake of Luther's break but did not completely agree with the Lutherans. Before long, religious division engulfed the German states and reached into Switzerland, France, and England. In response, Catholics undertook their own renewal, which strengthened the Catholic church and propagated Catholicism in the New World and in Asia. Catholicism might have been threatened inside Europe, but Catholic missionaries dominated efforts to convert indigenous peoples for a century or more.

The combined prospect of new riches abroad and growing confrontations over religion at home reshaped the long-standing rivalries between princes. The most powerful ruler of the age, Spanish king and Holy Roman Emperor Charles V, ruled over an expanding worldwide empire. His possessions in the New World brought in staggering sums of gold and silver, and he needed every penny. He fought his fellow Catholic French monarchs in Italy, frantically held back the Muslim Ottomans who pushed through Hungary all the way to the gates of Vienna, and at the same time battled German Protestant princes. These two new factors—overseas colonies and divisions between Catholics and Protestants—would together determine the course of European history for several generations.

CHAPTER FOCUS How did the conquest of the New World and the Protestant Reformation transform European governments and societies in this era?

The Discovery of New Worlds

The maritime explorations of Portugal and Spain brought Europe to the attention of the rest of the world. Fourteenth-century Mongols had been more interested in conquering China and Persia—lands with sophisticated cultures—than in invading Europe; Persian historians of the early fifteenth century dismissed Europeans as "barbaric Franks"; and China's Ming dynasty rulers, who sent naval expeditions to Southeast Asia and East Africa around 1400, seemed uninterested in the Europeans, even though Marco Polo and other Italian merchants had appeared at the court of the preceding Mongol Yuan dynasty. By the end of the fifteenth century, in contrast, Europeans could no longer be ignored. The Portuguese and Spanish, inspired by a crusad-

1492 Columbus reaches the Americas

1494 Italian Wars begin; Treaty of Tordesillas divides Atlantic world between Portugal and Spain

1516 Erasmus publishes Greek edition of the New Testament

1517 Luther composes ninety-five theses to challenge Catholic church

1519 Cortés captures Aztec capital of Tenochtitlán

1520 Luther publishes three treatises; Zwingli breaks from Rome

1525 German Peasants' War

1490 1500 1510 1520

ing spirit against Islam and by riches to be won through trade in spices and gold, sailed across the Atlantic, Indian, and Pacific Oceans. The English, French, and Dutch followed later in the sixteenth century, creating a new global exchange of people, crops, and diseases that would shape the modern world. As a result of these European expeditions, the people of the Americas for the first time confronted forces that threatened to destroy not only their culture but even their existence.

Portuguese Explorations

The first phase of European overseas expansion began in 1433 with Portuguese exploration of the West African coast and culminated in 1519–1522 with Spanish circumnavigation of the globe. Looking back, the sixteenth-century Spanish historian Francisco López de Gómora described the Iberian maritime voyages to the East and West Indies as "the greatest event since the creation of the world, apart from the incarnation and death of him who created it."

The Portuguese hoped to find a sea route to the spice-producing lands of South and Southeast Asia in order to bypass the Ottoman Turks, who controlled the traditional land routes between Europe and Asia. Rumors of vast gold mines in West Africa and a mysterious Christian kingdom established by the legendary Prester John and surrounded by Muslims drew sailors to voyages despite the possibilities of shipwreck and death. Success in the voyages of exploration depended on several technological breakthroughs, including the caravel, a small, easily maneuvered three-masted ship that used triangular lateen sails adapted from the Arabs. (The sails permitted a ship to tack against headwinds.) Prince Henry the Navigator of Portugal (1394–1460) personally financed many voyages with revenues from a noble crusading order. The first triumphs of the Portuguese attracted a host of Christian, Jewish, and even Arab sailors, astronomers, and cartographers to the service of Prince Henry and King John II (r. 1481–1495). They compiled better tide calendars and books of sailing directions for pilots that enabled sailors to venture farther into the oceans and reduced — though did not eliminate — the dangers of sea travel.

Searching for gold and then slaves, the Portuguese gradually established forts down the West African coast. In 1487–1488, they reached the Cape of Good Hope at the tip of Africa; ten years later, Vasco da Gama led a Portuguese fleet around the cape and reached as far as Calicut, India, the center of the spice trade. His return to Lisbon with twelve pieces of Chinese porcelain for the Portuguese king set off two centuries of porcelain mania. Until the early eighteenth century, only the Chinese knew how to produce porcelain (in vases or dinnerware), so over the next two hundred years Western merchants would import no fewer than seventy million pieces of porcelain, still known today as "china." By 1517, a chain of Portuguese forts dotted the Indian Ocean — at Mozambique, Hormuz (at the mouth of the Persian Gulf), Goa (in India), Colombo (in modern Sri Lanka), and Malacca (modern Malaysia) (Map 14.1). In 1519, Ferdinand Magellan, a Portuguese sailor in Spanish service, led the first expedition to circumnavigate the globe.

The Voyages of Columbus

One of many sailors inspired by the Portuguese explorations, **Christopher Columbus** (1451–1506) opened an entirely new direction for discovery. Most likely born in Genoa of Italian parents, Columbus sailed the West African coast in Portuguese service

---

Christopher Columbus: An Italian sailor (1451–1506) who opened up the New World by sailing west across the Atlantic in search of a route to Asia.

1527 Charles V's imperial troops sack Rome

1529 Colloquy of Marburg addresses disagreements between German and Swiss church reformers

1530

1534 Henry VIII breaks with Rome; Affair of the Placards in France

1536 Calvin publishes *Institutes of the Christian Religion*

1540 Jesuits established as new Catholic order

1540

1545–1563 Catholic Council of Trent condemns Protestant beliefs, confirms Catholic doctrine

1547 Charles V defeats Protestants at Mühlberg

1550

1555 Peace of Augsburg ends religious wars and recognizes Lutheran church in German states

1559 Treaty of Cateau-Cambrésis ends wars between Habsburg and Valois rulers

1560

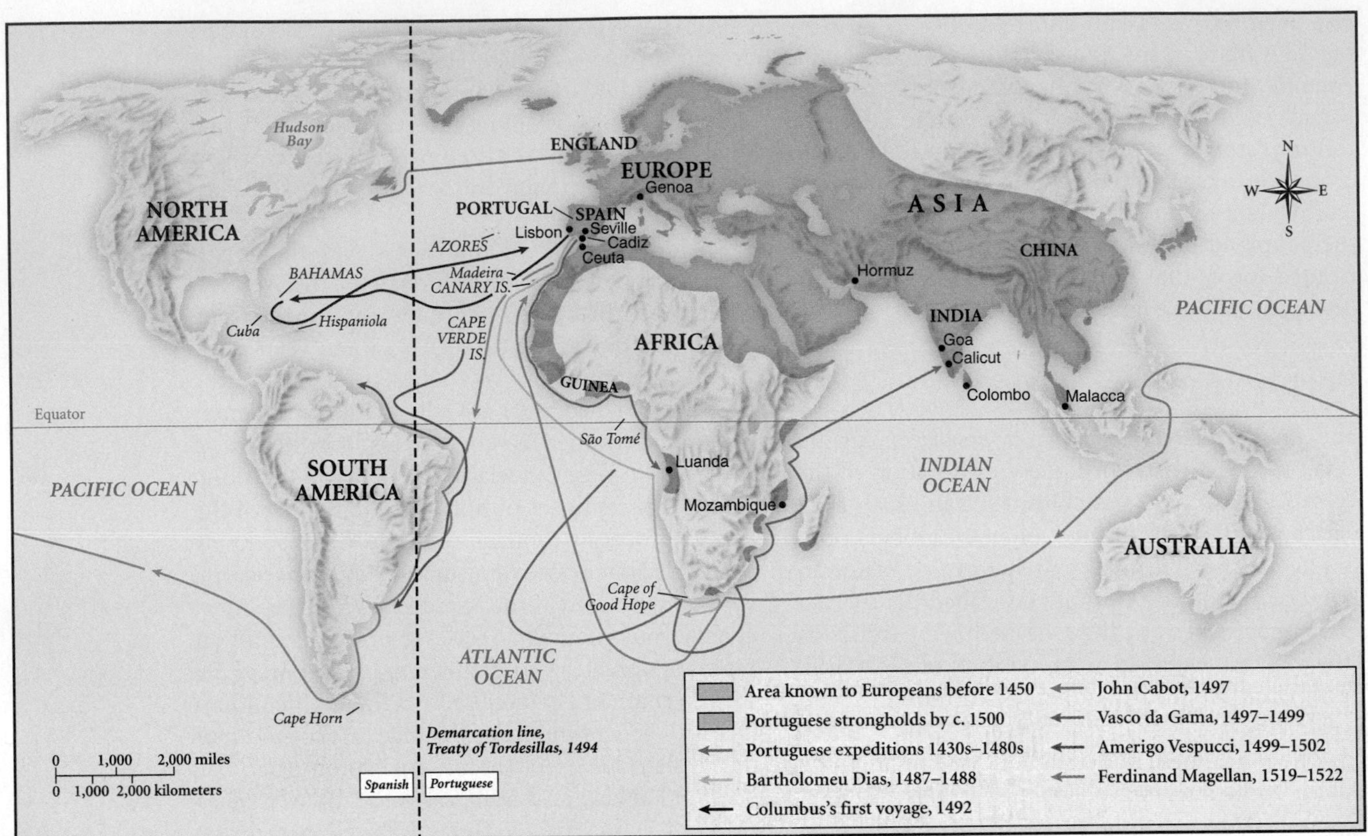

MAP 14.1 Early Voyages of World Exploration
Over the course of the fifteenth and early sixteenth centuries, European shipping dominated the Atlantic Ocean after the pioneering voyages of the Portuguese, who also first sailed around the Cape of Good Hope to the Indian Ocean and Cape Horn to the Pacific. The search for spices and the need to circumnavigate the Ottoman Empire inspired these voyages.

between 1476 and 1485. Fifteenth-century Europeans already knew that the world was round (see "Seeing History," page 455). Columbus had studied *The Travels of Marco Polo*, written more than a century earlier, and wanted to sail west to reach "the lands of the Great Khan," unaware that the Mongol Empire had already collapsed in eastern Asia. Hugely underestimating the distance of such a voyage, Columbus dreamed of finding a new route to the East's gold and spices. After the Portuguese refused to fund his plan, Columbus turned to the Spanish monarchs Isabella of Castile and Ferdinand of Aragon, who agreed to finance his venture.

On August 3, 1492, with ninety men on board two caravels and one larger merchant ship for carrying supplies, Columbus set sail westward. His contract stipulated that he would claim Castilian sovereignty over any new land and inhabitants and share any profits with the crown. Reaching what is today the Bahamas on October 12, Columbus mistook the islands to be part of the East Indies, not far from Japan. As the Spaniards explored the Caribbean islands, they encountered communities of peaceful Indians, the Arawaks, who were awed by the Europeans' military technology, not to mention their appearance. Although many positive entries in the ship's log testified to Columbus's personal goodwill toward the Indians, the Europeans' objectives were clear: find gold, subjugate the Indians, and propagate Christianity. (See Document, "Columbus Describes His First Voyage," page 456.)

Excited by the prospect of easy riches, many flocked to join Columbus's second voyage. When Columbus departed the Spanish port of Cádiz in September 1493, he commanded a fleet of seventeen ships carrying some fifteen hundred men, many of whom believed that all they had to do was "to load the gold into the ships." Failing to find the imagined gold mines and spices, Columbus and his crew began capturing Caribs, enemies of the Arawaks, with the intention of bringing them back as slaves. In 1494, Columbus proposed setting up a regular slave trade based on the West Indian island of Hispaniola. The Spaniards exported enslaved Indians to Spain, and slave traders sold them in Seville. When the Spanish monarchs realized the vast potential for material gain from their new dominions, they asserted direct royal authority by sending officials and priests

SEEING HISTORY

Expanding Geographic Knowledge: World Maps in an Age of Exploration

On the eve of Christopher Columbus's voyages, most Europeans knew that the world was round and many shared Columbus's view that new routes to Asia and its riches could be found by sailing west. Beyond that, however, geographic knowledge of what precisely lay on the other side of the Atlantic was sketchy at best. Even those regions familiar to Europe through trade and exploration—Africa and parts of Asia—were often shown inaccurately on maps of the day.

The hand-colored map at the top produced by a German geographer, Henricus Martellus, depicts the world as Europeans knew it just before Columbus's first voyage. The map reflects the new knowledge of the West African coast gained by Portuguese explorers, but it does not include the Americas, which Europeans had not yet discovered.

By 1570, when Abraham Ortelius's map was printed, European knowledge of world geography had grown by leaps and bounds thanks to the voyages of exploration. Ortelius, a well-traveled and prominent geographer and cartographer, included this map in his Theatrum Orbis Terrarum (Theater of the World), considered to be the first modern atlas.

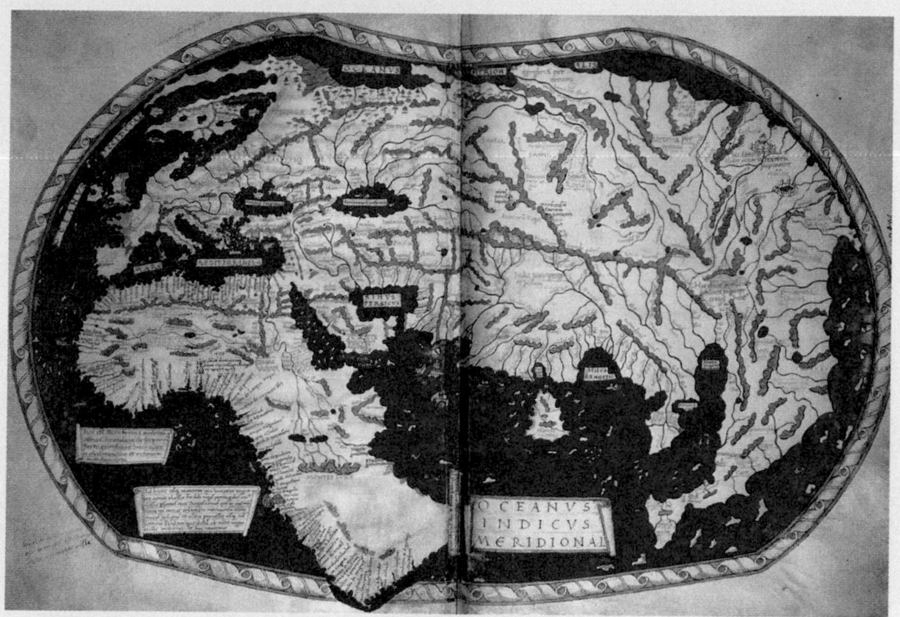

World Map by Henricus Martellus, 1489. *(The Art Archive/British Library.)*

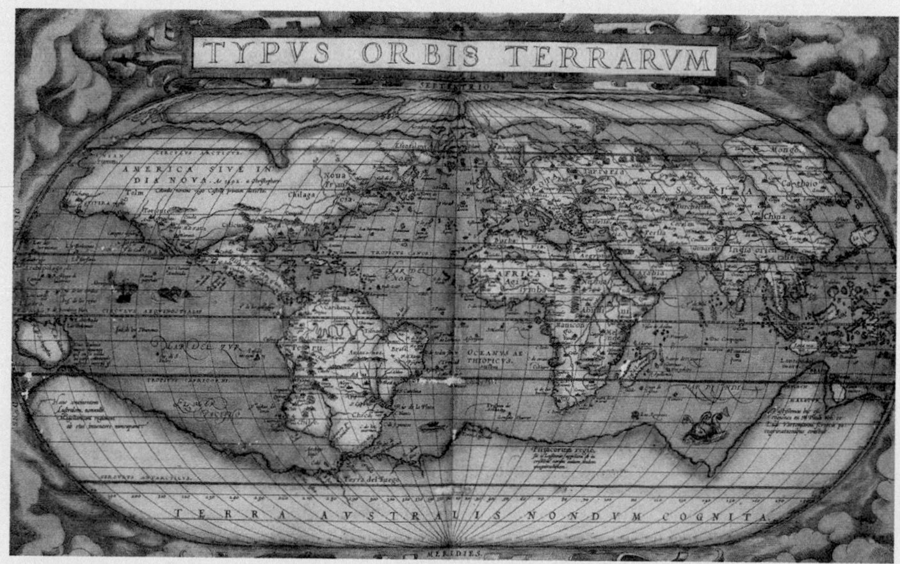

World Map by Abraham Ortelius, 1570. *(By permission of the British Library © British Library Board. All Rights Reserved. MAPS C. 2.c.3.)*

Questions to Consider

1. How accurate is the Martellus map's rendition of Europe, the Mediterranean, and Africa?
2. How does the Martellus map help explain Columbus's mistake about where he had landed in 1492?
3. What new knowledge had been gained by the time of Ortelius and what impact did that knowledge have on Europeans?

to the Americas, which were named after the Italian navigator Amerigo Vespucci, who led a voyage across the Atlantic in 1499–1502.

To head off looming conflicts between the Spanish and the Portuguese, Pope Alexander VI helped negotiate the Treaty of Tordesillas of 1494. It divided the Atlantic world between the two maritime powers, reserving for Portugal the West African coast and the route to India and giving Spain the oceans and lands to the west (see Map 14.1). The agreement

DOCUMENT

Columbus Describes His First Voyage (1493)

In this famous letter to Raphael Sanchez, treasurer to his patrons, Ferdinand and Isabella, Columbus recounts his initial journey to the Bahamas, Cuba, and Hispaniola (today Haiti and the Dominican Republic), and tells of his achievements. This passage reflects the first contact between native Americans and Europeans; already the themes of trade, subjugation, gold, and conversion emerge in Columbus's own words.

Indians would give whatever the seller required; . . . Thus they bartered, like idiots, cotton and gold for fragments of bows, glasses, bottles, and jars; which I forbad as being unjust, and myself gave them many beautiful and acceptable articles which I had brought with me, taking nothing from them in return; I did this in order that I might the more easily conciliate them, that they might be led to become Christians, and be inclined to entertain a regard for the King and Queen, our Princes and all Spaniards, and that I might induce them to take an interest in seeking out, and collecting, and delivering to us such things as they possessed in abundance, but which we greatly needed. They practise no kind of idolatry, but have a firm belief that all strength and power, and indeed all good things, are in heaven, and that I had descended from thence with these ships and sailors, and under this impression was I received after they had thrown aside their fears. Nor are they slow or stupid, but of very clear understanding; and those men who have crossed to the neighbouring islands give an admirable description of everything they observed; but they never saw any people clothed, nor any ships like ours. On my arrival at that sea, I had taken some Indians by force from the first island that I came to, in order that they might learn our language, and communicate to us what they know respecting the country; which plan succeeded excellently, and was a great advantage to us, for in a short time, either by gestures and signs, or by words, we were enabled to understand each other. These men are still travelling with me, and although they have been with us now a long time, they continue to entertain the idea that I have descended from heaven.

Source: Christopher Columbus, *Four Voyages to the New World*, trans. R. H. Major (New York: Corinth Books, 1961), 8–9.

Question to Consider

- **In what ways were Columbus's early impressions of native Americans both respectful and condescending?**

allowed Portugal to claim Brazil in 1500, when it was accidentally "discovered" by Pedro Alvares Cabral (1467–1520) on a voyage to India.

A New Era in Slavery

The European voyages of discovery initiated a new era in slavery, both by expanding the economic scale of slave labor and by attaching race and color to servitude. Slavery had existed since antiquity and flourished in many parts of the world. Some slaves were captured in war or by piracy; others—Africans—were sold by other Africans and Bedouin traders to Christian buyers; in western Asia, parents sold their children out of poverty into servitude; and many in the Balkans became slaves when their land was devastated by Ottoman invasions. Slaves could be Greek, Slav, European, African, or Turkish. Many served as domestics in European cities of the Mediterranean such as Barcelona or Venice. Others sweated as galley slaves in Ottoman and Christian fleets. Still others worked as agricultural laborers on Mediterranean islands. In the Ottoman army, slaves even formed an important elite contingent.

From the fifteenth century onward, Africans increasingly filled the ranks of slaves. Exploiting warfare between groups within West Africa, the Portuguese traded in gold and "pieces," as African slaves were called, a practice condemned at home by some conscientious clergy. The Portuguese priest Manoel Severim de Faria, for example, observed that "one cannot yet see any good effect resulting from so much butchery; for this is not the way in which commerce can flourish and the preaching of the gospel progress." Critical voices, however, could not deny the potential for profits that the slave trade brought to Portugal. Most slaves toiled in the sugar plantations that the Portuguese established on the Atlantic islands and in Brazil. A fortunate few had somewhat easier lives as domestic servants in Portugal, where African freedmen and slaves—some thirty-five thousand in the early sixteenth century—constituted almost 3 percent of the population, a percentage that was much higher than in other European countries.

In the Americas, slavery would expand enormously in the following centuries. Even outspoken critics of colonial brutality toward indigenous peoples defended the development of African slavery. The Spanish Dominican Bartolomé de Las Casas (1474–1566), for example, argued that Africans were constitutionally more suitable for labor than native Americans and should therefore be im-

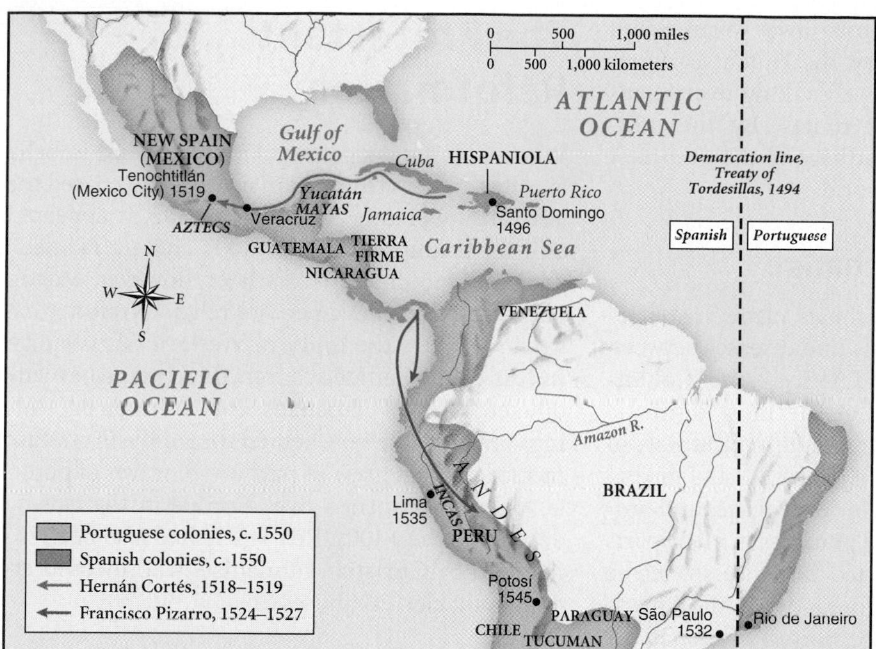

MAP 14.2 Spanish and Portuguese Colonies in the Americas, 1492–1560
The discovery of precious metals fueled the Spanish and Portuguese explorations and settlements of Central and South America, establishing the foundations of European colonial empires in the New World.

ported to the plantations in the Americas to relieve the indigenous peoples, who were being worked to death.

Conquering the New World

In 1500, on the eve of European invasion, the native peoples of the Americas lived in a great diversity of social and political arrangements. Some were nomads roaming large, sparsely inhabited territories; others practiced agriculture in complexly organized states. Among the settled peoples, the largest groupings could be found in the Mexican and Peruvian highlands. Combining an elaborate religious culture with a strict social and political hierarchy, the Aztecs in Mexico and the Incas in Peru ruled over subjugated Indian populations in their respective empires. From their large urban capitals, the Aztecs and Incas controlled large swaths of land and could be ruthless as conquerors.

The Spanish explorers organized their expeditions to the mainland of the Americas from a base in the Caribbean (Map 14.2). Two prominent commanders, **Hernán Cortés** (1485–1547) and Francisco Pizarro (c. 1475–1541), gathered men and arms and set off in search of gold. With them came Catholic priests intending to bring Christianity to supposedly uncivilized peoples. When Cortés first landed on the Mexican coast in 1519, the natives greeted him with gifts, thinking that he might be an ancient god returning to reclaim his kingdom. Some natives who resented their subjugation by the Aztecs joined Cortés and his soldiers. With a band of fewer than two hundred men, Cortés captured the Aztec capital, Tenochtitlán (present-day Mexico City), in 1519. Two years later, Mexico, then named New Spain, was added to the empire of the new ruler of Spain, Charles V, grandson of Ferdinand and Isabella. To the south, Pizarro conquered the Peruvian highlands in 1532–1533. The Spanish Empire was now the largest in the world, stretching from Mexico to Chile.

The Aztecs and Incas fell to the superior war technology of the Spanish conquistadores. Next the conquistadores subdued the Mayas on the Yucatán peninsula, a people with a sophisticated knowledge of cosmology and arithmetic. The gold and silver mines in Mexico proved a treasure trove for the Spanish crown, but the real prize was the discovery of vast silver deposits in Potosí (today in Bolivia). When the Spaniards began importing the gold and silver they found in the New World, inflation soared in a fashion never before witnessed in Europe.

Not to be outdone by the Spaniards, other European powers joined the scramble for gold in the New World. In North America, the French went in search of a "northwest passage" to China. The French wanted to establish settlements in what became Canada, but the climate and the hostility of the indigenous peoples defeated them. Permanent European settlements in Canada and the present-day United States would succeed only in the seventeenth century, and by then the English had entered the contest for world mastery. Even before the French and the English, the Dutch entered the colonial

Hernán Cortés: The Spanish explorer (1485–1547) who captured the Aztec capital, Tenochtitlán (present-day Mexico City), in 1519.

competition. After they broke away from Spain late in the sixteenth century, the Dutch set about systematically and aggressively taking over Spanish and Portuguese trade routes. By the mid-seventeenth century, they had become the wealthiest people (per capita) in the world.

The Columbian Exchange

The movement of peoples, animals, plants, manufactured goods, precious metals, and diseases between Europe, the New World, and Africa — the "Columbian exchange" — was one of the most dramatic transformations of ecology, agriculture, and ways of life in all of human history. It stretched out long beyond the years of Columbus's own voyages and profoundly altered customs and practices in many parts of the world. Columbus started the process when he brought with him firearms, unknown in the Americas, and on his second voyage, horses, which had become extinct in the Americas, as well as pigs, cows, chickens, goats, sheep, cattle, and various plants including wheat, melons, and sugarcane. Enslaved Africans, first brought to the Caribbean in 1503–1505, worked on sugarcane plantations, foreshadowing the development of a massive slave economy in the seventeenth and eighteenth centuries (see Chapter 17).

The Europeans also brought with them diseases. Amerindians died in catastrophic numbers because they lacked natural immunity from previous exposure. Smallpox first appeared in the New World in 1518; it and other epidemic diseases killed as many as 90 percent of natives in some places (though the precise numbers are unknown). Syphilis, or a genetic predecessor to it, came back with the explorers to Europe.

The Spanish also brought back tobacco, cacao (chocolate), sweet potatoes, maize, and tomato seeds, changing consumption patterns in Europe. Their native American wives, concubines, and domestics taught them to drink chocolate in the native fashion: frothy, red in color, and flavored with peppers. At the same time, Spanish and Portuguese slave traders brought these crops and others — such as manioc, capsicum peppers, pineapples, cashew nuts, and peanuts — from the Americas to West Africa, where their cultivation altered local agriculture and diets. The slavers bought African yams, sorghum, millet, and especially rice to feed the slaves in transit, and the slaves then grew those crops in the Americas. Thus the exchange went in every conceivable direction.

REVIEW QUESTION Which European countries led the way in maritime exploration and what were their motives?

The Protestant Reformation

When Columbus's patrons Ferdinand and Isabella expelled all Jews from Spain in 1492 and chased the last Muslims from Granada in 1502, it appeared as if the triumph of the Catholic church had been assured. Only fifteen years later, however, Martin Luther started a movement for religious reform that would fracture the unity of Western Christianity. Instead of one Catholic church, there would be many different kinds of Christians. The invention of printing with movable type helped spread the Protestant message, which grew in part out of waves of popular piety that washed over Europe in the closing decades of the 1400s. Reformers had also been influenced by Christian humanists who focused attention on clerical abuses.

The Invention of Printing

Printing with movable type, first developed in Europe in the 1440s by Johannes Gutenberg, a German goldsmith, marked a revolutionary departure from the old practice of copying works by hand or stamping pages with individually carved wood blocks. The Chinese invented movable type in the eleventh century, but they preferred woodblock printing because it was more suitable to the Chinese language, with its thousands of different characters. In Europe, with only twenty-six letters to the alphabet, movable type allowed entire manuscripts to be printed more quickly than ever before. Single letters, made in metal molds, could be emptied out of a frame and new ones inserted to print each new page. (See the illustration on page 459.) In 1467, two German printers established the first press in Rome; within five years, they had produced twelve thousand volumes, a feat that in the past would have required a thousand scribes working full-time. Printing also depended on the large-scale production of paper. Papermaking came to Europe from China via Arab intermediaries. By the fourteenth century, paper mills in Italy were producing paper that was more fragile but also much cheaper than parchment or vellum, the animal skins that Europeans had previously used for writing.

In the 1490s, the German city of Frankfurt became an international meeting place for printers and booksellers, establishing a book fair that remains an unbroken tradition to this day. Early printed books attracted an elite audience; their expense made them inaccessible to most literate people, who made up a minority of the population in any case. Gutenberg's famous two-volume Latin Bible was a luxury item, and only 185 copies were printed.

Printing Press
This illustration from a French manuscript of 1537 depicts typical printing equipment of the sixteenth century. An artisan is using the screw press to apply the inked type to the paper. Also shown are the composed type secured in a chase, the printed sheet (four pages of text printed on one sheet) held by the seated proofreader, and the bound volume. When two pages of text were printed on one standard-sized sheet, the bound book was called a folio. A bound book with four pages of text on one sheet was called a quarto ("in four"), and a book with eight pages of text on one sheet was called an octavo ("in eight"). The octavo is a pocket-size book, smaller than today's paperback. *(The Granger Collection, New York—All rights reserved.)*

Gutenberg Bibles remain today a treasure that only the greatest libraries possess.

The invention of mechanical printing dramatically increased the speed at which knowledge could be transmitted and freed individuals from having to memorize everything they learned. Printed books and pamphlets, even one-page flyers, would create a wider community of scholars no longer dependent on personal patronage or church sponsorship for texts. Printing thus encouraged the free expression and exchange of ideas, and its disruptive potential did not go unnoticed by political and religious authorities. Rulers and bishops in the German states, the birthplace of the printing industry, moved quickly to issue censorship regulations, but their efforts could not prevent the outbreak of the Protestant Reformation.

Popular Piety and Christian Humanism

The Christianizing of Europe had taken many centuries to complete, but by 1500 most people in Europe believed devoutly. However, the vast majority of them had little knowledge of Catholic doctrine. More popular forms of piety such as processions, festivals, and marvelous tales of saints' miracles captivated ordinary believers.

Urban merchants and artisans, more likely than the general population to be literate and critical of their local priests, yearned for a faith more meaningful to their daily lives and for a clergy more responsive to their needs. They wanted priests to preach edifying sermons, to administer the sacraments conscientiously, and to lead moral lives, so they generously donated money to establish new preaching positions for university-trained clerics. The merchants resented the funneling of the Catholic church's rich endowments to the younger children of the nobility who took up religious callings to protect the wealth of their families. The young, educated clerics funded by the merchants often came from cities themselves. They formed the backbone of **Christian humanism** and sometimes became reformers, too.

Humanism originated during the Renaissance in Italy among highly educated individuals attached to the personal households of prominent rulers. North of the Alps, however, humanists focused more on religious revival and the inculcation of Christian piety, especially through the schools of the Brethren of the Common Life. The Brethren preached religious self-discipline, specialized in the copying of manuscripts, and were among the first to print the ancient classics. Their most influential pupil was

Christian humanism: A general intellectual trend in the sixteenth century that coupled love of classical learning, as in Renaissance humanism, with an emphasis on Christian piety.

Albrecht Dürer, *The Knight, Death, and the Devil*
Dürer's 1513 engraving of the knight depicts a grim and determined warrior advancing past death (wearing a crown entwined with a serpent and holding out an hourglass) and the devil (the pig-snouted horned figure wielding a menacing pike). An illustration for Erasmus's *The Handbook of the Militant Christian*, this scene is often interpreted as portraying a Christian clad in the armor of righteousness on a path through life beset by death and demonic temptations. Yet the knight in early-sixteenth-century Germany had become a mercenary, selling his martial skills to princes. Some knights waylaid merchants, robbed rich clerics, and held citizens for ransom. The most notorious of these robber-knights, Franz von Sickingen, was declared an outlaw by the emperor and murdered in 1522. *(Bridgeman-Giraudon/Art Resource, NY.)*

the Dutch Christian humanist Desiderius Erasmus (c. 1466–1536). The illegitimate son of a man who became a priest, Erasmus joined the Augustinian order of monks, but the pope allowed him to leave the monastery and pursue the life of an independent scholar. An intimate friend of kings and popes, he became known across Europe. He devoted years to preparing a critical edition of the New Testament in Greek with a translation into Latin, which was finally published in 1516. Just as Cicero had dominated ancient Roman letters, Erasmus towered over the humanist world of early-sixteenth-century Europe.

Only through education, Erasmus believed, could individuals reform themselves and society. He strove for a unified, peaceful Christendom in which charity and good works, not empty ceremonies, would mark true religion and in which learning and piety would dispel the darkness of ignorance. He elaborated many of these ideas in his *Handbook of the Militant Christian* (1503), an eloquent plea for a simple religion devoid of greed and the lust for power. In *The Praise of Folly* (1509), Erasmus satirized values held dear by his contemporaries. Modesty, humility, and poverty represented the true Christian virtues in a world that worshipped pomposity, power, and wealth. The wise appeared foolish, he concluded, for their wisdom and values were not of this world.

Erasmus instructed the young future emperor Charles V to rule as a just Christian prince and avoid making war just for the sake of taxing his subjects. A man of peace and moderation, Erasmus soon found himself challenged by angry younger men and radical ideas once the Reformation took hold; he eventually chose Christian unity over reform and schism. His dream of Christian pacifism crushed, he lived to see dissenters executed — by Catholics and Protestants alike — for speaking their conscience. Erasmus spent his last years in Freiburg and Basel, isolated from the Protestant community, his writings condemned by many in the Catholic church. After the Protestant Reformation had been secured, the saying arose that "Erasmus laid the egg that Luther hatched." Some blamed the humanists for the emergence of Luther and Protestantism, despite the humanists' decision to remain in the Catholic church.

Martin Luther's Challenge

The crisis of faith of one man, **Martin Luther** (1483–1546), started the international movement known as the Protestant Reformation. Luther was an improbable spiritual revolutionary. Son of a miner and a deeply pious mother, he began his studies in the law. Caught in a thunderstorm on a lonely road one summer night, the young student begged the help of St. Anne, the mother of the Virgin Mary, and promised to enter a monastery if she protected him. Luther abandoned his law studies and, like Erasmus, entered the Augustinian order. There he experienced his religious crisis: despite fervent prayers, fasting, intense reading of the Bible, a personal pilgrimage to Rome (on foot), and study

Martin Luther: A German monk (1483–1546) who started the Protestant Reformation in 1517 by challenging the practices and doctrines of the Catholic church and advocating salvation through faith alone.

that led to a doctorate in theology, Luther did not feel saved.

Luther found peace inside himself when he became convinced that sinners were saved only through faith and that faith was a gift freely given by God. Shortly before his death, Luther recalled his crisis:

> Though I lived as a monk without reproach, I felt that I was a sinner before God with an extremely disturbed conscience. I could not believe that he was placated by my satisfaction [in penance]. I did not love, yes, I hated the righteous God who punishes sinners, and secretly . . . I was angry with God. . . . At last, by the mercy of God, meditating day and night, I gave heed to the context of the words, namely, "In [the gospel] the righteousness of God is revealed, as it is written, 'He who through faith is righteous shall live.'" There I began to understand that the righteousness of God is that by which the righteous live by a gift of God, namely by faith.

No amount of good works, Luther believed, could produce the faith on which salvation depended.

Just as Luther was working out his own personal search for salvation, a priest named Johann Tetzel arrived in Wittenberg, where Luther was a university professor, to sell indulgences. In the sacrament of penance, according to Catholic church doctrine, the sinner confessed his or her sin to a priest, who offered absolution and imposed a penance. Penance normally consisted of spiritual duties (prayers, pilgrimages), but the church also sold monetary substitutions, called indulgences. A person could even buy indulgences for a deceased relative to reduce that person's time in purgatory and release his or her soul for heaven. Like Erasmus and many other critics, Luther denounced the sale of indulgences as a corrupt practice. But Luther took his criticism a step further: he declared that indulgences, like the sacrament of penance itself, were ultimately useless unless one had faith.

Armed with his sense of God's justice and grace, Luther composed ninety-five theses for academic debate in 1517. Among them were attacks on the sale of indulgences and the purchase of church offices. Printed, the theses became public and unleashed a torrent of pent-up resentment and frustration among the laypeople. What began as a theological debate in a provincial university soon engulfed the Holy Roman Empire. (See "Contrasting Views," page 462.) Luther's earliest supporters included younger Christian humanists and clerics who shared his critical attitude toward the church establishment. None of these Evangelicals, as they called themselves, came from the upper echelons of the church; many were from urban middle-class backgrounds, and most were university trained. The Evangelicals represented social groups most ready to challenge clerical authority—merchants, artisans, and literate urban laypeople. But illiterate artisans and peasants also rallied to Luther, sometimes with an almost fanatical zeal. They and he believed they were living in the last days of the world. Luther and his cause might be a sign of the approaching Last Judgment.

Initially, Luther presented himself as the pope's "loyal opposition," but in 1520 he burned his bridges with the publication of three fiery treatises. In *Freedom of a Christian*, written in Latin for the learned and addressed to Pope Leo X, Luther argued that faith, not good works, saved sinners from damnation, and he sharply distinguished between true Gospel teachings and invented church doctrines. Luther advocated "the priesthood of all believers," insisting that the Bible provided all the teachings necessary for Christian living and that a professional caste of clerics should not hold sway over laypeople. *Freedom of a Christian* circulated widely in an immediate German translation. Its principles "by faith alone," "by Scripture alone," and "the priesthood of all believers" became central features of the reform movement.

In his second treatise, *To the Nobility of the German Nation*, written in German, Luther appealed to German identity and to the nobles as the natural leaders of any reform movement. He denounced the corrupt Italians in Rome who were cheating and exploiting his compatriots and called on the German princes to defend their nation and reform the church. Luther's third treatise, *On the Babylonian Captivity of the Church*, condemned the papacy as the embodiment of the Antichrist.

From Rome's perspective, the "Luther Affair," as church officials called it, concerned only one unruly monk. When the pope ordered him to obey his superiors and keep quiet, Luther tore up the decree. Spread by the printing press, Luther's ideas circulated throughout the Holy Roman Empire, letting loose forces that neither the church nor Luther could control. Social, nationalist, and religious protests fused with lower-class resentments, much as in the Czech movement that Jan Hus had inspired a century earlier. Like Hus, Luther appeared before an emperor: in 1521, he defended his faith at the Imperial Diet of Worms before **Charles V** (r. 1519–

Charles V: Holy Roman Emperor (r. 1519–1556) and the most powerful ruler in sixteenth-century Europe; he reigned over the Low Countries, Spain, Spain's Italian and New World dominions, and the Austrian Habsburg lands.

CONTRASTING VIEWS

Martin Luther: Holy Man or Heretic?

When Martin Luther criticized the papacy and the Catholic church, some hailed him as a godly prophet and others condemned him as a heretic. Both Protestants and Catholics used popular propaganda to argue their cause. They spread their message to a largely illiterate or semiliterate society through pamphlets, woodcuts, and broadsheets in which visual images took on increasing importance, to appeal to a wide public. These polemical works were distributed in the thousands to cities and market towns throughout the Holy Roman Empire. A few were even translated into Latin to reach an audience outside of Germany.

The 1521 woodcut by Matthias Gnidias represents Luther standing above his Catholic opponent, the Franciscan friar Thomas Murner, who is depicted here as a crawling dragon, the biblical monster Leviathan (Document 1). Another positive image of Luther, also published in 1521, depicts him as inspired by the Holy Spirit (Document 2). An anti-Luther image from a few years later represents him as a seven-headed monster (Document 3), signifying that the reformer is the source of discord within Christianity. This image appeared in a book published in 1529 by the Dominican friar Johannes Cochlaeus, one of Luther's vociferous opponents.

Visual examples of religious propaganda worked effectively to demonize enemies and to contrast good and evil. The 1520s saw the most intense production of these cheap polemical visual prints, but the use of visual propaganda would continue for more than a century in the religious conflict.

Luther and Leviathan

1. Matthias Gnidias's Representation of Luther and Leviathan (1521)

Dressed in a friar's robes, the Murner-Leviathan monster breathes "ignis, fumus, & sulphur"—fire, smoke, and sulfur. The good friar, Luther, holds the Bible in his hands and is represented here as a prophet (foretelling the end of the world). The vertical Latin caption declares that the Lord will visit the earth with his sword and kill the Leviathan monster; he will trample underfoot lions and dragons; and the dragon, with a halter around its nostrils, will be dragged away on a hook.

2. Luther as Monk, Doctor, Man of the Bible, and Saint (1521)

This woodcut by an anonymous artist appeared in a volume that the Strasbourg printer Johann Schott published in 1521. In addition to being one of the major centers of printing, Strasbourg was also a strong-

1556), the newly elected Holy Roman Emperor who, at the age of nineteen, ruled over the Low Countries, Spain, Spain's Italian and New World dominions, and the Austrian Habsburg lands. Luther shocked Germans by declaring his admiration for the Czech heretic. But unlike Hus, Luther enjoyed the protection of his lord, Frederick the Wise, the elector of Saxony , and therefore did not suffer martyrdom. Frederick was one of the seven electors whom Charles V had bribed to become Holy Roman Emperor, and Charles had to treat him with respect. The emperor soon had cause to regret his reluctance to punish Luther.

Lutheran propaganda flooded German towns and villages. Hundreds of pamphlets lambasted the papacy and the Catholic clergy; others simplified the message of Luther for the common folk. Sometimes only a few pages in length, these broadsheets were often illustrated with crude satirical cartoons. Magistrates began to curtail clerical privileges and subordinate the clergy to municipal authority. Luther's message — that each Christian could appeal directly to God for salvation — spoke to townspeople's spiritual needs and social vision. From Wittenberg, the reform movement quickly swelled and threatened to swamp all before it. Lutheranism soon spread northward to Scandinavia when reformers who studied in Germany brought back the faith and converted the kings.

Protestantism Spreads and Divides

Other Protestant reformers soon challenged Luther's doctrines even while applauding his break from the Catholic church. In 1520, just three years after Luther's initial rupture with Rome, the chief preacher *hold of the reform movement. Note the use of traditional symbols to signify Luther's holiness: the Bible in his hands, the halo, the Holy Spirit in the form of a dove, and his friar's robes. Although the cult of saints and monasticism came under severe criticism during the Reformation, the representation of Luther in traditional symbols of sanctity stressed his conservative values instead of his radical challenge to church authorities.*

Luther as Monk. *(The Granger Collection, New York.)*

3. The Seven-Headed Martin Luther by Johannes Cochlaeus (1529)

The seven heads are labeled (from left to right) doctor, Martin, Luther, ecclesiast, enthusiast, visitirer, and Barrabas. Enthusiast *was a term of abuse, applied usually by the Catholic church to Anabaptists and religious radicals of all sorts.* Visitirer *is a pun in German on the word* Tier, *meaning "animal." Cochlaeus also mocks the new practice of Protestant clergy visiting parishes to check up on pastors' and parishioners' adherence to Reformed church doctrines and rituals in order to enforce Christian discipline. From left to right, Luther's many heads gradually reveal him to be a rebel: according to the Bible, the Romans had condemned the rabble-rouser Barrabas to die but instead freed him and crucified Jesus in his place. The number seven also alludes to the seven deadly sins.*

Seven-Headed Luther. *(The Granger Collection, New York.)*

Questions to Consider

1. **Why did Johannes Cochlaeus condemn Martin Luther? How did he construct a negative image of Luther?**
2. **Evaluate the visual representations of Luther as a godly man. Which one is more effective?**

of Zurich, Huldrych Zwingli (1484–1531), openly declared himself a reformer. Like Luther, Zwingli attacked corruption in the Catholic church hierarchy, and he also questioned fasting and clerical celibacy. Under Zwingli's leadership, Zurich served as the center for the Swiss and southern German reform movement. Zwingli disagreed with Luther on the question of the Eucharist, the central Christian sacrament that Christians partook of in communion. Catholic doctrine held that when the priest consecrated the bread and wine of communion, they actually turned into the body and blood of Christ. Luther insisted that the bread and wine did not change their nature: they were simultaneously bread and wine and the body and blood of Christ. Zwingli, however, viewed the Eucharistic bread and wine as symbols of Christ's union with believers, not the real blood and body of Christ. This issue aroused such strong feelings because it concerned the role of the priest and the church in shaping the relationship between God and the believer.

In 1529, troubled by these differences and other disagreements, Evangelical princes and magistrates assembled the major reformers in the Colloquy of Marburg, in central Germany. After several days of intense discussions, the reformers managed to resolve some differences over doctrine, but Luther and Zwingli failed to agree on the meaning of the Eucharist. The issue of the Eucharist would soon divide Lutherans and Calvinists as well.

Under the leadership of **John Calvin** (1509–1564), another wave of reform challenged Catholic

---

John Calvin: French-born Christian humanist (1509–1564) and founder of Calvinism, one of the major branches of the Protestant Reformation; he led the reform movement in Geneva, Switzerland, from 1541 to 1564.

authority. Born in Picardy, in northern France, Calvin studied in Paris and Orléans, where he took a law degree. A gifted intellectual attracted to humanism, Calvin could have enjoyed a brilliant career in government or the church. Instead, experiencing a crisis of faith, like Luther, he sought salvation through intense theological study. Calvin read the works of the leading French humanists who sought to reform the church from within, and he also examined Luther's writings. Gradually, he, too, came to question fundamental Catholic teachings.

On Sunday, October 18, 1534, Parisians found church doors posted with ribald broadsheets denouncing the Catholic Mass. Smuggled into France from the Protestant and French-speaking parts of Switzerland, the broadsheets provoked a wave of royal repression in the capital. In response to this so-called Affair of the Placards, the government arrested hundreds of French Protestants, executed some of them, and forced many more, including Calvin, to flee abroad.

Calvin made his way to Geneva, the French-speaking Swiss city-state where he would find his life's work. Genevans had renounced their allegiance to the Catholic bishop, and local supporters of reform begged Calvin to stay and labor there. Although it took some time for Calvin to solidify his position in the city, his supporters eventually triumphed and he remained in Geneva until his death in 1564.

Under Calvin's leadership, Geneva became a Christian republic on the model set out in his *Institutes of the Christian Religion*, first published in 1536. No reformer prior to Calvin had expounded on the doctrines, organization, history, and practices of Christianity in such a systematic, logical, and coherent manner. Calvin followed Luther's doctrine of salvation to its ultimate logical conclusion: if God is almighty and humans cannot earn their salvation by good works, then no Christian can be certain of salvation. Developing the doctrine of **predestination**, Calvin argued that God had ordained every man, woman, and child to salvation or damnation—even before the creation of the world. Thus, in Calvin's theology, God saved only the "elect" (a small group) and knew their identity eternally.

Predestination could terrify, but it could also embolden. A righteous life might be a sign of a person's having been chosen for salvation. Thus, Calvinist doctrine demanded rigorous discipline. The knowledge that only the elect would be saved should guide the actions of the godly in an uncertain world. Fusing church and society into what followers named the Reformed church, Geneva became a theocratic city-state dominated by Calvin and the elders of the Reformed church. Its people were rigorously monitored; detractors said that they were bullied. (See Document, "Ordinances for Calvinist Churches," page 465.) From its base in Geneva, the Calvinist movement spread to France, the Low Countries, England, Scotland, the German states, Poland, Hungary, and eventually New England, becoming the established form of the Reformation in many of these countries.

In Geneva, Calvin tolerated no dissent. While passing through the city in 1553, the Spanish physician Michael Servetus was arrested because he had published books attacking Calvin and questioning the doctrine of the Trinity, the belief that there are three persons in one God—the Father, the Son (Christ), and the Holy Spirit. Upon Calvin's advice, the authorities executed Servetus. Calvin was not alone in persecuting dissenters. Each religious group believed that its doctrine was absolutely true and grounded in the Bible and that therefore violence in its defense was not only justified but required. Catholic and Protestant polemicists alike castigated their critics in the harshest terms, but they often saved their cruelest words for the Jews. Calvin, for example, called the Jews "profane, unholy, sacrilegious dogs," but Luther went even further and advocated burning down their houses and their synagogues. Religious toleration was still far in the future.

The Contested Church of England

England followed yet another path, with reform led by the king rather than by men trained as Catholic clergy. Despite a tradition of religious dissent that went back to John Wycliffe, Protestantism gained few English adherents in the 1520s. King **Henry VIII** (r. 1509–1547) changed that when he broke with the Roman Catholic church for reasons that were both personal and political. The resulting Church of England retained many aspects of Catholic worship but nonetheless aligned itself in the Protestant camp.

At first, Henry opposed the Reformation, even receiving the title Defender of the Faith from Pope

---

predestination: John Calvin's doctrine that God preordained salvation or damnation for each person before creation; those chosen for salvation were considered the "elect."

Henry VIII: The English king (r. 1509–1547) who first opposed the Protestant Reformation and then broke with the Catholic church, naming himself head of the Church of England in the Act of Supremacy of 1534.

DOCUMENT

Ordinances for Calvinist Churches (1547)

The Calvinist churches, like others during the Protestant Reformation, emphasized the need for strict moral regulation of individual behavior. These ordinances placed on churches in Geneva and surrounding areas show how all aspects of behavior, including popular entertainments, were subject to scrutiny.

Concerning the Times of Assembling at Church

That the temples be closed for the rest of the time [outside the time of services], in order that no one shall enter therein out of hours, impelled thereto by superstition; and if anyone be found engaged in any special act of devotion therein or nearby he shall be admonished for it: if it be found to be of a superstitious nature for which simple correction is inadequate then he shall be chastised.

Blasphemy.

Whoever shall have blasphemed, swearing by the body or by the blood of our Lord, or in similar manner, he shall be made to kiss the earth for the first offence; for the second to pay 5 sous, and for the third 6 sous, and for the last offence be put in the pillory for one hour.

Drunkenness.

1. That no one shall invite another to drink under penalty of 3 sous.
2. That taverns shall be closed during the sermon, under penalty that the tavern-keeper shall pay 3 sous, and whoever may be found therein shall pay the same amount.
3. If anyone be found intoxicated he shall pay for the first offence 3 sous and shall be remanded to the consistory [church council or governing body]; for the second offence he shall be held to pay the sum of 6 sous, and for the third 10 sous and be put in prison.
4. That no one shall make roiaumes [popular festivals] under penalty of 10 sous.

Songs and Dances.

If anyone sings immoral, dissolute or outrageous songs, or dance the virollet or other dance, he shall be put in prison for three days and then sent to the consistory.

Usury.

That no one shall take upon interest or profit more than five per cent., upon penalty of confiscation of the principal and of being condemned to make restitution as the case may demand.

Games.

That no one shall play at any dissolute game or at any game whatsoever it may be, neither for gold nor silver nor for any excessive stake [i.e., gambling], upon penalty of 5 sous and forfeiture of stake played for.

Source: George L. Burns, ed., in *Translations and Reprints from the Original Sources of European History*, 6 vols. (Philadelphia: University of Pennsylvania History Department, 1898–1912), 1:2–5.

Question to Consider

■ **To what extent do these ordinances suggest specific difficulties in maintaining a strict moral discipline in Calvinist Geneva during this era?**

Leo X for a treatise Henry wrote against Luther. An ambitious and well-educated man, Henry wanted to make his mark on history and, with the aid of his chancellors Cardinal Thomas Wolsey and Thomas More, he vigorously suppressed Protestantism and executed its leaders. More had made a reputation as a Christian humanist, publishing a controversial novel about an imaginary island called Utopia (1516), the source of the modern word for an ideal community. Unlike his friend Erasmus, More chose to serve the state directly and became personal secretary to Henry VIII, Speaker of the House of Commons, and finally Lord Chancellor.

By 1527, the king wanted to annul his marriage to Catherine of Aragon (d. 1536), the daughter of Ferdinand and Isabella of Spain and the aunt of Charles V. The eighteen-year marriage had produced a daughter, Mary (known as Mary Tudor), but Henry desperately needed a male heir to consolidate the rule of the still-new Tudor dynasty. Moreover, he had fallen in love with Anne Boleyn, a lady at court and a supporter of the Reformation. Henry claimed that his marriage to Catherine had never been valid because she was the widow of his older brother, Arthur. Arthur and Catherine's marriage, which apparently was never consummated, had been annulled by Pope Julius II to allow the marriage between Henry and Catherine to take place. Now Henry asked the reigning pope, Clement VII, to declare his marriage to Catherine invalid.

Around "the king's great matter" unfolded a struggle for political and religious control. When Cardinal Wolsey failed to secure papal approval of the annulment, Henry dismissed him and had him arrested. Wolsey died before he could be tried, and More took his place. However, More resigned in 1532 because he opposed Henry's new direction and was executed as a traitor in 1535. Henry now turned

The Progress of The Reformation

1517	Martin Luther disseminates ninety-five theses attacking the sale of indulgences and other church practices
1520	Reformer Huldrych Zwingli breaks with Rome
1525	Peasants' War in German states divides reform movement
1529	Lutheran German princes protest the condemnation of religious reform by Charles V
1534	The Act of Supremacy establishes King Henry VIII as head of the Church of England, severing ties to Rome
1534–1535	Anabaptists take over the German city of Münster in a failed experiment to create a holy community
1541	John Calvin establishes himself permanently in Geneva, making that city a model of Christian reform and discipline

to two Protestants, Thomas Cromwell (1485–1540) as chancellor and Thomas Cranmer (1489–1556) as archbishop of Canterbury. Under their leadership, the English Parliament passed a number of acts that severed ties between the English church and Rome. The most important of these, the Act of Supremacy of 1534, made Henry the head of the Church of England. Other legislation invalidated the claims of Mary Tudor to the throne, recognized Henry's marriage to Anne Boleyn, and allowed the English crown to embark on the dissolution of the monasteries. In an effort to consolidate support behind his version of the Reformation, Henry sold off monastic lands to the local gentry and aristocracy. His actions prompted an uprising in 1536 in the north of the country called the Pilgrimage of Grace. Though suppressed, it revealed that many people remained deeply Catholic in their sympathies.

Henry grew tired of Anne Boleyn, who had given birth to a daughter, the future Queen Elizabeth I, but had produced no sons. He ordered Anne beheaded in 1536 on the charge of adultery. The king would go on to marry four other wives but father only one son, Edward. When Henry died in 1547, the principle of royal supremacy in religious matters was firmly established, but much would now depend on who held the crown. Henry himself held ambiguous views on religion: he considered himself Catholic but would not accept the supremacy of the pope; he closed the monasteries and removed shrines but kept the Mass and believed in clerical celibacy.

REVIEW QUESTION How did Luther, Zwingli, Calvin, and Henry VIII each challenge the Roman Catholic church?

Reshaping Society through Religion

The religious upheavals of the sixteenth century affected European society in contradictory ways: the reformers and their followers challenged political authority and the social order, yet in reaction to the more extreme manifestations of the first, they underlined the need for discipline in worship and social behavior. Some Protestants wanted to push the Reformation in a more populist direction. They took the phrase "priesthood of all believers" quite literally and sided with the poor and the downtrodden. Like Catholics, Protestant authorities then became alarmed by the subversive potential of religious reforms. They viewed the Reformation not as a political and social movement, but as a way of instilling greater discipline in individual worship and church organization. Bible reading became a potent tool in the creation of this new, internally motivated person. At the same time, the Roman Catholic church undertook reforms of its own and launched an offensive against the Protestant Reformation that is sometimes called the Counter-Reformation.

Protestant Challenges to the Social Order

When Luther described the freedom of the Christian, he meant an entirely spiritual freedom. But others interpreted his call for freedom in social and political terms. In 1525, peasants and urban artisans rose up against the Catholic church and landed nobility and armed themselves to pursue their goals. Anabaptists experimented with new social and political doctrines. Most Anabaptists rejected violence, but one group tried to create a perfect Christian community in the German town of Münster. The results were disastrous.

The Peasants' War of 1525 Luther's and Zwingli's anticlerical messages struck home with peasants who paid taxes to both their lord and the Catholic church. In the spring of 1525, peasants in southern and central Germany rose in rebellion and attacked nobles' castles, convents, and monasteries, claiming to be following the word of God (Map 14.3). Urban workers joined them, and together they looted church properties in the towns. In Thuringia (central/eastern Germany), the rebels followed an ex-priest, Thomas Müntzer (1468?–1525), who promised to chastise the wicked and thus clear the way for the Last Judgment.

The Peasants' War split the reform movement. Princes and city officials, ultimately supported by Luther, turned against the rebels. Catholic and Protestant princes joined hands to crush Müntzer and his supporters. All over the empire, princes trounced peasant armies, hunted down their leaders, and uprooted all opposition. By the end of the year, more than 100,000 rebels had been killed and many others maimed, imprisoned, or exiled. Initially, Luther had tried to mediate the conflict, criticizing the princes for their brutality toward the peasants but also warning the rebels against mixing religion and social protest. Luther believed that God ordained rulers, who must therefore be obeyed even if they were tyrants. The kingdom of God belonged not to this world but to the next, he insisted. Luther considered Müntzer's mixing of religion and politics the greatest danger to the Reformation, nothing less than "the devil's work."

Fundamentally conservative in its political philosophy, the Lutheran church henceforth depended on established political authority for its protection. It lost supporters in rural areas and became an increasingly urban phenomenon. The ultimate

German Peasants' War of 1525
This woodcut depicts peasants attacking the pope, a monk, and a nobleman during the rural uprisings against the church that took place in Germany in 1525. Even the heavens show signs of trouble: a comet and clouds in the shape of a goat signify bloodshed and sin. *(The Granger Collection, New York—All rights reserved.)*

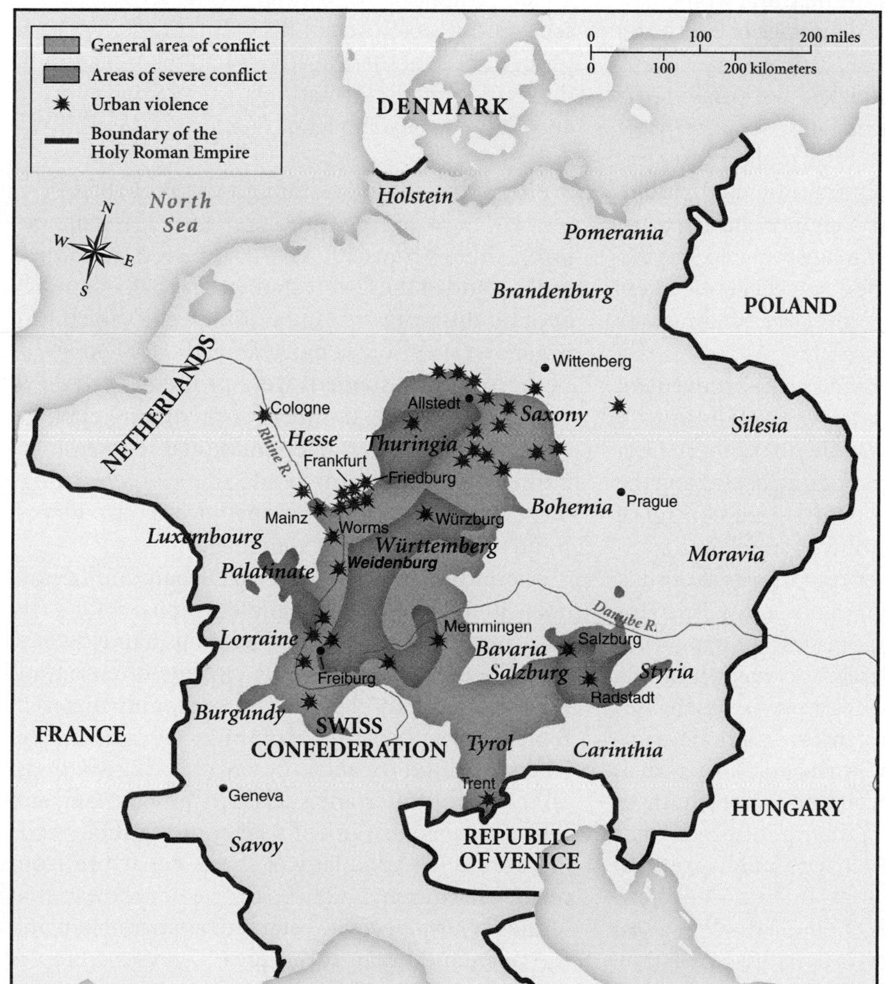

MAP 14.3 The Peasants' War of 1525
The centers of uprisings clustered in southern and central Germany, where the density of cities encouraged the spread of discontent and allowed for alliances between urban masses and rural rebels. The proximity to the Swiss Confederation, a stronghold of the Reformation movement, also inspired antiestablishment uprisings.

victors were the German princes. They defeated the peasants, sided with Luther, and confronted the Holy Roman Emperor, Charles V, who declared Roman Catholicism the empire's only legitimate religion. The fragmentation of the Holy Roman Empire only increased as people came to support their Protestant princes against Charles's Catholic orthodoxy.

Anabaptists | While Zwingli challenged the Roman Catholic church in public, some laypeople in Zurich secretly pursued their own path to reform. Taking their cue from the New Testament's descriptions of the first Christian community, these men and women believed that true faith came only to those with reason and free will. How could a baby knowingly choose Christ? Only adults could believe and accept baptism; hence, the **Anabaptists** ("rebaptizers") rejected the validity of infant baptism and called for adult rebaptism. Many were pacifists who also refused to acknowledge the authority of law courts and considered themselves a community of true Christians unblemished by sin. The Anabaptist movement drew its leadership primarily from the artisan class and its members from the middle and lower classes — men and women attracted by a simple but radical message of peace and salvation.

Zwingli immediately attacked the Anabaptists for their refusal to bear arms and swear oaths of allegiance, sensing accurately that they were repudiating his theocratic (church-directed) order. When persuasion failed to convince the Anabaptists, Zwingli urged Zurich magistrates to impose the death sentence. Thus, the evangelical reformers themselves created the Reformation's first martyrs of conscience.

Despite condemnation in 1529 of the movement by the Holy Roman Emperor, Anabaptism spread rapidly from Zurich to many cities in southern Germany. In 1534, one Anabaptist group, believing the end of the world was imminent, seized control of the city of Münster. Proclaiming themselves a community of saints, the Münster Anabaptists abolished private property in imitation of the early Christians and dissolved traditional marriages, allowing men, like Old Testament patriarchs, to have multiple wives, to the consternation of many women. Besieged by a combined Protestant and Catholic army, the city fell in June 1535. The Anabaptist leaders died in battle or were executed, their bodies hung in cages affixed to the church tower. Their punishment was intended as a warning to all who might want to take the Reformation away from the Protestant authorities and hand it to the people. The Anabaptist movement in northwestern Europe nonetheless survived under the determined pacifist leadership of the Dutch reformer Menno Simons (1469–1561), whose followers were eventually named Mennonites.

Anabaptists: Sixteenth-century Protestants who believed that only adults could truly have faith and accept baptism.

New Forms of Discipline

Faced with the social firestorms ignited by religious reform, the middle-class urbanites who supported the Protestant Reformation urged greater religious conformity and stricter moral behavior. To gain more control over religious ferment, Protestant rulers and clergy encouraged Bible reading and a new work ethic. Ordinary men and women who learned how to behave as virtuous Christians at home and in Sunday worship applied what they learned in their households and their businesses. Protestants did not have monasteries or convents or saints' lives to set examples; they sought moral examples in their own homes, in the sermons of their preachers, and in their own reading of the Bible. The new emphasis on self-discipline led to growing impatience with the poor, now viewed as lacking personal virtue, and greater emphasis on regulation of marriage, now seen as critical to social discipline in general. Although some of these attitudes had medieval roots, the Protestant Reformation fostered their spread and Catholics soon began to embrace them.

Reading the Bible | Although the Bible had been translated into German before, Luther's translations — of the New Testament in 1522 and of the Old Testament in 1534 — quickly became authoritative. A new Bible-centered culture began to take root, as more than 200,000 copies of Luther's New Testament were printed over twelve years, an immense number for the time. Peppered with witty phrases and colloquial expressions, Luther's Bible not only made the sacred writings more accessible to ordinary people but also helped standardize the German language.

Found for the most part in urban and literate households, the German Bible occupied a central place in a family's history. Generations handed down valuable editions, and pious citizens often bound Bibles with family papers or other reading material. Bible reading became a common pastime undertaken in solitude or at family and church gatherings. To counter Protestant success, Catholic German Bibles soon appeared, thus sanctioning Bible reading by the Catholic laity, a sharp departure from medieval church practice. In the same year that Luther's German New Testament appeared in print, the French humanist Jacques Lefèvre d'Étaples

(c. 1455–1536) translated the Vulgate (Latin) New Testament into French.

Catholic authorities did not always welcome translations, however. Sensing a potentially dangerous association between the vernacular Bible and heresy, England's Catholic church hierarchy had reacted swiftly against English-language Bibles. When William Tyndale (1495–1536) translated the Bible into English, he was burned at the stake as a heretic. After Henry VIII's break with Rome and adoption of the Reformation, in contrast, his government promoted an English Bible based on Tyndale's translation.

Public Relief for the Poor In the early sixteenth century, secular governments began to take over institutions of public charity from the church. This development, which took place in both Catholic and Protestant Europe, grew out of two trends: a new upsurge in poverty brought about by population growth and spiraling inflation, and the rise of a work ethic that included growing hostility toward the poor.

By 1500, the cycle of demographic collapse and economic depression triggered by the Black Death of 1346–1353 had passed. Between 1500 and 1560, rapid economic and population growth created prosperity for some and stress — caused or heightened by increased inflation — for many. Wanderers and urban beggars were by no means novel, but the reaction to poverty was. Sixteenth-century moralists decried the crime and sloth of vagabonds and rejected the notion that the poor played a central role in the Christian idea of salvation.

The Reformation provided an opportunity to restructure relief for the poor. Instead of decentralized, private initiatives often overseen by religious orders, Protestant magistrates appointed officials to head urban agencies that would certify the genuine poor and distribute welfare funds to them. This development progressed rapidly in urban areas, where poverty was most visible, and transcended religious divisions. During the 1520s, cities in the Low Countries, Italy, and Spain passed ordinances that prohibited begging and instituted public charity. In 1526, the Spanish humanist Juan Luis Vives, a Catholic, wrote *On the Support of the Poor*, a Latin treatise urging authorities to establish public poor relief; the work was soon translated into French, Italian, German, and English. National laws followed. In 1531, Henry VIII asked justices of the peace (unpaid local magistrates) to license the poor in England and to differentiate between those who could work and those who could not. In 1540, Charles V imposed a welfare tax in Spain to augment that country's inadequate system of private charity.

Euangelion Sanct I.
Matthes.

I.
DJs iſt das buch von der
geburt Jheſu Chriſti/der da iſt ein ſon
Dauids des ſons Abraham.
Abraham zeugete Jſaac.
Jſaac zeugete Jacob.
Jacob zeugete Juda vnd ſeine brůder.
Juda zeugete Pharez vnd Saram/von
der Thamar.
Pharez zeugete Hezron.
Hezron zeugete Ram.
Ram zeugete Aminadab.
Aminadab zeugete Nahaſſon.
Nahaſſon zeugete Salma.
Salma zeugete Boas/von der Rahab.
Boas zeugete Obed/von der Ruth.
Obed zeugete Jeſſe.
Jeſſe zeugete den kőnig Dauid.
Der kőnig Dauid zeugete Salomon/von dem weibe des Vrie.
Salomon zeugete Roboam.
Roboam zeugete Abia.
Abia zeugete Aſſa.
Aſſa zeugete Joſaphat.
Joſaphat zeugete Joram.

Abraham vnd Dauid werdẽ furnemlich angezogen/darumb das den ſelben Chriſtus ſonderlich verheiſſen iſt.

A Joram

Luther's Bible
This opening page from the Gospel of St. Matthew is taken from Luther's 1522 translation into German of the New Testament. The woodcut illustrations by Lucas Cranach, and Luther's decision to use a style of German that could be widely understood, made the book accessible to a wide audience. Bible reading became a central family activity for Protestants. *(Bible Society, London, UK / The Bridgeman Art Library International.)*

Reforming Marriage In their effort to establish order and discipline, Protestant reformers denounced sexual immorality and glorified the family. The early Protestant reformers like Luther championed the end of clerical celibacy and embraced marriage. Luther, once a celibate priest himself, married a former nun. Protestant magistrates closed brothels and established marriage courts to handle disputes over promises of marriage, child support, and divorce, allowed by Protestants in some rare situations. The magistrates also levied fines or ordered imprisonment for violent behavior, fornication, and adultery.

Prior to the Reformation, despite the legislation of church councils, marriages had largely been private affairs between families; some couples never even registered with the church. The Catholic church recognized any promise made between two consenting adults (with the legal age of twelve for females, fourteen for males) in the presence of two witnesses as a valid marriage. Many couples simply lived together as common-law husband and wife. Young men sometimes promised marriage in a passionate moment, only to renege later. Protestants proved more effective than the late medieval church in suppressing common-law marriages. They did so by asserting government control over marriage, and Catholic governments followed suit. A marriage was legitimate only if registered by both a government official and a member of the clergy.

In the fervor of the early Reformation years, the first generation of Protestant women attained greater marital equality than those of subsequent generations. Katharina Zell, wife of the reformer Matthew Zell, defended her equality by citing a Bible verse when a critic used St. Paul to support his argument that women should remain silent in church. Katharina retorted, "I would remind you of the word of this same apostle that in Christ there is no male nor female." Katharina helped feed and clothe the thousands of refugees who flooded Strasbourg after their defeat in the Peasants' War. In 1534, she published a collection of hymns. For the most part, however, women's position in society did not change: if anything, the closing of convents meant that their roles in Protestant areas were more than ever confined to the household and family.

Catholic Renewal

Like a slumbering giant finally awakened, the Catholic church decided in the 1540s to undertake drastic action to fend off the Protestant threat. Pope Paul III convened a general council of the church in 1545 at Trent, a town on the border between the Holy Roman Empire and Italy. Meeting sporadically over nearly twenty years (1545–1563), the **Council of Trent** effectively set the course of Catholicism until the 1960s. Catholic leaders sought renewal of religious devotion and reform of clerical morality as well as clarification of church doctrine. New religious orders set out to win converts overseas or to reconvert Catholics who had turned to Protestantism. Catholic clergy emphasized the pageantry of ritual and the decoration of churches in order to counter the austerity of Protestant worship. At the same time, the church did not hesitate to root out dissent by giving greater powers to the Inquisition, including the power to censor books. The papal Index, or list of prohibited books, was established in 1557 and not abolished until 1966.

The Council of Trent Italian and Spanish clergy predominated among the 255 bishops, archbishops, and cardinals attending the Council of Trent. Though its deliberations were interrupted first by an outbreak of the plague and then by warfare, the council came up with a remarkably wide-ranging series of decisions. It condemned the central doctrines of Protestantism. Salvation depended on faith and good works, not faith alone. On the sacrament of the Eucharist, the council reaffirmed that the bread of communion "really, truly" becomes Christ's body—a rejection of all Protestant positions on this issue so emphatic as to preclude compromise. It reasserted the supremacy of clerical authority over the laity; the church's interpretation of the Bible could not be challenged, and the Latin Vulgate was the only authoritative version. The council rejected divorce and reaffirmed the legitimacy of indulgences. It also called for reform from within, however, insisting that bishops henceforth reside in their dioceses and decreeing that seminaries for the training of priests be established in every diocese.

The Council of Trent marked a watershed; henceforth, the schism between Protestant and Catholic remained permanent, and all hopes of reconciliation faded. The focus of the Catholic church turned now to rolling back the tide of dissent.

New Religious Orders The energy of the Catholic renewal expressed itself most vigorously in the founding of new religious orders such as the Theatines, Barnabites, and for women, the Ursulines. The most important of these, the Society of Jesus, or **Jesuits**, was established by a Spanish nobleman, Ignatius of Loyola (1491–1556). Inspired by tales of chivalric romances and the national glory of the *reconquista*, Ignatius eagerly sought to prove himself as a soldier. In 1521, while defending a Spanish border fortress against French attack, he sustained a severe injury. During his convalescence, Ignatius read lives of the saints; once he recovered, he abandoned his quest for military glory in favor of serving the church.

Council of Trent: A general council of the Catholic church that met at Trent between 1545 and 1563 to set Catholic doctrine, reform church practices, and defend the church against the Protestant challenge.

Jesuits: Members of the Society of Jesus, a Catholic religious order founded by Ignatius of Loyola (1491–1556) and approved by the pope in 1540. Jesuits served as missionaries and educators all over the world.

Attracted by his activist piety, young men gravitated to this charismatic figure. Thanks to a cardinal's intercession, Ignatius gained a hearing before the pope, and in 1540 the church recognized his small band. With Ignatius as its first general, the Jesuits became the most vigorous defenders of papal authority. The society quickly expanded; by the time of Ignatius's death in 1556, Europe had one thousand Jesuits. They established hundreds of colleges throughout the Catholic world, educating future generations of Catholic leaders. Jesuit missionaries played a key role in the Spanish and Portuguese empires and brought Roman Catholicism to Africans, Asians, and native Americans. Together with other new religious orders, the Jesuits restored the confidence of the faithful in the dedication and power of the Catholic church. They also acquired a reputation for bringing controversy in their wake and for being drawn to power as counselors to powerful nobles and kings.

Missionary Zeal | To win new souls, Catholic missionaries set sail throughout the globe. They saw their effort as proof of the truth of Roman Catholicism and the success of their missions as a sign of divine favor, both particularly important in the face of Protestant challenge. But the missionary zeal of Catholics brought conflicting messages to indigenous peoples: for some, the message of a repressive and coercive alien religion; for others, a sweet sign of reason and faith. Frustrated in his efforts to convert Brazilian Indians, a Jesuit missionary wrote to his superior in Rome in 1563 that "for this kind of people it is better to be preaching with the sword and rod of iron." Yet others insisted that faith could not be forced; conversion had to be voluntary.

To ensure rapid Christianization, Catholic missionaries focused initially on winning over local elites. They learned the local languages and set up schools for the sons of conquered nobles. Once Christianized, those students wrote prayer and confessional manuals, sermons, and histories in their native languages. After an initial period of relatively little racial discrimination, the Catholic church in the Americas and Africa adopted strict rules based on color. For example, the first Mexican Ecclesiastical Provincial Council in 1555 declared that holy orders were not to be conferred on Indians, mestizos (people of mixed European-Indian

The Portuguese in Japan

In this sixteenth-century Japanese black-lacquer screen painting of Portuguese missionaries, the Jesuits are dressed in black and the Franciscans (members of another Catholic religious order) in brown. At the lower left corner is a Portuguese nobleman depicted with exaggerated "Western" features. The Japanese considered themselves lighter in skin color than the Portuguese, whom they classified as "barbarians." In turn, the Portuguese classified Japanese (and Chinese) as "whites." The perception of ethnic differences in the sixteenth century, however, depended less on skin color than on clothing, eating habits, and other cultural signals. Color classifications were unstable and changed over time: by the late seventeenth century, Europeans no longer regarded Asians as "whites." *(The Granger Collection, New York—All rights reserved.)*

parentage), or mulattoes (people of mixed European-African heritage); along with descendants of Muslims, Jews, and persons who had been sentenced by the Spanish Inquisition, these groups were deemed "inherently unworthy of the sacerdotal [priestly] office."

In East Asia, as in the Americas, Catholic missionaries under Portuguese protection concentrated their efforts on the elites, preaching the Gospel to Confucian scholar-officials in China and to the samurai (the warrior aristocracy) in Japan. European missionaries in Asia greatly admired Chinese and Japanese civilization and thus used the sermon rather than the sword to win converts. (See the illustration on page 471.) The Jesuit Francis Xavier preached in India and Japan, his work greatly assisted by a network of Portuguese trading stations. He died in 1552, awaiting permission to travel to China. A pioneer missionary in Asia, Xavier had prepared the ground for future missionary successes in Japan and China. The efforts of the Catholic missionaries seemed highly successful: vast multitudes of native Americans had become nominal Christians by the second half of the sixteenth century, and thirty years after Francis Xavier's 1549 landing in Japan, the Jesuits could claim more than 100,000 Japanese converts.

REVIEW QUESTION How did the forces for radical change unleashed by the Protestant Reformation interact with the urge for social order and stability?

Striving for Mastery

Although the riches of the New World and the conflicts generated by the Reformation raised the stakes of international politics, life at court did not change all at once. Princes and popes continued to sponsor the arts and literature of the Renaissance. Henry VIII, for example, hired the German artist Hans Holbein as king's painter; Holbein also painted a portrait of Erasmus. While Protestantism was taking root, Catholic monarchs still fought one another and constantly battled the powerful Ottoman Empire. Holy Roman Emperor Charles V dominated the political scene with his central position in Europe and his rising supply of gold and silver from the New World. Yet even his wealth proved insufficient to subdue all his challengers. Religious difference led to violence in every country, even Spain, where there were almost no Protestants but many Muslims who were forced to convert by Charles V in 1526. For the most part, violence failed to settle religious differences. By 1560, an exhausted Europe had achieved a provisional peace, but one sowed with the seeds of future conflict.

Courtiers and Princes

At the center of art patronage, dynastic competition, and religious division lay the court, the focus of princely power and intrigue and the agent of state building. Kings, princes, and popes alike used their courts to keep an eye on their leading courtiers (cardinals in the case of popes) and impress their other subjects. Briefly defined, the court was the ruler's household. Around the prince gathered a community of household servants, noble attendants, councilors, officials, artists, and soldiers. Renaissance culture had been promoted by this political elite, and that culture now entered its "high," or most sophisticated, phase. Its acclaimed representative was Michelangelo Buonarroti (1475–1564), an immensely talented Italian artist who sculpted a gigantic nude *David* for officials in Florence and then painted the ceiling of the Sistine Chapel for the recently elected Pope Julius II.

Italian artists also flocked to the French court of Francis I (r. 1515–1547), which swelled to the largest in Europe. In addition to the king's own household, the queen and the queen mother each had her own staff of maids and chefs, as did each of the royal children. The royal household employed officials to handle finances and provide guard duty, clothing, and food; in addition, physicians, librarians, musicians, dwarfs, animal trainers, and a multitude of hangers-on bloated its size. By 1535, the French court numbered 1,622 members. Although Francis built a magnificent Renaissance palace at Fontainebleau, where he hired Italian artists to produce paintings and sculpture, the French court often moved from palace to palace. It took no fewer than eighteen thousand horses to transport the people, furniture, and documents—not to mention the dogs and falcons for the royal hunt. Hunting was no mere diversion; it represented a form of mock combat, essential in the training of a military elite. Francis himself loved war games and almost lost his own life when, storming a house during one mock battle, he was hit on the head by a burning log.

Two Italian writers helped define the new culture of courtesy, or proper court behavior, that developed in such a setting: Ludovico Ariosto (1474–1533), in service at the Este court in Ferrara, and Baldassare Castiglione (1478–1529), a servant of the duke of Urbino and the pope. Considered one of the greatest Renaissance poets, Ariosto composed a long epic

King Francis I and His Court
In this illustration from a 1534 manuscript, the king of France is shown with his three sons listening to the reading of a translated ancient text. The translator, Antoine Macault, was the king's secretary and is shown wearing the black of officials. Renaissance kings took pride in sponsoring revivals of classical texts (in this case Diodorus of Sicily, a Greek historian from the first century B.C.E.). *(The Granger Collection, New York—All rights reserved.)*

poem, *Orlando Furioso*, which represented court culture as the highest synthesis of Christian and classical values. The poem's captivating tales of combat, valor, love, and magic ranged across Europe, Africa, Asia, and even the moon. Although set in the late 700s during Charlemagne's battles with the Arabs, the poem praises Christopher Columbus and Charles V. In *The Courtier*, Castiglione's characters debate the qualities of an ideal courtier in a series of eloquent dialogues. The true courtier, Castiglione asserts, is a gentleman who speaks in a refined language and carries himself with nobility and dignity in the service of his prince and his lady.

Courtesy was recommended to courtiers, but not always to princes. The Italian politician and writer Niccolò Machiavelli (1469–1527) helped found modern political science by treating the maintenance of power as an end in itself. In his provocative essay *The Prince*, he underlined the need for pragmatic, even cold calculation. Was it better, he asked, for a prince to be feared by his people or loved?

> It may be answered that one should wish to be both, but, because it is difficult to unite them in one person, is much safer to be feared than loved. . . . Because this is to be asserted in general of men, that they are ungrateful, fickle, false, cowardly, covetous, and as long as you succeed they are yours entirely; they will offer you their blood, property, life and children . . . when the need is far distant; but when it approaches they turn against you.

Machiavelli insisted that princes could benefit their subjects only by keeping a firm grip on power, if necessary through deceit and manipulation. *Machiavellian* has remained ever since a term for using cunning and duplicity to achieve one's ends.

Dynastic Wars

Even as the Renaissance developed in the princely courts and the Reformation began in the German states, the Habsburgs (the ruling family in Spain

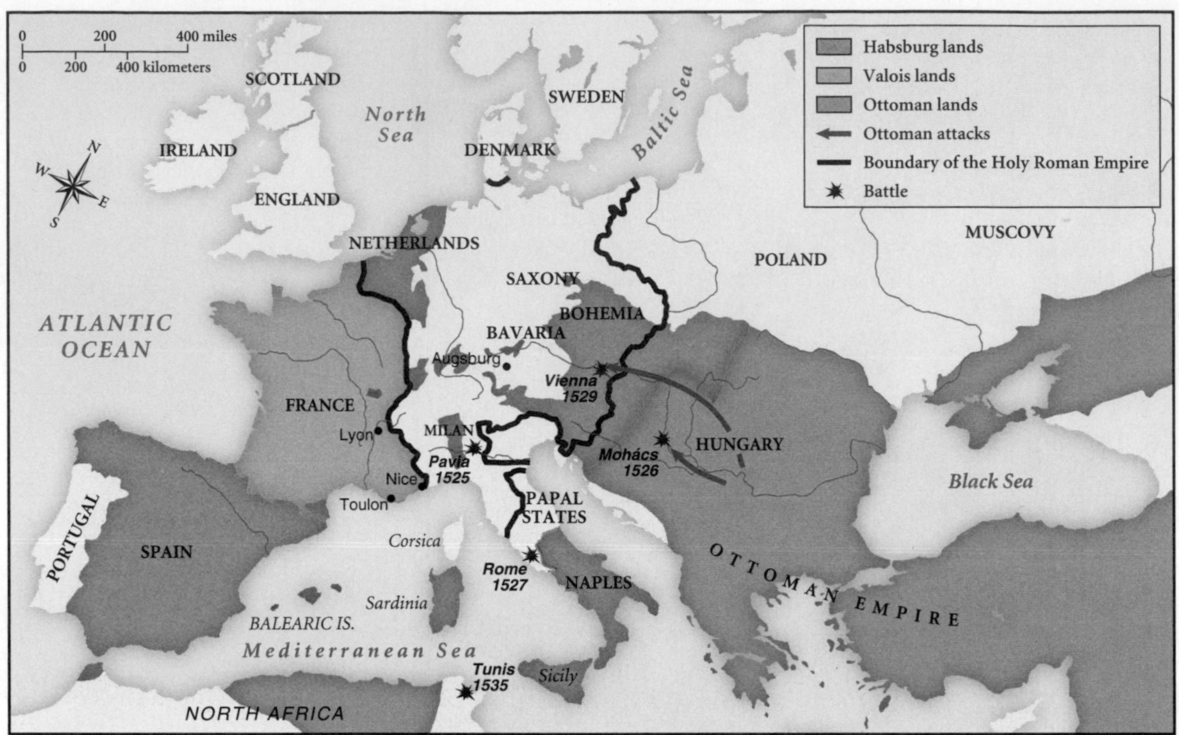

MAP 14.4 Habsburg-Valois-Ottoman Wars, 1494–1559
As the dominant European power, the Habsburg dynasty fought on two fronts: a religious war against the Islamic Ottoman Empire and a political war against the French Valois, who challenged Habsburg hegemony. The Mediterranean, the Balkans, and the Low Countries all became theaters of war.

and then the Holy Roman Empire) and the Valois (the ruling family in France) fought each other for domination of Europe (Map 14.4). French claims provoked the Italian Wars in 1494, which soon escalated into a general conflict that involved the major Christian monarchs and the Muslim Ottoman sultan as well. From 1494 to 1559, the Valois and Habsburg dynasties, both Catholic, remained implacable enemies. The fighting raged in Italy and the Low Countries. During the 1520s, the Habsburgs enjoyed the upper hand. In 1525, the troops of Charles V crushed the French army at Pavia, Italy, counting among their captives the French king himself, Francis I. Forced to renounce all claims to Italian territory to gain his freedom, Francis furiously repudiated the treaty the moment he reached France, reigniting the conflict.

In 1527, Charles's troops captured and sacked Rome because the pope had allied with the French. Many of the imperial troops were German Protestant mercenaries, who pillaged Catholic churches and brutalized the Catholic clergy. Protestants and Catholics alike interpreted the sack of Rome by imperial forces as a punishment of God; even the Catholic church read it as a sign that reform was necessary. Finally, in 1559, the French gave up their claims in Italy and signed the Treaty of Cateau-Cambrésis, ending the conflict. As was common in such situations, marriage sealed the peace between rival dynasties; the French king Henry II married his sister to the duke of Savoy, an ally of the Habsburgs, and his daughter to the Habsburg king of Spain, Philip II, who had succeeded his father Charles V in 1556.

The dynastic struggle (Valois versus Habsburg ruling family) had drawn in many other belligerents, who fought on one side or the other for their own benefit. Some acted purely out of power considerations, such as England, first siding with the Valois and then with the Habsburgs. Others fought for their independence, such as the papacy and the Italian states, which did not want any one power to dominate Italy. Still others chose sides for religious reasons, such as the Protestant princes in Germany, who exploited the Valois-Habsburg conflict to extract religious concessions from the emperor in 1555. The Ottoman Turks saw in this fight an opportunity to expand their territory.

The Ottoman Empire reached its height of power under Sultan Suleiman I, known as **Suleiman the Magnificent** (r. 1520–1566). In 1526, a Turkish expedition destroyed the Hungarian army at Mohács. Three years later, the Ottomans laid siege to Vienna; though unsuccessful, the attack sent shock waves throughout Christian Europe. (See the illustration on page 476.) In 1535, Charles V led a campaign to capture Tunis, the lair of North African pirates loyal to the Ottomans. Desperate to overcome Charles's superior Habsburg forces, the French king Francis I forged an alliance with the Turkish sultan. Coming to the aid of the French, the Turkish fleet besieged the Habsburg troops holding Nice, on the southern coast of France. Francis even ordered all inhabitants of nearby Toulon to vacate the town so that he could turn it into a Muslim colony for eight months, complete with a mosque and a slave market. The French alliance with the Turks scandalized many Christians, but it reflected the spirit of the times: the age-old idea of the Christian crusade against Islam now had to compete with a new political strategy that considered religion only one factor among many in power politics. Religion could be sacrificed, if need be, on the altar of state building.

Constantly distracted by the challenges of the Ottomans to the east and the German Protestants at home, Charles V could not crush the French with one swift blow. Years of conflict drained the treasuries of all rulers, because warfare was becoming more expensive. The formula that war raises revenues that in turn build governments could devolve into an absurdity if wars could not be won. The race for battlefield superiority was on.

Charles V and Francis I Make Peace
This fresco from the Palazzo Farnese in the town of Caprarola, north of Rome, shows French king Francis I and Holy Roman Emperor Charles V agreeing to the Truce of Nice in 1538, one of many peace agreements made and then broken during the wars between the Habsburgs and the Valois. Pope Paul III, who negotiated the truce, stands behind and between them. Charles is on the right pointing to Francis. The truce is the one celebrated in the Tlaxcala pageant described at the start of this chapter. *(The Art Archive/Palazzo Farnese Caprarola/Gianni Dagli Orti.)*

Financing War

The sixteenth century marked the beginning of superior Western military technology. All armies grew in size and their firepower became ever more deadly, increasing the cost of war. Heavier artillery pieces meant that the rectangular walls of medieval cities had to be transformed into fortresses with jutting ramparts and gun emplacements. Royal revenues could not keep up with war expenditures. To pay their bills, governments routinely devalued their coinage (the sixteenth-century equivalent of printing more paper money), causing prices to rise rapidly.

Charles V boasted the largest army in Europe, supported by the gold and silver coming in from the New World. Immediately after conquest, the Spanish looted gold and silver objects, melted them down, and sent the precious metals to Spain. Mining began with forced Indian labor in the 1520s, and the amount of silver extracted in Mexico and sent to Spain increased twentyfold in the 1530s and 1540s. Nevertheless, Charles could never make ends meet because of his extravagant war costs: his debt of 37 million ducats accumulated during his forty years in power exceeded by 2 million ducats all the gold and silver brought from the Americas. His opponents fared even worse. On his death in 1547, Francis I owed the bankers of Lyon almost 7 million French pounds — approximately the entire royal income for that year. The European powers thus fought themselves into bankruptcy. Taxation, the sale of offices, and outright confiscation failed to bring in enough money to satisfy the war machine. Both the Habsburg and the Valois kings looked to the leading bankers to finance their costly wars.

Foremost among these financiers was the Fugger bank, the largest such enterprise in sixteenth-century

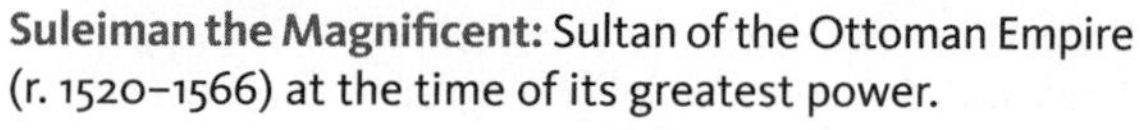

Suleiman the Magnificent: Sultan of the Ottoman Empire (r. 1520–1566) at the time of its greatest power.

The Siege of Vienna, 1529
This illustration from an Ottoman manuscript of 1588 depicts the Turkish siege of Vienna (the siege guns can be seen toward the top of the picture). Sultan Suleiman I (Suleiman the Magnificent) led an army of more than 100,000 men against Vienna, capital of the Austrian Habsburg lands. Several attacks on the city failed, and the Ottomans withdrew in October 1529. They maintained control over Hungary, but the logistics of moving so many men and horses kept them from advancing farther westward into Europe. *(The Art Archive/Topkapi Museum Istanbul/Gianni Dagli Orti.)*

Europe. Based in the southern German imperial city of Augsburg, the Fugger family and their associates built an international financial empire that helped to make kings. The enterprise began with Jakob Fugger (1459–1525), who became personal banker to Charles V's grandfather Maximilian I. Constantly short of cash, Maximilian granted the Fugger family numerous mining and minting concessions. To pay for the service of providing and accepting bills of exchange, the Fuggers charged substantial fees and made handsome profits. By the end of his life, Maximilian was so deeply in debt to Jakob Fugger that he had to pawn the royal jewels.

In 1519, Fugger assembled a consortium of German and Italian bankers to secure the election of Charles V as Holy Roman Emperor. For the next three decades, the alliance between Europe's biggest international bank and its largest empire remained very close. Between 1527 and 1547, the Fugger bank's assets more than doubled; more than half came from interest on loans to the Habsburgs. Charles stayed barely one step ahead of his creditors; in 1531, for example, he had to grant to the Fuggers eight years of mining rights in Spanish lands south of Peru (present-day Bolivia and Chile).

Divided Realms

European rulers viewed religious division as a dangerous challenge to the unity and stability of their rule. Subjects who considered their rulers heretics or blasphemers could only cause trouble, and religious differences encouraged the formation of competing noble factions, which easily led to violence when weak monarchs or children ruled.

France King Francis I tolerated Protestants until the Affair of the Placards in 1534. Even then, the government did not try to root out Protestantism, and the Reformed (Calvinist) church grew steadily. During the 1540s and 1550s, many French noble families—including some of the most powerful—converted to Calvinism and afforded the Protestants a measure of protection, especially in southern and western France. Francis and his successor, Henry II (r. 1547–1559), succeeded in maintaining a balance of power between Catholics and Calvinists, but after Henry's death the weakened monarchy could no longer hold together the fragile realm. The real drama of the Reformation in France took place after 1560, when the country plunged into four decades of religious wars, whose savagery was unparalleled elsewhere in Europe (see Chapter 15).

England and Scotland Religious divisions at the very top threatened the control of the English and Scottish rulers. Before his death in 1547, Henry VIII had succeeded in making himself head of the Church of England, but the nature of that church remained ambiguous. The advisers of the boy king Edward VI (r. 1547–1553) furthered the Protestant cause by welcoming prominent religious refugees from the continent. The refugees had been deeply influenced by Calvinism and wanted to see England move in that austere direction. But Edward died at age fifteen, opening the way to his Catholic half sister, Mary Tudor, who had been restored to the line of succession by an act of Parliament under Henry VIII in 1544.

When Mary (r. 1553–1558) came to the throne, she restored Catholicism and persecuted Protestants. Nearly three hundred Protestants perished at the stake, and more than eight hundred fled to the Protestant German states and Switzerland. Finally, when Anne Boleyn's daughter, Elizabeth, succeeded her half sister Mary, becoming Queen Elizabeth I (r. 1558–1603), the English Protestant cause again gained momentum. Under Elizabeth's leadership, Protestantism came to define the character of the English nation, though the influence of Calvinism within it was still a cause for dispute. Catholics were tolerated only if they kept their opinions on religion and politics to themselves. A tentative but nonetheless real peace returned to England.

Still another pattern of religious politics unfolded in Scotland, where powerful noble clans directly challenged royal power. Protestants formed a small minority in Scotland until the 1550s. The most prominent Scottish reformer, John Knox (1514–1572), spent many of his early years in exile in England and on the continent because of his devout Calvinism. At the center of Scotland's conflict over religion stood Mary of Guise, a French native and Catholic married to the king of Scotland, James V. After he died in 1542, she surrounded herself and her daughter Mary Stuart, also a Catholic and heir to the throne, with French advisers. When Mary Stuart married Francis, the son of Henry II and the heir to the French throne, in 1558 many Scottish noblemen, alienated by this pro-French atmosphere, joined the pro-English, anti-French Protestant cause.

John Knox helped bring matters to a head when he published in 1558 a diatribe against both Mary Tudor of England and Mary of Guise. The era's suspicion of female rulers and regents also played a part in the work, *The First Blast of the Trumpet against the Monstrous Regiment [Rule] of Women*. In 1560, Protestant nobles gained control of the Scottish Parliament and dethroned the regent Mary of Guise. Eventually they forced her daughter, Mary, by then known as queen of Scots, to flee to England, and installed Mary's infant son, James, as king. Scotland would turn toward the Calvinist version of the Reformation and thus establish the potential for conflict with England.

The German States In the German states, the Protestant princes and cities formed the Schmalkaldic League in 1531. Headed by the elector of Saxony and Philip of Hesse (the two leading Protestant princes), the league included most of the imperial cities. Opposing the league were Emperor Charles V, the bishops, and the few remaining Catholic princes. Although Charles had to concentrate on fighting the French and the Turks during the 1530s, he eventually secured the western Mediterranean and then turned his attention back home to central Europe to try to resolve the growing religious differences in his lands.

In 1541, Charles convened the Imperial Diet of Regensburg in an effort to mediate between Protestants and Catholics, only to see negotiations between the two sides rapidly break down. Rather than accept a permanent religious schism, Charles prepared to fight the Protestant Schmalkaldic League. War broke out in 1547, the year after Martin Luther's death. Using seasoned Spanish veterans and German allies, Charles occupied the German imperial cities in the south, restoring Catholic elites and suppressing the Reformation. When Protestant commanders could not agree on a joint strategy, Charles crushed the Schmalkaldic League's armies at Mühlberg in Saxony and captured the leading Lutheran princes. Jubilant, Charles restored Catholics' right to worship in Protestant lands while permitting Lutherans to keep their own rites. Protestant resistance to the declaration was deep and widespread: many pastors went into exile, and riots broke out in many cities. Charles's success did not last long. The Protestant princes regrouped, declared war in 1552, and chased

MAPPING THE WEST

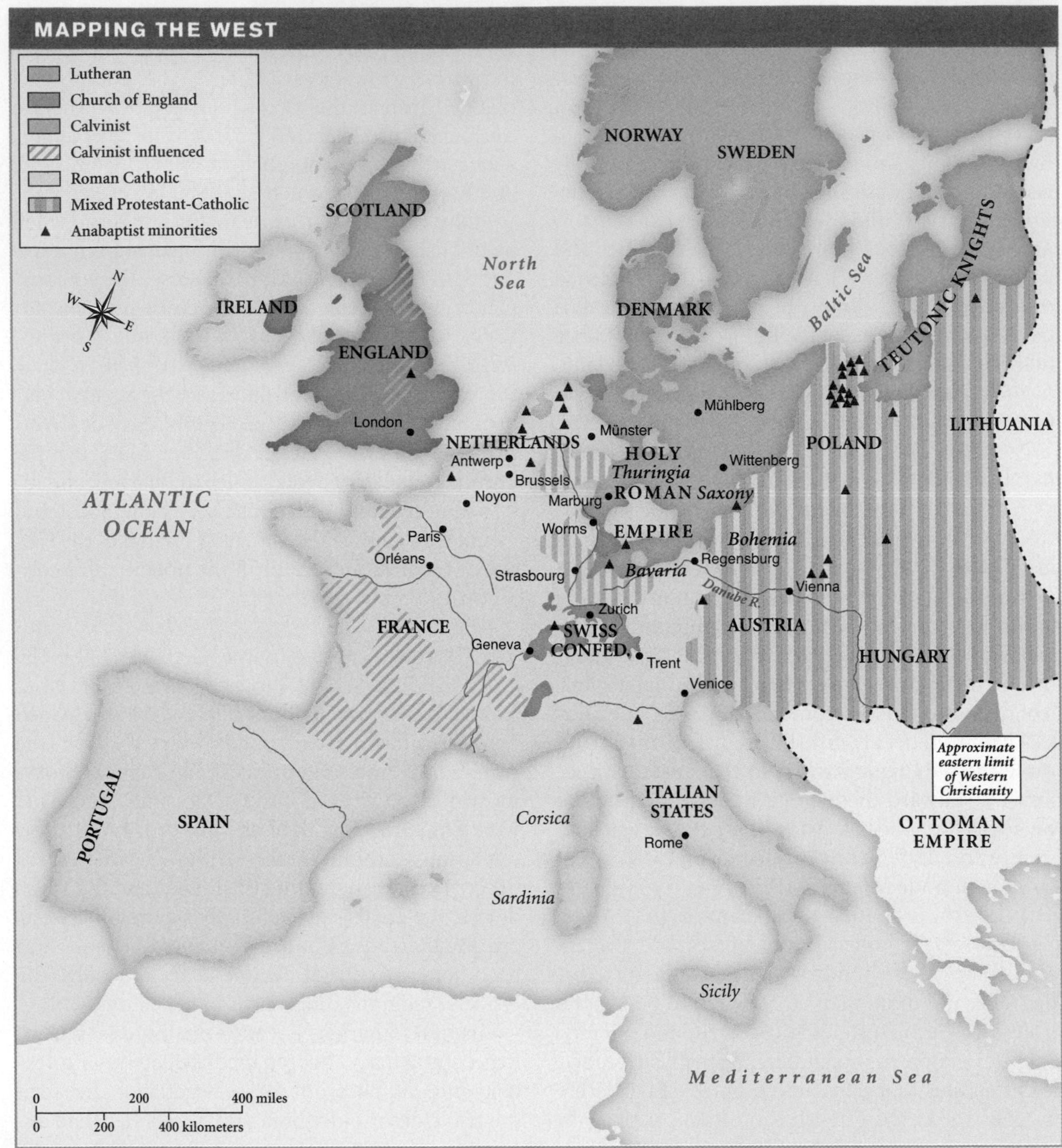

Reformation Europe, c. 1560

The fortunes of Roman Catholicism were at their lowest point around 1560. Northern Germany and Scandinavia owed allegiance to the Lutheran church; England broke away under a national church headed by its monarchs; and the Calvinist Reformation extended across large areas of western, central, and eastern Europe. Southern Europe remained solidly Catholic.

a surprised, unprepared, and practically bankrupt emperor back to Italy.

Forced to compromise, Charles V agreed to the **Peace of Augsburg** in 1555. The settlement recognized the Lutheran church in the empire; accepted the secularization of church lands but "reserved" the remaining ecclesiastical territories for Catholics; and, most important, established the principle that all princes, whether Catholic or Lutheran, enjoyed the sole right to determine the religion of their lands and subjects. Significantly, Calvinist, Anabaptist, and other dissenting groups were excluded from the settlement. Ironically, the religious revolt of the common people had culminated in a princes' reformation. As the constitutional framework for the Holy Roman Empire, the Augsburg settlement preserved a fragile peace in central Europe until 1618, but the exclusion of Calvinists would prompt future conflict.

Exhausted by decades of war and disappointed by the disunity in Christian Europe, Emperor Charles V resigned his many thrones in 1555 and 1556, leaving his Netherlandish-Burgundian and Spanish dominions to his son, Philip II, and his Austrian lands to his brother, Ferdinand (who was also elected Holy Roman Emperor to succeed Charles). Retiring to a monastery in southern Spain, the most powerful of the Christian monarchs spent his last years quietly seeking salvation.

Peace of Augsburg: The treaty of 1555 that settled disputes between Holy Roman Emperor Charles V and his Protestant princes. It recognized the Lutheran church and established the principle that all Catholic or Lutheran princes enjoyed the sole right to determine the religion of their lands and subjects.

REVIEW QUESTION **How did religious divisions complicate the efforts of rulers to maintain political stability and build stronger states?**

Conclusion

Charles V's decision to divide his empire reflected the tensions pulling Europe in different directions. Even as Charles's kingdom of Spain joined Portugal as a global power with new conquests overseas, Luther, Calvin, and a host of others sought converts to competing branches of Protestantism within the Holy Roman Empire. The reformers disagreed on many points of doctrine and church organization, but they all broke definitively from the Roman Catholic church. The pieces were never put together again. Portugal and Spain, the leaders in global exploration and conquest, remained resolutely Catholic, but as ruler of the Holy Roman Empire, where the Reformation began, Charles could not stifle the growing religious ferment. In the decades to come, Protestantism would spread, religious conflict would turn even more deadly, and emerging Protestant powers would begin to contest the global reach of Spain and Portugal.

FOR FURTHER EXPLORATION

- **For additional primary-source material from this period**, see *Sources of the Making of the West*, Fourth Edition.
- **For Web sites, images, and documents related to topics in this chapter**, visit *Make History* at bedfordstmartins.com/hunt.

Chapter 14 Review

Online Study Guide bedfordstmartins.com/hunt

Key Terms and People

In the grid below, identify the term or person and explain its historical significance. (To do this exercise online, go to bedfordstmartins.com/hunt.)

Term	Who or What & When	Why It Matters
Christopher Columbus (p. 453)		
Hernán Cortés (p. 457)		
Christian humanism (p. 459)		
Martin Luther (p. 460)		
Charles V (p. 461)		
John Calvin (p. 463)		
predestination (p. 464)		
Henry VIII (p. 464)		
Anabaptists (p. 468)		
Council of Trent (p. 470)		
Jesuits (p. 470)		
Suleiman the Magnificent (p. 475)		
Peace of Augsburg (p. 479)		

Review Questions

1. Which European countries led the way in maritime exploration and what were their motives?
2. How did Luther, Zwingli, Calvin, and Henry VIII each challenge the Roman Catholic church?
3. How did the forces for radical change unleashed by the Protestant Reformation interact with the urge for social order and stability?
4. How did religious divisions complicate the efforts of rulers to maintain political stability and build stronger states?

Making Connections

1. In what ways did the discovery of the Americas affect Europe?
2. Why was Charles V ultimately unable to prevent religious division in his lands?
3. How did the different religious groups respond to the opportunity presented by the printing press?
4. What motives besides religious differences caused war in this period?

Important Events

Date	Event
1492	Columbus reaches the Americas
1494	Italian Wars begin; Treaty of Tordesillas divides Atlantic world between Portugal and Spain
1516	Erasmus publishes Greek edition of the New Testament
1517	Luther composes ninety-five theses to challenge Catholic church
1519	Cortés captures Aztec capital of Tenochtitlán
1520	Luther publishes three treatises; Zwingli breaks from Rome
1525	German Peasants' War
1527	Charles V's imperial troops sack Rome
1529	Colloquy of Marburg addresses disagreements between German and Swiss church reformers
1534	Henry VIII breaks with Rome; Affair of the Placards in France
1536	Calvin publishes *Institutes of the Christian Religion*
1540	Jesuits established as new Catholic order
1545–1563	Catholic Council of Trent condemns Protestant beliefs, confirms Catholic doctrine
1547	Charles V defeats Protestants at Mühlberg
1555	Peace of Augsburg ends religious wars and recognizes Lutheran church in German states
1559	Treaty of Cateau-Cambrésis ends wars between Habsburg and Valois rulers

- Consider three events: **Luther publishes three treatises (1520), German Peasants' War (1525),** and **Catholic Council of Trent condemns Protestant beliefs, confirms Catholic doctrine (1545–1563).** How did Luther's treatises inspire the uprising of peasants and urban artisans? How did the changes wrought by the first two events prompt the Council of Trent, its goals, and its decisions?

SUGGESTED REFERENCES

A more global historical perspective is reshaping the study of both the European voyages of exploration and conquest and the Reformation, especially the Catholic renewal, which included a global missionary effort.

Christopher Columbus: http://www.ibiblio.org/expo/1492.exhibit/Intro.html

Crosby, Alfred W. *The Colombian Exchange: Biological and Cultural Consequences of 1492.* 2003.

Donnelly, John Patrick. *Ignatius of Loyola: Founder of the Jesuits.* 2004.

Holder, R. Ward. *Crisis and Renewal: The Era of the Reformations.* 2009.

Hsia, R. Po-chia. *A Companion to the Reformation World.* 2006.

Knecht, Robert Jean. *The French Renaissance Court, 1483–1589.* 2008.

Luther's life and thought: http://www.luther.de/en

Marshall, Peter. *Religious Identities in Henry VIII's England.* 2006.

*Müntzer, Thomas. *Revelation and Revolution: Basic Writings of Thomas Müntzer.* 1993.

O'Malley, John W. *Trent and All That: Renaming Catholicism in the Early Modern Era.* 2002.

Reston, James. *Defenders of the Faith: Charles V, Suleyman the Magnificent, and the Battle for Europe, 1520–1536.* 2009.

*Schwartz, Stuart B. *Victors and Vanquished: Spanish and Nahua Views of the Conquest of Mexico.* 2000.

Stjerna, Kirsi. *Women and the Reformation.* 2009.

Subrahmanyam, Sanjay. *The Career and Legend of Vasco da Gama.* 1997.

*Symcox, Geoffrey, and Blair Sullivan. *Christopher Columbus and the Enterprise of the Indies: A Brief History with Documents.* 2005.

Yoran, Hanan. *Between Utopia and Dystopia: Erasmus, Thomas More, and the Humanist Republic of Letters.* 2010.

Zell, Katharina, and Elsie Anne McKee. *Church Mother: The Writings of a Protestant Reformer in Sixteenth-Century Germany.* 2006.

*Primary source.

ANTORFF
Der Spanier große tÿrannej
Verursachet diese wütterej
Da durch Antorff im niderlant
Der weitter welt gar wolbekant
Verdorben wirt, vnd gar verbrent,
Beraubt, vnd jungfrauwen geschent
Vil tausendt leuth vnschuldigs bloit
Vergoßen wirt, vnd grosse noit
Sigtt man mitt elendigem karmen
O Gott will dich ein mhal erbarmen
Deren so ietz seind im elend,
Damitt das morden neem ein endt.

Wars of Religion and the Clash of Worldviews

CHAPTER 15

1560–1648

In November 1576 Spain's soldiers sacked Antwerp, the commercial, artistic, and printing center of the Netherlands and Europe's wealthiest city. In eleven days of horror known as the Spanish Fury, the troops rampaged through the city, slaughtering seven to eight thousand people and burning down a thousand buildings, including the city hall. The king of Spain had sent an army of ten thousand men in 1566 to occupy his rebellious northern domains and punish Calvinists, who had smashed stained-glass windows and statues of the Virgin Mary in Catholic churches. By 1575, however, the king had run out of funds, and his men rioted after being unpaid for months. The Spanish Fury was far from an isolated incident in this time of religious upheaval. It showed, moreover, that violence often exploded from a dangerous mixture of religious, political, and economic motives.

When Martin Luther started the Protestant Reformation in 1517, he unknowingly set into motion cycles of religious bloodshed that slowed down at times only to intensify again and again. The first two generations of battles ended with the Peace of Augsburg in 1555. That agreement helped maintain a relative calm in the lands of the Holy Roman Empire by granting each ruler the right to determine the religion of his territory. In western Europe, however, religious strife multiplied after 1560 as Calvinists made inroads in France, the Netherlands, and England. In 1618, fighting broke out again in the Holy Roman Empire—and before it ended in 1648, the Thirty Years' War involved most of the European powers and desolated lands and peoples across central Europe. All in all, nearly constant warfare marked the century between 1560 and 1648. Like the Spanish Fury, these struggles began as religious disputes but soon revealed other motives; political ambitions,

Atrocities in Antwerp
The sixteenth-century Netherlandish artist Franz Hogenberg produced this engraving of the Spanish sack of Antwerp not long after the events took place. It shows the kinds of atrocities—rape, murder, pillage, and burning of houses—that would be committed repeatedly on both sides of the conflict between Catholics and Protestants. *(akg-images.)*

long-standing rivalries between the leading powers, and greed all raised the stakes of conflict.

Suffering only increased when a major economic downturn in the early seventeenth century led to food shortages, famine, and disease in much of Europe. These catastrophes hit especially hard in the central European lands devastated by the fighting of the Thirty Years' War and helped shift the balance of economic power to northwestern Europe, away from the Mediterranean and central Europe. Intellectual life did not stand still in this time of turbulence. A new understanding of the motion of the planets in the heavens and of mechanics on earth developed among experimenters in "natural philosophy," that is, what came to be called science. This scientific revolution ultimately reshaped Western attitudes in virtually every field of knowledge, but at its beginnings it still had to compete with traditional religious views and popular beliefs in magic and witchcraft.

CHAPTER FOCUS What were the long-term political, economic, and intellectual consequences of the conflicts over religious belief in this era?

Religious Conflicts Threaten State Power, 1560–1618

The Peace of Augsburg made Lutheranism a legal religion in the predominantly Catholic Holy Roman Empire, but it did not extend recognition to Calvinists. Although the followers of Martin Luther (Lutherans) and those of John Calvin (Calvinists) similarly refused the authority of the Catholic church, they disagreed with each other about religious doctrine and church organization. The rapid expansion of Calvinism after 1560 threatened to alter the religious balance of power in much of Europe. Calvinists challenged Catholic dominance in France, the Spanish-ruled Netherlands, Scotland, and Poland-Lithuania. In England, they sought to influence the new Protestant monarch, Elizabeth I. Calvinists were not the only source of religious contention, however. Philip II of Spain fought the Muslim Ottoman Turks in the Mediterranean and expelled the remnants of the Muslim population in Spain. To the east, the Russian tsar Ivan IV fought to make Muscovy the center of an empire based on Russian Orthodox Christianity.

French Wars of Religion, 1562–1598

Calvinism spread in France after 1555, when the Genevan Company of Pastors sent missionaries supplied with false passports and often disguised as merchants. Calvinist nobles provided military protection to local congregations and helped set up a national organization for the French Calvinist—or Huguenot—church. In 1562, rival Huguenot and Catholic armies began fighting a series of wars that threatened to tear the French nation into shreds (Map 15.1).

Religious Division in the Nobility By the end of the 1560s, nearly one-third of the nobles had joined the Huguenots, and they raised their own armies. Conversion to Calvinism in French noble families often began with the noblewomen. Charlotte de Bourbon, for example, fled from a Catholic convent and eventually married William of Orange, the leader of the anti-Spanish resistance in the Netherlands. Calvinist noblewomen protected pastors, provided money and advice, and helped found schools and establish relief for the poor.

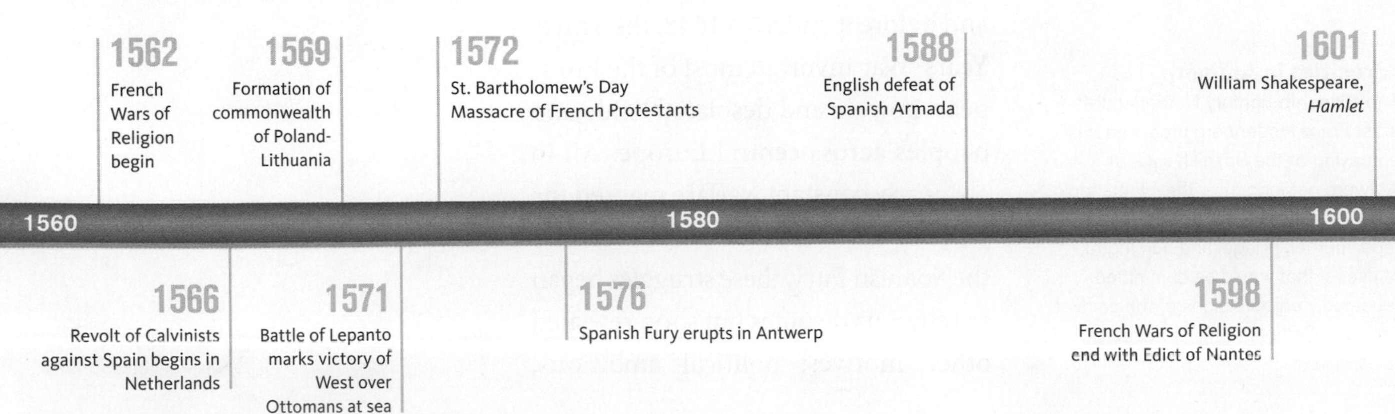

1562 French Wars of Religion begin
1569 Formation of commonwealth of Poland-Lithuania
1572 St. Bartholomew's Day Massacre of French Protestants
1588 English defeat of Spanish Armada
1601 William Shakespeare, *Hamlet*
1560
1580
1600
1566 Revolt of Calvinists against Spain begins in Netherlands
1571 Battle of Lepanto marks victory of West over Ottomans at sea
1576 Spanish Fury erupts in Antwerp
1598 French Wars of Religion end with Edict of Nantes

A series of family tragedies prevented the French kings from acting decisively to prevent the spread of Calvinism. King Henry II was accidentally killed during a jousting tournament in 1559, and his fifteen-year-old son, Francis, died soon after. Ten-year-old Charles IX (r. 1560–1574) became king, with his mother, **Catherine de Médicis**, as regent, or acting ruler. An ambassador commented on the weakness of Catherine's hold: "It is sufficient to say that she is a woman, a foreigner, and a Florentine to boot, born of a simple house, altogether beneath the dignity of the Kingdom of France." The Huguenots followed the lead of the Bourbon family, who were close relatives of the French king and stood first in line to inherit the throne if the Valois kings failed to produce a male heir. The most militantly Catholic nobles took their cues from the Guise family, who aimed to block Bourbon ambitions. Catherine tried to play the Bourbon and Guise factions against each other, but civil war erupted in 1562. Both sides committed terrible atrocities. Priests and pastors were murdered, and massacres of whole congregations became frighteningly commonplace.

St. Bartholomew's Day Massacre, 1572 Although a Catholic herself, Catherine feared the rise of Guise influence, so she arranged the marriage of the king's Catholic sister, Marguerite de Valois, to Henry of Navarre, a Huguenot

MAP 15.1 Protestant Churches in France, 1562
Calvinist missionaries took their message from their headquarters in Geneva across the border into France. The strongest concentration of Protestants was in southern France. The Bourbons, leaders of the Protestants in France, had their family lands in Navarre, a region in southwestern France that had been divided between France and Spain.

Catherine de Médicis: Italian-born mother of French king Charles IX (r. 1560–1574); she served as regent and tried but failed to prevent religious warfare between Calvinists and Catholics.

1618 Thirty Years' War begins

1625 Hugo Grotius publishes *The Laws of War and Peace*

1633 Galileo Galilei forced to recant his support of heliocentrism

1635 French join the Thirty Years' War by declaring war on Spain

1648 Peace of Westphalia ends Thirty Years' War

1620 1640 1660

and Bourbon. Just four days after the wedding, in August 1572, an assassin tried but failed to kill one of the Huguenot leaders. Violence against Calvinists spiraled out of control. On St. Bartholomew's Day, August 24, a bloodbath began, fueled by years of growing animosity between Catholics and Protestants. In three days, Catholic mobs murdered some three thousand Huguenots in Paris. Wherever Calvinists lacked military protection, they were at risk. Ten thousand Huguenots died in the provinces over the next six weeks. The pope joyfully ordered the church bells rung throughout Catholic Europe; Spain's Philip II wrote Catherine that it was "the best and most cheerful news which at present could come to me."

The massacre settled nothing. Huguenot pamphleteers now proclaimed their right to resist a tyrant who worshipped idols (a practice that Calvinists equated with Catholicism). This right of resistance was linked to a political notion of contract; upholding the true religion was part of the contract imagined as binding the ruler to his subjects. Both the right of resistance and the idea of a contract fed into the larger doctrine of constitutionalism — that a government's legitimacy rested on its upholding a constitution or contract between ruler and ruled. Constitutionalism was used to justify resistance movements from the sixteenth century onward. Protestants and Catholics alike now saw the religious conflict as an international struggle for survival that required aid to their fellow Catholics or Protestants in other countries. In this way, the French Wars of Religion paved the way for wider international conflicts over religion in the decades to come.

Henry IV and the Edict of Nantes

The religious division in France grew even more dangerous when Charles IX died and his brother Henry III (r. 1574–1589) became king. Like his brothers before him, Henry III failed to produce an heir. Next in line to the throne was none other than the Protestant Bourbon leader Henry of Navarre, a distant cousin of the Valois ruling family and brother-in-law of Charles and Henry. Convinced that Henry III lacked the will to root out Protestantism, the Guises formed the Catholic League, which requested help from Spanish king Philip II. Henry III responded with a fatal trick: in 1588, he summoned the two Guise leaders to a meeting and had his men kill them. A few months later, a fanatical Catholic monk stabbed Henry III to death, and Henry of Navarre became Henry IV (r. 1589–1610), despite Philip II's attempt to block his ascension with military intervention.

Henry IV soon concluded that to establish control over war-weary France he had to place the interests of the French state ahead of his Protestant faith. With the Catholic League threatening to declare his succession invalid, Henry publicly embraced Catholicism, reputedly explaining his conversion with the statement "Paris is worth a Mass." Within a few years he defeated the ultra-Catholic opposition and drove out the Spanish. In 1598, he made peace with Spain and issued the **Edict of Nantes**, in which he granted the Huguenots a large measure of religious toleration. The approximately 1.25 million Huguenots became a legally protected minority within an officially Catholic kingdom of some 20 million people. Protestants were free to worship in specified towns and were allowed their own troops, fortresses, and even courts.

Few believed in religious toleration as an ideal, but Henry IV followed the advice of those moderate Catholics and Calvinists — together called ***politiques*** — who urged him to give priority to the development of a durable state. Although their opponents, both Catholic and Protestant, hated them for their compromising spirit, the politiques believed that religious disputes could be resolved only in the peace provided by strong government. The French Catholic writer Michel de Montaigne (1533–1592) went even further than this pragmatic position and revived the ancient doctrine of skepticism, which held that total certainty is never attainable. On the beams of his study he painted the statement "All that is certain is that nothing is certain." Like toleration of religious differences, such skepticism was repugnant to Protestants and Catholics alike, both of whom were certain that their religion was the right one. Montaigne also questioned the common European habit of calling the native peoples of the New World barbarous and savage: "Everyone gives the title of barbarism to everything that is not in use in his own country."

The Edict of Nantes ended the French Wars of Religion, but Henry still needed to reestablish monarchical authority and hold the fractious nobles in check. He allowed rich merchants and lawyers to buy offices and, in exchange for an annual payment, pass their positions on to their heirs to sell them to someone else. This new social elite was known as the "nobility of the robe" (named after the robes that magistrates wore, much like those judges wear

---

Edict of Nantes: The decree issued by French king Henry IV in 1598 that granted the Huguenots a large measure of religious toleration.

politiques (poh lih TEEK)**:** Political advisers during the sixteenth-century French Wars of Religion who argued that compromise in matters of religion would strengthen the monarchy.

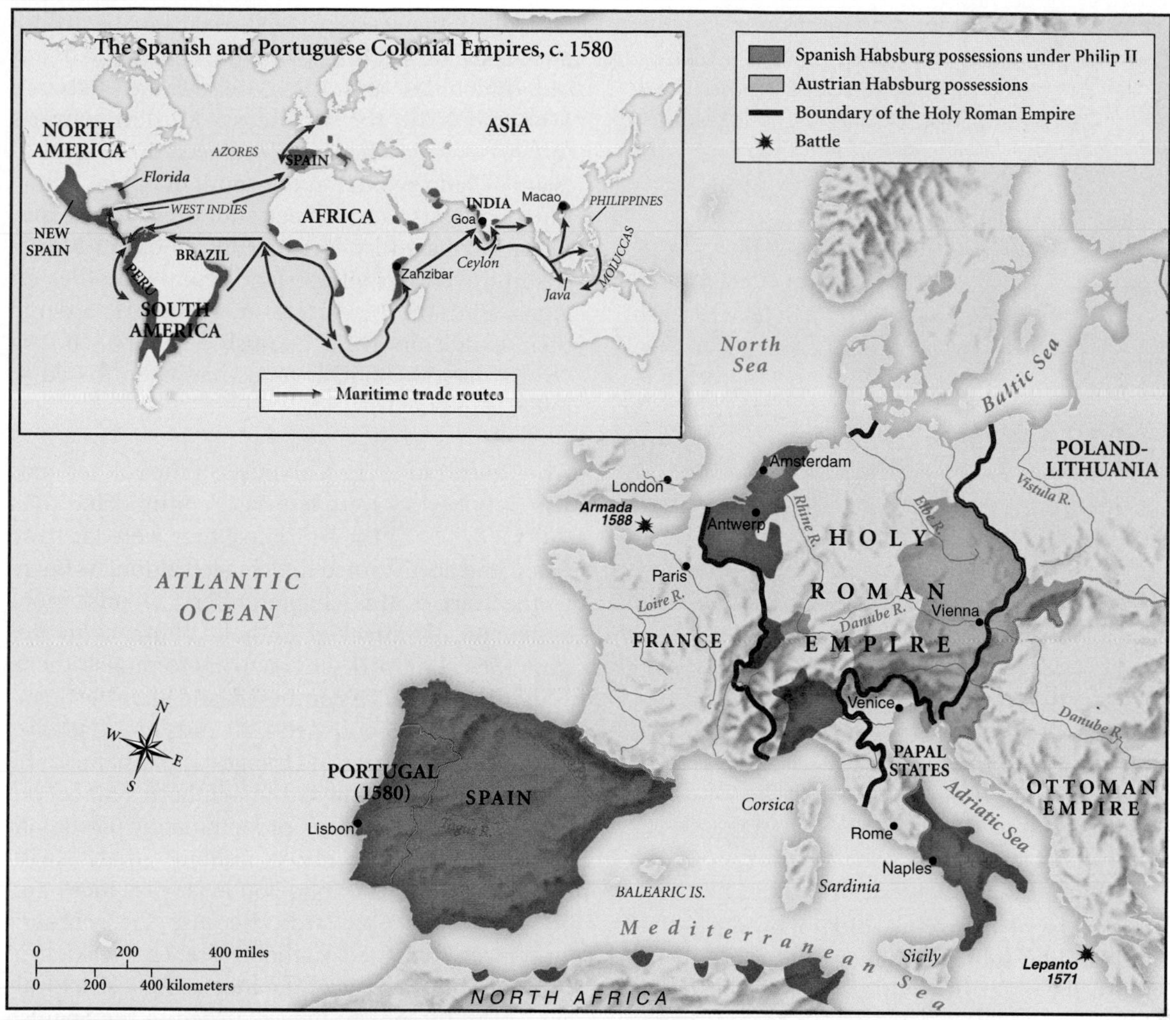

MAP 15.2 The Empire of Philip II, r. 1556–1598
Spanish king Philip II drew revenues from a truly worldwide empire. In 1580, he was the richest European ruler, but the demands of governing and defending his control of such far-flung territories eventually drained his resources.

today). Income raised by the increased sale of offices reduced the state debt and also helped Henry strengthen the monarchy. His efforts did not, however, prevent his enemies from assassinating him in 1610 after nineteen unsuccessful attempts.

Dutch Revolt against Spain

Although he failed to prevent Henry IV from taking the French throne in 1589, Philip II of Spain (r. 1556–1598) was the most powerful ruler in Europe (Map 15.2). In addition to the western Habsburg lands in Spain and the Netherlands, Philip had inherited from his father, Charles V, all the Spanish colonies recently settled in the New World of the Americas. Gold and silver funneled from the colonies supported his campaigns against the Ottoman Turks and the French and the English Protestants. But all of the money of the New World could not prevent Philip's eventual defeat in the Netherlands, where Calvinist rebels established the independent Dutch Republic, which soon vied with Spain, France, and England for commercial supremacy.

Philip II, the Catholic King A deeply devout Catholic, **Philip II** came to the Spanish throne at age twenty-eight determined to restore Catholic unity in Europe and lead the Christian defense against the Muslims. In his quest Philip benefited, ironically, from a series of misfortunes. His four wives all died, but through them he became part of four royal families: Portuguese, English, French, and Austrian. His brief marriage to Mary

Philip II: King of Spain (r. 1556–1598) and the most powerful ruler in Europe; he reigned over the western Habsburg lands and all the Spanish colonies recently settled in the New World.

The Battle of Lepanto
The Greek artist Antonio Vassilacchi painted this mural in 1600 to celebrate the Christian victory at the Battle of Lepanto. Vassilacchi was working in Venice, which was one of the main Christian allies in the campaign against the Turks. The victory was considered so important that it was celebrated in writings, medals, paintings, and sculptures. The mural captures the violence and confusion of the battle. *(Villa Barbarigo, Noventa Vicentina, Italy/Giraudon/The Bridgeman Art Library International.)*

Tudor (Mary I of England) did not produce an heir, but it and his subsequent marriage to Elisabeth de Valois, the sister of Charles IX and Henry III of France, gave him reason enough for involvement in English and French affairs. In 1578, the king of Portugal died fighting Muslims in Morocco, and two years later Philip took over this neighboring realm with its rich empire in Africa, India, and the Americas.

The Netherlands during the Revolt, c. 1580

Philip insisted on Catholic unity in his own possessions and worked to forge an international Catholic alliance against the Ottoman Turks. In 1571, he achieved the single greatest military victory of his reign when he joined with Venice and the papacy to defeat the Turks in a great sea battle off the Greek coast at **Lepanto**. Seventy thousand sailors and soldiers fought on the allied side, and eight thousand died. The Turks lost thirty thousand men. Spain now controlled the western Mediterranean but could not pursue its advantage because of chronic financial difficulties and threats elsewhere. Between 1568 and 1570, the Moriscos—Muslim converts to Christianity who remained secretly faithful to Islam—had revolted in the south of Spain, killing ninety priests and fifteen hundred Christians. Philip retaliated by forcing fifty thousand Moriscos to leave their villages and resettle in other regions. In 1609, his successor, Philip III, ordered their expulsion from Spanish territory, and by 1614 some 300,000 Moriscos had been forced to relocate to North Africa.

The Revolt of the Calvinists

The Calvinists of the Netherlands were less easily intimidated than the Moriscos: they were far from Spain and accustomed to being left alone. As noted at the start of this chapter, after Calvinist mobs systematically attacked Catholic churches in August 1566, Philip II sent an army to punish them. Calvinist resistance continued, and after the Spanish Fury of 1576 outraged Calvinists and Catholics alike, Prince William of Orange (whose name came from the lands he owned in southern France) led the Netherlands' seven predominantly Protestant northern provinces into a military alliance with the ten mostly Catholic southern provinces and drove out the Spaniards. Because the southern provinces remained Catholic, French-speaking in parts, and suspicious of the increasingly strict Calvinism in the north, they returned to the Spanish fold in 1579. Despite the assassination in 1584 of William of Orange, Spanish troops never regained control in the north. Spain would not formally recognize Dutch independence until 1648, but by the end of the sixteenth century the Dutch Republic (sometimes called Holland after the most populous of its seven provinces) was a self-governing state sheltering a variety of religious groups.

Religious toleration in the Dutch Republic developed for pragmatic reasons: the central government did not have the power to enforce religious orthodoxy. Urban merchant and professional families known as regents controlled the towns and provinces. Each province governed itself and sent delegates to the one common institution, the States General, which carried out the wishes of the strongest individual provinces and their ruling families. Although the princes of Orange resembled a ruling family, their powers paled next to those of local elites. One-

Lepanto: A site off the Greek coast where, in 1571, the allied Catholic forces of Spain's king Philip II, Venice, and the papacy defeated the Ottoman Turks in a great sea battle; the victory gave the Christian powers control of the Mediterranean.

Philip II of Spain
The king of Spain is shown here (kneeling in black) with his allies at the battle of Lepanto, the doge of Venice on his left and Pope Pius V on his right. El Greco painted this canvas, sometimes called *The Dream of Philip II*, in 1578 or 1579. The painting is typically mannerist in the way it crowds figures into every available space, uses larger-than-life or elongated bodies, and creates new and often bizarre visual effects. What can we conclude about Philip II's character from the way he is depicted here? *(© The National Gallery, London/Art Resource, NY.)*

third of the Dutch population remained Catholic, and local authorities allowed them to worship as they chose in private. The Dutch Republic also had a relatively large Jewish population because many Jews had settled there after being driven out of Spain and Portugal. From 1597, Jews could worship openly in their synagogues. This openness to various religions would help make the Dutch Republic one of Europe's chief intellectual and scientific centers in the seventeenth and eighteenth centuries.

Well situated for maritime commerce, the Dutch Republic developed a thriving economy based on shipping and shipbuilding. Dutch merchants favored free trade in Europe because they could compete at an advantage. Whereas elites in other countries focused on their landholdings, the Dutch looked for investments in trade. After the Dutch gained independence, Amsterdam became the main European money market for two centuries. The city was also a primary commodities market and a chief supplier of arms — to allies, neutrals, and even enemies. Dutch entrepreneurs produced goods at lower prices than competitors and marketed them more efficiently. The Dutch controlled many overseas markets thanks to their preeminence in seaborne commerce: by 1670, the Dutch commercial fleet was larger than the English, French, Spanish, Portuguese, and Austrian fleets combined.

Elizabeth I's Defense of English Protestantism

As the Dutch revolt unfolded, Philip II became increasingly infuriated with **Elizabeth I** (r. 1558–1603), who had succeeded her half sister Mary Tudor as queen of England. Philip had been married to Mary and had enthusiastically seconded Mary's efforts to return England to Catholicism. When Mary died in 1558, Elizabeth rejected Philip's proposal of marriage and promptly brought Protestantism back to England. Eventually, she provided funds and troops to the Dutch Protestant cause. As Elizabeth moved to solidify her personal power and the authority of the Church of England, she had to squash uprisings by Catholics in the north and at least two serious plots against her life. In the long run, however, her greatest challenges came from the Calvinist Puritans and Philip II.

Puritanism and the Church of England The **Puritans** were strict Calvinists who opposed all vestiges of Catholic ritual in the Church of England. After Elizabeth became queen, many Puritans returned from exile abroad, but Elizabeth resisted their demands for drastic

Elizabeth I: English queen (r. 1558–1603) who oversaw the return of the Protestant Church of England and, in 1588, the successful defense of the realm against the Spanish Armada.

Puritans: Strict Calvinists who in the sixteenth and seventeenth centuries opposed all vestiges of Catholic ritual in the Church of England.

Queen Elizabeth I of England
The Church of England's Prayerbook of 1569 included a hand-colored print of Elizabeth I saying her prayers. As queen, Elizabeth was also "supreme governor" of the Church of England; she named bishops and made final decisions about every aspect of church governance. The scepter or sword at her feet symbolizes her power. *(HIP/Art Resource, NY.)*

changes in church ritual and governance. The Church of England's Thirty-Nine Articles of Religion, issued under her authority in 1563, incorporated elements of Catholic ritual along with Calvinist doctrines. Puritan ministers angrily denounced the Church of England's "popish attire and foolish disguising, . . . tithings, holy days, and a thousand more abominations." To accomplish their reforms, Puritans tried to undercut the crown-appointed bishops' authority by placing control of church administration in the hands of a local presbytery, that is, a group made up of the minister and the elders of the congregation. Elizabeth rejected this Calvinist presbyterianism.

The Puritans nonetheless steadily gained influence. Known for their emphasis on strict moral lives, the Puritans tried to close England's theaters and Sunday fairs. Every Puritan father—with the help of his wife—was to "make his house a little church" by teaching the children to read the Bible. Believing themselves God's elect—those whom God has chosen for mercy and salvation—and England an "elect nation," the Puritans also pushed Elizabeth to help Protestants on the continent. Elizabeth initially resisted, but after Philip II annexed Portugal and began to interfere in French affairs, she sent funds to the Dutch rebels and in 1585 dispatched seven thousand soldiers to help them.

Triumph over Spain Although enraged by Elizabeth's aid to the Dutch rebels against his rule, Philip II bided his time as long as Elizabeth remained unmarried and her Catholic cousin Mary Stuart, better known as Mary, queen of Scots, stood next in line to inherit the English throne. In 1568, Scottish Calvinists forced Mary to abdicate the throne of Scotland in favor of her one-year-old son James (eventually James I of England), who was then raised as a Protestant. After her abdication, Mary spent nearly twenty years under house arrest in England. In 1587, when a letter from Mary offering her succession rights to Philip was discovered, Elizabeth overcame her reluctance to execute a fellow monarch and ordered Mary's beheading.

Now determined to act, Philip II sent his armada (Spanish for "fleet") of 130 ships from Lisbon toward the English Channel in May 1588. The English scattered the Spanish Armada by sending blazing fire ships into its midst. A great gale then forced the Spanish to flee around Scotland. When the armada limped home in September, half the ships had been lost and thousands of sailors were dead or starving. Protestants throughout Europe rejoiced. Philip and Catholic Spain had suffered a crushing psychological blow. A Spanish monk lamented, "Almost the whole of Spain went into mourning."

By the time Philip II died in 1598, his great empire had begun to lose its luster. The costs of fighting the Ottomans, Dutch, English, and French mounted inexorably and finally bankrupted the treasury. In his novel *Don Quixote* (1605), the Spanish writer Miguel de Cervantes captured the disappointment of thwarted ambitions. Cervantes himself had been wounded at Lepanto. His novel's hero, a minor nobleman, reads so many romances and books of chivalry that he loses his sense of proportion and wanders the countryside futilely trying to mimic the heroic deeds he has come across in his reading. Philip's empire declined, but Cervantes's novel captured the imagination of readers ever after.

England could never have defeated Spain in a head-to-head battle on land, but Elizabeth made the most of her limited means and consolidated the country's position as a Protestant power. In her early years, she held out the prospect of marriage to many political suitors; but in order to maintain her—and England's—independence, she never married. Her successor, James I (r. 1603–1625), came to the throne as king of both Scotland and England. Shakespeare's tragedies *Hamlet* (1601), *King Lear* (1605), and *Macbeth* (1606), written around the time of James's succession, might all be read as commentaries on the uncertainties faced by Elizabeth and James. But Elizabeth's story, unlike Shakespeare's tragedies, had a happy ending; she left James secure in a kingdom of growing weight in world politics.

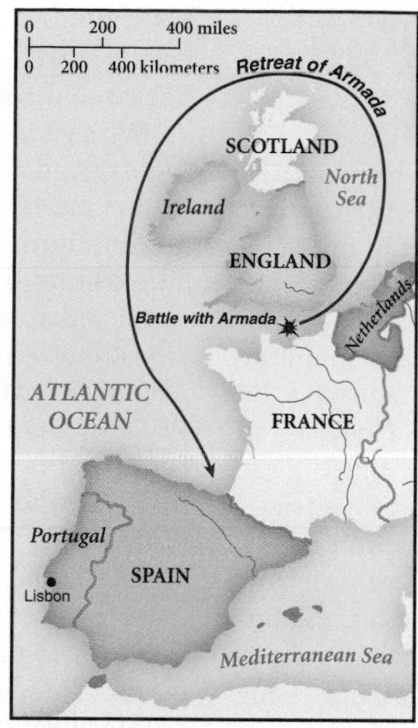

Retreat of the Spanish Armada, 1588

The Clash of Faiths and Empires in Eastern Europe

In the east, the most contentious border divided Christian Europe from the Islamic realm of the Ottoman Turks. Even after their defeat at Lepanto in 1571, the Ottomans continued their attacks, seizing Venetian-held Cyprus in 1573. In the Balkans, rather than forcibly converting their Christian subjects to Islam, the Turks allowed them to cling to the Orthodox faith. They also tolerated many prosperous Jewish communities, which grew with the influx of Jews expelled from Spain.

The Muscovite tsars officially protected the Russian Orthodox church, which faced no competition within Russian lands. Building on the base laid by his grandfather Ivan III, Tsar Ivan IV (r. 1533–1584) stopped at nothing in his endeavor to make Muscovy (the grand duchy centered on Moscow) the heart of a mighty Russian empire. Given to unpredictable fits of rage, Ivan tortured priests, killed numerous *boyars* (nobles), and murdered his own son with an iron rod during a quarrel. His epithet "the Terrible" reflects not only the terror he unleashed but also the awesome impression he evoked. Cunning and cruel, Ivan came to embody barbarism in the eyes of Westerners. One English visitor commented disapprovingly that the Russian government "is very similar to the Turkish, which they apparently try to imitate."

Ivan initiated Russian expansion eastward into Siberia and also tried to gain new territory to the west, when he attempted, unsuccessfully, to seize parts of present-day Estonia and Latvia to provide Russia direct access to the Baltic Sea. Two formidable foes blocked Ivan's plans for expansion: Sweden (which then included much of present-day Finland) and Poland-Lithuania. Their rulers hoped to annex the eastern Baltic provinces themselves. Poland and the grand duchy of Lithuania united into a single commonwealth in 1569 and controlled an extensive territory stretching from the Baltic Sea to deep within present-day Ukraine and Belarus. Poland-Lithuania, like the Dutch Republic, was one of the great exceptions to the general trend toward greater monarchical authority; the country's nobles elected their king and placed severe limits on his authority. Noble converts to Lutheranism or Calvinism feared religious persecution by the Catholic majority, so the Polish-Lithuanian nobles insisted that their kings accept the principle of religious toleration as a prerequisite for election.

Poland-Lithuania threatened the rule of Ivan's successors in Russia. After Ivan IV died in 1584, a terrible period of chaos known as the Time of Troubles ensued, during which the king of Poland-Lithuania tried to put his son on the Russian throne. In 1613, an army of nobles, townspeople, and peasants finally expelled the intruders and put on the throne a nobleman, Michael Romanov (r. 1613–1645), who established an enduring new dynasty. With the return of peace, Muscovite Russia resumed the process of state building.

Russia, Poland-Lithuania, and Sweden in the Late 1500s

REVIEW QUESTION How did state power depend on religious unity at the end of the sixteenth century and start of the seventeenth?

The Thirty Years' War, 1618–1648

Although the eastern states managed to avoid civil wars over religion in the early seventeenth century, the rest of Europe was drawn into the final and most deadly of the wars of religion, the Thirty Years' War. It began in 1618 with conflicts between Catholics and Protestants within the Holy Roman Empire and eventually involved most European states. By its end in 1648, many central European lands lay in ruins and the balance of power had shifted away from the Habsburg powers — Spain and Austria — toward France, England, and the Dutch Republic. Prolonged warfare created turmoil and suffering, but it also fostered the growth of armies and bureaucracies; out of the carnage would emerge centralized and powerful states that made increasing demands on ordinary people.

Origins and Course of the War

The fighting that devastated central Europe had its origins in a combination of religious dispute, ethnic competition, and political weakness. The Austrian Habsburgs officially ruled over the huge Holy Roman Empire, which comprised eight major ethnic groups. The emperor and four of the seven electors who chose him were Catholic; the other three electors were Protestants. The Peace of Augsburg of 1555 (see Chapter 14) was supposed to maintain the balance between Catholics and Lutherans, but it had no mechanism for resolving conflicts; tensions rose as the new Catholic religious order, the Jesuits, won many Lutheran cities back to Catholicism and as Calvinism, unrecognized under the peace, made inroads into Lutheran areas. By 1613, two of the three Protestant electors had become Calvinists.

These conflicts came to a head when the Catholic Habsburg heir Archduke Ferdinand was crowned king of Bohemia (present-day Czech Republic) in 1617. The Austrian Habsburgs held not only the imperial crown of the Holy Roman Empire but also a collection of separately administered royal crowns, of which Bohemia was one. Once crowned, Ferdinand began to curtail the religious freedom previously granted to Czech Protestants. When Ferdinand was elected emperor (as Ferdinand II, r. 1619–1637), the rebellious Czechs deposed him and chose in his place the young Calvinist Frederick V of the Palatinate (r. 1616–1623). A quick series of clashes ended in 1620 when the imperial armies defeated the outmanned Czechs at the battle of White Mountain, near Prague. Like the martyrdom of the religious reformer Jan Hus in 1415, White Mountain became an enduring symbol of the Czechs' desire for self-determination. They would not gain their independence until 1918.

White Mountain did not end the war, which soon spread to the German lands of the empire. Private mercenary armies (armies for hire) began to form during the fighting, and the emperor had little control over them. The meteoric rise of one commander, Albrecht von Wallenstein (1583–1634), showed how political ambition could trump religious conviction. A Czech Protestant by birth, Wallenstein offered in 1625 to raise an army for Ferdinand II and soon had in his employ 125,000 soldiers, who occupied and plundered much of Protestant Germany with the emperor's approval.

The Lutheran king of Denmark, Christian IV (r. 1596–1648), responded by invading northern Germany to protect the Protestants and to extend his own influence. Despite Dutch and English encouragement, Christian lacked adequate military support, and Wallenstein's forces defeated him. Emboldened by his general's victories, Ferdinand issued the Edict of Restitution in 1629, which outlawed Calvinism in the empire and reclaimed Catholic church properties confiscated by the Lutherans.

With Protestant interests in serious jeopardy, Gustavus Adolphus (r. 1611–1632) of Sweden marched into Germany in 1630. Declaring his support for the Protestant cause, he also intended to gain control over trade in northern Europe. His highly trained army of some 100,000 soldiers made Sweden, with a population of only one million, the supreme power of northern Europe. Hoping to block Spanish intervention in the war and win influence and perhaps territory in the Holy Roman Empire, the French monarchy's chief minister, Cardinal Richelieu (1585–1642), offered to subsidize the Lutheran Gustavus. This agreement between the Swedish Lutheran and French Catholic powers to fight the Catholic Habsburgs showed that state interests could outweigh religious considerations.

Gustavus defeated the imperial army and occupied the Catholic parts of southern Germany before he was killed at the battle of Lützen in 1632. Once again the tide turned, but this time it swept Wallenstein with it. Because Wallenstein was rumored to be negotiating with Protestant powers, Ferdinand dismissed his general and had him assassinated.

France openly joined the fray in 1635 by declaring war on Spain and soon after forged an alliance with the Calvinist Dutch to aid them in their ongoing struggle for official independence from Spain. Religion took a backseat to dynastic rivalry as the Catholic powers France and Spain pummeled each other. Advised by his minister Richelieu, who

The Violence of the Thirty Years' War
Toward the end of the Thirty Years' War, the German artist Hans Ulrich Franck began producing a series of twenty-five etchings aimed at capturing the horrors of the conflict. This wood engraving based on one such etching shows how violence was directed at women in particular. Unlike the print that opens this chapter, which shows a whole panorama of atrocities committed in a city, Franck's etchings focused on crimes committed by soldiers against civilians in small rural villages. *(akg-images.)*

held the high rank of cardinal in the Catholic church, the French king Louis XIII (r. 1610–1643) hoped to profit from the troubles of Spain in the Netherlands and from the conflicts between the Austrian emperor and his Protestant subjects. The Swedes kept up their pressure in Germany, the Dutch attacked the Spanish fleet, and a series of internal revolts shook the perennially cash-strapped Spanish crown. In 1640, peasants in the rich northeastern province of Catalonia rebelled, overrunning Barcelona and killing the viceroy; the Catalans resented government confiscation of their crops and demands that they house and feed soldiers on their way to the French frontier. The Portuguese revolted in 1640 and proclaimed independence like the Dutch. In 1643, the Spanish suffered their first major defeat at French hands. Although the Spanish were forced to concede independence to Portugal (annexed to Spain only since 1580), they eventually suppressed the Catalan revolt.

France, too, finally faced exhaustion after years of rising taxes and recurrent revolts. Richelieu died in 1642. Louis XIII followed him a few months later and was succeeded by his five-year-old son, Louis XIV. With yet another foreign queen mother—she was the daughter of the Spanish king—serving as regent and an Italian cardinal, Mazarin, providing advice, French politics once again moved into a period of instability, rumor, and crisis. All sides were ready for peace.

The Effects of Constant Fighting

When peace negotiations began in the 1640s, they did not come a moment too soon for the ordinary people of Europe. Some towns had faced up to ten or eleven prolonged sieges during the decades of fighting. Even worse suffering took place in the countryside. Peasants fled their villages, which were often burned down (see Document, "The Horrors of the Thirty Years' War, 1626," page 494). At times, desperate peasants revolted and attacked nearby castles and monasteries. War and intermittent outbreaks of plague cost some German towns one-third or more of their population. One-third of the inhabitants of Bohemia also perished.

Soldiers did not fare all that much better. An Englishman who fought for the Dutch army in 1633 described how he slept on the wet ground, got his boots full of water, and "at peep of day looked like a drowned ratt." Governments increasingly short of funds often failed to pay the troops, and frequent mutinies, looting, and pillaging resulted. Armies attracted all sorts of displaced people desperately in need of provisions. In the last year of the Thirty Years' War, the Imperial-Bavarian Army had 40,000 men entitled to draw rations—and more than 100,000 wives, prostitutes, servants, children, and other camp followers forced to scrounge for their own food.

DOCUMENT

The Horrors of the Thirty Years' War, 1626

A Lutheran weaver and churchwarden named Asmus Teufel, who lived in the North German town of Münden, recorded his memories of the fighting he saw in June 1626. More than two thousand people were killed when the emperor's army stormed the small town. Sieges and attacks on towns with military garrisons took place frequently during the war.

At your request I will write, at least as much as I can remember, about the terrible, unmentionable blood bath in this city. Much has gone forgotten because of my often difficult situation, and therefore it is not possible to describe everything.

. . . In the days of the siege there was an unceasing firing of large cannon from several places where they had batteries, and they killed many. On Tuesday 748 shots, including 200 exploding shells, horrible fire balls, which I recorded with my own hand. Then came the assault and the slaughter with halberds [poles with ax blades], and neither young nor old, not even the child in its mother's womb was spared. The truly blind, crippled, and dumb were cut down, even 8 preachers who had fled to the city from the villages. . . .

And although some people wanted to save their lives with money, and gave up hundreds, even thousands [of florins], the bloody murderers took the money from them, but then others came, who received nothing, and they cut them down. It's easy to imagine how they dealt with the womenfolk, many of whom they took back to their camp with them.

You can imagine what a wailing and screaming there was up at the castle, where they threw living and dead from the roof and out of the windows, even mothers with their children, so that in the trench behind the moat there was later more than enough evidence. They also cut people down, so that their blood flowed down the steps [of the castle], and at present there is still blood to see on the walls and on the tapestries.

Source: Asmus Teufel, *The Siege and Capture of Münden* (1626). Text discovered in the Münden town archive by Thomas Kossert, translated by Hans Medick and Benjamin Marschke.

Question to Consider

- **Why did the Thirty Years' War spark such gruesome violence, even against women, children, and the disabled?**

The Peace of Westphalia, 1648

The comprehensive settlement provided by the **Peace of Westphalia**—named after the German province where negotiations took place—would serve as a model for resolving future conflicts among warring European states. For the first time, a diplomatic congress convened to address international disputes, and those signing the treaties guaranteed the resulting settlement. A method still in use, the congress was the first to bring *all* parties together, rather than two or three at a time.

The Winners and Losers France and Sweden gained most from the Peace of Westphalia. Although France and Spain continued fighting until 1659, France acquired parts of Alsace and replaced Spain as the prevailing power on the continent. Baltic conflicts would not be resolved until 1661, but Sweden took several northern territories from the Holy Roman Empire (Map 15.3).

Peace of Westphalia: The settlement (1648) of the Thirty Years' War; it established enduring religious divisions in the Holy Roman Empire by which Lutheranism would dominate in the north, Calvinism in the area of the Rhine River, and Catholicism in the south.

The Habsburgs lost the most. The Spanish Habsburgs recognized Dutch independence after eighty years of war. The Swiss Confederation and the German princes demanded autonomy from the Austrian Habsburg rulers of the Holy Roman Empire. Each German prince gained the right to establish Lutheranism, Catholicism, or Calvinism in his state, a right denied to Calvinist rulers by the Peace of Augsburg in 1555. The independence ceded to German princes sustained political divisions that would remain until the nineteenth century and prepared the way for the emergence of a new power, the Hohenzollern Elector of Brandenburg, who increased his territories and developed a small but effective standing army. After losing considerable territory in the west, the Austrian Habsburgs turned eastward to concentrate on restoring Catholicism to Bohemia and wresting Hungary from the Turks.

The Peace of Westphalia settled the distributions of the main religions in the Holy Roman Empire: Lutheranism would dominate in the north, Calvinism in the area of the Rhine River, and Catholicism in the south. Most of the territorial changes in Europe remained intact until the nineteenth century. In the future, international warfare would be undertaken for reasons of national security, commercial ambition, or dynastic pride rather

MAP 15.3 The Thirty Years' War and the Peace of Westphalia, 1648
The Thirty Years' War involved many of the major continental European powers. The arrows marking invasion routes show that most of the fighting took place in central Europe in the lands of the Holy Roman Empire. The German states and Bohemia sustained the greatest damage during the fighting. None of the combatants emerged unscathed because even ultimate winners such as Sweden and France depleted their resources of men and money.

than to enforce religious uniformity. As the politiques of the late sixteenth century had hoped, state interests now outweighed motivations of faith in political affairs.

Growth of State Authority Warfare increased the reach of states: as armies grew to bolster the war effort, governments needed more money and more supervisory officials. The rate of land tax paid by French peasants doubled in the eight years after France joined the war. In addition to raising taxes, governments deliberately depreciated the value of the currency, which often resulted in inflation and soaring prices. Rulers also sold new offices and manipulated the embryonic stock and bond markets. When all else failed, they declared bankruptcy. The Spanish government, for example, did so three times in the first half of the seventeenth century. From Portugal to Muscovy, ordinary people resisted new taxes by forming makeshift armies and battling royal forces. With their colorful banners, unlikely leaders, strange names (the Nu-Pieds, or "Barefooted," in France, for instance), and crude weapons, the rebels usually proved no match for state armies, but they did keep officials worried and troops occupied.

To meet these new demands, monarchs relied on advisers who took on the role of modern prime ministers. Continuity in Swedish affairs, especially after the death of Gustavus Adolphus, largely depended on Axel Oxenstierna, who held office for more than forty years. Louis XIII's chief minister, Cardinal Richelieu, proclaimed the priority of ***raison d'état*** ("reason of state"), that is, the state's interest above all else. He silenced Protestants within France because they had become too independent, and he crushed noble and popular resistance to Louis's policies. He set up intendants — delegates from the king's

raison d'état **(ray ZOHN day TAH): French for "reason of state," the political doctrine, first proposed by Cardinal Richelieu of France, which held that the state's interests should prevail over those of religion.**

The Arts and State Power
In this enigmatic painting from 1656 called *Las Meninas* ("Maids of Honor"), the Spanish artist Diego Velázquez depicts Spanish King Philip IV's five-year-old daughter Margarita with her maids of honor, chaperone, bodyguard, a dwarf, and a large dog. The painter himself is working at a large canvas in the rear of the room. In the background on the left, a mirror reflects the upper bodies of the king and queen, who are presumably watching the scene. Which of these many figures is the real center of the painting? Like most monarchs of the time, Philip employed court painters like Velázquez to paint their portraits and contribute to their prestige. Ten years later Margarita would marry Holy Roman Emperor Leopold I, who was her uncle. *(Detail,* Las Meninas, *by Diego Velazquez [1599–1660]. Prado, Madrid, Spain / Giraudon / The Bridgeman Art Library International.)*

council dispatched to the provinces — to oversee police, army, and financial affairs.

To justify the growth of state authority and the expansion of government bureaucracies, rulers carefully cultivated their royal images. (See the illustration above.) James I of England argued that he ruled by divine right and was accountable only to God: "The state of monarchy is the supremest thing on earth; for kings are not only God's lieutenant on earth, but even by God himself they are called gods." He advised his son to maintain a manly appearance (some courtiers complained of his behavior toward certain male favorites): "Eschew to be effeminate in your clothes, in perfuming, preening, or such like." Appearance counted for so much that most rulers regulated who could wear which kinds of cloth and decoration, reserving the richest and rarest, such as ermine and gold, for themselves.

REVIEW QUESTION Why did a war fought over religious differences result in stronger states?

Economic Crisis and Realignment

The devastation caused by the Thirty Years' War deepened an economic crisis that was already under way. After a century of rising prices, caused partly by massive transfers of gold and silver from the New World and partly by population growth, in the early 1600s prices began to level off and even to drop, and in most places population growth slowed. With fewer goods being produced, international trade fell into recession. Agricultural yields

TAKING MEASURE

Precious Metals and the Spanish Colonies, 1550–1800

The graph shows that the production of gold and silver spurted upward between 1550 and 1590 and then declined until the beginning of the eighteenth century, paralleling the inflation of the last half of the sixteenth century and the following period of decline and depression. The graph also makes an important distinction between what was produced in the colonies, what was imported into Spain, and what the Spanish crown actually got as its share.

Source: From Timothy R. Walton, *The Spanish Treasure Fleets* (Sarasota, FL: Pineapple Press, 1994), 221.

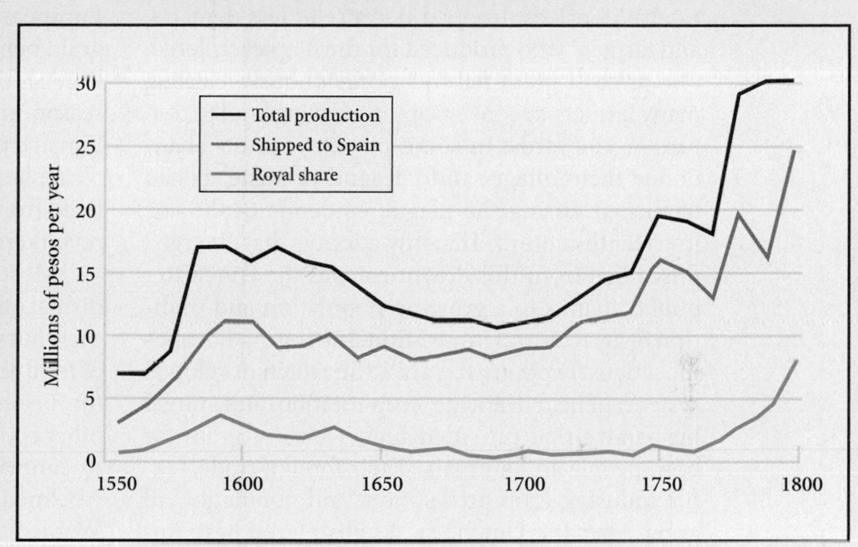

Question to Consider

■ **What can we conclude from this graph about the resources available to the Spanish king?**

also declined, and peasants and townspeople alike were less able to pay the escalating taxes needed to finance the wars. Famine and disease trailed grimly behind economic crisis and war, in some areas causing large-scale uprisings and revolts. Behind the scenes, the economic balance of power gradually shifted as northwestern Europe began to dominate international trade and broke the stranglehold of Spain and Portugal in the New World.

From Growth to Recession

Population grew and prices rose in the second half of the sixteenth century. Even though religious and political turbulence led to population decline in some cities, such as Antwerp, overall rates of growth remained impressive: in the sixteenth century, England's population grew by 70 percent and in parts of Spain the population grew by 100 percent (that is, it doubled). The supply of precious metals from the New World reached its height in the 1590s. (See "Taking Measure," above.) This flood of precious metals combined with population growth to fuel an astounding inflation in food prices in western Europe—400 percent in the sixteenth century—and a more moderate rise in the cost of manufactured goods. Wages rose much more slowly, at about half the rate of the increase in food prices. Governments always overspent revenues, and by 1600 most of Europe's rulers faced deep deficits.

Recession did not strike everywhere at the same time, but the warning signs were unmistakable. Foreign trade slumped as war and an uncertain money supply made business riskier. Imports of gold and silver declined, in part because so many of the native Americans who worked in Spanish colonial mines died from disease. Textile production fell in many countries and in some places nearly collapsed, largely because of decreased demand and a shrinking labor force. The trade in African slaves grew steadily between 1580 and 1630 and then it, too, declined by a third, though its growth would resume after 1650 and skyrocket after 1700. African slaves were first transported to the new colony of Virginia in 1619, foreshadowing a major transformation of economic life in the New World colonies.

Demographic slowdown also signaled economic trouble. Despite population growth in some areas,

Europe's total population may actually have declined, from 85 million in 1550 to 80 million in 1650. In the Mediterranean, growth had already stopped in the 1570s. The most sudden reversal occurred in central Europe as a result of the Thirty Years' War: one-fourth of the inhabitants of the Holy Roman Empire perished in the 1630s and 1640s. Population growth continued only in England, the Dutch Republic and the Spanish Netherlands, and Scandinavia.

Where the population stagnated or declined, agricultural prices dropped because of less demand, and farmers who produced for the market suffered. The price of grain fell most precipitously, causing many farmers to convert grain-growing land to pasture or vineyards. In some places, peasants abandoned their villages and left land to waste, as had happened during the plague epidemic of the late fourteenth century. The only country that emerged unscathed from this downturn was the Dutch Republic, thanks to a growing population and tradition of agricultural innovation. Inhabiting Europe's most densely populated area, the Dutch developed systems of field drainage, crop rotation, and animal husbandry that provided high yields of grain for both people and animals. Their foreign trade, textile industry, crop production, and population all grew. After the Dutch, the English fared best; unlike the Spanish, the English never depended on infusions of New World gold and silver to shore up their economy, and unlike most continental European countries, England escaped the direct impact of the Thirty Years' War.

Historians have long disagreed about the causes of the early-seventeenth-century recession. Some cite the inability of agriculture to support a growing population by the end of the sixteenth century; others blame the Thirty Years' War, the states' demands for more taxes, the irregularities in money supply resulting from rudimentary banking practices, or the waste caused by middle-class expenditures in the desire to emulate the nobility. To this list of causes, recent researchers have added climatic changes. (See "New Sources, New Perspectives," page 499.) Cold winters and wet summers meant bad harvests, and these natural disasters ushered in a host of social catastrophes. When the harvest was bad, prices shot back up and many could not afford to feed themselves.

Consequences for Daily Life

The recession of the early 1600s had both short-term and long-term effects. In the short term, it aggravated the threat of food shortages, increased the outbreaks of famine and disease, and caused people to leave their families and homes. In the long term, it deepened the division between prosperous and poor peasants and fostered the development of a new pattern of late marriages and smaller families.

Famine and Disease When grain harvests fell short, peasants immediately suffered because, outside of England and the Dutch Republic, grain had replaced more expensive meat as the essential staple of most Europeans' diets. By the end of the sixteenth century, the average adult European ate more than four hundred pounds of grain per year. Peasants lived on bread, soup with a little fat or oil, peas or lentils, garden vegetables in season, and only occasionally a piece of meat or fish. Usually the adverse years differed from place to place, but from 1594 to 1597 most of Europe suffered from shortages; the resulting famine triggered revolts from Ireland to Muscovy.

Most people, however, did not respond to their dismal circumstances by rebelling. They simply left their huts and hovels and took to the road in search of food and charity. Men left their families to search for better conditions in other parishes or even other countries. Those left behind might be reduced to eating chestnuts, roots, bark, and grass. Overwhelmed officials recorded pitiful tales of suffering. Women and children died while waiting in line for food at convents or churches. In eastern France in 1637, a witness reported, "The roads were paved with people. . . . Finally it came to cannibalism." Compassion sometimes gave way to fear when hungry vagabonds, who sometimes banded together to beg for bread, became more aggressive, occasionally threatening to burn a barn if they were not given food.

Successive bad harvests led to malnutrition, which weakened people and made them more susceptible to such epidemic diseases as the plague, typhoid fever, typhus, dysentery, smallpox, and influenza. Disease did not spare the rich, although many epidemics hit the poor hardest. The plague was feared most: in one year it could cause the death of up to half of a town's or village's population, and it struck with no discernible pattern. Nearly 5 percent of France's entire population died just in the plague of 1628–1632.

The Changing Status of the Peasantry Economic crisis widened the gap between rich and poor. Peasants paid rent to their landlords as well as fees for inheriting or selling land and tolls for using mills, wine presses, or ovens. States collected direct taxes on land and sales taxes on such consumer goods as salt, an essential preservative. Protestant and Catholic churches alike exacted a tithe (a tax equivalent to one-tenth of the

NEW SOURCES, NEW PERSPECTIVES

Tree Rings and the Little Ice Age

Global cooling helped bring about the economic crisis of the seventeenth century. Glaciers advanced, average temperatures fell, and winters were often exceptionally severe. Canals and rivers essential to markets froze over. Great storms disrupted ocean traffic — in fact, one storm changed the escape route of the Spanish Armada. Even in the valleys far from the mountain glaciers, cooler weather meant lower crop yields, which quickly translated into hunger and greater susceptibility to disease, leading in turn to population decline. Some historians of climate refer to the entire period 1600–1850 as the little ice age because glaciers advanced during this time and retreated only after 1850; others argue that the period 1550–1700 was the coldest, but either time frame includes the seventeenth century. Given the current debates about global warming, how can we sift through the evidence to come up with a reliable interpretation? Since systematic records of European temperatures were kept only from the 1700s onward, how do historians know that the weather was cooler?

Information about climate comes from various sources. The advance of glaciers can be seen in letters complaining to the authorities. In 1601, for example, panic-stricken villagers in Savoy (in the French Alps) wrote, "We are terrified of the glaciers . . . which are moving forward all the time and have just buried two of our villages." Yearly temperature fluctuations can be determined from the dates of wine harvests; growers harvested their grapes earliest when the weather was warmest and latest when it was coolest. Scientists study ice cores taken from Greenland to determine temperature variations; such studies seem to indicate that the coolest times were the periods 1160–1300, 1600–1700, and 1820–1850. The period 1730–1800 appears to have been warmer. Recently, scientists have developed techniques for sampling corals in the tropics and sediments on oceanic shelves to provide evidence of climate change.

But the most striking data come from dendrochronology, also called dendroclimatology: the science of dating events based on the study of tree rings. Dendrochronologists have taken timber samples from very old oak trees and also from ancient beams in buildings and archaeological digs and from logs left long undisturbed in northern bogs and riverbeds. In cold summers, trees lay down thin growth rings; in warm ones, thick rings. Information about tree rings confirms the conclusions drawn from wine harvest and ice core samples: the seventeenth century was relatively cold. Recent tree ring studies have shown that some of the coldest summers were caused by volcanic eruptions; according to a study of more than one hundred sites in North America and Europe, the five coldest summers in the past four hundred years were in 1601, 1641, 1669, 1699, and 1912 (four out of five in the seventeenth century), and all but the summer of 1699 came in years following recorded eruptions.

Questions to Consider

1. What were the historical consequences of global cooling in the seventeenth century?
2. Why would trees be especially valuable sources of information about climate?

Further Reading

Behringer, Wolfgang, *A Cultural History of Climate*. 2010.

Climate of the Past: http://www.clim-past.net

The Frozen Thames

This painting by Abraham Hondius of the frozen Thames River in London dates to 1677. The Thames froze several times in the 1670s and 1680s. Diarists recorded that shopkeepers even set up their stalls on the ice. The expected routines of daily life changed during the cooling down of the seventeenth century, and contemporaries were shocked enough by the changes to record them for posterity. *(© Museum of London.)*

The Life of the Poor
This mid-seventeenth-century painting by the Dutch artist Adriaen Pietersz van de Venne depicts the poor peasant weighed down by his wife and child. An empty food bowl signifies their hunger. In reality, many poor men abandoned their homes in search of work, leaving their wives behind to cope with hungry children and what remained of the family farm. What did the artist intend to convey about women? *(Allen Memorial Art Museum, Oberlin College, Mrs. F. F. Prentiss Fund, 1960.)*

parishioner's annual income); often the clergy took their tithe in the form of crops and collected it directly during the harvest. Any reversal of fortune could force peasants into the homeless world of vagrants and beggars, who numbered as much as 2 percent of the total population.

In England, the Dutch Republic, northern France, and northwestern Germany, the peasantry was disappearing. Improvements gave some peasants the means to become farmers who rented substantial holdings, produced for the market, and in good times enjoyed relative comfort and higher status. Those who could not afford to plant new crops such as maize (American corn) or to use techniques that ensured higher yields became simple laborers with little or no land of their own. One-half to four-fifths of the peasants did not have enough land to support a family. They descended deeper into debt during difficult times and often lost their land to wealthier farmers or to city officials intent on developing rural estates.

As the recession deepened, women lost some of their economic opportunities. Widows who had been able to take over their late husbands' trade now found themselves excluded by the urban guilds or limited to short tenures. Many women went into domestic service until they married, some for their entire lives. When town governments began to fear the effects of increased mobility from country to town and town to town, they carefully regulated the work of female servants, requiring women to stay in their positions unless they could prove mistreatment by a master.

Effects on Marriage and Childbearing European families reacted to economic downturn by postponing marriage and having fewer children. When hard times passed, more people married and had more children. But even in the best of times, one-fifth to one-quarter of all children died in their first year, and half died before age twenty. Childbirth still carried great risks for women, about 10 percent of whom died in the process. Even in the richest and most enlightened homes, childbirth often occasioned an atmosphere of panic. To allay their fears, women sometimes depended on magic stones, special pilgrimages, or prayers. Midwives delivered most babies; physicians were scarce, and even those who did attend births were generally less helpful than midwives. The Englishwoman Alice Thornton described in her diary how a doctor bled her to prevent a miscarriage after a fall (bloodletting, often by the application of leeches, was a common medical treatment); her son died anyway in a breech birth that almost killed her, too.

It might be assumed that families would have more children to compensate for high death rates, but beginning in the early seventeenth century and continuing until the end of the eighteenth, families in all ranks of society started to limit the number of children. Because methods of contraception were not widely known, they did this for the most part by marrying later; the average age at marriage during the seventeenth century rose from the early twenties to the late twenties. The average family had about four children. Poorer families seem to have had fewer children, wealthier ones more. Peasant couples, especially in eastern and southeastern Europe, had more children than urban couples because cultivation still required intensive manual labor—and having children was the most economical means of securing enough laborers.

The consequences of late marriage were profound. Young men and women were expected to put off marriage (and sexual intercourse) until their mid- to late twenties — if they were among the lucky 50 percent who lived that long and not among the 10 percent who never married. Because both Protestant and Catholic clergy alike stressed sexual fidelity and abstinence before marriage, the number of births out of wedlock was relatively small (2–5 percent of births); premarital intercourse was generally tolerated only after a couple had announced their engagement.

The Economic Balance of Power

Just as the recession of the early seventeenth century produced winners and losers among ordinary people, so too it created winners and losers among the competing states of Europe. The economies of southern Europe declined during this period, whereas those of the northwest emerged stronger. Competition in the New World reflected and reinforced this shift as the English, Dutch, and French rushed to establish trading outposts and permanent settlements to compete with the Spanish and Portuguese.

Regional Differences The new powers of northwestern Europe with their growing Atlantic trade gradually displaced the Mediterranean economies, which had dominated European commerce since the time of the Greeks and Romans. With expanding populations and geographical positions that promoted Atlantic trade, England and the Dutch Republic vied with France to become the leading mercantile and slave-trading powers. Northern Italian industries were eclipsed; Spanish commerce with the New World dropped. Amsterdam replaced Seville, Venice, Genoa, and Antwerp as the center of European trade and commerce. Even the plague contributed to this difference. Whereas central Europe and the Mediterranean countries took generations to recover from its ravages, northwestern Europe quickly replaced its lost population, no doubt because this area's people had suffered less from the effects of the Thirty Years' War and from the malnutrition related to the economic crisis.

All but the remnants of serfdom had disappeared in western Europe, yet in eastern Europe nobles reinforced their dominance over peasants, and the burden of serfdom increased. The price rise of the sixteenth century prompted Polish and eastern German nobles to increase their holdings and step up their production of grain for western markets. They demanded more rent and dues from their peasants, whom the government decreed must stay in their villages. In the economic downturn of the first half of the seventeenth century, peasants who were already dependent became serfs — completely tied to the land. A local official might complain of "this barbaric and as it were Egyptian servitude," but he had no power to fight the nobles. In Muscovy, the complete enserfment of the peasantry would eventually be recognized in the Code of Laws in 1649. Although enserfment produced short-term profits for landlords, in the long run it retarded economic development in eastern Europe and kept most of the population in a stranglehold of illiteracy and hardship.

Competition in the New World Economic realignment also took place across the Atlantic Ocean. Because Spain and Portugal had divided between themselves the rich spoils of South America, other prospective colonizers had to carve niches in seemingly less hospitable places, especially North America and the Caribbean (Map 15.4). Eventually, the English, French, and Dutch would dominate commerce with these colonies. Many European states, including Sweden and Denmark, rushed to join the colonial competition as a way of increasing national wealth. To this end, they chartered private joint-stock companies to enrich investors by

"Savages" of the New World
Scenes of cannibalism fascinated and horrified Europeans and they also helped justify brutal treatment of indigenous peoples. This 1564 colored engraving is the work of Theodore de Bry, a Flemish artist forced to flee Frankfurt because he was Protestant. De Bry also produced countless images of Spanish cruelty to the native peoples. Can you identify the Europeans in this engraving? *(Service Historique de la Marine, Vincennes, France / Giraudon / The Bridgeman Art Library International.)*

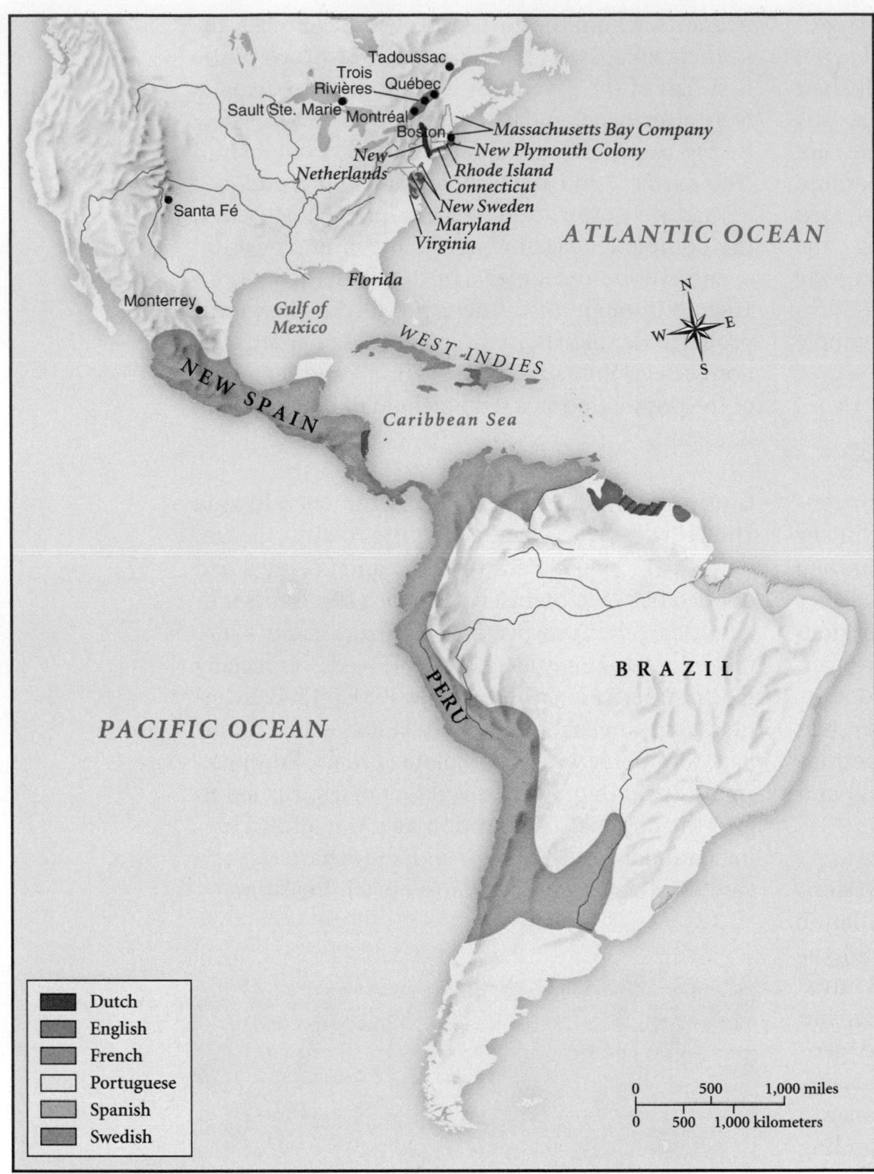

MAP 15.4 European Colonization of the Americas, c. 1640
Europeans coming to the Americas established themselves first in coastal areas. The English, French, and Dutch set up most of their colonies in the Caribbean and North America because the Spanish and Portuguese had already colonized the easily accessible regions in South America. Vast inland areas still remained unexplored and uncolonized in 1640.

importing fish, furs, tobacco, and precious metals, if they could be found, and to develop new markets for European products. British, French, Dutch, and Danish companies also began trading slaves.

In establishing permanent colonies, the Europeans created whole new communities across the Atlantic. Careful plans could not always surmount the hazards of transatlantic shipping, however. Originally, the warm climate of Virginia made it an attractive destination for the Pilgrims, a small English sect that attempted to separate from the Church of England. But in 1620 the *Mayflower*, which had sailed for Virginia with Pilgrim emigrants, landed far to the north in Massachusetts, where the settlers founded New Plymouth Colony. By the 1640s, the British North American colonies had more than fifty thousand people, of whom perhaps a thousand were Africans. Those numbers did not include the Indians native to the area, whose numbers had been decimated in epidemics and wars.

In contrast, French Canada had only about three thousand European inhabitants by 1640. Though thin in numbers, the French rapidly moved into the Great Lakes region. Fur traders sought beaver pelts to make the hats that had taken Paris fashion by storm. Jesuit missionaries lived with native American groups, learning their languages and describing their ways of life.

Both England and France turned some attention as well to the Caribbean in the 1620s and 1630s when they occupied the islands of the West Indies after driving off the native Caribs. These islands would prove ideal for a plantation economy of African slaves tending sugarcane and tobacco crops under the supervision of European settlers.

Even as the British and French moved into North America and the Caribbean, Spanish explorers traveled the Pacific coast up to what is now northern California and pushed into New Mexico. On the other side of the world, in the Philippines, the Spanish competed with local Muslim rulers and indigenous tribal leaders to extend their control. Catholic missionaries printed tracts in Spanish and the islands' native Tagalog and established a university in 1611. Spanish officials worked closely with the missionaries to rule over a colony composed of indigenous peoples, Spaniards, and some Chinese merchants.

REVIEW QUESTION What were the consequences of economic recession in the early 1600s?

The Rise of Science and a Scientific Worldview

The countries that moved ahead economically in the first half of the seventeenth century—England, the Dutch Republic, and to some extent France—turned out to be the most receptive to the rise of science and a scientific worldview. In the long-term process known as **secularization**, religion gradually became a matter of private conscience rather than public policy. Secularization did not entail a loss of religious faith, but it did prompt a search for nonreligious explanations for political authority and natural phenomena. During the late sixteenth and early seventeenth centuries, science, political theory, and even art began to break their long-standing bonds with religion. Scientists and scholars sought laws in nature to explain politics as well as movements in the heavens and on earth. The visual arts more frequently depicted secular subjects. A scientific revolution was in the making. Yet traditional attitudes did not disappear. Belief in magic and witchcraft pervaded every level of society. People of all classes believed that the laws of nature reflected a divine plan for the universe. They accepted supernatural explanations for natural phenomena, a view only gradually and partially undermined by new ideas.

The Scientific Revolution

Although the Catholic and Protestant churches encouraged the study of science and many prominent scientists were themselves clerics, the search for a secular, scientific method of determining the laws of nature undermined traditional accounts of natural phenomena. Christian doctrine had incorporated the scientific teachings of ancient philosophers, especially Ptolemy and Aristotle; now these came into question. A revolution in astronomy contested the Ptolemaic view, endorsed by the Catholic church, which held that the sun revolved around the earth. Startling breakthroughs took place in medicine, too, which laid the foundations for modern anatomy and pharmacology. Supporters of these new developments argued for a **scientific method** that would combine experimental observation and mathematical deduction. The use of scientific method culminated in the astounding breakthroughs of Isaac Newton at the end of the seventeenth century. Newton's ability to explain the motion of the planets, as well as everyday objects on earth, gave science enormous new prestige.

secularization: The long-term trend toward separating state power and science from religious faith, making the latter a private domain; begun in the seventeenth century, it prompted a search for nonreligious explanations for political authority and natural phenomena.

scientific method: The combination of experimental observation and mathematical deduction used to determine the laws of nature; first developed in the seventeenth century, it became the secular standard of truth.

The Revolution in Astronomy The traditional account of the movement of the heavens derived from the second-century Greek astronomer Ptolemy, who put the earth at the center of the cosmos. Above the earth were fixed the moon, the stars, and the planets in concentric crystalline spheres; beyond these fixed spheres dwelt God and the angels. The planets revolved around the earth at the command of God. In this view, the sun revolved around the earth; the heavens were perfect and unchanging, and the earth was "corrupted." Ptolemy insisted that the planets revolved in perfectly circular orbits (because circles were more "perfect" than other figures). To account for the actual elliptical paths that could be observed and calculated, he posited orbits within orbits, or epicycles.

In 1543, the Polish clergyman Nicolaus Copernicus (1473–1543) began the revolution in astronomy by publishing his treatise *On the Revolution of the Celestial Spheres*. Copernicus attacked the Ptolemaic account, arguing that the earth and planets revolved around the sun, a view known as **heliocentrism** (a sun-centered universe). He discovered that by placing the sun instead of the earth at the center of the system of spheres, he could eliminate many epicycles from the calculations. In other words, he claimed that the heliocentric view simplified the mathematics. Copernicus died soon after publishing his theories, but when the Italian monk Giordano Bruno (1548–1600) taught heliocentrism, the Catholic Inquisition (set up to seek out heretics) arrested him and burned him at the stake.

Copernicus's views began to attract widespread attention in the early 1600s, when astronomers systematically collected evidence that undermined the Ptolemaic view. A leader among them was the Danish astronomer Tycho Brahe (1546–1601), who designed his own instruments and observed a new star in 1572 and a comet in 1577. These discoveries called into question the traditional view that the universe was unchanging. Brahe still rejected heliocentrism, but the assistant he employed when he moved to Prague in 1599, Johannes Kepler (1571–1630), was converted to the Copernican view. Kepler continued Brahe's collection of planetary observations and used the evidence to develop his three laws of planetary motion, published between 1609 and 1619. Kepler's laws provided mathematical backing for heliocentrism and directly challenged the claim long held, even by Copernicus, that planetary motion was circular. Kepler's first law stated that the orbits of the

heliocentrism: The view articulated by Polish clergyman Nicolaus Copernicus that the earth and planets revolve around the sun.

The Trial of Galileo
In this anonymous painting of the trial held in 1633, Galileo appears seated on a chair in the center facing the church officials who accused him of heresy for insisting that the sun, not the earth, was the center of the universe (heliocentrism). Catholic officials forced him to recant or suffer the death penalty. Undated, the painting probably comes from a later time because contemporary paintings rarely included so many different figures each occupied in their own fashion. *(Erich Lessing/Art Resource, NY.)*

planets are ellipses, with the sun always at one focus of the ellipse.

The Italian astronomer Galileo Galilei (1564–1642) provided more evidence to support the heliocentric view and also challenged the doctrine that the heavens were perfect and unchanging. After learning in 1609 that two Dutch astronomers had built a telescope, Galileo built a better one and observed the earth's moon, four satellites of Jupiter, the phases of Venus (a cycle of changing physical appearances), and sunspots. The moon, the planets, and the sun were no more perfect than the earth, he insisted, and the shadows he could see on the moon could only be the product of hills and valleys like those on earth. Galileo portrayed the earth as a moving part of a larger system, only one of many planets revolving around the sun, not as the fixed center of a single, closed universe.

Because he recognized the utility of the new science for everyday projects, Galileo published his work in Italian, rather than Latin. But he meant only to instruct an educated elite of merchants and aristocrats. The new science, he claimed, suited "the minds of the wise," not "the shallow minds of the common people." After all, his discoveries challenged the commonsensical view that it is the sun that rises and sets while the earth stands still. If the Bible was wrong about motion in the universe, as Galileo's position implied, the error came from the Bible's use of common language to appeal to the lower orders. The Catholic church was not mollified by this explanation. In 1616, the church forbade Galileo to teach that the earth moves; then, in 1633, it accused him of not obeying the earlier order. Forced to appear before the Inquisition, he agreed to publicly recant his assertion about the movement of the earth to save himself from torture and death. (See Document, "Sentence Pronounced against Galileo," page 505, and the illustration above.) Afterward, Galileo lived under house arrest and could publish his work only in the Dutch Republic, which had become a haven for scientists and thinkers who challenged conventional ideas.

Breakthroughs in Medicine

Just as astronomical knowledge was based on Ptolemy's work, medical knowledge in Europe was, until the mid-sixteenth century, based on the writings of the second-century Greek physician Galen, Ptolemy's contemporary. Galen derived his knowledge of the anatomy of the human body from partial dissections. In the same year that Copernicus challenged the traditional account in astronomy (1543), the Flemish scientist Andreas Vesalius (1514–1564) did the same for anatomy. Drawing on public dissections (which had been condemned by the Catholic church since 1300) he performed himself, Vesalius refuted Galen's work in his illustrated anatomical text, *On the Construction of the Human Body*. The German physician Paracelsus (1493–1541) went even further than Vesalius. In 1527, he burned Galen's text at the University of Basel, where he was a professor of medicine. Though at the time most academic physicians taught medical theory, not practice, Paracelsus performed operations. He also pursued his interests in magic, alchemy,

DOCUMENT

Sentence Pronounced against Galileo (1633)

In 1633, the Roman Inquisition, a committee of cardinals of the Catholic church, considered the case against Galileo and pronounced its final judgment. It found Galileo guilty of heresy against Catholic doctrine for defending heliocentrism but allowed him to recant and thus avoid the death penalty usual in cases of heresy. Nearly 350 years later, in 1980, Pope John Paul II appointed a commission to review the evidence and verdict. After four years, the commission published its findings and concluded that the judges who condemned Galileo were wrong.

We say, pronounce, sentence, and declare that you, the above-mentioned Galileo, because of the things deduced in the trial and confessed by you as above, have rendered yourself according to this Holy Office [Inquisition] vehemently suspected of heresy, namely of having held and believed a doctrine which is false and contrary to the divine and Holy Scripture: that the sun is the center of the world and does not move from east to west, and the earth moves and is not the center of the world, and that one may hold and defend as probable an opinion after it has been declared and defined contrary to Holy Scripture. Consequently you have incurred all the censures and penalties imposed and promulgated by the sacred canons and all particular and general laws against such delinquents. We are willing to absolve you from them provided that first, with a sincere heart and unfeigned faith, in front of us you abjure, curse, and detest the above-mentioned errors and heresies, and every other error and heresy contrary to the Catholic and Apostolic Church, in the manner and form we will prescribe to you.

Furthermore, so that this serious and pernicious error and transgression of yours does not remain completely unpunished, and so that you will be more cautious in the future and an example for others to abstain from similar crimes, we order that the book *Dialogue* [*Dialogue Concerning the Two Chief World Systems*, published in 1632] by Galileo Galilei be prohibited by public edict.

Source: Maurice A. Finocchiaro, ed., *The Galileo Affair: A Documentary History* (Berkeley: University of California Press, 1989), 291.

Question to Consider

■ **Why did the Catholic church go to such dramatic lengths to repress Galileo's scientific argument in support of heliocentrism?**

and astrology, and he experimented with new drugs and thus helped establish the modern science of pharmacology.

Like Vesalius, the English physician William Harvey (1578–1657) used dissection to examine the circulation of blood within the body, demonstrating how the heart worked as a pump. The heart and its valves were "a piece of machinery," Harvey insisted. They obeyed mechanical laws just as the planets and earth revolved around the sun in a mechanical universe. Nature, he said, could be understood by experiment and rational deduction, not by following traditional authorities.

Scientific Method: Bacon and Descartes In the 1630s, the European intellectual elite began to accept the new scientific views. Ancient learning, the churches and their theologians, and long-standing popular beliefs all seemed to be undercut by the scientific method. Two men were chiefly responsible for spreading the reputation of the scientific method in the first half of the seventeenth century: the English Protestant politician Sir Francis Bacon (1561–1626) and the French Catholic mathematician and philosopher René Descartes (1596–1650). They represented the two essential halves of the scientific method: inductive reasoning through observation and experimental research, and deductive reasoning from self-evident principles.

In *The Advancement of Learning* (1605), Bacon attacked reliance on ancient writers and optimistically predicted that the scientific method would lead to social progress. The minds of the medieval scholars, he said, had been "shut up in the cells of a few authors (chiefly Aristotle, their dictator) as their persons were shut up in the cells of monasteries and colleges," and they could therefore produce only "cobwebs of learning" that were "of no substance or profit." Advancement would take place only through the collection, comparison, and analysis of information. Knowledge, in Bacon's view, must be empirically based (that is, gained by observation and experiment). Claiming that God had called the Catholic church "to account for their degenerate manners and ceremonies," Bacon looked to the Protestant English state, which he served as lord chancellor, for leadership on the road to scientific advancement.

Although Descartes agreed with Bacon's denunciation of traditional learning, he saw that the attack on tradition might only replace the dogmatism of the churches with the skepticism of Montaigne— that nothing at all was certain. Descartes aimed to establish the new science on more secure philosophical foundations, those of mathematics and logic. In his *Discourse on Method* (1637), he argued that mathematical and mechanical principles provided the key to understanding all of nature, including the actions of people and states. All prior assumptions must be repudiated in favor of one elementary principle: "I think, therefore I am." Everything else could—and should—be doubted, but even doubt showed the certain existence of someone thinking. Begin with the simple and go on to the complex, Descartes asserted, and believe only those ideas that present themselves "clearly and distinctly." He insisted that human reason could not only unravel the secrets of nature but also prove the existence of God. Although he hoped to secure the authority of both church and state, his reliance on human reason rather than faith irritated authorities, and his books were banned in many places. He moved to the Dutch Republic to work in peace. Scientific research, like economic growth, became centered in the northern, Protestant countries, where it was less constrained by church control than in the Catholic south.

Newton and the Consolidation of the Scientific Revolution The power of the new scientific method was dramatically confirmed in the grand synthesis of the laws of movement developed by the English natural philosopher Isaac Newton (1642–1727). Born five years after the publication of Descartes's *Discourse on Method* and educated at Cambridge University, where he later became a professor, Newton attacked an astounding variety of problems in mathematics, mechanics, and optics. For example, he established the basis for the new mathematics of moving bodies, the infinitesimal calculus. After years of labor, he finally brought his most significant mathematical and mechanical discoveries together in his masterwork, *Principia Mathematica* (1687). In it, he developed his law of universal gravitation, which explained both movement on earth and the motion of the planets. His law held that every body in the universe exerts over every other body an attractive force directly proportional to the product of their masses and inversely proportional to the square of the distance between them. This law of universal gravitation explained Kepler's elliptical planetary orbits just as it accounted for the way an apple fell to the ground.

To establish his law of universal gravitation, Newton first applied mathematical principles to formulate three fundamental physical laws: (1) in the absence of force, motion continues in a straight line; (2) the rate of change in the motion of an object is a result of the forces acting on it; and (3) the action of one object on another has an equal and opposite reaction. Newtonian physics thus combined mass, inertia, force, velocity, and acceleration—all key concepts in modern science—and made them quantifiable. Newton knew that the stakes were high: "From the same principles [of motion] I now demonstrate the frame of the System of the World."

Once set in motion, in Newton's view, the universe operated like a masterpiece made possible by the ingenuity of God. Newton saw no conflict between faith and science. He believed that by demonstrating that the physical universe followed rational principles, natural philosophers could prove the existence of God and so liberate humans from doubt and the fear of chaos. Even while laying the foundation for modern physics, optics, and mechanics, Newton spent long hours trying to calculate the date of the beginning of the world and its end with the second coming of Jesus. Others, less devout than Newton, envisioned a clockwork universe that had no need for God's continuing intervention.

Some scientists, especially those on the continent, were reluctant to accept Newton's planetary theories. The Dutch scientist Christian Huygens, for example, declared the concept of attraction (action at a distance) "absurd." But within a couple of generations, Newton's work had gained widespread assent, partly because of experimental verification.

The Natural Laws of Politics

In reaction to the religious wars, writers not only began to defend the primacy of state interests over those of religious conformity but also insisted on secular explanations for politics. The Italian political theorist Machiavelli had pointed in this direction with his advice to Renaissance princes in the early sixteenth century, but this secular intellectual movement gathered steam in the aftermath of the religious violence unleashed by the Reformation. Jean Bodin started the search for those principles, and Hugo Grotius developed ideas on government that would influence John Locke and the American revolutionaries of the eighteenth century.

Bodin The French Catholic lawyer and politique Jean Bodin (1530–1596) sought systematic secular answers to the problem of disorder in *The Six Books of the Republic* (1576). Comparing the different forms of government throughout history, he concluded that there were three basic types of sovereignty: monarchy, aristocracy, and democracy. Only strong monarchical power offered hope for maintaining order, he insisted. Bodin rejected any doctrine of the right to resist tyrannical authority: "I denied that it was the function of a good man or of a good citizen to offer violence to his prince for any reason, however great a tyrant he might be" (and, it might be added, whatever his ideas on religion). While Bodin's ideas helped lay the foundation for absolutism, the idea that the monarch should be the sole and uncontested source of power, his systematic discussion of types of governments implied that they might be subject to choice and undercut the notion that monarchies were ordained by God, as most rulers maintained.

Grotius and Natural Law During the Dutch revolt against Spain, the legal scholar Hugo Grotius (1583–1645) furthered secular thinking by attempting to systematize the notion of "natural law"—laws of nature that give legitimacy to government and stand above the actions of any particular ruler or religious group. Grotius argued that natural law stood beyond the reach of either secular or divine authority; it would be valid even if God did not exist (though Grotius himself believed in God). By this account, natural law—not scripture, religious authority, or tradition—should govern politics. Such ideas got Grotius into trouble with both Catholics and Protestants. His work *The Laws of War and Peace* (1625) was condemned by the Catholic church, while the Dutch Protestant government arrested him for taking part in religious controversies. Grotius's wife helped him escape prison by hiding him in a chest of books. He fled to Paris, where he got a small pension from Louis XIII and served as his ambassador to Sweden. The Swedish king Gustavus Adolphus claimed that he kept Grotius's book under his pillow even while at battle. Grotius was one of the first to argue that international conventions should govern the treatment of prisoners of war and the making of peace treaties.

Grotius's conception of natural law also challenged the widespread use of torture. Most states and the courts of the Catholic church used torture when a serious crime had been committed and the evidence seemed to point to a particular defendant but no definitive proof had been established. The judges ordered torture—hanging the accused by the hands with a rope thrown over a beam, pressing the legs in a leg screw, or just tying the hands very tightly—to extract a confession, which had to be given with a medical expert and notary present and had to be repeated without torture. Children, pregnant women, the elderly, aristocrats, kings, and even professors were exempt.

To be in accord with natural law, Grotius argued, governments had to defend natural rights, which he defined as life, body, freedom, and honor. Grotius did not encourage rebellion in the name of natural law or rights, but he did hope that someday all governments would adhere to these principles and stop killing their own and one another's subjects in the name of religion. Natural law and natural rights would play an important role in the founding of constitutional governments from the 1640s forward and in the establishment of various charters of human rights in our own time.

The Arts in an Age of Crisis

Two new forms of artistic expression—professional theater and opera—provided an outlet for secular values in an age of conflict over religious beliefs. William Shakespeare never referred to religious disputes in his plays, and he always set his most personal reflections on political turmoil and uncertainty in faraway times or places. Religion played an important role in the new mannerist and baroque styles of painting, however, even though many rulers commissioned paintings on secular subjects for their own uses.

Theater in the Age of Shakespeare The first professional acting companies performed before paying audiences in London, Seville, and Madrid in the 1570s. In previous centuries, traveling companies made their living by playing at major religious festivals and by repeating their performances in small towns and villages along the way. A huge outpouring of playwriting followed upon the formation of permanent professional theater companies. The Spanish playwright Lope de Vega (1562–1635) alone wrote more than fifteen hundred plays. Theaters were extremely popular despite Puritan opposition in England and Catholic objections in Spain. Shopkeepers, apprentices, lawyers, and court nobles crowded into open-air theaters to see everything from bawdy farces to profound tragedies.

The most enduring and influential playwright of the time—in fact, the man considered the greatest playwright of the English language—was William Shakespeare (1564–1616), who wrote three dozen plays (including histories, comedies, and tragedies) and was a member of a chief acting troupe. Although none of Shakespeare's plays were set in contemporary England, they reflected the concerns of his age: the nature of power and the crisis of authority. His tragedies in particular show the uncertainty and even chaos that result when power is misappropriated or misused. In *Hamlet* (1601), for example, the Danish prince Hamlet's mother marries the man who murdered his royal father and usurped the crown. In the end, Hamlet, his mother, and the usurper all die. One character in the final act describes Prince Hamlet's tragic story as one "Of carnal, bloody, and unnatural acts; / Of accidental judgments, casual slaughters; /

Of deaths put on by cunning and forced cause." Like many real-life people, Shakespeare's tragic characters found little peace in the turmoil of their times.

Mannerism and the Baroque in Art Although painting did not always touch broad popular audiences in the ways that theater could, new styles in art and especially church architecture helped shape ordinary people's experience of religion. In the late sixteenth century, the artistic style known as mannerism emerged in the Italian states and soon spread across Europe. Mannerism was an almost theatrical style that allowed painters to distort perspective to convey a message or emphasize a theme. The most famous mannerist painter, called El Greco because he was of Greek origin, trained in Venice and Rome before he moved to Spain in the 1570s. The religious intensity of El Greco's pictures found a ready audience in Catholic Spain, which had proved immune to the Protestant suspicion of ritual and religious imagery (see the illustration on page 489).

The most important new style was the **baroque**, which, like mannerism, originated in the Italian states. In place of the Renaissance emphasis on harmonious design, unity, and clarity, the baroque featured curves, exaggerated lighting, intense emotions, release from restraint, and even a kind of artistic sensationalism. Like many other historical designations, the word *baroque* ("irregularly shaped") was not used as a label by people living at the time; art critics in the eighteenth century coined the word to mean shockingly bizarre, confused, and extravagant, and until the late nineteenth century, art historians and collectors largely disdained the baroque.

Closely tied to Catholic resurgence after the Reformation, the baroque melodramatically reaffirmed the emotional depths of the Catholic faith and glorified both church and monarchy (see "Seeing History," page 509). The style spread from Rome to other Italian states and then into central Europe. The Catholic Habsburg territories, including Spain and the Spanish Netherlands, embraced the style. The Spanish built baroque churches in their American colonies as part of their massive conversion campaign.

Opera A new secular musical form, the opera, grew up parallel to the baroque style in the visual arts. First influential in the Italian states, opera combined music, drama, dance, and scenery in a grand sensual display, often with themes chosen to please the ruler and the aristocracy. Operas could be based on typically baroque sacred subjects or on traditional stories. Like many playwrights, including Shakespeare, opera composers often turned to familiar stories their audiences would recognize and readily follow. One of the most innovative composers of opera was Claudio Monteverdi (1567–1643), whose work contributed to the development of both opera and the orchestra. His earliest operatic production, *Orfeo* (1607), was based on Greek mythology. It required an orchestra of about forty instruments, and unlike previous composers, Monteverdi wrote parts for specific instruments as well as voices.

Magic and Witchcraft

Although the artists, political thinkers, and scientific experimenters increasingly pursued secular goals, most remained as devout in their religious beliefs as ordinary people. Shakespeare's plays showed, moreover, that audiences still believed in magic, witchcraft, and ghosts. Many scholars, like Paracelsus and Newton, studied alchemy alongside their scientific pursuits. Elizabeth I maintained a court astrologer who was also a serious mathematician, and many writers distinguished between "natural magic," which was close to experimental science, and demonic "black magic." The astronomer Tycho Brahe defended his studies of alchemy and astrology as part of natural magic.

Learned and ordinary people alike also firmly believed in witchcraft, that is, the exercise of magical powers gained by a pact with the devil. The same Jean Bodin who argued against religious fanaticism insisted on death for witches—and for those magistrates who would not prosecute them. In France alone, 345 books and pamphlets on witchcraft appeared between 1550 and 1650. Trials of witches peaked in Europe between 1560 and 1640, the very time of the celebrated breakthroughs of the new science. Montaigne was one of the few to speak out against executing accused witches: "It is taking one's conjectures rather seriously to roast someone alive for them," he wrote in 1580.

Belief in witches was not new in the sixteenth century. Witches had long been blamed for destroying crops and causing personal catastrophes ranging from miscarriage to madness. What was new was official persecution by state and religious authorities. In a time of economic crisis, plague, warfare, and the clash of religious differences, witchcraft trials provided an outlet for social stress and anxiety, legitimated by state power. Denunciation and persecution of witches coincided with the spread of reform, both Protestant and Catholic. Witch trials concentrated especially in the German lands of

---

baroque (buh ROHK): An artistic style of the seventeenth century that featured curves, exaggerated lighting, intense emotions, release from restraint, and even a kind of artistic sensationalism.

SEEING HISTORY

Religious Differences in Painting of the Baroque Period: Rubens and Rembrandt

Although the arts rarely reflect rigid religious or political divisions, artists do respond to the times in which they live. Protestant artists could not ignore the growing influence of the baroque style, but they also sought to distinguish themselves from it because of its association with the Catholic Counter-Reformation. The baroque style emphasized intense emotions, monumental decors, and even a kind of artistic sensationalism. Protestant artists, like Protestant preachers, wanted to produce strong reactions, too, but they placed more emphasis on the inner experience than on public display.

Here you see two paintings on the same biblical theme, one by Peter Paul Rubens (1577–1640), the great Catholic pioneer of the baroque style, and one by Rembrandt van Rijn (1606–1669), a Dutch Protestant. The subject of the paintings, taken from the Old Testament, is a scandalous one: when King David saw Bathsheba bathing, he fell in love with her, seduced her, and arranged for her husband to be killed in battle so that he might marry her.

Even though the central figure is the same in each painting, the artists' treatments are not. Look at the differences in settings, the number of people in the pictures, the colors, the lighting, and especially the facial expressions. In the Rubens, Bathsheba is about to receive a letter of summons from King David (shown on the balcony above), whereas in the Rembrandt she has just read the letter. Do not assume, however, that every difference in approach can be attributed to religious differences. Rembrandt created his own sensation by depicting Bathsheba almost entirely nude (and using his own mistress as the model).

Questions to Consider

1. **What are the differences in feeling conveyed in the two depictions of Bathsheba?**
2. **Why would Rembrandt draw attention to the sadness felt by Bathsheba, and how might this relate to the Protestant emphasis on each person's individual relationship to God? How do the setting and the lighting reinforce this emphasis on inwardness in the Rembrandt painting?**

Peter Paul Rubens, *Bathsheba at the Fountain*, c. 1635. *(Gemaeldegalerie Alte Meister, Dresden, Germany/© Staaliche Kunstsammlungen Dresden/The Bridgeman Art Library International.)*

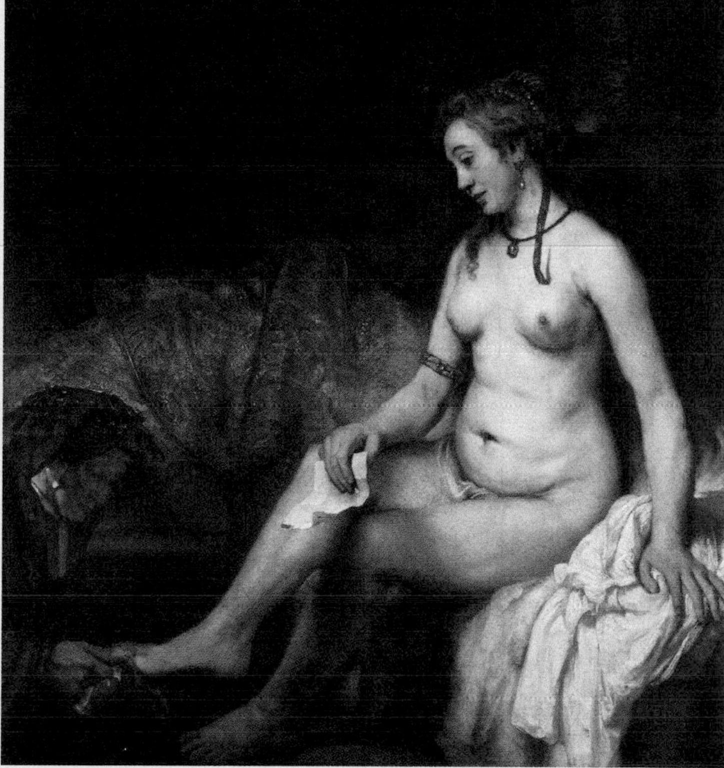

Rembrandt van Rijn, *Bathsheba at Her Bath*, 1654. *(Louvre, Paris, France/Giraudon/The Bridgeman Art Library International.)*

Witches' Kiss
In this hand-colored print from *The Compendium of Witches* (1608), a witch kisses the backside of the devil himself. The author of the compendium, Francesco Maria Guazzo, was an Italian priest in Milan. His compendium provided detailed descriptions of pacts between witches and the devil. *(© Charles Walker/Topham/The Image Works.)*

the Holy Roman Empire, the boiling cauldron of the Thirty Years' War.

The victims of the persecution were overwhelmingly female: women accounted for 80 percent of the accused witches in about 100,000 trials in Europe and North America during the sixteenth and seventeenth centuries. About one-third were sentenced to death. Before 1400, when witchcraft trials were rare, nearly half of those accused had been men. Why did attention now shift to women? Some official descriptions of witchcraft oozed lurid details of sexual orgies, in which women acted as the devil's sexual slaves. Social factors help explain the prominence of women among the accused. Accusers were almost always better off than those they accused. The poorest and most socially marginal people in most communities were elderly spinsters and widows. Because they were thought likely to hanker after revenge on those more fortunate, they were singled out as witches.

Witchcraft trials declined when scientific thinking about causes and effects raised questions about the evidence used in court: How could judges or jurors be certain that someone was a witch? The tide turned when physicians, lawyers, judges, and even clergy came to suspect that accusations were based on superstition and fear. As early as the 1640s, French courts ordered the arrest of witch-hunters and released suspected witches. In 1682, a French royal decree treated witchcraft as fraud and imposture, meaning that the law did not recognize anyone as a witch. In 1693, the jurors who had convicted twenty witches in Salem, Massachusetts, recanted, claiming: "We confess that we ourselves were not capable to understand. . . . We justly fear that we were sadly deluded and mistaken." The Salem jurors had not stopped believing in witches; they had simply lost confidence in their ability to identify them. This was a general pattern. Popular attitudes had not changed; what had changed was the attitudes of the elites. When physicians and judges had believed in witches and carried out official persecutions, with torture, those accused of witchcraft had gone to their deaths in record numbers. But when the same groups distanced themselves from popular beliefs, the trials and the executions stopped.

REVIEW QUESTION How could belief in witchcraft and the rising prestige of scientific method coexist?

Conclusion

The witchcraft persecutions reflected the traumas of these times of religious war, economic decline, and crises of political and intellectual authority. Faced with new threats, some people blamed poor widows or struggling neighbors for their problems; others joined desperate revolts, and still others emigrated to the New World to seek a better life. Even rulers confronted frightening choices: forced abdication, death in battle, or assassination often accompanied their religious decisions, and economic shocks could threaten the stability of their governments.

Deep differences over religion shaped the destinies of every European power in this period. These quarrels came to a head in the Thirty Years' War (1618–1648), which cut a path of destruction through central Europe and involved most of the European powers. Repulsed by the effects of religious violence on international relations, European rulers agreed to a peace that effectively removed disputes between Catholics and Protestants from the international arena. The growing separation of political motives from religious ones did not mean that violence or conflict had ended, however. Struggles for religious uniformity within states would continue, though on a smaller scale. Larger armies required more state involvement, and almost everywhere rulers emerged from these decades of war with expanded powers that they would seek to extend further in the second half of the seventeenth century. The growth of state power directly changed the lives of ordinary people: more men went into the armies, and most families paid higher taxes. The constant extension of state power is one of the defining themes of modern history; religious warfare gave it a jump-start.

MAPPING THE WEST

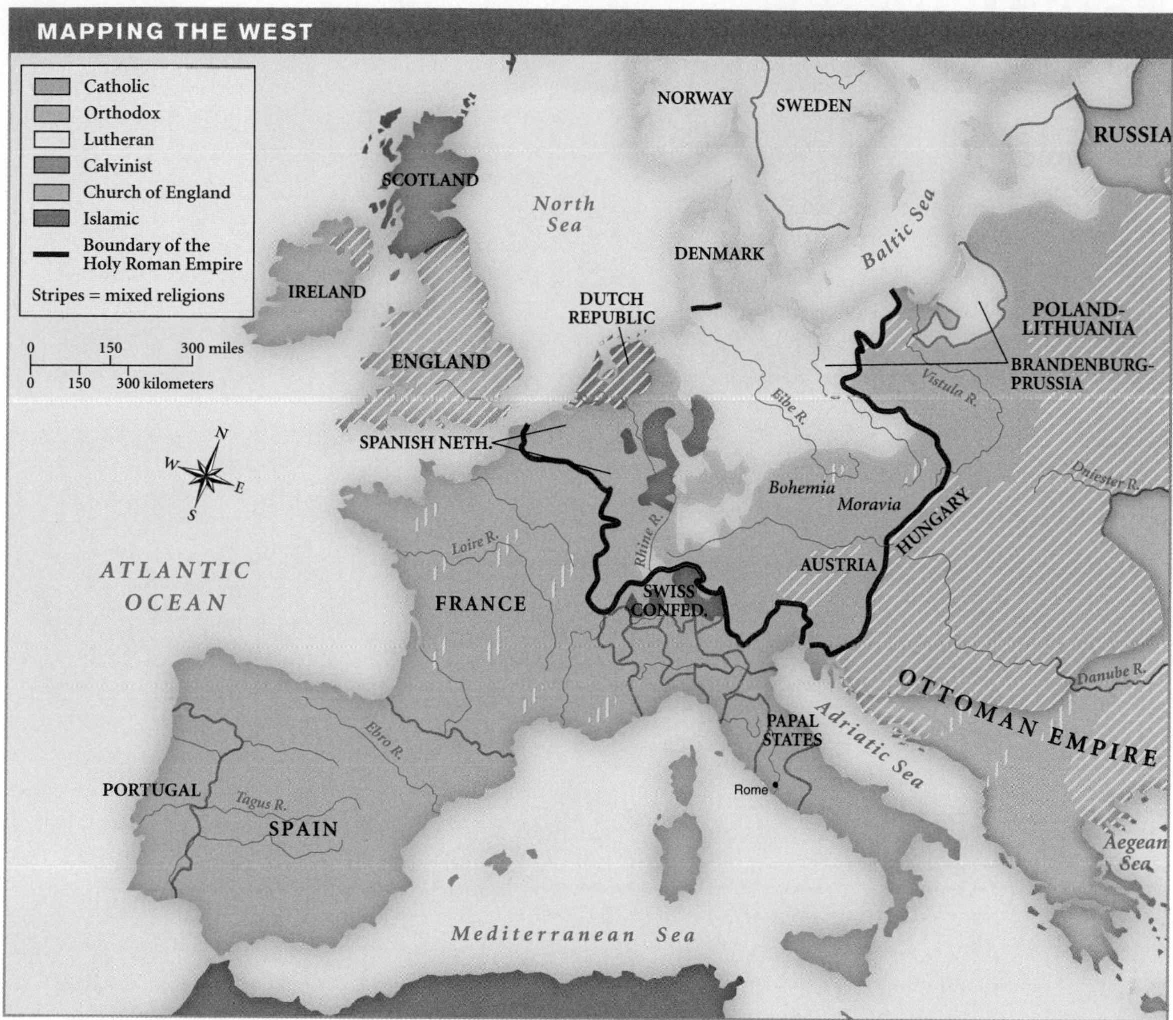

The Religious Divisions of Europe, c. 1648

The Peace of Westphalia recognized major religious divisions within Europe that have endured for the most part to the present day. Catholicism dominated in southern Europe, Lutheranism had its stronghold in northern Europe, and Calvinism flourished along the Rhine River. In southeastern Europe, the Islamic Ottoman Turks accommodated the Greek Orthodox Christians under their rule but bitterly fought the Catholic Austrian Habsburgs for control of Hungary.

For all their power and despite repeated efforts, rulers could not control economic, social, or intellectual trends. The economic downturn of the seventeenth century produced unexpected consequences for European states even while it made life miserable for many ordinary people; economic power and vibrancy shifted from the Mediterranean world to northwestern Europe because, in comparison, England, France, and the Dutch Republic suffered less from the fighting of the Thirty Years' War and recovered more quickly from the loss of population and production during bad times. They would become even more powerful in the decades to come.

Although it would be foolish to claim that everyone's mental universe changed because of the clash between religious and scientific worldviews, a truly monumental shift in attitudes had begun. Secularization encompassed the establishment of the scientific method as the standard of truth; the search for nonreligious foundations of political authority; and the growing popularity of nonreligious forms of art, such as theater and opera. Proponents of these changes did not renounce their religious beliefs or even hold them less fervently, but they did insist that attention to state interests and scientific knowledge could diminish religious violence and popular superstitions.

FOR FURTHER EXPLORATION

- **For additional primary-source material from this period**, see *Sources of the Making of the West*, Fourth Edition.
- **For Web sites, images, and documents related to topics in this chapter**, visit *Make History* at bedfordstmartins.com/hunt.

Chapter 15 Review

Online Study Guide bedfordstmartins.com/hunt

Key Terms and People

In the grid below, identify the term or person and explain its historical significance. (To do this exercise online, go to bedfordstmartins.com/hunt.)

Term	Who or What & When	Why It Matters
Catherine de Médicis (p. 485)		
Edict of Nantes (p. 486)		
politiques (p. 486)		
Philip II (p. 487)		
Lepanto (p. 488)		
Elizabeth I (p. 489)		
Puritans (p. 489)		
Peace of Westphalia (p. 494)		
raison d'état (p. 495)		
secularization (p. 503)		
scientific method (p. 503)		
heliocentrism (p. 503)		
baroque (p. 508)		

Review Questions

1. How did state power depend on religious unity at the end of the sixteenth century and start of the seventeenth?
2. Why did a war fought over religious differences result in stronger states?
3. What were the consequences of economic recession in the early 1600s?
4. How could belief in witchcraft and the rising prestige of scientific method coexist?

Making Connections

1. How did the balance of power shift in Europe between 1560 and 1648? What were the main reasons for the shift?
2. What were the limits to the growth of secularization?
3. What was the influence of New World colonies on Europe from 1560 to 1648?
4. How did religious conflict mix with political concerns in this period?

Important Events

Date	Event
1562	French Wars of Religion begin
1566	Revolt of Calvinists against Spain begins in Netherlands
1569	Formation of commonwealth of Poland-Lithuania
1571	Battle of Lepanto marks victory of West over Ottomans at sea
1572	St. Bartholomew's Day Massacre of French Protestants
1576	Spanish Fury erupts in Antwerp
1588	English defeat of Spanish Armada
1598	French Wars of Religion end with Edict of Nantes
1601	William Shakespeare, *Hamlet*
1618	Thirty Years' War begins
1625	Hugo Grotius publishes *The Laws of War and Peace*
1633	Galileo Galilei forced to recant his support of heliocentrism
1635	French join the Thirty Years' War by declaring war on Spain
1648	Peace of Westphalia ends Thirty Years' War

- Consider two events: **Thirty Years' War begins (1618)** and **Hugo Grotius publishes *The Laws of War and Peace* (1625)**. How does the latter event represent an effort to grapple with the climate of religious violence?

SUGGESTED REFERENCES

Religious conflict, the Thirty Years' War, science, witchcraft, and the travails of everyday life have all been the subject of groundbreaking research, yet the personalities of individual rulers still make for great stories, too.

Braudel, Fernand. *The Mediterranean and the Mediterranean World in the Age of Philip the Second.* Trans. Siân Reynolds. 2 vols. 1972, 1973.

Brown, Jonathan, and John Huxtable Elliott. *A Palace for a King: The Buen Retiro and the Court of Philip IV.* 2003.

*Diefendorf, Barbara B. *The Saint Bartholomew's Day Massacre: A Brief History with Documents.* 2008.

Elliott, John Huxtable. *Empires of the Atlantic World: Britain and Spain in America 1492–1830.* 2007.

Galileo Project: http://galileo.rice.edu

*Jacob, Margaret. *The Scientific Revolution: A Brief History with Documents.* 2010.

Konstam, Angus. *Lepanto 1571: The Greatest Naval Battle of the Renaissance.* 2003.

Levack, Brian P. *The Witch-Hunt in Early Modern Europe.* 2006.

Lynn, John A. *Women, Armies, and Warfare in Early Modern Europe.* 2008.

Madariaga, Isabel De. *Ivan the Terrible.* 2006.

Patterson, Benton Rain. *With the Heart of a King: Elizabeth I of England, Philip II of Spain, and the Fight for a Nation's Soul and Crown.* 2007.

Pitts, Vincent J. *Henri IV of France: His Reign and Age.* 2008.

Tracy, James D. *The Founding of the Dutch Republic: War, Finance, and Politics in Holland, 1572–1588.* 2008.

Wiesner-Hanks, Merry. *Women and Gender in Early Modern Europe.* 2008.

Wilson, Peter H. *The Thirty Years War: Europe's Tragedy.* 2009.

*Primary source.

CHAPTER 16

Absolutism, Constitutionalism, and the Search for Order

1640–1700

In May 1664, King Louis XIV of France organized the first of many spectacular entertainments for his court at Versailles, where he had recently begun construction of a magnificent new palace. More than six hundred members of his court attended the weeklong series of parades, races, ballets, plays, and fireworks displays called "The Delights of the Enchanted Island." Dressed in bright red and riding a horse whose bridle was studded with precious metals and stones, the king himself played the role of the romantic hero taken from Ariosto's sixteenth-century poem *Orlando Furioso* (see Chapter 14). In the opening parade, Louis was accompanied by an eighteen-foot-high float in the form of a chariot dedicated to Apollo, Greek god of the sun and Louis's personally chosen emblem. The king's favorite writers and musicians presented works specially prepared for the occasion, and each evening ended with a candlelit banquet served by masked and costumed servants. To the astonishment of everyone present, an Italian stage manager even created a huge floating whale and two whale calves on which rode the women playing the central heroine and her servants. Every detail of the festivities appeared in an official program that was published the same year to impress everyone with the king's grandeur and brilliance.

Louis XIV designed his pageants to awe those most dangerous to him, the leading nobles of his kingdom. To make his authority and glory concrete, the king relentlessly increased the power of his bureaucracy, expanded his army, and insisted on Catholic orthodoxy. This model of state building was known as **absolutism**, a system of government in which the ruler claims sole and uncontestable power. Other mid-seventeenth-century rulers followed Louis XIV's

Louis XIV and His Bodyguards
One of Louis XIV's court painters, the Flemish artist Adam Frans van der Meulen, depicted the king arriving at the palace of Versailles, still under construction. The painting dates from 1669, when none of the gardens, pools, or statues had yet been installed. Louis is the only figure facing the viewer, and his dress is much more colorful than that of anyone else in the painting. *(Réunion des Musées Nationaux/Art Resource, NY.)*

absolutism: A system of government in which the ruler claims sole and uncontestable power.

example or explicitly rejected it, but they could not afford to ignore it.

Although absolutism exerted great influence beginning in the mid-1600s, it faced competition from **constitutionalism**, a system in which the ruler shares power with an assembly of elected representatives. Constitutionalism provided a strong foundation for state power in England, the Dutch Republic, and the British North American colonies, while absolutism dominated in central and eastern Europe. Constitutionalism triumphed in England, however, only after one king had been executed as a traitor and another had been deposed. The English conflicts over the nature of authority found their most enduring expression in the writings of Thomas Hobbes and John Locke, which laid the foundations of modern political science.

The search for order took place not only in government and politics but also in intellectual, cultural, and social life. Artists sought means of glorifying power and expressing order and symmetry in new ways. As states consolidated their power, elites endeavored to distinguish themselves more clearly from the lower orders. The upper classes emulated the manners developed at court and tried in every way to distance themselves from anything viewed as vulgar or lower class. Officials, clergy, and laypeople all worked to reform the poor, now seen as a major source of disorder. Whether absolutist or constitutionalist, seventeenth-century states all aimed to extend control over their subjects' lives.

CHAPTER FOCUS What were the most important differences between absolutism and constitutionalism, and how did each system establish order?

constitutionalism: A system of government in which rulers share power with parliaments made up of elected representatives.

Louis XIV: Absolutism and Its Limits

French king **Louis XIV** (r. 1643–1715) personified the absolutist ruler, who in theory shared his power with no one. Louis personally made all important state decisions and left no room for dissent. In 1655, he reputedly told the Paris high court of justice, *"L'état, c'est moi"* ("I am the state"), emphasizing that state authority rested in him personally. Louis cleverly manipulated the affections and ambitions of his courtiers, chose as his ministers middle-class men who owed everything to him, built up Europe's largest army, and snuffed out every hint of religious or political opposition. Yet the absoluteness of his power should not be exaggerated. Like all other rulers of his time, Louis depended on the cooperation of many people: local officials who enforced his decrees, peasants and artisans who joined his armies and paid his taxes, creditors who loaned crucial funds, clergy who preached his notion of Catholicism, and nobles who joined court festivities rather than staying home and causing trouble.

The Fronde, 1648–1653

Louis XIV's absolutism built on a long French tradition of increasing centralization of state authority, but before he could establish his preeminence he had to weather a series of revolts known as the Fronde. Derived from the French word for a child's slingshot, the term was used by critics to signify that the revolts were mere child's play. In fact, however, they posed an unprecedented threat to the French crown.

Louis XIV: French king (r. 1643–1715) who in theory personified absolutism but in practice had to gain the cooperation of nobles, local officials, and even the ordinary subjects who manned his armies and paid his taxes.

1642–1646 English civil war between Charles I and Parliament

1648 Peace of Westphalia ends Thirty Years' War; Fronde revolt challenges royal authority in France; Ukrainian Cossack warriors rebel against king of Poland-Lithuania; Spain formally recognizes independence of Dutch Republic

1649 Charles I of England executed; new Russian legal code assigns all to hereditary class

1651 Thomas Hobbes publishes *Leviathan*

1660 Monarchy restored in England

1661 Slave code set up in Barbados

1640 — 1650 — 1660

Louis was only five when he came to the throne in 1643 upon the death of his father, Louis XIII, who with his chief minister, Cardinal Richelieu, had steered France through increasing involvement in the Thirty Years' War, rapidly climbing taxes, and innumerable tax revolts. Louis XIV's mother, Anne of Austria, and her Italian-born adviser and rumored lover, Cardinal Mazarin (1602–1661), ruled in the young monarch's name.

To meet the financial pressure of fighting the Thirty Years' War, Mazarin sold new offices, raised taxes, and forced creditors to extend loans to the government. In 1648, a coalition of his opponents presented him with a charter of demands that, if granted, would have given the parlements (high courts) a form of constitutional power with the right to approve new taxes. Mazarin responded by arresting the leaders of the parlements. He soon faced the series of revolts that at one time or another involved nearly every social group in France.

The Fronde posed an immediate menace to the young king. Fearing for his safety, his mother and members of his court took Louis and fled Paris. With civil war threatening, Mazarin and Anne agreed to compromise with the parlements. The nobles saw an opportunity to reassert their claims to power against the weakened monarchy and renewed their demands for greater local control, which they had lost when the French Wars of Religion ended in 1598. Leading noblewomen often played key roles in the opposition to Mazarin, carrying messages and forging alliances, especially when male family members were in prison. While the nobles sought to regain power and local influence, the middle and lower classes chafed at the repeated tax increases. Conflicts erupted throughout the kingdom as nobles, parlements, and city councils all raised their own armies to fight either the crown or each other, and rampaging soldiers devastated rural areas and disrupted commerce. The urban poor, such as those in the southwestern city of Bordeaux, sometimes revolted as well.

Louis XIV, Conqueror of the Fronde

In this painting of 1654, Louis XIV is depicted as the Roman god Jupiter, who crushes the discord of the Fronde (represented on the shield by the Medusa's head, made up of snakes). When the Fronde began, Louis was only ten years old; at the time of this painting, he was sixteen. The propaganda about his divine qualities had already begun. *(Réunion des Musées Nationaux/Art Resource, NY.)*

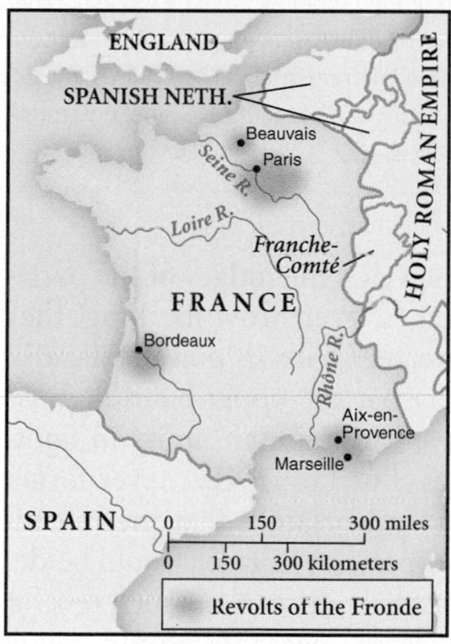

The Fronde, 1648–1653

1667 Louis XIV begins first of many wars that continue throughout his reign

1670

1678 Madame de Lafayette anonymously publishes *The Princess of Clèves*

1680

1683 Austrian Habsburgs break Turkish siege of Vienna

1685 Louis XIV revokes Edict of Nantes

1688 Parliament deposes James II; William, prince of Orange, and Mary take the throne

1690 John Locke publishes *Two Treatises of Government and Essay Concerning Human Understanding*

Louis XIV Visits the Royal Tapestry Workshop
This tapestry was woven at the Gobelins tapestry workshop between 1673 and 1680. It shows Louis XIV (at left, wearing a red hat) and his minister Jean-Baptiste Colbert (behind Louis, holding his hat) visiting the workshop on the outskirts of Paris. The workshop artisans scurry to show Louis all the luxury objects they manufacture. Louis bought the workshop in 1662 and made it a national enterprise for making tapestries and furniture. *(Réunion des Musées Nationaux/Art Resource, NY.)*

Neither the nobles nor the judges of the parlements really wanted to overthrow the king; they simply wanted a greater share in power. Mazarin and Anne eventually got the upper hand because their opponents failed to maintain unity in fighting the king's forces. But Louis XIV never forgot the humiliation and uncertainty that marred his childhood. His own policies as ruler would be designed to prevent the recurrence of any such revolts. Yet, for all his success, peasants would revolt against the introduction of new taxes on at least five more occasions in the 1660s and 1670s, requiring tens of thousands of soldiers to reestablish order. Absolutism was in part a fervent hope and not always a reality.

Court Culture as an Element of Absolutism

When Cardinal Mazarin died in 1661, Louis XIV, then twenty-two years old, decided to rule without a first minister. He described the dangers of his situation in memoirs he wrote later for his son's instruction: "Everywhere was disorder. My Court as a whole was still very far removed from the sentiments in which I trust you will find it." Louis listed many other problems in the kingdom, but none occupied him more than his attempts to control France's leading nobles, some of whom came from families that had opposed him militarily during the Fronde.

Typically quarrelsome, the French nobles had long exercised local authority by maintaining their own fighting forces, meting out justice on their estates, arranging jobs for underlings, and resolving their own conflicts through dueling. Louis set out to domesticate the warrior nobles by replacing violence with court ritual, such as the festivities at Versailles described at the beginning of this chapter. Using a systematic policy of bestowing pensions, offices, honors, gifts, and the threat of disfavor or punishment, Louis induced the nobles to cooperate with him and made himself the center of French power and culture. The aristocracy increasingly vied for his favor, attended the ballets and theatricals he put on, and learned the rules of etiquette he supervised — in short, became his clients, dependent on him for advancement. Great nobles competed for the honor of holding his shirt when he

DOCUMENT

Marie de Sévigné, Letter Describing the French Court (1675)

Marie de Rabutin-Chantal, marquise de Sévigné (1626–1696), was the most famous letter writer of her time. A noblewoman born in Paris, she frequented court circles and wrote about her experiences to her friends and relatives, especially her daughter. Although not published in her lifetime, her letters soon gained fame and were copied and read by those in her circle. She wrote her later letters with this audience in mind and so downplayed her own personal feelings, except those of missing her daughter, to whom she was deeply attached. This letter from 1675 to her daughter recounts court intrigue surrounding Louis XIV's mistress and the shock when one of France's leading generals was killed in battle. Though Sévigné enjoyed spending time at Louis XIV's court, she could also write about it with biting wit.

They [the king and his court] were to set off today for Fontainebleau [one of the king's castles near Paris], where the entertainments were to become boring by their very multiplicity. Everything was ready when a bolt fell from the blue that shattered the joy. The populace says it is on account of *Quantova* [Sévigné's nickname for the king's mistress, Madame de Montespan, with whom Louis XIV fathered seven children], the attachment is still intense. Enough fuss is being made to upset the curé [priest] and everybody else, but perhaps not enough for her, for in her visible triumph there is an underlying sadness. You talk of the pleasures of Versailles, and at the time when they were off to Fontainebleau to plunge into joys, lo and behold M. De Turenne [commander of the French armies during the Dutch War] killed, general consternation, Monsieur le Prince [de Condé, another leading general], rushing off to Germany, France in desolation. Instead of seeing the end of the campaigns and having your brother back [Sévigné's son served in the army], we don't know where we are. There you have the world in its triumph and, since you like them, surprising events.

Source: *Madame de Sévigné: Selected Letters*, trans. Leonard Tancock (New York: Penguin, 1982), 165.

Question to Consider

■ **How did Turenne's death reflect the limits to which order could be imposed by Louis XIV?**

dressed, foreign ambassadors squabbled for places near him, and royal mistresses basked in the glow of his personal favor. Far from the court, however, nobles could still make considerable trouble for the king, and royal officials learned to compromise with them.

Those who did come to the king's court were kept on their toes. The preferred styles changed without notice, and the tiniest lapse in attention to etiquette could lead to ruin. Marie-Madeleine Pioche de La Vergne, known as Madame de Lafayette, described the court in her novel *The Princess of Clèves* (1678): "The Court gravitated around ambition. Nobody was tranquil or indifferent—everybody was busily trying to better his or her position by pleasing, by helping, or by hindering somebody else." Elisabeth Charlotte, duchess of Orléans, the German-born sister-in-law of Louis, complained that "everything here is pure self-interest and deviousness." (See Document, "Marie de Sévigné, Letter Describing the French Court," above.)

Politics and the Arts | Louis XIV appreciated the political uses of every form of art. Mock battles, extravaganzas, theatrical performances, even the king's dinner—Louis's daily life was a public performance designed to enhance his prestige. Calling himself the Sun King, after Apollo, Greek god of the sun, Louis stopped at nothing to burnish this radiant image. He played Apollo in ballets performed at court; posed for portraits with the emblems of Apollo (laurel, lyre, and tripod); and adorned his palaces with statues of the god. He also emulated the style and methods of ancient Roman emperors. At a celebration for the birth of his first son in 1662, Louis dressed in Roman attire, and many engravings and paintings showed him as a Roman emperor. Commissioned histories vaunted his achievements, and coins and medals spread his likeness throughout the realm.

The king's officials treated the arts as a branch of government. The king gave pensions to artists who worked for him and sometimes protected writers from clerical critics. The most famous of these was the playwright Molière (the pen name of Jean-Baptiste Poquelin, 1622–1673), whose comedy *Tartuffe* (1664) made fun of religious hypocrites and was loudly condemned by church leaders. Louis forced Molière to delay public performances of the play after its premiere at the festivities of May 1664 but resisted calls for his dismissal. Louis's ministers not only set up royal academies of dance, painting, architecture, music, and science but also took control of the Académie française (French Academy), which to this day decides on correct usage of the French language. Louis's government regulated the number and locations of theaters and closely censored all forms of publication.

Music and theater enjoyed special prominence. Louis commissioned operas to celebrate royal marriages, baptisms, and military victories. His favorite composer, Jean-Baptiste Lully, wrote sixteen operas for court performances as well as many ballets. Louis himself danced in the ballets if a role seemed especially important. Playwrights often presented their new plays first to the court. Pierre Corneille and Jean Racine wrote tragedies set in Greece or Rome that celebrated the new aristocratic virtues that Louis aimed to inculcate: a reverence for order and self-control. All the characters were regal or noble, all the language lofty, all the behavior aristocratic.

The Palace of Versailles Louis glorified his image as well through massive public works projects. Veterans' hospitals and new fortified towns on the frontiers represented his military might. Urban improvements, such as the reconstruction of the Louvre palace in Paris, proved his wealth. But his most ambitious project was the construction of a new palace at Versailles, twelve miles from the turbulent capital. (See the illustration below.)

Building began in the 1660s. By 1685, the frenzied effort engaged thirty-six thousand workers, not including the thousands of troops who diverted a local river to supply water for pools and fountains. The gardens designed by landscape architect André Le Nôtre reflected the spirit of Louis XIV's rule: their geometrical arrangements and clear lines showed that art and design could tame nature and that order and control defined the exercise of power. Le Nôtre's geometrical landscapes were later imitated in places as far away as St. Petersburg and Washington, D.C. Versailles symbolized Louis's success in reining in the nobility and dominating Europe, and other monarchs eagerly mimicked French fashion and often conducted their business in French.

Yet for all its apparent luxury and frivolity, life at Versailles was often cramped and cold. Fifteen thousand people crowded into the palace's apartments, including all the highest military officers, the ministers of state, and the separate households of each member of the royal family. Refuse collected in the corridors during the incessant building, and thieves and prostitutes overran the grounds. By the time Louis actually moved from the Louvre to Versailles in 1682, he had reigned as monarch for thirty-nine years. After his wife's death in 1683, he secretly married his mistress, Françoise d'Aubigné, marquise de Maintenon, and conducted most state affairs from her apartments at the palace. Her opponents at court complained that she controlled all the appointments, but her efforts focused on her own projects, including her favorite: the founding in 1686

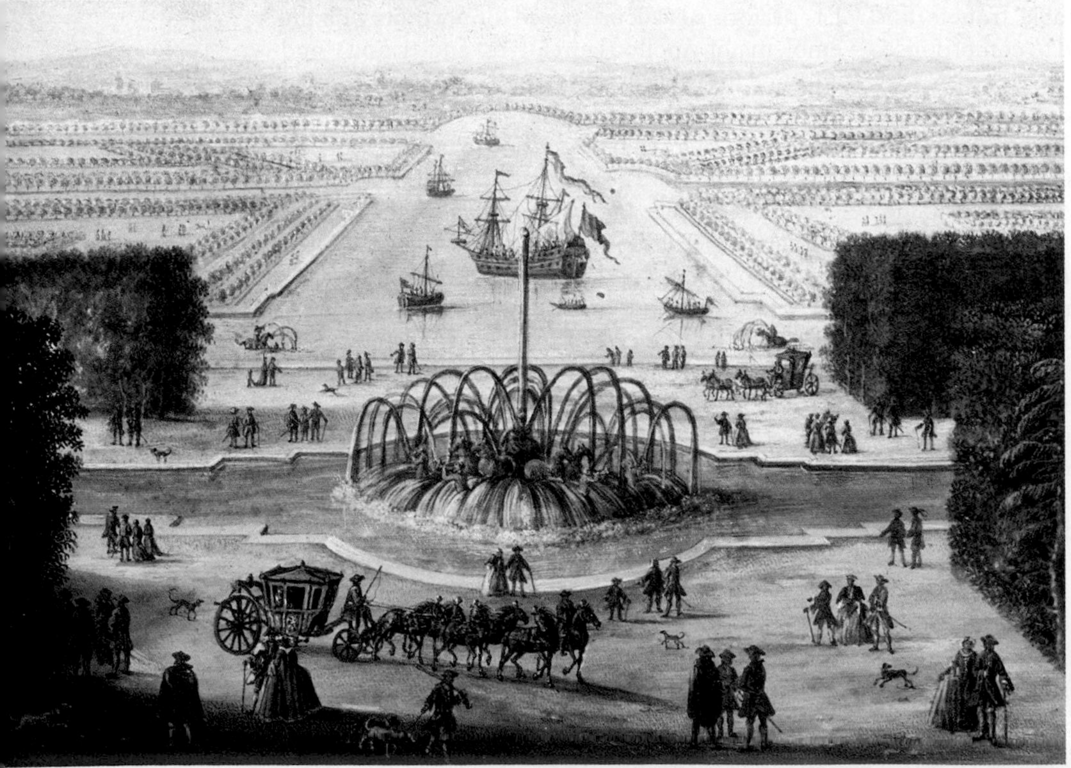

A View of the Grounds at Versailles
This late-seventeenth-century gouache on paper (gouache is a type of watercolor) shows the grand canal at Versailles with a statue dedicated to the Greek god of the sun, Apollo, in the pool in the foreground. Louis XIV put representations of Apollo everywhere to recall his favorite image of himself as the "sun king." Here Apollo is shown at the reins of his horse-drawn golden chariot. The ships in the canal remind the viewer of the size and magnificence of Louis XIV's newest castle. The king liked to have mock naval battles fought there during his most spectacular festivals. It took eleven years to build the canal and the pool. The canal alone is more than a mile long. *(Chateau de Versailles, France/Flammarion/The Bridgeman Art Library International.)*

of a royal school for girls from impoverished noble families. She also inspired Louis XIV to increase his devotion to Catholicism.

Enforcing Religious Orthodoxy

Louis believed that he reigned by divine right. As Bishop Jacques-Benigne Bossuet (1627–1704) explained, "We have seen that kings take the place of God, who is the true father of the human species. We have also seen that the first idea of power which exists among men is that of the paternal power; and that kings are modeled on fathers." The king, like a father, should instruct his subjects in the true religion, or at least make sure that others did so. In religious questions, too, the king's endeavors to gain more complete control showed both his wide-ranging ambition and the nature of the obstacles he faced.

Louis's campaign for religious conformity first focused on the Jansenists, Catholics whose doctrines and practices resembled some aspects of Protestantism. Following the posthumous publication of the book *Augustinus* (1640) by the Flemish theologian Cornelius Jansen (1585–1638), the Jansenists stressed the need for God's grace in achieving salvation. They emphasized the importance of original sin and resembled the English Puritans in their austere religious practice. Prominent among the Jansenists was Blaise Pascal (1623–1662), a mathematician of genius, who wrote his *Provincial Letters* (1656–1657) to defend Jansenism against charges of heresy. Many judges in the parlements likewise endorsed Jansenist doctrine.

Some questioned Louis's understanding of the finer points of doctrine: according to his sister-in-law, Louis himself "has never read anything about religion, nor the Bible either, and just goes along believing whatever he is told." But Louis rejected any doctrine that gave priority to considerations of individual conscience over the demands of the official church hierarchy, especially when that doctrine had been embraced by some noble supporters of the Fronde. Louis preferred teachings that stressed obedience to authority. Therefore, in 1660 he began enforcing various papal bulls (decrees) against Jansenism and closed down Jansenist theological centers. Jansenists were forced underground for the rest of his reign.

After many years of escalating pressure on the Calvinist Huguenots, Louis decided to eliminate all of the Calvinists' rights. Louis considered the Edict of Nantes (1598), by which his grandfather Henry IV granted the Protestants religious freedom and a degree of political independence, a temporary measure, and he fervently hoped to reconvert the Huguenots to Catholicism. In 1685, his **revocation of the Edict of Nantes** closed Calvinist churches and schools, forced all pastors to leave the country, and ordered the conversion of all Calvinists. Children of Calvinists could be taken away from their parents and raised Catholic. Tens of thousands of Huguenots responded by illegally fleeing to England, Brandenburg-Prussia, the Dutch Republic, or North America. Many now wrote for publications attacking Louis XIV's absolutism. Protestant European countries were shocked by this crackdown on religious dissent and would cite it in justification of their wars against Louis.

Extending State Authority at Home and Abroad

Louis XIV could not have enforced his religious policies without the services of a nationwide bureaucracy. **Bureaucracy** — a network of state officials carrying out orders according to a regular and routine line of authority — comes from the French word *bureau*, for "desk," which came to mean "office," both in the sense of a physical space and a position of authority. Louis personally supervised the activities of his bureaucrats and worked to ensure his supremacy in all matters. But he always had to negotiate with nobles and local officials who sometimes thwarted his will.

Bureaucracy and Mercantilism Louis extended the bureaucratic forms his predecessors had developed, especially the use of intendants, officials granted positions directly by the king rather than buying them, as crown officials had traditionally done. Louis handpicked an intendant for each region to represent his rule against entrenched local interests such as the parlements, provincial estates, and noble governors; they supervised the collection of taxes, the financing of public works, and the provisioning of the army. In 1673, Louis decreed that the parlements could no longer vote against his proposed laws or even speak against them.

Louis's success in consolidating his authority depended on hard work, an eye for detail, and an

---

revocation of the Edict of Nantes: French king Louis XIV's 1685 decision to eliminate the rights of Calvinists granted in the edict of 1598; Louis banned all Calvinist public activities and forced those who refused to embrace the state religion to flee.

bureaucracy: A network of state officials carrying out orders according to a regular and routine line of authority.

ear to the ground. In his memoirs he described the tasks he set for himself:

> to learn each hour the news concerning every province and every nation, the secrets of every court, the mood and weaknesses of each Prince and of every foreign minister; to be well-informed on an infinite number of matters about which we are supposed to know nothing; to elicit from our subjects what they hide from us with the greatest care; to discover the most remote opinions of our courtiers and the most hidden interests of those who come to us with quite contrary professions [claims].

To gather all this information, Louis relied on a series of talented ministers, usually of modest origins, who gained fame, fortune, and even noble status from serving the king. Most important among them was Jean-Baptiste Colbert (1619–1683), the son of a wool merchant turned royal official. Colbert had managed Mazarin's personal finances and worked his way up under Louis XIV to become head of royal finances, public works, and the navy. He founded a family dynasty that eventually produced five ministers of state, an archbishop, two bishops, and three generals.

Colbert used the bureaucracy to establish a new economic doctrine, **mercantilism**. According to mercantilist policy, governments must intervene to increase national wealth by whatever means possible. Such government intervention inevitably increased the role and eventually the number of bureaucrats needed. Under Colbert, the French government established overseas trading companies, granted manufacturing monopolies, and standardized production methods for textiles, paper, and soap. A government inspection system regulated the quality of finished goods and compelled all craftsmen to organize into guilds, in which masters could supervise the work of the journeymen and apprentices. To protect French production, Colbert rescinded many internal customs fees but enacted high foreign tariffs, which cut imports of competing goods. To compete more effectively with England and the Dutch Republic, Colbert also subsidized shipbuilding, a policy that dramatically expanded the number of seaworthy vessels. Such mercantilist measures aimed to ensure France's prominence in world markets and to provide the resources needed to fight wars against the nation's increasingly long list of enemies. Although later economists questioned the value of this state intervention in the economy, virtually every government in Europe embraced mercantilism.

mercantilism: The economic doctrine that governments must intervene to increase national wealth by whatever means possible.

Colbert's mercantilist projects shaped life in the colonies, too. He forbade colonial businesses from manufacturing anything already produced in mainland France. In 1663 he took control of the trading company that had founded New France (Canada). With the goal of establishing permanent settlements like those in the British North American colonies, he transplanted several thousand peasants from western France to the present-day province of Quebec, which France had claimed since 1608. He also tried to limit expansion westward, without success. Despite initial interruption of French fur-trading convoys by the Iroquois, in 1672 fur trader Louis Jolliet and Jesuit missionary Jacques Marquette reached the upper Mississippi River and traveled downstream as far as Arkansas. In 1684, French explorer Sieur de La Salle went all the way down to the Gulf of Mexico, claiming a vast territory for Louis XIV and calling it Louisiana after him. Colbert's successors embraced the expansion he had resisted, thinking it crucial to competing successfully with the English and the Dutch in the New World.

The Army and War | Colonial settlement occupied only a small portion of Louis XIV's attention, however, for his main foreign policy goal was to extend French power in Europe. In pursuing this purpose, he first came up against the Spanish and Austrian Habsburgs, whose lands encircled his, and then the Dutch and the English, with their competing commercial ambitions. To expand the army, Louis's minister of war centralized the organization of French troops. Barracks built in major towns received supplies—among which were uniforms to reinforce discipline—from a central distribution system. Louis's wartime army could field a force as large as that of all his enemies combined.

Absolutist governments always tried to increase their territorial holdings, and as Louis extended his reach, he gained new enemies. In 1667–1668, in the War of Devolution (so called because Louis claimed that lands in the Spanish Netherlands should devolve to him since the Spanish king had failed to pay the dowry of Louis's Spanish bride), Louis defeated the Spanish armies but had to make peace when England, Sweden, and the Dutch Republic joined the war. In the Treaty of Aix-la-Chapelle in 1668, he gained control of a few towns on the border of the Spanish Netherlands. Pamphlets sponsored by the Habsburgs accused Louis of aiming for "universal monarchy," or domination of Europe.

In 1672, Louis XIV opened hostilities against the Dutch because they stood in the way of his acquisition of more territory in the Spanish Netherlands. He declared war again on Spain in 1673. By now the Dutch had allied themselves with their former Spanish masters to hold off the French. Louis also marched his troops into territories of the Holy Roman Empire, provoking many of the German princes to join with the emperor, the Spanish, and the Dutch in an alliance against Louis, now denounced as a "Christian Turk" for his imperialist ambitions. Faced with bloody but inconclusive results on the battlefield, the parties agreed to the Treaty of Nijmegen of 1678–1679, which ceded several Flemish towns and the Franche-Comté region to Louis, linking Alsace to the rest of France. French government deficits soared, and in 1675 increases in taxes touched off the most serious antitax revolt of Louis's reign.

Louis had no intention of standing still. Heartened by the Habsburgs' seeming weakness, he pushed eastward, seizing the city of Strasbourg in 1681 and invading the province of Lorraine in 1684. In 1688, he attacked some of the small German cities of the Holy Roman Empire. His armies laid waste to German cities such as Mannheim; his government ordered the local military commander to "kill all those who would still wish to build houses there." So obsessed was Louis with his military standing that he had miniature battle scenes painted on his high heels and commissioned tapestries showing his military processions into conquered cities, even those he did not take by force (Map 16.1). It took a large coalition known as the League of Augsburg—made up of England, Spain, Sweden, the Dutch Republic, the Austrian emperor, and various German

MAP 16.1 Louis XIV's Acquisitions, 1668–1697

Every ruler in Europe hoped to extend his or her territorial control, and war was often the result. Louis XIV steadily encroached on the Spanish Netherlands to the north and the lands of the Holy Roman Empire to the east. Although coalitions of European powers reined in Louis's grander ambitions, he nonetheless incorporated many neighboring territories into the French crown.

Wars of Louis XIV

1667–1668	**War of Devolution** *Enemies:* Spain, Dutch Republic, England, Sweden Ended by Treaty of Aix-la-Chapelle in 1668, with France gaining towns in Spanish Netherlands (Flanders)
1672–1678	**Dutch War** *Enemies:* Dutch Republic, Spain, Holy Roman Empire Ended by Treaty of Nijmegen, 1678–1679, which gave several towns in Spanish Netherlands and Franche-Comté to France
1688–1697	**War of the League of Augsburg** *Enemies:* Holy Roman Empire, Sweden, Spain, England, Dutch Republic Ended by Peace of Rijswijk, 1697, with Louis returning all his conquests made since 1678 except Strasbourg
1701–1713	**War of the Spanish Succession** *Enemies:* Holy Roman Empire, England, Dutch Republic, Prussia Ended by Peace of Utrecht, 1713–1714, with Louis ceding territories in North America to the British

princes—to hold back the French king. When hostilities between Louis and the League of Augsburg ended in the Peace of Rijswijk in 1697, Louis returned many of his conquests made since 1678 with the exception of Strasbourg.

Four years later, Louis embarked on his last and most damaging war, the War of the Spanish Succession (1701–1713). It was caused by disagreement over who would inherit the throne of Spain when the Spanish king died without an heir. Before he died, Spanish king Charles II (r. 1665–1700) named Louis XIV's second grandson, Philip, duke of Anjou, as his heir, but the Austrian emperor Leopold I refused to accept this extension of French influence and the British and the Dutch supported his refusal. In the ensuing war, the French lost several major battles and had to accept disadvantageous terms in the Peace of Utrecht of 1713–1714; France ceded possessions in North America (Newfoundland, the Hudson Bay area, and most of Nova Scotia) to Britain. Although Philip was recognized as king of Spain, he had to renounce any future claim to the French crown, thus barring unification of the two kingdoms. Spain surrendered its territories in Italy and the Netherlands to the Austrians and Gibraltar to the British. Lying on his deathbed in 1715, the seventy-six-year-old Louis XIV watched helplessly as his accomplishments began to unravel.

Louis XIV's policy of absolutism fomented bitter hostility among his own subjects. Nobles resented his promotions of commoners to high office. The duke of Saint-Simon complained that "falseness, servility, admiring glances, combined with a dependent and cringing attitude, above all, an appearance of being nothing without him, were the only ways of pleasing him." Ordinary people suffered the most for Louis's ambitions. By the end of the Sun King's reign, one in six Frenchmen had served in the military. Louis XIV's armies swelled to twice the size of the armies France fielded during the Thirty Years' War. In addition to the higher taxes paid by everyone, those who lived on the routes leading to the battlefields had to house and feed soldiers; only nobles were exempt from this requirement. Louis himself advised his successor, "Do not imitate my love of building nor my liking for war."

REVIEW QUESTION How "absolute" was the power of Louis XIV?

Constitutionalism in England

Of the two models of state building, absolutism and constitutionalism, the first seemed unquestionably more powerful because Louis XIV could raise such large armies and tax his subjects without much consultation. In the end, however, Louis could not defeat the coalition led by England's constitutional monarch. Constitutionalism had its own distinctive strengths, which came from the ruler sharing power through a representative assembly such as the English houses of Parliament. But the English rulers themselves hoped to follow Louis XIV's lead and install their own absolutist policies. Two revolutions, in 1642–1660 and 1688–1689, overturned two kings and confirmed the constitutional powers of an elected parliament, laying the foundation for the idea that government must guarantee certain rights to the people under the law.

England Turned Upside Down, 1642–1660

Disputes about the right to levy taxes and the nature of authority in the Church of England had long troubled the relationship between the English crown and Parliament. For more than a hundred years, wealthy English landowners had been accustomed to participating in government through Parliament and expected to be consulted on royal policy. Although England had no single constitutional document, it did have a variety of laws, judicial decisions, customary procedures, and charters and petitions granted by the king that all regulated relations between king and Parliament. When Charles I tried to assert his authority over Parliament, a civil war broke out. That war set in motion an unpredictable chain of events, which included an extraordinary ferment of religious and political ideas. Some historians view the English civil war of 1642–1646 as the last great war of religion because it pitted Puritans against those trying to push the Church of England toward Catholicism; others see in it the first modern revolution because it gave birth to democratic political and religious movements.

Charles I versus Parliament When Charles I (r. 1625–1649) succeeded his father, James I, he faced an increasingly aggressive Parliament that resisted new taxes and resented the king's efforts to extend his personal control. In 1628, Parliament forced Charles to agree to the Petition of Right, by which he promised not to levy taxes without Parliament's consent. Charles hoped to avoid further interference with his plans by simply refusing to call Parliament into session between 1629 and 1640. Without it, the king's ministers had to find every loophole possible to raise revenues. They tried to turn "ship money," a levy on seaports in times of emergency, into an annual tax collected everywhere in the country. The crown won the ensuing court case, but many subjects still refused to pay what they considered to be an illegal tax.

Religious tensions brought conflicts over the king's authority to a head. The Puritans had long agitated for the removal of any vestiges of Catholicism, but Charles, married to a French Catholic, moved in the opposite direction in the 1630s. With Charles's encouragement, the archbishop of Canterbury, William Laud (1573–1645), imposed increasingly elaborate ceremonies on the Church of England. Angered by these moves toward "popery," the Puritans poured forth reproving pamphlets and sermons. In response, Laud hauled them before the feared Court of Star Chamber, which the king personally controlled. The court ordered harsh sentences for Laud's Puritan critics; they were whipped, pilloried, branded, and even had their ears cut off and their noses split. When Laud tried to apply his policies to Scotland, however, they backfired completely: the stubborn Presbyterian Scots rioted against the imposition of the Book of Common Prayer and in 1640 they invaded the north of England. To raise money to fight the war, Charles called Parliament into session and unwittingly opened the door to a constitutional and religious crisis.

The Parliament of 1640 did not intend revolution, but reformers in the House of Commons (the lower house of Parliament) wanted to undo what

The World Turned Upside Down
This print from 1647 conveys the anxieties many people felt in the midst of religious and political upheaval. Nothing is as it should be: the feet are where the hands should be, the cart comes before the horse, a fish flies, and the wheelbarrow pushes the person. *(John Taylor [d. 1651]), British Library, London, UK / © British Library Board. All rights reserved. / The Bridgeman Art Library International.)*

they saw as the royal tyranny of the 1630s. Parliament removed Laud from office, ordered the execution of an unpopular royal commander, abolished the Court of Star Chamber, repealed recently levied taxes, and provided for a parliamentary assembly at least once every three years, thus establishing a constitutional check on royal authority. Moderate reformers expected to stop there and resisted Puritan pressure to abolish bishops and eliminate the Church of England prayer book. They also faced a rebellion in Ireland by native Catholics against the English and Scottish settlers who had taken over their lands. The reformers in Parliament feared that the Irish Catholics would make common cause with Charles to reestablish Catholicism as the religion of England and Scotland. Their hand was forced in January 1642, when Charles and his soldiers invaded Parliament and tried unsuccessfully to arrest those leaders who had moved to curb his power. Faced with mounting opposition within London, Charles quickly withdrew from the city and organized an army.

Civil War and the Challenge to All Authorities

The ensuing civil war between king and Parliament lasted four years (1642–1646) and divided the country. The king's army of royalists, known as Cavaliers, enjoyed the most support in northern and western England. The parliamentary forces, called Roundheads because they cut their hair short, had their stronghold in the southeast, including London. Although Puritans dominated on the parliamentary side, they were divided among themselves about the proper form of church government: the Presbyterians wanted a Calvinist church with some central authority, whereas the Independents favored entirely autonomous congregations free from other church government (hence the term *congregationalism*, often associated with the Independents). The Puritans put aside their differences for the sake of military unity and united under an obscure member of the House of Commons, the country gentleman Oliver Cromwell (1599–1658), who sympathized with the Independents. After Cromwell skillfully reorganized the parliamentary troops, his New Model Army defeated the Cavaliers at the battle of Naseby in 1645. Charles surrendered in 1646.

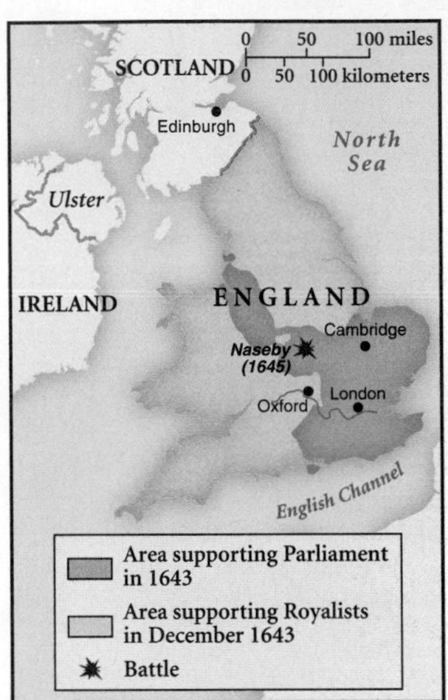

England during the Civil War

Although the civil war between king and Parliament had ended in victory for Parliament, divisions within the Puritan ranks now came to the fore: the Presbyterians dominated Parliament, but the Independents controlled the army. The disputes between the leaders drew lower-class groups into the debate. (See "Contrasting Views," page 528.) When Parliament tried to disband the New Model Army in 1647, disgruntled soldiers protested. Called **Levellers** because of their insistence on leveling social differences, the soldiers took on their officers in a series of debates about the nature of political authority. The Levellers demanded that Parliament meet annually, that members be paid so as to allow common people to participate, and that all male heads of households be allowed to vote. Their ideal of political participation excluded servants, the propertyless, and women but offered access to artisans, shopkeepers, and modest farmers. Cromwell and other army leaders rejected the Levellers' demands as threatening to property owners. Speaking to his advisers, Cromwell insisted, "You have no other way to deal with these men but to break them in pieces. . . . If you do not break them they will break you."

Just as political differences between Presbyterians and Independents helped spark new political movements, so too their conflicts over church organization fostered the emergence of new religious sects that emphasized the "inner light" of individual religious inspiration and a disdain for hierarchical authority. The Baptists, for example, insisted on adult baptism because they believed that Christians should choose their own church and that every child should not automatically become a member of the Church of England. The Religious Society of Friends, who came to be called Quakers, demonstrated their beliefs in equality and the inner light by refusing to doff their hats to men in authority. Manifesting their religious experience by trembling, or "quaking," the Quakers believed that anyone — man or woman — inspired by a direct experience of God could preach. In keeping with their notions of equality and individual inspiration, many of the new sects provided opportunities for women to become preachers and prophets.

Parliamentary leaders feared that the new sects would overturn the whole social hierarchy. The outspoken women in new sects like the Quakers underscored the threat of a social order turning upside down. Rumors abounded, for example, of naked Quakers running through the streets waiting for "a sign." Some sects did advocate sweeping change. The Diggers promoted rural communism — collective ownership of all property. Seekers and Ranters questioned just about everything. One notorious Ranter, John Robins, even claimed to be God. A few men advocated free love. These developments convinced the political elite that tolerating the new sects would lead to skepticism, anarchism, and debauchery.

Oliver Cromwell

At the heart of the continuing political struggle was the question of what to do with the king, who tried to negotiate with the Presbyterians in Parliament. In late 1648, Independents in the army purged the Presbyterians from Parliament, leaving a "rump" of about seventy members. This Rump Parliament then created a high court to try Charles I. The court found him guilty of attempting to establish "an unlimited and tyrannical power" and pronounced a death sentence. On January 30, 1649, Charles was beheaded before an enormous crowd, which reportedly groaned as one when the ax fell. Although many had objected to Charles's autocratic rule, few had wanted him killed. For royalists, Charles immedi-

Levellers: Disgruntled soldiers in Oliver Cromwell's New Model Army who in 1647 wanted to "level" social differences and extend political participation to all male property owners.

ately became a martyr, and reports of miracles, such as the curing of blindness by the touch of a handkerchief soaked in his blood, soon circulated.

The Rump Parliament abolished the monarchy and the House of Lords (the upper house of Parliament) and set up a Puritan republic with Oliver Cromwell (see the illustration below) as chairman of the Council of State. Cromwell did not tolerate dissent from his policies. He saw the hand of God in events and himself as God's agent. Pamphleteers and songwriters ridiculed his red nose and accused him of wanting to be king, but few challenged his leadership. When his agents discovered plans for mutiny within the army, they executed the perpetrators; new decrees silenced the Levellers. Although Cromwell allowed the various Puritan sects to worship rather freely and permitted Jews with needed skills to return to England for the first time since the thirteenth century, Catholics could not worship publicly, nor could adherents of the Church of England use the Book of Common Prayer, thought to be too Catholic. The elites were troubled by Cromwell's religious policies but pleased to see some social order reestablished.

The new regime aimed to extend state power just as Charles I had before. Cromwell laid the foundation for a Great Britain made up of England, Ireland, and Scotland by reconquering Scotland and brutally subduing Ireland. When his position was secured in 1649, Cromwell went to Ireland with a large force and easily defeated the rebels, massacring whole garrisons and their priests. He encouraged expropriating more lands of the Irish "barbarous wretches," and Scottish immigrants resettled the northern county of Ulster. This seventeenth-century English conquest left a legacy of bitterness that the Irish even today call "the curse of Cromwell." In 1651, Parliament turned its attention overseas, putting mercantilist ideas into practice in the first Navigation Act, which allowed imports only if they were carried on English ships or came directly from the producers of goods. The Navigation Act was aimed at the Dutch, who dominated world trade; Cromwell tried to carry the policy further by waging naval war on the Dutch from 1652 to 1654.

Execution of Charles I
This print depicting the execution of English king Charles I appeared on the first page of the fictitious confessions of his executioner, Richard Brandon, who supposedly claimed to feel pains in his own neck from the moment he cut off Charles's head. *(British Library, London, UK/© British Library Board. All rights reserved./The Bridgeman Art Library International.)*

Portrait of Oliver Cromwell (1599–1658)
In this painting by Thomas Wyck, Cromwell's pose on horseback mirrors that of King Charles I in a painting of 1633. Cromwell therefore appears quite literally as Charles's successor. The setting, however, is different. Cromwell is attended by a black servant with a backdrop that suggests North Africa. The artist may be referring to Cromwell's 1655 foray against the pirates who attacked English merchant ships from their headquarters on the Tunisian coast. Cromwell sent twenty ships to bombard the pirates' fortifications and destroy their fleet. *(Private Collection/Photo © Philip Mould Ltd., London/The Bridgeman Art Library International.)*

CONTRASTING VIEWS

The English Civil War

The civil war between Charles I and Parliament (1642–1646) excited furious debates about the proper forms of political authority, debates that influenced political thought for two centuries or more. The Levellers, who served in the parliamentary army, wanted Parliament to be more accountable to ordinary men like themselves (Document 1). In his statement rejecting Parliament's jurisdiction over him, Charles I reiterated the key positions of royalism (Document 2). Thomas Hobbes, in his famous political treatise Leviathan *(1651), develops the consequences of the civil war for political theory (Document 3).*

1. The Levellers, "The Agreement of the People, as Presented to the Council of the Army" (October 28, 1647)

Note especially two things about this document: (1) it focuses on Parliament as the chief instrument of reform, and (2) it claims that government depends on the consent of the people.

Since, therefore, our former oppressions and scarce-yet-ended troubles have been occasioned, either by want of frequent national meetings in Council [Parliament], or by rendering those meetings ineffectual, we are fully agreed and resolved to provide that hereafter our representatives be neither left to an uncertainty for the time nor made useless to the ends for which they are intended. In order whereunto we declare:—That the people of England, being at this day very unequally distributed by Counties, Cities, and Borough for the election of their deputies in Parliament, ought to be more indifferently [equally] proportioned according to the number of the inhabitants. . . . That the power of this, and all future Representatives of this Nation, is inferior only to theirs who choose them, and doth extend, without the consent or concurrence of any other person or persons [the king], to the enacting, altering, and repealing of laws, to the erecting and abolishing of offices and courts, to the appointing, removing, and calling to account magistrates and officers of all degrees, to the making of war and peace, to the treating with foreign States [in other words, Parliament is the supreme power, not the king]. . . . These things we declare to be our native rights, and therefore are agreed and resolved to maintain them with our utmost possibilities against all opposition whatsoever.

Source: Samuel Rawson Gardiner, ed., *The Constitutional Documents of the Puritan Revolution, 1625–1660* (Oxford: Clarendon Press, 1906), 333–35.

2. Charles I's Rejection of the Jurisdiction of Parliament (1649)

In January 1649, the English Parliament voted to try Charles I for treason. Previous monarchs had been on occasion overthrown and murdered but never tried by an act of Parliament. Charles rejected the right of Parliament to try him and refused to enter a plea. He was nonetheless convicted and executed as a traitor.

Having already made my protestations, not only against the illegality of this pretended Court, but also, that no earthly power can justly call me (who am your King) in question as a delinquent, I would not any more open my mouth upon this occasion, more than to refer myself to what I have spoken, were I in this case alone concerned: but the duty I owe to God in the preservation of the true liberty of my people will not suffer me at this time to be silent: for, how can any freeborn subject of England call life or anything he possesseth his own, if power without right daily make new, and abrogate the old fundamental laws of the land which I now take to be the present

At home, however, Cromwell faced growing resistance. His wars required a budget twice the size of Charles I's, and his increases in property taxes and customs duties alienated landowners and merchants. The conflict reached a crisis in 1653: Parliament considered disbanding the army, whereupon Cromwell abolished the Rump Parliament in a military coup and made himself Lord Protector. He now silenced his critics by banning newspapers and using networks of spies to read mail and keep tabs on his enemies. When Cromwell died in 1658, the diarist John Evelyn claimed, "There were none that cried but dogs." Cromwell intended that his son should succeed him, but his death only revived the prospect of civil war and political chaos. In 1660, a newly elected Parliament invited Charles II, the son of the executed king, to return from exile.

Restoration and Revolution Again

The traditional monarchical form of government was restored in 1660, and Charles II (r. 1660–1685) moved quickly to reestablish royal authority. More than a thousand Puritan ministers lost their positions, and attending a service other than one conforming with the Book of Common Prayer was illegal after 1664. Two natural disasters in quick succession posed new challenges. The plague struck in 1665, claiming more than thirty thousand victims in just a few months and forcing Charles and Parliament to flee from London. Then in 1666, the Great Fire (see the illustration on page 530) swept the city. Some saw these disasters as punishment for the sins of the Cromwell era, while case! . . . There is no proceeding just against any man, but what is warranted either by God's laws or the municipal laws of the country where he lives. Now I am most confident this day's proceeding cannot be warranted by God's laws; for, on the contrary, the authority of obedience unto Kings is clearly warranted, and strictly commanded in both the Old and New Testament, which, if denied, I am ready instantly to prove.

. . . Then for the law of this land, I am no less confident, that no learned lawyer will affirm that an impeachment can lie against the King, they all going in his name: and one of their maxims is, that the King can do no wrong. . . . And admitting, but not granting, that the people of England's commission could grant your pretended power, I see nothing you can show for that; for certainly you never asked the question of the tenth man in the kingdom, and in this way you manifestly wrong even the poorest ploughman, if you demand not his free consent. . . . Thus you see that I speak not for my own right alone, as I am your King, but also for the true liberty of all my subjects, which consists not in the power of government, but in living under such laws, such a government, as may give themselves the best assurance of their lives, and property of their goods.

Source: Samuel Rawson Gardiner, ed., *The Constitutional Documents of the Puritan Revolution, 1625–1660* (Oxford: Clarendon Press, 1906), 374–75.

3. Thomas Hobbes, *Leviathan* (1651)

In this excerpt, Hobbes depicts the anarchy of a society without a strong central authority, but he leaves open the question of whether that authority should be vested in "one Man" or "one Assembly of men," that is, a king or a parliament.

During the time men live without a common Power to keep them all in awe, they are in that condition which is called Warre [war]; and such a warre, as is of every man, against every man. . . . In such condition, there is no place for Industry; because the fruit thereof is uncertain: and consequently no Culture of the Earth; no Navigation, nor use of the commodities that may be imported by Sea; no commodious Building; no Instrument of moving, and removing such things as require much force; no Knowledge of the face of the Earth; no account of Time; no Arts; no Letters; no Society; and which is worst of all, continuall feare, and danger of violent death; and the life of man, solitary, poore, nasty, brutish, and short. The only way to erect such a Common Power, as may be able to defend them from the invasion of Forraigners, and the injuries of one another, and thereby to secure them in such sort, as that by their owne industrie, and by the Fruites of the Earth, they may nourish themselves and live contentedly; is, to conferre all their power and strength upon one Man, or upon one Assembly of men, that may reduce all their wills, by plurality of voices, unto one Will. . . . This is more than Consent, or Concord; it is a reall Unitie of them all, in one and the same Person, made by Covenant of every man with every man. . . . This done, the Multitude so united in one Person, is called a COMMON-WEALTH, in latine CIVITAS. This is the Generation of that great LEVIATHAN, or rather (to speake more reverently) of that *Mortall God*, to which wee owe under the *Immortall God*, our peace and defence.

Source: Thomas Hobbes, *Leviathan*, ed. Richard E. Flathman and David Johnston (New York: Norton, 1997), 70, 95.

Questions to Consider

1. **Why would both the king and the parliamentary leaders have found the Levellers' views disturbing?**
2. **What are the chief differences between the king's arguments and those of the Levellers and Hobbes?**
3. **Why did Hobbes's arguments about political authority upset supporters of both monarchy and Parliament?**

others perceived them as an ill omen for Charles's reign.

Many in Parliament feared that Charles wanted to emulate Louis XIV. In 1670, Charles II made a secret agreement, soon leaked, with Louis in which he promised to announce his conversion to Catholicism in exchange for money for a war against the Dutch. Charles never proclaimed himself a Catholic, but in his Declaration of Indulgence (1673) he did suspend all laws against Catholics and Protestant dissenters. Parliament refused to continue funding the Dutch war unless Charles rescinded his Declaration of Indulgence. Asserting its authority further, Parliament passed the Test Act in 1673, requiring all government officials to profess allegiance to the Church of England and in effect disavow Catholic doctrine. Then in 1678, Parliament precipitated the so-called Exclusion Crisis by explicitly denying the throne to a Roman Catholic. This action was aimed at the king's brother and heir, James, an open convert to Catholicism. Charles refused to allow it to become law.

The dynastic crisis over the succession of a Catholic gave rise to two distinct factions in Parliament: the Tories, who supported a strong, hereditary monarchy and the restored ceremony of the Church of England, and the Whigs, who advocated parliamentary supremacy and toleration of Protestant dissenters such as Presbyterians. Both labels were originally derogatory: *Tory* meant an Irish Catholic bandit; *Whig* was the Irish Catholic designation for a Presbyterian Scot. The Tories favored James's succession despite his Catholicism, whereas the Whigs opposed a Catholic monarch. The loose moral

Great Fire of London, 1666

This view of London shows the three-day fire at its height. The writer John Evelyn described the scene in his diary: "All the sky was of a fiery aspect, like the top of a burning oven, and the light seen above 40 miles round about for many nights. God grant mine eyes may never behold the like, who now saw above 10,000 houses all in one flame; the noise and cracking and thunder of people, the fall of towers, houses, and churches, was like an hideous storm." Everyone in London at the time felt overwhelmed by the catastrophe, and many deemed it God's punishment for the upheavals of the 1640s and 1650s. *(Photo © Museum of London, UK/The Bridgeman Art Library International.)*

atmosphere of Charles's court also offended some Whigs, who complained tongue in cheek that Charles was father of his country in much too literal a fashion (he had fathered more than one child by his mistresses but produced no legitimate heir).

When James II (r. 1685–1688) succeeded his brother, he seemed determined to force Catholicism on his subjects. Tories and Whigs joined together when a male heir—who would take precedence over James's two adult Protestant daughters—was born to James's second wife, an Italian Catholic, in 1688. They invited the Dutch ruler **William, prince of Orange**, and his wife, James's older daughter, Mary, to invade England. Mary was brought up as a Protestant and was willing to act with her husband against her father's pro-Catholic policies. James fled to France, and Parliament offered the throne jointly to William (r. 1689–1702) and Mary (r. 1689–1694) on the condition that they accept a bill of rights guaranteeing Parliament's full partnership in a constitutional government.

William, prince of Orange: Dutch ruler who, with his Protestant wife, Mary (daughter of James II), ruled England after the Glorious Revolution of 1688.

In the Bill of Rights (1689), William and Mary agreed not to raise a standing army or to levy taxes without Parliament's consent. They also agreed to call meetings of Parliament at least every three years, to guarantee free elections to parliamentary seats, and to abide by Parliament's decisions and not suspend duly passed laws. The agreement gave England's constitutional government a written, legal basis by formally recognizing Parliament as a self-contained, independent body that shared power with the rulers. Victorious supporters of the coup declared it the **Glorious Revolution** because it was achieved with so little bloodshed (at least in England).

The propertied classes who controlled Parliament prevented any resurgence of the popular turmoil of the 1640s. The Toleration Act of 1689 granted all Protestants freedom of worship, though non-Anglicans (those not in the Church of England)

Glorious Revolution: The events of 1688 when Tories and Whigs replaced England's monarch James II with his Protestant daughter, Mary, and her husband, Dutch ruler William of Orange; William and Mary agreed to a Bill of Rights that guaranteed rights to Parliament.

were still excluded from the universities; Catholics got no rights but were more often left alone to worship privately. When the Catholics in Ireland rose to defend James II, William and Mary's troops savagely suppressed them. With the Whigs in power and the Tories in opposition, wealthy landowners now controlled political life throughout the realm. The factions' differences, however, were minor; essentially, the Tories merely had less access to the king's patronage. A contemporary reported that King William had said "that if he had good places [honors and land] enough to bestow, he should soon unite the two parties."

Social Contract Theory: Hobbes and Locke

Out of the turmoil of the English revolutions came a major rethinking of the foundations of all political authority. Although Thomas Hobbes and John Locke wrote in response to the upheavals of their times, they offered opposing arguments that were applicable to any place and any time, not just England of the seventeenth century. Hobbes justified absolute authority; Locke provided the rationale for constitutionalism. Yet both argued that all authority came not from divine right but from a **social contract** among citizens. The Dutch scholar Hugo Grotius (see Chapter 15) had originated the idea of a social contract, but conceived of it in a more limited way. For Locke, in particular, the social contract implied that government rested on the consent of the governed.

Hobbes | Thomas Hobbes (1588–1679) was a royalist who sat out the English civil war of the 1640s in France, where he tutored the future king Charles II. Returning to England in 1651, he published his masterpiece, *Leviathan* (1651), in which he argued for unlimited authority in a ruler. Absolute authority could be vested in either a king or a parliament; it had to be absolute, Hobbes insisted, in order to overcome the defects of human nature. Believing that people are essentially self-centered and driven by the "right to self-preservation," Hobbes made his case by referring to science, not religion. To Hobbes, human life in a state of nature—that is, any situation without firm authority—was "solitary, poor, nasty, brutish, and short." He believed that the desire for power and natural greed would inevitably lead to unfettered competition. Only the assurance of social order could make people secure enough to act according to law; consequently, giving up personal liberty, he maintained, was the price of collective security. Rulers derived their power, he concluded, from a contract in which absolute authority protects people's rights.

Hobbes's notion of rule by an absolute authority left no room for political dissent or nonconformity, and it infuriated both royalists and supporters of Parliament. He enraged royalists by arguing that authority came not from divine right but from the social contract. Parliamentary supporters resisted Hobbes's claim that rulers must possess absolute authority to prevent the greater evil of anarchy; they believed that a constitution should guarantee shared power between king and Parliament, and protect individual rights under the law. Like Machiavelli before him, Hobbes became associated with a cynical, pessimistic view of human nature, and future political theorists often began their arguments by refuting Hobbes.

Locke | Rejecting both Hobbes and the more traditional royalist defenses of absolute authority, John Locke (1632–1704) used the notion of a social contract to provide a foundation for constitutionalism. Locke experienced political life firsthand as physician, secretary, and intellectual companion to the earl of Shaftesbury, a leading English Whig. In 1683, during the Exclusion Crisis, Locke fled with Shaftesbury to the Dutch Republic. There he continued work on his *Two Treatises of Government*, which, when published in 1690, served to justify the revolution of 1688. Locke's position was thoroughly anti-absolutist. He denied the divine right of kings and ridiculed the common royalist idea that political power in the state mirrored the father's authority in the family. Like Hobbes, he posited a state of nature that applied to all people. Unlike Hobbes, however, he thought people were reasonable and the state of nature peaceful.

Locke insisted that government's only purpose was to protect life, liberty, and property, a notion that linked economic and political freedom. Ultimate authority rested in the will of a majority of men who owned property, and government should be limited to its basic purpose of protection. A ruler who failed to uphold his part of the social contract between the ruler and the populace could be justifiably resisted, an idea that would become crucial for the leaders of the American Revolution a century later. For England's seventeenth-century landowners, however, Locke helped validate a revolution

---

social contract: The doctrine, originated by Hugo Grotius and argued by both Thomas Hobbes and John Locke, that all political authority derives not from divine right but from an implicit contract between citizens and their rulers.

that consolidated their interests and ensured their privileges in the social hierarchy.

Locke defended his optimistic view of human nature in the immensely influential *Essay Concerning Human Understanding* (1690). He denied the existence of any innate ideas and asserted instead that each human is born with a mind that is a tabula rasa (blank slate). Not surprisingly, Locke devoted considerable energy to rethinking educational practices; he believed that education crucially shaped the human personality by channeling all sensory experience. Everything humans know, he claimed, comes from sensory experience, not from anything inherent in human nature. Locke's views promoted the belief that "all men are created equal," a belief that challenged absolutist forms of rule and ultimately raised questions about women's roles as well. Although Locke himself owned shares in the Royal African Company and justified slavery, his writings were later used by abolitionists in their campaign against slavery.

REVIEW QUESTION What differences over religion and politics caused the conflict between king and Parliament in England?

Outposts of Constitutionalism

When William and Mary came to the throne in England in 1689, the Dutch and the English put aside the rivalries that had brought them to war against each other in 1652–1654, 1665–1667, and 1672–1674. Under William, the Dutch and the English together led the coalition that blocked Louis XIV's efforts to dominate continental Europe. The English and Dutch had much in common: oriented toward commerce, especially overseas, they both had developed representative forms of government. Also among the few outposts of constitutionalism in the seventeenth century were the British North American colonies, which developed representative government while the English were preoccupied with their revolutions at home. Constitutionalism was not the only factor shaping this Atlantic world; as constitutionalism developed in the colonies, so too did the enslavement of black Africans as a new labor force.

The Dutch Republic

When the Dutch Republic gained formal independence from Spain in 1648, it had already established a decentralized, constitutional state. Rich merchants called regents effectively controlled the internal affairs of each province and (through the Estates General) named the *stadholder*, the executive officer responsible for defense and for representing the state at all ceremonial occasions. They almost always chose one of the princes of the house of Orange, but the stadholder resembled a president more than a king.

The decentralized state encouraged and protected trade, and the Dutch Republic soon became Europe's financial capital. The Bank of Amsterdam offered borrowers lower interest rates than those available in England and France. Praised for their industriousness, thrift, and cleanliness — and maligned as greedy, dull, and fat — the Dutch dominated overseas commerce with their shipping (Map 16.2). They imported products from all over the world: spices, tea, and silk from Asia; sugar and tobacco from the Americas; wool from England and Spain; timber and furs from Scandinavia; grain from eastern Europe. A widely reprinted history of Amsterdam that appeared in 1662 described the city as "risen through the hand of God to the peak of prosperity and greatness. . . . The whole world stands amazed at its riches and from east and west, north and south they come to behold it."

The Dutch rapidly became the most prosperous and best-educated people in Europe. Middle-class people supported the visual arts, especially painting, to an unprecedented degree. Artists and engravers produced thousands of works, and Dutch artists were among the first to sell to a mass market. Whereas in other countries kings, nobles, and churches bought art, Dutch buyers were merchants, artisans, and shopkeepers. Engravings, illustrated histories, and oil paintings were all relatively inexpensive. One foreigner commented that "pictures are very common here, there being scarce an ordinary tradesman whose house is not decorated with them." Dutch artists focused on familiar daily details because for them ordinary people had religious as well as political significance; even children at play could be infused with radiant beauty. The family household, not the royal court, determined the moral character of this intensely commercial society. Relative prosperity decreased the need for married women to work, so Dutch society developed the clear contrast between middle-class male and female roles that would become prevalent elsewhere in Europe and in America more than a century later. As one contemporary Dutch writer explained, "The husband must be on the street to practice his trade; the wife must stay at home to be in the kitchen."

Extraordinarily high levels of urbanization and literacy created a large reading public. Dutch presses printed books censored elsewhere (printers or authors censored in one province simply shifted op-

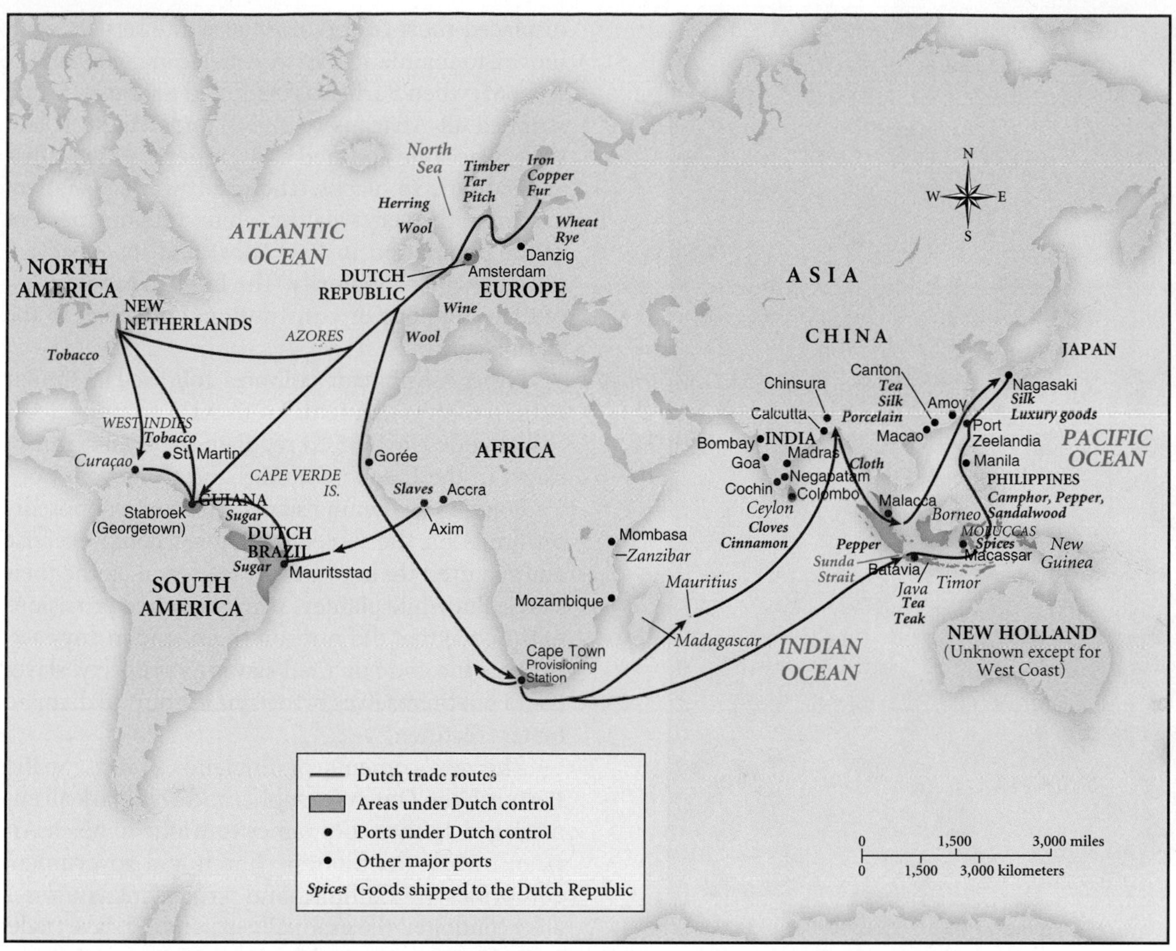

MAP 16.2 Dutch Commerce in the Seventeenth Century
Even before gaining formal independence from the Spanish in 1648, the Dutch had begun to compete with the Spanish and Portuguese all over the world. In 1602, a group of merchants established the Dutch East India Company, which soon offered investors an annual rate of return of 35 percent on the trade in spices with countries located on the Indian Ocean. Global commerce gave the Dutch the highest standard of living in Europe and soon attracted the envy of the French and the English.

erations to another), and the University of Leiden attracted students and professors from all over Europe. Dutch tolerance extended to the works of Benedict Spinoza (1633–1677), a Jewish philosopher and biblical scholar who was expelled by his synagogue for alleged atheism but left alone by the Dutch authorities. Spinoza strove to reconcile religion with science and mathematics, but his work scandalized many Christians and Jews because he seemed to equate God and nature. Like nature, Spinoza's God followed unchangeable laws and could not be influenced by human actions, prayers, or faith.

Dutch learning, painting, and commerce all enjoyed wide renown in the seventeenth century, but this luster proved hard to maintain. The Dutch lived in a world of international rivalries in which strong central authority gave their enemies an advantage. Though inconclusive, the naval wars with England between 1652 and 1674 drained the state's revenues. Even more dangerous were the land wars with France, which lasted until 1713. The Dutch survived these direct military challenges but began to lose their position in international trade as both the British and French limited commerce with their colonies to merchants from their own nations. At the end of the seventeenth century, as the Dutch began to put their savings into foreign investments rather than their own trade, the Dutch elites became more exclusive, more preoccupied with ostentation, and less tolerant of deviations from strict Calvinism. The Dutch "golden age" was over.

Freedom and Slavery in the New World

The Dutch also lost ground to the French and English in the New World colonies. The French and English established settler colonies in North America and the Caribbean that would eventually provide

A Typical Dutch Scene from Daily Life
Dutch artist Jan Steen painted *The Baker Arent Oostward and His Wife* in 1658. Steen ran a brewery and tavern in addition to painting, and he was known for his interest in the details of daily life. Dutch artists popularized this kind of "genre" painting, which showed ordinary people at work and play. *(Rijksmuseum, Amsterdam.)*

fabulous revenues to the home countries. The Dutch, in contrast, lost their only settler colony in North America, New Netherland (present-day New York, New Jersey, Delaware, and Connecticut), to the English in 1674. The Dutch, English, and French all competed with other European nations for their share of the burgeoning slave trade, and slavery began to take clear institutional form in the New World in this period. While whites found in the colonies greater political and religious freedom than in Europe, they subjected black Africans to the most degrading forms of bondage.

The Rise of the Slave Trade After the Spanish and Portuguese had shown that African slaves could be transported and forced to labor in South and Central America, the English and French endeavored to set up similar labor systems in their new Caribbean island colonies. White planters with large tracts of land bought African slaves to work fields of sugarcane; and as they gradually built up their holdings, the planters displaced most of the original white settlers, who moved to mainland North American colonies. After 1661, when Barbados instituted a slave code that stripped all Africans of rights under English law, slavery became codified as an inherited status that applied only to blacks. The result was a society of extremes: the very wealthy whites (about 7 percent of the population in Barbados) and the enslaved, powerless black majority. The English brought few of their religious or constitutional practices to the Caribbean.

Other Caribbean colonies followed a similar pattern of development. Louis XIV promulgated a "black code" in 1685 to regulate the legal status of slaves in the French colonies and to prevent non-Catholics from owning slaves. The code supposedly set limits on the violence planters could exercise and required them to house, feed, and clothe their slaves. But white planters simply ignored provisions of the code that did not suit them, and in any case, because the code defined slaves as property, slaves could not themselves bring suit in court to demand better treatment.

The governments of England, France, Spain, Portugal, the Dutch Republic, and Denmark all encouraged private companies to traffic in black Africans, while the highest church and government authorities in Catholic and Protestant countries alike condoned the gradually expanding slave trade. In 1600, seventy-six hundred Africans were exported annually from Africa to the New World; by 1700, this number had increased more than fourfold to thirty-three thousand. Historians advance several different ideas about which factors increased the slave trade: some claim that improvements in muskets made European slavers more effective; others cite the rising price for slaves, which made their sale more attractive for Africans; still others focus on factors internal to Africa such as the increasing size of African armies and their use of muskets in fighting and capturing other Africans for sale as slaves. What is clear is that a combination of factors prepared the way for the development of an Atlantic economy based on slavery.

Constitutional Freedoms in the English Colonies Virtually left to themselves during the upheavals in England, the fledgling English colonies in North America developed representative government on their own. Almost every colony had a governor and a two-house legislature. The colonial legislatures constantly sought to increase their power and resisted the efforts of Charles II and James II to reaffirm royal control. William and Mary reluctantly allowed emerging colonial elites more control over local affairs. The social and political elite among the settlers hoped to impose an English social hierarchy dominated by rich landowners. Ordinary immigrants to the colonies, however, took advantage of plentiful land to carve out their own farms using white servants and, later, in some colonies, African slaves.

For native Americans, the expanding European presence meant something else altogether. They faced death through disease, warfare, and the accelerating loss of their homelands. Unlike white settlers, many native Americans believed that land was a divine gift provided for their collective use and not subject to individual ownership. Europeans' claims that they owned exclusive land rights consequently resulted in frequent skirmishes. In 1675–1676, for instance, three tribes allied under Metacomet (called King Philip by the English) threatened the survival of New England settlers, who savagely repulsed the attacks and sold their captives as slaves. Whites could portray native Americans as "noble savages," but when threatened they often depicted them as conspiring villains and sneaky heathens who were akin to Africans in their savagery. The benefits of constitutionalism were reserved for Europeans.

REVIEW QUESTION Why did constitutionalism thrive in the Dutch Republic and the British North American colonies, even as their participation in the slave trade grew?

Absolutism in Central and Eastern Europe

Constitutionalism had an outpost in central and eastern Europe, too, but there it collapsed in failure. A long crisis in Poland-Lithuania virtually destroyed central state authority and pulled much of eastern Europe into its turbulent wake. Most central and eastern European rulers followed Louis XIV's model of absolutist state building, though they did not blindly emulate him, in part because they confronted conditions peculiar to their regions. Everywhere in eastern Europe, nobles lorded over their serfs but owed almost slavish obedience in turn to their rulers.

Poland-Lithuania Overwhelmed

In the version of constitutionalism in Poland-Lithuania, the great nobles dominated the Sejm (parliament). To maintain an equilibrium among themselves, these nobles each wielded an absolute veto power. This "free veto" constitutional system deadlocked parliamentary government. The monarchy lost its room to maneuver and, with it, much of its remaining power.

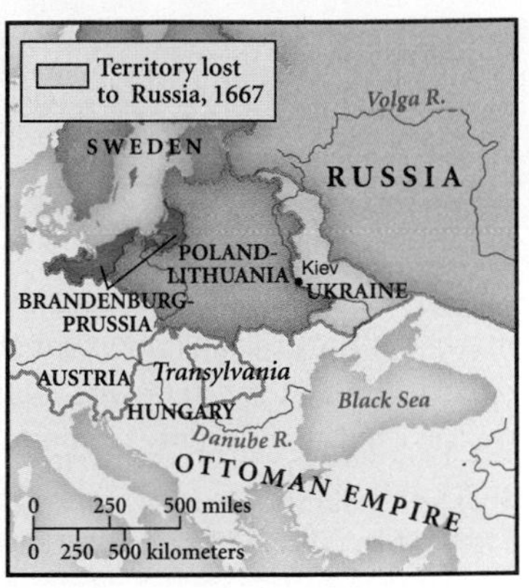

Poland-Lithuania in the Seventeenth Century

In 1648, Ukrainian Cossack warriors revolted against the king of Poland-Lithuania, inaugurating two decades of tumult known as the Deluge. *Cossack* was the name given to runaway serfs and poor nobles who formed outlaw bands in the no-man's-land of southern Russia and Ukraine. The Polish nobles who claimed this potentially rich land scorned the Cossacks as troublemakers, but to the Ukrainian peasant population they were liberators. In 1654, the Cossacks offered Ukraine to Russian rule, provoking a Russo-Polish war that ended in 1667 when the tsar annexed eastern Ukraine and Kiev. Neighboring powers tried to profit from the chaos in Poland-Lithuania: Sweden, Brandenburg-Prussia, and Transylvania sent armies to seize territory.

Many towns were destroyed in the fighting, and as much as a third of the Polish population perished. The once prosperous Jewish and Protestant minorities suffered greatly: some fifty-six thousand Jews were killed by the Cossacks, the Polish peasants, or the Russian troops, and thousands more had to flee or convert to Christianity. One rabbi wrote, "We were slaughtered each day, in a more agonizing way than cattle: they are butchered quickly, while we were being executed slowly." Surviving Jews moved from towns to shtetls (Jewish villages), where they took up petty trading, moneylending, tax gathering, and tavern leasing—activities that fanned peasant anti-Semitism. Desperate for protection amid the war, most Polish Protestants backed the violently anti-Catholic Swedes, and the victorious Catholic majority branded them as traitors. Some Protestant refugees fled to the Dutch Republic and England. In Poland-Lithuania it came to be assumed that a good Pole was a Catholic. The commonwealth had ceased to be an outpost of toleration.

The commonwealth revived briefly when a man of ability and ambition, Jan Sobieski (r. 1674–1696), was elected king. He gained a reputation throughout Europe when he led twenty-five thousand Polish cavalrymen into battle in the siege of Vienna in 1683. His cavalry helped rout the Turks and turned the tide against the Ottomans. Married to a politically shrewd French princess, Sobieski openly admired Louis XIV's France. Despite his efforts to rebuild the monarchy, he could not halt Poland-Lithuania's decline into powerlessness. The Polish

TAKING MEASURE

The Seventeenth-Century Army

The figures in this chart are only approximate, but they tell an important story. Take special note of the relative weight of the military in the different European states.

Source: From André Corvisier, *Armées et sociétés en Europe de 1494 à 1789* (Paris: Presses Universitaires de France, 1976), 126.

Questions to Consider

1. Why would England's army be so much smaller than that of the other European states?
2. Is the absolute or the relative size of the military the most important indicator of a state's power? Explain the reasons for your answer.

State	*Soldiers*	*Population*	*Ratio of soldiers/ total population*
France	300,000	20 million	1:66
Russia	220,000	14 million	1:64
Austria	100,000	8 million	1:80
Sweden	40,000	1 million	1:25
Brandenburg-Prussia	30,000	2 million	1:66
England	24,000	10 million	1:410

*Figures for the end of the seventeenth century, ranging from 1688 for Prussia to 1710 for France

version of constitutionalism fatally weakened the state and made it prey to neighboring powers.

Brandenburg-Prussia: Militaristic Absolutism

The contrast between Poland-Lithuania and Brandenburg-Prussia could not have been more extreme. The first was huge in territory, constitutional in government, and in the end a failed state. The second was puny, made up of disparate and far-flung territories, moving toward absolutism, and in the nineteenth century would unify the different German states into modern-day Germany. The ruler of Brandenburg was an elector, one of the seven German princes entitled to select the Holy Roman Emperor. Since the sixteenth century the ruler of Brandenburg had also controlled the duchy of East Prussia; after 1618, the state was called Brandenburg-Prussia. Despite meager resources, **Frederick William of Hohenzollern**, who was the Great Elector of Brandenburg-Prussia (r. 1640–1688), succeeded in welding his scattered lands into an absolutist state.

Frederick William of Hohenzollern: The Great Elector of Brandenburg-Prussia (r. 1640–1688) who brought his nation through the end of the Thirty Years' War and then succeeded in welding his scattered lands into an absolutist state.

Pressured first by the necessities of fighting the Thirty Years' War and then by the demands of reconstruction, Frederick William was determined to force his territories' estates (representative assemblies) to grant him a dependable income. The Great Elector struck a deal with the Junkers (nobles) of each province: in exchange for allowing him to collect taxes, he gave them complete control over their enserfed peasants and exempted them from taxation. The tactic worked. By the end of Frederick William's reign, the estates met only on ceremonial occasions.

Supplied with a steady income, Frederick William could devote his attention to military and bureaucratic consolidation. In the course of forty years he expanded his army from eight thousand to thirty thousand men. (See "Taking Measure," above.) The army mirrored the rigid domination of nobles over peasants that characterized Brandenburg-Prussian society: peasants filled the ranks, and Junkers became officers. Nobles also took positions as bureaucratic officials, but military needs always had priority. The elector named special war commissars to take charge not only of military affairs but also of tax collection. To hasten military dispatches, he also established one of Europe's first state postal systems.

As a Calvinist ruler, Frederick William avoided the ostentation of the French court, even while following the absolutist model of centralizing state power. He boldly rebuffed Louis XIV by welcoming twenty thousand French Huguenot refugees after Louis's revocation of the Edict of Nantes. In pursuing foreign and domestic policies that promoted state power and prestige, Frederick William adroitly switched sides in Louis's wars and would stop at almost nothing to crush resistance at home. In 1701, his son Frederick I (r. 1688–1713) persuaded Holy Roman Emperor Leopold I to grant him the title "king in Prussia" in exchange for support in the War of the Spanish Succession. Until then, there was only one kingdom in the Holy Roman Empire, the kingdom of Bohemia. Prussia had arrived as an important power.

An Uneasy Balance: Austrian Habsburgs and Ottoman Turks

Holy Roman Emperor Leopold I (r. 1658–1705) ruled over a variety of territories of different ethnicities, languages, and religions, yet in ways similar to his French and Prussian counterparts, he gradually consolidated his power. In addition to holding Louis XIV in check on his western frontiers, Leopold confronted the ever-present challenge of the Ottoman Turks to the east.

The Siege of Vienna, 1683
This detail from a painting by Franz Geffels shows the camp of the Ottoman Turks. The Turkish armies had surrounded Vienna since July 14, 1683. Jan Sobieski led an army of Poles who joined with Austrians and Germans to beat back the Turks on September 12, 1683. As with their earlier siege of Vienna in 1529, the Turks were again forced to withdraw. *(Photo © Alfredo Dagli Orti/The Art Archive/Corbis.)*

The Austrian Version of Absolutism Like all the Holy Roman Emperors since 1438, Leopold was an Austrian Habsburg. He was simultaneously duke of Upper and Lower Silesia, count of Tyrol, archduke of Upper and Lower Austria, king of Bohemia, king of Hungary and Croatia, and ruler of Styria and Moravia (Map 16.3). Some of these territories were provinces in the Holy Roman Empire; others were simply ruled from Vienna as Habsburg family holdings.

In response to the weakening of the Holy Roman Empire by the ravages of the Thirty Years' War, the emperor and his closest officials took control over recruiting, provisioning, and strategic planning and worked to replace the mercenaries hired during the war with a permanent standing army that promoted professional discipline. To pay for the army and staff his growing bureaucracy, Leopold gained the support of local aristocrats and chipped away at provincial institutions' powers.

Intent on replacing Bohemian nobles who had supported the 1618 revolt against Austrian authority, the Habsburgs promoted a new nobility made up of Czechs, Germans, Italians, Spaniards, and even Irish who used German as their common tongue, professed Catholicism, and loyally served the Austrian dynasty. Bohemia became a virtual Austrian colony. "Woe to you," lamented a Czech Jesuit in 1670, addressing Leopold. "The nobles you have oppressed, great cities made small. Of smiling towns you have made straggling villages." Austrian censors prohibited publication of this protest for over a century.

Battle for Hungary Austria had fought the Turks for control of Hungary for more than 150 years. In 1682, when war broke out again, Leopold controlled the northwest section of Hungary; the Turks occupied the center; and in the east, the Turks demanded tribute from the Hungarian princes who ruled Transylvania. As they had in 1529, the Turks in 1683 pushed all the way to the gates of Vienna and laid siege to the Austrian capital. With the help of Polish cavalry, the Austrians finally broke the siege and turned the tide in a major counteroffensive. (See the illustration above.) By the Treaty of Karlowitz of 1699, the Ottoman Turks surrendered almost all of Hungary to the Austrians,

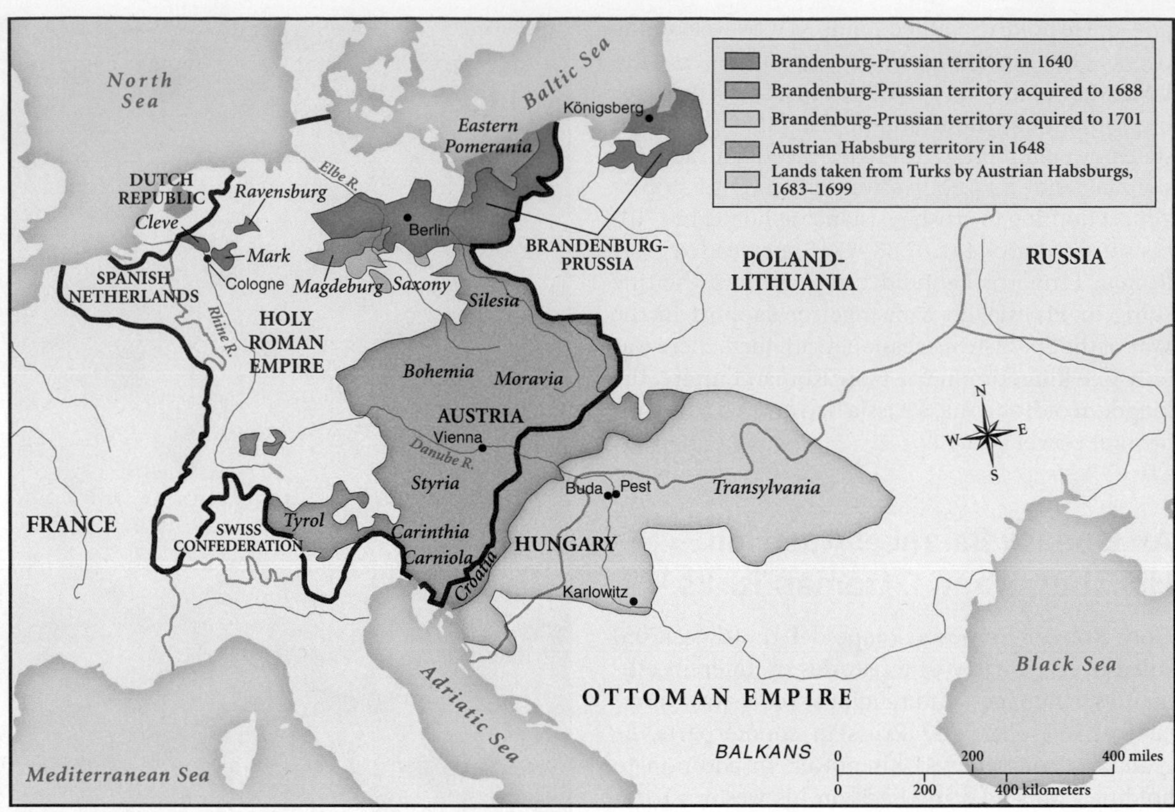

MAP 16.3 State Building in Central and Eastern Europe, 1648–1699
The Austrian Habsburgs had long contested the Ottoman Turks for dominance of eastern Europe, and by 1699 they had pushed the Turks out of Hungary. In central Europe, the Austrian Habsburgs confronted the growing power of Brandenburg-Prussia, which had emerged from relative obscurity after the Thirty Years' War to begin an aggressive program of expanding its military and its territorial base. As emperor of the Holy Roman Empire, the Austrian Habsburg ruler governed a huge expanse of territory, but the emperor's control was in fact only partial because of guarantees of local autonomy.

marking the beginning of the decline of Ottoman power.

Hungary's "liberation" from the Turks came at a high price. The fighting laid waste vast stretches of Hungary's central plain, and the population may have declined by as much as 65 percent in the seventeenth century. Once the Turks had been beaten back, Austrian rule over Hungary tightened. In 1687, the Habsburg dynasty's hereditary right to the Hungarian crown was acknowledged by the Hungarian diet, a parliament revived by Leopold in 1681 to gain the cooperation of Hungarian nobles. The diet was dominated by a core of pro-Habsburg Hungarian aristocrats who would support the dynasty until it fell in 1918; Austrians and Hungarians looked down on the other ethnic groups, such as Croats and Romanians, who had enjoyed considerable autonomy under the Ottoman Turks. To root out remaining Turkish influence and assert Austrian superiority, Leopold systematically destroyed Turkish buildings and rebuilt Catholic churches, monasteries, roadside shrines, and monuments in the flamboyant Austrian baroque style.

Ottoman State Authority The Ottoman Turks also pursued state consolidation, but in a very different fashion from Leopold I and other European rulers. The Ottoman state extended its authority through a combination of settlement and military control. Hundreds of thousands of Turkish families had moved with Turkish soldiers into the Balkan peninsula in the 1400s and 1500s. As locals converted to Islam, administration passed gradually into their hands. The Ottoman state, ultimately, would last longer than the French absolutist monarchy. Nevertheless, the seventeenth century marked a period of cultural decline in the eyes of the Turks themselves.

The Ottoman rulers, the sultans, were often challenged by mutinous army officers, but they rarely faced peasant revolts. Rather than resisting state authorities, Ottoman peasants periodically worked for the state as mercenaries. The sultans played off elites against one another, absorbing some into the state bureaucracy and pitting one level of authority against another. Despite frequent palace coups and assassinations of sultans, the Ottoman state survived. This constantly shifting social and political system explains how the Ottoman state could appear weak in Western eyes and still pose a massive military threat on Europe's southeastern borders.

Russia: Setting the Foundations of Bureaucratic Absolutism

Seventeenth-century Russia seemed a world apart from the Europe of Leopold I and Louis XIV. Straddling Europe and Asia, the Russian lands stretched across Siberia to the Pacific Ocean. Western visitors either sneered or shuddered at the "barbarism" of Russian life, and Russians reciprocated by nursing deep suspicions of everything foreign. But under the surface, Russia was evolving as an absolutist state; the tsars wanted to claim unlimited autocratic power, but like their European counterparts they had to surmount internal disorder and come to an accommodation with noble landlords.

Serfdom and the Code of 1649 When the Russian tsar Alexei (r. 1645–1676) tried to extend state authority by imposing new administrative structures and taxes in 1648, Moscow and other cities erupted in bloody rioting. The government immediately quelled the riots. In 1649, Alexei convened the Assembly of the Land (consisting of noble delegates from the provinces) to consult on a sweeping law code to organize Russian society in a strict social hierarchy. The code of 1649—which held for nearly two centuries—assigned all subjects to a hereditary class according to their current occupation or state needs. Slaves and free peasants were merged into a serf class. As serfs, they could not change occupations or move; they were tightly tied to the soil and to their noble masters. To prevent tax evasion, the code also forbade townspeople to move from the community where they resided. Nobles owed absolute obedience to the tsar and were required to serve in the army, but in return no other group could own estates worked by serfs. Serfs became the chattel of their lord, who could sell them like horses or land. Their lives differed little from those of the slaves on the plantations in the Americas.

Some peasants resisted enserfment. In 1667, **Stenka Razin**, the head of a powerful band of pirates and outlaws in southern Russia, led a rebellion that promised liberation from "the traitors and bloodsuckers of the peasant communes"—the great noble landowners, local governors, and Moscow courtiers. Captured four years later by the tsar's army, Razin was taken to Moscow, where he was dismembered in front of the public and his body thrown to the dogs. Thousands of his followers also suffered grisly deaths, but Razin's memory lived on in folk songs and legends. Landlords successfully petitioned for the use of state agents in searching for runaways, harsh penalties against those who harbored runaways, and the abolition of the statute of limitations on runaway serfs. The increase in Russian state authority went hand in hand with the enforcement of serfdom.

Stenka Razin: Leader of the 1667 rebellion that promised Russian peasants liberation from noble landowners and officials; he was captured by the tsar's army in 1671 and publicly executed in Moscow.

Stenka Razin in Captivity

After leading a revolt of thousands of serfs, peasants, and members of non-Russian tribes of the middle and lower Volga region, Stenka Razin was captured by Russian forces and led off to Moscow, as shown here, where he was executed in 1671. He has been the subject of songs, legends, and poems ever since. *(© Imagno/ullstein bild/The Image Works.)*

The Tsar's Absolute Powers To extend his power and emulate his western rivals, Tsar Alexei wanted a bigger army, exclusive control over state policy, and a greater say in religious matters. The size of the army increased dramatically from 35,000 in the 1630s to 220,000 by the end of the century. The Assembly of the Land, once an important source of consultation for the nobles, never met again after 1653. Alexei also imposed firm control over the Russian Orthodox church. In 1666, a church council reaffirmed the tsar's role as God's direct representative on earth. The state-dominated church took action against a religious group called the Old Believers, who rejected church efforts to bring Russian worship in line with Byzantine tradition. Whole communities of Old Believers starved or burned themselves to death rather than submit. Religious schism opened a gulf between the Russian people and the crown.

Nevertheless, modernizing trends prevailed. As the state bureaucracy expanded, adding more officials and establishing regulations and routines, the government intervened more and more in daily life. Decrees not only regulated tobacco smoking, card playing, and alcohol consumption but even dictated how people should leash and fence their pet dogs. Tsar Alexei set up the first Western-style theater in the Kremlin, and his daughter Sophia translated French plays. The most adventurous nobles began to wear German-style clothing. Some even argued that service, not just birth, should determine rank. Russia's long struggle over Western influences had begun.

REVIEW QUESTION Why did absolutism flourish everywhere in eastern Europe except Poland-Lithuania?

The Search for Order in Elite and Popular Culture

The state could intervene in daily life, as it did in Russia and all other states, even if subjects obeyed and order was maintained. In the period of state building from 1640 to 1715, questions about obedience, order, and the limits of state power occupied poets, painters, architects, and men of science as much as they did rulers and their ministers. How much freedom of expression could be allowed? How did the individual's needs and aspirations fit with the requirements of state authority? The greatest thinkers and writers wrestled with these issues and helped frame debates for generations to come. They did not have in mind people of the lower classes or slaves in the colonies. Elites worked to distinguish themselves from the lower classes by developing new codes of correct behavior and teaching order and discipline to their social inferiors. Their repeated efforts show, however, that popular culture had its own dynamics that resisted control from above.

Freedom and Constraint in the Arts and Sciences

Most Europeans feared disorder above all else. The French mathematician Blaise Pascal vividly captured their worries in his *Pensées* (Thoughts) of 1660: "I look on all sides, and I see only darkness everywhere." Though Pascal made important contributions to the mathematical theory of probabilities, he was skeptical about the human ability to forge order out of chaos: "Nature presents to me nothing which is not a matter of doubt and concern. . . . It is incomprehensible that God should exist, and incomprehensible that He should not exist." Pascal urged his readers to accept the wager that God existed. Reason could not determine whether God existed or not, Pascal concluded. Poets, painters, and architects all grappled with similar issues of faith, reason, and authority, but most of them came to more positive conclusions than Pascal about human capacities.

Milton The English Puritan poet John Milton (1608–1674) wrestled with the inevitable limitations on individual liberty. In 1643, in the midst of the civil war between king and Parliament, he published writings in favor of divorce. When Parliament enacted a censorship law aimed at such literature, Milton responded in 1644 with one of the first defenses of freedom of the press, *Areopagitica*. (See Document, "John Milton, Defense of Freedom of the Press," page 542.) In it, he argued that even controversial books about religion should be allowed because the state could not command religious belief. Milton favored limited religious toleration; that is, he wanted religious freedom for the many varieties of Protestants, but not for Catholics or non-Christians. Milton served as secretary to the Council of State during Cromwell's rule and earned the enmity of Charles II by writing a justification for the execution of his father, Charles I.

Forced into retirement after the restoration of the monarchy, Milton published his epic poem *Paradise Lost* in 1667. He used the biblical Adam and Eve's fall from grace to meditate on human freedom and the tragedies of rebellion. Although Milton wanted to "justify the ways of God to man," his Satan, the proud angel who challenges God and is cast out of heaven, is so compelling as to be heroic. In the end, Adam and Eve embrace moral responsibility for their actions. Individuals learn the limits to their freedom, yet personal liberty remains essential to their humanity.

The Varieties of Artistic Style The dominant artistic styles of the time — the baroque and the classical — both submerged the ordinary individual in a grander design. The baroque style proved to be especially suitable for public displays of faith and power that awed individual beholders. The combination of religious and political purposes in baroque art is best exemplified in the architecture and sculpture of Gian Lorenzo Bernini (1598–1680), the papacy's official artist. His architectural masterpiece was the gigantic square facing St. Peter's Basilica in Rome. Bernini's use of freestanding colonnades and a huge open space was meant to impress the individual observer with the power of the popes and the Catholic religion. He also sculpted tombs for the popes and a large statue of Constantine, the first Christian emperor of Rome — perfect examples of the marriage of power and religion.

Although France was a Catholic country, French painters, sculptors, and architects, like their patron Louis XIV, preferred the standards of **classicism** to those of the baroque. French artists developed classicism to be a French national style, distinct from the baroque style closely associated with France's enemies, the Austrian and Spanish Habsburgs. As its name suggests, classicism reflected the ideals of the art of antiquity: geometric shapes, order, and harmony of lines took precedence over the sensuous, exuberant, and emotional forms of the baroque. Rather than being overshadowed by the sheer power of emotional display, in classicism the individual could be found at the intersection of converging, symmetrical, straight lines. (See the illustration on page 543.) These influences were apparent in the work of the leading French painters of the period, Nicolas Poussin (1594–1665) and Claude Lorrain (1600–1682), both of whom worked in Rome and tried to re-create classical Roman values in their mythological scenes and Roman landscapes.

Art could also serve the interests of science. One of the most skilled illustrators of insects and flowers was Maria Sibylla Merian (1646–1717), a German-born painter-scholar whose engravings were widely celebrated for their brilliant realism and microscopic clarity. Merian eventually separated from her husband and joined a sect called the Labadists (after its French founder, Jean de Labadie), whose members did not believe in formal marriage ties. After moving with her daughters to the Labadists' community in the northern Dutch province of Friesland, Merian went with missionaries from the sect to the Dutch colony of Surinam, in South America, and painted watercolors (see the illustration on page 544) of the exotic flowers, birds, and insects she found in the jungle around the cocoa and sugarcane plantations. Many women during this time became known for their still lifes and especially their paintings of flowers.

classicism: A seventeenth-century style of painting and architecture that reflected the ideals of the art of antiquity; in classicism, geometric shapes, order, and harmony of lines took precedence over the sensuous, exuberant, and emotional forms of the baroque.

Gian Lorenzo Bernini, *Ecstasy of St. Teresa of Ávila* (c. 1650)
This ultimate statement of baroque sculpture captures all the drama and even sensationalism of a mystical religious faith. Bernini based his figures on a vision reported by St. Teresa in which she saw an angel: "In his hands I saw a great golden spear, and at the iron tip there appeared to be a point of fire. This he plunged into my heart several times so that it penetrated my entrails. When he pulled it out I felt that he took them with it, and left me utterly consumed by the great love of God." *(Scala/Art Resource, NY.)*

Public Interest in Science Despite the initial religious controversies associated with the scientific revolution, absolutist rulers quickly saw the potential of the new science for enhancing their prestige and glory. Frederick William, the Great Elector of Brandenburg-Prussia, for example, set up agricultural experiments in front of his Berlin palace, and various German princes supported the work of Gottfried Wilhelm Leibniz (1646–1716), who claimed that he, and not Isaac Newton, had invented modern calculus. A lawyer, diplomat, mathematician, and scholar who wrote about metaphysics, cosmology, and history, Leibniz also helped establish scientific societies in the German states.

Government involvement in science was greatest in France, where science became an arm of

DOCUMENT

John Milton, Defense of Freedom of the Press (1644)

In Areopagitica *(1644), the English poet John Milton rebuked Parliament for passing a bill to restrict freedom of the press by requiring licensing of every publication. The title came from Areopagus, the name of a court in ancient Athens. Milton argued that freedom of thought was essential to human dignity.*

I deny not but that it is of greatest concernment in the church and commonwealth to have a vigilant eye how books demean themselves as well as men; and thereafter to confine, imprison, and do sharpest justice on them as malefactors. For books are not absolutely dead things, but do contain a potency of life in them to be as active as that soul was whose progeny they are; nay, they do preserve as in a vial the purest efficacy and extraction of that living intellect that bred them. I know they are as lively and as vigorously productive as those fabulous dragon's teeth; and being sown up and down, may chance to spring up armed men. And yet, on the other hand, unless wariness be used, as good almost kill a man as kill a good book: who kills a man kills a reasonable creature, God's image; but he who destroys a good book, kills reason itself, kills the image of God, as it were, in the eye. Many a man lives a burden to the earth; but a good book is the precious lifeblood of a master spirit, embalmed and treasured up on purpose to a life beyond life. 'Tis true, no age can restore a life, whereof perhaps there is no great loss; and revolutions of ages do not oft recover the loss of a rejected truth, for the want of which whole nations fare the worse. We should be wary, therefore, what persecution we raise against the living labors of public men, how we spill that seasoned life of man preserved and stored up in books; since we see a kind of homicide may be thus committed, sometimes a martyrdom; and if it extend to the whole impression, a kind of massacre, whereof the execution ends not in the slaying of an elemental life, but strikes at that ethereal and fifth essence, the breath of reason itself, slays an immortality rather than a life. But lest I should be condemned of introducing license, while I oppose licensing, I refuse not the pains to be so much historical as will serve to show what hath been done by ancient and famous commonwealths against this disorder, till the very time that this project of licensing crept out of the Inquisition, was caught up by our prelates, and hath caught some of our presbyters. . . . As therefore the state of man now is, what wisdom can there be to choose, what continence to forbear without the knowledge of evil? He that can apprehend and consider vice with all her baits and seeming pleasures, and yet abstain, and yet distinguish, and yet prefer that which is truly better, he is the true warfaring Christian. I cannot praise a fugitive and cloistered virtue, unexercised and unbreathed, that never sallies out and sees her adversary, but slinks out of the race where that immortal garland is to be run for, not without dust and heat. Assuredly we bring not innocence into the world, we bring impurity much rather: that which purifies us is trial, and trial is by what is contrary.

Source: John Milton, *Milton's Prose Writing* (London: J. M. Dant, 1961), 149–50, 158.

Question to Consider

- **Why does Milton oppose censorship of books?**

mercantilist policy; in 1666, Jean-Baptiste Colbert founded the Royal Academy of Sciences, which supplied fifteen scientists with government stipends. It met in the King's Library in Paris, where for the first years the members devoted themselves to alchemical experiments and the study of mechanical devices.

Constitutional states supported science informally but provided an environment that encouraged its spread. The Royal Society of London, the counterpart to the one in Paris, grew out of informal meetings of scientists at London and Oxford rather than direct government involvement. It received a royal charter in 1662 but maintained complete independence. The society's secretary described its business to be "in the first place, to scrutinize the whole of Nature and to investigate its activity and powers by means of observations and experiments; and then in course of time to hammer out a more solid philosophy and more ample amenities of civilization." Whether the state paid for the work or not, thinkers of the day now tied science explicitly to social progress.

Because of their exclusion from most universities, women only rarely participated in the new scientific discoveries. In 1667, nonetheless, the Royal Society of London invited Margaret Cavendish, a writer of poems, essays, letters, and philosophical treatises, to attend a meeting to watch the exhibition of experiments. Labeled "mad" by her critics, she attacked the use of telescopes and microscopes because she detected in the new experimentalism a mechanistic view of the world that exalted masculine prowess and challenged the Christian belief in freedom of the will. Yet she urged the formal education of women, complaining that "we are kept like birds in cages to hop up and down in our houses." "Many of our Sex may have as much wit, and be capable of

French Classicism
This painting by Nicolas Poussin, *Discovery of Achilles on Skyros* (1649–1650), shows the French interest in classical themes and ideals. In the Greek story, Thetis dresses her son Achilles as a young woman and hides him on the island of Skyros so he would not have to fight in the Trojan War. When a chest of treasures is offered to the women, Achilles reveals himself (he is the figure on the far right) because he cannot resist the sword. In telling the story, Poussin emphasizes harmony and almost a sedateness of composition, avoiding the exuberance and emotionalism of the baroque style. *(Nicolas Poussin, French [active in Rome], 1594–1665. Oil on canvas, 97.5 x 131.1 cm. [38⅜ x 51⅝ in.], William I. Koch Gallery, Museum of Fine Arts, Boston, Juliana Cheney Edwards Collection, 46.463. Photograph © 2011 Museum of Fine Arts, Boston.)*

Learning as well as men," she insisted, "but since they want Instructions [lack education], it is not possible they should attain to it."

Women and Manners

Although excluded from the universities and the professions, women played important roles not only in the home but also in more formal spheres of social interaction, such as the courts of rulers. Women often took the lead in teaching manners or social etiquette. Women's importance in refining social relationships quickly became a subject of controversy.

The Cultivation of Manners The court had long been a central arena for the development of manners. Under the tutelage of their mothers and wives, nobles learned to hide all that was crass and to maintain a fine sense of social distinction. In some ways, aristocratic men were expected to act more like women; just as women had long been expected to please men, now aristocratic men had to please their monarch or patron by displaying proper manners and conversing with elegance and wit. The art of pleasing included foreign languages (especially French), dance, a taste for fine music, and attention to dress.

As part of the evolution of new aristocratic ideals, nobles learned to disdain all that was lowly. The upper classes began to reject popular festivals and fairs in favor of private theaters, where seats were relatively expensive and behavior was formal. Clowns and buffoons now seemed vulgar; the last king of England to keep a court fool was Charles I. Some tastes spread downward from the upper classes, however. Chivalric romances like Ariosto's *Orlando Furioso* that had long entranced the nobility now appeared in simplified form in cheap booklets printed for lower-class readers.

Molière, the greatest French playwright of the seventeenth century, wrote sparkling comedies of manners that revealed much about the new aristocratic behavior. His play *The Middle-Class Gentleman*, first performed for Louis XIV in 1670, revolves around the yearning of a rich middle-class Frenchman, Monsieur Jourdain, to learn to act like a *gentilhomme* (both "gentleman" and "nobleman"). Monsieur Jourdain buys fancy clothes; hires private instructors in dancing, music, fencing, and philosophy; and lends money to a debt-ridden noble in hopes that the noble will marry his daughter. Only his sensible wife and his daughter's love for a worthier commoner stand in his way. The message for the king's courtiers seemed to be a reassuring one: only born nobles can hope to act like nobles. But the play also showed how the middle classes were learning to emulate the nobility; if one could learn to act nobly through self-discipline, could not anyone with some education and money pass himself off as noble?

As Molière's play demonstrated, new attention to manners trickled down from the court to the middle class. A French treatise on manners written in 1672 explained proper behavior:

> If everyone is eating from the same dish, you should take care not to put your hand into it before those of higher rank have done so. . . . Formerly one was permitted . . . to dip one's bread into the sauce, provided only that one

> had not already bitten it. Nowadays that would be a kind of rusticity. Formerly one was allowed to take from one's mouth what one could not eat and drop it on the floor, provided it was done skillfully. Now that would be very disgusting.

The key words *rusticity* and *disgusting* reveal the association of unacceptable social behavior with the peasantry, dirt, and repulsion. Similar rules governed spitting and blowing one's nose in public. Once the elite had successfully distinguished itself from the lower classes through manners, scholars became more interested in studying popular expressions. They avidly collected proverbs, folktales, and songs—all of these now curiosities.

Debates about Women's Roles Courtly manners often permeated the upper reaches of society by means of the **salon**, an informal gathering held regularly in a private home and presided over by a socially eminent woman. In 1661, one French author claimed to have identified 251 Parisian women as hostesses of salons. The French government occasionally worried that these gatherings might challenge its authority, but the three main topics of conversation were love, literature, and philosophy. Hostesses often worked hard to encourage the careers of budding authors. Before publishing a manuscript, many authors, including court favorites like Pierre Corneille and Jean Racine, would read their compositions to a salon gathering.

Some women went beyond encouraging male authors and began to write on their own, but they faced many obstacles. Madame de Lafayette wrote several short novels that were published anonymously because it was considered inappropriate for aristocratic women to appear in print. Following the publication of *The Princess of Clèves* in 1678, she denied having written it. Hannah Woolley, the English author of many books on domestic conduct, published under the name of her first husband. Women were known for writing wonderful letters, but the correspondence circulated only in handwritten form. In the 1650s, despite these limitations, French women began to turn out best sellers of a new type of literary form, the novel. Their success prompted the philosopher Pierre Bayle to remark in 1697 that "our best French novels for a long time have been written by women."

salon: An informal gathering held regularly in a private home and presided over by a socially eminent woman; salons spread from France in the seventeenth century to other countries in the eighteenth century.

European Fascination with Products of the New World

In this painting of a banana plant, Maria Sibylla Merian offers a scientific study of one of the many exotic plants and animals found by Europeans who traveled to the colonies overseas. In 1699, Merian traveled to the Dutch South American colony of Surinam with her daughter. *(Courtesy of Hunt Institute for Botanical Documentation, Carnegie Mellon University, Pittsburgh, Pennsylvania.)*

The new importance of women in the world of manners and letters did not sit well with everyone. Although the French writer François Poulain de la Barre, in a series of works published in the 1670s, used the new science to assert the equality of women's minds, most men resisted the idea. Clergy, lawyers, scholars, and playwrights attacked women's growing public influence. Women, they complained, were corrupting forces and needed restraint. Only marriage, "this salutary yoke," could control their passions and weaknesses. Women were accused of raising "the banner of prostitution in the salons, in the promenades, and in the streets." Molière wrote plays denouncing women's pretension to judge literary merit. English playwrights derided learned women by creating characters with names such as Lady Knowall, Lady Meanwell, and Mrs. Lovewit.

A real-life target of the English playwrights was Aphra Behn (1640–1689), one of the first professional woman authors, who supported herself by journalism, wrote plays and poetry, and translated scientific works. Her short novel *Oroonoko* (1688) told the story of an African prince mistakenly sold into slavery. The story was so successful that it was adapted by playwrights and performed repeatedly in England and France for the next hundred years.

Women also played important roles in the new colonies. To establish more permanent and settled colonies, governments promoted the emigration of women so that male colonists would set up orderly white Christian households rather than pursuing sexual relations with native or slave women. Since many fewer women than men emigrated to the colonies, however, sexual relations between male colonists and native and slave women continued to be a vexed issue.

Reforming Popular Culture

Controversies over female influence had little effect on the unschooled peasants who made up most of Europe's population. Their culture had three main elements: their religion, which shaped every aspect of life and death; the knowledge needed to work at farming or in a trade; and popular forms of entertainment such as village fairs and dances. What changed most noticeably in the seventeenth century was the social elites' attitude toward lower-class culture. The division between elite and popular culture widened as elites insisted on their difference from the lower orders and tried to instill new forms of discipline in their social inferiors. These efforts did not always succeed, however, as villagers tenaciously clung to their own traditions.

Popular Religion

In the seventeenth century, Protestant and Catholic churches alike pushed hard to change popular religious practices. Their campaigns against popular "paganism" began during the sixteenth-century Protestant Reformation and Catholic Counter-Reformation but reached much of rural Europe only in the seventeenth century. Puritans in England tried to root out maypole dances, Sunday village fairs, gambling, taverns, and bawdy ballads because they interfered with sober observance of the Sabbath. In Lutheran Norway, pastors denounced a widespread belief in the miracle-working powers of St. Olaf. The word *superstition* previously meant "false religion" (Protestantism was a superstition for Catholics, Catholicism for Protestants); in the seventeenth century it took on its modern meaning of irrational fears, beliefs, and practices, which anyone educated or refined would avoid.

The Catholic campaign against superstitious practices found a ready ally in Louis XIV. While the Sun King reformed the nobles at court through etiquette and manners, Catholic bishops in the French provinces trained parish priests to reform their flocks by using catechisms in local dialects and insisting that parishioners attend Mass. The church faced a formidable challenge. One bishop in France complained in 1671, "Can you believe that there are in this diocese entire villages where no one has even heard of Jesus Christ?" In some places, believers sacrificed animals to the Virgin, prayed to the new moon, and worshipped at the sources of streams as in pre-Christian times.

Like its Protestant counterpart, the Catholic campaign against ignorance and superstition helped extend state power. Clergy, officials, and local police worked together to limit carnival celebrations, to regulate pilgrimages to shrines, and to replace "indecent" images of saints with more restrained and decorous ones. In Catholicism, the cult of the Virgin Mary and devotions closely connected with Jesus, such as the Holy Sacrament and the Sacred Heart, took precedence over the celebration of popular saints who seemed to have pagan origins or were credited with unverified miracles. Reformers everywhere tried to limit the number of feast days on the grounds that they encouraged lewd behavior.

New Attitudes toward Poverty

The campaign for more disciplined religious practices helped generate a new attitude toward the poor. Poverty previously had been closely linked with charity and virtue in Christianity; it was a Christian duty to give alms to the poor, and Jesus and many of the saints had purposely chosen lives of poverty. In the sixteenth and seventeenth centuries, the upper classes, the church, and the state increasingly regarded the poor as dangerous, deceitful, and lacking in character. "Criminal laziness is the source of all their vices," wrote a Jesuit "expert" on the poor. The courts had previously expelled beggars from cities; now local leaders, both Catholic and Protestant, tried to reform their character. Municipal magistrates collected taxes for poor relief, and local notables organized charities; together they transformed hospitals into houses of confinement for beggars. In Catholic France, upper-class women's religious associations, known as confraternities, set up asylums that confined prostitutes (by arrest if necessary) and rehabilitated them. Confraternities also founded hospices where orphans learned proper behavior and respect for their betters. Such groups advocated harsh discipline as the cure for poverty.

As hard times increased the numbers of the poor and the rates of violent crime as well, attitudes toward the poor hardened. The elites tried to separate the very poor from society either to change them or to keep them from contaminating others. Hospitals became holding pens for society's unwanted members; in them, the poor joined the disabled, the incurably diseased, and the insane. The founding of hospitals demonstrates the connection between elites' attitudes and state building. In 1676, Louis XIV ordered every French city to establish a hospital, and his government took charge of the finances. Other rulers soon followed the same path.

Popular Resistance to Reform Even as elites set themselves apart and reformers from church and state tried to regulate popular activities, villagers and townspeople pushed back with reassertions of their own values. For hundreds of years, peasants had maintained their own forms of village justice—called variously "rough music," "ride on a donkey," "skimmington," "charivari," or in North America, "shivaree." If a young man married a much older woman for her money, for example, villagers would serenade the couple by ringing bells, playing crude flutes, banging pots and pans, and shooting muskets. If a man was rumored to have been physically assaulted by his wife, a reversal of the usual sex roles, he (or effigies of him and his wife) might be ridden on a donkey facing backward (to signify the role reversal) and pelted with dung before being ducked in a nearby pond or river. Anyone who transgressed the local customs governing family life—adulterers, for example—might suffer a similar fate. Processions sometimes included the display of horned animal heads (a symbol of adultery) or obscene drawings, and people made up mocking rhymes and songs for various occasions. Some villagers singled out rebellious women, wife beaters, and fathers deemed excessively cruel to their children. Others directed their mockery at tax officials, gamekeepers on big estates who tried to keep villagers from hunting, or unpopular preachers.

No matter how much care went into controlling religious festivals, such events almost invariably opened the door to popular reinterpretation and sometimes drunken celebration. When the Spanish introduced Corpus Christi processions to their colony in Peru in the seventeenth century, elite Incas dressed in royal costumes to carry the banners of their parishes. Their clothing and ornaments combined Christian symbols with their own indigenous ones. They thus signaled their conversion to Catholicism but also reasserted their own prior identities. The Corpus Christi festival, held in late May or early June, conveniently took place about the same time as Inca festivals from the pre-Spanish era. Carnival, the days preceding Lent on the Christian calendar (Mardi Gras, or Fat Tuesday, is the last of them), offered the occasion for public revelry of all sorts. Although Catholic clergy worked hard to clamp down on the more riotous aspects of Carnival, many towns and villages still held parades, like those of modern New Orleans or Rio de Janeiro, that included companies of local men dressed in special costumes and gigantic stuffed figures, sometimes with animal skins or heads, or elaborate masks.

REVIEW QUESTION How did elite and popular culture become more separate in the seventeenth century?

Conclusion

The search for order took place on various levels, from the reform of the disorderly poor to the establishment of bureaucratic routines in government. The absolutist government of Louis XIV served as a model for all those who aimed to increase the power of the central state. Even Louis's rivals—such as the Holy Roman Emperor Leopold I and Frederick William, the Great Elector of Brandenburg-Prussia—followed his lead in centralizing authority and building up their armies. Whether absolutist or constitutionalist in form, seventeenth-century states aimed to penetrate more deeply into the lives of their subjects. They wanted more men for their armed forces; higher taxes to support their proj-

Mixing the Old World and the New
This ritual drinking vessel from Peru from the mid-seventeeenth century shows an Inca dignitary preceded by two musicians: a European trumpet player and an African drummer, both wearing cloaks and feathered hats. The decoration is one of the earliest indigenous representations of an African in Latin America. *(From the British Museum/photo © Werner Forman/HIP/The Image Works.)*

ects; and more control over foreign trade, religious dissent, and society's unwanted.

Some tears had begun to appear, however, in the seamless fabric of state power. The civil war between Charles I and Parliament in England in the 1640s opened the way to new demands for political participation. When Parliament overthrew James II in 1688, it also insisted that the new king and queen, William and Mary, agree to a Bill of Rights. Left on their own during the turmoil in England, the English North American colonies developed distinctive forms of representative government. In the eighteenth century, new levels of economic growth and the appearance of new social groups would exert pressures on the European state system. The success of seventeenth-century rulers created the political and economic conditions in which their critics would flourish.

FOR FURTHER EXPLORATION

- **For additional primary-source material from this period**, see *Sources of the Making of the West*, Fourth Edition.
- **For Web sites, images, and documents related to topics in this chapter**, visit *Make History* at bedfordstmartins.com/hunt.

MAPPING THE WEST

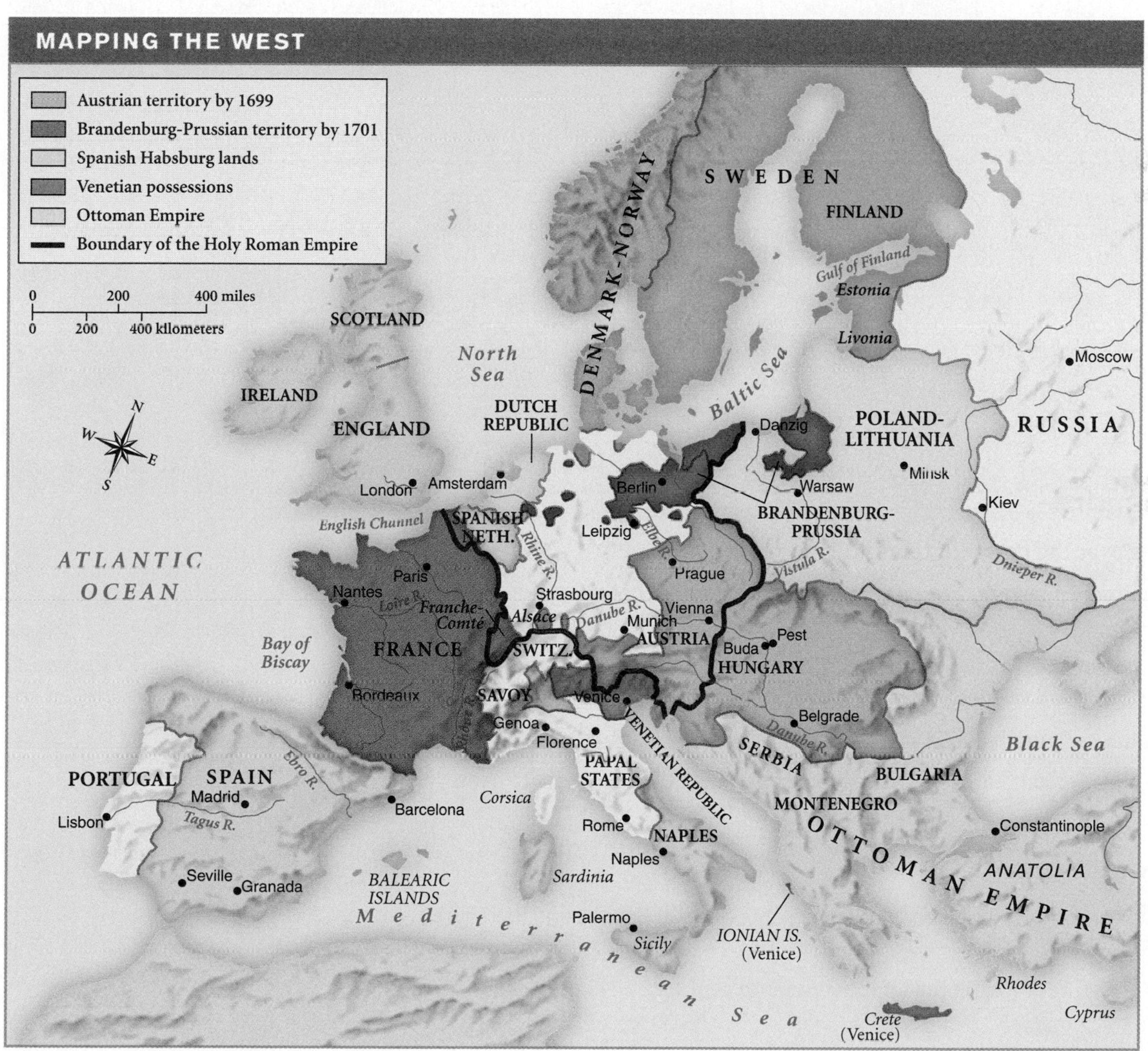

Europe at the End of the Seventeenth Century

Size was not necessarily an advantage in the late 1600s. Poland-Lithuania, a large country on the map, had been fatally weakened by internal conflicts. In the next century it would disappear entirely. While the Ottoman Empire still controlled an extensive territory, outside of Anatolia its rule depended on intermediaries. The Austrian Habsburgs had pushed the Turks out of Hungary and back into the Balkans. The tiny Dutch Republic, meanwhile, had become very rich through international commerce and was the envy of far larger nations.

Chapter 16 Review

Online Study Guide bedfordstmartins.com/hunt

Key Terms and People

In the grid below, identify the term or person and explain its historical significance. (To do this exercise online, go to bedfordstmartins.com/hunt.)

Term	Who or What & When	Why It Matters
absolutism (p. 515)		
constitutionalism (p. 516)		
Louis XIV (p. 516)		
revocation of the Edict of Nantes (p. 521)		
bureaucracy (p. 521)		
mercantilism (p. 522)		
Levellers (p. 526)		
William, prince of Orange (p. 530)		
Glorious Revolution (p. 530)		
social contract (p. 531)		
Frederick William of Hohenzollern (p. 536)		
Stenka Razin (p. 539)		
classicism (p. 541)		
salon (p. 544)		

Review Questions

1. How "absolute" was the power of Louis XIV?
2. What differences over religion and politics caused the conflict between king and Parliament in England?
3. Why did constitutionalism thrive in the Dutch Republic and the British North American colonies, even as their participation in the slave trade grew?
4. Why did absolutism flourish everywhere in eastern Europe except Poland-Lithuania?
5. How did elite and popular culture become more separate in the seventeenth century?

Making Connections

1. What accounts for the success of absolutism in some parts of Europe and its failure in others?
2. How did religious differences in the late seventeenth century still cause political conflict?
3. What were the chief differences between eastern and western Europe in this period?
4. Why was the search for order a major theme in science, politics, and the arts during this period?

Important Events

Date	Event	Date	Event
1642–1646	English civil war between Charles I and Parliament	1678	Madame de Lafayette anonymously publishes *The Princess of Clèves*
1648	Peace of Westphalia ends Thirty Years' War; Fronde revolt challenges royal authority in France; Ukrainian Cossack warriors rebel against king of Poland-Lithuania; Spain formally recognizes independence of Dutch Republic	1683	Austrian Habsburgs break Turkish siege of Vienna
1649	Charles I of England executed; new Russian legal code assigns all to hereditary class	1685	Louis XIV revokes Edict of Nantes
1651	Thomas Hobbes publishes *Leviathan*	1688	Parliament deposes James II; William, prince of Orange, and Mary take the throne
1660	Monarchy restored in England	1690	John Locke publishes *Two Treatises of Government and Essay Concerning Human Understanding*
1661	Slave code set up in Barbados		
1667	Louis XIV begins first of many wars that continue throughout his reign		

- Consider three events: **Thomas Hobbes publishes *Leviathan* (1651)**, **Madame de Lafayette anonymously publishes *The Princess of Clèves* (1678)**, and **John Locke publishes *Two Treatises of Government* (1690)**. How did Hobbes's new doctrine of absolute political authority, de Lafayette's novel, and Locke's emphasis on a social contract represent both an effort to create order and a challenge to the established order?

SUGGESTED REFERENCES

Recent studies have insisted that absolutism could never be entirely absolute because rulers depended on collaboration to enforce their policies. Studies of constitutional governments have emphasized the limitations of freedoms for the lower classes and especially for slaves.

Adamson, J. S. A. *The English Civil War: Conflict and Contexts, 1640–49.* 2009.

Barkey, Karen. *Empire of Difference: The Ottomans in Comparative Perspective.* 2008.

*Beik, William. *Louis XIV and Absolutism: A Brief Study with Documents.* 2000.

Boucher, Philip P. *France and the American Tropics to 1700: Tropics of Discontent?* 2008.

Brook, Timothy. *Vermeer's Hat: The Seventeenth Century and the Dawn of the Global World.* 2008.

Cromwell, Oliver: http://www.olivercromwell.org/

Davies, Brian L. *Warfare, State and Society on the Black Sea Steppe, 1500–1700.* 2007.

Davis, Natalie Zemon. *Women on the Margins: Three Seventeenth-Century Lives.* 1995.

*Forster, Elborg, trans. *A Woman's Life in the Court of the Sun King: Elisabeth Charlotte, Duchesse d'Orléans.* 1984.

France in America (site of the Library of Congress on French colonies in North America): http://international.loc.gov/intldl/fiahtml/fiatheme.html#track1

McKay, Derek. *The Great Elector.* 2001.

Michels, Georg Bernhard. *At War with the Church: Religious Dissent in Seventeenth-Century Russia.* 1999.

Nolan, Cathal J. *Wars of the Age of Louis XIV, 1650–1715: An Encyclopedia of Global Warfare and Civilization.* 2008.

*Pincus, Steven C. A. *England's Glorious Revolution, 1688–1689: A Brief History with Documents.* 2006.

Soll, Jacob. *The Information Master: Jean-Baptiste Colbert's Secret State Intelligence System.* 2009.

Stoye, John. *The Siege of Vienna: The Last Great Trial Between Cross and Crescent.* 2006.

Versailles castle: http://en.chateauversailles.fr/homepage

*Primary source.

CHAPTER 17

The Atlantic System and Its Consequences

1700–1750

The Atlantic System and the World Economy 552
- Slavery and the Atlantic System
- World Trade and Settlement
- The Birth of Consumer Society

New Social and Cultural Patterns 561
- Agricultural Revolution
- Social Life in the Cities
- New Tastes in the Arts
- Religious Revivals

Consolidation of the European State System 567
- A New Power Alignment
- British Rise and Dutch Decline
- Russia's Emergence as a European Power
- Continuing Dynastic Struggles
- The Power of Diplomacy and the Importance of Population

The Birth of the Enlightenment 576
- Popularization of Science and Challenges to Religion
- Travel Literature and the Challenge to Custom and Tradition
- Raising the Woman Question

In 1699 a few coffee plants changed the history of the world. European travelers at the end of the sixteenth century noticed Middle Eastern people drinking a "black drink" called *kavah*, but few Europeans sampled the drink at first, and the Arab monopoly on its production kept prices high. This all changed in 1699, when Dutch traders brought a few coffee plants from the east coast of India to their colony of Java (now Indonesia), which proved ideal for growing the beans. Within two decades, the trickle of beans going from Java to Europe became a flood of 200,000 pounds a year. Soon that figure rose to millions of pounds a year. After a shoot from a Dutch plant offered to Louis XIV as a present made its way to the Caribbean island of Martinique in 1721, coffee plants quickly spread throughout the Caribbean, where African slaves provided the plantation labor.

In Europe, imported coffee spurred the development of a new kind of meeting place: the first coffeehouse had opened in London in 1652, and the idea spread quickly to other European cities. Men began gathering in coffeehouses to drink, read newspapers, and talk politics. As a London newspaper commented in 1737, "There's scarce an Alley in City and Suburbs but has a Coffeehouse in it, which may be called the School of Public Spirit, where every Man over Daily and Weekly Journals, a Mug, or a Dram . . . devotes himself to that glorious one, his Country."

European consumption of coffee, tea, chocolate, and other novelties increased dramatically as European nations forged worldwide economic links. At the center of this new global economy was the **Atlantic system**, the web of trade routes that bound together western Europe, Africa, and

London Coffeehouse
This gouache (a variant on watercolor painting) from about 1725 depicts a scene from a London coffeehouse located in the courtyard of the Royal Exchange (merchants' bank). Middle-class men (wearing wigs) read newspapers, drink coffee, smoke pipes, and discuss the news of the day. The coffeehouse has drawn them out of their homes into a new public space. *(The British Museum, London, UK/The Bridgeman Art Library International.)*

Atlantic system: The network of trade established in the 1700s that bound together western Europe, Africa, and the Americas. Europeans sold slaves from western Africa and bought commodities that were produced by the new colonial plantations in North and South America and the Caribbean.

the Americas. Europeans bought slaves in western Africa, transported them to be sold in the colonies in North and South America and the Caribbean, bought raw commodities such as coffee and sugar that were produced by the new colonial plantations, and then sold those commodities in European ports for refining and reshipment. This Atlantic system, which first took clear shape in the early eighteenth century, became the hub of European expansion throughout the world.

Coffee drinking is just one example of the many new social and cultural patterns that took root between 1700 and 1750. Improvements in agricultural production at home reinforced the effects of trade overseas; Europeans now had more disposable income for extras, and they spent their money not only in the new coffeehouses and cafés that sprang up all over Europe but also on newspapers, musical concerts, paintings, and novels. A new middle-class public began to make its presence felt in every domain of culture and social life.

Although the rise of the Atlantic system gave Europe new prominence in the global context, European rulers still focused most of their political, diplomatic, and military energies on their rivalries within Europe. A coalition of countries had succeeded in containing French aggression under Louis XIV, and a more balanced diplomatic system emerged. In eastern Europe, Prussia and Austria had to contend with the rising power of Russia under Peter the Great. In western Europe, both Spain and the Dutch Republic declined in influence but continued to vie with Britain and France for colonial spoils across the globe. The more evenly matched competition among the great powers encouraged the development of diplomatic skills and drew attention to public health as a way of encouraging population growth.

In the aftermath of Louis XIV's revocation of the Edict of Nantes in 1685, a new intellectual movement known as the Enlightenment began to germinate. An initial impetus came from French Protestant refugees who published works critical of absolutism in politics and religion. Increased prosperity, the growth of a middle-class public, and the decline in warfare after Louis XIV's death in 1715 helped fuel this new critical spirit. Fed by the popularization of science and the growing interest in travel literature, the early Enlightenment encouraged greater skepticism about religious and state authority. Eventually, the movement would question almost every aspect of social and political life in Europe. The Enlightenment began in western Europe in those countries—Britain, France, and the Dutch Republic—most affected by the new Atlantic system. It, too, was a product of the age of coffee.

CHAPTER FOCUS What were the most important consequences of the growth of the Atlantic system?

The Atlantic System and the World Economy

Although their ships had been circling the globe since the early 1500s, Europeans did not draw most of the world into their economic orbit until the 1700s. Western European trading nations sent ships loaded with goods to buy slaves from local rulers on the western coast of Africa; the slaves were then transported to the colonies in North and South America and the Caribbean and sold to the owners of plantations producing coffee, sugar, cotton, and tobacco. Money from the slave trade was used to buy the raw commodities produced in the colonies and ship them back to Europe, where they were refined or processed and then sold within Europe and around the world. The Atlantic system and the growth of international trade thus helped create a new consumer society.

1700s Beginning of rapid development of plantations in Caribbean

1703 Peter the Great begins construction of St. Petersburg, founds first Russian newspaper

1713–1714 Peace of Utrecht treaties end War of Spanish Succession

1714 Elector of Hanover becomes King George I of England

1715 Death of Louis XIV

1719 Daniel Defoe publishes *Robinson Crusoe*

1720 Last outbreak of bubonic plague in western Europe

1721 Great Northern War ends; Montesquieu publishes *Persian Letters* anonymously in the Dutch Republic

1700 1710 1720

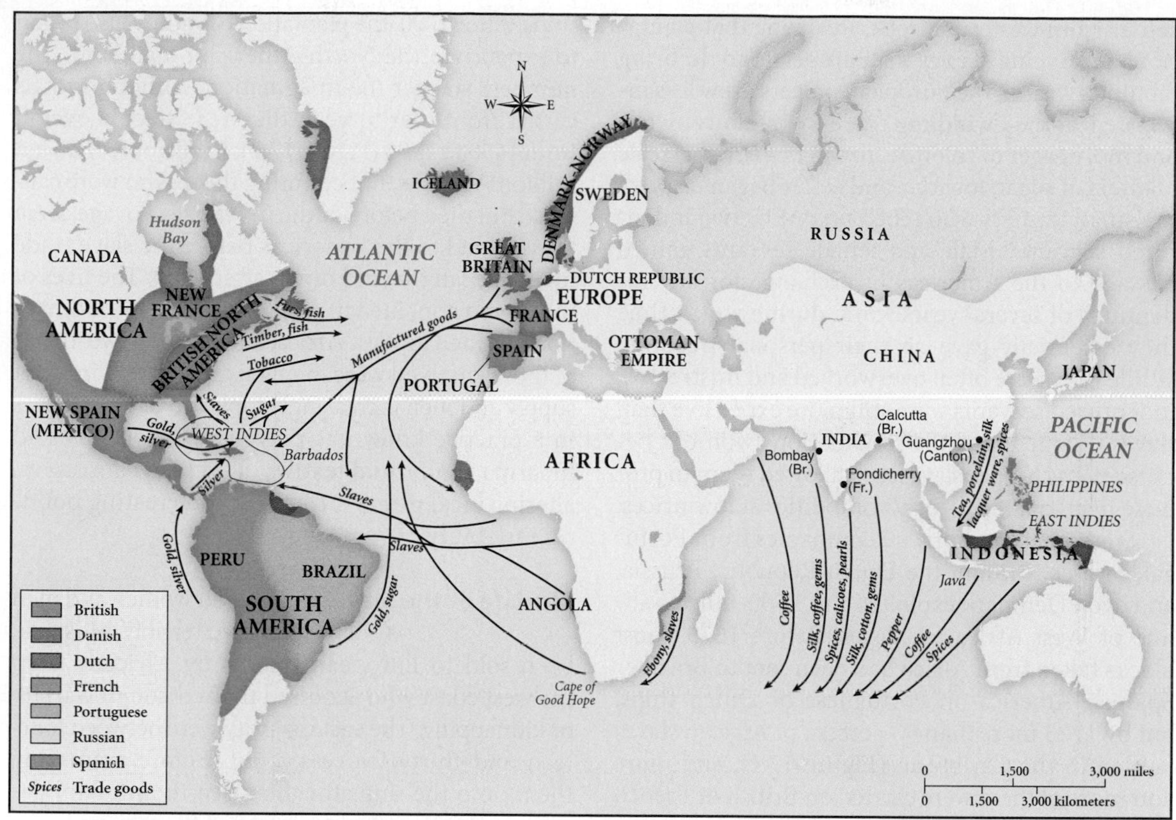

MAP 17.1 European Trade Patterns, c. 1740
By 1740, the European powers had colonized much of North and South America and incorporated their colonies there into a worldwide system of commerce centered on the slave trade and plantation production of staple crops. Europeans still sought spices and luxury goods in China and the East Indies, but outside of Java, few Europeans had settled permanently in these areas. | **How did control over colonies determine dominance in international trade in this period?**

Slavery and the Atlantic System

Spain and Portugal dominated Atlantic trade in the sixteenth and seventeenth centuries, but in the eighteenth century European trade in the Atlantic rapidly expanded and became more systematically interconnected (Map 17.1). By 1650, Portugal had already sent forty thousand African slaves to Brazil to work on the new plantations, which were producing some fifteen thousand tons of sugar a year. A **plantation** was a large tract of land that produced a staple crop such as sugar, coffee, or tobacco; was farmed by slave labor; and was owned by a colonial

plantation: A large tract of land that produced staple crops such as sugar, coffee, and tobacco; was farmed by slave labor; and was owned by a colonial settler.

1733 War of the Polish Succession; Voltaire's *Letters Concerning the English Nation* attacks French intolerance and narrow-mindedness

1741 George Frideric Handel composes *Messiah*

1730 — 1740 — 1750

1740–1748 War of the Austrian Succession

1748 Montesquieu publishes *The Spirit of Laws*

settler from western Europe. Realizing that plantations producing staples for Europeans could bring fabulous wealth, the European powers grew less interested in the dwindling trade in precious metals and more eager to colonize. In the 1700s, large-scale planters of sugar, tobacco, and coffee began displacing small farmers who relied on one or two indentured servants. Male and female servants gained passage to the Americas in exchange for an "indenture" of several years work, during which time they essentially gave up their personal freedom. While they were often overworked and mistreated, indentured servants were still more expensive than slaves. Planters and their plantations won out because even cheaper slave labor allowed them to produce mass quantities of commodities at low prices.

State-chartered private companies from Portugal, France, Britain, the Dutch Republic, Prussia, and even Denmark exploited the 3,500-mile coastline of West Africa for slaves. Before 1675, most blacks taken from Africa had been sent to Brazil or Spanish America on Portuguese or Dutch ships, but by 1725 more than 60 percent of African slaves landed in the Caribbean (Figure 17.1), and more and more of them were carried on British or French ships. After 1700, the plantation economy also began to expand on the North American mainland. The numbers stagger the imagination. Although totals varied from year to year, they rose steeply overall from 1650 to 1800 (Figure 17.2). In all, more than ten million Africans, not counting those who were captured but died before or during the sea voyage, were transported to the Americas before the slave trade finally began to wind down after 1850. The lives of those who remained in Africa changed, too. Population declined in West Africa, and because two-thirds of those enslaved were men, husbands were in short supply and men increasingly took two or more wives in a practice known as polygyny. Europeans sold firearms, liquor, and textiles in exchange for slaves, altering local power structures and creating political instability.

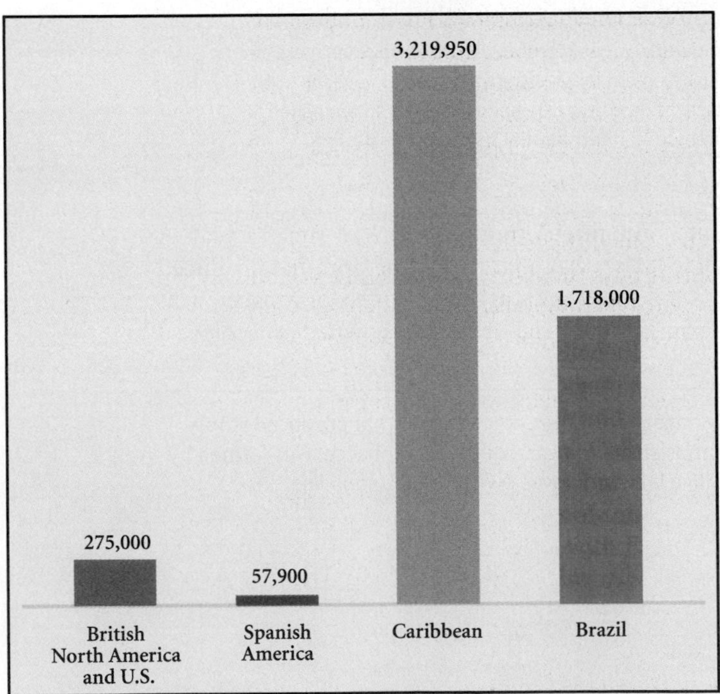

FIGURE 17.1 African Slaves Imported into American Territories, 1701–1810

During the eighteenth century, planters in the newly established Caribbean colonies imported millions of African slaves to work the new plantations that produced sugar, coffee, indigo, and cotton for the European market. The vast majority of African slaves transported to the Americas ended up in either the Caribbean or Brazil. Why were so many slaves transported to the Caribbean islands, which are relatively small compared to Spanish or British North America? *(Adapted from http://www.slavevoyages.org/.)*

The Life of the Slaves

Enslaved women and men suffered terribly. Most had been sold to European traders by Africans from the west coast who acquired them through warfare or kidnapping. The vast majority were between fourteen and thirty-five years old. Before cramming them onto the ships for the three-month trip, slavers shaved their heads, stripped them naked, and branded some with red-hot irons. They separated men and women, and shackled men with leg irons. Sailors and officers raped the women whenever they wished and beat those who refused their advances. In the cramped and appalling conditions of the voyage, as many as one-fourth of the slaves died.

Those who survived the transit were forced into degrading and oppressive conditions. Upon purchase, masters gave slaves new names, often only first names, and in some colonies branded them as personal property. Slaves had no social identities of their own; they were expected to learn their master's language and to do any job assigned. Slaves worked fifteen- to seventeen-hour days and were fed only enough to keep them on their feet. Brazilian slaves consumed more calories than the poorest Brazilians do today, but that hardly made them well fed. The death rate among slaves was high, especially on the sugar plantations, where slaves had to cut and haul sugarcane to the grinders and boilers before it spoiled. During the harvest, grinding and boiling went on around the clock. Because so many slaves died in the sugar-growing regions, more and more slaves, especially strong males, had to be imported. In North America, in contrast, where sugar was a minor crop, the slave population increased tenfold by 1863 through natural growth.

Not surprisingly, despite the threat of torture or death on recapture, slaves sometimes ran away.

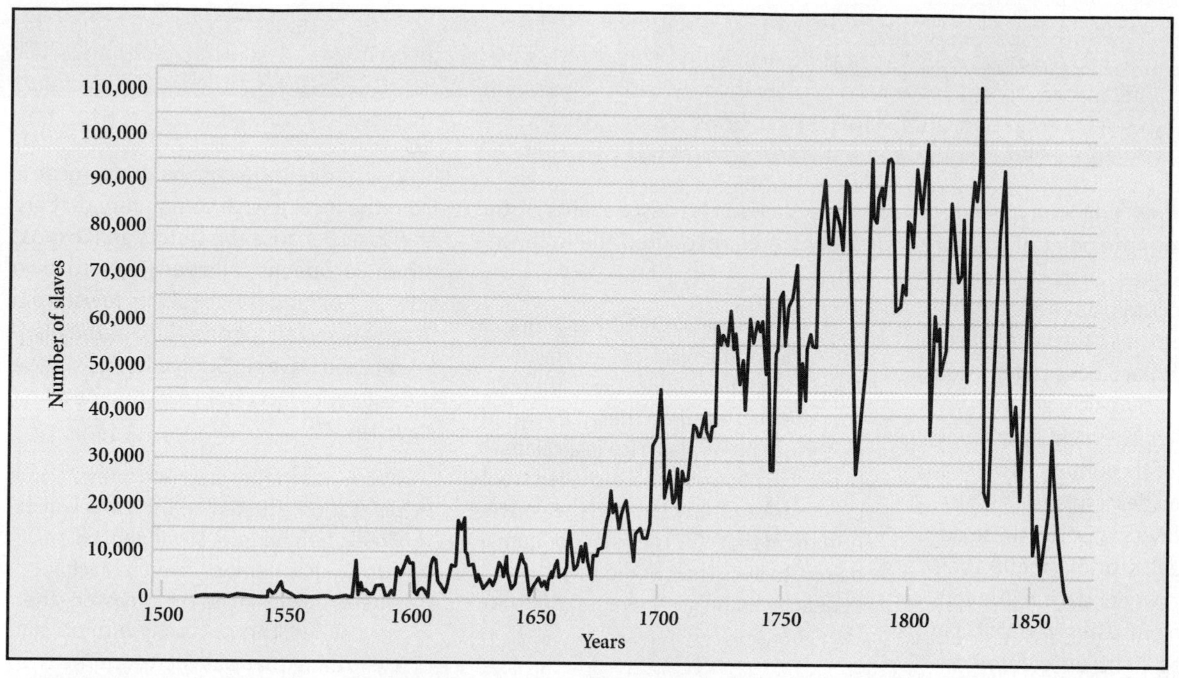

FIGURE 17.2 Annual Imports in the Atlantic Slave Trade, 1450–1870
The importation of slaves to the American territories increased overall from 1650 until 1800 and did not finally collapse until after 1850. *(Adapted from http://www.slavevoyages.org/.)*

(See "New Sources, New Perspectives," page 556.) In Brazil, runaways found *quilombos* ("hideouts") in the forests or backcountry. When it was discovered and destroyed in 1695, the quilombo of Palmares had thirty thousand fugitives who had formed their own social organization, complete with elected kings and councils of elders. Outright revolt was uncommon, especially before the nineteenth century, but other forms of resistance included stealing food, breaking tools, and feigning illness or stupidity. Slaveholders' fears about conspiracy and revolt lurked beneath the surface of every slave-based society. In 1710, the royal governor of Virginia reminded the colonial legislature of the need for unceasing vigilance: "We are not to Depend on Either Their Stupidity, or that Babel of Languages among 'em; freedom Wears a Cap which Can Without a Tongue, Call Together all Those

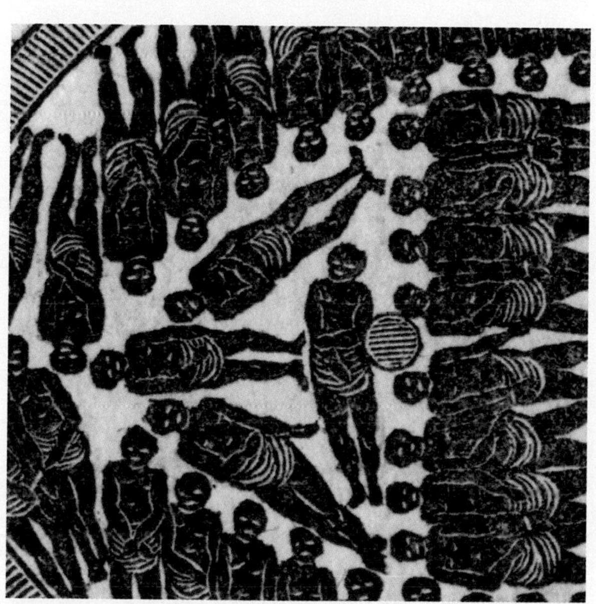

Conditions on Board a Slave Ship
Visual representations of the horrible conditions on slave ships appeared in the late 1700s as part of the emerging campaign for the abolition of the slave trade. This 1789 wood engraving shows a cross section of an English slave ship built in Liverpool in 1780–1781 for the merchant Joseph Brooks. In 1783 the ship carried more than 600 enslaved Africans across the Atlantic in a space designed for 451 people. Abolitionists showed members of Parliament a model of this ship to convince them of the brutality of the slave trade. *(Detail, © The Trustees of the British Museum/Art Resource, NY.)*

NEW SOURCES, NEW PERSPECTIVES

Oral History and the Life of Slaves

Historians have found it difficult to reconstruct slave life from the point of view of the slaves themselves, in part because slaves newly imported from Africa to the New World did not speak the language of their captors. Scholars have attempted to fill in this blank by using a variety of overlapping sources. The most interesting and controversial of these sources are oral histories taken from descendants of slaves. In some former slave societies, these descendants still tell stories about their ancestors' first days under slavery. The controversy comes from using present-day memories to shed light on eighteenth-century lives.

One of the regions most intensively studied in this fashion is Suriname (formerly Dutch Guiana), on the northeast coast of South America between present-day Guyana and French Guiana. This region is a good source of oral histories because 10 percent of the African slaves transported there between the 1680s and the 1750s escaped from the plantations and fled into the nearby rain forests. There they set up their own societies and developed their own language, in which they carried on the oral traditions of the first runaway slaves. The descendants of the runaway slaves recounted the following details:

> In slavery, there was hardly anything to eat. It was at the place called Providence Plantation. They whipped you there till your ass was burning. Then they would give you a bit of plain rice in a calabash [a bowl made from a hard-shelled tropical American fruit]. . . . And the gods told them that this is no way for human beings to live. They would help them. Let each person go where he could. So they ran.

From other sources, historians have learned that there was a major slave rebellion at Providence Plantation in Suriname in 1693.

By comparing such oral histories to written accounts of plantation owners, missionaries, and Dutch colonial officials, historians have been able to paint a richly detailed picture not only of slavery but also of runaway slave societies, which were especially numerous in South America. At the end of the eighteenth century, a Portuguese-speaking Jew named David de Ishak Cohen Nassy wrote his own history of plantation life based on records from the local Jewish community that are now lost. Because the Dutch, unlike most other Europeans, allowed Jews to own slaves, Portuguese-speaking Jews from Brazil owned about one-third of the plantations and slaves in Suriname. Nassy gave the following account of Suriname's first slave revolt:

> There was in the year 1690 a revolt on a plantation situated on the Cassewinica Creek, behind Jews Savannah, belonging to a Jew named Imanuël Machado, where, having killed their master, [the slaves] fled, carrying away with them everything that was there. . . . The Jews . . . in an expedition which they undertook against the rebels, killed many of them and brought back several who were punished by death on the very spot.

The oral histories told about the revolt from the runaway slaves' perspective:

> There had been a great council meeting [of runaway slaves] in the forest. . . . They decided to burn a different one of [Machado's] plantations from the place where he had whipped Lanu [one of the runaway slaves] because they

who Long to Shake off the fetters of Slavery." Masters defended whipping and other forms of physical punishment as essential to maintaining discipline. Laws called for the castration of a slave who struck a white person.

The balance of white and black populations in the New World colonies was determined by the staples produced. Because they did not own plantations, New England merchants and farmers bought few slaves. Blacks—both slave and free—made up only 3 percent of the population in eighteenth-century New England, compared with 60 percent in South Carolina. On the whole, the British North American colonies contained a higher proportion of African Americans from 1730 to 1765 than at any other time in American history. The imbalance of whites and blacks was even more extreme in the Caribbean, where most indigenous people had already died fighting Europeans or the diseases brought by them. By 1713, the French Caribbean colony of St. Domingue (on the western part of Hispaniola, present-day Haiti) had four times as many black slaves as whites; by 1754, slaves there outnumbered whites more than ten to one.

Effects of the Slave Trade on Europe Plantation owners often left their colonial possessions in the care of agents and merely collected the revenue so that they could live as wealthy landowners back home, where they built opulent mansions and gained influence in local and national politics. William Beckford, for example, had been sent from Jamaica to school in England as a young boy. When he inherited sugar plantations

would find more tools there. This was the Cassewinica Plantation, which had many slaves. They knew all about this plantation from slavery times. So, they attacked. It was at night. They killed the head of the plantation, a white man. They took all the things, everything they needed.

The runaway slaves saw the attack as part of their ongoing effort to build a life in the rain forest, away from the whites.

Over the next decades, the runaway slaves fought a constant series of battles with plantation owners and Dutch officials. Finally, in 1762, the Dutch granted the runaway slaves their freedom in a peace agreement and allowed them to trade in the main town of the colony in exchange for agreeing to return all future runaways. The runaways had not destroyed the slave system, but they had gained their own independence alongside it. From their oral histories it is possible to retrace their efforts to build new lives in a strange place, in which they combined African practices with New World experiences.

Source: Richard Price, *Alabi's World* (Baltimore: Johns Hopkins University Press, 1990), 17, 9.

Questions to Consider

1. **What did the runaway slaves mentioned in these accounts aim to accomplish when they attacked plantations?**
2. **Why would runaway slaves make an agreement with the Dutch colonial officials to return future runaways?**
3. **Can oral histories recorded in the twentieth century be considered accurate versions of events that took place in the eighteenth century? How can they be tested?**

Further Reading

Price, Richard. *Alabi's World*. 1990.

Stedman, John Gabriel. *Narrative of a Five Years' Expedition Against the Revolted Negroes of Surinam*. Edited, and with an introduction and notes, by Richard Price and Sally Price. 1988.

Slaves of Suriname in the 1770s

John Gabriel Stedman published an account of his participation in a five-year expedition against the runaway slaves of Suriname that took place in the 1770s. He provided drawings such as the one reproduced here, which shows Africans who have just come off a slave ship. *(The New York Public Library/Art Resource, NY.)*

and shipping companies from his father and older brother, he moved the headquarters of the family business to London in the 1730s to be close to the government and financial markets. His holdings formed the single most powerful economic interest in Jamaica, but he preferred to live in England, where he could buy works of art for his many luxurious homes, hold political office (he was lord mayor of London and a member of Parliament), and even lend money to the government.

The slave trade permanently altered consumption patterns for ordinary people. Sugar had been prescribed as a medicine before the end of the sixteenth century, but the development of plantations in Brazil and the Caribbean made it a standard food item. By 1700, the British were sending home fifty million pounds of sugar a year, a figure that doubled by 1730. During the French Revolution of the 1790s, sugar shortages would become a cause for rioting in Paris. Equally pervasive was the spread of tobacco; by the 1720s, Britain was importing two hundred shiploads of tobacco from Virginia and Maryland annually, and men of every country and class smoked pipes or took snuff.

The Origins of Modern Racism

The traffic in slaves disturbed many Europeans. As a government memorandum to the Spanish king explained in 1610: "Modern theologians in published books commonly report on, and condemn as unjust, the acts of enslavement which take place in provinces of this Royal Empire." Between 1667 and 1671, the French Dominican monk Father Du Tertre published three volumes in which he denounced the mistreatment of slaves in the French colonies.

In the 1700s, however, slaveholders began to justify their actions by demeaning the mental and spiritual qualities of the enslaved Africans. White Europeans and colonists sometimes described black slaves as animal-like, akin to apes. A leading New England Puritan asserted about the slaves: "Indeed their *Stupidity* is a *Discouragement*. It may seem, unto as little purpose, to *Teach*, as to *wash an Aethiopian* [Ethiopian]." One of the great paradoxes of this time was that talk of liberty and rights, especially prevalent in Britain and its North American colonies, coexisted with the belief that some people were meant to be slaves. Although Christians believed in principle in a kind of spiritual equality between blacks and whites, the churches often defended or at least did not oppose the inequities of slavery.

World Trade and Settlement

The Atlantic system helped extend European trade relations across the globe. The textiles that Atlantic shippers exchanged for slaves on the west coast of Africa, for example, were manufactured in India and exported by the British and French East India Companies. As much as one-quarter of the British exports to Africa in the eighteenth century were actually re-exports from India. To expand its trade in the rest of the world, Europeans seized territories and tried to establish permanent settlements. The eighteenth-century extension of European power prepared the way for western global domination in the nineteenth and twentieth centuries.

The Americas In contrast to the sparsely inhabited trading outposts in Asia and Africa, the colonies in the Americas bulged with settlers. The British North American colonies, for example, contained about 1.5 million nonnative (that is, white settler and black slave) residents by 1750. While the Spanish competed with the Portuguese for control of South America, the French competed with the British for control of North America. Spanish and British settlers came to blows over the boundary between the British colonies and Florida, which was held by Spain.

Local economies shaped colonial social relations; men in French trapper communities in Canada, for example, had little in common with the men and women of the plantation societies in Barbados or Brazil. Racial attitudes also differed from place to place. The Spanish and Portuguese tolerated intermarriage with the native populations in both America and Asia. Though mixed-race people could be found everywhere, sexual contact (both inside and outside marriage) fostered greater racial variety in the Spanish and Portuguese colonies than in the French or the English territories. By 1800, **mestizos**, people born to a Spanish father and an Indian mother, accounted for more than a quarter of the population in the Spanish colonies, and many of them aspired to join the local elite. However, greater racial diversity seems not to have improved the treatment of slaves.

Where intermarriage between colonizers and natives was common, conversion to Christianity proved most successful. Even while maintaining their native religious beliefs, many Indians in the Spanish colonies had come to consider themselves devout Catholics by 1700. Indian carpenters and artisans in the villages produced innumerable altars, retables (painted panels), and sculpted images to adorn their local churches, and individual families put up domestic shrines. Yet the clergy remained overwhelmingly Spanish: the church hierarchy concluded that the Indians' humility and innocence made them unsuitable for the priesthood.

In the early years of American colonization, many more men than women emigrated from Europe. Although the sex imbalance began to decline at the end of the seventeenth century, it remained substantial; two and a half times more men than women were among the immigrants leaving Liverpool, England, between 1697 and 1707, for example. Women who emigrated as indentured servants ran great risks: many died of disease during the voyage, at least one in five gave birth to an illegitimate child, and many others were virtually sold into marriage. Upper-class women were often kept in seclusion, especially in the Spanish and Portuguese colonies.

The uncertainties of life in the American colonies provided new opportunities for European women and men willing to live outside the law, however. In the 1500s and 1600s, the English and Dutch governments had routinely authorized pirates to prey on the ships of their rivals, the Spanish and Portuguese. Then, in the late 1600s, English, French, and Dutch bands made up of deserters and crews from wrecked vessels began to form their own associations of pirates, especially in the Caribbean. Called **buccaneers** from their custom of curing strips of beef, called *boucan* by the native Caribs of the islands, the pirates governed themselves and preyed on everyone's shipping without regard to national origin. After 1700, the colonial governments tried to stamp out piracy. As one British judge argued in 1705, "A pirate is in perpetual war with

---

mestizo: A person born to a Spanish father and a native American mother.

buccaneers: Pirates of the Caribbean who governed themselves and preyed on international shipping.

every individual and every state. . . . They are worse than ravenous beasts."

Africa and Asia White settlements in Africa and Asia remained small and almost insignificant, except for their long-term potential. Europeans had little contact with East Africa and almost none with Africa's vast interior. A handful of Portuguese trading posts in Angola and a few Dutch farms on the Cape of Good Hope provided the only toeholds for future expansion. In China, the emperors had welcomed Catholic missionaries at court in the seventeenth century, but the priests' credibility diminished as they squabbled among themselves and associated with European merchants, whom the Chinese considered pirates. "The barbarians [Europeans] are like wild beasts," one Chinese official concluded. In 1720, only one thousand Europeans resided in Guangzhou (Canton), the sole place where foreigners could legally trade for spices, tea, and silk (see Map 17.1, page 553).

Europeans exercised more influence in Java (in what was then called the East Indies) and in India. Many Dutch settled in Java to oversee coffee production and Asian trade. Dutch, English, French, Portuguese, and Danish companies competed in India for spices, cotton, and silk; by the 1740s, the English and French had become the leading rivals in India, just as they were in North America. Both countries extended their power as India's Muslim rulers lost control to local Hindu princes, rebellious Sikhs, invading Persians, and their own provincial governors. A few thousand Europeans lived in India, though many thousand more soldiers were stationed there to protect them. The staple of trade with India in the early 1700s was calico—lightweight, brightly colored cotton cloth that caught on as a fashion in Europe. (See the illustration below.) English and French slave traders sold calico to the Africans in exchange for slaves.

Europeans who visited India were especially struck by what they viewed as exotic religious practices. In a book published in 1696 of his travels to western India, an Anglican minister described the fakirs (religious mendicants, or beggars of alms), "some of whom show their devotion by a shameless appearance, walking naked, without the least rag of clothes to cover them." Such writings increased European interest in the outside world but also fed a European sense of superiority that helped excuse the more violent forms of colonial domination. (See the illustration on page 560.)

The Birth of Consumer Society

As worldwide colonization produced new supplies of goods, from coffee to calico, population growth in Europe fueled demand for them. Beginning first in Britain, then in France and the Italian states, and finally in eastern Europe, population surged, growing by about 20 percent between 1700 and 1750. The gap between a fast-growing northwest and a more stagnant south and central Europe now diminished as regions that had lost population dur-

India Cottons and Trade with the East
This colored cotton cloth (now faded with age) was painted and embroidered in Madras, in southern India, sometime in the late 1600s. The male figure with a mustache may be a European, but the female figures are clearly Asian. Europeans—especially the British—discovered that they could make big profits on the export of Indian cotton cloth to Europe. They also traded Indian cottons in Africa for slaves and sold large quantities in the colonies. *(Detail, Victoria and Albert Museum, London, UK/The Bridgeman Art Library International.)*

The Exotic as Consumer Item

This painting by the Venetian artist Rosalba Carriera (1675–1757) is titled *Africa*. The young black girl wearing a turban represents the African continent. Carriera was known for her use of pastels. In 1720, she journeyed to Paris, where she became an associate of Antoine Watteau and helped inaugurate the rococo style in painting. Why might the artist have chosen to paint an African girl? *(Gemäldegalerie Alte Meister, Staatliche Kunstsammlungen Dresden.)*

ing the seventeenth-century downturn recovered. Cities, in particular, grew. Between 1600 and 1750, Paris's population more than doubled and London's more than tripled.

Although contemporaries could not have realized it then, this was the start of the modern population explosion. It appears that a decline in the death rate, rather than a rise in the birthrate, explains the turnaround. Three main factors contributed to increased longevity: better weather and hence more bountiful harvests, improved agricultural techniques, and the plague's disappearance after 1720.

By the early eighteenth century, the effects of economic expansion and population growth brought about a **consumer revolution**. For example, the British East India Company began to import into Britain huge quantities of calico; British imports of tobacco doubled between 1672 and 1700; and at Nantes, the center of the French sugar trade, imports quadrupled between 1698 and 1733. Tea, chocolate, and coffee became virtual necessities. In the 1670s, only a trickle of tea reached London, but by 1720 the East India Company had sent nine million pounds to England — a figure that rose to thirty-seven million pounds by 1750. In 1700, England had two thousand coffeehouses; by 1740, every English country town had at least two. Paris got its first cafés at the end of the seventeenth century, and Berlin opened its first coffeehouse in 1714.

A new economic dynamic steadily took shape that has influenced all of subsequent history. More and more people escaped the confines of a subsistence economy, in which peasants produced barely enough to support themselves from year to year. As ordinary people gained more disposable income, demand for nonessential consumer goods rose (see Document, "The Social Effects of Growing Consumption," page 561). These included not only the new colonial products such as coffee and tea but also tables, chairs, sheets, chamber pots, lamps, and mirrors — and for the better off still, coffee- and teapots, china, cutlery, chests of drawers, desks, clocks, and pictures for the walls. Rising demand created more jobs and more income and yet more purchasing power in a mutually reinforcing cycle. In the English economic literature of the 1690s, writers reacted to these developments by expressing a new view of humans as consuming animals with boundless appetites. Many authors attacked the new doctrine of consumerism, but they could not hold back the fast-growing market for consumption. Change did not occur all at once, however. The consumer revolution spread from the cities to the countryside, from England to the continent, and from western Europe to eastern Europe only over the long run.

The distinctiveness of Europe should not be exaggerated. China's population grew even faster — it may have tripled during the 1700s — and there, too, consumption of cloth, furniture, tea, sugar, and tobacco all increased. In China, these goods could be locally produced, and China did not pursue colonization of far-flung lands. Still, foreign trade also increased, especially with lands on China's borders. In the nineteenth century, however, China lost its edge as population growth strained resources and the country came increasingly under the influence of European merchants.

consumer revolution: The rapid increase in consumption of new staples produced in the Atlantic system as well as of other items of daily life that were previously unavailable or beyond the reach of ordinary people.

REVIEW QUESTION How was consumerism related to slavery in the early eighteenth century?

DOCUMENT

The Social Effects of Growing Consumption (1728)

Daniel Defoe's adventures in real life are matched only by those of his famous fictional characters Robinson Crusoe and Moll Flanders. Though never shipwrecked like Crusoe, Defoe spent time in bankruptcy, in exile, and in prison (for writing a pamphlet satirizing Anglican treatment of dissenters). He turned his hand to various forms of commerce, in hosiery, woolens, wine, and political secrets, but most of all to mad scribbling on almost any topic imaginable. He published hundreds of books and pamphlets. In the 395-page book from which this excerpt is taken, he describes the recent fabulous growth in the import and export trade of Great Britain and contrasts the wealth gained by the "industrious" classes to the contempt shown them by the aristocracy (Gentry or Gentlemen).

Our People in general being in good Circumstances, I mean the middling, trading, and industrious People, living tolerably well, their well-faring gives Occasion to the vast Consumption of the foreign, as well as home Produce, the like of which is not to be equalled by any Nation in the World; the Particulars we shall enquire into in their Order.

How far the Multitudes of our People are encreased by these very Articles, and that to such a Degree as is scarce conceivable, is worth our Enquiry, were it not too tedious for this Place. What populous Towns are rais'd by our Manufactures, from with few Years! How are our Towns built into Cities, and small Villages (hardly known in ancient Times) grown up into populous Towns! . . .

Well might I say, as in the foregoing Chapter, That it is a Scandal upon the Understanding of the Gentry, to think contemptibly of the trading part of the Nation; seeing however the Gentlemen may value themselves upon their Birth and Blood, the Case begins to turn against them so evidently, as to Fortune and Estate, that tho' they say, the Tradesmen cannot be made Gentlemen; yet the Tradesmen are, at this Time, able to buy the Gentlemen almost in every part of the Kingdom. . . .

The ancient Families, who having wasted and exhausted their Estates, and being declin'd and decay'd in Fortune by Luxury and high Living, have restor'd and rais'd themselves again, by mixing Blood with the despis'd Tradesmen, marrying the Daughters of such Tradesmen. . . .

I might add here, that it would be worth the while for those Gentlemen, who talk so much of their antient Family Merit, and look so little at preserving the Stock, by encreasing their own: I say, it would be worth their while to look into the Roll of our Gentry, and enquire what is become of the Estates and those prodigious Numbers of lost and extinct Families, which now even the Heralds themselves can hardly find; let them tell us if those Estates are not now purchased by Tradesmen and Citizens, or the Posterity of such; and whether those Tradesmens Posterity do not now fill up the Vacancies, the Gaps, and Chasmes in the great Roll or Lift of Families, as well of the Gentry, as of the Nobility themselves; and whether there are many Families left, who have not been either restored *as in our first Head*, or supply'd, *as in the second*, by the Succession of Wealth, and new Branches from the growing Greatness of Trade.

Trade, in a word, raises antient Families when sunk and decay'd: And plants new Families, where the old ones are lost and extinct.

Source: Daniel Defoe, *A Plan of the English Commerce. Being a complete prospect of the trade of this nation, as well home as foreign. In three parts*, 2nd ed. (London, 1737), 79–83.

Question to Consider

- **Why do you think Defoe views the rise of English trade with such enthusiasm?**

New Social and Cultural Patterns

The rise of consumption in Europe was fueled in part by a revolution in agricultural techniques that made it possible to produce larger quantities of food with a smaller agricultural workforce. As population increased, more people moved to the cities, where they found themselves caught up in innovative urban customs such as attending musical concerts and reading novels. Along with a general increase in literacy, these activities helped create a public that responded to new writers and artists. As always, people's experiences varied depending on whether they lived in wealth or poverty, in urban or rural areas, or in eastern or western Europe.

Agricultural Revolution

Although Britain, France, and the Dutch Republic shared the enthusiasm for consumer goods, Britain's domestic market grew most quickly. In Britain, as agricultural output increased by 43 percent over the course of the 1700s, the population increased by 70 percent. The British imported grain to feed the growing population, but they also benefited from the development of techniques that together constituted an **agricultural revolution**. No new machinery propelled this revolution—just increasingly aggressive attitudes toward investment and management. The Dutch and the Flemish had pioneered many of these techniques in the 1600s, but the British took them further.

Four major changes occurred in British agriculture that eventually spread to other countries. First, farmers increased the amount of land under cultivation by draining wetlands and by growing crops on previously uncultivated common lands (acreage maintained by the community for grazing). Second, those farmers who could afford it consolidated small, scattered plots into larger, more efficient units. Third, livestock raising became more closely linked to crop growing, and the yields of each increased. (See "Taking Measure," page 563.) For centuries, most farmers had rotated their fields in and out of production to replenish the soil. Now farmers planted carefully chosen fodder crops such as clover and turnips that added nutrients to the soil, thereby eliminating the need to leave a field fallow (unplanted) every two or three years. With more fodder available, farmers could raise more livestock, which in turn produced more manure to fertilize grain fields. Fourth, selective breeding of animals combined with the increase in fodder to improve the quality and size of herds. New crops had only a slight impact; potatoes, for example, were introduced to Europe from South America in the 1500s, but because people feared they might cause leprosy, tuberculosis, or fevers, they were not grown in quantity until the late 1700s. By the 1730s and 1740s, agricultural output had increased dramatically, and prices for food had fallen because of these interconnected innovations.

Changes in agricultural practices did not benefit all landowners equally. The biggest British landowners consolidated their holdings in the "enclosure movement." They put pressure on small farmers and villagers to sell their land or give up their common lands. The big landlords then fenced off (enclosed) their property. Because enclosure eliminated community grazing rights, it frequently sparked a struggle between the big landlords and villagers, and in Britain it normally required an act of Parliament. Such acts became increasingly common in the second half of the eighteenth century, and by the century's end six million acres of common lands had been enclosed and developed. "Improvers" produced more food more efficiently than small farmers could and thus supported a growing population.

agricultural revolution: Increasingly aggressive attitudes toward investment in and management of land that increased production of food in the 1700s.

Contrary to the fears of contemporaries, small farmers and cottagers (those with little or no property) were not forced off the land all at once. But most villagers could not afford the litigation involved in resisting enclosure, and small landholders consequently had to sell out to landlords or farmers with larger plots. Landlords with large holdings leased their estates to tenant farmers at constantly increasing rents, and the tenant farmers in turn employed the cottagers as salaried agricultural workers. In this way the English peasantry largely disappeared, replaced by a more hierarchical society of big landlords, enterprising tenant farmers, and poor agricultural laborers.

The new agricultural techniques spread slowly from Britain and the Low Countries (the Dutch Republic and the Austrian Netherlands) to the rest of western Europe. Outside a few pockets in northern France and the western German states, however, subsistence agriculture (producing just enough to get by rather than surpluses for the market) continued to dominate farming in western Europe and Scandinavia. In southwestern Germany, for example, 80 percent of the peasants produced no surplus be-

Treatment of Serfs in Russia

Visitors from western Europe often remarked on the cruel treatment of serfs in Russia. This drawing by one such visitor shows the punishment that could be inflicted by landowners. Serfs could be whipped for almost any reason, even for making a soup too salty or neglecting to bow when the lord's family passed by. Their condition worsened in the 1700s, as landowners began to sell serfs much like slaves. Although life for Russian serfs was more brutal than for peasants elsewhere, upper classes in every country regarded the serfs as dirty, deceitful, and brutish. *(New York Public Library/Art Resource, NY.)*

cause their plots were too small. Unlike the populations of the highly urbanized Low Countries (where half the people lived in towns and cities), most Europeans, western and eastern, eked out their existence in the countryside and could barely participate in the new markets for consumer goods.

In eastern Europe, the condition of peasants worsened in the areas where landlords tried hardest to improve crop yields. To produce more for the Baltic grain market, aristocratic landholders in Prussia, Poland, and parts of Russia drained wetlands, cultivated moors, and built dikes. They also forced peasants off lands that the peasants had worked for themselves, increased compulsory labor services (the critical element in serfdom), and began to manage their estates directly. Some eastern landowners grew fabulously wealthy. The Potocki family in the Polish Ukraine, for example, owned three million acres of land and had 130,000 serfs. In parts of Poland and Russia, the serfs hardly differed from slaves in status, and their "masters" ran their huge estates much like American plantations. (See the illustration on page 562.)

Social Life in the Cities

Because of emigration from the countryside, cities grew in population and consequently exercised a growing influence on culture and social life. Between 1650 and 1750, cities with at least ten thousand inhabitants increased in population by 44 percent. From the eighteenth century onward, urban growth would be continuous. Along with the general growth of cities, an important south-to-north shift occurred in the pattern of urbanization. Around 1500, half of the people in cities of at least ten thousand residents could be found in the Italian states, Spain, or Portugal; by 1700, the urbanization of northwestern and southern Europe was roughly equal. Eastern Europe, despite the huge cities of Istanbul and Moscow, was still less urban than western Europe. London was by far the most populous European city, with 675,000 inhabitants in 1750; Berlin had 90,000 people, Warsaw only 23,000.

Urban Social Classes | Many landowners kept a residence in town, so the separation between rural and city life was not as extreme as might be imagined, at least not for the very rich. At the top of the ladder in the big cities were the landed nobles. Some of them filled their lives only with conspicuous consumption of fine food, extravagant clothing, coaches, books, and opera; others held key political, administrative, or judicial offices. However they spent their time, these rich families employed thousands of artisans, shopkeepers, and domestic servants. Many English peers (highest-ranking nobles) had thirty or forty servants at each of their homes.

The middle classes of officials, merchants, professionals, and landowners occupied the next rung down on the social ladder. London's population, for example, included about twenty thousand middle-

TAKING MEASURE

Relationship of Crop Harvested to Seed Used, 1400–1800

The impact and even the timing of the agricultural revolution can be determined by this figure, based on yield ratios (the number of grains produced for each seed planted). Britain, the Dutch Republic, and the Austrian Netherlands all experienced huge increases in crop yields after 1700. Other European regions lagged behind right into the 1800s.

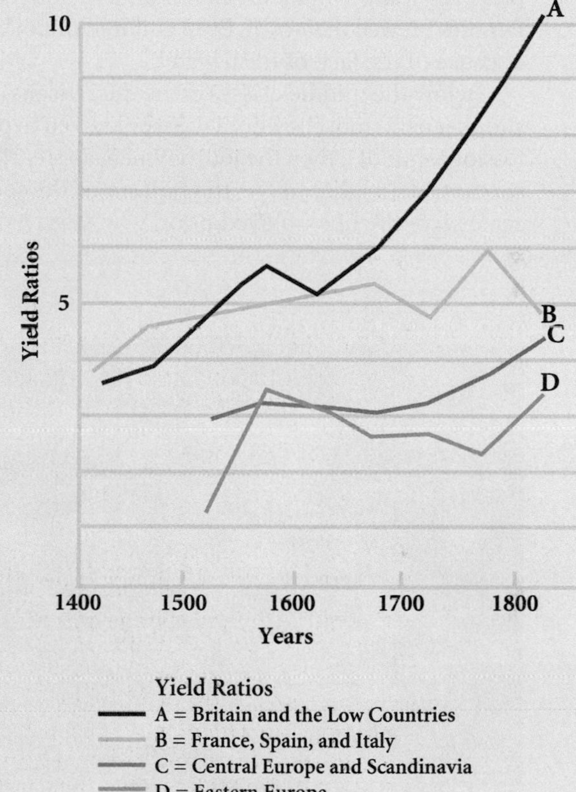

Source: Peter J. Hugill, *World Trade since 1431: Geography, Technology, and Capitalism* (Baltimore: Johns Hopkins University Press, 1995), 56.

Questions to Consider

1. **Why is crop yield such an important measure of a country's agricultural output?**
2. **How would crop yields in this era impact a country's overall population and trading opportunities?**

class families (constituting, at most, one-sixth of the city's population). In this period the middle classes began to develop distinctive ways of life that set them apart from both the rich noble landowners and the lower classes. Unlike the rich nobles, the middle classes lived primarily in the cities and towns, even if they owned small country estates. They ate more moderately than nobles but much better than peasants or laborers. For breakfast the British middle classes ate toast and rolls and, after 1700, drank tea. Dinner, served midday, consisted of roasted or boiled beef or mutton, poultry or pork, and vegetables. Supper was a light meal of bread and cheese with cake or pie. Beer was the main drink in London, and many families brewed their own. Even children drank beer because of the lack of fresh water.

Below the middle classes came the artisans and shopkeepers (most of whom were organized in professional guilds), then the journeymen, apprentices, servants, and laborers. At the bottom of the social scale were the unemployed poor, who survived by intermittent work and charity. Women married to artisans and shopkeepers often kept the accounts, supervised employees, and ran the household as well. Every middle-class and upper-class family employed servants; artisans and shopkeepers frequently hired them too. Women from poorer families usually worked as domestic servants until they married. Four out of five domestic servants in the city were female. In large cities such as London, the servant population grew faster than the population of the city as a whole.

Signs of Social Distinction Social status in the cities was readily visible. Wide, spacious streets graced rich districts; the houses had gardens, and the air was relatively fresh. In poor districts, the streets were narrow, dirty, dark, humid, and smelly, and the houses were damp and crowded. The poorest people were homeless, sleeping under bridges or in abandoned buildings. A Neapolitan prince described his homeless neighbors as

Vauxhall Gardens, London
This hand-colored print from the mid-eighteenth century shows the newly refurbished gardens near the Thames River. Prosperous families show off their brightly colored clothes and listen to a public concert by the orchestra seated just above them. These activities helped form a more self-conscious public. *(Bibliothèque des Arts Décoratifs, Paris, France/Archives Charmet/The Bridgeman Art Library.)*

"lying like filthy animals, with no distinction of age or sex." In some districts, rich and poor lived in the same buildings; the poor clambered up to shabby, cramped apartments on the top floors.

Like shelter, clothing was a reliable social indicator. The poorest workingwomen in Paris wore woolen skirts and blouses of dark colors over petticoats, a bodice, and a corset. They also donned caps of various sorts, cotton stockings, and shoes (probably their only pair). Workingmen dressed even more drably. Many occupations could be recognized by their dress: no one could confuse lawyers in their dark robes with masons or butchers in their special aprons, for example. People higher on the social ladder were more likely to sport a variety of fabrics, colors, and unusual designs in their clothing and to own many different outfits. Social status was not an abstract idea; it permeated every detail of daily life.

The Growth of a Literate Public The ability to read and write also reflected social differences. People in the upper classes were more literate than those in the lower classes; city people were more literate than peasants. Protestant countries appear to have been more successful at promoting education and literacy than Catholic countries, perhaps because of the Protestant emphasis on Bible reading. Widespread literacy among the lower classes was first achieved in the Protestant areas of Switzerland and in Presbyterian Scotland, and rates were also very high in the New England colonies and the Scandinavian countries. In France, literacy doubled in the eighteenth century thanks to the spread of parish schools, but still only one in two men and one in four women could read and write. Most peasants remained illiterate. Although some Protestant German states encouraged primary education, schooling remained woefully inadequate almost everywhere in Europe: few schools existed, teachers received low wages, and no country had yet established a national system of control or supervision.

Despite the deficiencies of primary education, a new literate public arose especially among the middle classes of the cities. More books and periodicals were published than ever before, another aspect of the consumer revolution. The trend began in the 1690s in Britain and the Dutch Republic and gradually accelerated. In 1695, the British government allowed the licensing system, through which it controlled publications, to lapse, and new newspapers and magazines appeared almost immediately. The first London daily newspaper came out in 1702, and in 1709 Joseph Addison and Richard Steele published the first literary magazine, *The Spectator*. They devoted their magazine to the cultural improvement of the increasingly influential middle class. By the 1720s, twenty-four provincial newspapers were published in England. In the London coffeehouses, an edition of a single newspaper might reach ten thousand male readers. Women did their reading at home. Except in the Dutch Republic, newspapers on the continent lagged behind and often consisted mainly of advertising with little critical commentary. France, for example, had no daily paper until 1777.

New Tastes in the Arts

The new literate public did not just read newspapers; its members now pursued an interest in painting, attended concerts, and besieged booksellers in search of popular novels. Because increased trade and prosperity put money into the hands of the growing middle classes, a new urban audience began to compete with the churches, rulers, and courtiers as chief patrons for new work. As the public for the arts expanded, printed commentary on them emerged, setting the stage for the appearance of political and social criticism. New artistic tastes thus had effects far beyond the realm of the arts.

Rococo Painting Developments in painting reflected the tastes of the new public, as the **rococo** style challenged the hold of the baroque and classical schools, especially in France. Like the baroque, the rococo emphasized irregularity and asymmetry, movement and curvature, but it did so on a much smaller, subtler scale. Many rococo paintings depicted scenes of intimate sensuality rather than the monumental, emotional grandeur favored by classical and baroque painters. Personal portraits and pastoral paintings took the place of heroic landscapes and grand, ceremonial canvases. Rococo paintings adorned homes as well as palaces and served as a form of interior decoration rather than as a statement of piety. Its decorative quality made rococo art an ideal complement to newly discovered materials such as stucco and porcelain, especially the porcelain vases now imported from China.

Rococo, like *baroque*, was an invented word (from the French word *rocaille*, "shellwork") and originally a derogatory label, meaning "frivolous decoration." But the great French rococo painters, such as Antoine Watteau (1684–1721) and François Boucher (1703–1770), were much more than mere

---

rococo: A style of painting that emphasized irregularity and asymmetry, movement and curvature, but on a smaller, more intimate scale than the baroque.

Rococo Painting
The rococo emphasis on interiors, on decoration, and on intimacy rather than monumental grandeur are evident in François Boucher's painting *The Luncheon* (1739). The painting also draws attention to new consumer items, from the mirror and the clock to chocolate, children's toys, a small Buddha statue, and the intricately designed furniture. *(The Art Archive/Musée du Louvre, Paris/Collection Dagli Orti.)*

decorators. Although both emphasized the erotic in their depictions, Watteau captured the melancholy side of a passing aristocratic style of life, and Boucher painted middle-class people at home during their daily activities. Both painters thereby contributed to the emergence of new sensibilities in art that increasingly attracted a middle-class public.

Music for the Public The first public music concerts were performed in England in the 1670s, becoming much more regular and frequent in the 1690s. City concert halls typically seated about two hundred, but the relatively high price of tickets limited attendance to the better-off. Music clubs provided entertainment in smaller towns and villages. On the continent, Frankfurt organized the first regular public concerts in 1712; Hamburg and Paris began holding them within a few years. Opera continued to spread in the eighteenth century; Venice had sixteen public opera houses by 1700, and the Covent Garden opera house opened in London in 1732.

The growth of a public that appreciated and supported music had much the same effect as the extension of the reading public: like authors, composers could now begin to liberate themselves from court patronage and work for a paying audience. This development took time to solidify, however, and court or church patrons still commissioned much eighteenth-century music. Johann Sebastian Bach (1685–1750), a German Lutheran, wrote his *St. Matthew Passion* for Good Friday services in 1729 while he was organist and choirmaster for the leading church in Leipzig. He composed secular works for the public and for a variety of private patrons.

The composer George Frideric Handel (1685–1759) was among the first to grasp the new directions in music. A German by birth, he wrote operas in Italy and then moved in 1710 to Britain, where he wrote music for the court and began composing oratorios. The oratorio, a form Handel introduced in Britain, combined the drama of opera with the majesty of religious and ceremonial music and featured the chorus over the soloists. The "Hallelujah Chorus" from Handel's oratorio *Messiah* (1741) is perhaps the single best-known piece of Western classical music. It reflected the composer's personal, deeply felt piety but also his willingness to combine musical materials into a dramatic form that captured the enthusiasm of the new public. In 1740, a poem about Handel published in the *Gentleman's Magazine* exulted: "His art so modulates the sounds in all, / Our passions, as he pleases, rise and fall." Music had become an integral part of the new middle-class public's culture.

Novels Nothing captured the imagination of the new public more than the novel, the literary genre whose very name underscored the eighteenth-century taste for novelty. More than three hundred French novels appeared between 1700 and 1730. During this unprecedented explosion, the novel took on its modern form and became more concerned with individual psychology and social description than with the adventure tales popular earlier (such as Miguel de Cervantes's *Don Quixote*). The novel's popularity was closely tied to the expansion of the reading public, and novels were available in serial form in periodicals or from the many booksellers who served the new market.

Women figured prominently in novels as characters, and women writers abounded. The English novel *Love in Excess* (1719) quickly reached a sixth printing, and its author, Eliza Haywood (1693?–

1756), earned her living turning out a stream of novels with titles such as *Persecuted Virtue, Constancy Rewarded*, and *The History of Betsy Thoughtless*— all showing a concern for the proper place of women as models of virtue in a changing world. When her husband deserted her and her two children, Haywood first worked as an actress but soon turned to writing plays and novels. In the 1740s, she began publishing a magazine, *The Female Spectator*, which argued in favor of higher education for women.

Haywood's male counterpart was Daniel Defoe (1660–1731), a merchant's son who had a diverse and colorful career as a manufacturer, political spy, novelist, and social commentator (see Document, "The Social Effects of Growing Consumption," page 561). Defoe wrote about schemes for national improvement, the state of English trade, the economic condition of the countryside, the effects of the plague, and the history of pirates; he is most well known, however, for his novels *Robinson Crusoe* (1719) and *Moll Flanders* (1722). The story of the adventures of a shipwrecked sailor, *Robinson Crusoe* portrayed the new values of the time: to survive, Crusoe had to employ fearless entrepreneurial ingenuity. He had to be ready for the unexpected and be able to improvise in every situation. He was, in short, the model for the new man in an expanding economy. Crusoe's patronizing attitude toward the black man Friday now draws much critical attention, but his discovery of Friday shows how the fate of blacks and whites had become intertwined in the new colonial environment.

Religious Revivals

Despite the novel's growing popularity, religious books and pamphlets still sold in huge numbers, and most Europeans remained devout, even as their religions were changing. In this period, a Protestant revivalist movement known as **Pietism** rocked the complacency of the established churches in the German Lutheran states, the Dutch Republic, and Scandinavia. Pietists believed in a mystical religion of the heart; they wanted a deeply emotional, even ecstatic religion. They urged intense Bible study, which in turn promoted popular education and contributed to the increase in literacy. Many Pietists attended catechism instruction every day and also went to morning and evening prayer meetings in addition to regular Sunday services. Although Pietism appealed to both Lutherans and Calvinists, it had the greatest impact in Lutheran Prussia, where it taught the virtues of hard work, obedience, and devotion to duty.

Catholicism also had its versions of religious revival, especially in France. A Frenchwoman, Jeanne Marie Guyon (1648–1717), attracted many noblewomen and a few leading clergymen to her own Catholic brand of Pietism, known as Quietism. Claiming miraculous visions and astounding prophecies, she urged a mystical union with God through prayer and simple devotion. Despite papal condemnation and intense controversy within Catholic circles in France, Guyon had followers all over Europe.

Even more influential were the Jansenists, who gained many new adherents to their austere form of Catholicism despite Louis XIV's harassment and repeated condemnation by the papacy. Under the pressure of religious and political persecution, Jansenism took a revivalist turn in the 1720s. At the funeral of a Jansenist priest in Paris in 1727, the crowd who flocked to the grave claimed to witness a series of miraculous healings. Within a few years, a cult formed around the priest's tomb and clandestine Jansenist presses were reporting new miracles to the reading public. When the French government tried to suppress the cult, one enraged wit placed a sign at the tomb that read, "By order of the king, God is forbidden to work miracles here." Some believers fell into frenzied convulsions, claiming to be inspired by the Holy Spirit through the intercession of the dead priest. After midcentury, Jansenism became even more politically active as its adherents joined in opposition to the crown's policies on religion.

REVIEW QUESTION How were new social trends reflected in cultural life in the early 1700s?

Consolidation of the European State System

The spread of Pietism and Jansenism reflected the emergence of a middle-class public that now participated in every new development, including religion. The middle classes could pursue these interests because the European state system gradually stabilized despite the increasing competition for wealth in the Atlantic system. Warfare settled three main issues between 1700 and 1750: a coalition of powers held France in check on the continent, Great Britain emerged from the wars against France as the

---

Pietism: A Protestant revivalist movement of the early eighteenth century that emphasized deeply emotional individual religious experience.

preeminent maritime power, and Russia defeated Sweden in the contest for supremacy in the Baltic. After Louis XIV's death in 1715, Europe enjoyed the fruits of a more balanced diplomatic system, in which warfare became less frequent and less widespread. States could then spend their resources establishing and expanding control over their own populations, both at home and in their colonies.

A New Power Alignment

The peace treaties that ended the War of the Spanish Succession (1701–1713) signaled a new alignment of power in western Europe (see Chapter 16). Spain began a long decline, French ambitions for dominance were thwarted, and Great Britain emerged as the new nodal point in the balance of power. A coalition led by Britain and joined by most of the European powers had confronted Louis XIV's French forces across Europe. The conflict extended to the Caribbean and North and South America as well. The casualties mounted inexorably: in the battle of Blenheim in southern Germany in 1704, 108,000 soldiers fought and 33,000 were killed or wounded—in just one day. At Malplaquet, near the northern French border, a great battle in 1709 engaged 166,000 soldiers and cavalrymen, and 36,000 of them were killed or wounded. Those allied against Louis won at Malplaquet, but they lost twice as many men as the French did and could not pursue their advantage. Everyone rejoiced when peace came (Map 17.2).

By the terms of the peace, Louis XIV's grandson was confirmed as king Philip V of Spain (r. 1700–1746) but only on the condition that he renounce any claim to the French throne. None of the other powers could countenance a joint French-Spanish monarchy. Philip introduced French-style academies, French dress, and Italian opera, thus opening Spain more to the rest of Europe. He also stabilized the currency, but he could not revive Spain's military prestige or commercial position. Spain consistently imported more from Britain and France than it exported to them. A country created by the campaign against Muslims within its boundaries, Spain remained firmly in the grip of the Catholic clergy, which insisted on the censorship of dissident or heretical ideas. Although the capital city, Madrid, had 200,000 inhabitants, it was against the law to smoke, play cards, read newspapers, or talk politics in the cafés and inns of the city—precisely the activities flourishing in England, France, and the Dutch Republic.

When French king Louis XIV died in 1715, his five-year-old great-grandson succeeded him as Louis XV (r. 1715–1774) with the duke of Orléans (1674–1723), nephew of the dead king, serving as regent for the young boy. The regent revived some of the parlements' powers and tried to give leading nobles a greater say in political affairs. To raise much-needed funds, in 1719 the regent encouraged the Scottish financier John Law to set up an official trading company for North America and a state bank that issued paper money and stock (without them, trade depended on the available supply of gold and silver). The bank was supposed to offer lower interest rates to the state, thus cutting the cost of financing the government's debts. The value of the stock rose rapidly in a frenzy of speculation, only to crash a few months later. With it vanished any hope of establishing a state bank or issuing paper money for nearly a century.

France finally achieved a measure of financial stability under the leadership of Cardinal Hercule de Fleury (1653–1743), the most powerful member of the government after the death of the regent. Fleury aimed to avoid adventure abroad and keep social peace at home; he balanced the budget and carried out a large project for road and canal construction. Colonial trade boomed. Peace and the acceptance of limits on territorial expansion inaugurated a century of French prosperity.

British Rise and Dutch Decline

The British and the Dutch had formed a coalition against Louis XIV under their joint ruler William III, who was simultaneously stadholder (elected head) of the Dutch Republic and, with his English wife, Mary (d. 1694), ruler of England, Wales, and Scotland. After William's death in 1702, the British and Dutch went their separate ways. Over the next decades, England incorporated Scotland and subjugated Ireland, becoming "Great Britain." At the same time, Dutch imperial power declined; by 1700, Great Britain dominated the seas, and the Dutch, with their small population of less than two million, came to depend on alliances with bigger powers.

From England to Great Britain English relations with Scotland and Ireland were complicated by the problem of succession: William and Mary had no children. To ensure a Protestant succession, Parliament ruled that Mary's sister, Anne, would succeed William and Mary and that the Protestant House of Hanover in Germany would succeed Anne if she had no surviving heirs. Catholics were excluded. When Queen Anne (r. 1702–1714) died leaving no children, the elector of Hanover, a Protestant great-grandson of James I, consequently became King George I (r. 1714–1727). The house of

MAP 17.2 Europe, c. 1715

Although Louis XIV succeeded in putting his grandson Philip on the Spanish throne, France emerged considerably weakened from the War of the Spanish Succession. France ceded large territories in Canada to Britain, which also gained key Mediterranean outposts from Spain as well as a monopoly on providing slaves to the Spanish colonies. Spanish losses were catastrophic. Philip had to renounce any future claim to the French crown and give up considerable territories in the Netherlands and Italy to the Austrians. | **How did the competing English and French claims in North America around 1715 create potential conflicts for the future?**

Hanover—renamed the house of Windsor during World War I—still occupies the British throne.

Support from the Scots and Irish for this solution did not come easily, because many in Scotland and Ireland supported the claims to the throne of the deposed Catholic king, James II, and, after his death in 1701, his son James Edward. Out of fear of this Jacobitism (from the Latin *Jacobus* for "James"), Scottish Protestant leaders agreed to the Act of Union of 1707, which abolished the Scottish

Parliament and affirmed the Scots' recognition of the Protestant Hanoverian succession. The Scots agreed to obey the Parliament of Great Britain, which would include Scottish members in the House of Commons and the House of Lords. A Jacobite rebellion in Scotland in 1715, aiming to restore the Stuart line, was suppressed (see Map 17.2, page 569). The threat of Jacobitism nonetheless continued into the 1740s.

The Irish — 90 percent of whom were Catholic — proved even more difficult to subdue. When James II had gone to Ireland in 1689 to raise a Catholic rebellion against the new monarchs of England, William III responded by taking command of the joint English and Dutch forces and defeating James's Irish supporters. James fled to France, and the Catholics in Ireland faced yet more confiscation and legal restrictions. By 1700, Irish Catholics, who in 1640 had owned 60 percent of the land in Ireland, owned just 14 percent. The Protestant-controlled Irish Parliament passed a series of laws limiting the rights of the Catholic majority: Catholics could not bear arms, send their children abroad for education, establish Catholic schools at home, or marry Protestants. Catholics could not sit in Parliament, nor could they vote for its members unless they took an oath renouncing Catholic doctrine. These and a host of other laws reduced Catholic Ireland to the status of a colony; one English official commented in 1745, "The poor people of Ireland are used worse than negroes." Most of the Irish were peasants who lived in primitive housing and subsisted on a meager diet that included no meat.

The Parliament of Great Britain was soon dominated by the Whigs. In Britain's constitutional system, the monarch ruled with Parliament. The crown chose the ministers, directed policy, and supervised administration, while Parliament raised revenue, passed laws, and represented the interests of the people to the crown. The powers of Parliament were reaffirmed by the Triennial Act in 1694, which provided that Parliaments meet at least once every three years (this was extended to seven years in 1716, after the Whigs had established their ascendancy). Only 200,000 propertied men could vote, out of a population of more than five million, and, not surprisingly, most members of Parliament came from the landed gentry. In fact, a few hundred families controlled all the important political offices.

George I and George II (r. 1727–1760) relied on one man, Sir **Robert Walpole** (1676–1745), to help them manage their relations with Parliament. From his position as First Lord of the Treasury, Walpole made himself into the first, or "prime," minister, leading the House of Commons from 1721 to 1742. (See the illustration on page 571.) Although appointed initially by the king, Walpole established an enduring pattern of parliamentary government in which a prime minister from the leading party guided legislation through the House of Commons. Walpole also built a vast patronage machine that dispensed government jobs to win support for the crown's policies. Walpole's successors relied more and more on the patronage system and eventually alienated not only the Tories but also the middle classes in London and even the North American colonies.

The partisan division between the Whigs, who supported the Hanoverian succession and the rights of dissenting Protestants, and the Tories, who had backed the Stuart line and the Church of England, did not hamper Great Britain's pursuit of economic, military, and colonial power. In this period, Great Britain became a great power on the world stage by virtue of its navy and its ability to finance major military involvement in wars. The founding in 1694 of the Bank of England — which, unlike the French bank, endured — enabled the government to raise money at low interest for foreign wars. By the 1740s, the government could borrow more than four times what it could in the 1690s.

The Dutch Eclipse When William of Orange (William III of England) died in 1702, he left no heirs, and for forty-five years the Dutch lived without a stadholder. The merchant ruling class of some two thousand families dominated the Dutch Republic more than ever, but they presided over a country that counted for less in international power politics. In some areas, Dutch decline was only relative: the Dutch population was not growing as fast as others, for example, and the Dutch share of the Baltic trade decreased from 50 percent in 1720 to less than 30 percent by the 1770s. After 1720, the Baltic countries — Prussia, Russia, Denmark, and Sweden — began to ban imports of manufactured goods to protect their own industries, and Dutch trade in particular suffered. The output of Leiden textiles dropped to one-third of its 1700 level by 1740. Shipbuilding, paper manufacturing, tobacco processing, salt refining, and pottery production all dwindled as well. The Dutch East India Company saw its political and military grip loosened in India, Ceylon, and Java.

The biggest exception to the downward trend was trade with the New World, which increased with escalating demands for sugar and tobacco. The Dutch shifted their interest away from great power

---

Robert Walpole: The first, or "prime," minister (1721–1742) of the House of Commons of Great Britain's Parliament. Although appointed initially by the king, through his long period of leadership he effectively established the modern pattern of parliamentary government.

Sir Robert Walpole at a Cabinet Meeting
Sir Robert Walpole and George II developed the institution of a cabinet, which brought together the important heads of departments. Their cabinet was the ancestor of modern cabinets in both Great Britain and the United States. Because of its modest size, its similarities to modern forms should not be overstated, however. How would discussions in the new coffeehouses (shown in the opening illustration to this chapter) influence the kinds of decisions made by Walpole and his cabinet? *(British Museum, London, UK/The Bridgeman Art Library International.)*

rivalries toward those areas of international trade and finance where they could establish an enduring presence.

Russia's Emergence as a European Power

The commerce and shipbuilding of the Dutch and British so impressed Russian tsar Peter I (r. 1689–1725) that he traveled incognito to their shipyards in 1697 to learn their methods firsthand. Known to history as **Peter the Great**, he dragged Russia kicking and screaming all the way to great-power status. Although he came to the throne while still a minor (on the eve of his tenth birthday), grew up under the threat of a palace coup, and enjoyed little formal education, his accomplishments soon matched his seven-foot-tall stature. Peter transformed public life in Russia and established an absolutist state on the Western model. His attempts to create a society patterned after western Europe, known as **Westernization**, ignited an enduring controversy: Did Peter set Russia on a course of inevitable Westernization required to compete with the West? Or did he forever and fatally disrupt Russia's natural evolution into a distinctive Slavic society?

Westernization To pursue his goal of Westernizing Russian culture, Peter set up the first greenhouses, laboratories, and technical schools and founded the Russian Academy of Sciences. He ordered translations of Western classics and hired a German theater company to perform the French plays of Molière. He replaced the

Peter the Great: Russian tsar Peter I (r. 1689–1725), who undertook the Westernization of Russia and built a new capital city named after himself, St. Petersburg.

Westernization: The effort, especially in Peter the Great's Russia, to make society and social customs resemble counterparts in western Europe, especially France, Britain, and the Dutch Republic.

Peter the Great Modernizes Russia

In this popular print, a barber forces a protesting noble to conform to Western fashions. Peter the Great ordered all nobles, merchants, and middle-class professionals to cut off their beards or pay a huge tax to keep them. An early biographer of Peter claimed that those who lost their beards saved them to put in their coffins, in fear that they would not enter heaven without them. Most western Europeans applauded these attempts to modernize Russia, but many Russians deeply resented the attack on traditional ways. Why was everyday appearance such a contested issue in Russia? *(Visual Connection Archive.)*

traditional Russian calendar with the Western one,[1] introduced Arabic numerals, and brought out the first public newspaper. He ordered his officials and the nobles to shave their beards (see the illustration above) and dress in Western fashion, and he even issued precise regulations about the suitable style of jacket, boots, and cap (generally French or German).

Peter encouraged foreigners to move to Russia to offer their advice and skills, especially for building the capital city. Named St. Petersburg after the tsar, the new capital symbolized Russia's opening to the West. Construction began in 1703 in a Baltic province that had been recently conquered from Sweden. By the end of 1709, thirty thousand recruits a year found themselves assigned to the work. Peter ordered skilled workers to move to the new city and commanded all landowners possessing more than forty serf households to build houses there. In the 1720s, a German minister described St. Petersburg "as a wonder of the world, considering its magnificent palaces, . . . and the short time that was employed in the building of it." By 1710, the permanent population of the capital reached eight thousand. At Peter's death in 1725, it had forty thousand residents.

As a new city far from the Russian heartland around Moscow, St. Petersburg represented a decisive break with Russia's past. Peter widened that gap by every means possible. At his new capital he tried to improve the traditionally denigrated, secluded status of women by ordering them to dress in European styles and appear publicly at his dinners for diplomatic representatives. Imitating French manners, he decreed that women attend his new social salons of officials, officers, and merchants for conversation and dancing. A foreigner headed every one of Peter's new technical and vocational schools, and for its first eight years the new Academy of Sciences included no Russians. Every ministry was assigned a foreign adviser. Upper-class Russians learned French or German, which they spoke even at home. Such changes affected only the very top of Russian society, however; the mass of the population had no contact with the new ideas and ended up paying for the innovations either in ruinous new taxation or by building St. Petersburg, a project that cost the lives of thousands of workers. Serfs remained tied to the land, completely dominated by their noble lords.

Peter the Great's Brand of Absolutism

Peter also reorganized government and finance on Western models and, like other absolute rulers, strengthened his army. With ruthless recruiting methods, which included branding a cross on every recruit's left hand to prevent desertion, he forged an army of 200,000 men and equipped it with modern weapons. He not only built the first navy in Russian history but also created schools for artillery, engineering, and military medicine. Not surprisingly, taxes tripled.

The tsar allowed nothing to stand in his way. He did not hesitate to use torture, and he executed thousands. He allowed a special guard regiment unprecedented power to expedite cases against those suspected of rebellion, espionage, pretensions to the throne, or just "unseemly utterances" against him. Opposition to his policies reached into his own family: because his only son, Alexei, had allied him-

[1]Peter introduced the Julian calendar, then still used in Protestant but not Catholic countries. Later in the eighteenth century, Protestant Europe abandoned the Julian for the Gregorian calendar. Not until 1918 was the Gregorian calendar adopted in Russia, at which point Russia's calendar had fallen thirteen days behind Europe's.

self with Peter's critics, the tsar threw him into prison, where the young man mysteriously died.

To control the often restive nobility, Peter insisted that all noblemen engage in state service. The Table of Ranks (1722) classified them into military, administrative, and court categories, a codification of social and legal relationships in Russia that would last for nearly two centuries. All social and material advantages now depended on serving the crown. Because the nobles lacked a secure independent status, Peter could command them to a degree that was unimaginable in western Europe. State service was not only compulsory but also permanent. Moreover, the male children of those in service had to be registered by the age of ten and begin serving at fifteen. To increase his authority over the Russian Orthodox church, Peter allowed the office of patriarch (supreme head) to remain vacant, and in 1721 he replaced it with the Holy Synod, a bureaucracy of laymen under his supervision. To many devout Russians, Peter was the devil incarnate.

Changes in the Balance of Power in the East Peter the Great's success in building up state power changed the balance of power in eastern Europe. Overcoming initial military setbacks, Russia eventually defeated Sweden and took its place as the leading power in the Baltic region. Russia could then compete with Prussia, Austria, and France in the rivalries between great powers.

Sweden had dominated the Baltic region since the Thirty Years' War (1618–1648), and though the monarchy lost some of its power under Queen Christina (r. 1632–1654), the daughter of Gustavus Adolphus, the Swedish kings quickly recovered their position. When Peter the Great joined an anti-Swedish coalition in 1700 with Denmark, Saxony, and Poland, Sweden's Charles XII (r. 1697–1718) stood up to the test. Still in his teens at the beginning of the Great Northern War (1700–1721), Charles first defeated Denmark, then destroyed the new Russian army, and quickly marched into Poland and Saxony. After defeating the Poles and occupying Saxony, Charles invaded Russia. Here Peter's rebuilt army finally defeated the Swedish king at the battle of Poltava (1709), taking twenty-three thousand Swedish soldiers prisoner and marking the end of Swedish imperial ambitions in the Baltic (Map 17.3). Charles fled to Ottoman territory (in present-day Moldova) and died in battle in 1718 when he tried to renew the fight against Denmark.

Prussia had to make the most of every military opportunity because it was much smaller in size and population than Russia, Austria, or France. King Frederick William I (r. 1713–1740) doubled the size of the Prussian army; though still smaller than those of his rivals, it was the best-trained and most up-to-date force in Europe. In 1715, Frederick William joined the Russian side against Sweden in the Great Northern War and gained new territories. By 1750, Prussia had Europe's highest proportion of men at arms (1 of every 28 people, versus 1 in 157 in France and 1 in 64 in Russia) and the highest proportion of nobles in the military (1 in 7 noblemen, as compared with 1 in 33 in France and 1 in 50 in Russia).

The army so dominated life in Prussia that the country earned the label "a large army with a small state attached." Frederick William, known as the "Sergeant King," was one of the first rulers to wear a military uniform as his everyday dress. He subordinated the entire domestic administration to the army's needs. He also installed a system for recruiting soldiers by local district quotas. He financed the army's growth by subjecting all the provinces to an excise tax on food, drink, and manufactured goods and by increasing rents on crown lands. Prussia was

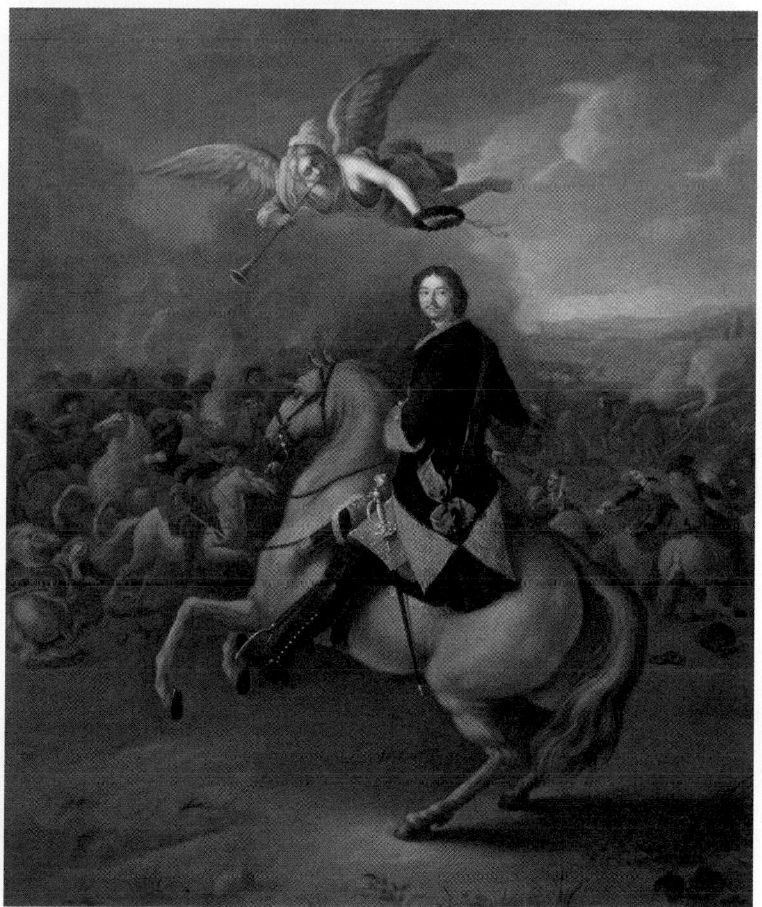

Peter the Great

In this painting by Gottfried Danhauer (1680–1733/7), the Russian tsar appears against the background of his most famous battle, Poltava. The angel holds a laurel wreath, symbol of victory, over his head. *(Tretyakov Gallery, Moscow, Russia/The Bridgeman Art Library International.)*

MAP 17.3 Russia and Sweden after the Great Northern War, 1721
After the Great Northern War, Russia supplanted Sweden as the major power in the north. Although Russia had a much larger population from which to draw its armies, Sweden made the most of its advantages and gave way only after a great military struggle.

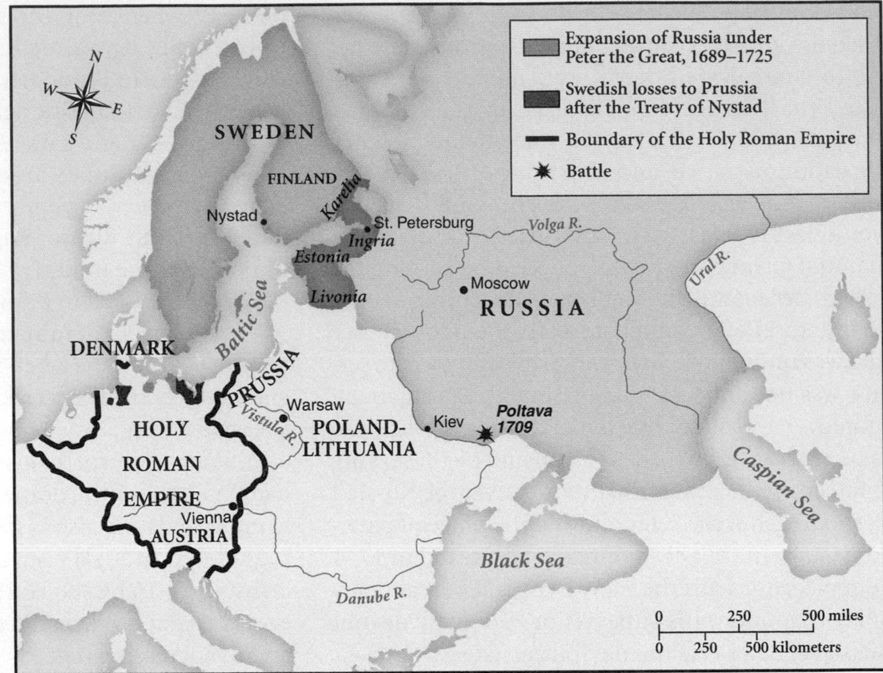

now poised to become one of the major players on the continent, but given the size of its forces, it could not enter into military engagements foolishly; the Prussians therefore chose to sit on the sidelines during the next conflict.

Continuing Dynastic Struggles

War broke out again in 1733 when the king of Poland-Lithuania died. France, Spain, and Sardinia joined in the War of Polish Succession (1733–1735) against Austria and Russia, each side supporting rival claimants to the Polish throne. Although Peter the Great had been followed by a series of weak rulers, Russian forces were still strong enough to drive the French candidate out of Poland-Lithuania, prompting France to accept the Austrian candidate. In exchange, Austria gave the province of Lorraine to the French candidate, the father-in-law of Louis XV, with the promise that the province would pass to France on his death. France and Britain went back to pursuing their colonial rivalries. Prussia and Russia concentrated on shoring up their influence within Poland-Lithuania.

Because its armies still faced the Turks on its southeastern border, Austria did not want to become mired in a long struggle in Poland-Lithuania. Even though the Austrians had forced the Turks to recognize their rule over all of Hungary and Transylvania in 1699 and occupied Belgrade in 1717, the Turks did not stop fighting. In the 1730s, the Turks retook Belgrade, and Russia now claimed a role in the struggle against the Turks. Moreover, Hungary, though "liberated" from Turkish rule, proved less than enthusiastic about submitting to Austria. In 1703, the wealthiest Hungarian noble landlord, Ferenc Rákóczi (1676–1735), raised an army of seventy thousand men who fought for "God, Fatherland, and Liberty" until 1711. They forced the Austrians to recognize local Hungarian institutions, grant amnesty, and restore confiscated estates in exchange for confirming hereditary Austrian rule.

When Holy Roman Emperor Charles VI died without a male heir in 1740, another war of succession, the **War of the Austrian Succession** (1740–1748), began.

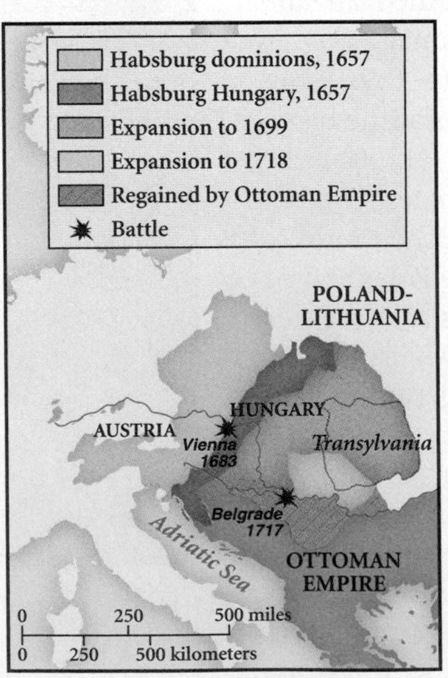

Austrian Conquest of Hungary, 1657–1730

War of the Austrian Succession: The war (1740–1748) over the succession to the Habsburg throne that pitted France and Prussia against Austria and Britain and provoked continuing hostilities between French and British settlers in the North American colonies.

Most European rulers recognized the emperor's chosen heiress, his daughter Maria Theresa, because Charles's Pragmatic Sanction of 1713 had given a woman the right to inherit the Habsburg crown lands. The new king of Prussia, Frederick II, who had just succeeded his father a few months earlier in 1740, saw his chance to grab territory and immediately invaded the rich Austrian province of Silesia. France joined Prussia in an attempt to further humiliate its traditional enemy Austria, and Great Britain allied with Austria to prevent the French from taking the Austrian Netherlands. The war soon expanded to the overseas colonies of Great Britain and France. French and British colonials in North America fought each other all along their boundaries, enlisting native American auxiliaries. Britain tried but failed to isolate the French Caribbean colonies during the war, and hostilities broke out in India, too.

Maria Theresa (r. 1740–1780) survived only by conceding Silesia to Prussia in order to split the Prussians off from France. The Peace of Aix-la-Chapelle (1748) recognized Maria Theresa as the heiress to the Austrian lands; her husband, Francis I, became Holy Roman Emperor, thus reasserting the integrity of the Austrian Empire. The peace of 1748 failed to resolve the colonial conflicts between Britain and France, however, and fighting for domination continued unofficially.

The Power of Diplomacy and the Importance of Population

No single power emerged from the wars of the first half of the eighteenth century clearly superior to the others, and the Peace of Utrecht explicitly declared that maintaining a balance of power was crucial to maintaining peace in Europe. In 1720 a British pamphleteer wrote, "There is not, I believe, any doctrine in the law of nations, of more certain truth . . . than this of the balance of power." Diplomacy helped maintain the balance, but in the end this system of equilibrium often rested on military force, such as the coalition against Sweden in the Great Northern War. The ongoing needs for a ready military had an interesting side effect: in the search for ever larger armies, states could not afford to ignore the general health of their populations.

Diplomatic Services To meet the new demands placed on it, the diplomatic service, like the military and financial bureaucracies before it, had to develop regular procedures. The French set a pattern that the other European states soon imitated. By 1685, France had embassies in all the important capitals. Nobles of ancient families served as ambassadors to Rome, Madrid, Vienna, and London, whereas royal officials were chosen for Switzerland, the Dutch Republic, and Venice. The ambassador selected and paid for his own staff. This practice could make the journey to a new post cumbersome, because the staff might be as large as eighty people, and they brought along all their own furniture, pictures, silverware, and tapestries. It took one French ambassador ten weeks to get from Paris to Stockholm.

Despite a new emphasis on honest and informed negotiation, rulers still employed secret agents and often sent covert instructions that negated the official ones sent by their own foreign offices. This behind-the-scenes diplomacy had some advantages because it allowed rulers to break with past alliances, but it also led to confusion and sometimes scandal, for the rulers often engaged unreliable adventurers as their confidential agents. Still, the diplomatic system in the early eighteenth century proved successful enough to ensure a continuation of the principles of the Peace of Westphalia (1648); in the midst of every crisis and war, the great powers would convene and hammer out a written agreement detailing the requirements for peace.

Public Health Adroit diplomacy could smooth the road toward peace, but success in war still depended on sheer numbers—of men and of muskets. Because each state's strength depended largely on the size of its army, the growth and health of the population increasingly entered into government calculations. William Petty's *Political Arithmetick* (1690) offered statistical estimates of human capital—that is, of population and wages—to determine Britain's national wealth. A large, growing population could be as vital to a state's future as access to silver mines or overseas trade, so government officials devoted increased effort to the statistical estimation of total population and rates of births, deaths, and marriages. In 1727, Frederick William I of Prussia founded two university chairs to encourage population studies, and textbooks and handbooks advocated state intervention to improve the population's health and welfare.

Physicians used the new population statistics to explain the environmental causes of disease, another new preoccupation in this period. Petty devised a quantitative scale that distinguished healthy from unhealthy places largely on the basis of air quality, an early precursor of modern environmental studies. Cities were the unhealthiest places because excrement (animal and human) and garbage accumulated where people lived densely packed together. The Irish writer Jonathan Swift described what happened in London after a big rainstorm: "Filths of all hues and colors . . . sweepings from butchers' stalls, dung, guts and blood . . . dead cats and turniptops come tumbling down the flood." Reacting to newly collected data on climate, disease, and population, local governments undertook such measures as draining low-lying areas, burying refuse, and cleaning wells, all of which eventually helped lower the death rates from epidemic diseases.

Not all changes came from direct government intervention. Hospitals, founded originally as charities concerned foremost with the moral worthiness of the poor, gradually evolved into medical institutions that defined patients by their diseases. The process of diagnosis changed as physicians began to use specialized Latin terms for illnesses. The gap between medical experts and their patients increased, as physicians now also relied on postmortem dissections in the hospital to gain better knowledge, a practice most patients' families resented. Press reports of body snatching and grave robbing by surgeons and their apprentices outraged the public well into the 1800s.

Despite the change in hospitals, the medical profession, with nationwide organizations and licensing, had not yet emerged, and no clear line separated trained physicians from quacks. Individual health care remained something of a free-for-all in which physicians competed with bloodletters, itinerant venereal-disease doctors, bonesetters, druggists, midwives, and "cunning women," who specialized in home remedies. In any case trained physicians were few, and almost none existed outside cities.

Even patients in a hospital were as likely to catch a deadly disease as to be cured there. Antiseptics were virtually unknown. Because doctors believed most insanity was caused by disorders in the system of bodily "humors," their prescribed treatments included blood transfusions; ingestion of bitter substances such as coffee, quinine, and soap; immersion in water; various forms of exercise; and burning or cauterizing the body to allow black vapors to escape.

Hardly any infectious diseases could be cured, though inoculation against smallpox spread from the Middle East to Europe in the early eighteenth century, thanks largely to the efforts of Lady Mary Wortley Montagu (1689–1762). In 1716, Montagu accompanied her husband to Constantinople, where he took up a post as British ambassador to the Ottoman Empire. She returned in 1718, having witnessed firsthand the Turkish use of inoculation. When a new smallpox epidemic threatened England in 1721, she called on her physician to inoculate her daughter. Two patients died after inoculation in the following months, prompting clergymen and physicians to attack the practice, which remained in dispute for decades. Inoculation against smallpox began to spread more widely after 1796, when the English physician Edward Jenner developed a serum based on cowpox, a milder disease. However, many other diseases spread quickly in the unsanitary conditions of urban life. Ordinary people washed or changed clothes rarely, lived in overcrowded housing with poor ventilation, and got their water from contaminated sources such as refuse-filled rivers.

Public bathhouses had disappeared from cities in the sixteenth and seventeenth centuries because they seemed a source of disorderly behavior and epidemic illness. In the eighteenth century, even private bathing came into disfavor because people feared the effects of contact with water. Fewer than one in ten newly built private mansions in Paris had baths. Bathing was hazardous, physicians insisted, because it opened the body to disease. One manners manual of 1736 admonished, "It is correct to clean the face every morning by using a white cloth to cleanse it. It is less good to wash with water, because it renders the face susceptible to cold in winter and sun in summer." The upper classes associated cleanliness not with baths but with frequently changed linens, powdered hair, and perfume, which was thought to strengthen the body and refresh the brain by counteracting corrupt and foul air.

REVIEW QUESTION What events and developments led to greater stability and more limited warfare within Europe?

The Birth of the Enlightenment

Economic expansion, the emergence of a new consumer society, and the stabilization of the European state system all generated optimism about the future. The intellectual corollary was the **Enlightenment**, a term used later in the eighteenth century to describe the loosely knit group of writers and scholars who believed that human beings could apply a critical, reasoning spirit to every problem they encountered in this world. The new secular, scientific, and critical attitude first emerged in the 1690s, scrutinizing everything from the absolutism of Louis XIV

Enlightenment: The eighteenth-century intellectual movement whose proponents believed that human beings could apply a critical, reasoning spirit to every problem.

TERMS OF HISTORY

Progress

Believing as they did in the possibilities of improvement, many Enlightenment writers preached a new doctrine about the meaning of human history. They challenged the traditional Christian belief that the original sin of Adam and Eve condemned human beings to unhappiness in this world and offered instead an optimistic vision: human nature, they claimed, was inherently good, and progress would be continuous if education developed human capacities to the utmost. Science and reason could bring happiness in this world. The idea of novelty or newness itself now seemed positive rather than threatening. Europeans began to imagine that they could surpass all those who preceded them in history, and they began to think of themselves as more "advanced" than the "backward" cultures they encountered in other parts of the world.

More than an intellectual concept, the idea of progress included a new conception of historical time and of Europeans' place within world history. Europeans stopped looking back, whether to a lost Garden of Eden or to the writings of Greek and Roman antiquity. Growing prosperity, European dominance overseas, and the scientific revolution oriented them toward the future. To distinguish it from the Middle Ages (a new term), Europeans began to apply the word *modern* to their epoch—and they considered their modern period superior in achievement. Consequently, Europeans took it as their mission to bring their modern, enlightened ways of progress to the areas they colonized.

The economic and ecological catastrophes, destructive wars, and genocides of the twentieth century cast much doubt on this rosy vision of continuing progress. As the philosopher George Santayana (1863–1952) complained, "The cry was for vacant freedom and indeterminate progress: *Vorwarts! Avanti! Onward! Full Speed Ahead!*, without asking whether directly before you was a bottomless pit." Historians are now chastened in their claims about progress. They would no longer side with the German philosopher Georg W. F. Hegel, who proclaimed in 1832, "The history of the world is none other than the progress of the consciousness of freedom." They worry about the nationalistic claims inherent, for example, in the English historian Thomas Babington Macaulay's insistence that "the history of England is emphatically the history of progress" (1843). As with many other historical questions, the final word is not yet in: Is there a direction in human history that can correctly be called progress? Or is history, as many in ancient times thought, a set of repeating cycles?

to the traditional role of women in society. After 1750, criticism took a more systematic turn as writers provided new theories for the organization of society and politics; but as early as the 1720s, established authorities realized they faced a new set of challenges. Even while slavery expanded in the Atlantic system, Enlightenment writers began to insist on the need for new freedoms in Europe.

Popularization of Science and Challenges to Religion

The writers of the Enlightenment glorified the geniuses of the new science and championed the scientific method as the solution for all social problems. (See "Terms of History," above.) One of the most influential popularizations was the French writer Bernard de Fontenelle's *Conversations on the Plurality of Worlds* (1686). Presented as a dialogue between an aristocratic woman and a man of the world, the book made the Copernican, heliocentric view of the universe available to the literate public. By 1700, mathematics and science had become fashionable topics in high society, and the public flocked to lectures explaining scientific discoveries. Journals complained that scientific learning had become the passport to female affection: "There were two young ladies in Paris whose heads had been so turned by this branch of learning that one of them declined to listen to a proposal of marriage unless the candidate for her hand undertook to learn how to make telescopes." Such writings poked fun at women with intellectual interests, but they also demonstrated that women now participated in discussions of science.

The New Skepticism Interest in science spread in literate circles because it offered a model for all forms of knowledge. As the prestige of science increased, some developed a skeptical attitude toward attempts to enforce religious conformity. A French Huguenot refugee from Louis XIV's persecutions, Pierre Bayle (1647–1706) launched an internationally influential campaign against religious intolerance from his safe haven in the Dutch Republic. His *News from the Republic of Letters* (first published in 1684) bitterly criticized the policies of Louis XIV and was quickly banned

A Budding Scientist
In this engraving, *Astrologia*, by the Dutch artist Jacob Gole (c. 1660–1723), an upper-class woman looks through a telescope to do her own astronomical investigations. Women with intellectual interests were often disparaged by men, and women were not allowed to attend university classes in any European country. Yet because many astronomical observatories were set up in private homes rather than public buildings or universities, wives and daughters of scientists could make observations and even publish their own findings. *(Bibliothèque nationale de France.)*

in Paris and condemned in Rome. After attacking Louis XIV's anti-Protestant policies, Bayle took a more general stand in favor of religious toleration. No state in Europe officially offered complete tolerance, though the Dutch Republic came closest with its tacit acceptance of Catholics, dissident Protestant groups, and open Jewish communities. In 1697, Bayle published his *Historical and Critical Dictionary*, which cited all the errors and delusions that he could find in past and present writers of all religions. Even religion must meet the test of reasonableness: "Any particular dogma, whatever it may be, whether it is advanced on the authority of the Scriptures, or whatever else may be its origins, is to be regarded as false if it clashes with the clear and definite conclusions of the natural understanding [reason]."

Although Bayle claimed to be a believer himself, his insistence on rational investigation seemed to challenge the authority of faith. As one critic complained, "It is notorious that the works of M. Bayle have unsettled a large number of readers, and cast doubt on some of the most widely accepted principles of morality and religion." Bayle asserted, for example, that atheists might possess moral codes as effective as those of the devout. Bayle's *Dictionary* became a model of critical thought in the West.

Other scholars challenged the authority of the Bible by subjecting it to historical criticism. Discoveries in geology in the early eighteenth century showed that marine fossils dated immensely further back than the biblical flood. Investigations of miracles, comets, and oracles — like the growing literature against belief in witchcraft— urged the use of reason to combat superstition and prejudice. Writers noted that comets, for example, should not be considered evil omens just because earlier generations had passed down such a belief. Defenders of church and state published books warning of the new skepticism's dangers. The spokesman for Louis XIV's absolutism, the bishop Jacques-Bénigne Bossuet, warned that "reason is the guide of their choice, but reason only brings them face to face with vague conjectures and baffling perplexities." Human beings, the traditionalists held, were simply incapable of subjecting everything to reason, especially in the realm of religion.

State authorities found religious skepticism equally unsettling because it threatened to undermine state power, too. The extensive literature of criticism was not limited to France, but much of it was published in French, and the French government took the lead in suppressing the more outspoken works. Forbidden books were then often published in the Dutch Republic, Britain, or Switzerland and smuggled back across the border to a public whose appetite was only whetted by censorship.

The Young Voltaire | The most influential writer of the early Enlightenment was a Frenchman born into the upper middle class, François-Marie Arouet, known by his pen name, **Voltaire** (1694–1778). Voltaire took inspiration from Bayle, once giving him the following tongue-in-cheek description: "He gives facts with such odious fidelity, he exposes the arguments for and against with such dastardly impartiality, he is so intolerably intelligible, that he leads people of only ordinary common sense to judge and even to doubt." In his early years, Voltaire suffered arrest, imprisonment, and exile, but he eventually achieved wealth and ac-

Voltaire: The pen name of François-Marie Arouet (1694–1778), who was the most influential writer of the early Enlightenment.

claim. His tangles with church and state began in the early 1730s, when he published his *Letters Concerning the English Nation* (the English version appeared in 1733), in which he devoted several chapters to Newton and Locke and used the virtues of the British as a way to attack Catholic bigotry and government rigidity in France. Impressed by British toleration of religious dissent (at least among Protestants), Voltaire spent two years in exile in Britain when the French state responded to his book with yet another order for his arrest.

Voltaire also popularized Newton's scientific discoveries in his *Elements of the Philosophy of Newton* (1738). The French state and many European theologians considered Newtonianism threatening because it glorified the human mind and seemed to reduce God to an abstract, external, rationalistic force. So sensational was the success of Voltaire's book on Newton that a hostile Jesuit reported, "The great Newton, was, it is said, buried in the abyss, in the shop of the first publisher who dared to print him. . . . M. de Voltaire finally appeared, and at once Newton is understood or is in the process of being understood; all Paris resounds with Newton, all Paris stammers Newton, all Paris studies and learns Newton." The success was international, too. Before long, Voltaire was elected a fellow of the Royal Society in London and in Edinburgh, as well as being admitted to twenty other scientific academies. Voltaire's fame continued to grow, reaching truly astounding proportions in the 1750s and 1760s.

A Jesuit Missionary in China
Father Ferdinand Verbiest (1623–1688), shown here in a colored German engraving from the late 1600s, was a Flemish (Belgian) Jesuit who worked in China as a missionary and astronomer from 1660 until his death in Beijing in 1688. After winning an astronomy contest with the leading Chinese astronomer in 1669, he became a close friend of the new Chinese emperor, helped correct the Chinese calendar, and directed the astronomical observatory in Beijing. Relations were not always so friendly, however. The Jesuits lost an earlier contest in 1664 and were nearly executed. In the eighteenth century the Catholic church authorities worried that collaboration with the Chinese had become too close, and they insisted that converts refuse to participate in traditional Chinese ceremonies. *(Bibliothèque des Fontaines, Chantilly, France/Archives Charmet/The Bridgeman Art Library International.)*

Travel Literature and the Challenge to Custom and Tradition

Just as scientific method could be used to question religious and even state authority, a more general skepticism also emerged from the expanding knowledge about the world outside of Europe. During the seventeenth and eighteenth centuries, the number of travel accounts dramatically increased as travel writers used the contrast between their home societies and other cultures to criticize the customs of European society.

Visitors to the new colonies sought something resembling "the state of nature," that is, ways of life that preceded sophisticated social and political organization — although they often misinterpreted different forms of society and politics as having no organization at all. Travelers to the Americas found "noble savages" (native peoples) who appeared to live in conditions of great freedom and equality; they were "naturally good" and "happy" without taxes, lawsuits, or much organized government. In China, in contrast, travelers found a people who enjoyed prosperity and an ancient civilization. Christian missionaries made little headway in China, and visitors had to admit that China's religious systems had flourished for four or five thousand years with no input from Europe or from Christianity. The basic lesson of travel literature in the 1700s, then, was that customs varied: justice, freedom, property, good government, religion, and morality all were relative to the place. One critic complained that travel

DOCUMENT

Montesquieu, *Persian Letters*: Letter 37 (1721)

Charles-Louis de Secondat, baron of Montesquieu (1689–1755), was one of the leading figures of the early Enlightenment. In Persian Letters, *he offered a kind of reverse travel account in which fictional Persians comment on what they see in France. Politics, religion, and social customs all came under critical scrutiny. Letter 37 points to one of his and other early Enlightenment authors' main targets: the French king, Louis XIV (r. 1643–1715), and his absolutist state. Written by one of the book's two main characters, a Persian named Usbek, to a friend back home, the letter explicitly criticizes the king's vanity, ostentation, and life at court. The letter implicitly passes even more serious judgment on the aging ruler in noting his esteem for "oriental policies." Montesquieu condemns these same policies elsewhere in his letters as inhumane and unjust.*

The King of France is old. We have no examples in our histories of such a long reign as his. It is said that he possesses in a very high degree the faculty of making himself obeyed: he governs with equal ability his family, his court, and his kingdom: he has often been heard to say, that, of all existing governments, that of the Turks, or that of our august Sultan, pleased him best: such is his high opinion of Oriental statecraft.[1]

I have studied his character, and I have found certain contradictions which I cannot reconcile. For example, he has a minister who is only eighteen years old,[2] and a mistress [Madame de Maintenon] who is fourscore; he loves his religion, and yet he cannot abide those [the Jansenists] who assert that it ought to be strictly observed; although he flies from the noise of cities, and is inclined to be reticent, from morning till night he is engaged in getting himself talked about; he is fond of trophies and victories, but he has as great a dread of seeing a good general at the head of his own troops, as at the head of an army of his enemies. It has never I believe happened to anyone but himself, to be burdened with more wealth than even a prince could hope for, and yet at the same time steeped in such poverty as a private person could ill brook.

He delights to reward those who serve him; but he pays as liberally the assiduous indolence of his courtiers, as the labors in the field of his captains; often the man who undresses him, or who hands him his serviette at table, is preferred before him who has taken cities and gained battles; he does not believe that the greatness of a monarch is compatible with restriction in the distribution of favors; and, without examining into the merit of a man, he will heap benefits upon him, believing that his selection makes the recipient worthy; accordingly, he has been known to bestow a small pension upon a man who had run off two leagues from the enemy, and a good government on another who had gone four.

Paris, the 7th of the moon of Maharram, 1713.

[1]When Louis XIV was in his sixteenth year, some courtiers discussed in his presence the absolute power of the Sultans, who dispose as they like of the goods and the lives of their subjects. "That is something like being a king," said the young monarch. Marshal d'Estrées, alarmed at the tendency revealed in that remark, rejoined, "But, sire, several of these emperors have been strangled even in my time."

[2]Barbezieux, son of Louvois, Louis's youngest minister, held office at twenty-three, not eighteen; and he was dead in 1713.

Source: Montesquieu, *Persian Letters*, trans. John Davidson (London: Privately printed, 1892), 1:85–86.

Question to Consider

- **In the commentary of the fictional character of Usbek in this letter, in what ways is Montesquieu criticizing both Louis XIV's personal style and absolutism in general?**

encouraged free thinking and the destruction of religion: "Some complete their demoralization by extensive travel, and lose whatever shreds of religion remained to them. Every day they see a new religion, new customs, new rites."

Travel literature turned explicitly political in Montesquieu's *Persian Letters* (1721). Charles-Louis de Secondat, baron of Montesquieu (1689–1755), the son of an eminent judicial family, was a high-ranking judge in a French court. He published *Persian Letters* anonymously in the Dutch Republic, and the book went into ten printings in just one year—a best seller for the times. Montesquieu tells the fictional story of two Persians, Rica and Usbek, who leave their country "for love of knowledge" and travel to Europe. They visit France in the last years of Louis XIV's reign and write home with their impressions. (See Document, "*Persian Letters*: Letter 37," above.) By imagining an outsider's perspective, Montesquieu could satirize French customs and politics without taking them on directly. Beneath the satire, however, was a serious investigation into the foundation of good government and morality. Montesquieu chose Persians for his travelers because they came from what was widely considered the most despotic of all governments, in which rulers had life-and-death powers over their subjects. In the book, the Persians constantly compare France to Persia, suggesting that the French monarchy might verge on despotism.

Montesquieu's anonymity did not last long, and soon Parisian society lionized him. In the late 1720s, he sold his judgeship and traveled extensively in Europe, staying eighteen months in Britain. In 1748, he published a widely influential work on comparative government, *The Spirit of Laws*. Like the politique Jean Bodin before him (see Chapter 15), Montesquieu examined the various types of government, but unlike Bodin he did not favor absolute power in a monarchy. His time in Britain made him much more favorable to constitutional forms of government. The Vatican soon listed both *Persian Letters* and *The Spirit of Laws* on its Index (its list of forbidden books).

Raising the Woman Question

Many of the letters exchanged in *Persian Letters* focused on women, marriage, and the family because Montesquieu considered the position of women a sure indicator of the nature of government and morality. Although Montesquieu was not a feminist, his depiction of Roxana, the favorite wife in Usbek's harem, struck a chord with many women. Roxana revolts against the authority of Usbek's eunuchs and writes a final letter to her husband announcing her impending suicide: "I may have lived in servitude, but I have always been free, I have amended your laws according to the laws of nature, and my mind has always remained independent." Women writers used the same language of tyranny and freedom to argue for concrete changes in their status. Feminist ideas were not entirely new, but they were presented systematically for the first time during the Enlightenment and represented a fundamental challenge to the ways of traditional societies.

The most systematic of these women writers was the English author Mary Astell (1666–1731), the daughter of a businessman and herself a supporter of the Tory party and the Anglican religious establishment. In 1694, she published *A Serious Proposal to the Ladies*, in which she advocated founding a private women's college to remedy women's lack of education. Addressing women, she asked, "How can you be content to be in the World like Tulips in a Garden, to make a fine *shew* [show] and be good for nothing?" Astell argued for intellectual training based on Descartes's principles, in which reason, debate, and careful consideration of the issues took priority over custom or tradition. Her book was an immediate success: five printings appeared by 1701. In later works such as *Reflections upon Marriage* (1706), Astell criticized the relationship between the sexes within marriage: "If absolute sovereignty be not necessary in a state, how comes it to be so in a family? . . . *If all men are born free*, how is it that all women are born slaves?" Her critics accused her of promoting subversive ideas and of contradicting the Bible.

Astell's work inspired other women to write in a similar vein. The anonymous *Essay in Defence of the Female Sex* (1696) attacked "the Usurpation of Men; and the Tyranny of Custom," which prevented women from getting an education. In the introduction to the work of one of the best-known female poets, Elizabeth Singer Rowe, a friend of the author complained of the "notorious Violations on the Liberties of Freeborn English Women" that came from "a plain and an open design to render us meer [mere] Slaves, perfect Turkish Wives."

Most male writers unequivocally stuck to the traditional view of women, which held that women were less capable of reasoning than men and therefore did not need systematic education. Such opinions often rested on biological suppositions. The long-dominant Aristotelian view of reproduction held that only the male seed carried spirit and individuality. At the beginning of the eighteenth century, however, scientists began to undermine this belief. Physicians and surgeons began to champion the doctrine of *ovism*—that the female egg was essential in making new humans. During the decades that followed, male Enlightenment writers would continue to debate women's nature and appropriate social roles.

REVIEW QUESTION What were the major issues in the early decades of the Enlightenment?

Conclusion

Europeans crossed a major threshold in the first half of the eighteenth century. They moved silently but nonetheless momentously from an economy governed by scarcity and the threat of famine to one of ever-increasing growth and the prospect of continuing improvement. Expansion of colonies overseas and economic development at home created greater wealth, longer life spans, and higher expectations for the future. In these better times for many, a spirit of optimism prevailed. People could now spend money on newspapers, novels, and travel literature as well as on coffee, tea, and cotton cloth. The growing literate public avidly followed the latest trends in religious debates, art, and music. Not everyone shared equally in the benefits, however: slaves toiled in misery for their masters in the Americas,

MAPPING THE WEST

Europe in 1750

By 1750, Europe had achieved a kind of diplomatic equilibrium in which no one power predominated despite repeated wars over dynastic succession. Spain, the Dutch Republic, Poland-Lithuania, and Sweden had all declined in power and influence while Great Britain, Russia, and Prussia gained prominence. France's ambitions to dominate had been thwarted, but its combination of a big army and rich overseas possessions made it a major player for a long time to come. In the War of the Austrian Succession, Austria lost its rich province of Silesia to Prussia.

eastern European serfs found themselves ever more closely bound to their noble lords, and rural folk almost everywhere tasted few fruits of consumer society.

Politics changed, too, as population and production increased and cities grew. Experts urged government intervention to improve public health, and states found it in their interest to settle many international disputes by diplomacy, which itself became more regular and routine. The consolidation of the European state system allowed a tide of criticism and new thinking about society to swell in Great Britain and France and begin to spill throughout Europe. Ultimately, the combination of the Atlantic system and the Enlightenment would give rise to a series of Atlantic revolutions.

FOR FURTHER EXPLORATION

- **For additional primary-source material from this period**, see *Sources of the Making of the West*, Fourth Edition.
- **For Web sites, images, and documents related to topics in this chapter**, visit *Make History* at bedfordstmartins.com/hunt.

Chapter 17 Review

Online Study Guide bedfordstmartins.com/hunt

Key Terms and People

In the grid below, identify the term or person and explain its historical significance. (To do this exercise online, go to bedfordstmartins.com/hunt.)

Term	Who or What & When	Why It Matters
Atlantic system (p. 551)		
plantation (p. 553)		
mestizo (p. 558)		
buccaneers (p. 558)		
consumer revolution (p. 560)		
agricultural revolution (p. 562)		
rococo (p. 565)		
Pietism (p. 567)		
Robert Walpole (p. 570)		
Peter the Great (p. 571)		
Westernization (p. 571)		
War of the Austrian Succession (p. 574)		
Enlightenment (p. 576)		
Voltaire (p. 578)		

Review Questions

1. How was consumerism related to slavery in the early eighteenth century?
2. How were new social trends reflected in cultural life in the early 1700s?
3. What events and developments led to greater stability and more limited warfare within Europe?
4. What were the major issues in the early decades of the Enlightenment?

Making Connections

1. How did the rise of slavery and the plantation system change European politics and society?
2. Why was the Enlightenment born just at the moment that the Atlantic system took shape?
3. What were the major differences between the wars of the first half of the eighteenth century and those of the seventeenth century? (Refer to Chapters 15 and 16.)
4. During the first half of the eighteenth century, what were the major issues affecting peasants in France and serfs in Poland and Russia?

Important Events

Date	Event	Date	Event
1700s	Beginning of rapid development of plantations in Caribbean	1720	Last outbreak of bubonic plague in western Europe
1703	Peter the Great begins construction of St. Petersburg, founds first Russian newspaper	1721	Great Northern War ends; Montesquieu publishes *Persian Letters* anonymously in the Dutch Republic
1713–1714	Peace of Utrecht treaties end War of Spanish Succession	1733	War of the Polish Succession; Voltaire's *Letters Concerning the English Nation* attacks French intolerance and narrow-mindedness
1714	Elector of Hanover becomes King George I of England	1740–1748	War of the Austrian Succession
1715	Death of Louis XIV	1741	George Frideric Handel composes *Messiah*
1719	Daniel Defoe publishes *Robinson Crusoe*	1748	Montesquieu publishes *The Spirit of Laws*

- Consider three events: **Beginning of rapid development of plantations in Caribbean (1700s)**, **Daniel Defoe publishes *Robinson Crusoe* (1719)**, and **Montesquieu publishes *Persian Letters* anonymously in the Dutch Republic (1721)**. In what ways were these two works of literature responses to the new global economy?

SUGGESTED REFERENCES

A new Web site on the slave trade offers the most up-to-date information about the workings of the Atlantic system, and another allows the viewer to trace the growth of certain cities over time. The definitive study of the early Enlightenment is the book by Hazard, but many others have contributed biographies of individual figures or studies of women writers.

Black, Jeremy. *European Warfare in a Global Context, 1660–1815.* 2007.

Blackburn, Robin. *The Making of New World Slavery: From the Baroque to the Modern, 1492–1800.* 1997.

Brewer, John. *The Sinews of Power: War, Money, and the English State, 1688–1783.* 1990.

Cracraft, James. *The Revolution of Peter the Great.* 2003.

Dickson, Peter, George Muir, and Christopher Storrs, eds. *The Fiscal-Military State in Eighteenth-Century Europe.* 2009.

Englund, Peter. *The Battle That Shook Europe: Poltava and the Birth of the Russian Empire.* 2003.

Handel's Messiah: The New Interactive Edition (CD-ROM). 1997.

Hazard, Paul. *The European Mind: The Critical Years, 1680–1715.* 1990.

*Hill, Bridget. *The First English Feminist: Reflections upon Marriage and Other Writings by Mary Astell.* 1986.

Hypercities project (includes Berlin): http://hypercities.ats.ucla.edu/

Israel, Jonathan. *A Revolution of the Mind: Radical Enlightenment and the Intellectual Origins of Modern Democracy.* 2010.

*Jacob, Margaret C. *The Enlightenment: A Brief History with Selected Readings.* 2000.

Norton, Marcy. *Sacred Gifts, Profane Pleasures: A History of Tobacco and Chocolate in the Atlantic World.* 2010.

Pearson, Roger. *Voltaire Almighty: A Life in Pursuit of Freedom.* 2005.

Sarti, Raffaella, and Allan Cameron. *Europe at Home: Family and Material Culture, 1500–1800.* 2004.

Slave trade: http://www.slavevoyages.org/tast/index.faces

*Primary source.

The Promise of Enlightenment

CHAPTER

18

1750–1789

In the summer of 1766, Empress Catherine II ("the Great") of Russia wrote to Voltaire, one of the leaders of the Enlightenment:

> It is a way of immortalizing oneself to be the advocate of humanity, the defender of oppressed innocence. . . . You have entered into combat against the enemies of mankind: superstition, fanaticism, ignorance, quibbling, evil judges, and the powers that rest in their hands. Great virtues and qualities are needed to surmount these obstacles. You have shown that you have them: you have triumphed.

Over a fifteen-year period, Catherine corresponded regularly with Voltaire, a writer who, at home in France, found himself in constant conflict with authorities of church and state. Her admiring letter shows how influential Enlightenment ideals had become by the middle of the eighteenth century. Even an absolutist ruler such as Catherine endorsed many aspects of the Enlightenment call for reform; she, too, wanted to be an "advocate of humanity."

Catherine's letter aptly summed up Enlightenment ideals: progress for humanity could be achieved only by rooting out the wrongs left by superstition, religious fanaticism, ignorance, and outmoded forms of justice. Enlightenment writers used every means at their disposal—from encyclopedias to novels to personal interaction with rulers—to argue for reform. Everything had to be examined in the cold light of reason, and anything that did not promote the improvement of humanity was to be jettisoned. As a result, Enlightenment writers supported religious toleration, attacked the legal use of torture to extract confessions, and criticized censorship by state or church. The book trade and new places for urban socializing, such as coffeehouses and learned societies, spread these ideas within a new elite of middle- and upper-class men and women.

The lower classes had little contact with Enlightenment ideas. Their lives

Catherine the Great
In this portrait (c. 1762) by the Danish painter Vigilius Eriksen, the Russian empress Catherine the Great is shown on horseback, much like any male ruler of the time. Born Sophia Augusta Frederika of Anhalt-Zerbst in 1729, Catherine was the daughter of a minor German prince. When she married the future tsar Peter III in 1745, she promptly learned Russian and adopted Russian Orthodoxy. Peter, physically and mentally frail, proved no match for her; in 1762 she staged a coup against him and took his place when he was killed. *(Erich Lessing/Art Resource, NY.)*

were shaped more profoundly by an increasing population, rising food prices, and ongoing wars among the great powers. States had to balance conflicting social pressures: rulers pursued Enlightenment reforms that they believed might enhance state power, but they feared changes that might unleash popular discontent. For example, Catherine aimed to bring Western ideas, culture, and reforms to Russia, but when faced with a massive uprising of the serfs, she not only suppressed the revolt but also increased the powers of the nobles over their serfs. All reform-minded rulers faced similar potential challenges to their authority.

Even if the movement for reform had its limits, governments needed to respond to a new force: "public opinion." Rulers wanted to portray themselves as modern, open to change, and responsive to those who were reading newspapers and closely following political developments. Enlightenment writers appealed to public opinion, but they still looked to rulers to effect reform. Writers such as Voltaire expressed little interest in the future of peasants or the lower classes; they favored neither revolution nor political upheaval. Yet their ideas paved the way for something much more radical and unexpected. The American Declaration of Independence in 1776 showed how Enlightenment ideals could be translated into democratic political practice. After 1789, democracy would come to Europe as well.

CHAPTER FOCUS How did the Enlightenment influence Western politics, culture, and society?

The Enlightenment at Its Height

The Enlightenment emerged as an intellectual movement before 1750 but reached its peak in the second half of the eighteenth century. (See "Terms of History," page 596.) The writers of the Enlightenment called themselves **philosophes**; the word is French for "philosophers," but that definition is somewhat misleading. Whereas philosophers concern themselves with abstract theories, the philosophes were public intellectuals dedicated to solving the real problems of the world. They wrote on subjects ranging from current affairs to art criticism, and they wrote in every conceivable format. The Swiss philosophe Jean-Jacques Rousseau, for example, wrote political tracts, a treatise on education, a constitution for Poland, an analysis of the effects of the theater on public morals, a best-selling novel, an opera, and a notorious autobiography. The philosophes wrote for a broad educated public of readers who snatched up every Enlightenment book they could find at their local booksellers, even when rulers or churches tried to forbid such works. Between 1750 and 1789, the Enlightenment acquired its name and, despite heated conflicts between the philosophes and state and religious authorities, gained support in the highest reaches of government.

Men and Women of the Republic of Letters

Although *philosophe* is a French word, the Enlightenment was distinctly cosmopolitan; philosophes could be found from Philadelphia to St. Petersburg. The philosophes considered themselves part of a grand "republic of letters" that transcended national political boundaries. They were not republicans in the usual sense, that is, people who supported representative government and opposed monarchy. What united them were the ideals of reason, reform, and freedom. In 1784, the German philosopher

philosophes (fee luh SAWF): French for "philosophers"; public intellectuals of the Enlightenment who wrote on subjects ranging from current affairs to art criticism with the goal of furthering reform in society.

1751–1772 *Encyclopedia* published in France

1762 Jean-Jacques Rousseau, *The Social Contract* and *Émile*

1764 Voltaire, *Philosophical Dictionary*

1772 First partition of Poland

1750 — 1760 — 1770

1756–1763 Seven Years' War fought in Europe, India, and the American colonies

1763 Wilkes affair begins in Great Britain

1771 Louis XV of France fails to break power of French law courts

Immanuel Kant summed up the program of the Enlightenment in two Latin words: *sapere aude* ("dare to know")—have the courage to think for yourself.

The philosophes used reason to attack superstition, bigotry, and religious fanaticism, which they considered the chief obstacles to free thought and social reform. Voltaire took religious fanaticism as his chief target: "Once fanaticism has corrupted a mind, the malady is almost incurable. . . . The only remedy for this epidemic malady is the philosophical spirit." Enlightenment writers did not necessarily oppose organized religion, but they strenuously objected to religious intolerance. They believed that the systematic application of reason could do what religious belief could not: improve the human condition by pointing to needed reforms. Reason meant critical, informed, scientific thinking about social issues and problems. Many Enlightenment writers collaborated on the multivolume *Encyclopedia* (published 1751–1772), which aimed to gather together knowledge about science, religion, industry, and society. The ancestor of all modern encyclopedias from the *Encyclopædia Britannica* to Wikipedia online, the Enlightenment version differed by using knowledge to criticize defects in society. The chief editor of the *Encyclopedia*, Denis Diderot (1713–1784), explained the goal: "All things must be examined, debated, investigated without exception and without regard for anyone's feelings." (See Document, "Denis Diderot, 'Encyclopedia,'" page 590.)

The philosophes believed that the spread of knowledge would encourage reform in every aspect of life, from the grain trade to the penal system. Chief among their desired reforms was intellectual freedom—the freedom to use one's own reason to conduct studies and to publish the results. The philosophes wanted freedom of the press and freedom of religion, which they considered "natural rights" guaranteed by "natural law." In their view, progress depended on these freedoms.

Most philosophes, like Voltaire, came from the upper classes, yet Rousseau's father was a modest watchmaker in Geneva, and Diderot was the son of a cutlery maker. Rarely were women philosophes; one, however, was the French noblewoman Émilie du Châtelet (1706–1749), who wrote extensively

Science in Action

In September 1783 the Montgolfier brothers demonstrated their newly invented hot air balloon at Versailles with the royal family in attendance. The flight reached an altitude of 1500 feet, covered two miles, and lasted eight minutes. The passengers—a sheep, a duck, and a rooster—landed safely. Hydrogen balloons were developed at the same time and quickly replaced the hot air versions because they could fly higher and longer. Thousands of people flocked to see the launches. *(Private Collection/The Bridgeman Art Library International.)*

1773 Pugachev rebellion of Russian peasants

1775 Flour War in France

1776 American Declaration of Independence from Great Britain; Adam Smith, *The Wealth of Nations*

1780 Joseph II of Austria undertakes a wide-reaching reform program

1781 Immanuel Kant, *The Critique of Pure Reason*

1784 Pierre-Augustin Caron de Beaumarchais, *The Marriage of Figaro*

1785 Catherine the Great's Charter of the Nobility grants nobles exclusive control over their serfs in exchange for subservience to the state

1787 Delegates from the states draft the U.S. Constitution

1780 — 1790

DOCUMENT

Denis Diderot, "Encyclopedia" (1755)

Denis Diderot (1713–1784) led the multinational team that produced the Encyclopedia, *a work much more radical in its aims than its bland name suggests. Seventeen volumes of text and eleven volumes of illustrative plates were published between 1751 and 1772, despite the efforts of French authorities to censor the work. The volumes covered every branch of human knowledge from the tools of artisans to the finest points of theology. Diderot and his collaborators used the occasion to lay out the principles of the Enlightenment as an intellectual movement and to challenge the authority, in particular, of the Catholic church. The article "Encyclopedia" summarized the goals of the project.*

ENCYCLOPEDIA (Philosophy). This word means the *interrelation of all knowledge*; it is made up of the Greek prefix *en*, in, and the nouns *kyklos*, circle, and *paideia*, instruction, science, knowledge. In truth, the aim of an *encyclopedia* is to collect all the knowledge scattered over the face of the earth, to present its general outlines and structure to the men with whom we live, and transmit this to those who will come after us, so that the work of the past centuries may be useful to the following centuries, that our children, by becoming more educated, may at the same time become more virtuous and happier, and that we may not die without having deserved well of the human race. . . .

We have seen that our *Encyclopedia* could only have been the endeavor of a philosophical century; that this age has dawned, and that fame, while raising to immortality the names of those who will perfect man's knowledge in the future, will perhaps not disdain to remember our own names. . . .

I have said that it could only belong to a philosophical age to attempt an *encyclopedia*; and I have said this because such a work constantly demands more intellectual daring than is commonly found in ages of pusillanimous [timid] taste. All things must be examined, debated, investigated without exception and without regard for anyone's feelings. . . . We must ride roughshod over all these ancient puerilities [childish sillinesses], overturn the barriers that reason never erected, give back to the arts and sciences the liberty that is so precious to them. . . . We have for quite some time needed a reasoning age when men would no longer seek the rules in classical authors but in nature.

Source: Margaret C. Jacob, *The Enlightenment: A Brief History with Documents* (Boston: Bedford/St. Martin's, 2001), 157–58.

Question for Consideration

- **Why would the Catholic church and the French state find Diderot's vision for the *Encyclopedia* so threatening?**

about the mathematics and physics of Gottfried Wilhelm Leibniz and Isaac Newton. (Châtelet's lover Voltaire learned much of his science from her.) Few of the leading writers held university positions, except those who were German or Scottish. Universities in France were dominated by the Catholic clergy and unreceptive to Enlightenment ideals.

Enlightenment ideas developed instead through printed books and pamphlets; through hand-copied letters that were circulated and sometimes published; and through informal readings of manuscripts. Salons — informal gatherings, usually sponsored by middle-class or aristocratic women — gave intellectual life an anchor outside the royal court and the church-controlled universities. Seventeenth-century salons had been tame affairs. In the Parisian salons of the eighteenth century, in contrast, the philosophes could discuss ideas they might hesitate to put into print, testing public opinion and even pushing it in new directions. Best known was the Parisian salon of Madame Marie-Thérèse Geoffrin (1699–1777), a wealthy middle-class widow who had been raised by her grandmother and married off at fourteen to a much older man. (See the illustration on page 591.) She brought together the most exciting thinkers and artists of the time and provided a forum for new ideas and an opportunity to establish new intellectual contacts. Madame Geoffrin corresponded extensively with influential people across Europe, including Catherine the Great. One Italian visitor commented, "There is no way to make Naples resemble Paris unless we find a woman to guide us, organize us, *Geoffrinize* us."

Women's salons provoked criticism from men who resented their power. (See "Contrasting Views," page 594.) Nevertheless, the gatherings helped galvanize intellectual life and reform movements all over Europe. Wealthy Jewish women created nine of the fourteen salons in Berlin at the end of the eighteenth century, and Princess Zofia Czartoryska gathered around her in Warsaw the reform leaders of Poland-Lithuania. Some of the aristocratic women in Madrid who held salons had lived in France, and they combined an interest in French culture and ideas with their efforts to promote the new ideas in Spain. Salons could be tied

Madame Geoffrin's Salon in 1755
This 1812 painting by Anicet Charles Lemonnier claims to depict the best-known Parisian salon of the 1750s. Lemonnier was only twelve years old in 1755 and so could not have based his rendition on firsthand knowledge. Madame Geoffrin is the figure in blue on the right facing the viewer. The bust is of Voltaire. Rousseau is the fifth person to the left of the bust (facing right), and behind him (facing left) is Guillaume Raynal. *(Réunion des Musées Nationaux/Art Resource, NY.)*

closely to the circles of power: in France, for example, Louis XV's mistress, Jeanne-Antoinette Poisson, first made her reputation as hostess of a salon frequented by Voltaire and Montesquieu. When she became Louis XV's mistress in 1745, she gained the title marquise de Pompadour and turned her attention to influencing artistic styles by patronizing architects and painters.

Conflicts with Church and State

Madame Geoffrin did not approve of discussions that attacked the Catholic church, but elsewhere voices against organized religion could be heard. Criticisms of religion required daring because the church, whatever its denomination, wielded enormous power in society, and most influential people considered religion an essential foundation of good society and government. Defying such opinion, the Scottish philosopher David Hume (1711–1776) boldly argued in *The Natural History of Religion* (1755) that belief in God rested on superstition and fear rather than on reason. At a dinner party in Paris, Hume questioned whether there were really any atheists. His host responded that of the eighteen guests present, "fifteen were atheists, and three had not quite made up their minds."

Hume was right to be dubious because at the time most Europeans believed in God. After Newton, however, and despite Newton's own deep religiosity, people could conceive of the universe as an eternally existing, self-perpetuating machine, in which God's intervention was unnecessary. In short, such people could become either atheists (people who do not believe in God) or **deists** (people who believe in God but give him no active role in earthly affairs). For the first time, writers claimed the label *atheist* and disputed the common view that atheism led inevitably to immorality.

Deists continued to believe in a benevolent, all-knowing God who had designed the universe and set it in motion. But they usually rejected the idea that God directly intercedes in the functioning of the universe, and they often criticized the churches for their dogmatic intolerance of dissenters. Voltaire was a deist, and in his influential *Philosophical Dictionary* (1764) he attacked most of the claims of organized Christianity, both Catholic and Protestant. Christianity, he argued, had been the prime source of fanaticism and brutality among humans. Throughout his life, Voltaire's motto was *Écrasez l'infâme*—"Crush the infamous thing" (the "thing" being bigotry and intolerance). French authorities publicly burned his *Philosophical Dictionary.*

Criticism of religious intolerance involved more than simply attacking the churches. Critics also had to confront the states to which churches were closely tied. In 1762, a judicial case in Toulouse provoked an outcry throughout France that Voltaire soon joined. When the son of a local Calvinist was found hanged (he had probably committed suicide), magistrates accused the father, Jean Calas, of murdering him

---

deists: Those who believe in God but give him no active role in human affairs. Deists of the Enlightenment believed that God had designed the universe and set it in motion but no longer intervened in its functioning.

to prevent his conversion to Catholicism. (Since Louis XIV's revocation of the Edict of Nantes in 1685, it had been illegal to practice Calvinism publicly in France.) The all-Catholic parlement of Toulouse tried to extract the names of accomplices through torture—using a rope to pull up Calas's arm while weighing down his feet and then pouring water down his throat—but Calas refused to confess. The torturers then executed him by breaking every bone in his body with an iron rod. Voltaire launched a successful crusade to rehabilitate Calas's good name and to restore the family's properties, which had been confiscated after his death. Voltaire's efforts eventually helped bring about the extension of civil rights to French Protestants and encouraged campaigns to abolish the judicial use of torture.

Critics also assailed state and church support for European colonization and slavery. One of the most popular books of the time was the *Philosophical and Political History of European Colonies and Commerce in the Two Indies*, published in 1770 by the abbé Guillaume Raynal (1713–1796), a French Catholic clergyman. Raynal and his collaborators described in excruciating detail the destruction of native populations by Europeans and denounced the slave trade. Despite the criticism, the slave trade continued. So did European exploration. British explorer James Cook (1728–1779) charted the coasts of New Zealand and Australia, discovered New Caledonia, and visited the ice fields of Antarctica.

Cook's adventures captivated European readers. When he arrived on the Kona coast of Hawaii in 1779, Cook thought that the natives considered him godlike, but in a confrontation he fired his gun and killed a man, provoking an attack in which he and some of his men were killed. Like Cook, many Enlightenment writers held conflicting views of natives: to some, they were innocent because primitive, but to others they seemed untrustworthy because savage. Views of Africans could be especially negative. Hume, for example, judged blacks to be "naturally inferior to the whites," concluding, "There never was a civilized nation of any other complexion than white."

Nevertheless, the Enlightenment belief in natural rights helped fuel the antislavery movement, which began to organize political campaigns against slavery in Britain, France, and the new United States in the 1780s. Advocates of the abolition of slavery encouraged freed slaves to write the story of their enslavement. One such freed slave, Olaudah Equiano, wrote of his kidnapping and enslavement in Africa and his long effort to free himself. *The Interesting Narrative of the Life of Olaudah Equiano*, published in 1788, became an international best seller. Armed with such firsthand accounts of slavery, **abolitionists** began to petition their governments for the abolition of the slave trade and then of slavery itself.

Enlightenment critics of church and state usually advocated reform, not revolution. For example, though he resided near the French-Swiss border in case he had to flee, Voltaire made a fortune in financial speculations and ended up being celebrated in his last years as a national hero even by many former foes. Other philosophes also believed that published criticism, rather than violent action, would bring about necessary reforms. As Diderot said, "We will speak against senseless laws until they are reformed; and, while we wait, we will abide by them." The philosophes generally regarded the lower classes—"the people"—as ignorant, violent, and prone to superstition; as a result, they pinned their hopes on educated elites and enlightened rulers.

The Individual and Society

The controversy created by the conflicts between the philosophes and the various churches and states of Europe drew attention away from a subtle but profound transformation in worldviews. In previous centuries, questions of theological doctrine and church organization had been the main focus of intellectual and even political interest. The Enlightenment writers shifted attention away from religious questions and toward the secular (nonreligious) study of society and the individual's role in it. Religion did not drop out of sight, but the philosophes tended to make religion a private affair of individual conscience, even while rulers and churches still considered religion very much a public concern.

The Enlightenment interest in secular society produced two major results: it advanced the secularization of European political life that had begun after the French Wars of Religion of the sixteenth and seventeenth centuries, and it laid the foundations for the social sciences of the modern era. Not surprisingly, then, many historians and philosophers consider the Enlightenment to be the origin of modernity, which they define as the belief that human reason, rather than theological doctrine, should set the patterns of social and political life. This belief in reason as the sole foundation for secular authority has often been contested, but it has also proved to be a powerful force for change.

Although most of the philosophes believed that human reason could understand and even remake

---

abolitionists: Advocates of the abolition of the slave trade and of slavery.

society and politics, they disagreed about what reason revealed. Among the many different approaches were two that proved enduringly influential, those of the Scottish philosopher Adam Smith and the Swiss writer Jean-Jacques Rousseau. Smith provided a theory of modern capitalist society and devoted much of his energy to defending free markets as the best way to make the most of individual efforts. The modern discipline of economics took shape around the questions raised by Smith. Rousseau, by contrast, emphasized the needs of the community over those of the individual. His work, which led both toward democracy and toward communism, continues to inspire heated debate in political science and sociology.

Adam Smith Adam Smith (1723–1790) optimistically believed that individual interests naturally harmonized with those of the whole society. To explain how this natural harmonization worked, he published *An Inquiry into the Nature and Causes of the Wealth of Nations* in 1776. Smith insisted that individual self-interest, even greed, was quite compatible with society's best interest: the laws of supply and demand served as an "invisible hand" ensuring that individual interests would be synchronized with those of the whole society. Market forces — "the propensity to truck, barter, and exchange one thing for another" — naturally brought individual and social interests in line.

Smith rejected the prevailing mercantilist views that the general welfare would be served by accumulating national wealth through agriculture or the hoarding of gold and silver. Instead, he argued that the division of labor in manufacturing increased productivity and generated more wealth for society and well-being for the individual. Using the example of the ordinary pin, Smith showed that when the manufacturing process was broken down into separate operations — one man to draw out the wire, another to straighten it, a third to cut it, a fourth to point it, and so on — workers who could make only one pin a day on their own could make thousands by pooling their labor.

To maximize the effects of market forces and the division of labor, Smith endorsed a concept called **laissez-faire** (that is, to leave alone) to free the economy from government intervention and control. He insisted that governments eliminate all restrictions on the sale of land, remove restraints on the grain trade, and abandon duties on imports. Free international trade, he argued, would stimulate production everywhere and thus ensure the growth of national wealth: "The natural effort of every individual to better his own condition, when suffered to exert itself with freedom and security, is so powerful a principle that it is alone, and without any assistance, not only capable of carrying the society to wealth and prosperity, but of surmounting a hundred impertinent obstructions with which the folly of human laws too often encumbers its operations." Governments, he continued, should restrict themselves to providing "security," that is, national defense, internal order, and public works. Smith recognized that government had an important role in providing a secure framework for market activity, but he placed most emphasis on freeing individual endeavor from what he saw as excessive government interference.

Jean-Jacques Rousseau
This eighteenth-century engraving of Rousseau shows him in his favorite place, outside in nature, where he walks, reads, and in this case collects plants. Rousseau claimed that he came to his most important insights while taking long walks, and in *Émile* he underlines the importance of physical activity for children. *(Private Collection/Roger Viollet, Paris, France/The Bridgeman Art Library International.)*

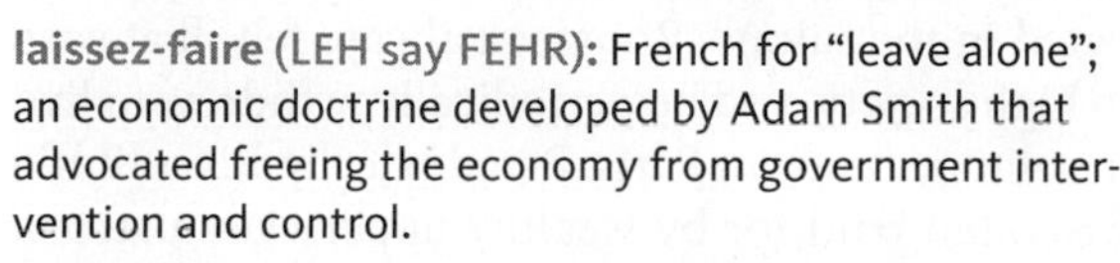

laissez-faire (LEH say FEHR): French for "leave alone"; an economic doctrine developed by Adam Smith that advocated freeing the economy from government intervention and control.

CONTRASTING VIEWS

Women and the Enlightenment

During the Enlightenment, women's roles in society became the subject of heated debates. Some men resented what they saw as the growing power of women, especially in the salons. Rousseau railed against their corrupting influence: "Every woman at Paris gathers in her apartment a harem of men more womanish than she." Rousseau's Émile *(Document 1) offered his own influential answer to the question of how women should be educated. The* Encyclopedia *ignored the contributions of salon women and praised women who stayed at home; in the words of one typical contributor, women "constitute the principal ornament of the world. . . . May they, through submissive discretion and through simple, adroit, artless cleverness, spur us [men] on to virtue." Many women objected to these characterizations. The editor of a prominent newspaper for women, Madame de Beaumer, wrote editorials blasting the masculine sense of superiority (Document 2). Many prominent women writers specifically targeted Rousseau's book because it proved to be the most influential educational treatise of the time (Document 3). Their ideas formed the core of nineteenth-century feminism.*

1. Jean-Jacques Rousseau, *Émile* (1762)

Rousseau used the character of Émile's wife-to-be, Sophie, to discuss his ideas about women's education. Sophie is educated for a domestic role as wife and mother, and she is taught to be obedient, always helpful to her husband and family, and removed from any participation in the public world. Despite his insistence on the differences between men's and women's roles, many women enthusiastically embraced Rousseau's ideas, for he placed great emphasis on maternal affections, breast-feeding, and child rearing. Rousseau's own children, however, suffered the contradictions that characterized his life. By his own admission, he abandoned to a foundling hospital all the children he had by his lower-class common-law wife because he did not think he could support them properly; if their fate was like that of most abandoned children of the day, they met an early death.

There is no parity between man and woman as to the importance of sex. The male is only a male at certain moments; the female all her life, or at least throughout her youth, is incessantly reminded of her sex and in order to carry out its functions she needs a corresponding constitution. She needs to be careful during pregnancy; she needs rest after childbirth; she needs a quiet and sedentary life while she nurses her children; she needs patience and gentleness in order to raise them; a zeal and affection that nothing can discourage. . . .

On the good constitution of mothers depends primarily that of the children; on the care of women depends the early education of men; and on women, again, depend their morals, their passions, their tastes, their pleasures, and even their happiness. Thus the whole education of women ought to be relative to men. To please them, to be useful to them, to make themselves loved and honored by them, to educate them when young, to care for them when grown, to counsel them, to console them, and to make life agreeable and sweet to them—these are the duties of women at all times, and should be taught them from their infancy.

Source: Susan Groag Bell and Karen M. Offen, *Women, the Family, and Freedom: The Debate in Documents*, vol. 1, *1750–1880* (Stanford: Stanford University Press, 1983), 46–49.

2. Madame de Beaumer, Editorial in *Le Journal des Dames* (1762)

Madame de Beaumer (d. 1766) was the first of three women editors of Le Journal des Dames *(The Ladies' Journal). She ran it for two years and published many editorials defending women against their male critics.*

The success of the *Journal des Dames* allows us to triumph over those frivolous persons who have regarded this periodical as a petty work containing only a few

Jean-Jacques Rousseau

Much more pessimistic about the relation between individual self-interest and the good of society was **Jean-Jacques Rousseau** (1712–1778). In Rousseau's view, society itself threatened natural rights or freedoms: "Man is born free, and everywhere he is in chains." Rousseau first gained fame by writing a prize-winning essay in 1749 in which he argued that the revival of science and the arts had corrupted social morals, not improved them. This startling conclusion seemed to oppose some of the Enlightenment's most cherished beliefs. Rather than improving society, he claimed, science and art raised artificial barriers between people and their natural state. Rousseau's works extolled the simplicity of rural life over urban society. Although he participated in the salons, Rousseau always felt ill at ease in high society, and he periodically withdrew to live in solitude far from Paris. Paradoxically, his solitude was often paid for by wealthy upper-class patrons

Jean-Jacques Rousseau (zhahn zhahk roo SOH): One of the most important philosophes (1712–1778); he argued that only a government based on a social contract among the citizens could make people truly moral and free.

bagatelles suited to help them kill time. In truth, Gentlemen, you do us much honor to think that we could not provide things that unite the useful to the agreeable. To rid you of your error, we have made our Journal historical, with a view to putting before the eyes of youth striking images that will guide them toward virtue. . . . An historical *Journal des Dames*! these Gentlemen reasoners reply. How ridiculous! How out of character with the nature of this work, which calls only for little pieces to amuse [ladies] during their toilette. . . . Please, Gentlemen *beaux esprits* [wits], mind your own business and let us write in a manner worthy of our sex; I love this sex, I am jealous to uphold its honor and its rights. If we have not been raised up in the sciences as you have, it is you who are the guilty ones.

Source: Susan Groag Bell and Karen M. Offen, *Women, the Family, and Freedom: The Debate in Documents*, vol. 1, *1750–1880* (Stanford: Stanford University Press, 1983), 27–28.

3. Catharine Macaulay, *Letters on Education* (1787)

Catharine Sawbridge Macaulay-Graham (1731–1791) was one of the best-known English writers of the 1700s. She wrote immensely popular histories of England and also joined in the debate provoked by Rousseau's Émile.

There is another prejudice . . . which affects yet more deeply female happiness, and female importance; a prejudice, which ought ever to have been confined to the regions of the east, because [of the] state of slavery to which female nature in that part of the world has been ever subjected, and can only suit with the notion of a positive inferiority in the intellectual powers of the female mind. You will soon perceive, that the prejudice which I mean, is that degrading difference in the culture of the understanding, which has prevailed for several centuries in all European societies. . . .

Among the most strenuous asserters of a sexual difference in character, Rousseau is the most conspicuous, both on account of that warmth of sentiment which distinguishes all his writing, and the eloquence of his compositions: but never did enthusiasm and the love of paradox, those enemies of philosophical disquisition, appear in more strong opposition to plain sense than in Rousseau's definition of this difference. He sets out with a supposition, that Nature intended the subjection of the one sex to the other; that consequently there must be an inferiority of intellect in the subjected party; but as man is a very imperfect being, and apt to play the capricious tyrant, Nature, to bring things nearer to an equality, bestowed on the woman such attractive graces, and such an insinuating address, as to turn the balance on the other scale. . . .

The situation and education of women . . . is precisely that which must necessarily tend to corrupt and debilitate both the powers of mind and body. From a false notion of beauty and delicacy, their system of nerves is depraved before they come out of the nursery; and this kind of depravity has more influence over the mind, and consequently over morals, than is commonly apprehended.

Source: Susan Groag Bell and Karen M. Offen, *Women, the Family, and Freedom: The Debate in Documents*, vol. 1, *1750–1880* (Stanford: Stanford University Press, 1983), 54–55.

Questions to Consider

1. Why would women in the eighteenth century read Rousseau with such interest and even enthusiasm?

2. Why does Madame de Beaumer address herself to male readers if the *Journal des Dames* is intended for women?

3. Why would Macaulay focus so much of her analysis on Rousseau? Why does she not just ignore him?

4. In what ways did Enlightenment ideas appeal to women?

who lodged him on their estates, even as his writings decried the upper-class privilege that made his efforts possible.

Rousseau explored the tension between the individual and society in a best-selling novel (*The New Heloise*, 1761); in an influential work on education (*Émile*, 1762); and in a treatise on political theory (*The Social Contract*, 1762). He wrote *Émile* in the form of a novel to make his educational theories easily comprehensible. Free from the supervision of the clergy, who controlled most schools, the boy Émile works alone with his tutor to develop practical skills and independent ways of thinking. After developing his individuality, Émile joins society through marriage to Sophie, who received the education Rousseau thought appropriate for women. (See "Contrasting Views," above.)

Whereas earlier Rousseau had argued that society corrupted the individual by taking him out of nature, in *The Social Contract* he aimed to show that the right kind of political order could make people truly moral and free. Individual moral freedom could be achieved only by learning to subject one's individual interests to "the general will," that is, the good of the community. Individuals did this by entering into a social contract not with their rulers,

TERMS OF HISTORY

Enlightenment

In 1784, in an essay titled "What Is Enlightenment?," the German philosopher Immanuel Kant gave widespread currency to a term that had been in the making for several decades. The term *enlightened century* had become common in the 1760s. The Enlightenment thus gave itself its own name, and the name clearly had propaganda value. The philosophes associated Enlightenment with philosophy, reason, and humanity; religious tolerance; natural rights; and criticism of outmoded customs and prejudices. They tied Enlightenment to "progress" and to the "modern," and it came into question, just as these other terms did, when events cast doubt on the benefits of progress and the virtues of modernity. Although some opposed the Enlightenment from the very beginning as antireligious, undermining of authority, and even atheistic and immoral, the French Revolution of 1789 galvanized the critics of Enlightenment who blamed every excess of revolution on Enlightenment principles.

For most of the nineteenth and twentieth centuries, condemnation of the Enlightenment came from right-wing sources. Some of the more extreme of these critics denounced a supposed "Jewish-Masonic conspiracy," believing that Jews and Freemasons benefited most from the spread of Enlightenment principles and worked in secret to jointly undermine Christianity and established monarchical authorities. Adolf Hitler and his followers shared these suspicions, and during World War II the Germans confiscated the records of Masonic lodges in every country they occupied. They sent the documents back to Berlin so that a special office could trace the links of this supposed conspiracy. They found nothing.

After the catastrophes of World War II, the Enlightenment came under attack from left-wing critics. They denounced the Enlightenment as "self-destructive" and even "totalitarian" because its belief in reason led not to freedom but to greater bureaucratic control. They asked why mankind was sinking into "a new kind of barbarism," and they answered, "Because we have trusted too much in the Enlightenment and its belief in reason and science." The Nazis used bureaucratic control and technology to kill millions of Jews and others they deemed inferior. Science gave us the atomic bomb and factories that pollute the atmosphere. These criticisms of the Enlightenment show how central the Enlightenment remains to the very definition of modern history.

but with one another. If everyone followed the general will, then all would be equally free and equally moral because they lived under a law to which they had all consented.

These arguments threatened the legitimacy of eighteenth-century governments. Like Hobbes and Locke before him, Rousseau derived his social contract from human nature, not from history, tradition, or the Bible. He went much further than Hobbes or Locke, however, when he implied that people would be most free and moral under a republican form of government with direct democracy. Neither Hobbes nor Locke favored republics. Moreover, Rousseau roundly condemned slavery: "To decide that the son of a slave is born a slave is to decide that he is not born a man." Not surprisingly, authorities in both Geneva and Paris banned *The Social Contract* for undermining political authority. Rousseau's works would become a kind of political bible for the French revolutionaries of 1789, and his attacks on private property inspired the communists of the nineteenth century such as Karl Marx. Rousseau's rather mystical concept of the general will remains controversial. The "greatest good of all," according to Rousseau, was liberty combined with equality, but he also insisted that the individual could be "forced to be free" by the terms of the social contract. His ideas provided no legal protections for individual rights. Rousseau's version of democracy did not preserve the individual freedoms so important to Adam Smith.

Spreading the Enlightenment

The Enlightenment flourished in places where an educated middle class provided an eager audience for ideas of constitutionalism and reform. (See "Terms of History," above.) It therefore found its epicenter in the triangle formed by London, Amsterdam, and Paris and diffused outward to eastern and southern Europe and North America. Where constitutionalism and guarantees of individual freedoms were most advanced, as in Great Britain and the Dutch Republic, the movement had less of an edge because there was, in a sense, less need for it. John Locke had already written extensively about constitutionalism in the 1690s. As a result, Scottish and English writers concentrated on economics, philosophy, and history rather than on politics or social relations. The English historian Edward Gibbon, for example, portrayed Christianity in a negative light in his immensely influential work *The History of the Decline and Fall of the Roman Empire* (1776–1788), but when he served as a member of Parliament he never even gave a speech. At the other extreme, in places with small middle classes, such as Spain and Russia, Enlightenment ideas did not get much traction because governments successfully suppressed writings they did not like. France was the Enlightenment hot spot because the French monarchy alternated between encouraging ideas for reform and harshly censuring criticisms it found too threatening.

The French Enlightenment French writers published the most daring critiques of church and state, and they often suffered harassment and persecution as a result. Voltaire, Diderot, and Rousseau all faced arrest, exile, or even imprisonment. The Catholic church and royal authorities routinely forbade the publication of their books, and the police arrested booksellers who ignored the warnings. Yet the French monarchy was far from the most autocratic in Europe, and Voltaire, Diderot, and Rousseau all ended their lives as cultural heroes. France seems to have been curiously caught in the middle during the Enlightenment: with fewer constitutional guarantees of individual freedom than Great Britain, it still enjoyed much higher levels of prosperity and cultural development than most other European countries. In short, French elites had reason to complain, the means to make their complaints known, and a government torn between the desire to censor dissident ideas and the desire to appear open to modernity and progress. Publishing was controlled in France—where all books had to get official permissions—but not as tightly as in Spain, where the Catholic Inquisition made up its own list of banned books, or in Russia, where Catherine the Great allowed no opposition.

By the 1760s, the French government regularly ignored the publication of many works once thought offensive or subversive. In addition, a growing flood of works printed abroad poured into France and circulated underground. Private companies in Dutch and Swiss cities made fortunes smuggling illegal books into France over mountain passes and back roads. Foreign printers provided secret catalogs of their offerings and sold their products through booksellers who were willing to market forbidden books for a high price—among them not only philosophical treatises of the Enlightenment but also pornographic books and pamphlets (some by Diderot) lampooning the Catholic clergy and leading members of the royal court. In the 1770s and 1780s, lurid descriptions of sexual promiscuity at the French court helped undermine the popularity of the throne.

The German Enlightenment Whereas the French philosophes often took a violently anticlerical and combative tone, their German counterparts avoided direct political confrontations with authorities. Gotthold Lessing (1729–1781) complained in 1769 that Prussia was still "the most slavish society in Europe" in its lack of freedom to criticize government policies. As a playwright, literary critic, and philosopher, Lessing promoted religious toleration for the Jews and spiritual emancipation of Germans from foreign, especially French, models of culture, which still dominated. Lessing also introduced the German Jewish writer Moses Mendelssohn (1729–1786) into Berlin salon society. Mendelssohn labored to build bridges between German and Jewish culture by arguing that Judaism was a rational and undogmatic religion. He believed that persecution and discrimination against the Jews would end as reason triumphed.

Reason was also the chief focus of the most influential German thinker of the Enlightenment, Immanuel Kant (1724–1804). A university professor who lectured on everything from economics to astronomy, Kant wrote one of the most important works in the history of Western philosophy, *The Critique of Pure Reason* (1781). Kant admired Adam Smith and especially Rousseau, whose portrait he displayed proudly in his lodgings. Just as Smith founded modern economics and Rousseau modern political theory, Kant in *The Critique of Pure Reason* set the foundations for modern philosophy. In this complex book, Kant established the doctrine of idealism, the belief that true understanding can come only from examining the ways in which ideas are formed in the mind. Ideas are shaped, Kant argued, not just by sensory information (a position central to empiricism, a philosophy based on John Locke's writings) but also by the operation on that information of mental categories such as space and time. In Kant's philosophy, these "categories of understanding" were neither sensory nor supernatural; they were entirely ideal and abstract and located in the human mind. For Kant, the supreme philosophical questions—Does God exist? Is personal immortality possible? Do humans have free will?—were unanswerable by reason alone. But like Rousseau, Kant insisted that true moral freedom could be achieved only by living in society and obeying its laws.

Major Works of the Enlightenment

1751	Beginning of publication of the French *Encyclopedia*
1755	David Hume, *The Natural History of Religion*
1762	Jean-Jacques Rousseau, *The Social Contract* and *Émile*
1764	Voltaire, *Philosophical Dictionary*
1770	Abbé Guillaume Raynal, *Philosophical and Political History of European Colonies and Commerce in the Two Indies*
1776	Adam Smith, *An Inquiry into the Nature and Causes of the Wealth of Nations*
1781	Immanuel Kant, *The Critique of Pure Reason*

The Limits of Reason: Roots of Romanticism and Religious Revival

As Kant showed, reason had its limits: it could not answer all of life's pressing questions. In reaction to what some saw as the Enlightenment's excessive reliance on the authority of human reason, a new artistic movement called **romanticism** took root. Although it would not fully flower until the early nineteenth century, romanticism traced its emphasis on individual genius, deep emotion, and the joys of nature to thinkers like Rousseau who had scolded the philosophes for ignoring those aspects of life that escaped and even conflicted with the power of reason. Rousseau's autobiographical *Confessions*, published posthumously in 1782, caused an immediate sensation because it revealed so much about his inner emotional life, including his sexual longings and his almost paranoid distrust of other Enlightenment figures.

A novel by the young German writer Johann Wolfgang von Goethe (1749–1832) captured the early romantic spirit with its glorification of emotion. *The Sorrows of Young Werther* (1774) told of a young man who loves nature and rural life and is unhappy in love. When the woman he loves marries someone else, he falls into deep melancholy and eventually kills himself. Reason cannot save him. The book spurred a veritable Werther craze: in addition to Werther costumes, engravings, embroidery, and medallions, there was even a perfume called Eau de Werther. The young Napoleon Bonaparte, who was to build an empire for France, claimed to have read Goethe's novel seven times.

Religious revivals underlined the limits of reason in a different way. Much of the Protestant world experienced an "awakening" in the 1740s. In the German states, Pietist groups founded new communities; and in the British North American colonies, revivalist Protestant preachers drew thousands of fervent believers in a movement called the Great Awakening. In North America, bitter conflicts between revivalists and their opponents in the established churches prompted the leaders on both sides to set up new colleges to support their beliefs. These included Princeton, Columbia, Brown, and Dartmouth, all founded between 1746 and 1769.

Revivalism also stirred eastern European Jews at about the same time. Israel ben Eliezer (1698–1760) laid the foundation for Hasidism in the 1740s and 1750s. He traveled the Polish countryside offering miraculous cures and became known as the Ba'al Shem Tov ("Master of the Good Name") because he used divine names to effect healing and bring believers into closer personal contact with God. He emphasized mystical contemplation of the divine, rather than study of Jewish law, and his followers, the Hasidim (Hebrew for "most pious" Jews), often expressed their devotion through music, dance, and fervent prayer. Their practices soon spread all over Poland-Lithuania.

Most of the waves of Protestant revivalism ebbed after the 1750s, but in Great Britain one movement continued to grow through the end of the century. John Wesley (1703–1791), the Oxford-educated son of a cleric in the Church of England, founded **Methodism**, a term evoked by Wesley's insistence on strict self-discipline and a methodical approach to religious study and observance. In 1738, Wesley began preaching a new brand of Protestantism that emphasized an intense personal experience of salvation and a life of thrift, abstinence, and hard work. Traveling all over the British Isles, Wesley would mount a table or a box to speak to the ordinary people of the village or town. He slept in his followers' homes, ate their food, and treated their illnesses with various remedies, including small electric shocks for nervous diseases (Wesley eagerly followed Benjamin Franklin's experiments with electricity). In fifty years, Wesley preached forty thousand sermons, an average of fifteen a week. Not surprisingly, his preaching disturbed the Church of England's authorities, who refused to let him preach in the churches. In response, Wesley began to ordain his own clergy. While radical in religious views,

---

romanticism: An artistic movement of the late eighteenth and early nineteenth centuries that glorified nature, emotion, genius, and imagination.

Methodism: A religious movement founded by John Wesley (1703–1791) that broke with the Church of England and insisted on strict self-discipline and a "methodical" approach to religious study and observance.

George Whitefield
This colored etching depicts one of the most prominent preachers of the Great Awakening in the British North American colonies, the English Methodist George Whitefield, preaching in the American colonies. Whitefield visited the North American colonies seven times, sometimes for long periods, and drew tens of thousands of people to his dramatic and emotional open-air sermons, which moved many listeners to tears of repentance. Whitefield was a celebrity in his time and is considered by many to be the founder of the Evangelical movement. *(The Granger Collection, New York—All rights reserved.)*

the Methodist leadership remained politically conservative during Wesley's lifetime; Wesley himself wrote many pamphlets urging order, loyalty, and submission to higher authorities.

REVIEW QUESTION What were the major differences between the Enlightenment in France, Great Britain, and the German states?

Society and Culture in an Age of Enlightenment

Religious revivals and the first stirrings of romanticism show that not all intellectual currents of the eighteenth century were flowing in the same channel. Some social and cultural developments manifested the influence of Enlightenment ideas, but others did not. The traditional leaders of European societies—the nobles—responded to Enlightenment ideals in contradictory fashion: many simply reasserted their privileges and resisted the influence of the Enlightenment, but an important minority embraced change and actively participated in reform efforts. The expanding middle classes saw in the Enlightenment a chance to make their claim for joining society's governing elite. They bought Enlightenment books, joined Masonic lodges, and patronized new styles in art, music, and literature. The lower classes were more affected by economic growth than by ideas. Trade boomed and the population grew, but people did not benefit equally. The ranks of the poor swelled, too, and with greater mobility, births to unmarried mothers also increased.

The Nobility's Reassertion of Privilege

Nobles made up about 3 percent of the European population, but their numbers and ways of life varied greatly from country to country. At least 10 percent of the population in Poland and 7 to 8 percent in Spain was noble, in contrast to only 2 percent in Russia and between 1 and 2 percent in the rest of western Europe. Many Polish and Spanish nobles lived in poverty; titles did not guarantee wealth. Still, the wealthiest European nobles luxuriated in almost unimaginable opulence. Many of the English peers, for example, owned more than ten thousand acres of land; invested widely in government bonds and trading companies; kept several country residences with scores of servants as well as houses in London; and occasionally even had their own private orchestras to complement libraries of expensive books, greenhouses for exotic plants, kennels of pedigreed dogs, and collections of antiques, firearms, and scientific instruments.

To support an increasingly expensive lifestyle in a period of inflation, European aristocrats sought to cash in on their remaining legal rights, called seigneurial dues (from the French *seigneur*, "lord"). Peasants felt the squeeze as a result. French landlords required their peasants to pay dues to grind grain at the lord's mill, bake bread in his oven, press grapes at his winepress, or even pass on their own land as inheritance. In addition, peasants had to work without compensation for a specified number of days every year on the public roads. They also paid taxes to the government on salt, an essential preservative, and on the value of their land; customs duties if they sold produce or wine in town; and the tithe on their grain (one-tenth of the crop) to the church.

In Britain, the landed gentry could not claim these same onerous dues from their tenants, but they tenaciously defended their exclusive right to hunt game. The game laws kept the poor from eating meat and helped protect the social status of the rich. The gentry enforced the game laws themselves by hiring gamekeepers who hunted down poachers and even set traps for them in the forests. According to the law, anyone who poached deer or rabbits while armed or disguised could be sentenced to death. After 1760, the number of arrests for breaking the game laws increased dramatically. In most other countries, too, hunting was the special right of the nobility, a cause of deep popular resentment.

Even though Enlightenment writers sharply criticized nobles' insistence on special privileges, most aristocrats maintained their marks of distinction. The male court nobility continued to sport swords, plumed hats, makeup, and elaborate wigs, while middle-class men wore simpler and more somber clothing. Aristocrats had their own seats in church and their own quarters in the universities. Frederick II ("the Great") of Prussia (r. 1740–1786) made sure that nobles dominated both the army officer corps and the civil bureaucracy. Russia's Catherine the Great (r. 1762–1796) granted the nobility vast tracts of land, the exclusive right to own serfs, and exemption from personal taxes and corporal punishment. Her Charter of the Nobility of 1785 codified these privileges in exchange for the nobles' political subservience to the state. In Austria, Spain, the Italian states, Poland-Lithuania, and Russia, most nobles consequently cared little about Enlightenment ideas; they did not read the books of the philosophes and feared reforms that might challenge their dominance of rural society.

In France, Britain, and the western German states, however, the nobility proved more open to the new ideas. Among those who personally corresponded with Rousseau, for example, half were nobles, as were 20 percent of the 160 contributors to the *Encyclopedia*. It had not escaped their notice that Rousseau had denounced inequality. In his view, it was "manifestly contrary to the law of nature . . . that a handful of people should gorge themselves with superfluities while the hungry multitude goes in want of necessities." The nobles of western Europe sometimes married into middle-class families and formed with them a new mixed elite, united by common interests in reform and new cultural tastes.

The Middle Class and the Making of a New Elite

The Enlightenment offered middle-class people an intellectual and cultural route to social improvement. The term *middle class* referred to the middle position on the social ladder; middle-class families did not have legal titles like the nobility above them, but neither did they work with their hands like the peasants, artisans, or laborers below them. Most middle-class people lived in towns or cities and earned their living in the professions—as doctors, lawyers, or lower-level officials—or through investment in land, trade, or manufacturing (see "Taking Measure," page 601). In the eighteenth century, the ranks of the middle class—also known as the bourgeoisie (from *bourgeois*, French for "city dweller")—grew steadily in western Europe as a result of economic expansion. In France, for example, the overall population grew by about one-third in the 1700s, but the bourgeoisie nearly tripled in size. Although middle-class people had many reasons to resent the nobles, they also aspired to be like them.

Lodges and Learned Societies Nobles and middle-class professionals mingled in Enlightenment salons and joined the new Masonic lodges and local learned societies. The Masonic lodges began as social clubs organized around elaborate secret rituals of stonemasons' guilds. They called their members **Freemasons** because that was the term given to apprentice masons

Freemasons: Members of Masonic lodges, where nobles and middle-class professionals (and even some artisans) shared interest in the Enlightenment and reform.

TAKING MEASURE

European Urbanization, 1750–1800

The bar graph shows that northwestern Europe was the most urbanized region, followed by the Mediterranean countries. Central and eastern Europe were much less urbanized, which meant that they had much smaller middle classes.

Questions to Consider

1. What are the possible consequences of these differences in urbanization?
2. What would urban consumers be more likely to purchase that rural consumers likely could not or would not?
3. How would urbanization contribute to the spread of the Enlightenment?

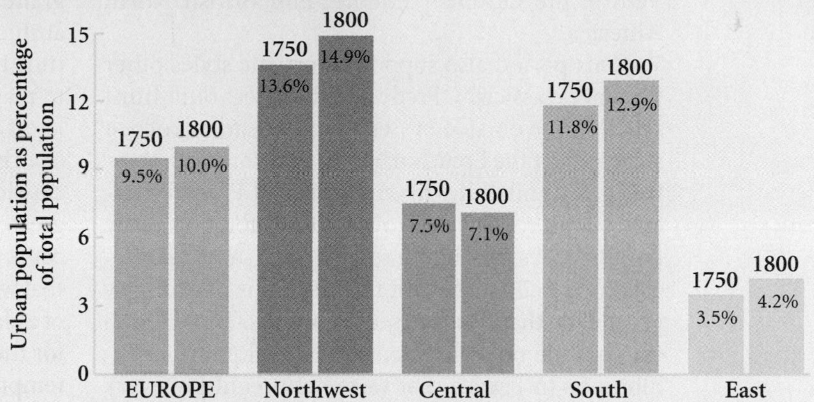

Source: Adapted from Andrew Lees and Lynn Hollen Lees, *Cities and the Making of Modern Europe, 1750–1914* (Cambridge: Cambridge University Press), 2008.

when they were deemed "free" to practice as masters of their guild. Although not explicitly political in aim, the lodges encouraged equality among members, and both aristocrats and middle-class men could join. Members wrote constitutions for their lodges and elected their own officers, thus promoting a direct experience of constitutional government.

Freemasonry arose in Great Britain and spread eastward: the first French and Italian lodges opened in 1726; Prussia's Frederick the Great founded a lodge in 1740; and after 1750, Freemasonry spread in Poland, Russia, and British North America. In France, women set up their own Masonic lodges. Despite the papacy's condemnation of Freemasonry in 1738 as subversive of religious and civil authority, lodges continued to multiply throughout the eighteenth century because they offered a place for socializing outside of the traditional channels and a way of declaring one's interest in the Enlightenment and reform. In short, Freemasonry offered a kind of secular religion. After 1789 and the outbreak of the French Revolution, conservatives would blame the lodges for every kind of political upheaval, but in the 1700s many high-ranking nobles became active members and saw no conflict with their privileged status.

Nobles and middle-class professionals also met in local learned societies, which greatly increased in number in this period. They gathered to discuss such practical issues as new scientific innovations or methods to eliminate poverty. The societies, sometimes called academies, brought the Enlightenment down from the realm of books and ideas to the level of concrete reforms. They sponsored essay contests, such as the one won by Rousseau in 1749 and the one set by the society in Metz in 1785 on the question "Are there means for making the Jews happier and more useful in France?" The Metz society approved essays that argued for granting civil rights to Jews.

New Cultural Styles

Shared tastes in travel, architecture, the arts, and even reading helped strengthen the links between nobles and members of the middle class. "Grand tours" of Europe often led upper-class youths to recently discovered Greek and Roman ruins at Pompeii, Herculaneum, and Paestum in Italy. These excavations aroused enthusiasm for the neoclassical style in architecture and painting, which began pushing aside the rococo and the long-dominant baroque. Urban residences, government buildings, furniture, fabrics, wallpaper, and even pottery soon reflected the neoclassical emphasis on purity and clarity of forms. As one German writer noted, with considerable exaggeration, "Everything in Paris is in the Greek style." Employing neoclassical motifs, the English potter Josiah Wedgwood (1730–1795) almost single-handedly created a mass market for domestic crockery and appealed to middle-class desires to emulate the rich and royal. His designs of special tea sets for the British queen, for Catherine the Great of Russia, and for leading aristocrats allowed him to advertise his wares as fashionable. By 1767, he claimed that his Queensware pottery had "spread over the whole Globe," and indeed by then his pottery was being marketed in France, Russia, Venice, the Ottoman Empire, and British North America.

This period also supported artistic styles other than neoclassicism. Frederick the Great built himself a palace outside of Berlin in the earlier rococo style, gave it the French name of Sanssouci ("worry-free"), and filled it with the works of French masters of the rococo. A growing taste for moralistic family scenes in painting reflected the same middle-class preoccupation with the emotions of ordinary private life that could be seen in novels. The middle-class public now attended the official painting exhibitions in France that were held regularly every other year after 1737. Court painting nonetheless remained much in demand. Marie-Louise-Élizabeth Vigée-Lebrun (1755–1842), who painted portraits at the French court, reported that in the 1780s "it was difficult to get a place on my waiting list. . . . I was the fashion."

Although wealthy nobles still patronized Europe's leading musicians, music, too, began to reflect the broadening of the elite and the spread of Enlightenment ideals as classical forms replaced the baroque style. Complex polyphony gave way to melody, which made music more accessible to ordinary listeners. Large sections of string instruments became the backbone of professional orchestras, which now played to large audiences of well-to-do listeners in sizable concert halls. The public concert gradually displaced the private recital, and a new attitude toward "the classics" developed: for the first time in the 1770s and 1780s, concert groups began to play older music rather than simply playing the latest commissioned works.

This laid the foundation for what we still call classical music today—that is, a repertory of the greatest music of the eighteenth and early nineteenth centuries. Because composers now created works that would be performed over and over again as part of a classical repertory, rather than occasional pieces for the court or noble patrons, they deliberately attempted to write lasting works. As a result, the major composers began to produce fewer symphonies: the Austrian composer Franz Joseph Haydn (1732–1809) wrote more than a hundred symphonies, but his successor Ludwig van Beethoven (1770–1827) would create only nine.

The two supreme masters of the new musical style of the eighteenth century show that the transition from noble patronage to classical concerts was far from complete. Haydn and his fellow Austrian Wolfgang Amadeus Mozart (1756–1791) both wrote for noble patrons, but by the early 1800s their com-

Neoclassical Style
In this Georgian interior of Syon House on the outskirts of London, various neoclassical motifs are readily apparent: Greek columns, Greek-style statuary on top of the columns, and Roman-style mosaics in the floor. The Scottish architect Robert Adam created this room for the duke of Northumberland in the 1760s. Adam had spent four years in Italy and returned in 1758 to London to decorate homes in the "Adam style," meaning the neoclassical manner. *(Syon House, Middlesex, UK / The Bridgeman Art Library International.)*

Jean-Baptiste Greuze, *Broken Eggs* (1756)
Greuze made his reputation as a painter of moralistic family scenes. In this one, an old woman (perhaps the mother) confronts the lover of a young girl and points to the eggs that have fallen out of a basket, a symbol of lost virginity. Diderot praised Greuze's work as "morality in paint," but the paintings often had an erotic subtext. *(© Francis G. Mayer/Corbis.)*

positions had been incorporated into the canon of concert classics all over Europe. Incredibly prolific, both excelled in combining lightness, clarity, and profound emotion. Both also wrote numerous Italian operas, a genre whose popularity continued to grow: in the 1780s, the Papal States alone boasted forty opera houses. Haydn spent most of his career working for a Hungarian noble family, the Eszterházys. Asked once why he had written no string quintets (at which Mozart excelled), he responded simply: "No one has ordered any."

Interest in reading, like attending public concerts, took hold of the middle classes and fed a frenzied increase in publication. By the end of the eighteenth century, six times as many books were being published in the German states, for instance, as at the beginning. One Parisian author commented that "people are certainly reading ten times as much in Paris as they did a hundred years ago." Provincial towns in western Europe published their own newspapers; by 1780, thirty-seven English towns had local newspapers. Lending libraries and book clubs multiplied. Despite the limitations of women's education, which emphasized domestic skills, women benefited as much as men from the spread of print. As one Englishman observed, "By far the greatest part of ladies now have a taste for books." Women also wrote them. Catherine Macaulay (1731–1791) published best-selling histories of Britain, and in France Stéphanie de Genlis (1746–1830) wrote children's books — a genre that was growing in importance as middle-class parents became more interested in education. The universities had little impact on these new tastes. An Austrian reformer complained about the universities in his country: "Critical history, natural sciences — which are supposed to make enlightenment general and combat prejudice — were neglected or wholly unknown."

Life on the Margins

Booming foreign trade fueled a dramatic economic expansion — French colonial trade increased tenfold in the 1700s — but the results did not necessarily trickle all the way down the social scale. The population of Europe grew by nearly 30 percent, with especially striking gains in England, Ireland, Prussia, and Hungary. Even though food production increased, shortages and crises still occurred periodically. Prices went up in many countries after the 1730s and continued to rise gradually until the early nineteenth century; wages in many trades rose as well, but less quickly than prices. Some people prospered — for example, peasants who produced surpluses to sell in local markets and shopkeepers and artisans who could increase their sales to meet growing demand. But those at the bottom of the social ladder — day laborers in the cities and peasants with small holdings — lived on the edge of dire poverty, and when they lost their land or work, they either migrated to the cities or wandered the roads in search of food and work. In France alone, 200,000 workers left their homes every year in search of seasonal employment elsewhere. At least 10 percent of Europe's urban population depended on some form of charity.

The growing numbers of poor overwhelmed local governments. In some countries, beggars and vagabonds had been locked up in workhouses since the mid-1600s. The expenses for running these overcrowded institutions increased by 60 percent in England between 1760 and 1785. After 1740, most German towns created workhouses that were part workshop, part hospital, and part prison. Such institutions also appeared for the first time in Boston, New York, and Philadelphia. To supplement the inadequate system of religious charity, offices for the poor, public workshops, and workhouse hospitals, the French government created *dépôts de mendicité* ("beggar houses") in 1767. The government sent people to these new workhouses to labor in manufacturing, but most were too weak or sick to work, and 20 percent of them died within a few months of incarceration. The ballooning number of poor people created fears about rising crime. To officials, beggars seemed more aggressive than ever. The handful of police assigned to keep order in each town or district found themselves confronted with increasing incidents of rural banditry and crimes against property.

The Persistence of Popular Culture

Those who were able to work or keep their land fared better: an increase in literacy, especially in the cities, allowed some lower-class people to participate in new tastes and ideas. One French observer insisted, "These days, you see a waiting-maid in her backroom, a lackey in an anteroom reading pamphlets. People can read in almost all classes of society." In France, only 50 percent of men and 27 percent of women could read and write in the 1780s, but that was twice the rate of a century earlier. Literacy rates were higher in England and the Dutch Republic, much lower in eastern Europe. About one in four Parisians owned books, but the lower classes overwhelmingly read religious books, as they had in the past.

Whereas the new elite might attend salons, concerts, or art exhibitions, peasants enjoyed their traditional forms of popular entertainment, such as fairs and festivals, and the urban lower classes relaxed in cabarets and taverns. Sometimes pleasures were cruel. In Britain, bullbaiting, bearbaiting, dogfighting, and cockfighting were all common forms of entertainment that provided opportunities for organized gambling. "Gentle" sports frequented by the upper classes had their violent side, too, showing that the upper classes had not become as different as they sometimes thought. Cricket matches, whose rules were first laid down in 1744, were often accompanied by brawls among fans (not unlike soccer matches today, though on a much smaller scale). Many Englishmen enjoyed what one observer called a "battle royal with sticks, pebbles and hog's dung."

Changes in Sexual Behavior

As population increased and villagers began to move to cities to better their prospects, sexual behavior changed, too. The rates of births out of wedlock soared, from less than 5 percent of all births in the seventeenth century to nearly 20 percent at the end of the eighteenth. Historians have disagreed about the causes and meanings of this change. Some detect in this pattern a sign of sexual liberation and the beginnings of a modern sexual revolution: as women moved out of the control of their families, they began to seek their own sexual fulfillment. Others view this change more bleakly, as a story of seduction and betrayal: family and community pressure had once forced a man to marry a woman pregnant with his child, but now a man could abandon a pregnant lover by simply moving away.

Increased mobility brought freedom for some women, but it also aggravated the vulnerability of those newly arrived in cities from the countryside. Desperation, not reason, often ruled their choices. Women who came to the city as domestic servants had little recourse against masters or fellow servants who seduced or raped them. The result was a startling rise in abandoned babies. Most European cities established foundling hospitals in the 1700s, but infant and child mortality was 50 percent higher in such institutions than for children brought up at home. Some women tried herbs, laxatives, or crude surgical means of abortion; a few, usually servants who would lose their jobs if their employers discovered they had borne a child, resorted to infanticide.

European states had long tried to regulate sexual behavior; every country had laws against prostitution, adultery, fornication, sodomy, and infanticide. Reformers criticized the harshness of laws against infanticide, but they showed no mercy for "sodomites" (as male homosexuals were called), who in some places, in particular the Dutch Republic, were systematically persecuted and imprisoned or even executed. Male homosexuals attracted the attention of authorities because they had begun to develop networks and special meeting places. The stereotype of the effeminate, exclusively homosexual male seems to have appeared for the first time in the eighteenth century, perhaps as part of a growing emphasis on separate roles for men and women.

The Enlightenment's emphasis on reason, self-control, and childhood innocence made parents increasingly anxious about their children's sexuality. Moralists and physicians wrote books about the evils of masturbation, "proving" that it led to physical and mental degeneration and even madness.

While the Enlightenment thus encouraged excessive concern about children being left to their own devices, it nevertheless taught the middle and upper classes to value their children and to expect their improvement through education. Writers such as de Genlis and Rousseau drew attention to children, who were no longer viewed only as little sinners in need of harsh discipline. Paintings now showed individual children playing at their favorite activities rather than formally posed with their families. Books about and for children became popular. *The Newtonian System of the Universe Digested for Young Minds*, by "Tom Telescope," was published in Britain in 1761 and reprinted many times. Toys, jigsaw puzzles, and clothing designed for children all appeared for the first time in the 1700s. Children were no longer considered miniature adults.

REVIEW QUESTION What were the major differences in the impact of the Enlightenment on the nobility, the middle classes, and the lower classes?

State Power in an Era of Reform

Rulers turned to Enlightenment-inspired reforms to improve life for their subjects and to gain commercial or military advantage over rival states. Historians label many of the sovereigns of this time **enlightened despots** or enlightened absolutists, for they aimed to promote Enlightenment reforms without giving up their absolutist powers. Catherine the Great's admiring relationship with Voltaire showed how even the most absolutist rulers championed reform when it suited their own goals. Foremost among those goals was the expansion of a ruler's territory.

War and Diplomacy

Europeans no longer fought devastating wars over religion that killed hundreds of thousands of civilians; instead, professional armies and navies battled for control of overseas empires and for dominance on the European continent. Rulers continued to expand their armies: the Prussian army, for example, nearly tripled in size between 1740 and 1789. Widespread use of flintlock muskets required deployment in long lines, usually three men deep, with each line in turn loading and firing on command. Military strategy became cautious and calculating, but this did not prevent the outbreak of hostilities. Between 1750 and 1775, the instability of the European balance of power resulted in a diplomatic reversal of alliances, a major international conflict, and the partition of Poland-Lithuania among Russia, Austria, and Prussia.

The Seven Years' War, 1756–1763 In 1756, a major reversal of alliances—what historians call the Diplomatic Revolution—reshaped relations among the great powers. Prussia and Great Britain signed a defensive alliance, prompting Austria to overlook two centuries of hostility and ally with France. Russia and Sweden soon joined the Franco-Austrian alliance. When Frederick the Great invaded Saxony, an ally of Austria, with his bigger and better-disciplined army, the long-simmering hostilities between Great Britain and France over colonial boundaries flared into a general war that became known as the **Seven Years' War** (1756–1763).

Fighting soon raged around the world (Map 18.1). The French and British battled on land and sea in North America (where the conflict was called the French and Indian War), the West Indies, and India. The two coalitions also fought each other in central Europe. At first, in 1757, Frederick the Great surprised Europe with a spectacular victory at Rossbach in Saxony over a much larger Franco-Austrian army. But in time, Russian and Austrian armies encircled his troops. Frederick despaired: "I believe all is lost. I will not survive the ruin of my country." A fluke of history saved him. Empress Elizabeth of Russia (r. 1741–1762) died and was succeeded by the mentally unstable Peter III, a fanatical admirer of Frederick and things Prussian. Peter withdrew Russia from the war. (This was practically his only accomplishment as tsar. He was soon mysteriously

---

enlightened despots: Rulers—such as Catherine the Great of Russia, Frederick the Great of Prussia, and Joseph II of Austria—who tried to promote Enlightenment reforms without giving up their own supreme political power; also called enlightened absolutists.

Seven Years' War: A worldwide series of battles (1756–1763) between Austria, France, Russia, and Sweden on one side and Prussia and Great Britain on the other.

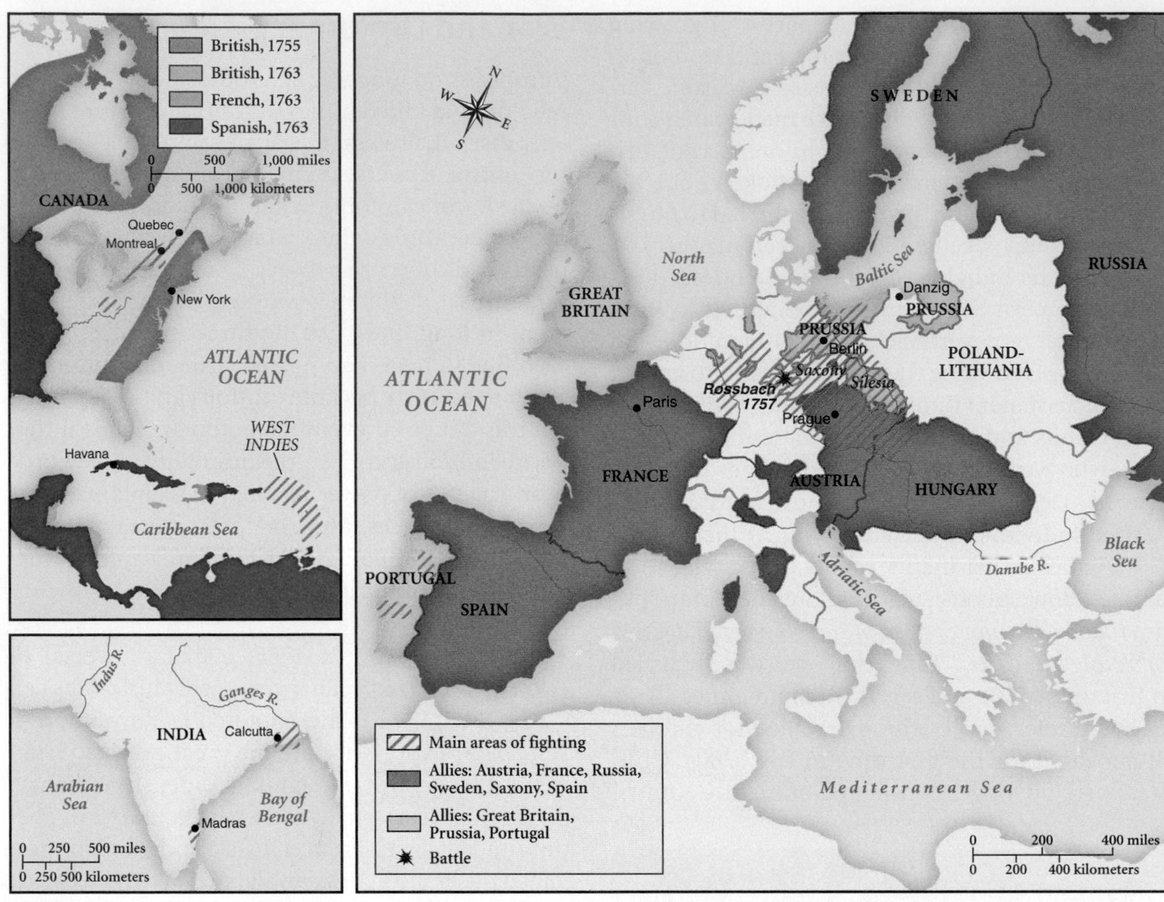

MAP 18.1 The Seven Years' War, 1756–1763
In what might justly be called the first worldwide war, the French and British fought each other in Europe, the West Indies, North America, and India. Skirmishing in North America helped precipitate the war, which became more general when Austria, France, and Russia allied to check Prussian influence in central Europe. The treaty between Austria and Prussia simply restored the status quo in Europe, but the changes overseas were much more dramatic. Britain gained control over Canada and India but gave back to France the West Indian islands of Guadeloupe and Martinique. Britain was now the dominant power of the seas.

murdered, probably at the instigation of his wife, Catherine the Great.) In a separate peace treaty Frederick kept all his territory, including Silesia, that had been conquered in the War of the Austrian Succession (1740–1748).

The Anglo-French overseas conflicts ended more decisively than the continental land wars. British naval superiority, fully achieved only in the 1750s, enabled Great Britain to rout the French in North America, India, and the West Indies. In the Treaty of Paris of 1763, France ceded Canada to Great Britain and agreed to remove its armies from India, in exchange for keeping its rich West Indian islands. Eagerness to avenge this defeat would motivate France to support the British North American colonists in their War of Independence just fifteen years later.

Prussia's Rise and the First Partition of Poland Although Prussia suffered great losses in the Seven Years' War—some 160,000 Prussian soldiers died either in action or of disease—the army helped vault Prussia to the rank of leading powers. In 1733, Frederick II's father, Frederick William I, had instituted the "canton system," which enrolled peasant youths in each canton (or district) in the army, gave them two or three months of training annually, and allowed them to return to their family farms the rest of the year. They remained "cantonists" (reservists) as long as they were able-bodied. In this fashion, the Prussian military steadily grew in size; by 1740, Prussia had the third or fourth largest army in Europe even though it was tenth in population and thirteenth in land area. Under Frederick II, Prussia's military expenditures rose to two-thirds of the state's revenue. Virtually every nobleman served in the army, paying for his own support as officer and buying a position as company commander. Once retired, the officers returned to their estates, coordinated the canton system, and served as local of-

Dividing Poland, 1772
In this contemporary depiction, Catherine the Great, Joseph II, and Frederick the Great point on the map to the portion of Poland-Lithuania each plans to take. The artist makes it clear that Poland's fate rested in the hands of neighboring rulers, not its own people. Can you infer the sentiments of the artist from the content of this engraving? *(Hulton Archive/Getty Images.)*

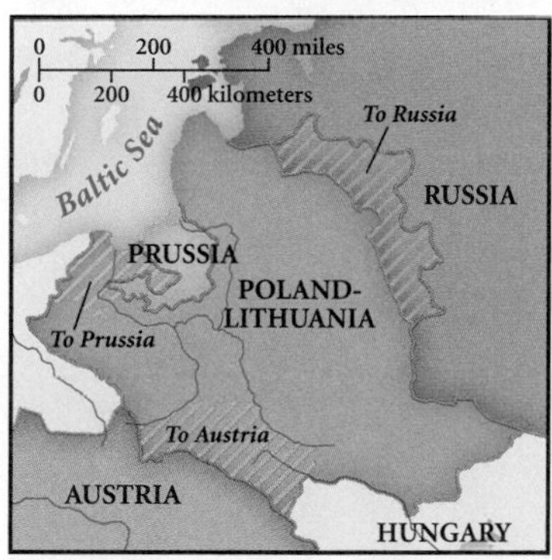

The First Partition of Poland, 1772

ficials. In this way, the military permeated every aspect of rural society, fusing army and agrarian organization. The army gave the state great power, but the militarization of Prussian society also had a profoundly conservative effect: it kept the peasants enserfed to their lords and blocked the middle classes from access to estates or high government positions.

Prussia's power grew so dramatically that in 1772 Frederick the Great proposed that large chunks of Poland-Lithuania be divided among Austria, Prussia, and Russia. Although the Austrian empress Maria Theresa protested that the partition would spread "a stain over my whole reign," she agreed to the first **partition of Poland**, splitting one-third of Poland-Lithuania's territory and half of its people among the three powers. Austria feared growing Russian influence in Poland and in the Balkans, where Russia had been successfully battling the Ottoman Empire. Conflicts between Catholics, Protestants, and Orthodox Christians in Poland were used to justify this cynical move. Russia took over most of Lithuania, effectively ending the large but weak Polish-Lithuanian commonwealth.

partition of Poland: Division of one-third of Poland-Lithuania's territory between Prussia, Russia, and Austria in 1772.

State-Sponsored Reform

In the aftermath of the Seven Years' War, all the belligerents faced pressing needs for more money to fund their growing armies, to organize navies to wage overseas conflicts, and to counter the impact of inflation. To make tax increases more palatable to public opinion, rulers appointed reform-minded ministers and gave them a mandate to modernize government. As one adviser to the Austrian ruler Joseph II put it, "A properly constituted state must be exactly analogous to a machine . . . and the ruler must be the foreman, the mainspring . . . which sets everything else in motion." Such reforms always threatened the interests of traditional groups, however, and the spread of Enlightenment ideas aroused sometimes unpredictable desires for more change.

Administrative and Legal Reforms

Reforming monarchs did not invent government bureaucracy, but they did insist on greater attention to merit, hard work, and professionalism, which made bureaucrats more like modern civil servants. In this view, the ruler should be a benevolent, enlightened administrator who worked for the general well-being of his or her people. Frederick II of Prussia, who drove himself as hard as he drove his officials, boasted, "I am the first servant of the state." A freemason and supporter

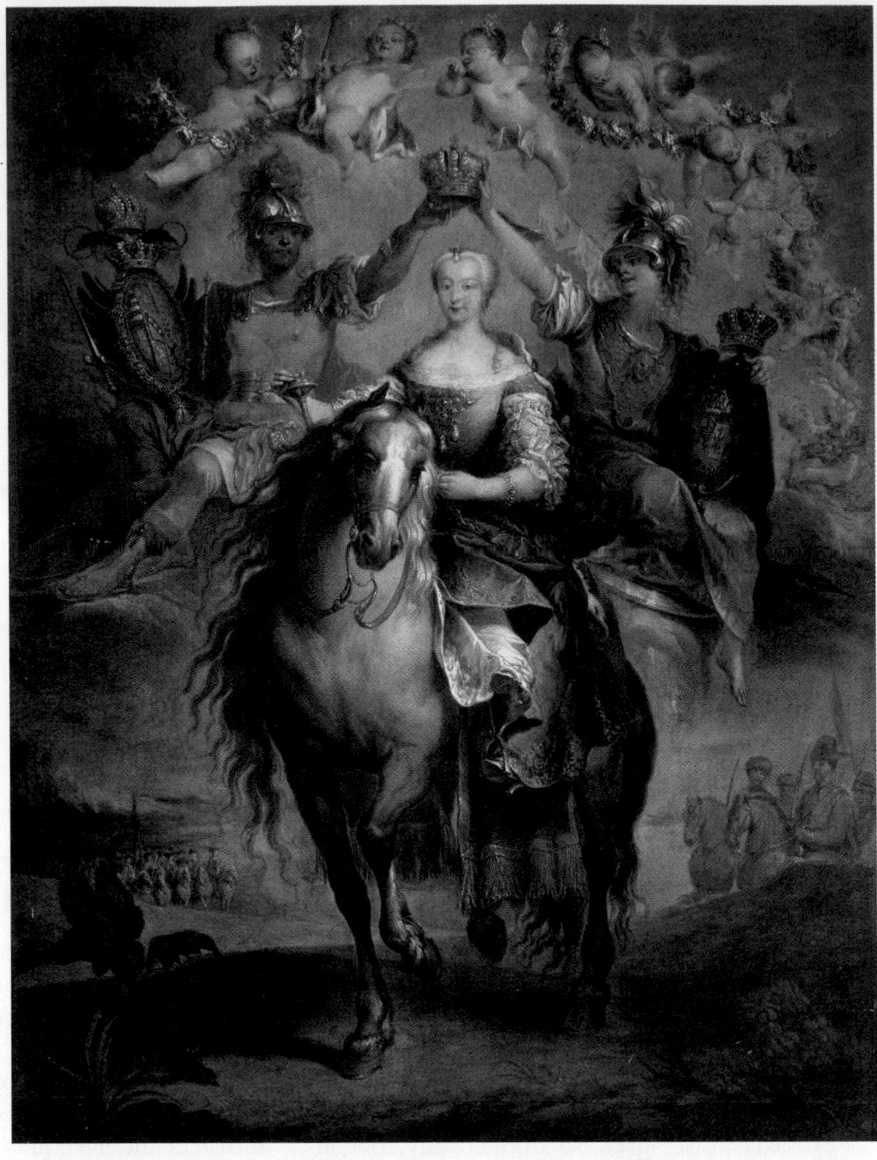

Maria Theresa
Like Catherine the Great, Maria Theresa had herself painted on horseback to emphasize her sovereign position, which the crown over her head makes apparent. This portrait from 1757 does not make her seem warlike, however, as she carries no sword. She had sixteen children, two of whom became Holy Roman Emperor (Joseph II and Leopold II) and two of whom became queens (Marie-Antoinette of France and Maria Carolina of Naples). *(Scala/White Images/Art Resource, NY.)*

of religious toleration, Frederick abolished torture, reorganized taxation, and hosted leading French philosophes at his court. The Prussian king also composed more than a hundred original pieces of music.

Legal reform, both of the judicial system and of the often disorganized and irregular law codes, was central to the work of many reform-minded monarchs. Like Frederick the Great, Joseph II of Austria (r. 1780–1790) ordered the compilation of a unified law code, a project that required many years for completion. Catherine the Great began such an undertaking even more ambitiously. In 1767, she called together a legislative commission of 564 deputies and asked them to consider a long document called the *Instruction*, which represented her hopes for legal reform based on the ideas of Montesquieu and the Italian jurist Cesare Beccaria. Montesquieu had insisted that punishment should fit the crime; he criticized the use of torture and brutal corporal punishment. In his influential book *On Crimes and Punishments* (1764), Beccaria argued that justice should be administered in public, that judicial torture should be abolished as inhumane, and that the accused should be presumed innocent until proven guilty. He also advocated eliminating the death penalty. Despite much discussion and hundreds of petitions and documents about local problems, little came of Catherine's commission because the monarch herself—despite her regard for Voltaire and his fellow philosophes—proved ultimately unwilling to see through far-reaching legal reform.

The Church, Education, and Religious Toleration

Rulers everywhere wanted more control over church affairs, and they used Enlightenment criticisms of the organized churches to get their way. In Catholic countries, many government officials resented the influence of the Jesuits, the major Catholic teaching order. The Jesuits trained the Catholic intellectual elite, ran a worldwide missionary network, enjoyed close ties to the papacy, and amassed great wealth. Critics mounted campaigns against the Jesuits in many countries, and by the early 1770s the Society of Jesus had been dissolved in Portugal, France, and Spain. In 1773, Pope Clement XIV (r. 1769–1774) agreed under pressure to disband the order, an edict that held until a reinvigorated papacy restored the society in 1814. Joseph II of Austria not only applauded the suppression of the Jesuits but also required Austrian bishops to swear fidelity and submission to him. Joseph had become Holy Roman Emperor and co-regent with his mother, Maria Theresa, in 1765. After her death in 1780, he initiated a wide-ranging program of reform. Under him, the Austrian state supervised Catholic seminaries, abolished contemplative monastic orders, and confiscated monastic property to pay for education and poor relief.

Joseph II launched the most ambitious educational reforms of the period. In 1774, once the Jesuits had been disbanded, the General School Ordinance in Austria ordered state subsidies for local schools, which the state would regulate. By 1789, one-quarter of the school-age children attended school. In Prussia, the school code of 1763 required all children between the ages of five and thirteen to attend school. Although not enforced uniformly, the Prussian law demonstrated Frederick the Great's belief that modernization depended on education. Catherine the Great also tried to expand elementary education — and the education of women in particular — and founded engineering schools.

No ruler pushed the principle of religious toleration as far as Joseph II of Austria, who in 1781 granted freedom of religious worship to Protestants, Orthodox Christians, and Jews. For the first time, these groups were allowed to own property, build schools, enter the professions, and hold political and military offices. The efforts of other rulers to extend religious toleration proved more limited. Louis XVI signed an edict in 1787 restoring French Protestants' civil rights — but still, Protestants could not hold political office. Great Britain continued to deny Catholics freedom of open worship and the right to sit in Parliament. Most European states limited the rights and opportunities available to Jews. In Russia, only wealthy Jews could hold municipal office, and in the Papal States, the pope encouraged forced baptism. Even in Austria, where Joseph encouraged toleration, the laws forced Jews to take German-sounding names. The leading philosophes opposed persecution of the Jews in theory but often treated them with undisguised contempt. Diderot's comment was all too typical: the Jews, he said, bore "all the defects peculiar to an ignorant and superstitious nation."

Limits of Reform

When enlightened absolutist leaders introduced reforms, they often ran into resistance from groups threatened by the proposed changes. The most contentious area of reform was agricultural policy. Whereas Catherine the Great reinforced the authority of Russian nobles over their serfs, Joseph II tried to remove the burdens of serfdom in the Habsburg lands. In 1781, he abolished the personal aspects of serfdom: serfs could now move freely, enter trades, or marry without their lords' permission. Joseph abolished the tithe to the church, shifted more of the tax burden to the nobility, and converted peasants' labor services into cash payments.

The Austrian nobility furiously resisted these far-reaching reforms. When Joseph died in 1790, his brother Leopold II had to revoke most reforms to appease the nobles. Prussia's Frederick the Great, like Joseph, encouraged such agricultural innovations as planting potatoes and turnips (new crops that could help feed a growing population), experimenting with cattle breeding, draining swamplands, and clearing forests. But Prussia's noble landlords, called *Junkers* in German, continued to expand their estates at the expense of poorer peasants and thwarted Frederick's attempts to improve the status of serfs.

Reforming ministers also tried to stimulate agricultural improvement in France. Unlike most other western European countries, France still had about a hundred thousand serfs; though their burdens weighed less heavily on them than on those in eastern Europe, serfdom did not entirely disappear until 1789. A group of economists called the physiocrats urged the French government to deregulate the grain trade and make the tax system more equitable to encourage agricultural productivity. In the interest of establishing a free market, they also insisted that urban guilds be abolished because the guilds prevented free entry into the trades. Their proposed reforms applied the Enlightenment emphasis on individual liberties to the economy; Adam Smith took up many of the physiocrats' ideas in his writing in favor of free markets. The French government heeded some of this advice and gave up its system of price controls on grain in 1763, but it had to reverse the decision in 1770 when grain shortages caused a famine.

A conflict with the parlements, the thirteen high courts of law, prompted Louis XV to go even further in 1771. He replaced the parlements with courts in which the judges no longer owned their offices and thus could not sell them or pass them on as an inheritance. Justice would then presumably be more impartial. The displaced judges of the parlements succeeded in arousing widespread opposition to what they portrayed as tyrannical royal policy. The furor calmed down only when Louis XV died in 1774 and his successor, Louis XVI (r. 1774–1792), yielded to aristocratic demands and restored the old parlements.

Louis XVI tried to carry out part of the program suggested by the physiocrats, and he chose one of their disciples, Jacques Turgot (1727–1781), as his chief minister. A contributor to the *Encyclopedia*, Turgot pushed through several edicts that again freed the grain trade, suppressed guilds, converted the peasants' forced labor on roads into a money tax payable by all landowners, and reduced court expenses. He also began making plans to introduce a system of elected local assemblies, which would have increased representation in the government. Faced with broad-based resistance led by the parlements and his own courtiers, as well as with riots against rising grain prices, Louis XVI dismissed Turgot, and one of the last possibilities to overhaul France's government collapsed.

The failure of reform in France paradoxically reflected the power of Enlightenment thinkers; everyone now endorsed Enlightenment ideas but used them for different ends. The nobles in the parlements blocked the French monarchy's reform efforts using the very same Enlightenment language spoken by the crown's ministers. France's large and growing middle-class public felt increasingly frustrated by the failure to institute social change, a failure that ultimately helped undermine the monarchy itself. Where Frederick the Great, Catherine the Great, and even Joseph II used reform to bolster the efficiency of absolutist government, attempts at change in France backfired. French kings found that their ambitious programs for reform succeeded only in arousing unrealistic hopes.

REVIEW QUESTION What prompted enlightened absolutists to undertake reforms in the second half of the eighteenth century?

Rebellions against State Power

Although traditional forms of popular discontent had not disappeared, Enlightenment ideals and reforms changed the rules of the game in politics. Governments had become accountable for their actions to a much wider range of people than ever before. In Britain and France, ordinary people rioted when they perceived government as failing to protect them against food shortages. The growth of informed public opinion had its most dramatic consequences in the North American colonies, where a struggle over the British Parliament's right to tax turned into a full-scale war for independence. The American War of Independence showed that, once put into practice, Enlightenment ideals could have revolutionary implications.

Food Riots and Peasant Uprisings

Population growth, inflation, and the extension of the market system put added pressure on the already beleaguered poor. Seventeenth-century peasants and townspeople had rioted to protest new taxes. In the last half of the eighteenth century, the food supply became the focus of political and social conflict. Poor people in the villages and the towns believed that it was the government's responsibility to ensure they had enough food, and many governments did stockpile grain to make up for the occasional bad harvest. At the same time, in keeping with Adam Smith's and the French physiocrats' free-market proposals, governments wanted to allow grain prices to rise with market demand, because higher profits would motivate producers to increase the overall supply of food.

Free trade in grain meant selling to the highest bidder even if that bidder was a foreign merchant. In the short run, in times of scarcity, big landowners and farmers could make huge profits by selling grain outside their hometowns or villages. This practice enraged poor farmers, agricultural workers, and urban wageworkers, who could not afford the higher prices. Lacking the political means to affect policy, they could enforce their desire for old-fashioned price regulation only by rioting. Most did not pillage or steal grain but rather forced the sale of grain or flour at a "just" price and blocked the shipment of grain out of their villages to other markets. Women often led these "popular price fixings," as they were called in France, in desperate attempts to protect the food supply for their children.

Such food riots occurred regularly in Britain and France in the last half of the eighteenth century. One of the most turbulent was the so-called Flour War in France in 1775. Turgot's deregulation of the grain trade in 1774 caused prices to rise in several provincial cities. Rioting spread from there to the Paris region, where villagers attacked grain convoys heading to the capital city. Local officials often ordered merchants and bakers to sell at the price the rioters demanded, only to find themselves arrested by the central government for overriding free trade. The government brought in troops to restore order and introduced the death penalty for rioting.

Frustrations with serfdom and hopes for a miraculous transformation provoked the **Pugachev rebellion** in Russia beginning in 1773. An army deserter from the southeast frontier region, Emelian Pugachev (1742–1775) claimed to be Tsar Peter III, the dead husband of Catherine the Great. Pugachev's appearance seemed to confirm peasant hopes for a "redeemer tsar" who would save the people from oppression. He rallied around him Cossacks like himself who resented the loss of their old tribal independence. Now increasingly enserfed or forced to pay taxes and endure army service, these nomadic bands joined with other serfs, rebellious mine workers, and Muslim minorities. Catherine dispatched a large army to squelch the uprising, but Pugachev eluded them and the fighting spread. Nearly three million people eventually participated, making this the largest single rebellion in the history of tsarist Russia. When Pugachev urged the peasants to attack the nobility and seize their estates, hundreds of noble families perished. Foreign newspapers called it "the revolution in southern Russia" and offered fantastic stories about Pugachev's life history. Finally, the army captured the rebel leader and brought him in an iron cage to Moscow, where he was tortured and executed. In the aftermath, Catherine tightened the nobles' control over their serfs with the Charter of the Nobility and harshly punished those who dared to criticize serfdom.

Area of rebellion
Pugachev's route
0 150 300 miles
0 150 300 kilometers
Moscow
RUSSIA
Volga R.
Don R.
Black Sea
Caspian Sea
Aral Sea

The Pugachev Rebellion, 1773

Public Opinion and Political Opposition

Peasant uprisings might briefly shake even a powerful monarchy, but the rise of public opinion as a force independent of court society caused more enduring changes in European politics. Across much of Europe and in the North American colonies, demands for broader political participation reflected Enlightenment notions about individual rights. Aristocratic bodies such as the French parlements, which had no legislative role like that of the British Parliament, insisted that the monarch consult them on the nation's affairs, and the new educated elite wanted more influence, too. Newspapers began to cover daily political affairs, and the public learned the basics of political life, despite the strict limits on political participation in most countries. Monarchs turned to public opinion to seek support against aristocratic groups that opposed reform. Gustavus III of Sweden (r. 1771–1792) called himself "the first citizen of a free people" and promised to deliver the country from "insufferable aristocratic despotism." Shortly after com-

A Cossack

Emelian Pugachev and many of his followers were Cossacks, Ukrainians who set up nomadic communities of horsemen to resist outside control, whether from Turks, Poles, or Russians. This eighteenth-century painting captures the common view of Cossacks as horsemen always ready for battle but with a fondness for music, too. *(© Odessa Fine Arts Museum, Ukraine/The Bridgeman Art Library International.)*

Pugachev (poo guh CHAWF) rebellion: A massive revolt of Russian Cossacks and serfs in 1773 against local nobles and the armies of Catherine the Great; its leader, Emelian Pugachev, was eventually captured and executed.

ing to the throne, Gustavus proclaimed a new constitution that divided power between the king and the legislature, abolished the use of torture in the judicial process, and assured some freedom of the press.

The Wilkes affair in Great Britain showed that public opinion could be mobilized to challenge a government. In 1763, during the reign of George III (r. 1760–1820), John Wilkes, a member of Parliament, attacked the government in his newspaper, *North Briton*, and sued the crown when he was arrested. He won his release as well as damages. When he was reelected, Parliament denied him his seat, not once but three times.

The Wilkes episode soon escalated into a major campaign against the corruption and social exclusiveness of Parliament, complaints the Levellers had first raised during the English Revolution of the late 1640s. Newspapers, magazines, pamphlets, handbills, and cheap editions of Wilkes's collected works all helped promote his cause. Those who could not vote demonstrated for Wilkes. In one incident eleven people died when soldiers broke up a huge gathering of his supporters. The slogan "Wilkes and Liberty" appeared on walls all over London. Middle-class voters formed the Society of Supporters of the Bill of Rights, which circulated petitions for Wilkes; they gained the support of about one-fourth of all the voters. The more determined Wilkesites proposed sweeping reforms of Parliament, including more frequent elections, more representation for the counties, elimination of "rotten boroughs" (election districts so small that they could be controlled by one big patron), and restrictions of pensions used by the crown to gain support. These demands would be at the heart of agitation for parliamentary reform in Britain for decades to come.

Popular demonstrations did not always support reforms. In 1780, the Gordon riots devastated London. They were named after the fanatical anti-Catholic crusader Lord George Gordon, who helped organize huge marches and petition campaigns against a bill the House of Commons passed to grant limited toleration to Catholics. The demonstrations culminated in a seven-day riot that left fifty buildings destroyed and three hundred people dead. Despite the continuing limitation on voting rights in Great Britain, British politicians were learning that they could ignore public opinion only at their peril.

Political opposition also took artistic forms, particularly in countries where governments restricted organized political activity. A striking example of a play with a political message was *The Marriage of Figaro* (1784) by Pierre-Augustin Caron de Beaumarchais (1732–1799), who at one time or another worked as a watchmaker, a judge, a gunrunner in the American War of Independence, and a French spy in Britain. *The Marriage of Figaro* was first a hit at the French court, when Queen Marie-Antoinette had it read for her friends. But when her husband, Louis XVI, read it, he forbade its production on the grounds that "this man mocks at everything that should be respected in government." When finally performed publicly, the play caused a sensation. The chief character, Figaro, is a clever servant who gets the better of his noble employer. When speaking of the count, he cries, "What have you done to deserve so many rewards? You went to the trouble of being born, and nothing more." Two years later, Mozart based an equally famous but somewhat tamer opera on Beaumarchais's story. Looking back, Napoleon would say that the play was the "revolution in action."

Revolution in North America

Oppositional forms of public opinion came to a head in Great Britain's North American colonies, where the result was American independence and the establishment of a republican constitution that stood in stark contrast to most European regimes. Many Europeans saw the American War of Independence, or the American Revolution, as a triumph for Enlightenment ideas. As one German writer exclaimed in 1777, American victory would give "greater scope to the Enlightenment, new keenness to the thinking of peoples and new life to the spirit of liberty."

The American revolutionary leaders had been influenced by a common Atlantic civilization; they participated in the Enlightenment and shared political ideas with the opposition Whigs in Britain. Supporters demonstrated for Wilkes in South Carolina and Boston, and the South Carolina legislature donated a substantial sum to the Society of Supporters of the Bill of Rights. In the 1760s and 1770s, both British and American opposition leaders became convinced that the British government was growing increasingly corrupt and despotic. British radicals wanted to reform Parliament so that the voices of a broader, more representative segment of the population would be heard. The colonies had no representatives in Parliament, and colonists claimed that "no taxation without representation" should be allowed. Indeed, they denied that Parliament had any jurisdiction over the colonies, insisting that the king govern them through colonial legislatures and recognize their traditional British liberties. The failure of the "Wilkes and Liberty" campaign to produce concrete results convinced many Americans that Parliament was hopelessly tainted and that they

DOCUMENT

Thomas Jefferson, Declaration of Independence (July 4, 1776)

Although others helped revise the Declaration of Independence of the thirteen North American colonies from Great Britain, Jefferson wrote the original draft himself. A Virginia planter and lawyer, Jefferson went on to become governor of Virginia, minister to France, secretary of state, vice president, and president of the United States (1801–1809). The Declaration begins with a stirring expression of the belief in natural or human rights.

When in the Course of human events, it becomes necessary for one people to dissolve the political bands which have connected them with another, and to assume among the powers of the earth, the separate and equal station to which the Laws of Nature and of Nature's God entitle them, a decent respect to the opinions of mankind requires that they should declare the causes which impel them to the separation.

We hold these truths to be self-evident, that all men are created equal, that they are endowed by their Creator with certain unalienable Rights, that among these are Life, Liberty and the pursuit of Happiness.—That to secure these rights, Governments are instituted among Men, deriving their just powers from the consent of the governed,—That whenever any Form of Government becomes destructive of these ends, it is the Right of the People to alter or to abolish it, and to institute new Government, laying its foundation on such principles and organizing its powers in such form, as to them shall seem most likely to effect their Safety and Happiness. Prudence, indeed, will dictate that Governments long established should not be changed for light and transient causes; and accordingly all experience hath shewn, that mankind are more disposed to suffer, while evils are sufferable, than to right themselves by abolishing the forms to which they are accustomed. But when a long train of abuses and usurpations, pursuing invariably the same Object evinces a design to reduce them under absolute Despotism, it is their right, it is their duty, to throw off such Government, and to provide new Guards for their future security.—Such has been the patient sufferance of these Colonies; and such is now the necessity which constrains them to alter their former Systems of Government. The history of the present King of Great Britain is a history of repeated injuries and usurpations, all having in direct object the establishment of an absolute Tyranny over these States.

Source: U.S. National Archives and Records Administration, Washington, D.C.

Question for Consideration

- **In what ways does the Declaration of Independence express the ideas of the Enlightenment?**

would have to stand up for their rights as British subjects.

The British colonies remained loyal to the crown until Parliament's encroachment on their autonomy and the elimination of the French threat at the end of the Seven Years' War transformed colonial attitudes. Unconsciously, perhaps, the colonies had begun to form a separate nation; their economies generally flourished in the eighteenth century, and between 1750 and 1776 their population almost doubled. With the British clamoring for lower taxes and the colonists paying only a fraction of the tax rate paid by the Britons at home, Parliament passed new taxes, including the Stamp Act in 1765, which required a special tax stamp on all legal documents and publications. After violent rioting in the colonies, the British repealed the tax, but in 1773 the new Tea Act revived colonial resistance, which culminated in the so-called Boston Tea Party of 1773. Colonists dressed as Indians boarded British ships and dumped the imported tea (by this time an enormously popular beverage) into Boston's harbor.

Political opposition in the American colonies turned belligerent when Britain threatened to use force to maintain control. In 1774, the First Continental Congress convened, composed of delegates from the colonies, and unsuccessfully petitioned the crown for redress. The next year the Second Continental Congress organized an army with George Washington in command. After actual fighting had begun, in 1776, the congress issued the Declaration of Independence. An eloquent statement of the American cause written by the Virginia planter and lawyer Thomas Jefferson, the Declaration of Independence was couched in the language of universal human rights, which enlightened Europeans could be expected to understand. (See Document, "Declaration of Independence," above.) George III denounced the American "traitors and rebels." But European newspapers enthusiastically reported on every American response to "the cruel acts of oppression they have been made to suffer." In 1778, France boosted the American cause by entering on the colonists' side. Spain, too, saw an opportunity to

Resistance to British Rule
To demonstrate their resistance to the 1765 Stamp Act, Boston citizens tar and feather a tax collector. The Stamp Act is nailed upside-down to a tree. *(Private Collection/Peter Newark Pictures/The Bridgeman Art Library International.)*

check the growing power of Britain, though without actually endorsing American independence out of fear of the response of its Latin American colonies. Spain declared war on Britain in 1779; in 1780, Great Britain declared war on the Dutch Republic in retaliation for Dutch support of the rebels. The worldwide conflict that resulted was more than Britain could handle. The American colonies achieved their independence in the peace treaty of 1783.

The newly independent states still faced the challenge of republican self-government. The Articles of Confederation, drawn up in 1777 as a provisional constitution, proved weak because they gave the central government few powers. In 1787, a constitutional convention met in Philadelphia to draft a new constitution. It established a two-house legislature, an indirectly elected president, and an independent judiciary. The U.S. Constitution's preamble insisted explicitly, for the first time in history, that government derived its power solely from the people and did not depend on divine right or on the tradition of royalty or aristocracy. The new educated elite of the eighteenth century had now created government based on a "social contract" among male, property-owning, white citizens. It was by no means a complete democracy (women and slaves were excluded from political participation), but the new government represented a radical departure from European models. In 1791, the Bill of Rights was appended to the Constitution outlining the essential rights (such as freedom of speech) that the government could never overturn. Although slavery continued in the American republic, the new emphasis on rights helped fuel the movement for its abolition in both Britain and the United States.

Interest in the new republic was greatest in France. The U.S. Constitution and various state constitutions were published in French with commentary by leading thinkers. Even more important in the long run were the effects of the American war. Dutch losses to Great Britain aroused a widespread movement for political reform in the Dutch Republic, and debts incurred by France in supporting the American colonies would soon force the French monarchy to the edge of bankruptcy and then to revolution. Ultimately, the entire European system of royal rule would be challenged.

REVIEW QUESTION Why did public opinion become a new factor in politics in the second half of the eighteenth century?

Conclusion

When Thomas Jefferson looked back many years later on the Declaration of Independence, he said he hoped it would be "the signal of arousing men to burst the chains under which monkish ignorance

MAPPING THE WEST

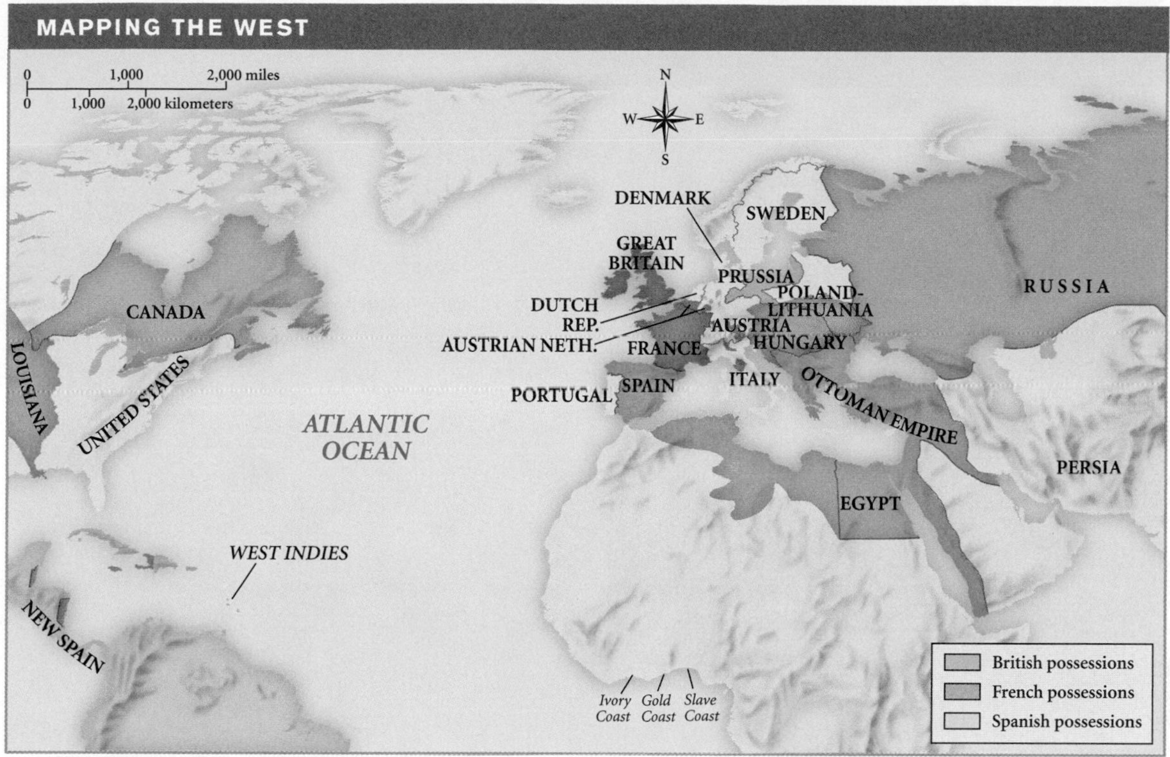

Europe and the World, c. 1780

Although Great Britain lost control over part of its North American colonies, which became the new United States, European influence on the rest of the world grew dramatically in the eighteenth century. The slave trade linked European ports to African slave-trading outposts and to plantations in the Caribbean, South America, and North America. The European countries on the Atlantic Ocean benefited most from this trade. Yet almost all of Africa, China, Japan, and large parts of India still resisted European incursion, and the Ottoman Empire, with its massive territories, still presented Europe with a formidable military challenge.

and superstition had persuaded them to bind themselves." What began as a cosmopolitan movement of a few intellectuals in the first half of the eighteenth century had reached a relatively wide audience among the educated elite of men and women by the 1770s and 1780s. The spirit of Enlightenment swept from the salons, coffeehouses, and Masonic lodges into the halls of government from Philadelphia to Vienna. Scientific inquiry into the causes of social misery and laws defending individual rights and freedoms gained adherents even among the rulers and ministers responsible for censoring Enlightenment works.

For most Europeans, however, the promise of the Enlightenment did not become a reality. Rulers such as Catherine the Great had every intention of retaining their full, often unchecked, powers, even as they corresponded with leading philosophes and entertained them at their courts. Moreover, would-be reformers often found themselves blocked by the resistance of nobles, by the priorities rulers gave to waging wars, or by popular resistance to deregulation of trade that increased the uncertainties of the market. Yet even the failure of reform contributed to the ferment in Europe after 1770. Peasant rebellions in eastern Europe, the "Wilkes and Liberty" campaign in Great Britain, the struggle over reform in France, and the revolution in America all occurred around the same time, and their conjunction convinced many Europeans that change was brewing. Just how much could change, and whether change made life better or worse, would come into question in the next ten years.

FOR FURTHER EXPLORATION

- **For additional primary-source material from this period**, see *Sources of the Making of the West*, Fourth Edition.
- **For Web sites, images, and documents related to topics in this chapter**, visit *Make History* at bedfordstmartins.com/hunt.

Chapter 18 Review

Online Study Guide bedfordstmartins.com/hunt

Key Terms and People

In the grid below, identify the term or person and explain its historical significance. (To do this exercise online, go to bedfordstmartins.com/hunt.)

Term	Who or What & When	Why It Matters
philosophes (p. 588)		
deists (p. 591)		
abolitionists (p. 592)		
laissez-faire (p. 593)		
Jean-Jacques Rousseau (p. 594)		
romanticism (p. 598)		
Methodism (p. 598)		
Freemasons (p. 600)		
enlightened despots (p. 605)		
Seven Years' War (p. 605)		
partition of Poland (p. 607)		
Pugachev rebellion (p. 611)		

Review Questions

1. What were the major differences between the Enlightenment in France, Great Britain, and the German states?
2. What were the major differences in the impact of the Enlightenment on the nobility, the middle classes, and the lower classes?
3. What prompted enlightened absolutists to undertake reforms in the second half of the eighteenth century?
4. Why did public opinion become a new factor in politics in the second half of the eighteenth century?

Making Connections

1. Why would rulers feel ambivalent about the Enlightenment, supporting reform on the one hand, while clamping down on political dissidents on the other hand?
2. Which major developments in this period ran counter to the influence of the Enlightenment?
3. In what ways had politics changed, and in what ways did they remain the same during the Enlightenment?
4. Explain how Catherine the Great of Russia could be taken as a symbol of both the promise and the limitations of the Enlightenment.

Important Events

Date	Event
1751–1772	*Encyclopedia* published in France
1756–1763	Seven Years' War fought in Europe, India, and the American colonies
1762	Jean-Jacques Rousseau, *The Social Contract* and *Émile*
1763	Wilkes affair begins in Great Britain
1764	Voltaire, *Philosophical Dictionary*
1771	Louis XV of France fails to break power of French law courts
1772	First partition of Poland
1773	Pugachev rebellion of Russian peasants
1775	Flour War in France
1776	American Declaration of Independence from Great Britain; Adam Smith, *The Wealth of Nations*
1780	Joseph II of Austria undertakes a wide-reaching reform program
1781	Immanuel Kant, *The Critique of Pure Reason*
1784	Pierre-Augustin Caron de Beaumarchais, *The Marriage of Figaro*
1785	Catherine the Great's Charter of the Nobility grants nobles exclusive control over their serfs in exchange for subservience to the state
1787	Delegates from the states draft the U.S. Constitution

- Consider three events: ***Encyclopedia* published in France (1751–1772)**, **Wilkes affair begins in Great Britain (1763)**, and **American Declaration of Independence from Great Britain (1776).** In what ways did the same Enlightenment ideals inform these events?

SUGGESTED REFERENCES

Gay's interpretive study of the Enlightenment remains useful, but the Kors volumes offer the most up-to-date views on the Enlightenment. Readers can find different perspectives in studies of individual rulers, their routes to power, and their reactions to the Enlightenment.

Beales, Derek. *Joseph II: In the Shadow of Maria Theresa: 1741–1780.* 2008.

Cash, Arthur H. *John Wilkes: The Scandalous Father of Civil Liberty.* 2006.

Catherine the Great: http://russia.nypl.org/home.html

Gay, Peter. *The Enlightenment: An Interpretation.* 2 vols. 1966, 1969.

Kors, Alan Charles, ed. *Encyclopedia of the Enlightenment.* 4 vols. 2003.

*Lessing, Gotthold Ephraim. *Nathan the Wise.* Ed. Ronald Schechter. 2004.

Mozart Project: http://www.mozartproject.org

Rounding, Virginia. *Catherine the Great: Love, Sex, and Power.* 2008.

*Rousseau, Jean-Jacques. *Discourse on the Origin and Foundations of Inequality among Men.* Ed. Helena Rosenblatt. 2011.

Schumann, Matt, and Karl W. Schweizer. *The Seven Years War: A Transatlantic History.* 2008.

Seven Years' War: http://www.historyworld.net/wrldhis/PlainTextHistories.asp?historyid=aa66

Venturi, Franco. *The End of the Old Regime in Europe, 1768–1776: The First Crisis.* Trans. R. Burr Litchfield. 1989.

Wilson, Peter H. *A Companion to Eighteenth-Century Europe.* 2008.

*Primary source.

CHAPTER

19

The Cataclysm of Revolution

1789–1799

On October 5, 1789, a crowd of several thousand women marched in a drenching rain from the center of Paris to Versailles, a distance of twelve miles. They demanded the king's help in securing more grain for the hungry and his reassurance that he did not intend to resist the emerging revolutionary movement. Joined the next morning by thousands of men who came from Paris to reinforce them, they broke into the royal family's private apartments, killing two of the royal bodyguards. To prevent further bloodshed, the king agreed to move his family and his government to Paris. A dramatic procession of the royal family guarded by throngs of ordinary men and women made its slow way back to the capital. The people's proud display of cannons and pikes underlined the fundamental transformation that was occurring. Ordinary people had forced the king of France to respond to their grievances. The French monarchy was in danger, and if such a powerful and long-lasting institution could come under fire, then could any monarch of Europe rest easy?

Although even the keenest political observer did not predict its eruption in 1789, the French Revolution had its immediate origins in a constitutional crisis provoked by a growing government deficit, traceable to French involvement in the American War of Independence. The constitutional crisis had come to a head on July 14, 1789, when armed Parisians captured the Bastille, a royal fortress and symbol of monarchical authority in the center of the capital. The fall of the Bastille, like the women's march to Versailles three months later, showed the determination of the common people to put their mark on events.

Women's March to Versailles
Thousands of prints broadcast the events of the French Revolution to the public in France and elsewhere. This colored engraving shows a crowd of armed women marching to Versailles on October 5, 1789, to confront the king. The sight of armed women frightened many observers and demonstrated that the Revolution was not only a men's affair. Note the middle-class woman on the left being forced to join with the others. *(The Granger Collection, New York—All rights reserved.)*

The French Revolution first grabbed the attention of the entire world because it seemed to promise universal human rights, constitutional government, and broad-based political participation. Its most famous slogan pledged "Liberty, Equality, and

Fraternity" for all. An enthusiastic German wrote, "One of the greatest nations in the world, the greatest in general culture, has at last thrown off the yoke of tyranny." The revolutionaries used a blueprint based on the Enlightenment idea of reason to remake all of society and politics: they executed the king and queen, established a republic for the first time in French history, abolished the nobility, and gave the vote to all adult men.

Even as the Revolution promised democracy, however, it also inaugurated a cycle of violence and intimidation. When the revolutionaries encountered resistance to their programs, they set up a government of terror to compel obedience. Some historians therefore see in the French Revolution the origins of modern totalitarianism — that is, governments that try to control every aspect of life, including daily activities, while limiting all forms of political dissent. As events unfolded after 1789, the French Revolution became the model of modern revolution; republicanism, democracy, terrorism, nationalism, and military dictatorship all took their modern forms during the French Revolution.

The Revolution might have remained a strictly French affair if war had not involved the rest of Europe. After 1792, huge French republican armies, fueled by patriotic nationalism, marched across Europe, promising liberation from traditional monarchies but often delivering old-fashioned conquest and annexation. French victories spread revolutionary ideas far and wide, from Poland to the colonies in the Caribbean, where the first successful slave revolt established the republic of Haiti.

The breathtaking succession of regimes in France between 1789 and 1799 and the failure of the republican experiment after ten years of upheaval raised disturbing questions about the relationship between rapid political change and violence: Do all revolutions inevitably degenerate into terror or wars of conquest? Is a regime democratic if it does not allow poor men, women, or blacks to vote? Such questions resonated in many countries because the French Revolution seemed to be only the most extreme example of a much broader political and social movement at the end of the eighteenth century.

CHAPTER FOCUS What was so revolutionary about the French Revolution?

The Revolutionary Wave, 1787–1789

Between 1787 and 1789, revolts in the name of liberty broke out in the Dutch Republic, the Austrian Netherlands (present-day Belgium and Luxembourg), and Poland as well as in France. At the same time, the newly independent United States of America was preparing a new federal constitution. Historians have sometimes referred to these revolts as the Atlantic revolutions because so many protest movements arose in countries on both shores of the North Atlantic. These revolutions were the product of long-term prosperity and high expectations, created in part by the spread of the Enlightenment. Europeans in general were wealthier, healthier, more numerous, and better educated than they had ever been before; and the Dutch, Belgian, and French societies were among the wealthiest and best educated within Europe. The French Revolution nonetheless differed greatly from the others. Not only was France the richest, most powerful, and most populous state in western Europe, but its revolution was also more violent, more long-lasting, and ultimately more influential. (See "Terms of History," page 621.)

Protesters in the Low Countries and Poland

Political protests in the Dutch Republic attracted European attention because Dutch banks still controlled a hefty portion of the world's capital at the

1787 Dutch Patriot revolt stifled by Prussian invasion

1788 Beginning of Austrian Netherlands resistance against reforms of Joseph II; opening of reform parliament in Poland

1789 French Revolution begins

1790 Internal divisions lead to collapse of resistance in Austrian Netherlands

1791 Beginning of slave revolt in St. Domingue (Haiti)

1787 1789 1791

TERMS OF HISTORY

Revolution

Revolution had previously meant cyclical change that brought life back to a starting point, as a planet makes a revolution around the sun. Revolutions could come and go, by this definition, and change nothing fundamental in the structure of society. After 1789, *revolution* came to mean a self-conscious attempt to leap into the future by reshaping society and politics and even the human personality. A revolutionary official analyzed the meaning of the word in 1793: "A revolution is never made by halves; it must either be total or it will abort. . . . *Revolutionary* means outside of all forms and all rules." In short, *revolution* soon had an all-or-nothing meaning; you were either for the revolution or against it. There could be no in between.

Revolution still has the same meaning given it by the French revolutionaries, but it is now an even more contested term because of its association with communist theory. In the nineteenth century, Karl Marx incorporated the French Revolution into his new doctrine of communism. In his view, the middle-class French revolutionaries had overthrown the monarchy and the "feudal" aristocracy to pave the way for capitalist development. In the future, the proletariat (industrial workers) would overthrow the capitalist middle class to install a communist government that would abolish private property. Since Marxists claimed the French Revolution as the forerunner of the communist revolution in the nineteenth and twentieth centuries, it was perhaps inevitable that those who opposed communism would also criticize the French Revolution.

The most influential example of this view is that of the French scholar François Furet. An ex-communist, Furet argued that the French Revolution can be seen as the origin of totalitarianism because it incarnated what Furet calls "the illusion of politics," that is, the belief that people can transform social and economic relationships through political revolution. The French revolutionaries became totalitarian, in Furet's view, because they wanted to establish a kind of political and social utopia (a perfect society), in which reason alone determined the shape of political and social life. Because this dream is impossible given human resistance to rapid change, the revolutionaries had to use force to achieve their goals. In other words, revolution itself was a problematic idea, according to Furet. *Revolution* as a term remains as contested as the events that gave rise to it.

end of the eighteenth century, even though the Dutch Republic's role in international politics had diminished. Revolts also broke out in the neighboring Austrian Netherlands and Poland. Although none of these movements ultimately succeeded, they showed how quickly political discontent could boil over in this era of rising economic and political expectations.

The Dutch Patriot Revolt, 1787 The Dutch Patriots, as they called themselves, wanted to reduce the powers of the prince of Orange, the kinglike stadholder who favored close ties with Great Britain. Government-sponsored Dutch banks owned 40 percent of the British national debt, and by 1796 they held the entire foreign debt of the United States. Relations with the British deteriorated during the American War of Independence, however, and by the middle of the 1780s, agitation in favor of the Americans had boiled over into an attack on the stadholder.

Building on support among middle-class bankers and merchants, the Dutch Patriots soon gained a more popular audience by demanding

1792 Beginning of war between France and rest of Europe; second revolution of August 10 overthrows monarchy

1793 Second partition of Poland by Austria and Russia; Louis XVI of France executed for treason

1794 Abolition of slavery in French colonies; Robespierre's government by terror falls

1795 Third (final) partition of Poland; France annexes Austrian Netherlands

1797–1798 Creation of "sister republics" in Italian states and Switzerland

1793 1795 1797

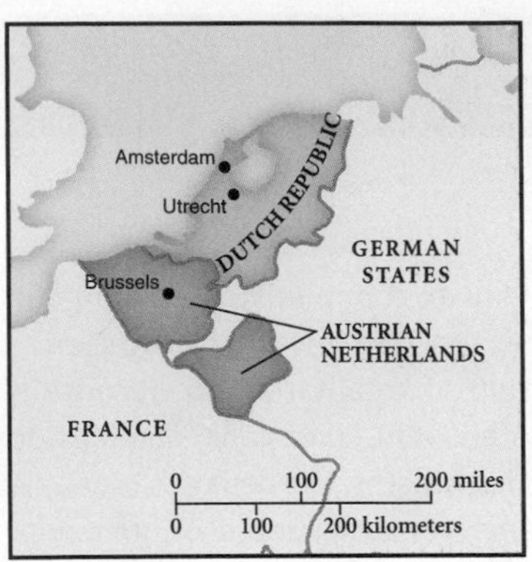

The Low Countries in 1787

political reforms and organizing armed citizen militias of men, called Free Corps. Town by town the Patriots forced local officials to set up new elections to replace councils that had been packed with Orangist supporters through patronage or family connections. Before long, the Free Corps took on the troops of the prince of Orange and got the upper hand. In response, Frederick William II of Prussia, whose sister had married the stadholder, intervened in 1787 with tacit British support. Thousands of Prussian troops soon occupied Utrecht and Amsterdam, and the house of Orange regained its former position.

Social divisions among the rebels paved the way for the success of this outside intervention. Many of the Patriots from the richest merchant families feared the growing power of the Free Corps. The Free Corps wanted a more democratic form of government, and to get it they encouraged the publication of pamphlets and cartoons attacking the prince and his wife, promoted the rapid spread of clubs and societies made up of common people, and organized crowd-pleasing public ceremonies, such as parades and bonfires, that sometimes turned into riots. In the aftermath of the Prussian invasion in September 1787, the Orangists got their revenge: lower-class mobs pillaged the houses of prosperous Dutch Patriot leaders, forcing many to flee to the United States, France, or the Austrian Netherlands. Those Patriots who remained nursed their grievances until the French republican armies invaded in 1795.

The Belgian Independence Movement If Austrian emperor Joseph II had not tried to introduce Enlightenment-inspired reforms, the Belgians of the ten provinces of the Austrian Netherlands might have remained tranquil. Just as he had done previously in his own crown lands (see Chapter 18), Joseph abolished torture, decreed toleration for Jews and Protestants (in this resolutely Catholic area), and suppressed monasteries. His reorganization of the administrative and judicial systems eliminated many offices that belonged to nobles and lawyers, sparking resistance among the upper classes in 1788.

Upper-class protesters intended only to defend historic local liberties against an overbearing government. Nonetheless, their resistance galvanized democrats, who wanted a more representative government and organized clubs to give voice to their demands. At the end of 1788, a secret society formed armed companies to prepare an uprising. By late 1789, each province had separately declared its independence, and the Austrian administration had collapsed. Delegates from the various provinces declared themselves the United States of Belgium, a clear reference to the American precedent.

Once again, however, social divisions doomed the rebels. When the democrats began to challenge noble authority, aristocratic leaders drew to their side the Catholic clergy and peasants, who had little sympathy for the democrats of the cities. Every Sunday in May and June 1790, thousands of peasant men and women, led by their priests, streamed into Brussels carrying crucifixes, nooses, and pitchforks to intimidate the democrats and defend the church. Faced with the choice between the Austrian emperor and "our current tyrants," the democrats chose to support the return of the Austrians under Emperor Leopold II (r. 1790–1792), who had succeeded his brother.

Polish Patriots A reform party calling itself the Patriots also emerged in Poland, which had been shocked by the loss of a third of its territory in the first partition of 1772. The Patriots sought to overhaul the weak commonwealth along modern western European lines and looked to King Stanislaw August Poniatowski (r. 1764–1795) to lead them. A nobleman who owed his crown solely to the dubious honor of being Catherine the Great's discarded lover but who was also a favorite correspondent of the Parisian salon hostess Madame Geoffrin, Poniatowski saw in moderate reform the only chance for his country to escape the consequences of a century's misgovernment and cultural decline. Ranged against the Patriots stood most of the aristocrats and the formidable Catherine the Great, determined to uphold imperial Russian influence.

Pleased to see Russian influence waning in Poland, Austria and Prussia allowed the reform movement to proceed. In 1788, the Patriots got their golden chance. Bogged down in war with the Ottoman Turks, Catherine could not block the summoning of a reform-minded parliament, which eventually enacted the constitution of May 3, 1791. It established a hereditary monarchy with somewhat strengthened authority, ended the veto power that each aristocrat had over legislation, granted townspeople limited political rights, and vaguely promised future Jewish emancipation. Abolishing serfdom was hardly mentioned. Within a year, however, Catherine II had turned her attention to Poland and engineered the downfall of the Patriots.

Origins of the French Revolution, 1787–1789

Many French enthusiastically greeted the American experiment in republican government and supported the Dutch, Belgian, and Polish Patriots. But they did not expect the United States and the Dutch Republic to provide them a model. Montesquieu and Rousseau, the leading political theorists of the Enlightenment, taught that republics suited only small countries, not big ones like France. After suffering humiliation at the hands of the British in the Seven Years' War (1756–1763), the French had regained international prestige by supporting the victorious Americans, and the monarchy had shown its eagerness to promote reforms. In 1787, for example, the French crown granted civil rights to Protestants. Yet by the late 1780s, the French monarchy faced a serious fiscal crisis caused by a mounting deficit. The fiscal crisis soon provoked a constitutional crisis of epic proportions.

Fiscal Crisis France's fiscal problems stemmed from the nation's support of the Americans against the British in the American War of Independence. About half of the French national budget went to paying interest on the debt that had accumulated. In contrast to Great Britain, which had a national bank to help raise loans for the government, the French government lived off relatively short-term, high-interest loans from private sources including Swiss banks, government annuities, and advances from tax collectors.

For years the French government had been trying unsuccessfully to modernize the tax system to make it more equitable. The peasants bore the greatest burden of taxes, whereas the nobles and clergy were largely exempt from them. Tax collection was also far from systematic: private contractors collected many taxes and pocketed a large share of the proceeds. With the growing support of public opinion, the bond and annuity holders from the middle and upper classes now demanded a clearer system of fiscal accountability.

In a monarchy, the ruler's character is always crucial. Many complained that **Louis XVI** (r. 1774–1792) showed more interest in hunting or in his hobby of making locks than in the problems of government. His wife, **Marie-Antoinette**, was blond, beautiful, and much criticized for her extravagant taste in clothes, elaborate hairdos, and supposed indifference to popular misery. It was reported that, when told the poor had no bread, the queen gave a reply that has come to epitomize oblivious coldheartedness: "Let them eat cake." "The Austrian bitch," as underground writers called her, had been the target of an increasingly nasty pamphlet campaign in the 1780s. By 1789, Marie-Antoinette had become an object of popular hatred. The king's ineffectiveness and the queen's growing unpopularity helped undermine the monarchy as an institution.

Queen Marie-Antoinette (detail)
Marie-Louise-Élizabeth Vigée-Lebrun painted this portrait of the French queen Marie-Antoinette and her children in 1788. The queen appears in the most stylish and lavish fashions of the day. When her eldest son (not shown in this detail) died in 1789, her second son (on her lap here) became heir to the throne. Known to supporters of the monarch as Louis XVII, the child died in prison in 1795 and never ruled. Vigée-Lebrun fled France in 1789 and returned only in 1805. *(Chateau de Versailles, France / Giraudon / The Bridgeman Art Library International.)*

Faced with a mounting deficit, in 1787 Louis submitted a package of reforms to the Assembly of Notables, a group of handpicked nobles, clergymen, and officials. When this group refused to endorse his program, the king presented his proposals for a more uniform land tax to his old rival the parlement

Louis XVI: French king (r. 1774–1792) who was tried for treason during the French Revolution; he was executed on January 21, 1793.

Marie-Antoinette: Wife of Louis XVI and queen of France who was tried for treason during the French Revolution and executed in October 1793.

of Paris. When it, too, refused, he ordered the parlement judges into exile in the provinces. Overnight, the judges (members of the nobility because of the offices they held) became popular heroes for resisting the king's "tyranny"; in reality, however, the judges, like the notables, wanted reform only on their own terms. Louis finally gave in to demands that he call a meeting of the Estates General, which had last met 175 years before.

The Estates General The calling of the Estates General electrified public opinion. Who would determine the fate of the nation? The **Estates General** was a body of deputies from the three estates, or orders, of France. The deputies in the First Estate represented some 100,000 clergy of the Catholic church, which owned about 10 percent of the land and collected a 10 percent tax (the tithe) on peasants. The deputies of the Second Estate represented the nobility, about 400,000 men and women who owned about 25 percent of the land, enjoyed many tax exemptions, and collected seigneurial dues and rents from their peasant tenants. The deputies of the Third Estate, mostly middle-class lawyers or officials, represented everyone else, at least 95 percent of the nation. Included in the Third Estate were the vast mass of peasants, some 75 percent of the population, and the *sans-culottes* ("without breeches") and middle classes of the cities. The sans-culottes were those who worked with their hands and wore long trousers rather than the knee breeches of the upper classes.

At the last meeting of the Estates General in 1614, each order had deliberated and voted separately. Before the elections to the Estates General in 1789, the king agreed to double the number of deputies for the Third Estate (making those deputies equal in number to the other two orders' combined), but he refused to mandate voting by individual head rather than by order. Voting by order, allowing each order to have one vote, would conserve the traditional powers of the clergy and nobility; voting by head, allowing each deputy one vote, would give the Third Estate an advantage since many clergymen and even some nobles sympathized with the Third Estate.

As the state's censorship apparatus broke down, pamphleteers by the hundreds denounced the traditional privileges of the nobility and clergy and called for voting by head rather than by order. In the most vitriolic of all the pamphlets, *What Is the Third Estate?*, the middle-class *abbé* ("abbot") Emmanuel-Joseph Sieyès charged that the nobility contributed nothing at all to the nation's well-being; they were, he said, "a malignant disease which preys upon and tortures the body of a sick man." In the winter and spring of 1789, villagers and townspeople alike held meetings to elect deputies and write down their grievances. The effect was immediate. Although educated men dominated the meetings at the regional level, the humblest peasants voted in their villages and burst forth with complaints, especially about taxes. As one villager lamented, "The last crust of bread has been taken from us." The long series of meetings raised expectations that the Estates General would help the king solve all the nation's ills.

These new hopes soared just at the moment France experienced an increasingly rare but always dangerous food shortage. Bad weather had damaged the harvest of 1788, causing bread prices to soar in many places in the spring and summer of 1789 and threatening starvation for the poorest people. In addition, a serious slump in textile production had been causing massive unemployment since 1786. Hundreds of thousands of textile workers were out of work and hungry, adding another volatile element to an already tense situation.

When some twelve hundred deputies journeyed to the king's palace of Versailles for the opening of the Estates General in May 1789, many readers avidly followed the developments in newspapers that sprouted overnight. Although most nobles insisted on voting by order, the deputies of the Third Estate refused to proceed on that basis. After six weeks of stalemate, on June 17, 1789, the deputies of the Third Estate took unilateral action and declared themselves and whoever would join them the National Assembly, in which each deputy would vote as an individual. Two days later, the clergy voted by a narrow margin to join them. Suddenly denied access to their meeting hall on June 20, the deputies met on a nearby tennis court and swore an oath not to disband until they had given France a constitution that reflected their newly declared authority. This "tennis court oath" expressed the determination of the Third Estate to carry through a constitutional revolution.

July 14, 1789: The Fall of the Bastille At first, Louis XVI appeared to agree to the new National Assembly, but he also ordered thousands of soldiers to march to Paris. The deputies who supported the Assembly feared a plot by the king and high-ranking nobles to arrest them and disperse the Assembly. "Everyone is convinced that the approach of the troops covers some violent design," one deputy wrote home. Their fears were

---

Estates General: A body of deputies from the three estates, or orders, of France: the clergy (First Estate), the nobility (Second Estate), and everyone else (Third Estate).

Fall of the Bastille

A central moment from the storming of the Bastille prison on July 14, 1789, is depicted in this colored print of a 1793 painting by Charles Thévenin. The insurgents have won the battle and are arresting the governor of the prison; in the next moments, they will cut off his head and parade it on a pike. The artist expresses his ambivalence about the violence by showing an insurgent in the right foreground brutally killing one of the defenders even though the battle is over. *(Réunion des Musées Nationaux/Art Resource, NY.)*

confirmed when, on July 11, the king fired Jacques Necker, the Swiss Protestant finance minister and the one high official regarded as sympathetic to the deputies' cause.

The popular reaction in Paris to Necker's dismissal and the threat of military force changed the course of the French Revolution. When the news spread, the sans-culottes in Paris began to arm themselves and attack places where either grain or arms were thought to be stored. A deputy in Versailles reported home: "Today all of the evils overwhelm France, and we are between despotism, carnage, and famine." On July 14, 1789, an armed crowd marched on the Bastille, a huge fortified prison that symbolized royal authority even though only a few prisoners were actually incarcerated there. After a chaotic battle in which a hundred armed citizens died, the prison officials surrendered.

The fall of the Bastille (an event now commemorated as the French national holiday) set an important precedent. The common people showed themselves willing to intervene violently at a crucial political moment. (See the illustration above.) All over France, food riots turned into revolts. Local governments were forced out of power and replaced by committees of "patriots" loyal to the revolutionary cause. The king's government began to crumble. To restore order, the patriots relied on newly formed

The Third Estate Awakens

This colored etching, produced after the fall of the Bastille (note the heads on pikes outside the prison), shows a clergyman (First Estate) and a noble (Second Estate) alarmed by the awakening of the commoners (Third Estate). The Third Estate breaks the chains of oppression and arms itself. In what ways does this print draw attention to the social conflicts that lay behind the political struggles in the Estates General? *(Réunion des Musées Nationaux/Art Resource, NY.)*

National Guard units composed of civilians. In Paris, the Marquis de Lafayette, a hero of the American War of Independence and a noble deputy in the National Assembly, became commander of the new National Guard. One of Louis XVI's brothers and many other leading aristocrats fled into exile. The Revolution thus had its first heroes, its first victims, and its first enemies.

REVIEW QUESTION How did the beginning of the French Revolution resemble the other revolutions of 1787–1789?

From Monarchy to Republic, 1789–1793

Until July 1789, the French Revolution followed a course much like that of the protest movements in the Low Countries. After July 1789, however, events in France escalated at a pace never before seen in history, leaving witnesses to them breathless with anticipation, anxiety, even shock. The French revolutionaries first tried to establish a constitutional monarchy based on the Enlightenment principles of human rights and rational government. This effort failed when the king attempted to flee and raise a counterrevolutionary army. When war broke out in 1792 and foreign soldiers invaded, a popular uprising on August 10, 1792, led to the arrest of the king and, for the first time in French history, the establishment of a republic.

The Revolution of Rights and Reason

Before drafting a constitution in 1789, the deputies of the National Assembly had to confront growing violence in the countryside. Most peasants could barely make ends meet but still had to pay taxes to the state, the tithe to the Catholic church, and a host of seigneurial dues to their lords, whether for using the lords' mills to grind wheat or to ensure their ability to give their land as inheritance to their children. As food shortages spread, peasants feared that the beggars and vagrants crowding the roads might be part of an aristocratic plot to starve the people by burning crops or barns. In many places, the **Great Fear** (the term used by historians to describe this rural panic) turned into peasant attacks on aristocrats or on the records of peasants' dues kept in the lord's château. Peasants now refused to pay dues to their lords, and the persistence of peasant violence raised alarms about the potential for a general peasant insurrection.

The Great Fear, 1789

The End of Feudalism | Alarmed by peasant unrest, the National Assembly decided to make sweeping changes. On the night of August 4, 1789, noble deputies announced their willingness to give up their tax exemptions and seigneurial dues. By the end of the night, amid wild enthusiasm, dozens of deputies had come to the podium to relinquish the tax exemptions of their own professional groups, towns, or provinces. The National Assembly decreed the abolition of what it called "the feudal regime"—that is, it freed the remaining serfs and eliminated all special privileges in matters of taxation, including all seigneurial dues on land. (A few days later the deputies insisted on financial compensation for some of these dues, but most peasants refused to pay.) Peasants had achieved their goals. The Assembly also mandated equality of opportunity in access to government positions. Talent, rather than birth, was to be the key to success. Enlightenment principles were beginning to become law.

The Declaration of the Rights of Man and Citizen | Three weeks later, the deputies to the National Assembly drew up the **Declaration of the Rights of Man and Citizen** as the preamble to a new constitution. In words reminiscent of the American Declaration of Independence, whose author, Thomas Jefferson, was in Paris at the time, it proclaimed, "Men are born and remain free and equal in rights." The Declaration granted freedom of religion, freedom of the press, equality of taxation, and equality before the law. It established the principle of national sovereignty: since "all sovereignty rests essentially in the nation," it said, the king derived his authority henceforth

---

Great Fear: The term used by historians to describe the French rural panic of 1789, which led to peasant attacks on aristocrats or on seigneurial records of peasants' dues.

Declaration of the Rights of Man and Citizen: The preamble to the French constitution drafted in August 1789; it established the sovereignty of the nation and equal rights for citizens.

DOCUMENT

The Rights of Minorities (1789)

When the National Assembly passed the Declaration of the Rights of Man and Citizen on August 26, 1789, it opened the way to discussion of the rights of various groups, from actors (considered ineligible for voting under the monarchy because they impersonated other people as part of their profession) to women, free blacks, mulattoes, and slaves. Count Stanislas de Clermont-Tonnerre, a nobleman and freemason, gave a speech on December 23, 1789, in which he advocated ending exclusions based on profession or religion, though not on gender or race. He was killed in the uprising of August 10, 1792, because he supported the monarchy.

Sirs, in the declaration that you believed you should put at the head of the French constitution you have established, consecrated, the rights of man and citizen. In the constitutional work that you have decreed relative to the organization of the municipalities, a work accepted by the King, you have fixed the conditions of eligibility that can be required of citizens. It would seem, Sirs, that there is nothing else left to do and that prejudices should be silent in the face of the language of the law; but an honorable member has explained to us that the *non-Catholics* of some provinces still experience harassment based on former laws, and seeing them excluded from the elections and public posts, another honorable member has protested against the effect of prejudice that persecutes some professions. This prejudice, these laws, force you to make your position clear. I have the honor to present you with the draft of a decree, and it is this draft that I defend here. I establish in it the principle that professions and religious creed can never become reasons for ineligibility. . . .

Every creed has only one test to pass in regard to the social body: it has only one examination to which it must submit, that of its morals. It is here that the adversaries of the Jewish people attack me. This people, they say, is not sociable. They are commanded to loan at usurious rates; they cannot be joined with us either in marriage or by the bonds of social interchange; our food is forbidden to them; our tables prohibited; our armies will never have Jews serving in the defense of the fatherland. The worst of these reproaches is unjust; the others are only specious. Usury is not commanded by their laws; loans at interest are forbidden between them and permitted with foreigners. . . .

But, they say to me, the Jews have their own judges and laws. I respond that is your fault and you should not allow it. We must refuse everything to the Jews as a nation and accord everything to Jews as individuals. We must withdraw recognition from their judges; they should only have our judges. We must refuse legal protection to the maintenance of the so-called laws of their Judaic organization; they should not be allowed to form in the state either a political body or an order. They must be citizens individually. But, some will say to me, they do not want to be citizens. Well then! If they do not want to be citizens, they should say so, and then, we should banish them. It is repugnant to have in the state an association of non-citizens, and a nation within the nation. . . . In short, Sirs, the presumed status of every man resident in a country is to be a citizen.

Source: *Archives parlementaires* 10 (Paris, 1878): 754–57. Translation by Lynn Hunt.

Question to Consider

■ **To what extent is this speech in defense of minority rights a reflection of the revolutionary spirit?**

from the nation rather than from tradition or divine right.

By pronouncing all *men* free and equal, the Declaration immediately created new dilemmas. Did women have equal rights with men? What about free blacks in the colonies? How could slavery be justified if all men were born free? Did religious toleration of Protestants and Jews include equal political rights? Women never received the right to vote during the French Revolution, though Protestant and Jewish men did. Women were theoretically citizens under civil law but without the right to full political participation. (See Document, "The Rights of Minorities," above.)

Some women did not accept their exclusion, viewing it as a betrayal of the promised new order. In addition to joining demonstrations, such as the march to Versailles in October 1789 (see chapter opener), women wrote petitions, published tracts, and organized political clubs to demand more participation (see the illustration on page 628). In her Declaration of the Rights of Women of 1791, writer and political activist Olympe de Gouges (1748–1793) played on the language of the official Declaration to make the point that women should also be included. She announced in Article I, "Woman is born free and lives equal to man in her rights." She also insisted that since "woman has the right to mount the scaffold," she must "equally have the right to mount the rostrum." De Gouges linked her complaints to a program of social reform in which women would have equal rights to property and public office and equal responsibilities in taxes and criminal punishment.

A Women's Club

In this gouache by the Lesueur brothers, *The Patriotic Women's Club*, the club president urges the members to contribute funds for poor patriot families. Women's clubs focused on philanthropic work but also discussed revolutionary legislation. The colorful but sober dress indicates that the women are of the middle class. *(Snark/Art Resource, NY.)*

The Constitution and the Church Unresponsive to calls for women's equality, the National Assembly turned to preparing France's first written constitution. As debates in the Assembly revealed deep political divisions, the deputies began to use terms—*left* and *right*—that would have an impact on political discussion to this day. The left—those who favored more far-reaching changes—sat on the left-hand side of the speaker's podium; the right—those who wanted to conserve elements of the old order and slow the pace of change—sat on the right-hand side. Left and right were evenly balanced in 1789, but left-wing politicians became increasingly prominent over time. The deputies gave voting rights only to white men who passed a test of wealth. Despite these limitations, France became a constitutional monarchy in which the king served as the leading state functionary. A one-house legislature was responsible for making laws. The king could postpone enactment of laws but not veto them. The deputies abolished all the old administrative divisions of the provinces and replaced them with a national system of eighty-three departments with identical administrative and legal structures (Map 19.1). All officials were elected; no offices could be bought or sold. The deputies also abolished the old taxes and replaced them with new ones that were supposed to be uniformly levied. The National Assembly had difficulty collecting taxes, however, because many people had expected a substantial cut in the tax rate. The new administrative system survived, nonetheless, and the departments are still the basic units of the French state today.

When the deputies turned to reforming the Catholic church, they created enduring conflicts. Convinced that monastic life encouraged idleness and a decline in the nation's population, the deputies outlawed any future monastic vows and encouraged monks and nuns to return to private life by offering state pensions. Motivated partly by the ongoing financial crisis, the National Assembly confiscated all the church's property and promised to pay clerical salaries in return. The Civil Constitution of the Clergy, passed in July 1790, set pay scales for the clergy and provided that the voters elect their own parish priests and bishops just as they elected other officials. The impounded property served as a guarantee for the new paper money, called assignats, issued by the government. The assignats soon became subject to inflation because the government began to sell the church lands to the highest bidders in state auctions. The sales increased the landholdings of wealthy city dwellers and prosperous peasants but cut the value of the paper money.

Faced with resistance to these changes, the National Assembly in November 1790 required all clergy to swear an oath of loyalty to the Civil Constitution of the Clergy. Pope Pius VI in Rome condemned the constitution, and half of the French clergy refused to take the oath. The oath of allegiance permanently divided the Catholic population, which had to choose between loyalty to the old church and commitment to the Revolution with its "constitutional" church. The revolutionary government lost many supporters by passing laws against the clergy who refused the oath and by forcing them into exile, deporting them forcibly, or executing them as traitors. Riots and demonstrations led by women greeted many of the oath-taking priests who replaced those who refused.

The End of Monarchy

The reorganization of the Catholic church offended Louis XVI and gave added weight to those pushing him to organize resistance. On June 20, 1791, the royal family escaped in disguise from Paris and fled toward the eastern border of France, where they hoped to gather support from Austrian emperor Leopold II, the brother of Marie-Antoinette. The plans went awry when a postmaster recognized the king from his portrait on the new French money, and the royal family was arrested at Varennes, forty miles from the Austrian Netherlands border. The National Assembly tried to depict the departure as a kidnapping, but the "flight to Varennes" touched off demonstrations in Paris against the royal family,

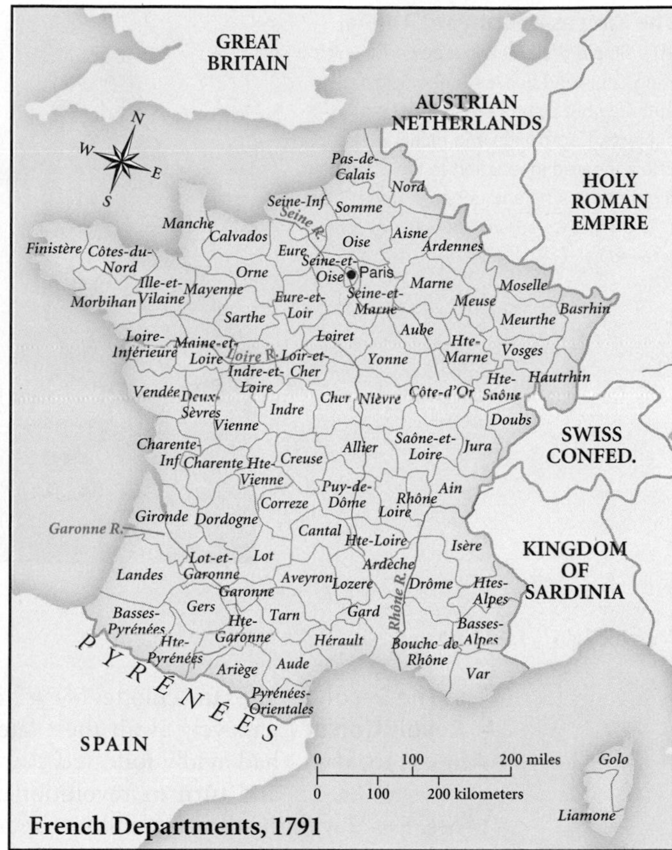

MAP 19.1 Redrawing the Map of France, 1789–1791

Before 1789, France had been divided into provinces named after the territories owned by dukes and counts in the Middle Ages. Many provinces had their own law codes and separate systems of taxation. As it began its deliberations, the new National Assembly determined to install uniform administrations and laws for the entire country. Discussion of the administrative reforms began in October 1789 and became law on February 15, 1790, when the Assembly voted to divide the provinces into eighty-three departments, with names based on their geographical characteristics: Basses-Pyrénées for the Pyrénées Mountains, Haute-Marne for the Marne River, and so on. | **How did this redrawing of the administrative map reflect the deputies' emphasis on reason over history?**

whom some now regarded as traitors. Cartoons circulated depicting the royal family as animals being returned "to the stable."

War with Austria and Prussia The constitution, finally completed in 1791, provided for the immediate election of a new legislature. In a rare act of self-denial, the deputies of the National Assembly declared themselves ineligible for the new one. Those who had experienced the Revolution firsthand now departed from the scene, opening the door to men with little previous experience in national politics. The status of the king might have remained uncertain if war had not intervened, but by early 1792 everyone seemed intent on war with Austria. Louis and Marie-Antoinette hoped that such a war would lead to the defeat of the Revolution, whereas the deputies who favored a republic believed that war would lead to the king's downfall. On April 21, 1792, Louis declared war on Austria. Prussia immediately entered on the Austrian side. Thousands of French aristocrats, including two-thirds of the army officer corps, had already emigrated, including both the king's brothers, and they were gathering along France's eastern border in expectation of joining a counterrevolutionary army.

When fighting broke out in 1792, all the powers expected a brief and relatively contained war. Instead, it would continue despite brief interruptions for the next twenty-three years. War had an immediate radicalizing effect on French politics. When the French armies proved woefully unprepared for battle, the authority of the new legislature came under fire. In June 1792, an angry crowd invaded the hall of the legislature in Paris and threatened the royal family. The Prussian commander, the duke of Brunswick, issued a manifesto announcing that Paris would be totally destroyed if the royal family suffered any violence.

The King as a Farmyard Animal
This simple print makes a powerful point: King Louis XVI has lost not only his authority but also the respect of his subjects. Engravings and etchings like this one appeared in reaction to the attempted flight of the king and queen in June 1791. *(The Granger Collection, New York—All rights reserved.)*

The Second Revolution of August 10, 1792

The sans-culottes of Paris did not passively await their fate. They had avidly followed every twist and turn in revolutionary fortunes. Faced with the threat of military retaliation and frustrated with the inaction of the deputies, on August 10, 1792, the sans-culottes organized an insurrection and attacked the Tuileries palace, the residence of the king. The king and his family had to seek refuge in the meeting room of the legislature, where the frightened deputies ordered elections for a constitutional convention. By abolishing the property qualifications for voting, the deputies instituted universal male suffrage for the first time.

When it met, the National Convention abolished the monarchy and on September 22, 1792, established the first republic in French history. The republic would answer only to the people, not to any royal authority. Many of the deputies in the Convention belonged to the devotedly republican (and therefore left-wing) **Jacobin Club**, named after the former monastery in Paris where the club first met. The Jacobin Club in Paris headed a national political network of clubs that linked all the major towns and cities. Lafayette and other liberal aristocrats who had supported the constitutional monarchy fled into exile.

Violence soon exploded again when early in September 1792 the Prussians approached Paris. Hastily gathered mobs stormed the overflowing prisons to seek out traitors who might help the enemy. In an atmosphere of near hysteria, eleven hundred inmates were killed, including many ordinary and completely innocent people. The princess of Lamballe, one of the queen's favorites, was hacked to pieces and her mutilated body displayed beneath the windows where the royal family was kept under guard. These "September massacres" showed the dark side of popular revolution, in which the common people demanded instant revenge on supposed enemies and conspirators.

The Execution of the King

The National Convention faced a dire situation. It needed to write a new constitution for the republic while fighting a war with external enemies and confronting increasing resistance at home. Many thought the Revolution had gone too far when it confiscated the properties of the church, eliminated titles of nobility, and deposed the king. The French people had never known any government other than monarchy. Only half the population could read and write at even a basic level. In this situation, symbolic actions became very important. Any public sign of monarchy was at risk, and revolutionaries soon pulled down statues of kings and burned reminders of the former regime.

The fate of Louis XVI and the future direction of the republic divided the deputies elected to the National Convention. Most of the deputies were middle-class lawyers and professionals who had developed their ardent republican beliefs in the network of Jacobin Clubs. After the fall of the monarchy in August 1792, however, the Jacobins divided into

---

Jacobin Club: A French political club formed in 1789 that inspired the formation of a national network whose members dominated the revolutionary government during the Terror.

The Execution of King Louis XVI
Louis XVI was executed by order of the National Convention on January 21, 1793. In this print, the executioner shows the severed head to the National Guards standing in orderly silence around the scaffold. *(Mary Evans Picture Library.)*

two factions. The Girondins (named after a department in southwestern France, the Gironde, which provided some of its leading orators) met regularly at the salon of Jeanne Roland, the wife of a minister. They resented the growing power of Parisian militants and tried to appeal to the departments outside of Paris. The Mountain (so called because its deputies sat in the highest seats of the National Convention), in contrast, was closely allied with the Paris militants.

The first showdown between the Girondins and the Mountain occurred during the trial of the king in December 1792. Although the Girondins agreed that the king was guilty of treason, many of them argued for clemency, exile, or a popular referendum on his fate. After a long and difficult debate, the National Convention supported the Mountain and voted by a very narrow majority to execute the king. Louis XVI went to the guillotine on January 21, 1793, sharing the fate of Charles I of England in 1649. "We have just convinced ourselves that a king is only a man," wrote one newspaper, "and that no man is above the law."

REVIEW QUESTION Why did the French Revolution turn in an increasingly radical direction after 1789?

Terror and Resistance

The execution of the king did not solve the new regime's problems. The continuing war required even more men and money, and the introduction of a national draft provoked massive resistance in some parts of France. In response to growing pressures, the National Convention named the Committee of Public Safety to supervise food distribution, direct the war effort, and root out counterrevolutionaries. The leader of the committee, **Maximilien Robespierre** (1758–1794), wanted to go beyond these stopgap measures and create a "republic of virtue," in which the government would teach, or force, citizens to become virtuous republicans through a massive program of political reeducation. Thus began the **Terror**, in which the guillotine became the

---

Maximilien Robespierre (roh behs PYEHR)**:** A lawyer from northern France who, as leader of the Committee of Public Safety, laid out the principles of a republic of virtue and of the Terror; his arrest and execution in July 1794 brought an end to the Terror.

Terror: The policy established under the direction of the Committee of Public Safety during the French Revolution to arrest dissidents and execute opponents in order to protect the republic from its enemies.

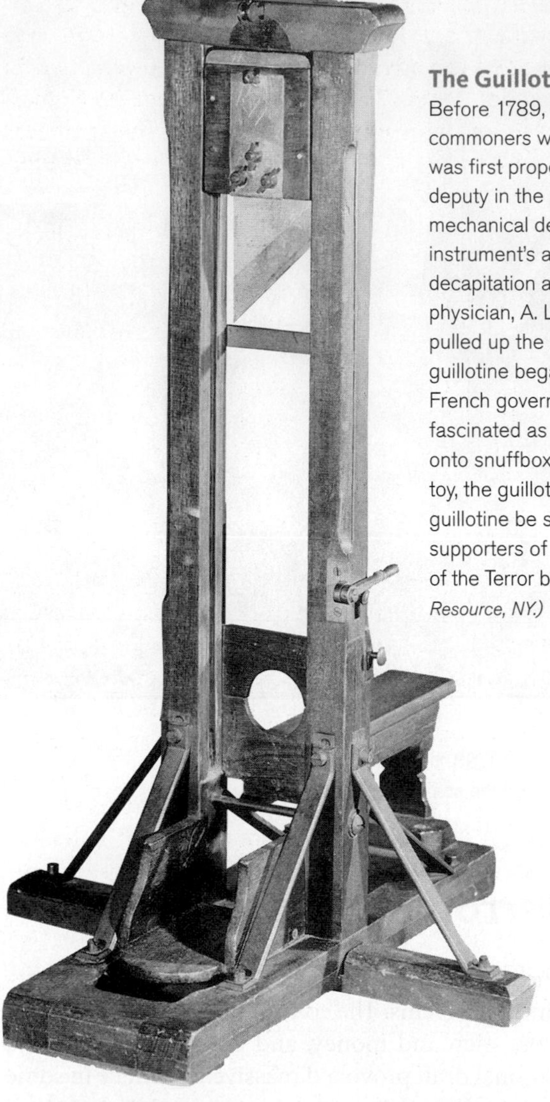

The Guillotine
Before 1789, only nobles were decapitated if condemned to death; commoners were usually hanged. Equalization of the death penalty was first proposed by J. I. Guillotin, a professor of anatomy and a deputy in the National Assembly. He also suggested that a mechanical device be constructed for decapitation, leading to the instrument's association with his name. The Assembly decreed decapitation as the death penalty in June 1791 and another physician, A. Louis, actually invented the guillotine. The executioner pulled up the blade by a cord and then released it. Use of the guillotine began in April 1792 and did not end until 1981, when the French government abolished the death penalty. The guillotine fascinated as much as it repelled. Reproduced in miniature, painted onto snuffboxes and china, worn as jewelry, and even serving as a toy, the guillotine became a part of popular culture. How could the guillotine be simultaneously celebrated as the people's avenger by supporters of the Revolution and vilified as the preeminent symbol of the Terror by opponents? *(Réunion des Musées Nationaux/Art Resource, NY.)*

most terrifying instrument of a government that suppressed almost every form of dissent (see the illustration above). These policies only increased divisions, which ultimately led to Robespierre's fall from power and to a dismantling of government by terror.

Robespierre and the Committee of Public Safety

The conflict between the more moderate Girondins and the more radical Mountain came to a head in spring 1793. Militants in Paris agitated for the removal of the deputies who had proposed a referendum on the king, and in retaliation the Girondins engineered the arrest of Jean-Paul Marat, a deputy allied with the Mountain who in his newspaper had been calling for more and more executions. Marat was acquitted, and Parisian militants marched into the National Convention on June 2, 1793, forcing the deputies to decree the arrest of their twenty-nine Girondin colleagues. The Convention consented to the establishment of paramilitary bands called "revolutionary armies" to hunt down political suspects and hoarders of grain. The deputies also agreed to speed up the operation of special revolutionary courts.

Setting the course for government and the war increasingly fell to the twelve-member Committee of Public Safety. When Robespierre was elected to the committee in July 1793, he became its guiding spirit and in effect the chief spokesman of the Revolution. A lawyer from northern France known as "the incorruptible" for his stern honesty and fierce dedication to democratic ideals, Robespierre remains one of the most controversial figures in world history because of his association with the Terror. Although he originally opposed the death penalty and the war, he was convinced that the emergency situation of 1793 required severe measures, including death for those, such as the Girondins, who opposed the committee's policies.

Like many other educated eighteenth-century men, Robespierre had read the classics of republicanism from the ancient Roman writers Tacitus and Plutarch to the Enlightenment thinkers Montesquieu and Rousseau. But he took them a step further. He defined "the theory of revolutionary government" as "the war of liberty against its enemies." He defended the people's right to democratic government, while in practice he supported many emergency measures that restricted their liberties. He personally favored a free-market economy, as did almost all middle-class deputies, but in this time of crisis he was willing to enact price controls and requisitioning. In an effort to stabilize prices, the National Convention established the General Maximum on September 29, 1793, which set limits on the prices of thirty-nine essential commodities and on wages. In a speech to the Convention, Robespierre explained the necessity of government by terror: "The first maxim of your policies must be to lead the people by reason and the people's enemies by terror. . . . Without virtue, terror is deadly; without terror, virtue is impotent." *Terror* was not an idle term; it seemed to imply that the goal of democracy justified what we now call totalitarian means, that is, the suppression of all dissent.

Through a series of desperate measures, the Committee of Public Safety set the machinery of the Terror in motion. It sent deputies out "on mission" to purge unreliable officials and organize the war effort. Revolutionary tribunals set up in Paris and provincial centers tried political suspects. In October 1793, the Revolutionary Tribunal in Paris convicted Marie-Antoinette of treason and sent her to the guillotine. The Girondin leaders and Jeanne Roland were also guillotined, as was Olympe de Gouges. The government confiscated all the property of convicted traitors.

The new republic won its greatest success on the battlefield. As of April 1793, France faced war with Austria, Prussia, Great Britain, Spain, Sardinia, and the Dutch Republic—all fearful of the impact of revolutionary ideals on their own populations. The execution of Louis XVI, in particular, galvanized European governments; according to William Pitt, the British prime minister, it was "the foulest and most atrocious act the world has ever seen." To face this daunting coalition of forces, the French republic ordered the first universal draft of men in history. Every unmarried man and childless widower between the ages of eighteen and twenty-five was declared eligible for conscription. The government also tapped a new and potent source of power—nationalist pride—in decrees mobilizing young and old alike:

> The young men will go to battle; married men will forge arms and transport provisions; women will make tents and clothing and serve in hospitals; children will make bandages; old men will get themselves carried to public places to arouse the courage of warriors and preach hatred of kings and unity of the republic.

Forges were set up in the parks and gardens of Paris to produce thousands of guns, and citizens everywhere helped collect saltpeter to make gunpowder. By the end of 1793, the French nation in arms had stopped the advance of the allied powers, and in the summer of 1794 it invaded the Austrian Netherlands and crossed the Rhine River. The army was ready to carry the gospel of revolution and republicanism to the rest of Europe.

The Republic of Virtue, 1793–1794

The program of the Terror went beyond pragmatic measures to fight the war and internal enemies to include efforts to "republicanize everything"—in other words, to effect a cultural revolution. While censoring writings deemed counterrevolutionary, the government encouraged republican art, set up civic festivals, and in some places directly attacked the churches in a campaign known as de-Christianization. In addition to drawing up plans for a new program of elementary education, the republic set about politicizing aspects of daily life, including even the measurement of space and time.

Republican Culture Refusing to tolerate opposition, the republic left no stone unturned in its endeavor to get its message across. Songs—especially the new national anthem, "La Marseillaise"—and placards, posters, pamphlets, books, engravings, paintings, sculpture, even everyday crockery, chamber pots, and playing cards conveyed revolutionary slogans and symbols. Foremost among the symbols was the figure of Liberty, which appeared on coins and bills, on letterheads and seals, and as statues in festivals. Hundreds of new plays were produced and old classics revised. To encourage the production of patriotic and republican works, the government sponsored state competitions for artists. Works of art were supposed to "awaken the public spirit and make clear how atrocious and ridiculous were the enemies of liberty and of the Republic."

At the center of this elaborate cultural campaign were the revolutionary festivals modeled on Rousseau's plans for a civic religion. The festivals first emerged in 1789 with the spontaneous planting of liberty trees in villages and towns. The Festival of Federation on July 14, 1790, marked the first anniversary of the fall of the Bastille. Under the National Convention, the well-known painter Jacques-Louis David (1748–1825), who was a deputy and an associate of Robespierre, took over festival planning. David aimed to destroy the mystique of monarchy and to make the republic sacred. His Festival of Unity on August 10, 1793, for example, celebrated the first

Representing Liberty
Liberty was represented by a female figure because in French the noun is feminine (*la liberté*). This painting from 1793–1794, by Jeanne-Louise (Nanine) Vallain, captures the usual attributes of Liberty: she is soberly seated, wearing a Roman-style toga and holding a pike with a Roman liberty cap on top. Her Roman appearance signals that she represents an abstract quality. The fact that she holds an instrument of battle suggests that women might be active participants. The Statue of Liberty in New York harbor, given by the French to the United States, is a late-nineteenth-century version of the same figure, but without any suggestion of battle. *(Nanine Vallain,* La Liberté, *Huile sur toile, 1794. Musée de la Révolution française, Vizille. © Conseil général de l'Isère/Domaine de Vizille.)*

anniversary of the overthrow of the monarchy. In front of the statue of Liberty built for the occasion, a bonfire consumed crowns and scepters symbolizing royalty while a cloud of three thousand white doves rose into the sky. This was all part of preaching the "moral order of the Republic . . . that will make us a people of brothers, a people of philosophers."

De-Christianization Some revolutionaries hoped the festival system would replace the Catholic church altogether. They initiated a campaign of **de-Christianization** that included closing churches (Protestant as well as Catholic), selling many church buildings to the highest bidder, and trying to force even those clergy who had taken the oath of loyalty to abandon their clerical vocations and marry. Great churches became storehouses for arms or grain, or their stones were sold off to contractors. The medieval statues of kings on the facade of Notre Dame cathedral were beheaded. Church bells were dismantled and church treasures melted down for government use.

In the ultimate step in de-Christianization, extremists tried to establish what they called the Cult of Reason to supplant Christianity. In Paris in the fall of 1793, a goddess of Liberty, played by an actress, presided over the Festival of Reason in Notre Dame cathedral. Local militants in other cities staged similar festivals, which alarmed deputies in the National Convention, who were wary of turning rural, devout populations against the republic. Robespierre objected to the de-Christianization campaign's atheism; he favored a Rousseau-inspired deistic religion without the supposedly superstitious trappings of Catholicism. The Committee of Public Safety halted the de-Christianization campaign, and Robespierre, with David's help, tried to institute an alternative, the Cult of the Supreme Being, in June 1794. Neither the Cult of Reason nor the Cult of the Supreme Being attracted many followers, but both show the depth of the commit-

---

de-Christianization: During the French Revolution, the campaign of extremist republicans against organized churches and in favor of a belief system based on reason.

ment to overturning the old order and all its traditional institutions.

Politicizing Daily Life In principle, the best way to ensure the future of the republic was through the education of the young. The deputy Georges-Jacques Danton (1759–1794), Robespierre's main competitor as theorist of the Revolution, maintained that "after bread, the first need of the people is education." The National Convention voted to make primary schooling free and compulsory for both boys and girls. It took control of education away from the Catholic church and tried to set up a system of state schools at both the primary and secondary levels, but it lacked trained teachers to replace those the Catholic religious orders had provided. As a result, opportunities for learning how to read and write may have diminished. In 1799, only one-fifth as many boys enrolled in the state secondary schools as had studied in church schools ten years earlier.

Although many of the ambitious republican programs failed, colors, clothing, and daily speech were all politicized. The tricolor—the combination of red, white, and blue that was to become the flag of France—was devised in July 1789, and by 1793 everyone had to wear a cockade (a badge made of ribbons) with the colors. Using the formal forms of speech—*vous* for "you"—or the title *monsieur* or *madame* might identify someone as an aristocrat; true patriots used the informal *tu* and *citoyen* or *citoyenne* ("citizen") instead. Some people changed their names or gave their children new kinds of names. Biblical and saints' names such as John, Peter, Joseph, and Mary gave way to names recalling heroes of the ancient Roman republic (Brutus, Gracchus, Cornelia), revolutionary heroes, or flowers and plants. Such changes symbolized adherence to the republic and to Enlightenment ideals rather than to Catholicism.

Even the measures of time and space were revolutionized. In October 1793, the National Convention introduced a new calendar to replace the Christian one. Its bases were reason and republican principles. Year I dated from the beginning of the republic on September 22, 1792. Twelve months of exactly thirty days each received new names derived from nature—for example, Pluviôse (roughly equivalent to February) recalled the rain (*la pluie*) of late winter. Instead of seven-day weeks, ten-day *décades* provided only one day of rest every ten days and pointedly eliminated the Sunday of the Christian calendar. The five days left at the end of the calendar year were devoted to special festivals called *sans-culottides*. The calendar remained in force for twelve years despite continuing resistance to it. More enduring was the new metric system based on units of ten that was invented to replace the hundreds of local variations in weights and measures. Other countries in Europe and throughout the world eventually adopted the metric system.

Revolutionary laws also changed the rules of family life. The state took responsibility for all family matters away from the Catholic church: people now registered births, deaths, and marriages at city hall, not the parish church. Marriage became a civil contract and as such could be broken and thereby nullified. The new divorce law of September 1792 was the most far-reaching in Europe: a couple could divorce by mutual consent or for reasons such as insanity, abandonment, battering, or criminal conviction. Thousands of men and women took advantage of the law to dissolve unhappy marriages, even though the pope had condemned the measure. (In 1816, the government revoked the right to divorce, and not until the 1970s did French divorce laws return to the principles of the 1792 legislation.) In one of its most influential actions, the National Convention passed a series of laws that created equal inheritance among all children in the family, including girls. The father's right to favor one child, especially the oldest male, was considered aristocratic and hence antirepublican.

Resisting the Revolution

By intruding into religion, culture, and daily life, the republic inevitably provoked resistance. Shouting curses against the republic, uprooting liberty trees, carrying statues of the Virgin Mary in procession, hiding a priest who would not take the oath, singing a royalist song—all these expressed dissent with the new symbols, rituals, and policies. Resistance also took more violent forms, from riots over food shortages or religious policies to assassination and full-scale civil war.

Women's Resistance Many women, in particular, suffered from the hard conditions of life that persisted in this time of war, and they had their own ways of voicing discontent. Long bread lines in the cities exhausted the patience of women, and police spies reported their constant grumbling, which occasionally turned into spontaneous demonstrations or riots over high prices or food shortages. Women also organized their fellow parishioners to refuse to hear Mass offered by the "constitutional" priests, and they protected the priests who would not sign the oath of loyalty.

Other forms of resistance were more individual. One young woman, Charlotte Corday, assassinated the outspoken deputy Jean-Paul Marat in July 1793.

Corday fervently supported the Girondins, and she considered it her patriotic duty to kill the deputy who, in the columns of his paper, had constantly demanded more heads and more blood. Marat was immediately eulogized as a great martyr, and Corday went to the guillotine vilified as a monster but confident that she had "avenged many innocent victims."

Rebellion and Civil War Organized resistance broke out in many parts of France. The arrest of the Girondin deputies in June 1793 sparked insurrections in several departments. After the government retook the city of Lyon, one of the centers of the revolt, the deputy on mission ordered sixteen hundred houses demolished and the name of the city changed to Liberated City. Special courts sentenced almost two thousand people to death.

In the Vendée region of western France, resistance turned into a bloody and prolonged civil war. Between March and December 1793, peasants, artisans, and weavers joined under noble leadership to form a "Catholic and Royal Army." One rebel group explained its motives: "They [the republicans] have killed our king, chased away our priests, sold the goods of our church, eaten everything we have and now they want to take our bodies [in the draft]." The uprising took two different forms: in the Vendée itself, a counterrevolutionary army organized to fight the republic; in nearby Brittany, resistance took the form of guerrilla bands, which united to attack a target and then quickly melted into the countryside. Great Britain provided money and underground contacts for these attacks, which were almost always aimed at towns. In many ways this was a civil war between town and country, for the townspeople were the ones who supported the Revolution and bought church lands for themselves. The peasants had gained most of what they wanted in 1789 with the abolition of seigneurial dues, and they resented the government's demands for money and manpower and actions taken against their local clergy.

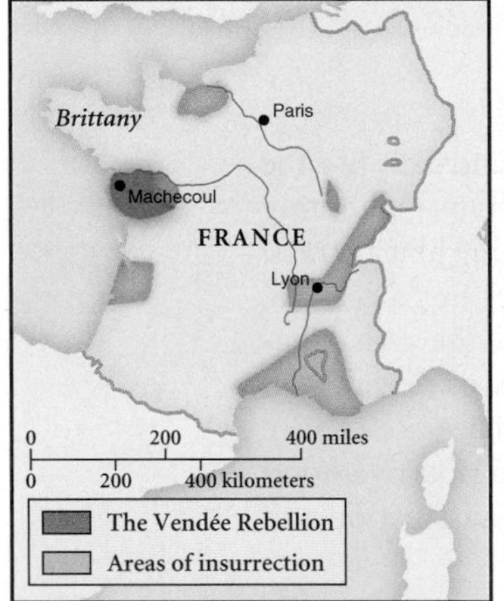

The Vendée Rebellion, 1793

For several months in 1793, the Vendée rebels stormed the largest towns in the region. Both sides committed horrible atrocities. At the small town of Machecoul, for example, the rebels massacred five hundred republicans, including administrators and National Guard members; many were tied together, shoved into freshly dug graves, and shot. By the fall, however, republican soldiers had turned back the rebels. A republican general wrote to the Committee of Public Safety claiming, "There is no more Vendée, citizens, it has perished under our free sword along with its women and children. . . . Following the orders that you gave me I have crushed children under the feet of horses, massacred women who at least . . . will engender no more brigands." His claims of complete victory soon turned hollow, however, as fighting continued.

"Infernal columns" of republican troops marched through the region to restore control, military courts ordered thousands executed, and republican soldiers massacred thousands of others. In one especially gruesome incident, the deputy Jean-Baptiste Carrier supervised the drowning of some two thousand Vendée rebels, including a number of priests. Barges loaded with prisoners were floated into the Loire River near Nantes and then sunk. Controversy still rages about the rebellion's death toll because no accurate count could be taken. Estimates of rebel deaths alone range from about 20,000 to higher than 250,000. Many thousands of republican soldiers and civilians also lost their lives in fighting that continued on and off for years. Even the low estimates reveal the carnage of this catastrophic confrontation between the republic and its opponents.

The Fall of Robespierre and the End of the Terror

In the atmosphere of fear of conspiracy that the outbreaks of rebellion fueled, Robespierre tried simultaneously to exert the National Convention's control over popular political activities and to weed out opposition among the deputies. As a result, the Terror intensified until July 1794, when a group of deputies joined within the Convention to order the arrest and execution of Robespierre and his followers. The Convention then ordered elections and drew up a new republican constitution that gave executive power to five directors. This "Directory government" maintained power during four years of seesaw battles between royalists and former Jacobins.

The Revolution Devours Its Own In the fall of 1793, the National Convention cracked down on popular clubs and societies. First to be suppressed were women's political clubs. Founded in early 1793, the Society of Revolutionary Republican Women played a very active part in sans-culottes politics. The society urged harsher measures against the republic's enemies and insisted that women have a voice in politics even if they did not have the vote. Women had set up their own clubs in many provincial towns and also attended the meetings of local men's organizations. Using traditional arguments about women's inherent unsuitability for politics, the deputies abolished women's political clubs. The closing of women's clubs marked an important turning point in the Revolution. From then on, the sans-culottes and their political organizations came increasingly under the thumb of the Jacobin deputies in the National Convention.

In the spring of 1794, the Committee of Public Safety moved against its critics among leaders in Paris and deputies in the National Convention itself. First, a handful of "ultrarevolutionaries"—a collection of local Parisian politicians—were arrested and executed. Next came the other side, the "indulgents," so called because they favored a moderation of the Terror. Included among them was the deputy Danton, himself once a member of the Committee of Public Safety and a friend of Robespierre. Danton was the Revolution's most flamboyant orator and, unlike Robespierre, a high-living, high-spending, excitable politician. At every critical turning point in national politics, his booming voice had swayed opinion. Now, under pressure from the Committee of Public Safety, the Revolutionary Tribunal convicted him and his friends of treason and sentenced them to death.

"The Revolution," as one of the Girondin victims of 1793 had remarked, "was devouring its own children." Even after the major threats to the Committee of Public Safety's power had been eliminated, the Terror not only continued but worsened. A law passed in June 1794 denied the accused the right of legal counsel, reduced the number of jurors necessary for conviction, and allowed only two judgments: acquittal or death. The category of political crimes expanded to include "slandering patriotism" and "seeking to inspire discouragement." Ordinary people risked the guillotine if they expressed any discontent. The rate of executions in Paris rose from five a day in the spring of 1794 to twenty-six a day in the summer. The political atmosphere darkened even though the military situation improved. At the end of June, the French armies decisively defeated the main Austrian army and advanced through the Austrian Netherlands to Brussels and Antwerp. The emergency measures for fighting the war were working, yet Robespierre and his inner circle had made so many enemies that they could not afford to loosen the grip of the Terror.

The Terror hardly touched many parts of France, but overall the experience was undeniably traumatic. Across the country, the official Terror cost the lives of at least 40,000 French people, most of them living in the regions of major insurrections or near the borders with foreign enemies, where suspicion of collaboration ran high. As many as 300,000 French people—1 out of every 50—went to prison as suspects between March 1793 and August 1794. The toll for the aristocracy and the clergy was especially high. Many leading nobles perished under the guillotine, and thousands emigrated. Thirty thousand to forty thousand clergy who refused the oath left the country, at least two thousand (including many nuns) were executed, and thousands were imprisoned. The clergy were singled out in particular in the

Major Events of the French Revolution

May 5, 1789	The Estates General opens at Versailles
June 17, 1789	The Third Estate decides to call itself the National Assembly
June 20, 1789	"Tennis court oath" shows determination of deputies to carry out a constitutional revolution
July 14, 1789	Fall of the Bastille
August 4, 1789	National Assembly abolishes "feudalism"
August 26, 1789	National Assembly passes Declaration of the Rights of Man and Citizen
October 5–6, 1789	Women march to Versailles and are joined by men in bringing the royal family back to Paris
July 12, 1790	Civil Constitution of the Clergy
June 20, 1791	Louis and Marie-Antoinette attempt to flee in disguise and are captured at Varennes
April 20, 1792	Declaration of war on Austria
August 10, 1792	Insurrection in Paris and attack on Tuileries palace lead to removal of king's authority
September 2–6, 1792	Murder of prisoners in "September massacres" in Paris
September 22, 1792	Establishment of the republic
January 21, 1793	Execution of Louis XVI
March 11, 1793	Beginning of uprising in the Vendée
May 31–June 2, 1793	Insurrection leading to arrest of the Girondins
July 27, 1793	Robespierre named to the Committee of Public Safety
September 29, 1793	Convention establishes General Maximum on prices and wages
October 16, 1793	Execution of Marie-Antoinette
February 4, 1794	Slavery abolished in the French colonies
March 13–24, 1794	Arrest, trial, and executions of so-called ultrarevolutionaries
March 30–April 5, 1794	Arrest, trial, and executions of Danton and his followers
July 27, 1794	Arrest of Robespierre and his supporters (executed July 28–29); beginning of end of the Terror
October 26, 1795	Directory government takes office
April 1796–October 1797	Succession of Italian victories by Bonaparte

civil war zones: 135 priests were massacred at Lyon in November 1793, and 83 were shot in one day during the Vendée revolt. Yet many victims of the Terror were peasants or sans-culottes.

The final crisis of the Terror came in July 1794. Conflicts within the Committee of Public Safety and the National Convention left Robespierre isolated. On July 27, 1794 (the ninth of Thermidor, Year II, according to the revolutionary calendar), Robespierre appeared before the Convention with yet another list of deputies to be arrested. Many feared they would be named, and they shouted him down and ordered him arrested along with his followers on the committee, the president of the Revolutionary Tribunal in Paris, and the commander of the Parisian National Guard. An armed uprising led by the Paris city government failed to save Robespierre when most of the National Guard took the side of the Convention. Robespierre tried to kill himself with a pistol but only broke his jaw. The next day he and scores of followers went to the guillotine.

The Thermidorian Reaction and the Directory, 1794–1799

The men who led the attack on Robespierre in Thermidor (July 1794) did not intend to reverse all his policies, but that happened nonetheless because of a violent backlash known as the **Thermidorian Reaction**. As most of the instruments of terror were dismantled, newspapers attacked the Robespierrists as "tigers thirsting for human blood." The new government released hundreds of suspects and arranged a temporary truce in the Vendée. It purged Jacobins from local bodies and replaced them with their opponents. It arrested some of the most notorious "terrorists" in the National Convention, such as Carrier, and put them to death. Within the year, the new leaders abolished the Revolutionary Tribunal and closed the Jacobin Club in Paris. Popular demonstrations met severe repression. In southeastern France, in particular, the "White Terror" replaced the Jacobins' "Red Terror." Former officials and local Jacobin leaders were harassed, beaten, and often murdered by paramilitary bands who had tacit support from the new authorities. Those who remained in the National Convention prepared yet another constitution in 1795, setting up a two-house legislature and an executive body—the Directory, headed by five directors.

The Directory regime tenuously held on to power for four years, all the while trying to fend off challenges from the remaining Jacobins and the resurgent royalists. The puritanical atmosphere of the Terror gave way to the pursuit of pleasure—low-cut dresses of transparent materials, the reappearance of prostitutes in the streets, fancy dinner parties, and "victims' balls" where guests wore red ribbons around their necks as reminders of the guillotine. Bands of young men dressed in knee breeches and rich fabrics picked fights with known Jacobins and disrupted theater performances with loud antirevolutionary songs. All over France, people petitioned to reopen churches closed during the Terror. If necessary, they broke into a church to hold services with a priest who had been in hiding or a lay schoolteacher who was willing to say Mass.

Although the Terror had ended, the revolution had not. In 1794, the most democratic and most repressive phases of the Revolution both ended at once. Between 1795 and 1799, the republic endured in France, but it directed a war effort abroad that would ultimately bring to power the man who would dismantle the republic itself.

REVIEW QUESTION What factors can explain the Terror? To what extent was it simply a response to a national emergency or a reflection of deeper problems within the French Revolution?

Revolution on the March

War raged almost constantly from 1792 to 1815. At one time or another, and sometimes all at once, France faced every principal power in Europe. The French republic—and later the French Empire under its supreme commander, Emperor Napoleon Bonaparte—proved an even more formidable opponent than the France of Louis XIV. New means of mobilizing and organizing soldiers enabled the French to dominate Europe for a generation. The influence of the French Revolution as a political model and the threat of French military conquest combined to challenge the traditional order in Europe and offer new prospects to the rest of the world as well.

Arms and Conquests

The powers allied against France squandered their best chance to triumph in early 1793, when the French armies verged on chaos because of the emi-

Thermidorian Reaction: The violent backlash against the rule of Robespierre that dismantled the Terror and punished Jacobins and their supporters.

gration of noble army officers and the problems of integrating new draftees. By the end of 1793, the French had a huge and powerful fighting force of 700,000 men. But the army still faced many problems in the field. As many as a third of the recent draftees deserted before or during battle. At times the soldiers were fed only moldy bread, and if their pay was late, they sometimes resorted to pillaging and looting. Generals might pay with their lives if they lost a key battle and their loyalty to the Revolution came under suspicion.

France nevertheless had one overwhelming advantage: those soldiers who agreed to serve fought for a revolution that they and their brothers and sisters had helped make. The republic was their government, and the army was in large measure theirs, too; many officers had risen through the ranks by skill and talent rather than by inheriting or purchasing their positions. One young peasant boy wrote to his parents, "Either you will see me return bathed in glory, or you will have a son who is a worthy citizen of France who knows how to die for the defense of his country."

When the French armies invaded the Austrian Netherlands and crossed the Rhine in the summer of 1794, they proclaimed a war of liberation. Middle-class people near the northern and eastern borders of France reacted most positively to the French invasion (Map 19.2). In the Austrian Netherlands, Mainz, Savoy, and Nice, French officers organized Jacobin Clubs that attracted locals. The clubs petitioned for annexation to France, and French legislation was then introduced, including the abolition of seigneurial dues. As the French annexed more and more territory, however, "liberated" people in many places began to view them as an army of occupation. Despite resistance, especially in the Austrian Netherlands, these areas remained part of France until 1815, and the legal changes were permanent.

The Directory government that came to power in 1795 launched an even more aggressive policy of creating semi-independent "sister republics" wherever the armies succeeded. When Prussia declared neutrality in 1795, the French armies swarmed into the Dutch Republic, abolished the stadholderate, and—with the revolutionary penchant for

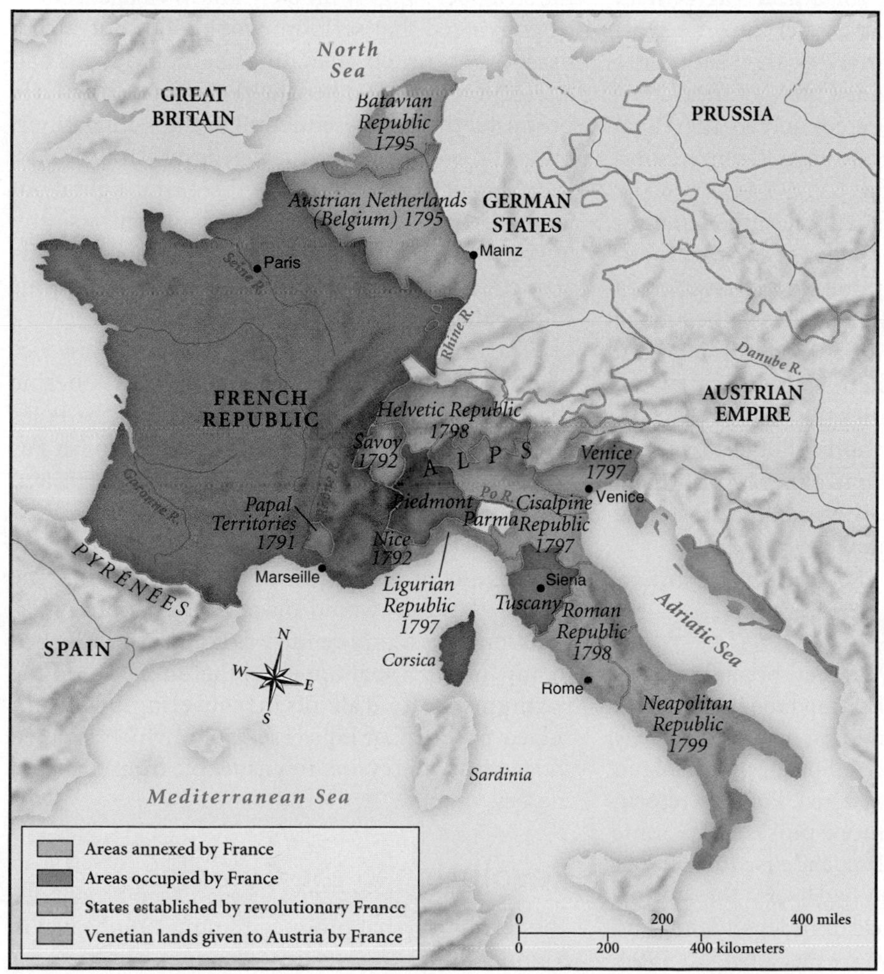

MAP 19.2 French Expansion, 1791–1799
The influence of the French Revolution on neighboring territories is dramatically evident in this map. The French directly annexed the papal territories in southern France in 1791, Nice and Savoy in 1792, and the Austrian Netherlands in 1795. They set up a series of sister republics in the former Dutch Republic and in various Italian states. Local people did not always welcome these changes. For example, the French made the Dutch pay a huge war indemnity, support a French occupying army of 25,000 soldiers, and give up some southern territories. The sister republics faced a future of subordination to French national interests.

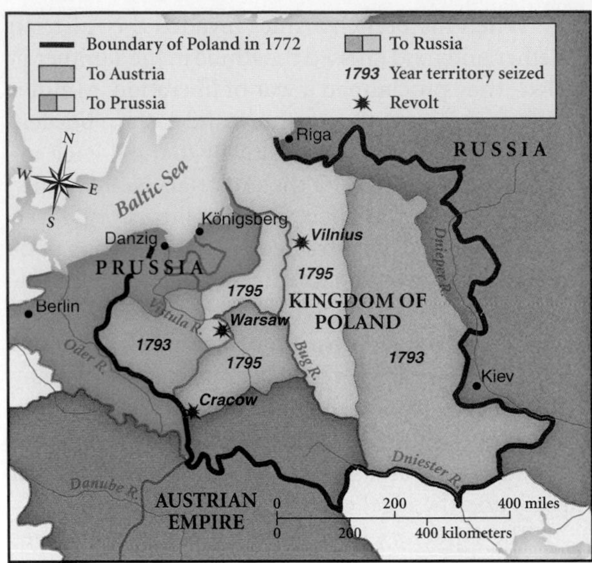

MAP 19.3 The Second and Third Partitions of Poland, 1793 and 1795
In 1793, Prussia took over territory that included 1.1 million Poles while Russia gained 3 million new inhabitants. Austria gave up any claims to Poland in exchange for help from Russia and Prussia in acquiring Bavaria. In the final division of 1795, Prussia absorbed an additional 900,000 Polish subjects, including those in Warsaw; Austria incorporated 1 million Poles and the city of Cracow; Russia gained another 2 million Poles. The three powers determined never to use the term *Kingdom of Poland* again. | **How had Poland become such a prey to the other powers?**

renaming—created the new Batavian Republic, a satellite of France. The brilliant young general Napoleon Bonaparte gained a reputation by defeating the Austrian armies in northern Italy in 1797 and then created the Cisalpine Republic. Next he overwhelmed Venice and then handed it over to the Austrians in exchange for a peace agreement that lasted less than two years. After the French attacked the Swiss cantons in 1798, they set up the Helvetic Republic and curtailed many of the Catholic church's privileges. They conquered the Papal States in 1798 and installed a Roman Republic, forcing the pope to flee to Siena.

The revolutionary wars had an immediate impact on European life at all levels of society. Thousands of men died in every country involved, with perhaps as many as 200,000 casualties in the French armies alone in 1794 and 1795. More soldiers died in hospitals as a result of their wounds than on the battlefields. Constant warfare hampered world commerce and especially disrupted French overseas shipping. Times were now hard almost everywhere, because the dislocations of internal and external commerce provoked constant shortages.

Poland Extinguished, 1793–1795

France had survived in 1793 in part because its enemies were busy elsewhere. Fearing French influence, Prussia joined Russia in dividing up generous new slices of territory in the second partition of Poland (Map 19.3). As might be expected, Poland's reform movement became even more pro-French. Some leaders fled abroad, including Tadeusz Kościuszko (1746–1817), an officer who had been a foreign volunteer in the War of American Independence and who now escaped to Paris. In the spring of 1794, Kościuszko returned from France to lead a nationalist revolt.

The Polish cities of Cracow and Warsaw, and the old Lithuanian capital, Vilnius, responded with uprisings. Kościuszko faced an immediate, insoluble dilemma. He could win only if the peasants joined the struggle—highly unlikely unless villagers could be convinced that serfdom would end. But such a drastic step risked alienating the nobles who had started the revolt. So Kościuszko compromised. He promised the serfs a reduction of their obligations, but not freedom itself. A few peasant bands joined the insurrection, but most let their lords fight it out alone. Urban workers displayed more enthusiasm; at Warsaw, for example, a mob hanged several Russian collaborators, including an archbishop in his full regalia.

The uprising failed. Kościuszko won a few victories, but when the Russian empress Catherine the Great's forces regrouped, they routed the Poles and Lithuanians. Kościuszko and other Polish Patriot leaders languished for years in Russian and Austrian prisons. Taking no further chances, Russia, Prussia, and Austria wiped Poland completely from the map in the third partition (1795). "The Polish question" would plague international relations for more than a century as Polish rebels flocked to any international upheaval that might undo the partitions. Beyond all this maneuvering lay the unsolved problem of Polish serfdom, which isolated the nation's gentry and townspeople from the rural masses.

Revolution in the Colonies

The revolution that produced so much upheaval in continental Europe transformed life in France's

DOCUMENT

Address on Abolishing the Slave Trade (February 5, 1790)

Founded in 1788, the Society of the Friends of Blacks agitated for the abolition of the slave trade. Among its members were many who became leaders of the French Revolution. In a pamphlet titled Address to the National Assembly in Favor of the Abolition of the Slave Trade, *the Friends of Blacks denied that they wanted to abolish slavery altogether and argued only for the abolition of the slave trade. The pamphlet raised the prospect of a slave revolt, which in fact broke out in St. Domingue in 1791. As a consequence, many planters and their allies accused the society of fomenting the revolt.*

You have declared them, these rights; you have engraved on an immortal monument that all men are born and remain free and equal in rights; you have restored to the French people these rights that despotism had for so long despoiled; . . . you have broken the chains of feudalism that still degraded a good number of our fellow citizens; you have announced the destruction of all the stigmatizing distinctions that religious or political prejudices introduced into the great family of humankind. . . .

We are not asking you to restore to French blacks those political rights which alone, nevertheless, attest to and maintain the dignity of man; we are not even asking for their liberty. No; slander, bought no doubt with the greed of the shipowners, ascribes that scheme to us and spreads it everywhere; they want to stir up everyone against us, provoke the planters and their numerous creditors, who take alarm even at gradual emancipation. They want to alarm all the French, to whom they depict the prosperity of the colonies as inseparable from the slave trade and the perpetuity of slavery.

. . . The immediate emancipation of the blacks would not only be a fatal operation for the colonies; it would even be a deadly gift for the blacks, in the state of abjection and incompetence to which cupidity has reduced them. It would be to abandon to themselves and without assistance children in the cradle or mutilated and impotent beings.

It is therefore not yet time to demand that liberty; we ask only that one cease butchering thousands of blacks regularly every year in order to take hundreds of captives; we ask that henceforth cease the prostitution, the profaning of the French name, used to authorize these thefts, these atrocious murders; we demand in a word the abolition of the slave trade. . . .

In regard to the colonists, we will demonstrate to you that if they need to recruit blacks in Africa to sustain the population of the colonies at the same level, it is because they wear out the blacks with work, whippings, and starvation; that, if they treated them with kindness and as good fathers of families, these blacks would multiply and that this population, always growing, would increase cultivation and prosperity. . . .

If some motive might on the contrary push them [the blacks] to insurrection, might it not be the indifference of the National Assembly about their lot? Might it not be the insistence on weighing them down with chains, when one consecrates everywhere this eternal axiom: *that all men are born free and equal in rights*. So then therefore there would only be fetters and gallows for the blacks while good fortune glimmers only for the whites? Have no doubt, our happy revolution must re-electrify the blacks whom vengeance and resentment have electrified for so long, and it is not with punishments that the effect of this upheaval will be repressed. From one insurrection badly pacified will twenty others be born, of which one alone can ruin the colonists forever.

Source: *Adresse à l'Assemblée Nationale, pour l'abolition de la traite des noirs* (Paris: La Société des Amis des Noirs de Paris, February 1790), 1–4, 10–11, 17, 19–22. Translation by Lynn Hunt.

Question to Consider

- **Why did the authors of this pamphlet support an end to the slave trade but oppose an immediate, outright end to slavery itself? How do you respond to that aspect of their argument?**

Caribbean colonies, too. These colonies were crucial to the French economy. Twice the size in land area of the neighboring British colonies, they also produced nearly twice as much revenue in exports. The slave population had doubled in the French colonies in the twenty years before 1789. St. Domingue (present-day Haiti) was the most important French colony. Occupying the western half of the island of Hispaniola, it was inhabited not only by 465,000 slaves and 30,000 whites but also by 28,000 free people of color, whose primary job was to apprehend runaway slaves and ensure plantation security.

Despite the efforts of a Paris club called the Friends of Blacks, most French revolutionaries did not consider slavery a pressing problem. As one deputy explained, "This regime [in the colonies] is oppressive, but it gives a livelihood to several million Frenchmen. This regime is barbarous but a still greater barbarity will result if you interfere with it without the necessary knowledge." (See Document, "Address on Abolishing the Slave Trade," above.)

In August 1791, however, the slaves in northern St. Domingue, inspired by the slogan "Listen to the voice of Liberty which speaks in the hearts of all," organized a large-scale revolt. To restore authority over the slaves, the deputies in Paris granted civil and political rights to the free blacks. This action infuriated white planters and merchants, who in 1793 signed an agreement with Great Britain, now France's enemy in war, declaring British sovereignty over St. Domingue. To complicate matters further, Spain, which controlled the rest of the island and had entered on Great Britain's side in the war with France, offered freedom to individual slave rebels who joined the Spanish armies as long as they agreed to maintain the slave regime for the other blacks.

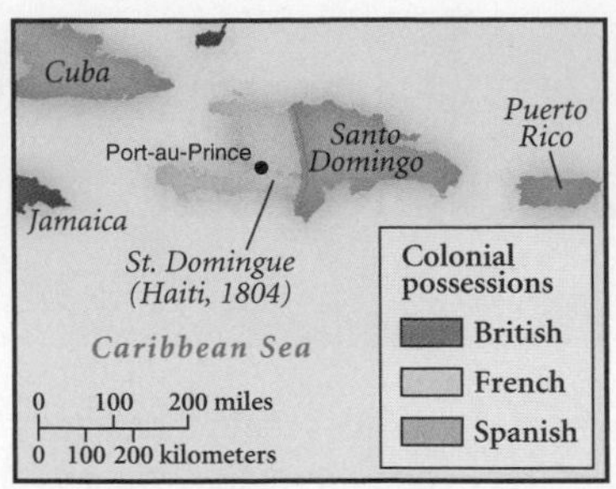

St. Domingue on the Eve of the Revolt, 1791

The few thousand French republican troops on St. Domingue were outnumbered, and to prevent complete military disaster, the French commissioner freed all the slaves in his jurisdiction in August 1793 without permission from the government in Paris. In February 1794, the National Convention formally abolished slavery and granted full rights to all black men in the colonies. These actions had the desired effect. One of the ablest black generals allied with the Spanish, the ex-slave François Dominique Toussaint L'Ouverture (1743–1803), changed sides and committed his troops to the French (see the illustration below). The French eventually appointed Toussaint governor of St. Domingue as a reward for his efforts. As former plantation owners fled to the new United States, slave owners there feared the prospect of spreading revolt.

The vicious fighting and the flight of whites left St. Domingue's economy in ruins. In 1800, the plantations produced one-fifth of what they had in 1789. In the zones Toussaint controlled, army officers or government officials took over the great estates and kept all those working in agriculture under military discipline. The former slaves were bound to their estates like serfs and forced to work the plantations in exchange for an autonomous family life and the right to maintain personal garden plots.

Toussaint remained in charge until 1802, when Napoleon sent French armies to regain control of the island. They arrested Toussaint and transported him to France, where he died in prison. His arrest prompted the English poet William Wordsworth to write of him:

> There's not a breathing of the common wind
> That will forget thee; thou hast great allies;
> Thy friends are exultations, agonies,
> And love, and man's unconquerable mind.

Toussaint L'Ouverture

The leader of the St. Domingue slave uprising appears on horseback, in his general's uniform, sword in hand. His depiction in this colored print from the early nineteenth century makes him seem much like other military heroes from the time, including Napoleon Bonaparte. *(Bibliothèque nationale, Paris, France/Archives Charmet/The Bridgeman Art Library International.)*

The English Rebuttal

In this caricature, James Gillray satirizes the French version of liberty. Gillray produced thousands of political caricatures. How would you interpret the message of this print? *(© The Trustees of the British Museum/Art Resource, NY.)*

Toussaint became a hero to abolitionists everywhere, a potent symbol of black struggles to win freedom. Napoleon attempted to restore slavery, as he had in the other French Caribbean colonies of Guadeloupe and Martinique, but the remaining black generals defeated his armies and in 1804 proclaimed the Republic of Haiti.

Worldwide Reactions to Revolutionary Change

As the example of the colonies shows, the French Revolution inflamed politics and social relations far beyond Europe. Citizens of the new United States witnessed more celebrations of the French Revolution between 1792 and 1796 than of Washington's birthday or even Independence Day, but the French Revolution soon became one of the most divisive issues in American politics. Thomas Jefferson wrote in January 1793 that "the liberty of the whole earth" depended on its success; John Adams, in contrast, believed that the French Revolution had set back human progress hundreds of years. In India, the ruler of the southern kingdom of Mysore, Tipu Sultan, planted a liberty tree and set up a Jacobin Club in the futile hope of gaining French allies against the British. Most other Muslim rulers, however, viewed the conflict as an obscure dispute between Christians. Views within Europe and the Americas evolved over time, and more and more people came to see the Revolution and especially the Terror as deeply problematic. (See "Contrasting Views," page 644.)

Many had greeted the events of 1789 with unabashed enthusiasm. The English Unitarian minister Richard Price had exulted, "Behold, the light . . . after setting AMERICA free, reflected to FRANCE, and there kindled into a blaze that lays despotism in ashes, and warms and illuminates EUROPE." Democrats and reformers from many countries flooded

CONTRASTING VIEWS

Perspectives on the French Revolution

Contemporaries instantly grasped the cataclysmic significance of the French Revolution and began to argue about its lessons for their own countries. A member of the British Parliament, Edmund Burke ignited a firestorm of controversy with his Reflections on the Revolution in France *(Document 1). He condemned the French revolutionaries for attempting to build a government on abstract reasoning rather than taking historical traditions and customs into account; his book provided a foundation for the doctrine known as conservatism, which argued for "conserving" the traditional foundations of society and avoiding the pitfalls of radical or revolutionary change. Burke's views provoked a strong response from the English political agitator Thomas Paine. Paine's pamphlet* Common Sense *(1776) had helped inspire the British North American colonies to demand independence from Great Britain. In* The Rights of Man *(Document 2), written fifteen years later, Paine attacked the traditional order as fundamentally unjust and defended the idea of a revolution to uphold rights. Joseph de Maistre, an aristocratic opponent of both the Enlightenment and the French Revolution, put the conservative attack on the French Revolution into a deeply religious and absolutist framework (Document 3). In contrast, Anne-Louise-Germaine de Staël, an opponent of Napoleon and one of the most influential intellectuals of the early nineteenth century, took the view that the violence of the Revolution had been the product of generations of superstition and arbitrary rule, that is, rule by an absolutist Catholic church and monarchical government (Document 4).*

1. Edmund Burke, *Reflections on the Revolution in France* (1790)

An Irish-born supporter of the American colonists in their opposition to the British Parliament, Edmund Burke (1729–1797) opposed the French Revolution. He argued the case for tradition, continuity, and gradual reform based on practical experience—what he called "a sure principle of conservation."

Can I now congratulate the same nation [France] upon its freedom? Is it because liberty in the abstract may be classed amongst the blessings of mankind, that I am seriously to felicitate a madman, who has escaped from the protecting restraint and wholesome darkness of his cell, on his restoration to the enjoyment of light and liberty? Am I to congratulate an highwayman and murderer, who has broke prison, upon the recovery of his natural rights? . . .

Government is not made in virtue of natural rights, which may and do exist in total independence of it; and exist in much greater clearness, and in a much greater degree of abstract perfection: but their abstract perfection is their practical defect. By having a right to every thing they want every thing. . . . The science of constructing a commonwealth, or renovating it, or reforming it, is, like every other experimental science, not to be taught *a priori* [based on theory rather than on experience]. Nor is it a short experience that can instruct us in that practical science; because the real effects of moral causes are not always immediate; but that which in the first instance is prejudicial may be excellent in its remoter operation; and its excellence may arise even from the ill effects it produces in the beginning. . . .

In the groves of *their* academy, at the end of every visto [vista], you see nothing but the gallows. Nothing is left which engages the affections on the part of the commonwealth. . . . To make us love our country, our country ought to be lovely.

Source: *Two Classics of the French Revolution:* Reflections on the Revolution in France *(Edmund Burke) and* The Rights of Man *(Thomas Paine)* (New York: Doubleday Anchor Books, 1973), 19, 71–74, 90–91.

2. Thomas Paine, The Rights of Man (1791)

In his reply to Burke, The Rights of Man, *which sold 200,000 copies in two years, Thomas Paine (1737–1809) defended the idea of reform based on reason, advocated a concept of universal human rights, and attacked the excesses of privilege and tradition in Great Britain. Elected as a deputy to the French National Convention in 1793 in recognition of his writings in favor of the French Revolution, Paine narrowly escaped condemnation as an associate of the Girondins.*

Before anything can be reasoned upon to a conclusion, certain facts, principles, or data, to reason from, must be established, admitted, or denied. Mr. Burke, with his usual outrage, abuses the *Declaration of the Rights of Man*, published by the National Assembly of France, as the basis on which the Constitution of France is built. This he calls "paltry and blurred sheets of paper about the rights of man."

Does Mr. Burke mean to deny that *man* has any rights? If he does, then he must mean that there are no such things as rights any where, and that he has none himself; for who is there in the world but man? . . .

Hitherto we have spoken only (and that but in part) of the natural rights of man. We have now to consider the civil rights of man, and to show how the one originates from the other. Man did not enter into society to become *worse* than he was before, nor to have fewer rights than he had before, but to have those rights better secured. His natural rights are the foundation of all his civil rights. . . .

A constitution is not a thing in name only, but in fact. It has not an ideal, but a real existence; and wherever it cannot be produced in a visible form, there is none. A constitution is a thing *antecedent* to a government, and a government is only the creature of a constitution. The constitution of a country is not the act of its government, but of the people constituting a government. . . .

Can then Mr. Burke produce the English Constitution? If he cannot, we may fairly conclude, that though it has been so much talked about, no such thing as a constitution exists, or ever did exist, and consequently that the people have yet a constitution to form.

Source: *Two Classics of the French Revolution:* Reflections on the Revolution in France *(Edmund Burke) and* The Rights of Man *(Thomas Paine)* (New York: Doubleday Anchor Books, 1973), 302, 305–6, 309.

3. Joseph De Maistre, *Considerations on France* (1797)

An aristocrat born in Savoy, Joseph de Maistre (1753–1821) believed in reform but he passionately opposed both the Enlightenment and the French Revolution as destructive to good order. He believed that Protestants, Jews, lawyers, journalists, and scientists all threatened the social order because they questioned the need for absolute obedience to authority in matters both religious and political. De Maistre set the foundations for reactionary conservatism, a conservatism that defended throne and altar.

This consideration especially makes me think that the French Revolution is a great epoch and that its consequences, in all kinds of ways, will be felt far beyond the time of its explosion and the limits of its birthplace. . . .

There is a satanic quality to the French Revolution that distinguishes it from everything we have ever seen or anything we are ever likely to see in the future. Recall the great assemblies, Robespierre's speech against the priesthood, the solemn apostasy [renunciation of vows] of the clergy, the desecration of objects of worship, the installation of the goddess of reason, and that multitude of extraordinary actions by which the provinces sought to outdo Paris. All this goes beyond the ordinary circle of crime and seems to belong to another world.

Source: Joseph de Maistre, *Considerations on France*, trans. Richard A. Lebrun (Cambridge: Cambridge University Press, 1994), 21, 41.

4. Anne-Louise-Germaine de Staël, *Considerations on the Main Events of the French Revolution* (1818)

De Staël published her views long after the Revolution was over, but she had lived through the events herself. She was the daughter of Jacques Necker, Louis XVI's Swiss Protestant finance minister. Necker's dismissal in July 1789 had sparked the attack on the Bastille. De Staël published novels, literary tracts, and memoirs and became one of the best-known writers of the nineteenth century. In her writings she defended the Enlightenment; though she opposed the violence unleashed by the Revolution, she traced it back to the excesses of monarchical government. (See her portrait on page 659.)

Once the people were freed from their harness there is no doubt that they were in a position to commit any kind of crime. But how can we explain their depravity? The government we are now supposed to miss so sorely [the former monarchy] had had plenty of time to form this guilty nation. The priests whose teaching, example, and wealth were supposed to be so good for us had supervised the childhood of the generation that broke out against them. The class that revolted in 1789 must have been accustomed to the privileges of feudal nobility which, as we are also assured, are so peculiarly agreeable to those on whom they weigh [the peasants]. How does it happen, then, that the seed of so many vices was sown under the ancient institutions? . . . What can we conclude from this, then?—That no people had been as unhappy for the preceding century as the French. If the Negroes of Saint-Domingue have committed even greater atrocities, it is because they had been even more greatly oppressed.

Source: Vivian Folkenflik, ed., *An Extraordinary Woman: Selected Writings of Germaine de Staël* (New York: Columbia University Press, 1987), 365–66.

Questions to Consider

1. **Which aspect of the French Revolution most disturbed these commentators?**
2. **How would you align each of these writers on a spectrum running from extreme right to extreme left in politics?**
3. **How would each of these writers judge the Enlightenment that preceded the French Revolution?**

MAPPING THE WEST

Europe in 1799

France's expansion during the revolutionary wars threatened to upset the balance of power in Europe. A century earlier, the English and Dutch had allied and formed a Europe-wide coalition to check the territorial ambitions of Louis XIV. Thwarting French ambitions after 1799 would prove to be even more of a challenge to the other European powers. The Dutch had been reduced to satellite status, as had most of the Italian states. Even Austria and Prussia would suffer devastating losses to the French on the battlefield. Only a new coalition of European powers could stop France in the future.

to Paris to witness events firsthand. Supporters of the French Revolution in Great Britain joined constitutional and reform societies that sprang up in many cities. Pro-French feeling ran even stronger in Ireland. Catholics and Presbyterians, both excluded from the vote, came together in 1791 in the Society of United Irishmen, which eventually pressed for secession from England.

European elites became alarmed when the French abolished monarchy and nobility and encouraged popular participation in politics. The British government, for example, quickly suppressed the corresponding societies and harassed their leaders, charging that their ideas and their contacts with the French were seditious. (See the illustration on page 643 for a negative English view.) When the Society of United Irishmen timed a rebellion to coincide with an attempted French invasion in 1798, the British mercilessly repressed them, killing thirty thousand rebels. To put down the rebellion, Britain required seventy thousand regular troops, twice as many as fought in any of the major continental battles.

Elites sometimes found allies in opposing the French. Peasants in the German and Italian states met the French occupation with resistance, often in the form of banditry. Because the French offered Jews religious toleration and civil and political rights wherever they conquered, anti-French groups sometimes attacked Jews. Many leading intellectuals in the German states, including the philosopher Immanuel Kant, initially supported the revolutionary cause, but after 1793 most of them turned against the popular violence and military aggressiveness of the Revolution. The German states, still run by many separate rulers, experienced a profound artistic and intellectual revival, which eventually connected with anti-French nationalism. This renaissance included a resurgence of intellectual life in the universities, a thriving press (1,225 journals were launched in the 1780s alone), and the multiplication of Masonic lodges and literary clubs.

Despite the turn in opinion, European rulers still dreaded the mere mention of revolution. Although Swedish king Gustavus III (r. 1771–1792) was assassinated by a nobleman, his son Gustavus IV (r. 1792–1809) was convinced that the French Jacobins had sanctioned the killing. Spain's royal government simply suppressed all news from France, fearing that it might ignite the spirit of revolt. Despite similar government controls on news in Russia, 278 outbreaks of peasant unrest occurred there between 1796 and 1798. A Russian landlord explained, "This is the self-same . . . spirit of insubordination and independence, which has spread through all Europe." When insubordination did turn revolutionary, as in Naples under French influence in 1799, the retribution could be awful: 100 republicans, including leading intellectuals, were executed when the royalists returned to power.

REVIEW QUESTION **Why did some groups outside of France embrace the French Revolution while others resisted it?**

Conclusion

Growing out of aspirations for freedom that also inspired the Dutch, Belgians, and Poles, the revolution that shook France permanently altered the political landscape of the Western world. Between 1789 and 1799, monarchy as a form of government gave way in France to a republic whose leaders were elected. Aristocracy based on rank and birth was undermined in favor of civil equality and the promotion of merit. The people who marched in demonstrations, met in clubs, and, in the case of men, voted in national elections for the first time insisted that government respond to them. Thousands of men held elective office. A revolutionary government tried to teach new values with a refashioned calendar, state festivals, and a civic religion. Its example inspired would-be revolutionaries everywhere.

But the French Revolution also had its darker side. The divisions created by the Revolution within France endured in many cases until after World War II. Even now, French public-opinion surveys ask if it was right to execute the king in 1793 (most believe that Louis XVI was guilty of treason but should not have been executed). The revolutionaries proclaimed human rights and democratic government as universal goals, but they also explicitly excluded women, even though they admitted Protestant, Jewish, and eventually black men. They used the new spirit of national pride to inspire armies and then used those armies to conquer other peoples. Their ideals of universal education, religious toleration, and democratic participation could not prevent the institution of new forms of government terror to persecute, imprison, and kill dissidents. These paradoxes created an opening for Napoleon Bonaparte, who rushed in with his remarkable military and political skills to push France — and with it all of Europe — in new directions.

FOR FURTHER EXPLORATION

- **For additional primary-source material from this period**, see *Sources of the Making of the West*, Fourth Edition.
- **For Web sites, images, and documents related to topics in this chapter**, visit *Make History* at bedfordstmartins.com/hunt.

Chapter 19 Review

Online Study Guide bedfordstmartins.com/hunt

Key Terms and People

In the grid below, identify the term or person and explain its historical significance. (To do this exercise online, go to bedfordstmartins.com/hunt.)

Term	Who or What & When	Why It Matters
Louis XVI (p. 623)		
Marie-Antoinette (p. 623)		
Estates General (p. 624)		
Great Fear (p. 626)		
Declaration of the Rights of Man and Citizen (p. 626)		
Jacobin Club (p. 630)		
Maximilien Robespierre (p. 631)		
Terror (p. 631)		
de-Christianization (p. 634)		
Thermidorian Reaction (p. 638)		

Review Questions

1. How did the beginning of the French Revolution resemble the other revolutions of 1787–1789?
2. Why did the French Revolution turn in an increasingly radical direction after 1789?
3. What factors can explain the Terror? To what extent was it simply a response to a national emergency or a reflection of deeper problems within the French Revolution?
4. Why did some groups outside of France embrace the French Revolution while others resisted it?

Making Connections

1. Should the French Revolution be viewed as the origin of democracy or the origin of totalitarianism (a government in which no dissent is allowed)? Explain.
2. Why did other European rulers find the French Revolution so threatening?
3. What made the French revolutionary armies so powerful in this period?
4. How was the French Revolution related to the Enlightenment that preceded it?

Important Events

Date	Event
1787	Dutch Patriot revolt stifled by Prussian invasion
1788	Beginning of Austrian Netherlands resistance against reforms of Joseph II; opening of reform parliament in Poland
1789	French Revolution begins
1790	Internal divisions lead to collapse of resistance in Austrian Netherlands
1791	Beginning of slave revolt in St. Domingue (Haiti)
1792	Beginning of war between France and rest of Europe; second revolution of August 10 overthrows monarchy
1793	Second partition of Poland by Austria and Russia; Louis XVI of France executed for treason
1794	Abolition of slavery in French colonies; Robespierre's government by terror falls
1795	Third (final) partition of Poland; France annexes Austrian Netherlands
1797–1798	Creation of "sister republics" in Italian states and Switzerland

- Consider three events: **Dutch patriot revolt stifled by Prussian invasion (1787)**, **French Revolution begins (1789)**, and **Beginning of slave revolt in St. Domingue (Haiti) (1791)**. How would you explain the relationships between these three uprisings? How were they similar and different in their inspirations, ideologies, tactics, and results?

SUGGESTED REFERENCES

The most influential book on the meaning of the French Revolution is still the classic study by Tocqueville, who insisted that the Revolution continued the process of state centralization undertaken by the monarchy. The revolutions in the colonies are now the subject of many new and important studies.

Andress, David. *The Terror: The Merciless War for Freedom in Revolutionary France.* 2006.

Armitage, David, and Sanjay Subrahmanyam, eds. *The Age of Revolutions in Global Context, c. 1760–1840.* 2010.

Censer, Jack R., and Lynn Hunt. *Liberty, Equality, Fraternity: Exploring the French Revolution* (includes CD-ROM of images and music). 2001. See also the accompanying Web site: http://www.chnm.gmu.edu/revolution

Chickering, Roger, and Stig Förster, eds. *War in an Age of Revolution, 1775–1815.* 2010.

Desan, Suzanne. *The Family on Trial in Revolutionary France.* 2006.

*Dubois, Laurent, and John D. Garrigus, eds. *Slave Revolution in the Caribbean, 1789–1804: A Brief History with Documents.* 2006.

Furet, François. *Interpreting the French Revolution.* Trans. Elborg Forster. 1981.

Godineau, Dominique. *The Women of Paris and Their French Revolution.* Trans. Katherine Streip. 1998.

*Hunt, Lynn, ed. *The French Revolution and Human Rights: A Brief Documentary History.* 1996.

*Levy, Darline Gay, Harriet Branson Applewhite, and Mary Durham Johnson, eds. *Women in Revolutionary Paris, 1789–1795.* 1979.

Palmer, R. R. *The Age of the Democratic Revolution: A Political History of Europe and America, 1760–1800.* Vol. 2, *The Struggle.* 1964.

*Popkin, Jeremy D. *Facing Racial Revolution: Eyewitness Accounts of the Haitian Insurrection.* 2007.

——. *You Are All Free: The Haitian Revolution and the Abolition of Slavery.* 2010.

Schechter, Ronald, ed. *The French Revolution: The Essential Readings.* 2001.

Scurr, Ruth. *Fatal Purity: Robespierre and the French Revolution.* 2007.

Tocqueville, Alexis de. *The Old Regime and the French Revolution.* Trans. Stuart Gilbert. 1856; repr. 1955.

*Primary source.

DAVID L'AN
BONAPARTE

CHAPTER

20

Napoleon and the Revolutionary Legacy

1800–1830

In her novel *Frankenstein* (1818), the prototype for modern thrillers, Mary Shelley tells the story of a Swiss technological genius who creates a humanlike monster in his pursuit of scientific knowledge. The monster, "so scaring and unearthly in his ugliness," terrifies all who encounter him and ends by destroying Dr. Frankenstein's own loved ones. Despite desperate chases across deserts and frozen landscapes, Frankenstein never manages to trap the monster, who is last seen hunched over his creator's deathbed.

Frankenstein's monster can be taken as a particularly horrifying incarnation of the fears of the postrevolutionary era, but which fears did Shelley have in mind? Did the monster represent the French Revolution, which had devoured its own children in the Terror? Shelley was the daughter of Mary Wollstonecraft, an English feminist who had defended the French Revolution and died in childbirth when Mary was born in 1797. Mary Shelley was also the wife of the romantic poet Percy Bysshe Shelley, who often wrote against the ugliness of contemporary life and in opposition to the conservative politics that had triumphed in Great Britain after Napoleon's fall. Whatever the meaning — and Mary Shelley may well have intended more than one — *Frankenstein* makes the forceful point that humans cannot always control their own creations. The Enlightenment and the French Revolution had celebrated the virtues of human creativity, but Shelley's novel shows that innovation often has a dark and uncontrollable side.

Napoleon as Military Hero
In this painting from 1800–1801, *Napoleon Crossing the Alps at St. Bernard*, Jacques-Louis David reminds the French of Napoleon's heroic military exploits. Napoleon is a picture of calm and composure while his horse shows the fright and energy of the moment. David painted this propagandistic image shortly after one of his former students went to the guillotine on a trumped-up charge of plotting to assassinate the new French leader. The former organizer of republican festivals during the Terror had become a kind of court painter for the new regime. *(Réunion des Musées Nationaux/Art Resource, NY.)*

Those who witnessed Napoleon Bonaparte's stunning rise to European dominance might have cast him as either Frankenstein or his monster. Like the scientist Frankenstein, Bonaparte created something dramatically new: the French Empire with himself as emperor. Like the former kings of France, he ruled under his first name. This Corsican artillery officer who spoke French with an Italian accent ended the French Revolution even while maintaining some of its most important innovations. Bonaparte transformed France from a republic with democratically elected leaders to an empire with a new aristocracy based on military service. But he kept the revolutionary administration and most of the laws that ensured equal treatment of citizens. Although he tolerated no opposition at home, he prided himself on bringing French-style changes to peoples elsewhere.

Bonaparte continued his revolutionary policy of conquest and annexation until it reached grotesque dimensions. His foreign policies made many see him as a monster hungry for dominion; he turned the sister republics of the revolutionary era into kingdoms personally ruled by his relatives, and he exacted tribute wherever he triumphed. Eventually, resistance to the French armies and the ever-mounting costs of military glory toppled Napoleon. The powers allied against him met and agreed to restore the monarchical governments that had been overthrown by the French, shrink France back to its prerevolutionary boundaries, and maintain this settlement against future demands for change.

Although the people of Europe longed for peace and stability in the aftermath of the Napoleonic whirlwind, they lived in a deeply unsettled world. Profoundly affected by French military occupation, many groups of people organized to demand ethnic and cultural autonomy, first from Napoleon and then from the restored governments after 1815. In 1830, a new round of revolutions broke out in France, Belgium, Poland, and some of the Italian states. The revolutionary legacy was far from exhausted.

CHAPTER FOCUS How did Napoleon Bonaparte's actions force other European rulers to change their policies?

The Rise of Napoleon Bonaparte

In 1799, a charismatic young general took over the French republic and set France on a new course. Within a year, **Napoleon Bonaparte** (1769–1821) had effectively ended the French Revolution and steered France toward an authoritarian state. As emperor after 1804, he dreamed of European integration in the tradition of Augustus and Charlemagne, but he also mastered the details of practical administration. To achieve his goals, he compromised with the Catholic church and with exiled aristocrats willing to return to France. His most enduring accomplishment, the new Civil Code, tempered the principles of the Enlightenment and the Revolution with an insistence on the powers of fathers over children, husbands over wives, and employers over workers. His influence spread into many spheres as he personally patronized scientific inquiry and encouraged artistic styles in line with his vision of imperial greatness.

A General Takes Over

It would have seemed astonishing in 1795 that the twenty-six-year-old son of a noble family from the island of Corsica off the Italian coast would within four years become the supreme ruler of France and one of the greatest military leaders in world history. That year, Bonaparte was a penniless artillery officer, only recently released from prison as a presumed Robespierrist. Thanks to some early military suc-

---

Napoleon Bonaparte: The French general who became First Consul in 1799 and emperor (Napoleon I) in 1804; after losing the battle of Waterloo in 1815, he was exiled to the island of St. Helena.

1799 Coup against Directory government in France; Napoleon Bonaparte named First Consul

1801 Napoleon signs concordat with the pope

1804 Napoleon crowned emperor of France, issues new Civil Code

1805 British naval forces defeat French at the battle of Trafalgar; Napoleon wins his greatest victory at the battle of Austerlitz

1807–1814 French invade and occupy Spain and Portugal

1812 Napoleon invades Russia

1814–1815 Congress of Vienna

1815 Napoleon defeated at Waterloo and exiled to island of St. Helena, where he dies in 1821

cesses and links to Parisian politicians, however, he was named commander of the French army in Italy in 1796.

Bonaparte's astounding success in the Italian campaigns of 1796–1797 launched his meteoric career. With an army of fewer than fifty thousand men, he defeated the Piedmontese and the Austrians. In quick order, he established client republics dependent on his own authority, negotiated with the Austrians himself, and molded the army into his personal force by paying the soldiers in cash taken as tribute from the newly conquered territories. He pleased the Directory government by sending home wagonloads of Italian masterpieces of art, which were added to Parisian museum collections (most are still there) after being paraded in victory festivals.

In 1798, the Directory set aside its plans to invade England, gave Bonaparte command of the army raised for that purpose, and sent him across the Mediterranean Sea to Egypt. The Directory government hoped that French occupation of Egypt would strike a blow at British trade by cutting the route to India. Although the French immediately defeated a much larger Egyptian army, the British admiral Lord Horatio Nelson destroyed the French fleet while it was anchored in Aboukir Bay, cutting the French off from home. In the face of determined resistance and an outbreak of the bubonic plague, Bonaparte's armies retreated from a further expedition in Syria. But the French occupation of Egypt lasted long enough for that largely Muslim country to experience the same kinds of Enlightenment-inspired legal reforms that had been introduced in Europe: the French abolished torture, introduced equality before the law, eliminated religious taxes, and proclaimed religious toleration.

Even the failures of the Egyptian campaign did not dull Bonaparte's luster. Bonaparte had taken France's leading scientists with him on the expedition, and his soldiers had discovered a slab of black basalt dating from 196 B.C.E. written in both hieroglyphic and Greek. Called the Rosetta stone after a nearby town, it enabled scholars to finally decipher the hieroglyphs used by the ancient Egyptians.

With his army pinned down by Nelson's victory at sea, Bonaparte slipped out of Egypt and made his way secretly to southern France in October 1799. He arrived home at just the right moment: the war in Europe was going badly. The territories of the former Austrian Netherlands had revolted against French conscription laws, and deserters swelled the ranks of rebels in western France. Amid increasing political instability, generals in the field had become virtually independent, and the troops felt more loyal to their units and generals than to the republic. Disillusioned members of the government saw in Bonaparte's return an occasion to overturn the constitution of 1795.

On November 9, 1799, the conspirators persuaded the legislature to move out of Paris to avoid an imaginary Jacobin plot. But when Bonaparte stomped into the new meeting hall the next day and demanded immediate changes in the constitution, he was greeted by cries of "Down with the dictator!" His quick-thinking brother Lucien, president of the Council of Five Hundred (the lower house), saved Bonaparte's coup by summoning troops guarding the hall and claiming that some deputies had tried to assassinate the popular general. The soldiers ejected those who opposed Bonaparte and left the remaining ones to vote to abolish the Directory and establish a new three-man executive called the consulate.

Bonaparte became **First Consul**, a title revived from the ancient Roman republic. He promised to

---

First Consul: The most important of the three consuls established by the French Constitution of 1800; the title, given to Napoleon Bonaparte, was taken from ancient Rome.

1818
Mary Shelley, *Frankenstein*

1820
Revolt of liberal army officers against Spanish crown

1824
Ludwig van Beethoven, Ninth Symphony

1825
Russian army officers demand constitutional reform in Decembrist Revolt

1830
Greece gains its independence from Ottoman Turks; rebels overthrow Charles X of France and install Louis-Philippe; rebellion in Poland against Russia fails

1832
English Parliament passes Reform Bill; Johann Wolfgang von Goethe, *Faust*

1820 1825 1830 1835

be a man above party and to restore order to the republic. A new constitution—with no declaration of rights—was submitted to the voters. Millions abstained from voting, and the government falsified the results to give an appearance of even greater support to the new regime. Inside France, political apathy had overtaken the original enthusiasm for revolutionary ideals. Altogether it was an unpromising beginning; yet within five years, Bonaparte would crown himself Napoleon I, emperor of the French. The French armies would recover from their reverses of 1799 to push the frontiers of French influence even farther eastward.

From Republic to Empire

Napoleon had no long-range plans to establish himself as emperor and conquer most of Europe. The deputies of the legislature who engineered the coup d'état of November 1799 picked him as one of three provisional consuls only because he was a famous general. Napoleon immediately asserted his leadership over the other two consuls in the process of drafting another constitution—the fourth since 1789. He then set about putting his stamp on every aspect of French life, building monuments and institutions that in some cases have endured to the present day.

The End of the Republic When the constitution of 1799 made Napoleon the First Consul, it gave him the right to pick the Council of State, which drew up all laws. He exerted control by choosing men loyal to him. Government was no longer representative in any real sense: the new constitution eliminated direct elections for deputies and granted no independent powers to the three houses of the legislature. Napoleon and his advisers chose the legislature's members out of a small pool of "notables." Almost all men over twenty-one could vote in the plebiscite (referendum) to approve the constitution, but their only option was to choose *yes* or *no*.

Napoleon's most urgent task was to reconcile to his regime Catholics who had been alienated by revolutionary policies. Although nominally Catholic, Napoleon held no deep religious convictions. "How can there be order in the state without religion?" he asked cynically. "When a man is dying of hunger beside another who is stuffing himself, he cannot accept this difference if there is not an authority who tells him: 'God wishes it so.' " In 1801, a concordat with Pope Pius VII (r. 1800–1823) ended a decade of church-state conflict in France. The pope validated all sales of church lands, and the government agreed to pay the salaries of bishops and priests who would swear loyalty to the state. Catholicism was officially recognized as the religion of "the great majority of French citizens." (The state also paid Protestant pastors' salaries.) Thus, the pope brought the huge French Catholic population back into the fold and Napoleon gained the pope's support for his regime.

Napoleon continued the centralization of state power that had begun under the absolutist monarchy of Louis XIV and resumed under the Terror. As First Consul, he appointed prefects who directly supervised local affairs in every department in the country. He created the Bank of France to facilitate government borrowing and relied on gold and silver coinage rather than paper money. He improved tax collection but balanced the budget only by exacting tribute from the territories he conquered.

To achieve order and end the upheavals of ten years of revolutionary turmoil, the regime severely limited political expression. Napoleon never relied on mass executions to maintain control, but he refused to allow those who opposed him to meet in clubs, influence elections, or publish newspapers. A decree reduced the number of newspapers in Paris from seventy-three to thirteen (and then finally to four), and the newspapers that remained became government organs. Government censors had to approve all operas and plays, and they banned "offensive" artistic works even more frequently than their royal predecessors had. The minister of police, Joseph Fouché, once a leading figure in the Terror of 1793–1794, imposed house arrest, arbitrary imprisonment, and surveillance of political dissidents. Political contest and debate shriveled to almost nothing. When a bomb attack on Napoleon's carriage failed in 1800, Fouché suppressed the evidence of a royalist plot and instead arrested hundreds of former Jacobins. More than one hundred of them were deported and seven hundred imprisoned.

When it suited him, Napoleon also struck against royalist conspirators. In 1804, he ordered his police to kidnap the duke d'Enghien from his residence in Germany. Napoleon had intelligence, which proved to be false, that d'Enghien had joined a plot in Paris against him. Even when he learned the truth, he insisted that a military tribunal try d'Enghien, a close relative of the dead king Louis XVI. After a summary trial, d'Enghien was shot on the spot.

By then, Napoleon's political intentions had become clear. He had named himself First Consul for life in 1802, and in 1804, with the pope's blessing, he crowned himself emperor. Once again, plebiscites approved his decisions but only yes/no alternatives

Napoleon's Coronation as Emperor
In this detail from *The Coronation of Napoleon and Josephine* (1805–1807), Jacques-Louis David shows Napoleon crowning his wife at the ceremony of 1804. Napoleon orchestrated the entire event and took the only active role in it: Pope Pius VII gave his blessing to the ceremony (he can be seen seated behind Napoleon), but Napoleon crowned himself. What is the significance of Napoleon crowning himself? *(Erich Lessing/Art Resource, NY.)*

were offered. Still, though the democratic political aims of the French Revolution had been trampled, some aspects of daily life continued to be affected by egalitarian ideals (see "Seeing History," page 656).

Imperial Rule Napoleon's outsize personality dominated the new regime. His face and name adorned coins, engravings, histories, paintings, and public monuments. His favorite painters embellished his legend by depicting him as a warrior-hero of mythic proportions even though he was short and physically unimpressive in person. Believing that "what is big is always beautiful," Napoleon embarked on ostentatious building projects that would outshine even those of Louis XIV. Government-commissioned architects built the Arc de Triomphe, the Stock Exchange, fountains, and even slaughterhouses. Most of the emperor's new construction reflected his neoclassical taste for monumental buildings set in vast empty spaces.

Napoleon worked hard at establishing his reputation as an efficient administrator with broad intellectual interests: he met frequently with scientists, jurists, and artists, and stories abounded of his unflagging energy. When not on military campaigns, he worked on state affairs, usually until 10:00 p.m., taking only a few minutes for each meal. "Authority," declared his adviser the abbé Sieyès, "must come from above and confidence from below." To establish his authority, Napoleon relied on men who had served with him in the army. His chief of staff Alexandre Berthier, for example, became minister of war, and the chemist Claude Berthollet, who had organized the scientific part of the expedition to Egypt, became vice president of the Senate in 1804. Napoleon's bureaucracy was based on a patron-client relationship, with Napoleon as the ultimate patron. Some of Napoleon's closest associates married into his family.

Combining aristocratic and revolutionary values in a new social hierarchy that rewarded merit and talent, Napoleon personally chose as senators the nation's most illustrious generals, ministers, prefects, scientists, rich men, and former nobles. Intending to replace both the old nobility of birth and the republic's strict emphasis on equality, in 1802 he

SEEING HISTORY

The Clothing Revolution: The Social Meaning of Changes in Postrevolutionary Fashion

Some revolutions take place in the realm of social life and culture rather than politics. One of the most striking of these social and cultural revolutions was the wearing of trousers. Before the French Revolution of 1789, men of the middle classes and nobility wore knee breeches, stockings, and buckled shoes, as can be seen in the colored engraving from 1778. Trousers (long pants) were worn only by working-class men, who needed them to protect themselves on the job and from the mud in the streets.

From Napoleon onward, a shift toward trousers took place across Europe, not all at once but slowly and surely. Napoleon himself wore close-fitting pantaloons (from which the word *pants* is derived) until he became too fat and reverted back to knee breeches. The colored engraving of a middle-class couple in 1830 shows how long pants had become the fashion for men. In line with political changes that installed equality under the law and careers open to merit rather than birth, men began to dress more alike; all men wore trousers. Taking a closer look at the men in both pictures, do you see any other changes in style and accessories that might reflect a less class-conscious society?

Women's dress, in contrast, maintained and even underlined social distinctions after the Revolution. In the nineteenth century, middle- and upper-class women continued to wear dresses with such long and full skirts that they could not possibly be imagined working. Working women wore simpler blouses and skirts that allowed the movements necessary to labor at home or in manufacturing.

Questions to Consider

1. **Compare the pre-Revolution fashion shown with that of the woman in the 1830 engraving. Does one outfit look more comfortable than the other? Why or why not? What other differences (or similarities) do you notice?**
2. **Why do you think women's fashion failed to become more uniform the way men's did in the decades following the Revolution?**

Gentleman Proposing to a Lady, 1778. *(Private Collection/The Stapleton Collection/The Bridgeman Art Library International.)*

Fashion for Men and Women, 1830. *(Musée de la Ville de Paris, Musée Carnavalet, Paris, France/Lauros/Giraudon/The Bridgeman Art Library International.)*

took the first step toward creating a new nobility by founding the Legion of Honor. (Members of the legion received lifetime pensions along with their titles.) Napoleon usually equated honor with military success; by 1814, the legion had thirty-two thousand members, only 5 percent of them civilians.

In 1808, Napoleon introduced a complete hierarchy of noble titles, ranging from princes down to barons and chevaliers. All Napoleonic nobles had served the state. Titles could be inherited but had to be supported by wealth—a man could not be a duke without a fortune of 200,000 francs or a chevalier without 3,000 francs. To go along with their new titles, Napoleon gave his favorite generals huge fortunes, often in the form of estates in the conquered territories.

Napoleon's own family reaped the greatest benefits. He made his older brother, Joseph, ruler of the newly established kingdom of Naples in 1806, the same year he installed his younger brother Louis as king of Holland. He proclaimed his twenty-three-year-old stepson, Eugène de Beauharnais, viceroy of Italy in 1805 and established his sister Caroline and brother-in-law General Joachim Murat as king and queen of Naples in 1808 when he moved Joseph to the throne of Spain. Napoleon wanted to establish an imperial succession, but he lacked an heir. In thirteen years of marriage, his wife, Josephine, had borne no children, so in 1809 he divorced her and in 1810 married the eighteen-year-old princess Marie-Louise of Austria. The next year Marie-Louise gave birth to a son, to whom Napoleon immediately gave the title king of Rome.

Emperor Napoleon in His Study
In this portrait painted by Jacques-Louis David in 1812, Napoleon is shown in his general's uniform, sword by his side. He stands by his desk covered with papers to show how hard he works for the country. *(Erich Lessing/Art Resource, NY.)*

The New Paternalism: The Civil Code

As part of his restoration of order, Napoleon brought a paternalistic model of power to his state. Previous governments had tried to unify and standardize France's multiple legal codes, but only Napoleon successfully established a new one, partly because he personally presided over the commission that drafted the new **Civil Code**, completed in 1804. Called the Napoleonic Code as a way of further exalting the emperor's image, it reasserted the Old Regime's patriarchal system of male domination over women and insisted on a father's control over his children, which revolutionary legislation had limited. For example, a child under age sixteen who refused to follow his or her father's commands could be sent to prison for up to a month with no hearing of any sort. Yet the code also required fathers to provide for their children's welfare. Moreover, the Civil Code protected many of the gains of the French Revolution by defining and ensuring property rights, guaranteeing religious liberty, and establishing a uniform system of law that provided equal treatment for all adult males and affirmed the right of men to choose their professions. Napoleon wanted to discourage abortion and infanticide, not uncommon among the poorest classes in the fast-growing urban areas, so he helped set up private charities to help indigent mothers and made it easier for women to abandon their children anonymously to a government foundling hospital.

Civil Code: The French legal code formulated by Napoleon in 1804; it ensured equal treatment under the law to all men and guaranteed religious liberty, but it curtailed many rights of women.

Although the code maintained the equal division of family property between all children, both male and female, it sharply curtailed women's rights in other respects. Napoleon wanted to restrict women to the private sphere of the home. One of his leading jurists remarked, "Women need protection because they are weaker; men are free because they are stronger." The law obligated a husband to support his wife, but the husband alone controlled any property held in common; a wife could not sue in court, sell or mortgage her own property, or contract a debt without her husband's consent. Divorce was severely restricted. A wife could petition for divorce only if her husband brought his mistress to live in the family home. In contrast, a wife convicted of adultery could be imprisoned for up to two years. The code's framers saw these discrepancies as a way to reinforce the family and make women responsible for private virtue, while leaving public decisions to men. The French code was imitated in many European and Latin American countries and in the French colony of Louisiana, where it had a similar negative effect on women's rights. Not until 1965 did French wives gain legal status equal to that of their husbands.

Napoleon took little interest in girls' education, believing that girls should spend most of their time at home learning religion, manners, and such "female occupations" as sewing and music. For boys, by contrast, the government set up a new system of lycées, state-run secondary schools in which students wore military uniforms and drumrolls signaled the beginning and end of classes. The lycées offered wider access to education and thus helped achieve Napoleon's goal of opening careers to those with talent, regardless of their social origins. (The lycées have dropped the military trappings and are now coeducational, but they are still the heart of the French educational system.)

The new paternalism extended to relations between employers and employees. The state required all workers to carry a work card attesting to their good conduct, and it prohibited all workers' organizations. The police considered workers without cards to be vagrants or criminals and could send them to a workhouse or prison. After 1806, arbitration boards settled labor disputes, but they took employers at their word while treating workers as minors, demanding that foremen and shop superintendents represent them. Occasionally strikes broke out, led by secret, illegal journeymen's associations, yet many employers laid off employees when times were hard, deducted fines from their wages, and dismissed them without appeal for being absent or making errors. These limitations on workers' rights won Napoleon the support of French business.

Patronage of Science and Intellectual Life

Napoleon did everything possible to promote French scientific inquiry, especially that which could serve practical ends. He closely monitored the research institutes established during the Revolution, sometimes intervening personally to achieve political conformity. An impressive outpouring of new theoretical and practical scientific work rewarded the state's efforts. Experiments with balloons led to the discovery of laws about the expansion of gases, and research on fossil shells prepared the way for new theories of evolutionary change later in the nineteenth century. The surgeon Dominique-Jean Larrey developed new techniques of battlefield amputation and medical care during Napoleon's wars, winning an appointment as an officer in the Legion of Honor and becoming a baron with a pension.

Napoleon aimed to modernize French society through science, but he could not tolerate criticism. Napoleon considered most writers useless or dangerous, "good for nothing under any government." Some of the most talented French writers of the time had to live in exile. The best-known expatriate was Anne-Louise-Germaine de Staël (1766–1817), the daughter of Louis XVI's finance minister, Jacques Necker. When explaining his desire to banish her, Napoleon exclaimed, "She is a machine in motion who stirs up the salons." While exiled in the German states, de Staël wrote *Corinne* (1807), a novel whose heroine is a brilliant woman thwarted by a patriarchal system, and *On Germany* (1810), an account of the important new literary currents east of the Rhine. Her books were banned in France.

Although Napoleon restored the strong authority of state and religion in France, many royalists and Catholics still criticized him as an impious usurper. (See "Contrasting Views," page 666.) François-René de Chateaubriand (1768–1848) admired Napoleon as "the strong man who has saved us from the abyss," but he preferred monarchy. In his view, Napoleon had not properly understood the need to defend Christian values against the Enlightenment's excessive reliance on reason. Chateaubriand wrote his *Genius of Christianity* (1802) to draw attention to the power and mystery of faith. He warned, "It is to the vanity of knowledge that we owe almost all our misfortunes. . . . The learned ages have always been followed by ages of destruction." Chateaubriand's book appeared during a rare lull in wars that soon engulfed much of Europe.

REVIEW QUESTION In what ways did Napoleon continue the French Revolution, and in what ways did he break with it?

Germaine de Staël
One of the most fascinating intellectuals of her time, Anne-Louise-Germaine de Staël seemed to irritate Napoleon more than any other person did. Daughter of Louis XVI's Swiss Protestant finance minister, Jacques Necker, and wife of a Swedish diplomat, Madame de Staël frequently criticized Napoleon's policies. She published best-selling novels and influential literary criticism, and whenever allowed to reside in Paris she encouraged the intellectual and political dissidents from Napoleon's regime. In this painting from 1809, Elisabeth Vigée-Lebrun depicts her as Corinne, the heroine of one of her novels. *(Musée d'Art et d'Histoire, Geneva, Switzerland/The Bridgeman Art Library International.)*

"Europe Was at My Feet": Napoleon's Conquests

Building on innovations introduced by the republican governments before him, Napoleon revolutionized the art of war with tactics and strategies based on a highly mobile army. By 1812, he ruled a European empire more extensive than any since ancient Rome (Map 20.1). Yet that empire had already begun to crumble, and with it went Napoleon's power at home. Napoleon's empire failed because it was based on a contradiction: Napoleon tried to reduce virtually all nations of Europe to the status of colonial dependents when Europe had long consisted of independent states. The result, inevitably, was a great upsurge in nationalist feeling that has dominated European politics to the present.

The Grand Army and Its Victories, 1800–1807

Napoleon attributed his military success "three-quarters to morale" and the rest to leadership and superiority of numbers at the point of attack. Conscription provided the large numbers: 1.3 million men ages twenty to twenty-four were drafted between 1800 and 1812, another 1 million in 1813–1814. Many willingly served because the republic had taught them to identify the army with the nation. Military service was both a patriotic duty and a means of social mobility. The men who rose through the ranks to become officers were young, ambitious, and accustomed to the new ways of war. Consequently, the French army had higher morale than the armies of other powers, most of which rejected conscription as too democratic and continued to restrict their officer corps to the nobility. Only in 1813–1814, when the military tide turned against Napoleon, did French morale plummet.

When Napoleon came to power in 1799, desertion was rampant and the generals competed with one another for predominance. Napoleon ended the squabbling by uniting all the armies into one Grand Army under his personal command. By 1812, he was commanding 700,000 troops; while 250,000 soldiers fought in Spain, others remained garrisoned in France. In any given battle, between 70,000 and 180,000 men, not all of them French, fought for France. Life on campaign was no picnic — ordinary soldiers slept in the rain, mud, and snow and often

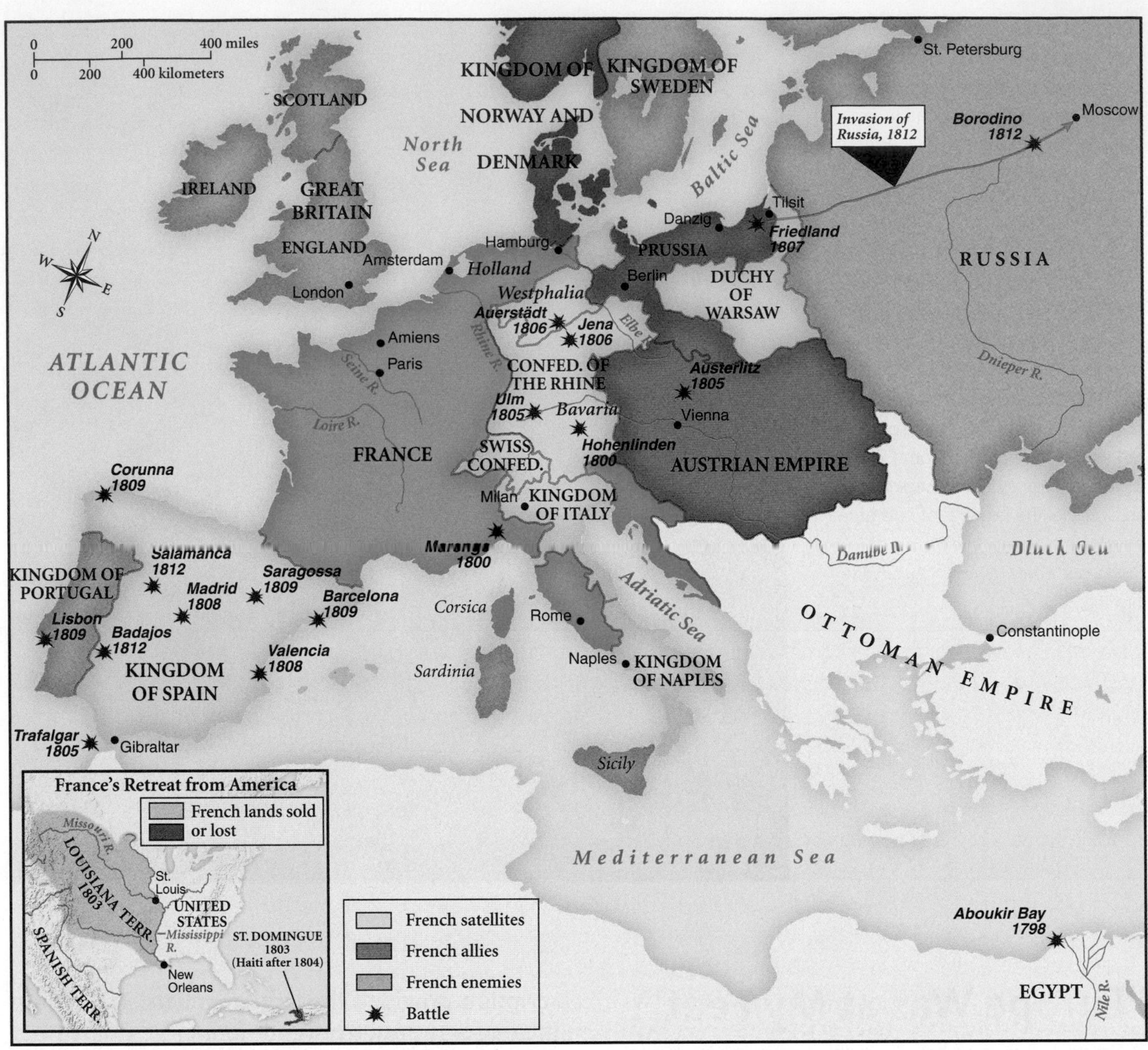

MAP 20.1 Napoleon's Empire at Its Height, 1812
In 1812, Napoleon had at least nominal control of almost all of western Europe. Even before he made his fatal mistake of invading Russia, however, his authority had been undermined in Spain and seriously weakened in the Italian and German states. Still earlier, he had given up his dreams of a worldwide empire. French armies withdrew from Egypt in 1801 and from Saint Domingue (Haiti) in 1802. In 1803 Napoleon sold the Louisiana Territory to the United States.

had to forage for food—but Napoleon nonetheless inspired almost fanatical loyalty. He fought alongside his soldiers in some sixty battles and had nineteen horses shot from under him. One opponent said that Napoleon's presence alone was worth fifty thousand men.

A brilliant strategist who carefully studied the demands of war, Napoleon outmaneuvered virtually all his opponents. He had a pragmatic and direct approach to strategy: he went for the main body of the opposing army and tried to crush it in a lightning campaign. He gathered the largest possible army for one great and decisive battle and then followed with a relentless pursuit to break enemy morale altogether. His military command, like his rule within France, was personal and highly centralized. He essentially served as his own operations officer: "I alone know what I have to do," he insisted. This style worked as long as Napoleon could be on the battlefield, but he failed to train independent subordinates to take over in his absence. He also faced constant difficulties in supplying a rapidly moving army, which, because of its size, could not always live off the land.

One of Napoleon's greatest advantages was the lack of coordination among his enemies. Britain dominated the seas but did not want to field huge land armies. On the continent, the French republic had already set up satellites in the Netherlands and Italy, which served as a buffer against the big powers to the east—Austria, Prussia, and Russia. By maneuvering diplomatically and militarily, Napoleon could usually take these on one by one. After reorganizing the French armies in 1799, for example, Napoleon won striking victories against the Austrians at Marengo and Hohenlinden in 1800, forcing them to agree to peace terms. Once the Austrians had withdrawn, Britain agreed to the Treaty of Amiens in 1802, effectively ending hostilities on the continent. Napoleon considered the peace with Great Britain merely a truce, however, and it lasted only until 1803.

Napoleon used the breathing space not only to consolidate his position before taking up arms again but also to send an expeditionary force to the Caribbean colony of St. Domingue to regain control of the island. Continuing resistance among the black population and an epidemic of yellow fever forced Napoleon to withdraw his troops from St. Domingue and abandon his plans to extend his empire to the Western Hemisphere. As part of his retreat, he sold the Louisiana Territory to the United States in 1803.

When war resumed in Europe, the British navy once more proved its superiority by blocking an attempted French invasion and by defeating the French and their Spanish allies in a huge naval battle at Trafalgar in 1805. France lost many ships; the British lost no vessels, but their renowned admiral Lord Horatio Nelson died in the battle.

On land, Napoleon remained invincible. In 1805, Austria took up arms again when Napoleon demanded that it declare neutrality in the conflict with Britain. Napoleon promptly captured twenty-five thousand Austrian soldiers at Ulm, in Bavaria, in 1805. After marching on to Vienna, he again trounced the Austrians, who had been joined by their new ally, Russia. The battle of Austerlitz, often considered Napoleon's greatest victory, was fought on December 2, 1805, the first anniversary of his coronation.

After maintaining neutrality for a decade, Prussia now declared war on France. In 1806, the French routed the Prussian army at Jena and Auerstädt. In 1807, Napoleon defeated the Russians at Friedland. Personal negotiations between Napoleon and the young tsar Alexander I (r. 1801–1825) resulted in a humiliating settlement imposed on Prussia, which paid the price for temporary reconciliation between France and Russia; the Treaties of Tilsit turned Prussian lands west of the Elbe River into the kingdom of Westphalia under Napoleon's brother Jerome, and Prussia's Polish provinces became the duchy of Warsaw. Napoleon once again had turned the divisions among his enemies to his favor.

The Impact of French Victories

Wherever the Grand Army conquered, Napoleon's influence followed soon after. By annexing some territories and setting up others as satellite kingdoms with much-reduced autonomy, Napoleon attempted to colonize large parts of Europe (see Map 20.1, page 660). But even where he did not rule directly or through his relatives, his startling string of victories forced the other powers to reconsider their own methods of rule.

Rule in the Colonized Territories Napoleon brought the disparate German and Italian states together so that he could rule them more effectively and exploit their resources for his own ends. In 1803, he consolidated the tiny German states by abolishing some of them and

Napoleon Visiting the Battlefield
Antoine-Jean Gros painted this scene of the battle of Eylau (now in northwestern Russia, then in East Prussia) shortly after Napoleon's victory against the Russian army in 1807. The painter aims to show the compassion of Napoleon for his men, but he also draws attention to the sheer carnage of war. Each side lost 25,000 men, killed or wounded, in this battle. What would you conclude from the way the ordinary soldiers are depicted here? *(Louvre, Paris, France/The Bridgeman Art Library International.)*

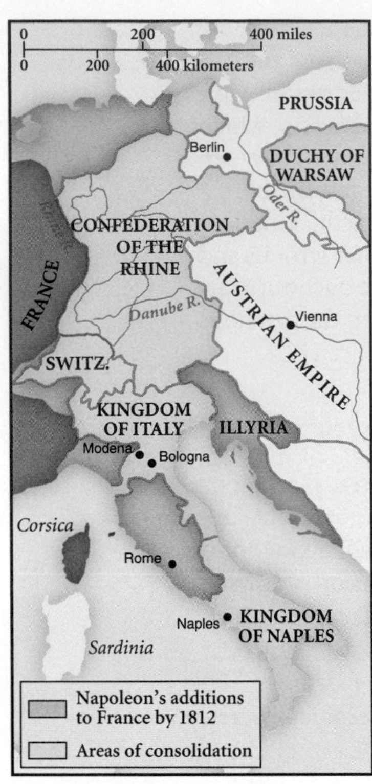

Consolidation of German and Italian States, 1812

attaching them to larger units. In July 1806, he established the Confederation of the Rhine, which soon included almost all the German states except Austria and Prussia. The Holy Roman Emperor gave up his title, held since the thirteenth century, and became simply the emperor of Austria. Napoleon established three units in Italy: the territories directly annexed to France and the satellite kingdoms of Italy and Naples. Italy had not been so unified since the Roman Empire.

Napoleon forced French-style reforms on both the annexed territories, which were ruled directly from France, and the satellite kingdoms, which were usually ruled by one or another of Napoleon's relatives but with a certain autonomy. French-style reforms included abolishing serfdom, eliminating seigneurial dues, introducing the Napoleonic Code, suppressing monasteries, and subordinating church to state, as well as extending civil rights to Jews and other religious minorities. Napoleon's chosen rulers often made real improvements in roads, public works, law codes, and education. The removal of internal tariffs fostered economic growth by opening up the domestic market for goods, especially textiles. By 1814, Bologna had five hundred factories and Modena four hundred. Yet almost everyone had some cause for complaint. Republicans regretted Napoleon's conversion of the sister republics into kingdoms. Tax increases and ever-rising conscription quotas fomented discontent as well. The annexed territories and satellite kingdoms paid half the cost of Napoleon's wars.

Almost everywhere, conflicts arose between Napoleon's desire for a standardized, centralized government and local insistence on maintaining customs and traditions. Sometimes his own relatives sided with the countries they ruled. Napoleon's brother Louis, for instance, would not allow conscription in the Netherlands because the Dutch had never had compulsory military service. When Napoleon tried to introduce an economic policy banning trade with Great Britain, Louis's lax enforcement infuriated the emperor, and Napoleon annexed the satellite kingdom in 1810.

Pressure for Reform in Prussia and Russia

Napoleon's victories forced defeated rulers to rethink their political and cultural assumptions. After the crushing defeat of Prussia in 1806 left his country greatly reduced in territory, Frederick William III (r. 1797–1840) appointed a reform commission, and on its recommendation he abolished serfdom and allowed non-nobles to buy and enclose land. Peasants gained their personal independence from their noble landlords, who could no longer sell them to pay gambling debts, for example, or refuse them permission to marry. Yet the lives of the former serfs remained bleak; they were left without land, and their landlords no longer had to care for them in hard times. The king's advisers also overhauled the army to make the high command more efficient and to open the way to the appointment of middle-class officers. Prussia instituted these reforms to try to compete with the French, not to promote democracy. As one reformer wrote to Frederick William, "We must do from above what the French have done from below."

Reform received lip service in Russia. Tsar Alexander I had gained his throne after an aristocratic coup deposed and killed his autocratic and capricious father, Paul (r. 1796–1801), and in the early years of his reign the remorseful young ruler created Western-style ministries, lifted restrictions on importing foreign books, and founded six new universities. In addition, reform commissions studied abuses, nobles were encouraged voluntarily to free their serfs (a few actually did so), and there was even talk of drafting a constitution. But none of these efforts reached beneath the surface of Russian life, and by the second decade of his reign Alexander began to reject the Enlightenment spirit that his grandmother Catherine the Great had instilled in him.

The Continental System

The one power always standing between Napoleon and total dominance of Europe was Great Britain. The British ruled the seas and financed anyone who would oppose Napoleon. In an effort to bankrupt this "nation of shopkeepers" by choking its trade, Napoleon inaugurated the **Continental System** in 1806. It prohibited all commerce between Great Britain and France or France's dependent states and allies. At first, the system worked: in 1807–1808, British exports dropped by 20 percent and manufacturing by 10 percent; unemployment

---

Continental System: The boycott of British goods in France and its satellites ordered by Napoleon in 1806; it had success but was later undermined by smuggling.

and a strike of sixty thousand workers in northern England resulted. The British retaliated by confiscating merchandise on ships, even those of powers neutral in the wars, that sailed into or out of ports from which the British were excluded by the system.

In the midst of continuing wars, moreover, the Continental System proved impossible to enforce, and widespread smuggling brought British goods into the European market. British growth continued, despite some setbacks; calico-printing works, for example, quadrupled their production, and imports of raw cotton increased by 40 percent. At the same time, French and other continental industries benefited from the temporary protection from British competition.

Resistance to French Rule, 1807–1812 Smuggling British goods was only one way of opposing the French. Almost everywhere in Europe, resistance began as local opposition to French demands for money or draftees but eventually prompted a more nationalistic patriotic defense. In southern Italy, gangs of bandits harassed the French army and local officials, who arrested thirty-three thousand Italian bandits in 1809 alone. But resistance continued via a network of secret societies called the *carbonari* ("charcoal burners"), which got its name from the practice of marking each new member's forehead with a charcoal mark. Throughout the nineteenth century, the carbonari played a leading role in Italian nationalism. In the German states, intellectuals wrote passionate defenses of the virtues of the German nation and of the superiority of German literature.

No nations bucked under Napoleon's reins more than Spain and Portugal. In 1807, Napoleon sent 100,000 troops through Spain to invade Portugal, Great Britain's ally. The royal family fled to the Portuguese colony of Brazil, but fighting continued, aided by a British army. When Napoleon got his brother Joseph named king of Spain in place of the senile Charles IV (r. 1788–1808), the Spanish clergy and nobles raised bands of peasants to fight the French occupiers. Even Napoleon's taking personal command of the French forces failed to quell the Spanish, who for six years fought a war of national

French Atrocities in Spain

In 1814 the Spanish painter Francisco Jose de Goya y Lucientes was inspired to depict a popular rebellion that took place in Madrid in 1808. The Spanish rebelled against the invading French when they learned that the French armies were forcing members of the Spanish royal family to leave Madrid. In this detail of the painting *The Second of May, 1808*, Mamelukes of the French army charge the rioting Spanish. (Mamelukes were Muslim soldiers who had originally been slaves.) *(Image © Francis G. Mayer/Corbis.)*

independence that pinned down thousands of French soldiers. Germaine de Staël commented that Napoleon "never understood that a war might be a crusade. . . . He never reckoned with the one power that no arms could overcome — the enthusiasm of a whole people."

More than a new feeling of nationalism was aroused in Spain. Peasants hated French requisitioning of their food supplies and sought to defend their priests against French anticlericalism. Spanish nobles feared revolutionary reforms and were willing to defend the old monarchy in the person of the young Ferdinand VII, heir to Charles IV, even while Ferdinand himself was congratulating Napoleon on his victories. The Spanish Catholic church spread anti-French propaganda that equated Napoleon with heresy. As the former archbishop of Seville wrote to the archbishop of Granada in 1808, "You realize that we must not recognize as king a freemason, heretic, Lutheran, as are all the Bonapartes and the French nation." In this tense atmosphere, the Spanish peasant rebels, assisted by the British, countered every French massacre with atrocities of their own. They tortured their French prisoners (boiling one general alive) and lynched collaborators.

From Russian Winter to Final Defeat, 1812–1815

Despite opposition, Napoleon ruled over an extensive empire by 1812. Only two major European states remained fully independent — Great Britain and Russia — but once allied they would successfully challenge his dominion and draw many other states to their side. Britain sent aid to the Portuguese and Spanish rebels, while Russia once again prepared for war. Tsar Alexander I made peace with Turkey and allied himself with Great Britain and Sweden. In 1812, Napoleon invaded Russia with 250,000 horses and 600,000 men, including contingents of Italians, Poles, Swiss, Dutch, and Germans. This daring move proved to be his undoing.

Invasion of Russia, 1812 Napoleon followed his usual strategy of trying to strike quickly, but the Russian generals avoided confrontation and retreated eastward, destroying anything that might be useful to the invaders. In September, on the road to Moscow, Napoleon finally engaged the main Russian force in the gigantic battle of Borodino (see Map 20.1, page 660). French casualties numbered 30,000 men, including 47 generals; the Russians lost 45,000. The French soldiers had nothing to celebrate around their campfires: as one soldier wrote, "Everyone . . . wept for some dead friend." Once again the Russians retreated, leaving Moscow undefended. Napoleon entered the deserted city, but the victory turned hollow because the departing Russians had set the wooden city on fire. Within a week, three-fourths of it had burned to the ground. Still Alexander refused to negotiate, and French morale plunged with worsening problems of supply. Weeks of constant marching in the dirt and heat had worn down the foot soldiers, who were dying of disease or deserting in large numbers (see Document, "An Ordinary Soldier on Campaign with Napoleon," page 665).

In October, Napoleon began his retreat; in November came the cold. A German soldier in the Grand Army described trying to cook fistfuls of raw bran with snow to make something like bread. For him, the retreat was "the indescribable horror of all possible plagues." Within a week the Grand Army lost 30,000 horses and had to abandon most of its artillery and food supplies. Russian forces harassed the retreating army, now more pathetic than grand. By December only 100,000 troops remained, one-sixth the original number, and the retreat had turned into a rout: the Russians had captured 200,000 soldiers, including 48 generals and 3,000 other officers.

Napoleon had made a classic military mistake that would be repeated by Adolf Hitler in World War II: fighting a war on two distant fronts simultaneously. The Spanish war tied down 250,000 French troops and forced Napoleon to bully Prussia and Austria into supplying soldiers of dubious loyalty for the Moscow campaign; those soldiers deserted at the first opportunity. The fighting in Spain and Portugal also exacerbated the already substantial logistical and communications problems involved in marching to Moscow.

The End of Napoleon's Empire Napoleon's humiliation might have been temporary if the British and Russians had not successfully organized a coalition to complete the job. Napoleon still had resources at his command; by the spring of 1813, he had replenished his army with another 250,000 men. With British financial support, Russian, Austrian, Prussian, and Swedish armies met the French outside Leipzig in October 1813 and defeated Napoleon in the Battle of the Nations. One by one, Napoleon's German allies deserted him to join the German nationalist "war of liberation." The Confederation of the Rhine dissolved, and the Dutch revolted and restored the prince of Orange. Joseph Bonaparte fled Spain, and a combined Spanish-Portuguese army under British command invaded France. In only a few months, the allied powers crossed the Rhine and marched

DOCUMENT

An Ordinary Soldier on Campaign with Napoleon (1812)

Jakob Walter (1788–1864) recorded his experience as a soldier in the Napoleonic armies marching to Moscow in 1812. He wrote his account sometime after the events took place, though exactly when is not known. Walter was a German conscripted into military service from one of the many western German states controlled by Napoleon. The selection here describes the Napoleonic armies still on the offensive moving toward Moscow. But the seeds of future problems are already germinating.

On August 19, the entire army moved forward, and pursued the Russians with all speed. Four or five hours' farther up the river another battle started, but the enemy did not hold out long, and the march now led to Moshaisk [near Borodino], the so-called "Holy Valley." From Smolensk to Moshaisk the war displayed its horrible work of destruction: all the roads, fields, and woods lay as though sown with people, horses, wagons, burned villages and cities; everything looked like the complete ruin of all that lived. In particular, we saw ten dead Russians to one of our men, although every day our numbers fell off considerably. In order to pass through woods, swamps, and narrow trails, trees which formed barriers in the woods had to be removed, and wagon barricades of the enemy had to be cleared away. . . . The march up to there, as far as it was a march, is indescribable and inconceivable for people who have not seen anything of it. The very great heat, the dust which was like a thick fog, the closed line of march in columns, and the putrid water from holes filled with dead people and cattle brought everyone close to death; and eye pains, fatigue, thirst, and hunger tormented everybody. God! How often I remembered the bread and beer which I had enjoyed at home with such an indifferent pleasure! Now, however, I must struggle, half wild, with the dead and living. How gladly would I renounce for my whole life the warm food so common at home if I only did not lack good bread and beer now! I would not wish for more all my life. But these were empty, helpless thoughts. Yes, the thought of my brothers and sisters so far away added to my pain! Wherever I looked, I saw the soldiers with dead, half-desperate faces.

Source: Marc Raeff, ed., *Jakob Walter: The Diary of a Napoleonic Foot Soldier* (New York: Doubleday, 1991), 52–53.

Question to Consider

- **Do you think Walter's account of his experiences with Napoleon's army was clouded by the fact that he was a German conscript?**

toward Paris. In March 1814, the French Senate deposed Napoleon, who abdicated when his remaining generals refused to fight. Napoleon went into exile on the island of Elba off the Italian coast. His wife, Marie-Louise, refused to accompany him. The allies restored to the throne Louis XVIII (r. 1814–1824), the brother of Louis XVI, beheaded during the Revolution. (Louis XVI's son was known as Louis XVII even though he died in prison in 1795 without ever ruling.)

Because Louis XVIII lacked a solid base of support, Napoleon had one last chance to regain power. The new king tried to steer a middle course through a charter that established a British-style monarchy with a two-house legislature and guaranteed civil rights. But he was caught between nobles returning from exile, who demanded a complete restoration of their lands and powers, and the vast majority of ordinary people, who had supported either the republic or Napoleon during the previous twenty-five years. Sensing an opportunity, Napoleon escaped from Elba in early 1815 and, landing in southern France, made swift and unimpeded progress to Paris. Although he had left in ignominy, now crowds cheered him and former soldiers volunteered to serve him. The period eventually known as the Hundred Days (the length of time between Napoleon's escape and his final defeat) had begun. Louis XVIII fled across the border, waiting for help from France's enemies.

Napoleon quickly moved his reconstituted army of 74,000 men into present-day Belgium. At first, it seemed that he might succeed in separately fighting the two armies arrayed against him—a Prussian army of some 60,000 men and a joint force of 68,000 Belgian, Dutch, German, and British troops led by British general Sir Arthur Wellesley (1769–1852), duke of Wellington. The decisive **battle of Waterloo** took place on June 18, 1815, less than ten miles from Brussels. Napoleon's forces attacked Wellington's men first with infantry and then with cavalry, but the French failed to dislodge their opponents. Late in the afternoon, the Prussians arrived and the rout was complete. Napoleon had no

battle of Waterloo: The final battle lost by Napoleon; it took place near Brussels on June 18, 1815, and led to the deposed emperor's final exile.

CONTRASTING VIEWS

Napoleon: For and Against

After his final exile, Napoleon presented himself as a martyr to the cause of liberty whose goal was to create a European "federation of free people." Few were convinced by this "gospel according to St. Helena" (Document 1). Followers such as Emmanuel de Las Cases burnished the Napoleonic legend, but detractors such as Benjamin Constant viewed him as a tyrant (Document 2). For all his defects, Napoleon fascinated even those who were too young to understand his rise and fall. The French romantic poet Victor Hugo celebrated both the glory and the tragedy of Napoleonic ambitions (Document 3).

1. Napoleon's Own View from Exile

As might be expected, Napoleon put the most positive possible construction on his plans for France. In exile he wrote letters and talked at length to Emmanuel de Las Cases (1766–1842), an aristocratic officer in the royal navy who rallied to Napoleon in 1802, served in the Council of State, and later accompanied him to St. Helena. Much of what we know about Napoleon's views comes from a book published by Las Cases in 1821.

March 3, 1817:

In spite of all the libels, I have no fear whatever about my fame. Posterity will do me justice. The truth will be known; and the good I have done will be compared with the faults I have committed. I am not uneasy as to the result. Had I succeeded, I would have died with the reputation of the greatest man that ever existed. As it is, although I have failed, I shall be considered as an extraordinary man: my elevation was unparalleled, because unaccompanied by crime. I have fought fifty pitched battles, almost all of which I have won. I have framed and carried into effect a code of laws that will bear my name to the most distant posterity. I raised myself from nothing to be the most powerful monarch in the world. Europe was at my feet. I have always been of the opinion that the sovereignty lay in the people. In fact, the imperial government was a kind of republic. Called to the head of it by the voice of the nation, my maxim was, *la carrière est ouverte aux talents* ["careers open to talent"] without distinction of birth or fortune, and this system of equality is the reason that your oligarchy hates me so much.

Source: R. M. Johnston, *The Corsican: A Diary of Napoleon's Life in His Own Words* (Boston: Houghton Mifflin, 1921), 492.

2. Benjamin Constant, Spokesman for the Liberal Opposition to Napoleon

Benjamin Constant (1767–1830) came from an old French Calvinist family that had fled to Switzerland to escape persecution. Constant spent the early years of the French Revolution in a minor post at a minor German court. He moved to Paris in 1795 and became active in French politics during the Directory. Under Napoleon he went into exile, where he published a romantic novel, Adolphe *(1806), and pamphlets like this one attacking Napoleon. He reconciled to Napoleon during the Hundred Days and then opposed the restored Bourbon monarchy. In this selection, written during his exile, he expresses his hostility to Napoleon as a usurper dependent on war to maintain himself in power.*

Surely, Bonaparte is a thousand times more guilty than those barbarous conquerors who, ruling over barbarians, were by no means at odds with their age. Unlike them, he has chosen barbarism; he has preferred it. In the midst of enlightenment, he has sought to bring back the night. He has chosen to transform into greedy and bloodthirsty nomads a mild and polite people: his crime lies in this premeditated intention, in his obstinate effort to rob us of the heritage of all the enlightened generations who have preceded us on this earth. But why have we given him the right to conceive such a project?

When he first arrived here, alone, out of poverty and obscurity, and until he was twenty-four, his greedy gaze wandering over the country around him, why did we show him a country in which any religious idea was the object of irony? [Constant refers here to de-Christianization during the French Revolution.] When he listened to what was professed in our circles, why did serious thinkers tell him that man had no other motivation than his own interest? . . .

Because immediate usurpation was easy, he believed it could be durable, and

choice but to abdicate again. This time the victorious allies banished him permanently to the remote island of St. Helena, far off the coast of West Africa, where he died in 1821 at the age of fifty-two.

The cost of Napoleon's rule was high: 750,000 French soldiers and 400,000 others from annexed and satellite states died between 1800 and 1815. Yet his impact on world history was undeniable. (See "Contrasting Views," above.) Napoleon's plans for a united Europe, his insistence on spreading the legal reforms of the French Revolution, his social welfare programs, and even his inadvertent awakening of national sentiment set the agenda for European history in the modern era.

REVIEW QUESTION Why was Napoleon able to gain control over so much of Europe's territory?

once he became a usurper, he did all that usurpation condemns a usurper to do in our century.

It was necessary to stifle inside the country all intellectual life: he banished discussion and proscribed the freedom of the press.

The nation might have been stunned by that silence: he provided, extorted or paid for acclamation which sounded like the national voice. . . . War flung onto distant shores that part of the French nation that still had some real energy. It prompted the police harassment of the timid, whom it could not force abroad. It struck terror into men's hearts, and left there a certain hope that chance would take responsibility for their deliverance: a hope agreeable to fear and convenient to inertia. How many times have I heard men who were pressed to resist tyranny postponing this, during wartime till the coming of peace, and in peacetime until war commences!

I am right therefore in claiming that a usurper's sole resource is uninterrupted war. Some object: what if Bonaparte had been pacific? Had he been pacific, he would never have lasted for twelve years. Peace would have re-established communication among the different countries of Europe. These communications would have restored to thought its means of expression. Works published abroad would have been smuggled into the country. The French would have seen that they did not enjoy the approval of the majority of Europe.

Source: Benjamin Constant, "Further Reflections on Usurpation," in *Political Writings*, trans. Biancamaria Fontana (Cambridge: Cambridge University Press, 1988), 161–63.

3. Victor Hugo, "The Two Islands" (1825)

Victor Hugo (1802–1885) was France's greatest romantic poet and novelist, author of The Hunchback of Notre Dame *and* Les Misérables. *His father was a Napoleonic general, but his mother was an equally ardent royalist. In this early poem, Hugo compares Napoleon to one of Napoleon's favorite icons, the eagle, symbol of empire. The two islands of the title are Corsica, Napoleon's birthplace, and St. Helena, his place of final exile and death.*

These Isles, where Ocean's shattered spray
Upon the ruthless rocks is cast,
Seem like two treacherous ships of prey,
Made by eternal anchors fast.
The hand that settled bleak and black
Those shores on their unpeopled rack,
And clad in fear and mystery,
Perchance thus made them tempest-torn,
That Bonaparte might there be born,
And that Napoleon there might die. . . .
He his imperial nest hath built so far and high,
He seems to us to dwell within that tranquil sky,
Where you shall never see the angry tempest break.
'Tis but beneath his feet the growling storms are sped,
And thunders to assault his head
Must to their highest source go back.
The bolt flew upwards: from his eyrie [nest] riven,
Blazing he falls beneath the stroke of heaven;
Then kings their tyrant foe reward—
They chain him, living, on that lonely shore;
And earth captive giant handed o'er
To ocean's more resistless guard. . . .
Shame, hate, misfortune, vengeance, curses sore,
On him let heaven and earth together pour:
Now, see we dashed the vast Colossus low.
May he forever rue, alive and dead,
All tears he caused mankind to shed,
And all the blood he caused to flow.

Source: Henry Carrington, *Translations from the Poems of Victor Hugo* (London: Walter Scott, 1885), 34–41.

Questions to Consider

1. **Which of these views of Napoleon has the most lasting value as opposed to immediate dramatic effect?**
2. **According to these selections, what was Napoleon's greatest accomplishment? His greatest failure?**
3. **Victor Hugo called Napoleon "the vast Colossus." Why did he pick this larger-than-life metaphor even when writing lines critical of Napoleon's legacy of tears and bloodshed?**

The "Restoration" of Europe

Even while Napoleon was making his last desperate bid for power, his enemies were meeting in the Congress of Vienna (1814–1815) to decide the fate of postrevolutionary, post-Napoleonic Europe. Although interrupted by the Hundred Days, the **Congress of Vienna** settled the boundaries of European states, determined who would rule each nation, and established a new framework for international

Congress of Vienna: Face-to-face negotiations (1814–1815) between the great powers to settle the boundaries of European states and determine who would rule each nation after the defeat of Napoleon.

relations based on periodic meetings, or congresses, between the major powers. The doctrine of conservatism bolstered this post-Napoleonic order and in some places went hand in hand with a revival of religion.

The Congress of Vienna, 1814–1815

The Vienna settlement established a new equilibrium that relied on cooperation among the major powers while guaranteeing the status of smaller states. The revolutionary and Napoleonic wars had produced a host of potentially divisive issues. In addition to determining the boundaries of France, the congress had to decide the fate of Napoleon's duchy of Warsaw, the German province of Saxony, the Netherlands, the states once part of the Confederation of the Rhine, and various Italian territories. All had either changed hands or been created during the wars. These issues were resolved by face-to-face negotiations among representatives of the five major powers: Austria, Russia, Prussia, Britain, and France. With its aim to establish a long-lasting, negotiated peace endorsed by all parties, both winners and losers, the Congress of Vienna provided a model for the twentieth-century League of Nations and United Nations. The congress system, or "concert of Europe," helped prevent another major war until the 1850s, and no conflict comparable to the Napoleonic wars would occur again until 1914.

Austria's chief negotiator, Prince **Klemens von Metternich** (1773–1859), took the lead in devising the settlement and shaping the post-Napoleonic order. A well-educated nobleman who spoke five languages, Metternich served as a minister in the Austrian cabinet from 1809 to 1848. Although his penchant for womanizing made him a security risk in the eyes of the British Foreign Office (he even had an affair with Napoleon's younger sister), he worked with the British prime minister Robert Castlereagh (1769–1822) to ensure a moderate agreement that would check French aggression yet maintain France's great-power status. Metternich and Castlereagh believed that French aggression must be contained, because it had threatened the European peace since the days of Louis XIV, but at the same time that France must remain a major player to prevent any one European power from dominating the others. In this way, France could help Austria and Britain counter the ambitions of Prussia and Russia. Castlereagh hoped to make Britain the arbiter of European affairs, but he knew this could be accomplished only through adroit diplomacy because the British consti-

Klemens von Metternich (KLAY mehnts fawn MEH tur nihk): An Austrian prince (1773–1859) who took the lead in devising the post-Napoleonic settlement arranged by the Congress of Vienna (1814–1815).

Congress of Vienna

An unknown French engraver caricatured the efforts of the diplomats at the Congress of Vienna, complaining that they used the occasion to divide the spoils of European territory. What elements in this engraving make it a caricature? *(Photo: akg-images.)*

MAP 20.2 Europe after the Congress of Vienna, 1815
The Congress of Vienna forced France to return to its 1789 borders. The Austrian Netherlands and the Dutch Republic were united in a new kingdom of the Netherlands, the German states were joined in a German Confederation that built on Napoleon's Confederation of the Rhine, and Napoleon's duchy of Warsaw became the kingdom of Poland with the tsar of Russia as king. To compensate for its losses in Poland, Prussia gained territory in Saxony and on the left bank of the Rhine. Austria reclaimed the Italian provinces of Lombardy and Venetia and the Dalmatian coast.

tutional monarchy had little in common with most of its more absolutist continental counterparts.

The task of ensuring France's status at the Congress of Vienna fell to Prince Charles Maurice de Talleyrand (1754–1838), an aristocrat and former bishop who had embraced the French Revolution, served as Napoleon's foreign minister, and ended as foreign minister to Louis XVIII after helping arrange the emperor's overthrow. Informed of Talleyrand's betrayal, Napoleon called him "excrement in silk stockings." When the French army failed to oppose Napoleon's return to power in the Hundred Days, the allies took away all territory conquered since 1790, levied an indemnity against France, and required it to support an army of occupation until it had paid.

The goal of the Congress of Vienna was to achieve postwar stability by establishing secure states with guaranteed borders (Map 20.2). Because the congress aimed to "restore" as many regimes as possible to their former rulers, this epoch is sometimes labeled the **restoration**. But simple restoration was not always feasible, and in those cases the congress rearranged territory to balance the competing interests of the great powers. Thus, the congress turned the duchy of Warsaw into a new Polish kingdom but made the tsar of Russia its king. (Poland would not regain its independence until 1918.) The former Dutch Republic and the Austrian Netherlands, both annexed to France, were now united as the new kingdom of the Netherlands under the restored stadholder. Austria took charge of the German Confederation, which replaced the defunct Holy Roman Empire and also included Prussia.

---

restoration: The epoch after the fall of Napoleon, in which the Congress of Vienna aimed to "restore" as many regimes as possible to their former rulers.

The lesser powers were not forgotten. The kingdom of Piedmont-Sardinia took Genoa, Nice, and part of Savoy. Sweden obtained Norway from Denmark but had to accept Russia's conquest of Finland. Finally, various international trade issues were also resolved. Great Britain, which had abolished its slave trade in 1807, urged the congress to condemn that trade for other nations. The congress agreed in principle; in reality, however, the slave trade continued in many places until 1850. Nearly three million Africans were sold into slavery between 1800 and 1850, and most were transported on either Portuguese or Brazilian slave ships.

To impart spiritual substance to this very calculated settlement of political affairs, Tsar Alexander proposed the Holy Alliance, which called on divine assistance in upholding religion, peace, and justice. Prussia and Austria signed the agreement, but Great Britain refused to accede to what Castlereagh called "a piece of sublime mysticism and nonsense." Despite the reassertion of traditional religious principles, the congress had in fact given birth to a new diplomatic order: in the future, the legitimacy of states depended on the treaty system, not on divine right.

The Emergence of Conservatism

The French Revolution and Napoleonic domination of Europe had shown contemporaries that government could be changed overnight, that the old hierarchies could be overthrown in the name of reason, and that even Christianity could be written off or at least profoundly altered with the stroke of a pen. The potential for rapid change raised many questions about the proper sources of authority. Kings and churches could be restored and former revolutionaries locked up or silenced, but the old order no longer commanded automatic obedience. The old order was now merely *old*, no longer "natural" and "timeless." It had been ousted once and therefore might fall again. People insisted on having reasons to believe in their "restored" governments. The political doctrine that justified the restoration was **conservatism**.

Conservatives benefited from the disillusionment that permeated Europe after 1815. In the eyes of most Europeans, Napoleon had become a tyrant who ruled in his own interests. Conservatives saw a logical progression in recent history: the Enlightenment, based on reason, led to the French Revolution, with its bloody guillotine and horrifying Terror, which in turn spawned the authoritarian and militaristic Napoleon. Therefore, those who espoused conservatism rejected both the Enlightenment and the French Revolution. They favored monarchies over republics, tradition over revolution, and established religion over Enlightenment skepticism.

The original British critic of the French Revolution, Edmund Burke (1729–1797), inspired many of the conservatives who followed. He had argued that the revolutionaries erred in thinking they could construct an entirely new government based on reason. Government, Burke said, had to be rooted in long experience, which evolved over generations. All change must be gradual and must respect national and historical traditions. Like Burke, later conservatives believed that religious and other major traditions were an essential foundation for any society. Most of them took their resistance to change even further, however, and tried to restore the pre-1789 social order.

Conservatives blamed the French Revolution's attack on religion on the skepticism and anticlericalism of such Enlightenment thinkers as Voltaire, and they defended both hereditary monarchy and the authority of the church, whether Catholic or Protestant. Louis de Bonald, an official under the restored French monarchy, insisted that "the revolution began with the declaration of the rights of man and will only finish when the rights of God are declared." The declaration of rights, he asserted, represented the evil influence of Enlightenment philosophy and with it atheism, Protestantism, and freemasonry, which he lumped together. In this view, an enduring social order could be constructed only on the foundations provided by the church, the state, and the patriarchal family. Faith, sentiment, history, and tradition must fill the vacuum left by the failures of reason and excessive belief in individual rights. Across Europe, these views were taken up and elaborated by government advisers, professors, and writers. Not surprisingly, they had their strongest appeal in ruling circles and guided the politics of men such as Metternich in Austria, Alexander I in Russia, and the restored Bourbons in France.

The restored French monarchy provided a major test for conservatism because the returning Bourbons had to confront the legacy of twenty-five years of upheaval. Louis XVIII tried to ensure a measure of continuity by maintaining Napoleon's Civil Code. He also guaranteed the rights of ownership to church lands sold during the revolutionary period and created a parliament composed of the Chamber of Peers, nominated by the king, and the Chamber of Deputies, elected by very restricted suf-

---

conservatism: A political doctrine that emerged after 1789 and took hold after 1815; it rejected much of the Enlightenment and the French Revolution, preferring monarchies over republics, tradition over revolution, and established religion over Enlightenment skepticism.

frage (fewer than 100,000 voters in a population of 30 million). In making these concessions, the king tried to follow a moderate course of compromise, but the Ultras (ultraroyalists) pushed for complete repudiation of the revolutionary past. When Louis returned to power after Napoleon's final defeat, armed royalist bands attacked and murdered hundreds of Bonapartists and former revolutionaries. In 1816, the Ultras insisted on abolishing divorce and set up special courts to punish opponents of the regime. When an assassin killed Louis XVIII's nephew in 1820, the Ultras successfully demanded even more extreme measures.

The Revival of Religion

The experience of revolutionary upheaval and nearly constant warfare prompted many to renew their religious faith once peace returned. In France, the Catholic church sent missionaries to hold open-air "ceremonies of reparation" to express repentance for the outrages of revolution. In Rome, the papacy reestablished the Jesuit order, which had been disbanded during the Enlightenment. In the Italian states and Spain, governments used religious societies of laypeople to combat the influence of reformers and nationalists such as the Italian carbonari.

Revivalist movements, especially in Protestant countries, could on occasion challenge the status quo rather than supporting it. In parts of Protestant Germany and Britain, religious revival had begun in the eighteenth century with the rise of Pietism and Methodism, movements that stressed individual religious experience rather than reason as the true path to moral and social reform. The English Methodists followed John Wesley (1703–1791), who had preached an emotional, morally austere, and very personal "method" of gaining salvation.

The Methodists, or Wesleyans, gradually separated from the Church of England and in the early decades of the nineteenth century attracted thousands of members in huge revival meetings that lasted for days. Shopkeepers, artisans, agricultural laborers, miners, and workers in cottage industries, both male and female, flocked to the new denomination, even though at first Methodism seemed to emphasize conservative political views: Methodist statutes of 1792 had insisted that "none of us shall either in writing or in conversation speak lightly or irreverently of the government." In their hostility to rigid doctrine and elaborate ritual and their encouragement of popular preaching, however, the Methodists in England fostered a sense of democratic community and even a rudimentary sexual equality. From the beginning, women preachers traveled on horseback to preach in barns, town halls, and textile dye houses. The Methodist Sunday schools that taught thousands of poor children to read and write eventually helped create greater demands for working-class political participation.

The religious revival was not limited to Europe. In the United States, the second Great Awakening began around 1790 with huge camp meetings that brought together thousands of worshippers and scores of evangelical preachers, many of them Methodist. (The original Great Awakening took place in the 1730s and 1740s, sparked by the preaching of George Whitefield, a young English evangelist and follower of John Wesley.) Men and women danced to exhaustion, fell into trances, and spoke in tongues. During this period, Protestant sects began systematic missionary activity in other parts of the world. In the British colony of India, for example, Protestant missionaries pushed the British administration to abolish the Hindu custom of *sati*—the burning of widows on the funeral pyres of their

A Protestant Missionary in India
This colored engraving shows the English Baptist missionary William Carey (1761–1834) baptizing his first Hindu convert. Carey went to India in 1793 and spent forty years there as a teacher and a preacher. He led efforts to get the British governor general to outlaw the Hindu rite of *sati*, the burning of widows with their husbands. He became professor of Indian languages at Fort William College, established in Calcutta for training British officials, and supervised the translation of the Bible into more than forty local languages. *(The Granger Collection, New York—All rights reserved.)*

husbands—in 1829. The missionaries hoped such actions would make Indians more likely to embrace Christianity. Missionary activity by Protestants and Catholics would become one of the arms of European imperialism and cultural influence in the nineteenth century.

REVIEW QUESTION To what extent did the Congress of Vienna restore the old order?

Challenges to the Conservative Order

Conservatives hoped to clamp a lid on European affairs, but the lid kept threatening to fly off. Drawing on the turmoil in society and politics was romanticism, the burgeoning international movement in the arts and literature that dominated artistic expression in the first half of the nineteenth century. Although romantics shared with conservatives a distrust of the Enlightenment's emphasis on reason, romanticism did not translate into a unified political position. It did, however, heighten the general discontent with the conservative Vienna settlement. Isolated revolts threatened the hold of some conservative governments in the 1820s, but most of these rebellions were quickly bottled up. Then in 1830, successive uprisings briefly overwhelmed the established order. Across Europe, angry protesters sought constitutional guarantees of individual liberties and national unity and autonomy. The revolutionary legacy came back to life again.

Romanticism

As an artistic movement, romanticism encompassed poetry, music, painting, history, and literature. (See Chapter 18 for the origins of romanticism.) It glorified nature, emotion, genius, and imagination as antidotes to the Enlightenment and to classicism in the arts, challenging the reliance on reason, symmetry, and cool geometric spaces. Classicism idealized models from Roman history; romanticism turned to folklore and medieval legends. Classicism celebrated orderly, crisp lines; romantics sought out all that was wild, fevered, and disorderly. Chief among the arts of romanticism were poetry, music, and painting, which captured the deep-seated emotion characteristic of romantic expression. Romantics might take any political position, but they exerted the most political influence when they expressed nationalist feelings.

Romantic Poetry Romantic poetry celebrated overwhelming emotion and creative imagination. George Gordon, Lord Byron (1788–1824), explained his aims in writing poetry:

> For what is Poesy but to create
> From overfeeling, Good and Ill, and aim
> At an external life beyond our fate,
> And be the new Prometheus of new man.

Prometheus was the mythological figure who brought fire from the Greek gods to human beings. Byron did not seek the new Prometheus among political leaders or military men; he sought him within his own "overfeeling," his own intense emotions. Byron became a romantic hero himself when he rushed off to act on his emotions by fighting and dying in the Greek war for independence from

Romantic Painting
Johann Heinrich Fuseli painted *The Nightmare* in 1781, and it instantly became controversial because of the pose of the woman and the accompanying nightmarish figures. Are they actually present in the room, or are they only in the mind of the sleeper? Mary Shelley based a scene in *Frankenstein* on the painting; her parents were close friends of Fuseli. In what ways does this painting capture the themes of romanticism? *(Oil on canvas, 1781, Johann Heinrich Fussli [1741–1825]. Detroit Institute of Arts, USA / Founders Society purchase with Mr. and Mrs. Bert L. Smokler and Mr. and Mrs. Lawrence A. Fleischman funds / The Bridgeman Art Library International.)*

DOCUMENT

Wordsworth's Poetry (1798)

The son of a lawyer, William Wordsworth (1770–1850) studied at Cambridge University and then traveled to France during the early years of the French Revolution. He returned to England and began publishing the poetry that for many scholars marks the beginning of romanticism with its emphasis on the sublime beauties of nature. This excerpt from "Lines Composed a Few Miles above Tintern Abbey" (1798) shows the influence of his extensive walking tours through the English countryside. But the passage also captures the melancholy and nostalgia that characterized much of romantic poetry.

And now, with gleams of half-extinguished thought,
With many recognitions dim and faint,
And somewhat of a sad perplexity,
The picture of the mind revives again:
While here I stand, not only with the sense
Of present pleasure, but with pleasing thoughts
That in this moment there is life and food
For future years. And so I dare to hope,
Though changed, no doubt, from what I was when first
I came among these hills; when like a roe
I bounded o'er the mountains, by the sides
Of the deep rivers, and the lonely streams,
Wherever nature led: more like a man
Flying from something that he dreads, than one
Who sought the thing he loved. For nature then
(The coarser pleasures of my boyish days,
And their glad animal movements all gone by)
To me was all in all.—I cannot paint
What then I was. The sounding cataract
Haunted me like a passion: the tall rock,
The mountain, and the deep and gloomy wood,
Their colours and their forms, were then to me
An appetite; a feeling and a love,
That had no need of a remoter charm,
By thought supplied, nor any interest
Unborrowed from the eye.—That time is past.

Source: Paul Davis, ed., *Bedford Anthology of World Literature.* Book 5: *The Nineteenth Century, 1800–1900* (Boston: Bedford/St. Martin's, 2003), 246–47.

Question to Consider

- **In its specific imagery and overall message, how does Wordsworth's poem reflect a different sensibility about the world than writing associated with the Enlightenment?**

the Turks. An English aristocrat, Byron nonetheless claimed, "I have simplified my politics into a detestation of all existing governments."

Romantic poetry elevated the wonders of nature almost to the supernatural. In a poem that became one of the most beloved exemplars of romanticism, "Tintern Abbey" (1798), the English poet William Wordsworth (1770–1850) compared himself to a deer even while making nature seem filled with human emotions (see Document, "Wordsworth's Poetry," above). Like many poets of his time, Wordsworth greeted the French Revolution with joy; in his poem "French Revolution" (1809), he remembered his early enthusiasm: "Bliss was it in that dawn to be alive." But gradually he became disenchanted with the revolutionary experiment and celebrated British nationalism instead; in 1816, he published a poem to commemorate the "intrepid sons of Albion [England]" who died at the battle of Waterloo.

Their emphasis on authentic self-expression at times drew romantics to exotic, mystical, or even reckless experiences. Some romantics depicted the artist as possessed by demons and obsessed with hallucinations. This more nightmarish side was captured, and perhaps criticized, by Mary Shelley in *Frankenstein*. The aged German poet Johann Wolfgang von Goethe (1749–1832) likewise denounced the extremes of romanticism, calling it "everything that is sick." In his tragic play *Faust* (1808–1832), he seemed to warn of the same dangers Shelley portrayed in her novel. In Goethe's retelling of a sixteenth-century legend, Faust offers his soul to the devil in return for a chance to taste all human experience—from passionate love to the heights of power—in his effort to reshape nature for humanity's benefit. Faust's striving, like Frankenstein's, leaves a wake of suffering and destruction.

Romantic Painting and Music Romanticism in painting similarly idealized nature and the individual of deep feelings. The German romantic painter Caspar David Friedrich (1774–1840) depicted scenes—often far away in the mountains—that captured the romantic fascination with the sublime power of nature. His melancholy individual figures looked lost in the vastness of an overpowering nature. Friedrich hated the modern world. His landscapes

Eugène Delacroix, *Massacre at Chios* (1824)
More than any other painter associated with romanticism, Delacroix focused on dramatic events of his time. Here he shows sick and dying Greek civilians about to be massacred by the Turks. He aims to elicit sympathy for the Greek campaign for independence, a cause that had many followers in France and the rest of Europe.
(Oil on canvas, 1824/The Granger Collection, New York—All rights reserved.)

often had religious meaning as well, as in his controversial painting *The Cross in the Mountains* (1808), which showed a Christian cross standing alone in a mountain scene. It symbolized the steadfastness of faith but seemed to separate religion from the churches and attach it to mystical experience.

Many other artists developed similar themes. The English painter Joseph M. W. Turner (1775–1851) depicted his vision of nature in mysterious, misty seascapes, anticipating later artists by blurring the outlines of objects. The French painter Eugène Delacroix (1798–1863) chose contemporary as well as medieval scenes of great turbulence to emphasize light and color and break away from what he saw as "the servile copies repeated *ad nauseum* in academies of art." Critics denounced his techniques as "painting with a drunken broom." To broaden his experience of light and color, Delacroix traveled in the 1830s to North Africa and painted many exotic scenes in Morocco and Algeria.

The towering presence of the German composer **Ludwig van Beethoven** (1770–1827) in early-nineteenth-century music helped establish the direction for musical romanticism. His music, according to one leading German romantic, "sets in motion the lever of fear, of awe, of horror, of suffering, and awakens just that infinite longing which is the essence of Romanticism." Beethoven transformed the symphony into a connected work with recurring and evolving musical themes. Romantic symphonies conveyed the impression of growth, a metaphor for the organic process with an emphasis on the natural that was dear to the romantics. For example, Beethoven's Sixth Symphony, the *Pastoral* (1808), used a variety of instruments to represent sounds heard in the country. Beethoven's work—ranging from religious works to symphonies, sonatas, and concertos—showed remarkable diversity. Some of his work was explicitly political; his Ninth Symphony (1824) employed a chorus to sing the German poet Friedrich Schiller's verses in praise of universal human solidarity. Beethoven had admired Napoleon and even dedicated his Third Symphony, the *Eroica* (1804), to him, but when he learned of Napoleon's decision to name himself emperor, he tore up the dedication in disgust.

Romantic Nationalism

If romantics had any common political thread, it was the support of nationalist aspirations, especially through the search for the historical origins of national identity. In the German states, the Austrian Empire, Russia and other Slavic lands, and Scandinavia, romantic poets and writers collected old legends and folktales that expressed a shared cultural and linguistic heritage stretching back to the Middle Ages. These collections showed that Germany, for example, had always existed even if it did not currently take the form of a single unified state. Italian nationalists took *The Betrothed* (1825–1827), a novel by Alessandro Manzoni (1785–1873), as a kind of bible. Manzoni, the grandson of the Italian Enlightenment hero Cesare Beccaria, set his novel in the seventeenth century, when Spain controlled Italy's destiny, but his readers understood that he intended to attack the Austrians who controlled northern Italy in his own day. By writing this book (the first historical novel in Italian literature) in the Tuscan dialect, Manzoni achieved two aims: he helped create a standard national language and popularized Italian history for a people long divided by different dialects and competing rulers.

Ludwig van Beethoven: The German composer (1770–1827) who helped set the direction of musical romanticism; his music used recurring and evolving themes to convey the impression of natural growth.

William Blake, *The Circle of the Lustful* (1824)
An English romantic poet, painter, engraver, and printmaker, Blake always sought his own way. Self-taught, he began writing poetry at age twelve and apprenticed himself to an engraver at fourteen. His works incorporate many otherworldly attributes; they are quite literally visionary—imagining other worlds. In this engraving of hell, the twisting, turning figures are caught up in a kind of spiritual ether. Can you find elements in this engraving that reflect a criticism of Enlightenment ideals? *(© Birmingham Museums and Art Gallery, Birmingham, UK/The Bridgeman Art Library International.)*

Manzoni had been inspired to write his novel by the most influential of all historical novelists, **Sir Walter Scott** (1771–1832). While working as a lawyer and then judge in Scotland, Scott first collected and published traditional Scottish ballads that he heard as a child. After achieving immediate success with his own poetry, especially *The Lady of the Lake* (1810), he switched to historical novels. His novels are almost all renditions of historical events, from *Rob Roy* (1817), with its account of Scottish resistance to the English in the early eighteenth century, to *Ivanhoe* (1819), with its tales of medieval England. One contemporary critic claimed, "There is more history in the novels of Walter Scott than in half of the historians." Scott captured the truths of human nature rather than sticking to the bare facts recorded by historians.

Political Revolts in the 1820s

The restoration of regimes after Napoleon's fall disappointed those who dreamed of constitutional freedoms and national independence. Membership grew in secret societies such as the carbonari, attracting tens of thousands of members, including physicians, lawyers, officers, and students. Revolts broke out in the 1820s in Spain, Italy, Russia, and Greece (see Map 20.3 on page 678), as well as across the Atlantic in the Spanish and Portuguese colonies of Latin America. Most revolts failed, but those in Greece and Latin America succeeded, largely because they did not threaten the conservative order in Europe.

Sir Walter Scott: A prolific author (1771–1832) of popular historical novels; he also collected and published traditional Scottish ballads and wrote poetry.

Uprisings in Spain and Italy When Ferdinand VII regained the Spanish crown in 1814, he quickly restored the prerevolutionary nobility, church, and monarchy. He had foreign books and newspapers confiscated at the frontier and allowed the publication of only two newspapers. Not surprisingly, such repressive policies disturbed the middle class, especially the army officers who had encountered French ideas. Many responded by joining secret societies. In 1820, disgruntled soldiers demanded that Ferdinand proclaim his adherence to the constitution of 1812, which he had abolished in 1814. When the revolt spread, Ferdinand convened the *cortes* (parliament), which could agree on virtually nothing. Ferdinand bided his time, and in 1823 a French army invaded and restored him to absolute power. The French acted with the consent of the other great powers. The restored Spanish government tortured and executed hundreds of rebels; thousands were imprisoned or forced into exile.

Hearing of the Spanish uprising, rebellious soldiers in the kingdom of Naples joined forces with the carbonari and demanded a constitution. When a new parliament met, it too broke down over internal disagreements. The promise of reform sparked rebellion in the northern Italian kingdom of Piedmont-Sardinia, where rebels urged Charles Albert, the young heir to the Piedmont throne, to fight the Austrians for Italian unification. He vacillated; but in 1821, after the rulers of Austria, Prussia, and Russia met and agreed on intervention, the

Austrians defeated the rebels in Naples and Piedmont. Liberals were arrested in many Italian states, and the pope condemned the secret societies as "devouring wolves." Despite the opposition of Great Britain, which condemned the indiscriminate suppression of revolutionary movements, Metternich convinced the other powers to agree to his muffling of the Italian opposition to Austrian rule.

Metternich acted quickly to suppress any sign of dissent closer to home. University students had formed nationalist student societies called *Burschenschaften*, and in 1817 they held a mass rally at which they burned books they did not like, including Napoleon's Civil Code. Their leader was Friedrich Ludwig Jahn, who hoped to create a nationally unified Germany through education. He advocated gymnastics (he invented the parallel bars, the balance beam, gymnastics rings, the vaulting horse, and the horizontal bar) and study of all things German in order to create a stronger German "breed." Jahn favored the formation of a huge, racially pure German nation encompassing Switzerland, the Low Countries, Denmark, Prussia, and Austria. He also spouted such xenophobic (antiforeign) slogans as "If you let your daughter learn French, you might just as well train her to become a whore." Metternich did not mind the anti-French slant, but he was convinced—incorrectly—that the Burschenschaften in the German states and the carbonari in Italy were linked in an international conspiracy. In 1819, when a student assassinated the playwright August Kotzebue because he had ridiculed the student movement, Metternich convinced the leaders of the biggest German states to pass the Carlsbad Decrees, dissolving the student societies and more strictly censoring the press. Professors who criticized their rulers were immediately fired. Metternich considered any form of public criticism to be potentially subversive.

The Decembrist Revolt in Russia

Aspirations for constitutional government surfaced in Russia when Alexander I died suddenly in 1825. On a day in December when the troops assembled in St. Petersburg to take an oath of loyalty to Alexander's brother Nicholas as the new tsar, rebel officers insisted that the crown belonged to another brother, Constantine, whom they hoped would be more favorable to constitutional reform. Constantine, though next in the line of succession after Alexander, had refused the crown. The soldiers nonetheless raised the cry "Long live Constantine, long live the Constitution!" (Some troops apparently thought that "the Constitution" was Constantine's wife.) Soldiers loyal to Nicholas easily suppressed the Decembrist Revolt (so called after the month of the uprising), since the Decembrists were so outnumbered that they had no realistic chance to succeed. The subsequent trial, however, made the rebels into legendary heroes. Of their imprisonment at hard labor, the Russian poet Alexander Pushkin (1799–1837) wrote:

> The heavy-hanging chains will fall,
> The walls will crumble at a word,
> And Freedom greet you in the light,
> And brothers give you back the sword.

Pushkin would not live to see this freedom. For the next thirty years, Nicholas I (r. 1825–1855) used a new political police, the Third Section, to spy on potential opponents and stamp out rebelliousness.

Greek Independence from the Turks

The Ottoman Turks faced growing nationalist challenges in the Balkans, but the European powers feared that supporting such opposition would encourage a seditious spirit at home. The Serbs revolted against Turkish rule and won virtual independence by 1817. A Greek general in the Russian army, Prince Alexander Ypsilanti, tried to lead a revolt against the Turks in 1820 but failed when the tsar, urged on by Metternich, disavowed him. Metternich feared rebellion even by Christians against their Turkish rulers. A second revolt, this time by Greek peasants, sparked a wave of atrocities in 1821 and 1822. The Greeks killed every Turk who did not escape; in retaliation, the Turks hanged the Greek patriarch of Constantinople and, in the areas they still controlled, pillaged churches, massacred thousands of men, and sold the women into slavery.

Western opinion turned against the Turks; Greece, after all, was the birthplace of Western civilization. While the great powers negotiated, Greeks and pro-Greece committees around the world sent food and military supplies; like the English poet Byron, a few enthusiastic European and American volunteers joined the Greeks. The Greeks

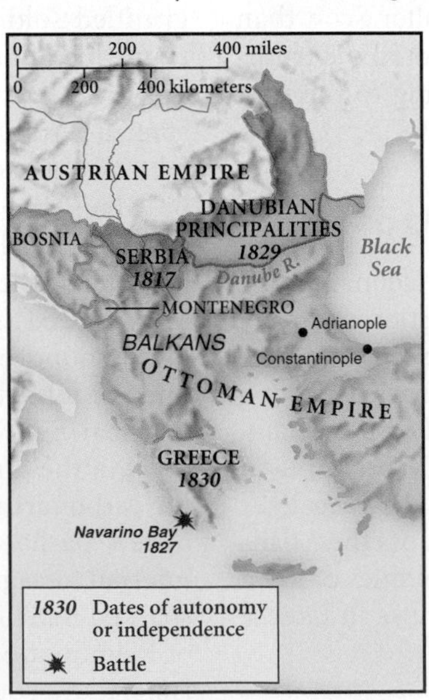

Nationalistic Movements in the Balkans, 1815–1830

Greek Independence
From 1836 to 1839, the Greek painter Panagiotis Zographos worked with his two sons on a series of scenes from the Greek struggle for independence from the Turks. Response was so favorable that one Greek general ordered lithographic reproductions for popular distribution. Nationalistic feeling could be thus encouraged even among those who were not directly touched by the struggle. Here Turkish sultan Mehmet the Conqueror, exulting over the fall of Constantinople in 1453, views a row of Greeks under the yoke, a sign of submission. *(Visual Connection Archive.)*

held on until the great powers were willing to intervene. In 1827, a combined force of British, French, and Russian ships destroyed the Turkish fleet at Navarino Bay; and in 1828, Russia declared war on Turkey and advanced close to Constantinople. The Treaty of Adrianople of 1829 gave Russia a protectorate over the Danubian principalities in the Balkans and provided for a conference among representatives of Britain, Russia, and France, all of whom had broken with Austria in support of the Greeks. In 1830, Greece was declared an independent kingdom under the guarantee of the three powers; in 1833, the second son of King Ludwig of Bavaria became Otto I of Greece. Nationalism, with the support of European public opinion, had made its first breach in Metternich's system.

Wars of Independence in Latin America

Across the Atlantic, national revolts also succeeded after a series of bloody wars of independence. Taking advantage of the upheavals in Spain and Portugal that began under Napoleon, restive colonists from Mexico to Argentina rebelled. One leader who stood out was **Simón Bolívar** (1783–1830), born in Caracas (present-day Venezuela) to an aristocratic slave-owning family of Spanish descent. He was educated in Europe on the works of Voltaire and Rousseau. Although Bolívar fancied himself a Latin American Napoleon, he had to acquiesce to the formation of a series of independent republics between 1821 and 1823, even in Bolivia, which is named after him.

By 1825, Portugal had lost all its American colonies, including Brazil, and Spain was left with only Cuba and Puerto Rico (Map 20.4). Brazil declared its independence under the banner of the Portuguese king's own son and therefore maintained a monarchical form of government along with slavery. In contrast, the new republics freed those slaves who fought on their side, abolished the slave trade, and gradually eliminated slavery. Because the struggles for independence required arms and armed forces, the new Spanish American republics

---

Simón Bolívar (1783–1830): The Venezuelan-born, European-educated aristocrat who became one of the leaders of the Latin American independence movement in the 1820s. Bolivia is named after him.

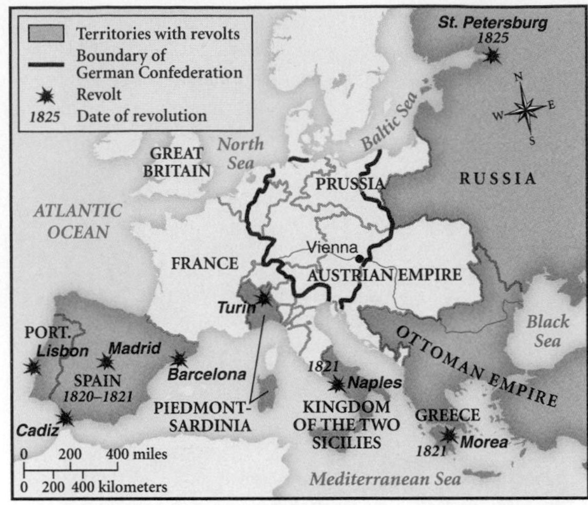

MAP 20.3 Revolutionary Movements of the 1820s
The revolts of the 1820s took place on the periphery of Europe, in Spain, Italy, Greece, Russia, and in the Spanish and Portuguese colonies of Latin America. Rebels in Spain and Russia wanted constitutional reforms. Although the Italian revolts failed, as did the uprisings in Spain and Russia, the Greek and Latin American independence movements eventually succeeded.

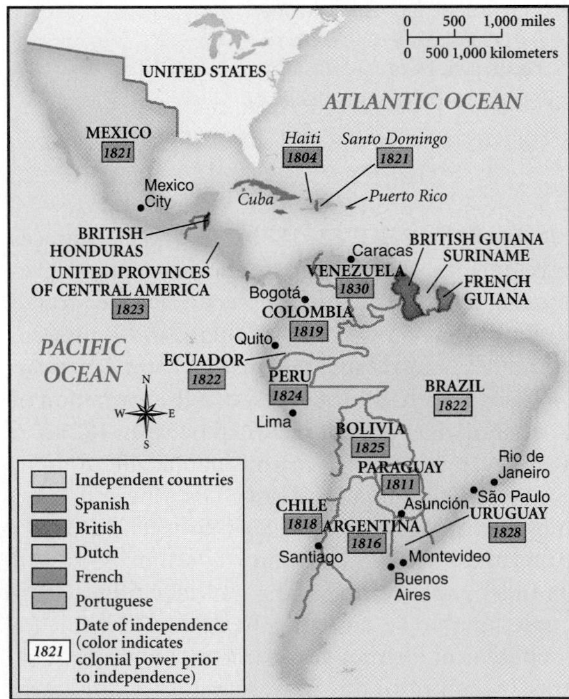

MAP 20.4 Latin American Independence, 1804–1830
Napoleon's occupation of Spain and Portugal seriously weakened those countries' hold on their Latin American colonies. Despite the restoration of the Spanish and Portuguese rulers in 1814, most of their colonies successfully broke away in a wave of rebellions between 1811 and 1830.

faced the prospect of internal violence for years afterward. Soldiers and militiamen refused to lay down their arms and sometimes fought on behalf of local interests against the new national governments. The United States and Great Britain recognized the new states, and in 1823 President James Monroe announced his Monroe Doctrine, closing the Americas to European intervention—a prohibition that depended on British naval power and British willingness to declare neutrality.

Revolution and Reform, 1830–1832

In 1830, a new wave of liberal and nationalist revolts broke against the bulwark of conservatism. The revolts of the 1820s had served as warning shots but had been largely confined to the peripheries of Europe. Now revolution once again threatened the established order in western Europe.

The French Revolution of 1830 Louis XVIII's younger brother and successor, Charles X (r. 1824–1830), brought about his own downfall by steering the monarchy in an increasingly repressive direction. In 1825, the Law of Indemnity compensated nobles who had emigrated during the French Revolution for the loss of their estates, and the Law of Sacrilege in the same year imposed the death penalty for such offenses as stealing religious objects from churches. Charles enraged liberals when he dissolved the legislature, removed many wealthy and powerful voters from the rolls, and imposed strict censorship. Spontaneous demonstrations in Paris led to fighting on July 26, 1830. After three days of street battles in which 500 citizens and 150 soldiers died, a group of moderate liberal leaders, fearing the reestablishment of a republic, agreed to give the crown to Charles X's cousin Louis-Philippe, duke of Orléans.

Charles X went into exile in England, and the new king extended political liberties and voting rights. Although the number of voting men nearly doubled, it remained minuscule—approximately 170,000 in a country of 30 million. Such reforms did little for the poor and working classes, who had manned the barricades in July. Dissatisfaction with the 1830 settlement boiled over in Lyon in 1831, when a silk-workers' strike over wages turned into a rebellion that died down only when the army arrived. Revolution had broken the hold of those who wanted to restore the pre-1789 monarchy and nobility, but it had gone no further this time than installing a more liberal, constitutional monarchy.

Simón Bolívar
This watercolor by Fernandez Luis Cancino celebrates Bolívar's promise to abolish slavery in territories he freed from Spanish rule. Although Bolívar liberated his own slaves in 1820, he was unable to persuade the legislators of the newly independent countries to act immediately. They insisted on gradual emancipation. *(Watercolor on paper by Luis Fernandez Cancino [nineteenth century], Casa-Museo 20 de Julio de 1810, Bogota, Colombia / Giraudon / The Bridgeman Art Library International.)*

Belgian Independence from the Dutch

News of the July revolution in Paris ignited the Belgians, whose country had been annexed to the kingdom of the Netherlands in 1815. Differences in traditions, language, and religion separated the largely Catholic Belgians from the Dutch. An opera about a seventeenth-century insurrection in Naples provided the spark, and students in Brussels rioted, shouting "Down with the Dutch!"

The riot turned into revolt. King William of the Netherlands appealed to the great powers to intervene; after all, the Congress of Vienna had established his kingdom. But Great Britain and France opposed intervention and invited Russia, Austria, and Prussia to a conference that guaranteed Belgium independence in exchange for its neutrality in international affairs. Belgian neutrality would remain a cornerstone of European diplomacy for a century. After much maneuvering, the crown of the new kingdom of Belgium was offered to a German prince, Leopold of Saxe-Coburg, in 1831. The choice, like that of Otto I of Greece, ensured the influence of the great European powers without favoring any one of them in particular. Belgium, like France and Britain, now had a constitutional monarchy.

Revolts in Italy and Poland

The Austrian emperor and the Russian tsar would have supported intervention in Belgium had they not been preoccupied with their own revolts. In the south, rebels in Naples and Palermo demanded constitutional government; in the north, rebels in Piedmont fought for an Italy independent of Austria. Metternich sent Austrian armies to quell the unrest.

The Polish revolt was more serious. When set up in 1815, the "congress kingdom" (so called because the Congress of Vienna had created it) was given a constitution that provided for an elected Polish parliament, a national army, and guarantees of free speech and a free press. But by 1818, its ruler, the Russian tsar Alexander I, had begun retracting these concessions. Polish students and military officers responded by forming secret nationalist societies to plot for change by illegal means. The government then cracked down, arresting student leaders and dismissing professors who promoted reforms. In 1830, in response to news of revolution in France, students raised the banner of rebellion. Polish aristocrats formed a provisional government, but it got no support from Britain or France and was defeated by the Russian army. In reprisal, Tsar Nicholas abolished the Polish constitution that his brother Alexander had granted and ordered thousands of Poles executed or banished. The independence movements in Poland and Italy went underground only to reemerge later.

The British Reform Bill of 1832

The British had long been preoccupied with two subjects: the royal family and elections for control of Parliament. In 1820, the domestic quarrels between the new king, George IV (r. 1820–1830), and his German wife, Caroline, seemed to threaten the future of the monarchy.

When George IV came to the throne, he tried to divorce Caroline, and he refused to have her crowned queen. He hoped to use rumors of her love affairs on the continent to win his case, but the divorce trial provoked massive demonstrations in support of Caroline. Women's groups gathered thousands of signatures on petitions supporting her, and popular songs and satires portrayed George as a fat, drunken libertine. Caroline's death a few months after George's coronation ended the Queen Caroline Affair. The monarchy survived, but with a tarnished reputation.

The demonstrations in the Queen Caroline Affair followed on the heels of a huge political rally held just the year before. In August 1819, sixty thousand people attended an illegal political meeting held in St. Peter's Fields in Manchester. They wanted reform of parliamentary elections, which had long been controlled by aristocratic landowners. When the local authorities sent the cavalry to arrest the speaker, panic resulted; eleven people were killed and many hundreds injured. Punsters called it the battle of Peterloo or the Peterloo massacre. An alarmed government passed the Six Acts, which forbade large political meetings and restricted press criticism.

In the 1820s, however, new men came into government. Sir Robert Peel (1788–1850), the secretary for home affairs, revised the criminal code to reduce the number of crimes punishable by death and introduced a municipal police force in London, called the Bobbies after him. In 1824, the laws prohibiting labor unions were repealed, and though restrictions on strikes remained, workers could now organize themselves legally to confront their employers collectively. In 1828, the appointment of the

MAPPING THE WEST

Europe in 1830

By 1830, the fragilities of the Congress of Vienna settlement had become apparent. Rebellion in Poland failed, but Belgium won its independence from the kingdom of the Netherlands, and a French revolution in July chased out the Bourbon ruler and installed Louis-Philippe, who promised constitutional reform. Most European rulers held on to their positions in this period of ferment, but they had to accommodate new desires for constitutional guarantees of rights and growing nationalist sentiment.

duke of Wellington, the hero of Waterloo, as prime minister kept the Tories in power, and his government pushed through a bill in 1829 allowing Catholics to sit in Parliament and hold most public offices.

When in 1830, and again in 1831, the Whigs in Parliament proposed an extension of the right to vote, Tory diehards, principally in the House of Lords, dug in their heels and predicted that even the most modest proposals would doom civilization itself. Even though the proposed law would grant only limited, not universal, male suffrage, mass demonstrations in favor of it took place in many cities. One supporter of reform described the scene: "Meetings of almost every description of persons were held in cities, towns, and parishes; by journeymen tradesmen in their clubs, and by common workmen who had no trade clubs or associations of any kind." In this "state of diseased and feverish excitement" (according to its opponents), the **Reform Bill of 1832** passed, after the king threatened to create enough new peers to obtain its passage in the House of Lords.

Although the Reform Bill altered Britain's political structure in significant ways, the gains were not revolutionary. One of the bill's foremost backers, historian and member of Parliament Thomas Macaulay, explained, "I am opposed to Universal Suffrage, because I think that it would produce a destructive revolution. I support this plan, because I am sure that it is our best security against a revolution." Although the number of male voters increased by about 50 percent, only one in five Britons could now vote, and voting still depended on holding property. Nevertheless, the bill gave representation to new cities in the north for the first time and set a precedent for widening suffrage further. Exclusive aristocratic politics now gave way to a mixed middle-class and aristocratic structure that would prove more responsive to the problems of a fast-growing society. Those disappointed with the outcome would organize with renewed vigor in the 1830s and 1840s.

REVIEW QUESTION Why were independence movements thwarted in Italy and Poland in this era, but not in Greece, Belgium, and Latin America?

Reform Bill of 1832: A measure passed by the British Parliament to increase the number of male voters by about 50 percent and give representation to new cities in the north; it set a precedent for widening suffrage.

Conclusion

The agitations and uprisings of the 1820s and early 1830s showed that the revolutionary legacy still smoldered and might erupt into flames again at any moment. Napoleon Bonaparte had kept the legacy alive by insisting on fundamental reforms wherever his armies triumphed. His imperial rule galvanized supporters and opponents alike; no one could be indifferent to his impact on European and even world affairs. He reshaped French institutions and left a lasting imprint in many European countries. Moreover, like Frankenstein's monster, he seemed to bounce back from every reversal; between the French retreat from Moscow in 1812 and his final defeat at Waterloo in 1815, Napoleon lost many battles yet managed to raise an army again and again.

The French emperor's attempt to colonize much of Europe ultimately failed. Germans, Italians, Russians, and Spaniards all resisted and in the process discovered new national feelings that would have an impact throughout modern times. Unlike Frankenstein's monster, Napoleon could not hide from his enemies and was forced into exile until his death. The powers who eventually defeated Napoleon tried to maintain the European peace by shoring up monarchical governments and damping down aspirations for constitutional freedoms and national autonomy. They sometimes fell short. Belgium separated from the Netherlands, Greece achieved independence from the Turks, Latin American countries shook off the rule of Spain and Portugal, and the French installed a more liberal monarchy than the one envisioned by the Congress of Vienna. Yet Metternich's vision of a conservative Europe still held, and most efforts at revolt failed. In the next two decades, however, dramatic social changes would raise the stakes of political contests and prompt a new and much more deadly round of revolutions.

FOR FURTHER EXPLORATION

- **For additional primary-source material from this period**, see *Sources of the Making of the West*, Fourth Edition.
- **For Web sites, images, and documents related to topics in this chapter**, visit *Make History* at bedfordstmartins.com/hunt.

Chapter 20 Review

Online Study Guide bedfordstmartins.com/hunt

Key Terms and People

In the grid below, identify the term or person and explain its historical significance. (For a printable version of this grid, visit bedfordstmartins.com/hunt.)

Term	Who or What & When	Why It Matters
Napoleon Bonaparte (p. 652)		
First Consul (p. 653)		
Civil Code (p. 657)		
Continental System (p. 662)		
battle of Waterloo (p. 665)		
Congress of Vienna (p. 667)		
Klemens von Metternich (p. 668)		
restoration (p. 669)		
conservatism (p. 670)		
Ludwig van Beethoven (p. 674)		
Sir Walter Scott (p. 675)		
Simón Bolívar (p. 677)		
Reform Bill of 1832 (p. 681)		

Review Questions

1. In what ways did Napoleon continue the French Revolution, and in what ways did he break with it?
2. Why was Napoleon able to gain control over so much of Europe's territory?
3. To what extent did the Congress of Vienna restore the old order?
4. Why were independence movements thwarted in Italy and Poland in this era, but not in Greece, Belgium, and Latin America?

Making Connections

1. What was the long-term significance of Napoleon for Europe?
2. What best explains Napoleon's fall from power: apathy at home, resistance to his rule, or military defeat?
3. In what ways did Metternich succeed in holding back the revolutionary legacy? In what ways did he fail?
4. How did the revolts and rebellions of the 1820s reflect the revolutionary legacy? In what ways did they move in new directions?

Important Events

Date	Event
1799	Coup against Directory government in France; Napoleon Bonaparte named First Consul
1801	Napoleon signs concordat with the pope
1804	Napoleon crowned emperor of France, issues new Civil Code
1805	British naval forces defeat French at the battle of Trafalgar; Napoleon wins his greatest victory at the battle of Austerlitz
1807–1814	French invade and occupy Spain and Portugal
1812	Napoleon invades Russia
1814–1815	Congress of Vienna
1815	Napoleon defeated at Waterloo and exiled to island of St. Helena, where he dies in 1821

Date	Event
1818	Mary Shelley, *Frankenstein*
1820	Revolt of liberal army officers against Spanish crown
1824	Ludwig van Beethoven, Ninth Symphony
1825	Russian army officers demand constitutional reform in Decembrist Revolt
1830	Greece gains its independence from Ottoman Turks; rebels overthrow Charles X of France and install Louis-Philippe; rebellion in Poland against Russia fails
1832	English Parliament passes Reform Bill; Johann Wolfgang von Goethe, *Faust*

- Consider three events: **Congress of Vienna (1814–1815), Mary Shelley, *Frankenstein* (1818),** and **Ludwig van Beethoven, Ninth Symphony (1824).** How did the peace established by the Congress of Vienna help to foster these works? How might things have been different if Napoleon had not been defeated?

SUGGESTED REFERENCES

Napoleon and his wars have always been the subject of great interest, but recent scholars have devoted more attention to the long-term influence of the wars. The years between 1815 and 1830 have not attracted as much scholarship, even though those years are arguably even more significant than the Napoleonic era for their long-term cultural and political effects.

Bell, David A. *The First Total War: Napoleon's Europe and the Birth of Warfare as We Know It.* 2007.

Black, Jeremy. *The Battle of Waterloo.* 2010.

*Blaufarb, Rafe. *Napoleon: A Symbol for an Age. A Brief Biography with Documents.* 2008.

Breckman, Warren. *European Romanticism: A Brief History with Documents.* 2007.

Brewer, David. *The Greek War of Independence: The Struggle for Freedom from Ottoman Oppression and the Birth of the Modern Greek Nation.* 2003.

Cole, Juan. *Napoléon's Egypt: Invading the Middle East.* 2007.

Englund, Steven. *Napoleon: A Political Life.* 2004.

Fregosi, Paul. *Dreams of Empire: Napoleon and the First World War 1792–1815.* 1989.

Hobsbawm, E. J. *The Age of Revolution, 1789–1848.* 1996.

Johnson, Paul. *The Birth of the Modern: World Society, 1815–1830.* 1991.

Laven, David, and Lucy Riall, eds. *Napoleon's Legacy: Problems of Government in Restoration Europe.* 2000.

Napoleon Foundation: http://www.napoleon.org

Romantic Chronology: http://english.ucsb.edu:591/rchrono

Sandeman, G. A. C. *Metternich.* 2006.

Schroeder, Paul W. *The Transformation of European Politics 1763–1848.* 1996.

*Primary source.

CHAPTER 21

Industrialization and Social Ferment

1830–1850

In 1830, the Liverpool and Manchester Railway Line opened to the cheers of crowds and the congratulations of government officials, including the duke of Wellington, the hero of Waterloo who had been named British prime minister. In the excitement, some of the dignitaries gathered on a parallel track. Another engine, George Stephenson's *Rocket*, approached at high speed — the engine could go as fast as twenty-seven miles per hour. Most of the gentlemen scattered to safety, but former cabinet minister William Huskisson fell and was hit. A few hours later he died, the first official casualty of the newfangled railroad.

Dramatic and expensive, railroads were the most striking symbol of the new industrial age. Industrialization and its by-product of rapid urban growth fundamentally changed political conflicts, social relations, cultural concerns, and even the landscape. So great were the changes that they are collectively labeled the Industrial Revolution. Although this revolution did not take place in a single decade like the French Revolution, the introduction of steam-driven machinery, large factories, and a new working class transformed life in the Western world. Peasants and workers streamed into the cities. London's population grew by 130,000 in the 1830s alone; Berlin's more than doubled between 1819 and 1849; and Paris's expanded by 120,000 just between 1841 and 1846. To many observers, overcrowding, disease, prostitution, crime, and alcohol consumption all seemed to be on the increase as a result.

The shock of industrial and urban growth generated an outpouring of commentary on the need for social reforms. Painters, poets, and especially novelists joined in the chorus warning about rising tensions. Many who wrote on social issues expected middle-class women to organize their homes as a domestic haven from the heartless process of upheaval. Yet despite the emphasis on domesticity, middle-class women participated in

Inauguration of the Railway Line from Naples to Portici, Italy, 1839
People of all classes flocked to the inauguration of new railway lines. This lithograph by the Italian artist Salvatore Fergola depicts the opening of the first railway line in Italy, which ran from Naples to Portici, a town five miles south of Naples. Portici housed a royal palace and offered access to Herculaneum, an important classical ruin visited by many foreigners. *(By Salvatore Fergola, Museum San Martino, Naples, photo © Roger Viollet/The Image Works.)*

public issues, too: they set up reform societies that fought prostitution and helped poor mothers, they agitated for temperance (abstention from alcohol), and they joined the campaigns to abolish slavery. Middle-class men and women frequently denounced the lower classes' appetites for drink, tobacco, and cockfighting, but they remained largely silent when British traders received government support in forcing the Chinese to accept imports of the addictive drug opium.

Social ferment set the ideological pots to a boil. A word coined during the French Revolution, **ideology** refers to a coherent set of beliefs about the way the social and political order should be organized. The dual impact of the French Revolution and the Industrial Revolution prompted the development of a whole spectrum of ideologies to explain the meaning of the changes taking place. Nationalists, liberals, socialists, and communists offered competing visions of the social order they desired: they all agreed that change was necessary, but they disagreed about both the means and the ends of change. Their contest came to a head in 1848 when the rapid transformation of European society led to a new set of revolutionary outbreaks, more consuming than any since 1789. As in 1789, food shortages and constitutional crises fueled rebellions, but now class tensions and nationalist impulses fanned the flames in capitals across Europe, not only in Paris. Although the revolutionaries of 1848 eventually went down to defeat, the demands they raised shaped the political agenda for decades to come.

CHAPTER FOCUS How did the Industrial Revolution create new social and political conflicts?

ideology: A word coined during the French Revolution to refer to a coherent set of beliefs about the way the social and political order should be organized.

The Industrial Revolution

French and English writers of the 1820s invented the term **Industrial Revolution** to capture the drama of contemporary change and to draw a parallel with the French Revolution. The chief components of the Industrial Revolution, industrialization and urbanization, are long-term processes that have continued to the present; unlike the French upheaval, they do not have precise beginning and ending dates. The Industrial Revolution began in England in the 1770s and 1780s in textile manufacturing and spread from there across the continent. In the 1830s and 1840s, industrialization and urbanization both accelerated quite suddenly, as governments across Europe encouraged railroad construction and the mechanization of manufacturing. States exercised little control over the consequences of industrial and urban growth, however, and many officials, preachers, and intellectuals worried that unchecked growth would destroy traditional social relationships and create disorder. Some held out the constancy of rural life as an antidote to the ravages of industrialization and urbanization, but population growth produced new tensions in the countryside, too.

Roots of Industrialization

British inventors had been steadily perfecting steam engines for five decades before George Stephenson built his *Rocket*. A key breakthrough took place in 1776 when James Watt developed an efficient steam engine that could be used to pump water from coal mines or drive machinery in textile factories. Since

Industrial Revolution: The transformation of life in the Western world over several decades in the late eighteenth and early nineteenth centuries as a result of the introduction of steam-driven machinery, large factories, and a new working class.

1830–1832
Cholera epidemic sweeps across Europe
1832
George Sand, *Indiana*
1834
German *Zollverein* established under Prussian leadership
1839
Beginning of Opium War; invention of photography
1830
1835
1840
1830
France invades and begins conquest of Algeria
1833
Factory Act regulates work of children in Great Britain; abolition of slavery in British Empire
1835
Belgium opens first continental railway built with state funds

coal fired the steam engines that drove new textile machinery, innovations tended to reinforce one another. This kind of synergy built on previous changes in the textile industry. In 1733, the Englishman John Kay had patented the flying shuttle, which enabled weavers to "throw" yarn across the loom rather than draw it back and forth by hand. When the flying shuttle came into widespread use in the 1760s, weavers began producing cloth more quickly than spinners could produce the thread. The resulting shortage of spun thread propelled the invention of the spinning jenny, a multispool spinning wheel that enabled one worker to run eight spools at once. In the following decades, increasingly mechanized forms of spinning yarn replaced thousands of women working at home by hand. The increased output of yarn then stimulated the mechanization of weaving. Using the engines produced by James Watt and his partner Matthew Boulton, Edmund Cartwright designed a mechanized loom in the 1780s that, when perfected, could be run by a small boy and yet yield fifteen times the output of a skilled adult working a handloom. By the end of the century, manufacturers were assembling new power machinery in large factories that hired semiskilled men, women, and children to replace skilled weavers.

Several factors interacted to make England the first site of the Industrial Revolution. Because population increased by more than 50 percent in England in the second half of the eighteenth century, manufacturers had an incentive to produce more and cheaper cotton cloth. England had a good supply of private investment capital from overseas trade and commercial profits, ready access to raw cotton from the plantations of its Caribbean colonies and the southern United States, and the necessary natural resources at home such as coal and iron. Good opportunities for social mobility and relative political stability in the eighteenth century provided an environment that fostered the pragmatism of the English and Scottish inventors who designed the machinery. These early industrialists shared a culture of informal scientific education through learned societies and popular lectures (one of the prominent forms of the Enlightenment in Britain). Manufacturers proved eager to introduce steam-driven machinery to increase output and gradually established factories to house the new machines and concentrate the labor of their workers. The agricultural revolution of the eighteenth century had enabled England to produce food more efficiently, freeing some agricultural workers to move to the new sites of manufacturing. Cotton textile production skyrocketed.

Elsewhere in Europe, textile manufacturing—long a linchpin in the European economy—expanded even without the introduction of new machines and factories because of the spread of the "putting-out," or "domestic," system. Under the putting-out system, manufacturers supplied the raw materials, such as woolen or cotton fibers, to families working at home. The mother and her children washed, carded, and combed the fibers. Then the mother and oldest daughters spun them into thread. The father, assisted by the children, wove the cloth. The cloth was then finished (bleached, dyed, smoothed, and so on) under the supervision of the manufacturer in a large workshop, located either in town or in the countryside. This system had existed in the textile industry for hundreds of years, but it grew dramatically in the eighteenth century, and the manufacture of other products—such as glassware, baskets, nails, and guns—followed suit. The spread of the putting-out system of manufacturing is sometimes called proto-industrialization to signify that the process helped pave the way for the full-scale Industrial Revolution. Because of the increase in textile production, ordinary people began to wear underclothes and nightclothes, both rare in the past. White, red, blue, yellow, green, and even pastel shades of cotton now replaced the black, gray, or brown of traditional wool.

1841
Charles Dickens, *The Old Curiosity Shop*

1846
Famine strikes Ireland; Corn Laws repealed in England; peasant insurrection in Austrian province of Galicia

1848
Revolutions of 1848 throughout Europe; last great wave of Chartist demonstrations in Britain; Karl Marx and Friedrich Engels, *The Communist Manifesto*; abolition of slavery in French colonies; end of serfdom in Austrian Empire

1851
Crystal Palace exhibition in London

1845 1850 1855

TAKING MEASURE

Railroad Lines, 1830–1850

Great Britain quickly extended its lead in the building of railroads. The extension of commerce and, before long, the ability to wage war would depend on the development of effective railroad networks. These statistics might be taken as predicting a realignment of power within Europe after 1850.

Source: B. R. Mitchell, *European Historical Statistics 1750–1970* (New York: Columbia University Press, 1975), F1.

Question to Consider

- **What do the numbers shown in this graph say about the relative positions of Germany (the German states, including Prussia but excluding Austria), the Austrian Empire, and France?**

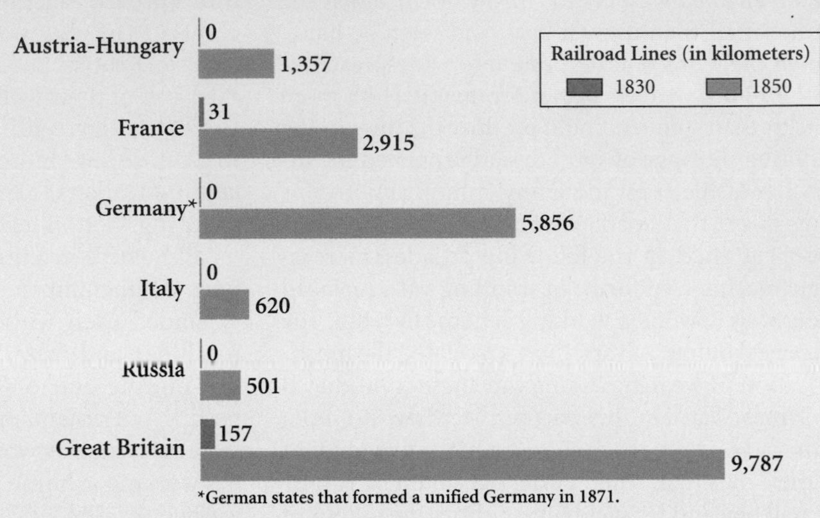

Workers in the textile industry, whether in the putting-out system or in factories, enjoyed few protections against fluctuations in the market. Whenever demand for cloth declined, manufacturers simply did not buy from the families producing it. Hundreds of thousands of families might be reduced to bankruptcy in periods of food shortage or overproduction. Handloom weavers sometimes violently resisted the establishment of the factory power looms that would force them out of work. In England in 1811 and 1812, for example, bands of handloom weavers wrecked factory machinery and burned mills in the Midlands, Yorkshire, and Lancashire. To restore order and protect industry, the government sent in an army of twelve thousand regular soldiers and made machine wrecking punishable by death. The rioters were called Luddites after the fictitious figure Ned Ludd, whose signature appeared on their manifestos. (The term is still used to describe those who resist new technology.)

Engines of Change

Steam-driven engines took on a dramatic new form in the 1820s when the English engineer George Stephenson perfected an engine to pull wagons along rail tracks. In the 1830s and 1840s, every major country in Europe hurried to set up a railroad system, pushing industrialization from west to east across Europe (see "Taking Measure," above). Although the new industries employed only a small percentage of workers, the working class that took shape in them immediately attracted the attention of social commentators and government officials. Rulers could not afford to ignore the social problems that came from industrialization.

The Rise of the Railroad The idea of a railroad was not new: iron tracks had been used since the seventeenth century to haul coal from mines in wagons pulled by horses. A railroad system as a mode of transport, however, developed only after Stephenson's invention of a steam-powered locomotive. Placed on the new tracks, steam-driven carriages could transport people and goods to the cities and link coal and iron deposits to the new factories. In the 1840s alone, railroad track mileage more than doubled in Great Britain, and British investment in railways jumped tenfold. The British also began to build railroads in India. Private investment that had been going into the building of thousands of miles of canals now went into railroads. Britain's success with rail transportation led other countries to develop their own projects. Railroads grew spectacularly in the United States in the 1830s and 1840s, reaching 9,000 miles of track by midcentury. In 1835, Belgium, newly independent in 1830, opened the first continental European railroad with state bonds backed by British capital. By 1850, the world had 23,500 miles of track, most of it in western Europe.

Railroad building spurred both industrial development and state power (Map 21.1). Governments everywhere participated in the construction of railroads, which depended on private and state funds to pay for the massive amounts of iron, coal, heavy machinery, and human labor required to build and run them. Demand for iron products accelerated industrial development. Until the 1840s, cotton had led industrial production; between 1816 and 1840, cotton output more than quadrupled in Great Britain. But from 1830 to 1850, Britain's output of iron and coal doubled (Table 21.1). Similarly, Austrian output of iron doubled between the 1820s and the 1840s. One-third of all investment in the German states in the 1840s went into railroads.

Steam-powered engines made Britain the world leader in manufacturing. By midcentury, more than half of Britain's national income came from manufacturing and trade. The number of steamboats in Great Britain rose from two in 1812 to six hundred in 1840. Between 1840 and 1850, steam-engine power doubled in Great Britain and increased even more rapidly elsewhere in Europe, as those adopting British inventions strove to catch up. The power applied in German manufacturing, for example, grew sixfold during the 1840s but still amounted to only a little more than a quarter of the British figure. German coal and iron outputs were only 6 or 7 percent of the British outputs.

Industrialization Moves Eastward Although Great Britain consciously strove to protect its industrial supremacy, thousands of British engineers defied laws against the export of

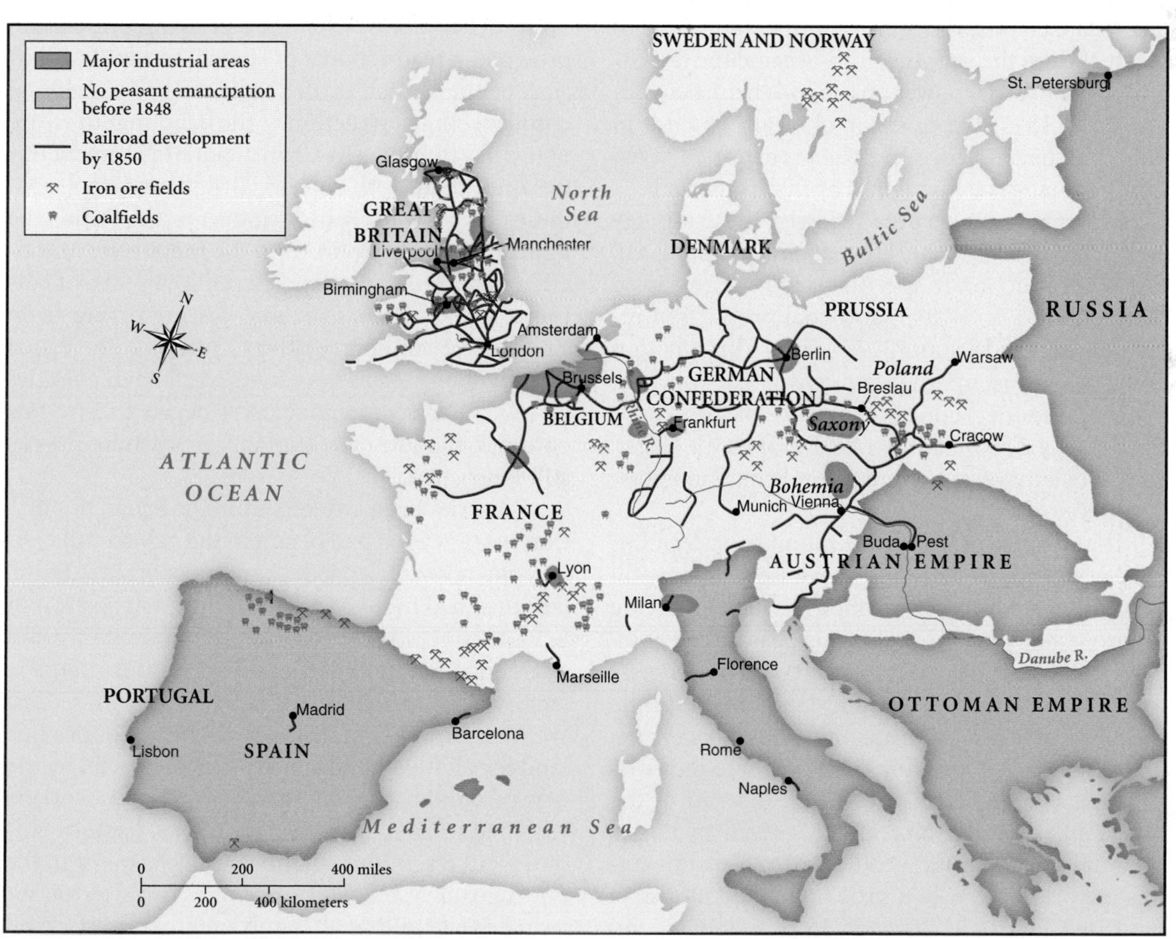

MAP 21.1 Industrialization in Europe, c. 1850
Industrialization (mainly mechanized textile production) first spread in a band across northern Europe that included Great Britain, northern France, Belgium, the northern German states, the region around Milan in northern Italy, and Bohemia. Although railroads were not the only factor in promoting industrialization, the map makes clear the interrelationship between railroad building and the development of new industrial sites of coal mining and textile production.

TABLE 21.1 Coal Output, 1830–1850*

Like the numbers for railroad mileage given in Taking Measure, page 688, these figures for coal production show the economic dominance of Great Britain throughout the period 1830–1850. As long as coal remained the essential fuel of industrialization, Britain enjoyed a clear advantage.

	Austria	Belgium	France	German States (including Prussia)	Great Britain
1830	214	**	1,863	1,800	22,800
1835	251	2,639	2,506	2,100	28,100
1840	473	3,930	3,003	3,200	34,200
1845	689	4,919	4,202	4,400	46,600
1850	877	5,821	4,434	5,100	50,200

*In thousands of metric tons.
**Data not available.

Source: B. R. Mitchell, *European Historical Statistics, 1750–1970* (New York: Columbia University Press, 1975), D2.

machinery or the emigration of artisans. Only slowly, thanks to the pirating of British methods and to new technical schools, did most continental countries begin closing the gap. Belgium became the fastest-growing industrial power on the continent: between 1830 and 1844, the number of steam engines in Belgium quadrupled, and Belgians exported seven times as many steam engines as they imported.

Industrialization spread slowly east from key areas in Prussia (near Berlin), Saxony, and Bohemia. Cotton production in the Austrian Empire tripled between 1831 and 1845, and coal production increased fourfold from 1827 to 1847. Both cotton growing and coal mining were centered in Bohemia, which was more productive than Prussia or Saxony. Even so, by 1850, continental Europe still lagged almost twenty years behind Great Britain in industrial development.

The advance of industrialization in eastern Europe was slow, in large part because serfdom still survived there, hindering labor mobility and tying up investment capital: as long as peasants were legally tied to the land as serfs, they could not migrate to the new factory towns and landlords felt little incentive to invest their income in manufacturing. The problem was worst in Russia, where industrialization would not take off until the end of the nineteenth century. Nevertheless, even in Russia signs of industrialization could be detected: raw cotton imports (a sign of a growing textile industry) increased sevenfold between 1831 and 1848, and the number of factories doubled along with the size of the industrial workforce.

Factories and Workers Despite the spread of industrialization, factory workers remained a minority everywhere. In the 1840s, factories in England employed only 5 percent of the workers; in France, 3 percent; in Prussia, 2 percent. The putting-out system remained strong, employing two-thirds of the manufacturing workers in Prussia and Saxony, for example, in the 1840s. Many peasants kept their options open by combining factory work or putting-out work with agricultural labor. From Switzerland to Russia, people worked in agriculture during the spring and summer and in manufacturing in the fall and winter. Unstable industrial wages made such arrangements essential. In addition, some new industries idled periodically: for example, iron forges stopped for several months when the water level in streams dropped, and blast furnaces shut down for repairs several weeks every year.

Even though factories employed only a small percentage of the population, they attracted much attention. Already by 1830, more than a million people in Britain depended on the cotton industry for employment, and cotton cloth constituted 50 percent of the country's exports. Factories sprang up in urban areas, where the growing population provided a ready source of labor. The rapid expansion of the British textile industry had a colonial corollary: the destruction of the hand manufacture of textiles in India. The British put high import duties on Indian cloth entering Britain and kept such duties very low for British cloth entering India. The figures are dramatic: in 1813, the Indian city of Calcutta exported to England £2 million worth of cotton cloth; by 1830, Calcutta was importing from England £2 million worth of cotton cloth. When Britain abolished slavery in its Caribbean colonies in 1833, British manufacturers began to buy raw cotton in the southern United States, where slavery still flourished.

Factories drew workers from the urban population surge, which had begun in the eighteenth century and now accelerated. The number of agricultural laborers also increased during industrialization in Britain, suggesting that a growing birthrate created a larger population and fed workers into the new factory system. The new workers came from several sources: families of farmers who could not provide land for all their children, artisans displaced by the new machinery, and children of the earliest workers who had moved to the factory towns. Factory employment resembled labor on family farms or in the putting-out system: entire families came to toil for a single wage, although family members performed different tasks. Workdays of twelve to seventeen hours were typical, even for children, and the work was grueling.

As urban factories grew, their workers gradually came to constitute a new socioeconomic class with a distinctive culture and traditions. The term *working class*, like *middle class*, came into use for the first time in the early nineteenth century. It referred to the laborers in the new factories. In the past, urban workers had labored in isolated trades: water and wood carrying, gardening, laundry, and building. In contrast, factories brought working people together with machines, under close supervision by their employers. Soon developing a sense of common interests, they organized societies for mutual help and political reform. From these would come the first labor unions.

Factories produced wealth without regard to the pollution they caused or the exhausted state of their workers; industry created unheard-of riches and new forms of poverty all at once. "From this foul drain the greatest stream of human industry flows out to fertilize the whole world," wrote the French aristocrat Alexis de Tocqueville after visiting the new English industrial city of Manchester in the 1830s. "From this filthy sewer pure gold flows. Here humanity attains its most complete development and its most brutish, here civilization works its miracles and civilized man is turned almost into a savage." Studies by physicians set the life expectancy of workers in Manchester at just seventeen years (partly because of high rates of infant mortality), whereas the average life expectancy in England was forty years in 1840. (See "New Sources, New Perspectives," page 692.) One American visitor in Britain in the late 1840s described how "in the manufacturing town, the fine soot or *blacks* darken the day, give white sheep the color of black sheep, discolor the human saliva, contaminate the air, poison many plants, and corrode monuments and buildings." In some parts of Europe, city leaders banned factories, hoping to insulate their towns from the effects of industrial growth.

As factory production expanded, local and national governments collected information about the workers. Investigators detailed their pitiful condition. A French physician in the eastern town of Mulhouse described the "pale, emaciated women who walk barefooted through the dirt" to reach the factory. The young children who worked in the factory appeared "clothed in rags which are greasy with the oil from the looms and frames." A report to the city government in Lille, France, in 1832 described "dark cellars" where the cotton workers lived: "the air is never renewed, it is infected; the walls are plastered with garbage."

Government inquiries often focused on women and children. In Great Britain, the Factory Act of 1833 outlawed the employment of children under the age of nine in textile mills (except in the lace and silk industries); it also limited the workdays for those ages nine to thirteen to nine hours a day, and those ages thirteen to eighteen to twelve hours. Adults worked even longer hours. Investigating commissions showed that women and young children, sometimes under age six, hauled coal trucks through low, cramped passageways in coal mines. One nine-year-old girl, Margaret Gomley, described her typical day in the mines as beginning at 7:00 a.m. and ending at 6:00 p.m.: "I get my dinner at 12 o'clock, which is a dry muffin, and sometimes butter on, but have no time allowed to stop to eat it, I eat it while I am thrusting the load. . . . They flog us down in the pit, sometimes with their hand upon my bottom, which hurts me very much." In response to the investigations, the British Parliament in 1842 passed the Mines Act, which prohibited the employment of women and girls underground. In 1847, the Central Short Time Committee, one of Britain's many social reform organizations, successfully pressured Parliament to limit the workday of women and

Child Labor in Coal Mines

The passage of legislation in 1842 against women and girls working underground did nothing to prevent boys from continuing to perform essential tasks in cramped spaces in British coal mines. Lithographs such as this one from 1844 accompanied campaigns against these practices. *(akg-images.)*

NEW SOURCES, NEW PERSPECTIVES

Statistics and the Standard of Living of the Working Class

From the very beginning of industrialization, experts argued about whether industrialization improved or worsened the standard of living of the working class. There was a counterclaim for every claim, and most often these claims came in the form of statistics. Some experts argued that factories offered higher-paying jobs to workers; others countered that factories took work away from artisans such as handloom weavers and left them on the verge of starvation. Supporters of industrialization maintained that factories gave women paying work; opponents insisted that factories destroyed the family by taking women away from the home. Through mass production, industrialization made goods cheaper and therefore more available; by polluting the air, it destroyed health, lowered life expectancy, and ruined the environment. Karl Marx and Friedrich Engels would give the debate even more of an edge by tying it to the ideology of communism. In 1844, Engels described to Marx his aim in writing *The Condition of the Working Class in England*: "I shall present the English with a fine bill of indictment. At the bar of world opinion I charge the English middle classes with mass murder, wholesale robbery and all the other crimes in the calendar." The stakes of the argument were not small.

The controversy about the benefits and costs of industrialization has continued right down to the present, in part because it is an argument directly inspired by the ideologies—liberalism, socialism, communism—that emerged as explanations of and blueprints for economic and social change. In the 1830s and 1840s, liberals insisted that industrialization would promote greater prosperity for everyone, whereas conservatives complained that it destroyed traditional ways of life and socialists warned that it exaggerated inequality and class division. In the 1950s and 1960s, defenders of capitalist free enterprise still advanced the argument about prosperity, but now they were opposed by communists who argued that state control of production could sidestep the horrors of early capitalist exploitation. Newly developing countries looked to the history of the 1830s and 1840s for lessons about the likely impact of industrialization on their countries in the 1950s and beyond. The scholarly debates therefore attracted worldwide attention, and all sides called on statistics to make their competing cases.

Unfortunately, the statistics can be interpreted in many different ways. Did it matter more that wages for factory workers went up or that life expectancy went down? If an increase in sugar consumption in Great Britain from 207,000 tons in 1844 to 290,000 tons in 1847 meant an overall increase in the standard of living, how does that square with the hundreds of thousands of deaths in Ireland at the same time or the increasing disparity throughout Great Britain between rich and poor? Some convergence of opinion has taken place, however. Most now agree that by sometime between 1820 and 1845 (the exact date depending on the scholar), conditions in Great Britain had become better than before the Industrial Revolution. And there is no doubt that the debate itself has had one major positive effect: since making one's point depends on having statistics to prove it, the debate itself has encouraged a staggering amount

children to ten hours. The continental countries followed the British lead, but since most did not insist on government inspection, enforcement was lax.

Urbanization and Its Consequences

Industrial development spurred urban growth, yet even cities with little industry grew as well. **Urbanization** is the growth of towns and cities due to the movement of people from rural to urban areas. Here, too, Great Britain led the way: half the population of England and Wales was living in towns by 1850, while in France and the German states only about a quarter of the total population was urban. Both old and new cities teemed with rising numbers in the 1830s and 1840s; the population of Vienna ballooned by 125,000 between 1827 and 1847, and the new industrial city of Manchester grew by 70,000 just in the 1830s.

Massive rural emigration, rather than births to women already living in cities, accounted for this remarkable increase. Agricultural improvements had increased the food supply and hence the rural population, but the land could no longer support the people living on it. City life and new factories beckoned those faced with hunger and poverty, including immigrants from other lands: thousands of Irish emigrated to English cities, Italians went to

---

urbanization: The growth of towns and cities due to the movement of people from rural to urban areas, a trend that was encouraged by the development of factories and railroads.

of research into quantitative measures of just about everything imaginable, from measures of wages and prices to rates of mortality and even average heights (height being correlated, it is thought, to economic well-being). British soldiers in the nineteenth century were taller on average than those in any other country except the United States, and people who believe that industrialization improved the standard of living are happy to seize on this as evidence for their case.

The graph shown here, adapted from a recent study by Charles H. Feinstein, compares money earnings with the cost-of-living index to determine "real" earnings, that is, what the money earned would actually be able to buy in Great Britain. Feinstein developed an index of money earnings for both men and women for twenty different occupations and a cost-of-living index based on the price of twelve types of food as well as coal, candles, beer, footwear, clothing, and rent.

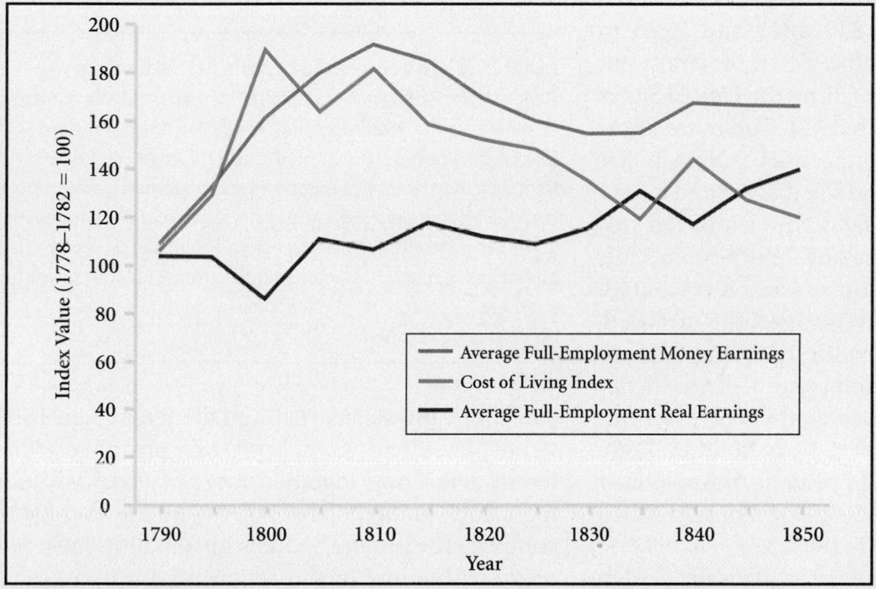

Annual Indexes of Money Earnings, the Cost of Living, and Real Earnings

(From Charles H. Feinstein, "Pessimism Perpetuated: Real Wages and the Standard of Living in Britain during and after the Industrial Revolution," Journal of Economic History *58, no. 3 [September 1998]: 625–58, table on 652–53.)*

Questions to Consider

1. **At what point according to this table did real earnings increase in significant fashion?**
2. **Looking back to Chapter 20, why might the cost of living have gone up so dramatically between 1800 and 1814?**
3. **What are the virtues of using statistical measures to determine the standard of living? What are the defects?**

Further Reading

Thompson, Noel W. *The Real Rights of Man: Political Economies for the Working Class, 1775–1850.* 1998.

Williamson, Jeffrey G., and Jeff Williamson. *Did British Capitalism Breed Inequality?* 2006.

French cities, and Poles flocked to German cities. Settlements sprang up outside the old city limits but gradually became part of the urban area. Cities incorporated parks, cemeteries, zoos, and greenways—all imitations of the countryside, which itself was being industrialized by railroads and factories. "One can't even go to one's land for the slightest bit of gardening," grumbled a French citizen, annoyed by new factories in town, "without being covered with a black powder that spoils every plant that it touches."

Overcrowding and Disease The rapid influx of people caused serious overcrowding in the cities because the housing stock expanded much more slowly than population growth and wages were not high enough for many workers to afford city rents. In Paris, thirty thousand workers lived in lodging houses, eight or nine to a room, with no separation of the sexes. In 1847 in St. Giles, the Irish quarter of London, 461 people lived in just twelve houses. Men, women, and children with no money for fuel huddled together for warmth on piles of filthy rotting straw or potato peels.

Severe crowding worsened already dire sanitation conditions. Residents dumped refuse into streets or courtyards, and human excrement collected in cesspools under apartment houses. At midcentury, London's approximately 250,000 cesspools were emptied only once or twice a year. Water was scarce and had to be fetched daily from nearby fountains. Despite the diversion of water from provincial rivers to Paris and a tripling of the number of public fountains, Parisians had enough water for only two baths annually per person (the upper classes enjoyed more baths, of course; the lower classes, fewer).

In London, private companies that supplied water turned on pumps in the poorer sections for only a few hours three days a week. In rapidly growing British industrial cities such as Manchester, one-third of the houses contained no latrines. Human waste ended up in the rivers that supplied drinking water. The horses that provided transportation inside the cities left droppings everywhere, and city dwellers often kept chickens, ducks, goats, pigs, geese, and even cattle, as well as dogs and cats, in their houses. The result was a "universal atmosphere of filth and stink," as one observer recounted.

Such conditions made cities prime breeding grounds for disease. In 1830–1832 and again in 1847–1851, devastating outbreaks of cholera swept across Asia and Europe, touching the United States as well in 1849–1850 (Map 21.2). Today we know that a waterborne bacterium causes cholera, but at the time no one understood the disease and everyone feared it. The usually fatal illness induced violent vomiting and diarrhea and left the skin blue, eyes sunken and dull, and hands and feet ice cold. While cholera particularly ravaged the crowded, filthy neighborhoods of rapidly growing cities, it also claimed many rural and some well-to-do victims. In Paris, 18,000 people died in the 1832 epidemic and 20,000 in that of 1849; in London, 7,000 died in each epidemic; and in Russia, the epidemic was catastrophic, claiming 250,000 victims in 1831–1832 and 1 million in 1847–1851.

Rumors and panic followed in the wake of each cholera epidemic. Everywhere the downtrodden imagined conspiracies: in Paris in April 1832, a crowd of workers attacked a central hospital, believing the doctors were poisoning the poor but using cholera as a hoax to cover up the conspiracy. Eastern European peasants burned estates and killed physicians and officials. Although devastating, cholera did not kill as many people as tuberculosis, Europe's number-one deadly disease. But tuberculosis took its victims gradually, one by one, and therefore had less impact on social relations.

Middle-Class Fears | Epidemics revealed the social tensions lying just beneath the surface of urban life. The middle and upper classes lived in large, well-appointed apartments or houses with more light, more air, and more water than in lower-class dwellings. But the lower classes lived nearby, sometimes in the cramped upper floors of the same apartment houses. Middle-class reformers often considered the poor to be morally degenerate because of the circumstances of urban life. In their view, overcrowding led to sexual promiscuity and illegitimacy. They depicted the lower classes as dangerously lacking in sexual self-

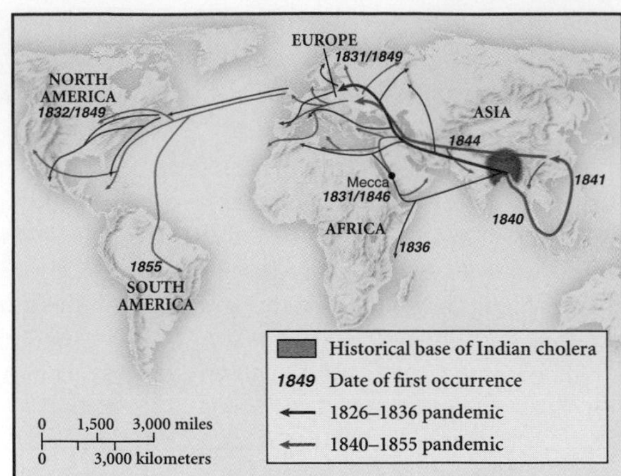

MAP 21.2 The Spread of Cholera, 1826–1855
Contemporaries did not understand the causes of the cholera epidemics in the 1830s and the 1840s in Europe. Western Europeans knew only that the disease marched progressively from east to west across Europe. Nothing seemed able to stop it. It appeared and died out for reasons that could not be grasped at the time. Nevertheless, the cholera epidemics prompted authorities in most European countries to set up public health agencies to coordinate the response and study sanitation conditions in the cities.

control. A physician visiting Lille, France, in 1835 wrote of "individuals of both sexes and of very different ages lying together, most of them without nightshirts and repulsively dirty. . . . The reader will complete the picture. . . . His imagination must not recoil before any of the disgusting mysteries performed on these impure beds, in the midst of obscurity and drunkenness."

Officials collected statistics on illegitimacy that seemed to bear out these fears: one-quarter to one-half of the babies born in the big European cities in the 1830s and 1840s were illegitimate, and alarmed medical men wrote about thousands of infanticides. Between 1815 and the mid-1830s in France, thirty-three thousand babies were abandoned at foundling hospitals every year; 27 percent of births in Paris in 1850 were illegitimate, compared with only 4 percent of rural births. By collecting such statistics, physicians and administrators in the new public health movement hoped to promote legislation to better the living conditions for workers, but at the same time they helped stereotype workers as immoral and out of control.

Sexual disorder seemed to go hand in hand with drinking and crime. Beer halls and pubs dotted the urban landscape. By the 1830s, Hungary's twin cities of Buda and Pest had eight hundred beer and wine houses for the working classes. One London street boasted twenty-three pubs in three hundred yards. Police officials estimated that London had seventy thousand thieves and eighty thousand prostitutes. In many cities, nearly half the population lived at the level of bare subsistence, and increasing numbers depended on public welfare, charity, or criminality to make ends meet.

Everywhere reformers warned of a widening separation between rich and poor and a growing sense of hostility between the classes. The French poet Amédée Pommier wrote of "These leagues of laborers who have no work, / These far too many arms, these starving mobs." Clergymen joined physicians and humanitarians in making dire predictions. A Swiss pastor noted: "A new spirit has arisen among the workers. Their hearts seethe with hatred of the well-to-do; their eyes lust for a share of the wealth about them; their mouths speak unblushingly of a coming day of retribution." In 1848, it would seem that that day of retribution had arrived.

Agricultural Perils and Prosperity

Rising populations created increased demand for food and spurred changes in the countryside, too. Peasants and farmers planted fallow land, chopped down forests, and drained marshes to increase their farming capacity. Still, Europe's ability to feed its expanding population remained questionable: although agricultural yields increased by 30 to 50 percent in the first half of the nineteenth century, population grew by nearly 100 percent. Railroads and canals improved food distribution, but much of Europe — particularly in the east — remained isolated from markets and vulnerable to famines.

Most people still lived on the land, and the upper classes still dominated rural society. Successful businessmen bought land avidly, seeing it not only as the ticket to respectability but also as a hedge against hard times. Hardworking, crafty, or lucky commoners sometimes saved enough to purchase holdings that they had formerly rented or slowly acquired slivers of land from less fortunate neighbors. In France at midcentury, almost two million economically independent peasants tended their own small properties. But in England, southern Italy, Prussia, and eastern Europe, large landowners, usually noblemen, consolidated and expanded their estates by buying up the land of less successful nobles or peasants. As agricultural prices rose, the big landowners pushed for legislation to allow them to continue converting common land to private property.

Wringing a living from the soil under such conditions put pressure on traditional family life. For example, men often migrated seasonally to earn cash in factories or as village artisans, while their wives, sisters, and daughters did the traditional "men's work" of tending crops. In France, Napoleon's Civil Code provided for an equal distribution of inheritance among all heirs; as a result, land was divided over generations into such small parcels that less than 25 percent of all French landowners could support themselves. In the past, population growth had been contained by postponing marriage (leaving fewer years for childbearing) and by high rates of death in childbirth as well as infant mortality. Now, as child mortality declined outside the industrial cities and people without property began marrying earlier, Europeans became more aware of birth control methods. Contraceptive techniques improved; for example, the vulcanization of rubber in the 1840s improved the reliability of condoms. When such methods failed and population increase left no options open at home, people emigrated, often to the United States. Some 800,000 Germans had moved out of central Europe by 1850, while in the 1840s famine drove hundreds of thousands of Irish abroad. Between 1816 and 1850, five million Europeans left their home countries for new lives overseas. When France colonized Algeria in the 1830s and 1840s, officials tried to attract settlers by emphasizing the fertility of the land; they offered the prospect of agricultural prosperity in the colony as an alternative to the rigors of industrialization and urbanization at home.

Despite all the challenges to established ways of life, rural political power remained in the hands of traditional elites. The biggest property owners dominated their tenants, sharecroppers, and serfs, often demanding a greater yield without making improvements that would enhance productivity. They controlled the political assemblies as well and often personally selected local officials. Such power provoked resentment. One Italian critic wrote, "Great landowner is often the synonym for great ignoramus." Nowhere did the old rural social order seem more impregnable than in Russia. Most Russian serfs remained tied to the land, and troops easily suppressed serfs' uprisings in 1831 and 1842. Yet in the 1850s railroad construction would begin to transform life in Russia too, and the railroads would bring with them the same social problems — urbanization, the beginning of industrialization, and a growing awareness of social disparities — that threatened the social and political order in western Europe in the 1830s and 1840s. These new social problems demanded a response. But would that response be reform or revolution?

REVIEW QUESTION What dangers did the Industrial Revolution pose to both urban and rural life?

Reforming the Social Order

The experience of dramatic economic and social changes prompted artists and writers to focus on emerging social problems, even when they rejected the influence of the new industrial way of life. Their literary and artistic depictions of social problems helped inspire the creation of new organizations for social reform. Middle-class women often took the lead in establishing charitable organizations that tried to bring religious faith, educational uplift, and the reform of manners to the lower classes. The middle class, both men and women, expected women to soften the rigors of a rapidly changing society, but this expectation led to some confusion about women's proper role: Should they devote themselves to social reform in the world or to their own domestic spaces? Many hoped to apply the same zeal for reform to the colonial peoples living in places administered by Europeans.

Cultural Responses to the Social Question

The *social question*, an expression reflecting the widely shared concern about social changes arising from industrialization and urbanization, pervaded all forms of art and literature. The dominant artistic movement of the time, romanticism, generally took a dim view of industrialization. The English-born American painter Thomas Cole (1801–1848) complained in 1836: "In this age . . . a meager utilitarianism seems ready to absorb every feeling and sentiment, and what is sometimes called improvement in its march makes us fear that the bright and tender flowers of the imagination shall all be crushed beneath its iron tramp." Yet culture itself underwent important changes as the growing capitals of Europe attracted flocks of aspiring painters and playwrights; the 1830s and 1840s witnessed an explosion in culture as the number of would-be artists increased dramatically and new technologies such as photography and lithography (see the illustration on the top of page 698) brought art to the masses. Many of these new intellectuals would support the revolutions of 1848.

Romantic Concerns about Industrial Life

Because romanticism tended to glorify nature and reject industrial and urban growth, romantics often gave vivid expression to the problems created by rapid economic and social transformation. The English poet Elizabeth Barrett Browning, best known for her love poems, denounced child labor in "The Cry of the Children" (1843). Architects of the period sometimes sought to recapture a preindustrial world. When the British Houses of Parliament were rebuilt after they burned down in 1834, the architect Sir Charles Barry constructed them in a Gothic style reminiscent of the Middle Ages. This medievalism was taken even further by A. W. N. Pugin, who contributed some of the designs for the Houses of Parliament. In his polemical book *Contrasts* (1836), Pugin denounced modern conditions and compared them unfavorably with those in the 1400s. To underline his view, Pugin wore medieval clothes at home.

Romantic painters specialized in landscape as a way of calling attention to the sublime wonders of nature, but sometimes even landscapes showed the power of new technologies. In *Rain, Steam, and Speed: The Great Western Railway* (1844), the leading English romantic painter, Joseph M. W. Turner (1775–1851), portrayed the struggle between the forces of nature and the means of economic growth. Turner was fascinated by steamboats: in *The Fighting "Téméraire" Tugged to Her Last Berth to Be Broken Up* (1838; see the illustration on page 697), he featured the victory of steam power over more conventional sailing ships. An admirer described the painting as an "almost prophetic idea of smoke, soot, iron, and steam, coming to the front in all naval matters."

The Depiction of Social Conditions in Novels

Increased literacy, the spread of reading rooms and lending libraries, and serialization in newspapers and journals gave novels a large reading public. Unlike the fiction of the eighteenth century, which had focused on individual personalities, the great novels of the 1830s and 1840s specialized in the portrayal of social life in all its varieties. Manufacturers, financiers, starving students, workers, bureaucrats, prostitutes, underworld figures, thieves, and aristocratic men and women filled the pages of works by popular writers. Hoping to get out of debt, the French writer Honoré de Balzac (1799–1850) pushed himself to exhaustion and a premature death by cranking out ninety-five novels and many short stories. He aimed to catalog the social types that could be found in French society. Many of his characters, like himself, were driven by the desire to climb higher in the social order.

The English fiction writer Charles Dickens (1812–1870) worked with a similar frenetic energy and for much the same reason. When his father was imprisoned for debt in 1824, the young Dickens took a job in a shoe-polish factory. In 1836, he published a series of literary sketches of daily life in London to accompany a volume of caricatures by the

Joseph M. W. Turner, *The Fighting "Téméraire" Tugged to Her Last Berth to Be Broken Up* (1838)
In this painting a steamer belching smoke tows a wooden sailing ship to its last berth, where it will be destroyed. Turner muses about the passing of old ways but also displays his mastery of color in the final blaze of sunset, itself another sign of the passing of time. Turner was an avid reader of the romantic poets, especially Byron. British opinion polls have rated this painting the best of all British paintings. How does the painting capture the clash of old and new? *(© The National Gallery, London, UK/Art Resource, NY.)*

artist George Cruikshank. Dickens then produced a series of novels that appeared in monthly installments and attracted thousands of readers. In them, he paid close attention to the distressing effects of industrialization and urbanization. In *The Old Curiosity Shop* (1841), for example, he depicts the Black Country, the manufacturing region west and northwest of Birmingham, as a "cheerless region," a "mournful place," in which tall chimneys "made foul the melancholy air." In addition to publishing such enduring favorites as *Oliver Twist* (1838) and *A Christmas Carol* (1843), he ran charitable organizations and pressed for social reforms. For Dickens, the ability to portray the problems of the poor went hand in hand with a personal commitment to reform.

Novels by women often revealed the bleaker side of women's situations. Charlotte Brontë's *Jane Eyre* (1847) describes the difficult life of an orphaned girl who becomes a governess, the only occupation open to most single middle-class women. The French novelist Amandine-Aurore-Lucile Dupin Dudevant (1804–1876), writing under the pen name **George Sand**, took her social criticism a step further. She announced her independence in the 1830s by dressing like a man and smoking cigars. Though she published her work under a male pseudonym, as did many other women writers of the time, she created female characters who prevail in difficult circumstances through romantic love and moral idealism. Sand's novel *Indiana* (1832), about an unhappily married woman, was read all over Europe. Her notoriety—she became the lover of the Polish pianist and composer Frédéric Chopin, among others, and threw herself into socialist politics—made the term *George-Sandism* a common expression of disdain for independent women.

George Sand: The pen name of French novelist Amandine-Aurore-Lucile Dupin Dudevant (1804–1876), who showed her independence in the 1830s by dressing like a man and smoking cigars. The term *George-Sandism* became an expression of disdain for independent women.

George Sand

In this lithograph by Alcide Lorentz of 1842, George Sand is shown in one of her notorious male costumes standing on a cloud created by the cigar in her left hand. Sand published numerous works, including novels (*Indiana* is shown at her feet), plays, essays, travel writing, and an autobiography. She advocated setting up a Chamber of Mothers to go alongside the Chamber of Deputies (her right arm rests on sheets with those words on them), and she actively participated in the revolution of 1848 in France, writing pamphlets in support of the new republic. Disillusioned by the rise to power of Louis-Napoleon Bonaparte, she withdrew to her country estate and devoted herself exclusively to her writing. *(The Granger Collection, New York—All rights reserved.)*

The First Daguerreotype

Jacques Daguerre experimented extensively with producing an image on a metal plate before he came up with a viable photographic process in 1837. He called this first daguerreotype *Still Life*, a common title for paintings. In 1839, the French government bought the rights and made the process freely available. *(Louis Daguerre, Time & Life Pictures / Getty Images.)*

The Explosion of Culture

As artists became more interested in society and social relations, ordinary citizens crowded cultural events. Museums opened to the public across Europe, and the middle classes began collecting art. Popular theaters in big cities drew thousands from the lower and middle classes every night; in London, for example, some twenty-four thousand people attended eighty "penny theaters" nightly. The audience for print culture also multiplied. In the German states, for example, the production of new literary works doubled between 1830 and 1843, as did the number of periodicals and newspapers and the number of booksellers. Thirty or forty private lending libraries offered books in Berlin in the 1830s, and reading rooms in pastry shops stocked political newspapers and satirical journals. Young children and ragpickers sold cheap prints and books door-to-door or in taverns.

The advent of photography in 1839 provided an amazing new medium for artists. The daguerreotype, named after its inventor, French painter Jacques Daguerre (1787–1851), prompted one artist to claim that "from today, painting is dead." Although this prediction was highly exaggerated, photography did open up new ways of portraying reality. It did so only gradually, however, as early photographs required exposure times of twenty to thirty minutes, making it impossible to capture anything or anyone in movement.

Culture expanded its reach in part because the number of artists and writers swelled. Estimates suggest that the number of painters and sculptors in France, the undisputed center of European art at the time, grew sixfold between 1789 and 1838. Not everyone could succeed in this hothouse atmosphere, in which writers and artists furiously competed for public attention. Their own troubles made some of them more keenly aware of the hardships faced by the poor. A satirical article in one of the many bitingly critical journals and booklets published in Berlin proclaimed: "In Ipswich in England a mechanical genius has invented a stomach, whose extraordinary efficient construction is remarkable. This artificial stomach is intended for factory workers there and is adjusted so that it is fully satisfied with three lentils or peas; one potato is enough for an entire week."

The Varieties of Social Reform

Lithographs, novels, and even joke booklets helped drive home the need for social reform, but religious conviction also inspired efforts to help the poor. Moral reform societies, Bible groups, Sunday schools, and temperance groups aimed to turn the poor into respectable people. In 1844, for example, 450 different relief organizations operated in London alone. States supported these efforts by encouraging education and enforcing laws against the vagrant poor.

The Religious Impulse for Social Reform Religiously motivated reformers first had to overcome the perceived indifference of the working classes. Protestant and Catholic clergy complained that workers had no interest in religion; less than 10 percent of the workers in the cities attended religious services. In a report on the state of religion in England and Wales in 1851, the head of the census commented that "the masses of our working population . . . are *unconscious secularists*. . . . These are never, or but seldom seen in our religious congregations." To combat such indifference, British religious groups launched the Sunday school movement, which reached its zenith in the 1840s. By 1851, more than half of all working-class children ages five to fifteen were attending Sunday school, even though very few of their parents regularly went to religious services. The Sunday schools taught children how to read at a time when few working-class children could go to school during the week.

Women took a more prominent role than ever before in charitable work. Catholic religious orders, which by 1850 enrolled many more women than men, ran schools, hospitals, leper colonies, insane asylums, and old-age homes. The Catholic church established new orders, especially for women, and increased missionary activity overseas. Protestant women in Great Britain and the United States established Bible, missionary, and female reform societies by the hundreds. Chief among their concerns was prostitution, and many societies dedicated themselves to reforming "fallen women" and castigating men who visited prostitutes. As a pamphlet of the Boston Female Moral Reform Society explained, "Our mothers, our sisters, our daughters are sacrificed by the thousands every year on the altar of sin, and who are the agents in this work of destruction: Why, our fathers, our brothers, and our sons."

Catholics and Protestants alike promoted the temperance movement. In Ireland, England, the German states, and the United States, temperance societies organized to fight the "pestilence of hard liquor." The first societies had appeared in the United States as early as 1813, and by 1835 the American Temperance Society claimed 1.5 million members. Temperance advocates saw drunkenness as a sign of moral weakness and a threat to social order. Industrialists pointed to the loss of worker productivity, and efforts to promote temperance often reflected middle- and upper-class fears of the lower classes' lack of discipline. One German temperance advocate insisted, "One need not be a prophet to know that all efforts to combat the widespread and rapidly spreading pauperism will be unsuccessful as long as the common man fails to realize that the principal source of his degradation and misery is his fondness of drink." Yet temperance societies also attracted working-class people who shared the desire for respectability.

Education and Reform of the Poor Social reformers saw education as one of the main prospects for uplifting the poor and the working class. In addition to setting up Sunday schools, British churches founded organizations such as the British and Foreign School Society. More secular in intent were the Mechanics Institutes, which provided education for workers in the big cities. In 1833, the French government passed an education law that required every town to maintain a primary school, pay a teacher, and provide free education to poor boys. As the law's author, François Guizot, argued, "Ignorance renders the masses turbulent and ferocious." Girls' schools were optional, although hundreds of women taught at the primary level, most of them in private, often religious schools. Despite these efforts, only one out of every thirty children went to school in France, many fewer than in Protestant states such as Prussia, where 75 percent of children were in primary school by 1835. Popular education remained woefully undeveloped in most of eastern Europe. Peasants were specifically excluded from the few primary schools in Russia, where Tsar Nicholas I blamed the Decembrist Revolt of 1825 on education.

Above all else, the elite sought to impose discipline and order on working people. Popular sports, especially blood sports such as cockfighting and bearbaiting, suggested a lack of control, and longstanding efforts in Great Britain to eliminate these recreations now gained momentum through organizations such as the Society for the Prevention of Cruelty to Animals. By the end of the 1830s, bullbaiting had been abandoned in Great Britain. "This useful animal," rejoiced one reformer in 1839, "is no longer tortured amidst the exulting yells of those who are a disgrace to our common form and nature." The other blood sports died out more slowly, and efforts in other countries generally lagged behind those of the British.

When private charities failed to meet the needs of the poor, governments often intervened. Great Britain sought to control the costs of public welfare by passing a new poor law in 1834, called by its critics the Starvation Act. The law required that all able-bodied persons receiving relief be housed together in workhouses, with husbands separated from wives

Class Differences

In 1841 a new satirical weekly in London called *Punch* began publishing "cartoons" (humorous drawings). This one from 1843 depicts the dramatic differences between the life experiences of those with money ("Capital") and those who worked with their hands ("Labour"). *(From* Punch, *vol. 5, London, 1843, cartoon number 5/akg-images.)*

and parents from children. Workhouse life was designed to be as unpleasant as possible so that poor people would move on to regions of higher employment. British women from all social classes organized anti–poor law societies to protest the separation of mothers from their children in the workhouses.

Domesticity and the Subordination of Women

Many women viewed charitable work as the extension of their domestic roles: they promoted virtuous behavior and morality in their efforts to improve society. In one widely read advice book, Englishwoman Sarah Lewis suggested in 1839 that "women may be the prime agents in the regeneration of mankind." But women's social reform activities concealed a paradox. According to the ideology that historians call **domesticity**, women were to live their lives entirely within the domestic sphere, devoting themselves to their families and the home. The English poet Alfred, Lord Tennyson, captured this view in a popular poem published in 1847: "Man for the field and woman for the hearth; / Man for the sword and for the needle she. / . . . All else confusion." Many believed that maintaining proper and distinct roles for men and women was critically important to maintaining social order in general.

Most women had little hope of economic independence. The notion that they belonged in a separate, domestic sphere prevented women from pursuing higher education, work in professional careers, or participation in politics through voting or holding office — all activities deemed appropriate only to men. Laws everywhere codified the subordination of women. Many countries followed the model of Napoleon's Civil Code, which classified married women as legal incompetents along with children, the insane, and criminals. In Great Britain, which had no national law code, the courts upheld the legality of a husband's complete control. For example, a court ruled in 1840 that "there can be no doubt of the general dominion which the law of England attributes to the husband over the wife." In some countries, such as France and Austria, unmarried women enjoyed some rights over property, but elsewhere laws explicitly defined them as perpetual minors under paternal control.

Distinctions between men and women were most noticeable in the privileged classes. Whereas boys attended secondary schools, most middle- and upper-class girls still received their education at home or in church schools, where they were taught to be religious, obedient, and accomplished in music and languages. As men's fashions turned practical — long trousers and short jackets of solid, often dark colors; no makeup (previously common for aristocratic men); and simply cut hair — women continued to dress for decorative effect, now with tightly corseted waists that emphasized the differences between female and male bodies. Middle- and upper-class women favored long hair that required hours of brushing and pinning up, and they wore long, cumbersome skirts. Advice books written by women detailed the tasks that such women undertook in the home: maintaining household accounts, supervising servants, and organizing social events.

Scientists reinforced stereotypes. Once considered sexually insatiable, women were now described as incapacitated by menstruation and largely uninterested in sex, an attitude that many equated with moral superiority. Thus was born the "Victorian" woman (the epoch gets its name from England's

---

domesticity: An ideology prevailing in the nineteenth century that women should devote themselves to their families and the home.

Queen Victoria—see page 716), a figment of the largely male medical imagination. Physicians and scholars considered women mentally inferior. In 1839, Auguste Comte, an influential early French sociologist, wrote, "As for any functions of government, the radical inaptitude of the female sex is there yet more marked . . . and limited to the guidance of the mere family."

Some women denounced the ideology of domesticity and separate spheres; the English writer Ann Lamb, for example, proclaimed that "the duty of a wife *means* the obedience of a Turkish slave." Middle-class women who did not marry, however, had few options for earning a living; they often worked as governesses or ladies' companions for the well-to-do. Most lower-class women worked because of financial necessity; as the wives of peasants, laborers, or shopkeepers, they had to supplement the family's meager income by working on the farm, in a factory, or in a shop. Domesticity might have been an ideal for them, but rarely was it a reality. Families crammed into small spaces had no time or energy for separate spheres.

Abuses and Reforms Overseas

Like the ideal of domesticity, the ideal of colonialism often conflicted with the reality of economic interests. In the first half of the nineteenth century, those economic interests changed as European colonialism underwent a subtle but momentous transformation. Colonialism became **imperialism**—a word coined only in the mid-nineteenth century—as Europeans turned their interest away from the plantation colonies of the Caribbean and toward new colonies in Asia and Africa. Colonialism had most often led to the establishment of settler colonies, direct rule by Europeans, the introduction of slave labor from Africa, and the wholesale destruction of indigenous peoples; in contrast, imperialism usually meant more indirect forms of economic exploitation and political rule. Europeans still profited from their colonies, but now they also aimed to re-form colonial peoples in their own image—when it did not conflict too much with their economic interests to do so.

Abolition of Slavery

Colonialism—as opposed to imperialism—rose and fell with the enslavement of black Africans. British religious groups, especially the Quakers, had taken the lead in forming antislavery societies. The contradiction between calling for more liberty at home and maintaining slavery in the West Indies seemed intolerable to them. One English abolitionist put the matter in these terms: "[God] has given to us an unexampled portion of civil liberty; and we in return drag his rational creatures into a most severe and perpetual bondage." Such groups as the London Society for Effecting the Abolition of the Slave Trade gained a first victory in 1807 when the British House of Lords voted to abolish the slave trade (though not the institution of slavery itself). The new Latin American republics abolished slavery in the 1820s and 1830s after they defeated the Spanish with armies that included many slaves. British missionary and evangelical groups continued to condemn the conquest, enslavement, and exploitation of native African populations and successfully blocked British annexations in central and southern Africa in the 1830s.

British reformers finally obtained the abolition of slavery in the British Empire in 1833. Antislavery petitions to Parliament bore 1.5 million signatures, including those of 350,000 women on one petition alone. In France, the new government of Louis-Philippe took strong measures against clandestine slave traffic, virtually ending French participation during the 1830s. Slavery was abolished in the remaining French Caribbean colonies in 1848.

Neither slavery nor the slave trade disappeared immediately just because the British and French had given it up. Because of increased participation by Spanish and Portuguese traders, almost as many slaves were traded in the 1820s as in the 1780s and the overall traffic did not dwindle until the 1850s. Human bondage continued unabated in Brazil, Cuba (still a Spanish colony), and the United States. Some American reformers supported abolition, but they remained a minority. Like serfdom in Russia, slavery in the Americas involved a quagmire of economic, political, and moral problems that worsened as the nineteenth century wore on.

Economic and Political Imperialism

Despite the abolition of slavery, Britain and France had not lost interest in overseas colonies. Using the pretext of an insult to its envoy, France invaded Algeria in 1830 and, after a long military campaign, established political control over most of the country in the next two decades. By 1848, more than seventy thousand French, Italian, and Maltese colonists had settled there with government encouragement, often confiscating the lands of native peoples. In that year, the French government officially incorporated Algeria as part of France. Eventually, the French embarked on a policy of

---

imperialism: European dominance of the non-West through economic exploitation and political rule; the word (as distinct from *colonialism*, which usually implied establishment of settler colonies, often with slavery) was coined in the mid-nineteenth century.

Opium Den in London (c. 1870)
This woodcut by Gustave Doré shows that opium smoking persisted in Britain at least to the 1870s. Doré was a French book illustrator who came to London in 1869–1871 and produced illustrations of the poorer neighborhoods in the city. His taste for the grotesque is apparent in the figures watching the smokers. *(Snark/Art Resource, NY.)*

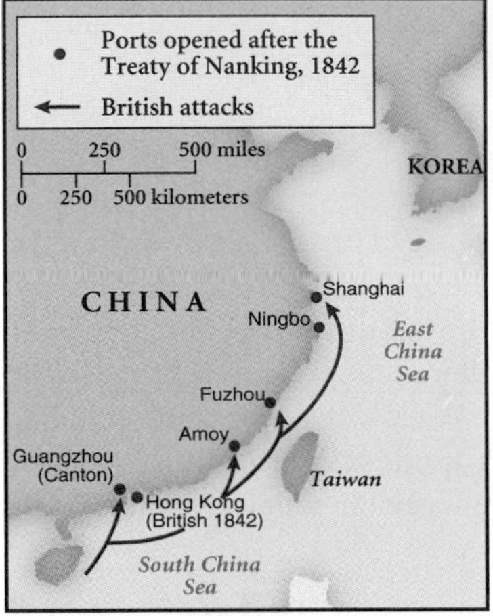

The Opium War, 1839–1842

assimilating the native population into French culture, but their efforts proved less than completely successful. France also imposed a protectorate government over the South Pacific island of Tahiti.

Although the British granted Canada greater self-determination in 1839, they extended their dominion elsewhere by annexing Singapore (1819), an island off the Malay peninsula, and New Zealand (1840). They also increased their control in India through the administration of the East India Company, a private group of merchants chartered by the British crown. The British educated a native elite to take over much of the day-to-day business of administering the country, and they used native soldiers to augment their military control. By 1850, only one in six soldiers serving Britain in India was European.

The East India Company also tried to establish a regular trade with China in opium, long known for its medicinal uses but increasingly bought in China as a recreational drug. The Chinese government forbade Western merchants to venture outside the southern city of Guangzhou (Canton) and banned the import of opium, but these measures failed. Through smuggling Indian opium into China and bribing local officials, British traders built up a flourishing market, and by the mid-1830s they were pressuring the British government to force an expanded opium trade on the Chinese. When the Chinese authorities expelled British merchants from southern China in 1839, Britain retaliated by bombarding Chinese coastal cities. The **Opium War** ended in 1842, when Britain dictated to a defeated China the Treaty of Nanking, by which four more Chinese ports were opened to Europeans and the British took sovereignty over the island of Hong Kong, received a substantial war indemnity, and were assured of a continuation of the opium trade. In this case, reform took a backseat to economic interest, despite the complaints of religious groups in Britain. In general, reform organizations aimed to improve the lives of the downtrodden, not overturn the basic structures of the political order or social hierarchy. Faced with continuing conflicts and unrest, some intellectuals and activists began to look for more systematic solutions to the social problems of the time.

REVIEW QUESTION In which areas did reformers trying to address the social problems created by industrialization and urbanization succeed, and in which did they fail?

Opium War: War between China and Great Britain (1839–1842) that resulted in the opening of four Chinese ports to Europeans and British sovereignty over Hong Kong.

Ideologies and Political Movements

Although reform organizations grew rapidly in the 1830s and 1840s, many Europeans found them insufficient to answer the questions raised by industrialization and urbanization. How did the new social order differ from the earlier one, which was less urban and less driven by commercial concerns? Who should control this new order? Should governments try to moderate or accelerate the pace of change? New ideologies such as liberalism and socialism offered competing answers to these questions and provided the platform for new political movements. Established governments faced challenges not only from liberals and socialists but also from the most potent of the new doctrines, nationalism. Nationalists looked past social problems to concentrate on achieving political autonomy and self-determination for groups identified by ethnicity rather than by class.

The Spell of Nationalism

According to the doctrine of **nationalism**, all peoples derive their identities from their nations, which are defined by common language, shared cultural traditions, and sometimes religion. When such nations do not coincide with state boundaries, nationalism can produce violence and warfare as different national groups compete for control over territory (Map 21.3).

Nationalist aspirations were especially explosive for the Austrian Empire, which included a variety of peoples united only by their enforced allegiance to the Habsburg emperor. The empire included three main national groups: the Germans, who made up one-fourth of the population; the Magyars of Hungary (which included Transylvania and Croatia); and the Slavs, who together formed the largest group in the population but were divided into different ethnic groups such as Poles, Czechs, Croats, and Serbs. The Austrian Empire also included Italians in Lombardy and Venetia, and Romanians in Transylvania. Efforts to govern such diverse peoples preoccupied Prince Klemens von Metternich, chief minister to the weak Habsburg emperor Francis I (r. 1792–1835). Metternich's domestic policy aimed to restrain nationalist impulses, and it largely succeeded until the 1840s. He set up a secret police organization on the Napoleonic model that opened letters of even the highest officials. Censorship in the Italian provinces was so strict that even the works of Dante were expurgated. Metternich announced that "the Lombards must forget that they are Italians."

Metternich's policies forced the leading Italian nationalist, **Giuseppe Mazzini** (1805–1872), into exile in France in 1831. There Mazzini founded Young Italy, a secret society that attracted thousands with its message that Italy would touch off a European-wide revolutionary movement. The conservative order throughout Europe felt threatened by Mazzini's charismatic leadership and conspiratorial scheming, but he lacked both European allies against Austria and widespread support among the Italian masses.

Since so many different ethnic groups lived within the borders of the Austrian Empire, neither the emperor nor Metternich favored aspirations for German unification. Economic unification in the German states nonetheless took a step forward with the foundation in 1834, under Prussian leadership, of the *Zollverein* ("customs union"). Austria was not part of the Zollverein. German nationalists sought a government uniting German-speaking peoples, but they could not agree on its boundaries: Would the unified German state include both Prussia and the Austrian Empire? If it included Austria, what about the non-German territories of the Austrian Empire? And could the powerful, conservative kingdom of Prussia coexist in a unified German state with other, more liberal but smaller states? These questions would vex German history for decades to come.

Polish nationalism became more self-conscious after the collapse of the revolt in 1830 against Russian domination. Ten thousand Poles, mostly noble army officers and intellectuals, fled Poland in 1830 and 1831. Most of them took up residence in western European capitals, especially Paris, where they mounted a successful public relations campaign for worldwide support. Their intellectual hero was the poet Adam Mickiewicz (1798–1855), whose mystical writings portrayed the Polish exiles as martyrs of a crucified nation with an international Christian mission: "Your endeavors are for all men, not only for yourselves. You will achieve a new Christian civilization."

Mickiewicz formed the Polish Legion to fight for national restoration, but rivalries and divisions among the Polish nationalists prevented united

---

nationalism: An ideology that arose in the nineteenth century and that holds that all peoples derive their identities from their nations, which are defined by common language, shared cultural traditions, and sometimes religion.

Giuseppe Mazzini: An Italian nationalist (1805–1872) who founded Young Italy, a secret society to promote Italian unity. He believed that a popular uprising would create a unified Italy.

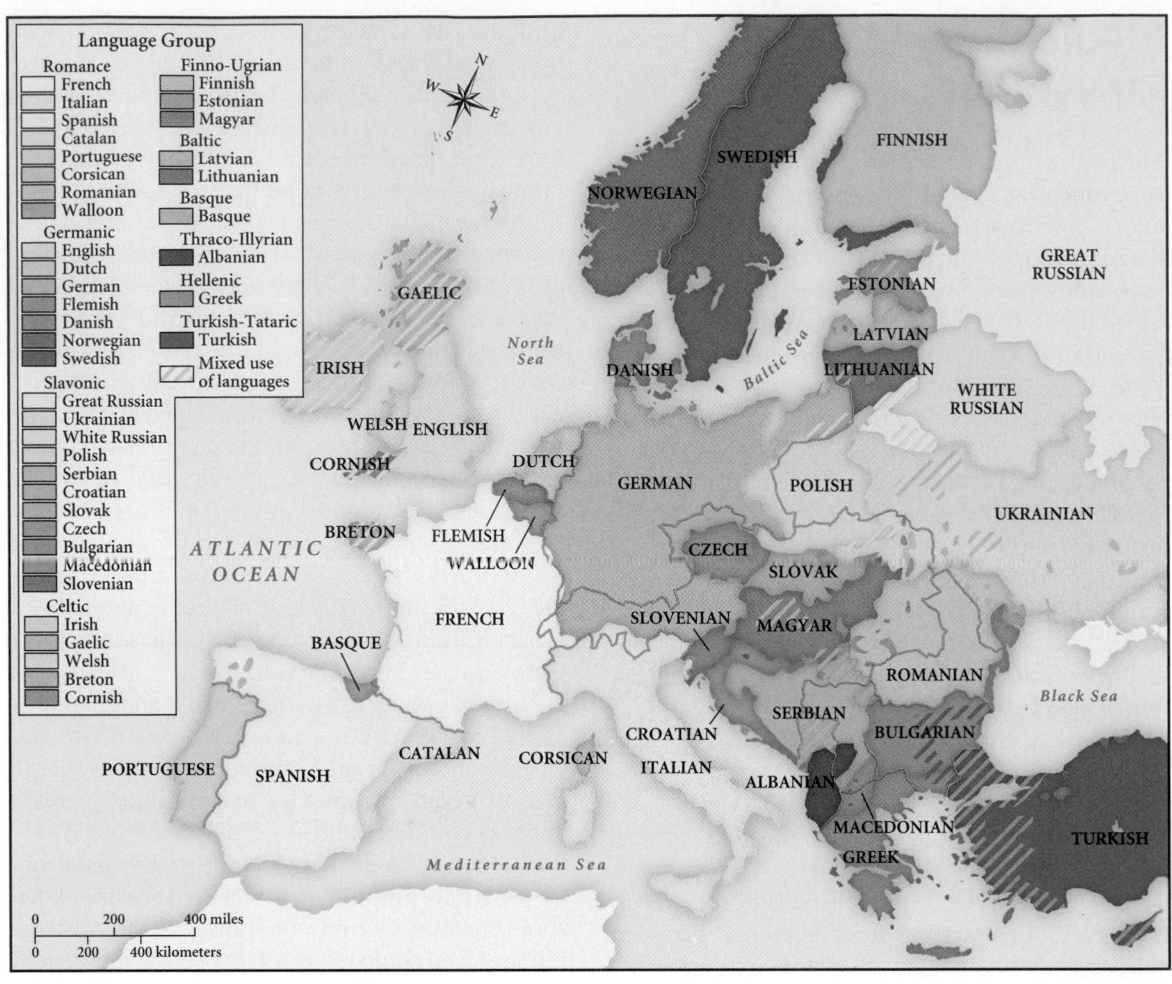

MAP 21.3 Languages of Nineteenth-Century Europe

Even this detailed map of linguistic diversity understates the number of different languages and dialects spoken in Europe. In Italy, for example, few people spoke Italian as their first language. Instead, they spoke local dialects such as Piedmontese or Ligurian, and some might speak better French than Italian if they came from the regions bordering France. How does the map underline the inherent contradictions of nationalism in Europe? What were the consequences of linguistic diversity within national borders? Keep in mind that even in Spain, France, and Great Britain, linguistic diversity continued right up to the beginning of the 1900s.

action until 1846, when Polish exiles in Paris tried to launch a coordinated insurrection for Polish independence. Plans for an uprising in the Polish province of Galicia in the Austrian Empire collapsed when peasants instead revolted against their noble Polish masters. Slaughtering some two thousand aristocrats, a desperate rural population served the Austrian government's end by defusing the nationalist challenge. Class interests and national identity worked against each other.

In Russia, nationalism took the form of opposition to Western ideas. Russian nationalists, or Slavophiles (lovers of the Slavs), opposed the Westernizers, who wanted Russia to follow Western models of industrial development and constitutional government. The Slavophiles favored maintaining rural traditions infused by the values of the Russian Orthodox church. Only a return to Russia's basic historical principles, they argued, could protect the country against the corrosion of rationalism and materialism. Slavophiles sometimes criticized the regime, however, because they believed the state exerted too much power over the church. The conflict between Slavophiles and Westernizers has continued to shape Russian cultural and intellectual life to the present day.

The most significant nationalist movement in western Europe could be found in Ireland. The Irish had struggled for centuries against English occupation, but Irish nationalists developed strong organizations only in the 1840s. In 1842, a group of writers founded the Young Ireland movement, which aimed to recover Irish traditions and preserve the Gaelic language (spoken by at least one-third of the peasantry). Daniel O'Connell (1775–1847), a Catholic lawyer and landowner who sat in the British House of Commons, hoped to force the British Parliament to repeal the Act of Union of 1801, which had made Ireland part of Great Britain. In 1843, London newspapers reported "monster meetings" that drew crowds of as many as 300,000 people in support of repeal of the union. In response, the British government arrested O'Connell and convicted him of conspiracy. As the Irish example shows, nationalism could turn social tensions into a political movement against an outside oppressor and make independence seem to be the only solution to social injustice. In 1848, when revolutions broke out all over Europe, nationalism often worked against the other political ideologies of the time.

Liberalism in Economics and Politics

As an ideology, **liberalism** had a longer lineage than nationalism but enjoyed less influence among the common people. Liberalism traced its origins to the writings of John Locke in the seventeenth century and the Enlightenment philosophy in the eighteenth. The adherents of liberalism defined themselves in opposition to conservatives on one end of the political spectrum and revolutionaries on the other. Unlike conservatives, liberals supported the Enlightenment ideals of constitutional guarantees of personal liberty and free trade in economics, believing that greater liberty in politics and economic matters would promote social improvement and economic growth. For that reason, they also generally applauded the social and economic changes produced by the Industrial Revolution, while opposing the violence and excessive state power promoted by the French Revolution. The leaders of the expanding middle class composed of manufacturers, merchants, and professionals favored liberalism.

British Liberalism The rapid industrialization and urbanization of Great Britain created a receptive environment for liberalism. Its foremost proponent in the early nineteenth century was the philosopher and jurist Jeremy Bentham (1748–1832). He called his brand of liberalism utilitarianism because he held that the best policy is the one that produces "the greatest good for the greatest number" and is thus the most useful, or utilitarian. Bentham's criticisms spared no institution; he railed against the injustices of the British parliamentary process, the abuses of the prisons and the penal code, and the educational system. In his zeal for social engineering, Bentham proposed elaborate schemes for managing the poor and model prisons that would emphasize rehabilitation through close supervision rather than corporal punishment. British liberals like Bentham wanted government involvement, including deregulation of trade, but they shied away from any association with revolutionary violence.

British liberals wanted government to limit its economic role to maintaining the currency, enforcing contracts, and financing major enterprises like the military and the railroads. As historian and member of Parliament Thomas Macaulay (1800–1859) explained in 1830:

> Our rulers will best promote the improvement of the nation by strictly confining themselves to their own legitimate duties, by leaving capital to find its most lucrative course, commodities their fair price, industry and intelligence their natural reward, idleness and folly their natural punishment, by maintaining peace, by defending property, by diminishing the price of law, and by observing strict economy in every department of the State.

British liberals sought to lower or eliminate British tariffs, especially through repeal of the **Corn Laws**, which benefited landowners by preventing the import of cheap foreign grain while keeping the price of food artificially high for the workers. When landholders in the House of Commons thwarted efforts to lower grain tariffs, two Manchester cotton manufacturers set up the Anti–Corn Law League. The league appealed to the middle class against the landlords, who were labeled "a bread-taxing oligarchy" and "blood-sucking vampires," and attracted thousands of workers to its meetings. League members established local branches, published newspapers and the journal *The Economist* (founded in 1843 and now one of the world's most influential periodicals), and campaigned in elections. They

liberalism: An economic and political ideology that—tracing its roots to John Locke in the seventeenth century and Enlightenment philosophers in the eighteenth—emphasized free trade and the constitutional guarantees of individual rights such as freedom of speech and religion; its adherents stood between conservatives on the right and revolutionaries on the left in the nineteenth century.

Corn Laws: Tariffs on grain in Great Britain that benefited landowners by preventing the import of cheap foreign grain; they were repealed by the British government in 1846.

finally won the support of the Tory prime minister Sir Robert Peel, whose government repealed the Corn Laws in 1846.

Liberalism on the Continent Free trade had less appeal in continental Europe than in England because continental industries needed protection against British industrial dominance. As a consequence, liberals on the continent focused on constitutional reform. French liberals, for example, agitated for greater press freedoms and a broadening of the vote. Louis-Philippe's government brutally repressed working-class and republican insurrections in Lyon and Paris in the early 1830s and forced the republican opposition underground. The French king's increasingly restrictive governments also thwarted liberals' hopes for reforms by suppressing many political organizations and reestablishing censorship.

Repression muted criticism in most other European states as well. Nevertheless, liberal reform movements grew up in pockets of industrialization in Prussia, the smaller German states, and the Austrian Empire. Some state bureaucrats, especially university-trained middle-class officials, favored economic liberalism. Hungarian count Stephen Széchenyi (1791–1860) personally campaigned for the introduction of British-style changes. He introduced British agricultural techniques on his own lands, helped start up steamboat traffic on the Danube, encouraged the importation of machinery and technicians for steam-driven textile factories, and pushed the construction of Hungary's first railway line, from Budapest to Vienna.

In the 1840s, however, Széchenyi's efforts paled before those of the flamboyant Magyar nationalist Lajos Kossuth (1802–1894). After spending four years in prison for sedition, Kossuth grabbed every opportunity to publicize American democracy and British political liberalism, all in a fervent nationalist spirit. In 1844, he founded the Protective Association, whose members bought only Hungarian products; to Kossuth, boycotting Austrian goods was crucial to ending "colonial dependence" on Austria. Born of a lesser landowning family without a noble title, Kossuth did not hesitate to attack "the cowardly selfishness of the landowner class."

Even in Russia, signs of liberal opposition appeared in the 1830s and 1840s. Small circles of young noblemen serving in the army or bureaucracy met in cities, especially Moscow, to discuss the latest Western ideas and to criticize the Russian state: "The world is undergoing a transformation, while we vegetate in our hovels of wood and clay," wrote one. Out of these groups came such future revolutionaries as Alexander Herzen (1812–1870), described by the police as "a daring free-thinker, extremely dangerous to society." Tsar Nicholas I (r. 1825–1855) banned Western liberal writings as well as all books about the United States. He sent nearly ten thousand people a year into exile in Siberia as punishment for their political activities.

Socialism and the Early Labor Movement

The newest ideology, **socialism**, took up where liberalism left off: socialists believed that the liberties advocated by liberals benefited only the middle class—the owners of factories and businesses—not the workers. They sought to reorganize society totally rather than to reform it piecemeal through political measures. They envisioned a future society in which workers would share a harmonious, cooperative, and prosperous life. Building on the theoretical and practical ideas laid out in the early nineteenth century by thinkers and reformers such as Count Henri de Saint-Simon, Charles Fourier, and Robert Owen, the socialists of the 1830s and 1840s hoped that economic planning and working-class organization would solve the problems caused by industrial growth, including the threat of increasingly mechanical, unfeeling social relations.

Origins of Socialism Early socialists criticized the emerging Industrial Revolution for dividing society into two classes: the new middle class, or capitalists (who owned the wealth), and the working class, their downtrodden and impoverished employees. As their name suggests, the socialists aimed to restore harmony and cooperation through social reorganization. Robert Owen (1771–1858), a successful Welsh-born manufacturer, founded British socialism. In 1800, he bought a cotton mill in New Lanark, Scotland, and began to set up a model factory town, where workers labored only ten hours a day (instead of seventeen, as was common) and children between the ages of five and ten attended school rather than working. To put his principles once more into action, Owen moved to the United States in the 1820s and founded a community named New Harmony in Indiana. The experiment collapsed after three years, a victim of internal squabbling. But out of Owen's experiments

---

socialism: A social and political ideology, originating in the early nineteenth century, that advocated the reorganization of society to overcome the new tensions created by industrialization and restore social harmony through communities based on cooperation.

and writings, such as *The Book of the New Moral World* (1820), would come the movement for producer cooperatives (businesses owned and controlled by their workers), consumers' cooperatives (stores in which consumers owned shares), and a national trade union.

Claude Henri de Saint-Simon (1760–1825) and Charles Fourier (1772–1837) were Owen's counterparts in France. Saint-Simon was a noble who had served as an officer in the War of American Independence and lost a fortune speculating in national property during the French Revolution. Fourier traveled as a salesman for a Lyon cloth merchant. Both shared Owen's alarm about the effects of industrialization on social relations. Saint-Simon—who coined the terms *industrialism* and *industrialist* to define the new economic order and its chief animators—believed that work was the central element in the new society and that it should be controlled not by politicians but by scientists, engineers, artists, and industrialists themselves. To correct the abuses of the new industrial order, Fourier urged the establishment of communities that were part garden city and part agricultural commune; all jobs would be rotated to maximize happiness. Fourier hoped that a network of small, decentralized communities would replace the state.

Socialism and Women

The emancipation of women was essential to Fourier's vision of a harmonious community: "The extension of the privileges of women is the fundamental cause of all social progress." After Saint-Simon's death in 1825, some of his followers established a quasi-religious cult with elaborate rituals and a "he-pope" and "she-pope," or ruling father and mother. Saint-Simonians lived and worked together in cooperative arrangements and scandalized some by advocating free love. They set up branches in the United States and Egypt. In 1832, some Saint-Simonian women founded a feminist newspaper, *The Free Woman*, asserting that "with the emancipation of woman will come the emancipation of the worker."

In Great Britain, many women joined the Owenites and helped form cooperative societies and unions. They defended women's working-class organizations against the complaints of men in the new societies and trade unions. One woman wrote, "Do not say the unions are only for men. . . . 'Tis a wrong impression, forced on our minds to keep us slaves!" As women became more active, Owenites agitated for women's rights, marriage reform, and popular education. The French activist Flora Tristan (1801–1844) devoted herself to reconciling the interests of male and female workers. She had seen the "frightful reality" of London's poverty and made a reputation reporting on British working conditions. Tristan published a stream of books and pamphlets urging male workers to address women's unequal status, arguing that "the emancipation of male workers is *impossible* so long as women remain in a degraded state."

Collectivists and Communists

Even though most male socialists ignored Tristan's plea for women's participation, they did strive to create working-class associations. The French socialist Louis Blanc (1811–1882) explained the importance of working-class associations in his book *Organization of Labor* (1840), which deeply influenced the French labor movement. Similarly, the printer turned journalist Pierre-Joseph Proudhon (1809–1865) urged workers to form producers' associations so that the workers could control the work process and eliminate profits made by capitalists. His 1840 book *What Is Property?* argues that property is theft: labor alone is productive, and rent, interest, and profit unjust.

After 1840, some socialists began to call themselves **communists**, emphasizing their desire to replace private property by communal, collective ownership. The Frenchman Étienne Cabet (1788–1856) was the first to use the word *communist*. In 1840, he published *Travels in Icaria*, a novel describing a communist utopia in which a popularly elected dictatorship efficiently organized work, reduced the workday to seven hours, and made work tasks "short, easy, and attractive."

Out of the churning of socialist ideas of the 1840s emerged two men whose collaboration would change the definition of socialism and remake it into an ideology that would shake the world for the next 150 years. Karl Marx (1818–1883) had studied philosophy at the University of Berlin, edited a liberal newspaper until the Prussian government suppressed it, and then left for Paris, where he met Friedrich Engels (1820–1895). While working in the offices of his wealthy family's cotton manufacturing interests in Manchester, England, Engels had been shocked into writing *The Condition of the Working Class in England in 1844* (1845), a sympathetic depiction of industrial workers' dismal lives. In Paris, where German and eastern European intellectuals could pursue their political interests more freely than at home, Marx and Engels organized the Communist League, in whose name they published *The Communist Manifesto* in 1848 (see

---

communists: Those socialists who after 1840 (when the word was first used) advocated the abolition of private property in favor of communal, collective ownership.

DOCUMENT

Marx and Engels, *The Communist Manifesto* (1848)

Karl Marx (1818–1883) and Friedrich Engels (1820–1895) were both sons of prosperous German-Jewish families that had converted to Christianity. In the manifesto for the Communist League, they laid out many of the central principles that would guide Marxist revolution in the future: they insisted that all history is shaped by class struggle and that in future revolutions the working class would overthrow the bourgeoisie, or middle class, and replace capitalism and private property with a communist state in which all property is collectively rather than individually owned. As this selection shows, Marx and Engels always placed more emphasis on class struggle than on the state that would result from the ensuing revolution.

The history of all hitherto existing society is the history of class struggles.

Freeman and slave, patrician and plebeian, lord and serf, guild-master and journeyman, in a word, oppressor and oppressed, stood in constant opposition to one another, carried on an uninterrupted, now hidden, now open fight, a fight that each time ended, either in a revolutionary reconstitution of society at large, or in the common ruin of the contending classes. . . .

The modern bourgeois society that has sprouted from the ruins of feudal society has not done away with class antagonisms. It has but established new classes, new conditions of oppression, new forms of struggle in place of the old ones.

Our epoch, the epoch of the bourgeoisie, possesses, however, this distinctive feature: It has simplified the class antagonisms: Society as a whole is more and more splitting up into two great hostile camps, into two great classes directly facing each other: Bourgeoisie [middle class] and Proletariat [working class]. . . .

The weapons with which the bourgeoisie felled feudalism to the ground are now turned against the bourgeoisie itself.

But not only has the bourgeoisie forged the weapons that bring death to itself; it has also called into existence the men who are to wield those weapons—the modern working class—the proletarians. . . .

The essential condition for the existence, and for the sway of the bourgeois class, is the formation and augmentation of capital; the condition for capital is wage-labour. Wage-labour rests exclusively on competition between labourers. The advance of industry, whose involuntary promoter is the bourgeoisie, replaces the isolation of the labourers, due to competition, by their revolutionary combination, due to association. The development of Modern Industry, therefore, cuts from under its feet the very foundation on which the bourgeoisie produces and appropriates products. What the bourgeoisie, therefore, produces, above all, is its own gravediggers. Its fall and the victory of the proletariat are equally inevitable.

Source: Karl Marx and Friedrich Engels, *The Communist Manifesto*. Translated by Samuel Moore (*Manifesto of the Communist Party*; London: William Reeves, 1888).

Question to Consider

- **According to Marx and Engels, what are the consequences of "Modern Industry"?**

Document, "Marx and Engels, *The Communist Manifesto*," above).

It eventually became the touchstone of Marxist and communist revolutions all over the world. Communists, the *Manifesto* declared, must aim for "the downfall of the bourgeoisie [capitalist class] and the ascendancy of the proletariat [working class], the abolition of the old society based on class conflicts and the foundation of a new society without classes and without private property." Marx and Engels embraced industrialization because they believed it would eventually bring on the proletarian revolution and thus lead inevitably to the abolition of exploitation, private property, and class society.

Working-Class Organization Socialism accompanied, and in some places incited, an upsurge in working-class organization in western Europe. British workers founded cooperative societies, local trade unions, and so-called friendly societies for mutual aid—all of which frightened the middle classes. A newspaper exclaimed in 1834, "The trade unions are, we have no doubt, the most dangerous institutions that were ever permitted to take root."

Many British workers joined in **Chartism**, which aimed to transform Britain into a democracy. In 1838, political radicals drew up the People's Charter, which demanded universal manhood suffrage, vote by secret ballot, equal electoral districts, annual elec-

Chartism: The British movement of supporters of the People's Charter (1838), which demanded universal manhood suffrage, vote by secret ballot, equal electoral districts, and other reforms.

tions, and the elimination of property qualifications for and the payment of stipends to members of Parliament. Chartists denounced their opponents as seeking "to keep the people in social slavery and political degradation." Many women took part by founding female political unions, setting up Chartist Sunday schools, organizing boycotts of unsympathetic shopkeepers, and joining Chartist temperance associations. Nevertheless, the People's Charter refrained from calling for woman suffrage because the movement's leaders feared that doing so would alienate potential supporters.

The Chartists organized a massive campaign during 1838 and 1839, with large public meetings, fiery speeches, and torchlight parades. Presented with petitions for the People's Charter signed by more than a million people, the House of Commons refused to act. In response to this rebuff from middle-class liberals, the Chartists allied themselves in the 1840s with working-class strike movements in the manufacturing districts and associated with various European revolutionary movements. But at the same time they—like their British and continental allies—distanced themselves from women workers.

Continental workers were less well organized because trade unions and strikes were illegal everywhere except Great Britain. Nevertheless, artisans and skilled workers in France formed mutual aid societies that provided insurance, death benefits, and education. In eastern and central Europe, socialism and labor organization—like liberalism—had less impact than in western Europe. Cooperative societies and workers' newspapers did not appear in the German states until 1848. In general, labor organization tended to flourish where urbanization and industrialization were most advanced; even though factory workers rarely organized, skilled artisans did so in order to resist mechanization and wage cuts. When revolutions broke out in 1848, artisans and workers played a prominent—and controversial—role.

REVIEW QUESTION Why did ideologies have such a powerful appeal in the 1830s and 1840s?

The Revolutions of 1848

Food shortages, overpopulation, and unemployment helped turn ideological turmoil into revolution. In 1848, demonstrations and uprisings toppled governments, forced rulers and ministers to flee, and offered revolutionaries an opportunity to put liberal, socialist, and nationalist ideals into practice (Map 21.4). In the end, the revolutions failed because the various ideological movements quarreled, leaving an opening for rulers and their armies to return to power. Rulers returned, but they now faced populations with greater expectations for political participation, national unification, and government responsiveness to social problems.

The Hungry Forties

Beginning in 1845, crop failures across Europe caused food prices to shoot skyward. In the best of times, urban workers paid 50 to 80 percent of their income for a diet consisting largely of bread; now even bread was beyond their means. Overpopulation hastened famine in some places, especially Ireland, where blight destroyed the staple crop, potatoes, first in 1846 and again in 1848 and 1851. Irish peasants had planted potatoes because a family of four might live off one acre of potatoes but would require at least two acres of grain. The Irish often sought security in large families, trusting that their children would help work the land and care for them in old age. By the 1840s, Ireland was especially vulnerable to the potato blight. Out of a population of

The Irish Famine
Contemporary depictions drew attention to the plight of the Irish peasants when a blight infected potato plants, destroying the single most important staple crop. The young girl on the left and the old woman on the right appear too weak with hunger even to move. *(The Granger Collection, New York—All rights reserved.)*

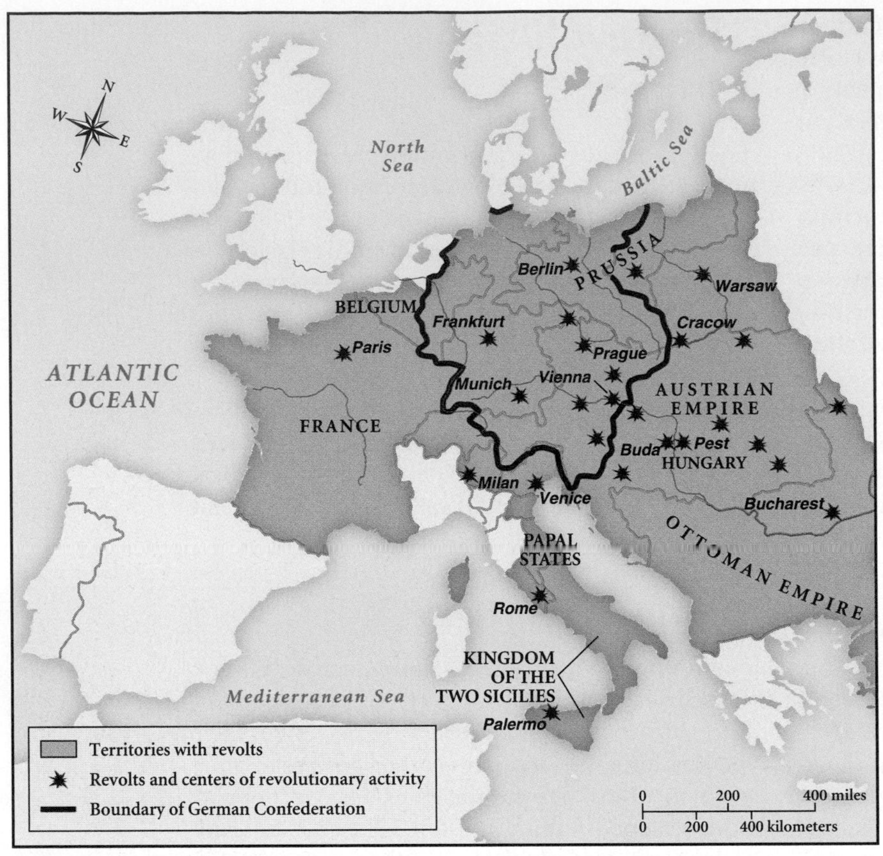

MAP 21.4 The Revolutions of 1848

The attempts of rulers to hold back the forces of change collapsed suddenly in 1848 when once again the French staged a revolution that inspired many others in Europe. This time, cities all over central and eastern Europe joined in as the spirit of revolt inflamed one capital after another. Although all of these revolutions eventually failed because of social and political divisions, the sheer scale of rebellion forced rulers to reconsider their policies.

eight million, as many as one million people died of starvation or disease. Corpses lay unburied on the sides of roads, and whole families were found dead in their cottages, half-eaten by dogs. Hundreds of thousands emigrated to England, the United States, and Canada.

Throughout Europe, famine jeopardized social peace. In age-old fashion, rumors circulated about farmers hoarding grain to drive up prices. Believing that governments should ensure fair prices, crowds took to the streets to protest, often attacking markets or bakeries. They threatened officials with retribution. "If the grain merchants do not cease to take away grains . . . we will go to your homes and cut your throats and those of the three bakers . . . and burn the whole place down." So went one threat from French villagers in the hungry winter of 1847. Although harvests improved in 1848, by then many people had lost their land or become hopelessly indebted.

High food prices also drove down the demand for manufactured goods, resulting in increased unemployment. Industrial workers' wages had been rising—in the German states, for example, wages rose by an average of 5.5 percent in the 1830s and 10.5 percent in the 1840s—but the cost of living rose by about 16 percent each decade, canceling out wage increases. Seasonal work and regular unemployment were already the norm when the crisis of the late 1840s exacerbated the uncertainties of urban life. "The most miserable class that ever sneaked its way into history" is how Friedrich Engels described underemployed and starving workers in 1847.

Another French Revolution

The specter of hunger amplified the voices criticizing established rulers. A Parisian demonstration in favor of reform turned violent on February 23, 1848, when panicky soldiers opened fire on the crowd, killing forty or fifty demonstrators. The next day, faced with fifteen hundred barricades and a furious populace, King Louis-Philippe abdicated and fled to England. A hastily formed provisional government declared France a republic once again.

The new republican government issued liberal reforms—an end to the death penalty for political crimes, the abolition of slavery in the colonies, and freedom of the press—and agreed to introduce universal adult male suffrage despite misgivings about political participation by peasants and unemployed workers. The government allowed Paris officials to organize a system of "national workshops" to provide the unemployed with construction work. When women protested their exclusion, the city set up a few workshops for women workers, albeit with wages lower than men's. To meet a mounting deficit, the provisional government then levied a 45 percent surtax on property taxes, alienating peasants and landowners.

While peasants grumbled, scores of newspapers and political clubs inspired grassroots democratic fervor in Paris and other cities. Meeting in concert halls, theaters, and government auditoriums, the clubs became a regular evening attraction for the citizenry. Women also formed clubs, published women's newspapers, and demanded representation in national politics.

This street-corner activism alarmed middle-class liberals and conservatives. To ensure its control, the republican government paid some unemployed youths to join a mobile guard with its own uniforms and barracks. Tension between the government and the workers in the national workshops rose. Faced with rising radicalism in Paris and other big cities, the voters elected a largely conservative National Assembly in April 1848; most of the deputies chosen were middle-class professionals or landowners who favored either a restoration of the monarchy or a moderate republic. The Assembly immediately appointed a five-man executive committee to run the government and pointedly excluded known supporters of workers' rights. Suspicious of all demands for rapid change, the deputies dismissed a petition to restore divorce and voted down woman suffrage by 899 to 1. When the numbers enrolled in the national workshops in Paris rocketed from a predicted 10,000 to 110,000, the government ordered the workshops closed to new workers, and on June 21 it directed that those already enrolled move to the provinces or join the army.

The workers exploded in anger. In the June Days, as the following week came to be called, the government summoned the army, the National Guard, and the newly recruited mobile guard to fight the workers. Alexis de Tocqueville breathed a sigh of relief: "The Red Republic [red being associated with demands for socialism] is lost forever; all France has joined against it. The National Guard, citizens, and peasants from the remotest parts of the country have come pouring in." (See Document, "Alexis de Tocqueville Describes the June Days in Paris," page 713.) The government forces crushed the workers: more than 10,000 people, most of them workers, were killed or injured; 12,000 were arrested; and 4,000 eventually were convicted and deported.

French Women Activists in 1848

The French artist Honoré Daumier spared no one in his satires. In the early 1830s, one of his lithographs ridiculing the French king landed him in prison for six months. During the revolution of 1848, Daumier published several series mocking women activists. This one is from the series *The Divorcers*, and its caption proclaimed, "Lady Citizens . . . they say that divorce is about to be refused to us . . . let us continue meeting and declare that the country is in danger!" Divorce had been abolished in 1816 and was not reinstated in France until 1884. *(Bibliothèque nationale, Paris, France/ Giraudon/The Bridgeman Art Library International.)*

After the National Assembly adopted a new constitution calling for a presidential election in which all adult men could vote, the electorate chose **Louis-Napoleon Bonaparte** (1808–1873), nephew of the dead emperor. Bonaparte got more than 5.5 million votes out of some 7.4 million cast. He had lived most of his life outside of France, and the leaders of the republic expected him to follow their tune. In uncertain times, the Bonaparte name promised something to everyone. Even many workers supported him because he had no connection with the blood-drenched June Days.

In reality, Bonaparte's election spelled the end of the Second Republic, just as his uncle had dismantled the first one established in 1792. In 1852, on the forty-eighth anniversary of Napoleon I's coronation as emperor, Louis-Napoleon declared himself Emperor Napoleon III, thus inaugurating the Second Empire. (Napoleon I's son died and never became Napoleon II, but Napoleon III wanted to create a sense of legitimacy and so used the Roman numeral III.) Political division and class conflict had proved fatal to the Second Republic. Although the revolution of 1848 never had a period of terror like that in 1793–1794, it nonetheless ended in similar fashion, with an authoritarian government that tried to play monarchists and republicans off against each other.

Nationalist Revolution in Italy

In January 1848, a revolt broke out in Palermo, Sicily, against the Bourbon ruler. Then came the electrifying news of the February revolution in Paris. In

---

Louis-Napoleon Bonaparte (1808–1873): Nephew of Napoleon I; he was elected president of France in 1848, declared himself Emperor Napoleon III in 1852, and ruled until 1870.

The Violence of Revolution
Their red flag of revolt is all that is left to these victims at a barricade thrown up in Paris during the uprising of June 1848. What was the intention of artist Louis Adolphe Hervier when he chose to paint this scene? *(Oil on panel by Louis Adolphe Hervier, Private Collection/Archives Charmet/The Bridgeman Art Library International.)*

Milan, a huge nationalist demonstration quickly degenerated into battles between Austrian forces and armed demonstrators. In Venice, an uprising drove out the Austrians. Peasants in the south occupied large landowners' estates. Across central Italy, revolts mobilized the poor and unemployed against local rulers. Peasants demanded more land, and artisans and workers called for higher wages, restrictions on the use of machinery, and unemployment relief.

But class divisions and regional differences stood in the way of national unity. Property owners, businessmen, and professionals wanted liberal reforms and national unification under a conservative regime; intellectuals, workers, and artisans dreamed of democracy and social reforms. Some nationalists favored a loose federation; others wanted a monarchy under Charles Albert of Piedmont-Sardinia; still others urged rule by the pope; a few shared Mazzini's vision of a republic with a strong central government. Many leaders of national unification spoke standard Italian only as a second language; most Italians spoke regional dialects.

As king of the most powerful Italian state, Charles Albert (r. 1831–1849) inevitably played a central role. After some hesitation caused by fears of French intervention, he led a military campaign against Austria. It soon failed, partly because of dissension over goals and tactics among the nationalists. Although Austrian troops defeated Charles Albert in the north in the summer of 1848, democratic and nationalist forces prevailed at first in the south. In the fall, the Romans drove the pope from the city and declared Rome a republic. For the next few months, republican leaders, such as Giuseppe Mazzini and Giuseppe Garibaldi (1807–1882), congregated in Rome to organize the new republic. These efforts eventually faltered when foreign powers intervened. The new president of republican France, Louis-Napoleon Bonaparte, sent an expeditionary force to secure the papal throne for Pius IX. Mazzini and Garibaldi fled. Although revolution had been defeated in Italy, the memory of the Roman republic and the commitment to unification remained, and they would soon emerge again with new force.

Revolt and Reaction in Central Europe

News of the revolution in Paris also provoked popular demonstrations in central and eastern Europe. When the Prussian army tried to push back a crowd gathered in front of Berlin's royal palace on March 18, 1848, their actions provoked panic and street fighting. The next day the crowd paraded wagons loaded with dead bodies under the window of the Prussian king Frederick William IV (r. 1840–1860), forcing him to salute the victims killed by his own army. In a state of near collapse, the king promised to call an assembly to draft a constitution and adopted the German nationalist flag of black, red, and gold.

The Divisions of Italy, 1848

The goal of German unification soon took precedence over social reform or constitutional changes within the separate states. In March and April, most

DOCUMENT

Alexis de Tocqueville Describes the June Days in Paris (1848)

Alexis de Tocqueville (1805–1859) was a noble landowner, well-known writer, and deputy in the National Assembly elected in April 1848. As a political liberal, he supported the new republican government against the uprising of workers in the National Workshops. His description of the June Days comes from a memoir he wrote in 1850 about the events of the 1848 revolution. Although a fierce opponent of socialism, Tocqueville detected class struggle in the insurrection.

Now at last I have come to that insurrection in June which was the greatest and the strangest that had ever taken place in our history, or perhaps in that of any other nation: the greatest because for four days more than a hundred thousand men took part in it, and there were five generals killed; the strangest, because the insurgents were fighting without a battle cry, leaders, or flag, and yet they showed wonderful powers of co-ordination and a military expertise that astonished the most experienced officers.

Another point that distinguished it from all other events of the same type during the last sixty years was that its object was not to change the form of the government, but to alter the organization of society. In truth it was not a political struggle (in the sense in which we have used the word "political" up to now), but a class struggle, a sort of "Servile War." It stood in the same relation to the facts of the February Revolution as the theory of socialism stood to its ideas; or rather it sprang naturally from those ideas, as a son from his mother; and one should not see it only as a brutal and blind, but as a powerful effort of the workers to escape from the necessities of their condition, which had been depicted to them as an illegitimate depression, and by the sword to open up a road towards that imaginary well-being that had been shown to them in the distance as a right. It was this mixture of greedy desires and false theories that engendered the insurrection and made it so formidable. These poor people had been assured that the goods of the wealthy were in some way the result of a theft committed against themselves. They had been assured that inequalities of fortune were as much opposed to morality and the interests of society, as to nature. This obscure and mistaken conception of right, combined with brute force, imparted to it an energy, tenacity and strength it would never have had on its own.

One should note, too, that this terrible insurrection was not the work of a certain number of conspirators, but was the revolt of one whole section of the population against another. The women took as much part in it as the men. While the men fought, the women got the ammunition ready and brought it up. And when in the end they had to surrender, the women were the last to yield. . . .

Down all the roads not held by the insurgents, thousands of men were pouring in from all parts of France to aid us. Thanks to the railways, those from fifty leagues [150 miles] off were already arriving, although the fighting had begun only in the evening of the previous day. The next day and the days following, they were to arrive from one and two hundred leagues [300–600 miles] away. These men were drawn without distinction from all classes of society; among them there were great numbers of peasants, bourgeois, large landowners and nobles, all jumbled up together in the same ranks.

Source: Alexis de Tocqueville, *Recollections*, ed. J. P. Mayer and A. P. Kerr, trans. George Lawrence (Garden City, NY: Doubleday, 1970), 136–37, 152.

Question to Consider

- **Why is Tocqueville so dismissive of the goals of those who participated in the June Days revolt in Paris in 1848?**

of the German states agreed to elect delegates to a federal parliament at Frankfurt that would attempt to unite Germany. Local princes and even the more powerful kings of Prussia and Bavaria seemed to totter. Yet the revolutionaries' weaknesses soon became apparent. The eight hundred delegates to the Frankfurt parliament had little practical political experience and no access to an army. Unemployed artisans and workers smashed machines; peasants burned landlords' records and occasionally attacked Jewish moneylenders; women set up clubs and newspapers to demand their emancipation from "perfumed slavery."

The advantage lay with the princes, who bided their time. While the Frankfurt parliament laboriously prepared a liberal constitution for a united Germany—one that denied self-determination to Czechs, Poles, and Danes within its proposed German borders—Frederick William recovered his confidence. First, his army crushed the revolution in Berlin in the fall of 1848. Prussian troops then intervened to help other local rulers put down the last wave of democratic and nationalist insurrections in the spring of 1849. When the Frankfurt parliament finally concluded its work, offering the emperorship of a constitutional, federal Germany to the king of Prussia, Frederick William contemptuously refused this "crown from the gutter."

Events followed a similar course in the Austrian Empire. Just as Italians were driving the

Revolution of 1848 in Eastern Europe
This painting by an unknown artist shows a group of Romanian revolutionaries in Transylvania marching in opposition to Russian rule. Leading them is a woman identified as Ana Ipatescu. In April 1848, local landowners began to organize meetings. Paris-educated nationalists spearheaded the movement, which demanded the end of Russian control and various legal and political reforms. By August, the movement had split between those who wanted independence only and those who pushed for the end of serfdom and for universal manhood suffrage. In response, the Russians invaded Moldavia and the Turks moved into Walachia. By October, the uprising was over. Russia and Turkey agreed to control the provinces jointly. *(The Art Archive/National Museum, Bucharest/Collection Dagli Orti.)*

Austrians out of their lands in northern Italy and Magyar nationalists were demanding political autonomy for Hungary, a student-led demonstration for political reform on March 13, 1848, in Vienna turned into rioting, looting, and machine breaking. Metternich resigned, escaping to England in disguise. Emperor Ferdinand promised a constitution, an elected parliament, and the end of censorship. The beleaguered authorities in Vienna could not refuse Magyar demands for home rule, and Széchenyi and Kossuth both became ministers in the new Hungarian government. The Magyars were the largest ethnic group in Hungary but still did not make up 50 percent of the population, which included Croats, Romanians, Slovaks, and Slovenes, all of whom preferred Austrian rule to domination by local Magyars.

The ethnic divisions in Hungary foreshadowed the many political and social divisions that would doom the revolutionaries. Fears of peasant insurrection prompted the Magyar nationalists around Kossuth to abolish serfdom. This measure alienated the largest noble landowners. The new government alienated the other nationalities when it imposed the Magyar language on them. In Prague, Czech nationalists convened a Slav congress as a counter to the Germans' Frankfurt parliament and called for a reorganization of the Austrian Empire that would recognize the rights of ethnic minorities. Such assertiveness by non-German peoples provoked German nationalists to protest on behalf of German-speaking people in areas with a Czech or Magyar majority.

The Austrian government took advantage of these divisions. To quell peasant discontent and appease liberal reformers, it abolished all remaining peasant obligations to the nobility in March 1848. Rejoicing country folk soon lost interest in the revolution. Military force finally broke up the revolutionary movements. The first blow fell in Prague in June 1848; General Prince Alfred von Windischgrätz, the military governor, bombarded the city into submission when a demonstration led to violence (including the shooting death of his wife, watching from a window). After another uprising in Vienna a few months later, Windischgrätz marched seventy thousand soldiers into the capital and set up direct military rule. In December, the Austrian monarchy came back to life when the eighteen-year-old Francis Joseph (r. 1848–1916), unencumbered by promises extracted by the revolutionaries from his now feeble uncle Ferdinand, assumed the imperial crown after intervention by leading court officials. In the spring of 1849, General Count Joseph Radetzky defeated the last Italian challenges to Austrian power in northern Italy, and his army moved east, joining with Croats and Serbs to take on the Hungarian rebels. The Austrian army teamed up with Tsar Nicholas I, who marched into Hungary with more than 300,000 Russian troops. Hungary was put under brutal martial law. Széchenyi went mad, and Kossuth found refuge in the United States. Social conflicts and ethnic divisions weakened the revolutionary movements from the inside and gave the Austrian government the opening it needed to restore its position.

Aftermath to 1848: Reimposing Authority

Although the revolutionaries of 1848 failed to achieve their goals, their efforts left a profound mark on the political and social landscape. Between 1848 and 1851, the French served a kind of republican apprenticeship that prepared the population for another, more lasting republic after 1870. In Italy, the failure of unification did not stop the spread of nationalist ideas and the rooting of demands for democratic participation. In the German states, the revolutionaries of 1848 turned nationalism from an idea of professors and writers into a popular enthusiasm and even a practical reality. The initiation of artisans, workers, and journeymen into democratic clubs increased political awareness in the lower classes and helped prepare them for broader political participation. Almost all the German states had a constitution and a parliament after 1850. The spectacular failures of 1848 thus hid some important underlying successes.

The absence of revolution in 1848 was just as significant as its presence. No revolution occurred in Great Britain, the Netherlands, or Belgium, the three places where industrialization and urbanization had developed most rapidly. In Great Britain, the prospects for revolution actually seemed quite good: the Chartist movement took inspiration from the European revolutions in 1848 and mounted several gigantic demonstrations to force Parliament into granting all adult males the vote. But even though Parliament refused, no uprising occurred—in part because the government had already proved its responsiveness: the middle classes in Britain had been co-opted into the established order by the Reform Bill of 1832, and the working classes had won parliamentary regulation of children's and women's work.

The other notable exception to revolution among the great powers was Russia, where Tsar Nicholas I maintained a tight grip through police surveillance and censorship. The Russian schools, limited to the upper classes, taught Nicholas's three most cherished principles: autocracy (the unlimited power of the tsar), orthodoxy (obedience to the church in religion and morality), and nationality (devotion to Russian traditions). These provided no space for political dissent. Social conditions also fostered political passivity: serfdom continued in force, and the sluggish rate of industrial and urban growth created little discontent.

Although much had changed, the aristocracy remained the dominant power almost everywhere. As army officers, aristocrats put down revolutionary forces. As landlords, they continued to dominate the rural scene and control parliamentary bodies. They also held many official positions in the state bureaucracies. One Italian princess explained, "There are doubtless men capable of leading the nation . . . but their names are unknown to the people, whereas those of noble families . . . are in every memory." Aristocrats kept their authority by adapting to change: they entered the bureaucracy and professions, turned their estates into moneymaking enterprises, and learned how to invest shrewdly.

The reassertion of conservative rule hardened gender definitions. Women everywhere had participated in the revolutions, especially in the Italian states, where they joined armies in the tens of thousands and applied household skills toward making bandages, clothing, and food. As conservatives returned to power, all signs of women's political activism disappeared. The French feminist movement, the most advanced in Europe, fell apart when, after the June Days, the increasingly conservative republican government forbade women to form political clubs and arrested and imprisoned two of the most outspoken women leaders for their socialist activities. As rulers reimposed their authority in the years after 1848, many socialists, communists, and nationalists suffered a similar fate; if they did not fall in battle or go to prison, they fled into exile, waiting for another opportunity to voice their demands.

Revolutions of 1848

1848	
January	Uprising in Palermo, Sicily
February	Revolution in Paris; proclamation of republic
March	Insurrections in Vienna, German cities, Milan, and Venice; autonomy movement in Hungary; Charles Albert of Piedmont-Sardinia declares war on Austrian Empire
May	Frankfurt parliament opens
June	Austrian army crushes revolutionary movement in Prague; June Days end in defeat of workers in Paris
July	Austrians defeat Charles Albert and Italian forces
November	Insurrection in Rome
December	Francis Joseph becomes Austrian emperor; Louis-Napoleon elected president in France
1849	
February	Rome declared a republic
April	Frederick William of Prussia rejects crown of united Germany offered by Frankfurt parliament
July	Roman republic overthrown by French intervention
August	Russian and Austrian armies combine to defeat Hungarian forces

REVIEW QUESTION **Why did the revolutions of 1848 fail?**

The Crystal Palace, 1851

George Baxter's lithograph (above) shows the exterior of the main building for the Great Exhibition of the Works of Industry of All Nations in London. It was designed by Sir Joseph Paxton to gigantic dimensions: 1,848 feet long by 456 feet wide; 135 feet high; 772,784 square feet of ground-floor area covering no less than 18 acres. The lithograph by Peter Mabuse (below) offers a view of one of the colonial displays at the Great Exhibition. The tented room and carved ivory throne are meant to recall India, Britain's premier colony. *(Above: © Maidstone Museum and Art Gallery, Kent, UK/The Bridgeman Art Library. Below: Private Collection/The Stapleton Collection/The Bridgeman Art Library International.)*

Conclusion

In 1851, Europe's most important female monarch presided over a midcentury celebration of peace and industrial growth that helped dampen the still-smoldering fires of revolutionary passion. In the place of revolutionary fervor was a government-sponsored spectacle of what industry, hard work, and technological imagination could produce. Queen Victoria (r. 1837–1901), who herself promoted the notion of domesticity as women's sphere, opened the Great Exhibition of the Works of Industry of All Nations in London on May 1. A huge iron-and-glass building housed the display. Soon people referred to it as the Crystal Palace; its nine hundred tons of glass created an aura of fantasy, and the abundant goods from around the world inspired satisfaction and pride. One German visitor described the structure as "this miracle which has so suddenly appeared to dazzle the inhabitants of our globe." Many of the six million people who visited the Crystal Palace display came on the new railroads, the foremost symbol of the age of industrial transformation. Along with the railroads, the application of steam engines to textile manufacturing set in motion a host of economic and social changes: cities burgeoned with rapidly growing populations; factories concentrated laborers who formed a new working class; manufacturers now challenged landed elites for political leadership; and social problems galvanized reform organizations and governments alike. The Crystal Palace presented the rosy view of modern, industrial, urban life, but the housing shortages, in-

MAPPING THE WEST

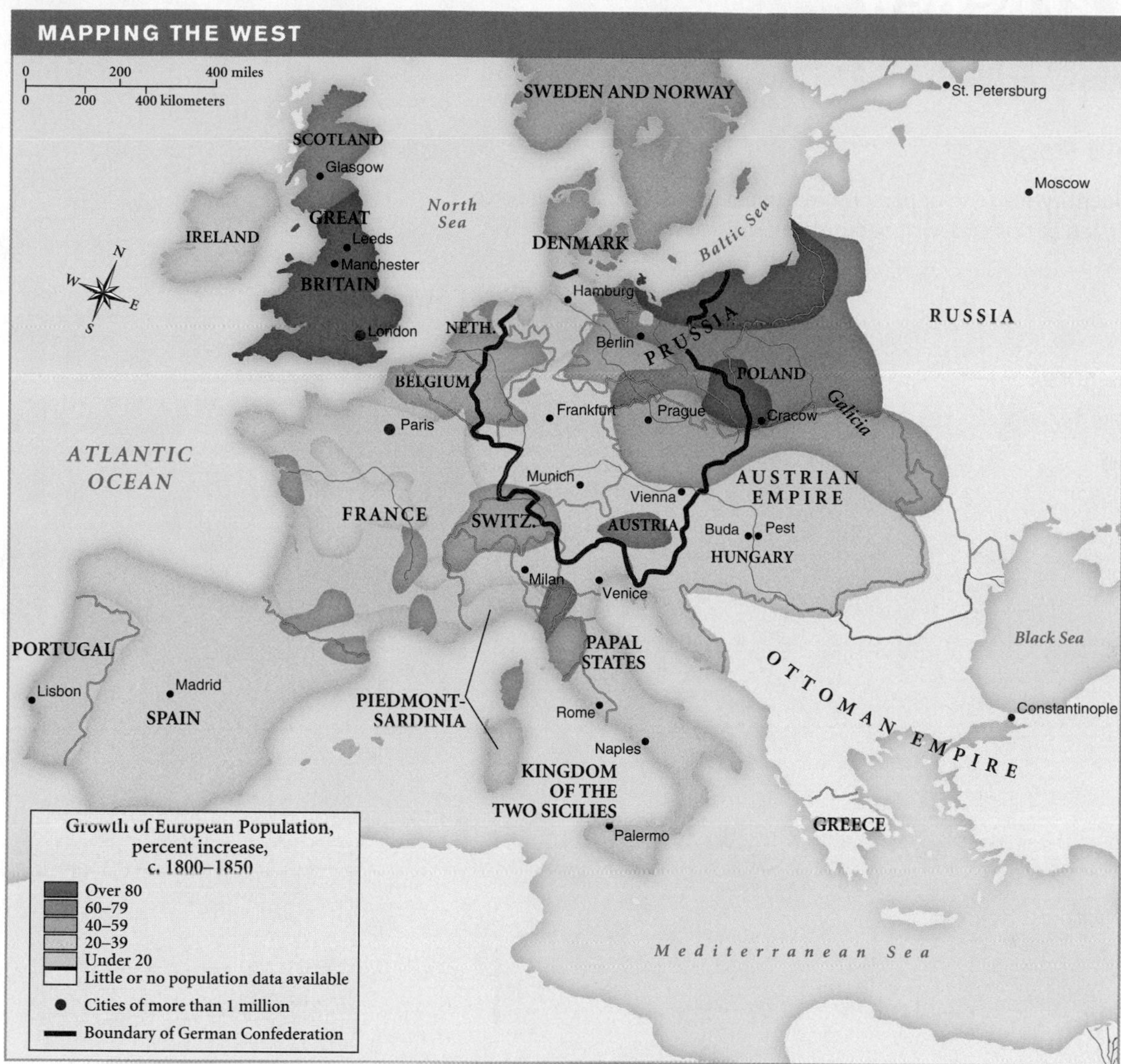

Europe in 1850

This map of population growth between 1800 and 1850 reveals important trends that would not otherwise be evident. Although population growth correlated for the most part with industrialization, population also grew in more agricultural regions such as East Prussia, Poland, and Ireland. Ireland's rapid population growth does not appear on this map because the famine of 1846–1851 killed more than 10 percent of the population and forced many others to emigrate. | **Compare this map to Map 21.1: Which areas experienced both industrialization and population increase?**

adequacy of water supplies, and recurrent epidemic diseases had not disappeared.

Although the revolutions of 1848 brought to the surface the profound tensions within a European society in transition toward industrialization and urbanization, they did not resolve those tensions. The Industrial Revolution continued, workers developed more extensive organizations, and liberals and socialists fought over the pace of reform. Confronted with the menace of revolution, conservative elites now sought alternatives that would be less threatening to the established order and still permit some change. This search for alternatives became immediately evident in the question of national unification in Germany and Italy. National unification would hereafter depend not on speeches and parliamentary resolutions, but rather on what the Prussian leader Otto von Bismarck would call "iron and blood."

FOR FURTHER EXPLORATION

- **For additional primary-source material from this period**, see *Sources of the Making of the West*, Fourth Edition.
- **For Web sites, images, and documents related to topics in this chapter**, visit *Make History* at bedfordstmartins.com/hunt.

Chapter 21 Review

Online Study Guide bedfordstmartins.com/hunt

Key Terms and People

In the grid below, identify the term or person and explain its historical significance. (For a printable version of this grid, visit bedfordstmartins.com/hunt.)

Term	Who or What & When	Why It Matters
ideology (p. 686)		
Industrial Revolution (p. 686)		
urbanization (p. 692)		
George Sand (p. 697)		
domesticity (p. 700)		
imperialism (p. 701)		
Opium War (p. 702)		
nationalism (p. 703)		
Giuseppe Mazzini (p. 703)		
liberalism (p. 705)		
Corn Laws (p. 705)		
socialism (p. 706)		
communists (p. 707)		
Chartism (p. 708)		
Louis-Napoleon Bonaparte (p. 711)		

Review Questions

1. What dangers did the Industrial Revolution pose to both urban and rural life?
2. In which areas did reformers trying to address the social problems created by industrialization and urbanization succeed, and in which did they fail?
3. Why did ideologies have such a powerful appeal in the 1830s and 1840s?
4. Why did the revolutions of 1848 fail?

Making Connections

1. Which of the ideologies of this period had the greatest impact on political events? How can you explain this?
2. In what ways might industrialization be considered a force for peaceful change rather than a revolution? (Hint: Think about the situation in Great Britain.)
3. In what ways did the revolutions of 1848 repeat elements of the French revolutions in 1789 and 1830, and in what ways did they break with those precedents?
4. Neither Great Britain nor Russia had a revolution in 1848. How is the absence of revolution in those two countries related to their history in the preceding decades?

Important Events

Date	Event
1830–1832	Cholera epidemic sweeps across Europe
1830	France invades and begins conquest of Algeria
1832	George Sand, *Indiana*
1833	Factory Act regulates work of children in Great Britain; abolition of slavery in British Empire
1834	German *Zollverein* established under Prussian leadership
1835	Belgium opens first continental railway built with state funds
1839	Beginning of Opium War; invention of photography
1841	Charles Dickens, *The Old Curiosity Shop*
1846	Famine strikes Ireland; Corn Laws repealed in England; peasant insurrection in Austrian province of Galicia
1848	Revolutions of 1848 throughout Europe; last great wave of Chartist demonstrations in Britain; Karl Marx and Friedrich Engels, *The Communist Manifesto*; abolition of slavery in French colonies; end of serfdom in Austrian Empire
1851	Crystal Palace exhibition in London

- Consider three events: **Charles Dickens, *The Old Curiosity Shop* (1841), Revolutions of 1848 throughout Europe (1848),** and **Karl Marx and Friedrich Engels, *The Communist Manifesto* (1848)**. How do these events represent different responses to the changes wrought by the Industrial Revolution?

SUGGESTED REFERENCES

The spread of industrialization has elicited much more historical interest than the process of urbanization because the analysis of industrialization occupied a central role in Marxism. The Web site Gallica, produced by the National Library of France, offers a wealth of imagery and information on French cultural history.

Berend, Tibor Iván. *History Derailed: Central and Eastern Europe in the Long Nineteenth Century.* 2003.

Clark, Anna. *The Struggle for the Breeches: Gender and the Making of the British Working Class.* 1997.

Davidoff, Leonore, and Catherine Hall. *Family Fortunes: Men and Women of the English Middle Class, 1780–1850.* 2002.

Dickens Project: http://dickens.ucsc.edu/

Gallica: Images and Texts from Nineteenth-Century French-Speaking Culture: http://gallica.bnf.fr

Hanes, W. Travis, and Frank Sanello. *The Opium Wars: The Addiction of One Empire and the Corruption of Another.* 2004.

Hobsbawm, E. J. *The Age of Revolution, 1789–1848.* 1996.

Kahan, Alan S. *Liberalism in Nineteenth-Century Europe: The Political Culture of Limited Suffrage.* 2003.

Kinealy, Christine. *Repeal and Revolution: 1848 in Ireland.* 2009.

Kostantaras, Dean J. *Nationalism and Revolution in Europe, 1815–1848.* 2010.

Lees, Andrew, and Lynn Hollen Lees. *Cities and the Making of Modern Europe, 1750–1914.* 2007.

*Marx, Karl, and Frederick Engels. *The Communist Manifesto: With Related Documents.* Ed. John E. Toews. 1848; repr. 1999.

Mokyr, Joel. *The Enlightened Economy: An Economic History of Britain, 1700–1850.* 2009.

*Pollard, S., and C. Holmes. *Documents of European Economic History. Vol. 1, The Process of Industrialization, 1750–1870.* 1968.

Rapport, Mike. *1848, Year of Revolution.* 2009.

Thompson, E. P. *The Making of the English Working Class.* 1964.

*Primary source.

VENEZIA
TEATRO LA FENICE
IN OCCASIONE DEL
CONGRESSO GEOGRAFICO INTERNAZIONALE
IMPRESA CESARE TREVISAN
DALL'11 AL 22 SETTEMBRE SI DARANNO 7 RAPPRESENTAZIONI DELLA GRANDIOSA OPERA-BALLO
AIDA
MUSICA DEL COMM.RE GIUSEPPE VERDI
ESEGUITA DAI SEGUENTI ARTISTI
PRIME DONNE
EMMA TUROLLA — GIUSEPPINA PASQUA
PRIMO TENORE
GIOVANNI SANI
PRIMO BARITONO
COMM.RE GOTTARDO ALDIGHIERI
PRIMI BASSI
ENRICO SERBOLINI ✦ FRANCESCO PANARI
MAESTRO DIRETTORE D'ORCHESTRA
CAV.RE FRANCO FACCIO
ALTRO MAESTRO
RAFAELE BRACÂLE
TENORE COMPRIMARIO
GIUSEPPE CINQUANTA
M.O ISTRUTTORE DEI CORI
LORENZO POLI
SUGGERITORE
ANTONIO RENIER
COREOGRAFO
RINALDO ROSSI
N. 70 PROFESSORI D'ORCHESTRA. N. 80 CORISTI E CORISTE. N. 24 BALLERINE. N. 6 TROMBE EGIZIANE BANDA
Direttore
RINALDO ROSSI
Direttore delle masse
GAETANO ARCHINTI
Pittore Scenografo
CESARE RECANATINI
Direttore di Macchinismo
LUIGI CAPRARA
L. ZAMPERONI
Attrezzista proprietà
CROCE e FIGLIO
Fornitore della luce
ANTONIO TREVISAN
Parrucchiere
G. GASPEROTTO
R. MAVEROFFER
Biglietto d'ingresso alla platea e palchi (in sere ordinarie) L. 5.—
detto al loggione (id) 2.—
Poltrona a bracciuoli, oltre l'ingresso 10.—
Posti riservati in platea (scanni in velluto) 5.—
Posti riservati in Galleria (Loggione) 1.50
Abbonamento per le sette rappresent.ni (compresa quella di gala) 25.—
detto limitato a N.o 40 Poltrone 50.—
detto ai posti riservati (scanni) 25.—
Le suddette 7 rappresentazioni sono finora stabilite nelle sere dell' 11-13-15-17-18-20-22 Settembre
Proprietà dello spartito Tito di Gio. Ricordi

CHAPTER

Politics and Culture of the Nation-State 22

1850–1870

In 1859, the name *VERDI* suddenly appeared scrawled on walls across the disunited cities of the Italian peninsula. The graffiti seemed to celebrate the composer Giuseppe Verdi, whose operas thrilled crowds of Europeans. Among Italians, Verdi was a particular hero; his stories of downtrodden groups struggling against tyrannical government seemed to refer specifically to them. As his operatic choruses thundered out calls to rebellion in the name of the nation, Italian audiences were sure that Verdi was telling them to throw off Austrian and papal rule and unite in a newborn Roman Empire. The graffiti had a second political message: *VERDI* also formed an acronym for *V*ittorio *E*mmanuele *R*e *d'I*talia ("Victor Emmanuel, King of Italy"), and in 1859 it summoned Italians to unite under Victor Emmanuel II, king of Sardinia and Piedmont — the one Italian leader with a nationalist, modernizing profile. The graffiti was good publicity, for the very next year Italy united as a result of warfare and hard bargaining by political realists.

After the failed revolutions of 1848, European statesmen and the politically conscious public increasingly rejected idealism in favor of **Realpolitik** — a politics of tough-minded realism aimed at strengthening the state and tightening social order. Realpolitikers disliked the romanticism and high-minded ideas of the revolutionaries. Instead, they put their faith in power politics and even the use of violence to attain their goals. Two particularly skilled practitioners of Realpolitik, the Italian Camillo di Cavour and the Prussian Otto von Bismarck, succeeded in unifying Italy and Germany not by romantic slogans but by war and diplomacy. Most leading figures of the decades 1850–1870, enmeshed like

***Aïda* Poster**
Aïda (1871), Giuseppe Verdi's opera of human passion and state power among people of different nations, became a staple of Western culture, bringing people across Europe into a common cultural orbit. Written to celebrate the opening of the Suez Canal, *Aïda* also celebrated the improvement of Europe's access to Asian resources provided by the new waterway. The opera was a prime example of the surge of interest in Egyptian styles and objects that followed the opening of the canal. *(Madeline Grimoldi.)*

Realpolitik (ray AHL poh lih teek): Policies developed after the revolutions of 1848 and initially associated with nation building; they were based on realism rather than on the romantic notions of earlier nationalists. The term has come to mean any policy based on considerations of power alone.

Verdi's operatic heroes in power politics, strengthened their states by harnessing the forces of nationalism and liberalism that had led to earlier romantic revolts. Their achievements changed the face of Europe.

Making modern nation-states was complicated and called for more than winning wars. Economic development was crucial, as was using government policy and culture to create a sense of national identity and common purpose. As productivity and wealth increased, governments took vigorous steps to improve rapidly growing cities, promote public health, and boost national loyalty. State support for cultural institutions such as public schools helped establish a common fund of knowledge and even shared political beliefs. Authoritarian leaders like Bismarck and the new French emperor Napoleon III believed that a better quality of life would not only make the state more stable by calming revolutionary impulses of years past but also silence liberal critics.

Culture built a sense of belonging. Reading novels, attending operas and art exhibitions, and visiting the newly fashionable world's fairs gave ordinary people a stronger sense of being French or German or British and even of being European. Like politicians, artists and writers also came to reject romanticism, featuring instead harsher, more realistic aspects of everyday life. Artists painted nudes in shockingly blunt ways, eliminating romantic hues and dreamy poses. The Russian author Leo Tolstoy depicted the bleak life of soldiers in the Crimean War, which erupted in 1853 between the Russian and Ottoman Empires, while other authors wrote about ordinary people suffering poverty or turning to crime. Alongside the tough-minded nation-building policies there arose tough-minded art, not just mirroring Realpolitik but encouraging it.

In their quest to build strong nations, Western politicians did not shy away from using violence or causing harm. They sent armies to distant areas to stamp out resistance to their continuing global expansion. At home, governments uprooted neighborhoods to construct public buildings, roads, and parks. The process of nation building was often brutal, bringing foreign wars, arrests, and even civil war—all the centerpieces of many Verdi operas. In 1871, an uprising of Parisians challenged the central government's intrusion into everyday life and its failure to count the costs. Thus, for the most part, the powerful Western nation-state did not arise spontaneously. Instead, its growth and the tighter unification of peoples depended on shrewd policy, deliberate warfare, and new inroads into societies around the world. Realpolitik relied on all these factors, as well as on a general climate of modern opinion that valued realism, hard facts, and shrewd deeds.

CHAPTER FOCUS How did the creation and strengthening of nation-states change European politics, society, and culture in the mid-nineteenth century?

The End of the Concert of Europe

The revolutions of 1848 had weakened the concert of Europe, driving out its architect, Austrian foreign minister Klemens von Metternich, and allowing the forces of nationalism to flourish. It became more difficult for countries to control their competing ambitions and act together. In addition, the dreaded revival of Bonapartism in the person of Louis-Napoleon Bonaparte, the nephew of Napoleon I, added to European instability as France reasserted itself. One of Louis-Napoleon's targets was Russia, formerly a mainstay of the concert of Europe. To limit Russia's and Austria's grip on power, France helped engineer the Crimean War, which not only changed the distribution of European power but

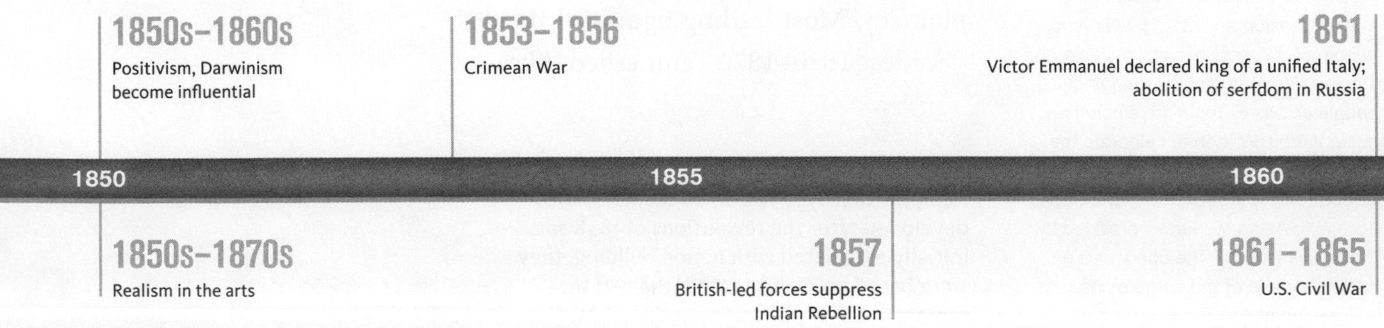
1850s–1860s
Positivism, Darwinism become influential
1853–1856
Crimean War
1861
Victor Emmanuel declared king of a unified Italy; abolition of serfdom in Russia
1850
1855
1860
1850s–1870s
Realism in the arts
1857
British-led forces suppress Indian Rebellion
1861–1865
U.S. Civil War

Napoleon III and Eugénie Receive the Siamese Ambassadors, 1864
At a splendid gathering of their court, the emperor Napoleon III, his consort Eugénie, and their son and heir greet ambassadors from Siam, whose exoticism and servility before the imperial family are the centerpiece of this depiction by Jean-Léon Gerome. How might a middle-class French citizen react to this scene? *(Bridgeman-Giraudon / Art Resource, NY.)*

also resulted in the end of serfdom in Russia and the birth of new European nations.

Napoleon III and the Quest for French Glory

Louis-Napoleon Bonaparte, who declared himself Napoleon III in 1852, encouraged the revival of French grandeur and the cult of his famous uncle as part of nation building. "A man of destiny," he called himself. Napoleon III acted as Europe's schoolmaster, showing its leaders how to combine economic liberalism and nationalism with authoritarian rule. To the public, he claimed to represent "your families, your property — rich and poor alike," but he closed cafés where men might discuss politics and established a rubber-stamp legislature, the Corps législatif, that made representative government a charade. Imperial style replaced republican simplicity (see the illustration above). Napoleon's opulent court dazzled the public, and the emperor (like his namesake) cultivated a masculine image of strength and majesty by wearing military uniforms and by conspicuously maintaining mistresses. In contrast, Napoleon's wife, Empress Eugénie, followed middle-class norms by playing up her domestic role as devoted mother to her only son and supporting many charities. The authoritarian, apparently old-fashioned order imposed by Napoleon satisfied the many peasants that the radicalism of 1848 was under control.

Napoleon III was nonetheless a modernizer. He promoted a strong economy and public works

1867 Second Reform Bill in England; Austro-Hungarian monarchy

1868 Meiji Restoration begins in Japan

1869 Suez Canal opens

1869–1871 Women's colleges founded at Cambridge University

1870–1871 Franco-Prussian War

1871 German Empire proclaimed at Versailles; self-governing Paris Commune established

1865 — 1870 — 1875

programs, luring the middle and working classes away from radical politics with jobs. The magnificent rebuilding of Paris made France prosper as Europe recovered from the hard times of the late 1840s. Empress Eugénie wore lavish gowns, encouraging French silk production and keeping Paris at the center of the lucrative fashion trade. The regime also reached a free-trade agreement with Britain and backed the establishment of innovative investment banks. Such new institutions led the way in financing railroad expansion, and railway mileage increased fivefold during Napoleon III's reign. During the economic downturn of the late 1850s, he wooed support by allowing working-class organizations to form and introducing features of democratic government. Although some historians have judged Napoleon III to be devious because of these abrupt changes, he gave practical responses to economic change.

On the international scene, Napoleon III's main goals were to overcome the containment of France imposed by the Congress of Vienna and to acquire international glory like a true Bonaparte. To reshape European politics in France's favor, Napoleon pitted France first against Russia in the Crimean War, then against Austria in the War of Italian Unification (1860–1861), and finally against Prussia in the Franco-Prussian War (1870–1871). Beyond Europe, Napoleon's army continued to enforce French rule in Algeria and Southeast Asia. He attempted to install Maximilian, the brother of Habsburg emperor Francis Joseph, as emperor of Mexico and ultimately of all Central America. The attempt ended in a show of French weakness when Mexicans rebelled and executed Maximilian in 1867.

Despite this glaring failure, Napoleon successfully encouraged the construction of the Suez Canal to connect the Mediterranean and the Red Sea, and his foreign policy broke down the international order established at the Congress of Vienna. His push for worldwide influence eventually destroyed him, however: the French overthrew him after Prussia easily defeated his army in 1870.

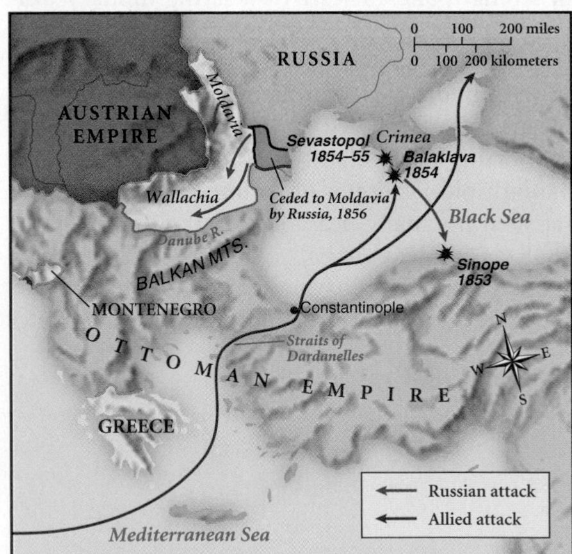

MAP 22.1 The Crimean War, 1853–1856
The most destructive war in Europe between the Napoleonic Wars and World War I, the Crimean War drew attention to the conflicting ambitions around territories of the declining Ottoman Empire. The war fractured the alliance of conservative forces from the Congress of Vienna, allowing Italy and Germany to come into being as unified states.

The Crimean War, 1853–1856: Turning Point in European Affairs

Napoleon III first flexed his diplomatic muscle in the Crimean War (1853–1856), which began as a conflict between the Russian and Ottoman Empires but ended as a war with long-lasting consequences for much of Europe. While professing to uphold the status quo, Russia had been expanding into Asia and the Middle East. In particular, Tsar Nicholas I wanted territory in the Ottoman Empire, fast becoming known as "the sick man of Europe" because of its disintegrating authority. Napoleon encouraged Nicholas to be even more aggressive in his expansionism — a maneuver that provoked war in October 1853 between the two eastern empires (Map 22.1). The war disrupted the united Austrian and Russian front that kept France in check. Other consequences would be the end of serfdom in Russia and the birth of new European nations.

The war drew in other states and upset Europe's balance of power as set in the Congress of Vienna. Napoleon III convinced Austria to remain neutral during the war, thus splitting the conservative Russian-Austrian coalition that had checked French ambitions since 1815. The Austrian government was concerned that the defeat of the Ottomans would bring Russian expansion into the Balkans. To protect its Mediterranean routes to East Asia, Britain prodded the Ottomans to stand up to Russia, but in the fall of 1853, the Russians blasted the Turkish wooden ships to bits at the Ottoman port of Sinope on the Black Sea. The Russians justified their actions as a necessary defense of Christians in the Ottoman Empire. In 1854, France and Great Britain, though enemies in war for more than a century, allied to declare war on Russia and defend the Ottoman Empire's sovereignty and territories.

Faced with attacking the massive Russian Empire, the British and French allies settled for the lim-

Nurse Tending Wounded Man
The Crimean War exposed the backward, and lethal, sanitary conditions of warfare—conditions that became intolerable to nation-states concerned with the well-being of their citizen soldiers. Women's contribution as nurses during both the Crimean War (shown in the image here) and the U.S. Civil War helped improve the situation, but voluntary assistance was not enough to prevent horrific death rates from disease and lack of coordinated medical attention. *(Private Collection/The Bridgeman Art Library International.)*

ited military goal of capturing the Russian naval base at Sevastopol, on the Crimea, a peninsula jutting into the Black Sea. Even so, the Crimean War was spectacularly bloody. British and French troops landed in the Crimea in September 1854 and waged a long siege at Sevastopol, which fell only after a year of savage and costly combat. Generals on both sides demonstrated their incompetence, and governments failed to provide combatants with even minimal supplies, sanitation, or medical care. Hospitals had no beds, no dishes, and no water. As a result, the war claimed a massive toll. A million men died, more than two-thirds from disease or starvation.

In the midst of this unfolding catastrophe, **Alexander II** (r. 1855–1881) ascended the Russian throne after the death of Nicholas I, his father. With casualties mounting, the new tsar asked for peace. As a result of the Treaty of Paris, signed in March 1856, Russia lost the right to base its navy in the Strait of Dardanelles and the Black Sea, which were declared neutral waters. Moldavia and Wallachia (which soon merged to form Romania) became autonomous Turkish provinces under the victors' protection, drastically reducing Russian influence in that region, too.

Some historians have called the Crimean War one of the most senseless conflicts in modern history because competing claims in southeastern Europe could have been settled by diplomacy had it not been for Napoleon III's driving ambition to disrupt the peace. Yet the war was full of consequence. New technologies were introduced into warfare: the railroad, shell-firing cannons, breech-loading rifles, and steam-powered ships. The relationship of the home front to the battlefront was beginning to change with the use of the telegraph and increased press coverage. Home audiences received news from the Crimean front lines more rapidly and in more detail than ever before. Reports of incompetence, poor sanitation, and the huge death toll outraged the public, inspiring some civilians, such as **Florence Nightingale**, to head for the front lines to help. Nightingale seized the moment to escape the confines of middle-class domesticity by organizing a battlefield nursing service to care for the British sick and wounded. Through her tough-minded organization of nursing units, she pioneered nursing as a profession and made sanitary conditions for soldiers a new and enduring priority. (See Document, "Mrs. Seacole: The *Other* Florence Nightingale," page 726.)

More immediately, the war accomplished Napoleon III's goal of severing the alliance between

---

Alexander II: Russian tsar (r. 1855–1881) who initiated the age of Great Reforms and emancipated the serfs in 1861.

Florence Nightingale: The Englishwoman who in the nineteenth century pioneered the professionalization of nursing and the use of statistics in the study of public health and the well-being of the military.

DOCUMENT

Mrs. Seacole: The *Other* Florence Nightingale

Another highly skilled medical worker besides Florence Nightingale made an impact on the battlefields in Crimea. Mary Seacole (1805–1881), daughter of a free black Jamaican woman and a Scottish army officer, had learned about medicine from her mother and from doctors who passed through Kingston, staying at the family's boardinghouse. In addition to a gift for healing, Mrs. Seacole (as she was always called) had a passion for travel—to Europe, the United States, and Panama—which she supported by tending other travelers. When the Crimean War broke out, she chafed—like Nightingale herself—to be at the battlefront. Arriving in Crimea in 1855, Mrs. Seacole saved many desperately ill soldiers who lacked all medical care. The text describes the mid-nineteenth century as an age of professionalization, domesticity for women, and lack of opportunity for many colonized people. Mrs. Seacole may be the exception that proves the rule, or it may be that society was more open and fluid than commonly believed.

[Sick soldiers] could and did get at my store sick-comforts and nourishing food, which the heads of the medical staff would sometimes find it difficult to procure. These reasons, with the additional one that I was very familiar with the diseases which they suffered most from and successful in their treatment (I say this in no spirit of vanity), were quite sufficient to account for the numbers who came daily to the British Hotel for medical treatment.

That the officers were glad of me as a doctress and nurse may be easily understood. When a poor fellow lay sickening in his cheerless hut and sent down to me, he knew very well that I should not ride up in answer to his message empty-handed. And although I did not hesitate to charge him with the value of the necessaries I took him, still he was thankful enough to be able to *purchase* them. When we lie ill at home surrounded with comfort, we never think of feeling any special gratitude for the sick-room delicacies which we accept as a consequence of our illness; but the poor officer lying ill and weary in his crazy hut, dependent for the merest necessaries of existence upon a clumsy, ignorant soldier-cook, who would almost prefer eating his meat raw to having the troubles of cooking it (our English soldiers are bad campaigners), often finds his greatest troubles in the want of those little delicacies with which a weak stomach must be humoured into retaining nourishment.

Source: Mary Grant Seacole, *Wonderful Adventures of Mrs. Seacole in Many Lands* (London: James Blackwood, 1857).

Question for Consideration

- **By her own account, why was Seacole successful in her profession? How might professionalizing medical people and city planners have viewed her?**

Austria and Russia, the two conservative powers on which the Congress of Vienna peace settlement had rested since 1815. It thus ended Austria's and Russia's grip on European affairs and undermined their ability to contain the forces of liberalism and nationalism. Russia's catastrophic defeat forced it to embark on some long-overdue reforms.

Reform in Russia

Defeat in the Crimean War not only blocked Russia's territorial ambition but also made clear the need for meaningful reform. Hundreds of peasant insurrections had erupted in the decade before the Crimean War. Serf defiance ranged from malingering at forced labor to boycotting vodka in protest of its heavy taxation. "Our own and neighboring households were gripped with fear," one aristocrat reported, because of potential serf violence. Although economic development spread in parts of eastern Europe, the Russian economy stagnated compared with that of western Europe. Old-fashioned farming techniques depleted soil and led to food shortages, and the nobility was often contemptuous of the suffering caused by malnutrition and hard labor.

Artists made their own call for reform with their sympathetic portrayals of serfs and condemnations of brutal masters, as in *A Hunter's Sketches* (1852) by novelist Ivan Turgenev. A Russian translation of American author Harriet Beecher Stowe's antislavery novel *Uncle Tom's Cabin* (1852) also hit home. When Russia lost the Crimean War, the educated public, including some government officials, found the poor performance of serf armies a disgrace and the system of serf labor a glaring problem.

Emancipation of the Serfs Confronted with the need for change, Tsar Alexander II acted. Well educated and more widely traveled than his father, Alexander ushered in what came to be known as the Great Reforms, granting Russians new rights from above as a way of pre-

Emancipation of the Russian Serfs
This trading card was used as a marketing gimmick to promote canned meat. Cards like these were given away by the thousands and traded just as baseball cards are today. Historical scenes were popular subjects for the cards—this one shows the 1861 emancipation of the serfs in Russia. Note that the caption is in French, the language of the European upper classes, including those in Russia, who would have consumed this product. The emancipation is presented as a wholly beneficial act with no strings attached. *(Mary Evans Picture Library.)*

venting violent action from below that might force change. The most dramatic reform was the emancipation of almost fifty million serfs beginning in 1861. By the terms of emancipation, communities of newly freed serfs, headed by male village elders, received grants of land. The community itself, traditionally called a **mir**, had full power to allocate this land among individuals and to direct their economic activity. Although emancipation partially laid the groundwork for a modern labor force in Russia, communal landowning and decision making meant that individual peasants could not simply sell their parcel of land and leave their rural communities to work in factories, as laborers had been doing in western Europe.

The condition attached to the so-called land grants in Russia was that peasants were not *given* land along with their personal freedom: they were forced to "redeem" the land they farmed by paying off long-term loans from the government, which in land remained in the hands of the nobility, and most peasants ended up with less land than they had farmed as serfs. These conditions, especially the huge burden of debt and communal regulations, slowed Russian agricultural development for decades. Even so, idealistic reformers believed that the emancipation of the serfs, once treated by the nobility virtually as livestock, had produced miraculous results. As one of them put it, "The people are without any exaggeration transfigured from head to foot. . . . The look, the walk, the speech, everything is changed."

The state also reformed local administration, the judiciary, and the military. The government compensated the nobility for loss of peasant services and set up zemstvos—regional councils through which aristocrats could control local affairs such as education, public health, and welfare. Aristocratic control ensured that the zemstvos would remain conservative, but they became a new political force with the potential for challenging the authoritarian central government. Some aristocrats took advantage of newly relaxed rules on travel to see how the rest of Europe was governed. Their vision broadened as they observed different ways of solving social and economic problems. The principle of equality of all persons before the law, regardless of social rank, was introduced in Russia for the first time, as judicial reform gave all Russians access to modern civil courts. Even serfs were no longer left to the mercy of a landowner's version of justice. Military reform followed in 1874 when the government reduced the twenty-five-year period of service to a six-year term and began focusing on educating troops in an effort to match the efficiency and fitness of soldiers in western Europe.

From Reform to Rebellion

Alexander's reforms helped landowners be more effective in the market, just as enclosures and emancipation had done much earlier for landowners in western Europe. At the same time, the changes reduced the privileges of the nobility, weakening their authority and sparking family conflict. "An epidemic seemed to seize upon [noble] children . . . an

---

mir (mihr): A Russian farm community that provided for holding land in common and regulating the movements of any individual member by the group.

DOCUMENT

Education of a Mathematical Genius in Russia

Sofya Kovalevskaya (1850–1891) grew up in a privileged household with a governess and plenty of servants. Her education was supposed to include needlework, deportment, and other "womanly" subjects, but from childhood she developed tricks and practiced outright disobedience so that she could study math, a subject with which a favorite uncle helped her. Later, to get to universities in central and western Europe, she contracted a phony marriage with a young man with similar aspirations and then went to Göttingen and Berlin, where she had problems at first getting accepted as a student because she was a woman. Kovalevskaya finally found a university teaching position in Sweden and published some of the most important mathematical treatises of modern times. In this excerpt from her autobiographical sketch, she describes her girlhood determination to learn math.

Not until I grew somewhat more familiar with [algebra] did I begin to feel an attraction to mathematics so intense that I started to neglect my other studies. Observing the direction I was taking, my father—who in any case harbored a strong prejudice against learned women—decided that it was high time to put a stop to my mathematics lessons. . . . But somehow I managed to wheedle out of my teacher a copy of Bourdon's *Algebra Course* and began studying it with diligence.

Since I was under my governess's strict surveillance, I was forced to practice some cunning in this matter. At bedtime I used to put the book under my pillow and then, when everyone was asleep, I would read the night through under the dim light of the icon-lamp or the night lamp. . . .

My mathematical knowledge would likely have remained confined to the contents of Bourdon's *Algebra* if I had not been aided by the following incident, which motivated my father to reassess his views on my education to some degree.

One of our neighboring landowners, Professor Tyrtov, bought us the textbook of elementary physics he had written. I made an attempt to read it, but in the section on optics, to my chagrin, I encountered trigonometric formulas, sines, cosines and tangents.

Then trying to cope with the formulas contained in the book I tried to explain it for myself. *[Kovalevskaya's old teacher did not know these either. — Ed.]*

Some time later I was having a conversation with Professor Tyrtov about his book, and he expressed doubt at first that I could have understood it. To my declaration that I had read it with great interest he said, "Come, now—aren't you bragging?" But when I told him the means I had used to explain the trigonometric formulas he completely changed his tone. He went straight to my father, heatedly arguing the necessity of providing me with the most serious kind of instruction, and even comparing me to Pascal.

Source: Sofya Kovalevskaya, *A Russian Childhood* (New York: Springer-Verlag, 1978), 216–18.

Question to Consider

- **Describe Sofya Kovalevskaya's intellectual challenges. How does she address the prevailing idea that women should not study math?**

epidemic of fleeing from the parental roof," one observer noted. Rejecting aristocratic leisure, youthful rebels from the upper class valued practical activity and sometimes identified with peasants and workers instead of their own class. Some formed communes where they hoped to do humble manual labor; others turned to higher education, especially the sciences. Daughters of the nobility opposed their parents by cutting their hair short, wearing black, and escaping from home through phony marriages so they could study in western European universities. (See Document, "Education of a Mathematical Genius in Russia," above.) This rejection of traditional society led these young people to be labeled as nihilists (from the Latin for "nothing")—implying a lack of belief in any values whatsoever. In fact, they represented a defiant spirit percolating not just at the bottom but also at the top of Russian society.

Reform and an atmosphere of change also inspired resistance among the more than one hundred Russian-dominated ethnic groups in the Russian Empire. Aristocratic and upper-class nationalist Poles staged an uprising in 1863, demanding full national independence for their country. By 1864, however, Alexander II's army had regained control of the Russian section of Poland, using the promise of reform to win peasant help in defeating the rebels. The government then swiftly clamped down on other nationalist uprisings and enforced **Russification**—a tactic meant to reduce the threat of future rebellion by insisting that ethnic minorities within the empire adopt Russian language and culture. Despite these measures, the tsarist regime in this era of the

---

Russification: A program for the integration of Russia's many nationality groups that involved the forced learning of the Russian language and the practice of Russian Orthodox religion as well as the settlement of ethnic Russians among other nationality groups.

Great Reforms only partially succeeded in developing the administrative, economic, and civic institutions that made the nation-state strong elsewhere in Europe. The tsar and his inner circle tightly controlled the government, allowing few to share in power. In imperial Russia, autocracy and continued abuse of many in the population slowed the development of the sense of common citizenship forming elsewhere in the West, while the urge to revolt grew.

REVIEW QUESTION What were the main results of the Crimean War?

War and Nation Building

Dynamic leaders in the German and Italian states used the opportunity provided by the weakened concert of Europe to unify their fragmented countries through warfare. When national disunity threatened, the United States waged a bloody civil war to maintain its integrity, which opened the way for further expansion and vigorous economic growth. The rise of powerful **nation-states** such as Italy, Germany, and the United States was accompanied by a sense of pride in national identity—or nationalism—among their peoples (see "Terms of History," at right). This was not an inevitable or universal trend in the West, however. Millions of individuals in the Austrian Empire, Ireland, and elsewhere maintained a regional, local, or distinct ethnic identity even as the nation-state was strengthening and national sentiment was on the rise.

Cavour, Garibaldi, and the Process of Italian Unification

Despite the failure of the revolutions of 1848 in the Italian states, hope for national unification remained strong, aided by diplomatic instability across Europe. The kingdom of Piedmont-Sardinia, in the economically modernizing north of Italy, drove the unification process that came to be called the Risorgimento ("rebirth"). Italians rallied to the operas of Verdi, but it was railroads, a modern army, and the military support of France against the Austrian Empire, which still dominated the peninsula, that made political unification possible.

---

nation-state: An independent political unit of modern times based on representing a united people.

TERMS OF HISTORY

Nationalism

The word *nationalism* is associated with a sense of a common identity among people within geographically defined nation-states. Nationalism simultaneously promotes the nation-state around which that common identity develops. A phenomenon of the past two to three centuries, it became increasingly important to politics from the nineteenth century on. Strongly held feelings of a common national identity grew in the years after 1750, and this sense of national identification increasingly competed in people's minds with religious, regional, and local loyalties.

In an early version of nationalism, the eighteenth-century British took pride in the fact that as Protestants they had defeated the Catholic French king in the global trade wars in Asia and the New World. At about the same time, the German author Johann Gottfried Herder concluded from his studies that a common language—along with its folktales, history, and laws—also served as the basis for a shared national identity. Herder's emphasis on past accomplishments and traditions connects this kind of nationalism to themes in the romantic movement. In 1789, French revolutionary politicians set out in the Declaration of the Rights of Man and Citizen that all men were citizens—not subjects—and that as citizens they had rights. The Declaration thus proclaimed that common identity could be based on the rule of law. By the beginning of the nineteenth century, some of the major components of nationalism had developed: pride in military conquest (militaristic nationalism); pride in a common culture developed over centuries (sometimes called romantic nationalism); and belief in citizenship and the rule of law, with its guarantee of civil rights and other freedoms (civic nationalism).

In the nineteenth century, nationalism became a force in domestic and international politics. From the 1820s on, nationalistic politicians took to the battlefield, as in the fight for Greek independence or in the wars of Italian and German unification. Some Italian nationalists expected that unification would strengthen national identity by providing the kind of common citizenship and freedom that the Americans and French had won through their revolutions.

After 1848, realists like Bismarck and Cavour promoted nationalism as the work of "iron and blood"—national strength backed by military might. Nationalism became a matter of pride in a people's toughness and realism in a competitive world. After their wars of unification, both Germany and Italy continued to promote the vision of the nation triumphant in battle. This differed from the French revolutionary ideal of being triumphant in battle in order to bring rights and constitutions to oppressed peoples—a civic nationalism. By the end of the nineteenth century, the basis of nationalism had shifted from pride in democratic institutions to pride in a nation's military power. With growing racism in the nineteenth century, there came to be a form of nationalism based on purity of blood. Today, the word *nationalism* usually combines a wide array of ingredients, prompting politicians to appeal to common religion, laws, customs, language, ethnicity, race, and history to build national pride.

Cavour, Architect of the New Italy

The pragmatic **Camillo di Cavour** (1810–1861), prime minister of the kingdom of Piedmont-Sardinia from 1852 until his death, had a Realpolitiker's vision of how to unify the Italian states. A rebel in his youth, Cavour in his maturity organized steamship companies, played the stock market, and inhaled the heady air of modernization during his travels to Paris and London. He promoted economic development rather than idealistic uprisings as the means to achieve a united Italy. As a skilled prime minister, Cavour helped the less capable king, Victor Emmanuel II (r. Piedmont-Sardinia 1849–1861, r. Italy 1861–1878), achieve a strong Piedmontese economy, a modern army, and a liberal political climate as the foundation for Piedmont's claim to lead the unification process (Map 22.2).

To unify Italy, however, Piedmont would have to confront Austria, which governed the provinces of Lombardy and Venetia and exerted strong influence over most of the peninsula. Cavour turned for help to Napoleon III, who at a meeting in the summer of 1858 promised French assistance in exchange for the city of Nice and the region of Savoy. Napoleon III additionally expected that France rather than Austria would influence the peninsula thereafter. Sure of French help, Cavour provoked the Austrians to invade northern Italy in April 1859. The cause of Piedmont-Sardinia's monarchy now became the cause of nationalist Italians everywhere, even those who had supported romantic republicanism in 1848, and they rose up on the side of Piedmont. The French and Piedmontese armies used the newly built Piedmontese railroad to move troops and thereby achieved rapid victories. Suddenly fearing the growth of Piedmont as a potential competing force, Napoleon independently signed a peace treaty with Austria that gave Lombardy,

Camillo di Cavour: Prime minister (1852–1861) of the kingdom of Piedmont-Sardinia and architect of a united Italy.

MAP 22.2 Unification of Italy, 1859–1870

The many states of the Italian peninsula had different languages, ways of life, and economic interests. The northern kingdom of Sardinia, which included the commercially advanced state of Piedmont, had much to gain from a unified market and a more extensive pool of labor. Although the armies of King Victor Emmanuel II and Giuseppe Garibaldi brought the Italian states together as a single country, it would take decades to construct a culturally, socially, and economically unified nation.

but not Venetia, to Piedmont. The rest of Italy remained disunited, leaving Cavour's nationalist ambitions not yet realized.

Garibaldi, Symbol of Italian Freedom Napoleon III's plan to keep Italy disunited was soon derailed. Support for Piedmont continued to swell among Italians, while a financially strapped Austria stood by, unable to keep control of events on the peninsula. Citizens of the rest of the northern and central Italian states (except Rome, which French troops had occupied) ousted their leaders and elected to join Piedmont. Giuseppe Garibaldi (1807–1882), a committed republican and veteran of the revolutions of 1848, set sail from Genoa in May 1860 with a thousand red-shirted volunteers (many of them teenage boys) to liberate Sicily, where peasants were rebelling against their landlords and the corrupt government in anticipation of the Risorgimento. In the autumn of that year, Victor Emmanuel II's victorious forces descending from the north and Garibaldi's moving up from the south met in Naples. Although some of his followers still clamored for a republic, Garibaldi threw his support to the king. In 1861, the kingdom of Italy was proclaimed with Victor Emmanuel as its ruler.

Exhausted by a decade of overwork, Cavour died within months of leading the unification, leaving lesser men to organize the new Italy. The task ahead was enormous and complex: There was still no common Italian language; 90 percent of the peninsula's inhabitants spoke local dialects. Moreover, consensus among Italy's elected political leaders was often difficult to reach after the war, and admirers of Cavour, such as Verdi (who had been made senator), quit the quarrelsome political stage. Politicians from the wealthy commercial north and the impoverished agricultural south disagreed over issues like taxation and development, as they do even today. Finally, Italian borders did not yet seem complete because Venetia and Rome remained outside them, under Austrian and French control, respectively. Holding the new nation together amid these difficulties was the romanticized retelling of the Italian struggle for freedom from foreign and domestic tyrants, under the daring leadership of Garibaldi and his Red Shirts. The legend of Garibaldi papered over Cavour's economic and military Realpolitik, but the story became the centerpiece of a new and unifying national pride.

Bismarck and the Realpolitik of German Unification

The most momentous act of nation building for Europe and the world was the creation of a united Germany in 1871. This, too, was the product of Realpolitik, undertaken once the concert of Europe was smashed and the champions of the status quo defeated. Employing the old military caste to wage war, yet enjoying support from industrialists, merchants, and financiers who saw profits in a single national market, the Prussian state brought a vast array of cities and kingdoms under its control within a single decade. From then on, Germany prospered, continuing to consolidate its economic and political might. By the end of the nineteenth century, it would be the foremost continental power.

Seamstresses of the Red Shirts
Sewing uniforms and making battle flags, European women like these Italian volunteers saw themselves as contributors to the nation. Many nineteenth-century women participated in nation building as "republican mothers" by donating their domestic skills and raising the next generation of citizens to be patriotic. *(Oil on canvas, Florence/Private Collection/© Electa/akg-images/The Image Works.)*

King William I of Prussia and His Generals
Realpolitik politicians used warfare to create new nations like the unified Germany, which led other states in using up-to-date weaponry and transportation. Nonetheless, horses, swords, and flashing helmets such as those worn by King William I and the generals of Prussia were still a major feature of developing modern warfare. *(Reproduction of a painting by G. Koch/Mary Evans Picture Library/Everett Collection.)*

Bismarck's Rise to Power

The architect of the unified Germany was **Otto von Bismarck** (1815–1898). Bismarck came from a traditional Junker (Prussian landed nobility) family on his father's side; his mother's family included high-ranking bureaucrats and literati of the middle class. At university, the young Bismarck had gambled and womanized. After failing in the civil service, he worked to modernize operations on his landholdings while leading an otherwise decadent life. His marriage to a pious Lutheran woman gave him new seriousness. In the 1850s, his diplomatic service to the Prussian state made him increasingly angry at the Habsburg grip on German affairs. Establishing Prussia as the most respected and dominant German power became Bismarck's cause.

Otto von Bismarck (1815–1898): Leading Prussian politician and German chancellor who waged war in order to create a united German Empire, which was established in 1871.

In 1862, William I (king of Prussia, r. 1861–1888; German emperor, r. 1871–1888) appointed Bismarck prime minister in hopes that he would crush the growing power of the liberals in the Prussian parliament. The liberals, representing the prosperous professional and business classes, had gained parliamentary strength at the expense of conservative landowners during the decades of industrial expansion. Indeed, the liberals' wealth was crucial to the Prussian state's ability to augment its power, but liberals wanted Prussia to be like other parts of western Europe, with political rights for citizens and increased civilian control of the military. William I, along with members of the traditional Prussian elite such as Bismarck, rejected the western European model. Acting on his conservative beliefs, Bismarck rammed through programs to build the army and prevent civilian control. "Germany looks not to Prussia's liberalism, but to its power," he proclaimed. "The great questions of the day will not be settled by speeches and majority decisions — that was the great mistake of 1848 and 1849 — but by iron and blood."

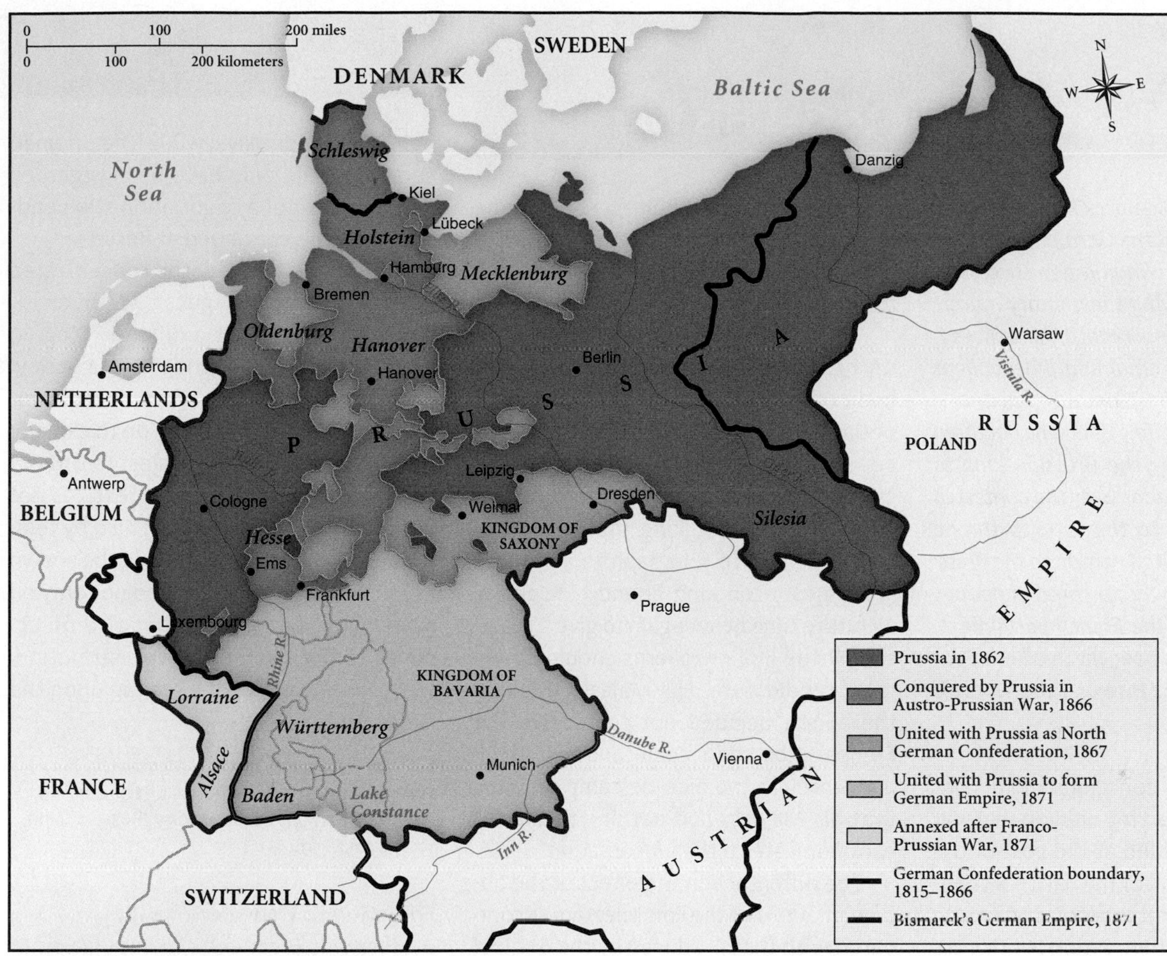

MAP 22.3 Unification of Germany, 1862–1871
In a complex series of diplomatic maneuvers, Prussian leader Otto von Bismarck welded disunited kingdoms and small states into a major continental power independent of the other dominant German dynasty, the Habsburg monarchy. That unity almost immediately unleashed the new nation's economic and industrial potential, but an aristocratic and agrarian elite remained firmly in power.

Prussia's Wars of Unification

After his triumph over the parliament, Bismarck led Prussia into a series of wars: against Denmark in 1864, Austria in 1866, and France in 1870. Using war as a political tactic, he kept the disunited German states from choosing Austrian leadership and instead united them around Prussia. Bismarck drew Austria into the 1864 war over Denmark's proposed incorporation of the provinces of Schleswig and Holstein, with their partially German population. The Prussian-Austrian victory resulted in an agreement that Prussia would administer Schleswig, and Austria, Holstein. That arrangement stretched Austria's geographic interests far from its central European base: "We were very honorable, but very dumb," Emperor Francis Joseph later said of being drawn into the Schleswig-Holstein debacle.

Austria proved weaker than Prussia, because the empire lagged in economic development and was beset by the discontent of its many national minorities. Bismarck, however, so encouraged Austria's pretensions to grandeur and influence that it disputed the administration of Schleswig and Holstein and in the summer of 1866 confidently declared war on Prussia itself. Within seven weeks, the modernized Prussian army, using railroads and breech-loading rifles against the outdated Austrian military, won a decisive victory that allowed Bismarck to drive Austria from the German Confederation and create the North German Confederation, led by Prussia (Map 22.3).

To bring the remaining German states into Prussia's expanding orbit, Bismarck next moved to provoke France into war. The atmosphere became charged when Spain proposed a Prussian prince to fill its vacant royal throne. This candidacy at once threatened France with Prussian rulers on two of its borders and inflated Prussian pride at the possibility of its princely lines ruling grand states. To get nationalist sentiments onto the news pages in

DOCUMENT

Bismarck Tricks the Public to Get His War

By 1870, Otto von Bismarck had gained the allegiance of most of the German states (excluding Austria) by waging two successful wars and thus showing the military muscle of Prussia. Defeating France, he believed, would pull in the remaining independent German states—most notably Bavaria—and unite Germany. To this end he doctored a document sent by the Prussian king to the French ambassador over the contested issue of succession to the Spanish throne and released the edited version to the press. He knew that its newly contrived imperious tone would offend the French parliament. Realpolitik, then as now, involved manipulating the press. Here Bismarck describes his actions.

All considerations, conscious and unconscious, strengthened my opinion that war could only be avoided at the cost of the honor of Prussia and of the national confidence in her. Under this conviction I made use of the royal authorization . . . to publish the contents of the telegram; and in the presence of my two guests [General Moltke and General Roon] I reduced the telegram by striking out words, but without adding or altering anything, to the following form:

"After the news of the renunciation of the hereditary prince of Hohenzollern had been officially communicated to the imperial government of France by the royal government of Spain, the French ambassador at Ems made the further demand of his Majesty the king that he should authorize him to telegraph to Paris that his Majesty the king bound himself for all future time never again to give his consent if the Hohenzollerns should renew their candidature. His Majesty the king thereupon decided not to receive the French ambassador again, and sent to tell him, through the aide-de-camp on duty, that his Majesty had nothing further to communicate to the ambassador."

The difference in the effect of the abbreviated text of the Ems telegram as compared with that produced by the original was not the result of stronger words, but of the form, which made this announcement appear decisive, while [the original] version would only have been regarded as a fragment of a negotiation still pending and to be continued at Berlin.

After I had read out the concentrated edition to my two guests, Moltke remarked: "Now it has a different ring; in its original form it sounded like a parley; now it is like a flourish of trumpets in answer to a challenge." I went on to explain: "If, in execution of his Majesty's order, I at once communicate this text, . . . not only to the newspapers, but also by telegraph to all our embassies, it will be known in Paris before midnight, and not only on account of its contents, but also on account of the manner of its distribution, will have the effect of a red rag upon the Gallic bull."

Source: Otto von Bismarck, *Memoirs*, in James Harvey Robinson and Charles Beard, eds., *Readings in Modern European History* (Boston: Ginn, 1909), 2:158–59.

Question to Consider

- **How was Bismarck's manipulation of the Ems telegram an example of Realpolitik at work?**

both countries, Bismarck edited a diplomatic communication (the so-called Ems telegram, named after the spa town in which it was issued) to make it look as if the king of Prussia had insulted France over the issue of the vacant throne. Publication of the revised telegram inflamed the French into demanding war. (See Document, "Bismarck Tricks the Public to Get His War," above.) The parliament gladly declared it on July 19, 1870, setting in motion the alliances Prussia had created with the other German states and launching the Franco-Prussian War. The Prussians captured Napoleon III with his army on September 2, 1870, and France's Second Empire fell two days later.

Birth of the German Empire Prussian forces were still besieging Paris when, in January 1871 in the Hall of Mirrors at Versailles, King William of Prussia was proclaimed kaiser ("emperor") of the new German Reich ("empire"). The peace terms ending the Franco-Prussian War, signed in May, required France to cede the rich industrial provinces of Alsace and Lorraine to Germany and to pay a multibillion-franc indemnity. Without French protection for the papacy, Rome became part of Italy. Germany was now poised to dominate continental politics.

Prussian military might served as the foundation for German nation building, and a complex constitution for the German Empire ensured the continued political dominance of the aristocracy and monarchy—despite the growing wealth and influence of the liberal business classes. Kaiser William, who remained Prussia's king, controlled the military and appointed Bismarck to the powerful position of chancellor for the Reich. Individual German states were represented in a council called the Bundesrat, while the Reichstag was an assembly elected by universal male suffrage. The Reichstag ratified all budgets but had little power to initiate programs. In framing this political settlement, Bismarck accorded rights such as suffrage in the belief that the masses would uphold conservatism and the monarchy out of their fear of modernizing businessmen, whom Bismarck opposed as "liberal power." Taking no chances, he balanced this move with an electoral system in Prussia in which the votes from the upper classes counted more than those from the lower. He had little to fear from liberals, however. Dizzy with German military success, they came to support the blend of economic progress, constitutional government, and militaristic nationalism that Bismarck represented.

Francis Joseph and the Creation of the Austro-Hungarian Monarchy

The Austrian monarchy took a different approach to nation building, proving that there was no one blueprint for the modern nation-state. Just as the Crimean War left Russia searching for solutions to its social and political problems, so the confrontations with Cavour and Bismarck left the Habsburg Empire struggling to keep its standing in a rapidly changing Europe. The Habsburg Empire had emerged from the revolutions of 1848 renewed by the ascension of the young monarch Francis Joseph (r. 1848–1916), who favored absolutist rule. A tireless worker, Francis Joseph enhanced his authority through stiff court ceremonies, playing to the popular fascination with celebrity and power. Though the emperor stubbornly resisted reform, official standards of honesty and efficiency improved, and the government promoted local education. The administration used the German language and the schools taught it, but the government respected the rights of national minorities — Czechs and Poles, for instance — to receive education and communicate with officials in their native tongue. Above all, the government abolished most internal customs barriers, boosted railway construction, and attracted foreign capital. Like Paris, the capital city of Vienna underwent extensive rebuilding, and as industrialization progressed, if unevenly, people found jobs.

In the fast-moving nineteenth century, the absolutist Austrian emperor could not match Bismarck in nation building. Too much of the old regime remained as a roadblock: the Catholic church controlled education and civil institutions such as marriage, prosperous liberals lacked representation in such important policy matters as taxation and finance, and police informers swarmed around them. Wanting truly representative government and free speech, the liberals prevented measures — such as providing funds for modernizing the military — that would have strengthened the reactionary government. Unlike Bismarck in Prussia, there was no one to override the liberals to bring about change.

After Prussia's 1866 victory over Austria, the vast, wealthy kingdom of Hungary became the key to the Habsburg Empire's existence. The leaders of the Hungarian agrarian elites forced the Austrian

Muslim Quarter and Bazaar
Nineteenth-century Europeans were a diverse people, composed of many religions, ethnicities, and ways of life. In the Balkans, many were Muslims, as this marketplace in Sarajevo, Bosnia, illustrates. The goal of finding a common cultural ground eluded the peoples of the Balkans. The Habsburg monarchy, which annexed Bosnia-Herzegovina in 1908, exerted its influence in the area to keep peoples divided and to play one against the other. *(Albertina, Vienna.)*

emperor to accept a **dual monarchy**—that is, one in which the Magyars had home rule over the Hungarian kingdom within the Habsburg lands. This agreement restored the Hungarian parliament and gave it control of internal policy (including the right to decide how to treat Hungary's national minorities). Although the Habsburg emperor Francis Joseph was crowned king of Hungary and Austro-Hungarian foreign policy was coordinated from Vienna, the Hungarians mostly ruled themselves after 1867 and hammered out common policies such as tariffs with the government in Vienna. These negotiations were mostly bitter, weakening the process of nation building in the empire.

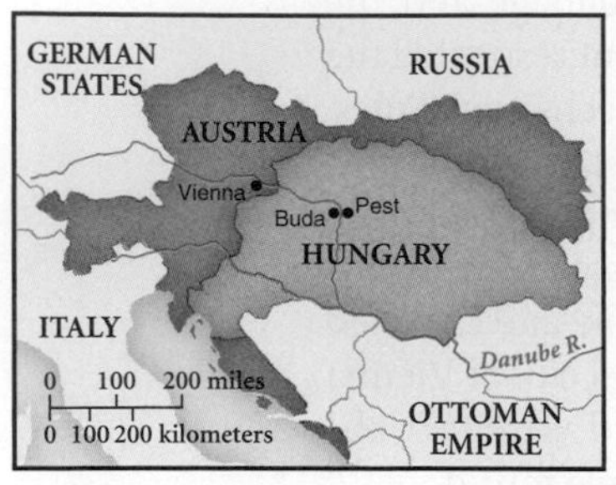

The Austro-Hungarian Monarchy, 1867

A second weakness in the compromise that created the dual monarchy was that, although designed specifically to address the Hungarian demands, the dual monarchy led to claims by Czechs, Slovaks, and other national groups in the Habsburg Empire for a similar kind of self-rule. Czechs who had helped the empire advance industrially, for example, wanted Hungarian-style liberties. More menacing, other leaders of dissatisfied ethnic groups turned to **Pan-Slavism**—that is, the transnational loyalty of all ethnic Slavs whose common heritage, they believed, transcended current national boundaries. Instead of looking toward Vienna, they turned to the largest Slavic country—Russia—as key to achieving the unity of all Slavs outside the Habsburg Empire. With so many competing ethnicities, the Austro-Hungarian monarchy remained a dynastic state in which people could show loyalty to the Habsburg dynasty but had increasing difficulty relating to one another as members of a single nation.

Political Stability through Gradual Reform in Great Britain

In contrast to the nations in turmoil on the continent, Britain appeared the ideal of liberal progress. By the 1850s, the monarchy symbolized domestic tranquillity and propriety. Unlike their predecessors, Queen Victoria (r. 1837–1901) and her husband, Prince Albert, portrayed themselves as models of morality, British stability, and middle-class virtues (see "Seeing History," page 738). Britain's parliamentary system steadily brought more men into the political process. Economic prosperity supported peaceful political reform, except that politicians did little to relieve Ireland's continued suffering. A flexible party system helped smooth governmental decision making: the Tories evolved into the Conservatives, who favored a more status-oriented politics but still went along with the emerging liberal consensus around economic development and representative government. The Whigs became the Liberals, so named for their commitment to the same values on which the term *liberal* had taken shape in the first place: progress and free, expansive trade, and appreciating active industrialists as much as the entrenched aristocracy. In 1867, the Conservatives, led by Benjamin Disraeli (1804–1881), passed the Second Reform Bill, which extended voting rights to a million more men. Disraeli proposed, like Bismarck somewhat later, that the working classes would choose "the most conservative interests in the country"—not the business ones. Thus more men voting and deferring to their aristocratic betters would build his party, not that of the Liberals.

Both political parties supported reforms because citizens had formed pressure groups to influence national policies. Women's groups advocated the Matrimonial Causes Act of 1857, which facilitated divorce, and the Married Women's Property Act of 1870, which allowed married women to own property and keep the wages they earned. The Reform League, another pressure organization, had held mass demonstrations in London to bring about passage of the Second Reform Bill. Plush royal ceremonies united critics and activists and masked political conflict but, more important, involved all social classes. Whereas previous monarchs' sexual infidelities had incited mobs to riot, Queen Victoria and Prince Albert, with their newly devised celebrations of royal marriages, anniversaries, and births, drew respectful crowds. Promoting the monarchy in this way was so successful that the term *Victorian* came to symbolize almost the entire nineteenth century and could refer to anything from manners to political beliefs.

The aristocracy, maintaining power despite the rising wealth of liberal businessmen, built gigantic country houses in traditional English architectural styles such as Queen Anne and Georgian, thus using the monarchical heritage to anchor the modern age. Yet Britain's politicians were as devoted to

---

dual monarchy: The shared power arrangement between the Habsburg Empire and Hungary after the Prussian defeat of the Austrian Empire in 1866–1867.

Pan-Slavism: The nineteenth-century movement calling for the unity of all Slavs across national and regional boundaries.

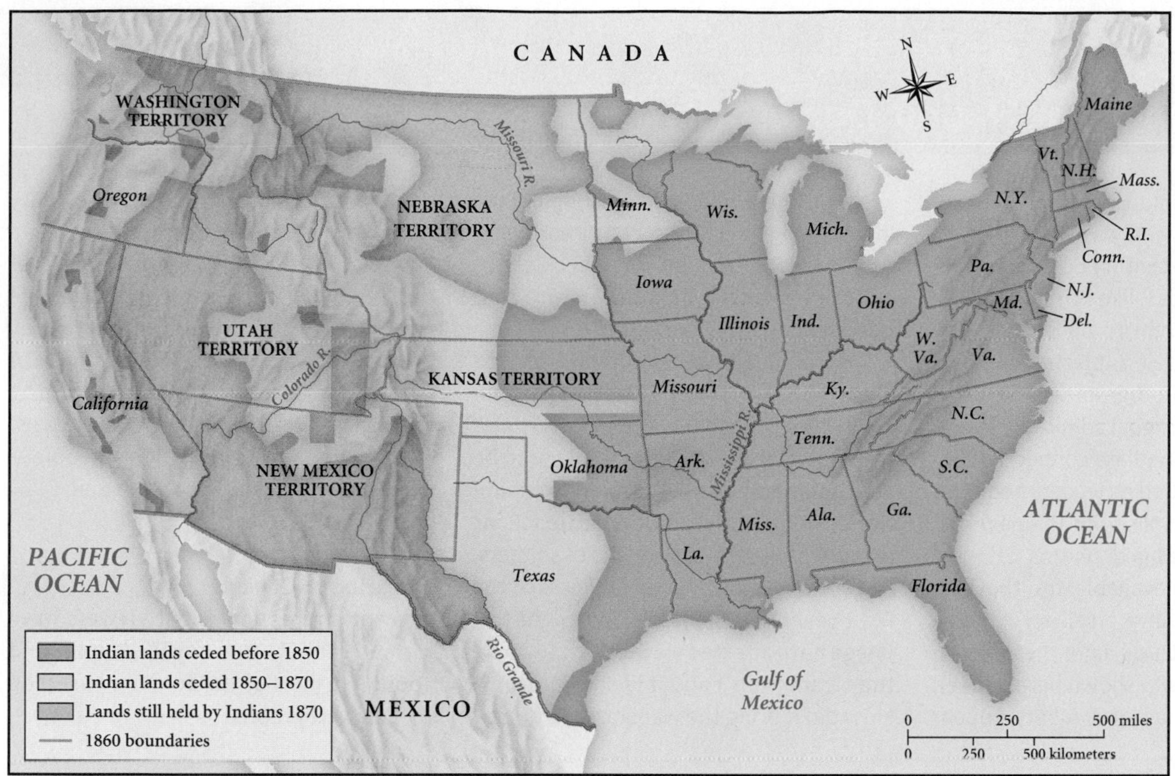

MAP 22.4 U.S. Expansion, 1850–1870
Like Russia, the United States expanded into adjacent regions to create a continental nation-state. In taking over territories, however, the United States differed from Russia by herding native peoples into small confined spaces called reservations so that settlers could acquire thousands of square miles for farming and other enterprises. The U.S. government granted full citizenship for all native Americans only in 1925.

Realpolitik as those in Germany, Italy, or France. Their policies included the use of violence to expand their overseas empire and, increasingly, to control Ireland, where reform stopped short. This violence occurred beyond the view of most British people, however, allowing them to imagine their nation as peaceful, advanced, and united.

Nation Building in North America

Nation building in the midcentury United States involved unprecedented and destructive upheaval. The young nation had a far more democratic political culture than that of Europe, and nationalism was on the rise. Virtually universal white male suffrage, a rambunctiously independent press, and mass political parties reflected a common belief that sovereignty derived from the people. From the beginning, a combative public politics shaped America.

The United States continued to expand westward (Map 22.4). In 1848, victory in the Mexican-American War almost doubled the size of the country: the United States officially annexed Texas, and large portions of California and the Southwest extended U.S. borders into formerly Mexican land. Politicians and citizens alike favored banning native Americans from these western lands and confining them to reservations. There was no agreement, however, on whether slavery would be allowed in the new western territories. The issue polarized the country. In the North, politicians in the new Republican Party ran on a platform of "free soil, free labor, free men," although few Republicans actually endorsed the abolitionists' demand to end slavery.

After Republican Abraham Lincoln was elected president in 1860, most of the slaveholding states seceded to form the Confederate States of America. Civil war broke out in 1861 when, under Lincoln's leadership, the North fought to preserve the Union. The future of nation building in the United States hung in the balance. Lincoln did not initially aim to abolish slavery, but his Emancipation Proclamation of January 1863, issued as a wartime measure, officially freed all slaves in the Confederacy and turned the war into a fight not only for union but also for an end to human bondage. After the summer of 1863, the North's superior industrial strength and military might overpowered and physically

SEEING HISTORY

Photographing the Nation: Domesticity and War

Fostering a common national identity among their citizens was important to many nineteenth-century European leaders, especially those, like Britain's Queen Victoria, who sought to build unity and loyalty among their subjects. The new technology of photography, developed in 1839, served this goal admirably by enabling a more immediate connection between the public and its leaders and their policies. For example, with the new medium, carefully staged photos of royal families became available for the first time, circulating in a small format like today's baseball cards among eager collectors. In the photo shown here, Queen Victoria and her husband, Albert, appear as an ordinary middle-class couple. Posing for many such photos, Victoria and Albert helped develop modern celebrity culture but also a national culture that transcended local identities.

The Crimean War was another shared experience for Britons, many of whom avidly collected photos from the front, for the conflict was one of the first ever to be photographed. Crowds flocked to exhibitions in major cities to view battle scenes (usually staged) and portraits of soldiers, like the one shown here of officers of the Fifty-seventh Regiment. How might this image have affected viewers? What could they learn from it about life on the front? How did it bring the war closer to home?

Both war photography and photography of national leaders, including U.S. president Abraham Lincoln with his wife, Mary Todd Lincoln, or France's Napoleon III and Eugénie, were major ingredients of nation building. The new technology made lofty leaders and the faraway wars they prosecuted accessible — indeed, a part of everyday life — to individuals across the West and beyond. As millions of eyes gazed on these images, the nation's people — wherever they lived — became one.

Question to Consider

■ **What impression might viewers have formed about the royal couple and about the lives of the soldiers based on these photographs?**

Portrait of Queen Victoria and Prince Albert at Buckingham Palace, May 15, 1860. *(Hulton Archive / Getty Images.)*

Roger Fenton, Officers of the 57th Regiment, 1855. *(Library of Congress, Prints and Photographs Division. LC-USZC4-9132.)*

destroyed much of the South. By April 1865, the North had prevailed, though a Confederate sympathizer assassinated Lincoln. Constitutional amendments ended slavery and promised full political rights to African American men.

Northerners hailed their victory as the triumph of American values, but racism remained entrenched throughout the Union. By 1871, northern interest in promoting African American political rights was waning, and whites began regaining control of state politics in the South, often by organized violence and intimidation. The end of northern occupation of the South in 1877 was a setback in obtaining rights for blacks. Nonetheless, in ending slavery, the Union victory opened the way to stronger national government and to economic advancement no longer tied to the old Atlantic plantation system.

The North's triumph had profound effects elsewhere in North America. It allowed the reunited United States to contribute to Napoleon III's defeat in Mexico in 1867. The United States also threatened the annexation of Canada to punish Britain, whose dependence on cotton had led it to support the Confederacy. To prevent the loss of their largest territory, the British government allowed Canadians to form a united dominion — that is, a self-governing unit of the empire — in 1867. Dominion status answered Canadians' appeal for home rule, weakened the cause of those opposing Britain's control of Canada, and strengthened Canadian national unity.

REVIEW QUESTION What role did warfare play in the various nineteenth-century nation-building efforts?

Nation Building through Social Order

Government officials and reformers worked to establish social unity and order as a way of making political unity stronger. With new improvements, they also hoped to offset the violent changes of the nation-building process. Population rose dramatically and cities grew crowded as the nineteenth century progressed, leading officials across Europe to promote public health and safety. Many liberal theorists wanted a laissez-faire government that left social and economic life largely to private enterprise. In contrast, bureaucrats and reformers took direct action to improve citizens' lives and, along with missionaries and explorers, worked more actively to establish social order and to extend European power to the farthest reaches of the globe. Some of these efforts met violent resistance both within Europe and outside it.

Bringing Order to the Cities

European cities became the backdrop for displays of state power and accomplishment. Governments focused on improving capital cities such as Vienna and Rome, although many noncapital cities also acquired handsome parks, widened streets, stately museums, and massive city halls. In 1857, Austrian emperor Francis Joseph ordered the old Viennese city walls to be replaced with concentric boulevards lined with major public buildings such as the opera house and government offices (see the illustration on page 740). Opera houses and ministries were concrete evidence of national wealth and power, and the broad boulevards allowed crowds to observe royal pageantry. The wide roads were also easier for troops to navigate than the twisted, narrow medieval streets that in 1848 had concealed insurrectionists in cities like Paris and Vienna — an advantage that convinced some otherwise reluctant officials to approve the expense. Impressive parks and public gardens showed the state's control of nature, ordered people's leisure time, and inspired respect for the nation-state's achievements.

One effect of renovated cities was to highlight class differences. Construction first required destruction. Buildings and entire neighborhoods that had intermingled rich and poor disappeared, and thousands of city dwellers were dislocated. The boulevards often served as boundaries marking the newly built rich quarters from the poor sections of the city. In Paris, the process of urban change was called Haussmannization, named for the prefect Georges-Eugène Haussmann, who implemented a grand design that included eighty-five miles of new streets, many lined with showy dwellings for the wealthy. In London, the spaciousness and ornamentation of the many new banks and insurance companies, one architect believed, "help[ed] the impression of stability." The civic pride resulting from urban rebuilding would replace rebelliousness and disunity.

Yet amid redevelopment and beautification, serious problems menaced the urban population. Repeated epidemics of diseases such as cholera killed alarming numbers of city dwellers and gave the strong impression of social decay, not national power. Poor sanitation allowed typhoid bacteria to spread through sewage and into water supplies, infecting rich and poor alike. In 1861, Britain's Prince

Albert—the beloved husband of Queen Victoria—reputedly died of typhoid fever, commonly known as a "filth disease." Heaps of animal excrement in chicken coops, pigsties, and stables; unregulated urban slaughterhouses and tanneries; and piles of human waste alongside buildings were breeding grounds for disease. In cities the stench alone—not to mention the disorder it suggested—made sanitation a top priority.

Scientific research, increasingly undertaken in publicly financed laboratories and hospitals, provided the means to promote public health and control disease. France's Louis Pasteur, three of whose young daughters had also died of typhoid, advanced the germ theory of disease. Seeking a method to prevent wine from spoiling, Pasteur found that the growth of living organisms caused fermentation in wine, and he suggested that certain organisms—bacteria and parasites—might be responsible for human and animal diseases. Pasteur demonstrated that heating foods such as wine and milk to a certain temperature, a process that soon became known as pasteurization, killed these organisms and made food safe. English surgeon Joseph Lister applied Pasteur's germ theory of disease to infection and developed antiseptics for treating wounds and preventing puerperal fever, a condition, caused by the dirty hands of physicians and midwives, that killed innumerable women after childbirth.

Governments undertook projects to modernize sewer and other sanitary systems, including the straightening of rivers to eliminate marshes and other stagnant pools of water that could breed disease. Citizens often prized such improvements as signs of national superiority. In Paris, sewage flowed into newly built, watertight underground collectors (see the illustration on page 741). In addition, Haussmann piped in water from uncontaminated sources in the countryside to provide each household with a secure supply. These improvements were imitated across Europe: the Russian Empire's port city Riga (now in Latvia), for example, organized its first water company in 1863. To prevent devastating floods and to eliminate disease-ridden marshlands, governments rerouted and straightened rivers such as the Rhine and built canals. Improved sanitation testified to the activist state's ability to bring about progress.

Citizens responded positively to improvements in everyday life and came to expect that cities could and should change for the better. When sanitary public toilets for men became a feature of modern cities, women petitioned governments for similar facilities. More aware of dirt, disease, and smells, the

Museums and Nation Building

The Kunsthistorisches Museum (Museum of Fine Arts) in Vienna was part of a huge rebuilding project that adorned the city with wide boulevards and grand public buildings. Art museums such as Vienna's represented the cultural wealth of the state and allowed citizens to take pride in this wealth while they routinely gathered collectively to view it. *(ullstein—imagebroker.net.)*

Touring a National Treasure: The Sewers of Paris
The enlargement of sewage systems was so grand an undertaking in urban capitals that they attracted visitors. Many had a curiosity about what technology could achieve and flocked to the new sewers to enjoy tours—a pastime that continues to this day in cities like Paris. *(© Leonard de Selva/Corbis.)*

middle classes bathed more regularly, sometimes even once a week. One Russian city dweller complained to a Moscow newspaper of "an enormous cloud of white dust constantly over the city" that injured the eyes and lungs. Such individual concerns for refinement and health mirrored governments' pursuit of order.

Expanding Government Bureaucracy

Building an orderly national community meant a more active role for the state, and bureaucracies expanded in these years to direct nation building and the push for social order. The nation-state required citizens to follow a growing catalog of regulations as government authority reached further into everyday life. The censuses that Britain, France, and the United States had begun in the late eighteenth century became routine in most other countries as well. Censuses provided the state with personal details of citizens' lives such as age, occupation, residence, marital status, and number of children. Governments then used these data for everything from setting quotas for military conscription to predicting the need for new prisons. Reformers like Florence Nightingale, who gathered medical, public health, and other statistics to support sanitary reform, believed that such quantitative information would help government base decisions on facts rather than on influence peddling or ill-informed hunches, and thus make it less susceptible to corruption and inefficiency. In 1860, Sweden introduced the income tax, which opened private citizens' earnings from work or investment to government scrutiny.

To bring about their vision of social order, many governments also expanded the regulation of prostitution. Venereal disease, especially syphilis, was common, and like typhoid fever, it infected individuals and whole families. Officials blamed prostitutes, not their clients, for its spread. The police picked up suspect women, who were examined for syphilis and, if infected, confined for treatment. As states began monitoring prostitution and other social matters like public health and housing, they had to add departments and agencies. In 1867, Hungary's bureaucracy handled fewer than 250,000 individual cases ranging from health to poverty issues; twenty years later, it handled more than 1 million.

Schooling and Professionalizing Society

Emphasis on empirical knowledge and objective standards changed the professions and raised their status. Growing numbers of middle-class doctors, lawyers, managers, professors, and journalists employed solid information in their work. The middle classes argued that jobs in government should be awarded according to talent and skill rather than aristocratic birth or political connections. In Britain, a civil service law passed in 1870 required competitive examinations to ensure competency in government posts—a system long used in China. Governments began to allow professionals to influence state policy and to determine rules for admission to their fields. Such legislation had both positive and negative effects: groups could set high standards, but otherwise qualified people were sometimes prohibited from working because they lacked the established credentials. The medical profession, for example, gained the authority to license physicians, but it tried to block experienced midwives from attending childbirths. Science became the province of the trained specialist rather than the knowledgeable amateur. Newly employed at government-financed institutions, professors of science often viewed their work as part of a national struggle for prestige and superiority.

Nation building required major improvements in the education of all citizens, professional or not. "We have made Italy," one Italian official announced. "Now we have to make Italians." Education was one way of bringing citizens to hold common beliefs and values. Bureaucrats and professionals called for radical changes in the curriculum and faculty of schools—from kindergarten to university—to make the general population more fit for citizenship and able to further economic progress. Expansion of the electorate and lower-class activism prompted one British aristocrat to say of the common people, whom he feared as they gained influence, "We must now educate our masters!" Governments introduced compulsory schooling to reduce illiteracy rates, which were more than 65 percent in Italy and Spain in the 1870s and even higher in eastern Europe. As ordinary people were allowed to vote, books taught them about the responsibilities of citizenship and provided the practical knowledge necessary for contributing to industrial society.

Educational reform was not easy. At midcentury, religious authorities supervised schools and charged tuition, making primary education an option chosen only by prosperous or religious parents. After the 1850s, national politicians felt that their states could not afford masses of ignorant peasants, whose backwardness one French official blamed on parish priests, specifically "their lack of intelligence [and] the narrowness of their views." His statement was extreme, but more measured critics also questioned the relevance of religion in the curricula of modern schools. In 1861, an English commission on education concluded that instead of knowledge of the Bible, "the knowledge most important to a labouring man is that of the causes which regulate the amount of his wages, the hours of his work, the regularity of his employment, and the prices of what he consumes." To feel part of a nation, the young had to learn its language, literature, and history. Replacing religion was a challenge for the secular and increasingly knowledge-based state.

Enforcing school attendance was another challenge. Although the Netherlands, Sweden, and Switzerland had functioning primary-school systems before midcentury, rural parents in these and other countries resisted sending their children to school. Farm families depended on children to perform chores and believed that work in the fields or the household provided the best and most useful education. Urban homemakers from the lower classes needed their children to fetch water, dispose of waste, tend younger children, and scavenge for household necessities such as stale bread from bakers or soup from local missions. Yet some of the working poor developed a craze for learning, which made traveling lecturers, public forums, reading groups, and debating societies popular among the middle and working classes.

Secondary education also expanded through the creation of more lycées (high schools) and technical schools yet remained even more of a luxury. In authoritarian countries such as Russia, advanced knowledge, including education in science and technology, was suspect because it empowered the young with information and taught them to think for themselves. Reformers pushed for more advanced and more complex courses for young women as part of nation building. The rationale was that modern knowledge in history and science, for example, would make them more interesting wives and better mothers of future citizens. In Britain, the founders of two women's colleges—Girton (1869) and Newnham (1871)—at Cambridge University believed, and were later proved right, that exacting standards and a modern curriculum in women's higher education would inspire improvements in the men's colleges of Cambridge and Oxford. Nonetheless, higher education for women remained a hotly contested issue; the vast majority of people felt that knowledge of religion, sewing, and manners was adequate for women.

Education also opened professional doors to women, who came to attend universities — in particular, medical schools — in Zurich and Paris in the 1860s. Despite complaints by those who wanted to maintain separate spheres for men and women, women doctors argued that they could not only bring feminine values to health care but also get better results because women patients would be more open with them than with male doctors. The need for educated citizens also offered opportunities for large numbers of women to enter teaching, a field once dominated by men. Thousands of women founded nursery schools and kindergartens based on the Enlightenment idea that developmental processes start at an early age. In a newly unified Italy, women opened schools as a way to expand knowledge and teach lessons in citizenship. Yet many men opposed the idea of women teaching. "I shudder at philosophic women," wrote one critic of female kindergarten teachers. Seen as radical because it enticed middle-class women out of the home, the push for early childhood education was as controversial as other educational reforms.

Spreading National Power and Order beyond the West

In an age of nation building, colonies took on new importance because they seemed to add to the power of the nation-state. This benefit led Great Britain, France, and Russia to expand their political control and rule colonies directly instead of through trading companies. Sometimes the colonial powers offered social and cultural services, such as schools. For instance, in the 1850s and 1860s provincial governors and local officials promoted the extension of Russian borders to gain control over nomadic tribes in central and eastern Asia. Russian officials then instituted common educational and religious policies, such as instruction in the Russian language and in the principles of the Russian Orthodox church as a means to social order.

British Rule in India

Great Britain, the era's mightiest imperial power, made a dramatic change of course toward direct political rule abroad as part of nation building. Before the 1850s, British liberals desired commercial profits from colonies, but, believing in laissez-faire, they kept political involvement in colonial affairs minimal. Since the eighteenth century, the East India Company had been gaining control over various kingdoms on the Indian subcontinent, whose princes awarded the company trading and tax collection rights, and then began building railroads throughout the countryside to make commerce and revenue collecting more efficient. As commerce with Britain grew, many Indian businessmen, including traders and tax collectors for the company, became wealthy. Other local men served in the colonial army, which became one of the largest standing armies in the world.

European expansion, including Britain's, sometimes met resistance. In 1857, a contingent of Indian troops, both Muslim and Hindu, violently rebelled when a rumor spread that Britain would force them to use cartridges greased with cow and pig fat, which violated the Hindu ban on beef and the Muslim prohibition of pork. This was not their main grievance, however. The soldiers, more generally angered at widening British control such as the imposition of a heavy tax on salt, overran the old Moghul capital at Delhi and declared the independence of the Indian nation — an uprising that became known as the Indian Rebellion of 1857.

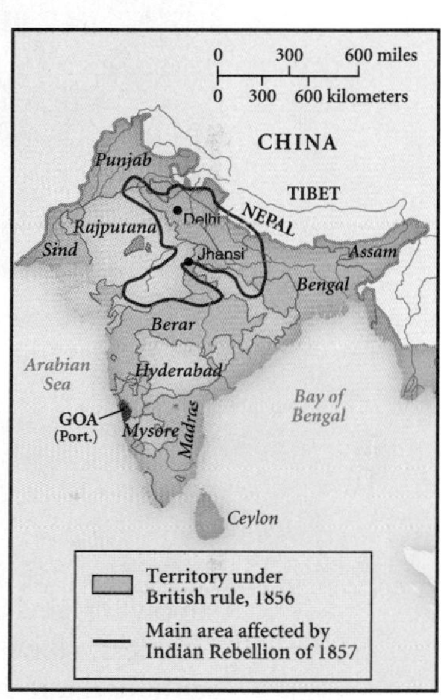

Indian Resistance, 1857

Simultaneously, uprisings erupted among displaced local rulers and their followers, who condemned "the tyranny and oppression of the infidel and treacherous English." Lakshmibai, the *rani* ("queen") of the state of Jhansi in central India, led a separate military revolt when the East India Company tried to take over her lands after her husband died. Even as the British brutally crushed the rebels, Indian nationalism was born. Victorious, the British government took direct control of India in 1858, and the British Parliament declared Queen Victoria the empress of India in 1876.

A system of rule took shape in which close to half a million South Asians, supervised by a few thousand British men, governed a region of once-independent states now called India. Local people continued to collect taxes and distribute patronage. Colonial rule meant both outright domination and subtle intervention in everyday life. For example, British taxes on high-quality Indian textiles aimed to divert the colonized Indian population away from domestically produced goods in favor of cheap British cottons. Artisans were directed instead to farm raw materials such as wheat, cotton, and jute to

An English View of the Indian Rebellion

Drawings such as this of the Indian Rebellion of 1857 show noble English families under savage attack by rebels. Artists emphasized the innocence of English victims and thus provided a rationale for the rule of superior Europeans over depraved non-Westerners. These drawings also united citizens around the expansion of the nation-state. *(The Granger Collection, New York—All rights reserved.)*

supply Britain's industry and feed its workers. Nevertheless, some Indians benefited from improved sanitation and medicine and chose to accept British arguments against Indian customs such as child marriage and *sati*—a widow who self-immolates on her husband's funeral pyre. Others found Europe's scientific values attractive and came to appreciate that British rule, ironically, brought a kind of unity to India's many separate princedoms, thus laying the foundation for an Indian nation. Soon the resulting nationalism would turn against British domination.

French Overseas Expansion French political expansion was similarly complex. The French government pushed to establish its dominion over Cochin China (modern southern Vietnam) in the 1860s. Missionaries in the area, ambitious French naval officers, and even some local peoples—much like Indian merchants and financiers—pulled the French government farther into the region. Like the British, the French brought improvements such as the Mekong Delta project, which increased the amount of cultivable land and spurred growth in the food supply. Sanitation and public health programs proved a mixed blessing, because they led to a rise in population that strained resources. Furthermore, landowners and French imperialists siphoned off most of the profits from economic improvement. The French also undertook a cultural mission to transform cities like Saigon with tree-lined boulevards and other signs of Western life similar to those of Paris. French literature, theater, and art were popular not only with colonial officials but also with upper-class local people.

In this age of Realpolitik, the Crimean War had shown the great powers the importance of the Mediterranean basin. Napoleon III, remembering his uncle's campaign in Egypt, took an interest in building the Suez Canal, which would connect the Mediterranean with the Red Sea and the Indian Ocean and thus dramatically shorten the route from Europe to Asia. Following the canal's completion in 1869, "canal fever" spread: Verdi composed the opera *Aïda* (set in ancient Egypt), and people across the West applied Egyptian designs to textiles, furniture, art, and even public monuments in cities.

The rest of the Mediterranean and the Ottoman Empire felt the heightened presence of the European powers. The French army had occupied all of Algeria by 1870, when the number of European immigrants to the region reached one-quarter million. French rule in Algeria, as elsewhere, was aided by local people's attraction to European goods and technology and by the opportunity to make money. Merchants and local leaders cooperated in building railroads, sought trade with the French, and sent their children to European-style schools. Other local peoples, however, resisted the invasions by continuing to attack soldiers and settlers. European-spread diseases killed many others; by 1872, the native population in Algeria had declined by more than 20 percent from five years earlier.

European Inroads in China Its vastness allowed China to escape complete takeover, but the Qing Empire was rapidly losing its position as the world's most prosperous economy. Traders and Christian missionaries from Europe made inroads for the Western powers. Missionaries directed the Christian message to a population of 430 million, which had nearly doubled since the last century, but defeat in the Opium War caused an economic slump and helped generate the mass movement known as the Taiping ("Heavenly Kingdom"). Headed by a leader who claimed to be the brother of Jesus, the Taiping's millions of adherents wanted an end to the ruling Qing dynasty, the expulsion of foreigners, more equal treatment of women, and land reform. By the mid-1850s, the Taiping controlled half of China. The threatened Qing regime promised the British and French greater influence in exchange for aid in defeating the Taiping. More than 20 million Chinese died in the resulting civil war (compared with 600,000 dead in the U.S. Civil War). When peace finally came in 1864, Western governments controlled much of the Chinese customs service and had virtually unlimited access to the country.

The Meiji Restoration in Japan Japan alone in East Asia was able to escape Western domination, but it did not escape Western influence. Through Dutch traders at Nagasaki, the Japanese had become keenly aware of the industrial, military, and commercial innovations taking place in the West. In 1854, the Japanese agreed to open the country to foreign trade; contacts with Europe had already given the Japanese a healthy appetite for Western goods, including the West's superior weaponry. Japanese reformers in 1867 overthrew a government that resisted change and in 1868 enacted the Meiji Restoration. The word *Meiji* pointed to the "enlightened rule" of the new emperor whose power reformers had restored. The goal was to combine "Western science and Eastern values" as a way of "making new"—hence, a combination of restoration and innovation. The new regime set the stage for Japan to become a modern, technologically powerful state free from Western control.

Challenging the Nation-State's Order at Home

Europeans did not simply sit by as the growing nation-state changed and often disrupted their lives. A better-informed urban working class protested the upheavals in everyday life caused when cities were ripped apart for improvements and when the growth of factories destroyed artisans' livelihoods. Political theorists such as Pierre-Joseph Proudhon and Karl Marx analyzed what was wrong with society, and their ideas spread among disgruntled citizens. Unions sprang up, calling for strikes and other actions against both employers and the government. In the spring of 1871, the people of Paris, blaming the centralized state for the French surrender to the Prussians, declared Paris a commune—a community of equals without bureaucrats and politicians. Reacting to the Paris Commune, the middle classes and politicians feared for the stability of the rising nation-state.

The Rise of Marxism New theories arose to explain the growing power of the nation-state and the spread of industry on which the state depended. Increasingly educated by public schools, urban workers frequented cafés and pubs to hear news and discuss economic and political events. After the post-1848 repression of worker organizations, unions gradually started to take shape, sometimes in secret because of continuing opposition from governments. Many of the most outspoken labor activists were artisans struggling to survive in the new industrializing climate. They were attracted at first by the ideas of former printer Pierre-Joseph Proudhon (1809–1865). In the 1840s, Proudhon proclaimed, "Property is theft," suggesting that property ownership robbed people of their rightful share of the earth's benefits. He opposed the centralized state and proposed that society be organized instead around natural groupings of men in artisans' workshops. (Women, he believed, should work in seclusion at home for their husbands' comfort.) These workshops and a central bank crediting each worker for his labor would replace government and would lead to a "mutualist" social organization.

As the nation-state expanded its power, workers were also drawn to **anarchism**, which maintained that the existence of the state was the root of social injustice. According to Russian nobleman and anarchist leader Mikhail Bakunin (1814–1876), the slightest infringement on freedom, especially by the central state and its laws, was unacceptable. Anarchism thus advocated the destruction of all state power. Its appeal grew as government grew in the second half of the nineteenth century.

Political theorist and labor organizer Karl Marx (1818–1883) opposed both mutualism and anarchism. These doctrines, he insisted, were emotional and wrongheaded, lacking the sound, scientific basis of his own theory, subsequently called **Marxism**. Marx's analysis, appearing most notably in *Das Kapital* (*Capital*), adopted the liberal idea, dating back to John Locke in the seventeenth century, that human existence was defined by the necessity to work to fulfill basic needs such as food, clothing, and shelter. Published between 1867 and 1894, *Das Kapital* was based on mathematical calculations of production and profit that would justify Realpolitik for the working classes. Marx held that the fundamental organization of any society, including its politics and culture, derived from the relationships arising from work or production. This idea, known as *materialism*, meant that the foundation of a society rested on class relationships—such as those between serf and medieval lord, slave and master, or worker and capitalist. Marx called the class relationships that developed around work the *mode of production*—for instance, feudalism, slavery, or capitalism. He rejected the liberal focus on individual rights and emphasized instead the unequal class relations caused by those who had taken from workers control of the means of production—that is, the capital, land, tools, or factories that allowed basic human needs to be met.

Marx, like the politicians around him, took a tough-minded and realistic look at the economy, discarding the romantic views of the utopian socialists. Unlike them, he saw struggle, not warmhearted cooperation, as the means for bringing about change. Workers' awareness of their oppression would produce class consciousness, he argued, leading them to revolt against their exploiters. Capitalism would be overthrown by these workers—the proletariat—who would then form a socialist society. Marx rejected the liberal Enlightenment view that society was basically harmonious, maintaining instead that social progress could occur only through conflict.

anarchism: The belief that people should not have government; it was popular among some peasants and workers in the last half of the nineteenth century and the first decades of the twentieth.

Marxism: A body of thought about the organization of production, social inequality, and the processes of revolutionary change as devised by the philosopher and economist Karl Marx.

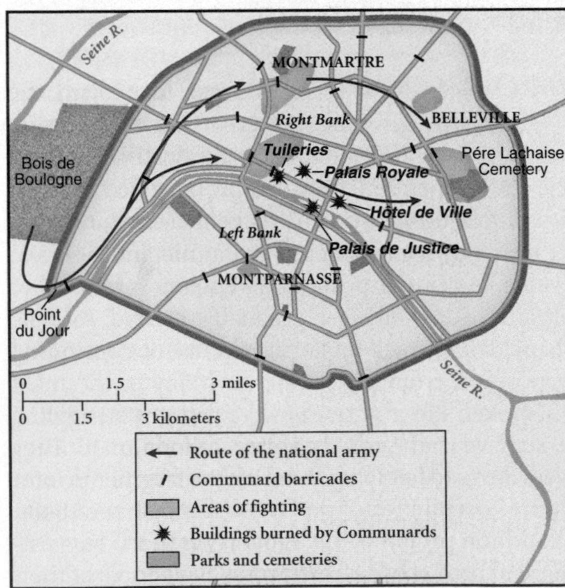

MAP 22.5 The Paris Commune, 1871
The war between the French government and the Paris Commune took place on the streets of Paris and resulted in widespread destruction of major buildings, most notably the Tuileries palace adjacent to the Louvre. Combatants destroyed many government records in what some saw as a civil war; bitterness, like destruction of property, was great on both sides.

The Paris Commune versus the French State

As the Franco-Prussian War ended, revolution and civil war erupted not only in Paris but also in other French cities—catching the attention of Marx as a sign that his predictions were coming true. As the Prussians laid siege to Paris in the winter of 1870–1871, causing death from starvation and bitter cold, Parisians rose up and demanded new republican liberties, new systems of work, and a more balanced distribution of power between the central government and localities. On March 28, 1871, to counter what they saw as the despotism of the centralized government, they declared themselves a self-governing commune (Map 22.5). One issue behind the unrest was the nation-state's takeover of city life. As urban renovation had displaced tens of thousands of workers, homelessness and general chaos had embittered many Parisians against the state. Citizens in other French municipalities also orga-

The Commune

A sympathetic artist chose a ferocious woman to represent the Paris Commune. He shows her defending the people of France by driving off politicians who had negotiated the disastrous peace treaty with Germany and who wanted to bring back kings and emperors. The artist depicts those selling out the nation as wasps. *(© Bibliothèque nationale, Paris, France/Giraudon/The Bridgeman Art Library International.)*

nized themselves in an attempt to form a decentralized state of independent, confederated communes run by local citizens, not bureaucrats.

In the Paris Commune's two months of existence, its forty-member council, its National Guard, and its many other improvised offices found themselves at cross-purposes. Trying to maintain "communal" instead of "national" values, Parisians quickly developed a wide array of political clubs, local ceremonies, and self-managed workshops. Women workers, for example, banded together to make National Guard uniforms on a cooperative rather than a for-profit basis. Beyond liberal political equality, the Commune proposed to liberate the worker and ensure "the absolute equality of women laborers." Thus, a *commune*—in contrast to a *republic*—was meant to bring about social revolution. Communards, however, often disagreed on how to change society. Mutualism, anticlericalism, feminism, socialism, and anarchism were but a few of the proposed routes to social justice.

In the meantime, the provisional government that succeeded the defeated Napoleon III struck back to reinstitute national order. It quickly stamped out similar uprisings in other French cities. On May 21, the army entered Paris. In a week of fighting, both Communards and the army set the city ablaze (the Communards did so to slow the progress of government troops) and both sides executed hostages. Ultimately, the well-supplied national army won. In the wake of victory, the army shot tens of thousands of citizens on the streets. Parisian rebels, one citizen commented, "deserved no better judge than a soldier's bullet."

In an age of growing national power, the Communards had promoted a kind of antistate in an age of rising state power. Soon a different interpretation of the Commune emerged: it was the work of the *pétroleuse* ("woman incendiary")—a case of frenzied women running amok through the streets. While revolutionary men became heroes in the history books, writers were soon blaming the burning of Paris on women—"shameless slatterns, half-naked women, who kindled courage and breathed life into arson."

Defeat in the Franco-Prussian War, the rise of the Paris Commune, and the civil war were all horrendous blows to the French state. Key to restoring order in France after 1870 were instilling family virtues, fortifying religion, and claiming that the

Commune had resulted from the disorder women caused when they left the domestic sphere to influence politics. Karl Marx disagreed: he analyzed the Commune as a class struggle of workers attacking the propertied capitalists. The centralized state grew larger, in his mind, to protect the interests of those wealthy citizens alone. In the struggle against the Commune, the nation-state once again showed its strengthening muscle. Executions and deportations by the thousands followed, and fear of workers spread across Europe.

REVIEW QUESTION How did Europe's expanding nation-states attempt to impose social order within and beyond Europe, and what resistance did they face?

The Culture of Social Order

Artists and writers of the mid-nineteenth century had complex reactions to the state's expanding reach and the economic growth that sustained it. After 1848, many artists and writers criticized the resulting political repression as well as—paradoxically—the extension of the right to vote to working-class men. They saw daily life as filled with commercial values and organized by mindless officials. Ordinary people no longer appeared heroic, as they had during the revolutionary years. "How tired I am of the ignoble workman, the inept bourgeois, the stupid peasant, and the odious priest," wrote the French novelist Gustave Flaubert. Rejecting romanticism, he described ordinary people in a harsh new style called **realism**. Intellectuals of the time proposed scientific theories that also took a cold, hard look at human life in society and used their new insights to challenge fervent religious belief. Theirs was a detached point of view similar to that applied by statesmen to politics.

The Arts Confront Social Reality

Culture helped the cause of national unity. A hungry reading public devoured biographies of political leaders, past and present, and credited daring heroes with creating the triumphant nation-state. As the development of schooling spread literacy, all classes of readers responded to the mid-nineteenth-century novel and to an increasing number of artistic, scientific, and natural history exhibitions sponsored by the nation-state. While exalting hard-headed heroes of war and peace, citizens came to appreciate the artistic style called realism and, more generally, to embrace the shared national heritage they had begun learning about in school.

The Realist Novel In response to the craving for realism—that is, true-to-life portrayals of society without romantic or idealistic overtones—a well-financed press and commercially minded publishers produced an age of best sellers. Newspapers published the novels of Charles Dickens in serial form, and each installment attracted buyers eager for the latest plot twist. Drawn from contemporary English society, Dickens's characters included starving orphans, grasping lawyers, greedy bankers, and ruthless opportunists. *Hard Times* (1854) depicts the grinding poverty and ill health of workers alongside the heartlessness of businessmen. Novelist **George Eliot** (the pen name of Mary Ann Evans) deeply probed private, real-life dilemmas in *The Mill on the Floss* (1860) and *Middlemarch* (1871–1872). Describing rural society—high and low—Eliot allowed her readers to see one another's predicaments, wherever they lived. She knew the pain of ordinary life from her own experience: despite her fame, she was a social outcast because she lived with a married man. Popular novels that showed a hard reality helped form a shared culture among people in distant parts of a nation much as state institutions did.

French writers also scorned dreams of utopian, trouble-free societies and ideal beauty. Gustave Flaubert's novel *Madame Bovary* (1857) tells the story of a doctor's wife who longs to escape her provincial surroundings. Filled with romantic fantasies, she has two love affairs to escape her boredom, becomes hopelessly indebted buying gifts for her lovers, and commits suicide by swallowing arsenic. *Madame Bovary* scandalized French society with its frank picture of women's sexuality, but it attracted a wide readership. Poet Charles-Pierre Baudelaire, called satanic by his critics, wrote explicitly about sex. In his 1857 collection, *Les Fleurs du mal* (*Flowers of Evil*), he expressed drug- and alcohol-induced passions—some focused on the brown body of his

---

realism: An artistic style that arose in the mid-nineteenth century and was dedicated to depicting society realistically without romantic or idealistic overtones.

George Eliot: The pen name of English novelist Mary Ann Evans (1819–1880), who described the harsh reality of many ordinary people's lives in her works.

African mistress—and spun out visions that critics condemned as perverse. French authorities brought charges of obscenity against both Flaubert and Baudelaire. At issue was social and artistic order: "Art without rules is no longer art," maintained the prosecutor.

During the era of Alexander II's Great Reforms, Russian writers debated whether western European values were harming Russian culture. Adopting one viewpoint, Ivan Turgenev created a powerful novel of Russian life, *Fathers and Sons* (1862), a story of nihilistic children rejecting not only parental authority but also their parents' spiritual values in favor of science and facts. Fyodor Dostoevsky, in contrast, portrayed nihilists as dark, ridiculous, and neurotic. His novels made Turgenev look like a soft-headed romantic. The highly intelligent characters in Dostoevsky's *Crime and Punishment* (1866) are personally tormented and condemned to lead absurd, even criminal lives. Dostoevsky used antiheroes to emphasize spirituality and traditional Russian values but added a "realistic" spin by planting such values in ordinary, often seedy people. Just as people were drawn together by the innovations of the nation-state, the Russian public was drawn together in discussing these novels and the issues they raised about Russian identity.

Age of Great Books

1851	Auguste Comte, *System of Positive Politics*
1852	Harriet Beecher Stowe, *Uncle Tom's Cabin*
1854	Charles Dickens, *Hard Times*
1857	Gustave Flaubert, *Madame Bovary*; Charles Baudelaire, *Les Fleurs du mal*
1859	Charles Darwin, *On the Origin of Species*; John Stuart Mill, *On Liberty*
1862	Ivan Turgenev, *Fathers and Sons*
1866	Fyodor Dostoevsky, *Crime and Punishment*
1867	Karl Marx, *Das Kapital*
1869	John Stuart Mill, *The Subjection of Women*
1871–1872	George Eliot, *Middlemarch*

Painting | While writers of realism depended on sales to thousands of readers, painters usually depended on government support. Leaders such as Prince Albert of Great Britain actively patronized the arts and purchased works for official collections and for themselves. Having their artwork chosen for display at government-sponsored exhibitions was another way for artists to earn a living. Officially appointed juries selected works of art to be exhibited and then chose prizewinners from among them. Hundreds of thousands from all social classes attended, though not all could afford to buy the art.

After the revolutions of 1848, artists began rejecting the romantic idealizing of ordinary folk or grand historic events even though government purchasers continued to favor these topics. Instead, painters like Gustave Courbet portrayed groaning laborers at backbreaking work because, as he stated, an artist should "never permit sentiment to overthrow logic." The renovated city, artists found, had become a visual spectacle; its wide new boulevards served as a stage on which urban residents performed. *Universal Exhibition* (1867) by Édouard Manet used the world's fair of 1867 as its background; figures from all social classes promenaded in the foreground, gazing at the Paris scene and observing one another to learn correct modern behavior. Manet also broke with romantic conventions of the nude. His *Olympia* (1865) depicts a white courtesan lying on her bed, attended by a black woman (see the illustration on page 750). This disregard for the classical tradition of showing women in mythical or idealized settings was too much for the critics: "A sort of female gorilla," one wrote of *Olympia*, as debate raged. Shocking at first, graphic portrayals that shattered romantic illusions were a feature of realism and the subject of discussion among a broad public.

Opera | Unlike most of the visual arts, opera was commercially profitable, accessible to most classes of society, and thus an effective means of reaching the nineteenth-century public. Verdi used musical theater to contrast noble ideals with the deadly effects of power and the lure of passion with the need for social order. The German Richard Wagner, the most musically innovative composer of the era, hoped to revolutionize opera by fusing music and drama to arouse the audience's fear, awe, and engagement with his productions. A gigantic cycle of four operas, *The Ring of the Nibelungen* reshaped ancient German myths into a modern, nightmarish story of a world doomed by its obsessive pursuit of money and power and saved only through unselfish love. His opera *The Mastersingers of Nuremberg* (*Die Meistersinger von Nürnberg*), composed between 1862 and 1867, was a tribute to German culture. The piece was said to be implicitly anti-Semitic because of its rejection of influences other than German ones in the arts. Wagner's flair for publicity and musical innovation made him a major force in philosophy, politics, and the arts across Europe. To his fellow citizens, however, his operas stood for Germany.

Daumier, *The Burden*
Artists painted stark images of ordinary people as they struggled to survive in an industrializing age. Despite romantic views of a secluded separate sphere for women that was protected from life's realities, the majority of women hardly enjoyed such an existence, as shown by this depiction of a weighted-down working woman and her child. Daumier was one of the artists who captured that reality. *(National Gallery, Prague, Czech Republic / photo by Erich Lessing / Art Resource, NY.)*

A Realist View of the Nude
Manet's *Olympia* (1865) was one of the most shocking works of art of its day. The central woman is not glamorously dressed or posed erotically; rather, she stares candidly and boldly at the viewer. The black maid offers the woman—obviously a courtesan—flowers from an admirer. This scene was far too modern in its style and subject matter for most critics. *(Musée d'Orsay, Paris, France / Giraudon / The Bridgeman Art Library International.)*

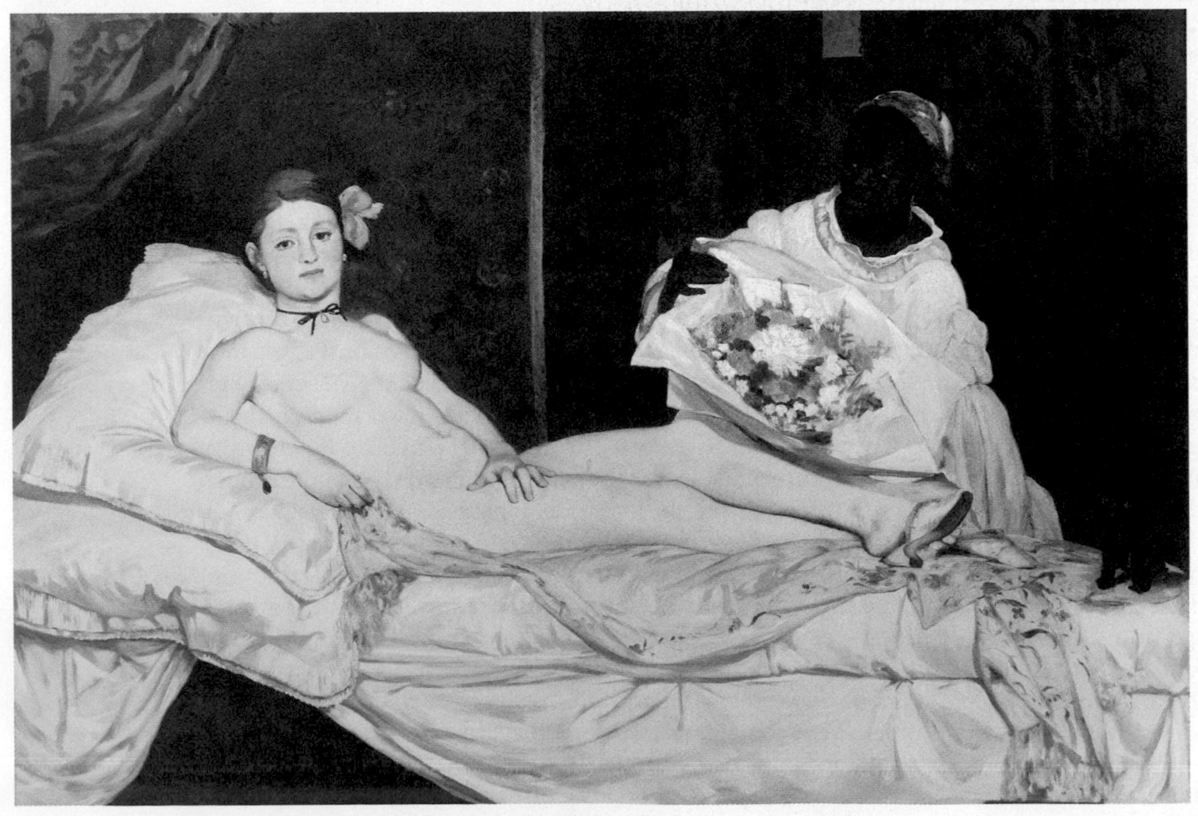

All of the arts, no matter how controversial, shaped the cultural attitudes of the decades 1850–1870. Employing the realist values of the nation builders, the arts provided visions that helped unite isolated individuals into a public with a shared, if debated, cultural experience. Artists both implicitly (like George Eliot) and more explicitly (like Richard Wagner) promoted nation building even as they experimented with new forms.

Religion and National Order

The expansion of state power set the stage for clashes over the role of organized religion in the nation-state. Should religion have the same hold on government and public life as in the past, thus competing with loyalty to the nation? In the 1850s, many politicians supported religious institutions and attended public church rituals because they were another source of order. Simultaneously, some nation builders, intellectuals, and economic liberals came to reject the religious worldview of established churches, particularly Roman Catholicism, as harmful to the nation because it was based in faith, not reason. Bismarck was one of those who believed that religious loyalties slowed the growth of nationalist sentiment.

Bismarck mounted a full-blown **Kulturkampf** ("culture war") against religion. The German government expelled the Jesuits from Germany in 1872, increased state power over the clergy in Prussia in 1873, and introduced a civil ceremony as an obligatory part of marriage in 1875. Bismarck had bragged, "I am the master of Germany in all but name," but he miscalculated his ability to manipulate politics. The pope fought back, sending a public letter to bishops to resist Bismarck's attack: "One must obey God more than men," he ordered. German Catholics rebelled against policies of religious repression as part of nation building, and even conservative Protestants thought Bismarck wrongheaded in attacking religion. Competition between church and state for power and influence heated up in the age of Realpolitik.

Catholic Reaction The Catholic church felt assaulted by the spread across Europe of rational and scientific thought that appeared to be replacing religious faith. It saw nation building in Italy and Germany as competition for people's traditional loyalty to Catholicism. In addition, nation builders had extended liberal rights to Jews, whom many Christians considered enemies. Attacking changing values, Pope Pius IX issued *The Syllabus of Errors* (1864), which found fault "with progress, with liberalism, and with modern civilization." In 1870, the First Vatican Council approved the dogma of papal infallibility. This teaching proclaimed that the pope spoke divinely revealed truth on issues of morality and faith. Eight years later, a new pope, Leo XIII, began reconciling the church to modern politics by encouraging up-to-date scholarship in Catholic institutes and universities and by accepting aspects of representative democracy. Leo's ideas marked a dramatic turn, ending the Kulturkampf between church and state and making it easier for the faithful to be both Catholic and patriotic.

Religion continued to have powerful popular appeal, but the place of organized religion in society was changing. While many in the upper and middle classes and most of the peasantry remained faithful, church attendance declined among workers and artisans. There was a religious gender gap, too. Women's spiritual beliefs became more intense, with both Roman Catholic and Russian Orthodox women's religious orders increasing in size and number; men, by contrast, were falling away from religious devotion. Many urban Jews abandoned religious practices and assimilated instead to secular, national cultures. The social composition of the faithful had come to take a distinctly different shape from the days when religion included everyone.

In 1854, the pope's announcement of the doctrine of the Immaculate Conception (stating that Mary, alone among all humans, had been born without original sin) was followed by an outburst of popular religious fervor, especially among women. In 1858, a young peasant girl, Bernadette Soubirous, began having visions of the Virgin Mary at Lourdes in southern France. In these visions, Mary told Soubirous to drink from the ground, at which point a spring appeared. Crowds, mostly of women, flocked to Lourdes, believing that its waters could cure their ailments. In 1867, less than ten years later, a new railroad line to Lourdes enabled millions of pilgrims to visit the shrine on church-organized trips. The Catholic church thus showed that it, too, could use such modern means as railroads, shopping centers, and medical verifications of miraculous cures to make the religious experience more up-to-date. Traditional institutions like churches began taking steps to make themselves as effective as the nation-state.

Kulturkampf: Literally, "culture war"; a term used in the 1870s by German chancellor Otto von Bismarck to describe his fight to weaken the power of the Catholic church.

The Challenge from Natural Science

At about the time of Soubirous's vision, the English naturalist **Charles Darwin** (1809–1882) published *On the Origin of Species* (1859). In this book and in later writings, Darwin argued that life had taken shape over countless millions of years before humans existed and that human life was but the result of this slow development, called evolution. For many, this theory directly challenged the Judeo-Christian dogma that humanity was the unique creation of God. Instead of God miraculously bringing the universe and all life into being in six days as described in the Bible, Darwin held that life developed from lower forms through a primal battle for survival and through the sexual selection of mates — a process he called natural selection. A respectable Victorian gentleman, Darwin shockingly announced in later writing that the Bible gave a "manifestly false history of the world." Darwin's theories also undermined certain liberal, secular beliefs. Enlightenment principles, for example, had not only glorified nature as tranquil and noble but also viewed human beings as essentially rational. The theory of natural selection, in which the fittest survive, suggested a different kind of human society, one composed of warlike individuals and groups constantly fighting one another to triumph over hostile surroundings.

Charles Darwin: The English naturalist (1809–1882) who popularized the theory of evolution by means of natural selection and thereby challenged the biblical story of creation.

Darwin's findings and other innovative biological research placed religious views of reproduction under attack. Working with pea plants in his monastery garden in the 1860s, the Austrian monk Gregor Mendel (1822–1884) discovered the principles of heredity, from which the science of genetics later developed. Investigation into the female reproductive cycle led German scientists to discover the principle of spontaneous ovulation — the automatic release of the egg by the ovary independent of sexual intercourse. This discovery caused theorists to conclude that men had strong sexual drives because reproduction depended on their

"Gentlemen, We Are Descended from Monkeys," Spain, Late Nineteenth Century

Darwin's scientific ideas aroused anger, admiration, and even mirth, as shown in this engraving some decades after the publication of his major works. As you consider this image, what message would you say the artist is trying to convey about evolution? *(The Art Archive/Bibliothèque des Arts Décoratifs/Alfredo Dagli Orti.)*

sexual arousal. In contrast, the spontaneous release of the egg each month independent of arousal indicated that women were passive and lacked sexual feeling.

Many other ideas disturbed the status quo. Even before Darwin, the influential writer Herbert Spencer (1820–1903) had written that the "unfit" should be allowed to perish in the name of progress — thus challenging the biblical teaching that the poor were valued. On these grounds Spencer opposed public education and any other attempt to soften the harshness of the struggle for existence. Darwin continued this line of argument when he claimed that white European men in the nineteenth century were wealthier and better because more highly evolved than white women or people of color. Despite recognizing a common ancestor for all humans, Darwin held that people of color, or "lower races," were far behind whites in intelligence and civilization. As for women, one could observe that they were in a lower state because any individual man achieved "a higher eminence in whatever he takes up." A school of thought known as Social Darwinism grew out of Darwin's and Spencer's ideas. In the years to come, Social Darwinists used their own version of evolutionary theory to lobby against traditional Christian charity and fairness and instead to promote racist, sexist, and other discriminatory policies as a way of strengthening the nation-state.

From the Natural Sciences to Social Science

In an age influenced by Realpolitik, Darwin's revolutionary thought was part of a quest to find alternatives to the idea that the social order was created by God. French thinker Auguste Comte (1798–1857) developed **positivism** — a theory claiming that careful study of facts would generate accurate and useful, or "positive," laws of society. Comte's *System of Positive Politics, or Treatise on Sociology* (1851) proposed that social scientists construct knowledge of the political order as they would an understanding of the natural world — that is, through observation and objective study. This idea inspired people to believe they could solve the problems resulting from economic and social changes. To accomplish this goal, tough-minded reformers founded study groups and scientifically oriented associations to dig up social facts such as statistics on poverty or the conditions of working-class life. Comte encouraged women's participation in reform because he deemed "womanly" compassion and love as fundamental to social harmony as scientific public policy was. Positivism led not only to women's increased public activism but also to the development of the social sciences in this period. Sociology was primary among the influential new disciplines that brought science and a new realism to the study of human society.

The celebrated English philosopher John Stuart Mill (1806–1873) used Comte's theories to advocate widespread reform and mass education. In his political treatise *On Liberty* (1859), Mill advocated the improvement of society generally, but he also expressed concern that superior people not be brought down by the will of the masses. Influenced not only by Comte but also by his wife, Harriet Taylor Mill, he argued for women's rights and introduced a woman suffrage bill into the House of Commons after her death. The bill's defeat led Mill to publish *The Subjection of Women* (1869), a work summarizing his studies with his wife. Translated into many languages and influential in eastern Europe, Scandinavia, and the Americas, *The Subjection of Women* showed the family as a despotic institution, lacking modern values such as rights and freedom. Mill called women's cheerful obedience in marriage a sham. To make a woman appear "not a forced slave, but a willing one," he said, she was trained from childhood not to value her own talent and independence but to welcome her own "submission" and "control" by men. Critiquing the century's basic beliefs about women's inferiority, *The Subjection of Women* became an internationally celebrated guide for a growing movement committed to obtaining basic rights for women.

The progressive side of Mill's social thought was soon lost in a flood of Social Darwinist theories and became one among several visions of social order believed to be scientific and thus true. The theories of Mill, Comte, Darwin, and others influenced later national debates over policy in the West. Inspired by the social sciences, policymaking came to rely on statistics and fact-gathering to produce realistic appraisals for the purpose of building strong, unified nations.

positivism: A theory developed in the mid-nineteenth century that the study of facts would generate accurate, or "positive," laws of society and that these laws could, in turn, help in the formulation of policies and legislation.

REVIEW QUESTION How did cultural expression and scientific and social thought help produce the hardheaded and realistic values of the mid-nineteenth century?

Conclusion

Throughout modern history, the development of nation-states has been neither inevitable nor uniform nor peaceful. This was especially true in the nineteenth century, when ambitious politicians, shrewd monarchs, and determined bureaucrats used a variety of methods and policies to transform very different countries into effective nation-states. Nation building was most dramatic in Germany and Italy, where states unified through military force and where people of opposing political opinions ultimately agreed that national unity should be the primary goal. Compelled by military defeat to shake off centuries of tradition, the Austrian and Russian monarchs instituted reforms as a way of keeping their systems in place. The Habsburg Empire became a dual monarchy, an arrangement that gave the Hungarians virtual home rule and raised the level of disunity. Reforms in Russia left the authoritarian monarchy intact and only partially transformed the social order.

After decades of romantic fervor, no-nonsense realism in politics — Realpolitik — became a much touted principle. Proponents of realism such as Darwin and Marx developed theories disturbing to those who maintained an Enlightenment faith in social and political harmony. Realist novels and artworks jarred polite society, and, like the operas of Verdi, portrayed dilemmas of the times. Growing government administrations set policies that were meant to bring order but often brought disorder, including the destruction of entire neighborhoods and violence toward people in far-off lands. In the long term, schooling taught the lower classes to be orderly citizens, and urban renewal ultimately improved cities and public health to complement nation building.

Objections arose to the expanding power of the nation-state. The Indian Rebellion of 1857 against Britain and the Paris Commune of 1871 against the French state were but two examples where violent actions raised difficult questions about nation-building methods. How far should the power of the state extend in both domestic and international affairs? Would nationalism be a force for war or for peace? In the face of state power, would ordinary people have any say in their destiny? As these issues ripened, the next decades saw extraordinary economic advances and an unprecedented surge in Europe's global power — much of it the result of successes in nation building.

FOR FURTHER EXPLORATION

- **For additional primary-source material from this period**, see *Sources of the Making of the West*, Fourth Edition.
- **For Web sites, images, and documents related to topics in this chapter**, visit *Make History* at bedfordstmartins.com/hunt.

MAPPING THE WEST

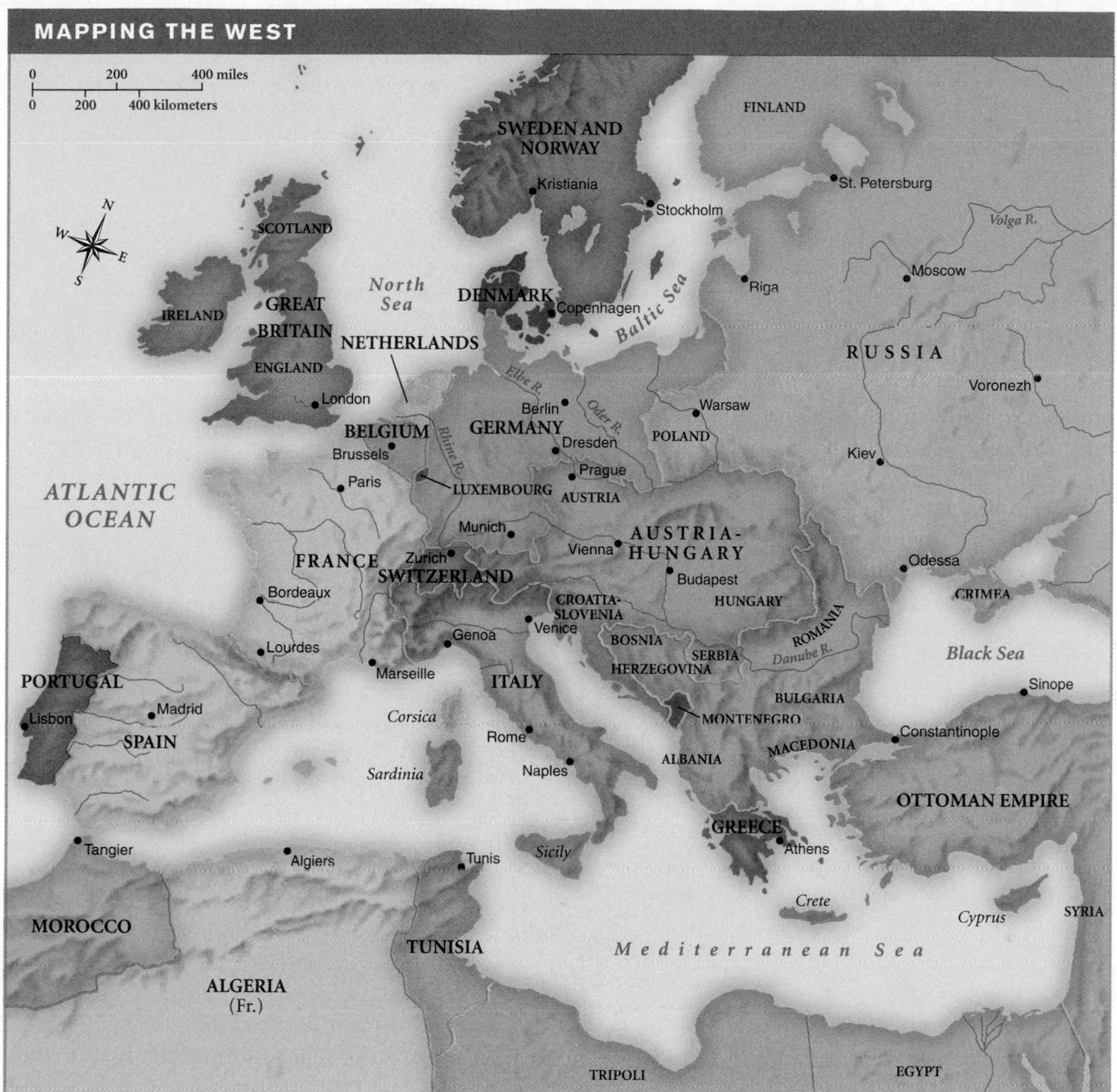

Europe and the Mediterranean, 1871

European nation-states consolidated their power by building unified state structures and by developing the means for the diverse peoples within their borders to become socially and culturally integrated. Nation-states were also rapidly expanding outside their boundaries, extending their economic and political reach. North Africa and the Middle East—parts of the declining Ottoman Empire—particularly appealed to European governments because of their resources and their potential for further European settlement. They offered a gateway to the rest of the world. | **Compare this map of Europe with that from two decades earlier (page 717) to explain the progress of nation building. What aspects of nation building do not appear on this map?**

Chapter 22 Review

Online Study Guide bedfordstmartins.com/hunt

Key Terms and People

In the grid below, identify the term or person and explain its historical significance. (To do this exercise online, go to bedfordstmartins.com/hunt.)

Term	Who or What & When	Why It Matters
Realpolitik (p. 721)		
Alexander II (p. 725)		
Florence Nightingale (p. 725)		
mir (p. 727)		
Russification (p. 728)		
nation-state (p. 729)		
Camillo di Cavour (p. 730)		
Otto von Bismarck (p. 732)		
dual monarchy (p. 736)		
Pan-Slavism (p. 736)		
anarchism (p. 746)		
Marxism (p. 746)		
realism (p. 748)		
George Eliot (p. 748)		
Kulturkampf (p. 751)		
Charles Darwin (p. 752)		
positivism (p. 753)		

Review Questions

1. What were the main results of the Crimean War?
2. What role did warfare play in the various nineteenth-century nation-building efforts?
3. How did Europe's expanding nation-states attempt to impose social order within and beyond Europe, and what resistance did they face?
4. How did cultural expression and scientific and social thought help produce the hard-headed and realistic values of the mid-nineteenth century?

Making Connections

1. What were the main methods of nation building in the mid-nineteenth century, and how did they differ from those of state building in the early modern period?
2. How did realism in social thought break with Enlightenment values?
3. In what ways did religion emerge as an issue (both within and outside Europe) during the course of nation building?
4. How was the Paris Commune related to earlier revolutions in France? How did it differ from them? How was it related to nation building?

Important Events

Date	Event	Date	Event
1850s–1860s	Positivism, Darwinism become influential	1867	Second Reform Bill in England; Austro-Hungarian monarchy
1850s–1870s	Realism in the arts	1868	Meiji Restoration begins in Japan
1853–1856	Crimean War	1869	Suez Canal opens
1857	British-led forces suppress Indian Rebellion	1869–1871	Women's colleges founded at Cambridge University
1861	Victor Emmanuel declared king of a unified Italy; abolition of serfdom in Russia	1870–1871	Franco-Prussian War
1861–1865	U.S. Civil War	1871	German Empire proclaimed at Versailles; self-governing Paris Commune established

- Consider three events: **Positivism, Darwinism become influential (1850s–1860s)**, **Realism in the arts (1850s–1870s)**, and **German Empire proclaimed at Versailles (1871)**. How is this era's quest for practicality, order and stability shown in each of these events?

SUGGESTED REFERENCES

Nation building took many forms in the nineteenth century, including wars, urban improvement, mythmaking, and the development of scientific and realistic attitudes—all of these themes are found in the books below.

Barnes, David S. *The Great Stink of Paris and the Nineteenth-Century Struggle against Filth and Germs.* 2006.

Berra, Tim M. *Charles Darwin: The Concise Story of an Extraordinary Man.* 2009.

Blackbourn, David. *The Conquest of Nature: Water, Landscape, and the Making of Modern Germany.* 2006.

Gross, Michael B. *The War against Catholicism: Liberalism and the Anti-Catholic Imagination in Nineteenth-Century Germany.* 2005.

Heretz, Leonid. *Russia on the Eve of Modernity: Popular Religion and Traditional Culture under the Last Tsars.* 2008.

Kaufman, Suzanne. *Consuming Visions: Mass Culture and the Lourdes Shrine.* 2005.

Parker, Kate, and Julia Shone, eds. *The Austro-Hungarian Dual Monarchy, 1867–1918.* 2008.

Reid, Brian Holden. *The Civil War and the Wars of the Nineteenth Century.* 2006.

Riall, Lucy. *Garibaldi: The Invention of a Hero.* 2007.

Roy, Tapti. *The Raj of the Rani.* 2007.

*Seacole, Mary. *Wonderful Adventures of Mrs. Seacole in Many Lands.* 1857.

Unowsky, Daniel L. *The Pomp and Politics of Patriotism: Imperial Celebrations in Habsburg Austria, 1848–1916.* 2005.

The Victorian Web: http://www.victorianweb.org

Wetzel, David. *A Duel of Giants: Bismarck, Napoleon III, and the Origins of the Franco-Prussian War.* 2001.

Wirtschafter, Elise Kimerling. *Russia's Age of Serfdom 1649–1861.* 2008.

*Primary source.

CHAPTER

23

Empire, Industry, and Everyday Life

1870–1890

In the mid-1880s, Frieda von Bülow, a young German woman of aristocratic birth, joined several activist groups interested in promoting German colonial expansion in Africa. Like other women in these pro-imperial organizations, von Bülow was eager to help German settlers—and even some Africans—in East Africa, which Germany was in the process of colonizing. She also met adventurous men such as Carl Peters, a nationalist zealot and leading figure in imperialist circles. As Europeans competed to take over the African continent, von Bülow and Peters headed for Zanzibar and other distant cities not only to conquer them but also to carry on a passionate romance. Once in Africa, von Bülow basked in the freedom from her society's restrictions on women and developed an even stronger sense of German superiority in comparison to local African peoples. For his part, Peters followed his usual pattern of tricking Africans into giving up their lands and bullying them, using guns, rape, and other violence to get his way. Peters seduced one African woman and then had her executed because of her relationship with another man. Though Peters's womanizing caused von Bülow to break up with him, she maintained both her racism and her German nationalism, learning to shoot a gun on behalf of colonial conquest, writing popular novels about empire and white superiority, and setting up a plantation in Southeast Africa.

European Immigrants Arriving in New York
This calm image of an immigrant ship arriving in New York harbor hardly captures the emotions the immigrants had (as we know from their letters and diaries) on leaving their communities and facing an unknown life in the United States or other parts of the Western Hemisphere. Many came from agricultural regions and would soon be the labor behind the advance of industry; others would become settlers, driving out Native Americans and thus becoming agents of empire. *(The Granger Collection, New York—All rights reserved.)*

Von Bülow and Peters were just two of the tens of thousands of Europeans pursuing imperial adventure, as the search for lands to colonize reached a feverish pitch after the 1870s. Those involved in imperialism had a variety of motives and, like Peters, were often swaggering and violent. The rapid expansion of Western takeovers was called the "new imperialism" because the race for empire now aimed at political rather than mere economic power. Europeans had been acquiring global territory since the late fifteenth century; the new imperialism was actually the final gulp in this process. In their rush for empire, Europeans like Frieda von Bülow and Carl Peters worked to control whole societies instead of dominating coastal trade until, by the beginning of the twentieth century, Western nations claimed jurisdiction over vast stretches of the world's surface. Beyond political control, Europeans tried to stamp other continents with European-style place-names, architecture, clothing, languages, and domestic customs. They used culture to secure their empires just as they used it to forge the nation-state.

Millions of people traveled vast distances in the nineteenth century—a time of greatly increased mobility and migration, much of which was made possible by an expansion of industry and colonization. Some migrated temporarily to serve in colonial governments or to find business opportunities. Others relocated permanently within Europe or outside it. In search of a better life, they migrated to Australia and to North and South America. Such migration changed the everyday life of both Europeans and non-Europeans: it uprooted tens of millions of people, disrupted social and family networks, and often inflicted terrible violence on native peoples dislocated by European migrants.

The decades from 1870 to 1890 were also an era of expanding industry in the West. Empire and industry fed on each other as raw materials from conquered areas supplied Western factories and as innovations in weaponry, transportation, medicine, and communication allowed imperialism to thrive. Manufacturing soared in the West as industrialization spread from Britain to central and eastern Europe and brought a continuous new supply of products to the market. A growing appetite for these products, many of them for household consumption, changed the fabric of everyday life for Europeans. New industry attracted people to cities, where common experiences of neighborhood and work life drew them closer together. As they became more educated and enjoyed a mushrooming variety of colonial goods, people learned to take pride in their nations' conquests. Urban workers began demanding greater participation in the political process. Proud Europeans brimmed with confidence and hope, while the grimmer aspects of empire and industrialization played themselves out in distant colonies, urban slums, and declining standards of living in rural areas.

Marianne North, *Pitcher Plant*
Wealthy Europeans increasingly traveled overseas in the quest for knowledge and adventure. As the West prospered, travel and world tourism did, too. An amateur artist, Marianne North initially gained an audience for her scientific drawings, reports, and specimens only because she traveled in the "best circles." Scientists later prized her drawings, like this one of a pitcher plant. *(Reproduced with the kind permission of the Director and the Board of Trustees, Royal Botanic Gardens, Kew.)*

1860s–1890s Impressionism flourishes in the arts; absorption of Asian influences

1870s–1890s Vast emigration from Europe continues; the new imperialism

1871 Franco-Prussian War ends

1873 Extended economic recession begins with global impact

1876 British Parliament declares Victoria empress; invention of telephone

1878 Treaty of San Stefano

1879 Dual Alliance formed between Germany and Austria-Hungary

1860s | 1870 | 1875 | 1880

CHAPTER FOCUS How were imperial conquest and industrial advances related, and how did they affect Western society, culture, and politics in the late nineteenth century?

The New Imperialism

Imperialism surged in the last third of the nineteenth century. Industrial demand for raw materials and heated business rivalry for new markets fueled competition for territory in Africa and Asia, and European nations, the United States, and Japan now aimed to rule sizable portions of the world directly. The British government declared itself an empire in 1876 after taking control of India from the East India Company, and other governments followed the British model. National pride also grew with imperial expansion. "Nations are not great except for the activities they undertake," declared a French advocate of imperialism in 1885. Conquering foreign territory and developing wealth through industry appeared to heap glory on the nation-state. Although some missionaries and reformers involved in the new imperialism aimed to spread Western religions and culture as a benefit to colonized peoples, the expansion of the West increased the subjugation of those peoples, inflicted violence on them, and radically altered their lives.

Taming the Mediterranean

European countries had always viewed the African and Asian shores of the Mediterranean as areas where they could profit through trade and investment. In the late nineteenth century, they aimed for political control of the region as well. Egypt, a convenient and profitable stop on the way to Asia, was an early target. Modernizing rulers had made Cairo into a bustling metropolis with lively commercial and manufacturing enterprises. Egyptians also increased their production of raw materials, such as cotton for European textile mills. Europeans invested heavily in the region, first in ventures such as building the Suez Canal in the 1860s, then in laying thousands of miles of railroad track, improving harbors, creating telegraph systems, and finally and most important, loaning money at exorbitant rates of interest.

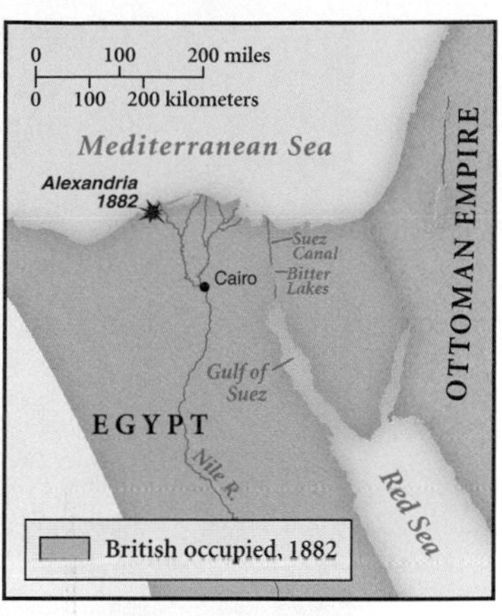

The Suez Canal and British Invasion of Egypt, 1882

In 1879, the British and the French took over the Egyptian treasury, allegedly to guarantee profits from their investments and the repayment of loans. In 1882, they invaded the country with the excuse of squashing Egyptian nationalists who protested the takeover of the treasury. The British next seized control of the government as a whole and forcibly reshaped the Egyptian economy from a system based on multiple crops that maintained the country's self-sufficiency to one that emphasized the production of a few crops—mainly cotton, raw silk, wheat, and rice—that cheaply fed both European manufacturing and the European working classes. Businessmen from the colonial powers, Egyptian landowners, and local merchants profited from these agricultural changes, while the bulk of the rural population barely eked out an existence.

Claiming a need to protect its stake in Algeria, France occupied neighboring Tunisia in 1881. Farther to the east, businessmen from Britain, France, and Germany flooded Asia Minor and the Middle East with cheap goods, driving artisans from their trades and into low-paid work building railroads or processing tobacco. Instead of basing wage rates on gender (as they did at home), Europeans used ethnicity and religion, paying Muslims less than Christians, and Arabs less than other ethnic

1881 Tsar Alexander II assassinated; France occupies Tunisia

1882 Triple Alliance formed between Germany, Austria-Hungary, and Italy; Britain invades Egypt

1882–1884 Bismarck sponsors social welfare legislation

1884 British Parliament passes the Reform Act, doubling size of male electorate

1884–1885 European nations carve up Africa at Berlin conference

1885 Invention of workable gasoline engine; formation of Indian National Congress

1889 Japan adopts constitution based on European models; socialists meet in Paris and establish Second International

1891 Construction of Trans Siberian Railroad begins

1885 1890

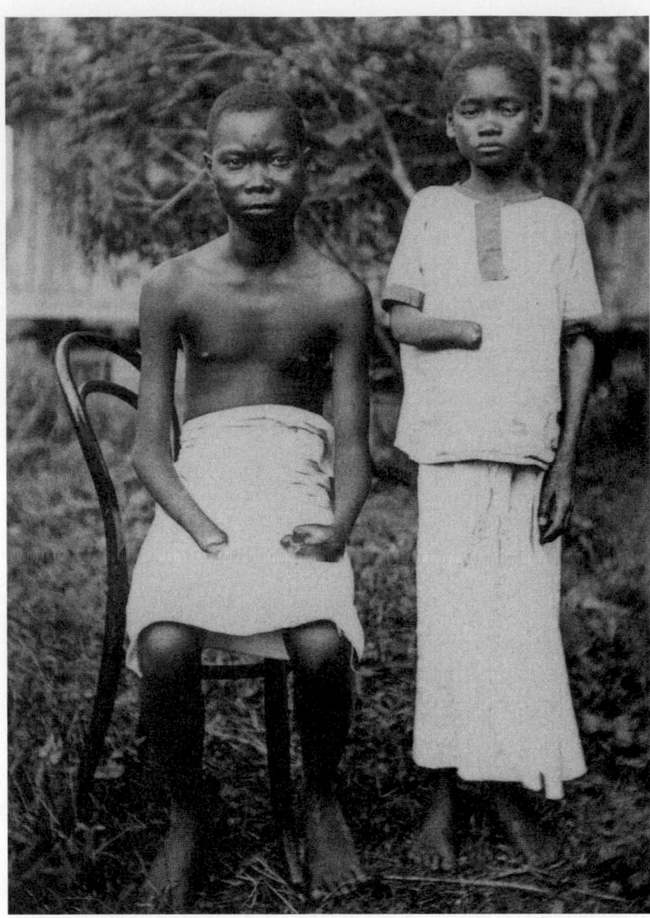

The Violence of Colonization
King Leopold II, ruler of the Belgian Congo, was so greedy and ruthless that his agents squeezed the last drop of rubber and other resources from local peoples. Missionaries reported and photographed such atrocities as the killing of workers whose quotas were even slightly short or the amputation of hands for the same offense. Belgian agents collected amputated hands and sent them to government officials to show Leopold that they were enforcing his kind of discipline. *(Anti-Slavery International.)*

groups. Such practices planted the seeds for anticolonial movements and long-lasting hatred.

The Scramble for Africa

After the British takeover of the Egyptian government, Europeans turned their attention to sub-Saharan Africa. In the past, contact between Europe and Africa had principally involved the trade of African slaves for manufactured goods from around the world. By this time, however, the European slave trade had virtually ended and the Europeans' objective had shifted to acquiring Africa's raw materials, such as palm oil, cotton, metals, diamonds, cocoa, and rubber. Additionally, Britain wanted the southern and eastern coasts of Africa for stopover ports on the route to Asia and its empire in India.

Except for the French conquest of Algeria, Europeans had rarely connected commerce with political control of Africa. Yet in the 1880s, European military forces conquered one African territory after another (Map 23.1). The British, French, Belgians, Portuguese, Italians, and Germans jockeyed to dominate peoples, land, and resources—"the magnificent cake of Africa," as King **Leopold II** of Belgium (r. 1865–1909) put it. Insatiable greed drove Leopold to claim the Congo region of central Africa, initiating competition with France for that territory and inflicting on its peoples unparalleled acts of cruelty (see the illustration on the left). German chancellor Otto von Bismarck, who saw colonies mostly as political bargaining chips, established German control over Cameroon and a section of East Africa, to which Frieda von Bülow and Carl Peters headed. Faced with competition, the British poured millions of pounds into conquering the continent "from Cairo to Cape Town," as the slogan went, and the French cemented their hold on large portions of western Africa.

The scramble for Africa escalated tensions in Europe and prompted Bismarck to call a conference of interested nations at Berlin. The European nations represented at the conference, held in a series of meetings in 1884 and 1885, decided that control of settlements along the African coast guaranteed rights to internal territory. This agreement led to the strictly linear dissection of the continent—a dissection that cut across indigenous boundaries of African culture and ethnic life. The Berlin conference also banned the sale of alcohol and controlled the flow of arms to indigenous peoples. In theory, the meeting was supposed to reduce bloodshed and ambitions for territory in Africa. In reality, the agreement simply accelerated conquest of the continent and left everyone on edge over the threat of more violence. Newspaper accounts depicted the struggle for foreign lands, whetting the popular appetite for more takeovers. Music hall audiences rose to their feet and cheered at the sound of popular songs about imperial heroes of the day.

The lust for conquest had perhaps its greatest effect in southern Africa, where farmers of European descent and immigrant prospectors, rather than military personnel, battled the Xhosa, Zulu, and other African peoples for control of their land. The Dutch had moved into the area in the seventeenth

---

Leopold II: King of Belgium (r. 1865–1909) who sponsored the takeover of the Congo in Africa, which he ran with great violence against native peoples.

century, but by 1815 the British had gained control. Thereafter, descendants of the Dutch, called Boers (Dutch for "farmers"), and British immigrants joined together in their fight to wrest farmland and mineral resources from local peoples. British businessman and politician Cecil Rhodes, sent to South Africa for his health just as diamonds were being discovered in 1870, cornered the diamond market and claimed a huge amount of African territory hundreds of miles into the interior. His ambition for Britain and for himself was boundless: "I contend that we are the finest race in the world," he

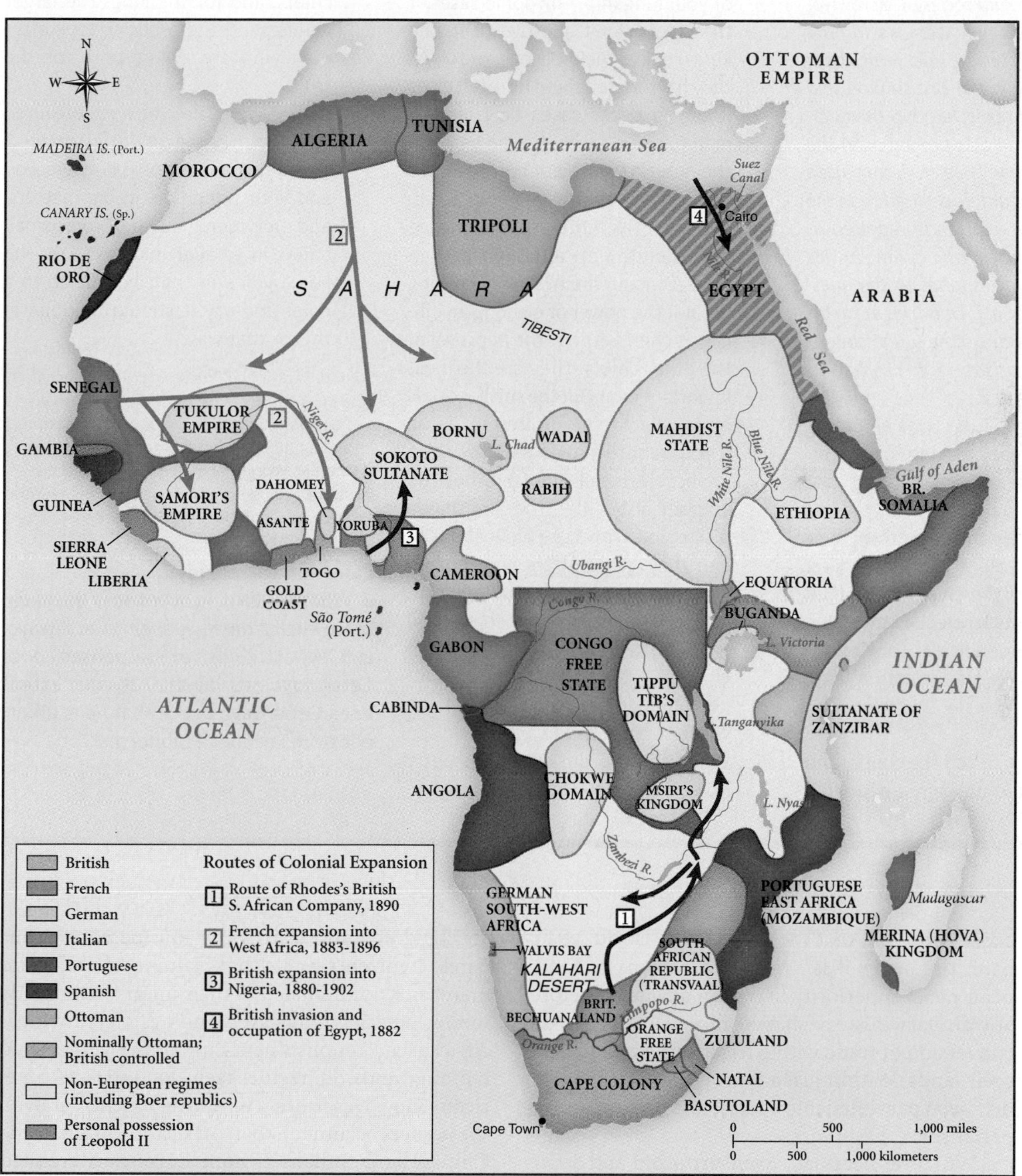

MAP 23.1 Africa, c. 1890

The scramble for Africa entailed a change in European trading practices, which generally had been limited to the coastline. Trying to penetrate economically and rule the interior ultimately resulted in a map of the continent that made sense only to the imperial powers, for it divided ethnic groups and made territorial unities that had nothing to do with Africans' sense of geography or patterns of settlement. This map shows the unfolding of that process and the political and ethnic groupings to be conquered.

DOCUMENT

An African King Describes His Government

The British engaged in bloody warfare against the king of Zulu society, Cetshwayo, on the grounds that they were freeing the Zulu from a cruel tyrant who kept them enslaved. Ultimately, the British won and sent Cetshwayo into exile, but they then subjected him to official questioning as to the nature of his tyranny. They were convinced that the Zulu were far less civilized than the British and utterly ignorant of representative government or the rule of law. In this passage Cetshwayo responds to the questions of the judge, Sir J. D. Barry, at an official hearing in 1881 as the judge sought proof of Zulu barbarism.

144. As king of the Zulus, was all power invested in you, as king, over your subjects?—In conjunction with the chiefs of the land.

145. How did the chiefs derive their power from you as king?—The king calls together the chiefs of the land when he wants to elect a new chief, and asks their advice as to whether it is fit to make such a man a large chief, and if they say "yes" the chief is made.

146. If you had consulted the chiefs, and found they did not agree with you, could you appoint a chief by virtue of your kingship?—In some cases, if the chiefs don't approve of it, the king requires their reasons, and when they have stated them he often gives it up. In other cases he tries the man to see whether he can perform the duties required of him or not.

147. In fact, you have the power to act independently of the chiefs in making an appointment, although you always consult them?—No, the king has not the power of electing an official as chief without the approval of the other chiefs. They are the most important men. But the smaller chiefs he can elect at his discretion. . . .

168. If you want to make a new law, to be applicable to all Zululand, how do you set about it?—The king has a discussion with the chiefs about it, and they give out the law, but he cannot make a law without their consent. He consults the chiefs and gives his reasons, and if they conclude to agree to it, it is the law, but he cannot make a law against the wishes of his chiefs. . . .

180. What are the duties of the petty [lower] chiefs?—They principally superintend work for their superior chiefs, and for the king. The larger chiefs send them out to look after men who are doing work for the king. . . .

183. The people are never consulted about either big or little matters? The only consultation is between you and your big chiefs in big matters, and between you and your small chiefs in smaller matters?—Yes, he has a voice in that; he can go to a chief and say it should be done in this or that way.

Source: *Report and Proceedings with Appendices of the Government Commission on Native Laws and Customs, Cape of Good Hope Parliamentary Paper*, G4, 1883, Part 1, 523–30, excerpted in William H. Worger et al., eds., *Africa and the West: A Documentary History*, 2 vols. (New York: Oxford University Press, 2010) 1:108–9.

Question to Consider

- **What kinds of answers does the judge try to elicit from former king Cetshwayo, and what kinds of responses does Cetshwayo provide him? To what extent does Cetshwayo prove that he is different from European monarchs?**

explained, "and that the more of the world we inhabit the better it is." Although notions of European racial superiority had been advanced before, Social Darwinism reshaped racism to justify the conversion of trade with Africans into conquest of their lands. Within just a few decades, Darwinism had been perverted into a racist justification for imperialism.

Wherever necessary to ensure profit and domination, Europeans either destroyed African economic and political systems or transformed them into instruments of their rule. A British governor of the West African region known as the Gold Coast put the matter succinctly in 1886: the British would "rule the country as if there were no inhabitants." Indeed, most Europeans considered Africans barely civilized, despite the wealth local rulers and merchants accumulated in their international trade in raw materials and slaves, and despite individual Africans' accomplishments in fabric dyeing, road building, and architecture (see Document, "An African King Describes His Government," above). Westerners claimed that Africans—unlike the Chinese and Indians, whom Europeans credited with a scientific and artistic heritage—were capable only of manual labor. They felt this justified their confiscation of land from Africans, who were then forced to work for them to pay European-imposed taxes. Agriculture to support families, often performed by women and slaves, declined in

Nigerian Brass Bust
This brass depiction of an *oni* or king in one region of what is now Nigeria shows the sophisticated skill of African artists. Although Westerners collected such statuary and proudly displayed it, many considered themselves to be far superior to Africans, whom they viewed as virtually without cultural talent and thus useful only for hard physical labor. *(The Granger Collection, New York—All rights reserved.)*

favor of mining and farming cash crops. Men were made to leave their homes to work in mines or to build railroads. Family and community networks, though upset by the new arrangements, helped support Africans during this upheaval in everyday life.

Acquiring Territory in Asia

Britain justified its invasion of African countries as strategically necessary for acquiring stopover ports to resupply Asian-bound ships and thus help to preserve its control over India's quarter of a billion people. In reality the expansion of imperial power from the 1870s on was occurring around the world, not just Africa. Much of Asia, with India as the centerpiece, was integrated into Western empires. At the same time, resistance to outside domination was also growing. Discriminated against but educated, the Indian elite in 1885 founded the Indian National Congress. Some of its members accepted British liberalism in economic and social policy, welcoming opportunities for trade, education, and social advancement. Others went further, however, challenging Britain's right to rule India at all. In the next century, the Congress would develop into a mass movement.

To the east, British military forces took control of the Malay peninsula in 1874 and of the interior of Burma in 1885. In both areas, political instability often threatened secure trade. The British depended on the region's tin, oil, rice, teak, and rubber as well as its access to the numerous interior trade routes of China. British troops guaranteed the order necessary to expand railroads for more efficient export of raw materials and the development of Western systems of communication. The British also built factories and hoped to use its Burmese and Malaysian base to expand industrially into China.

The British added to their holdings in Asia partly to counter Russian and French annexations. Since 1865, Russia had been absorbing the small Muslim states of central Asia, including provinces of Afghanistan (see Map 23.2). Besides extending into the Ottoman Empire, Russian tentacles reached into Persia, India, and China, often encountering British competition. The Trans-Siberian Railroad allowed

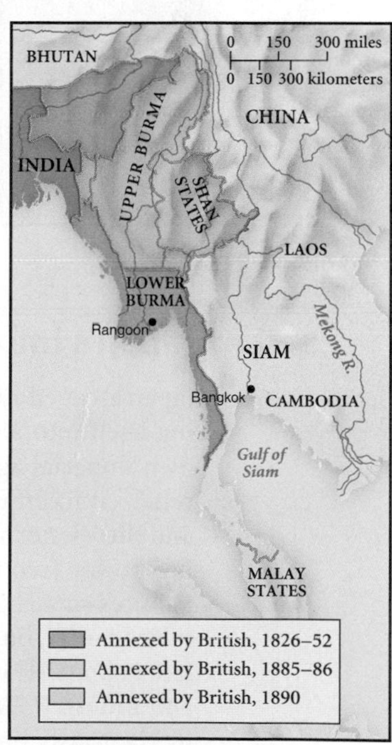

British Colonialism in the Malay Peninsula and Burma, 1826–1890

MAP 23.2 Expansion of Russia in Asia, 1865–1895

Russian administrators and military men continued enlarging Russia, bringing in Asians of many different ethnicities, ways of life, and religions. Land-hungry peasants in western Russia followed the path of expansion into Siberia and Muslim territories to the south. In some cases they drove native peoples from their lands, but in others they settled unpopulated frontier areas. As in all cases of imperial expansion, local peoples resisted any expropriation of their livelihood, while the central government tried various policies for integration.

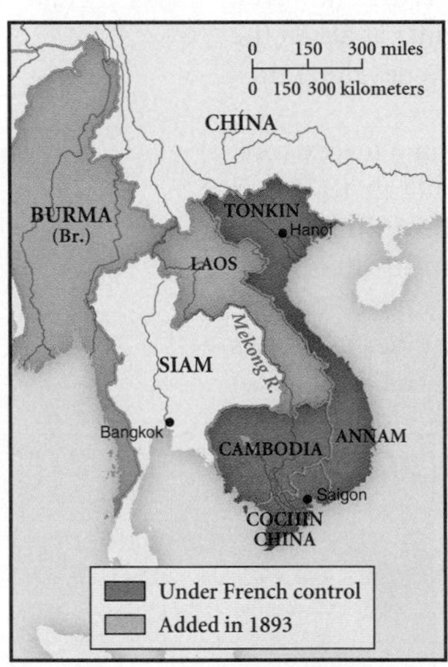

The Union of Indochina, 1893

Russia to begin integrating Siberia—considered a distant colony in the eighteenth and early nineteenth centuries. Hundreds of thousands of hungry peasants moved to the region, and trade routes to cities in the west expanded. France meanwhile used the threat of military action to negotiate favorable treaties with Indochinese rulers, creating the Union of Indochina from the ancient states of Cambodia, Tonkin, Annam, and Cochin China in 1887 (the latter three now constitute Vietnam). Laos was added to Indochina in 1893.

Japan's Imperial Agenda

Japan escaped European rule by rapidly transforming itself into a modern industrial nation with its own imperial agenda. A Japanese print of the late nineteenth century illustrates both traditional ways and the Western influence behind Japan's burgeoning power (see the illustration on page 767). The picture's small boats might have been rendered centuries earlier, but the steaming locomotive symbolizes change. The Japanese embraced foreign trade and industry. "All classes high and low shall unite in vigorously promoting the economy and welfare of the nation," ran one of the first pronouncements of the Meiji regime that had come to power in 1868. The Japanese government directed the country's turn toward modern industry, and state support led daring innovators like Iwasaki Yataro, founder of the Mitsubishi firm, to develop heavy industries such as mining and shipping. The Japanese sent students, entrepreneurs, and government officials to the West to bring back as much new knowledge as they could. Unlike China, Japan endorsed Western-style modernization in preparation for gaining its own empire.

Change was the order of the day in Japan. Japanese legal scholars, following German models, helped draft a constitution in 1889 that emphasized state power rather than individual rights. Western dress became the rule at the imperial court, and when fire destroyed Tokyo in 1872, a European planner directed the rebuilding in Western architectural style. The Japanese adapted samurai traditions such as spiritual discipline to create a large and technologically modern military. In the 1870s, Japan ordered naval ships from Britain and began conquering adjacent islands, including Okinawa. In the 1880s, it used its new naval strength to begin imposing favorable trade treaties on Korea, preliminary to a more complete takeover on the horizon.

The Paradoxes of Imperialism

Imperialism ignited constant, sometimes heated debate because of its many paradoxes. Although it was meant to make European nations more economically secure, imperialism intensified distrust in international politics and thus threatened everyone. Countries vied with one another for a share of world influence. In securing India's borders, for example, the British faced Russian expansion in Afghanistan and along the borders of China. Imperial competition even made areas of Europe more volatile than ever: Austria-Hungary, Russia, and rival ethnic groups disputed control of the Balkans as the Ottoman Empire's grip weakened in the region.

The Costs and Profits of Empire Politicians claimed that empire would bring great riches, but the costs of empire were high. Opponents claimed that empire was more costly than profitable to societies as a whole. Britain, for example, spent enormous amounts of tax revenue to maintain its empire even as its industrial lead began to slip. Yet for certain businesses, colonies provided crucial markets and large profits: late in the century, French colonies bought 65 percent of France's exports of soap and 41 percent of its metallurgical exports. Imperialism provided huge numbers of jobs to people in European port cities, but taxpayers in all parts of a nation — whether they benefited or not — paid for colonial armies, increasingly costly weaponry, and administrators.

The Civilizing Mission To those who opposed colonial expansion as "spending our money on distant adventures," advocates of imperialism pointed out that whites had a "civilizing mission." The French thus taught some of their colonial subjects French language, literature, and history. The emphasis was always on European, not local, culture. In Germany's African colonies, an exam for students in a school run by missionaries asked them to write on "Germany's most important mountains" and "the reign of William I and the wars he waged." The deeds of Africa's great rulers and the accomplishments of its kingdoms disappeared from the curriculum. While Europeans believed in instructing colonial subjects, they did not believe that Africans and Asians were as capable as Europeans of great achievements.

So imperialism's goal of "civilizing" was also in conflict. French advocates argued that their nation "must keep its role as the soldier of civilization." But it was unclear whether imperialism should emphasize soldiering (that is, the conquest and murder of local peoples) or civilizing (the education of local peoples in the European tradition). The French tried both in Indochina, building a legacy of resistance that continued unabated until the mid-twentieth century and another legacy of French culture among the people of that region.

Inferiority and Superiority The paradoxes of imperialism extended to Europeans' study of other cultures. Western scholars and travelers had long studied Asian and African languages, art, and literature, and had gathered and used botanical and other scientific knowledge. Yet even the best scholars' appreciation of foreign cultures was tinged with bias, misinterpretation, and error. European scholars of Islam characterized Muhammad as an inferior imitation of Jesus, for example. Confident in their cultural superiority, many Europeans considered Asians and Africans as low types, variously characterizing them as lying, lazy, self-indulgent, or irrational. One English official proclaimed that "accuracy is abhorrent to the Oriental mind." At the height of imperialism, such beliefs offered still another justification for conquest: that inferior colonized peoples would ultimately be grateful for what Europe had brought them.

Modernization in Japan

Like the West, Japan bustled with commerce and industry thanks to improved and expanding transportation. Railroads, ships, and a range of new inventions such as the rickshaw speeded goods and individuals within cities, across the country, and ultimately to new, foreign destinations. The Japanese traveled widely to learn about ongoing technological innovation. *(Rue des Archives/The Granger Collection, New York—All rights reserved.)*

***An ABC for Baby Patriots* (1899)**
Pride in empire began at an early age, when learning the alphabet from this kind of book helped develop an imperial sensibility. The subject of geography became important in schools during the decades between 1870 and 1890 and helped young people know what possessions they could claim as citizens. In British schools, the young celebrated the holiday Empire Day with ceremonies and festivities emphasizing imperial power. *(Bodleian Library, University of Oxford. Mary F. Ames, shelfmark 2523 c. 24 [1899].)*

Hoping to spread the religion they believed superior, European missionaries ventured to newly secured areas of Africa and Asia with attitudes full of contradictions. A woman missionary reflected a common view when she remarked that the Tibetans with whom she worked were "going down, down into hell, and there is no one but me . . . to witness for Jesus amongst them." Many people under colonial rule did accept Christianity, often blending their local religious practices with Christian ones. Christianizing entire populations and making them obedient proved impossible, however. When native people resisted, "civilizers," including missionaries, often supported brutal military measures against them, willing to see them slaughtered in the name of imparting Christian values and Western order.

Yet other Europeans—from novelists to military men—held quite opposite views of conquered peoples, considering them better than Europeans because they were unspoiled by civilization. "At last some local color," enthused one colonial officer, fresh from the industrial cities of Europe, on seeing Constantinople. This romantic vision of an ancient center of culture, similar to eighteenth-century condescension toward the "noble savage," had little to do with the reality of conquered peoples' lives.

The paradoxes of imperialism are clear in hindsight, but at the time European self-confidence hid many of them. There was the belief that through imperialist ventures "a country exhibits before the world its strength or weakness as a nation," as one French politician announced. Some in government, however, worried that imperialism—because of its expense and the constant possibility of war—might weaken rather than strengthen the nation-state. The most glaring paradox of all was that Western peoples who believed in nation building and national independence invaded the territory of others thousands of miles away and refused them the right to rule themselves.

REVIEW QUESTION What were the goals of the new imperialism, and how did Europeans accomplish those goals?

The Industry of Empire

Behind the expansion of Western empires lay dramatic developments in economic and technological power. Fed by raw materials from around the world, industry turned out a cornucopia of new products, including the increasingly powerful guns that served imperial conquest, and many workers' wages increased. Beginning in 1873, however, downturns in business threatened both entrepreneurs and the working class. Businesspeople sought remedies in new technology, managerial techniques, and a revolutionary marketing institution—the department store. Governments played their part by changing business law and supporting the drive for raw materials and global profits. The steady advance of industry, global trade, and the consumer economy further transformed people's daily lives.

Industrial Innovation

In nineteenth-century Europe, an abundance of industrial, technological, and commercial innovation backed the ambitions of the nation-state and the drive for empire. Alongside the new inventions and discoveries that benefited European society and ultimately the world were innovations in medicines and firearms that speeded European conquest of Africa and Asia. Innovation remained uneven, however, as older leaders lagged and new leaders emerged in the contest for industrial prosperity.

In the last third of the nineteenth century, new products ranging from the bicycle, the typewriter, and the telephone to the internal combustion engine provided striking proof of industrial progress. In 1885, sophisticated German engineer Karl Benz devised a workable gasoline engine; six years later, France's Armand Peugeot constructed a car and tested it by chasing a bicycle race. Electricity became more widely used after 1880, providing power to light everything from private drawing rooms to government office buildings. Like the many bridges, skyscrapers, and railroad stations with their skeletal frames, the Eiffel Tower, constructed in Paris for the Universal Exposition of 1889, stood as a monument to the age's engineering wizardry. Visitors rode to the Eiffel Tower's summit in electric elevators.

To fuel the West's explosive industrial growth, the leading industrial nations mined and produced massive quantities of coal, iron, and steel in the 1870s and 1880s. Production of iron increased from 11 million to 23 million tons annually. Steel output in the industrial nations grew just as impressively, increasing from 500,000 to 11 million tons annually in these decades. Manufacturers used the metal to build the more than 100,000 locomotives that pulled trains — trains that transported two billion people a year.

The Spread of Factories and Innovations in Agriculture

Historians used to contrast a "second" Industrial Revolution, with a concentration on heavy industrial products like iron and steel, to the "first" one of the eighteenth and early nineteenth centuries, in which innovations in the manufacture of textiles and the use

The Invention of Electric Lighting

By the 1890s, residents of major European cities could see many fresh inventions in a single walk down the newly widened boulevards. In this illustration of Piccadilly in London, electric lighting illuminates the way for modern bicycles and automobiles as well as horse-drawn carriages. By the turn of the century, streets had also become crowded with electric trams. *(Mary Evans Picture Library.)*

of steam energy predominated. Many historians now believe this distinction mainly applies to Britain, where industrialization did rise in two stages. In countries where industrialization came later, the two developments occurred simultaneously. Numerous and increasingly advanced textile mills were installed on the European continent later than in Britain, for instance, at the same time that blast furnaces were being constructed. Although industrialization led to the decline of traditional crafts like weaving, home industry—or **outwork**, the process of having some aspects of industrial work done outside factories in individual homes (similar to the putting-out system described on page 687)—persisted in garment making, metalwork, and porcelain painting. Industrial production occurring simultaneously in homes, small workshops, and factories has continued through the entire history of modern manufacturing down to the present day.

Industrial innovations also changed agriculture. Chemical fertilizers boosted crop yields, and reapers and threshers mechanized harvesting. In the 1870s, Sweden produced a cream separator, a first step toward mechanizing dairy farming. Wire fencing and barbed wire replaced wooden fencing and stone walls, both of which required intensive labor to construct. Refrigeration, developed during this period, allowed fruits, vegetables, and meat to be transported without spoiling, thus diversifying and increasing the urban food supply. Tin from colonies facilitated large-scale commercial canning, which made many foods available year-round to people in the cities and thus improved their health.

The Tools of Empire Industrial technology combined with scientific breakthroughs to provide the powerful guns, railroads, steamships, and medicines that accelerated Western penetration of Asia and Africa. The steam-powered gunboats that forced the Chinese to open their borders to opium in the 1830s continued to play a crucial role in European expansion. Improvements in steamboat technology helped in the conquest of the African interior, but the scientific development of quinine was also crucial. Before the development of medicinal quinine in the 1840s and 1850s, the deadly tropical disease malaria decimated many a European party embarking on exploration or military conquest, giving Africa the nickname "White Man's Grave." The use of quinine, extracted from cinchona bark from the Andes, radically cut deaths from malaria among soldiers, missionaries, adventurers, traders, and bureaucrats.

Drought and famine plagued large stretches of both Africa and Asia in these decades, thus weakening local peoples' ability to resist. Europeans kept their health, thanks to quinine, and then their weapons did the work of definitively destroying self-sufficiency and self-rule. Improvements to the breech-loading rifle and the development of the machine gun, or "repeater," between 1862 and the 1880s dramatically increased firepower. Europeans carried on a brisk trade selling outmoded guns at bargain prices to peoples needing protection both from their internal enemies and from the Europeans themselves. In contrast, Europeans crushed African resistance with rapid, accurate, and blazing gunfire: "The whites did not seize their enemy as we do by the body, but thundered from afar," claimed one local African resister. "Death raged everywhere—like the death vomited forth from the tempest."

Challenges to British Dominance Despite innovation and global expansion, Britain's rate of industrial growth slowed as its entrepreneurs remained wedded to older technologies. Great Britain increased its trade, profited from its investments worldwide, and consolidated its global power in the late nineteenth century but shifted its focus to expanding both its global rule and the military means to protect it. Meanwhile, Germany and the United States began surpassing Britain in research, technical education, and innovation—and ultimately in overall rates of economic growth.

Following the Franco-Prussian War, Germany annexed Alsace and Lorraine, territories with both textile industries and rich iron deposits. Investing heavily in research, German businesses devised new industrial processes and began to mass-produce goods. Germany also spent as much money on education as on its military in the 1870s and 1880s. This investment resulted in highly skilled engineers and technical workers who sent German industrial productivity soaring. The United States began intensive exploitation of its vast natural resources, including coal, metal ores, gold, and oil. The value of U.S. industrial goods jumped from $5 billion in 1880 to $13 billion by 1900. Whereas German productivity rested more on state promotion of industrial efforts, U.S. growth often involved innovative entrepreneurs, such as Andrew Carnegie in iron and steel and John D. Rockefeller in oil. Most other countries trailed the three leaders in the pervasiveness of industry.

---

outwork: The nineteenth-century process of having some aspects of industrial work done outside factories in individual homes.

Sukharev Market, Moscow (c. 1890)
For all their modernization, cities also offered their products in dozens of centuries-old food and flea markets such as this one in Russia. Rural farmers brought fresh produce to the cities, while urban market women sold clothing and household items. *(© Austrian Archives/Corbis.)*

Areas of Slower Industrialization French industry grew steadily, but French businesses remained smaller than those in Germany and the United States. In Spain, Austria-Hungary, and Italy, industrial development was primarily a local phenomenon. Austria-Hungary, for example, had densely industrialized areas around Vienna and in Styria and Bohemia, but the rest of the country remained tied to traditional, nonmechanized agriculture. Italy industrialized in the north while remaining rural and agricultural in the south. The Italian government spent more on building Rome into a grand capital than it invested in economic growth. A mere 1.4 percent of Italy's 1872 budget went to education and science, compared with 10.8 percent in Germany. Scandinavian countries, poor in coal and ore, lagged behind those with greater natural resources. The commercial use of electricity eventually helped them to industrialize in the last third of the nineteenth century and become leaders in the use of hydroelectric power.

Russia's road to industrialization was tortuous, slowed partly by its relatively small urban labor force. The terms of serf emancipation bound many Russian peasants, who may have wished to find opportunities in factory work, to the mir, or landed community. Some villages sent men and women to cities, but on the condition that they return for plowing and harvesting. Nevertheless, by the 1890s, Moscow, St. Petersburg, and a few other cities had substantial working-class populations. The Russian government attracted foreign capital, entrepreneurs, and engineers to help construct railroads, including the Trans-Siberian Railroad (1891–1916), which upon completion stretched 5,787 miles from Moscow to Vladivostok. Russia's industrial and military power increased, but its peasants bore the main burden of paying for the state's financing of industry, mostly in the form of higher taxes on vodka. Russia offered a prime example of the uneven benefits of industrialization: neither Russian peasants nor underpaid urban workers could afford to buy the goods their country produced.

Facing Economic Crisis

Economic conditions were far from rosy throughout the 1870s and 1880s despite industrial innovation. In 1873, prosperity suddenly gave way to a severe economic depression, followed by almost three decades of economic fluctuations, featuring sharp downturns. People of all classes lost their jobs or businesses and faced long stretches of unemployment or bankruptcy. Because economic ties bound industrialized western Europe to international markets, the downturns affected economies around the world: Australia, South Africa, California, Newfoundland, and the West Indies.

By the 1870s, as industry gained in influence, industrial and financial setbacks — not agricultural ones as in the past — were capable of sending the economy into a long tailspin. Innovation created new or modernized industries on an unprecedented scale, but economic uncertainty accompanied the forward march of Western industrial development, and businesspeople faced real problems. First, the start-up costs of new enterprises skyrocketed. The early textile mills had required relatively small amounts of capital in comparison to the new factories producing steel and iron. **Capital-intensive industry**, which required huge financial investment for the purchase of expensive machinery, replaced labor-intensive production, which relied on the hiring of more workers. Second, the distribution and consumption of goods failed to keep pace with industrial growth, in part because businessmen kept wages so low that workers could afford little besides food. For them, purchasing the new industrial goods was impossible. The series of slumps turned industrialists' attention to finding ways to enhance sales and distribution and to control markets and prices.

Governments took steps to address the economic crisis. New laws spurred the development of the **limited liability corporation**, which protected investors from personal responsibility for a firm's debt and thus encouraged investment. Before limited liability, owners or investors were personally responsible for the debts of a bankrupt business. In one case in England, a former partner who had failed to have his name removed from a legal document after leaving the business remained responsible to creditors when the company went bankrupt. He lost everything he owned except a watch and the equivalent of one hundred dollars. By reducing personal risk, limited liability made investors more confident about financing business ventures, which led to the growth of stock markets. These stock markets raised money from a larger pool of private capital than before and gave businesses the funds to innovate. At the center of an international economy linked by telegraph, telephone, railways, and steamships, the London Stock Exchange in 1882 traded industrial shares worth £54 million, a value that surged to £443 million by 1900.

capital-intensive industry: A mid- to late-nineteenth-century development in industry that required great investments of money for machinery and infrastructure to make a profit.

limited liability corporation: A legal entity, such as a factory or other enterprise, developed in the second half of the nineteenth century whose owners were liable for only restricted (limited) amounts of money owed to creditors in the case of financial failure.

Another way in which businesses met the crisis that began in 1873 was to band together in cartels and trusts. Cartels — combinations of industries formed to control prices and competition — flourished particularly in German chemical, iron, coal, and electric industries. A single German coal cartel, founded in the 1880s, eventually dominated more than 95 percent of coal production in Germany, allowing it to restrict output and set prices. Trusts — similar to cartels in their power to control prices but different in structure — appeared first in the United States in 1882, when John D. Rockefeller created the Standard Oil Trust by acquiring stock from many different oil companies and placing it under the direction of trustees. The trustees then controlled so much of the companies' stock that they could set prices for the entire industry and even dictate to the railroads the rates for transporting the oil. While expressing their belief in free trade, those who set up cartels and trusts were actually restricting the free market. Governments did the same by imposing import taxes, in the belief that doing so would help protect domestic industries.

Much of Europe had adopted free trade after midcentury, but during the recessions of the 1870s and 1880s the resulting huge trade deficits — caused when imports exceeded exports — soured many Europeans on the concept. Countries with trade deficits had less capital available to invest internally, slowing the growth of job opportunities and increasing the chance of social unrest. Farmers in many European countries suffered when improvements in transportation made it possible to import perishable food, such as cheap grain from the United States and Ukraine. With broad popular support, governments approved tariffs to make foreign goods more expensive. Farmers, capitalists, and even many workers backed taxes on imports to prevent competition from outside. By the early 1890s, all but Belgium, Britain, and the Netherlands had ended free trade.

Revolution in Business Practices

Industrialists also tried to minimize the damage of economic downturns by revolutionizing the everyday conduct of their businesses. A generation earlier, factory owners had been directly involved in every aspect of their businesses and often learned to run their firms through trial and error. In the late 1800s, industrialists began to hire managers to run their increasingly complex day-to-day operations. Managers who specialized in a particular aspect of a business — such as sales and distribution, finance, or the purchase of raw materials — made

Berlin Telephone Operators
Middle-class women needing jobs embraced the opportunities offered by the growing service sector in telephone, telegraph, and office work and other "respectable" employment. These Berlin telephone operators probably earned less than women factory workers, as service sector employers took advantage of an untapped educated pool of labor to advance industrial development. *(akg-images.)*

decisions in their area of expertise, assisted by workers in the new service sector.

The White-Collar Sector A "white-collar" service sector, composed of workers with mathematical skills and literacy acquired in the new public primary schools, emerged as part of the development of management. Businesses employed secretaries, file clerks, and typists to guide the flow of business information. Banks that accepted savings from the general public and that invested those funds heavily in business needed tellers and clerks; railroads, insurance companies, and government-run telegraph and telephone companies all needed armies of office workers.

Women, responding to the availability of clean, respectable work, formed the bulk of service employees. At the beginning of the nineteenth century, middle-class women still tended businesses with their husbands. In the next few decades, however, the new ideology of domesticity became so strong that male employers were unwilling to hire married women, and women in the lower-middle and middle classes were themselves ashamed to work outside the home. But by the late nineteenth century, the costs of middle-class family life had increased, especially because children, who were now forced by law to get an education, were no longer working and contributing to family resources. Instead, the family needed more money to support them. Whether to help pay family expenses or to support themselves, both unmarried and married women of the respectable middle class increasingly took jobs despite the ideal of domesticity. Employers found, as one put it, a "quickness of eye and ear, and the delicacy of touch" in the new women workers.

By hiring women for newly created clerical jobs, business and government contributed to a dual labor market in which certain categories of jobs were predominantly male and others were overwhelmingly female. Since society had come to believe that women were not meant to work or even not fit to work, businesses made greater profits by paying women in the service sector chronically low wages—

Interior of Au Coin de la Rue (c. 1870)
This Parisian department store, not the grandest or first of its kind, shows the typical cascade of goods displayed on railings and balconies. The abundance of textiles and carpets sparked the shopper's imagination, inciting her to let go of thrift and wander wherever her fancy took her among the many counters and displays until she had overspent. *(© Stefano Bianchetti/Corbis.)*

much less than they would have had to pay men for doing the same tasks.

The Department Store The drive to boost consumption led to a new development in merchandising—the emergence of the department store. Founded after mid-century in the largest cities, department stores gathered an impressive variety of goods in one place in imitation of the Middle Eastern bazaar. Created by daring entrepreneurs such as Aristide and Marguerite Boucicaut of the Bon Marché in Paris and John Wanamaker of Wanamaker's in Philadelphia, department stores eventually replaced stores selling single lines of goods such as dishware or fabrics.

Single-item stores that people entered knowing clearly what they wanted to purchase were often small, somber shops, miniature by comparison with the modern shopping palaces built of marble and filled with lights and mirrors. In the department store, luxurious silks, delicate laces, and richly embellished tapestries spilled over railings and counters, not in neat order reflecting rational, middle-class ideas, but in glorious disarray to stimulate consumer desires. Shoppers no longer limited their purchases to necessities but rather reacted to sales, a new marketing technique that could incite a buying frenzy. Because most men lacked the time for shopping expeditions, department stores became the domain of women, who came out of their domestic sphere into a new public role. Attractive salesgirls, another variety of service workers, were hired to inspire customers to buy. Department-store shopping also took place outside of cities: glossy mail order catalogs from the Bon Marché or Sears, Roebuck in Chicago arrived regularly in rural areas, with both necessities and exotic items from the faraway dream world of the city.

Consumerism was shaped by empire. Travelers like Frieda von Bülow and Carl Peters journeyed on speedier ocean liners, carrying quinine, antiseptics, and other medicines as well as cameras, revolvers, and the latest in rubber goods and apparel. Consumption of colonial products such as coffee, tea, sugar, tobacco, cocoa, and cola became more widespread for the stimulation they offered hardworking Westerners. Tons of palm oil from Africa were turned into both margarine and soap, allowing even ordinary people in the West to see themselves as cleaner and more civilized than those in other parts of the world, including areas from which those raw materials came. Empire and industry jointly shaped everyday life by exciting the desire to own things—whether industrial goods or products from the colonies.

REVIEW QUESTION What were the major changes in Western industry and business in the last third of the nineteenth century?

Imperial Society and Culture

The spread of empire not only made the world an interconnected marketplace but also transformed everyday culture and society. Success in manufacturing and foreign ventures created millionaires, and the expansion of a professional middle class and development of a service sector meant that more people were affluent enough to own property, see some of the world, and give their children a quality education. Many Europeans grew healthier, partly because of improved diet and partly because of government-sponsored programs aimed at promoting the fitness necessary for citizens of imperial powers. At the same time, the uncertainties of life in a rapidly changing society drove millions of poor Europeans to migrate in search of opportunities around the world—even in the colonies—while artists found exciting new subject matter in those same industrial and imperial changes around them.

The "Best Circles" and the Expanding Middle Class

Profits from empire and industrial growth added new members to the upper class, or "best circles," so called at the time because of their members' wealth, education, and social status. People in the best circles often came from the aristocracy, which remained powerful and was still widely seen as a model of style. Increasingly, however, aristocrats had to share their social position with new millionaires from the ranks of the upper middle class, or bourgeoisie. In fact, the very distinction between aristocrat and bourgeois became blurred, as monarchs gratefully bestowed aristocratic titles on wealthy businesspeople and as aristocrats financed global business ventures. Poorer aristocrats approved marriages between their children and those of the newly rich. Such arrangements brought much-needed money to old, established families and the glamour of an aristocratic title to newly wealthy families. Thus, Jeanette Jerome, daughter of a wealthy New York financier, married England's Lord Randolph Churchill (their son Winston later became England's prime minister). Millionaires discarded the thrifty ways of a century earlier to build palatial country homes and villas and engage in flashy displays of wealth. To justify their success, the wealthy often quoted Social Darwinist principles, maintaining that their prosperity resulted from their natural superiority over the poor.

Empire reshaped the way people in the best circles spent their leisure time. Upper-class men bonded over big-game hunting in Asia and Africa, which replaced age-old traditions of fox and bird hunting. European hunters forced native Africans, who had depended on hunting for income, food, and group unity, to work as guides, porters, and domestics on hunts. Collectors brought exotic specimens back to Europe for zoological exhibits, natural history museums, and traveling displays, all of which flourished during this period. Wealthy Europeans brought empire into their homes with displays of stags' heads, elephant tusks, and animal skins.

People in the best circles saw themselves as an imperial elite, and upper-class women devoted themselves to maintaining its standards of social conduct. Members of the upper class did their best to exclude inferiors by controlling their children's social lives, especially by preventing girls' sexual activity and relationships with the lower classes. Upper-class men regularly seduced lower-class women because a double standard saw promiscuity as normal for men and as immoral for women. Parents arranged many marriages directly, and "visiting days"—a kind of regulated open house—brought eligible young people together to help ensure correct matrimonial decisions.

Instead of working for pay, upper-class women devoted themselves to raising children and directing staffs of servants. They took their role seriously, keeping detailed accounts of their expenditures and monitoring their children's religious and intellectual development. Furnishings in fashionable homes displayed imperial treasures such as Persian-inspired textiles, Oriental carpets, bamboo furniture, and Chinese porcelains. With the importation of azaleas, rhododendrons, and other plants from around the world, lavish flower gardens replaced parks and lawns. Being an active consumer of fashionable clothing was also a time-consuming activity for women. In contrast to men's plain garments, upper-class women wore elaborate costumes—

Tiger Hunting in the Punjab
Big-game hunting became the imperial sport of choice, as this Indian work of art shows. European and American hunters took the place of local Asians and Africans who had previously depended on the hunt for their livelihood. Western manliness was coming to depend on such seemingly heroic feats as big-game hunting, and imperialists scorned those who continued the old aristocratic fox hunt as effeminate. Though not apparent in this illustration, some Western women enjoyed hunting, too. *(V & A Images, London/Art Resource, NY.)*

featuring constricting corsets, voluminous skirts, bustles, and low-cut necklines for evening wear—that made them symbols of elite leisure. Women offset the grim side of imperial and industrial society with the rigorous practice of art and music. One Hungarian observer wrote, "The piano mania has become almost an epidemic in Budapest as well as Vienna." Its keys made of ivory from Africa, the piano symbolized the imperial elite's accomplishments and superiority.

Below the best circles, or upper crust, the solid middle class of businesspeople and professionals such as lawyers was expanding, most notably in western and central Europe. In eastern Europe, this expansion did not happen naturally, and the Russian government often sought out foreigners to build its professional and business classes. Although middle-ranked businessmen and professionals could sometimes mingle with those at the top of society, their lives remained more modest. They did, however, employ at least one servant, which might give the appearance of leisure to the middle-class woman in the home. Professional men working at home did so from a well-appointed, if not lavish, room. Middle-class women did many household chores themselves, and middle-class domesticity substituted cleanliness and polish for the imperial grandeur of upper-class life.

Working People's Strategies

For centuries, working people had migrated from countryside to city and from country to country to make a living. After the middle of the nineteenth century, empire and industry were powerful factors in migration. Established European cities like Riga, Marseille, and Hamburg offered secure new industrial jobs and opportunities for work in global trade, while new colonies provided land, jobs for administrators, and the possibility of unheard-of wealth in diamonds, gold, and other natural resources.

Working People Leave Europe

Europeans who left their native lands moved for a variety of reasons (see "Contrasting Views," page 778). In parts of Europe, the land simply could not produce enough to support a rapidly expanding population. Greek shipbuilding in ancient times had stripped the vast forests of Sicily, leaving the soil eroded and nearly worthless. By the end of the nineteenth century, hundreds of thousands of Sicilians were leaving, often temporarily, to find work in the industrial cities of North and South America. One-third of all European immigrants came from the British Isles, especially Ireland between 1840 and 1920, first because of the potato famine and then because English landlords drove them from their farms to get higher rents by simply changing tenants. Between 1886 and 1900, half a million Swedes out of a population of 4.75 million quit their country (see "Taking Measure," page 777). Millions of rural Jews, especially from eastern Europe, left their villages for economic reasons, but Russian Jews also fled vicious anti-Semitism. Russian mobs brutally attacked Jewish communities, destroying homes and businesses and even murdering some Jews. These ritualized attacks, called pogroms, were scenes of horror. "People who saw such things never smiled anymore, no matter how long they lived," recalled one Russian Jewish woman who migrated to the United States in the early 1890s.

Commercial and imperial development determined destinations. Most migrants who left Europe

TAKING MEASURE

European Emigration, 1870–1890

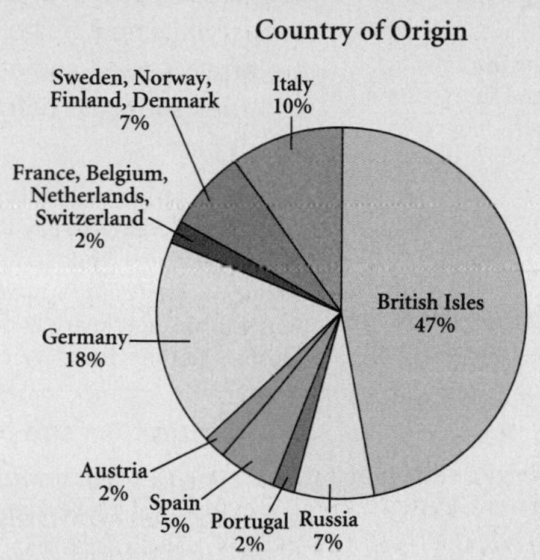

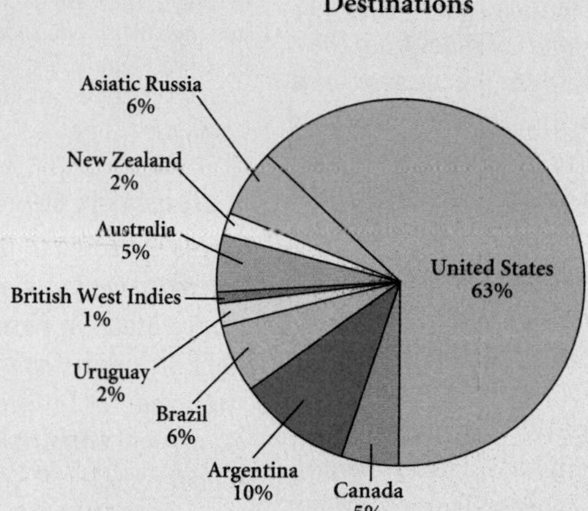

The suffering caused by economic change and by political persecution motivated people from almost every European country to leave their homes for greater security elsewhere. North America attracted more than two-thirds of these migrants, many of whom followed reports of vast quantities of available land in both Canada and the United States. Both countries were known for following the rule of law and for providing economic opportunity in urban as well as rural areas.

Source: Theodore Hamerow, *The Birth of New Europe: State and Society in the Nineteenth Century* (Chapel Hill: University of North Carolina Press, 1983), 169.

Question for Consideration

- **Where did the majority of these migrants originate? What historical factors prompted them to leave their homelands?**

went to North and South America, Australia, and New Zealand, as news of opportunity reached Europe. The railroad and steamship made journeys across and out of Europe more affordable and faster, though most workers traveled in steerage with few comforts. Once established elsewhere, migrants frequently sent money back home; the funds could be used to pay for education or to set up family members in small businesses, thus improving their condition. European farm families often received a good deal of their income from husbands or grown sons and daughters who had left. Cash-starved peasants in eastern and central Europe welcomed the arrival of "magic dollars" from their kin. Migrants themselves appreciated the chance to begin anew without the harsh conditions of the Old World. One settler in the United States was relieved to escape the meager peasant meal of rye bread and herring: "God save us from . . . all that is Swedish," he wrote home sourly.

Migration out of Europe often meant an end to the old way of life. Workers immediately had to learn new languages and compete for jobs in growing cities where they formed the cheapest pool of labor, often in factories or sweatshops. Emigrant women who worked as homemakers, however, tended to keep to themselves, preserving traditional ways. More insulated, they might never learn the new language or put their peasant dresses away. Their children and husbands more often left their past behind as they built a life in schools and factories of the New World.

More common than international migration was internal migration from rural areas to European cities, accelerating the urbanization of Europe. The most urbanized countries were Great Britain and Belgium, followed by Germany, France, and the Netherlands. In Russia, only 7 percent of the population lived in cities of ten thousand or more; in Portugal the figure was 12 percent. Many who moved to the cities were seasonal migrants who worked as masons, cabdrivers, or factory hands to supplement declining income from agriculture. When they returned to the countryside, they provided hands for the harvest. In villages across Europe, independent artisans such as handloom

CONTRASTING VIEWS

Experiences of Migration

In the nineteenth century, millions of migrants moved thousands of miles from their homelands. The vast distances traveled and the permanent relocation of these migrants were among the issues generating a wide range of responses. Among observers, government officials, migrants themselves, and those they left behind, reactions varied from acceptance and enthusiasm to opposition and anger. The conflicting reactions appeared in official reports, local newspapers, poems, and personal letters. While officials pointed to the benefits of emigration (Document 1), others in the home country had mixed views and opinions (Document 2). Migrants themselves had vastly differing experiences, adding to the debate over migration (Documents 3, 4, and 5).

1. The Government View

The preamble to the Hungarian census for 1890 was blunt and unambiguous on the subject of migration at a time when population growth was said to be a good thing. It offered a clear assessment of emigration.

Emigration has proved to be a veritable boom. The impoverished populace has been drawn off to where it has found lucrative employment; the position of those left behind, their work opportunities and standard of living, have undoubtedly improved thanks to the rise in wages, and thanks to the substantial financial aid coming into the country: sums of from 300,000 to 1,500,000 florints.

Source: Quoted in Julianna Puskas, "Consequences of Overseas Migration for the Country of Origin: The Case of Hungary," in Dirk Hoerder and Inge Blank, eds., *Roots of the Transplanted: Late 19th Century East Central and Southeastern Europe* (Boulder: East European Monographs, 1994), 1:397.

2. Those Left Behind

Teofila Borkowska, from Warsaw, Poland, reacted to her husband's resettlement in the United States in two letters from 1893 and 1894. Stripped of a family group, Borkowska struggled to survive, and her husband, Wladyslaw Borkowski, never did return or send for her.

1893. Dear Husband: Up to the present I live with the Rybickis. I am not very well satisfied, perhaps because I was accustomed to live for so many years quietly, with you alone. And today you are at one end of the world and I at the other, so when I look at strange corners [surroundings], I don't know what to do from longing and regret. I comfort myself only that you won't forget me, that you will remain noble as you have been. . . . I have only the sort of friends who think that I own thousands and from time to time someone comes to me, asking me to lend her a dozen roubles.

1894. Up to the present I thought and rejoiced that you would still come back to Warsaw, but since you write that you won't come I comply with the will of God and with your will. I shall now count the days and weeks [until you take me to America]. . . . Such a sad life! I go almost to nobody, for as long as you were in Warsaw everything was different. Formerly we had friends, and everybody was glad to see us, while now, if I go to anybody, they are afraid I need something from them and they show me beforehand an indifferent face.

Source: Letters from Teofila Borkowska to Wladyslaw Borkowski, July 21, 1893, and April 12, 1894, in William I. Thomas and Florian Znaniecki, *The Polish Peasant in Europe and America*, Vol. 2, Primary-Group Organization (Boston: Gorham Press, 1920), 348–49.

3. Migration Defended

In some cases, emigrants were said to be unpatriotic and cowardly for leaving their homeland just to avoid hard economic times. To charges against Swedish emigrants, journalist Isador Kjelberg responded with the following explanation.

Patriotism? Let us not misuse so fine a word! Does patriotism consist of withholding the truth from the workingman by claiming that "things are bad in America"? I want nothing to do with such patriotism! If patriotism consists of seeking, through lies, to persuade the poorest classes to remain under the yoke, like mindless beasts, so that we others should be so much better off, then I am lacking in patriotism. I love my country, as such, but even more I love and sympathize with the human being, the worker. . . . Among those who most sternly condemn emigration are those who least value the human and civic value of the workingman. . . . They demand that he remain here. What are they prepared to give him to compensate the deprivations this requires? . . . It is only cowardly, unmanly,

weavers often supported their unprofitable livelihoods by sending their wives and daughters to work in industrial cities.

Adaptation to Industrial Change Changes in technology and management practices eliminated outmoded jobs and often made factory work more stressful. Workers complained that new machinery speeded up the pace of work to an unrealistic level. For example, employers at a foundry in suburban Paris required workers using new furnaces to turn out 50 percent more metal per day than they had produced using the old furnaces. Stepped-up productivity demanded much more physical exertion, but workers received no additional pay for their extra efforts. Workers heartless, to let oneself become a slave under deplorable circumstances which one *can* overcome.

Source: Quoted in H. Arnold Barton, *A Folk Divided: Homeland Swedes and Swedish Americans, 1840–1940* (Carbondale: Southern Illinois University Press, 1994), 72–73.

This anonymous Swedish poem combined a political explanation of migration with an economic one.

I'm bound for young America,
Farewell old Scandinavia.
I've had my fill of cold and toil,
All for the love of mother soil.
You poets with your rocks and rills
Can stay and starve—on words, no frills.
There, out west, a man breathes free,
While here one slaves, a tired bee,
Gathering honey to fill the hive
Of wise old rulers, on us they thrive.
In toil we hover before their thrones,
While they take to slumber, like lazy drones.
Drunk with our nectar they've set us afright,
But opportunity has knocked, and we'll take our flight.

Source: Quoted in H. Arnold Barton, *A Folk Divided: Homeland Swedes and Swedish Americans, 1840–1940* (Carbondale: Southern Illinois University Press, 1994), 137.

4. The Perils of Migration

A contrasting view of emigration to the United States appeared in the following Slovak song.

My fellow countryman, Rendek from Senica, the son of poor parents
Went out into the wide world. In Pittsburgh he began to toil.
From early morning till late at night he filled the furnaces with coal.
Faster, faster, roared the foreman, every day. . . .
Rendek toiled harder
So as to see his wife.
But alas! He was careless
And on Saturday evening late
He received his injuries. At home his widow waited
For the card which would never come.
I, his friend, write this song
To let you know
What a hard life we have here.

Source: Quoted in Frantisek Bielik, Horst Hogh, and Anna Stvrtecka, "Slovak Images of the New World: 'We Could Pay Off Our Debts,'" in Dirk Hoerder and Inge Blank, eds., *Roots of the Transplanted: Late 19th Century East Central and Southeastern Europe* (Boulder: East European Monographs, 1994), 1:388.

5. The Lure of Latin America

The following letter, written in 1883 by an English migrant to his family, shows why, despite hardship, Europeans fled their homelands for places such as Argentina, where this immigrant settled. Original spelling has been preserved.

SAUCE GRANDE, SOUTH AMERICA, MARCH 28, 1883

MY DR BROTHER AND SISTERS

I received your kind and welcome letters and was glad to hear from you after so long a time. Since I last wrote you I have left my situation where I was for three years past and have sold my share of sheep which counted 300 at 34$ pr head I have also got my Wool and sheepskins for sale in Buenos Aires for which I expect to get about 8.000$. Last year I made about 13.000$ clear money.

I suppose you know that one thousand dollars amount to about 8£ in English money. Sheep are very cheap and plentiful in this country. Thousands are sold at 30$ pr head. I have the pleasure to inform you that I have got 1.500 sheep on thirds from Messrs Samuel & Bo. I am now living in a house alone with my flock of sheep and it is rather lonesome but as soon as I receive my wool money I intend to get married. My intended wife is a Miss Victoria Smith, who is born in this country but of English parents and speaks very good English. . . .

Hoping this will find you all well as, I am happy to say, it leaves me at presant I remain your Effectionate Brother

Willie X

Source: Fordham Modern History Sourcebook: Immigration. http://web.archive.org/web/19981203161408/www.signature.pair.com/letters/archive/argentina.html

Questions to Consider

1. What are the different views of migration represented in these documents?
2. What interests and points of view do these contrasting opinions represent?
3. How do we draw an accurate view of migration from such contrasting views and experiences?
4. Given these differing views, why would people consider leaving Europe and why would governments promote it?

also grumbled about the increased number of managers; many believed that foremen, engineers, and other supervisors interfered with their work. For women, supervision sometimes brought on-the-job harassment, as in the case of female workers in a German food-canning plant who kept their jobs only in return for granting sexual favors to the male manager.

Many in the urban and rural labor force continued to do outwork at home. In Russia, workers made bricks, sieves, shawls, lace, and locks during the slow winter season. Every branch of industry, from metallurgy to toy manufacturing to food processing, also employed urban women at home—and their work was essential to the family economy. They painted tin soldiers, wrapped chocolate, made cheese boxes, and polished metal. Factory owners liked the system because low piece rates made outworkers desperate for income under any conditions and thus willing to work extremely long days. A German seamstress at her new sewing machine reported that she "pedaled at a stretch from six o'clock in the morning until midnight. . . . At four o'clock I got up and did the housework and prepared meals." Owners could lay off women at home during slack times and rehire them whenever needed with little fear of organized protest.

Economic change and the periodic return of hard times had uneven consequences for people's everyday lives. In the late nineteenth century, joblessness and destitution threatened. Some city workers prospered by comparison to those in rural areas, though a growing number lost the steadiness of traditional artisanal work. By and large, however, urban workers were better informed and more connected to the progress of industry and empire than their rural counterparts were.

National Fitness: Reform, Sports, and Leisure

Many in the urban working class suffered from the stresses of industrial modernization and the upheaval of migration. In an age of Social Darwinist concerns about national fitness in the international struggle to survive, middle- and upper-class reformers founded organizations for social improvement. Officials also promoted competitive sports and healthy leisure-time activities to build national fitness and provide some relief from the stresses of daily life.

Reform for the Working Classes Settlement houses, clinics, and maternal and child health centers sprang up overnight in cities. Young middle- and upper-class men and women, often from universities, eagerly took up residence in poor neighborhoods to study and help the people there. Belief in the scientific approach to solving social problems, as well as compassion for the poor, led these reformers to seek the causes of social problems and their solutions. The Fabian Society, a small organization established in London in 1884, undertook studies to devise reforms based on planning rather than socialist revolution. In 1893, the Fabians helped found the Labour Party to make social improvement a political cause. Religious faith also shaped these efforts: "There is Christ's own work to be done," wrote one woman who volunteered to inspect workhouse conditions. Catholics and Protestants alike countered the decline in religious observance with missionary efforts among the working poor. The Catholic church in Hungary, for example, ministered to those experiencing rural poverty as agriculture came under the stresses of global competition.

To make the poor more fit in a competitive world, philanthropists and government officials intervened in the lives of working-class families. The worry was that the poor, as one reformer put it, "were permanently stranded on lower levels of evolution." Intervening more in the lives of poor families was seen as a way to "quicken evolution." Reformers sponsored health clinics and milk centers to provide good medical care and food for children and instructed mothers in child-care techniques, including breast-feeding to promote infant health. Some schools distributed free lunches, medicine, and clothing and inspected the health and appearance of their students. Yet the poor were also pressured to follow new standards they could ill afford, such as finding children respectable shoes, and reformers believed they had the right to enter working-class apartments whenever they chose to inspect them.

A few professionals began to distribute birth-control information in the belief that smaller families could better survive the challenges of urban life. In the 1880s, Aletta Jacobs (1851–1929), a Dutch physician, opened the first birth-control clinic, which specialized in promoting the new, German-invented diaphragm. Jacobs wanted to help women in Amsterdam slums who were worn out by numerous pregnancies and whose lives, she believed, would be greatly improved by limiting their fertility. Working-class women used these clinics, and knowledge of birth-control techniques spread by word of mouth among workers. The churches adamantly opposed this trend, and even reformers wondered whether birth control would increase the sexual exploitation of women if the threat of pregnancy were removed.

Another government reform effort consisted of measures said to protect women from certain kinds of work. Legislation across Europe barred women from night work and from such "dangerous" professions as florist and bartender—allegedly for health reasons. Additionally, medical statistics demonstrated that women in even the most strenuous jobs became sick less often than men. But lawmakers and workingmen claimed that women were not producing healthy enough children and were stealing jobs from men. Women who had worked in trades newly defined as dangerous were forced to find other, lower-paying jobs or remain at home. The new laws did not prevent women from holding jobs, but they made earning

Anglo-Indian Polo Team
Team sports underwent rapid development during the imperial years as spectators rooted for the success of their football team in the same spirit they rooted for their armies abroad. Some educators believed that team sports molded the male character so that men could be more effective soldiers against peoples of other races. In the instance of polo, as illustrated by the team photo here, the English learned from the Indians what would soon be seen as a typically English sport. *(Hulton Archive/Getty Images.)*

a living harder. Social Darwinists justified these measures as making the population fit for the struggle to survive.

Sports and Leisure As nations competed for territory and global trade, male athletes turned away from village games and created sports teams. Soccer, rugby, and cricket drew mass followings that welded the lower and higher classes into a common, competitive culture. Large audiences drawn from all classes backed their favorite teams, and competitive sports began to be seen as signs of national strength and spirit. Newspapers reported the results of all sorts of new contests, whether they concerned nations vying for colonies or bicyclists participating in cross-country races such as the Tour de France, sponsored by tire makers who wanted to prove the superiority of their product. "The Battle of Waterloo was won on the playing fields of Eton," ran the wisdom of the day, suggesting that the games played in school could mold the strength of an army—an army that competed with those of other nations in pursuit of empire.

Team sports—like civilian military service—helped differentiate male and female spheres and thus promoted a social order based on distinction between the sexes. Reformers introduced exercise and gymnastics into schools for girls, often with the idea that these would strengthen them for motherhood and thus help build the nation-state. Some team sports for women emerged—soccer, field hockey, and rowing—but women generally were encouraged to engage in individual sports. "Riding [horses] improves the temper, the spirits and the appetite," wrote one sportswoman. As knowledge of the world developed, some women began to practice yoga.

The middle classes thought that leisure pursuits such as mountain climbing built mental and physical skills, and they even crossed the empire to challenge themselves. As a Swedish editor explained, "The passion for mountain-climbing can only be understood by those who realize that it is the step-by-step achievement of a goal which is the real pleasure of the world." Working-class people adopted middle-class habits by joining clubs for such pursuits as bicycling, touring, and hiking. Clubs that sponsored trips often had names like the Patriots or the Nationals, making a clear association between physical fitness and national strength. The emphasis on healthy recreation gave people a greater sense of individual might and promoted an imperial citizenship based less on constitutions and rights than on an individual nation's exercise of raw power. A farmer's son in the 1890s boasted that with a bicycle, "I was king of the road, since I was faster than a horse."

Artistic Responses to Empire and Industry

In the 1870s and 1880s, the arts explored the process of global expansion and economic innovation, often in the same gloomy Darwinistic terms that made reformers anxious. Darwin's theory held out the possibility that strong civilizations, if they failed to adapt to changing conditions, could weaken and collapse. French writer Émile Zola, influenced by fears of social decay, produced a series of novels set

DOCUMENT

Henrik Ibsen, From *A Doll's House*

Norwegian playwright Henrik Ibsen helped create the global marketplace of ideas with such plays as A Doll's House, *an 1879 work critical of traditional gender roles, as this conversation between Torvald Helmer and his wife, Nora, reveals. With women like Frieda von Bülow traveling the globe, Ibsen increasingly believed that the middle-class housewife did not develop as a full human being. His plays were performed in many countries—not only in Europe but also in Egypt, the United States, and as far away as Japan.* A Doll's House *sparked fierce debate around the world, especially about the condition of women. If European artists and writers borrowed from other cultures, Europe's cultural influence also spread beyond its borders.*

Helmer: Nora, how can you be so unreasonable and ungrateful? Haven't you been happy here?

Nora: No; never. I used to think I was; but I haven't ever been happy.

Helmer: Not—not happy?

Nora: No. I've just had fun. You've always been very kind to me. But our home has never been anything but a playroom. I've been your doll-wife, just as I used to be Papa's doll-child. And the children have been my dolls. I used to think it was fun when you came in and played with me, just as they think it's fun when I go in and play games with them. That's all our marriage has been, Torvald.

Helmer: There may be a little truth in what you say, though you exaggerate and romanticize. But from now on it'll be different. Playtime is over. Now the time has come for education.

Nora: Whose education? Mine or the children's?

Helmer: Both yours and the children's, my dearest Nora.

Nora: Oh, Torvald, you're not the man to educate me into being the right wife for you.

Helmer: How can you say that?

Nora: And what about me? Am I fit to educate the children?

Helmer: Nora!

Nora: Didn't you say yourself a few minutes ago that you dare not leave them in my charge?

Helmer: In a moment of excitement. Surely you don't think I meant it seriously?

Nora: Yes. You were perfectly right. I'm not fitted to educate them. There's something else I must do first. I must educate myself. And you can't help me with that. It's something I must do by myself. That's why I'm leaving you.

Helmer (jumps up): What did you say?

Nora: I must stand on my own feet if I am to find out the truth about myself and about life. So I can't go on living here with you any longer.

Helmer: Nora, Nora!

Nora: I'm leaving you now, at once. Christine will put me up for tonight—

Helmer: You're out of your mind! You can't do this! I forbid you!

Nora: It's no use your trying to forbid me any more. I shall take with me nothing but what is mine. I don't want anything from you, now or ever.

Helmer: What kind of madness is this?

Nora: Tomorrow I shall go home—I mean, to where I was born. It'll be easiest for me to find some kind of a job there.

Helmer: But you're blind! You've no experience of the world—

Nora: I must try to get some, Torvald.

Helmer: But to leave your home, your husband, your children! Have you thought what people will say?

Nora: I can't help that. I only know that I must do this.

Helmer: But this is monstrous! Can you neglect your most sacred duties?

Nora: What do you call my most sacred duties?

Helmer: Do I have to tell you? Your duties towards your husband, and your children.

Nora: I have another duty which is equally sacred.

Helmer: You have not. What on earth could that be?

Nora: My duty towards myself.

Source: Henrik Ibsen, *A Doll's House* (New York: Anchor, 1966), 96–97.

Question to Consider

- **How do Helmer's attempts to convince Nora to stay reveal his ideas about women and their proper roles in society?**

in industrializing France about a family plagued by alcoholism and madness. Zola's characters, who led violent strikes and in one case even castrated an oppressive grocer, raised questions about the future of civilization. Zola had a dark vision of how industrial society affected individuals: his novel *Women's Paradise* (1883) depicts the upper class shopper who abandons rational decision making as a consumer for the frenzy of the new department stores. Other fictional heroines were equally upsetting because they violated other long-standing rules. The character Nora in the drama *A Doll's House* (1879) by Norwegian playwright Henrik Ibsen undermines civilized values and the health of society by leaving an oppressive marriage (see Document, "From *A Doll's House*," above).

Writers envisioned a widespread deterioration of behavior pervading urban and rural life. The stories of Emilia Pardo Bazán are tales of incest and murder among wealthy landowning families in rural Spain. The heroine of Olive Schreiner's *The Story of an African Farm* (1889) rejects the role of submissive wife in rural Africa, describing the British Empire as a "dirty little world, full of confusion." Schreiner became celebrated among opponents of empire for her grim portrayals. Novelists addressed the burning issues of their times and echoed the Social Darwinism that was in the air.

Decorative arts of this period featured a countertrend away from stark realism. Country people used mass-produced textiles to create traditional-looking costumes and developed ceremonies based on a mythical past. Such invented customs, romanticized as old and authentic, brought tourists from the cities to villages. So-called folk motifs caught the eye of modern urban architects and industrial designers, who copied rustic styles when creating household goods and decorative objects. The influence of empire is apparent in the traditional Persian and Indian motifs used by English designers William Morris (1834–1896) and his daughter May Morris (1862–1938) in their designs of fabrics, wallpaper, and household items based on such natural imagery as the silhouettes of plants. They wanted to replace "dead" and "ornate" styles of the early industrial years with the simple crafts of the past. Their work gave birth to the arts and crafts style, which paradoxically attracted consumers benefiting from the industrial age.

Industrial developments also influenced the work of painters, who by the 1870s felt intense competition from a popular industrial invention—the camera. Photographers could produce cheap copies of paintings and create more realistic portraits than painters could, at affordable prices. In response, painters altered their style, employing new and varying techniques to distinguish their art from the photographic realism of the camera. Claude Monet, for example, was fascinated by the way light transformed an object, and he often portrayed the same place—a bridge or a railroad station—at different times of day.

This daring style of art generally came to be called **impressionism**. It emphasizes the artist's attempt to capture a single moment by focusing on the ever-changing light and color found in ordinary scenes. Using splotches and dots, impressionists moved away from the precise realism of earlier painters and challenged artistic norms. Vincent Van Gogh used vibrant colors in great swirls to capture sunflowers, haystacks, and the starry evening sky. Distortions made the impressionists' visual style seem outrageous to those accustomed to realism, but a few enthusiastically greeted impressionism's luminous quality. Closely following the impressionists, French painter Georges Seurat depicted with thousands of dots and dabs the Parisian suburbs' newly created parks with their Sunday bicyclists and office workers in their store-bought clothing, carrying books or newspapers and parading like the well-to-do. Industry contributed to the new styles of painting, as factories produced a range of pigments that allowed artists to use a wider and more intense spectrum of colors than ever before. Both new industrial products such as the camera and chemically based paints gave birth to a rebellion in the arts.

An increasingly global vision also influenced painting in the age of empire. In both composition and style, impressionists borrowed heavily from Asian art and architecture. The impressionist goal of portraying the fleetingness of light or human situations came from an ancient Japanese concept—*mono no aware* ("sensitivity to the fleetingness of life"). The color, line, and delicacy of Japanese art (which many impressionists collected) is evident, for example, in Monet's later paintings of water lilies, his studies of wisteria, and even his re-creation of a Japanese garden at his home in France as the subject for artistic study. Similarly, the American expatriate Mary Cassatt used the two-dimensionality of Japanese art in *The Letter* (1890–1891) and other paintings. Van Gogh sometimes filled the background of portraits with copies of intensely colored Japanese prints, even imitating classic Japanese woodcuts. The graphic arts advanced the West's ongoing borrowing from around the globe, while responding to the changes brought about by industry.

REVIEW QUESTION How did empire and industry influence art and everyday life?

The Birth of Mass Politics

Ordinary people struggled for political voice, especially through the vote, as they watched the wealth and influence of industry and empire increase. By bringing more people into closer contact with one another in cities, the growth of industries helped

---

impressionism: A mid- to late-nineteenth-century artistic style that captured the sensation of light in images, derived from Japanese influences and in opposition to the realism of photographs.

Mary Cassatt, *The Letter* (c. 1890)
Mary Cassatt, an American artist who spent much of her time in Europe, was one of the many Western artists smitten by Japanese prints. Like many other Western artists of her day, she learned Japanese techniques for printmaking, but she also reshaped her painting style to follow Japanese conventions in composition, perspective, and the use of color. Cassatt is known for her many depictions of Western mothers and children and of individual women. In this painting, the woman herself even looks Japanese. *(Worcester Art Museum, Worcester, Massachusetts, USA / The Bridgeman Art Library International.)*

develop networks of political communication and a stronger national consciousness. The railroad, for example, took high-ranking officials such as British prime minister William Gladstone on campaigns to win votes before national audiences. Such events made workers more politically aware and active, leading western European governments to allow more men to vote. Although only men profited from electoral reform, the era's expanding franchise marked the beginning of mass politics — a major feature of the twentieth-century West. Women could not vote, but they participated in public life by forming auxiliary groups to support political parties. Among the authoritarian monarchies, Germany had male suffrage, but in more autocratic states to the east — for instance, Russia — violence and ethnic conflict shaped political systems. In such places, the harsh rule from above often resembled the control imposed on colonized peoples rather than participation of voting citizens.

Workers, Politics, and Protest

Workers in the 1870s–1890s joined together politically to exert pressure on governments and businesses. Strikes and worker activism were reactions to workplace hardships, but they depended on community bonds forged in neighborhoods. With the backing of their neighbors and fellow laborers, workers formed effective unions and powerful political parties — many of them based on a Marxist platform. Unions served to protect workers from the often brutal pace of industrial change and to guarantee that they received a fair wage. Workers banded together both in grassroots organizations, such as clubs and reading societies, and in transnational organizations, such as the Second International, across their individual nation-state's boundaries. Such organizations aimed to combat the growing nationalism and imperial competition that separated workers rather than binding them in a common cause.

Unions and Strikes | As the nineteenth century entered its final decades, workers organized formal unions, which attracted the allegiance of millions. Unions demanded a say in working conditions and aimed, as one union's rule book put it, "to ensure that wages never suffer illegitimate reductions and that they always follow the rises in the price of basic commodities." Businessmen and governments viewed striking workers simply as rebels, threatening political unrest and destructive violence. Even so, strong unions appealed to some industrialists because a union could make strikes more predictable (or even prevent them) and present worker demands coherently instead of piecemeal by groups of angry workers.

From the 1880s on, the pace of collective action for better pay, lower prices, and better working conditions accelerated. In 1888, for example, hundreds of young women who made matches, the so-called London matchgirls, went on strike to end the fining system, under which they could be penalized an entire day's wage for being a minute or two late to work. The fines, the matchgirls maintained, helped companies reap profits of more than 20 percent. Newspapers and philanthropists picked up the strikers' story, condemning "respectable" owners "who suck wealth out of the starvation of helpless girls." In 1890, sixty thousand workers took to the streets of Budapest to agitate for safer working conditions and the vote; the next year, day laborers on Hungarian farms struck, too. Across Europe between 1888 and 1890, the number of strikes and major demonstrations rose by more than 50 percent, from 188 to 289.

Housewives, who often acted in support of strikers, carried out their own protests against high food prices. They confiscated merchants' goods and sold them at what they considered a fair price. "There should no longer be either rich or poor," argued Italian peasant women. "All should have bread for themselves and for their children. We should all be equal." They took other kinds of action as well: housewives often hid neighbors' truant children from school officials so that the children could continue to help with work at home. When landlords evicted tenants, women gathered in the streets to return the ousted families' household goods as fast as they were removed. Meeting on doorsteps or at fountains, laundries, and markets, women initiated rural newcomers into urban ways. In doing so, they helped cement the working-class unity created by workers in the factory.

Governments increasingly responded to strikes by calling out troops or armed police, even though most strikes were about working conditions and not about political revolution. Even in the face of government force, unions did not back down or lose their commitment to solidarity. Craft-based unions of skilled artisans, such as carpenters and printers, were the most active and cohesive, but from the mid-1880s on, a movement known as **new unionism** attracted transport workers, miners, matchgirls, and dockworkers. These new unions were nationwide groups with salaried managers who could plan a widespread general strike across the trades, focusing on such common goals as the eight-hour workday and also paralyzing an entire nation through work stoppages. Although the small, local workers' associations remained important, the large unions of the industrialized countries of western Europe had more potential for challenging large industries, cartels, and trusts.

Political Parties Working-class political parties developed from unions. Workingmen helped create the Labour Party in England, the Socialist Party in France, and the Social Democratic Parties of Sweden, Hungary, Austria, and Germany—most of them inspired by Marxist theories. Germany was home to the largest socialist party in Europe after 1890. Socialist parties held out hope that newly enfranchised male working-class voters could become a collective force in national elections, even triumphing because of their numbers over the power of the upper class.

Those who accepted Marx's assertion that "workingmen have no country" also founded an international movement to address workers' common interests across national boundaries. In 1889, some four hundred socialists from across Europe met to form the **Second International**, a federation of working-class organizations and political parties that replaced the First International, founded by Marx before the Paris Commune. The Second International adopted a Marxist revolutionary program, but it also advocated suffrage (in countries where it still did not exist) and better working conditions.

Members of the Second International determined to rid the organization of anarchists, who flourished in the less industrial parts of Europe—Russia, Italy, and Spain. In these countries, anarchism drew strong support from peasants, small property owners, and agricultural day laborers, for whom Marxist theories of worker-controlled factories had less appeal. In an age of tough international competition in agriculture, many rural people sought a life free from the domination of large landowners and governments that backed the landowners' interests. Many advocated extreme tactics, including physical violence and even murder. "We want to overthrow the government . . . with violence since it is by the use of violence that they force us to obey," wrote one Italian anarchist. In the 1880s, anarchists bombed stock exchanges, parliaments, and businesses. Members of the Second International felt that such random violence was counterproductive.

Workingwomen joined unions and workers' political parties, but in much smaller numbers than men. Unable to vote in national elections and usually responsible for housework in addition to their

new unionism: A nineteenth-century development in labor organizing that replaced local craft-based unions with those that extended membership to all kinds of workers.

Second International: A transnational organization of workers established in 1889, mostly committed to Marxian socialism.

paying jobs, women had little time for party meetings. In addition, their low wages hardly allowed them to survive, much less pay party or union dues. Many workingmen also opposed women's presence in unions. Contact with women would mean "suffocation," one Russian workingman believed, and end male union members' sense of being "comrades in the revolutionary cause." Unions glorified the heroic struggles of a male proletariat against capitalism. Marxist leaders maintained that capitalism alone caused injustice to women and thus that the creation of a socialist society would automatically end gender inequality. As a result, although the new political organizations wanted women's support, they dismissed women's concerns about lower wages and sexual harassment.

Popular community activities that intertwined politics with everyday life also built worker solidarity. The gymnastics and musical societies that had once united Europeans in nationalistic fervor now served working-class goals. Socialist gymnastics, bicycling, and marching societies rejected competition and prizes as middle-class preoccupations, but they valued physical fitness because it could help workers in the "struggle for existence"—a reflection of the spread of Darwinian thinking to all levels of society. Workers also held festivals and cheerful parades, most notably on May 1—a centuries-old holiday that the Second International now claimed as a labor holiday. Like religious processions of an earlier time, parades fostered unity, and as a result, governments frequently banned such public gatherings, calling them a public danger.

Expanding Political Participation in Western Europe

Ordinary people everywhere in the West were becoming aware of politics through newspapers, which, combined with industrial and imperial progress, were important in developing a sense of citizenship in a nation. Western European countries moved toward mass politics more rapidly than did countries to the east. In western Europe, people's access to newspapers and their political participation meant that the will of the people was increasingly important and the power of small cliques relatively less so in determining election outcomes. In eastern Europe, in contrast, conservative elites opposed the integration of citizens as active participants in a national community that was the trend in western Europe.

Mass Journalism The rise of mass journalism after 1880 was the product of imperial and industrial development. The invention of automatic typesetting and the production of newsprint from wood pulp lowered the costs of printing; the telephone allowed reporters to communicate news to their papers almost instantly. Once literary in content, many daily newspapers now emphasized sensational news, using banner headlines, dramatic pictures, and gruesome or lurid details—particularly about murders and sexual scandals—to sell papers. In the hustle and bustle of industrial society, one editor wrote, "you must strike your reader right between the eyes." A series of articles in 1885 in London's *Pall Mall Gazette* on the "white slave trade" warned the innocent not to read further. The author then proceeded to describe how young women were "snared, trapped," and otherwise forced into prostitution in distant lands through sexual violation and drugs. Stories of imperial adventurers and exaggerated accounts of wasted women workers and their unborn babies similarly drew ordinary people to the mass press.

Journalism created a national community of up-to-date citizens, whether or not they could vote. Unlike the book, the newspaper was meant not for quiet reflection at home or in the upper-class club but for quick reading of attention-grabbing stories on mass transportation and on the streets. Elites complained that the sensationalist press was a sign of social decay, but for up-and-coming people from the working and middle classes, journalism provided an avenue to success. As London, Paris, Vienna, Berlin, and St. Petersburg became centers not only of politics but also of news, a number of European politicians got their start working for daily newspapers. In western Europe, increasing political literacy opened the political process to wider participation.

British Political Reforms A change in political campaigning was one example of this widening participation. In the fall of 1879, **William Gladstone** (1809–1898), leader of the British Liberals, whose party was then out of power, took a train trip across Britain to campaign for a seat in the House of Commons. During his campaign, Gladstone addressed thousands of workers, arguing for the people of India and Africa to have more rights and summoning his audiences to "honest, manful, humble effort" in the middle-class tradition of "hard work." Newspapers around the country reported on his trip and these accounts, along with mass meetings, fueled public interest in

William Gladstone (1809–1898): Liberal politician and prime minister of Great Britain who innovated in popular campaigning and who criticized British imperialism.

politics. Gladstone's campaign was successful, and he took the post of prime minister for the second of the four nonconsecutive terms he served between 1868 and 1894.

Other changes fostered the growth of mass politics in Britain. The Ballot Act of 1872 made voting secret, a reform that reduced the ability of landlords and employers to control how their workers voted. The **Reform Act of 1884** doubled the electorate to around 4.5 million men, enfranchising many urban workers and artisans and thus further diminishing traditional aristocratic influence in the countryside. To win the votes of the newly enfranchised, Liberal and Conservative parties alike established national political clubs to build party loyalty. These clubs competed with small cliques of parliamentary elites who had controlled party politics. Broadly based interest groups such as unions and national political clubs opened up politics by appealing to many more voters.

British political reforms immediately affected Irish politics by arming poor tenant farmers with the secret ballot. The political climate in Ireland was explosive mainly because of the repressive tactics of absentee landlords, many of them English and Protestant, who drove tenants from their land in order to charge higher rents to newcomers. In 1879, opponents of these landlords' attacks on Irish well-being formed the Irish National Land League and launched fiery protests. Irish tenants elected a solid bloc of nationalist representatives to the British Parliament.

The Irish members of Parliament began voting as a group, which gave them sufficient strength to defeat either the Conservatives or the Liberals. Irish leader **Charles Stewart Parnell** (1846–1891) demanded British support for **home rule**—a system giving Ireland its own parliament—in return for Irish votes. As prime minister, Gladstone accommodated Parnell with bills on home rule and tenant security. But Conservatives called home rule "a conspiracy against the honor of Britain," and when they were in power (1885–1886 and 1886–1892), they cracked down on Irish activism. Scandals reported in the press, some of them totally invented, weakened Parnell's influence. In 1890, the news broke of

Parnell Cartoon

Passions ran high among the English over demands for Irish home rule. A special target of outrage was the Irish leader Charles Stewart Parnell, whom the British government and media spied upon and lied about. Here Parnell is depicted as the evil murderer Mr. Hyde, from the popular tale of Dr. Jekyll and Mr. Hyde, out to destroy Prime Minister William Gladstone and by implication the well-being of the entire British Empire. *(Hulton Archive/Getty Images.)*

his affair with a married woman, and he died in disgrace soon after, as cultural values and the media determined politics. Irish home rule remained a heated political issue in the British Parliament, a powerful sign, some said, of the determination to end Ireland's colonial status.

France's Third Republic

Prussia's defeat of Napoleon III in 1871 led to the creation of the **Third Republic** to replace the Second Empire. The republic was shaky at the start because the monarchist political factions—Bonapartist,

---

Reform Act of 1884: British legislation that granted the right to vote to a mass male citizenry.

Charles Stewart Parnell: Irish politician (1846–1891) whose advocacy of home rule was a thorn in the side of the British establishment.

home rule: The right to an independent parliament demanded by the Irish and resisted by the British from the second half of the nineteenth century on.

Third Republic: The French government that succeeded Napoleon III's Second Empire after its defeat in the Franco-Prussian War of 1870–1871. It lasted until France's defeat by Germany in 1940.

Orléanist, and Bourbon—all struggled to restore their respective families to power. But the republican form of government, which French supporters had been trying to solidify for almost a century, survived when the monarchists' compromise candidate for king, the comte de Chambord, stubbornly refused to accept the tricolored flag devised during the French Revolution. Associating the tricolor with the killing of Louis XVI, Chambord would accept only the white flag adorned with the fleur-de-lis of the Bourbons. He thus lost the chance to revive the monarchy, and in 1875 a new constitution created a ceremonial presidency and a premier (prime minister) dependent on support from the elected Chamber of Deputies. An alliance of businessmen, shopkeepers, professionals, and rural property owners hoped the new system would prevent the kind of strongman politics that had seen previous republics give way to the rule of emperors and the return of monarchs.

Fragile at birth, the Third Republic would remain so until World War II. Economic downturns, widespread corruption, and growing anti-Semitism, fueled by a highly partisan press, kept the Third Republic on shaky ground. Newspaper stories about members of the Chamber of Deputies selling their votes to business interests and about the alleged trickery of Jewish businessmen manipulating the economy added to the instability. As a result, the public also blamed Jews for the failures of republican government and the economy. With the support of those disgusted by the messiness of parliamentary politics, Georges Boulanger, a dashing and highly popular general, began a coup to take over the government. He soon lost his nerve, however, saving the French from rule by another strongman. Boulanger's popularity showed that in hard economic times, liberal values based on constitutions, elections, and the rights of citizens could be called into question by someone promising easy solutions.

Republican leaders attempted to strengthen citizen loyalty by instituting compulsory and free public education in the 1880s. In public schools, secular teachers who supported republicanism replaced the Catholic clergy, who usually favored a return to monarchy. A centralized curriculum—identical in every schoolhouse in the country—featured patriotic reading books and courses in French geography, literature, and history. To perpetuate republican ideals, the government established secular public high schools for young women, seen as the educators of future citizens. Mandatory military service for men in the republic's army inculcated national pride in place of regional and rural loyalties that were often centered on the Catholic church. In short, schools and the army both turned peasants into Frenchmen.

Political Liberalism Rejected Although many western European leaders believed in economic liberalism, constitutions, and efficient government, these ideals did not always translate into universal male suffrage and citizens' rights in the less powerful western European countries. Spain and Belgium abruptly awarded suffrage to all men in 1890 and 1893, respectively, but both governments remained monarchies. An alliance of conservative landowners and the Catholic church dominated Spain, although there was increasingly lively urban activism in the industrial centers of Barcelona and Bilbao. Denmark and Sweden continued to limit political participation, and reform in the Netherlands increased male suffrage to only 14 percent by the mid-1890s. An 1887 law in Italy gave the vote to all men who had a primary school education, or 14 percent of the male population.

In Italy, the process of unification left a towering debt and huge pockets of discontented people, including Catholic supporters of the pope and impoverished citizens in the south. Without receiving the benefits of nation building—education, urban improvements, industrial progress, and the vote—the average Italian in the south felt less loyalty to the new nation than fear of the devastating effects of national taxes and the draft on the family economy. Italians' growing unhappiness with constitutional government would have dramatic implications in the twentieth century.

Power Politics in Central and Eastern Europe

Germany, Austria-Hungary, and Russia diverged from the political paths taken by western European countries in the decades 1870–1890. These countries industrialized at varying rates—Germany rapidly and Russia far more slowly. Literacy and the development of a civic, urban culture were more advanced in Germany and Austria-Hungary than in Russia. Even Russia, however, saw the development of a modern press, although with a far smaller readership than elsewhere. In all three countries, conservative large landowners remained powerful, often blocking improvements in transport, sanitation, and tariff policy that would support a growing urban population.

Bismarck's Germany Bismarck had upset the European balance of power, first by humiliating France in the Franco-Prussian War and then by creating a powerful, unified Germany, with explosive economic growth and rapid development of every aspect of the nation-state, from transport to the thriving capital city of Berlin (Map 23.3). His goals achieved, Bismarck now desired stability built on diplomacy instead of war. Fearing that France would soon seek revenge against the new Reich and needing peace to consolidate the nation, he pronounced Germany "satisfied," meaning that it sought no new territory in Europe. To ensure Germany's long-term security, in 1873 Bismarck forged the Three Emperors' League — an alliance of Germany, Austria-Hungary, and Russia. The three conservative powers shared a commitment to maintaining the political status quo.

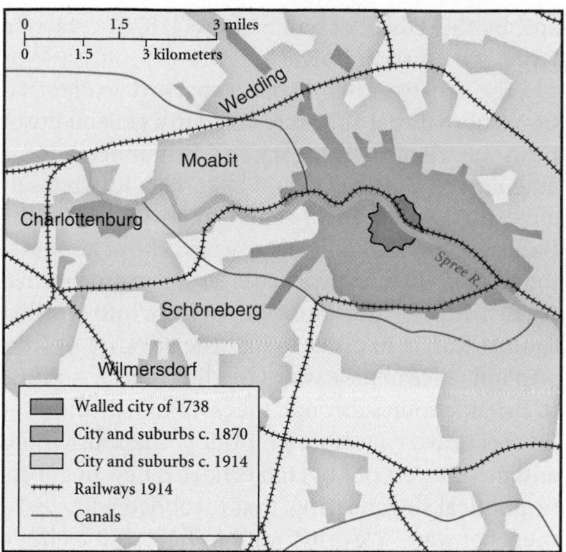

MAP 23.3 Expansion of Berlin to 1914
"A capital city is essential for the state to act as a pivot for its culture," the German historian Heinrich von Treitschke asserted. No other capital city grew as dramatically as Berlin after German unification in 1871. Industrialists and bankers set themselves up in the new capital, while workers migrated there for jobs, swelling the population. The city was newly dotted with military monuments and with museums to show off its culture.

At home, Bismarck, who owned land and invested heavily in industry, joined with the liberals to create a variety of financial institutions, including a central bank to advance German commerce and industry. After religious leaders defeated his Kulturkampf against Catholicism, Bismarck turned to attacking socialists and liberals instead of Catholics as enemies of the regime. He used unsuccessful assassination attempts on Emperor William I as a pretext to outlaw the workers' Social Democratic Party in 1878. Hoping to lure the working class away from socialism, between 1882 and 1884 Bismarck sponsored an accident and disability insurance program — the first of its kind in Europe and an important step in broadening the role of government to encompass social welfare. In 1879, he put through tariffs protecting German agriculture and industry from foreign competition but also raising the prices of consumer goods for ordinary people. Ending his support for laissez-faire economics, Bismarck broke with political liberals while simultaneously increasing the power of the agrarian conservatives by attacking the interests of Germany's industrial sector.

Authoritarian Austria-Hungary

Austria-Hungary, like Germany, frequently employed liberal economic policies and practices. From the 1860s, liberal businessmen succeeded in industrializing parts of the empire, and the prosperous middle classes erected conspicuously large homes, giving themselves a prominence in urban life that rivaled the aristocracy's. They persuaded the government to enact free-trade provisions in the 1870s and to search out foreign investment to build up infrastructure, such as railroads.

Despite these measures, Austria-Hungary remained monarchist and authoritarian. Liberals in Austria — most of them ethnic Germans — saw their influence weaken under the leadership of Count Edouard von Taaffe, Austrian prime minister from 1879 to 1893. Building a coalition of clergy, conservatives, and Slavic parties, Taaffe used its power to weaken the liberals. In Bohemia, for example, he designated Czech as an official language of the bureaucracy and school system, thus breaking the German speakers' monopoly on officeholding. Reforms outraged individuals at whose expense other ethnic groups received benefits, yet those who won concessions, such as the Czechs, clamored for even greater autonomy. By playing nationalities off one another, the government ensured the monarchy's central role in holding together competing interest groups in an era of rapid change. Emperor Francis Joseph and his ministers still feared the influence of the most powerful Slavic nation — Russia — on the ethnic minorities living within Austria-Hungary.

Nationalists in the Balkans demanded independence from the declining Ottoman Empire, raising Austro-Hungarian fears and ambitions. In 1876, Slavs in Bulgaria and Bosnia-Herzegovina revolted against Turkish rule, killing Ottoman officials. As the Ottomans slaughtered thousands of Bulgarians in turn, two other small Balkan states, Serbia and Montenegro, rebelled against the sultan, too. Russian Pan-Slavic organizations sent aid to the Balkan rebels and so pressured the tsar's government that Russia declared war on Turkey in 1877 in the name of protecting Orthodox Christians. With help from Romania and Greece, Russia defeated the Ottomans and by the Treaty of San Stefano (1878) created a large, pro-Russian Bulgaria.

The Treaty of San Stefano sparked an international uproar that almost resulted in a general European war. Austria-Hungary and Britain feared that an enlarged Bulgaria would become a Russian satellite that would enable the tsar to dominate the Balkans. Austrian officials worried about an uprising of their own restless Slavs. British prime minister Benjamin Disraeli moved warships into position against Russia in order to halt the advance of Russian influence in the eastern Mediterranean, so close to Britain's routes through the Suez Canal. The public was drawn into foreign policy: the music halls and newspapers of England echoed a new jingoism, or political sloganeering, that throbbed with sentiments of war: "We don't want to fight, but by jingo if we do, / We've got the ships, we've got the men, we've got the money too!"

The other great powers, however, did not want a Europe-wide war, and in 1878 they attempted to revive the concert of Europe by meeting at Berlin under the auspices of Bismarck, who was a calming presence on the diplomatic scene. The Congress of Berlin rolled back the Russian victory by partitioning the large Bulgarian state that Russia had carved out of Ottoman territory and denying any part of Bulgaria full independence from the Ottomans (Map 23.4). Austria occupied (but did not annex) Bosnia and Herzegovina as a way of gaining clout in the Balkans; Serbia and Montenegro became fully independent. Nonetheless, the Balkans remained a site of political unrest, teeming ambition for independence, and great-power rivalries.

Following the Congress of Berlin, the European powers attempted to guarantee stability through a complex series of alliances and treaties. Anxious about the Balkans, Austria-Hungary forged a defensive alliance with Germany in 1879. The **Dual Alliance**, as it was called, offered protection against Russia and its potential for inciting Slav rebellions. In 1882, Italy joined this partnership (henceforth called the Triple Alliance), largely because of Italy's imperial rivalries with France. Tensions between Russia and Austria-Hungary remained high, so Bismarck replaced the Three Emperors League with the Reinsurance Treaty (1887) with Russia to

---

Dual Alliance: A defensive alliance between Germany and Austria-Hungary created in 1879 as part of Bismarck's system of alliances to prevent or limit war. It was joined by Italy in 1882 as a third partner and then called the Triple Alliance.

MAP 23.4 The Balkans, c. 1878

After midcentury, the map of the Balkans was almost constantly redrawn. This resulted in part from the weakness of the dominant Ottoman Empire, but also from the ambitions of inhabitants themselves and from great power rivalry. In tune with the growing sense of national identities based on shared culture, history, and ethnicity, various Balkan peoples sought to emphasize local, small-group identities rather than merging around a single dominant group such as the Serbs. Yet there was also a move by some intellectuals to transcend borders and create a southern Slav culture.

keep the Habsburgs from recklessly starting a war over Pan-Slavism.

Unrest in Russia Besides its expansionist moves and setbacks, Russia was beset by domestic problems in the 1870s and 1880s. It remained almost the only European country without a constitutional government, and young Russians were turning to revolutionary groups for solutions to political and social problems. One such group, the Populists, wanted to rouse debt-ridden peasants to revolt. Other people formed terrorist bands with the goal of forcing change by assassinating public officials. The secret police, relying on informers, rounded up hundreds of members of one of the largest groups, Land and Liberty, and subjected them to brutal torture, show trials, and imprisonment. When in 1877 a young radical, Vera Zasulich, tried unsuccessfully to assassinate the chief of the St. Petersburg police, the people of the capital city applauded her act and acquittal, so great was their outrage at government treatment of young radicals from respectable families.

Russia: The Pale of Settlement in the Nineteenth Century

Writers added to the debate over Russia's future, often by specifically discussing these political issues and mobilizing public opinion. Novelists Leo Tolstoy, author of the epic *War and Peace* (1869), and Fyodor Dostoevsky, a former radical, believed that Russia above all required spiritual regeneration—not revolution. Tolstoy's novel *Anna Karenina* (1877) tells the story of an impassioned, adulterous love affair, but it also weaves in the spiritual quest of Levin, a former "progressive" landowner who, like Tolstoy, idealizes the peasantry's tradition of stoic endurance. Dostoevsky satirized Russia's radicals in *The Possessed* (1871), a novel in which a group of revolutionaries murders one of its own members. In Dostoevsky's view, the radicals were simply destructive, offering no solutions whatsoever to Russia's ills.

Despite the influential critiques published by Tolstoy and Dostoevsky, violent action rather than spiritual uplift remained the foundation of radicalism. In 1881, the People's Will, a splinter group of Land and Liberty impatient with its failure to mobilize the peasantry, killed Tsar Alexander II in a bomb attack. His death, however, failed to provoke the general uprising the terrorists expected. Alexander III (r. 1881–1894) unleashed a new wave of oppression against religious and ethnic minorities and gave the police virtually unchecked power. Popular books and drawings depicted Tatars, Poles, Ukrainians, and others as horrifying and uncivilized—and thus a menace to Russian culture. The five million Russian Jews, confined to the eighteenth-century Pale of Settlement (the name for the restricted territory in which they were permitted to live), endured particularly severe oppression. Local officials instigated pogroms against Jews, whose distinctive language, dress, and isolation in ghettos made them easy targets. Government administrators encouraged people to blame Jews for rising living costs—though the true cause was the high taxes levied on peasants to pay for industrialization.

As the tsar inflicted even greater repression across Russia, Bismarck's delicate system of alliances of the three conservative powers was coming apart. A brash but deeply insecure young kaiser, William II (r. 1888–1918), came to the German throne in 1888. William resented Bismarck's power, and his advisers flattered the young man into thinking that his own talent made Bismarck an unnecessary rival. William dismissed Bismarck in 1890 and let the Reinsurance Treaty with Russia lapse in favor of a pro-German relationship with Austria-Hungary. He thus destabilized the diplomatic scene just as imperial rivalries were intensifying antagonisms among the European nation-states and empires.

REVIEW QUESTION What were the major changes in political life from the 1870s to the 1890s, and which areas of Europe did they most affect?

Conclusion

The period from the 1870s to the 1890s has been called the age of empire and industry because Western society pursued both these ends in a way that rapidly transformed Europe and the world. Much of Europe thrived due to industrial innovation, becoming more populous and more urbanized. Using the innovative weapons streaming from Europe's factories, the great powers undertook a new imperialism that established political rule over foreign peoples. As they tightened connections with the rest

Torah Scrolls

After the assassination of Alexander II in 1881, the government unleashed pogroms against the Jews of the Russian Empire. The pogroms involved violent acts such as murder, beatings, and the destruction of property on a grand scale. In this image, Jewish men survey the damage done to the sacred texts of their religion during one such vicious attack. *(© From the Jewish Chronicle Archive/Heritage Images/The Image Works.)*

of the globe, Europeans proudly spread their supposedly superior culture throughout the world and, like Frieda von Bülow and Carl Peters, sought out whatever distant peoples could offer in terms of power and wealth.

Imperial expansion and industrial change affected all social classes. The upper class attempted to maintain its position of social and political dominance, while an expanding middle class was gaining power and influence. Working-class people often suffered from the effects of rapid industrial change when their labor was replaced by machinery. Millions relocated to escape poor conditions in the countryside and to find new opportunities. Political reform, especially the expansion of suffrage, helped working-class men gain a political voice. Workers formed unions and political parties to protect their interests, but governments often responded to workers' activism with repression.

As workers struck for improved wages and conditions and the impoverished migrated to find a better life, Western society showed that troubles existed in the new imperial and industrial age. Newspapers informed people about disturbing national and international events overnight. By the 1890s, the advance of empire and industry was bringing unprecedented tensions to national politics, the international scene, and everyday life. Racism, anti-Semitism, and ethnic chauvinism were spreading, and many were questioning the costs of empire both to their own nation and conquered peoples. Politics in the authoritarian countries of central and eastern Europe was taking a more conservative turn, resisting participation and reform. The rising tensions of modern life would soon have grave consequences for the West as a whole.

FOR FURTHER EXPLORATION

- **For additional primary-source material from this period**, see *Sources of the Making of the West*, Fourth Edition.
- **For Web sites, images, and documents related to topics in this chapter**, visit *Make History* at bedfordstmartins.com/hunt.

MAPPING THE WEST

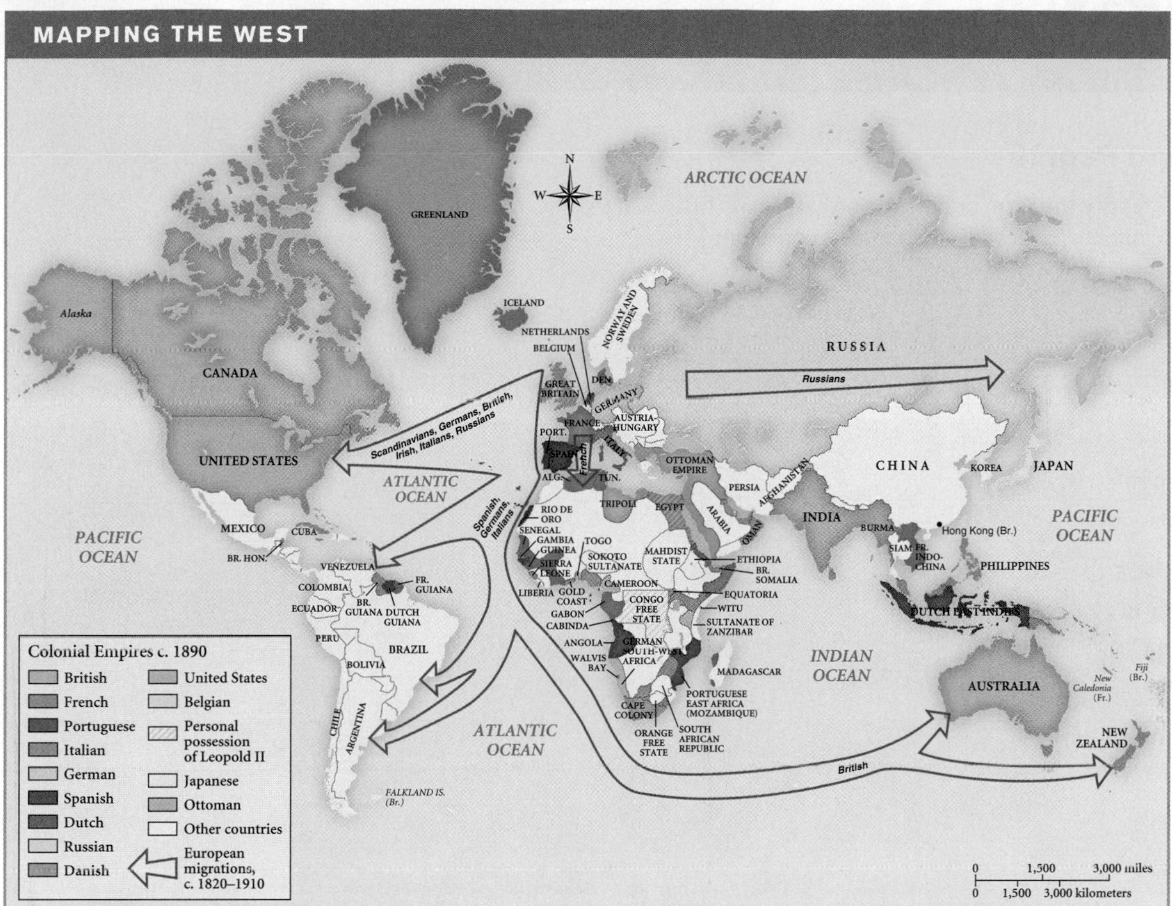

The West and the World, c. 1890

In the late nineteenth century, European trade and political reach spanned the globe. Needing markets for the vast quantities of goods that poured from European factories and access to raw materials to produce the goods, governments asserted that the Western way of life should be spread to the rest of the world and that resources would be best used by Europeans. Explorations and scientific discoveries continued both to build the knowledge base of Western nations and to enhance their ability for greater conquest. Simultaneously, millions of Europeans left their homes to find a better life elsewhere.

Chapter 23 Review

Online Study Guide **bedfordstmartins.com/hunt**

Key Terms and People

In the grid below, identify the term or person and explain its historical significance. (To do this exercise online, go to bedfordstmartins.com/hunt.)

Term	Who or What & When	Why It Matters
Leopold II (p. 762)		
outwork (p. 770)		
capital-intensive industry (p. 772)		
limited liability corporation (p. 772)		
impressionism (p. 783)		
new unionism (p. 785)		
Second International (p. 785)		
William Gladstone (p. 786)		
Reform Act of 1884 (p. 787)		
Charles Stewart Parnell (p. 787)		
home rule (p. 787)		
Third Republic (p. 787)		
Dual Alliance (p. 790)		

Review Questions

1. What were the goals of the new imperialism, and how did Europeans accomplish those goals?
2. What were the major changes in Western industry and business in the last third of the nineteenth century?
3. How did empire and industry influence art and everyday life?
4. What were the major changes in political life from the 1870s to the 1890s, and which areas of Europe did they most affect?

Making Connections

1. How did the new imperialism differ from European expansion of two centuries earlier? Of four centuries earlier?
2. Describe the effects of imperialism on European politics and society as a whole in 1870–1890.
3. Compare the political and social goals of the newly enfranchised male electorate with those of people from the "best circles."

Important Events

Date	Event	Date	Event
1860s–1890s	Impressionism flourishes in the arts; absorption of Asian influences	1882	Triple Alliance formed between Germany, Austria-Hungary, and Italy; Britain invades Egypt
1870s–1890s	Vast emigration from Europe continues; the new imperialism	1882–1884	Bismarck sponsors social welfare legislation
1871	Franco-Prussian War ends	1884	British Parliament passes the Reform Act, doubling size of male electorate
1873	Extended economic recession begins with global impact	1884–1885	European nations carve up Africa at Berlin conference
1876	British Parliament declares Victoria empress; invention of telephone	1885	Invention of workable gasoline engine; formation of Indian National Congress
1878	Treaty of San Stefano	1889	Japan adopts constitution based on European models; socialists meet in Paris and establish Second International
1879	Dual Alliance formed between Germany and Austria-Hungary	1891	Construction of Trans-Siberian Railroad begins
1881	Tsar Alexander II assassinated; France occupies Tunisia		

- Consider three events: **Impressionism flourishes in the arts (1860s–1890s)**, **Vast emigration from Europe continues (1870s–1890s)**, and **Bismarck sponsors social welfare legislation (1882–1884)**. How were all of these related to empire and industry?

SUGGESTED REFERENCES

The literature on imperialism is becoming increasingly exciting, especially as authors such as Burbank and Cooper show imperialism's relationship with the nation-state. Others show its confusions and chaotic nature.

Brewer, John, and Frank Trentmann, eds. *Consuming Cultures, Global Perspectives: Historical Trajectories, Transnational Exchanges*. 2006.

Burbank, Jane, and Frederick Cooper. *Empires in World History: Power and the Politics of Difference*. 2010.

Cain, P. J., and A. G. Hopkins, *British Imperialism, 1688–2000*. 2002.

Davis, Mike. *Late Victorian Holocausts: El Niño Famines and the Making of the Third World*. 2001.

Eley, Geoff. *Forging Democracy: A History of the Left in Europe, 1850–2000*. 2002.

Headrick, Daniel R. *Power over Peoples: Technology, Environments, and Western Imperialism 1400 to the Present*. 2010.

Lorcin, Patricia M. E., ed. *Algeria and France 1800–2000: Identity, Memory, Nostalgia*. 2006.

Manning, Patrick. *Migration in World History*. 2005.

Maynes, Mary Jo, et al. *Secret Gardens, Satanic Mills: Placing Girls in European History, 1750–1960*. 2005.

Rappaport, Erika. *Shopping for Pleasure: Women in the Making of London's West End*. 2000.

Reeder, Linda. *Widows in White: Migration and the Transformation of Rural Italian Women, Sicily, 1880–1920*. 2003.

Reid, Richard J. *A History of Modern Africa*. 2009.

Smith, Michael S. *The Emergence of Modern Business Enterprise in France, 1800–1930*. 2005.

Streets, Heather. *Martial Races: The Military, Race, and Masculinity in British Imperial Culture, 1857–1918*. 2004.

Weaver, Stewart, and Maurice Isserman. *Fallen Giants: A History of Himalayan Mountaineering from the Age of Empire to the Age of Extremes*. 2008.

Wildenthal, Lora. *German Women for Empire, 1884–1945*. 2001.

Modernity and the Road to War

CHAPTER 24

1890–1914

In the first decade of the twentieth century, a wealthy young Russian man traveled from one country to another to find relief from a common malady of the time called neurasthenia. Its symptoms included fatigue, lack of interest in life, depression, and sometimes physical illness. In 1910, the young man consulted Sigmund Freud, a Viennese physician whose unconventional treatment—eventually called psychoanalysis—took the form of a conversation about the patient's dreams, sexual experiences, and everyday life. Over the course of four years, Freud uncovered his patient's deeply hidden fear of castration, which was disguised as a fear of wolves—thus the name Wolf-Man, by which he is known to us. Freud worked his cure, as the Wolf-Man himself put it, "by bringing repressed ideas into consciousness" through extensive talking.

In many ways, the Wolf-Man could be said to represent his time. Born into a family that owned vast estates, he reflected Europe's growing prosperity, though on a grander scale than most. Countless individuals were troubled, even mentally disturbed like the Wolf-Man, and suicides were not uncommon. The Wolf-Man's own sister and father died from intentional drug overdoses. As the twentieth century opened, Europeans raised questions about family, gender relationships, empire, religion, and the consequences of technology. Every sign of imperial wealth brought on an apparently irrational sense of Europe's decline. British writer H. G. Wells saw in this era "humanity upon the wane . . . the sunset of mankind." Gloom filled the pages of many a book and upset the lives of individuals like the Wolf-Man.

Conflict rattled the world as a growing number of powers, including Japan and the United States, fought their way into even more territories. The nations of Europe had lurched from one diplomatic crisis to another

Edvard Munch, *The Scream* (1893)
In some of his paintings, Norwegian artist Edvard Munch captured a certain spirit of the turn of the century, depicting in soft pastel colors the newly leisured life of people strolling in the countryside. But modern life also had a tortured side, which Munch was equally capable of portraying. *The Scream* is taken as emblematic of the torments of modernity as the individual turns inward, beset by neuroses, self-destructive impulses, and even madness. It can also be suggested that the screamer, like Europe, travels the road to World War I. *(Scala/Art Resource, NY/© 2011 The Munch Museum/The Munch-Ellingsen Group/Artists Rights Society [ARS], New York.)*

over access to global resources and control of territory—both within Europe and outside it. As the great powers fought to dominate people around the world, competition for empire fueled an arms race that threatened to turn Europe—the most civilized region of the world, according to its leaders—into a savage battleground. In domestic politics, militant nationalism fueled ethnic hatreds and anti-Semitism, even leading to physical violence. Women suffragists along with politically disadvantaged groups such as the Slavs and Irish demanded full rights, even as political assassinations and public brutality swept away the liberal values of tolerance and human rights.

These were just some of the conflicts associated with modernity, a term often used to describe the rise of mass politics, the spread of technology, the faster pace of life, and the decline of a rural social order—all of which were visible in the West from the late nineteenth century on (see "Terms of History," page 799). The word *modern* was also applied to art, music, science, and philosophy of this period. Although many people today admire the brilliant, innovative qualities of modern art, music, and dance, people of the time were offended, even outraged, by the new styles and sounds. Freud's theory that sexual drives exist in even the youngest children shocked people. Every advance in science and the arts simultaneously undermined middle-class faith in the stability of Western civilization.

That faith was further tested when the heir to the Austro-Hungarian throne was assassinated in June 1914. Few gave much thought to the global significance of the event, least of all the Wolf-Man, whose treatment with Freud was just ending. He viewed the fateful day of June 28 simply as the day he "could now leave Vienna a healthy man." Yet the assassination put the spark to the powder keg of international discord that had been building for several decades. The resulting disastrous war, World War I, like the insights of Freud, would transform life in the West.

CHAPTER FOCUS How did developments in social life, art, intellectual life, and politics at the turn of the twentieth century produce instability and set the backdrop for war?

Public Debate over Private Life

At the beginning of the twentieth century, an increasing number of people could aspire to a comfortable family life because of Europe's improved standard of living. Yet as the twentieth century opened, traditional social norms such as heterosexual marriage and woman's domestic role as wife and mother came under attack by what were seen as the forces of modernity. The falling birthrate, rising divorce rate, and growing activism for marriage reform provoked heated accusations that changes in private life were endangering national health. Discussions about sexual identity became a political issue. Middle-class women took jobs and became active in public to such an extent that some feared the disappearance of distinct gender roles. Women's visibility in public life prompted one British songster in the late 1890s to write:

> Rock-a-bye baby, for father is near
> Mother is "biking" she never is here!
> Out in the park she's scorching all day
> Or at some meeting is talking away!

Discussions of gender roles and private life contributed to rising social tensions because they challenged so many traditional ideals. Freud and other scientists tried to be dispassionate in their study of such phenomena—sexuality, for example—and to formulate treatments for "modern" ailments such as those afflicting the Wolf-Man. Public discussions of private life, especially when they became inter-

1894–1895 Japan defeats China in Sino-Japanese War

1894–1899 Dreyfus Affair exposes anti-Semitism in France

1895

1899–1902 South African War fought between Dutch descendants and British in South African states

1900 Sigmund Freud publishes *The Interpretation of Dreams*

1900

1901 Irish National Theater established by Maud Gonne and William Butler Yeats; death of Queen Victoria

1903 Emmeline Pankhurst founds Women's Social and Political Union

1904–1905 Japan defeats Russia in Russo-Japanese War

TERMS OF HISTORY

Modern

The word *modernus* was introduced into Latin in the sixth century; after that, the claim to being modern occurred in many centuries and cultures. Shakespeare, for example, referred to "modern ideas" in his plays, and historians have long debated where "modern" history begins: with Abraham? with Charlemagne? with the Renaissance?

Despite the claims of many ages to being modern, the term has fastened itself most firmly on the period from the end of the nineteenth century through the first half of the twentieth. Its most specific historical use has been to describe the art, music, and dance that flourished at that time. When used in this sense, *modern* indicates a sharp break with lyrical, romantic music and dance and with the tradition of realism in the arts. The blurred images of the impressionists and the jarring music of Arnold Schoenberg are part of modern art because they break with accepted forms. The sexual rawness of Gustave Flaubert's *Madame Bovary* (see Chapter 22) or of Sigmund Freud's analysis of the Wolf-Man's dreams added to the multifaceted meanings of the word *modern*. Sometimes this intellectual break with the cultural past is referred to as modernism.

At the end of the nineteenth century, the word *modern* also referred to social phenomena. Women who went to work or entered universities or began careers were called modern women. They believed that, by showing themselves capable and rational, they could end restrictions placed on them. They lived different lives from those women who confined themselves to the domestic sphere. This departure from tradition also made them appear modern.

In seeking an education, these women were invoking a meaning of the words *modern* and *modernity* dating back to the Enlightenment. Rational thought and science have also been taken as the bedrock of the modern. *Modernization*—another derivative of the word *modern*—refers to the kind of scientific and technological progress that rational observation produced. Industry and its products—indoor plumbing, electricity, telephones, and automobiles—were signs of *modernity*. This focus on the term *modern* to indicate technological advance made it useful as a way to celebrate the West's modernity in contrast to other people's backwardness. Its association with new (and therefore superior) thinking and forward advancement became central to the justification for imperial rule, especially as Western empires were increasingly contested by 1900.

The many meanings of the word *modern* and those words deriving from it make it a multipurpose term. Complex, paradoxical, and dense with meaning, *modern* may not always be precise. But its very breadth explains why *modern* remains a much-debated term of history.

twined with politics, demonstrated the close connection of private and public concerns.

Population Pressure

From the 1890s on, European politicians and the public hotly discussed urgent concerns over trends in population, marriage, and sexuality. The staggering population increases of the eighteenth century continued through the nineteenth century, and rural people and migrants crowded into cities. Alarmed by the urban masses, Social Darwinists became louder in their warnings about racial decay. Reformers and politicians saw both the quantity and quality of population as looming national crises.

1905
Nicholas II establishes the Duma after revolution erupts in Russia; Albert Einstein publishes his special theory of relativity

1906
Women receive vote in Finland

1907
Pablo Picasso launches cubist painting with *Les Demoiselles d'Avignon*

1908
Young Turks revolt against rule by sultan in Ottoman Empire

1911–1912
Revolutionaries overthrow Qing dynasty and declare China a republic

1914
Assassination of Austrian archduke Francis Ferdinand and his wife by Serbian nationalist precipitates World War I

1905 1910 1915

Soaring Population The European population continued to grow as the twentieth century opened. Germany increased in size from 41 million people in 1871 to 64 million in 1910, and tiny Denmark grew from 1.7 million people in 1870 to 2.7 million in 1911. Improvements in sanitation and public health that extended the human life span and reduced infant mortality contributed to the increase. Following the earlier examples of Vienna and Paris, planners tore apart and rebuilt Berlin, Budapest, and Moscow to house their swelling populations. The German government pulled down eighteenth-century Berlin and reconstructed the city with new roadways and mass-transport systems as the capital's population grew to over 4 million. Less-powerful states also rebuilt cities to absorb population growth: the Balkan capitals of Sofia, Belgrade, and Bucharest gained tree-lined boulevards and improved sanitation facilities. As the number of urban residents surpassed that of the rural population in a number of countries, ruling elites from the countryside protested the activism and unruliness of urban dwellers.

Alarm over the Falling Birthrate While the absolute size of the population was rising in the West, the birthrate (measured in births per thousand people) was falling. The birthrate had been decreasing in France since the eighteenth century; other European countries began experiencing the decline late in the nineteenth century. The Swedish birthrate dropped from thirty-five births per thousand people in 1859 to twenty-four per thousand in 1911; Germany went from forty births per thousand in 1875 to twenty-seven per thousand in 1913.

Industrialization and urbanization helped bring about this change. Farm families needed fewer hands because new agricultural machinery was taking the place of human laborers. In cities, individual couples were free to make their own decisions about limiting family size, learning from neighbors or, for those with enough money and education, from pamphlets and advice books about birth-control practices, including coitus interruptus (the withdrawal method of preventing pregnancy). Industrial technology played a further role in curtailing reproduction: condoms, improved after the vulcanization of rubber in the 1840s, proved fairly reliable in preventing conception, as did the diaphragm. Abortions were also common.

The wider use of birth control stirred controversy. Critics accused middle-class women, whose fertility was falling most rapidly, of holding a "birth strike." Meeting early in the twentieth century, bishops in the Church of England condemned family limitation as "demoralizing to character and hostile to national welfare." Politicians worried that the drop in the birthrate was due to a crisis in masculinity, which would put military strength at risk. In the United States, Theodore Roosevelt, who became president in 1901, blamed middle-class women's selfishness for the population decline, calling family limitation "one of the most unpleasant and unwholesome features of modern life." The "quality" of those being born worried activists: If the "best" classes had fewer children, politicians asked, what would society look like if only the "worst" classes grew in number?

Racism and nationalism shaped the debate over population. The decline in fertility, one German nationalist warned, would fill the country with "alien peoples, above all Slavs and probably East European Jews as well." Nationalist groups promoting large, "racially fit" families sprang up in France, Germany, Britain, and elsewhere, and they inflamed the political climate with racial hatreds. Instead of building consensus to create an integrated political community, politicians won votes by rais-

Large Czech Family
This photograph of a rural family in Czechoslovakia shows the differences that were coming to distinguish urban from rural people. Although even a farm family, especially in eastern Europe, might proudly display technology such as a new phonograph, it might not practice family limitation, which was gradually reducing the size of urban households. In eastern Europe, several generations lived together more commonly in rural areas than in cities. How many generations do you see in this image? (*© Scheufler Collection/Corbis.*)

ing fears of ethnic minorities, the poor, and women who limited family size.

Reforming Marriage

Reformers thought that improving conditions within marriage would raise both the quality and quantity of children born. Many educated Europeans believed in eugenics — a set of ideas about producing "superior" people through selective breeding. A famed Italian criminologist declared that "lower" types of people were not humans but "orangutans." Eugenicists wanted increased childbearing for "the fittest" and decreased childbearing — even sterilization — for "degenerates": the disabled, criminals, and others deemed inferior. Women of the "better" classes, reformers also believed, would have more children if marriage were made more equal. One step would be to allow married women to keep their wages and to own property, both of which in the traditional system legally belonged to their husbands. Another step would be to allow women rights to their own children, and given the legal limits, reformers suggested, married women were reluctant to have more than one or two children.

Reformers worked to improve marriage laws in order to boost the birthrate, while feminists sought to improve the lot of mothers and their children. Sweden made men's and women's control over property equal in marriage and allowed married women to work without their husband's permission. Other countries, among them France (1884), legalized divorce and made it less complicated to obtain. Reformers reasoned that divorce would allow unhappy couples to separate and undertake more loving and thus more fertile marriages. By the early twentieth century, several countries had passed legislation that provided government subsidies for medical care and child support in order to encourage motherhood among the lower classes. Concerns regarding population partially laid the foundations for the welfare state — that is, a nation-state whose policies addressed not just military defense, foreign policy, and political processes but also the social and economic well-being of its people.

The conditions of women's lives varied across Europe. For example, a greater number of legal reforms occurred in western versus eastern Europe, but women could get university degrees in Austria-Hungary long before they could at Oxford or Cambridge. However, in much of rural eastern Europe, the father's power over the extended family remained almost dictatorial. According to a survey of family life in eastern Europe in the early 1900s, fathers married off their children so young that 25 percent of women in their early forties had been pregnant more than ten times. Yet reform of everyday customs did occur. For instance, in some Balkan villages a traditional family system called the *zadruga*, in which all individual families within an extended family shared a common great house, survived from earlier times. Yet by the late nineteenth century, individual couples gained privacy by building small sleeping dwellings surrounding the great house. In addition, among the middle and upper classes of eastern Europe, many grown children were coming to believe that they had a right to select a marriage partner instead of accepting the spouse their parents chose for them.

New Women, New Men, and the Politics of Sexual Identity

Rapid social change set the stage for even bolder behaviors among some middle-class women. Adventurous women traveled the globe on their own to promote Christianity, make money, or learn about other cultures. The increasing availability of white collar jobs for educated women meant that more of them could adopt an independent way of life. The so-called **new woman** dressed more practically, with

new woman: A woman who, from the 1880s on, dressed practically, moved about freely, and often supported herself.

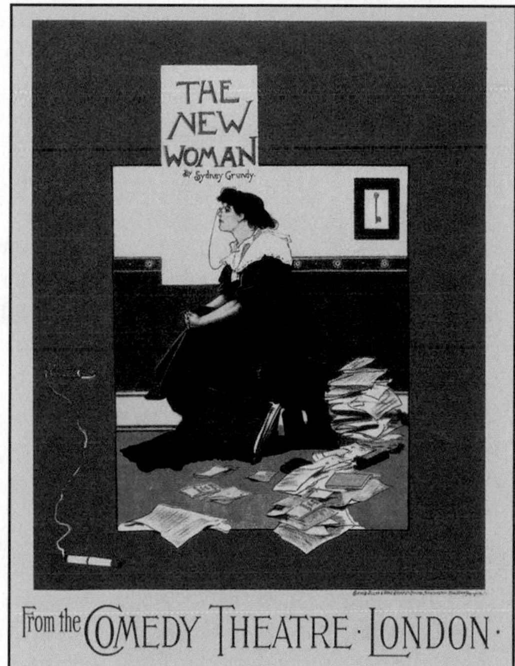

Sydney Grundy, *The New Woman* (1900)
By the opening of the twentieth century, the "new woman" had become a much-discussed phenomenon. Artists painted portraits of this independent creature, while novelists and playwrights like Henrik Ibsen depicted her ambition to throw off the wifely role — or at least to shape that role more to her own personality. In this lithograph, she also smokes. *(© Private Collection/The Stapleton Collection/The Bridgeman Art Library.)*

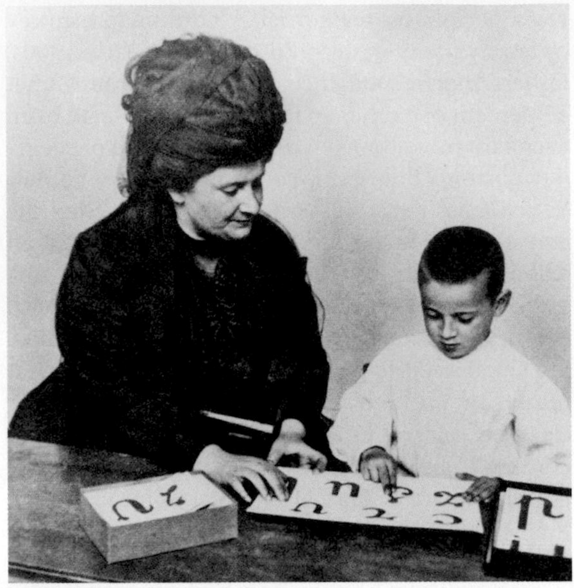

Maria Montessori

Maria Montessori, famous today for the global network of schools that bear her name, was the perfect example of a "new woman." Her work outside the home with children was controversial; she was also a highly skilled medical doctor and, secretly, an unwed mother. While she developed a set of sophisticated theories for the advancement of young children generally, others cared for her own son. *(akg-images/ullstein bild.)*

Oscar Wilde

The Irish-born writer Oscar Wilde symbolized the persecution experienced by homosexuals in the late nineteenth century. Convicted of indecency for having sexual relations with another man, Wilde served time in prison—a humiliation for the husband, father, acclaimed author, and witty playwright. *(Library of Congress, Prints and Photographs Division. LC-USZ62 914833.)*

fewer petticoats and looser corsets, biked down city streets and country lanes, lived apart from her family in a women's club or an apartment, and supported herself (see the illustration on page 801). Italian educator Maria Montessori (1870–1952), the first woman in Italy to earn a medical degree and the founder of an educational system that still bears her name, secretly gave birth to an illegitimate child. Other new women lived openly with their lovers. The growing number of new women challenged accepted views of women's dependence and seclusion in the home. Not surprisingly, there was loud criticism: the new woman, German philosopher Friedrich Nietzsche wrote, had led to the "uglification of Europe."

Sexual identity also fueled debate. A popular book in the new field of "sexology," which studied sex scientifically, was *Sexual Inversion* (1896) by Havelock Ellis. Ellis, a British medical doctor, claimed that there was a new personality type—the homosexual—identifiable by such traits as effeminate behavior and attraction to the arts (in males) and physical affection for members of their own sex (in both males and females). Homosexuals joined the discussion, calling for recognition that they composed a natural "third sex" and were not just people behaving sinfully. Some maintained that homosexuals were members of an "intermediate sex," possessing both male and female traits and thus marking "a higher order" on the scale of human evolution. The discussion of homosexuality started the trend toward seeing sexuality in general as a basic part of human identity.

The issue became explosive in the spring of 1895, when Irish playwright Oscar Wilde (1854–1900) was convicted of indecency—a charge that referred to his sexual affairs with young men (see the illustration on the left)—and sentenced to two years in prison. "Open the windows! Let in the fresh air!" one newspaper rejoiced at the conviction. Between 1907 and 1909, German newspapers broadcast the courts-martial of military men in Kaiser William II's closest circle who were condemned for homosexuality and transvestitism. Amid growing concern over population and family values, the government had to assure the public that William's own family life was "a fine model" for the German nation. Heterosexuality thus took on patriotic overtones: accused homosexuals among the elite in Germany were said by journalists to be out to "emasculate our courageous master race." Despite the harsh judgments against homosexuals, these cases paved the way for growing sexual openness in the next generations. Yet they also made sexual issues regular weapons in politics.

Sciences of the Modern Self

Scientists and Social Darwinists found cause for alarm not only in the poor condition of the working class but also in modern society's mental complaints such as those of the Wolf-Man. Medical people decided that most mental illnesses originated in the "nerves," which were troubled by the hectic pace of urban living. New sciences of the mind such as psychology and psychoanalysis aimed to treat everyone, not just the insane.

New Approaches to Mental Ailments A number of books in the 1890s presented arguments on causes and cures for modern nervous ailments. *Degeneration* (1892–1893), by Hungarian-born physician Max Nordau, blamed overstimulation for both individual and national deterioration. According to Nordau, male and female nervous complaints and the increasingly bizarre art world reflected a general downturn in the human species. The Social Darwinist remedy for such mental decline was imperial adventure for men and increased childbearing for both sexes because it would restore men's virility and women's femininity.

Investigations into the working of the mind led to new fields of study. Scientific study of the origins of criminal behavior developed into the field of criminology. French psychologist Alfred Binet designed intelligence tests he claimed could measure the capacity of the human mind more accurately than a schoolteacher could. In Russia, physiologist Ivan Pavlov proposed that behavior could be controlled by conditioning mental reflexes. Pavlov's experiments in changing behavior, especially his success in getting a dog to salivate upon hearing a bell, became part of the toolkit of modern psychology.

Freud and Psychoanalysis **Sigmund Freud** (1856–1939) devised an approach to treating modern anxieties and mental problems that challenged the widespread liberal belief, dating from the Enlightenment, in a rational self that consistently acts in its own best interest. Dreams, he explained in *The Interpretation of Dreams* (1900), reveal an unseen, repressed, and powerful part of one's personality—the "unconscious"—where all sorts of desires are more or less hidden from one's rational understanding. Freud also believed that the human psyche is made up of

---

Sigmund Freud: Viennese medical doctor and founder, in the late nineteenth century, of psychoanalysis, a theory of mental processes and problems and a method of treating them.

Freud's Office and Collection
Sigmund Freud surrounded himself with imperial trophies such as Oriental rugs and African art objects in his study and therapy room in Vienna. Freud was fascinated by cures brought about through shamanism, trances, and other practices of non-Western medicine. Despite his successes, Freud, like other Jews, was a target of anti-Semitism from Nazis and others; he eventually escaped Vienna for exile in London in 1938. *(ullstein bild/The Granger Collection, NYC—All rights reserved.)*

NEW SOURCES, NEW PERSPECTIVES

Psychohistory and Its Lessons

In the last fifty years, historians have radically changed the way they write history. In the nineteenth century, history books mostly recounted the deeds of kings and emperors, discussed royal genealogy, and listed wars and peace treaties. Determined to be factual, historians not only laid out the fine points of laws, charters, and treaties but also checked their sources in archives. They would often characterize historical actors as brave, evil, determined, or weak.

Much has changed since then, partly because of the rise of psychology and psychoanalysis as the twentieth century opened. Confronted with strikes, mass demonstrations, anarchist deeds, anti-Semitism, and other forms of political violence, some observers tried to explain a phenomenon they called crowd psychology. According to this view, psychological states are important factors in shaping some public events. Scholars began pursuing deeper insights and more systematic ways of analyzing the character and motivation of important people from the past.

Not surprisingly, Sigmund Freud studied great historic figures like Leonardo da Vinci from a psychoanalytic perspective, exploring the connection between repressed childhood fantasies and later towering accomplishments. Freud also explained the outbreak of World War I as more of a psychological than a diplomatic event. He saw the war as a collective death wish. He subjected both individuals and entire societies to psychoanalytic probing. Few historians followed Freud's lead.

In 1957, William Langer, president of the American Historical Association, charged his fellow scholars with being foolishly backward in their methods. Unlike scientists, he claimed, historians did not develop scientific systems or explore new techniques such as psychoanalysis that might advance their understanding of the past. Weren't such characterizations as ambition, greed, hate, and great intelligence simply commonsensical and not at all rigorously analytical? But what was the "scientific" depth in such characterizations? Another criticism by those interested in psychology and psychoanalysis was that historians often saw people as acting rationally in their self-interest. Trauma, irrational or uncontrollable drives, and unconscious motivations played no role in understanding historical figures.

Psychohistory was born of these discussions. Psychoanalyst Erik Erikson, in *Young Man Luther* (1958), announced that the Protestant Reformation originated in the childhood traumas of Martin Luther. Identity crises stemming from his relationship with his father caused Luther to search for and reject father figures, including the pope. Erikson's book caused a stir among historians, changing the way people understood Luther and starting an entirely new school of historical thought.

Some of the most compelling examples of psychohistory have focused on the lives of individuals whose leadership has appeared abnormal or even psychotic. Historians interested in psychoanalysis have examined Kaiser William II's childhood for explanations of his rejection of Bismarck, his turn to an aggressive foreign policy, and his participation in World War I. Analyses of Adolf Hitler's followers have attributed the blind worship of these dictators to mass psychic needs and traumas, while the brutality of Hitler's father and the adoration of his mother have been seen to play a role in the future dictator's development.

Psychohistory remains controversial. While its practitioners expand the field of historical explanation, its critics find that fitting the behavior of historical characters into Freud's schema can be a formulaic process. Other critics find that psychohistory is too imprecise and speculative because it is not based on the same kinds of hard, documentary evidence that

three competing parts: the ego, the part that is most in touch with the need to work and survive—that is, reality; the id (or libido), the part that contains instincts and sexual energies; and the superego, the part that serves as the conscience. Freud's theory of human mental processes and his method for treating their malfunctioning came to be called psychoanalysis.

Freud demanded that sexual life should be understood objectively, free from religious or moral judgments. He shocked many of his contemporaries by insisting, for example, that all children have sexual drives from the moment of birth. He believed that for the individual to attain maturity and for society to remain civilized, sexual desires—such as impulses toward incest—had to be rigorously repressed. Freud claimed that adult gender identity does not result from anatomy alone but rather develops over the course of a person's life experiences. Although gender is more complicated than biology alone would suggest, certain aspects of gender roles—such as motherhood—are normal. Freud's psychoanalytic theory maintained that girls and women have powerful sexual feelings, an idea that broke sharply with existing beliefs that women were passionless.

historians have been trained to use. Nonetheless, psychohistorians have made a good case that if we are going to look at personalities, character, and relationships, we should do so in the most informed way possible and not rely simply on clichés.

Questions to Consider

1. What are the advantages and disadvantages of psychohistory?
2. How would you set out to investigate the psychological reasons for the actions of William II, Emmeline Pankhurst, Marie Curie, or Gavrilo Princip? Would you look at their social background, their childhood, their character, or other parts of their lives?
3. Can we write history without talking about the emotions, mental habits, and human relationships of major figures? To what extent should we either embrace or avoid psychologizing when thinking about the past?

Further Reading

Binion, Rudolph. *Hitler among the Germans*. 1984.
Erikson, Erik. *Young Man Luther: A Study in Psychoanalysis and History*. 1958.
Kohut, Thomas A. *Wilhelm II and the Germans: A Study in Leadership*. 1991.

Kaiser William and Edward VII's Family
Psychotherapy aimed to cure troubled individuals in large part by discussing family relationships and the fantasies built around them. Psychohistory often draws its analyses from these same relationships. The royal families of Europe are ripe for such analysis because Russian, German, British, and other monarchs were closely related. (In this photo Britain's Edward VII is at right, and Germany's Kaiser William is second from right.) Psychohistorians may therefore view the outbreak of World War I as the work of complex family dynamics. *(Hulton Archive/Getty Images.)*

The influence of psychoanalysis became pervasive in the twentieth century (see "New Sources, New Perspectives," above). For example, Freud's "talking cure," as his method of treatment was quickly labeled, gave rise to a general acceptance of talking out one's problems. As psychoanalysis gained respect as a means of restoring mental health, terms such as *neurotic* and *unconscious* came into widespread use. Freud attributed girls' complaints about sexual harassment or abuse to fantasy caused by "penis envy," an idea that led members of the new profession of social work to believe that most instances of such abuse had not actually occurred. A meticulous scientist, Freud closely observed symptoms and paid attention to the most minute evidence from everyday life. Like Darwin, he rejected optimistic views of the world, claiming that humans were motivated by irrational drives toward death and destruction. These urges, he believed, shaped society's collective actions.

REVIEW QUESTION How did ideas about the self and about personal life change at the beginning of the twentieth century?

Modernity and the Revolt in Ideas

Toward the beginning of the twentieth century, intellectuals and artists so completely rejected longstanding beliefs and traditional artistic forms that they ushered in a new era. In science, the theories of Albert Einstein and other researchers established new truths in physics. Art and music became unrecognizable. Artists and musicians who produced deliberately shocking works were, like Freud, heavily influenced by advances in science and the progress of empire. Their blending of the scientific and the irrational, and of Western and non-Western styles, helped launch the disorienting revolution in ideas and creative expression that we now identify collectively as **modernism**.

The Opposition to Positivism

Late in the nineteenth century, many philosophers and social thinkers suddenly rejected the century-old belief that using scientific methods would uncover enduring social laws. This belief, called positivism, had emphasized the permanent nature of fundamental laws and had motivated reformers' attempts to perfect legislation based on studies of society. Challenging positivism, some critics declared that because human experience is ever changing, there are no constant or enduring social laws. German political theorist Max Weber (1864–1920) maintained that the sheer number of facts involved in policymaking would often make decisive action by bureaucrats impossible. In times of crisis, a charismatic leader might usurp power because of his ability to act simply on intuition. These turn-of-the-century thinkers, called relativists and pragmatists, influenced thinking about society and government throughout the twentieth century.

The most radical among the scholars was the German philosopher **Friedrich Nietzsche** (1844–1900), who distinguished between the "Apollonian," or rational, side of human existence and the "Dionysian" side, with its expression of more primal urges. Nietzsche believed that people generally prefer the rational, Apollonian explanations of life because the powerful Dionysian sense of death and love, such as that found in Greek tragedy, is too disturbing. He asserted that truth is not certain but rather a human representation of reality. Neither scientists nor other careful observers, he said, can have knowledge of nature that is not filtered through human perception.

Rather than writing the long, sustained type of argument common to traditional Western philosophy, Nietzsche used aphorisms — short, disconnected statements of truth or opinion — to convey the impression that his ideas were a single individual's unique perspective instead of a universal and absolute truth. Nietzsche was convinced that late-nineteenth-century Europe was witnessing the decline of absolute truths such as those found in religion. Thus, he announced, "God is dead, we have killed him." Far from arousing dread, however, the death of God, according to Nietzsche, would give birth to a joyful quest for new "poetries of life" to replace worn-out religious and middle-class rules. Nietzsche believed that an uninhibited, dynamic "superman," free from traditional religious and moral values, would replace the rule-bound middle-class person.

Nietzsche thought that each individual had within a vital life energy that he called "the will to power." The idea inspired many at the time, including his students. As a teacher, Nietzsche was so vibrant — like his superman — that his first students thought they were hearing another Socrates. Nietzsche's teaching career, however, was short-lived: he contracted syphilis and was insane in the last eleven years of his life, cared for by his sister. She edited his attacks on middle-class values into attacks on Jews, and after his death she revised his complicated concepts of the will to power and of superman to appeal to nationalists, anti-Semites, and militarists, all of whom he actually hated.

The Revolution in Science

While Nietzsche and other philosophers questioned the ability of traditional science to provide timeless truths, scientific inquiry itself flourished and the sciences gained in prestige. Around the turn of the century, however, discoveries by pioneering researchers shook the foundations of scientific certainty and challenged accepted knowledge. In 1896, French physicist Antoine Becquerel discovered radioactivity. He also suggested the mutability of elements by the rearrangement of their atoms. French chemist Marie Curie and her husband, Pierre Curie, isolated the elements polonium and radium, which

---

modernism: Artistic styles around the turn of the twentieth century that featured a break with realism in art and literature and with lyricism in music.

Friedrich Nietzsche: Late-nineteenth-century German philosopher who called for a new morality in the face of God's death at the hands of science and whose theories were reworked by his sister to emphasize militarism and anti-Semitism.

are more radioactive than the uranium Becquerel used. From these and other discoveries, scientists concluded that atoms are not solid, as had long been believed, but are composed of subatomic particles moving about a core. In a paper published in 1900, German physicist Max Planck announced his quantum theory, stating that energy is delivered not in a steady stream but in discrete packets, which he later called quanta.

In this atmosphere of discovery, physicist **Albert Einstein** (1879–1955) proclaimed his special theory of relativity in 1905. According to this theory, space and time are not absolute categories but instead vary according to the vantage point of the observer. Only the speed of light is constant. That same year, Einstein suggested that the solution to problems in Planck's theory lay in considering light both as little packets *and* as waves. Einstein later proposed yet another blurring of two distinct physical properties, mass and energy. He expressed this equivalence in the equation $E = mc^2$, or energy equals mass times the square of the speed of light. In 1916, Einstein published his general theory of relativity, which connected the force, or gravity, of an object with its mass and proposed a fourth mathematical dimension to the universe. Much more lay ahead once Einstein's theories of energy were applied to technology: television; nuclear power; and, within forty years, nuclear bombs.

The findings of Planck, Einstein, and others were not readily accepted, because long-standing scientific truths were at stake. Both Einstein and Planck struggled against mainstream science and its professional institutions. Other factors were at work: Marie Curie faced such resistance from the scientific establishment that even after she became the first person ever to receive a second Nobel Prize (1911), the prestigious French Academy of Science turned down her candidacy for membership. It claimed that a woman simply could not have done such outstanding work. Acceptance of these scientists' discoveries gradually came, and Max Planck Institutes were established in German cities, streets across Europe were named after Marie Curie, and Einstein's name became synonymous with *genius*. These scientists achieved what historians call a paradigm shift—that is, in the face of considerable resistance, they transformed the foundations of science as their findings and theories came to replace those of earlier pioneers.

Albert Einstein: Scientist whose theory of relativity (1905) revolutionized modern physics and other fields of thought.

Marie and Pierre Curie
Pierre and Marie Curie shared a Nobel Prize in Physics in 1903, and after Pierre's death in 1906, Marie went on to win a Nobel Prize in Chemistry in 1911. Their daughter Irène Joliot-Curie followed in her parents' footsteps; like her mother, she died of leukemia because of long exposure to radioactive material during experiments. *(Mary Evans Picture Library/AISA Media.)*

Modern Art

Conflicts between traditional values and new ideas also raged in the arts as artists distanced themselves further from classical Western styles. Some modern artists defied the historic and realistic scenes still favored, for example, by the powerful German monarchy and public museums. Modernism in the arts not only challenged time-honored standards but also led to an increase in competing artistic styles that continues today.

A Variety of Styles Abandoning the soft colors of impressionism as too subtle for a dynamic industrial society, a group of Parisian artists exhibiting in 1905 combined blues, greens, reds, and oranges so intensely that they were called *fauves* ("wild beasts"). A leader of the short-lived fauvism, Henri Matisse soon struck out in a new direction, targeting the expanding class of white-collar workers. Matisse saw his art as meant "for every mental worker, be he businessman or writer, like an appeasing influence, like a mental soother, something like a good armchair in which to rest from physical fatigue." His colorful depictions of domestic interiors, North African scenes, and family life departed from strict realism, yet they appealed to viewers in part because of their calming qualities.

French artist Paul Cézanne initiated one of the most powerful trends in modern art by using rectangular daubs of paint to portray his geometric vision of dishes, fruit, drapery, and the human body. Cézanne's art accentuated structure—the lines and planes found in nature—instead of presenting nature as it appeared in everyday life. Following in Cézanne's footsteps, Spanish artist Pablo Picasso (1881–1973) developed a style called cubism. Its radical emphasis on planes and surfaces converted his models into bizarre, almost unrecognizable forms. Picasso's painting *Les Demoiselles d'Avignon* (1907), for example, showed the bodies of the *demoiselles* ("young ladies" or in this case "prostitutes") as fragmented and angular, with their heads modeled on African masks. Picasso's work showed the profound influences of African, Asian, and South American arts, but his use of these features was less decorative and more brutal than Matisse's, for example. Like imperialists who recounted their brutal exploits in speeches and memoirs, he brought knowledge of the empire home in a disturbing style that captured the jarring uncertainties of society and politics in these decades.

Duchamp's *Bicycle Wheel*

French artist Marcel Duchamp's *Bicycle Wheel* exemplifies the kind of modern art that outraged patrons and museumgoers. To many it appeared to mock the careful work of great Western artists in the past and to stand for nothing at all—that is, a kind of artistic nihilism. In fact, Duchamp closely studied Asian thought and religions, and many of his works reflect his engagement. In this case, the bicycle wheel stood for the wheel of dharma and thus represented an object of meditation. *(Marcel Duchamp [1887–1968]/The Israel Museum, Jerusalem, Israel/ © DACS/Vera and Arturo Schwarz Collection of Dada and Surrealist Art/The Bridgeman Art Library International/© 2011 Artists Rights Society [ARS], New York/ADAGP, Paris/Succession Marcel Duchamp.)*

Art as Political Criticism

Across Europe, artists mixed political criticism, even outrage, with the stylistic changes in their work. "Show the people how hideous is their actual life," anarchists challenged. Picasso, who had spent his youth in working-class Barcelona, a hotbed of anarchist thought, aimed to present the plain truth about industrial society in his art. In 1912, Picasso and French painter Georges Braque devised a new kind of collage that incorporated bits of newspaper stories, string, and various useless objects. The effect was a work of art that appeared to be made of trash. The newspaper clippings Picasso included described battles and murders, suggesting that Western civilization was not as refined as it claimed to be. In eastern and central Europe, artists criticized the growing nationalism that determined royal purchases of sculpture and painting: "The whole empire is littered with monuments to soldiers and monuments to Kaiser William," one German artist complained. Groups of avant-garde artists in Vienna and Berlin produced other types of art, much of it critical of boastful nationalism.

Scandinavian and eastern European artists produced works expressing the torment many felt at the time. Like the ideas of Freud, their style of portraying inner feelings—called expressionism—broke with middle-class optimism. Norwegian painter

Edvard Munch aimed "to make the emotional mood ring out again as happens on a gramophone." His painting *The Scream* (1893), shown in the chapter opening illustration, used twisting lines and a tortured skeletal human form to convey the horror of modern life that many artists perceived. The Blue Rider group of artists, led by German painter Gabriele Münter and Russian painter Wassily Kandinsky, used geometric forms and striking colors to express an inner, spiritual truth. Kandinsky is often credited with producing the first fully abstract paintings around 1909; shapes in these paintings no longer bear any resemblance whatsoever to physical objects or reality but are meant to express deep feelings. The expressionism of Oskar Kokoschka, who worked in Vienna, was even more intense, displaying ecstasy, horror, and hallucinations. As a result, his work—like that of other expressionists and cubists before World War I—was a commercial failure in an increasingly complex marketplace run not only by museum curators but by professional dealers—"experts"—like the professionals in medicine and law.

Art Nouveau Only one innovative style of this period was an immediate commercial success. That style, **art nouveau** ("new art"), won approval from government, critics, and the masses. Designers manufactured everything from dishes, calendars, and advertising posters to streetlamps and even entire buildings in this new style. As one French official said about the first art nouveau coins issued in 1895, "Soon even the most humble among us will be able to have a masterpiece in his pocket." Adapting elements from Asian design, art nouveau attempted to offset the harshness of industrial work and office routine with flowing lines and images depicting intertwined elements from nature. The impersonality of machines was replaced by vines and flowers and the softly curving bodies of female nudes intended to soothe the individual viewer. This idea directly contrasted with Picasso's artistic vision. Art nouveau was the notable exception to the public outcries over innovations in the visual arts.

Art Nouveau Objects
Alone among the new art at the turn of the twentieth century, art nouveau was a commercial success, producing objects such as this picture frame, mirror, and ashtray that well-to-do consumers bought in quantity. As it became a global style, art nouveau also influenced travel posters, stained-glass windows, and large pieces of furniture. *(Private Collection/The Bridgeman Art Library International.)*

The Revolt in Music and Dance

"Astonish me!" was the motto of modern dance and music, both of which shocked audiences in the concert halls of Europe. American dancer Isadora Duncan took Europe by storm at the turn of the century when, draped in a flowing garment, she appeared barefoot in one of the first performances of modern dance. Her sophisticated style was called "primitive" because it no longer followed the steps of classical ballet. Experimentation with forms of bodily expression animated the Russian Ballet's 1913 performance of *The Rite of Spring*, by Igor Stravinsky, the tale of an orgiastic dance to the death performed to ensure a plentiful harvest. The dance troupe struck awkward poses and danced to rhythms intended to sound primitive. At the work's premiere in Paris, one journalist reported that "the audience began shouting its indignation. . . . Fighting actually broke out among some of the spectators." Such controversy made *The Rite of Spring* a box office hit, although critics called its choreographer a "lunatic" and the music itself "the most discordant composition ever written."

Composers had been rebelling against Western traditions for several decades, producing music that was disturbing rather than pretty. Having heard Asian musicians at international expositions, French composer Claude Debussy transformed his style to reflect non-European musical patterns and wrote

---

art nouveau: An early-twentieth-century artistic style in graphics, fashion, and household design that featured flowing, sinuous lines, borrowed in large part from Asian art.

articles in praise of Asian harmonies. Italian composer Giacomo Puccini used non-Western subject matter for his opera *Madame Butterfly*, which debuted in 1904. Listeners were jarred when they heard non-Western tonalities. Like the bizarre representation of reality in cubism, the works of Austrian composer Richard Strauss added to the revolution in music by using several musical keys simultaneously, thus distorting familiar musical patterns. Strauss's operas *Salome* (1905) and *Elektra* (1909) reflected the modern fascination with violence and obsessive passion. A newspaper critic claimed that Strauss's dissonant works "spit and scratch and claw each other like enraged panthers."

The early orchestral work of Austrian composer Arnold Schoenberg, who also wrote cabaret music to earn a living, shocked even Strauss. In *Theory of Harmony* (1911), Schoenberg proposed eliminating tonality altogether; a decade later, he devised a new twelve-tone scale. "I am aware of having broken through all the barriers of a dated aesthetic ideal," Schoenberg wrote of his music. But new aesthetic models distanced artists like Schoenberg from their audiences, who found this music unpleasant and incomprehensible. The artistic elite and the social elite parted ranks. "Anarchist! Nihilist!" shouted Schoenberg's audiences, using political terms to show their distaste for modernist music.

REVIEW QUESTION How did modernism transform the arts and the world of ideas?

Growing Tensions in Mass Politics

Alongside disturbances in intellectual life, the political atmosphere grew charged. On the one hand, liberal opinions led to political representation for workingmen. Networks of communication, especially the development of journalism, created a common fund of political knowledge that made mass politics possible. On the other hand, many political activists were no longer satisfied with the liberal rights such as the vote sought by earlier reformers, and some strenuously opposed them. Militant nationalists, anti-Semites, socialists, suffragists, and others demanded changes that challenged liberal values. Traditional elites, resentful of the rising middle classes and urban peoples, aimed to overturn constitutional processes and crush city life. Politics soon threatened national unity, especially in central and eastern Europe, where governments often answered reformers' demands with repression.

The Expanding Power of Labor

European leaders worried about the rise of working-class political power late in the nineteenth century. Laboring people's growing confidence came in part from expanding educational opportunities. Workers in England, for example, avidly read works by Shakespeare and took literally his calls for political action in the cause of justice that rang out in plays such as *Julius Caesar*. Unions gained members among factory workers, while the labor and socialist parties won seats in parliaments as men in the lower classes received the vote. In Germany, Kaiser William II had allowed antisocialist laws to lapse after dismissing Bismarck as chancellor in 1890. Through grassroots organizing at the local level, the Social Democratic Party, founded by German socialists in 1875, became the largest parliamentary group in the Reichstag by 1912. Other socialist parties across Europe helped elect workers' representatives into parliaments, where they focused on passing legislation that benefited workers and their families.

Winning elections actually raised problems among socialists. Some felt uncomfortable sitting in parliaments alongside the upper classes—in Marxism, the enemies of working people. Others worried that accepting high public offices would weaken socialists' commitment to the ultimate goal of revolution. These issues divided socialist organizations. Between 1900 and 1904, the Second International wrestled with the question of revisionism—that is, whether socialists should work from within governments to improve the daily lives of laborers or push for a violent revolution to overthrow governments. Powerful German Marxists argued that settling for reform rather than revolution would only buttress capitalism. The wealthy would continue to rule unchallenged while throwing small crumbs to a few working-class politicians. Stormy discussions divided these German purists, whom the German aristocracy held in contempt, from the socialist delegates of France, England, and Belgium who had gained influential government posts.

Police persecution forced some working-class parties to operate in exile. The Russian government, for instance, outlawed political parties, imprisoned activists, and gave the vote to only a limited number of men when it finally introduced a parliament in 1905. Thus, Russian activist V. I. Lenin (1870–1924), who would take power during the Russian Revolution of 1917 and whose brother was executed for plotting the tsar's assassination, was a journalist and Marxist theorist operating outside the country. Lenin advanced the theory that a highly disciplined socialist elite—rather than the working class as a whole—would lead a lightly industrialized Russia into socialism. At a 1903 party meeting of Russian Marxists, he maneuvered his opponents into walking out of the proceedings so that his supporters gained control of the party. Thereafter, his faction was known as the Bolsheviks, so named after the Russian word for "majority," which they had temporarily formed. They struggled to suppress the Mensheviks ("minority"), who had been the dominant voice in Russian Marxism until Lenin outmaneuvered them. Neither of these factions, however, had as large a constituency within Russia as the Socialist Revolutionaries, whose objective was to politicize peasants, rather than industrial workers, to bring about revolution. All of these groups prepared for the revolutionary moment through study, propaganda efforts, and secret organizing—not through the electoral politics successfully employed elsewhere in Europe.

During this same period, anarchists, along with some trade union members known as syndicalists, kept Europe in a panic with their terrorist acts. In the 1880s, anarchists had bombed stock exchanges, parliaments, and businesses; by the 1890s, they were assassinating heads of state: the Spanish premier in 1897, the empress of Austria-Hungary in 1898, the king of Italy in 1900, and the president of the United States in 1901, to name a few famous victims. Syndicalists advocated the use of direct action, such as general strikes and sabotage, to paralyze the economy and give labor unions more power. Not unexpectedly, the upper and middle classes watched these developments with alarm, while politicians from the old landowning and military elites of eastern and central Europe worked to reverse the trend toward constitutionalism and mass political participation.

Rights for Women and the Battle for Suffrage

Women continued to agitate for the benefits of liberalism such as the right to vote and to own their wages if married. Laws in France, Austria, and Germany even made women's attendance at political meetings a crime. There were many battlefields besides the one for legal rights. German women focused on widening opportunities for female education. Their activism aimed to achieve the German cultural ideal of *Bildung*—the belief that education can build character and that individual development has public importance. In several countries, women monitored the regulation of prostitution. Their goal was to prevent prostitutes from being imprisoned on suspicion of having syphilis when men with syphilis faced no such incarceration. Other women took up pacifism as their cause. Many of them were inspired by Bertha von Suttner's popular book *Lay Down Your Arms* (1889), which emphasized how war inflicted terror on women and families. (Later, von Suttner would influence Alfred Nobel to institute a peace prize and then win the prize herself in 1903.)

By the 1890s, many women activists decided to focus their efforts on a single issue—suffrage (the right to vote)—as the most effective way to correct the many problems caused by male privilege. Thereafter, suffragists created major organizations involving millions of activists, paid officials, and permanent offices out of the earlier reform groups and women's clubs. British suffrage leader Millicent Garrett Fawcett (1847–1929) pressured members of Parliament for women's right to vote and participated in national and international congresses on behalf of suffrage. Across the Atlantic, American Susan B. Anthony (1820–1906) traveled the country to speak at mass suffrage rallies, edited a suffragist newspaper, and founded the International Woman Suffrage Alliance in 1904. Its leadership argued that despite men's promises to protect women in exchange for their inequality, the system of male chivalry had led to exploitation and abuse. "So long as the subjection of women endures, and is confirmed by law and custom, . . . women will be victimized," a leading British suffragist claimed. Other activists believed that women had attributes needed to balance masculine qualities that dominated society. The characteristics associated with mothering, they asserted, were as necessary in shaping a country's destiny as were qualities that stemmed from industry and commerce.

Women's rights activists were predominantly, though not exclusively, from the middle class. Free from the need to earn a living, they simply had more time to be activists and to read the works of feminist theorists such as Harriet Taylor and John Stuart Mill. They attended theater productions of Norwegian playwright Henrik Ibsen's jarring plays about rebellious middle-class heroines, such as *A Doll's House* (see page 782). But working-class women also participated in the suffrage movement, though many distrusted the middle class and believed suffrage to be less crucial than women's pressing economic concerns. Textile workers of Manchester, England, for example, put together a vigorous movement for the vote, seeing it as essential to improved working conditions.

In 1906 in Finland, suffragists achieved their first major victory when the Finnish parliament granted women the vote. The failure of parliaments elsewhere in Europe to enact similar legislation pro-

Woman Suffrage in Finland

In 1906, Finnish women became the first in Europe to receive the vote in national elections when the socialist party there—usually opposed to feminism as a middle-class rather than a working-class project—supported woman suffrage. The Finnish vote encouraged activists in the West, now linked together by many international organizations and ties, because it showed that more than a century of lobbying for reform could lead to gains. *(Mary Evans Picture Library.)*

voked some suffragists to violence. British suffragist **Emmeline Pankhurst** (1858–1928) and her daughters founded the Women's Social and Political Union (WSPU) in 1903 in the belief that women would accomplish nothing unless they threatened men's property. Starting in 1907, members of the WSPU held parades in English cities, and in 1909 they began a campaign of violence, blowing up railroad stations, slashing works of art, and chaining themselves to the gates of Parliament. Disguising themselves as ordinary shoppers, they carried little hammers in their hand warmers to smash the plate-glass windows of department stores and shops. Parades and demonstrations made suffrage a public spectacle, and outraged men responded by attacking the marchers. Arrested for disturbing the peace, the marchers went on hunger strikes in prison. Like striking workers, these women were willing to use confrontational tactics to obtain rights, and, like anarchists, they were not afraid to damage property or add to the tensions of urban life.

Liberalism Tested

Governments in western Europe, where liberal institutions were seemingly well entrenched, sought to control turn-of-the-century conflicts with pragmatic policies that often struck at liberalism's very foundations. Beyond ending the policy of free trade at the heart of economic liberalism, politicians decided that government needed to expand social welfare programs—another break with the liberal idea that societies should develop freely without government interference. Although the programs were few and addressed urban needs only in part, they added to the growing apparatus of the welfare state in which governments actively promoted social well-being.

Revising Liberalism in Britain

Political parties in Britain discovered that the recently enfranchised voter wanted solid benefits in exchange for his support. In 1905, the British Liberal Party won a majority in the House of Commons and pushed for social legislation aimed at the working class. "We are keenly in sympathy with the representatives of Labour," one Liberal politician announced. "We have too few of them in the House of Commons." The National Insurance Act of 1911 instituted a program of unemployment assistance funded by new taxes on the wealthy. When Conservatives in the House of Lords resisted the higher taxation, the Liberal government threatened to add to the number of lords and thus dilute the power of the nobility. The newcomers, unlike the defiant Conservatives, would be sure to vote for reform. Under this threat, the lords approved the Parliament Bill of 1911, which eliminated their veto power.

Emmeline Pankhurst (1858–1928): Organizer of a militant branch of the British suffrage movement, working actively for women's right to vote.

The Irish question further tested Britain's commitment to such liberal values as autonomy, opportunity, and individual rights. In the 1890s, new groups formed to foster Irish culture as a way of heightening the political challenge to what they saw as Britain's continuing colonization of the country. In 1901, the circle around poet William Butler Yeats and actress Maud Gonne founded the Irish National Theater to present Irish rather than English plays. Gonne took Irish politics into everyday life by opposing British efforts to gain the loyalty of the young. Every time an English monarch visited Ireland, he or she held special receptions for children. Gonne and other Irish volunteers sponsored competing events, handing out candies and other treats for patriotic youngsters. "Dublin never witnessed anything so marvelous," enthused one home rule supporter, "as the procession . . . of thirty thousand school children who refused to be bribed into parading before the Queen of England."

Promoters of an "Irish way of life" encouraged speaking Irish Gaelic instead of English, singing songs in Irish, and rallying in support of Catholicism instead of the Church of England. This cultural agenda gained political force with the founding in 1905 of Sinn Féin ("We Ourselves"), a group that strove for complete Irish independence. In 1913, Parliament approved home rule for Ireland. While the outbreak of World War I prevented the legislation from taking effect, it hardly killed dreams of independence.

Unrest in Italy Italian nation builders, left with a towering debt from unification and with widespread pockets of discontent, drifted rapidly from liberalism's moorings in solid industrial development and the rule of law. Corruption plagued Italy's constitutional monarchy, which had not yet developed either the secure parliamentary system of England or the authoritarian monarchy of Germany to guide its growth. To forge national unity in the 1890s, prime ministers used patriotic rhetoric and imperial adventure, notably a second unsuccessful attempt to conquer Ethiopia in 1896. Riots and strikes, followed by armed government repression, erupted, until Giovanni Giolitti, who served as prime minister for three terms between 1903 and 1914, adopted a policy known as *trasformismo* (from the word for "transform"). Following this policy, he used bribes, public works programs, and other benefits to localities to gain support from their deputies in parliament. Political opponents called Giolitti the "Minister of the Underworld" and accused him of preferring to buy the votes of local bosses rather than spending money to develop the Italian economy. In a wave of protest, urban workers in the industrial cities of Turin and Milan and rural laborers in the depressed agrarian south demanded change, especially of the suffrage laws that allowed only three million of more than eight million adult men to vote. Giolitti appeased the protesters by instituting social welfare programs and, in 1912, virtually complete manhood suffrage. These reforms, however, did not signal a full commitment either to a liberal constitutional system or to economic development across the nation.

Anti-Semitism, Nationalism, and Zionism in Mass Politics

The real crisis for liberal political values of equal citizenship and tolerance came in the two decades leading up to World War I when politicians used anti-Semitism and militant nationalism to win elections. They told voters that Jews were responsible for the difficulties of everyday life and that anti-Semitism and increased patriotism would fix all problems. Voters from many levels of society responded enthusiastically, agreeing that Jews were villains and the nation-state was the hero in the struggle to survive. In both republics and monarchies, anti-Semitism and militant nationalism played key roles in mass politics by providing those on the radical right with a platform to gain working-class votes and thus combat the radical left of social democracy. This new radical right shattered the older notion of nationalism based on liberal ideas of the rule of law and the equality of all citizens. Liberals had hoped that voting by the masses would make politics more harmonious as parliamentary debate and compromise smoothed out class and other differences. The new politics as shaped by right-wing leaders — usually representatives of the agrarian nobility, aristocrats who controlled the military, and highly placed clergy — dashed those hopes by making politics loud, emotional, and hateful and thus a distinct departure from liberal consensus and rational debate.

Authoritarianism in Russia A strong tradition of anti-Semitism existed in Russian politics. Russian tsar **Nicholas II** (r. 1894–1917) believed firmly in Russian orthodox religion, autocratic politics, and anti-Semitic social values. Taught as a child to hate Jews, Nicholas blamed them for any failure in Russian policy. Many high officials eagerly endorsed anti-

---

Nicholas II: Tsar of Russia (r. 1894–1917) who promoted anti-Semitism and resisted reform in the empire.

The Humiliation of Alfred Dreyfus
French captain Alfred Dreyfus was sent to a harsh exile after being convicted of spying for Germany. Before he was taken to Devil's Island, he was subjected to the extreme humiliation of having his officer's insignia and ribbons stripped from his uniform and his sword broken before hundreds of troops and a mob of screaming anti-Semites. We can only imagine what this meant to a man in his mid-thirties who, despite being Jewish, had worked his way through an elite military school and up the ranks of the army. What do you see in his bearing? *(The Granger Collection, New York.)*

Semitism to gain the tsar's favor. Pogroms became a regular threat to Russian Jews, especially as Nicholas was adamant that he would never order soldiers to "fire on Christians to protect Jews." Nicholas increasingly limited where Jews could live and how they could earn a living. This tradition of anti-Semitism was integral to Russian autocracy and religion.

The Dreyfus Affair in France Principles of equal citizenship and tolerance were sorely tested in France, where the Dreyfus Affair marked the most notorious instance of anti-Semitism in mass politics. The fragile Third Republic was backed by a liberal alliance of businessmen, shopkeepers, professionals, and rural property owners but opposed by powerful forces in the aristocracy, the military, and the Catholic church. They hoped that this republic, like earlier ones, could be overthrown. Economic downturns, widespread corruption, and attempted coups made the republic more vulnerable, and the press attributed failures of almost any kind to Jews, who, it said, controlled all businesses and even the republic itself. Despite an excellent system of primary education promoting literacy and rational thinking, the public tended to agree, while the clergy and monarchists kept hammering the message that the republic was nothing but a conspiracy of Jews.

Amid rising anti-Semitism, a Jewish captain in the French army, Alfred Dreyfus, was charged with spying for Germany in 1894. From a well-respected family, Dreyfus had worked his way through the military, whose upper echelons were traditionally aristocratic, Catholic, and monarchist. The military produced manufactured "evidence" to gain Dreyfus's conviction and exile to the harsh fortress on Devil's Island. Even though the espionage continued after his arrest, the republican government stubbornly upheld Dreyfus's guilt. Then several newspapers received proof that the army had fabricated documents to convict Dreyfus. In 1898, the celebrated French novelist Émile Zola published an article titled *"J'accuse"* (I accuse) on the front page of a Paris daily, exposing the web of perjury that had created the impression of Dreyfus's guilt.

The article named the truly guilty parties and called for a return to government based on honesty and the rule of law. "I have but one passion, that of Enlightenment," wrote Zola. *"J'accuse"* led to public riots, quarrels among families and friends, and denunciations of the army, which eroded confidence in the republic and in French institutions. The government finally pardoned Dreyfus in 1899, dismissed the aristocratic and Catholic officers held responsible, and ended religious teaching orders to ensure a secular public school system that honored toleration and the rule of law. In the final analysis, however, the Dreyfus Affair made anti-Semitism and official lies a standard tool of politics by showing the effectiveness of hate-filled slogans on the public.

Nationalist and Anti-Semitic Politics in Germany The ruling elites in Germany also used anti-Semitism to win support from those who feared the consequences of Germany's sudden and overwhelming industrialization. The agrarian elites, who still controlled the highest reaches of government, lost ground as agriculture (from which they drew their fortunes) declined as a force in Germany's economy. Its share of the gross national product fell from 37 percent in the 1880s to only 25 percent early in the 1900s. As industrialists grew wealthier and new opportunities drew rural workers to the cities, where they would be free from the landowner's grip, the agrarian elites came to loathe industry for challenging their traditional authority. A Berlin newspaper noted, "The agrarians' hate for cities . . . blinds them to the simplest needs and the most natural demands of the urban population."

Principal Ethnic Groups in Austria-Hungary, c. 1900

In contrast to Bismarck's astute wooing of the masses through social programs, William II's aristocracy often encouraged anti-Semitism as its political tool. Conservatives and a growing radical right claimed that Jews, who made up less than 1 percent of the German population, were responsible for destroying traditional society. In the 1890s, nationalist and anti-Semitic political pressure groups flourished, hurling diatribes against Jews, new women, and Social Democrats, whom they branded as internationalist and unpatriotic. They played to the fears of small farmers by accusing Jews of causing agricultural booms and busts. Political campaigns came to feature hate-filled speeches and nationalist ranting rather than rational programs to meet the problems of economic change. This new right invented a modern politics that rejected the liberal value of parliamentary consensus, relying instead on inventing enemies and thus dividing what was supposed to be a unified nation-state.

Ethnic Politics in Austria-Hungary Politicians in the dual monarchy of Austria-Hungary also used militant nationalism and anti-Semitism to win votes, but here the presence of many ethnic groups meant competing nationalisms and thus greater complexity in the politics of hate. Foremost among the nationalists were the Hungarians, who wanted autonomy for themselves while forcibly imposing Hungarian language and culture on all other, supposedly inferior, ethnic groups in Hungary. Nationalist claims for greater Hungarian influence (or Magyarization, from Magyars, the principal ethnic group) rested on two pieces of evidence: Budapest was a thriving industrial city, and the export of Hungarian grain from the vast estates of the Magyar nobility saved the monarchy's finances. The nationalists disrupted the Hungarian parliament so regularly that it weakened the orderly functioning of the government.

Although capable of causing trouble for the empire, Hungarian nationalists, who mostly represented agrarian wealth, were themselves vulnerable. Hungary's exploited ethnic groups—Slovaks, Romanians, and Ruthenians—resisted Magyarization. Industrial workers struck to protest horrendous labor conditions, and 100,000 activists gathered in the fall of 1905 in front of the Hungarian parliament to demonstrate for the vote. In response, Hungarians intensified Magyarization, even decreeing that all tombstones be engraved in Magyar. Emperor Francis Joseph temporarily quieted the Hungarian nationalists by threatening to introduce universal manhood suffrage, which would allow both the Magyars' lower-class and non-Magyar opponents to vote. Although many assimilated Magyar ways, discriminatory policies toward these groups and scorn for the imperial government in Vienna made for instability throughout Austria-Hungary.

Nationalities across the Dual Monarchy intensified their demands for rights. Croats, Serbs, and other Slavic groups in the south called for equality with the Hungarians. The central government allowed the Czechs a greater number of Czech officials in the government because of the growing industrial prosperity of their region. But every step favoring the Czechs provoked outrage from the traditionally dominant ethnic Germans. When Austria-Hungary decreed in 1897 that government officials in the Czech region of the empire would have to speak Czech as well as German, the Germans rioted—further straining unity in the empire.

Tensions mounted as German politicians in Vienna linked the growing power of Hungarians and Czechs to Jews. Karl Lueger, whose newly formed Christian Social Party attracted members from among the aristocracy, Catholics, artisans, shopkeepers, and white-collar workers, had great success with this new brand of politics. In hate-filled speeches that hurled abuse at Jews and other non-German groups, Lueger appealed to those for whom modern life meant a loss of privilege and security, and he was elected mayor of Vienna in 1895. Lueger's ethnic nationalism and anti-Semitism threatened the multinationalism on which Austria-Hungary was based. His attacks were so effective at getting votes, however, that a widening group of politicians made anti-Semitism an integral part of their election campaigns, calling Jews the "sucking vampire" of modernity and blaming them for the tumult of migration, the economy, and just about

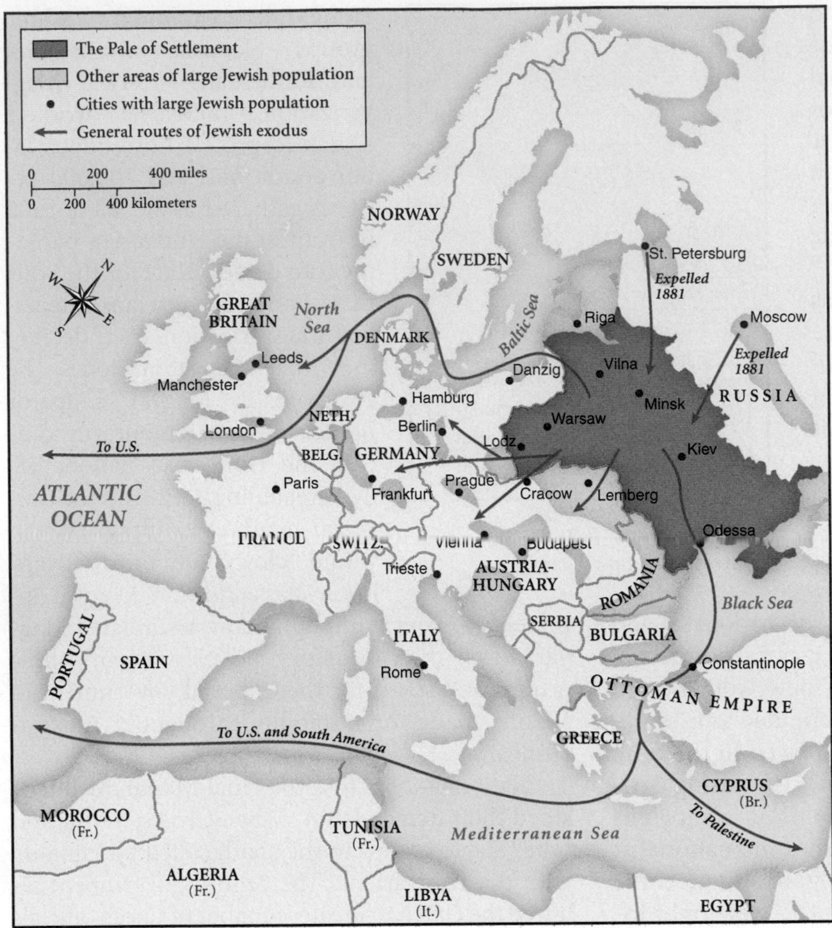

MAP 24.1 Jewish Migrations in the Late Nineteenth Century
Pogroms in eastern Europe, increasingly violent anti-Semitism across the continent, and the search for opportunity motivated Jews to migrate to many parts of the world. Between 1890 and 1914, some five million Jews left Russia alone. They moved to European cities; to North and South America; and, as Zionism progressed, to Palestine.

anything else people found disturbing. Politics became a thing not of debate in parliaments but of violent racism in the streets.

The Jewish Response to Anti-Liberal Politics

Anti-Semites lumped Jewish people into one hated group, but like members of any other religion, Jews were divided by social class and education. Jews in western Europe had responded to increased legal tolerance in the nineteenth century by moving out of Jewish neighborhoods, intermarrying with Christians, and in some cases converting to Christianity—practices known as assimilation. Many well-educated Jews favored the classical culture of the German Empire because it seemed more rational and liberal than the ritualistic Catholicism of Austria-Hungary. Still, many accomplished and prosperous Jews, like the pioneer of psychoanalysis, Sigmund Freud, flourished amid the cosmopolitan urban culture of Vienna or Budapest despite escalating anti-Semitism. By contrast, less educated and less prosperous Jews, such as those in Russia and Romania, were increasingly singled out for persecution, legally disadvantaged, and forced to live in ghettos. Jews from these countries might seek refuge in the nearby cities of central and eastern Europe where they could eke out a living as day laborers or artisans. Jewish migration to the United States and other countries also swelled (Map 24.1). By 1900, many Jews were prominent in cultural and economic affairs in cities across the continent even as far more were discriminated against and victimized elsewhere.

Amid vast migration and continued persecution, a spirit of Jewish nationalism arose. "Why should we be any less worthy than any other . . . people?" one Jewish leader asked. "What about our nation, our language, our land?" Jews began organizing resistance to pogroms and anti-Semitic politics, and intellectuals drew on Jewish folklore, language, customs, and history to establish a national identity parallel to that of other Europeans. In the 1880s, the Ukrainian physician Leon Pinsker, seeing the Jews' lack of national territory as fundamental to the persecution heaped on them, advocated the migration of Jews to Palestine. (See Document, "Leon Pinsker Calls for a Jewish State," page 817.) In 1896, Theodor Herzl, strongly influ-

DOCUMENT

Leon Pinsker Calls for a Jewish State

In 1882, the Ukrainian physician Leon Pinsker published a pamphlet called Auto-Emancipation *in which he analyzed the situation of the Jews in Europe. This pamphlet convinced some in Europe—most notably Theodor Herzl—that Jews could never be assimilated into European culture no matter how many dropped their religion in favor of Christian ways. This pamphlet ultimately led some Jews to migrate to Palestine, despite Pinsker's own conviction that the Middle East was not necessarily the right place for creating a Jewish nation.*

This is the kernel of the problem, as we see it: *the Jews comprise a distinctive element among the nations under which they dwell, and as such can neither assimilate nor be readily digested by any nation*. . . .

A fear of the Jewish ghost has passed down the generations and the centuries. First a breeder of prejudice, later . . . it culminated in Judeophobia. Judeophobia is a psychic aberration. As a psychic aberration it is hereditary, and as a disease transmitted for two thousand years it is incurable. . . .

The Jews are aliens who can have no representatives, because they have no country. Because they have none, because their home has no boundaries within which they can be entrenched, their misery too is boundless. . . .

. . . If we would have a secure home, give up our endless life of wandering and rise to the dignity of a nation in our own eyes and in the eyes of the world, we must, above all, not dream of restoring ancient Judaea. We must not attach ourselves to the place where our political life was once violently interrupted and destroyed. The goal of our present endeavors must be not the "Holy Land," but a land of our own. We need nothing but a large tract of land for our poor brothers, which shall remain our property and from which no foreign power can expel us. There we shall take with us the most sacred possessions which we have saved from the shipwreck of our former country, the *God-idea* and the *Bible*. It is these alone which have made our old fatherland the Holy Land, and not Jerusalem or the Jordan. Perhaps the Holy Land will again become ours. If so, all the better, but *first of all*, we must determine—and this is the crucial point—what country is accessible to us, and at the same time adapted to offer the Jews of all lands who must leave their homes a secure and indisputed refuge, capable of productivization.

Source: Robert Chazan and Marc Lee Raphael, eds., *Modern Jewish History: A Source Reader* (New York: Schocken Books, 1974), 161, 163, 165–66, 169–71, 171–74.

Question to Consider

- **According to Pinsker, why must Jews find "a land of our own"? What is most important in determining the appropriate location for that homeland?**

enced by Pinsker, published *The Jewish State*, a book that called not simply for migration but for the creation of a Jewish nation-state, the goal of a movement known as **Zionism**. A Hungarian-born Jew, Herzl experienced anti-Semitism firsthand as a Viennese journalist and a writer in Paris during the Dreyfus Affair. He scoured Europe for financial backing, but many prosperous Jews who had assimilated thought his ideas mad. However, backed by poorer eastern European Jews, he organized the first International Zionist Congress (1897). By 1914, some eighty-five thousand Jews had moved into Palestine.

REVIEW QUESTION What were the points of tension in European political life at the beginning of the twentieth century?

Zionism: A movement that began in the late nineteenth century among European Jews to found a Jewish state.

European Imperialism Challenged

Anti-Semitism was only one sign that the conditions of modern life were deeply troubling and that the rule of law and other liberal values like tolerance were threatened. Militant nationalism across the West made it difficult for nations to calm international tensions. This nationalist atmosphere heated up, making imperial rivalries among the European powers alarmingly worse. As colonized peoples challenged European control, Japan's growth as an Asian power also threatened stability: in 1904–1905, Japanese expansionism came close to toppling the mighty Russian Empire.

The Trials of Empire

After centuries of global expansion, imperial adventure soured for Britain and France at the beginning of the twentieth century. Newcomers Italy and Germany now fought for a place at the imperial table, and the tense atmosphere among nations raised questions about the future. "Where thirty years ago there existed one sensitive spot in our relations with France, or Germany, or Russia," the British economist J. A. Hobson wrote in 1902, "diplomatic strains are of almost monthly occurrence between the Powers." Mounting tensions exploded violently when Japan and Russia went to war in 1904.

The South African War Everyone was quick to violence when it came to empire, and Britain in its pursuit of the **South African War** (or Boer War) of 1899–1902 was no exception. In 1896, Cecil Rhodes, then prime minister of the Cape Colony in southern Africa, directed a raid into the neighboring territory of the Transvaal in hopes of stirring up trouble between the Boers, descendants of early Dutch settlers, and the more recent immigrants from Britain who had come to southern Africa in search of gold and other riches. In Rhodes's scheme, the turmoil caused by the raid would justify a British takeover of the Transvaal and the Orange Free State, which the Boers independently controlled. The Boers, however, easily routed the raiders, dealing Britain a bloody defeat and forcing Rhodes to resign in disgrace.

The stunned British government did not accept defeat easily, especially when other Europeans gloated over the British loss. In 1899, Britain began full-scale operations against the Boers. Foreign correspondents covering the South African War reported on appalling bloodshed, heavy casualties, and the unfit condition of the average British soldier. Most alarmingly to those who liked to think of Britain as the most civilized country in the world, news arrived back in London of rampant disease and inhumane treatment of South Africans herded into an unfamiliar institution — the concentration camp, which became the graveyard of tens of thousands, mostly women and children. Britain finally annexed the area after defeating the Boers in 1902, but the cost of war in money, destruction, demoralization, and loss of life was enormous (Map 24.2). Prominent citizens began to call imperialism not the work of civilization but an act of barbarism.

South African War: The war (1899–1902) between Britain and the Boer (originally Dutch) inhabitants of South Africa for control of the region; also called the Boer War.

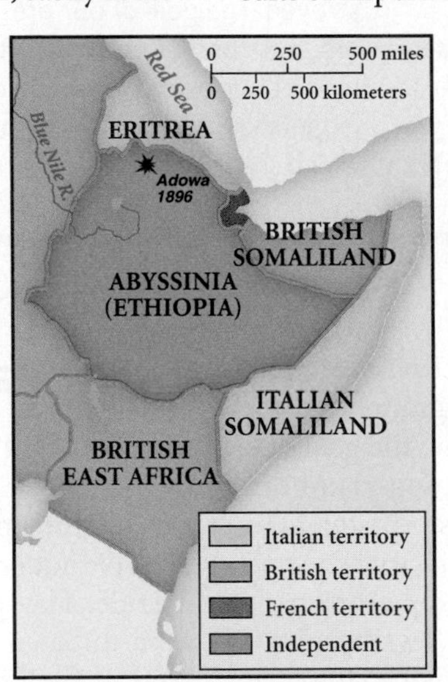

The Struggle for Ethiopia, 1896

Newcomers Face Setbacks Nearly simultaneously with the South African War, the United States defeated Spain in the Spanish-American War in 1898 and took Cuba, Puerto Rico, and the Philippines as its trophies. Experienced in empire, the United States had successfully crushed native Americans, killing many and confining survivors to reservations. However, its imperial reach had generally been continental until its annexation of Hawaii in 1898. Both Cuba and the Philippines had begun vigorous efforts to free themselves from Spanish rule before the war. Urged on by the expansionist-minded Theodore Roosevelt (then assistant secretary of the navy) and the inflammatory daily press, the United States went to war against Spain, claiming it was doing so to help the independence movements. Instead of allowing the independence that victory promised, however, the U.S. government annexed Puerto Rico and Guam and bought the Philippines from Spain. Cuba was theoretically independent, but the United States monitored its activities.

Both Spain and the United States found the results of imperialism uncertain. Spain lost its territories, and the triumphant United States next had to wage a bloody war against the Filipinos, who wanted independence, not another imperial ruler. British poet Rudyard Kipling had encouraged the United States to "take up the white man's burden" by bringing the benefits of Western civilization to those liberated from Spain. However, reports of American brutality in the Philippines, where some 200,000 local people were slaughtered, disillusioned the Western public, who liked to imagine native peoples joyously welcoming the bearers of civilization.

Despite these setbacks, the newly unified countries had an emotional stake in gaining colonies. In the early twentieth century, Italian public figures bragged about Italians becoming Nietzschean supermen by conquering Africa and restoring Italy to its ancient position of world domination. After a disastrous war against Ethiopia in 1896, Italy won a costly victory over the Ottoman Empire in Libya. These wars stirred the military spirit in Italians, and hopes rose for imperial grandeur in the future.

Germany likewise joined the imperial contest, demanding an end to British-French domination as colonial powers. Under Bismarck, Germany had

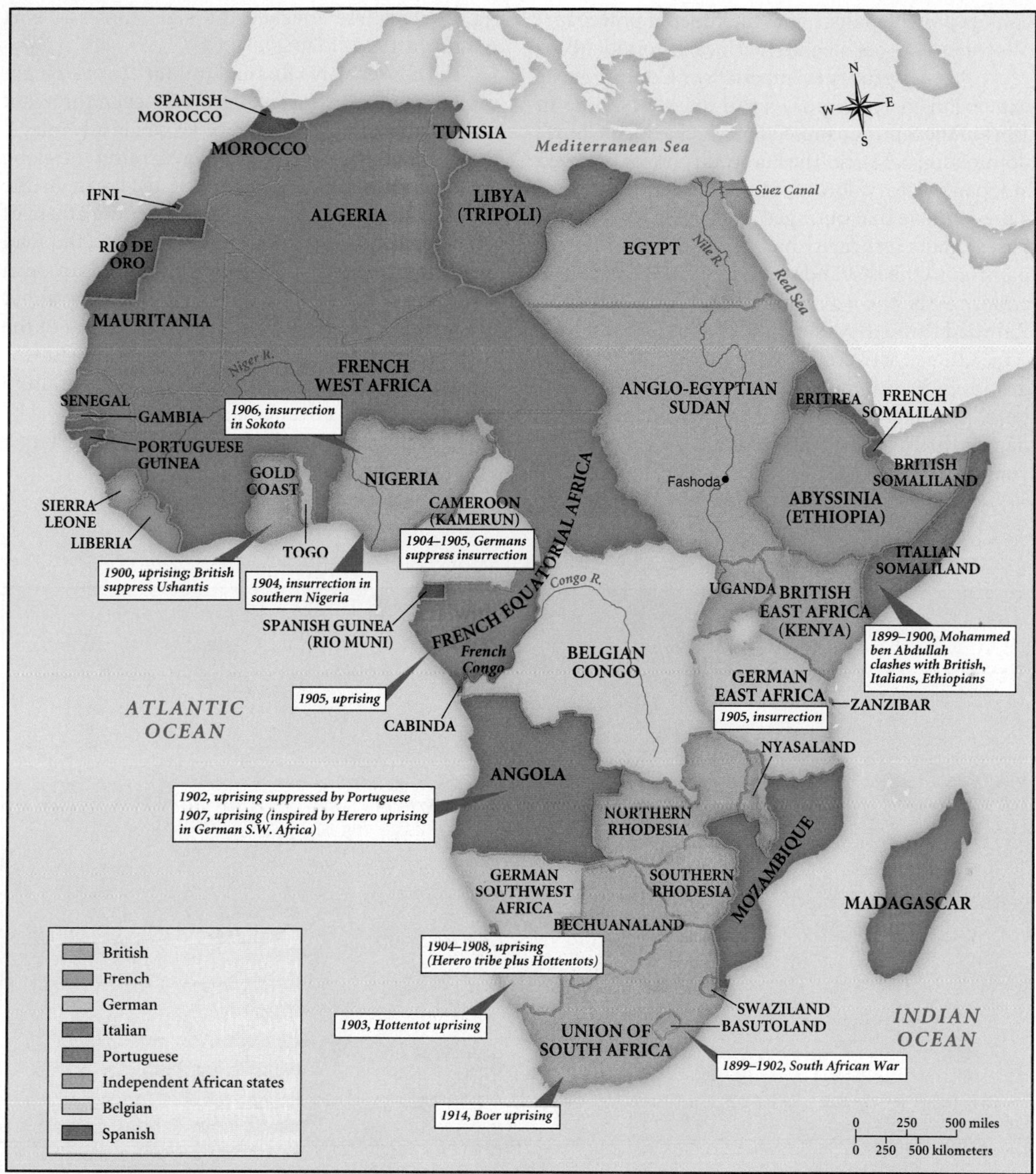

MAP 24.2 Africa in 1914

Uprisings intensified in Africa in the early twentieth century as Europeans tried both to consolidate their rule and to extract more wealth from the Africans. As Europeans were putting down rebellions against their rule, a pan-African movement arose, attempting to unite Africans as one people.

begun its imperial expansion, and German bankers and businessmen were active across Asia, the Middle East, and Latin America. By the turn of the century, Germany had colonies in Southwest Africa, the Cameroons, Togoland, and East Africa and sent linguists, ethnographers, and museum curators to study these cultures and obtain their treasures. Despite these successes, Germany, too, met humiliation and faced constant problems, especially in its dealings with Britain and France and with local peoples in Africa and elsewhere who resisted the German takeover. As Italy and Germany joined the aggressive pursuit of new territory, the confident rule-setting for imperialism at the Berlin Conference a generation earlier gave way to general anxiety, heated rivalry, and nationalist passion.

Japan Victorious

Japan's rise as an imperial power further ate into Europeans' confident approach to imperialism. Continuing its expansion in the region, Japan defeated China in 1894 in the Sino-Japanese War, which ended China's domination of Korea. The European powers, alarmed at Japan's victory, forced it to relinquish most of its gains, a move that outraged and affronted the Japanese. Japan's insecurity had risen with Russian expansion to the east and south in Asia. Pushing into eastern Asia, the Russians built the Trans-Siberian Railroad through Manchuria, sent millions of Russian settlers eastward, and sponsored anti-Japanese groups in Korea, making the Korean peninsula appear, as a Japanese military leader put it, like "a dagger thrust at the heart of Japan." Angered by the continuing presence of Russian troops in Manchuria, the Japanese attacked the tsar's forces at Port Arthur in 1904 (Map 24.3).

The conservative Russian military proved inept in the ensuing Russo-Japanese War, even though it often had better equipment or strategic advantage. Russia's Baltic Fleet sailed halfway around the globe only to be completely destroyed by Japan in the battle of Tsushima Strait (1905). Opening an era of Japanese domination in East Asian politics, the solid victory of a non-European nation over a European great power gave the West reason to worry about the future. As one English general observed of the Russian defeat: "I have today seen the most stupendous spectacle it is possible for the mortal brain to conceive—Asia advancing, Europe falling back." Japan annexed Korea in 1910 and began to target other areas for colonization.

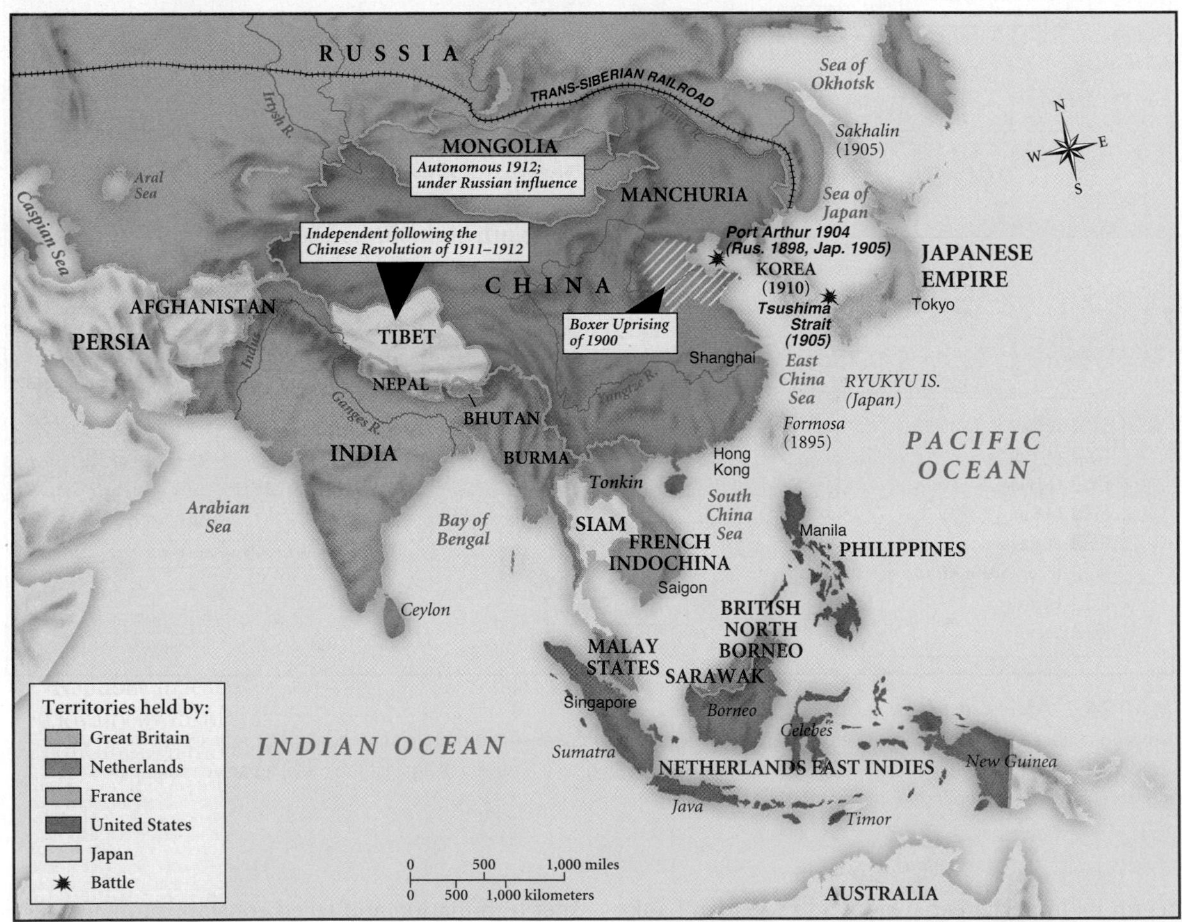

MAP 24.3 Imperialism in Asia, 1894–1914

The established imperialists came to blows in East Asia as they struggled for influence in China and as they met a formidable new rival—Japan. Simultaneously, liberation groups like the Boxers were taking shape, committed to throwing off restraints imposed by foreign powers and eliminating these interlopers altogether. In 1911, revolutionary Sun Yat-sen overthrew the Qing dynasty, which had left China unprepared to resist foreign takeover, and started the country on a different course.

The Russian Empire Threatened

Alongside the humiliating loss to Japan, revolution erupted in Russia in 1905, and the empire tottered on the brink of chaos. Having expanded southward in Asia and settled much of Siberia during the nineteenth century, the mighty Russian Empire had concealed its weaknesses well. State-sponsored industrialization in the 1890s had made the country appear modern to outside observers, and the Russification policy imitated Western-style nation building by attempting to impose a unified national culture on Russia's diverse population. Burdened by heavy taxes to pay for industrialization and by debts owed for the land they acquired during emancipation, peasants revolted in isolated uprisings at the turn of the century. Unrest occurred in the cities, too, as Marxist and union activists incited workers to demand better conditions. In 1903, skilled workers led strikes in Baku; the unity of Armenians and Tatars in these strikes showed how Russification made political cooperation possible among the various ethnicities. Growing worker activism, along with Japan's victory, challenged the autocratic regime.

The Revolution of 1905 On a Sunday in January 1905, a crowd gathered outside the tsar's Winter Palace in St. Petersburg to march in a demonstration to make Nicholas II aware of the brutal working conditions they suffered. Nicholas had often traveled the empire, displaying himself as the divinely ordained "father" of his people; therefore, his "children" thought it natural to appeal to him for aid. Leading the demonstration was a priest who, unknown to the crowd, was a police informant and agitator. Instead of allowing the marchers to pass, troops guarding the palace shot into the trusting crowd, killing hundreds and wounding thousands. Thus began the Revolution of 1905, as news of "Bloody Sunday" moved outraged workers elsewhere to rebel.

In almost a year of turmoil across Russia, urban workers struck over wages, hours, and factory conditions and demanded political representation in the government. Delegates from revolutionary parties such as the Social Democrats and the Socialist Revolutionaries encouraged more direct blows against the central government, but workers also organized their own councils, called soviets. In February, the uncle of the tsar was assassinated; in June, sailors on the battleship *Potemkin* mutinied; in October, a massive railroad strike brought rail transportation to a halt; and in November, uprisings broke out in Moscow. The tsar's forces kept killing protesters, but their deaths only produced more protest.

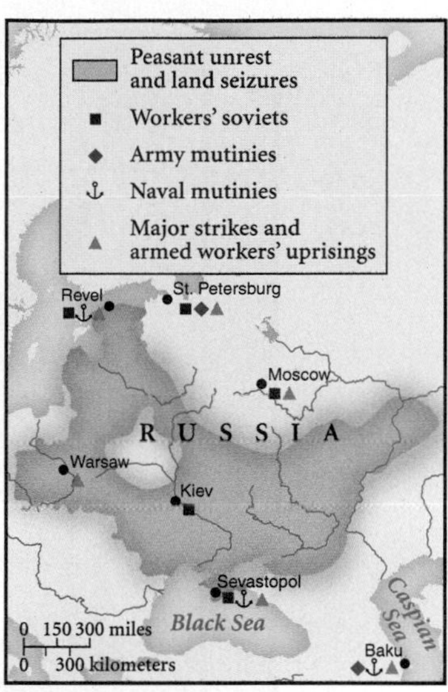

Russian Revolution of 1905

Anger at Nicholas II's absolute rule brought together an opposing group of artisans and industrial workers, peasants, professionals, and upper-class reformers. Women joined the fray, many demanding an end to discriminatory laws such as those firing women teachers who married. Using the unrest to press their goals, liberals from the zemstvos (local councils) and the intelligentsia (a Russian word for well-educated elites) demanded political reform, in particular the creation of a constitutional monarchy and representative legislature. They believed that the reliance on censorship and the secret police, characteristic of Russian imperial rule, marked the empire as backward. Nicholas's halfhearted responses triggered more street fighting. In the words of one protester, the tsar's attitude turned "yesterday's benighted slaves into decisive warriors."

Attempts at Political Reform The tsar finally yielded to the violence by creating a representative body called the **Duma**. Although very few Russians could vote for representatives to the Duma, its mere existence, along with the new right of open public debate, liberalized government and allowed people to present their grievances to a responsive body. Political parties committed to parliamentary rather than revolutionary programs also took shape during this time. When these newly formed constitutional parties backed the reforms, revolutionary activity finally stopped.

People soon wondered, however, if anything had really changed. From 1907 to 1917, the Duma convened, but twice when the tsar disliked its recommendations he simply sent the delegates home. Nicholas did have an able administrator in Prime Minister Pyotr Stolypin (1863–1911), who was determined to eliminate the sources of discontent. He ended the mir system of communal farming and canceled the land redemption payments that had burdened the peasants since their emancipation in

---

Duma: The Russian parliament set up in the aftermath of the outbreak of the Revolution of 1905.

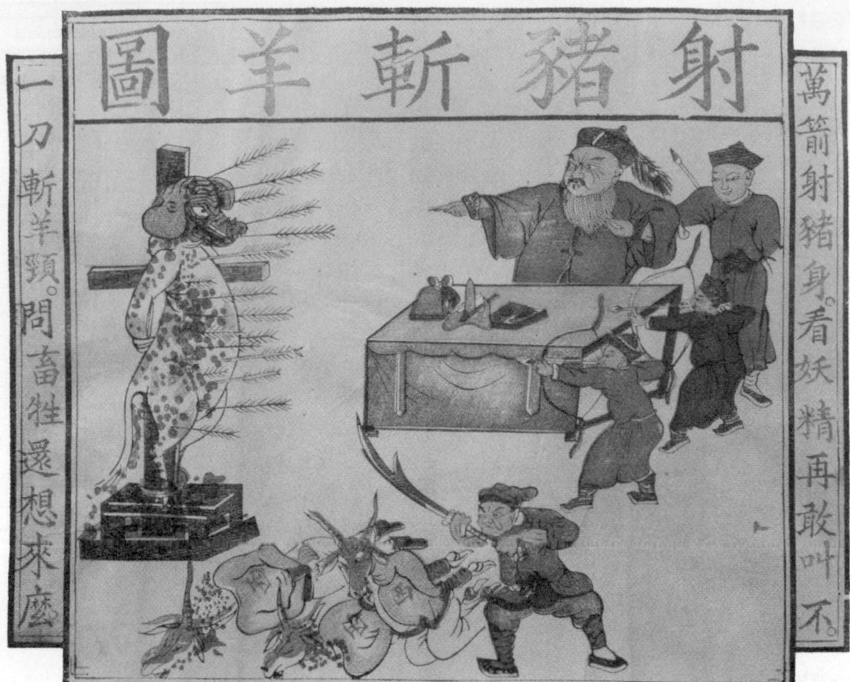

The Foreign Pig Is Put to Death
The Boxers used brightly colored placards to spread information about their movement in order to build wide support among the Chinese population. They felt that the presence of foreigners had caused a series of disasters, including the defection of the Chinese from traditional religion, the flow of wealth from the country, and a string of natural disasters such as famine. This depiction shows the harsh judgment of the Boxers toward foreigners and their Chinese allies—they are pigs to be killed. *(Private Collection/The Bridgeman Art Library International.)*

1861. He also made government loans available to peasants, who were then able to purchase land and thus to own farms outright. These reforms allowed people to move to the cities in search of jobs and created a larger group of independent peasants.

Stolypin was determined to restore law and order. He clamped down on revolutionary organizations, sentencing so many of their members to death by hanging that nooses were nicknamed "Stolypin neckties." The government urged more pogroms and stepped up Russification to crush ethnic dissent. But rebels continued to assassinate government officials—four thousand were killed or wounded in 1906–1907. Stolypin himself was assassinated in 1911. Stolypin's reforms promoted peasant well-being, which encouraged what one historian has called a "new peasant assertiveness." The industrial workforce also grew, but more strikes broke out, culminating in a general strike in St. Petersburg in 1914. The imperial government and the conservative nobility still had no solution to the ongoing activism in the streets, and their refusal to share power through the Duma left the way open to an even greater upheaval in 1917.

Growing Resistance to Colonial Domination

Japanese military victories over the Qing in China and the Romanovs in Russia upset the status quo in both countries. In addition, colonized peoples gained confidence from the Japanese victory to act more forcefully against imperialism. The ability of Russian revolutionaries to force a great European power to reform, however slightly, encouraged nationalist protests throughout the globe, further setting the West on edge.

Revolution in China Uprisings began in China after its 1895 defeat by Japan led the Western powers to force more economic concessions from the Qing dynasty. Nonhuman factors also stepped in as drought and famine came to plague the empire. Despairing peasants organized into secret societies to expel the foreigners and restore Chinese dignity and power. One organization was the Society of the Righteous and Harmonious Fists, commonly called the Boxers, whose members maintained that ritual boxing would protect them from a variety of evils, including bullets. Encouraged by the Qing ruler, the dowager empress Tz'u-hsi (Cixi; 1835–1908), the Boxers rebelled in 1900, massacring the missionaries and Chinese Christians to whom they attributed China's troubles. Seven of the colonial powers united to put down the Boxer Uprising and encouraged their troops to devastate the areas in which the Boxers operated. Defeated once more, the Chinese had to pay a huge indemnity for damages done to foreign property and allow even greater foreign military occupation.

The Boxer Uprising thoroughly discredited the Qing dynasty, leading a group of revolutionaries to overthrow the dynasty in 1911 and to declare China a republic the next year. Their leader, Sun Yat-sen (1866–1925), who had been educated in Hawaii and Japan, combined Western ideas and Chinese values in his Three Principles of the People: "national-

DOCUMENT

Turkish Nationalism

Both old and new empires experienced waves of nationalist sentiment during the years 1890–1914. Turks dominated the Ottoman Empire and their newfound nationalism was directed at the European powers trying to encroach on Ottoman lands. Turkish nationalism, however, was also announced as the unifying force and dominant value of the multinational Ottoman empire and thus met with resistance from the many groups such as Slavs, Arabs, and others within the empire. The poem below, "Going to Battle," expresses Turkish nationalism and is now well known to children across Turkey. Mehmed Emin was twenty-eight when he published the work in 1897. His devotion to nationalism prompted him to adopt the name Yurdakul, meaning "slave to the homeland." After World War I, Mehmed Emin became a prominent politician in the new Turkish nation.

Going to Battle

I am a Turk, my religion, my race are great,
My breast, my soul are filled with fire.
He who is a man is the servant of his fatherland.
The Turkish child does not stay at home—I go.

I do not allow the book of Muhammad to be abolished,
I do not suffer the flag of Osman to be taken away,
I do not permit the enemy to attack my fatherland
The House of God will not be destroyed—I go.

The earth is the home of my ancestors;
My house, my village are a corner of this place.
Here is the homeland, here is the lap of God.
The fatherland needs sons—I go.

My god is witness that I will keep my word,
All my love for my country deep in my heart,
In my eyes nothing but my fatherland.
The enemy shall not take my native soil—I go.

I wipe my tears with a white shirt,
I whet my knife with a black stone.
I desire grandeur for my fatherland;
No one stays in this world forever—I go.

Source: Robert G. Landen, ed., *The Emergence of the Modern Middle East: Selected Readings* (New York: Van Nostrand Reinhold, 1970), 120.

Question to Consider

- **In what ways do the nationalist sentiments of the poem resemble those of Western nations, and in what ways do they differ?**

ism, democracy, and socialism." For example, Sun's socialism included the Chinese belief that all people should have enough food, and his Nationalist Party called for revival of the Chinese tradition of correctness in behavior between governors and the governed, modern economic reform, and an end to Western domination of trade. Sun's stirring leadership and the changes brought about by the 1911 revolution helped weaken Western imperialism.

Nationalists in India

In India, the Japanese victory over Russia and the Revolution of 1905 stimulated politicians to take a more radical course than that offered by the Indian National Congress. The anti-British Hindu leader B. G. Tilak, less moderate than Congress reformers, urged noncooperation: "We shall not give them assistance to collect revenue and keep peace. We shall not assist them in fighting beyond the frontiers or outside India with Indian blood and money." Tilak promoted Hindu customs, asserted the distinctiveness of Hindu values from British ways, and inspired violent rebellion against the British. This brand of nationalism contrasted with that based on assimilating to British culture and promoting gradual change. Trying to stop Tilak, the British sponsored a rival nationalist group, the Muslim League, in a blatant attempt to divide Muslims from Hindus in the Congress.

Faced with political activism on many fronts, however, Britain conceded to Indians' representation in ruling councils and their right to vote based on property ownership. Because the independence movement had not fully reached the masses, some of these small concessions to the elites temporarily prevented an explosion of anger among colonized Indians as a whole. But discontent also mounted, sometimes silently, as did worries among the most clear-sighted imperialists about the future.

Young Turks in the Ottoman Empire

Revolutionary nationalism was simultaneously weakening the Ottoman Empire, which for centuries had controlled much of the Mediterranean. Rebellions plagued Ottoman rule, and this resistance allowed European influence to grow even as Ottoman reformers aimed to strengthen the government. Sultan Abdul Hamid II (r. 1876–1909) tried to revitalize the multiethnic empire by using Islam to counteract the rising nationalism of

DOCUMENT

Vietnamese Resistance and the Importance of Becoming Modern

There was growing resistance to imperialism, using both weapons and words. Phan Boi Chau, an educated Vietnamese, chose words and formed one of the first important movements against the French in 1904. He wrote a torrent of pamphlets and essays describing the crimes of French occupiers of his homeland and proposing that the Vietnamese would become great and independent once they became more modern. Here is an excerpt from his essay "The New Vietnam" (1907). In 1925, the French condemned him to death for his ideas but ultimately allowed him to spend the rest of his life under police guard.

After a thousand kilometers of railroads have been laid, merchandise to be exchanged would reach its destination in hours; sprawling cities and large villages would promptly communicate with one another, then even if we were to relax in a sculpted house or if we were just to sit on a flowered mat, it would still feel as though we have scaled mountains and crossed rivers. What a wonderful sensation that will be! . . .

Ever since France came to protect us, Frenchmen hold every lever of power; they hold the power of life and death over everyone. The life of thousands of Vietnamese people is not worth that of a French dog; the moral prestige of hundreds of our officials does not prevail over that of a French woman. Look at those men with blue eyes and yellow beards. They are not our fathers, nor are they our brothers. How can they squat here, defecating on our heads? Are the men from Vietnam not ashamed of that situation? As long as our bodies remain able, we should try to flatten the crest of the open ocean; we should be determined to kill the enemy in order to raise the energy of the yellow race of ours.

After modernization we shall determine the domestic as well as foreign affairs of our country. The work of civilization will go on, day after day, and our country's status in the world will be heightened. We shall have three million infantrymen, as fierce as tigers, looking into the four corners of the universe. . . . All the shame and humiliation we have suffered previously . . . will become potent medicine to help us build up this feat of modernization. . . . The wind of freedom will blow fiercely, refreshing in one single sweep the entire five continents. Such will be the victory of our race.

Source: "The New Vietnam" (1907), quoted in Truong Buu Lam, *Colonialism Experienced: Vietnamese Writings on Colonialism 1900–1931* (Ann Arbor: University of Michigan Press, 2000), 105–8.

Question to Consider

- **What are Phan Boi Chau's charges against the French, and how does he see the future of Vietnam?**

the Serbs, Bulgarians, and Macedonians. Instead, he unintentionally provoked Turkish nationalism in Constantinople itself. Turkish nationalists rejected the sultan's pan-Islamic solution and built their movement on the uniqueness of their culture, history, and language, as many European ethnic groups were also doing (see Document, "Turkish Nationalism," page 823). They first traced the history and culture of the group they called Turks to change the word *Turk* from one of derision to one of pride. The Japanese defeat of Russia in 1904–1905 electrified these nationalists with the vision of a modern Turkey becoming "the Japan of the Middle East," as they called it. In 1908, a group of nationalists called the Young Turks took control of the government in Constantinople, which had been increasingly weakened by nationalist agitation and by the empire's growing indebtedness to Western financiers and businessmen.

The Young Turks' triumph motivated other ethnic groups in the Middle East and the Balkans to demand an end to Ottoman domination in their regions. These nationalists adopted Western values and political platforms, and some, such as the Egyptians, had strong contingents of feminist-nationalists who mobilized women to work for independence. The Young Turks, often aided by European powers with financial interests in the region, brutally repressed nationalist uprisings in Egypt, Syria, and the Balkans that their own success had encouraged.

The rebellions became part of the turmoil in global relations during the years just before World War I. Empires, whether old or young, were the scene of growing opposition in the wake of Japanese, Russian, and Turkish events. In German East Africa, colonial forces responded to native resistance in 1905 with a scorched-earth policy of destroying homes, livestock, food, and other resources, killing more than 100,000 Africans there. To maintain their grip on Indochina, the French closed the University of Hanoi, executed Indochinese intellectuals, and deported thousands of suspected nationalists (see Document, "Vietnamese Resistance and the Importance of Becoming Modern," above).

A French general stationed there summed up the fears of many colonial rulers: "The gravest fact of our actual political situation in Indochina is not the recent trouble in Tonkin [or] the plots undertaken against us but in the muted but growing hatred that our subjects show toward us." At home and abroad, Western political ambitions revolved around violence in speech and deed.

REVIEW QUESTION How and why did events in overseas empires from the 1890s on challenge Western faith in imperialism?

Roads to War

Internationally, competition intensified among the great powers and drove Western nationalists to become similarly more aggressive. In the spring of 1914, U.S. president Woodrow Wilson (1856–1924) sent his trusted adviser Colonel Edward House to Europe to observe the rising tensions there. "It is militarism run stark mad," House reported, adding that he foresaw an "awful cataclysm" ahead. Government spending on what people called the arms race had stimulated European economies. While stockpiles of arms temporarily promoted economic growth, however, they menaced the future. As early as the mid-1890s, one socialist had called the situation a "cold war" because the hostile atmosphere made war seem a certainty. By 1914, the air was even more charged, with militant nationalism in the Balkan states and politics—both at home and worldwide—propelling Europeans toward mass destruction.

Competing Alliances and Clashing Ambitions

As the twentieth century opened, the Triple Alliance that Bismarck had negotiated among Germany, Austria-Hungary, and Italy confronted an opposing alliance between France and Russia, created in the 1890s. The wild card in the diplomatic scenario was Great Britain, traditional enemy of France, especially in the contest for global power. Britain and France—constant rivals in Africa—edged to the brink of war in 1898 over competing claims to Fashoda, a town in the Sudan. The threat of conflict led France to withdraw, showing both nations as embracing a truce out of mutual self-interest. To prevent another Fashoda, they entered into secret agreements, the first of which (1904) recognized British claims in Egypt and French claims in Morocco. This agreement marked the beginning of the British-French alliance called the **Entente Cordiale**. Still, Britain's response to a future European war remained in question. Even French statesmen feared that, should war break out, their ally might decide to remain neutral.

Germany's Imperial Demands Kaiser William II inflamed the diplomatic atmosphere just as France and Britain were developing the Entente Cordiale. After victory in the Franco-Prussian War, Bismarck had proclaimed Germany a "satisfied" nation and worked to balance great-power interests in order to avoid further wars. William II, in contrast, was emboldened by Germany's growing industrial might and announced in 1901 that Germany needed greater global power to be achieved by "friendly conquests." His actions, however, were far from friendly. Believing in Britain's fundamental hostility toward France, William II used the opportunity presented by the defeat of France's ally Russia in 1904–1905 to contest French advances in Morocco. A boastful, blustery man who was easily prodded to rash actions by his advisers, William landed in Morocco in 1905 to block the French. To resolve what became known as the First Moroccan Crisis, an international conference met in Spain in 1906. Germany confidently expected to gain concessions and global influence, but instead the powers, now including the United States, upheld French claims in North Africa. France and Britain, seeing German interference in Morocco, drew closer together.

Germany found itself weak internationally and strong economically, a situation that made its leaders more determined to compete for territory abroad. When the French took over Morocco completely in 1911, Germany triggered the Second Moroccan Crisis by sending a gunboat to the port of Agadir and again demanding concessions from the French. This time no power—not even Austria-Hungary—backed Germany. No one acknowledged this dominant country's might or its right to influence in the region. The British and French now made binding military provisions for the deployment of their forces in case of war, thus strengthening the Entente Cordiale. Smarting from its setbacks on the world stage, Germany refocused its sights on its continental role and on its own alliances.

Entente Cordiale: An alliance between Britain and France that began with an agreement in 1904 to honor colonial holdings.

Crises in the Balkans Germany's bold territorial claims, along with public uncertainty about the binding force of alliances, unsettled Europe, particularly the Balkans. German statesmen began envisioning the creation of a **Mitteleuropa**—a term that literally meant "central Europe" but that in their minds also included the Balkans and Turkey. The Habsburgs, firmly backed by Germany, judged that their own expansion into the Balkans and the resulting addition of even more ethnic groups would weaken the claims of any single ethnic minority in the Dual Monarchy. Russia, however, saw *itself* as the protector of Slavs in the region and wanted to replace the Ottomans as the dominant Balkan power, especially since Japan had crushed Russian hopes for expansion to the east. Austria's swift annexation of Bosnia-Herzegovina during the Young Turks' revolt in 1908 enraged not only the Russians but the Serbs as well, who wanted Bosnia as part of an enlarged Serbia. The Balkans thus whetted many appetites (Map 24.4).

Even without the greedy eyes cast on the Balkans, the situation would have been extremely volatile. The nineteenth century had seen the rise of nationalism and ethnicity as the basis for the unity of the nation-state, and by late in the century, ethnic loyalty challenged the dynastic rule of the Habsburgs and Ottomans in the Balkans. Greece, Serbia, Bulgaria, Romania, and Montenegro emerged as autonomous states, almost all of them composed of several ethnicities as well as several faiths: Or-

Mitteleuropa (miht el oy ROH pah): Literally, "central Europe," but used by military leaders in Germany before World War I to refer to land in both central and eastern Europe that they hoped to acquire.

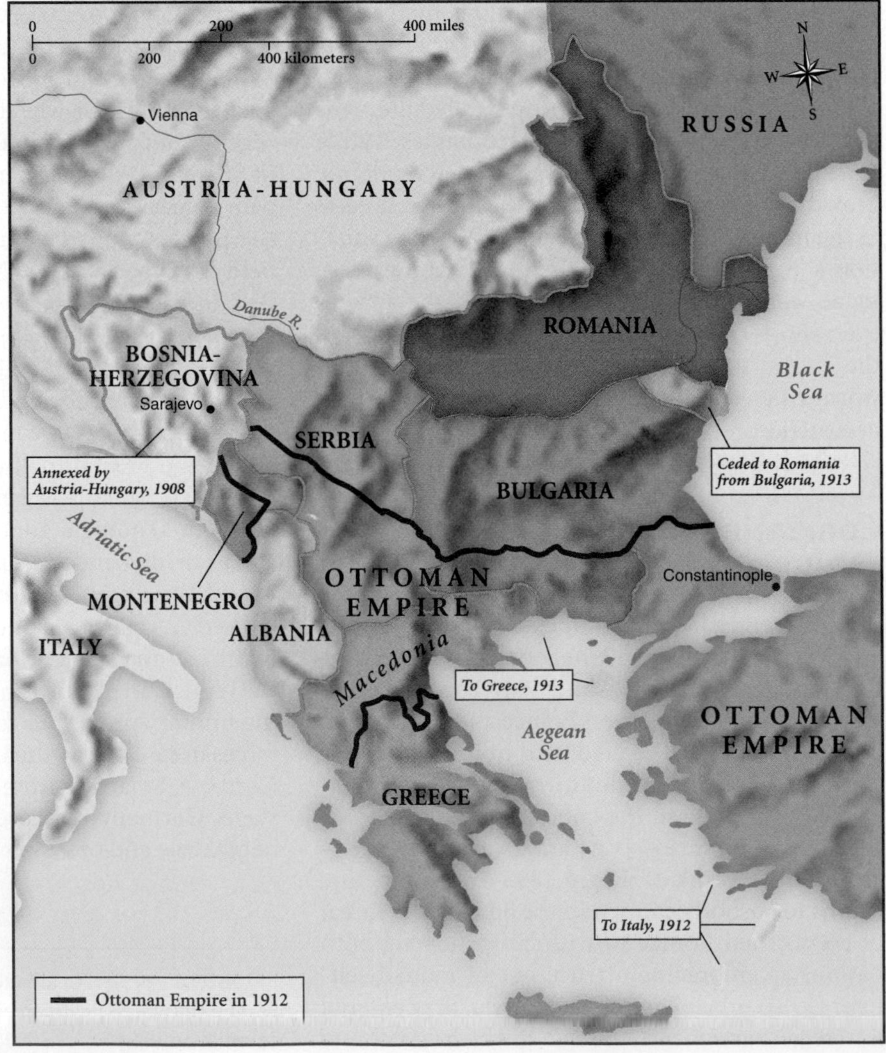

MAP 24.4 The Balkans, 1908–1914
Balkan peoples—mixed in religion, ethnicity, and political views—were successful in asserting their desire for independence, especially in the First Balkan War, which claimed territory from the Ottoman Empire. Their increased autonomy sparked rivalries among them and continued to attract attention from the great powers. Three empires in particular—the Russian, Ottoman, and Austro-Hungarian—simultaneously wanted influence for themselves in the region, which became a powder keg of competing ambitions.

thodox Christian, Roman Catholic, and Muslim. All these states sought more Ottoman and Habsburg territory to cement a common ethnicity—an impossible desire given the intermingling of ethnicities throughout the region. Nonetheless, war for territory was on these nationalists' agenda.

In the First Balkan War, in 1912, Serbia, Bulgaria, Greece, and Montenegro joined forces to gain Macedonia and Albania from the Ottomans. The victors divided up their booty, with Bulgaria gaining the most territory, but in the Second Balkan War, in 1913, Serbia, Greece, and Montenegro contested Bulgarian gains. The quick victory of these allies increased Austria's concern at Serbia's rising power. Grievances between the Habsburgs and the Serbs seemed stalemated as each aimed for greater influence in the Balkans. The region had become perilous: both Austria-Hungary (as ruler of many Slavs) and Russia (as their would-be protector) stationed increasing numbers of troops along the borders. The situation led strategists to think hopefully that a quick war there—something like Bismarck's wars—could resolve tension and uncertainty.

The Race to Arms

In the nineteenth century, global rivalries and aspirations for national greatness made constant readiness for war seem increasingly necessary. On the seas and in foreign lands, the colonial powers battled to establish control, and violence became an everyday occurrence in the drive for empire. The powers developed railroad, telegraph, and telephone networks everywhere to control their conquests and to move troops as well as to trade. Governments began to draft ordinary citizens for periods of two to six years into large standing armies, in contrast to the smaller forces that had served the more limited military goals of the eighteenth century. By 1914, escalating tensions in Europe boosted the annual intake of draftees: Germany, France, and Russia called up 250,000 or more troops each year. The per capita expenditure on the military rose in all the major powers between 1890 and 1914; the proportion of national budgets devoted to defense in 1910 was lowest in Austria-Hungary (at 10 percent) and highest in Germany (at 45 percent).

The modernization of weaponry also transformed warfare. Swedish arms manufacturer Alfred Nobel patented dynamite and developed a kind of gunpowder that improved the accuracy of guns and produced a clearer battlefield environment by reducing firearm smoke. Breakthroughs in the chemical industry led to improvements in long-range artillery, which by 1914 could fire on targets as far as six miles away. Munitions factories across Europe manufactured ever-growing stockpiles of howitzers, Mauser rifles, and Hotchkiss machine guns. Used in the Russo-Japanese and South African wars, these new weapons had shown that military offensives were more difficult to win than in the past because neither side could overcome such accurate firepower. Military leaders devised new strategies to protect their armies from the heavy firepower and deadly accuracy of the new weapons: in the Russo-Japanese War, trenches and barbed wire blanketed the front around Port Arthur.

Naval construction figured in both the arms race and the rising nationalism in politics. To defend against powerful weaponry, ships built after the mid-nineteenth century were made of metal rather than wood. Launched in 1905, HMS *Dreadnought*, a warship with unprecedented firepower, was the centerpiece of the British navy's plan to construct at least seven battleships per year. Germany also built up its navy and made itself a great land and sea power. Military men followed the writings of the American naval theorist Alfred Thayer Mahan, who argued that command of the seas determined international power. Germany thus planned naval bases as far away as the Pacific, but its drive to build battleships strengthened Britain's alliance with France in the Entente Cordiale and boosted the annual naval spending of those countries as well (see "Taking Measure," page 828). The Germans described their fleet buildup as "a peaceful policy," but, like British naval expansion, it only fed the hostile international climate and intense competition in weapons manufacture.

Public relations campaigns encouraged military buildup. When critics of the arms race suggested a temporary "naval holiday" to stop British and German building, British officials sent out news releases warning that such a cutback "would throw innumerable men on the pavement." Advocates of imperial expansion and nationalist groups lobbied for military spending as boosting national pride, while businessmen promoted large navies as beneficial to international trade and domestic industry. When Germany's Social Democrats questioned the use of taxes and their heavy burden on workers, the press criticized the party for lack of patriotism. The Conservative Party in Great Britain, eager for more battleships, made popular the slogan "We want eight and we won't wait." Public enthusiasm for arms buildups, militant nationalism, and growing international competition set the stage for war. The remarks of a French military leader were typical of sentiments at the time, even among the public at large. When asked in 1912 about his predictions for

TAKING MEASURE

The Growth in Armaments, 1890–1914

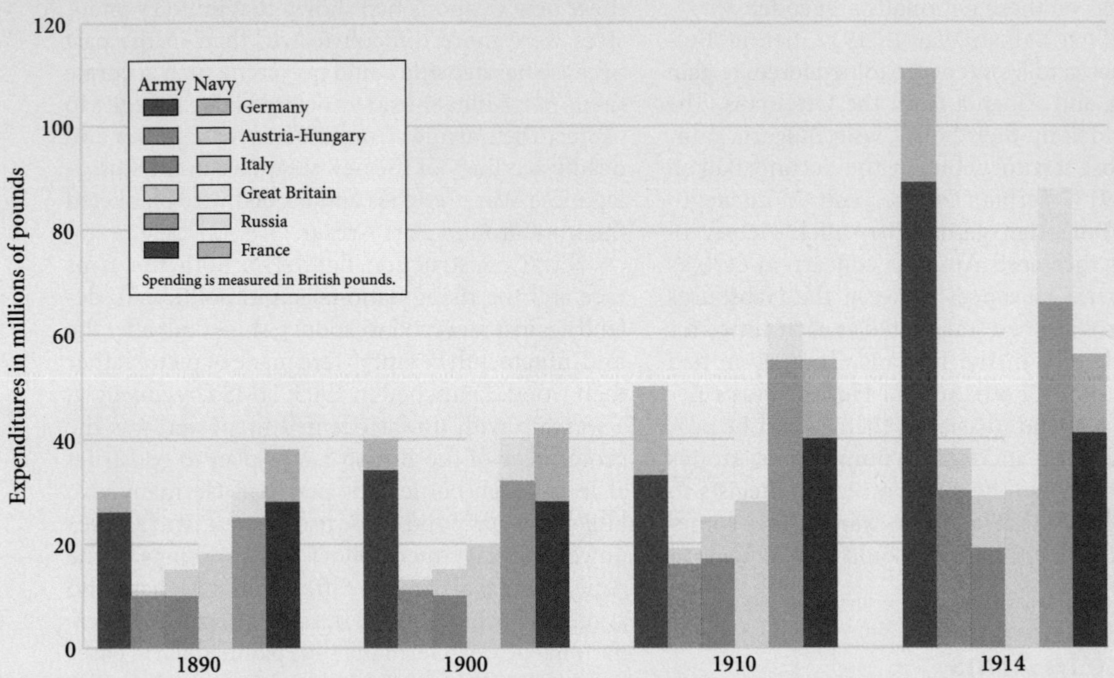

At the beginning of the twentieth century, the European powers engaged in a massive arms race that was part of industrial innovation. Even as sophisticated weaponry was one key to advancing global conquest, it also became part of national rivalries including economic, military, and imperial ones. Several comparisons offer themselves, not only in terms of the rates of increase but in terms of the military sectors that saw those increases. There is no doubt that the arms race stoked the fires of war, but historians often ask whether better diplomacy could have prevented the outbreak of the global conflict in 1914. The enormous military buildup, however, made some people living in the early twentieth century, as well as some later historians, see war as inevitable.

Source: *The Hammond Atlas of the Twentieth Century* (London: Times Books, 1996), 29.

Question to Consider

■ Which nations experienced the greatest rates of military buildup between 1890 and 1914, and which lagged behind? How do you account for the individual differences among the rates of military expansion?

war and peace, he responded enthusiastically, "We shall have war. I will make it. I will win it."

1914: War Erupts

June 28, 1914, began as an ordinary, even happy day not only for Freud's patient the Wolf-Man but also for the Austrian archduke and heir to the Habsburg throne, Francis Ferdinand, and his wife, Sophie, as they ended a state visit to Sarajevo in Bosnia. The archduke, in full military regalia, was riding in a motorcade when a group of young Serb nationalists threw bombs in an unsuccessful assassination attempt. The danger did not register; after a stop, the archduke and his wife set out again. In the crowd was another nationalist, Gavrilo Princip, who had traveled in secret for several weeks to reach this destination, dreaming of reuniting his homeland of Bosnia-Herzegovina with Serbia and smuggling weapons with him to accomplish his end. Princip shot dead the unprotected and unsuspecting Austrian couple.

Some in the Habsburg government saw the assassination as an opportunity to put down the Serbians once and for all. Evidence showed that Princip had received arms and information from Serbian

Arrest of the Assassin

Gavrilo Princip belonged to the Young Bosnians, a group devoted to killing Habsburgs in revenge for the Austro-Hungarian monarchy's having sent workers to colonize their homeland. In June 1914, at the age of nineteen, Princip lived out his dream, killing the heir to the Habsburg throne and his wife. Here Princip is shown being apprehended. He spent the rest of his life in prison and was appalled at the carnage of World War I. *(© Bettmann/Corbis.)*

officials, who directed a terrorist organization from within the government. Endorsing a quick defeat of Serbia, German statesmen and military leaders urged the Austrians to be unyielding and promised support in case of war. The Austrians sent an ultimatum to the Serbian government, demanding suppression of terrorist groups and the participation of Austrian officials in an investigation of the crime, among other things. "You are setting Europe ablaze," the Russian foreign minister remarked of the Austrians' humiliating demands made on a sovereign state. Yet the Serbs were conciliatory, accepting all the terms except the presence of Austrian officials in the investigation. Kaiser William was pleased: "A great moral success for Vienna! All reason for war is gone." His relief proved unfounded. Austria-Hungary, confident of German backing, used the Serbs' resistance to one demand as the pretext for declaring war against them on July 28.

Some statesmen tried desperately to avoid war. The tsar and the kaiser sent pleading letters to one another not to start a European war. The British foreign secretary proposed an all-European conference, but without success. Germany displayed firm support for Austria in hopes of convincing the French and British to stay out of the war. The failure of either to fight, German officials believed, would keep Russia from mobilizing. Additionally, German military leaders had become fixed on fighting a short, preemptive war that would provide territorial gains leading toward the goal of a Mitteleuropa. As conservatives, they planned to impose martial law the minute war began, using it as an excuse for arresting the leadership of the German Social Democratic Party, which threatened their rule.

The European press caught the war fever of nationalist and pro-war organizations, and military leaders, especially in Germany and Austria-Hungary, promoted mobilization rather than diplomacy in the last days of July. The Austrians declared war and then ordered mobilization on July 31 in full confidence of German military aid, because as early as 1909 Germany had promised to defend Austria-Hungary, even if that country took the offensive. The thought was that Russia would not dare to intervene against an Austria-Hungary backed by Germany military power, but Nicholas II ordered the mobilization in defense of the Serbs—Russia's Slavic allies. Encouraging the Austrians to attack Serbia, the German general staff mobilized on August 1. France declared war by virtue of its agreement to aid its ally Russia, and when Germany violated Belgian neutrality on its way to invade France, Britain entered the war on the side of France and Russia.

REVIEW QUESTION What were the major factors leading to the outbreak of World War I?

Conclusion

Rulers soon forgot their last-minute hesitations when in some capitals celebration erupted with the declaration of war. "A mighty wonder has taken place," wrote a Viennese actor after watching the troops march off amid public enthusiasm. "We have become *young*." Both sides exulted, certain of victory as militant nationalism led many Europeans to favor war over peace. There were advantages to war: disturbances in private life and challenges to established truths would disappear, it was believed, in the crucible of war. A short conflict, people maintained, would resolve tensions ranging from the rise of the working class to political problems caused by global imperial competition. German military men saw war as an opportune moment to round up social democrats and reestablish the traditional power of an agrarian aristocracy. Liberal government based on rights and constitutions, some believed, had simply gone too far in allowing new groups full citizenship and political influence.

Modernity helped blaze the path to war. New technology, mass armies, and new techniques of persuasion supported the military buildup. *The Rite of Spring*, the ballet that opened in Paris on the eve of war in 1913, had taken as its theme humans' ritualistic attraction of death. Facing continuing violence in politics, chaos in the arts, and problems in the industrial order, there was a belief that war would save nations from the modern perils they faced. The nervous pessimism that characterized the years before 1914 would end, replaced by patriotism. "Like men longing for a thunderstorm to relieve them of the summer's sultriness," wrote an Austrian official, "so the generation of 1914 believed in the relief that war might bring." Tragically, any hope of relief soon faded. Instead of bringing the refreshment of summer rain, war opened an era of political turmoil, widespread suffering, massive human slaughter, and even greater doses of modernity.

FOR FURTHER EXPLORATION

- **For additional primary-source material from this period**, see *Sources of the Making of the West*, Fourth Edition.
- **For Web sites, images, and documents related to topics in this chapter**, visit *Make History* at bedfordstmartins.com/hunt.

MAPPING THE WEST

Europe at the Outbreak of World War I, August 1914

All the powers expected a great, swift victory when war broke out. Many saw war as a chance to increase their territories; as rivals for trade and empire, almost all believed that war would bring them many advantages. But if European nations appeared well prepared and invincible at the start of the war, relatively few would survive the conflict intact.

Chapter 24 Review

Online Study Guide bedfordstmartins.com/hunt

Key Terms and People

In the grid below, identify the term or person and explain its historical significance. (To do this exercise online, go to bedfordstmartins.com/hunt.)

Term	Who or What & When	Why It Matters
new woman (p. 801)		
Sigmund Freud (p. 803)		
modernism (p. 806)		
Friedrich Nietzsche (p. 806)		
Albert Einstein (p. 807)		
art nouveau (p. 809)		
Emmeline Pankhurst (p. 812)		
Nicholas II (p. 813)		
Zionism (p. 817)		
South African War (p. 818)		
Duma (p. 821)		
Entente Cordiale (p. 825)		
Mitteleuropa (p. 826)		

Review Questions

1. How did ideas about the self and about personal life change at the beginning of the twentieth century?
2. How did modernism transform the arts and the world of ideas?
3. What were the points of tension in European political life at the beginning of the twentieth century?
4. How and why did events in overseas empires from the 1890s on challenge Western faith in imperialism?
5. What were the major factors leading to the outbreak of World War I?

Making Connections

1. How did changes in society at the turn of the twentieth century affect the development of mass politics?
2. How was culture connected to the world of politics in the years 1890–1914?
3. How had nationalism changed since the French Revolution?
4. In what ways were imperial wars from the 1890s to 1914 relevant to the outbreak of World War I?

Important Events

Date	Event
1894–1895	Japan defeats China in Sino-Japanese War
1894–1899	Dreyfus Affair exposes anti-Semitism in France
1899–1902	South African War fought between Dutch descendants and British in South African states
1900	Sigmund Freud publishes *The Interpretation of Dreams*
1901	Irish National Theater established by Maud Gonne and William Butler Yeats; death of Queen Victoria
1903	Emmeline Pankhurst founds Women's Social and Political Union
1904–1905	Japan defeats Russia in Russo-Japanese War
1905	Nicholas II establishes the Duma after revolution erupts in Russia; Albert Einstein publishes his special theory of relativity
1906	Women receive vote in Finland
1907	Pablo Picasso launches cubist painting with *Les Demoiselles d'Avignon*
1908	Young Turks revolt against rule by sultan in Ottoman Empire
1911–1912	Revolutionaries overthrow Qing dynasty and declare China a republic
1914	Assassination of Austrian archduke Francis Ferdinand and his wife by Serbian nationalist precipitates World War I

- Consider three events: **Sigmund Freud publishes *The Interpretation of Dreams* (1900)**, **Emmeline Pankhurst founds Women's Social and Political Union (1903)**, and **Pablo Picasso launches cubist painting with *Les Demoiselles d'Avignon* (1907)**. How did these events help to bring about modernity?

SUGGESTED REFERENCES

The cultural ferment, social turmoil, and actual violence of the pre–World War I years come alive in the works listed here.

Adamson, Walter L. *Embattled Avant-Gardes: Modernism's Resistance to Commodity Culture in Europe*. 2007.

Anderson, Margaret L. *Practicing Democracy: Elections and Political Culture in Imperial Germany*. 2000.

Childs, Peter. *Modernism*. 2008.

Forth, Christopher E. *The Dreyfus Affair and the Crisis of French Manhood*. 2005.

Frevert, Ute. *A Nation of Barracks: Modern Germany, Military Conscription and Civil Society*. 2004.

Hull, Isabel. *Absolute Destruction: Military Culture and the Practices of War in Imperial Germany*. 2005.

Hunt, Nancy Rose. *A Nervous State: Violence, Sterility, and Healing Movements in Colonial Congo*. 2011.

Kaplan, Morris B. *Sodom on the Thames: Sex, Love, and Scandal in Wilde Times*. 2005.

Marchand, Suzanne, and David Lindenfeld, eds. *Germany at the Fin-de-Siècle*. 2004.

Meir, Natan M. *Kiev, Jewish Metropolis: A History, 1859–1914*. 2010.

Nolan, Michael E. *The Inverted Mirror: Mythologizing the Enemy in France and Germany, 1898–1914*. 2005.

Reagin, Nancy R. *Sweeping the German Nation: Domesticity and National Identity in Germany, 1870–1945*. 2006.

Stanford Encyclopedia of Philosophy: http://plato.stanford.edu

Stanislawski, Michael. *Zionism and the Fin-de-Siècle: Cosmopolitanism and Nationalism from Nordau to Jabotinsky*. 2001.

Thompson, J. Lee. *Theodore Roosevelt Abroad: Nature, Empire and the Journey of an American President*. 2010.

Willmott, H. P. *The Last Century of Sea Power: From Port Arthur to Chanak, 1894–1922*. 2009.

CHAPTER

25

World War I and Its Aftermath

1914–1929

Jules Amar found his true vocation as a result of war. A French expert on improving the efficiency of industrial work, Amar switched his focus after 1914. As hundreds of thousands of soldiers returned from the battlefront missing body parts, plastic surgery and the construction of masks and other devices to hide deformities developed rapidly. Amar devised artificial limbs that would allow the wounded soldier to return to normal life by "making up for a function lost, or greatly reduced." The artificial arms featured hooks, magnets, and other mechanisms with which veterans could hold a cigarette, play a violin, and, most important, work with tools such as typewriters. Those who had been mangled by the weapons of modern technological warfare would be made whole, it was thought, by technology such as Amar's.

Amar dealt with the human tragedy of the Great War, so named by contemporaries because of its staggering human toll—forty million wounded or killed in battle. The Great War did not settle problems or restore social order as the European powers hoped it would. Instead, the war produced political chaos, overturning the Russian, German, Ottoman, and Austro-Hungarian Empires. The burden of war crushed the European powers and accelerated the rise of the United States, while colonized peoples who served in the war intensified their demands for independence. In fact, the armistice in 1918 did not truly end conflict: many soldiers remained actively fighting long into what was supposed to be peacetime, and others had been so militarized that they longed for a life that was more like wartime.

World War I transformed society, too. A prewar feeling of doom and decline gave way to postwar cynicism. Many Westerners turned their backs on politics and in the Roaring Twenties attacked life with wild gaiety,

Grieving Parents
Before World War I, the German artist Käthe Kollwitz gained her artistic reputation with woodcuts of handloom weavers whose livelihoods were threatened by industrialization. From 1914 on, she depicted the suffering and death that swirled around her and never with more sober force than in these two monuments to her son Peter, who died on the western front in the first months of battle. Today one can still travel to his burial place in Vladslo, Belgium, to see this father and mother mourning their loss, like millions across Europe in those heartbreaking days. *(photo © John Parker Picture Library. © 2011 Artists Rights Society [ARS], New York/VG Bild-Kunst, Bonn.)*

shopping for new consumer goods, enjoying once forbidden personal freedoms, and taking pleasure in the entertainment provided by films and radio. Others found reason for hope in the new political systems the war made possible: Soviet communism and Italian fascism. Modern communication technologies such as radio gave politicians the means to promote a utopian mass politics that, ironically, was antidemocratic, militaristic, and violent—like the war itself. Total war further weakened the gentlemanly political tone of British prime minister William Gladstone's day and perhaps even totally devastated it.

A war that was long anticipated and even welcomed in some quarters as a remedy for modernity destabilized Europe far into the following decades. From statesmen to ordinary citizens, many Europeans, including Jules Amar and those he helped, would spend the next decade dealing with the violent aftermath of war. While some tried to make war-ravaged society function normally, others kept alive the forces of militarism that the war had so glorified. It became clear that prewar normality was gone forever and that war and its values were shaping the 1920s.

CHAPTER FOCUS What political, social, and economic impact did World War I have during the conflict, immediately after it, and through the 1920s?

The Great War, 1914–1918

When war erupted in August 1914, two months after the assassination of the Austrian archduke and his wife at Sarajevo, there already existed long-standing alliances, well-defined strategies, and a stockpile of military technologies such as heavy artillery, machine guns, and airplanes. Most people felt that this would be a short, decisive conflict similar to Prussia's rapid victories in the 1860s and 1870–1871 and Japan's swift defeat of Russia in 1904–1905. In fact, the unexpected happened: the war lasted for more than four long years. It was also what historians call a **total war**, meaning one built on the full mobilization of entire societies—soldiers and civilians—and the industrial capacities of the nations involved. It was the war's unexpected and unprecedented horror that made World War I "great."

Blueprints for War

World War I's two sets of opponents were formed roughly out of the alliances developed during the previous fifty years. On one side stood the Central Powers (Austria-Hungary and Germany), which had evolved from Bismarck's Triple Alliance. On the other side were the Allies (France, Great Britain, and Russia), which had emerged as a bloc from the Entente Cordiale between France and Great Britain and the 1890s treaties between France and Russia. In 1915, Italy, originally part of the Triple Alliance, switched sides and joined the Allies in hopes of postwar gain. The war soon exploded globally: in late August 1914, Japan, eager to extend its empire into China, went over to the Allies, while in the fall the Ottoman Empire united with the Central Powers against its traditional enemy, Russia (Map 25.1).

Both sides fought with the same ferocious hunger for power, prestige, and prosperity that had inspired imperialism. Of the Central Powers, Germany wanted a bigger empire, to be gained by annexing Russian territory and incorporating parts of Belgium,

---

total war: A war built on the full mobilization of soldiers, civilians, and technology of the nations involved. The term also refers to a highly destructive war of ideologies.

1912 | **1915** | **1918**

1913–1925 Suffrage for women expands in much of Europe

1914 August: World War I begins

1916 Irish nationalists stage Easter Uprising against British rule

1917 March: Revolution in Russia overturns tsarist autocracy
April: United States enters World War I
November: Bolshevik Revolution in Russia

1918 November: Armistice ends fighting of World War I; revolutionary turmoil throughout Germany; kaiser abdicates

1918–1922 Civil war in Russia

A French Regiment Leaves for the Front, August 1914
Bands played, crowds cheered, and bicyclists led the way as bayonet-equipped soldiers marched eagerly to war. Some viewed the outbreak of war more soberly, and this mood became more common as machine guns and poison chemicals brought the bravest men down. People in cities, working to provide munitions and supplies, soon felt the pinch of inflation; later, many lacked food. Countless men returned physically disabled or mentally deranged from their experience. *(Roger Viollet/Getty Images.)*

France, and Luxembourg. Some German leaders wanted to annex Austria-Hungary as well. Austria-Hungary hoped to keep its great-power status despite the competing nationalisms of ethnic groups within its borders. Among the Allies, Russia wished to reassert its status as a great power and as the protector of the Slavs by adding a reunified Poland to the Russian Empire and by taking formal leadership of other Slavic peoples. The French, too, craved territory, especially the return of Alsace and Lorraine, ceded to Germany after the Franco-Prussian War of 1870–1871. The British wanted to cement their hold on Egypt and the Suez Canal and keep the rest of their world empire secure. By the Treaty of London (1915), France and Britain promised Italy territory in Africa, Asia Minor, the Balkans, and elsewhere in return for joining the Allies.

The colonies participated too, providing massive assistance and serving as battlegrounds. Some one million Africans, one million Indians, and more than a million men from the British commonwealth countries fought on the battlefronts. The imperial powers also conscripted uncounted numbers of colonists as forced laborers: a million Kenyans and Tanzanians alone are estimated to have been conscripted for menial labor in the battle for East Africa. Colonial troops played a major role in the fighting across north and sub-Saharan Africa. Using Arab, African, and Indian troops, the British waged successful war in the Ottoman lands of the Middle East. In sub-Saharan Africa, the vicious campaign for East Africa cost many lives, not only among the African troops used against one another on behalf of the imperialist powers but also among the civilian population whose resources were confiscated and whose villages were burned. As one of the Allies, Japan seized German-controlled territories in China and imposed its rule there.

1919 Weimar Republic established

1922 Eliot, "The Waste Land"; Joyce, *Ulysses*

1924–1929 Period of general economic prosperity and stability

1921 — 1924 — 1927

1919–1920 Paris Peace Conference redraws map of Europe

1922 Ireland gains independence; Fascists march on Rome; Mussolini becomes prime minister; Hitler builds Nazi Party

1924 Lenin dies; Stalin and Trotsky contend for power

1929 October: Stock market crash in United States

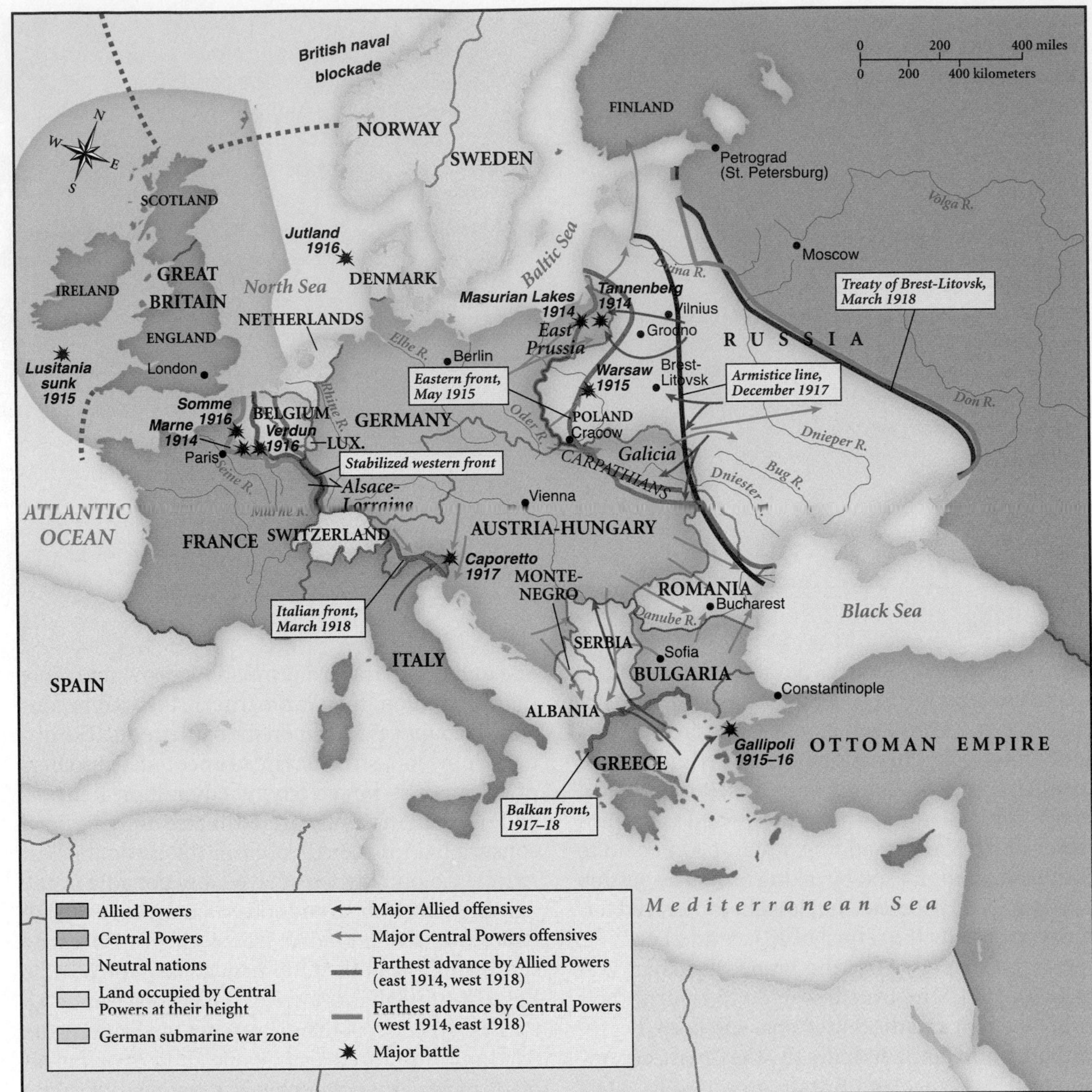

MAP 25.1 The Fronts of World War I, 1914–1918
Because the western front remained relatively stationary, devastation of land and resources was intense. All fronts, however, destroyed segments of Europe's hard-won industrial and agricultural capacity, while the immobile trenches increased military casualties whenever heavy artillery fire pounded them. Men long engaged in trench warfare developed an intense camaraderie based on their mutual suffering and deprivation.

Unprecedented use of machinery determined the course of war. In August 1914, machine guns, fast breech-loading rifles, and military vehicles such as airplanes, battleships, submarines, and motorized transport (cars and trains) were all at the armies' disposal. New technologies such as chlorine gas, tanks, and bombs developed between 1914 and 1918. Countries differed, however, in their experience with and access to large quantities of these technologies. British generals knew the destructive capacity of the weapons because of their colonial wars; the Germans were far more advanced in strategy and weaponry than either the Russians or the Austrians. The war itself became a lethal testing ground, as both new and old weapons were used, often ineffectively. Many officers on both sides believed in a **cult of the offensive**, which called for spirited attacks against the enemy and high troop

cult of the offensive: A military strategy of constantly attacking the enemy that was believed to be the key to winning World War I but that brought great loss of life while failing to bring decisive victory.

morale. Despite the availability of newer, more powerful war technology, an old-fashioned, heroic vision of war made many officers unwilling to abandon the more familiar sabers, lances, and bayonets. In the face of massive firepower, the cult of the offensive would cost millions of lives.

The Battlefronts

The first months of the war crushed any hope of a quick victory. All the major armies mobilized rapidly. The Germans were guided by the **Schlieffen Plan**, named after its author, Alfred von Schlieffen, a former chief of the general staff. The plan essentially outlined a way to combat enemies on two fronts by concentrating on one foe at a time. It called for a concentrated blow to the west against France, which would lead to that nation's defeat in six weeks, accompanied by a light holding action against Russia to the east. The attack on France was to proceed without resistance through neutral Belgium. Once France had fallen, Germany's western armies would move against Russia, which, it was believed, would mobilize far more slowly. None of the great powers expected that war would turn into the prolonged massacre of their nations' youth.

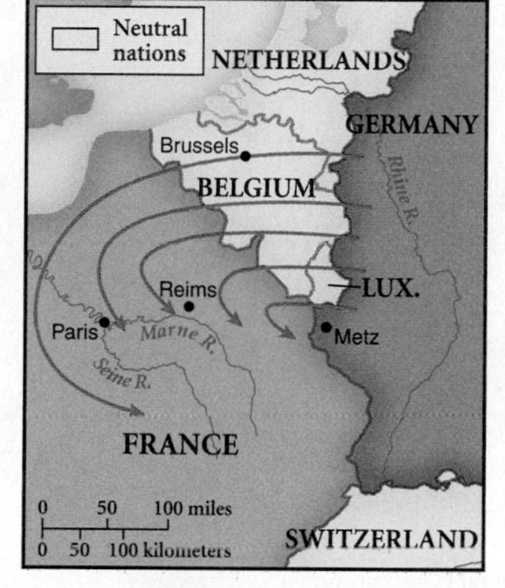

The Schlieffen Plan

Indecisive Offensives: 1914–1915 When German troops reached Belgium and Luxembourg at the beginning of August 1914, the Belgians surprisingly mounted a vigorous defense, which slowed the German advance. This allowed British and French troops, the latter based on France's eastern border, to reach the northern front. In September, the British and French armies engaged the Germans along the Marne River in France. Neither side could defeat the other, and casualties were shocking: in the first three months of war, more than 1.5 million men fell on the western front alone. Guns like the 75-millimeter howitzer, accurate at long range, turned what was supposed to be an offensive war of movement into a stationary standoff along a line that stretched from the North Sea through Belgium and northern France to Switzerland (Map 25.2). Deep within opposing lines of trenches dug along this front, millions of soldiers lived in nightmarish conditions.

On the eastern front, the Russian steam-roller—named thus because of the number of men mobilized, some twelve million in all—drove far more quickly than expected into East Prussia in mid-August. The Russians believed that no army could stand up to the massive number of their soldiers, regardless of how badly equipped and poorly trained those soldiers were. Their success was short-lived. The Germans overwhelmed the tsar's army in East Prussia and then turned south to Galicia. Victory made heroes of the German military leaders Paul von Hindenburg (1847–1934) and Erich Ludendorff (1865–1937), who demanded more troops for the eastern front. However, the German triumphs in the east had only temporarily halted the Russians and had also undermined the Schlieffen Plan by removing forces from the west before the western front had been won.

War at sea proved equally indecisive. Confident of Britain's superior naval power, the Allies blockaded ports to prevent supplies from reaching Germany and Austria-Hungary. Kaiser William and his advisers planned a massive U-boat (*Unterseeboot*, "underwater boat," or submarine) campaign against Allied and neutral shipping around Britain and France. In May 1915, U-boats sank the British passenger ship *Lusitania* and killed 1,198 people, including 124 Americans. Despite U.S. outrage, President Woodrow Wilson maintained a policy of neutrality; Germany, unwilling to provoke Wilson further, called off unrestricted submarine warfare. In May 1916, the navies of Germany and Britain finally clashed in the North Sea at Jutland. This inconclusive battle demonstrated that the German fleet could not master British seapower.

Ideas of a negotiated peace were discarded: "No peace before England is defeated and destroyed," William II stormed against his cousin King George V. "Only amidst the ruins of London will I forgive Georgy." French leaders called for a "war to the death." General staffs on both sides continued to prepare fierce attacks several times a year. Campaigns opened with heavy artillery pounding enemy trenches and gun emplacements. Troops then responded to the order to go "over the top" by scrambling out of their trenches and into battle, usually to be mowed down by machine-gun fire

Schlieffen Plan: The Germans' strategy in World War I that called for attacks on two fronts—concentrating first on France to the west and then turning east to attack Russia.

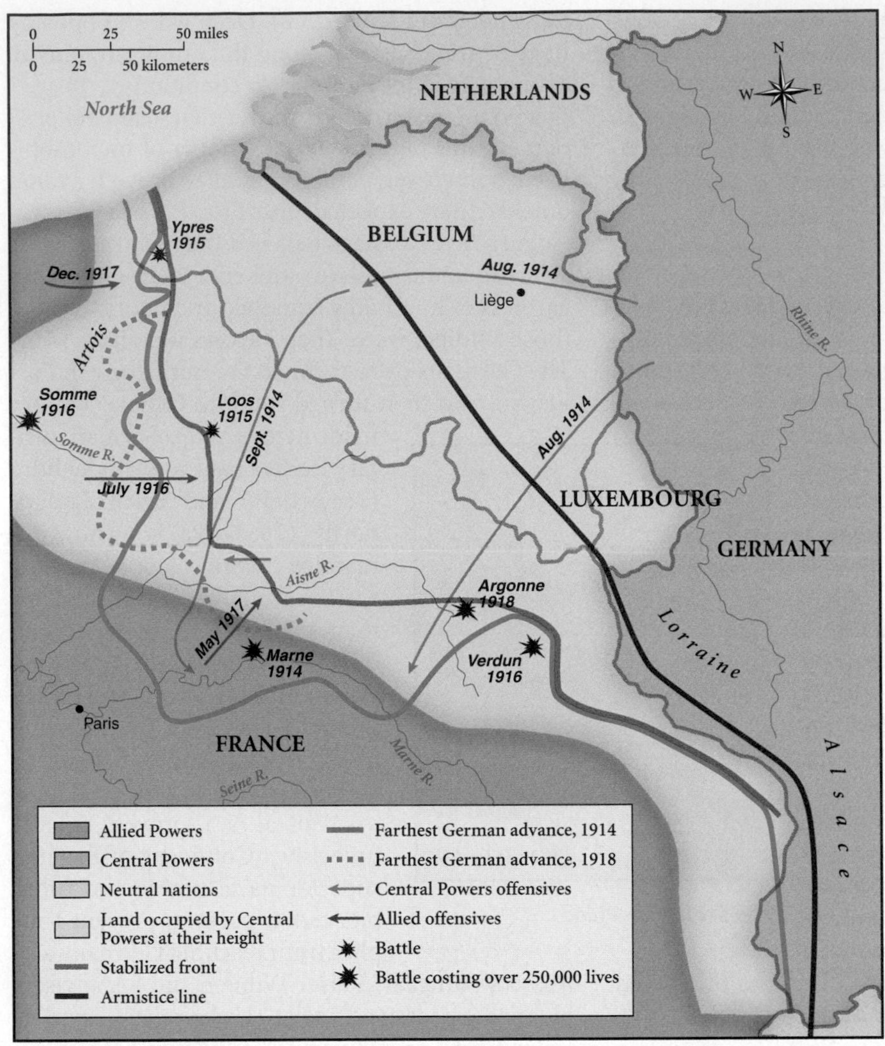

MAP 25.2
The Western Front
The western front occupied some of the richest parts of France, with long-lasting consequences. Destruction of French villages, roads, bridges, livestock, and property was the worst in Europe, while the trauma of the French people endured for generations. The effects of horrendous casualties, ever-present artillery fire, provisioning and hospital needs, and the demands of military and medical personnel changed everyone's way of life.

from defenders secure in their own trenches. On the western front, the French assaulted the Germans throughout 1915 to drive them from industrial regions. They accomplished little, and casualties of 100,000 and more for a single campaign became commonplace. On the eastern front, Russian armies captured parts of Galicia in the spring of 1915 and lumbered toward Hungary. The Central Powers struck back in Poland later that year, bringing the front closer to Petrograd (formerly St. Petersburg), the Russian capital.

Mounting Catastrophe: 1916 The next year's battles were even more disastrous and futile. To cripple French morale, the Germans launched massive assaults on the fortress at Verdun, firing as many as a million shells in a single day. Combined French and German losses totaled close to a million men. Nonetheless, the French held. Hoping to relieve their allies, the British unleashed an artillery pounding of German trenches in the Somme region in June 1916. In several months of battle at the Somme, 1.25 million men were killed or wounded, but the final result was stalemate. By the end of 1916, the French had suffered more than 3.5 million casualties. To help the Allies engaged at Verdun and the Somme, the Russians struck again, driving into the Carpathian Mountains, recouping territory, and menacing Austria-Hungary. The German army stopped the advance, as the German general staff decided it would take over Austrian military operations. The war was sapping Europe's strength and national independence.

The Soldiers' War Had military leaders thoroughly dominated the scene, historians judge, all armies would have been utterly demolished by the end of 1915. Yet ordinary soldiers in this war were not automatons in the face of what seemed to them suicidal orders. Informal agreements among troops to avoid battles allowed some battalions to go for long stretches with hardly a casualty. Enemies facing each other across the trenches frequently ate their meals in peace, even though the trenches were within hand-

War in the Trenches
Men at the front developed close friendships while they lived with daily discomfort, death, and the horrors of modern technological warfare. Some of the complexities of trench warfare appear in this image showing soldiers rescuing their fallen comrades after fighting at Bagatelle in northern France. *(Hulton Archive/Getty Images.)*

grenade reach. Throughout the war, soldiers on both fronts fraternized with one another. They played an occasional game of soccer, shouted across the trenches, and made gestures of agreement not to fight. A British veteran of the trenches explained to a new recruit that the Germans "don't want to fight any more than we do, so there's a kind of understanding between us. Don't fire at us and we'll not fire at you." Burying enemy dead in common graves with their own fallen comrades, many ordinary soldiers came to feel more warmly toward enemies who shared the trench experience than toward civilians back home.

Male camaraderie relieved some of the misery of trench life and aided survival. Sharing danger and deprivation on the front lines weakened traditional class distinctions. In some cases, upper-class officers and working-class recruits became friends in that "wholly masculine way of life uncomplicated by women," as another soldier put it. Soldiers picked lice from one another's bodies and clothes, tended one another's blistered feet, and came to love one another, sometimes even passionately. This sense of frontline community survived the war and influenced postwar politics.

Troops of colonized soldiers from Asia and Africa had different experiences. Often these soldiers were put in the very front ranks, where the risks were greatest. They suffered from the rigors of an unfamiliar climate and strange food as well as from Western war technology. Yet, like class divisions, racial barriers sometimes fell: a European might give extra blankets and clothing to soldiers from warmer regions. The perspectives of colonial troops changed, too: "What miserable crowned head was able to order such horrors?" wrote one corporal from West Africa. These troops saw their "masters"

War in the Skies (1914)
As the war started, aviators and the machines they piloted became symbols of the human potential to transcend time and space. The Great War, however, featured the airplane as the new weapon in what British writer H. G. Wells called the "headlong sweep to death." Daring pilots, or "aces," took the planes on reconnaissance flights and guided them in the totally new practice of aerial combat, as shown in this engraving from an Italian newspaper of a French airplane shooting down a German one. *(The Art Archive/Domenica del Corriere/Gianni Dagli Orti.)*

completely undone and "uncivilized," for when fighting did break out, trenches became a veritable hell of shelling and sniping, flying body parts, blinding gas, and rotting cadavers. Some soldiers became hysterical or shell-shocked through the stress and violence of battle. Some soldiers lost hope entirely: "It might be me tomorrow," a young British soldier wrote his mother in 1916. "Who cares?" Soldiers had gone to war to escape ordinary life in industrial society. They learned, however, as one German put it, "that in the modern war . . . the triumph of the machine over the individual is carried to its most extreme form." They took this hard-won knowledge into battle, pulling their comrades back when an offensive seemed lost or too costly.

The Home Front

World War I took place off the battlefield, too. Total war demanded the involvement of civilians in war industry: manufacturing the shells, the machine guns, the poisonous gases, the bombs, the airplanes, and eventually the tanks that were the backbone of technological warfare. Increased production of coffins, canes, wheelchairs, and artificial limbs (devised by the likes of Jules Amar) was also required. Because the war would have utterly failed without them, civilians had to work overtime, believe in, and sacrifice for victory. To keep the war machine operating smoothly, governments oversaw factories, transportation systems, and resources ranging from food to coal to textiles. Before the war, such tight government control would have outraged many liberals, but now it was accepted as necessary to win the war.

Politics Suspended At first, most political parties put aside their differences. Many socialists and working-class people who had formerly criticized the military buildup announced their support for the war. For decades, socialist parties had preached that "the worker has no country" and that nationalism was an ideology meant to keep workers disunited and subjected to the will of their employers. In August 1914, however, most socialists became as patriotic as the rest of society. Feminists divided over whether to maintain their traditional pacifism or to support the war. Although many feminists actively opposed the conflict, the British suffrage leader Emmeline Pankhurst and her daughter Christabel were among those who became militant nationalists, even changing the name of their suffrage paper to *Britannia.* Parties representing the middle classes dropped their distrust of the socialists and working classes. In the name of victory, national leaders wanted to end political division of all kinds: "I no longer recognize [political] parties," William II declared on August 4, 1914. "I recognize only Germans." Ordinary people, even those who had been at the receiving end of discrimination, came to believe that a new day of unity was dawning. One rabbi proudly echoed the kaiser: "In the German fatherland there are no longer any Christians and Jews, any believers and disbelievers, there are only Germans."

Mobilization of the People Governments mobilized the home front with varying degrees of success. All countries were caught without replacements for their heavy losses of military equipment and soon felt the shortage of food and labor as well. War ministries set up boards to allocate labor on both the home front and the battlefront and to give industrialists financial incentives to encourage productivity. The Russian bureaucracy, however, only cooperated halfheartedly with industrialists and other groups that could aid the war effort. In several countries, emergency measures allowed the drafting of both men and women for military or industrial service. Desperate for factory workers, the Germans forced Belgian citizens to move to Germany, housing them in prison camps. In the face of rationing, municipal governments set up canteens and day-care centers. Rural Russia, Austria-Hungary, Bulgaria, and Serbia, where youths, women, and old men struggled to sustain farms, had no such relief programs.

Governments throughout Europe passed sedition laws that made it a crime to criticize war-related policies. To ensure civilian acceptance of longer working hours and shortages of consumer goods, governments created propaganda agencies to advertise the war as a patriotic mission to resist villainous enemies (see "Seeing History," page 843). British propagandists fabricated some of the atrocities that the Germans, whom they called Huns (referring to the nomadic tribe of ancient times), supposedly committed against Belgians, and German propagandists warned that French African troops would rape German women if Germany were defeated. In Russia, Tsar Nicholas II had changed the German-sounding name of the capital St. Petersburg to the Russian Petrograd as a patriotic move. Maintaining that Armenians in the Ottoman Empire were plotting against the Central Powers, the Ottomans drove those Armenians living in Turkey from their homes, forcing them onto long marches or into concentration camps where they simply died or were murdered. The Allies also caused the deaths of civilians en masse by creating famines, blockading the Syrian provinces of the Ottoman Empire in hopes that the people there would rebel or die of starvation.

SEEING HISTORY

Portraying Soldiers in World War I

During World War I, photography captured the reality of life for soldiers in the trenches and riveted the public's attention. Because weaponry was so powerful, censorship in all combatant countries prevented the worst images—such as body parts lying around a battlefield or hanging from trees—from being printed. Some people created images that only suggested what war was like and tried to stir patriotism in heroic posters, while others, like Jules Amar, showed designs for prosthetics to add to veterans' bodies. Soldiers themselves also portrayed life at the front in a variety of artistic ways.

Visual propaganda was crucial in mobilizing civilian populations to join the military; work overtime on the home front; and willingly sacrifice food, health, and even their lives. Propaganda specialists who had promoted the arms buildups before the war now joined with graphic artists to produce emotionally compelling images, often of a savage enemy threatening helpless white women and their children. Celebrated Australian artist Norman Lindsay excelled in this genre as in others. The poster shown here, "The Trumpet Calls" (1918), suggested the transformation of ordinary men into muscular, brave soldiers. Indeed, Australian soldiers fought in large numbers in some of World War I's most celebrated battles, including the battle of Gallipoli (1915), and, like soldiers from every country, became symbols of patriotism and national strength as a result.

German artilleryman and artist Otto Dix was one of thousands of wartime volunteers, and his depictions of soldiers' reality was starkly different. Asked why he had signed up for the war, he replied: "I had to experience how someone beside me suddenly falls over and is dead and the bullet has hit him squarely. I had to experience that quite directly. I wanted it. I'm therefore not a pacifist at all—or am I? Perhaps I was an inquisitive person." His etching *Wounded Soldier* (completed in 1916 at the battle of the Somme and published in 1924) captures another side of war, one that many soldiers recalled in their postwar nightmares. Australian nurses described a similar reality for the wounded men in their diaries. As one put it more emotionally, "[I] shall not describe their wounds, they were too awful. One loses sight of all the honour and the glory in the work we are doing." Another said that she only wished the wounded who would eventually die had been "killed outright," so great was their agony. Competing visions of war shaped postwar culture and almost immediately influenced the course of politics.

Question to Consider

■ Compare these visual depictions of soldiers, the motivations that might have led to their production, and the effects they might have had on the viewing public. Which image do you think more powerful, and why?

Norman Lindsay, "The Trumpet Calls" (1918).
(The Trumpet Calls, by Norman Lindsay. Library of Congress, Prints and Photographs Division, LC-USZC4-12164.)

Otto Dix, *Wounded Soldier* (1924).
(Otto Dix [1891–1969], photo © ARS, NY. Wounded Man, Autumn 1916, Bapaume *from the portfolio* The War *[Verwundeter, Herbst 1916, Bapaume aus der Mappe Der Krieg]. 1924. Etching and aquatint from a portfolio of twenty etching, aquatint and drypoints, fourteen etching and aquatints, nine etching and drypoints, four etchings, and one drypoint and aquatint plate: $7\frac{3}{4} \times 11\frac{7}{16}$" [19.7 x 29 cm.]; sheet: $13\frac{3}{4} \times 18\frac{11}{16}$" [35 x 47.4 cm.]. Publisher: Karl Nierendorf, Berlin. Printer: Otto Felsing, Berlin. Gift of Abby Aldrich Rockefeller. [159.1934.6]. The Museum of Modern Art, New York, NY, USA. Digital Image © The Museum of Modern Art/Licensed by SCALA/Art Resource, NY/© 2011 Artists Rights Society [ARS], New York/VG Bild-Kunst, Bonn.)*

A New Workforce in Wartime
With men at the front, women (at right in this French photograph) moved into factory work at jobs from which they had been unofficially barred before the war. In addition, tens of thousands of forced laborers from the colonies were moved to Europe also to replace men sent to the front. The European experience of forced labor and service at the front politicized colonial subjects, fortifying independence movements in the postwar period. *(Roger Viollet/Getty Images.)*

Despite widespread popular support for the war, some individuals worked to bring about a negotiated peace. In 1915, activists in the international women's movement met in The Hague to call for an end to the war. "We can no longer endure . . . brute force as the only solution of international disputes," declared Dutch physician Aletta Jacobs. The women had no success, though many brought their cause to individual heads of state. In Austria-Hungary, nationalist groups agitating for ethnic self-determination hampered the empire's war effort. The Czechs undertook a vigorous anti-Habsburg campaign at home, while Croats, Slovenes, and Serbs in the Balkans formed a committee to plan a southern Slavic state independent of Austria-Hungary. The Allies encouraged such independence movements as part of their strategy to defeat Austria-Hungary.

The Civilians' War The war upset the social order as well as the political one. In the war's early days, many women lost their jobs when luxury shops, textile factories, and other nonessential businesses closed. But governments and businesses soon recognized the amount of labor it would take to wage technological war. As more and more men left for the trenches, women who had lost their jobs elsewhere joined with low-paid domestic workers to take over higher-paying jobs in munitions and metallurgical industries. In Warsaw women drove trucks, and in London they conducted streetcars. Some young women drove ambulances and nursed the wounded near the front lines.

The press praised women's patriotism in adapting to the wartime emergency, but women's assumption of men's jobs looked to many like a sign of social disorder. In the words of one metalworker, women were "sending men to the slaughter." Men feared that women would remain in the workforce after the war, robbing men of the breadwinner role. Others, even some women, objected to women's loss of femininity. "The feminine in me decreased more and more, and I did not know whether to be sad or glad about this," wrote one Russian nurse about wearing rough male clothing near the battlefield. Others criticized young female munitions workers for squandering their pay on ribbons and jewelry. The heated prewar debates over the "new woman" and gender roles returned.

Although soldiers from different backgrounds often felt bonds of solidarity in the trenches, difficult wartime conditions increasingly pitted civilians

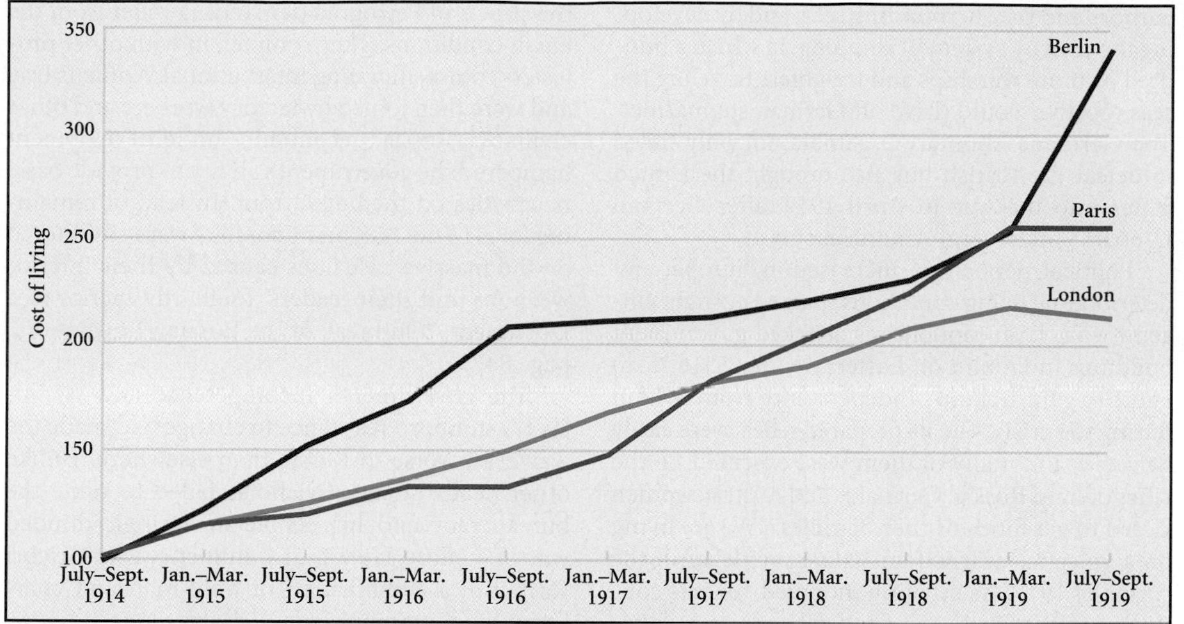

FIGURE 25.1 The Rising Cost of Living During World War I
The diversion of resources to the military resulted in a soaring cost of living for civilians. As men went to the front and as some remaining agricultural workers could find higher pay in factories, a decline in agricultural output led to scarcity and thus rising prices for food. Finally, housing came to be in short supply as resources were directed to the war effort rather than used to construct needed buildings. Even after the war, prices rose in Germany because the Allies maintained their blockade to keep the pressure on the peacemaking process. *(Jay Winter and Jean-Louis Robert,* Capital Cities at War: Paris, London, Berlin, 1914–1919 *[Cambridge: Cambridge University Press, 1997], 259.)*

against one another on the home front. Workers toiled long hours with less to eat, while many in the upper classes bought fancy food and fashionable clothing on the black market (outside the official system of rationing). Governments allowed many businesses high rates of profit, a policy that made the cost of living surge and thus contributed to social tensions (Figure 25.1). Shortages of staples like bread, sugar, and meat occurred across Europe. The Germans, in fact, called the brutal winter of 1916–1917 the turnip winter, because turnips were often the only food available. A German roof workers' association pleaded for relief: "We can no longer go on. Our children are starving." Reviving prewar anti-Semitism, some blamed Jews for the shortages. Colonial populations suffered oppressive conditions as well. The French forcibly transported some 100,000 Vietnamese to work in France for the war effort. Africans also faced grueling forced labor along with skyrocketing taxes and prices. Civilian suffering during the war, whether in the colonies or in Europe, laid the groundwork for ordinary people to take political action.

REVIEW QUESTION In what ways was World War I a total war?

Protest, Revolution, and War's End, 1917–1918

By 1917, the situation was becoming desperate for everyone—politicians, the military, and civilians. Discontent on the home front started shaping the course of the war. Neither patriotic slogans before the war nor propaganda during it had prepared people for wartime devastation. Civilians rebelled in cities across Europe. While soldiers in some armies mutinied, nationalist struggles continued to plague Britain and Austria-Hungary. Soon full-fledged revolution was sweeping Europe, toppling the Russian dynasty, and threatening not just war but civil war as well.

War Protest

On February 1, 1917, the German government, hard-pressed by the public clamor over mounting casualties and by the military's growing control, resumed full-scale submarine warfare. The military promised that this campaign would end the war in six months by cutting off food and military supplies to Britain and thus forcing the island nation to surrender. The British responded by mining their harbors and the surrounding seas, and by developing the convoy system of shipping, in which a hundred or more warships and freighters traveling the seas together could drive off German submarines. The Germans' submarine gamble not only failed to defeat the British but also brought the United States into the war in April 1917, after German U-boats sank several American ships.

Political opposition increased in Europe, and deteriorating living conditions sparked outright citizen revolt. Irish republicans attacked government buildings in Dublin on Easter Monday 1916 in an effort to gain Ireland's independence from Britain during the crisis. The ill-prepared rebels were easily defeated, and many of them were executed. In the cities of Italy, Russia, Germany, and Austria, women rioted to get food for their families. "We are living on a volcano," warned an Italian politician in the spring of 1917. As inflation mounted, tenants conducted rent strikes, and factory hands and white-collar workers alike walked off the job.

Amid these protests, Austria-Hungary secretly asked the Allies for a negotiated peace to avoid a total collapse of the empire. In the summer of 1917, the German Reichstag also made overtures for a "peace of understanding and permanent reconciliation of peoples." In January 1918, President Woodrow Wilson issued his **Fourteen Points**, a blueprint for a nonvindictive peace settlement held out to the war-weary citizens of the Central Powers. By that time, however, French soldiers had already mutinied against further bloody and useless offensives, and in Russia, protest had turned into outright revolution.

Revolution in Russia

Of all the warring nations, Russia sustained the greatest number of casualties — 7.5 million by 1917. Slaughter on the eastern front drove hundreds of thousands of peasants into the Russian interior, spreading hunger, homelessness, and disease. In March 1917,[1] crowds of workingwomen swarmed the streets of Petrograd demanding relief from the harsh conditions. They soon fell in with other protesters commemorating International Women's Day and were then joined by factory workers and other civilians. Russia's economic underdevelopment hampered the government's ability to provide basic necessities on the home front. Instead of remaining loyal to the tsar, many soldiers were embittered by the massive casualties caused by their inferior weapons and their leaders' foolhardy tactics (see Document, "Outbreak of the Russian Revolution," page 847).

The government's incompetence and Nicholas II's stubborn resistance to change had made the war even worse in Russia than elsewhere. Unlike other heads of state, Nicholas failed to unite the bureaucracy and his people in a single-minded wartime effort. He was also influenced by Grigori Rasputin, a combination of holy man and charlatan who manipulated Nicholas and his wife, Alexandra, by claiming to control the hemophilia of their son and heir. Rasputin's disastrous impact on state matters led influential leaders to question rather than support the government. "Is this stupidity or treason?" one member of the Duma asked of the corrupt wartime administration. When the riots erupted in March 1917, Nicholas finally realized the situation was hopeless. He abdicated, bringing the three-hundred-year-old Romanov dynasty to a sudden end.

The Provisional Government Aristocratic and middle-class politicians from the old Duma formed a new administration called the Provisional Government. At first, hopes were high that under the Provisional Government, as one revolutionary poet put it, "our false, filthy, boring, hideous life should become a just, pure, merry, and beautiful life." To survive, the Provisional Government had to pursue the war successfully, manage internal affairs better, and set the government on a firm constitutional footing. However, it did not rule alone, because other political forces had also strengthened during the revolution. Among them, the **soviets** — councils elected from workers and soldiers — competed with the government for political support. Born during the Revolution of 1905, the soviets in 1917 campaigned to end the deference usually given to the wealthy and to military officers, urged respect for workers and

[1]Until February 1918, Russia observed the Julian calendar, which was thirteen days behind the Gregorian calendar used by the rest of Europe. Hence, the first phase of the revolution occurred in March according to the Gregorian calendar (but February in the Julian calendar), the later phase in November on the Gregorian calendar (October according to the Julian). All dates used in this book follow the Gregorian calendar.

Fourteen Points: U.S. president Woodrow Wilson's World War I peace proposal; based on settlement rather than on conquest, it encouraged the surrender of the Central Powers.

soviets: Councils of workers and soldiers first formed in Russia in the Revolution of 1905; they were revived to represent the people in the early days of the 1917 Russian Revolution.

DOCUMENT

Outbreak of the Russian Revolution

It is clear only in retrospect when a full-fledged and sustainable revolution has broken out. Here an eighteen-year-old student describes what happened when news of the St. Petersburg revolt reached Moscow in the late winter of 1917. Crowds had already formed when the young man decided to see what was happening in the streets.

In the crowd were many students who explained that a revolution had begun in St. Petersburg. The news swept through them like a breeze and created an extraordinary atmosphere. People began to embrace and kiss; strangers became close friends; some wept for joy. In five to ten minutes people seemed reborn. A pretty girl came up to me and took me by the hand, as though we had known each other for ages. Then hand-in-hand, in a warm embrace, and without asking each other's name, we proceeded toward the Krutitskie barracks. . . .

The crowd grew bigger and bigger, and somewhere in the distance one could hear the well-known refrain of a revolutionary song. By this time it was so crowded that it was quite impossible to get to one side or the other. We continued to hold hands, as though we might get lost. Slowly, barely perceptibly, the human stream moved toward the Red Gates, where I knew there was another barracks. It was the same scene there, except that the soldiers were shouting loudly, waving and greeting us. We couldn't make out what they said. Near Pokrovka we ran into a group of police officers, but instead of greeting them with good-natured jokes, thousands of voices yelled fierce, threatening cries: "Pharaohs! Your time is up! Get away for your own good!"

. . . We moved slowly and could see neither the front nor the back of the crowd, for the street was blocked solid. For the first time in my life I sensed that atmosphere of joy, when everyone you meet seems close to you, your flesh and blood, when people look at one another with eyes full of love. To call it mass hypnosis is not quite right, but the mood of the crowd was transmitted from one to another like conduction, like a spontaneous burst of laughter, joy, or anger.

The majority of the crowd consisted of people who that morning had been praying for the good health of the imperial family. Now they were shouting, "Down with the Tsar!" and not disguising their joyful contempt. My companion was a good example. She showered me with questions: Where are we going? Why are we marching? Why is there a revolution? How will we manage without a tsar? It seemed like a mere holiday to her—Sunday's carnival procession, complete with mass participation. Tomorrow—Monday—humdrum working life would begin again, just as usual. Without asking a question, as though talking to herself, she suddenly said: "How good it would be if there was another revolution tomorrow!" What could I say? Tomorrow? Probably tomorrow the police would arrest us. But today there was a festival on the streets.

Source: Eduard Dune, *Notes of a Red Guard*, trans. and ed. Dianne Koenker and S. A. Smith (Champaign: University of Illinois Press, 1993), 32, 34.

Question to Consider

- **What is the mood of the crowd in Moscow? What was happening in Russia that would make them react this way to news of the revolt?**

the poor, and temporarily gave an air of celebration and carnival to the political upheaval. The peasants, also competing for power, began to confiscate landed estates and withhold produce from the market because there were no consumer goods for which to exchange food. As a result, urban food shortages worsened, threatening the Provisional Government.

In hopes of adding to the turmoil in Russia, the Germans in April 1917 provided safe rail transportation for **V. I. Lenin** (1870–1924) and other prominent Bolsheviks to return to Russia through German territory. Lenin had devoted his entire existence to bringing about socialism through the force of his small band of Bolsheviks. Upon his return to Petrograd, he issued the April Theses, a radical document that called for Russia to withdraw from the war, for the soviets to seize power on behalf of workers and poor peasants, and for all private land to be nationalized. As the Bolsheviks aimed to supplant the Provisional Government, they employed such slogans as "All power to the soviets" and "Peace, land, and bread."

The Bolshevik Takeover Time was running out for the Provisional Government, which saw a battlefield victory as the only way to ensure its survival. On July 1, the Russian army attacked the Austrians in Galicia but was defeated once again. The new prime minister, Aleksandr Kerensky, used his commanding oratory to arouse patriotism, but he lacked the political skills needed to create an effective wartime government. Under the Provisional Government, the army itself

---

V. I. Lenin: Bolshevik leader who executed the Bolshevik Revolution in the fall of 1917, took Russia out of World War I, and imposed communism in Russia.

Revolution in Russia

1917	March 8	International Women's Day, strikes and demonstrations
	March 12	Establishment of Provisional Government
	March 15	Nicholas II abdicates
	April	Lenin and other Bolshevik leaders return to Russia
	May	Turmoil in the Provisional Government
	Late June–early July	Russian offensive against Germany fails
	Mid-July	Attempted popular uprising fails; Kerensky is prime minister
	September	Military coup fails
	November 6–7	Bolsheviks seize power on behalf of soviets
	November 25	Constituent assembly elections held
1918	January	Constituent assembly closed down by Bolsheviks
	March 2	Treaty of Brest-Litovsk
1918–1922		Civil war
1923		Union of Soviet Socialist Republics established
1924		Death of Lenin
1928–1929		Stalin takes full power

had become, as one critic put it, "a huge crowd of tired, poorly clad, poorly fed, embittered men"—eager for radical change.

The Bolshevik leadership, urged on by Lenin, attacked and overthrew the weakened Provisional Government in November 1917, an event called the **Bolshevik Revolution**. In January 1918, elections for a constituent assembly failed to give the Bolsheviks a plurality, so the party used troops to take over the new government completely. The Bolsheviks also seized town and city administrations, and in the winter of 1918–1919, their new government, observing Marxist doctrine, abolished private property and nationalized factories in order to stimulate production. The Provisional Government had allowed both men and women to vote in 1917, making Russia the first great power to legalize universal suffrage. This soon became a hollow privilege once the Bolsheviks limited the candidates to chosen members of the Communist Party.

The Bolsheviks asked Germany for peace and agreed to the Treaty of Brest-Litovsk (March 1918), which placed vast regions of the old Russian Empire under German occupation. Because the loss of millions of square miles to the Germans put Petrograd at risk, the Bolsheviks relocated the capital to Moscow and formally adopted the name Communists (taken from Karl Marx's writings) to distinguish themselves from the socialists/social democrats who had voted for the disastrous war in the first place. Lenin called the catastrophic terms of the treaty "obscene." However, he accepted them—not only because he had promised to bring peace to Russia but also because he believed that the rest of Europe would soon rebel against the war and overthrow the capitalist order.

Civil War in Russia A full-blown civil war now broke out in Russia, with the pro-Bolsheviks (or "Reds") pitted against an array of forces (the "Whites") who wanted to turn back the revolution (Map 25.3). Among the Whites were three distinct groups: the tsarist military leadership, composed mainly of landlords and supporters of aristocratic rule; the liberal educated class, including businessmen whose property had been nationalized; and non-Russian nationalities who had been brought into the empire through force and Russification and who fought the Bolsheviks because they saw their chance for independence. In addition, before World War I ended, Russia's former allies—notably the United States, Britain, France, and Japan—landed troops in the country both to block the Germans and to fight the Bolsheviks. The counterrevolutionary groups lacked a strong leader and unified goals, however. Instead, they competed with one another: the pro-tsarist forces, for example, alienated groups seeking independent nation-state status, such as the Ukrainians, Estonians, and Lithuanians, by stressing the goal of restoring the Russian Empire. Even with the presence of Allied troops, the opponents of revolution could not defeat the Bolsheviks without a common purpose or an effective, unified command.

The civil war shaped Russian communism. Leon Trotsky (1879–1940), Bolshevik commissar of war, built the highly disciplined army by ending democratic procedures, such as the election of officers, that had originally attracted soldiers to Bolshevism. Lenin and Trotsky introduced the policy of war communism, whereby urban workers and troops moved through the countryside, seizing grain from the peasantry to feed the civil war army and workforce. The Cheka (secret police) imprisoned political opponents and black marketers and often shot them without trial. As the bureaucracy, the Cheka, and the Red Army all grew in size and strength, the result was a more authoritarian government—a development that broke Marx's promise that revolution would bring a "withering away" of the state.

As the Bolsheviks clamped down on their opponents during the bloody civil war, they organized their supporters to foster revolutionary Marxism across Europe. In March 1919, they founded the

---

Bolshevik Revolution: The overthrow of Russia's Provisional Government in the fall of 1917 by V. I. Lenin and his Bolshevik forces.

Third International, also known as the Communist International (Comintern), to replace the Second International with a centralized organization dedicated to preaching communism. By mid-1921, the Red Army had defeated the Whites in the Crimea, the Caucasus, and the Muslim borderlands in central Asia. After ousting the Japanese from Siberia in 1922, the Bolsheviks governed a state as multinational as the old Russian Empire had been. Although the revolution had turned out the inept Romanovs and the privileged aristocracy, the civil war and the resulting hunger and disease took millions of lives. Meanwhile, the Bolsheviks had made brutality their political style, one at odds with socialist promises for a humane and flourishing society.

Ending the War, 1918

With Russia out of the war, Europe's leaders faced a new balance of military forces. In the spring of 1918, the Central Powers made one final attempt to smash through the Allied lines using a new offensive strategy. It consisted of concentrated forces piercing single points of the enemy's defense lines and then wreaking havoc from the rear. Using these tactics, the Central Powers overwhelmed the Italian army at Caporetto in the fall of 1917, but a similar offensive on the western front in the spring of 1918

Lenin Addressing Soldiers
Lenin mobilized the masses with his oratory, but he also used traditional weapons of the Russian Empire such as secret police, imprisonment and torture, and executions. At the time of the civil war it was more than ever important to keep soldiers loyal. Understanding this, Lenin, with the crucial aid of Leon Trotsky, began building the Red Army into a formidable fighting force. *(Rue des Archives/The Granger Collection, New York—All rights reserved.)*

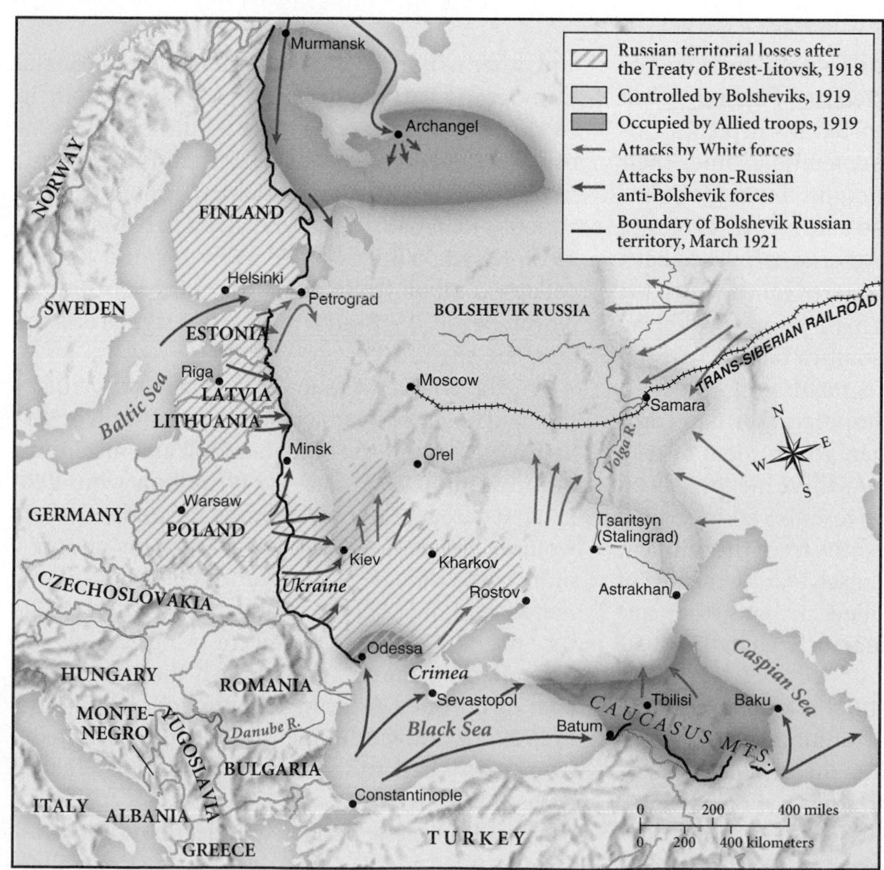

MAP 25.3 The Russian Civil War, 1917–1922
Nationalists, aristocrats, middle-class citizens, and property-owning peasants tried to combine their interests to defeat the Bolsheviks, but they failed to create an effective political consensus. As fighting covered the countryside, ordinary people suffered, especially when their grain was confiscated by armies on both sides. The Western powers and Japan also sent in troops to put down this threatening revolution.

TAKING MEASURE

The Victims of Influenza, 1918–1919

The influenza pandemic that broke out among soldiers and civilians during World War I was devastating, claiming between 50 and 100 million lives worldwide. Not only was the death toll unprecedented, but the victims of the flu differed significantly from those in the general population who had normally died from influenza and pneumonia. The graph at right, showing the "terrible W" shape of flu deaths, illustrates that difference. (*Specific death rate* refers to a method of calculating mortality rates from a specified cause.)

Question to Consider

- **What was the difference among victims of the flu pandemic during and immediately after World War I and those who had died of flu before the war? Why was this difference so alarming to officials and ordinary people alike?**

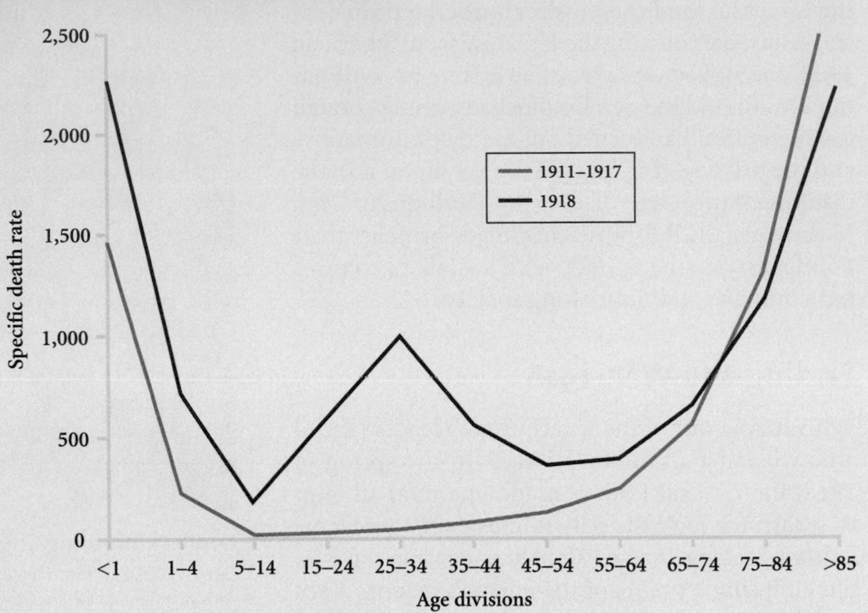

Source: Jeffrey K. Taubenberger and David Morens, "1918 Influenza: The Mother of All Pandemics," *Emerging Infectious Diseases* 12, no. 1 (2006): 15–22.

ground to a bloody halt within weeks. By then, the British and French had started making limited but effective use of tanks supported by airplanes. Although the first tanks were cumbersome, their ability to withstand machine-gun fire made offensive attacks winnable. In the summer of 1918, the Allies, now fortified by the Americans, pushed back the Germans all along the western front and headed toward Germany. The German armies, suffering more than two million casualties between spring and summer, rapidly disintegrated.

By October 1918, the desperate German command helped create a civilian government to take over rule of the home front. As these inexperienced politicians took power, they were also taking blame for the defeat. Shifting the blame from the military, the generals proclaimed themselves fully capable of winning the war. Weak-willed civilians, they announced, had dealt the military a "stab in the back" by forcing a surrender. Amid this outright lying, naval officers called for a final sea battle. Having spent years watching high-ranking officers enjoy champagne-filled meals while they themselves survived on turnips and thin soup, sailors rebelled against what they saw as a suicide mission. The sailors' revolt spread to workers in Berlin, Munich, and other major cities. The uprisings led the Social Democratic Party to declare a German republic in an effort to prevent revolution. At the end of October, Czechs and Slovaks declared an independent state, while the Croatian parliament simultaneously announced Croatia's independence. On November 9, 1918, Kaiser William II fled as the Central Powers collapsed on all fronts. Finally, on the morning of November 11, 1918, an armistice was signed and the guns fell silent.

In the course of four years, European civilization had been sorely tested, if not shattered. Conservative figures put the battlefield toll at a minimum of ten million dead and thirty million wounded, incapacitated, or doomed eventually to die of their wounds. In every European combatant country, industrial and agricultural production had plummeted, and much of the reduced output filled military needs. Asia, Africa, and the Americas, which depended on European trade, felt the painful impact of Europe's declining production. From 1918 to 1919, a worldwide influenza epidemic left as many as one hundred million more dead (see "Taking Measure," above).

Besides illness, hunger, and death, moral questioning filled media and private discussions alike.

Soldiers returning home in 1918 and 1919 flooded the book market with their memoirs, trying to give meaning to their experiences. Some twenty-five hundred war poets published in Britain alone. Whereas many had begun by emphasizing heroism and glory, others were cynical and bitter by war's end. They insisted that the fighting had been absolutely meaningless. Total war had not only drained society of resources and population but also sown the seeds of further catastrophe.

REVIEW QUESTION Why did people rebel during World War I, and what turned rebellion into outright revolution in Russia?

The Search for Peace in an Era of Revolution

World War I, like many other wars in the past, had unforeseen and dramatic consequences. Revolutionary fervor now swept the continent, especially in the former empires of Germany and Austria-Hungary. Until 1921, socialist victory seemed plausible; many of the newly independent peoples of eastern and central Europe strongly supported socialist principles. The revolutionary mood infected workers and peasants in Germany, too. In contrast, many activists on both the left and the right hoped for a political order based on military authority of the kind they had relied on during the war. Faced with both liberal and right-wing uprisings, diplomats from around the world arrived in Paris in January 1919 to negotiate the terms of peace, though without fully recognizing the fact that the war was still going on not only in city streets, where soldiers were bringing the war home, but also in people's hearts.

Europe in Turmoil

Urban citizens and returning soldiers ignited the protests that swept Europe in 1918 and 1919. In January 1919, the red flag of socialist revolution flew from the city hall in Glasgow, Scotland, while in cities of the collapsing Austro-Hungarian monarchy, workers set up councils to take over factory production and direct politics. Many soldiers did not disband at the armistice but formed volunteer armies, preventing the return to peacetime politics. Germany was especially unstable, partly because of the shock of defeat. Independent socialist groups and workers' councils fought for control of the government, and workers and veterans filled the streets, demanding food and back pay. Whereas in 1848, revolutionaries had marched to city hall or the king's residence, these protesters took over newspapers and telegraph offices to control the flow of information. One of the most radical socialist factions was the Spartacists, led by cofounders Karl Liebknecht (1871–1919) and Rosa Luxemburg (1870–1919). Unlike Lenin, the two leading Spartacists wanted any uprisings to give workers political experience instead of simply following an all-knowing party leadership on a set course.

German conservatives had believed that the war would put an end to Social Democratic influence; instead, it brought German socialists to power. Social Democratic leader Friedrich Ebert, who headed the new German government, rejected revolution and supported the creation of a parliamentary republic to replace the monarchy. He appeared to back the idea of settling political differences with military solutions by calling on the German army and the Freikorps—a roving paramilitary band of students, demobilized soldiers, and others—to suppress the workers' councils and demonstrators. "The enthusiasm is marvelous," wrote one young soldier. "No mercy's shown. We shoot even the wounded. . . . We were much more humane against the French in the field." Members of the Freikorps hunted down Luxemburg and Liebknecht, among others, and murdered them.

Violence continued even as an assembly meeting in the city of Weimar in February 1919 approved a constitution and founded a parliamentary republic called the **Weimar Republic**. This time the right rebelled, for the military leadership dreamed of a restored monarchy: "As I love Germany, so I hate the Republic," wrote one officer. To defeat a military coup by Freikorps officers, Ebert called for a general strike. This action cut short a takeover of the new republic by showing the clear lack of popular support for a military regime. But in so doing, the Weimar Republic had set a dangerous precedent: it had relied on street violence, paramilitary groups, and protests rather than parliaments to solve political problems.

Revolutionary activism surged and was smashed in many parts of Europe. Late in the winter of 1919, leftists proclaimed "soviet republics"—governments led by workers' councils—in Bavaria and Hungary. Volunteer armies and troops soon put the soviets down. The Bolsheviks tried to establish a Marxist regime in Poland in the belief that its people wanted a workers' revolution. Instead, the Poles resisted and drove the Red Army back in 1920, while the Allied powers rushed supplies and advisers to Warsaw.

Weimar Republic: The parliamentary republic established in 1919 in Germany to replace the monarchy.

Though they failed, the various revolts provided further proof that total war had let loose the forces of political chaos. War, it seemed, continued.

The Paris Peace Conference, 1919–1920

As political turmoil engulfed peoples from Berlin to Moscow, the Paris Peace Conference opened in January 1919. Visions of communism spreading westward haunted the deliberations, but the assembled statesmen were also focused on the reconstruction of a secure Europe and the status of Germany. Leaders such as French premier Georges Clemenceau had to satisfy angry citizens who were demanding revenge or, at the very least, money to rebuild and pay their nation's war debts. France had lost 1.3 million people — almost an entire generation of young men — and more than a million buildings, six thousand bridges, and thousands of miles of railroad lines and roads. Great Britain's representative, Prime Minister David Lloyd George, caught the mood of the British public by campaigning in 1918 with such slogans as "Hang the kaiser." The Italians arrived on the scene demanding the territory promised to them in the 1915 Treaty of London. Meanwhile, U.S. president Woodrow Wilson (1856–1924), head of the new world power that had helped achieve the Allied victory, had his own agenda. His Fourteen Points, on which the truce had been based, were steeped in the language of freedom and called for open diplomacy, arms reduction, and the right of nationality groups to determine their own government.

The Fourteen Points did not represent the mood of the victors. Allied propaganda had made the Germans seem like inhuman monsters, and many citizens demanded a harsh peace. In addition, some military experts feared that Germany was using the armistice only to regroup for more warfare. Indeed, Germans widely refused to admit that their army had lost the war. Eager for army support, Ebert had given returning soldiers a rousing welcome: "As you return unconquered from the field of battle, I salute you." Wilson's former allies campaigned to make him look naive and unrealistic. "Wilson bores me with his Fourteen Points," Clemenceau complained. "Why, the good Lord himself has only ten."

Nevertheless, Wilson's plan persuaded Germans that the settlement would not be vindictive. His commitment to *settlement* as opposed to *surrender* wisely recognized that Germany was still the strongest state on the continent, and he pushed for a treaty that balanced the strengths and interests of various European powers. Economists and other specialists accompanying Wilson to Paris agreed that, harshly dealt with and humiliated, Germany might soon become vengeful and chaotic — a lethal combination.

The Peace of Paris Treaties

After six months, the statesmen and their teams of experts produced the **Peace of Paris** (1919–1920), composed of a cluster of individual treaties that shocked the countries that had to accept them. The treaties separated Austria from Hungary, reduced Hungary by almost two-thirds of its inhabitants and three-quarters of its territory, broke up the Ottoman Empire, and treated Germany severely. They replaced the Habsburg Empire with a group of small, internally divided, and economically weak states: Czechoslovakia; Poland; and the Kingdom of the Serbs, Croats, and Slovenes (soon renamed Yugoslavia). After a century and a half of partition, Poland was reconstructed from parts of Russia, Germany, and Austria-Hungary — leaving one-third of its population ethnically non-Polish. The statesmen in Paris also created the Polish Corridor, which connected Poland to the Baltic Sea and separated East Prussia from the rest of Germany (Map 25.4). Austria and Hungary were both left reeling at their drastic loss of territory and resources.

The Treaty of Versailles, the centerpiece of the Peace of Paris, specifically dealt with Germany. In it, France recovered Alsace and Lorraine, and the Allies would temporarily occupy the left, or western, bank of the Rhine and the coal-bearing Saar basin. Wilson accepted his allies' expectations that Germany would pay substantial reparations for civilian damage during the war. The specific amount was set in 1921 at the crushing sum of 132 billion gold marks. Germany also had to reduce its army, almost eliminate its navy, stop manufacturing offensive weapons, and deliver a large amount of free coal each year to Belgium and France. Furthermore, it was forbidden to have an air force and had to give up its colonies. The average German saw in these terms an unmerited humiliation that was compounded by Article 231 of the treaty, which described Germany's "responsibility" for damage caused "by the aggression of Germany and her allies." Outraged Germans interpreted this as a **war guilt clause**, which blamed Germany for the war and allowed the victors to collect reparations from their economi-

---

Peace of Paris: The series of peace treaties (1919–1920) that provided the settlement of World War I. The Treaty of Versailles with Germany was the centerpiece of the Peace of Paris.

war guilt clause: The part of the Treaty of Versailles that assigned blame for World War I to Germany.

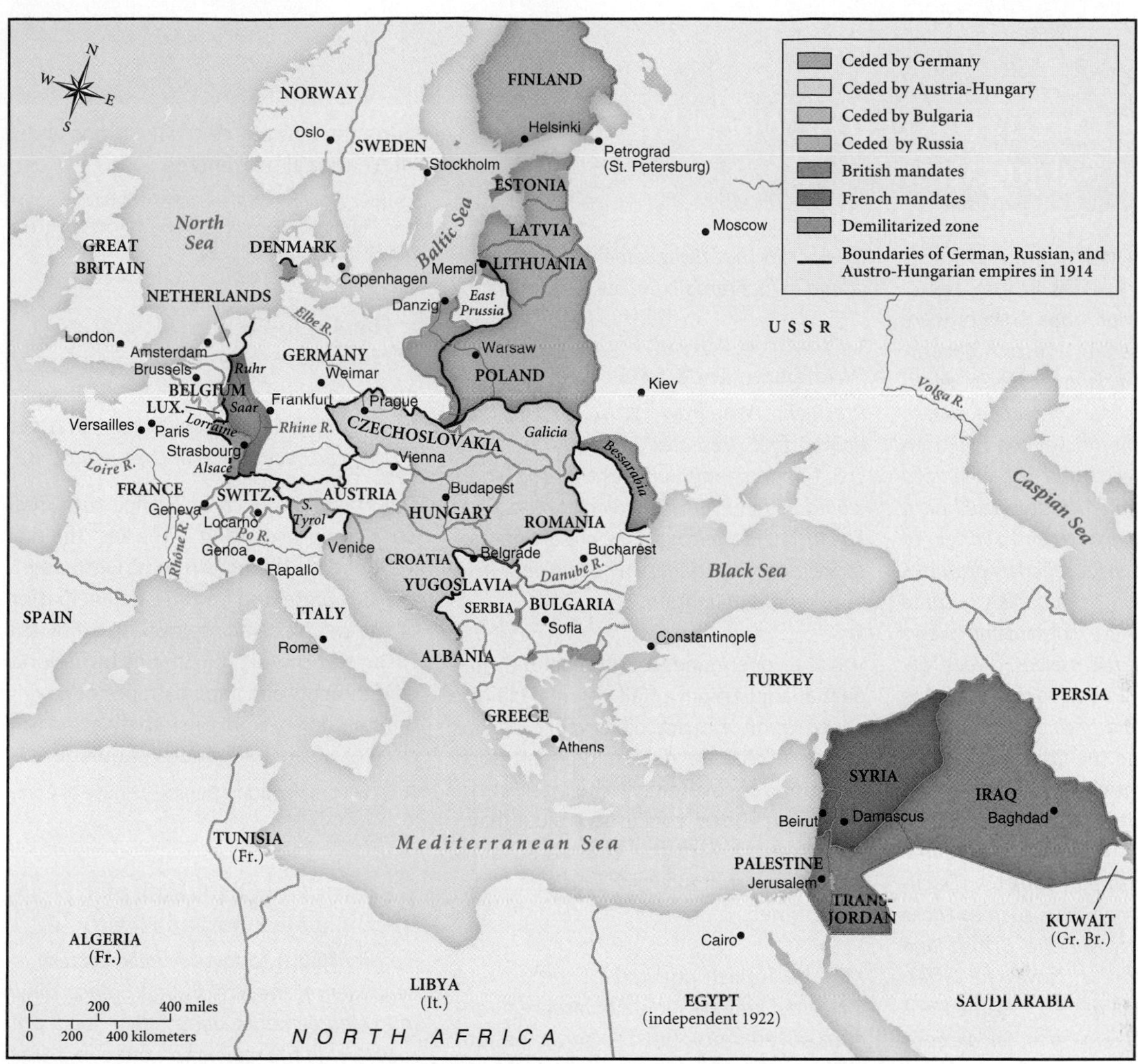

MAP 25.4 Europe and the Middle East after the Peace Settlements of 1919–1920
The political landscape of central, east, and east-central Europe changed dramatically as a result of the Russian Revolution and the Peace of Paris. The Ottoman, German, Russian, and Austro-Hungarian Empires were either broken up into multiple small states or territorially reduced. The settlement left resentments among Germans and Hungarians and created a group of weak, struggling nations in the heartland of Europe. The victorious powers took over much of the oil-rich Middle East. | **Why is it significant that the postwar geopolitical changes were so concentrated in one section of Europe?**

cally developed country rather than from ruined Austria. War guilt made Germans feel like outcasts in the community of nations.

The League of Nations Besides redrawing the map of Europe, the Peace of Paris set up an organization called the **League of Nations**, whose members had a joint responsibility for maintaining peace—a principle called collective security. It was supposed to replace the divisive secrecy of prewar power politics. As part of Wilson's vision, the league would guide the world toward disarmament and arbitrate its members' disputes. The U.S. Senate, rejecting the idea of collective security, failed to ratify the peace settlement and refused to join the league. Moreover, Germany and Russia initially were excluded from the league and were thus blocked from working cooperatively with the league. The absence of these three important powers weakened the league as a global peacekeeper from the outset.

League of Nations: The international organization set up following World War I to maintain peace by arbitrating disputes and promoting collective security.

CONTRASTING VIEWS

The Middle East at the End of World War I: Freedom or Subjugation?

The end of World War I aroused hopes around the world. In Paris in 1919, representatives of the victorious powers were besieged by outsiders to Western government, each making a claim for special attention to their needs or for concrete action to realize the noble rhetoric of the Fourteen Points. The conquered and the colonized expected a fair-minded treaty based on a range of Allied agreements, and a variety of other peoples were encouraged by promises of self-determination. Yet it quickly became clear that there were contrasting views among the Allies themselves. Woodrow Wilson's Fourteen Points articulated one position on the future of colonized areas of the world, including the Ottoman Empire (Document 1). As the war drew to a close in November 1918, Britain and France seemed to endorse Wilson's position when it came to freedom for Ottoman subjects (Document 2). Other agreements, such as those dividing up oil between the British and French in the Middle East, gave a far different impression (Document 3). At the Paris Peace Conference in 1919–1920, Middle Eastern leaders lobbied for their independence. The emir Faisal was one of these, after having led pro-Allied troops to bring about freedom from the Ottomans and to achieve Arab unity (Document 4). When the mandate system was drawn up, however, it became clear that those under Ottoman rule would in fact remain unfree (Document 5).

1. Woodrow Wilson, Fourteen Points, January 8, 1918

President Woodrow Wilson's Fourteen Points, first presented in a speech to the U.S. Congress, raised hopes that the world would be fairer after the war than before. The fifth and twelfth points, presented here, spoke especially to those who had been held in colonial subjugation.

V. A free, openminded, and absolutely impartial adjustment of all colonial claims, based upon a strict observance of the principle that in determining all such questions of sovereignty the interests of the populations concerned must have equal weight with the equitable claims of the government whose title is to be determined.

XII. The Turkish portions of the present Ottoman Empire should be assured a secure sovereignty, but the other nationalities which are now under Turkish rule should be assured an undoubted security of life and an absolutely unmolested opportunity of autonomous development, and the Dardanelles should be permanently opened as a free passage to the ships and commerce of all nations under international guarantees.

Source: Woodrow Wilson, "Speech on the Fourteen Points," *Congressional Record*, 65th Congress, 2nd Session, 1918, 680–81.

2. The Anglo-French Declaration of November 7, 1918

As World War I reached its end in the autumn of 1918, the French and British issued this official declaration of their war aims.

The object aimed at by France and Great Britain in prosecuting in the East the War let loose by the ambition of Germany is the complete and definite emancipation of the peoples so long oppressed by the Turks and the establishment of national governments and administrations deriving their authority from the initiative and free choices of the indigenous populations.

Source: Parliamentary Debates, House of Commons, 5, cxlv, 351.

3. British-French Division of the Oil in Mesopotamia (Iraq)

Despite claims to favor Middle Eastern independence, the British and French made many agreements about their joint prerogatives in the region, this one concerning oil, which the war had shown to be an increasingly indispensable commodity.

The British Government undertake to grant to the French Government or its nominee twenty-five percent of the net

The League of Nations also organized the administration of the former colonies and territories of Germany and the Ottoman Empire — such as Togo, Cameroon, Syria, and Palestine — through systems of political control called mandates (see "Contrasting Views," above). The victorious powers exercised political control or mandates over these territories, while local leaders retained limited authority. The league justified the **mandate system** as providing governance by "advanced nations" over territories "not yet able to stand by themselves under the strenuous conditions of the modern world." But colonized people, many of whom had fought and received promises of political rights and independence for doing so, challenged these claims. They had seen how savage and degraded the people who claimed to be racially and politically superior could be. "Never again will the darker people of the world occupy just the place they had before," the African American leader W. E. B. Du Bois predicted in 1918. Yet the mandate system not only kept imperialism alive at a time when the powers were bankrupt and weak but also, like the Peace of Paris, aroused anger and resistance.

mandate system: The political control over the former colonies and territories of the German and Ottoman Empires granted to the victors of World War I by the League of Nations.

output of crude oil at current market rates which His Majesty's Government may secure from the Mesopotamian oilfields in the event of their being developed by Government action; or in the event of a private petroleum company being used to develop the Mesopotamian oilfields the British Government will place at the disposal of the French Government a share of twenty-five percent in such company.

Source: *Memorandum of Agreement between M. Philippe Berthelot, Directeur des Affaires Politiques et Commerciles au Ministère des Affaires Etrangères, and Professor Sir John Cadman, Director in Charge of His Majesty's Petroleum Department,* in Cmd. 675 of 1920 and in *U.S. Foreign Relations 1920*, ii, 655–58.

4. Claiming Independence for the Middle East

Arabs had hotly debated whether to assist the Allied colonizers in World War I, but promises of independence won them over. Some Arabs argued for independence of individual areas in the Middle East and for resolutions to competing claims of the Arabs and of new Jewish settlers in the region. Emir Faisal, who had commanded Arab forces in the war, presented the pan-Arab ideal.

The aim of the Arab nationalist movement is to unite the Arabs eventually into one nation. . . . I came to Europe on behalf of my father and the Arabs of Asia to say that they are expecting the powers at the Conference not to attach undue importance to superficial differences of condition among us and not to consider them only from the low ground of existing European material interests and supposed spheres of influence. They expect the powers to think of them as one potential people, jealous of their language and liberty, and they ask that no step be taken inconsistent with the prospect of an eventual union of these areas under one sovereign government.

Source: Stephen Bonsal, *Suitors and Suppliants: The Little Nations at Versailles* (Port Washington: Kennikat Press, 1969), 32–33.

5. Resolution of the Syrian Congress at Damascus, July 2, 1919

In 1919, a commission from the Paris Peace Conference was established to investigate the political conditions in the Middle East. The Syrian Congress met to prepare this statement for the commission.

Considering the fact that the Arabs inhabiting the Syrian area are not naturally less gifted than other more advanced races and that they are by no means less developed than the Bulgarians, Serbians, Greeks, and Roumanians at the beginning of their independence, we protest against Article 22 of the Covenant of the League of Nations placing us among the nations in their middle stage of development which stand in need of a mandatory power.

We oppose the pretentions of the Zionists to create a Jewish commonwealth in the southern part of Syria, known as Palestine, and oppose zionist migration to any part of our country. . . . Our Jewish compatriots shall enjoy our common rights and assume the common responsibilities.

We also have the fullest confidence that the Peace Conference will realize that we would not have risen against the Turks with whom we had participated in all civil, political, and representative privileges . . . and so will grant us our desires in full in order that our political rights may not be less after the war than they were before, since we have shed so much blood in the cause of our liberty and independence.

Source: Quoted in J. C. Hurewitz, ed., *The Middle East and North Africa in World Politics: A Documentary Record*, 2nd ed. 2 vols. (New Haven: Yale University Press, 1979), 2:180–81.

Questions to Consider

1. **Describe the various claims of the official combatant powers. How do you explain these differing positions?**
2. **How were the competing positions at the peace conference related to the politics and conditions of World War I?**
3. **Does any one or two of the demands seem more justifiable in addressing the peacetime needs of Europe and the world?**
4. **What was the position of the Arabs?**
5. **How do you explain the fact that the Arabs lost the argument so completely?**

Economic and Diplomatic Consequences of the Peace

Just as wartime conditions, including military action, continued long after the armistice, so the Peace of Paris posed problems into the 1920s and beyond. Western leaders faced two related issues in the aftermath of the war. The first was economic recovery and its relationship to war debts and German reparation payments. The second was ensuring that peace actually came about and lasted.

Economic Dilemmas France, hardest hit by wartime destruction and billions of dollars in debt to the United States, estimated that Germany owed it at least $200 billion. Britain, by contrast, had not been physically devastated and was worried instead about maintaining its empire and restoring trade with Germany, not exacting huge reparations to rebuild. Nevertheless, both France and Britain were dependent on some German payments to settle their war debts to the United States because Europe's income from world trade had plunged during the war.

Germany claimed that the demand for reparations strained its government, already facing political upheaval. But Germany's economic problems had begun long before the Peace of Paris with the kaiser's policy of not raising taxes—especially on the rich—to pay for the war, leaving the new

Inflation and the German Elections
The extraordinary inflation that struck the German economy in 1923 haunted those who lived through it and lost their life savings as money became worthless. The disaster gravely affected both the social and political order, leaving a legacy of fear and outrage. In this poster, the German Democratic Party rouses terror with its highly charged image of inflation as a monstrous enemy of the nation in the election campaign of 1924. *(© Photo 12/The Image Works.)*

republic with a staggering debt. Now this republic, an experiment in democracy, needed to win over its citizens, and hiking taxes to pay Germany's debt would only anger them. In 1921, when Germans refused to present a realistic plan for paying reparations, the French occupied several cities in the Ruhr until a settlement was reached.

At odds with the powers to the west, the German government turned to eastern Europe for support. In the Treaty of Rapallo (1922), it reached an agreement establishing economic ties with Russia, which was desperate for Western trade. Meanwhile, Germany's relations with powers to the west continued to deteriorate. In 1923, after Germany defaulted on coal deliveries, the French and the Belgians sent troops into the Ruhr basin, planning to seize its resources to pay for wartime expenditures. Urged on by the government, Ruhr citizens shut down industry by staying home from work. The German government printed trillions of marks to support the workers and to pay its own war debts with practically worthless currency. The result was a staggering inflation in Germany that gravely threatened the international economy: at one point, a single U.S. dollar cost 4.42 trillion marks, and wheelbarrows of money were required to buy a turnip. Negotiations to resolve this economic chaos resulted in the Dawes Plan (1924) and the Young Plan (1929), which reduced reparations to more realistic levels and restored the value of German currency. Before that happened, however, the inflation had wiped out people's savings and turned many more Germans against their democratic government.

Making Peace In addition to economic recovery, a second burning issue involved making the peace take hold and last. Statesmen determined that peace needed disarmament, a return of Germany to the community of nations, and security for the new countries of eastern Europe. Hard diplomatic bargaining produced two plans in Germany's favor. At the Washington Conference in 1921, the United States, Great Britain, Japan, France, and Italy agreed to reduce their number of battleships and to stop constructing new ones for ten years. Four years later, in 1925, the League of Nations sponsored a meeting of the great powers, including Germany, at Locarno, Switzerland. The Treaty of Locarno provided Germany with a seat in the league as of 1926. In return, Germany agreed not to violate the borders of France and Belgium and to keep the nearby Rhineland demilitarized—that is, unfortified by troops.

To the east, statesmen feared a German attempt to regain territory lost to Poland, to merge with Austria, or to launch any attack on states spun off from Austria-Hungary. To meet this threat, Czechoslovakia, Yugoslavia, and Romania formed the Little Entente in 1920–1921, a collective security agreement intended to protect them from Germany and Russia. Between 1924 and 1927, France allied itself with the Little Entente and with Poland. In 1928, sixty nations, including the major European powers, Japan, and the United States, signed the Kellogg-

0 100 200 miles
0 100 200 kilometers
GERMANY
POLAND
USSR
CZECHOSLOVAKIA
AUSTRIA
HUNGARY
ROMANIA
YUGOSLAVIA
BULGARIA
ALBANIA

The Little Entente

Briand Pact, which formally rejected international violence. The pact lacked any mechanism for enforcement and thus resembled, as one critic put it, "an international kiss."

The publicity surrounding the international agreements of the 1920s sharply contrasted with old-style diplomacy, which had been conducted in secret and subject to little public scrutiny. The development of a system of open, collective security suggested a diplomatic revolution that would promote international peace. Yet openness allowed diplomats to feed the press information designed to provoke the masses. For example, the press and opposition parties whipped the German populace into a nationalist fury whenever Germany's diplomats appeared to compromise, even though these compromises worked to undo the Treaty of Versailles. Right-wing journalists who hated republican government used international meetings such as the one at Locarno to fire up political hatreds rather than promote peace or rational public discussion.

REVIEW QUESTION What were the major outcomes of the postwar peacemaking process?

A Decade of Recovery: Europe in the 1920s

Even after the armistice and the peace treaties, the wartime spirit endured. Towns and villages built their monuments to the fallen, and battlefield tourism sprang up for veterans and their families in search of a relative's final resting place. Words and phrases from the battlefield became part of everyday speech. Before the war the word *lousy* had meant "lice-infested," but English-speaking soldiers returning from the trenches now applied it to anything bad. Raincoats became *trenchcoats*, and terms like *bombarded* and *rank and file* entered civilian talk. Maimed, disfigured veterans were present everywhere, and while some received prostheses designed by Jules Amar, others without limbs were sometimes carried in baskets—hence the expression *basket case.*

Total war had generally strengthened the military spirit and authoritarian government. Four autocratic governments had collapsed as a result of the war, but whether these states would become workable democracies remained an open question. During the war, the European economy lost many of its international markets to India, Canada, Australia, Japan, and the United States. Now worldwide economic competition with these new players also threatened European recovery. Returning veterans crowded hospitals and mental institutions, and family life centered on their care. Although contemporaries referred to the 1920s as the Roaring Twenties or the Jazz Age, the sense of cultural excitement masked the serious problem of restoring stability and implementing democracy. The real challenge of the 1920s was coming to terms with the grim legacy of the war.

Women Gain Suffrage in the West

1906	Finland
1913	Norway
1915	Denmark, Iceland
1917	Netherlands, Russia
1918	Czechoslovakia, Great Britain (limited suffrage)
1919	Germany
1920	Austria, United States
1921	Poland
1925	Hungary (limited suffrage)
1945	Italy, France
1971	Switzerland

Changes in the Political Landscape

The collapse of autocratic governments and the widespread extension of suffrage to women brought political turmoil as well as the expansion of democracy. Women's suffrage resulted in part from decades of activism, but many men in government claimed that suffrage was a "reward" for women's war efforts. Women were voted into parliaments in the first postwar elections, and the impression grew that they had also made extraordinary gains in the workplace. French men pointedly denied women the vote, however, threatening that women voters would bring back the rule of kings and priests. (Only at the end of World War II would France and Italy extend suffrage to women.) The welfare state also expanded, with payments being made to veterans and victims of workplace accidents. These benefits stemmed from the belief that more evenly distributed wealth—sometimes called economic democracy—would prevent the outbreak of revolution.

The trend toward economic democracy was not easy to maintain, however, because the cycles of boom and bust that had characterized the late nineteenth century reemerged. A short postwar economic boom prompted by reconstruction and consumer spending was followed by an economic downturn that was most severe between 1920 and 1922. By the mid-1920s, many of the economic opportunities for women had disappeared and women made up a smaller percentage of the workforce than in 1913. Skyrocketing unemployment produced more discontent with governments. Veterans were especially angered by economic insecurity after their years of enduring the war's horrors, and unemployment resulted in more anger toward governments.

Eastern Europe The new republics of eastern Europe were unprepared for hard economic times and poorly equipped to compete in the world market. None but Czechoslovakia had a mature industrial sector, and agricultural techniques were often primitive. Additionally, vast migrations occurred as some 1 million citizens escaped the civil war in Russia and 800,000 soldiers from the defeated Whites searched for safety. Two million people fled Turkey, Greece, and Bulgaria because the postwar settlement called for the new nations to be built along "nationality" lines. One statesman called the chaotic postwar settlement "a great unmixing of populations." Hundreds of thousands landed in new nations with populations largely composed of their own ethnic group: Hungary, for example, had to receive 300,000 people of Magyar ethnicity who were no longer welcome in Romania, Czechoslovakia, or Yugoslavia. Most of these millions of refugees lacked land or jobs. They had nothing to do "but loaf and starve," one English journalist observed of refugees in Bulgaria. The influx of people brought more conflict in various parts of eastern Europe. Romania, Czechoslovakia, and the Kingdom of the Serbs, Croats, and Slovenes invaded Hungary, for instance, to gain more land.

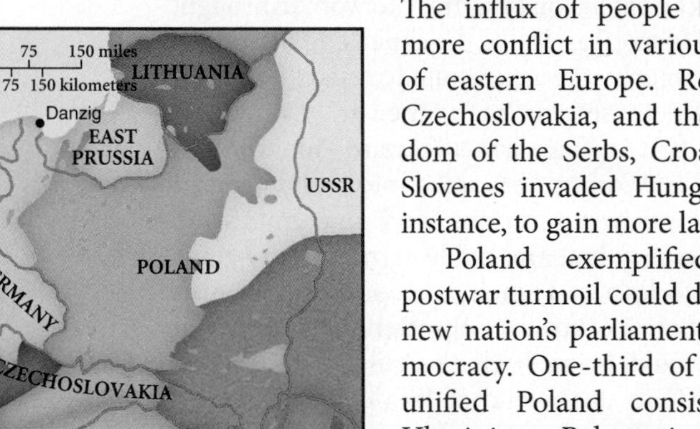

National Minorities in Postwar Poland

Poland exemplified how postwar turmoil could destroy a new nation's parliamentary democracy. One-third of the reunified Poland consisted of Ukrainians, Belorussians, Germans, and other ethnic minorities—many of whom had grievances against the dominant Poles. Varying religious and cultural traditions also divided the Poles, who for 150 years had been split among Austria, Germany, and Russia. Polish reunification occurred without a common currency, political structure, or language—even the railroad tracks were not a standard size. Under a new constitution that professed equal rights for all ethnicities and religions, the Sejm (parliament) tried to redistribute large estates among the peasantry. However, declining crop prices and overpopulation (two-thirds of the population lived by subsistence farming) made life in the countryside difficult. The economic downturn brought strikes and violence in 1922–1923. Ultimately former military leader Jozef Pilsudski took power via a coup in 1926 because of the government's inability to bring about prosperity. In postwar east-central Europe, military solutions to economic hardship became common, demonstrating the endurance of war long after the peace had officially begun.

Central Europe Germany was a different case, though it, too, received a flood of refugees from the east. Although Germany's economy picked up and the nation became a center of experimentation in the arts, political life remained unstable because so many people, nostalgic for imperial glory, associated defeat with the new Weimar Republic. Extremist politicians heaped daily abuse on Weimar's parliamentary political system. A wealthy newspaper and film tycoon called anyone cooperating with the parliamentary system "a moral cripple." Right-wing parties favored violence rather than consensus building, and nationalist thugs murdered democratic leaders and Jews. Communists were not shy about jumping into street brawls, either.

Support for the far right came from wealthy landowners and businessmen, white-collar workers whose standard of living had dropped during the war, and members of the lower-middle and middle classes hurt by inflation. Bands of disaffected youth and veterans multiplied, among them a group called the Brown Shirts. Their leader was an ex-soldier and political newcomer named Adolf Hitler (1889–1945)—a favorite among antigovernment crowds. In the wake of the Ruhr occupation of 1923, Hitler and German military hero Erich Ludendorff launched a coup d'état—or *putsch* in German—from a beer hall in Munich. Government troops suppressed the Beer Hall Putsch and arrested its leaders, but Ludendorff was acquitted and Hitler spent less than a year in jail. To conservative judges, former aristocrats, and most of the prewar bureaucrats who still staffed the government, such men were national heroes.

Western Europe In France and Britain, parties on the right were less effective than in Germany because representative institutions were better established and the upper classes were not plotting to restore an authoritarian monarchy. In France, politicians from the conservative right and moderate left successively formed coalitions and rallied general support to rebuild war-torn regions and to force Germany to pay for the reconstruction. Hoping to stimulate population growth after the devastating loss of life, the French parliament made distributing birth-control information illegal and abortion a severely punished crime.

Britain encountered postwar boom-and-bust cycles and continuing conflict in Ireland. Ramsay

MacDonald (1866–1937), elected the first Labour prime minister in 1924, represented the political strength of workers. Like other postwar British leaders, he had to face the unpleasant truth that although Britain had the largest world empire, many of its industries were obsolete or in poor condition. A showdown came in the ailing coal industry, where prices fell and wages plunged once the Ruhr mines again offered tough postwar competition to British mines. On May 3, 1926, workers launched a nine-day general strike against wage cuts and dangerous conditions in the mines. The strike provoked unprecedented middle-class resistance. University students, homemakers, and businessmen shut down the strike by driving trains, working on docks, and replacing workers in other jobs. Citizens from many walks of life revived the wartime spirit to defeat those who appeared to them to be attacking the national economy.

In Ireland, the British government's continuing failure to implement home rule provoked bloody confrontations. In January 1919, republican leaders declared Ireland's independence and created a separate parliament. The British government refused to recognize the parliament and sent in the Black and Tans, a volunteer army of demobilized soldiers named for the color of their uniforms. Terror reigned in Ireland, as both the pro-independence forces and the Black and Tans waged guerrilla warfare, taking hostages, blowing up buildings, and even shooting into crowds at soccer matches. By 1921, public outrage forced the British to negotiate a treaty, one that reversed the Irish declaration of independence and made the Irish Free State a self-governing dominion owing allegiance to the British crown. Northern Ireland, a group of six northern counties containing a majority of Protestants, gained a separate status: it was self-governing but still had representation in the British Parliament. This settlement left bitter discontent, and violence soon erupted again.

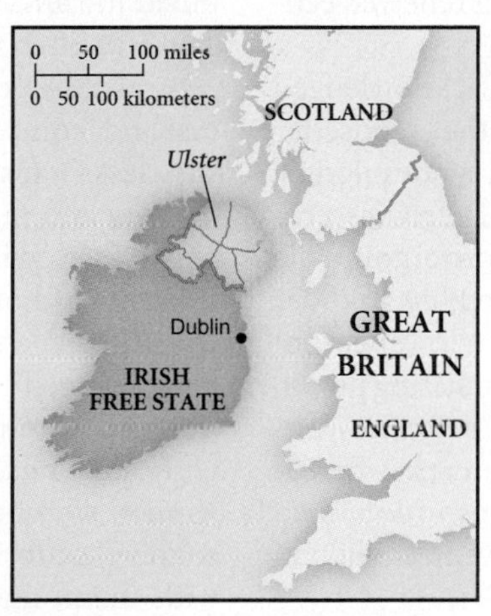

The Irish Free State and Ulster, 1921

The Colonies | War had also changed everything in the colonies. European politicians and military recruiters had promised colonized peoples the vote and other reforms, even independence, in exchange for their support during the war. However, these peoples' political activism—now enhanced by increasing education, trade, and experience with the West—mostly met with a brutal response. British forces massacred protesters at Amritsar, India, in 1919 and put down revolts against the mandate system in Egypt and Iran in the early 1920s. The Dutch jailed political leaders in Indonesia; the French punished Indochinese nationalists. For many Western governments, maintaining empires abroad was crucial to ensuring democracy at home, for any hint of declining national prestige fed antidemocratic forces.

Despite resistance, the 1920s marked the high tide of imperialism. Britain and France, enjoying new access to Germany's colonies in Africa and the territories of the fallen Ottoman Empire in the Middle East, were at the height of their global power. No matter how battered by the war, all the imperial powers took advantage of the growing profitability that enterprise around the world could bring. Middle Eastern and Indonesian oil, for instance, increasingly heated homes and fueled the West's growing number of automobiles, airplanes, trucks, ships, and buses. Products like chocolate and tropical fruit became regular items in Westerners' diets, and some Westerners built fortunes processing and selling products from the colonies.

The balance of power among the imperial nations was shifting, however. The most important change was Japan's surging competition for markets, resources, influence, and ultimately colonies. During the war, Japanese output of industrial goods such as metal and ships grew dramatically because the Western powers outsourced their wartime needs for such products. As Japan took business from Britain and France, its prosperity skyrocketed, allowing the country to become the dominant power in China. The Japanese government advertised its success as a sign of hope for non-Westerners. Japan's prosperity, the country's politicians claimed, would end the West's domination in the competition for land and resources. Ardently nationalist, the Japanese government was not yet strong enough to challenge the Western powers militarily. Thus, although outraged when the Western powers at Paris refused a nondiscrimination clause in the charter of the League of Nations, Japan cooperated in the Anglo-American–dominated peace. It agreed to the settlement at the naval conference in Washington that set the ratio of English, American, and Japanese shipbuilding at 5:5:3. "Rolls Royce, Rolls Royce, Ford," a Japanese official commented bitterly.

Reconstructing the Economy

The war had weakened European economies and allowed newcomers and rivals—Japan, India, the United States, Australia, and Canada—to flourish in their place. At the same time, the war had forced European manufacturing to become more efficient and had expanded the demand for automotive and air transport, electrical products, and synthetic goods. The prewar pattern of mergers and cartels continued after 1918, giving rise to gigantic food-processing firms such as Nestlé in Switzerland and petroleum enterprises such as Royal Dutch Shell. Owners of these large manufacturing conglomerates wielded more financial and political power than entire small countries. By the late 1920s, Europe had overcome the wild economic swings of the immediate postwar years and was enjoying renewed economic prosperity.

Some European businesspeople acknowledged that the United States had become the trendsetter in economic modernization, and they made pilgrimages to the Ford Motor Company's Detroit assembly line, which by 1929 produced a Ford automobile every ten seconds. Increased productivity, founder Henry Ford pointed out, resulted in a lower cost of living and thus increased workers' purchasing power. Rising productivity helped some American workers afford such expensive goods as cars: whereas French, German, and British citizens in total had fewer than two million cars, some seventeen million cars were on U.S. streets in 1925.

Scientific management also helped raise productivity. American efficiency expert Frederick Taylor (1856–1915) had developed methods to streamline workers' tasks and bodily motions for maximum productivity. European industrialists adopted Taylor's methods during the war and after, but they were also influenced by European psychologists who emphasized the mental aspects of productivity and thus the need to balance work and leisure activities. In theory, increased productivity not only produced prosperity for all but also united workers and management, avoiding Russian-style worker revolution. For many workers, however, the emphasis on efficiency seemed inhumane; in some businesses restrictions were so severe that workers were allowed to use the bathroom only on a fixed schedule. "When I left the factory, it followed me," wrote one worker. "In my dreams I was a machine."

The managerial sector in industry had expanded during the war and continued to do so thereafter. Workers' experience became devalued, with managers alone seen as creative and innovative. Managers reorganized work procedures and classified workers' skills. They categorized jobs held by women as requiring less skill—whether they did or not—and therefore deserving of lower wages. With male workers' jobs increasingly threatened by labor-saving machinery, unions usually agreed that women should receive lower wages to keep them from competing with men for scarce high-paying jobs. Like the managerial sector, a complex union bureaucracy had ballooned during World War I to help monitor labor's part in the war. Playing a key role in everyday political life, unions could mobilize masses of people, as evidenced by their actions against coups in Weimar Germany and by the general strike in Great Britain in 1926.

Restoring Society

Civilians met the returning millions of brutalized, incapacitated, and shell-shocked veterans with combined joy and apprehension—and that apprehension was often valid. Tens of thousands of German, central European, and Italian soldiers refused to disband; some British veterans vandalized university classrooms and assaulted women streetcar conductors and factory workers. Many veterans were angry that civilians had protested wartime conditions instead of enduring them. Patriotic when the war erupted, civilians, especially women, sometimes felt estranged from the returning warriors who had inflicted so much death and who had lived daily with filth, rats, and decaying human flesh. While women who had served on the front had seen the soldiers' suffering firsthand and could sympathize with them, many British suffragists, for instance, who had fought for equality in men's and women's lives before the war, now embraced separate spheres for men and women, so fearful were they of returning veterans.

For their part, veterans returned to a world that differed from the home they had left. They found that the war had blurred class distinctions, giving rise to expectations that life would be fairer afterward. Massive battlefield casualties had made it possible for commoners to move up to the ranks of officers, positions often monopolized by the prewar aristocracy. British author Rudyard Kipling, whose only son had been killed on the western front, was among those who influenced the decision that all memorials to individual soldiers would be the same for rich and poor, just as the experience of the trenches had been. Wealth, he maintained, should not allow some to "proclaim their grief above other people's grief" when rich and poor had died for the same cause. The identical, evenly spaced markers of military cemeteries kept all the dead equal, as did the mass "brothers' graves" at the battlefront where all ranks lay side by side in a single burial pit.

Despite their expectations, veterans often had few or no jobs open to them, and some found that their wives and sweethearts had abandoned them. Many found, too, that women's roles had gone through other changes: middle-class women did their own housework because former servants could earn more money in factories, and greater numbers of women worked outside the home. Women of all classes cut their hair short, wore sleeker clothes, smoked, and had money of their own because of war work.

Focusing on veterans' needs, governments tried to make civilian life as comfortable as possible to reintegrate men into society and reduce the appeal of communism. Politicians believed in the calming power of family life and supported social programs such as veterans' pensions and housing and benefits for out-of-work men. The new housing—"homes for heroes," as politicians called the program—was a considerable improvement over nineteenth-century working-class tenements. In Vienna, Frankfurt, Berlin, and Stockholm, modern housing projects provided common laundries, day-care centers, and rooms for socializing. They featured gardens, terraces, and balconies to provide a soothing, country ambience that offset the hectic nature of industrial life. Inside, they boasted modern kitchens and bathrooms, central heating, and electricity.

Despite government efforts to restore traditional family life, war had dissolved other middle-class conventions, among them attempts to keep unmarried young men and women apart. Freer relationships and more open discussions of sex characterized the 1920s. Middle-class youths of both sexes visited jazz clubs and attended movies together. Revealing bathing suits, short skirts, and body-hugging clothing emphasized women's sexuality, seeming to invite men and women to join together and replenish the postwar population. In the long run, however, the context for sexuality remained marriage. British scientist Marie Stopes published the best seller *Married Love* in 1918, and Dutch author Theodor van de Velde published the wildly successful *Ideal Marriage: Its Physiology and Technique* in 1927. Both authors described sex in glowing terms and offered precise information about birth control and sexual physiology. Changing ideas about sex were not limited to the middle and upper classes. One Viennese reformer described working-class marriage as "an erotic-comradely relationship of equals" rather than the economic partnership of past centuries. Meanwhile, such writers as the Briton D. H. Lawrence and the American Ernest Hemingway glorified men's sexual vigor in, respectively, *Women in Love* (1920) and *The Sun Also Rises* (1926). Mass culture's focus on heterosexuality encouraged the return to normality after the gender disorder that had troubled the prewar and war years.

As images of men and women changed, people paid more attention to bodily improvement. The increasing use of toothbrushes and toothpaste, safety and electric razors, and deodorants reflected new standards for personal hygiene and grooming. For

New Housing in Vienna
Politicians saw to the building of "homes for heroes" across postwar Europe, and Vienna was one leader in constructing modern housing for the working class. With many veterans enraged by the war experience and with socialist revolution a looming threat, new housing, it was hoped, would help return men to peaceful civilian life.
(© Bettmann/Corbis.)

The Flapper
This modern workingwoman smoking her cigarette stood for all that had changed—or was said to have changed—in the postwar world. Women had worked and had money of their own, they were out in public and could vote in many countries, and they were liberated from old constraints on their sexual and other behavior. *(Hulton Archive/Getty Images.)*

Western women, a multibillion-dollar cosmetics industry sprang up almost overnight. Women went to beauty parlors regularly to have their short hair cut, set, dyed, conditioned, straightened, or curled. They also tweezed their eyebrows, applied makeup, and even submitted to cosmetic surgery. Ordinary women "painted" their faces (something only prostitutes had done formerly) and competed in beauty contests. Instead of wanting to look plump and pale, people aimed to become thin and tan, often through exercise and playing sports. Consumers' new focus on personal health coincided with industry's need for a physically fit workforce.

As prosperity returned in the mid-1920s, people could afford to buy more consumer goods. Middle- and upper-class families snapped up sleek modern furniture, washing machines, and vacuum cleaners. Other modern conveniences such as electric irons and gas stoves appeared in better-off working-class households. Installment buying, popularized from the 1920s on, helped people finance these purchases. Housework became more mechanized, and family intimacy increasingly depended on machines of mass communication like radios, phonographs, and even automobiles. These new products not only transformed private life but also brought changes in the public world of mass culture and mass politics.

REVIEW QUESTION What were the major political, social, and economic problems facing postwar Europe, and how did governments attempt to address them?

Mass Culture and the Rise of Modern Dictators

Wartime propaganda had aimed to unite all classes against a common enemy. In the 1920s, new technology made the process of integrating diverse groups into a single Western or mass culture easier. The tools of mass culture—primarily radio, film, and newspapers—expanded their influence in the 1920s. Whereas some intellectuals urged elites to form an experimental avant-garde that refused to cater to "the drab mass of society," others wanted to use modern media and art to reach and even control the masses. The media had the potential for creating an informed citizenry and thus strengthening democracy. At the same time, it allowed authoritarian rulers and would-be dictators such as Benito Mussolini, Joseph Stalin, and Adolf Hitler to shape a uniform political thought and to control citizens' behavior far beyond what previous rulers had been able to do.

Culture for the Masses

The media received a big boost from the war. Bulletins from the battlefront whetted the public's craving for news and real-life stories, and sales of nonfiction books soared. After years of deprivation, people were driven to achieve material success, and they devoured books about how to gain it. A biography of Henry Ford, telling his story of upward mobility and technological accomplishment, became a best seller in Germany. With postwar readers avidly pursuing practical knowledge, institutes and night schools became popular, and school systems promoted the study of geography, science, and history. Phonographs, radio programs, and movies also widened the scope of national culture.

In the 1920s, film evolved from an experimental medium to a thriving international business in which large corporations set up theater chains and marketed movies worldwide. Specialization emerged, with directors, producers, marketers, film editors, and many others subdividing the process. A "star" system turned film personalities into celebrities who were promoted by publicists and lived like royalty.

Films of literary classics and political events developed people's sense of a common heritage and were often sponsored by governments. Bolshevik leaders backed the inventive work of director Sergei Eisenstein, whose films *Potemkin* (1925) and *Ten Days That Shook the World* (1927–1928) presented a Bolshevik view of history to Russian and international audiences.

Films incorporated familiar elements from everyday life. The piano accompaniment of silent films derived from music halls; comic characters and slapstick humor were borrowed from street or burlesque shows and from trends in postwar living. The popular comedies of the 1920s made the flapper more visible to the masses and poked fun at men's and women's inept attempts at marriage and emotional intimacy. Lavish cinema houses attracted some hundred million weekly viewers, the majority of them women. As popular films and books crossed national borders, a global culture for an international audience flourished.

Films also played to postwar fantasies and fears. In Germany, the influential hit *The Cabinet of Doctor Caligari* (1919) depicted frightening events in an insane asylum as horrifying symbols of state power. Popular detective and cowboy films portrayed heroes who could restore wholeness to the disordered world of murder, crime, and injustice. The plight of gangsters appealed to veterans, who had been exposed to the cheap value of modern life in the trenches. English comedian Charlie Chaplin (1889–1977) created the character of the Little Tramp, who won international popularity as the anonymous down-and-out hero trying to preserve his dignity in a mechanized world. Films featured characters from around the world and were often set in faraway deserts and mountain ranges; newsreels showed athletic, soldier-like bodies in sporting events like boxing.

Like film, radio evolved from an experimental medium to an instrument of mass culture during the 1920s. Developed from the wireless technology of Italian inventor Guglielmo Marconi, radio broadcasts in the first half of the 1920s were heard by mass audiences in public halls (much like movie houses) and featured orchestra performances and songs followed by audience discussion. The radio quickly became an affordable consumer item, allowing the public concert or lecture to penetrate the individual's private living space. Specialized programming for men (such as sports reporting) and for women (such as advice on home management) attracted listeners. Through radio, disabled veterans found ways to participate in public events and keep up-to-date. By the 1930s, radio helped politicians to reach the masses wherever they might be — even alone at home.

Cultural Debates over the Future

Cultural leaders in the 1920s either were obsessed with the horrendous experience of war or held high hopes for creating a fresh, utopian future that would have little relation to the past. German artists, especially, produced bleak or violent visions. The sculpture and woodcuts of German artist Käthe Kollwitz (1867–1945), whose son had died in the war, portrayed bereaved parents, starving children, and other heart-wrenching antiwar images (see page 834). Others thought that Europeans needed to search for answers in far-off cultures. Seeing Europe as decadent, some turned to the spiritual richness of Asian philosophies and religions. An "Asiatic fever" seemed to grip intellectuals, including the British writer Virginia Woolf, who drew on ideas of reincarnation in her novel *Orlando* (1928), and the filmmaker Sergei Eisenstein, who modeled the new techniques of juxtaposing film shots (montage) on Japanese calligraphy.

Other artists used satire and contempt to express postwar rage at civilization's wartime failure. George Grosz (1893–1959), stunned by the war's carnage, joined Dada, an artistic and literary movement that had emerged during the war. With a meaningless name, Dada produced works marked by nonsense and shrieking expressions of alienation. Grosz's paintings and cartoons of maimed soldiers and brutally murdered women reflected his wartime trauma and his self-proclaimed desire "to bellow back." In the postwar years, the modernist practice of shocking audiences became more savage and often more contemptuous of ordinary people. Portrayals of seedy everyday life flourished in cabarets and theaters in the 1920s and reinforced veterans' beliefs in civilian decadence.

The art world itself became a battlefield, especially in defeated Germany, where it paralleled the Weimar Republic's contentious politics. Popular writers such as veteran Ernst Jünger glorified life in the trenches and called for the militarization of society to restore order. In contrast, Erich Maria Remarque, also a veteran, cried out for an end to war in his controversial novel *All Quiet on the Western Front* (1928). This international best seller depicted the life shared by enemies on the battlefield, thus aiming to overcome the national hatred aroused by wartime propaganda. Remarque's novel was part of a flood of popular, and often bitter, literature appearing on the tenth anniversary of the war's end. It coincided with an interest in "Great War tourism" such as visiting battlefields. (See Document, "Memory and Battlefield Tourism," page 865.)

George Grosz, "Twilight" from the Series *Ecce Homo* (1922)
George Grosz's series of postwar art was named after a book by Friedrich Nietzsche, *Ecce Homo* (*Behold the Man*). The "man" to behold was the veteran, opportunistically called a hero by postwar politicians to get their votes but in fact living a grim reality, as Grosz saw it. Surrounded by prosperous businessmen, fashionable women, and strutting military officers, the veteran was pushed to the background, gray and lonely amid the colorful peacetime society. *(bpk, Berlin/Kunstbibliothek, Staaliche Museen, Berlin, Germany/photo by Kund Petersen/Art Resource, NY/Art © Estate of George Grosz/Licensed by VAGA, New York, NY.)*

Poets reflected on postwar conditions in more general terms, using styles that rejected the comforting rhymes or accessible metaphors of earlier verse. T. S. Eliot, an American-born poet who had studied Buddhism and Sanskrit and for a time worked as a banker in Britain, portrayed postwar life as petty and futile in "The Waste Land" (1922) and "The Hollow Men" (1925). The Irish poet William Butler Yeats joined Eliot in mourning the replacement of traditional society, with its religious and moral convictions, with a new, superficial generation gaily dancing to jazz and engaging in promiscuous sex. Both poets had an uneasy relationship with the modern world and at times advocated authoritarianism rather than democracy.

The postwar arts produced many a utopian fantasy turned upside down; dystopias of life in a war-traumatized Europe multiplied. In the bizarre stories of Franz Kafka, who worked by day in a large insurance company in Prague, the world is a vast, impersonal machine. His novels *The Trial* (1925) and *The Castle* (1926) show the hopeless condition of individuals caught between the cogs of society's relentlessly turning gears. His theme seemed to capture for civilian life the helplessness that soldiers had felt at the front. As an old social order collapsed in the face of political and technological innovation, other writers depicted the complex, sometimes nightmarish inner life of individuals.

Irish writer James Joyce portrayed this interior self built on memories and sensations, many of them from the war. Joyce's *Ulysses* (1922) illuminates the fast-moving inner lives of its characters in the course of a single day. In one of the most celebrated passages in *Ulysses*, a long interior monologue traces a woman's lifetime of erotic and emotional sensations. The technique of using a character's thoughts to propel a story was called stream of consciousness. Virginia Woolf, too, used this technique in her novel *Mrs. Dalloway* (1925). For Woolf, the war had dissolved the solid society from which absorbing stories and fascinating characters were once fashioned. Her characters experience fragmented conversations and incomplete relationships. Woolf's novel *Orlando* also reflected the postwar attention to women. In the novel, the hero Orlando lives hundreds of years and in the course of his long life is eventually transformed into a woman.

There was another side to the postwar story, however—one based not on the interior life of a traumatized society, but on the promise of technology. Before the war, avant-garde artists had celebrated the new, the futuristic, the utopian. After the war, like Jules Amar crafting prostheses for shattered limbs, many postwar artists were optimistic that technology could make an entire wounded society whole. The aim of art, observed one of them, "is not to decorate our life but to organize it." German artists, calling themselves the Bauhaus (after the idea of a craft association, or *Bauhütte*), created streamlined office buildings and designed functional furniture and utensils, many of them inspired by forms from "untainted" East Asia and Africa. Russian artists, temporarily caught up in the communist experiment, optimistically wrote novels about cement factories and created ballets about steel.

Artists fascinated by technology and machinery were drawn to the most modern of all countries—the United States. Hollywood films, glossy advertisements, and the bustling metropolis of New York tempted careworn Europeans. They loved films and

DOCUMENT

Memory and Battlefield Tourism

World War I left deep wounds in the survivors, including the families of those who had died, and memories of the war and their loved ones filled everyday life. Like the English writer Vera Brittain, many relatives roamed the battlefields of Europe, in hopes of cementing their memories and understanding what had happened to their loved ones—and to Western civilization as a whole. During the war, Brittain had served as a nurse while suffering the loss of her brother, fiancé, and friends. Whereas organized tours of battlefields had begun almost immediately after the war, in 1921 Brittain went on her own to find her brother's grave high up in the remote mountains of Italy. She recounted this visit in a memoir of her early life.

"How strange, how strange it is," I reflected, as I looked, with an indefinable pain stabbing my chest, for Edward's name among those neat rows of oblong stones, "that all my past years—the childhood of which I have no one, now, to share the remembrance, the bright fields at Uppingham, the restless months in Buxton, the hopes and ambitions of Oxford, the losses and long-drawn agonies of the War—should be buried in this grave on the top of a mountain, in the lofty silence, the singing unearthly stillness, of these remote forests! At every turn of every future road I shall want to ask him questions, to recall to him memories, and he will not be there. Who could have dreamed that the little boy born in such uneventful security to an ordinary provincial family would end his brief days in a battle among the high pine-woods of an unknown Italian plateau?"

Close to the wall, in the midst of a group of privates from the Sherwood Foresters who had all died on June 15th, I found his name: "Captain E. H. Brittain, M.C., 11th Notts. And Derby Regt. Killed in action June 15th, 1918. Aged 22." In Venice I had bought some rosebuds and a small asparagus fern in a pot; the shopkeeper had told me that it would last a long time, and I planted it in the rough grass beside the grave.

"How trivial my life has been since the War!" I thought, as I smoothed the earth over the fern. "How mean they are, these little strivings, these petty ambitions of us who are left, now that all of you are gone! How can the future achieve, through us, the sombre majesty of the past? Oh, Edward, you're so lonely up here; why can't I stay for ever and keep your grave company, far from the world and its vain endeavours to rebuild civilisation, on this Plateau where alone there is dignity and peace?"

Source: Vera Brittain, *Testament of Youth* (1933; repr. London: Virago, 1978), 525–27.

Question to Consider

- **In what ways are memory and historical facts important in this account of the postwar world? How do memory and facts shape Brittain's analysis of the future?**

stories about the Wild West or the carefree "modern girl." They were especially attracted to jazz, the improvisational music developed by African Americans. Performers like Josephine Baker (1906–1976) and Louis Armstrong (1900–1971) became international sensations when they toured Europe's capital cities. Like jazz, the New York skyscraper pointed to the future, not to the grim wartime past.

The Communist Utopia

Communism also promised a shining future and a modern, technological culture. As the Bolsheviks met powerful resistance, however, they became ever more ruthless and authoritarian. In the early 1920s, peasant bands called Green Armies revolted against the Bolshevik policy of war communism that confiscated their crops. Industrial production stood at only 13 percent of prewar levels, shortages of housing affected the entire population, and millions of refugees clogged the cities and roamed the countryside. In the early spring of 1921, workers in Petrograd and sailors at the naval base at Kronstadt revolted, protesting their short rations and the privileged standard of living that Bolshevik supervisors enjoyed. They called for "soviets without Communists"—that is, a worker state without elite leaders.

The Bolsheviks had many of the rebels shot, but the Kronstadt revolt pushed Lenin to institute reform. His New Economic Policy (NEP) returned parts of the economy to the free market, a temporary retreat to capitalist methods that allowed peasants to sell their grain and others to trade consumer goods freely. Although the state still controlled large industries and banking, the NEP encouraged people to produce, sell, and even, in the spirited slogan of one official, "get rich." As a result, consumer goods and more food became available. Although many people remained impoverished, some peasants and merchants prospered. The rise of these wealthy "NEPmen," who bought and furnished splendid homes, broke the Bolshevik promise of a classless utopia.

Further protests erupted within Communist ranks. At the 1921 party congress, a group called

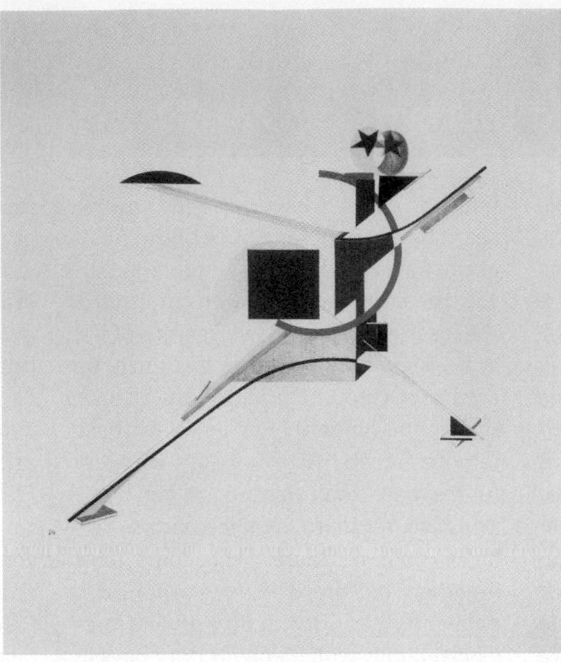

The New Man
There was a sense in the postwar world that people were entering a new age after the horrors of war. Nowhere was this feeling stronger than among Communists in Russia, where it was also believed that communism would create the "new man." In this work by Eli Lissitsky, *Victory over the Sun: The New Man* (1923), note the energy in the figure as it stretches its reach in all directions. The use of pure lines and geometric forms symbolized the higher reality that the new man would reach once the messiness and corruption of ordinary reality had been eliminated. *(Tate, London/Art Resource, NY/© 2011 Artists Rights Society [ARS], New York/VG Bild-Kunst, Bonn.)*

the Worker Opposition objected to the party's takeover of economic control from worker organizations and pointed out that the NEP was not a proletarian program for workers. In response, Lenin suppressed the Worker Opposition and set up procedures for purging opponents — a policy that would become a deadly feature of Communist rule. Bolshevik leaders also worked to make the Communist revolution a cultural reality in people's lives and thinking. The Communist Party set up classes in a variety of political and social subjects throughout the countryside, and volunteers struggled to improve the literacy rate — which was only 40 percent on the eve of World War I. To create social equality between the sexes, which had been part of the Marxist vision of the future, the state made birth control, abortion, and divorce readily available. As commissar for public welfare, **Aleksandra Kollontai** (1872–1952) promoted birth-control education for adults and day care for children of working parents. To encourage literacy, she wrote simply worded novels about love and work in the new socialist state for ordinary readers.

The bureaucracy swelled to bring modern ways to every corner of life, and *hygiene* and *efficiency* became watchwords, as they were in the rest of Europe. Agencies such as the Zhenotdel ("Women's Bureau") taught women about sanitary housekeeping and their rights under communism. Efficiency experts aimed to replace tsarist backwardness with technological modernity based on American techniques. The short-lived government agency Proletkult tried to develop proletarian culture through such undertakings as workers' universities, a workers' theater, and workers' publishing. Russian artists experimented with blending high art and technology in mass culture. Poet Vladimir Mayakovsky wrote verse praising his Communist passport and essays promoting toothbrushing, while composers punctuated their music with the sound of train or factory whistles. The early days of Bolshevik rule saw interesting experiments in all of the arts and in mass culture.

As with war communism, many resisted efforts to change everyday life and culture. As Zhenotdel workers moved into the countryside, for example, they attempted to teach women to behave as men's equals. Peasant families, still strongly patriarchal, often resisted. In Islamic regions of central Asia, incorporated from the old Russian Empire into the new Communist one, Bolsheviks urged Muslim women to remove their veils, change their way of life by learning their rights, and generally to become more "modern," but fervent Muslims often attacked both Zhenotdel workers and women who followed their advice.

In the spring of 1922, Lenin suffered a debilitating stroke, and amid ongoing cultural experimentation and factional fighting, this architect of the Bolshevik Revolution died in January 1924. The party congress declared the day of his death a permanent holiday, changed the name of Petrograd to Leningrad, and elevated the deceased leader into a secular god. After Lenin's death, no one was allowed to criticize anything associated with his name, a situation that opened the way for future abuses of power by Communist leaders.

Joseph Stalin (1879–1953), who served in the powerful post of general secretary of the Communist Party, was the chief mourner at Lenin's funeral, using the occasion to hand out good jobs and other patronage. He advertised his role in joining Russian and non-Russian regions into the Union of Soviet Socialist Republics (USSR) in 1923 as an example of his leadership skills. Concerned with Stalin's influence and ruthlessness, Lenin in his last

---

Aleksandra Kollontai: A Russian activist and minister of public welfare in the Bolshevik government who promoted social programs such as birth control and day care for children of working parents.

Mussolini and the Black Shirts, 1922
Mussolini always struck a tough, military pose, even when not in uniform, as in this photo taken in 1922 with his Black Shirt supporters, many also without uniforms. Once in power, Mussolini continued the militarization of society that had begun during World War I, instilling a cult of obedience and submission to state authority that he viewed as more important than fancy theories of politics and government. *(The Granger Collection, New York—All rights reserved.)*

will and testament had asked that "the comrades find a way to remove Stalin." Stalin, however, prevented Lenin's will from being publicized and discredited his chief rival, Trotsky, as an unpatriotic internationalist. With the blessing of Trotsky's other rivals, Stalin had him exiled. Simultaneously, Stalin organized the Lenin cult, which included the public display of Lenin's embalmed corpse—still on view today. Bringing in several hundred thousand new party members who owed their positions in government and industry to him, Stalin had achieved virtually complete control of the USSR by 1929.

Fascism on the March in Italy

In Italy, the rise to power of a political journalist who had turned from socialism to the radical right—**Benito Mussolini** (1883–1945)—kept the war alive. Italians raged when the Allies at Paris refused to honor the territorial promises of the Treaty of London, and peasants and workers protested their economic plight during the slump of the early 1920s. Since the late nineteenth century, many Europeans had come to blame parliaments and constitutions for their troubles, so Italians backed Mussolini when he built a personal army (the Black Shirts) of veterans and the unemployed to overturn parliamentary government. In 1922, his supporters, known as the Fascists, started a march on Rome, forcing King Victor Emmanuel III (r. 1900–1946) to make Mussolini prime minister.

The Fascist movement flourished because of poverty and wounded national pride. Like the Bolsheviks, Mussolini promised an efficient military utopia and the restoration of men's warrior status. The Black Shirts attracted many young men who felt cheated of wartime glory and many veterans who missed the vigor of military life. The fasces, an ancient Roman symbol depicting a bundle of sticks wrapped around an ax with the blade exposed (representing both unity and force), served as the movement's emblem and provided its name: **fascism**. Unlike Marxism, fascism scoffed at coherent ideology: "Fascism is not a church," Mussolini announced upon taking power in 1922. "It is more like a training ground." The Fascist Party was defined by deeds—specifically its promotion of male

Benito Mussolini: Leader of Italian fascist movement and, after the March on Rome in 1922, dictator of Italy.

fascism: A doctrine that emphasizes violence and glorifies the state over the people and their individual or civil rights; in Italy, the Fascist Party took hold in the 1920s as Mussolini consolidated power.

violence and its attacks on parliamentary rule and the socialist movement.

Mussolini consolidated his power by criminalizing any criticism of the state and by using violence against opponents in parliament. Bands of men from the Fascist Party wrecked socialist newspaper offices, attacked striking workers, used their favorite tactic of forcing castor oil (which caused diarrhea) down the throats of socialists, and even murdered rivals. Yet this brutality and the sight of the Black Shirts marching through the streets like disciplined soldiers signaled to many Italians that their country was orderly and modern. Large landowners and businessmen approved the Fascists' attacks on strikers and therefore financed the movement. Their generous funding allowed Mussolini to build a large staff by hiring the unemployed, creating the illusion that Fascists could rescue the economy when no one else could.

Like a wartime leader, Mussolini used mass propaganda to build support for a kind of military campaign to remake Italy. Peasant men huddled around radios to hear him call for a "battle of wheat" to enhance farm productivity. Peasant women, responding to his praise for maternal duty, adored him for appearing to value womanhood. In the cities the government launched avant-garde architectural projects and used public relations promoters to advertise its achievements. The modern city became a stage set for Fascist spectacle: old residential neighborhoods fell to the wrecking machines, allowing room for broad avenues for Fascist parades, captured by newsreel cameras and broadcast by radio. Mussolini claimed that he made the trains run on time, and this triumph of modern technology fanned people's hopes that he could restore order, even if it was military order.

Mussolini added a strong dose of traditional values and prejudices to his modern order. Although an atheist himself, he recognized the importance of Catholicism in Italian life. In 1929, the Lateran Agreement between the Italian government and the church made the Vatican an independent state under papal sovereignty. The government recognized the church's right to determine marriage and family policy and supported its role in education. In return, the church ended its criticism of Fascist tactics. Mussolini also introduced a "corporate" state that denied individual political rights in favor of duty to the state, as in wartime. Corporatist decrees in 1926 outlawed labor unions, replacing them with organized groups or corporations of employers, workers, and professionals to settle grievances and determine conditions of work. Mussolini drew praise from business leaders when he announced cuts in women's wages; later he won the approval of civil servants, lawyers, and professors by banning women from those professions. Mussolini did not want women out of the workforce altogether, but he aimed to confine them to low-paying jobs as part of his scheme for reinvigorating men by boosting male privileges.

Mussolini's numerous admirers across the West included Adolf Hitler, who throughout the 1920s had been building a paramilitary group of storm troopers and a political organization called the National Socialist German Workers' Party (the Nazi Party). During his brief stint in jail for the 1923 Beer Hall Putsch, Hitler wrote *Mein Kampf* (My Struggle); in the book, he expressed both his vicious anti-Semitism and his political psychology for manipulating the masses. Hitler was fascinated by the details of Mussolini's success: the Black Shirts' dramatic march on Rome, Mussolini's legal accession to power, and his triumph over all opposition. Late in the 1920s, however, the conditions that had allowed Mussolini to rise to power in 1922 no longer existed in Germany. Although Hitler was welding the Nazi Party into a strong political instrument, the Weimar parliamentary government was actually functioning better as the decade wore on.

REVIEW QUESTION **How did the postwar atmosphere influence cultural expression and encourage the trend toward dictatorship?**

Conclusion

The year 1929 was to prove just as fateful as 1914 had been. In 1914, World War I began an orgy of death, causing tens of millions of casualties, the destruction of major dynasties, and the collapse of aristocratic classes. For four years, the war promoted military technology, fierce nationalism, and the control of everyday life by bureaucracy. While dynasties fell, the centralization of power increased the scope of the nation-state. The Peace of Paris treaties of 1919–1920 left Germans bitterly resentful, while in eastern and central Europe the intermingling of ethnicities, religions, and languages in the new states created by the treaties failed to guarantee a peaceful future. Massive migrations produced additional chaos, as some new nations expelled minority groups.

War furthered the development of mass society. It leveled social classes on the battlefield and in the graveyard, standardized political thinking through

MAPPING THE WEST

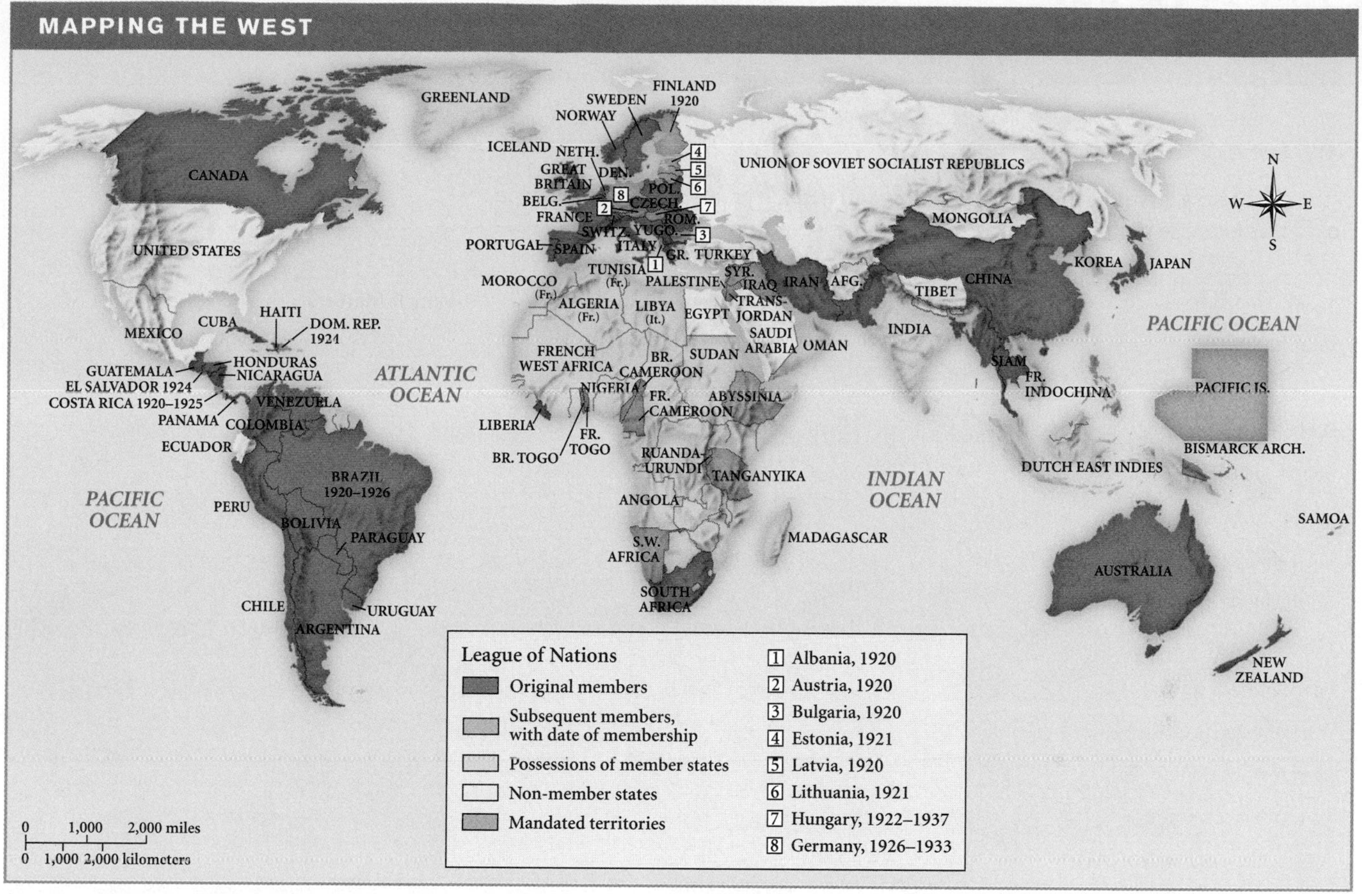

Europe and the World in 1929

The map reflects the partitions and nations that came into being as a result of war and revolution, while it obscures the increasing movement toward throwing off colonial rule. This was the true high point of empire: the drive for empire would diminish after 1929 except for Italy, which still craved colonies, and Japan, which continued searching for more land and resources to fuel its rapid growth. | **Observe the League of Nations membership as depicted in the map. What common bonds, if any, united these member nations?**

wartime propaganda, and extended many political rights to women. Production techniques, improved during wartime, were used in peacetime for manufacturing consumer goods. Technological innovations from the prostheses built by Jules Amar to air transport, cinema, and radio transmission became available to more people. Modernity in the arts intensified, probing the nightmarish war that continued to haunt the population.

By the end of the 1920s, the war had so militarized the population that strongmen had come to power in several countries, including the Soviet Union and Italy, with Adolf Hitler waiting in the wings in Germany. These strongmen and their followers kept alive the wartime commitment to violence. Many Westerners were impressed by the tough, modern efficiency of Fascists and Communists who made parliaments and citizen rule seem out of date, even effeminate. When the U.S. stock market crashed in 1929 and economic disaster circled the globe, authoritarian solutions and militarism continued to look appealing. What followed was a series of catastrophes even more devastating than those of World War I.

FOR FURTHER EXPLORATION

- **For additional primary-source material from this period**, see *Sources of the Making of the West*, Fourth Edition.
- **For Web sites, images, and documents related to topics in this chapter**, visit *Make History* at bedfordstmartins.com/hunt.

Chapter 25 Review

Online Study Guide bedfordstmartins.com/hunt

Key Terms and People

In the grid below, identify the term or person and explain its historical significance. (To do this exercise online, go to bedfordstmartins.com/hunt.)

Term	Who or What & When	Why It Matters
total war (p. 836)		
cult of the offensive (p. 838)		
Schlieffen Plan (p. 839)		
Fourteen Points (p. 846)		
soviets (p. 846)		
V. I. Lenin (p. 847)		
Bolshevik Revolution (p. 848)		
Weimar Republic (p. 851)		
Peace of Paris (p. 852)		
war guilt clause (p. 852)		
League of Nations (p. 853)		
mandate system (p. 854)		
Aleksandra Kollontai (p. 866)		
Benito Mussolini (p. 867)		
fascism (p. 867)		

Review Questions

1. In what ways was World War I a total war?
2. Why did people rebel during World War I, and what turned rebellion into outright revolution in Russia?
3. What were the major outcomes of the postwar peacemaking process?
4. What were the major political, social, and economic problems facing postwar Europe, and how did governments attempt to address them?
5. How did the postwar atmosphere influence cultural expression and encourage the trend toward dictatorship?

Making Connections

1. How did the experience of war shape postwar mass politics?
2. What social changes from World War I carried over into the postwar years and why?
3. How did postwar artistic and cultural innovations build on the modern movements that developed between 1890 and 1914?
4. What changes did the war bring to relationships between European countries and their colonies?

Important Events

Date	Event
1913–1925	Suffrage for women expands in much of Europe
1914	*August:* World War I begins
1916	Irish nationalists stage Easter Uprising against British rule
1917	*March:* Revolution in Russia overturns tsarist autocracy *April:* United States enters World War I *November:* Bolshevik Revolution in Russia
1918	*November:* Armistice ends fighting of World War I; revolutionary turmoil throughout Germany; kaiser abdicates
1918–1922	Civil war in Russia
1919	Weimar Republic established
1919–1920	Paris Peace Conference redraws map of Europe
1922	Ireland gains independence; Fascists march on Rome; Mussolini becomes prime minister; Eliot, "The Waste Land"; Joyce, *Ulysses*; Hitler builds Nazi Party
1924	Lenin dies; Stalin and Trotsky contend for power
1924–1929	Period of general economic prosperity and stability
1929	October: Stock market crash in United States

- Consider three events: **Eliot, "The Waste Land" (1922)**, **Fascists march on Rome (1922)**, and **Period of general economic prosperity and stability (1924–1929)**. How do these events illustrate the complexities of postwar life?

SUGGESTED REFERENCES

Readers of history and scholars continue to explore the gripping and tragic events of World War I. Martha Hanna's work captures the often heartrending relationship between the battlefront and home front.

Barry, John. *The Great Influenza: The Epic Story of the Greatest Plague in History.* 2004.

Hanna, Martha. *Your Death Would Be Mine: Paul and Marie Pireaud in the Great War.* 2006.

Healy, Maureen. *Vienna and the Fall of the Habsburg Empire: Total War and Everyday Life in World War I.* 2004.

Holquist, Peter. *Making War, Forging Revolution: Russia's Continuum of Crisis, 1914–1921.* 2002.

Horne, John, ed. *State, Society, and Mobilization in Europe during the First World War.* 2002.

Jensen, Eric N. *Body by Weimar: Athletes, Gender and German Modernity.* 2010.

Kent, Susan Kingsley. *Aftershocks: The Politics of Trauma in Britain, 1918–1931.* 2009.

Liulevicius, Vejas Gabriel. *War Land on the Eastern Front: Culture, National Identity and German Occupation in World War I.* 2000.

Makaman, Douglas, and Michael Mays, eds. *World War I and the Cultures of Modernity.* 2000.

Marks, Sally. *The Ebbing of European Ascendancy: An International History of the World.* 2002.

Northrup, Douglas. *Veiled Empire: Gender and Power in Stalinist Central Asia.* 2004.

Panchasi, Roxanne. *Future Tense: The Culture of Anticipation in France Between the Wars.* 2009.

Robb, George. *British Culture and the First World War.* 2002.

Roshwald, Aviel. *Ethnic Nationalism and the Fall of Empires: Central Europe, Russia and the Middle East, 1914–1923.* 2001.

Scales, Rebecca. "Radio Broadcasting, Disabled Veterans, and Politics of National Recovery in Interwar France." *French Historical Studies.* 2008.

Weitz, Eric D. *Weimar Germany: Promise and Tragedy.* 2009.

World War I Document Archive: http://www.lib.byu.edu/%7Erdh/wwi

The Great Depression and World War II

CHAPTER 26

1929–1945

When Etty Hillesum moved to Amsterdam from the Dutch provinces in 1932 to attend law school, an economic depression gripped the world. A resourceful young woman, Hillesum pieced together a living as a housekeeper and part-time language teacher so that she could continue her studies. Absorbed by the pressures and pleasures of her everyday life, she took little note of Adolf Hitler's spectacular rise to power in Germany, even when he demonized her fellow Jews as responsible for the economic slump and for virtually every other problem Germany faced. In 1939, the outbreak of World War II awakened her to the reality of what was happening. The German conquest of the Netherlands in 1940 led to the persecution of Dutch Jews, bringing Hillesum to a shattering realization, noted in her diary: "What they are after is our total destruction." The Nazis started relocating Jews to camps in Germany and Poland. Hillesum went to work for Amsterdam's Jewish Council, which was forced to organize the transport of Jews to the death camps in eastern Europe. Changing from self-absorbed student to heroine, she did what she could to help other Jews and began carefully recording the deportations. When she and her family were captured and deported in turn, she smuggled out letters from the transit camps along the route to Poland, describing the inhumane conditions and brutal treatment of the Jews. "I wish I could live for a long time so that one day I may know how to explain it," she wrote. Etty Hillesum never got her wish: she died at Auschwitz in November 1943.

Nazis on Parade
By the time Hitler came to power in 1933, Germany was mired in the Great Depression. Hated by Communists, Nazis, and conservatives alike, the Weimar Republic had few supporters. Hitler took his cue from Mussolini by promising an end to democracy and tolerance and by using the visual power of Nazi soldiers marching through the streets during the depression to win support for overthrowing the government. *(Hugo Jaeger/Time & Life Pictures/Getty Images.)*

The economic recovery of the late 1920s came to a halt with the U.S. stock market crash in 1929. Financial collapse in the United States was part of the worldwide Great Depression. Economic distress intensified social grievances. In Europe, many people turned to military-style strongmen for solutions to their problems. Among these dictators was Adolf Hitler, who called on the German masses to restore the national glory that had been damaged by defeat in 1918. He urged Germans to scorn democratic rights and root out those he considered to be inferior people: Jews, Slavs, and Sinti and Roma (often called Gypsies), among others. Militaristic and fascist regimes spread to Spain, Poland, Hungary, Japan, and countries of Latin America, crushing representative institutions. In the Soviet Union, Joseph Stalin justified the killing of millions of citizens as necessary for the USSR's industrialization and the survival of communism. For millions of hard-pressed people in the 1930s, dictatorship had great appeal.

Elected leaders in the democracies reacted cautiously to both economic depression and the dictators' aggression. In an age of mass media, leaders following democratic principles appeared timid, while dictators dressed in uniforms looked bold and decisive. Only the German invasion of Poland in 1939 pushed the democracies to strong action, as World War II erupted in Europe. By 1941, the war had spread across the globe with the United States, Great Britain, the Soviet Union, and many other nations united in combat against Germany, Italy, Japan, and their allies. Tens of millions would perish in this war because both technology and ideology had become more deadly than they had been just two decades earlier. More than half the dead were civilians, among them Etty Hillesum, whose only crime was being Jewish.

CHAPTER FOCUS **What were the main economic, social, and political challenges of the years 1929–1945, and how did governments and individuals respond to them?**

The Great Depression

The U.S. stock market crash of 1929 and economic developments around the world triggered the Great Depression of the 1930s. Rural and urban folk alike suffered as tens of millions lost their jobs and livelihoods. The whole world felt the depression's impact: commerce and investment in industry fell off, social life and gender roles were upset, and the birthrate plummeted. From peasants in Asia to industrial workers in Germany and the United States, the Great Depression shattered the lives of millions.

Economic Disaster Strikes

In the 1920s, U.S. corporations and banks as well as millions of individual Americans had not only invested all their money but also borrowed funds to invest in the stock market, which seemed to deliver endless profits. Confident that stock prices would continue to rise, they used easy credit to buy shares in popular companies based on electric, automotive, and other new technologies. By the end of the decade, the Federal Reserve Bank—the nation's central bank, which controlled financial policy—tried to slow speculation by limiting credit availability. To meet the new restrictions, brokers had to demand that their clients immediately pay back the money they had borrowed to buy stock. As stocks were sold to raise the necessary cash, the market collapsed. Between early October and mid-November 1929, the value of businesses listed on the U.S. stock exchange dropped from $87 billion to $30 billion. For individuals and for the economy as a whole, it was the beginning of catastrophe.

The crash helped bring on a global depression that unfolded over the course of several years. The

1929 U.S. stock market crashes; global depression begins; Soviet war against kulaks

1930

1931 Japan invades Manchuria; Spanish republicans overthrow monarchy

1933 Hitler comes to power

1935 Nuremberg Laws; Italy invades Ethiopia

1936 Purges and show trials in USSR; Spanish Civil War begins

1937 Japan attacks China

1938 Germany annexes Austria; European leaders meet to negotiate with Hitler; Kristallnacht

United States had financed the international economic growth of the previous five years, so when the suddenly strapped U.S. banks cut back on loans and called in debts, they undermined businesses at home and abroad. As jobs dwindled, Europe and other parts of the world faced a decline in consumer buying, overproduction, and competition from low-cost U.S. and Japanese goods—all of which slowed the European economy, including the young businesses of eastern Europe.

The Great Depression left no sector of the world economy unscathed, but government actions made the depression worse. To try to spur their economies, governments cut budgets and set high tariffs against foreign goods; these policies discouraged the consumer spending and international trade needed to spark the economy. Officials in charge of global money flows that fostered commerce desperately guarded their own supplies of gold. Unemployment soared: Great Britain—with its outdated textile, steel, and coal industries—had close to three million unemployed in 1932. By 1933, almost six million German workers, or about one-third of the workforce, were unemployed. Even in France, which had a more self-sufficient economy based on small businesses, firms began to fail, and by the mid-1930s more than 800,000 French people had lost their jobs.

Agricultural prices had been declining for several years because of technological advances and abundant harvests around the world. With their incomes slashed, millions of small farmers had no money to buy the chemical fertilizers and motorized machinery they needed to remain competitive. Now creditors confiscated farms. Eastern and southern European peasants, who had pressed for the redistribution of land after World War I, could not afford to operate their newly acquired farms, and they, too, went under. In Poland, many of the

Unemployed in Germany (1932)
"I'm looking for work of any kind," this respectably dressed unemployed man announces on his sign. Germans were among those hardest hit by the Great Depression, and when demogogues pointed to such sights as evidence that democracy didn't work, it helped pull down the rule of constitutions, representative government, and guaranteed rights. *(ullstein bild/The Granger Collection, New York.)*

1939 Germany invades Czechoslovakia, Poland; Spanish Civil War ends; Nazi-Soviet Pact; Britain, France declare war on Germany; World War II begins

1940 France falls to German army

1940–1941 Battle of Britain

1941 Germany invades USSR; Japan attacks Pearl Harbor; U.S. enters war

1941–1945 The Holocaust

1942–1943 Siege of Stalingrad

1944 Allied forces land at Normandy

1945 Fall of Berlin; U.S. drops atomic bombs on Japan; World War II ends

1940 — 1945

700,000 new landowners fell into debt trying to upgrade their farms. Eastern European governments often ignored the farmers' plight while pouring available funds into industrialization — a policy that increased tensions in rural society.

Social Effects of the Depression

The Great Depression had complex effects on society. First, life was not uniformly bleak, and despite the slump, modernization continued. Bordering English slums, one traveler in the mid-1930s noticed, were "filling stations and factories that look like exhibition buildings, giant cinemas and dance halls and cafés, bungalows with tiny garages, cocktail bars, Woolworth's [and] swimming pools." Municipal and national governments continued road construction and sanitation projects. Running water, electricity, and sewage pipes were installed in many homes for the first time. New factories manufactured synthetic fabrics, automobiles, and electrical products such as stoves — all of them in demand. With government assistance, eastern European industry developed: Romanian industrial production, for example, increased by 55 percent between 1929 and 1939.

Second, the majority of Europeans and Americans had jobs throughout the 1930s, and people with steady employment benefited from a drastic drop in prices. Service workers, managers, and business magnates often prospered. In contrast, towns with heavy industry often saw more than half the population out of work. In England in the mid-1930s, close to 20 percent of the population lacked adequate food, clothing, or housing. In a 1932 school assignment, a German youth wrote: "My father has been out of work for two and a half years. He thinks that I'll never find a job." Despite the prosperity of many people, the Great Depression spread fear beyond the unemployed. (See Document, "A Family Copes with Unemployment," page 877.)

Economic catastrophe upset gender relations and weakened social ties. Women often found low-paying jobs doing laundry and cleaning house, while unemployed men sometimes stayed home all day and took over housekeeping chores. Some, however, felt that this "women's work" demeaned their masculinity, and as many women became breadwinners, albeit for low wages, men could be seen standing on street corners begging — a change in gender expectations that fed discontent. Young men in cities faced severe unemployment; with nothing to do but loiter in parks, they became ripe for movements like Nazism. As the number of farmworkers in western Europe decreased, rural men also faced a decline in male authority, once responsible for directing farm labor. Demagogues everywhere attacked democracy's failure to stop the collapse of traditional life. Their complaints helped clear the way for Nazi and Fascist politicians who promised to create jobs and thus restore male dignity.

Politicians drew attention to the declining birthrates during the slump as still another national problem. In difficult economic times, which had plagued the West on and off since World War I, people in the 1930s chose to have fewer children than ever before. In addition, compulsory education and more years of required schooling, enforced more strictly after the war, reduced the income once earned by children. Working-class children now cost their families money while they went to school. Family-planning centers opened, receiving many clients, and knowledge of birth control spread across the working and lower-middle classes. The situation, leaders believed, was ominous.

Politicians from all parties threatened that declining fertility along with a depressed economy would lead to a national collapse in morale and military readiness. Many politicians also used the population "crisis" to gain votes by igniting racism: "superior" peoples were selfishly failing to breed, politicians charged, while "inferior" peoples were just waiting to take their place. This racism took a particularly violent form in eastern Europe, where the rural population also rose because of increased life expectancy despite the declining birthrate. As financial hardships continued, political parties across eastern Europe blamed Jewish bankers for farm foreclosures and Jewish civil servants (of whom there were actually very few) for inadequate relief programs. Thus, population issues along with economic misery produced discord, especially in the form of ethnic hatred and anti-Semitism, opening the way still further for dictators who promised that eliminating "undesirables" would restore prosperity.

The Great Depression beyond the West

The effects of the depression extended beyond the West, spreading discontent in European empires. World War I and postwar investment had produced economic growth, a rising population, and explosive urbanization in Asia, Africa, and Latin America. Japan in particular had become a formidable industrial rival. The depression, however, cut the demand for copper, tin, and other raw materials and for the finished products made in urban factories worldwide. Rising agricultural productivity drove down the price of foodstuffs like rice and coffee, a disaster for colonial peoples who had been forced to grow a single cash crop. One French official in Algeria said that the collapse of agricultural prices

DOCUMENT

A Family Copes with Unemployment

Austria and Germany were incredibly hard hit by the depression. The trauma was made worse because of the catastrophic defeat and dismemberment of both the Austrian and German Empires. In 1931, sociologists visited a small industrial town called Marienthal, an hour outside of Vienna, to report on the psychological and physical condition of the hundreds of families left penniless by the closing of the textile mills.

The father was sitting on a low stool with a pile of worn-out children's shoes in front of him that he was trying to mend with roofing felt. The children were sitting together motionless on a box, in stockinged feet, waiting for their shoes to be finished. The father explained with embarrassment, "... On Sundays I have to patch the shoes up a bit so that the children can go to school again on Monday." He held up the completely dilapidated shoes of the eldest boy. "I just don't know what I can do with these. On holidays he can't go out of the house any more. . . ."

The youngest child caught our attention. His face was feverish and puffy and swollen around the nose. He breathed heavily with his mouth open. The mother explained: "He always has a cold. He ought to have his tonsils and adenoids out, but we can't afford the trip to the hospital. . . ." The father told us that things had been going terribly badly these last few days. All they had been able to buy was bread, and not enough of that. The children kept coming into the kitchen asking for another piece; they were always hungry. His wife sat in the kitchen crying.

Source: Marie Jahoda et al., eds., *Marienthal: The Sociography of an Unemployed Community*, trans. John Reginall and Thomas Elsaesser (1933; repr. Chicago: Aldine-Atherton, 1971), 87–88.

Question to Consider

- **How does the situation of this Austrian family illustrate why Europeans might have willingly followed Nazi and Fascist politicians in the 1930s?**

"endanger[ed] the entire colonial project." Just as in Europe, however, the economic picture in the colonies was uneven. For instance, established Indian industries such as the textile business gained strength, with India no longer needing British cloth.

Economic distress fueled anger, and anger led to action. Colonial farmers withheld produce like cocoa from imperial trade, and colonial workers went on strike to protest the wage cuts imposed by imperial landlords. Discontent ran deep. Millions of African and Asian colonial troops had fought for Britain and France in World War I, but the imperialist countries had given little back to their colonial populations. In fact, the League of Nations charter had pointedly omitted any reference to the principle of racial equality demanded by people of color at the Paris peace conference. Fortified by these wrongs, by the model of Japan's growing power, and by their own industrial development, more colonial peoples than ever before resolved to win independence.

In India, anger toward colonialism boiled over. Millions of working people, including hundreds of thousands of veterans, joined with the upper-class Indians, who had organized to gain rights from Britain in the late nineteenth century. Mohandas K. Gandhi (1869–1948), called Mahatma ("great-souled"), emerged as the charismatic leader for Indian independence. Trained in England as a Western-style lawyer, Gandhi preached Hindu self-denial and rejected British love of material wealth. He wore simple clothing made of thread he had spun himself and advocated **civil disobedience**—deliberately but peacefully breaking the law—a tactic he claimed to have taken from the British suffragists and from the teachings of spiritual leaders like Jesus and Buddha. Boycotting British-made goods and disobeying British laws, Gandhi aimed to end Indian deference to the British. The British jailed Gandhi repeatedly and tried to split the independence movement by promoting Hindu-Muslim antagonism. Instead, commitment to independence grew.

The end of the Ottoman Empire following World War I led to efforts to build new independent nations in the Middle East. Mustafa Kemal (1881–1938), who later took the name Atatürk ("first among Turks"), led the Turks to found an independent republic in 1923 and to craft a capitalist economy. In an effort to Westernize Turkish culture and promote the new Turkish state, Kemal moved the capital from Constantinople to Ankara in 1923, officially changed the name Constantinople to the Turkish name Istanbul in 1930, mandated Western dress for men and women, introduced the Latin alphabet, and abolished polygamy. In 1936, Turkish women

---

civil disobedience: The act of deliberately but peacefully breaking the law, a tactic used by Mohandas Gandhi in India and earlier by British suffragists to protest oppression and obtain political change.

Gandhi Speaks to Women and Children
Mohandas K. Gandhi, an English-trained lawyer, was central to making the Indian independence movement a mass phenomenon. He made Indians see the superior values in their own culture in contrast to those of the West. The West, he maintained, including the United States, valued only money. Gandhi riveted his audiences, addressing women and children as well as men. *(akg-images/Archiv Peter Rühe.)*

received the vote and were made eligible to serve in the parliament. Persia, which changed its name to Iran in 1935, similarly loosened the European grip on its economy by updating its government and by forcing the negotiation of oil contracts that kept Western countries from taking the oil for virtually nothing.

Anticolonial activism thrived in French colonies, too, but the government made few concessions. Like all imperial countries during the depression, France depended increasingly on the profits it could take from its empire; therefore, its trade with its colonies increased as trade with Europe lagged. France also depended on the colonies for sheer numbers of people, and the growing colonial population bolstered French optimism. One official estimated what colonial numbers could mean for national security: "One hundred and ten million strong, France can stand up to Germany." Ho Chi Minh, founder of the Indochinese Communist Party, rallied his people to protest French imperialism, but in 1930 the French government brutally crushed the peasant uprising he led. Needing their empires, Britain and France increased the number of their troops stationed around the world. As a result, fascism spread largely unchecked in Europe during the 1930s.

REVIEW QUESTION How did the Great Depression affect society and politics?

Totalitarian Triumph

Representative government collapsed in many countries under the sheer weight of social and economic crisis. After 1929, Mussolini in Italy, Stalin in the USSR, and Hitler in Germany were able to mobilize vast support for their regimes. Many admired Mussolini and Hitler for the discipline they brought to social and economic life. Desperate for economic relief, many citizens supported political violence as key to restoring well-being. Scholars have classified the Fascist, Nazi, and Communist regimes of the 1930s as totalitarian. The term *totalitarianism* refers to highly centralized systems of government that attempt to control society and ensure obedience through a single party and police terror. Born during World War I and gaining support in its aftermath, totalitarian governments broke with liberal principles of freedom and natural rights and came to wage war on their own citizens. But there were important differences among totalitarian states, especially between Fascist and Communist states. Whereas communism denounced private ownership of property and economic inequality, fascism supported them as crucial to national might (see Terms of History, page 879).

The Rise of Stalinism

In the 1930s, **Joseph Stalin** (1879–1953) led the transformation of the USSR from a rural society into an industrial power. Stalin ended Lenin's New Economic Policy, which had allowed individuals to profit from trade and agriculture, and in 1929 laid out the first of several ambitious five-year plans for industrializing the country. Coercion and violence were crucial components of this gigantic undertaking.

Transforming the Economy Stalin's **five-year plans** outlined a program for huge increases in the output of coal, iron ore, steel, and industrial goods over successive five-year periods. Without an end to economic backwardness, Stalin warned, "the advanced countries . . . will crush us."

Joseph Stalin: Leader of the USSR who, with considerable backing, formed a brutal dictatorship in the 1930s and forcefully converted the country into an industrial power.

five-year plans: Centralized programs for economic development begun in 1929 by Joseph Stalin and copied by Adolf Hitler; these plans set production priorities and gave production targets for individual industries and agriculture.

TERMS OF HISTORY

Fascism

Fascism was, along with communism and liberalism, one of the dominant ideologies of the twentieth century. It began in the 1920s as Benito Mussolini's movement in Italy, taking its name from *fasces*—a Latin word for the bundle of rods with hatchet symbolizing Roman magisterial authority. Under Mussolini, the concept placed the value of the national community above that of individuals and the laws and rights that protected them.

The term was then broadened to apply generally to the various authoritarian political parties (such as the Nazis) and their leaders, who came to power in Italy, Germany, Spain, eastern Europe, and other parts of the world before World War II. As an outgrowth of World War I, fascism applauded violence and military struggle on the state's behalf and denied the value of peace and pacifism. Fascism was also explicitly and fundamentally antidemocratic: both Mussolini and Hitler loudly rejected democratic values, with Mussolini arguing that the twentieth century would be the century of "authority" and of the "state"—not the century of democracy and hard-won consensus, which he saw as outmoded.

The expansion of fascism as a general political concept passed through several phases, moving from a "rooting" stage of growth and mobilization, to the seizure and exercise of brutal state power, to a violent expansion that culminated in radical action such as war and genocide. The rooting stage required popular support, which Fascist leaders solicited through programs with mass appeal: just after World War I, Mussolini issued a First Fascist Program that included votes for women, the eight-hour day, taxation of war profits, confiscation of church lands, and workers' participation in industrial management. Once in power, however, Fascists cast aside the principles that had won them popular support. By 1935, fascism had come to focus on the powers of one charismatic leader: Hitler, Franco, and Mussolini, in their military-garbed persons, became living embodiments of the all-powerful state. Japan also joined the fascist Axis powers after its attack on the United States in 1941, in part because Japan's military had come to embrace the same violence-driven ambitions.

Underlying fascist actions was the core belief that racial superiority fostered a strong national community. Fascists argued that a regimented society would strengthen the "master race," with Germany and Japan slaughtering millions toward that end. Believing that militarization strengthens the state and transforms the people, fascists also eagerly pursued war as an important end in itself. Through regimentation, militarization, and violent action, fascists sought to eliminate those deemed inferior or subversive and cause the emergence of an idealized "man of steel."

This emphasis on inequality distinguished the fascist from the Soviet totalitarian state. While fascism valued inequality and the triumphs of the wealthy, Soviets did not. Thus, Germany and Italy supported the actions of the rebel chief Francisco Franco in the Spanish Civil War, seeing this as part of the drive to overthrow rights-based, equal-opportunity democracies in the name of an absolutist state where the wealthy and powerful flourished. Fascist ideology also affected areas such as Romania, Bulgaria, Albania, and Greece.

Today, the term *fascist* has lost its clear definition and is regularly used to characterize any opponent with whom one disagrees. In this regard, similar use is made of terms like *socialist* and *liberal*—words that once had a precise meaning, but now have become epithets among the uninformed.

He thus established economic planning—that is, government direction of the economy used on both sides in World War I and increasingly implemented around the world. Between 1928 and 1940, the number of Soviet workers in industry, construction, and transport grew from 4.6 million to 12.6 million and factory output soared. Stalin's first five-year plan helped make the USSR a leading industrial nation.

A new bureaucratic elite implemented the plans, and the number of managers—mostly party officials and technical experts—in heavy industry grew by almost 500 percent between 1929 and 1935. Despite limited rights to change jobs or even move from place to place, skilled workers benefited from the privileges that went along with their new industrial role. Compared with people working the land, both managers and industrial workers had better housing and wages. Communist officials received additional rewards such as country homes, good food, and luxurious vacations.

New or unskilled workers enjoyed no such benefits. Newcomers from the countryside were herded into barracks or tents and subjected to dangerous factory conditions. Despite the hardships, many took pride in their new skills. "We mastered this profession—completely new to us—with great pleasure," a female lathe operator recalled. More often, however, workers fresh from the countryside lacked the technical skills necessary to accomplish goals of the five-year plans. Because meeting these goals had top priority as a measure of progress toward a Communist utopia, official lying about productivity became part of the economic system. The attempt to turn an illiterate peasant society into an advanced industrial economy in a single decade brought intense suffering, but hardship was tolerated because, as one worker put it, Soviet workers believed in the need for "constant struggle, struggle, and struggle" to achieve a Communist society.

In country and city alike, politics influenced work. Stalin demanded more output from industry and more grain from peasants both to feed the urban workforce and to provide exports whose sale abroad would finance industrialization. Some peasants resisted government demands by withholding produce from the market, prompting Stalin to demand a "liquidation of the kulaks." The word *kulak*, which literally means "fist," was a negative term for prosperous peasants, but in practice it applied to anyone who opposed Stalin's plans to end independent farming. Party workers began searching villages, seizing grain, and forcing villagers to identify the kulaks among them. Propagandists followed to stir up hatred. One Russian remembered believing the kulaks were "bloodsuckers, cattle, swine, loathsome, repulsive: they had no souls; they stank." Denounced as "enemies of the state," whole families were robbed of their possessions, left to starve, or even murdered outright. Confiscated kulak land formed the basis for the new collective farms, or kolkhoz, where the remaining peasants were forced to share facilities and modern machinery. Traditional peasant life was brought to a violent end.

Transforming Society Once the state had defined work life as central to communism, economic failure took on political meaning. Such failure was common because factory workers, farmers, and party officials alike were too inexperienced with advanced industrialization to meet quotas. The experiment with collectivization, combined with the murder of farmers, resulted in a drop in the grain harvest from 83 million tons in 1930 to 67 million in 1934. Soviet citizens starved. Blaming failure on "wreckers" deliberately plotting against communism, Stalin instituted **purges**—that is, state violence in the form of widespread arrests, imprisonments in labor camps, and executions—to rid society of these "villains." The purges touched all segments of society, beginning with engineers who were condemned for causing low productivity.

Beginning in 1936, the government charged prominent Bolshevik leaders with conspiring to overthrow Soviet rule. In a series of "show trials"—trials based on trumped-up charges, fabricated evidence, and coerced confessions—Bolshevik leaders were tortured and forced to confess in court. Most of those found guilty were shot. Some of the top leaders accepted their fate, seeing the purges as good for the future of socialism. Just before his execution, one Bolshevik loyalist and former editor of the party newspaper *Pravda* wrote to Stalin praising the "great and bold political idea behind the general purge." While there was resistance to Stalin, there were many sincere believers who sought to serve what they considered his noble work.

The spirit of purge swept through society, eventually reaching the Soviet power structure. One woman poet described the scene in towns and cities: "Great concert and lecture halls were turned into public confessionals. . . . People did penance for [everything]. . . . Beating their breasts, the 'guilty' would lament that they had 'shown political shortsightedness' and 'lack of vigilance' . . . and were full of 'rotten liberalism.'" In 1937 and 1938, military leaders were arrested and executed without public trials; some ranks were entirely wiped out. Although the massacre of military leaders appeared suicidal at a time when Hitler threatened war, thousands of high military posts became open to new talent. Stalin would not have to worry about an officer corps wedded to old ideas, as had happened in World War I. Simultaneously, the government expanded the system of prison camps, founded under Lenin, into an extensive network stretching several thousand miles from Moscow to Siberia. Called the Gulag—an acronym for the government department that ran the camps—the system held millions of prisoners under lethal conditions. Prisoners aided the economy by doing every kind of work from digging canals to building apartment buildings. Some one million died annually as a result of the harsh conditions, which included insufficient food, inadequate housing, and twelve- to sixteen-hour days of crushing physical labor. Regular beatings and murders of prisoners rounded out Gulag life, which became another aspect of totalitarian violence.

As social and sexual experimentation disappeared in the 1930s, toleration in Soviet social life ended. The birthrate in the USSR, like that in the rest of Europe, declined rapidly. The Soviet Union also needed to replace the millions of people lost since 1914. To meet this need, Stalin restricted access to birth-control information and abortion. Lavish wedding ceremonies came back into fashion,

---

purges: The series of attacks on citizens of the USSR accused of being "wreckers," or saboteurs of communism, in the 1930s and later.

divorces became difficult to obtain, and the state made homosexuality a crime. Whereas Bolsheviks had once attacked the family as a capitalist institution, propaganda now referred to the family as a "school for socialism." At the same time, women in rural areas made gains in literacy and received improved health care. Positions in the lower ranks of the party opened to women as the purges continued, and more women were accepted into the professions. However, women in the industrial workforce faced increased stress. After long hours in factories, workingwomen stood in lines for scarce consumer goods and still performed all household and child-care tasks.

Avant-garde experimentation in the arts ended under Stalin. He called artists and writers "engineers of the soul" and, thus recognizing their influence, controlled their output through the Union of Soviet Writers. The union not only assigned housing, office space, equipment, and secretarial help but also determined the types of books authors could write. In return, the "comrade artist" adhered to the official style of "socialist realism," derived from the 1920s focus on the common worker as a hero. Although some writers and artists went underground, secretly creating works that are still coming to light, many others found ways to adjust their talents to the state's demands. The composer Sergei Prokofiev, for example, wrote music both for the delightful *Peter and the Wolf* and for Sergei Eisenstein's 1938 film *Alexander Nevsky*, a work that flatteringly compared Stalin to the medieval rulers of the Russian people. Aided by adaptable artists, workers, and bureaucrats, Stalin stood triumphant as the 1930s drew to a close. He was, as two different workers put it, "our beloved Leader" and "a god on earth."

Hitler's Rise to Power

A different but ultimately no less violent system emerged when **Adolf Hitler** (1889–1945) and his followers put an end to democracy in Germany. Since the early 1920s, Hitler had harangued the German masses to destroy the Weimar Republic and drummed at a message of anti-Semitism and the rebirth of the German "race." When the Great Depression struck Germany in 1929, his Nazi Party began to outstrip its rivals in elections, thanks in part to financial support from big business. Film and press tycoon Alfred Hugenberg helped, constantly slamming the Weimar government as responsible for the disastrous economy and for the loss of German pride after World War I. Nazi supporters took to the streets, attacking young Communist groups who agitated just as loudly on behalf of the new Soviet experiment. Hugenberg's newspapers always reported such incidents as the work of Communist thugs who had assaulted blameless Nazis, thus building sympathy for the Nazis among the middle classes.

Parliamentary government practically ground to a halt during the depression, adding to unrest and the sense of disorder. The Reichstag, or German assembly, failed to approve emergency plans to improve the economy, first because its members disagreed over policies and second because Nazi and Communist deputies disrupted its sessions. Its failure to act discredited democracy among the German people. Hitler's followers made parliamentary government look incapable of providing basic law and order by rampaging unchecked through the streets and attacking Jews, Communists, and Social Democrats. By targeting all these as a single, monolithic group of "Bolshevik" enemies, the Nazis won wide approval. They were seen as fearlessly confronting those within Germany responsible for the depression. Many thought it was time to replace democratic government with a bold new leader who would take on these enemies military-style, without concern for constitutions, laws, or individual rights. It was time for war at home.

Every age group and class of people supported Hitler, though like Stalin, he especially attracted young people. In 1930, 70 percent of Nazi Party members were under forty and many had never thought of war except as exciting games they played as children during World War I. They believed that a better world was possible under Hitler's command. The largest number of supporters came from the industrial working class, but many white-collar workers and members of the lower-middle class also joined the party in percentages out of proportion with their numbers in the population. The inflation that had wiped out savings left them especially bitter and open to Hitler's rhetoric. In the deepening economic crisis, the Nazi Party, which had received little more than 2 percent of the vote in 1928, won almost 20 percent in the Reichstag elections of 1930 and more than twice that in 1932 (see "Contrasting Views," page 882).

Hitler used modern propaganda techniques to build up his following. Nazi Party members passed

---

Adolf Hitler (1889–1945): Chancellor of Germany (1933–1945) who, with considerable backing, overturned democratic government, created the Third Reich, persecuted millions, and ultimately led Germany and the world into World War II.

CONTRASTING VIEWS

Nazism and Hitler: For and Against

Today Hitler is uniformly regarded as a dictator while his followers are seen as perpetrating great harm on German and other societies, especially by causing the deaths of tens of millions of people. In the 1930s, however, there was a division of opinion about Nazism and Hitler even before the coming of the Third Reich and its deadly programs.

1. An Author Opposes Nazism

Journalist, playwright, and novelist Lion Feuchtwanger was an early critic of Nazism, tagging it as a movement operating against the goals of democracy and clear thinking. Luckily, when the Nazis came to power in early 1933, Feuchtwanger was on a tour of the United States. The Nazis ransacked his house and burned his writings. On his return to Europe, Feuchtwanger went into exile but was temporarily imprisoned in France when the Nazis invaded. He eventually escaped to the United States, where he continued to write. This critique of Nazism dates from early 1931.

The war [World War I] liberated the barbarian instincts of the individual and society to a degree that was previously unimaginable. National Socialism has skillfully organized the barbarity. Among the intellectuals it is called OBG: Organized Barbarity of Germany.

Anti-logical and anti-intellectual in its being and ideology, National Socialism strives to depose reason and install in its place emotion and drive—to be precise, barbarity. Just because intellect and art are transnational, National Socialism distrusts and hates them to the extreme. . . .

Source: Lion Feuchtwanger, "How Do We Struggle against a Third Reich," January 21, 1931, in Anton Kaes et al., eds., *Weimar Republic Sourcebook* (Berkeley: University of California Press, 1994), 167.

2. Hitler Defends National Socialist Street Activism

Before and after the Nazis took power, storm troopers took to the streets at night, engaging in brawls, beating up Communists (who fought as well), and generally making their noisy presence felt. Their activism reassured some people that something was being done to protect Germany, while others believed that the Nazis were a menace. In this speech to the Industry Club in January 1932, Hitler explained the paramilitary activity and praised the storm troopers.

I know quite well, gentlemen, that when National Socialists march through the streets and suddenly in the evening a tumult and commotion arises, then the bourgeois draws back the window-curtain, looks out, and says: Once more my night's rest disturbed: no more sleep for me. Why must the Nazis always be so provocative and run about the place at night? Gentlemen, if everyone thought like that, then no one's sleep at night would be disturbed, it is true. But then the bourgeois today could not venture out into the street. If everyone thought in that way, if these young folk had no ideal to move them and drive them forward, then certainly they would gladly be rid of these nocturnal fights. But remember that it means sacrifice when today many hundreds of thousands of SA and SS men of the National Socialist movement every day have to mount their trucks, protect meetings, undertake marches, sacrifice themselves night after night, and then come back in the gray dawn either to workshop and factory or as unemployed to take the pittance of the dole. . . . Believe me, there is already in all this the force of an ideal—a great ideal! And if the whole German nation today had the same faith in its vocation as these hundreds of thousands, if the whole nation possessed

out thousands of recordings of Hitler's speeches and other Nazi mementos to German citizens. Teenagers painted their fingernails with swastikas, and soldiers flashed metal match covers with Nazi insignia. Nazi rallies were carefully planned displays in which Hitler captivated the crowds, who saw him as their strong, vastly superior *Führer* ("leader"). Frenzied and inspirational, he seemed neither a calculating politician nor a wooden bureaucrat but a "creative element," as one poet put it. In actuality, however, Hitler regarded the masses with contempt, and in *Mein Kampf* he discussed how to deal with them:

> The receptivity of the great masses is very limited, their intelligence is small. In consequence of these facts, all effective propaganda must be limited to a very few points and must harp on those in slogans until the last member of the public understands what you want him to understand.

Hitler's media techniques were so successful that they continue to influence political campaigns today, particularly in the use of sound bites and simple messages often filled with hate or threats.

In the 1932 elections, both Nazis and Communists did very well, making the leader of one of these two parties the logical choice as chancellor. Influential conservative politicians loathed the Communists for their opposition to private property and favored Hitler as someone they could easily con-this idealism, Germany would stand in the eyes of the world otherwise than she stands now!

Source: Adolf Hitler, "Address to the Industry Club," January 27, 1932, in Anton Kaes et al., eds., *The Weimar Republic Sourcebook* (Berkeley: University of California Press, 1994), 141.

3. A Professor against Hitler

Victor Klemperer was a professor of literature and a Protestant, though his father had been a Jewish rabbi. Once Hitler came to power, Klemperer, a veteran of World War I who was married to an "Aryan" woman, found himself unable to publish his writings and dismissed from his teaching position. During the Third Reich, he kept a journal tracking not only his own mounting difficulties but also the emigration, dismissals, poverty, and suicides of his family and friends. He had clear opinions about Hitler, whom he listened to on the radio, and firm beliefs about the Nazis and Communists.

November 11, 1933 . . . more than forty minutes of Hitler. A mostly hoarse, strained, agitated voice, long passages in the whining tone of the sectarian preachers. . . . "Jews!" want to set nations of millions at one another's throat. I want only peace, I have risen from the common people. I want nothing for myself. . . . etc. in no proper order, impassioned; every sentence mendacious, but I almost believe unconsciously mendacious. The man is a blinkered fanatic.

November 14, 1933 . . . All Germany prefers Hitler to the Communists. And I see no difference between either of the two movements; both are materialistic and lead to slavery.

Source: Victor Klemperer, *I Will Bear Witness: A Diary of the Nazi Years, 1933–1941*, trans. Martin Chalmers (New York: Random House, 1998), 41–42.

4. Praise for Nazis

A year after Hitler came to power, Paula Müller-Otfried, a former deputy to the Reichstag who had opposed both communism and liberalism, sent out this New Year's card.

When I wrote a year ago and saw only a glimmer of hope, I could not possibly have believed . . . my plea would be so richly fulfilled. . . . The vast majority of the *Volk* joyfully summoned the national regime, with its drive to purify public life, to combat unemployment, hunger, and need. . . . We prayed and the answer arrived. May God grant our rulers wisdom. May the "steel-hardened man" for whom we cried out a year ago . . . retain his power.

Source: Quoted in Claudia Koonz, *Mothers in the Fatherland: Women, the Family, and Nazi Politics* (New York: St. Martin's, 1987), 234.

5. Hitler in Prayers

Children in Germany recited the following bedtime prayer, addressed not to God but to Hitler. It expressed a clear view of who Hitler was and what he meant to Germany.

Führer, my Führer, sent to me from God, protect and maintain me throughout my life. Thou who has saved Germany from Deepest need, I thank thee today for my daily bread. Remain at my side and never leave me, Führer, my Führer. My Faith. My light. *Heil, mein Führer!*

Source: Quoted in Claudia Koonz, *Mothers in the Fatherland: Women, the Family, and Nazi Politics* (New York: St. Martin's, 1987), 287.

Questions to Consider

1. **What are the positive qualities attributed to Nazis and their leader?**
2. **What are the major criticisms of Hitler and the Nazis by the opposition?**
3. **To what do you attribute the different opinions about Hitler and the Nazis?**
4. **What aspects of pro-Nazi ideas made them so persuasive and appealing?**

trol. When Hitler was invited to become chancellor in January 1933, he accepted.

The Nazification of German Politics

Millions of Germans celebrated Hitler's ascent to power. "My father went down to the cellar and brought up our best bottles of wine. . . . And my mother wept for joy," one German recalled. "Now everything will be all right." Yet instead of being easy to control, Hitler took command brutally, quickly closing down representative government with an ugly show of force. Tens of thousands of his paramilitary supporters—the Stürmabteilung (SA), or "storm troopers"—paraded through the streets with blazing torches.

Terror in the Nazi State Within a month of Hitler's taking power, the Nazi state was in place. When the Reichstag building was gutted by fire in February 1933, Nazis used the fire as the excuse for suspending civil rights, censoring the press, and prohibiting meetings of other political parties. Hitler had always claimed to hate democracy and diverse political opinions. "Our opponents complain that we National Socialists, and I in particular, are intolerant," he declared. "They are right, we are intolerant! I have set myself one task, namely to sweep those parties out of Germany."

Toys Depicting Nazis
As a totalitarian ideology, Nazism was part of everyday life. Nazi insignia decorated clothing, dishes, cigarette lighters, and even fingernails. Parents sent young people to Nazi clubs and organizations and bought Nazi toys like these for their children's playtime. Nazi songs, Nazi parades and festivals, and Nazi radio programs filled leisure hours. *(Imperial War Museum, London.)*

The storm troopers' violence became a way of life, silencing democratic politicians but also making those who participated in the violence feel part of a glorious whole. At the end of March, intimidated Reichstag delegates let pass the **Enabling Act**, which suspended the constitution for four years and allowed Nazi laws to take effect without parliamentary approval. Solid middle-class Germans approved the Enabling Act as a way to advance the creation of a *Volksgemeinschaft* ("people's community") of like-minded, racially pure Germans—Aryans, the Nazis named them. Heinrich Himmler headed the elite Schutzstaffel (SS), Hitler's "protection squadron," and he commanded the Reich's political police system. The Gestapo, the secret police force run by Hermann Goering, also enforced obedience to Nazism. These organizations had vast powers to arrest people and either execute them or imprison them in concentration camps, the first of which opened at Dachau, near Munich, in March 1933. The Nazis filled it and later camps with political enemies like socialists, and then with Jews, homosexuals, and others said to be enemies of the Volksgemeinschaft. As one Nazi leader proclaimed:

> [National socialism] does not believe that one soul is equal to another, one man equal to another. It does not believe in rights as such. It aims to create the German man of strength, its task is to protect the German people, and all . . . must be subordinate to this goal.

Hitler deliberately blurred authority in the government and party to encourage confusion and competition. He then settled disputes, often with violence. When Ernst Roehm, leader of the SA and Hitler's longtime collaborator, called for a "second revolution" to end the business and military elites' continuing influence on top Nazis, Hitler ordered Roehm's assassination. The bloody Night of the Long Knives (June 30, 1934), during which hundreds of SA leaders and innocent civilians were killed, strengthened the support of the conservative upper classes for the Nazi regime. They saw that Hitler would deal ruthlessly with those favoring a leveling-out of social privilege. Nazism's terrorist politics served as the foundation of Hitler's Third Reich—a German empire grandly advertised as the successor to the First Reich of Charlemagne and the Second Reich of Bismarck and William II.

Nazi Economic and Social Programs

Like violence, new economic programs, especially those putting people back to work, were crucial to the survival of Nazism. Economic revival built popular support, which in turn strengthened the call for German expansion. The Nazi government pursued **pump priming**—that is, stimulating the economy through government spending on tanks and airplanes and on public works programs such as building the Autobahn, or highway system. Unemployment declined from a peak of almost 6 million in 1932 to 1.6 million by 1936. As labor shortages appeared in some sectors, the government drafted single women into forced service as farmworkers and domestics. The Nazi Party closed down labor unions, and government managers determined work procedures and set pay levels, rating women's jobs lower than men's regardless of the level of expertise required. Imitating Stalin, Hitler announced a four-year plan in 1936 with the secret aim of preparing Germany for war by 1940. His programs produced large budget deficits, but he was already planning to conquer and loot neighboring countries to cover the costs.

Enabling Act: The legislation passed in 1933 suspending constitutional government for four years in order to meet the crisis in the German economy.

pump priming: An economic policy used by governments, including the Nazis in Germany, to stimulate the economy through public works programs and other infusions to public funds.

Nazi officials devised policies to control everyday life, including gender roles. In June 1933, a bill took effect that encouraged Aryans (those people defined as racially German) to marry and have children. The bill provided for loans to Aryan newlyweds, but only if the wife left the workforce. The loans were forgiven on the birth of the pair's fourth child. The ideal woman gave up her job, gave birth to many children, and completely surrendered her will to that of her husband, allowing him to feel powerful despite military defeat and economic depression. A good wife "joyfully sacrifices and fulfills her fate," one Nazi leader explained of women's contribution to rebuilding the community.

The government also controlled culture, destroying the rich creativity of the Weimar years. Although 70 percent of households had radios by 1938, programs were severely censored. Books like Erich Maria Remarque's *All Quiet on the Western Front* were banned, and in May 1933 a huge book-burning ceremony rid libraries of works by Jews, socialists, homosexuals, and modernist writers. Modern art in museums and private collections was either destroyed or confiscated. In the Hitler Youth, which boys and girls over age ten were required to join, children learned to report those adults they suspected of disloyalty to the Third Reich, even their own parents. People boasted that they could leave their bicycles out at night without fear of robbery, but their world was filled with informers—some 100,000 of them on the Nazi payroll. In general, the improved economy led many to inflate their belief in Hitler's powers. They saw him working an economic miracle while restoring pride in Germany and strengthening the Aryan community. For hundreds of thousands if not millions of Germans, however, Nazi rule in the 1930s brought anything but harmony and community.

Nazi Racism

The Nazis defined Jews as an inferior "race" dangerous to the superior Aryan "race" and responsible for most of Germany's problems, including defeat in World War I and the economic depression. The reasons for targeting Jews were, Hitler insisted, scientific. "National Socialism is a cool and highly reasoned approach to reality based on the greatest of scientific knowledge," he declared in a 1938 speech. Hitler attacked many ethnic and social groups, but he took anti-Semitism to new and frightening heights. In the rhetoric of Nazism, Jews were "vermin," "abscesses," and "Bolsheviks." They were enemies, biologically weakening the race and plotting Germany's destruction—all of this, given scientific knowledge then and now, utterly false. Thus building community meant eliminating as well as including. By branding Jews both as evil businessmen and as working-class Bolsheviks, Hitler fashioned an enemy for many segments of the population to hate.

Nazis insisted that terms such as *Aryan* and *Jewish* (a religious category) were scientific racial classifications that could be determined by physical characteristics such as the shape of the nose. In 1935, the government enacted the **Nuremberg Laws**, legislation that deprived Jews of citizenship and prohibited marriage between Jews and other Germans. Abortions and birth-control information were readily available to enemy outcast groups, including Jews, Slavs, Sinti and Roma, and mentally or physically disabled people, but were forbidden to women classified as Aryan. In the name of improving the Aryan race, doctors helped organize the T4 project, which used carbon monoxide poisoning and other means to kill large numbers of people—200,000 handicapped and elderly—late in the 1930s. The murder of the disabled aimed to eliminate those whose disability or "racial inferiority" endangered the Aryans. These murders prepared the way for even larger mass exterminations in the future.

Jews were forced into slave labor, evicted from their apartments, and prevented from buying most clothing and food. In 1938, a Jewish teenager, reacting to the harassment of his parents, killed a German official. In retaliation, Nazis and other Germans attacked some two hundred synagogues, smashed windows of Jewish-owned stores, ransacked apartments of known or suspected Jews, and threw more than twenty thousand Jews into prisons and camps. The night of November 9–10 became known as Kristallnacht, or the Night of Broken Glass. Faced with this relentless persecution, more than half of Germany's 500,000 Jews had emigrated by the outbreak of World War II in 1939. Their enormous emigration fees helped finance Germany's economic recovery, while neighbors and individual Nazis used anti-Semitism to justify stealing Jewish property and taking the jobs Jews were forced to leave. Identifying a group as a menacing foe had been an ideological tactic used to foster unity in wartime, but it now became a peacetime tactic that allowed those who stole from Jews to believe they were doing a patriotic service.

REVIEW QUESTION What role did violence play in the Soviet and Nazi regimes?

Nuremberg Laws: Legislation enacted by the Nazis in 1935 that deprived Jewish Germans of their citizenship and imposed many other hardships on them.

Democracies on the Defensive

Nazism, communism, and fascism offered bold new approaches to modern politics. These ideologies maintained that democracy was effeminate and that it wasted precious time in building consensus among all citizens. Totalitarian leaders' energetic military style of mobilizing the masses made representative government and the democratic values of the United States, France, and Great Britain appear feeble—a sign that these societies were on the decline. The appeal of totalitarianism to citizens around the world put democracies on the defensive as they aimed to restore the well-being of citizens while still upholding individual rights and the rule of law.

Confronting the Economic Crisis

As the depression wore on through the 1930s, some governments experimented with ways to solve social and economic crises democratically. The United States and Sweden were among the most successful in facing the double-barreled assault of economic depression and fascism. Other countries, such as France, had less consistently good results, but its short-lived Popular Front government made antifascism and the preservation of democracy its special cause. In the new nations of eastern Europe, however, the economic crisis took such a toll on individual lives that parliamentary government and the rule of law often gave way to dictatorship and worse.

The United States | In the early days of the economic slump, U.S. president Herbert Hoover opposed direct help to the unemployed and even ordered the army to drive away jobless veterans who had marched on Washington, D.C. With unemployment close to fifteen million, Franklin Delano Roosevelt (1882–1945), the wealthy governor of New York, defeated Hoover in the presidential election of 1932 on the promise of relief and recovery. Roosevelt, or FDR as he became known, pushed through a torrent of legislation: relief for businesses, price supports for hard-pressed farmers, and public works programs for unemployed youth. The Social Security Act of 1935 set up a fund to which employers and employees contributed. It provided retirement benefits for workers, unemployment insurance, and payments to dependent mothers, their children, and people with disabilities.

These programs advanced a new kind of state taking shape not only in the United States but elsewhere across the West: the welfare state—that is, a state in which the government guarantees a certain level of economic well-being for individuals and businesses. Roosevelt's "New Deal" angered businesspeople and the wealthy, who saw it as socialist. Even though the depression remained severe, Roosevelt maintained widespread support. Like other successful politicians of the 1930s, he was an expert at using the new mass media, especially in his series of "fireside chats" broadcast by radio to the American people. Unlike Mussolini and Hitler, however, Roosevelt's public statements promoted rather than attacked faith in democratic rights and popular government. The participation of First Lady Eleanor Roosevelt sharply contrasted with the antiwoman ideology of Nazis and Fascists, and the Roosevelts insisted that justice and human rights for all must not be surrendered in difficult times. "We Americans of today . . . are characters in the living book of democracy," Roosevelt told a group of teenagers in 1939. "But we are also its author." Lynchings and other racial violence continued to cause great suffering in the United States during the Roosevelt administration, and the economy did not fully recover, yet the president's new programs and media success were able to keep most Americans' faith in democracy strong.

Sweden | Sweden also developed a coherent program for solving economic and population problems, assigning the government a central role in promoting social welfare and economic democracy. Sweden devalued its currency to make Swedish exports more attractive on the international market. Thanks to pump-priming programs, Swedish productivity rose by 20 percent between 1929 and 1935, a time when other democracies were still experiencing decline.

Sweden addressed the population problem with government programs, but without the racism and coercion of Nazism. Alva Myrdal, a leading member of Sweden's parliament, believed that boosting childbirth depended both on the economy and on individual well-being. It was undemocratic, she maintained, that "the bearing of a child should mean economic distress" to parents. Acting on Myrdal's advice to promote "voluntary parenthood," the government introduced prenatal care, free childbirth in a hospital, a food relief program, and subsidized housing for large families. By the end of the decade, almost 50 percent of all mothers in Sweden received government aid, most effectively in the form of a **family allowance** to help cover the costs of raising children. Long a concern of feminists and other

---

family allowance: Government funds given to families with children to boost the birthrate in democratic countries (e.g., Sweden during the Great Depression) and totalitarian ones alike.

A Fireside Chat with FDR
President Franklin Delano Roosevelt was a master of words, inspiring Americans during the depression and World War II. Aware of its growing power in making politicians look dynamic, the press never showed that Roosevelt was actually confined to a wheelchair (after being paralyzed by polio). Instead, FDR became a symbol of U.S. resolve and might. Here he addresses the nation over a radio hookup on August 23, 1938, while First Lady Eleanor Roosevelt and the president's mother, Sara, observe—a far different image from that of Hitler and Mussolini. *(Hulton Archive/Getty Images.)*

social reformers, support of families became a new feature of the modern state, which now involved itself in promoting citizen well-being. Because all families—rural and urban, poor or prosperous—received these social benefits, there was widespread approval for developing a welfare state.

Britain and France The most powerful democracy, the United States, had withdrawn from world leadership by refusing to participate in the League of Nations, leaving Britain and France with greater responsibility for international peace and well-being than their postwar resources could sustain. When the Great Depression hit, British prime minister Ramsay MacDonald faced a drop in government income. Though leader of the Labour Party, MacDonald reduced payments to the unemployed, and Parliament denied unemployment insurance to women even though they had contributed to the unemployment fund. To protect jobs, the government imposed huge tariffs on imported goods, but these only discouraged a revival of international trade and did not relieve British misery. Finally, in 1933, with the economy continuing to worsen, the government began to take effective steps with massive programs of slum clearance, new housing construction, and health insurance for the needy. British leaders rejected pump-priming methods of stimulating the economy as foolish and thus resorted to them only when all else had failed.

Depression struck later in France, but the country endured a decade of public strife in the 1930s due to postwar demoralization and stagnant population growth. Deputies with opposing solutions to the economic crisis frequently came to blows in the Chamber of Deputies, and administrations were voted in and out with dizzying speed. Parisians took to the streets to protest the government's budget cuts, and Nazi-style paramilitary groups flourished, attracting the unemployed, students, and veterans to the cause of ending representative government. In February 1934, the paramilitary groups joined Communists and other outraged citizens in riots around the parliament building. "Let's string up the deputies," chanted the crowd. "And if we can't string them up, let's beat in their faces, let's reduce them to a pulp." Hundreds of demonstrators were wounded and killed, but the right-wing enemies of democratic government lacked both substantial support outside Paris and a charismatic leader like Hitler or Mussolini to follow.

Shocked into action by fascist violence, French liberals, socialists, and Communists established an antifascist coalition known as the **Popular Front**. Until that time, such a merging of groups had been impossible because Stalin had directed Communists across Europe not to cooperate with other political parties. As fascism attracted followers around the world, however, Stalin reversed his earlier position and allowed Communists to join efforts to protect

---

Popular Front: An alliance of political parties (initially led by Léon Blum in France) in the 1930s to resist fascism despite philosophical differences.

democracy. For just over a year in 1936–1937 and again briefly in 1938, the French Popular Front led the government, with the socialist leader Léon Blum as premier. Like the American New Dealers and the Swedish reformers, the Popular Front instituted social-welfare programs, including family subsidies. Blum appointed women to his government (though women in France were still not allowed to vote). In June 1936, the government guaranteed workers two-week paid vacations, a forty-hour workweek, and the right to bargain collectively. Working people would long remember Blum as the man who improved their living standards and provided them with the right to vacations.

During its brief life, the Popular Front offered citizens a youthful but democratic political culture. "In 1936 everyone was twenty years old," one man recalled, evoking the atmosphere of idealism. To express their opposition to fascism, the French celebrated democratic holidays like Bastille Day with new enthusiasm. Not everyone liked the Popular Front, however, and despite support from workers, Léon Blum's government was politically weak. Bankers and industrialists sent their money out of the country in protest, leaving France financially strapped. "Better Hitler than Blum" was the slogan of the upper classes. Blum's government fell when it lost crucial support for refusing to aid the fight against fascism in Spain. Because of antiwar sentiment, France, like Britain, kept military budgets small and refused any form of military confrontation, even to help the new Spanish republic survive. The collapse of the antifascist Popular Front showed the difficulties that democratic societies had facing the revival of militarism during hard economic times.

Central and Eastern Europe Fledgling democracies in central Europe, hit hard by the depression, also fought the twin struggle for economic survival and representative government, but with little success. In 1932, Engelbert Dollfuss came to power in Austria, dismissing the parliament and ruling briefly as a dictator. Despite his authoritarian stance, Dollfuss would not submit to the Nazis, who stormed his office and assassinated him in 1934 in an unsuccessful coup attempt. In Hungary, where outrage over the Peace of Paris remained intense, a crippled economy allowed right-wing general Gyula Gömbös to take over in 1932. Gömbös reoriented his country's foreign policy toward Mussolini and Hitler. He stirred up anti-Semitism and ethnic hatreds and left considerable pro-Nazi feeling after his death in 1936. In democratic Czechoslovakia, the Slovaks, who were both poorer and less educated than the urbanized Czechs, built a strong Slovak Fascist Party. In many of the new states created by the Peace of Paris, ethnic tensions simmered and the appeal of fascism grew during the Great Depression.

Cultural Visions in Hard Times

Responding to the crisis of hard times and political menace, cultural leaders produced art that captured the spirit of everyday struggle. Some sympathized with the situations of factory workers, homemakers, and shopgirls straining to support themselves and their families; others looked to interpret the lives of an ever-growing number of unemployed and destitute. Artists portrayed the inhuman, regimented, heartless side of modern life. In 1931, French director René Clair's film *Give Us Liberty* likened the routine of prison to work on a factory assembly line. In the film *Modern Times* (1936), the Little Tramp character created by **Charlie Chaplin** is a factory worker so molded by his monotonous job that he assumes anything he can see, even a coworker's body, needs mechanical adjustment.

Media sympathy poured out to other victims of the crisis, with women portrayed alternately as the cause and as the cure for society's problems. *The Blue Angel* (1930), a German film starring Marlene Dietrich, contrasted a powerfully seductive woman with an impractical, bumbling professor, showing how mixed-up gender roles could destroy men — and civilization. Such films worked to strengthen fascist claims. In comedies and musicals, by comparison, heroines behaved bravely, pulling their men out of the depths of despair and setting things right again. In such films as *Keep Smiling* (1938), the British comedienne Gracie Fields portrayed spunky working-class women who remained cheerful despite the challenges of living in hard times. Two years later, Chaplin mocked Hitler in his classic satire *The Great Dictator* (1940), which took a beleaguered Jewish woman as its heroine.

To drive home their antifascist, pacifist, or pro-worker beliefs, writers created realistic studies of human misery and the threat of war that haunted life in the 1930s. The British writer George Orwell described his experiences among the poor of Paris and London, wrote investigative pieces about the unemployed in the north of England, and published an account of atrocities committed by both sides during the Spanish Civil War (1936–1939). German writer Thomas Mann, a Christian, was so

---

Charlie Chaplin (1889–1977): Major entertainment leader, whose sympathetic portrayals of the common man and satires of Hitler helped preserve democratic values in the 1930s and 1940s.

Gracie Fields Keeps Smiling
Like Roosevelt and many cultural leaders during the Great Depression, British star Gracie Fields in the hit film *Shipyard Sally* (1939) urged viewers to be courageous and maintain their respect as workers and citizens despite hard times. This was in stark contrast to fascist advocacy of conquest, war, and violence toward neighbors at home and abroad. *(20th Century Fox/The Kobal Collection.)*

outraged at Hitler's ascent to power that he went into voluntary exile. Mann's series of novels based on the Old Testament hero Joseph convey the struggle between humane values and barbarism. The fourth volume, *Joseph the Provider* (1944), praised Joseph's welfare state, in which the granaries were full and the rich paid taxes so that the poor might live decent lives. In *Three Guineas* (1938), one of her last works, English writer Virginia Woolf attacked militarism, poverty, and the oppression of women, claiming they were interconnected parts of a single, devastating ethos undermining Europe in the 1930s.

While writers revived moral concerns, scientists in research institutes and universities pointed out limits to human understanding—limits that seemed at odds with the megalomaniacal pronouncements of dictators. Astronomer Edwin Hubble in California determined in the early 1930s that the universe was an expanding entity and thus an unpredictably changing one. Czech mathematician Kurt Gödel maintained that all mathematical systems contain some propositions that are undecidable. The German physicist Werner Heisenberg developed the uncertainty, or indeterminacy, principle in physics. Scientific observation of atomic behavior, according to this theory, itself disturbs the atom and thereby makes precise formulations impossible. Even scientists, Heisenberg asserted, had to settle for statistical probability. Approximation, probability, and limits to understanding were not concepts that military dictators welcomed, and even people in democracies had a difficult time reconciling these new ideas with science's reputation for certainty.

Religious leaders helped foster a spirit of resistance to dictatorship among the faithful. Some prominent clergymen hoped for a re-Christianization of ordinary people so that they might choose religious values rather than fascist ones. The Swiss theologian Karl Barth encouraged opposition to the Nazis, teaching that religious people had to take seriously biblical calls for resistance to oppression. In his 1931 address to the world on social issues, Pope Pius XI (r. 1922–1939) condemned the failure of modern societies to provide their citizens with a decent, moral life. To critics, the proclamation seemed an endorsement of the heavy-handed intervention of the fascists. In Germany, nonetheless, German Catholics opposed Hitler, and religious commitment inspired many other individuals to oppose the rising tide of fascism and protect Jews and other fellow citizens whose lives were now threatened.

REVIEW QUESTION **How did the democracies' responses to the twin challenges of economic depression and the rise of fascism differ from those of totalitarian regimes?**

The Road to Global War

The economic crash intensified competition among the major powers and made external colonies more important than ever. Governments did not let up on the collection of taxes in the colonies. As Britain, France, and other imperial powers guarded their holdings, Hitler, Mussolini, and Japan's military leaders believed that their nation's destiny was to rule a far larger territory. At first, statesmen in Britain and France hoped that sanctions imposed by the League of Nations would stop these aggressors. Other people, still traumatized by memories of the past war, wanted to turn a blind eye both to Japanese, Italian, and German expansionism and to the fascist attack on the Spanish republic. The unchecked brutality of these states in the 1930s led to another, more deadly global war.

A Surge in Global Imperialism

The global imperialism of the 1930s ultimately produced a thoroughly global war. The French, Dutch, British, and Belgians increased their control over their colonies, while in Palestine European Jews continued to arrive and claim the area from local peoples especially as Hitler enacted his harsh anti-Jewish policies in 1933. To prevent the arrival of Jews in their own countries, the major European states encouraged emigration to Palestine even as local leaders there regarded the soaring number of immigrants as a major threat. Straining like the colonial powers for resources, including food, at a time of modernization and growing need, Japan, Germany, and Italy escalated the competition for land and wealth—both close at hand and far away.

Japan's Expansionism Japan, which had once borrowed from European institutions to become modern and powerful, now decided to chase Europeans from Asia. Japan's military and business leaders longed to control more of the continent and saw China, the Soviet Union, and the Western powers as obstacles to the empire's prosperity and the fulfillment of its destiny. Japan suffered from a weak monarchy in the person of Hirohito, just twenty-five years old when he became emperor in 1926, which led military and other groups to seek control of the government. Nationalists encouraged these leaders to pursue military success for Japan as the basis of a new world order. They viewed an expanded empire as key to pulling agriculture and small business from the depths of economic depression. A belief in racial superiority and in the right to take the lands of "inferior" peoples linked Japan with Germany and Italy in the 1930s. The groundwork was being laid for a powerful global alliance.

The Japanese army swung into action in 1931, when Japanese officers blew up a train in the Chinese province of Manchuria, where Japanese businesses had invested heavily. The army made the explosion look like a Chinese plot and used it as an excuse to take over the territory, set up a puppet government, and push farther into China (Map 26.1). The Japanese public agreed with journalistic calls for aggressive expansion, and from 1931 on, Japan continued to attack China, angering the United States, on which Japan depended for natural resources and markets. The Japanese military leadership saw its expansionism as fully justified because of unfair Western domination in East Asia. "Unequal distribution of land and resources causes war," an adviser to Hirohito announced to an enthusiastic Japanese public. Advocating Asian conquest as part of Japan's "divine mission," the military solidified its influence in the government. By 1936–1937, Japan was spending 47 percent of its budget on arms.

The situation in East Asia affected international politics. Japanese military success added to the threat Japan posed to the West, because the conquest of new regions gave Japanese goods bigger markets in Asia. The League of Nations condemned the invasion of Manchuria but imposed no sanctions. The league's condemnation outraged Japanese citizens and goaded the government to ally with Hitler and Mussolini. In 1937, Japan attacked China again, justifying its offensive as a first step toward liberating the region from Western imperialism. Hundreds of thousands of Chinese were massacred in the Rape of Nanjing—an atrocity so named because of the Japanese soldiers' brutality, especially toward girls and women. President Roosevelt immediately announced a U.S. embargo on the exportation of airplane parts to Japan and later drastically cut the flow of the crucial raw materials that supplied Japanese industry. Nonetheless, the Western powers, including the Soviet Union, did not effectively resist Japan's territorial expansion in Asia and the Pacific (see Document, "The Greater East Asia Co-Prosperity Sphere," page 892).

Germany and Italy Contest the Status Quo Like Japanese leaders, Mussolini and Hitler called their countries "have-nots" and demanded land and resources more in line with the other imperial powers. Mussolini threatened "permanent conflict" to expand Italy's borders. Hitler's agenda included disregarding the Versailles treaty's restrictions and gaining

MAP 26.1 The Expansion of Japan, 1931–1941
Japanese expansion in the twentieth century approximated that of Russia and the United States in the nineteenth century; that is, it incorporated neighboring regions of Korea, Taiwan, and Manchuria with the vast area of China an inviting target. Japan's ambition upset the United States' own Pacific goals and made these two powers suddenly become deadly rivals.

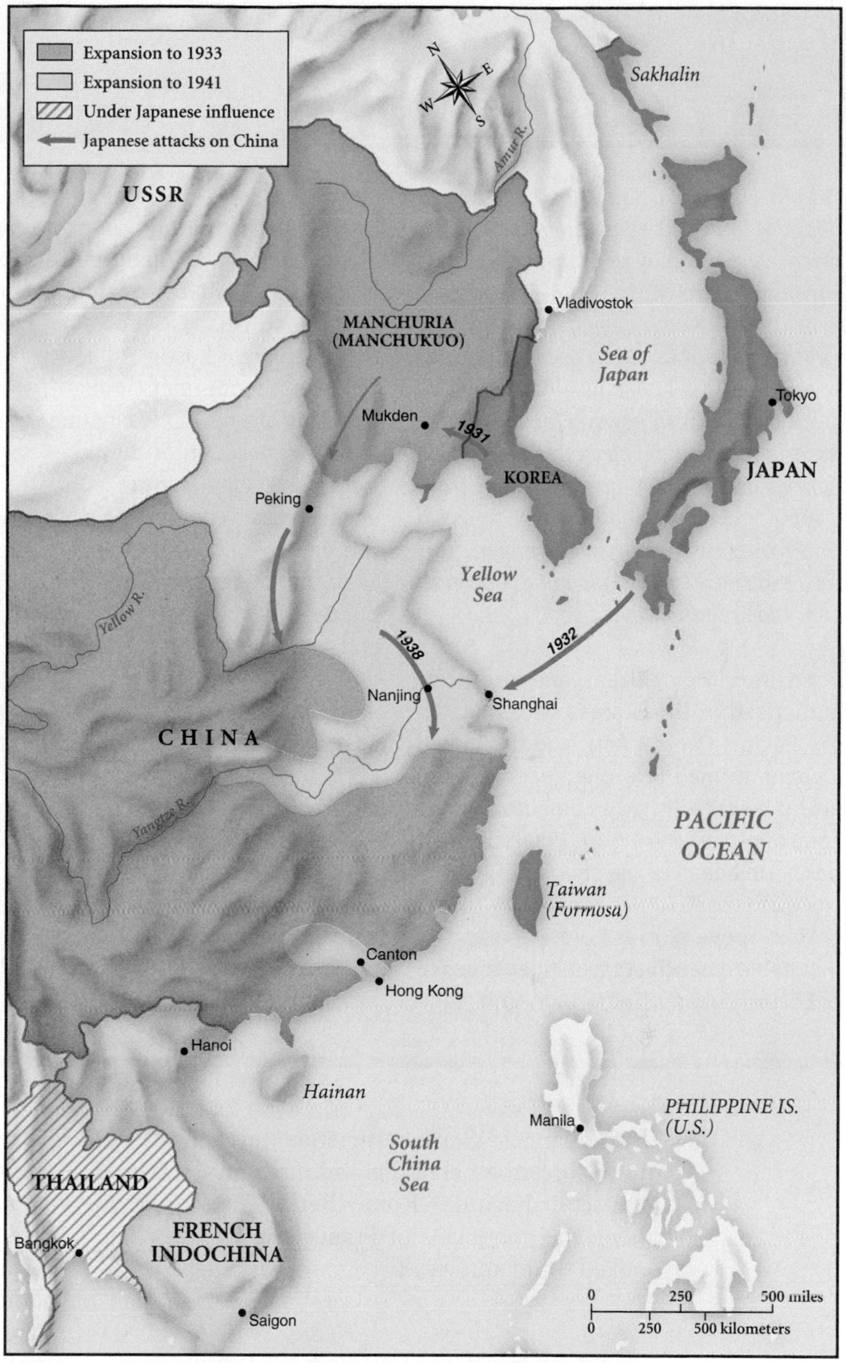

Lebensraum, or living space, in which "superior" Aryans could thrive. This space would be taken from the "inferior" Slavic peoples and Bolsheviks, who would be moved to Siberia or would serve as slaves. The two dictators portrayed themselves as peace-loving men who resorted to extreme measures only to benefit their country and humanity. Their anticommunism appealed to statesmen across the West, and Hitler's anti-Semitism also had widespread support. Many thus favored these two dictators' demands to take land and resources that belonged to others.

Germany and Italy now moved to plunder other countries openly. In the autumn of 1933, Hitler announced Germany's withdrawal from the League of Nations. In 1935, he loudly rejected the clauses of the Treaty of Versailles that limited German military strength. Germany had been rearming in secret for years, but now it started doing so openly. Mussolini chose 1935 to invade Ethiopia, one of the few African states not overwhelmed by European imperialism. He wanted to demonstrate his regime's youth and vigor and to raise Italy's standing in the world. "The Roman legionnaires are again on the march," one soldier exulted. The poorly equipped Ethiopians resisted, but their capital, Addis Ababa, fell in the spring of 1936. Although the League of Nations voted to impose sanctions against Italy, Britain and France opposed an embargo with teeth in it—that is, one including oil—and thus kept the sanctions from being effective while also suggesting a lack of resolve to fight aggression. The fall of Ethiopia and Italy's boastful assertions of African racial inferiority strengthened the resolve of African nationalists.

While the world focused on Italy's Ethiopian campaign, in March 1936 Hitler defiantly sent his troops into what was supposed to be a permanently demilitarized zone in the Rhineland bordering France. The inhabitants greeted the arrival with wild enthusiasm, and the French, whose security was most endangered by this action, protested to the League of Nations instead of occupying the region, as they had done in the Ruhr in 1923. The British simply accepted the German military move.

Lebensraum: Literally, "living space"; the land that Hitler proposed to conquer so that the people he defined as true Aryans might have sufficient space to live their noble lives.

DOCUMENT

The Greater East Asia Co-Prosperity Sphere

During the 1930s, Japan entered a new phase of imperial expansion in the Pacific, after having already taken over Korea and Formosa before World War I. To keep pace with its rapidly developing industrial and military capacities, Japan needed access to raw materials and markets blocked by the U.S. and European powers. Japan justified its expansion in China and other Pacific nations as a move to liberate Asians from Western imperialism and form the so-called Co-Prosperity Sphere for the region. This secret 1942 government planning paper outlines Japan's expansionist goals.

The states, their citizens, and resources, comprised in those areas pertaining to the Pacific, Central Asia, and the Indian Oceans formed into one general union are to be established as an autonomous zone of peaceful living and common prosperity on behalf of the peoples of the nations of East Asia. . . .

The above purpose presupposes the inevitable emancipation or independence of Eastern Siberia, China, Indo-China, the South Seas, Australia, and India. . . . It is intended that the unification of Japan, Manchoukuo, and China in neighborly friendship be realized by the settlement of the Sino-Japanese problems through the crushing of hostile influences in the Chinese interior, and through the construction of a new China in tune with the rapid construction of the Inner Sphere. Aggressive American and British influences in East Asia shall be driven out of the area of Indo-China and the South Seas, and this area shall be brought into our defense sphere. The war with Britain and America shall be prosecuted for that purpose.

The Russian aggressive influence in East Asia will be driven out. Eastern Siberia shall be cut off from the Soviet regime and included in our defense sphere. For this purpose, a war with the Soviets is expected. It is considered possible that this Northern problem may break out before the general settlement of the present Sino-Japanese and the Southern problems if the situation renders this unavoidable. Next the independence of Australia, India, etc. shall gradually be brought about. For this purpose, a recurrence of war with Britain and her allies is expected. . . . Occidental individualism and materialism shall be rejected and a moral world view, the basic principle of whose morality shall be the Imperial Way, shall be established. The ultimate object to be achieved is not exploitation but co-prosperity and mutual help, not competitive conflict but mutual assistance and mild peace, not a formal view of equality but a view of order based on righteous classification, not an idea of rights but an idea of service, and not several world views but one unified world view.

Source: Ryusaku Tsunoda, William Theodore de Bary, and Donald Keene, *Sources of Japanese Tradition* (New York: Columbia University Press, 1958) 802–3, 805.

Question to Consider

- **Although the Japanese government claimed to be acting in the interest of other Asian countries, what language in this document suggests that it had different motives in mind?**

The Italian and German dictators thus appeared as powerful heroes, creating, in Mussolini's muscular phrase, a dynamic "Rome–Berlin Axis." Next to them, the politicians of France and Great Britain looked timid and weak.

The Spanish Civil War, 1936–1939

Spain seemed to be headed toward democracy early in the 1930s. In 1931, Spanish republicans overthrew the monarchy and the dictatorship that ruled in its name. For centuries, the Spanish state had backed the domination of large landowners and the Catholic clergy in the countryside. With some cities, like Barcelona and Bilbao, industrializing, these ruling elites kept an impoverished peasantry in their grip, making Spain a country of economic extremes. Urban people reacted enthusiastically to the end of the dictatorship and began debating the course of change, with constitutionalists, socialists, anarchists, Communists, and other splinter groups disagreeing on how to create a democratic nation. For republicans, the air was electric with promise. As public debate developed, one woman recalled, people sat for hours dreaming dreams: "We saw a backward country suddenly blossoming out into a modern state. We saw peasants living like decent human beings. We saw men allowed freedom of conscience. We saw life, instead of death, in Spain."

With little political experience, however, democratic groups so battled one another to get their way that the republic had a hard time putting in place a political program that would gain support in the countryside. Instead of building popular loyalty and reducing the strength of the right wing by enacting land reform, the various antimonarchist factions struggled among themselves to shape the new government. They wanted political and economic modernization, but they failed to mount a unified effort against their reactionary opponents. The republicans resorted instead to symbolic acts such as releasing political prisoners and handing out coveted mu-

Bombing of Barcelona, 1938
The Spanish Civil War gave fair warning that major wars to come would target civilians as well as soldiers. The forces aiming to overthrow the republic, with the aid of their Fascist allies in Germany and Italy, bombed cities large and small without regard to civilians. This indiscriminate bombing shocked the democracies, though not enough for any of them to intervene. *(AP Photo.)*

nicipal jobs to the urban unemployed. In 1936, growing monarchist opposition frightened the pro-republican forces into forming a Popular Front coalition to win elections and prevent the republic from collapsing.

In response to the Popular Front victory, the forces of the right drew closer together, using their considerable wealth to undermine the government. In 1936, a group of army officers led by General **Francisco Franco** (1892–1975) staged an uprising against the republic in Madrid. The rebels, who included monarchist landowners, the clergy, and the fascist Falange Party, soon had the help of fascists in other parts of Europe. Pro-republican citizens—male and female—fought back, forming armed volunteer units to meet the grave military challenge. In their minds, citizen armies symbolized republicanism, while professional troops followed the aristocratic rebels against democracy. As civil war gripped the country, the republicans generally held Madrid, Barcelona, and other commercial and industrial areas. The right-wing rebels took the agricultural west and south (Map 26.2).

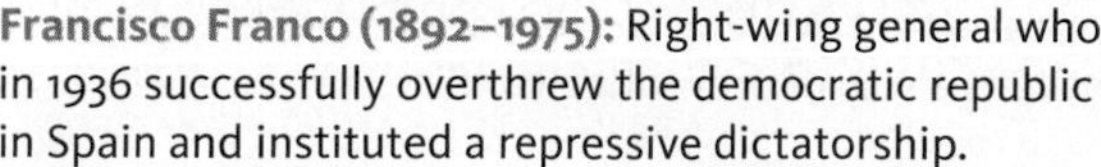

Francisco Franco (1892–1975): Right-wing general who in 1936 successfully overthrew the democratic republic in Spain and instituted a repressive dictatorship.

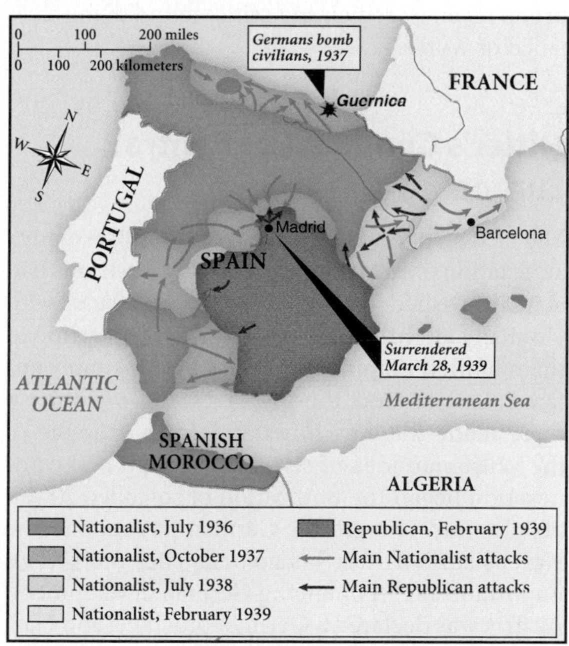

MAP 26.2 The Spanish Civil War, 1936–1939
Republican and antirepublican forces bitterly fought one another to determine whether Spain would be a democracy or an authoritarian state. Germany and Italy sent military assistance to the rebels, notably airplanes to experiment with bombing civilians, while volunteers from around the world arrived to fight for the republic. Defeating the ill-organized republican groups, General Francisco Franco instituted a pro-fascist government that sent many to jail and into exile.

Spain became a training ground for World War II. Hitler and Mussolini sent military personnel in support of Franco, gaining the opportunity to test new weapons and to practice the terror bombing of civilians. In 1937, German planes attacked the town of Guernica, mowing down civilians in the streets. This useless slaughter inspired Pablo Picasso's memorial mural to the dead, *Guernica* (1937), in which the intense suffering is starkly displayed in monochromatic grays and whites. The Spanish republic appealed everywhere for assistance, but only the Soviet Union answered. Stalin withdrew his troops and tanks in 1938 as the republican ranks floundered, however, while Britain and France refused to provide aid despite the outpouring of popular support for the cause of democracy. Instead, a few thousand volunteers from a variety of countries—including many students, journalists, and artists—fought for the republic. With Hitler and Mussolini on a rampage in Europe, "Spain was the place to stop fascism," these volunteers believed. The conflict was bitter and bloody, with widespread atrocities committed on both sides. The splinter groups and random armies with which the Republic defended itself could not hold, however. The aid Franco received helped his professional armies defeat the republicans in 1939, strengthening the cause of military authoritarianism in Europe. Tens of thousands fled Franco's brutal revenge; remaining critics found themselves jailed or worse.

Hitler's Conquest of Central Europe, 1938–1939

The next step toward World War II was Germany's annexation of Austria in 1938. Many Austrians had actually wished for a merger, or *Anschluss*, with Germany after the Paris peace settlement stripped them of their empire. So Hitler's troops simply entered Austria, and the joy of Nazi sympathizers there made the Anschluss appear an example of the Wilsonian idea of self-determination. The annexation began the unification of so-called Aryan peoples into one greater German nation, and the Nazi seizure of Austria's gold supplies marked an important step in financing German development. Austria was declared a German province, and Nazi thugs ruled once-cosmopolitan Vienna. An observer later commented on the scene:

> University professors were obliged to scrub the streets with their naked hands, pious white-bearded Jews were dragged into the synagogue by hooting youths and forced to do knee-exercises and to shout "Heil Hitler" in chorus.

Nazis gained additional support in Austria by attacking the stubborn problem of unemployment—especially among the young and out-of-work rural migrants to the cities. Factories sprang up overnight, mostly to foster rearmament, and new "Hitler housing" was made available to workers. "We were given work!" Austrians continued to say long afterward, defending their enthusiasm for the Third Reich. German policies eliminated some of the pain Austrians had suffered when their empire had been reduced to a small country after World War I.

With Austria firmly in his grasp, Hitler turned next to Czechoslovakia and its rich resources. Conquering this democracy looked more difficult, however, because Czechoslovakia had a large army, strong border defenses, and efficient armament factories—and most Czech citizens were prepared to fight for their country. The Nazi propaganda machine swung into action, accusing Czechoslovakia of persecuting its German minority. By October 1, 1938, Hitler warned, Czechoslovakia would have to grant autonomy (amounting to Nazi rule) to the German-populated border region, the Sudetenland, or face German invasion.

Hitler gambled correctly that the other Western powers would choose **appeasement**, the prevention of conflict by making concessions for grievances (in this case, the treatment of Germany in the Treaty of Versailles). As the October deadline approached, British prime minister Neville Chamberlain, French premier Edouard Daladier, and Mussolini met with Hitler at Munich and agreed not to oppose Germany's claim to the Sudetenland. Appeasement was widely seen as positive at the time, and the Munich Pact prompted Chamberlain to announce that he had secured "peace in our time." Having portrayed himself as a man of peace, Hitler waited until March 1939 to invade the rest of Czechoslovakia (Map 26.3). Britain and France responded by promising military support to Poland, Romania, Greece, and Turkey in case of Nazi invasion. In May 1939, Hitler and Mussolini countered this agreement by signing a pledge of mutual assistance called the Pact of Steel.

Some historians have sharply criticized the Munich Pact because it bought Hitler time to build his army and seemed to give him the green light for further aggression. They believe that a confrontation might have stopped Hitler and that even if war had resulted, the democracies would have triumphed at less cost than they later did. According to this view, each military move by Germany, Italy,

---

appeasement: Making concessions in the face of grievances as a way of preventing conflict.

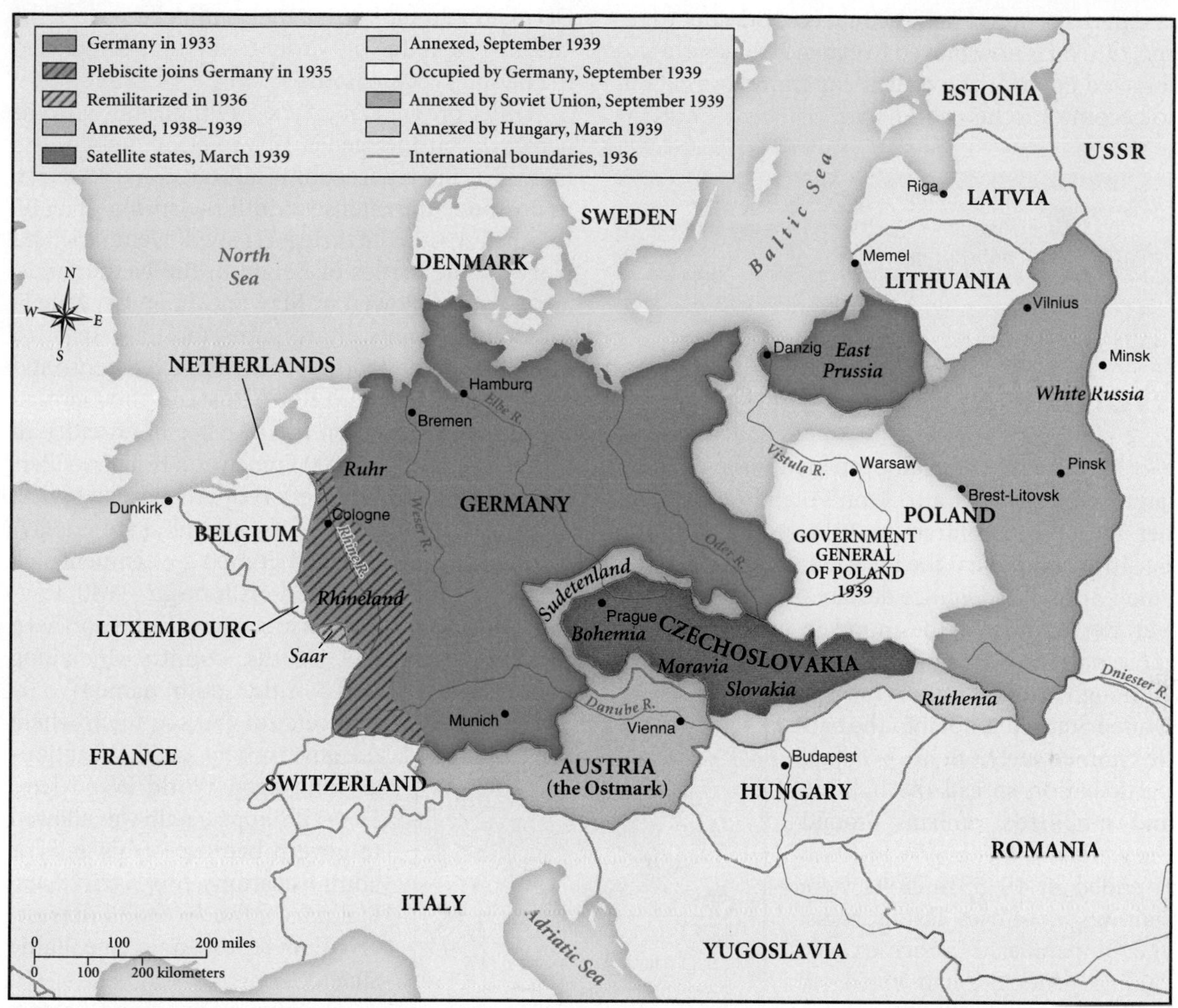

MAP 26.3 The Growth of Nazi Germany, 1933–1939
German expansion was rapid and surprising, as Hitler's forces and Nazi diplomacy achieved the annexation of several new states of central and eastern Europe. Although committed to defending the independence of these states through the League of Nations, French and British diplomats were more concerned with satisfying Hitler in the mistaken belief that doing so would prevent his claiming more of Europe. In the process, Hitler acquired the human and material resources of adjacent countries to support his Third Reich. | **What is the relationship between Germany's expansion during the 1930s and the terms of the Treaty of Versailles after World War I?**

and Japan should have been met with stiff opposition, and the Soviet Union should have been made a partner to this resistance. Others counter that appeasement provided France and Britain precious time to beef up their own armies, which the Munich Pact led them to do.

Stalin, excluded from the Munich deliberations, saw that the democracies were not going to fight to protect eastern Europe. He took action. To the astonishment of people in the West, on August 23, 1939, Germany and the USSR signed a nonaggression agreement. The **Nazi-Soviet Pact** provided that if one country became embroiled in war, the other country would remain neutral. Moreover, the two dictators secretly agreed to divide Poland and the Baltic states—Latvia, Estonia, and Lithuania—at some future date. The Nazi-Soviet Pact ensured that, should war come, the democracies would be fighting a Germany that feared no attack on its eastern borders. The pact also benefited the USSR. Despite Hitler's threats to wipe Bolshevism from the face of the earth, the pact allowed Stalin extra time to reconstitute his officer corps, which had been wiped out by the purges. In the belief that Great Britain

Nazi-Soviet Pact: The agreement reached in 1939 by Germany and the Soviet Union in which both agreed not to attack the other in case of war and to divide any conquered territories.

and perhaps even France would continue not to resist, the Nazis now moved to expand even more and targeted Poland. The contest for empire was about to become another world war.

REVIEW QUESTION How did the aggression of Japan, Germany, and Italy create the conditions for global war?

World War II, 1939–1945

World War II officially opened when Hitler launched an all-out attack on Poland on September 1, 1939. In contrast to 1914, no jubilation in Berlin accompanied the invasion; when Britain and France declared war two days later, the mood in those nations was similarly grim. Although Japan, Italy, and the United States did not join the battle immediately, their eventual participation spread the fighting and mobilized civilians around the world. By the time World War II ended in 1945, millions were starving; countries lay in ruins; and unparalleled atrocities, including genocide, had killed six million Jews and six million Slavs, Sinti and Roma, homosexuals, and other civilian targets of fascism.

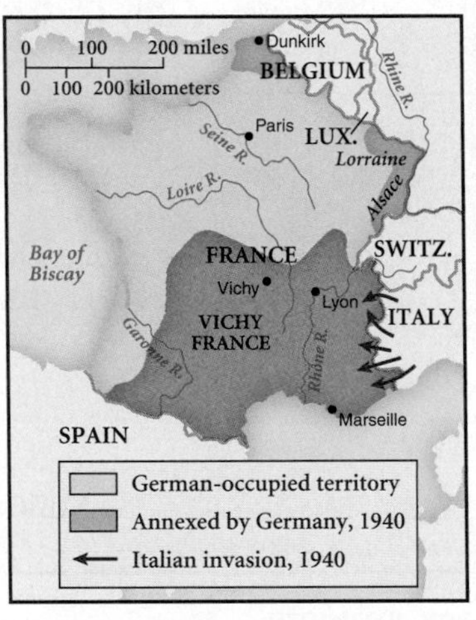

The Division of France, 1940

The German Onslaught

German forces quickly defeated the ill-equipped Polish troops by launching a **Blitzkrieg** ("lightning war"), in which they concentrated airplanes, tanks, and motorized infantry to encircle Polish defenders and capture the capital, Warsaw, with overpowering force and blinding speed. Allowing the army to conserve supplies, Blitzkrieg suggested to Germans at home that the costs of gaining Lebensraum would be low. On September 17, 1939, the Soviets invaded Poland from the east. By the end of the month, the Polish army was in shambles and the victors had divided the country according to the Nazi-Soviet Pact. Nazi propagandists frightened Germans into supporting the conflict because of the "warlike menace" of world Jewry that threatened the nation's very existence.

Hitler ordered an attack on France for November 1939, but his generals, who feared that Germany was ill prepared for total war, convinced him to postpone the offensive until the spring of 1940. In April 1940, Blitzkrieg crushed Denmark and Norway; the battles of Belgium, the Netherlands, and France followed in May and June. On June 5, Mussolini, eyeing future gains for Italy, invaded France from the southeast. The French defense and its British allies could not withstand the German onslaught. Trapped on the beaches of Dunkirk in northern France, 370,000 French and British soldiers were rescued in a heroic effort by an improvised fleet of naval ships, fishing boats, and pleasure craft. A dejected French government surrendered on June 22, 1940, leaving Germany to rule the northern half of the country, including Paris. In the south, named Vichy France after the spa town where the government sat, the reactionary and aged World War I hero Henri Philippe Pétain was allowed to govern because of his and his administration's pro-Nazi values. Stalin used the diversion in western Europe to annex the Baltic states.

Britain now stood alone. Blaming Germany's rapid victories on Chamberlain's policy of appeasement, the British swept him out of office and installed as prime minister Winston Churchill (1874–1965), an early campaigner for resistance to Hitler. After Hitler ordered the bombardment of Britain in the summer of 1940, Churchill rallied the nation by radio — now in millions of British homes — to protect the ideals of liberty with their "blood, toil, tears, and sweat." In the battle of Britain — or Blitz, as the British called it — the German Luftwaffe ("air force") bombed monuments, public buildings, weapons depots, and industry. Using the wealth of its colonies, Britain poured resources into antiaircraft weapons, its highly successful code-breaking group called Ultra, and further development of radar. At year's end, the British air industry was outproducing the Germans by 50 percent.

By the fall of 1940, German air losses forced Hitler to abandon his plan for a naval invasion of Britain. By forcing Hungary, Romania, and Bulgaria to join the Axis powers, Germany gained access to more food, oil, and other resources. He then made

---

Blitzkrieg: Literally, "lightning war"; a strategy for the conduct of war (used by the Germans in World War II) in which motorized firepower quickly and overwhelmingly attacks the enemy, leaving it unable to resist psychologically or militarily.

his fatal decision to attack the Soviet Union — the "center of judeobolshevism," he called it. In June 1941, the German army crossed the Soviet border, breaking the Nazi-Soviet Pact, and Hitler promised to "raze Moscow and Leningrad to the ground." Three million German and other troops quickly penetrated Soviet lines along a two-thousand-mile front, and by July, the German army had rolled to within two hundred miles of Moscow. Using a strategy of rapid encirclement, German troops killed, captured, or wounded more than half the 4.5 million Soviet soldiers defending the border.

Amid success, Hitler blundered. Considering himself a military genius and the Slavic people inferior, he proposed attacking Leningrad, the Baltic states, and the Ukraine simultaneously, even though his generals wanted to concentrate on Moscow. Hitler's grandiose strategy cost precious time without achieving a decisive victory, and driven by Stalin and local party members, the Soviet people fought back. The onset of winter turned Nazi soldiers into frostbitten wretches because Hitler had feared that equipping his army for Russian conditions would suggest to civilians that a long campaign lay ahead. Yet Hitler remained so convinced of a quick victory in the USSR that he switched German production from making tanks and artillery to making battleships and airplanes for war beyond the Soviet Union. Consequently, Germany's poorly supplied armies fell victim not only to the weather but also to a shortage of equipment. As the war became worldwide, Germany had an inflated view of its own power even though the Russian campaign demonstrated that this view was a fantasy.

War Expands: The Pacific and Beyond

With the outbreak of war in Europe, Japan occupied territories of the British Empire and invaded French Indochina to procure raw materials for its industrial and military expansion. The militarist Japanese government decided to settle matters once and for all with the United States, which was blocking Japan's access to technology and resources in an attempt to stop its expansionism. On December 7, 1941, it launched an all-out attack on the United States at Pearl Harbor in Hawaii. After bombing Pearl Harbor, Japanese planes then decimated a fleet of airplanes in the Philippines. Roosevelt immediately summoned the U.S. Congress to declare war on Japan. By the spring of 1942, the Japanese had conquered Guam, the Philippines, Malaya, Burma, Indonesia, Singapore, and much of the southwestern Pacific. Like Hitler's early conquests, the Japanese victories strengthened the military's confidence: "The era of democracy is finished," the foreign minister announced. Officials marketed Emperor Hirohito to conquered peoples as the pan-Asian monarch who would liberate Asians everywhere.

Germany quickly joined its Japanese ally and declared war on the United States — an enemy, Hitler proclaimed, that was "half Judaized and the other half Negrified." Mussolini followed suit. The United States was not prepared for a prolonged struggle at the time, partly because isolationist sentiment remained strong. Its armed forces numbered only 1.6 million, and no plan existed for producing the necessary guns, tanks, and airplanes. In addition, the United States and the Soviet Union mistrusted each other. Yet despite these obstacles to cooperation, Hitler's four enemies came together in the Grand Alliance of Great Britain, the Free French (an exile government in London led by General Charles de Gaulle), the Soviet Union, and the United States.

The Grand Alliance formed a larger coalition with twenty other countries — known collectively as the Allies. It had to overcome animosity and competing interests among its members in its struggle against the Axis powers — Germany, Italy, and Japan. Yet in the long run, the Allies had advantages: greater manpower and resources and access to goods from their global empires. The globalization of the war brought into play Britain's traditional naval strength and its leaders' and troops' experience in combat on many continents. Meeting frequently, Allied leaders worked hard to wage effective war against the Axis powers, whose rulers were fanatically committed to global conquest at any price.

The War against Civilians

Far more civilians than soldiers died in World War II. The Axis powers and Allies alike bombed cities simply to destroy civilian will to resist — a tactic that seemed to backfire by inspiring defiance rather than surrender. Two such Allied attacks were the firebombing of Dresden and Tokyo, which killed tens of thousands of civilians, though Axis attacks were more widespread. The British people, not British soldiers, were the target of the battle of Britain, and as the German army swept through eastern Europe, it slaughtered Jews, Communists, Slavs, and others Nazi ideology defined as "racial inferiors" and enemies. In Poland and Ukraine, the SS murdered hundreds of thousands of Polish citizens or relocated them to forced-labor camps. Confiscated Polish land and homes were given to "racially pure" Aryans from Germany and other central European countries. In the name of collectivization, Soviet

Life in the Warsaw Ghetto
The occupying Nazis resettled Warsaw's Jews into a minuscule area of the city in order, the Germans explained, to bring moral purification and to keep Germans from being infected by these "carriers of the bacteria of epidemics." Living with bare amounts of food, Warsaw's Jews died daily on the streets. Corpses were a regular sight for the average citizen—young or old. *(ullstein bild/The Granger Collection, New York.)*

forces perpetuated the same violence in the same area of eastern Europe, which has been called the Bloodlands for the millions who died there at the hands of both Nazis and Soviets.

Nazi and Soviet leaders saw literate people in the conquered areas as leading members of the civil society that they wanted to destroy. A ploy of the Nazis was to test captured people's reading skills, suggesting that those who could read would be given clerical jobs while those who could not would be relegated to hard labor. Those who could read, however, were lined up and shot. Because many in the German army initially rebelled at this inhuman mission, special Gestapo forces took up the charge of herding their victims into woods, to ravines, or even against town walls where they would be shot en masse. The Japanese did the same in China, in Southeast Asia, and on the islands in the Pacific. The number of casualties in China alone has been estimated at thirty million, with untold millions murdered elsewhere.

The Holocaust On the eve of war in 1939, Hitler had predicted "the destruction of the Jewish race in Europe." The Nazis' initial plan for reducing the Jewish population included driving Jews into urban ghettos, stripping them of their possessions, and making people live on minimal rations until they died of starvation or disease. There was also direct murder. Around Soviet towns, Jews were usually shot in pits, some of which they had been forced to dig themselves. After making people shed their clothes, which were put in ordered piles for later use, the Nazis killed ten thousand or more at a time, often with the help of local anti-Semitic volunteers. In Jedwabne, Poland, and surrounding towns in 1941, some eight hundred citizens on their own initiative beat and burned their Jewish neighbors to death and took their property—evidence that the Holocaust was not simply a Nazi initiative. However, the "Final Solution"—the Nazis' plan to murder all of Europe's Jews more systematically—was not yet fully under way.

An organized, technological system for rounding up Jews and transporting them to extermination sites had taken shape by the fall of 1941 and was formalized at a meeting in Wannsee, Germany, in January 1942. Although Hitler did not attend the meeting at Wannsee, his responsibility for the Holocaust is clear: he discussed the Final Solution's progress, issued oral directives for it, and made violent anti-Semitism a basis for Nazism from the beginning. Scientists, doctors, lawyers, government workers, and Nazi officials took initiative in making the Holocaust work. Six camps in Poland were developed specifically for the purposes of mass murder, though some, like Auschwitz-Birkenau, served as both extermination and labor camps (Map 26.4). Using techniques developed in the T4 project, which killed disabled and elderly people, the camp at Chelmno first gassed Christian Poles and Soviet prisoners of war. Specially designed crematoria for the mass burning of corpses started functioning in 1943. By then, Auschwitz had the capacity to burn

MAP 26.4 Concentration Camps and Extermination Sites in Europe

This map shows the major extermination sites and concentration camps in Europe, but the entire continent was dotted with thousands of lesser camps to which the victims of Nazism were transported. Some of these lesser camps were merely way stations on the path to ultimate extermination. In focusing on the major camps, historians often lose sight of the ways in which evidence of deportation and extermination blanketed Europe.

Children in Concentration Camps, c. 1945

When Germany undertook the Holocaust and ethnic cleansing, children of outcast groups were generally automatic victims, unless they seemed useful for medical experiments. Great numbers of children died of starvation in occupied and besieged areas or were killed when the Germans exacted reprisals for acts of resistance. Teenagers were used as slave laborers; the children in this picture may be older than they look because of starvation. *(Mary Evans/Alinari Archives.)*

1.7 million bodies per year. About 60 percent of new arrivals—particularly children, women, and old people—were selected for immediate murder in the gas chambers; the other 40 percent labored until, utterly used up, they too were gassed.

Death and Life in the Camps Victims from all over Europe were sent to extermination camps. In the ghettos of various European cities, councils of Jewish leaders, such as the one in Amsterdam where Etty Hillesum worked, were to choose those to be sent for "resettlement in the east"—a phrase used to mask the Nazis' true plans. For weakened, poorly armed ghetto inhabitants, open resistance meant certain death. When Jews rose up against their Nazi captors in Warsaw in 1943, they were mercilessly butchered. The Nazis also took pains to cloak the purpose of the extermination camps. Bands played to greet incoming trainloads of victims, and survivors later noted that the purpose of the camps was so unthinkable that potential victims could not begin to imagine their fate. Those not chosen for immediate murder had their heads shaved, were disinfected, and were then given prison garments—many of them used and so thin that they offered no protection against winter cold and rain. So began life in "a living hell," as one survivor wrote.

The camps were scenes of struggle for life in the face of torture and death. Instead of the minimum calories needed to keep an adult in good health, overworked inmates usually received less than five hundred calories per day, leaving them vulnerable to the diseases that swept through the camps. Prisoners sometimes went mad, as did many of the guards. In the name of advancing "racial science," doctors performed unbelievably cruel medical experiments with no anesthesia on pregnant women, twins, and other innocent people. Despite the harsh conditions, however, some people maintained their spirit: prisoners forged new friendships, and women in particular observed religious holidays and celebrated birthdays—all of which helped the struggle for survival. Thanks to those sharing a bread ration, wrote the Auschwitz survivor Primo Levi, "I managed not to forget that I myself was a man." In the end, six million Jews, the vast majority from eastern Europe—along with an estimated five to six million Slavs, Sinti and Roma, homosexuals, and countless others—were murdered in the Nazi genocidal fury. The bureaucratic organization of this vast crime perpetrated by apparently civilized people still shocks and outrages the world. (See "New Sources, New Perspectives," page 901.)

Societies at War

Even more than World War I, World War II depended on industrial productivity aimed at war and mass killings. The Axis countries remained at a disadvantage throughout the war despite their initial conquests, for the Allies simply outproduced them (Figure 26.1). Even while Germany occupied the Soviet industrial heartland and besieged many of its cities, the USSR increased its production of weapons. Both Japan and Germany made the most of their lower output, especially in the use of Blitzkrieg, but they faced other problems: Hitler had to avoid imposing wartime austerity because he had come to power promising prosperity, not more economic suffering. The use of vast quantities of stolen resources and of millions of slave laborers said to be inferior helped, but both Japan's and Germany's belief in their racial superiority worked against them by preventing them from accurately assessing the capabilities of an enemy they held in contempt.

Allied governments were overwhelmingly successful in mobilizing civilians, especially women. In Germany and Italy, where government policy particularly exalted motherhood and kept women from good jobs, officials began to realize that women were desperately needed in the workforce. Nazis changed their propaganda to emphasize the need for everyone to take a job, but their messages were not effective enough to convince women to take the low-paid work offered them. In contrast, Soviet women constituted more than half the workforce by war's end, and 800,000 volunteered for the military, even serving as pilots. As the Germans invaded, Soviet citizens moved entire factories eastward. In a dramatic about-face, the government encouraged devotion to the Russian Orthodox church as a way of boosting morale and patriotism.

Even more than in World War I, civilians faced huge amounts of propaganda when they listened to the radio or went to the movies. People were glued to their radios for war news, but much of it was tightly controlled. The totalitarian powers often withheld news of military defeats and large casualty numbers in order to keep civilian support. Wartime films focused on aviation heroes and infantrymen as well as on the self-sacrificing workingwomen and wives on the home front. Government agencies practiced censorship by allocating supplies only to films whose scripts they liked.

Between 1939 and 1945, governments organized many aspects of everyday life — a necessity because resources such as food had to be shifted away from civilians toward the military. In most countries, it

FIGURE 26.1 Weapons Production of the Major Powers, 1939–1945
World War II devoured people and weapons, necessitating dramatic changes in the workforce and everyday life. Because agricultural production was often hit hard by invading forces, people lived on reduced rations. Raw materials were channeled into the manufacture of weapons, and it was the real difference in productivity that spelled victory for the Allies: Germany and Japan were outproduced in almost every category. *(From* The Hammond Atlas of the Twentieth Century *[London: Times Books, 1996], 103.)*

	1939	1940	1941	1942	1943	1944	1945
Aircraft							
Great Britain	7,940	15,049	20,094	23,672	26,263	26,461	12,070
United States	5,856	12,804	26,277	47,826	85,998	96,318	49,761
USSR	10,382	10,565	15,735	25,436	34,900	40,300	20,900
Germany	8,295	10,247	11,776	15,409	24,807	39,807	7,540
Japan	4,467	4,768	5,088	8,861	16,693	28,180	11,066
Major Vessels							
Great Britain	57	148	236	239	224	188	64
United States	—	—	544	1,854	2,654	2,247	1,513
USSR	—	33	62	19	13	23	11
Germany (U-boats only)	15	40	196	244	270	189	0
Japan	21	30	49	68	122	248	51
Tanks							
Great Britain	969	1,399	4,841	8,611	7,476	5,000	2,100
United States	—	c. 400	4,052	24,997	29,497	17,565	11,968
USSR	2,950	2,794	6,590	24,446	24,089	28,963	15,400
Germany	c. 1,300	2,200	5,200	9,200	17,300	22,100	4,400
Japan	c. 200	1,023	1,024	1,191	790	401	142

NEW SOURCES, NEW PERSPECTIVES

Museums and Memory

Historical monuments and museums that house historical artifacts are testimonials to historical events because they provide records of those events and show that people were deeply moved by them. But is the impression conveyed by a tragic photo or the memory of an event the same as its history? For the most part, historians regard photographs and oral testimony as legitimate kinds of evidence. However, many judge institutions such as Holocaust museums to be only partially about the history of the Holocaust. Instead, a Holocaust museum tells a great deal about the nation or group that builds it. It tells about the "memory" that the nation or group wants people to have of the Holocaust.

The complicated development of Holocaust memorials is instructive to historians. Some Holocaust memory sites sprang up spontaneously in concentration camps as memorials constructed by survivors themselves. Stones, writings, plaques, flowers and plants, and other objects were used to testify to what had happened in the camp. In many cases, these initial memorials were replaced when local and national governments stepped in to take over the site, sometimes waiting years between destroying the spontaneous memorials and replacing them with an official one. The concentration camp at Dachau, near Munich, fell into disrepair until a group of survivors, including many Catholic clergy, demanded that the camp be made into a permanent museum and memorial, with the crematorium and other grisly features preserved. Although townspeople and local government resisted, Dachau and its crematorium became one of the most visited camps and indeed came to symbolize the Holocaust in all its horror. Yet Dachau was not primarily an extermination site for Jews, Slavs, and Sinti and Roma but rather a grim concentration camp where Hitler put political prisoners, many of them Catholic clergy. It is so often visited because it is on the tourist route, close to a beautiful city. Indeed, one of the plaques in this on-site museum invites visitors to tour other cultural institutions and scenery of the area while another asks them to remember that vast numbers of those interned at Dachau were Polish and Catholic. Historians need to take into account all of these factors in the politics of memories—official and unofficial, competing and contested.

In the case of Holocaust museums, official memories can clash with memories of actual survivors who, for instance, may not like what is often the most aesthetic or avant-grade in terms of art and architecture. Survivors have generally rejected abstract art, feeling that a more realistic depiction of their suffering is more authentic. The architectural design of the American Holocaust Museum was redone so that it would not look grimly out of place but would instead fit in with the tranquil style of the central museum mall in Washington, D.C., and thus be another tourist attraction. Historians question the way certain objects like shoes or eyeglasses are displayed to create a certain memory effect. They note that costume designers puff up prison uniforms to make them look more lifelike and to stir people emotionally.

Holocaust museums offer a powerful, vivid, and emotionally charged experience of history. In contrast, historians pride themselves on eliminating emotions and biases in ascertaining facts, calculating cause and effect, and reaching historical judgments. Though each provides an important representation of the past, the relationship between memory and history remains fraught with questions—and never more so than in the case of the Holocaust.

Questions to Consider

1. What is the difference between a history textbook and a historical monument?
2. Do you trust a history book more than you trust a museum? How do people compare and evaluate the presentation of the past in either one?
3. Why might museums and public exhibitions of art and artifacts arouse more debate than history books might?

Further Reading

Marcuse, Harold. *Legacies of Dachau: The Uses and Abuses of a Concentration Camp, 1933–2001*. 2001.

Sherman, Daniel J., and Irit Rogoff, eds. *Museum Culture: Histories, Discourses, Spectacles*. 1994.

Young, James Edward. *At Memory's Edge: After-Images of the Holocaust in Contemporary Art and Architecture*. 2000.

Jewish Museum Berlin

Among the latest of the museums dedicated to the Holocaust was this one, which opened in 2001 in Berlin—the heart of Nazi Germany. Architect Daniel Libeskind, a Polish Jew who lost many family members in the Holocaust, hoped the museum would serve not only as a memorial to Jewish deaths but also as a celebration of Jewish life and culture. What features on the museum's exterior stand out? *(© Jewish Museum Berlin. Photo: Jens Ziehe.)*

was simply taken for granted that civilians would not receive what they needed to survive in good health. Soviet children and old people were at the greatest risk, a high proportion of them among the one million residents who starved to death during the siege of Leningrad. Statisticians and other specialists in government regulated the production and distribution of food, clothing, and household products, all of which were rationed and generally of lower quality than before the war. They gave hints for meals without meat, sugar, and fat and urged women and children to embrace deprivation so that their fighting men would have more. With governments standardizing such items as food, clothing, and entertainment, World War II furthered the development of mass society in which people lived and thought in similar ways.

On both sides, propaganda and government policies promoted racial thinking. Since the early 1930s, the German government had published ugly caricatures of Jews and Slavs. Similarly, Allied propaganda during the war depicted Germans as perverts and the "Japs" as insectlike fanatics. The U.S. government forced citizens of Japanese origin into internment camps, while Muslims and minority ethnic groups in the Soviet Union were uprooted and relocated away from the front lines as potential Nazi collaborators. As in World War I, both sides drew colonized peoples into the war through forced labor and conscription into the armies. Some two million Indian men served the Allied cause, as did several hundred thousand Africans. As the Japanese swept through the Pacific and parts of East Asia, they, too, conscripted local men into their army.

Hidden Revolver

Resistance to Nazism took many forms, from the uprising in Warsaw to small acts of protest to assassinations of Nazi officers and collaborators. In a militarized state with informers everywhere, retaliation against Nazis sparked human ingenuity, whether in obtaining enough food or killing the enemy. Weapons were hidden in baby carriages, under clothing, or in books—as in this example from the Dutch resistance. *(Erich Lessing/Art Resource, NY.)*

From Resistance to Allied Victory

Resistance to fascism began early in the war. Having escaped from France to London in 1940, General Charles de Gaulle directed from a distance the Free French government and its forces—a mixed organization of troops of colonized Asians and Africans, soldiers who had escaped via Dunkirk, and volunteers from other occupied countries. Meanwhile, Allied forces started tightening a noose around the Axis powers in mid-1942 (Map 26.5), and Allied victory began to look certain by 1943. At the same time, civilian resistance in the Nazi-occupied areas further pressured the Axis. Still, Hitler and Nazi officials continued to promote an unrealistic expectation of German victory, announcing, for example, that the United States was "a big bluff." Bluster could not win the war, however, and the Allies, squeezing Germany from east and west and crushing the Japanese in the Pacific, brought the war to an end in 1945.

Civilian Resistance Less well-known than the Free French, resisters in occupied Europe fought in Communist-dominated groups, some of which gathered information to aid the Allied invasion of the continent. Rural groups called partisans, or in France the *maquis*, planned assassinations of traitors and German officers and bombed bridges, rail lines, and military facilities. Although the Catholic church supported Mussolini in Italy and endorsed the Croatian puppet government's slaughter of a million Serbs, Catholic and Protestant clergy and their parishioners were among those who set up resistance networks, often hiding Jews and fugitives. The Polish resistance worked tirelessly against the Nazis, as did individuals such as Swedish diplomat Raoul Wallenberg, whose dealings with Nazi officials saved thousands of Hungarian Jews.

People also fought back through everyday activities. Homemakers circulated newsletters urging demonstrations at prisons where civilians were detained. In central Europe, hikers smuggled Jews and others over dangerous mountain passes. Danish villagers created vast escape networks, and countless thousands across Europe volunteered to be part of escape routes. Women resisters used stereotypes to good advantage, often carrying weapons to assassination sites in the correct belief that Nazis would rarely suspect or search them. They also seduced and murdered enemy officers. "Naturally the Germans didn't think that a woman could have carried a bomb," explained one Italian resister, "so this became the woman's task." Resistance kept

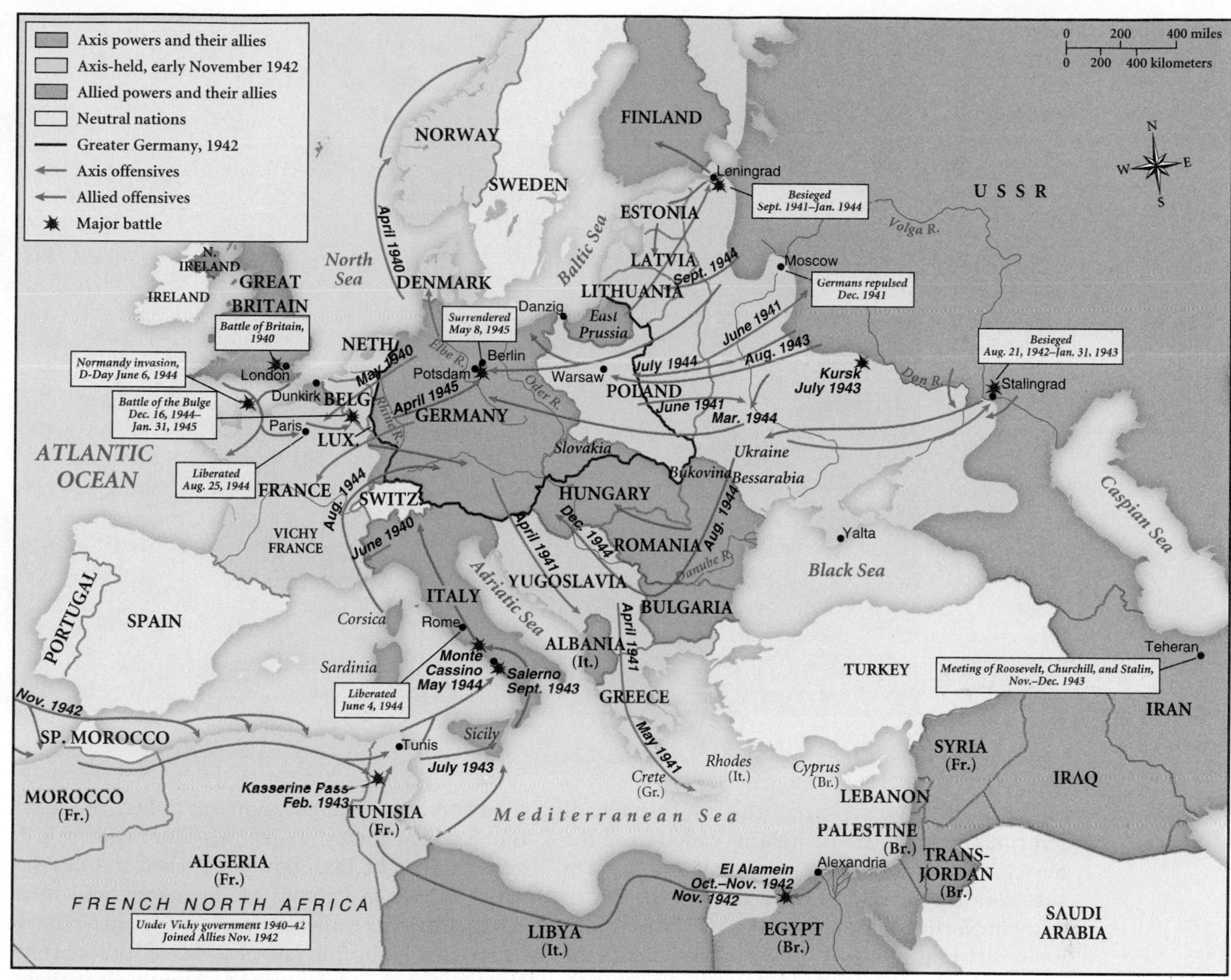

MAP 26.5 World War II in Europe and Africa
World War II inflicted massive loss of life and destruction of property on civilians, armies, and all the infrastructure—including factories, equipment, and agriculture—needed to wage total war. Thus, the war swept the European continent as well as areas in Africa colonized by or allied with the major powers. Ultimately the Allies crushed the Axis powers by moving from east, west, and south to inflict a total defeat.

alive the liberal ideal of individual action in the face of tyranny.

Both subtle and dramatically visible resistance took place in the fascist countries. Couples in Germany and Italy limited family size in defiance of pro-birth policies. German teenagers danced the forbidden American jitterbug, thus disobeying the Nazis and forcing the use of scarce manpower to police their groups. More spectacularly, in July 1944, a group of German military officers, fearing their country's military humiliation, tried but failed to assassinate Hitler—one of several such attempts. Wounded and shaken, Hitler mercilessly tortured and killed hundreds of conspirators, innocent friends, and family members. Some ask whether the assassination attempt came too late in the war to count as resistance. However, some five million Germans alone, and millions more of other nationalities, lost their lives in the last nine months of the war. Had Hitler died even as late as the summer of 1944, the relief to humanity would have been considerable.

The Axis Crushed in Europe

Amid civilian resistance, Allied forces turned the frontline war against the Axis powers beginning with the battle of Stalingrad in 1942–1943. The German army had as its goal the eventual access to

Fighting in the Streets of Budapest, 1945
House-to-house fighting characterized many battles in World War II (including Stalingrad) despite the "high-tech" nature of the war. As resisters saw the Allies undermining the Axis hold on their cities and towns, they shot from windows, threw bombs at enemy soldiers, and blew up or dismantled train tracks. The history of warfare from World War II to the present has thrown the invincibility of even the most powerful military forces into question. *(© Sovfoto.)*

Soviet oil through capturing this city. Months of ferocious house-to-house fighting ended when the Soviet army captured the ninety thousand German survivors in February 1943. Meanwhile, the British army in North Africa held against German troops under Erwin Rommel, a skilled practitioner of the new kind of mobile warfare who aimed to capture the Suez Canal and thus access to Middle Eastern oil. Although Rommel let his tanks improvise creatively, moving hundreds of miles from supply lines, the Allies' access to secret German communications because of their code-breaking capacity ultimately helped them block the capture of Egypt and take Morocco and Algeria in the fall of 1942. After driving Rommel out of Africa, the Allies landed in Sicily in July 1943, provoking a German invasion during which they took over the war effort from the Italians. A slow, bitter fight for the Italian peninsula followed, lasting until April 1945, when Allied forces finally triumphed. After Italy's liberation, partisans shot Mussolini and his mistress and hung their dead bodies for public display.

The victory at Stalingrad marked the beginning of the Soviet drive westward, during which the Soviets bore the brunt of the Nazi war machine. From the air, Britain and the United States bombed German cities, aiming to demoralize ordinary Germans and destroy war industries. But it was an invasion from the west that Stalin wanted from his allies. Finally, on June 6, 1944, known as D-Day, the combined Allied forces, under the command of U.S. general Dwight Eisenhower, attacked the heavily fortified French beaches of Normandy and then fought their way through the German-held territory of western France. In late July, Allied forces broke through German defenses and a month later helped liberate Paris. The Soviets meanwhile captured the Baltic states and entered Poland, pausing for desperately needed supplies. The Germans took advantage of the pause to put down an uprising of the Polish resistance in August 1944, which gave the Soviets a freer hand in eastern Europe after the war. Facing more than twice as many troops as on the western front, the Soviet army took Bulgaria and Romania at the end of August, then faced fierce German fighting in Hungary during the winter of 1944–1945. British, Canadian, U.S., and other Allied forces simultaneously fought their way eastward to join the Soviets in squeezing the Third Reich to its final defeat.

As the Allies advanced, Hitler decided that Germans were proving themselves unworthy of his greatness and deserved to perish in a total and bloody downfall. He thus refused all negotiations that might have spared them further death and destruction from the relentless bombing. As the Soviet army took Berlin, Hitler and his wife, Eva Braun, committed suicide. Although many soldiers remained loyal to the Third Reich, Germany finally surrendered on May 8, 1945.

The Atomic Bomb and the Defeat of Japan The Allies had followed a "Europe first" strategy in conducting the war. They had nonetheless pursued the Japanese in the Pacific without pause. In 1940 and 1941, Japan had ousted the Europeans from many colonial holdings in Asia, but the Allies turned the tide in 1942 by destroying some of Japan's formidable navy in battles at Midway Island and Guadalcanal (Map 26.6). Japan had far less industrial capacity and manpower than the United States alone, to say nothing of the global resources of the Allies.

Allied forces stormed one Pacific island after another, where they found many inhabitants just as disillusioned by Japanese policies of forced labor and military conscription as they were by similar policies of the Western powers. This island-hopping gained the Allies bases from which to cut off the importation of supplies and to launch bombers toward Japan itself. Short of men and weapons, the Japanese military resorted to kamikaze tactics, in which pilots deliberately crashed their planes into Allied ships, killing themselves in the process. In response, the Allies stepped up their bombing of major cities, killing more than 100,000 civilians in their spring 1945 firebombing of Tokyo. The Japanese leadership still ruled out surrender.

Meanwhile a U.S.-based international team of more than 100,000 workers, including scientists and technicians, had been working on the Manhattan Project, the code name for a secret project to develop an atomic bomb. The Japanese practice of dying almost to the man rather than surrendering caused Allied military leaders to calculate that defeating Japan might cost the lives of hundreds of thousands of Allied soldiers (and even more Japanese). On August 6 and 9, 1945, the U.S. government therefore unleashed the new atomic weapons on Hiroshima and Nagasaki, killing 140,000 people

Hiroshima, 1945

This photo captures what little remained of the city of Hiroshima after the United States dropped an atomic bomb on August 6, 1945. Without the bomb, the U.S. military foresaw a long and costly struggle to defeat Japan, given that country's overall strategy of fighting to the last person and in the process inflicting the maximum number of enemy casualties. Some claim that the United States dropped the bomb to menace the Soviet Union, its opponent in the cold war just beginning. Others point to the fact that no such bomb was ever dropped on a Caucasian population. *(The Everett Collection, Inc.)*

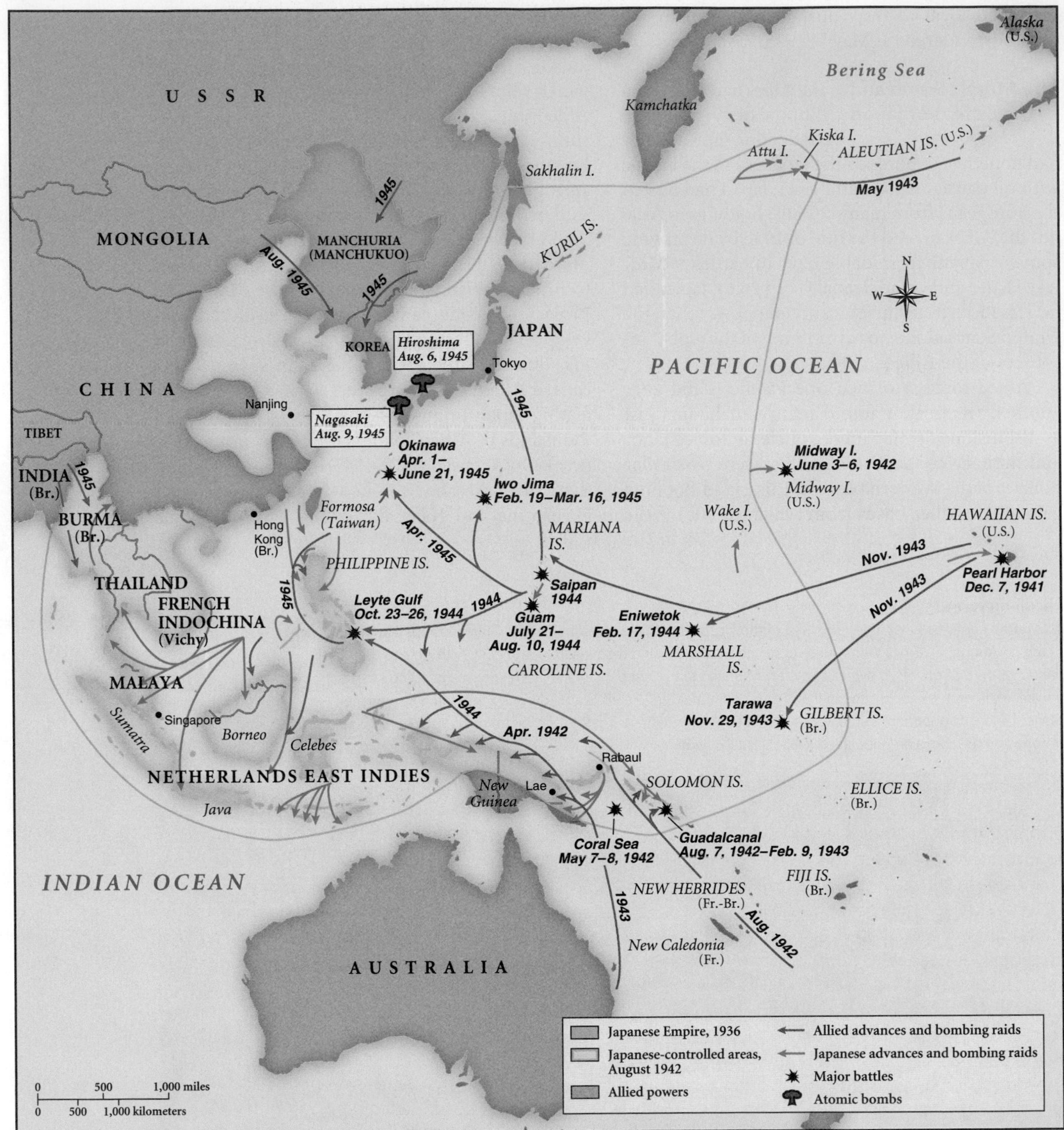

MAP 26.6 World War II in the Pacific

As in Europe, the early days of World War II gave the advantage to the Axis power Japan as it took the offensive in conquering islands in the Pacific and territories in Asia—many of them colonies of European states. Britain countered by mobilizing a vast Indian army, while the United States, after the disastrous losses at Pearl Harbor and in the Philippines, gradually gained the upper hand by costly assaults, island by island. The Japanese strategy of fighting to the last person instead of surrendering when a loss was in sight was one factor in President Truman's decision to drop the atomic bomb in August 1945.

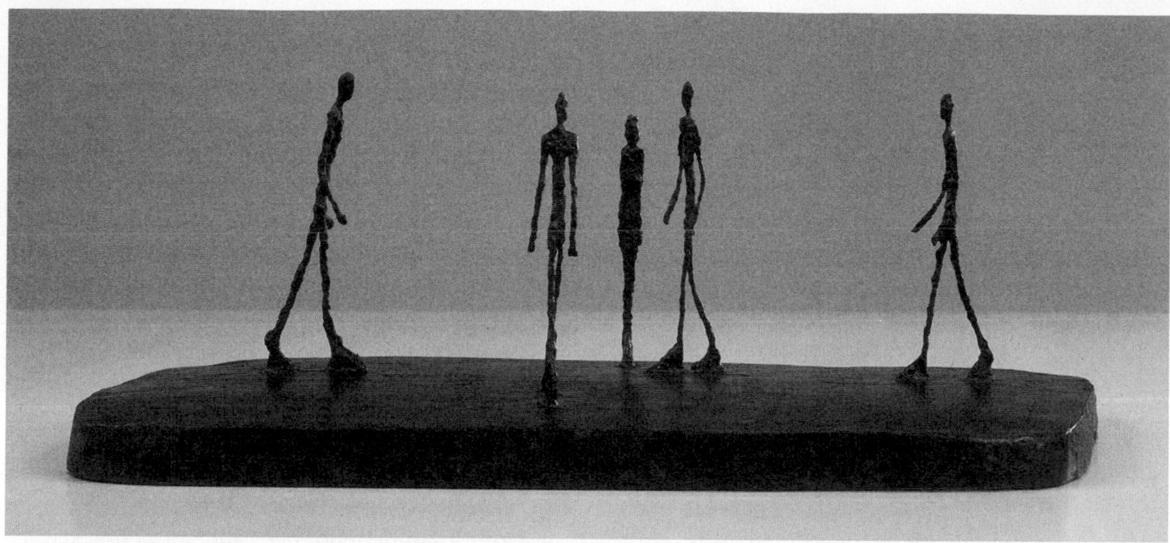

Alberto Giacometti, *The Square II* (1948–1949)
Swiss Artist Alberto Giacometti began making sculptures featuring thin, elongated figures in the 1940s. They appear to be moving forward, striving and active, but at the same time their spareness evokes the skeletal shape of concentration camp survivors. What kind of statement do you see Giacometti making about the times? *(bpk, Berlin/Nationalgalerie, Museum Berggruen, Staaliche Museen, Berlin, Germany/Art Resource, NY/© 2011 Succession Giacometti/Artists Rights Society [ARS], New York/ADAGP, Paris.)*

instantly; tens of thousands later died from burns, wounds, and other afflictions. Hardliners in the Japanese military wanted to continue the war, but on August 14, 1945, Japan surrendered.

An Uneasy Postwar Settlement

Throughout the war, Allied leaders had met not only to plan strategy but also to resolve postwar issues. Unlike World War I, however, there would be neither a celebrated peace conference nor a formal agreement among all the Allies about the final terms for peace. Yet peace and recovery were more important than ever: Europe lay in ruins, and tens of millions were starving, many of them wandering the continent in search of food, shelter, and personal safety. Because the victorious Allies distrusted one another to varying degrees, with the United States and the Soviet Union moving toward another war, the future looked grim.

Wartime Agreements about the Peace

Wartime agreements among members of the Grand Alliance about the future reflected their differences and became the subject of intense postwar debate. In 1941, Roosevelt and Churchill crafted the Atlantic Charter, which condemned aggression and endorsed collective security and the right of all people to choose their governments. Not only did the Allies come to support these ideals, but so did colonized peoples to whom, Churchill said, the charter was not meant to apply. In October 1944, Churchill and Stalin agreed on the postwar distribution of territories. The Soviet Union would control Romania and Bulgaria, Britain would control Greece, and they would jointly oversee Hungary and Yugoslavia. These agreements went against Roosevelt's faith in collective security, self-determination, and open doors in trade. In February 1945, the "Big Three"—Roosevelt, Churchill, and Stalin—met in the Crimean town of Yalta. Roosevelt advocated for the formation of the United Nations to replace the League of Nations as a global peace mechanism, and he supported future Soviet influence in Korea, Manchuria, and the Sakhalin and Kurile Islands. The last meeting of the Allied leaders, with President Harry S. Truman replacing Roosevelt, who had died in April, took place at Potsdam, Germany, in the summer of 1945. At Potsdam, they agreed to give the Soviets control of eastern Poland, to give a large stretch of eastern Germany to Poland, and to finalize a temporary four-way occupation of Germany that would include France as one of the supervising powers.

The War's Grim Legacy

The Great Depression had inflicted global suffering, while the Second World War left an estimated 100 million dead, more than 50 million refugees without homes, and one of the most abominable moral legacies in human history. Conscripted into armies or into labor camps for war production, colonial peoples in Vietnam, Algeria, India, and elsewhere were in full rebellion or close to it. For a second time in three decades, they had seen their imperial masters killing one another with the very technology that was supposed to prove European superiority. Deference to Europe was virtually finished, with independence a matter of time.

The war weakened and even destroyed standards of decency and truth. Democratic Europe had succumbed to continuous wartime values, and it was this Europe that George Orwell captured in his novel *1984* (1949). Orwell had worked for the wartime Ministry of Information (called the Ministry of Truth in the novel) and made up phony war news and threats for civilian audiences. Truth hardly mattered, and words changed meaning during the war to sound better: *battle fatigue* substituted for *insanity*, and *liberating* a country could mean invading it and slaughtering its civilians. Hungry, careworn people walking in ragged clothing along grimy streets characterized both wartime London and Orwell's fictional state of Oceania. Millions cheered the demise of Nazi evil in 1945, but Orwell saw the war as ending prosperity, deadening creativity, and bringing big government into everyday life. For Orwell, bureaucratic domination depended on continuing conflict, and fresh conflict was indeed brewing even before the war ended. As Allied powers competed for territory, a new struggle called the cold war was beginning.

REVIEW QUESTION How and where was World War II fought, and what were its major consequences?

Conclusion

The Great Depression, which brought fear, hunger, and joblessness to millions, created a setting in which dictators thrived because they promised to restore economic prosperity by destroying democracy and representative government. Desperate people believed the promises of these dynamic new leaders—Mussolini, Stalin, and Hitler—and often embraced the brutality of their regimes. In the USSR, Stalin's program of rapid industrialization cost the lives of millions as he inspired Communist believers to purge enemies—real and imagined. With the democracies preoccupied with economic recovery while preserving the rule of law and still haunted by memories of World War I, Hitler, Mussolini, and their millions of supporters went on to menace Europe unchallenged. At the same time, Japan embarked on a program of conquest aimed at ending Western domination in Asia and taking more of Asia for itself. The coalition of Allies that finally formed to stop the Axis powers of Germany, Italy, and Japan was an uneasy alliance among Britain, Free France, the Soviet Union, and the United States. World War II ended European dominance. Its economies were shattered, its colonies were on the verge of independence, and its peoples were starving and homeless.

The costs of a bloody war—one waged against civilians as much as armies—taught the victorious powers different lessons. The United States, Britain, and France were convinced that a minimum of citizen well-being was necessary to prevent a recurrence of fascism. The devastation of the USSR's population and resources made Stalin increasingly obsessed with national security and compensation for the damage inflicted by the Nazis. Britain and France faced the end of their imperial might, underscoring Orwell's insight that the war had utterly transformed society. The militarization of society and the deliberate murder of millions of innocent citizens like Etty Hillesum were tragedies that permanently injured the West's claims to being an advanced civilization. Nonetheless, backed by vast supplies of sophisticated weaponry, the United States and the Soviet Union used their opposing views on a postwar settlement to justify threatening one another—and the world—with another horrific war.

FOR FURTHER EXPLORATION

- **For additional primary-source material from this period**, see *Sources of the Making of the West*, Fourth Edition.
- **For Web sites, images, and documents related to topics in this chapter**, visit *Make History* at bedfordstmartins.com/hunt.

MAPPING THE WEST

Europe at War's End, 1945

The damage of World War II left scars that would last for decades. Major German cities were bombed to bits, while the Soviet Union suffered an unimaginable toll of perhaps as many as forty-five million deaths due to the war alone. In addition to the vast civilian and military losses shown on this map, historians estimate that no less than twelve million people were murdered in the Nazi death camps. Everything from politics to family life needed rebuilding, adding to the chaos. *(From* The Hammond Atlas of the Twentieth Century *[London: Times Books, 1996], 102.)*

Chapter 26 Review

Online Study Guide bedfordstmartins.com/hunt

Key Terms and People

In the grid below, identify the term or person and explain its historical significance. (To do this exercise online, go to bedfordstmartins.com/hunt.)

Term	Who or What & When	Why It Matters
civil disobedience (p. 877)		
Joseph Stalin (p. 878)		
five-year plans (p. 878)		
purges (p. 880)		
Adolf Hitler (p. 881)		
Enabling Act (p. 884)		
pump priming (p. 884)		
Nuremberg Laws (p. 885)		
family allowance (p. 886)		
Popular Front (p. 887)		
Charlie Chaplin (p. 888)		
Lebensraum (p. 891)		
Francisco Franco (p. 893)		
appeasement (p. 894)		
Nazi-Soviet Pact (p. 895)		
Blitzkrieg (p. 896)		

Review Questions

1. How did the Great Depression affect society and politics?
2. What role did violence play in the Soviet and Nazi regimes?
3. How did the democracies' responses to the twin challenges of economic depression and the rise of fascism differ from those of totalitarian regimes?
4. How did the aggression of Japan, Germany, and Italy create the conditions for global war?
5. How and where was World War II fought, and what were its major consequences?

Making Connections

1. Compare fascist ideas of the individual with the idea of individual rights that inspired the American and French Revolutions.
2. What are the major differences between World War I and World War II?
3. What explains the bleak view of writers like George Orwell after the Allied victory over the Axis powers?
4. What connections can you make between the Great Depression and the coming of World War II?

Important Events

Date	Event	Date	Event
1929	U.S. stock market crashes; global depression begins; Soviet leadership initiates "liquidation of the kulaks"; Stalin's first five-year plan officially begins	1940	France falls to German army
1931	Japan invades Manchuria; Spanish republicans overthrow monarchy	1940–1941	British air force fends off German attacks in the battle of Britain
1933	Hitler comes to power in Germany	1941	Germany invades Soviet Union; Japan attacks Pearl Harbor; United States enters war
1935	German government enacts Nuremberg Laws; Italy invades Ethiopia	1941–1945	The Holocaust
1936	Purges and show trials begin in USSR; Hitler remilitarizes Rhineland; Spanish Civil War begins	1942–1943	Siege of Stalingrad
1937	Japan attacks China	1944	Allied forces land at Normandy, France
1938	Germany annexes Austria; European leaders meet in Munich to negotiate with Hitler; Kristallnacht in Germany	1945	The fall of Berlin; United States drops atomic bombs on Hiroshima and Nagasaki; World War II ends
1939	Germany invades Czechoslovakia; Spanish Civil War ends; Nazi-Soviet Pact; Germany invades Poland; Britain and France declare war on Germany; World War II begins		

- Consider three events: **Global depression begins (1929), Stalin's first five-year plan officially begins (1929)**, and **Hitler comes to power in Germany (1933)**. How did the global depression contribute to the success of these leaders?

SUGGESTED REFERENCES

This grim period in human history has yielded an ever-growing crop of excellent books, some of them coldly examining the worst aspects of the Great Depression and World War II and others looking at resistance, survival, and intellectual breakthroughs.

Alvarez, Luis. *The Power of the Zoot: Youth Culture and Resistance during World War II*. 2008.

Clavin, Patricia. *The Great Depression in Europe, 1929–1939*. 2000.

Collingham, Lizzie. *The Taste of War: World War II and the Battle for Food*. 2011.

Friedlander, Saul. *The Years of Extermination: Nazi Germany and the Jews, 1939–1945*. 2007.

*Gandhi, Mohandas. *Hind Swaraj and Other Writings*. 2009.

Gross, Jan. *Neighbors: The Destruction of the Jewish Community in Jedwabne, Poland*. 2001.

Hellbeck, Jochen. *Revolution on My Mind: Writing a Diary under Stalin*. 2006.

Imlay, Talbot C. *Facing the Second World War: Strategy, Politics, and Economics in Britain and France 1938–1940*. 2003.

Kaplan, Marion. *Between Dignity and Despair: Jewish Life in Nazi Germany*. 1998.

Maas, Ad, and Hans Hooijijers, eds. *Scientific Research in World War II: What Scientists Did in the War*. 2009.

Miner, Steven Merritt. *Stalin's Holy War: Religion, Nationalism, and Alliance Politics, 1941–1945*. 2003.

Naimark, Norman M. *Stalin's Genocides*. 2010.

Seidman, Michael. *Republic of Egos: A Social History of the Spanish Civil War*. 2002.

Snyder, Timothy. *Bloodlands: Europe between Hitler and Stalin*. 2010.

Stoltzfus, Nathan, et al., eds. *Courageous Resistance: The Power of Ordinary People*. 2007.

Tierney, Robert T. *Tropics of Savagery: The Culture of Japanese Empire in Comparative Frame*. 2010.

Viola, Lynn, ed. *Contending with Stalinism: Soviet Power and Popular Resistance in the 1930s*. 2003.

Weinberg, Gerhard. *A World at Arms: A Global History of World War II*. 2005.

Wildt, Michel. *An Uncompromising Generation: The Nazi Leadership of the Reich Security Main Office*. 2009.

*Primary source.

A LOVE CAUGHT IN THE FIRE OF REVOLUTION

Turbulent were the times
and fiery was
the love story
of Zhivago,
his wife...
and the
passionate,
tender
Lara.

METRO-GOLDWYN-MAYER PRESENTS A CARLO PONTI PRODUCTION

DAVID LEAN'S FILM OF BORIS PASTERNAKS

DOCTOR ZHIVAGO

STARRING

GERALDINE CHAPLIN · JULIE CHRISTIE · TOM COURTENAY
ALEC GUINNESS · SIOBHAN McKENNA · RALPH RICHARDSON
OMAR SHARIF (AS ZHIVAGO) ROD STEIGER · RITA TUSHINGHAM

WINNER OF
6
ACADEMY
AWARDS!

SCREEN PLAY BY
ROBERT BOLT · DIRECTED BY
DAVID LEAN IN PANAVISION® AND METROCOLOR

MGM

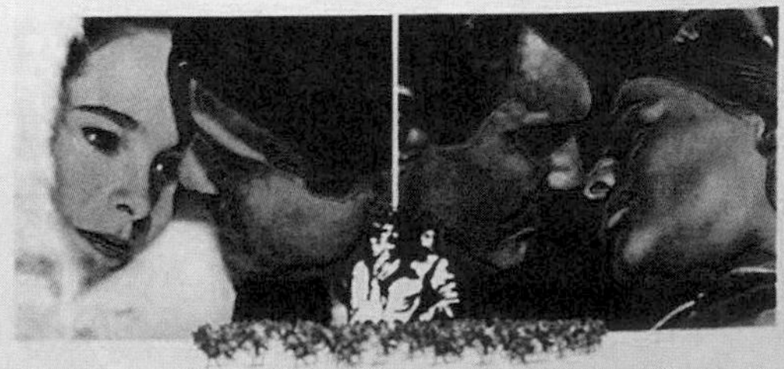

CHAPTER

27

The Cold War and the Remaking of Europe

1945–1960s

Late in 1945, with the USSR still reeling from the devastation of World War II, Soviet poet Boris Pasternak began a new project—*Doctor Zhivago*, a novel about a thoughtful medical man caught up in the whirlwind of the Russian Revolution. Like others in the USSR, Pasternak expected the postwar era to usher in, as he put it, "a great renewal of Russian life," ending the violence and famine of the past three decades. So he struggled on with his complex epic even as the cold war tensions between the United States and the USSR unfolded. In 1953, Joseph Stalin's sudden death raised Pasternak's hopes that a more tolerant political climate would allow his masterpiece to receive a warm reception; those hopes were dashed, however, when the Soviets forbade the book's publication.

A determined Pasternak bypassed the Soviet authorities and allowed *Doctor Zhivago* to come out first in 1957 in Italy—now an anti-Soviet ally of the United States in the cold war. The book became a best seller, showing its readers that the Russian Revolution was far from perfect and so angering the Soviet leadership that Stalin's successor, Nikita Khrushchev, forced Pasternak to decline the Nobel Prize for Literature awarded him in 1958. But if the cold war prompted the Soviets to denounce *Doctor Zhivago* and frighten people into denouncing its author, it was the cold war that allowed *Doctor Zhivago* to live on. Soon after the novel appeared, the famed Hollywood studio MGM bought the rights to the book and turned it into a blockbuster film (1965), seen by tens of millions. By that time, however, Pasternak was dead—a broken victim of cold war persecutions that haunted the world long after the calamitous years of war and genocide had ended.

***Doctor Zhivago* Poster**
As soon as Boris Pasternak's forbidden novel *Doctor Zhivago* was published in Italy in 1957, Hollywood's MGM studio went after the rights for the film. Finally completed in 1965, the movie was a cold war blockbuster—an epic of life and love in postrevolutionary Russia. The opening scene, invented for the movie, was a grim Soviet factory, while the story itself was more or less symbolized in this advertising poster highlighting two incredibly attractive people who fall in love and are torn apart by the crushing Bolshevik system. *(MGM/The Kobal Collection.)*

Following World War II, people in Europe, Japan, and much of East and Southeast Asia were starving and homeless. Evidence of genocide and other inhumanity was everywhere; and nuclear annihilation menaced the world. The old international order was gone, replaced by the rivalry of the United States and the Soviet Union for control of Europe, whose political, social, and economic order was shattered. The nuclear arsenals of these two superpowers—a term coined in 1947—grew massively in the 1950s, but they were enemies who did not fight outright. Thus, their terrifying rivalry was called the **cold war**. The cold war divided the West and led to political persecution in many areas, even in the wealthy and secure United States.

At the same time, the defeat of Nazism inspired cautious optimism and a revival of thoughtful reflection like Pasternak's. Heroic effort had defeated fascism, and that defeat raised hopes that a new age would begin. Atomic science promised advances in medicine, and nuclear energy was seen as a replacement for coal and oil. The creation of the United Nations in 1945 heralded an era of international cooperation. Around the globe, colonial peoples won independence from European masters, while in the United States the civil rights movement grew in strength. The welfare state expanded, and by the end of the 1950s, economic rebirth had made much of Europe more prosperous than ever before. An "economic miracle" had occurred; just a decade after the war, many Europeans and Americans were beginning to enjoy the highest standard of living they had ever known, which included the ability to buy quantities of consumer goods and to enjoy simple pleasures such as films like *Doctor Zhivago*.

The postwar period was one of open redefinition, as the experience of total war transformed both society and the international order. Gone was the definition of a West comprising Europe and its cultural offshoots such as the United States and of an East comprising Asian countries like India, China, and Japan. During the cold war, the word *West* came to stand for the United States and its dependent allies in western Europe, while *East* meant the Soviet Union and its tightly controlled bloc in eastern Europe. Still another set of terms arose in the 1950s, one that divided the globe into the first world, or capitalist bloc of countries; the second world, or socialist bloc; and the third world, or countries emerging from imperial domination. This last term was meant to compare favorably those rising nations to the Third Estate—that is, the rising citizens of the French Revolution—but is now considered an insulting term. As the world's people redefined themselves, the superpowers took the world to the brink of nuclear disaster when the United States discovered Soviet missile sites on the island of Cuba. From the dropping of the atomic bomb on Japan in 1945 to the Cuban missile crisis of 1962, fear and personal anguish like that suffered by Pasternak gripped much of the world, even in the midst of prosperity and Europe's rebirth.

CHAPTER FOCUS How did the cold war shape the politics, economy, social life, and culture of post–World War II Europe?

World Politics Transformed

World War II ended Europe's global leadership. Many countries lay in ruins in the summer of 1945, and conditions would deteriorate before they im-

cold war: The rivalry between the United States and the Soviet Union from 1945 to 1989 that led to massive growth in nuclear weapons on both sides.

1945 Cold war begins

1947 India and Pakistan win independence from Britain

1948 State of Israel established

1949 Mao Zedong leads Communist revolution in China; Simone de Beauvoir publishes *The Second Sex*

1950 Korean War begins

1953 Stalin dies; Korean War ends

1954 *Brown v. Board of Education* prohibits segregated schools in the United States; Vietnamese forces defeat French at Dien Bien Phu proved. Though victorious, bombed and bankrupt Britain could not feed its people, and continuing turmoil destroyed the lives of millions in central and eastern Europe. In contrast, the United States, whose territory was virtually untouched in the war, emerged as the world's sole economic giant, while the Soviet Union, despite suffering immense devastation, retained formidable military might. Occupying Europe as part of the victorious alliance against Nazism and fascism, the two superpowers used Germany—at the heart of the continent and its politics—to divide Europe in two. By the late 1940s, the USSR had imposed Communist rule throughout most of eastern Europe, as it gained control of the territory that the Nazis had desired for German settlement. Western Europeans found themselves at least partially controlled by the very U.S. economic power that helped them rebuild, especially because the United States maintained air bases and nuclear weapons sites on their soil. The new age of bipolar world politics made Europe its testing ground.

Chaos in Europe

In contrast to the often stationary trench warfare of World War I, armies in World War II had fought a war of movement on the ground and in the air. Massive bombing had leveled thousands of square miles of territory, and whole cities were clogged with rubble. On the Rhine River, almost no bridge remained standing; in the Soviet Union, seventy thousand villages and more than a thousand cities lay in shambles. Everywhere people were suffering. In the Netherlands, the severity of Nazi occupation left the Dutch population close to death, relieved only by a U.S. airlift of food. In Britain, many died in the bitterly cold winter of 1946–1947 because of a shortage of fuel. To control scarce supplies, Italian bakers sold bread by the slice. Allied troops in Germany were almost the sole source of food: "To see the children fighting for food," remarked one British soldier handing out supplies, "was like watching animals being fed in a zoo." There was social disarray, even chaos, at the war's end but no mass uprisings as after World War I. Until the late 1940s, people were too absorbed by the struggle for bare survival.

The tens of millions of refugees suffered the most, as they wandered a continent where resources were slim and the dangers of assault, robbery, and ethnic violence great. An estimated thirty million Europeans, many of German ethnicity, were forcibly expelled from Poland, Czechoslovakia, and Hungary. Many refugees fled to western Europe, but others ultimately found homes in countries that experienced little or no war damage, such as Denmark, Sweden, Canada, and Australia. Following the exodus of refugees from the east, western Europe became one of the world's most densely populated regions (Map 27.1). The USSR lobbied hard for the return of several million Soviet prisoners of war and forced laborers, and the Allies transported millions of Soviet refugees home. The Allies slowed the process when they discovered that Soviet leaders had ordered the execution of many of the returnees for being "contaminated" by Western ideas. Hundreds of thousands of Soviet citizens thus joined the ocean of destitute refugees.

Survivors of the concentration camps discovered that their suffering had not ended with Germany's defeat. Many returned home diseased and disoriented, while others had no home to return to, as property had been confiscated. Anti-Semitism—official policy under the Nazis—lingered in popular attitudes, and people used it to justify their claim to Jewish property and to jobs vacated by Jews. The fascist use of violence as a means of upward mobility remained common throughout eastern Europe. In the summer of 1946, a vicious crowd in Kielce, Poland, assaulted some 250 Jewish survivors, killing at least 40. Meanwhile, some officials across Europe

1956 General Abdel Nasser nationalizes Suez Canal; uprising in Hungary against USSR

1957 Boris Pasternak publishes *Doctor Zhivago*; USSR launches *Sputnik*; Treaty of Rome establishes European Economic Community (Common Market)

1958 Fifth Republic begins in France

1962 United States and USSR face off in the Cuban missile crisis

1955 — 1960 — 1965

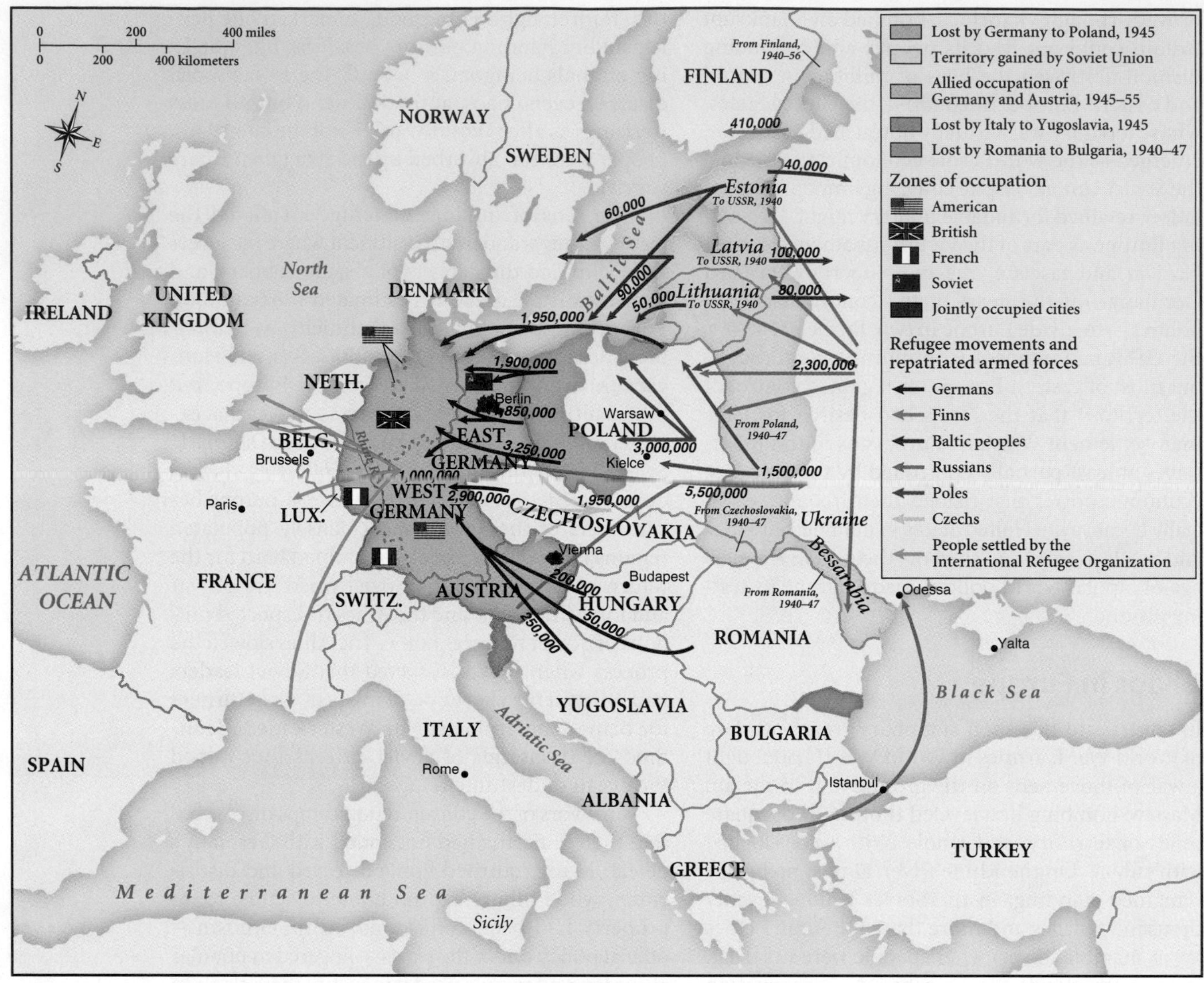

MAP 27.1 The Impact of World War II on Europe
European governments, many of them struggling to provide food and other necessities for their populations, found themselves responsible for hundreds of thousands, if not millions, of new refugees. Simultaneously, millions of prisoners of war, servicemen, and slave laborers were returned to the Soviet Union, many of them by force. This situation unfolded amid political instability and even violence. | **What does the movement of peoples shown on the map suggest about social conditions in post–World War II Europe?**

even denied that unprecedented atrocities had been committed and refused Jews any help. Survivors therefore fled to the port cities of Italy and other Mediterranean countries, eventually leaving Europe for Palestine, where Zionists had been settling for half a century. Unwilling to help Hitler's victims, many Europeans had simply lost their moral bearings.

New Superpowers: The United States and the Soviet Union

Only two countries were still powerful in 1945: the United States and the Soviet Union. The United States was now the richest nation in the world. Its industrial output had increased by a remarkable 15 percent annually between 1940 and 1944. By 1947, the United States controlled almost two-thirds of the world's gold bullion and launched more than half of the world's commercial shipping. Continued spending on industrial and military research added to postwar prosperity, bolstering the confident mood that now swept the United States. In contrast to the post–World War I policy of isolationism, Americans embraced global leadership. Many had learned about the world while tracking the war's progress; hundreds of thousands of soldiers, government officials, and relief workers had direct experience of Europe, Africa, and Asia. Despite the fear of nuclear annihilation that troubled many, a wave of suburban housing development and consumer spending kept the economy buoyant. Temporarily reversing the trend toward lower birthrates, a baby boom exploded from the late 1940s through the early 1960s in response to prosperity.

The Soviets also emerged from the war with a well-justified sense of accomplishment. Despite horrendous losses, they had resisted the most massive onslaught ever launched against a nation. Instead of being outcasts as they had been after World War I, Soviet officials expected to have influence on the world stage, and indeed many Europeans and Americans gratefully acknowledged the Soviet contribution to Hitler's defeat. Ordinary Soviet citizens believed that a victory that had cost the USSR as many as forty-five million lives would lead to improvement in everyday conditions and a continuation of the war's relatively relaxed politics. Rumors spread among the peasants that the collective farms would be divided and returned to them as individual property now that the war had been won and agriculture modernized. "Life will become pleasant," one writer prophesied. "There will be much coming and going, and a lot of contacts with the West." The Stalinist goals of industrialization and defense against Nazism had been won, and thus many Soviets, among them Boris Pasternak, anticipated an end to decades of hardship and repression.

Stalin took a different view and, despite his personal exhaustion from the wartime effort, moved ruthlessly to reassert control. In 1946, his new five-year plan set increased production goals and mandated more stringent collectivization of agriculture. For him, rapid recovery meant more work, not less, and more order, not greater freedom. Stalin cut back the army by two-thirds to beef up the labor force and also turned his attention to the low birthrate, a result of wartime male casualties and women's long, arduous working days, which discouraged them from adding child care to their already heavy responsibilities. He introduced an intense propaganda campaign emphasizing that women should hold down jobs and also fulfill their "true nature" by producing many children. A crackdown on freedom took place, and a new round of purges began in which people were told that enemies among them were threatening the state. Jews were especially targeted, and in 1953 the government announced that doctors — most of them Jews — had long been assassinating Soviet leaders, murdering newborns and patients in hospitals, and plotting to poison water supplies. Hysteria gripped the nation, as people feared for their lives. "I am a simple worker and not an anti-Semite," one Moscow resident wrote, "but I say . . . it's time to clean these people out." With this rebirth of Stalinism, an atmosphere of fear returned to feed the cold war.

Origins of the Cold War

The cold war between the United States and the Soviet Union, which began in 1945, would afflict the world for more than four decades. No peace treaty officially ended World War II to document what went wrong, as in the Peace of Paris of 1919–1920. As a result, the origins of the cold war remain a matter of debate, with historians faulting both sides for starting the dangerous rivalry (see "New Sources, New Perspectives," page 918). Some point to consistent U.S., British, and French hostility to the Soviets that began as far back as the Bolshevik Revolution of 1917 and continued through the depression and World War II. These powers opposed the Communists' abolition of private property and Russia's withdrawal from World War I. Others stress Stalin's aggressive policies, notably the 1939 Nazi-Soviet Pact and Stalin's quick claims on the Baltic states and Polish territory when World War II broke out. In this view, other countries naturally feared Soviet expansionism.

Suspicion ran deep among the Allied leadership during the war, and the alliance was always a troubled one. Stalin believed that Churchill and Roosevelt were deliberately letting the USSR bear the brunt of Hitler's rampage across the continent as part of their anti-Communist policy. He rightly viewed Churchill in particular as interested primarily in preserving Britain's imperial power, no matter what the cost in Soviet lives. At the time, some Americans believed that dropping the atomic bomb on Japan would also frighten the Soviets and discourage them from making any more land grabs. In addition, the new U.S. president, Harry Truman, was far tougher than Roosevelt with regard to Soviet needs. He cut off aid to the USSR almost the instant the last gun was fired, fueling Stalin's belief that the United States was aiming for the Soviet Union's utter collapse. Seeing a threat from the West, especially from a revived Germany, Stalin completed what he had begun in the war: the takeover of eastern Europe with the goal of collectivizing agriculture and providing the USSR with a permanent "buffer zone" of loyal European states. Across the Atlantic, Truman viewed the Soviet occupation of eastern Europe as opening an era of Communist takeovers around the world. Members of the U.S. State Department fueled U.S. fears by depicting Stalin as another in a long line of neurotic Asian tyrants thirsting for world domination.

The cold war thus became a series of moves and countermoves in the shared occupation of a rich European heartland that had fallen into chaos. In line with the view of its political needs, the USSR repressed democratic coalition governments of liberals, socialists, Communists, and peasant parties

NEW SOURCES, NEW PERSPECTIVES

Government Archives and the Truth about the Cold War

As the modern nation-state grew in the nineteenth century, historians came increasingly to rely on official government archives to answer questions arising from ideological disputes. The cold war was one such battle of charges and countercharges. Government archives have thrown light on the accusations of both sides. Participants and eyewitnesses, it is believed, are not reliable because of their bias. Instead, trained scholars, ridding themselves of bias, carefully examine government records, preserved in official repositories where tampering cannot take place.

The opening of the Soviet Union's archives in the late 1980s and 1990s after the fall of Soviet communism gave answers to many cold war questions. In 1956, in the midst of superpower rivalry, Nikita Khrushchev first threw official light on the slaughter connected with Stalin's regime. In Khrushchev's partial revelation of truths, V. I. Lenin and Joseph Stalin were presented as distinctly different political beings, with Lenin an ideologue and benefactor, and Stalin a creature of excess. The Soviet archives, however, revealed a more vicious Lenin, one who demanded from the start of the Bolshevik regime the kind of brutality that Khrushchev had pinned on Stalin alone. Lenin and his contemporaries started the reliance on wholesale massacre of the upper classes, peasants, dissenters, and even ordinary citizens. At the same time, the archives discredited the U.S. claim that the Soviet Union in the 1950s was out to conquer the world. Instead, scholars found both Stalin and Khrushchev fearful of a U.S. nuclear attack and eager to come to terms.

Much official U.S. archival material still remains closed to scholars, but the Freedom of Information Act (1966, amended 1974) allows historians to press for access and at times to obtain it. Official U.S. documents have opened up debate about the dropping of the atomic bomb, with some scholars concluding that it was not merely a matter of ending the war with Japan in the most expeditious way. Instead, brandishing atomic weapons served the United States' desire to scare the Soviets. Tapes released from John F. Kennedy's administration have shown the president differing from his generals, most of whom wanted a nuclear war during the Cuban missile crisis. Kennedy, far from being the consistent cold warrior he sought to portray, pulled back from the brink.

For all that new archival evidence can reveal, reliance on this material has many pitfalls. First, one train of thought leads to the mistaken belief that if an archive contains no written evidence of an event, the event is open to question. For instance, if there is no written order from Adolf Hitler to start the Holocaust, some have argued, it means that he did not know about the event or even that it did not occur. Second, archives are susceptible to evidence tampering, including forgery and document planting, as has happened with some Russian documents of the 1990s. Finally, excessive faith in archival documents, some critics say, skews history by suggesting that the most important kind of history comes from official government sources. Important historical evidence lies as well in sources ranging from newspapers, family account books, diaries, and personal letters to novels, paintings, and architecture, especially when many kinds of sources are used to verify one another.

Questions to Consider

1. **Are archives overseen by government officials more or less likely to be biased than other sources? How can we know the extent to which archives contain the truth?**
2. **What are the most reliable sources for discovering historical truth? Make a list and provide reasons for your counting these sources as reliable.**

Further Reading

Andrew, Christopher, and Vasili Mitrokhin. *The Mitrokhin Archive: The KGB in Europe and the West*. 1999.

Courtois, Stephane, et al. *The Black Book of Communism: Crimes, Terror, Repression*. Trans. Jonathan Murphy and Mark Kramer. 1999.

Zubok, Vladislav, and Constantine Pleshakov. *Inside the Kremlin's Cold War: From Stalin to Khrushchev*. 1996.

Russian Secret Archives

The opening of archives across the former Soviet bloc had many consequences. In the former East Germany, for instance, names of secret police informers were made public and many people had their reputations utterly tarnished. The opening of the archives also exposed the cases of those convicted with trumped-up evidence (some pictured here), most of them sent to camps and to their deaths long since. The probable existence of such secret archives around the world has made historians and the families of victims fight for access. Simultaneously, politicians in the democracies are struggling to keep their archives closed, especially to scholars trained to assess them. *(© Sovfoto.)*

in central and eastern Europe between 1945 and 1949. It imposed Communist rule almost immediately in Bulgaria and Romania. In Romania, Stalin cited citizen violence in 1945 as the excuse to demand an ouster of all non-Communists from the civil service and cabinet. In Poland, the Communists fixed the election results of 1945 and 1946 to create the illusion of approval for communism. Nevertheless, the Communists had to share power between 1945 and 1947 with the popular Peasant Party, which had a large constituency of rural workers and peasant landowners. The Allies protested many of these moves by the Communists as the cold war advanced.

The United States put its new interventionist spirit to work, promoting American influence. It acknowledged Soviet authority in USSR-occupied areas of central and eastern Europe but worried that Communist power would spread to western Europe. The Communists' promises of better conditions appealed to hungry workers, while memories of Communist leadership in the resistance to fascism gave it powerful appeal. In Greece, for example, Communist insurgents had enough of a following to threaten the right-wing monarchy the British had installed in 1944.

In March 1947, Truman reacted to the Communist threat in Greece by announcing what quickly became known as the **Truman Doctrine**, the use of economic and military aid to block communism. The president requested $400 million in military aid for Greece and Turkey, where the Communists were also exerting pressure. Fearing that Americans would balk at backing an un-democratic Greece, the U.S. Congress said it would agree to the program only if, as one congressman put it, Truman would "scare the hell out of the country." Truman thus publicized the expensive aid program as a necessary first step to prevent Soviet conquest of the world. The show of American support made the Communists back off, and in 1949 the Greek rebels declared a cease-fire.

In 1947, the United States also devised the **Marshall Plan**—a program of massive economic aid to Europe—to relieve the daily hardships that were making communism attractive to Europeans.

The Cold War

1945–1949	USSR establishes satellite states in eastern Europe
1947	Truman Doctrine announces American commitment to contain communism; U.S. Marshall Plan provides massive aid to rebuild Europe
1948–1949	Soviet troops blockade Berlin; United States airlifts provisions to Berliners
1949	West Germany and East Germany formed; Western nations form North Atlantic Treaty Organization (NATO); Soviet bloc establishes Council for Mutual Economic Assistance (COMECON); USSR tests its first nuclear weapon
1950–1953	Korean War
1950–1954	U.S. senator Joseph McCarthy leads hunt for American Communists
1953	Stalin dies
1955	USSR and eastern bloc countries form military alliance, the Warsaw Pact
1956	Khrushchev denounces Stalin in "secret speech" to Communist Party Congress; Hungarians revolt unsuccessfully against Soviet domination
1959	Fidel Castro comes to power in Cuba
1961	Berlin Wall erected
1962	Cuban missile crisis

"The seeds of totalitarian regimes are nurtured by misery and want," Truman warned. Named after Secretary of State George C. Marshall, who proposed the plan, the program's direct aid would immediately improve everyday life, while its loans and financial credits would restart international trade. The government claimed that the Marshall Plan was not directed "against any country or doctrine but against hunger, poverty, desperation, and chaos." By the early 1950s, the United States had sent Europe more than $12 billion in food, equipment, and services, reducing communism's appeal in the countries of western Europe that received the aid.

Stalin saw the Marshall Plan as a U.S. political trick because the devastated USSR had little aid to offer client countries in eastern and central Europe. He thus clamped down still harder on eastern European governments, preventing them from responding to the U.S. offer of assistance and eliminating the last scraps of democracy in Hungary and Poland. In the autumn of 1947, a purge of non-Communist officials began in Czechoslovakia; by June 1948, Czechoslovakia's socialist president, Edvard Beneš, had resigned and been replaced by a Communist figurehead. The populace accepted the change so passively that Communist leaders said the takeover was "like cutting butter with a knife."

The only exception to the Soviet sweep in eastern Europe came in Yugoslavia, under the Commu-

---

Truman Doctrine: The policy devised by U.S. president Harry Truman to limit communism after World War II by countering political crises with economic and military aid.

Marshall Plan: A post–World War II program funded by the United States to get Europe back on its feet economically and thereby reduce the appeal of communism. It played an important role in the rebirth of European prosperity in the 1950s.

Marshall Plan Poster
The Marshall Plan was a major factor in both western European recovery and the cold war. This poster in Italian advertises the plan as "Aid from America" and specifies that it includes "grain, coal, food, and medical supplies." Given both the image and the text, what would you judge the poster's effect to be? *(Archivio GBB/CONTRASTO/Redux.)*

nist ruler known as Tito (Josip Broz, 1892–1980). During the war, Tito had led the powerful anti-Nazi Yugoslav "partisans." After the war, he drew on support from Serbs, Croats, and Muslims to mount a Communist revolution. His revolution, however, was explicitly meant to avoid Soviet influence. Eager for Yugoslavia to develop industrially rather than simply serve Soviet needs, Tito remarked, "We study and take as an example the Soviet system, but we are developing socialism in our country in somewhat different forms." Stalin was furious; in his eyes, commitment to communism meant obedience to him. Nonetheless, Yugoslavia emerged from its Communist revolution as a culturally diverse federation of six republics and two independent provinces within Serbia. Tito's break with

Yugoslavia after the Revolution

Stalin intensified the purges in the USSR because the Soviet government could point to Tito as a menacing example of the treachery supposedly at work even in the heart of the Communist world. Tito used his forceful personality and strong organization to hold diverse groups of southern Slavs together until his death in 1980 and to keep the Soviets at bay.

The Division of Germany

The superpower struggle for control of Germany took the cold war to a menacing level. The agreements reached at the Yalta and Potsdam conferences in 1945 provided for Germany's division into four zones, each of which was controlled by one of the four principal victors in World War II — the United States, the Soviet Union, Britain, and France — and occupied by troops from those nations. However, the superpowers disagreed on how to treat Germany. Many in the United States had come to believe that there was something wrong with the character of Germans — a permanently evil flaw responsible for two world wars and the Holocaust. After the war, the U.S. occupation forces undertook to reprogram German attitudes by controlling the press and censoring all media in the U.S. zone to ensure that they did not express fascist values. In contrast, Stalin believed that Nazism was an extreme form of capitalism. His solution was to confiscate the estates of wealthy Germans and redistribute them to ordinary people and supporters.

A second disagreement, concerning the economy, led to Germany's partition. According to the American plan for coordinating the various segments of the German economy, surplus crops from the Soviet-occupied areas would feed urban populations in the western zones; in turn, industrial goods would be sent to the USSR. The Soviets upset this plan. Following the Allied agreement that the USSR would receive reparations from German resources, the Soviets dismantled industries and seized German equipment on their own, shipping it all to the Soviet Union. They transported skilled German workers, engineers, and scientists to the USSR to work as forced laborers. The Soviets also manipulated the currency in their zone, enabling the USSR to buy German goods at unfairly low prices.

The struggle between the superpowers escalated still more when the western Allies agreed to merge their zones into a West German state. Instead of limiting German power, as wartime agreements called for, the United States began an economic buildup of the western zone under the Marshall Plan in order to make that zone a strong buffer against the Soviets. By 1948, notions of a permanently weakened Germany had ended, and the United States enlisted many former Nazi officials as spies and bureaucrats to jump-start the economy and pursue the cold war.

On July 24, 1948, Stalin retaliated by using Soviet troops to blockade Germany's capital, Berlin. Like Germany as a whole, the city—located more than one hundred miles deep into the Soviet zone and thus cut off from western territory—had been divided into four occupation zones. Expecting the United States and its allies to give up on Berlin, the Soviets declared that the city was now part of their zone of occupation and refused to allow western vehicles to travel through the Soviet zone to reach it. The United States responded decisively with the Berlin airlift—Operation Vittles, as U.S. pilots called it—flying in millions of tons of provisions to Berliners. During the winter of 1948–1949, the Berlin airlift even funneled in coal to warm some two million isolated citizens (Map 27.2). Given the limited number of available transport planes, pilots kept the plane engines on to achieve a rapid turnaround that would ensure the delivery of enough provisions. The Soviets ended their blockade in May 1949, but cold war rhetoric made the divided capital an enduring symbol of the capitalist-communist divide—of good versus evil.

The creation of competing institutions, military alliances, and entirely new countries added to cold war tensions (Map 27.3). A few months after the establishment of the West German state in 1948, the USSR formed an East German state. In 1949, the United States, Canada, and their allies in western Europe and Scandinavia formed the **North Atlantic Treaty Organization (NATO)**, which provided a unified military force for its member countries. In 1955, after the United States forced France and Britain to invite West Germany to join NATO, the Soviet Union retaliated by establishing with its satellite countries the military organization commonly called the **Warsaw Pact**. By that time, both the United States and the USSR had accelerated arms buildups: the Soviets had exploded their own atomic bomb in 1949, and both nations then tested increasingly powerful nuclear weapons. These two

MAP 27.2 Divided Germany and the Berlin Airlift, 1946–1949

Berlin—controlled by the United States, Great Britain, France, and the Soviet Union—was deep in the Soviet zone of occupation and became a major point of contention among the former allies. When the USSR blockaded the western half of the city, the United States responded with a massive airlift. To stop movement between the two zones, the USSR built a wall in 1961 and used troops to patrol it.

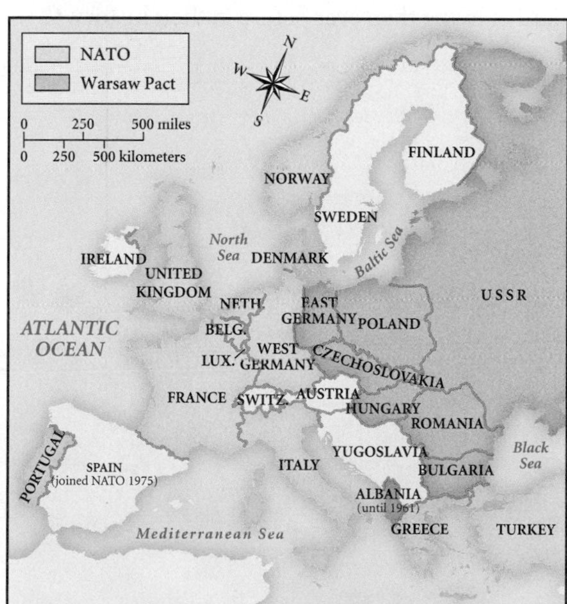

MAP 27.3 European NATO Members and the Warsaw Pact in the 1950s

The two superpowers intensified their rivalry by creating large military alliances: NATO, formed in 1949, and the Warsaw Pact, formed in 1955 after NATO invited West German membership. International politics revolved around these two alliances, which faced off in the heart of Europe. War games for the two sides often assumed a massive war concentrated in central Europe over control of Germany.

North Atlantic Treaty Organization (NATO): The security alliance formed in 1949 to provide a unified military force for the United States, Canada, and their allies in western Europe and Scandinavia.

Warsaw Pact: A security alliance of the Soviet Union and its allies formed in 1955, in retaliation for NATO's admittance of West Germany.

massive regional alliances, armed to the teeth, backed cold war politics with military muscle, definitively outstripping the individual might of the formerly dominant European powers.

REVIEW QUESTION What were the major events in the development of the cold war?

Political and Economic Recovery in Europe

The clash between the United States and the Soviet Union served as a background to the remarkable recovery that took place in Europe. The first two items on the political agenda were the eradication of the Nazi past and the establishment of stable governments. While western Europe revived its democratic political structures, its individualistic culture, and its productive capabilities, eastern Europe was far less prosperous and far more repressive under the Stalinism of the immediate postwar period. Even to the east, however, the conditions of everyday life improved as peasant societies were forced to modernize and some consumer goods industries and basic health services were restored. By 1960, people across the continent were enjoying a higher standard of living than ever before in their history. Governments took increasing responsibility for the health and well-being of citizens, making the cold war era also the age of the welfare state.

Dealing with Nazism

In May 1945, Europeans lived under a confusing system in which local resistance leaders, Allied armies of occupation, international relief workers, and the remnants of bureaucracies — among them Nazi sympathizers — vied for authority. The goals of feeding civilians, dealing with millions of refugees, purging Nazis, and setting up peacetime governments all needed attention. Governments-in-exile returned to reclaim power, but they often ran up against occupying armies that were a law unto themselves. The Soviets were especially feared for inflicting rape and robbery on Germans — abuses they justified by pointing to the tens of millions of worse atrocities committed by the Nazis. Adding to the sense of disorder was the lively trade in sex for food among starving civilians and well-supplied soldiers in all armies. The desire for revenge against Nazis hardened with the discovery of the death camps' skeletal survivors and the remains of the millions murdered there. Employing swift vigilante justice, civilians released pent-up rage and punished collaborators for their participation in genocide and occupation crimes. In France, villagers often shaved the heads of women suspected of associating with

Polish Refugees
These refugees, a handful among millions, are waiting for a train that might carry them to a safer destination. The refugee situation was appalling, as ethnic Poles, Germans, Hungarians, Croats, Czechs, and others were driven from areas where in some cases their families had lived for centuries. The goal of many postwar governments was to "ethnically cleanse" regions along the line of thought that grew up with Wilson's Fourteen Points: that national ethnicities should determine the kind of society and government they would have. *(Photo by Fred Ramage / Keystone / Getty Images.)*

Women Clearing Berlin The amount of destruction caused by World War II was staggering, requiring the mobilization of the civilian population in Berlin, where women were conscripted to sort the rubble and clear it away. Scenes like this were ultimately used as propaganda in the cold war to make it seem as if the Germans were the victims rather than the perpetrators of the war. That German soldiers held in Soviet camps were only slowly repatriated added to the image of Soviet rather than German aggression in World War II. *(akg-images.)*

Germans and made some of them parade naked through the local streets. Members of the resistance executed tens of thousands of Nazi officers and collaborators on the spot and without trial.

Allied representatives undertook what they claimed to be a systematic "denazification" that ranged from forcing German civilians to view the death camps to investigating and bringing to trial suspected local collaborators. The trials conducted at Nuremberg, Germany, by the victorious Allies in the fall of 1945 used the Nazis' own documents to reveal a horrifying panorama of crimes by Nazi leaders. Although international law lacked any definition of genocide as a crime, the judges at Nuremberg found sufficient cause to impose death sentences on half of the twenty-four defendants, among them Hitler's closest associates, and to give prison terms to the remainder. The Nuremberg trials introduced today's notion of prosecution for crimes against humanity.

Allied prosecution of the Axis leadership was hardly thorough, however. Some of those most responsible for war crimes disappeared and were not pursued, leaving many Germans skeptical about Allied intentions. As women in Germany faced violence at the hands of occupying troops, endured starvation, and were forced to do the rough manual labor of clearing rubble, Germans came to believe that they themselves were the main victims of the war. German civilians also interpreted the trials of Nazis as simple payback by victors rather than a just punishment of the guilty. Distrust mounted when Allied officials, eager to restore government services and make western Europe more efficient than Soviet-controlled eastern Europe, began to hire former high-ranking Fascists and Nazis. Soon the new West German government proclaimed that the war's real casualties were the German prisoners of war still held in Soviet camps.

Rebirth of the West

Following the immediate postwar chaos, Europe's revival accelerated in the 1950s. In western Europe, reform-minded civilian governments reflected the broad coalitions of the resistance movements and other opposition to the Axis powers. They conspicuously emphasized democratic values to show their rejection of the totalitarian regimes that had earlier attracted so many Europeans. Rebuilding devastated towns and cities spurred industrial recovery, while bold projects for economic cooperation — like the European Common Market and the conversion of wartime technology to peacetime use — produced a brisk trade in consumer goods and services in western Europe by the late 1950s. Memories of the war remained vivid, but prosperity restored confidence and hope for a better future.

Democratic Politics Restored Resistance leaders made the first claims on political office in postwar western Europe. In France, the leader of the Free French, General Charles de Gaulle, governed briefly as chief of state, and the French approved a constitution in 1946 that established the Fourth Republic and finally granted the vote to French women. De Gaulle wanted a more conservative political system with a strong executive and, failing to achieve that, soon resigned in favor of centrist and left-wing parties. Meanwhile, Italy replaced its constitutional monarchy with a republic that also allowed women the vote for the first time. As in France, a resistance-based government initially took control. Then, late in 1945, the socialist and labor politicians were replaced by a coalition headed by the conservative **Christian Democrats**, descended from the traditional Catholic centrist parties of the prewar period. Other countries likewise saw the growing influence of Christian politicians because of their participation in the resistance.

Still other voters in western Europe favored the Communist Party. Symbol of the common citizen, the Soviet soldier was a hero to many western Europeans outside occupied Germany. So were the resistance leaders, who were themselves often Communist. Some establishment politicians had decided late in the war to join what looked to be a certain resistance victory, and they, too, received credit. People still remembered the hardships of the depression of the 1930s. Therefore, in Britain, despite the wartime successes of Winston Churchill's Conservative Party leadership, the government of longtime Labour Party leader Clement Attlee—though not Communist—appeared most likely to fulfill promises to share prosperity equitably among the classes. The extreme difficulties of the immediate postwar years provided further support for governments that would represent the millions of ordinary citizens who had suffered, fought, and worked incredibly hard during the war.

In West Germany, however, with the Communist takeovers occurring directly to the east and with memories of the millions of German soldiers who had died at the hands of the Red Army, communism and the left in general had little appeal. In 1949, centrist politicians came to power in the new state, officially named the German Federal Republic, whose constitution aimed to prevent the emergence of a dictator and to guarantee individual rights. West Germany's first chancellor was the seventy-three-year-old Catholic anti-Communist Konrad Adenauer, who allied himself with the economist Ludwig Erhard. Erhard stabilized the postwar German currency so that people would have enough confidence in its soundness to resume normal trade, manufacturing, and other economic activity crucial to society's revival. Successfully guiding Germany away from both fascism and communism and using large amounts of U.S. Marshall Plan aid, the economist and the politician restored the representative government that Hitler had overthrown.

Paradoxically, given its leadership in the fight against fascism, the United States was a country in which individual freedom and democracy were imperiled after the war. Two events in 1949—the Soviet Union's successful test of an atomic bomb and the Communist revolution in China—brought to the fore Joseph McCarthy, a U.S. senator foreseeing a reelection struggle. To strengthen his following and win the election, McCarthy warned of a great conspiracy to overthrow the U.S. government. As during the Soviet purges, people of all occupations—including government workers, film stars, and union leaders—were called before congressional panels to confess, testify against friends, and say whether they had ever had Communist sympathies. The atmosphere was electric with confusion, for only five years before, the mass media had run glowing stories about Stalin and the Soviet system. During the war, the American public was told to think of Stalin as a friendly "Uncle Joe." By 1952, however, millions of Americans had been investigated, imprisoned, or fired from their jobs. McCarthy had works like Thomas Paine's *Common Sense*, written in the eighteenth century to support the American Revolution, removed from U.S. agency shelves at home and abroad, and he personally oversaw book burnings. Although the Senate finally voted to censure McCarthy in the winter of 1954, the assault on freedom had been devastating. Even as democracy was restored, fearfulness and anticommunism had come to dominate political life.

An Economic Surge Given the wartime destruction, the economic rebirth of western Europe was even more surprising than the revival of democracy. In the first weeks and months after the war, the job of rebuilding often involved menial physical labor that mobilized entire populations for such jobs as clearing the

---

Christian Democrats: Powerful center to center-right political parties that evolved in the late 1940s from former Catholic parties of the pre–World War II period.

massive urban rubble by hand. Initially, governments diverted labor and capital into rebuilding infrastructure—transportation, communications, industrial capacity—and away from producing consumer goods. However, the scarcity of household goods sparked unrest. Communism held some attraction because it seemed less interested in the revival of big business and more concerned with ensuring ordinary people a decent standard of living. In the midst of this growing discontent, the Marshall Plan suddenly boosted recovery with American dollars; food and consumer goods became more plentiful; and demand for automobiles, washing machines, and vacuum cleaners accelerated economic growth. Increased productivity wiped out most unemployment.

Helping the postwar recovery was the continuation of military spending for the cold war and the adaptation of wartime technology to meet consumer needs. Civilian travel expanded as nations organized their own airlines based on improved airplane technology. Developed to relieve wartime shortages, synthetic goods such as nylon now became part of peacetime civilian life. Factories churned out a vast assortment of plastic products, ranging from pipes to rainwear. In the climate of cold war, however, military needs remained high: governments ordered bombs, fighter planes, tanks, and missiles (Figure 27.1) and sponsored military research. The outbreak of the Korean War in 1950 (see page 931) increased U.S. orders for manufactured goods to wage that war, further sustaining economic growth in Europe. Ultimately, the cold war prevented a repeat of the 1920s, when reduced military spending threw people out of jobs and fed the growth of fascism.

Large and small states alike developed and redeveloped modern economies in short order. In the twelve principal countries of western Europe, the annual rate of economic growth had been 1.3 percent per inhabitant between 1870 and 1913. Those countries almost tripled that rate between 1950 and 1973, attaining an annual per capita growth rate of 3.8 percent. Among the larger powers, West Germany surprisingly became the economic leader, achieving by the 1960s a stunning revival called the "economic miracle." The smaller Scandinavian countries also achieved a notable recovery: Sweden succeeded in the development of automobile, truck, and shipbuilding industries. Finland modernized its industry in order to pay the reparations demanded by the Soviet Union for resisting its invasion. It also modernized its agriculture, which in turn forced the surplus farm population to seek factory work. Scandinavian women joined the workforce in record numbers, which also boosted economic growth and expanded prosperity. The thirty years after World War II were a golden age of European economic growth.

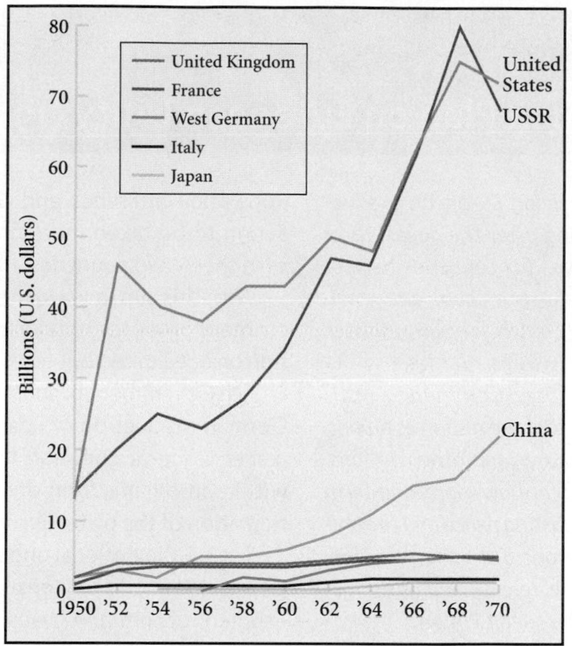

FIGURE 27.1 Military Spending and the Cold War Arms Race, 1950–1970
As soon as the war ended, the United States and the Soviet Union started a massive arms buildup that would continue into the 1980s. Because it had not suffered destruction during the war, the United States could afford to spend hundreds of billions of dollars on weapons. The Soviet Union could not, so its military expenditures deprived Soviet citizens of consumer goods. By the end of the twentieth century, the United States and Russia held vast arsenals of nuclear and other weapons and, along with France, led the way in selling arms that fueled war and genocide around the world.

Birth of the Common Market The creation of the Common Market, which evolved over time to become the European Union, was the final ingredient in the postwar recovery. The Marshall Plan demanded as a condition for assistance that recipient nations undertake far-reaching economic cooperation. In 1951, Italy, France, West Germany, Belgium, Luxembourg, and the Netherlands took a major step toward cooperation when they formed the European Coal and Steel Community (ECSC)—an organization to manage the joint production of basic resources. Importantly, it arranged for West Germany's abundant output of coal and steel to benefit all of western Europe. According to the ECSC's principal architect, Robert

DOCUMENT

The Schuman Plan on European Unity (1950)

One method of reviving European productivity and well-being after the devastation of World War II was for countries to pool natural resources such as coal and steel. Robert Schuman, French foreign minister from 1948 to 1953, was an architect of the European Coal and Steel Community, instituted after the war to share resources among France, West Germany, and other nations. Schuman, however, foresaw more long-term benefits, including lasting peace and the unification of all of Europe. The Schuman Plan, excerpted here, is widely viewed as a blueprint for today's European Union.

World peace can only be safeguarded if constructive efforts are made proportionate to the dangers which threaten it. . . . Europe will not be made all at once, nor according to a single, general plan. It will be formed by taking measures which work primarily to bring about real solidarity. The gathering of the European nations requires the elimination of the age-old opposition of France and Germany. The action to be taken must first of all concern these two countries.

With this aim in view, the French Government proposes to take immediate action on one limited but decisive point. The French Government proposes that Franco-German production of coal and steel be placed under a common high authority within an organisation open to the participation of the other European nations.

The pooling of coal and steel production will immediately ensure the establishment of common bases for economic development as a first step in the federation of Europe, and will change the destinies of those regions which have long been devoted to the manufacture of arms, to which they themselves were the constant victims.

The common production thus established will make it plain that any war between France and Germany becomes not only unthinkable, but materially impossible. The establishment of this powerful entity, open to all countries willing to take part, and eventually capable of making available on equal terms the fundamental elements of industrial production, will give a real foundation to their economic unification. . . .

By pooling basic production and by creating a new high authority whose decisions will be binding on France, Germany and the other countries that may subsequently join, these proposals will lay the first concrete foundation for a European Federation which is so indispensable to the preservation of peace.

Source: U.S. Department of State Bulletin, June 12, 1959, 936–37. Reprinted in A. G. Harryvan and J. van der Harst, eds., *Documents on European Union* (New York: St. Martin's, 1997), 61–62.

Question to Consider

- **What are the goals of the Schuman Plan and how realistic do they seem in retrospect?**

Schuman, the cooperation created by the organization would make another war "materially impossible." Simply put, ties created by joint productivity and trade would keep France and Germany from another cataclysmic war. (See Document, "The Schuman Plan on European Unity," above.)

The success of the ECSC led to the next momentous step: in 1957, the six ECSC members signed the Treaty of Rome, which provided for a more general trading partnership called the **European Economic Community (EEC)**, known popularly as the **Common Market**. The EEC reduced tariffs among the six partners and developed common trade policies. It brought under one cooperative economic umbrella more than two hundred million consumers and would eventually add several hundred million more. According to one of its founders, the EEC aimed to "prevent the race of nationalism, which is the true curse of the modern world." Increased cooperation produced great economic rewards for the six members, whose rates of economic growth soared.

Britain pointedly refused to join the partnership at first, since membership would have required it to surrender certain imperial trading rights among its Commonwealth partners such as Australia and Canada. Since 1945, British politicians had shunned the developing continental trading bloc because, as one of them put it, participation would make Britain "just another European country." Even without Britain, the rising prosperity of a new western Europe joined in the Common Market was striking.

Economic planning and coordination by specialists (as developed during wartime) shaped the Common Market. Called technocrats, specialists working for the Common Market were to base decisions on expertise rather than on personal interest and on the goals of the organization as a whole

---

European Economic Community (EEC or Common Market): A consortium of six European countries established in 1957 to promote free trade and economic cooperation among its members; its membership and activities expanded over the years, and it later evolved into the European Union (EU).

rather than on the demands of any one nation. The aim was to reduce the potential for irrationality and violence in politics, both domestic and international. Administered by a commission of technocrats based in Brussels, Belgium, the Common Market transcended the borders of the nation-state and thus exceeded the power of elected politicians. Some critics insisted (and some still insist today) that expert planning would diminish democracy by transferring decision making from legislators to a transnational bureaucracy. Defenders were just as insistent that planning and cooperation would be the surest tools of prosperity and lasting peace.

The Welfare State in Action, 1947
The Danish creche, or day-care center, here shows the welfare state in action. Government programs to maintain the well-being of citizens became almost universally available in Europe, Canada, and (to a lesser extent) the United States. Children were seen as particularly important, given the loss of life in the war, so governments encouraged couples to reproduce through up-to-date health care systems, day-care centers, and generous family allowances to support family growth. *(Hulton Archive/Getty Images.)*

The Welfare State: Common Ground East and West

On both sides of the cold war divide, governments channeled new resources into state-financed programs such as pensions, disability insurance, and national health care. These social programs taken as a whole became known as the **welfare state**, indicating that states were no longer interested solely in maintaining order and augmenting their power. Veterans' pensions and programs were primary, but the welfare state extended beyond those who had sacrificed in wartime and in part became a weapon in the cold war. Because the European population had declined during the war, almost all countries now desperately wanted to boost the birthrate and thus gave couples direct financial aid for having children. Imitating the social security programs initiated under Bismarck and the more sweeping Swedish programs of the 1930s, nations expanded or created family allowances, health care and medical benefits, and programs for pregnant women and new mothers. The French gave larger family allowances for each birth after the first; for many French families, this allowance provided as much as a third of the household income. Countries east and west vied to show their support of citizens.

Some welfare-state policies had a strong gender bias against women. Britain's maternity benefits and child allowances favored women who did not work outside the home by providing little coverage for workingwomen. The West German government passed strict legislation that forced employers to give women maternity leave, thus discouraging them from hiring women. It also cut back or eliminated pensions and benefits to married women. In fact, West Germans bragged about removing women from the workforce, claiming that doing so distinguished democratic practices from Communist ones. The refusal to build day-care centers or to allow stores to remain open in the evening so that workingwomen could buy food for their families led West Germany to have among the lowest rates of female employment of any industrial country. Another result of West Germany's discriminatory policies was a high rate of female poverty in old age.

By contrast, in eastern Europe and the Soviet Union, where wartime loss of life had been enormous, women worked nearly full-time and usually

---

welfare state: A system (developed on both sides during the cold war) comprising government-sponsored social programs to provide health care, family allowances, disability insurance, and pensions for veterans and retired workers.

outnumbered men in the workforce. As in many western European countries, however, child-care programs, family allowances, and maternity benefits were designed to encourage pregnancies by workingwomen. A national health program provided medical services, as in most countries to the west, but the hardships of everyday life undermined the drive to increase population. The scarcity of consumer goods, the housing shortages, and the lack of household conveniences discouraged workingwomen in Communist countries from having large families no matter what the government wanted. Because women bore the sole burden of domestic duties under such conditions on top of their paying jobs, they rarely wanted more children. As a result, birthrates in the eastern bloc stagnated.

Across Europe, welfare-state programs aimed to improve people's health. State-funded health care systems covered medical needs in most industrial nations except the United States. The combination of better material conditions and state provision of health care dramatically extended life expectancy and lowered rates of infant mortality. Contributing to the overall progress, the number of doctors and dentists more than doubled between the end of World War I and 1950, and vaccines greatly reduced the death toll from such diseases as tuberculosis, diphtheria, measles, and polio. In England, schoolchildren stood an inch taller, on average, than children the same age had a decade earlier.

State initiatives in other areas played a role in raising the standard of living. A growing network of government-built atomic power plants brought more thorough electrification of eastern Europe and the Soviet Union. Governments legislated more leisure time for workers. Beginning in 1955, Italian workers received twenty-eight paid holidays annually; in Sweden, workers received twenty-nine vacation days, a number that grew in the 1960s. Housing shortages brought on by three decades of economic depression and destructive war meant that postwar Europeans often lived with three generations sharing one or two rooms. To rebuild, governments sponsored a postwar housing boom. New suburbs and even entire cities formed around the edges of major urban areas in both East and West. Many buildings went up slapdash, and although some suburbs ultimately were seen as a blight on the environment, they dramatically improved living conditions for postwar refugees, workers, and immigrants.

Recovery in the East

To create a Soviet bloc according to Stalin's vision, Communists revived the harsh methods that had transformed peasant economies earlier in the century. In eastern Europe, Stalin not only continued to collectivize agriculture but also brought about badly needed industrialization through the nationalization of private property. In Hungary, for example, Communists seized and reapportioned all estates over twelve hundred acres. Having gained

Propaganda for Collective Farming
Dramatic changes were in store for people in eastern Europe who fell under Communist control after World War II. Most objectionable was the policy of collective farming, which stripped farmers of their lands and forced them to farm state property as a group. The poster aims to show Czechs that farming will bring huge benefits, including personal satisfaction. How do you interpret this poster, and why does a woman figure so prominently? *(The Art Archive/German Poster Museum, Essen/Marc Charmet.)*

support of the poorer peasants through this redistribution, the Communists later dispossessed those peasants of their prized lands and pushed them into cooperative farming, though less thoroughly than in the USSR. In Poland, a substantial number of private farms remained.

The process of collectivization was brutal, and rural people later looked back on the 1950s as dreadful. But some workers in the countryside felt that ultimately their lives and their children's lives had improved. "Before we peasants were dirty and poor, we worked like dogs. . . . Was that a good life? No sir, it wasn't. . . . I was a miserable sharecropper and my son is an engineer," said one Romanian peasant. Despite modernization, government investment in agriculture was never high enough to produce the bumper crops of western Europe, and even the USSR depended on produce from the small plots that enterprising farmers cultivated on the side.

Constructing the Soviet Bloc Stalin admired American industrial know-how and prodded the Communist economies to match U.S. productivity. The Soviet Union formed regional organizations like those in the West, instituting the Council for Mutual Economic Assistance (COMECON) in 1949 to coordinate economic relations among the satellite countries and Moscow. The terms of the COMECON relationship worked against the satellite states, however, for the USSR was allowed to buy goods from its clients at bargain prices and sell goods to them at exorbitant ones. Nonetheless, these formerly peasant states became oriented toward technology and industrial economies directed by bureaucrats, who touted the virtues of steel plants and modern transport.

To escape collectivization, rural people moved to cities, where they received education, health care, and ultimately jobs, albeit at the price of repression. The Roman Catholic church often protested the imposition of communism, but the government crushed it as much as possible or used agents to infiltrate it. The government also discriminated against former members of the elite, including professionals, and even imprisoned them or forced them into hard labor in uranium and other dangerous mines. This policy cleared away opposition—real and imagined—to the Communist takeover of eastern Europe.

Culture, along with science, was a building block of Stalinism in both the USSR and satellite countries. State-instituted programs aimed to build loyalty to the modernizing regime; thus, citizens were obliged to attend adult education classes, women's groups, and public ceremonies. An intense program of Russification and de-Christianization forced non-Russian students in eastern Europe to read histories of the war that ignored their own country's resistance and gave the Red Army sole credit for fighting the Nazis. Rigid censorship resulted in what even one Communist writer in the USSR characterized as "a dreary torrent of colorless, mediocre literature." Stalin also purged prominent wartime leaders to ensure obedience and conformity. Marshal Zhukov, a popular leader of the Soviet armed forces, was shipped to a distant command, while Anna Akhmatova, the widely admired poet who championed wartime resistance to the Nazis, was confined to a crowded hospital room because she refused to glorify Stalin in her postwar poetry.

The Death of Stalin In March 1953, amid growing repression, Stalin died, and it soon became clear that the old ways would not hold. Political prisoners in the labor camps rebelled, leading to the release of more than a million people from the Gulag. In June 1953, workers in East German cities, many of them socialists and antifascist activists from before the war, protested the rise of privileged Communists in a series of strikes that spread like wildfire. At the other end of the social order, Soviet officials, despite enjoying luxury goods and plentiful food, had come to distrust Stalinism and now favored change. To calm protests across the Soviet bloc, governments stepped up the production of consumer goods—a policy called goulash communism (after the Hungarian stew) because it resulted in more food for ordinary people. The future after Stalin remained uncertain, however.

In 1955, **Nikita Khrushchev** (1894–1971), an illiterate coal miner before the Bolshevik Revolution, outmaneuvered other rivals to become the undisputed leader of the Soviet Union—but he did so without the Stalinist practice of executing his opponents. Khrushchev listened to popular complaints in both city and countryside and then made the surprising move of attacking Stalin. At a party congress in 1956, Khrushchev denounced the "cult of personality" Stalin had built about himself and announced that Stalinism did not equal communism. Khrushchev thus cleverly attributed problems with communism to a single individual. The "secret speech"—it was not published in the USSR but became known fairly quickly—was a bombshell. People experienced, in the words of one writer, "a

---

Nikita Khrushchev (nyih KEE tuh kroosh CHAWF): Leader of the USSR from c. 1955 until his dismissal in 1964; known for his speech denouncing Stalin, creation of the "thaw," and participation in the Cuban missile crisis.

holiday of the soul." Debates broke out in public, and books appeared championing the ordinary worker against the party bureaucracy. The climate of relative tolerance for free expression after Stalin's death was called the thaw.

Protest erupted once more in early summer 1956, when discontented Polish railroad workers struck for better wages. Inspired by the Polish example and angry at living under communism, Hungarians rebelled against forced collectivization in October 1956—"the golden October," they would call their uprising. As in Poland, economic issues, especially announcements of reduced wages, and reports of Stalin's crimes contributed to the outbreak of violence that soon targeted the entire Communist system. Tens of thousands of protesters filled the streets of Budapest and succeeded in returning a popular hero, Imre Nagy, to power. When Nagy announced that Hungary might leave the Warsaw Pact, however, Soviet troops moved in, killing tens of thousands and causing hundreds of thousands more to flee to the West. Nagy was hanged. Crushing the Hungarian Revolution vividly displayed the limits to the thaw. Despite a rhetoric of democracy, the United States refused to intervene in Hungary, choosing not to risk World War III by challenging the Soviet sphere of influence.

The failure of eastern European uprisings overshadowed significant changes since Stalin's death. While defeating his rivals, Khrushchev ended the Stalinist purges and reformed the courts, which came to function according to procedures instead of staging the show trials of the past. The secret police lost many of its arbitrary powers. "It has become more interesting to visit and see people," Boris Pasternak said of the changes. "It has become easier to work." In 1957, the Soviets successfully launched the first artificial earth satellite, *Sputnik*, and in 1961 they put the first cosmonaut, Yuri Gagarin, in orbit around the earth. The Soviets' edge in space technology shocked the western bloc and motivated the creation of the U.S. National Aeronautics and Space Administration (NASA). For Soviet citizens, such successes indicated that the USSR had achieved Stalin's goal of modernization and might inch further toward freedom.

Khrushchev, however, was inconsistent, showing himself open to changes in Soviet culture at one moment and then bullying honest writers at another. After assaulting Pasternak because his novel *Doctor Zhivago* cast doubt on communism and affirmed the value of the individual, in 1961 he allowed the publication of Aleksandr Solzhenitsyn's *One Day in the Life of Ivan Denisovitch*. This chilling account of life in the Gulag was useful, however, in underscoring Khrushchev's denunciation of Stalin's crimes and excesses. Under the thaw, Khrushchev made several trips to the West and was more widely seen by the public than Stalin. More confident and more affluent, the Soviets took steps to reduce their diplomacy's paranoid style and to expand communism's appeal in the new nations of Asia, Africa, and Latin America emerging from colonialism. Despite the USSR's more relaxed posture, however, the cold war advanced and the superpowers moved closer to the nuclear brink.

REVIEW QUESTION What factors drove recovery in western Europe and in eastern Europe?

Decolonization in a Cold War Climate

After World War II, activists in colonized regions in Asia, Africa, and the Middle East used the postwar chaos in Europe and the uncertainties of the cold war to achieve their long-held goal of liberation. At war's end, the colonial powers repressed nationalist groups and futilely attempted to reimpose their control as if they were still dominant around the world. Yet colonized peoples had been on the front lines defending the West; and as in World War I, they had witnessed the full barbarism of Western warfare. Like African American soldiers in the U.S. army, they experienced discrimination even while saving the West. Excluded from victory parades so that the great powers could maintain the illusion of white and Western supremacy, colonial veterans returning home did not receive the rights of citizenship promised them. Moreover, successive wars had allowed local industries in the colonies to develop, while industry in the imperial homelands fell into decline. As a result of the war, colonized peoples, often steeped in Western values and experienced in war and business, were committed to independence.

The path to independence—a process called **decolonization**—was paved with difficulties. In Africa, a continent whose peoples spoke more than five thousand languages and dialects, the European creation of convenient administrative units such as Nigeria and Rhodesia had cut across ethnic lines and undermined local cultures. Religion played a divisive role in independence movements. In India,

---

decolonization: The process—whether violent or peaceful—by which colonies gained their independence from the imperial powers after World War II.

Hindus and Muslims battled one another even though they shared the goal of eliminating the British. In the Middle East and North Africa, pan-Arab and pan-Islamic movements — that is, those wanting to bring together all Arabs or all Muslims as the basis for decolonization — might seem to have been unifying forces. Yet many Muslims were not Arab, not all Arabs were Muslim, and Islam itself encompassed a range of beliefs. Differences among religious beliefs, ethnic groups, and cultural practices — many of them invented or promoted by the colonizers to divide and rule — worked against political unity. Despite these complications, various peoples in what was coming to be called the third world succeeded in overthrowing imperialism, while the United States and the Soviet Union rushed in to co-opt them for the cold war.

The End of Empire in Asia

At the end of World War II, leaders in Asia succeeded in mobilizing mass discontent to drive out foreign rulers. Declining from an imperial power to a small island nation, Britain was the biggest loser. In 1947, it parted with India, whose independence it had promised in the 1930s. While some two million Indian men were mobilized to fight in the Middle East and Asia, local Indian industry became an important supplier of war goods, and Indian business leaders bought out British entrepreneurs short of cash. Now, armed with economic might and an effective military, Indians began to face off with the British in strikes and other protests.

Britain quickly faced reality. So great was the mistrust it had incited between the Indian National Congress and the Muslim League that Britain decreed that two countries should emerge from the old colony. The partition of 1947 created India for Hindus and Pakistan (itself later divided into two parts) for Muslims. During the independence year, political tensions exploded among opposing members of the two religions. Still another religious group, the Sikhs, felt totally ignored in the settlement and therefore also contributed to the violence. Hundreds of thousands of people overall were massacred in the great shift of populations between India and Pakistan. In 1948, a radical Hindu assassinated Gandhi, who though a Hindu himself had continued to champion religious reconciliation. Elsewhere, as some half a billion Asians gained their independence, Britain's sole remaining Asian colony of note was Hong Kong.

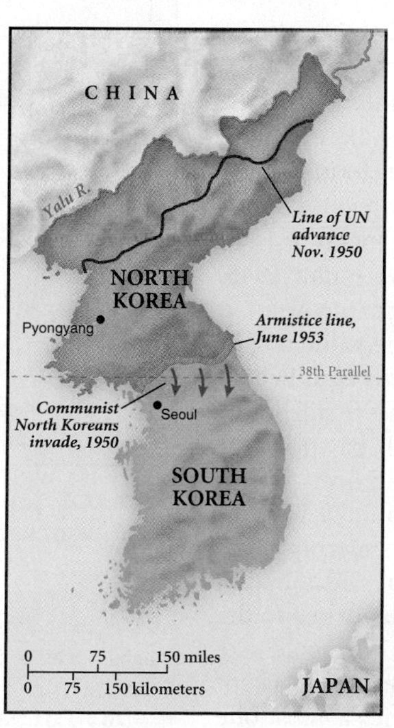

The Korean War, 1950–1953

In 1949, after prolonged fighting, a Communist takeover in China brought in a government led by Mao Zedong (1893–1976). Chinese communism in the new People's Republic of China emphasized above all that the country was no longer the plaything of the colonial powers and that its goal was the welfare of the peasantry rather than the industrial proletariat — a departure from both Marxism and Stalinism. At the same time, Mao instituted reforms such as civil equality for women but also imposed Soviet-style collectivization, rapid industrialization, and brutal repression of the privileged classes.

The United States and the Soviet Union were deeply interested in East Asia, the United States because of the region's economic importance and the USSR because of its shared borders. The victory of the Chinese Communists spurred both to increase their involvement in Asian politics. The superpowers faced off first in Korea, which had been split at the thirty-eighth parallel after World War II. In 1950, the North Koreans, with the support of the Soviet Union, invaded U.S.-backed South Korea, whose agents had themselves been stirring up tensions with raids across the border. The United States maneuvered the Security Council of the United Nations into approving a "police action" against the North, and its forces quickly drove well into North Korean territory, where they were met by the Chinese army. After two and a half years of a horribly destructive stalemate, the opposing sides finally agreed to a settlement in 1953: Korea would remain split at its prewar border, the thirty-eighth parallel. As a result of the Korean War, the United States increased its military spending from almost $11 billion in 1948 to almost $60 billion in 1953. The expansion of the cold war to Asia prompted the creation of an Asian counterpart to NATO: the U.S.-backed Southeast Asia Treaty Organization (SEATO), established in 1954. Another effect of the Korean War was the rapid reindustrialization of Japan to provide the United States with supplies.

The cold war then spread to Indochina, where nationalists had been struggling against the postwar revival of French imperi-

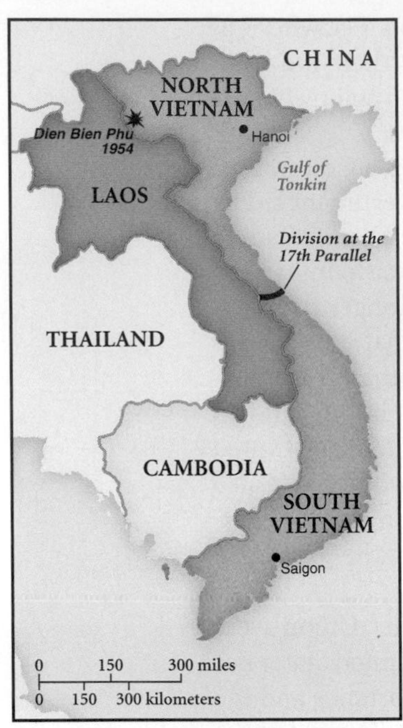

Indochina, 1954

alism. Their leader, the European-educated Ho Chi Minh (1890–1969), built a powerful organization, the Viet Minh, to fight colonial rule. He advocated the redistribution of land held by big landowners, especially in the rich agricultural area in southern Indochina where some six thousand owners possessed more than 60 percent of the land. Viet Minh peasant guerrillas ultimately defeated the technologically superior French army, which was receiving aid from the United States, in the bloody battle of Dien Bien Phu in 1954. Later that year, the Geneva Conference carved out an independent Laos and divided Vietnam along the seventeenth parallel into North and South, each free from French control. The Communist-backed Viet Minh, under Ho Chi Minh as president, ruled in the north, while the United States supported the landowner-backed regime of Ngo Dinh Diem (1901–1963) in the south. Continued superpower intervention undermined the peace agreement, as the two countries fought the cold war in small foreign nations—conflicts now referred to as proxy wars.

The Struggle for Identity in the Middle East

Independence struggles in the Middle East highlighted the world's growing need for oil and often showed the ability of small countries to maneuver between the superpowers. As in other regions dominated by the West, Middle Eastern peoples resisted attempts to reimpose imperial control after 1945. Weakened by the war, British oil companies wanted to tighten their grip on profits as the value of this energy source soared. To achieve this end, British leaders arrogantly behaved as if they were still dominant. For example, Winston Churchill, paying a visit to Saudi Arabia during negotiations over the renewal of Britain's oil rights in the country, insisted that he be served drinks and cigars, sneering at the Islamic prohibitions against alcohol and tobacco. Outraged by this insult, Saudi Arabia turned to the United States, saying that the superpower could take over the oil consortium so long as Britain was kept out. By playing the Western countries against one another, Middle Eastern leaders gained their independence and simultaneously renegotiated higher payments for drilling rights.

The legacy of the Holocaust complicated the Middle Eastern political scene. Since early in the century Western backing for a Jewish settlement in the Middle East had stirred up Arabs' determination not to be pushed out of their ancient homeland. When World War II broke out, 600,000 Jewish settlers and twice as many Arabs lived, tensely, in British-controlled Palestine. In 1947, an exhausted Britain ceded Palestine to the newly created United Nations, which voted to partition Palestine into an Arab region and a Jewish one (Map 27.4). Hostility turned to open war, which Jewish military forces won, and on May 14, 1948, the state of Israel came into being. "The dream had come true," Golda Meir, the future prime minister of Israel, remembered, but "too late to save those who had perished in the Holocaust." Israel opened its gates to immigrants, pitting its expansionist ambitions against those of its Arab neighbors.

One of those neighbors, Egypt, gained its independence from Britain at the end of the war. Britain, however, still dominated shipping to Asia through its control of the Suez Canal, which was owned by a

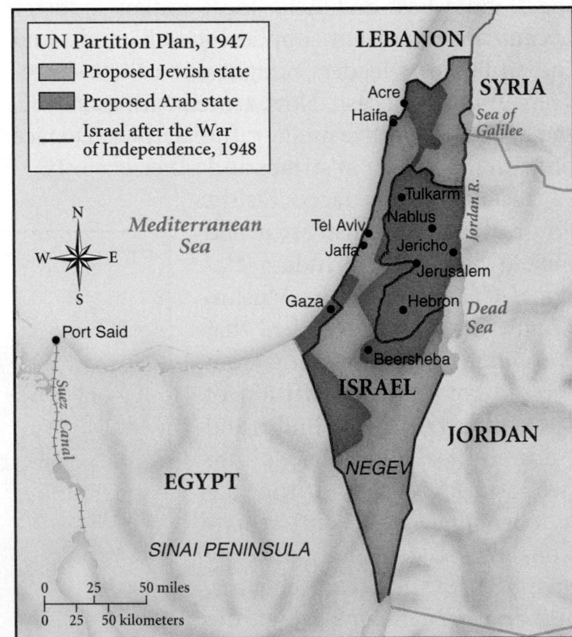

MAP 27.4 The Partition of Palestine and the Creation of Israel, 1947–1948

The creation of the Jewish state of Israel in 1948 against a backdrop of ongoing wars among Jews and indigenous Arab peoples turned the Middle East into a powder keg, a situation that has lasted until the present day. The struggle for resources and for securing the borders of viable nation-states was at the heart of these bitter contests, threatening to pull the superpowers into a third world war.

British-run company. In 1952, Colonel Gamal Abdel Nasser (1918–1970) became Egypt's president on a platform of economic modernization and true national independence—meaning Egyptian control of the canal. In July 1956, Nasser nationalized the canal: "I am speaking in the name of every Egyptian Arab," he remarked in his speech explaining the takeover, "and in the name of all free countries and of all those who believe in liberty and are ready to defend it." Nasser became a heroic figure to Arabs in the region, especially when Britain, supported by Israel and France, attacked Egypt, bringing the Suez crisis to a head while the Hungarian Revolution (see page 930) was in full swing. The British branded Nasser another Hitler and hoped that the events in Hungary would distract the superpowers. The United States, however, fearing that Egypt would turn to the USSR, made the British back down. Nasser's triumph inspired confidence that colonized peoples around the world could gain true independence.

Emerging Nations in the Cold War
Emerging nations could be the playthings of the superpowers during the cold war, but they could also benefit from the rivalry. When Egyptian president Gamal Abdel Nasser refused U.S. military aid in the 1950s because of the supervision the U.S. demanded, Nasser turned to the Soviets and received not only military support but also a low-interest loan for the Aswan Dam—the kind of development project undertaken by emerging nations to provide power and water for both agriculture and industry. In 1964, Nasser (right), Soviet leader Nikita Krushchev, and Algerian president Ahmed Ben Bella inaugurated the opening of the dam. *(Rue des Archives/The Granger Collection, New York—)*

New Nations in Africa

In sub-Saharan Africa, nationalist leaders roused their people to challenge Europe's increasing demands for resources and labor—demands that resulted in poverty for African peoples. "The European Merchant is my shepherd, and I am in want," went one African version of the Twenty-third Psalm. During World War II, many Africans had flocked to urban shantytowns, where they kept themselves alive by doing menial labor for whites and by scavenging. At the war's end, veterans returned home and protest mounted. Kwame Nkrumah (1909–1972), for example, led the inhabitants of the British-controlled West African Gold Coast in Gandhi-inspired civil disobedience, finally driving the British to withdraw and bringing the state of Ghana into being in 1957. Nigeria, the most populous African region, achieved independence in 1960, and many other African states also became free (Map 27.5).

In mixed-race territory with large settler populations the independence struggle was often fierce and bloody. The eastern coast and southern and central areas of Africa had numerous European settlers, who resisted giving up their control. In British East Africa, where white settlers ruled in splendor and where blacks lacked both land and economic opportunity, fighting erupted in the 1950s. African men formed rebel groups named the Land Freedom Army but nicknamed Mau Mau. With women serving as provisioners, messengers, and weapon stealers, Mau Mau bands, composed mostly of war veterans from the Kikuyu ethnic group, tried to recover land from whites. In 1964, the Land Freedom Army's resistance helped Kenya gain formal independence, but only after the British had put hundreds of thousands of Kikuyus in concentration camps—called a "living hell" and a "British gulag" by those tortured there. The British slaughtered tens of thousands more.

France—although eager to regain its great-power status after its humiliating defeat and occupation in World War II—followed the British pattern of granting independence with relatively little blood shed to territories such as Tunisia, Morocco, and West Africa, where there were few white settlers. In Algeria, however, which had one million settlers of European descent, the French fought bitterly to keep control. In the final days of World War II, the French army massacred tens of thousands of Algerian nationalists seeking independence; however, the liberation movement resurfaced with new intensity in 1954 as the Front for National Liberation

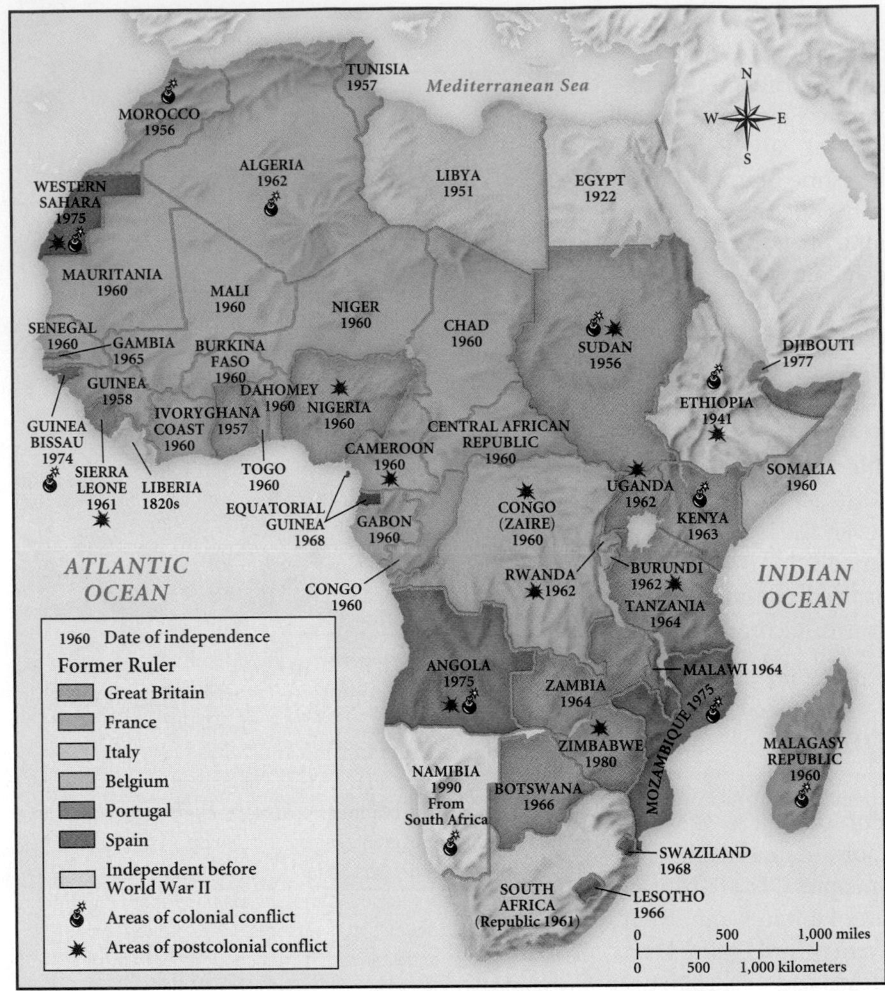

MAP 27.5 The Decolonization of Africa, 1951–1990
The liberation of Africa from European rule was an uneven process, sometimes occurring peacefully and at other times demanding armed struggle to drive out European settlers, governments, and armies. The difficult—and costly—process of nation building following liberation involved setting up state institutions, including educational and other services. Creating national unity out of many ethnicities also took work, except where the struggle against colonialism had already brought people together.

(FNL). The French dug in, sending more than 400,000 troops. Neither side fought according to the rules of warfare: the French savagely tortured Algerian Arabs; Algerian women, shielded from suspicion by gender stereotypes, planted bombs in European cafés and carried weapons to assassination sites. "The loss of Algeria," warned one statesman, defending French savagery, "would be an unprecedented national disaster," while the FNL, far less powerful and smaller in number, took its case to the court of world opinion. Reports of the French army's barbarous practices against Algeria's Muslim population prompted protests in Paris and around the globe. (See Document, "Torture in Algeria," page 935.)

France's Fourth Republic collapsed over Algeria, and wartime leader Charles de Gaulle returned to power in 1958. While promising an end to the Algerian nightmare, he demanded the creation of a new republican government, one with a strong president who chose the prime minister and could exercise emergency power. As de Gaulle's plans to decolonize Algeria unfolded, the French military launched a campaign of terrorism within France itself. By 1962, de Gaulle had negotiated independence with the Algerian nationalists, and hundreds of thousands of *pieds noirs* ("black feet")—as the French condescendingly called Europeans in Algeria—as well as their Arab supporters fled to France.

Violent resistance to the reimposition of colonial rule also ended the empires of the Dutch and Belgians. As newly independent nations emerged in Asia, Africa, and the Middle East, structures arose to promote international security and worldwide deliberations that included representation from the new states. Foremost among these was the **United Nations (UN)**, convened for the first time in 1945. One notable change ensured the UN a greater chance of success than the League of Nations: both the United States and the Soviet Union were active

---

United Nations (UN): An organization set up in 1945 for collective security and for the resolution of international conflicts through both deliberation and the use of force.

DOCUMENT

Torture in Algeria

Torture was common in the Algerian War, and both the French and the pro-independence forces advertised the brutality of the other side. The French had the greatest means available to pick up and torture not just suspected opponents to their rule but also their neighbors, families, and even bystanders in buildings and on the street. The Algerians printed accounts by the score and circulated them around the world, eventually prompting a broad segment of global public opinion, some of it already shocked by the record of Axis torture and genocide, to oppose French colonialism. As the cases were verified, many more came to light. Here is a published account of the torture of a young woman, Djamila Boupacha, from her sworn deposition against the French. We have edited out some of the most horrific acts done to her.

On the night of 10th and 11th of February 1960, the police, Arab collaborators, and police inspectors—about fifty in all—got out of their jeeps and military trucks . . . and stopped at my parents' house where I lived in Algiers. . . .

On the spot and without being taken away, I was beaten savagely. My brother-in-law Abedelli Ahmed who was also there, suffered the same fate as did my father Boupacha Abdelaziz, 70 years of age.

We were taken to the triage center El-Biar. There I received terrible blows which made me fall to the ground. That was when the soldiers, led by a parachutist captain, crushed my ribs with their boots. I still suffer today from deviated ribs on the left.

After four or five days, I was transferred to Hussein-Dey. It was, they told me, to receive "the second degree." I soon found out what that meant: electric torture to begin with (the electrodes placed on my breasts did not stick so one of the torturers glued them to my skin with scotch tape), then they burned me in the same way on my legs, groin, genitals, and face. Electric torture alternated with cigarette burns, punches with fists, and water torture: suspended over a full bathtub, I was made to drink until suffocating.

Source: Sworn testimony, published in *El Moudjahid* 66 (June 20, 1960), reprinted in *La Femme algerienne dans la revolution. Textes et témoignages inédits* (Alger: ENAG/EDITIONS), 68–69. Translated by Bonnie G. Smith.

Question to Consider

- **What might have been the reaction of various groups, ethnicities, political parties, and regions of European and U.S. society to this testimony?**

members from the outset. The UN's charter outlined a collective global authority that would resolve conflicts and provide military protection if any members were threatened by aggression. In 1955, the Indonesian president Sukarno, who had succeeded in wrenching Indonesian independence from the Dutch, sponsored the Bandung Convention of nonaligned nations to set a common policy for achieving modernization and facing the superpowers. Newly independent countries viewed the future with hope but still had to contend with the high costs of nation building and problems left from decades of colonial exploitation. Both UN deliberations and meetings such as the Bandung Conference began raising major global issues such as human rights and inequities between the countries of the north, which had prospered through colonial plunder, and those of the south, which had been plundered.

Newcomers Arrive in Europe

Amid the uncertainties of wars of independence, people from the former colonies began migrating to Europe—a reversal of the nineteenth-century trend of migration out of Europe. The first non-Europeans came from Britain's Caribbean possessions right after the war. Next, labor shortages in Germany, France, Switzerland, and elsewhere drove governments to negotiate with southern European countries for temporary workers. The German situation was particularly dire; in 1950, the working-age population (people between the ages of fifteen and sixty-four) was composed of 15.5 million men and 18 million women. In an ideological climate that wanted women out of the workforce, the government desperately needed immigrants. Germany and France next turned to North African and then to sub-Saharan countries in the 1960s. Countries in the Soviet bloc took refugees from war-torn Southeast Asia. Scandinavia received immigrants from around the world who flocked there because of reportedly greater opportunity and social programs to integrate newcomers. By the 1980s, some 8 percent of the European population was foreign-born, compared with 6 percent in the United States.

According to negotiated agreements, immigrant workers would have only temporary resident status, with a regular process of return to their homeland. Turks and Algerians would arrive in Germany or France, for example, to work for a set period of

Newcomers to Europe
World War II disrupted everyday life and patterns of trade not only in Europe but also around the globe. Some of the first people to immigrate to Europe in search of postwar opportunity were from the Caribbean (like these men photographed in London in 1956) and South Asia. An expanding welfare state hired some of them to do menial work in hospitals, clinics, and construction, no matter what their qualifications. Governments and businesses in western Europe needed these new laborers to rebuild after World War II, and though some objected, many of these workers—and their wives and children—became not only citizens but political, economic, and cultural leaders as well. *(© Hulton-Deutsch Collection/Corbis.)*

time, return home temporarily to see their families, then head back to Europe for another period as guest workers. Initially, these workers were housed in barracks and few Europeans paid any attention to the quality of their lives. They were welcomed because they took few social services, not even needing education because they came as adults. For businesspeople and policymakers alike, temporary workers made good economic sense. Virtually none of the welfare-state benefits would apply to them; often their menial work was off the books. "As they are young," one French business publication explained, "the immigrants often pay more in taxes than they receive in allowances." Most immigrants did jobs that people in the West were not likely to want: they collected garbage, built roads, and cleaned homes. Although men predominated among migrant workers, women performed similar chores for even less pay.

Immigrants came to see Europe as a land of relatively good government, wealth, and opportunity. Living conditions, too, seemed decent to many. As one Chinese immigrant to Spain put it: "If you want to be a millionaire, you must go to Singapore; if you want to be rich, you must go to Germany; but if you want good weather and an easy life, go to Spain." The advantages of living in Europe, especially the higher wages, made many decide to stay and soon attracted clandestine workers. In the late 1970s, clandestine workers from Africa and Asia began entering countries like Italy that had formerly exported labor. As empires collapsed, European populations became more diverse in terms of race, religion, ethnicity, and social life. Across Europe and North America, many newcomers eventually became citizens and their children achieved good positions in government, business, education, and the professions.

REVIEW QUESTION What were the results of decolonization?

Daily Life and Culture in the Shadow of Nuclear War

Both World War II and the cold war shaped postwar culture. People engaged in heated debate over responsibility for Nazism, ethnic and racial justice, and the merits of the two superpowers. During this period of intense self-scrutiny, Europeans discussed the Americanization that seemed to accompany the influx of U.S. dollars, consumer goods, and cultural media. The quality of private life, so torn by war and totalitarianism, gained attention across the cold war divide. As Europeans examined their war-filled past and their newfound prosperity, the cold war menaced hopes for peace and stability. In 1961, the USSR demanded the construction of a massive wall that physically divided the city of Berlin in half. In October 1962, the world held its breath while the leaders of the Soviet Union and the United States nearly provoked nuclear conflagration over the issue of missiles on the island of Cuba. In hindsight, the existence of extreme nuclear threat in an age of unprecedented prosperity seems utterly bewildering, but for those who lived with the threat of global annihilation, the dangers were all too real.

Restoring "Western" Values

After the depravity of fascism, cultural currents in Europe and the United States reemphasized universal values and spiritual renewal. Some saw the churches as central to the restoration of values through an active commitment to re-Christianizing both the West and the world without concern for national boundaries or imperial competition. Responding to what he saw as a crisis in faith caused by affluence and secularism, Pope John XXIII (r. 1958–1963) in 1962 convened the Second Vatican Council. Known as **Vatican II**, this council modernized the liturgy, democratized many church procedures, and at the last session in 1965 renounced church doctrine that condemned the Jewish people as guilty of killing Jesus. Vatican II promoted ecumenism—that is, mutual cooperation among the world's faiths—and outreach to the world different from the old practice of missionary crusading to expand empires.

The trend toward a more secular culture continued despite reform in the churches. In the early postwar years, people in the U.S. bloc emphasized the triumph of a Western heritage, a Western civilization, and Western values over fascism, and they characterized the war as one "to defend civilization [from] a conspiracy against man." This definition of *West* often emphasized the heritage of Greece and Rome and the rise of national governments in England, France, and western Europe as they encountered "barbaric" forces, a concept that included nomadic tribes, Nazi armies, Communist agents, or national liberation movements in Asia and Africa. Many white Europeans looked back nostalgically on their imperial history and produced exotic films and novels about conquest and its pageantry. University courses in Western civilization flourished after the war to reaffirm these values.

Holocaust and Resistance Literature Readers around the world snapped up memoirs of the death camps and tales of the resistance. Rescued from the Third Reich in 1940, Nelly Sachs won the Nobel Prize for Literature in 1966 for her poetry about the Holocaust. Anne Frank's *Diary of a Young Girl* (1947), the moving record of a teenager hidden with her family in the back of an Amsterdam house, showed the survival of Western values in the face of Nazi persecution. Amid the menacing evils of Nazism, Frank, who died near the end of the war in the Bergen-Belsen camp, wrote that she never stopped believing that "people are really good at heart." Governments erected permanent plaques at spots where resisters had been killed, and organizations of resisters publicly commemorated their role in winning the war, hiding the fact of widespread collaboration in the heroism of resistance. Thus, French filmmakers, for instance, avoided the subject for decades after the war. Many a politician with a Nazi past returned easily to the new cultural mainstream even as the stories of resistance took on mythical qualities.

Existential Philosophy At the end of the 1940s, **existentialism** became the rage among the cultural elites and students in universities. This philosophy explored the meaning of human existence in a world where evil flourished. Two of existentialism's leaders, Albert Camus and Jean-Paul Sartre, had written for the resistance during the war, and in its aftermath they confronted the question of "being," given what they perceived as the absence of God and the tragic breakdown of morality. Their answer was that being, or existing, was not the automatic process either of God's creation or of birth into the natural world. One was not born with spiritual goodness in the image of a creator, but instead created an "authentic" existence through action and choice. Camus's novels, such as *The Stranger* (1942) and *The Plague* (1947), pondered the responsibility of humans living under an evil and corrupt political order. Sartre's writings emphasized political activism and resistance under totalitarianism. Even though they had never confronted the enormous problems of making choices while living under fascism, young people in the

---

Vatican II: A Catholic Council held between 1962 and 1965 to modernize some aspects of church teachings (such as condemnation of Jews), to update the liturgy, and to promote cooperation among the faiths (i.e., ecumenism).

existentialism: A philosophy prominent after World War II developed primarily by Jean-Paul Sartre to stress the importance of action in the creation of an authentic self.

Jean-Paul Sartre and Simone de Beauvoir
The postwar period saw the rise of glossy, richly illustrated weekly magazines featuring news and pop culture. The faces of even the most complex philosophers became well known to the public, while their private lives intrigued readers. The public story of these two existentialists, who were seen to promote the revival of human values after the nightmare of fascism, hid the twisted relationship Sartre and Beauvoir actually had. *(David E. Sherman/Time & Life Pictures/Getty Images.)*

1950s found existentialism compelling and made it the most fashionable philosophy of the day.

In 1949, **Simone de Beauvoir**, Sartre's lifetime companion, published the twentieth century's most important work on the condition of women, *The Second Sex*. Beauvoir believed that most women had failed to take the kind of action necessary to lead authentic lives. Instead, they lived in the world of biological necessity, devoting themselves exclusively to having children. Failing to create an authentic self through action and accomplishment, they had become its opposite—an object, or "Other." Moreover, instead of struggling to define themselves and assert their freedom, women passively accepted their lives as defined by men. Beauvoir's now classic book was a smash hit, and people wrote her thousands of letters asking for advice. Both Sartre and Beauvoir became celebrities, for the media spread the new commitment to humane values just as it had previously spread support for Nazism or for other political ideas.

Simone de Beauvoir (see MAWN duh bohv WAHR): Author of *The Second Sex* (1949), a globally influential work that created an interpretation of women's age-old inferior status from existentialist philosophy.

Race and Human Rights People of color in Africa and Asia contributed new theories of humanity by exploring the topics of liberation and racial difference. During the 1950s, Frantz Fanon, a black psychiatrist from the French colony of Martinique, began analyzing liberation movements, gaining his insights from his participation in the Algerian war of liberation and other struggles at the time. He wrote that the mental functioning of the colonized person was "traumatized" by the brutal imposition of an outside culture. Ruled by guns, the colonized person knew only violence and would thus naturally decolonize by means of violence. Translated into many languages, Fanon's *Black Skin, White Masks* (1952) and *The Wretched of the Earth* (1961) posed the question of how to decolonize one's culture and mind.

Simultaneous with decolonization, the commitment to the cause of civil rights of such longstanding organizations as the National Association for the Advancement of Colored People (NAACP), founded in 1909, intensified in the 1950s. African Americans had fought in World War II to defeat the Nazi idea of white racial superiority; as civilians, they now hoped to advance that ideal in the United States. With its ruling in *Brown v. Board of Education* (1954), the U.S. Supreme Court declared that segregated education violated the U.S. Constitution. The next step in the civil rights movement came in December 1955, in Montgomery, Alabama, when Rosa Parks, a seamstress and part-time secretary for the local branch of the NAACP, boarded a city bus and took the first available seat in the "colored" section. When a white man found himself without a seat, the driver screamed at Parks, "Nigger, move back." She refused to move, and her studied use of civil disobedience led to a boycott of public transportation in Montgomery and eventually to widespread nonviolent disobedience among African Americans throughout the South.

Civil rights groups boycotted discriminatory businesses, held sit-ins at segregated facilities, and registered black voters disfranchised by local regulations. Talented leaders emerged, foremost among them the great orator Martin Luther King Jr. (1929–1968), a Baptist pastor from Georgia, whose speeches roused activists to nonviolent resistance despite brutal white retaliation. Strongly influenced by Gandhi's life and practice of nonviolent resistance, King advocated "soulforce"—Gandhi's *satyagraha* ("holding to truth")—to counter aggression. The postwar culture of nonviolence shaped the early years of the civil rights movement until the influence of Fanon and other third world activists turned it toward more violent activism in pursuit of rights.

Frantz Fanon
Caribbean psychiatrist Frantz Fanon fought in the French army and studied medicine in Paris; he was also influenced by the existential thinking of his time. His experiences with the French put him on the side of those fighting for national liberation, especially in Algeria. Fanon died of leukemia at age thirty-six, but in his brief lifespan he became a towering intellectual figure for his explanation of the need to decolonize the mind and to use violence to defeat the colonial powers. *(© Everett Collection Inc./Alamy.)*

Zbigniew Cybulski, the Polish James Dean
Zbigniew Cybulski depicted a tortured young resistance fighter in the film *Ashes and Diamonds* (1958) by Andrzej Wajda. Cybulski's character is to assassinate a Communist resistance leader on what turns out to be the last day of World War II, and his human dilemma around the act is set amid the chaos in Poland at war's end. Like existentialist philosophers and other film directors at the time, Wajda captured the debate over human values and the interest in young heroes of the postwar era. *(Photofest.)*

Cold War Consumerism and Shifting Gender Norms

Government spending on Europe's reconstruction and welfare after World War II helped prevent the kind of upheaval that had followed World War I. Meanwhile, the rising birthrate and bustling youth culture led to an upsurge in consumer spending—a contrast to wartime, during which the lack of con sumer goods had made for an absence of spending. Increased emphasis on consumer needs created jobs for veterans. Nonetheless, the war had affected men's roles and sense of themselves. Young men who had missed World War II adopted the rough, violent style of soldiers, and roaming gangs posed as tough military types. While Soviet youth admired aviator aces, elsewhere groups such as the "teddy boys" in England (named after their Edwardian style of dressing) and the *gamberros* ("hooligans") in Spain took their cues from pop culture in rock-and-roll music and film. (See Document, "Popular Culture, Youth Consumerism, and the Birth of the Generation Gap," page 940.)

The leader of rock-and-roll style was the American singer Elvis Presley. Sporting slicked-back hair and an aviator-style jacket, Presley bucked his hips and sang sexual lyrics to screaming and devoted fans. Rock-and-roll concerts and movies galvanized youth across Europe, including the Soviet bloc, where teens demanded the production of blue jeans and leather jackets. In a German nightclub late in the 1950s, members of a British rock group of Elvis fans called the Quarrymen performed, yelling at and fighting with one another as part of their show. They would soon become known as the Beatles. Rebellious young American film stars like James Dean in *Rebel Without a Cause* (1955) and Marlon Brando in *The Wild One* (1953) created the beginnings of a postwar youth culture in which the ideal was to be a bad boy.

The rebellious and rough masculine style appeared also in literature, for example in James Watson's autobiography, *The Double Helix* (1968), in which he described how he and Francis Crick had discovered the structure of the DNA molecule

DOCUMENT

Popular Culture, Youth Consumerism, and the Birth of the Generation Gap

A new development put young people at the cutting edge of consumerism and other aspects of Americanization and economic revival. The generation gap, so much talked about in the 1960s, took shape in the preceding decade because of youthful openness on matters of the body and sexuality. Not so mired in the war as their parents, the young were ready for adventure—and adults worried about the consequences. Here an Austrian working-class woman (born in 1933) who sewed for a living describes her consumerism and youth more generally around 1955.

I bought myself records, American blues and jazz, Benny Goodman and Louis Armstrong. I was happy dancing the boogie-woogie. . . .

In fashion I was always very much in opposition to my mother. First, there was the craze around nylon stockings, which were very expensive, and which almost everyone bought. We wore long checked skirts, not made of sheep's wool but of a "mixed" wool that was produced out of rags. Then came a short skirt, just above the knee. When I went dancing, however, everyone wore tight, fashionable skirts. One really had to get oneself into them with a shoehorn, and one's backside stood out. I then sewed a kind of cascade on one side, and thus attired, I proudly went dancing.

At first one wore hair long. But my boss was at me so much about it that I had it cut. Then with the new permanents from America one got a totally new look which was flat in the back with a garland of curls around the rest. But fashion changed fast, at one minute such a hairdo was modern, but then one had to put a comb in to push it up higher.

My home was very nice, with a great deal of love, and because of that my parents gave me a lot of freedom although my mother was always concerned. Above everything she always worried: "What will the neighbors think?"

We only spoke about sex with our schoolmates. Certainly nothing about it came from my parents, nothing either from the school. No, one could not ask about such things. . . . Everything was taboo. And boys and girls were strictly segregated from one another in the school. I remember at carnival time a boy came to school dressed as a girl and was sent right home.

Source: Birgit Bolognese-Leuchtenmüller et al., eds., *Frauen der ersten Stunde 1945–1955* (Vienna: Medieninhaber Europaverlag, 1985), 20–21. Translation by Bonnie G. Smith.

Question to Consider

- **How does this woman's account reflect the clash of ideas between the older and younger generations?**

by stealing other people's findings. The German novelist Heinrich Böll, who decades later admitted to having been a Nazi soldier, protested that West Germany's postwar goal of respectability had allowed the reappearance of the types of people who had produced Nazism. In Böll's novel *The Clown* (1963), the young middle-class hero leaves home and takes up life as a vagabond clown, amusing audiences with clever pantomimes about the folly of their lives. Not a breadwinner but a bum, he ends up a model bad boy begging in a railroad station. American "beat" poets and writers vehemently rejected the traditional ideals of the upright male breadwinner and family man.

Both high and low culture revealed that two horrendous world wars had upset the Enlightenment view of men as rational, responsible achievers. The 1953 inaugural issue of the American magazine *Playboy*, and the hundreds of magazines that came to imitate it across Europe, ushered in a startling depiction of a changed male identity. This new media presented modern man as sexually aggressive and independent of dull domestic life—just as he had been in the war. Breadwinning for a family destroyed a man's freedom and sense of self, this new male culture claimed. The definition of men's citizenship had come to include not just political and economic rights but also sexual freedom outside the restrictions of marriage.

In contrast, Western society promoted a postwar model for women that differed from their wartime roles, adopting instead the fascist notion of women's inferiority. Rather than being essential workers and heads of families in the absence of their men, postwar women were to symbolize the return to normalcy by leading a domestic and submissive life at home. Late in the 1940s, the fashion house of Christian Dior launched a clothing style called the "new look." It featured pinched waists, tightly fitting bodices, and voluminous skirts. This restoration of the nineteenth-century female silhouette invited a renewal of clearly defined gender roles. Women's magazines publicized the new look and urged women to give up ambitions for themselves. Even in the hard-pressed Soviet Union, domesticity flourished; recipes for homemade face creams, for

Rock and Roll

Rock and roll, born in the 1950s, swept cities around the world with unprecedented energy and speed. Teen women wore the voluminous skirts that the "new look" had made fashionable in the late 1940s, and young men sported hairdos like those of Elvis Presley or Zbigniew Cybulski. East and west, teens thronged and even rioted to attend rock concerts and would continue to do so despite public criticism and even police action against the movement. *(ullstein bild/The Granger Collection, New York—All rights reserved.)*

example, passed from woman to woman, and beauty parlors did a brisk business. In the West, household products such as refrigerators and washing machines raised standards for housekeeping by giving women the means to be "perfect" housewives.

However, new-look propaganda did not necessarily mesh with reality or even with all social norms. Dressmaking fabric was still being rationed in the late 1940s; even in the next decade, women could not always get enough of it to make voluminous skirts. In Europe, where people had barely enough to eat, the underwear needed for new-look contours simply did not exist—although for many, unfortunately, the semistarved look was not achieved by choice. In Spain, women were said to perform their role best by being religious and concerned with the spiritual well-being of their families. Spanish advertising, however, emphasized the physical beauty available through cosmetics and clothing; it urged women to buy things that would make their families look better, too.

Despite welfare-state policies intended to promote childbearing, European women continued to work outside the home after the war; indeed, mature women and mothers were working more than ever before—especially in the Soviet bloc (Figure 27.2). Across the Soviet sphere consumer goods were always in short supply, but opinion makers stressed to these women the importance of a tasteful and up-to-date domestic interior. East and West, the female workforce was going through a profound revolution as it gradually became populated by wives and mothers who would hold jobs all their lives despite being bombarded with images of nineteenth-century femininity.

The advertising business presided over the creation of these cultural messages as part of both the return of consumerism and the cold war. Guided by marketing experts, western Europeans imitated Americans by drinking Coca-Cola; using American detergents, toothpaste, and soap; and driving some forty million motorized vehicles, including motorbikes, cars, buses, and trucks. While many Europeans embraced American business practices, the cold war was ever present: the Communist Party in France led a successful campaign to ban Coca-Cola for a time in the 1950s, and tastemakers in the Soviet sphere initiated competing products and styles.

Radio remained the most influential medium in the 1950s, carrying much of the postwar consumer advertising and making the connection between cold war and consumerism. Even as the number of radios in homes grew steadily, television loomed on the horizon. In the United States, two-thirds of the population had TV sets in the early 1950s, while in Britain only one-fifth did. Only in the 1960s did television become an important consumer item for most Europeans. In radio and television, though, both East and West tried to exceed the other in advertising their values. Russian programs stressed a uniform Communist culture, often emphasizing the importance of family values and practical, if aesthetically pleasing, household tips for women. The United States, by contrast, emphasized diverse programming, promoted debate about current affairs, and filled the airwaves with

	Member Countries of Council of Mutual Economic Assistance[1]		Member Countries of European Economic Community[2]	
	1950	1960	1950	1960
Female as % of total population	54.9	53.9	51.8	51.6
Female labor force as % of total labor force	48.5	48.7	31.1	31.4
Distribution of female labor force (%):				
Agriculture	63.3	50.0	26.1	16.8
Industry	16.9	22.6	29.3	31.3
Services	19.8	27.4	44.6	51.9

[1]Albania, Bulgaria, Czechoslovakia, East Germany, Hungary, Poland, Romania, and USSR

[2]Belgium, Denmark, France, West Germany, Ireland, Italy, Luxembourg, Netherlands, and United Kingdom

FIGURE 27.2 Women in the Workforce, 1950–1960
In contrast to the situation after World War I, women did not leave the workforce in great numbers after World War II. In fact, Europe faced labor shortages. In Soviet-bloc countries, women vastly outnumbered men because so many men had died in the war, and the task of rebuilding demanded every available worker. In western Europe, women's workforce participation was lower, and countries like West Germany tried to keep women out of the labor pool to distinguish themselves from the Communist bloc. Note the increase in women's service-sector employment in just one decade. *(From* World Employment 1996–1997: National Policies in a Global Context *[Geneva: International Labour Office, 1996], 7.)*

advertising for consumer goods. The cold war was thus a consumer as well as a military phenomenon.

The Three Graces
French artist Niki de Saint Phalle's compositions often tried to capture the vibrancy of non-Western art, especially that created by women, whose spirit and style she hoped to duplicate in her own work. Saint Phalle's sculptures decorate public places across the West. *(Washington Post/Getty Images.)*

The Culture of Cold War

Films, books, and other cultural productions also promoted the cold war even when they conveyed an antiwar message. Books like George Orwell's *1984* (1949) were claimed by both sides in the cold war as supporting their position. Ray Bradbury's popular *Fahrenheit 451* (1953), whose title refers to the temperature at which books would burn, condemned restrictions on intellectual freedom on both sides of the cold war divide. In the USSR, official writers churned out spy stories, and espionage novels topped best-seller lists in the West. *Casino Royale* (1953), by the British author Ian Fleming, introduced the fictional British intelligence agent James Bond, who tested his wit and physical prowess against Communist and other political villains. Soviet pilots would not take off for flights when the work of Yulian Simyonov, the Russian counterpart of Ian Fleming, was playing on radio or television. Reports, fictional and real, of Soviet- and U.S.-bloc characters facing one another down became part of everyday life.

High culture also operated in a cold-war climate. Europe's major cities rebuilt their war-ravaged opera houses and museums, and both sides tried to win the cold war by pouring vast sums of money into high culture. The United States did so by secretly channeling government money into foundations to award fellowships to artists or promote favorable journalism around the world. As leadership of the art world passed to the United States, art became part of the cold war. Abstract expressionists such as American artist Jackson Pollock produced nonrepresentational works by dripping and spattering paint; they also spoke of the importance of the artist's self-discovery in the process of painting. "If I stretch my arms next to the rest of myself and wonder where my fingers are, that is all the space I need as a painter," commented Dutch-born artist Willem de Kooning on his relationship with his canvas. Said to exemplify Western freedom, such painters were awarded commissions at the secret direction of the U.S. Central Intelligence Agency.

The USSR more openly promoted an official Communist culture. When a show of abstract art opened in the Soviet Union, Khrushchev yelled that it was "dog shit." Pro-Soviet critics in western Europe saw U.S.-style abstract art as "an infantile sickness" and supported socialist realist art with "human content," showing the condition of the workers and the oppressed races in the United States. The Italian filmmakers Roberto Rossellini, in *Open City* (1945), and Vittorio De Sica, in *The Bicycle Thief* (1948), developed the neorealist technique that challenged lush Hollywood-style sets and costumes by using ordinary characters living in devastated, impoverished cities. By depicting stark conditions, neorealist directors conveyed their distance both from middle-class prosperity and from fascist bombast. "We are in rags? Let's show everyone our rags," said one Italian director. Many of these left-leaning directors associated support for the suffering masses with the Communist cause, while on the pro-American side, the film *Doctor Zhivago* became a hit celebrating individualism and condemning the Communist way of life. Overtly or covertly, the cold war affected virtually all aspects of cultural life.

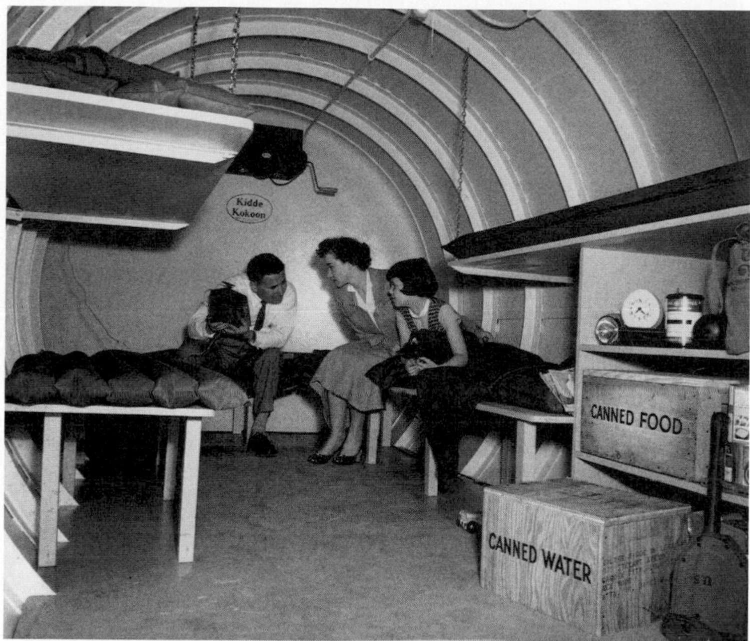

Bomb Shelter

Americans expressed their fear of nuclear annihilation by building tens of thousands of individual bomb shelters. Stocked with several months' supply of canned food and other goods, the shelters were to protect a family from the nuclear blast itself and from the disorder that might follow nuclear war. The government also prepared shelters to shield top officials and to ensure the continuation of civil society despite vast casualties and massive destruction. *(© Bettman/Corbis.)*

The Atomic Brink

The 1950s were a time of emotional terror for people at the center of the cold war. Radio bombarded the public with messages about the threat of nuclear annihilation at the hands of the villainous superpower enemy. As superpower rivalry heated up, radio's propaganda function remained as strong as it had been in wartime, and it was soon joined by television. During the late 1940s and 1950s, the Voice of America, with its main studio in Washington, D.C., broadcast in thirty-eight languages from one hundred transmitters and provided an alternative source of news as well as menacing messages for people in eastern Europe. Its Soviet counterpart broadcast in Russian around the clock but initially spent much of its wattage jamming U.S. programming. The public also heard reports of nuclear buildups, and tests of emergency power facilities sent them scurrying for cover. Children rehearsed at school for nuclear war, while at home families built bomb shelters in their backyards. Fear gripped people's emotions in these decades.

In this upsetting climate of cold war, **John Fitzgerald Kennedy** (1917–1963) was elected U.S. president in 1960. Kennedy represented American affluence and youth, yet he also confirmed the nation's commitment to the cold war. Kennedy's media advisers recognized how perfect a match their articulate, good-looking president was for the power of television. A war hero and an early fan of the fictional cold war spy James Bond, Kennedy par-

---

John Fitzgerald Kennedy: U.S. president (1961–1963) who faced off with Soviet leader Nikita Khrushchev in the Cuban missile crisis.

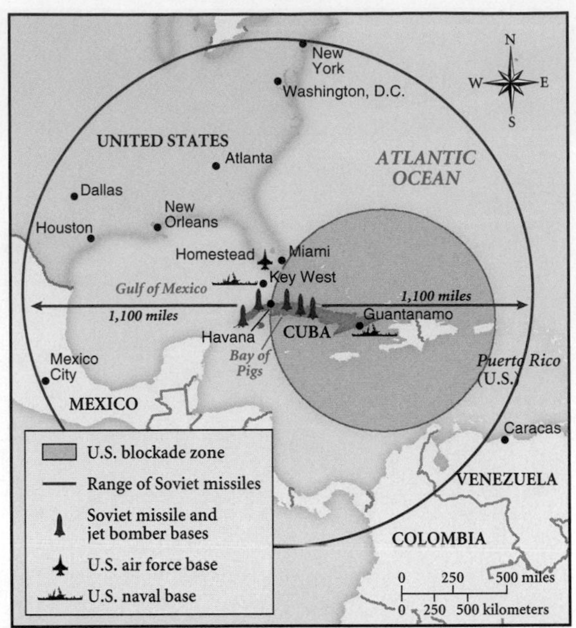

MAP 27.6 The Cuban Missile Crisis, 1962
Just off the coast of the southeastern United States, Cuba posed a threat to North American security once the Soviet Union began stocking the island with silos for missiles. The United States reacted vigorously, insisting that the USSR dismantle the missile sites. Although his generals were prepared for nuclear war with the Soviet Union, President Kennedy refused to take this step, and Soviet premier Khrushchev similarly backed down from a military confrontation. | **Explain the placement of missiles in Cuba and the U.S. reaction to it.**

ticipated in the escalating cold war. Some of this escalation occurred over the nearby island of Cuba, where in 1959 the Communist leader Fidel Castro (1926–) had come to power by overthrowing the corrupt government of the dictator Fulgencio Batista. After being rebuffed by the United States, Castro aligned his new government with the Soviet Union. In the spring of 1961, Kennedy, assured by the Central Intelligence Agency (CIA) of success, launched an invasion of Cuba at the Bay of Pigs intended to overthrow Castro. The invasion failed miserably and humiliated the United States.

Cold war tensions increased. In the summer of 1961, the East German government directed workers to stack bales of barbed wire across miles of the city's east–west border as the beginning of the Berlin Wall. The divided city had served as an escape route by which some three million people, including skilled workers and professionals, had fled to the West. Kennedy responded by calling for more defense spending. In October 1962, tensions came to a head in the **Cuban missile crisis**, when the CIA reported the installation of silos to house Soviet medium-range missiles in Cuba (Map 27.6). Kennedy acted forcefully, ordering a naval blockade of ships headed for Cuba and demanding removal of the installations. For several days, the world stood on the brink of nuclear war. Then, between October 25 and 27, Khrushchev and Kennedy negotiated an end to the crisis. Kennedy spent the remainder of his short life working to improve nuclear diplomacy; Khrushchev did the same. In the summer of 1963, less than a year after the shock of the Cuban missile crisis, the United States and the Soviet Union signed a test-ban treaty outlawing the explosion of nuclear weapons in the atmosphere and in the seas. Allowing the superpowers to back away from the brink, the treaty held out hope that the cold war and its culture would give way to something better.

REVIEW QUESTION | **How were everyday culture and social life part of the cold war?**

Conclusion

Nikita Khrushchev was ousted in 1964 for his erratic policies and for the Cuban missile crisis. In his forced retirement, he expressed regret at his brutal treatment of Boris Pasternak: "We shouldn't have banned [*Doctor Zhivago*]. There's nothing anti-Soviet in it." But the postwar decades were grim times. Two superpowers—the Soviet Union and the United States—each controlling atomic arsenals, overshadowed European leadership and engaged in a menacing cold war, complete with the threat of nuclear annihilation. The cold war saturated everyday life, giving birth to bomb shelters, spies, purges, and witch hunts—all of them creating a culture of anxiety that kept people in constant fear of imminent war. Cold war diplomacy divided Europe into an eastern bloc dominated by the Soviets and a freer western bloc mostly allied with the United States. In this bleak atmosphere, starving, homeless, and refugee people joined the task of rebuilding a devastated Europe.

Despite the chaos at the end of 1945, both halves of Europe recovered almost miraculously in little more than a decade. Eastern Europe, where wartime devastation and ongoing violence were greatest, experienced less prosperity. In the West, wartime technology served as the basis for new consumer

Cuban missile crisis: The confrontation in 1962 between the United States and the USSR over Soviet installation of missile sites off the U.S. coast in Cuba.

MAPPING THE WEST

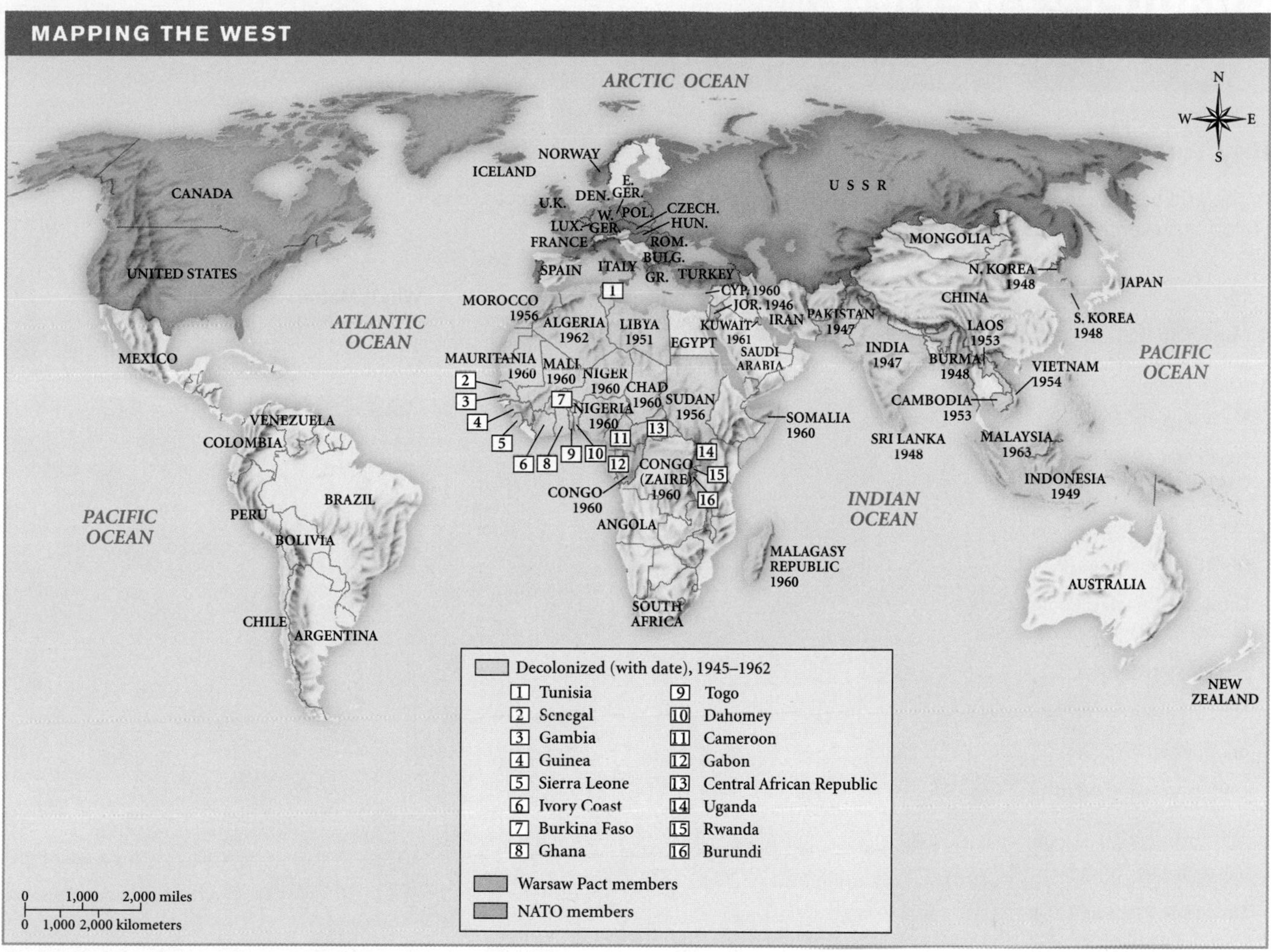

The Cold War World, c. 1960

Superpower rivalry between the United States and the Soviet Union resulted in the division of much of the industrial world into cold war alliances. Simultaneously, the superpowers vied for the allegiance of the newly decolonized countries of Asia and Africa by providing military, economic, and technological assistance. Wars such as those in Vietnam and Korea were also products of the cold war. | **How might this map be said to convey the idea that a first world, a second world, and a third world existed? How does this map differ from the map on page 793?**

goods and welfare-state planning improved health. Spurred on by aid from the United States, western Europe formed the successful Common Market, which became the foundation for greater European unity in the future. As a result of World War II and the cold war, Germany recovered as two countries, not one. The war so weakened the European powers that they lost their colonies to thriving independence movements. Newly independent nations emerged in Asia and Africa, leaving in question whether there would be further change in the balance of global power. These new countries were often caught in the competition for cold war allies and faced the additional problems of creating stable political structures and a sound economic future. As the West as a whole grew in prosperity, its cultural life focused paradoxically on reviving Western values while enjoying the new phenomenon of mass consumerism. Above all, the West—and the rest of the world—had to survive the atomic rivalry of the superpowers.

FOR FURTHER EXPLORATION

- **For additional primary-source material from this period**, see *Sources of the Making of the West*, Fourth Edition.
- **For Web sites, images, and documents related to topics in this chapter**, visit *Make History* at bedfordstmartins.com/hunt.

Chapter 27 Review

Online Study Guide bedfordstmartins.com/hunt

Key Terms and People

In the grid below, identify the term or person and explain its historical significance. (To do this exercise online, go to bedfordstmartins.com/hunt.)

Term	Who or What & When	Why It Matters
cold war (p. 914)		
Truman Doctrine (p. 919)		
Marshall Plan (p. 919)		
North Atlantic Treaty Organization (NATO) (p. 921)		
Warsaw Pact (p. 921)		
Christian Democrats (p. 924)		
European Economic Community (EEC or Common Market) (p. 926)		
welfare state (p. 927)		
Nikita Khrushchev (p. 929)		
decolonization (p. 930)		
United Nations (UN) (p. 934)		
Vatican II (p. 937)		
existentialism (p. 937)		
Simone de Beauvoir (p. 938)		
John Fitzgerald Kennedy (p. 943)		
Cuban missile crisis (p. 944)		

Review Questions

1. What were the major events in the development of the cold war?
2. What factors drove recovery in western Europe and in eastern Europe?
3. What were the results of decolonization?
4. How were everyday culture and social life part of the cold war?

Making Connections

1. What was the political climate after World War II, and how did it differ from the political climate after World War I?
2. What were the relative strengths of the two European blocs in the cold war?
3. What were the main developments of postwar cultural life?
4. Why did decolonization follow World War II so immediately?

Important Events

Date	Event	Date	Event
1945	Cold war begins	1954	*Brown v. Board of Education* prohibits segregated schools in the United States; Vietnamese forces defeat French at Dien Bien Phu
1947	India and Pakistan win independence from Britain	1956	General Abdel Nasser nationalizes Suez Canal; uprising in Hungary against USSR
1948	State of Israel established	1957	Boris Pasternak publishes *Doctor Zhivago*; USSR launches *Sputnik*; Treaty of Rome establishes European Economic Community (Common Market)
1949	Mao Zedong leads Communist revolution in China; Simone de Beauvoir publishes *The Second Sex*	1958	Fifth Republic begins in France
1950	Korean War begins	1962	United States and USSR face off in the Cuban missile crisis
1953	Stalin dies; Korean War ends		

- Consider three events: **India and Pakistan win independence from Britain (1947)**, **Simone de Beauvoir publishes *The Second Sex* (1949)**, and ***Brown v. Board of Education* prohibits segregated schools in the United States (1954)**. How did colonized peoples, women, and African Americans use the experience of war to seek liberation and civil rights?

SUGGESTED REFERENCES

New nationhood and the postwar era are charted in exciting new books that study veterans, youth, and daily life in the aftermath of Nazism and an age of cold war. Historians are also focusing on the complexities of decolonization.

Chin, Rita, et al., eds. *After the Nazi Racial State: Difference and Democracy in Germany and Europe*. 2009.

De Grazia, Victoria. *Irresistible Empire: America's Advance through 20th-Century Europe*. 2005.

Edele, Mark. *Soviet Veterans of World War II: A Popular Movement in an Authoritarian Society, 1941–1991*. 2008.

Frommer, Benjamin. *National Cleansing: Retribution against Nazi Collaborators in Postwar Czechoslovakia*. 2005.

Gaddis, John. *The Cold War: A New History*. 2006.

Grossman, Atina. *Jews, Germans, and Allies: Close Encounters in Occupied Germany, 1945–1949*. 2007.

Jobs, Richard I. *Riding the New Wave: Youth and the Rejuvenation of France after World War II*. 2007.

Milward, Alan S. *The United Kingdom and the Economic Community*. 2002.

Moeller, Robert. *War Stories: The Search for a Usable Past in the Federal Republic of Germany*. 2001.

Nord, Philip. *France's New Deal: From the Thirties to the Postwar Era*. 2010.

Pence, Katherine, and Paul Betts, eds. *Socialist Modern: East German Everyday Culture and Politics*. 2008.

Poiger, Uta. *Jazz, Rock, and Rebels: Cold War Politics and American Culture in a Divided Germany*. 2000.

Shepard, Todd. *The Invention of Decolonization: The Algerian War and the Remaking of France*. 2006.

Shipway, Martin. *Decolonization and Its Impact: A Comparative Approach to the End of the Colonial Empires*. 2008.

Smith, Andrea L., ed. *Europe's Invisible Migrants*. 2003.

Smith, Mark B. *Property of Communists: The Urban Housing Program from Stalin to Khrushchev*. 2010.

Statler, Andrea, and Andrew Johns, eds. *The Eisenhower Administration, the Third World, and the Globalization of the Cold War*. 2006.

Velký výklad víry, kap. V, 1420
si do smrti, neboť pravda tě vysvobodí
OZNAMUJEME, ŽE DNE 19. LEDNA 1969 OD NÁS
NÁS SYN A BRATR, STUDENT
FAKULTY UNIVERSITY KARLOVY
PALACH
NEJČISTŠÍMI A NEJHUMANNĚJŠÍMI LIDSKÝMI
SVÉMU LIDU A SVÉ ZKOUŠENÉ
VLASTI.
Pan prezident
Havel
DNES 1.1.1990
Tvým hlasem
NEZAPOMENEM
NÁROD

CHAPTER

28

Postindustrial Society and the End of the Cold War Order

1960s–1989

In January 1969, Jan Palach, a twenty-one-year-old philosophy student, drove to a main square in Prague, doused his body with gasoline, and set himself ablaze. Before that, he had put aside his coat with a message in it demanding an end to Communist repression in Czechoslovakia. It promised more such suicides unless the government lifted state censorship. The manifesto was signed "Torch No. 1." Jan Palach's suicide stunned his nation. Black flags hung from windows, and close to a million people flocked to his funeral. In the next months, more Czech youth followed Palach's grim example and became torches for freedom.

Before his self-immolation, Jan Palach was an ordinary, well-educated citizen of an increasingly technological society. Having recovered from World War II, the West shifted from a manufacturing economy based on heavy industry to a service economy that depended on technical knowledge in such fields as engineering, health care, and finance. This new service economy has been labeled "postindustrial." To staff it, institutions of higher education sprang up at a dizzying rate and attracted more students than ever before. Young men like Jan Palach—along with women, minorities, and many other activists in the 1960s and 1970s—far from being satisfied with their rising status, struck out against war and cold war, inequality and repression, and even against technology itself. From Czechoslovakia to the United States and around the world, protesters warned that postindustrial nations in general and the superpowers in particular were becoming technological and political monsters. Before long, countries in both the Soviet and U.S. blocs were on the verge of political revolution.

Shrine to Jan Palach
Jan Palach was a martyr to the cause of an independent Czechoslovakia. His self-immolation on behalf of that cause roused the nation. As makeshift shrines sprang up and multiplied throughout the 1970s and 1980s, they served as common rallying points that ultimately contributed to the overthrow of Communist rule. Václav Havel, the future president of a liberated Czechoslovakia, was arrested early in the momentous year of 1989 for commemorating Palach's sacrifice at a shrine. In light of so many other deaths in the Soviet bloc, why did Jan Palach's death become so powerful a force? *(© Marc Garanger/Corbis.)*

The challenges posed by young reformers came at a bad time for the superpowers and other leading European states. An agonizing war in Vietnam weakened the United States, and China confronted the Soviet Union on its borders. In a dramatic turn of events, the oil-producing states of the Middle East formed a cartel and reduced the export of oil to the leading Western nations in the 1970s. The resulting price increases helped bring on a recession, threatening the ballooning postindustrial economy. Extremists turned to terrorism to achieve their goals, while despite their wealth and military might, the superpowers could not guarantee that they would emerge victorious in this age of increasingly global competition. As the USSR experienced decay in a climate of postindustrial innovation across the West, a reform-minded leader—Mikhail Gorbachev—directed his nation to change course and initiated new policies of economic and political freedom. It was too late: in 1989, the Soviet bloc collapsed, an event brought about in part by countless acts of protest, not least of them the individual heroism of Jan Palach and his fellow human torches.

CHAPTER FOCUS How did technological, economic, and social change contribute to increased activism, and what were the political results of that activism?

The Revolution in Technology

The protests of the 1960s began in the midst of astonishing technological advances. These advances steadily boosted prosperity and changed daily life in the West, where people awoke to instantaneous radio and television news, worked with computers, and used new forms of contraceptives to control reproduction. Satellites orbiting the earth relayed telephone signals and collected military intelligence, while around the world nuclear energy powered economies. Smaller gadgets—electric popcorn poppers, portable radios and tape players, automatic garage door openers—made life more pleasant. The increased use of machines led one philosopher to insist that people were no longer self-sufficient individuals, but rather cyborgs—that is, humans who needed machines to sustain ordinary life processes.

The Information Age: Television and Computers

Information technology powered change in the postindustrial period that began in the 1960s, just as innovations in textile making and the spread of railroads had in the nineteenth century. This technology's ability to transmit knowledge, culture, and political information globally made it even more revolutionary. In the first half of the twentieth century, mass journalism, film, and radio had begun to forge a more uniform society based on shared information and images. In the last third of the century, television, computers, and telecommunications made information even more accessible and, some critics said, made culture more standardized. Once-remote villages were linked to urban capitals on the other side of the world thanks to videocassettes, satellite television, and telecommunications. Because of technology, protests became media events worldwide.

Television Americans embraced television in the 1950s; following the postwar recovery, it was Europe's turn. Between the mid-1950s and the mid-1970s, Europeans rapidly adopted television as a major entertainment and communications medium. In 1954, just 1 percent of French households had television; by 1974, almost 80 percent did. With the average viewer tuning in about

1963
Betty Friedan publishes *The Feminine Mystique*
1967
First successful human heart transplant
1968
Revolution in Czechoslovakia; student uprisings throughout Europe and the United States
1973
End of Vietnam War; OPEC raises price of oil and imposes oil embargo on the West
1965
1970
1975
1966
Willy Brandt becomes West German foreign minister and develops Ostpolitik
1969
U.S. astronauts walk on the moon's surface
1972
SALT I between the United States and Soviet Union
1973–1976
Aleksandr Solzhenitsyn publishes *The Gulag Archipelago*

four and a half hours a day, the audience for newspapers and theater declined. "We devote more . . . hours per year to television than [to] any other single artifact," one sociologist commented in 1969. As with radio, European governments funded television broadcasting with tax dollars and controlled TV programming to avoid what they perceived as the substandard fare offered by American commercial TV; instead they featured drama, ballet, concerts, variety shows, and news. The welfare state, in Europe at least, thereby gained more power to shape daily life.

The emergence of communications satellites and video recorders in the 1960s brought competition to state-sponsored television. Worldwide audiences enjoyed broadcasts from throughout the West as satellite technology allowed for the global transmission of sports broadcasts and other programming. What statesmen and intellectuals considered the junk programming of the United States — soap operas, game shows, sitcoms — arrived dubbed in the native language. Feature films on videotape became readily available to television stations (although not yet to individuals) and competed with made-for-television movies and other programs. The competition increased in 1969 when the Sony Corporation introduced the first affordable color videocassette recorder to the consumer market. Critics complained that, although TV provided more information than had ever been available before, the resulting shared culture represented the lowest common denominator.

East and west, television exercised a powerful political and cultural influence. Even in a rural area of the Soviet Union, more than 70 percent of the inhabitants watched television regularly in the late 1970s. Educational programming united the far-flung population of the USSR by broadcasting shows designed to advance Soviet culture. At the same time, with travel impossible or forbidden to many, shows about foreign lands were among the most popular — as were postcards from these lands, which became household decorations. Heads of state could usually bump regular programming. In the 1960s, French president Charles de Gaulle appeared frequently on television, using the grandiose gestures of an imperial ruler to stir patriotism. As electoral success in western Europe increasingly depended on cultivating a successful media image, political staffs needed media experts as much as they did policy experts.

Computers | Just as revolutionary as television, the computer reshaped work in science, defense, and ultimately industry. Computers had evolved dramatically since the first electronic ones, like the Colossus used by the British in 1943 to decode Nazi military and diplomatic messages. Several countries had devised these machines, all of them primitive by later standards in being gigantic, slow, noisy, and able only to decode. From the 1940s to the 1980s, computing machines shrank from the size of a gymnasium to that of an attaché case. They also became both far less expensive and fantastically more powerful, thanks to the development of increasingly sophisticated digital electronic circuitry implanted on tiny silicon chips, which replaced clumsy radio tubes. Within a few decades, the computer could perform hundreds of millions of operations per second and the price of the integrated circuit at the heart of computer technology would fall to less than a dollar.

Computers changed the pace and patterns of work not only by speeding up tasks but also by performing many operations that workers had once done themselves. In garment making, for example, experienced workers no longer painstakingly figured out how to arrange patterns on cloth for maximum economy. Instead, a computer specified instructions for the best positioning of pattern pieces, and trained workers, usually women, followed the machine's directions. Soon, like outworkers of the eighteenth

1978 The first test-tube baby is born in England

1981 Ronald Reagan becomes U.S. president

1985 Mikhail Gorbachev becomes Soviet premier

1986 Explosion at Chernobyl nuclear plant; Spain joins the Common Market

1980 — 1985 — 1990

1978–1979 Islamic revolution in Iran; hostages taken at U.S. embassy in Teheran

1980 Solidarity organizes resistance to Polish communism; British prime minister Margaret Thatcher begins dismantling the welfare state

1989 Chinese students revolt in Tiananmen Square; Communist governments ousted in eastern Europe; Berlin Wall demolished

The Space Age

1957	Soviet Union launches the first artificial satellite, *Sputnik*
1961	Soviet cosmonaut Yuri Gagarin orbits the earth; capsule carrying Alan Shepard Jr. makes first U.S. suborbital flight
1965	United States launches first commercial communications satellite, *Intelsat I*
1969	U.S. astronauts Neil Armstrong and Edwin "Buzz" Aldrin walk on moon's surface
1970s–present	Soviet Union and United States individually and in collaboration with various countries perform space station maneuvers, lunar probes, and other scientific experiments
1971	Soviet Union attempts unsuccessfully to put the space station *Salyut 1* into orbit
1973	United States puts the experimental space station *Skylab* into orbit
1976	*Viking* spacecraft explores Mars
1979–1986	Spacecraft *Voyager* makes successful flybys of Jupiter, Saturn, and Uranus

century, people could work for large industries at home, connected to a central mainframe. In 1981, the French phone company launched a public Internet server, the Minitel—a forerunner of the World Wide Web—through which individuals could make reservations, perform stock transactions, and obtain information.

Whereas during the Industrial Revolution mechanical power replaced humans' physical energy, the computer technology of the information revolution added to brainpower and thus advanced the postindustrial age. Many observers believed that computers would profoundly expand mental capacity, providing, in the words of one scientist, "boundless opportunities . . . to resolve the puzzles of cosmology, of life, and of the society of man." Others countered that computers programmed people, reducing human initiative and the ability to solve problems. The information revolution was under way.

Valentina Tereshkova, Russian Cosmonaut
People sent into space were heroes, representing modern values of courage, strength, and well-honed skills. Insofar as the space age was part of the cold war race for superpower superiority, the USSR held the lead during the first decade. The Soviets trained both women and men, and the 1963 flight of Valentina Tereshkova—the first woman in space—supported Soviet claims of gender equality in contrast to the all-male superstar image of the early U.S. space program.
(Hulton Archive/Getty Images.)

The Space Age

The "space race" between the United States and the Soviet Union, also made possible by computers, began when the Soviets launched the satellite *Sputnik* in 1957. The competition led to increasingly complex space flights that tested humans' ability to survive the process of space exploration, including weightlessness. Astronauts walked in space, endured weeks (and later months) in orbit, docked with other craft, fixed satellites, and carried out experiments for the military and private industry. In addition, a series of unmanned rockets launched weather, television, intelligence, and other communications satellites into orbit around the earth. In July 1969, a worldwide television audience watched as U.S. astronauts Neil Armstrong and Edwin "Buzz" Aldrin walked on the moon's surface—the climactic moment in the space race.

The space race also influenced Western culture. Astronauts and cosmonauts were perhaps the era's most admired heroes: Yuri Gagarin, John Glenn, and Valentina Tereshkova—the first woman in space—topped the list. A whole new fantasy world developed. Children's toys and games revolved increasingly around space. Films such as *2001: A Space Odyssey* (1968) portrayed space explorers answering questions about life that were formerly the domain of church leaders. Polish author Stanislaw Lem's popular novel *Solaris* (1961), later made into a film, described space-age individuals engaged in personal quests and drew readers and ultimately viewers into a futuristic fantasy.

The space age grew out of cold war concerns, and advances in rocket technology not only launched vehicles into space but also powered destructive missiles. At the same time, the space age promoted and even depended on global cooperation. From the 1960s on, U.S. spaceflights often involved the participation of other countries. In 1965, an international consortium headed by the United States launched the first commercial communications satellite, *Intelsat I*—a feat envisioned since early in the postwar period. By the 1970s, some 150 countries were working together at more than four hundred stations worldwide to maintain global satellite communications. Although some 50 percent of satellites were for spying purposes, the rest made international communication and the global transmission of data possible. Transnational collaboration was more than ever a necessity.

Pure science flourished amid the space race. Astronomers used mineral samples from the moon to calculate the age of the solar system with unprecedented precision. Unmanned spacecraft provided data on cosmic radiation, magnetic fields, and infrared sources. Although the media depicted the space age as one of warrior astronauts conquering space, breakthroughs depended on the products of technology, including the radio telescope, which depicted space by receiving, measuring, and calculating nonvisible rays. These findings reinforced the so-called big bang theory of the origin of the universe, first outlined in the 1930s by American astronomer Edwin Hubble and given crucial support in the 1950s by the discovery of low-level radiation permeating the universe in all directions. The big bang theory proposes that the universe originated from the explosion of superdense, superhot matter some ten to twenty billion years ago.

The Nuclear Age

Scientists, government officials, and engineers put the force of the atom to economic use, especially in the form of nuclear power, and the dramatic boost in available energy helped continue postwar economic expansion into the 1960s and beyond. The USSR built the first nuclear plant to produce electricity in Obinsk in 1954, followed by Britain and the United States. During the 1960s and 1970s, nuclear power for industrial and household use multiplied a hundredfold—a growth that did not include the nuclear-powered submarines and aircraft carriers, which also multiplied in this period.

Because of the vast costs and complex procedures involved in building, supplying, running, and safeguarding nuclear reactors, governments provided substantial aid and even financed nuclear power plants almost entirely. "A state does not count," announced French president Charles de Gaulle, "if it does not . . . contribute to the technological progress of the world." The watchword for all governments building nuclear reactors was technological development—a new function for the modern state. The USSR sponsored plants throughout the Soviet bloc as part of the drive to modernize, but it was not alone—Western nations, too, continued to rely on nuclear power. In 2006, France produced some 80 percent of its energy, and the United States 20 percent, via nuclear power plants. More than thirty countries had substantial nuclear installations in the twenty-first century, with new ones under construction.

Revolutions in Biology and Reproductive Technology

A revolution in the life sciences brought about dramatic health benefits and ultimately changed reproduction itself. In 1952, scientists Francis Crick, an Englishman, and James Watson, an American, discovered the structure of deoxyribonucleic acid **(DNA)**, the material in a cell's chromosomes that carries hereditary information. Simultaneously, other scientists were working on "the pill"—an oral contraceptive for women that capped more than a century of scientific work in the field of birth control. Still other breakthroughs in biology lay ahead, including ones that revolutionized conception and made possible the scientific duplication of species (cloning).

Understanding DNA | Crick and Watson solved the mystery of biological inheritance when they demonstrated the structure of DNA. They showed how the double helix of the DNA molecule splits in cellular reproduction to form the basis of each new cell. This genetic material, biologists concluded, provides a chemical pattern for an individual organism's life. Beginning in the 1960s, genetics and the new field of molecular biology progressed rapidly. Growing understanding of nucleic acids and proteins not only led to increased knowledge about viruses and bacteria but also effectively ended in the West such diseases as polio, mumps, measles, tetanus, and syphilis through the development of new vaccines.

Scientists used their understanding of DNA to alter the makeup of plants and to bypass natural

---

DNA: The genetic material that forms the basis of each cell; the discovery of its structure in 1952 revolutionized genetics, molecular biology, and other scientific and medical fields.

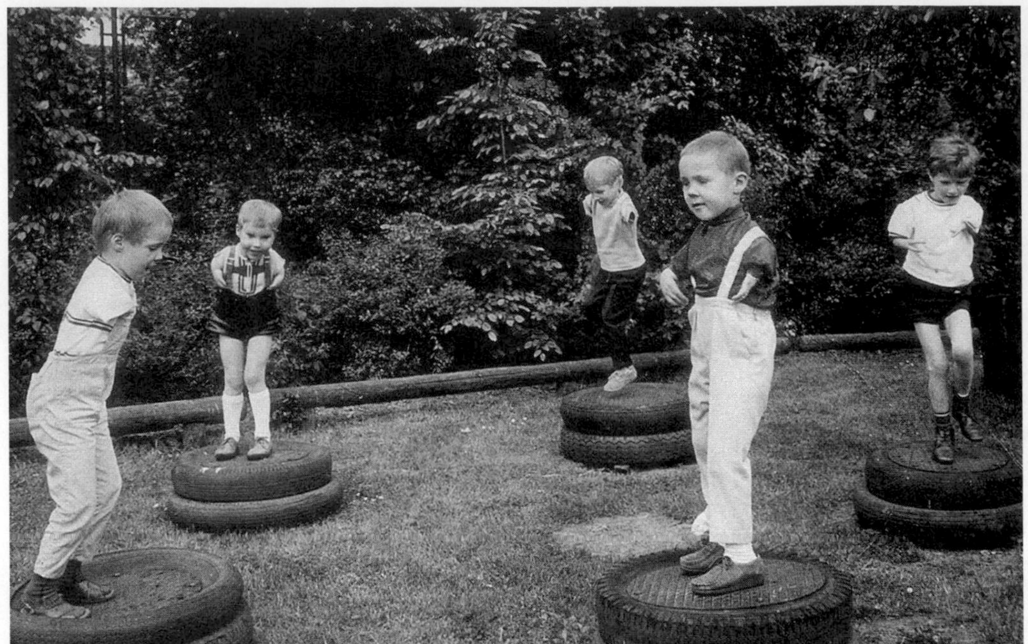

Thalidomide Children
In the last third of the twentieth century, increasingly destructive side effects of powerful medicines became apparent. Women who had taken the drug thalidomide gave birth to children with severe disabilities, a result of the race to profit from scientific and technological developments. Children affected by thalidomide, once they became adults, were among those who launched the disability rights movement. *(DPA/LANDOV.)*

animal reproduction in a process called cloning—obtaining the cells of an organism and dividing or reproducing them in an exact copy in a laboratory. In 1997, the process had so evolved that one group of British researchers produced a cloned sheep named Dolly, though she suffered an array of disabilities and died six years later. Cloning raised questions about whether scientists should interfere with so basic and essential a process as reproduction. Similarly, the possibility of genetically altering plant and animal species and even creating new ones (for instance, to control agricultural pests) led to concern about how such actions would affect the balance of nature.

In 1967, Dr. Christiaan Barnard of South Africa performed the first successful heart transplant. Other researchers later developed both immunosuppressants (to prevent rejection of the transplant) and an artificial heart. As major advances like these occurred, commentators began to ask whether the enormous cost of new medical technology to save a few people would be better spent on helping the many who lacked even basic medical care.

Transforming Reproduction Technology also influenced the most intimate areas of human relations—sexuality and procreation. Matching family size to agricultural productivity no longer shaped sexual behavior in the industrialized and urbanized West. With reliable birth-control devices more readily available, young people began sexual relations earlier, with less risk of pregnancy. These trends accelerated in the 1960s when the birth-control pill, the result of research around the world, was first marketed in the United States. The pill was initially tested on American medical students in Puerto Rico and then on a larger scale among Puerto Rican nurses, many of whom were eager for reliable contraception. By 1970, the pill's use was spreading around the world. Millions also sought out voluntary surgical sterilization through tubal ligations and vasectomies. New techniques brought abortion, traditionally performed by amateurs, into the hands of medical professionals, making it a safe procedure for the first time.

Childbirth and conception were similarly transformed. Whereas only a small minority of Western births took place in hospitals in 1920, more than 90 percent did by 1970. Obstetricians now performed much of the work midwives had once done. As pregnancy and birth became a medical process, new procedures and equipment made it possible to monitor women and fetuses throughout pregnancy, labor, and delivery. The number of medical interventions such as cesarean births rose.

In 1978, the first "test-tube baby," Louise Brown, was born to an English couple. She had been conceived when her mother's eggs were fertilized with her father's sperm in a laboratory dish and then implanted in her mother's uterus—a complex process called **in vitro fertilization**. If a woman could

in vitro fertilization: A process developed in the 1970s by which human eggs are fertilized with sperm outside the body and then implanted in a woman's uterus.

not carry a child to term, the laboratory-fertilized embryo could be implanted in the uterus of a surrogate, or substitute, mother. Researchers even began working on an artificial womb to allow for reproduction entirely outside the body—from storage bank to artificial embryonic environment. In reproductive technology, as in other areas, the revolution in biology was dramatically changing human life, improving health, and even making new life possible.

REVIEW QUESTION What were the technological and scientific advances of the 1960s and 1970s, and how did they change human life and society?

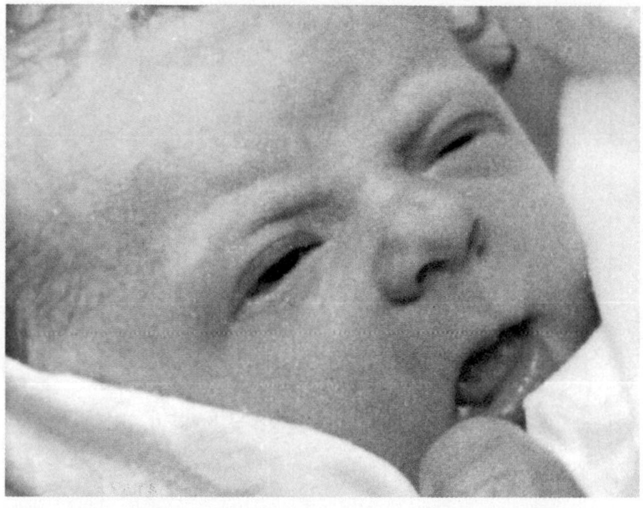

The First Test-Tube Baby
The birth in Britain in 1978 of Louise Brown, the first baby conceived by in vitro fertilization, caused a sensation worldwide. The new procedure was just one of the many medical breakthroughs of the late twentieth century and gave hope to would-be parents around the world that science might make infertility a thing of the past. *(Getty Images.)*

Postindustrial Society and Culture

Soaring investments in science and the spread of technology put Western countries on what has been labeled a postindustrial course. Instead of being centered on manufacturing and heavy industry, a postindustrial economy emphasized the distribution of services such as health care and education. The service sector was the leading force in the economy, and this meant that intellectual work, not industrial or manufacturing work, was central to creating jobs and profits. Moreover, all parts of society and industry interlocked, forming a system constantly in need of complex analysis, as in the nuclear industry. These characteristics of postindustrial society and culture would carry over from the 1960s and 1970s into the next century.

Multinational Corporations

A major development of the postindustrial era was the growth of the **multinational corporation**. Multinationals produced goods and services for a global market and conducted business worldwide, but unlike older kinds of international firms, they established major factories and managerial centers in countries other than their home base. For example, of the five hundred largest businesses in the United States in 1970, more than one hundred did over a quarter of their business abroad, with IBM operating in more than one hundred countries. Although U.S.-based corporations led the way, European and Japanese multinationals like Volkswagen, Shell, Nestlé, and Sony also had a broad global reach.

Some multinational corporations had bigger revenues than entire nations. They appeared to burst the bounds of the nation-state as they set up shop in whatever part of the world offered cheap labor. In the first years after World War II, multinationals preferred European employees, who constituted a highly educated labor pool and had well-developed consumer habits. Then, beginning in the 1960s, multinationals moved more of their operations to the emerging economies of formerly colonized states to reduce labor costs and avoid taxes. Although multinational corporations provided jobs in developing areas, profits usually went out of those areas to enrich foreign stockholders. Multinational corporations lacked the interest in the well-being of localities or nations that earlier industrialists had often shown. Thus, this system of business looked to some like imperialism in a new form.

Firms believed that they could stay competitive only by expanding, merging with other companies, or partnering with governments. In France, for example, a massive glass conglomerate merged with a metallurgical company to form a new group specializing in all phases of construction—a wise move given the postwar building boom. Firms also increased their investment in research and used international cooperation to produce major new products. Beginning with its first commercial flight in 1976, the British-French Concorde supersonic aircraft flew from London to New York in under four

---

multinational corporation: A business that operates in many foreign countries by sending large segments of its manufacturing, finance, sales, and other business components abroad.

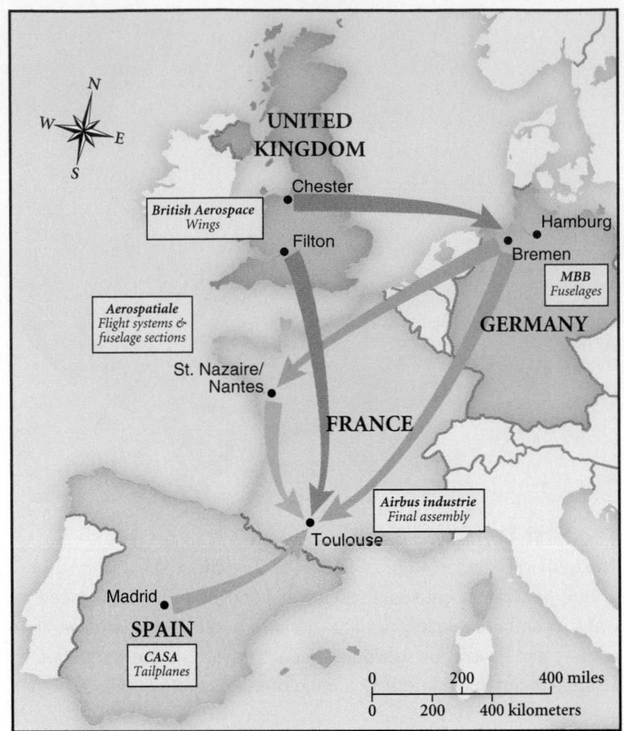

MAP 28.1 The Airbus Production System
Aircraft manufacturer Airbus began as an international consortium, marking an important step in the economic and industrial integration of Europe and the revitalization of its national economies. Today, Airbus is a global enterprise with locations offering parts and service around the world, including the United States, China, and India. Its orders for and deliveries of planes have exceeded those of its top competitor over the past few years.

hours. Another venture was the Airbus, a more practical series of passenger jets inaugurated in 1972 by a consortium of European firms. Both projects grew from the strong relationships among government, business, and science as well as from the international cooperation in manufacturing among members of the Common Market (Map 28.1). Such relationships allowed European businesses to compete successfully with U.S.-based and other multinational giants.

The New Worker

In the early years of industry, workers often labored to exhaustion and lived in poor conditions. These conditions changed fundamentally in postwar Europe with the reduction of the blue-collar workforce, the growth of off-shore manufacturing, and increased automation of industrial work. Manufacturing was simply cleaner and less dangerous than ever before. Within firms, the relationship of workers to bosses shifted as management started grouping workers into teams that set their own production quotas, determined and assigned tasks, and competed with other teams to produce more. As workers took on responsibilities once assigned to managers, union membership declined.

In both the U.S. and Soviet blocs, a new working class of white-collar service personnel emerged. Its rise undermined economic distinctions based on the way a person worked, for those who performed service work or had managerial titles were not necessarily better paid than blue-collar laborers. The ranks of service workers swelled with researchers, planners, health care and medical staff, and government functionaries. As emphasis on service grew, entire categories of employees such as flight attendants devoted much of their skill to the psychological well-being of customers. The consumer economy provided more jobs in restaurants and personal health, fitness and grooming, and hotels and tourism. By 1969, the percentage of service-sector employees had passed that of manufacturing workers in several industrial countries: 61.1 percent versus 33.7 percent in the United States, and 48.8 percent versus 41.1 percent in Sweden (see "Taking Measure," page 957).

Postindustrial work life differed somewhat in the Soviet bloc. There, the percentage of farmers remained higher than in western Europe. A huge difference between professional occupations and those involving physical work also remained in socialist countries because of declining investment in advanced machinery and cleaner work processes. Men in both blocs generally earned higher pay and had better jobs than women. Uniquely in the Soviet bloc, however, women's badly paying jobs included street cleaning, garbage collection, heavy labor on farms, general medicine, and dentistry. Somewhere between 80 and 95 percent of women in socialist countries worked, mostly under difficult conditions.

Farming changed as well, consolidating and becoming more scientific. Small landowners sold family plots to farmers and corporations engaged in agribusiness — that is, vast acreage devoted to commercial rather than peasant farming. Governments, farmers' cooperatives, and planning agencies shaped the decision making of the individual farmer; they set production quotas and handled an array of marketing transactions. Genetic research that yielded pest-resistant seeds and the skyrocketing use of pesticides, fertilizers, and machinery contributed to economic growth. Between 1965 and 1979, the number of tractors in Germany more than tripled from 384,000 to 1.34 million.

Technical planners played a crucial role in transforming agriculture. For example, in the 1970s, a woman named Fernande Pelletier owned a hundred-acre farm in southwestern France in the new set-

TAKING MEASURE

Postindustrial Occupational Structure, 1984

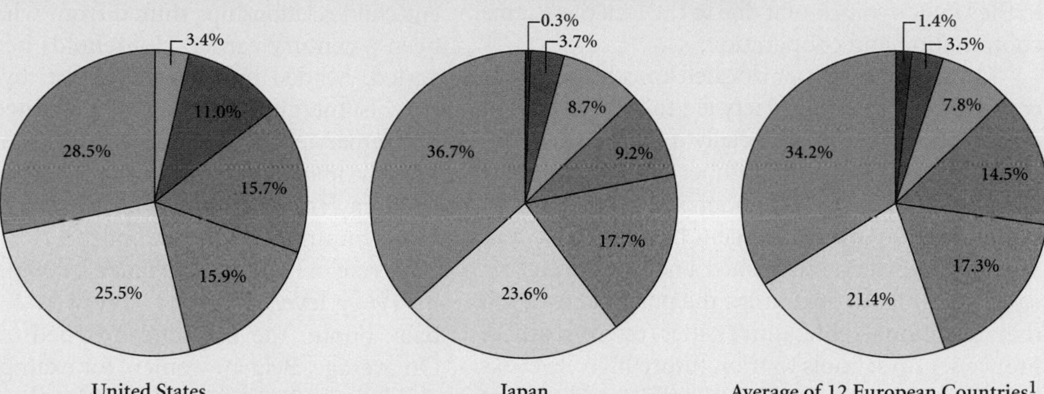

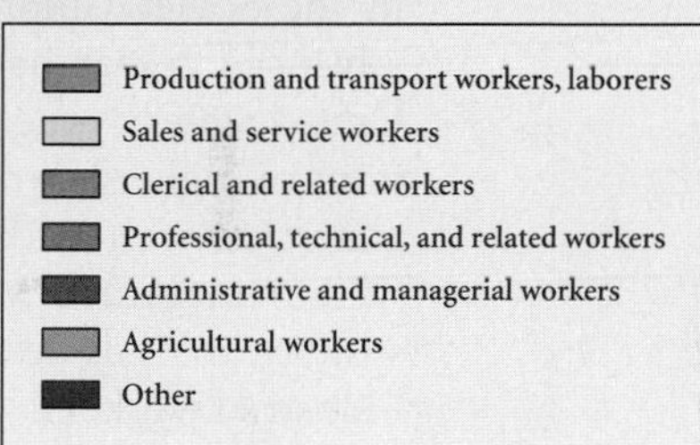

[1]Austria, Belgium, West Germany, Denmark, Spain, Finland, Greece, Ireland, Netherlands, Norway, Portugal, and Sweden.

Striking changes occurred in the composition of the workforce in the postwar period. Agriculture continued to decline as a source of jobs; by the 1980s, the percentage of agricultural workers in the most advanced industrial countries had dropped well below 10 percent. The most striking development was the expansion of the service sector, which came to employ more than half of all workers. In the United States, the agricultural and industrial sectors (represented by production and transportation workers), which had dominated a century earlier, now offered less than a third of all jobs.

Source: *Yearbook of Labour Statistics* (Geneva: International Labour Office, 1992), Table 2.7.

Question to Consider

■ **What difference does it make to ordinary people that jobs in service work predominate? What does the rise of the service sector mean for the economy and society as a whole?**

ting of international agribusiness. On the advice of a government expert to produce whatever foods might sell competitively in the Common Market, Pelletier switched from lamb and veal to foie gras and walnuts, and she joined with other farmers in her region to buy heavy machinery and to bring products to market. Agricultural prosperity required as much managerial and technical know-how as did success in other parts of the economy.

The Boom in Education and Research

Education and research were key to running postindustrial society and had now become the means by which nations maintained their economic and military might. In the West, common sense, hard work, and creative intuition had launched the earliest successes of the Industrial Revolution. By the late twentieth century, success in business or government demanded a wide variety of expertise and ever-growing staffs of researchers—"the accumulation of knowledge, not of wealth," as one official put it.

Investment in research fueled military and industrial leadership. The United States funneled more than 20 percent of its gross national product (a measure of the total value of goods and services a nation produced in a year) into research in the 1960s, attracting many of Europe's leading intellectuals and technicians to move to the United States in a so-called brain drain. Complex systems required intricate coordination and professional oversight—nuclear power generation, for example, included scientific conceptualization, plant construction, and the publicly supervised disposal of radioactive waste. Scientists and bureaucrats frequently made more crucial decisions than did elected politicians in the realm of space programs, weapons development, and economic policy. Here east–west differences became important: Soviet-bloc nations proved less adept at linking their considerable achievements in science to real-life applications because of bureaucratic red tape. In the 1960s, some 40 percent of scientific findings in the Soviet bloc became obsolete before the government approved them for application to technology. An invisible backsliding from superpower effectiveness and leadership had begun in the USSR—much of it due to the lack of systems coordination and cooperation.

The centrality of sophisticated knowledge to success in postindustrial society led to unprecedented growth in education, especially in universities and scientific institutes. The number of university students in Sweden rose by about 580 percent and in West Germany by 250 percent between 1950 and 1969. Great Britain established a network of technical universities to encourage the practical research that traditional elite universities often scorned. France set up schools to train future high-level experts in administration. The scientific establishment in the Soviet Union grew so rapidly that Soviet advanced researchers outnumbered those in the United States by the late 1970s. Meanwhile, institutions of higher learning, particularly in the United States and western Europe, added courses in business management, information technology, and systems analysis designed for the new pool of postindustrial workers.

The Rolling Stones (1976)
The Rolling Stones were more energetic, sexual, and flamboyant than the earlier British rock sensation, the Beatles. Astute marketing experts for big record companies helped such rock groups target youth successfully. What exactly was the appeal of the Beatles, the Rolling Stones, and the other celebrated rock stars who followed in their wake? *(Getty Images.)*

Changing Family Life and the Generation Gap

Just as education changed to meet the needs of postindustrial society, family structures and parent-child relationships shifted from what they had been a century earlier. Households became more varied, headed by a single parent, by remarried parents merging two sets of unrelated children, by unmarried couples cohabitating, or by traditionally married couples who had few—or no—children. Households of same-sex partners became more common. At the end of the 1970s, the marriage rate in the West had fallen by 30 percent from its 1960s level, and after almost two decades of baby boom, the birthrate dropped significantly. On average, Belgian women, for example, bore 2.6 children in 1960 but only 1.8 by the end of the 1970s. In the Soviet bloc, the birthrate was even lower. Although the birthrate fell, the percentage of children born outside of marriage soared.

Daily life within the family also changed. Technological consumer items filled the home, with radio and television often forming the basis of the household's common social life. Appliances such as dishwashers, washing machines, and clothes dryers became more affordable and more widespread, especially in the western bloc, raising standards of cleanliness and reducing (in theory) the time women had to devote to household work. More women worked outside the home during these years to pay for the prolonged economic dependence of children, but working mothers still did the housework and provided child care almost entirely themselves.

Whereas earlier the family had organized labor, taught craft skills, and monitored reproductive behavior of young people, the modern family seemed to have a primarily psychological mission, providing emotional nurturance for children who acquired their intellectual skills in school. Parents turned to psychologists, social workers, and other social service experts for advice on rearing their children. Television and other media also offered much-heeded instruction and models of how people should deal with life in postindustrial society.

Postindustrial society changed teenagers' lives most dramatically, creating strong differences between adolescents and adults. A century earlier, teens had been full-time wage earners like their parents; now, in the new knowledge-based society, most were students and some were financially dependent on their parents into their twenties. Despite teenagers' longer financial childhood, sexual activity began at an ever younger age, and people talked more openly about sex, prompting the Western media to announce the arrival of a "sexual revolution."

With rising prosperity after the war, youth simultaneously gained new roles as consumers. Seeing baby boomers as a multibillion-dollar market, advertisers and industrialists wooed them with consumer items associated with rock music — records, portable radios, and stereos. Rock music celebrated youthful rebellion against adult culture in biting, critical, and often explicitly sexual lyrics. Sex roles for the young did not change, however. Despite the popularity of a few individual women rockers, promoters focused on groups of male musicians, whom they depicted as heroic, surrounded by worshipping female "groupies." The new models for youth such as the Beatles were themselves the products of advanced technology and savvy marketing for mass consumption. "What's your message for American teenagers?" the Beatles were asked. "Buy some more Beatles records," they responded. The mixture of high-tech music, pop-star marketing, and the sexual openness of fans contributed to a sense that there was a unique youth culture separating the young from their parents — the so-called generation gap.

Pop Art

Claes Oldenburg excelled in highlighting objects of everyday life, such as this hamburger (*Floor Burger*, 1962). He also modeled vacuum cleaners, shuttlecocks, telephones, and many other much-used things — a feature of pop art, which often contained humor in addition. Can you spot the humor in this creation? *(Claes Oldenburg,* Floor Burger, *1962. Canvas filled with foam rubber and cardboard boxes, painted with latex and Liquitex, 4 ft. 4 in. [1.32 m] high; 7 ft. [2.13 m] diameter. Collection Art Gallery of Ontario, Toronto, Canada, Purchase 1967. Photo courtesy the Oldenburg van Bruggen Studio. Copyright © 1962 Claes Oldenburg. Photo provided by The Bridgeman Art Library International.)*

Art, Ideas, and Religion in a Technocratic Society

Cultural trends developed alongside the march of consumer society and technological breakthroughs. Artists and scholars of the postindustrial age addressed the growing consumerism and the new world of space, electronics, and computers in their art and thought. As colonies threw off the imperialist yoke and became new nations, the influence of their culture on the West remained strong. Like the new multinational corporations, many artists and scholars enjoyed increasing international recognition and reached global markets. Social scientists gained influence by employing complex statistical and other scientific methods made possible by increasingly sophisticated and powerful computers.

The Visual Arts A new style in the visual arts was called **pop art**. It featured images from everyday life and employed the glossy techniques and products of what these artists called admass, or mass advertising. Like advertising itself, art leadership passed from Europe to the United States. U.S. pop artist Robert Rauschenberg, for example, made collages from comic strips, magazine clippings, and fabric to fulfill his vision that "a picture is more like the real world when it's made out of the real world." Maverick American artists such as Andy Warhol (1928–1987) made pop art a financial success with their parodies of modern commercialism. Through images of actress Marilyn Monroe and former first lady Jacqueline Kennedy, Warhol showed, for example, how depictions of women were used to sell everything mass culture had to offer in the 1960s and 1970s. He depicted Campbell's soup cans as they appeared in advertisements and sold these works as elite artistic creations.

Swedish-born artist Claes Oldenburg (1929–) portrayed the grotesque aspects of ordinary consumer products in *Giant Hamburger with Pickle Attached* (1962) and *Lipstick Ascending on Caterpillar Tractor* (1967). Capturing this mocking world of

pop art: A style in the visual arts that mimicked advertising and consumerism and that used ordinary objects as a part of paintings and other compositions.

art, German artist Sigmar Polke did cartoon-like drawings of products and of those who craved them. Others practicing this "high art" added "low" objects such as scraps of metal, cigarette butts, dirt, and even excrement to their work. The Swiss sculptor Jean Tinguely used rusted parts of old machines—the junk of industrial society—to make fountains that could move. His partner Niki de Saint Phalle (1930–2002) then decorated them with huge, gaudy figures—many of them inspired by the folk traditions of the Caribbean and Africa (see Chapter 27, page 942). Their colorful, mobile fountains adorned main squares in Stockholm, Paris, and other cities.

Music The American composer John Cage (1912–1992) worked in a similar vein when he added to his musical scores sounds produced by such everyday items as combs, pieces of wood, and radio noise. Buddhist influence led Cage to incorporate silence in music and to compose by randomly tossing coins and then choosing notes by the corresponding numbers in the ancient Chinese *I Ching* (Book of Changes). These techniques continued the trend away from classical melody that had begun with modernism. Other composers, called minimalists, simplified music by featuring repetition and sustained notes instead of producing the lush melodies of nineteenth-century symphonies and piano music. Estonian composer Arvo Pärt wrote minimalist pieces in the 1970s using only three or four notes in total; he called this style "starvation" music to emphasize the lack of both freedom and goods in the Soviet bloc. Such innovation in classical music continued to produce sounds that many listeners found unpleasant. Yet improved recording technology and mass marketing brought music of all varieties to a wider home audience than ever before.

Social Science The social sciences reached the peak of their prestige in the postindustrial era, often because of the increasing use of statistical models made possible by advanced electronic computations. Sociologists and psychologists produced detailed studies that claimed to demonstrate rules for understanding individual and group behavior. Those who gained knowledge of such rules over the course of their university education would thus be fit to govern an increasingly complex postindustrial population. Anthropology was among the most exciting of the social sciences, for it brought young university students information about societies that seemed untouched by modern technology and industry. Colorful ethnographic films revealed different lifestyles and seemingly exotic practices. While studying people who came to be called "the other," students had their sense of freedom reinforced by the vision of going back to nature. Whatever their discipline, social scientists announced that, like technicians and engineers, their specialized methods and factual knowledge were key to managing the complexities of postindustrial society and setting policy for developing nations.

At the same time, the social sciences undermined Enlightenment beliefs that individuals had true freedom. French anthropologist Claude Lévi-Strauss (1908–2009) developed a theory called structuralism, which insisted that all societies function within controlling structures—kinship and exchange, for example. While challenging existentialism's claim that humans could create a free existence, structuralism also attacked the social sciences' faith in rationality. Lévi-Strauss's book *The Savage Mind* (1966) demonstrated that people outside the West, even though they did not use scientific methods, had their own extremely effective systems of problem solving. In the 1960s and 1970s, the findings of some social scientists additionally echoed concerns that technology and highly managed bureaucratic systems were creating a society in which people lacked individuality and freedom.

Religion Religious leaders and parishioners responded to the changing times in a variety of ways. Pope Paul VI (r. 1963–1978) opposed artificial birth control as it became more prevalent, while also becoming the first pontiff to carry out the global vision of Vatican II by visiting Africa, Asia, and South America. In some places, grassroots religious fervor surged in the face of advancing science and the threat of nuclear annihilation. Growing numbers of U.S. Protestants, for example, joined sects that stressed the literal truth of the Bible and denied the validity of past scientific discoveries such as the age of the universe and the evolution of the species. In western Europe, however, Christian churchgoing remained at a low ebb. In the 1970s, for example, only 10 percent of the British population went to religious services—about the same number that attended live soccer matches. Most striking was the changing composition of the Western religious public. Immigration of people from former colonies and other parts of the world increased the strength of non-Christian religions such as Islam and varieties of Hindu faiths. Mosques, Buddhist temples, and shrines to other creeds appeared in a greater number of cities and towns. New religious values sometimes mixed tensely with western European Judeo-Christianity and the antireligious culture of the Soviet bloc.

REVIEW QUESTION How did Western society and culture change in the postindustrial age?

Protesting Cold War Conditions

The United States and the Soviet Union reached new heights of power in the 1960s, but trouble was brewing for the superpowers. By 1965, the six-nation Common Market had temporarily replaced the United States as the leader in worldwide trade, and its members often acted in their own self-interest, not in the interests of the superpowers. In 1973, Britain's membership in the Common Market, followed by Ireland and Denmark, boosted the market's exports to almost three times those of the United States. The USSR faced challenges, too. Communist China, along with countries in eastern Europe, contested Soviet leadership, and many decolonizing regions refused to ally with either of the superpowers. The struggle for an independent Vietnamese nation continued, too, and by the mid-1960s, the United States was waging a devastating war in Vietnam in order to block the Communist independence movement there. Rising citizen discontent, sometimes expressed in dramatic acts of protest like that of Jan Palach, presented another serious challenge to the cold war order. From the 1960s until 1989, people rose up against technology, the lack of fundamental rights, and the potential for nuclear holocaust.

Cracks in the Cold War Order

Across the social and political spectrum came calls to reduce cold war tensions in this age of unprecedented technological advance. In the Soviet Union, the new middle class of bureaucrats and managers demanded a better standard of living and a reduction in the cold war hostility that made everyday life so menacing. Voters in western European countries elected politicians who promoted an increasing array of social programs designed to ensure the economic democracy of the welfare state and to promote technological development. A significant minority of voters shifted their allegiance from the centrist Christian Democratic coalitions that supported U.S. political goals to Socialist, Labor, and Social Democratic parties that endorsed policies to bridge the cold war divide.

Germany and France The German and French governments both made solid and highly visible changes in policy, which, though different, upset the cold war order. In Germany, Social Democratic politicians had enough influence to shift money from cold war defense spending to domestic programs. Willy Brandt (1913–1992), the Socialist mayor of West Berlin, became foreign minister in 1966 and worked to improve frigid relations with Communist East Germany in order to open up trade. This anti–cold war policy, known as **Ostpolitik**, gave West German business leaders what they wanted: "the depoliticization of Germany's foreign trade," as one industrialist put it, and an opening of consumerism in the Soviet bloc. West German trade with eastern Europe grew rapidly, but it left the relatively poorer countries of the Soviet bloc strapped with mounting debt — some $45 billion annually by 1970. Nonetheless, commerce began building bridges across the U.S.-Soviet cold war divide.

To break the superpowers' stranglehold on international politics, French president Charles de Gaulle poured huge sums into French nuclear development, withdrew French forces from NATO, and signed trade treaties with the Soviet bloc. Communist China and France also drew closer through trade and diplomatic ties. However, de Gaulle protected France's good relations with Germany to prevent further encroachments from the Soviet bloc. At home, de Gaulle's government sponsored the construction of modern housing and ordered the exterior cleaning of all Parisian buildings — a massive project taking years — to wipe away more than a century of industrial grime and to demonstrate community, not cold war, values. With his haughty pursuit of French grandeur, de Gaulle offered the European public an alternative to obeying the superpowers.

The Soviet Union Brandt's Ostpolitik and de Gaulle's independence had their echoes in Soviet-bloc reforms. After the ouster of Soviet premier Nikita Khrushchev in 1964, the new leadership of Leonid Brezhnev (1909–1982) and Alexei Kosygin (1904–1980) initially continued attempts at reform, encouraging plant managers to turn a profit and allowing the production of televisions, household appliances, and cheap housing to alleviate the discontent of an increasingly better-educated and better-informed citizenry. The government also allowed more cultural and scientific meetings with Westerners, another move that relaxed the cold war atmosphere in the mid-1960s. Like the French, the Soviets set up "technopoles" — new cities devoted to research and technological innovation. The Soviet satellites in eastern Europe seized the economic opportunity presented by Moscow's relaxed posture. For example, Hungarian leader János Kádár introduced elements of a market system into the national economy by encouraging

---

Ostpolitik: A policy initiated by West German foreign minister Willy Brandt in the late 1960s in which West Germany sought better economic relations with the Communist countries of eastern Europe.

small businesses and trade to develop outside the Communist-controlled state network.

Soviet-bloc writers sought to break the hold of socialist realism on the arts and reduce their praise for the Soviet past. Dissident artists' paintings rejected brightly colored scenes and heroic figures and instead depicted Soviet citizens as worn and tired in grays and other monochromatic color schemes (see "Seeing History," page 963). Ukrainian poet Yevgeny Yevtushenko exposed Soviet complicity in the Holocaust in *Babi Yar* (1961), a passionate protest against the slaughter of tens of thousands of Jews near Kiev during World War II. East Berlin writer Christa Wolf challenged the celebratory nature of socialist art when she showed a couple tragically divided by the Berlin Wall in her novel *Divided Heaven* (1965). Repression of artistic expression returned in the later 1960s and 1970s, as the Soviet government took to bulldozing outdoor art shows, thereby forcing visual artists to hold secret exhibitions, announced at the very last minute by word of mouth. For their part, writers relied on **samizdat** culture, a form of protest activity in which individuals reproduced government-suppressed publications by hand and passed them from reader to reader, thus building a foundation for the successful resistance of the 1980s.

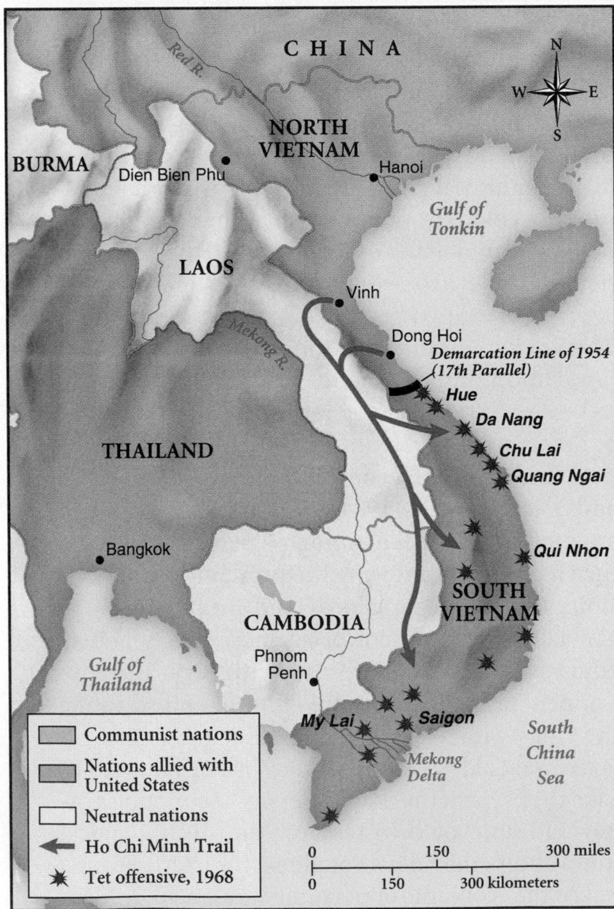

MAP 28.2 The Vietnam War, 1954–1975
The local peoples of Southeast Asia had long resisted incursions by their neighbors. The Vietnamese beat the French colonizers in the battle of Dien Bien Phu in 1954. But the Americans soon became involved, trying to stem what they saw as the tide of Communist influence behind the Vietnamese liberation movement. The ensuing war in Vietnam in the 1960s and 1970s spread into neighboring countries, making the region the scene of vast destruction.

The United States Other issues challenged U.S. leadership of the western bloc during the cold war. The assassination of President John F. Kennedy in November 1963 shocked the nation and the world, but only momentarily did it halt the escalating demands for civil rights for African Americans and other minorities. White segregationists murdered and brutalized those attempting to integrate lunch counters, register black voters, or simply march on behalf of freedom. This violent racism was a weak point in the American claim to moral superiority in the cold war. In response to the murders and destruction, Kennedy had introduced civil rights legislation and forced the desegregation of schools and universities. Lyndon B. Johnson (1908–1973), Kennedy's successor, steered the Civil Rights Act through Congress in 1964. This legislation forbade segregation in public facilities and created the Equal Employment Opportunity Commission (EEOC) to fight job discrimination based on "race, color, national origin, religion, and sex." Southern conservatives had tacked on the provision outlawing discrimination against women in the vain hope that it would doom the bill. Modeling himself on his hero Franklin Roosevelt, Johnson envisioned what he called the Great Society, in which new government programs would improve the lot of the forty million Americans living in poverty. Johnson's many reform programs included Project Head Start for educating disadvantaged preschool children and the Job Corps for training youth. Black novelist Ralph Ellison called Johnson "the greatest American president for the poor and the Negroes."

Still, the cold war did not go away, and the United States became increasingly embroiled in Vietnam (Map 28.2). After the Geneva Conference of 1954, which divided Vietnam into North and South, the United States increased its support for the corrupt leaders of non-Communist South Vietnam. North

---

samizdat: A key form of dissident activity across the Soviet bloc in which individuals reproduced government-suppressed publications by hand and passed them from reader to reader, thus building a foundation for the successful resistance of the 1980s.

SEEING HISTORY

Critiquing the Soviet System: Dissident Art in the 1960s and 1970s

Artists, writers, composers, and performers in the USSR were supposed to follow Communist Party directives, creating uplifting works that spread Communist ideals, despite the political repression and economic hardships that plagued the system. Numerous dissident artists sought to undermine the Communist message and criticize the regime through their work, thus helping to prepare the ground for a full-scale revolt against the Soviet system in the late 1980s. The Soviet government persecuted these artists and their families and often destroyed subversive works that were displayed in public. Yet dissident artists bravely forged ahead, displaying their art and even selling it to foreign dealers to smuggle out of the country.

Dissident artists employed a range of techniques, both subtle and explicit, to critique the Soviet regime. Eric Bulatov often made use of the officially approved Soviet style of socialist realism in his works to slyly criticize the system. His painting *Krasikov Street*, shown here, shows Lenin walking forward and refers to Lenin's much-repeated motto meant to inspire Soviet citizens: "Always forward, never backward." How does Bulatov use motion and color here to comment on both Soviet society and the Communist establishment? What messages is he conveying?

In his work *The General*, Boris Orlov used sculpture to lampoon one of the mainstays of Soviet society during the cold war. As the heroes of World War II and protectors of communism, generals were officially revered, parading on Soviet holidays and at commemorative events. Their uniforms feature oak and laurel leaves—common symbols of strength and victory. What are the general's main features as portrayed by Orlov? What adjectives would you use to describe this work? How would you characterize the tone and purpose of Orlov's depiction?

Question to Consider

- **As you reflect on these two works of art, what in your opinion would have made them dangerous to the survival of Soviet communism?**

Boris Orlov, *The General*, 1970. *(Collection of the Jane Voorhees Zimmerli Art Museum, Rutgers, The State University of New Jersey, The Norton and Nancy Dodge Collection of Nonconformist Art from the Soviet Union. Photograph by Jack Abraham. 14194 © Boris Orlov/RAO, Moscow/VAGA, New York, NY.)*

Eric Bulatov, *Krasikov Street*, 1977. *(Erik Bulatov, Krasikov Street, 1977. Oil on canvas 150 x 198.5 cm. Collection of the Zimmerli Art Museum at Rutgers University, Norton and Nancy Dodge Collection of Nonconformist Art from the Soviet Union, 1991.0877/05125. Photograph by Jack Abraham. © 2011 Artists Rights Society [ARS], New York/ADAGP, Paris.)*

Vietnam, China, and the Soviet Union backed the rebel Vietcong, or South Vietnamese Communists. By 1966, the United States had more than half a million soldiers in South Vietnam, yet the strength of the Vietcong seemed to grow daily. Despite massive bombings by the United States, the insurgents, who had struggled against colonialism for decades, rejected a negotiated peace even as Johnson's advisers regularly appeared on television claiming that the United States was winning the war. Faced with mounting casualties, growing antiwar sentiment, and increasing military costs, Johnson announced in March 1968 that he would not run for president again.

The Growth of Citizen Activism

In the midst of cold war conflict and technological advance, a new activism emerged. Prosperity and the rising benefits of a postindustrial, service-oriented economy made people ever more eager for peace. University students did not want their lives to end on faraway battlefields. Other activists — among them minorities, women, and homosexuals — simply wanted a fair chance at education, jobs, and some political voice. Students, blacks and other minorities, Soviet-bloc citizens, women, environmentalists, and homosexuals brought various Western societies to the brink of revolution during what became increasingly fiery protests in the late 1960s.

Civil Rights The U.S. civil rights movement broadened, as other minorities joined African Americans in demanding fair treatment. In 1965, César Chávez (1927–1993) led Mexican American migrant workers in the California grape agribusiness to strike for better wages and working conditions. Meanwhile, beginning in 1965, urban riots erupted across the United States out of African Americans' frustration in their struggle for equal rights. The issue blacks faced was one they felt they had in common with decolonizing peoples: how to shape an identity different from that imposed on them by white oppressors. Some chose to celebrate their race under the banner "black is beautiful," and some urged a push for "black power" to reclaim rights forcefully instead of "begging" for them nonviolently. Separatism, not integration, became the goal of others. Small cadres of militants like the Black Panthers took up arms, believing that, like decolonizing peoples elsewhere, they needed to protect themselves against the violent whites around them.

From the 1950s on, homosexuals had also lobbied for the decriminalization of their sexual lives and practices. Propaganda equated male homosexuality with a lack of militaristic manliness needed to protect the nation-state on either side of the cold war divide. In June 1969, gay men in the Stonewall area of Greenwich Village, New York, rioted against the police and more general persecution, as had African Americans, both to assert their civil rights and to affirm their identity. The gay liberation movement born in that time came to span the globe and to include not only men but gay women, too.

Student Activism As a result of the new turn in black efforts for change, white American university students who had participated in the early stages of the civil rights movement found themselves excluded from leadership positions. Many of them soon joined the swelling protests against technological change, consumerism, and the Vietnam War. European youth were also feverish for reform. In the mid-1960s, university students in Rome occupied an administration building after right-wing opponents assassinated one of their number during a protest against the 200-to-1 student–teacher ratio. In 1966, Prague students, chanting "The only good Communist is a dead one," held carnival-like processions to commemorate the tenth anniversary of the 1956 Hungarian uprisings. The "situationists" in France used shocking graffiti and street theater to call on students to wake up from the slumbering pace of consumer society.

Throughout the 1960s, students criticized the traditional university curriculum and flaunted their own countercultural values. They questioned how studying Plato or Dante would help them after graduation. "How to Train Stuffed Geese" was French students' satirical version of the teaching methods inflicted on them. "No professors over forty" and "Don't trust anyone over thirty" were powerful slogans of the day. Long hair, communal living, scorn for personal cleanliness, and ridicule for sexual chastity were part of students' rejection of middle-class values. Widespread use of the pill and open promiscuity made the sexual revolution explicit and public. Marijuana use became common among students, and amphetamines and barbiturates added to the drug culture, which had its own rituals, music, and gathering places. Hated by students, big business nonetheless made billions of dollars by selling everything from blue jeans to natural foods as well as by packaging and managing the rock stars of the counterculture.

The Women's Movement Women's activism erupted across the political spectrum (see "Contrasting Views," page 966). Working for reproductive rights, women in France helped end the nation's ban on birth control in 1965. More

Second-Wave Feminists on the March
Like turn-of-the-century feminists, women in the 1960s and 1970s took to the streets to protest their condition. This march in Paris features signs showing a clock fixed at 7:30 and a list of chores including "breakfast for husband," "wake the children," and "hurry." For many citizens, the sight of "unladylike" women demonstrating in public was a shock—which was the point for many activists. *(© Rue des Archives/AGIP/The Granger Collection, New York—All rights reserved.)*

politically conventional middle class women eagerly responded to the international best seller *The Feminine Mystique* (1963) by American journalist Betty Friedan. Pointing to the stagnating talents of many housewives, Friedan helped organize the National Organization for Women (NOW) in 1966 "to bring women into full participation in the mainstream of American society now." NOW advocated equal pay for equal work and a variety of other legal and economic reforms. In Sweden, women lobbied to make tasks both at home and in the workplace less gender-segregated, and in these same years a few Soviet women began speaking out against their low-paid and unpaid work that kept the USSR running.

Women engaged in the civil rights and student movements soon realized that many protest organizations devalued women just as society at large did. Male activists adopted the leather-jacketed machismo style of their film and rock heroes, but women in the movements were often judged by the status of their male-protester lovers. "A woman was to 'inspire' her man," African American activist Angela Davis complained, adding that women seeking equality were accused of wanting "to rob [male activists] of their manhood." West German women students tossed tomatoes at male protest leaders in defiance of male domination of the movement and of standards set by society for ladylike behavior.

1968: Year of Crisis

Calls for reform finally boiled over in 1968. In January, on the first day of Tet, the Vietnamese New Year, the Vietcong and the North Vietnamese attacked more than one hundred South Vietnamese towns and American bases, inflicting heavy casualties. The Tet offensive, as it came to be called, led many in the United States and across the West to conclude that the war might be unwinnable and fueled the antiwar movement around the world. Students in Paris, Tokyo, Mexico City, and other major capitals took to the streets against the war, often in violent protest. Meanwhile, in Czechoslovakia, a quieter movement against Soviet cold war domination had taken shape, but the atmosphere in that country, as elsewhere, became explosive when the Soviets invaded to put down reform.

The Outbreak of Violence

On April 4, 1968, a white racist assassinated civil rights leader Martin Luther King Jr. Riots erupted in more than a hundred cities in the United States as African Americans vented their anguish and rage. Rejecting King's policy of nonviolence, black leaders turned to violence: "Burn, baby, burn," chanted rioters as they rampaged through grim inner cities. On campuses, bitter clashes over the inter-

CONTRASTING VIEWS

Feminist Debates

The feminist movement of the late twentieth century provoked the most pronounced and widespread debate over gender in recorded history. Discussion often reached a heated pitch, as it did in other reform movements of the day. Feminists had a variety of concerns, often depending on their nationality, ethnicity, race, religion, sexual orientation, and class. Opinion on these issues could produce conflict among activists and serious divisions on goals and policies, as the authors of the Combahee River Statement demonstrated (Document 1). At times, concerns over issues like equal opportunity in the workplace were directed at government policies, as in the case of the Soviet worker (Document 2). Italian feminists saw all the disabilities imposed by government as characteristic of larger problems (Document 3), while Germans explicitly connected the cause of feminism to that of environmentalism (Document 4). With the advances in global travel and televised news, comparisons came to the fore as well (Document 5).

1. Criticizing White Feminism

In the United States, black women, like several other minority groups, found themselves marginalized in both the feminist and civil rights movements. In 1977, some of them issued the Combahee River Statement.

Black, other third world, and working women have been involved in the feminist movement from its start, but both outside reactionary forces and racism and elitism within the movement itself have served to obscure our participation. . . .

Black feminist politics also have an obvious connection to movements for Black liberation, particularly those of the 1960s and 1970s. . . . It was our experience and disillusionment within these liberation movements, as well as experience on the periphery of the white male left, that led to the need to develop a politics that was antiracist, unlike those of white women, and antisexist, unlike those of Black and white men. . . .

Above all else, our politics initially sprang from the shared belief that Black women are inherently valuable, that our liberation is a necessity not as an adjunct to somebody else's but because of our need as human persons for autonomy.

Source: "The Combahee River Collective Statement," in *Feminism in Our Time: The Essential Writings, World War II to the Present*, ed. Miriam Schneir (New York: Vintage, 1994), 177–79.

2. Criticizing Socialism

Official policy in the Soviet Union stated that socialism had brought women full equality, eliminating the need for feminism. In the 1970s, however, clusters of Russian women announced their dissatisfaction with so-called equality under socialism. Tatyana Mamonova, the editor of a collection of Russian women's writings such as this from a railroad worker, was ultimately expelled from the USSR.

It is becoming increasingly clear that the current equality means only giving women the right to perform heavy labor. . . . [I]n our day the woman, still not freed from the incredible burden of the family, strains herself even harder in the service of society. The situation . . . is true not only in large cities but also in villages. On collective and state farms, women do the hardest and most exhausting work while the men are employed as administrators, agronomists, accountants, warehouse managers, or high-paid tractor and combine drivers. In other words, men do the work that is more interesting and more profitable and does not damage their health.

Source: Tatyana Mamonova, ed., *Women and Russia: Feminist Writings from the Soviet Union* (Boston: Beacon Press, 1984), 8.

3. Policy and Patriarchy

In Italy, as in the Soviet Union, feminism had an underground quality involving mimeographed tracts and graffiti on buildings; women formed their own bookshops and published small newspapers. But others lobbied hard to get legislation on divorce and abortion changed, while in 1976 the Feminist Movement of Rome issued this article in its paper.

Patriarchal society is based on authoritarian-exploitative relationships, and its sexuality is sadomasochistic. The values of power, of the domination of man over the other [woman], are reflected in sexu-

twined issues of war, technology, racism, and sexism closed down classes.

Similar student unrest erupted across the globe, most dramatically in France. In January, students at the university in Nanterre, outside of Paris, had gone on strike, invading administration offices to protest what they saw as a second-rate education. They called themselves a proletariat — an exploited working class — as worker activists had done for more than a century. They did not embrace Soviet communism but rather considered themselves part of the New Left, not the old Communist or Socialist left. When students at the prestigious Sorbonne in Paris also took to the streets in protest, police assaulted them. The Parisian middle classes reacted with unexpected, if temporary, sympathy to the student uprising because of their own resentment of bureaucracy. They were also horrified at seeing the police force beating middle-class students and even passersby who expressed their support.

French workers joined in the protest. Some nine million went on strike, occupying factories and call-

ality, where historically woman is given to man for his use. . . .

The idea of woman as man's property is fundamental to her oppression and she is often the only possession that dominant men allow exploited men to keep. . . .

In other words woman is given to the (exploited) man as compensation for his lack of possessions. . . .

We denounce as the latest form of woman's oppression the idea of a "sexual revolution" where woman is forced to go from being one man's object to being everybody's object, and where sadomasochistic pornography in films, in magazines, in all the forms of mass media that brutalize and violate woman, is bandied about as a triumph of sexual liberty.

Source: "Male Sexuality—Perversion," *Movimento Femminista Romano* (1976), quoted in *Italian Feminist Thought: A Reader*, eds. Paola Bono and Sandra Kemp (Oxford: Blackwell, 1991), 68–69.

4. Feminism and Environmentalism

Environmentally aware feminists took a different approach, such as announced in this "Manifesto of the 'Green' Women." It was originally a 1975 speech made in West Germany in the context of the moon landing and other accomplishments in space.

Man has actually landed on the moon—an admirable feat. . . . We "Green" women . . . believe that men belong to our environment. In order to rescue that environment for our children, we want to confront this man, this adventurer and moon explorer. A female cosmonaut from a so-called socialist republic doesn't justify this energy-wasting enterprise for us at a time when three-fourths of the earth's population is suffering from malnutrition.

Our inability to solve immediate problems may tempt us into escape—to the moon, into careerism, escape into ideologies, into alcohol or other drugs. But one group cannot escape completely: women, society's potential mothers, who must give birth to children, willingly or unwillingly, in this polluted world of ours.

Source: Delphine Brox-Brochot, "Manifesto of the 'Green' Women," in *German Feminism: Readings in Politics and Literature*, eds. Edith Hoshino Altbach et al. (Albany: State University of New York Press, 1984), 314.

5. Comparing the Situation of European and African Women

In an age when communications technology was bringing greater knowledge of conditions around the world, there were more frequent comparisons of situations faced by Western women with those faced by women in distant regions. The Malian politician Awa Thiam offered such an analysis in her Speak Out, Black Sisters *(1986).*

In any European country, when a husband goes in for that form of semi-condoned polygamy that consists of taking a mistress—or several—the wife can have recourse to the law by instituting action for divorce, or at least obtain support for better treatment from him. Such a course of action is not possible for a Muslim woman, who grows up in a system of institutionalized polygamy, where this is not permitted. What is more, such action would appear aberrant in a Black African context, in which marriage is generally religious, not civil. And this is the main basis for our claim that the Black woman's struggle is of a different nature from that of her White sister. The majority of European women do not lack essentials, whereas Black women are fighting for survival as much in the field of institutions as in the manner of her daily existence.

Source: Awa Thiam, *Speak Out, Black Sisters: Feminism and Oppression in Black Africa*, quoted in *Daughters of Africa: An International Anthology of Words and Writings by Women of African Descent from Ancient Egypt to the Present*, ed. Margaret Busby (New York: Ballantine Books, 1994), 477–78.

Questions to Consider

1. **What was the relationship between ideas within the feminist movement of the 1960s and 1970s and the thinking of other reform movements of the day?**
2. **In what ways was feminism in these decades a unified movement in terms of its thinking, and in what ways was it a set of multiple movements?**
3. **What issues do these activists raise?**
4. **What possibilities for consensus do you see in the differing positions?**

ing not only for higher wages but also for participation in everyday decision making. The combined revolt of youth and workers looked as if it might spiral into another French revolution, so unified were the expressions of political anger. The normally decisive president Charles de Gaulle seemed paralyzed at first, but he soon sent tanks into Paris. In June, he announced a raise for workers, and businesses offered them more involvement in decision making. Many citizens, having grown tired of the street violence, the destruction of so much private property, and the breakdown of services such as garbage collection, began to sympathize with the government instead of the students. Although demonstrations continued throughout June, the student movement in France at least had been closed down. The revolutionary moment had passed.

The Prague Spring By contrast, the 1968 revolt in Prague began within the Czechoslovak Communist Party itself. At a party congress in the autumn of 1967, Alexander Dubček,

Invasion Puts Down the Prague Spring
When the Soviet Union and other Warsaw Pact members cracked down on the Prague Spring, they met determined citizen resistance. People refused assistance of any kind to the invaders and personally talked to them about the Czech cause. Despite the repression, protests small and large continued until the final fall of Communist rule two decades later. *(© Bettmann/Corbis.)*

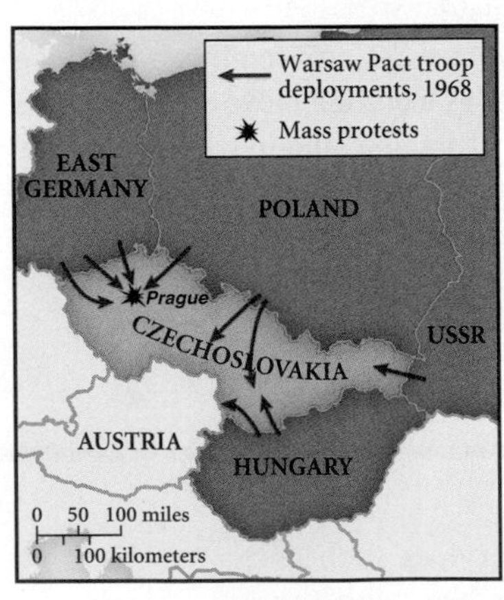

Prague Spring, 1968

head of the Slovak branch of the party, had called for more social and political openness. Attacked as an inferior Slovak by the Communist leadership, Dubček nonetheless struck a chord among frustrated party officials, technocrats, and intellectuals. Czech citizens began to dream of creating a new society—one based on "socialism with a human face." Reform-minded party delegates elevated Dubček to the top position, and he quickly changed the Communist style of government by ending censorship, instituting the secret ballot for party elections, and allowing competing political groups to form. "Look!" one little girl in the street remarked as the new government took power. "Everyone's smiling today." The Prague Spring had begun—"an orgy of free expression," one Czech journalist called it. People bought uncensored publications, packed uncensored theater productions, and engaged in nonstop political debate.

Dubček faced the enormous problem of negotiating policies acceptable to the USSR, the party bureaucracy, and reform-minded citizens. His government handed down reforms with warnings about maintaining "discipline" and showing "wise behavior." Fearing change, the Polish, East German, and Soviet regimes threatened the reform government daily. When Dubček failed to attend a meeting of Warsaw Pact leaders, Soviet threats intensified until finally, in August 1968, Soviet tanks rolled into Prague in a massive show of force. Citizens tried to halt the return to Communist orthodoxy through sabotage: they painted graffiti on the tanks and removed street signs to confuse invading troops. Illegal radio stations broadcast testimonials of resistance, and merchants refused to sell food or other commodities to Soviet troops. These actions did not stop the determined Soviet leadership, which gradually removed reformers from power. Jan Palach and other university students immolated themselves the following January, but the moment of reform-minded change eventually ended here, too. Around the world, governments worked to stamp out criticism of the cold war order.

The Superpowers Restore Order The protests of 1968 challenged the political direction of Western societies, but little turned out the way reformers hoped as governments turned to conservative solutions. In November 1968, the Soviets announced the Brezhnev Doctrine, which stated that reform movements, as a "common problem" of all socialist countries, would face swift repression. In the early 1970s, the hard-liner Brezhnev clamped down on critics, crushing the morale of dissidents in the USSR. "The shock of our tanks crushing the Prague Spring . . . convinced us that the Soviet colossus was invincible," explained one pessimistic liberal. Other voices persisted, however. In 1974, Brezhnev expelled author Aleksandr Solzhenitsyn from the USSR after the publication of the first volume of *The Gulag Archipelago* (1973–1976) in the U.S.-led bloc. Solzhenitsyn documented the story of the Gulag (the Soviet system of internment and forced-labor camps) with firsthand reports and other sources of information about the deadly conditions prisoners endured. More than any other single work, *The Gulag Archipelago* disillusioned loyal Communists around the world.

The USSR and other Communist countries used both persecution of ordinary citizens and the "soft" power of the new medium of television to reestablish order. Soviet psychologists, working with the government, certified the "mental illness" of people who did not play by the rules; thus, dissidents wound up as virtual prisoners in mental institutions. In a revival of tsarist Russia's anti-Semitism, Jews faced educational restrictions (especially in university admissions), severe job discrimination, and constant assault on their religious practice. Soviet officials commonly accused Jews of being "unreliable." One said, "They think only of emigrating. . . . It's madness to give them an education, because it's state money wasted." Simultaneously the new medium of television was enlisted to restore calm. In Czechoslovakia, where by 1970 some 80 percent of households had TV, government writers created a new batch of soap operas after the uprisings. These featured heroines who taught their families to replace activism in the public sphere with the contentment of private life. Heroes selflessly traveled to the West for their jobs, only to return disillusioned by its faults.

Despite these efforts, the brain drain of eastern European intellectuals to the West and of Jews to Israel or the United States increased into the 1970s and beyond. The modernist composer György Ligeti had left Hungary in 1956, after which his work was celebrated in concert halls and in such classic films as *2001: A Space Odyssey*. From exile in Paris, Czech writer Milan Kundera enthralled audiences with *The Book of Laughter and Forgetting* (1979) and *The Unbearable Lightness of Being* (1984). His novels chronicled his own path from enthusiasm for communism to despair shaped by bitter humor. Kundera claimed that the Soviet regime in Czechoslovakia depended on making people forget. The memory of fallen leaders was ruthlessly erased from history books, for instance, and individuals tried to block out grim reality by engaging in lots of sexual activity. Like the migrants from fascist Germany and Italy in the 1930s, newcomers—from noted intellectuals to skilled craftspeople and dancers—enriched the culture of those countries in the West that welcomed them.

In the United States, the reaction against activists was different, though restoring order ultimately succeeded there, too. Elected in 1968, President **Richard Nixon** (1913–1994) promised to bring peace to Southeast Asia, but in 1970 he ordered U.S. troops to invade Cambodia, the site of North Vietnamese bases. Campuses erupted again in protest, and on May 4 the National Guard killed four students and wounded eleven others at a demonstration at Kent State University in Ohio. Nixon called the victims "bums," and a growing reaction against the counterculture led many Americans to agree with one citizen who declared that the guardsmen "should have fired sooner and longer." The United States and North Vietnam agreed to peace in January 1973, but warfare continued. In 1975, a determined North Vietnamese offensive defeated South Vietnam and its U.S. allies and forcibly reunified the country. The United States reeled from the defeat, having suffered loss of young lives, turbulence at home, vast military costs, and a weakening of its reputation around the world. Yet a strong current of public opinion turned against activists, born of the sense that somehow they—not the war, government corruption, or the huge war debt—had brought down the United States. Both superpowers were being tested, almost to the limits, creating a climate of uncertainty not only about politics but also about the future of postindustrial prosperity.

REVIEW QUESTION What were the main issues for protesters in the 1960s, and how did governments address them?

Richard Nixon: U.S. president (1969–1974) who escalated the Vietnam War, worked for accommodation with China, and resigned from the presidency after trying to block free elections.

The Testing of Superpower Domination and the End of the Cold War

Protesters like Jan Palach left a lasting legacy that continued to motivate those seeking political change, particularly in the Soviet bloc. As order was restored, some disillusioned reformers in the West turned to open terrorism, and like every other political occurrence in these days, television broadcast the events. New forces also emerged from beyond Europe and the United States to challenge superpower dominance. The 1970s brought an era of détente — a lessening of tensions — during which both superpowers limited the nuclear arms race in order to deal with crises at home. Even so, internal corruption, the threat of terrorism, competition from the oil-producing states, and the pursuit of warfare beyond their borders all threw the superpowers and their allies off balance, allowing reform-minded heads of state to come to the fore. The two most famous innovators were Margaret Thatcher in Britain and Mikhail Gorbachev in the USSR, who introduced drastic new policies in the 1980s to keep their economies moving forward. But in the Soviet bloc, postindustrial prosperity was simply unattainable by trying to refine the old system. Gorbachev's reforms actually contributed to the collapse of the Soviet system and the end of the cold war in 1989.

A Changing Balance of World Power

After being tested by protest at home, the superpowers found themselves facing a changing balance in world power. In 1972, the United States pulled off a foreign policy triumph over the USSR when it opened relations with the other Communist giant — China. But it was hit hard by a Middle Eastern oil embargo that followed on the heels of that victory. As the situation in the Middle East grew ever bloodier, militants in Iran took U.S. embassy personnel hostage. The relationship of the United States to the Middle East began to weaken the U.S. bloc and to compete with the cold war as a major global issue.

From Nixon in China to Détente In the midst of turmoil at home and the draining war in Vietnam, Henry Kissinger, Nixon's secretary of state and a believer — like Otto von Bismarck — in Realpolitik, decided to take advantage of the ongoing rivalry between the USSR and China. After the Communist Revolution in 1949, Mao Zedong, China's new leader, undertook foolish experiments in both manufacturing and agriculture that caused famine and massive suffering. In the Cultural Revolution of the 1960s, Mao encouraged students to attack officials, teachers, and other authorities to prevent — he claimed — the development of a Soviet-style bureaucracy. As internal problems grew in both the Soviet Union and China, the two Communist giants skirmished along their shared borders and in diplomatic arenas. In 1972, President Nixon visited China, linking, if only tentatively, two very different great nations both facing disorder at home. Within China, Nixon's visit helped slow the brutality and excesses of Mao's Cultural Revolution. It also advanced the careers of Chinese pragmatists who were interested in technology, trade, and relations with the West and who laid the groundwork for China's boom that started later in the century.

The diplomatic success of the visit also sped up the process of détente between the United States and the Soviet Union. Fearful of the Chinese diplomatic advantage and similarly confronted by popular protest, the Soviets made their own overtures to the U.S.-led bloc. In 1972, the superpowers signed the first Strategic Arms Limitation Treaty (SALT I), which set a cap on the number of antimissile defenses each country could have. In 1975, in the Helsinki accords on human rights, the western bloc officially acknowledged Soviet territorial gains in World War II in exchange for the Soviet bloc's guarantee of basic human rights.

Despite these diplomatic successes, the war in Vietnam left the United States billions of dollars in debt to other countries. The international currency system collapsed under the weight of this imbalance. In the face of the resulting global economic chaos, Common Market countries united to force the United States to relinquish its single-handed direction of Western economic strategy. Another blow to U.S. leadership followed when it was revealed that Nixon's office had threatened the U.S. system of free elections by authorizing the burglary and wiretapping of Democratic Party headquarters at Washington's Watergate building during the 1972 presidential campaign. The Watergate scandal forced Nixon to resign in disgrace in the summer of 1974 — the first U.S. president ever to do so. Nixon's downfall was one more weak spot in U.S. superpower status in the 1960s and 1970s.

Oil and Stagflation Amid the instability in the United States in the 1960s and 1970s, the Middle East's oil-producing nations dealt Western dominance still another major blow. Tensions between Israel and the Arab world pro-

The Middle East and the Politics of Oil
When Middle Eastern countries took control of the price and volume of oil they sold, Western leaders were taken aback, so thoroughly accustomed were the United States and its allies to setting the conditions of trade. OPEC leaders were lampooned in cartoons as the global economic crisis unfolded. Stagflation hit Western economies hard, while everyone came to terms with the new force of oil in international politics. *(© Copyright 1977 by Hy Rosen/Albany Times-Union, Albany, New York.)*

vided the catalyst. In 1967, Israeli forces, responding to Palestinian guerrilla attacks, quickly seized Gaza and the Sinai peninsula from Egypt, the Golan Heights from Syria, and the West Bank from Jordan. Israel's stunning victory in this action, which came to be called the Six-Day War, was followed in 1973 by a joint Egyptian and Syrian attack on Israel on Yom Kippur, the most holy day in the Jewish calendar. Israel, with material assistance from the United States, stopped the assault.

Israel after the Six-Day War, 1967

Having failed militarily, the Arabs turned to economic clout. They struck at the West's weakest point—its dependence on Middle Eastern oil for its advanced industries and postindustrial lifestyle. Arab nations in the **Organization of Petroleum Exporting Countries (OPEC)**, a relatively loose consortium before the Yom Kippur War, combined to quadruple the price of their oil and impose an embargo, cutting off all exports of oil to the United States and its allies because they backed Israel. For the first time since imperialism's heyday, the producers of raw materials—not the industrial powers—controlled the flow of commodities and set prices to their own advantage. The West was now mired in an oil crisis.

Throughout the 1970s, oil-dependent Westerners watched in astonishment as OPEC upset the balance of economic power and helped provoke a recession in the West (Figure 28.1). The oil embargo and price hike not only caused unemployment to rise by more than 50 percent in Europe and the United States but also caused inflation to soar. By the end of 1973, the inflation rate jumped to over 8 percent in West Germany, 12 percent in France, and 20 percent in Portugal. Eastern-bloc countries, dependent on Soviet oil, fared little better because the West could no longer afford their products and the Soviets boosted the price of their own oil. Skyrocketing interest rates discouraged both industrial investment and consumer buying. With prices, unemployment, and interest rates all rising—an unusual combination of economic conditions called **stagflation**—some in the West came to realize that both energy resources and economic growth had limits. Western Europe drastically cut back on its oil dependence by undertaking conservation, enhancing public trans-

---

Organization of Petroleum Exporting Countries (OPEC): A consortium that regulated the supply and export of oil and that acted with more unanimity after the United States supported Israel against the Arabs in the wars of the late 1960s and early 1970s.

stagflation: The combination of a stagnant economy and soaring inflation; a period of stagflation occurred in the West in the 1970s as a result of an OPEC embargo on oil.

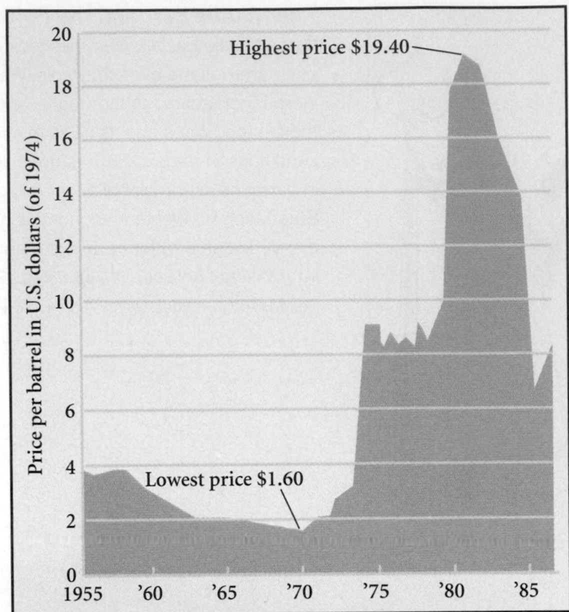

FIGURE 28.1 Fluctuating Oil Prices, 1955–1985
Colonization allowed the Western imperial powers to obtain raw materials at advantageous prices or even without paying at all. OPEC's oil embargo and price hikes of the 1970s were signs of change, which included the exercise of decolonized countries' control over their own resources. OPEC's action led to a decade of painful economic downturn, but it also encouraged some European governments to improve public transportation, encourage the production of fuel-efficient cars, and make individual consumers cut back their dependence on oil.

portation, and raising the price of gasoline to encourage the development of fuel-efficient cars.

The U.S. bloc took further blows. Elected U.S. president in 1976, Jimmy Carter—a successful peanut farmer and governor of Georgia—was unable to return the economy to its pre–Vietnam War and pre–oil embargo prosperity. His administration also faced an insurmountable crisis in the Middle East. In the late 1970s, students, clerics, shopkeepers, and unemployed men in Iran began a religious uprising that brought to power the Islamic ayatollah (a Shi'ite religious leader) Ruhollah Khomeini (1902–1989). Using the new medium of audiocassette recordings to spread his message, Khomeini called for a transformation of Iran into a truly Islamic society, which meant the renunciation of the Western ways advocated by the American-backed shah, who as a result was deposed. In the autumn of 1979, revolutionary supporters of Khomeini took hostages at the U.S. embassy in Teheran and held them for 444 days, even as images of the captives' stricken faces were sent around the globe via satellites. The United States was essentially paralyzed in the face of Islamic militancy, further OPEC price hikes, and a downwardly spiraling economy.

The Western Bloc Meets Challenges with Reform

As the 1980s opened, the first agenda item for non-Communist governments in the West was to put their economic houses in order. Second was to confront the growing phenomenon of terrorism—that is, coordinated and targeted political violence by opposition groups. The mix of terrorism, the energy crisis, soaring unemployment, and double-digit inflation sparked the election of conservative politicians, who maintained that decades of supporting a welfare state were at the heart of economic problems. Across the West, people came to feel that the unemployed and new immigrants from around the world were responsible for the downturn in the postindustrial economy. Nineteenth-century emphases on competitiveness, individualism, and revival of privilege for the "best circles" replaced the twentieth-century trend toward advancing economic democracy to combat totalitarianism. Postindustrial society changed political course.

Terrorism The terrorism at the U.S. embassy in Iran was part of a trend that had actually begun in the West. In the 1970s, terrorist bands of young people in Europe responded to the suppression of activism and the worsening economic conditions with kidnappings, bank robberies, bombings, and assassinations. In West Germany, the Red Army Faction—eager to bring down the Social Democratic coalition that had led the country through the 1970s—assassinated prominent businessmen, judges, and other public officials. Practiced in assassinations of public figures and random shootings of pedestrians, Italy's Red Brigades kidnapped and then murdered the head of the dominant Christian Democrats in 1978. Advocates of independence for the Basque nation in northern Spain assassinated Spanish politicians and police officers.

In the 1970s, Catholics in Northern Ireland pitted themselves against the dominant Protestants to protest job discrimination and a lack of civil rights. Demonstrators urged union with the Irish Republic, and with protest escalating, the British government sent in troops. On January 30, 1972, which became known as Bloody Sunday, British troops fired at demonstrators and killed thirteen, setting off a cycle of violence that left five hundred dead in that year alone. Protestants fearful of losing their dominant position combated a reinvigorated Irish Republican Army (IRA), which carried out bombings and assassinations to press for the union of the two Irelands and an end to the oppression of Catholics.

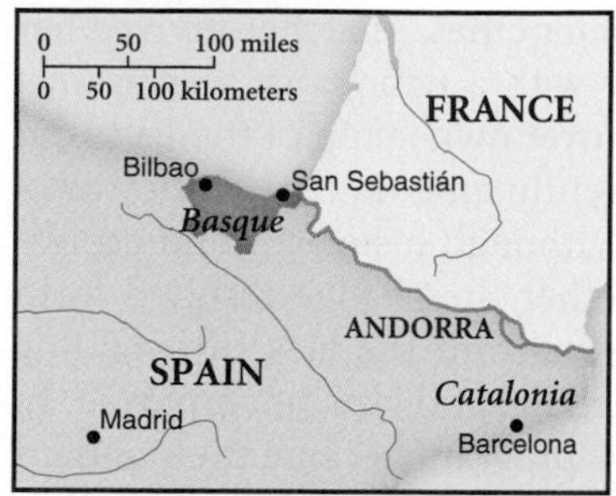

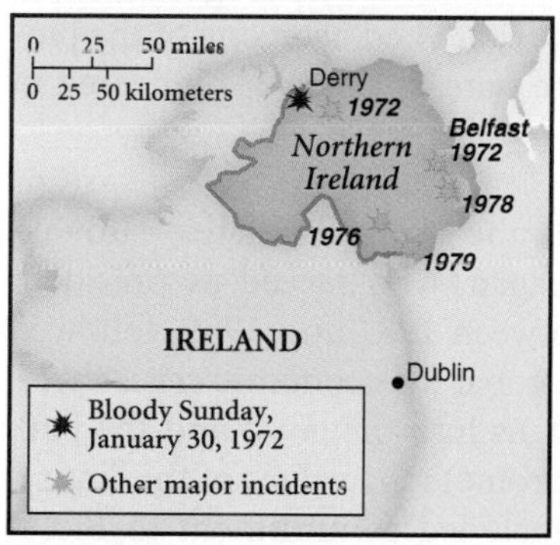

Nationalist Movements of the 1970s

Soldiers and Civilians in Northern Ireland

Separatist, civil rights, and terrorist movements increasingly directed their violence against ordinary people, following the lead of soldiers in World War II. In Northern Ireland, British troops fought to put down the Irish Republican Army, but civilians were also their target. However, this image from Derry in 1969 shows that civilians resisted, fighting with homemade weapons. It was only late in the 1990s that both sides called a halt to the killing and agreed to negotiate. *(Getty Images.)*

Terrorists failed in their goal of overturning the existing democracies, and, battered as it was, parliamentary government scored a few important successes in the 1970s. Spain and Portugal, suffering under dictatorships since the 1930s, set out on a course of political openness and greater prosperity. The death of Spain's Francisco Franco in 1975 ended more than three decades of dictatorial rule. Franco's handpicked successor, King Juan Carlos, surprisingly steered his nation to Western-style constitutional monarchy, facing down threatened military coups. Portugal and Greece also ousted right-wing dictators, thus paving the way for their integration into western Europe and for economic growth. Despite these democratic advances, economic crisis and political terrorism weighed on the West.

Thatcher Reshapes Politics More than anyone else, **Margaret Thatcher**, the leader of Britain's Conservative Party and prime minister from 1979 to 1990, reshaped the West's political and economic ideas to meet the crisis. Coming to power amid continuing economic decline, revolt in Northern Ireland, and labor unrest, the combative prime minister rejected the politics of consensus building. She believed that only business could revive the sluggish British economy, so she lashed out at union leaders, Labour Party politicians, and people who received welfare-state benefits, calling them enemies of British prosperity. Her policies against the welfare state sounded a revolutionary chord, and she called herself "a nineteenth-century liberal" in reference to the economic individualism of that age. In her view, business leaders were the key members of society. She characterized immigrants, whose low wages contributed greatly to business profits, as inferior. Under Thatcher, even workers blamed labor leaders or newcomers for Britain's troubles.

The policies of "Thatcherism" were based on monetarist, or supply-side, economic theory. According to monetarist theory, inflation results when government pumps money into the economy at a rate higher than the nation's economic growth rate. Monetarists thus believe that the government should keep a tight rein on the money supply to prevent prices from rising rapidly. Supply-side economists maintain that the economy as a whole flourishes when businesses grow and their prosperity "trickles down" throughout society. To implement these

---

Margaret Thatcher: Prime minister of Britain (1979–1990) who set a new tone for British politics by promoting neoliberal economic policies and criticizing poor people, union members, and racial minorities as worthless, even harmful citizens.

On the World Stage: Margaret Thatcher and Mohammed Anwar al-Sadat
Margaret Thatcher, Great Britain's conservative prime minister, and Egyptian president Mohammed Anwar al-Sadat met in London in August 1981, just two months before Sadat was assassinated for participating in the Egyptian-Israeli peace accord. Thatcher's term in office was as memorable as Sadat's: she went on to launch a new conservatism in politics and economics that would sweep the world in the 1980s and 1990s. *(Mary Evans Picture Library/Marx Memorial Library.)*

theories, the British government cut income taxes on the wealthy as a way of encouraging investment and increased sales taxes to compensate for the lost revenue. The result was a greater burden on working people, who bore the brunt of the higher sales tax. Thatcher also vigorously cut government's role in the economy: she sold publicly owned businesses and utilities such as British Airways, refused to prop up "outmoded" industries such as coal mining, and slashed education and health programs. As Thatcher's package of economic policies spread through the West and the world, it came to be known as **neoliberalism** (see Document, "Margaret Thatcher's Economic Vision," page 975).

In the first three years of Thatcher's government, the British economy did not respond well to her shock treatment. The quality of universities, public transportation, highways, and hospitals deteriorated, and leading scholars and scientists left the country in a renewal of the brain drain. In addition, social unity fragmented as she pitted the lower classes against one another. In 1981, blacks and Asians rioted in major cities. Thatcher revived her sagging popularity with a nationalist war against Argentina in 1982 over ownership of the Falkland Islands off the Argentinian coast. Stagflation ultimately dissipated, although historians and economists debated whether the change resulted from Thatcher's policies or from the lack of spending power that burdened the poor and unemployed. In any case, Thatcher's program became the standard for those facing the challenge of stagflation and economic decline. Britain had been one of the pioneers of the welfare state, and now it pioneered in changing course.

In Thatcher's Footsteps In the United States, Ronald Reagan, who served as president between 1981 and 1989, followed a similar road to combat the economic crisis there. Dividing U.S. citizens into the good and the bad, Reagan vowed to promote the values of the "moral majority," which included commitment to Bible-based religion, dedication to work, and unquestioned patriotism. He blasted so-called spendthrift and immoral "liberals" when introducing "Reaganomics"—a program of whopping income tax cuts for the wealthy combined with massive reductions in federal spending for student loans, school lunch programs, and mass transit. Like Thatcher, Reagan believed that cutting programs for the poor and taxes for the wealthy would help the economy. Federal funding of social programs, he felt, only encouraged bad Americans to be lazy.

In foreign policy, Reagan warned of the Communist threat from the Soviet Union—which he called the "evil empire"—and thus rolled back détente. He demanded huge military budgets to counter the Soviets and announced the Strategic Defense Initiative (SDI), known popularly as Star Wars, a costly plan to put lasers in space to defend the United States against a nuclear attack. The combination of tax cuts and military expansion had pushed the federal budget deficit to $200 billion by 1986. As in Britain, inflation was brought under control and business picked up.

Other western European leaders also limited welfare-state benefits in the face of stagflation, though without Thatcher's and Reagan's socially divisive rhetoric. West German leader Helmut Kohl, who took power in 1982, reduced welfare spending, froze government wages, and cut corporate taxes. By 1984, the inflation rate was only 2 percent and West Germany had acquired a 10 percent share of world trade. Unlike Thatcher, Kohl did not fan class and racial hatreds. Such a strategy would have been particularly unwise in Germany, where terrorism on the left and on the right continued to flourish.

---

neoliberalism: A theory first promoted by British prime minister Margaret Thatcher, calling for a return to liberal principles of the nineteenth century, including the reduction of welfare-state programs and the cutting of taxes for the wealthy to promote economic growth.

DOCUMENT

Margaret Thatcher's Economic Vision

Margaret Thatcher, Britain's longest-serving prime minister, changed Western thinking about the welfare state. Many Europeans saw the welfare state as a mainstay of democracy, which would alleviate the hardships that had turned workers toward either socialism, from Bismarck's time onward, or toward Mussolini's and Hitler's fascism during the difficult interwar years. Thatcher, however, believed that programs to provide health care, education, and housing coddled the lazy. She thought the money for such programs should be invested in private industry, to produce a profit and to encourage more investment and greater productivity. Here she outlines her thoughts on public spending to members of the Conservative Party.

I and my colleagues say that to add to public spending takes away the very money and resources that industry needs to stay in business, let alone to expand. Higher public spending, far from curing unemployment, can be the very vehicle that loses jobs and causes bankruptcies in trade and commerce. That is why we warned local authorities that since rates [taxes] are frequently the biggest tax that industry now faces, increases in them can cripple local businesses. . . .

That is why I stress that if those who work in public authorities take for themselves large pay increases, they leave less to be spent on equipment and new buildings. That in turn deprives the private sector of the orders it needs, especially some of those industries in the hard pressed regions. Those in the public sector have a duty to those in the private sector not to take out so much in pay that they cause others' unemployment. That is why we point out that every time high wage settlements in nationalised monopolies lead to higher charges for telephones, electricity, coal, and water, they can drive companies out of business and cost other people their jobs.

If spending money like water was the answer to our country's problems, we would have no problems right now. If ever a nation has spent, spent, spent, and spent again, ours has. Today that dream is over. All of that money has got us nowhere, but it still has to come from somewhere. Those who urge us to relax the squeeze, to spend yet more money indiscriminately in the belief that it will help the unemployed and the small businessman, are not being kind or compassionate or caring. They are not the friends of the unemployed or the small business. They are asking us to do again the very things that caused the problems in the first place. . . .

I am accused of lecturing or preaching about this. I suppose it is a critic's way of saying, "Well, we know it is true, but we have to carp at something." I do not care about that. But I do care about the future of free enterprise, the jobs and exports it provides, and the independence it brings to our people.

Source: Juliet S. Thompson and Wayne C. Thompson, ed., *Margaret Thatcher: Prime Minister Indomitable* (Boulder: Westview, 1994), 230–31.

Question to Consider

- **According to Thatcher, how does public spending harm the private sector and the citizens of Great Britain as a whole?**

Moreover, the legacy of Nazism loomed menacingly. When an unemployed German youth said of immigrant Turkish workers, "Let's gas 'em," the revival of Nazi hate speech appalled many in Germany's middle class.

By 1981, stagflation had put more than 1.5 million people out of work in France, but the French took a different political path to deal with the economic crisis. They elected a Socialist president, François Mitterrand, who nationalized banks and certain industries and increased wages and social spending to stimulate the economy—the opposite of Thatcherism. New public buildings like museums and libraries arose along with new subway lines and improved public transport. When conservative Jacques Chirac succeeded Mitterrand as president in 1995, he adopted neoliberal policies. Socially divisive politics that had unfolded during hard economic times grew in appeal. From the 1980s on, the racist National Front Party won 10 percent and sometimes more of the French vote with promises to deport African and Middle Eastern immigrants.

Prosperity in Smaller States

At the same time, smaller European states without heavy defense commitments began to thrive, some of them by slashing welfare programs. Spain joined the Common Market in 1986 and used Common Market investment and tourist dollars to help rebuild its sagging infrastructure as in the southern cities of Granada and Córdoba. In Ireland, new investment in education for high-tech jobs combined with low wage rates attracted business to the country in the 1990s. Prosperity and the rising death toll led to a political rapprochement between Ireland and Northern Ireland in 1999. Austria prospered, too, in part by reducing government pensions and aid to business. Austrian chancellor Franz Vranitsky summed up the changed focus of government in the 1980s and 1990s: "In Austria, the shelter that the state has given to almost everyone—employee as well as entrepreneur—has led . . . a lot of people [to] think not only what they can do to solve a problem but what the state can do. . . . This needs to change." The century-long growth of the welfare state slowed by the 1990s as new economic and political theories took hold.

Almost alone, Sweden maintained a full array of social programs for everyone. The government offered each immigrant a choice of subsidized housing in neighborhoods inhabited primarily by Swedes or primarily by people from the immigrant's native land. Such programs were expensive: the tax rate on income over $46,000 was 80 percent. Despite a highly productive workforce, Sweden dropped from fourth to fourteenth place among nations in per capita income by 1998. Although the Swedes reduced their costly dependence on foreign oil by cutting consumption in half between 1976 and 1986, their welfare state came to seem extreme to many citizens. As elsewhere, immigrants were cast as the source of the country's problems—past, present, and future: "How long will it be before our Swedish children will have to turn their faces toward Mecca?" ran one politician's campaign speech in 1993.

Collapse of Communism in the Soviet Bloc

Beginning in 1985, reform came to the Soviet Union as well, but instead of fortifying the economy, it helped bring about the collapse of the Soviet bloc. The need for reform was evident. In 1979, the USSR became embroiled against Islam in Afghanistan when it supported a coup by a Communist faction against the government: casualties were 800,000 for the Soviets alone and 3 million for Afghans. Further, global communications technology, international trade, and the ongoing protests of workers, artists, and intellectuals showed Soviet citizens that another way of life was possible. Citizens could see that the Soviet system of corrupt economic management produced a deteriorating standard of living. After working a full day, Soviet homemakers stood in long lines to obtain basic commodities. Shortages necessitated the three-generation household, in which grandparents took over tedious homemaking tasks from their working children and grandchildren. "There is no special skill to this," a seventy-three-year-old grandmother and former garbage collector remarked. "You just stand in line and wait." Even so, people often went away empty handed as basic household supplies like soap disappeared instantly from stores. One cheap and readily available product—vodka—often formed the center of people's social lives. Alcoholism reached crisis levels, diminishing productivity and tremendously straining the nation's morale.

Mikhail Gorbachev, Soviet Reformer

In 1985, a new leader, **Mikhail Gorbachev**, unexpectedly opened an era of change in hopes of remedying all these ills. The son of peasants, Gorbachev had risen through Communist Party ranks as an agricultural specialist and had traveled abroad to observe life in the West. At home, he saw the consequences of that economic stagnation: in much of the USSR, ordinary people decided not to have children. The Soviet Union was forced to import massive amounts of grain because 20 to 30 percent of the grain that was produced in the USSR rotted before it could be harvested or shipped to market, so great was the inefficiency of the state-directed economy. Industrial pollution had reached scandalous proportions because state-run enterprises cared only about meeting production quotas. A massive and privileged party bureaucracy feared innovation and failed to achieve socialism's professed goal of a decent standard of living for working people. To match U.S. military growth, the Soviet Union diverted 15 to 20 percent of its gross national product (more than double the U.S. proportion) to armaments, further crippling the economy's chances of raising living standards. As these problems grew, a new cynical generation was coming of age that had no memory of World War II or Stalin's purges. "They believe in nothing," a mother said of Soviet youth in 1984.

Gorbachev knew from experience and from his travels to western Europe that the Soviet system was completely inadequate, and he quickly proposed several unusual programs. A crucial economic reform, **perestroika** ("restructuring"), aimed to reinvigorate the Soviet economy by improving productivity, increasing investment, encouraging the use of up-to-date technology, and gradually introducing such market features as prices and profits. The complement to economic change was the policy

---

Mikhail Gorbachev: Leader of the Soviet Union (1985–1991) who instituted reforms such as glasnost and perestroika, thereby contributing to the collapse of Communist rule in the Soviet bloc and the USSR.

perestroika: Literally, "restructuring"; an economic policy instituted in the 1980s by Soviet premier Mikhail Gorbachev calling for the introduction of market mechanisms and the achievement of greater efficiency in manufacturing, agriculture, and services.

of **glasnost** (usually translated as "openness" or "publicity"), which called for disseminating "wide, prompt, and frank information" and for allowing Soviet citizens new measures of free speech. When officials complained that glasnost threatened their status, Gorbachev replaced more than a third of the Communist Party's leadership in the first months of his administration. The pressing need for glasnost became most evident after the Chernobyl catastrophe in 1986, when a nuclear reactor exploded and spewed radioactive dust into the atmosphere. Bureaucratic cover-ups delayed the spread of information about the accident, with lethal consequences for people living near the plant.

After Chernobyl, even the Communist Party and Marxism-Leninism were opened to public criticism. Party meetings suddenly included complaints about the highest leaders and their policies. Television shows adopted the outspoken methods of American investigative reporting; one program exposed the plight of Leningrad's homeless children — an admission of communism's failings. Instead of publishing made-up letters praising the great Soviet state, newspapers were flooded with real ones complaining of shortages and abuse. One outraged "mother of two" protested that the cost-cutting policy of reusing syringes in hospitals was a source of AIDS. "Why should little kids have to pay for the criminal actions of our Ministry of Health?" she asked. Debate and factions arose across the political spectrum (see Document, "A Citizen's Experience of Gorbachev's Reforms," page 978). In the fall of 1987, one of Gorbachev's allies, Boris Yeltsin, quit the government after denouncing perestroika as insufficient to produce real reform. Yeltsin's political daring, which in the past would have consigned him to oblivion (or Siberia), inspired others to organize in opposition to crumbling Communist rule. In the spring of 1989, in a remarkably free balloting in Moscow's local elections, not a single Communist was chosen.

Glasnost and perestroika dramatically changed superpower relations. Recognizing how severely the cold war arms race was draining Soviet resources, Gorbachev almost immediately began scaling back missile production. His unilateral actions gradually won over Ronald Reagan. In 1985, the two leaders initiated a personal relationship and began defusing the cold war. "I bet the hard-liners in both our countries are bleeding when we shake hands," said the jovial Reagan at the conclusion of one meeting. In early 1989, Gorbachev withdrew the last of his country's forces from the debilitating war in Afghanistan, and the United States started to cut back its own vast military buildup.

Mikhail and Raisa Gorbachev
Mikhail Gorbachev and his wife, Raisa, gave a fresh look to Soviet politics. They traveled, made friends abroad, and were fashionable and modern. While the Gorbachevs became part of Western celebrity culture, however, average citizens back home in the USSR saw the Gorbachevs' privileged lifestyle as simply the continuation of the Communist government's disregard for ordinary people. *(© Peter Turnley/Corbis.)*

Rebellion in Poland

As Gorbachev's reforms in the USSR started spiraling out of his control, dissent was rising across the Soviet bloc, beginning in Poland, where resistance to the Soviet takeover had existed for decades. In the summer of 1980, Poles had gone on strike to protest government-increased food prices. As the protest spread, workers at the Gdańsk shipyards, led by electrician Lech Walesa and crane operator Anna Walentynowicz, created an independent labor movement called **Solidarity**. The organization soon embraced much of the adult population, including a million members of the Communist Party. Both intellectuals and the Catholic church, long in the forefront of opposition to antireligious communism,

---

glasnost: Literally, "openness" or "publicity"; a policy instituted in the 1980s by Soviet premier Mikhail Gorbachev calling for greater openness in speech and in thinking, which translated to the reduction of censorship in publishing, radio, television, and other media.

Solidarity: A Polish labor union founded in 1980 by Lech Walesa and Anna Walentynowicz that contested Communist Party programs and eventually succeeded in ousting the party from the Polish government.

DOCUMENT

A Citizen's Experience of Gorbachev's Reforms

Some people—especially in the U.S. bloc—interpreted Gorbachev's reforms as noble and enlightened, opening the way to free markets and free speech. In particular, the policy of glasnost offered the possibility of free speech, leading to lively television programming and newspaper investigations. In 1987 the weekly Ogonyok, *whose name means "A Small Fire," began publishing letters to the editor from actual readers. Before that, most letters to newspapers and magazines in the Soviet Union had been written by editors to tow the proper political line. The feature became so popular that within two years the magazine was receiving as many as 150,000 letters a year covering every situation imaginable—from corruption to waiting in line, from privileges given to officials to the shortcomings of Gorbachev's reforms themselves. Presented here is a letter from a schoolteacher writing in 1988 about her own experience of glasnost.*

As a member of the "Knowledge" Society and a deputy to the local soviet, I was asked to prepare a speech for the evening in honor of the Seventieth Anniversary of the October Revolution. I studied M. S. Gorbachev's speech, "the October Revolution and *Perestroika*: The Revolution Continues," thoroughly and collected material about exemplary production workers in our village. In my speech I pointed out not only the successes, but also the shortcomings of our village, district and school. I gave the speech on November 6, and a week later I was called into the Executive Committee of the village society. I was accused of being apolitical [disloyal] and told that I would not be allowed onto the podium . . . because I was airing dirty linen in public.

. . . [A]fter a rebuke like that I have lost my desire to tell the truth, especially since the Party organization of the Cheremkhovsky collective farm and the chairman of the village soviet have suffered because of me. They were both reprimanded for not checking my speech, and for letting me onto the podium. Apparently, *glasnost* and *perestroika* have not reached us yet.

Source: Letter of Z. I. Kupriyanova, January 1988, in *Small Fires: Letters from the Soviet People to* Ogonyok *Magazine 1987–1990*, ed. Christopher Cerf and Marina Albee (New York: Summit Books, 1990), 60.

Question to Consider

- **What aspects of Gorbachev's policy does the speaker address in her letter, and what is the letter's tone?**

supported Solidarity workers as they occupied factories in protest against the deteriorating conditions of everyday life. The members of Solidarity waved Polish flags and paraded giant portraits of the Virgin Mary and Pope John Paul II—a Polish native.

Global media coverage encouraged Solidarity leaders to demand government recognition of the union's legitimacy. As food became scarce and prices rose, tens of thousands of women joined in with marches, crying "We're hungry!" They also protested working conditions, but as both workers and the only caretakers of home life, it was the scarcity of food that sent them into the streets. The Communist Party teetered on the edge of collapse, until the police and the army, with Soviet support, imposed a military government and in the winter of 1981 outlawed Solidarity. The stern and puritanical head of the new regime, Wojciech Jaruzelski, could not push repression too far: he needed new loans from the U.S.-led bloc to keep the sinking Polish economy afloat. Using world communications networks, dissidents kept Solidarity alive both inside and outside of Poland. Workers kept meeting, creating a new culture outside the official Soviet arts and newscasts. Poets read dissident verse to overflow crowds, and university professors lectured to Solidarity members on such forbidden topics as Polish resistance in World War II. Activism in Poland and the news about it set the stage for communism's downfall across the Soviet bloc.

The Revolutions of 1989 The year 1989 saw the sudden and unexpected disintegration of Communist power in eastern Europe, but uprisings were occurring around the world—in Chile, the Philippines, Haiti, South Africa, and China, for example. In 1980 the global news network CNN was established, linking many individual movements for democratic change through its twenty-four-hour coverage of world events. The most surprising and widely covered of these was the attack on the Communist state in China. Inspired by Gorbachev's visit to Beijing, in the spring of 1989 thousands of Chinese students massed in the city's Tiananmen Square, the world's largest public square, to demand democracy. They used telex machines and e-mail to rush their messages to the international community, and they effectively conveyed their goals through the cameras that Western television, broadcasting via satellite, trained on them. China's aged Communist leaders, while pushing economic modernization, refused to consider the introduction of democracy. As workers began joining the pro-democracy forces, the government crushed the movement and executed as many as a thousand rebels.

News of the protests in Tiananmen Square was galvanizing to those in eastern Europe, who were inspired in their long-standing tradition of resistance. In June 1989, the Polish government, weakened by its own bungling of the economy and lacking Soviet support for further repression, held free parliamentary elections. Solidarity candidates overwhelmingly defeated the Communists, and Walesa became president in early 1990, hastening Poland's rocky transition to a market economy. Gorbachev openly reversed the Brezhnev Doctrine, refusing to interfere in the political course of another nation. When it became clear that the Soviet Union would not intervene in Poland, the fall of communism repeated itself across the Soviet bloc.

Communism collapsed first in Poland and then in Hungary, in part because of those countries' early introduction of free-market measures. In Hungary, which had experimented with "market socialism" since the 1960s, even officials began to realize that political democracy had to accompany economic freedom. Citizens were already protesting the government, lobbying, for example, against ecologically unsound projects like the construction of a new dam. They encouraged boycotts of Communist holidays, and on March 15, 1989, they boldly commemorated the anniversary of the Hungarian uprising. Finally, these popular demands for liberalization led the Parliament in the fall of 1989 to dismiss the Communist Party as the official ruling institution; people across the country tore down Soviet and Communist symbols.

The most potent symbol of a divided Europe—the Berlin Wall—stood in the midst of a divided Germany. East Germans had attempted to escape over the wall for decades, and since the early 1980s dissidents had held peace vigils in cities across East Germany. In the summer of 1989, crowds of East Germans flooded the borders to escape the crumbling Soviet bloc, and hundreds of thousands of protesters rallied throughout the fall against the regime. Satellite television brought them visions of postindustrial prosperity and of free and open public debate in West Germany. Crowds of demonstrators greeted Gorbachev, taken as a hero by many, when he visited the country in October. On November 9, guards at the Berlin Wall allowed free passage to the west, turning protest into a festive holiday: West Berliners greeted the Easterners with bananas, a consumer good that had been in short supply in the Eastern zone, and that fruit became the unofficial symbol of a newfound liberation. As they strolled freely in the streets, East Berliners saw firsthand the goods available in a successful postindustrial society.

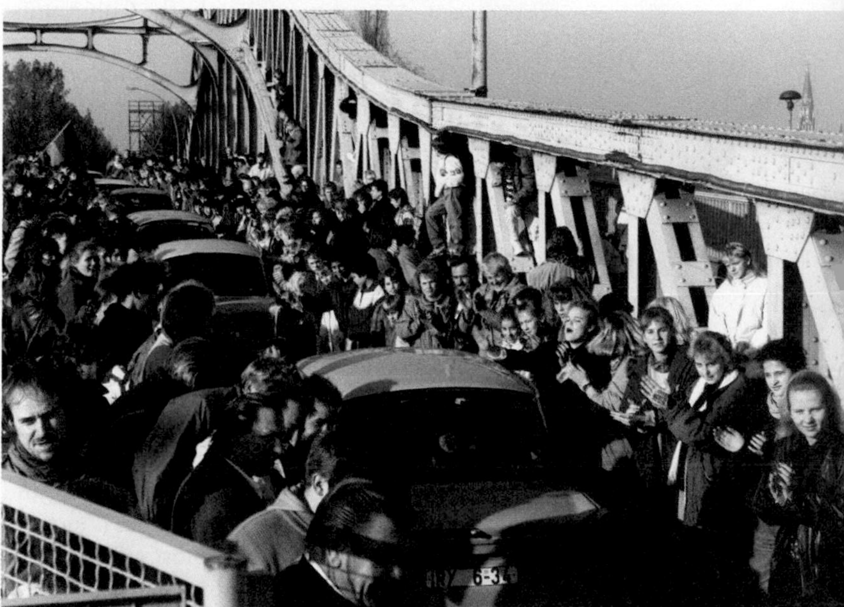

November 1989: East Germany Meets West Germany
The fall of the Berlin Wall and the "iron curtain" separating the Soviet from the western bloc was a joyous occasion across Europe, but nowhere more so than in Germany. Divided from one another into two countries after World War II, Germans would later find that reunification was a problem, bringing unemployment and social dislocation. In November 1989, however, West Germans lined up to welcome their fellow citizens traveling from the east to see what life was like beyond the Soviet sphere. *(ullstein bild/Bildarchiv/The Granger Collection, New York—All rights reserved.)*

Soon thereafter, citizens—east and west—released years of frustration by assaulting the Berlin Wall with sledgehammers. The government finished the wall's destruction in 1990.

In Czechoslovakia, where both Soviet-style "softer" cultural policies aimed to maintain order since 1968, people also watched televised news of glasnost expectantly. Persecuted dissidents had maintained their critique of Communist rule. In an open letter to the Czechoslovak Communist Party leadership, playwright Václav Havel accused Marxist-Leninist rule of making people materialistic and indifferent to civic life. In 1977, Havel, along with a group of fellow intellectuals and workers, signed Charter 77, a public protest against the regime that resulted in the arrest of the signers. In the mid-1980s, they and the wider population heard Gorbachev on television calling for free speech, though never mentioning reform in Czechoslovakia. Protesters clamored for democracy, but the government turned the police on them, arresting activists in January 1989 for commemorating the death of Jan Palach. The turning point came in November 1989 when, in response to police beatings of students, Alexander Dubček, leader of the Prague Spring of 1968, addressed the crowds in Prague's Wenceslas Square with a call to oust the Stalinists from the government. Almost immediately, the Communist leadership resigned. Capping what became known as the "velvet revolution" for its lack of bloodshed, the formerly Communist-dominated parliament elevated Havel to the presidency.

The world's attention next fastened on the unfolding political drama in Romania. From the mid-1960s on, Nicolae Ceaușescu had ruled as the harshest dictator in Communist Europe since Stalin. In the name of modernization, he destroyed whole villages; to build up the population, he outlawed contraceptives and abortions, a restriction that led to the abandonment of tens of thousands of children. He preached the virtues of a very slim body so that he could cut rations and use the savings on his pet projects such as buying up private castles and other property. Most Romanians lived in utter poverty as Ceaușescu channeled almost all the country's resources into building himself an enormous palace in Bucharest. To this end, he tore down entire neighborhoods and dozens of historical buildings and crushed opponents of the gaudy project to make it appear popular. Yet in early December 1989, an opposition movement rose up: workers demonstrated against the dictatorial government, and the army turned on Ceaușescu loyalists. On Christmas Day, viewers watched on television as the dictator and his wife were tried by a military court and then executed. For many, the death of Ceaușescu meant that the very worst of communism was over.

Homeless Romanian Children (1995)
These children were among the many who lived without families around the railroad station in Romania's capital city, Bucharest. Nicolae Ceaușescu's regime prohibited birth control and abortion in order to increase the supply of workers while simultaneously cutting back on food rations. Children were the victims of this policy, even after Ceaușescu was overthrown, as families simply abandoned children they could not support. In order to survive, the children scavenged, stole, and begged. *(© Barry Lewis/Corbis.)*

REVIEW QUESTION How and why did the balance of world power change during the 1980s?

Conclusion

The fall of the Berlin Wall in 1989 symbolized the end of the cold war, even though the USSR still stood as a bulwark of communism. Collapse of communism in the Soviet satellites was an utter surprise around the world, for U.S.-bloc analysts had reported throughout the 1980s that the Soviet empire was in dangerously robust health. But no one should have been unaware of dissent or economic discontent. Since the 1960s, rebellious youth, ethnic and racial minorities, and women had all been condemning conditions across the West, along with criticizing the threat posed by the cold war. By the early 1980s, wars in Vietnam and Afghanistan, protests against privations in the Soviet bloc, the power of oil-producing states, and the growing political force of Islam had cost the superpowers their resources and reputations. Margaret Thatcher in Britain, Ronald Reagan in the United States, and Mikhail Gorbachev in the Soviet Union tried with varying degrees of success to put their postindustrial and cold war houses in order. The first two were successful, while Gorbachev's policies of glasnost and perestroika — aimed at political and economic improvements — brought on collapse.

Glasnost and perestroika were supposed to bring about the high levels of postindustrial prosperity enjoyed outside the Soviet bloc. Across the West, including the USSR, an unprecedented set of technological developments had transformed businesses, space exploration, and the functioning of government. Technological advances also had an enormous impact on everyday life. Work changed as society reached a stage called postindustrial, in which the service sector predominated. New patterns of family life, new relationships among the generations, and revised standards for sexual behavior also characterized these years, leading to youth rebellions. It was only in the United States and western Europe, however, that the full consumer benefits of postindustrialization reached ordinary people, for the attainment of a thoroughgoing consumer, service, and high-tech society demanded levels of efficiency, coordination, and cooperation unknown in the Soviet bloc.

MAPPING THE WEST

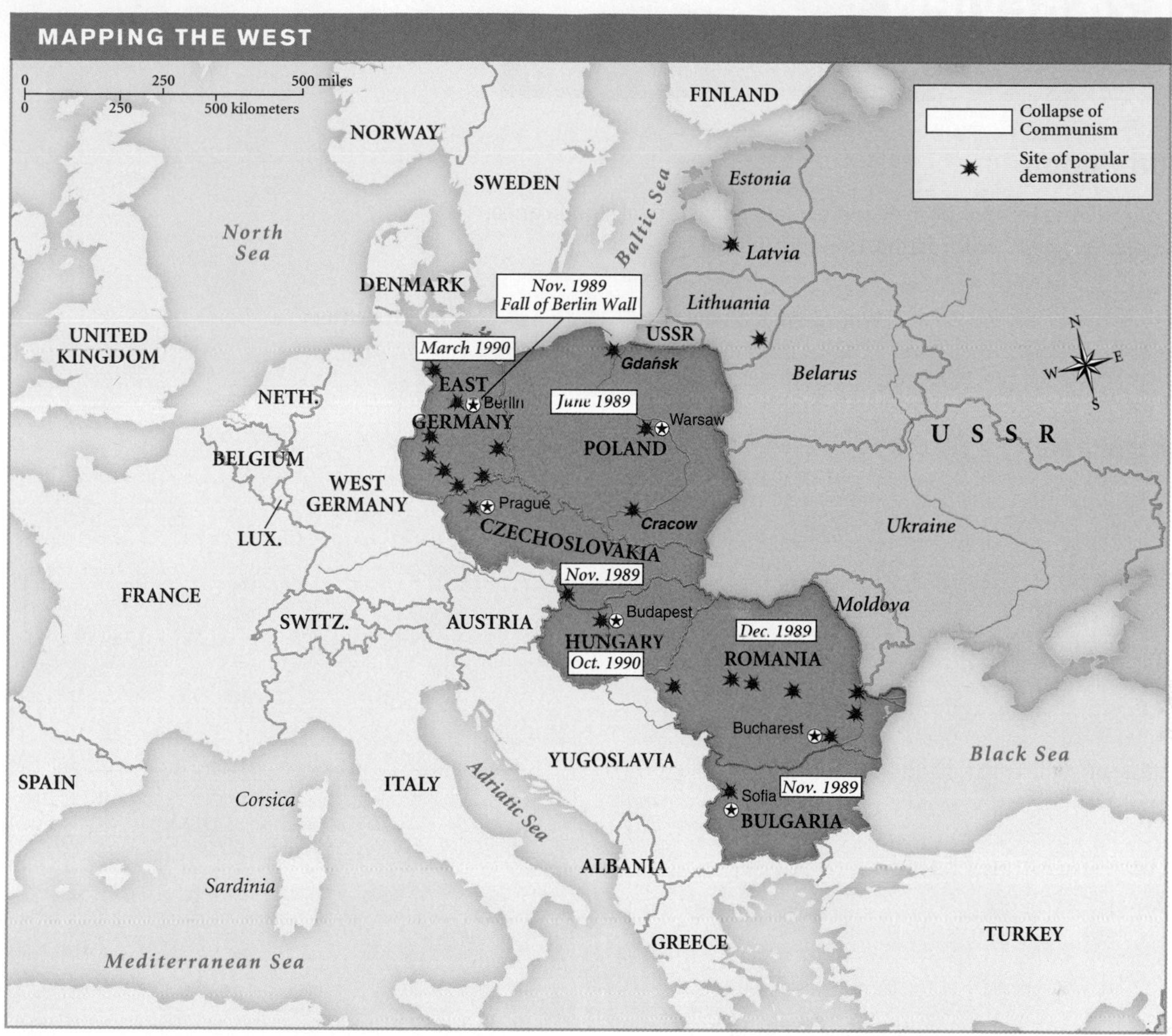

The Collapse of Communism in Europe, 1989–1990

The 1989 overthrow of the Communist Party in the USSR satellite countries of eastern Europe occurred with surprising rapidity. The transformation began when Polish voters tossed out Communist Party leaders in June 1989, and then accelerated in September when thousands of East Germans fled to Hungary, Poland, and Czechoslovakia. Between October and December, Communist regimes were replaced in East Germany, Czechoslovakia, Bulgaria, and Romania. Within three years, the Baltic states would declare their independence, the USSR itself would dissolve, and the breakup of Yugoslavia would lead to war in the Balkans.

Many complained, nonetheless, about the dramatic changes resulting from postindustrial development. The protesters of the late 1960s addressed postindustrial society's stubborn problems: concentrations of bureaucratic and industrial power (often enabled by technology), social inequality, environmental degradation, and even uncertainty about humankind's future. In the Soviet sphere, protests were continuous but were little heeded until the collapse of Soviet domination of eastern Europe in 1989. Soon communism would be overturned in the USSR itself. However, the triumph of democracy in the former Soviet empire opened an era of painful adjustment, impoverishment, and even violence for hundreds of millions of people. Amid this rapid political change was the growing awareness—via technology's instantaneous coverage of the fall of repressive governments across the globe—that the world's peoples were more tightly connected than ever before.

FOR FURTHER EXPLORATION

- **For additional primary-source material from this period**, see *Sources of the Making of the West*, Fourth Edition.
- **For Web sites, images, and documents related to topics in this chapter**, visit *Make History* at bedfordstmartins.com/hunt.

Chapter 28 Review

Online Study Guide bedfordstmartins.com/hunt

Key Terms and People

In the grid below, identify the term or person and explain its historical significance. (To do this exercise online, go to bedfordstmartins.com/hunt.)

Term	Who or What & When	Why It Matters
DNA (p. 953)		
in vitro fertilization (p. 954)		
multinational corporation (p. 955)		
pop art (p. 959)		
Ostpolitik (p. 961)		
samizdat (p. 962)		
Richard Nixon (p. 969)		
Organization of Petroleum Exporting Countries (OPEC) (p. 971)		
stagflation (p. 971)		
Margaret Thatcher (p. 973)		
neoliberalism (p. 974)		
Mikhail Gorbachev (p. 976)		
perestroika (p. 976)		
glasnost (p. 977)		
Solidarity (p. 977)		

Review Questions

1. What were the technological and scientific advances of the 1960s and 1970s, and how did they change human life and society?
2. How did Western society and culture change in the postindustrial age?
3. What were the main issues for protesters in the 1960s, and how did governments address them?
4. How and why did the balance of world power change during the 1980s?

Making Connections

1. What were the differences between industrial society of the late nineteenth century and postindustrial society of the late twentieth century?
2. Why were there so many protests, acts of terrorism, and uprisings across the West in the decades between 1960 and 1990?
3. What have been the long-term consequences of Communist rule in the Soviet bloc between 1917 and 1989?
4. How did technology shape politics over the course of the twentieth century?

Important Events

Date	Event	Date	Event
1963	Betty Friedan publishes *The Feminine Mystique*	1978	The first test-tube baby is born in England
1966	Willy Brandt becomes West German foreign minister and develops Ostpolitik	1978–1979	Islamic revolution in Iran; hostages taken at U.S. embassy in Teheran
1967	First successful human heart transplant	1980	Solidarity organizes resistance to Polish communism; British prime minister Margaret Thatcher begins dismantling the welfare state
1968	Revolution in Czechoslovakia; student uprisings throughout Europe and the United States	1981	Ronald Reagan becomes U.S. president
1969	U.S. astronauts walk on the moon's surface	1985	Mikhail Gorbachev becomes Soviet premier
1972	SALT I between the United States and Soviet Union	1986	Explosion at Chernobyl nuclear plant; Spain joins the Common Market
1973	End of Vietnam War; OPEC raises price of oil and imposes oil embargo on the West	1989	Chinese students revolt in Tiananmen Square; Communist governments ousted in eastern Europe; Berlin Wall demolished
1973–1976	Aleksandr Solzhenitsyn publishes *The Gulag Archipelago*		

- Consider three events: **Betty Friedan publishes *The Feminine Mystique* (1963)**, **Aleksandr Solzhenitsyn publishes *The Gulag Archipelago* (1973–1976)**, and **British prime minister Margaret Thatcher begins dismantling the welfare state (1980)**. How can all of these be considered responses to postindustrial society?

SUGGESTED REFERENCES

The history-changing events of the 1960s to 1989 ran the gamut from life-changing technology to dramatic political upheavals—all of them chronicled in the innovative books below. The story of television in post-uprising Czechoslovakia illustrates that even dictatorships used this new technology to "soften" its control.

Bauer, Martin W., and George Gaskell, eds. *Biotechnology: The Making of a Global Controversy*. 2002.

Bren, Paulina. *The Greengrocer and His TV: The Culture of Communism after the 1968 Prague Spring*. 2010.

Carter, David. *Stonewall: The Riots That Sparked the Gay Rights Movement*. 2011.

Chaplin, Tamara. *Turning on the Mind: French Philosophers on Television*. 2007.

Dahl, Henne Marlene, and Tine Rask Eriksen, eds. *Dilemmas of Care in the Nordic Welfare State: Continuity and Change*. 2005.

Fink, Carole, et al. *1968: The World Transformed*. 1998.

*Freedman, Estelle B. *The Essential Feminist Reader*. 2007.

Green Parties Worldwide: http://www.greens.org

Hadley, Louisa, and Elizabeth Ho, eds. *Thatcher & After: Margaret Thatcher and Her Afterlife in Contemporary Culture*. 2011.

Harvey, Brian. *Europe's Space Program: To Ariane and Beyond*. 2003.

Horn, Gerd-Rainer. *The Spirit of 68: Rebellion in Western Europe and North America, 1956–1976*. 2007.

Kenney, Padraic. *Carnival of Revolution: Central Europe, 1989*. 2002.

Kotkin, Steven. *Armageddon Averted: Soviet Collapse, 1970–2000*. 2008.

Martin Luther King Jr. Papers Project at Stanford University: http://mlk-kpp01.stanford.edu/

Natalicchi, Giorgio. *Wiring Europe: Reshaping the European Telecommunications Regime*. 2001.

Ouimet, Matthew J. *The Rise and Fall of the Brezhnev Doctrine in Soviet Foreign Policy*. 2003.

Siani-Davies, Peter. *The Romanian Revolution of December 1989*. 2005.

Suri, Jeremy. *Power and Protest: Global Revolution and the Rise of Détente*. 2003.

Varon, Jeremy. *Bringing the War Home: The Weather Underground, the Red Army Faction, and Revolutionary Violence in the Sixties and Seventies*. 2004.

*Primary source.

CHAPTER

29

A New Globalism

1989 to the Present

Thérèse is a Congolese immigrant to Paris who arrived there in the late 1970s with the help of a brother who worked for an airline. Thérèse had been well-known in Africa as the teenage girlfriend of pop singer Bozi Boziana, who wrote a hit song about her. But Congo's political instability made her search for safety in Paris. Once there, Thérèse remained famous among African immigrants because she ran *nganda*, or informal bars, for them. Like Thérèse, the immigrants who frequent her nganda are often Congolese and other Africans who have settled in Paris, many of them illegally. They flock to her nganda because they like her stylish dress, the African food she cooks, the African music she plays, and the African products she sells. Many of Thérèse's small bars and eateries have flourished, only to be closed down by landlords who want more of her handsome profits or who object to her running an unlicensed café. Despite such obstacles, Thérèse keeps business going by moving her faithful clientele around her Paris neighborhood from basement to shop front to spare room. Thérèse is a new global citizen, counting on networks back home for supplies, constantly on the move because she lives on the margins of legality, and always striving to make a good living for herself and her family.

Thérèse is just one concrete example of the ways in which people in the post–cold war world crossed national boundaries while maintaining crucial ties around the globe. The end of the cold war rivalry between the superpowers and their allies paved the way for a more intimately connected world. In the 1990s, globalization advanced further with the dramatic collapse of communism in Yugoslavia and then of the Soviet Union itself. The world was no longer divided in two by the heavily guarded borders and hostile cold war propaganda. Now, instead of being forced to follow one superpower or the other, nations and individuals around the

Global Citizens
The world's migrants at the turn of the millennium sought safety, education, or jobs in the West's manufacturing and service occupations. Like these young immigrants from Senegal who are sharing a meal at a café in Paris, they also appreciated Western amenities. Children of immigrants were sometimes disillusioned, however, not wanting the life of extreme sacrifice that their parents had lived. Their frustrations at not being accepted as full citizens occasionally erupted into protest and even violence. (© Directphoto.org/Alamy.)

world had more opportunity to trade and interact freely. The Common Market transformed itself into the European Union, which from 2004 on admitted many states from the former Soviet bloc. The telecommunication systems put in place in the 1960s advanced **globalization**, binding peoples and cultures together in an ever more complicated social and economic web.

The global age brought the vast national and international migration of tens of millions of people, an expanding global marketplace, and rapid cultural exchange of popular music, books, films, and television shows. On the negative side, the new globalization also brought lethal disasters such as epidemic diseases, environmental deterioration, genocide, and terrorism. Nations in the West faced competition from the rising economic power of Japan, China, India, and Latin America. International business mergers accelerated in the 1990s, advancing efficiencies but often threatening jobs. As millions of workers found new but sometimes unsatisfying jobs in an interlinked economy, they discovered that the global age was one of opportunities but also insecurities (see "Terms of History," page 988).

While the end of superpower rivalry made global exchange easier, it also resulted in the dominance of a single power, the United States, in world affairs. As the United States sought to exercise global power through warfare, however, the West itself seemed to fragment. European states started to resist the United States just as the Soviet satellites had pulled away from the USSR. New forces arose to rival those of the West: not only did the economic power of Asian, Middle Eastern, and other countries create new centers of influence, but so did the cultural might of Islam. Some observers predicted a huge "clash of civilizations" because of sharp differences between Western civilization and cultures beyond the West. Others, however, saw a different clash — one between a Europe reborn after decades of disastrous wars as a peace-seeking group of nations confronting an imperial United States that, like Europe in the nineteenth century, was increasingly at war around the world. Instead of bringing connections and understanding, globalization in either of these scenarios could bring global splintering, even catastrophic warfare.

Such a dire future was not on most Westerners' minds, but globalization did bring economic struggles for many. Beginning in 2007, the global economy collapsed, resulting in widespread hardship. As Asia and other non-Western parts of the world recovered beginning in 2010, it became apparent that a reenergizing of Western capacities was needed. Illegal immigrants began leaving Europe and the United States as unemployment climbed. Whether Thérèse was among them, we do not know.

globalization: The interconnection of labor, capital, ideas, services, and goods around the world. Although globalization has existed for hundreds of years, the late twentieth and early twenty-first centuries are seen as more global because of the speed with which people, goods, and ideas travel the world.

CHAPTER FOCUS How has globalization been both a unifying and a divisive influence on the West in the twenty-first century?

Collapse of the Soviet Union and Its Aftermath

Following the fall of communist regimes in eastern Europe, rejection of communism spread in the 1990s, turning events in unpredictable, even violent directions. Yugoslavia and then the Soviet Union itself fell apart, as nationality groups in the USSR began to demand independence. The USSR had held together more than one hundred ethnic groups,

1989 Chinese students revolt in Tiananmen Square; fall of the Berlin Wall

1990

1990–1991 War in Persian Gulf

1990s Internet revolution

1991 Civil war erupts in former Yugoslavia; failed coup by Communist hard-liners in Soviet Union

1992 Soviet Union is dissolved

1993 Toni Morrison wins Nobel Prize for Literature; Czechoslovakia splits into Czech Republic and Slovakia

1994 Nelson Mandela elected president of South Africa; Russian troops invade Chechnya; European Union (EU) officially formed

1995

1999 European Union introduces the euro; world population reaches six billion

MAP 29.1 Eastern Europe in the 1990s
In the 1990s, the countries of eastern Europe tried to forge their own destiny free from the direction of either Russia or the United States. The transition was far from easy. States like Czechoslovakia fragmented, and many state borders were contested. Turning from Russia, the leadership of these countries began to look to western Europe, most of them eventually opting for membership in the European Union.

and the five republics of Soviet Central Asia were home to fifty million Muslims. For more than a century, successive governments had attempted to instill Russian and Soviet culture, although some cultural autonomy was allowed. The policy of Russification failed to build any heartfelt allegiance, leading to a swift collapse of the USSR. In Yugoslavia, Communist rulers had also enforced unity among religious and ethnic groups, and intermarriage among them occurred regularly. Beginning in the unstable years of the early 1990s, however, ambitious politicians seeking to build a following whipped up ethnic hatreds (Map 29.1). Throughout the decade, the use of ethnic violence as a political tool made it unclear whether peaceful, democratic nations would emerge. The additional uncertainty of who would control the massive Soviet arsenal of nuclear weapons posed an even more dangerous threat.

The Breakup of Yugoslavia

Ethnic nationalism shaped the post-Communist future in Yugoslavia. Tensions erupted there in 1990 after Serbia's president **Slobodan Milosevic** began to promote control of the entire Yugoslav federation by ethnic Serbs as a replacement for communism. Other ethnic groups in Yugoslavia resisted Milosevic's militant pro-Serb nationalism and called for secession. "Slovenians . . . have one more reason to say they are in favor of independence," warned one of them in the face of rising

Slobodan Milosevic: President of Serbia (1989–1997) who pushed for Serb control of post-Communist Yugoslavia; in 2002, he was tried for crimes against humanity in the ethnic cleansing that accompanied the dissolution of the Yugoslav state.

2000
Vladimir Putin becomes president of Russia

2001
September 11 terrorist attacks; United States declares "war against terrorism," attacks Afghanistan

2003
United States invades Iraq; the West divides on this policy

2004
Ten countries join European Union

2005
Emissions reductions of Kyoto Protocol go into effect

2007
Bulgaria and Romania admitted to European Union; world economic crisis begins

2009
Barack Obama becomes the first African American president of the United States

2010
China overtakes Japan to become world's second largest economy

2000 2005 2010

TERMS OF HISTORY

Globalization

Globalization refers to the worldwide connections linking peoples, economies, cultures, and politics. A globalized world today means a world without borders, in which human activities flow without—or in spite of—official restrictions. The current definition of *globalization* includes economic policies such as free trade and outsourcing of work, collective security mechanisms such as the United Nations, and environmental agreements such as the Kyoto Protocol. Flows of information, migration, disease, and fashions also make up globalization.

When globalization began is a matter of opinion. Commonly the idea is that globalization began some twenty years ago when the Internet allowed economic activity to operate more globally. The rise of economic competitors to the West is seen as a recent phenomenon. This view also holds that the fall of the Soviet Union contributed to globalization because it stopped the division of the world into two competing spheres of influence. The cold war blocked the free exchange not only of ideas but also of goods and services. It hindered cooperation in politics as well as effective activity by nongovernmental organizations (NGOs) and the United Nations.

Historians, however, tend to date globalization in the distant past: some put it in the fifteenth century when Europeans crossed the Atlantic and began exploiting their new connections with the Western Hemisphere. Other historians look back further, to large-scale regional exchanges: the Indus Valley civilizations, the Hellenistic Age, the Islamic Golden Age, and the reign of the Mongol khans have all been cited as examples of globalization. In both these longer views, large-scale, high-speed exchanges are not defining factors in globalization; rather, constant dealings outside of a specific political and economic center are key.

In the broadest definition of *globalization*, the phenomenon has had mixed results for the West. Early globalization promoted enriched diets and biological diversity as plants and animals spread from the Middle East and North Africa to Europe. Goods traveled across Asia to Europe via the early Silk Road, and Christianity and Judaism were notable non-Western religions that changed European culture. Migrants from Asia and Africa also appeared in the West before European pathfinders set out on their voyages. In fact, knowledge of African gold and Asian riches inspired those voyages in the first place. On the negative side, plagues also traveled these routes before the age of Columbus, devastating populations in and beyond Europe. Groups of Asian nomads often wreaked havoc on European centers, and Europeans later brought devastation to them.

Globalization even in ancient times included attempts to see the world as a whole. From the ancient Hellenic author Polybius, who traveled the Mediterranean, to the English scholar Arnold Toynbee, historians have tried to write universal history and to rise above the parochial, local, and temporary with the goal of viewing humanity altogether. The end of the cold war provided the most recent incentive to achieve a universal perspective. For some thinkers, the search for a broader view seems part of a new millennium aiming toward cosmopolitanism, as expressed in the slogan "Think globally, act locally." Globalization is founded on the condition of plural and often conflicting values, aims, and outcomes. Whether in debates over outsourcing, migration, or the role of the World Bank, globalization means complexity, contradictions, and a willingness to deal with the advantages and disadvantages of relationships at a great distance. It is a difficult concept, but one that appears permanently to be with us.

Serb claims for domination of the small republics that made up Yugoslavia (Map 29.2). In the summer of 1991, two of these republics, Slovenia and Croatia, countered Milosevic's call for a Serb-dominated centralized state by seceding. Croatia, however, lost almost a quarter of its territory when the Yugoslav army, eager to enforce Serbian supremacy, invaded. A devastating civil war broke out in Bosnia-Herzegovina when the republic's Muslim majority tried to create a multicultural and multiethnic state. With the covert military support of Milosevic's government, Bosnian Serb men formed a guerrilla army and gained the upper hand. A United Nations (UN) arms embargo prevented the Bosnian Muslims from equipping their forces adequately to defend themselves even though the Serbs at the time were massacring them.

Violence in the Balkans was relentless—inflicted on neighbors in the name of creating "ethnically pure" states in a region where ethnic mixture, not ethnic purity, was the norm. During the 1990s, civilians died by the tens of thousands, as Serbs under Milosevic's leadership pursued a policy they called **ethnic cleansing**—that is, genocide—against the other ethnicities or nationalities. They raped women

ethnic cleansing: The mass murder—genocide—of people according to ethnicity or nationality; it can also include eliminating all traces of the murdered people's past. Examples include the post–World War I elimination of minorities in eastern and central Europe and the rape and murders that resulted from the breakup of Yugoslavia in the 1990s.

MAP 29.2 The Former Yugoslavia, c. 2000
After a decade of destructive civil war, UN forces and UN-brokered agreements attempted to protect the civilians of the former Yugoslavia from the brutal consequences of post-Communist rule. Ambitious politicians, most notably Slobodan Milosevic, used the twentieth-century Western strategy of fostering ethnic and religious hatred as a powerful tool to build support for themselves while making those favoring peace look softhearted and unfit to rule. | **What issues of national identity does the breakup of Yugoslavia indicate?**

to leave them pregnant with Serb babies as another form of conquest. In 1995, Croatian forces murdered Serbs who had helped seize land from Croatia. That same year, the Serbs retaliated by slaughtering eight thousand Muslim boys and men in the town of Srebrenica. "Kill the lot," the commander of the Serb forces ordered at Srebrenica. The Serbs buried the bodies in mass graves, then reburied them to conceal the massacre. Military units on all sides destroyed libraries and museums, architectural treasures like the Mostar Bridge, and cities rich with history such as Dubrovnik. Ethnic cleansing thus entailed eliminating both actual people and all traces of their complex past. Many in the West explained violence in the Balkans as part of "age-old" blood feuds typical of a backward, "almost Asian" society. Others saw using genocide to achieve national power as nothing more than a modern political practice that had been employed by the imperial powers and by other politicians, including Adolf Hitler.

Destruction of the Mostar Bridge in Yugoslavia, 1990
In modern history, the construction of a nation-state has depended on the growth of institutions such as armies and bureaucracies and the promotion of a common national culture. In an effort to dominate Bosnia and Croatia, Serbs in the 1990s destroyed non-Serb art, books, and architecture, including such symbols as the sixteenth-century bridge. *(Top and bottom: © Cardinale Stephane/Corbis-Sygma.)*

As with German, Italian, and Japanese aggression in the 1930s, no one stepped in to stop the violence in the former Yugoslavia. Peacekeepers were put in place, but they turned their backs on such atrocities as the Srebrenica massacre and let them proceed to their horrific end. Late in the 1990s, Serb forces moved to attack Muslims of Albanian ethnicity living in the Yugoslav province of Kosovo. From 1997 to 1999, crowds of Albanian Kosovars fled their homes as Serb militias and the Yugoslav army slaughtered the civilian population. North Atlantic Treaty Organization (NATO) pilots bombed the region to drive back the army and Serb militias. UN peacekeeping forces finally intervened to enforce an interethnic truce, but people throughout the world felt that this intervention came far too late to protect human rights and human lives.

Alongside the independent republics of Bosnia and Croatia, a new regime emerged in Serbia, and Milosevic was turned over to the International Court of Justice, or World Court, in the Netherlands to be tried for crimes against humanity. In 2003, Milosevic loyalists, many of them due to be rounded up for trial in the World Court, assassinated the new Serbian prime minister. Across a fragmenting eastern Europe, hateful racial, ethnic, and religious rhetoric influenced political agendas in the post-Communist states.

The Soviet Union Comes Apart

In less than three years after the overthrow of communism in its eastern European satellites, the once powerful Soviet Union itself fell apart. Perestroika had failed to revitalize the Soviet economy; people confronted corruption, soaring prices, the specter of unemployment, and even greater scarcity of goods than in the past. Although Soviet leader Mikhail Gorbachev announced late in 1990 that there was "no alternative to the transition to the market [economy]," his plan satisfied no one. In 1991, the Russian parliament elected Boris Yeltsin as president of the Russian Republic over a Communist candidate.

Yeltsin's election was the last straw for a group of eight antireform hard-liners, including the powerful head of the Soviet secret police, or KGB, who attempted a coup to overthrow the government. As coup leaders held Gorbachev under house arrest and claimed to be rescuing the Soviet Union from the "mortal danger" posed by "extremist forces," Yeltsin defiantly stood atop a tank outside the Russian parliament building and called for mass resistance. Residents of Moscow and Leningrad filled the streets, and units of the army defected to protect Yeltsin's headquarters. People used fax machines and computers to coordinate internal resistance and send messages to the rest of the world. Citizen action defeated the coup and prevented a return to the Communist past.

Yeltsin Defeats the Communists After the failed coup, the Soviet Union disintegrated. People tore down statues of Soviet heroes; Yeltsin outlawed the Communist Party newspaper, *Pravda*, and sealed the KGB's files. At the end of August 1991, the Soviet parliament suspended operations of the Communist Party itself. The Baltic states of Estonia, Latvia, and Lithuania declared their independence in September; other republics within the USSR followed their lead. Bloody ethnic conflicts erupted in the disintegrating Soviet world. In the Soviet republic of Tajikistan, native Tajiks rioted against Armenians living there; in the Baltic states, anti-Semitism revived as a political tool. The USSR finally dissolved on January 1, 1992. Twelve of the fifteen former Soviet republics banded together as the Commonwealth of Independent States (CIS), but that hardly ended the disintegration of Russian power (Map 29.3).

Weakened by the coup attempt, Gorbachev abandoned politics. Yeltsin stepped in and accelerated the change to a market economy, introducing new problems as he did so. Plagued by corruption, the Russian economy entered an ever-deepening crisis. Yeltsin's political allies bought up national resources, stripped them of their value, and sent billions of dollars out of the country, as a new class of superwealthy Russians called oligarchs was born. Managers, military officers, and bureaucrats took whatever goods they could lay their hands on, including weaponry, and sold it.

By 1999, Yeltsin's own family appeared to be deeply implicated in stealing the wealth once seen as belonging to all the people. To build support by appealing to nationalist anti-ethnic sentiments in Russia, Yeltsin launched a destructive military action against the resource-rich province of Chechnya, which wanted independence. Meanwhile social disorder prevailed as organized criminals interfered in the distribution of goods and services and assassinated legitimate entrepreneurs, legislators, and anyone who criticized them. The Russian parliament pursued an investigation into the business dealings of Yeltsin, his family, and his allies, leading Yeltsin to resign on December 31, 1999. He appointed a new protégé, **Vladimir Putin**, as interim president.

Vladimir Putin: President of Russia elected in 2000 and prime minister as of 2008; he has worked to reestablish Russia as a world power through control of the country's resources and military capabilities.

MAP 29.3 Countries of the Former Soviet Union, c. 2000

Following an agreement of December 1991, twelve of the countries of the former Soviet Union formed the Commonwealth of Independent States (CIS). Dominated by Russia and with Ukraine often disputing this domination, the CIS worked to bring about common economic and military policies. As nation-states dissolved rapidly in the late twentieth century, regional alliances and coordination were necessary to meet the political and economic challenges of the global age.

Vladimir Putin Takes Charge

Putin was a little-known functionary in Russia's new security apparatus, which had evolved from the old KGB. In the presidential elections of spring 2000, Putin surprised everyone when the electorate voted him in. Though associated with the Yeltsin family corruption, he declared himself committed to legality. "Democracy," he announced, "is the dictatorship of law." With a solid mandate, Putin proceeded to drive from power the biggest figures in regional and central government, usually the henchmen of the oligarchs. Faced with a desperate economic situation, Putin claimed he would restore "strong government" and end the influence of a "handful of billionaires with only egotistical concerns." Putin's popularity rose even higher when the government arrested the billionaire head of the Yukos Oil Company in 2003. The pillaging of the country—the source of ordinary citizens' recent suffering—was finally being punished. According to critics, however, Putin was merely transferring Russia's natural resources and other assets to himself and his own cronies. He also continued the destructive war in Chechnya, causing casualties, atrocities, disease, and the physical devastation of Chechen cities.

Toward a Market Economy

Developing free markets and republican governments initially brought misery to Russia and the rest of eastern Europe. The conditions of everyday life grew increasingly dire as salaries went unpaid, food remained in short supply, and essential services disintegrated. In 1994, inflation soared at a rate of 14 percent a month in Russia, while industrial production dropped by 15 percent. People took drastic steps to stay alive. Hotel lobbies became clogged with prostitutes because women were the first people fired as governments privatized industry and cut service jobs. Unpaid soldiers sold their services to the Russian Mafia. Ordinary citizens lined the sidewalks of major cities selling their household possessions. "Anything and everything is for sale," one critic noted at the time. Simultaneously, pent-up demand was unleashed for items never before available. An enormous underground economy existed in goods such as automobiles stolen from people in other countries and then driven or shipped to Russia.

There were, of course, many pluses to the new system of government. People with enough money were able to travel freely for the first time, and the media were initially more open than ever before. Some workers, many of them young and highly educated, profited from contacts with technology and business. However, their frequent emigration to more prosperous parts of the world further depleted the human resources of the former Communist states. At the same time, as the different republics that had once composed the Soviet Union became independent, the hundreds of thousands of ethnic Russians who had earlier been sent by the state to colonize these regions returned to Russia as refugees, putting further demands on the chaotic Russian economy but occasionally reuniting families. The dismantling of communism was more complicated and painful than anyone had imagined it would be.

The Economic Agenda For many in the former Soviet bloc, the first priority was getting their economies running again—but on new terms. Replacing a state-controlled economy with a market one could not happen naturally or automatically, but rather required government guidance. Given the spiraling misery, however, many opposed the introduction of new market-oriented measures. In Russia, members of collective farms fought to preserve them as a means of security in a rapidly changing world. With the farms up for sale, most collective farmers faced landlessness and starvation. The countries that experienced the most success were those in which administrators had already introduced ingredients of free trade, such as allowing farmers to sell their produce on the open market or encouraging independent entrepreneurs or even government factories to deal in international trade. Hungary and Poland thus emerged from the transition with less strain, because both had adopted some free-market practices early on and had hired advisers to speed the transformation of the economy. They set up business schools and worked to attract foreign capital, anchoring themselves securely to the world economy.

Elsewhere the transition to a market economy happened differently. The former Soviet Union itself became, in the words of one critic, a vast "kleptocracy" in the 1990s as the country's resources—theoretically the property of all the people—were stolen for individual gain. An economist described the new scene as "piratization" rather than privatization. In this regard, one Polish adviser noted, democracy and a successful economic transition went hand in hand, for without a powerful representative government, former officials would simply operate as criminals. Corruption fed on the Soviet system of off-the-books dealing, tax evasion, bribery, and outright theft. In addition to corruption, the Soviet policy of removing the economy from global developments further hindered the transition. Industry had not benefited from technological change. Because plants and personnel were hopelessly out of date, the introduction of competition and free trade often meant closing factories and firing all the workers.

Talent Flees the Region A final element in post-Soviet economic difficulties was a region-wide brain drain. The economic chaos that followed the fall of communism set off a rush of migration from eastern Europe to western Europe, often involving those with marketable skills. Mi-

Post-Soviet Shopping
The economy of the former Soviet bloc changed dramatically after the fall of communism. Insiders and Western firms bought up out-of-date factories and natural resources for very little money, often installing modern labor-saving equipment. As prosperity grew, megastores and luxury malls sprang up for eager consumers. Located in the suburbs of Moscow, the megastore shown here is part of Europe's largest shopping mall. *(© TASS/Sovoto.)*

grants left for several reasons, including the lack of jobs, the upsurge of ethnic hatreds, and the availability of higher salaries for well-educated workers in other countries. "I knew in my heart that communism would collapse," said one Romanian ex-dissident, commenting sadly on the exodus of youth from his country, "but it never crossed my mind that the future would look like this." Escaping anti-Semitism also played a role. Post-Communist politicians used the rallying cry of hatred of Jews to build a following, just as Hitler and many others had done so effectively in the past. Unchecked banditry and violence inflicted by organized crime added to the disadvantages of remaining in eastern Europe.

The everyday advantages of living in western Europe included safe water, better housing, personal safety, and at least a minimal level of social services. Although western Europe was now on a firm neoliberal course of reducing spending on welfare state programs, most benefits had disappeared entirely in former Communist countries. Pensions for veterans and retired workers were rarely paid, and even when paid were often worthless given the soaring inflation. Day-care centers, kindergartens, and homes for the elderly closed their doors, and health care deteriorated. In these circumstances, the benefits of citizenship in western European countries were a powerful attraction.

International Politics and the New Russia

Although Gorbachev had pulled the Soviet Union out of its disastrous war with Afghanistan, his successors opened another war to prevent the secession of oil-rich Chechnya and to provide a nationalist rallying cry to build domestic support for the administration during the difficult transition. For decades, Chechens had been integrated into the Soviet bureaucracy and military, but in the fall of 1991, the National Congress of the Chechen People took over the government of the region from the USSR to gain the same kind of independence achieved by other former Soviet states. In June 1992, Chechen rebels got control of massive numbers of Russian weapons, including airplanes, tanks, and some forty thousand automatic weapons and machine guns.

In December 1994, the Russian government sealed the Chechen borders and invaded. A high Russian official defended the war as crucial to bolstering Yeltsin's position: "We now need a small victorious war. . . . We must raise the President's rating." Despite the Russian population's opposition to the war, Chechnya's capital city of Grozny was pounded to bits. Casualties mounted not only among Chechen civilians but also among Russians. In 2002, Chechen loyalists took hundreds of hostages in a Moscow theater; Chechen suicide bombers blew up airplanes, buses, and apartment buildings. Putin pursued the Chechen war into the twenty-first century, weakening the reputation of the post-Communist government.

Putin expanded Soviet influence in Ukraine, Belarus, India, and China as well by taking advantage of the politics of energy. Russia had the commodities—especially oil and gas—needed to sustain the fantastic growth of emerging industries around the world, and by 2005 surging commodity prices were making Russia once again a real player in global politics—now because of its economic strength. Democratic values, however, were not put

Chechnya, 1999
Russia justified its war in Chechnya in the 1990s and early 2000s as part of a struggle against Muslim terrorists. During the war, the Russian military kidnapped and murdered Chechen rebels while pummeling cities with gunfire and harassing the population, as this photo of civilians being checked shows. In retaliation, Chechens brought terrorism to Russia, setting off bombs and blowing up planes. Even with the new administration of Vladimir Putin, the bloodshed continued. *(© Reuters/Corbis.)*

Assassination in Moscow
In 2009, Russian citizens honored journalist and human rights activist Anna Politkovskaya, assassinated three years earlier in her Moscow apartment building. Politkovskaya relentlessly investigated the atrocities during the war in Chechnya as well as the corruption in the Putin government. Honest journalism in post-Soviet Russia was dangerous; scores of journalists were murdered in the twenty years following the collapse of communism, and many of Politkovskaya's collaborators were also killed. Several men were arrested, tried, and acquitted in the Politkovskaya case. *(AP Photo/Pavel Golovkin.)*

into practice. Putin's critics were mercilessly assassinated, newspapers and broadcast media were closed down, and a general distrust of politics grew among people who had never really experienced sustained political exchange of views. Yet Putin's popularity was steady, especially as the Russian government used its new wealth to refurbish cities and everyday life grew easier.

REVIEW QUESTION What were the major issues facing the former Soviet bloc in the 1990s and early 2000s?

The Nation-State in a Global Age

Although the end of the Soviet system fractured one large regional economy, it gave a boost to European unification. In the 1990s and early 2000s, the European Economic Community (Common Market), which renamed itself the European Community in 1993, was healthy compared with other regions of the world, especially those plagued with civil wars and violence. It was also economically robust compared with former Soviet-bloc countries, many of which applied for membership to benefit from tying themselves to a powerful transnational organization. The relatively harmonious operation of the European Community and its economic success provoked the formation of the North American Free Trade Agreement (NAFTA), which established a free-trade zone of the United States, Canada, and Mexico. The nationalist function of cities diminished as major urban areas like London and Paris became packed with people from other countries, who brought with them new ideas and new customs. Organizations for world governance grew in influence alongside the strength of large regional economic blocs. There was resistance to these trends from those who wanted to preserve their own traditions and who felt the loss of a secure, face-to-face, local way of life.

The Euro

The euro went into circulation on January 1, 2002. The euro bills' designer used architectural imagery of windows and bridges to suggest openness, light, connectedness, and boundary crossing. Reflecting the compromise between Europe and individual states, the head sides of euro coins bear a common image, while the tail sides contain symbols chosen by individual nations within the euro zone. *(Royalty Free/Corbis.)*

Europe Looks beyond the Nation-State

From the 1990s on, Europeans worked to strengthen their shared institutions beyond those of the traditional nation-state, first by expanding the range of their common efforts. The Common Market of the 1950s had opened the pathway to unified supranational policy in economic matters; its evolution into the European Community and then the European Union (EU) in the 1990s extended cooperation in political and cultural matters. Then, in 2004 and 2007, nations from the former Soviet bloc joined the EU, suggesting that power might shift eastward if some of these new EU members built thriving economies, too.

From Common Market to European Union

The Common Market changed dramatically after the demise of European communism. In 1992, the twelve countries of the Common Market ended national distinctions in certain business activities, border controls, and transportation, effectively closing down passport controls at their shared borders. Citizens of the member countries carried a uniform burgundy-colored passport, and governments, whether municipal or national, had to treat all member nations' firms the same. In 1994, by the terms of the **Maastricht Treaty**, the European Community (EC) became the **European Union (EU)**, and in 1999 a common currency—the **euro**—came into being, first for transactions among financial institutions and then in 2002 for general use by the public. Common policies governed everything from the number of American soap operas aired on television to pollution controls on automobiles to the health warnings on cigarette packages. The EU parliament convened regularly in Strasbourg, France, while subgroups met to negotiate further cultural, economic, and social policies. With the adoption of a common currency, an EU central bank came into being to guide interest rates and economic policy.

The EU was seen as the key to a peaceful Europe. "People with the same money don't go to war with one another," said a French nuclear scientist about the introduction of the euro. Greece pushed for the admission of its traditional enemy Turkey in 2002 and 2003 despite the warnings of a former president of France that a predominantly Muslim country could never fit in with the Christian traditions of EU members. Both Greece and Turkey stood to benefit by having their disputes adjudicated by the larger body of European members, principally because they would be able to cut that part of

---

Maastricht Treaty: The agreement among the members of the European Community to have a closer alliance, including the use of common passports and eventually the development of a common currency; by the terms of this treaty, the European Community became the European Union (EU) in 1994.

European Union (EU): Formerly the European Economic Community (EEC, or Common Market), and then the European Community (EC); formed in 1994 by the terms of the Maastricht Treaty. Its members have political ties through the European parliament as well as long-standing common economic, legal, and business mechanisms.

euro: The common currency in seventeen member states of the European Union (EU) and of EU institutions. It went into effect gradually, used first in business transactions in 1999 and entering public circulation in 2002.

MAP 29.4 The European Union in 2011
The European Union (EU) appeared to increase the economic health of its members despite the rocky start of its common currency, the euro. The EU helped end the traditional competition between its members and facilitated trade and worker migration by providing common passports and business laws, and open borders. But many critics feared a loss of cultural distinctiveness among peoples in an age of mass communications.

their defense budget used for weapons directed against each other. Like the rivalry between Germany and France, that between Turkey and Greece, it was hoped, would dissolve if bound by the strong economic and political ties of the EU. As of 2011, however, Turkey was still awaiting progress on its application.

Drawbacks to EU membership remained. The EU enforced no common regulatory practices, and the common economic policies demanding cooperation among its members were not always observed. Individual governments set up hurdles and barriers for businesses, such as obstructing transnational mergers they did not like. One government might block the acquisition of a company based on its own soil no matter what the advantages to shareholders, the economy, the workforce, or the consumers of unified Europe. Nonetheless, countries of eastern Europe clamored to join, working hard to meet not only the EU's fiscal requirements but also those pertaining to human rights and social policy (Map 29.4).

East Joins West That the EU became attractive to eastern Europe is demonstrated in the case of Greece, long considered the poor relative of the other member countries. Greece joined the European Community in 1981; its per capita gross domestic product was 64 percent of the European average in 1985. However, Greek leaders and the EU made a real effort during the 1990s to bring the country closer to EU norms. Hoping for similar gains, the countries to the east moved toward EU membership throughout the 1990s. The collapse of the Soviet system advanced privatization of eastern European industry, as governments sold basic services to the highest bidder. Often, only companies in the wealthy western countries of the EU could afford to purchase eastern European assets. For example, the Czech Republic in 2001 sold its major energy distributor Transgaz and eight other regional distributors for 4.1 billion euros to a German firm. Lower wages and costs of doing business in eastern Europe attracted foreign investment, especially to Poland, the Czech Republic, Hungary, and Slovenia — the most developed state spun off from Yugoslavia. There were hopes that membership would encourage further investment and advance modernization. (See Document, "Václav Havel, 'Czechoslovakia Is Returning to Europe,'" page 997.)

In 2004, the EU admitted ten new members — the Czech Republic, Cyprus, Estonia, Hungary, Latvia, Lithuania, Malta, Poland, Slovakia, and

DOCUMENT

Václav Havel, "Czechoslovakia Is Returning to Europe"

Czech playwright and longtime anti-Communist activist Václav Havel became the first president of his country after the Communist Party was ousted in 1989. Havel was an idealist who believed that the people of eastern Europe had gained important insights from their experience of Soviet domination. This speech provides a backdrop to the admission of eastern European countries to the European Union in 2004. Despite fears among more prosperous EU countries that the lower standard of living in eastern Europe will drag the EU down, there is also a strong sense that the EU is incomplete without them. Havel details what eastern Europeans have to offer, even to those who have long enjoyed greater freedom and prosperity, including the Congress of the United States, before which the speech was given.

Czechoslovakia is returning to Europe. . . . We are doing what we can so that Europe will be capable of really accepting us, its wayward children. Which means that it may open itself to us, and may begin to transform its structures—which are formally European but de facto Western European. . . .

The Communist type of totalitarian system has left . . . all the nations of the Soviet Union and the other countries the Soviet Union subjugated in its time, a legacy of countless dead, an infinite spectrum of human suffering, profound economic decline, and above all enormous human humiliation. It has brought us horrors that fortunately you have not known.

At the same time, however—unintentionally, of course—it has given us something positive: a special capacity to look, from time to time, somewhat further than someone who has not undergone this bitter experience. A person who cannot move and live a somewhat normal life because he is pinned under a boulder has more time to think about his hopes than someone who is not trapped that way. . . .

For this reason, the salvation of the human world lies nowhere else than in the human heart, in the human power to reflect, in human meekness and in human responsibility. . . . If we are no longer threatened by world war, or by the danger that the absurd mountains of accumulated nuclear weapons might blow up the world, this does not mean that we have definitively won. We are in fact far from the final victory. . . .

In other words, we still don't know how to put morality ahead of politics, science and economics. We are still incapable of understanding that the only genuine backbone of all our actions—if they are to be moral—is responsibility. Responsibility to something higher than my family, my country, my company, my success. Responsibility to the order of Being, where all our actions are indelibly recorded. . . .

I end where I began: history has accelerated. I believe that once again it will be the human mind that will notice this acceleration, give it a name, and transform those words into deeds.

Source: From speech delivered to the Joint Session of Congress, Washington, D.C., on February 21, 1990. Reprinted in *Vital Speeches of the Day*, March 15, 1990, 329–30.

Question to Consider

- **What argument is Havel making, and why did he choose to make it to politicians in the United States?**

Slovenia—and in 2007 it welcomed Bulgaria and Romania. Just before Poland's admission to the EU, its standard of living was 39 percent of EU standards, up from 33 percent in 1995. The Czech Republic and Hungary were at 55 and 50 percent, respectively. In all three cases these figures masked the discrepancy between the ailing countryside and thriving cities. Citizens in eastern Europe were not always happy at the prospect of joining the EU. A retiree foresaw the cost of beer going up and added, "If I wanted to join anything in the West, I would have defected." Still others felt that having just established an independent national identity, they should not allow themselves to be swallowed up once again. People in older member states were having second thoughts, too: in the spring of 2005, a majority of voters in France and the Netherlands rejected a complex draft constitution that would have strengthened EU ties. Commentators attributed the rejection to popular anger at the EU bureaucracy's failure to consult ordinary people in this and other decision making.

Although still weak by comparison with most of western Europe, the economic life of eastern Europe had in fact picked up considerably by 2000. In contrast to the massive layoffs, soaring inflation, and unpaid salaries of the first post-Communist years, in 2002 residents of Poland, Slovenia, and Estonia had purchasing power some 40 percent higher than in 1989. Outsourcing by international companies began to flourish across the region, increasing opportunities for those with language and commercial skills. Even in countries with the weakest economies—Latvia, Bulgaria, and Romania—a greater number of residents enjoyed such modern conveniences as freezers, computers, and portable telephones. Shopping malls sprang up mostly around capital cities, testifying both to the urban nature of the benefits of the free economy and to the allure of this great new market of 100 million customers. Superstores like the furniture giant IKEA and the electronics firm Electroworld were a consumer's paradise to those long starved of goods. "When Electroworld opened in Budapest [April 2002], it provoked a riot. Two hundred thousand people crowded to get in the doors," reported one amazed observer. Critics worried that eastern Europeans had fallen prey to "consumania," that is, uncontrolled materialism and frenzied shopping. Consumers themselves, however, saw shopping as "a social act, indicating that one had joined consumer society," as one eastern European businessman put it. Learning to read labels and to compare prices offered by superstores was a sign of belonging to a global community of those free and prosperous enough to consume. Proudly, many believed they had left Communist poverty behind.

Globalizing Cities and Fragmenting Nations

After the collapse of communism, the West changed still further. One notable change was the globalization of major cities. These were cities whose institutions, functions, and visions were overwhelmingly global rather than regional or national. They contained stock markets, legal firms, insurance companies, financial service organizations, and other enterprises that operated worldwide and that were linked to similar enterprises in other global cities. Within these cities, high-level decision makers set global economic policy and enacted global business. The presence of high-powered and high-income global businesspeople made urban life extremely costly, driving middle managers and engineers to lower-priced living quarters in the suburbs, which nonetheless provided good schools and other amenities for well-educated white-collar earners. Crowded into the slums of global cities and the poorer suburbs were the lowest paid of service providers — the maintenance, domestic, and other workers whose menial labor was essential around the clock to the needs and comfort of those at the top.

Global cities often had the best transport or telecommunication facilities and thus became centers for migration for highly skilled and more modest workers alike. Paris, London, Moscow, and New York were not just cosmopolitan but global spaces in direct and constant contact with institutions, businesses, and governments around the world. In contrast, citizens of more locally oriented cities took pride in maintaining a distinctive national culture or local sense of community and often denounced global cities as rootless. Critics also pointed out that their concentrated wealth came at the expense of poorer people in southern countries and that their citizens lacked patriotic focus on national causes. Global cities were often the base for diasporas of prosperous migrants, such as the estimated ninety thousand Japanese in England in the mid-1990s who staffed Japan's thriving global businesses. Because these migrants did not aim to become citizens, they made no economic or political claims on the adopted country and were thus sometimes called invisible migrants. As a result, global cities were said to produce a "deterritorialization of identities" — meaning that many city dwellers lacked both a national and a local sense of themselves, so much did they travel the world or deal worldwide.

Ironically, as globalization took hold economically and culturally, there came to be more nation-states in Europe in 2000 than there had been in 1945. Claims of ethnic distinctiveness caused individual nation-states to break apart and separatist movements — like that in Chechnya — to grow. Despite two centuries aimed at unification of the Slavs, for example, Slavs separated themselves from one another in the 1990s and early twenty-first century. Yugoslavia came apart into several states, as discussed earlier in this chapter, and in 1993, Czechoslovakia split into the Czech Republic and Slovakia (see Map 29.1, page 987).

Activists launched movements for regional independence in France, Italy, and Spain. Some Bretons (residents of the historical French province of Brittany) and Corsicans demanded independence from France, the Corsicans violently attacking national officials. Sharp cultural differences threatened to split Belgium in two. Basque nationalists in northern Spain assassinated tourists, police, and other public servants in an effort to gain autonomy, and although in 2005 they publicly renounced terrorism, violence often resurfaced. The push for an independent northern Italy began somewhat halfheartedly, but when politicians saw its attractiveness to voters, they loudly publicized the urgent need for secession. As cities globalized and nations fragmented, new combinations of local, national, and global identities took shape. Basque separatists in Spain promoted a common identity with Basques in France and other parts of the world — not with other Spaniards. Nganda manager Thérèse simultaneously enjoyed her neighborhood in Paris, her identity as a migrant to France, and contact with friends and family in Congo. Such changing identities, plus the overall expansion of the EU, called the nation-state into question.

Global Organizations

Supranational organizations, some of them regulating international politics and others addressing finance and social issues, had been in place for decades. By the twenty-first century, the interconnectedness of industry, finance, and government had made these organizations both more plentiful and influential. The World Bank, the International Monetary Fund (IMF), and the World Trade Organization (WTO) raised money from national governments and dealt, for example, with the terms of trade among countries and the economic well-being of individual peoples. The IMF made loans to developing countries on the condition that they restructure their economies according to neoliberal principles. Other supranational organizations were charitable foundations, think tanks, or service-based organizations acting independently of governments, many of them based in Europe and the United States; they were called **nongovernmental organizations (NGOs)**. Because some—the Rockefeller Foundation, the Ford Foundation, and the Open Society Foundation, for example—controlled so much money, NGOs often had considerable international power. After the fall of the Soviet bloc, NGOs used their resources to shape economic and social policy and even the course of political transformation. Some charitable and activist NGOs, like the French-based Doctors Without Borders, depended on global contributions and used them to provide medical attention in such places as the former Yugoslavia, where people facing war had no other medical help. Small, locally based NGOs excelled at inspiring grassroots activism. All of these organizations, small and large, were in tune with the globalization process. As with the EU, the larger NGOs were often criticized for influencing government policies with no regard for democratic processes.

Not everyone supported or was pleased with the process of globalization; some people formed activist groups to attack globalization or to influence its course. In 1998, the Association for the Taxation of Financial Transactions and Aid to Citizens (ATTAC) worked to block the control of globalization by the forces of high finance, declaring: "Commercial totalitarianism is not free trade." ATTAC had as its major policy goal to tax international financial transactions (just as the purchase of household necessities was taxed) and to create with the tax a fund for people living in poor countries. With members from more than forty nations, the organization held well-attended conferences to find new directions for countries suffering from global development. French farmer José Bové, a globally known activist, protested the opening of McDonald's chains in France and destroyed stocks of genetically modified seeds: "The only regret I have now," Bové claimed at his trial in 2003, "is that I didn't destroy more of it." Bové went to jail, but he remained a hero to antiglobalism activists who saw him as an enemy of standardization and an honest champion, in his own words, of "good food."

REVIEW QUESTION What trends suggest that the nation-state was a declining institution at the beginning of the twenty-first century?

An Interconnected World's New Challenges

The rising tide of globalization ushered in as many challenges as opportunities. First, the health of the world's peoples and their environment came under a multipronged attack from nuclear disaster, acid rain, and surging population. Second, economic prosperity and physical safety continued to elude great masses of people, especially in the southern half of the globe. Third, as suprastate organizations developed, transnational allegiances and religious and ethnic movements vied for power and influence. Growing prosperity in some regions outside the West and a devastating economic crisis that rippled from Wall Street across the globe challenged the traditional economic leadership of the United States and Europe. The crisis, along with their newfound wealth, led leaders in Asia, the Middle East, and Latin America to suggest that the West give up its claims to dominance.

The Problems of Pollution

By the early years of the twenty-first century, many people had become aware of the dangers of industrial growth—once seen as an unqualified blessing. Despite growing ecological awareness, technological development continued to threaten the environment. In the aftermath of the 1986 nuclear explosion at Chernobyl, which killed thirty-one people instantly, levels of radioactivity rose for hundreds of miles in all directions and some fifteen thousand

---

nongovernmental organizations (NGOs): Charitable foundations and activist groups such as Doctors Without Borders that work outside of governments, often on political, economic, and relief issues; also, philanthropic organizations such as the Rockefeller, Ford, and Open Society Foundations that shape economic and social policy and the course of political reform.

Smart Cars in Europe
The havoc caused by the oil crisis of the 1970s and the growing awareness of climate change in the latter part of the twentieth century spurred many European states to encourage the development of alternate sources of energy and transportation. Thus, by the twenty-first century, the landscape was dotted not only with windmills but also with tiny, highly fuel-efficient automobiles like the Smart car shown here. European governments also heavily taxed gasoline with the result that it cost twice as much or more than in the United States, thus further encouraging people to buy the Smart car rather than an SUV—a far rarer sight in Europe than in the United States. *(© David Cooper/Toronto Star/ZUMA/Corbis.)*

people perished over time from the effects of radiation. Moreover, as Russia opened up, it became clear that Soviet managers and officials had thrown toxic waste into thousands of square miles of lakes and rivers. Used nuclear fuel had been dumped in neighboring seas, and many nuclear and other tests had left entire regions of Asia unfit for human, animal, and plant life.

Other environmental problems had devastating global effects. Pollutants from fossil fuels such as natural gas, coal, and oil mixed with atmospheric moisture to produce acid rain, a poisonous brew that destroyed forests in industrial areas. In eastern Europe, the unchecked use of fossil fuels turned trees into brown skeletons and inflicted ailments such as chronic bronchial disease on children. In other areas, clearing the world's rain forests to develop the land for cattle grazing or for cultivation of cash crops depleted the global oxygen supply. By the late 1980s, scientists determined that the use of chlorofluorocarbons (CFCs), chemicals found in aerosol and refrigeration products, had blown a hole in the earth's ozone layer, the part of the blanket of atmospheric gases that prevents harmful ultraviolet rays from reaching the planet. Simultaneously, automobile and industrial emissions of chemicals were infusing that thermal blanket. The buildup of CFCs, carbon dioxide, and other atmospheric pollutants produced what is known as a greenhouse effect that results in **global warming**, an increase in the temperature of the earth's lower atmosphere. Already in the 1990s, the Arctic pack ice was breaking up, allowing Finland by 2002 to ship oil along a once-iced-over route. Scientists predicted dire consequences: the rate of global ice melting, which had more than doubled since 1988, would raise sea levels by more than ten inches by 2100, flooding coastal areas, disturbing fragile ecosystems, and harming the freshwater supply. Other results of the greenhouse effect included not only climatic extremes such as alternating periods of drought and drenching rain but also dramatic weather events such as severe storms.

Activism against unbridled industrial growth took decades to develop as an effective political force. An escapee from Nazi Germany, E. F. "Fritz" Schumacher, produced one of the bibles of the environmental movement, *Small Is Beautiful* (1973), which spelled out how technology and industrialization threatened the earth and its inhabitants. Rachel Carson's powerful critique, *Silent Spring* (1962), advocated the immediate rescue of rivers, forests, and the soil from the ravages of factories and chemical farming in the United States. In West Germany, environmentalism united members of older and younger generations around a political tactic called citizen initiatives, in which groups of people blocked plans for urban growth that menaced forests and farmland. In 1979, the **Green Party** was founded in West Germany; soon the emergence of Green Party candidates across Europe forced other politicians to voice their concern for the environment. (See Document, "The Green Parties Unite Transnationally and Announce Common Goals," page 1001.)

global warming: An increase in the temperature of the earth's lower atmosphere resulting from a buildup of chemical emissions.

Green Party: A political party first formed in West Germany in 1979 to bring about environmentally sound policies. It spread across Europe and around the world thereafter.

DOCUMENT

The Green Parties Unite Transnationally and Announce Common Goals (2006)

In 1993, members of Green Parties across Europe formed the European Federation of Green Parties, which came to include members from twenty-nine European countries. The federation also made global connections with parties in Australia, Taiwan, the United States, and elsewhere in the world. In 2004, the federation formally became the European Green Party, which in 2006 adopted a charter endorsing not only environmental responsibility but a range of other values as well. Following is the opening statement of the charter. Even as it was written, the charter became outdated, for in 2006 China passed the United States as the world's leading emitter of greenhouse gases.

The European Greens proudly stand for the sustainable development of humanity on planet Earth, a mode of development respectful of human rights and built upon the values of environmental responsibility, freedom, justice, diversity and non-violence.

Green political movements emerged in Europe while the continent was divided by the Cold War and amidst the energy crises of the mid-seventies. At that time, it became clear that the pattern of economic development was unsustainable and was putting the planet and its inhabitants in grave environmental, social and economic dangers. Existing political parties were incapable of dealing with this challenge.

Our origins lie in many social movements: environmentalists and anti-nuclear activists concerned with the growing damages to our planet; non-violent peace activists promoting alternative ways to resolve conflicts; feminists, struggling for real equality between women and men; freedom and human rights movements fighting against dictatorial and authoritarian regimes; third-world solidarity movements supporting the end of colonization and more economically balanced relations between the North and the South of our planet; activists campaigning against poverty and for social justice within our own societies.

Question to Consider

- **What examples about the social and political situations around the world do the charter's authors provide to show the importance of their cause?**

Spurred by successful Green Party campaigns, Europeans attacked environmental problems on local and global levels. Some European cities—Frankfurt, for example—developed car-free zones, and in Paris, whenever automobile emissions reached dangerous levels, cars were banned from city streets until the emission levels receded. The Smart, a very small car using reduced amounts of fuel, became fashionable in Europe. European cities also developed bicycle lanes on major city streets, and the United States did the same in the twenty-first century. To reduce dependence on fossil fuels, parts of Europe developed wind power to such an extent that 20 percent of some countries' electricity was generated by wind. Many cities in the West undertook extensive recycling of waste materials. These were success stories, involving changing habits and dependencies in some of the most industrialized countries in the world. By 1999, some eighty-four countries, including EU members, had signed the Kyoto Protocol, an international treaty whose signatories agreed to reduce their levels of emissions and other pollutants to specified targets. However, the United States, the world's second leading polluter after China, rejected this partnership. The Kyoto emissions reductions finally went into effect in February 2005, but the United States' refusal to join its former allies to protect the environment suggested that the West was fragmenting around basic values.

Population, Health, and Disease

The issue of population was as difficult in the early twenty-first century as it had been in the 1930s. Nations with less-developed economies struggled with the pressing problem of surging population, while Europe experienced negative growth (that is, more deaths than births) after 1995. The less industrially developed countries accounted for 98 percent of worldwide population growth, in part because the spread of Western medicine enabled people there to live much longer than before. By late 1999, the earth's population had reached six billion, with a doubling forecast for 2045 (see "Taking Measure," page 1002). Yet because many European countries were not replacing their population, they were facing problems related to an aging citizenry and a shortage of younger people to bring new ideas and promote change. In fact, Europe as a region had the lowest fertility in the world. The fertility rate in Italy and Spain was only 1.3 children per woman of reproductive age, far below the replacement level of 2.1 needed to maintain a steady population number.

TAKING MEASURE

World Population Growth, 1950–2010

A major question in the twenty-first century is whether the global environment can sustain billions of people indefinitely. In the early modern period, local communities had lived according to unwritten rules that balanced population size with the productive capacities of individual farming regions. Centuries later, the same need for balance had reached global proportions. As fertility dropped around the planet because of contraception, population continued to grow because of improved health.

Question to Consider

- **Which areas have the strongest rate of growth? What are the potential causes and implications of this growth?**

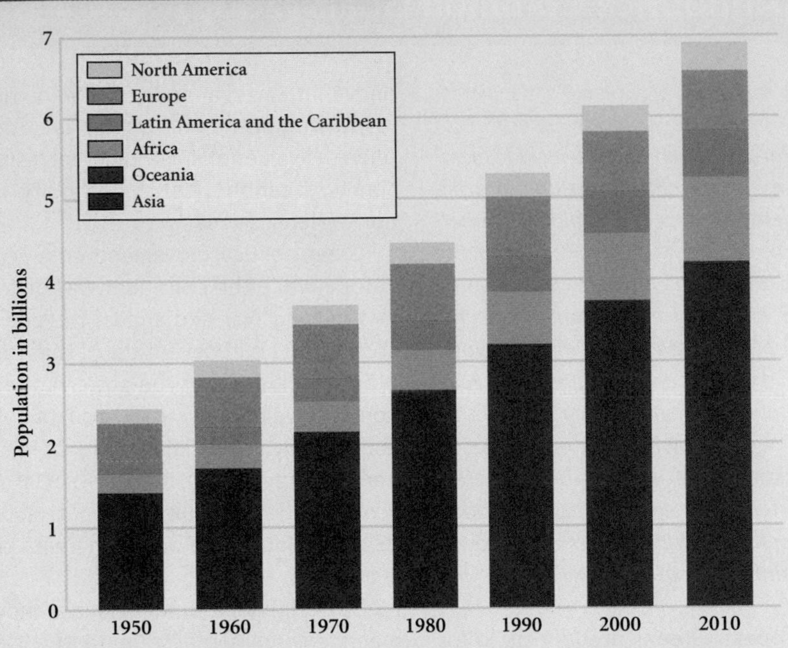

Some forecasters predicted that this low rate meant that by 2050 the population of Europe would fall from 725 to 600 million. Economists saw as a consequence fewer young workers paying into the social security system to fund retirees' pensions and health care.

Population problems were especially urgent in Russia, where life expectancy was declining at a catastrophic rate from a peak of seventy years for Russian men in the mid-1970s to fifty-one years at the beginning of the twenty-first century. Heart disease and cancer were the leading causes of male death, and these stark death rates were generally attributed to increased drinking (one in seven men was an alcoholic in Russia), smoking, drug use, poor diet, and general stress. Between 1992 and 2010, the Russian population declined from 149 to 142 million, with predictions that by 2050 it would fall below 100 million. Meanwhile, fertility rates in the former Soviet bloc were also declining: the lowest levels of fertility in 2003 were in the Czech Republic and Ukraine (1.1 children per woman of reproductive age), and children in eastern Europe lived on average twelve years less than their counterparts in western Europe.

Good health was spread unevenly around the world. Western medicine brought better health to many in the less-developed world through the increased use of vaccines and drugs for diseases such as malaria and smallpox. However, half of all Africans lacked the basic ingredients of well-being such as safe drinking water. Drought and poverty, along with the corruption of politicians in some cases, spread famine in Sudan, Somalia, Ethiopia, and elsewhere. Around the world, the poor and the unemployed suffered more chronic illnesses than those who were better off, but they received less care. Whereas in many parts of the world people still died from malnutrition and infectious diseases, in the West noncontagious illnesses (heart disease, autoimmune diseases, stroke, cancer, and depression) were more lethal. The distribution of health services—for example, heart transplants for the wealthy versus preventive health care for a wider range of clients—became a hotly debated issue.

Disease, like population and technology, operated on a global terrain, though there were many regional differences. In the early 1980s, both Western values and Western technological expertise were challenged by the spread of a global epidemic disease: acquired immunodeficiency syndrome (AIDS). An incurable, highly virulent killer that effectively shuts down the body's entire immune system, AIDS initially afflicted heterosexuals in central Africa; the disease later turned up in Haitian immigrants to the United States and in homosexual men worldwide. Within a decade, AIDS became a global epidemic. The disease spread especially quickly and widely among the heterosexual populations of Africa and Asia, passed mainly by men to and through women, but in 2010 the U.S. capital, Washington D.C., had a rate of infection as high as that in Africa. By 2010, a cure seemed to be on the medical horizon; in the meantime protease-inhibiting drugs helped alleviate the symptoms. The mounting global death toll made some equate AIDS with the Black Death. Treatment was often not provided to poor people living in sub-Saharan Africa and the slums of Asian cities, but global NGOs worked to get life-saving drugs to these people. In addition to the AIDS pandemic, the deadly Ebola virus and dozens of other viruses smoldered like a global conflagration in the making. In the twenty-first century, an avian flu virus called severe acute respiratory syndrome (SARS) and swine flu — both potentially deadly to humans — traveled the world even as health professionals worked to contain them. Diseases as much as environmental dangers underscored the interconnectedness of the world's peoples.

North versus South?

During the 1980s and 1990s, world leaders tried to address the differences between the earth's northern and southern regions. Other than Australians and New Zealanders, southern peoples generally suffered lower living standards and measures of health than northerners. Emerging from colonial rule and economic exploitation by northerners, citizens in the southern regions could not yet count on their governments to provide welfare services or education. Funding for such programs generally came from the wealth of the northern countries; international organizations like the World Bank and the International Monetary Fund provided loans for economic development. However, the conditions tied to those loans, such as cutting government spending for education and health care, led to criticism that ordinary citizens gained no real benefit. Some twenty-first-century leaders from both North and South advocated that wealthy countries simply give southern countries the money they needed as reparation for centuries of imperial plunder.

Southern regions experienced different kinds of barriers to economic development. Latin American nations grappled with government corruption, multibillion-dollar debt, widespread crime, and grinding poverty, though some countries — prominent among them Brazil — began to strengthen their economies by marketing their oil and other natural resources more effectively and by valuing administrative expertise among government officials. In contrast, Africa suffered from drought, famine, and civil war. In countries such as Rwanda, Somalia, and Sudan, the military rule, ideological factionalism, and ethnic antagonism encouraged under imperialism produced a lethal mixture of conflict and genocide in the 1990s and early 2000s. Millions perished; others were left starving and homeless due to kleptocracies that drained revenues. In Africa, too, nations began turning away from violence and military dictatorship toward constitutional government at the same time that uneven economic development and the scourge of AIDS and other unchecked diseases added to the weight of the continent's problems.

Radical Islam Meets the West

North–South antagonisms became evident in the rise of radical Islam, which often flourished where democracy and prosperity for the masses were missing. The Iranian hostage crisis that began in 1979 and commanded the world's attention revealed the nationalism and anti-Western sentiment among Islamic fundamentalists. The charismatic leaders of the 1980s and 1990s — the ayatollah Ruhollah Khomeini in Iran; Libya's Muammar Qaddafi; Iraq's Saddam Hussein; and **Osama bin Laden**, a Saudi Arabian by birth and leader of the transnational terrorist organization al-Qaeda — variously promoted a pan-Islamic or (outside Iran) pan-Arabic world order that gathered increasing support. Khomeini's program — "Neither East, nor West, only the Islamic Republic" — had wide appeal. Renouncing the Westernization that had flourished under the shah, Khomeini's regime in Iran (whose population is predominantly Persian, not Arabic) required women once again to cover their bodies almost totally in special clothing, restricted their access to divorce, and eliminated a range of other rights for men and women alike. Buoyed by the prosperity that oil had brought, Islamic revolutionaries believed that a strict theocracy would restore the pride and Islamic identity that imperialism had stripped from Middle Eastern men. Khomeini built widespread support among Shi'ite Muslims by proclaiming the ascendancy of the Shi'ite clergy. Although they were numerous, even constituting the majority in parts

Osama bin Laden: Wealthy leader of the militant Islamic group al-Qaeda, which executed terrorist plots, including the September 11, 2001, attacks on the United States, to end the presence of U.S. forces in his home country, Saudi Arabia.

of the Middle East, the Shi'ites had long been discriminated against by the Sunnis.

Power in the Middle East remained fragmented, however, and Islamic leaders did not achieve their unifying goals. Instead, war plagued the region. In 1980, Saddam Hussein, fearing a rebellion from Shi'ites in Iraq, attacked Iran, in hopes of channeling Shi'ite discontent with a patriotic crusade against non-Arab Iranians. The United States provided Iraq with massive aid in the struggle against Iran, but eight years of combat, with extensive loss of life on both sides, ended in stalemate. In 1990, Saddam tested the post–cold war waters by invading neighboring Kuwait in hopes of annexing the oil-rich country to debt-ridden Iraq. A United Nations coalition led by the United States stopped the invasion and defeated the Iraqi army, but discontent mounted in the region (Map 29.5).

To the east, the Taliban—a militant Islamic group initially funded by the United States, China, Saudi Arabia, and Pakistan during the cold war—took over the government of Afghanistan in the late 1990s. Its leaders imposed a regime that forbade girls from attending schools and women from leaving their homes without a male escort and demanded from men strict adherence to its rules for dress.

To the west, conflict between the Israelis and the Palestinians continued. As Israeli settlers took more Palestinian land, Palestinian suicide bombers

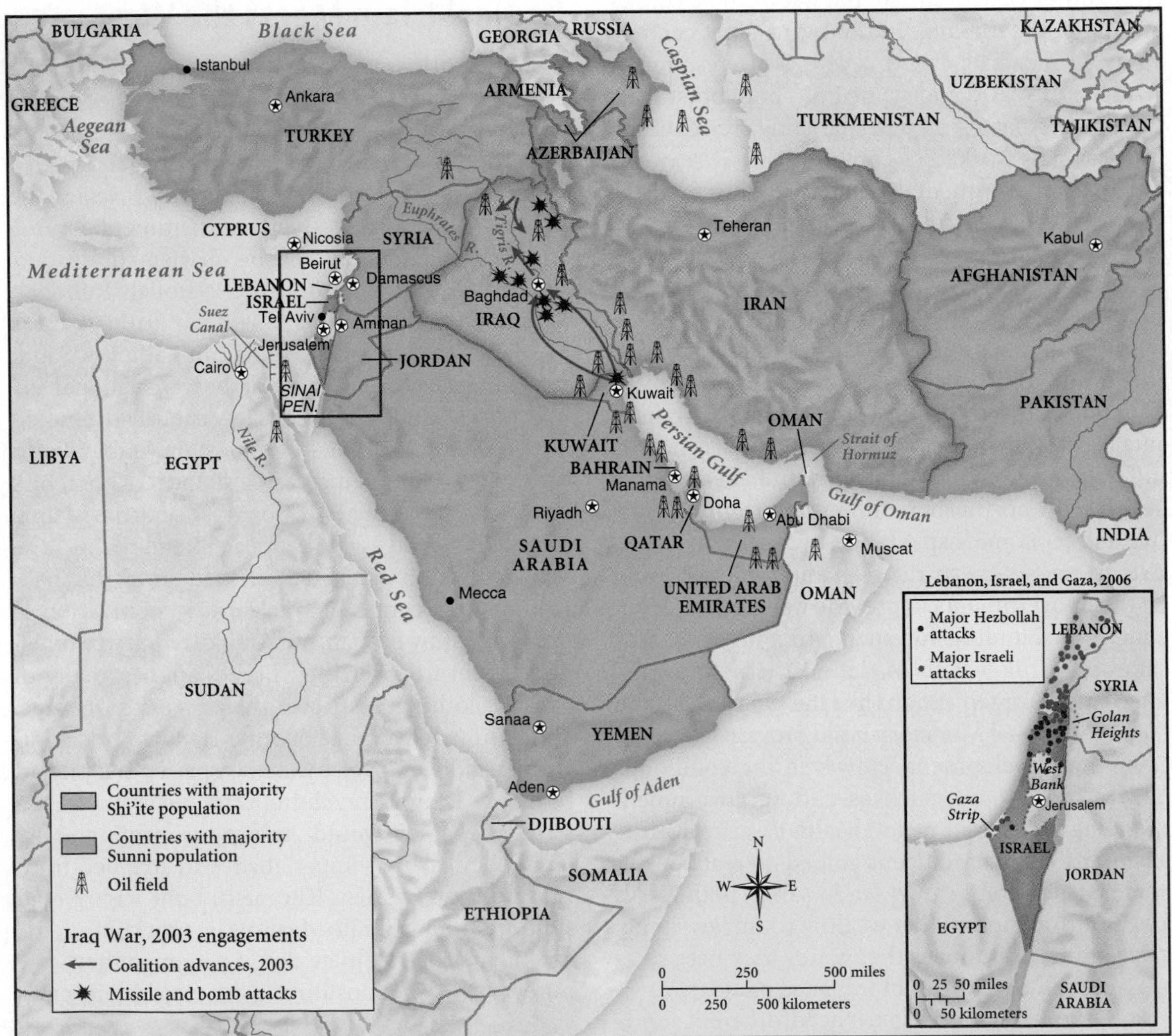

MAP 29.5 The Middle East in the Twenty-First Century
Tensions among states in the Middle East, especially the ongoing conflict between the Palestinians and Israelis and animosities among Shi'ites and Sunnis, became more complicated from the 1990s on. The situation in the Middle East grew more uncertain in 2003 when a U.S.- and British-led invasion of Iraq deteriorated into escalating violence among competing religious and ethnic groups in the country. Additionally, for thirty-four days in the summer of 2006, Israel bombed Lebanon, including its capital city and refugee camps, with fire returned by Hezbollah and Hamas forces in the region.

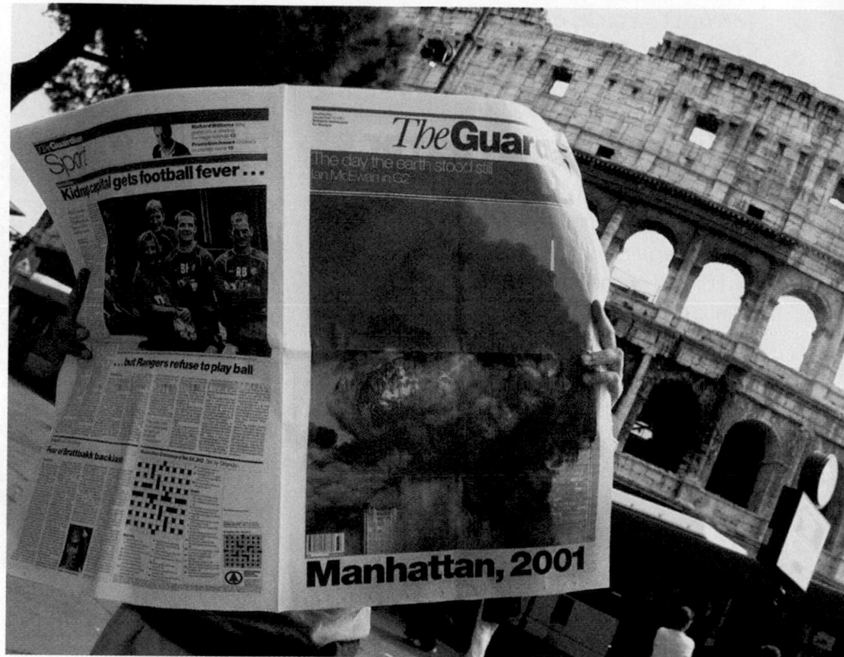

Europeans React to September 11 Terror Attacks
On September 11, 2001, terrorists killed thousands of people from dozens of countries in airplane attacks on the World Trade Center and the Pentagon. Throughout the world, people expressed their shock and sorrow in vigils, and like this British tourist in Rome, they remained glued to the latest news. Terrorism, which had plagued Europeans for several decades, easily traveled the world in the days of more open borders, economic globalization, and cultural exchange. *(© Alberto Pizzoli/Corbis-Sygma.)*

began murdering Israeli civilians in the late 1990s. The Israeli government retaliated with missiles, machine guns, and tanks, often killing Palestinian civilians in turn. In 2006, the Israelis, responding to the political militia Hezbollah's kidnapping of Israeli soldiers, attacked Lebanon, destroying infrastructure, sending missiles into its capital city of Beirut, and killing hundreds of civilians. In 2009, Israel's invasion and bombing of Gaza had similar results.

Beginning in the 1980s and continuing into the 2000s, terrorists from the Middle East and North Africa planted bombs in European cities, blew airplanes out of the sky, and bombed the Paris subway system. These attacks, causing widespread destruction and loss of life, were said to be punishment for the West's support both for Israel and for the dictatorships in the other Middle Eastern countries.

On September 11, 2001, the ongoing terrorism in Europe and around the world caught the full attention of the United States. In an unprecedented act, Muslim militants hijacked four planes in the United States and flew two of them into the World Trade Center in New York City and one into the Pentagon in Virginia. The fourth plane, en route to the Capitol, crashed in Pennsylvania when passengers forced the hijackers to lose control of the aircraft. The hijackers, most of whom were from Saudi Arabia, were inspired by the wealthy radical leader of al-Qaeda, Osama bin Laden, who sought to end the presence of U.S. forces in Saudi Arabia. They had trained in bin Laden's terrorist camps in Afghanistan and learned to pilot planes in the United States. The loss of more than three thousand lives led the United States to declare a "war against terrorism." In the wake of the September 11 attacks, the administration of U.S. president George W. Bush forged a multinational coalition, which included the vital cooperation of Islamic countries such as Pakistan, with the main goals of driving the ruling Taliban out of Afghanistan. After some initial coalition success, the war dragged on inconclusively and, as of 2011, the Taliban was making a comeback.

At first, the September 11 attacks and other lethal terrorist attacks around the world promoted global cooperation. European countries rounded up suspected terrorists and conducted the first successful trials of them in the spring of 2003. Ultimately, however, the West became divided when the United States claimed that Saddam Hussein was concealing weapons of mass destruction in Iraq and suggested ties between him and bin Laden's terrorist group. Great Britain, Spain, and Poland were among those who joined the coalition of invading forces, but powerful European states, including Germany, Russia, and France, refused, sparking the anger of many Americans, some of whom sported bumper stickers with the demand "First Iraq, Next France" or participated in happy hours devoted to "French bashing."

U.S. war fever mounted with the suggestion that Syria and Iran should also be invaded, while the rest of the world condemned what seemed a sudden American blood lust. Europeans in general, including the British public, accused the United States of becoming a world military dictatorship in order to preserve its only remaining value—wasteful consumerism. The United States countercharged that the Europeans were too selfishly enjoying their democracy and creature comforts to help fund the military defense of freedom under attack. The Spanish withdrew from the U.S. occupation of Iraq after terrorists linked to al-Qaeda bombed four Madrid commuter trains on March 11, 2004. The British, too, reeled when terrorists exploded bombs in three subway cars and a bus in central London in July 2005. Barack Obama, who was elected the first African American U.S. president in 2008, promised to bring home all the troops. As of 2011, however, the United States still maintained a military presence in Iraq, though alone among western nations since others in the initial coalition had all withdrawn their forces.

Terrorist Attacks on Spanish Commuter Trains, 2004
Terrorism became more widespread from the 1970s onward, taking many forms and espousing many causes. Although terrorists of the 1970s and early 1980s often targeted prominent individuals, later ones engineered wider attacks on random citizens to increase the loss of life. On March 11, 2004, foreign terrorists who opposed Spain's participation in the U.S.-led invasion of Iraq used bombs planted on commuter trains to kill 191 people and injure more than 2,000. Spanish voters ousted the prime minister and installed one who pulled Spanish forces out of Iraq. *(Christophe Simon/AFP/Getty Images.)*

The Promise and Problems of a World Economy

Amid the violence, an incredible rise in industrial entrepreneurship and technological development took place outside the West. Just as economic change in the early modern period had redirected European affairs from the Mediterranean to the Atlantic, so explosive productivity from Japan to Singapore in the 1980s and 1990s spread economic power from the Atlantic region to the Pacific. By the twenty-first century the economies of Brazil, Russia, India, and China—sometimes called the BRICs—were also developing rapidly, bringing new prosperity to their people. When the world economic collapse began in 2007, these newcomers were less indebted and less threatened than the West.

The Pacific Economic Surge

The rise of the Pacific was almost imperceptible from one year to the next, but in 1982, the Asian-Pacific nations accounted for 16.4 percent of global gross domestic product, a figure that had doubled since the 1960s. By 1989, East Asia's share of world production had grown to more than 25 percent as that of the West declined. By 2006, China alone was achieving economic growth rates of over 10 percent per year, and in 2010 it overtook Japan as the second largest national economy after the United States, with Germany falling to fourth place.

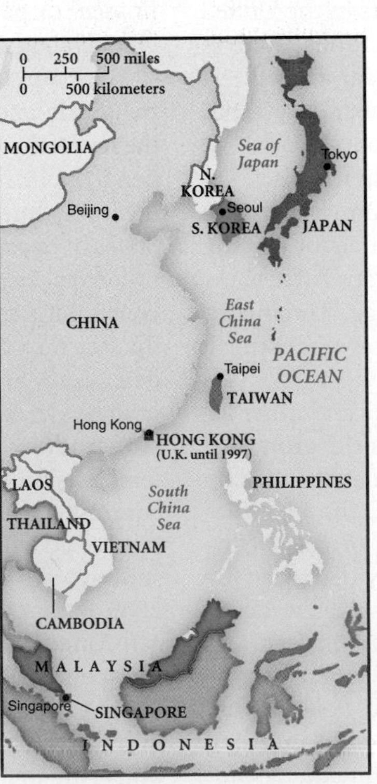

Tigers of the Pacific Rim, c. 1995

South Korea, Taiwan, Singapore, and Hong Kong were popularly called **Pacific tigers** for the ferocity of their growth in the 1980s and 1990s. By the 1990s, China, pursuing a policy of economic modernization and market orientation, had joined the surge in productivity and even surpassed all the others. Japan, however, led the initial charge of Asian economies with investment in high-tech consumer industries driving the Japanese economy. For example, in 1982, Japan had thirty-two thousand industrial robots in operation; western Europe employed only nine thousand, and the United States had seven thousand. In 1989, the Japanese government and private businesses invested $549 billion to modernize industrial capacity, a full $36 billion more than in the United States. Such spending paid off substantially, as buyers around the world snapped up automobiles, televisions, videocassette recorders, and computers from Japanese or other Asian-Pacific companies. As the United States poured vast sums into its military budgets and a series of wars, Asian and

Pacific tigers: Countries of East Asia so named because of their massive economic growth, much of it from the 1980s on; foremost among these were Japan and China.

Middle Eastern governments purchased U.S. government bonds, thus financing America's ballooning national debt. Forty years after its total defeat in World War II, Japan was bankrolling its former conqueror. By 2000, China had become the largest creditor of the United States.

Despite rising national prosperity, individual workers, particularly outside of Japan, often paid dearly for this newly created wealth. For example, safety standards in China were abominable, leading to horrendous mining disasters among other catastrophes. Women in South Korea, Taiwan, and Central America labored in sweatshops to produce clothing for U.S.-based companies. Using the lure of a low-paid and docile female workforce, governments were able to attract electronics and other industries. However, educational standards rose, along with access to birth control and other medical care for these women, and many valued the escape from rural poverty.

Other Emerging Economies

Other emerging economies in the Southern Hemisphere as a whole continued to increase their share of the world's gross domestic product during the 1980s and 1990s, and some achieved political gains as well. In South Africa, native peoples began winning the struggle for political rights when, in 1990, the moderate government of F. W. de Klerk released political leader Nelson Mandela, imprisoned for almost three decades because of his anti-apartheid activism. After holding free elections in 1994, which Mandela won, South Africa—like Brazil, Russia, Iran, Saudi Arabia, Nigeria, and Chile—profited from the need for vast quantities of raw materials such as oil and ores to feed global expansion. India made strides in education, women's rights, and local cooperation (calming bitter rivalries), but assassinations of prime ministers raised the question of whether India would be able to attract investment and thus to continue modernization. After the brief rule of a Hindu nationalist government that often blocked development, India's economy also achieved soaring growth early in the twenty-first century, taking business from Western firms and making global acquisitions that gave it, for example, the world's largest steel industry. Although Western firms faced the challenge of competition, they also profited from prosperity that was more widely spread around the world by the 1990s.

World Economic Collapse

There was a downside to global economic interconnectedness. Beginning in 1997, when speculators brought down the Thai baht, and continuing with the collapse of the Russian ruble in 1998 and the bursting of the technology bubble in the early 2000s, the global economy suffered a series of shocks. Then in 2008, the real estate bubble burst in the United States, setting in motion a financial crisis of enormous proportions. For several years, lenders had been making home mortgages available to U.S. consumers who could not afford them. The boom in housing made the economy as a whole look robust. Bankers then sold their bad housing debt around the world to those who hoped to make handsome profits based on rate increases written into the mortgage contracts. When people were unable to make their monthly mortgage payments and pay their ballooning credit card debt, credit became unavailable both to ordinary people and to banks and industry. A credit collapse followed, just as it had in the stock market crash of

Protesting Reform amid Economic Crisis
By 2010 and 2011, global economic crisis and the attempts to repair the damage had led to massive government debt. To remedy the situation, governments cut back on jobs, benefits, and services while giving banks and businesses huge bailouts. Here, on the island of Cyprus, unions and NGOs sponsored this demonstration against the policy of simultaneously heaping money on banks and taking it from ordinary citizens. *(EPA/Katia Christodouloul/Landov.)*

1929. Beginning in the United States and continuing around the world, banks and industries became insolvent, forcing governments to set common policies to prop up failing banks with billions of dollars. Unemployment rose as businesses and consumers alike stopped purchasing goods.

By 2011, their more prudent management helped Asian economies as well as that of Brazil to recover, even as governments in the West faced bankruptcy and horrific rates of unemployment, such as the 20 percent of Spain's population who were out of work. It looked to some as if the European Union itself might collapse as the richer nations such as Germany and France were threatened by backing the debt of the poorer ones such as Greece, Ireland, Portugal, and even Italy. The globalization of economic crises was another of the perils faced by the world's population.

REVIEW QUESTION What were the principal challenges facing the West at the beginning of the twenty-first century?

Global Culture and Society in the Twenty-First Century

Amid warfare, booms, and crises, increased migration and growing global communications were changing culture and society, prompting many to ask what would become of national cultures and Western civilization itself. Would the world become a homogeneous mass with everyone wearing the same kind of clothing, eating the same kind of food, watching the same films, and communicating with the same smartphones? Some critics predicted a clash of civilizations in which increasingly incompatible religions and cultures would lead to a global holocaust. Others asked whether the West would fragment as the United States wore itself down waging war while much of Europe distanced itself from its former ally.

The migration that had accelerated since the 1990s, the spread of disease, global climate change, the information revolution, and the global sharing of culture argued against the cultural purity of any group, Western or otherwise. "Civilizations," Indian economist and Nobel Prize winner Amartya Sen wrote after the terrorist attacks of September 11, "are hard to partition . . . given the diversities within each society as well as the linkages among different countries and cultures."

Through global communication and migration, Western society changed even more rapidly in the 1980s and 1990s than it had hundreds of years earlier when it came into intense contact with the rest of the globe. In addition, national boundaries in the traditional European center of the West were weakening, given the open borders within the EU and the influx of migrants. Culture knew no national boundaries, as East, West, North, and South became saturated with one another's cultural products via satellite television, films, telecommunications, and computer technology. Consequently some observers labeled the new century an era of denationalization — meaning that national cultures as well as national boundaries were becoming less distinct. There is no denying that even while the West absorbed peoples and cultures, it continued to exercise not only economic but also cultural influence over the rest of the globe. Yet Western influence was also being contested as Westerners absorbed the cultures of other regions.

Redefining the West: The Impact of Global Migration

The global movement of people was massive in the last third of the twentieth century and into the twenty-first. Uneven economic development, political persecution, and warfare (which claimed more than 100 million victims after 1945) sent tens of millions in search of opportunity and safety. By 2010, France had between five and eight million Muslims within its borders and Europe as a whole had between thirty-five and fifty million. Other parts of the world were as full as the West of migrants from other cultures. The oil-producing nations of the Middle East employed millions of foreign workers, who generally constituted one-third of the labor force. Violence in Africa sent Rwandans, Congolese, and others to South Africa, as its government abandoned all-white rule. Wars in Afghanistan increased the number of refugees to Iran to nearly two million in 1995, while the Iraq-Iran War and the U.S. invasion of Iraq in 2003 sent millions more fleeing. In 2010, there were more than 200 million migrants worldwide, with many of them headed to the West.

Migrants often earned desperately needed income for family members who remained in the native country, and in some cases they propped up the economies of entire nations. In countries as different as the Yugoslav republics, Egypt, Spain, Mexico, and Pakistan, money sent home from abroad constituted up to 60 percent of national income. Sometimes migration was coerced: many eastern European and Asian prostitutes were held in international sex rings that controlled their passports, wages, and lives. Others came to the West voluntarily, seeking op-

Headscarf Controversy in Germany
Western countries have long debated the relationship between religion and the nation-state, especially in public education. In an age of global migration, the issue of religion in the schools resurfaced, this time focusing on the headscarves worn by many Muslim women. In 2003, a German court upheld the right of teacher Fereshta Ludin, pictured here, to wear her headscarf while teaching on the grounds of religious freedom. Note the justices' own different clothing. *(© Vincent Kessler/Reuters/Corbis.)*

portunity and a better life: "I do not want to go back to China," said one woman restaurant owner in Hungary in the 1990s. "Some of my relatives there also have restaurants. . . . They have to have good relations with officials, . . . and sometimes they have to bribe somebody. . . . I would not be happy living like that." Like the illegal Congolese café proprietor Thérèse, whose story opens this chapter, many lived on the margins of the law, supporting networks of family and maintaining global economic ties from a new base in the West.

Foreign workers were often scapegoats for native peoples suffering from economic woes such as unemployment caused by downsizing. On the eve of EU enlargement in 2004, the highly respected weekly magazine *The Economist* included an article entitled "The Coming Hordes," which warned of Britain's being overrun by Roma (Gypsies) from eastern Europe. Political parties with racist programs sprang to life in Europe, aided by celebrities: the Moscow rock band Corroded Metals campaigned for anti-immigrant candidates with hate-filled songs and chants in English of "Kill, kill, kill, kill the bloody foreigners" running in the background. Even citizens of immigrant descent often had a difficult time being accepted. In Austria, France, the Netherlands, Sweden, and many other Western countries, thriving anti-immigrant and white supremacist politicians challenged centrist parties. In Austria and the Netherlands, anti-immigration candidates were elected to head the government. (See "Contrasting Views," page 1010.) Nonetheless, because employers sought out illegal immigrants for the low wages they could be paid, the West remained a place of opportunity.

Global Networks and the Economy

Like migration, rapid technological change also weakened traditional political, cultural, and economic borders and to some extent even made borders obsolete. In 1969, the U.S. Department of Defense developed a computer network to carry communications in case of nuclear war. This system and others like it in universities, government, and business grew into an unregulated system of more than ten thousand networks worldwide. These came to be known as the Internet—shorthand for *internetworking*. By 1995, users in more than 137 countries were connected to the Internet, creating new "communities" via the World Wide Web based on business needs, shared cultural interests, or other factors that transcended common citizenship in a particular nation-state. By 2011, some two billion people—one-third of the world's population—used the Internet, creating an online marketplace that offered goods and services ranging from advanced weaponry to organ transplants. While enthusiasts claimed that the Internet could promote world democracy, critics charged that communications technology favored elites and disadvantaged those without computer skills or the financial resources needed to access computers. In fact, wealthy North America, Europe, and Australia/Oceania had the highest percentage of users.

By 2000, as postindustrial skills spread, the Internet had brought service jobs to countries that had heretofore suffered unemployment and real poverty. One of the first countries to recognize the possibilities of computing and help-desk services was Ireland, which pushed computer literacy to attract business. In 2003, U.S. firms spent $8.3 bil-

CONTRASTING VIEWS

The Dutch Debate Globalization, Muslim Immigrants, and Turkey's Admission to the EU

Early in the twenty-first century, Westerners debated a series of intertwined issues springing from conditions created by the new globalized world. The issue of immigration and the accommodation of peoples from outside the West was one of them. The Netherlands was one of the European countries that began debating whether globalization hadn't gone too far in this direction. The debate came to the fore in the Netherlands after an animal rights activist in 2002 assassinated Pim Fortuyn, a candidate for prime minister who ran on a popular anti-immigrant platform and proclaimed, "Holland is full." When, in 2004, a Muslim radical assassinated filmmaker Theo van Gogh, who took special pride in insulting Islam, the Dutch debate over globalization fixated on the presence of foreigners, especially Muslims, in the Netherlands and the admission of Turkey to the European Union.

1. The View from Everyday Life

Leon was a Rotterdam window cleaner who did not want his last name revealed. Here is his opinion of the main problem of Dutch life brought about by globalization.

There are too many people coming here who don't want to work. Before long there will be more foreigners than Dutch people, and Dutch people won't be the boss of their own country. That's why this has to be stopped.

Source: Jennifer Ehrlich, "Liberal Netherlands Grows Less So on Immigration," *Christian Science Monitor*, December 19, 2003.

2. Too Much Islamic Architecture

Many immigrants and their descendants, all of whom could become Dutch citizens, often lived in cities where there was economic opportunity. Although mosques existed in many cities, most were tucked away in obscure and shabby parts of town near the ghettos where many Muslim immigrant families lived. When the Muslim community in Rotterdam proposed building a stately mosque with 164-foot minarets, many in Rotterdam opposed the project. Ronald Sorenson, a member of Rotterdam's city council, objected in particular to the design of the proposed mosque and its cultural connotations.

There's no reason the minarets have to be that high — it will not be Rotterdam; it will be Mecca on the Maas [River].

Source: Jennifer Ehrlich, "Liberal Netherlands Grows Less So on Immigration," *Christian Science Monitor*, December 19, 2003.

3. Opposing Immigration and Turkey's Membership in the European Union

Acceptance of new members has made the EU the largest economic power in the world. In the first decade of the twenty-first century, some Europeans looked to the integration of Turkey into the EU as further expansion of EU influence. Others, however, opposed it, as the issue of EU enlargement had implications for immigration. Geert Wilders, member of Dutch parliament, voiced his opposition. In 2010, he was put on trial for inciting hatred against Muslims.

Turkey is an Islamic country and as such doesn't belong in the EU. The flow [of Turks] is already too big. . . . There is a big problem with the integration of immigrants already in Holland. They top the list in terms of criminality, unemployment, welfare payments, domestic violence. . . . Let us concentrate on solving the problems with the immigrants already here properly.

Source: *Expatica*, October 5, 2004.

4. A Student's Thoughts on Muslims in the Netherlands

Loubna el Morabet, a PhD candidate in social science at Leiden University, gave this reaction to Geert Wilders's pronouncements on Muslims and to the media's coverage of him and his political party.

lion on outsourcing to Ireland and $7.7 billion on outsourcing to India. In that same year, the United States bought $77.38 billion in services from foreign countries and sold $131.01 billion to them, meaning in fact that more was insourced than outsourced. Thus, the Internet allowed for jobs to be apportioned anywhere. Moroccans did help-desk work for French or Spanish speakers, and in the twenty-first century Estonia, Hungary, and the Czech Republic as well as India and the Philippines were rebuilding their economies successfully by providing call center and other business services. The Internet allowed service industries to globalize just as the manufacturing sector had done much earlier through multinational corporations.

Globalization of the economy affected the West in complex ways. Those who worked in outsourcing enterprises were more likely than those in domestic firms to participate in the global consumer economy, much of it for Western goods. Benefiting from the booming global economy of the 1990s, the Irish and eastern Europeans became integrated into the Western consumer economy, and by the 2000s Asians and South Americans were integrated, too. Their new disposable income allowed them to purchase luxury automobiles, CD players, and per-

This is an ongoing process. Muslims in the Netherlands are already very Dutch. I have done research in the Netherlands and England and learnt that Muslim students here have adopted the Dutch mentality. This is their country.

Of course I feel threatened when I hear Wilders speaking. But if I take a step back, I realize he will never be able to carry out his ideas. Taxing headscarves is nonsense and halting immigration from Islamic countries is discrimination. The principle of equality is deeply embedded in Dutch law.

I think it is ridiculous that media pay so much attention to a party that has garnered a handful of seats in the municipal elections. [Left-wing liberal party] D66 was the real winner of the local elections and that happens to be the one party that tells Wilders: "You are shutting people out, you discriminate." That gets relatively little attention.

Source: "Muslims Quietly Take Wilders' Abuse," Radio Netherlands Worldwide, March 25, 2010.

5. An Evaluation of Dutch Values

Popular Amsterdam actress Funda Müjde admitted to being called a "filthy Turk" during the debates over immigration and ethnic violence in the city.[1] *In her online stage performances and journalism, she gave sharp-witted responses to the anti-immigration furor around her.*

"Do aliens actually love Holland?" This question woke me up with a start. After work (a workshop at the Employment Office) I traveled back [home from the job] with a colleague because he needed to be in Amsterdam. We have been working together for a while now and I notice that our conversations are always about something substantial.

Now it seemed as if he was even bolder in asking all kinds of questions.

Hurray! Do we aliens (read: mainly the first-generation Moroccans and Turks) really love Holland? Immediately I want to answer this question with another question. "Does Holland really love aliens?" Just in time, I bite my tongue.

Source: Funda Müjde Web site, http://www.fundam.nl/English/fundas-column-telegraaf-daily-newspaper-04.htm.

[1] Ian Buruma, *Murder in Amsterdam: The Death of Theo van Gogh and the Limits of Tolerance* (New York: Penguin, 2006), 175.

6. Encouragement for Religious Tolerance in the EU

On July 21, 2004, Dutch prime minister Jan Peter Balkenende gave a speech before the European Parliament that called on Europeans to reconsider their position on immigration.

We must not allow ourselves to be guided by fear, for example, of Islam. The raising of barriers to any particular religion is not consistent with Europe's shared values. Our opposition should be directed not against religions, but against people and groups misusing their religion to get their way by force. Islam is not the problem.

Source: European Stability Initiative, "Speech by the President, Jan Peter Balkenende, to the European Parliament, in Strasbourg on 21 July 2004," http://www.esiweb.org.

Questions to Consider

1. **What are the main points of view in the debate over Muslims, immigration, and the admission of Turkey to the European Union?**
2. **How do you evaluate the strength of each position?**
3. **Given that globalization brought about a wide variety of changes, why would Muslim immigration and Turkish EU membership become such heated issues?**
4. **What sense do you get of the Muslim reaction to hostility and discrimination?**

sonal computers that would have been far beyond their means a decade earlier. Non-Westerners may have taken jobs from the West, but they often sent funds back. For example, a twenty-one-year old Indian woman, working for a service provider in Bangalore under the English name Sharon, used her salary to buy Western consumer items, such as a cell phone from the Finnish company Nokia. "As a teenager I wished for so many things," she said. "Now I'm my own Santa Claus." Ordinary Western workers often discovered that this global revolution threatened their jobs. In Germany, where taxes for social security and other welfare-state financing comprised 42 percent of payroll costs in 2003, the incentive for businesses to downsize or to move to countries with lower costs was strong. Globalization redistributed jobs across the West and reworked economic networks to operate worldwide.

A New Global Culture?

Despite the sense that national boundaries are weakening, cultural exchange flowing in many directions goes back millennia. In the ancient world, Greek philosophers and traders knew distant Asian religious beliefs, and Middle Eastern religions such as

Judaism and Christianity were influenced by them. In the eighteenth and nineteenth centuries, Western scholars immersed themselves in Asian philosophy and languages. By the early 1990s, visitors from around the world had made tourism the largest single industry in Britain and in many other Western countries, promoting cultural exchange. Chinese students in Tiananmen Square in 1989 testified to the power of the West in the world's imagination when in the name of freedom they rallied around their own representation of the Statue of Liberty (which itself was a gift from France to the United States). In Japan, businesspeople wore Western-style clothing and watched soccer, baseball, and other Western sports using English terms, while Europeans and Americans wore flip-flops, carried umbrellas, and practiced yoga — all imports from beyond the West.

Remarkable innovations in communications integrated cultures and made the earth seem a much smaller place, though possibly one with a Western flavor. Videotapes and satellite-beamed telecasts transported American television shows to Hong Kong and Japanese movies to Europe and North America. American rock music sold briskly in Russia and elsewhere in the former Soviet bloc. When more than 100,000 Czechoslovakian rock fans, including President Václav Havel, attended a Rolling Stones concert in Prague in 1990, it was clear that despite half a century of supposed isolation under communism, Czechs and Slovaks had been well tuned in to the larger world. Young black immigrants forged transnational culture when they created hip-hop and other pop music styles by combining elements of Africa, the Caribbean, Afro-America, and Europe. Athletes like the Brazilian soccer player Ronaldo and Japanese baseball star Ichiro Suzuki became better known to countless people than their own national leaders were. Film entrepreneurs marketed such international blockbusters as the Chinese *Crouching Tiger, Hidden Dragon* (2000). With their messages conveyed around the world, even today's moral leaders — the Nobel Peace Prize winners Nelson Mandela, former president of South Africa; the Dalai Lama, the spiritual leader of Tibet; and Aung San Suu Kyi, opposition leader in Burma — are global figures.

Culture from beyond the West

As it had done for centuries, the West continued to devour material from other cultures — whether Hong Kong films, African textiles, Indian music, or Latin American pop culture. One of the most important influences in the West came from what was called the boom in Latin American literature. Latin American authors developed a style known as magical realism that melded everyday events with Latin American history and geography, while also incorporating elements of myth, magic, and religion. The novels of Colombian-born Nobel Prize winner Gabriel García Márquez were translated into dozens of languages. His lush fantasies, including *One Hundred Years of Solitude* (1967), *Love in the Time of Cholera* (1988), and many later works, portray people of titanic ambitions and passions who endure war and all manner of personal trials. García Márquez narrated the tradition of dictators in Latin America, but he also paid close attention to the effects of global business. *One Hundred Years of Solitude*, for example, closes with the machine-gunning in 1928 of thousands of workers for the American United Fruit company because they asked for one day off per week and breaks to use the toilet. Wherever they lived, readers snapped up the book, which sold thirty million copies worldwide. García Márquez's work inspired a host of other outstanding novels in the magical realism tradition, including Laura Esquivel's *Like Water for*

Tourism, Migration, and the Mixing of Cultures
Tourism was a major economic boon to the West, and Western countries were the top tourist destinations in the world. Spreading prosperity allowed for greater leisure and travel to distant spots. Curiosity grew about other cultures. This Scottish bagpiper in London clearly arouses the interest of passersby, whether visitors from afar or citizens of his own country. *(© Will van Overbeek. All Rights Reserved.)*

Chocolate (1989). In the 1990s, the work was translated into two dozen languages and became a hit film because of its setting in a Mexican kitchen during the revolution of 1910, where cooking, sexuality, and brutality are intertwined. The Latin American boom continued into the early twenty-first century, with innumerable authors in the West adopting aspects of García Márquez's style.

Magical realism influenced a range of Western writers, including those migrating to Europe. Some described how the experience of Western culture felt to the transnational person. British-born Zadie Smith, daughter of a Jamaican mother, became a prizewinning author with her novel *White Teeth* (2000), which describes postimperial Britain through the lives of often bizarre and larger-than-life characters from many ethnic backgrounds. Odd science fiction technology, deep emotional wounds, and weird but hilarious situations guide a plot full of heartbreak. Equally drawn to aspects of the magical realist style, Indian-born **Salman Rushdie** published the novel *The Satanic Verses* (1988), which outraged Muslims around the world because it appeared to blaspheme the Prophet Muhammad. From Iran, the ayatollah Khomeini issued a fatwa (decree) promising both a monetary reward and salvation in the afterlife to anyone who would assassinate the writer. Rushdie's Italian and Japanese translators were murdered, while his Norwegian publisher survived an assassination attempt. In a display of Western cultural unity, international leaders took bold steps to protect Rushdie until the threat to his life was lifted a decade later.

As groups outside the accepted circles engaged in artistic production, battles over culture erupted. U.S. novelist **Toni Morrison** became, in 1993, the first African American woman to win the Nobel Prize for Literature. In works such as *Beloved* (1987), *Jazz* (1992), and *A Mercy* (2008), Morrison describes the nightmares, daily experiences, achievements, and dreams of those who were brought as slaves to the United States and their descendants. But some parents objected to the inclusion of Morrison's work in school curricula alongside Shakespeare and other authors of the accepted canon. Critics charged that unlike Shakespeare's universal Western truth, the writing of African Americans, Native Americans, and women represented only propaganda, not great literature. In both the United States and Europe, politicians on the right saw the presence of multiculturalism as a sign of national decay similar to that brought about by immigration.

Toni Morrison, Recipient of the Nobel Prize
Toni Morrison, shown here receiving the Nobel Prize for Literature in 1993, was the first African American woman to receive the Nobel Prize. Morrison uses her literary talent to depict the condition of blacks under slavery and after emancipation. She also publishes insightful essays on social, racial, and gender issues. *(AP Photo.)*

Salman Rushdie: Immigrant British author, whose novel *The Satanic Verses* (1988) led the ayatollah Ruhollah Khomeini of Iran to issue a fatwa calling for Rushdie's murder.

Toni Morrison: The first African American woman to win the Nobel Prize for Literature; her works include *Beloved* (1987), *Jazz* (1992), and *A Mercy* (2008).

Building Post-Soviet Culture

In the former Soviet bloc, artists and writers faced unique challenges. After the Soviet Union collapsed, celebrated writers like Mikhail Bulgakov (1891–1940), famous in the West for his novel *The Master and Margarita* (published posthumously in 1966–1967), became known in his homeland. At the same time, the collapse put literary dissidents out of business. In helping bring down the Soviet regime, they had lost their subject matter—the critique of a tyrannical system. State-supported authors suddenly lost their jobs. Eastern-bloc writers who formerly found both critical and financial success in the West seemed less heroic—and less talented—in the wide-open post-Soviet world. The work of Czech writer Milan Kundera, for example, lost its luster. It had been, according to one critic, merely about Western publishers' hype, not literature but merely a "line of business." To make matters worse, there was no idea of what the post-Communist arts should be.

New literature aimed at rethinking the communist experience and eastern Europe's cultural relationship to western Europe and the West more generally. Andrei Makine, an expatriate Russian author, became popular worldwide for his poignant yet disturbing novels of the collapse of communism. He described the attraction of western European culture and the role of the war and the Gulag on the imaginations of eastern-bloc people, including teenagers. Both *Dreams of My Russian Summers* (1995) and *Once Upon the River Love* (1994) describe young people bred to fantasize about the wealth, sexiness, and material goods of western Europe and America. Victor Pelevin wrote more satirically and bitingly in such works as *The Life of Insects* (1993), in which insect-humans buzz around Russia trying to discover who they are in the post-Soviet world. Pelevin, a Buddhist and former engineer, wrote hilarious send-ups of politicians and the almost sacred Soviet space program, depicting it as a media sham run from the depths of the Moscow subway system in which hundreds of cosmonaut-celebrities are killed to prevent the truth from getting out. For him, "any politician is a TV program, and this doesn't change from one government to another." So one simply judged them by haircuts, ties, and other aspects of personal style, as he showed in his novel *Homo Zapiens* (1999), in which politicians are all "virtual"—that is, produced by technical effects and scriptwriters.

In music and the other arts, much energy was spent on recovering and absorbing all the underground works that had been hidden since 1917. For example, music lovers were astonished as the work of first-rate composers emerged. Those composers had written their classical works in private for fear that they might contain phrasings, sounds, and rhythms that would be called subversive. Meanwhile, they had often earned a living writing for films, as did Giya Kancheli, who wrote immensely popular music for more than forty films but was in addition a gifted composer of classical music. Other work could now become even better known. Alfred Schnittke (1934–1998) produced dozens of operas, symphonies, chamber music pieces, concertos, and other works that were extremely sad, punctuated with anger in loud bursts of dissonance, and set in a somber bass register. Alongside great artists, ordinary people in eastern Europe rethought the past, creating ceremonies honoring Gulag victims and those purged by Stalin, all the while trying to sort out what Communism had meant to their lives and to history.

U.S. Cultural Dominance Even as the cold war ended and as the post-Soviet world tried to rethink its cultural values, the global power of the United States gave its culture an edge. The United States's success in marketing its culture, along with the legacy of British imperialism, helped make English the dominant international language by the end of the twentieth century. Such English words as *stop*, *shopping*, *parking*, *okay*, *weekend*, and *rock* infiltrated dozens of non-English vocabularies. English became one of the official languages of the European Union; across Europe, it served as the main language of higher education, science, and tourism. Already in the 1960s, French president Charles de Gaulle, fearing the corruption of the French language, had banned such new words as *computer* in government documents, and succeeding administrations followed his path. The ban did not stop the influx of English into scientific, diplomatic, and daily life. Nonetheless, in another sign of cultural divide, the EU's parliament and national cultural ministries regulated the amount of American programming on television and in cinemas.

American influence in film was dominant: films such as *The Matrix Reloaded* (2003) and *Avatar* (2009) earned hundreds of millions of dollars from global audiences. Simultaneously, however, the United States itself welcomed films from around the world—whether the Mexican *Y Tu Mamá También* (2001) or the British *Slumdog Millionaire* (2009). "Bollywood" films—happy, lavish films from the Indian movie industry—had a huge following in all Western countries, even influencing the plots of some American productions. The fastest-growing media sector in the United States in the twenty-first century was Spanish-language television, just one more indication that even in the United States culture was based on mixture and global exchange.

Postmodernism Some have called the global culture of the late twentieth and early twenty-first centuries **postmodernism**, defined in part as intense stylistic mixing in the arts without following an elite set of standards. Striking examples of postmodern art abounded in Western society, including the AT&T Building (now known as the Sony Building) in New York City, which looks sleek and modern. Its entryway, however, is a Roman arch, and its cloud-piercing top suggests eighteenth-century Chippendale furniture. Postmodern buildings used elements from the past, drawing from cultural styles that spanned millennia and continents without valuing one style above others. The Guggenheim Museum in Bilbao, Spain, designed by American Frank Gehry and considered bizarre

postmodernism: A term applied in the late twentieth century to both an intense stylistic mixture in the arts without a central unifying theme or elite set of standards and a critique of Enlightenment and scientific beliefs in rationality and the possibility of certain knowledge.

by classical or even modern standards, includes forms, materials, and perspectives that, by rules of earlier decades, did not belong together. Architects from around the world working in a variety of hybrid styles completed the postunification rebuilding of Berlin. One crowning achievement was the rebuilding of the Reichstag, whose traditional facade was given a modern dome of glass and steel. To add to the changing reality, all of these postmodern buildings could be visited virtually on the World Wide Web.

Some intellectuals defined postmodernism in political terms as part of the decline of the eighteenth-century Enlightenment ideals of human rights, individualism, and personal freedom, which were seen as modern (see page 799). This political postmodernism included the decline of the Western nation-state. A structure like the Bilbao Guggenheim was simply an international tourist attraction rather than an institution reflecting Spanish traditions or national purpose. It embodied consumption, global technology, mass communications, and international migration rather than citizenship, nationalism, and rights. These qualities made it a rootless structure, unlike the Louvre in Paris, for example, which was built by the French monarchy to serve its own purposes. Critics saw the Bilbao Guggenheim as drifting, more like the nomadic businesswoman Thérèse, who moved between nations and cultures with no set identity. Cities and nations alike were losing their function as places providing social roots, personal identity, or human rights. For postmodernists of a political bent, computers had replaced the autonomous, free self and bureaucracy had rendered representative government obsolete.

The German Reichstag: Reborn and Green
Nothing better symbolizes the end of the postwar era and the new millennium than the restoration of the Reichstag, the parliament building in Berlin. Like other manifestations of postmodernism, the restoration—designed by a British architect—preserves the old, while adding a new dome of glass, complete with solar panels that make the building self-sufficient in its energy needs. Visitors can walk around the glass dome, looking at their elected representatives deliberating below. *(© Svenja-Foto/Corbis.)*

REVIEW QUESTION What social and cultural questions has globalization raised?

Conclusion

Postmodernist thinking has not eclipsed humane values in the global age. The urge to find practical solutions to the daunting problems of contemporary life — population explosion, scarce resources, pollution, global warming, ethnic hatred, North-South inequities, and terrorism — through the careful assessment of facts still guides public policy. Some of these global problems were briefly overshadowed by the collapse of the Soviet empire, which initially produced human misery, rising criminality, and the flight of population during the 1990s and even into the 2000s. Reformers who sought improved conditions of life by bringing down Soviet and Yugoslav communism saw unexpected bloodshed and even genocide. What appeared an economic boom resulting from globalization and the collapse of communism itself had disadvantages, as a series of crises beginning in Thailand in 1997 and finally exploding in the more sustained crisis from 2007 on cost jobs and harmed human well-being.

Yet the past twenty-five years have also seen great improvements. Events from South Africa and Latin America, for example, indicated that there could be progress toward democracy, prosperity, and an end to oppression. Human health gradually improved even as scientists sought to cure the victims of global pandemics and even to prevent them altogether. The global age ushered in by the Soviet collapse unexpectedly brought denationalization to many regions of the world, leading to weakening of borders and cooperation among former enemies. The expansion of the European Union and the tight-

MAPPING THE WEST

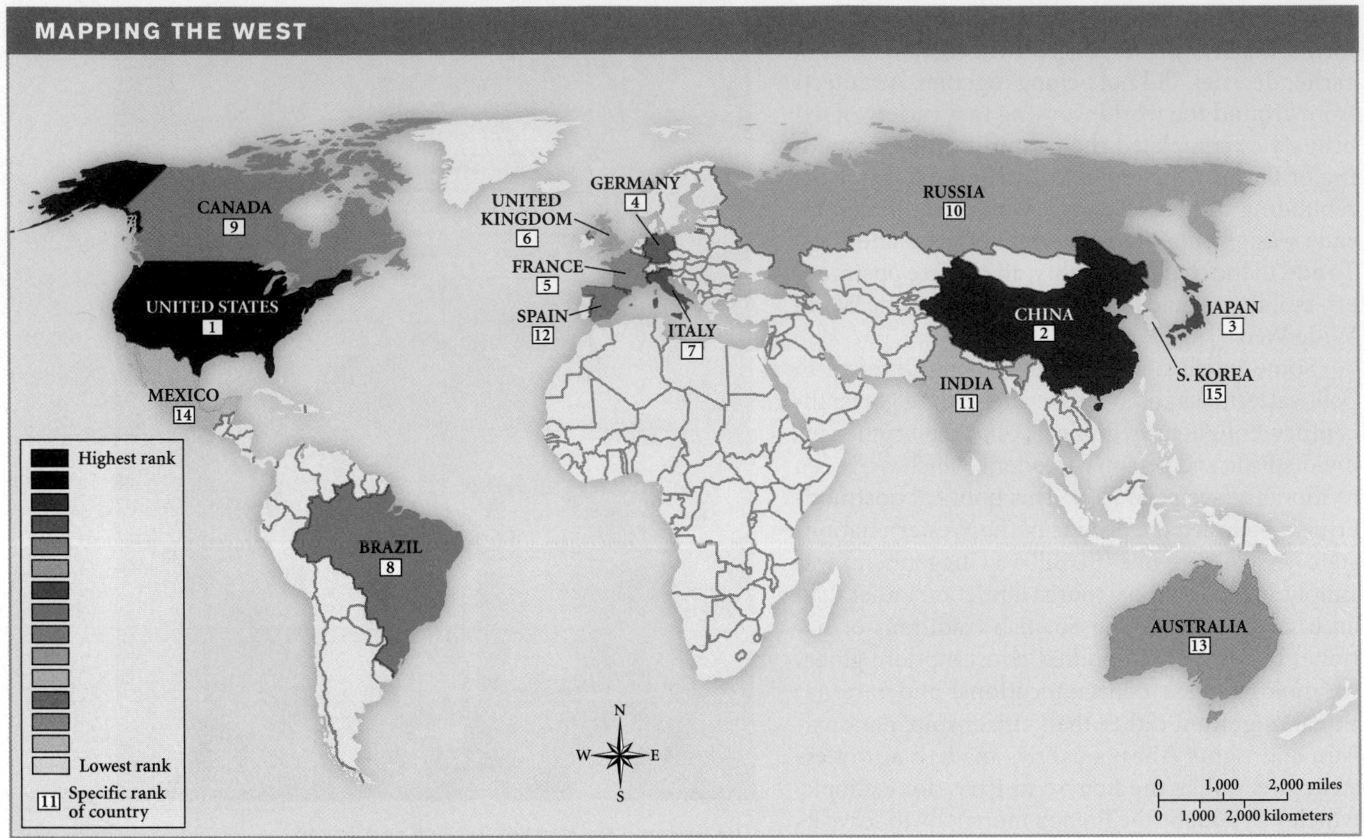

The World's Top Fifteen Economies as of 2010

From the nineteenth to the twenty-first centuries, the comparative economic strength of individual nations changed considerably. In the nineteenth century, India and China had the largest economies; they were eclipsed by the European powers as the Industrial Revolution progressed. The European powers in turn were eventually overtaken by the United States. By the end of the twentieth century, the reemergence of non-Western economic powerhouses marked another transformation. | **How would you describe economic dynamism in the twenty-first century as shown in the map?**

ening of relationships within it are the best example of this development.

Some consequences of increasing globalization are still being determined. The Internet and migration suggest that people's empathy for one another grew worldwide. One commentator claimed that there was little bloodshed in the collapse of the Soviet empire because fax machines and television circulated images of events globally, which discouraged the excessive violence often associated with political revolution. At the same time, militants from Saudi Arabia, Egypt, Indonesia, the Philippines, North Africa, Britain, and elsewhere unleashed unprecedented terrorism on the world in an attempt to push back global forces. Nor did powerful countries hesitate to wage wars against Chechnya, Kuwait, Iraq, Afghanistan, Lebanon, and other nations around the world. On a different level, even as globalization raised standards of living and education in many parts of the world, in other areas—such as poorer regions in Africa and Asia—people faced disease and the dramatic social and economic crises specifically associated with the global age. In contrast, the most hopeful development in recent globalization was communication in the arts and in culture more generally—most visible in the exchange of books, music, and ideas around the world—and the cooperation that nations undertook with one another in the realm of health, economics, and politics. Events from the recent past thus show that both opportunities and challenges lie ahead for citizens of the West and of the world as they make the transition to what some are calling the digital age.

FOR FURTHER EXPLORATION

- **For additional primary-source material from this period**, see *Sources of the Making of the West*, Fourth Edition.
- **For Web sites, images, and documents related to topics in this chapter**, visit *Make History* at bedfordstmartins.com/hunt.

Chapter 29 Review

Online Study Guide bedfordstmartins.com/hunt

Key Terms and People

In the grid below, identify the term or person and explain its historical significance. (To do this exercise online, go to bedfordstmartins.com/hunt.)

Term	Who or What & When	Why It Matters
globalization (p. 986)		
Slobodan Milosevic (p. 987)		
ethnic cleansing (p. 988)		
Vladimir Putin (p. 990)		
Maastricht Treaty (p. 995)		
European Union (EU) (p. 995)		
euro (p. 995)		
nongovernmental organizations (NGOs) (p. 999)		
global warming (p. 1000)		
Green Party (p. 1000)		
Osama bin Laden (p. 1003)		
Pacific tigers (p. 1006)		
Salman Rushdie (p. 1013)		
Toni Morrison (p. 1013)		
postmodernism (p. 1014)		

Review Questions

1. What were the major issues facing the former Soviet bloc in the 1990s and early 2000s?
2. What trends suggest that the nation-state was a declining institution at the beginning of the twenty-first century?
3. What were the principal challenges facing the West at the beginning of the twenty-first century?
4. What social and cultural questions has globalization raised?

Making Connections

1. In what ways were global connections at the beginning of the twenty-first century different from the global connections at the beginning of the twentieth century?
2. How did the Western nation-state of the early twenty-first century differ from the Western nation-state at the opening of the twentieth century?
3. Migration has been a major factor across the human past. How has it affected the West differently in the twenty-first century?
4. Economic crises caused by changes in weather, the spread of disease, and trade and financial disturbances have been constants throughout history. How does the economic crisis that began in 2007 compare with earlier crises?

Important Events

Date	Event	Date	Event
1989	Chinese students revolt in Tiananmen Square; fall of the Berlin Wall	2000	Vladimir Putin becomes president of Russia
1990s	Internet revolution	2001	September 11 terrorist attacks; United States declares "war against terrorism," attacks Afghanistan
1990–1991	War in Persian Gulf	2003	United States invades Iraq; the West divides on this policy
1991	Civil war erupts in former Yugoslavia; failed coup by Communist hard-liners in Soviet Union	2004	Ten countries join European Union
1992	Soviet Union is dissolved	2005	Emissions reductions of Kyoto Protocol go into effect
1993	Toni Morrison wins Nobel Prize for Literature; Czechoslovakia splits into Czech Republic and Slovakia	2007	Bulgaria and Romania admitted to European Union; world economic crisis begins
1994	Nelson Mandela elected president of South Africa; Russian troops invade Chechnya; European Union (EU) officially formed	2009	Barack Obama becomes the first African American president of the United States
1999	European Union introduces the euro; world population reaches six billion	2010	China overtakes Japan to become world's second largest economy

- Consider three events: **Internet revolution (1990s)**, **Soviet Union is dissolved (1992)**, and **European Union (EU) officially formed (1994)**. How did each of these events help to bring about a more interconnected, globalized world?

SUGGESTED REFERENCES

Studies of the globalized world describe both hopeful efforts to cure disease and survive migration and devastating effects of terrorism and ethnic conflict. Interesting works portray politics and everyday life in post-Soviet Russia and eastern Europe.

Bass, Gary J. *Freedom's Battle: The Origins of Humanitarian Intervention*. 2008.

Bess, Michael. *The Light-Green Society: Economic and Technological Modernity in France*. 2003.

Brier, Jennifer. *Infectious Ideas: U.S. Political Response to the AIDS Crisis*. 2009.

Bucur, Maria. *Heroes and Victims: Remembering the War in Twentieth-Century Romania*. 2009.

Burleigh, Michael. *Blood and Rage: A Cultural History of Terrorism*. 2008.

Burrett, Tina. *Television and Presidential Power in Putin's Russia*. 2010.

*Emecheta, Buchi. *The New Tribe*. 1996.

*Gorbachev, Mikhail. *Memoirs*. 1996.

Hoerder, Dirk. *Cultures in Contact: World Migrations in the 2nd Millennium*. 2002.

Hsu, Roland, ed. *Ethnic Europe: Mobility, Identity, and Conflict in a Globalized World*. 2010.

Humphrey, Caroline. *The Unmaking of Soviet Life: Everyday Economies after Socialism*. 2002.

Kavoori, Anandam P., and Aswin Punathambekar, eds. *Global Bollywood*. 2008.

Kenney, Padraic. *The Burdens of Freedom: Eastern Europe since 1989*. 2006.

MacGaffey, Janet, et al. *Congo-Paris: Transnational Traders on the Margins of the Law*. 2000.

Osumare, Halifu. *The Africanist Aesthetic in Global Hip-Hop: Power Moves*. 2007.

Ried, T. R. *The United States of Europe: The New Superpower and the End of American Supremacy*. 2005.

Rosefielde, Steven. *Russia in the 21st Century: The Prodigal Superpower*. 2006.

Sinno, Abdulkader H., ed. *Muslims in Western Politics*. 2008.

United Nations. *Overcoming Barriers: Human Mobility and Development*. 2009.

United Nations population data: http://www.unfpa.org/swp/swpmain.htm

*Primary source.

Epilogue

The Making of the West Continues in the Digital Age

Were you born digital? If you are reading this book between 2012 and 2015, the answer to this question for many of you is most likely yes. You have been able to access the Internet since you were four or five years old; you probably keep in touch with friends through Facebook and are a skillful and frequent texter; and you are likely to download music and videos onto a range of digital equipment, including your iPod, iPhone, or iPad. Online research is easy for you, and you may even be accessing this book online.

We refer to your own possible life experience to ask whether the West and the world have entered a new age comparable to the Stone Age, the Iron Age, the Commercial Revolution of the Middle Ages, the Agricultural Revolution, the Industrial Revolution, or the Global Age — all of these distinct times in history characterized by profound, if sometimes invisible, transformations in the way humans live. Many suspect that we in the West, and to a large extent the world, have entered such a transformative period — a new and distinct episode in human history. That new age is the Digital Age, and you are a major player in it. Let's use this brief epilogue to consider how this development relates to events and trends that you have studied in this book.

For historians, understanding trends in the recent past is a challenge in itself. Every day is filled with news, and never more so than after September 11, 2001. Global communication technology makes reporting virtually instantaneous — but unlike journalists, who are pressed for an immediate story, historians try to judge which items from the unfiltered mass of instant news will be important in the long run. Historians identify social, cultural, and political events that are uniquely important or generally significant for people's everyday lives, and they need time to collect facts from multiple sources. They make the most reliable evaluations when events are no longer news — that is, after a substantial amount of time has shown the events' lasting influence and importance.

When we wrote the first edition of this book, we held our breath in the face of rapidly changing events and judged that the fall of communism and the increasing interconnectedness of the world's peoples and cultures were the challenges not only of the moment but also of history.

Today we persist in that judgment, knowing that the fall of communism and the coming of globalism have brought even greater opportunities and perils than we saw only a few years earlier. Now, after we made our first selections of important trends, we judge the potential for the unification of the entire European continent as momentous. We also see both the rising economic development around the world and the forces of terrorism as still important historical influences. As an experiment in history, you might note the important events during the months in which you take this course, put your list away for several years or more, and then see if those events — along with the events discussed in this epilogue — stand the test of time.

We imagine that you would probably put that list of important events away digitally rather than on hard copy. From there you can share it with friends on a social networking site. In contrast, previous generations would have written their list on paper and put it in a drawer, where it would exist privately. In our first version of this book on the West, we missed the transformative effects of the Digital Age, and it has only slowly dawned on us in watching our students and doing our research that a major revolution in human life may be under way. The Internet has been around for more than forty years, and the World Wide Web for nearly twenty, but only recently has the full import of digitization become apparent: entire cultures are being changed, beginning most thoroughly with the current generation, by this process. Let's consider how the Digital Age may be yielding new patterns in some of the major categories that help us describe the past. We encourage you to add to the list.

Social Transformation

In studying the history of the West, we see how social structures have frequently been transformed by technological innovations. Developments in stone and iron capacity, for example, revolutionized human life and consequently reshaped social patterns. The Industrial Revolution prompted another massive social shift: in preindustrial society, those who controlled both agriculture and labor were, on the whole, the people able to cultivate learning and participate in politics. Those who worked the land, whether slave or free, often (though not always) led difficult lives with little social or political influence. The coming of manufacturing altered that social situation, as we saw in the rise of industrial society and the more democratic politics that often made it a success. Increasingly, education and knowledge determined social structure, giving influence, power, and wealth to those who had the intellectual tools to innovate — or at least the knowledge to coordinate or operate — technology and services.

The Digital Age is no less filled with meaning for society. Today, social status and social class are determined largely by access to digital technology. One's ability to secure a good job often depends on one's skill with this technology — but one can only acquire such skill with the proper equipment and access. In this regard, the West remains a privileged place to be born. As a principal site of wealth and technology, the West has more "digital natives" than other parts of the world do — though people in places like South Korea, Japan, China, Egypt, and Libya are rapidly accessing digital technology, and those with digital skills are advancing in their societies. A large gap remains — similar to older wealth-, class-, and status-based differences — between those who are adept with digital media and those who are not.

The Digital Age also allows for social identities that are more fluid than ever before. Fundamental characteristics such as gender, age, and appearance — as well as other traits such as skills and abilities, likes and dislikes, or professional experience — can be manipulated, refashioned, or fabricated in new and hard-to-detect ways. Moreover, with digitization, people's identities have become public in entirely new ways. Those with access to digital technology can create social networks and participate in various types of information sharing. Concerns for privacy and individuality that developed in the West from the seventeenth century onward may no longer be relevant when many aspects of people's identity are available to corporations, governments, online pirates, and a significant portion of the population.

Finally, although gender discrimination is rampant around the world — evidenced especially by the fact that 80 percent of the world's poor are women and children — digital skills seem to know no gender. Many of the first computer programmers in Europe were women. Then computers took off, and programming became an essential, highly paid job primarily held by men. The gender-neutral potential of the Digital Age has not yet been fully realized.

Economic Transformations

Over the last two chapters of this book, we have looked at the economic impact of digitization. As explained earlier, computer technology has allowed for a great advance in the globalization of economies in all parts of the world. The surprising rise of economies in Brazil, Russia, India, and China, for example, has appeared as a challenge to the West's overwhelming lead in the modern global economy (see the map below). Oddly enough, although the Digital Age began in the West and although many of the world's foremost digital innovators are also Westerners, the emerging nations may be the powerhouses of the future, especially as they increasingly develop their digital capabilities. Companies and individuals alike are investing in emerging markets and are seeing the first industrial nations as falling behind.

The Digital Age has thus had mixed effects on economic well-being. Service jobs demanding literacy and technological skills have migrated to new places such as Ireland and eastern Europe. Jobs have also left the West, finding new homes in areas where skills are high and wages low—for example, in India and Southeast Asia. Thus, skills are being built around the world, especially as non-Westerners become polylingual and technologically adept. The number of highly educated engineers, lawyers, and other top members of the service sector is soaring outside the West even as the building of modern skills across the population is declining in the center of technological innovation. In this respect one wonders whether digital technology is fundamentally changing the Western economy—which remains predominantly capitalist—as much as it is changing skill levels, boosting human capacities everywhere.

Digitization has also affected worldwide patterns of commerce, as new jobs have helped the number of consumers buying the products of Western innovation to soar. At the same time, commercial behavior has been changing: On a micro level, individuals are banking online, engaging in real-time stock trading, changing their consumption patterns in ways that impact business massively (consider, for example, the amount of e-commerce that now takes place during holiday seasons), and becoming the subjects of ever more targeted advertising campaigns. On a more global scale, online transactions—from an eBay purchase by a New

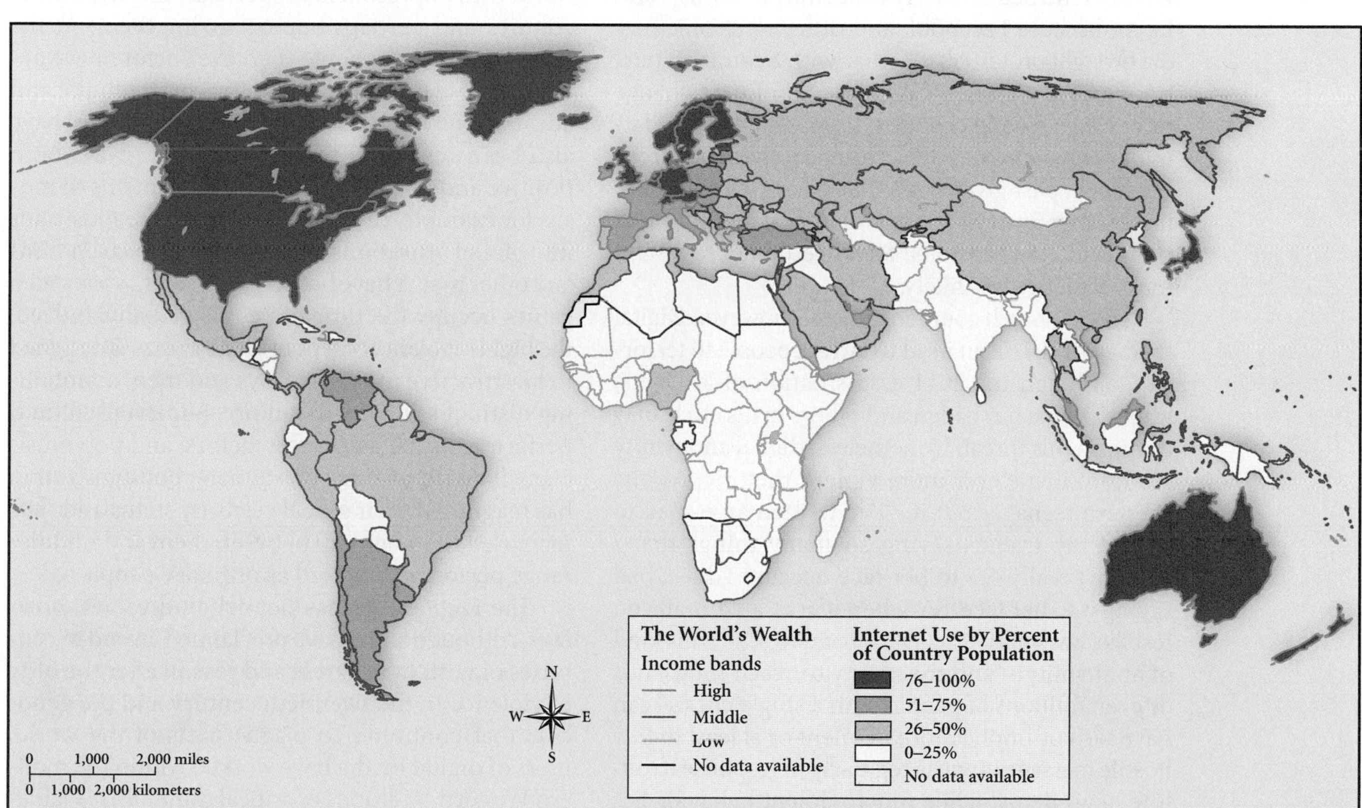

The World in the New Millennium

By the twenty-first century, the Internet had transformed communications and economic organization into an interconnected global network. Observers now think in terms of a North/South divide rather than an East/West one. People in the North had greater access to the communications network and for the most part enjoyed greater wealth than those in the South. But despite greater inequalities and lower Internet usage (compared with those in the North), Africa, the Middle East, and Latin America have seen an acceleration of Internet access. | **In what ways does this map indicate a closely connected world?**

Yorker of an antique poster in Australia to the trade in foreign currencies — are facilitating the immediate purchase of anything, anywhere, at any time, linking global economies in a way never before possible.

War, Peace, and Politics

Whether digitization will lead to a more peaceful world remains an open question. The evidence is mixed. There is the positive example from the relatively calm revolutions, mobilized in part by new communications, that overthrew communism across eastern Europe. In comparison with the civil war that erupted during the English Revolution, the Terror during the French Revolution, and the horrific civil war following the Russian Revolution of 1917, the events of 1989 were pacific — except for the civil war in Yugoslavia in the 1990s, where there was less Internet access and other communication infrastructure than elsewhere. In 2011, governments were overturned relatively peacefully in Tunisia and Egypt because Facebook and other electronic media brought protesters together with a common purpose, using communication to coordinate change rather than having change accompanied by escalating expressions of public violence. Evidence from the recent past gives hope that an era of even more instantaneous news feeds and digital communications will ease tensions, advance democracy, and make violence less likely.

There is much counterevidence, however. Digital media has also been used to attract people to terrorism, although the 2011 assassination of al-Qaeda leader Osama bin Laden and others in his circle may diminish this threat. Nonetheless, digital anonymity seems to invite ever more violent rhetoric. As one Western teenager put it: "I've written an e-mail to one of my friends saying so many things that I wouldn't really say to her face because I'd feel bad saying it to her face. So, when it's . . . an e-mail you just feel less guilty." On a more macro scale, this kind of anonymity — and the ability to reach thousands or even millions of people with a single click — can have serious implications. Violent or at least highly hostile messages appear regularly in response to online news items, while much violent behavior has been previewed in warnings on Web sites and elsewhere from young and older perpetrators.

Questions also arise about the Digital Age and the evolution of politics. It has become apparent around the world that digitization has altered politics, bringing in young people — especially those who were born digital. Whereas the selection of political leaders once took place among a select few in England or France, followed by mass campaigning by train and increasingly in the print media, today politics appears to be in the process of transformation. Digital media played a significant role in twenty-first-century political campaigns in Ukraine and other parts of eastern Europe, elections in the United States, and reform movements in the Middle East — to name a few. Protests are launched, supporters meet in chat forums, speeches are livestreamed, and money is raised via the Internet, shaping public opinion on a near constant basis and uniting ordinary people across nations and around the world.

Culture and Intellectual Creativity

Simultaneously, our culture itself has become digitized. Digitization has allowed cultural products such as film, music, art, and sports to travel the world with unprecedented speed, uniting the world's cultures and perhaps homogenizing them. At the same time, more people than ever before have access to these products, which can brighten life and advance knowledge. The products themselves have also been reworked by digitization, in ways both positive and negative: digital enhancements to music, for example, can transform mediocre musicians into global sensations. Superhuman effects in films and other media have become the norm, while video games occupy the time of people globally. Indeed, the highly violent content of video games is designed to be attractive mostly to boys and men, maintaining distinct sex roles in culture. Superstar cultural performers such as athletes, actors, and pop musicians flourish as our entertainers, but digitization has magnified their global celebrity status and thus increased the wage gap between them and middle-range performers as well as ordinary people.

The Digital Age has not eclipsed values, however. Although some have proclaimed an end to centuries of faith in progress and reason after the orgy of violence in the twentieth century and the genocide that continues to plague parts of the world, users of digital media have worked within the modern Western traditions of critical thinking, reevaluation, and problem solving. Digital media, and their enabling of widespread information sharing and fact checking, have allowed individuals and organizations to spread awareness of the daunting problems of contemporary life — population explosion, scarce resources, North–South inequities, global pollution, ethnic hatred, and global terrorism — which demand, more than ever, the exercise of humane values and rational thought. Yet through digitization we have become ever more aware that attempts at rational decision making fall short because of the issue of unintended consequences — that is, one cannot know in advance the consequences of an act. Who would have predicted, for example, the human misery and rising criminality resulting initially from the fall of communism across eastern Europe?

The West in the Digital World

Indeed, it is during the Digital Age that we have been made aware of the paradoxes in the momentous events around us. The collapse of communism signaled the eclipse of an ideology that was perhaps noble in its theory of making life better for the average person but deadly in practice. Events in South Africa and Northern Ireland have indicated that certain long-feuding groups can rationally put aside decades of bloodshed and work toward peace; in contrast, those reformers rationally seeking improved conditions by bringing down Soviet and Yugoslav communism unleashed bloodshed, sickness, unprecedented corruption, assassinations, and even genocide. The globalization ushered in by both the Digital Age and the Soviet collapse has unexpectedly brought denationalization to many regions of the world.

What, then, will become of Western traditions in an increasingly digitized world? A 2010 poll suggested that the places where the Digital Age has settled in the fastest have the *lowest* level of optimism about the future: only 31 percent of Britons, 30 percent of Americans, and 26 percent of French citizens believe that their nations are moving in the right direction and are content with their lot. In contrast, 87 percent of Chinese, 50 percent of Brazilians, and 45 percent of Indians have higher expectations for the future of their country.[1] Despite relative discontent among Europeans and Americans, Western traditions of democracy, human rights, and economic well-being still have much to offer. Although these were initially intended for a limited number of people — white men in powerful Western nations — global debates about their value and relevance are more widespread than ever, thanks in large part to digitization. The nation-state, which protected those values for the privileged and denied them to many others, is another legacy of the West that is being rethought in an age of transnationalism and instant communication. Migrants, for example, demand the dignity of national citizenship, but opponents of immigration often use the Internet to resist those demands. Moreover, it is often supranational organizations, rather than the nation-state, that have advocated for the expansion of citizenship, prosperity, and humane values in electronic forums and political activism.

At the same time, the West faces questions of its own unity and cultural identity — an identity that more than ever includes people from Asia, Africa, and the Americas — areas far from Europe, the traditional center of the West. Will the Digital Age help resolve the tensions and problems brought on by the West's greater complexity? Throughout history, non-Westerners of all kinds have challenged, criticized, refashioned, and made enormous contributions to Western culture; they have also served the West's citizens as slaves, servants, and menial workers. One of the greatest challenges to the West and the world in this global millennium is to determine how diverse peoples and cultures can live together on terms that are fair for everyone. We hope that the growing capacities of the Digital Age will provide answers. As we saw in the final chapter of this book, supranational organizations, both governmental and nongovernmental, have attempted to meet the challenges created by increased globalism, but the long-term effects of their efforts to achieve such benefits as human rights are not yet known.

The consequences of increasing globalization are still being determined. While the Internet and migration suggest that people will and often do have empathy for one another worldwide, militants — using the most advanced technology to build global networks — have unleashed unprecedented terrorism on the world in an attempt to push back global forces. Even as globalization has raised standards of living and education in many parts of the world, in other areas — such as poorer regions in Africa and Asia — people face disease and the dramatic social and economic deterioration associated with the global age. Rational results of planning and inexplicable consequences coexist in our present, global, digitized world.

Conclusion

A final challenge to the West involves the inventive human spirit. Over the past five hundred years, the West has benefited from its scientific and technological advances and perhaps never more so than

[1]Pew Research Council, quoted in *The Economist*, December 18, 2010, 13.

in the Digital Age. Longevity and improved material well-being have spread to many places, and in the past century, communication and information technology have brought people closer to one another than ever before. However, through the use of technology, the period from the last century to the present one has also become the bloodiest era in human history—and one during which the use of technology has threatened, and still threatens, the future of the earth as a home for the human race. Technology has facilitated war, genocide, terrorism, and environmental deterioration, all of which pose great challenges to the West and to the world. The use of digital media to promote violent causes, inflame others, and network with and recruit new followers has made some of these challenges even more significant. Yet digitization has simultaneously made us more aware than ever of the dangers we face. The making of the West has been a constantly inventive undertaking, but also a deadly one. The question is, How will the human race adapt to the creativity the Digital Age has unleashed? How will the West and the world manage both the promises and the challenges of Digital Age technology to protect the human race in the years ahead?

Appendix

Useful Facts and Figures

Prominent Roman Emperors

Julio-Claudians

27 B.C.E.–14 C.E.	Augustus
14–37	Tiberius
37–41	Gaius (Caligula)
41–54	Claudius
54–68	Nero

Flavian Dynasty

69–79	Vespasian
79–81	Titus
81–96	Domitian

Golden Age Emperors

96–98	Nerva
98–117	Trajan
117–138	Hadrian
138–161	Antoninus Pius
161–180	Marcus Aurelius

Severan Emperors

193–211	Septimius Severus
211–217	Antoninus (Caracalla)
217–218	Macrinus
222–235	Severus Alexander

Period of Instability

235–238	Maximinus Thrax
238–244	Gordian III
244–249	Philip the Arab
249–251	Decius
251–253	Trebonianus Gallus
253–260	Valerian
270–275	Aurelian
275–276	Tacitus
276–282	Probus
283–285	Carinus

Dominate

284–305	Diocletian
306	Constantius
306–337	Constantine I
337–340	Constantine II
337–350	Constans I
337–361	Constantius II
361–363	Julian
363–364	Jovian
364–375	Valentinian I
364–378	Valens
367–383	Gratian
375–392	Valentinian II
378–395	Theodosius I (the Great)

The Western Empire

395–423	Honorius
406–407	Marcus
407–411	Constantine III
409–411	Maximus
411–413	Jovinus
412–413	Sebastianus
423–425	Johannes
425–455	Valentinian III
455–456	Avitus
457–461	Majorian
461–465	Libius Severus
467–472	Anthemius
473–474	Glycerius
474–475	Julius Nepos
475–476	Romulus Augustulus

Prominent Byzantine Emperors

Dynasty of Theodosius

395–408	Arcadius
408–450	Theodosius II
450–457	Marcian

Dynasty of Leo

457–474	Leo I
474	Leo II
474–491	Zeno
475–476	Basiliscus
484–488	Leontius
491–518	Anastasius

Dynasty of Justinian

518–527	Justin
527–565	Justinian I
565–578	Justin II
578–582	Tiberius II
578–582	Tiberius II (I) Constantine
582–602	Maurice
602–610	Phocas

Dynasty of Heraclius

610–641	Heraclius
641	Heraclonas
641	Constantine III
641–668	Constans II
646–647	Gregory
649–653	Olympius
669	Mezezius
668–685	Constantine IV
685–695	Justinian II (banished)
695–698	Leontius
698–705	Tiberius III (II)
705–711	Justinian II (restored)
711–713	Bardanes
713–716	Anastasius II
716–717	Theodosius III

Isaurian Dynasty

717–741	Leo III
741–775	Constantine V Copronymus
775–780	Leo IV
780–797	Constantine VI
797–802	Irene
802–811	Nicephorus I
811	Strauracius
811–813	Michael I
813–820	Leo V

Phrygian Dynasty

820–829	Michael II
821–823	Thomas
829–842	Theophilus
842–867	Michael III

Macedonian Dynasty

867–886	Basil I
869–879	Constantine
887–912	Leo VI
912–913	Alexander
913–959	Constantine VII Porphrogenitos
920–944	Romanus I Lecapenus
921–931	Christopher
924–945	Stephen
959–963	Romanus II
963–969	Nicephorus II Phocas
976–1025	Basil II
1025–1028	Constantine VIII (IX) alone
1028–1034	Romanus III Argyrus
1034–1041	Michael IV the Paphlagonian
1041–1042	Michael V Calaphates
1042	Zoe and Theodora
1042–1055	Constantine IX Monomachus
1055–1056	Theodora alone
1056–1057	Michael VI Stratioticus

Prelude to the Comnenian Dynasty

1057–1059	Isaac I Comnenos
1059–1067	Constantine X (IX) Ducas
1068–1071	Romanus IV Diogenes
1071–1078	Michael VII Ducas
1078–1081	Nicephorus III Botaniates
1080–1081	Nicephorus Melissenus

Comnenian Dynasty

1081–1118	Alexius I
1118–1143	John II
1143–1180	Manuel I
1180–1183	Alexius II
1183–1185	Andronieus I
1183–1191	Isaac, Emperor of Cyprus

Dynasty of the Angeli

1185–1195	Isaac II
1195–1203	Alexius III
1203–1204	Isaac II (restored) with Alexius IV
1204	Alexius V Ducas Murtzuphlus

Lascarid Dynasty in Nicaea

1204–1222	Theodore I Lascaris
1222–1254	John III Ducas Vatatzes
1254–1258	Theodore II Lascaris
1258–1261	John IV Lascaris

Dynasty of the Paleologi

1259–1289	Michael VIII Paleologus
1282–1328	Andronicus II
1328–1341	Andronicus III
1341–1391	John V
1347–1354	John VI Cantancuzenus
1376–1379	Andronicus IV
1379–1391	John V (restored)
1390	John VII
1391–1425	Manuel II
1425–1448	John VIII
1449–1453	Constantine XI (XIII) Dragases

Prominent Popes

314–335	Sylvester
440–461	Leo I
590–604	Gregory I (the Great)
687–701	Sergius I
741–752	Zachary
858–867	Nicholas I
1049–1054	Leo IX
1059–1061	Nicholas II
1073–1085	Gregory VII
1088–1099	Urban II
1099–1118	Paschal II
1159–1181	Alexander III
1198–1216	Innocent III
1227–1241	Gregory IX
1243–1254	Innocent IV
1294–1303	Boniface VIII
1316–1334	John XXII
1447–1455	Nicholas V
1458–1464	Pius II
1492–1503	Alexander VI
1503–1513	Julius II
1513–1521	Leo X
1534–1549	Paul III
1555–1559	Paul IV
1585–1590	Sixtus V
1623–1644	Urban VIII
1831–1846	Gregory XVI
1846–1878	Pius IX
1878–1903	Leo XIII
1903–1914	Pius X
1914–1922	Benedict XV
1922–1939	Pius XI
1939–1958	Pius XII
1958–1963	John XXIII
1963–1978	Paul VI
1978	John Paul I
1978–2005	John Paul II
2005–	Benedict XVI

The Carolingian Dynasty

687–714	Pepin of Heristal, Mayor of the Palace
715–741	Charles Martel, Mayor of the Palace
741–751	Pepin III, Mayor of the Palace
751–768	Pepin III, King
768–814	Charlemagne, King
800–814	Charlemagne, Emperor
814–840	Louis the Pious

West Francia

840–877	Charles the Bald, King
875–877	Charles the Bald, Emperor
877–879	Louis II, King
879–882	Louis III, King
879–884	Carloman, King

Middle Kingdoms

840–855	Lothair, Emperor
855–875	Louis (Italy), Emperor
855–863	Charles (Provence), King
855–869	Lothair II (Lorraine), King

East Francia

840–876	Ludwig, King
876–880	Carloman, King
876–882	Ludwig, King
876–887	Charles the Fat, Emperor

German Kings Crowned Emperor

Saxon Dynasty

962–973	Otto I
973–983	Otto II
983–1002	Otto III
1002–1024	Henry II

Franconian Dynasty

1024–1039	Conrad II
1039–1056	Henry III
1056–1106	Henry IV
1106–1125	Henry V
1125–1137	Lothair II (Saxony)

Hohenstaufen Dynasty

1138–1152	Conrad III
1152–1190	Frederick I (Barbarossa)
1190–1197	Henry VI
1198–1208	Philip of Swabia
1198–1215	Otto IV (Welf)
1220–1250	Frederick II
1250–1254	Conrad IV

Interregnum, 1254–1273: Emperors from Various Dynasties

1273–1291	Rudolf I (Habsburg)
1292–1298	Adolf (Nassau)
1298–1308	Albert I (Habsburg)
1308–1313	Henry VII (Luxemburg)
1314–1347	Ludwig IV (Wittelsbach)
1347–1378	Charles IV (Luxemburg)
1378–1400	Wenceslas (Luxemburg)
1400–1410	Rupert (Wittelsbach)
1410–1437	Sigismund (Luxemburg)

Habsburg Dynasty

1438–1439	Albert II
1440–1493	Frederick III
1493–1519	Maximilian I
1519–1556	Charles V
1556–1564	Ferdinand I
1564–1576	Maximilian II
1576–1612	Rudolf II
1612–1619	Matthias
1619–1637	Ferdinand II
1637–1657	Ferdinand III
1658–1705	Leopold I
1705–1711	Joseph I
1711–1740	Charles VI
1742–1745	Charles VII (not a Habsburg)
1745–1765	Francis I
1765–1790	Joseph II
1790–1792	Leopold II
1792–1806	Francis II

Rulers of France

Capetian Dynasty

987–996	Hugh Capet
996–1031	Robert II
1031–1060	Henry I
1060–1108	Philip I
1108–1137	Louis VI
1137–1180	Louis VII
1180–1223	Philip II (Augustus)
1223–1226	Louis VIII
1226–1270	Louis IX (St. Louis)
1270–1285	Philip III
1285–1314	Philip IV
1314–1316	Louis X
1316–1322	Philip V
1322–1328	Charles IV

Valois Dynasty

1328–1350	Philip VI
1350–1364	John
1364–1380	Charles V
1380–1422	Charles VI
1422–1461	Charles VII
1461–1483	Louis XI
1483–1498	Charles VIII
1498–1515	Louis XII
1515–1547	Francis I
1547–1559	Henry II
1559–1560	Francis II
1560–1574	Charles IX
1574–1589	Henry III

Bourbon Dynasty

1589–1610	Henry IV
1610–1643	Louis XIII
1643–1715	Louis XIV
1715–1774	Louis XV
1774–1792	Louis XVI

After 1792

1792–1799	First Republic
1799–1804	Napoleon Bonaparte, First Consul
1804–1814	Napoleon I, Emperor
1814–1824	Louis XVIII (Bourbon Dynasty)
1824–1830	Charles X (Bourbon Dynasty)
1830–1848	Louis Philippe
1848–1852	Second Republic
1852–1870	Napoleon III, Emperor
1870–1940	Third Republic
1940–1944	Vichy government, Pétain regime
1944–1946	Provisional government
1946–1958	Fourth Republic
1958–	Fifth Republic

Monarchs of England and Great Britain

Anglo-Saxon Monarchs

829–839	Egbert
839–858	Ethelwulf
858–860	Ethelbald
860–866	Ethelbert
866–871	Ethelred I
871–899	Alfred the Great
899–924	Edward the Elder
924–939	Ethelstan
939–946	Edmund I
946–955	Edred
955–959	Edwy
959–975	Edgar
975–978	Edward the Martyr
978–1016	Ethelred the Unready
1016–1035	Canute (Danish nationality)
1035–1040	Harold I
1040–1042	Hardicanute
1042–1066	Edward the Confessor
1066	Harold II

Norman Monarchs

1066–1087	William I (the Conqueror)
1087–1100	William II
1100–1135	Henry I

House of Blois

1135–1154	Stephen

House of Plantagenet

1154–1189	Henry II
1189–1199	Richard I
1199–1216	John
1216–1272	Henry III
1272–1307	Edward I
1307–1327	Edward II
1327–1377	Edward III
1377–1399	Richard II

House of Lancaster

1399–1413	Henry IV
1413–1422	Henry V
1422–1461	Henry VI

House of York

1461–1483	Edward IV
1483	Edward V
1483–1485	Richard III

House of Tudor

1485–1509	Henry VII
1509–1547	Henry VIII
1547–1553	Edward VI
1553–1558	Mary
1558–1603	Elizabeth I

House of Stuart

1603–1625	James I
1625–1649	Charles I

Commonwealth and Protectorate (1649–1660)

1653–1658	Oliver Cromwell
1658–1659	Richard Cromwell

House of Stuart (Restored)

1660–1685	Charles II
1685–1688	James II
1689–1694	William III and Mary II
1694–1702	William III (alone)
1702–1714	Anne

House of Hanover

1714–1727	George I
1727–1760	George II
1760–1820	George III
1820–1830	George IV
1830–1837	William IV
1837–1901	Victoria

House of Saxe-Coburg-Gotha

1901–1910	Edward VII

House of Windsor

1910–1936	George V
1936	Edward VIII
1936–1952	George VI
1952–	Elizabeth II

Prime Ministers of Great Britain

Term	Prime Minister	Government
1721–1742	Sir Robert Walpole	Whig
1742–1743	Spencer Compton, Earl of Wilmington	Whig
1743–1754	Henry Pelham	Whig
1754–1756	Thomas Pelham-Holles, Duke of Newcastle	Whig
1756–1757	William Cavendish, Duke of Devonshire	Whig
1757–1761	William Pitt (the Elder), Earl of Chatham	Whig
1761–1762	Thomas Pelham-Holles, Duke of Newcastle	Whig
1762–1763	John Stuart, Earl of Bute	Tory
1763–1765	George Grenville	Whig
1765–1766	Charles Watson-Wentworth, Marquess of Rockingham	Whig
1766–1768	William Pitt, Earl of Chatham (the Elder)	Whig
1768–1770	Augustus Henry Fitzroy, Duke of Grafton	Whig
1770–1782	Frederick North (Lord North)	Tory
1782	Charles Watson-Wentworth, Marquess of Rockingham	Whig
1782–1783	William Petty FitzMaurice, Earl of Shelburn	Whig
1783	William Henry Cavendish Bentinck, Duke of Portland	Whig
1783–1801	William Pitt (the Younger)	Tory
1801–1804	Henry Addington	Tory
1804–1806	William Pitt (the Younger)	Tory
1806–1807	William Wyndham Grenville (Baron Grenville)	Whig
1807–1809	William Henry Cavendish Bentinck, Duke of Portland	Tory
1809–1812	Spencer Perceval	Tory
1812–1827	Robert Banks Jenkinson, Earl of Liverpool	Tory
1827	George Canning	Tory
1827–1828	Frederick John Robinson (Viscount Goderich)	Tory
1828–1830	Arthur Wellesley, Duke of Wellington	Tory
1830–1834	Charles Grey (Earl Grey)	Whig
1834	William Lamb, Viscount Melbourne	Whig
1834–1835	Sir Robert Peel	Tory
1835–1841	William Lamb, Viscount Melbourne	Whig
1841–1846	Sir Robert Peel	Tory
1846–1852	John Russell (Lord)	Whig
1852	Edward Geoffrey–Smith Stanley Derby, Earl of Derby	Whig
1852–1855	George Hamilton Gordon Aberdeen, Earl of Aberdeen	Peelite
1855–1858	Henry John Temple Palmerston, Viscount Palmerston	Tory
1858–1859	Edward Geoffrey–Smith Stanley Derby, Earl of Derby	Whig
1859–1865	Henry John Temple Palmerston, Viscount Palmerston	Tory
1865–1866	John Russell (Earl)	Liberal
1866–1868	Edward Geoffrey–Smith Stanley Derby, Earl of Derby	Tory
1868	Benjamin Disraeli, Earl of Beaconfield	Conservative
1868–1874	William Ewart Gladstone	Liberal
1874–1880	Benjamin Disraeli, Earl of Beaconfield	Conservative
1880–1885	William Ewart Gladstone	Liberal
1885–1886	Robert Arthur Talbot, Marquess of Salisbury	Conservative
1886	William Ewart Gladstone	Liberal
1886–1892	Robert Arthur Talbot, Marquess of Salisbury	Conservative
1892–1894	William Ewart Gladstone	Liberal
1894–1895	Archibald Philip–Primrose Rosebery, Earl of Rosebery	Liberal
1895–1902	Robert Arthur Talbot, Marquess of Salisbury	Conservative
1902–1905	Arthur James Balfour, Earl of Balfour	Conservative
1905–1908	Sir Henry Campbell-Bannerman	Liberal
1908–1915	Herbert Henry Asquith	Liberal
1915–1916	Herbert Henry Asquith	Coalition
1916–1922	David Lloyd George, Earl Lloyd-George of Dwyfor	Coalition
1922–1923	Andrew Bonar Law	Conservative
1923–1924	Stanley Baldwin, Earl Baldwin of Bewdley	Conservative
1924	James Ramsay MacDonald	Labour
1924–1929	Stanley Baldwin, Earl Baldwin of Bewdley	Conservative
1929–1931	James Ramsay MacDonald	Labour
1931–1935	James Ramsay MacDonald	Coalition
1935–1937	Stanley Baldwin, Earl Baldwin of Bewdley	Coalition
1937–1940	Neville Chamberlain	Coalition
1940–1945	Winston Churchill	Coalition
1945	Winston Churchill	Conservative
1945–1951	Clement Attlee, Earl Attlee	Labour
1951–1955	Sir Winston Churchill	Conservative
1955–1957	Sir Anthony Eden, Earl of Avon	Conservative
1957–1963	Harold Macmillan, Earl of Stockton	Conservative
1963–1964	Sir Alec Frederick Douglas-Home, Lord Home of the Hirsel	Conservative
1964–1970	Harold Wilson, Lord Wilson of Rievaulx	Labour
1970–1974	Edward Heath	Conservative
1974–1976	Harold Wilson, Lord Wilson of Rievaulx	Labour
1976–1979	James Callaghan, Lord Callaghan of Cardiff	Labour
1979–1990	Margaret Thatcher (Baroness)	Conservative
1990–1997	John Major	Conservative
1997–2007	Tony Blair	Labour
2007–2010	Gordon Brown	Labour
2010–	David Cameron	Conservative

Rulers of Prussia and Germany

1701–1713	*Frederick I
1713–1740	*Frederick William I
1740–1786	*Frederick II (the Great)
1786–1797	*Frederick William II
1797–1840	*Frederick William III
1840–1861	*Frederick William IV
1861–1888	*William I (German emperor after 1871)
1888	Frederick III
1888–1918	*William II
1918–1933	Weimar Republic
1933–1945	Third Reich (Nazi dictatorship under Adolf Hitler)
1945–1952	Allied occupation
1949–1990	Division of Federal Republic of Germany in west and German Democratic Republic in east
1990–	Federal Republic of Germany (reunited)

*King of Prussia.

Rulers of Austria and Austria-Hungary

1493–1519	*Maximilian I (Archduke)
1519–1556	*Charles V
1556–1564	*Ferdinand I
1564–1576	*Maximilian II
1576–1612	*Rudolf II
1612–1619	*Matthias
1619–1637	*Ferdinand II
1637–1657	*Ferdinand III
1658–1705	*Leopold I
1705–1711	*Joseph I
1711–1740	*Charles VI
1740–1780	Maria Theresa
1780–1790	*Joseph II
1790–1792	*Leopold II
1792–1835	*Francis II (emperor of Austria as Francis I after 1804)
1835–1848	Ferdinand I
1848–1916	Francis Joseph (after 1867 emperor of Austria and king of Hungary)
1916–1918	Charles I (emperor of Austria and king of Hungary)
1918–1938	Republic of Austria (dictatorship after 1934)
1945–1956	Republic restored, under Allied occupation
1956–	Free Republic

*Also bore title of Holy Roman Emperor.

Leaders of Post–World War II Germany

West Germany (Federal Republic of Germany), 1949–1990

Years	*Chancellor*	*Party*
1949–1963	Konrad Adenauer	Christian Democratic Union (CDU)
1963–1966	Ludwig Erhard	Christian Democratic Union (CDU)
1966–1969	Kurt Georg Kiesinger	Christian Democratic Union (CDU)
1969–1974	Willy Brandt	Social Democratic Party (SPD)
1974–1982	Helmut Schmidt	Social Democratic Party (SPD)
1982–1990	Helmut Kohl	Christian Democratic Union (CDU)

East Germany (German Democratic Republic), 1949–1990

Years	*Communist Party Leader*
1946–1971	Walter Ulbricht
1971–1989	Erich Honecker
1989–1990	Egon Krenz

Federal Republic of Germany (reunited), 1990–

Years	*Chancellor*	*Party*
1990–1998	Helmut Kohl	Christian Democratic Union (CDU)
1998–2005	Gerhard Schroeder	Social Democratic Party (SPD)
2005–	Angela Merkel	Christian Democratic Union (CDU)

Rulers of Russia, the USSR, and the Russian Federation

c. 980–1015	Vladimir
1019–1054	Yaroslav the Wise
1176–1212	Vsevolod III
1462–1505	Ivan III
1505–1553	Vasily III
1553–1584	Ivan IV
1584–1598	Theodore I
1598–1605	Boris Godunov
1605	Theodore II
1606–1610	Vasily IV
1613–1645	Michael
1645–1676	Alexius
1676–1682	Theodore III
1682–1689	Ivan V and Peter I
1689–1725	Peter I (the Great)
1725–1727	Catherine I
1727–1730	Peter II
1730–1740	Anna
1740–1741	Ivan VI
1741–1762	Elizabeth
1762	Peter III
1762–1796	Catherine II (the Great)
1796–1801	Paul
1801–1825	Alexander I
1825–1855	Nicholas I
1855–1881	Alexander II
1881–1894	Alexander III
1894–1917	Nicholas II

Union of Soviet Socialist Republics (USSR)*

1917–1924	Vladimir Ilyich Lenin
1924–1953	Joseph Stalin
1953–1964	Nikita Khrushchev
1964–1982	Leonid Brezhnev
1982–1984	Yuri Andropov
1984–1985	Konstantin Chernenko
1985–1991	Mikhail Gorbachev

Russian Federation

1991–1999	Boris Yeltsin
1999–2008	Vladimir Putin
2008–	Dmitry Medvedev

*USSR established in 1922.

Rulers of Spain

1479–1504	Ferdinand and Isabella
1504–1506	Ferdinand and Philip I
1506–1516	Ferdinand and Charles I
1516–1556	Charles I (Holy Roman Emperor Charles V)
1556–1598	Philip II
1598–1621	Philip III
1621–1665	Philip IV
1665–1700	Charles II
1700–1746	Philip V
1746–1759	Ferdinand VI
1759–1788	Charles III
1788–1808	Charles IV
1808	Ferdinand VII
1808–1813	Joseph Bonaparte
1814–1833	Ferdinand VII (restored)
1833–1868	Isabella II
1868–1870	Republic
1870–1873	Amadeo
1873–1874	Republic
1874–1885	Alfonso XII
1886–1931	Alfonso XIII
1931–1939	Republic
1939–1975	Fascist dictatorship under Francisco Franco
1975–	Juan Carlos I

Rulers of Italy

1861–1878	Victor Emmanuel II
1878–1900	Humbert I
1900–1946	Victor Emmanuel III
1922–1943	Fascist dictatorship under Benito Mussolini (maintained in northern Italy until 1945)
1946 (May 9–June 13)	Humbert II
1946–	Republic

Secretaries-General of the United Nations

Years	Secretary-General	Nationality
1946–1952	Trygve Lie	Norway
1953–1961	Dag Hammarskjöld	Sweden
1961–1971	U Thant	Myanmar
1972–1981	Kurt Waldheim	Austria
1982–1991	Javier Pérez de Cuéllar	Peru
1992–1996	Boutros Boutros-Ghali	Egypt
1997–2006	Kofi A. Annan	Ghana
2007–	Ban Kimoon	South Korea

United States Presidential Administrations

Term(s)	President	Political Party
1789–1797	George Washington	No party designation
1797–1801	John Adams	Federalist
1801–1809	Thomas Jefferson	Democratic-Republican
1809–1817	James Madison	Democratic-Republican
1817–1825	James Monroe	Democratic-Republican
1825–1829	John Quincy Adams	Democratic-Republican
1829–1837	Andrew Jackson	Democratic
1837–1841	Martin Van Buren	Democratic
1841	William H. Harrison	Whig
1841–1845	John Tyler	Whig
1845–1849	James K. Polk	Democratic
1849–1850	Zachary Taylor	Whig
1850–1853	Millard Filmore	Whig
1853–1857	Franklin Pierce	Democratic
1857–1861	James Buchanan	Democratic
1861–1865	Abraham Lincoln	Republican
1865–1869	Andrew Johnson	Republican
1869–1877	Ulysses S. Grant	Republican
1877–1881	Rutherford B. Hayes	Republican
1881	James A. Garfield	Republican
1881–1885	Chester A. Arthur	Republican
1885–1889	Grover Cleveland	Democratic
1889–1893	Benjamin Harrison	Republican
1893–1897	Grover Cleveland	Democratic
1897–1901	William McKinley	Republican
1901–1909	Theodore Roosevelt	Republican
1909–1913	William H. Taft	Republican
1913–1921	Woodrow Wilson	Democratic
1921–1923	Warren G. Harding	Republican
1923–1929	Calvin Coolidge	Republican
1929–1933	Herbert C. Hoover	Republican
1933–1945	Franklin D. Roosevelt	Democratic
1945–1953	Harry S. Truman	Democratic
1953–1961	Dwight D. Eisenhower	Republican
1961–1963	John F. Kennedy	Democratic
1963–1969	Lyndon B. Johnson	Democratic
1969–1974	Richard M. Nixon	Republican
1974–1977	Gerald R. Ford	Republican
1977–1981	Jimmy Carter	Democratic
1981–1989	Ronald W. Reagan	Republican
1989–1993	George H. W. Bush	Republican
1993–2001	William J. Clinton	Democratic
2001–2009	George W. Bush	Republican
2009–	Barack Obama	Democratic

Major Wars of the Modern Era

1546–1555	German Wars of Religion
1526–1571	Ottoman wars
1562–1598	French Wars of Religion
1566–1609, 1621–1648	Revolt of the Netherlands
1618–1648	Thirty Years' War
1642–1648	English Civil War
1652–1678	Anglo-Dutch Wars
1667–1697	Wars of Louis XIV
1683–1697	Ottoman wars
1689–1697	War of the League of Augsburg
1702–1714	War of Spanish Succession
1702–1721	Great Northern War
1714–1718	Ottoman wars
1740–1748	War of Austrian Succession
1756–1763	Seven Years' War
1775–1781	American Revolution
1796–1815	Napoleonic wars
1846–1848	Mexican-American War
1853–1856	Crimean War
1861–1865	United States Civil War
1870–1871	Franco-Prussian War
1894–1895	Sino-Japanese War
1898	Spanish-American War
1904–1905	Russo-Japanese War
1914–1918	World War I
1939–1945	World War II
1946–1975	Vietnam wars
1950–1953	Korean War
1990–1991	Persian Gulf War
1991–1997	Civil War in the former Yugoslavia
2001–	War in Afghanistan
2003–	Iraq War

Glossary of Key Terms and People

This glossary contains definitions of terms and people that are central to your understanding of the material covered in this textbook. Each term or person in the glossary is in boldface in the text when it is first defined, then listed again in the corresponding Chapter Review section to signal its importance. We have also included the page number on which the full discussion of the term or person appears so that you can easily locate the complete explanation to strengthen your historical vocabulary.

For words or names not defined here, two additional resources may be useful: the index, which will direct you to many more topics discussed in the text, and a good dictionary.

Abbasids (283): The dynasty of caliphs that, in 750, took over from the Umayyads in all of the Islamic realm except for Spain (al-Andalus). From their new capital at Baghdad, they presided over a wealthy realm until the late ninth century.

abolitionists (592): Advocates of the abolition of the slave trade and of slavery.

absolutism (515): A system of government in which the ruler claims sole and uncontestable power.

agora (83): The central market square of a Greek city-state, a popular gathering place for conversation.

agricultural revolution (562): Increasingly aggressive attitudes toward investment in and management of land that increased production of food in the 1700s.

Alexander II (725): Russian tsar (r. 1855–1881) who initiated the age of Great Reforms and emancipated the serfs in 1861.

Alexander the Great (116): The fourth-century B.C.E. Macedonian king whose conquest of the Persian Empire led to the greatly increased cultural interactions of Greece and the Near East in the Hellenistic Age.

Alexius I (Alexius Comnenus) (330): The Byzantine emperor (r. 1081–1118) whose leadership marked a new triumph of the *dynatoi*. His request to Pope Urban II for troops to fight the Turks turned into the First Crusade.

Alfred the Great (303): King of Wessex (r. 871–899) and the first king to rule over most of England. He organized a successful defense against Viking invaders, had key Latin works translated into the vernacular, and wrote a law code for the whole of England.

Anabaptists (468): Sixteenth-century Protestants who believed that only adults could truly have faith and accept baptism.

anarchism (746): The belief that people should not have government; it was popular among some peasants and workers in the last half of the nineteenth century and the first decades of the twentieth.

Anatolia (7): The large peninsula that is today the nation of Turkey.

apostolic succession (193): The principle by which Christian bishops traced their authority back to the apostles of Jesus.

appeasement (894): Making concessions in the face of grievances as a way of preventing conflict.

apprentices (316): Boys (and occasionally girls) placed under the tutelage of a master craftsman in the Middle Ages. Normally unpaid, they were expected to be servants of their masters, with whom they lived, at the same time as they were learning their trade.

aretê (49): The Greek value of competitive individual excellence.

Arianism (219): The Christian doctrine named after Arius, who argued that Jesus was "begotten" by God and did not have an identical nature with God the Father.

Aristotle (114): Greek philosopher famous for his scientific investigations, development of logical argument, and practical ethics.

art nouveau (809): An early-twentieth-century artistic style in graphics, fashion, and household design that featured flowing, sinuous lines, borrowed in large part from Asian art.

asceticism (222): The practice of self-denial, especially through spiritual discipline; a doctrine for Christians emphasized by Augustine.

Atlantic system (551): The network of trade established in the 1700s that bound together western Europe, Africa, and the Americas. Europeans sold slaves from western Africa and bought commodities that were produced by the new colonial plantations in North and South America and the Caribbean.

Augustine (218): Bishop in North Africa whose writings defining religious orthodoxy made him the most influential theologian in Western civilization.

Augustus (173): The honorary name meaning "divinely favored" that the Roman Senate bestowed on Octavian; it became shorthand for "Roman imperial ruler."

Avignon papacy (401): The period (1309–1378) during which the popes ruled from Avignon rather than from Rome.

baroque (508): An artistic style of the seventeenth century that featured curves, exaggerated lighting, intense emotions, release from restraint, and even a kind of artistic sensationalism.

Basil II (281): The Byzantine emperor (r. 976–1025) who presided over the end of the Bulgar threat (earning the name Bulgar-Slayer) and the conversion of Kievan Russia to Christianity.

battle of Hastings (336): The battle of 1066 that replaced the Anglo-Saxon king with a Norman one and thus tied England to the rest of Europe as never before.

battle of Waterloo (665): The final battle lost by Napoleon; it took place near Brussels on June 18, 1815, and led to the deposed emperor's final exile.

Beauvoir, Simone de (938): Author of *The Second Sex* (1949), a globally influential work that created an interpretation of women's age-old inferior status from existentialist philosophy.

Beethoven, Ludwig van (674): The German composer (1770–1827) who helped set the direction of musical romanticism; his music used recurring and evolving themes to convey the impression of natural growth.

bin Laden, Osama (1003): Wealthy leader of the militant Islamic group al-Qaeda, which executed terrorist plots, including the September 11, 2001, attacks on the United States, to end the presence of U.S. forces in his home country, Saudia Arabia.

Bismarck, Otto von (732): 1815–1898. Leading Prussian politician and German chancellor who waged war in order to create a united German Empire, which was established in 1871.

Black Death (412): The term historians give to the disease that swept through Europe in 1347–1352.

Blitzkrieg (896): Literally, "lightning war"; a strategy for the conduct of war (used by the Germans in World War II) in which motorized firepower quickly and overwhelmingly attacks the enemy, leaving it unable to resist psychologically or militarily.

blood libel (388): The charge that Jews used the blood of Christian children in their Passover ritual; though false, it led to massacres of Jews in cities in England, France, Spain, and Germany in the thirteenth century.

Bolívar, Simón (677): 1783–1830. The Venezuelan-born, European-educated aristocrat who became one of the leaders of the Latin American independence movement in the 1820s. Bolivia is named after him.

Bolshevik Revolution (848): The overthrow of Russia's Provisional Government in the fall of 1917 by V. I. Lenin and his Bolshevik forces.

Bonaparte, Louis-Napoleon (711): 1808–1873. Nephew of Napoleon I; he was elected president of France in 1848, declared himself Emperor Napoleon III in 1852, and ruled until 1870.

Bonaparte, Napoleon (652): The French general who became First Consul in 1799 and emperor (Napoleon I) in 1804; after losing the battle of Waterloo in 1815, he was exiled to the island of St. Helena.

Boniface VIII (400): The pope (r. 1294–1303) whose clash with King Philip the Fair of France left the papacy considerably weakened.

buccaneers (558): Pirates of the Caribbean who governed themselves and preyed on international shipping.

bureaucracy (521): A network of state officials carrying out orders according to a regular and routine line of authority.

Calvin, John (463): French-born Christian humanist (1509–1564) and founder of Calvinism, one of the major branches of the Protestant Reformation; he led the reform movement in Geneva, Switzerland, from 1541 to 1564.

Capetian dynasty (304): A long-lasting dynasty of French kings, taking their name from Hugh Capet (r. 987–996).

capital-intensive industry (772): A mid- to late-nineteenth-century development in industry that required great investments of money for machinery and infrastructure to make a profit.

capitalism (317): The modern economic system characterized by an entrepreneurial class of property owners who employ others and produce (or provide services) for a market in order to make a profit.

Carolingian (287): The Frankish dynasty that ruled a western European empire from 751 to the late 800s; its greatest vigor was in the time of Charlemagne (r. 768–814) and Louis the Pious (r. 814–840).

castellan (300): The holder of a castle. In the tenth and eleventh centuries, castellans became important local lords. They mustered men for military service, collected taxes, and administered justice.

Catherine de Médicis (485): Italian-born mother of French king Charles IX (r. 1560–1574); she served as regent and tried but failed to prevent religious warfare between Calvinists and Catholics.

Cavour, Camillo di (730): Prime minister (1852–1861) of the kingdom of Piedmont-Sardinia and architect of a united Italy.

chansons de geste (368): Epic poems of the twelfth century about knightly and heroic deeds.

Chaplin, Charlie (888): 1899–1977. Major entertainment leader, whose sympathetic portrayals of the common man and satires of Hitler helped preserve democratic values in the 1930s and 1940s.

Charlemagne (287): The Carolingian king (r. 768–814) whose conquests greatly expanded the Frankish kingdom. He was crowned emperor on December 25, 800.

Charles V (461): Holy Roman Emperor (r. 1519–1556) and the most powerful ruler in sixteenth-century Europe; he reigned over the Low Countries, Spain, Spain's Italian and New World dominions, and the Austrian Habsburg lands.

Chartism (708): The British movement of supporters of the People's Charter (1838), which demanded universal manhood suffrage, vote by secret ballot, equal electoral districts, and other reforms.

chivalry (369): An ideal of knightly comportment that included military prowess, bravery, fair play, piety, and courtesy.

Christ (190): Greek for "anointed one," in Hebrew *Mashiach* or in English *Messiah*; in apocalyptic thought, God's agent sent to conquer the forces of evil.

Christian Democrats (924): Powerful center to center-right political parties that evolved in the late 1940s from former Catholic parties of the pre–World War II period.

Christian humanism (459): A general intellectual trend in the sixteenth century that coupled love of classical learning, as in Renaissance humanism, with an emphasis on Christian piety.

Cicero (156): Rome's most famous orator and author of the doctrine of *humanitas*.

city-state (8): An urban center exercising political and economic control over the surrounding countryside.

Civil Code (657): The French legal code formulated by Napoleon in 1804; it ensured equal treatment under the law to all men and guaranteed religious liberty, but it curtailed many rights of women.

civil disobedience (877): The act of deliberately but peacefully breaking the law, a tactic used by Mohandas Gandhi in India and earlier by British suffragists to protest oppression and obtain political change.

civilization (4): A way of life based in cities with dense populations organized as political states, large buildings constructed for communal activities, the production of food, diverse economies, a sense of local identity, and some knowledge of writing.

classicism (541): A seventeenth-century style of painting and architecture that reflected the ideals of the art of antiquity; in classicism, geometric shapes, order, and harmony of lines took precedence over the sensuous, exuberant, and emotional forms of the baroque.

cold war (914): The rivalry between the United States and the Soviet Union from 1945 to 1989 that led to massive growth in nuclear weapons on both sides.

coloni (212): Literally, "cultivators"; tenant farmers in the Roman Empire who became bound by law to the land they worked and whose children were legally required to continue to farm the same land.

Colosseum (183): Rome's fifty-thousand-seat amphitheater built by the Flavian dynasty for gladiatorial combats and other spectacles.

Columbus, Christopher (453): An Italian sailor (1451–1506) who opened up the New World by sailing west across the Atlantic in search of a route to Asia.

commercial revolution (312): A term for the western European development (starting around 1050) of a money economy centered in urban areas but affecting the countryside as well.

common law (357): Begun by Henry II (r. 1154–1189), the English royal law carried out by the king's justices in eyre (traveling justices). It applied to the entire kingdom and thus was "common" to all.

commune (318): In a medieval town, a sworn association of citizens who formed a legal corporate body. The commune appointed or elected officials, made laws, kept the peace, and administered justice.

communists (707): Those socialists who after 1840 (when the word was first used) advocated the abolition of private property in favor of communal, collective ownership.

Concordat of Worms (322): The agreement between pope and emperor in 1122 that ended the Investiture Conflict.

Congress of Vienna (667): Face-to-face negotiations (1814–1815) between the great powers to settle the boundaries of European states and determine who would rule each nation after the defeat of Napoleon.

conservatism (670): A political doctrine that emerged after 1789 and took hold after 1815; it rejected much of the Enlightenment and the French Revolution, preferring monarchies over republics, tradition over revolution, and established religion over Enlightenment skepticism.

constitutionalism (516): A system of government in which rulers share power with parliaments made up of elected representatives.

consumer revolution (560): The rapid increase in consumption of new staples produced in the Atlantic system as well as of other items of daily life that were previously unavailable or beyond the reach of ordinary people.

Continental System (662): The boycott of British goods in France and its satellites ordered by Napoleon in 1806; it had success but was later undermined by smuggling.

Corn Laws (705): Tariffs on grain in Great Britain that benefited landowners by preventing the import of cheap foreign grain; they were repealed by the British government in 1846.

cortes (399): The earliest European representative institution, called initially to consent to royal wishes; first convoked in 1188 by the king of Castile-León.

Cortés, Hernán (457): The Spanish explorer (1485–1547) who captured the Aztec capital, Tenochtitlán (present-day Mexico City), in 1519.

Council of Trent (470): A general council of the Catholic church that met at Trent between 1545 and 1563 to set Catholic doctrine, reform church practices, and defend the church against the Protestant challenge.

Cuban missile crisis (944): The confrontation in 1962 between the United States and the USSR over Soviet installation of missile sites off the U.S. coast in Cuba.

cult (57): In ancient Greece, a set of official, publicly funded religious activities for a deity overseen by priests and priestesses.

cult of the offensive (838): A military strategy of constantly attacking the enemy that was believed to be the key to winning World War I but that brought great loss of life while failing to bring decisive victory.

cuneiform (11): The earliest form of writing, invented in Mesopotamia and done with wedge-shaped characters.

curials (212): The social elite in Roman empires' cities and towns, most of whom were obliged to serve as decurions on municipal Senates and collect taxes for the imperial government, paying any shortfalls themselves.

Cyrus (41): Founder of the Persian Empire.

Darwin, Charles (752): The English naturalist (1809–1882) who popularized the theory of evolution by means of natural selection and thereby challenged the biblical story of creation.

debasement of coinage (198): Putting less silver in a coin without changing its face value, a failed financial strategy during the third-century C.E. crisis in Rome.

de-Christianization (634): During the French Revolution, the campaign of extremist republicans against organized churches and in favor of a belief system based on reason.

Declaration of the Rights of Man and Citizen (626): The preamble to the French constitution drafted in August 1789; it established the sovereignty of the nation and equal rights for citizens.

decolonization (930): The process — whether violent or peaceful — by which colonies gained their independence from the imperial powers after World War II.

decurions (185): Municipal Senate members in the Roman Empire responsible for collecting local taxes.

deists (626): Those who believe in God but give him no active role in human affairs. Deists of the Enlightenment believed that God had designed the universe and set it in motion but no longer intervened in its functioning.

Delian League (80): The naval alliance led by Athens in the Golden Age that became the basis for the Athenian Empire.

demes (68): The villages and city neighborhoods that formed the constituent political units of Athenian democracy in the late Archaic Age.

demography (P-9): The study of the size, growth, density, distribution, and vital statistics of the human population.

Diaspora (47): The dispersal of the Jewish population from their homeland.

DNA (953): The genetic material that forms the basis of each cell; the discovery of its structure in 1952 revolutionized genetics, molecular biology, and other scientific and medical fields.

domesticity (700): An ideology prevailing in the nineteenth century that women should devote themselves to their families and the home.

dominate (207): The openly authoritarian style of Roman rule from Diocletian (r. 284–305) onward; the word was derived from *dominus* ("master" or "lord") and contrasted with *principate*.

Dual Alliance (790): A defensive alliance between Germany and Austria-Hungary created in 1879 as part of Bismarck's system of alliances to prevent or limit war. It was joined by Italy in 1882 as a third partner and then called the Triple Alliance.

dual monarchy (736): The shared power arrangement between the Habsburg Empire and Hungary after the Prussian defeat of the Austrian Empire in 1866–1867.

dualism (113): The philosophical idea that the human soul (or mind) and body are separate.

Duma (821): The Russian parliament set up in the aftermath of the outbreak of the Revolution of 1905.

dynatoi (280): The "powerful men" who dominated the countryside of the Byzantine Empire in the tenth and eleventh centuries, and to some degree challenged the authority of the emperor.

Edict of Milan (213): The proclamation of Roman co-emperors Constantine and Licinius decreeing free choice of religion in the empire.

Edict of Nantes (486): The decree issued by French king Henry IV in 1598 that granted the Huguenots a large measure of religious toleration.

Einstein, Albert (807): Scientist whose theory of relativity (1905) revolutionized modern physics and other fields of thought.

Eliot, George (748): The pen name of English novelist Mary Ann Evans (1819–1880), who described the harsh reality of many ordinary people's lives in her works.

Elizabeth I (489): English queen (r. 1558–1603) who oversaw the return of the Protestant Church of England and, in 1588, the successful defense of the realm against the Spanish Armada.

empire (12): A political state in which one or more formerly independent territories or peoples are ruled by a single sovereign power.

Enabling Act (884): The legislation passed in 1933 suspending constitutional government for four years in order to meet the crisis in the German economy.

enlightened despots (605): Rulers — such as Catherine the Great of Russia, Frederick the Great of Prussia, and Joseph II of Austria — who tried to promote Enlightenment reforms without giving up their own supreme political power; also called enlightened absolutists.

Enlightenment (576): The eighteenth-century intellectual movement whose proponents believed that human beings could apply a critical, reasoning spirit to every problem.

Entente Cordiale (825): An alliance between Britain and France that began with an agreement in 1904 to honor colonial holdings.

Epicureanism (129): The philosophy founded by Epicurus of Athens to help people achieve a life of true pleasure, by which he meant "absence of disturbance."

epigrams (127): Short poems written by women in the Hellenistic Age; many were about other women and the writer's personal feelings.

equites (159): Literally, "equestrians" or "knights"; wealthy Roman businessmen who chose not to pursue a government career.

Estates General (624): A body of deputies from the three estates, or orders, of France: the clergy (First Estate), the nobility (Second Estate), and everyone else (Third Estate).

ethnic cleansing (988): The mass murder — genocide — of people according to ethnicity or nationality; it can also include eliminating all traces of the murdered people's past. Examples include the post–World War I elimination of minorities in eastern and central Europe and the rape and murders that resulted from the breakup of Yugoslavia in the 1990s.

euro (995): The common currency in seventeen member states of the European Union (EU) and of EU institutions. It went into effect gradually, used first in business transactions in 1999 and entering public circulation in 2002.

European Economic Community (EEC or Common Market) (926): A consortium of six European countries established in 1957 to promote free trade and economic cooperation among its members; its membership and activities expanded over the years, and it later evolved into the European Union (EU).

European Union (EU) (995): Formerly the European Economic Community (EEC, or Common Market), and then the European Community (EC); formed in 1994 by the terms of the Maastricht Treaty. Its members have political ties through the European parliament as well as long-standing common economic, legal, and business mechanisms.

existentialism (937): A philosophy prominent after World War II developed primarily by Jean-Paul Sartre to stress the importance of action in the creation of an authentic self.

family allowance (886): Government funds given to families with children to boost the birthrate in democratic countries (e.g., Sweden during the Great Depression) and totalitarian ones alike.

fascism (867): A doctrine that emphasizes violence and glorifies the state over the people and their individual or civil rights; in Italy, the Fascist Party took hold in the 1920s as Mussolini consolidated power.

Fatimids (284): Members of the tenth-century Shi'ite dynasty who derived their name from Fatimah, the daughter of Muhammad and wife of Ali; they dominated in parts of North Africa, Egypt, and even Syria.

feudalism (297): The whole complex of lords, vassals, and fiefs (from the Latin *feodum*) as an institution. The nature of that institution varied from place to place, and in some regions it did not exist at all.

fiefs (297): Grants of land, theoretically temporary, from lords to their noble dependents (*fideles* or, later, vassals) given in recognition of services, usually military, done or expected in the future; also called *benefices*.

First Consul (653): The most important of the three consuls established by the French Constitution of 1800; the title, given to Napoleon Bonaparte, was taken from ancient Rome.

First Crusade (331): The massive armed pilgrimage to Jerusalem that lasted from 1096 to 1099. It resulted in the massacre of Jews in the Rhineland (1095), the sack of Jerusalem (1099), and the setting up of the crusader states.

First Triumvirate (164): The coalition formed in 60 B.C.E. by Pompey, Crassus, and Caesar. (The word *triumvirate* means "group of three.")

Five Pillars of Islam (247): The five essential practices of Islam, namely, the *zakat* (alms); the fast of Ramadan; the *hajj* (pilgrimage to Mecca); the *salat* (formal worship); and the *shahadah* (profession of faith).

five-year plans (878): Centralized programs for economic development begun in 1929 by Joseph Stalin and copied by Adolf Hitler; these plans set production priorities and gave production targets for individual industries and agriculture.

Fourteen Points (846): U.S. president Woodrow Wilson's World War I peace proposal; based on settlement rather than on conquest, it encouraged the surrender of the Central Powers.

Fourth Crusade (372): The crusade that lasted from 1202 to 1204; its original goal was to recapture Jerusalem, but the crusaders ended up conquering Constantinople instead.

Fourth Lateran Council (383): The council that met in 1215 and covered the important topics of Christianity, among them the nature of the sacraments, the obligations of the laity, and policies toward heretics and Jews.

Franciscans (369): The religious order founded by St. Francis (c. 1182–1226) and dedicated to poverty and preaching, particularly in towns and cities.

Franco, Francisco (893): 1892–1975. Right-wing general who in 1936 successfully overthrew the democratic republic in Spain and instituted a repressive dictatorship.

Frederick I (Barbarossa) (362): King of Germany (r. 1152–1190) and emperor (crowned 1155) who tried to cement the power of the German king through conquest (for example, of northern Italy) and the bonds of vassalage.

Frederick II (397): The grandson of Barbarossa who became king of Sicily and Germany, as well as emperor (r. 1212–1250), who allowed the German princes a free hand as he battled the pope for control of Italy.

Frederick William of Hohenzollern (536): The Great Elector of Brandenburg-Prussia (r. 1640–1688) who brought his nation through the end of the Thirty Years' War and then succeeded in welding his scattered lands into an absolutist state.

Freemasons (600): Members of Masonic lodges, where nobles and middle-class professionals (and even some artisans) shared interest in the Enlightenment and reform.

Freud, Sigmund (803): Viennese medical doctor and founder, in the late nineteenth century, of psychoanalysis, a theory of mental processes and problems and a method of treating them.

Gladstone, William (786): 1809–1898. Liberal politician and prime minister of Great Britain who innovated in popular campaigning and who criticized British imperialism.

glasnost (977): Literally, "openness" or "publicity"; a policy instituted in the 1980s by Soviet premier Mikhail Gorbachev calling for greater openness in speech and in thinking, which translated to the reduction of censorship in publishing, radio, television, and other media.

global warming (1000): An increase in the temperature of the earth's lower atmosphere resulting from a buildup of chemical emissions.

globalization (986): The interconnection of labor, capital, ideas, services, and goods around the world. Although globalization has existed for hundreds of years, the late twentieth and early twenty-first centuries are seen as more global because of the speed with which people, goods, and ideas travel the world.

Glorious Revolution (530): The events of 1688 when Tories and Whigs replaced England's monarch James II with his Protestant daughter, Mary, and her husband, Dutch ruler William of Orange; William and Mary agreed to a Bill of Rights that guaranteed rights to Parliament.

Golden Horde (403): The political institution set up by the Mongols in Russia, lasting from the thirteenth to the fifteenth century.

Gorbachev, Mikhail (976): Leader of the Soviet Union (1985–1991) who instituted reforms such as glasnost and perestroika, thereby contributing to the collapse of Communist rule in the Soviet bloc and the USSR.

Gothic architecture (351): The style of architecture that started in the Île-de-France in the twelfth century and eventually became the quintessential cathedral style of the Middle Ages, characterized by pointed arches, ribbed vaults, and stained-glass windows.

Great Famine (403): The shortage of food and accompanying social ills that besieged northern Europe between 1315 and 1322.

Great Fear (626): The term used by historians to describe the French rural panic of 1789, which led to peasant attacks on aristocrats or on seigneurial records of peasants' dues.

Great Persecution (213): The violent program initiated by Diocletian in 303 to make Christians convert to traditional religion or risk confiscation of their property and even death.

Great Schism (424): The papal dispute of 1378–1417 when the church had two and even (between 1409 and 1417) three popes. The Great Schism was ended by the Council of Constance.

Green Party (1000): A political party first formed in West Germany in 1979 to bring about environmentally sound policies. It spread across Europe and around the world thereafter.

Gregorian reform (321): The papal movement for church reform associated with Gregory VII (r. 1073–1085); its ideals included ending three practices: the purchase of church offices, clerical marriage, and lay investiture.

Gregory of Tours (260): Bishop of Tours (in Gaul) from 573 to 594, the chief source for the history and culture of the Merovingian kingdoms.

Gregory the Great (266): The pope (r. 590–604) who sent missionaries to Anglo-Saxon England, wrote influential books, tried to reform the church, and had contact with the major ruling families of Europe and Byzantium.

guild (316): A trade organization within a city or town that controlled product quality and cost and outlined members' responsibilities. Guilds were also social and religious associations.

Hammurabi (14): King of Babylonia in the eighteenth century B.C.E., famous for his law code.

Hanseatic League (437): A league of northern European cities formed in the fourteenth century to protect their mutual interests in trade and defense.

heliocentrism (503): The view articulated by Polish clergyman Nicolaus Copernicus that the earth and planets revolve around the sun.

Hellenistic (120): An adjective meaning "Greek-like" that is today used as a chronological term for the period 323–30 B.C.E.

helot (64): A slave owned by the Spartan city-state; such slaves came from parts of Greece conquered by the Spartans.

Henry II (354): King of England (r. 1154–1189) who ended the period of civil war there and affirmed and expanded royal powers. He is associated with the creation of common law in England.

Henry IV (321): King of Germany (r. 1056–1106), crowned emperor in 1084. From 1075 until his death, he was embroiled in the Investiture Conflict with Pope Gregory VII.

Henry VIII (464): The English king (r. 1509–1547) who first opposed the Protestant Reformation and then broke with the Catholic church, naming himself head of the Church of England in the Act of Supremacy of 1534.

Heraclius (252): The Byzantine emperor who reversed the fortunes of war with the Persians in the first quarter of the seventh century.

heresy (194): False doctrine; specifically, the beliefs banned for Christians by councils of bishops.

hetaira (91): A witty and attractive woman who charged fees to entertain at a symposium.

hierarchy (P-5): The system of ranking people in society according to their status and authority.

hieroglyphic (18): The ancient Egyptian pictographic writing system for official texts.

Hijra (246): The emigration of Muhammad from Mecca to Medina. Its date, 622, marks year 1 of the Islamic calendar.

Hitler, Adolf (881): 1899–1945. Chancellor of Germany (1933–1945) who, with considerable backing, overturned democratic government, created the Third Reich, persecuted millions, and ultimately led Germany and the world into World War II.

home rule (787): The right to an independent parliament demanded by the Irish and resisted by the British from the second half of the nineteenth century on.

Homer (49): Greece's first and most famous author, who composed *The Iliad* and *The Odyssey*.

Homo sapiens sapiens (P-3): The scientific name (in Latin) of the type of early human being identical to people today; it means "wise, wise human being."

hoplite (58): A heavily armed Greek infantryman. Hoplites constituted the main strike force of a city-state's militia.

hubris (99): The Greek term for violent arrogance.

humanism (428): A literary and linguistic movement cultivated in particular during the Renaissance (1350–1600) and founded on reviving classical Latin and Greek texts, styles, and values.

humanitas (156): The Roman orator Cicero's ideal of "humaneness," meaning generous and honest treatment of others based on natural law.

Hundred Years' War (417): The long war between England and France, 1337–1453 (actually 116 years); it produced numerous social upheavals yet left both states more powerful than before.

hunter-gatherers (P-3): Human beings who roam to hunt and gather food in the wild and do not live in permanent, settled communities.

iconoclasm (256): Literally, "icon breaking"; referring to the destruction of icons, or images of holy people. Byzantine emperors banned icons from 726 to 787; a modified ban was revived in 815 and lasted until 843.

icons (256): Images of holy people such as Jesus, Mary, and the saints. Controversy arose in Byzantium over the meaning of such images. The iconoclasts considered them "idols," but those who adored icons maintained that they manifested the physical form of those who were holy.

ideology (686): A word coined during the French Revolution to refer to a coherent set of beliefs about the way the social and political order should be organized.

imperialism (701): European dominance of the non-West through economic exploitation and political rule; the word (as distinct from *colonialism*, which usually implied establishment of settler colonies, often with slavery) was coined in the mid-nineteenth century.

impressionism (783): A mid- to late-nineteenth-century artistic style that captured the sensation of light in images, derived from Japanese influences and in opposition to the realism of photographs.

in vitro fertilization (954): A process developed in the 1970s by which human eggs are fertilized with sperm outside the body and then implanted in a woman's uterus.

indulgence (425): A step beyond confession and penance, an indulgence (normally granted by popes or bishops) lifted the temporal punishment still necessary for a sin already forgiven. Normally, that punishment was said to take place in purgatory. But it could be remitted through good works (including prayers and contributing money to worthy causes).

Industrial Revolution (686): The transformation of life in the Western world over several decades in the late eighteenth and early nineteenth centuries as a result of the introduction of steam-driven machinery, large factories, and a new working class.

Innocent III (382): The pope (r. 1198–1216) who called the Fourth Lateran Council; he was the most powerful, respected, and prestigious of medieval popes.

Investiture Conflict (322): The confrontation between Pope Gregory VII and Emperor Henry IV that began in 1075 over the appointment of prelates in some Italian cities and grew into a dispute over the nature of church leadership. It ended in 1122 with the Concordat of Worms.

Jacobin Club (630): A French political club formed in 1789 that inspired the formation of a national network whose members dominated the revolutionary government during the Terror.

Jacquerie (421): The 1358 uprising of French peasants against the nobles amid the Hundred Years' War; it was brutally put down.

Jesuits (470): Members of the Society of Jesus, a Catholic religious order founded by Ignatius of Loyola (1491–1556) and approved by the pope in 1540. Jesuits served as missionaries and educators all over the world.

jihad (247): In the Qur'an, the word means "striving in the way of God." This can mean both striving to live righteously and striving to confront unbelievers, even through holy war.

Joan of Arc (417): A peasant girl (1412–1431) whose conviction that God had sent her to save France in fact helped France win the Hundred Years' War.

journeymen/journeywomen (316): Laborers in the Middle Ages whom guildmasters hired for a daily wage to help them produce their products.

Julian the Apostate (215): The Roman emperor (r. 361–363), who rejected Christianity and tried to restore traditional religion as the state religion. *Apostate* means "renegade from the faith."

Julio-Claudians (181): The ruling family of the early principate from Augustus through Nero, descended from the aristocratic families of the Julians and the Claudians.

Justinian and Theodora (233): Sixth-century emperor and empress of the eastern Roman Empire, famous for waging costly wars to reunite the empire.

Kennedy, John Fitzgerald (943): U.S. president (1961–1963) who faced off with Soviet leader Nikita Khrushchev in the Cuban missile crisis.

Khrushchev, Nikita (929): Leader of the USSR from c. 1955 until his dismissal in 1964; known for his speech denouncing Stalin, creation of the "thaw," and participation in the Cuban missile crisis.

Koine (132): The "common" or "shared" form of the Greek language that became the international language in the Hellenistic period.

Kollontai, Aleksandra (866): A Russian activist and minister of public welfare in the Bolshevik government who promoted social programs such as birth control and day care for children of working parents.

Kulturkampf (751): Literally, "culture war"; a term used in the 1870s by German chancellor Otto von Bismarck to describe his fight to weaken the power of the Catholic church.

ladder of offices (149): The series of Roman elective government offices from quaestor to aedile to praetor to consul.

laissez-faire (593): French for "leave alone"; an economic doctrine developed by Adam Smith that advocated freeing the economy from government intervention and control.

lay investiture (320): The installation of clerics into their offices by lay rulers.

League of Nations (853): The international organization set up following World War I to maintain peace by arbitrating disputes and promoting collective security.

Lebensraum (891): Literally, "living space"; the land that Hitler proposed to conquer so that the people he defined as true Aryans might have sufficient space to live their noble lives.

Lenin, V. I. (847): Bolshevik leader who executed the Bolshevik Revolution in the fall of 1917, took Russia out of World War I, and imposed communism in Russia.

Leopold II (762): King of Belgium (r. 1865–1909) who sponsored the takeover of the Congo in Africa, which he ran with great violence against native peoples.

Lepanto (488): A site off the Greek coast where, in 1571, the allied Catholic forces of Spain's king Philip II, Venice, and the papacy defeated the Ottoman Turks in a great sea battle; the victory gave the Christian powers control of the Mediterranean.

leprosy (388): A bacterial disease that causes skin lesions and attacks peripheral nerves. In the Middle Ages, lepers were isolated from society.

Levellers (526): Disgruntled soldiers in Oliver Cromwell's New Model Army who in 1647 wanted to "level" social differences and extend political participation to all male property owners.

liberalism (705): An economic and political ideology that—tracing its roots to John Locke in the seventeenth century and Enlightenment philosophers in the eighteenth—emphasized free trade and the constitutional guarantees of individual rights such as freedom of speech and religion; its adherents stood between conservatives on the right and revolutionaries on the left in the nineteenth century.

limited liability corporation (772): A legal entity, such as a factory or other enterprise, developed in the second half of the nineteenth century whose owners were liable for only restricted (limited) amounts of money owed to creditors in the case of financial failure.

Linear B (30): The Mycenaeans' pictographic script for writing Greek.

Lombards (252): The people who settled in Italy during the sixth century, following Justinian's reconquest. A king ruled the north of Italy, while dukes ruled the south. In between was the papacy, which felt threatened both by Lombard Arianism and by the Lombards' proximity to Rome.

Louis IX (398): A French king (r. 1226–1270) revered as a military leader and a judge; he was declared a saint after his death.

Louis XIV (516): French king (r. 1643–1715) who in theory personified absolutism but in practice had to gain the cooperation of nobles, local officials, and even the ordinary subjects who manned his armies and paid his taxes.

Louis XVI (623): French king (r. 1774–1792) who was tried for treason during the French Revolution; he was executed on January 21, 1793.

Luther, Martin (460): A German monk (1483–1546) who started the Protestant Reformation in 1517 by challenging the practices and doctrines of the Catholic church and advocating salvation through faith alone.

Lyceum (114): The school for research and teaching in a wide range of subjects founded by Aristotle in Athens in 335 B.C.E.

Maastricht Treaty (995): The agreement among the members of the European Community to have a closer alliance, including the use of common passports and eventually the development of a common currency; by the terms of this treaty, the European Community became the European Union (EU) in 1994.

Maat (20): The Egyptian goddess embodying truth, justice, and cosmic order. (The word *maat* means "what is right.")

Magna Carta (359): Literally, "Great Charter"; the charter of baronial liberties that King John was forced to agree to in 1215. It implied that royal power was subject to custom and law.

mandate system (854): The political control over the former colonies and territories of the German and Ottoman Empires granted to the victors of World War I by the League of Nations.

Marie-Antoinette (623): Wife of Louis XVI and queen of France who was tried for treason during the French Revolution and executed in October 1793.

Marshall Plan (919): A post–World War II program funded by the United States to get Europe back on its feet economically and thereby reduce the appeal of communism. It played an important role in the rebirth of European prosperity in the 1950s.

martyr (193): Greek for "witness," the term for someone who dies for his or her religious beliefs.

Marxism (746): A body of thought about the organization of production, social inequality, and the processes of revolutionary change as devised by the philosopher and economist Karl Marx.

masters (316): Men (and occasionally women) who, having achieved expertise in a craft, ran the guilds in the Middle Ages. They had to be rich enough to have their own shop and tools and to pay an entry fee into the guild. Often their positions were hereditary.

materialism (128): A philosophical doctrine of the Hellenistic Age that denied metaphysics and claimed instead that only things consisting of matter truly exist.

Mazzini, Giuseppe (703): An Italian nationalist (1805–1872) who founded Young Italy, a secret society to promote Italian unity. He believed that a popular uprising would create a unified Italy.

Medici (443): The ruling family of Florence during much of the fifteenth to the seventeenth centuries.

Mediterranean polyculture (28): The cultivation of olives, grapes, and grains in a single, interrelated agricultural system.

Mehmed II (423): The sultan under whom the Ottoman Turks conquered Constantinople in 1453.

mercantilism (522): The economic doctrine that governments must intervene to increase national wealth by whatever means possible.

Merovingian dynasty (258): The royal dynasty that ruled Gaul from about 486 to 751.

mestizo (558): A person born to a Spanish father and a native American mother.

metaphysics (113): Philosophical ideas about the ultimate nature of reality beyond the reach of human senses.

Methodism (598): A religious movement founded by John Wesley (1703–1791) that broke with the Church of England and insisted on strict self-discipline and a "methodical" approach to religious study and observance.

metic (87): A foreigner granted permanent residence status in Athens in return for paying taxes and serving in the military.

Metternich, Klemens von (668): An Austrian prince (1773–1859) who took the lead in devising the post-Napoleonic settlement arranged by the Congress of Vienna (1814–1815).

Milosevic, Slobodan (987): President of Serbia (1989–1997) who pushed for Serb control of post-Communist Yugoslavia; in 2002, he was tried for crimes against humanity in the ethnic cleansing that accompanied the dissolution of the Yugoslav state.

mir (727): A Russian farm community that provided for holding land in common and regulating the movements of any individual member by the group.

Mitteleuropa (826): Literally, "central Europe," but used by military leaders in Germany before World War I to refer to land in both central and eastern Europe that they hoped to acquire.

modernism (806): Artistic styles around the turn of the twentieth century that featured a break with realism in art and literature and with lyricism in music.

monotheism (6): The belief in and worship of only one god, as in Judaism, Christianity, and Islam.

moral dualism (43): The belief that the world is the arena for an ongoing battle for control between divine forces of good and evil.

Morrison, Toni (1013): The first African American woman to win the Nobel Prize for Literature; her works include *Beloved* (1987), *Jazz* (1992), and *A Mercy* (2008).

mos maiorum (140): Literally, "the way of the elders"; the set of Roman values handed down from the ancestors.

Muhammad (244): The prophet of Islam (c. 570–632). He united a community of believers around his religious tenets, above all that there was one God whose words had been revealed to him by the angel Gabriel. Later, written down, these revelations became the Qur'an.

multinational corporation (955): A business that operates in many foreign countries by sending large segments of its manufacturing, finance, sales, and other business components abroad.

Mussolini, Benito (867): Leader of Italian fascist movement and, after the March on Rome in 1922, dictator of Italy.

mystery cults (87): Religious worship that provided initiation into secret knowledge and divine protection, including hope for a better afterlife.

nationalism (703): An ideology that arose in the nineteenth century and that holds that all peoples derive their identities from their nations, which are defined by common language, shared cultural traditions, and sometimes religion.

nation-state (729): An independent political unit of modern times based on representing a united people.

Nazi-Soviet Pact (895): The agreement reached in 1939 by Germany and the Soviet Union in which both agreed not to attack the other in case of war and to divide any conquered territories.

neoliberalism (974): A theory first promoted by British prime minister Margaret Thatcher, calling for a return to liberal principles of the nineteenth century, including the reduction of welfare-state programs and the cutting of taxes for the wealthy to promote economic growth.

Neolithic Age (P-2): The "New Stone" Age, dating from around 10,000 to 4000 B.C.E.

Neolithic Revolution (P-6): The invention of agriculture, the domestication of animals, and the consequent changes in human society that occurred about 10,000–8000 B.C.E. in the Near East.

Neoplatonism (196): Plotinus's spiritual philosophy, based mainly on Plato's ideas, which was very influential for Christian intellectuals.

new unionism (785): A nineteenth-century development in labor organizing that replaced local craft-based unions with those that extended membership to all kinds of workers.

new woman (801): A woman who, from the 1880s on, dressed practically, moved about freely, and often supported herself.

Nicene Creed (220): The doctrine agreed on by the council of bishops convened by Constantine at Nicaea in 325 to defend orthodoxy against Arianism. It declared that God the Father and Jesus were *homoousion* ("of one substance").

Nicholas II (813): Tsar of Russia (r. 1894–1917) who promoted anti-Semitism and resisted reform in the empire.

Nietzsche, Friedrich (806): Late-nineteenth-century German philosopher who called for a new morality in the face of God's death at the hands of science and whose theories were reworked by his sister to emphasize militarism and anti-Semitism.

Nightingale, Florence (725): The Englishwoman who in the nineteenth century pioneered the professionalization of nursing and the use of statistics in the study of public health and the well-being of the military.

Nixon, Richard (969): U.S. president (1969–1974) who escalated the Vietnam War, worked for accommodation with China, and resigned from the presidency after trying to block free elections.

nongovernmental organizations (NGOs) (999): Charitable foundations and activist groups such as Doctors Without Borders that work outside of governments, often on political, economic, and relief issues; also, philanthropic organizations such as the Rockefeller, Ford, and Open Society Foundations that shape economic and social policy and the course of political reform.

North Atlantic Treaty Organization (NATO) (921): The security alliance formed in 1949 to provide a unified military force for the United States, Canada, and their allies in western Europe and Scandinavia.

Nuremberg Laws (885): Legislation enacted by the Nazis in 1935 that deprived Jewish Germans of their citizenship and imposed many other hardships on them.

Opium War (702): War between China and Great Britain (1839–1842) that resulted in the opening of four Chinese ports to Europeans and British sovereignty over Hong Kong.

optimates (159): The Roman political faction supporting the "best," or highest, social class; established during the late republic.

orders (148): The two groups of people in the Roman republic—**patricians** (aristocratic families) and **plebeians** (all other citizens).

Organization of Petroleum Exporting Countries (OPEC) (971): A consortium that regulated the supply and export of oil and that acted with more unanimity after the United States supported Israel against the Arabs in the wars of the late 1960s and early 1970s.

orthodoxy (194): True doctrine; specifically, the beliefs defined for Christians by councils of bishops.

Ostpolitik (961): A policy initiated by West German foreign minister Willy Brandt in the late 1960s in which West Germany sought better economic relations with the Communist countries of eastern Europe.

ostracism (82): An annual procedure in Athenian radical democracy by which a man could be voted out of the city-state for ten years; its purpose was to prevent tyranny.

Ottonian kings (304): The tenth- and early-eleventh-century kings of Germany; beginning with Otto I (r. 936–973), they claimed the imperial crown and worked closely with their bishops to rule a vast territory.

outwork (770): The nineteenth-century process of having some aspects of industrial work done outside factories in individual homes.

Pacific tigers (1006): Countries of East Asia so named because of their massive economic growth, much of it from the 1980s on; foremost among these were Japan and China.

palace society (28): Minoan and Mycenaean social and political organization centered on multichambered buildings housing the rulers and the administration of the state.

Paleolithic Age (P-2): The "Old Stone" Age, dating from around 200,000 to 10,000 B.C.E.

Pankhurst, Emmeline (812): 1858–1928. Organizer of a militant branch of the British suffrage movement, working actively for women's right to vote.

Pan-Slavism (736): The nineteenth-century movement calling for the unity of all Slavs across national and regional boundaries.

Parnell, Charles Stewart (787): Irish politician (1846–1891) whose advocacy of home rule was a thorn in the side of the British establishment.

Parthenon (84): The massive temple to Athena as a warrior goddess built atop the Athenian acropolis in the Golden Age of Greece.

partition of Poland (607): Division of one-third of Poland-Lithuania's territory between Prussia, Russia, and Austria in 1772.

patria potestas (142): Literally, "father's power"; the legal power a Roman father possessed over the children and slaves in his family, including owning all their property and having the right to punish them, even with death.

patriarchy (P-13): Dominance by men in society and politics.

patricians: *See* orders.

patrilineal (301): Relating to or tracing descent through the paternal line (for example, through the father and grandfather).

patron-client system (142): The interlocking network of mutual obligations between Roman patrons (social superiors) and clients (social inferiors).

Pax Romana (172): Literally, "Roman Peace"; the two centuries of relative peace and prosperity in the Roman Empire under the early principate begun by Augustus.

Peace of Augsburg (479): The treaty of 1555 that settled disputes between Holy Roman Emperor Charles V and his Protestant princes. It recognized the Lutheran church and established the principle that all Catholic or Lutheran princes enjoyed the sole right to determine the religion of their lands and subjects.

Peace of God (302): A movement begun by bishops in the south of France around 990, first to limit the violence done to property and to the unarmed, and later, with the Truce of God, to limit fighting between warriors.

Peace of Paris (852): The series of peace treaties (1919–1920) that provided the settlement of World War I. The Treaty of Versailles with Germany was the centerpiece of the Peace of Paris.

Peace of Westphalia (494): The settlement (1648) of the Thirty Years' War; it established enduring religious divisions in the Holy Roman Empire by which Lutheranism would dominate in the north, Calvinism in the area of the Rhine River, and Catholicism in the south.

perestroika (976): Literally, "restructuring"; an economic policy instituted in the 1980s by Soviet premier Mikhail Gorbachev calling for the introduction of market mechanisms and the achievement of greater efficiency in manufacturing, agriculture, and services.

Pericles (81): Athens's political leader during the Golden Age.

Peter the Great (571): Russian tsar Peter I (r. 1689–1725), who undertook the Westernization of Russia and built a new capital city named after himself, St. Petersburg.

Petrarch, Francis (429): An Italian poet (1304–1374) who revived the styles of classical authors; he is considered the first Renaissance humanist.

Philip II (487): King of Spain (r. 1556–1598) and the most powerful ruler in Europe; he reigned over the western Habsburg lands and all the Spanish colonies recently settled in the New World.

Philip II (Philip Augustus) (358): King of France (r. 1180–1223) who bested the English king John and won most of John's continental territories, thus immeasurably strengthening the power of the Capetian dynasty.

philosophes (588): French for "philosophers"; public intellectuals of the Enlightenment who wrote on subjects ranging from current affairs to art criticism with the goal of furthering reform in society.

Pietism (567): A Protestant revivalist movement of the early eighteenth century that emphasized deeply emotional individual religious experience.

plantation (553): A large tract of land that produced staple crops such as sugar, coffee, and tobacco; was farmed by slave labor; and was owned by a colonial settler.

Plato (112): A follower of Socrates who became Greece's most famous philosopher.

plebeians: *See* orders.

plebiscites (150): Resolutions passed by the Plebeian Assembly; such resolutions gained the force of law in 287 B.C.E.

polis (51): The Greek city-state, an independent community of citizens not ruled by a king.

political states (P-2): People living in a defined territory with boundaries and organized under a system of government with powerful officials, leaders, and judges.

politiques (486): Political advisers during the sixteenth-century French Wars of Religion who argued that compromise in matters of religion would strengthen the monarchy.

polytheism (6): The belief in and worship of multiple gods.

pop art (959): A style in the visual arts that mimicked advertising and consumerism and that used ordinary objects as a part of paintings and other compositions.

popolo (401): Literally, "people"; a communal faction, largely made up of merchants, that demanded (and often obtained) power in thirteenth-century Italian cities.

Popular Front (887): An alliance of political parties (initially led by Léon Blum in France) in the 1930s to resist fascism despite philosophical differences.

populares (159): The Roman political faction supporting the common people; established during the late republic.

positivism (753): A theory developed in the mid-nineteenth century that the study of facts would generate accurate, or "positive," laws of society and that these laws could, in turn, help in the formulation of policies and legislation.

postmodernism (1014): A term applied in the late twentieth century to both an intense stylistic mixture in the arts without a central unifying theme or elite set of standards and a critique of Enlightenment and scientific beliefs in rationality and the possibility of certain knowledge.

praetorian guard (174): The group of soldiers stationed in Rome under the emperor's control; first formed by Augustus.

predestination (464): John Calvin's doctrine that God preordained salvation or damnation for each person before creation; those chosen for salvation were considered the "elect."

primogeniture (301): An inheritance practice that left all property to the oldest son.

principate (173): Roman political system invented by Augustus as a disguised monarchy with the *princeps* ("first man") as emperor.

proletarians (159): In the Roman republic, the mass of people so poor they owned no property.

Pugachev rebellion (611): A massive revolt of Russian Cossacks and serfs in 1773 against local nobles and the armies of Catherine the Great; its leader, Emelian Pugachev, was eventually captured and executed.

pump priming (884): An economic policy used by governments, including the Nazis in Germany, to stimulate the economy through public works programs and other infusions to public funds.

purges (880): The series of attacks on citizens of the USSR accused of being "wreckers," or saboteurs of communism, in the 1930s and later.

Puritans (489): Strict Calvinists who in the sixteenth and seventeenth centuries opposed all vestiges of Catholic ritual in the Church of England.

Putin, Vladimir (990): President of Russia elected in 2000 and prime minister as of 2008; he has worked to reestablish Russia as a world power through control of the country's resources and military capabilities.

Qur'an (246): The holy book of Islam, considered the word of Allah ("the God") as revealed to the Prophet Muhammad.

radical democracy (81): The Athenian system of democracy established in the 460s and 450s B.C.E. that extended direct political power and participation in the court system to all adult male citizens.

raison d'état (495): French for "reason of state," the political doctrine, first proposed by Cardinal Richelieu of France, which held that the state's interests should prevail over those of religion.

rationalism (70): The philosophic idea that people must justify their claims by logic and reason, not myth.

Razin, Stenka (539): Leader of the 1667 rebellion that promised Russian peasants liberation from noble landowners and officials; he was captured by the tsar's army in 1671 and publicly executed in Moscow.

realism (748): An artistic style that arose in the mid-nineteenth century and was dedicated to depicting society realistically without romantic or idealistic overtones.

Realpolitik (721): Policies developed after the revolutions of 1848 and initially associated with nation building; they were based on realism rather than on the romantic notions of earlier nationalists. The term has come to mean any policy based on considerations of power alone.

reconquista (321): The collective name for the wars waged by the Christian princes of Spain against the Muslim-ruled regions to their south. These wars were considered holy, akin to the crusades.

redistributive economy (14): A system in which state officials control the production and distribution of goods.

Reform Act of 1884 (787): British legislation that granted the right to vote to a mass male citizenry.

Reform Bill of 1832 (681): A measure passed by the British Parliament to increase the number of male voters by about 50 percent and give representation to new cities in the north; it set a precedent for widening suffrage.

res publica (145): Literally, "the people's matter" or "the public business"; the Romans' name for their republic and the source of our word *republic*.

restoration (669): The epoch after the fall of Napoleon, in which the Congress of Vienna aimed to "restore" as many regimes as possible to their former rulers.

revocation of the Edict of Nantes (521): French king Louis XIV's 1685 decision to eliminate the rights of Calvinists granted in the edict of 1598; Louis banned all Calvinist public activities and forced those who refused to embrace the state religion to flee.

Robespierre, Maximilien (631): A lawyer from northern France who, as leader of the Committee of Public Safety, laid out the principles of a republic of virtue and of the Terror; his arrest and execution in July 1794 brought an end to the Terror.

rococo (565): A style of painting that emphasized irregularity and asymmetry, movement and curvature, but on a smaller, more intimate scale than the baroque.

Romanesque (350): An architectural style that flourished in Europe between about 1000 and 1150. It is characterized by solid, heavy forms and semicircular arches and vaults. Romanesque buildings were often decorated with fanciful sculpture and wall paintings.

Romanization (185): The spread of Roman law and culture in the provinces of the Roman Empire.

romanticism (598): An artistic movement of the late eighteenth and early nineteenth centuries that glorified nature, emotion, genius, and imagination.

Rousseau, Jean-Jacques (594): One of the most important philosophes (1712–1778); he argued that only a government based on a social contract among the citizens could make people truly moral and free.

ruler cults (133): Cults that involved worship of a Hellenistic ruler as a savior god.

Rushdie, Salman (1013): Immigrant British author, whose novel *The Satanic Verses* (1988) led the ayatollah Ruhollah Khomeini of Iran to issue a fatwa calling for Rushdie's murder.

Russification (728): A program for the integration of Russia's many nationality groups that involved the forced learning of the Russian language and the practice of Russian Orthodox religion as well as the settlement of ethnic Russians among other nationality groups.

sacraments (323): In the Catholic church, the institutionalized means by which God's heavenly grace is transmitted to Christians. Examples of sacraments include baptism, the Eucharist (communion), and marriage.

salon (544): An informal gathering held regularly in a private home and presided over by a socially eminent woman; salons spread from France in the seventeenth century to other countries in the eighteenth century.

samizdat (962): A key form of dissident activity across the Soviet bloc in which individuals reproduced government-suppressed publications by hand and passed them from reader to reader, thus building a foundation for the successful resistance of the 1980s.

Sand, George (697): The pen name of French novelist Amandine-Aurore-Lucile Dupin Dudevant (1804–1876), who showed her independence in the 1830s by dressing like a man and smoking cigars. The term *George-Sandism* became an expression of disdain for independent women.

Sappho (69): The most famous woman lyric poet of ancient Greece, a native of Lesbos.

Schlieffen Plan (839): The Germans' strategy in World War I that called for attacks on two fronts — concentrating first on France to the west and then turning east to attack Russia.

scholasticism (389): The method of logical inquiry used by the scholastics, the scholars of the medieval universities; it applied Aristotelian logic to biblical and other authoritative texts in an attempt to summarize and reconcile all knowledge.

scientific method (503): The combination of experimental observation and mathematical deduction used to determine the laws of nature; first developed in the seventeenth century, it became the secular standard of truth.

Scott, Sir Walter (675): A prolific author (1771–1832) of popular historical novels; he also collected and published traditional Scottish ballads and wrote poetry.

Sea Peoples (31): The diverse groups of raiders who devastated the eastern Mediterranean region in the period of violence 1200–1000 B.C.E.

Second International (785): A transnational organization of workers established in 1889, mostly committed to Marxian socialism.

secularization (503): The long-term trend toward separating state power and science from religious faith, making the latter a private domain; begun in the seventeenth century, it prompted a search for nonreligious explanations for political authority and natural phenomena.

Seven Years' War (605): A worldwide series of battles (1756–1763) between Austria, France, Russia, and Sweden on one side and Prussia and Great Britain on the other.

Shi'ite (250): A Muslim of the "party of Ali" and his descendants. Shi'ites are thus opposed to the Sunni Muslims, who reject the authority of Ali.

simony (320): The sin of giving gifts or paying money to get a church office.

social contract (531): The doctrine, originated by Hugo Grotius and argued by both Thomas Hobbes and John Locke, that all political authority derives not from divine right but from an implicit contract between citizens and their rulers.

socialism (706): A social and political ideology, originating in the early nineteenth century, that advocated the reorganization of society to overcome the new tensions created by industrialization and restore social harmony through communities based on cooperation.

Socratic method (96): The Athenian philosopher Socrates' method of teaching through conversation, in which he asked probing questions to make his listeners examine their most cherished assumptions.

Solidarity (977): A Polish labor union founded in 1980 by Lech Walesa and Anna Walentynowicz that contested Communist Party programs and eventually succeeded in ousting the party from the Polish government.

Solon (67): Athenian political reformer whose changes promoted early democracy.

Sophists (94): Competitive intellectuals and teachers in ancient Greece who offered expensive courses in persuasive public speaking and new ways of philosophic and religious thinking beginning around 450 B.C.E.

South African War (818): The war (1899–1902) between Britain and the Boer (originally Dutch) inhabitants of South Africa for control of the region; also called the Boer War.

soviets (846): Councils of workers and soldiers first formed in Russia in the Revolution of 1905; they were revived to represent the people in the early days of the 1917 Russian Revolution.

St. Bernard (327): The most important Cistercian abbot (early twelfth century) and the chief preacher of the Second Crusade.

stagflation (971): The combination of a stagnant economy and soaring inflation; a period of stagflation occurred in the West in the 1970s as a result of an OPEC embargo on oil.

Stalin, Joseph (878): Leader of the USSR who, with considerable backing, formed a brutal dictatorship in the 1930s and forcefully converted the country into an industrial power.

Statute in Favor of the Princes (397): A statute finalized by Frederick II in 1232 that gave the German princes sovereign power within their own principalities.

Stoicism (130): The Hellenistic philosophy whose followers believed in fate but also in pursuing excellence (virtue) by cultivating good sense, justice, courage, and temperance.

Suleiman the Magnificent (475): Sultan of the Ottoman Empire (r. 1520–1566) at the time of its greatest power.

Synod of Whitby (266): The meeting of churchmen and King Oswy of Northumbria in 664 that led to the adoption of the Roman brand of Christianity in England.

Terror (631): The policy established under the direction of the Committee of Public Safety during the French Revolution to arrest dissidents and execute opponents in order to protect the republic from its enemies.

tetrarchy (209): The "rule by four," consisting of two co-emperors and two assistant emperors/designated successors, initiated by Diocletian to subdivide the ruling of the Roman Empire into four regions.

Thatcher, Margaret (973): Prime minister of Britain (1979–1990) who set a new tone for British politics by promoting neoliberal economic policies and criticizing poor people, union members, and racial minorities as worthless, even harmful citizens.

theme (255): A military district in Byzantium. The earliest themes were created in the seventh century and served mainly defensive purposes.

Themistocles (77): Athens's leader during the great Persian invasion of Greece.

Theodosius I (216): The Roman emperor (r. 379–395) who made Christianity the state religion by ending public sacrifices in the traditional cults and closing their temples. In 395 he also divided the empire into western and eastern halves to be ruled by his sons.

Thermidorian Reaction (638): The violent backlash against the rule of Robespierre that dismantled the Terror and punished Jacobins and their supporters.

Third Republic (787): The French government that succeeded Napoleon III's Second Empire after its defeat in the Franco-Prussian War of 1870–1871. It lasted until France's defeat by Germany in 1940.

Torah (45): The first five books of the Hebrew Bible, also referred to as the Pentateuch. It contains early Jewish law.

total war (836): A war built on the full mobilization of soldiers, civilians, and technology of the nations involved. The term also refers to a highly destructive war of ideologies.

Treaty of Verdun (292): The treaty that, in 843, split the Carolingian Empire into three parts; its borders roughly outline modern western European states.

triremes (80): Greek wooden warships rowed by 170 oarsmen sitting on three levels and equipped with a battering ram at the bow.

troubadours (366): Vernacular poets in southern France in the twelfth and early thirteenth centuries who sang of love, longing, and courtesy.

Truman Doctrine (919): The policy devised by U.S. president Harry Truman to limit communism after World War II by countering political crises with economic and military aid.

Twelve Tables (149): The first written Roman law code, enacted between 451 and 449 B.C.E.

Umayyad caliphate (250): The caliphs (successors of Muhammad) who traced their ancestry to Umayyah, a member of Muhammad's tribe. The dynasty lasted from 661 to 750.

United Nations (UN) (934): An organization set up in 1945 for collective security and for the resolution of international conflicts through both deliberation and the use of force.

Urban II (330): The pope (r. 1088–1099) responsible for calling the First Crusade in 1095.

urbanization (692): The growth of towns and cities due to the movement of people from rural to urban areas, a trend that was encouraged by the development of factories and railroads.

Vatican II (937): A Catholic Council held between 1962 and 1965 to modernize some aspects of church teachings (such as condemnation of Jews), to update the liturgy, and to promote cooperation among the faiths (i.e., ecumenism).

Visigoths (229): The name given to the barbarians whom Alaric united and led on a military campaign into the western Roman Empire to establish a new kingdom; they sacked Rome in 410.

Voltaire (578): The pen name of François-Marie Arouet (1694–1778), who was the most influential writer of the early Enlightenment.

Walpole, Robert (570): The first, or "prime," minister (1721–1742) of the House of Commons of Great Britain's Parliament. Although appointed initially by the king, through his long period of leadership he effectively established the modern pattern of parliamentary government.

war guilt clause (852): The part of the Treaty of Versailles that assigned blame for World War I to Germany.

War of the Austrian Succession (574): The war (1740–1748) over the succession to the Habsburg throne that pitted France and Prussia against Austria and Britain and provoked continuing hostilities between French and British settlers in the North American colonies.

Warsaw Pact (921): A security alliance of the Soviet Union and its allies formed in 1955, in retaliation for NATO's admittance of West Germany.

Weimar Republic (851): The parliamentary republic established in 1919 in Germany to replace the monarchy.

welfare state (927): A system (developed on both sides during the cold war) comprising government-sponsored social programs to provide health care, family allowances, disability insurance, and pensions for veterans and retired workers.

wergild (231): Under Frankish law, the payment that a murderer had to make as compensation for the crime, to prevent feuds of revenge.

Westernization (571): The effort, especially in Peter the Great's Russia, to make society and social customs resemble counterparts in western Europe, especially France, Britain, and the Dutch Republic.

William, prince of Orange (530): Dutch ruler who, with his Protestant wife, Mary (daughter of James II), ruled England after the Glorious Revolution of 1688.

wisdom literature (22): Texts giving instructions for proper behavior by officials.

ziggurats (8): Mesopotamian temples of massive size built on a stair-step design.

Zionism (817): A movement that began in the late nineteenth century among European Jews to found a Jewish state.

Additional Credits

Chapter 1, page 15: "Hammurabi's Laws for Physicians." From James Pritchard, *Ancient Near Eastern Texts Relating to the Old Testament,* Third Edition with Supplement. Copyright © 1950, 1955, 1969, renewed 1978 by Princeton University Press. Reprinted by permission of Princeton University Press. **Page 25:** "Declaring Innocence on Judgment Day in Ancient Egypt." From "The Declaration to the Forty-two Gods" in *The Book of the Dead,* reprinted in Miriam Lichtheim, trans., *Ancient Egyptian Literature: A Book of Readings,* vol. 2, *The New Kingdom.* Copyright © 1978 by the Regents of the University of California. Reprinted by permission of the University of California Press.

Chapter 3, page 95: "Sophists Argue Both Sides of a Case." Excerpt from *Dissoi Logio* 1.1–6. Translation adapted from *The Older Sophists,* edited by Rosamond Kent Sprague. Copyright © 1972 by Rosamond Kent Sprague. Reprinted by permission of the University of South Carolina Press.

Chapter 6, page 188: "Tertullian's Defense of His Fellow Christians, 197 C.E." Reprinted by permission of the publishers and the Trustees of the Loeb Classical Library from *Tertullian,* Loeb Classical Library Volume 250, translated by T. R. Glover, Cambridge, Mass.: Harvard University Press. Copyright © 1931 by the President and Fellows of Harvard College. The Loeb Classical Library ® is a registered trademark of the President and Fellows of Harvard College. **Page 188:** "Pliny on Early Imperial Policy toward Christians, c. 112 C.E." From *The Letters of the Younger Pliny,* translated with an introduction by Betty Radice (Penguin Classics, 1963; repr., 1969), Book 10, nos. 96 and 97. Copyright © Betty Radice, 1963, 1969. Reproduced by permission of Penguin Books Ltd.

Chapter 8, page 247: "The Fatihah of the Qur'an." From *Approaching the Qur'án: The Early Revelations,* introduced and translated by Michael Sells. Copyright © 1999 by White Cloud Press. Reprinted by permission of White Cloud Press. **Page 249:** The Pact of Umar." From "Umar II and the 'Protected People'" in *Classical Islam: A Sourcebook of Religious Literature,* edited and translated by Norman Calder, Jawid Mojaddedi, and Andrew Rippin. Copyright © 2003 Routledge. Reproduced by permission of Taylor & Francis Books UK.

Chapter 9, page 286: "When She Approached" by Ibn Darraj al-Quastali. From "Andalusi Poetry: The Golden Period" in *The Legacy of Muslim Spain,* edited by Salma Khadra Jayyusi, 2 volumes (Leiden: Brill, 1994), 1:335. Copyright © 1994 by Brill. Reprinted by permission of Koninklijke Brill NV. **Page 290:** "Charles as Emperor." From *Charlemagne's Courtier: The Complete Einhard,* edited and translated by Paul Edward Dutton. Copyright © 1998 by Paul Edward Dutton. Broadview Press (University of Toronto Press Higher Education Division). Reprinted with permission of the publisher. **Page 290:** "The 'Father of Europe.'" From *Carolingian Civilization: A Reader,* 2nd edition, edited by Paul Edward Dutton. Copyright © 2004 by Paul Edward Dutton. Broadview Press (University of Toronto Press Higher Education Division). Reprinted with permission of the publisher. **Page 291:** "The Chief Bishop." From *Two Lives of Charlemagne* by Einhard and Notker the Stammerer, translated with an introduction by Professor Lewis Thorpe (Penguin Classics, 1969). Copyright © Professor Lewis Thorpe, 1969. Reproduced by permission of Penguin Books Ltd.

Chapter 10, page 314: "Peppercorns as Money." From *Medieval Trade in the Mediterranean World: Illustrative Documents,* translated by Robert S. Lopez and Irving W. Raymond. Copyright © 1955, 1990, 2001 Columbia University Press. Reprinted with permission of the publisher. **Page 324:** "Anonymous Account of Henry's Minority." From *The Life of the Emperor Henry IV* in *Imperial Lives and Letters of the Eleventh Century,* translated by Theodor E. Mommsen and Karl F. Morrison. Copyright © 2000 Columbia University Press. Reprinted by permission of the publisher and Karl F. Morrison. **Page 324:** "Gregory VII Admonishes Henry." From *The Correspondence of Pope Gregory VII: Selected Letters from the Registrum,* translated by Ephraim Emerton. Copyright © 1932, 1960, 1990 Columbia University Press. Reprinted by permission of the publisher. **Page 325:** "Henry's Response to Gregory's Admonition." Excerpt from *The Letters of Henry IV* in *Imperial Lives and Letters of the Eleventh Century,* trans. Theodor E. Mommsen and Karl F. Morrison. Copyright © 2000 Columbia University Press. Reprinted by permission of the publisher and Karl F. Morrison. **Page 334:** "Excerpt from a letter by Yahya, c. 1100." From Mark R. Cohen, *The Voice of the Poor in the Middle Ages.* Copyright © 2005 Princeton University Press. Reprinted by permission of Princeton University Press. **Page 338:** "Penances for the Invaders." From *English Historical Documents,* vol. 2, *1042–1189,* edited by David C. Douglas and George W. Greenaway, 2nd ed. Copyright © 1996 Routledge. Reproduced by permission of Taylor & Francis Books UK.

Chapter 11, page 360: Magna Carta (excerpt). From *English Historical Documents,* vol. 3, *1189–1327,* edited by Harry Rothwell. Copyright © 1975 Routledge. Reproduced by permission of Taylor & Francis Books UK. **Page 361:** "The Barons at Parliament Refuse to Give the King an Aid, 1242." From *English Historical Documents,* vol. 3, *1189–1327,* edited by Harry Rothwell. Copyright © 1975 Routledge. Reproduced by permission of Taylor & Francis Books UK. **Page 363:** "Frederick I's Reply to the Romans." Reprinted with the permission of Simon & Schuster, Inc., from *The Crisis of Church and State, 1050–1300* by Brian Tierney. Copyright © 1964 by Prentice-Hall, Inc.; copyright renewed © 1992 by Brian Tierney. All rights reserved. **Page 367:** "Troubadour Song: I Never Died for Love" by Peire Vidal. From *Songs of the Troubadours and Trouveres/1,* edited by Samuel N. Rosenberg, Margaret Switten, and Gerard Le Vot (Routledge, 1998). Copyright © 1997 by Samuel N. Rosenberg, Margaret Switten, and Gerard Le Vot. Reprinted by permission of Taylor & Francis Group LLC Books. **Page 368:** "Bertran de Born, 'I love the joyful time of Easter.'" From *Lyrics of the Troubadours and Trouvères,* translated by Frederick Goldin. Copyright © 1973 by Frederick Goldin. Used by permission of Doubleday, a division of Random House, Inc. **Page 373:** "The Children's Crusade." From *Medieval Popular Religion, 1000–1500: A Reader,* edited and translated by John Shinners. Copyright © 1997 by John Shinners. Broadview Press (University of Toronto Press Higher Education Division). Reprinted with permission of the publisher.

Chapter 12, page 387: "Raymond de l'Aire's Testimony." Excerpted from "The Inquisitorial Register of Jacques Fournier" in *Heresy and Authority in Medieval Europe: Documents in Translation,* edited by Edward Peters. Copyright © 1980 University of Pennsylvania Press. Reprinted with permission of the University of Pennsylvania Press. **Page 391:** "Thomas Aquinas Writes about Sex." From "The Reason Why Simple Fornication Is a Sin According to Divine Law, and That Matrimony Is Natural" in Saint Thomas Aquinas, *Summa Contra Gentiles,* Book 3: *Providence,* Part II, translated by Vernon J. Bourke (Notre Dame, Ind.: University of Notre Dame Press, 1975). Copyright © 1975. Reprinted by permission of the University of Notre Dame Press. **Page 392:** "The Debate between Reason and the Lover." From *The Romance of the Rose* by Guillaume de Lorris and Jean de Meun, edited by Charles W. Dunn and translated by Harry W. Robbins. Copyright © 1962 by Florence L. Robbins. Used by permission of Dutton, a division of Penguin Group (USA) Inc. and Charlotte G. Larmee.

Chapter 13, page 418: "Joan the Visionary," "Messenger of God?" and "Normal Girl?" Excerpted from *Joan of Arc: La Pucelle,* translated and annotated by Craig Taylor. Copyright © 2006 by Manchester University Press. Reprinted by permission of Manchester University Press. **Page 440:** "The Ducal Entry into Ghent" (1458). From *Court and Civic Society in the Burgundian Low Countries, c. 1420–1530,* ed. Andrew Brown and Graeme Small. Copyright © 2007 by Manchester University Press. Reprinted by permission of Manchester University Press.

Chapter 15, page 494: "The Horrors of the Thirty Years' War." From Asmus Teufel, *The Siege and Capture of Münden* (1626). Text discovered in the Münden town archive by Thomas Kossert, translated by Hans Medick and Benjamin Marschke. Reprinted by permission. **Page 505:** "Sentence Pronounced against Galileo." From *The Galileo Affair: A Documentary History,* edited by Maurice A. Finocchiaro. Copyright © 1989 University of California Press. Reprinted by permission of University of California Press.

Chapter 16, page 519: "Marie de Sévigné, Letter Describing the French Court (1675)." From *Madame de Sévigné: Selected Letters,* translated with an introduction by Leonard Tancock (Penguin Classics, 1982). Copyright © Leonard Tancock, 1982. Reproduced by permission of Penguin Books Ltd. **Page 529:** "Thomas Hobbes, *Leviathan* (1651)." From Thomas Hobbes, *Leviathan* (Norton Critical Edition, edited by Richard E. Flathman and David Johnston. Copyright © 1997 by W. W. Norton & Company, Inc. Used by permission of W. W. Norton & Company, Inc.

Chapter 17, page 556: "Oral History and the Life of Slaves." From *Alabi's World* by Richard Price. Copyright © 1990 by Richard Price. Reprinted with permission of The Johns Hopkins University Press.

Chapter 18, page 590: "Denis Diderot, 'Encyclopedia' (1755)." From *Denis Diderot, The Encyclopedia: Selections,* edited and translated by Stephen J. Gendzier. Harper & Row Publishers, Inc. 1967, copyright Stephen J. Gendzier. Reprinted by permission of Stephen J. Gendzier. **Page 594:** "Jean-Jacques Rousseau, *Émile* (1762)." From *Women, the Family, and Freedom: The Debate in Documents,* Volume 1, *1750–1880*, edited by Susan Groag Bell and Karen M. Offen. Copyright © 1983 by the Board of Trustees of the Leland Stanford Junior University. All rights reserved. Used with the permission of Stanford University Press, www.sup.org. **Page 594:** "Madame de Beaumer, Editorial in *Le Journal des Dames.*" From *Women, the Family, and Freedom: The Debate in Documents,* Volume 1, *1750–1880*, edited by Susan Groag Bell and Karen M. Offen. Copyright © 1983 by the Board of Trustees of the Leland Stanford Junior University. All rights reserved. Used with the permission of Stanford University Press, www.sup.org.

Chapter 19, page 645: "Anne-Louise-Germaine de Staël, *Considerations on the Main Events of the French Revolution* (1818)." From *An Extraordinary Woman: Selected Writings of Germaine de Staël*, edited by Vivian Folkenflik. Copyright © 1987 Columbia University Press. Reprinted with permission of the publisher.

Chapter 20, page 666: "Benjamin Constant, Spokesman for the Liberal Opposition to Napoleon." From "Further Reflections on Usurpation" in *Constant: Political Writings,* edited and translated by Biancamaria Fontana. Copyright © 1988 by Cambridge University Press. Reprinted with the permission of Cambridge University Press.

Chapter 21, page 713: "Alexis de Tocqueville Describes the June Days in Paris (1848)." From Alexis de Tocqueville, *Recollections: The French Revolution of 1848,* edited by J. P. Mayer and A. P. Kerr, translated by George Lawrence. Copyright © 1986 by Transaction Publishers. Reprinted by permission of the publisher.

Chapter 23, page 764: "An African King Describes His Government." From *Report and Proceedings with Appendices of the Government Commission on Native Laws and Customs, Cape of Good Hope Parliamentary Paper, G4,* 1883, Part 1, 523–30, excerpted in William H. Worger, Nancy L. Clark, and Edward A. Alpers, eds. *Africa and the West: A Documentary History,* 2nd ed., vol. 1, *From the Slave Trade to Conquest, 1441–1905* (New York: Oxford University Press, 2010), 208, 209. Copyright (c) 2001, 2010 by William H. Worger, Nancy L. Clark, and Edward A. Alpers. By permission of Oxford University Press. **Page 778:** "The Government View." Quoted in Julianna Puskas, "Consequences of Overseas Migration for the Country of Origin: The Case of Hungary," in *Roots of the Transplanted,* vol. 1, *Late 19th Century East Central and Southeastern Europe*, edited by Dirk Hoerder and Inge Blank (Boulder: East European Monographs, 1994), 397. Copyright © 1994 by Dirk Hoerder and Inge Blank. Reprinted by permission of Dirk Hoerder. **Page 778:** "Migration Defended." From H. Arnold Barton, *A Folk Divided: Homeland Swedes and Swedish Americans, 1840–1940* (Carbondale: Southern Illinois University Press, 1994), 72–73, 137. Copyright © 1994 by the Board of Trustees, Southern Illinois University. Reprinted by permission of the publisher. **Page 779:** "The Perils of Migration." Quoted in Frantisek Bielik, Horst Hogh, and Anna Stvrtecka, "Slovak Images of the New World: 'We Could Pay Off Our Debts,'" in *Roots of the Transplanted,* vol. 1, *Late 19th Century East Central and Southeastern Europe*, edited by Dirk Hoerder and Inge Blank (Boulder: East European Monographs, 1994), 388. Copyright © 1994 by Dirk Hoerder and Inge Blank. Reprinted by permission of Dirk Hoerder. **Page 782:** "Henrik Ibsen, From *A Doll's House.*" From *A Doll's House/Ghost/An Enemy of the People/Rosmersholm* by Henrik Ibsen and newly translated by Michael Meyer. Copyright © 1966 by Michael Meyer. Copyright renewed 1994 by Michael Meyer. Reprinted by permission of Harold Ober Associates Incorporated.

Chapter 24, page 817: "Leon Pinsker Calls for a Jewish State." From Robert Chazan and Marc Lee Raphael, eds., *Modern Jewish History: A Source Reader* (New York: Schocken Books, 1974). Copyright © 1974. Reprinted by permission of Marc Lee Raphael. **Page 823:** "Turkish Nationalism." Mehmed Emin, "Going to Battle," from Robert G. Landen, ed., *The Emergence of the Modern Middle East: Selected Readings* (New York: Van Nostrand Reinhold Company, 1970), 120. Copyright © 1970. Reprinted by permission. **Page 824:** "Vietnamese Resistance and the Importance of Becoming Modern." Excerpted from Phan Boi Chau, "The New Vietnam" (1907), as quoted in Truong Buu Lam, *Colonialism Experienced: Vietnamese Writings on Colonialism, 1900–1931*. Copyright © by the University of Michigan 2000. Reprinted by permission of the publisher.

Chapter 25, page 847: "Outbreak of the Russian Revolution." From Eduard Dune, *Notes of a Red Guard,* translated and edited by Dianne Koenker and S. A. Smith. Copyright © 1933 by Dianne Koenker and S. A. Smith. Reprinted by permission of the University of Illinois Press. **Page 865:** "Memory and Battlefield Tourism." From Vera Brittain, *Testament of Youth*. Copyright © 1978, Virago Press. Extracts from Vera Brittain are reproduced by permission of Mark Bostridge and T. J. Brittain-Catlin, literary executors for the Vera Brittain Estate, 1970.

Chapter 26, page 877: "A Family Copes with Unemployment." From Marie Jahoda, Paul Lazarsfeld, and Hans Zeisel, *Marienthal: The Sociography of an Unemployed Community*, translated by John Reginall and Thomas Elsaesser (Chicago: Aldine, Atherton, 1933; repr., 1971), pps. 87–88. Copyright © 2002 Transaction Publishers. Reprinted by permission of Transaction Publishers. **Page 882:** "An Author Opposes Nazism." From Lion Feuchtwanger, "How Do We Struggle against a Third Reich?" January 21, 1931, in *The Weimar Republic Sourcebook*, edited by Anton Kaes, Martin Jay, and Edward Dimendberg. Copyright © 1994. Reprinted by permission of the University of California Press. **Page 883:** A Professor against Hitler." From Victor Klemperer, *I Will Bear Witness: A Diary of the Nazi Years, 1933–1941,* translated by Martin Chalmers. Copyright © 1998 by Martin Chalmers. Used by permission of Random House, Inc. **Page 883:** "Praise for Nazis" and "Hitler in Prayers." From Claudia Koonz, *Mothers in the Fatherland: Women, the Family, and Nazi Politics.* Copyright © 1987 by Claudia Koonz. Reprinted by permission of St. Martin's Press, Inc. **Page 892:** "The Greater East Asia Co-Prosperity Sphere." Excerpted from "Draft of Basic Plan for Establishment of Greater East Asia Co-Prosperity Sphere" in *Sources of Japanese Tradition*, compiled by Ryusaku Tsunoda, William Theodore de Bary, and Donald Keene (New York: Columbia University Press, 1958), 802–3, 805. Copyright © 1958 by Ryusaku Tsunoda, William Theodore de Bary, and Donald Keene. Reprinted with permission of the publisher.

Chapter 28, page 966: "Criticizing White Feminism (The Combahee River Collective Statement)." From *Feminism in Our Time: The Essential Writings, World War II to the Present,* edited by Miriam Schneir (New York: Vintage, 1994), 177–79. Copyright © 1994 Vintage. Reprinted by permission of Monthly Review Foundation. **Page 966:** "Criticizing Socialism." From *Women and Russia: Feminist Writings from the Soviet Union*, edited by Tatyana Mamonova. Copyright © 1984 by Tatyana Mamonova. Reprinted by permission of Beacon Press, Boston. **Page 967:** "Comparing the Situation of European and African Women." From Awa Thiam, *Black Sisters, Speak Out: Feminism and Oppression in Black Africa,* translated by Dorothy S. Blair. Copyright © 1986 by Awa Thiam. Reprinted by permission of Pluto Press. **Page 975:** "Margaret Thatcher's Economic Vision." From a speech given by Margaret Thatcher to the Conservative Party Conference, Brighton, October 10, 1980. Copyright © Margaret Thatcher Foundation. All Rights Reserved. Reprinted by permission of the Margaret Thatcher Foundation, info@margaretthatcher.org. **Page 978:** "A Citizen's Experience of Gorbachev's Reforms." From a letter by Z. I. Kupriyanova, January 1988. Reprinted with the permission of Simon & Schuster, Inc., and Ed Victor Ltd. Literary Agency from Christopher Cerf and Marina Albee, *Small Fires: Letters from the Soviet People to* Ogonyok *Magazine, 1987–1990.* Copyright © 1990 by Christopher Cerf and Marina Albee. All rights reserved.

Chapter 29, page 1010: "The View from Everyday Life" and "Too Much Islamic Architecture." From Jennifer Ehrlich, "Liberal Netherlands Grows Less So on Immigration," *Christian Science Monitor,* December 19, 2003. Copyright © 2003. Reprinted by permission of Jennifer Ehrlich. **Page 1010:** "Opposing Immigration and Turkey's Membership in the European Union." Geert Wilders quoted in "'Turkey in the EU? Never!'" *Expatica,* October 5, 2004, http://www.expatica.com/nl/news/news_focus/turkey-in-the-eu-never-12536_60600.html. Reprinted by permission of Expatica Communications.

Page 1010: "A Student's Thoughts on Muslims in the Netherlands." Loubna el Morabet quoted in "Muslims Quietly Take Wilders' Abuse" by Sheila Kamerman and Dirk Vlasblom, Radio Netherlands Worldwide Africa Desk, March 26, 2010, http://www.rnw.nl/africa/article/muslims-quietly-take-wilders-abuse-0. **Page 1011:** "An Evaluation of Dutch Values." Funda Müjde, from "Holland," posted on the Funda Müjde Web site: http://www.fundam.nl/english/fundas-column-telegraaf-daily-newspaper-04.htm. Reprinted by permission of Müjde Productions Amsterdam.

Index

A note about the index:
Names of individuals appear in bold face; biographical dates are included for major historical figures.
Letters in parentheses following pages refer to:
(i) illustrations, including photographs and artifacts
(f) figures, including charts, graphs, and tables
(m) maps
(b) boxed features (such as "Contrasting Views")

About the authors

Lynn Hunt (Ph.D., Stanford University) is Eugen Weber Professor of Modern European History at the University of California, Los Angeles. She is the author or editor of several books, including most recently *Bernard Picart and the First Global Vision of Religion; The Book That Changed Europe: Picart and Bernard's Religious Ceremonies of the World; Measuring Time, Making History;* and *Inventing Human Rights.*

Thomas R. Martin (Ph.D., Harvard University) is Jeremiah O'Connor Professor in Classics at the College of the Holy Cross. He is the author of *Ancient Greece* and *Sovereignty and Coinage in Classical Greece* and is one of the originators of *Perseus: Interactive Sources and Studies on Ancient Greece* (www.perseus.tufts.edu). He is currently conducting research on the career of Pericles as a political leader in classical Athens as well as on the text of Josephus's *Jewish War.*

Barbara H. Rosenwein (Ph.D., University of Chicago) is professor of history at Loyola University Chicago. She is the author or editor of several books including *A Short History of the Middle Ages* and *Emotional Communities in the Early Middle Ages.* She is currently working on a general history of the emotions in the West.

Bonnie G. Smith (Ph.D., University of Rochester) is Board of Governors Professor of History at Rutgers University. She is the author or editor of several books including *The Oxford Encyclopedia of Women in World History; The Gender of History: Men, Women and Historical Practice;* and *Ladies of the Leisure Class.* Currently she is studying the globalization of European culture and society since the seventeenth century.

About the cover image

Giuseppe De Nittis, *Westminster,* 1875

Italian painter Giuseppe De Nittis (1846–1884) was trained in Naples, but eventually settled and made his career in Paris. There, he spent time with many of the most prominent impressionist painters of the period, striking up a good friendship with Edgar Degas. The impressionist influence is apparent in this work, created during a trip to London. The artist captures a single moment in time, as men smoke, talk, and stare out at the Thames River from Westminster Bridge. De Nittis emphasizes the effects of light and fog to create a dreamy, luminous depiction of an otherwise ordinary scene from daily life. It was this focus on the everyday and the fleeting moment that characterized the impressionist style.

Make History

Free Maps, Images, Documents, and Web Links

bedfordstmartins.com/makehistory

Make History combines the best Web resources with hundreds of maps and images to make finding the source material you need simple. Browse the collection of thousands of resources by course or by topic, date, and type. Each item has been carefully chosen and helpfully annotated to make it easy to find exactly what you need. You can also create collections of *Make History* content to save or use later.

- ***DocLinks*** Over 900 annotated links to important primary documents
- ***HistoryLinks*** Over 800 annotated links to history-related Web sites
- **The Bedford Image Library** Over 500 annotated images
- ***MapCentral*** Over 600 full-color maps
- **Outline Maps** Over 100 maps to use for review
- **History Research and Writing Help**

80°N
60°N
40°N
20°N
0°
Equator
20°S
40°S
60°S
80°S
160°W
140°W
120°W
100°W
80°W
60°W
40°W
20°W
Alaska (U.S.)
CANADA
Greenland (Den.)
ICELAND
UNITED STATES
ATLANTIC OCEAN
Azores (Port.)
Madeira (Port.)
Canary Is. (Sp.)
Western Sahara (Mor.)
Hawaii (U.S.)
MEXICO
BAHAMAS
DOMINICAN REPUBLIC
HAITI
CUBA
JAMAICA
BELIZE
HONDURAS
GUATEMALA
EL SALVADOR
NICARAGUA
COSTA RICA
PANAMA
Puerto Rico (U.S.)
ST. KITTS AND NEVIS
ANTIGUA AND BARBUDA
Guadeloupe (Fr.)
DOMINICA
Martinique (Fr.)
ST. VINCENT AND THE GRENADINES
ST. LUCIA
BARBADOS
GRENADA
TRINIDAD AND TOBAGO
VENEZUELA
GUYANA
SURINAME
French Guiana (Fr.)
CAPE VERDE
SENEGAL
GAMBIA
GUINEA-BISSAU
GUINEA
SIERRA LEONE
LIBERIA
PACIFIC OCEAN
COLOMBIA
ECUADOR
Galápagos Is. (Ec.)
BRAZIL
PERU
BOLIVIA
PARAGUAY
CHILE
URUGUAY
ARGENTINA
SAMOA
TONGA
Easter I. (Chile)
ATLANTIC OCEAN
Falkland Is. (U.K.)
0 1,500 3,000 miles
0 1,500 3,000 kilometers